Holy Bible
The American Standard Version
Yahweh Edition

Devoted Publishing
Email: devotedpub@hotmail.com
Facebook: @DevotedPublishing
Woodstock, Ontario, 2017

Table of Contents

Holy Bible, The American Standard Version, Yahweh Edition

Layout and Formatting by Anthony Uyl and is Copyright 2017 Devoted Publishing.
ISBN: 978-1-77356-042-7

Table of Contents

Old Testament 3
   The First Book of Moses, called Genesis 3
   The Second Book of Moses, Called Exodus 23
   The Third Book of Moses, commonly called Leviticus 40
   The Fourth Book of Moses, called Numbers 52
   The Fifth Book of Moses, called Deuteronomy 70
   The Book of Joshua 85
   The Book of Judges 95
   The Book of Ruth 105
   The First Book of Samuel 107
   The Second Book of Samuel 120
   The First Book of the Kings 131
   The Second Book of the Kings 143
   The First Book of the Chronicles 155
   The Second Book of the Chronicles 167
   Ezra 180
   The Book of Nehemiah 184
   The Book of Esther 190
   The Book of Job 193
The Book of Psalms 207
   The Proverbs 242
   Ecclesiastes or, The Preacher 254
   The Song of Songs, Which is Solomon's 257
   The Book of the Prophet Isaiah 260
   The Book of the Prophet Jeremiah 279
   The Lamentations of Jeremiah 300
   The Book of the Prophet Ezekiel 303
   The Book of Daniel 322
   Hosea 328
   Joel 331
   Amos 333
   Obadiah 336
   Jonah 337
   Micah 338
   Nahum 340
   Habakkuk 341
   Zephaniah 342
   Haggai 343
   Zechariah 344
   Malachi 348
New Testament 349
   The Gospel According to St. Matthew 349
   The Gospel According to St. Mark 362
   The Gospel According to St. Luke 370
   The Gospel According to St. John 384
   The Acts of the Apostles 394
   The Epistle of Paul the Apostle to the Romans 407
   The First Epistle of Paul the Apostle to the Corinthians 413
   The Second Epistle of Paul the Apostle to the Corinthians 419
   The Epistle of Paul the Apostle to the Galatians 423
   The Epistle of Paul the Apostle to the Ephesians 425
   The Epistle of Paul the Apostle to the Philippians 427
   The Epistle of Paul the Apostle to the Colossians 429
   The First Epistle of Paul to the Thessalonians 431
   The Second Epistle of Paul the Apostle to the Thessalonians . 433
   The First Epistle of Paul the Apostle to Timothy 434
   The Second Epistle of Paul the Apostle to Timothy 436
   The Epistle of Paul to Titus 437
   The Epistle of Paul to Philemon 438
   The Epistle to the Hebrews 439
   The General Epistle of James 444
   The First Epistle General of Peter 446
   The Second Epistle General of Peter 448
   The First Epistle General of John 449
   The Second Epistle of John 451
   The Third Epistle of John 452
   The General Epistle of Jude 453
   The Revelation to St. John 454

Old Testament

The First Book of Moses, called Genesis

Chapter 1

1In the beginning God created the heavens and the earth.

2And the earth was waste and void; and darkness was upon the face of the deep: and the Spirit of God moved upon the face of the waters

3And God said, Let there be light: and there was light.

4And God saw the light, that it was good: and God divided the light from the darkness.

5And God called the light Day, and the darkness he called Night. And there was evening and there was morning, one day.

6And God said, Let there be a firmament in the midst of the waters, and let it divide the waters from the waters.

7And God made the firmament, and divided the waters which were under the firmament from the waters which were above the firmament: and it was so.

8And God called the firmament Heaven. And there was evening and there was morning, a second day.

9And God said, Let the waters under the heavens be gathered together unto one place, and let the dry land appear: and it was so.

10And God called the dry land Earth; and the gathering together of the waters called he Seas: and God saw that it was good.

11And God said, Let the earth put forth grass, herbs yielding seed, and fruit-trees bearing fruit after their kind, wherein is the seed thereof, upon the earth: and it was so.

12And the earth brought forth grass, herbs yielding seed after their kind, and trees bearing fruit, wherein is the seed thereof, after their kind: and God saw that it was good.

13And there was evening and there was morning, a third day.

14And God said, Let there be lights in the firmament of heaven to divide the day from the night; and let them be for signs, and for seasons, and for days and years:

15and let them be for lights in the firmament of heaven to give light upon the earth: and it was so.

16And God made the two great lights; the greater light to rule the day, and the lesser light to rule the night: he made the stars also.

17And God set them in the firmament of heaven to give light upon the earth,

18and to rule over the day and over the night, and to divide the light from the darkness: and God saw that it was good.

19And there was evening and there was morning, a fourth day.

20And God said, Let the waters swarm with swarms of living creatures, and let birds fly above the earth in the open firmament of heaven.

21And God created the great sea-monsters, and every living creature that moveth, wherewith the waters swarmed, after their kind, and every winged bird after its kind: and God saw that it was good.

22And God blessed them, saying, Be fruitful, and multiply, and fill the waters in the seas, and let birds multiply on the earth.

23And there was evening and there was morning, a fifth day.

24And God said, Let the earth bring forth living creatures after their kind, cattle, and creeping things, and beasts of the earth after their kind: and it was so.

25And God made the beasts of the earth after their kind, and the cattle after their kind, and everything that creepeth upon the ground after its kind: and God saw that it was good.

26And God said, Let us make man in our image, after our likeness: and let them have dominion over the fish of the sea, and over the birds of the heavens, and over the cattle, and over all the earth, and over every creeping thing that creepeth upon the earth.

27And God created man in his own image, in the image of God created he him; male and female created he them.

28And God blessed them: and God said unto them, Be fruitful, and multiply, and replenish the earth, and subdue it; and have dominion over the fish of the sea, and over the birds of the heavens, and over every living thing that moveth upon the earth.

29And God said, Behold, I have given you every herb yielding seed, which is upon the face of all the earth, and every tree, in which is the fruit of a tree yielding seed; to you it shall be for food:

30and to every beast of the earth, and to every bird of the heavens, and to everything that creepeth upon the earth, wherein there is life, I have given every green herb for food: and it was so.

31And God saw everything that he had made, and, behold, it was very good. And there was evening and there was morning, the sixth day.

Chapter 2

1And the heavens and the earth were finished, and all the host of them.

2And on the seventh day God finished his work which he had made; and he rested on the seventh day from all his work which he had made.

3And God blessed the seventh day, and hallowed it; because that in it he rested from all his work which God had created and made.

4These are the generations of the heavens and of the earth when they were created, in the day that Yahweh God made earth and heaven.

5And no plant of the field was yet in the earth, and no herb of the field had yet sprung up; for Yahweh God had not caused it to rain upon the earth: and there was not a man to till the ground;

6but there went up a mist from the earth, and watered the whole face of the ground.

7And Yahweh God formed man of the dust of the ground, and breathed into his nostrils the breath of life; and man became a living soul.

8And Yahweh God planted a garden eastward, in Eden; and there he put the man whom he had formed.

9And out of the ground made Yahweh God to grow every tree that is pleasant to the sight, and good for food; the tree of life also in the midst of the garden, and the tree of the knowledge of good and evil.

10And a river went out of Eden to water the garden; and from thence it was parted, and became four heads.

11The name of the first is Pishon: that is it which compasseth the whole land of Havilah, where there is gold;

12and the gold of that land is good: there is bdellium and the onyx stone.

13And the name of the second river is Gihon: the same is it that compasseth the whole land of Cush.

14And the name of the third river is Hiddekel: that is it which goeth in front of Assyria. And the fourth river is the Euphrates.

15And Yahweh God took the man, and put him into the garden of Eden to dress it and to keep it.

16And Yahweh God commanded the man, saying, Of every tree of the garden thou mayest freely eat:

17but of the tree of the knowledge of good and evil, thou shalt not eat of it: for in the day that thou eatest thereof thou shalt surely die.

18And Yahweh God said, It is not good that the man should be alone; I will make him a help meet for him.

19And out of the ground Yahweh God formed every beast of the field, and every bird of the heavens; and brought them unto the man to see what he would call them: and whatsoever the man called every living creature, that was the name thereof.

20And the man gave names to all cattle, and to the birds of the heavens, and to every beast of the field; but for man there was not found a help meet for him.

21And Yahweh God caused a deep sleep to fall upon the man, and he slept; and he took one of his ribs, and closed up the flesh instead thereof:

22and the rib, which Yahweh God had taken from the man, made he a woman, and brought her unto the man.

23And the man said, This is now bone of my bones, and flesh of my flesh: she shall be called Woman, because she was taken out of Man.

24Therefore shall a man leave his father and his mother, and shall cleave unto his wife: and they shall be one flesh.

25And they were both naked, the man and his wife, and were not ashamed.

Chapter 3

1Now the serpent was more subtle than any beast of the field which Yahweh God had made. And he said unto the woman, Yea, hath God said, Ye shall not eat of any tree of the garden?

2And the woman said unto the serpent, Of the fruit of the trees of the garden we may eat:

3but of the fruit of the tree which is in the midst of the garden, God hath said, Ye shall not eat of it, neither shall ye touch it, lest ye die:

4And the serpent said unto the woman, Ye shall not surely die:

5for God doth know that in the day ye eat thereof, then your eyes shall be opened, and ye shall be as God, knowing good and evil.

6And when the woman saw that the tree was good for food, and that it was a delight to the eyes, and that the tree was to be desired to make one wise, she took of the fruit thereof, and did eat; and she gave also unto her husband with her, and he did eat.

7And the eyes of them both were opened, and they knew that they were naked; and they sewed fig-leaves together, and made themselves aprons.

8And they heard the voice of Yahweh God walking in the garden in the cool of the day: and the man and his wife hid themselves from the presence of Yahweh God amongst the trees of the garden.

9And Yahweh God called unto the man, and said unto him, Where art thou?

10And he said, I heard thy voice in the garden, and I was afraid, because I was naked; and I hid myself.

11And he said, Who told thee that thou wast naked? Hast thou eaten of the tree, whereof I commanded thee that thou shouldest not eat?

12And the man said, The woman whom thou gavest to be with me, she gave me of the tree, and I did eat.

13And Yahweh God said unto the woman, What is this thou hast done? And the woman said, The serpent beguiled me, and I did eat.

14And Yahweh God said unto the serpent, Because thou hast done this, cursed art thou above all cattle, and above every beast of the field; upon thy belly shalt thou go, and dust shalt thou eat all the days of thy life:

15and I will put enmity between thee and the woman, and between thy seed and her seed: he shall bruise thy head, and thou shalt bruise his heel.

16Unto the woman he said, I will greatly multiply thy pain and thy conception; in pain thou shalt bring forth children; and thy desire shall be to thy husband, and he shall rule over thee.

17And unto Adam he said, Because thou hast hearkened unto the voice of thy wife, and hast eaten of the tree, of which I commanded thee, saying, Thou shalt not eat of it: cursed is the ground for thy sake; in toil shalt thou eat of it all the days of thy life;

Genesis

18thorns also and thistles shall it bring forth to thee; and thou shalt eat the herb of the field;

19in the sweat of thy face shalt thou eat bread, till thou return unto the ground; for out of it wast thou taken: for dust thou art, and unto dust shalt thou return.

20And the man called his wife's name Eve; because she was the mother of all living.

21And Yahweh God made for Adam and for his wife coats of skins, and clothed them.

22And Yahweh God said, Behold, the man is become as one of us, to know good and evil; and now, lest he put forth his hand, and take also of the tree of life, and eat, and live for ever-

23therefore Yahweh God sent him forth from the garden of Eden, to till the ground from whence he was taken.

24So he drove out the man; and he placed at the east of the garden of Eden the Cherubim, and the flame of a sword which turned every way, to keep the way of the tree of life.

Chapter 4

1And the man knew Eve his wife; and she conceived, and bare Cain, and said, I have gotten a man with the help of Yahweh.

2And again she bare his brother Abel. And Abel was a keeper of sheep, but Cain was a tiller of the ground.

3And in process of time it came to pass, that Cain brought of the fruit of the ground an offering unto Yahweh.

4And Abel, he also brought of the firstlings of his flock and of the fat thereof. And Yahweh had respect unto Abel and to his offering:

5but unto Cain and to his offering he had not respect. And Cain was very wroth, and his countenance fell.

6And Yahweh said unto Cain, Why art thou wroth? and why is thy countenance fallen?

7If thou doest well, shall it not be lifted up? and if thou doest not well, sin coucheth at the door: and unto thee shall be its desire, but do thou rule over it.

8And Cain told Abel his brother. And it came to pass, when they were in the field, that Cain rose up against Abel his brother, and slew him.

9And Yahweh said unto Cain, Where is Abel thy brother? And he said, I know not: am I my brother's keeper?

10And he said, What hast thou done? the voice of thy brother's blood crieth unto me from the ground.

11And now cursed art thou from the ground, which hath opened its mouth to receive thy brother's blood from thy hand;

12when thou tillest the ground, it shall not henceforth yield unto thee its strength; a fugitive and a wanderer shalt thou be in the earth.

13And Cain said unto Yahweh, My punishment is greater than I can bear.

14Behold, thou hast driven me out this day from the face of the ground; and from thy face shall I be hid; and I shall be a fugitive and a wanderer in the earth; and it will come to pass, that whosoever findeth me will slay me.

15And Yahweh said unto him, Therefore whosoever slayeth Cain, vengeance shall be taken on him sevenfold. And Yahweh appointed a sign for Cain, lest any finding him should smite him.

16And Cain went out from the presence of Yahweh, and dwelt in the land of Nod, on the east of Eden.

17And Cain knew his wife; and she conceived, and bare Enoch: and he builded a city, and called the name of the city, after the name of his son, Enoch.

18And unto Enoch was born Irad: and Irad begat Mehujael: and Mehujael begat Methushael; and Methushael begat Lamech.

19And Lamech took unto him two wives: the name of the one was Adah, and the name of the other Zillah.

20And Adah bare Jabal: he was the father of such as dwell in tents and have cattle.

21And his brother's name was Jubal: he was the father of all such as handle the harp and pipe.

22And Zillah, she also bare Tubal-cain, the forger of every cutting instrument of brass and iron: and the sister of Tubal-cain was Naamah.

23And Lamech said unto his wives:
Adah and Zillah, hear my voice;
Ye wives of Lamech, hearken unto my speech:
For I have slain a man for wounding me,
And a young man for bruising me:

24If Cain shall be avenged sevenfold,
Truly Lamech seventy and sevenfold.

25And Adam knew his wife again; and she bare a son, and called his name Seth. For, said she, God hath appointed me another seed instead of Abel; for Cain slew him.

26And to Seth, to him also there was born a son; and he called his name Enosh. Then began men to call upon the name of Yahweh.

Chapter 5

1This is the book of the generations of Adam. In the day that God created man, in the likeness of God made he him;

2male and female created he them, and blessed them, and called their name Adam, in the day when they were created.

3And Adam lived a hundred and thirty years, and begat a son in his own likeness, after his image; and called his name Seth:

4and the days of Adam after he begat Seth were eight hundred years: and he begat sons and daughters.

5And all the days that Adam lived were nine hundred and thirty years: and he died.

6And Seth lived a hundred and five years, and begat Enosh:

7and Seth lived after he begat Enosh eight hundred and seven years, and begat sons and daughters:

8and all the days of Seth were nine hundred and twelve years: and he died.

9And Enosh lived ninety years, and begat Kenan.

10and Enosh lived after he begat Kenan eight hundred and fifteen years, and begat sons and daughters:

11and all the days of Enosh were nine hundred and five years: and he died.

12And Kenan lived seventy years, and begat Mahalalel:

13and Kenan lived after he begat Mahalalel eight hundred and forty years, and begat sons and daughters:

14and all the days of Kenan were nine hundred and ten years: and he died.

15And Mahalalel lived sixty and five years, and begat Jared:

16And Mahalalel lived after he begat Jared eight hundred and thirty years, and begat sons and daughters:

17and all the days of Mahalalel were eight hundred ninety and five years: and he died.

18And Jared lived a hundred sixty and two years, and begat Enoch:

19and Jared lived after he begat Enoch eight hundred years, and begat sons and daughters:

20And all the days of Jared were nine hundred sixty and two years: and he died.

21And Enoch lived sixty and five years, and begat Methuselah:

22and Enoch walked with God after he begat Methuselah three hundred years, and begat sons and daughters:

23and all the days of Enoch were three hundred sixty and five years:

24and Enoch walked with God: and he was not; for God took him.

25And Methuselah lived a hundred eighty and seven years, and begat Lamech:

26and Methuselah lived after he begat Lamech seven hundred eighty and two years, and begat sons and daughters.

27And all the days of Methuselah were nine hundred sixty and nine years: and he died.

28And Lamech lived a hundred eighty and two years, and begat a son:

29and he called his name Noah, saying, This same shall comfort us in our work and in the toil of our hands, which cometh because of the ground which Yahweh hath cursed.

30And Lamech lived after he begat Noah five hundred ninety and five years, and begat sons and daughters.

31And all the days of Lamech were seven hundred seventy and seven years: and he died.

32And Noah was five hundred years old: And Noah begat Shem, Ham, and Japheth.

Chapter 6

1And it came to pass, when men began to multiply on the face of the ground, and daughters were born unto them,

2that the sons of God saw the daughters of men that they were fair; and they took them wives of all that they chose.

3And Yahweh said, My spirit shall not strive with man for ever, for that he also is flesh: yet shall his days be a hundred and twenty years.

4The Nephilim were in the earth in those days, and also after that, when the sons of God came unto the daughters of men, and they bare children to them: the same were the mighty men that were of old, the men of renown.

5And Yahweh saw that the wickedness of man was great in the earth, and that every imagination of the thoughts of his heart was only evil continually.

6And it repented Yahweh that he had made man on the earth, and it grieved him at his heart.

7And Yahweh said, I will destroy man whom I have created from the face of the ground; both man, and beast, and creeping things, and birds of the heavens; for it repenteth me that I have made them.

8But Noah found favor in the eyes of Yahweh.

9These are the generations of Noah. Noah was a righteous man, and perfect in his generations: Noah walked with God.

10And Noah begat three sons, Shem, Ham, and Japheth.

11And the earth was corrupt before God, and the earth was filled with violence.

12And God saw the earth, and, behold, it was corrupt; for all flesh had corrupted their way upon the earth.

13And God said unto Noah, The end of all flesh is come before me; for the earth is filled with violence through them; and, behold, I will destroy them with the earth.

14Make thee an ark of gopher wood; rooms shalt thou make in the ark, and shalt pitch it within and without with pitch.

15And this is how thou shalt make it: the length of the ark three hundred cubits, the breadth of it fifty cubits, and the height of it thirty cubits.

16A light shalt thou make to the ark, and to a cubit shalt thou finish it upward; and the door of the ark shalt thou set in the side thereof; with lower, second, and third stories shalt thou make it.

17And I, behold, I do bring the flood of waters upon this earth, to destroy all flesh, wherein is the breath of life, from under heaven; everything that is in the earth shall die.

18But I will establish my covenant with thee; and thou shalt come into the ark, thou, and thy sons, and thy wife, and thy sons' wives with thee.

19And of every living thing of all flesh, two of every sort shalt thou bring into the ark, to keep them alive with thee; they shall be male and female.

20Of the birds after their kind, and of the cattle after their kind, of every creeping thing of the ground after its kind, two of every sort shall come unto thee, to keep them alive.

21And take thou unto thee of all food that is eaten, and gather it to thee; and it shall be for food for thee, and for them.

22Thus did Noah; according to all that God commanded him, so did he.

Chapter 7

1And Yahweh said unto Noah, Come thou and all thy house into the ark; for thee have I seen righteous before me in this generation.

2Of every clean beast thou shalt take to thee seven and seven, the male and his female; and of the beasts that are not clean two, the male and his female:

3of the birds also of the heavens, seven and seven, male and female, to keep seed alive upon the face of all the earth.

4For yet seven days, and I will cause it to rain upon the earth forty days and forty nights; and every living thing that I have made will I destroy from off the face of the ground.

5And Noah did according unto all that Yahweh commanded him.

6And Noah was six hundred years old when the flood of waters was upon the earth.

7And Noah went in, and his sons, and his wife, and his sons' wives with him, into the ark, because of the waters of the flood.

8Of clean beasts, and of beasts that are not clean, and of birds, and of everything that creepeth upon the ground,

9there went in two and two unto Noah into the ark, male and female, as God commanded Noah.

10And it came to pass after the seven days, that the waters of the flood were upon the earth.

11In the six hundredth year of Noah's life, in the second month, on the seventeenth day of the month, on the same day were all the fountains of the great deep broken up, and the windows of heaven were opened.

12And the rain was upon the earth forty days and forty nights.

13In the selfsame day entered Noah, and Shem, and Ham, and Japheth, the sons of Noah, and Noah's wife, and the three wives of his sons with them, into the ark;

14they, and every beast after its kind, and all the cattle after their kind, and every creeping thing that creepeth upon the earth after its kind, and every bird after its kind, every bird of every sort.

15And they went in unto Noah into the ark, two and two of all flesh wherein is the breath of life.

16And they that went in, went in male and female of all flesh, as God commanded him: and Yahweh shut him in.

17And the flood was forty days upon the earth; and the waters increased, and bare up the ark, and it was lifted up above the earth.

18And the waters prevailed, and increased greatly upon the earth; and the ark went upon the face of the waters.

19And the waters prevailed exceedingly upon the earth; and all the high mountains that were under the whole heaven were covered.

20Fifteen cubits upward did the waters prevail; and the mountains were covered.

21And all flesh died that moved upon the earth, both birds, and cattle, and beasts, and every creeping thing that creepeth upon the earth, and every man:

22all in whose nostrils was the breath of the spirit of life, of all that was on the dry land, died.

23And every living thing was destroyed that was upon the face of the ground, both man, and cattle, and creeping things, and birds of the heavens; and they were destroyed from the earth: and Noah only was left, and they that were with him in the ark.

24And the waters prevailed upon the earth a hundred and fifty days.

Chapter 8

1And God remembered Noah, and all the beasts, and all the cattle that were with him in the ark: and God made a wind to pass over the earth, and the waters assuaged;

2the fountains also of the deep and the windows of heaven were stopped, and the rain from heaven was restrained;

3and the waters returned from off the earth continually: and after the end of a hundred and fifty days the waters decreased.

4And the ark rested in the seventh month, on the seventeenth day of the month, upon the mountains of Ararat.

5And the waters decreased continually until the tenth month: in the tenth month, on the first day of the month, were the tops of the mountains seen.

6And it came to pass at the end of forty days, that Noah opened the window of the ark which he had made:

7and he sent forth a raven, and it went forth to and fro, until the waters were dried up from off the earth.

8And he sent forth a dove from him, to see if the waters were abated from off the face of the ground;

9but the dove found no rest for the sole of her foot, and she returned unto him to the ark; for the waters were on the face of the whole earth: and he put forth his hand, and took her, and brought her in unto him into the ark.

10And he stayed yet other seven days; and again he sent forth the dove out of the ark;

11and the dove came in to him at eventide; and, lo, in her mouth an olive-leaf plucked off: so Noah knew that the waters were abated from off the earth.

12And he stayed yet other seven days, and sent forth the dove; and she returned not again unto him any more.

13And it came to pass in the six hundred and first year, in the first month, the first day of the month, the waters were dried up from off the earth: and Noah removed the covering of the ark, and looked, and, behold, the face of the ground was dried.

14And in the second month, on the seven and twentieth day of the month, was the earth dry.

15And God spake unto Noah, saying,

16Go forth from the ark, thou, and thy wife, and thy sons, and thy sons' wives with thee.

17Bring forth with thee every living thing that is with thee of all flesh, both birds, and cattle, and every creeping thing that creepeth upon the earth; that they may breed abundantly in the earth, and be fruitful, and multiply upon the earth.

18And Noah went forth, and his sons, and his wife, and his sons' wives with him:

19every beast, every creeping thing, and every bird, whatsoever moveth upon the earth, after their families, went forth out of the ark.

20And Noah builded an altar unto Yahweh, and took of every clean beast, and of every clean bird, and offered burnt-offerings on the altar.

21And Yahweh smelled the sweet savor; and Yahweh said in his heart, I will not again curse the ground any more for man's sake, for that the imagination of man's heart is evil from his youth; neither will I again smite any more everything living, as I have done.

22While the earth remaineth, seedtime and harvest, and cold and heat, and summer and winter, and day and night shall not cease.

Chapter 9

1And God blessed Noah and his sons, and said unto them, Be fruitful, and multiply, and replenish the earth.

2And the fear of you and the dread of you shall be upon every beast of the earth, and upon every bird of the heavens; With all wherewith the ground teemeth, and all the fishes of the sea, into your hand are they delivered.

3Every moving thing that liveth shall be food for you; As the green herb have I given you all.

4But flesh with the life thereof, which is the blood thereof, shall ye not eat.

5And surely your blood, the blood of your lives, will I require; At the hand of every beast will I require it. And at the hand of man, even at the hand of every man's brother, will I require the life of man.

6Whoso sheddeth man's blood, by man shall his blood be shed: For in the image of God made he man.

7And you, be ye fruitful, and multiply; Bring forth abundantly in the earth, and multiply therein.

8And God spake unto Noah, and to his sons with him, saying,

9And I, behold, I establish my covenant with you, and with your seed after you;

10and with every living creature that is with you, the birds, the cattle, and every beast of the earth with you. Of all that go out of the ark, even every beast of the earth.

11And I will establish my covenant with you; neither shall all flesh be cut off any more by the waters of the flood; neither shall there any more be a flood to destroy the earth.

12And God said, This is the token of the covenant which I make between me and you and every living creature that is with you, for perpetual generations:

13I do set my bow in the cloud, and it shall be for a token of a covenant between me and the earth.

14And it shall come to pass, when I bring a cloud over the earth, that the bow shall be seen in the cloud,

15and I will remember my covenant, which is between me and you and every living creature of all flesh; and the waters shall no more become a flood to destroy all flesh.

16And the bow shall be in the cloud; and I will look upon it, that I may remember the everlasting covenant between God and every living creature of all flesh that is upon the earth.

17And God said unto Noah, This is the token of the covenant which I have established between me and all flesh that is upon the earth.

18And the sons of Noah, that went forth from the ark, were Shem, and Ham, and Japheth: and Ham is the father of Canaan.

19These three were the sons of Noah: and of these was the whole earth overspread.

20And Noah began to be a husbandman, and planted a vineyard:

21and he drank of the wine, and was drunken. And he was uncovered within his tent.

22And Ham, the father of Canaan, saw the nakedness of his father, and told his two brethren without.

23And Shem and Japheth took a garment, and laid it upon both their shoulders, and went backward, and covered the nakedness of their father. And their faces were backward, and they saw not their father's nakedness.

24And Noah awoke from his wine, and knew what his youngest son had done unto him.

25And he said,
Cursed be Canaan;
A servant of servants shall he be unto his brethren.
26And he said,
Blessed be Yahweh, the God of Shem;
And let Canaan be his servant.
27God enlarge Japheth,
And let him dwell in the tents of Shem;
And let Canaan be his servant.

28And Noah lived after the flood three hundred and fifty years.

29And all the days of Noah were nine hundred and fifty years: And he died.

Genesis
Chapter 10

1Now these are the generations of the sons of Noah, namely, of Shem, Ham, and Japheth: and unto them were sons born after the flood.

2The sons of Japheth: Gomer, and Magog, and Madai, and Javan, and Tubal, and Meshech, and Tiras.

3And the sons of Gomer: Ashkenaz, and Riphath, and Togarmah.

4And the sons of Javan: Elishah, and Tarshish, Kittim, and Dodanim.

5Of these were the isles of the nations divided in their lands, every one after his tongue, after their families, in their nations.

6And the sons of Ham: Cush, and Mizraim, and Put, and Canaan.

7And the sons of Cush: Seba, and Havilah, and Sabtah, and Raamah, and Sabteca; and the sons of Raamah: Sheba, and Dedan.

8And Cush begat Nimrod: he began to be a mighty one in the earth.

9He was a mighty hunter before Yahweh: wherefore it is said, Like Nimrod a mighty hunter before Yahweh.

10And the beginning of his kingdom was Babel, and Erech, and Accad, and Calneh, in the land of Shinar.

11Out of that land he went forth into Assyria, and builded Nineveh, and Rehoboth-ir, and Calah,

12and Resen between Nineveh and Calah (the same is the great city).

13And Mizraim begat Ludim, and Anamim, and Lehabim, and Naphtuhim,

14and Pathrusim, and Casluhim (whence went forth the Philistines), and Caphtorim.

15And Canaan begat Sidon his first-born, and Heth,

16and the Jebusite, and the Amorite, and the Girgashite,

17and the Hivite, and the Arkite, and the Sinite,

18and the Arvadite, and the Zemarite, and the Hamathite: and afterward were the families of the Canaanite spread abroad.

19And the border of the Canaanite was from Sidon, as thou goest toward Gerar, unto Gaza; as thou goest toward Sodom and Gomorrah and Admah and Zeboiim, unto Lasha.

20These are the sons of Ham, after their families, after their tongues, in their lands, in their nations.

21And unto Shem, the father of all the children of Eber, the elder brother of Japheth, to him also were children born.

22The sons of Shem: Elam, and Asshur, and Arpachshad, and Lud, and Aram.

23And the sons of Aram: Uz, and Hul, and Gether, and Mash.

24And Arpachshad begat Shelah; and Shelah begat Eber.

25And unto Eber were born two sons: The name of the one was Peleg. For in his days was the earth divided. And his brother's name was Joktan.

26And Joktan begat Almodad, and Sheleph, and Hazarmaveth, and Jerah,

27and Hadoram, and Uzal, and Diklah,

28and Obal, and Abimael, and Sheba,

29and Ophir, and Havilah, and Jobab: all these were the sons of Joktan.

30And their dwelling was from Mesha, as thou goest toward Sephar, the mountain of the east.

31These are the sons of Shem, after their families, after their tongues, in their lands, after their nations.

32These are the families of the sons of Noah, after their generations, in their nations: and of these were the nations divided in the earth after the flood.

Chapter 11

1And the whole earth was of one language and of one speech.

2And it came to pass, as they journeyed east, that they found a plain in the land of Shinar; and they dwelt there.

3And they said one to another, Come, let us make brick, and burn them thoroughly. And they had brick for stone, and slime had they for mortar.

4And they said, Come, let us build us a city, and a tower, whose top may reach unto heaven, and let us make us a name; lest we be scattered abroad upon the face of the whole earth.

5And Yahweh came down to see the city and the tower, which the children of men builded.

6And Yahweh said, Behold, they are one people, and they have all one language; and this is what they begin to do: and now nothing will be withholden from them, which they purpose to do.

7Come, let us go down, and there confound their language, that they may not understand one another's speech.

8So Yahweh scattered them abroad from thence upon the face of all the earth: and they left off building the city.

9Therefore was the name of it called Babel; because Yahweh did there confound the language of all the earth: and from thence did Yahweh scatter them abroad upon the face of all the earth.

10These are the generations of Shem. Shem was a hundred years old, and begat Arpachshad two years after the flood.

11and Shem lived after he begat Arpachshad five hundred years, and begat sons and daughters.

12And Arpachshad lived five and thirty years, and begat Shelah.

13and Arpachshad lived after he begat Shelah four hundred and three years, and begat sons and daughters.

14And Shelah lived thirty years, and begat Eber:

15and Shelah lived after he begat Eber four hundred and three years, and begat sons and daughters.

16And Eber lived four and thirty years, and begat Peleg:

17and Eber lived after he begat Peleg four hundred and thirty years, and begat sons and daughters.

18And Peleg lived thirty years, and begat Reu:

19and Peleg lived after he begat Reu two hundred and nine years, and begat sons and daughters.

20And Reu lived two and thirty years, and begat Serug:

21and Reu lived after he begat Serug two hundred and seven years, and begat sons and daughters.

22And Serug lived thirty years, and begat Nahor:

23and Serug lived after he begat Nahor two hundred years, and begat sons and daughters.

24And Nahor lived nine and twenty years, and begat Terah:

25and Nahor lived after he begat Terah a hundred and nineteen years, and begat sons and daughters.

26And Terah lived seventy years, and begat Abram, Nahor, and Haran.

27Now these are the generations of Terah. Terah begat Abram, Nahor, and Haran. And Haran begat Lot.

28And Haran died before his father Terah in the land of his nativity, in Ur of the Chaldees.

29And Abram and Nahor took them wives: The name of Abram's wife was Sarai; and the name of Nahor's wife, Milcah, the daughter of Haran, the father of Milcah, and the father of Iscah.

30And Sarai was barren; She had no child.

31And Terah took Abram his son, and Lot the son of Haran, his son's son, and Sarai his daughter-in-law, his son Abram's wife; and they went forth with them from Ur of the Chaldees, to go into the land of Canaan; and they came unto Haran, and dwelt there.

32And the days of Terah were two hundred and five years: and Terah died in Haran.

Chapter 12

1Now Yahweh said unto Abram, Get thee out of thy country, and from thy kindred, and from thy father's house, unto the land that I will show thee:

2and I will make of thee a great nation, and I will bless thee, and make they name great; and be thou a blessing;

3and I will bless them that bless thee, and him that curseth thee will I curse: and in thee shall all the families of the earth be blessed.

4So Abram went, as Yahweh had spoken unto him; and Lot went with him: and Abram was seventy and five years old when he departed out of Haran.

5And Abram took Sarai his wife, and Lot his brother's son, and all their substance that they had gathered, and the souls that they had gotten in Haran; and they went forth to go into the land of Canaan; and into the land of Canaan they came.

6And Abram passed through the land unto the place of Shechem, unto the oak of Moreh. And the Canaanite was then in the land.

7And Yahweh appeared unto Abram, and said, Unto thy seed will I give this land: and there builded he an altar unto Yahweh, who appeared unto him.

8And he removed from thence unto the mountain on the east of Beth-el, and pitched his tent, having Beth-el on the west, and Ai on the east: and there he builded an altar unto Yahweh, and called upon the name of Yahweh.

9And Abram journeyed, going on still toward the South.

10And there was a famine in the land: and Abram went down into Egypt to sojourn there; for the famine was sore in the land.

11And it came to pass, when he was come near to enter into Egypt, that he said unto Sarai his wife, Behold now, I know that thou art a fair woman to look upon:

12and it will come to pass, when the Egyptians shall see thee, that they will say, This is his wife: and they will kill me, but they will save thee alive.

13Say, I pray thee, thou art my sister; that it may be well with me for thy sake, and that my soul may live because of thee.

14And it came to pass, that, when Abram was come into Egypt, the Egyptians beheld the woman that she was very fair.

15And the princes of Pharaoh saw her, and praised her to Pharaoh: and the woman was taken into Pharaoh's house.

16And he dealt well with Abram for her sake: and he had sheep, and oxen, and he-asses, and men-servants, and maid-servants, and she-asses, and camels.

17And Yahweh plagued Pharaoh and his house with great plagues because of Sarai, Abram's wife.

18And Pharaoh called Abram, and said, What is this that thou hast done unto me? why didst thou not tell me that she was thy wife?

19why saidst thou, She is my sister, so that I took her to be my wife? now therefore behold thy wife, take her, and go thy way.

20And Pharaoh gave men charge concerning him: and they brought him on the way, and his wife, and all that he had.

Chapter 13

1And Abram went up out of Egypt, he, and his wife, and all that he had, and Lot with him, into the South.

2And Abram was very rich in cattle, in silver, and in gold.

3And he went on his journeys from the South even to Beth-el, unto the place where his tent had been at the beginning, between Beth-el and Ai,

4unto the place of the altar, which he had made there at the first: and there Abram called on the name of Yahweh.

5And Lot also, who went with Abram, had flocks, and herds, and tents.

6And the land was not able to bear them, that they might dwell together: for their substance was great, so that they could not dwell together.

7And there was a strife between the herdsmen of Abram's cattle and the herdsmen of Lot's cattle: and the Canaanite and the Perizzite dwelt then in the land.

8And Abram said unto Lot, Let there be no strife, I pray thee, between me and thee, and between my herdsmen and thy herdsmen; for we are brethren.

9Is not the whole land before thee? separate thyself, I pray thee, from me. If thou wilt take the left hand, then I will go to the right. Or if thou take the right hand, then I will go to the left.

10And Lot lifted up his eyes, and beheld all the Plain of the Jordan, that it was well watered every where, before Yahweh destroyed Sodom and Gomorrah, like the garden of Yahweh, like the land of Egypt, as thou goest unto Zoar.

11So Lot chose him all the Plain of the Jordan; and Lot journeyed east: and they separated themselves the one from the other.

12Abram dwelt in the land of Canaan, and Lot dwelt in the cities of the Plain, and moved his tent as far as Sodom.

13Now the men of Sodom were wicked and sinners against Yahweh exceedingly.

14And Yahweh said unto Abram, after that Lot was separated from him, Lift up now thine eyes, and look from the place where thou art, northward and southward and eastward and westward:

15for all the land which thou seest, to thee will I give it, and to thy seed for ever.

16And I will make thy seed as the dust of the earth: So that if a man can number the dust of the earth, then may thy seed also be numbered.

17Arise, walk through the land in the length of it and in the breadth of it; for unto thee will I give it.

18And Abram moved his tent, and came and dwelt by the oaks of Mamre, which are in Hebron, and built there an altar unto Yahweh.

Chapter 14

1And it came to pass in the days of Amraphel king of Shinar, Arioch king of Ellasar, Chedorlaomer king of Elam, and Tidal king of Goiim,

2that they made war with Bera king of Sodom, and with Birsha king of Gomorrah, Shinab king of Admah, and Shemeber king of Zeboiim, and the king of Bela (the same is Zoar).

3All these joined together in the vale of Siddim (the same is the Salt Sea).

4Twelve years they served Chedorlaomer, and in the thirteenth year they rebelled.

5And in the fourteenth year came Chedorlaomer, and the kings that were with him, and smote the Rephaim in Ashteroth-karnaim, and the Zuzim in Ham, and the Emim in Shaveh-kiriathaim,

6and the Horites in their mount Seir, unto Elparan, which is by the wilderness.

7And they returned, and came to En-mishpat (the same is Kadesh), and smote all the country of the Amalekites, and also the Amorites, that dwelt in Hazazon-tamar.

8And there went out the king of Sodom, and the king of Gomorrah, and the king of Admah, and the king of Zeboiim, and the king of Bela (the same is Zoar); and they set the battle in array against them in the vale of Siddim;

9against Chedorlaomer king of Elam, and Tidal king of Goiim, and Amraphel king of Shinar, and Arioch king of Ellasar; four kings against the five.

10Now the vale of Siddim was full of slime pits; and the kings of Sodom and Gomorrah fled, and they fell there, and they that remained fled to the mountain.

11And they took all the goods of Sodom and Gomorrah, and all their victuals, and went their way.

12And they took Lot, Abram's brother's son, who dwelt in Sodom, and his goods, and departed.

13And there came one that had escaped, and told Abram the Hebrew: now he dwelt by the oaks of Mamre, the Amorite, brother of Eshcol, and brother of Aner; and these were confederate with Abram.

14And when Abram heard that his brother was taken captive, he led forth his trained men, born in his house, three hundred and eighteen, and pursued as far as Dan.

15And he divided himself against them by night, he and his servants, and smote them, and pursued them unto Hobah, which is on the left hand of Damascus.

16And he brought back all the goods, and also brought back his brother Lot, and his goods, and the women also, and the people.

17And the king of Sodom went out to meet him, after his return from the slaughter of Chedorlaomer and the kings that were with him, at the vale of Shaveh (the same is the King's Vale).

18And Melchizedek king of Salem brought forth bread and wine: and he was priest of God Most High.

19And he blessed him, and said, Blessed be Abram of God Most High, possessor of heaven and earth:

20and blessed be God Most High, who hath delivered thine enemies into thy hand. And he gave him a tenth of all.

21And the king of Sodom said unto Abram, Give me the persons, and take the goods to thyself.

22And Abram said to the king of Sodom, I have lifted up my hand unto Yahweh, God Most High, possessor of heaven and earth,

23that I will not take a thread nor a shoe-latchet nor aught that is thine, lest thou shouldest say, I have made Abram rich:

24save only that which the young men have eaten, and the portion of the men that went with me, Aner, Eshcol, and Mamre. Let them take their portion.

Chapter 15

1After these things the word of Yahweh came unto Abram in a vision, saying, Fear not, Abram: I am thy shield, and thy exceeding great reward.

2And Abram said, O Lord Yahweh, what wilt thou give me, seeing I go childless, and he that shall be possessor of my house is Eliezer of Damascus?

3And Abram said, Behold, to me thou hast given no seed: and, lo, one born in my house is mine heir.

4And, behold, the word of Yahweh came unto him, saying, This man shall not be thine heir; But he that shall come forth out of thine own bowels shall be thine heir.

5And he brought him forth abroad, and said, Look now toward heaven, and number the stars, if thou be able to number them: and he said unto him, So shall thy seed be.

6And he believed in Yahweh; and he reckoned it to him for righteousness.

7And he said unto him, I am Yahweh that brought thee out of Ur of the Chaldees, to give thee this land to inherit it.

8And he said, O Lord Yahweh, whereby shall I know that I shall inherit it?

9And he said unto him, Take me a heifer three years old, and a she-goat three years old, and a ram three years old, and a turtle-dove, and a young pigeon.

10And he took him all these, and divided them in the midst, and laid each half over against the other: but the birds divided he not.

11And the birds of prey came down upon the carcasses, and Abram drove them away.

12And when the sun was going down, a deep sleep fell upon Abram; and, lo, a horror of great darkness fell upon him.

13And he said unto Abram, Know of a surety that thy seed shall be sojourners in a land that is not theirs, and shall serve them; and they shall afflict them four hundred years;

14and also that nation, whom they shall serve, will I judge: and afterward shall they come out with great substance.

15But thou shalt go to thy fathers in peace; thou shalt be buried in a good old age.

16And in the fourth generation they shall come hither again; for the iniquity of the Amorite is not yet full.

17And it came to pass, that, when the sun went down, and it was dark, behold, a smoking furnace, and a flaming torch that passed between these pieces.

18In that day Yahweh made a covenant with Abram, saying, Unto thy seed have I given this land, from the river of Egypt unto the great river, the river Euphrates:

19the Kenite, and the Kenizzite, and the Kadmonite,

20and the Hittite, and the Perizzite, and the Rephaim,

21and the Amorite, and the Canaanite, and the Girgashite, and the Jebusite.

Chapter 16

1Now Sarai, Abram's wife, bare him no children: and she had a handmaid, an Egyptian, whose name was Hagar.

2And Sarai said unto Abram, Behold now, Yahweh hath restrained me from bearing; go in, I pray thee, unto my handmaid; it may be that I shall obtain children by her. And Abram hearkened to the voice of Sarai.

3And Sarai, Abram's wife, took Hagar the Egyptian, her handmaid, after Abram had dwelt ten years in the land of Canaan, and gave her to Abram her husband to be his wife.

4And he went in unto Hagar, and she conceived: and when she saw that she had conceived, her mistress was despised in her eyes.

5And Sarai said unto Abram, My wrong be upon thee: I gave my handmaid into they bosom; and when she saw that she had conceived, I was despised in her eyes: Yahweh judge between me and thee.

6But Abram said unto Sarai, Behold, thy maid is in thy hand; do to her that which is good in thine eyes. And Sarai dealt hardly with her, and she fled from her face.

7And the angel of Yahweh found her by a fountain of water in the wilderness, by the fountain in the way to Shur.

8And he said, Hagar, Sarai's handmaid, whence camest thou? and whither goest thou? And she said, I am fleeing from the face of my mistress Sarai.

9And the angel of Yahweh said unto her, Return to thy mistress, and submit thyself under her hands.

10And the angel of Yahweh said unto her, I will greatly multiply thy seed, that it shall not be numbered for multitude.

11And the angel of Yahweh said unto her, Behold, thou art with child, and shalt bear a son; and thou shalt call his name Ishmael, because Yahweh hath heard thy affliction.

12And he shall be as a wild ass among men; his hand shall be against every man, and every man's hand against him; and he shall dwell over against all his brethren.

13And she called the name of Yahweh that spake unto her, Thou art a God that seeth: for she said, Have I even here looked after him that seeth me?

14Wherefore the well was called Beer-lahai-roi; behold, it is between Kadesh and Bered.

15And Hagar bare Abram a son: and Abram called the name of his son, whom Hagar bare, Ishmael.

16And Abram was fourscore and six years old, when Hagar bare Ishmael to Abram.

Chapter 17

1And when Abram was ninety years old and nine, Yahweh appeared to Abram, and said unto him, I am God Almighty; walk before me, and be thou perfect.

2And I will make my covenant between me and thee, and will multiply thee exceedingly.

3And Abram fell on his face: and God talked with him, saying,

4As for me, behold, my covenant is with thee, and thou shalt be the father of a multitude of nations.

5Neither shall thy name any more be called Abram, but thy name shall be Abraham; for the father of a multitude of nations have I made thee.

6And I will make thee exceeding fruitful, and I will make nations of thee,

Genesis

and kings shall come out of thee.

7And I will establish my covenant between me and thee and thy seed after thee throughout their generations for an everlasting covenant, to be a God unto thee and to thy seed after thee.

8And I will give unto thee, and to thy seed after thee, the land of thy sojournings, all the land of Canaan, for an everlasting possession; and I will be their God.

9And God said unto Abraham, And as for thee, thou shalt keep my covenant, thou, and thy seed after thee throughout their generations.

10This is my covenant, which ye shall keep, between me and you and thy seed after thee: every male among you shall be circumcised.

11And ye shall be circumcised in the flesh of your foreskin; and it shall be a token of a covenant betwixt me and you.

12And he that is eight days old shall be circumcised among you, every male throughout your generations, he that is born in the house, or bought with money of any foreigner that is not of thy seed.

13He that is born in thy house, and he that is bought with thy money, must needs be circumcised: and my covenant shall be in your flesh for an everlasting covenant.

14And the uncircumcised male who is not circumcised in the flesh of his foreskin, that soul shall be cut off from his people; he hath broken my covenant.

15And God said unto Abraham, As for Sarai thy wife, thou shalt not call her name Sarai, but Sarah shall her name be.

16And I will bless her, and moreover I will give thee a son of her: yea, I will bless her, and she shall be a mother of nations; kings of peoples shall be of her.

17Then Abraham fell upon his face, and laughed, and said in his heart, Shall a child be born unto him that is a hundred years old? and shall Sarah, that is ninety years old, bear?

18And Abraham said unto God, Oh that Ishmael might live before thee!

19And God said, Nay, but Sarah thy wife shall bear thee a son; and thou shalt call his name Isaac: and I will establish my covenant with him for an everlasting covenant for his seed after him.

20And as for Ishmael, I have heard thee: behold, I have blessed him, and will make him fruitful, and will multiply him exceedingly; twelve princes shall he beget, and I will make him a great nation.

21But my covenant will I establish with Isaac, whom Sarah shall bear unto thee at this set time in the next year.

22And he left off talking with him, and God went up from Abraham.

23And Abraham took Ishmael his son, and all that were born in his house, and all that were bought with his money, every male among the men of Abraham's house, and circumcised the flesh of their foreskin in the selfsame day, as God had said unto him.

24And Abraham was ninety years old and nine, when he was circumcised in the flesh of his foreskin.

25And Ishmael his son was thirteen years old, when he was circumcised in the flesh of his foreskin.

26In the selfsame day was Abraham circumcised, and Ishmael his son.

27And all the men of his house, those born in the house, and those bought with money of a foreigner, were circumcised with him.

Chapter 18

1And Yahweh appeared unto him by the oaks of Mamre, as he sat in the tent door in the heat of the day;

2and he lifted up his eyes and looked, and, lo, three men stood over against him: and when he saw them, he ran to meet them from the tent door, and bowed himself to the earth,

3and said, My lord, if now I have found favor in thy sight, pass not away, I pray thee, from thy servant:

4let now a little water be fetched, and wash your feet, and rest yourselves under the tree:

5and I will fetch a morsel of bread, and strengthen ye your heart; after that ye shall pass on: forasmuch as ye are come to your servant. And they said, So do, as thou hast said.

6And Abraham hastened into the tent unto Sarah, and said, Make ready quickly three measures of fine meal, knead it, and make cakes.

7And Abraham ran unto the herd, and fetched a calf tender and good, and gave it unto the servant; and he hasted to dress it.

8And he took butter, and milk, and the calf which he had dressed, and set it before them; and he stood by them under the tree, and they did eat.

9And they said unto him, Where is Sarah thy wife? And he said, Behold, in the tent.

10And he said, I will certainly return unto thee when the season cometh round; and, lo, Sarah thy wife shall have a son. And Sarah heard in the tent door, which was behind him.

11Now Abraham and Sarah were old, and well stricken in age; it had ceased to be with Sarah after the manner of women.

12And Sarah laughed within herself, saying, After I am waxed old shall I have pleasure, my lord being old also?

13And Yahweh said unto Abraham, Wherefore did Sarah laugh, saying, Shall I of a surety bear a child, who am old?

14Is anything too hard for Yahweh? At the set time I will return unto thee, when the season cometh round, and Sarah shall have a son.

15Then Sarah denied, saying, I laughed not; for she was afraid. And he said, Nay; but thou didst laugh.

16And the men rose up from thence, and looked toward Sodom: and Abraham went with them to bring them on the way.

17And Yahweh said, Shall I hide from Abraham that which I do;

18seeing that Abraham had surely become a great and mighty nation, and all the nations of the earth shall be blessed in him?

19For I have known him, to the end that he may command his children and his household after him, that they may keep the way of Yahweh, to do righteousness and justice; to the end that Yahweh may bring upon Abraham that which he hath spoken of him.

20And Yahweh said, Because the cry of Sodom and Gomorrah is great, and because their sin is very grievous;

21I will go down now, and see whether they have done altogether according to the cry of it, which is come unto me; and if not, I will know.

22And the men turned from thence, and went toward Sodom: but Abraham stood yet before Yahweh.

23And Abraham drew near, and said, Wilt thou consume the righteous with the wicked?

24Peradventure there are fifty righteous within the city: wilt thou consume and not spare the place for the fifty righteous that are therein?

25That be far from thee to do after this manner, to slay the righteous with the wicked, that so the righteous should be as the wicked; that be far from thee: shall not the Judge of all the earth do right?

26And Yahweh said, If I find in Sodom fifty righteous within the city, then I will spare all the place for their sake.

27And Abraham answered and said, Behold now, I have taken upon me to speak unto the Lord, who am but dust and ashes:

28peradventure there shall lack five of the fifty righteous: wilt thou destroy all the city for lack of five? And he said, I will not destroy it, if I find there forty and five.

29And he spake unto him yet again, and said, Peradventure there shall be forty found there. And he said, I will not do it for the forty's sake.

30And he said, Oh let not the Lord be angry, and I will speak: peradventure there shall thirty be found there. And he said, I will not do it, if I find thirty there.

31And he said, Behold now, I have taken upon me to speak unto the Lord: peradventure there shall be twenty found there. And he said, I will not destroy it for the twenty's sake.

32And he said, Oh let not the Lord be angry, and I will speak yet but this once: peradventure ten shall be found there. And he said, I will not destroy it for the ten's sake.

33And Yahweh went his way, as soon as he had left off communing with Abraham: and Abraham returned unto his place.

Chapter 19

1And the two angels came to Sodom at even; and Lot sat in the gate of Sodom: and Lot saw them, and rose up to meet them; and he bowed himself with his face to the earth;

2and he said, Behold now, my lords, turn aside, I pray you, into your servant's house, and tarry all night, and wash your feet, and ye shall rise up early, and go on your way. And they said, Nay; but we will abide in the street all night.

3And he urged them greatly; and they turned in unto him, and entered into his house; and he made them a feast, and did bake unleavened bread, and they did eat.

4But before they lay down, the men of the city, even the men of Sodom, compassed the house round, both young and old, all the people from every quarter;

5and they called unto Lot, and said unto him, Where are the men that came in to thee this night? bring them out unto us, that we may know them.

6And Lot went out unto them to the door, and shut the door after him.

7And he said, I pray you, my brethren, do not so wickedly.

8Behold now, I have two daughters that have not known man; let me, I pray you, bring them out unto you, and do ye to them as is good in your eyes: only unto these men do nothing, forasmuch as they are come under the shadow of my roof.

9And they said, Stand back. And they said, This one fellow came in to sojourn, and he will needs be a judge: now will we deal worse with thee, than with them. And they pressed sore upon the man, even Lot, and drew near to break the door.

10But the men put forth their hand, and brought Lot into the house to them, and shut to the door.

11And they smote the men that were at the door of the house with blindness, both small and great, so that they wearied themselves to find the door.

12And the men said unto Lot, Hast thou here any besides? son-in-law, and thy sons, and thy daughters, and whomsoever thou hast in the city, bring them out of the place:

13for we will destroy this place, because the cry of them is waxed great before Yahweh: and Yahweh hath sent us to destroy it.

14And Lot went out, and spake unto his sons-in-law, who married his daughters, and said, Up, get you out of this place; for Yahweh will destroy the city. But he seemed unto his sons-in-law as one that mocked.

15And when the morning arose, then the angels hastened Lot, saying, Arise, take thy wife, and thy two daughters that are here, lest thou be consumed in the iniquity of the city.

16But he lingered; and the men laid hold upon his hand, and upon the hand of his wife, and upon the hand of his two daughters, Yahweh being merciful unto him; and they brought him forth, and set him without the city.

17And it came to pass, when they had brought them forth abroad, that he said, Escape for thy life; look not behind thee, neither stay thou in all the Plain; escape to the mountain, lest thou be consumed.

18And Lot said unto them, Oh, not so, my lord:

19behold now, thy servant hath found favor in thy sight, and thou hast magnified thy lovingkindness, which thou hast showed unto me in saving my life; and I cannot escape to the mountain, lest evil overtake me, and I die:

20behold now, this city is near to flee unto, and it is a little one. Oh let me escape thither (is it not a little one?), and my soul shall live.

21And he said unto him, See, I have accepted thee concerning this thing also, that I will not overthrow the city of which thou hast spoken.

22Haste thee, escape thither; for I cannot do anything till thou be come thither. Therefore the name of the city was called Zoar.

23The sun was risen upon the earth when Lot came unto Zoar.

24Then Yahweh rained upon Sodom and upon Gomorrah brimstone and fire from Yahweh out of heaven;

25and he overthrew those cities, and all the Plain, and all the inhabitants of the cities, and that which grew upon the ground.

26But his wife looked back from behind him, and she became a pillar of salt.

27And Abraham gat up early in the morning to the place where he had stood before Yahweh:

28and he looked toward Sodom and Gomorrah, and toward all the land of the Plain, and beheld, and, lo, the smoke of the land went up as the smoke of a furnace.

29And it came to pass, when God destroyed the cities of the Plain, that God remembered Abraham, and sent Lot out of the midst of the overthrow, when he overthrew the cities in which Lot dwelt.

30And Lot went up out of Zoar, and dwelt in the mountain, and his two daughters with him; for he feared to dwell in Zoar: and he dwelt in a cave, he and his two daughters.

31And the first-born said unto the younger, Our father is old, and there is not a man in the earth to come in unto us after the manner of all the earth:

32come, let us make our father drink wine, and we will lie with him, that we may preserve seed of our father.

33And they made their father drink wine that night: and the first-born went in, and lay with her father; and he knew not when she lay down, nor when she arose.

34And it came to pass on the morrow, that the first-born said unto the younger, Behold, I lay yesternight with my father: let us make him drink wine this night also; and go thou in, and lie with him, that we may preserve seed of our father.

35And they made their father drink wine that night also: and the younger arose, and lay with him; and he knew not when she lay down, nor when she arose.

36Thus were both the daughters of Lot with child by their father.

37And the first-born bare a son, and called his name Moab: the same is the father of the Moabites unto this day.

38And the younger, she also bare a son, and called his name Ben-ammi: the same is the father of the children of Ammon unto this day.

Chapter 20

1And Abraham journeyed from thence toward the land of the South, and dwelt between Kadesh and Shur. And he sojourned in Gerar.

2And Abraham said of Sarah his wife, She is my sister. And Abimelech king of Gerar sent, and took Sarah.

3But God came to Abimelech in a dream of the night, and said to him, Behold, thou art but a dead man, because of the woman whom thou hast taken. For she is a man's wife.

4Now Abimelech had not come near her. And he said, Lord, wilt thou slay even a righteous nation?

5Said he not himself unto me, She is my sister? And she, even she herself said, He is my brother. In the integrity of my heart and the innocency of my hands have I done this.

6And God said unto him in the dream, Yea, I know that in the integrity of thy heart thou has done this, and I also withheld thee from sinning against me. Therefore suffered I thee not to touch her.

7Now therefore restore the man's wife. For he is a prophet, and he shall pray for thee, and thou shalt live. And if thou restore her not, know thou that thou shalt surely die, thou, and all that are thine.

8And Abimelech rose early in the morning, and called all his servants, and told all these things in their ear. And the men were sore afraid.

9Then Abimelech called Abraham, and said unto him, What hast thou done unto us? And wherein have I sinned against thee, that thou hast brought on me and on my kingdom a great sin? Thou hast done deeds unto me that ought not to be done.

10And Abimelech said unto Abraham, What sawest thou, that thou hast done this thing?

11And Abraham said, Because I thought, Surely the fear of God is not in this place. And they will slay me for my wife's sake.

12And moreover she is indeed my sister, the daughter of my father, but not the daughter of my mother; and she became my wife.

13and it came to pass, when God caused me to wander from my father's house, that I said unto her, This is thy kindness which thou shalt show unto me. At every place whither we shall come, say of me, He is my brother.

14And Abimelech took sheep and oxen, and men-servants and women-servants, and gave them unto Abraham, and restored him Sarah his wife.

15And Abimelech said, Behold, my land is before thee. Dwell where it pleaseth thee.

16And unto Sarah he said, Behold, I have given thy brother a thousand pieces of silver. Behold, it is for thee a covering of the eyes to all that are with thee. And in respect of all thou art righted.

17And Abraham prayed unto God. And God healed Abimelech, and his wife, and his maid-servants. And they bare children.

18For Yahweh had fast closed up all the wombs of the house of Abimelech, because of Sarah, Abraham's wife.

Chapter 21

1And Yahweh visited Sarah as he had said, and Yahweh did unto Sarah as he had spoken.

2And Sarah conceived, and bare Abraham a son in his old age, at the set time of which God had spoken to him.

3And Abraham called the name of his son that was born unto him, whom Sarah bare to him, Isaac.

4And Abraham circumcised his son Isaac when he was eight days old, as God had commanded him.

5And Abraham was a hundred years old, when his son Isaac was born unto him.

6And Sarah said, God hath made me to laugh. Every one that heareth will laugh with me.

7And she said, Who would have said unto Abraham, that Sarah should give children suck? For I have borne him a son in his old age.

8And the child grew, and was weaned. And Abraham made a great feast on the day that Isaac was weaned.

9And Sarah saw the son of Hagar the Egyptian, whom she had borne unto Abraham, mocking.

10Wherefore she said unto Abraham, Cast out this handmaid and her son. For the son of this handmaid shall not be heir with my son, even with Isaac.

11And the thing was very grievous in Abraham's sight on account of his son.

12And God said unto Abraham, Let it not be grievous in thy sight because of the lad, and because of thy handmaid. In all that Sarah saith unto thee, hearken unto her voice. For in Isaac shall thy seed be called.

13And also of the son of the handmaid will I make a nation, because he is thy seed.

14And Abraham rose up early in the morning, and took bread and a bottle of water, and gave it unto Hagar, putting it on her shoulder, and gave her the child, and sent her away. And she departed, and wandered in the wilderness of Beer-sheba.

15And the water in the bottle was spent, and she cast the child under one of the shrubs.

16And she went, and sat her down over against him a good way off, as it were a bowshot. For she said, Let me not look upon the death of the child. And she sat over against him, and lifted up her voice, and wept.

17And God heard the voice of the lad. And the angel of God called to Hagar out of heaven, and said unto her, What aileth thee, Hagar? Fear not. For God hath heard the voice of the lad where he is.

18Arise, lift up the lad, and hold him in thy hand. For I will make him a great nation.

19And God opened her eyes, and she saw a well of water. And she went, and filled the bottle with water, and gave the lad drink.

20And God was with the lad, and he grew. And he dwelt in the wilderness, and became, as he grew up, an archer.

21And he dwelt in the wilderness of Paran. And his mother took him a wife out of the land of Egypt.

22And it came to pass at that time, that Abimelech and Phicol the captain of his host spake unto Abraham, saying, God is with thee in all that thou doest.

23Now therefore swear unto me here by God that thou wilt not deal falsely with me, nor with my son, nor with my son's son. But according to the kindness that I have done unto thee, thou shalt do unto me, and to the land wherein thou hast sojourned.

24And Abraham said, I will swear.

25And Abraham reproved Abimelech because of the well of water, which Abimelech's servants had violently taken away.

26And Abimelech said, I know not who hath done this thing. Neither didst thou tell me, neither yet heard I of it, but to-day.

27And Abraham took sheep and oxen, and gave them unto Abimelech. And they two made a covenant.

28And Abraham set seven ewe lambs of the flock by themselves.

29And Abimelech said unto Abraham, What mean these seven ewe lambs which thou hast set by themselves?

30And he said, These seven ewe lambs shalt thou take of my hand, that it may be a witness unto me, that I have digged this well.

31Wherefore he called that place Beer-sheba. Because there they sware both of them.

32So they made a covenant at Beer-sheba. And Abimelech rose up, and Phicol the captain of his host, and they returned into the land of the Philistines.

33And Abraham planted a tamarisk tree in Beer-sheba, and called there on the name of Yahweh, the Everlasting God.

34And Abraham sojourned in the land of the Philistines many days.

Chapter 22

1And it came to pass after these things, that God did prove Abraham, and said unto him, Abraham. And he said, Here am I.

2And he said, Take now thy son, thine only son, whom thou lovest, even Isaac, and get thee into the land of Moriah. And offer him there for a burnt-offering upon one of the mountains which I will tell thee of.

3And Abraham rose early in the morning, and saddled his ass, and took two of his young men with him, and Isaac his son. And he clave the wood for the burnt-offering, and rose up, and went unto the place of which God had told him.

4On the third day Abraham lifted up his eyes, and saw the place afar off.

5And Abraham said unto his young men, Abide ye here with the ass, and I and the lad will go yonder; and we will worship, and come again to you.

6And Abraham took the wood of the burnt-offering, and laid it upon Isaac his son. And he took in his hand the fire and the knife. And they went both of

Genesis

them together.

7And Isaac spake unto Abraham his father, and said, My father. And he said, Here am I, my son. And he said, Behold, the fire and the wood. But where is the lamb for a burnt-offering?

8And Abraham said, God will provide himself the lamb for a burnt-offering, my son. So they went both of them together.

9And they came to the place which God had told him of. And Abraham built the altar there, and laid the wood in order, and bound Isaac his son, and laid him on the altar, upon the wood.

10And Abraham stretched forth his hand, and took the knife to slay his son.

11And the angel of Yahweh called unto him out of heaven, and said, Abraham, Abraham. And he said, Here I am.

12And he said, Lay not thy hand upon the lad, neither do thou anything unto him. For now I know that thou fearest God, seeing thou hast not withheld thy son, thine only son, from me.

13And Abraham lifted up his eyes, and looked, and behold, behind him a ram caught in the thicket by his horns. And Abraham went and took the ram, and offered him up for a burnt-offering in the stead of his son.

14And Abraham called the name of that place Yahweh-jireh. As it is said to this day, In the mount of Yahweh it shall be provided.

15And the angel of Yahweh called unto Abraham a second time out of heaven,

16and said, By myself have I sworn, saith Yahweh, because thou hast done this thing, and hast not withheld thy son, thine only son,

17that in blessing I will bless thee, and in multiplying I will multiply thy seed as the stars of the heavens, and as the sand which is upon the seashore. And thy seed shall possess the gate of his enemies.

18And in thy seed shall all the nations of the earth be blessed. Because thou hast obeyed my voice.

19So Abraham returned unto his young men, and they rose up and went together to Beer-sheba. And Abraham dwelt at Beer-sheba.

20And it came to pass after these things, that it was told Abraham, saying, Behold, Milcah, she also hath borne children unto they brother Nahor.

21Uz his first-born, and Buz his brother, and Kemuel the father of Aram.

22And Chesed, and Hazo, and Pildash, and Jidlaph, and Bethuel.

23And Bethuel begat Rebekah. These eight did Milcah bear to Nahor, Abraham's brother.

24And his concubine, whose name was Reumah, she also bare Tebah, and Gaham, and Tahash, and Maacah.

Chapter 23

1And the life of Sarah was a hundred and seven and twenty years. These were the years of the life of Sarah.

2And Sarah died in Kiriath-arba (the same is Hebron), in the land of Canaan. And Abraham came to mourn for Sarah, and to weep for her.

3And Abraham rose up from before his dead, and spake unto the children of Heth, saying,

4I am a stranger and a sojourner with you. Give me a possession of a burying-place with you, that I may bury my dead out of my sight.

5And the children of Heth answered Abraham, saying unto him,

6Hear us, my lord. Thou art a prince of God among us. In the choice of our sepulchres bury thy dead. None of us shall withhold from thee his sepulchre, but that thou mayest bury thy dead.

7And Abraham rose up, and bowed himself to the people of the land, even to the children of Heth.

8And he communed with them, saying, If it be your mind that I should bury my dead out of my sight, hear me, and entreat for me to Ephron the son of Zohar,

9that he may give me the cave of Machpelah, which he hath, which is in the end of his field. For the full price let him give it to me in the midst of you for a possession of a burying-place.

10Now Ephron was sitting in the midst of the children of Heth. And Ephron the Hittite answered Abraham in the audience of the children of Heth, even of all that went in at the gate of his city, saying,

11Nay, my lord, hear me. The field give I thee, and the cave that is therein, I give it thee. In the presence of the children of my people give I it thee. Bury thy dead.

12And Abraham bowed himself down before the people of the land.

13And he spake unto Ephron in the audience of the people of the land, saying, But if thou wilt, I pray thee, hear me. I will give the price of the field. Take it of me, and I will bury my dead there.

14And Ephron answered Abraham, saying unto him,

15My lord, hearken unto me. A piece of land worth four hundred shekels of silver, what is that betwixt me and thee? Bury therefore thy dead.

16And Abraham hearkened unto Ephron. And Abraham weighed to Ephron the silver which he had named in the audience of the children of Heth, four hundred shekels of silver, current money with the merchant.

17So the field of Ephron, which was in Machpelah, which was before Mamre, the field, and the cave which was therein, and all the trees that were in the field, that were in all the border thereof round about, were made sure

18unto Abraham for a possession in the presence of the children of Heth, before all that went in at the gate of his city.

19And after this, Abraham buried Sarah his wife in the cave of the field of Machpelah before Mamre (the same is Hebron), in the land of Canaan.

20And the field, and the cave that is therein, were made sure unto Abraham for a possession of a burying-place by the children of Heth.

Chapter 24

1And Abraham was old, and well stricken in age. And Yahweh had blessed Abraham in all things.

2And Abraham said unto his servant, the elder of his house, that ruled over all that he had, Put, I pray thee, thy hand under my thigh.

3And I will make thee swear by Yahweh, the God of heaven and the God of the earth, that thou wilt not take a wife for my son of the daughters of the Canaanites, among whom I dwell.

4But thou shalt go unto my country, and to my kindred, and take a wife for my son Isaac.

5And the servant said unto him, Peradventure the woman will not be willing to follow me unto this land. Must I needs bring thy son again unto the land from whence thou camest?

6And Abraham said unto him, Beware thou that thou bring not my son thither again.

7Yahweh, the God of heaven, who took me from my father's house, and from the land of my nativity, and who spake unto me, and who sware unto me, saying, Unto thy seed will I give this land. He will send his angel before thee, and thou shalt take a wife for my son from thence.

8And if the woman be not willing to follow thee, then thou shalt be clear from this my oath. Only thou shalt not bring my son thither again.

9And the servant put his hand under the thigh of Abraham his master, and sware to him concerning this matter.

10And the servant took ten camels, of the camels of his master, and departed, having all goodly things of his master's in his hand. And he arose, and went to Mesopotamia, unto the city of Nahor.

11And he made the camels to kneel down without the city by the well of water at the time of evening, the time that women go out to draw water.

12And he said, O Yahweh, the God of my master Abraham, send me, I pray thee, good speed this day, and show kindness unto my master Abraham.

13Behold, I am standing by the fountain of water. And the daughters of the men of the city are coming out to draw water.

14And let it come to pass, that the damsel to whom I shall say, Let down thy pitcher, I pray thee, that I may drink. And she shall say, Drink, and I will give thy camels drink also. Let the same be she that thou hast appointed for thy servant Isaac. And thereby shall I know that thou hast showed kindness unto my master.

15And it came to pass, before he had done speaking, that, behold, Rebekah came out, who was born to Bethuel the son of Milcah, the wife of Nahor, Abraham's brother, with her pitcher upon her shoulder.

16And the damsel was very fair to look upon, a virgin, neither had any man known her. And she went down to the fountain, and filled her pitcher, and came up.

17And the servant ran to meet her, and said, Give me to drink, I pray thee, a little water from thy pitcher.

18And she said, Drink, my lord. And she hasted, and let down her pitcher upon her hand, and gave him drink.

19And when she had done giving him drink, she said, I will draw for thy camels also, until they have done drinking.

20And she hasted, and emptied her pitcher into the trough, and ran again unto the well to draw, and drew for all his camels.

21And the man looked stedfastly on her, holding his peace, to know whether Yahweh had made his journey prosperous or not.

22And it came to pass, as the camels had done drinking, that the man took a golden ring of half a shekel weight, and two bracelets for her hands of ten shekels weight of gold,

23and said, Whose daughter art thou? Tell me, I pray thee. Is there room in thy father's house for us to lodge in?

24And she said unto him, I am the daughter of Bethuel the son of Milcah, whom she bare unto Nahor.

25She said moreover unto him, We have both straw and provender enough, and room to lodge in.

26And the man bowed his head, and worshipped Yahweh.

27And he said, Blessed be Yahweh, the God of my master Abraham, who hath not forsaken his lovingkindness and his truth toward my master. As for me, Yahweh hath led me in the way to the house of my master's brethren.

28And the damsel ran, and told her mother's house according to these words.

29And Rebekah had a brother, and his name was Laban: and Laban ran out unto the man, unto the fountain.

30And it came to pass, when he saw the ring, and the bracelets upon his sister's hands, and when he heard the words of Rebekah his sister, saying, Thus spake the man unto me. That he came unto the man. And, behold, he was standing by the camels at the fountain.

31And he said, Come in, thou blessed of Yahweh. Wherefore standest thou without? For I have prepared the house, and room for the camels.

32And the man came into the house, and he ungirded the camels. And he gave straw and provender for the camels, and water to wash his feet and the feet of the men that were with him.

33And there was set food before him to eat. But he said, I will not eat, until I have told mine errand. And he said, Speak on.

34And he said, I am Abraham's servant.

35And Yahweh hath blessed my master greatly. And he is become great. And he hath given him flocks and herds, and silver and gold, and men-servants and maid-servants, and camels and asses.

36And Sarah my master's wife bare a son to my master when she was old. And unto him hath he given all that he hath.

37And my master made me swear, saying, Thou shalt not take a wife for my son of the daughters of the Canaanites, in whose land I dwell.

38But thou shalt go unto my father's house, and to my kindred, and take a wife for my son.

39And I said unto my master, Peradventure the woman will not follow me.

40And he said unto me, Yahweh, before whom I walk, will send his angel with thee, and prosper thy way. And thou shalt take a wife for my son of my kindred, and of my father's house.

41Then shalt thou be clear from my oath, when thou comest to my kindred. And if they give her not to thee, thou shalt be clear from my oath.

42And I came this day unto the fountain, and said, O Yahweh, the God of my master Abraham, if now thou do prosper my way which I go.

43Behold, I am standing by the fountain of water. And let it come to pass, that the maiden that cometh forth to draw, to whom I shall say, Give me, I pray thee, a little water from thy pitcher to drink.

44And she shall say to me, Both drink thou, and I will also draw for thy camels. Let the same be the woman whom Yahweh hath appointed for my master's son.

45And before I had done speaking in my heart, behold, Rebekah came forth with her pitcher on her shoulder. And she went down unto the fountain, and drew. And I said unto her, Let me drink, I pray thee.

46And she made haste, and let down her pitcher from her shoulder, and said, Drink, and I will give thy camels drink also. So I drank, and she made the camels drink also.

47And I asked her, and said, Whose daughter art thou? And she said, The daughter of Bethuel, Nahor's son, whom Milcah bare unto him. And I put the ring upon her nose, and the bracelets upon her hands.

48And I bowed my head, and worshipped Yahweh, and blessed Yahweh, the God of my master Abraham, who had led me in the right way to take my master's brother's daughter for his son.

49And now if ye will deal kindly and truly with my master, tell me. And if not, tell me. That I may turn to the right hand, or to the left.

50Then Laban and Bethuel answered and said, The thing proceedeth from Yahweh. We cannot speak unto thee bad or good.

51Behold, Rebekah is before thee, take her, and go, and let her be thy master's son's wife, as Yahweh hath spoken.

52And it came to pass, that, when Abraham's servant heard their words, he bowed himself down to the earth unto Yahweh.

53And the servant brought forth jewels of silver, and jewels of gold, and raiment, and gave them to Rebekah. He gave also to her brother and to her mother precious things.

54And they did eat and drink, he and the men that were with him, and tarried all night. And they rose up in the morning, and he said, Send me away unto my master.

55And her brother and her mother said, Let the damsel abide with us a few days, at the least ten. After that she shall go.

56And he said unto them, Hinder me not, seeing Yahweh hath prospered my way. Send me away that I may go to my master.

57And they said, We will call the damsel, and inquire at her mouth.

58And they called Rebekah, and said unto her, Wilt thou go with this man? And she said, I will go.

59And they sent away Rebekah their sister, and her nurse, and Abraham's servant, and his men.

60And they blessed Rebekah, and said unto her, Our sister, be thou the mother of thousands of ten thousands, and let thy seed possess the gate of those that hate them.

61And Rebekah arose, and her damsels, and they rode upon the camels, and followed the man. And the servant took Rebekah, and went his way.

62And Isaac came from the way of Beer-lahai-roi. For he dwelt in the land of the South.

63And Isaac went out to meditate in the field at the eventide. And he lifted up his eyes, and saw, and, behold, there were camels coming.

64And Rebekah lifted up her eyes, and when she saw Isaac, she alighted from the camel.

65And she said unto the servant, What man is this that walketh in the field to meet us? And the servant said, It is my master. And she took her veil, and covered herself.

66And the servant told Isaac all the things that he had done.

67And Isaac brought her into his mother Sarah's tent, and took Rebekah, and she became his wife. And he loved her. And Isaac was comforted after his mother's death.

Chapter 25

1And Abraham took another wife, and her name was Keturah.

2And she bare him Zimran, and Jokshan, and Medan, and Midian, and Ishbak, and Shuah.

3And Jokshan begat Sheba, and Dedan. And the sons of Dedan were Asshurim, and Letushim, and Leummim.

4And the sons of Midian: Ephah, and Epher, and Hanoch, and Abida, and Eldaah. All these were the children of Keturah.

5And Abraham gave all that he had unto Isaac.

6But unto the sons of the concubines, that Abraham had, Abraham gave gifts. And he sent them away from Isaac his son, while he yet lived, eastward, unto the east country.

7And these are the days of the years of Abraham's life which he lived, a hundred threescore and fifteen years.

8And Abraham gave up the ghost, and died in a good old age, an old man, and full of years, and was gathered to his people.

9And Isaac and Ishmael his sons buried him in the cave of Machpelah, in the field of Ephron the son of Zohar the Hittite, which is before Mamre.

10The field which Abraham purchased of the children of Heth. There was Abraham buried, and Sarah his wife.

11And it came to pass after the death of Abraham, that God blessed Isaac his son. And Isaac dwelt by Beer-lahai-roi.

12Now these are the generations of Ishmael, Abraham's son, whom Hagar the Egyptian, Sarah's handmaid, bare unto Abraham.

13And these are the names of the sons of Ishmael, by their names, according to their generations: the first-born of Ishmael, Nebaioth, and Kedar, and Adbeel, and Mibsam,

14And Mishma, and Dumah, and Massa,

15Hadad, and Tema, Jetur, Naphish, and Kedemah.

16These are the sons of Ishmael, and these are their names, by their villages, and by their encampments. Twelve princes according to their nations.

17And these are the years of the life of Ishmael, a hundred and thirty and seven years. And he gave up the ghost and died, and was gathered unto his people.

18And they dwelt from Havilah unto Shur that is before Egypt, as thou goest toward Assyria. He abode over against all his brethren.

19And these are the generations of Isaac, Abraham's son. Abraham begat Isaac.

20And Isaac was forty years old when he took Rebekah, the daughter of Bethuel the Syrian of Paddan-aram, the sister of Laban the Syrian, to be his wife.

21And Isaac entreated Yahweh for his wife, because she was barren. And Yahweh was entreated of him, and Rebekah his wife conceived.

22And the children struggled together within her. And she said, If it be so, wherefore do I live? And she went to inquire of Yahweh.

23And Yahweh said unto her,
Two nations are in thy womb,
And two peoples shall be separated from thy bowels.
And the one people shall be stronger than the other people.
And the elder shall serve the younger.

24And when her days to be delivered were fulfilled, behold, there were twins in her womb.

25And the first came forth red, all over like a hairy garment. And they called his name Esau.

26And after that came forth his brother, and his hand had hold on Esau's heel. And his name was called Jacob. And Isaac was threescore years old when she bare them.

27And the boys grew. And Esau was a skilful hunter, a man of the field. And Jacob was a quiet man, dwelling in tents.

28Now Isaac loved Esau, because he did eat of his venison. And Rebekah loved Jacob.

29And Jacob boiled pottage. And Esau came in from the field, and he was faint.

30And Esau said to Jacob, Feed me, I pray thee, with that same red pottage. For I am faint. Therefore was his name called Edom.

31And Jacob said, Sell me first thy birthright.

32And Esau said, Behold, I am about to die. And what profit shall the birthright do to me?

33And Jacob said, Swear to me first. And he sware unto him. And he sold his birthright unto Jacob.

34And Jacob gave Esau bread and pottage of lentils. And he did eat and drink, and rose up, and went his way. So Esau despised his birthright.

Chapter 26

1And there was a famine in the land, besides the first famine that was in the days of Abraham. And Isaac went unto Abimelech king of the Philistines, unto Gerar.

2And Yahweh appeared unto him, and said, Go not down into Egypt. Dwell in the land which I shall tell thee of.

3Sojourn in this land, and I will be with thee, and will bless thee. For unto thee, and unto thy seed, I will give all these lands, and I will establish the oath which I sware unto Abraham thy father.

4And I will multiply thy seed as the stars of heaven, and will give unto thy seed all these lands. And in thy seed shall all the nations of the earth be blessed.

5Because that Abraham obeyed my voice, and kept my charge, my commandments, my statutes, and my laws.

6And Isaac dwelt in Gerar.

7And the men of the place asked him of his wife. And he said, She is my sister. For he feared to say, My wife. Lest, said he, the men of the place should kill me for Rebekah. Because she was fair to look upon.

8And it came to pass, when he had been there a long time, that Abimelech king of the Philistines looked out at a window, and saw, and, behold, Isaac was sporting with Rebekah his wife.

9And Abimelech called Isaac, and said, Behold, of a surety she is thy wife. And how saidst thou, She is my sister? And Isaac said unto him, Because I said, Lest I die because of her.

10And Abimelech said, What is this thou hast done unto us? One of the people might easily have lain with thy wife, and thou wouldest have brought guiltiness upon us.

11And Abimelech charged all the people, saying, He that toucheth this man or his wife shall surely be put to death.

12And Isaac sowed in that land, and found in the same year a hundredfold. And Yahweh blessed him.

13And the man waxed great, and grew more and more until he became very great.

14And he had possessions of flocks, and possessions of herds, and a great household. And the Philistines envied him.

15Now all the wells which his father's servants had digged in the days of Abraham his father, the Philistines had stopped, and filled with earth.

16And Abimelech said unto Isaac, Go from us. For thou art much mightier than we.

17And Isaac departed thence, and encamped in the valley of Gerar, and

Genesis

dwelt there.

18And Isaac digged again the wells of water, which they had digged in the days of Abraham his father. For the Philistines had stopped them after the death of Abraham. And he called their names after the names by which his father had called them.

19And Isaac's servants digged in the valley, and found there a well of springing water.

20And the herdsmen of Gerar strove with Isaac's herdsmen, saying, The water is ours. And he called the name of the well Esek, because they contended with him.

21And they digged another well, and they strove for that also. And he called the name of it Sitnah.

22And he removed from thence, and digged another well. And for that they strove not. And he called the name of it Rehoboth. And he said, For now Yahweh hath made room for us, and we shall be fruitful in the land.

23And he went up from thence to Beer-sheba.

24And Yahweh appeared unto him the same night, and said, I am the God of Abraham thy father. Fear not, for I am with thee, and will bless thee, and multiply thy seed for my servant Abraham's sake.

25And he builded an altar there, and called upon the name of Yahweh, and pitched his tent there. And there Isaac's servants digged a well.

26Then Abimelech went to him from Gerar, and Ahuzzath his friend, and Phicol the captain of his host.

27And Isaac said unto them, Wherefore are ye come unto me, seeing ye hate me, and have sent me away from you?

28And they said, We saw plainly that Yahweh was with thee. And we said, Let there now be an oath betwixt us, even betwixt us and thee, and let us make a covenant with thee,

29that thou wilt do us no hurt, as we have not touched thee, and as we have done unto thee nothing but good, and have sent thee away in peace. Thou art now the blessed of Yahweh.

30And he made them a feast, and they did eat and drink.

31And they rose up betimes in the morning, and sware one to another. And Isaac sent them away, and they departed from him in peace.

32And it came to pass the same day, that Isaac's servants came, and told him concerning the well which they had digged, and said unto him, We have found water.

33And he called it Shibah. Therefore the name of the city is Beer-sheba unto this day.

34And when Esau was forty years old he took to wife Judith the daughter of Beeri the Hittite, and Basemath the daughter of Elon the Hittite.

35And they were a grief of mind unto Isaac and to Rebekah.

Chapter 27

1And it came to pass, that when Isaac was old, and his eyes were dim, so that he could not see, he called Esau his elder son, and said unto him, My son. And he said unto him, Here am I.

2And he said, Behold now, I am old, I know not the day of my death.

3Now therefore take, I pray thee, thy weapons, thy quiver and thy bow, and go out to the field, and take me venison.

4And make me savory food, such as I love, and bring it to me, that I may eat. That my soul may bless thee before I die.

5And Rebekah heard when Isaac spake to Esau his son. And Esau went to the field to hunt for venison, and to bring it.

6And Rebekah spake unto Jacob her son, saying, Behold, I heard thy father speak unto Esau thy brother, saying,

7Bring me venison, and make me savory food, that I may eat, and bless thee before Yahweh before my death.

8Now therefore, my son, obey my voice according to that which I command thee.

9Go now to the flock, and fetch me from thence two good kids of the goats. And I will make them savory food for thy father, such as he loveth.

10And thou shalt bring it to thy father, that he may eat, so that he may bless thee before his death.

11And Jacob said to Rebekah his mother, Behold, Esau my brother is a hairy man, and I am a smooth man.

12My father peradventure will feel me, and I shall seem to him as a deceiver. And I shall bring a curse upon me, and not a blessing.

13And his mother said unto him, Upon me be thy curse, my son. Only obey my voice, and go fetch me them.

14And he went, and fetched, and brought them to his mother. And his mother made savory food, such as his father loved.

15And Rebekah took the goodly garments of Esau her elder son, which were with her in the house, and put them upon Jacob her younger son.

16And she put the skins of the kids of the goats upon his hands, and upon the smooth of his neck.

17And she gave the savory food and the bread, which she had prepared, into the hand of her son Jacob.

18And he came unto his father, and said, My father. And he said, Here am I. Who art thou, my son?

19And Jacob said unto his father, I am Esau thy first-born; I have done according as thou badest me: arise, I pray thee, sit and eat of my venison, that thy soul may bless me.

20And Isaac said unto his son, How is it that thou hast found it so quickly, my son? And he said, Because Yahweh thy God sent me good speed.

21And Isaac said unto Jacob, Come near, I pray thee, that I may feel thee, my son, whether thou be my very son Esau or not.

22And Jacob went near unto Isaac his father. And he felt him, and said, The voice is Jacob's voice, but the hands are the hands of Esau.

23And he discerned him not, because his hands were hairy, as his brother Esau's hands. So he blessed him.

24And he said, Art thou my very son Esau? And he said, I am.

25And he said, Bring it near to me, and I will eat of my son's venison, that my soul may bless thee. And he brought it near to him, and he did eat. And he brought him wine, and he drank.

26And his father Isaac said unto him, Come near now, and kiss me, my son.

27And he came near, and kissed him. And he smelled the smell of his raiment, and blessed him, and said,

See, the smell of my son
Is as the smell of a field which Yahweh hath blessed.
28And God give thee of the dew of heaven,
And of the fatness of the earth,
And plenty of grain and new wine.
29Let peoples serve thee,
And nations bow down to thee.
Be lord over thy brethren,
And let thy mother's sons bow down to thee.
Cursed be every one that curseth thee,
And blessed be every one that blesseth thee.

30And it came to pass, as soon as Isaac had made an end of blessing Jacob, and Jacob was yet scarce gone out from the presence of Isaac his father, that Esau his brother came in from his hunting.

31And he also made savory food, and brought it unto his father. And he said unto his father, Let my father arise, and eat of his son's venison, that thy soul may bless me.

32And Isaac his father said unto him, Who art thou? And he said, I am thy son, thy first-born, Esau.

33And Isaac trembled very exceedingly, and said, Who then is he that hath taken venison, and brought it me, and I have eaten of all before thou camest, and have blessed him? Yea, and he shall be blessed.

34When Esau heard the words of his father, he cried with an exceeding great and bitter cry, and said unto his father, Bless me, even me also, O my father.

35And he said, Thy brother came with guile, and hath taken away thy blessing.

36And he said, Is not he rightly name Jacob? for he hath supplanted me these two time. He took away my birthright. And, behold, now he hath taken away my blessing. And he said, Hast thou not reserved a blessing for me?

37And Isaac answered and said unto Esau, Behold, I have made him thy lord, and all his brethren have I given to him for servants. And with grain and new wine have I sustained him. And what then shall I do for thee, my son?

38And Esau said unto his father, Hast thou but one blessing, my father? Bless me, even me also, O my father. And Esau lifted up his voice, and wept.

39And Isaac his father answered and said unto him,
Behold, of the fatness of the earth shall be thy dwelling,
And of the dew of heaven from above.
40And by thy sword shalt thou live, and thou shalt serve thy brother.
And it shall come to pass, when thou shalt break loose,
That thou shalt shake his yoke from off thy neck.

41And Esau hated Jacob because of the blessing wherewith his father blessed him. And Esau said in his heart, The days of mourning for my father are at hand. Then will I slay my brother Jacob.

42And the words of Esau her elder son were told to Rebekah. And she sent and called Jacob her younger son, and said unto him, Behold, thy brother Esau, as touching thee, doth comfort himself, purposing to kill thee.

43Now therefore, my son, obey my voice. And arise, flee thou to Laban my brother to Haran.

44And tarry with him a few days, until thy brother's fury turn away.

45Until thy brother's anger turn away from thee, and he forget that which thou hast done to him. Then I will send, and fetch thee from thence. Why should I be bereaved of you both in one day?

46And Rebekah said to Isaac, I am weary of my life because of the daughters of Heth. If Jacob take a wife of the daughters of Heth, such as these, of the daughters of the land, what good shall my life do me?

Chapter 28

1And Isaac called Jacob, and blessed him, and charged him, and said unto him, Thou shalt not take a wife of the daughters of Canaan.

2Arise, go to Paddan-aram, to the house of Bethuel thy mother's father. And take thee a wife from thence of the daughters of Laban thy mother's brother.

3And God Almighty bless thee, and make thee fruitful, and multiply thee, that thou mayest be a company of peoples.

4And give thee the blessing of Abraham, to thee, and to thy seed with thee. That thou mayest inherit the land of thy sojournings, which God gave unto Abraham.

5And Isaac sent away Jacob. And he went to Paddan-aram unto Laban, son of Bethuel the Syrian, the brother of Rebekah, Jacob's and Esau's mother.

6Now Esau saw that Isaac had blessed Jacob and sent him away to Paddan-aram, to take him a wife from thence. And that as he blessed him he gave him a charge, saying, Thou shalt not take a wife of the daughters of Canaan.

7And that Jacob obeyed his father and his mother, and was gone to Paddan-aram.

8And Esau saw that the daughters of Canaan pleased not Isaac his father.

9And Esau went unto Ishmael, and took, besides the wives that he had, Mahalath the daughter of Ishmael Abraham's son, the sister of Nebaioth, to be his wife.

10And Jacob went out from Beer-sheba, and went toward Haran.

11And he lighted upon a certain place, and tarried there all night, because the sun was set. And he took one of the stones of the place, and put it under his head, and lay down in that place to sleep.

¹²And he dreamed. And behold, a ladder set up on the earth, and the top of it reached to heaven. And behold, the angels of God ascending and descending on it.

¹³And, behold, Yahweh stood above it, and said, I am Yahweh, the God of Abraham thy father, and the God of Isaac. The land whereon thou liest, to thee will I give it, and to thy seed.

¹⁴And thy seed shall be as the dust of the earth, and thou shalt spread abroad to the west, and to the east, and to the north, and to the south. And in thee and in thy seed shall all the families of the earth be blessed.

¹⁵And, behold, I am with thee, and will keep thee, whithersoever thou goest, and will bring thee again into this land. For I will not leave thee, until I have done that which I have spoken to thee of.

¹⁶And Jacob awaked out of his sleep, and he said, Surely Yahweh is in this place. And I knew it not.

¹⁷And he was afraid, and said, How dreadful is this place! This is none other than the house of God, and this is the gate of heaven.

¹⁸And Jacob rose up early in the morning, and took the stone that he had put under his head, and set it up for a pillar, and poured oil upon the top of it.

¹⁹And he called the name of that place Beth-el. But the name of the city was Luz at the first.

²⁰And Jacob vowed a vow, saying, If God will be with me, and will keep me in this way that I go, and will give me bread to eat, and raiment to put on,

²¹so that I come again to my father's house in peace, and Yahweh will be my God,

²²then this stone, which I have set up for a pillar, shall be God's house. And of all that thou shalt give me I will surely give the tenth unto thee.

Chapter 29

¹Then Jacob went on his journey, and came to the land of the children of the east.

²And he looked, and behold, a well in the field, and, lo, three flocks of sheep lying there by it. For out of that well they watered the flocks. And the stone upon the well's mouth was great.

³And thither were all the flocks gathered. And they rolled the stone from the well's mouth, and watered the sheep, and put the stone again upon the well's mouth in its place.

⁴And Jacob said unto them, My brethren, whence are ye? And they said, Of Haran are we.

⁵And he said unto them, Know ye Laban the son of Nahor? And they said, We know him.

⁶And he said unto them, Is it well with him? And they said, It is well. And, behold, Rachel his daughter cometh with the sheep.

⁷And he said, Lo, it is yet high day, neither is it time that the cattle should be gathered together. Water ye the sheep, and go and feed them.

⁸And they said, We cannot, until all the flocks be gathered together, and they roll the stone from the well's mouth. Then we water the sheep.

⁹While he was yet speaking with them, Rachel came with her father's sheep. For she kept them.

¹⁰And it came to pass, when Jacob saw Rachel the daughter of Laban his mother's brother, and the sheep of Laban his mother's brother, that Jacob went near, and rolled the stone from the well's mouth, and watered the flock of Laban his mother's brother.

¹¹And Jacob kissed Rachel, and lifted up his voice, and wept.

¹²And Jacob told Rachel that he was her father's brother, and that he was Rebekah's son. And she ran and told her father.

¹³And it came to pass, when Laban heard the tidings of Jacob his sister's son, that he ran to meet him, and embraced him, and kissed him, and brought him to his house. And he told Laban all these things.

¹⁴And Laban said to him, Surely thou art my bone and my flesh. And he abode with him the space of a month.

¹⁵And Laban said unto Jacob, Because thou art my brother, shouldest thou therefore serve me for nought? Tell me, what shall thy wages be?

¹⁶And Laban had two daughters. The name of the elder was Leah, and the name of the younger was Rachel.

¹⁷And Leah's eyes were tender. But Rachel was beautiful and well favored.

¹⁸And Jacob loved Rachel. And he said, I will serve thee seven years for Rachel thy younger daughter.

¹⁹And Laban said, It is better that I give her to thee, than that I should give her to another man. Abide with me.

²⁰And Jacob served seven years for Rachel. And they seemed unto him but a few days, for the love he had to her.

²¹And Jacob said unto Laban, Give me my wife, for my days are fulfilled, that I may go in unto her.

²²And Laban gathered together all the men of the place, and made a feast.

²³And it came to pass in the evening, that he took Leah his daughter, and brought her to him. And he went in unto her.

²⁴And Laban gave Zilpah his handmaid unto his daughter Leah for a handmaid.

²⁵And it came to pass in the morning that, behold, it was Leah. And he said to Laban, What is this thou hast done unto me? Did not I serve with thee for Rachel? Wherefore then hast thou beguiled me?

²⁶And Laban said, It is not so done in our place, to give the younger before the first-born.

²⁷Fulfil the week of this one, and we will give thee the other also for the service which thou shalt serve with me yet seven other years.

²⁸And Jacob did so, and fulfilled her week. And he gave her Rachel his daughter to wife.

²⁹And Laban gave to Rachel his daughter Bilhah his handmaid to be her handmaid.

³⁰And he went in also unto Rachel, and he loved also Rachel more than Leah, and served with him yet seven other years.

³¹And Yahweh saw that Leah was hated, and he opened her womb. But Rachel was barren.

³²And Leah conceived, and bare a son, and she called his name Reuben. For she said, Because Yahweh hath looked upon my affliction. For now my husband will love me.

³³And she conceived again, and bare a son: and said, Because Yahweh hath heard that I am hated, he hath therefore given me this son also. And she called his name Simeon.

³⁴And she conceived again, and bare a son. And said, Now this time will my husband be joined unto me, because I have borne him three sons. Therefore was his name called Levi.

³⁵And she conceived again, and bare a son. And she said, This time will I praise Yahweh. Therefore she called his name Judah. And she left off bearing.

Chapter 30

¹And when Rachel saw that she bare Jacob no children, Rachel envied her sister; and she said unto Jacob, Give me children, or else I die.

²And Jacob's anger was kindled against Rachel: and he said, Am I in God's stead, who hath withheld from thee the fruit of the womb?

³And she said, Behold, my maid Bilhah, go in unto her; that she may bear upon my knees, and I also may obtain children by her.

⁴And she gave him Bilhah her handmaid to wife: and Jacob went in unto her.

⁵And Bilhah conceived, and bare Jacob a son.

⁶And Rachel said, God hath judged me, and hath also heard my voice, and hath given me a son: therefore called she his name Dan.

⁷And Bilhah Rachel's handmaid conceived again, and bare Jacob a second son.

⁸And Rachel said, With mighty wrestlings have I wrestled with my sister, and have prevailed: and she called his name Naphtali.

⁹When Leah saw that she had left off bearing, she took Zilpah her handmaid, and gave her to Jacob to wife.

¹⁰And Zilpah Leah's handmaid bare Jacob a son.

¹¹And Leah said, Fortunate! and she called his name Gad.

¹²And Zilpah Leah's handmaid bare Jacob a second son.

¹³And Leah said, Happy am I! for the daughters will call me happy: and she called his name Asher.

¹⁴And Reuben went in the days of wheat harvest, and found mandrakes in the field, and brought them unto his mother Leah. Then Rachel said to Leah, Give me, I pray thee, of thy son's mandrakes.

¹⁵And she said unto her, Is it a small matter that thou hast taken away my husband? and wouldest thou take away my son's mandrakes also? And Rachel said, Therefore he shall lie with thee to-night for thy son's mandrakes.

¹⁶And Jacob came from the field in the evening, and Leah went out to meet him, and said, Thou must come in unto me; for I have surely hired thee with my son's mandrakes. And he lay with her that night.

¹⁷And God hearkened unto Leah, and she conceived, and bare Jacob a fifth son.

¹⁸And Leah said, God hath given me my hire, because I gave my handmaid to my husband: and she called his name Issachar.

¹⁹And Leah conceived again, and bare a sixth son to Jacob.

²⁰And Leah said, God hath endowed me with a good dowry; now will my husband dwell with me, because I have borne him six sons: and she called his name Zebulun.

²¹And afterwards she bare a daughter, and called her name Dinah.

²²And God remembered Rachel, and God hearkened to her, and opened her womb.

²³And she conceived, and bare a son: and said, God hath taken away my reproach:

²⁴and she called his name Joseph, saying, Yahweh add to me another son.

²⁵And it came to pass, when Rachel had borne Joseph, that Jacob said unto Laban, Send me away, that I may go unto mine own place, and to my country.

²⁶Give me my wives and my children for whom I have served thee, and let me go: for thou knowest my service wherewith I have served thee.

²⁷And Laban said unto him, If now I have found favor in thine eyes, tarry: for I have divined that Yahweh hath blessed me for thy sake.

²⁸And he said, Appoint me thy wages, and I will give it.

²⁹And he said unto him, Thou knowest how I have served thee, and how thy cattle have fared with me.

³⁰For it was little which thou hadst before I came, and it hath increased unto a multitude; and Yahweh hath blessed thee whithersoever I turned: and now when shall I provide for mine own house also?

³¹And he said, What shall I give thee? And Jacob said, Thou shalt not give me aught: if thou wilt do this thing for me, I will again feed thy flock and keep it.

³²I will pass through all thy flock to-day, removing from thence every speckled and spotted one, and every black one among the sheep, and the spotted and speckled among the goats: and of such shall be my hire.

³³So shall my righteousness answer for me hereafter, when thou shalt come concerning my hire that is before thee: every one that is not speckled and spotted among the goats, and black among the sheep, that if found with me, shall be counted stolen.

³⁴And Laban said, Behold, I would it might be according to thy word.

³⁵And he removed that day the he-goats that were ringstreaked and spotted, and all the she-goats that were speckled and spotted, every one that had white in it, and all the black ones among the sheep, and gave them into the hand of his sons;

³⁶and he set three days' journey betwixt himself and Jacob: and Jacob fed

Genesis

the rest of Laban's flocks.

37And Jacob took him rods of fresh poplar, and of the almond and of the plane-tree. And peeled white streaks in them, and made the white appear which was in the rods.

38And he set the rods which he had peeled over against the flocks in the gutters in the watering-troughs where the flocks came to drink; and they conceived when they came to drink.

39And the flocks conceived before the rods, and the flocks brought forth ringstreaked, speckled, and spotted.

40And Jacob separated the lambs, and set the faces of the flocks toward the ringstreaked and all the black in the flock of Laban: and he put his own droves apart, and put them not unto Laban's flock.

41And it came to pass, whensoever the stronger of the flock did conceive, that Jacob laid the rods before the eyes of the flock in the gutters, that they might conceive among the rods;

42but when the flock were feeble, he put them not in: so the feebler were Laban's, and the stronger Jacob's.

43And the man increased exceedingly, and had large flocks, and maid-servants and men-servants, and camels and asses.

Chapter 31

1And he heard the words of Laban's sons, saying, Jacob hath taken away all that was our father's; and of that which was our father's hath he gotten all this glory.

2And Jacob beheld the countenance of Laban, and, behold, it was not toward him as beforetime.

3And Yahweh said unto Jacob, Return unto the land of thy fathers, and to thy kindred; and I will be with thee.

4And Jacob sent and called Rachel and Leah to the field unto his flock,

5and said unto them, I see your father's countenance, that it is not toward me as beforetime; but the God of my father hath been with me.

6And ye know that will all my power I have served your father.

7And your father hath deceived me, and changed my wages ten times; but God suffered him not to hurt me.

8If he said thus, The speckled shall be thy wages; then all the flock bare speckled: and if he said thus, The ringstreaked shall be thy wages; then bare all the flock ringstreaked.

9Thus God hath taken away the cattle of your father, and given them to me.

10And it came to pass at the time that the flock conceive, that I lifted up mine eyes, and saw in a dream, and, behold, the he-goats which leaped upon the flock were ringstreaked, speckled, and grizzled.

11And the angel of God said unto me in the dream, Jacob: and I said, Here am I.

12And he said, Lift up now thine eyes, and see, all the he-goats which leap upon the flock are ringstreaked, speckled, and grizzled: for I have seen all that Laban doeth unto thee.

13I am the God of Beth-el, where thou anointedst a pillar, where thou vowedst a vow unto me: now arise, get thee out from this land, and return unto the land of thy nativity.

14And Rachel and Leah answered and said unto him, Is there yet any portion or inheritance for us in our father's house?

15Are we not accounted by him as foreigners? for he hath sold us, and hath also quite devoured our money.

16For all the riches which God hath taken away from our father, that is ours and our children's: now then, whatsoever God hath said unto thee, do.

17Then Jacob rose up, and set his sons and his wives upon the camels;

18and he carried away all his cattle, and all his substance which he had gathered, the cattle of his getting, which he had gathered in Paddan-aram, to go to Isaac his father unto the land of Canaan.

19Now Laban was gone to shear his sheep: and Rachel stole the teraphim that were her father's.

20And Jacob stole away unawares to Laban the Syrian, in that he told him not that he fled.

21So he fled with all that he had; and he rose up, and passed over the River, and set his face toward the mountain of Gilead.

22And it was told Laban on the third day that Jacob was fled.

23And he took his brethren with him, and pursued after him seven days' journey; and he overtook him in the mountain of Gilead.

24And God came to Laban the Syrian in a dream of the night, and said unto him, Take heed to thyself that thou speak not to Jacob either good or bad.

25And Laban came up with Jacob. Now Jacob had pitched his tent in the mountain: and Laban with his brethren encamped in the mountain of Gilead.

26And Laban said to Jacob, What hast thou done, that thou hast stolen away unawares to me, and carried away my daughters as captives of the sword?

27Wherefore didst thou flee secretly, and steal away from me, and didst not tell me, that I might have sent thee away with mirth and with songs, with tabret and with harp;

28and didst not suffer me to kiss my sons and my daughters? now hast thou done foolishly.

29It is in the power of my hand to do you hurt: but the God of your father spake unto me yesternight, saying, Take heed to thyself that thou speak not to Jacob either good or bad.

30And now, though thou wouldest needs be gone, because thou sore longedst after thy father's house, yet wherefore hast thou stolen my gods?

31And Jacob answered and said to Laban, Because I was afraid: for I said, Lest thou shouldest take thy daughters from me by force.

32With whomsoever thou findest thy gods, he shall not live: before our brethren discern thou what is thine with me, and take it to thee. For Jacob knew not that Rachel had stolen them.

33And Laban went into Jacob's tent, and into Leah's tent, and into the tent of the two maid-servants; but he found them not. And he went out of Leah's tent, and entered into Rachel's tent.

34Now Rachel had taken the teraphim, and put them in the camel's saddle, and sat upon them. And Laban felt about all the tent, but found them not.

35And she said to her father, Let not my lord be angry that I cannot rise up before thee; for the manner of women is upon me. And he searched, but found not the teraphim.

36And Jacob was wroth, and chode with Laban: and Jacob answered and said to Laban, What is my trespass? what is my sin, that thou hast hotly pursued after me?

37Whereas thou hast felt about all my stuff, what hast thou found of all thy household stuff? Set it here before my brethren and thy brethren, that they may judge betwixt us two.

38These twenty years have I been with thee; thy ewes and thy she-goats have not cast their young, and the rams of thy flocks have I not eaten.

39That which was torn of beasts I brought not unto thee; I bare the loss of it; of my hand didst thou require it, whether stolen by day or stolen by night.

40Thus I was; in the day the drought consumed me, and the frost by night; and my sleep fled from mine eyes.

41These twenty years have I been in thy house; I served thee fourteen years for thy two daughters, and six years for thy flock: and thou hast changed my wages ten times.

42Except the God of my father, the God of Abraham, and the Fear of Isaac, had been with me, surely now hadst thou sent me away empty. God hath seen mine affliction and the labor of my hands, and rebuked thee yesternight.

43And Laban answered and said unto Jacob, The daughters are my daughters, and the children are my children, and the flocks are my flocks, and all that thou seest is mine: and what can I do this day unto these my daughters, or unto their children whom they have borne?

44And now come, let us make a covenant, I and thou; and let it be for a witness between me and thee.

45And Jacob took a stone, and set it up for a pillar.

46And Jacob said unto his brethren, Gather stones; and they took stones, and made a heap: and they did eat there by the heap.

47And Laban called it Jegar-saha-dutha: but Jacob called it Galeed.

48And Laban said, This heap is witness between me and thee this day. Therefore was the name of it called Galeed:

49and Mizpah, for he said, Yahweh watch between me and thee, when we are absent one from another.

50If thou shalt afflict my daughters, and if thou shalt take wives besides my daughters, no man is with us; see, God is witness betwixt me and thee.

51And Laban said to Jacob, Behold this heap, and behold the pillar, which I have set betwixt me and thee.

52This heap be witness, and the pillar be witness, that I will not pass over this heap to thee, and that thou shalt not pass over this heap and this pillar unto me, for harm.

53The God of Abraham, and the God of Nahor, the God of their father, judge betwixt us. And Jacob sware by the Fear of his father Isaac.

54And Jacob offered a sacrifice in the mountain, and called his brethren to eat bread: and they did eat bread, and tarried all night in the mountain.

55And early in the morning Laban rose up, and kissed his sons and his daughters, and blessed them: and Laban departed and returned unto his place.

Chapter 32

1And Jacob went on his way, and the angels of God met him.

2And Jacob said when he saw them, This is God's host: and he called the name of that place Mahanaim.

3And Jacob sent messengers before him to Esau his brother unto the land of Seir, the field of Edom.

4And he commanded them, saying, Thus shall ye say unto my lord Esau: Thus saith thy servant Jacob, I have sojourned with Laban, and stayed until now:

5and I have oxen, and asses, and flocks, and men-servants, and maid-servants: and I have sent to tell my lord, that I may find favor in thy sight.

6And the messengers returned to Jacob, saying, We came to thy brother Esau, and moreover he cometh to meet thee, and four hundred men with him.

7Then Jacob was greatly afraid and was distressed: and he divided the people that were with him, and the flocks, and the herds, and the camels, into two companies;

8and he said, If Esau come to the one company, and smite it, then the company which is left shall escape.

9And Jacob said, O God of my father Abraham, and God of my father Isaac, O Yahweh, who saidst unto me, Return unto thy country, and to thy kindred, and I will do thee good:

10I am not worthy of the least of all the lovingkindnesses, and of all the truth, which thou hast showed unto thy servant; for with my staff I passed over this Jordan; and now I am become two companies.

11Deliver me, I pray thee, from the hand of my brother, from the hand of Esau: for I fear him, lest he come and smite me, the mother with the children.

12And thou saidst, I will surely do thee good, and make thy seed as the sand of the sea, which cannot be numbered for multitude.

13And he lodged there that night, and took of that which he had with him a present for Esau his brother:

14two hundred she-goats and twenty he-goats, two hundred ewes and twenty rams,

15thirty milch camels and their colts, forty cows and ten bulls, twenty she-asses and ten foals.

16And he delivered them into the hand of his servants, every drove by itself, and said unto his servants, Pass over before me, and put a space betwixt drove and drove.

17And he commanded the foremost, saying, When Esau my brother meeteth thee, and asketh thee, saying, Whose art thou? and whither goest thou? and whose are these before thee?

18then thou shalt say They are thy servant Jacob's; it is a present sent unto my lord Esau: and, behold, he also is behind us.

19And he commanded also the second, and the third, and all that followed the droves, saying, On this manner shall ye speak unto Esau, when ye find him;

20and ye shall say, Moreover, behold, thy servant Jacob is behind us. For he said, I will appease him with the present that goeth before me, and afterward I will see his face; peradventure he will accept me.

21So the present passed over before him: and he himself lodged that night in the company.

22And he rose up that night, and took his two wives, and his two handmaids, and his eleven children, and passed over the ford of the Jabbok.

23And he took them, and sent them over the stream, and sent over that which he had.

24And Jacob was left alone; and there wrestled a man with him until the breaking of the day.

25And when he saw that he prevailed not against him, he touched the hollow of his thigh; and the hollow of Jacob's thigh was strained, as he wrestled with him.

26And he said, Let me go, for the day breaketh. And he said, I will not let thee go, except thou bless me.

27And he said unto him, What is thy name? And he said, Jacob.

28And he said, Thy name shall be called no more Jacob, but Israel: for thou hast striven with God and with men, and hast prevailed.

29And Jacob asked him, and said, Tell me, I pray thee, thy name. And he said, Wherefore is it that thou dost ask after my name? And he blessed him there.

30And Jacob called the name of the place Peniel: for, said he, I have seen God face to face, and my life is preserved.

31And the sun rose upon him as he passed over Penuel, and he limped upon his thigh.

32Therefore the children of Israel eat not the sinew of the hip which is upon the hollow of the thigh, unto this day: because he touched the hollow of Jacob's thigh in the sinew of the hip.

Chapter 33

1And Jacob lifted up his eyes, and looked, and, behold, Esau was coming, and with him four hundred men. And he divided the children unto Leah, and unto Rachel, and unto the two handmaids.

2And he put the handmaids and their children foremost, and Leah and her children after, and Rachel and Joseph hindermost.

3And he himself passed over before them, and bowed himself to the ground seven times, until he came near to his brother.

4And Esau ran to meet him, and embraced him, and fell on his neck, and kissed him: and they wept.

5And he lifted up his eyes, and saw the women and the children; and said, Who are these with thee? And he said, The children whom God hath graciously given thy servant.

6Then the handmaids came near, they and their children, and they bowed themselves.

7And Leah also and her children came near, and bowed themselves: and after came Joseph near and Rachel, and they bowed themselves.

8And he said, What meanest thou by all this company which I met? And he said, To find favor in the sight of my lord.

9And Esau said, I have enough, my brother; let that which thou hast be thine.

10And Jacob said, Nay, I pray thee, if now I have found favor in thy sight, then receive my present at my hand; forasmuch as I have seen thy face, as one seeth the face of God, and thou wast pleased with me.

11Take, I pray thee, my gift that is brought to thee; because God hath dealt graciously with me, and because I have enough. And he urged him, and he took it.

12And he said, Let us take our journey, and let us go, and I will go before thee.

13And he said unto him, My lord knoweth that the children are tender, and that the flocks and herds with me have their young: and if they overdrive them one day, all the flocks will die.

14Let my lord, I pray thee, pass over before his servant: and I will lead on gently, according to the pace of the cattle that are before me and according to the pace of the children, until I come unto my lord unto Seir.

15And Esau said, Let me now leave with thee some of the folk that are with me. And he said, What needeth it? let me find favor in the sight of my lord.

16So Esau returned that day on his way unto Seir.

17And Jacob journeyed to Succoth, and built him a house, and made booths for his cattle: therefore the name of the place is called Succoth.

18And Jacob came in peace to the city of Shechem, which is in the land of Canaan, when he came from Paddan-aram; and encamped before the city.

19And he bought the parcel of ground, where he had spread his tent, at the hand of the children of Hamor, Shechem's father, for a hundred pieces of money.

20And he erected there an altar, and called it El-elohe-israel.

Chapter 34

1And Dinah the daughter of Leah, whom she bare unto Jacob, went out to see the daughters of the land.

2And Shechem the son of Hamor the Hivite, the prince of the land, saw her; And he took her, and lay with her, and humbled her.

3And his soul clave unto Dinah the daughter of Jacob, and he loved the damsel, and spake kindly unto the damsel.

4And Shechem spake unto his father Hamor, saying, Get me this damsel to wife.

5Now Jacob heard that he had defiled Dinah his daughter; and his sons were with his cattle in the field: and Jacob held his peace until they came.

6And Hamor the father of Shechem went out unto Jacob to commune with him.

7And the sons of Jacob came in from the field when they heard it: and the men were grieved, and they were very wroth, because he had wrought folly in Israel in lying with Jacob's daughter; which thing ought not to be done.

8And Hamor communed with them, saying, The soul of my son Shechem longeth for your daughter: I pray you, give her unto him to wife.

9And make ye marriages with us; give your daughters unto us, and take our daughters unto you.

10And ye shall dwell with us: and the land shall be before you; dwell and trade ye therein, and get you possessions therein.

11And Shechem said unto her father and unto her brethren, Let me find favor in your eyes, and what ye shall say unto me I will give.

12Ask me never so much dowry and gift, and I will give according as ye shall say unto me: but give me the damsel to wife.

13And the sons of Jacob answered Shechem and Hamor his father with guile, and spake, because he had defiled Dinah their sister,

14and said unto them, We cannot do this thing, to give our sister to one that is uncircumcised; for that were a reproach unto us.

15Only on this condition will we consent unto you: if ye will be as we are, that every male of you be circumcised;

16then will we give our daughters unto you, and we will take your daughters to us, and we will dwell with you, and we will become one people.

17But if ye will not hearken unto us, to be circumcised; then will we take our daughter, and we will be gone.

18And their words pleased Hamor, and Shechem Hamor's son.

19And the young man deferred not to do the thing, because he had delight in Jacob's daughter: and he was honored above all the house of his father.

20And Hamor and Shechem his son came unto the gate of their city, and communed with the men of their city, saying,

21These men are peaceable with us; therefore let them dwell in the land, and trade therein; for, behold, the land is large enough for them; let us take their daughters to us for wives, and let us give them our daughters.

22Only on this condition will the men consent unto us to dwell with us, to become one people, if every male among us be circumcised, as they are circumcised.

23Shall not their cattle and their substance and all their beasts be ours? only let us consent unto them, and they will dwell with us.

24And unto Hamor and unto Shechem his son hearkened all that went out of the gate of his city; and every male was circumcised, all that went out of the gate of his city.

25And it came to pass on the third day, when they were sore, that two of the sons of Jacob, Simeon and Levi, Dinah's brethren, took each man his sword, and came upon the city unawares, and slew all the males.

26And they slew Hamor and Shechem his son with the edge of the sword, and took Dinah out of Shechem's house, and went forth.

27The sons of Jacob came upon the slain, and plundered the city, because they had defiled their sister.

28They took their flocks and their herds and their asses, and that which was in the city, and that which was in the field;

29and all their wealth, and all their little ones and their wives, took they captive and made a prey, even all that was in the house.

30And Jacob said to Simeon and Levi, Ye have troubled me, to make me odious to the inhabitants of the land, among the Canaanites and the Perizzites: and, I being few in number, they will gather themselves together against me and smite me; and I shall be destroyed, I and my house.

31And they said, Should he deal with our sister as with a harlot?

Chapter 35

1And God said unto Jacob, Arise, go up to Beth-el, and dwell there: and make there an altar unto God, who appeared unto thee when thou fleddest from the face of Esau thy brother.

2Then Jacob said unto his household, and to all that were with him, Put away the foreign gods that are among you, and purify yourselves, and change your garments:

3and let us arise, and go up to Beth-el; and I will make there an altar unto God, who answered me in the day of my distress, and was with me in the way which I went.

4And they gave unto Jacob all the foreign gods which were in their hand, and the rings which were in their ears; and Jacob hid them under the oak which was by Shechem.

5And they journeyed: and a terror of God was upon the cities that were round about them, and they did not pursue after the sons of Jacob.

6So Jacob came to Luz, which is in the land of Canaan (the same is Beth-el), he and all the people that were with him.

7And he built there an altar, and called the place El-beth-el; because there God was revealed unto him, when he fled from the face of his brother.

8And Deborah Rebekah's nurse died, and she was buried below Beth-el under the oak: and the name of it was called Allon-bacuth.

9And God appeared unto Jacob again, when he came from Paddan-aram, and blessed him.

10And God said unto him, Thy name is Jacob: thy name shall not be called any more Jacob, but Israel shall be thy name: and he called his name Israel.

11And God said unto him, I am God Almighty: be fruitful and multiply; a nation and a company of nations shall be of thee, and kings shall come out of thy loins;

12and the land which I gave unto Abraham and Isaac, to thee I will give it, and to thy seed after thee will I give the land.

13And God went up from him in the place where he spake with him.

14And Jacob set up a pillar in the place where he spake with him, a pillar of stone: and he poured out a drink-offering thereon, and poured oil thereon.

15And Jacob called the name of the place where God spake with him, Beth-el.

16And they journeyed from Beth-el; and there was still some distance to come to Ephrath: and Rachel travailed, and she had hard labor.

17And it came to pass, when she was in hard labor, that the midwife said unto her, Fear not; for now thou shalt have another son.

18And it came to pass, as her soul was departing (for she died), that she called his name Ben-oni: but his father called him Benjamin.

19And Rachel died, and was buried in the way to Ephrath (the same is Beth-lehem).

20And Jacob set up a pillar upon her grave: the same is the Pillar of Rachel's grave unto this day.

21And Israel journeyed, and spread his tent beyond the tower of Eder.

22And it came to pass, while Israel dwelt in that land, that Reuben went and lay with Bilhah his father's concubine: and Israel heard of it.

Now the sons of Jacob were twelve:

23The sons of Leah: Reuben, Jacob's first-born, and Simeon, and Levi, and Judah, and Issachar, and Zebulun;

24the sons of Rachel: Joseph and Benjamin;

25and the sons of Bilhah, Rachel's handmaid: Dan and Naphtali;

26and the sons of Zilpah, Leah's handmaid: Gad and Asher: these are the sons of Jacob, that were born to him in Paddan-aram.

27And Jacob came unto Isaac his father to Mamre, to Kiriath-arba (the same is Hebron), where Abraham and Isaac sojourned.

28And the days of Isaac were a hundred and fourscore years.

29And Isaac gave up the ghost, and died, and was gathered unto his people, old and full of days: and Esau and Jacob his sons buried him.

Chapter 36

1Now these are the generations of Esau (the same is Edom).

2Esau took his wives of the daughters of Canaan: Adah the daughter of Elon the Hittite, and Oholibamah the daughter of Anah, the daughter of Zibeon the Hivite,

3and Basemath Ishmael's daughter, sister of Nebaioth.

4And Adah bare to Esau Eliphaz; and Basemath bare Reuel;

5and Oholibamah bare Jeush, and Jalam, and Korah: these are the sons of Esau, that were born unto him in the land of Canaan.

6And Esau took his wives, and his sons, and his daughters, and all the souls of his house, and his cattle, and all his beasts, and all his possessions, which he had gather in the land of Canaan; and went into a land away from his brother Jacob.

7For their substance was too great for them to dwell together; and the land of their sojournings could not bear them because of their cattle.

8And Esau dwelt in mount Seir: Esau is Edom.

9And these are the generations of Esau the father of the Edomites in mount Seir:

10these are the names of Esau's sons: Eliphaz the son of Adah the wife of Esau, Reuel the son of Basemath the wife of Esau.

11And the sons of Eliphaz were Teman, Omar, Zepho, and Gatam, and Kenaz.

12And Timna was concubine to Eliphaz Esau's son; and she bare to Eliphaz Amalek: these are the sons of Adah, Esau's wife.

13And these are the sons of Reuel: Nahath, and Zerah, Shammah, and Mizzah: these were the sons of Basemath, Esau's wife.

14And these were the sons of Oholibamah the daughter of Anah, the daughter of Zibeon, Esau's wife: and she bare to Esau Jeush, and Jalam, and Korah.

15These are the chiefs of the sons of Esau: the sons of Eliphaz the first-born of Esau: chief Teman, chief Omar, chief Zepho, chief Kenaz,

16chief Korah, chief Gatam, chief Amalek: these are the chiefs that came of Eliphaz in the land of Edom; these are the sons of Adah.

17And these are the sons of Reuel, Esau's son: chief Nahath, chief Zerah, chief Shammah, chief Mizzah: these are the chiefs that came of Reuel in the land of Edom; these are the sons of Basemath, Esau's wife.

18And these are the sons of Oholibamah, Esau's wife: chief Jeush, chief Jalam, chief Korah: these are the chiefs that came of Oholibamah the daughter of Anah, Esau's wife.

19These are the sons of Esau, and these are their chiefs: the same is Edom.

20These are the sons of Seir the Horite, the inhabitants of the land: Lotan and Shobal and Zibeon and Anah,

21and Dishon and Ezer and Dishan: these are the chiefs that came of the Horites, the children of Seir in the land of Edom.

22And the children of Lotan were Hori and Heman. And Lotan's sister was Timna.

23And these are the children of Shobal: Alvan and Manahath and Ebal, Shepho and Onam.

24And these are the children of Zibeon: Aiah and Anah; this is Anah who found the hot springs in the wilderness, as he fed the asses of Zibeon his father.

25And these are the children of Anah: Dishon and Oholibamah the daughter of Anah.

26And these are the children of Dishon: Hemdan and Eshban and Ithran and Cheran.

27These are the children of Ezer: Bilhan and Zaavan and Akan.

28These are the children of Dishan: Uz and Aran.

29These are the chiefs that came of the Horites: chief Lotan, chief Shobal, chief Zibeon, chief Anah,

30chief Dishon, chief Ezer, chief Dishan: these are the chiefs that came of the Horites, according to their chiefs in the land of Seir.

31And these are the kings that reigned in the land of Edom, before there reigned any king over the children of Israel.

32And Bela the son of Beor reigned in Edom; and the name of his city was Dinhabah.

33And Bela died, and Jobab the son of Zerah of Bozrah reigned in his stead.

34And Jobab died, and Husham of the land of the Temanites reigned in his stead.

35And Husham died, and Hadad the son of Bedad, who smote Midian in the field of Moab, reigned in his stead: and the name of his city was Avith.

36And Hadad died, and Samlah of Masrekah reigned in his stead.

37And Samlah died, and Shaul of Rehoboth by the River reigned in his stead.

38And Shaul died, and Baal-hanan the son of Achbor reigned in his stead.

39And Baal-hanan the son of Achbor died, and Hadar reigned in his stead: and the name of his city was Pau; and his wife's name was Mehetabel, the daughter of Matred, the daughter of Me-zahab.

40And these are the names of the chiefs that came of Esau, according to their families, after their places, by their names: chief Timna, chief Alvah, chief Jetheth,

41chief Oholibamah, chief Elah, chief Pinon,

42chief Kenaz, chief Teman, chief Mibzar,

43chief Magdiel, chief Iram: these are the chiefs of Edom, according to their habitations in the land of their possession. This is Esau, the father of the Edomites.

Chapter 37

1And Jacob dwelt in the land of his father's sojournings, in the land of Canaan.

2These are the generations of Jacob. Joseph, being seventeen years old, was feeding the flock with his brethren; and he was a lad with the sons of Bilhah, and with the sons of Zilpah, his father's wives: and Joseph brought the evil report of them unto their father.

3Now Israel loved Joseph more than all his children, because he was the son of his old age: and he made him a coat of many colors.

4And his brethren saw that their father loved him more than all his brethren; and they hated him, and could not speak peaceably unto him.

5And Joseph dreamed a dream, and he told it to his brethren: and they hated him yet the more.

6And he said unto them, Hear, I pray you, this dream which I have dreamed:

7for, behold, we were binding sheaves in the field, and, lo, my sheaf arose, and also stood upright; and, behold, your sheaves came round about, and made obeisance to my sheaf.

8And his brethren said to him, Shalt thou indeed reign over us? Or shalt thou indeed have dominion over us? And they hated him yet the more for his dreams, and for his words.

9And he dreamed yet another dream, and told it to his brethren, and said, Behold, I have dreamed yet a dream: and, behold, the sun and the moon and eleven stars made obeisance to me.

10And he told it to his father, and to his brethren; and his father rebuked him, and said unto him, What is this dream that thou hast dreamed? Shall I and thy mother and thy brethren indeed come to bow down ourselves to thee to the earth?

11And his brethren envied him; but his father kept the saying in mind.

12And his brethren went to feed their father's flock in Shechem.

13And Israel said unto Joseph, Are not thy brethren feeding the flock in Shechem? Come, and I will send thee unto them. And he said to him, Here am I.

14And he said to him, Go now, see whether it is well with thy brethren, and well with the flock; and bring me word again. So he sent him out of the vale of Hebron, and he came to Shechem.

15And a certain man found him, and, behold, he was wandering in the field: and the man asked him, saying, What seekest thou?

16And he said, I am seeking my brethren: tell me, I pray thee, where they are feeding the flock.

17And the man said, They are departed hence; for I heard them say, Let us go to Dothan. And Joseph went after his brethren, and found them in Dothan.

18And they saw him afar off, and before he came near unto them, they conspired against him to slay him.

19And they said one to another, Behold, this dreamer cometh.

20Come now therefore, and let us slay him, and cast him into one of the pits, and we will say, And evil beast hath devoured him: and we shall see what will become of his dreams.

21And Reuben heard it, and delivered him out of their hand, and said, Let us not take his life.

22And Reuben said unto them, Shed no blood; cast him into this pit that is in the wilderness, but lay no hand upon him: that he might deliver him out of their hand, to restore him to his father.

23And it came to pass, when Joseph was come unto his brethren, that they stripped Joseph of his coat, the coat of many colors that was on him;

24and they took him, and cast him into the pit: and the pit was empty, there was no water in it.

25And they sat down to eat bread: and they lifted up their eyes and looked, and, behold, a caravan of Ishmaelites was coming from Gilead, with their camels bearing spicery and balm and myrrh, going to carry it down to Egypt.

26And Judah said unto his brethren, What profit is it if we slay our brother and conceal his blood?

27Come, and let us sell him to the Ishmaelites, and let not our hand be upon him; for he is our brother, our flesh. And his brethren hearkened unto him.

28And there passed by Midianites, merchantmen; and they drew and lifted up Joseph out of the pit, and sold Joseph to the Ishmaelites for twenty pieces of silver. And they brought Joseph into Egypt.

29And Reuben returned unto the pit; and, behold, Joseph was not in the pit; and he rent his clothes.

30And he returned unto his brethren, and said, The child is not; and I, whither shall I go?

31And they took Joseph's coat, and killed a he-goat, and dipped the coat in the blood;

32and they sent the coat of many colors, and they brought it to their father, and said, This have we found: know now whether it is thy son's coat or not.

33And he knew it, and said, It is my son's coat: an evil beast hath devoured him; Joseph is without doubt torn in pieces.

34And Jacob rent his garments, and put sackcloth upon his loins, and mourned for his son many days.

35And all his sons and all his daughters rose up to comfort him; but he refused to be comforted; and he said, For I will go down to Sheol to my son mourning. And his father wept for him.

36And the Midianites sold him into Egypt unto Potiphar, an officer of Pharaoh's, the captain of the guard.

Chapter 38

1And it came to pass at that time, that Judah went down from his brethren, and turned in to a certain Adullamite, whose name was Hirah.

2And Judah saw there a daughter of a certain Canaanite whose name was Shua. And he took her, and went in unto her.

3And she conceived, and bare a son; and he called his name Er.

4And she conceived again, and bare a son; and she called his name Onan.

5And she yet again bare a son, and called his name Shelah: and he was at Chezib, when she bare him.

6And Judah took a wife for Er his first-born, and her name was Tamar.

7And Er, Judah's first-born, was wicked in the sight of Yahweh. And Yahweh slew him.

8And Judah said unto Onan, Go in unto thy brother's wife, and perform the duty of a husband's brother unto her, and raise up seed to thy brother.

9And Onan knew that the seed would not be his; and it came to pass, when he went in unto his brother's wife, that he spilled it on the ground, lest he should give seed to his brother.

10And the thing which he did was evil in the sight of Yahweh: and he slew him also.

11Then said Judah to Tamar his daughter-in-law, Remain a widow in thy father's house, till Shelah my son be grown up; for he said, Lest he also die, like his brethren. And Tamar went and dwelt in her father's house.

12And in process of time Shua's daughter, the wife of Judah, died; and Judah was comforted, and went up unto his sheep-shearers to Timnah, he and his friend Hirah the Adullamite.

13And it was told Tamar, saying, Behold, thy father-in-law goeth up to Timnah to shear his sheep.

14And she put off from her the garments of her widowhood, and covered herself with her veil, and wrapped herself, and sat in the gate of Enaim, which is by the way to Timnah; for she saw that Shelah was grown up, and she was not given unto him to wife.

15When Judah saw her, he thought her to be a harlot; for she had covered her face.

16And he turned unto her by the way, and said, Come, I pray thee, let me come in unto thee: for he knew not that she was his daughter-in-law. And she said, What wilt thou give me, that thou mayest come in unto me?

17And he said, I will send thee a kid of the goats from the flock. And she said, Wilt thou give me a pledge, till thou send it?

18And he said, What pledge shall I give thee? And she said, Thy signet and thy cord, and thy staff that is in thy hand. And he gave them to her, and came in unto her, and she conceived by him.

19And she arose, and went away, and put off her veil from her, and put on the garments of her widowhood.

20And Judah sent the kid of the goats by the hand of his friend the Adullamite, to receive the pledge from the woman's hand: but he found her not.

21Then he asked the men of her place, saying, Where is the prostitute, that was at Enaim by the wayside? And they said, There hath been no prostitute here.

22And he returned to Judah, and said, I have not found her; and also the men of the place said, There hath been no prostitute here.

23And Judah said, Let her take it to her, lest we be put to shame: behold, I sent this kid, and thou hast not found her.

24And it came to pass about three months after, that it was told Judah, saying, Tamar thy daughter-in-law hath played the harlot; and moreover, behold, she is with child by whoredom. And Judah said, Bring her forth, and let her be burnt.

25When she was brought forth, she sent to her father-in-law, saying, By the man, whose these are, am I with child: and she said, Discern, I pray thee, whose are these, the signet, and the cords, and the staff.

26And Judah acknowledged them, and said, She is more righteous than I; forasmuch as I gave her not to Shelah my son. And he knew her again no more.

27And it came to pass in the time of her travail, that, behold, twins were in her womb.

28And it came to pass, when she travailed, that one put out a hand; and the midwife took and bound upon his hand a scarlet thread, saying, This came out first.

29And it came to pass, as he drew back his hand, that, behold, his brother came out: and she said, Wherefore hast thou made a breach for thyself? Therefore his name was called Perez.

30And afterward came out his brother, that had the scarlet thread upon his hand: and his name was called Zerah.

Chapter 39

1And Joseph was brought down to Egypt; and Potiphar, an officer of Pharaoh's, the captain of the guard, an Egyptian, bought him of the hand of the Ishmaelites, that had brought him down thither.

2And Yahweh was with Joseph, and he was a prosperous man; and he was in the house of his master the Egyptian.

3And his master saw that Yahweh was with him, and that Yahweh made all that he did to prosper in his hand.

4And Joseph found favor in his sight, and he ministered unto him: and he made him overseer over his house, and all that he had he put into his hand.

5And it came to pass from the time that he made him overseer in his house, and over all that he had, that Yahweh blessed the Egyptian's house for Joseph's sake; and the blessing of Yahweh was upon all that he had, in the house and in the field.

6And he left all that he had in Joseph's hand; and he knew not aught that was with him, save the bread which he did eat. And Joseph was comely, and well-favored.

7And it came to pass after these things, that his master's wife cast her eyes upon Joseph; and she said, Lie with me.

8But he refused, and said unto his master's wife, Behold, my master knoweth not what is with me in the house, and he hath put all that he hath into my hand:

9he is not greater in this house than I; neither hath he kept back anything from me but thee, because thou art his wife: how then can I do this great wickedness, and sin against God?

10And it came to pass, as she spake to Joseph day by day, that he hearkened not unto her, to lie by her, or to be with her.

11And it came to pass about this time, that he went into the house to do his work; and there was none of the men of the house there within.

12And she caught him by his garment, saying, Lie with me: and he left his garment in her hand, and fled, and got him out.

13And it came to pass, when she saw that he had left his garment in her hand, and was fled forth,

14that she called unto the men of her house, and spake unto them, saying, See, he hath brought in a Hebrew unto us to mock us: he came in unto me to lie with me, and I cried with a loud voice:

15and it came to pass, when he heard that I lifted up my voice and cried, that he left his garment by me, and fled, and got him out.

16And she laid up his garment by her, until his master came home.

17And she spake unto him according to these words, saying, The Hebrew servant, whom thou hast brought unto us, came in unto me to mock me:

18and it came to pass, as I lifted up my voice and cried, that he left his garment by me, and fled out.

19And it came to pass, when his master heard the words of his wife, which she spake unto him, saying, After this manner did thy servant to me; that his wrath was kindled.

20And Joseph's master took him, and put him into the prison, the place where the king's prisoners were bound: and he was there in the prison.

21But Yahweh was with Joseph, and showed kindness unto him, and gave him favor in the sight of the keeper of the prison.

22And the keeper of the prison committed to Joseph's hand all the prisoners that were in the prison; and whatsoever they did there, he was the doer of it.

23The keeper of the prison looked not to anything that was under his hand, because Yahweh was with him; and that which he did, Yahweh made it prosper.

Chapter 40

1And it came to pass after these things, that the butler of the king of Egypt and his baker offended their lord the king of Egypt.

2And Pharaoh was wroth against his two officers, against the chief of the butlers, and against the chief of the bakers.

3And he put them in ward in the house of the captain of the guard, into the prison, the place where Joseph was bound.

4And the captain of the guard charged Joseph with them, and he ministered unto them: and they continued a season in ward.

5And they dreamed a dream both of them, each man his dream, in one night, each man according to the interpretation of his dream, the butler and the baker of the king of Egypt, who were bound in the prison.

6And Joseph came in unto them in the morning, and saw them, and, behold, they were sad.

7And he asked Pharaoh's officers that were with him in ward in his master's house, saying, Wherefore look ye so sad to-day?

8And they said unto him, We have dreamed a dream, and there is none that can interpret it. And Joseph said unto them, Do not interpretations belong to God? tell it me, I pray you.

9And the chief butler told his dream to Joseph, and said to him, In my dream, behold, a vine was before me;

10and in the vine were three branches: and it was as though it budded, and its blossoms shot forth; and the clusters thereof brought forth ripe grapes:

11and Pharaoh's cup was in my hand; and I took the grapes, and pressed them into Pharaoh's cup, and I gave the cup into Pharaoh's hand.

12And Joseph said unto him, This is the interpretation of it: the three branches are three days;

13within yet three days shall Pharaoh lift up thy head, and restore thee unto

Genesis

thine office: and thou shalt give Pharaoh's cup into his hand, after the former manner when thou wast his butler.

14But have me in thy remembrance when it shall be well with thee, and show kindness, I pray thee, unto me, and make mention of me unto Pharaoh, and bring me out of this house:

15for indeed I was stolen away out of the land of the Hebrews: and here also have I done nothing that they should put me into the dungeon.

16When the chief baker saw that the interpretation was good, he said unto Joseph, I also was in my dream, and, behold, three baskets of white bread were on my head:

17and in the uppermost basket there was of all manner of baked food for Pharaoh; and the birds did eat them out of the basket upon my head.

18And Joseph answered and said, This is the interpretation thereof: the three baskets are three days;

19within yet three days shall Pharaoh lift up thy head from off thee, and shall hang thee on a tree; and the birds shall eat thy flesh from off thee.

20And it came to pass the third day, which was Pharaoh's birthday, that he made a feast unto all his servants: and he lifted up the head of the chief butler and the head of the chief baker among his servants.

21And he restored the chief butler unto his butlership again; and he gave the cup into Pharaoh's hand:

22but he hanged the chief baker: as Joseph had interpreted to them.

23Yet did not the chief butler remember Joseph, but forgat him.

Chapter 41

1And it came to pass at the end of two full years, that Pharaoh dreamed: and, behold, he stood by the river.

2And, behold, there came up out of the river seven kine, well-favored and fat-fleshed; and they fed in the reed-grass.

3And, behold, seven other kine came up after them out of the river, ill-favored and lean-fleshed, and stood by the other kine upon the brink of the river.

4And the ill-favored and lean-fleshed kine did eat up the seven well-favored and fat kine. So Pharaoh awoke.

5And he slept and dreamed a second time: and, behold, seven ears of grain came up upon one stalk, rank and good.

6And, behold, seven ears, thin and blasted with the east wind, sprung up after them.

7And the thin ears swallowed up the seven rank and full ears. And Pharaoh awoke, and, behold, it was a dream.

8And it came to pass in the morning that his spirit was troubled; and he sent and called for all the magicians of Egypt, and all the wise men thereof: and Pharaoh told them his dream; but there was none that could interpret them unto Pharaoh.

9Then spake the chief butler unto Pharaoh, saying, I do remember my faults this day:

10Pharaoh was wroth with his servants, and put me in ward in the house of the captain of the guard, me and the chief baker:

11and we dreamed a dream in one night, I and he; we dreamed each man according to the interpretation of his dream.

12And there was with us there a young man, a Hebrew, servant to the captain of the guard; and we told him, and he interpreted to us our dreams; to each man according to his dream he did interpret.

13And it came to pass, as he interpreted to us, so it was; me he restored unto mine office, and him he hanged.

14Then Pharaoh sent and called Joseph, and they brought him hastily out of the dungeon: and he shaved himself, and changed his raiment, and came in unto Pharaoh.

15And Pharaoh said unto Joseph, I have dreamed a dream, and there is none that can interpret it: and I have heard say of thee, that when thou hearest a dream thou canst interpret it.

16And Joseph answered Pharaoh, saying, It is not in me: God will give Pharaoh an answer of peace.

17And Pharaoh spake unto Joseph, In my dream, behold, I stood upon the brink of the river:

18and, behold, there came up out of the river seven kine, fat-fleshed and well-favored: and they fed in the reed-grass:

19and, behold, seven other kine came up after them, poor and very ill-favored and lean-fleshed, such as I never saw in all the land of Egypt for badness:

20and the lean and ill-favored kine did eat up the first seven fat kine:

21and when they had eaten them up, it could not be known that they had eaten them; but they were still ill-favored, as at the beginning. So I awoke.

22And I saw in my dream, and, behold, seven ears came up upon one stalk, full and good:

23and, behold, seven ears, withered, thin, and blasted with the east wind, sprung up after them:

24and the thin ears swallowed up the seven good ears: and I told it unto the magicians; but there was none that could declare it to me.

25And Joseph said unto Pharaoh, The dream of Pharaoh is one: what God is about to do he hath declared unto Pharaoh.

26The seven good kine are seven years; and the seven good ears are seven years: the dream is one.

27And the seven lean and ill-favored kine that came up after them are seven years, and also the seven empty ears blasted with the east wind; they shall be seven years of famine.

28That is the thing which I spake unto Pharaoh: what God is about to do he hath showed unto Pharaoh.

29Behold, there come seven years of great plenty throughout all the land of Egypt:

30and there shall arise after them seven years of famine; and all the plenty shall be forgotten in the land of Egypt; and the famine shall consume the land;

31and the plenty shall not be known in the land by reason of that famine which followeth; for it shall be very grievous.

32And for that the dream was doubled unto Pharaoh, it is because the thing is established by God, and God will shortly bring it to pass.

33Now therefore let Pharaoh look out a man discreet and wise, and set him over the land of Egypt.

34Let Pharaoh do this, and let him appoint overseers over the land, and take up the fifth part of the land of Egypt in the seven plenteous years.

35And let them gather all the food of these good years that come, and lay up grain under the hand of Pharaoh for food in the cities, and let them keep it.

36And the food shall be for a store to the land against the seven years of famine, which shall be in the land of Egypt; that the land perish not through the famine.

37And the thing was good in the eyes of Pharaoh, and in the eyes of all his servants.

38And Pharaoh said unto his servants, Can we find such a one as this, a man in whom the spirit of God is?

39And Pharaoh said unto Joseph, Forasmuch as God hath showed thee all of this, there is none so discreet and wise as thou:

40thou shalt be over my house, and according unto thy word shall all my people be ruled: only in the throne will I be greater than thou.

41And Pharaoh said unto Joseph, See, I have set thee over all the land of Egypt.

42And Pharaoh took off his signet ring from his hand, and put it upon Joseph's hand, and arrayed him in vestures of fine linen, and put a gold chain about his neck;

43and he made him to ride in the second chariot which he had; and they cried before him, Bow the knee: and he set him over all the land of Egypt.

44And Pharaoh said unto Joseph, I am Pharaoh, and without thee shall no man lift up his hand or his foot in all the land of Egypt.

45And Pharaoh called Joseph's name Zaphenath-paneah; and he gave him to wife Asenath, the daughter of Poti-phera priest of On. And Joseph went out over the land of Egypt.

46And Joseph was thirty years old when he stood before Pharaoh king of Egypt. And Joseph went out from the presence of Pharaoh, and went throughout all the land of Egypt.

47And in the seven plenteous years the earth brought forth by handfuls.

48And he gathered up all the food of the seven years which were in the land of Egypt, and laid up the food in the cities: the food of the field, which was round about every city, laid he up in the same.

49And Joseph laid up grain as the sand of the sea, very much, until he left off numbering; for it was without number.

50And unto Joseph were born two sons before the year of famine came, whom Asenath, the daughter of Potiphera priest of On, bare unto him.

51And Joseph called the name of the first-born Manasseh: For, said he, God hath made me forget all my toil, and all my father's house.

52And the name of the second called he Ephraim: For God hath made me fruitful in the land of my affliction.

53And the seven years of plenty, that was in the land of Egypt, came to an end.

54And the seven years of famine began to come, according as Joseph had said: and there was famine in all lands; but in all the land of Egypt there was bread.

55And when all the land of Egypt was famished, the people cried to Pharaoh for bread: and Pharaoh said unto all the Egyptians, Go unto Joseph; what he saith to you, do.

56And the famine was over all the face of the earth: and Joseph opened all the store-houses, and sold unto the Egyptians; and the famine was sore in the land of Egypt.

57And all countries came into Egypt to Joseph to buy grain, because the famine was sore in all the earth.

Chapter 42

1Now Jacob saw that there was grain in Egypt, and Jacob said unto his sons, Why do ye look one upon another?

2And he said, Behold, I have heard that there is grain in Egypt: get you down thither, and buy for us from thence; that we may live, and not die.

3And Joseph's ten brethren went down to buy grain from Egypt.

4But Benjamin, Joseph's brother, Jacob sent not with his brethren; for he said, Lest Peradventure harm befall him.

5And the sons of Israel came to buy among those that came: for the famine was in the land of Canaan.

6And Joseph was the governor over the land; he it was that sold to all the people of the land. And Joseph's brethren came, and bowed down themselves to him with their faces to the earth.

7And Joseph saw his brethren, and he knew them, but made himself strange unto them, and spake roughly with them; and he said unto them, Whence come ye? And they said, From the land of Canaan to buy food.

8And Joseph knew his brethren, but they knew not him.

9And Joseph remembered the dreams which he dreamed of them, and said unto them, Ye are spies; to see the nakedness of the land ye are come.

10And they said unto him, Nay, my lord, but to buy food are thy servants come.

11We are all one man's sons; we are true men, thy servants are no spies.

12And he said unto them, Nay, but to see the nakedness of the land ye are come.

13And they said, We thy servants are twelve brethren, the sons of one man in the land of Canaan; and, behold, the youngest is this day with our father, and one is not.

¹⁴And Joseph said unto them, That is it that I spake unto you, saying, Ye are spies:

¹⁵hereby ye shall be proved: by the life of Pharaoh ye shall not go forth hence, except your youngest brother come hither.

¹⁶Send one of you, and let him fetch your brother, and ye shall be bound, that your words may be proved, whether there be truth in you: or else by the life of Pharaoh surely ye are spies.

¹⁷And he put them all together into ward three days.

¹⁸And Joseph said unto them the third day, This do, and live: for I fear God:

¹⁹if ye be true men, let one of your brethren be bound in your prison-house; but go ye, carry grain for the famine of your houses:

²⁰and bring your youngest brother unto me; so shall your words be verified, and ye shall not die. And they did so.

²¹And they said one to another, We are verily guilty concerning our brother, in that we saw the distress of his soul, when he besought us, and we would not hear; therefore is this distress come upon us.

²²And Reuben answered them, saying, Spake I not unto you, saying, Do not sin against the child; and ye would not hear? therefore also, behold, his blood is required.

²³And they knew not that Joseph understood them; for there was an interpreter between them.

²⁴And he turned himself about from them, and wept; and he returned to them, and spake to them, and took Simeon from among them, and bound him before their eyes.

²⁵Then Joseph commanded to fill their vessels with grain, and to restore every man's money into his sack, and to give them provisions for the way: and thus was it done unto them.

²⁶And they laded their asses with their grain, and departed thence.

²⁷And as one of them opened his sack to give his ass provender in the lodging-place, he espied his money; and, behold, it was in the mouth of his sack.

²⁸And he said unto his brethren, My money is restored; and, lo, it is even in my sack: and their heart failed them, and they turned trembling one to another, saying, What is this that God hath done unto us?

²⁹And they came unto Jacob their father unto the land of Canaan, and told him all that had befallen them, saying,

³⁰The man, the lord of the land, spake roughly with us, and took us for spies of the country.

³¹And we said unto him, We are true men; and we are no spies:

³²we are twelve brethren, sons of our father; one is not, and the youngest is this day with our father in the land of Canaan.

³³And the man, the lord of the land, said unto us, Hereby shall I know that ye are true men: leave one of your brethren with me, and take grain for the famine of your houses, and go your way:

³⁴and bring your youngest brother unto me: then shall I know that ye are no spies, but that ye are true men: so will I deliver you your brother, and ye shall traffic in the land.

³⁵And it came to pass as they emptied their sacks, that, behold, every man's bundle of money was in his sack: and when they and their father saw their bundles of money, they were afraid.

³⁶And Jacob their father said unto them, Me have ye bereaved of my children: Joseph is not, and Simeon is not, and ye will take Benjamin away: all these things are against me.

³⁷And Reuben spake unto his father, saying, Slay my two sons, if I bring him not to thee: deliver him into my hand, and I will bring him to thee again.

³⁸And he said, My son shall not go down with you; for his brother is dead, and he only is left: if harm befall him by the way in which ye go, then will ye bring down my gray hairs with sorrow to Sheol.

Chapter 43

¹And the famine was sore in the land.

²And it came to pass, when they had eaten up the grain which they had brought out of Egypt, their father said unto them, Go again, buy us a little food.

³And Judah spake unto him, saying, The man did solemnly protest unto us, saying, Ye shall not see my face, except your brother be with you.

⁴If thou wilt send our brother with us, we will go down and buy thee food:

⁵but if thou wilt not send him, we will not go down; for the man said unto us, Ye shall not see my face, except your brother be with you.

⁶And Israel said, Wherefore dealt ye so ill with me, as to tell the man whether ye had yet a brother?

⁷And they said, The man asked straitly concerning ourselves, and concerning our kindred, saying, Is your father yet alive? have ye another brother? and we told him according to the tenor of these words: could we in any wise know that he would say, Bring your brother down?

⁸And Judah said unto Israel his father, Send the lad with me, and we will arise and go; that we may live, and not die, both we, and thou, and also our little ones.

⁹I will be surety for him; of my hand shalt thou require him: if I bring him not unto thee, and set him before thee, then let me bear the blame for ever:

¹⁰for except we had lingered, surely we had now returned a second time.

¹¹And their father Israel said unto them, If it be so now, do this: take of the choice fruits of the land in your vessels, and carry down the man a present, a little balm, and a little honey, spicery and myrrh, nuts, and almonds;

¹²and take double money in your hand; and the money that was returned in the mouth of your sacks carry again in your hand; peradventure it was an oversight:

¹³take also your brother, and arise, go again unto the man:

¹⁴and God Almighty give you mercy before the man, that he may release unto you your other brother and Benjamin. And if I be bereaved of my children, I am bereaved.

¹⁵And the men took that present, and they took double money in their hand, and Benjamin; and rose up, and went down to Egypt, and stood before Joseph.

¹⁶And when Joseph saw Benjamin with them, he said to the steward of his house, Bring the men into the house, and slay, and make ready; for the men shall dine with me at noon.

¹⁷And the man did as Joseph bade; and the man brought the men to Joseph's house.

¹⁸And the men were afraid, because they were brought to Joseph's house; and they said, Because of the money that was returned in our sacks at the first time are we brought in; that he may seek occasion against us, and fall upon us, and take us for bondmen, and our asses.

¹⁹And they came near to the steward of Joseph's house, and they spake unto him at the door of the house,

²⁰and said, Oh, my lord, we came indeed down at the first time to buy food:

²¹and it came to pass, when we came to the lodging-place, that we opened our sacks, and, behold, every man's money was in the mouth of his sack, our money in full weight: and we have brought it again in our hand.

²²And other money have we brought down in our hand to buy food: we know not who put our money in our sacks.

²³And he said, Peace be to you, fear not: your God, and the God of your father, hath given you treasure in your sacks: I had your money. And he brought Simeon out unto them.

²⁴And the man brought the men into Joseph's house, and gave them water, and they washed their feet. And he gave their asses provender.

²⁵And they made ready the present against Joseph's coming at noon: for they heard that they should eat bread there.

²⁶And when Joseph came home, they brought him the present which was in their hand into the house, and bowed down themselves to him to the earth.

²⁷And he asked them of their welfare, and said, Is your father well, the old man of whom ye spake? Is he yet alive?

²⁸And they said, Thy servant our father is well, he is yet alive. And they bowed the head, and made obeisance.

²⁹And he lifted up his eyes, and saw Benjamin his brother, his mother's son, and said, Is this your youngest brother, of whom ye spake unto me? And he said, God be gracious unto thee, my son.

³⁰And Joseph made haste; for his heart yearned over his brother: and he sought where to weep; and he entered into his chamber, and wept there.

³¹And he washed his face, and came out; and he refrained himself, and said, Set on bread.

³²And they set on for him by himself, and for them by themselves, and for the Egyptians, that did eat with him, by themselves: because the Egyptians might not eat bread with the Hebrews; for that is an abomination unto the Egyptians.

³³And they sat before him, the first-born according to his birthright, and the youngest according to his youth: and the men marvelled one with another.

³⁴And he took and sent messes unto them from before him: but Benjamin's mess was five times so much as any of theirs. And they drank, and were merry with him.

Chapter 44

¹And he commanded the steward of his house, saying, Fill the men's sacks with food, as much as they can carry, and put every man's money in his sack's mouth.

²And put my cup, the silver cup, in the sack's mouth of the youngest, and his grain money. And he did according to the word that Joseph had spoken.

³As soon as the morning was light, the men were sent away, they and their asses.

⁴And when they were gone out of the city, and were not yet far off, Joseph said unto his steward, Up, follow after the men; and when thou dost overtake them, say unto them, Wherefore have ye rewarded evil for good?

⁵Is not this that in which my lord drinketh? and whereby he indeed divineth? ye have done evil in so doing.

⁶And he overtook them, and he spake unto them these words.

⁷And they said unto him, Wherefore speaketh my lord such words as these? Far be it from thy servants that they should do such a thing.

⁸Behold, the money, which we found in our sacks' mouths, we brought again unto thee out of the land of Canaan: how then should we steal out of thy lord's house silver or gold?

⁹With whomsoever of thy servants it be found, let him die, and we also will be my lord's bondmen.

¹⁰And he said, Now also let it be according unto your words: he with whom it is found shall be my bondman; and ye shall be blameless.

¹¹Then they hasted, and took down every man his sack to the ground, and opened every man his sack.

¹²And he searched, and began at the eldest, and left off at the youngest: and the cup was found in Benjamin's sack.

¹³Then they rent their clothes, and laded every man his ass, and returned to the city.

¹⁴And Judah and his brethren came to Joseph's house; and he was yet there: and they fell before him on the ground.

¹⁵And Joseph said unto them, What deed is this that ye have done? know ye not that such a man as I can indeed divine?

¹⁶And Judah said, What shall we say unto my lord? what shall we speak? or how shall we clear ourselves? God hath found out the iniquity of thy servants: behold, we are my lord's bondmen, both we, and he also in whose hand the cup is found.

¹⁷And he said, Far be it from me that I should do so: the man in whose hand the cup is found, he shall be my bondman; but as for you, get you up in peace unto your father.

Genesis

18Then Judah came near unto him, and said, Oh, my lord, let thy servant, I pray thee, speak a word in my lord's ears, and let not thine anger burn against thy servant; for thou art even as Pharaoh.

19My lord asked his servants, saying, Have ye a father, or a brother?

20And we said unto my lord, We have a father, an old man, and a child of his old age, a little one; and his brother is dead, and he alone is left of his mother; and his father loveth him.

21And thou saidst unto thy servants, Bring him down unto me, that I may set mine eyes upon him.

22And we said unto my lord, The lad cannot leave his father: for if he should leave his father, his father would die.

23And thou saidst unto thy servants, Except your youngest brother come down with you, ye shall see my face no more.

24And it came to pass when we came up unto thy servant my father, we told him the words of my lord.

25And our father said, Go again, buy us a little food.

26And we said, We cannot go down: if our youngest brother be with us, then will we go down: for we may not see the man's face, expect our youngest brother be with us.

27And thy servant my father said unto us, Ye know that my wife bare me two sons:

28and the one went out from me, and I said, Surely he is torn in pieces; and I have not seen him since:

29and if ye take this one also from me, and harm befall him, ye will bring down my gray hairs with sorrow to Sheol.

30Now therefore when I come to thy servant my father, and the lad is not with us; seeing that his life is bound up in the lad's life;

31it will come to pass, when he seeth that the lad is not with us, that he will die: and thy servants will bring down the gray hairs of thy servant our father with sorrow to Sheol.

32For thy servant became surety for the lad unto my father, saying, If I bring him not unto thee, then shall I bear the blame to my father for ever.

33Now therefore, let thy servant, I pray thee, abide instead of the lad a bondman to my lord; and let the lad go up with his brethren.

34For how shall I go up to my father, if the lad be not with me? lest I see the evil that shall come on my father.

Chapter 45

1Then Joseph could not refrain himself before all them that stood before him; and he cried, Cause every man to go out from me. And there stood no man with him, while Joseph made himself known unto his brethren.

2And he wept aloud: and the Egyptians heard, and the house of Pharaoh heard.

3And Joseph said unto his brethren, I am Joseph; doth my father yet live? And his brethren could not answer him; for they were troubled at his presence.

4And Joseph said unto his brethren, Come near to me, I pray you. And they came near. And he said, I am Joseph your brother, whom ye sold into Egypt.

5And now be not grieved, nor angry with yourselves, that ye sold me hither: for God did send me before you to preserve life.

6For these two years hath the famine been in the land: and there are yet five years, in which there shall be neither plowing nor harvest.

7And God sent me before you to preserve you a remnant in the earth, and to save you alive by a great deliverance.

8So now it was not you that sent me hither, but God: and he hath made me a father to Pharaoh, and lord of all his house, and ruler over all the land of Egypt.

9Haste ye, and go up to my father, and say unto him, Thus saith thy son Joseph, God hath made me lord of all Egypt: come down unto me, tarry not;

10and thou shalt dwell in the land of Goshen, and thou shalt be near unto me, thou, and thy children, and thy children's children, and thy flocks, and thy herds, and all that thou hast:

11and there will I nourish thee; for there are yet five years of famine; lest thou come to poverty, thou, and thy household, and all that thou hast.

12And, behold, your eyes see, and the eyes of my brother Benjamin, that it is my mouth that speaketh unto you.

13And ye shall tell my father of all my glory in Egypt, and of all that ye have seen: and ye shall haste and bring down my father hither.

14And he fell upon his brother Benjamin's neck, and wept; and Benjamin wept upon his neck.

15And he kissed all his brethren, and wept upon them: and after that his brethren talked with him.

16And the report thereof was heard in Pharaoh's house, saying, Joseph's brethren are come: and it pleased Pharaoh well, and his servants.

17And Pharaoh said unto Joseph, Say unto thy brethren, This do ye: lade your beasts, and go, get you unto the land of Canaan;

18and take your father and your households, and come unto me: and I will give you the good of the land of Egypt, and ye shall eat the fat of the land.

19Now thou art commanded, this do ye: take you wagons out of the land of Egypt for your little ones, and for your wives, and bring your father, and come.

20Also regard not your stuff; for the good of all the land of Egypt is yours.

21And the sons of Israel did so: and Joseph gave them wagons, according to the commandment of Pharaoh, and gave them provision for the way.

22To all of them he gave each man changes of raiment; but to Benjamin he gave three hundred pieces of silver, and five changes of raiment.

23And to his father he sent after this manner: ten asses laden with the good things of Egypt, and ten she-asses laden with grain and bread and provision for his father by the way.

24So he sent his brethren away, and they departed: and he said unto them, See that ye fall not out by the way.

25And they went up out of Egypt, and came into the land of Canaan unto Jacob their father.

26And they told him, saying, Joseph is yet alive, and he is ruler over all the land of Egypt. And his heart fainted, for he believed them not.

27And they told him all the words of Joseph, which he had said unto them: and when he saw the wagons which Joseph had sent to carry him, the spirit of Jacob their father revived:

28and Israel said, It is enough; Joseph my son is yet alive: I will go and see him before I die.

Chapter 46

1And Israel took his journey with all that he had, and came to Beer-sheba, and offered sacrifices unto the God of his father Isaac.

2And God spake unto Israel in the visions of the night, and said, Jacob, Jacob. And he said, Here am I.

3And he said, I am God, the God of thy father: fear not to go down into Egypt; for I will there make of thee a great nation.

4I will go down with thee into Egypt; and I will also surely bring thee up again: and Joseph shall put his hand upon thine eyes.

5And Jacob rose up from Beer-sheba: and the sons of Israel carried Jacob their father, and their little ones, and their wives, in the wagons which Pharaoh had sent to carry him.

6And they took their cattle, and their goods, which they had gotten in the land of Canaan, and came into Egypt, Jacob, and all his seed with him:

7his sons, and his sons' sons with him, his daughters, and his sons's daughters, and all his seed brought he with him into Egypt.

8And these are the names of the children of Israel, who came into Egypt, Jacob and his sons: Reuben, Jacob's first-born.

9And the sons of Reuben: Hanoch, and Pallu, and Hezron, and Carmi.

10And the sons of Simeon: Jemuel, and Jamin, and Ohad, and Jachin, and Zohar, and Shaul the son of a Canaanitish woman.

11And the sons of Levi: Gershon, Kohath, and Merari.

12And the sons of Judah: Er, and Onan, and Shelah, and Perez, and Zerah; but Er and Onan died in the land of Canaan. And the sons of Perez were Hezron and Hamul.

13And the sons of Issachar: Tola, and Puvah, and Iob, and Shimron.

14And the sons of Zebulun: Sered, and Elon, and Jahleel.

15These are the sons of Leah, whom she bare unto Jacob in Paddan-aram, with his daughter Dinah: all the souls of his sons and his daughters were thirty and three.

16And the sons of Gad: Ziphion, and Haggi, Shuni, and Ezbon, Eri, and Arodi, and Areli.

17And the sons of Asher: Imnah, and Ishvah, and Ishvi, and Beriah, and Serah their sister; and the sons of Beriah: Heber, and Malchiel.

18These are the sons of Zilpah, whom Laban gave to Leah his daughter; and these she bare unto Jacob, even sixteen souls.

19The sons of Rachel Jacob's wife: Joseph and Benjamin.

20And unto Joseph in the land of Egypt were born Manasseh and Ephraim, whom Asenath, the daughter of Poti-phera priest of On, bare unto him.

21And the sons of Benjamin: Bela, and Becher, and Ashbel, Gera, and Naaman, Ehi, and Rosh, Muppim, and Huppim, and Ard.

22These are the sons of Rachel, who were born to Jacob: all the souls were fourteen.

23And the sons of Dan: Hushim.

24And the sons of Naphtali: Jahzeel, and Guni, and Jezer, and Shillem.

25These are the sons of Bilhah, whom Laban gave unto Rachel his daughter, and these she bare unto Jacob: all the souls were seven.

26All the souls that came with Jacob into Egypt, that came out of his loins, besides Jacob's sons' wives, all the souls were threescore and six;

27and the sons of Joseph, who were born to him in Egypt, were two souls: all the souls of the house of Jacob, that came into Egypt, were threescore and ten.

28And he sent Judah before him unto Joseph, to show the way before him unto Goshen; and they came into the land of Goshen.

29And Joseph made ready his chariot, and went up to meet Israel his father, to Goshen; and he presented himself unto him, and fell on his neck, and wept on his neck a good while.

30And Israel said unto Joseph, Now let me die, since I have seen thy face, that thou art yet alive.

31And Joseph said unto his brethren, and unto his father's house, I will go up, and tell Pharaoh, and will say unto him, My brethren, and my father's house, who were in the land of Canaan, are come unto me;

32and the men are shepherds, for they have been keepers of cattle; and they have brought their flocks, and their herds, and all that they have.

33And it shall come to pass, when Pharaoh shall call you, and shall say, What is your occupation?

34that ye shall say, Thy servants have been keepers of cattle from our youth even until now, both we, and our fathers: that ye may dwell in the land of Goshen; for every shepherd is an abomination unto the Egyptians.

Chapter 47

1Then Joseph went in and told Pharaoh, and said, My father and my brethren, and their flocks, and their herds, and all that they have, are come out of the land of Canaan; and, behold, they are in the land of Goshen.

2And from among his brethren he took five men, and presented them unto Pharaoh.

3And Pharaoh said unto his brethren, What is your occupation? And they said unto Pharaoh, Thy servants are shepherds, both we, and our fathers.

4And they said unto Pharaoh, To sojourn in the land are we come; for there is no pasture for thy servants' flocks; for the famine is sore in the land of Canaan:

now therefore, we pray thee, let thy servants dwell in the land of Goshen.

5And Pharaoh spake unto Joseph, saying, Thy father and thy brethren are come unto thee:

6the land of Egypt is before thee; in the best of the land make thy father and thy brethren to dwell; in the land of Goshen let them dwell: and if thou knowest any able men among them, then make them rulers over my cattle.

7And Joseph brought in Jacob his father, and set him before Pharaoh: and Jacob blessed Pharaoh.

8And Pharaoh said unto Jacob, How many are the days of the years of thy life?

9And Jacob said unto Pharaoh, The days of the years of my pilgrimage are a hundred and thirty years: few and evil have been the days of the years of my life, and they have not attained unto the days of the years of the life of my fathers in the days of their pilgrimage.

10And Jacob blessed Pharaoh, and went out from the presence of Pharaoh.

11And Joseph placed his father and his brethren, and gave them a possession in the land of Egypt, in the best of the land, in the land of Rameses, as Pharaoh had commanded.

12And Joseph nourished his father, and his brethren, and all his father's household, with bread, according to their families.

13And there was no bread in all the land; for the famine was very sore, so that the land of Egypt and the land of Canaan fainted by reason of the famine.

14And Joseph gathered up all the money that was found in the land of Egypt, and in the land of Canaan, for the grain which they bought: and Joseph brought the money into Pharaoh's house.

15And when the money was all spent in the land of Egypt, and in the land of Canaan, all the Egyptians came unto Joseph, and said, Give us bread: for why should we die in thy presence? for our money faileth.

16And Joseph said, Give your cattle; and I will give you for your cattle, if money fail.

17And they brought their cattle unto Joseph; and Joseph gave them bread in exchange for the horses, and for the flocks, and for the herds, and for the asses: and he fed them with bread in exchange for all their cattle for that year.

18And when that year was ended, they came unto him the second year, and said unto him, We will not hide from my lord, how that our money is all spent; and the herds of cattle are my lord's; there is nought left in the sight of my lord, but our bodies, and our lands:

19wherefore should we die before thine eyes, both we and our land? buy us and our land for bread, and we and our land will be servants unto Pharaoh: and give us seed, that we may live, and not die, and that the land be not desolate.

20So Joseph bought all the land of Egypt for Pharaoh; for the Egyptians sold every man his field, because the famine was sore upon them: and the land became Pharaoh's.

21And as for the people, he removed them to the cities from one end of the border of Egypt even to the other end thereof.

22Only the land of the priests bought he not: for the priests had a portion from Pharaoh, and did eat their portion which Pharaoh gave them; wherefore they sold not their land.

23Then Joseph said unto the people, Behold, I have bought you this day and your land for Pharaoh: lo, here is seed for you, and ye shall sow the land.

24And it shall come to pass at the ingatherings, that ye shall give a fifth unto Pharaoh, and four parts shall be your own, for seed of the field, and for your food, and for them of your households, and for food for your little ones.

25And they said, Thou hast saved our lives: let us find favor in the sight of my lord, and we will be Pharaoh's servants.

26And Joseph made it a statute concerning the land of Egypt unto this day, that Pharaoh should have the fifth; only the land of the priests alone became not Pharaoh's.

27And Israel dwelt in the land of Egypt, in the land of Goshen; and they gat them possessions therein, and were fruitful, and multiplied exceedingly.

28And Jacob lived in the land of Egypt seventeen years: so the days of Jacob, the years of his life, were a hundred forty and seven years.

29And the time drew near that Israel must die: and he called his son Joseph, and said unto him, If now I have found favor in thy sight, put, I pray thee, thy hand under my thigh, and deal kindly and truly with me: bury me not, I pray thee, in Egypt;

30but when I sleep with my fathers, thou shalt carry me out of Egypt, and bury me in their burying-place. And he said, I will do as thou hast said.

31And he said, Swear unto me: and he sware unto him. And Israel bowed himself upon the bed's head.

Chapter 48

1And it came to pass after these things, that one said to Joseph, Behold, thy father is sick: and he took with him his two sons, Manasseh and Ephraim.

2And one told Jacob, and said, Behold, thy son Joseph cometh unto thee: and Israel strengthened himself, and sat upon the bed.

3And Jacob said unto Joseph, God Almighty appeared unto me at Luz in the land of Canaan, and blessed me,

4and said unto me, Behold, I will make thee fruitful, and multiply thee, and I will make of thee a company of peoples, and will give this land to thy seed after thee for an everlasting possession.

5And now thy two sons, who were born unto thee in the land of Egypt before I came unto thee into Egypt, are mine; Ephraim and Manasseh, even as Reuben and Simeon, shall be mine.

6And thy issue, that thou begettest after them, shall be thine; they shall be called after the name of their brethren in their inheritance.

7And as for me, when I came from Paddan, Rachel died by me in the land of Canaan in the way, when there was still some distance to come unto Ephrath: and I buried her there in the way to Ephrath (the same is Beth-lehem).

8And Israel beheld Joseph's sons, and said, Who are these?

9And Joseph said unto his father, They are my sons, whom God hath given me here. And he said, Bring them, I pray thee, unto me, and I will bless them.

10Now the eyes of Israel were dim for age, so that he could not see. And he brought them near unto him; and he kissed them, and embraced them.

11And Israel said unto Joseph, I had not thought to see thy face: and, lo, God hath let me see thy seed also.

12And Joseph brought them out from between his knees; and he bowed himself with his face to the earth.

13And Joseph took them both, Ephraim in his right hand toward Israel's left hand, and Manasseh in his left hand toward Israel's right hand, and brought them near unto him.

14And Israel stretched out his right hand, and laid it upon Ephraim's head, who was the younger, and his left hand upon Manasseh's head, guiding his hands wittingly; for Manasseh was the first-born.

15And he blessed Joseph, and said, The God before whom my fathers Abraham and Isaac did walk, the God who hath fed me all my life long unto this day,

16the angel who hath redeemed me from all evil, bless the lads; and let my name be named on them, and the name of my fathers Abraham and Isaac; and let them grow into a multitude in the midst of the earth.

17And when Joseph saw that his father laid his right hand upon the head of Ephraim, it displeased him: and he held up his father's hand, to remove it from Ephraim's head unto Manasseh's head.

18And Joseph said unto his father, Not so, my father; for this is the first-born; put thy right hand upon his head.

19And his father refused, and said, I know it, my son, I know it. He also shall become a people, and he also shall be great: howbeit his younger brother shall be greater than he, and his seed shall become a multitude of nations.

20And he blessed them that day, saying, In thee will Israel bless, saying, God make thee as Ephraim and as Manasseh: and he set Ephraim before Manasseh.

21And Israel said unto Joseph, Behold, I die: but God will be with you, and bring you again unto the land of your fathers.

22Moreover I have given to thee one portion above thy brethren, which I took out of the hand of the Amorite with my sword and with my bow.

Chapter 49

49 1And Jacob called unto his sons, and said: gather yourselves together, that I may tell you that which shall befall you in the latter days.

2Assemble yourselves, and hear, ye sons of Jacob;
And hearken unto Israel your father.
3Reuben, thou art my first-born, my might, and the beginning of my strength;
The pre-eminence of dignity, and the pre-eminence of power.
4Boiling over as water, thou shalt not have the pre-eminence;
Because thou wentest up to thy father's bed;
Then defiledst thou it: he went up to my couch.
5Simeon and Levi are brethren;
Weapons of violence are their swords.
6O my soul, come not thou into their council;
Unto their assembly, my glory, be not thou united;
For in their anger they slew a man,
And in their self-will they hocked an ox.
7Cursed be their anger, for it was fierce;
And their wrath, for it was cruel:
I will divide them in Jacob,
And scatter them in Israel.
8Judah, thee shall thy brethren praise:
Thy hand shall be on the neck of thine enemies;
Thy father's sons shall bow down before thee.
9Judah is a lion's whelp;
From the prey, my son, thou art gone up:
He stooped down, he couched as a lion,
And as a lioness; who shall rouse him up?
10The sceptre shall not depart from Judah,
Nor the ruler's staff from between his feet,
Until Shiloh come:
And unto him shall the obedience of the peoples be.
11Binding his foal unto the vine,
And his ass's colt unto the choice vine;
He hath washed his garments in wine,
And his vesture in the blood of grapes:
12His eyes shall be red with wine,
And his teeth white with milk.
13Zebulun shall dwell at the haven of the sea;
And he shall be for a haven of ships;
And his border shall be upon Sidon.
14Issachar is a strong ass,
Couching down between the sheepfolds:
15And he saw a resting-place that it was good,
And the land that it was pleasant;
And he bowed his shoulder to bear,
And became a servant under taskwork.
16Dan shall judge his people,
As one of the tribes of Israel.
17Dan shall be a serpent in the way,
An adder in the path,
That biteth the horse's heels,

Genesis

So that his rider falleth backward.
18I have waited for thy salvation, O Yahweh.
19Gad, a troop shall press upon him;
But he shall press upon their heel.
20Out of the Asher his bread shall be fat,
And he shall yield royal dainties.
21Naphtali is a hind let loose:
He giveth goodly words.
22Joseph is a fruitful bough,
A fruitful bough by a fountain;
His branches run over the wall.
23The archers have sorely grieved him,
And shot at him, and persecute him:
24But his bow abode in strength,
And the arms of his hands were made strong,
By the hands of the Mighty One of Jacob,
(From thence is the shepherd, the stone of Israel),
25Even by the God of thy father, who shall help thee,
And by the Almighty, who shall bless thee,
With blessings of heaven above,
Blessings of the deep that coucheth beneath,
Blessings of the breasts, and of the womb.
26The blessings of thy father
Have prevailed above the blessings of my progenitors
Unto the utmost bound of the everlasting hills:
They shall be on the head of Joseph,
And on the crown of the head of him that was separate from his brethren.
27Benjamin is a wolf that raveneth:
In the morning she shall devour the prey,
And at even he shall divide the spoil.

28All these are the twelve tribes of Israel: and this is it that their father spake unto them and blessed them; every one according to his blessing he blessed them.

29And he charged them, and said unto them, I am to be gathered unto my people: bury me with my fathers in the cave that is in the field of Ephron the Hittite,

30in the cave that is in the field of Machpelah, which is before Mamre, in the land of Canaan, which Abraham bought with the field from Ephron the Hittite for a possession of a burying-place.

31there they buried Abraham and Sarah his wife; there they buried Isaac and Rebekah his wife; and there I buried Leah:

32the field and the cave that is therein, which was purchased from the children of Heth.

33And when Jacob made an end of charging his sons, he gathered up his feet into the bed, and yielded up the ghost, and was gathered unto his people.

Chapter 50

1And Joseph fell upon his father's face, and wept upon him, and kissed him.

2And Joseph commanded his servants the physicians to embalm his father: and the physicians embalmed Israel.

3And forty days were fulfilled for him; for so are fulfilled the days of embalming: and the Egyptians wept for him three-score and ten days.

4And when the days of weeping for him were past, Joseph spake unto the house of Pharaoh, saying, If now I have found favor in your eyes, speak, I pray you, in the ears of Pharaoh, saying,

5My father made me swear, saying, Lo, I die: in my grave which I have digged for me in the land of Canaan, there shalt thou bury me. Now therefore let me go up, I pray thee, and bury my father, and I will come again.

6And Pharaoh said, Go up, and bury thy father, according as he made thee swear.

7And Joseph went up to bury his father; and with him went up all the servants of Pharaoh, the elders of his house, and all the elders of the land of Egypt,

8and all the house of Joseph, and his brethren, and his father's house: only their little ones, and their flocks, and their herds, they left in the land of Goshen.

9And there went up with him both chariots and horsemen: and it was a very great company.

10And they came to the threshing-floor of Atad, which is beyond the Jordan, and there they lamented with a very great and sore lamentation: and he made a mourning for his father seven days.

11And when the inhabitants of the land, the Canaanites, saw the mourning in the floor of Atad, they said, This is a grievous mourning to the Egyptians: wherefore the name of it was called Abel-mizraim, which is beyond the Jordan.

12And his sons did unto him according as he commanded them:

13for his sons carried him into the land of Canaan, and buried him in the cave of the field of Machpelah, which Abraham bought with the field, for a possession of a burying-place, of Ephron the Hittite, before Mamre.

14And Joseph returned into Egypt, he, and his brethren, and all that went up with him to bury his father, after he had buried his father.

15And when Joseph's brethren saw that their father was dead, they said, It may be that Joseph will hate us, and will fully requite us all the evil which we did unto him.

16And they sent a message unto Joseph, saying, Thy father did command before he died, saying,

17So shall ye say unto Joseph, Forgive, I pray thee now, the transgression of thy brethren, and their sin, for that they did unto thee evil. And now, we pray thee, forgive the transgression of the servants of the God of thy father. And Joseph wept when they spake unto him.

18And his brethren also went and fell down before his face; and they said, Behold, we are thy servants.

19And Joseph said unto them, Fear not: for am I in the place of God?

20And as for you, ye meant evil against me; but God meant it for good, to bring to pass, as it is this day, to save much people alive.

21Now therefore fear ye not: I will nourish you, and your little ones. And he comforted them, and spake kindly unto them.

22And Joseph dwelt in Egypt, he, and his father's house: and Joseph lived a hundred and ten years.

23And Joseph saw Ephraim's children of the third generation: the children also of Machir the son of Manasseh were born upon Joseph's knees.

24And Joseph said unto his brethren, I die; but God will surely visit you, and bring you up out of this land unto the land which he sware to Abraham, to Isaac, and to Jacob.

25And Joseph took an oath of the children of Israel, saying, God will surely visit you, and ye shall carry up my bones from hence.

26So Joseph died, being a hundred and ten years old: and they embalmed him, and he was put in a coffin in Egypt.

The Second Book of Moses, Called Exodus

Chapter 1

1Now these are the names of the sons of Israel, who came into Egypt (every man and his household came with Jacob):

2Reuben, Simeon, Levi, and Judah,

3Issachar, Zebulun, and Benjamin,

4Dan and Naphtali, Gad and Asher.

5And all the souls that came out of the loins of Jacob were seventy souls: and Joseph was in Egypt already.

6And Joseph died, and all his brethren, and all that generation.

7And the children of Israel were fruitful, and increased abundantly, and multiplied, and waxed exceeding mighty; and the land was filled with them.

8Now there arose a new king over Egypt, who knew not Joseph.

9And he said unto his people, Behold, the people of the children of Israel are more and mightier than we:

10come, let us deal wisely with them, lest they multiply, and it come to pass, that, when there falleth out any war, they also join themselves unto our enemies, and fight against us, and get them up out of the land.

11Therefore they did set over them taskmasters to afflict them with their burdens. And they built for Pharaoh store-cities, Pithom and Raamses.

12But the more they afflicted them, the more they multiplied and the more they spread abroad. And they were grieved because of the children of Israel.

13And the Egyptians made the children of Israel to serve with rigor:

14and they made their lives bitter with hard service, in mortar and in brick, and in all manner of service in the field, all their service, wherein they made them serve with rigor.

15And the king of Egypt spake to the Hebrew midwives, of whom the name of the one was Shiphrah, and the name of the other Puah:

16and he said, When ye do the office of a midwife to the Hebrew women, and see them upon the birth-stool; if it be a son, then ye shall kill him; but if it be a daughter, then she shall live.

17But the midwives feared God, and did not as the king of Egypt commanded them, but saved the men-children alive.

18And the king of Egypt called for the midwives, and said unto them, Why have ye done this thing, and have saved the men-children alive?

19And the midwives said unto Pharaoh, Because the Hebrew women are not as the Egyptian women; for they are lively, and are delivered ere the midwife come unto them.

20And God dealt well with the midwives: and the people multiplied, and waxed very mighty.

21And it came to pass, because the midwives feared God, that he made them households.

22And Pharaoh charged all his people, saying, Every son that is born ye shall cast into the river, and every daughter ye shall save alive.

Chapter 2

1And there went a man of the house of Levi, and took to wife a daughter of Levi.

2And the woman conceived, and bare a son: and when she saw him that he was a goodly child, she hid him three months.

3And when she could not longer hide him, she took for him an ark of bulrushes, and daubed it with slime and with pitch; and she put the child therein, and laid it in the flags by the river's brink.

4And his sister stood afar off, to know what would be done to him.

5And the daughter of Pharaoh came down to bathe at the river; and her maidens walked along by the river-side; and she saw the ark among the flags, and sent her handmaid to fetch it.

6And she opened it, and saw the child: and, behold, the babe wept. And she had compassion on him, and said, This is one of the Hebrews' children.

7Then said his sister to Pharaoh's daughter, Shall I go and call thee a nurse of the Hebrew women, that she may nurse the child for thee?

8And Pharaoh's daughter said to her, Go. And the maiden went and called the child's mother.

9And Pharaoh's daughter said unto her, Take this child away, and nurse it for me, and I will give thee thy wages. And the woman took the child, and nursed it.

10And the child grew, and she brought him unto Pharaoh's daughter, and he became her son. And she called his name Moses, and said, Because I drew him out of the water.

11And it came to pass in those days, when Moses was grown up, that he went out unto his brethren, and looked on their burdens: and he saw an Egyptian smiting a Hebrew, one of his brethren.

12And he looked this way and that way, and when he saw that there was no man, he smote the Egyptian, and hid him in the sand.

13And he went out the second day, and, behold, two men of the Hebrews were striving together: and he said to him that did the wrong, Wherefore smitest thou thy fellow?

14And he said, Who made thee a prince and a judge over us? Thinkest thou to kill me, as thou killedst the Egyptian? And Moses feared, and said, Surely the thing is known.

15Now when Pharaoh heard this thing, he sought to slay Moses. But Moses fled from the face of Pharaoh, and dwelt in the land of Midian: and he sat down by a well.

16Now the priest of Midian had seven daughters: and they came and drew water, and filled the troughs to water their father's flock.

17And the shepherds came and drove them away; but Moses stood up and helped them, and watered their flock.

18And when they came to Reuel their father, he said, How is it that ye are come so soon to-day?

19And they said, An Egyptian delivered us out of the hand of the shepherds, and moreover he drew water for us, and watered the flock.

20And he said unto his daughters, And where is he? Why is it that ye have left the man? Call him, that he may eat bread.

21And Moses was content to dwell with the man: and he gave Moses Zipporah his daughter.

22And she bare a son, and he called his name Gershom; for he said, I have been a sojourner in a foreign land.

23And it came to pass in the course of those many days, that the king of Egypt died: and the children of Israel sighed by reason of the bondage, and they cried, and their cry came up unto God by reason of the bondage.

24And God heard their groaning, and God remembered his covenant with Abraham, with Isaac, and with Jacob.

25And God saw the children of Israel, and God took knowledge of them.

Chapter 3

1Now Moses was keeping the flock of Jethro his father-in-law, the priest of Midian: and he led the flock to the back of the wilderness, and came to the mountain of God, unto Horeb.

2And the angel of Yahweh appeared unto him in a flame of fire out of the midst of a bush: and he looked, and, behold, the bush burned with fire, and the bush was not consumed.

3And Moses said, I will turn aside now, and see this great sight, why the bush is not burnt.

4And when Yahweh saw that he turned aside to see, God called unto him out of the midst of the bush, and said, Moses, Moses. And he said, Here am I.

5And he said, Draw not nigh hither: put off thy shoes from off thy feet, for the place whereon thou standest is holy ground.

6Moreover he said, I am the God of thy father, the God of Abraham, the God of Isaac, and the God of Jacob. And Moses hid his face; for he was afraid to look upon God.

7And Yahweh said, I have surely seen the affliction of my people that are in Egypt, and have heard their cry by reason of their taskmasters; for I know their sorrows;

8and I am come down to deliver them out of the hand of the Egyptians, and to bring them up out of that land unto a good land and a large, unto a land flowing with milk and honey; unto the place of the Canaanite, and the Hittite, and the Amorite, and the Perizzite, and the Hivite, and the Jebusite.

9And now, behold, the cry of the children of Israel is come unto me: moreover I have seen the oppression wherewith the Egyptians oppress them.

10Come now therefore, and I will send thee unto Pharaoh, that thou mayest bring forth my people the children of Israel out of Egypt.

11And Moses said unto God, Who am I, that I should go unto Pharaoh, and that I should bring forth the children of Israel out of Egypt?

12And he said, Certainly I will be with thee; and this shall be the token unto thee, that I have sent thee: when thou hast brought forth the people out of Egypt, ye shall serve God upon this mountain.

13And Moses said unto God, Behold, when I come unto the children of Israel, and shall say unto them, The God of your fathers hath sent me unto you; and they shall say to me, What is his name? What shall I say unto them?

14And God said unto Moses, I AM THAT I AM: and he said, Thus shalt thou say unto the children of Israel, I AM hath sent me unto you.

15And God said moreover unto Moses, Thus shalt thou say unto the children of Israel, Yahweh, the God of your fathers, the God of Abraham, the God of Isaac, and the God of Jacob, hath sent me unto you: this is my name forever, and this is my memorial unto all generations.

16Go, and gather the elders of Israel together, and say unto them, Yahweh, the God of your fathers, the God of Abraham, of Isaac, and of Jacob, hath appeared unto me, saying, I have surely visited you, and seen that which is done to you in Egypt:

17and I have said, I will bring you up out of the affliction of Egypt unto the land of the Canaanite, and the Hittite, and the Amorite, and the Perizzite, and the Hivite, and the Jebusite, unto a land flowing with milk and honey.

18And they shall hearken to thy voice: and thou shalt come, thou and the elders of Israel, unto the king of Egypt, and ye shall say unto him, Yahweh, the God of the Hebrews, hath met with us: and now let us go, we pray thee, three days' journey into the wilderness, that we may sacrifice to Yahweh our God.

19And I know that the king of Egypt will not give you leave to go, no, not by a mighty hand.

20And I will put forth my hand, and smite Egypt with all my wonders which I will do in the midst thereof: and after that he will let you go.

21And I will give this people favor in the sight of the Egyptians: and it shall come to pass, that, when ye go, ye shall not go empty.

22But every woman shall ask of her neighbor, and of her that sojourneth in her house, jewels of silver, and jewels of gold, and raiment: and ye shall put them upon your sons, and upon your daughters; and ye shall despoil the Egyptians.

Exodus
Chapter 4

1And Moses answered and said, But, behold, they will not believe me, nor hearken unto my voice; for they will say, Yahweh hath not appeared unto thee.

2And Yahweh said unto him, What is that in thy hand? And he said, A rod.

3And he said, Cast in on the ground. And he cast it on the ground, and it became a serpent; and Moses fled from before it.

4And Yahweh said unto Moses, Put forth thy hand, and take it by the tail: (and he put forth his hand, and laid hold of it, and it became a rod in his hand:)

5That they may believe that Yahweh, the God of their fathers, the God of Abraham, the God of Isaac, and the God of Jacob, hath appeared unto thee.

6And Yahweh said furthermore unto him, Put now thy hand into thy bosom. And he put his hand into his bosom: and when he took it out, behold, his hand was leprous, as white as snow.

7And he said, Put thy hand into thy bosom again. (And he put his hand into his bosom again; and when he took it out of his bosom, behold, it was turned again as his other flesh.)

8And it shall come to pass, if they will not believe thee, neither hearken to the voice of the first sign, that they will believe the voice of the latter sign.

9And it shall come to pass, if they will not believe even these two signs, neither hearken unto thy voice, that thou shalt take of the water of the river, and pour it upon the dry land: and the water which thou takest out of the river shall become blood upon the dry land.

10And Moses said unto Yahweh, Oh, Lord, I am not eloquent, neither heretofore, nor since thou hast spoken unto thy servant; for I am slow of speech, and of a slow tongue.

11And Yahweh said unto him, Who hath made man's mouth? Or who maketh a man dumb, or deaf, or seeing, or blind? Is it not I, Yahweh?

12Now therefore go, and I will be with thy mouth, and teach thee what thou shalt speak.

13And he said, Oh, Lord, send, I pray thee, by the hand of him whom thou wilt send.

14And the anger of Yahweh was kindled against Moses, and he said, Is there not Aaron thy brother the Levite? I know that he can speak well. And also, behold, he cometh forth to meet thee: and when he seeth thee, he will be glad in his heart.

15And thou shalt speak unto him, and put the words in his mouth: and I will be with thy mouth, and with his mouth, and will teach you what ye shall do.

16And he shall be thy spokesman unto the people; and it shall come to pass, that he shall be to thee a mouth, and thou shalt be to him as God.

17And thou shalt take in thy hand this rod, wherewith thou shalt do the signs.

18And Moses went and returned to Jethro his father-in-law, and said unto him, Let me go, I pray thee, and return unto my brethren that are in Egypt, and see whether they be yet alive. And Jethro said to Moses, Go in peace.

19And Yahweh said unto Moses in Midian, Go, return into Egypt; for all the men are dead that sought thy life.

20And Moses took his wife and his sons, and set them upon an ass, and he returned to the land of Egypt: and Moses took the rod of God in his hand.

21And Yahweh said unto Moses, When thou goest back into Egypt, see that thou do before Pharaoh all the wonders which I have put in thy hand: but I will harden his heart and he will not let the people go.

22And thou shalt say unto Pharaoh, Thus saith Yahweh, Israel is my son, my first-born:

23and I have said unto thee, Let my son go, that he may serve me; and thou hast refused to let him go: behold, I will slay thy son, thy first-born.

24And it came to pass on the way at the lodging-place, that Yahweh met him, and sought to kill him.

25Then Zipporah took a flint, and cut off the foreskin of her son, and cast it at his feet; and she said, Surely a bridegroom of blood art thou to me.

26So he let him alone. Then she said, A bridegroom of blood art thou, because of the circumcision.

27And Yahweh said to Aaron, Go into the wilderness to meet Moses. And he went, and met him in the mountain of God, and kissed him.

28And Moses told Aaron all the words of Yahweh wherewith he had sent him, and all the signs wherewith he had charged him.

29And Moses and Aaron went and gathered together all the elders of the children of Israel:

30and Aaron spake all the words which Yahweh had spoken unto Moses, and did the signs in the sight of the people.

31And the people believed: and when they heard that Yahweh had visited the children of Israel, and that he had seen their affliction, then they bowed their heads and worshipped.

Chapter 5

1And afterward Moses and Aaron came, and said unto Pharaoh, Thus saith Yahweh, the God of Israel, Let my people go, that they may hold a feast unto me in the wilderness.

2And Pharaoh said, Who is Yahweh, that I should hearken unto his voice to let Israel go? I know not Yahweh, and moreover I will not let Israel go.

3And they said, The God of the Hebrews hath met with us: let us go, we pray thee, three days' journey into the wilderness, and sacrifice unto Yahweh our God, lest he fall upon us with pestilence, or with the sword.

4And the king of Egypt said unto them, Wherefore do ye, Moses and Aaron, loose the people from their works? get you unto your burdens.

5And Pharaoh said, Behold, the people of the land are now many, and ye make them rest from their burdens.

6And the same day Pharaoh commanded the taskmasters of the people, and their officers, saying,

7Ye shall no more give the people straw to make brick, as heretofore: let them go and gather straw for themselves.

8And the number of the bricks, which they did make heretofore, ye shall lay upon them; ye shall not diminish aught thereof: for they are idle; therefore they cry, saying, Let us go and sacrifice to our God.

9Let heavier work be laid upon the men, that they may labor therein; and let them not regard lying words.

10And the taskmasters of the people went out, and their officers, and they spake to the people, saying, Thus saith Pharaoh, I will not give you straw.

11Go yourselves, get you straw where ye can find it: for nought of your work shall be diminished.

12So the people were scattered abroad throughout all the land of Egypt to gather stubble for straw.

13And the taskmasters were urgent saying, Fulfil your works, your daily tasks, as when there was straw.

14And the officers of the children of Israel, whom Pharaoh's taskmasters had set over them, were beaten, and demanded, Wherefore have ye not fulfilled your task both yesterday and to-day, in making brick as heretofore?

15Then the officers of the children of Israel came and cried unto Pharaoh, saying, Wherefore dealest thou thus with thy servants?

16There is no straw given unto thy servants, and they say to us, Make brick: and, behold, thy servants are beaten; but the fault it in thine own people.

17But he said, Ye are idle, ye are idle: therefore ye say, Let us go and sacrifice to Yahweh.

18Go therefore now, and work; for there shall no straw be given you, yet shall ye deliver the number of bricks.

19And the officers of the children of Israel did see that they were in evil case, when it was said, Ye shall not diminish aught from your bricks, your daily tasks.

20And they met Moses and Aaron, who stood in the way, as they came forth from Pharaoh:

21and they said unto them, Yahweh look upon you, and judge: because ye have made our savor to be abhorred in the eyes of Pharaoh, and in the eyes of his servants, to put a sword in their hand to slay us.

22And Moses returned unto Yahweh, and said, Lord, wherefore hast thou dealt ill with this people? why is it that thou hast sent me?

23For since I came to Pharaoh to speak in thy name, he hath dealt ill with this people; neither hast thou delivered thy people at all.

Chapter 6

1And Yahweh said unto Moses, Now shalt thou see what I will do to Pharaoh: for by a strong hand shall he let them go, and by a strong hand shall he drive them out of his land.

2And God spake unto Moses, and said unto him, I am Yahweh:

3and I appeared unto Abraham, unto Isaac, and unto Jacob, as God Almighty; but by my name Yahweh I was not known to them.

4And I have also established my covenant with them, to give them the land of Canaan, the land of their sojournings, wherein they sojourned.

5And moreover I have heard the groaning of the children of Israel, whom the Egyptians keep in bondage; and I have remembered my covenant.

6Wherefore say unto the children of Israel, I am Yahweh, and I will bring you out from under the burdens of the Egyptians, and I will rid you out of their bondage, and I will redeem you with an outstretched arm, and with great judgments:

7and I will take you to me for a people, and I will be to you a God; and ye shall know that I am Yahweh your God, who bringeth you out from under the burdens of the Egyptians.

8And I will bring you in unto the land which I sware to give to Abraham, to Isaac, and to Jacob; and I will give it you for a heritage: I am Yahweh.

9And Moses spake so unto the children of Israel: but they hearkened not unto Moses for anguish of spirit, and for cruel bondage.

10And Yahweh spake unto Moses, saying,

11Go in, speak unto Pharaoh king of Egypt, that he let the children of Israel go out of his land.

12And Moses spake before Yahweh, saying, Behold, the children of Israel have not hearkened unto me; how then shall Pharaoh hear me, who am of uncircumcised lips?

13And Yahweh spake unto Moses and unto Aaron, and gave them a charge unto the children of Israel, and unto Pharaoh king of Egypt, to bring the children of Israel out of the land of Egypt.

14These are the heads of their fathers' houses. The sons of Reuben the first-born of Israel: Hanoch, and Pallu, Hezron, and Carmi; these are the families of Reuben.

15And the sons of Simeon: Jemuel, and Jamin, and Ohad, and Jachin, and Zohar, and Shaul the son of a Canaanitish woman; these are the families of Simeon.

16And these are the names of the sons of Levi according to their generations: Gershon, and Kohath, and Merari; and the years of the life of Levi were a hundred thirty and seven years.

17The sons of Gershon: Libni and Shimei, according to their families.

18And the sons of Kohath: Amram, and Izhar, and Hebron, and Uzziel; and the years of the life of Kohath were a hundred thirty and three years.

19And the sons of Merari: Mahli and Mushi. These are the families of the Levites according to their generations.

20And Amram took him Jochebed his father's sister to wife; and she bare him Aaron and Moses: and the years of the life of Amram were a hundred and thirty and seven years.

21And the sons of Izhar: Korah, and Nepheg, and Zichri.

22And the sons of Uzziel: Mishael, and Elzaphan, and Sithri.

23And Aaron took him Elisheba, the daughter of Amminadab, the sister of Nahshon, to wife; and she bare him Nadab and Abihu, Eleazar and Ithamar.

24And the sons of Korah: Assir, and Elkanah, and Abiasaph; these are the families of the Korahites.

25And Eleazar Aaron's son took him one of the daughters of Putiel to wife; and she bare him Phinehas. These are the heads of the fathers' houses of the Levites according to their families.

26These are that Aaron and Moses, to whom Yahweh said, Bring out the children of Israel from the land of Egypt according to their hosts.

27These are they that spake to Pharaoh king of Egypt, to bring out the children of Israel from Egypt: these are that Moses and Aaron.

28And it came to pass on the day when Yahweh spake unto Moses in the land of Egypt,

29that Yahweh spake unto Moses, saying, I am Yahweh: speak thou unto Pharaoh king of Egypt all that I speak unto thee.

30And Moses said before Yahweh, Behold, I am of uncircumcised lips, and how shall Pharaoh hearken unto me?

Chapter 7

1And Yahweh said unto Moses, See, I have made thee as God to Pharaoh; and Aaron thy brother shall be thy prophet.

2Thou shalt speak all that I command thee; and Aaron thy brother shall speak unto Pharaoh, that he let the children of Israel go out of his land.

3And I will harden Pharaoh's heart, and multiply my signs and my wonders in the land of Egypt.

4But Pharaoh will not hearken unto you, and I will lay my hand upon Egypt, and bring forth my hosts, my people the children of Israel, out of the land of Egypt by great judgments.

5And the Egyptians shall know that I am Yahweh, when I stretch forth my hand upon Egypt, and bring out the children of Israel from among them.

6And Moses and Aaron did so; as Yahweh commanded them, so did they.

7And Moses was fourscore years old, and Aaron fourscore and three years old, when they spake unto Pharaoh.

8And Yahweh spake unto Moses and unto Aaron, saying,

9When Pharaoh shall speak unto you, saying, Show a wonder for you; then thou shalt say unto Aaron, Take thy rod, and cast it down before Pharaoh, that it become a serpent.

10And Moses and Aaron went in unto Pharaoh, and they did so, as Yahweh had commanded: and Aaron cast down his rod before Pharaoh and before his servants, and it became a serpent.

11Then Pharaoh also called for the wise men and the sorcerers: and they also, the magicians of Egypt, did in like manner with their enchantments.

12For they cast down every man his rod, and they became serpents: but Aaron's rod swallowed up their rods.

13And Pharaoh's heart was hardened, and he hearkened not unto them; as Yahweh had spoken.

14And Yahweh said unto Moses, Pharaoh's heart is stubborn, he refuseth to let the people go.

15Get thee unto Pharaoh in the morning; lo, he goeth out unto the water; and thou shalt stand by the river's brink to meet him; and the rod which was turned to a serpent shalt thou take in thy hand.

16And thou shalt say unto him, Yahweh, the God of the Hebrews, hath sent me unto thee, saying, Let my people go, that they may serve me in the wilderness: and, behold, hitherto thou hast not hearkened.

17Thus saith Yahweh, In this thou shalt know that I am Yahweh: behold, I will smite with the rod that is in my hand upon the waters which are in the river, and they shall be turned to blood.

18And the fish that are in the river shall die, and the river shall become foul; and the Egyptians shall loathe to drink water from the river.

19And Yahweh said unto Moses, Say unto Aaron, Take thy rod, and stretch out thy hand over the waters of Egypt, over their rivers, over their streams, and over their pools, and over all their ponds of water, that they may become blood; and there shall be blood throughout all the land of Egypt, both in vessels of wood and in vessels of stone.

20And Moses and Aaron did so, as Yahweh commanded; and he lifted up the rod, and smote the waters that were in the river, in the sight of Pharaoh, and in the sight of his servants; and all the waters that were in the river were turned to blood.

21And the fish that were in the river died; and the river became foul, and the Egyptians could not drink water from the river; and the blood was throughout all the land of Egypt.

22And the magicians of Egypt did in like manner with their enchantments: and Pharaoh's heart was hardened, and he hearkened not unto them; as Yahweh had spoken.

23And Pharaoh turned and went into his house, neither did he lay even this to heart.

24And all the Egyptians digged round about the river for water to drink; for they could not drink of the water of the river.

25And seven days were fulfilled, after that Yahweh had smitten the river.

Chapter 8

1And Yahweh spake unto Moses, Go in unto Pharaoh, and say unto him, Thus saith Yahweh, Let my people go, that they may serve me.

2And if thou refuse to let them go, behold, I will smite all thy borders with frogs:

3and the river shall swarm with frogs, which shall go up and come into thy house, and into thy bedchamber, and upon thy bed, and into the house of thy servants, and upon thy people, and into thine ovens, and into thy kneading-troughs:

4and the frogs shall come up both upon thee, and upon thy people, and upon all thy servants.

5And Yahweh said unto Moses, Say unto Aaron, Stretch forth thy hand with thy rod over the rivers, over the streams, and over the pools, and cause frogs to come up upon the land of Egypt.

6And Aaron stretched out his hand over the waters of Egypt; and the frogs came up, and covered the land of Egypt.

7And the magicians did in like manner with their enchantments, and brought up frogs upon the land of Egypt.

8Then Pharaoh called for Moses and Aaron, and said, Entreat Yahweh, that he take away the frogs from me, and from my people; and I will let the people go, that they may sacrifice unto Yahweh.

9And Moses said unto Pharaoh, Have thou this glory over me: against what time shall I entreat for thee, and for thy servants, and for thy people, that the frogs be destroyed from thee and thy houses, and remain in the river only?

10And he said, Against to-morrow. And he said, Be it according to thy word; that thou mayest know that there is none like unto Yahweh our God.

11And the frogs shall depart from thee, and from thy houses, and from thy servants, and from thy people; they shall remain in the river only.

12And Moses and Aaron went out from Pharaoh: and Moses cried unto Yahweh concerning the frogs which he had brought upon Pharaoh.

13And Yahweh did according to the word of Moses; and the frogs died out of the houses, out of the courts, and out of the fields.

14And they gathered them together in heaps; and the land stank.

15But when Pharaoh saw that there was respite, he hardened his heart, and hearkened not unto them, as Yahweh had spoken.

16And Yahweh said unto Moses, Say unto Aaron, Stretch out thy rod, and smite the dust of the earth, that is may become lice throughout all the land of Egypt.

17And they did so; and Aaron stretched out his hand with his rod, and smote the dust of the earth, and there were lice upon man, and upon beast; all the dust of the earth became lice throughout all the land of Egypt.

18And the magicians did so with their enchantments to bring forth lice, but they could not: and there were lice upon man, and upon beast.

19Then the magicians said unto Pharaoh, This is the finger of God: and Pharaoh's heart was hardened, and he hearkened not unto them; as Yahweh had spoken.

20And Yahweh said unto Moses, Rise up early in the morning, and stand before Pharaoh; lo, he cometh forth to the water; and say unto him, Thus saith Yahweh, Let my people go, that they may serve me.

21Else, if thou wilt not let my people go, behold, I will send swarms of flies upon thee, and upon they servants, and upon thy people, and into thy houses: and the houses of the Egyptians shall be full of swarms of flies, and also the ground whereon they are.

22And I will set apart in that day the land of Goshen, in which my people dwell, that no swarms of flies shall be there; to the end thou mayest know that I am Yahweh in the midst of the earth.

23And I will put a division between my people and thy people: by to-morrow shall this sign be.

24And Yahweh did so; and there came grievous swarms of flies into the house of Pharaoh, and into his servants' houses: and in all the land of Egypt the land was corrupted by reason of the swarms of flies.

25And Pharaoh called for Moses and for Aaron, and said, Go ye, sacrifice to your God in the land.

26And Moses said, It is not meet so to do; for we shall sacrifice the abomination of the Egyptians to Yahweh our God: lo, shall we sacrifice the abomination of the Egyptians before their eyes, and will they not stone us?

27We will go three days' journey into the wilderness, and sacrifice to Yahweh our God, as he shall command us.

28And Pharaoh said, I will let you go, that ye may sacrifice to Yahweh your God in the wilderness; only ye shall not go very far away: entreat for me.

29And Moses said, Behold, I go out from thee, and I will entreat Yahweh that the swarms of flies may depart from Pharaoh, from his servants, and from his people, to-morrow: only let not Pharaoh deal deceitfully any more in not letting the people go to sacrifice to Yahweh.

30And Moses went out from Pharaoh, and entreated Yahweh.

31And Yahweh did according to the word of Moses; and he removed the swarms of flies from Pharaoh, from his servants, and from his people; there remained not one.

32And Pharaoh hardened his heart this time also, and he did not let the people go.

Chapter 9

1Then Yahweh said unto Moses, Go in unto Pharaoh, and tell him, Thus saith Yahweh, the God of the Hebrews, Let my people go, that they may serve me.

2For if thou refuse to let them go, and wilt hold them still,

3behold, the hand of Yahweh is upon thy cattle which are in the field, upon the horses, upon the asses, upon the camels, upon the herds, and upon the flocks: there shall be a very grievous murrain.

4And Yahweh shall make a distinction between the cattle of Israel and the cattle of Egypt; and there shall nothing die of all that belongeth to the children of Israel.

5And Yahweh appointed a set time, saying, To-morrow Yahweh shall do this thing in the land.

6And Yahweh did that thing on the morrow; and all the cattle of Egypt died; but of the cattle of the children of Israel died not one.

7And Pharaoh sent, and, behold, there was not so much as one of the cattle of the Israelites dead. But the heart of Pharaoh was stubborn, and he did not let the

Exodus

people go.

8 And Yahweh said unto Moses and unto Aaron, Take to you handfuls of ashes of the furnace, and let Moses sprinkle it toward heaven in the sight of Pharaoh.

9 And it shall become small dust over all the land of Egypt, and shall be a boil breaking forth with blains upon man and upon beast, throughout all the land of Egypt.

10 And they took ashes of the furnace, and stood before Pharaoh; and Moses sprinkled it up toward heaven; and it became a boil breaking forth with blains upon man and upon beast.

11 And the magicians could not stand before Moses because of the boils; for the boils were upon the magicians, and upon all the Egyptians.

12 And Yahweh hardened the heart of Pharaoh, and he hearkened not unto them, as Yahweh had spoken unto Moses.

13 And Yahweh said unto Moses, Rise up early in the morning, and stand before Pharaoh, and say unto him, Thus saith Yahweh, the God of the Hebrews, Let my people go, that they may serve me.

14 For I will this time send all my plagues upon thy heart, and upon thy servants, and upon thy people; that thou mayest know that there is none like me in all the earth.

15 For now I had put forth my hand, and smitten thee and thy people with pestilence, and thou hadst been cut off from the earth:

16 but in very deed for this cause have I made thee to stand, to show thee my power, and that my name may be declared throughout all the earth.

17 As yet exaltest thou thyself against my people, that thou wilt not let them go?

18 Behold, to-morrow about this time I will cause it to rain a very grievous hail, such as hath not been in Egypt since the day it was founded even until now.

19 Now therefore send, hasten in thy cattle and all that thou hast in the field; for every man and beast that shall be found in the field, and shall not be brought home, the hail shall come down upon them, and they shall die.

20 He that feared the word of Yahweh among the servants of Pharaoh made his servants and his cattle flee into the houses.

21 And he that regarded not the word of Yahweh left his servants and his cattle in the field.

22 And Yahweh said unto Moses, Stretch forth thy hand toward heaven, that there may be hail in all the land of Egypt, upon man, and upon beast, and upon every herb of the field, throughout the land of Egypt.

23 And Moses stretched forth his rod toward heaven: and Yahweh sent thunder and hail, and fire ran down unto the earth; and Yahweh rained hail upon the land of Egypt.

24 So there was hail, and fire mingled with the hail, very grievous, such as had not been in all the land of Egypt since it became a nation.

25 And the hail smote throughout all the land of Egypt all that was in the field, both man and beast; and the hail smote every herb of the field, and brake every tree of the field.

26 Only in the land of Goshen, where the children of Israel were, was there no hail.

27 And Pharaoh sent, and called for Moses and Aaron, and said unto them, I have sinned this time: Yahweh is righteous, and I and my people are wicked.

28 Entreat Yahweh; for there hath been enough of these mighty thunderings and hail; and I will let you go, and ye shall stay no longer.

29 And Moses said unto him, As soon as I am gone out of the city, I will spread abroad my hands unto Yahweh; the thunders shall cease, neither shall there be any more hail; that thou mayest know that the earth is Yahweh's.

30 But as for thee and thy servants, I know that ye will not yet fear Yahweh God.

31 And the flax and the barley were smitten: for the barley was in the ear, and the flax was in bloom.

32 But the wheat and the spelt were not smitten: for they were not grown up.

33 And Moses went out of the city from Pharaoh, and spread abroad his hands unto Yahweh: and the thunders and hail ceased, and the rain was not poured upon the earth.

34 And when Pharaoh saw that the rain and the hail and the thunders were ceased, he sinned yet more, and hardened his heart, he and his servants.

35 And the heart of Pharaoh was hardened, and he did not let the children of Israel go, as Yahweh had spoken by Moses.

Chapter 10

1 And Yahweh said unto Moses, Go in unto Pharaoh: for I have hardened his heart, and the heart of his servants, that I may show these my signs in the midst of them,

2 and that thou mayest tell in the ears of thy son, and of thy son's son, what things I have wrought upon Egypt, and my signs which I have done among them; that ye may know that I am Yahweh.

3 And Moses and Aaron went in unto Pharaoh, and said unto him, Thus saith Yahweh, the God of the Hebrews, How long wilt thou refuse to humble thyself before me? let my people go, that they may serve me.

4 Else, if thou refuse to let my people go, behold, to-morrow will I bring locusts into thy border:

5 and they shall cover the face of the earth, so that one shall not be able to see the earth: and they shall eat the residue of that which is escaped, which remaineth unto you from the hail, and shall eat every tree which groweth for you out of the field:

6 and thy houses shall be filled, and the houses of all thy servants, and the houses of all the Egyptians; as neither thy fathers nor thy fathers' fathers have seen, since the day that they were upon the earth unto this day. And he turned, and went out from Pharaoh.

7 And Pharaoh's servants said unto him, How long shall this man be a snare unto us? let the men go, that they may serve Yahweh their God: knowest thou not yet that Egypt is destroyed?

8 And Moses and Aaron were brought again unto Pharaoh: and he said unto them, Go, serve Yahweh your God; but who are they that shall go?

9 And Moses said, We will go with our young and with our old; with our sons and with our daughters, with our flocks and with our herds will we go; for we must hold a feast unto Yahweh.

10 And he said unto them, So be Yahweh with you, as I will let you go, and your little ones: look to it; for evil is before you.

11 Not so: go now ye that are men, and serve Yahweh; for that is what ye desire. And they were driven out from Pharaoh's presence.

12 And Yahweh said unto Moses, Stretch out thy hand over the land of Egypt for the locusts, that they may come up upon the land of Egypt, and eat every herb of the land, even all that the hail hath left.

13 And Moses stretched forth his rod over the land of Egypt, and Yahweh brought an east wind upon the land all that day, and all the night; and when it was morning, the east wind brought the locusts.

14 And the locusts went up over all the land of Egypt, and rested in all the borders of Egypt; very grievous were they; before them there were no such locusts as they, neither after them shall be such.

15 For they covered the face of the whole earth, so that the land was darkened; and they did eat every herb of the land, and all the fruit of the trees which the hail had left: and there remained not any green thing, either tree or herb of the field, through all the land of Egypt.

16 Then Pharaoh called for Moses and Aaron in haste; and he said, I have sinned against Yahweh your God, and against you.

17 Now therefore forgive, I pray thee, my sin only this once, and entreat Yahweh your God, that he may take away from me this death only.

18 And he went out from Pharaoh, and entreated Yahweh.

19 And Yahweh turned an exceeding strong west wind, which took up the locusts, and drove them into the Red Sea; there remained not one locust in all the border of Egypt.

20 But Yahweh hardened Pharaoh's heart, and he did not let the children of Israel go.

21 And Yahweh said unto Moses, Stretch out thy hand toward heaven, that there may be darkness over the land of Egypt, even darkness which may be felt.

22 And Moses stretched forth his hand toward heaven; and there was a thick darkness in all the land of Egypt three days;

23 they saw not one another, neither rose any one from his place for three days: but all the children of Israel had light in their dwellings.

24 And Pharaoh called unto Moses, and said, Go ye, serve Yahweh; only let your flocks and your herds be stayed: let your little ones also go with you.

25 And Moses said, Thou must also give into our hand sacrifices and burnt-offerings, that we may sacrifice unto Yahweh our God.

26 Our cattle also shall go with us; there shall not a hoof be left behind: for thereof must we take to serve Yahweh our God; and we know not with what we must serve Yahweh, until we come thither.

27 But Yahweh hardened Pharaoh's heart, and he would not let them go.

28 And Pharaoh said unto him, Get thee from me, take heed to thyself, see my face no more; for in the day thou seest my face thou shalt die.

29 And Moses said, Thou hast spoken well. I will see thy face again no more.

Chapter 11

1 And Yahweh said unto Moses, Yet one plague more will I bring upon Pharaoh, and upon Egypt; afterwards he will let you go hence: when he shall let you go, he shall surely thrust you out hence altogether.

2 Speak now in the ears of the people, and let them ask every man of his neighbor, and every woman of her neighbor, jewels of silver, and jewels of gold.

3 And Yahweh gave the people favor in the sight of the Egyptians. Moreover the man Moses was very great in the land of Egypt, in the sight of Pharaoh's servants, and in the sight of the people.

4 And Moses said, Thus saith Yahweh, About midnight will I go out into the midst of Egypt:

5 and all the first-born in the land of Egypt shall die, from the first-born of Pharaoh that sitteth upon his throne, even unto the first-born of the maid-servant that is behind the mill; and all the first-born of cattle.

6 And there shall be a great cry throughout all the land of Egypt, such as there hath not been, nor shall be any more.

7 But against any of the children of Israel shall not a dog move his tongue, against man or beast: that ye may know how that Yahweh doth make a distinction between the Egyptians and Israel.

8 And all these thy servants shall come down unto me, and bow down themselves unto me, saying, Get thee out, and all the people that follow thee: and after that I will go out. And he went out from Pharaoh in hot anger.

9 And Yahweh said unto Moses, Pharaoh will not hearken unto you; that my wonders may be multiplied in the land of Egypt.

10 And Moses and Aaron did all these wonders before Pharaoh: and Yahweh hardened Pharaoh's heart, and he did not let the children of Israel go out of his land.

Chapter 12

1 And Yahweh spake unto Moses and Aaron in the land of Egypt, saying,

2 This month shall be unto you the beginning of months: it shall be the first month of the year to you.

3 Speak ye unto all the congregation of Israel, saying, In the tenth day of this month they shall take to them every man a lamb, according to their fathers' houses, a lamb for a household:

4and if the household be too little for a lamb, then shall he and his neighbor next unto his house take one according to the number of the souls; according to every man's eating ye shall make your count for the lamb.

5Your lamb shall be without blemish, a male a year old: ye shall take it from the sheep, or from the goats:

6and ye shall keep it until the fourteenth day of the same month; and the whole assembly of the congregation of Israel shall kill it at even.

7And they shall take of the blood, and put it on the two side-posts and on the lintel, upon the houses wherein they shall eat it.

8And they shall eat the flesh in that night, roast with fire, and unleavened bread; with bitter herbs they shall eat it.

9Eat not of it raw, nor boiled at all with water, but roast with fire; its head with its legs and with the inwards thereof.

10And ye shall let nothing of it remain until the morning; but that which remaineth of it until the morning ye shall burn with fire.

11And thus shall ye eat it: with your loins girded, your shoes on your feet, and your staff in your hand; and ye shall eat it in haste: it is Yahweh's passover.

12For I will go through the land of Egypt in that night, and will smite all the first-born in the land of Egypt, both man and beast; and against all the gods of Egypt I will execute judgments; I am Yahweh.

13And the blood shall be to you for a token upon the houses where ye are: and when I see the blood, I will pass over you, and there shall no plague be upon you to destroy you, when I smite the land of Egypt.

14And this day shall be unto you for a memorial, and ye shall keep it a feast to Yahweh: throughout your generations ye shall keep it a feast by an ordinance for ever.

15Seven days shall ye eat unleavened bread; even the first day ye shall put away leaven out of your houses: for whosoever eateth leavened bread from the first day until the seventh day, that soul shall be cut off from Israel.

16And in the first day there shall be to you a holy convocation, and in the seventh day a holy convocation; no manner of work shall be done in them, save that which every man must eat, that only may be done by you.

17And ye shall observe the feast of unleavened bread; for in this selfsame day have I brought your hosts out of the land of Egypt: therefore shall ye observe this day throughout your generations by an ordinance for ever.

18In the first month, on the fourteenth day of the month at even, ye shall eat unleavened bread, until the one and twentieth day of the month at even.

19Seven days shall there be no leaven found in your houses: for whosoever eateth that which is leavened, that soul shall be cut off from the congregation of Israel, whether he be a sojourner, or one that is born in the land.

20Ye shall eat nothing leavened; in all your habitations shall ye eat unleavened bread.

21Then Moses called for all the elders of Israel, and said unto them, Draw out, and take you lambs according to your families, and kill the passover.

22And ye shall take a bunch of hyssop, and dip it in the blood that is in the basin, and strike the lintel and the two side-posts with the blood that is in the basin; and none of you shall go out of the door of his house until the morning.

23For Yahweh will pass through to smite the Egyptians; and when he seeth the blood upon the lintel, and on the two side-posts, Yahweh will pass over the door, and will not suffer the destroyer to come in unto your houses to smite you.

24And ye shall observe this thing for an ordinance to thee and to thy sons for ever.

25And it shall come to pass, when ye are come to the land which Yahweh will give you, according as he hath promised, that ye shall keep this service.

26And it shall come to pass, when your children shall say unto you, What mean ye by this service?

27that ye shall say, It is the sacrifice of Yahweh's passover, who passed over the houses of the children of Israel in Egypt, when he smote the Egyptians, and delivered our houses. And the people bowed the head and worshipped.

28And the children of Israel went and did so; as Yahweh had commanded Moses and Aaron, so did they.

29And it came to pass at midnight, that Yahweh smote all the first-born in the land of Egypt, from the first-born of Pharaoh that sat on his throne unto the first-born of the captive that was in the dungeon; and all the first-born of cattle.

30And Pharaoh rose up in the night, he, and all his servants, and all the Egyptians; and there was a great cry in Egypt, for there was not a house where there was not one dead.

31And he called for Moses and Aaron by night, and said, Rise up, get you forth from among my people, both ye and the children of Israel; and go, serve Yahweh, as ye have said.

32Take both your flocks and your herds, as ye have said, and be gone; and bless me also.

33And the Egyptians were urgent upon the people, to send them out of the land in haste; for they said, We are all dead men.

34And the people took their dough before it was leavened, their kneading-troughs being bound up in their clothes upon their shoulders.

35And the children of Israel did according to the word of Moses; and they asked of the Egyptians jewels of silver, and jewels of gold, and raiment.

36And Yahweh gave the people favor in the sight of the Egyptians, so that they let them have what they asked. And they despoiled the Egyptians.

37And the children of Israel journeyed from Rameses to Succoth, about six hundred thousand on foot that were men, besides children.

38And a mixed multitude went up also with them; and flocks, and herds, even very much cattle.

39And they baked unleavened cakes of the dough which they brought forth out of Egypt; for it was not leavened, because they were thrust out of Egypt, and could not tarry, neither had they prepared for themselves any victuals.

40Now the time that the children of Israel dwelt in Egypt was four hundred and thirty years.

41And it came to pass at the end of four hundred and thirty years, even the selfsame day it came to pass, that all the hosts of Yahweh went out from the land of Egypt.

42It is a night to be much observed unto Yahweh for bringing them out from the land of Egypt: this is that night of Yahweh, to be much observed of all the children of Israel throughout their generations.

43And Yahweh said unto Moses and Aaron, This is the ordinance of the passover: there shall no foreigner eat thereof;

44but every man's servant that is bought for money, when thou hast circumcised him, then shall he eat thereof.

45A sojourner and a hired servant shall not eat thereof.

46In one house shall it be eaten; thou shalt not carry forth aught of the flesh abroad out of the house; neither shall ye break a bone thereof.

47All the congregation of Israel shall keep it.

48And when a stranger shall sojourn with thee, and will keep the passover to Yahweh, let all his males be circumcised, and then let him come near and keep it; and he shall be as one that is born in the land: but no uncircumcised person shall eat thereof.

49One law shall be to him that is home-born, and unto the stranger that sojourneth among you.

50Thus did all the children of Israel; as Yahweh commanded Moses and Aaron, so did they.

51And it came to pass the selfsame day, that Yahweh did bring the children of Israel out of the land of Egypt by their hosts.

Chapter 13

1And Yahweh spake unto Moses, saying,

2Sanctify unto me all the first-born, whatsoever openeth the womb among the children of Israel, both of man and of beast: it is mine.

3And Moses said unto the people, Remember this day, in which ye came out from Egypt, out of the house of bondage; for by strength of hand Yahweh brought you out from this place: there shall no leavened bread be eaten.

4This day ye go forth in the month Abib.

5And it shall be, when Yahweh shall bring thee into the land of the Canaanite, and the Hittite, and the Amorite, and the Hivite, and the Jebusite, which he sware unto thy fathers to give thee, a land flowing with milk and honey, that thou shalt keep this service in this month.

6Seven days thou shalt eat unleavened bread, and in the seventh day shall be a feast to Yahweh.

7Unleavened bread shall be eaten throughout the seven days; and there shall no leavened bread be seen with thee, neither shall there be leaven seen with thee, in all thy borders.

8And thou shalt tell thy son in that day, saying, It is because of that which Yahweh did for me when I came forth out of Egypt.

9And it shall be for a sign unto thee upon thy hand, and for a memorial between thine eyes, that the law of Yahweh may be in thy mouth: for with a strong hand hath Yahweh brought thee out of Egypt.

10Thou shalt therefore keep this ordinance in its season from year to year.

11And it shall be, when Yahweh shall bring thee into the land of the Canaanite, as he sware unto thee and to thy fathers, and shall give it thee,

12that thou shalt set apart unto Yahweh all that openeth the womb, and every firstling which thou hast that cometh of a beast; the males shall be Yahweh's.

13And every firstling of an ass thou shalt redeem with a lamb; and if thou wilt not redeem it, then thou shalt break its neck: and all the first-born of man among thy sons shalt thou redeem.

14And it shall be, when thy son asketh thee in time to come, saying, What is this? that thou shalt say unto him, By strength of hand Yahweh brought us out from Egypt, from the house of bondage:

15and it came to pass, when Pharaoh would hardly let us go, that Yahweh slew all the first-born in the land of Egypt, both the first-born of man, and the first-born of beast: therefore I sacrifice to Yahweh all that openeth the womb, being males; but all the first-born of my sons I redeem.

16And it shall be for a sign upon thy hand, and for frontlets between thine eyes: for by strength of hand Yahweh brought us forth out of Egypt.

17And it came to pass, when Pharaoh had let the people go, that God led them not by the way of the land of the Philistines, although that was near; for God said, Lest peradventure the people repent when they see war, and they return to Egypt:

18but God led the people about, by the way of the wilderness by the Red Sea: and the children of Israel went up armed out of the land of Egypt.

19And Moses took the bones of Joseph with him: for he had straitly sworn the children of Israel, saying, God will surely visit you; and ye shall carry up my bones away hence with you.

20And they took their journey from Succoth, and encamped in Etham, in the edge of the wilderness.

21And Yahweh went before them by day in a pillar of cloud, to lead them the way, and by night in a pillar of fire, to give them light, that they might go by day and by night:

22the pillar of cloud by day, and the pillar of fire by night, departed not from before the people.

Chapter 14

1And Yahweh spake unto Moses, saying,

2Speak unto the children of Israel, that they turn back and encamp before Pihahiroth, between Migdol and the sea, before Baal-zephon: over against it shall ye encamp by the sea.

3And Pharaoh will say of the children of Israel, They are entangled in the

Exodus

land, the wilderness hath shut them in.

4And I will harden Pharaoh's heart, and he shall follow after them; and I will get me honor upon Pharaoh, and upon all his host: and the Egyptians shall know that I am Yahweh. And they did so.

5And it was told the king of Egypt that the people were fled: and the heart of Pharaoh and of his servants was changed towards the people, and they said, What is this we have done, that we have let Israel go from serving us?

6And he made ready his chariot, and took his people with him:

7and he took six hundred chosen chariots, and all the chariots of Egypt, and captains over all of them.

8And Yahweh hardened the heart of Pharaoh king of Egypt, and he pursued after the children of Israel: for the children of Israel went out with a high hand.

9And the Egyptians pursued after them, all the horses and chariots of Pharaoh, and his horsemen, and his army, and overtook them encamping by the sea, beside Pihahiroth, before Baal-zephon.

10And when Pharaoh drew nigh, the children of Israel lifted up their eyes, and, behold, the Egyptians were marching after them; and they were sore afraid: and the children of Israel cried out unto Yahweh.

11And they said unto Moses, Because there were no graves in Egypt, hast thou taken us away to die in the wilderness? wherefore hast thou dealt thus with us, to bring us forth out of Egypt?

12Is not this the word that we spake unto thee in Egypt, saying, Let us alone, that we may serve the Egyptians? For it were better for us to serve the Egyptians, than that we should die in the wilderness.

13And Moses said unto the people, Fear ye not, stand still, and see the salvation of Yahweh, which he will work for you to-day: for the Egyptians whom ye have seen to-day, ye shall see them again no more for ever.

14Yahweh will fight for you, and ye shall hold your peace.

15And Yahweh said unto Moses, Wherefore criest thou unto me? speak unto the children of Israel, that they go forward.

16And lift thou up thy rod, and stretch out thy hand over the sea, and divide it: and the children of Israel shall go into the midst of the sea on dry ground.

17And I, behold, I will harden the hearts of the Egyptians, and they shall go in after them: and I will get me honor upon Pharaoh, and upon all his host, upon his chariots, and upon his horsemen.

18And the Egyptians shall know that I am Yahweh, when I have gotten me honor upon Pharaoh, upon his chariots, and upon his horsemen.

19And the angel of God, who went before the camp of Israel, removed and went behind them; and the pillar of cloud removed from before them, and stood behind them:

20and it came between the camp of Egypt and the camp of Israel; and there was the cloud and the darkness, yet gave it light by night: and the one came not near the other all the night.

21And Moses stretched out his hand over the sea; and Yahweh caused the sea to go back by a strong east wind all the night, and made the sea dry land, and the waters were divided.

22And the children of Israel went into the midst of the sea upon the dry ground: and the waters were a wall unto them on their right hand, and on their left.

23And the Egyptians pursued, and went in after them into the midst of the sea, all Pharaoh's horses, his chariots, and his horsemen.

24And it came to pass in the morning watch, that Yahweh looked forth upon the host of the Egyptians through the pillar of fire and of cloud, and discomfited the host of the Egyptians.

25And he took off their chariot wheels, and they drove them heavily; so that the Egyptians said, Let us flee from the face of Israel; for Yahweh fighteth for them against the Egyptians.

26And Yahweh said unto Moses, Stretch out thy hand over the sea, that the waters may come again upon the Egyptians, upon their chariots, and upon their horsemen.

27And Moses stretched forth his hand over the sea, and the sea returned to its strength when the morning appeared; and the Egyptians fled against it; and Yahweh overthrew the Egyptians in the midst of the sea.

28And the waters returned, and covered the chariots, and the horsemen, even all the host of Pharaoh that went in after them into the sea; there remained not so much as one of them.

29But the children of Israel walked upon dry land in the midst of the sea; and the waters were a wall unto them on their right hand, and on their left.

30Thus Yahweh saved Israel that day out of the hand of the Egyptians; and Israel saw the Egyptians dead upon the sea-shore.

31And Israel saw the great work which Yahweh did upon the Egyptians, and the people feared Yahweh: and they believed in Yahweh, and in his servant Moses.

Chapter 15

1Then sang Moses and the children of Israel this song unto Yahweh, and spake, saying,

I will sing unto Yahweh, for he hath triumphed gloriously;
The horse and his rider hath he thrown into the sea.

2Yahweh is my strength and song,
And he is become my salvation:
This is my God, and I will praise him;
My father's God, and I will exalt him.

3Yahweh is a man of war:
Yahweh is his name.

4Pharaoh's chariots and his host hath he cast into the sea;
And his chosen captains are sunk in the Red Sea.

5The deeps cover them:
They went down into the depths like a stone.

6Thy right hand, O Yahweh, is glorious in power,
Thy right hand, O Yahweh, dasheth in pieces the enemy.

7And in the greatness of thine excellency thou overthrowest them that rise up against thee: Thou sendest forth thy wrath, it consumeth them as stubble.

8And with the blast of thy nostrils the waters were piled up,
The floods stood upright as a heap;
The deeps were congealed in the heart of the sea.

9The enemy said, I will pursue, I will overtake, I will divide the spoil;
My desire shall be satisfied upon them;
I will draw my sword, my hand shall destroy them.

10Thou didst blow with thy wind, the sea covered them:
They sank as lead in the mighty waters.

11Who is like unto thee, O Yahweh, among the gods?
Who is like thee, glorious in holiness,
Fearful in praises, doing wonders?

12Thou stretchedst out thy right hand,
The earth swallowed them.

13Thou in thy lovingkindness hast led the people that thou hast redeemed:
Thou hast guided them in thy strength to thy holy habitation.

14The peoples have heard, they tremble:
Pangs have taken hold on the inhabitants of Philistia.

15Then were the chiefs of Edom dismayed;
The mighty men of Moab, trembling taketh hold upon them:
All the inhabitants of Canaan are melted away.

16Terror and dread falleth upon them;
By the greatness of thine arm they are as still as a stone;
Till thy people pass over, O Yahweh,
Till the people pass over that thou hast purchased.

17Thou wilt bring them in, and plant them in the mountain of thine inheritance,
The place, O Yahweh, which thou hast made for thee to dwell in,
The sanctuary, O Lord, which thy hands have established.

18Yahweh shall reign for ever and ever.

19For the horses of Pharaoh went in with his chariots and with his horsemen into the sea, and Yahweh brought back the waters of the sea upon them; but the children of Israel walked on dry land in the midst of the sea.

20And Miriam the prophetess, the sister of Aaron, took a timbrel in her hand; and all the women went out after her with timbrels and with dances.

21And Miriam answered them,
Sing ye to Yahweh, for he hath triumphed gloriously;
The horse and his rider hath he thrown into the sea.

22And Moses led Israel onward from the Red Sea, and they went out into the wilderness of Shur; and they went three days in the wilderness, and found no water.

23And when they came to Marah, they could not drink of the waters of Marah, for they were bitter: therefore the name of it was called Marah.

24And the people murmured against Moses, saying, What shall we drink?

25An he cried unto Yahweh; And Yahweh showed him a tree, and he cast it into the waters, and the waters were made sweet. There he made for them a statute and an ordinance, and there he proved them;

26and he said, If thou wilt diligently hearken to the voice of Yahweh thy God, and wilt do that which is right in his eyes, and wilt give ear to his commandments, and keep all his statutes, I will put none of the diseases upon thee, which I have put upon the Egyptians: for I am Yahweh that healeth thee.

27And they came to Elim, where were twelve springs of water, and threescore and ten palm-trees: and they encamped there by the waters.

Chapter 16

1And they took their journey from Elim, and all the congregation of the children of Israel came unto the wilderness of Sin, which is between Elim and Sinai, on the fifteenth day of the second month after their departing out of the land of Egypt.

2And the whole congregation of the children of Israel murmured against Moses and against Aaron in the wilderness:

3and the children of Israel said unto them, Would that we had died by the hand of Yahweh in the land of Egypt, when we sat by the flesh-pots, when we did eat bread to the full; for ye have brought us forth into this wilderness, to kill this whole assembly with hunger.

4Then said Yahweh unto Moses, Behold, I will rain bread from heaven for you; and the people shall go out and gather a day's portion every day, that I may prove them, whether they will walk in my law, or not.

5And it shall come to pass on the sixth day, that they shall prepare that which they bring in, and it shall be twice as much as they gather daily.

6And Moses and Aaron said unto all the children of Israel, At even, then ye shall know that Yahweh hath brought you out from the land of Egypt;

7and in the morning, then ye shall see the glory of Yahweh; for that he heareth your murmurings against Yahweh: and what are we, that ye murmur against us?

8And Moses said, This shall be, when Yahweh shall give you in the evening flesh to eat, and in the morning bread to the full; for that Yahweh heareth your murmurings which ye murmur against him: and what are we? your murmurings are not against us, but against Yahweh.

9And Moses said unto Aaron, Say unto all the congregation of the children of Israel, Come near before Yahweh; for he hath heard your murmurings.

10And it came to pass, as Aaron spake unto the whole congregation of the children of Israel, that they looked toward the wilderness, and, behold, the glory of Yahweh appeared in the cloud.

11And Yahweh spake unto Moses, saying,

12I have heard the murmurings of the children of Israel: speak unto them, saying, At even ye shall eat flesh, and in the morning ye shall be filled with bread:

and ye shall know that I am Yahweh your God.

¹³And it came to pass at even, that the quails came up, and covered the camp: and in the morning the dew lay round about the camp.

¹⁴And when the dew that lay was gone up, behold, upon the face of the wilderness a small round thing, small as the hoar-frost on the ground.

¹⁵And when the children of Israel saw it, they said one to another, What is it? For they knew not what it was. And Moses said unto them, It is the bread which Yahweh hath given you to eat.

¹⁶This is the thing which Yahweh hath commanded, Gather ye of it every man according to his eating; an omer a head, according to the number of your persons, shall ye take it, every man for them that are in his tent.

¹⁷And the children of Israel did so, and gathered some more, some less.

¹⁸And when they measured it with an omer, he that gathered much had nothing over, and he that gathered little had no lack; they gathered every man according to his eating.

¹⁹And Moses said unto them, Let no man leave of it till the morning.

²⁰Notwithstanding they hearkened not unto Moses; but some of them left of it until the morning, and it bred worms, and became foul: and Moses was wroth with them.

²¹And they gathered it morning by morning, every man according to his eating: and when the sun waxed hot, it melted.

²²And it came to pass, that on the sixth day they gathered twice as much bread, two omers for each one: and all the rulers of the congregation came and told Moses.

²³And he said unto them, This is that which Yahweh hath spoken, Tomorrow is a solemn rest, a holy sabbath unto Yahweh: bake that which ye will bake, and boil that which ye will boil; and all that remaineth over lay up for you to be kept until the morning.

²⁴And they laid it up till the morning, as Moses bade: and it did not become foul, neither was there any worm therein.

²⁵And Moses said, Eat that to-day; for to-day is a sabbath unto Yahweh: to-day ye shall not find it in the field.

²⁶Six days ye shall gather it; but on the seventh day is the sabbath, in it there shall be none.

²⁷And it came to pass on the seventh day, that there went out some of the people to gather, and they found none.

²⁸And Yahweh said unto Moses, How long refuse ye to keep my commandments and my laws?

²⁹See, for that Yahweh hath given you the sabbath, therefore he giveth you on the sixth day the bread of two days; abide ye every man in his place, let no man go out of his place on the seventh day.

³⁰So the people rested on the seventh day.

³¹And the house of Israel called the name thereof Manna: and it was like coriander seed, white; and the taste of it was like wafers made with honey.

³²And Moses said, This is the thing which Yahweh hath commanded, Let an omerful of it be kept throughout your generations, that they may see the bread wherewith I fed you in the wilderness, when I brought you forth from the land of Egypt.

³³And Moses said unto Aaron, Take a pot, and put an omerful of manna therein, and lay it up before Yahweh, to be kept throughout your generations.

³⁴As Yahweh commanded Moses, so Aaron laid it up before the Testimony, to be kept.

³⁵And the children of Israel did eat the manna forty years, until they came to a land inhabited; they did eat the manna, until they came unto the borders of the land of Canaan.

³⁶Now an omer is the tenth part of an ephah.

Chapter 17

¹And all the congregation of the children of Israel journeyed from the wilderness of Sin, by their journeys, according to the commandment of Yahweh, and encamped in Rephidim: and there was no water for the people to drink.

²Wherefore the people stove with Moses, and said, Give us water that we may drink. And Moses said unto them, Why strive ye with me? Wherefore do ye tempt Yahweh?

³And the people thirsted there for water; and the people murmured against Moses, and said, Wherefore hast thou brought us up out of Egypt, to kill us and our children and our cattle with thirst?

⁴And Moses cried unto Yahweh, saying, What shall I do unto this people? They are almost ready to stone me.

⁵And Yahweh said unto Moses, Pass on before the people, and take with thee of the elders of Israel; and they rod, wherewith thou smotest the river, take in thy hand, and go.

⁶Behold, I will stand before thee there upon the rock in Horeb; and thou shalt smite the rock, and there shall come water out of it, that the people may drink. And Moses did so in the sight of the elders of Israel.

⁷And he called the name of the place Massah, and Meribah, because of the striving of the children of Israel, and because they tempted Yahweh, saying, Is Yahweh among us, or not?

⁸Then came Amalek, and fought with Israel in Rephidim.

⁹And Moses said unto Joshua, Choose us out men, and go out, fight with Amalek: to-morrow I will stand on the top of the hill with the rod of God in my hand.

¹⁰So Joshua did as Moses had said to him, and fought with Amalek: and Moses, Aaron, and Hur went up to the top of the hill.

¹¹And it came to pass, when Moses held up his hand, that Israel prevailed; and when he let down his hand, Amalek prevailed.

¹²But Moses' hands were heavy; and they took a stone, and put it under him, and he sat thereon; and Aaron and Hur stayed up his hands, the one on the one side, and the other on the other side; And his hands were steady until the going down of the sun.

¹³And Joshua discomfited Amalek and his people with the edge of the sword.

¹⁴And Yahweh said unto Moses, Write this for a memorial in a book, and rehearse it in the ears of Joshua: that I will utterly blot out the remembrance of Amalek from under heaven.

¹⁵And Moses built an altar, and called the name of it Yahweh-nissi;

¹⁶And he said, Yahweh hath sworn: Yahweh will have war with Amalek from generation to generation.

Chapter 18

¹Now Jethro, the priest of Midian, Moses' father-in-law, heard of all that God had done for Moses, and for Israel his people, how that Yahweh had brought Israel out of Egypt.

²And Jethro, Moses' father-in-law, took Zipporah, Moses' wife, after he had sent her away,

³and her two sons; of whom the name of the one was Gershom; for he said, I have been a sojourner in a foreign land:

⁴and the name of the other was Eliezer; for he said, The God of my father was my help, and delivered me from the sword of Pharaoh.

⁵And Jethro, Moses' father-in-law, came with his sons and his wife unto Moses into the wilderness where he was encamped, at the mount of God:

⁶and he said unto Moses, I, thy father-in-law Jethro, am come unto thee, and thy wife, and her two sons with her.

⁷And Moses went out to meet his father-in-law, and did obeisance, and kissed him: and they asked each other of their welfare; and they came into the tent.

⁸And Moses told his father-in-law all that Yahweh had done unto Pharaoh and to the Egyptians for Israel's sake, all the travail that had come upon them by the way, and how Yahweh delivered them.

⁹And Jethro rejoiced for all the goodness which Yahweh had done to Israel, in that he had delivered them out of the hand of the Egyptians.

¹⁰And Jethro said, Blessed be Yahweh, who hath delivered you out of the hand of the Egyptians, and out of the hand of Pharaoh; who hath delivered the people from under the hand of the Egyptians.

¹¹Now I know that Yahweh is greater than all gods; yea, in the thing wherein they dealt proudly against them.

¹²And Jethro, Moses' father-in-law, took a burnt-offering and sacrifices for God: and Aaron came, and all the elders of Israel, to eat bread with Moses' father-in-law before God.

¹³And it came to pass on the morrow, that Moses sat to judge the people: and the people stood about Moses from the morning unto the evening.

¹⁴And when Moses' father-in-law saw all that he did to the people, he said, What is this thing that thou doest to the people? why sittest thou thyself alone, and all the people stand about thee from morning unto even?

¹⁵And Moses said unto his father-in-law, Because the people come unto me to inquire of God:

¹⁶when they have a matter, they come unto me; and I judge between a man and his neighbor, and I make them know the statutes of God, and his laws.

¹⁷And Moses' father-in-law said unto him, The thing that thou doest is not good.

¹⁸Thou wilt surely wear away, both thou, and this people that is with thee: for the thing is too heavy for thee; thou art not able to perform it thyself alone.

¹⁹Hearken now unto my voice, I will give thee counsel, and God be with thee: be thou for the people to God-ward, and bring thou the causes unto God:

²⁰and thou shalt teach them the statutes and the laws, and shalt show them the way wherein they must walk, and the work that they must do.

²¹Moreover thou shalt provide out of all the people able men, such as fear God, men of truth, hating unjust gain; and place such over them, to be rulers of thousands, rulers of hundreds, rulers of fifties, and rulers of tens:

²²and let them judge the people at all seasons: and it shall be, that every great matter they shall bring unto thee, but every small matter they shall judge themselves: so shall it be easier for thyself, and they shall bear the burden with thee.

²³If thou shalt do this thing, and God command thee so, then thou shalt be able to endure, and all this people also shall go to their place in peace.

²⁴So Moses hearkened to the voice of his father-in-law, and did all that he had said.

²⁵And Moses chose able men out of all Israel, and made them heads over the people, rulers of thousands, rulers of hundreds, rulers of fifties, and rulers of tens.

²⁶And they judged the people at all seasons: the hard causes they brought unto Moses, but every small matter they judged themselves.

²⁷And Moses let his father-in-law depart; and he went his way into his own land.

Chapter 19

¹In the third month after the children of Israel were gone forth out of the land of Egypt, the same day came they into the wilderness of Sinai.

²And when they were departed from Rephidim, and were come to the wilderness of Sinai, they encamped in the wilderness; and there Israel encamped before the mount.

³And Moses went up unto God, and Yahweh called unto him out of the mountain, saying, Thus shalt thou say to the house of Jacob, and tell the children of Israel:

⁴Ye have seen what I did unto the Egyptians, and how I bare you on eagles' wings, and brought you unto myself.

⁵Now therefore, if ye will obey my voice indeed, and keep my covenant, then ye shall be mine own possession from among all peoples: for all the earth is

Exodus

mine:

6and ye shall be unto me a kingdom of priests, and a holy nation. These are the words which thou shalt speak unto the children of Israel.

7And Moses came and called for the elders of the people, and set before them all these words which Yahweh commanded him.

8And all the people answered together, and said, All that Yahweh hath spoken we will do. And Moses reported the words of the people unto Yahweh.

9And Yahweh said unto Moses, Lo, I come unto thee in a thick cloud, that the people may hear when I speak with thee, and may also believe thee for ever. And Moses told the words of the people unto Yahweh.

10And Yahweh said unto Moses, Go unto the people, and sanctify them to-day and to-morrow, and let them wash their garments,

11and be ready against the third day; for the third day Yahweh will come down in the sight of all the people upon mount Sinai.

12And thou shalt set bounds unto the people round about, saying, Take heed to yourselves, that ye go not up into the mount, or touch the border of it: whosoever toucheth the mount shall be surely put to death:

13no hand shall touch him, but he shall surely be stoned, or shot through; whether it be beast or man, he shall not live: when the trumpet soundeth long, they shall come up to the mount.

14And Moses went down from the mount unto the people, and sanctified the people; and they washed their garments.

15And he said unto the people, Be ready against the third day: come not near a woman.

16And it came to pass on the third day, when it was morning, that there were thunders and lightnings, and a thick cloud upon the mount, and the voice of a trumpet exceeding loud; and all the people that were in the camp trembled.

17And Moses brought forth the people out of the camp to meet God; and they stood at the nether part of the mount.

18And mount Sinai, the whole of it, smoked, because Yahweh descended upon it in fire; and the smoke thereof ascended as the smoke of a furnace, and the whole mount quaked greatly.

19And when the voice of the trumpet waxed louder and louder, Moses spake, and God answered him by a voice.

20And Yahweh came down upon mount Sinai, to the top of the mount: and Yahweh called Moses to the top of the mount; and Moses went up.

21And Yahweh said unto Moses, Go down, charge the people, lest they break through unto Yahweh to gaze, and many of them perish.

22And let the priests also, that come near to Yahweh, sanctify themselves, lest Yahweh break forth upon them.

23And Moses said unto Yahweh, The people cannot come up to mount Sinai: for thou didst charge us, saying, Set bounds about the mount, and sanctify it.

24And Yahweh said unto him, Go, get thee down; and thou shalt come up, thou, and Aaron with thee: but let not the priests and the people break through to come up unto Yahweh, lest he break forth upon them.

25So Moses went down unto the people, and told them.

Chapter 20

1And God spake all these words, saying,

2I am Yahweh thy God, who brought thee out of the land of Egypt, out of the house of bondage.

3Thou shalt have no other gods before me.

4Thou shalt not make unto thee a graven image, nor any likeness of any thing that is in heaven above, or that is in the earth beneath, or that is in the water under the earth.

5Thou shalt not bow down thyself unto them, nor serve them, for I Yahweh thy God am a jealous God, visiting the iniquity of the fathers upon the children, upon the third and upon the fourth generation of them that hate me,

6and showing lovingkindness unto thousands of them that love me and keep my commandments.

7Thou shalt not take the name of Yahweh thy God in vain; for Yahweh will not hold him guiltless that taketh his name in vain.

8Remember the sabbath day, to keep it holy.

9Six days shalt thou labor, and do all thy work;

10but the seventh day is a sabbath unto Yahweh thy God: in it thou shalt not do any work, thou, nor thy son, nor thy daughter, thy man-servant, nor thy maid-servant, nor thy cattle, nor thy stranger that is within thy gates:

11for in six days Yahweh made heaven and earth, the sea, and all that in them is, and rested the seventh day: wherefore Yahweh blessed the sabbath day, and hallowed it.

12Honor thy father and thy mother, that thy days may be long in the land which Yahweh thy God giveth thee.

13Thou shalt not kill.

14Thou shalt not commit adultery.

15Thou shalt not steal.

16Thou shalt not bear false witness against thy neighbor.

17Thou shalt not covet thy neighbor's house, thou shalt not covet thy neighbor's wife, nor his man-servant, nor his maid-servant, nor his ox, nor his ass, nor anything that is thy neighbor's.

18And all the people perceived the thunderings, and the lightnings, and the voice of the trumpet, and the mountain smoking: and when the people saw it, they trembled, and stood afar off.

19And they said unto Moses, Speak thou with us, and we will hear; but let not God speak with us, lest we die.

20And Moses said unto the people, Fear not: for God is come to prove you, and that his fear may be before you, that ye sin not.

21And the people stood afar off, and Moses drew near unto the thick darkness where God was.

22And Yahweh said unto Moses, Thus thou shalt say unto the children of Israel, Ye yourselves have seen that I have talked with you from heaven.

23Ye shall not make other gods with me; gods of silver, or gods of gold, ye shall not make unto you.

24An altar of earth thou shalt make unto me, and shalt sacrifice thereon thy burnt-offerings, and thy peace-offerings, thy sheep, and thine oxen: in every place where I record my name I will come unto thee and I will bless thee.

25And if thou make me an altar of stone, thou shalt not build it of hewn stones; for if thou lift up thy tool upon it, thou hast polluted it.

26Neither shalt thou go up by steps unto mine altar, that thy nakedness be not uncovered thereon.

Chapter 21

21 1Now these are the ordinances which thou shalt set before them.

2If thou buy a Hebrew servant, six years he shall serve: and in the seventh he shall go out free for nothing.

3If he come in by himself, he shall go out by himself: if he be married, then his wife shall go out with him.

4If his master give him a wife and she bear him sons or daughters; the wife and her children shall be her master's, and he shall go out by himself.

5But if the servant shall plainly say, I love my master, my wife, and my children; I will not go out free:

6then his master shall bring him unto God, and shall bring him to the door, or unto the door-post; and his master shall bore his ear through with an awl; and he shall serve him for ever.

7And if a man sell his daughter to be a maid-servant, she shall not go out as the men-servants do.

8If she please not her master, who hath espoused her to himself, then shall he let her be redeemed: to sell her unto a foreign people he shall have no power, seeing he hath dealt deceitfully with her.

9And if he espouse her unto his son, he shall deal with her after the manner of daughters.

10If he take him another wife; her food, her raiment, and her duty of marriage, shall he not diminish.

11And if he do not these three things unto her, then shall she go out for nothing, without money.

12He that smiteth a man, so that he dieth, shall surely be put to death.

13And if a man lie not in wait, but God deliver him into his hand; then I will appoint thee a place whither he shall flee.

14And if a man come presumptuously upon his neighbor, to slay him with guile; thou shalt take him from mine altar, that he may die.

15And he that smiteth his father, or his mother, shall be surely put to death.

16And he that stealeth a man, and selleth him, or if he be found in his hand, he shall surely be put to death.

17And he that curseth his father or his mother, shall surely be put to death.

18And if men contend, and one smite the other with a stone, or with his fist, and he die not, but keep his bed;

19if he rise again, and walk abroad upon his staff, then shall he that smote him be quit: only he shall pay for the loss of his time, and shall cause him to be thoroughly healed.

20And if a man smite his servant, or his maid, with a rod, and he die under his hand; he shall surely be punished.

21Notwithstanding, if he continue a day or two, he shall not be punished: for he is his money.

22And if men strive together, and hurt a woman with child, so that her fruit depart, and yet no harm follow; he shall be surely fined, according as the woman's husband shall lay upon him; and he shall pay as the judges determine.

23But if any harm follow, then thou shalt give life for life,

24eye for eye, tooth for tooth, hand for hand, foot for foot,

25burning for burning, wound for wound, stripe for stripe.

26And if a man smite the eye of his servant, or the eye of his maid, and destroy it; he shall let him go free for his eye's sake.

27And if he smite out his man-servant's tooth, or his maid-servant's tooth, he shall let him go free for his tooth's sake.

28And if an ox gore a man or a woman to death, the ox shall be surely stoned, and its flesh shall not be eaten; but the owner of the ox shall be quit.

29But if the ox was wont to gore in time past, and it hath been testified to its owner, and he hath not kept it in, but it hath killed a man or a woman, the ox shall be stoned, and its owner also shall be put to death.

30If there be laid on him a ransom, then he shall give for the redemption of his life whatsoever is laid upon him.

31Whether it have gored a son, or have gored a daughter, according to this judgment shall it be done unto him.

32If the ox gore a man-servant or a maid-servant, there shall be given unto their master thirty shekels of silver, and the ox shall be stoned.

33And if a man shall open a pit, or if a man shall dig a pit and not cover it, and an ox or an ass fall therein,

34the owner of the pit shall make it good; he shall give money unto the owner thereof, and the dead beast shall be his.

35And if one man's ox hurt another's, so that it dieth, then they shall sell the live ox, and divide the price of it: and the dead also they shall divide.

36Or if it be known that the ox was wont to gore in time past, and its owner hath not kept it in, he shall surely pay ox for ox, and the dead beast shall be his own.

Chapter 22

1If a man shall steal an ox, or a sheep, and kill it, or sell it; he shall pay five oxen for an ox, and four sheep for a sheep.

2If the thief be found breaking in, and be smitten so that he dieth, there shall be no bloodguiltiness for him.

3If the sun be risen upon him, there shall be bloodguiltiness for him; he shall make restitution: if he have nothing, then he shall be sold for his theft.

4If the theft be found in his hand alive, whether it be ox, or ass, or sheep, he shall pay double.

5If a man shall cause a field or vineyard to be eaten, and shall let his beast loose, and it feed in another man's field; of the best of his own field, and of the best of his own vineyard, shall he make restitution.

6If fire break out, and catch in thorns, so that the shocks of grain, or the standing grain, or the field are consumed; he that kindled the fire shall surely make restitution.

7If a man shall deliver unto his neighbor money or stuff to keep, and it be stolen out of the man's house; if the thief be found, he shall pay double.

8If the thief be not found, then the master of the house shall come near unto God, to see whether he have not put his hand unto his neighbor's goods.

9For every matter of trespass, whether it be for ox, for ass, for sheep, for raiment, or for any manner of lost thing, whereof one saith, This is it, the cause of both parties shall come before God; he whom God shall condemn shall pay double unto his neighbor.

10If a man deliver unto his neighbor an ass, or an ox, or a sheep, or any beast, to keep; and it die, or be hurt, or driven away, no man seeing it:

11the oath of Yahweh shall be between them both, whether he hath not put his hand unto his neighbor's goods; and the owner thereof shall accept it, and he shall not make restitution.

12But if it be stolen from him, he shall make restitution unto the owner thereof.

13If it be torn in pieces, let him bring it for witness: he shall not make good that which was torn.

14And if a man borrow aught of his neighbor, and it be hurt, or die, the owner thereof not being with it, he shall surely make restitution.

15If the owner thereof be with it, he shall not make it good: if it be a hired thing, it came for its hire.

16And if a man entice a virgin that is not betrothed, and lie with her, he shall surely pay a dowry for her to be his wife.

17If her father utterly refuse to give her unto him, he shall pay money according to the dowry of virgins.

18Thou shalt not suffer a sorceress to live.

19Whosoever lieth with a beast shall surely be put to death.

20He that sacrificeth unto any god, save unto Yahweh only, shall be utterly destroyed.

21And a sojourner shalt thou not wrong, neither shalt thou oppress him: for ye were sojourners in the land of Egypt.

22Ye shall not afflict any widow, or fatherless child.

23If thou afflict them at all, and they cry at all unto me, I will surely hear their cry;

24and my wrath shall wax hot, and I will kill you with the sword; and your wives shall be widows, and your children fatherless.

25If thou lend money to any of my people with thee that is poor, thou shalt not be to him as a creditor; neither shall ye lay upon him interest.

26If thou at all take thy neighbor's garment to pledge, thou shalt restore it unto him before the sun goeth down:

27for that is his only covering, it is his garment for his skin: wherein shall he sleep? And it shall come to pass, when he crieth unto me, that I will hear; for I am gracious.

28Thou shalt not revile God, nor curse a ruler of thy people.

29Thou shalt not delay to offer of thy harvest, and of the outflow of thy presses. The first-born of thy sons shalt thou give unto me.

30Likewise shalt thou do with thine oxen, and with thy sheep: seven days it shall be with its dam; on the eighth day thou shalt give it me.

31And ye shall be holy men unto me: therefore ye shall not eat any flesh that is torn of beasts in the field; ye shall cast it to the dogs.

Chapter 23

1Thou shalt not take up a false report: put not thy hand with the wicked to be an unrighteous witness.

2Thou shalt not follow a multitude to do evil; neither shalt thou speak in a cause to turn aside after a multitude to wrest justice:

3neither shalt thou favor a poor man in his cause.

4If thou meet thine enemy's ox or his ass going astray, thou shalt surely bring it back to him again.

5If thou see the ass of him that hateth thee lying under his burden, thou shalt forbear to leave him, thou shalt surely release it with him.

6Thou shalt not wrest the justice due to thy poor in his cause.

7Keep thee far from a false matter; and the innocent and righteous slay thou not: for I will not justify the wicked.

8And thou shalt take no bribe: for a bribe blindeth them that have sight, and perverteth the words of the righteous.

9And a sojourner shalt thou not oppress: for ye know the heart of a sojourner, seeing ye were sojourners in the land of Egypt.

10And six years thou shalt sow thy land, and shalt gather in the increase thereof:

11but the seventh year thou shalt let it rest and lie fallow; that the poor of thy people may eat: and what they leave the beast of the field shall eat. In like manner thou shalt deal with thy vineyard, and with thy oliveyard.

12Six days thou shalt do thy work, and on the seventh day thou shalt rest; that thine ox and thine ass may have rest, and the son of thy handmaid, and the sojourner, may be refreshed.

13And in all things that I have said unto you take ye heed: and make no mention of the name of other gods, neither let it be heard out of thy mouth.

14Three times thou shalt keep a feast unto me in the year.

15The feast of unleavened bread shalt thou keep: seven days thou shalt eat unleavened bread, as I commanded thee, at the time appointed in the month Abib (for in it thou camest out from Egypt); and none shall appear before me empty:

16and the feast of harvest, the first-fruits of thy labors, which thou sowest in the field: and the feast of ingathering, at the end of the year, when thou gatherest in thy labors out of the field.

17Three times in the year all thy males shall appear before the Lord Yahweh.

18Thou shalt not offer the blood of my sacrifice with leavened bread; neither shall the fat of my feast remain all night until the morning.

19The first of the first-fruits of thy ground thou shalt bring into the house of Yahweh thy God. Thou shalt not boil a kid in it mother's milk.

20Behold, I send an angel before thee, to keep thee by the way, and to bring thee into the place which I have prepared.

21Take ye heed before him, and hearken unto his voice; provoke him not; for he will not pardon your transgression: for my name is in him.

22But if thou shalt indeed hearken unto his voice, and do all that I speak; then I will be an enemy unto thine enemies, and an adversary unto thine adversaries.

23For mine angel shall go before thee, and bring thee in unto the Amorite, and the Hittite, and the Perizzite, and the Canaanite, the Hivite, and the Jebusite: and I will cut them off.

24Thou shalt not bow down to their gods, nor serve them, nor do after their works; but thou shalt utterly overthrow them, and break in pieces their pillars.

25And ye shall serve Yahweh your God, and he will bless thy bread, and thy water; and I will take sickness away from the midst of thee.

26There shall none cast her young, nor be barren, in thy land: the number of thy days I will fulfil.

27I will send my terror before thee, and will discomfit all the people to whom thou shalt come, and I will make all thine enemies turn their backs unto thee.

28And I will send the hornet before thee, which shall drive out the Hivite, the Canaanite, and the Hittite, from before thee.

29I will not drive them out from before thee in one year, lest the land become desolate, and the beasts of the field multiply against thee.

30By little and little I will drive them out from before thee, until thou be increased, and inherit the land.

31And I will set thy border from the Red Sea even unto the sea of the Philistines, and from the wilderness unto the River: for I will deliver the inhabitants of the land into your hand: and thou shalt drive them out before thee.

32Thou shalt make no covenant with them, nor with their gods.

33They shall not dwell in thy land, lest they make thee sin against me; for if thou serve their gods, it will surely be a snare unto thee.

Chapter 24

1And he said unto Moses, Come up unto Yahweh, thou, and Aaron, Nadab, and Abihu, and seventy of the elders of Israel; and worship ye afar off:

2and Moses alone shall come near unto Yahweh; but they shall not come near; neither shall the people go up with him.

3And Moses came and told the people all the words of Yahweh, and all the ordinances: and all the people answered with one voice, and said, All the words which Yahweh hath spoken will we do.

4And Moses wrote all the words of Yahweh, and rose up early in the morning, and builded an altar under the mount, and twelve pillars, according to the twelve tribes of Israel.

5And he sent young men of the children of Israel, who offered burnt-offerings, and sacrificed peace-offerings of oxen unto Yahweh.

6And Moses took half of the blood, and put it in basins; and half of the blood he sprinkled on the altar.

7And he took the book of the covenant, and read in the audience of the people: and they said, All that Yahweh hath spoken will we do, and be obedient.

8And Moses took the blood, and sprinkled it on the people, and said, Behold the blood of the covenant, which Yahweh hath made with you concerning all these words.

9Then went up Moses, and Aaron, Nadab, and Abihu, and seventy of the elders of Israel.

10And they saw the God of Israel; and there was under his feet as it were a paved work of sapphire stone, and as it were the very heaven for clearness.

11And upon the nobles of the children of Israel he laid not his hand: and they beheld God, and did eat and drink.

12And Yahweh said unto Moses, Come up to me into the mount, and be there: and I will give thee the tables of stone, and the law and the commandment, which I have written, that thou mayest teach them.

13And Moses rose up, and Joshua his minister: and Moses went up into the mount of God.

14And he said unto the elders, Tarry ye here for us, until we come again unto you: and, behold, Aaron and Hur are with you: whosoever hath a cause, let him come near unto them.

15And Moses went up into the mount, and the cloud covered the mount.

16And the glory of Yahweh abode upon mount Sinai, and the cloud covered it six days: and the seventh day he called unto Moses out of the midst of the cloud.

17And the appearance of the glory of Yahweh was like devouring fire on the

Exodus

top of the mount in the eyes of the children of Israel.

18And Moses entered into the midst of the cloud, and went up into the mount: and Moses was in the mount forty days and forty nights.

Chapter 25

1And Yahweh spake unto Moses, saying,

2Speak unto the children of Israel, that they take for me an offering: of every man whose heart maketh him willing ye shall take my offering.

3And this is the offering which ye shall take of them: gold, and silver, and brass,

4and blue, and purple, and scarlet, and fine linen, and goats' hair,

5and rams' skins dyed red, and sealskins, and acacia wood,

6oil for the light, spices for the anointing oil, and for the sweet incense,

7onyx stones, and stones to be set, for the ephod, and for the breastplate.

8And let them make me a sanctuary, that I may dwell among them.

9According to all that I show thee, the pattern of the tabernacle, and the pattern of all the furniture thereof, even so shall ye make it.

10And they shall make an ark of acacia wood: two cubits and a half shall be the length thereof, and a cubit and a half the breadth thereof, and a cubit and a half the height thereof.

11And thou shalt overlay it with pure gold, within and without shalt thou overlay it, and shalt make upon it a crown of gold round about.

12And thou shalt cast four rings of gold for it, and put them in the four feet thereof; and two rings shall be on the one side of it, and two rings on the other side of it.

13And thou shalt make staves of acacia wood, and overlay them with gold.

14And thou shalt put the staves into the rings on the sides of the ark, wherewith to bear the ark.

15The staves shall be in the rings of the ark: they shall not be taken from it.

16And thou shalt put into the ark the testimony which I shall give thee.

17And thou shalt make a mercy-seat of pure gold: two cubits and a half shall be the length thereof, and a cubit and a half the breadth thereof.

18And thou shalt make two cherubim of gold; of beaten work shalt thou make them, at the two ends of the mercy-seat.

19And make one cherub at the one end, and one cherub at the other end: of one piece with the mercy-seat shall ye make the cherubim on the two ends thereof.

20And the cherubim shall spread out their wings on high, covering the mercy-seat with their wings, with their faces one to another; toward the mercy-seat shall the faces of the cherubim be.

21And thou shalt put the mercy-seat above upon the ark; and in the ark thou shalt put the testimony that I shall give thee.

22And there I will meet with thee, and I will commune with thee from above the mercy-seat, from between the two cherubim which are upon the ark of the testimony, of all things which I will give thee in commandment unto the children of Israel.

23And thou shalt make a table of acacia wood: two cubits shall be the length thereof, and a cubit the breadth thereof, and a cubit and a half the height thereof.

24And thou shalt overlay it with pure gold, and make thereto a crown of gold round about.

25And thou shalt make unto it a border of a handbreadth round about; and thou shalt make a golden crown to the border thereof round about.

26And thou shalt make for it four rings of gold, and put the rings in the four corners that are on the four feet thereof.

27Close by the border shall the rings be, for places for the staves to bear the table.

28And thou shalt make the staves of acacia wood, and overlay them with gold, that the table may be borne with them.

29And thou shalt make the dishes thereof, and the spoons thereof, and the flagons thereof, and the bowls thereof, wherewith to pour out: of pure gold shalt thou make them.

30And thou shalt set upon the table showbread before me alway.

31And thou shalt make a candlestick of pure gold: of beaten work shall the candlestick be made, even its base, and its shaft; its cups, its knops, and its flowers, shall be of one piece with it.

32And there shall be six branches going out of the sides thereof; three branches of the candlestick out of the one side thereof, and three branches of the candlestick out of the other side thereof:

33three cups made like almond-blossoms in one branch, a knop and a flower; and three cups made like almond-blossoms in the other branch, a knop and a flower: so for the six branches going out of the candlestick:

34and in the candlestick four cups made like almond-blossoms, the knops thereof, and the flowers thereof;

35and a knop under two branches of one piece with it, and a knop under two branches of one piece with it, and a knop under two branches of one piece with it, for the six branches going out of the candlestick.

36Their knops and their branches shall be of one piece with it; the whole of it one beaten work of pure gold.

37And thou shalt make the lamps thereof, seven: and they shall light the lamps thereof, to give light over against it.

38And the snuffers thereof, and the snuffdishes thereof, shall be of pure gold.

39Of a talent of pure gold shall it be made, with all these vessels.

40And see that thou make them after their pattern, which hath been showed thee in the mount.

Chapter 26

1Moreover thou shalt make the tabernacle with ten curtains; of fine twined linen, and blue, and purple, and scarlet, with cherubim the work of the skilful workman shalt thou make them.

2The length of each curtain shall be eight and twenty cubits, and the breadth of each curtain four cubits: all the curtains shall have one measure.

3Five curtains shall be coupled together one to another; and the other five curtains shall be coupled one to another.

4And thou shalt make loops of blue upon the edge of the one curtain from the selvedge in the coupling; and likewise shalt thou make in the edge of the curtain that is outmost in the second coupling.

5Fifty loops shalt thou make in the one curtain, and fifty loops shalt thou make in the edge of the curtain that is in the second coupling; the loops shall be opposite one to another.

6And thou shalt make fifty clasps of gold, and couple the curtains one to another with the clasps: and the tabernacle shall be one whole.

7And thou shalt make curtains of goats' hair for a tent over the tabernacle: eleven curtains shalt thou make them.

8The length of each curtain shall be thirty cubits, and the breadth of each curtain four cubits: the eleven curtains shall have one measure.

9And thou shalt couple five curtains by themselves, and six curtains by themselves, and shalt double over the sixth curtain in the forefront of the tent.

10And thou shalt make fifty loops on the edge of the one curtain that is outmost in the coupling, and fifty loops upon the edge of the curtain which is outmost in the second coupling.

11And thou shalt make fifty clasps of brass, and put the clasps into the loops, and couple the tent together, that it may be one.

12And the overhanging part that remaineth of the curtains of the tent, the half curtain that remaineth, shall hang over the back of the tabernacle.

13And the cubit on the one side, and the cubit on the other side, of that which remaineth in the length of the curtains of the tent, shall hang over the sides of the tabernacle on this side and on that side, to cover it.

14And thou shalt make a covering for the tent of rams' skins dyed red, and a covering of sealskins above.

15And thou shalt make the boards for the tabernacle of acacia wood, standing up.

16Ten cubits shall be the length of a board, and a cubit and a half the breadth of each board.

17Two tenons shall there be in each board, joined one to another: thus shalt thou make for all the boards of the tabernacle.

18And thou shalt make the boards for the tabernacle, twenty boards for the south side southward.

19And thou shalt make forty sockets of silver under the twenty boards; two sockets under one board for its two tenons, and two sockets under another board for its two tenons.

20And for the second side of the tabernacle, on the north side, twenty boards,

21and their forty sockets of silver; two sockets under one board, and two sockets under another board.

22And for the hinder part of the tabernacle westward thou shalt make six boards.

23And two boards shalt thou make for the corners of the tabernacle in the hinder part.

24And they shall be double beneath, and in like manner they shall be entire unto the top thereof unto one ring: thus shall it be for them both; they shall be for the two corners.

25And there shall be eight boards, and their sockets of silver, sixteen sockets; two sockets under one board, and two sockets under another board.

26And thou shalt make bars of acacia wood: five for the boards of the one side of the tabernacle,

27and five bars for the boards of the other side of the tabernacle, and five bars for the boards of the side of the tabernacle, for the hinder part westward.

28And the middle bar in the midst of the boards shall pass through from end to end.

29And thou shalt overlay the boards with gold, and make their rings of gold for places for the bars: and thou shalt overlay the bars with gold.

30And thou shalt rear up the tabernacle according to the fashion thereof which hath been showed thee in the mount.

31And thou shalt make a veil of blue, and purple, and scarlet, and fine twined linen: with cherubim the work of the skilful workman shall it be made.

32And thou shalt hang it upon four pillars of acacia overlaid with gold; their hooks shall be of gold, upon four sockets of silver.

33And thou shalt hang up the veil under the clasps, and shalt bring in thither within the veil the ark of the testimony: and the veil shall separate unto you between the holy place and the most holy.

34And thou shalt put the mercy-seat upon the ark of the testimony in the most holy place.

35And thou shalt set the table without the veil, and the candlestick over against the table on the side of the tabernacle toward the south: and thou shalt put the table on the north side.

36And thou shalt make a screen for the door of the Tent, of blue, and purple, and scarlet, and fine twined linen, the work of the embroiderer.

37And thou shalt make for the screen five pillars of acacia, and overlay them with gold: their hooks shall be of gold: and thou shalt cast five sockets of brass for them.

Chapter 27

1 And thou shalt make the altar of acacia wood, five cubits long, and five cubits broad; the altar shall be foursquare: and the height thereof shall be three cubits.

2 And thou shalt make the horns of it upon the four corners thereof; the horns thereof shall be of one piece with it: and thou shalt overlay it with brass.

3 And thou shalt make its pots to take away its ashes, and its shovels, and its basins, and its flesh-hooks, and its firepans: all the vessels thereof thou shalt make of brass.

4 And thou shalt make for it a grating of network of brass: and upon the net shalt thou make four brazen rings in the four corners thereof.

5 And thou shalt put it under the ledge round the altar beneath, that the net may reach halfway up the altar.

6 And thou shalt make staves for the altar, staves of acacia wood, and overlay them with brass.

7 And the staves thereof shall be put into the rings, and the staves shall be upon the two sides of the altar, in bearing it.

8 Hollow with planks shalt thou make it: as it hath been showed thee in the mount, so shall they make it.

9 And thou shalt make the court of the tabernacle: for the south side southward there shall be hangings for the court of fine twined linen a hundred cubits long for one side:

10 and the pillars thereof shall be twenty, and their sockets twenty, of brass; the hooks of the pillars and their fillets shall be of silver.

11 And likewise for the north side in length there shall be hangings a hundred cubits long, and the pillars thereof twenty, and their sockets twenty, of brass; the hooks of the pillars, and their fillets, of silver.

12 And for the breadth of the court on the west side shall be hangings of fifty cubits; their pillars ten, and their sockets ten.

13 And the breadth of the court on the east side eastward shall be fifty cubits.

14 The hangings for the one side of the gate shall be fifteen cubits; their pillars three, and their sockets three.

15 And for the other side shall be hangings of fifteen cubits; their pillars three, and their sockets three.

16 And for the gate of the court shall be a screen of twenty cubits, of blue, and purple, and scarlet, and fine twined linen, the work of the embroiderer; their pillars four, and their sockets four.

17 All the pillars of the court round about shall be filleted with silver; their hooks of silver, and their sockets of brass.

18 The length of the court shall be a hundred cubits, and the breadth fifty every where, and the height five cubits, of fine twined linen, and their sockets of brass.

19 All the instruments of the tabernacle in all the service thereof, and all the pins thereof, and all the pins of the court, shall be of brass.

20 And thou shalt command the children of Israel, that they bring unto thee pure olive oil beaten for the light, to cause a lamp to burn continually.

21 In the tent of meeting, without the veil which is before the testimony, Aaron and his sons shall keep it in order from evening to morning before Yahweh: it shall be a statue for ever throughout their generations on the behalf of the children of Israel.

Chapter 28

1 And bring thou near unto thee Aaron thy brother, and his sons with him, from among the children of Israel, that he may minister unto me in the priest's office, even Aaron, Nadab and Abihu, Eleazar and Ithamar, Aaron's sons.

2 And thou shalt make holy garments for Aaron thy brother, for glory and for beauty.

3 And thou shalt speak unto all that are wise-hearted, whom I have filled with the spirit of wisdom, that they make Aaron's garments to sanctify him, that he may minister unto me in the priest's office.

4 And these are the garments which they shall make: a breastplate, and an ephod, and a robe, and a coat of checker work, a mitre, and a girdle: and they shall make holy garments for Aaron thy brother, and his sons, that he may minister unto me in the priest's office.

5 And they shall take the gold, and the blue, and the purple, and the scarlet, and the fine linen.

6 And they shall make the ephod of gold, of blue, and purple, scarlet, and fine twined linen, the work of the skilful workman.

7 It shall have two shoulder-pieces joined to the two ends thereof, that it may be joined together.

8 And the skilfully woven band, which is upon it, wherewith to gird it on, shall be like the work thereof and of the same piece; of gold, of blue, and purple, and scarlet, and fine twined linen.

9 And thou shalt take two onyx stones, and grave on them the names of the children of Israel:

10 six of their names on the one stone, and the names of the six that remain on the other stone, according to their birth.

11 With the work of an engraver in stone, like the engravings of a signet, shalt thou engrave the two stones, according to the names of the children of Israel: thou shalt make them to be inclosed in settings of gold.

12 And thou shalt put the two stones upon the shoulder-pieces of the ephod, to be stones of memorial for the children of Israel: and Aaron shall bear their names before Yahweh upon his two shoulders for a memorial.

13 And thou shalt make settings of gold,

14 and two chains of pure gold; like cords shalt thou make them, of wreathen work: and thou shalt put the wreathen chains on the settings.

15 And thou shalt make a breastplate of judgment, the work of the skilful workman; like the work of the ephod thou shalt make it; of gold, of blue, and purple, and scarlet, and fine twined linen, shalt thou make it.

16 Foursquare it shall be and double; a span shall be the length thereof, and a span the breadth thereof.

17 And thou shalt set in it settings of stones, four rows of stones: a row of sardius, topaz, and carbuncle shall be the first row;

18 and the second row an emerald, a sapphire, and a diamond;

19 and the third row a jacinth, an agate, and an amethyst;

20 and the fourth row a beryl, and an onyx, and a jasper: they shall be inclosed in gold in their settings.

21 And the stones shall be according to the names of the children of Israel, twelve, according to their names; like the engravings of a signet, every one according to his name, they shall be for the twelve tribes.

22 And thou shalt make upon the breastplate chains like cords, of wreathen work of pure gold.

23 And thou shalt make upon the breastplate two rings of gold, and shalt put the two rings on the two ends of the breastplate.

24 And thou shalt put the two wreathen chains of gold in the two rings at the ends of the breastplate.

25 And the other two ends of the two wreathen chains thou shalt put on the two settings, and put them on the shoulder-pieces of the ephod in the forepart thereof.

26 And thou shalt make two rings of gold, and thou shalt put them upon the two ends of the breastplate, upon the edge thereof, which is toward the side of the ephod inward.

27 And thou shalt make two rings of gold, and shalt put them on the two shoulder-pieces of the ephod underneath, in the forepart thereof, close by the coupling thereof, above the skilfully woven band of the ephod.

28 And they shall bind the breastplate by the rings thereof unto the rings of the ephod with a lace of blue, that it may be upon the skilfully woven band of the ephod, and that the breastplate be not loosed from the ephod.

29 And Aaron shall bear the names of the children of Israel in the breastplate of judgment upon his heart, when he goeth in unto the holy place, for a memorial before Yahweh continually.

30 And thou shalt put in the breastplate of judgment the Urim and the Thummim; and they shall be upon Aaron's heart, when he goeth in before Yahweh: and Aaron shall bear the judgment of the children of Israel upon his heart before Yahweh continually.

31 And thou shalt make the robe of the ephod all of blue.

32 And it shall have a hole for the head in the midst thereof: it shall have a binding of woven work round about the hole of it, as it were the hole of a coat of mail, that it be not rent.

33 And upon the skirts of it thou shalt make pomegranates of blue, and of purple, and of scarlet, round about the skirts thereof; and bells of gold between them round about:

34 a golden bell and a pomegranate, a golden bell and a pomegranate, upon the skirts of the robe round about.

35 And it shall be upon Aaron to minister: and the sound thereof shall be heard when he goeth in unto the holy place before Yahweh, and when he cometh out, that he die not.

36 And thou shalt make a plate of pure gold, and grave upon it, like the engravings of a signet, HOLY TO YAHWEH.

37 And thou shalt put it on a lace of blue, and it shall be upon the mitre; upon the forefront of the mitre it shall be.

38 And it shall be upon Aaron's forehead, and Aaron shall bear the iniquity of the holy things, which the children of Israel shall hallow in all their holy gifts; and it shall be always upon his forehead, that they may be accepted before Yahweh.

39 And thou shalt weave the coat in checker work of fine linen, and thou shalt make a mitre of fine linen, and thou shalt make a girdle, the work of the embroiderer.

40 And for Aaron's sons thou shalt make coats, and thou shalt make for them girdles, and head-tires shalt thou make for them, for glory and for beauty.

41 And thou shalt put them upon Aaron thy brother, and upon his sons with him, and shalt anoint them, and consecrate them, and sanctify them, that they may minister unto me in the priest's office.

42 And thou shalt make them linen breeches to cover the flesh of their nakedness; from the loins even unto the thighs they shall reach:

43 And they shall be upon Aaron, and upon his sons, when they go in unto the tent of meeting, or when they come near unto the altar to minister in the holy place; that they bear not iniquity, and die: it shall be a statute for ever unto him and unto his seed after him.

Chapter 29

1 And this is the thing that thou shalt do unto them to hallow them, to minister unto me in the priest's office: take one young bullock and two rams without blemish,

2 and unleavened bread, and cakes unleavened mingled with oil, and wafers unleavened anointed with oil: of fine wheaten flour shalt thou make them.

3 And thou shalt put them into one basket, and bring them in the basket, with the bullock and the two rams.

4 And Aaron and his sons thou shalt bring unto the door of the tent of meeting, and shalt wash them with water.

5 And thou shalt take the garments, and put upon Aaron the coat, and the robe of the ephod, and the ephod, and the breastplate, and gird him with the skilfully woven band of the ephod;

6 and thou shalt set the mitre upon his head, and put the holy crown upon the mitre.

7 Then shalt thou take the anointing oil, and pour it upon his head, and anoint him.

Exodus

8And thou shalt bring his sons, and put coats upon them.

9And thou shalt gird them with girdles, Aaron and his sons, and bind head-tires on them: and they shall have the priesthood by a perpetual statute: and thou shalt consecrate Aaron and his sons.

10And thou shalt bring the bullock before the tent of meeting: and Aaron and his sons shall lay their hands upon the head of the bullock.

11And thou shalt kill the bullock before Yahweh, at the door of the tent of meeting.

12And thou shalt take of the blood of the bullock, and put it upon the horns of the altar with thy finger; and thou shalt pour out all the blood at the base of the altar.

13And thou shalt take all the fat that covereth the inwards, and the caul upon the liver, and the two kidneys, and the fat that is upon them, and burn them upon the altar.

14But the flesh of the bullock, and its skin, and it dung, shalt thou burn with fire without the camp: it is a sin-offering.

15Thou shalt also take the one ram; and Aaron and his sons shall lay their hands upon the head of the ram.

16And thou shalt slay the ram, and thou shalt take its blood, and sprinkle it round about upon the altar.

17And thou shalt cut the ram into its pieces, and wash its inwards, and its legs, and put them with its pieces, and with its head.

18And thou shalt burn the whole ram upon the altar: it is a burnt-offering unto Yahweh; it is a sweet savor, an offering made by fire unto Yahweh.

19And thou shalt take the other ram; and Aaron and his sons shall lay their hands upon the head of the ram.

20Then shalt thou kill the ram, and take of its blood, and put it upon the tip of the right ear of Aaron, and upon the tip of the right ear of his sons, and upon the thumb of their right hand, and upon the great toe of their right foot, and sprinkle the blood upon the altar round about.

21And thou shalt take of the blood that is upon the altar, and of the anointing oil, and sprinkle it upon Aaron, and upon his garments, and upon his sons, and upon the garments of his sons with him: and he shall be hallowed, and his garments, and his sons, and his sons' garments with him.

22Also thou shalt take of the ram the fat, and the fat tail, and the fat that covereth the inwards, and the caul of the liver, and the two kidneys, and the fat that is upon them, and the right thigh (for it is a ram of consecration),

23and one loaf of bread, and one cake of oiled bread, and one wafer, out of the basket of unleavened bread that is before Yahweh.

24And thou shalt put the whole upon the hands of Aaron, and upon the hands of his sons, and shalt wave them for a wave-offering before Yahweh.

25And thou shalt take them from their hands, and burn them on the altar upon the burnt-offering, for a sweet savor before Yahweh: it is an offering made by fire unto Yahweh.

26And thou shalt take the breast of Aaron's ram of consecration, and wave it for a wave-offering before Yahweh: and it shall be thy portion.

27And thou shalt sanctify the breast of the wave-offering, and the thigh of the heave-offering, which is waved, and which is heaved up, of the ram of consecration, even of that which is for Aaron, and of that which is for his sons:

28and it shall be for Aaron and his sons as their portion for ever from the children of Israel; for it is a heave-offering: and it shall be a heave-offering from the children of Israel of the sacrifices of their peace-offerings, even their heave-offering unto Yahweh.

29And the holy garments of Aaron shall be for his sons after him, to be anointed in them, and to be consecrated in them.

30Seven days shall the son that is priest in his stead put them on, when he cometh into the tent of meeting to minister in the holy place.

31And thou shalt take the ram of consecration, and boil its flesh in a holy place.

32And Aaron and his sons shall eat the flesh of the ram, and the bread that is in the basket, at the door of the tent of meeting.

33And they shall eat those things wherewith atonement was made, to consecrate and to sanctify them: but a stranger shall not eat thereof, because they are holy.

34And if aught of the flesh of the consecration, or of the bread, remain unto the morning, then thou shalt burn the remainder with fire: it shall not be eaten, because it is holy.

35And thus shalt thou do unto Aaron, and to his sons, according to all that I have commanded thee: seven days shalt thou consecrate them.

36And every day shalt thou offer the bullock of sin-offering for atonement: and thou shalt cleanse the altar, when thou makest atonement for it; and thou shalt anoint it, to sanctify it.

37Seven days thou shalt make atonement for the altar, and sanctify it: and the altar shall be most holy; whatsoever toucheth the altar shall be holy.

38Now this is that which thou shalt offer upon the altar: two lambs a year old day by day continually.

39The one lamb thou shalt offer in the morning; and the other lamb thou shalt offer at even:

40and with the one lamb a tenth part of an ephah of fine flour mingled with the fourth part of a hin of beaten oil, and the fourth part of a hin of wine for a drink-offering.

41And the other lamb thou shalt offer at even, and shalt do thereto according to the meal-offering of the morning, and according to the drink-offering thereof, for a sweet savor, an offering made by fire unto Yahweh.

42It shall be a continual burnt-offering throughout your generations at the door of the tent of meeting before Yahweh, where I will meet with you, to speak there unto thee.

43And there I will meet with the children of Israel; and the Tent shall be sanctified by my glory.

44And I will sanctify the tent of meeting, and the altar: Aaron also and his sons will I sanctify, to minister to me in the priest's office.

45And I will dwell among the children of Israel, and will be their God.

46And they shall know that I am Yahweh their God, that brought them forth out of the land of Egypt, that I might dwell among them: I am Yahweh their God.

Chapter 30

1And thou shalt make an altar to burn incense upon: of acacia wood shalt thou make it.

2A cubit shall be the length thereof, and a cubit the breadth thereof; foursquare shall it be; and two cubits shall be the height thereof: the horns thereof shall be of one piece with it.

3And thou shalt overlay it with pure gold, the top thereof, and the sides thereof round about, and the horns thereof; and thou shalt make unto it a crown of gold round about.

4And two golden rings shalt thou make for it under the crown thereof; upon the two ribs thereof, upon the two sides of it shalt thou make them; and they shall be for places for staves wherewith to bear it.

5And thou shalt make the staves of acacia wood, and overlay them with gold.

6And thou shalt put it before the veil that is by the ark of the testimony, before the mercy-seat that is over the testimony, where I will meet with thee.

7And Aaron shall burn thereon incense of sweet spices: every morning, when he dresseth the lamps, he shall burn it.

8And when Aaron lighteth the lamps at even, he shall burn it, a perpetual incense before Yahweh throughout your generations.

9Ye shall offer no strange incense thereon, nor burnt-offering, nor meal-offering; and ye shall pour no drink-offering thereon.

10And Aaron shall make atonement upon the horns of it once in the year; with the blood of the sin-offering of atonement once in the year shall he make atonement for it throughout your generations: it is most holy unto Yahweh.

11And Yahweh spake unto Moses, saying,

12When thou takest the sum of the children of Israel, according to those that are numbered of them, then shall they give every man a ransom for his soul unto Yahweh, when thou numberest them; that there be no plague among them, when thou numberest them.

13This they shall give, every one that passeth over unto them that are numbered, half a shekel after the shekel of the sanctuary; (the shekel is twenty gerahs;) half a shekel for an offering to Yahweh.

14Every one that passeth over unto them that are numbered, from twenty years old and upward, shall give the offering of Yahweh.

15The rich shall not give more, and the poor shall not give less, than the half shekel, when they give the offering of Yahweh, to make atonement for your souls.

16And thou shalt take the atonement money from the children of Israel, and shalt appoint it for the service of the tent of meeting; that it may be a memorial for the children of Israel before Yahweh, to make atonement for your souls.

17And Yahweh spake unto Moses, saying,

18Thou shalt also make a laver of brass, and the base thereof of brass, whereat to wash. And thou shalt put it between the tent of meeting and the altar, and thou shalt put water therein.

19And Aaron and his sons shall wash their hands and their feet thereat:

20when they go into the tent of meeting, they shall wash with water, that they die not; or when they come near to the altar to minister, to burn an offering made by fire unto Yahweh.

21So they shall wash their hands and their feet, that they die not: and it shall be a statute for ever to them, even to him and to his seed throughout their generations.

22Moreover Yahweh spake unto Moses, saying,

23Take thou also unto thee the chief spices: of flowing myrrh five hundred shekels, and of sweet cinnamon half so much, even two hundred and fifty, and of sweet calamus two hundred and fifty,

24and of cassia five hundred, after the shekel of the sanctuary, and of olive oil a hin.

25And thou shalt make it a holy anointing oil, a perfume compounded after the art of the perfumer: it shall be a holy anointing oil.

26And thou shalt anoint therewith the tent of meeting, and the ark of the testimony,

27and the table and all the vessels thereof, and the candlestick and the vessels thereof, and the altar of incense,

28and the altar of burnt-offering with all the vessels thereof, and the laver and the base thereof.

29And thou shalt sanctify them, that they may be most holy: whatsoever toucheth them shall be holy.

30And thou shalt anoint Aaron and his sons, and sanctify them, that they may minister unto me in the priest's office.

31And thou shalt speak unto the children of Israel, saying, This shall be a holy anointing oil unto me throughout your generations.

32Upon the flesh of man shall it not be poured, neither shall ye make any like it, according to the composition thereof: it is holy, and it shall be holy unto you.

33Whosoever compoundeth any like it, or whosoever putteth any of it upon a stranger, he shall be cut off from his people.

34And Yahweh said unto Moses, Take unto thee sweet spices, stacte, and onycha, and galbanum; sweet spices with pure frankincense: of each shall there be a like weight;

35and thou shalt make of it incense, a perfume after the art of the perfumer, seasoned with salt, pure and holy:

36and thou shalt beat some of it very small, and put of it before the testimony in the tent of meeting, where I will meet with thee: it shall be unto you most holy.

37And the incense which thou shalt make, according to the composition thereof ye shall not make for yourselves: it shall be unto thee holy for Yahweh.

38Whosoever shall make like unto that, to smell thereof, he shall be cut off from his people.

Chapter 31

1And Yahweh spake unto Moses, saying,

2See, I have called by name Bezalel the son of Uri, the son of Hur, of the tribe of Judah:

3and I have filled him with the Spirit of God, in wisdom, and in understanding, and in knowledge, and in all manner of workmanship,

4to devise skilful works, to work in gold, and in silver, and in brass,

5and in cutting of stones for setting, and in carving of wood, to work in all manner of workmanship.

6And I, behold, I have appointed with him Oholiab, the son of Ahisamach, of the tribe of Dan; and in the heart of all that are wise-hearted I have put wisdom, that they may make all that I have commanded thee:

7the tent of meeting, and the ark of the testimony, and the mercy-seat that is thereupon, and all the furniture of the Tent,

8and the table and its vessels, and the pure candlestick with all its vessels, and the altar of incense,

9and the altar of burnt-offering with all its vessels, and the laver and its base,

10and the finely wrought garments, and the holy garments for Aaron the priest, and the garments of his sons, to minister in the priest's office,

11and the anointing oil, and the incense of sweet spices for the holy place: according to all that I have commanded thee shall they do.

12And Yahweh spake unto Moses, saying,

13Speak thou also unto the children of Israel, saying, Verily ye shall keep my sabbaths: for it is a sign between me and you throughout your generations; that ye may know that I am Yahweh who sanctifieth you.

14Ye shall keep the sabbath therefore; for it is holy unto you: every one that profaneth it shall surely be put to death; for whosoever doeth any work therein, that soul shall be cut off from among his people.

15Six days shall work be done, but on the seventh day is a sabbath of solemn rest, holy to Yahweh: whosoever doeth any work on the sabbath day, he shall surely be put to death.

16Wherefore the children of Israel shall keep the sabbath, to observe the sabbath throughout their generations, for a perpetual covenant.

17It is a sign between me and the children of Israel for ever: for in six days Yahweh made heaven and earth, and on the seventh day he rested, and was refreshed.

18And he gave unto Moses, when he had made an end of communing with him upon mount Sinai, the two tables of the testimony, tables of stone, written with the finger of God.

Chapter 32

1And when the people saw that Moses delayed to come down from the mount, the people gathered themselves together unto Aaron, and said unto him, Up, make us gods, which shall go before us; for as for this Moses, the man that brought us up out of the land of Egypt, we know not what is become of him.

2And Aaron said unto them, Break off the golden rings, which are in the ears of your wives, of your sons, and of your daughters, and bring them unto me.

3And all the people brake off the golden rings which were in their ears, and brought them unto Aaron.

4And he received it at their hand, and fashioned it with a graving tool, and made it a molten calf: and they said, These are thy gods, O Israel, which brought thee up out of the land of Egypt.

5And when Aaron saw this, he built an altar before it; and Aaron made proclamation, and said, To-morrow shall be a feast to Yahweh.

6And they rose up early on the morrow, and offered burnt-offerings, and brought peace-offerings; and the people sat down to eat and to drink, and rose up to play.

7And Yahweh spake unto Moses, Go, get thee down; for thy people, that thou broughtest up out of the land of Egypt, have corrupted themselves:

8they have turned aside quickly out of the way which I commanded them: they have made them a molten calf, and have worshipped it, and have sacrificed unto it, and said, These are thy gods, O Israel, which brought thee up out of the land of Egypt.

9And Yahweh said unto Moses, I have seen this people, and, behold, it is a stiffnecked people:

10now therefore let me alone, that my wrath may wax hot against them, and that I may consume them: and I will make of thee a great nation.

11And Moses besought Yahweh his God, and said, Yahweh, why doth thy wrath wax hot against thy people, that thou hast brought forth out of the land of Egypt with great power and with a mighty hand?

12Wherefore should the Egyptians speak, saying, For evil did he bring them forth, to slay them in the mountains, and to consume them from the face of the earth? Turn from thy fierce wrath, and repent of this evil against thy people.

13Remember Abraham, Isaac, and Israel, thy servants, to whom thou swarest by thine own self, and saidst unto them, I will multiply your seed as the stars of heaven, and all this land that I have spoken of will I give unto your seed, and they shall inherit it for ever.

14And Yahweh repented of the evil which he said he would do unto his people.

15And Moses turned, and went down from the mount, with the two tables of the testimony in his hand; tables that were written on both their sides; on the one side and on the other were they written.

16And the tables were the work of God, and the writing was the writing of God, graven upon the tables.

17And when Joshua heard the noise of the people as they shouted, he said unto Moses, There is a noise of war in the camp.

18And he said, It is not the voice of them that shout for mastery, neither is it the voice of them that cry for being overcome; but the noise of them that sing do I hear.

19And it came to pass, as soon as he came nigh unto the camp, that he saw the calf and the dancing: and Moses' anger waxed hot, and he cast the tables out of his hands, and brake them beneath the mount.

20And he took the calf which they had made, and burnt it with fire, and ground it to powder, and strewed it upon the water, and made the children of Israel drink of it.

21And Moses said unto Aaron, What did this people unto thee, that thou hast brought a great sin upon them?

22And Aaron said, Let not the anger of my lord wax hot: thou knowest the people, that they are set on evil.

23For they said unto me, Make us gods, which shall go before us; for as for this Moses, the man that brought us up out of the land of Egypt, we know not what is become of him.

24And I said unto them, Whosoever hath any gold, let them break it off: so they gave it me; and I cast it into the fire, and there came out this calf.

25And when Moses saw that the people were broken loose, (for Aaron had let them loose for a derision among their enemies,)

26then Moses stood in the gate of the camp, and said, Whoso is on Yahweh's side, let him come unto me. And all the sons of Levi gathered themselves together unto him.

27And he said unto them, Thus saith Yahweh, the God of Israel, Put ye every man his sword upon his thigh, and go to and fro from gate to gate throughout the camp, and slay every man his brother, and every man his companion, and every man his neighbor.

28And the sons of Levi did according to the word of Moses: and there fell of the people that day about three thousand men.

29And Moses said, Consecrate yourselves to-day to Yahweh, yea, every man against his son, and against his brother; that he may bestow upon you a blessing this day.

30And it came to pass on the morrow, that Moses said unto the people, Ye have sinned a great sin: and now I will go up unto Yahweh; peradventure I shall make atonement for your sin.

31And Moses returned unto Yahweh, and said, Oh, this people have sinned a great sin, and have made them gods of gold.

32Yet now, if thou wilt forgive their sin-; and if not, blot me, I pray thee, out of thy book which thou hast written.

33And Yahweh said unto Moses, Whosoever hath sinned against me, him will I blot out of my book.

34And now go, lead the people unto the place of which I have spoken unto thee: behold, mine angel shall go before thee; nevertheless in the day when I visit, I will visit their sin upon them.

35And Yahweh smote the people, because they made the calf, which Aaron made.

Chapter 33

1And Yahweh spake unto Moses, Depart, go up hence, thou and the people that thou hast brought up out of the land of Egypt, unto the land of which I sware unto Abraham, to Isaac, and to Jacob, saying, Unto thy seed will I give it.

2and I will send an angel before thee; and I will drive out the Canaanite, the Amorite, and the Hittite, and the Perizzite, the Hivite, and the Jebusite:

3unto a land flowing with milk and honey: for I will not go up in the midst of thee, for thou art a stiffnecked people, lest I consume thee in the way.

4And when the people heard these evil tidings, they mourned: and no man did put on him his ornaments.

5And Yahweh said unto Moses, Say unto the children of Israel, Ye are a stiffnecked people; if I go up into the midst of thee for one moment, I shall consume thee: therefore now put off thy ornaments from thee, that I may know what to do unto thee.

6And the children of Israel stripped themselves of their ornaments from mount Horeb onward.

7Now Moses used to take the tent and to pitch it without the camp, afar off from the camp; and he called it, The tent of meeting. And it came to pass, that every one that sought Yahweh went out unto the tent of meeting, which was without the camp.

8And it came to pass, when Moses went out unto the Tent, that all the people rose up, and stood, every man at his tent door, and looked after Moses, until he was gone into the Tent.

9And it came to pass, when Moses entered into the Tent, the pillar of cloud descended, and stood at the door of the Tent: and Yahweh spake with Moses.

10And all the people saw the pillar of cloud stand at the door of the Tent: and all the people rose up and worshipped, every man at his tent door.

11And Yahweh spake unto Moses face to face, as a man speaketh unto his friend. And he turned again into the camp: but his minister Joshua, the son of Nun, a young man, departed not out of the Tent.

12And Moses said unto Yahweh, See, thou sayest unto me, Bring up this people: and thou hast not let me know whom thou wilt send with me. Yet thou hast said, I know thee by name, and thou hast also found favor in my sight.

13Now therefore, I pray thee, if I have found favor in thy sight, show me now thy ways, that I may know thee, to the end that I may find favor in thy sight: and consider that this nation is thy people.

14And he said, My presence shall go with thee, and I will give thee rest.

Exodus

15 And he said unto him, If thy presence go not with me, carry us not up hence.

16 For wherein now shall it be known that I have found favor in thy sight, I and thy people? is it not in that thou goest with us, so that we are separated, I and thy people, from all the people that are upon the face of the earth?

17 And Yahweh said unto Moses, I will do this thing also that thou hast spoken; for thou hast found favor in my sight, and I know thee by name.

18 And he said, Show me, I pray thee, thy glory.

19 And he said, I will make all my goodness pass before thee, and will proclaim the name of Yahweh before thee; and I will be gracious to whom I will be gracious, and will show mercy on whom I will show mercy.

20 And he said, Thou canst not see my face; for man shall not see me and live.

21 and Yahweh said, Behold, there is a place by me, and thou shalt stand upon the rock:

22 and it shall come to pass, while my glory passeth by, that I will put thee in a cleft of the rock, and will cover thee with my hand until I have passed by:

23 and I will take away my hand, and thou shalt see my back; but my face shall not be seen.

Chapter 34

1 And Yahweh said unto Moses, Hew thee two tables of stone like unto the first: and I will write upon the tables the words that were on the first tables, which thou brakest.

2 And be ready by the morning, and come up in the morning unto mount Sinai, and present thyself there to me on the top of the mount.

3 And no man shall come up with thee; neither let any man be seen throughout all the mount; neither let the flocks nor herds feed before that mount.

4 And he hewed two tables of stone like unto the first; and Moses rose up early in the morning, and went up unto mount Sinai, as Yahweh had commanded him, and took in his hand two tables of stone.

5 And Yahweh descended in the cloud, and stood with him there, and proclaimed the name of Yahweh.

6 And Yahweh passed by before him, and proclaimed, Yahweh, Yahweh, a God merciful and gracious, slow to anger, and abundant in lovingkindness and truth,

7 keeping lovingkindness for thousands, forgiving iniquity and transgression and sin; and that will by no means clear the guilty, visiting the iniquity of the fathers upon the children, and upon the children's children, upon the third and upon the fourth generation.

8 And Moses made haste, and bowed his head toward the earth, and worshipped.

9 And he said, If now I have found favor in thy sight, O Lord, let the Lord, I pray thee, go in the midst of us; for it is a stiffnecked people; and pardon our iniquity and our sin, and take us for thine inheritance.

10 And he said, Behold, I make a covenant: before all thy people I will do marvels, such as have not been wrought in all the earth, nor in any nation; and all the people among which thou art shall see the work of Yahweh; for it is a terrible thing that I do with thee.

11 Observe thou that which I command thee this day: behold, I drive out before thee the Amorite, and the Canaanite, and the Hittite, and the Perizzite, and the Hivite, and the Jebusite.

12 Take heed to thyself, lest thou make a covenant with the inhabitants of the land whither thou goest, lest it be for a snare in the midst of thee:

13 but ye shall break down their altars, and dash in pieces their pillars, and ye shall cut down their Asherim;

14 for thou shalt worship no other god: for Yahweh, whose name is Jealous, is a jealous God:

15 lest thou make a covenant with the inhabitants of the land, and they play the harlot after their gods, and sacrifice unto their gods, and one call thee and thou eat of his sacrifice;

16 and thou take of their daughters unto thy sons, and their daughters play the harlot after their gods, and make thy sons play the harlot after their gods.

17 Thou shalt make thee no molten gods.

18 The feast of unleavened bread shalt thou keep. Seven days thou shalt eat unleavened bread, as I commanded thee, at the time appointed in the month Abib; for in the month Abib thou camest out from Egypt.

19 All that openeth the womb is mine; and all thy cattle that is male, the firstlings of cow and sheep.

20 And the firstling of an ass thou shalt redeem with a lamb: and if thou wilt not redeem it, then thou shalt break its neck. All the first-born of thy sons thou shalt redeem. And none shall appear before me empty.

21 Six days thou shalt work, but on the seventh day thou shalt rest: in plowing time and in harvest thou shalt rest.

22 And thou shalt observe the feast of weeks, even of the first-fruits of wheat harvest, and the feast of ingathering at the year's end.

23 Three times in the year shall all thy males appear before the Lord Yahweh, the God of Israel.

24 For I will cast out nations before thee, and enlarge thy borders: neither shall any man desire thy land, when thou goest up to appear before Yahweh thy God three times in the year.

25 Thou shalt not offer the blood of my sacrifice with leavened bread; neither shall the sacrifice of the feast of the passover be left unto the morning.

26 The first of the first-fruits of thy ground thou shalt bring unto the house of Yahweh thy God. Thou shalt not boil a kid in its mother's milk.

27 And Yahweh said unto Moses, Write thou these words: for after the tenor of these words I have made a covenant with thee and with Israel.

28 And he was there with Yahweh forty days and forty nights; he did neither eat bread, nor drink water. And he wrote upon the tables the words of the covenant, the ten commandments.

29 And it came to pass, when Moses came down from mount Sinai with the two tables of the testimony in Moses' hand, when he came down from the mount, that Moses knew not that the skin of his face shone by reason of his speaking with him.

30 And when Aaron and all the children of Israel saw Moses, behold, the skin of his face shone; and they were afraid to come nigh him.

31 And Moses called unto them; and Aaron and all the rulers of the congregation returned unto him: and Moses spake to them.

32 And afterward all the children of Israel came nigh: and he gave them in commandment all that Yahweh had spoken with him in mount Sinai.

33 And when Moses had done speaking with them, he put a veil on his face.

34 But when Moses went in before Yahweh to speak with him, he took the veil off, until he came out; and he came out, and spake unto the children of Israel that which he was commanded.

35 And the children of Israel saw the face of Moses, that the skin of Moses' face shone: and Moses put the veil upon his face again, until he went in to speak with him.

Chapter 35

1 And Moses assembled all the congregation of the children of Israel, and said unto them, These are the words which Yahweh hath commanded, that ye should do them.

2 Six days shall work be done; but on the seventh day there shall be to you a holy day, a sabbath of solemn rest to Yahweh: whosoever doeth any work therein shall be put to death.

3 Ye shall kindle no fire throughout your habitations upon the sabbath day.

4 And Moses spake unto all the congregation of the children of Israel, saying, This is the thing which Yahweh commanded, saying,

5 Take ye from among you an offering unto Yahweh; whosoever is of a willing heart, let him bring it, Yahweh's offering: gold, and silver, and brass,

6 and blue, and purple, and scarlet, and fine linen, and goats' hair,

7 and rams' skins dyed red, and sealskins, and acacia wood,

8 and oil for the light, and spices for the anointing oil, and for the sweet incense,

9 and onyx stones, and stones to be set, for the ephod, and for the breastplate.

10 And let every wise-hearted man among you come, and make all that Yahweh hath commanded:

11 the tabernacle, its tent, and its covering, its clasps, and its boards, its bars, its pillars, and its sockets;

12 the ark, and the staves thereof, the mercy-seat, and the veil of the screen;

13 the table, and its staves, and all its vessels, and the showbread;

14 the candlestick also for the light, and its vessels, and its lamps, and the oil for the light;

15 and the altar of incense, and its staves, and the anointing oil, and the sweet incense, and the screen for the door, at the door of the tabernacle;

16 the altar of burnt-offering, with its grating of brass, it staves, and all its vessels, the laver and its base;

17 the hangings of the court, the pillars thereof, and their sockets, and the screen for the gate of the court;

18 the pins of the tabernacle, and the pins of the court, and their cords;

19 the finely wrought garments, for ministering in the holy place, the holy garments for Aaron the priest, and the garments of his sons, to minister in the priest's office.

20 And all the congregation of the children of Israel departed from the presence of Moses.

21 And they came, every one whose heart stirred him up, and every one whom his spirit made willing, and brought Yahweh's offering, for the work of the tent of meeting, and for all the service thereof, and for the holy garments.

22 And they came, both men and women, as many as were willing-hearted, and brought brooches, and ear-rings, and signet-rings, and armlets, all jewels of gold; even every man that offered an offering of gold unto Yahweh.

23 And every man, with whom was found blue, and purple, and scarlet, and fine linen, and goats' hair, and rams' skins dyed red, and sealskins, brought them.

24 Every one that did offer an offering of silver and brass brought Yahweh's offering; and every man, with whom was found acacia wood for any work of the service, brought it.

25 And all the women that were wise-hearted did spin with their hands, and brought that which they had spun, the blue, and the purple, the scarlet, and the fine linen.

26 And all the women whose heart stirred them up in wisdom spun the goats' hair.

27 And the rulers brought the onyx stones, and the stones to be set, for the ephod, and for the breastplate;

28 and the spice, and the oil; for the light, and for the anointing oil, and for the sweet incense.

29 The children of Israel brought a freewill-offering unto Yahweh; every man and woman, whose heart made them willing to bring for all the work, which Yahweh had commanded to be made by Moses.

30 And Moses said unto the children of Israel, See, Yahweh hath called by name Bezalel the son of Uri, the son of Hur, of the tribe of Judah.

31 And he hath filled him with the Spirit of God, in wisdom, in understanding, and in knowledge, and in all manner of workmanship;

32 and to devise skilful works, to work in gold, and in silver, and in brass,

33 and in cutting of stones for setting, and in carving of wood, to work in all manner of skilful workmanship.

34 And he hath put in his heart that he may teach, both he, and Oholiab, the son of Ahisamach, of the tribe of Dan.

35Them hath he filled with wisdom of heart, to work all manner of workmanship, of the engraver, and of the skilful workman, and of the embroiderer, in blue, and in purple, in scarlet, and in fine linen, and of the weaver, even of them that do any workmanship, and of those that devise skilful works.

Chapter 36

1And Bezalel and Oholiab shall work, and every wise-hearted man, in whom Yahweh hath put wisdom and understanding to know how to work all the work for the service of the sanctuary, according to all that Yahweh hath commanded.

2And Moses called Bezalel and Oholiab, and every wise-hearted man, in whose heart Yahweh had put wisdom, even every one whose heart stirred him up to come unto the work to do it:

3and they received of Moses all the offering which the children of Israel had brought for the work of the service of the sanctuary, wherewith to make it. And they brought yet unto him freewill-offerings every morning.

4And all the wise men, that wrought all the work of the sanctuary, came every man from his work which they wrought.

5And they spake unto Moses, saying, The people bring much more than enough for the service of the work which Yahweh commanded to make.

6And Moses gave commandment, and they caused it to be proclaimed throughout the camp, saying, Let neither man nor woman make any more work for the offering of the sanctuary. So the people were restrained from bringing.

7For the stuff they had was sufficient for all the work to make it, and too much.

8And all the wise-hearted men among them that wrought the work made the tabernacle with ten curtains; of fine twined linen, and blue, and purple, and scarlet, with cherubim, the work of the skilful workman, Bezalel made them.

9The length of each curtain was eight and twenty cubits, and the breadth of each curtain four cubits: all the curtains had one measure.

10And he coupled five curtains one to another: and the other five curtains he coupled one to another.

11And he made loops of blue upon the edge of the one curtain from the selvedge in the coupling: likewise he made in the edge of the curtain that was outmost in the second coupling.

12Fifty loops made he in the one curtain, and fifty loops made he in the edge of the curtain that was in the second coupling: the loops were opposite one to another.

13And he made fifty clasps of gold, and coupled the curtains one to another with the clasps: so the tabernacle was one.

14And he made curtains of goats' hair for a tent over the tabernacle: eleven curtains he made them.

15The length of each curtain was thirty cubits, and four cubits the breadth of each curtain: the eleven curtains had one measure.

16And he coupled five curtains by themselves, and six curtains by themselves.

17And he made fifty loops on the edge of the curtain that was outmost in the coupling, and fifty loops made he upon the edge of the curtain which was outmost in the second coupling.

18And he made fifty clasps of brass to couple the tent together, that it might be one.

19And he made a covering for the tent of rams' skins dyed red, and a covering of sealskins above.

20And he made the boards for the tabernacle, of acacia wood, standing up.

21Ten cubits was the length of a board, and a cubit and a half the breadth of each board.

22Each board had two tenons, joined one to another: thus did he make for all the boards of the tabernacle.

23And he made the boards for the tabernacle: twenty boards for the south side southward.

24And he made forty sockets of silver under the twenty boards; two sockets under one board for its two tenons, and two sockets under another board for its two tenons.

25And for the second side of the tabernacle, on the north side, he made twenty boards,

26and their forty sockets of silver; two sockets under one board, and two sockets under another board.

27And for the hinder part of the tabernacle westward he made six boards.

28And two boards made he for the corners of the tabernacle in the hinder part.

29And they were double beneath; and in like manner they were entire unto the top thereof unto one ring: thus he did to both of them in the two corners.

30And there were eight boards, and their sockets of silver, sixteen sockets; under every board two sockets.

31And he made bars of acacia wood; five for the boards of the one side of the tabernacle,

32and five bars for the boards of the other side of the tabernacle, and five bars for the boards of the tabernacle for the hinder part westward.

33And he made the middle bar to pass through in the midst of the boards from the one end to the other.

34And he overlaid the boards with gold, and made their rings of gold for places for the bars, and overlaid the bars with gold.

35And he made the veil of blue, and purple, and scarlet, and fine twined linen: with cherubim, the work of the skilful workman, made he it.

36And he made thereunto four pillars of acacia, and overlaid them with gold: their hooks were of gold; And he cast for them four sockets of silver.

37And he made a screen for the door of the Tent, of blue, and purple, and scarlet, and fine twined linen, the work of the embroiderer;

38and the five pillars of it with their hooks: and he overlaid their capitals and their fillets with gold; and their five sockets were of brass.

Chapter 37

1And Bezalel made the ark of acacia wood: two cubits and a half was the length of it, and a cubit and a half the breadth of it, and a cubit and a half the height of it:

2and he overlaid it with pure gold within and without, and made a crown of gold to it round about.

3And he cast for it four rings of gold, in the four feet thereof; even two rings on the one side of it, and two rings on the other side of it.

4And he made staves of acacia wood, and overlaid them with gold.

5And he put the staves into the rings on the sides of the ark, to bear the ark.

6And he made a mercy-seat of pure gold: two cubits and a half was the length thereof, and a cubit and a half the breadth thereof.

7And he made two cherubim of gold; of beaten work made he them, at the two ends of the mercy-seat;

8one cherub at the one end, and one cherub at the other end: of one piece with the mercy-seat made he the cherubim at the two ends thereof.

9And the cherubim spread out their wings on high, covering the mercy-seat with their wings, with their faces one to another; toward the mercy-seat were the faces of the cherubim.

10And he made the table of acacia wood: two cubits was the length thereof, and a cubit the breadth thereof, and a cubit and a half the height thereof:

11and he overlaid it with pure gold, and made thereto a crown of gold round about.

12And he made unto it a border of a handbreadth round about, and made a golden crown to the border thereof round about.

13And he cast for it four rings of gold, and put the rings in the four corners that were on the four feet thereof.

14Close by the border were the rings, the places for the staves to bear the table.

15And he made the staves of acacia wood, and overlaid them with gold, to bear the table.

16And he made the vessels which were upon the table, the dishes thereof, and the spoons thereof, and the bowls thereof, and the flagons thereof, wherewith to pour out, of pure gold.

17And he made the candlestick of pure gold: of beaten work made he the candlestick, even its base, and its shaft; its cups, it knops, and its flowers, were of one piece with it:

18and there were six branches going out of the sides thereof; three branches of the candlestick out of the one side thereof, and three branches of the candlestick out of the other side thereof:

19three cups made like almond-blossoms in one branch, a knop and a flower, and three cups made like almond-blossoms in the other branch, a knop and a flower: so for the six branches going out of the candlestick.

20And in the candlestick were four cups made like almond-blossoms, the knops thereof, and the flowers thereof;

21and a knop under two branches of one piece with it, and a knop under two branches of one piece with it, and a knop under two branches of one piece with it, for the six branches going out of it.

22Their knops and their branches were of one piece with it: the whole of it was one beaten work of pure gold.

23And he made the lamps thereof, seven, and the snuffers thereof, and the snuffdishes thereof, of pure gold.

24Of a talent of pure gold made he it, and all the vessels thereof.

25And he made the altar of incense of acacia wood: a cubit was the length thereof, and a cubit the breadth thereof, foursquare; and two cubits was the height thereof; the horns thereof were of one piece with it.

26And he overlaid it with pure gold, the top thereof, and the sides thereof round about, and the horns of it: and he made unto it a crown of gold round about.

27And he made for it two golden rings under the crown thereof, upon the two ribs thereof, upon the two sides of it, for places for staves wherewith to bear it.

28And he made the staves of acacia wood, and overlaid them with gold.

29And he made the holy anointing oil, and the pure incense of sweet spices, after the art of the perfumer.

Chapter 38

1And he made the altar of burnt-offering of acacia wood: five cubits was the length thereof, and five cubits the breadth thereof, foursquare; and three cubits the height thereof.

2And he made the horns thereof upon the four corners of it; the horns thereof were of one piece with it: and he overlaid it with brass.

3And he made all the vessels of the altar, the pots, and the shovels, and the basins, the flesh-hooks, and the firepans: all the vessels thereof made he of brass.

4And he made for the altar a grating of network of brass, under the ledge round it beneath, reaching halfway up.

5And he cast four rings for the four ends of the grating of brass, to be places for the staves.

6And he made the staves of acacia wood, and overlaid them with brass.

7And he put the staves into the rings on the sides of the altar, wherewith to bear it; he made it hollow with planks.

8And he made the laver of brass, and the base thereof of brass, of the mirrors of the ministering women that ministered at the door of the tent of meeting.

9And he made the court: for the south side southward the hangings of the court were of fine twined linen, a hundred cubits;

10their pillars were twenty, and their sockets twenty, of brass; the hooks of

Exodus

the pillars and their fillets were of silver.

11And for the north side a hundred cubits, their pillars twenty, and their sockets twenty, of brass; the hooks of the pillars, and their fillets, of silver.

12And for the west side were hangings of fifty cubits, their pillars ten, and their sockets ten; the hooks of the pillars, and their fillets, of silver.

13And for the east side eastward fifty cubits.

14The hangings for the one side of the gate were fifteen cubits; their pillars three, and their sockets three;

15and so for the other side: on this hand and that hand by the gate of the court were hangings of fifteen cubits; their pillars three, and their sockets three.

16All the hangings of the court round about were of fine twined linen.

17And the sockets for the pillars were of brass; the hooks of the pillars, and their fillets, of silver; and the overlaying of their capitals, of silver; and all the pillars of the court were filleted with silver.

18And the screen for the gate of the court was the work of the embroiderer, of blue, and purple, and scarlet, and fine twined linen: and twenty cubits was the length, and the height in the breadth was five cubits, answerable to the hangings of the court.

19And their pillars were four, and their sockets four, of brass; their hooks of silver, and the overlaying of their capitals, and their fillets, of silver.

20And all the pins of the tabernacle, and of the court round about, were of brass.

21This is the sum of the things for the tabernacle, even the tabernacle of the testimony, as they were counted, according to the commandment of Moses, for the service of the Levites, by the hand of Ithamar, the son of Aaron the priest.

22And Bezalel the son of Uri, the son of Hur, of the tribe of Judah, made all that Yahweh commanded Moses.

23And with him was Oholiab, the son of Ahisamach, of the tribe of Dan, an engraver, and a skilful workman, and an embroiderer in blue, and in purple, and in scarlet, and in fine linen.

24All the gold that was used for the work in all the work of the sanctuary, even the gold of the offering, was twenty and nine talents, and seven hundred and thirty shekels, after the shekel of the sanctuary.

25And the silver of them that were numbered of the congregation was a hundred talents, and a thousand seven hundred and threescore and fifteen shekels, after the shekel of the sanctuary:

26a beka a head, that is, half a shekel, after the shekel of the sanctuary, for every one that passed over to them that were numbered, from twenty years old and upward, for six hundred thousand and three thousand and five hundred and fifty men.

27And the hundred talents of silver were for casting the sockets of the sanctuary, and the sockets of the veil; a hundred sockets for the hundred talents, a talent for a socket.

28And of the thousand seven hundred seventy and five shekels he made hooks for the pillars, and overlaid their capitals, and made fillets for them.

29And the brass of the offering was seventy talents, and two thousand and four hundred shekels.

30And therewith he made the sockets to the door of the tent of meeting, and the brazen altar, and the brazen grating for it, and all the vessels of the altar,

31and the sockets of the court round about, and the sockets of the gate of the court, and all the pins of the tabernacle, and all the pins of the court round about.

Chapter 39

1And of the blue, and purple, and scarlet, they made finely wrought garments, for ministering in the holy place, and made the holy garments for Aaron; as Yahweh commanded Moses.

2And he made the ephod of gold, blue, and purple, and scarlet, and fine twined linen.

3And they did beat the gold into thin plates, and cut it into wires, to work it in the blue, and in the purple, and in the scarlet, and in the fine linen, the work of the skilful workman.

4They made shoulder-pieces for it, joined together; at the two ends was it joined together.

5And the skilfully woven band, that was upon it, wherewith to gird it on, was of the same piece and like the work thereof; of gold, of blue, and purple, and scarlet, and fine twined linen; as Yahweh commanded Moses.

6And they wrought the onyx stones, inclosed in settings of gold, graven with the engravings of a signet, according to the names of the children of Israel.

7And he put them on the shoulder-pieces of the ephod, to be stones of memorial for the children of Israel; as Yahweh commanded Moses.

8And he made the breastplate, the work of the skilful workman, like the work of the ephod; of gold, of blue, and purple, and scarlet, and fine twined linen.

9It was foursquare; they made the breastplate double: a span was the length thereof, and a span the breadth thereof, being double.

10And they set in it four rows of stones. A row of sardius, topaz, and carbuncle was the first row;

11and the second row, an emerald, a sapphire, and a diamond;

12and the third row, a jacinth, an agate, and an amethyst;

13and the fourth row, a beryl, an onyx, and a jaspar: they were inclosed in inclosings of gold in their settings.

14And the stones were according to the names of the children of Israel, twelve, according to their names; like the engravings of a signet, every one according to his name, for the twelve tribes.

15And they made upon the breastplate chains like cords, of wreathen work of pure gold.

16And they made two settings of gold, and two gold rings, and put the two rings on the two ends of the breastplate.

17And they put the two wreathen chains of gold in the two rings at the ends of the breastplate.

18And the other two ends of the two wreathen chains they put on the two settings, and put them on the shoulder-pieces of the ephod, in the forepart thereof.

19And they made two rings of gold, and put them upon the two ends of the breastplate, upon the edge thereof, which was toward the side of the ephod inward.

20And they made two rings of gold, and put them on the two shoulder-pieces of the ephod underneath, in the forepart thereof, close by the coupling thereof, above the skilfully woven band of the ephod.

21And they did bind the breastplate by the rings thereof unto the rings of the ephod with a lace of blue, that it might be upon the skilfully woven band of the ephod, and that the breastplate might not be loosed from the ephod; as Yahweh commanded Moses.

22And he made the robe of the ephod of woven work, all of blue.

23And the hole of the robe in the midst thereof, as the hole of a coat of mail, with a binding round about the hole of it, that it should not be rent.

24And they made upon the skirts of the robe pomegranates of blue, and purple, and scarlet, and twined linen.

25And they made bells of pure gold, and put the bells between the pomegranates upon the skirts of the robe round about, between the pomegranates;

26a bell and a pomegranate, a bell and a pomegranate, upon the skirts of the robe round about, to minister in; as Yahweh commanded Moses.

27And they made the coats of fine linen of woven work for Aaron, and for his sons,

28and the mitre of fine linen, and the goodly head-tires of fine linen, and the linen breeches of fine twined linen,

29and the girdle of fine twined linen, and blue, and purple, and scarlet, the work of the embroiderer; as Yahweh commanded Moses.

30And they made the plate of the holy crown of pure gold, and wrote upon it a writing, like the engravings of a signet, HOLY TO YAHWEH.

31And they tied unto it a lace of blue, to fasten it upon the mitre above; as Yahweh commanded Moses.

32Thus was finished all the work of the tabernacle of the tent of meeting: and the children of Israel did according to all that Yahweh commanded Moses; so did they.

33And they brought the tabernacle unto Moses, the Tent, and all its furniture, its clasps, its boards, it bars, and its pillars, and it sockets;

34and the covering of rams' skins dyed red, and the covering of sealskins, and the veil of the screen;

35the ark of the testimony, and the staves thereof, and the mercy-seat;

36the table, all the vessels thereof, and the showbread;

37the pure candlestick, the lamps thereof, even the lamps to be set in order, and all the vessels thereof, and the oil for the light;

38and the golden altar, and the anointing oil, and the sweet incense, and the screen for the door of the Tent;

39the brazen altar, and its grating of brass, its staves, and all its vessels, the laver and its base;

40the hangings of the court, its pillars, and its sockets, and the screen for the gate of the court, the cords thereof, and the pins thereof, and all the instruments of the service of the tabernacle, for the tent of meeting;

41the finely wrought garments for ministering in the holy place, and the holy garments for Aaron the priest, and the garments of his sons, to minister in the priest's office.

42According to all that Yahweh commanded Moses, so the children of Israel did all the work.

43And Moses saw all the work, and, behold, they had done it; as Yahweh had commanded, even so had they done it: and Moses blessed them.

Chapter 40

1And Yahweh spake unto Moses, saying,

2On the first day of the first month shalt thou rear up the tabernacle of the tent of meeting.

3And thou shalt put therein the ark of the testimony, and thou shalt screen the ark with the veil.

4And thou shalt bring in the table, and set in order the things that are upon it; and thou shalt bring in the candlestick, and light the lamps thereof.

5And thou shalt set the golden altar for incense before the ark of the testimony, and put the screen of the door to the tabernacle.

6And thou shalt set the altar of burnt-offering before the door of the tabernacle of the tent of meeting.

7And thou shalt set the laver between the tent of meeting and the altar, and shalt put water therein.

8And thou shalt set up the court round about, and hang up the screen of the gate of the court.

9And thou shalt take the anointing oil, and anoint the tabernacle, and all that is therein, and shalt hallow it, and all the furniture thereof: and it shall be holy.

10And thou shalt anoint the altar of burnt-offering, and all its vessels, and sanctify the altar: and the altar shall be most holy.

11And thou shalt anoint the laver and its base, and sanctify it.

12And thou shalt bring Aaron and his sons unto the door of the tent of meeting, and shalt wash them with water.

13And thou shalt put upon Aaron the holy garments; and thou shalt anoint him, and sanctify him, that he may minister unto me in the priest's office.

14And thou shalt bring his sons, and put coats upon them;

15and thou shalt anoint them, as thou didst anoint their father, that they may minister unto me in the priest's office: and their anointing shall be to them for an everlasting priesthood throughout their generations.

16Thus did Moses: according to all that Yahweh commanded him, so did he.

17And it came to pass in the first month in the second year, on the first day of the month, that the tabernacle was reared up.

18And Moses reared up the tabernacle, and laid its sockets, and set up the boards thereof, and put in the bars thereof, and reared up its pillars.

¹⁹And he spread the tent over the tabernacle, and put the covering of the tent above upon it; as Yahweh commanded Moses.

²⁰And he took and put the testimony into the ark, and set the staves on the ark, and put the mercy-seat above upon the ark:

²¹and he brought the ark into the tabernacle, and set up the veil of the screen, and screened the ark of the testimony; as Yahweh commanded Moses.

²²And he put the table in the tent of meeting, upon the side of the tabernacle northward, without the veil.

²³And he set the bread in order upon it before Yahweh; as Yahweh commanded Moses.

²⁴And he put the candlestick in the tent of meeting, over against the table, on the side of the tabernacle southward.

²⁵And he lighted the lamps before Yahweh; as Yahweh commanded Moses.

²⁶And he put the golden altar in the tent of meeting before the veil:

²⁷and he burnt thereon incense of sweet spices; as Yahweh commanded Moses.

²⁸And he put the screen of the door to the tabernacle.

²⁹And he set the altar of burnt-offering at the door of the tabernacle of the tent of meeting, and offered upon it the burnt-offering and the meal-offering; as Yahweh commanded Moses.

³⁰And he set the laver between the tent of meeting and the altar, and put water therein, wherewith to wash.

³¹And Moses and Aaron and his sons washed their hands and their feet thereat;

³²when they went into the tent of meeting, and when they came near unto the altar, they washed; as Yahweh commanded Moses.

³³And he reared up the court round about the tabernacle and the altar, and set up the screen of the gate of the court. So Moses finished the work.

³⁴Then the cloud covered the tent of meeting, and the glory of Yahweh filled the tabernacle.

³⁵And Moses was not able to enter into the tent of meeting, because the cloud abode thereon, and the glory of Yahweh filled the tabernacle.

³⁶And when the cloud was taken up from over the tabernacle, the children of Israel went onward, throughout all their journeys:

³⁷but if the cloud was not taken up, then they journeyed not till the day that it was taken up.

³⁸For the cloud of Yahweh was upon the tabernacle by day, and there was fire therein by night, in the sight of all the house of Israel, throughout all their journeys.

Leviticus

The Third Book of Moses, commonly called Leviticus

Chapter 1

1And Yahweh called unto Moses, and spake unto him out of the tent of meeting, saying,

2Speak unto the children of Israel, and say unto them, When any man of you offereth an oblation unto Yahweh, ye shall offer your oblation of the cattle, even of the herd and of the flock.

3If his oblation be a burnt-offering of the herd, he shall offer it a male without blemish: he shall offer it at the door of the tent of meeting, that he may be accepted before Yahweh.

4And he shall lay his hand upon the head of the burnt-offering; and it shall be accepted for him to make atonement for him.

5And he shall kill the bullock before Yahweh: and Aaron's sons, the priests, shall present the blood, and sprinkle the blood round about upon the altar that is at the door of the tent of meeting.

6And he shall flay the burnt-offering, and cut it into its pieces.

7And the sons of Aaron the priest shall put fire upon the altar, and lay wood in order upon the fire;

8and Aaron's sons, the priests, shall lay the pieces, the head, and the fat, in order upon the wood that is on the fire which is upon the altar:

9but its inwards and its legs shall he wash with water: and the priest shall burn the whole on the altar, for a burnt-offering, an offering made by fire, of a sweet savor unto Yahweh.

10And if his oblation be of the flock, of the sheep, or of the goats, for a burnt-offering; he shall offer it a male without blemish.

11And he shall kill it on the side of the altar northward before Yahweh: and Aaron's sons, the priests, shall sprinkle its blood upon the altar round about.

12And he shall cut it into its pieces, with its head and its fat; and the priest shall lay them in order on the wood that is on the fire which is upon the altar:

13but the inwards and the legs shall he wash with water; and the priest shall offer the whole, and burn it upon the altar: it is a burnt-offering, an offering made by fire, of a sweet savor unto Yahweh.

14And if his oblation to Yahweh be a burnt-offering of birds, then he shall offer his oblation of turtle-doves, or of young pigeons.

15And the priest shall bring it unto the altar, and wring off its head, and burn it on the altar; and the blood thereof shall be drained out on the side of the altar;

16and he shall take away its crop with the filth thereof, and cast it beside the altar on the east part, in the place of the ashes:

17and he shall rend it by the wings thereof, but shall not divide it asunder; and the priest shall burn it upon the altar, upon the wood that is upon the fire: it is a burnt-offering, an offering made by fire, of a sweet savor unto Yahweh.

Chapter 2

1And when any one offereth an oblation of a meal-offering unto Yahweh, his oblation shall be of fine flour; and he shall pour oil upon it, and put frankincense thereon:

2and he shall bring it to Aaron's sons the priests; and he shall take thereout his handful of the fine flour thereof, and of the oil thereof, with all the frankincense thereof; and the priest shall burn it as the memorial thereof upon the altar, an offering made by fire, of a sweet savor unto Yahweh.

3and that which is left of the meal-offering shall be Aaron's and his sons': it is a thing most holy of the offerings of Yahweh made by fire.

4And when thou offerest an oblation of a meal-offering baken in the oven, it shall be unleavened cakes of fine flour mingled with oil, or unleavened wafers anointed with oil.

5And if thy oblation be a meal-offering of the baking-pan, it shall be of fine flour unleavened, mingled with oil.

6Thou shalt part it in pieces, and pour oil thereon: it is a meal-offering.

7And if thy oblation be a meal-offering of the frying-pan, it shall be made of fine flour with oil.

8And thou shalt bring the meal-offering that is made of these things unto Yahweh: and it shall be presented unto the priest, and he shall bring it unto the altar.

9And the priest shall take up from the meal-offering the memorial thereof, and shall burn it upon the altar, an offering made by fire, of a sweet savor unto Yahweh.

10And that which is left of the meal-offering shall be Aaron's and his sons': it is a thing most holy of the offerings of Yahweh made by fire.

11No meal-offering, which ye shall offer unto Yahweh, shall be made with leaven; for ye shall burn no leaven, nor any honey, as an offering made by fire unto Yahweh.

12As an oblation of first-fruits ye shall offer them unto Yahweh: but they shall not come up for a sweet savor on the altar.

13And every oblation of thy meal-offering shalt thou season with salt; neither shalt thou suffer the salt of the covenant of thy God to be lacking from thy meal-offering: with all thine oblations thou shalt offer salt.

14And if thou offer a meal-offering of first-fruits unto Yahweh, thou shalt offer for the meal-offering of thy first-fruits grain in the ear parched with fire, bruised grain of the fresh ear.

15And thou shalt put oil upon it, and lay frankincense thereon: it is a meal-offering.

16And the priest shall burn the memorial of it, part of the bruised grain thereof, and part of the oil thereof, with all the frankincense thereof: it is an offering made by fire unto Yahweh.

Chapter 3

1And if his oblation be a sacrifice of peace-offerings; if he offer of the herd, whether male or female, he shall offer it without blemish before Yahweh.

2And he shall lay his hand upon the head of his oblation, and kill it at the door of the tent of meeting: and Aaron's sons the priests shall sprinkle the blood upon the altar round about.

3And he shall offer of the sacrifice of peace-offerings an offering made by fire unto Yahweh; the fat that covereth the inwards, and all the fat that is upon the inwards,

4and the two kidneys, and the fat that is on them, which is by the loins, and the caul upon the liver, with the kidneys, shall he take away.

5And Aaron's sons shall burn it on the altar upon the burnt-offering, which is upon the wood that is on the fire: it is an offering made by fire, of a sweet savor unto Yahweh.

6And if his oblation for a sacrifice of peace-offerings unto Yahweh be of the flock; male or female, he shall offer it without blemish.

7If he offer a lamb for his oblation, then shall he offer it before Yahweh;

8and he shall lay his hand upon the head of his oblation, and kill it before the tent of meeting: and Aaron's sons shall sprinkle the blood thereof upon the altar round about.

9And he shall offer of the sacrifice of peace-offerings an offering made by fire unto Yahweh; the fat thereof, the fat tail entire, he shall take away hard by the backbone; and the fat that covereth the inwards, and all the fat that is upon the inwards,

10and the two kidneys, and the fat that is upon them, which is by the loins, and the caul upon the liver, with the kidneys, shall he take away.

11And the priest shall burn it upon the altar: it is the food of the offering made by fire unto Yahweh.

12And if his oblation be a goat, then he shall offer it before Yahweh:

13and he shall lay his hand upon the head of it, and kill it before the tent of meeting; and the sons of Aaron shall sprinkle the blood thereof upon the altar round about.

14And he shall offer thereof his oblation, even an offering made by fire unto Yahweh; the fat that covereth the inwards, and all the fat that is upon the inwards,

15and the two kidneys, and the fat that is upon them, which is by the loins, and the caul upon the liver, with the kidneys, shall he take away.

16And the priest shall burn them upon the altar: it is the food of the offering made by fire, for a sweet savor; all the fat is Yahweh's.

17It shall be a perpetual statute throughout your generations in all your dwellings, that ye shall eat neither fat nor blood.

Chapter 4

1And Yahweh spake unto Moses, saying,

2Speak unto the children of Israel, saying, If any one shall sin unwittingly, in any of the things which Yahweh hath commanded not to be done, and shall do any one of them:

3if the anointed priest shall sin so as to bring guilt on the people, then let him offer for his sin, which he hath sinned, a young bullock without blemish unto Yahweh for a sin-offering.

4And he shall bring the bullock unto the door of the tent of meeting before Yahweh; and he shall lay his hand upon the head of the bullock, and kill the bullock before Yahweh.

5And the anointed priest shall take of the blood of the bullock, and bring it to the tent of meeting:

6and the priest shall dip his finger in the blood, and sprinkle of the blood seven times before Yahweh, before the veil of the sanctuary.

7And the priest shall put of the blood upon the horns of the altar of sweet incense before Yahweh, which is in the tent of meeting; and all the blood of the bullock shall he pour out at the base of the altar of burnt-offering, which is at the door of the tent of meeting.

8And all the fat of the bullock of the sin-offering he shall take off from it; the fat that covereth the inwards, and all the fat that is upon the inwards,

9and the two kidneys, and the fat that is upon them, which is by the loins, and the caul upon the liver, with the kidneys, shall he take away,

10as it is taken off from the ox of the sacrifice of peace-offerings: and the priest shall burn them upon the altar of burnt-offering.

11And the skin of the bullock, and all its flesh, with its head, and with its legs, and its inwards, and its dung,

12even the whole bullock shall he carry forth without the camp unto a clean place, where the ashes are poured out, and burn it on wood with fire: where the ashes are poured out shall it be burnt.

13And if the whole congregation of Israel err, and the thing be hid from the eyes of the assembly, and they have done any of the things which Yahweh hath commanded not to be done, and are guilty;

14when the sin wherein they have sinned is known, then the assembly shall offer a young bullock for a sin-offering, and bring it before the tent of meeting.

15And the elders of the congregation shall lay their hands upon the head of the bullock before Yahweh; and the bullock shall be killed before Yahweh.

16And the anointed priest shall bring of the blood of the bullock to the tent of meeting:

17and the priest shall dip his finger in the blood, and sprinkle it seven times before Yahweh, before the veil.

18And he shall put of the blood upon the horns of the altar which is before Yahweh, that is in the tent of meeting; and all the blood shall he pour out at the base of the altar of burnt-offering, which is at the door of the tent of meeting.

19And all the fat thereof shall he take off from it, and burn it upon the altar.

20Thus shall he do with the bullock; as he did with the bullock of the sin-offering, so shall he do with this; and the priest shall make atonement for them, and they shall be forgiven.

21And he shall carry forth the bullock without the camp, and burn it as he burned the first bullock: it is the sin-offering for the assembly.

22When a ruler sinneth, and doeth unwittingly any one of all the things which Yahweh his God hath commanded not to be done, and is guilty;

23if his sin, wherein he hath sinned, be made known to him, he shall bring for his oblation a goat, a male without blemish.

24And he shall lay his hand upon the head of the goat, and kill it in the place where they kill the burnt-offering before Yahweh: it is a sin-offering.

25And the priest shall take of the blood of the sin-offering with his finger, and put it upon the horns of the altar of burnt-offering; and the blood thereof shall he pour out at the base of the altar of burnt-offering.

26And all the fat thereof shall he burn upon the altar, as the fat of the sacrifice of peace-offerings; and the priest shall make atonement for him as concerning his sin, and he shall be forgiven.

27And if any one of the common people sin unwittingly, in doing any of the things which Yahweh hath commanded not to be done, and be guilty;

28if his sin, which he hath sinned, be made known to him, then he shall bring for his oblation a goat, a female without blemish, for his sin which he hath sinned.

29And he shall lay his hand upon the head of the sin-offering, and kill the sin-offering in the place of burnt-offering.

30And the priest shall take of the blood thereof with his finger, and put it upon the horns of the altar of burnt-offering; and all the blood thereof shall he pour out at the base of the altar.

31And all the fat thereof shall he take away, as the fat is taken away from off the sacrifice of peace-offerings; and the priest shall burn it upon the altar for a sweet savor unto Yahweh; and the priest shall make atonement for him, and he shall be forgiven.

32And if he bring a lamb as his oblation for a sin-offering, he shall bring it a female without blemish.

33And he shall lay his hand upon the head of the sin-offering, and kill it for a sin-offering in the place where they kill the burnt-offering.

34And the priest shall take of the blood of the sin-offering with his finger, and put it upon the horns of the altar of burnt-offering; and all the blood thereof shall he pour out at the base of the altar;

35and all the fat thereof shall he take away, as the fat of the lamb is taken away from the sacrifice of peace-offerings; and the priest shall burn them on the altar, upon the offerings of Yahweh made by fire; and the priest shall make atonement for him as touching his sin that he hath sinned, and he shall be forgiven.

Chapter 5

1And if any one sin, in that he heareth the voice of adjuration, he being a witness, whether he hath seen or known, if he do not utter it, then he shall bear his iniquity.

2Or if any one touch any unclean thing, whether it be the carcass of an unclean beast, or the carcass of unclean cattle, or the carcass of unclean creeping things, and it be hidden from him, and he be unclean, then he shall be guilty.

3Or if he touch the uncleanness of man, whatsoever his uncleanness be wherewith he is unclean, and it be hid from him; when he knoweth of it, then he shall be guilty.

4Or if any one swear rashly with his lips to do evil, or to do good, whatsoever it be that a man shall utter rashly with an oath, and it be hid from him; when he knoweth of it, then he shall be guilty in one of these things.

5And it shall be, when he shall be guilty in one of these things, that he shall confess that wherein he hath sinned:

6and he shall bring his trespass-offering unto Yahweh for his sin which he hath sinned, a female from the flock, a lamb or a goat, for a sin-offering; and the priest shall make atonement for him as concerning his sin.

7And if his means suffice not for a lamb, then he shall bring his trespass-offering for that wherein he hath sinned, two turtle-doves, or two young pigeons, unto Yahweh; one for a sin-offering, and the other for a burnt-offering.

8And he shall bring them unto the priest, who shall offer that which is for the sin-offering first, and wring off its head from its neck, but shall not divide it asunder:

9and he shall sprinkle of the blood of the sin-offering upon the side of the altar; and the rest of the blood shall be drained out at the base of the altar: it is a sin-offering.

10And he shall offer the second for a burnt-offering, according to the ordinance; and the priest shall make atonement for him as concerning his sin which he hath sinned, and he shall be forgiven.

11But if his means suffice not for two turtle-doves, or two young pigeons, then he shall bring his oblation for that wherein he hath sinned, the tenth part of an ephah of fine flour for a sin-offering: he shall put no oil upon it, neither shall he put any frankincense thereon; for it is a sin-offering.

12And he shall bring it to the priest, and the priest shall take his handful of it as the memorial thereof, and burn it on the altar, upon the offerings of Yahweh made by fire: it is a sin-offering.

13And the priest shall make atonement for him as touching his sin that he hath sinned in any of these things, and he shall be forgiven: and the remnant shall be the priest's, as the meal-offering.

14And Yahweh spake unto Moses, saying,

15If any one commit a trespass, and sin unwittingly, in the holy things of Yahweh; then he shall bring his trespass-offering unto Yahweh, a ram without blemish out of the flock, according to thy estimation in silver by shekels, after the shekel of the sanctuary, for a trespass-offering:

16and he shall make restitution for that which he hath done amiss in the holy thing, and shall add the fifth part thereto, and give it unto the priest; and the priest shall make atonement for him with the ram of the trespass-offering, and he shall be forgiven.

17And if any one sin, and do any of the things which Yahweh hath commanded not to be done; though he knew it not, yet is he guilty, and shall bear his iniquity.

18And he shall bring a ram without blemish out of the flock, according to thy estimation, for a trespass-offering, unto the priest; and the priest shall make atonement for him concerning the thing wherein he erred unwittingly and knew it not, and he shall be forgiven.

19It is a trespass-offering: he is certainly guilty before Yahweh.

Chapter 6

1And Yahweh spake unto Moses, saying,

2If any one sin, and commit a trespass against Yahweh, and deal falsely with his neighbor in a matter of deposit, or of bargain, or of robbery, or have oppressed his neighbor,

3or have found that which was lost, and deal falsely therein, and swear to a lie; in any of all these things that a man doeth, sinning therein;

4then it shall be, if he hath sinned, and is guilty, that he shall restore that which he took by robbery, or the thing which he hath gotten by oppression, or the deposit which was committed to him, or the lost thing which he found,

5or any thing about which he hath sworn falsely; he shall even restore it in full, and shall add the fifth part more thereto: unto him to whom it appertaineth shall he give it, in the day of his being found guilty.

6And he shall bring his trespass-offering unto Yahweh, a ram without blemish out of the flock, according to thy estimation, for a trespass-offering, unto the priest:

7and the priest shall make atonement for him before Yahweh; and he shall be forgiven concerning whatsoever he doeth so as to be guilty thereby.

8And Yahweh spake unto Moses, saying,

9Command Aaron and his sons, saying, This is the law of the burnt-offering: the burnt-offering shall be on the hearth upon the altar all night unto the morning; and the fire of the altar shall be kept burning thereon.

10And the priest shall put on his linen garment, and his linen breeches shall he put upon his flesh; and he shall take up the ashes whereto the fire hath consumed the burnt-offering on the altar, and he shall put them beside the altar.

11And he shall put off his garments, and put on other garments, and carry forth the ashes without the camp unto a clean place.

12And the fire upon the altar shall be kept burning thereon, it shall not go out; and the priest shall burn wood on it every morning: and he shall lay the burnt-offering in order upon it, and shall burn thereon the fat of the peace-offerings.

13Fire shall be kept burning upon the altar continually; it shall not go out.

14And this is the law of the meal-offering: the sons of Aaron shall offer it before Yahweh, before the altar.

15And he shall take up therefrom his handful, of the fine flour of the meal-offering, and of the oil thereof, and all the frankincense which is upon the meal-offering, and shall burn it upon the altar for a sweet savor, as the memorial thereof, unto Yahweh.

16And that which is left thereof shall Aaron and his sons eat: it shall be eaten without leaven in a holy place; in the court of the tent of meeting they shall eat it.

17It shall not be baken with leaven. I have given it as their portion of my offerings made by fire; it is most holy, as the sin-offering, and as the trespass-offering.

18Every male among the children of Aaron shall eat of it, as his portion for ever throughout your generations, from the offerings of Yahweh made by fire: whosoever toucheth them shall be holy.

19And Yahweh spake unto Moses, saying,

20This is the oblation of Aaron and of his sons, which they shall offer unto Yahweh in the day when he is anointed: the tenth part of an ephah of fine flour for a meal-offering perpetually, half of it in the morning, and half thereof in the evening.

21On a baking-pan it shall be made with oil; when it is soaked, thou shalt bring it in: in baken pieces shalt thou offer the meal-offering for a sweet savor unto Yahweh.

22And the anointed priest that shall be in his stead from among his sons shall offer it: by a statute for ever it shall be wholly burnt unto Yahweh.

23And every meal-offering of the priest shall be wholly burnt: it shall not be eaten.

24And Yahweh spake unto Moses, saying,

25Speak unto Aaron and to his sons, saying, This is the law of the sin-offering: in the place where the burnt-offering is killed shall the sin-offering be killed before Yahweh: it is most holy.

26The priest that offereth it for sin shall eat it: in a holy place shall it be eaten, in the court of the tent of meeting.

27Whatsoever shall touch the flesh thereof shall be holy; and when there is sprinkled of the blood thereof upon any garment, thou shalt wash that whereon it was sprinkled in a holy place.

28But the earthen vessel wherein it is boiled shall be broken; and if it be boiled in a brazen vessel, it shall be scoured, and rinsed in water.

29Every male among the priests shall eat thereof: it is most holy.

30And no sin-offering, whereof any of the blood is brought into the tent of meeting to make atonement in the holy place, shall be eaten: it shall be burnt with fire.

Leviticus
Chapter 7

1And this is the law of the trespass-offering: it is most holy.

2In the place where they kill the burnt-offering shall they kill the trespass-offering; and the blood thereof shall he sprinkle upon the altar round about.

3And he shall offer of it all the fat thereof: the fat tail, and the fat that covereth the inwards,

4and the two kidneys, and the fat that is on them, which is by the loins, and the caul upon the liver, with the kidneys, shall he take away;

5and the priest shall burn them upon the altar for an offering made by fire unto Yahweh: it is a trespass-offering.

6Every male among the priests shall eat thereof: it shall be eaten in a holy place: it is most holy.

7As is the sin-offering, so is the trespass-offering; there is one law for them: the priest that maketh atonement therewith, he shall have it.

8And the priest that offereth any man's burnt-offering, even the priest shall have to himself the skin of the burnt-offering which he hath offered.

9And every meal-offering that is baken in the oven, and all that is dressed in the frying-pan, and on the baking-pan, shall be the priest's that offereth it.

10And every meal-offering, mingled with oil, or dry, shall all the sons of Aaron have, one as well as another.

11And this is the law of the sacrifice of peace-offerings, which one shall offer unto Yahweh.

12If he offer it for a thanksgiving, then he shall offer with the sacrifice of thanksgiving unleavened cakes mingled with oil, and unleavened wafers anointed with oil, and cakes mingled with oil, of fine flour soaked.

13With cakes of leavened bread he shall offer his oblation with the sacrifice of his peace-offerings for thanksgiving.

14And of it he shall offer one out of each oblation for a heave-offering unto Yahweh; it shall be the priest's that sprinkleth the blood of the peace-offerings.

15And the flesh of the sacrifice of his peace-offerings for thanksgiving shall be eaten on the day of his oblation; he shall not leave any of it until the morning.

16But if the sacrifice of his oblation be a vow, or a freewill-offering, it shall be eaten on the day that he offereth his sacrifice; and on the morrow that which remaineth of it shall be eaten:

17but that which remaineth of the flesh of the sacrifice on the third day shall be burnt with fire.

18And if any of the flesh of the sacrifice of his peace-offerings be eaten on the third day, it shall not be accepted, neither shall it be imputed unto him that offereth it: it shall be an abomination, and the soul that eateth of it shall bear his iniquity.

19And the flesh that toucheth any unclean thing shall not be eaten; it shall be burnt with fire. And as for the flesh, every one that is clean shall eat thereof:

20but the soul that eateth of the flesh of the sacrifice of peace-offerings, that pertain unto Yahweh, having his uncleanness upon him, that soul shall be cut off from his people.

21And when any one shall touch any unclean thing, the uncleanness of man, or an unclean beast, or any unclean abomination, and eat of the flesh of the sacrifice of peace-offerings, which pertain unto Yahweh, that soul shall be cut off from his people.

22And Yahweh spake unto Moses, saying,

23Speak unto the children of Israel, saying, Ye shall eat no fat, of ox, or sheep, or goat.

24And the fat of that which dieth of itself, and the fat of that which is torn of beasts, may be used for any other service; but ye shall in no wise eat of it.

25For whosoever eateth the fat of the beast, of which men offer an offering made by fire unto Yahweh, even the soul that eateth it shall be cut off from his people.

26And ye shall eat no manner of blood, whether it be of bird or of beast, in any of your dwellings.

27Whosoever it be that eateth any blood, that soul shall be cut off from his people.

28And Yahweh spake unto Moses, saying,

29Speak unto the children of Israel, saying, He that offereth the sacrifice of his peace-offerings unto Yahweh shall bring his oblation unto Yahweh out of the sacrifice of his peace-offerings:

30his own hands shall bring the offerings of Yahweh made by fire; the fat with the breast shall he bring, that the breast may be waved for a wave-offering before Yahweh.

31And the priest shall burn the fat upon the altar; but the breast shall be Aaron's and his sons'.

32And the right thigh shall ye give unto the priest for a heave-offering out of the sacrifices of your peace-offerings.

33He among the sons of Aaron that offereth the blood of the peace-offerings, and the fat, shall have the right thigh for a portion.

34For the wave-breast and the heave-thigh have I taken of the children of Israel out of the sacrifices of their peace-offerings, and have given them unto Aaron the priest and unto his sons as their portion for ever from the children of Israel.

35This is the anointing-portion of Aaron, and the anointing-portion of his sons, out of the offerings of Yahweh made by fire, in the day when he presented them to minister unto Yahweh in the priest's office;

36which Yahweh commanded to be given them of the children of Israel, in the day that he anointed them. It is their portion for ever throughout their generations.

37This is the law of the burnt-offering, of the meal-offering, and of the sin-offering, and of the trespass-offering, and of the consecration, and of the sacrifice of peace-offerings;

38which Yahweh commanded Moses in mount Sinai, in the day that he commanded the children of Israel to offer their oblations unto Yahweh, in the wilderness of Sinai.

Chapter 8

1And Yahweh spake unto Moses, saying,

2Take Aaron and his sons with him, and the garments, and the anointing oil, and the bullock of the sin-offering, and the two rams, and the basket of unleavened bread;

3and assemble thou all the congregation at the door of the tent of meeting.

4And Moses did as Yahweh commanded him; and the congregation was assembled at the door of the tent of meeting.

5And Moses said unto the congregation, This is the thing which Yahweh hath commanded to be done.

6And Moses brought Aaron and his sons, and washed them with water.

7And he put upon him the coat, and girded him with the girdle, and clothed him with the robe, and put the ephod upon him, and he girded him with the skilfully woven band of the ephod, and bound it unto him therewith.

8And he placed the breastplate upon him: and in the breastplate he put the Urim and the Thummim.

9And he set the mitre upon his head; and upon the mitre, in front, did he set the golden plate, the holy crown; as Yahweh commanded Moses.

10And Moses took the anointing oil, and anointed the tabernacle and all that was therein, and sanctified them.

11And he sprinkled thereof upon the altar seven times, and anointed the altar and all its vessels, and the laver and its base, to sanctify them.

12And he poured of the anointing oil upon Aaron's head, and anointed him, to sanctify him.

13And Moses brought Aaron's sons, and clothed them with coats, and girded them with girdles, and bound head-tires upon them; as Yahweh commanded Moses.

14And he brought the bullock of the sin-offering: and Aaron and his sons laid their hands upon the head of the bullock of the sin-offering.

15And he slew it; and Moses took the blood, and put it upon the horns of the altar round about with his finger, and purified the altar, and poured out the blood at the base of the altar, and sanctified it, to make atonement for it.

16And he took all the fat that was upon the inwards, and the caul of the liver, and the two kidneys, and their fat; and Moses burned it upon the altar.

17But the bullock, and its skin, and its flesh, and its dung, he burnt with fire without the camp; as Yahweh commanded Moses.

18And he presented the ram of the burnt-offering: and Aaron and his sons laid their hands upon the head of the ram.

19And he killed it; and Moses sprinkled the blood upon the altar round about.

20And he cut the ram into its pieces; and Moses burnt the head, and the pieces, and the fat.

21And he washed the inwards and the legs with water; and Moses burnt the whole ram upon the altar: it was a burnt-offering for a sweet savor: it was an offering made by fire unto Yahweh; as Yahweh commanded Moses.

22And he presented the other ram, the ram of consecration: and Aaron and his sons laid their hands upon the head of the ram.

23And he slew it; and Moses took of the blood thereof, and put it upon the tip of Aaron's right ear, and upon the thumb of his right hand, and upon the great toe of his right foot.

24And he brought Aaron's sons; and Moses put of the blood upon the tip of their right ear, and upon the thumb of their right hand, and upon the great toe of their right foot: and Moses sprinkled the blood upon the altar round about.

25And he took the fat, and the fat tail, and all the fat that was upon the inwards, and the caul of the liver, and the two kidneys, and their fat, and the right thigh:

26and out of the basket of unleavened bread, that was before Yahweh, he took one unleavened cake, and one cake of oiled bread, and one wafer, and placed them on the fat, and upon the right thigh:

27and he put the whole upon the hands of Aaron, and upon the hands of his sons, and waved them for a wave-offering before Yahweh.

28And Moses took them from off their hands, and burnt them on the altar upon the burnt-offering: they were a consecration for a sweet savor: it was an offering made by fire unto Yahweh.

29And Moses took the breast, and waved it for a wave-offering before Yahweh: it was Moses' portion of the ram of consecration; as Yahweh commanded Moses.

30And Moses took of the anointing oil, and of the blood which was upon the altar, and sprinkled it upon Aaron, upon his garments, and upon his sons, and upon his sons' garments with him, and sanctified Aaron, his garments, and his sons, and his sons' garments with him.

31And Moses said unto Aaron and to his sons, Boil the flesh at the door of the tent of meeting: and there eat it and the bread that is in the basket of consecration, as I commanded, saying, Aaron and his sons shall eat it.

32And that which remaineth of the flesh and of the bread shall ye burn with fire.

33And ye shall not go out from the door of the tent of meeting seven days, until the days of your consecration be fulfilled: for he shall consecrate you seven days.

34As hath been done this day, so Yahweh hath commanded to do, to make atonement for you.

35And at the door of the tent of meeting shall ye abide day and night seven days, and keep the charge of Yahweh, that ye die not: for so I am commanded.

36And Aaron and his sons did all the things which Yahweh commanded by Moses.

Chapter 9

1And it came to pass on the eighth day, that Moses called Aaron and his sons, and the elders of Israel;

2and he said unto Aaron, Take thee a calf of the herd for a sin-offering, and a ram for a burnt-offering, without blemish, and offer them before Yahweh.

3And unto the children of Israel thou shalt speak, saying, Take ye a he-goat for a sin-offering; and a calf and a lamb, both a year old, without blemish, for a burnt-offering;

4and an ox and a ram for peace-offerings, to sacrifice before Yahweh; and a meal-offering mingled with oil: for to-day Yahweh appeareth unto you.

5And they brought that which Moses commanded before the tent of meeting: and all the congregation drew near and stood before Yahweh.

6And Moses said, This is the thing which Yahweh commanded that ye should do: and the glory of Yahweh shall appear unto you.

7And Moses said unto Aaron, Draw near unto the altar, and offer thy sin-offering, and thy burnt-offering, and make atonement for thyself, and for the people; and offer the oblation of the people, and make atonement for them; as Yahweh commanded.

8So Aaron drew near unto the altar, and slew the calf of the sin-offering, which was for himself.

9And the sons of Aaron presented the blood unto him; and he dipped his finger in the blood, and put it upon the horns of the altar, and poured out the blood at the base of the altar:

10but the fat, and the kidneys, and the caul from the liver of the sin-offering, he burnt upon the altar; as Yahweh commanded Moses.

11And the flesh and the skin he burnt with fire without the camp.

12And he slew the burnt-offering; and Aaron's sons delivered unto him the blood, and he sprinkled it upon the altar round about.

13And they delivered the burnt-offering unto him, piece by piece, and the head: and he burnt them upon the altar.

14And he washed the inwards and the legs, and burnt them upon the burnt-offering on the altar.

15And he presented the people's oblation, and took the goat of the sin-offering which was for the people, and slew it, and offered it for sin, as the first.

16And he presented the burnt-offering, and offered it according to the ordinance.

17And he presented the meal-offering, and filled his hand therefrom, and burnt it upon the altar, besides the burnt-offering of the morning.

18He slew also the ox and the ram, the sacrifice of peace-offerings, which was for the people: and Aaron's sons delivered unto him the blood, which he sprinkled upon the altar round about,

19and the fat of the ox and of the ram, the fat tail, and that which covereth the inwards, and the kidneys, and the caul of the liver:

20and they put the fat upon the breasts, and he burnt the fat upon the altar:

21and the breasts and the right thigh Aaron waved for a wave-offering before Yahweh; as Moses commanded.

22And Aaron lifted up his hands toward the people, and blessed them; and he came down from offering the sin-offering, and the burnt-offering, and the peace-offerings.

23And Moses and Aaron went into the tent of meeting, and came out, and blessed the people: and the glory of Yahweh appeared unto all the people.

24And there came forth fire from before Yahweh, and consumed upon the altar the burnt-offering and the fat: and when all the people saw it, they shouted, and fell on their faces.

Chapter 10

1And Nadab and Abihu, the sons of Aaron, took each of them his censer, and put fire therein, and laid incense thereon, and offered strange fire before Yahweh, which he had not commanded them.

2And there came forth fire from before Yahweh, and devoured them, and they died before Yahweh.

3Then Moses said unto Aaron, This is it that Yahweh spake, saying, I will be sanctified in them that come nigh me, and before all the people I will be glorified. And Aaron held his peace.

4And Moses called Mishael and Elzaphan, the sons of Uzziel the uncle of Aaron, and said unto them, Draw near, carry your brethren from before the sanctuary out of the camp.

5So they drew near, and carried them in their coats out of the camp, as Moses had said.

6And Moses said unto Aaron, and unto Eleazar and unto Ithamar, his sons, Let not the hair of your heads go loose, neither rend your clothes; that ye die not, and that he be not wroth with all the congregation: but let your brethren, the whole house of Israel, bewail the burning which Yahweh hath kindled.

7And ye shall not go out from the door of the tent of meeting, lest ye die; for the anointing oil of Yahweh is upon you. And they did according to the word of Moses.

8And Yahweh spake unto Aaron, saying,

9Drink no wine nor strong drink, thou, nor thy sons with thee, when ye go into the tent of meeting, that ye die not: it shall be a statute for ever throughout your generations:

10and that ye may make a distinction between the holy and the common, and between the unclean and the clean;

11and that ye may teach the children of Israel all the statutes which Yahweh hath spoken unto them by Moses.

12And Moses spake unto Aaron, and unto Eleazar and unto Ithamar, his sons that were left, Take the meal-offering that remaineth of the offerings of Yahweh made by fire, and eat it without leaven beside the altar; for it is most holy;

13and ye shall eat it in a holy place, because it is thy portion, and thy sons' portion, of the offerings of Yahweh made by fire: for so I am commanded.

14And the wave-breast and the heave-thigh shall ye eat in a clean place, thou, and thy sons, and thy daughters with thee: for they are given as thy portion, and thy sons' portion, out of the sacrifices of the peace-offerings of the children of Israel.

15The heave-thigh and the wave-breast shall they bring with the offerings made by fire of the fat, to wave it for a wave-offering before Yahweh: and it shall be thine, and thy sons' with thee, as a portion for ever; as Yahweh hath commanded.

16And Moses diligently sought the goat of the sin-offering, and, behold, it was burnt: and he was angry with Eleazar and with Ithamar, the sons of Aaron that were left, saying,

17Wherefore have ye not eaten the sin-offering in the place of the sanctuary, seeing it is most holy, and he hath given it you to bear the iniquity of the congregation, to make atonement for them before Yahweh?

18Behold, the blood of it was not brought into the sanctuary within: ye should certainly have eaten it in the sanctuary, as I commanded.

19And Aaron spake unto Moses, Behold, this day have they offered their sin-offering and their burnt-offering before Yahweh; and there have befallen me such things as these: and if I had eaten the sin-offering to-day, would it have been well-pleasing in the sight of Yahweh?

20And when Moses heard that, it was well-pleasing in his sight.

Chapter 11

1And Yahweh spake unto Moses and to Aaron, saying unto them,

2Speak unto the children of Israel, saying, These are the living things which ye may eat among all the beasts that are on the earth.

3Whatsoever parteth the hoof, and is clovenfooted, and cheweth the cud, among the beasts, that may ye eat.

4Nevertheless these shall ye not eat of them that chew the cud, or of them that part the hoof: the camel, because he cheweth the cud but parteth not the hoof, he is unclean unto you.

5And the coney, because he cheweth the cud but parteth not the hoof, he is unclean unto you.

6And the hare, because she cheweth the cud but parteth not the hoof, she is unclean unto you.

7And the swine, because he parteth the hoof, and is clovenfooted, but cheweth not the cud, he is unclean unto you.

8Of their flesh ye shall not eat, and their carcasses ye shall not touch; they are unclean unto you.

9These may ye eat of all that are in the waters: whatsoever hath fins and scales in the waters, in the seas, and in the rivers, that may ye eat.

10And all that have not fins and scales in the seas, and in the rivers, of all that move in the waters, and of all the living creatures that are in the waters, they are an abomination unto you,

11and they shall be an abomination unto you; ye shall not eat of their flesh, and their carcasses ye shall have in abomination.

12Whatsoever hath no fins nor scales in the waters, that is an abomination unto you.

13And these ye shall have in abomination among the birds; they shall not be eaten, they are an abomination: the eagle, and the gier-eagle, and the ospray,

14and the kite, and the falcon after its kind,

15every raven after its kind,

16and the ostrich, and the night-hawk, and the seamew, and the hawk after its kind,

17and the little owl, and the cormorant, and the great owl,

18and the horned owl, and the pelican, and the vulture,

19and the stork, the heron after its kind, and the hoopoe, and the bat.

20All winged creeping things that go upon all fours are an abomination unto you.

21Yet these may ye eat of all winged creeping things that go upon all fours, which have legs above their feet, wherewith to leap upon the earth.

22Even these of them ye may eat: the locust after its kind, and the bald locust after its kind, and the cricket after its kind, and the grasshopper after its kind.

23But all winged creeping things, which have four feet, are an abomination unto you.

24And by these ye shall become unclean: whosoever toucheth the carcass of them shall be unclean until the even;

25And whosoever beareth aught of the carcass of them shall wash his clothes, and be unclean until the even.

26Every beast which parteth the hoof, and is not clovenfooted, nor cheweth the cud, is unclean unto you: every one that toucheth them shall be unclean.

27And whatsoever goeth upon its paws, among all beasts that go on all fours, they are unclean unto you: whoso toucheth their carcass shall be unclean until the even.

28And he that beareth the carcass of them shall wash his clothes, and be unclean until the even: they are unclean unto you.

29And these are they which are unclean unto you among the creeping things that creep upon the earth: the weasel, and the mouse, and the great lizard after its kind,

30and the gecko, and the land-crocodile, and the lizard, and the sand-lizard, and the chameleon.

31These are they which are unclean to you among all that creep: whosoever doth touch them, when they are dead, shall be unclean until the even.

32And upon whatsoever any of them, when they are dead, doth fall, it shall be unclean; whether it be any vessel of wood, or raiment, or skin, or sack, whatsoever vessel it be, wherewith any work is done, it must be put into water, and it shall be unclean until the even; then shall it be clean.

Leviticus

33And every earthen vessel, whereinto any of them falleth, whatsoever is in it shall be unclean, and it ye shall break.

34All food therein which may be eaten, that on which water cometh, shall be unclean; and all drink that may be drunk in every such vessel shall be unclean.

35And every thing whereupon any part of their carcass falleth shall be unclean; whether oven, or range for pots, it shall be broken in pieces: they are unclean, and shall be unclean unto you.

36Nevertheless a fountain or a pit wherein is a gathering of water shall be clean: but that which toucheth their carcass shall be unclean.

37And if aught of their carcass fall upon any sowing seed which is to be sown, it is clean.

38But if water be put upon the seed, and aught of their carcass fall thereon, it is unclean unto you.

39And if any beast, of which ye may eat, die; he that toucheth the carcass thereof shall be unclean until the even.

40And he that eateth of the carcass of it shall wash his clothes, and be unclean until the even: he also that beareth the carcass of it shall wash his clothes, and be unclean until the even.

41And every creeping thing that creepeth upon the earth is an abomination; it shall not be eaten.

42Whatsoever goeth upon the belly, and whatsoever goeth upon all fours, or whatsoever hath many feet, even all creeping things that creep upon the earth, them ye shall not eat; for they are an abomination.

43Ye shall not make yourselves abominable with any creeping thing that creepeth, neither shall ye make yourselves unclean with them, that ye should be defiled thereby.

44For I am Yahweh your God: sanctify yourselves therefore, and be ye holy; for I am holy: neither shall ye defile yourselves with any manner of creeping thing that moveth upon the earth.

45For I am Yahweh that brought you up out of the land of Egypt, to be your God: ye shall therefore be holy, for I am holy.

46This is the law of the beast, and of the bird, and of every living creature that moveth in the waters, and of every creature that creepeth upon the earth;

47to make a distinction between the unclean and the clean, and between the living thing that may be eaten and the living thing that may not be eaten.

Chapter 12

1And Yahweh spake unto Moses, saying,

2Speak unto the children of Israel, saying, If a woman conceive seed, and bear a man-child, then she shall be unclean seven days; as in the days of the impurity of her sickness shall she be unclean.

3And in the eighth day the flesh of his foreskin shall be circumcised.

4And she shall continue in the blood of her purifying three and thirty days; she shall touch no hallowed thing, nor come into the sanctuary, until the days of her purifying be fulfilled.

5But if she bear a maid-child, then she shall be unclean two weeks, as in her impurity; and she shall continue in the blood of her purifying threescore and six days.

6And when the days of her purifying are fulfilled, for a son, or for a daughter, she shall bring a lamb a year old for a burnt-offering, and a young pigeon, or a turtle-dove, for a sin-offering, unto the door of the tent of meeting, unto the priest:

7and he shall offer it before Yahweh, and make atonement for her; and she shall be cleansed from the fountain of her blood. This is the law for her that beareth, whether a male or a female.

8And if her means suffice not for a lamb, then she shall take two turtle-doves, or two young pigeons; the one for a burnt-offering, and the other for a sin-offering: and the priest shall make atonement for her, and she shall be clean.

Chapter 13

1And Yahweh spake unto Moses and unto Aaron, saying,

2When a man shall have in the skin of his flesh a rising, or a scab, or a bright spot, and it become in the skin of his flesh the plague of leprosy, then he shall be brought unto Aaron the priest, or unto one of his sons the priests:

3and the priest shall look on the plague in the skin of the flesh: and if the hair in the plague be turned white, and the appearance of the plague be deeper than the skin of his flesh, it is the plague of leprosy; and the priest shall look on him, and pronounce him unclean.

4And if the bright spot be white in the skin of his flesh, and the appearance thereof be not deeper than the skin, and the hair thereof be not turned white, then the priest shall shut up him that hath the plague seven days:

5and the priest shall look on him the seventh day: and, behold, if in his eyes the plague be at a stay, and the plague be not spread in the skin, then the priest shall shut him up seven days more:

6and the priest shall look on him again the seventh day; and, behold, if the plague be dim, and the plague be not spread in the skin, then the priest shall pronounce him clean: it is a scab: and he shall wash his clothes, and be clean.

7But if the scab spread abroad in the skin, after that he hath showed himself to the priest for his cleansing, he shall show himself to the priest again:

8and the priest shall look; and, behold, if the scab be spread in the skin, then the priest shall pronounce him unclean: it is leprosy.

9When the plague of leprosy is in a man, then he shall be brought unto the priest;

10and the priest shall look; and, behold, if there be a white rising in the skin, and it have turned the hair white, and there be quick raw flesh in the rising,

11it is an old leprosy in the skin of his flesh, and the priest shall pronounce him unclean: he shall not shut him up, for he is unclean.

12And if the leprosy break out abroad in the skin, and the leprosy cover all the skin of him that hath the plague from his head even to his feet, as far as appeareth to the priest;

13then the priest shall look; and, behold, if the leprosy have covered all his flesh, he shall pronounce him clean that hath the plague: it is all turned white: he is clean.

14But whensoever raw flesh appeareth in him, he shall be unclean.

15And the priest shall look on the raw flesh, and pronounce him unclean: the raw flesh is unclean: it is leprosy.

16Or if the raw flesh turn again, and be changed unto white, then he shall come unto the priest;

17and the priest shall look on him; and, behold, if the plague be turned into white, then the priest shall pronounce him clean that hath the plague: he is clean.

18And when the flesh hath in the skin thereof a boil, and it is healed,

19and in the place of the boil there is a white rising, or a bright spot, reddish-white, then is shall be showed to the priest;

20and the priest shall look; and, behold, if the appearance thereof be lower than the skin, and the hair thereof be turned white, then the priest shall pronounce him unclean: it is the plague of leprosy, it hath broken out in the boil.

21But if the priest look on it, and, behold, there be no white hairs therein, and it be not lower than the skin, but be dim; then the priest shall shut him up seven days:

22And if it spread abroad in the skin, then the priest shall pronounce him unclean: it is a plague.

23But if the bright spot stay in its place, and be not spread, it is the scar of the boil; and the priest shall pronounce him clean.

24Or when the flesh hath in the skin thereof a burning by fire, and the quick flesh of the burning become a bright spot, reddish-white, or white;

25then the priest shall look upon it; and, behold, if the hair in the bright spot be turned white, and the appearance thereof be deeper than the skin; it is leprosy, it hath broken out in the burning: and the priest shall pronounce him unclean: it is the plague of leprosy.

26But if the priest look on it, and, behold, there be no white hair in the bright spot, and it be no lower than the skin, but be dim; then the priest shall shut him up seven days:

27and the priest shall look upon him the seventh day: if it spread abroad in the skin, then the priest shall pronounce him unclean: it is the plague of leprosy.

28And if the bright spot stay in its place, and be not spread in the skin, but be dim; it is the rising of the burning, and the priest shall pronounce him clean: for it is the scar of the burning.

29And when a man or woman hath a plague upon the head or upon the beard,

30then the priest shall look on the plague; and, behold, if the appearance thereof be deeper than the skin, and there be in it yellow thin hair, then the priest shall pronounce him unclean: it is a scall, it is leprosy of the head or of the beard.

31And if the priest look on the plague of the scall, and, behold, the appearance thereof be not deeper than the skin, and there be no black hair in it, then the priest shall shut up him that hath the plague of the scall seven days:

32And in the seventh day the priest shall look on the plague; and, behold, if the scall be not spread, and there be in it no yellow hair, and the appearance of the scall be not deeper than the skin,

33then he shall be shaven, but the scall shall he not shave; and the priest shall shut up him that hath the scall seven days more:

34and in the seventh day the priest shall look on the scall; and, behold, if the scall be not spread in the skin, and the appearance thereof be not deeper than the skin; then the priest shall pronounce him clean: and he shall wash his clothes, and be clean.

35But if the scall spread abroad in the skin after his cleansing,

36then the priest shall look on him; and, behold, if the scall be spread in the skin, the priest shall not seek for the yellow hair; he is unclean.

37But if in his eyes the scall be at a stay, and black hair be grown up therein; the scall is healed, he is clean: and the priest shall pronounce him clean.

38And when a man or a woman hath in the skin of the flesh bright spots, even white bright spots;

39then the priest shall look; and, behold, if the bright spots in the skin of their flesh be of a dull white, it is a tetter, it hath broken out in the skin; he is clean.

40And if a man's hair be fallen off his head, he is bald; yet is he clean.

41And if his hair be fallen off from the front part of his head, he is forehead bald; yet is he clean.

42But if there be in the bald head, or the bald forehead, a reddish-white plague; it is leprosy breaking out in his bald head, or his bald forehead.

43Then the priest shall look upon him; and, behold, if the rising of the plague be reddish-white in his bald head, or in his bald forehead, as the appearance of leprosy in the skin of the flesh;

44he is a leprous man, he is unclean: the priest shall surely pronounce him unclean; his plague is in his head.

45And the leper in whom the plague is, his clothes shall be rent, and the hair of his head shall go loose, and he shall cover his upper lip, and shall cry, Unclean, unclean.

46All the days wherein the plague is in him he shall be unclean; he is unclean: he shall dwell alone; without the camp shall his dwelling be.

47The garment also that the plague of leprosy is in, whether it be a woollen garment, or a linen garment;

48whether it be in warp, or woof; of linen, or of woollen; whether in a skin, or in anything made of skin;

49if the plague be greenish or reddish in the garment, or in the skin, or in the warp, or in the woof, or in anything of skin; it is the plague of leprosy, and shall be showed unto the priest.

50And the priest shall look upon the plague, and shut up that which hath the plague seven days:

51and he shall look on the plague on the seventh day: if the plague be spread in the garment, either in the warp, or in the woof, or in the skin, whatever service skin is used for; the plague is a fretting leprosy; it is unclean.

52And he shall burn the garment, whether the warp or the woof, in woollen or in linen, or anything of skin, wherein the plague is: for it is a fretting leprosy; it shall be burnt in the fire.

53And if the priest shall look, and, behold, the plague be not spread in the garment, either in the warp, or in the woof, or in anything of skin;

54then the priest shall command that they wash the thing wherein the plague is, and he shall shut it up seven days more:

55and the priest shall look, after that the plague is washed; and, behold, if the plague have not changed its color, and the plague be not spread, it is unclean; thou shalt burn it in the fire: it is a fret, whether the bareness be within or without.

56And if the priest look, and, behold, the plague be dim after the washing thereof, then he shall rend it out of the garment, or out of the skin, or out of the warp, or out of the woof:

57and if it appear still in the garment, either in the warp, or in the woof, or in anything of skin, it is breaking out: thou shalt burn that wherein the plague is with fire.

58And the garment, either the warp, or the woof, or whatsoever thing of skin it be, which thou shalt wash, if the plague be departed from them, then it shall be washed the second time, and shall be clean.

59This is the law of the plague of leprosy in a garment of woollen or linen, either in the warp, or the woof, or anything of skin, to pronounce it clean, or to pronounce it unclean.

Chapter 14

1And Yahweh spake unto Moses, saying,

2This shall be the law of the leper in the day of his cleansing: he shall be brought unto the priest:

3and the priest shall go forth out of the camp; and the priest shall look; and, behold, if the plague of leprosy be healed in the leper,

4then shall the priest command to take for him that is to be cleansed two living clean birds, and cedar wood, and scarlet, and hyssop:

5And the priest shall command to kill one of the birds in an earthen vessel over running water.

6As for the living bird, he shall take it, and the cedar wood, and the scarlet, and the hyssop, and shall dip them and the living bird in the blood of the bird that was killed over the running water:

7And he shall sprinkle upon him that is to be cleansed from the leprosy seven times, and shall pronounce him clean, and shall let go the living bird into the open field.

8And he that is to be cleansed shall wash his clothes, and shave off all his hair, and bathe himself in water; and he shall be clean: and after that he shall come into the camp, but shall dwell outside his tent seven days.

9And it shall be on the seventh day, that he shall shave all his hair off his head and his beard and his eyebrows, even all his hair he shall shave off: and he shall wash his clothes, and he shall bathe his flesh in water, and he shall be clean.

10And on the eighth day he shall take two he-lambs without blemish, and one ewe-lamb a year old without blemish, and three tenth parts of an ephah of fine flour for a meal-offering, mingled with oil, and one log of oil.

11And the priest that cleanseth him shall set the man that is to be cleansed, and those things, before Yahweh, at the door of the tent of meeting.

12And the priest shall take one of the he-lambs, and offer him for a trespass-offering, and the log of oil, and wave them for a wave-offering before Yahweh:

13and he shall kill the he-lamb in the place where they kill the sin-offering and the burnt-offering, in the place of the sanctuary: for as the sin-offering is the priest's, so is the trespass-offering: it is most holy:

14and the priest shall take of the blood of the trespass-offering, and the priest shall put it upon the tip of the right ear of him that is to be cleansed, and upon the thumb of his right hand, and upon the great toe of his right foot.

15And the priest shall take of the log of oil, and pour it into the palm of his own left hand;

16and the priest shall dip his right finger in the oil that is in his left hand, and shall sprinkle of the oil with his finger seven times before Yahweh:

17and of the rest of the oil that is in his hand shall the priest put upon the tip of the right ear of him that is to be cleansed, and upon the thumb of his right hand, and upon the great toe of his right foot, upon the blood of the trespass-offering:

18and the rest of the oil that is in the priest's hand he shall put upon the head of him that is to be cleansed: and the priest shall make atonement for him before Yahweh.

19And the priest shall offer the sin-offering, and make atonement for him that is to be cleansed because of his uncleanness; and afterward he shall kill the burnt-offering;

20and the priest shall offer the burnt-offering and the meal-offering upon the altar: and the priest shall make atonement for him, and he shall be clean.

21And if he be poor, and cannot get so much, then he shall take one he-lamb for a trespass-offering to be waved, to make atonement for him, and one tenth part of an ephah of fine flour mingled with oil for a meal-offering, and a log of oil;

22and two turtle-doves, or two young pigeons, such as he is able to get; and the one shall be a sin-offering, and the other a burnt-offering.

23And on the eighth day he shall bring them for his cleansing unto the priest, unto the door of the tent of meeting, before Yahweh:

24and the priest shall take the lamb of the trespass-offering, and the log of oil, and the priest shall wave them for a wave-offering before Yahweh:

25And he shall kill the lamb of the trespass-offering; and the priest shall take of the blood of the trespass-offering, and put it upon the tip of the right ear of him that is to be cleansed, and upon the thumb of his right hand, and upon the great toe of his right foot.

26And the priest shall pour of the oil into the palm of his own left hand:

27and the priest shall sprinkle with his right finger some of the oil that is in his left hand seven times before Yahweh:

28and the priest shall put of the oil that is in his hand upon the tip of the right ear of him that is to be cleansed, and upon the thumb of his right hand, and upon the great toe of his right foot, upon the place of the blood of the trespass-offering:

29and the rest of the oil that is in the priest's hand he shall put upon the head of him that is to be cleansed, to make atonement for him before Yahweh.

30And he shall offer one of the turtle-doves, or of the young pigeons, such as he is able to get,

31even such as he is able to get, the one for a sin-offering, and the other for a burnt-offering, with the meal-offering: and the priest shall make atonement for him that is to be cleansed before Yahweh.

32This is the law of him in whom is the plague of leprosy, who is not able to get that which pertaineth to his cleansing.

33And Yahweh spake unto Moses and unto Aaron, saying,

34When ye are come into the land of Canaan, which I give to you for a possession, and I put the plague of leprosy in a house of the land of your possession;

35then he that owneth the house shall come and tell the priest, saying, There seemeth to me to be as it were a plague in the house.

36And the priest shall command that they empty the house, before the priest goeth in to see the plague, that all that is in the house be not made unclean: and afterward the priest shall go in to see the house:

37and he shall look on the plague; and, behold, if the plague be in the walls of the house with hollow streaks, greenish or reddish, and the appearance thereof be lower than the wall;

38then the priest shall go out of the house to the door of the house, and shut up the house seven days.

39And the priest shall come again the seventh day, and shall look; and, behold, if the plague be spread in the walls of the house;

40then the priest shall command that they take out the stones in which the plague is, and cast them into an unclean place without the city:

41and he shall cause the house to be scraped within round about, and they shall pour out the mortar, that they scrape off, without the city into an unclean place:

42and they shall take other stones, and put them in the place of those stones; and he shall take other mortar, and shall plaster the house.

43And if the plague come again, and break out in the house, after that he hath taken out the stones, and after he hath scraped the house, and after it is plastered;

44then the priest shall come in and look; and, behold, if the plague be spread in the house, it is a fretting leprosy in the house: it is unclean.

45And he shall break down the house, the stones of it, and the timber thereof, and all the mortar of the house; and he shall carry them forth out of the city into an unclean place.

46Moreover he that goeth into the house all the while that it is shut up shall be unclean until the even.

47And he that lieth in the house shall wash his clothes; and he that eateth in the house shall wash his clothes.

48And if the priest shall come in, and look, and, behold, the plague hath not spread in the house, after the house was plastered; then the priest shall pronounce the house clean, because the plague is healed.

49And he shall take to cleanse the house two birds, and cedar wood, and scarlet, and hyssop:

50and he shall kill one of the birds in an earthen vessel over running water:

51and he shall take the cedar wood, and the hyssop, and the scarlet, and the living bird, and dip them in the blood of the slain bird, and in the running water, and sprinkle the house seven times:

52and he shall cleanse the house with the blood of the bird, and with the running water, and with the living bird, and with the cedar wood, and with the hyssop, and with the scarlet:

53but he shall let go the living bird out of the city into the open field: so shall he make atonement for the house; and it shall be clean.

54This is the law for all manner of plague of leprosy, and for a scall,

55and for the leprosy of a garment, and for a house,

56and for a rising, and for a scab, and for a bright spot;

57to teach when it is unclean, and when it is clean: this is the law of leprosy.

Chapter 15

1And Yahweh spake unto Moses and to Aaron, saying,

2Speak unto the children of Israel, and say unto them, When any man hath an issue out of his flesh, because of his issue he is unclean.

3And this shall be his uncleanness in his issue: whether his flesh run with his issue, or his flesh be stopped from his issue, it is his uncleanness.

4Every bed whereon he that hath the issue lieth shall be unclean; and everything whereon he sitteth shall be unclean.

5And whosoever toucheth his bed shall wash his clothes, and bathe himself in water, and be unclean until the even.

6And he that sitteth on anything whereon he that hath the issue sat shall wash his clothes, and bathe himself in water, and be unclean until the even.

7And he that toucheth the flesh of him that hath the issue shall wash his clothes, and bathe himself in water, and be unclean until the even.

8And if he that hath the issue spit upon him that is clean, then he shall wash his clothes, and bathe himself in water, and be unclean until the even.

9And what saddle soever he that hath the issue rideth upon shall be unclean.

10And whosoever toucheth anything that was under him shall be unclean

Leviticus

until the even: and he that beareth those things shall wash his clothes, and bathe himself in water, and be unclean until the even.

11And whomsoever he that hath the issue toucheth, without having rinsed his hands in water, he shall wash his clothes, and bathe himself in water, and be unclean until the even.

12And the earthen vessel, which he that hath the issue toucheth, shall be broken; and every vessel of wood shall be rinsed in water.

13And when he that hath an issue is cleansed of his issue, then he shall number to himself seven days for his cleansing, and wash his clothes; and he shall bathe his flesh in running water, and shall be clean.

14And on the eighth day he shall take to him two turtle-doves, or two young pigeons, and come before Yahweh unto the door of the tent of meeting, and give them unto the priest:

15and the priest shall offer them, the one for a sin-offering, and the other for a burnt-offering; and the priest shall make atonement for him before Yahweh for his issue.

16And if any man's seed of copulation go out from him, then he shall bathe all his flesh in water, and be unclean until the even.

17And every garment, and every skin, whereon is the seed of copulation, shall be washed with water, and be unclean until the even.

18The woman also with whom a man shall lie with seed of copulation, they shall both bathe themselves in water, and be unclean until the even.

19And if a woman have an issue, and her issue in her flesh be blood, she shall be in her impurity seven days: and whosoever toucheth her shall be unclean until the even.

20And everything that she lieth upon in her impurity shall be unclean: everything also that she sitteth upon shall be unclean.

21And whosoever toucheth her bed shall wash his clothes, and bathe himself in water, and be unclean until the even.

22And whosoever toucheth anything that she sitteth upon shall wash his clothes, and bathe himself in water, and be unclean until the even.

23And if it be on the bed, or on anything whereon she sitteth, when he toucheth it, he shall be unclean until the even.

24And if any man lie with her, and her impurity be upon him, he shall be unclean seven days; and every bed whereon he lieth shall be unclean.

25And if a woman have an issue of her blood many days not in the time of her impurity, or if she have an issue beyond the time of her impurity; all the days of the issue of her uncleanness she shall be as in the days of her impurity: she is unclean.

26Every bed whereon she lieth all the days of her issue shall be unto her as the bed of her impurity: and everything whereon she sitteth shall be unclean, as the uncleanness of her impurity.

27And whosoever toucheth those things shall be unclean, and shall wash his clothes, and bathe himself in water, and be unclean until the even.

28But if she be cleansed of her issue, then she shall number to herself seven days, and after that she shall be clean.

29And on the eighth day she shall take unto her two turtle-doves, or two young pigeons, and bring them unto the priest, to the door of the tent of meeting.

30And the priest shall offer the one for a sin-offering, and the other for a burnt-offering; and the priest shall make atonement for her before Yahweh for the issue of her uncleanness.

31Thus shall ye separate the children of Israel from their uncleanness, that they die not in their uncleanness, when they defile my tabernacle that is in the midst of them.

32This is the law of him that hath an issue, and of him whose seed of copulation goeth from him, so that he is unclean thereby;

33and of her that is sick with her impurity, and of him that hath an issue, of the man, and of the woman, and of him that lieth with her that is unclean.

Chapter 16

1And Yahweh spake unto Moses, after the death of the two sons of Aaron, when they drew near before Yahweh, and died;

2and Yahweh said unto Moses, Speak unto Aaron thy brother, that he come not at all times into the holy place within the veil, before the mercy-seat which is upon the ark; that he die not: for I will appear in the cloud upon the mercy-seat.

3Herewith shall Aaron come into the holy place: with a young bullock for a sin-offering, and a ram for a burnt-offering.

4He shall put on the holy linen coat, and he shall have the linen breeches upon his flesh, and shall be girded with the linen girdle, and with the linen mitre shall he be attired: they are the holy garments; and he shall bathe his flesh in water, and put them on.

5And he shall take of the congregation of the children of Israel two he-goats for a sin-offering, and one ram for a burnt-offering.

6And Aaron shall present the bullock of the sin-offering, which is for himself, and make atonement for himself, and for his house.

7And he shall take the two goats, and set them before Yahweh at the door of the tent of meeting.

8And Aaron shall cast lots upon the two goats; one lot for Yahweh, and the other lot for Azazel.

9And Aaron shall present the goat upon which the lot fell for Yahweh, and offer him for a sin-offering.

10But the goat, on which the lot fell for Azazel, shall be set alive before Yahweh, to make atonement for him, to send him away for Azazel into the wilderness.

11And Aaron shall present the bullock of the sin-offering, which is for himself, and shall make atonement for himself, and for his house, and shall kill the bullock of the sin-offering which is for himself:

12and he shall take a censer full of coals of fire from off the altar before Yahweh, and his hands full of sweet incense beaten small, and bring it within the veil:

13and he shall put the incense upon the fire before Yahweh, that the cloud of the incense may cover the mercy-seat that is upon the testimony, that he die not:

14and he shall take of the blood of the bullock, and sprinkle it with his finger upon the mercy-seat on the east; and before the mercy-seat shall he sprinkle of the blood with his finger seven times.

15Then shall he kill the goat of the sin-offering, that is for the people, and bring his blood within the veil, and do with his blood as he did with the blood of the bullock, and sprinkle it upon the mercy-seat, and before the mercy-seat:

16and he shall make atonement for the holy place, because of the uncleannesses of the children of Israel, and because of their transgressions, even all their sins: and so shall he do for the tent of meeting, that dwelleth with them in the midst of their uncleannesses.

17And there shall be no man in the tent of meeting when he goeth in to make atonement in the holy place, until he come out, and have made atonement for himself, and for his household, and for all the assembly of Israel.

18And he shall go out unto the altar that is before Yahweh, and make atonement for it, and shall take of the blood of the bullock, and of the blood of the goat, and put it upon the horns of the altar round about.

19And he shall sprinkle of the blood upon it with his finger seven times, and cleanse it, and hallow it from the uncleannesses of the children of Israel.

20And when he hath made an end of atoning for the holy place, and the tent of meeting, and the altar, he shall present the live goat:

21and Aaron shall lay both his hands upon the head of the live goat, and confess over him all the iniquities of the children of Israel, and all their transgressions, even all their sins; and he shall put them upon the head of the goat, and shall send him away by the hand of a man that is in readiness into the wilderness:

22and the goat shall bear upon him all their iniquities unto a solitary land: and he shall let go the goat in the wilderness.

23And Aaron shall come into the tent of meeting, and shall put off the linen garments, which he put on when he went into the holy place, and shall leave them there:

24and he shall bathe his flesh in water in a holy place, and put on his garments, and come forth, and offer his burnt-offering and the burnt-offering of the people, and make atonement for himself and for the people.

25And the fat of the sin-offering shall he burn upon the altar.

26And he that letteth go the goat for Azazel shall wash his clothes, and bathe his flesh in water, and afterward he shall come into the camp.

27And the bullock of the sin-offering, and the goat of the sin-offering, whose blood was brought in to make atonement in the holy place, shall be carried forth without the camp; and they shall burn in the fire their skins, and their flesh, and their dung.

28And he that burneth them shall wash his clothes, and bathe his flesh in water, and afterward he shall come into the camp.

29And it shall be a statute for ever unto you: in the seventh month, on the tenth day of the month, ye shall afflict your souls, and shall do no manner of work, the home-born, or the stranger that sojourneth among you:

30for on this day shall atonement be made for you, to cleanse you; from all your sins shall ye be clean before Yahweh.

31It is a sabbath of solemn rest unto you, and ye shall afflict your souls; it is a statute for ever.

32And the priest, who shall be anointed and who shall be consecrated to be priest in his father's stead, shall make the atonement, and shall put on the linen garments, even the holy garments:

33and he shall make atonement for the holy sanctuary; and he shall make atonement for the tent of meeting and for the altar; and he shall make atonement for the priests and for all the people of the assembly.

34And this shall be an everlasting statute unto you, to make atonement for the children of Israel because of all their sins once in the year. And he did as Yahweh commanded Moses.

Chapter 17

1And Yahweh spake unto Moses, saying,

2Speak unto Aaron, and unto his sons, and unto all the children of Israel, and say unto them: This is the thing which Yahweh hath commanded, saying,

3What man soever there be of the house of Israel, that killeth an ox, or lamb, or goat, in the camp, or that killeth it without the camp,

4and hath not brought it unto the door of the tent of meeting, to offer it as an oblation unto Yahweh before the tabernacle of Yahweh: blood shall be imputed unto that man; he hath shed blood; and that man shall be cut off from among his people:

5To the end that the children of Israel may bring their sacrifices, which they sacrifice in the open field, even that they may bring them unto Yahweh, unto the door of the tent of meeting, unto the priest, and sacrifice them for sacrifices of peace-offerings unto Yahweh.

6And the priest shall sprinkle the blood upon the altar of Yahweh at the door of the tent of meeting, and burn the fat for a sweet savor unto Yahweh.

7And they shall no more sacrifice their sacrifices unto the he-goats, after which they play the harlot. This shall be a statute forever unto them throughout their generations.

8And thou shalt say unto them, Whatsoever man there be of the house of Israel, or of the strangers that sojourn among them, that offereth a burnt-offering or sacrifice,

9and bringeth it not unto the door of the tent of meeting, to sacrifice it unto Yahweh; that man shall be cut off from his people.

10And whatsoever man there be of the house of Israel, or of the strangers that sojourn among them, that eateth any manner of blood, I will set my face against that soul that eateth blood, and will cut him off from among his people.

Leviticus

11For the life of the flesh is in the blood; and I have given it to you upon the altar to make atonement for your souls: for it is the blood that maketh atonement by reason of the life.

12Therefore I said unto the children of Israel, No soul of you shall eat blood, neither shall any stranger that sojourneth among you eat blood.

13And whatsoever man there be of the children of Israel, or of the strangers that sojourn among them, who taketh in hunting any beast or bird that may be eaten; he shall pour out the blood thereof, and cover it with dust.

14For as to the life of all flesh, the blood thereof is all one with the life thereof: therefore I said unto the children of Israel, Ye shall eat the blood of no manner of flesh; for the life of all flesh is the blood thereof: whosoever eateth it shall be cut off.

15And every soul that eateth that which dieth of itself, or that which is torn of beasts, whether he be home-born or a sojourner, he shall wash his clothes, and bathe himself in water, and be unclean until the even: then shall he be clean.

16But if he wash them not, nor bathe his flesh, then he shall bear his iniquity.

Chapter 18

1And Yahweh spake unto Moses, saying,

2Speak unto the children of Israel, and say unto them, I am Yahweh your God.

3After the doings of the land of Egypt, wherein ye dwelt, shall ye not do: and after the doings of the land of Canaan, whither I bring you, shall ye not do; neither shall ye walk in their statutes.

4Mine ordinances shall ye do, and my statutes shall ye keep, to walk therein: I am Yahweh your God.

5Ye shall therefore keep my statutes, and mine ordinances; which if a man do, he shall live in them: I am Yahweh.

6None of you shall approach to any that are near of kin to him, to uncover their nakedness: I am Yahweh.

7The nakedness of thy father, even the nakedness of thy mother, shalt thou not uncover: she is thy mother; thou shalt not uncover her nakedness.

8The nakedness of thy father's wife shalt thou not uncover: it is thy father's nakedness.

9The nakedness of thy sister, the daughter of thy father, or the daughter of thy mother, whether born at home, or born abroad, even their nakedness thou shalt not uncover.

10The nakedness of thy son's daughter, or of thy daughter's daughter, even their nakedness thou shalt not uncover: for theirs is thine own nakedness.

11The nakedness of thy father's wife's daughter, begotten of thy father, she is thy sister, thou shalt not uncover her nakedness.

12Thou shalt not uncover the nakedness of thy father's sister: she is thy father's near kinswoman.

13Thou shalt not uncover the nakedness of thy mother's sister: for she is thy mother's near kinswoman.

14Thou shalt not uncover the nakedness of thy father's brother, thou shalt not approach to his wife: she is thine aunt.

15Thou shalt not uncover the nakedness of thy daughter-in-law: she is thy son's wife; thou shalt not uncover her nakedness.

16Thou shalt not uncover the nakedness of thy brother's wife: it is thy brother's nakedness.

17Thou shalt not uncover the nakedness of a woman and her daughter; thou shalt not take her son's daughter, or her daughter's daughter, to uncover her nakedness; they are near kinswomen: it is wickedness.

18And thou shalt not take a wife to her sister, to be a rival to her, to uncover her nakedness, besides the other in her life-time.

19And thou shalt not approach unto a woman to uncover her nakedness, as long as she is impure by her uncleanness.

20And thou shalt not lie carnally with thy neighbor's wife, to defile thyself with her.

21And thou shalt not give any of thy seed to make them pass through the fire to Molech; neither shalt thou profane the name of thy God: I am Yahweh.

22Thou shalt not lie with mankind, as with womankind: it is abomination.

23And thou shalt not lie with any beast to defile thyself therewith; neither shall any woman stand before a beast, to lie down thereto: it is confusion.

24Defile not ye yourselves in any of these things: for in all these the nations are defiled which I cast out from before you;

25And the land is defiled: therefore I do visit the iniquity thereof upon it, and the land vomiteth out her inhabitants.

26Ye therefore shall keep my statutes and mine ordinances, and shall not do any of these abominations; neither the home-born, nor the stranger that sojourneth among you;

27(for all these abominations have the men of the land done, that were before you, and the land is defiled);

28that the land vomit not you out also, when ye defile it, as it vomited out the nation that was before you.

29For whosoever shall do any of these abominations, even the souls that do them shall be cut off from among their people.

30Therefore shall ye keep my charge, that ye practise not any of these abominable customs, which were practised before you, and that ye defile not yourselves therein: I am Yahweh your God.

Chapter 19

1And Yahweh spake unto Moses, saying,

2Speak unto all the congregation of the children of Israel, and say unto them, Ye shall be holy; for I Yahweh your God am holy.

3Ye shall fear every man his mother, and his father; and ye shall keep my sabbaths: I am Yahweh your God.

4Turn ye not unto idols, nor make to yourselves molten gods: I am Yahweh your God.

5And when ye offer a sacrifice of peace-offerings unto Yahweh, ye shall offer it that ye may be accepted.

6It shall be eaten the same day ye offer it, and on the morrow: and if aught remain until the third day, it shall be burnt with fire.

7And if it be eaten at all on the third day, it is an abomination; it shall not be accepted:

8but every one that eateth it shall bear his iniquity, because he hath profaned the holy thing of Yahweh: and that soul shall be cut off from his people.

9And when ye reap the harvest of your land, thou shalt not wholly reap the corners of thy field, neither shalt thou gather the gleaning of thy harvest.

10And thou shalt not glean thy vineyard, neither shalt thou gather the fallen fruit of thy vineyard; thou shalt leave them for the poor and for the sojourner: I am Yahweh your God.

11Ye shall not steal; neither shall ye deal falsely, nor lie one to another.

12And ye shall not swear by my name falsely, and profane the name of thy God: I am Yahweh.

13Thou shalt not oppress thy neighbor, nor rob him: the wages of a hired servant shall not abide with thee all night until the morning.

14Thou shalt not curse the deaf, nor put a stumblingblock before the blind; but thou shalt fear thy God: I am Yahweh.

15Ye shall do no unrighteousness in judgment: thou shalt not respect the person of the poor, nor honor the person of the mighty; but in righteousness shalt thou judge thy neighbor.

16Thou shalt not go up and down as a talebearer among thy people: neither shalt thou stand against the blood of thy neighbor: I am Yahweh.

17Thou shalt not hate thy brother in thy heart: thou shalt surely rebuke thy neighbor, and not bear sin because of him.

18Thou shalt not take vengeance, nor bear any grudge against the children of thy people; but thou shalt love thy neighbor as thyself: I am Yahweh.

19Ye shall keep my statutes. Thou shalt not let thy cattle gender with a diverse kind: thou shalt not sow thy field with two kinds of seed: neither shall there come upon thee a garment of two kinds of stuff mingled together.

20And whosoever lieth carnally with a woman, that is a bondmaid, betrothed to a husband, and not at all redeemed, nor freedom given her; they shall be punished; they shall not be put to death, because she was not free.

21And he shall bring his trespass-offering unto Yahweh, unto the door of the tent of meeting, even a ram for a trespass-offering.

22And the priest shall make atonement for him with the ram of the trespass-offering before Yahweh for his sin which he hath sinned: and the sin which he hath sinned shall be forgiven him.

23And when ye shall come into the land, and shall have planted all manner of trees for food, then ye shall count the fruit thereof as their uncircumcision: three years shall they be as uncircumcised unto you; it shall not be eaten.

24But in the fourth year all the fruit thereof shall be holy, for giving praise unto Yahweh.

25And in the fifth year shall ye eat of the fruit thereof, that it may yield unto you the increase thereof: I am Yahweh your God.

26Ye shall not eat anything with the blood: neither shall ye use enchantments, nor practise augury.

27Ye shall not round the corners of your heads, neither shalt thou mar the corners of thy beard.

28Ye shall not make any cuttings in your flesh for the dead, nor print any marks upon you: I am Yahweh.

29Profane not thy daughter, to make her a harlot; lest the land fall to whoredom, and the land become full of wickedness.

30Ye shall keep my sabbaths, and reverence my sanctuary; I am Yahweh.

31Turn ye not unto them that have familiar spirits, nor unto the wizards; seek them not out, to be defiled by them: I am Yahweh your God.

32Thou shalt rise up before the hoary head, and honor the face of the old man, and thou shalt fear thy God: I am Yahweh.

33And if a stranger sojourn with thee in your land, ye shall not do him wrong.

34The stranger that sojourneth with you shall be unto you as the home-born among you, and thou shalt love him as thyself; for ye were sojourners in the land of Egypt: I am Yahweh your God.

35Ye shall do no unrighteousness in judgment, in measures of length, of weight, or of quantity.

36Just balances, just weights, a just ephah, and a just hin, shall ye have: I am Yahweh your God, who brought you out of the land of Egypt.

37And ye shall observe all my statutes, and all mine ordinances, and do them: I am Yahweh.

Chapter 20

1And Yahweh spake unto Moses, saying,

2Moreover, thou shalt say to the children of Israel, Whosoever he be of the children of Israel, or of the strangers that sojourn in Israel, that giveth of his seed unto Molech; he shall surely be put to death: the people of the land shall stone him with stones.

3I also will set my face against that man, and will cut him off from among his people; because he hath given of his seed unto Molech, to defile my sanctuary,

Leviticus

and to profane my holy name.

4And if the people at the land do at all hide their eyes from that man, when he giveth of his seed unto Molech, and put him not to death;

5then I will set my face against that man, and against his family, and will cut him off, and all that play the harlot after him, to play the harlot with Molech, from among their people.

6And the soul that turneth unto them that have familiar spirits, and unto the wizards, to play the harlot after them, I will even set my face against that soul, and will cut him off from among his people.

7Sanctify yourselves therefore, and be ye holy; for I am Yahweh your God.

8And ye shall keep my statutes, and do them: I am Yahweh who sanctifieth you.

9For every one that curseth his father or his mother shall surely be put to death: he hath cursed his father or his mother; his blood shall be upon him.

10And the man that committeth adultery with another man's wife, even he that committeth adultery with his neighbor's wife, the adulterer and the adulteress shall surely be put to death.

11And the man that lieth with his father's wife hath uncovered his father's nakedness: both of them shall surely be put to death; their blood shall be upon them.

12And if a man lie with his daughter-in-law, both of them shall surely be put to death: they have wrought confusion; their blood shall be upon them.

13And if a man lie with mankind, as with womankind, both of them have committed abomination: they shall surely be put to death; their blood shall be upon them.

14And if a man take a wife and her mother, it is wickedness: they shall be burnt with fire, both he and they; that there be no wickedness among you.

15And if a man lie with a beast, he shall surely be put to death: and ye shall slay the beast.

16And if a woman approach unto any beast, and lie down thereto, thou shalt kill the woman, and the beast: they shall surely be put to death; their blood shall be upon them.

17And if a man shall take his sister, his father's daughter, or his mother's daughter, and see her nakedness, and she see his nakedness; it is a shameful thing; and they shall be cut off in the sight of the children of their people: he hath uncovered his sister's nakedness; he shall bear his iniquity.

18And if a man shall lie with a woman having her sickness, and shall uncover her nakedness; he hath made naked her fountain, and she hath uncovered the fountain of her blood: and both of them shall be cut off from among their people.

19And thou shalt not uncover the nakedness of thy mother's sister, nor of thy father's sister; for he hath made naked his near kin: they shall bear their iniquity.

20And if a man shall lie with his uncle's wife, he hath uncovered his uncle's nakedness: they shall bear their sin; they shall die childless.

21And if a man shall take his brother's wife, it is impurity: he hath uncovered his brother's nakedness; they shall be childless.

22Ye shall therefore keep all my statutes, and all mine ordinances, and do them; that the land, whither I bring you to dwell therein, vomit you not out.

23And ye shall not walk in the customs of the nation, which I cast out before you: for they did all these things, and therefore I abhorred them.

24But I have said unto you, Ye shall inherit their land, and I will give it unto you to possess it, a land flowing with milk and honey: I am Yahweh your God, who hath separated you from the peoples.

25Ye shall therefore make a distinction between the clean beast and the unclean, and between the unclean fowl and the clean: and ye shall not make your souls abominable by beast, or by bird, or by anything wherewith the ground teemeth, which I have separated from you as unclean.

26And ye shall be holy unto me: for I, Yahweh, am holy, and have set you apart from the peoples, that ye should be mine.

27A man also or a woman that hath a familiar spirit, or that is a wizard, shall surely be put to death: they shall stone them with stones; their blood shall be upon them.

Chapter 21

1And Yahweh said unto Moses, Speak unto the priests, the sons of Aaron, and say unto them, There shall none defile himself for the dead among his people;

2except for his kin, that is near unto him, for his mother, and for his father, and for his son, and for his daughter, and for his brother;

3and for his sister a virgin, that is near unto him, that hath had no husband; for her may he defile himself.

4He shall not defile himself, being a chief man among his people, to profane himself.

5They shall not make baldness upon their head, neither shall they shave off the corner of their beard, nor make any cuttings in their flesh.

6They shall be holy unto their God, and not profane the name of their God; for the offerings of Yahweh made by fire, the bread of their God, they do offer: therefore they shall be holy.

7They shall not take a woman that is a harlot, or profane; neither shall they take a woman put away from her husband: for he is holy unto his God.

8Thou shalt sanctify him therefore; for he offereth the bread of thy God: he shall be holy unto thee: for I Yahweh, who sanctify you, am holy.

9And the daughter of any priest, if she profane herself by playing the harlot, she profaneth her father: she shall be burnt with fire.

10And he that is the high priest among his brethren, upon whose head the anointing oil is poured, and that is consecrated to put on the garments, shall not let the hair of his head go loose, nor rend his clothes;

11neither shall he go in to any dead body, nor defile himself for his father, or for his mother;

12neither shall he go out of the sanctuary, nor profane the sanctuary of his God; for the crown of the anointing oil of his God is upon him: I am Yahweh.

13And he shall take a wife in her virginity.

14A widow, or one divorced, or a profane woman, a harlot, these shall he not take: but a virgin of his own people shall he take to wife.

15And he shall not profane his seed among his people: for I am Yahweh who sanctifieth him.

16And Yahweh spake unto Moses, saying,

17Speak unto Aaron, saying, Whosoever he be of thy seed throughout their generations that hath a blemish, let him not approach to offer the bread of his God.

18For whatsoever man he be that hath a blemish, he shall not approach: a blind man, or a lame, or he that hath a flat nose, or anything superfluous,

19or a man that is broken-footed, or broken-handed,

20or crook-backed, or a dwarf, or that hath a blemish in his eye, or is scurvy, or scabbed, or hath his stones broken;

21no man of the seed of Aaron the priest, that hath a blemish, shall come nigh to offer the offerings of Yahweh made by fire: he hath a blemish; he shall not come nigh to offer the bread of his God.

22He shall eat the bread of his God, both of the most holy, and of the holy:

23only he shall not go in unto the veil, nor come nigh unto the altar, because he hath a blemish; that he profane not my sanctuaries: for I am Yahweh who sanctifieth them.

24So Moses spake unto Aaron, and to his sons, and unto all the children of Israel.

Chapter 22

1And Yahweh spake unto Moses, saying,

2Speak unto Aaron and to his sons, that they separate themselves from the holy things of the children of Israel, which they hallow unto me, and that they profane not my holy name: I am Yahweh.

3Say unto them, Whosoever he be of all your seed throughout your generations, that approacheth unto the holy things, which the children of Israel hallow unto Yahweh, having his uncleanness upon him, that soul shall be cut off from before me: I am Yahweh.

4What man soever of the seed of Aaron is a leper, or hath an issue; he shall not eat of the holy things, until he be clean. And whoso toucheth anything that is unclean by the dead, or a man whose seed goeth from him;

5or whosoever toucheth any creeping thing, whereby he may be made unclean, or a man of whom he may take uncleanness, whatsoever uncleanness he hath;

6the soul that toucheth any such shall be unclean until the even, and shall not eat of the holy things, unless he bathe his flesh in water.

7And when the sun is down, he shall be clean; and afterward he shall eat of the holy things, because it is his bread.

8That which dieth of itself, or is torn of beasts, he shall not eat, to defile himself therewith: I am Yahweh.

9They shall therefore keep my charge, lest they bear sin for it, and die therein, if they profane it: I am Yahweh who sanctifieth them.

10There shall no stranger eat of the holy thing: a sojourner of the priest's, or a hired servant, shall not eat of the holy thing.

11But if a priest buy any soul, the purchase of his money, he shall eat of it; and such as are born in his house, they shall eat of his bread.

12And if a priest's daughter be married unto a stranger, she shall not eat of the heave-offering of the holy things.

13But if a priest's daughter be a widow, or divorced, and have no child, and be returned unto her father's house, as in her youth, she shall eat of her father's bread: but there shall no stranger eat thereof.

14And if a man eat of the holy thing unwittingly, then he shall put the fifth part thereof unto it, and shall give unto the priest the holy thing.

15And they shall not profane the holy things of the children of Israel, which they offer unto Yahweh,

16and so cause them to bear the iniquity that bringeth guilt, when they eat their holy things: for I am Yahweh who sanctifieth them.

17And Yahweh spake unto Moses, saying,

18Speak unto Aaron, and to his sons, and unto all the children of Israel, and say unto them, Whosoever he be of the house of Israel, or of the sojourners in Israel, that offereth his oblation, whether it be any of their vows, or any of their freewill-offerings, which they offer unto Yahweh for a burnt-offering;

19that ye may be accepted, ye shall offer a male without blemish, of the bullocks, of the sheep, or of the goats.

20But whatsoever hath a blemish, that shall ye not offer: for it shall not be acceptable for you.

21And whosoever offereth a sacrifice of peace-offerings unto Yahweh to accomplish a vow, or for a freewill-offering, of the herd or of the flock, it shall be perfect to be accepted; there shall be no blemish therein.

22Blind, or broken, or maimed, or having a wen, or scurvy, or scabbed, ye shall not offer these unto Yahweh, nor make an offering by fire of them upon the altar unto Yahweh.

23Either a bullock or a lamb that hath anything superfluous or lacking in his parts, that mayest thou offer for a freewill-offering; but for a vow it shall not be accepted.

24That which hath its stones bruised, or crushed, or broken, or cut, ye shall not offer unto Yahweh; neither shall ye do thus in your land.

25Neither from the hand of a foreigner shall ye offer the bread of your God of any of these; because their corruption is in them, there is a blemish in them: they shall not be accepted for you.

26And Yahweh spake unto Moses, saying,

27When a bullock, or a sheep, or a goat, is brought forth, then it shall be seven days under the dam; and from the eighth day and thenceforth it shall be accepted for the oblation of an offering made by fire unto Yahweh.

28And whether it be cow or ewe, ye shall not kill it and its young both in one day.

29And when ye sacrifice a sacrifice of thanksgiving unto Yahweh, ye shall sacrifice it that ye may be accepted.

30On the same day it shall be eaten; ye shall leave none of it until the morning: I am Yahweh.

31Therefore shall ye keep my commandments, and do them: I am Yahweh.

32And ye shall not profane my holy name; but I will be hallowed among the children of Israel: I am Yahweh who halloweth you,

33who brought you out of the land of Egypt, to be your God: I am Yahweh.

Chapter 23

1And Yahweh spake unto Moses, saying,

2Speak unto the children of Israel, and say unto them, The set feasts of Yahweh, which ye shall proclaim to be holy convocations, even these are my set feasts.

3Six days shall work be done: but on the seventh day is a sabbath of solemn rest, a holy convocation; ye shall do no manner of work: it is a sabbath unto Yahweh in all your dwellings.

4These are the set feasts of Yahweh, even holy convocations, which ye shall proclaim in their appointed season.

5In the first month, on the fourteenth day of the month at even, is Yahweh's passover.

6And on the fifteenth day of the same month is the feast of unleavened bread unto Yahweh: seven days ye shall eat unleavened bread.

7In the first day ye shall have a holy convocation: ye shall do no servile work.

8But ye shall offer an offering made by fire unto Yahweh seven days: in the seventh day is a holy convocation; ye shall do no servile work.

9And Yahweh spake unto Moses, saying,

10Speak unto the children of Israel, and say unto them, When ye are come into the land which I give unto you, and shall reap the harvest thereof, then ye shall bring the sheaf of the first-fruits of your harvest unto the priest:

11and he shall wave the sheaf before Yahweh, to be accepted for you: on the morrow after the sabbath the priest shall wave it.

12And in the day when ye wave the sheaf, ye shall offer a he-lamb without blemish a year old for a burnt-offering unto Yahweh.

13And the meal-offering thereof shall be two tenth parts of an ephah of fine flour mingled with oil, an offering made by fire unto Yahweh for a sweet savor; and the drink-offering thereof shall be of wine, the fourth part of a hin.

14And ye shall eat neither bread, nor parched grain, nor fresh ears, until this selfsame day, until ye have brought the oblation of your God: it is a statute for ever throughout your generations in all your dwellings.

15And ye shall count unto you from the morrow after the sabbath, from the day that ye brought the sheaf of the wave-offering; seven sabbaths shall there be complete:

16even unto the morrow after the seventh sabbath shall ye number fifty days; and ye shall offer a new meal-offering unto Yahweh.

17Ye shall bring out of your habitations two wave-loaves of two tenth parts of an ephah: they shall be of fine flour, they shall be baken with leaven, for first-fruits unto Yahweh.

18And ye shall present with the bread seven lambs without blemish a year old, and one young bullock, and two rams: they shall be a burnt-offering unto Yahweh, with their meal-offering, and their drink-offerings, even an offering made by fire, of a sweet savor unto Yahweh.

19And ye shall offer one he-goat for a sin-offering, and two he-lambs a year old for a sacrifice of peace-offerings.

20And the priest shall wave them with the bread of the first-fruits for a wave-offering before Yahweh, with the two lambs: they shall be holy to Yahweh for the priest.

21And ye shall make proclamation on the selfsame day; there shall be a holy convocation unto you; ye shall do no servile work: it is a statute for ever in all your dwellings throughout your generations.

22And when ye reap the harvest of your land, thou shalt not wholly reap the corners of thy field, neither shalt thou gather the gleaning of thy harvest: thou shalt leave them for the poor, and for the sojourner: I am Yahweh your God.

23And Yahweh spake unto Moses, saying,

24Speak unto the children of Israel, saying, In the seventh month, on the first day of the month, shall be a solemn rest unto you, a memorial of blowing of trumpets, a holy convocation.

25Ye shall do no servile work; and ye shall offer an offering made by fire unto Yahweh.

26And Yahweh spake unto Moses, saying,

27Howbeit on the tenth day of this seventh month is the day of atonement: it shall be a holy convocation unto you, and ye shall afflict your souls; and ye shall offer an offering made by fire unto Yahweh.

28And ye shall do no manner of work in that same day; for it is a day of atonement, to make atonement for you before Yahweh your God.

29For whatsoever soul it be that shall not be afflicted in that same day; he shall be cut off from his people.

30And whatsoever soul it be that doeth any manner of work in that same day, that soul will I destroy from among his people.

31Ye shall do no manner of work: it is a statute for ever throughout your generations in all your dwellings.

32It shall be unto you a sabbath of solemn rest, and ye shall afflict your souls: in the ninth day of the month at even, from even unto even, shall ye keep your sabbath.

33And Yahweh spake unto Moses, saying,

34Speak unto the children of Israel, saying, On the fifteenth day of this seventh month is the feast of tabernacles for seven days unto Yahweh.

35On the first day shall be a holy convocation: ye shall do no servile work.

36Seven days ye shall offer an offering made by fire unto Yahweh: on the eighth day shall be a holy convocation unto you; and ye shall offer an offering made by fire unto Yahweh: it is a solemn assembly; ye shall do no servile work.

37These are the set feasts of Yahweh, which ye shall proclaim to be holy convocations, to offer an offering made by fire unto Yahweh, a burnt-offering, and a meal-offering, a sacrifice, and drink-offerings, each on its own day;

38besides the sabbaths of Yahweh, and besides your gifts, and besides all your vows, and besides all your freewill-offerings, which ye give unto Yahweh.

39Howbeit on the fifteenth day of the seventh month, when ye have gathered in the fruits of the land, ye shall keep the feast of Yahweh seven days: on the first day shall be a solemn rest, and on the eighth day shall be a solemn rest.

40And ye shall take you on the first day the fruit of goodly trees, branches of palm-trees, and boughs of thick trees, and willows of the brook; and ye shall rejoice before Yahweh your God seven days.

41And ye shall keep it a feast unto Yahweh seven days in the year: it is a statute for ever throughout your generations; ye shall keep it in the seventh month.

42Ye shall dwell in booths seven days; all that are home-born in Israel shall dwell in booths;

43that your generations may know that I made the children of Israel to dwell in booths, when I brought them out of the land of Egypt: I am Yahweh your God.

44And Moses declared unto the children of Israel the set feasts of Yahweh.

Chapter 24

1And Yahweh spake unto Moses, saying,

2Command the children of Israel, that they bring unto thee pure olive oil beaten for the light, to cause a lamp to burn continually.

3Without the veil of the testimony, in the tent of meeting, shall Aaron keep it in order from evening to morning before Yahweh continually: it shall be a statute for ever throughout your generations.

4He shall keep in order the lamps upon the pure candlestick before Yahweh continually.

5And thou shalt take fine flour, and bake twelve cakes thereof: two tenth parts of an ephah shall be in one cake.

6And thou shalt set them in two rows, six on a row, upon the pure table before Yahweh.

7And thou shalt put pure frankincense upon each row, that it may be to the bread for a memorial, even an offering made by fire unto Yahweh.

8Every sabbath day he shall set it in order before Yahweh continually; it is on the behalf of the children of Israel, an everlasting covenant.

9And it shall be for Aaron and his sons; and they shall eat it in a holy place: for it is most holy unto him of the offerings of Yahweh made by fire by a perpetual statute.

10And the son of an Israelitish woman, whose father was an Egyptian, went out among the children of Israel; and the son of the Israelitish woman and a man of Israel strove together in the camp:

11and the son of the Israelitish woman blasphemed the Name, and cursed; and they brought him unto Moses. And his mother's name was Shelomith, the daughter of Dibri, of the tribe of Dan.

12And they put him in ward, that it might be declared unto them at the mouth of Yahweh.

13And Yahweh spake unto Moses, saying,

14Bring forth him that hath cursed without the camp; and let all that heard him lay their hands upon his head, and let all the congregation stone him.

15And thou shalt speak unto the children of Israel, saying, Whosoever curseth his God shall bear his sin.

16And he that blasphemeth the name of Yahweh, he shall surely be put to death; all the congregation shall certainly stone him: as well the sojourner, as the home-born, when he blasphemeth the name of Yahweh, shall be put to death.

17And he that smiteth any man mortally shall surely be put to death.

18And he that smiteth a beast mortally shall make it good, life for life.

19And if a man cause a blemish in his neighbor; as he hath done, so shall it be done to him:

20breach for breach, eye for eye, tooth for tooth; as he hath caused a blemish in a man, so shall it be rendered unto him.

21And he that killeth a beast shall make it good: and he that killeth a man shall be put to death.

22Ye shall have one manner of law, as well for the sojourner, as for the home-born: for I am Yahweh your God.

23And Moses spake to the children of Israel; and they brought forth him that had cursed out of the camp, and stoned him with stones. And the children of Israel did as Yahweh commanded Moses.

Chapter 25

1And Yahweh spake unto Moses in mount Sinai, saying,

2Speak unto the children of Israel, and say unto them, When ye come into the land which I give you, then shall the land keep a sabbath unto Yahweh.

3Six years thou shalt sow thy field, and six years thou shalt prune thy vineyard, and gather in the fruits thereof;

4but in the seventh year shall be a sabbath of solemn rest for the land, a sabbath unto Yahweh: thou shalt neither sow thy field, nor prune thy vineyard.

5That which groweth of itself of thy harvest thou shalt not reap, and the grapes of thy undressed vine thou shalt not gather: it shall be a year of solemn rest for the land.

6And the sabbath of the land shall be for food for you; for thee, and for thy servant and for thy maid, and for thy hired servant and for thy stranger, who

Leviticus

sojourn with thee.

7And for thy cattle, and for the beasts that are in thy land, shall all the increase thereof be for food.

8And thou shalt number seven sabbaths of years unto thee, seven times seven years; and there shall be unto thee the days of seven sabbaths of years, even forty and nine years.

9Then shalt thou send abroad the loud trumpet on the tenth day of the seventh month; in the day of atonement shall ye send abroad the trumpet throughout all your land.

10And ye shall hallow the fiftieth year, and proclaim liberty throughout the land unto all the inhabitants thereof: it shall be a jubilee unto you; and ye shall return every man unto his possession, and ye shall return every man unto his family.

11A jubilee shall that fiftieth year be unto you: ye shall not sow, neither reap that which groweth of itself in it, nor gather the grapes in it of the undressed vines.

12For it is a jubilee; it shall be holy unto you: ye shall eat the increase thereof out of the field.

13In this year of jubilee ye shall return every man unto his possession.

14And if thou sell aught unto thy neighbor, or buy of thy neighbor's hand, ye shall not wrong one another.

15According to the number of years after the jubilee thou shalt buy of thy neighbor, and according unto the number of years of the crops he shall sell unto thee.

16According to the multitude of the years thou shalt increase the price thereof, and according to the fewness of the years thou shalt diminish the price of it; for the number of the crops doth he sell unto thee.

17And ye shall not wrong one another; but thou shalt fear thy God: for I am Yahweh your God.

18Wherefore ye shall do my statutes, and keep mine ordinances and do them; and ye shall dwell in the land in safety.

19And the land shall yield its fruit, and ye shall eat your fill, and dwell therein in safety.

20And if ye shall say, What shall we eat the seventh year? Behold, we shall not sow, nor gather in our increase;

21then I will command my blessing upon you in the sixth year, and it shall bring forth fruit for the three years.

22And ye shall sow the eighth year, and eat of the fruits, the old store; until the ninth year, until its fruits come in, ye shall eat the old store.

23And the land shall not be sold in perpetuity; for the land is mine: for ye are strangers and sojourners with me.

24And in all the land of your possession ye shall grant a redemption for the land.

25If thy brother be waxed poor, and sell some of his possession, then shall his kinsman that is next unto him come, and shall redeem that which his brother hath sold.

26And if a man have no one to redeem it, and he be waxed rich and find sufficient to redeem it;

27then let him reckon the years of the sale thereof, and restore the overplus unto the man to whom he sold it; and he shall return unto his possession.

28But if he be not able to get it back for himself, then that which he hath sold shall remain in the hand of him that hath bought it until the year of jubilee: and in the jubilee it shall go out, and he shall return unto his possession.

29And if a man sell a dwelling-house in a walled city, then he may redeem it within a whole year after it is sold; for a full year shall he have the right of redemption.

30And if it be not redeemed within the space of a full year, then the house that is in the walled city shall be made sure in perpetuity to him that bought it, throughout his generations: it shall not go out in the jubilee.

31But the houses of the villages which have no wall round about them shall be reckoned with the fields of the country: they may be redeemed, and they shall go out in the jubilee.

32Nevertheless the cities of the Levites, the houses of the cities of their possession, may the Levites redeem at any time.

33And if one of the Levites redeem, then the house that was sold, and the city of his possession, shall go out in the jubilee; for the houses of the cities of the Levites are their possession among the children of Israel.

34But the field of the suburbs of their cities may not be sold; for it is their perpetual possession.

35And if thy brother be waxed poor, and his hand fail with thee; then thou shalt uphold him: as a stranger and a sojourner shall he live with thee.

36Take thou no interest of him or increase, but fear thy God; that thy brother may live with thee.

37Thou shalt not give him thy money upon interest, nor give him thy victuals for increase.

38I am Yahweh your God, who brought you forth out of the land of Egypt, to give you the land of Canaan, and to be your God.

39And if thy brother be waxed poor with thee, and sell himself unto thee; thou shalt not make him to serve as a bond-servant.

40As a hired servant, and as a sojourner, he shall be with thee; he shall serve with thee unto the year of jubilee:

41then he go out from thee, he and his children with him, and shall return unto his own family, and unto the possession of his fathers shall he return.

42For they are my servants, whom I brought forth out of the land of Egypt: they shall not be sold as bondmen.

43Thou shalt not rule over him with rigor, but shalt fear thy God.

44And as for thy bondmen, and thy bondmaids, whom thou shalt have; of the nations that are round about you, of them shall ye buy bondmen and bondmaids.

45Moreover of the children of the strangers that sojourn among you, of them shall ye buy, and of their families that are with you, which they have begotten in your land: and they shall be your possession.

46And ye shall make them an inheritance for your children after you, to hold for a possession; of them shall ye take your bondmen for ever: but over your brethren the children of Israel ye shall not rule, one over another, with rigor.

47And if a stranger or sojourner with thee be waxed rich, and thy brother be waxed poor beside him, and sell himself unto the stranger or sojourner with thee, or to the stock of the stranger's family;

48after that he is sold he may be redeemed: one of his brethren may redeem him;

49or his uncle, or his uncle's son, may redeem him, or any that is nigh of kin unto him of his family may redeem him; or if he be waxed rich, he may redeem himself.

50And he shall reckon with him that bought him from the year that he sold himself to him unto the year of jubilee: and the price of his sale shall be according unto the number of years; according to the time of a hired servant shall he be with him.

51If there be yet many years, according unto them he shall give back the price of his redemption out of the money that he was bought for.

52And if there remain but few years unto the year of jubilee, then he shall reckon with him; according unto his years shall he give back the price of his redemption.

53As a servant hired year by year shall he be with him: he shall not rule with rigor over him in thy sight.

54And if he be not redeemed by these means, then he shall go out in the year of jubilee, he, and his children with him.

55For unto me the children of Israel are servants; they are my servants whom I brought forth out of the land of Egypt: I am Yahweh your God.

Chapter 26

1Ye shall make you no idols, neither shall ye rear you up a graven image, or a pillar, neither shall ye place any figured stone in your land, to bow down unto it: for I am Yahweh your God.

2Ye shall keep my sabbaths, and reverence my sanctuary: I am Yahweh.

3If ye walk in my statutes, and keep my commandments, and do them;

4then I will give your rains in their season, and the land shall yield its increase, and the trees of the field shall yield their fruit.

5And your threshing shall reach unto the vintage, and the vintage shall reach unto the sowing time; and ye shall eat your bread to the full, and dwell in your land safely.

6And I will give peace in the land, and ye shall lie down, and none shall make you afraid: and I will cause evil beasts to cease out of the land, neither shall the sword go through your land.

7And ye shall chase your enemies, and they shall fall before you by the sword.

8And five of you shall chase a hundred, and a hundred of you shall chase ten thousand; and your enemies shall fall before you by the sword.

9And I will have respect unto you, and make you fruitful, and multiply you, and will establish my covenant with you.

10And ye shall eat old store long kept, and ye shall bring forth the old because of the new.

11And I will set my tabernacle among you: and my soul shall not abhor you.

12And I will walk among you, and will be your God, and ye shall be my people.

13I am Yahweh your God, who brought you forth out of the land of Egypt, that ye should not be their bondmen; and I have broken the bars of your yoke, and made you go upright.

14But if ye will not hearken unto me, and will not do all these commandments;

15and if ye shall reject my statutes, and if your soul abhor mine ordinances, so that ye will not do all my commandments, but break my covenant;

16I also will do this unto you: I will appoint terror over you, even consumption and fever, that shall consume the eyes, and make the soul to pine away; and ye shall sow your seed in vain, for your enemies shall eat it.

17And I will set my face against you, and ye shall be smitten before your enemies: they that hate you shall rule over you; and ye shall flee when none pursueth you.

18And if ye will not yet for these things hearken unto me, then I will chastise you seven times more for your sins.

19And I will break the pride of your power: and I will make your heaven as iron, and your earth as brass;

20and your strength shall be spent in vain; for your land shall not yield its increase, neither shall the trees of the land yield their fruit.

21And if ye walk contrary unto me, and will not hearken unto me, I will bring seven times more plagues upon you according to your sins.

22And I will send the beast of the field among you, which shall rob you of your children, and destroy your cattle, and make you few in number; and your ways shall become desolate.

23And if by these things ye will not be reformed unto me, but will walk contrary unto me;

24then will I also walk contrary unto you; and I will smite you, even I, seven times for your sins.

25And I will bring a sword upon you, that shall execute the vengeance of the covenant; and ye shall be gathered together within your cities: and I will send the pestilence among you; and ye shall be delivered into the hand of the enemy.

26When I break your staff of bread, ten women shall bake your bread in one oven, and they shall deliver your bread again by weight: and ye shall eat, and not be satisfied.

27And if ye will not for all this hearken unto me, but walk contrary unto me;

28then I will walk contrary unto you in wrath; and I also will chastise you seven times for your sins.

29And ye shall eat the flesh of your sons, and the flesh of your daughters shall ye eat.

30And I will destroy your high places, and cut down your sun-images, and cast your dead bodies upon the bodies of your idols; and my soul shall abhor you.

31And I will make your cities a waste, and will bring your sanctuaries unto desolation, and I will not smell the savor of your sweet odors.

32And I will bring the land into desolation; and your enemies that dwell therein shall be astonished at it.

33And you will I scatter among the nations, and I will draw out the sword after you: and your land shall be a desolation, and your cities shall be a waste.

34Then shall the land enjoy its sabbaths, as long as it lieth desolate, and ye are in your enemies' land; even then shall the land rest, and enjoy its sabbaths.

35As long as it lieth desolate it shall have rest, even the rest which it had not in your sabbaths, when ye dwelt upon it.

36And as for them that are left of you, I will send a faintness into their heart in the lands of their enemies: and the sound of a driven leaf shall chase them; and they shall flee, as one fleeth from the sword; and they shall fall when none pursueth.

37And they shall stumble one upon another, as it were before the sword, when none pursueth: and ye shall have no power to stand before your enemies.

38And ye shall perish among the nations, and the land of your enemies shall eat you up.

39And they that are left of you shall pine away in their iniquity in your enemies' lands; and also in the iniquities of their fathers shall they pine away with them.

40And they shall confess their iniquity, and the iniquity of their fathers, in their trespass which they trespassed against me, and also that, because they walked contrary unto me,

41I also walked contrary unto them, and brought them into the land of their enemies: if then their uncircumcised heart be humbled, and they then accept of the punishment of their iniquity;

42then will I remember my covenant with Jacob; and also my covenant with Isaac, and also my covenant with Abraham will I remember; and I will remember the land.

43The land also shall be left by them, and shall enjoy its sabbaths, while it lieth desolate without them: and they shall accept of the punishment of their iniquity; because, even because they rejected mine ordinances, and their soul abhorred my statutes.

44And yet for all that, when they are in the land of their enemies, I will not reject them, neither will I abhor them, to destroy them utterly, and to break my covenant with them; for I am Yahweh their God;

45but I will for their sakes remember the covenant of their ancestors, whom I brought forth out of the land of Egypt in the sight of the nations, that I might be their God: I am Yahweh.

46These are the statutes and ordinances and laws, which Yahweh made between him and the children of Israel in mount Sinai by Moses.

Chapter 27

1And Yahweh spake unto Moses, saying,

2Speak unto the children of Israel, and say unto them, When a man shall accomplish a vow, the persons shall be for Yahweh by thy estimation.

3And thy estimation shall be of the male from twenty years old even unto sixty years old, even thy estimation shall be fifty shekels of silver, after the shekel of the sanctuary.

4And if it be a female, then thy estimation shall be thirty shekels.

5And if it be from five years old even unto twenty years old, then thy estimation shall be of the male twenty shekels, and for the female ten shekels.

6And if it be from a month old even unto five years old, then thy estimation shall be of the male five shekels of silver, and for the female thy estimation shall be three shekels of silver.

7And if it be from sixty years old and upward; if it be a male, then thy estimation shall be fifteen shekels, and for the female ten shekels.

8But if he be poorer than thy estimation, then he shall be set before the priest, and the priest shall value him; according to the ability of him that vowed shall the priest value him.

9And if it be a beast, whereof men offer an oblation unto Yahweh, all that any man giveth of such unto Yahweh shall be holy.

10He shall not alter it, nor change it, a good for a bad, or a bad for a good: and if he shall at all change beast for beast, then both it and that for which it is changed shall be holy.

11And if it be any unclean beast, of which they do not offer an oblation unto Yahweh, then he shall set the beast before the priest;

12and the priest shall value it, whether it be good or bad: as thou the priest valuest it, so shall it be.

13But if he will indeed redeem it, then he shall add the fifth part thereof unto thy estimation.

14And when a man shall sanctify his house to be holy unto Yahweh, then the priest shall estimate it, whether it be good or bad: as the priest shall estimate it, so shall it stand.

15And if he that sanctified it will redeem his house, then he shall add the fifth part of the money of thy estimation unto it, and it shall be his.

16And if a man shall sanctify unto Yahweh part of the field of his possession, then thy estimation shall be according to the sowing thereof: the sowing of a homer of barley shall be valued at fifty shekels of silver.

17If he sanctify his field from the year of jubilee, according to thy estimation it shall stand.

18But if he sanctify his field after the jubilee, then the priest shall reckon unto him the money according to the years that remain unto the year of jubilee; and an abatement shall be made from thy estimation.

19And if he that sanctified the field will indeed redeem it, then he shall add the fifth part of the money of thy estimation unto it, and it shall be assured to him.

20And if he will not redeem the field, or if he have sold the field to another man, it shall not be redeemed any more:

21but the field, when it goeth out in the jubilee, shall be holy unto Yahweh, as a field devoted; the possession thereof shall be the priest's.

22And if he sanctify unto Yahweh a field which he hath bought, which is not of the field of his possession;

23then the priest shall reckon unto him the worth of thy estimation unto the year of jubilee: and he shall give thine estimation in that day, as a holy thing unto Yahweh.

24In the year of jubilee the field shall return unto him of whom it was bought, even to him to whom the possession of the land belongeth.

25And all thy estimations shall be according to the shekel of the sanctuary: twenty gerahs shall be the shekel.

26Only the firstling among beasts, which is made a firstling to Yahweh, no man shall sanctify it; whether it be ox or sheep, it is Yahweh's.

27And if it be of an unclean beast, then he shall ransom it according to thine estimation, and shall add unto it the fifth part thereof: or if it be not redeemed, then it shall be sold according to thy estimation.

28Notwithstanding, no devoted thing, that a man shall devote unto Yahweh of all that he hath, whether of man or beast, or of the field of his possession, shall be sold or redeemed: every devoted thing is most holy unto Yahweh.

29No one devoted, that shall be devoted from among men, shall be ransomed; he shall surely be put to death.

30And all the tithe of the land, whether of the seed of the land, or of the fruit of the tree, is Yahweh's: it is holy unto Yahweh.

31And if a man will redeem aught of his tithe, he shall add unto it the fifth part thereof.

32And all the tithe of the herd or the flock, whatsoever passeth under the rod, the tenth shall be holy unto Yahweh.

33He shall not search whether it be good or bad, neither shall he change it: and if he change it at all, then both it and that for which it is changed shall be holy; it shall not be redeemed.

34These are the commandments, which Yahweh commanded Moses for the children of Israel in mount Sinai.

Numbers

The Fourth Book of Moses, called Numbers

Chapter 1

1And Yahweh spake unto Moses in the wilderness of Sinai, in the tent of meeting, on the first day of the second month, in the second year after they were come out of the land of Egypt, saying,

2Take ye the sum of all the congregation of the children of Israel, by their families, by their fathers' houses, according to the number of the names, every male, by their polls;

3from twenty years old and upward, all that are able to go forth to war in Israel, thou and Aaron shall number them by their hosts.

4And with you there shall be a man of every tribe; every one head of his fathers' house.

5And these are the names of the men that shall stand with you. Of Reuben: Elizur the son of Shedeur.

6Of Simeon: Shelumiel the son of Zurishaddai.

7Of Judah: Nahshon the son of Amminadab.

8Of Issachar: Nethanel the son of Zuar.

9Of Zebulun: Eliab the son of Helon.

10Of the children of Joseph: Of Ephraim: Elishama the son of Ammihud. Of Manasseh: Gamaliel the son of Pedahzur.

11Of Benjamin: Abidan the son of Gideoni.

12Of Dan: Ahiezer the son of Ammishaddai.

13Of Asher: Pagiel the son of Ochran.

14Of Gad: Eliasaph the son of Deuel.

15Of Naphtali: Ahira the son of Enan.

16These are they that were called of the congregation, the princes of the tribes of their fathers; they were the heads of the thousands of Israel.

17And Moses and Aaron took these men that are mentioned by name:

18And they assembled all the congregation together on the first day of the second month; and they declared their pedigrees after their families, by their fathers' houses, according to the number of the names, from twenty years old and upward, by their polls.

19As Yahweh commanded Moses, so he numbered them in the wilderness of Sinai.

20And the children of Reuben, Israel's first-born, their generations, by their families, by their fathers' houses, according to the number of the names, by their polls, every male from twenty years old and upward, all that were able to go forth to war;

21those that were numbered of them, of the tribe of Reuben, were forty and six thousand and five hundred.

22Of the children of Simeon, their generations, by their families, by their fathers' houses, those that were numbered thereof, according to the number of the names, by their polls, every male from twenty years old and upward, all that were able to go forth to war;

23those that were numbered of them, of the tribe of Simeon, were fifty and nine thousand and three hundred.

24Of the children of Gad, their generations, by their families, by their fathers' houses, according to the number of the names, from twenty years old and upward, all that were able to go forth to war;

25those that were numbered of them, of the tribe of Gad, were forty and five thousand six hundred and fifty.

26Of the children of Judah, their generations, by their families, by their fathers' houses, according to the number of the names, from twenty years old and upward, all that were able to go forth to war;

27those that were numbered of them, of the tribe of Judah, were threescore and fourteen thousand and six hundred.

28Of the children of Issachar, their generations, by their families, by their fathers' houses, according to the number of the names, from twenty years old and upward, all that were able to go forth to war;

29those that were numbered of them, of the tribe of Issachar, were fifty and four thousand and four hundred.

30Of the children of Zebulun, their generations, by their families, by their fathers' houses, according to the number of the names, from twenty years old and upward, all that were able to go forth to war;

31those that were numbered of them, of the tribe of Zebulun, were fifty and seven thousand and four hundred.

32Of the children of Joseph, namely, of the children of Ephraim, their generations, by their families, by their fathers' houses, according to the number of the names, from twenty years old and upward, all that were able to go forth to war;

33those that were numbered of them, of the tribe of Ephraim, were forty thousand and five hundred.

34Of the children of Manasseh, their generations, by their families, by their fathers' houses, according to the number of the names, from twenty years old and upward, all that were able to go forth to war;

35those that were numbered of them, of the tribe of Manasseh, were thirty and two thousand and two hundred.

36Of the children of Benjamin, their generations, by their families, by their fathers' houses, according to the number of the names, from twenty years old and upward, all that were able to go forth to war;

37those that were numbered of them, of the tribe of Benjamin, were thirty and five thousand and four hundred.

38Of the children of Dan, their generations, by their families, by their fathers' houses, according to the number of the names, from twenty years old and upward, all that were able to go forth to war;

39those that were numbered of them, of the tribe of Dan, were threescore and two thousand and seven hundred.

40Of the children of Asher, their generations, by their families, by their fathers' houses, according to the number of the names, from twenty years old and upward, all that were able to go forth to war;

41those that were numbered of them, of the tribe of Asher, were forty and one thousand and five hundred.

42Of the children of Naphtali, their generations, by their families, by their fathers' houses, according to the number of the names, from twenty years old and upward, all that were able to go forth to war;

43those that were numbered of them, of the tribe of Naphtali, were fifty and three thousand and four hundred.

44These are they that were numbered, whom Moses and Aaron numbered, and the princes of Israel, being twelve men: they were each one for his fathers' house.

45So all they that were numbered of the children of Israel by their fathers' houses, from twenty years old and upward, all that were able to go forth to war in Israel;

46even all they that were numbered were six hundred thousand and three thousand and five hundred and fifty.

47But the Levites after the tribe of their fathers were not numbered among them.

48For Yahweh spake unto Moses, saying,

49Only the tribe of Levi thou shalt not number, neither shalt thou take the sum of them among the children of Israel;

50but appoint thou the Levites over the tabernacle of the testimony, and over all the furniture thereof, and over all that belongeth to it: they shall bear the tabernacle, and all the furniture thereof; and they shall minister unto it, and shall encamp round about the tabernacle.

51And when the tabernacle setteth forward, the Levites shall take it down; and when the tabernacle is to be pitched, the Levites shall set it up: and the stranger that cometh nigh shall be put to death.

52And the children of Israel shall pitch their tents, every man by his own camp, and every man by his own standard, according to their hosts.

53But the Levites shall encamp round about the tabernacle of the testimony, that there be no wrath upon the congregation of the children of Israel: and the Levites shall keep the charge of the tabernacle of the testimony.

54Thus did the children of Israel; according to all that Yahweh commanded Moses, so did they.

Chapter 2

1And Yahweh spake unto Moses and unto Aaron, saying,

2The children of Israel shall encamp every man by his own standard, with the ensigns of their fathers' houses: over against the tent of meeting shall they encamp round about.

3And those that encamp on the east side toward the sunrising shall be they of the standard of the camp of Judah, according to their hosts: and the prince of the children of Judah shall be Nahshon the son of Amminadab.

4And his host, and those that were numbered of them, were threescore and fourteen thousand and six hundred.

5And those that encamp next unto him shall be the tribe of Issachar: and the prince of the children of Issachar shall be Nethanel the son of Zuar.

6And his host, and those that were numbered thereof, were fifty and four thousand and four hundred.

7And the tribe of Zebulun: and the prince of the children of Zebulun shall be Eliab the son of Helon.

8And his host, and those that were numbered thereof, were fifty and seven thousand and four hundred.

9All that were numbered of the camp of Judah were a hundred thousand and fourscore thousand and six thousand and four hundred, according to their hosts. They shall set forth first.

10On the south side shall be the standard of the camp of Reuben according to their hosts: and the prince of the children of Reuben shall be Elizur the son of Shedeur.

11And his host, and those that were numbered thereof, were forty and six thousand and five hundred.

12And those that encamp next unto him shall be the tribe of Simeon: and the prince of the children of Simeon shall be Shelumiel the son of Zurishaddai.

13And his host, and those that were numbered of them, were fifty and nine thousand and three hundred.

14And the tribe of Gad: and the prince of the children of Gad shall be Eliasaph the son of Reuel.

15And his host, and those that were numbered of them, were forty and five thousand and six hundred and fifty.

16All that were numbered of the camp of Reuben were a hundred thousand and fifty and one thousand and four hundred and fifty, according to their hosts. And they shall set forth second.

17Then the tent of meeting shall set forward, with the camp of the Levites in the midst of the camps: as they encamp, so shall they set forward, every man in his place, by their standards.

18On the west side shall be the standard of the camp of Ephraim according to their hosts: and the prince of the children of Ephraim shall be Elishama the son of Ammihud.

19And his host, and those that were numbered of them, were forty thousand and five hundred.

20And next unto him shall be the tribe of Manasseh: and the prince of the children of Manasseh shall be Gamaliel the son of Pedahzur.

21And his host, and those that were numbered of them, were thirty and two thousand and two hundred.

22And the tribe of Benjamin: and the prince of the children of Benjamin shall be Abidan the son of Gideoni.

23And his host, and those that were numbered of them, were thirty and five thousand and four hundred.

24All that were numbered of the camp of Ephraim were a hundred thousand and eight thousand and a hundred, according to their hosts. And they shall set forth third.

25On the north side shall be the standard of the camp of Dan according to their hosts: and the prince of the children of Dan shall be Ahiezer the son of Ammishaddai.

26And his host, and those that were numbered of them, were threescore and two thousand and seven hundred.

27And those that encamp next unto him shall be the tribe of Asher: and the prince of the children of Asher shall be Pagiel the son of Ochran.

28And his host, and those that were numbered of them, were forty and one thousand and five hundred.

29And the tribe of Naphtali: and the prince of the children of Naphtali shall be Ahira the son of Enan.

30And his host, and those that were numbered of them, were fifty and three thousand and four hundred.

31All that were numbered of the camp of Dan were a hundred thousand and fifty and seven thousand and six hundred. They shall set forth hindmost by their standards.

32These are they that were numbered of the children of Israel by their fathers' houses: all that were numbered of the camps according to their hosts were six hundred thousand and three thousand and five hundred and fifty.

33But the Levites were not numbered among the children of Israel; as Yahweh commanded Moses.

34Thus did the children of Israel; according to all that Yahweh commanded Moses, so they encamped by their standards, and so they set forward, every one by their families, according to their fathers' houses.

Chapter 3

1Now these are the generations of Aaron and Moses in the day that Yahweh spake with Moses in mount Sinai.

2And these are the names of the sons of Aaron: Nadab the first-born, and Abihu, Eleazar, and Ithamar.

3These are the names of the sons of Aaron, the priests that were anointed, whom he consecrated to minister in the priest's office.

4And Nadab and Abihu died before Yahweh, when they offered strange fire before Yahweh, in the wilderness of Sinai, and they had no children; and Eleazar and Ithamar ministered in the priest's office in the presence of Aaron their father.

5And Yahweh spake unto Moses, saying,

6Bring the tribe of Levi near, and set them before Aaron the priest, that they may minister unto him.

7And they shall keep his charge, and the charge of the whole congregation before the tent of meeting, to do the service of the tabernacle.

8And they shall keep all the furniture of the tent of meeting, and the charge of the children of Israel, to do the service of the tabernacle.

9And thou shalt give the Levites unto Aaron and to his sons: they are wholly given unto him on the behalf of the children of Israel.

10And thou shalt appoint Aaron and his sons, and they shall keep their priesthood: and the stranger that cometh nigh shall be put to death.

11And Yahweh spake unto Moses, saying,

12And I, behold, I have taken the Levites from among the children of Israel instead of all the first-born that openeth the womb among the children of Israel; and the Levites shall be mine:

13for all the first-born are mine; on the day that I smote all the first-born in the land of Egypt I hallowed unto me all the first-born in Israel, both man and beast; mine they shall be: I am Yahweh.

14And Yahweh spake unto Moses in the wilderness of Sinai, saying,

15Number the children of Levi by their fathers' houses, by their families: every male from a month old and upward shalt thou number them.

16And Moses numbered them according to the word of Yahweh, as he was commanded.

17And these were the sons of Levi by their names: Gershon, and Kohath, and Merari.

18And these are the names of the sons of Gershon by their families: Libni and Shimei.

19And the sons of Kohath by their families: Amram, and Izhar, Hebron, and Uzziel.

20And the sons of Merari by their families: Mahli and Mushi. These are the families of the Levites according to their fathers' houses.

21Of Gershon was the family of the Libnites, and the family of the Shimeites: these are the families of the Gershonites.

22Those that were numbered of them, according to the number of all the males, from a month old and upward, even those that were numbered of them were seven thousand and five hundred.

23The families of the Gershonites shall encamp behind the tabernacle westward.

24And the prince of the fathers' house of the Gershonites shall be Eliasaph the son of Lael.

25And the charge of the sons of Gershon in the tent of meeting shall be the tabernacle, and the Tent, the covering thereof, and the screen for the door of the tent of meeting,

26and the hangings of the court, and the screen for the door of the court, which is by the tabernacle, and by the altar round about, and the cords of it for all the service thereof.

27And of Kohath was the family of the Amramites, and the family of the Izharites, and the family of the Hebronites, and the family of the Uzzielites: these are the families of the Kohathites.

28According to the number of all the males, from a month old and upward, there were eight thousand and six hundred, keeping the charge of the sanctuary.

29The families of the sons of Kohath shall encamp on the side of the tabernacle southward.

30And the prince of the fathers' house of the families of the Kohathites shall be Elizaphan the son of Uzziel.

31And their charge shall be the ark, and the table, and the candlestick, and the altars, and the vessels of the sanctuary wherewith they minister, and the screen, and all the service thereof.

32And Eleazar the son of Aaron the priest shall be prince of the princes of the Levites, and have the oversight of them that keep the charge of the sanctuary.

33Of Merari was the family of the Mahlites, and the family of the Mushites: these are the families of Merari.

34And those that were numbered of them, according to the number of all the males, from a month old and upward, were six thousand and two hundred.

35And the prince of the fathers' house of the families of Merari was Zuriel the son of Abihail: they shall encamp on the side of the tabernacle northward.

36And the appointed charge of the sons of Merari shall be the boards of the tabernacle, and the bars thereof, and the pillars thereof, and the sockets thereof, and all the instruments thereof, and all the service thereof,

37and the pillars of the court round about, and their sockets, and their pins, and their cords.

38And those that encamp before the tabernacle eastward, before the tent of meeting toward the sunrising, shall be Moses, and Aaron and his sons, keeping the charge of the sanctuary for the charge of the children of Israel; and the stranger that cometh nigh shall be put to death.

39All that were numbered of the Levites, whom Moses and Aaron numbered at the commandment of Yahweh, by their families, all the males from a month old and upward, were twenty and two thousand.

40And Yahweh said unto Moses, Number all the first-born males of the children of Israel from a month old and upward, and take the number of their names.

41And thou shalt take the Levites for me (I am Yahweh) instead of all the first-born among the children of Israel; and the cattle of the Levites instead of all the firstlings among the cattle of the children of Israel:

42and Moses numbered, as Yahweh commanded him, all the first-born among the children of Israel.

43And all the first-born males according to the number of names, from a month old and upward, of those that were numbered of them, were twenty and two thousand two hundred and threescore and thirteen.

44And Yahweh spake unto Moses, saying,

45Take the Levites instead of all the first-born among the children of Israel, and the cattle of the Levites instead of their cattle; and the Levites shall be mine: I am Yahweh.

46And for the redemption of the two hundred and threescore and thirteen of the first-born of the children of Israel, that are over and above the number of the Levites,

47thou shalt take five shekels apiece by the poll; after the shekel of the sanctuary shalt thou take them (the shekel is twenty gerahs):

48and thou shalt give the money, wherewith the odd number of them is redeemed, unto Aaron and to his sons.

49And Moses took the redemption-money from them that were over and above them that were redeemed by the Levites;

50from the first-born of the children of Israel took he the money, a thousand three hundred and threescore and five shekels, after the shekel of the sanctuary:

51and Moses gave the redemption-money unto Aaron and to his sons, according to the word of Yahweh, as Yahweh commanded Moses.

Chapter 4

1And Yahweh spake unto Moses and unto Aaron, saying,

2Take the sum of the sons of Kohath from among the sons of Levi, by their families, by their fathers' houses,

3from thirty years old and upward even until fifty years old, all that enter upon the service, to do the work in the tent of meeting.

4This is the service of the sons of Kohath in the tent of meeting, about the most holy things:

5when the camp setteth forward, Aaron shall go in, and his sons, and they shall take down the veil of the screen, and cover the ark of the testimony with it,

6and shall put thereon a covering of sealskin, and shall spread over it a cloth all of blue, and shall put in the staves thereof.

7And upon the table of showbread they shall spread a cloth of blue, and put thereon the dishes, and the spoons, and the bowls and the cups wherewith to pour out; and the continual bread shall be thereon:

8and they shall spread upon them a cloth of scarlet, and cover the same with a covering of sealskin, and shall put in the staves thereof.

9And they shall take a cloth of blue, and cover the candlestick of the light, and its lamps, and its snuffers, and its snuffdishes, and all the oil vessels thereof, wherewith they minister unto it:

10and they shall put it and all the vessels thereof within a covering of sealskin, and shall put it upon the frame.

11And upon the golden altar they shall spread a cloth of blue, and cover it with a covering of sealskin, and shall put in the staves thereof:

12and they shall take all the vessels of ministry, wherewith they minister in the sanctuary, and put them in a cloth of blue, and cover them with a covering of sealskin, and shall put them on the frame.

Numbers

13And they shall take away the ashes from the altar, and spread a purple cloth thereon:

14and they shall put upon it all the vessels thereof, wherewith they minister about it, the firepans, the flesh-hooks, and the shovels, and the basins, all the vessels of the altar; and they shall spread upon it a covering of sealskin, and put in the staves thereof.

15And when Aaron and his sons have made an end of covering the sanctuary, and all the furniture of the sanctuary, as the camp is set forward; after that, the sons of Kohath shall come to bear it: but they shall not touch the sanctuary, lest they die. These things are the burden of the sons of Kohath in the tent of meeting.

16And the charge of Eleazar the son of Aaron the priest shall be the oil for the light, and the sweet incense, and the continual meal-offering, and the anointing oil, the charge of all the tabernacle, and of all that therein is, the sanctuary, and the furniture thereof.

17And Yahweh spake unto Moses and unto Aaron, saying,

18Cut ye not off the tribe of the families of the Kohathites from among the Levites;

19but thus do unto them, that they may live, and not die, when they approach unto the most holy things: Aaron and his sons shall go in, and appoint them every one to his service and to his burden;

20but they shall not go in to see the sanctuary even for a moment, lest they die.

21And Yahweh spake unto Moses, saying,

22Take the sum of the sons of Gershon also, by their fathers' houses, by their families;

23from thirty years old and upward until fifty years old shalt thou number them; all that enter in to wait upon the service, to do the work in the tent of meeting.

24This is the service of the families of the Gershonites, in serving and in bearing burdens:

25they shall bear the curtains of the tabernacle, and the tent of meeting, its covering, and the covering of sealskin that is above upon it, and the screen for the door of the tent of meeting,

26and the hangings of the court, and the screen for the door of the gate of the court, which is by the tabernacle and by the altar round about, and their cords, and all the instruments of their service, and whatsoever shall be done with them: therein shall they serve.

27At the commandment of Aaron and his sons shall be all the service of the sons of the Gershonites, in all their burden, and in all their service; and ye shall appoint unto them in charge all their burden.

28This is the service of the families of the sons of the Gershonites in the tent of meeting: and their charge shall be under the hand of Ithamar the son of Aaron the priest.

29As for the sons of Merari, thou shalt number them by their families, by their fathers' houses;

30from thirty years old and upward even unto fifty years old shalt thou number them, every one that entereth upon the service, to do the work of the tent of meeting.

31And this is the charge of their burden, according to all their service in the tent of meeting: the boards of the tabernacle, and the bars thereof, and the pillars thereof, and the sockets thereof,

32and the pillars of the court round about, and their sockets, and their pins, and their cords, with all their instruments, and with all their service: and by name ye shall appoint the instruments of the charge of their burden.

33This is the service of the families of the sons of Merari, according to all their service, in the tent of meeting, under the hand of Ithamar the son of Aaron the priest.

34And Moses and Aaron and the princes of the congregation numbered the sons of the Kohathites by their families, and by their fathers' houses,

35from thirty years old and upward even unto fifty years old, every one that entered upon the service, for work in the tent of meeting:

36and those that were numbered of them by their families were two thousand seven hundred and fifty.

37These are they that were numbered of the families of the Kohathites, all that did serve in the tent of meeting, whom Moses and Aaron numbered according to the commandment of Yahweh by Moses.

38And those that were numbered of the sons of Gershon, their families, and by their fathers' houses,

39from thirty years old and upward even unto fifty years old, every one that entered upon the service, for work in the tent of meeting,

40even those that were numbered of them, by their families, by their fathers' houses, were two thousand and six hundred and thirty.

41These are they that were numbered of the families of the sons of Gershon, all that did serve in the tent of meeting, whom Moses and Aaron numbered according to the commandment of Yahweh.

42And those that were numbered of the families of the sons of Merari, by their families, by their fathers' houses,

43from thirty years old and upward even unto fifty years old, every one that entered upon the service, for work in the tent of meeting,

44even those that were numbered of them by their families, were three thousand and two hundred.

45These are they that were numbered of the families of the sons of Merari, whom Moses and Aaron numbered according to the commandment of Yahweh by Moses.

46All those that were numbered of the Levites, whom Moses and Aaron and the princes of Israel numbered, by their families, and by their fathers' houses,

47from thirty years old and upward even unto fifty years old, every one that entered in to do the work of service, and the work of bearing burdens in the tent of meeting,

48even those that were numbered of them, were eight thousand and five hundred and fourscore.

49According to the commandment of Yahweh they were numbered by Moses, every one according to his service, and according to his burden: thus were they numbered of him, as Yahweh commanded Moses.

Chapter 5

1And Yahweh spake unto Moses, saying,

2Command the children of Israel, that they put out of the camp every leper, and every one that hath an issue, and whosoever is unclean by the dead:

3both male and female shall ye put out, without the camp shall ye put them; that they defile not their camp, in the midst whereof I dwell.

4And the children of Israel did so, and put them out without the camp; as Yahweh spake unto Moses, so did the children of Israel.

5And Yahweh spake unto Moses, saying,

6Speak unto the children of Israel, When a man or woman shall commit any sin that men commit, so as to trespass against Yahweh, and that soul shall be guilty;

7then he shall confess his sin which he hath done: and he shall make restitution for his guilt in full, and add unto it the fifth part thereof, and give it unto him in respect of whom he hath been guilty.

8But if the man have no kinsman to whom restitution may be made for the guilt, the restitution for guilt which is made unto Yahweh shall be the priest's; besides the ram of the atonement, whereby atonement shall be made for him.

9And every heave-offering of all the holy things of the children of Israel, which they present unto the priest, shall be his.

10And every man's hallowed things shall be his: whatsoever any man giveth the priest, it shall be his.

11And Yahweh spake unto Moses, saying,

12Speak unto the children of Israel, and say unto them, If any man's wife go aside, and commit a trespass against him,

13and a man lie with her carnally, and it be hid from the eyes of her husband, and be kept close, and she be defiled, and there be no witness against her, and she be not taken in the act;

14and the spirit of jealousy come upon him, and he be jealous of his wife, and she be defiled: or if the spirit of jealousy come upon him, and he be jealous of his wife, and she be not defiled:

15then shall the man bring his wife unto the priest, and shall bring her oblation for her, the tenth part of an ephah of barley meal; he shall pour no oil upon it, nor put frankincense thereon; for it is a meal-offering of jealousy, a meal-offering of memorial, bringing iniquity to remembrance.

16And the priest shall bring her near, and set her before Yahweh:

17and the priest shall take holy water in an earthen vessel; and of the dust that is on the floor of the tabernacle the priest shall take, and put it into the water.

18And the priest shall set the woman before Yahweh, and let the hair of the woman's head go loose, and put the meal-offering of memorial in her hands, which is the meal-offering of jealousy: and the priest shall have in his hand the water of bitterness that causeth the curse.

19And the priest shall cause her to swear, and shall say unto the woman, If no man have lain with thee, and if thou have not gone aside to uncleanness, being under thy husband, be thou free from this water of bitterness that causeth the curse.

20But if thou have gone aside, being under thy husband, and if thou be defiled, and some man have lain with thee besides thy husband;

21then the priest shall cause the woman to swear with the oath of cursing, and the priest shall say unto the woman, Yahweh make thee a curse and an oath among thy people, when Yahweh doth make thy thigh to fall away, and thy body to swell;

22and this water that causeth the curse shall go into thy bowels, and make thy body to swell, and thy thigh to fall away. And the woman shall say, Amen, Amen.

23And the priest shall write these curses in a book, and he shall blot them out into the water of bitterness:

24and he shall make the woman drink the water of bitterness that causeth the curse; and the water that causeth the curse shall enter into her and become bitter.

25And the priest shall take the meal-offering of jealousy out of the woman's hand, and shall wave the meal-offering before Yahweh, and bring it unto the altar:

26and the priest shall take a handful of the meal-offering, as the memorial thereof, and burn it upon the altar, and afterward shall make the woman drink the water.

27And when he hath made her drink the water, then it shall come to pass, if she be defiled, and have committed a trespass against her husband, that the water that causeth the curse shall enter into her and become bitter, and her body shall swell, and her thigh shall fall away: and the woman shall be a curse among her people.

28And if the woman be not defiled, but be clean; then she shall be free, and shall conceive seed.

29This is the law of jealousy, when a wife, being under her husband, goeth aside, and is defiled;

30or when the spirit of jealousy cometh upon a man, and he is jealous of his wife; then shall he set the woman before Yahweh, and the priest shall execute upon her all this law.

31And the man shall be free from iniquity, and that woman shall bear her iniquity.

Chapter 6

1And Yahweh spake unto Moses, saying,

2Speak unto the children of Israel, and say unto them, When either man or woman shall make a special vow, the vow of a Nazirite, to separate himself unto Yahweh,

3he shall separate himself from wine and strong drink; he shall drink no vinegar of wine, or vinegar of strong drink, neither shall he drink any juice of grapes, nor eat fresh grapes or dried.

4All the days of his separation shall he eat nothing that is made of the grape-vine, from the kernels even to the husk.

5All the days of his vow of separation there shall no razor come upon his head: until the days be fulfilled, in which he separateth himself unto Yahweh, he shall be holy; he shall let the locks of the hair of his head grow long.

6All the days that he separateth himself unto Yahweh he shall not come near to a dead body.

7He shall not make himself unclean for his father, or for his mother, for his brother, or for his sister, when they die; because his separation unto God is upon his head.

8All the days of his separation he is holy unto Yahweh.

9And if any man die very suddenly beside him, and he defile the head of his separation; then he shall shave his head in the day of his cleansing, on the seventh day shall he shave it.

10And on the eighth day he shall bring two turtle-doves, or two young pigeons, to the priest, to the door of the tent of meeting:

11and the priest shall offer one for a sin-offering, and the other for a burnt-offering, and make atonement for him, for that he sinned by reason of the dead, and shall hallow his head that same day.

12And he shall separate unto Yahweh the days of his separation, and shall bring a he-lamb a year old for a trespass-offering; but the former days shall be void, because his separation was defiled.

13And this is the law of the Nazirite, when the days of his separation are fulfilled: he shall be brought unto the door of the tent of meeting:

14and he shall offer his oblation unto Yahweh, one he-lamb a year old without blemish for a burnt-offering, and one ewe-lamb a year old without blemish for a sin-offering, and one ram without blemish for peace-offerings,

15and a basket of unleavened bread, cakes of fine flour mingled with oil, and unleavened wafers anointed with oil, and their meal-offering, and their drink-offerings.

16And the priest shall present them before Yahweh, and shall offer his sin-offering, and his burnt-offering:

17and he shall offer the ram for a sacrifice of peace-offerings unto Yahweh, with the basket of unleavened bread: the priest shall offer also the meal-offering thereof, and the drink-offering thereof.

18And the Nazirite shall shave the head of his separation at the door of the tent of meeting, and shall take the hair of the head of his separation, and put it on the fire which is under the sacrifice of peace-offerings:

19And the priest shall take the boiled shoulder of the ram, and one unleavened cake out of the basket, and one unleavened wafer, and shall put them upon the hands of the Nazirite, after he hath shaven the head of his separation;

20and the priest shall wave them for a wave-offering before Yahweh; this is holy for the priest, together with the wave-breast and heave-thigh: and after that the Nazirite may drink wine.

21This is the law of the Nazirite who voweth, and of his oblation unto Yahweh for his separation, besides that which he is able to get: according to his vow which he voweth, so he must do after the law of his separation.

22And Yahweh spake unto Moses, saying,

23Speak unto Aaron and unto his sons, saying, On this wise ye shall bless the children of Israel: ye shall say unto them,

24Yahweh bless thee, and keep thee:

25Yahweh make his face to shine upon thee, and be gracious unto thee:

26Yahweh lift up his countenance upon thee, and give thee peace.

27So shall they put my name upon the children of Israel; and I will bless them.

Chapter 7

1And it came to pass on the day that Moses had made an end of setting up the tabernacle, and had anointed it and sanctified it, and all the furniture thereof, and the altar and all the vessels thereof, and had anointed them and sanctified them;

2that the princes of Israel, the heads of their fathers' houses, offered. These were the princes of the tribes, these are they that were over them that were numbered:

3and they brought their oblation before Yahweh, six covered wagons, and twelve oxen; a wagon for every two of the princes, and for each one an ox: and they presented them before the tabernacle.

4And Yahweh spake unto Moses, saying,

5Take it of them, that they may be used in doing the service of the tent of meeting; and thou shalt give them unto the Levites, to every man according to his service.

6And Moses took the wagons and the oxen, and gave them unto the Levites.

7Two wagons and four oxen he gave unto the sons of Gershon, according to their service:

8and four wagons and eight oxen he gave unto the sons of Merari, according unto their service, under the hand of Ithamar the son of Aaron the priest.

9But unto the sons of Kohath he gave none, because the service of the sanctuary belonged unto them; they bare it upon their shoulders.

10And the princes offered for the dedication of the altar in the day that it was anointed, even the princes offered their oblation before the altar.

11And Yahweh said unto Moses, They shall offer their oblation, each prince on his day, for the dedication of the altar.

12And he that offered his oblation the first day was Nahshon the son of Amminadab, of the tribe of Judah:

13and his oblation was one silver platter, the weight whereof was a hundred and thirty shekels, one silver bowl of seventy shekels, after the shekel of the sanctuary; both of them full of fine flour mingled with oil for a meal-offering;

14one golden spoon of ten shekels, full of incense;

15one young bullock, one ram, one he-lamb a year old, for a burnt-offering;

16one male of the goats for a sin-offering;

17and for the sacrifice of peace-offerings, two oxen, five rams, five he-goats, five he-lambs a year old: this was the oblation of Nahshon the son of Amminadab.

18On the second day Nethanel the son of Zuar, prince of Issachar, did offer:

19he offered for his oblation one silver platter, the weight whereof was a hundred and thirty shekels, one silver bowl of seventy shekels, after the shekel of the sanctuary; both of them full of fine flour mingled with oil for a meal-offering;

20one golden spoon of ten shekels, full of incense;

21one young bullock, one ram, one he-lamb a year old, for a burnt-offering;

22one male of the goats for a sin-offering;

23and for the sacrifice of peace-offerings, two oxen, five rams, five he-goats, five he-lambs a year old: this was the oblation of Nethanel the son of Zuar.

24On the third day Eliab the son of Helon, prince of the children of Zebulun.:

25his oblation was one silver platter, the weight whereof was a hundred and thirty shekels, one silver bowl of seventy shekels, after the shekel of the sanctuary; both of them full of fine flour mingled with oil for a meal-offering;

26one golden spoon of ten shekels, full of incense;

27one young bullock, one ram, one he-lamb a year old, for a burnt-offering;

28one male of the goats for a sin-offering;

29and for the sacrifice of peace-offerings, two oxen, five rams, five he-goats, five he-lambs a year old: this was the oblation of Eliab the son of Helon.

30On the fourth day Elizur the son of Shedeur, prince of the children of Reuben:

31his oblation was one silver platter, the weight whereof was a hundred and thirty shekels, one silver bowl of seventy shekels, after the shekel of the sanctuary; both of them full of fine flour mingled with oil for a meal-offering;

32one golden spoon of ten shekels, full of incense;

33one young bullock, one ram, one he-lamb a year old, for a burnt-offering;

34one male of the goats for a sin-offering;

35and for the sacrifice of peace-offerings, two oxen, five rams, five he-goats, five he-lambs a year old: this was the oblation of Elizur the son of Shedeur.

36On the fifth day Shelumiel the son of Zurishaddai, prince of the children of Simeon:

37his oblation was one silver platter, the weight whereof was a hundred and thirty shekels, one silver bowl of seventy shekels, after the shekel of the sanctuary; both of them full of fine flour mingled with oil for a meal-offering;

38one golden spoon of ten shekels, full of incense;

39one young bullock, one ram, one he-lamb a year old, for a burnt-offering;

40one male of the goats for a sin-offering;

41and for the sacrifice of peace-offerings, two oxen, five rams, five he-goats, five he-lambs a year old: this was the oblation of Shelumiel the son of Zurishaddai.

42On the sixth day Eliasaph the son of Deuel, prince of the children of Gad:

43his oblation was one silver platter, the weight whereof was a hundred and thirty shekels, one silver bowl of seventy shekels, after the shekel of the sanctuary; both of them full of fine flour mingled with oil for a meal-offering;

44one golden spoon of ten shekels, full of incense;

45one young bullock, one ram, one he-lamb a year old, for a burnt-offering;

46one male of the goats for a sin-offering;

47and for the sacrifice of peace-offerings, two oxen, five rams, five he-goats, five he-lambs a year old: this was the oblation of Eliasaph the son of Deuel.

48On the seventh day Elishama the son of Ammihud, prince of the children of Ephraim:

49his oblation was one silver platter, the weight whereof was a hundred and thirty shekels, one silver bowl of seventy shekels, after the shekel of the sanctuary; both of them full of fine flour mingled with oil for a meal-offering;

50one golden spoon of ten shekels, full of incense;

51one young bullock, one ram, one he-lamb a year old, for a burnt-offering;

52one male of the goats for a sin-offering;

53and for the sacrifice of peace-offerings, two oxen, five rams, five he-goats, five he-lambs a year old: this was the oblation of Elishama the son of Ammihud.

54On the eighth day Gamaliel the son of Pedahzur, prince of the children of Manasseh:

55his oblation was one silver platter, the weight whereof was a hundred and thirty shekels, one silver bowl of seventy shekels, after the shekel of the sanctuary; both of them full of fine flour mingled with oil for a meal-offering;

56one golden spoon of ten shekels, full of incense;

57one young bullock, one ram, one he-lamb a year old, for a burnt-offering;

58one male of the goats for a sin-offering;

59and for the sacrifice of peace-offerings, two oxen, five rams, five he-goats, five he-lambs a year old: this was the oblation of Gamaliel the son of Pedahzur.

60On the ninth day Abidan the son of Gideoni, prince of the children of Benjamin:

61his oblation was one silver platter, the weight whereof was a hundred and thirty shekels, one silver bowl of seventy shekels, after the shekel of the sanctuary; both of them full of fine flour mingled with oil for a meal-offering;

Numbers

62one golden spoon of ten shekels, full of incense;
63one young bullock, one ram, one he-lamb a year old, for a burnt-offering;
64one male of the goats for a sin-offering;
65and for the sacrifice of peace-offerings, two oxen, five rams, five he-goats, five he-lambs a year old: this was the oblation of Abidan the son of Gideoni.
66On the tenth day Ahiezer the son of Ammishaddai, prince of the children of Dan:
67his oblation was one silver platter, the weight whereof was a hundred and thirty shekels, one silver bowl of seventy shekels, after the shekel of the sanctuary; both of them full of fine flour mingled with oil for a meal-offering;
68one golden spoon of ten shekels, full of incense;
69one young bullock, one ram, one he-lamb a year old, for a burnt-offering;
70one male of the goats for a sin-offering;
71and for the sacrifice of peace-offerings, two oxen, five rams, five he-goats, five he-lambs a year old: this was the oblation of Ahiezer the son of Ammishaddai.
72On the eleventh day Pagiel the son of Ochran, prince of the children of Asher:
73his oblation was one silver platter, the weight whereof was a hundred and thirty shekels, one silver bowl of seventy shekels, after the shekel of the sanctuary; both of them full of fine flour mingled with oil for a meal-offering;
74one golden spoon of ten shekels, full of incense;
75one young bullock, one ram, one he-lamb a year old, for a burnt-offering;
76one male of the goats for a sin-offering;
77and for the sacrifice of peace-offerings, two oxen, five rams, five he-goats, five he-lambs a year old: this was the oblation of Pagiel the son of Ochran.
78On the twelfth day Ahira the son of Enan, prince of the children of Naphtali:
79his oblation was one silver platter, the weight whereof was a hundred a thirty shekels, one silver bowl of seventy shekels, after the shekel of the sanctuary; both of them full of fine flour mingled with oil for a meal-offering;
80one golden spoon of ten shekels, full of incense;
81one young bullock, one ram, one he-lamb a year old, for a burnt-offering;
82one male of the goats for a sin-offering;
83and for the sacrifice of peace-offerings, two oxen, five rams, five he-goats, five he-lambs a year old: this was the oblation of Ahira the son of Enan.
84This was the dedication of the altar, in the day when it was anointed, by the princes of Israel: twelve silver platters, twelve silver bowls, twelve golden spoons;
85each silver platter weighing a hundred and thirty shekels, and each bowl seventy; all the silver of the vessels two thousand and four hundred shekels, after the shekel of the sanctuary;
86the twelve golden spoons, full of incense, weighing ten shekels apiece, after the shekel of the sanctuary; all the gold of the spoons a hundred and twenty shekels;
87all the oxen for the burnt-offering twelve bullocks, the rams twelve, the he-lambs a year old twelve, and their meal-offering; and the males of the goats for a sin-offering twelve;
88and all the oxen for the sacrifice of peace-offerings twenty and four bullocks, the rams sixty, the he-goats sixty, the he-lambs a year old sixty. This was the dedication of the altar, after that it was anointed.
89And when Moses went into the tent of meeting to speak with him, then he heard the Voice speaking unto him from above the mercy-seat that was upon the ark of the testimony, from between the two cherubim: and he spake unto him.

Chapter 8

1And Yahweh spake unto Moses, saying,
2Speak unto Aaron, and say unto him, When thou lightest the lamps, the seven lamps shall give light in front of the candlestick.
3And Aaron did so; he lighted the lamps thereof so as to give light in front of the candlestick, as Yahweh commanded Moses.
4And this was the work of the candlestick, beaten work of gold; unto the base thereof, and unto the flowers thereof, it was beaten work: according unto the pattern which Yahweh had showed Moses, so he made the candlestick.
5And Yahweh spake unto Moses, saying,
6Take the Levites from among the children of Israel, and cleanse them.
7And thus shalt thou do unto them, to cleanse them: sprinkle the water of expiation upon them, and let them cause a razor to pass over all their flesh, and let them wash their clothes, and cleanse themselves.
8Then let them take a young bullock, and its meal-offering, fine flour mingled with oil; and another young bullock shalt thou take for a sin-offering.
9And thou shalt present the Levites before the tent of meeting: and thou shalt assemble the whole congregation of the children of Israel:
10and thou shalt present the Levites before Yahweh. And the children of Israel shall lay their hands upon the Levites:
11and Aaron shall offer the Levites before Yahweh for a wave-offering, on the behalf of the children of Israel, that it may be theirs to do the service of Yahweh.
12And the Levites shall lay their hands upon the heads of the bullocks: and offer thou the one for a sin-offering, and the other for a burnt-offering, unto Yahweh, to make atonement for the Levites.
13And thou shalt set the Levites before Aaron, and before his sons, and offer them for a wave-offering unto Yahweh.
14Thus shalt thou separate the Levites from among the children of Israel; and the Levites shall be mine.
15And after that shall the Levites go in to do the service of the tent of meeting: and thou shalt cleanse them, and offer them for a wave-offering.
16For they are wholly given unto me from among the children of Israel; instead of all that openeth the womb, even the first-born of all the children of Israel, have I taken them unto me.
17For all the first-born among the children of Israel are mine, both man and beast: on the day that I smote all the first-born in the land of Egypt I sanctified them for myself.
18And I have taken the Levites instead of all the first-born among the children of Israel.
19And I have given the Levites as a gift to Aaron and to his sons from among the children of Israel, to do the service of the children of Israel in the tent of meeting, and to make atonement for the children of Israel; that there be no plague among the children of Israel, when the children of Israel come nigh unto the sanctuary.
20Thus did Moses, and Aaron, and all the congregation of the children of Israel, unto the Levites: according unto all that Yahweh commanded Moses touching the Levites, so did the children of Israel unto them.
21And the Levites purified themselves from sin, and they washed their clothes: and Aaron offered them for a wave-offering before Yahweh; and Aaron made atonement for them to cleanse them.
22And after that went the Levites in to do their service in the tent of meeting before Aaron, and before his sons: as Yahweh had commanded Moses concerning the Levites, so did they unto them.
23And Yahweh spake unto Moses, saying,
24This is that which belongeth unto the Levites: from twenty and five years old and upward they shall go in to wait upon the service in the work of the tent of meeting:
25and from the age of fifty years they shall cease waiting upon the work, and shall serve no more,
26but shall minister with their brethren in the tent of meeting, to keep the charge, and shall do no service. Thus shalt thou do unto the Levites touching their charges.

Chapter 9

1And Yahweh spake unto Moses in the wilderness of Sinai, in the first month of the second year after they were come out of the land of Egypt, saying,
2Moreover let the children of Israel keep the passover in its appointed season.
3In the fourteenth day of this month, at even, ye shall keep it in its appointed season: according to all the statutes of it, and according to all the ordinances thereof, shall ye keep it.
4And Moses spake unto the children of Israel, that they should keep the passover.
5And they kept the passover in the first month, on the fourteenth day of the month, at even, in the wilderness of Sinai: according to all that Yahweh commanded Moses, so did the children of Israel.
6And there were certain men, who were unclean by reason of the dead body of a man, so that they could not keep the passover on that day: and they came before Moses and before Aaron on that day:
7and those men said unto him, We are unclean by reason of the dead body of a man: wherefore are we kept back, that we may not offer the oblation of Yahweh in its appointed season among the children of Israel?
8And Moses said unto them, Stay ye, that I may hear what Yahweh will command concerning you.
9And Yahweh spake unto Moses, saying,
10Speak unto the children of Israel, saying, If any man of you or of your generations shall be unclean by reason of a dead body, or be on a journey afar off, yet he shall keep the passover unto Yahweh.
11In the second month on the fourteenth day at even they shall keep it; they shall eat it with unleavened bread and bitter herbs:
12they shall leave none of it unto the morning, nor break a bone thereof: according to all the statute of the passover they shall keep it.
13But the man that is clean, and is not on a journey, and forbeareth to keep the passover, that soul shall be cut off from his people; because he offered not the oblation of Yahweh in its appointed season, that man shall bear his sin.
14And if a stranger shall sojourn among you, and will keep the passover unto Yahweh; according to the statute of the passover, and according to the ordinance thereof, so shall he do: ye shall have one statute, both for the sojourner, and for him that is born in the land.
15And on the day that the tabernacle was reared up the cloud covered the tabernacle, even the tent of the testimony: and at even it was upon the tabernacle as it were the appearance of fire, until morning.
16So it was alway: the cloud covered it, and the appearance of fire by night.
17And whenever the cloud was taken up from over the Tent, then after that the children of Israel journeyed: and in the place where the cloud abode, there the children of Israel encamped.
18At the commandment of Yahweh the children of Israel journeyed, and at the commandment of Yahweh they encamped: as long as the cloud abode upon the tabernacle they remained encamped.
19And when the cloud tarried upon the tabernacle many days, then the children of Israel kept the charge of Yahweh, and journeyed not.
20And sometimes the cloud was a few days upon the tabernacle; then according to the commandment of Yahweh they remained encamped, and according to the commandment of Yahweh they journeyed.
21And sometimes the cloud was from evening until morning; and when the cloud was taken up in the morning, they journeyed: or if it continued by day and by night, when the cloud was taken up, they journeyed.
22Whether it were two days, or a month, or a year, that the cloud tarried upon the tabernacle, abiding thereon, the children of Israel remained encamped, and journeyed not; but when it was taken up, they journeyed.
23At the commandment of Yahweh they encamped, and at the

commandment of Yahweh they journeyed: they kept the charge of Yahweh, at the commandment of Yahweh by Moses.

Chapter 10

1 And Yahweh spake unto Moses, saying,

2 Make thee two trumpets of silver; of beaten work shalt thou make them: and thou shalt use them for the calling of the congregation, and for the journeying of the camps.

3 And when they shall blow them, all the congregation shall gather themselves unto thee at the door of the tent of meeting.

4 And if they blow but one, then the princes, the heads of the thousands of Israel, shall gather themselves unto thee.

5 And when ye blow an alarm, the camps that lie on the east side shall take their journey.

6 And when ye blow an alarm the second time, the camps that lie on the south side shall take their journey: they shall blow an alarm for their journeys.

7 But when the assembly is to be gathered together, ye shall blow, but ye shall not sound an alarm.

8 And the sons of Aaron, the priests, shall blow the trumpets; and they shall be to you for a statute for ever throughout your generations.

9 And when ye go to war in your land against the adversary that oppresseth you, then ye shall sound an alarm with the trumpets; and ye shall be remembered before Yahweh your God, and ye shall be saved from your enemies.

10 Also in the day of your gladness, and in your set feasts, and in the beginnings of your months, ye shall blow the trumpets over your burnt-offerings, and over the sacrifices of your peace-offerings; and they shall be to you for a memorial before your God: I am Yahweh your God.

11 And it came to pass in the second year, in the second month, on the twentieth day of the month, that the cloud was taken up from over the tabernacle of the testimony.

12 And the children of Israel set forward according to their journeys out of the wilderness of Sinai; and the cloud abode in the wilderness of Paran.

13 And they first took their journey according to the commandment of Yahweh by Moses.

14 And in the first place the standard of the camp of the children of Judah set forward according to their hosts: and over his host was Nahshon the son of Amminadab.

15 And over the host of the tribe of the children of Issachar was Nethanel the son of Zuar.

16 And over the host of the tribe of the children of Zebulun was Eliab the son of Helon.

17 And the tabernacle was taken down; and the sons of Gershon and the sons of Merari, who bare the tabernacle, set forward.

18 And the standard of the camp of Reuben set forward according to their hosts: and over his host was Elizur the son of Shedeur.

19 And over the host of the tribe of the children of Simeon was Shelumiel the son of Zurishaddai.

20 And over the host of the tribe of the children of Gad was Eliasaph the son of Deuel.

21 And the Kohathites set forward, bearing the sanctuary: and the others did set up the tabernacle against their coming.

22 And the standard of the camp of the children of Ephraim set forward according to their hosts: and over his host was Elishama the son of Ammihud.

23 And over the host of the tribe of the children of Manasseh was Gamaliel the son of Pedahzur.

24 And over the host of the tribe of the children of Benjamin was Abidan the son of Gideoni.

25 And the standard of the camp of the children of Dan, which was the rearward of all the camps, set forward according to their hosts: and over his host was Ahiezer the son of Ammishaddai.

26 And over the host of the tribe of the children of Asher was Pagiel the son of Ochran.

27 And over the host of the tribe of the children of Naphtali was Ahira the son of Enan.

28 Thus were the journeyings of the children of Israel according to their hosts; and they set forward.

29 And Moses said unto Hobab, the son of Reuel the Midianite, Moses' father-in-law, We are journeying unto the place of which Yahweh said, I will give it you: come thou with us, and we will do thee good; for Yahweh hath spoken good concerning Israel.

30 And he said unto him, I will not go; but I will depart to mine own land, and to my kindred.

31 And he said, Leave us not, I pray thee; forasmuch as thou knowest how we are to encamp in the wilderness, and thou shalt be to us instead of eyes.

32 And it shall be, if thou go with us, yea, it shall be, that what good soever Yahweh shall do unto us, the same will we do unto thee.

33 And they set forward from the mount of Yahweh three days' journey; and the ark of the covenant of Yahweh went before them three days' journey, to seek out a resting-place for them.

34 And the cloud of Yahweh was over them by day, when they set forward from the camp.

35 And it came to pass, when the ark set forward, that Moses said, Rise up, O Yahweh, and let thine enemies be scattered; and let them that hate thee flee before thee.

36 And when it rested, he said, Return, O Yahweh, unto the ten thousands of the thousands of Israel.

Chapter 11

1 And the people were as murmurers, speaking evil in the ears of Yahweh: and when Yahweh heard it, his anger was kindled; and the fire of Yahweh burnt among them, and devoured in the uttermost part of the camp.

2 And the people cried unto Moses; and Moses prayed unto Yahweh, and the fire abated.

3 And the name of that place was called Taberah, because the fire of Yahweh burnt among them.

4 And the mixed multitude that was among them lusted exceedingly: and the children of Israel also wept again, and said, Who shall give us flesh to eat?

5 We remember the fish, which we did eat in Egypt for nought; the cucumbers, and the melons, and the leeks, and the onions, and the garlic:

6 but now our soul is dried away; there is nothing at all save this manna to look upon.

7 And the manna was like coriander seed, and the appearance thereof as the appearance of bdellium.

8 The people went about, and gathered it, and ground it in mills, or beat it in mortars, and boiled it in pots, and made cakes of it: and the taste of it was as the taste of fresh oil.

9 And when the dew fell upon the camp in the night, the manna fell upon it.

10 And Moses heard the people weeping throughout their families, every man at the door of his tent: and the anger of Yahweh was kindled greatly; and Moses was displeased.

11 And Moses said unto Yahweh, Wherefore hast thou dealt ill with thy servant? and wherefore have I not found favor in thy sight, that thou layest the burden of all this people upon me?

12 Have I conceived all this people? have I brought them forth, that thou shouldest say unto me, Carry them in thy bosom, as a nursing-father carrieth the sucking child, unto the land which thou swarest unto their fathers?

13 Whence should I have flesh to give unto all this people? for they weep unto me, saying, Give us flesh, that we may eat.

14 I am not able to bear all this people alone, because it is too heavy for me.

15 And if thou deal thus with me, kill me, I pray thee, out of hand, if I have found favor in thy sight; and let me not see my wretchedness.

16 And Yahweh said unto Moses, Gather unto me seventy men of the elders of Israel, whom thou knowest to be the elders of the people, and officers over them; and bring them unto the tent of meeting, that they may stand there with thee.

17 And I will come down and talk with thee there: and I will take of the Spirit which is upon thee, and will put it upon them; and they shall bear the burden of the people with thee, that thou bear it not thyself alone.

18 And say thou unto the people, Sanctify yourselves against to-morrow, and ye shall eat flesh; for ye have wept in the ears of Yahweh, saying, Who shall give us flesh to eat? for it was well with us in Egypt: therefore Yahweh will give you flesh, and ye shall eat.

19 Ye shall not eat one day, nor two days, nor five days, neither ten days, nor twenty days,

20 but a whole month, until it come out at your nostrils, and it be loathsome unto you; because that ye have rejected Yahweh who is among you, and have wept before him, saying, Why came we forth out of Egypt?

21 And Moses said, The people, among whom I am, are six hundred thousand footmen; and thou hast said, I will give them flesh, that they may eat a whole month.

22 Shall flocks and herds be slain for them, to suffice them? or shall all the fish of the sea be gathered together for them, to suffice them?

23 And Yahweh said unto Moses, Is Yahweh's hand waxed short? now shalt thou see whether my word shall come to pass unto thee or not.

24 And Moses went out, and told the people the words of Yahweh: and he gathered seventy men of the elders of the people, and set them round about the Tent.

25 And Yahweh came down in the cloud, and spake unto him, and took of the Spirit that was upon him, and put it upon the seventy elders: and it came to pass, that, when the Spirit rested upon them, they prophesied, but they did so no more.

26 But there remained two men in the camp, the name of the one was Eldad, and the name of the other Medad: and the Spirit rested upon them; and they were of them that were written, but had not gone out unto the Tent; and they prophesied in the camp.

27 And there ran a young man, and told Moses, and said, Eldad and Medad do prophesy in the camp.

28 And Joshua the son of Nun, the minister of Moses, one of his chosen men, answered and said, My lord Moses, forbid them.

29 And Moses said unto him, Art thou jealous for my sake? would that all Yahweh's people were prophets, that Yahweh would put his Spirit upon them!

30 And Moses gat him into the camp, he and the elders of Israel.

31 And there went forth a wind from Yahweh, and brought quails from the sea, and let them fall by the camp, about a day's journey on this side, and a day's journey on the other side, round about the camp, and about two cubits above the face of the earth.

32 And the people rose up all that day, and all the night, and all the next day, and gathered the quails: he that gathered least gathered ten homers: and they spread them all abroad for themselves round about the camp.

33 While the flesh was yet between their teeth, ere it was chewed, the anger of Yahweh was kindled against the people, and Yahweh smote the people with a very great plague.

34 And the name of that place was called Kibrothhattaavah, because there they buried the people that lusted.

35 From Kibrothhattaavah the people journeyed unto Hazeroth; and they abode at Hazeroth.

Numbers
Chapter 12
1And Miriam and Aaron spake against Moses because of the Cushite woman whom he had married; for he had married a Cushite woman.

2And they said, Hath Yahweh indeed spoken only with Moses? hath he not spoken also with us? And Yahweh heard it.

3Now the man Moses was very meek, above all the men that were upon the face of the earth.

4And Yahweh spake suddenly unto Moses, and unto Aaron, and unto Miriam, Come out ye three unto the tent of meeting. And they three came out.

5And Yahweh came down in a pillar of cloud, and stood at the door of the Tent, and called Aaron and Miriam; and they both came forth.

6And he said, Hear now my words: if there be a prophet among you, I Yahweh will make myself known unto him in a vision, I will speak with him in a dream.

7My servant Moses is not so; he is faithful in all my house:

8with him will I speak mouth to mouth, even manifestly, and not in dark speeches; and the form of Yahweh shall he behold: wherefore then were ye not afraid to speak against my servant, against Moses?

9And the anger of Yahweh was kindled against them; and he departed.

10And the cloud removed from over the Tent; and, behold, Miriam was leprous, as white as snow: and Aaron looked upon Miriam, and, behold, she was leprous.

11And Aaron said unto Moses, Oh, my lord, lay not, I pray thee, sin upon us, for that we have done foolishly, and for that we have sinned.

12Let her not, I pray, be as one dead, of whom the flesh is half consumed when he cometh out of his mother's womb.

13And Moses cried unto Yahweh, saying, Heal her, O God, I beseech thee.

14And Yahweh said unto Moses, If her father had but spit in her face, should she not be ashamed seven days? let her be shut up without the camp seven days, and after that she shall be brought in again.

15And Miriam was shut up without the camp seven days: and the people journeyed not till Miriam was brought in again.

16And afterward the people journeyed from Hazeroth, and encamped in the wilderness of Paran.

Chapter 13
1And Yahweh spake unto Moses, saying,

2Send thou men, that they may spy out the land of Canaan, which I give unto the children of Israel: of every tribe of their fathers shall ye send a man, every one a prince among them.

3And Moses sent them from the wilderness of Paran according to the commandment of Yahweh: all of them men who were heads of the children of Israel.

4And these were their names: Of the tribe of Reuben, Shammua the son of Zaccur.

5Of the tribe of Simeon, Shaphat the son of Hori.

6Of the tribe of Judah, Caleb the son of Jephunneh.

7Of the tribe of Issachar, Igal the son of Joseph.

8Of the tribe of Ephraim, Hoshea the son of Nun.

9Of the tribe of Benjamin, Palti the son of Raphu.

10Of the tribe of Zebulun, Gaddiel the son of Sodi.

11Of the tribe of Joseph, namely, of the tribe of Manasseh, Gaddi the son of Susi.

12Of the tribe of Dan, Ammiel the son of Gemalli.

13Of the tribe of Asher, Sethur the son of Michael.

14Of the tribe of Naphtali, Nahbi the son of Vophsi.

15Of the tribe of Gad, Geuel the son of Machi.

16These are the names of the men that Moses sent to spy out the land. And Moses called Hoshea the son of Nun Joshua.

17And Moses sent them to spy out the land of Canaan, and said unto them, Get you up this way by the South, and go up into the hill-country:

18and see the land, what it is; and the people that dwell therein, whether they are strong or weak, whether they are few or many;

19and what the land is that they dwell in, whether it is good or bad; and what cities they are that they dwell in, whether in camps, or in strongholds;

20and what the land is, whether it is fat or lean, whether there is wood therein, or not. And be ye of good courage, and bring of the fruit of the land. Now the time was the time of the first-ripe grapes.

21So they went up, and spied out the land from the wilderness of Zin unto Rehob, to the entrance of Hamath.

22And they went up by the South, and came unto Hebron; and Ahiman, Sheshai, and Talmai, the children of Anak, were there. (Now Hebron was built seven years before Zoan in Egypt.)

23And they came unto the valley of Eshcol, and cut down from thence a branch with one cluster of grapes, and they bare it upon a staff between two; they brought also of the pomegranates, and of the figs.

24That place was called the valley of Eshcol, because of the cluster which the children of Israel cut down from thence.

25And they returned from spying out the land at the end of forty days.

26And they went and came to Moses, and to Aaron, and to all the congregation of the children of Israel, unto the wilderness of Paran, to Kadesh; and brought back word unto them, and unto all the congregation, and showed them the fruit of the land.

27And they told him, and said, We came unto the land whither thou sentest us; and surely it floweth with milk and honey; and this is the fruit of it.

28Howbeit the people that dwell in the land are strong, and the cities are fortified, and very great: and moreover we saw the children of Anak there.

29Amalek dwelleth in the land of the South: and the Hittite, and the Jebusite, and the Amorite, dwell in the hill-country; and the Canaanite dwelleth by the sea, and along by the side of the Jordan.

30And Caleb stilled the people before Moses, and said, Let us go up at once, and possess it; for we are well able to overcome it.

31But the men that went up with him said, We are not able to go up against the people; for they are stronger than we.

32And they brought up an evil report of the land which they had spied out unto the children of Israel, saying, The land, through which we have gone to spy it out, is a land that eateth up the inhabitants thereof; and all the people that we saw in it are men of great stature.

33And there we saw the Nephilim, the sons of Anak, who come of the Nephilim: and we were in our own sight as grasshoppers, and so we were in their sight.

Chapter 14
1And all the congregation lifted up their voice, and cried; and the people wept that night.

2And all the children of Israel murmured against Moses and against Aaron: and the whole congregation said unto them, Would that we had died in the land of Egypt! or would that we had died in this wilderness!

3And wherefore doth Yahweh bring us unto this land, to fall by the sword? Our wives and our little ones will be a prey: were it not better for us to return into Egypt?

4And they said one to another, Let us make a captain, and let us return into Egypt.

5Then Moses and Aaron fell on their faces before all the assembly of the congregation of the children of Israel.

6And Joshua the son of Nun and Caleb the son of Jephunneh, who were of them that spied out the land, rent their clothes:

7and they spake unto all the congregation of the children of Israel, saying, The land, which we passed through to spy it out, is an exceeding good land.

8If Yahweh delight in us, then he will bring us into this land, and give it unto us; a land which floweth with milk and honey.

9Only rebel not against Yahweh, neither fear ye the people of the land; for they are bread for us: their defence is removed from over them, and Yahweh is with us: fear them not.

10But all the congregation bade stone them with stones. And the glory of Yahweh appeared in the tent of meeting unto all the children of Israel.

11And Yahweh said unto Moses, How long will this people despise me? and how long will they not believe in me, for all the signs which I have wrought among them?

12I will smite them with the pestilence, and disinherit them, and will make of thee a nation greater and mightier than they.

13And Moses said unto Yahweh, Then the Egyptians will hear it; for thou broughtest up this people in thy might from among them;

14and they will tell it to the inhabitants of this land. They have heard that thou Yahweh art in the midst of this people; for thou Yahweh art seen face to face, and thy cloud standeth over them, and thou goest before them, in a pillar of cloud by day, and in a pillar of fire by night.

15Now if thou shalt kill this people as one man, then the nations which have heard the fame of thee will speak, saying,

16Because Yahweh was not able to bring this people into the land which he sware unto them, therefore he hath slain them in the wilderness.

17And now, I pray thee, let the power of the Lord be great, according as thou hast spoken, saying,

18Yahweh is slow to anger, and abundant in lovingkindness, forgiving iniquity and transgression; and that will by no means clear the guilty, visiting the iniquity of the fathers upon the children, upon the third and upon the fourth generation.

19Pardon, I pray thee, the iniquity of this people according unto the greatness of thy lovingkindness, and according as thou hast forgiven this people, from Egypt even until now.

20And Yahweh said, I have pardoned according to thy word:

21but in very deed, as I live, and as all the earth shall be filled with the glory of Yahweh;

22because all those men that have seen my glory, and my signs, which I wrought in Egypt and in the wilderness, yet have tempted me these ten times, and have not hearkened to my voice;

23surely they shall not see the land which I sware unto their fathers, neither shall any of them that despised me see it:

24but my servant Caleb, because he had another spirit with him, and hath followed me fully, him will I bring into the land whereinto he went; and his seed shall possess it.

25Now the Amalekite and the Canaanite dwell in the valley: to-morrow turn ye, and get you into the wilderness by the way to the Red Sea.

26And Yahweh spake unto Moses and unto Aaron, saying,

27How long shall I bear with this evil congregation, that murmur against me? I have heard the murmurings of the children of Israel, which they murmur against me.

28Say unto them, As I live, saith Yahweh, surely as ye have spoken in mine ears, so will I do to you:

29your dead bodies shall fall in this wilderness, and all that were numbered of you, according to your whole number, from twenty years old and upward, that have murmured against me,

30surely ye shall not come into the land, concerning which I sware that I would make you dwell therein, save Caleb the son of Jephunneh, and Joshua the son of Nun.

31But your little ones, that ye said should be a prey, them will I bring in, and they shall know the land which ye have rejected.

32But as for you, your dead bodies shall fall in this wilderness.

33And your children shall be wanderers in the wilderness forty years, and shall bear your whoredoms, until your dead bodies be consumed in the wilderness.

34After the number of the days in which ye spied out the land, even forty days, for every day a year, shall ye bear your iniquities, even forty years, and ye shall know my alienation.

35I, Yahweh, have spoken, surely this will I do unto all this evil congregation, that are gathered together against me: in this wilderness they shall be consumed, and there they shall die.

36And the men, whom Moses sent to spy out the land, who returned, and made all the congregation to murmur against him, by bringing up an evil report against the land,

37even those men that did bring up an evil report of the land, died by the plague before Yahweh.

38But Joshua the son of Nun, and Caleb the son of Jephunneh, remained alive of those men that went to spy out the land.

39And Moses told these words unto all the children of Israel: and the people mourned greatly.

40And they rose up early in the morning, and gat them up to the top of the mountain, saying, Lo, we are here, and will go up unto the place which Yahweh hath promised: for we have sinned.

41And Moses said, Wherefore now do ye transgress the commandment of Yahweh, seeing it shall not prosper?

42Go not up, for Yahweh is not among you; that ye be not smitten down before your enemies.

43For there the Amalekite and the Canaanite are before you, and ye shall fall by the sword: because ye are turned back from following Yahweh, therefore Yahweh will not be with you.

44But they presumed to go up to the top of the mountain: nevertheless the ark of the covenant of Yahweh, and Moses, departed not out of the camp.

45Then the Amalekite came down, and the Canaanite who dwelt in that mountain, and smote them and beat them down, even unto Hormah.

Chapter 15

1And Yahweh spake unto Moses, saying,

2Speak unto the children of Israel, and say unto them, When ye are come into the land of your habitations, which I give unto you,

3and will make an offering by fire unto Yahweh, a burnt-offering, or a sacrifice, to accomplish a vow, or as a freewill-offering, or in your set feasts, to make a sweet savor unto Yahweh, of the herd, or of the flock;

4then shall he that offereth his oblation offer unto Yahweh a meal-offering of a tenth part of an ephah of fine flour mingled with the fourth part of a hin of oil:

5and wine for the drink-offering, the fourth part of a hin, shalt thou prepare with the burnt-offering, or for the sacrifice, for each lamb.

6Or for a ram, thou shalt prepare for a meal-offering two tenth parts of an ephah of fine flour mingled with the third part of a hin of oil:

7and for the drink-offering thou shalt offer the third part of a hin of wine, of a sweet savor unto Yahweh.

8And when thou preparest a bullock for a burnt-offering, or for a sacrifice, to accomplish a vow, or for peace-offerings unto Yahweh;

9then shall he offer with the bullock a meal-offering of three tenth parts of an ephah of fine flour mingled with half a hin of oil:

10and thou shalt offer for the drink-offering half a hin of wine, for an offering made by fire, of a sweet savor unto Yahweh.

11Thus shall it be done for each bullock, or for each ram, or for each of the he-lambs, or of the kids.

12According to the number that ye shall prepare, so shall ye do to every one according to their number.

13All that are home-born shall do these things after this manner, in offering an offering made by fire, of a sweet savor unto Yahweh.

14And if a stranger sojourn with you, or whosoever may be among you throughout your generations, and will offer an offering made by fire, of a sweet savor unto Yahweh; as ye do, so he shall do.

15For the assembly, there shall be one statute for you, and for the stranger that sojourneth with you, a statute for ever throughout your generations: as ye are, so shall the sojourner be before Yahweh.

16One law and one ordinance shall be for you, and for the stranger that sojourneth with you.

17And Yahweh spake unto Moses, saying,

18Speak unto the children of Israel, and say unto them, When ye come into the land whither I bring you,

19then it shall be, that, when ye eat of the bread of the land, ye shall offer up a heave-offering unto Yahweh.

20Of the first of your dough ye shall offer up a cake for a heave-offering: as the heave-offering of the threshing-floor, so shall ye heave it.

21Of the first of your dough ye shall give unto Yahweh a heave-offering throughout your generations.

22And when ye shall err, and not observe all these commandments, which Yahweh hath spoken unto Moses,

23even all that Yahweh hath commanded you by Moses, from the day that Yahweh gave commandment, and onward throughout your generations;

24then it shall be, if it be done unwittingly, without the knowledge of the congregation, that all the congregation shall offer one young bullock for a burnt-offering, for a sweet savor unto Yahweh, with the meal-offering thereof, and the drink-offering thereof, according to the ordinance, and one he-goat for a sin-offering.

25And the priest shall make atonement for all the congregation of the children of Israel, and they shall be forgiven; for it was an error, and they have brought their oblation, an offering made by fire unto Yahweh, and their sin-offering before Yahweh, for their error:

26and all the congregation of the children of Israel shall be forgiven, and the stranger that sojourneth among them; for in respect of all the people it was done unwittingly.

27And if one person sin unwittingly, then he shall offer a she-goat a year old for a sin-offering.

28And the priest shall make atonement for the soul that erreth, when he sinneth unwittingly, before Yahweh, to make atonement for him; and he shall be forgiven.

29Ye shall have one law for him that doeth aught unwittingly, for him that is home-born among the children of Israel, and for the stranger that sojourneth among them.

30But the soul that doeth aught with a high hand, whether he be home-born or a sojourner, the same blasphemeth Yahweh; and that soul shall be cut off from among his people.

31Because he hath despised the word of Yahweh, and hath broken his commandment, that soul shall utterly be cut off; his iniquity shall be upon him.

32And while the children of Israel were in the wilderness, they found a man gathering sticks upon the sabbath day.

33And they that found him gathering sticks brought him unto Moses and Aaron, and unto all the congregation.

34And they put him in ward, because it had not been declared what should be done to him.

35And Yahweh said unto Moses, The man shall surely be put to death: all the congregation shall stone him with stones without the camp.

36And all the congregation brought him without the camp, and stoned him to death with stones; as Yahweh commanded Moses.

37And Yahweh spake unto Moses, saying,

38Speak unto the children of Israel, and bid them that they make them fringes in the borders of their garments throughout their generations, and that they put upon the fringe of each border a cord of blue:

39and it shall be unto you for a fringe, that ye may look upon it, and remember all the commandments of Yahweh, and do them; and that ye follow not after your own heart and your own eyes, after which ye use to play the harlot;

40that ye may remember and do all my commandments, and be holy unto your God.

41I am Yahweh your God, who brought you out of the land of Egypt, to be your God: I am Yahweh your God.

Chapter 16

1Now Korah, the son of Izhar, the son of Kohath, the son of Levi, with Dathan and Abiram, the sons of Eliab, and On, the son of Peleth, sons of Reuben, took men:

2and they rose up before Moses, with certain of the children of Israel, two hundred and fifty princes of the congregation, called to the assembly, men of renown;

3and they assembled themselves together against Moses and against Aaron, and said unto them, Ye take too much upon you, seeing all the congregation are holy, every one of them, and Yahweh is among them: wherefore then lift ye up yourselves above the assembly of Yahweh?

4And when Moses heard it, he fell upon his face:

5and he spake unto Korah and unto all his company, saying, In the morning Yahweh will show who are his, and who is holy, and will cause him to come near unto him: even him whom he shall choose will he cause to come near unto him.

6This do: take you censers, Korah, and all his company;

7and put fire in them, and put incense upon them before Yahweh to-morrow: and it shall be that the man whom Yahweh doth choose, he shall be holy: ye take too much upon you, ye sons of Levi.

8And Moses said unto Korah, Hear now, ye sons of Levi:

9seemeth it but a small thing unto you, that the God of Israel hath separated you from the congregation of Israel, to bring you near to himself, to do the service of the tabernacle of Yahweh, and to stand before the congregation to minister unto them;

10and that he hath brought thee near, and all thy brethren the sons of Levi with thee? and seek ye the priesthood also?

11Therefore thou and all thy company are gathered together against Yahweh: and Aaron, what is he that ye murmur against him?

12And Moses sent to call Dathan and Abiram, the sons of Eliab; and they said, We will not come up:

13is it a small thing that thou hast brought us up out of a land flowing with milk and honey, to kill us in the wilderness, but thou must needs make thyself also a prince over us?

14Moreover thou hast not brought us into a land flowing with milk and honey, nor given us inheritance of fields and vineyards: wilt thou put out the eyes of these men? we will not come up.

15And Moses was very wroth, and said unto Yahweh, Respect not thou their offering: I have not taken one ass from them, neither have I hurt one of them.

16And Moses said unto Korah, Be thou and all thy company before Yahweh, thou, and they, and Aaron, to-morrow:

17and take ye every man his censer, and put incense upon them, and bring ye before Yahweh every man his censer, two hundred and fifty censers; thou also, and Aaron, each his censer.

18And they took every man his censer, and put fire in them, and laid incense thereon, and stood at the door of the tent of meeting with Moses and Aaron.

19And Korah assembled all the congregation against them unto the door of the tent of meeting: and the glory of Yahweh appeared unto all the congregation.

Numbers

20 And Yahweh spake unto Moses and unto Aaron, saying,

21 Separate yourselves from among this congregation, that I may consume them in a moment.

22 And they fell upon their faces, and said, O God, the God of the spirits of all flesh, shall one man sin, and wilt thou be wroth with all the congregation?

23 And Yahweh spake unto Moses, saying,

24 Speak unto the congregation, saying, Get you up from about the tabernacle of Korah, Dathan, and Abiram.

25 And Moses rose up and went unto Dathan and Abiram; and the elders of Israel followed him.

26 And he spake unto the congregation, saying, Depart, I pray you, from the tents of these wicked men, and touch nothing of theirs, lest ye be consumed in all their sins.

27 So they gat them up from the tabernacle of Korah, Dathan, and Abiram, on every side: and Dathan and Abiram came out, and stood at the door of their tents, and their wives, and their sons, and their little ones.

28 And Moses said, Hereby ye shall know that Yahweh hath sent me to do all these works; for I have not done them of mine own mind.

29 If these men die the common death of all men, or if they be visited after the visitation of all men; then Yahweh hath not sent me.

30 But if Yahweh make a new thing, and the ground open its mouth, and swallow them up, with all that appertain unto them, and they go down alive into Sheol; then ye shall understand that these men have despised Yahweh.

31 And it came to pass, as he made an end of speaking all these words, that the ground clave asunder that was under them;

32 and the earth opened its mouth, and swallowed them up, and their households, and all the men that appertained unto Korah, and all their goods.

33 So they, and all that appertained to them, went down alive into Sheol: and the earth closed upon them, and they perished from among the assembly.

34 And all Israel that were round about them fled at the cry of them; for they said, Lest the earth swallow us up.

35 And fire came forth from Yahweh, and devoured the two hundred and fifty men that offered the incense.

36 And Yahweh spake unto Moses, saying,

37 Speak unto Eleazar the son of Aaron the priest, that he take up the censers out of the burning, and scatter thou the fire yonder; for they are holy,

38 even the censers of these sinners against their own lives; and let them be made beaten plates for a covering of the altar: for they offered them before Yahweh; therefore they are holy; and they shall be a sign unto the children of Israel.

39 And Eleazar the priest took the brazen censers, which they that were burnt had offered; and they beat them out for a covering of the altar,

40 to be a memorial unto the children of Israel, to the end that no stranger, that is not of the seed of Aaron, come near to burn incense before Yahweh; that he be not as Korah, and as his company: as Yahweh spake unto him by Moses.

41 But on the morrow all the congregation of the children of Israel murmured against Moses and against Aaron, saying, Ye have killed the people of Yahweh.

42 And it came to pass, when the congregation was assembled against Moses and against Aaron, that they looked toward the tent of meeting: and, behold, the cloud covered it, and the glory of Yahweh appeared.

43 And Moses and Aaron came to the front of the tent of meeting.

44 And Yahweh spake unto Moses, saying,

45 Get you up from among this congregation, that I may consume them in a moment. And they fell upon their faces.

46 And Moses said unto Aaron, Take they censer, and put fire therein from off the altar, and lay incense thereon, and carry it quickly unto the congregation, and make atonement for them: for there is wrath gone out from Yahweh; the plague is begun.

47 And Aaron took as Moses spake, and ran into the midst of the assembly; and, behold, the plague was begun among the people: and he put on the incense, and made atonement for the people.

48 And he stood between the dead and the living; and the plague was stayed.

49 Now they that died by the plague were fourteen thousand and seven hundred, besides them that died about the matter of Korah.

50 And Aaron returned unto Moses unto the door of the tent of meeting: and the plague was stayed.

Chapter 17

1 And Yahweh spake unto Moses, saying,

2 Speak unto the children of Israel, and take of them rods, one for each fathers' house, of all their princes according to their fathers' houses, twelve rods: write thou every man's name upon his rod.

3 And thou shalt write Aaron's name upon the rod of Levi; for there shall be one rod for each head of their fathers' houses.

4 And thou shalt lay them up in the tent of meeting before the testimony, where I meet with you.

5 And it shall come to pass, that the rod of the man whom I shall choose shall bud: and I will make to cease from me the murmurings of the children of Israel, which they murmur against you.

6 And Moses spake unto the children of Israel; and all their princes gave him rods, for each prince one, according to their fathers' houses, even twelve rods: and the rod of Aaron was among their rods.

7 And Moses laid up the rods before Yahweh in the tent of the testimony.

8 And it came to pass on the morrow, that Moses went into the tent of the testimony; and, behold, the rod of Aaron for the house of Levi was budded, and put forth buds, and produced blossoms, and bare ripe almonds.

9 And Moses brought out all the rods from before Yahweh unto all the children of Israel: and they looked, and took every man his rod.

10 And Yahweh said unto Moses, Put back the rod of Aaron before the testimony, to be kept for a token against the children of rebellion; that thou mayest make an end of their murmurings against me, that they die not.

11 Thus did Moses: as Yahweh commanded him, so did he.

12 And the children of Israel spake unto Moses, saying, Behold, we perish, we are undone, we are all undone.

13 Every one that cometh near, that cometh near unto the tabernacle of Yahweh, dieth: shall we perish all of us?

Chapter 18

1 And Yahweh said unto Aaron, Thou and thy sons and thy fathers' house with thee shall bear the iniquity of the sanctuary; and thou and thy sons with thee shall bear the iniquity of your priesthood.

2 And thy brethren also, the tribe of Levi, the tribe of thy father, bring thou near with thee, that they may be joined unto thee, and minister unto thee: but thou and thy sons with thee shall be before the tent of the testimony.

3 And they shall keep thy charge, and the charge of all the Tent: only they shall not come nigh unto the vessels of the sanctuary and unto the altar, that they die not, neither they, nor ye.

4 And they shall be joined unto thee, and keep the charge of the tent of meeting, for all the service of the Tent: and a stranger shall not come nigh unto you.

5 And ye shall keep the charge of the sanctuary, and the charge of the altar; that there be wrath no more upon the children of Israel.

6 And I, behold, I have taken your brethren the Levites from among the children of Israel: to you they are a gift, given unto Yahweh, to do the service of the tent of meeting.

7 And thou and thy sons with thee shall keep your priesthood for everything of the altar, and for that within the veil; and ye shall serve: I give you the priesthood as a service of gift: and the stranger that cometh nigh shall be put to death.

8 And Yahweh spake unto Aaron, And I, behold, I have given thee the charge of my heave-offerings, even all the hallowed things of the children of Israel; unto thee have I given them by reason of the anointing, and to thy sons, as a portion for ever.

9 This shall be thine of the most holy things, reserved from the fire: every oblation of theirs, even every meal-offering of theirs, and every sin-offering of theirs, and every trespass-offering of theirs, which they shall render unto me, shall be most holy for thee and for thy sons.

10 As the most holy things shalt thou eat thereof; every male shall eat thereof: it shall be holy unto thee.

11 And this is thine: the heave-offering of their gift, even all the wave-offerings of the children of Israel; I have given them unto thee, and to thy sons and to thy daughters with thee, as a portion for ever; every one that is clean in thy house shall eat thereof.

12 All the best of the oil, and all the best of the vintage, and of the grain, the first-fruits of them which they give unto Yahweh, to thee have I given them.

13 The first-ripe fruits of all that is in their land, which they bring unto Yahweh, shall be thine; every one that is clean in thy house shall eat thereof.

14 Everything devoted in Israel shall be thine.

15 Everything that openeth the womb, of all flesh which they offer unto Yahweh, both of man and beast shall be thine: nevertheless the first-born of man shalt thou surely redeem, and the firstling of unclean beasts shalt thou redeem.

16 And those that are to be redeemed of them from a month old shalt thou redeem, according to thine estimation, for the money of five shekels, after the shekel of the sanctuary (the same is twenty gerahs).

17 But the firstling of a cow, or the firstling of a sheep, or the firstling of a goat, thou shalt not redeem; they are holy: thou shalt sprinkle their blood upon the altar, and shalt burn their fat for an offering made by fire, for a sweet savor unto Yahweh.

18 And the flesh of them shall be thine, as the wave-breast and as the right thigh, it shall be thine.

19 All the heave-offerings of the holy things, which the children of Israel offer unto Yahweh, have I given thee, and thy sons and thy daughters with thee, as a portion for ever: it is a covenant of salt for ever before Yahweh unto thee and to thy seed with thee.

20 And Yahweh said unto Aaron, Thou shalt have no inheritance in their land, neither shalt thou have any portion among them: I am thy portion and thine inheritance among the children of Israel.

21 And unto the children of Levi, behold, I have given all the tithe in Israel for an inheritance, in return for their service which they serve, even the service of the tent of meeting.

22 And henceforth the children of Israel shall not come nigh the tent of meeting, lest they bear sin, and die.

23 But the Levites shall do the service of the tent of meeting, and they shall bear their iniquity: it shall be a statute for ever throughout your generations; and among the children of Israel they shall have no inheritance.

24 For the tithe of the children of Israel, which they offer as a heave-offering unto Yahweh, I have given to the Levites for an inheritance: therefore I have said unto them, Among the children of Israel they shall have no inheritance.

25 And Yahweh spake unto Moses, saying,

26 Moreover thou shalt speak unto the Levites, and say unto them, When ye take of the children of Israel the tithe which I have given you from them for your inheritance, then ye shall offer up a heave-offering of it for Yahweh, a tithe of the tithe.

27 And your heave-offering shall be reckoned unto you, as though it were the grain of the threshing-floor, and as the fulness of the winepress.

28 Thus ye also shall offer a heave-offering unto Yahweh of all your tithes, which ye receive of the children of Israel; and thereof ye shall give Yahweh's

heave-offering to Aaron the priest.

29Out of all your gifts ye shall offer every heave-offering of Yahweh, of all the best thereof, even the hallowed part thereof out of it.

30Therefore thou shalt say unto them, When ye heave the best thereof from it, then it shall be reckoned unto the Levites as the increase of the threshing-floor, and as the increase of the wine-press.

31And ye shall eat it in every place, ye and your households: for it is your reward in return for your service in the tent of meeting.

32And ye shall bear no sin by reason of it, when ye have heaved from it the best thereof: and ye shall not profane the holy things of the children of Israel, that ye die not.

Chapter 19

1And Yahweh spake unto Moses and unto Aaron, saying,

2This is the statute of the law which Yahweh hath commanded, saying, Speak unto the children of Israel, that they bring thee a red heifer without spot, wherein is no blemish, and upon which never came yoke.

3And ye shall give her unto Eleazar the priest, and he shall bring her forth without the camp, and one shall slay her before his face:

4and Eleazar the priest shall take of her blood with his finger, and sprinkle her blood toward the front of the tent of meeting seven times.

5And one shall burn the heifer in his sight; her skin, and her flesh, and her blood, with her dung, shall he burn:

6and the priest shall take cedar-wood, and hyssop, and scarlet, and cast it into the midst of the burning of the heifer.

7Then the priest shall wash his clothes, and he shall bathe his flesh in water, and afterward he shall come into the camp, and the priest shall be unclean until the even.

8And he that burneth her shall wash his clothes in water, and bathe his flesh in water, and shall be unclean until the even.

9And a man that is clean shall gather up the ashes of the heifer, and lay them up without the camp in a clean place; and it shall be kept for the congregation of the children of Israel for a water for impurity: it is a sin-offering.

10And he that gathereth the ashes of the heifer shall wash his clothes, and be unclean until the even: and it shall be unto the children of Israel, and unto the stranger that sojourneth among them, for a statute for ever.

11He that toucheth the dead body of any man shall be unclean seven days:

12the same shall purify himself therewith on the third day, and on the seventh day he shall be clean: but if he purify not himself the third day, then the seventh day he shall not be clean.

13Whosoever toucheth a dead person, the body of a man that hath died, and purifieth not himself, defileth the tabernacle of Yahweh; and that soul shall be cut off from Israel: because the water for impurity was not sprinkled upon him, he shall be unclean; his uncleanness is yet upon him.

14This is the law when a man dieth in a tent: every one that cometh into the tent, and every one that is in the tent, shall be unclean seven days.

15And every open vessel, which hath no covering bound upon it, is unclean.

16And whosoever in the open field toucheth one that is slain with a sword, or a dead body, or a bone of a man, or a grave, shall be unclean seven days.

17And for the unclean they shall take of the ashes of the burning of the sin-offering; and running water shall be put thereto in a vessel:

18and a clean person shall take hyssop, and dip it in the water, and sprinkle it upon the tent, and upon all the vessels, and upon the persons that were there, and upon him that touched the bone, or the slain, or the dead, or the grave:

19and the clean person shall sprinkle upon the unclean on the third day, and on the seventh day: and on the seventh day he shall purify him; and he shall wash his clothes, and bathe himself in water, and shall be clean at even.

20But the man that shall be unclean, and shall not purify himself, that soul shall be cut off from the midst of the assembly, because he hath defiled the sanctuary of Yahweh: the water for impurity hath not been sprinkled upon him; he is unclean.

21And it shall be a perpetual statute unto them: and he that sprinkleth the water for impurity shall wash his clothes; and he that toucheth the water for impurity shall be unclean until even.

22And whatsoever the unclean person toucheth shall be unclean; and the soul that toucheth it shall be unclean until even.

Chapter 20

1And the children of Israel, even the whole congregation, came into the wilderness of Zin in the first month: and the people abode in Kadesh; and Miriam died there, and was buried there.

2And there was no water for the congregation: and they assembled themselves together against Moses and against Aaron.

3And the people strove with Moses, and spake, saying, Would that we had died when our brethren died before Yahweh!

4And why have ye brought the assembly of Yahweh into this wilderness, that we should die there, we and our beasts?

5And wherefore have ye made us to come up out of Egypt, to bring us in unto this evil place? it is no place of seed, or of figs, or of vines, or of pomegranates; neither is there any water to drink.

6And Moses and Aaron went from the presence of the assembly unto the door of the tent of meeting, and fell upon their faces: and the glory of Yahweh appeared unto them.

7And Yahweh spake unto Moses, saying,

8Take the rod, and assemble the congregation, thou, and Aaron thy brother, and speak ye unto the rock before their eyes, that it give forth its water; and thou shalt bring forth to them water out of the rock; so thou shalt give the congregation and their cattle drink.

9And Moses took the rod from before Yahweh, as he commanded him.

10And Moses and Aaron gathered the assembly together before the rock, and he said unto them, Hear now, ye rebels; shall we bring you forth water out of this rock?

11And Moses lifted up his hand, and smote the rock with his rod twice: and water came forth abundantly, and the congregation drank, and their cattle.

12And Yahweh said unto Moses and Aaron, Because ye believed not in me, to sanctify me in the eyes of the children of Israel, therefore ye shall not bring this assembly into the land which I have given them.

13These are the waters of Meribah; because the children of Israel strove with Yahweh, and he was sanctified in them.

14And Moses sent messengers from Kadesh unto the king of Edom, Thus saith thy brother Israel, Thou knowest all the travail that hath befallen us:

15how our fathers went down into Egypt, and we dwelt in Egypt a long time; and the Egyptians dealt ill with us, and our fathers:

16and when we cried unto Yahweh, he heard our voice, and sent an angel, and brought us forth out of Egypt: and, behold, we are in Kadesh, a city in the uttermost of thy border.

17Let us pass, I pray thee, through thy land: we will not pass through field or through vineyard, neither will we drink of the water of the wells: we will go along the king's highway; we will not turn aside to the right hand nor to the left, until we have passed thy border.

18And Edom said unto him, Thou shalt not pass through me, lest I come out with the sword against thee.

19And the children of Israel said unto him, We will go up by the highway; and if we drink of thy water, I and my cattle, then will I give the price thereof: let me only, without doing anything else, pass through on my feet.

20And he said, Thou shalt not pass through. And Edom came out against him with much people, and with a strong hand.

21Thus Edom refused to give Israel passage through his border: wherefore Israel turned away from him.

22And they journeyed from Kadesh: and the children of Israel, even the whole congregation, came unto mount Hor.

23And Yahweh spake unto Moses and Aaron in mount Hor, by the border of the land of Edom, saying,

24Aaron shall be gathered unto his people; for he shall not enter into the land which I have given unto the children of Israel, because ye rebelled against my word at the waters of Meribah.

25Take Aaron and Eleazar his son, and bring them up unto mount Hor;

26and strip Aaron of his garments, and put them upon Eleazar his son: and Aaron shall be gathered unto his people, and shall die there.

27And Moses did as Yahweh commanded: and they went up into mount Hor in the sight of all the congregation.

28And Moses stripped Aaron of his garments, and put them upon Eleazar his son; and Aaron died there on the top of the mount: and Moses and Eleazar came down from the mount.

29And when all the congregation saw that Aaron was dead, they wept for Aaron thirty days, even all the house of Israel.

Chapter 21

1And the Canaanite, the king of Arad, who dwelt in the South, heard tell that Israel came by the way of Atharim; and he fought against Israel, and took some of them captive.

2And Israel vowed a vow unto Yahweh, and said, If thou wilt indeed deliver this people into my hand, then I will utterly destroy their cities.

3And Yahweh hearkened to the voice of Israel, and delivered up the Canaanites; and they utterly destroyed them and their cities: and the name of the place was called Hormah.

4And they journeyed from mount Hor by the way to the Red Sea, to compass the land of Edom: and the soul of the people was much discouraged because of the way.

5And the people spake against God, and against Moses, Wherefore have ye brought us up out of Egypt to die in the wilderness? for there is no bread, and there is no water; and our soul loatheth this light bread.

6And Yahweh sent fiery serpents among the people, and they bit the people; and much people of Israel died.

7And the people came to Moses, and said, We have sinned, because we have spoken against Yahweh, and against thee; pray unto Yahweh, that he take away the serpents from us. And Moses prayed for the people.

8And Yahweh said unto Moses, Make thee a fiery serpent, and set it upon a standard: and it shall come to pass, that every one that is bitten, when he seeth it, shall live.

9And Moses made a serpent of brass, and set it upon the standard: and it came to pass, that if a serpent had bitten any man, when he looked unto the serpent of brass, he lived.

10And the children of Israel journeyed, and encamped in Oboth.

11And they journeyed from Oboth, and encamped at Iyeabarim, in the wilderness which is before Moab, toward the sunrising.

12From thence they journeyed, and encamped in the valley of Zered.

13From thence they journeyed, and encamped on the other side of the Arnon, which is in the wilderness, that cometh out of the border of the Amorites: for the Arnon is the border of Moab, between Moab and the Amorites.

14Wherefore it is said in the book of the Wars of Yahweh,
Vaheb in Suphah,
And the valleys of the Arnon,
15And the slope of the valleys
That inclineth toward the dwelling of Ar,
And leaneth upon the border of Moab.

16And from thence they journeyed to Beer: that is the well whereof Yahweh

Numbers

said unto Moses, Gather the people together, and I will give them water.

17Then sang Israel this song:
Spring up, O well; sing ye unto it:
18The well, which the princes digged,
Which the nobles of the people delved,
With the sceptre, and with their staves.
And from the wilderness they journeyed to Mattanah;
19and from Mattanah to Nahaliel; and from Nahaliel to Bamoth;
20and from Bamoth to the valley that is in the field of Moab, to the top of Pisgah, which looketh down upon the desert.

21And Israel sent messengers unto Sihon king of the Amorites, saying,
22Let me pass through thy land: we will not turn aside into field, or into vineyard; we will not drink of the water of the wells: we will go by the king's highway, until we have passed thy border.
23And Sihon would not suffer Israel to pass through his border: but Sihon gathered all his people together, and went out against Israel into the wilderness, and came to Jahaz; and he fought against Israel.
24And Israel smote him with the edge of the sword, and possessed his land from the Arnon unto the Jabbok, even unto the children of Ammon; for the border of the children of Ammon was strong.
25And Israel took all these cities: and Israel dwelt in all the cities of the Amorites, in Heshbon, and in all the towns thereof.
26For Heshbon was the city of Sihon the king of the Amorites, who had fought against the former king of Moab, and taken all his land out of his hand, even unto the Arnon.
27Wherefore they that speak in proverbs say,
Come ye to Heshbon;
Let the city of Sihon be built and established:
28For a fire is gone out of Heshbon,
A flame from the city of Sihon:
It hath devoured Ar of Moab,
The lords of the high places of the Arnon.
29Woe to thee, Moab!
Thou art undone, O people of Chemosh:
He hath given his sons as fugitives,
And his daughters into captivity,
Unto Sihon king of the Amorites.
30We have shot at them; Heshbon is perished even unto Dibon,
And we have laid waste even unto Nophah,
Which reacheth unto Medeba.
31Thus Israel dwelt in the land of the Amorites.
32And Moses sent to spy out Jazer; and they took the towns thereof, and drove out the Amorites that were there.
33And they turned and went up by the way of Bashan: and Og the king of Bashan went out against them, he and all his people, to battle at Edrei.
34And Yahweh said unto Moses, Fear him not: for I have delivered him into thy hand, and all his people, and his land; and thou shalt do to him as thou didst unto Sihon king of the Amorites, who dwelt at Heshbon.
35So they smote him, and his sons and all his people, until there was none left him remaining: and they possessed his land.

Chapter 22

1And the children of Israel journeyed, and encamped in the plains of Moab beyond the Jordan at Jericho.
2And Balak the son of Zippor saw all that Israel had done to the Amorites.
3And Moab was sore afraid of the people, because they were many: and Moab was distressed because of the children of Israel.
4And Moab said unto the elders of Midian, Now will this multitude lick up all that is round about us, as the ox licketh up the grass of the field. And Balak the son of Zippor was king of Moab at that time.
5And he sent messengers unto Balaam the son of Beor, to Pethor, which is by the River, to the land of the children of his people, to call him, saying, Behold, there is a people come out from Egypt: behold, they cover the face of the earth, and they abide over against me.
6Come now therefore, I pray thee, curse me this people; for they are too mighty for me: peradventure I shall prevail, that we may smite them, and that I may drive them out of the land: for I know that he whom thou blessest is blessed, and he whom thou cursest is cursed.
7And the elders of Moab and the elders of Midian departed with the rewards of divination in their hand; and they came unto Balaam, and spake unto him the words of Balak.
8And he said unto them, Lodge here this night, and I will bring you word again, as Yahweh shall speak unto me: and the princes of Moab abode with Balaam.
9And God came unto Balaam, and said, What men are these with thee?
10And Balaam said unto God, Balak the son of Zippor, king of Moab, hath sent unto me, saying,
11Behold, the people that is come out of Egypt, it covereth the face of the earth: now, come curse me them; peradventure I shall be able to fight against them, and shall drive them out.
12And God said unto Balaam, Thou shalt not go with them; thou shalt not curse the people; for they are blessed.
13And Balaam rose up in the morning, and said unto the princes of Balak, Get you into your land; for Yahweh refuseth to give me leave to go with you.
14And the princes of Moab rose up, and they went unto Balak, and said, Balaam refuseth to come with us.
15And Balak sent yet again princes, more, and more honorable than they.
16And they came to Balaam, and said to him, Thus saith Balak the son of Zippor, Let nothing, I pray thee, hinder thee from coming unto me:
17for I will promote thee unto very great honor, and whatsoever thou sayest unto me I will do: come therefore, I pray thee, curse me this people.
18And Balaam answered and said unto the servants of Balak, If Balak would give me his house full of silver and gold, I cannot go beyond the word of Yahweh my God, to do less or more.
19Now therefore, I pray you, tarry ye also here this night, that I may know what Yahweh will speak unto me more.
20And God came unto Balaam at night, and said unto him, If the men are come to call thee, rise up, go with them; but only the word which I speak unto thee, that shalt thou do.
21And Balaam rose up in the morning, and saddled his ass, and went with the princes of Moab.
22And God's anger was kindled because he went; and the angel of Yahweh placed himself in the way for an adversary against him. Now he was riding upon his ass, and his two servants were with him.
23And the ass saw the angel of Yahweh standing in the way, with his sword drawn in his hand; and the ass turned aside out of the way, and went into the field: and Balaam smote the ass, to turn her into the way.
24Then the angel of Yahweh stood in a narrow path between the vineyards, a wall being on this side, and a wall on that side.
25And the ass saw the angel of Yahweh, and she thrust herself unto the wall, and crushed Balaam's foot against the wall: and he smote her again.
26And the angel of Yahweh went further, and stood in a narrow place, where was no way to turn either to the right hand or to the left.
27And the ass saw the angel of Yahweh, and she lay down under Balaam: and Balaam's anger was kindled, and he smote the ass with his staff.
28And Yahweh opened the mouth of the ass, and she said unto Balaam, What have I done unto thee, that thou hast smitten me these three times?
29And Balaam said unto the ass, Because thou hast mocked me, I would there were a sword in my hand, for now I had killed thee.
30And the ass said unto Balaam, Am not I thine ass, upon which thou hast ridden all thy life long unto this day? was I ever wont to do so unto thee? and he said, Nay.
31Then Yahweh opened the eyes of Balaam, and he saw the angel of Yahweh standing in the way, with his sword drawn in his hand; and he bowed his head, and fell on his face.
32And the angel of Yahweh said unto him, Wherefore hast thou smitten thine ass these three times? behold, I am come forth for an adversary, because thy way is perverse before me:
33and the ass saw me, and turned aside before me these three times: unless she had turned aside from me, surely now I had even slain thee, and saved her alive.
34And Balaam said unto the angel of Yahweh, I have sinned; for I knew not that thou stoodest in the way against me: now therefore, if it displease thee, I will get me back again.
35And the angel of Yahweh said unto Balaam, Go with the men; but only the word that I shall speak unto thee, that thou shalt speak. So Balaam went with the princes of Balak.
36And when Balak heard that Balaam was come, he went out to meet him unto the City of Moab, which is on the border of the Arnon, which is in the utmost part of the border.
37And Balak said unto Balaam, Did I not earnestly send unto thee to call thee? wherefore camest thou not unto me? am I not able indeed to promote thee to honor?
38And Balaam said unto Balak, Lo, I am come unto thee: have I now any power at all to speak anything? the word that God putteth in my mouth, that shall I speak.
39And Balaam went with Balak, and they came unto Kiriath-huzoth.
40And Balak sacrificed oxen and sheep, and sent to Balaam, and to the princes that were with him.
41And it came to pass in the morning, that Balak took Balaam, and brought him up into the high places of Baal; and he saw from thence the utmost part of the people.

Chapter 23

1And Balaam said unto Balak, Build me here seven altars, and prepare me here seven bullocks and seven rams.
2And Balak did as Balaam had spoken; and Balak and Balaam offered on every altar a bullock and a ram.
3And Balaam said unto Balak, Stand by thy burnt-offering, and I will go: peradventure Yahweh will come to meet me; and whatsoever he showeth me I will tell thee. And he went to a bare height.
4And God met Balaam: and he said unto him, I have prepared the seven altars, and I have offered up a bullock and a ram on every altar.
5And Yahweh put a word in Balaam's mouth, and said, Return unto Balak, and thus thou shalt speak.
6And he returned unto him, and, lo, he was standing by his burnt-offering, he, and all the princes of Moab.
7And he took up his parable, and said, From Aram hath Balak brought me, The king of Moab from the mountains of the East: Come, curse me Jacob, And come, defy Israel.
8How shall I curse, whom God hath not cursed? And how shall I defy, whom Yahweh hath not defied?
9For from the top of the rocks I see him, And from the hills I behold him: lo, it is a people that dwelleth alone, And shall not be reckoned among the nations.
10Who can count the dust of Jacob, Or number the fourth part of Israel? Let me die the death of the righteous, And let my last end be like his!
11And Balak said unto Balaam, What hast thou done unto me? I took thee to curse mine enemies, and, behold, thou hast blessed them altogether.

12And he answered and said, Must I not take heed to speak that which Yahweh putteth in my mouth?

13And Balak said unto him, Come, I pray thee, with me unto another place, from whence thou mayest see them; thou shalt see but the utmost part of them, and shalt not see them all: and curse me them from thence.

14And he took him into the field of Zophim, to the top of Pisgah, and built seven altars, and offered up a bullock and a ram on every altar.

15And he said unto Balak, Stand here by thy burnt-offering, while I meet Yahweh yonder.

16And Yahweh met Balaam, and put a word in his mouth, and said, Return unto Balak, and thus shalt thou speak.

17And he came to him, and, lo, he was standing by his burnt-offering, and the princes of Moab with him. And Balak said unto him, What hath Yahweh spoken?

18And he took up his parable, and said,
Rise up, Balak, and hear;
Hearken unto me, thou son of Zippor:
19God is not a man, that he should lie,
Neither the son of man, that he should repent:
Hath he said, and will he not do it?
Or hath he spoken, and will he not make it good?
20Behold, I have received commandment to bless:
And he hath blessed, and I cannot reverse it.
21He hath not beheld iniquity in Jacob;
Neither hath he seen perverseness in Israel:
Yahweh his God is with him,
And the shout of a king is among them.
22God bringeth them forth out of Egypt;
He hath as it were the strength of the wild-ox.
23Surely there is no enchantment with Jacob;
Neither is there any divination with Israel:
Now shalt it be said of Jacob and of Israel,
What hath God wrought!
24Behold, the people riseth up as a lioness,
And as a lion doth he lift himself up:
He shall not lie down until he eat of the prey,
And drink the blood of the slain.

25And Balak said unto Balaam, Neither curse them at all, nor bless them at all.

26But Balaam answered and said unto Balak, Told not I thee, saying, All that Yahweh speaketh, that I must do?

27And Balak said unto Balaam, Come now, I will take thee unto another place; peradventure it will please God that thou mayest curse me them from thence.

28And Balak took Balaam unto the top of Peor, that looketh down upon the desert.

29And Balaam said unto Balak, Build me here seven altars, and prepare me here seven bullocks and seven rams.

30And Balak did as Balaam had said, and offered up a bullock and a ram on every altar.

Chapter 24

1And when Balaam saw that it pleased Yahweh to bless Israel, he went not, as at the other times, to meet with enchantments, but he set his face toward the wilderness.

2And Balaam lifted up his eyes, and he saw Israel dwelling according to their tribes; and the Spirit of God came upon him.

3And he took up his parable, and said,
Balaam the son of Beor saith,
And the man whose eye was closed saith;
4He saith, who heareth the words of God,
Who seeth the vision of the Almighty,
Falling down, and having his eyes open:
5How goodly are thy tents, O Jacob,
Thy tabernacles, O Israel!
6As valleys are they spread forth,
As gardens by the river-side,
As lign-aloes which Yahweh hath planted,
As cedar-trees beside the waters.
7Water shall flow from his buckets,
And his seed shall be in many waters,
And his king shall be higher than Agag,
And his kingdom shall be exalted.
8God bringeth him forth out of Egypt;
He hath as it were the strength of the wild-ox:
He shall eat up the nations his adversaries,
And shall break their bones in pieces,
And smite them through with his arrows.
9He couched, he lay down as a lion,
And as a lioness; who shall rouse him up?
Blessed be every one that blesseth thee,
And cursed be every one that curseth thee.

10And Balak's anger was kindled against Balaam, and he smote his hands together; and Balak said unto Balaam, I called thee to curse mine enemies, and, behold, thou hast altogether blessed them these three times.

11Therefore now flee thou to thy place: I thought to promote thee unto great honor; but, lo, Yahweh hath kept thee back from honor.

12And Balaam said unto Balak, Spake I not also to thy messengers that thou sentest unto me, saying,

13If Balak would give me his house full of silver and gold, I cannot go beyond the word of Yahweh, to do either good or bad of mine own mind; what Yahweh speaketh, that will I speak?

14And now, behold, I go unto my people: come, and I will advertise thee what this people shall do to thy people in the latter days.

15And he took up his parable, and said,
Balaam the son of Beor saith,
And the man whose eye was closed saith;
16He saith, who heareth the words of God,
And knoweth the knowledge of the Most High,
Who seeth the vision of the Almighty,
Falling down, and having his eyes open:
17I see him, but not now;
I behold him, but not nigh:
There shall come forth a star out of Jacob,
And a sceptre shall rise out of Israel,
And shall smite through the corners of Moab,
And break down all the sons of tumult.
18And Edom shall be a possession,
Seir also shall be a possession, who were his enemies;
While Israel doeth valiantly.
19And out of Jacob shall one have dominion,
And shall destroy the remnant from the city.
20And he looked on Amalek, and took up his parable, and said,
Amalek was the first of the nations;
But his latter end shall come to destruction.
21And he looked on the Kenite, and took up his parable, and said,
Strong is thy dwelling-place,
And thy nest is set in the rock.
22Nevertheless Kain shall be wasted,
Until Asshur shall carry thee away captive.
23And he took up his parable, and said,
Alas, who shall live when God doeth this?
24But ships shall come from the coast of Kittim,
And they shall afflict Asshur, and shall afflict Eber;
And he also shall come to destruction.

25And Balaam rose up, and went and returned to his place; and Balak also went his way.

Chapter 25

1And Israel abode in Shittim; and the people began to play the harlot with the daughters of Moab:

2for they called the people unto the sacrifices of their gods; and the people did eat, and bowed down to their gods.

3And Israel joined himself unto Baal-peor: and the anger of Yahweh was kindled against Israel.

4And Yahweh said unto Moses, Take all the chiefs of the people, and hang them up unto Yahweh before the sun, that the fierce anger of Yahweh may turn away from Israel.

5And Moses said unto the judges of Israel, Slay ye every one his men that have joined themselves unto Baal-peor.

6And, behold, one of the children of Israel came and brought unto his brethren a Midianitish woman in the sight of Moses, and in the sight of all the congregation of the children of Israel, while they were weeping at the door of the tent of meeting.

7And when Phinehas, the son of Eleazar, the son of Aaron the priest, saw it, he rose up from the midst of the congregation, and took a spear in his hand;

8and he went after the man of Israel into the pavilion, and thrust both of them through, the man of Israel, and the woman through her body. So the plague was stayed from the children of Israel.

9And those that died by the plague were twenty and four thousand.

10And Yahweh spake unto Moses, saying,

11Phinehas, the son of Eleazar, the son of Aaron the priest, hath turned my wrath away from the children of Israel, in that he was jealous with my jealousy among them, so that I consumed not the children of Israel in my jealousy.

12Wherefore say, Behold, I give unto him my covenant of peace:

13and it shall be unto him, and to his seed after him, the covenant of an everlasting priesthood; because he was jealous for his God, and made atonement for the children of Israel.

14Now the name of the man of Israel that was slain, who was slain with the Midianitish woman, was Zimri, the son of Salu, a prince of a fathers' house among the Simeonites.

15And the name of the Midianitish woman that was slain was Cozbi, the daughter of Zur; he was head of the people of a fathers' house in Midian.

16And Yahweh spake unto Moses, saying,

17Vex the Midianites, and smite them;

18for they vex you with their wiles, wherewith they have beguiled you in the matter of Peor, and in the matter of Cozbi, the daughter of the prince of Midian, their sister, who was slain on the day of the plague in the matter of Peor.

Chapter 26

1And it came to pass after the plague, that Yahweh spake unto Moses and unto Eleazar the son of Aaron the priest, saying,

2Take the sum of all the congregation of the children of Israel, from twenty years old and upward, by their fathers' houses, all that are able to go forth to war in Israel.

3And Moses and Eleazar the priest spake with them in the plains of Moab by the Jordan at Jericho, saying,

4Take the sum of the people, from twenty years old and upward; as Yahweh commanded Moses and the children of Israel, that came forth out of the land of Egypt.

5Reuben, the first-born of Israel; the sons of Reuben: of Hanoch, the family of the Hanochites; of Pallu, the family of the Palluites;

6of Hezron, the family of the Hezronites; of Carmi, the family of the Carmites.

7These are the families of the Reubenites; and they that were numbered of them were forty and three thousand and seven hundred and thirty.

8And the sons of Pallu: Eliab.

9And the sons of Eliab: Nemuel, and Dathan, and Abiram. These are that Dathan and Abiram, who were called of the congregation, who strove against Moses and against Aaron in the company of Korah, when they strove against Yahweh,

10and the earth opened its mouth, and swallowed them up together with Korah, when that company died; what time the fire devoured two hundred and fifty men, and they became a sign.

11Notwithstanding, the sons of Korah died not.

12The sons of Simeon after their families: of Nemuel, the family of the Nemuelites; of Jamin, the family of the Jaminites; of Jachin, the family of the Jachinites;

13of Zerah, the family of the Zerahites; of Shaul, the family of the Shaulites.

14These are the families of the Simeonites, twenty and two thousand and two hundred.

15The sons of Gad after their families: of Zephon, the family of the Zephonites; of Haggi, the family of the Haggites; of Shuni, the family of the Shunites;

16of Ozni, the family of the Oznites; of Eri, the family of the Erites;

17of Arod, the family of the Arodites; of Areli, the family of the Arelites.

18These are the families of the sons of Gad according to those that were numbered of them, forty thousand and five hundred.

19The sons of Judah: Er and Onan; and Er and Onan died in the land of Canaan.

20And the sons of Judah after their families were: of Shelah, the family of the Shelanites; of Perez, the family of the Perezites; of Zerah, the family of the Zerahites.

21And the sons of Perez were: of Hezron, the family of the Hezronites; of Hamul, the family of the Hamulites.

22These are the families of Judah according to those that were numbered of them, threescore and sixteen thousand and five hundred.

23The sons of Issachar after their families: of Tola, the family of the Tolaites; of Puvah, the family of the Punites;

24of Jashub, the family of the Jashubites; of Shimron, the family of the Shimronites.

25These are the families of Issachar according to those that were numbered of them, threescore and four thousand and three hundred.

26The sons of Zebulun after their families: of Sered, the family of the Seredites; of Elon, the family of the Elonites; of Jahleel, the family of the Jahleelites.

27These are the families of the Zebulunites according to those that were numbered of them, threescore thousand and five hundred.

28The sons of Joseph after their families: Manasseh and Ephraim.

29The sons of Manasseh: of Machir, the family of the Machirites; and Machir begat Gilead; of Gilead, the family of the Gileadites.

30These are the sons of Gilead: of Iezer, the family of the Iezerites; of Helek, the family of the Helekites;

31and of Asriel, the family of the Asrielites; and of Shechem, the family of the Shechemites;

32and of Shemida, the family of the Shemidaites; and of Hepher, the family of the Hepherites.

33And Zelophehad the son of Hepher had no sons, but daughters: and the names of the daughters of Zelophehad were Mahlah, and Noah, Hoglah, Milcah, and Tirzah.

34These are the families of Manasseh; and they that were numbered of them were fifty and two thousand and seven hundred.

35These are the sons of Ephraim after their families: of Shuthelah, the family of the Shuthelahites; of Becher, the family of the Becherites; of Tahan, the family of the Tahanites.

36And these are the sons of Shuthelah: of Eran, the family of the Eranites.

37These are the families of the sons of Ephraim according to those that were numbered of them, thirty and two thousand and five hundred. These are the sons of Joseph after their families.

38The sons of Benjamin after their families: of Bela, the family of the Belaites; of Ashbel, the family of the Ashbelites; of Ahiram, the family of the Ahiramites;

39of Shephupham, the family of the Shuphamites; of Hupham, the family of the Huphamites.

40And the sons of Bela were Ard and Naaman: of Ard, the family of the Ardites; of Naaman, the family of the Naamites.

41These are the sons of Benjamin after their families; and they that were numbered of them were forty and five thousand and six hundred.

42These are the sons of Dan after their families: of Shuham, the family of the Shuhamites. These are the families of Dan after their families.

43All the families of the Shuhamites, according to those that were numbered of them, were threescore and four thousand and four hundred.

44The sons of Asher after their families: of Imnah, the family of the Imnites; of Ishvi, the family of the Ishvites; of Beriah, the family of the Berites.

45Of the sons of Beriah: of Heber, the family of the Heberites; of Malchiel, the family of the Malchielites.

46And the name of the daughter of Asher was Serah.

47These are the families of the sons of Asher according to those that were numbered of them, fifty and three thousand and four hundred.

48The sons of Naphtali after their families: of Jahzeel, the family of the Jahzeelites; of Guni, the family of the Gunites;

49of Jezer, the family of the Jezerites; of Shillem, the family of the Shillemites.

50These are the families of Naphtali according to their families; and they that were numbered of them were forty and five thousand and four hundred.

51These are they that were numbered of the children of Israel, six hundred thousand and a thousand seven hundred and thirty.

52And Yahweh spake unto Moses, saying,

53Unto these the land shall be divided for an inheritance according to the number of names.

54To the more thou shalt give the more inheritance, and to the fewer thou shalt give the less inheritance: to every one according to those that were numbered of him shall his inheritance be given.

55Notwithstanding, the land shall be divided by lot: according to the names of the tribes of their fathers they shall inherit.

56According to the lot shall their inheritance be divided between the more and the fewer.

57And these are they that were numbered of the Levites after their families: of Gershon, the family of the Gershonites; of Kohath, the family of the Kohathites; of Merari, the family of the Merarites.

58These are the families of Levi: the family of the Libnites, the family of the Hebronites, the family of the Mahlites, the family of the Mushites, the family of the Korahites. And Kohath begat Amram.

59And the name of Amram's wife was Jochebed, the daughter of Levi, who was born to Levi in Egypt: and she bare unto Amram Aaron and Moses, and Miriam their sister.

60And unto Aaron were born Nadab and Abihu, Eleazar and Ithamar.

61And Nadab and Abihu died, when they offered strange fire before Yahweh.

62And they that were numbered of them were twenty and three thousand, every male from a month old and upward: for they were not numbered among the children of Israel, because there was no inheritance given them among the children of Israel.

63These are they that were numbered by Moses and Eleazar the priest, who numbered the children of Israel in the plains of Moab by the Jordan at Jericho.

64But among these there was not a man of them that were numbered by Moses and Aaron the priest, who numbered the children of Israel in the wilderness of Sinai.

65For Yahweh had said of them, They shall surely die in the wilderness. And there was not left a man of them, save Caleb the son of Jephunneh, and Joshua the son of Nun.

Chapter 27

1Then drew near the daughters of Zelophehad, the son of Hepher, the son of Gilead, the son of Machir, the son of Manasseh, of the families of Manasseh the son of Joseph; and these are the names of his daughters: Mahlah, Noah, and Hoglah, and Milcah, and Tirzah.

2And they stood before Moses, and before Eleazar the priest, and before the princes and all the congregation, at the door of the tent of meeting, saying,

3Our father died in the wilderness, and he was not among the company of them that gathered themselves together against Yahweh in the company of Korah: but he died in his own sin; and he had no sons.

4Why should the name of our father be taken away from among his family, because he had no son? Give unto us a possession among the brethren of our father.

5And Moses brought their cause before Yahweh.

6And Yahweh spake unto Moses, saying,

7The daughters of Zelophehad speak right: thou shalt surely give them a possession of an inheritance among their father's brethren; and thou shalt cause the inheritance of their father to pass unto them.

8And thou shalt speak unto the children of Israel, saying, If a man die, and have no son, then ye shall cause his inheritance to pass unto his daughter.

9And if he have no daughter, then ye shall give his inheritance unto his brethren.

10And if he have no brethren, then ye shall give his inheritance unto his father's brethren.

11And if his father have no brethren, then ye shall give his inheritance unto his kinsman that is next to him of his family, and he shall possess it: and it shall be unto the children of Israel a statute and ordinance, as Yahweh commanded Moses.

12And Yahweh said unto Moses, Get thee up into this mountain of Abarim, and behold the land which I have given unto the children of Israel.

13And when thou hast seen it, thou also shalt be gathered unto thy people, as Aaron thy brother was gathered;

14because ye rebelled against my word in the wilderness of Zin, in the strife of the congregation, to sanctify me at the waters before their eyes. (These are the waters of Meribah of Kadesh in the wilderness of Zin.)

15And Moses spake unto Yahweh, saying,

16Let Yahweh, the God of the spirits of all flesh, appoint a man over the congregation,

17who may go out before them, and who may come in before them, and who may lead them out, and who may bring them in; that the congregation of Yahweh be not as sheep which have no shepherd.

18And Yahweh said unto Moses, Take thee Joshua the son of Nun, a man in whom is the Spirit, and lay thy hand upon him;

19and set him before Eleazar the priest, and before all the congregation; and give him a charge in their sight.

20And thou shalt put of thine honor upon him, that all the congregation of the children of Israel may obey.

21And he shall stand before Eleazar the priest, who shall inquire for him by the judgment of the Urim before Yahweh: at his word shall they go out, and at his word they shall come in, both he, and all the children of Israel with him, even all the congregation.

22And Moses did as Yahweh commanded him; and he took Joshua, and set him before Eleazar the priest, and before all the congregation:

23and he laid his hands upon him, and gave him a charge, as Yahweh spake by Moses.

Chapter 28

1And Yahweh spake unto Moses, saying,

2Command the children of Israel, and say unto them, My oblation, my food for my offerings made by fire, of a sweet savor unto me, shall ye observe to offer unto me in their due season.

3And thou shalt say unto them, This is the offering made by fire which ye shall offer unto Yahweh: he-lambs a year old without blemish, two day by day, for a continual burnt-offering.

4The one lamb shalt thou offer in the morning, and the other lamb shalt thou offer at even;

5and the tenth part of an ephah of fine flour for a meal-offering, mingled with the fourth part of a hin of beaten oil.

6It is a continual burnt-offering, which was ordained in mount Sinai for a sweet savor, an offering made by fire unto Yahweh.

7And the drink-offering thereof shall be the fourth part of a hin for the one lamb: in the holy place shalt thou pour out a drink-offering of strong drink unto Yahweh.

8And the other lamb shalt thou offer at even: as the meal-offering of the morning, and as the drink-offering thereof, thou shalt offer it, an offering made by fire, of a sweet savor unto Yahweh.

9And on the sabbath day two he-lambs a year old without blemish, and two tenth parts of an ephah of fine flour for a meal-offering, mingled with oil, and the drink-offering thereof:

10this is the burnt-offering of every sabbath, besides the continual burnt-offering, and the drink-offering thereof.

11And in the beginnings of your months ye shall offer a burnt-offering unto Yahweh: two young bullocks, and one ram, seven he-lambs a year old without blemish;

12and three tenth parts of an ephah of fine flour for a meal-offering, mingled with oil, for each bullock; and two tenth parts of fine flour for a meal-offering, mingled with oil, for the one ram;

13and a tenth part of fine flour mingled with oil for a meal-offering unto every lamb; for a burnt-offering of a sweet savor, an offering made by fire unto Yahweh.

14And their drink-offerings shall be half a hin of wine for a bullock, and the third part of a hin for the ram, and the fourth part of a hin for a lamb: this is the burnt-offering of every month throughout the months of the year.

15And one he-goat for a sin-offering unto Yahweh; it shall be offered besides the continual burnt-offering, and the drink-offering thereof.

16And in the first month, on the fourteenth day of the month, is Yahweh's passover.

17And on the fifteenth day of this month shall be a feast: seven days shall unleavened bread be eaten.

18In the first day shall be a holy convocation: ye shall do no servile work;

19but ye shall offer an offering made by fire, a burnt-offering unto Yahweh: two young bullocks, and one ram, and seven he-lambs a year old; they shall be unto you without blemish;

20and their meal-offering, fine flour mingled with oil: three tenth parts shall ye offer for a bullock, and two tenth parts for the ram;

21a tenth part shalt thou offer for every lamb of the seven lambs;

22and one he-goat for a sin-offering, to make atonement for you.

23Ye shall offer these besides the burnt-offering of the morning, which is for a continual burnt-offering.

24After this manner ye shall offer daily, for seven days, the food of the offering made by fire, of a sweet savor unto Yahweh: it shall be offered besides the continual burnt-offering, and the drink-offering thereof.

25And on the seventh day ye shall have a holy convocation: ye shall do no servile work.

26Also in the day of the first-fruits, when ye offer a new meal-offering unto Yahweh in your feast of weeks, ye shall have a holy convocation; ye shall do no servile work;

27but ye shall offer a burnt-offering for a sweet savor unto Yahweh: two young bullocks, one ram, seven he-lambs a year old;

28and their meal-offering, fine flour mingled with oil, three tenth parts for each bullock, two tenth parts for the one ram,

29a tenth part for every lamb of the seven lambs;

30one he-goat, to make atonement for you.

31Besides the continual burnt-offering, and the meal-offering thereof, ye shall offer them (they shall be unto you without blemish), and their drink-offerings.

Chapter 29

1And in the seventh month, on the first day of the month, ye shall have a holy convocation; ye shall do no servile work: it is a day of blowing of trumpets unto you.

2And ye shall offer a burnt-offering for a sweet savor unto Yahweh: one young bullock, one ram, seven he-lambs a year old without blemish;

3and their meal-offering, fine flour mingled with oil, three tenth parts for the bullock, two tenth parts for the ram,

4and one tenth part for every lamb of the seven lambs;

5and one he-goat for a sin-offering, to make atonement for you;

6besides the burnt-offering of the new moon, and the meal-offering thereof, and the continual burnt-offering and the meal-offering thereof, and their drink-offerings, according unto their ordinance, for a sweet savor, an offering made by fire unto Yahweh.

7And on the tenth day of this seventh month ye shall have a holy convocation; and ye shall afflict your souls: ye shall do no manner of work;

8but ye shall offer a burnt-offering unto Yahweh for a sweet savor: one young bullock, one ram, seven he-lambs a year old; they shall be unto you without blemish;

9and their meal-offering, fine flour mingled with oil, three tenth parts for the bullock, two tenth parts for the one ram,

10a tenth part for every lamb of the seven lambs:

11one he-goat for a sin-offering; besides the sin-offering of atonement, and the continual burnt-offering, and the meal-offering thereof, and their drink-offerings.

12And on the fifteenth day of the seventh month ye shall have a holy convocation; ye shall do no servile work, and ye shall keep a feast unto Yahweh seven days;

13and ye shall offer a burnt-offering, an offering made by fire, of a sweet savor unto Yahweh; thirteen young bullocks, two rams, fourteen he-lambs a year old; they shall be without blemish;

14and their meal-offering, fine flour mingled with oil, three tenth parts for every bullock of the thirteen bullocks, two tenth parts for each ram of the two rams,

15and a tenth part for every lamb of the fourteen lambs;

16and one he-goat for a sin-offering, besides the continual burnt-offering, the meal-offering thereof, and the drink-offering thereof.

17And on the second day ye shall offer twelve young bullocks, two rams, fourteen he-lambs a year old without blemish;

18and their meal-offering and their drink-offerings for the bullocks, for the rams, and for the lambs, according to their number, after the ordinance;

19and one he-goat for a sin-offering; besides the continual burnt-offering, and the meal-offering thereof, and their drink-offerings.

20And on the third day eleven bullocks, two rams, fourteen he-lambs a year old without blemish;

21and their meal-offering and their drink-offerings for the bullocks, for the rams, and for the lambs, according to their number, after the ordinance;

22and one he-goat for a sin-offering; besides the continual burnt-offering, and the meal-offering thereof, and the drink-offering thereof.

23And on the fourth day ten bullocks, two rams, fourteen he-lambs a year old without blemish;

24their meal-offering and their drink-offerings for the bullocks, for the rams, and for the lambs, according to their number, after the ordinance;

25and one he-goat for a sin-offering; besides the continual burnt-offering, the meal-offering thereof, and the drink-offering thereof.

26And on the fifth day nine bullocks, two rams, fourteen he-lambs a year old without blemish;

27and their meal-offering and their drink-offerings for the bullocks, for the rams, and for the lambs, according to their number, after the ordinance;

28and one he-goat for a sin-offering, besides the continual burnt-offering, and the meal-offering thereof, and the drink-offering thereof.

29And on the sixth day eight bullocks, two rams, fourteen he-lambs a year old without blemish;

30and their meal-offering and their drink-offerings for the bullocks, for the rams, and for the lambs, according to their number, after the ordinance;

31and one he-goat for a sin-offering; besides the continual burnt-offering, the meal-offering thereof, and the drink-offerings thereof.

32And on the seventh day seven bullocks, two rams, fourteen he-lambs a year old without blemish;

33and their meal-offering and their drink-offerings for the bullocks, for the rams, and for the lambs, according to their number, after the ordinance;

34and one he-goat for a sin-offering; besides the continual burnt-offering, the meal-offering thereof, and the drink-offering thereof.

35On the eighth day ye shall have a solemn assembly: ye shall do no servile work;

36but ye shall offer a burnt-offering, an offering made by fire, of a sweet savor unto Yahweh: one bullock, one ram, seven he-lambs a year old without blemish;

37their meal-offering and their drink-offerings for the bullock, for the ram, and for the lambs, shall be according to their number, after the ordinance:

38and one he-goat for a sin-offering, besides the continual burnt-offering, and the meal-offering thereof, and the drink-offering thereof.

39These ye shall offer unto Yahweh in your set feasts, besides your vows, and your freewill-offerings, for your burnt-offerings, and for your meal-offerings, and for your drink-offerings, and for your peace-offerings.

40And Moses told the children of Israel according to all that Yahweh commanded Moses.

Numbers

Chapter 30

1And Moses spake unto the heads of the tribes of the children of Israel, saying, This is the thing which Yahweh hath commanded.

2When a man voweth a vow unto Yahweh, or sweareth an oath to bind his soul with a bond, he shall not break his word; he shall do according to all that proceedeth out of his mouth.

3Also when a woman voweth a vow unto Yahweh, and bindeth herself by a bond, being in her father's house, in her youth,

4and her father heareth her vow, and her bond wherewith she hath bound her soul, and her father holdeth his peace at her; then all her vows shall stand, and every bond wherewith she hath bound her soul shall stand.

5But if her father disallow her in the day that he heareth, none of her vows, or of her bonds wherewith she hath bound her soul, shall stand: and Yahweh will forgive her, because her father disallowed her.

6And if she be married to a husband, while her vows are upon her, or the rash utterance of her lips, wherewith she hath bound her soul,

7and her husband hear it, and hold his peace at her in the day that he heareth it; then her vows shall stand, and her bonds wherewith she hath bound her soul shall stand.

8But if her husband disallow her in the day that he heareth it, then he shall make void her vow which is upon her, and the rash utterance of her lips, wherewith she hath bound her soul: and Yahweh will forgive her.

9But the vow of a widow, or of her that is divorced, even everything wherewith she hath bound her soul, shall stand against her.

10And if she vowed in her husband's house, or bound her soul by a bond with an oath,

11and her husband heard it, and held his peace at her, and disallowed her not; then all her vows shall stand, and every bond wherewith she bound her soul shall stand.

12But if her husband made them null and void in the day that he heard them, then whatsoever proceeded out of her lips concerning her vows, or concerning the bond of her soul, shall not stand: her husband hath made them void; and Yahweh will forgive her.

13Every vow, and every binding oath to afflict the soul, her husband may establish it, or her husband may make it void.

14But if her husband altogether hold his peace at her from day to day, then he establisheth all her vows, or all her bonds, which are upon her: he hath established them, because he held his peace at her in the day that he heard them.

15But if he shall make them null and void after that he hath heard them, then he shall bear her iniquity.

16These are the statutes, which Yahweh commanded Moses, between a man and his wife, between a father and his daughter, being in her youth, in her father's house.

Chapter 31

31 1And Yahweh spake unto Moses, saying,

2Avenge the children of Israel of the Midianites: afterward shalt thou be gathered unto thy people.

3And Moses spake unto the people, saying, Arm ye men from among you for the war, that they may go against Midian, to execute Yahweh's vengeance on Midian.

4Of every tribe a thousand, throughout all the tribes of Israel, shall ye send to the war.

5So there were delivered, out of the thousands of Israel, a thousand of every tribe, twelve thousand armed for war.

6And Moses sent them, a thousand of every tribe, to the war, them and Phinehas the son of Eleazar the priest, to the war, with the vessels of the sanctuary and the trumpets for the alarm in his hand.

7And they warred against Midian, as Yahweh commanded Moses; and they slew every male.

8And they slew the kings of Midian with the rest of their slain: Evi, and Rekem, and Zur, and Hur, and Reba, the five kings of Midian: Balaam also the son of Beor they slew with the sword.

9And the children of Israel took captive the women of Midian and their little ones; and all their cattle, and all their flocks, and all their goods, they took for a prey.

10And all their cities in the places wherein they dwelt, and all their encampments, they burnt with fire.

11And they took all the spoil, and all the prey, both of man and of beast.

12And they brought the captives, and the prey, and the spoil, unto Moses, and unto Eleazar the priest, and unto the congregation of the children of Israel, unto the camp at the plains of Moab, which are by the Jordan at Jericho.

13And Moses, and Eleazar the priest, and all the princes of the congregation, went forth to meet them without the camp.

14And Moses was wroth with the officers of the host, the captains of thousands and the captains of hundreds, who came from the service of the war.

15And Moses said unto them, Have ye saved all the women alive?

16Behold, these caused the children of Israel, through the counsel of Balaam, to commit trespass against Yahweh in the matter of Peor, and so the plague was among the congregation of Yahweh.

17Now therefore kill every male among the little ones, and kill every woman that hath known man by lying with him.

18But all the women-children, that have not known man by lying with him, keep alive for yourselves.

19And encamp ye without the camp seven days: whosoever hath killed any person, and whosoever hath touched any slain, purify yourselves on the third day and on the seventh day, ye and your captives.

20And as to every garment, and all that is made of skin, and all work of goats' hair, and all things made of wood, ye shall purify yourselves.

21And Eleazar the priest said unto the men of war that went to the battle, This is the statute of the law which Yahweh hath commanded Moses:

22howbeit the gold, and the silver, the brass, the iron, the tin, and the lead,

23everything that may abide the fire, ye shall make to go through the fire, and it shall be clean; nevertheless it shall be purified with the water for impurity: and all that abideth not the fire ye shall make to go through the water.

24And ye shall wash your clothes on the seventh day, and ye shall be clean; and afterward ye shall come into the camp.

25And Yahweh spake unto Moses, saying,

26Take the sum of the prey that was taken, both of man and of beast, thou, and Eleazar the priest, and the heads of the fathers' houses of the congregation;

27and divide the prey into two parts: between the men skilled in war, that went out to battle, and all the congregation.

28And levy a tribute unto Yahweh of the men of war that went out to battle: one soul of five hundred, both of the persons, and of the oxen, and of the asses, and of the flocks:

29take it of their half, and give it unto Eleazar the priest, for Yahweh's heave-offering.

30And of the children of Israel's half, thou shalt take one drawn out of every fifty, of the persons, of the oxen, of the asses, and of the flocks, even of all the cattle, and give them unto the Levites, that keep the charge of the tabernacle of Yahweh.

31And Moses and Eleazar the priest did as Yahweh commanded Moses.

32Now the prey, over and above the booty which the men of war took, was six hundred thousand and seventy thousand and five thousand sheep,

33and threescore and twelve thousand oxen,

34and threescore and one thousand asses,

35and thirty and two thousand persons in all, of the women that had not known man by lying with him.

36And the half, which was the portion of them that went out to war, was in number three hundred thousand and thirty thousand and seven thousand and five hundred sheep;

37and Yahweh's tribute of the sheep was six hundred and threescore and fifteen.

38And the oxen were thirty and six thousand; of which Yahweh's tribute was threescore and twelve.

39And the asses were thirty thousand and five hundred; of which Yahweh's tribute was threescore and one.

40And the persons were sixteen thousand; of whom Yahweh's tribute was thirty and two persons.

41And Moses gave the tribute, which was Yahweh's heave-offering, unto Eleazar the priest, as Yahweh commanded Moses.

42And of the children of Israel's half, which Moses divided off from the men that warred

43(now the congregation's half was three hundred thousand and thirty thousand, seven thousand and five hundred sheep,

44and thirty and six thousand oxen,

45and thirty thousand and five hundred asses,

46and sixteen thousand persons),

47even of the children of Israel's half, Moses took one drawn out of every fifty, both of man and of beast, and gave them unto the Levites, that kept the charge of the tabernacle of Yahweh; as Yahweh commanded Moses.

48And the officers that were over the thousands of the host, the captains of thousands, and the captains of hundreds, came near unto Moses;

49and they said unto Moses, Thy servants have taken the sum of the men of war that are under our charge, and there lacketh not one man of us.

50And we have brought Yahweh's oblation, what every man hath gotten, of jewels of gold, ankle-chains, and bracelets, signet-rings, ear-rings, and armlets, to make atonement for our souls before Yahweh.

51And Moses and Eleazar the priest took the gold of them, even all wrought jewels.

52And all the gold of the heave-offering that they offered up to Yahweh, of the captains of thousands, and of the captains of hundreds, was sixteen thousand seven hundred and fifty shekels.

53(For the men of war had taken booty, every man for himself.)

54And Moses and Eleazar the priest took the gold of the captains of thousands and of hundreds, and brought it into the tent of meeting, for a memorial for the children of Israel before Yahweh.

Chapter 32

32 1Now the children of Reuben and the children of Gad had a very great multitude of cattle: and when they saw the land of Jazer, and the land of Gilead, that, behold, the place was a place for cattle;

2the children of Gad and the children of Reuben came and spake unto Moses, and to Eleazar the priest, and unto the princes of the congregation, saying,

3Ataroth, and Dibon, and Jazer, and Nimrah, and Heshbon, and Elealeh, and Sebam, and Nebo, and Beon,

4the land which Yahweh smote before the congregation of Israel, is a land for cattle; and thy servants have cattle.

5And they said, If we have found favor in thy sight, let this land be given unto thy servants for a possession; bring us not over the Jordan.

6And Moses said unto the children of Gad, and to the children of Reuben, Shall your brethren go to the war, and shall ye sit here?

7And wherefore discourage ye the heart of the children of Israel from going over into the land which Yahweh hath given them?

8Thus did your fathers, when I sent them from Kadesh-barnea to see the land.

9For when they went up unto the valley of Eshcol, and saw the land, they discouraged the heart of the children of Israel, that they should not go into the land which Yahweh had given them.

10And Yahweh's anger was kindled in that day, and he sware, saying,

11Surely none of the men that came up out of Egypt, from twenty years old and upward, shall see the land which I sware unto Abraham, unto Isaac, and unto Jacob; because they have not wholly followed me:

12save Caleb the son of Jephunneh the Kenizzite, and Joshua the son of Nun; because they have wholly followed Yahweh.

13And Yahweh's anger was kindled against Israel, and he made them wander to and fro in the wilderness forty years, until all the generation, that had done evil in the sight of Yahweh, was consumed.

14And, behold, ye are risen up in your fathers' stead, an increase of sinful men, to augment yet the fierce anger of Yahweh toward Israel.

15For if ye turn away from after him, he will yet again leave them in the wilderness; and ye will destroy all this people.

16And they came near unto him, and said, We will build sheepfolds here for our cattle, and cities for our little ones:

17but we ourselves will be ready armed to go before the children of Israel, until we have brought them unto their place: and our little ones shall dwell in the fortified cities because of the inhabitants of the land.

18We will not return unto our houses, until the children of Israel have inherited every man his inheritance.

19For we will not inherit with them on the other side of the Jordan, and forward; because our inheritance is fallen to us on this side of the Jordan eastward.

20And Moses said unto them, If ye will do this thing, if ye will arm yourselves to go before Yahweh to the war,

21and every armed man of you will pass over the Jordan before Yahweh, until he hath driven out his enemies from before him,

22and the land is subdued before Yahweh; then afterward ye shall return, and be guiltless towards Yahweh, and towards Israel; and this land shall be unto you for a possession before Yahweh.

23But if ye will not do so, behold, ye have sinned against Yahweh; and be sure your sin will find you out.

24Build you cities for your little ones, and folds for your sheep; and do that which hath proceeded out of your mouth.

25And the children of Gad and the children of Reuben spake unto Moses, saying, Thy servants will do as my lord commandeth.

26Our little ones, our wives, our flocks, and all our cattle, shall be there in the cities of Gilead;

27but thy servants will pass over, every man that is armed for war, before Yahweh to battle, as my lord saith.

28So Moses gave charge concerning them to Eleazar the priest, and to Joshua the son of Nun, and to the heads of the fathers' houses of the tribes of the children of Israel.

29And Moses said unto them, If the children of Gad and the children of Reuben will pass with you over the Jordan, every man that is armed to battle, before Yahweh, and the land shall be subdued before you; then ye shall give them the land of Gilead for a possession:

30but if they will not pass over with you armed, they shall have possessions among you in the land of Canaan.

31And the children of Gad and the children of Reuben answered, saying, As Yahweh hath said unto thy servants, so will we do.

32We will pass over armed before Yahweh into the land of Canaan, and the possession of our inheritance shall remain with us beyond the Jordan.

33And Moses gave unto them, even to the children of Gad, and to the children of Reuben, and unto the half-tribe of Manasseh the son of Joseph, the kingdom of Sihon king of the Amorites, and the kingdom of Og king of Bashan, the land, according to the cities thereof with their borders, even the cities of the land round about.

34And the children of Gad built Dibon, and Ataroth, and Aroer,

35and Atrothshophan, and Jazer, and Jogbehah,

36and Beth-nimrah, and Beth-haran: fortified cities, and folds for sheep.

37And the children of Reuben built Heshbon, and Elealeh, and Kiriathaim,

38and Nebo, and Baal-meon, (their names being changed,) and Sibmah: and they gave other names unto the cities which they builded.

39And the children of Machir the son of Manasseh went to Gilead, and took it, and dispossessed the Amorites that were therein.

40And Moses gave Gilead unto Machir the son of Manasseh; and he dwelt therein.

41And Jair the son of Manasseh went and took the towns thereof, and called them Havvoth-jair.

42And Nobah went and took Kenath, and the villages thereof, and called it Nobah, after his own name.

Chapter 33

33 1These are the journeys of the children of Israel, when they went forth out of the land of Egypt by their hosts under the hand of Moses and Aaron.

2And Moses wrote their goings out according to their journeys by the commandment of Yahweh: and these are their journeys according to their goings out.

3And they journeyed from Rameses in the first month, on the fifteenth day of the first month; on the morrow after the passover the children of Israel went out with a high hand in the sight of all the Egyptians,

4while the Egyptians were burying all their first-born, whom Yahweh had smitten among them: upon their gods also Yahweh executed judgments.

5And the children of Israel journeyed from Rameses, and encamped in Succoth.

6And they journeyed from Succoth, and encamped in Etham, which is in the edge of the wilderness.

7And they journeyed from Etham, and turned back unto Pihahiroth, which is before Baal-zephon: and they encamped before Migdol.

8And they journeyed from before Hahiroth, and passed through the midst of the sea into the wilderness: and they went three days' journey in the wilderness of Etham, and encamped in Marah.

9And they journeyed from Marah, and came unto Elim: and in Elim were twelve springs of water, and threescore and ten palm-trees; and they encamped there.

10And they journeyed from Elim, and encamped by the Red Sea.

11And they journeyed from the Red Sea, and encamped in the wilderness of Sin.

12And they journeyed from the wilderness of Sin, and encamped in Dophkah.

13And they journeyed from Dophkah, and encamped in Alush.

14And they journeyed from Alush, and encamped in Rephidim, where was no water for the people to drink.

15And they journeyed from Rephidim, and encamped in the wilderness of Sinai.

16And they journeyed from the wilderness of Sinai, and encamped in Kibroth-hattaavah.

17And they journeyed from Kibroth-hattaavah, and encamped in Hazeroth.

18And they journeyed from Hazeroth, and encamped in Rithmah.

19And they journeyed from Rithmah, and encamped in Rimmon-perez.

20And they journeyed from Rimmon-perez, and encamped in Libnah.

21And they journeyed from Libnah, and encamped in Rissah.

22And they journeyed from Rissah, and encamped in Kehelathah.

23And they journeyed from Kehelathah, and encamped in mount Shepher.

24And they journeyed from mount Shepher, and encamped in Haradah.

25And they journeyed from Haradah, and encamped in Makheloth.

26And they journeyed from Makheloth, and encamped in Tahath.

27And they journeyed from Tahath, and encamped in Terah.

28And they journeyed from Terah, and encamped in Mithkah.

29And they journeyed from Mithkah, and encamped in Hashmonah.

30And they journeyed from Hashmonah, and encamped in Moseroth.

31And they journeyed from Moseroth, and encamped in Bene-jaakan.

32And they journeyed from Bene-jaakan, and encamped in Hor-haggidgad.

33And they journeyed from Hor-haggidgad, and encamped in Jotbathah.

34And they journeyed from Jotbathah, and encamped in Abronah.

35And they journeyed from Abronah, and encamped in Ezion-geber.

36And they journeyed from Ezion-geber, and encamped in the wilderness of Zin (the same is Kadesh).

37And they journeyed from Kadesh, and encamped in mount Hor, in the edge of the land of Edom.

38And Aaron the priest went up into mount Hor at the commandment of Yahweh, and died there, in the fortieth year after the children of Israel were come out of the land of Egypt, in the fifth month, on the first day of the month.

39And Aaron was a hundred and twenty and three years old when he died in mount Hor.

40And the Canaanite, the king of Arad, who dwelt in the South in the land of Canaan, heard of the coming of the children of Israel.

41And they journeyed from mount Hor, and encamped in Zalmonah.

42And they journeyed from Zalmonah, and encamped in Punon.

43And they journeyed from Punon, and encamped in Oboth.

44And they journeyed from Oboth, and encamped in Iye-abarim, in the border of Moab.

45And they journeyed from Iyim, and encamped in Dibon-gad.

46And they journeyed from Dibon-gad, and encamped in Almon-diblathaim.

47And they journeyed from Almon-diblathaim, and encamped in the mountains of Abarim, before Nebo.

48And they journeyed from the mountains of Abarim, and encamped in the plains of Moab by the Jordan at Jericho.

49And they encamped by the Jordan, from Beth-jeshimoth even unto Abel-shittim in the plains of Moab.

50And Yahweh spake unto Moses in the plains of Moab by the Jordan at Jericho, saying,

51Speak unto the children of Israel, and say unto them, When ye pass over the Jordan into the land of Canaan,

52then ye shall drive out all the inhabitants of the land from before you, and destroy all their figured stones, and destroy all their molten images, and demolish all their high places:

53and ye shall take possession of the land, and dwell therein; for unto you have I given the land to possess it.

54And ye shall inherit the land by lot according to your families; to the more ye shall give the more inheritance, and to the fewer thou shalt give the less inheritance: wheresoever the lot falleth to any man, that shall be his; according to the tribes of your fathers shall ye inherit.

55But if ye will not drive out the inhabitants of the land from before you, then shall those that ye let remain of them be as pricks in your eyes, and as thorns in your sides, and they shall vex you in the land wherein ye dwell.

56And it shall come to pass, that, as I thought to do unto them, so will I do unto you.

Numbers

Chapter 34

34 1And Yahweh spake unto Moses, saying,

2Command the children of Israel, and say unto them, When ye come into the land of Canaan (this is the land that shall fall unto you for an inheritance, even the land of Canaan according to the borders thereof),

3then your south quarter shall be from the wilderness of Zin along by the side of Edom, and your south border shall be from the end of the Salt Sea eastward;

4and your border shall turn about southward of the ascent of Akrabbim, and pass along to Zin; and the goings out thereof shall be southward of Kadesh-barnea; and it shall go forth to Hazar-addar, and pass along to Azmon;

5and the border shall turn about from Azmon unto the brook of Egypt, and the goings out thereof shall be at the sea.

6And for the western border, ye shall have the great sea and the border thereof: this shall be your west border.

7And this shall be your north border: from the great sea ye shall mark out for you mount Hor;

8from mount Hor ye shall mark out unto the entrance of Hamath; and the goings out of the border shall be at Zedad;

9and the border shall go forth to Ziphron, and the goings out thereof shall be at Hazar-enan: this shall be your north border.

10And ye shall mark out your east border from Hazar-enan to Shepham;

11and the border shall go down from Shepham to Riblah, on the east side of Ain; and the border shall go down, and shall reach unto the side of the sea of Chinnereth eastward;

12and the border shall go down to the Jordan, and the goings out thereof shall be at the Salt Sea. This shall be your land according to the borders thereof round about.

13And Moses commanded the children of Israel, saying, This is the land which ye shall inherit by lot, which Yahweh hath commanded to give unto the nine tribes, and to the half-tribe;

14for the tribe of the children of Reuben according to their fathers' houses, and the tribe of the children of Gad according to their fathers' houses, have received, and the half-tribe of Manasseh have received, their inheritance;

15the two tribes and the half-tribe have received their inheritance beyond the Jordan at Jericho eastward, toward the sunrising.

16And Yahweh spake unto Moses, saying,

17These are the names of the men that shall divide the land unto you for inheritance: Eleazar the priest, and Joshua the son of Nun.

18And ye shall take one prince of every tribe, to divide the land for inheritance.

19And these are the names of the men: Of the tribe of Judah, Caleb the son of Jephunneh.

20And of the tribe of the children of Simeon, Shemuel the son of Ammihud.

21Of the tribe of Benjamin, Elidad the son of Chislon.

22And of the tribe of the children of Dan a prince, Bukki the son of Jogli.

23Of the children of Joseph: of the tribe of the children of Manasseh a prince, Hanniel the son of Ephod.

24And of the tribe of the children of Ephraim a prince, Kemuel the son of Shiphtan.

25And of the tribe of the children of Zebulun a prince, Elizaphan the son of Parnach.

26And of the tribe of the children of Issachar a prince, Paltiel the son of Azzan.

27And of the tribe of the children of Asher a prince, Ahihud the son of Shelomi.

28And of the tribe of the children of Naphtali a prince, Pedahel the son of Ammihud.

29These are they whom Yahweh commanded to divide the inheritance unto the children of Israel in the land of Canaan.

Chapter 35

1And Yahweh spake unto Moses in the plains of Moab by the Jordan at Jericho, saying,

2Command the children of Israel, that they give unto the Levites of the inheritance of their possession cities to dwell in; and suburbs for the cities round about them shall ye give unto the Levites.

3And the cities shall they have to dwell in; and their suburbs shall be for their cattle, and for their substance, and for all their beasts.

4And the suburbs of the cities, which ye shall give unto the Levites, shall be from the wall of the city and outward a thousand cubits round about.

5And ye shall measure without the city for the east side two thousand cubits, and for the south side two thousand cubits, and for the west side two thousand cubits, and for the north side two thousand cubits, the city being in the midst. This shall be to them the suburbs of the cities.

6And the cities which ye shall give unto the Levites, they shall be the six cities of refuge, which ye shall give for the manslayer to flee unto: and besides them ye shall give forty and two cities.

7All the cities which ye shall give to the Levites shall be forty and eight cities; them shall ye give with their suburbs.

8And concerning the cities which ye shall give of the possession of the children of Israel, from the many ye shall take many; and from the few ye shall take few: every one according to his inheritance which he inheriteth shall give of his cities unto the Levites.

9And Yahweh spake unto Moses, saying,

10Speak unto the children of Israel, and say unto them, When ye pass over the Jordan into the land of Canaan,

11then ye shall appoint you cities to be cities of refuge for you, that the manslayer that killeth any person unwittingly may flee thither.

12And the cities shall be unto you for refuge from the avenger, that the manslayer die not, until he stand before the congregation for judgment.

13And the cities which ye shall give shall be for you six cities of refuge.

14Ye shall give three cities beyond the Jordan, and three cities shall ye give in the land of Canaan; they shall be cities of refuge.

15For the children of Israel, and for the stranger and for the sojourner among them, shall these six cities be for refuge; that every one that killeth any person unwittingly may flee thither.

16But if he smote him with an instrument of iron, so that he died, he is a murderer: the murderer shall surely be put to death.

17And if he smote him with a stone in the hand, whereby a man may die, and he died, he is a murderer: the murderer shall surely be put to death.

18Or if he smote him with a weapon of wood in the hand, whereby a man may die, and he died, he is a murderer: the murderer shall surely be put to death.

19The avenger of blood shall himself put the murderer to death: when he meeteth him, he shall put him to death.

20And if he thrust him of hatred, or hurled at him, lying in wait, so that he died,

21or in enmity smote him with his hand, so that he died; he that smote him shall surely be put to death; he is a murderer: the avenger of blood shall put the murderer to death, when he meeteth him.

22But if he thrust him suddenly without enmity, or hurled upon him anything without lying in wait,

23or with any stone, whereby a man may die, seeing him not, and cast it upon him, so that he died, and he was not his enemy, neither sought his harm;

24then the congregation shall judge between the smiter and the avenger of blood according to these ordinances;

25and the congregation shall deliver the manslayer out of the hand of the avenger of blood, and the congregation shall restore him to his city of refuge, whither he was fled: and he shall dwell therein until the death of the high priest, who was anointed with the holy oil.

26But if the manslayer shall at any time go beyond the border of his city of refuge, whither he fleeth,

27and the avenger of blood find him without the border of his city of refuge, and the avenger of blood slay the manslayer; he shall not be guilty of blood,

28because he should have remained in his city of refuge until the death of the high priest: but after the death of the high priest the manslayer shall return into the land of his possession.

29And these things shall be for a statute and ordinance unto you throughout your generations in all your dwellings.

30Whoso killeth any person, the murderer shall be slain at the mouth of witnesses: but one witness shall not testify against any person that he die.

31Moreover ye shall take no ransom for the life of a murderer, that is guilty of death; but he shall surely be put to death.

32And ye shall take no ransom for him that is fled to his city of refuge, that he may come again to dwell in the land, until the death of the priest.

33So ye shall not pollute the land wherein ye are: for blood, it polluteth the land; and no expiation can be made for the land for the blood that is shed therein, but by the blood of him that shed it.

34And thou shalt not defile the land which ye inhabit, in the midst of which I dwell: for I, Yahweh, dwell in the midst of the children of Israel.

Chapter 36

1And the heads of the fathers' houses of the family of the children of Gilead, the son of Machir, the son of Manasseh, of the families of the sons of Joseph, came near, and spake before Moses, and before the princes, the heads of the fathers' houses of the children of Israel:

2and they said, Yahweh commanded my lord to give the land for inheritance by lot to the children of Israel: and my lord was commanded by Yahweh to give the inheritance of Zelophehad our brother unto his daughters.

3And if they be married to any of the sons of the other tribes of the children of Israel, then will their inheritance be taken away from the inheritance of our fathers, and will be added to the inheritance of the tribe whereunto they shall belong: so will it be taken away from the lot of our inheritance.

4And when the jubilee of the children of Israel shall be, then will their inheritance be added unto the inheritance of the tribe whereunto they shall belong: so will their inheritance be taken away from the inheritance of the tribe of our fathers.

5And Moses commanded the children of Israel according to the word of Yahweh, saying, The tribe of the sons of Joseph speaketh right.

6This is the thing which Yahweh doth command concerning the daughters of Zelophehad, saying, Let them be married to whom they think best; only into the family of the tribe of their father shall they be married.

7So shall no inheritance of the children of Israel remove from tribe to tribe; for the children of Israel shall cleave every one to the inheritance of the tribe of his fathers.

8And every daughter, that possesseth an inheritance in any tribe of the children of Israel, shall be wife unto one of the family of the tribe of her father, that the children of Israel may possess every man the inheritance of his fathers.

9So shall no inheritance remove from one tribe to another tribe; for the tribes of the children of Israel shall cleave every one to his own inheritance.

10Even as Yahweh commanded Moses, so did the daughters of Zelophehad:

11for Mahlah, Tirzah, and Hoglah, and Milcah, and Noah, the daughters of Zelophehad, were married unto their father's brothers' sons.

12 They were married into the families of the sons of Manasseh the son of Joseph; and their inheritance remained in the tribe of the family of their father.

13 These are the commandments and the ordinances which Yahweh commanded by Moses unto the children of Israel in the plains of Moab by the Jordan at Jericho.

Deuteronomy

The Fifth Book of Moses, called Deuteronomy

Chapter 1

1These are the words which Moses spake unto all Israel beyond the Jordan in the wilderness, in the Arabah over against Suph, between Paran, and Tophel, and Laban, and Hazeroth, and Di-zahab.

2It is eleven days' journey from Horeb by the way of mount Seir unto Kadesh-barnea.

3And it came to pass in the fortieth year, in the eleventh month, on the first day of the month, that Moses spake unto the children of Israel, according unto all that Yahweh had given him in commandment unto them;

4after he had smitten Sihon the king of the Amorites, who dwelt in Heshbon, and Og the king of Bashan, who dwelt in Ashtaroth, at Edrei.

5Beyond the Jordan, in the land of Moab, began Moses to declare this law, saying,

6Yahweh our God spake unto us in Horeb, saying, Ye have dwelt long enough in this mountain:

7turn you, and take your journey, and go to the hill-country of the Amorites, and unto all the places nigh thereunto, in the Arabah, in the hill-country, and in the lowland, and in the South, and by the sea-shore, the land of the Canaanites, and Lebanon, as far as the great river, the river Euphrates.

8Behold, I have set the land before you: go in and possess the land which Yahweh sware unto your fathers, to Abraham, to Isaac, and to Jacob, to give unto them and to their seed after them.

9And I spake unto you at that time, saying, I am not able to bear you myself alone:

10Yahweh your God hath multiplied you, and, behold, ye are this day as the stars of heaven for multitude.

11Yahweh, the God of your fathers, make you a thousand times as many as ye are, and bless you, as he hath promised you!

12How can I myself alone bear your cumbrance, and your burden, and your strife?

13Take you wise men, and understanding, and known, according to your tribes, and I will make them heads over you.

14And ye answered me, and said, The thing which thou hast spoken is good for us to do.

15So I took the heads of your tribes, wise men, and known, and made them heads over you, captains of thousands, and captains of hundreds, and captains of fifties, and captains of tens, and officers, according to your tribes.

16And I charged your judges at that time, saying, Hear the causes between your brethren, and judge righteously between a man and his brother, and the sojourner that is with him.

17Ye shall not respect persons in judgment; ye shall hear the small and the great alike; ye shall not be afraid of the face of man; for the judgment is God's: and the cause that is too hard for you ye shall bring unto me, and I will hear it.

18And I commanded you at that time all the things which ye should do.

19And we journeyed from Horeb, and went through all that great and terrible wilderness which ye saw, by the way to the hill-country of the Amorites, as Yahweh our God commanded us; and we came to Kadesh-barnea.

20And I said unto you, Ye are come unto the hill-country of the Amorites, which Yahweh our God giveth unto us.

21Behold, Yahweh thy God hath set the land before thee: go up, take possession, as Yahweh, the God of thy fathers, hath spoken unto thee; fear not, neither be dismayed.

22And ye came near unto me every one of you, and said, Let us send men before us, that they may search the land for us, and bring us word again of the way by which we must go up, and the cities unto which we shall come.

23And the thing pleased me well; and I took twelve men of you, one man for every tribe:

24and they turned and went up into the hill-country, and came unto the valley of Eshcol, and spied it out.

25And they took of the fruit of the land in their hands, and brought it down unto us, and brought us word again, and said, It is a good land which Yahweh our God giveth unto us.

26Yet ye would not go up, but rebelled against the commandment of Yahweh your God:

27and ye murmured in your tents, and said, Because Yahweh hated us, he hath brought us forth out of the land of Egypt, to deliver us into the hand of the Amorites, to destroy us.

28Whither are we going up? our brethren have made our heart to melt, saying, The people are greater and taller than we; the cities are great and fortified up to heaven; and moreover we have seen the sons of the Anakim there.

29Then I said unto you, Dread not, neither be afraid of them.

30Yahweh your God who goeth before you, he will fight for you, according to all that he did for you in Egypt before your eyes,

31and in the wilderness, where thou hast seen how that Yahweh thy God bare thee, as a man doth bear his son, in all the way that ye went, until ye came unto this place.

32Yet in this thing ye did not believe Yahweh your God,

33who went before you in the way, to seek you out a place to pitch your tents in, in fire by night, to show you by what way ye should go, and in the cloud by day.

34And Yahweh heard the voice of your words, and was wroth, and sware, saying,

35Surely there shall not one of these men of this evil generation see the good land, which I sware to give unto your fathers,

36save Caleb the son of Jephunneh: he shall see it; and to him will I give the land that he hath trodden upon, and to his children, because he hath wholly followed Yahweh.

37Also Yahweh was angry with me for your sakes, saying, Thou also shalt not go in thither:

38Joshua the son of Nun, who standeth before thee, he shall go in thither: encourage thou him; for he shall cause Israel to inherit it.

39Moreover your little ones, that ye said should be a prey, and your children, that this day have no knowledge of good or evil, they shall go in thither, and unto them will I give it, and they shall possess it.

40But as for you, turn you, and take your journey into the wilderness by the way to the Red Sea.

41Then ye answered and said unto me, We have sinned against Yahweh, we will go up and fight, according to all that Yahweh our God commanded us. And ye girded on every man his weapons of war, and were forward to go up into the hill-country.

42And Yahweh said unto me, Say unto them, Go not up, neither fight; for I am not among you; lest ye be smitten before your enemies.

43So I spake unto you, and ye hearkened not; but ye rebelled against the commandment of Yahweh, and were presumptuous, and went up into the hill-country.

44And the Amorites, that dwelt in that hill-country, came out against you, and chased you, as bees do, and beat you down in Seir, even unto Hormah.

45And ye returned and wept before Yahweh; but Yahweh hearkened not to your voice, nor gave ear unto you.

46So ye abode in Kadesh many days, according unto the days that ye abode there.

Chapter 2

1Then we turned, and took our journey into the wilderness by the way to the Red Sea, as Yahweh spake unto me; and we compassed mount Seir many days.

2And Yahweh spake unto me, saying,

3Ye have compassed this mountain long enough: turn you northward.

4And command thou the people, saying, Ye are to pass through the border of your brethren the children of Esau, that dwell in Seir; and they will be afraid of you: take ye good heed unto yourselves therefore;

5contend not with them; for I will not give you of their land, no, not so much as for the sole of the foot to tread on; because I have given mount Seir unto Esau for a possession.

6Ye shall purchase food of them for money, that ye may eat; and ye shall also buy water of them for money, that ye may drink.

7For Yahweh thy God hath blessed thee in all the work of thy hand; he hath known thy walking through this great wilderness: these forty years Yahweh thy God hath been with thee; thou hast lacked nothing.

8So we passed by from our brethren the children of Esau, that dwell in Seir, from the way of the Arabah from Elath and from Ezion-geber.

And we turned and passed by the way of the wilderness of Moab.

9And Yahweh said unto me, Vex not Moab, neither contend with them in battle; for I will not give thee of his land for a possession; because I have given Ar unto the children of Lot for a possession.

10(The Emim dwelt therein aforetime, a people great, and many, and tall, as the Anakim:

11these also are accounted Rephaim, as the Anakim; but the Moabites call them Emim.

12The Horites also dwelt in Seir aforetime, but the children of Esau succeeded them; and they destroyed them from before them, and dwelt in their stead; as Israel did unto the land of his possession, which Yahweh gave unto them.)

13Now rise up, and get you over the brook Zered. And we went over the brook Zered.

14And the days in which we came from Kadesh-barnea, until we were come over the brook Zered, were thirty and eight years; until all the generation of the men of war were consumed from the midst of the camp, as Yahweh sware unto them.

15Moreover the hand of Yahweh was against them, to destroy them from the midst of the camp, until they were consumed.

16So it came to pass, when all the men of war were consumed and dead from among the people,

17that Yahweh spake unto me, saying,

18Thou art this day to pass over Ar, the border of Moab:

19and when thou comest nigh over against the children of Ammon, vex them not, nor contend with them; for I will not give thee of the land of the children of Ammon for a possession; because I have given it unto the children of Lot for a possession.

20(That also is accounted a land of Rephaim: Rephaim dwelt therein aforetime; but the Ammonites call them Zamzummim,

21a people great, and many, and tall, as the Anakim; but Yahweh destroyed them before them; and they succeeded them, and dwelt in their stead;

22as he did for the children of Esau, that dwell in Seir, when he destroyed the Horites from before them; and they succeeded them, and dwelt in their stead even unto this day:

23and the Avvim, that dwelt in villages as far as Gaza, the Caphtorim, that came forth out of Caphtor, destroyed them, and dwelt in their stead.)

24Rise ye up, take your journey, and pass over the valley of the Arnon: behold, I have given into thy hand Sihon the Amorite, king of Heshbon, and his land; begin to possess it, and contend with him in battle.

25This day will I begin to put the dread of thee and the fear of thee upon the peoples that are under the whole heaven, who shall hear the report of thee, and shall tremble, and be in anguish because of thee.

26And I sent messengers out of the wilderness of Kedemoth unto Sihon king of Heshbon with words of peace, saying,

27Let me pass through thy land: I will go along by the highway, I will turn neither unto the right hand nor to the left.

28Thou shalt sell me food for money, that I may eat; and give me water for money, that I may drink: only let me pass through on my feet,

29as the children of Esau that dwell in Seir, and the Moabites that dwell in Ar, did unto me; until I shall pass over the Jordan into the land which Yahweh our God giveth us.

30But Sihon king of Heshbon would not let us pass by him; for Yahweh thy God hardened his spirit, and made his heart obstinate, that he might deliver him into thy hand, as at this day.

31And Yahweh said unto me, Behold, I have begun to deliver up Sihon and his land before thee: begin to possess, that thou mayest inherit his land.

32Then Sihon came out against us, he and all his people, unto battle at Jahaz.

33And Yahweh our God delivered him up before us; and we smote him, and his sons, and all his people.

34And we took all his cities at that time, and utterly destroyed every inhabited city, with the women and the little ones; we left none remaining:

35only the cattle we took for a prey unto ourselves, with the spoil of the cities which we had taken.

36From Aroer, which is on the edge of the valley of the Arnon, and from the city that is in the valley, even unto Gilead, there was not a city too high for us; Yahweh our God delivered up all before us:

37only to the land of the children of Ammon thou camest not near; all the side of the river Jabbok, and the cities of the hill-country, and wheresoever Yahweh our God forbade us.

Chapter 3

1Then we turned, and went up the way to Bashan: and Og the king of Bashan came out against us, he and all his people, unto battle at Edrei.

2And Yahweh said unto me, Fear him not; for I have delivered him, and all his people, and his land, into thy hand; and thou shalt do unto him as thou didst unto Sihon king of the Amorites, who dwelt at Heshbon.

3So Yahweh our God delivered into our hand Og also, the king of Bashan, and all his people: and we smote him until none was left to him remaining.

4And we took all his cities at that time; there was not a city which we took not from them; threescore cities, all the region of Argob, the kingdom of Og in Bashan.

5All these were cities fortified with high walls, gates, and bars; besides the unwalled towns a great many.

6And we utterly destroyed them, as we did unto Sihon king of Heshbon, utterly destroying every inhabited city, with the women and the little ones.

7But all the cattle, and the spoil of the cities, we took for a prey unto ourselves.

8And we took the land at that time out of the hand of the two kings of the Amorites that were beyond the Jordan, from the valley of the Arnon unto mount Hermon;

9(which Hermon the Sidonians call Sirion, and the Amorites call it Senir;)

10all the cities of the plain, and all Gilead, and all Bashan, unto Salecah and Edrei, cities of the kingdom of Og in Bashan.

11(For only Og king of Bashan remained of the remnant of the Rephaim; behold, his bedstead was a bedstead of iron; is it not in Rabbah of the children of Ammon? nine cubits was the length thereof, and four cubits the breadth of it, after the cubit of a man.)

12And this land we took in possession at that time: from Aroer, which is by the valley of the Arnon, and half the hill-country of Gilead, and the cities thereof, gave I unto the Reubenites and to the Gadites:

13and the rest of Gilead, and all Bashan, the kingdom of Og, gave I unto the half-tribe of Manasseh; all the region of Argob, even all Bashan. (The same is called the land of Rephaim.

14Jair the son of Manasseh took all the region of Argob, unto the border of the Geshurites and the Maacathites, and called them, even Bashan, after his own name, Havvoth-jair, unto this day.)

15And I gave Gilead unto Machir.

16And unto the Reubenites and unto the Gadites I gave from Gilead even unto the valley of the Arnon, the middle of the valley, and the border thereof, even unto the river Jabbok, which is the border of the children of Ammon;

17the Arabah also, and the Jordan and the border thereof, from Chinnereth even unto the sea of the Arabah, the Salt Sea, under the slopes of Pisgah eastward.

18And I commanded you at that time, saying, Yahweh your God hath given you this land to possess it: ye shall pass over armed before your brethren the children of Israel, all the men of valor.

19But your wives, and your little ones, and your cattle, (I know that ye have much cattle,) shall abide in your cities which I have given you,

20until Yahweh give rest unto your brethren, as unto you, and they also possess the land which Yahweh your God giveth them beyond the Jordan: then shall ye return every man unto his possession, which I have given you.

21And I commanded Joshua at that time, saying, Thine eyes have seen all that Yahweh your God hath done unto these two kings: so shall Yahweh do unto all the kingdoms whither thou goest over.

22Ye shall not fear them; for Yahweh your God, he it is that fighteth for you.

23And I besought Yahweh at that time, saying,

24O Lord Yahweh, thou hast begun to show thy servant thy greatness, and thy strong hand: for what god is there in heaven or in earth, that can do according to thy works, and according to thy mighty acts?

25Let me go over, I pray thee, and see the good land that is beyond the Jordan, that goodly mountain, and Lebanon.

26But Yahweh was wroth with me for your sakes, and hearkened not unto me; and Yahweh said unto me, Let it suffice thee; speak no more unto me of this matter.

27Get thee up unto the top of Pisgah, and lift up thine eyes westward, and northward, and southward, and eastward, and behold with thine eyes: for thou shalt not go over this Jordan.

28But charge Joshua, and encourage him, and strengthen him; for he shall go over before this people, and he shall cause them to inherit the land which thou shalt see.

29So we abode in the valley over against Beth-peor.

Chapter 4

1And now, O Israel, hearken unto the statutes and unto the ordinances, which I teach you, to do them; that ye may live, and go in and possess the land which Yahweh, the God of your fathers, giveth you.

2Ye shall not add unto the word which I command you, neither shall ye diminish from it, that ye may keep the commandments of Yahweh your God which I command you.

3Your eyes have seen what Yahweh did because of Baal-peor; for all the men that followed Baal-peor, Yahweh thy God hath destroyed them from the midst of thee.

4But ye that did cleave unto Yahweh your God are alive every one of you this day.

5Behold, I have taught you statutes and ordinances, even as Yahweh my God commanded me, that ye should do so in the midst of the land whither ye go in to possess it.

6Keep therefore and do them; for this is your wisdom and your understanding in the sight of the peoples, that shall hear all these statutes, and say, Surely this great nation is a wise and understanding people.

7For what great nation is there, that hath a god so nigh unto them, as Yahweh our God is whensoever we call upon him?

8And what great nation is there, that hath statutes and ordinances so righteous as all this law, which I set before you this day?

9Only take heed to thyself, and keep thy soul diligently, lest thou forget the things which thine eyes saw, and lest they depart from thy heart all the days of thy life; but make them known unto thy children and thy children's children;

10the day that thou stoodest before Yahweh thy God in Horeb, when Yahweh said unto me, Assemble me the people, and I will make them hear my words, that they may learn to fear me all the days that they live upon the earth, and that they may teach their children.

11And ye came near and stood under the mountain; and the mountain burned with fire unto the heart of heaven, with darkness, cloud, and thick darkness.

12And Yahweh spake unto you out of the midst of the fire: ye heard the voice of words, but ye saw no form; only ye heard a voice.

13And he declared unto you his covenant, which he commanded you to perform, even the ten commandments; and he wrote them upon two tables of stone.

14And Yahweh commanded me at that time to teach you statutes and ordinances, that ye might do them in the land whither ye go over to possess it.

15Take ye therefore good heed unto yourselves; for ye saw no manner of form on the day that Yahweh spake unto you in Horeb out of the midst of the fire.

16Lest ye corrupt yourselves, and make you a graven image in the form of any figure, the likeness of male or female,

17the likeness of any beast that is on the earth, the likeness of any winged bird that flieth in the heavens,

18the likeness of anything that creepeth on the ground, the likeness of any fish that is in the water under the earth;

19and lest thou lift up thine eyes unto heaven, and when thou seest the sun and the moon and the stars, even all the host of heaven, thou be drawn away and worship them, and serve them, which Yahweh thy God hath allotted unto all the peoples under the whole heaven.

20But Yahweh hath taken you, and brought you forth out of the iron furnace, out of Egypt, to be unto him a people of inheritance, as at this day.

21Furthermore Yahweh was angry with me for your sakes, and sware that I should not go over the Jordan, and that I should not go in unto that good land, which Yahweh thy God giveth thee for an inheritance:

22but I must die in this land, I must not go over the Jordan; but ye shall go over, and possess that good land.

23Take heed unto yourselves, lest ye forget the covenant of Yahweh your God, which he made with you, and make you a graven image in the form of anything which Yahweh thy God hath forbidden thee.

24For Yahweh thy God is a devouring fire, a jealous God.

25When thou shalt beget children, and children's children, and ye shall have been long in the land, and shall corrupt yourselves, and make a graven image in the form of anything, and shall do that which is evil in the sight of Yahweh thy God, to provoke him to anger;

26I call heaven and earth to witness against you this day, that ye shall soon utterly perish from off the land whereunto ye go over the Jordan to possess it; ye shall not prolong your days upon it, but shall utterly be destroyed.

27And Yahweh will scatter you among the peoples, and ye shall be left few in number among the nations, whither Yahweh shall lead you away.

28And there ye shall serve gods, the work of men's hands, wood and stone, which neither see, nor hear, nor eat, nor smell.

29But from thence ye shall seek Yahweh thy God, and thou shalt find him,

Deuteronomy

when thou searchest after him with all thy heart and with all thy soul.

30When thou art in tribulation, and all these things are come upon thee, in the latter days thou shalt return to Yahweh thy God, and hearken unto his voice:

31for Yahweh thy God is a merciful God; he will not fail thee, neither destroy thee, nor forget the covenant of thy fathers which he sware unto them.

32For ask now of the days that are past, which were before thee, since the day that God created man upon the earth, and from the one end of heaven unto the other, whether there hath been any such thing as this great thing is, or hath been heard like it?

33Did ever a people hear the voice of God speaking out of the midst of the fire, as thou hast heard, and live?

34Or hath God assayed to go and take him a nation from the midst of another nation, by trials, by signs, and by wonders, and by war, and by a mighty hand, and by an outstretched arm, and by great terrors, according to all that Yahweh your God did for you in Egypt before your eyes?

35Unto thee it was showed, that thou mightest know that Yahweh he is God; there is none else besides him.

36Out of heaven he made thee to hear his voice, that he might instruct thee: and upon earth he made thee to see his great fire; and thou heardest his words out of the midst of the fire.

37And because he loved thy fathers, therefore he chose their seed after them, and brought thee out with his presence, with his great power, out of Egypt;

38to drive out nations from before thee greater and mightier than thou, to bring thee in, to give thee their land for an inheritance, as at this day.

39Know therefore this day, and lay it to thy heart, that Yahweh he is God in heaven above and upon the earth beneath; there is none else.

40And thou shalt keep his statutes, and his commandments, which I command thee this day, that it may go well with thee, and with thy children after thee, and that thou mayest prolong thy days in the land, which Yahweh thy God giveth thee, for ever.

41Then Moses set apart three cities beyond the Jordan toward the sunrising;

42that the manslayer might flee thither, that slayeth his neighbor unawares, and hated him not in time past; and that fleeing unto one of these cities he might live:

43namely, Bezer in the wilderness, in the plain country, for the Reubenites; and Ramoth in Gilead, for the Gadites; and Golan in Bashan, for the Manassites.

44And this is the law which Moses set before the children of Israel:

45these are the testimonies, and the statutes, and the ordinances, which Moses spake unto the children of Israel, when they came forth out of Egypt,

46beyond the Jordan, in the valley over against Beth-peor, in the land of Sihon king of the Amorites, who dwelt at Heshbon, whom Moses and the children of Israel smote, when they came forth out of Egypt.

47And they took his land in possession, and the land of Og king of Bashan, the two kings of the Amorites, who were beyond the Jordan toward the sunrising;

48from Aroer, which is on the edge of the valley of the Arnon, even unto mount Sion (the same is Hermon),

49and all the Arabah beyond the Jordan eastward, even unto the sea of the Arabah, under the slopes of Pisgah.

Chapter 5

1And Moses called unto all Israel, and said unto them, Hear, O Israel, the statutes and the ordinances which I speak in your ears this day, that ye may learn them, and observe to do them.

2Yahweh our God made a covenant with us in Horeb.

3Yahweh made not this covenant with our fathers, but with us, even us, who are all of us here alive this day.

4Yahweh spake with you face to face in the mount out of the midst of the fire,

5(I stood between Yahweh and you at that time, to show you the word of Yahweh: for ye were afraid because of the fire, and went not up into the mount;) saying,

6I am Yahweh thy God, who brought thee out of the land of Egypt, out of the house of bondage.

7Thou shalt have no other gods before me.

8Thou shalt not make unto thee a graven image, nor any likeness of anything that is in heaven above, or that is in the earth beneath, or that is in the water under the earth:

9thou shalt not bow down thyself unto them, nor serve them; for I, Yahweh, thy God, am a jealous God, visiting the iniquity of the fathers upon the children, and upon the third and upon the fourth generation of them that hate me;

10and showing lovingkindness unto thousands of them that love me and keep my commandments.

11Thou shalt not take the name of Yahweh thy God in vain: for Yahweh will not hold him guiltless that taketh his name in vain.

12Observe the sabbath day, to keep it holy, as Yahweh thy God commanded thee.

13Six days shalt thou labor, and do all thy work;

14but the seventh day is a sabbath unto Yahweh thy God: in it thou shalt not do any work, thou, nor thy son, nor thy daughter, nor thy man-servant, nor thy maid-servant, nor thine ox, nor thine ass, nor any of thy cattle, nor thy stranger that is within thy gates; that thy man-servant and thy maid-servant may rest as well as thou.

15And thou shalt remember that thou wast a servant in the land of Egypt, and Yahweh thy God brought thee out thence by a mighty hand and by an outstretched arm: therefore Yahweh thy God commanded thee to keep the sabbath day.

16Honor thy father and thy mother, as Yahweh thy God commanded thee; that thy days may be long, and that it may go well with thee, in the land which Yahweh thy God giveth thee.

17Thou shalt not kill.

18Neither shalt thou commit adultery.

19Neither shalt thou steal.

20Neither shalt thou bear false witness against thy neighbor.

21Neither shalt thou covet thy neighbor's wife; neither shalt thou desire thy neighbor's house, his field, or his man-servant, or his maid-servant, his ox, or his ass, or anything that is thy neighbor's.

22These words Yahweh spake unto all your assembly in the mount out of the midst of the fire, of the cloud, and of the thick darkness, with a great voice: and he added no more. And he wrote them upon two tables of stone, and gave them unto me.

23And it came to pass, when ye heard the voice out of the midst of the darkness, while the mountain was burning with fire, that ye came near unto me, even all the heads of your tribes, and your elders;

24and ye said, Behold, Yahweh our God hath showed us his glory and his greatness, and we have heard his voice out of the midst of the fire: we have seen this day that God doth speak with man, and he liveth.

25Now therefore why should we die? for this great fire will consume us: if we hear the voice of Yahweh our God any more, then we shall die.

26For who is there of all flesh, that hath heard the voice of the living God speaking out of the midst of the fire, as we have, and lived?

27Go thou near, and hear all that Yahweh our God shall say: and speak thou unto us all that Yahweh our God shall speak unto thee; and we will hear it, and do it.

28And Yahweh heard the voice of your words, when ye spake unto me; and Yahweh said unto me, I have heard the voice of the words of this people, which they have spoken unto thee: they have well said all that they have spoken.

29Oh that there were such a heart in them, that they would fear me, and keep all my commandments always, that it might be well with them, and with their children for ever!

30Go say to them, Return ye to your tents.

31But as for thee, stand thou here by me, and I will speak unto thee all the commandment, and the statutes, and the ordinances, which thou shalt teach them, that they may do them in the land which I give them to possess it.

32Ye shall observe to do therefore as Yahweh your God hath commanded you: ye shall not turn aside to the right hand or to the left.

33Ye shall walk in all the way which Yahweh your God hath commanded you, that ye may live, and that it may be well with you, and that ye may prolong your days in the land which ye shall possess.

Chapter 6

1Now this is the commandment, the statutes, and the ordinances, which Yahweh your God commanded to teach you, that ye might do them in the land whither ye go over to possess it;

2that thou mightest fear Yahweh thy God, to keep all his statutes and his commandments, which I command thee, thou, and thy son, and thy son's son, all the days of thy life; and that thy days may be prolonged.

3Hear therefore, O Israel, and observe to do it; that it may be well with thee, and that ye may increase mightily, as Yahweh, the God of thy fathers, hath promised unto thee, in a land flowing with milk and honey.

4Hear, O Israel: Yahweh our God is one Yahweh:

5and thou shalt love Yahweh thy God with all thy heart, and with all thy soul, and with all thy might.

6And these words, which I command thee this day, shall be upon thy heart;

7and thou shalt teach them diligently unto thy children, and shalt talk of them when thou sittest in thy house, and when thou walkest by the way, and when thou liest down, and when thou risest up.

8And thou shalt bind them for a sign upon thy hand, and they shall be for frontlets between thine eyes.

9And thou shalt write them upon the door-posts of thy house, and upon thy gates.

10And it shall be, when Yahweh thy God shall bring thee into the land which he sware unto thy fathers, to Abraham, to Isaac, and to Jacob, to give thee, great and goodly cities, which thou buildest not,

11and houses full of all good things, which thou filledst not, and cisterns hewn out, which thou hewedst not, vineyards and olive-trees, which thou plantedst not, and thou shalt eat and be full;

12then beware lest thou forget Yahweh, who brought thee forth out of the land of Egypt, out of the house of bondage.

13Thou shalt fear Yahweh thy God; and him shalt thou serve, and shalt swear by his name.

14Ye shall not go after other gods, of the gods of the peoples that are round about you;

15for Yahweh thy God in the midst of thee is a jealous God; lest the anger of Yahweh thy God be kindled against thee, and he destroy thee from off the face of the earth.

16Ye shall not tempt Yahweh your God, as ye tempted him in Massah.

17Ye shall diligently keep the commandments of Yahweh your God, and his testimonies, and his statutes, which he hath commanded thee.

18And thou shalt do that which is right and good in the sight of Yahweh; that it may be well with thee, and that thou mayest go in and possess the good land which Yahweh sware unto thy fathers,

19to thrust out all thine enemies from before thee, as Yahweh hath spoken.

20When thy son asketh thee in time to come, saying, What mean the testimonies, and the statutes, and the ordinances, which Yahweh our God hath commanded you?

21then thou shalt say unto thy son, We were Pharaoh's bondmen in Egypt: and Yahweh brought us out of Egypt with a mighty hand;

22and Yahweh showed signs and wonders, great and sore, upon Egypt, upon

Pharaoh, and upon all his house, before our eyes;

23and he brought us out from thence, that he might bring us in, to give us the land which he sware unto our fathers.

24And Yahweh commanded us to do all these statutes, to fear Yahweh our God, for our good always, that he might preserve us alive, as at this day.

25And it shall be righteousness unto us, if we observe to do all this commandment before Yahweh our God, as he hath commanded us.

Chapter 7

1When Yahweh thy God shall bring thee into the land whither thou goest to possess it, and shall cast out many nations before thee, the Hittite, and the Girgashite, and the Amorite, and the Canaanite, and the Perizzite, and the Hivite, and the Jebusite, seven nations greater and mightier than thou;

2and when Yahweh thy God shall deliver them up before thee, and thou shalt smite them; then thou shalt utterly destroy them: thou shalt make no covenant with them, nor show mercy unto them;

3neither shalt thou make marriages with them; thy daughter thou shalt not give unto his son, nor his daughter shalt thou take unto thy son.

4For he will turn away thy son from following me, that they may serve other gods: so will the anger of Yahweh be kindled against you, and he will destroy thee quickly.

5But thus shall ye deal with them: ye shall break down their altars, and dash in pieces their pillars, and hew down their Asherim, and burn their graven images with fire.

6For thou art a holy people unto Yahweh thy God: Yahweh thy God hath chosen thee to be a people for his own possession, above all peoples that are upon the face of the earth.

7Yahweh did not set his love upon you, nor choose you, because ye were more in number than any people; for ye were the fewest of all peoples:

8but because Yahweh loveth you, and because he would keep the oath which he sware unto your fathers, hath Yahweh brought you out with a mighty hand, and redeemed you out of the house of bondage, from the hand of Pharaoh king of Egypt.

9Know therefore that Yahweh thy God, he is God, the faithful God, who keepeth covenant and lovingkindness with them that love him and keep his commandments to a thousand generations,

10and repayeth them that hate him to their face, to destroy them: he will not be slack to him that hateth him, he will repay him to his face.

11Thou shalt therefore keep the commandment, and the statutes, and the ordinances, which I command thee this day, to do them.

12And it shall come to pass, because ye hearken to these ordinances, and keep and do them, that Yahweh thy God will keep with thee the covenant and the lovingkindness which he sware unto thy fathers:

13and he will love thee, and bless thee, and multiply thee; he will also bless the fruit of thy body and the fruit of thy ground, thy grain and thy new wine and thine oil, the increase of thy cattle and the young of thy flock, in the land which he sware unto thy fathers to give thee.

14Thou shalt be blessed above all peoples: there shall not be male or female barren among you, or among your cattle.

15And Yahweh will take away from thee all sickness; and none of the evil diseases of Egypt, which thou knowest, will he put upon thee, but will lay them upon all them that hate thee.

16And thou shalt consume all the peoples that Yahweh thy God shall deliver unto thee; thine eye shall not pity them: neither shalt thou serve their gods; for that will be a snare unto thee.

17If thou shalt say in thy heart, These nations are more than I; how can I dispossess them?

18thou shalt not be afraid of them: thou shalt well remember what Yahweh thy God did unto Pharaoh, and unto all Egypt;

19the great trials which thine eyes saw, and the signs, and the wonders, and the mighty hand, and the outstretched arm, whereby Yahweh thy God brought thee out: so shall Yahweh thy God do unto all the peoples of whom thou art afraid.

20Moreover Yahweh thy God will send the hornet among them, until they that are left, and hide themselves, perish from before thee.

21Thou shalt not be affrighted at them; for Yahweh thy God is in the midst of thee, a great God and a terrible.

22And Yahweh thy God will cast out those nations before thee by little and little: thou mayest not consume them at once, lest the beasts of the field increase upon thee.

23But Yahweh thy God will deliver them up before thee, and will discomfit them with a great discomfiture, until they be destroyed.

24And he will deliver their kings into thy hand, and thou shalt make their name to perish from under heaven: there shall no man be able to stand before thee, until thou have destroyed them.

25The graven images of their gods shall ye burn with fire: thou shalt not covet the silver or the gold that is on them, nor take it unto thee, lest thou be snared therein; for it is an abomination to Yahweh thy God.

26And thou shalt not bring an abomination into thy house, and become a devoted thing like unto it: thou shalt utterly detest it, and thou shalt utterly abhor it; for it is a devoted thing.

Chapter 8

1All the commandment which I command thee this day shall ye observe to do, that ye may live, and multiply, and go in and possess the land which Yahweh sware unto your fathers.

2And thou shalt remember all the way which Yahweh thy God hath led thee these forty years in the wilderness, that he might humble thee, to prove thee, to know what was in thy heart, whether thou wouldest keep his commandments, or not.

3And he humbled thee, and suffered thee to hunger, and fed thee with manna, which thou knewest not, neither did thy fathers know; that he might make thee know that man doth not live by bread only, but by everything that proceedeth out of the mouth of Yahweh doth man live.

4Thy raiment waxed not old upon thee, neither did thy foot swell, these forty years.

5And thou shalt consider in thy heart, that, as a man chasteneth his son, so Yahweh thy God chasteneth thee.

6And thou shalt keep the commandments of Yahweh thy God, to walk in his ways, and to fear him.

7For Yahweh thy God bringeth thee into a good land, a land of brooks of water, of fountains and springs, flowing forth in valleys and hills;

8a land of wheat and barley, and vines and fig-trees and pomegranates; a land of olive-trees and honey;

9a land wherein thou shalt eat bread without scarceness, thou shalt not lack anything in it; a land whose stones are iron, and out of whose hills thou mayest dig copper.

10And thou shalt eat and be full, and thou shalt bless Yahweh thy God for the good land which he hath given thee.

11Beware lest thou forget Yahweh thy God, in not keeping his commandments, and his ordinances, and his statutes, which I command thee this day:

12lest, when thou hast eaten and art full, and hast built goodly houses, and dwelt therein;

13and when thy herds and thy flocks multiply, and thy silver and thy gold is multiplied, and all that thou hast is multiplied;

14then thy heart be lifted up, and thou forget Yahweh thy God, who brought thee forth out of the land of Egypt, out of the house of bondage;

15who led thee through the great and terrible wilderness, wherein were fiery serpents and scorpions, and thirsty ground where was no water; who brought thee forth water out of the rock of flint;

16who fed thee in the wilderness with manna, which thy fathers knew not; that he might humble thee, and that he might prove thee, to do thee good at thy latter end:

17and lest thou say in thy heart, My power and the might of my hand hath gotten me this wealth.

18But thou shalt remember Yahweh thy God, for it is he that giveth thee power to get wealth; that he may establish his covenant which he sware unto thy fathers, as at this day.

19And it shall be, if thou shalt forget Yahweh thy God, and walk after other gods, and serve them, and worship them, I testify against you this day that ye shall surely perish.

20As the nations that Yahweh maketh to perish before you, so shall ye perish; because ye would not hearken unto the voice of Yahweh your God.

Chapter 9

1Hear, O Israel: thou art to pass over the Jordan this day, to go in to dispossess nations greater and mightier than thyself, cities great and fortified up to heaven,

2a people great and tall, the sons of the Anakim, whom thou knowest, and of whom thou hast heard say, Who can stand before the sons of Anak?

3Know therefore this day, that Yahweh thy God is he who goeth over before thee as a devouring fire; he will destroy them, and he will bring them down before thee: so shalt thou drive them out, and make them to perish quickly, as Yahweh hath spoken unto thee.

4Speak not thou in thy heart, after that Yahweh thy God hath thrust them out from before thee, saying, For my righteousness Yahweh hath brought me in to possess this land; whereas for the wickedness of these nations Yahweh doth drive them out from before thee.

5Not for thy righteousness, or for the uprightness of thy heart, dost thou go in to possess their land; but for the wickedness of these nations Yahweh thy God doth drive them out from before thee, and that he may establish the word which Yahweh sware unto thy fathers, to Abraham, to Isaac, and to Jacob.

6Know therefore, that Yahweh thy God giveth thee not this good land to possess it for thy righteousness; for thou art a stiffnecked people.

7Remember, forget thou not, how thou provokedst Yahweh thy God to wrath in the wilderness: from the day that thou wentest forth out of the land of Egypt, until ye came unto this place, ye have been rebellious against Yahweh.

8Also in Horeb ye provoked Yahweh to wrath, and Yahweh was angry with you to destroy you.

9When I was gone up into the mount to receive the tables of stone, even the tables of the covenant which Yahweh made with you, then I abode in the mount forty days and forty nights; I did neither eat bread nor drink water.

10And Yahweh delivered unto me the two tables of stone written with the finger of God; and on them was written according to all the words, which Yahweh speak with you in the mount out of the midst of the fire in the day of the assembly.

11And it came to pass at the end of forty days and forty nights, that Yahweh gave me the two tables of stone, even the tables of the covenant.

12And Yahweh said unto me, Arise, get thee down quickly from hence; for thy people that thou hast brought forth out of Egypt have corrupted themselves; they are quickly turned aside out of the way which I commanded them; they have made them a molten image.

13Furthermore Yahweh spake unto me, saying, I have seen this people, and, behold, it is a stiffnecked people:

14let me alone, that I may destroy them, and blot out their name from under heaven; and I will make of thee a nation mightier and greater than they.

15So I turned and came down from the mount, and the mount was burning with fire: and the two tables of the covenant were in my two hands.

Deuteronomy

16And I looked, and, behold, ye had sinned against Yahweh your God; ye had made you a molten calf: ye had turned aside quickly out of the way which Yahweh had commanded you.

17And I took hold of the two tables, and cast them out of my two hands, and brake them before your eyes.

18And I fell down before Yahweh, as at the first, forty days and forty nights; I did neither eat bread nor drink water; because of all your sin which ye sinned, in doing that which was evil in the sight of Yahweh, to provoke him to anger.

19For I was afraid of the anger and hot displeasure, wherewith Yahweh was wroth against you to destroy you. But Yahweh hearkened unto me that time also.

20And Yahweh was very angry with Aaron to destroy him: and I prayed for Aaron also at the same time.

21And I took your sin, the calf which ye had made, and burnt it with fire, and stamped it, grinding it very small, until it was as fine as dust: and I cast the dust thereof into the brook that descended out of the mount.

22And at Taberah, and at Massah, and at Kibroth-hattaavah, ye provoked Yahweh to wrath.

23And when Yahweh sent you from Kadesh-barnea, saying, Go up and possess the land which I have given you; then ye rebelled against the commandment of Yahweh your God, and ye believed him not, nor hearkened to his voice.

24Ye have been rebellious against Yahweh from the day that I knew you.

25So I fell down before Yahweh the forty days and forty nights that I fell down, because Yahweh had said he would destroy you.

26And I prayed unto Yahweh, and said, O Lord Yahweh, destroy not thy people and thine inheritance, that thou hast redeemed through thy greatness, that thou hast brought forth out of Egypt with a mighty hand.

27Remember thy servants, Abraham, Isaac, and Jacob; look not unto the stubbornness of this people, nor to their wickedness, nor to their sin;

28lest the land whence thou broughtest us out say, Because Yahweh was not able to bring them into the land which he promised unto them, and because he hated them, he hath brought them out to slay them in the wilderness.

29Yet they are thy people and thine inheritance, which thou broughtest out by thy great power and by thine outstretched arm.

Chapter 10

1At that time Yahweh said unto me, Hew thee two tables of stone like unto the first, and come up unto me into the mount, and make thee an ark of wood.

2And I will write on the tables the words that were on the first tables which thou brakest, and thou shalt put them in the ark.

3So I made an ark of acacia wood, and hewed two tables of stone like unto the first, and went up into the mount, having the two tables in my hand.

4And he wrote on the tables, according to the first writing, the ten commandments, which Yahweh spake unto you in the mount out of the midst of the fire in the day of the assembly: and Yahweh gave them unto me.

5And I turned and came down from the mount, and put the tables in the ark which I had made; and there they are as Yahweh commanded me.

6(And the children of Israel journeyed from Beeroth Bene-jaakan to Moserah. There Aaron died, and there he was buried; and Eleazar his son ministered in the priest's office in his stead.

7From thence they journeyed unto Gudgodah; and from Gudgodah to Jotbathah, a land of brooks of water.

8At that time Yahweh set apart the tribe of Levi, to bear the ark of the covenant of Yahweh, to stand before Yahweh to minister unto him, and to bless in his name, unto this day.

9Wherefore Levi hath no portion nor inheritance with his brethren; Yahweh is his inheritance, according as Yahweh thy God spake unto him.)

10And I stayed in the mount, as at the first time, forty days and forty nights: and Yahweh hearkened unto me that time also; Yahweh would not destroy thee.

11And Yahweh said unto me, Arise, take thy journey before the people; and they shall go in and possess the land, which I sware unto their fathers to give unto them.

12And now, Israel, what doth Yahweh thy God require of thee, but to fear Yahweh thy God, to walk in all his ways, and to love him, and to serve Yahweh thy God with all thy heart and with all thy soul,

13to keep the commandments of Yahweh, and his statutes, which I command thee this day for thy good?

14Behold, unto Yahweh thy God belongeth heaven and the heaven of heavens, the earth, with all that is therein.

15Only Yahweh had a delight in thy fathers to love them, and he chose their seed after them, even you above all peoples, as at this day.

16Circumcise therefore the foreskin of your heart, and be no more stiffnecked.

17For Yahweh your God, he is God of gods, and Lord of lords, the great God, the mighty, and the terrible, who regardeth not persons, nor taketh reward.

18He doth execute justice for the fatherless and widow, and loveth the sojourner, in giving him food and raiment.

19Love ye therefore the sojourner; for ye were sojourners in the land of Egypt.

20Thou shalt fear Yahweh thy God; him shalt thou serve; and to him shalt thou cleave, and by his name shalt thou swear.

21He is thy praise, and he is thy God, that hath done for thee these great and terrible things, which thine eyes have seen.

22Thy fathers went down into Egypt with threescore and ten persons; and now Yahweh thy God hath made thee as the stars of heaven for multitude.

Chapter 11

1Therefore thou shalt love Yahweh thy God, and keep his charge, and his statutes, and his ordinances, and his commandments, alway.

2And know ye this day: for I speak not with your children that have not known, and that have not seen the chastisement of Yahweh your God, his greatness, his mighty hand, and his outstretched arm,

3and his signs, and his works, which he did in the midst of Egypt unto Pharaoh the king of Egypt, and unto all his land;

4and what he did unto the army of Egypt, unto their horses, and to their chariots; how he made the water of the Red Sea to overflow them as they pursued after you, and how Yahweh hath destroyed them unto this day;

5and what he did unto you in the wilderness, until ye came unto this place;

6and what he did unto Dathan and Abiram, the sons of Eliab, the son of Reuben; how the earth opened its mouth, and swallowed them up, and their households, and their tents, and every living thing that followed them, in the midst of all Israel:

7but your eyes have seen all the great work of Yahweh which he did.

8Therefore shall ye keep all the commandment which I command thee this day, that ye may be strong, and go in and possess the land, whither ye go over to possess it;

9and that ye may prolong your days in the land, which Yahweh sware unto your fathers to give unto them and to their seed, a land flowing with milk and honey.

10For the land, whither thou goest in to possess it, is not as the land of Egypt, from whence ye came out, where thou sowedst thy seed, and wateredst it with thy foot, as a garden of herbs;

11but the land, whither ye go over to possess it, is a land of hills and valleys, and drinketh water of the rain of heaven,

12a land which Yahweh thy God careth for: the eyes of Yahweh thy God are always upon it, from the beginning of the year even unto the end of the year.

13And it shall come to pass, if ye shall hearken diligently unto my commandments which I command you this day, to love Yahweh your God, and to serve him with all your heart and with all your soul,

14that I will give the rain of your land in its season, the former rain and the latter rain, that thou mayest gather in thy grain, and thy new wine, and thine oil.

15And I will give grass in thy fields for thy cattle, and thou shalt eat and be full.

16Take heed to yourselves, lest your heart be deceived, and ye turn aside, and serve other gods, and worship them;

17and the anger of Yahweh be kindled against you, and he shut up the heavens, so that there shall be no rain, and the land shall not yield its fruit; and ye perish quickly from off the good land which Yahweh giveth you.

18Therefore shall ye lay up these my words in your heart and in your soul; and ye shall bind them for a sign upon your hand, and they shall be for frontlets between your eyes.

19And ye shall teach them your children, talking of them, when thou sittest in thy house, and when thou walkest by the way, and when thou liest down, and when thou risest up.

20And thou shalt write them upon the door-posts of thy house, and upon thy gates;

21that your days may be multiplied, and the days of your children, in the land which Yahweh sware unto your fathers to give them, as the days of the heavens above the earth.

22For if ye shall diligently keep all this commandment which I command you, to do it, to love Yahweh your God, to walk in all his ways, and to cleave unto him;

23then will Yahweh drive out all these nations from before you, and ye shall dispossess nations greater and mightier than yourselves.

24Every place whereon the sole of your foot shall tread shall be yours: from the wilderness, and Lebanon, from the river, the river Euphrates, even unto the hinder sea shall be your border.

25There shall no man be able to stand before you: Yahweh your God shall lay the fear of you and the dread of you upon all the land that ye shall tread upon, as he hath spoken unto you.

26Behold, I set before you this day a blessing and a curse:

27the blessing, if ye shall hearken unto the commandments of Yahweh your God, which I command you this day;

28and the curse, if ye shall not hearken unto the commandments of Yahweh your God, but turn aside out of the way which I command you this day, to go after other gods, which ye have not known.

29And it shall come to pass, when Yahweh thy God shall bring thee into the land whither thou goest to possess it, that thou shalt set the blessing upon mount Gerizim, and the curse upon mount Ebal.

30Are they not beyond the Jordan, behind the way of the going down of the sun, in the land of the Canaanites that dwell in the Arabah, over against Gilgal, beside the oaks of Moreh?

31For ye are to pass over the Jordan to go in to possess the land which Yahweh your God giveth you, and ye shall possess it, and dwell therein.

32And ye shall observe to do all the statutes and the ordinances which I set before you this day.

Chapter 12

1These are the statutes and the ordinances which ye shall observe to do in the land which Yahweh, the God of thy fathers, hath given thee to possess it, all the days that ye live upon the earth.

2Ye shall surely destroy all the places wherein the nations that ye shall dispossess served their gods, upon the high mountains, and upon the hills, and under every green tree:

3and ye shall break down their altars, and dash in pieces their pillars, and burn their Asherim with fire; and ye shall hew down the graven images of their gods; and ye shall destroy their name out of that place.

4Ye shall not do so unto Yahweh your God.

5But unto the place which Yahweh your God shall choose out of all your tribes, to put his name there, even unto his habitation shall ye seek, and thither thou shalt come;

6and thither ye shall bring your burnt-offerings, and your sacrifices, and your tithes, and the heave-offering of your hand, and your vows, and your freewill-offerings, and the firstlings of your herd and of your flock:

7and there ye shall eat before Yahweh your God, and ye shall rejoice in all that ye put your hand unto, ye and your households, wherein Yahweh thy God hath blessed thee.

8Ye shall not do after all the things that we do here this day, every man whatsoever is right in his own eyes;

9for ye are not as yet come to the rest and to the inheritance, which Yahweh thy God giveth thee.

10But when ye go over the Jordan, and dwell in the land which Yahweh your God causeth you to inherit, and he giveth you rest from all your enemies round about, so that ye dwell in safety;

11then it shall come to pass that to the place which Yahweh your God shall choose, to cause his name to dwell there, thither shall ye bring all that I command you: your burnt-offerings, and your sacrifices, your tithes, and the heave-offering of your hand, and all your choice vows which ye vow unto Yahweh.

12And ye shall rejoice before Yahweh your God, ye, and your sons, and your daughters, and your men-servants, and your maid-servants, and the Levite that is within your gates, forasmuch as he hath no portion nor inheritance with you.

13Take heed to thyself that thou offer not thy burnt-offerings in every place that thou seest;

14but in the place which Yahweh shall choose in one of thy tribes, there thou shalt offer thy burnt-offerings, and there thou shalt do all that I command thee.

15Notwithstanding, thou mayest kill and eat flesh within all thy gates, after all the desire of thy soul, according to the blessing of Yahweh thy God which he hath given thee: the unclean and the clean may eat thereof, as of the gazelle, and as of the hart.

16Only ye shall not eat the blood; thou shalt pour it out upon the earth as water.

17Thou mayest not eat within thy gates the tithe of thy grain, or of thy new wine, or of thine oil, or the firstlings of thy herd or of thy flock, nor any of thy vows which thou vowest, nor thy freewill-offerings, nor the heave-offering of thy hand;

18but thou shalt eat them before Yahweh thy God in the place which Yahweh thy God shall choose, thou, and thy son, and thy daughter, and thy man-servant, and thy maid-servant, and the Levite that is within thy gates: and thou shalt rejoice before Yahweh thy God in all that thou puttest thy hand unto.

19Take heed to thyself that thou forsake not the Levite as long as thou livest in thy land.

20When Yahweh thy God shall enlarge thy border, as he hath promised thee, and thou shalt say, I will eat flesh, because thy soul desireth to eat flesh; thou mayest eat flesh, after all the desire of thy soul.

21If the place which Yahweh thy God shall choose, to put his name there, be too far from thee, then thou shalt kill of thy herd and of thy flock, which Yahweh hath given thee, as I have commanded thee; and thou mayest eat within thy gates, after all the desire of thy soul.

22Even as the gazelle and as the hart is eaten, so thou shalt eat thereof: the unclean and the clean may eat thereof alike.

23Only be sure that thou eat not the blood: for the blood is the life; and thou shalt not eat the life with the flesh.

24Thou shalt not eat it; thou shalt pour it out upon the earth as water.

25Thou shalt not eat it; that it may go well with thee, and with thy children after thee, when thou shalt do that which is right in the eyes of Yahweh.

26Only thy holy things which thou hast, and thy vows, thou shalt take, and go unto the place which Yahweh shall choose:

27and thou shalt offer thy burnt-offerings, the flesh and the blood, upon the altar of Yahweh thy God; and the blood of thy sacrifices shall be poured out upon the altar of Yahweh thy God; and thou shalt eat the flesh.

28Observe and hear all these words which I command thee, that it may go well with thee, and with thy children after thee for ever, when thou doest that which is good and right in the eyes of Yahweh thy God.

29When Yahweh thy God shall cut off the nations from before thee, whither thou goest in to dispossess them, and thou dispossessest them, and dwellest in their land;

30take heed to thyself that thou be not ensnared to follow them, after that they are destroyed from before thee; and that thou inquire not after their gods, saying, How do these nations serve their gods? even so will I do likewise.

31Thou shalt not do so unto Yahweh thy God: for every abomination to Yahweh, which he hateth, have they done unto their gods; for even their sons and their daughters do they burn in the fire to their gods.

32What thing soever I command you, that shall ye observe to do: thou shalt not add thereto, nor diminish from it.

Chapter 13

1If there arise in the midst of thee a prophet, or a dreamer of dreams, and he give thee a sign or a wonder,

2and the sign or the wonder come to pass, whereof he spake unto thee, saying, Let us go after other gods, which thou hast not known, and let us serve them;

3thou shalt not hearken unto the words of that prophet, or unto that dreamer of dreams: for Yahweh your God proveth you, to know whether ye love Yahweh your God with all your heart and with all your soul.

4Ye shall walk after Yahweh your God, and fear him, and keep his commandments, and obey his voice, and ye shall serve him, and cleave unto him.

5And that prophet, or that dreamer of dreams, shall be put to death, because he hath spoken rebellion against Yahweh your God, who brought you out of the land of Egypt, and redeemed thee out of the house of bondage, to draw thee aside out of the way which Yahweh thy God commanded thee to walk in. So shalt thou put away the evil from the midst of thee.

6If thy brother, the son of thy mother, or thy son, or thy daughter, or the wife of thy bosom, or thy friend, that is as thine own soul, entice thee secretly, saying, Let us go and serve other gods, which thou hast not known, thou, nor thy fathers;

7of the gods of the peoples that are round about you, nigh unto thee, or far off from thee, from the one end of the earth even unto the other end of the earth;

8thou shalt not consent unto him, nor hearken unto him; neither shall thine eye pity him, neither shalt thou spare, neither shalt thou conceal him:

9but thou shalt surely kill him; thy hand shall be first upon him to put him to death, and afterwards the hand of all the people.

10And thou shalt stone him to death with stones, because he hath sought to draw thee away from Yahweh thy God, who brought thee out of the land of Egypt, out of the house of bondage.

11And all Israel shall hear, and fear, and shall do not more any such wickedness as this is in the midst of thee.

12If thou shalt hear tell concerning one of thy cities, which Yahweh thy God giveth thee to dwell there, saying,

13Certain base fellows are gone out from the midst of thee, and have drawn away the inhabitants of their city, saying, Let us go and serve other gods, which ye have not known;

14then shalt thou inquire, and make search, and ask diligently; and, behold, if it be truth, and the thing certain, that such abomination is wrought in the midst of thee,

15thou shalt surely smite the inhabitants of that city with the edge of the sword, destroying it utterly, and all that is therein and the cattle thereof, with the edge of the sword.

16And thou shalt gather all the spoil of it into the midst of the street thereof, and shalt burn with fire the city, and all the spoil thereof every whit, unto Yahweh thy God: and it shall be a heap for ever; it shall not be built again.

17And there shall cleave nought of the devoted thing to thy hand; that Yahweh may turn from the fierceness of his anger, and show thee mercy, and have compassion upon thee, and multiply thee, as he hath sworn unto thy fathers;

18when thou shalt hearken to the voice of Yahweh thy God, to keep all his commandments which I command thee this day, to do that which is right in the eyes of Yahweh thy God.

Chapter 14

1Ye are the children of Yahweh your God: ye shall not cut yourselves, nor make any baldness between your eyes for the dead.

2For thou art a holy people unto Yahweh thy God, and Yahweh hath chosen thee to be a people for his own possession, above all peoples that are upon the face of the earth.

3Thou shalt not eat any abominable thing.

4These are the beasts which ye may eat: the ox, the sheep, and the goat,

5the hart, and the gazelle, and the roebuck, and the wild goat, and the pygarg, and the antelope, and the chamois.

6And every beast that parteth the hoof, and hath the hoof cloven in two, and cheweth the cud, among the beasts, that may ye eat.

7Nevertheless these ye shall not eat of them that chew the cud, or of them that have the hoof cloven: the camel, and the hare, and the coney; because they chew the cud but part not the hoof, they are unclean unto you.

8And the swine, because he parteth the hoof but cheweth not the cud, he is unclean unto you: of their flesh ye shall not eat, and their carcasses ye shall not touch.

9These ye may eat of all that are in the waters: whatsoever hath fins and scales may ye eat;

10and whatsoever hath not fins and scales ye shall not eat; it is unclean unto you.

11Of all clean birds ye may eat.

12But these are they of which ye shall not eat: the eagle, and the gier-eagle, and the ospray,

13and the glede, and the falcon, and the kite after its kind,

14and every raven after its kind,

15and the ostrich, and the night-hawk, and the sea-mew, and the hawk after its kind,

16the little owl, and the great owl, and the horned owl,

17and the pelican, and the vulture, and the cormorant,

18and the stork, and the heron after its kind, and the hoopoe, and the bat.

19And all winged creeping things are unclean unto you: they shall not be eaten.

20Of all clean birds ye may eat.

21Ye shall not eat of anything that dieth of itself: thou mayest give it unto

Deuteronomy

the sojourner that is within thy gates, that he may eat it; or thou mayest sell it unto a foreigner: for thou art a holy people unto Yahweh thy God. Thou shalt not boil a kid in its mother's milk.

22Thou shalt surely tithe all the increase of thy seed, that which cometh forth from the field year by year.

23And thou shalt eat before Yahweh thy God, in the place which he shall choose, to cause his name to dwell there, the tithe of thy grain, of thy new wine, and of thine oil, and the firstlings of thy herd and of thy flock; that thou mayest learn to fear Yahweh thy God always.

24And if the way be too long for thee, so that thou art not able to carry it, because the place is too far from thee, which Yahweh thy God shall choose, to set his name there, when Yahweh thy God shall bless thee;

25then shalt thou turn it into money, and bind up the money in thy hand, and shalt go unto the place which Yahweh thy God shall choose:

26and thou shalt bestow the money for whatsoever thy soul desireth, for oxen, or for sheep, or for wine, or for strong drink, or for whatsoever thy soul asketh of thee; and thou shalt eat there before Yahweh thy God, and thou shalt rejoice, thou and thy household.

27And the Levite that is within thy gates, thou shalt not forsake him; for he hath no portion nor inheritance with thee.

28At the end of every three years thou shalt bring forth all the tithe of thine increase in the same year, and shalt lay it up within thy gates:

29and the Levite, because he hath no portion nor inheritance with thee, and the sojourner, and the fatherless, and the widow, that are within thy gates, shall come, and shall eat and be satisfied; that Yahweh thy God may bless thee in all the work of thy hand which thou doest.

Chapter 15

1At the end of every seven years thou shalt make a release.

2And this is the manner of the release: every creditor shall release that which he hath lent unto his neighbor; he shall not exact it of his neighbor and his brother; because Yahweh's release hath been proclaimed.

3Of a foreigner thou mayest exact it: but whatsoever of thine is with thy brother thy hand shall release.

4Howbeit there shall be no poor with thee; (for Yahweh will surely bless thee in the land which Yahweh thy God giveth thee for an inheritance to possess it;)

5if only thou diligently hearken unto the voice of Yahweh thy God, to observe to do all this commandment which I command thee this day.

6For Yahweh thy God will bless thee, as he promised thee: and thou shalt lend unto many nations, but thou shalt not borrow; and thou shalt rule over many nations, but they shall not rule over thee.

7If there be with thee a poor man, one of thy brethren, within any of thy gates in thy land which Yahweh thy God giveth thee, thou shalt not harden thy heart, nor shut thy hand from thy poor brother;

8but thou shalt surely open thy hand unto him, and shalt surely lend him sufficient for his need in that which he wanteth.

9Beware that there be not a base thought in thy heart, saying, The seventh year, the year of release, is at hand; and thine eye be evil against thy poor brother, and thou give him nought; and he cry unto Yahweh against thee, and it be sin unto thee.

10Thou shalt surely give him, and thy heart shall not be grieved when thou givest unto him; because that for this thing Yahweh thy God will bless thee in all thy work, and in all that thou puttest thy hand unto.

11For the poor will never cease out of the land: therefore I command thee, saying, Thou shalt surely open thy hand unto thy brother, to thy needy, and to thy poor, in thy land.

12If thy brother, a Hebrew man, or a Hebrew woman, be sold unto thee, and serve thee six years; then in the seventh year thou shalt let him go free from thee.

13And when thou lettest him go free from thee, thou shalt not let him go empty:

14thou shalt furnish him liberally out of thy flock, and out of thy threshing-floor, and out of thy winepress; as Yahweh thy God hath blessed thee thou shalt give unto him.

15And thou shalt remember that thou wast a bondman in the land of Egypt, and Yahweh thy God redeemed thee: therefore I command thee this thing to-day.

16And it shall be, if he say unto thee, I will not go out from thee; because he loveth thee and thy house, because he is well with thee;

17then thou shalt take an awl, and thrust it through his ear unto the door, and he shall be thy servant for ever. And also unto thy maid-servant thou shalt do likewise.

18It shall not seem hard unto thee, when thou lettest him go free from thee; for to the double of the hire of a hireling hath he served thee six years: and Yahweh thy God will bless thee in all that thou doest.

19All the firstling males that are born of thy herd and of thy flock thou shalt sanctify unto Yahweh thy God: thou shalt do no work with the firstling of thy herd, nor shear the firstling of thy flock.

20Thou shalt eat it before Yahweh thy God year by year in the place which Yahweh shall choose, thou and thy household.

21And if it have any blemish, as if it be lame or blind, any ill blemish whatsoever, thou shalt not sacrifice it unto Yahweh thy God.

22Thou shalt eat it within thy gates: the unclean and the clean shall eat it alike, as the gazelle, and as the hart.

23Only thou shalt not eat the blood thereof; thou shalt pour it out upon the ground as water.

Chapter 16

1Observe the month of Abib, and keep the passover unto Yahweh thy God; for in the month of Abib Yahweh thy God brought thee forth out of Egypt by night.

2And thou shalt sacrifice the passover unto Yahweh thy God, of the flock and the herd, in the place which Yahweh shall choose, to cause his name to dwell there.

3Thou shalt eat no leavened bread with it; seven days shalt thou eat unleavened bread therewith, even the bread of affliction; for thou camest forth out of the land of Egypt in haste: that thou mayest remember the day when thou camest forth out of the land of Egypt all the days of thy life.

4And there shall be no leaven seen with thee in all thy borders seven days; neither shall any of the flesh, which thou sacrificest the first day at even, remain all night until the morning.

5Thou mayest not sacrifice the passover within any of thy gates, which Yahweh thy God giveth thee;

6but at the place which Yahweh thy God shall choose, to cause his name to dwell in, there thou shalt sacrifice the passover at even, at the going down of the sun, at the season that thou camest forth out of Egypt.

7And thou shalt roast and eat it in the place which Yahweh thy God shall choose: and thou shalt turn in the morning, and go unto thy tents.

8Six days thou shalt eat unleavened bread; and on the seventh day shall be a solemn assembly to Yahweh thy God; thou shalt do no work therein.

9Seven weeks shalt thou number unto thee: from the time thou beginnest to put the sickle to the standing grain shalt thou begin to number seven weeks.

10And thou shalt keep the feast of weeks unto Yahweh thy God with a tribute of a freewill-offering of thy hand, which thou shalt give, according as Yahweh thy God blesseth thee:

11and thou shalt rejoice before Yahweh thy God, thou, and thy son, and thy daughter, and thy man-servant, and thy maid-servant, and the Levite that is within thy gates, and the sojourner, and the fatherless, and the widow, that are in the midst of thee, in the place which Yahweh thy God shall choose, to cause his name to dwell there.

12And thou shalt remember that thou wast a bondman in Egypt: and thou shalt observe and do these statutes.

13Thou shalt keep the feast of tabernacles seven days, after that thou hast gathered in from thy threshing-floor and from thy winepress:

14and thou shalt rejoice in thy feast, thou, and thy son, and thy daughter, and thy man-servant, and thy maid-servant, and the Levite, and the sojourner, and the fatherless, and the widow, that are within thy gates.

15Seven days shalt thou keep a feast unto Yahweh thy God in the place which Yahweh shall choose; because Yahweh thy God will bless thee in all thine increase, and in all the work of thy hands, and thou shalt be altogether joyful.

16Three times in a year shall all thy males appear before Yahweh thy God in the place which he shall choose: in the feast of unleavened bread, and in the feast of weeks, and in the feast of tabernacles; and they shall not appear before Yahweh empty:

17every man shall give as he is able, according to the blessing of Yahweh thy God which he hath given thee.

18Judges and officers shalt thou make thee in all thy gates, which Yahweh thy God giveth thee, according to thy tribes; and they shall judge the people with righteous judgment.

19Thou shalt not wrest justice: thou shalt not respect persons; neither shalt thou take a bribe; for a bribe doth blind the eyes of the wise, and pervert the words of the righteous.

20That which is altogether just shalt thou follow, that thou mayest live, and inherit the land which Yahweh thy God giveth thee.

21Thou shalt not plant thee an Asherah of any kind of tree beside the altar of Yahweh thy God, which thou shalt make thee.

22Neither shalt thou set thee up a pillar; which Yahweh thy God hateth.

Chapter 17

1Thou shalt not sacrifice unto Yahweh thy God an ox, or a sheep, wherein is a blemish, or anything evil; for that is an abomination unto Yahweh thy God.

2If there be found in the midst of thee, within any of thy gates which Yahweh thy God giveth thee, man or woman, that doeth that which is evil in the sight of Yahweh thy God, in transgressing his covenant,

3and hath gone and served other gods, and worshipped them, or the sun, or the moon, or any of the host of heaven, which I have not commanded;

4and it be told thee, and thou hast heard of it, then shalt thou inquire diligently; and, behold, if it be true, and the thing certain, that such abomination is wrought in Israel,

5then shalt thou bring forth that man or that woman, who hath done this evil thing, unto thy gates, even the man or the woman; and thou shalt stone them to death with stones.

6At the mouth of two witnesses, or three witnesses, shall he that is to die be put to death; at the mouth of one witness he shall not be put to death.

7The hand of the witnesses shall be first upon him to put him to death, and afterward the hand of all the people. So thou shalt put away the evil from the midst of thee.

8If there arise a matter too hard for thee in judgment, between blood and blood, between plea and plea, and between stroke and stroke, being matters of controversy within thy gates; then shalt thou arise, and get thee up unto the place which Yahweh thy God shall choose;

9and thou shalt come unto the priests the Levites, and unto the judge that shall be in those days: and thou shalt inquire; and they shall show thee the sentence of judgment.

10And thou shalt do according to the tenor of the sentence which they shall show thee from that place which Yahweh shall choose; and thou shalt observe to do according to all that they shall teach thee:

11according to the tenor of the law which they shall teach thee, and according to the judgment which they shall tell thee, thou shalt do; thou shalt not turn aside from the sentence which they shall show thee, to the right hand, nor to the left.

12And the man that doeth presumptuously, in not hearkening unto the priest that standeth to minister there before Yahweh thy God, or unto the judge, even that man shall die: and thou shalt put away the evil from Israel.

13And all the people shall hear, and fear, and do no more presumptuously.

14When thou art come unto the land which Yahweh thy God giveth thee, and shalt possess it, and shalt dwell therein, and shalt say, I will set a king over me, like all the nations that are round about me;

15thou shalt surely set him king over thee, whom Yahweh thy God shall choose: one from among thy brethren shalt thou set king over thee; thou mayest not put a foreigner over thee, who is not thy brother.

16Only he shall not multiply horses to himself, nor cause the people to return to Egypt, to the end that he may multiply horses; forasmuch as Yahweh hath said unto you, Ye shall henceforth return no more that way.

17Neither shall he multiply wives to himself, that his heart turn not away: neither shall he greatly multiply to himself silver and gold.

18And it shall be, when he sitteth upon the throne of his kingdom, that he shall write him a copy of this law in a book, out of that which is before the priests the Levites:

19and it shall be with him, and he shall read therein all the days of his life; that he may learn to fear Yahweh his God, to keep all the words of this law and these statutes, to do them;

20that his heart be not lifted up above his brethren, and that he turn not aside from the commandment, to the right hand, or to the left: to the end that he may prolong his days in his kingdom, he and his children, in the midst of Israel.

Chapter 18

1The priests the Levites, even all the tribe of Levi, shall have no portion nor inheritance with Israel: they shall eat the offerings of Yahweh made by fire, and his inheritance.

2And they shall have no inheritance among their brethren: Yahweh is their inheritance, as he hath spoken unto them.

3And this shall be the priests' due from the people, from them that offer a sacrifice, whether it be ox or sheep, that they shall give unto the priest the shoulder, and the two cheeks, and the maw.

4The first-fruits of thy grain, of thy new wine, and of thine oil, and the first of the fleece of thy sheep, shalt thou give him.

5For Yahweh thy God hath chosen him out of all thy tribes, to stand to minister in the name of Yahweh, him and his sons for ever.

6And if a Levite come from any of thy gates out of all Israel, where he sojourneth, and come with all the desire of his soul unto the place which Yahweh shall choose;

7then he shall minister in the name of Yahweh his God, as all his brethren the Levites do, who stand there before Yahweh.

8They shall have like portions to eat, besides that which cometh of the sale of his patrimony.

9When thou art come into the land which Yahweh thy God giveth thee, thou shalt not learn to do after the abominations of those nations.

10There shall not be found with thee any one that maketh his son or his daughter to pass through the fire, one that useth divination, one that practiseth augury, or an enchanter, or a sorcerer,

11or a charmer, or a consulter with a familiar spirit, or a wizard, or a necromancer.

12For whosoever doeth these things is an abomination unto Yahweh: and because of these abominations Yahweh thy God doth drive them out from before thee.

13Thou shalt be perfect with Yahweh thy God.

14For these nations, that thou shalt dispossess, hearken unto them that practise augury, and unto diviners; but as for thee, Yahweh thy God hath not suffered thee so to do.

15Yahweh thy God will raise up unto thee a prophet from the midst of thee, of thy brethren, like unto me; unto him ye shall hearken;

16according to all that thou desiredst of Yahweh thy God in Horeb in the day of the assembly, saying, Let me not hear again the voice of Yahweh my God, neither let me see this great fire any more, that I die not.

17And Yahweh said unto me, They have well said that which they have spoken.

18I will raise them up a prophet from among their brethren, like unto thee; and I will put my words in his mouth, and he shall speak unto them all that I shall command him.

19And it shall come to pass, that whosoever will not hearken unto my words which he shall speak in my name, I will require it of him.

20But the prophet, that shall speak a word presumptuously in my name, which I have not commanded him to speak, or that shall speak in the name of other gods, that same prophet shall die.

21And if thou say in thy heart, How shall we know the word which Yahweh hath not spoken?

22when a prophet speaketh in the name of Yahweh, if the thing follow not, nor come to pass, that is the thing which Yahweh hath not spoken: the prophet hath spoken it presumptuously, thou shalt not be afraid of him.

Chapter 19

1When Yahweh thy God shall cut off the nations, whose land Yahweh thy God giveth thee, and thou succeedest them, and dwellest in their cities, and in their houses;

2thou shalt set apart three cities for thee in the midst of thy land, which Yahweh thy God giveth thee to possess it.

3Thou shalt prepare thee the way, and divide the borders of thy land, which Yahweh thy God causeth thee to inherit, into three parts, that every manslayer may flee thither.

4And this is the case of the manslayer, that shall flee thither and live: whoso killeth his neighbor unawares, and hated him not in time past;

5as when a man goeth into the forest with his neighbor to hew wood, and his hand fetcheth a stroke with the axe to cut down the tree, and the head slippeth from the helve, and lighteth upon his neighbor, so that he dieth; he shall flee unto one of these cities and live:

6lest the avenger of blood pursue the manslayer, while his heart is hot, and overtake him, because the way is long, and smite him mortally; whereas he was not worthy of death, inasmuch as he hated him not in time past.

7Wherefore I command thee, saying, Thou shalt set apart three cities for thee.

8And if Yahweh thy God enlarge thy border, as he hath sworn unto thy fathers, and give thee all the land which he promised to give unto thy fathers;

9if thou shalt keep all this commandment to do it, which I command thee this day, to love Yahweh thy God, and to walk ever in his ways; then shalt thou add three cities more for thee, besides these three:

10that innocent blood be not shed in the midst of thy land, which Yahweh thy God giveth thee for an inheritance, and so blood be upon thee.

11But if any man hate his neighbor, and lie in wait for him, and rise up against him, and smite him mortally so that he dieth, and he flee into one of these cities;

12then the elders of his city shall send and fetch him thence, and deliver him into the hand of the avenger of blood, that he may die.

13Thine eye shall not pity him, but thou shalt put away the innocent blood from Israel, that it may go well with thee.

14Thou shalt not remove thy neighbor's landmark, which they of old time have set, in thine inheritance which thou shalt inherit, in the land that Yahweh thy God giveth thee to possess it.

15One witness shall not rise up against a man for any iniquity, or for any sin, in any sin that he sinneth: at the mouth of two witnesses, or at the mouth of three witnesses, shall a matter be established.

16If an unrighteous witness rise up against any man to testify against him of wrong-doing,

17then both the men, between whom the controversy is, shall stand before Yahweh, before the priests and the judges that shall be in those days;

18and the judges shall make diligent inquisition: and, behold, if the witness be a false witness, and have testified falsely against his brother;

19then shall ye do unto him, as he had thought to do unto his brother: so shalt thou put away the evil from the midst of thee.

20And those that remain shall hear, and fear, and shall henceforth commit no more any such evil in the midst of thee.

21And thine eyes shall not pity; life shall go for life, eye for eye, tooth for tooth, hand for hand, foot for foot.

Chapter 20

1When thou goest forth to battle against thine enemies, and seest horses, and chariots, and a people more than thou, thou shalt not be afraid of them; for Yahweh thy God is with thee, who brought thee up out of the land of Egypt.

2And it shall be, when ye draw nigh unto the battle, that the priest shall approach and speak unto the people,

3and shall say unto them, Hear, O Israel, ye draw nigh this day unto battle against your enemies: let not your heart faint; fear not, nor tremble, neither be ye affrighted at them;

4for Yahweh your God is he that goeth with you, to fight for you against your enemies, to save you.

5And the officers shall speak unto the people, saying, What man is there that hath built a new house, and hath not dedicated it? let him go and return to his house, lest he die in the battle, and another man dedicate it.

6And what man is there that hath planted a vineyard, and hath not used the fruit thereof? let him go and return unto his house, lest he die in the battle, and another man use the fruit thereof.

7And what man is there that hath betrothed a wife, and hath not taken her? let him go and return unto his house, lest he die in the battle, and another man take her.

8And the officers shall speak further unto the people, and they shall say, What man is there that is fearful and faint-hearted? let him go and return unto his house, lest his brethren's heart melt as his heart.

9And it shall be, when the officers have made an end of speaking unto the people, that they shall appoint captains of hosts at the head of the people.

10When thou drawest nigh unto a city to fight against it, then proclaim peace unto it.

11And it shall be, if it make thee answer of peace, and open unto thee, then it shall be, that all the people that are found therein shall become tributary unto thee, and shall serve thee.

12And if it will make no peace with thee, but will make war against thee, then thou shalt besiege it:

13and when Yahweh thy God delivereth it into thy hand, thou shalt smite every male thereof with the edge of the sword:

14but the women, and the little ones, and the cattle, and all that is in the city,

Deuteronomy

even all the spoil thereof, shalt thou take for a prey unto thyself; and thou shalt eat the spoil of thine enemies, which Yahweh thy God hath given thee.

15Thus shalt thou do unto all the cities which are very far off from thee, which are not of the cities of these nations.

16But of the cities of these peoples, that Yahweh thy God giveth thee for an inheritance, thou shalt save alive nothing that breatheth;

17but thou shalt utterly destroy them: the Hittite, and the Amorite, the Canaanite, and the Perizzite, the Hivite, and the Jebusite; as Yahweh thy God hath commanded thee;

18that they teach you not to do after all their abominations, which they have done unto their gods; so would ye sin against Yahweh your God.

19When thou shalt besiege a city a long time, in making war against it to take it, thou shalt not destroy the trees thereof by wielding an axe against them; for thou mayest eat of them, and thou shalt not cut them down; for is the tree of the field man, that it should be besieged of thee?

20Only the trees of which thou knowest that they are not trees for food, thou shalt destroy and cut them down; and thou shalt build bulwarks against the city that maketh war with thee, until it fall.

Chapter 21

1If one be found slain in the land which Yahweh thy God giveth thee to possess it, lying in the field, and it be not known who hath smitten him;

2then thy elders and thy judges shall come forth, and they shall measure unto the cities which are round about him that is slain:

3and it shall be, that the city which is nearest unto the slain man, even the elders of that city shall take a heifer of the herd, which hath not been wrought with, and which hath not drawn in the yoke;

4and the elders of that city shall bring down the heifer unto a valley with running water, which is neither plowed nor sown, and shall break the heifer's neck there in the valley.

5And the priests the sons of Levi shall come near; for them Yahweh thy God hath chosen to minister unto him, and to bless in the name of Yahweh; and according to their word shall every controversy and every stroke be.

6And all the elders of that city, who are nearest unto the slain man, shall wash their hands over the heifer whose neck was broken in the valley;

7and they shall answer and say, Our hands have not shed this blood, neither have our eyes seen it.

8Forgive, O Yahweh, thy people Israel, whom thou hast redeemed, and suffer not innocent blood to remain in the midst of thy people Israel. And the blood shall be forgiven them.

9So shalt thou put away the innocent blood from the midst of thee, when thou shalt do that which is right in the eyes of Yahweh.

10When thou goest forth to battle against thine enemies, and Yahweh thy God delivereth them into thy hands, and thou carriest them away captive,

11and seest among the captives a beautiful woman, and thou hast a desire unto her, and wouldest take her to thee to wife;

12then thou shalt bring her home to thy house; and she shall shave her head, and pare her nails;

13and she shall put the raiment of her captivity from off her, and shall remain in thy house, and bewail her father and her mother a full month: and after that thou shalt go in unto her, and be her husband, and she shall be thy wife.

14And it shall be, if thou have no delight in her, then thou shalt let her go whither she will; but thou shalt not sell her at all for money, thou shalt not deal with her as a slave, because thou hast humbled her.

15If a man have two wives, the one beloved, and the other hated, and they have borne him children, both the beloved and the hated; and if the first-born son be hers that was hated;

16then it shall be, in the day that he causeth his sons to inherit that which he hath, that he may not make the son of the beloved the first-born before the son of the hated, who is the first-born:

17but he shall acknowledge the first-born, the son of the hated, by giving him a double portion of all that he hath; for he is the beginning of his strength; the right of the first-born is his.

18If a man have a stubborn and rebellious son, that will not obey the voice of his father, or the voice of his mother, and, though they chasten him, will not hearken unto them;

19then shall his father and his mother lay hold on him, and bring him out unto the elders of his city, and unto the gate of his place;

20and they shall say unto the elders of his city, This our son is stubborn and rebellious, he will not obey our voice; he is a glutton, and a drunkard.

21And all the men of his city shall stone him to death with stones: so shalt thou put away the evil from the midst of thee; and all Israel shall hear, and fear.

22And if a man have committed a sin worthy of death, and he be put to death, and thou hang him on a tree;

23his body shall not remain all night upon the tree, but thou shalt surely bury him the same day; for he that is hanged is accursed of God; that thou defile not thy land which Yahweh thy God giveth thee for an inheritance.

Chapter 22

1Thou shalt not see thy brother's ox or his sheep go astray, and hide thyself from them: thou shalt surely bring them again unto thy brother.

2And if thy brother be not nigh unto thee, or if thou know him not, then thou shalt bring it home to thy house, and it shall be with thee until thy brother seek after it, and thou shalt restore it to him.

3And so shalt thou do with his ass; and so shalt thou do with his garment; and so shalt thou do with every lost thing of thy brother's, which he hath lost, and thou hast found: thou mayest not hide thyself.

4Thou shalt not see thy brother's ass or his ox fallen down by the way, and hide thyself from them: thou shalt surely help him to lift them up again.

5A woman shall not wear that which pertaineth unto a man, neither shall a man put on a woman's garment; for whosoever doeth these things is an abomination unto Yahweh thy God.

6If a bird's nest chance to be before thee in the way, in any tree or on the ground, with young ones or eggs, and the dam sitting upon the young, or upon the eggs, thou shalt not take the dam with the young:

7thou shalt surely let the dam go, but the young thou mayest take unto thyself; that it may be well with thee, and that thou mayest prolong thy days.

8When thou buildest a new house, then thou shalt make a battlement for thy roof, that thou bring not blood upon thy house, if any man fall from thence.

9Thou shalt not sow thy vineyard with two kinds of seed, lest the whole fruit be forfeited, the seed which thou hast sown, and the increase of the vineyard.

10Thou shalt not plow with an ox and an ass together.

11Thou shalt not wear a mingled stuff, wool and linen together.

12Thou shalt make thee fringes upon the four borders of thy vesture, wherewith thou coverest thyself.

13If any man take a wife, and go in unto her, and hate her,

14and lay shameful things to her charge, and bring up an evil name upon her, and say, I took this woman, and when I came nigh to her, I found not in her the tokens of virginity;

15then shall the father of the damsel, and her mother, take and bring forth the tokens of the damsel's virginity unto the elders of the city in the gate;

16and the damsel's father shall say unto the elders, I gave my daughter unto this man to wife, and he hateth her;

17and, lo, he hath laid shameful things to her charge, saying, I found not in thy daughter the tokens of virginity; and yet these are the tokens of my daughter's virginity. And they shall spread the garment before the elders of the city.

18And the elders of that city shall take the man and chastise him;

19and they shall fine him a hundred shekels of silver, and give them unto the father of the damsel, because he hath brought up an evil name upon a virgin of Israel: and she shall be his wife; he may not put her away all his days.

20But if this thing be true, that the tokens of virginity were not found in the damsel;

21then they shall bring out the damsel to the door of her father's house, and the men of her city shall stone her to death with stones, because she hath wrought folly in Israel, to play the harlot in her father's house: so shalt thou put away the evil from the midst of thee.

22If a man be found lying with a woman married to a husband, then they shall both of them die, the man that lay with the woman, and the woman: so shalt thou put away the evil from Israel.

23If there be a damsel that is a virgin betrothed unto a husband, and a man find her in the city, and lie with her;

24then ye shall bring them both out unto the gate of that city, and ye shall stone them to death with stones; the damsel, because she cried not, being in the city; and the man, because he hath humbled his neighbor's wife: so thou shalt put away the evil from the midst of thee.

25But if the man find the damsel that is betrothed in the field, and the man force her, and lie with her; then the man only that lay with her shall die:

26but unto the damsel thou shalt do nothing; there is in the damsel no sin worthy of death: for as when a man riseth against his neighbor, and slayeth him, even so is this matter;

27for he found her in the field, the betrothed damsel cried, and there was none to save her.

28If a man find a damsel that is a virgin, that is not betrothed, and lay hold on her, and lie with her, and they be found;

29then the man that lay with her shall give unto the damsel's father fifty shekels of silver, and she shall be his wife, because he hath humbled her; he may not put her away all his days.

30A man shall not take his father's wife, and shall not uncover his father's skirt.

Chapter 23

1He that is wounded in the stones, or hath his privy member cut off, shall not enter into the assembly of Yahweh.

2A bastard shall not enter into the assembly of Yahweh; even to the tenth generation shall none of his enter into the assembly of Yahweh.

3An Ammonite or a Moabite shall not enter into the assembly of Yahweh; even to the tenth generation shall none belonging to them enter into the assembly of Yahweh for ever:

4because they met you not with bread and with water in the way, when ye came forth out of Egypt, and because they hired against thee Balaam the son of Beor from Pethor of Mesopotamia, to curse thee.

5Nevertheless Yahweh thy God would not hearken unto Balaam; but Yahweh thy God turned the curse into a blessing unto thee, because Yahweh thy God loved thee.

6Thou shalt not seek their peace nor their prosperity all thy days for ever.

7Thou shalt not abhor an Edomite; for he is thy brother: thou shalt not abhor an Egyptian, because thou wast a sojourner in his land.

8The children of the third generation that are born unto them shall enter into the assembly of Yahweh.

9When thou goest forth in camp against thine enemies, then thou shalt keep thee from every evil thing.

10If there be among you any man, that is not clean by reason of that which chanceth him by night, then shall he go abroad out of the camp, he shall not come within the camp:

11but it shall be, when evening cometh on, he shall bathe himself in water; and when the sun is down, he shall come within the camp.

12Thou shalt have a place also without the camp, whither thou shalt go forth abroad;

13and thou shalt have a paddle among thy weapons; and it shall be, when thou sittest down abroad, thou shalt dig therewith, and shalt turn back and cover that which cometh from thee:

14for Yahweh thy God walketh in the midst of thy camp, to deliver thee, and to give up thine enemies before thee; therefore shall thy camp be holy, that he may not see an unclean thing in thee, and turn away from thee.

15Thou shalt not deliver unto his master a servant that is escaped from his master unto thee:

16he shall dwell with thee, in the midst of thee, in the place which he shall choose within one of thy gates, where it pleaseth him best: thou shalt not oppress him.

17There shall be no prostitute of the daughters of Israel, neither shall there be a sodomite of the sons of Israel.

18Thou shalt not bring the hire of a harlot, or the wages of a dog, into the house of Yahweh thy God for any vow: for even both these are an abomination unto Yahweh thy God.

19Thou shalt not lend upon interest to thy brother; interest of money, interest of victuals, interest of anything that is lent upon interest:

20unto a foreigner thou mayest lend upon interest; but unto thy brother thou shalt not lend upon interest, that Yahweh thy God may bless thee in all that thou puttest thy hand unto, in the land whither thou goest in to possess it.

21When thou shalt vow a vow unto Yahweh thy God, thou shalt not be slack to pay it: for Yahweh thy God will surely require it of thee; and it would be sin in thee.

22But if thou shalt forbear to vow, it shall be no sin in thee.

23That which is gone out of thy lips thou shalt observe and do; according as thou hast vowed unto Yahweh thy God, a freewill-offering, which thou hast promised with thy mouth.

24When thou comest into thy neighbor's vineyard, then thou mayest eat of grapes thy fill at thine own pleasure; but thou shalt not put any in thy vessel.

25When thou comest into thy neighbor's standing grain, then thou mayest pluck the ears with thy hand; but thou shalt not move a sickle unto thy neighbor's standing grain.

Chapter 24

1When a man taketh a wife, and marrieth her, then it shall be, if she find no favor in his eyes, because he hath found some unseemly thing in her, that he shall write her a bill of divorcement, and give it in her hand, and send her out of his house.

2And when she is departed out of his house, she may go and be another man's wife.

3And if the latter husband hate her, and write her a bill of divorcement, and give it in her hand, and send her out of his house; or if the latter husband die, who took her to be his wife;

4her former husband, who sent her away, may not take her again to be his wife, after that she is defiled; for that is abomination before Yahweh: and thou shalt not cause the land to sin, which Yahweh thy God giveth thee for an inheritance.

5When a man taketh a new wife, he shall not go out in the host, neither shall he be charged with any business: he shall be free at home one year, and shall cheer his wife whom he hath taken.

6No man shall take the mill or the upper millstone to pledge; for he taketh a man's life to pledge.

7If a man be found stealing any of his brethren of the children of Israel, and he deal with him as a slave, or sell him; then that thief shall die: so shalt thou put away the evil from the midst of thee.

8Take heed in the plague of leprosy, that thou observe diligently, and do according to all that the priests the Levites shall teach you: as I commanded them, so ye shall observe to do.

9Remember what Yahweh thy God did unto Miriam, by the way as ye came forth out of Egypt.

10When thou dost lend thy neighbor any manner of loan, thou shalt not go into his house to fetch his pledge.

11Thou shalt stand without, and the man to whom thou dost lend shall bring forth the pledge without unto thee.

12And if he be a poor man, thou shalt not sleep with his pledge;

13thou shalt surely restore to him the pledge when the sun goeth down, that he may sleep in his garment, and bless thee: and it shall be righteousness unto thee before Yahweh thy God.

14Thou shalt not oppress a hired servant that is poor and needy, whether he be of thy brethren, or of thy sojourners that are in thy land within thy gates:

15in his day thou shalt give him his hire, neither shall the sun go down upon it; for he is poor, and setteth his heart upon it: lest he cry against thee unto Yahweh, and it be sin unto thee.

16The fathers shall not be put to death for the children, neither shall the children be put to death for the fathers: every man shall be put to death for his own sin.

17Thou shalt not wrest the justice due to the sojourner, or to the fatherless, nor take the widow's raiment to pledge:

18but thou shalt remember that thou wast a bondman in Egypt, and Yahweh thy God redeemed thee thence: therefore I command thee to do this thing.

19When thou reapest thy harvest in thy field, and hast forgot a sheaf in the field, thou shalt not go again to fetch it: it shall be for the sojourner, for the fatherless, and for the widow; that Yahweh thy God may bless thee in all the work of thy hands.

20When thou beatest thine olive-tree, thou shalt not go over the boughs again: it shall be for the sojourner, for the fatherless, and for the widow.

21When thou gatherest the grapes of thy vineyard, thou shalt not glean it after thee: it shall be for the sojourner, for the fatherless, and for the widow.

22And thou shalt remember that thou wast a bondman in the land of Egypt: therefore I command thee to do this thing.

Chapter 25

1If there be a controversy between men, and they come unto judgment, and the judges judge them; then they shall justify the righteous, and condemn the wicked;

2and it shall be, if the wicked man be worthy to be beaten, that the judge shall cause him to lie down, and to be beaten before his face, according to his wickedness, by number.

3Forty stripes he may give him, he shall not exceed; lest, if he should exceed, and beat him above these with many stripes, then thy brother should seem vile unto thee.

4Thou shalt not muzzle the ox when he treadeth out the grain.

5If brethren dwell together, and one of them die, and have no son, the wife of the dead shall not be married without unto a stranger: her husband's brother shall go in unto her, and take her to him to wife, and perform the duty of a husband's brother unto her.

6And it shall be, that the first-born that she beareth shall succeed in the name of his brother that is dead, that his name be not blotted out of Israel.

7And if the man like not to take his brother's wife, then his brother's wife shall go up to the gate unto the elders, and say, My husband's brother refuseth to raise up unto his brother a name in Israel; he will not perform the duty of a husband's brother unto me.

8Then the elders of his city shall call him, and speak unto him: and if he stand, and say, I like not to take her;

9then shall his brother's wife come unto him in the presence of the elders, and loose his shoe from off his foot, and spit in his face; and she shall answer and say, So shall it be done unto the man that doth not build up his brother's house.

10And his name shall be called in Israel, The house of him that hath his shoe loosed.

11When men strive together one with another, and the wife of the one draweth near to deliver her husband out of the hand of him that smiteth him, and putteth forth her hand, and taketh him by the secrets;

12then thou shalt cut off her hand, thine eye shall have no pity.

13Thou shalt not have in thy bag diverse weights, a great and a small.

14Thou shalt not have in thy house diverse measures, a great and a small.

15A perfect and just weight shalt thou have; a perfect and just measure shalt thou have: that thy days may be long in the land which Yahweh thy God giveth thee.

16For all that do such things, even all that do unrighteously, are an abomination unto Yahweh thy God.

17Remember what Amalek did unto thee by the way as ye came forth out of Egypt;

18how he met thee by the way, and smote the hindmost of thee, all that were feeble behind thee, when thou wast faint and weary; and he feared not God.

19Therefore it shall be, when Yahweh thy God hath given thee rest from all thine enemies round about, in the land which Yahweh thy God giveth thee for an inheritance to possess it, that thou shalt blot out the remembrance of Amalek from under heaven; thou shalt not forget.

Chapter 26

1And it shall be, when thou art come in unto the land which Yahweh thy God giveth thee for an inheritance, and possessest it, and dwellest therein,

2that thou shalt take of the first of all the fruit of the ground, which thou shalt bring in from thy land that Yahweh thy God giveth thee; and thou shalt put it in a basket, and shalt go unto the place which Yahweh thy God shall choose, to cause his name to dwell there.

3And thou shalt come unto the priest that shall be in those days, and say unto him, I profess this day unto Yahweh thy God, that I am come unto the land which Yahweh sware unto our fathers to give us.

4And the priest shall take the basket out of thy hand, and set it down before the altar of Yahweh thy God.

5And thou shalt answer and say before Yahweh thy God, A Syrian ready to perish was my father; and he went down into Egypt, and sojourned there, few in number; and he became there a nation, great, mighty, and populous.

6And the Egyptians dealt ill with us, and afflicted us, and laid upon us hard bondage:

7and we cried unto Yahweh, the God of our fathers, and Yahweh heard our voice, and saw our affliction, and our toil, and our oppression;

8and Yahweh brought us forth out of Egypt with a mighty hand, and with an outstretched arm, and with great terribleness, and with signs, and with wonders;

9and he hath brought us into this place, and hath given us this land, a land flowing with milk and honey.

10And now, behold, I have brought the first of the fruit of the ground, which thou, O Yahweh, hast given me. And thou shalt set it down before Yahweh thy God, and worship before Yahweh thy God:

11and thou shalt rejoice in all the good which Yahweh thy God hath given unto thee, and unto thy house, thou, and the Levite, and the sojourner that is in the midst of thee.

12When thou hast made an end of tithing all the tithe of thine increase in the third year, which is the year of tithing, then thou shalt give it unto the Levite, to the sojourner, to the fatherless, and to the widow, that they may eat within thy gates, and be filled.

13And thou shalt say before Yahweh thy God, I have put away the hallowed things out of my house, and also have given them unto the Levite, and unto the sojourner, to the fatherless, and to the widow, according to all thy commandment

Deuteronomy

which thou hast commanded me: I have not transgressed any of thy commandments, neither have I forgotten them:

14I have not eaten thereof in my mourning, neither have I put away thereof, being unclean, nor given thereof for the dead: I have hearkened to the voice of Yahweh my God; I have done according to all that thou hast commanded me.

15Look down from thy holy habitation, from heaven, and bless thy people Israel, and the ground which thou hast given us, as thou swarest unto our fathers, a land flowing with milk and honey.

16This day Yahweh thy God commandeth thee to do these statutes and ordinances: thou shalt therefore keep and do them with all thy heart, and with all thy soul.

17Thou hast avouched Yahweh this day to be thy God, and that thou wouldest walk in his ways, and keep his statutes, and his commandments, and his ordinances, and hearken unto his voice:

18and Yahweh hath avouched thee this day to be a people for his own possession, as he hath promised thee, and that thou shouldest keep all his commandments;

19and to make thee high above all nations that he hath made, in praise, and in name, and in honor; and that thou mayest be a holy people unto Yahweh thy God, as he hath spoken.

Chapter 27

1And Moses and the elders of Israel commanded the people, saying, Keep all the commandment which I command you this day.

2And it shall be on the day when ye shall pass over the Jordan unto the land which Yahweh thy God giveth thee, that thou shalt set thee up great stones, and plaster them with plaster:

3and thou shalt write upon them all the words of this law, when thou art passed over; that thou mayest go in unto the land which Yahweh thy God giveth thee, a land flowing with milk and honey, as Yahweh, the God of thy fathers, hath promised thee.

4And it shall be, when ye are passed over the Jordan, that ye shall set up these stones, which I command you this day, in mount Ebal, and thou shalt plaster them with plaster.

5And there shalt thou build an altar unto Yahweh thy God, an altar of stones: thou shalt lift up no iron tool upon them.

6Thou shalt build the altar of Yahweh thy God of unhewn stones; and thou shalt offer burnt-offerings thereon unto Yahweh thy God:

7and thou shalt sacrifice peace-offerings, and shalt eat there; and thou shalt rejoice before Yahweh thy God.

8And thou shalt write upon the stones all the words of this law very plainly.

9And Moses and the priests the Levites spake unto all Israel, saying, Keep silence, and hearken, O Israel: this day thou art become the people of Yahweh thy God.

10Thou shalt therefore obey the voice of Yahweh thy God, and do his commandments and his statutes, which I command thee this day.

11And Moses charged the people the same day, saying,

12These shall stand upon mount Gerizim to bless the people, when ye are passed over the Jordan: Simeon, and Levi, and Judah, and Issachar, and Joseph, and Benjamin.

13And these shall stand upon mount Ebal for the curse: Reuben, Gad, and Asher, and Zebulun, Dan, and Naphtali.

14And the Levites shall answer, and say unto all the men of Israel with a loud voice,

15Cursed be the man that maketh a graven or molten image, an abomination unto Yahweh, the work of the hands of the craftsman, and setteth it up in secret. And all the people shall answer and say, Amen.

16Cursed be he that setteth light by his father or his mother. And all the people shall say, Amen.

17Cursed be he that removeth his neighbor's landmark. And all the people shall say, Amen.

18Cursed be he that maketh the blind to wander out of the way. And all the people shall say, Amen.

19Cursed be he that wresteth the justice due to the sojourner, fatherless, and widow. And all the people shall say, Amen.

20Cursed be he that lieth with his father's wife, because he hath uncovered his father's skirt. And all the people shall say, Amen.

21Cursed be he that lieth with any manner of beast. And all the people shall say, Amen.

22Cursed be he that lieth with his sister, the daughter of his father, or the daughter of his mother. And all the people shall say, Amen.

23Cursed be he that lieth with his mother-in-law. And all the people shall say, Amen.

24Cursed be he that smiteth his neighbor in secret. And all the people shall say, Amen.

25Cursed be he that taketh a bribe to slay an innocent person. And all the people shall say, Amen.

26Cursed be he that confirmeth not the words of this law to do them. And all the people shall say, Amen.

Chapter 28

1And it shall come to pass, if thou shalt hearken diligently unto the voice of Yahweh thy God, to observe to do all his commandments which I command thee this day, that Yahweh thy God will set thee on high above all the nations of the earth:

2and all these blessings shall come upon thee, and overtake thee, if thou shalt hearken unto the voice of Yahweh thy God.

3Blessed shalt thou be in the city, and blessed shalt thou be in the field.

4Blessed shall be the fruit of thy body, and the fruit of thy ground, and the fruit of thy beasts, the increase of thy cattle, and the young of thy flock.

5Blessed shall be thy basket and thy kneading-trough.

6Blessed shalt thou be when thou comest in, and blessed shalt thou be when thou goest out.

7Yahweh will cause thine enemies that rise up against thee to be smitten before thee: they shall come out against thee one way, and shall flee before thee seven ways.

8Yahweh will command the blessing upon thee in thy barns, and in all that thou puttest thy hand unto; and he will bless thee in the land which Yahweh thy God giveth thee.

9Yahweh will establish thee for a holy people unto himself, as he hath sworn unto thee; if thou shalt keep the commandments of Yahweh thy God, and walk in his ways.

10And all the peoples of the earth shall see that thou art called by the name of Yahweh; and they shall be afraid of thee.

11And Yahweh will make thee plenteous for good, in the fruit of thy body, and in the fruit of thy cattle, and in the fruit of thy ground, in the land which Yahweh sware unto thy fathers to give thee.

12Yahweh will open unto thee his good treasure the heavens, to give the rain of thy land in its season, and to bless all the work of thy hand: and thou shalt lend unto many nations, and thou shalt not borrow.

13And Yahweh will make thee the head, and not the tail; and thou shalt be above only, and thou shalt not be beneath; if thou shalt hearken unto the commandments of Yahweh thy God, which I command thee this day, to observe and to do them,

14and shalt not turn aside from any of the words which I command you this day, to the right hand, or to the left, to go after other gods to serve them.

15But it shall come to pass, if thou wilt not hearken unto the voice of Yahweh thy God, to observe to do all his commandments and his statutes which I command thee this day, that all these curses shall come upon thee, and overtake thee.

16Cursed shalt thou be in the city, and cursed shalt thou be in the field.

17Cursed shall be thy basket and thy kneading-trough.

18Cursed shall be the fruit of thy body, and the fruit of thy ground, the increase of thy cattle, and the young of thy flock.

19Cursed shalt thou be when thou comest in, and cursed shalt thou be when thou goest out.

20Yahweh will send upon thee cursing, discomfiture, and rebuke, in all that thou puttest thy hand unto to do, until thou be destroyed, and until thou perish quickly; because of the evil of thy doings, whereby thou hast forsaken me.

21Yahweh will make the pestilence cleave unto thee, until he hath consumed thee from off the land, whither thou goest in to possess it.

22Yahweh will smite thee with consumption, and with fever, and with inflammation, and with fiery heat, and with the sword, and with blasting, and with mildew; and they shall pursue thee until thou perish.

23And thy heaven that is over thy head shall be brass, and the earth that is under thee shall be iron.

24Yahweh will make the rain of thy land powder and dust: from heaven shall it come down upon thee, until thou be destroyed.

25Yahweh will cause thee to be smitten before thine enemies; thou shalt go out one way against them, and shalt flee seven ways before them: and thou shalt be tossed to and from among all the kingdoms of the earth.

26And thy dead body shall be food unto all birds of the heavens, and unto the beasts of the earth; and there shall be none to frighten them away.

27Yahweh will smite thee with the boil of Egypt, and with the emerods, and with the scurvy, and with the itch, whereof thou canst not be healed.

28Yahweh will smite thee with madness, and with blindness, and with astonishment of heart;

29and thou shalt grope at noonday, as the blind gropeth in darkness, and thou shalt not prosper in thy ways: and thou shalt be only oppressed and robbed alway, and there shall be none to save thee.

30Thou shalt betroth a wife, and another man shall lie with her: thou shalt build a house, and thou shalt not dwell therein: thou shalt plant a vineyard, and shalt not use the fruit thereof.

31Thine ox shall be slain before thine eyes, and thou shalt not eat thereof: thine ass shall be violently taken away from before thy face, and shall not be restored to thee: thy sheep shall be given unto thine enemies, and thou shalt have none to save thee.

32Thy sons and thy daughters shall be given unto another people; and thine eyes shall look, and fail with longing for them all the day: and there shall be nought in the power of thy hand.

33The fruit of thy ground, and all thy labors, shall a nation which thou knowest not eat up; and thou shalt be only oppressed and crushed alway;

34so that thou shalt be mad for the sight of thine eyes which thou shalt see.

35Yahweh will smite thee in the knees, and in the legs, with a sore boil, whereof thou canst not be healed, from the sole of thy foot unto the crown of thy head.

36Yahweh will bring thee, and thy king whom thou shalt set over thee, unto a nation that thou hast not known, thou nor thy fathers; and there shalt thou serve other gods, wood and stone.

37And thou shalt become an astonishment, a proverb, and a byword, among all the peoples whither Yahweh shall lead thee away.

38Thou shalt carry much seed out into the field, and shalt gather little in; for the locust shall consume it.

39Thou shalt plant vineyards and dress them, but thou shalt neither drink of the wine, nor gather the grapes; for the worm shall eat them.

40Thou shalt have olive-trees throughout all thy borders, but thou shalt not anoint thyself with the oil; for thine olive shall cast its fruit.

41Thou shalt beget sons and daughters, but they shall not be thine; for they shall go into captivity.

42All thy trees and the fruit of thy ground shall the locust possess.

43The sojourner that is in the midst of thee shall mount up above thee higher and higher; and thou shalt come down lower and lower.

44He shall lend to thee, and thou shalt not lend to him: he shall be the head, and thou shalt be the tail.

45And all these curses shall come upon thee, and shall pursue thee, and overtake thee, till thou be destroyed; because thou hearkenedst not unto the voice of Yahweh thy God, to keep his commandments and his statutes which he commanded thee:

46and they shall be upon thee for a sign and for a wonder, and upon thy seed for ever.

47Because thou servedst not Yahweh thy God with joyfulness, and with gladness of heart, by reason of the abundance of all things;

48therefore shalt thou serve thine enemies that Yahweh shall send against thee, in hunger, and in thirst, and in nakedness, and in want of all things: and he shall put a yoke of iron upon thy neck, until he have destroyed thee.

49Yahweh will bring a nation against thee from far, from the end of the earth, as the eagle flieth; a nation whose tongue thou shalt not understand;

50a nation of fierce countenance, that shall not regard the person of the old, nor show favor to the young,

51and shall eat the fruit of thy cattle, and the fruit of thy ground, until thou be destroyed; that also shall not leave thee grain, new wine, or oil, the increase of thy cattle, or the young of thy flock, until they have caused thee to perish.

52And they shall besiege thee in all thy gates, until thy high and fortified walls come down, wherein thou trustedst, throughout all thy land; and they shall besiege thee in all thy gates throughout all thy land, which Yahweh thy God hath given thee.

53And thou shalt eat the fruit of thine own body, the flesh of thy sons and of thy daughters, whom Yahweh thy God hath given thee, in the siege and in the distress wherewith thine enemies shall distress thee.

54The man that is tender among you, and very delicate, his eye shall be evil toward his brother, and toward the wife of his bosom, and toward the remnant of his children whom he hath remaining;

55so that he will not give to any of them of the flesh of his children whom he shall eat, because he hath nothing left him, in the siege and in the distress wherewith thine enemy shall distress thee in all thy gates.

56The tender and delicate woman among you, who would not adventure to set the sole of her foot upon the ground for delicateness and tenderness, her eye shall be evil toward the husband of her bosom, and toward her son, and toward her daughter,

57and toward her young one that cometh out from between her feet, and toward her children whom she shall bear; for she shall eat them for want of all things secretly, in the siege and in the distress wherewith thine enemy shall distress thee in thy gates.

58If thou wilt not observe to do all the words of this law that are written in this book, that thou mayest fear this glorious and fearful name, YAHWEH THY GOD;

59then Yahweh will make thy plagues wonderful, and the plagues of thy seed, even great plagues, and of long continuance, and sore sicknesses, and of long continuance.

60And he will bring upon thee again all the diseases of Egypt, which thou wast afraid of; and they shall cleave unto thee.

61Also every sickness, and every plague, which is not written in the book of this law, them will Yahweh bring upon thee, until thou be destroyed.

62And ye shall be left few in number, whereas ye were as the stars of heaven for multitude; because thou didst not hearken unto the voice of Yahweh thy God.

63And it shall come to pass, that, as Yahweh rejoiced over you to do you good, and to multiply you, so Yahweh will rejoice over you to cause you to perish, and to destroy you; and ye shall be plucked from off the land whither thou goest in to possess it.

64And Yahweh will scatter thee among all peoples, from the one end of the earth even unto the other end of the earth; and there thou shalt serve other gods, which thou hast not known, thou nor thy fathers, even wood and stone.

65And among these nations shalt thou find no ease, and there shall be no rest for the sole of thy foot: but Yahweh will give thee there a trembling heart, and failing of eyes, and pining of soul;

66and thy life shall hang in doubt before thee; and thou shalt fear night and day, and shalt have no assurance of thy life.

67In the morning thou shalt say, Would it were even! and at even thou shalt say, Would it were morning! for the fear of thy heart which thou shalt fear, and for the sight of thine eyes which thou shalt see.

68And Yahweh will bring thee into Egypt again with ships, by the way whereof I said unto thee, Thou shalt see it no more again: and there ye shall sell yourselves unto your enemies for bondmen and for bondwomen, and no man shall buy you.

Chapter 29

1These are the words of the covenant which Yahweh commanded Moses to make with the children of Israel in the land of Moab, besides the covenant which he made with them in Horeb.

2And Moses called unto all Israel, and said unto them, Ye have seen all that Yahweh did before your eyes in the land of Egypt unto Pharaoh, and unto all his servants, and unto all his land;

3the great trials which thine eyes saw, the signs, and those great wonders:

4but Yahweh hath not given you a heart to know, and eyes to see, and ears to hear, unto this day.

5And I have led you forty years in the wilderness: your clothes are not waxed old upon you, and thy shoe is not waxed old upon thy foot.

6Ye have not eaten bread, neither have ye drunk wine or strong drink; that ye may know that I am Yahweh your God.

7And when ye came unto this place, Sihon the king of Heshbon, and Og the king of Bashan, came out against us unto battle, and we smote them:

8and we took their land, and gave it for an inheritance unto the Reubenites, and to the Gadites, and to the half-tribe of the Manassites.

9Keep therefore the words of this covenant, and do them, that ye may prosper in all that ye do.

10Ye stand this day all of you before Yahweh your God; your heads, your tribes, your elders, and your officers, even all the men of Israel,

11your little ones, your wives, and thy sojourner that is in the midst of thy camps, from the hewer of thy wood unto the drawer of thy water;

12that thou mayest enter into the covenant of Yahweh thy God, and into his oath, which Yahweh thy God maketh with thee this day;

13that he may establish thee this day unto himself for a people, and that he may be unto thee a God, as he spake unto thee, and as he sware unto thy fathers, to Abraham, to Isaac, and to Jacob.

14Neither with you only do I make this covenant and this oath,

15but with him that standeth here with us this day before Yahweh our God, and also with him that is not here with us this day

16(for ye know how we dwelt in the land of Egypt, and how we came through the midst of the nations through which ye passed;

17and ye have seen their abominations, and their idols, wood and stone, silver and gold, which were among them);

18lest there should be among you man, or woman, or family, or tribe, whose heart turneth away this day from Yahweh our God, to go to serve the gods of those nations; lest there should be among you a root that beareth gall and wormwood;

19and it come to pass, when he heareth the words of this curse, that he bless himself in his heart, saying, I shall have peace, though I walk in the stubbornness of my heart, to destroy the moist with the dry.

20Yahweh will not pardon him, but then the anger of Yahweh and his jealousy will smoke against that man, and all the curse that is written in this book shall lie upon him, and Yahweh will blot out his name from under heaven.

21And Yahweh will set him apart unto evil out of all the tribes of Israel, according to all the curses of the covenant that is written in this book of the law.

22And the generation to come, your children that shall rise up after you, and the foreigner that shall come from a far land, shall say, when they see the plagues of that land, and the sicknesses wherewith Yahweh hath made it sick;

23and that the whole land thereof is brimstone, and salt, and a burning, that it is not sown, nor beareth, nor any grass groweth therein, like the overthrow of Sodom and Gomorrah, Admah and Zeboiim, which Yahweh overthrew in his anger, and in his wrath:

24even all the nations shall say, Wherefore hath Yahweh done thus unto this land? what meaneth the heat of this great anger?

25Then men shall say, Because they forsook the covenant of Yahweh, the God of their fathers, which he made with them when he brought them forth out of the land of Egypt,

26and went and served other gods, and worshipped them, gods that they knew not, and that he had not given unto them:

27therefore the anger of Yahweh was kindled against this land, to bring upon it all the curse that is written in this book;

28and Yahweh rooted them out of their land in anger, and in wrath, and in great indignation, and cast them into another land, as at this day.

29The secret things belong unto Yahweh our God; but the things that are revealed belong unto us and to our children for ever, that we may do all the words of this law:

Chapter 30

1And it shall come to pass, when all these things are come upon thee, the blessing and the curse, which I have set before thee, and thou shalt call them to mind among all the nations, whither Yahweh thy God hath driven thee,

2and shalt return unto Yahweh thy God, and shalt obey his voice according to all that I command thee this day, thou and thy children, with all thy heart, and with all thy soul;

3that then Yahweh thy God will turn thy captivity, and have compassion upon thee, and will return and gather thee from all the peoples, whither Yahweh thy God hath scattered thee.

4If any of thine outcasts be in the uttermost parts of heaven, from thence will Yahweh thy God gather thee, and from thence will he fetch thee:

5and Yahweh thy God will bring thee into the land which thy fathers possessed, and thou shalt possess it; and he will do thee good, and multiply thee above thy fathers.

6And Yahweh thy God will circumcise thy heart, and the heart of thy seed, to love Yahweh thy God with all thy heart, and with all thy soul, that thou mayest live.

7And Yahweh thy God will put all these curses upon thine enemies, and on them that hate thee, that persecuted thee.

8And thou shalt return and obey the voice of Yahweh, and do all his commandments which I command thee this day.

9And Yahweh thy God will make thee plenteous in all the work of thy hand, in the fruit of thy body, and in the fruit of thy cattle, and in the fruit of thy ground, for good: for Yahweh will again rejoice over thee for good, as he rejoiced over thy fathers;

10if thou shalt obey the voice of Yahweh thy God, to keep his commandments and his statutes which are written in this book of the law; if thou turn unto Yahweh thy God with all thy heart, and with all thy soul.

11For this commandment which I command thee this day, it is not too hard

Deuteronomy

for thee, neither is it far off.

12It is not in heaven, that thou shouldest say, Who shall go up for us to heaven, and bring it unto us, and make us to hear it, that we may do it?

13Neither is it beyond the sea, that thou shouldest say, Who shall go over the sea for us, and bring it unto us, and make us to hear it, that we may do it?

14But the word is very nigh unto thee, in thy mouth, and in thy heart, that thou mayest do it.

15See, I have set before thee this day life and good, and death and evil;

16in that I command thee this day to love Yahweh thy God, to walk in his ways, and to keep his commandments and his statutes and his ordinances, that thou mayest live and multiply, and that Yahweh thy God may bless thee in the land whither thou goest in to possess it.

17But if thy heart turn away, and thou wilt not hear, but shalt be drawn away, and worship other gods, and serve them;

18I denounce unto you this day, that ye shall surely perish; ye shall not prolong your days in the land, whither thou passest over the Jordan to go in to possess it.

19I call heaven and earth to witness against you this day, that I have set before thee life and death, the blessing and the curse: therefore choose life, that thou mayest live, thou and thy seed;

20to love Yahweh thy God, to obey his voice, and to cleave unto him; for he is thy life, and the length of thy days; that thou mayest dwell in the land which Yahweh sware unto thy fathers, to Abraham, to Isaac, and to Jacob, to give them.

Chapter 31

1And Moses went and spake these words unto all Israel.

2And he said unto them, I am a hundred and twenty years old this day; I can no more go out and come in: and Yahweh hath said unto me, Thou shalt not go over this Jordan.

3Yahweh thy God, he will go over before thee; he will destroy these nations from before thee, and thou shalt dispossess them: and Joshua, he shall go over before thee, as Yahweh hath spoken.

4And Yahweh will do unto them as he did to Sihon and to Og, the kings of the Amorites, and unto their land; whom he destroyed.

5And Yahweh will deliver them up before you, and ye shall do unto them according unto all the commandment which I have commanded you.

6Be strong and of good courage, fear not, nor be affrighted at them: for Yahweh thy God, he it is that doth go with thee; he will not fail thee, nor forsake thee.

7And Moses called unto Joshua, and said unto him in the sight of all Israel, Be strong and of good courage: for thou shalt go with this people into the land which Yahweh hath sworn unto their fathers to give them; and thou shalt cause them to inherit it.

8And Yahweh, he it is that doth go before thee; he will be with thee, he will not fail thee, neither forsake thee: fear not, neither be dismayed.

9And Moses wrote this law, and delivered it unto the priests the sons of Levi, that bare the ark of the covenant of Yahweh, and unto all the elders of Israel.

10And Moses commanded them, saying, At the end of every seven years, in the set time of the year of release, in the feast of tabernacles,

11when all Israel is come to appear before Yahweh thy God in the place which he shall choose, thou shalt read this law before all Israel in their hearing.

12Assemble the people, the men and the women and the little ones, and thy sojourner that is within thy gates, that they may hear, and that they may learn, and fear Yahweh your God, and observe to do all the words of this law;

13and that their children, who have not known, may hear, and learn to fear Yahweh your God, as long as ye live in the land whither ye go over the Jordan to possess it.

14And Yahweh said unto Moses, Behold, thy days approach that thou must die: call Joshua, and present yourselves in the tent of meeting, that I may give him a charge. And Moses and Joshua went, and presented themselves in the tent of meeting.

15And Yahweh appeared in the Tent in a pillar of cloud: and the pillar of cloud stood over the door of the Tent.

16And Yahweh said unto Moses, Behold, thou shalt sleep with thy fathers; and this people will rise up, and play the harlot after the strange gods of the land, whither they go to be among them, and will forsake me, and break my covenant which I have made with them.

17Then my anger shall be kindled against them in that day, and I will forsake them, and I will hide my face from them, and they shall be devoured, and many evils and troubles shall come upon them; so that they will say in that day, Are not these evils come upon us because our God is not among us?

18And I will surely hide my face in that day for all the evil which they shall have wrought, in that they are turned unto other gods.

19Now therefore write ye this song for you, and teach thou it the children of Israel: put it in their mouths, that this song may be a witness for me against the children of Israel.

20For when I shall have brought them into the land which I sware unto their fathers, flowing with milk and honey, and they shall have eaten and filled themselves, and waxed fat; then will they turn unto other gods, and serve them, and despise me, and break my covenant.

21And it shall come to pass, when many evils and troubles are come upon them, that this song shall testify before them as a witness; for it shall not be forgotten out of the mouths of their seed: for I know their imagination which they frame this day, before I have brought them into the land which I sware.

22So Moses wrote this song the same day, and taught it the children of Israel.

23And he gave Joshua the son of Nun a charge, and said, Be strong and of good courage; for thou shalt bring the children of Israel into the land which I sware unto them: and I will be with thee.

24And it came to pass, when Moses had made an end of writing the words of this law in a book, until they were finished,

25that Moses commanded the Levites, that bare the ark of the covenant of Yahweh, saying,

26Take this book of the law, and put it by the side of the ark of the covenant of Yahweh your God, that it may be there for a witness against thee.

27For I know thy rebellion, and thy stiff neck: behold, while I am yet alive with you this day, ye have been rebellious against Yahweh; and how much more after my death?

28Assemble unto me all the elders of your tribes, and your officers, that I may speak these words in their ears, and call heaven and earth to witness against them.

29For I know that after my death ye will utterly corrupt yourselves, and turn aside from the way which I have commanded you; and evil will befall you in the latter days; because ye will do that which is evil in the sight of Yahweh, to provoke him to anger through the work of your hands.

30And Moses spake in the ears of all the assembly of Israel the words of this song, until they were finished.

Chapter 32

32 1Give ear, ye heavens, and I will speak;
And let the earth hear the words of my mouth.
2My doctrine shall drop as the rain;
My speech shall distil as the dew,
As the small rain upon the tender grass,
And as the showers upon the herb.
3For I will proclaim the name of Yahweh:
Ascribe ye greatness unto our God.
4The Rock, his work is perfect;
For all his ways are justice:
A God of faithfulness and without iniquity,
Just and right is he.
5They have dealt corruptly with him, they are not his children, it is their blemish;
They are a perverse and crooked generation.
6Do ye thus requite Yahweh,
O foolish people and unwise?
Is not he thy father that hath bought thee?
He hath made thee, and established thee.
7Remember the days of old,
Consider the years of many generations:
Ask thy father, and he will show thee;
Thine elders, and they will tell thee.
8When the Most High gave to the nations their inheritance,
When he separated the children of men,
He set the bounds of the peoples
According to the number of the children of Israel.
9For Yahweh's portion is his people;
Jacob is the lot of his inheritance.
10He found him in a desert land,
And in the waste howling wilderness;
He compassed him about, he cared for him,
He kept him as the apple of his eye.
11As an eagle that stirreth up her nest,
That fluttereth over her young,
He spread abroad his wings, he took them,
He bare them on his pinions.
12Yahweh alone did lead him,
And there was no foreign god with him.
13He made him ride on the high places of the earth,
And he did eat the increase of the field;
And he made him to suck honey out of the rock,
And oil out of the flinty rock;
14Butter of the herd, and milk of the flock,
With fat of lambs,
And rams of the breed of Bashan, and goats,
With the finest of the wheat;
And of the blood of the grape thou drankest wine.
15But Jeshurun waxed fat, and kicked:
Thou art waxed fat, thou art grown thick, thou art become sleek;
Then he forsook God who made him,
And lightly esteemed the Rock of his salvation.
16They moved him to jealousy with strange gods;
With abominations provoked they him to anger.
17They sacrificed unto demons, which were no God,
To gods that they knew not,
To new gods that came up of late,
Which your fathers dreaded not.
18Of the Rock that begat thee thou art unmindful,
And hast forgotten God that gave thee birth.
19And Yahweh saw it, and abhorred them,
Because of the provocation of his sons and his daughters.
20And he said, I will hide my face from them,
I will see what their end shall be:
For they are a very perverse generation,
Children in whom is no faithfulness.
21They have moved me to jealousy with that which is not God;
They have provoked me to anger with their vanities:
And I will move them to jealousy with those that are not a people;

I will provoke them to anger with a foolish nation.
22For a fire is kindled in mine anger,
And burneth unto the lowest Sheol,
And devoureth the earth with its increase,
And setteth on fire the foundations of the mountains.
23I will heap evils upon them;
I will spend mine arrows upon them:
24They shall be wasted with hunger, and devoured with burning heat
And bitter destruction;
And the teeth of beasts will I send upon them,
With the poison of crawling things of the dust.
25Without shall the sword bereave,
And in the chambers terror;
It shall destroy both young man and virgin,
The suckling with the man of gray hairs.
26I said, I would scatter them afar,
I would make the remembrance of them to cease from among men;
27Were it not that I feared the provocation of the enemy,
Lest their adversaries should judge amiss,
Lest they should say, Our hand is exalted,
And Yahweh hath not done all this.
28For they are a nation void of counsel,
And there is no understanding in them.
29Oh that they were wise, that they understood this,
That they would consider their latter end!
30How should one chase a thousand,
And two put ten thousand to flight,
Except their Rock had sold them,
And Yahweh had delivered them up?
31For their rock is not as our Rock,
Even our enemies themselves being judges.
32For their vine is of the vine of Sodom,
And of the fields of Gomorrah:
Their grapes are grapes of gall,
Their clusters are bitter:
33Their wine is the poison of serpents,
And the cruel venom of asps.
34Is not this laid up in store with me,
Sealed up among my treasures?
35Vengeance is mine, and recompense,
At the time when their foot shall slide:
For the day of their calamity is at hand,
And the things that are to come upon them shall make haste.
36For Yahweh will judge his people,
And repent himself for his servants;
When he seeth that their power is gone,
And there is none remaining, shut up or left at large.
37And he will say, Where are their gods,
The rock in which they took refuge;
38Which did eat the fat of their sacrifices,
And drank the wine of their drink-offering?
Let them rise up and help you,
Let them be your protection.
39See now that I, even I, am he,
And there is no god with me:
I kill, and I make alive;
I wound, and I heal;
And there is none that can deliver out of my hand.
40For I lift up my hand to heaven,
And say, As I live for ever,
41If I whet my glittering sword,
And my hand take hold on judgment;
I will render vengeance to mine adversaries,
And will recompense them that hate me.
42I will make mine arrows drunk with blood,
And my sword shall devour flesh;
With the blood of the slain and the captives,
From the head of the leaders of the enemy.
43Rejoice, O ye nations, with his people:
For he will avenge the blood of his servants,
And will render vengeance to his adversaries,
And will make expiation for his land, for his people.
44And Moses came and spake all the words of this song in the ears of the people, he, and Hoshea the son of Nun.
45And Moses made an end of speaking all these words to all Israel;
46And he said unto them, Set your heart unto all the words which I testify unto you this day, which ye shall command your children to observe to do, even all the words of this law.
47For it is no vain thing for you; because it is your life, and through this thing ye shall prolong your days in the land, whither ye go over the Jordan to possess it.
48And Yahweh spake unto Moses that selfsame day, saying,
49Get thee up into this mountain of Abarim, unto mount Nebo, which is in the land of Moab, that is over against Jericho; and behold the land of Canaan, which I give unto the children of Israel for a possession;
50and die in the mount whither thou goest up, and be gathered unto thy people, as Aaron thy brother died in mount Hor, and was gathered unto his people:
51because ye trespassed against me in the midst of the children of Israel at the waters of Meribah of Kadesh, in the wilderness of Zin; because ye sanctified me not in the midst of the children of Israel.
52For thou shalt see the land before thee; but thou shalt not go thither into the land which I give the children of Israel.

Chapter 33

1And this is the blessing, wherewith Moses the man of God blessed the children of Israel before his death.
2And he said,
Yahweh came from Sinai,
And rose from Seir unto them;
He shined forth from mount Paran,
And he came from the ten thousands of holy ones:
At his right hand was a fiery law for them.
3Yea, he loveth the people;
All his saints are in thy hand:
And they sat down at thy feet;
Every one shall receive of thy words.
4Moses commanded us a law,
An inheritance for the assembly of Jacob.
5And he was king in Jeshurun,
When the heads of the people were gathered,
All the tribes of Israel together.
6Let Reuben live, and not die;
Nor let his men be few.
7And this is the blessing of Judah: and he said,
Hear, Yahweh, the voice of Judah,
And bring him in unto his people.
With his hands he contended for himself;
And thou shalt be a help against his adversaries.
8And of Levi he said,
Thy Thummim and thy Urim are with thy godly one,
Whom thou didst prove at Massah,
With whom thou didst strive at the waters of Meribah;
9Who said of his father, and of his mother, I have not seen him;
Neither did he acknowledge his brethren,
Nor knew he his own children:
For they have observed thy word,
And keep thy covenant.
10They shall teach Jacob thine ordinances,
And Israel thy law:
They shall put incense before thee,
And whole burnt-offering upon thine altar.
11Bless, Yahweh, his substance,
And accept the work of his hands:
Smite through the loins of them that rise up against him,
And of them that hate him, that they rise not again.
12Of Benjamin he said,
The beloved of Yahweh shall dwell in safety by him;
He covereth him all the day long,
And he dwelleth between his shoulders.
13And of Joseph he said,
Blessed of Yahweh be his land,
For the precious things of heaven, for the dew,
And for the deep that coucheth beneath,
14And for the precious things of the fruits of the sun,
And for the precious things of the growth of the moons,
15And for the chief things of the ancient mountains,
And for the precious things of the everlasting hills,
16And for the precious things of the earth and the fulness thereof,
And the good will of him that dwelt in the bush.
Let the blessing come upon the head of Joseph,
And upon the crown of the head of him that was separate from his brethren.
17The firstling of his herd, majesty is his;
And his horns are the horns of the wild-ox:
With them he shall push the peoples all of them, even the ends of the earth:
And they are the ten thousands of Ephraim,
And they are the thousands of Manasseh.
18And of Zebulun he said,
Rejoice, Zebulun, in thy going out;
And, Issachar, in thy tents.
19They shall call the peoples unto the mountain;
There shall they offer sacrifices of righteousness:
For they shall suck the abundance of the seas,
And the hidden treasures of the sand.
20And of Gad he said,
Blessed be he that enlargeth Gad:
He dwelleth as a lioness,
And teareth the arm, yea, the crown of the head.
21And he provided the first part for himself,
For there was the lawgiver's portion reserved;
And he came with the heads of the people;
He executed the righteousness of Yahweh,
And his ordinances with Israel.
22And of Dan he said,
Dan is a lion's whelp,
That leapeth forth from Bashan.
23And of Naphtali he said,
O Naphtali, satisfied with favor,
And full with the blessing of Yahweh,

Deuteronomy

Possess thou the west and the south.
24And of Asher he said,
Blessed be Asher with children;
Let him be acceptable unto his brethren,
And let him dip his foot in oil.
25Thy bars shall be iron and brass;
And as thy days, so shall thy strength be.
26There is none like unto God, O Jeshurun,
Who rideth upon the heavens for thy help,
And in his excellency on the skies.
27The eternal God is thy dwelling-place,
And underneath are the everlasting arms.
And he thrust out the enemy from before thee,
And said, Destroy.
28And Israel dwelleth in safety,
The fountain of Jacob alone,
In a land of grain and new wine;
Yea, his heavens drop down dew.
29Happy art thou, O Israel:
Who is like unto thee, a people saved by Yahweh,
The shield of thy help,
And the sword of thy excellency!
And thine enemies shall submit themselves unto thee;
And thou shalt tread upon their high places.

Chapter 34

1And Moses went up from the plains of Moab unto mount Nebo, to the top of Pisgah, that is over against Jericho. And Yahweh showed him all the land of Gilead, unto Dan,

2and all Naphtali, and the land of Ephraim and Manasseh, and all the land of Judah, unto the hinder sea,

3and the South, and the Plain of the valley of Jericho the city of palm-trees, unto Zoar.

4And Yahweh said unto him, This is the land which I sware unto Abraham, unto Isaac, and unto Jacob, saying, I will give it unto thy seed: I have caused thee to see it with thine eyes, but thou shalt not go over thither.

5So Moses the servant of Yahweh died there in the land of Moab, according to the word of Yahweh.

6And he buried him in the valley in the land of Moab over against Beth-peor: but no man knoweth of his sepulchre unto this day.

7And Moses was a hundred and twenty years old when he died: his eye was not dim, nor his natural force abated.

8And the children of Israel wept for Moses in the plains of Moab thirty days: so the days of weeping in the mourning for Moses were ended.

9And Joshua the son of Nun was full of the spirit of wisdom; for Moses had laid his hands upon him: and the children of Israel hearkened unto him, and did as Yahweh commanded Moses.

10And there hath not arisen a prophet since in Israel like unto Moses, whom Yahweh knew face to face,

11in all the signs and the wonders, which Yahweh sent him to do in the land of Egypt, to Pharaoh, and to all his servants, and to all his land,

12and in all the mighty hand, and in all the great terror, which Moses wrought in the sight of all Israel.

The Book of Joshua

Chapter 1

1 Now it came to pass after the death of Moses the servant of Yahweh, that Yahweh spake unto Joshua the son of Nun, Moses' minister, saying,

2 Moses my servant is dead; now therefore arise, go over this Jordan, thou, and all this people, unto the land which I do give to them, even to the children of Israel.

3 Every place that the sole of your foot shall tread upon, to you have I given it, as I spake unto Moses.

4 From the wilderness, and this Lebanon, even unto the great river, the river Euphrates, all the land of the Hittites, and unto the great sea toward the going down of the sun, shall be your border.

5 There shall not any man be able to stand before thee all the days of thy life. as I was with Moses, so I will be with thee; I will not fail thee, nor forsake thee.

6 Be strong and of good courage; for thou shalt cause this people to inherit the land which I sware unto their fathers to give them.

7 Only be strong and very courageous, to observe to do according to all the law, which Moses my servant commanded thee: turn not from it to the right hand or to the left, that thou mayest have good success whithersoever thou goest.

8 This book of the law shall not depart out of thy mouth, but thou shalt meditate thereon day and night, that thou mayest observe to do according to all that is written therein: for then thou shalt make thy way prosperous, and then thou shalt have good success.

9 Have not I commanded thee? Be strong and of good courage; be not affrighted, neither be thou dismayed: for Yahweh thy God is with thee whithersoever thou goest.

10 Then Joshua commanded the officers of the people, saying,

11 Pass through the midst of the camp, and command the people, saying, Prepare you victuals; for within three days ye are to pass over this Jordan, to go in to possess the land, which Yahweh your God giveth you to possess it.

12 And to the Reubenites, and to the Gadites, and to the half-tribe of Manasseh, spake Joshua, saying,

13 Remember the word which Moses the servant of Yahweh commanded you, saying, Yahweh your God giveth you rest, and will give you this land.

14 Your wives, your little ones, and your cattle, shall abide in the land which Moses gave you beyond the Jordan; but ye shall pass over before your brethren armed, all the mighty men of valor, and shall help them;

15 until Yahweh have given your brethren rest, as he hath given you, and they also have possessed the land which Yahweh your God giveth them: then ye shall return unto the land of your possession, and possess it, which Moses the servant of Yahweh gave you beyond the Jordan toward the sunrising.

16 And they answered Joshua, saying, All that thou hast commanded us we will do, and whithersoever thou sendest us we will go.

17 According as we hearkened unto Moses in all things, so will we hearken unto thee: only Yahweh thy God be with thee, as he was with Moses.

18 Whosoever he be that shall rebel against thy commandment, and shall not hearken unto thy words in all that thou commandest him, he shall be put to death: only be strong and of good courage.

Chapter 2

1 And Joshua the son of Nun sent out of Shittim two men as spies secretly, saying, Go, view the land, and Jericho. And they went and came into the house of a harlot whose name was Rahab, and lay there.

2 And it was told the king of Jericho, saying, Behold, there came men in hither to-night of the children of Israel to search out the land.

3 And the king of Jericho sent unto Rahab, saying, Bring forth the men that are come to thee, that are entered into thy house; for they are come to search out all the land.

4 And the woman took the two men, and hid them; and she said, Yea, the men came unto me, but I knew not whence they were:

5 and it came to pass about the time of the shutting of the gate, when it was dark, that the men went out; whither the men went I know not: pursue after them quickly; for ye will overtake them.

6 But she had brought them up to the roof, and hid them with the stalks of flax, which she had laid in order upon the roof.

7 And the men pursued after them the way to the Jordan unto the fords: and as soon as they that pursued after them were gone out, they shut the gate.

8 And before they were laid down, she came up unto them upon the roof;

9 and she said unto the men, I know that Yahweh hath given you the land, and that the fear of you is fallen upon us, and that all the inhabitants of the land melt away before you.

10 For we have heard how Yahweh dried up the water of the Red Sea before you, when ye came out of Egypt; and what ye did unto the two kings of the Amorites, that were beyond the Jordan, unto Sihon and to Og, whom ye utterly destroyed.

11 And as soon as we had heard it, our hearts did melt, neither did there remain any more spirit in any man, because of you: for Yahweh your God, he is God in heaven above, and on earth beneath.

12 Now therefore, I pray you, swear unto me by Yahweh, since I have dealt kindly with you, that ye also will deal kindly with my father's house, and give me a true token;

13 and that ye will save alive my father, and my mother, and my brethren, and my sisters, and all that they have, and will deliver our lives from death.

14 And the men said unto her, Our life for yours, if ye utter not this our business; and it shall be, when Yahweh giveth us the land, that we will deal kindly and truly with thee.

15 Then she let them down by a cord through the window: for her house was upon the side of the wall, and she dwelt upon the wall.

16 And she said unto them, Get you to the mountain, lest the pursuers light upon you; and hide yourselves there three days, until the pursuers be returned: and afterward may ye go your way.

17 And the men said unto her, We will be guiltless of this thine oath which thou hast made us to swear.

18 Behold, when we come into the land, thou shalt bind this line of scarlet thread in the window which thou didst let us down by: and thou shalt gather unto thee into the house thy father, and thy mother, and thy brethren, and all thy father's household.

19 And it shall be, that whosoever shall go out of the doors of thy house into the street, his blood shall be upon his head, and we shall be guiltless: and whosoever shall be with thee in the house, his blood shall be on our head, if any hand be upon him.

20 But if thou utter this our business, then we shall be guiltless of thine oath which thou hast made us to swear.

21 And she said, According unto your words, so be it. And she sent them away, and they departed: and she bound the scarlet line in the window.

22 And they went, and came unto the mountain, and abode there three days, until the pursuers were returned: and the pursuers sought them throughout all the way, but found them not.

23 Then the two men returned, and descended from the mountain, and passed over, and came to Joshua the son of Nun; and they told him all that had befallen them.

24 And they said unto Joshua, Truly Yahweh hath delivered into our hands all the land; and moreover all the inhabitants of the land do melt away before us.

Chapter 3

1 And Joshua rose up early in the morning; and they removed from Shittim, and came to the Jordan, he and all the children of Israel; and they lodged there before they passed over.

2 And it came to pass after three days, that the officers went through the midst of the camp;

3 and they commanded the people, saying, When ye see the ark of the covenant of Yahweh your God, and the priests the Levites bearing it, then ye shall remove from your place, and go after it.

4 Yet there shall be a space between you and it, about two thousand cubits by measure: come not near unto it, that ye may know the way by which ye must go; for ye have not passed this way heretofore.

5 And Joshua said unto the people, Sanctify yourselves; for tomorrow Yahweh will do wonders among you.

6 And Joshua spake unto the priests, saying, Take up the ark of the covenant, and pass over before the people. And they took up the ark of the covenant, and went before the people.

7 And Yahweh said unto Joshua, This day will I begin to magnify thee in the sight of all Israel, that they may know that, as I was with Moses, so I will be with thee.

8 And thou shalt command the priests that bear the ark of the covenant, saying, When ye are come to the brink of the waters of the Jordan, ye shall stand still in the Jordan.

9 And Joshua said unto the children of Israel, Come hither, and hear the words of Yahweh your God.

10 And Joshua said, Hereby ye shall know that the living God is among you, and that he will without fail drive out from before you the Canaanite, and the Hittite, and the Hivite, and the Perizzite, and the Girgashite, and the Amorite, and the Jebusite.

11 Behold, the ark of the covenant of the Lord of all the earth passeth over before you into the Jordan.

12 Now therefore take you twelve men out of the tribes of Israel, for every tribe a man.

13 And it shall come to pass, when the soles of the feet of the priests that bear the ark of Yahweh, the Lord of all the earth, shall rest in the waters of the Jordan, that the waters of the Jordan shall be cut off, even the waters that come down from above; and they shall stand in one heap.

14 And it came to pass, when the people removed from their tents, to pass over the Jordan, the priests that bare the ark of the covenant being before the people;

15 and when they that bare the ark were come unto the Jordan, and the feet of the priests that bare the ark were dipped in the brink of the water (for the Jordan overfloweth all its banks all the time of harvest,)

16 that the waters which came down from above stood, and rose up in one heap, a great way off, at Adam, the city that is beside Zarethan; and those that went down toward the sea of the Arabah, even the Salt Sea, were wholly cut off: and the people passed over right against Jericho.

17 And the priests that bare the ark of the covenant of Yahweh stood firm on dry ground in the midst of the Jordan; and all Israel passed over on dry ground, until all the nation were passed clean over the Jordan.

Joshua
Chapter 4
1And it came to pass, when all the nation were clean passed over the Jordan, that Yahweh spake unto Joshua, saying,

2Take you twelve men out of the people, out of every tribe a man,

3and command ye them, saying, Take you hence out of the midst of the Jordan, out of the place where the priests' feet stood firm, twelve stones, and carry them over with you, and lay them down in the lodging-place, where ye shall lodge this night.

4Then Joshua called the twelve men, whom he had prepared of the children of Israel, out of every tribe a man:

5and Joshua said unto them, Pass over before the ark of Yahweh your God into the midst of the Jordan, and take you up every man of you a stone upon his shoulder, according unto the number of the tribes of the children of Israel;

6that this may be a sign among you, that, when your children ask in time to come, saying, What mean ye by these stones?

7then ye shall say unto them, Because the waters of the Jordan were cut off before the ark of the covenant of Yahweh; when it passed over the Jordan, the waters of the Jordan were cut off: and these stones shall be for a memorial unto the children of Israel for ever.

8And the children of Israel did so as Joshua commanded, and took up twelve stones out of the midst of the Jordan, as Yahweh spake unto Joshua, according to the number of the tribes of the children of Israel; and they carried them over with them unto the place where they lodged, and laid them down there.

9And Joshua set up twelve stones in the midst of the Jordan, in the place where the feet of the priests that bare the ark of the covenant stood: and they are there unto this day.

10For the priests that bare the ark stood in the midst of the Jordan, until everything was finished that Yahweh commanded Joshua to speak unto the people, according to all that Moses commanded Joshua: and the people hasted and passed over.

11And it came to pass, when all the people were clean passed over, that the ark of Yahweh passed over, and the priests, in the presence of the people.

12And the children of Reuben, and the children of Gad, and the half-tribe of Manasseh, passed over armed before the children of Israel, as Moses spake unto them:

13about forty thousand ready armed for war passed over before Yahweh unto battle, to the plains of Jericho.

14On that day Yahweh magnified Joshua in the sight of all Israel; and they feared him, as they feared Moses, all the days of his life.

15And Yahweh spake unto Joshua, saying,

16Command the priests that bear the ark of the testimony, that they come up out of the Jordan.

17Joshua therefore commanded the priests, saying, Come ye up out of the Jordan.

18And it came to pass, when the priests that bare the ark of the covenant of Yahweh were come up out of the midst of the Jordan, and the soles of the priests' feet were lifted up unto the dry ground, that the waters of the Jordan returned unto their place, and went over all its banks, as aforetime.

19And the people came up out of the Jordan on the tenth day of the first month, and encamped in Gilgal, on the east border of Jericho.

20And those twelve stones, which they took out of the Jordan, did Joshua set up in Gilgal.

21And he spake unto the children of Israel, saying, When your children shall ask their fathers in time to come, saying, What mean these stones?

22Then ye shall let your children know, saying, Israel came over this Jordan on dry land.

23For Yahweh your God dried up the waters of the Jordan from before you, until ye were passed over, as Yahweh your God did to the Red Sea, which he dried up from before us, until we were passed over;

24that all the peoples of the earth may know the hand of Yahweh, that it is mighty; that ye may fear Yahweh your God for ever.

Chapter 5
1And it came to pass, when all the kings of the Amorites, that were beyond the Jordan westward, and all the kings of the Canaanites, that were by the sea, heard how that Yahweh had dried up the waters of the Jordan from before the children of Israel, until we were passed over, that their heart melted, neither was there spirit in them any more, because of the children of Israel.

2At that time Yahweh said unto Joshua, Make thee knives of flint, and circumcise again the children of Israel the second time.

3And Joshua made him knives of lint, and circumcised the children of Israel at the hill of the foreskins.

4And this is the cause why Joshua did circumcise: all the people that came forth out of Egypt, that were males, even all the men of war, died in the wilderness by the way, after they came forth out of Egypt.

5For all the people that came out were circumcised; but all the people that were born in the wilderness by the way as they came forth out of Egypt, they had not circumcised.

6For the children of Israel walked forty years in the wilderness, till all the nation, even the men of war that came forth out of Egypt, were consumed, because they hearkened not unto the voice of Yahweh: unto whom Yahweh sware that he would not let them see the land which Yahweh sware unto their fathers that he would give us, a land flowing with milk and honey.

7And their children, whom he raised up in their stead, them did Joshua circumcise: for they were uncircumcised, because they had not circumcised them by the way.

8And it came to pass, when they had done circumcising all the nation, that they abode in their places in the camp, till they were whole.

9And Yahweh said unto Joshua, This day have I rolled away the reproach of Egypt from off you. Wherefore the name of that place was called Gilgal, unto this day.

10And the children of Israel encamped in Gilgal; and they kept the passover on the fourteenth day of the month at even in the plains of Jericho.

11And they did eat of the produce of the land on the morrow after the passover, unleavened cakes and parched grain, in the selfsame day.

12And the manna ceased on the morrow, after they had eaten of the produce of the land; neither had the children of Israel manna any more; but they did eat of the fruit of the land of Canaan that year.

13And it came to pass, when Joshua was by Jericho, that he lifted up his eyes and looked, and, behold, there stood a man over against him with his sword drawn in his hand: and Joshua went unto him, and said unto him, Art thou for us, or for our adversaries?

14And he said, Nay; but as prince of the host of Yahweh am I now come. And Joshua fell on his face to the earth, and did worship, and said unto him, What saith my lord unto his servant?

15And the prince of Yahweh's host said unto Joshua, Put off thy shoe from off thy foot; for the place whereon thou standest is holy. And Joshua did so.

Chapter 6
1Now Jericho was straitly shut up because of the children of Israel: none went out, and none came in.

2And Yahweh said unto Joshua, See, I have given into thy hand Jericho, and the king thereof, and the mighty men of valor.

3And ye shall compass the city, all the men of war, going about the city once. Thus shalt thou do six days.

4And seven priests shall bear seven trumpets of rams' horns before the ark: and the seventh day ye shall compass the city seven times, and the priests shall blow the trumpets.

5And it shall be, that, when they make a long blast with the ram's horn, and when ye hear the sound of the trumpet, all the people shall shout with a great shout; and the wall of the city shall fall down flat, and the people shall go up every man straight before him.

6And Joshua the son of Nun called the priests, and said unto them, Take up the ark of the covenant, and let seven priests bear seven trumpets of rams' horns before the ark of Yahweh.

7And they said unto the people, Pass on, and compass the city, and let the armed men pass on before the ark of Yahweh.

8And it was so, that, when Joshua had spoken unto the people, the seven priests bearing the seven trumpets of rams' horns before Yahweh passed on, and blew the trumpets: and the ark of the covenant of Yahweh followed them.

9And the armed men went before the priests that blew the trumpets, and the rearward went after the ark, the priests blowing the trumpets as they went.

10And Joshua commanded the people, saying, Ye shall not shout, nor let your voice be heard, neither shall any word proceed out of your mouth, until the day I bid you shout; then shall ye shout.

11So he caused the ark of Yahweh to compass the city, going about it once: and they came into the camp, and lodged in the camp.

12And Joshua rose early in the morning, and the priests took up the ark of Yahweh.

13And the seven priests bearing the seven trumpets of rams' horns before the ark of Yahweh went on continually, and blew the trumpets: and the armed men went before them; and the rearward came after the ark of Yahweh, the priests blowing the trumpets as they went.

14And the second day they compassed the city once, and returned into the camp: so they did six days.

15And it came to pass on the seventh day, that they rose early at the dawning of the day, and compassed the city after the same manner seven times: only on the day they compassed the city seven times.

16And it came to pass at the seventh time, when the priests blew the trumpets, Joshua said unto the people, Shout; for Yahweh hath given you the city.

17And the city shall be devoted, even it and all that is therein, to Yahweh: only Rahab the harlot shall live, she and all that are with her in the house, because she hid the messengers that we sent.

18But as for you, only keep yourselves from the devoted thing, lest when ye have devoted it, ye take of the devoted thing; so would ye make the camp of Israel accursed, and trouble it.

19But all the silver, and gold, and vessels of brass and iron, are holy unto Yahweh: they shall come into the treasury of Yahweh.

20So the people shouted, and the priests blew the trumpets; and it came to pass, when the people heard the sound of the trumpet, that the people shouted with a great shout, and the wall fell down flat, so that the people went up into the city, every man straight before him, and they took the city.

21And they utterly destroyed all that was in the city, both man and woman, both young and old, and ox, and sheep, and ass, with the edge of the sword.

22And Joshua said unto the two men that had spied out the land, Go into the harlot's house, and bring out thence the woman, and all that she hath, as ye sware unto her.

23And the young men the spies went in, and brought out Rahab, and her father, and her mother, and her brethren, and all that she had; all her kindred also they brought out; and they set them without the camp of Israel.

24And they burnt the city with fire, and all that was therein; only the silver, and the gold, and the vessels of brass and of iron, they put into the treasury of the house of Yahweh.

25But Rahab the harlot, and her father's household, and all that she had, did Joshua save alive; and she dwelt in the midst of Israel unto this day, because she hid the messengers, whom Joshua sent to spy out Jericho.

26And Joshua charged them with an oath at that time, saying, Cursed be the man before Yahweh, that riseth up and buildeth this city Jericho: with the loss of his first-born shall he lay the foundation thereof, and with the loss of his youngest son shall he set up the gates of it.

27So Yahweh was with Joshua; and his fame was in all the land.

Chapter 7

1But the children of Israel committed a trespass in the devoted thing; for Achan, the son of Carmi, the son of Zabdi, the son of Zerah, of the tribe of Judah, took of the devoted thing: and the anger of Yahweh was kindled against the children of Israel.

2And Joshua sent men from Jericho to Ai, which is beside Beth-aven, on the east side of Beth-el, and spake unto them, saying, Go up and spy out the land. And the men went up and spied out Ai.

3And they returned to Joshua, and said unto him, Let not all the people go up; but let about two or three thousand men go up and smite Ai; make not all the people to toil thither; for they are but few.

4So there went up thither of the people about three thousand men: and they fled before the men of Ai.

5And the men of Ai smote of them about thirty and six men; and they chased them from before the gate even unto Shebarim, and smote them at the descent; and the hearts of the people melted, and became as water.

6And Joshua rent his clothes, and fell to the earth upon his face before the ark of Yahweh until the evening, he and the elders of Israel; and they put dust upon their heads.

7And Joshua said, Alas, O Lord Yahweh, wherefore hast thou at all brought this people over the Jordan, to deliver us into the hand of the Amorites, to cause us to perish? would that we had been content and dwelt beyond the Jordan!

8Oh, Lord, what shall I say, after that Israel hath turned their backs before their enemies?

9For the Canaanites and all the inhabitants of the land will hear of it, and will compass us round, and cut off our name from the earth: and what wilt thou do for thy great name?

10And Yahweh said unto Joshua, Get thee up; wherefore art thou thus fallen upon thy face?

11Israel hath sinned; yea, they have even transgressed my covenant which I commanded them: yea, they have even taken of the devoted thing, and have also stolen, and dissembled also; and they have even put it among their own stuff.

12Therefore the children of Israel cannot stand before their enemies; they turn their backs before their enemies, because they are become accursed: I will not be with you any more, except ye destroy the devoted thing from among you.

13Up, sanctify the people, and say, Sanctify yourselves against tomorrow: for thus saith Yahweh, the God of Israel, There is a devoted thing in the midst of thee, O Israel; thou canst not stand before thine enemies, until ye take away the devoted thing from among you.

14In the morning therefore ye shall be brought near by your tribes: and it shall be, that the tribe which Yahweh taketh shall come near by families; and the family which Yahweh shall take shall come near by households; and the household which Yahweh shall take shall come near man by man.

15And it shall be, that he that is taken with the devoted thing shall be burnt with fire, he and all that he hath; because he hath transgressed the covenant of Yahweh, and because he hath wrought folly in Israel.

16So Joshua rose up early in the morning, and brought Israel near by their tribes; and the tribe of Judah was taken:

17and he brought near the family of Judah; and he took the family of the Zerahites: and he brought near the family of the Zerahites man by man; and Zabdi was taken:

18and he brought near his household man by man; and Achan, the son of Carmi, the son of Zabdi, the son of Zerah, of the tribe of Judah, was taken.

19And Joshua said unto Achan, My son, give, I pray thee, glory to Yahweh, the God of Israel, and make confession unto him; and tell me now what thou hast done; hide it not from me.

20And Achan answered Joshua, and said, Of a truth I have sinned against Yahweh, the God of Israel, and thus and thus have I done:

21when I saw among the spoil a goodly Babylonish mantle, and two hundred shekels of silver, and a wedge of gold of fifty shekels weight, then I coveted them, and took them; and, behold, they are hid in the earth in the midst of my tent, and the silver under it.

22So Joshua sent messengers, and they ran unto the tent; and, behold, it was hid in his tent, and the silver under it.

23And they took them from the midst of the tent, and brought them unto Joshua, and unto all the children of Israel; and they laid them down before Yahweh.

24And Joshua, and all Israel with him, took Achan the son of Zerah, and the silver, and the mantle, and the wedge of gold, and his sons, and his daughters, and his oxen, and his asses, and his sheep, and his tent, and all that he had: and they brought them up unto the valley of Achor.

25And Joshua said, Why hast thou troubled us? Yahweh shall trouble thee this day. And all Israel stoned him with stones; and they burned them with fire, and stoned them with stones.

26And they raised over him a great heap of stones, unto this day; and Yahweh turned from the fierceness of his anger. Wherefore the name of that place was called, The valley of Achor, unto this day.

Chapter 8

1And Yahweh said unto Joshua, Fear not, neither be thou dismayed: take all the people of war with thee, and arise, go up to Ai; see, I have given into thy hand the king of Ai, and his people, and his city, and his land;

2And thou shalt do to Ai and her king as thou didst unto Jericho and her king: only the spoil thereof, and the cattle thereof, shall ye take for a prey unto yourselves: set thou an ambush for the city behind it.

3So Joshua arose, and all the people of war, to go up to Ai: and Joshua chose out thirty thousand men, the mighty men of valor, and sent them forth by night.

4And he commanded them, saying, Behold, ye shall lie in ambush against the city, behind the city; go not very far from the city, but be ye all ready:

5and I, and all the people that are with me, will approach unto the city. And it shall come to pass, when they come out against us, as at the first, that we will flee before them;

6and they will come out after us, till we have drawn them away from the city; for they will say, They flee before us, as at the first: so we will flee before them;

7and ye shall rise up from the ambush, and take possession of the city: for Yahweh your God will deliver it into your hand.

8And it shall be, when ye have seized upon the city, that ye shall set the city on fire; according to the word of Yahweh shall ye do: see, I have commanded you.

9And Joshua sent them forth; and they went to the ambushment, and abode between Beth-el and Ai, on the west side of Ai: but Joshua lodged that night among the people.

10And Joshua arose up early in the morning, and mustered the people, and went up, he and the elders of Israel, before the people to Ai.

11And all the people, even the men of war that were with him, went up, and drew nigh, and came before the city, and encamped on the north side of Ai: now there was a valley between him and Ai.

12And he took about five thousand men, and set them in ambush between Beth-el and Ai, on the west side of the city.

13So they set the people, even all the host that was on the north of the city, and their liers-in-wait that were on the west of the city; and Joshua went that night into the midst of the valley.

14And it came to pass, when the king of Ai saw it, that they hasted and rose up early, and the men of the city went out against Israel to battle, he and all his people, at the time appointed, before the Arabah; but he knew not that there was an ambush against him behind the city.

15And Joshua and all Israel made as if they were beaten before them, and fled by the way of the wilderness.

16And all the people that were in the city were called together to pursue after them: and they pursued after Joshua, and were drawn away from the city.

17And there was not a man left in Ai or Beth-el, that went not out after Israel: and they left the city open, and pursued after Israel.

18And Yahweh said unto Joshua, Stretch out the javelin that is in thy hand toward Ai; for I will give it into thy hand. And Joshua stretched out the javelin that was in his hand toward the city.

19And the ambush arose quickly out of their place, and they ran as soon as he had stretched out his hand, and entered into the city, and took it; and they hasted and set the city on fire.

20And when the men of Ai looked behind them, they saw, and, behold, the smoke of the city ascended up to heaven, and they had no power to flee this way or that way: and the people that fled to the wilderness turned back upon the pursuers.

21And when Joshua and all Israel saw that the ambush had taken the city, and that the smoke of the city ascended, then they turned again, and slew the men of Ai.

22And the others came forth out of the city against them; so they were in the midst of Israel, some on this side, and some on that side: and they smote them, so that they let none of them remain or escape.

23And the king of Ai they took alive, and brought him to Joshua.

24And it came to pass, when Israel had made an end of slaying all the inhabitants of Ai in the field, in the wilderness wherein they pursued them, and they were all fallen by the edge of the sword, until they were consumed, that all Israel returned unto Ai, and smote it with the edge of the sword.

25And all that fell that day, both of men and women, were twelve thousand, even all the men of Ai.

26For Joshua drew not back his hand, wherewith he stretched out the javelin, until he had utterly destroyed all the inhabitants of Ai.

27Only the cattle and the spoil of that city Israel took for prey unto themselves, according unto the word of Yahweh which he commanded Joshua.

28So Joshua burnt Ai, and made it a heap for ever, even a desolation, unto this day.

29And the king of Ai he hanged on a tree until the eventide: and at the going down of the sun Joshua commanded, and they took his body down from the tree, and cast it at the entrance of the gate of the city, and raised thereon a great heap of stones, unto this day.

30Then Joshua built an altar unto Yahweh, the God of Israel, in mount Ebal,

31as Moses the servant of Yahweh commanded the children of Israel, as it is written in the book of the law of Moses, an altar of unhewn stones, upon which no man had lifted up any iron: and they offered thereon burnt-offerings unto Yahweh, and sacrificed peace-offerings.

32And he wrote there upon the stones a copy of the law of Moses, which he wrote, in the presence of the children of Israel.

33And all Israel, and their elders and officers, and their judges, stood on this side of the ark and on that side before the priests the Levites, that bare the ark of the covenant of Yahweh, as well the sojourner as the homeborn; half of them in front of mount Gerizim, and half of them in front of mount Ebal; as Moses the

Joshua

servant of Yahweh had commanded at the first, that they should bless the people of Israel.

34And afterward he read all the words of the law, the blessing and the curse, according to all that is written in the book of the law.

35There was not a word of all that Moses commanded, which Joshua read not before all the assembly of Israel, and the women, and the little ones, and the sojourners that were among them.

Chapter 9

1And it came to pass, when all the kings that were beyond the Jordan, in the hill-country, and in the lowland, and on all the shore of the great sea in front of Lebanon, the Hittite, and the Amorite, the Canaanite, the Perizzite, the Hivite, and the Jebusite, heard thereof;

2that they gathered themselves together, to fight with Joshua and with Israel, with one accord.

3But when the inhabitants of Gibeon heard what Joshua had done unto Jericho and to Ai,

4they also did work wilily, and went and made as if they had been ambassadors, and took old sacks upon their asses, and wine-skins, old and rent and bound up,

5and old and patched shoes upon their feet, and old garments upon them; and all the bread of their provision was dry and was become mouldy.

6And they went to Joshua unto the camp at Gilgal, and said unto him, and to the men of Israel, We are come from a far country: now therefore make ye a covenant with us.

7And the men of Israel said unto the Hivites, Peradventure ye dwell among us; and how shall we make a covenant with you?

8And they said unto Joshua, We are thy servants. And Joshua said unto them, Who are ye? and from whence come ye?

9And they said unto him, From a very far country thy servants are come because of the name of Yahweh thy God: for we have heard the fame of him, and all that he did in Egypt,

10and all that he did to the two kings of the Amorites, that were beyond the Jordan, to Sihon king of Heshbon, and to Og king of Bashan, who was at Ashtaroth.

11And our elders and all the inhabitants of our country spake to us, saying, Take provision in your hand for the journey, and go to meet them, and say unto them, We are your servants: and now make ye a covenant with us.

12This our bread we took hot for our provision out of our houses on the day we came forth to go unto you; but now, behold, it is dry, and is become mouldy:

13and these wine-skins, which we filled, were new; and, behold, they are rent: and these our garments and our shoes are become old by reason of the very long journey.

14And the men took of their provision, and asked not counsel at the mouth of Yahweh.

15And Joshua made peace with them, and made a covenant with them, to let them live: and the princes of the congregation sware unto them.

16And it came to pass at the end of three days after they had made a covenant with them, that they heard that they were their neighbors, and that they dwelt among them.

17And the children of Israel journeyed, and came unto their cities on the third day. Now their cities were Gibeon, and Chephirah, and Beeroth, and Kiriath-jearim.

18And the children of Israel smote them not, because the princes of the congregation had sworn unto them by Yahweh, the God of Israel. And all the congregation murmured against the princes.

19But all the princes said unto all the congregation, We have sworn unto them by Yahweh, the God of Israel: now therefore we may not touch them.

20This we will do to them, and let them live; lest wrath be upon us, because of the oath which we sware unto them.

21And the princes said unto them, Let them live: so they became hewers of wood and drawers of water unto all the congregation, as the princes had spoken unto them.

22And Joshua called for them, and he spake unto them, saying, Wherefore have ye beguiled us, saying, We are very far from you; when ye dwell among us?

23Now therefore ye are cursed, and there shall never fail to be of you bondmen, both hewers of wood and drawers of water for the house of my God.

24And they answered Joshua, and said, Because it was certainly told thy servants, how that Yahweh thy God commanded his servant Moses to give you all the land, and to destroy all the inhabitants of the land from before you; therefore we were sore afraid for our lives because of you, and have done this thing.

25And now, behold, we are in thy hand: as it seemeth good and right unto thee to do unto us, do.

26And so did he unto them, and delivered them out of the hand of the children of Israel, that they slew them not.

27And Joshua made them that day hewers of wood and drawers of water for the congregation, and for the altar of Yahweh, unto this day, in the place which he should choose.

Chapter 10

1Now it came to pass, when Adoni-zedek king of Jerusalem heard how Joshua had taken Ai, and had utterly destroyed it; as he had done to Jericho and her king, so he had done to Ai and her king; and how the inhabitants of Gibeon had made peace with Israel, and were among them;

2that they feared greatly, because Gibeon was a great city, as one of the royal cities, and because it was greater than Ai, and all the men thereof were mighty.

3Wherefore Adoni-zedek king of Jerusalem sent unto Hoham king of Hebron, and unto Piram king of Jarmuth, and unto Japhia king of Lachish, and unto Debir king of Eglon, saying,

4Come up unto me, and help me, and let us smite Gibeon; for it hath made peace with Joshua and with the children of Israel.

5Therefore the five kings of the Amorites, the king of Jerusalem, the king of Hebron, the king of Jarmuth, the king of Lachish, the king of Eglon, gathered themselves together, and went up, they and all their hosts, and encamped against Gibeon, and made war against it.

6And the men of Gibeon sent unto Joshua to the camp to Gilgal, saying, Slack not thy hand from thy servants; come up to us quickly, and save us, and help us: for all the kings of the Amorites that dwell in the hill-country are gathered together against us.

7So Joshua went up from Gilgal, he, and all the people of war with him, and all the mighty men of valor.

8And Yahweh said unto Joshua, Fear them not: for I have delivered them into thy hands; there shall not a man of them stand before thee.

9Joshua therefore came upon them suddenly; for he went up from Gilgal all the night.

10And Yahweh discomfited them before Israel, and he slew them with a great slaughter at Gibeon, and chased them by the way of the ascent of Beth-horon, and smote them to Azekah, and unto Makkedah.

11And it came to pass, as they fled from before Israel, while they were at the descent of Beth-horon, that Yahweh cast down great stones from heaven upon them unto Azekah, and they died: they were more who died with the hailstones than they whom the children of Israel slew with the sword.

12Then spake Joshua to Yahweh in the day when Yahweh delivered up the Amorites before the children of Israel; and he said in the sight of Israel,

Sun, stand thou still upon Gibeon;

And thou, Moon, in the valley of Aijalon.

13And the sun stood still, and the moon stayed,

Until the nation had avenged themselves of their enemies.

Is not this written in the book of Jashar? And the sun stayed in the midst of heaven, and hasted not to go down about a whole day.

14And there was no day like that before it or after it, that Yahweh hearkened unto the voice of a man: for Yahweh fought for Israel.

15And Joshua returned, and all Israel with him, unto the camp to Gilgal.

16And these five kings fled, and hid themselves in the cave at Makkedah.

17And it was told Joshua, saying, The five kings are found, hidden in the cave at Makkedah.

18And Joshua said, Roll great stones unto the mouth of the cave, and set men by it to keep them:

19but stay not ye; pursue after your enemies, and smite the hindmost of them; suffer them not to enter into their cities: for Yahweh your God hath delivered them into your hand.

20And it came to pass, when Joshua and the children of Israel had made an end of slaying them with a very great slaughter, till they were consumed, and the remnant which remained of them had entered into the fortified cities,

21that all the people returned to the camp to Joshua at Makkedah in peace: none moved his tongue against any of the children of Israel.

22Then said Joshua, Open the mouth of the cave, and bring forth those five kings unto me out of the cave.

23And they did so, and brought forth those five kings unto him out of the cave, the king of Jerusalem, the king of Hebron, the king of Jarmuth, the king of Lachish, the king of Eglon.

24And it came to pass, when they brought forth those kings unto Joshua, that Joshua called for all the men of Israel, and said unto the chiefs of the men of war that went with him, Come near, put your feet upon the necks of these kings. And they came near, and put their feet upon the necks of them.

25And Joshua said unto them, Fear not, nor be dismayed; be strong and of good courage: for thus shall Yahweh do to all your enemies against whom ye fight.

26And afterward Joshua smote them, and put them to death, and hanged them on five trees: and they were hanging upon the trees until the evening.

27And it came to pass at the time of the going down of the sun, that Joshua commanded, and they took them down off the trees, and cast them into the cave wherein they had hidden themselves, and laid great stones on the mouth of the cave, unto this very day.

28And Joshua took Makkedah on that day, and smote it with the edge of the sword, and the king thereof: he utterly destroyed them and all the souls that were therein; he left none remaining; and he did to the king of Makkedah as he had done unto the king of Jericho.

29And Joshua passed from Makkedah, and all Israel with him, unto Libnah, and fought against Libnah:

30and Yahweh delivered it also, and the king thereof, into the hand of Israel; and he smote it with the edge of the sword, and all the souls that were therein; he left none remaining in it; and he did unto the king thereof as he had done unto the king of Jericho.

31And Joshua passed from Libnah, and all Israel with him, unto Lachish, and encamped against it, and fought against it:

32and Yahweh delivered Lachish into the hand of Israel; and he took it on the second day, and smote it with the edge of the sword, and all the souls that were therein, according to all that he had done to Libnah.

33Then Horam king of Gezer came up to help Lachish; and Joshua smote him and his people, until he had left him none remaining.

34And Joshua passed from Lachish, and all Israel with him, unto Eglon; and they encamped against it, and fought against it;

35and they took it on that day, and smote it with the edge of the sword; and all the souls that were therein he utterly destroyed that day, according to all that he had done to Lachish.

36And Joshua went up from Eglon, and all Israel with him, unto Hebron; and they fought against it:

37and they took it, and smote it with the edge of the sword, and the king thereof, and all the cities thereof, and all the souls that were therein; he left none remaining, according to all that he had done to Eglon; but he utterly destroyed it, and all the souls that were therein.

38And Joshua returned, and all Israel with him, to Debir, and fought against it:

39and he took it, and the king thereof, and all the cities thereof; and they smote them with the edge of the sword, and utterly destroyed all the souls that were therein; he left none remaining: as he had done to Hebron, so he did to Debir, and to the king thereof; as he had done also to Libnah, and to the king thereof.

40So Joshua smote all the land, the hill-country, and the South, and the lowland, and the slopes, and all their kings: he left none remaining, but he utterly destroyed all that breathed, as Yahweh, the God of Israel, commanded.

41And Joshua smote them from Kadesh-barnea even unto Gaza, and all the country of Goshen, even unto Gibeon.

42And all these kings and their land did Joshua take at one time, because Yahweh, the God of Israel, fought for Israel.

43And Joshua returned, and all Israel with him, unto the camp to Gilgal.

Chapter 11

1And it came to pass, when Jabin king of Hazor heard thereof, that he sent to Jobab king of Madon, and to the king of Shimron, and to the king of Achshaph,

2and to the kings that were on the north, in the hill-country, and in the Arabah south of Chinneroth, and in the lowland, and in the heights of Dor on the west,

3to the Canaanite on the east and on the west, and the Amorite, and the Hittite, and the Perizzite, and the Jebusite in the hill-country, and the Hivite under Hermon in the land of Mizpah.

4And they went out, they and all their hosts with them, much people, even as the sand that is upon the sea-shore in multitude, with horses and chariots very many.

5And all these kings met together; and they came and encamped together at the waters of Merom, to fight with Israel.

6And Yahweh said unto Joshua, Be not afraid because of them; for to-morrow at this time will I deliver them up all slain before Israel: thou shalt hock their horses, and burn their chariots with fire.

7So Joshua came, and all the people of war with him, against them by the waters of Merom suddenly, and fell upon them.

8And Yahweh delivered them into the hand of Israel, and they smote them, and chased them unto great Sidon, and unto Misrephoth-maim, and unto the valley of Mizpeh eastward; and they smote them, until they left them none remaining.

9And Joshua did unto them as Yahweh bade him: he hocked their horses, and burnt their chariots with fire.

10And Joshua turned back at that time, and took Hazor, and smote the king thereof with the sword: for Hazor beforetime was the head of all those kingdoms.

11And they smote all the souls that were therein with the edge of the sword, utterly destroying them; there was none left that breathed: and he burnt Hazor with fire.

12And all the cities of those kings, and all the kings of them, did Joshua take, and he smote them with the edge of the sword, and utterly destroyed them; as Moses the servant of Yahweh commanded.

13But as for the cities that stood on their mounds, Israel burned none of them, save Hazor only; that did Joshua burn.

14And all the spoil of these cities, and the cattle, the children of Israel took for a prey unto themselves; but every man they smote with the edge of the sword, until they had destroyed them, neither left they any that breathed.

15As Yahweh commanded Moses his servant, so did Moses command Joshua: and so did Joshua; he left nothing undone of all that Yahweh commanded Moses.

16So Joshua took all that land, the hill-country, and all the South, and all the land of Goshen, and the lowland, and the Arabah, and the hill-country of Israel, and the lowland of the same;

17from mount Halak, that goeth up to Seir, even unto Baal-gad in the valley of Lebanon under mount Hermon: and all their kings he took, and smote them, and put them to death.

18Joshua made war a long time with all those kings.

19There was not a city that made peace with the children of Israel, save the Hivites the inhabitants of Gibeon: they took all in battle.

20For it was of Yahweh to harden their hearts, to come against Israel in battle, that he might utterly destroy them, that they might have no favor, but that he might destroy them, as Yahweh commanded Moses.

21And Joshua came at that time, and cut off the Anakim from the hill-country, from Hebron, from Debir, from Anab, and from all the hill-country of Judah, and from all the hill-country of Israel: Joshua utterly destroyed them with their cities.

22There was none of the Anakim left in the land of the children of Israel: only in Gaza, in Gath, and in Ashdod, did some remain.

23So Joshua took the whole land, according to all that Yahweh spake unto Moses; and Joshua gave it for an inheritance unto Israel according to their divisions by their tribes. And the land had rest from war.

Chapter 12

1Now these are the kings of the land, whom the children of Israel smote, and possessed their land beyond the Jordan toward the sunrising, from the valley of the Arnon unto mount Hermon, and all the Arabah eastward:

2Sihon king of the Amorites, who dwelt in Heshbon, and ruled from Aroer, which is on the edge of the valley of the Arnon, and the city that is in the middle of the valley, and half Gilead, even unto the river Jabbok, the border of the children of Ammon;

3and the Arabah unto the sea of Chinneroth, eastward, and unto the sea of the Arabah, even the Salt Sea, eastward, the way to Beth-jeshimoth; and on the south, under the slopes of Pisgah.

4and the border of Og king of Bashan, of the remnant of the Rephaim, who dwelt at Ashtaroth and at Edrei,

5and ruled in mount Hermon, and in Salecah, and in all Bashan, unto the border of the Geshurites and the Maacathites, and half Gilead, the border of Sihon king of Heshbon.

6Moses the servant of Yahweh and the children of Israel smote them: and Moses the servant of Yahweh gave it for a possession unto the Reubenites, and the Gadites, and the half-tribe of Manasseh.

7And these are the kings of the land whom Joshua and the children of Israel smote beyond the Jordan westward, from Baal-gad in the valley of Lebanon even unto mount Halak, that goeth up to Seir; and Joshua gave it unto the tribes of Israel for a possession according to their divisions;

8in the hill-country, and in the lowland, and in the Arabah, and in the slopes, and in the wilderness, and in the South; the Hittite, the Amorite, and the Canaanite, the Perizzite, the Hivite, and the Jebusite:

9the king of Jericho, one; the king of Ai, which is beside Bethel, one;

10the king of Jerusalem, one; the king of Hebron, one;

11the king of Jarmuth, one; the king of Lachish, one;

12the king of Eglon, one; the king of Gezer, one;

13the king of Debir, one; the king of Geder, one;

14the king of Hormah, one; the king of Arad, one;

15the king of Libnah, one; the king of Adullam, one;

16the king of Makkedah, one; the king of Bethel, one;

17the king of Tappuah, one; the king of Hepher, one;

18the king of Aphek, one; the king of Lassharon, one;

19the king of Madon, one; the king of Hazor, one;

20the king of Shimron-meron, one; the king of Achshaph, one;

21the king of Taanach, one; the king of Megiddo, one;

22the king of Kedesh, one; the king of Jokneam in Carmel, one;

23the king of Dor in the height of Dor, one; the king of Goiim in Gilgal, one;

24the king of Tirzah, one: all the kings thirty and one.

Chapter 13

1Now Joshua was old and well stricken in years; and Yahweh said unto him, Thou art old and well stricken in years, and there remaineth yet very much land to be possessed.

2This is the land that yet remaineth: all the regions of the Philistines, and all the Geshurites;

3from the Shihor, which is before Egypt, even unto the border of Ekron northward, which is reckoned to the Canaanites; the five lords of the Philistines; the Gazites, and the Ashdodites, the Ashkelonites, the Gittites, and the Ekronites; also the Avvim,

4on the south; all the land of the Canaanites, and Mearah that belongeth to the Sidonians, unto Aphek, to the border of the Amorites;

5and the land of the Gebalites, and all Lebanon, toward the sunrising, from Baal-gad under mount Hermon unto the entrance of Hamath;

6all the inhabitants of the hill-country from Lebanon unto Misrephoth-maim, even all the Sidonians; them will I drive out from before the children of Israel: only allot thou it unto Israel for an inheritance, as I have commanded thee.

7Now therefore divide this land for an inheritance unto the nine tribes, and the half-tribe of Manasseh.

8With him the Reubenites and the Gadites received their inheritance, which Moses gave them, beyond the Jordan eastward, even as Moses the servant of Yahweh gave them:

9from Aroer, that is on the edge of the valley of the Arnon, and the city that is in the middle of the valley, and all the plain of Medeba unto Dibon;

10and all the cities of Sihon king of the Amorites, who reigned in Heshbon, unto the border of the children of Ammon;

11and Gilead, and the border of the Geshurites and Maacathites, and all mount Hermon, and all Bashan unto Salecah;

12all the kingdom of Og in Bashan, who reigned in Ashtaroth and in Edrei (the same was left of the remnant of the Rephaim); for these did Moses smite, and drove them out.

13Nevertheless the children of Israel drove not out the Geshurites, nor the Maacathites: but Geshur and Maacath dwell in the midst of Israel unto this day.

14Only unto the tribe of Levi he gave no inheritance; the offerings of Yahweh, the God of Israel, made by fire are his inheritance, as he spake unto him.

15And Moses gave unto the tribe of the children of Reuben according to their families.

16And their border was from Aroer, that is on the edge of the valley of the Arnon, and the city that is in the middle of the valley, and all the plain by Medeba;

17Heshbon, and all its cities that are in the plain; Dibon, and Bamoth-baal, and Beth-baal-meon,

18and Jahaz, and Kedemoth, and Mephaath,

19and Kiriathaim, and Sibmah, and Zereth-shahar in the mount of the valley,

Joshua

20and Beth-peor, and the slopes of Pisgah, and Beth-jeshimoth,

21and all the cities of the plain, and all the kingdom of Sihon king of the Amorites, who reigned in Heshbon, whom Moses smote with the chiefs of Midian, Evi, and Rekem, and Zur, and Hur, and Reba, the princes of Sihon, that dwelt in the land.

22Balaam also the son of Beor, the soothsayer, did the children of Israel slay with the sword among the rest of their slain.

23And the border of the children of Reuben was the Jordan, and the border thereof. This was the inheritance of the children of Reuben according to their families, the cities and the villages thereof.

24And Moses gave unto the tribe of Gad, unto the children of Gad, according to their families.

25And their border was Jazer, and all the cities of Gilead, and half the land of the children of Ammon, unto Aroer that is before Rabbah;

26and from Heshbon unto Ramath-mizpeh, and Betonim; and from Mahanaim unto the border of Debir;

27and in the valley, Beth-haram, and Beth-nimrah, and Succoth, and Zaphon, the rest of the kingdom of Sihon king of Heshbon, the Jordan and the border thereof, unto the uttermost part of the sea of Chinnereth beyond the Jordan eastward.

28This is the inheritance of the children of Gad according to their families, the cities and the villages thereof.

29And Moses gave inheritance unto the half-tribe of Manasseh: and it was for the half-tribe of the children of Manasseh according to their families.

30And their border was from Mahanaim, all Bashan, all the kingdom of Og king of Bashan, and all the towns of Jair, which are in Bashan, threescore cities:

31and half Gilead, and Ashtaroth, and Edrei, the cities of the kingdom of Og in Bashan, were for the children of Machir the son of Manasseh, even for the half of the children of Machir according to their families.

32These are the inheritances which Moses distributed in the plains of Moab, beyond the Jordan at Jericho, eastward.

33But unto the tribe of Levi Moses gave no inheritance: Yahweh, the God of Israel, is their inheritance, as he spake unto them.

Chapter 14

1And these are the inheritances which the children of Israel took in the land of Canaan, which Eleazar the priest, and Joshua the son of Nun, and the heads of the fathers' houses of the tribes of the children of Israel, distributed unto them,

2by the lot of their inheritance, as Yahweh commanded by Moses, for the nine tribes, and for the half-tribe.

3For Moses had given the inheritance of the two tribes and the half-tribe beyond the Jordan: but unto the Levites he gave no inheritance among them.

4For the children of Joseph were two tribes, Manasseh and Ephraim: and they gave no portion unto the Levites in the land, save cities to dwell in, with the suburbs thereof for their cattle and for their substance.

5As Yahweh commanded Moses, so the children of Israel did; and they divided the land.

6Then the children of Judah drew nigh unto Joshua in Gilgal: and Caleb the son of Jephunneh the Kenizzite said unto him, Thou knowest the thing that Yahweh spake unto Moses the man of God concerning me and concerning thee in Kadesh-barnea.

7Forty years old was I when Moses the servant of Yahweh sent me from Kadesh-barnea to spy out the land; and I brought him word again as it was in my heart.

8Nevertheless my brethren that went up with me made the heart of the people melt; but I wholly followed Yahweh my God.

9And Moses sware on that day, saying, Surely the land whereon thy foot hath trodden shall be an inheritance to thee and to thy children for ever, because thou hast wholly followed Yahweh my God.

10And now, behold, Yahweh hath kept me alive, as he spake, these forty and five years, from the time that Yahweh spake this word unto Moses, while Israel walked in the wilderness: and now, lo, I am this day fourscore and five years old.

11As yet I am as strong this day as I as in the day that Moses sent me: as my strength was then, even so is my strength now, for war, and to go out and to come in.

12Now therefore give me this hill-country, whereof Yahweh spake in that day; for thou heardest in that day how the Anakim were there, and cities great and fortified: it may be that Yahweh will be with me, and I shall drive them out, as Yahweh spake.

13And Joshua blessed him; and he gave Hebron unto Caleb the son of Jephunneh for an inheritance.

14Therefore Hebron became the inheritance of Caleb the son of Jephunneh the Kenizzite unto this day; because that he wholly followed Yahweh, the God of Israel.

15Now the name of Hebron beforetime was Kiriath-arba; which Arba was the greatest man among the Anakim. And the land had rest from war.

Chapter 15

1And the lot for the tribe of the children of Judah according to their families was unto the border of Edom, even to the wilderness of Zin southward, at the uttermost part of the south.

2And their south border was from the uttermost part of the Salt Sea, from the bay that looketh southward;

3and it went out southward of the ascent of Akrabbim, and passed along to Zin, and went up by the south of Kadesh-barnea, and passed along by Hezron, and went up to Addar, and turned about to Karka;

4and it passed along to Azmon, and went out at the brook of Egypt; and the goings out of the border were at the sea: this shall be your south border.

5And the east border was the Salt Sea, even unto the end of the Jordan. And the border of the north quarter was from the bay of the sea at the end of the Jordan;

6and the border went up to Beth-hoglah, and passed along by the north of Beth-arabah; and the border went up to the stone of Bohan the son of Reuben;

7and the border went up to Debir from the valley of Achor, and so northward, looking toward Gilgal, that is over against the ascent of Adummim, which is on the south side of the river; and the border passed along to the waters of En-shemesh, and the goings out thereof were at En-rogel;

8and the border went up by the valley of the son of Hinnom unto the side of the Jebusite southward (the same is Jerusalem); and the border went up to the top of the mountain that lieth before the valley of Hinnom westward, which is at the uttermost part of the vale of Rephaim northward;

9and the border extended from the top of the mountain unto the fountain of the waters of Nephtoah, and went out to the cities of mount Ephron; and the border extended to Baalah (the same is Kiriath-jearim);

10and the border turned about from Baalah westward unto mount Seir, and passed along unto the side of mount Jearim on the north (the same is Chesalon), and went down to Beth-shemesh, and passed along by Timnah;

11and the border went out unto the side of Ekron northward; and the border extended to Shikkeron, and passed along to mount Baalah, and went out at Jabneel; and the goings out of the border were at the sea.

12And the west border was to the great sea, and the border thereof. This is the border of the children of Judah round about according to their families.

13And unto Caleb the son of Jephunneh he gave a portion among the children of Judah, according to the commandment of Yahweh to Joshua, even Kiriath-arba, which Arba was the father of Anak (the same is Hebron).

14And Caleb drove out thence the three sons of Anak: Sheshai, and Ahiman, and Talmai, the children of Anak.

15And he went up thence against the inhabitants of Debir: now the name of Debir beforetime was Kiriath-sepher.

16And Caleb said, He that smiteth Kiriath-sepher, and taketh it, to him will I give Achsah my daughter to wife.

17And Othniel the son of Kenaz, the brother of Caleb, took it: and he gave him Achsah his daughter to wife.

18And it came to pass, when she came unto him, that she moved him to ask of her father a field: and she alighted from off her ass; and Caleb said, What wouldest thou?

19And she said, Give me a blessing; for that thou hast set me in the land of the South, give me also springs of water. And he gave her the upper springs and the nether springs.

20This is the inheritance of the tribe of the children of Judah according to their families.

21And the uttermost cities of the tribe of the children of Judah toward the border of Edom in the South were Kabzeel, and Eder, and Jagur,

22and Kinah, and Dimonah, and Adadah,

23and Kedesh, and Hazor, and Ithnan,

24Ziph, and Telem, and Bealoth,

25and Hazor-hadattah, and Kerioth-hezron (the same is Hazor),

26Amam, and Shema, and Moladah,

27and Hazar-gaddah, and Heshmon, and Beth-pelet,

28and Hazar-shual, and Beer-sheba, and Biziothiah,

29Baalah, and Iim, and Ezem,

30and Eltolad, and Chesil, and Hormah,

31and Ziklag, and Madmannah, and Sansannah,

32and Lebaoth, and Shilhim, and Ain, and Rimmon: all the cities are twenty and nine, with their villages.

33In the lowland, Eshtaol, and Zorah, and Ashnah,

34and Zanoah, and En-gannim, Tappuah, and Enam,

35Jarmuth, and Adullam, Socoh, and Azekah,

36and Shaaraim, and Adithaim, and Gederah, and Gederothaim; fourteen cities with their villages.

37Zenan, and Hadashah, and Migdal-gad,

38and Dilean, and Mizpeh, and Joktheel,

39Lachish, and Bozkath, and Eglon,

40and Cabbon, and Lahmam, and Chitlish,

41and Gederoth, Beth-dagon, and Naamah, and Makkedah; sixteen cities with their villages.

42Libnah, and Ether, and Ashan,

43and Iphtah, and Ashnah, and Nezib,

44and Keilah, and Achzib, and Mareshah; nine cities with their villages.

45Ekron, with its towns and its villages;

46from Ekron even unto the sea, all that were by the side of Ashdod, with their villages.

47Ashdod, its towns and its villages; Gaza, its towns and its villages; unto the brook of Egypt, and the great sea, and the border thereof.

48And in the hill-country, Shamir, and Jattir, and Socoh,

49and Dannah, and Kiriath-sannah (the same is Debir),

50and Anab, and Eshtemoh, and Anim,

51and Goshen, and Holon, and Giloh; eleven cities with their villages.

52Arab, and Dumah, and Eshan,

53and Janim, and Beth-tappuah, and Aphekah,

54and Humtah, and Kiriath-arba (the same is Hebron), and Zior; nine cities with their villages.

55Maon, Carmel, and Ziph, and Jutah,

56and Jezreel, and Jokdeam, and Zanoah,

57Kain, Gibeah, and Timnah; ten cities with their villages.

58Halhul, Beth-zur, and Gedor,

59and Maarath, and Beth-anoth, and Eltekon; six cities with their villages.

60Kiriath-baal (the same is Kiriath-jearim), and Rabbah; two cities with their villages.

61In the wilderness, Beth-arabah, Middin, and Secacah,

62and Nibshan, and the City of Salt, and En-gedi; six cities with their villages.

63And as for the Jebusites, the inhabitants of Jerusalem, the children of Judah could not drive them out: but the Jebusites dwell with the children of Judah at Jerusalem unto this day.

Chapter 16

16 1And the lot came out for the children of Joseph from the Jordan at Jericho, at the waters of Jericho on the east, even the wilderness, going up from Jericho through the hill-country to Beth-el;

2and it went out from Beth-el to Luz, and passed along unto the border of the Archites to Ataroth;

3and it went down westward to the border of the Japhletites, unto the border of Beth-horon the nether, even unto Gezer; and the goings out thereof were at the sea.

4And the children of Joseph, Manasseh and Ephraim, took their inheritance.

5And the border of the children of Ephraim according to their families was thus: the border of their inheritance eastward was Ataroth-addar, unto Beth-horon the upper;

6and the border went out westward at Michmethath on the north; and the border turned about eastward unto Taanath-shiloh, and passed along it on the east of Janoah;

7and it went down from Janoah to Ataroth, and to Naarah, and reached unto Jericho, and went out at the Jordan.

8From Tappuah the border went along westward to the brook of Kanah; and the goings out thereof were at the sea. This is the inheritance of the tribe of the children of Ephraim according to their families;

9together with the cities which were set apart for the children of Ephraim in the midst of the inheritance of the children of Manasseh, all the cities with their villages.

10And they drove not out the Canaanites that dwelt in Gezer: but the Canaanites dwell in the midst of Ephraim unto this day, and are become servants to do taskwork.

Chapter 17

1And this was the lot for the tribe of Manasseh; for he was the first-born of Joseph. As for Machir the first-born of Manasseh, the father of Gilead, because he was a man of war, therefore he had Gilead and Bashan.

2So the lot was for the rest of the children of Manasseh according to their families: for the children of Abiezer, and for the children of Helek, and for the children of Asriel, and for the children of Shechem, and for the children of Hepher, and for the children of Shemida: these were the male children of Manasseh the son of Joseph according to their families.

3But Zelophehad, the son of Hepher, the son of Gilead, the son of Machir, the son of Manasseh, had no sons, but daughters: and these are the names of his daughters: Mahlah, and Noah, Hoglah, Milcah, and Tirzah.

4And they came near before Eleazar the priest, and before Joshua the son of Nun, and before the princes, saying, Yahweh commanded Moses to give us an inheritance among our brethren: therefore according to the commandment of Yahweh he gave them an inheritance among the brethren of their father.

5And there fell ten parts to Manasseh, besides the land of Gilead and Bashan, which is beyond the Jordan;

6because the daughters of Manasseh had an inheritance among his sons. And the land of Gilead belonged unto the rest of the sons of Manasseh.

7And the border of Manasseh was from Asher to Michmethath, which is before Shechem; and the border went along to the right hand, unto the inhabitants of En-tappuah.

8The land of Tappuah belonged to Manasseh; but Tappuah on the border of Manasseh belonged to the children of Ephraim.

9And the border went down unto the brook of Kanah, southward of the brook: these cities belonged to Ephraim among the cities of Manasseh: and the border of Manasseh was on the north side of the brook, and the goings out thereof were at the sea:

10southward it was Ephraim's, and northward it was Manasseh's, and the sea was his border; and they reached to Asher on the north, and to Issachar on the east.

11And Manasseh had in Issachar and in Asher Beth-shean and its towns, and Ibleam and its towns, and the inhabitants of Dor and its towns, and the inhabitants of En-dor and its towns, and the inhabitants of Taanach and its towns, and the inhabitants of Megiddo and its towns, even the three heights.

12Yet the children of Manasseh could not drive out the inhabitants of those cities; but the Canaanites would dwell in that land.

13And it came to pass, when the children of Israel were waxed strong, that they put the Canaanites to taskwork, and did not utterly drive them out.

14And the children of Joseph spake unto Joshua, saying, Why hast thou given me but one lot and one part for an inheritance, seeing I am a great people, forasmuch as hitherto Yahweh hath blessed me?

15And Joshua said unto them, If thou be a great people, get thee up to the forest, and cut down for thyself there in the land of the Perizzites and of the Rephaim; since the hill-country of Ephraim is too narrow for thee.

16And the children of Joseph said, The hill-country is not enough for us: and all the Canaanites that dwell in the land of the valley have chariots of iron, both they who are in Beth-shean and its towns, and they who are in the valley of Jezreel.

17And Joshua spake unto the house of Joseph, even to Ephraim and to Manasseh, saying, Thou art a great people, and hast great power; thou shalt not have one lot only:

18but the hill-country shall be thine; for though it is a forest, thou shalt cut it down, and the goings out thereof shall be thine; for thou shalt drive out the Canaanites, though they have chariots of iron, and though they are strong.

Chapter 18

1And the whole congregation of the children of Israel assembled themselves together at Shiloh, and set up the tent of meeting there: and the land was subdued before them.

2And there remained among the children of Israel seven tribes, which had not yet divided their inheritance.

3And Joshua said unto the children of Israel, How long are ye slack to go in to possess the land, which Yahweh, the God of your fathers, hath given you?

4Appoint for you three men of each tribe: and I will send them, and they shall arise, and walk through the land, and describe it according to their inheritance; and they shall come unto me.

5And they shall divide it into seven portions: Judah shall abide in his border on the south, and the house of Joseph shall abide in their border on the north.

6And ye shall describe the land into seven portions, and bring the description hither to me; and I will cast lots for you here before Yahweh our God.

7For the Levites have no portion among you; for the priesthood of Yahweh is their inheritance: and Gad and Reuben and the half-tribe of Manasseh have received their inheritance beyond the Jordan eastward, which Moses the servant of Yahweh gave them.

8And the men arose, and went: and Joshua charged them that went to describe the land, saying, Go and walk through the land, and describe it, and come again to me; and I will cast lots for you here before Yahweh in Shiloh.

9And the men went and passed through the land, and described it by cities into seven portions in a book; and they came to Joshua unto the camp at Shiloh.

10And Joshua cast lots for them in Shiloh before Yahweh: and there Joshua divided the land unto the children of Israel according to their divisions.

11And the lot of the tribe of the children of Benjamin came up according to their families: and the border of their lot went out between the children of Judah and the children of Joseph.

12And their border on the north quarter was from the Jordan; and the border went up to the side of Jericho on the north, and went up through the hill-country westward; and the goings out thereof were at the wilderness of Beth-aven.

13And the border passed along from thence to Luz, to the side of Luz (the same is Beth-el), southward; and the border went down to Ataroth-addar, by the mountain that lieth on the south of Beth-horon the nether.

14And the border extended thence, and turned about on the west quarter southward, from the mountain that lieth before Beth-horon southward; and the goings out thereof were at Kiriath-baal (the same is Kiriath-jearim), a city of the children of Judah: this was the west quarter.

15And the south quarter was from the uttermost part of Kiriath-jearim; and the border went out westward, and went out to the fountain of the waters of Nephtoah;

16and the border went down to the uttermost part of the mountain that lieth before the valley of the son of Hinnom, which is in the vale of Rephaim northward; and it went down to the valley of Hinnom, to the side of the Jebusite southward, and went down to En-rogel;

17and it extended northward, and went out at En-shemesh, and went out to Geliloth, which is over against the ascent of Adummim; and it went down to the stone of Bohan the son of Reuben;

18and it passed along to the side over against the Arabah northward, and went down unto the Arabah;

19and the border passed along to the side of Beth-hoglah northward; and the goings out of the border were at the north bay of the Salt Sea, at the south end of the Jordan: this was the south border.

20And the Jordan was the border of it on the east quarter. This was the inheritance of the children of Benjamin, by the borders thereof round about, according to their families.

21Now the cities of the tribe of the children of Benjamin according to their families were Jericho, and Beth-hoglah, and Emek-keziz,

22and Beth-arabah, and Zemaraim, and Beth-el,

23and Avvim, and Parah, and Ophrah,

24and Chephar-ammoni, and Ophni, and Geba; twelve cities with their villages:

25Gibeon, and Ramah, and Beeroth,

26and Mizpeh, and Chephirah, and Mozah,

27and Rekem, and Irpeel, and Taralah,

28and Zelah, Eleph, and the Jebusite (the same is Jerusalem), Gibeath, and Kiriath; fourteen cities with their villages. This is the inheritance of the children of Benjamin according to their families.

Chapter 19

1And the second lot came out for Simeon, even for the tribe of the children of Simeon according to their families: and their inheritance was in the midst of the inheritance of the children of Judah.

2And they had for their inheritance Beer-sheba, or Sheba, and Moladah,

3and Hazar-shual, and Balah, and Ezem,

4and Eltolad, and Bethul, and Hormah,

5and Ziklag, and Beth-marcaboth, and Hazar-susah,

6and Beth-lebaoth, and Sharuhen; thirteen cities with their villages:

7Ain, Rimmon, and Ether, and Ashan; four cities with their villages:

8and all the villages that were round about these cities to Baalath-beer, Ramah of the South. This is the inheritance of the tribe of the children of Simeon according to their families.

Joshua

9Out of the part of the children of Judah was the inheritance of the children of Simeon; for the portion of the children of Judah was too much for them: therefore the children of Simeon had inheritance in the midst of their inheritance.

10And the third lot came up for the children of Zebulun according to their families; and the border of their inheritance was unto Sarid;

11and their border went up westward, even to Maralah, and reached to Dabbesheth; and it reached to the brook that is before Jokneam;

12and it turned from Sarid eastward toward the sunrising unto the border of Chisloth-tabor; and it went out to Daberath, and went up to Japhia;

13and from thence it passed along eastward to Gath-hepher, to Eth-kazin; and it went out at Rimmon which stretcheth unto Neah;

14and the border turned about it on the north to Hannathon; and the goings out thereof were at the valley of Iphtah-el;

15and Kattath, and Nahalal, and Shimron, and Idalah, and Bethlehem: twelve cities with their villages.

16This is the inheritance of the children of Zebulun according to their families, these cities with their villages.

17The fourth lot came out for Issachar, even for the children of Issachar according to their families.

18And their border was unto Jezreel, and Chesulloth, and Shunem,

19and Hapharaim, and Shion, and Anaharath,

20and Rabbith, and Kishion, and Ebez,

21and Remeth, and Engannim, and En-haddah, and Beth-pazzez,

22and the border reached to Tabor, and Shahazumah, and Beth-shemesh; and the goings out of their border were at the Jordan: sixteen cities with their villages.

23This is the inheritance of the tribe of the children of Issachar according to their families, the cities with their villages.

24And the fifth lot came out for the tribe of the children of Asher according to their families.

25And their border was Helkath, and Hali, and Beten, and Achshaph,

26and Allammelech, and Amad, and Mishal; and it reached to Carmel westward, and to Shihor-libnath;

27and it turned toward the sunrising to Beth-dagon, and reached to Zebulun, and to the valley of Iphtah-el northward to Beth-emek and Neiel; and it went out to Cabul on the left hand,

28and Ebron, and Rehob, and Hammon, and Kanah, even unto great Sidon;

29and the border turned to Ramah, and to the fortified city of Tyre; and the border turned to Hosah; and the goings out thereof were at the sea by the region of Achzib;

30Ummah also, and Aphek, and Rehob: twenty and two cities with their villages.

31This is the inheritance of the tribe of the children of Asher according to their families, these cities with their villages.

32The sixth lot came out for the children of Naphtali, even for the children of Naphtali according to their families.

33And their border was from Heleph, from the oak in Zaanannim, and Adaminekeb, and Jabneel, unto Lakkum; and the goings out thereof were at the Jordan;

34and the border turned westward to Aznoth-tabor, and went out from thence to Hukkok; and it reached to Zebulun on the south, and reached to Asher on the west, and to Judah at the Jordan toward the sunrising.

35And the fortified cities were Ziddim, Zer, and Hammath, Rakkath, and Chinnereth,

36and Adamah, and Ramah, and Hazor,

37and Kedesh, and Edrei, and En-hazor,

38And Iron, and Migdal-el, Horem, and Beth-anath, and Beth-shemesh; nineteen cities with their villages.

39This is the inheritance of the tribe of the children of Naphtali according to their families, the cities with their villages.

40The seventh lot came out for the tribe of the children of Dan according to their families.

41And the border of their inheritance was Zorah, and Eshtaol, and Ir-shemesh,

42and Shaalabbin, and Aijalon, and Ithlah,

43and Elon, and Timnah, and Ekron,

44and Eltekeh, and Gibbethon, and Baalath,

45and Jehud, and Bene-berak, and Gath-rimmon,

46and Me-jarkon, and Rakkon, with the border over against Joppa.

47And the border of the children of Dan went out beyond them; for the children of Dan went up and fought against Leshem, and took it, and smote it with the edge of the sword, and possessed it, and dwelt therein, and called Leshem, Dan, after the name of Dan their father.

48This is the inheritance of the tribe of the children of Dan according to their families, these cities with their villages.

49So they made an end of distributing the land for inheritance by the borders thereof; and the children of Israel gave an inheritance to Joshua the son of Nun in the midst of them:

50according to the commandment of Yahweh they gave him the city which he asked, even Timnath-serah in the hill-country of Ephraim; and he built the city, and dwelt therein.

51These are the inheritances, which Eleazar the priest, and Joshua the son of Nun, and the heads of the fathers' houses of the tribes of the children of Israel, distributed for inheritance by lot in Shiloh before Yahweh, at the door of the tent of meeting. So they made an end of dividing the land.

Chapter 20

1And Yahweh spake unto Joshua, saying,

2Speak to the children of Israel, saying, Assign you the cities of refuge, whereof I spake unto you by Moses,

3that the manslayer that killeth any person unwittingly and unawares may flee thither: and they shall be unto you for a refuge from the avenger of blood.

4And he shall flee unto one of those cities, and shall stand at the entrance of the gate of the city, and declare his cause in the ears of the elders of that city; and they shall take him into the city unto them, and give him a place, that he may dwell among them.

5And if the avenger of blood pursue after him, then they shall not deliver up the manslayer into his hand; because he smote his neighbor unawares, and hated him not beforetime.

6And he shall dwell in that city, until he stand before the congregation for judgment, until the death of the high priest that shall be in those days: then shall the manslayer return, and come unto his own city, and unto his own house, unto the city from whence he fled.

7And they set apart Kedesh in Galilee in the hill-country of Naphtali, and Shechem in the hill-country of Ephraim, and Kiriath-arba (the same is Hebron) in the hill-country of Judah.

8And beyond the Jordan at Jericho eastward, they assigned Bezer in the wilderness in the plain out of the tribe of Reuben, and Ramoth in Gilead out of the tribe of Gad, and Golan in Bashan out of the tribe of Manasseh.

9These were the appointed cities for all the children of Israel, and for the stranger that sojourneth among them, that whosoever killeth any person unwittingly might flee thither, and not die by the hand of the avenger of blood, until he stood before the congregation.

Chapter 21

1Then came near the heads of fathers' houses of the Levites unto Eleazar the priest, and unto Joshua the son of Nun, and unto the heads of fathers' houses of the tribes of the children of Israel;

2and they spake unto them at Shiloh in the land of Canaan, saying, Yahweh commanded Moses to give us cities to dwell in, with the suburbs thereof for our cattle.

3And the children of Israel gave unto the Levites out of their inheritance, according to the commandment of Yahweh, these cities with their suburbs.

4And the lot came out for the families of the Kohathites: and the children of Aaron the priest, who were of the Levites, had by lot out of the tribe of Judah, and out of the tribe of the Simeonites, and out of the tribe of Benjamin, thirteen cities.

5And the rest of the children of Kohath had by lot out of the families of the tribe of Ephraim, and out of the tribe of Dan, and out of the half-tribe of Manasseh, ten cities.

6And the children of Gershon had by lot out of the families of the tribe of Issachar, and out of the tribe of Asher, and out of the tribe of Naphtali, and out of the half-tribe of Manasseh in Bashan, thirteen cities.

7The children of Merari according to their families had out of the tribe of Reuben, and out of the tribe of Gad, and out of the tribe of Zebulun, twelve cities.

8And the children of Israel gave by lot unto the Levites these cities with their suburbs, as Yahweh commanded by Moses.

9And they gave out of the tribe of the children of Judah, and out of the tribe of the children of Simeon, these cities which are here mentioned by name:

10and they were for the children of Aaron, of the families of the Kohathites, who were of the children of Levi; for theirs was the first lot.

11And they gave them Kiriath-arba, which Arba was the father of Anak (the same is Hebron), in the hill-country of Judah, with the suburbs thereof round about it.

12But the fields of the city, and the villages thereof, gave they to Caleb the son of Jephunneh for his possession.

13And unto the children of Aaron the priest they gave Hebron with its suburbs, the city of refuge for the manslayer, and Libnah with its suburbs,

14and Jattir with its suburbs, and Eshtemoa with its suburbs,

15and Holon with its suburbs, and Debir with its suburbs,

16and Ain with its suburbs, and Juttah with its suburbs, and Beth-shemesh with its suburbs; nine cities out of those two tribes.

17And out of the tribe of Benjamin, Gibeon with its suburbs, Geba with its suburbs,

18Anathoth with its suburbs, and Almon with its suburbs; four cities.

19All the cities of the children of Aaron, the priests, were thirteen cities with their suburbs.

20And the families of the children of Kohath, the Levites, even the rest of the children of Kohath, they had the cities of their lot out of the tribe of Ephraim.

21And they gave them Shechem with its suburbs in the hill-country of Ephraim, the city of refuge for the manslayer, and Gezer with its suburbs,

22and Kibzaim with its suburbs, and Beth-horon with its suburbs; four cities.

23And out of the tribe of Dan, Elteke with its suburbs, Gibbethon with its suburbs,

24Aijalon with its suburbs, Gath-rimmon with its suburbs; four cities.

25And out of the half-tribe of Manasseh, Taanach with its suburbs, and Gath-rimmon with its suburbs; two cities.

26All the cities of the families of the rest of the children of Kohath were ten with their suburbs.

27And unto the children of Gershon, of the families of the Levites, out of the half-tribe of Manasseh they gave Golan in Bashan with its suburbs, the city of refuge for the manslayer, and Be-eshterah with its suburbs; two cities.

28And out of the tribe of Issachar, Kishion with its suburbs, Daberath with its suburbs,

29Jarmuth with its suburbs, En-gannim with its suburbs; four cities.

30And out of the tribe of Asher, Mishal with its suburbs, Abdon with its suburbs,

31Helkath with its suburbs, and Rehob with its suburbs; four cities.

32And out of the tribe of Naphtali, Kedesh in Galilee with its suburbs, the city of refuge for the manslayer, and Hammoth-dor with its suburbs, and Kartan with its suburbs; three cities.

33All the cities of the Gershonites according to their families were thirteen cities with their suburbs.

34And unto the families of the children of Merari, the rest of the Levites, out of the tribe of Zebulun, Jokneam with its suburbs, and Kartah with its suburbs,

35Dimnah with its suburbs, Nahalal with its suburbs; four cities.

36And out of the tribe of Reuben, Bezer with its suburbs, and Jahaz with its suburbs,

37Kedemoth with its suburbs, and Mephaath with its suburbs; four cities.

38And out of the tribe of Gad, Ramoth in Gilead with its suburbs, the city of refuge for the manslayer, and Mahanaim with its suburbs,

39Heshbon with its suburbs, Jazer with its suburbs; four cities in all.

40All these were the cities of the children of Merari according to their families, even the rest of the families of the Levites; and their lot was twelve cities.

41All the cities of the Levites in the midst of the possession of the children of Israel were forty and eight cities with their suburbs.

42These cities were every one with their suburbs round about them: thus it was with all these cities.

43So Yahweh gave unto Israel all the land which he sware to give unto their fathers; and they possessed it, and dwelt therein.

44And Yahweh gave them rest round about, according to all that he sware unto their fathers: and there stood not a man of all their enemies before them; Yahweh delivered all their enemies into their hand.

45There failed not aught of any good thing which Yahweh had spoken unto the house of Israel; all came to pass.

Chapter 22

1Then Joshua called the Reubenites, and the Gadites, and the half-tribe of Manasseh,

2and said unto them, Ye have kept all that Moses the servant of Yahweh commanded you, and have hearkened unto my voice in all that I commanded you:

3ye have not left your brethren these many days unto this day, but have kept the charge of the commandment of Yahweh your God.

4And now Yahweh your God hath given rest unto your brethren, as he spake unto them: therefore now turn ye, and get you unto your tents, unto the land of your possession, which Moses the servant of Yahweh gave you beyond the Jordan.

5Only take diligent heed to do the commandment and the law which Moses the servant of Yahweh commanded you, to love Yahweh your God, and to walk in all his ways, and to keep his commandments, and to cleave unto him, and to serve him with all your heart and with all your soul.

6So Joshua blessed them, and sent them away; and they went unto their tents.

7Now to the one half-tribe of Manasseh Moses had given inheritance in Bashan; but unto the other half gave Joshua among their brethren beyond the Jordan westward; moreover when Joshua sent them away unto their tents, he blessed them,

8and spake unto them, saying, Return with much wealth unto your tents, and with very much cattle, with silver, and with gold, and with brass, and with iron, and with very much raiment: divide the spoil of your enemies with your brethren.

9And the children of Reuben and the children of Gad and the half-tribe of Manasseh returned, and departed from the children of Israel out of Shiloh, which is in the land of Canaan, to go unto the land of Gilead, to the land of their possession, whereof they were possessed, according to the commandment of Yahweh by Moses.

10And when they came unto the region about the Jordan, that is in the land of Canaan, the children of Reuben and the children of Gad and the half-tribe of Manasseh built there an altar by the Jordan, a great altar to look upon.

11And the children of Israel heard say, Behold, the children of Reuben and the children of Gad and the half-tribe of Manasseh have built an altar in the forefront of the land of Canaan, in the region about the Jordan, on the side that pertaineth to the children of Israel.

12And when the children of Israel heard of it, the whole congregation of the children of Israel gathered themselves together at Shiloh, to go up against them to war.

13And the children of Israel sent unto the children of Reuben, and to the children of Gad, and to the half-tribe of Manasseh, into the land of Gilead, Phinehas the son of Eleazar the priest,

14and with him ten princes, one prince of a fathers' house for each of the tribes of Israel; and they were every one of them head of their fathers' houses among the thousands of Israel.

15And they came unto the children of Reuben, and to the children of Gad, and to the half-tribe of Manasseh, unto the land of Gilead, and they spake with them, saying,

16Thus saith the whole congregation of Yahweh, What trespass is this that ye have committed against the God of Israel, to turn away this day from following Yahweh, in that ye have builded you an altar, to rebel this day against Yahweh?

17Is the iniquity of Peor too little for us, from which we have not cleansed ourselves unto this day, although there came a plague upon the congregation of Yahweh,

18that ye must turn away this day from following Yahweh? and it will be, seeing ye rebel to-day against Yahweh, that to-morrow he will be wroth with the whole congregation of Israel.

19Howbeit, if the land of your possession be unclean, then pass ye over unto the land of the possession of Yahweh, wherein Yahweh's tabernacle dwelleth, and take possession among us: but rebel not against Yahweh, nor rebel against us, in building you an altar besides the altar of Yahweh our God.

20Did not Achan the son of Zerah commit a trespass in the devoted thing, and wrath fell upon all the congregation of Israel? and that man perished not alone in his iniquity.

21Then the children of Reuben and the children of Gad and the half-tribe of Manasseh answered, and spake unto the heads of the thousands of Israel,

22The Mighty One, God, Yahweh, the Mighty One, God, Yahweh, he knoweth; and Israel he shall know: if it be in rebellion, or if in trespass against Yahweh (save thou us not this day,)

23that we have built us an altar to turn away from following Yahweh; or if to offer thereon burnt-offering or meal-offering, or if to offer sacrifices of peace-offerings thereon, let Yahweh himself require it;

24and if we have not rather out of carefulness done this, and of purpose, saying, In time to come your children might speak unto our children, saying, What have ye to do with Yahweh, the God of Israel?

25for Yahweh hath made the Jordan a border between us and you, ye children of Reuben and children of Gad; ye have no portion in Yahweh: so might your children make our children cease from fearing Yahweh.

26Therefore we said, Let us now prepare to build us an altar, not for burnt-offering, nor for sacrifice:

27but it shall be a witness between us and you, and between our generations after us, that we may do the service of Yahweh before him with our burnt-offerings, and with our sacrifices, and with our peace-offerings; that your children may not say to our children in time to come, Ye have no portion in Yahweh.

28Therefore said we, It shall be, when they so say to us or to our generations in time to come, that we shall say, Behold the pattern of the altar of Yahweh, which our fathers made, not for burnt-offering, nor for sacrifice; but it is a witness between us and you.

29Far be it from us that we should rebel against Yahweh, and turn away this day from following Yahweh, to build an altar for burnt-offering, for meal-offering, or for sacrifice, besides the altar of Yahweh our God that is before his tabernacle.

30And when Phinehas the priest, and the princes of the congregation, even the heads of the thousands of Israel that were with him, heard the words that the children of Reuben and the children of Gad and the children of Manasseh spake, it pleased them well.

31And Phinehas the son of Eleazar the priest said unto the children of Reuben, and to the children of Gad, and to the children of Manasseh, This day we know that Yahweh is in the midst of us, because ye have not committed this trespass against Yahweh: now have ye delivered the children of Israel out of the hand of Yahweh.

32And Phinehas the son of Eleazar the priest, and the princes, returned from the children of Reuben, and from the children of Gad, out of the land of Gilead, unto the land of Canaan, to the children of Israel, and brought them word again.

33And the thing pleased the children of Israel; and the children of Israel blessed God, and spake no more of going up against them to war, to destroy the land wherein the children of Reuben and the children of Gad dwelt.

34And the children of Reuben and the children of Gad called the altar Ed: For, said they, it is a witness between us that Yahweh is God.

Chapter 23

1And it came to pass after many days, when Yahweh had given rest unto Israel from all their enemies round about, and Joshua was old and well stricken in years;

2that Joshua called for all Israel, for their elders and for their heads, and for their judges and for their officers, and said unto them, I am old and well stricken in years:

3and ye have seen all that Yahweh your God hath done unto all these nations because of you; for Yahweh your God, he it is that hath fought for you.

4Behold, I have allotted unto you these nations that remain, to be an inheritance for your tribes, from the Jordan, with all the nations that I have cut off, even unto the great sea toward the going down of the sun.

5And Yahweh your God, he will thrust them out from before you, and drive them from out of your sight; and ye shall possess their land, as Yahweh your God spake unto you.

6Therefore be ye very courageous to keep and to do all that is written in the book of the law of Moses, that ye turn not aside therefrom to the right hand or to the left;

7that ye come not among these nations, these that remain among you; neither make mention of the name of their gods, nor cause to swear by them, neither serve them, nor bow down yourselves unto them;

8but cleave unto Yahweh your God, as ye have done unto this day.

9For Yahweh hath driven out from before you great nations and strong: but as for you, no man hath stood before you unto this day.

10One man of you shall chase a thousand; for Yahweh your God, he it is that fighteth for you, as he spake unto you.

11Take good heed therefore unto yourselves, that ye love Yahweh your God.

12Else if ye do at all go back, and cleave unto the remnant of these nations, even these that remain among you, and make marriages with them, and go in unto them, and they to you;

13know for a certainty that Yahweh your God will no more drive these nations from out of your sight; but they shall be a snare and a trap unto you, and a scourge in your sides, and thorns in your eyes, until ye perish from off this good land which Yahweh your God hath given you.

14And, behold, this day I am going the way of all the earth: and ye know in

Joshua

all your hearts and in all your souls, that not one thing hath failed of all the good things which Yahweh your God spake concerning you; all are come to pass unto you, not one thing hath failed thereof.

15And it shall come to pass, that as all the good things are come upon you of which Yahweh your God spake unto you, so will Yahweh bring upon you all the evil things, until he have destroyed you from off this good land which Yahweh your God hath given you.

16When ye transgress the covenant of Yahweh your God, which he commanded you, and go and serve other gods, and bow down yourselves to them; then will the anger of Yahweh be kindled against you, and ye shall perish quickly from off the good land which he hath given unto you.

Chapter 24

1And Joshua gathered all the tribes of Israel to Shechem, and called for the elders of Israel, and for their heads, and for their judges, and for their officers; and they presented themselves before God.

2And Joshua said unto all the people, Thus saith Yahweh, the God of Israel, Your fathers dwelt of old time beyond the River, even Terah, the father of Abraham, and the father of Nahor: and they served other gods.

3And I took your father Abraham from beyond the River, and led him throughout all the land of Canaan, and multiplied his seed, and gave him Isaac.

4And I gave unto Isaac Jacob and Esau: and I gave unto Esau mount Seir, to possess it: and Jacob and his children went down into Egypt.

5And I sent Moses and Aaron, and I plagued Egypt, according to that which I did in the midst thereof: and afterward I brought you out.

6And I brought your fathers out of Egypt: and ye came unto the sea; and the Egyptians pursued after your fathers with chariots and with horsemen unto the Red Sea.

7And when they cried out unto Yahweh, he put darkness between you and the Egyptians, and brought the sea upon them, and covered them; and your eyes saw what I did in Egypt: and ye dwelt in the wilderness many days.

8And I brought you into the land of the Amorites, that dwelt beyond the Jordan: and they fought with you; and I gave them into your hand, and ye possessed their land; and I destroyed them from before you.

9Then Balak the son of Zippor, king of Moab, arose and fought against Israel: and he sent and called Balaam the son of Beor to curse you;

10but I would not hearken unto Balaam; therefore he blessed you still: so I delivered you out of his hand.

11And ye went over the Jordan, and came unto Jericho: and the men of Jericho fought against you, the Amorite, and the Perizzite, and the Canaanite, and the Hittite, and the Girgashite, the Hivite, and the Jebusite; and I delivered them into your hand.

12And I sent the hornet before you, which drove them out from before you, even the two kings of the Amorites; not with thy sword, nor with thy bow.

13And I gave you a land whereon thou hadst not labored, and cities which ye built not, and ye dwell therein; of vineyards and oliveyards which ye planted not do ye eat.

14Now therefore fear Yahweh, and serve him in sincerity and in truth; and put away the gods which your fathers served beyond the River, and in Egypt; and serve ye Yahweh.

15And if it seem evil unto you to serve Yahweh, choose you this day whom ye will serve; whether the gods which your fathers served that were beyond the River, or the gods of the Amorites, in whose land ye dwell: but as for me and my house, we will serve Yahweh.

16And the people answered and said, Far be it from us that we should forsake Yahweh, to serve other gods;

17for Yahweh our God, he it is that brought us and our fathers up out of the land of Egypt, from the house of bondage, and that did those great signs in our sight, and preserved us in all the way wherein we went, and among all the peoples through the midst of whom we passed;

18and Yahweh drove out from before us all the peoples, even the Amorites that dwelt in the land: therefore we also will serve Yahweh; for he is our God.

19And Joshua said unto the people, Ye cannot serve Yahweh; for he is a holy God; he is a jealous God; he will not forgive your transgression nor your sins.

20If ye forsake Yahweh, and serve foreign gods, then he will turn and do you evil, and consume you, after that he hath done you good.

21And the people said unto Joshua, Nay; but we will serve Yahweh.

22And Joshua said unto the people, Ye are witnesses against yourselves that ye have chosen you Yahweh, to serve him. And they said, We are witnesses.

23Now therefore put away, said he, the foreign gods which are among you, and incline your heart unto Yahweh, the God of Israel.

24And the people said unto Joshua, Yahweh our God will we serve, and unto his voice will we hearken.

25So Joshua made a covenant with the people that day, and set them a statute and an ordinance in Shechem.

26And Joshua wrote these words in the book of the law of God; and he took a great stone, and set it up there under the oak that was by the sanctuary of Yahweh.

27And Joshua said unto all the people, Behold, this stone shall be a witness against us; for it hath heard all the words of Yahweh which he spake unto us: it shall be therefore a witness against you, lest ye deny your God.

28So Joshua sent the people away, every man unto his inheritance.

29And it came to pass after these things, that Joshua the son of Nun, the servant of Yahweh, died, being a hundred and ten years old.

30And they buried him in the border of his inheritance in Timnathserah, which is in the hill-country of Ephraim, on the north of the mountain of Gaash.

31And Israel served Yahweh all the days of Joshua, and all the days of the elders that outlived Joshua, and had known all the work of Yahweh, that he had wrought for Israel.

32And the bones of Joseph, which the children of Israel brought up out of Egypt, buried they in Shechem, in the parcel of ground which Jacob bought of the sons of Hamor the father of Shechem for a hundred pieces of money: and they became the inheritance of the children of Joseph.

33And Eleazar the son of Aaron died; and they buried him in the hill of Phinehas his son, which was given him in the hill-country of Ephraim.

The Book of Judges

Chapter 1

¹And it came to pass after the death of Joshua, that the children of Israel asked of Yahweh, saying, Who shall go up for us first against the Canaanites, to fight against them?

²And Yahweh said, Judah shall go up: behold, I have delivered the land into his hand.

³And Judah said unto Simeon his brother, Come up with me into my lot, that we may fight against the Canaanites; and I likewise will go with thee into thy lot. So Simeon went with him.

⁴And Judah went up; and Yahweh delivered the Canaanites and the Perizzites into their hand: and they smote of them in Bezek ten thousand men.

⁵And they found Adoni-bezek in Bezek; and they fought against him, and they smote the Canaanites and the Perizzites.

⁶But Adoni-bezek fled; and they pursued after him, and caught him, and cut off his thumbs and his great toes.

⁷And Adoni-bezek said, Threescore and ten kings, having their thumbs and their great toes cut off, gathered their food under my table: as I have done, so God hath requited me. And they brought him to Jerusalem, and he died there.

⁸And the children of Judah fought against Jerusalem, and took it, and smote it with the edge of the sword, and set the city on fire.

⁹And afterward the children of Judah went down to fight against the Canaanites that dwelt in the hill-country, and in the South, and in the lowland.

¹⁰And Judah went against the Canaanites that dwelt in Hebron (now the name of Hebron beforetime was Kiriath-arba); and they smote Sheshai, and Ahiman, and Talmai.

¹¹And from thence he went against the inhabitants of Debir. (Now the name of Debir beforetime was Kiriath-sepher.)

¹²And Caleb said, He that smiteth Kiriath-sepher, and taketh it, to him will I give Achsah my daughter to wife.

¹³And Othniel the son of Kenaz, Caleb's younger brother, took it: and he gave him Achsah his daughter to wife.

¹⁴And it came to pass, when she came unto him, that she moved him to ask of her father a field: and she alighted from off her ass; and Caleb said unto her, What wouldest thou?

¹⁵And she said unto him, Give me a blessing; for that thou hast set me in the land of the South, give me also springs of water. And Caleb gave her the upper springs and the nether springs.

¹⁶And the children of the Kenite, Moses' brother-in-law, went up out of the city of palm-trees with the children of Judah into the wilderness of Judah, which is in the south of Arad; and they went and dwelt with the people.

¹⁷And Judah went with Simeon his brother, and they smote the Canaanites that inhabited Zephath, and utterly destroyed it. And the name of the city was called Hormah.

¹⁸Also Judah took Gaza with the border thereof, and Ashkelon with the border thereof, and Ekron with the border thereof.

¹⁹And Yahweh was with Judah; and drove out the inhabitants of the hill-country; for he could not drive out the inhabitants of the valley, because they had chariots of iron.

²⁰And they gave Hebron unto Caleb, as Moses had spoken: and he drove out thence the three sons of Anak.

²¹And the children of Benjamin did not drive out the Jebusites that inhabited Jerusalem; but the Jebusites dwell with the children of Benjamin in Jerusalem unto this day.

²²And the house of Joseph, they also went up against Beth-el: and Yahweh was with them.

²³And the house of Joseph sent to spy out Beth-el. (Now the name of the city beforetime was Luz.)

²⁴And the watchers saw a man come forth out of the city, and they said unto him, Show us, we pray thee, the entrance into the city, and we will deal kindly with thee.

²⁵And he showed them the entrance into the city; and they smote the city with the edge of the sword; but they let the man go and all his family.

²⁶And the man went into the land of the Hittites, and built a city, and called the name thereof Luz, which is the name thereof unto this day.

²⁷And Manasseh did not drive out the inhabitants of Beth-shean and its towns, nor of Taanach and its towns, nor the inhabitants of Dor and its towns, nor the inhabitants of Ibleam and its towns, nor the inhabitants of Megiddo and its towns; but the Canaanites would dwell in that land.

²⁸And it came to pass, when Israel was waxed strong, that they put the Canaanites to taskwork, and did not utterly drive them out.

²⁹And Ephraim drove not out the Canaanites that dwelt in Gezer; but the Canaanites dwelt in Gezer among them.

³⁰Zebulun drove not out the inhabitants of Kitron, nor the inhabitants of Nahalol; but the Canaanites dwelt among them, and became subject to taskwork.

³¹Asher drove not out the inhabitants of Acco, nor the inhabitants of Sidon, nor of Ahlab, nor of Achzib, nor of Helbah, nor of Aphik, nor of Rehob;

³²but the Asherites dwelt among the Canaanites, the inhabitants of the land; for they did not drive them out.

³³Naphtali drove not out the inhabitants of Beth-shemesh, nor the inhabitants of Beth-anath; but he dwelt among the Canaanites, the inhabitants of the land: nevertheless the inhabitants of Beth-shemesh and of Beth-anath became subject to taskwork.

³⁴And the Amorites forced the children of Dan into the hill-country; for they would not suffer them to come down to the valley;

³⁵but the Amorites would dwell in mount Heres, in Aijalon, and in Shaalbim: yet the hand of the house of Joseph prevailed, so that they became subject to taskwork.

³⁶And the border of the Amorites was from the ascent of Akrabbim, from the rock, and upward.

Chapter 2

¹And the angel of Yahweh came up from Gilgal to Bochim. And he said, I made you to go up out of Egypt, and have brought you unto the land which I sware unto your fathers; and I said, I will never break my covenant with you:

²and ye shall make no covenant with the inhabitants of this land; ye shall break down their altars. But ye have not hearkened unto my voice: why have ye done this?

³Wherefore I also said, I will not drive them out from before you; but they shall be as thorns in your sides, and their gods shall be a snare unto you.

⁴And it came to pass, when the angel of Yahweh spake these words unto all the children of Israel, that the people lifted up their voice, and wept.

⁵And they called the name of that place Bochim: and they sacrificed there unto Yahweh.

⁶Now when Joshua had sent the people away, the children of Israel went every man unto his inheritance to possess the land.

⁷And the people served Yahweh all the days of Joshua, and all the days of the elders that outlived Joshua, who had seen all the great work of Yahweh that he had wrought for Israel.

⁸And Joshua the son of Nun, the servant of Yahweh, died, being a hundred and ten years old.

⁹And they buried him in the border of his inheritance in Timnath-heres, in the hill-country of Ephraim, on the north of the mountain of Gaash.

¹⁰And also all that generation were gathered unto their fathers: and there arose another generation after them, that knew not Yahweh, nor yet the work which he had wrought for Israel.

¹¹And the children of Israel did that which was evil in the sight of Yahweh, and served the Baalim;

¹²and they forsook Yahweh, the God of their fathers, who brought them out of the land of Egypt, and followed other gods, of the gods of the peoples that were round about them, and bowed themselves down unto them: and they provoked Yahweh to anger.

¹³And they forsook Yahweh, and served Baal and the Ashtaroth.

¹⁴And the anger of Yahweh was kindled against Israel, and he delivered them into the hands of spoilers that despoiled them; and he sold them into the hands of their enemies round about, so that they could not any longer stand before their enemies.

¹⁵Whithersoever they went out, the hand of Yahweh was against them for evil, as Yahweh had spoken, and as Yahweh had sworn unto them: and they were sore distressed.

¹⁶And Yahweh raised up judges, who saved them out of the hand of those that despoiled them.

¹⁷And yet they hearkened not unto their judges; for they played the harlot after other gods, and bowed themselves down unto them: they turned aside quickly out of the way wherein their fathers walked, obeying the commandments of Yahweh; but they did not so.

¹⁸And when Yahweh raised them up judges, then Yahweh was with the judge, and saved them out of the hand of their enemies all the days of the judge: for it repented Yahweh because of their groaning by reason of them that oppressed them and vexed them.

¹⁹But it came to pass, when the judge was dead, that they turned back, and dealt more corruptly than their fathers, in following other gods to serve them, and to bow down unto them; they ceased not from their doings, nor from their stubborn way.

²⁰And the anger of Yahweh was kindled against Israel; and he said, Because this nation have transgressed my covenant which I commanded their fathers, and have not hearkened unto my voice;

²¹I also will not henceforth drive out any from before them of the nations that Joshua left when he died;

²²that by them I may prove Israel, whether they will keep the way of Yahweh to walk therein, as their fathers did keep it, or not.

²³So Yahweh left those nations, without driving them out hastily; neither delivered he them into the hand of Joshua.

Chapter 3

¹Now these are the nations which Yahweh left, to prove Israel by them, even as many of Israel as had not known all the wars of Canaan;

²only that the generations of the children of Israel might know, to teach them war, at the least such as beforetime knew nothing thereof:

³namely, the five lords of the Philistines, and all the Canaanites, and the Sidonians, and the Hivites that dwelt in mount Lebanon, from mount Baal-hermon unto the entrance of Hamath.

⁴And they were left, to prove Israel by them, to know whether they would hearken unto the commandments of Yahweh, which he commanded their fathers by Moses.

⁵And the children of Israel dwelt among the Canaanites, the Hittites, and the Amorites, and the Perizzites, and the Hivites, and the Jebusites:

⁶and they took their daughters to be their wives, and gave their own daughters to their sons and served their gods.

⁷And the children of Israel did that which was evil in the sight of Yahweh, and forgat Yahweh their God, and served the Baalim and the Asheroth.

Judges

8Therefore the anger of Yahweh was kindled against Israel, and he sold them into the hand of Cushan-rishathaim king of Mesopotamia: and the children of Israel served Cushan-rishathaim eight years.

9And when the children of Israel cried unto Yahweh, Yahweh raised up a saviour to the children of Israel, who saved them, even Othniel the son of Kenaz, Caleb's younger brother.

10And the Spirit of Yahweh came upon him, and he judged Israel; and he went out to war, and Yahweh delivered Cushan-rishathaim king of Mesopotamia into his hand: and his hand prevailed against Cushan-rishathaim.

11And the land had rest forty years. And Othniel the son of Kenaz died.

12And the children of Israel again did that which was evil in the sight of Yahweh: and Yahweh strengthened Eglon the king of Moab against Israel, because they had done that which was evil in the sight of Yahweh.

13And he gathered unto him the children of Ammon and Amalek; and he went and smote Israel, and they possessed the city of palm-trees.

14And the children of Israel served Eglon the king of Moab eighteen years.

15But when the children of Israel cried unto Yahweh, Yahweh raised them up a saviour, Ehud the son of Gera, the Benjamite, a man left-handed. And the children of Israel sent tribute by him unto Eglon the king of Moab.

16And Ehud made him a sword which had two edges, a cubit in length; and he girded it under his raiment upon his right thigh.

17And he offered the tribute unto Eglon king of Moab: now Eglon was a very fat man.

18And when he had made an end of offering the tribute, he sent away the people that bare the tribute.

19But he himself turned back from the quarries that were by Gilgal, and said, I have a secret errand unto thee, O king. And he said, Keep silence. And all that stood by him went out from him.

20And Ehud came unto him; and he was sitting by himself alone in the cool upper room. And Ehud said, I have a message from God unto thee. And he arose out of his seat.

21And Ehud put forth his left hand, and took the sword from his right thigh, and thrust it into his body:

22and the haft also went in after the blade; and the fat closed upon the blade, for he drew not the sword out of his body; and it came out behind.

23Then Ehud went forth into the porch, and shut the doors of the upper room upon him, and locked them.

24Now when he was gone out, his servants came; and they saw, and, behold, the doors of the upper room were locked; and they said, Surely he is covering his feet in the upper chamber.

25And they tarried till they were ashamed; and, behold, he opened not the doors of the upper room: therefore they took the key, and opened them, and, behold, their lord was fallen down dead on the earth.

26And Ehud escaped while they tarried, and passed beyond the quarries, and escaped unto Seirah.

27And it came to pass, when he was come, that he blew a trumpet in the hill-country of Ephraim; and the children of Israel went down with him from the hill-country, and he before them.

28And he said unto them, Follow after me; for Yahweh hath delivered your enemies the Moabites into your hand. And they went down after him, and took the fords of the Jordan against the Moabites, and suffered not a man to pass over.

29And they smote of Moab at that time about ten thousand men, every lusty man, and every man of valor; and there escaped not a man.

30So Moab was subdued that day under the hand of Israel. And the land had rest fourscore years.

31And after him was Shamgar the son of Anath, who smote of the Philistines six hundred men with an ox-goad: and he also saved Israel.

Chapter 4

1And the children of Israel again did that which was evil in the sight of Yahweh, when Ehud was dead.

2And Yahweh sold them into the hand of Jabin king of Canaan, that reigned in Hazor; the captain of whose host was Sisera, who dwelt in Harosheth of the Gentiles.

3And the children of Israel cried unto Yahweh: for he had nine hundred chariots of iron; and twenty years he mightily oppressed the children of Israel.

4Now Deborah, a prophetess, the wife of Lappidoth, she judged Israel at that time.

5And she dwelt under the palm-tree of Deborah between Ramah and Beth-el in the hill-country of Ephraim: and the children of Israel came up to her for judgment.

6And she sent and called Barak the son of Abinoam out of Kedesh-naphtali, and said unto him, Hath not Yahweh, the God of Israel, commanded, saying, Go and draw unto mount Tabor, and take with thee ten thousand men of the children of Naphtali and of the children of Zebulun?

7And I will draw unto thee, to the river Kishon, Sisera, the captain of Jabin's army, with his chariots and his multitude; and I will deliver him into thy hand.

8And Barak said unto her, If thou wilt go with me, then I will go; but if thou wilt not go with me, I will not go.

9And she said, I will surely go with thee: notwithstanding, the journey that thou takest shall not be for thine honor; for Yahweh will sell Sisera into the hand of a woman. And Deborah arose, and went with Barak to Kedesh.

10And Barak called Zebulun and Naphtali together to Kedesh; and there went up ten thousand men at his feet: and Deborah went up with him.

11Now Heber the Kenite had separated himself from the Kenites, even from the children of Hobab the brother-in-law of Moses, and had pitched his tent as far as the oak in Zaanannim, which is by Kedesh.

12And they told Sisera that Barak the son of Abinoam was gone up to mount Tabor.

13And Sisera gathered together all his chariots, even nine hundred chariots of iron, and all the people that were with him, from Harosheth of the Gentiles, unto the river Kishon.

14And Deborah said unto Barak, Up; for this is the day in which Yahweh hath delivered Sisera into thy hand; is not Yahweh gone out before thee? So Barak went down from mount Tabor, and ten thousand men after him.

15And Yahweh discomfited Sisera, and all his chariots, and all his host, with the edge of the sword before Barak; and Sisera alighted from his chariot, and fled away on his feet.

16But Barak pursued after the chariots, and after the host, unto Harosheth of the Gentiles: and all the host of Sisera fell by the edge of the sword; there was not a man left.

17Howbeit Sisera fled away on his feet to the tent of Jael the wife of Heber the Kenite; for there was peace between Jabin the king of Hazor and the house of Heber the Kenite.

18And Jael went out to meet Sisera, and said unto him, Turn in, my lord, turn in to me; fear not. And he turned in unto her into the tent, and she covered him with a rug.

19And he said unto her, Give me, I pray thee, a little water to drink; for I am thirsty. And she opened a bottle of milk, and gave him drink, and covered him.

20And he said unto her, Stand in the door of the tent, and it shall be, when any man doth come and inquire of thee, and say, Is there any man here? that thou shalt say, No.

21Then Jael Heber's wife took a tent-pin, and took a hammer in her hand, and went softly unto him, and smote the pin into his temples, and it pierced through into the ground; for he was in a deep sleep; so he swooned and died.

22And, behold, as Barak pursued Sisera, Jael came out to meet him, and said unto him, Come, and I will show thee the man whom thou seekest. And he came unto her; and, behold, Sisera lay dead, and the tent-pin was in his temples.

23So God subdued on that day Jabin the king of Canaan before the children of Israel.

24And the hand of the children of Israel prevailed more and more against Jabin the king of Canaan, until they had destroyed Jabin king of Canaan.

Chapter 5

1Then sang Deborah and Barak the son of Abinoam on that day, saying,
2For that the leaders took the lead in Israel,
For that the people offered themselves willingly,
Bless ye Yahweh.
3Hear, O ye kings; give ear, O ye princes;
I, even I, will sing unto Yahweh;
I will sing praise to Yahweh, the God of Israel.
4Yahweh, when thou wentest forth out of Seir,
When thou marchedst out of the field of Edom,
The earth trembled, the heavens also dropped,
Yea, the clouds dropped water.
5The mountains quaked at the presence of Yahweh,
Even yon Sinai at the presence of Yahweh, the God of Israel.
6In the days of Shamgar the son of Anath,
In the days of Jael, the highways were unoccupied,
And the travellers walked through byways.
7The rulers ceased in Israel, they ceased,
Until that I Deborah arose,
That I arose a mother in Israel.
8They chose new gods;
Then was war in the gates:
Was there a shield or spear seen
Among forty thousand in Israel?
9My heart is toward the governors of Israel,
That offered themselves willingly among the people:
Bless ye Yahweh.
10Tell of it, ye that ride on white asses,
Ye that sit on rich carpets,
And ye that walk by the way.
11Far from the noise of archers, in the places of drawing water,
There shall they rehearse the righteous acts of Yahweh,
Even the righteous acts of his rule in Israel.
Then the people of Yahweh went down to the gates.
12Awake, awake, Deborah;
Awake, awake, utter a song:
Arise, Barak, and lead away thy captives, thou son of Abinoam.
13Then came down a remnant of the nobles and the people;
Yahweh came down for me against the mighty.
14Out of Ephraim came down they whose root is in Amalek;
After thee, Benjamin, among thy peoples;
Out of Machir came down governors,
And out of Zebulun they that handle the marshal's staff.
15And the princes of Issachar were with Deborah;
As was Issachar, so was Barak;
Into the valley they rushed forth at his feet.
By the watercourses of Reuben
There were great resolves of heart.
16Why sattest thou among the sheepfolds,
To hear the pipings for the flocks?
At the watercourses of Reuben
There were great searchings of heart.
17Gilead abode beyond the Jordan:
And Dan, why did he remain in ships?
Asher sat still at the haven of the sea,

And abode by his creeks.

18Zebulun was a people that jeoparded their lives unto the death,
And Naphtali, upon the high places of the field.

19The kings came and fought;
Then fought the kings of Canaan.
In Taanach by the waters of Megiddo:
They took no gain of money.

20From heaven fought the stars,
From their courses they fought against Sisera.

21The river Kishon swept them away,
That ancient river, the river Kishon.
O my soul, march on with strength.

22Then did the horsehoofs stamp
By reason of the prancings, the prancings of their strong ones.

23Curse ye Meroz, said the angel of Yahweh.
Curse ye bitterly the inhabitants thereof,
Because they came not to the help of Yahweh,
To the help of Yahweh against the mighty.

24Blessed above women shall Jael be,
The wife of Heber the Kenite;
Blessed shall she be above women in the tent.

25He asked water, and she gave him milk;
She brought him butter in a lordly dish.

26She put her hand to the tent-pin,
And her right hand to the workmen's hammer;
And with the hammer she smote Sisera, she smote through his head;
Yea, she pierced and struck through his temples.

27At her feet he bowed, he fell, he lay;
At her feet he bowed, he fell,
Where he bowed, there he fell down dead.

28Through the window she looked forth, and cried,
The mother of Sisera cried through the lattice,
Why is his chariot so long in coming?
Why tarry the wheels of his chariots?

29Her wise ladies answered her,
Yea, she returned answer to herself,

30Have they not found, have they not divided the spoil?
A damsel, two damsels to every man;
To Sisera a spoil of dyed garments,
A spoil of dyed garments embroidered,
Of dyed garments embroidered on both sides, on the necks of the spoil?

31So let all thine enemies perish, O Yahweh:
But let them that love him be as the sun when he goeth forth in his might.
And the land had rest forty years.

Chapter 6

1And the children of Israel did that which was evil in the sight of Yahweh: and Yahweh delivered them into the hand of Midian seven years.

2And the hand of Midian prevailed against Israel; and because of Midian the children of Israel made them the dens which are in the mountains, and the caves, and the strongholds.

3And so it was, when Israel had sown, that the Midianites came up, and the Amalekites, and the children of the east; they came up against them;

4and they encamped against them, and destroyed the increase of the earth, till thou come unto Gaza, and left no sustenance in Israel, neither sheep, nor ox, nor ass.

5For they came up with their cattle and their tents; they came in as locusts for multitude; both they and their camels were without number: and they came into the land to destroy it.

6And Israel was brought very low because of Midian; and the children of Israel cried unto Yahweh.

7And it came to pass, when the children of Israel cried unto Yahweh because of Midian,

8that Yahweh sent a prophet unto the children of Israel: and he said unto them, Thus saith Yahweh, the God of Israel, I brought you up from Egypt, and brought you forth out of the house of bondage;

9and I delivered you out of the hand of the Egyptians, and out of the hand of all that oppressed you, and drove them out from before you, and gave you their land;

10and I said unto you, I am Yahweh your God; ye shall not fear the gods of the Amorites, in whose land ye dwell. But ye have not hearkened unto my voice.

11And the angel of Yahweh came, and sat under the oak which was in Ophrah, that pertained unto Joash the Abiezrite: and his son Gideon was beating out wheat in the winepress, to hide it from the Midianites.

12And the angel of Yahweh appeared unto him, and said unto him, Yahweh is with thee, thou mighty man of valor.

13And Gideon said unto him, Oh, my lord, if Yahweh is with us, why then is all this befallen us? and where are all his wondrous works which our fathers told us of, saying, Did not Yahweh bring us up from Egypt? but now Yahweh hath cast us off, and delivered us into the hand of Midian.

14And Yahweh looked upon him, and said, Go in this thy might, and save Israel from the hand of Midian: have not I sent thee?

15And he said unto him, Oh, Lord, wherewith shall I save Israel? behold, my family is the poorest in Manasseh, and I am the least in my father's house.

16And Yahweh said unto him, Surely I will be with thee, and thou shalt smite the Midianites as one man.

17And he said unto him, If now I have found favor in thy sight, then show me a sign that it is thou that talkest with me.

18Depart not hence, I pray thee, until I come unto thee, and bring forth my present, and lay it before thee. And he said, I will tarry until thou come again.

19And Gideon went in, and made ready a kid, and unleavened cakes of an ephah of meal: the flesh he put in a basket, and he put the broth in a pot, and brought it out unto him under the oak, and presented it.

20And the angel of God said unto him, Take the flesh and the unleavened cakes, and lay them upon this rock, and pour out the broth. And he did so.

21Then the angel of Yahweh put forth the end of the staff that was in his hand, and touched the flesh and the unleavened cakes; and there went up fire out of the rock, and consumed the flesh and the unleavened cakes; and the angel of Yahweh departed out of his sight.

22And Gideon saw that he was the angel of Yahweh; and Gideon said, Alas, O Lord Yahweh! forasmuch as I have seen the angel of Yahweh face to face.

23And Yahweh said unto him, Peace be unto thee; fear not: thou shalt not die.

24Then Gideon built an altar there unto Yahweh, and called it Yahweh-shalom: unto this day it is yet in Ophrah of the Abiezrites.

25And it came to pass the same night, that Yahweh said unto him, Take thy father's bullock, even the second bullock seven years old, and throw down the altar of Baal that thy father hath, and cut down the Asherah that is by it;

26and build an altar unto Yahweh thy God upon the top of this stronghold, in the orderly manner, and take the second bullock, and offer a burnt-offering with the wood of the Asherah which thou shalt cut down.

27Then Gideon took ten men of his servants, and did as Yahweh had spoken unto him: and it came to pass, because he feared his father's household and the men of the city, so that he could not do it by day, that he did it by night.

28And when the men of the city arose early in the morning, behold, the altar of Baal was broken down, and the Asherah was cut down that was by it, and the second bullock was offered upon the altar that was built.

29And they said one to another, Who hath done this thing? And when they inquired and asked, they said, Gideon the son of Joash hath done this thing.

30Then the men of the city said unto Joash, Bring out thy son, that he may die, because he hath broken down the altar of Baal, and because he hath cut down the Asherah that was by it.

31And Joash said unto all that stood against him, Will ye contend for Baal? Or will ye save him? he that will contend for him, let him be put to death whilst it is yet morning: if he be a god, let him contend for himself, because one hath broken down his altar.

32Therefore on that day he called him Jerubbaal, saying, Let Baal contend against him, because he hath broken down his altar.

33Then all the Midianites and the Amalekites and the children of the east assembled themselves together; and they passed over, and encamped in the valley of Jezreel.

34But the Spirit of Yahweh came upon Gideon; and he blew a trumpet; and Abiezer was gathered together after him.

35And he sent messengers throughout all Manasseh; and they also were gathered together after him: and he sent messengers unto Asher, and unto Zebulun, and unto Naphtali; and they came up to meet them.

36And Gideon said unto God, If thou wilt save Israel by my hand, as thou hast spoken,

37behold, I will put a fleece of wool on the threshing-floor; if there be dew on the fleece only, and it be dry upon all the ground, then shall I know that thou wilt save Israel by my hand, as thou hast spoken.

38And it was so; for he rose up early on the morrow, and pressed the fleece together, and wrung the dew out of the fleece, a bowlful of water.

39And Gideon said unto God, Let not thine anger be kindled against me, and I will speak but this once: let me make trial, I pray thee, but this once with the fleece; let it now be dry only upon the fleece, and upon all the ground let there be dew.

40And God did so that night: for it was dry upon the fleece only, and there was dew on all the ground.

Chapter 7

1Then Jerubbaal, who is Gideon, and all the people that were with him, rose up early, and encamped beside the spring of Harod: and the camp of Midian was on the north side of them, by the hill of Moreh, in the valley.

2And Yahweh said unto Gideon, The people that are with thee are too many for me to give the Midianites into their hand, lest Israel vaunt themselves against me, saying, Mine own hand hath saved me.

3Now therefore proclaim in the ears of the people, saying, Whosoever is fearful and trembling, let him return and depart from mount Gilead. And there returned of the people twenty and two thousand; and there remained ten thousand.

4And Yahweh said unto Gideon, The people are yet too many; bring them down unto the water, and I will try them for thee there: and it shall be, that of whom I say unto thee, This shall go with thee, the same shall go with thee; and of whomsoever I say unto thee, This shall not go with thee, the same shall not go.

5So he brought down the people unto the water: and Yahweh said unto Gideon, Every one that lappeth of the water with his tongue, as a dog lappeth, him shalt thou set by himself; likewise every one that boweth down upon his knees to drink.

6And the number of them that lapped, putting their hand to their mouth, was three hundred men: but all the rest of the people bowed down upon their knees to drink water.

7And Yahweh said unto Gideon, By the three hundred men that lapped will I save you, and deliver the Midianites into thy hand; and let all the people go every man unto his place.

8So the people took victuals in their hand, and their trumpets; and he sent all the men of Israel every man unto his tent, but retained the three hundred men: and the camp of Midian was beneath him in the valley.

9And it came to pass the same night, that Yahweh said unto him, Arise, get thee down into the camp; for I have delivered it into thy hand.

10But if thou fear to go down, go thou with Purah thy servant down to the camp:

11and thou shalt hear what they say; and afterward shall thy hands be strengthened to go down into the camp. Then went he down with Purah his servant unto the outermost part of the armed men that were in the camp.

12And the Midianites and the Amalekites and all the children of the east lay along in the valley like locusts for multitude; and their camels were without number, as the sand which is upon the sea-shore for multitude.

13And when Gideon was come, behold, there was a man telling a dream unto his fellow; and he said, Behold, I dreamed a dream; and, lo, a cake of barley bread tumbled into the camp of Midian, and came unto the tent, and smote it so that it fell, and turned it upside down, so that the tent lay flat.

14And his fellow answered and said, This is nothing else save the sword of Gideon the son of Joash, a man of Israel: into his hand God hath delivered Midian, and all the host.

15And it was so, when Gideon heard the telling of the dream, and the interpretation thereof, that he worshipped; and he returned into the camp of Israel, and said, Arise; for Yahweh hath delivered into your hand the host of Midian.

16And he divided the three hundred men into three companies, and he put into the hands of all of them trumpets, and empty pitchers, with torches within the pitchers.

17And he said unto them, Look on me, and do likewise: and, behold, when I come to the outermost part of the camp, it shall be that, as I do, so shall ye do.

18When I blow the trumpet, I and all that are with me, then blow ye the trumpets also on every side of all the camp, and say, For Yahweh and for Gideon.

19So Gideon, and the hundred men that were with him, came unto the outermost part of the camp in the beginning of the middle watch, when they had but newly set the watch: and they blew the trumpets, and brake in pieces the pitchers that were in their hands.

20And the three companies blew the trumpets, and brake the pitchers, and held the torches in their left hands, and the trumpets in their right hands wherewith to blow; and they cried, The sword of Yahweh and of Gideon.

21And they stood every man in his place round about the camp; and all the host ran; and they shouted, and put them to flight.

22And they blew the three hundred trumpets, and Yahweh set every man's sword against his fellow, and against all the host; and the host fled as far as Beth-shittah toward Zererah, as far as the border of Abel-meholah, by Tabbath.

23And the men of Israel were gathered together out of Naphtali, and out of Asher, and out of all Manasseh, and pursued after Midian.

24And Gideon sent messengers throughout all the hill-country of Ephraim, saying, Come down against Midian, and take before them the waters, as far as Beth-barah, even the Jordan. So all the men of Ephraim were gathered together, and took the waters as far as Beth-barah, even the Jordan.

25And they took the two princes of Midian, Oreb and Zeeb; and they slew Oreb at the rock of Oreb, and Zeeb they slew at the winepress of Zeeb, and pursued Midian: and they brought the heads of Oreb and Zeeb to Gideon beyond the Jordan.

Chapter 8

1And the men of Ephraim said unto him, Why hast thou served us thus, that thou calledst us not, when thou wentest to fight with Midian? And they did chide with him sharply.

2And he said unto them, What have I now done in comparison with you? Is not the gleaning of the grapes of Ephraim better than the vintage of Abiezer?

3God hath delivered into your hand the princes of Midian, Oreb and Zeeb: and what was I able to do in comparison with you? Then their anger was abated toward him, when he had said that.

4And Gideon came to the Jordan, and passed over, he, and the three hundred men that were with him, faint, yet pursuing.

5And he said unto the men of Succoth, Give, I pray you, loaves of bread unto the people that follow me; for they are faint, and I am pursuing after Zebah and Zalmunna, the kings of Midian.

6And the princes of Succoth said, Are the hands of Zebah and Zalmunna now in thy hand, that we should give bread unto thine army?

7And Gideon said, Therefore when Yahweh hath delivered Zebah and Zalmunna into my hand, then I will tear your flesh with the thorns of the wilderness and with briers.

8And he went up thence to Penuel, and spake unto them in like manner; and the men of Penuel answered him as the men of Succoth had answered.

9And he spake also unto the men of Penuel, saying, When I come again in peace, I will break down this tower.

10Now Zebah and Zalmunna were in Karkor, and their hosts with them, about fifteen thousand men, all that were left of all the host of the children of the east; for there fell a hundred and twenty thousand men that drew sword.

11And Gideon went up by the way of them that dwelt in tents on the east of Nobah and Jogbehah, and smote the host; for the host was secure.

12And Zebah and Zalmunna fled; and he pursued after them; and he took the two kings of Midian, Zebah and Zalmunna, and discomfited all the host.

13And Gideon the son of Joash returned from the battle from the ascent of Heres.

14And he caught a young man of the men of Succoth, and inquired of him: and he described for him the princes of Succoth, and the elders thereof, seventy and seven men.

15And he came unto the men of Succoth, and said, Behold Zebah and Zalmunna, concerning whom ye did taunt me, saying, Are the hands of Zebah and Zalmunna now in thy hand, that we should give bread unto thy men that are weary?

16And he took the elders of the city, and thorns of the wilderness and briers, and with them he taught the men of Succoth.

17And he brake down the tower of Penuel, and slew the men of the city.

18Then said he unto Zebah and Zalmunna, What manner of men were they whom ye slew at Tabor? And they answered, As thou art, so were they; each one resembled the children of a king.

19And he said, They were my brethren, the sons of my mother: as Yahweh liveth, if ye had saved them alive, I would not slay you.

20And he said unto Jether his first-born, Up, and slay them. But the youth drew not his sword; for he feared, because he was yet a youth.

21Then Zebah and Zalmunna said, Rise thou, and fall upon us; for as the man is, so is his strength. And Gideon arose, and slew Zebah and Zalmunna, and took the crescents that were on their camels' necks.

22Then the men of Israel said unto Gideon, Rule thou over us, both thou, and thy son, and thy son's son also; for thou hast saved us out of the hand of Midian.

23And Gideon said unto them, I will not rule over you, neither shall my son rule over you: Yahweh shall rule over you.

24And Gideon said unto them, I would make a request of you, that ye would give me every man the ear-rings of his spoil. (For they had golden ear-rings, because they were Ishmaelites.)

25And they answered, We will willingly give them. And they spread a garment, and did cast therein every man the ear-rings of his spoil.

26And the weight of the golden ear-rings that he requested was a thousand and seven hundred shekels of gold, besides the crescents, and the pendants, and the purple raiment that was on the kings of Midian, and besides the chains that were about their camels' necks.

27And Gideon made an ephod thereof, and put it in his city, even in Ophrah: and all Israel played the harlot after it there; and it became a snare unto Gideon, and to his house.

28So Midian was subdued before the children of Israel, and they lifted up their heads no more. And the land had rest forty years in the days of Gideon.

29And Jerubbaal the son of Joash went and dwelt in his own house.

30And Gideon had threescore and ten sons of his body begotten; for he had many wives.

31And his concubine that was in Shechem, she also bare him a son, and he called his name Abimelech.

32And Gideon the son of Joash died in a good old age, and was buried in the sepulchre of Joash his father, in Ophrah of the Abiezrites.

33And it came to pass, as soon as Gideon was dead, that the children of Israel turned again, and played the harlot after the Baalim, and made Baal-berith their god.

34And the children of Israel remembered not Yahweh their God, who had delivered them out of the hand of all their enemies on every side;

35neither showed they kindness to the house of Jerubbaal, who is Gideon, according to all the goodness which he had showed unto Israel.

Chapter 9

1And Abimelech the son of Jerubbaal went to Shechem unto his mother's brethren, and spake with them, and with all the family of the house of his mother's father, saying,

2Speak, I pray you, in the ears of all the men of Shechem, Whether is better for you, that all the sons of Jerubbaal, who are threescore and ten persons, rule over you, or that one rule over you? remember also that I am your bone and your flesh.

3And his mother's brethren spake of him in the ears of all the men of Shechem all these words: and their hearts inclined to follow Abimelech; for they said, He is our brother.

4And they gave him threescore and ten pieces of silver out of the house of Baal-berith, wherewith Abimelech hired vain and light fellows, who followed him.

5And he went unto his father's house at Ophrah, and slew his brethren the sons of Jerubbaal, being threescore and ten persons, upon one stone: but Jotham the youngest son of Jerubbaal was left; for he hid himself.

6And all the men of Shechem assembled themselves together, and all the house of Millo, and went and made Abimelech king, by the oak of the pillar that was in Shechem.

7And when they told it to Jotham, he went and stood on the top of mount Gerizim, and lifted up his voice, and cried, and said unto them, Hearken unto me, ye men of Shechem, that God may hearken unto you.

8The trees went forth on a time to anoint a king over them; and they said unto the olive-tree, Reign thou over us.

9But the olive-tree said unto them, Should I leave my fatness, wherewith by me they honor God and man, and go to wave to and fro over the trees?

10And the trees said to the fig-tree, Come thou, and reign over us.

11But the fig-tree said unto them, Should I leave my sweetness, and my good fruit, and go to wave to and fro over the trees?

12And the trees said unto the vine, Come thou, and reign over us.

13And the vine said unto them, Should I leave my new wine, which cheereth God and man, and go to wave to and fro over the trees?

14Then said all the trees unto the bramble, Come thou, and reign over us.

15And the bramble said unto the trees, If in truth ye anoint me king over you, then come and take refuge in my shade; and if not, let fire come out of the bramble, and devour the cedars of Lebanon.

16Now therefore, if ye have dealt truly and uprightly, in that ye have made Abimelech king, and if ye have dealt well with Jerubbaal and his house, and have done unto him according to the deserving of his hands

17(for my father fought for you, and adventured his life, and delivered you out of the hand of Midian:

18and ye are risen up against my father's house this day, and have slain his sons, threescore and ten persons, upon one stone, and have made Abimelech, the son of his maid-servant, king over the men of Shechem, because he is your brother);

19if ye then have dealt truly and uprightly with Jerubbaal and with his house this day, then rejoice ye in Abimelech, and let him also rejoice in you:

20but if not, let fire come out from Abimelech, and devour the men of Shechem, and the house of Millo; and let fire come out from the men of Shechem, and from the house of Millo, and devour Abimelech.

21And Jotham ran away, and fled, and went to Beer, and dwelt there, for fear of Abimelech his brother.

22And Abimelech was prince over Israel three years.

23And God sent an evil spirit between Abimelech and the men of Shechem; and the men of Shechem dealt treacherously with Abimelech:

24that the violence done to the threescore and ten sons of Jerubbaal might come, and that their blood might be laid upon Abimelech their brother, who slew them, and upon the men of Shechem, who strengthened his hands to slay his brethren.

25And the men of Shechem set liers-in-wait for him on the tops of the mountains, and they robbed all that came along that way by them: and it was told Abimelech.

26And Gaal the son of Ebed came with his brethren, and went over to Shechem; and the men of Shechem put their trust in him.

27And they went out into the field, and gathered their vineyards, and trod the grapes, and held festival, and went into the house of their god, and did eat and drink, and cursed Abimelech.

28And Gaal the son of Ebed said, Who is Abimelech, and who is Shechem, that we should serve him? is not he the son of Jerubbaal? and Zebul his officer? serve ye the men of Hamor the father of Shechem: but why should we serve him?

29And would that this people were under my hand! then would I remove Abimelech. And he said to Abimelech, Increase thine army, and come out.

30And when Zebul the ruler of the city heard the words of Gaal the son of Ebed, his anger was kindled.

31And he sent messengers unto Abimelech craftily, saying, Behold, Gaal the son of Ebed and his brethren are come to Shechem; and, behold, they constrain the city to take part against thee.

32Now therefore, up by night, thou and the people that are with thee, and lie in wait in the field:

33and it shall be, that in the morning, as soon as the sun is up, thou shalt rise early, and rush upon the city; and, behold, when he and the people that are with him come out against thee, then mayest thou do to them as thou shalt find occasion.

34And Abimelech rose up, and all the people that were with him, by night, and they laid wait against Shechem in four companies.

35And Gaal the son of Ebed went out, and stood in the entrance of the gate of the city: and Abimelech rose up, and the people that were with him, from the ambushment.

36And when Gaal saw the people, he said to Zebul, Behold, there come people down from the tops of the mountains. And Zebul said unto him, Thou seest the shadow of the mountains as if they were men.

37And Gaal spake again and said, See, there come people down by the middle of the land, and one company cometh by the way of the oak of Meonenim.

38Then said Zebul unto him, Where is now thy mouth, that thou saidst, Who is Abimelech, that we should serve him? is not this the people that thou hast despised? go out now, I pray, and fight with them.

39And Gaal went out before the men of Shechem, and fought with Abimelech.

40And Abimelech chased him, and he fled before him, and there fell many wounded, even unto the entrance of the gate.

41And Abimelech dwelt at Arumah: and Zebul drove out Gaal and his brethren, that they should not dwell in Shechem.

42And it came to pass on the morrow, that the people went out into the field; and they told Abimelech.

43And he took the people, and divided them into three companies, and laid wait in the field; and he looked, and, behold, the people came forth out of the city; And he rose up against them, and smote them.

44And Abimelech, and the companies that were with him, rushed forward, and stood in the entrance of the gate of the city: and the two companies rushed upon all that were in the field, and smote them.

45And Abimelech fought against the city all that day; and he took the city, and slew the people that were therein: and he beat down the city, and sowed it with salt.

46And when all the men of the tower of Shechem heard thereof, they entered into the stronghold of the house of Elberith.

47And it was told Abimelech that all the men of the tower of Shechem were gathered together.

48And Abimelech gat him up to mount Zalmon, he and all the people that were with him; and Abimelech took an axe in his hand, and cut down a bough from the trees, and took it up, and laid it on his shoulder: and he said unto the people that were with him, What ye have seen me do, make haste, and do as I have done.

49And all the people likewise cut down every man his bough, and followed Abimelech, and put them to the stronghold, and set the stronghold on fire upon them; so that all the men of the tower of Shechem died also, about a thousand men and women.

50Then went Abimelech to Thebez, and encamped against Thebez, and took it.

51But there was a strong tower within the city, and thither fled all the men and women, and all they of the city, and shut themselves in, and gat them up to the roof of the tower.

52And Abimelech came unto the tower, and fought against it, and drew near unto the door of the tower to burn it with fire.

53And a certain woman cast an upper millstone upon Abimelech's head, and brake his skull.

54Then he called hastily unto the young man his armorbearer, and said unto him, Draw thy sword, and kill me, that men say not of me, A woman slew him. And his young man thrust him through, and he died.

55And when the men of Israel saw that Abimelech was dead, they departed every man unto his place.

56Thus God requited the wickedness of Abimelech, which he did unto his father, in slaying his seventy brethren;

57and all the wickedness of the men of Shechem did God requite upon their heads: and upon them came the curse of Jotham the son of Jerubbaal.

Chapter 10

1And after Abimelech there arose to save Israel Tola the son of Puah, the son of Dodo, a man of Issachar; and he dwelt in Shamir in the hill-country of Ephraim.

2And he judged Israel twenty and three years, and died, and was buried in Shamir.

3And after him arose Jair, the Gileadite; and he judged Israel twenty and two years.

4And he had thirty sons that rode on thirty ass colts, and they had thirty cities, which are called Havvoth-jair unto this day, which are in the land of Gilead.

5And Jair died, and was buried in Kamon.

6And the children of Israel again did that which was evil in the sight of Yahweh, and served the Baalim, and the Ashtaroth, and the gods of Syria, and the gods of Sidon, and the gods of Moab, and the gods of the children of Ammon, and the gods of the Philistines; and they forsook Yahweh, and served him not.

7And the anger of Yahweh was kindled against Israel, and he sold them into the hand of the Philistines, and into the hand of the children of Ammon.

8And they vexed and oppressed the children of Israel that year: eighteen years oppressed they all the children of Israel that were beyond the Jordan in the land of the Amorites, which is in Gilead.

9And the children of Ammon passed over the Jordan to fight also against Judah, and against Benjamin, and against the house of Ephraim; so that Israel was sore distressed.

10And the children of Israel cried unto Yahweh, saying, We have sinned against thee, even because we have forsaken our God, and have served the Baalim.

11And Yahweh said unto the children of Israel, Did not I save you from the Egyptians, and from the Amorites, from the children of Ammon, and from the Philistines?

12The Sidonians also, and the Amalekites, and the Maonites, did oppress you; and ye cried unto me, and I saved you out of their hand.

13Yet ye have forsaken me, and served other gods: wherefore I will save you no more.

14Go and cry unto the gods which ye have chosen; let them save you in the time of your distress.

15And the children of Israel said unto Yahweh, We have sinned: do thou unto us whatsoever seemeth good unto thee; only deliver us, we pray thee, this day.

16And they put away the foreign gods from among them, and served Yahweh; and his soul was grieved for the misery of Israel.

17Then the children of Ammon were gathered together, and encamped in Gilead. And the children of Israel assembled themselves together, and encamped in Mizpah.

18And the people, the princes of Gilead, said one to another, What man is he that will begin to fight against the children of Ammon? he shall be head over all the inhabitants of Gilead.

Chapter 11

1Now Jephthah the Gileadite was a mighty man of valor, and he was the son of a harlot: and Gilead begat Jephthah.

2And Gilead's wife bare him sons; and when his wife's sons grew up, they drove out Jephthah, and said unto him, Thou shalt not inherit in our father's house; for thou art the son of another woman.

3Then Jephthah fled from his brethren, and dwelt in the land of Tob: and there were gathered vain fellows to Jephthah, and they went out with him.

4And it came to pass after a while, that the children of Ammon made war against Israel.

5And it was so, that, when the children of Ammon made war against Israel, the elders of Gilead went to fetch Jephthah out of the land of Tob;

6and they said unto Jephthah, Come and be our chief, that we may fight with the children of Ammon.

7And Jephthah said unto the elders of Gilead, Did not ye hate me, and drive me out of my father's house? and why are ye come unto me now when ye are in distress?

8And the elders of Gilead said unto Jephthah, Therefore are we turned again to thee now, that thou mayest go with us, and fight with the children of Ammon; and thou shalt be our head over all the inhabitants of Gilead.

9And Jephthah said unto the elders of Gilead, If ye bring me home again to fight with the children of Ammon, and Yahweh deliver them before me, shall I be your head?

10And the elders of Gilead said unto Jephthah, Yahweh shall be witness between us; surely according to thy word so will we do.

11Then Jephthah went with the elders of Gilead, and the people made him head and chief over them: and Jephthah spake all his words before Yahweh in Mizpah.

12And Jephthah sent messengers unto the king of the children of Ammon,

Judges

saying, What hast thou to do with me, that thou art come unto me to fight against my land?

¹³And the king of the children of Ammon answered unto the messengers of Jephthah, Because Israel took away my land, when he came up out of Egypt, from the Arnon even unto the Jabbok, and unto the Jordan: now therefore restore those lands again peaceably.

¹⁴And Jephthah sent messengers again unto the king of the children of Ammon;

¹⁵and he said unto him, Thus saith Jephthah: Israel took not away the land of Moab, nor the land of the children of Ammon,

¹⁶but when they came up from Egypt, and Israel went through the wilderness unto the Red Sea, and came to Kadesh;

¹⁷then Israel sent messengers unto the king of Edom, saying, Let me, I pray thee, pass through thy land; but the king of Edom hearkened not. And in like manner he sent unto the king of Moab; but he would not: and Israel abode in Kadesh.

¹⁸Then they went through the wilderness, and went around the land of Edom, and the land of Moab, and came by the east side of the land of Moab, and they encamped on the other side of the Arnon; but they came not within the border of Moab, for the Arnon was the border of Moab.

¹⁹And Israel sent messengers unto Sihon king of the Amorites, the king of Heshbon; and Israel said unto him, Let us pass, we pray thee, through thy land unto my place.

²⁰But Sihon trusted not Israel to pass through his border; but Sihon gathered all his people together, and encamped in Jahaz, and fought against Israel.

²¹And Yahweh, the God of Israel, delivered Sihon and all his people into the hand of Israel, and they smote them: so Israel possessed all the land of the Amorites, the inhabitants of that country.

²²And they possessed all the border of the Amorites, from the Arnon even unto the Jabbok, and from the wilderness even unto the Jordan.

²³So now Yahweh, the God of Israel, hath dispossessed the Amorites from before his people Israel, and shouldest thou possess them?

²⁴Wilt not thou possess that which Chemosh thy god giveth thee to possess? So whomsoever Yahweh our God hath dispossessed from before us, them will we possess.

²⁵And now art thou anything better than Balak the son of Zippor, king of Moab? did he ever strive against Israel, or did he ever fight against them?

²⁶While Israel dwelt in Heshbon and its towns, and in Aroer and its towns, and in all the cities that are along by the side of the Arnon, three hundred years; wherefore did ye not recover them within that time?

²⁷I therefore have not sinned against thee, but thou doest me wrong to war against me: Yahweh, the Judge, be judge this day between the children of Israel and the children of Ammon.

²⁸Howbeit the king of the children of Ammon hearkened not unto the words of Jephthah which he sent him.

²⁹Then the Spirit of Yahweh came upon Jephthah, and he passed over Gilead and Manasseh, and passed over Mizpeh of Gilead, and from Mizpeh of Gilead he passed over unto the children of Ammon.

³⁰And Jephthah vowed a vow unto Yahweh, and said, If thou wilt indeed deliver the children of Ammon into my hand,

³¹then it shall be, that whatsoever cometh forth from the doors of my house to meet me, when I return in peace from the children of Ammon, it shall be Yahweh's, and I will offer it up for a burnt-offering.

³²So Jephthah passed over unto the children of Ammon to fight against them; and Yahweh delivered them into his hand.

³³And he smote them from Aroer until thou come to Minnith, even twenty cities, and unto Abelcheramim, with a very great slaughter. So the children of Ammon were subdued before the children of Israel.

³⁴And Jephthah came to Mizpah unto his house; and, behold, his daughter came out to meet him with timbrels and with dances: and she was his only child; besides her he had neither son nor daughter.

³⁵And it came to pass, when he saw her, that he rent his clothes, and said, Alas, my daughter! thou hast brought me very low, and thou art one of them that trouble me; for I have opened my mouth unto Yahweh, and I cannot go back.

³⁶And she said unto him, My father, thou hast opened thy mouth unto Yahweh; do unto me according to that which hath proceeded out of thy mouth, forasmuch as Yahweh hath taken vengeance for thee on thine enemies, even on the children of Ammon.

³⁷And she said unto her father, Let this thing be done for me: let me alone two months, that I may depart and go down upon the mountains, and bewail my virginity, I and my companions.

³⁸And he said, Go. And he sent her away for two months: and she departed, she and her companions, and bewailed her virginity upon the mountains.

³⁹And it came to pass at the end of two months, that she returned unto her father, who did with her according to his vow which he had vowed: and she knew not man. And it was a custom in Israel,

⁴⁰that the daughters of Israel went yearly to celebrate the daughter of Jephthah the Gileadite four days in a year.

Chapter 12

¹And the men of Ephraim were gathered together, and passed northward; and they said unto Jephthah, Wherefore passedst thou over to fight against the children of Ammon, and didst not call us to go with thee? we will burn thy house upon thee with fire.

²And Jephthah said unto them, I and my people were at great strife with the children of Ammon; and when I called you, ye saved me not out of their hand.

³And when I saw that ye saved me not, I put my life in my hand, and passed over against the children of Ammon, and Yahweh delivered them into my hand: wherefore then are ye come up unto me this day, to fight against me?

⁴Then Jephthah gathered together all the men of Gilead, and fought with Ephraim; and the men of Gilead smote Ephraim, because they said, Ye are fugitives of Ephraim, ye Gileadites, in the midst of Ephraim, and in the midst of Manasseh.

⁵And the Gileadites took the fords of the Jordan against the Ephraimites. And it was so, that, when any of the fugitives of Ephraim said, Let me go over, the men of Gilead said unto him, Art thou an Ephraimite? If he said, Nay,

⁶then said they unto him, Say now Shibboleth; and he said Sibboleth; for he could not frame to pronounce it right: then they laid hold on him, and slew him at the fords of the Jordan. And there fell at that time of Ephraim forty and two thousand.

⁷And Jephthah judged Israel six years. Then died Jephthah the Gileadite, and was buried in one of the cities of Gilead.

⁸And after him Ibzan of Beth-lehem judged Israel.

⁹And he had thirty sons; and thirty daughters he sent abroad, and thirty daughters he brought in from abroad for his sons. And he judged Israel seven years.

¹⁰And Ibzan died, and was buried at Beth-lehem.

¹¹And after him Elon the Zebulunite judged Israel; and he judged Israel ten years.

¹²And Elon the Zebulunite died, and was buried in Aijalon in the land of Zebulun.

¹³And after him Abdon the son of Hillel the Pirathonite judged Israel.

¹⁴And he had forty sons and thirty sons' sons, that rode on threescore and ten ass colts: and he judged Israel eight years.

¹⁵And Abdon the son of Hillel the Pirathonite died, and was buried in Pirathon in the land of Ephraim, in the hill-country of the Amalekites.

Chapter 13

¹And the children of Israel again did that which was evil in the sight of Yahweh; and Yahweh delivered them into the hand of the Philistines forty years.

²And there was a certain man of Zorah, of the family of the Danites, whose name was Manoah; and his wife was barren, and bare not.

³And the angel of Yahweh appeared unto the woman, and said unto her, Behold now, thou art barren, and bearest not; but thou shalt conceive, and bear a son.

⁴Now therefore beware, I pray thee, and drink no wine nor strong drink, and eat not any unclean thing:

⁵for, lo, thou shalt conceive, and bear a son; and no razor shall come upon his head; for the child shall be a Nazirite unto God from the womb: and he shall begin to save Israel out of the hand of the Philistines.

⁶Then the woman came and told her husband, saying, A man of God came unto me, and his countenance was like the countenance of the angel of God, very terrible; and I asked him not whence he was, neither told he me his name:

⁷but he said unto me, Behold, thou shalt conceive, and bear a son; and now drink no wine nor strong drink, and eat not any unclean thing; for the child shall be a Nazirite unto God from the womb to the day of his death.

⁸Then Manoah entreated Yahweh, and said, Oh, Lord, I pray thee, let the man of God whom thou didst send come again unto us, and teach us what we shall do unto the child that shall be born.

⁹And God hearkened to the voice of Manoah; and the angel of God came again unto the woman as she sat in the field: but Manoah her husband was not with her.

¹⁰And the woman made haste, and ran, and told her husband, and said unto him, Behold, the man hath appeared unto me, that came unto me the other day.

¹¹And Manoah arose, and went after his wife, and came to the man, and said unto him, Art thou the man that spakest unto the woman? And he said, I am.

¹²And Manoah said, Now let thy words come to pass: what shall be the ordering of the child, and how shall we do unto him?

¹³And the angel of Yahweh said unto Manoah, Of all that I said unto the woman let her beware.

¹⁴She may not eat of anything that cometh of the vine, neither let her drink wine or strong drink, nor eat any unclean thing; all that I commanded her let her observe.

¹⁵And Manoah said unto the angel of Yahweh, I pray thee, let us detain thee, that we may make ready a kid for thee.

¹⁶And the angel of Yahweh said unto Manoah, Though thou detain me, I will not eat of thy bread; and if thou wilt make ready a burnt-offering, thou must offer it unto Yahweh. For Manoah knew not that he was the angel of Yahweh.

¹⁷And Manoah said unto the angel of Yahweh, What is thy name, that, when thy words come to pass, we may do thee honor?

¹⁸And the angel of Yahweh said unto him, Wherefore askest thou after my name, seeing it is wonderful?

¹⁹So Manoah took the kid with the meal-offering, and offered it upon the rock unto Yahweh: and the angel did wondrously, and Manoah and his wife looked on.

²⁰For it came to pass, when the flame went up toward heaven from off the altar, that the angel of Yahweh ascended in the flame of the altar: and Manoah and his wife looked on; and they fell on their faces to the ground.

²¹But the angel of Yahweh did no more appear to Manoah or to his wife. Then Manoah knew that he was the angel of Yahweh.

²²And Manoah said unto his wife, We shall surely die, because we have seen God.

²³But his wife said unto him, If Yahweh were pleased to kill us, he would not have received a burnt-offering and a meal-offering at our hand, neither would he have showed us all these things, nor would at this time have told such things as these.

²⁴And the woman bare a son, and called his name Samson: and the child grew, and Yahweh blessed him.

25And the Spirit of Yahweh began to move him in Mahaneh-dan, between Zorah and Eshtaol.

Chapter 14

1And Samson went down to Timnah, and saw a woman in Timnah of the daughters of the Philistines.

2And he came up, and told his father and his mother, and said, I have seen a woman in Timnah of the daughters of the Philistines: now therefore get her for me to wife.

3Then his father and his mother said unto him, Is there never a woman among the daughters of thy brethren, or among all my people, that thou goest to take a wife of the uncircumcised Philistines? And Samson said unto his father, Get her for me; for she pleaseth me well.

4But his father and his mother knew not that it was of Yahweh; for he sought an occasion against the Philistines. Now at that time the Philistines had rule over Israel.

5Then went Samson down, and his father and his mother, to Timnah, and came to the vineyards of Timnah: and, behold, a young lion roared against him.

6And the Spirit of Yahweh came mightily upon him, and he rent him as he would have rent a kid; and he had nothing in his hand: but he told not his father or his mother what he had done.

7And he went down, and talked with the woman, and she pleased Samson well.

8And after a while he returned to take her; and he turned aside to see the carcass of the lion: and, behold, there was a swarm of bees in the body of the lion, and honey.

9And he took it into his hands, and went on, eating as he went; and he came to his father and mother, and gave unto them, and they did eat: but he told them not that he had taken the honey out of the body of the lion.

10And his father went down unto the woman: and Samson made there a feast; for so used the young men to do.

11And it came to pass, when they saw him, that they brought thirty companions to be with him.

12And Samson said unto them, Let me now put forth a riddle unto you: if ye can declare it unto me within the seven days of the feast, and find it out, then I will give you thirty linen garments and thirty changes of raiment;

13but if ye cannot declare it unto me, then shall ye give me thirty linen garments and thirty changes of raiment. And they said unto him, Put forth thy riddle, that we may hear it.

14And he said unto them,
Out of the eater came forth food,
And out of the strong came forth sweetness.
And they could not in three days declare the riddle.

15And it came to pass on the seventh day, that they said unto Samson's wife, Entice thy husband, that he may declare unto us the riddle, lest we burn thee and thy father's house with fire: have ye called us to impoverish us? is it not so?

16And Samson's wife wept before him, and said, Thou dost but hate me, and lovest me not: thou hast put forth a riddle unto the children of my people, and hast not told it me. And he said unto her, Behold, I have not told it my father nor my mother, and shall I tell thee?

17And she wept before him the seven days, while their feast lasted: and it came to pass on the seventh day, that he told her, because she pressed him sore; and she told the riddle to the children of her people.

18And the men of the city said unto him on the seventh day before the sun went down, What is sweeter than honey? and what is stronger than a lion? And he said unto them,
If ye had not plowed with my heifer,
Ye had not found out my riddle.

19And the Spirit of Yahweh came mightily upon him, and he went down to Ashkelon, and smote thirty men of them, and took their spoil, and gave the changes of raiment unto them that declared the riddle. And his anger was kindled, and he went up to his father's house.

20But Samson's wife was given to his companion, whom he had used as his friend.

Chapter 15

1But it came to pass after a while, in the time of wheat harvest, that Samson visited his wife with a kid; and he said, I will go in to my wife into the chamber. But her father would not suffer him to go in.

2And her father said, I verily thought that thou hadst utterly hated her; therefore I gave her to thy companion: is not her younger sister fairer than she? take her, I pray thee, instead of her.

3And Samson said unto them, This time shall I be blameless in regard of the Philistines, when I do them a mischief.

4And Samson went and caught three hundred foxes, and took firebrands, and turned tail to tail, and put a firebrand in the midst between every two tails.

5And when he had set the brands on fire, he let them go into the standing grain of the Philistines, and burnt up both the shocks and the standing grain, and also the oliveyards.

6Then the Philistines said, Who hath done this? And they said, Samson, the son-in-law of the Timnite, because he hath taken his wife, and given her to his companion. And the Philistines came up, and burnt her and her father with fire.

7And Samson said unto them, If ye do after this manner, surely I will be avenged of you, and after that I will cease.

8And he smote them hip and thigh with a great slaughter: and he went down and dwelt in the cleft of the rock of Etam.

9Then the Philistines went up, and encamped in Judah, and spread themselves in Lehi.

10And the men of Judah said, Why are ye come up against us? And they said, To bind Samson are we come up, to do to him as he hath done to us.

11Then three thousand men of Judah went down to the cleft of the rock of Etam, and said to Samson, Knowest thou not that the Philistines are rulers over us? what then is this that thou hast done unto us? And he said unto them, As they did unto me, so have I done unto them.

12And they said unto him, We are come down to bind thee, that we may deliver thee into the hand of the Philistines. And Samson said unto them, Swear unto me, that ye will not fall upon me yourselves.

13And they spake unto him, saying, No; but we will bind thee fast, and deliver thee into their hand: but surely we will not kill thee. And they bound him with two new ropes, and brought him up from the rock.

14When he came unto Lehi, the Philistines shouted as they met him: and the Spirit of Yahweh came mightily upon him, and the ropes that were upon his arms became as flax that was burnt with fire, and his bands dropped from off his hands.

15And he found a fresh jawbone of an ass, and put forth his hand, and took it, and smote a thousand men therewith.

16And Samson said,
With the jawbone of an ass, heaps upon heaps,
With the jawbone of an ass have I smitten a thousand men.

17And it came to pass, when he had made an end of speaking, that he cast away the jawbone out of his hand; and that place was called Ramath-lehi.

18And he was sore athirst, and called on Yahweh, and said, Thou hast given this great deliverance by the hand of thy servant; and now shall I die for thirst, and fall into the hand of the uncircumcised.

19But God clave the hollow place that is in Lehi, and there came water thereout; and when he had drunk, his spirit came again, and he revived: wherefore the name thereof was called En-hakkore, which is in Lehi, unto this day.

20And he judged Israel in the days of the Philistines twenty years.

Chapter 16

1And Samson went to Gaza, and saw there a harlot, and went in unto her.

2And it was told the Gazites, saying, Samson is come hither. And they compassed him in, and laid wait for him all night in the gate of the city, and were quiet all the night, saying, Let be till morning light, then we will kill him.

3And Samson lay till midnight, and arose at midnight, and laid hold of the doors of the gate of the city, and the two posts, and plucked them up, bar and all, and put them upon his shoulders, and carried them up to the top of the mountain that is before Hebron.

4And it came to pass afterward, that he loved a woman in the valley of Sorek, whose name was Delilah.

5And the lords of the Philistines came up unto her, and said unto her, Entice him, and see wherein his great strength lieth, and by what means we may prevail against him, that we may bind him to afflict him: and we will give thee every one of us eleven hundred pieces of silver.

6And Delilah said to Samson, Tell me, I pray thee, wherein thy great strength lieth, and wherewith thou mightest be bound to afflict thee.

7And Samson said unto her, If they bind me with seven green withes that were never dried, then shall I become weak, and be as another man.

8Then the lords of the Philistines brought up to her seven green withes which had not been dried, and she bound him with them.

9Now she had liers-in-wait abiding in the inner chamber. And she said unto him, The Philistines are upon thee, Samson. And he brake the withes, as a string of tow is broken when it toucheth the fire. So his strength was not known.

10And Delilah said unto Samson, Behold, thou hast mocked me, and told me lies: now tell me, I pray thee, wherewith thou mightest be bound.

11And he said unto her, If they only bind me with new ropes wherewith no work hath been done, then shall I become weak, and be as another man.

12So Delilah took new ropes, and bound him therewith, and said unto him, The Philistines are upon thee, Samson. And the liers-in-wait were abiding in the inner chamber. And he brake them off his arms like a thread.

13And Delilah said unto Samson, Hitherto thou hast mocked me, and told me lies: tell me wherewith thou mightest be bound. And he said unto her, If thou weavest the seven locks of my head with the web.

14And she fastened it with the pin, and said unto him, The Philistines are upon thee, Samson. And he awaked out of his sleep, and plucked away the pin of the beam, and the web.

15And she said unto him, How canst thou say, I love thee, when thy heart is not with me? thou hast mocked me these three times, and hast not told me wherein thy great strength lieth.

16And it came to pass, when she pressed him daily with her words, and urged him, that his soul was vexed unto death.

17And he told her all his heart, and said unto her, There hath not come a razor upon my head; for I have been a Nazirite unto God from my mother's womb: if I be shaven, then my strength will go from me, and I shall become weak, and be like any other man.

18And when Delilah saw that he had told her all his heart, she sent and called for the lords of the Philistines, saying, Come up this once, for he hath told me all his heart. Then the lords of the Philistines came up unto her, and brought the money in their hand.

19And she made him sleep upon her knees; and she called for a man, and shaved off the seven locks of his head; and she began to afflict him, and his strength went from him.

20And she said, The Philistines are upon thee, Samson. And he awoke out of his sleep, and said, I will go out as at other times, and shake myself free. But he knew not that Yahweh was departed from him.

21And the Philistines laid hold on him, and put out his eyes; and they brought him down to Gaza, and bound him with fetters of brass; and he did grind in the prison-house.

Judges

22Howbeit the hair of his head began to grow again after he was shaven.

23And the lords of the Philistines gathered them together to offer a great sacrifice unto Dagon their god, and to rejoice; for they said, Our god hath delivered Samson our enemy into our hand.

24And when the people saw him, they praised their god; for they said, Our god hath delivered into our hand our enemy, and the destroyer of our country, who hath slain many of us.

25And it came to pass, when their hearts were merry, that they said, Call for Samson, that he may make us sport. And they called for Samson out of the prison-house; and he made sport before them. And they set him between the pillars:

26and Samson said unto the lad that held him by the hand, Suffer me that I may feel the pillars whereupon the house resteth, that I may lean upon them.

27Now the house was full of men and women; and all the lords of the Philistines were there; and there were upon the roof about three thousand men and women, that beheld while Samson made sport.

28And Samson called unto Yahweh, and said, O Lord Yahweh, remember me, I pray thee, and strengthen me, I pray thee, only this once, O God, that I may be at once avenged of the Philistines for my two eyes.

29And Samson took hold of the two middle pillars upon which the house rested, and leaned upon them, the one with his right hand, and the other with his left.

30And Samson said, Let me die with the Philistines. And he bowed himself with all his might; and the house fell upon the lords, and upon all the people that were therein. So the dead that he slew at his death were more than they that he slew in his life.

31Then his brethren and all the house of his father came down, and took him, and brought him up, and buried him between Zorah and Eshtaol in the burying-place of Manoah his father. And he judged Israel twenty years.

Chapter 17

1And there was a man of the hill-country of Ephraim, whose name was Micah.

2And he said unto his mother, The eleven hundred pieces of silver that were taken from thee, about which thou didst utter a curse, and didst also speak it in mine ears, behold, the silver is with me; I took it. And his mother said, Blessed be my son of Yahweh.

3And he restored the eleven hundred pieces of silver to his mother; and his mother said, I verily dedicate the silver unto Yahweh from my hand for my son, to make a graven image and a molten image: now therefore I will restore it unto thee.

4And when he restored the money unto his mother, his mother took two hundred pieces of silver, and gave them to the founder, who made thereof a graven image and a molten image: and it was in the house of Micah.

5And the man Micah had a house of gods, and he made an ephod, and teraphim, and consecrated one of his sons, who became his priest.

6In those days there was no king in Israel: every man did that which was right in his own eyes.

7And there was a young man out of Beth-lehem-judah, of the family of Judah, who was a Levite; and he sojourned there.

8And the man departed out of the city, out of Beth-lehem-judah, to sojourn where he could find a place, and he came to the hill-country of Ephraim to the house of Micah, as he journeyed.

9And Micah said unto him, Whence comest thou? And he said unto him, I am a Levite of Beth-lehem-judah, and I go to sojourn where I may find a place.

10And Micah said unto him, Dwell with me, and be unto me a father and a priest, and I will give thee ten pieces of silver by the year, and a suit of apparel, and thy victuals. So the Levite went in.

11And the Levite was content to dwell with the man; and the young man was unto him as one of his sons.

12And Micah consecrated the Levite, and the young man became his priest, and was in the house of Micah.

13Then said Micah, Now know I that Yahweh will do me good, seeing I have a Levite to my priest.

Chapter 18

1In those days there was no king in Israel: and in those days the tribe of the Danites sought them an inheritance to dwell in; for unto that day their inheritance had not fallen unto them among the tribes of Israel.

2And the children of Dan sent of their family five men from their whole number, men of valor, from Zorah, and from Eshtaol, to spy out the land, and to search it; and they said unto them, Go, search the land. And they came to the hill-country of Ephraim, unto the house of Micah, and lodged there.

3When they were by the house of Micah, they knew the voice of the young man the Levite; and they turned aside thither, and said unto him, Who brought thee hither? and what doest thou in this place? and what hast thou here?

4And he said unto them, Thus and thus hath Micah dealt with me, and he hath hired me, and I am become his priest.

5And they said unto him, Ask counsel, we pray thee, of God, that we may know whether our way which we go shall be prosperous.

6And the priest said unto them, Go in peace: before Yahweh is your way wherein ye go.

7Then the five men departed, and came unto Laish, and saw the people that were therein, how they dwelt in security, after the manner of the Sidonians, quiet and secure; for there was none in the land, possessing authority, that might put them to shame in anything, and they were far from the Sidonians, and had no dealings with any man.

8And they came unto their brethren to Zorah and Eshtaol: and their brethren said unto them, What say ye?

9And they said, Arise, and let us go up against them; for we have seen the land, and, behold, it is very good: and are ye still? be not slothful to go and to enter in to possess the land.

10When ye go, ye shall come unto a people secure, and the land is large; for God hath given it into your hand, a place where there is no want of anything that is in the earth.

11And there set forth from thence of the family of the Danites, out of Zorah and out of Eshtaol, six hundred men girt with weapons of war.

12And they went up, and encamped in Kiriath-jearim, in Judah: wherefore they called that place Mahaneh-dan, unto this day; behold, it is behind Kiriath-jearim.

13And they passed thence unto the hill-country of Ephraim, and came unto the house of Micah.

14Then answered the five men that went to spy out the country of Laish, and said unto their brethren, Do ye know that there is in these houses an ephod, and teraphim, and a graven image, and a molten image? now therefore consider what ye have to do.

15And they turned aside thither, and came to the house of the young man the Levite, even unto the house of Micah, and asked him of his welfare.

16And the six hundred men girt with weapons of war, who were of the children of Dan, stood by the entrance of the gate.

17And the five men that went to spy out the land went up, and came in thither, and took the graven image, and the ephod, and the teraphim, and the molten image: and the priest stood by the entrance of the gate with the six hundred men girt with weapons of war.

18And when these went into Micah's house, and fetched the graven image, the ephod, and the teraphim, and the molten image, the priest said unto them, What do ye?

19And they said unto him, Hold thy peace, lay thy hand upon thy mouth, and go with us, and be to us a father and a priest: is it better for thee to be priest unto the house of one man, or to be priest unto a tribe and a family in Israel?

20And the priest's heart was glad, and he took the ephod, and the teraphim, and the graven image, and went in the midst of the people.

21So they turned and departed, and put the little ones and the cattle and the goods before them.

22When they were a good way from the house of Micah, the men that were in the houses near to Micah's house were gathered together, and overtook the children of Dan.

23And they cried unto the children of Dan. And they turned their faces, and said unto Micah, What aileth thee, that thou comest with such a company?

24And he said, ye have taken away my gods which I made, and the priest, and are gone away, and what have I more? and how then say ye unto me, What aileth thee?

25And the children of Dan said unto him, Let not thy voice be heard among us, lest angry fellows fall upon you, and thou lose thy life, with the lives of thy household.

26And the children of Dan went their way: and when Micah saw that they were too strong for him, he turned and went back unto his house.

27And they took that which Micah had made, and the priest whom he had, and came unto Laish, unto a people quiet and secure, and smote them with the edge of the sword; and they burnt the city with fire.

28And there was no deliverer, because it was far from Sidon, and they had no dealings with any man; and it was in the valley that lieth by Beth-rehob. And they built the city, and dwelt therein.

29And they called the name of the city Dan, after the name of Dan their father, who was born unto Israel: howbeit the name of the city was Laish at the first.

30And the children of Dan set up for themselves the graven image: and Jonathan, the son of Gershom, the son of Moses, he and his sons were priests to the tribe of the Danites until the day of the captivity of the land.

31So they set them up Micah's graven image which he made, all the time that the house of God was in Shiloh.

Chapter 19

1And it came to pass in those days, when there was no king in Israel, that there was a certain Levite sojourning on the farther side of the hill-country of Ephraim, who took to him a concubine out of Beth-lehem-judah.

2And his concubine played the harlot against him, and went away from him unto her father's house to Beth-lehem-judah, and was there the space of four months.

3And her husband arose, and went after her, to speak kindly unto her, to bring her again, having his servant with him, and a couple of asses: and she brought him into her father's house; and when the father of the damsel saw him, he rejoiced to meet him.

4And his father-in-law, the damsel's father, retained him; and he abode with him three days: so they did eat and drink, and lodged there.

5And it came to pass on the fourth day, that they arose early in the morning, and he rose up to depart: and the damsel's father said unto his son-in-law, Strengthen thy heart with a morsel of bread, and afterward ye shall go your way.

6So they sat down, and did eat and drink, both of them together: and the damsel's father said unto the man, Be pleased, I pray thee, to tarry all night, and let thy heart be merry.

7And the man rose up to depart; but his father-in-law urged him, and he lodged there again.

8And he arose early in the morning on the fifth day to depart; and the damsel's father said, Strengthen thy heart, I pray thee, and tarry ye until the day declineth; and they did eat, both of them.

9And when the man rose up to depart, he, and his concubine, and his servant, his father-in-law, the damsel's father, said unto him, Behold, now the day draweth toward evening, I pray you tarry all night: behold, the day groweth to an end, lodge here, that thy heart may be merry; and to-morrow get you early on your way, that thou mayest go home.

10But the man would not tarry that night, but he rose up and departed, and came over against Jebus (the same is Jerusalem): and there were with him a couple of asses saddled; his concubine also was with him.

11When they were by Jebus, the day was far spent; and the servant said unto his master, Come, I pray thee, and let us turn aside into this city of the Jebusites, and lodge in it.

12And his master said unto him, We will not turn aside into the city of a foreigner, that is not of the children of Israel; but we will pass over to Gibeah.

13And he said unto his servant, Come and let us draw near to one of these places; and we will lodge in Gibeah, or in Ramah.

14So they passed on and went their way; and the sun went down upon them near to Gibeah, which belongeth to Benjamin.

15And they turned aside thither, to go in to lodge in Gibeah: and he went in, and sat him down in the street of the city; for there was no man that took them into his house to lodge.

16And, behold, there came an old man from his work out of the field at even: now the man was of the hill-country of Ephraim, and he sojourned in Gibeah; but the men of the place were Benjamites.

17And he lifted up his eyes, and saw the wayfaring man in the street of the city; and the old man said, Whither goest thou? and whence comest thou?

18And he said unto him, We are passing from Beth-lehem-judah unto the farther side of the hill-country of Ephraim; from thence am I, and I went to Beth-lehem-judah: and I am now going to the house of Yahweh; and there is no man that taketh me into his house.

19Yet there is both straw and provender for our asses; and there is bread and wine also for me, and for thy handmaid, and for the young man that is with thy servants: there is no want of anything.

20And the old man said, Peace be unto thee; howsoever let all thy wants lie upon me; only lodge not in the street.

21So he brought him into his house, and gave the asses fodder; and they washed their feet, and did eat and drink.

22As they were making their hearts merry, behold, the men of the city, certain base fellows, beset the house round about, beating at the door; and they spake to the master of the house, the old man, saying, Bring forth the man that came into thy house, that we may know him.

23And the man, the master of the house, went out unto them, and said unto them, Nay, my brethren, I pray you, do not so wickedly; seeing that this man is come into my house, do not this folly.

24Behold, here is my daughter a virgin, and his concubine; them I will bring out now, and humble ye them, and do with them what seemeth good unto you: but unto this man do not any such folly.

25But the men would not hearken to him: so the man laid hold on his concubine, and brought her forth unto them; and they knew her, and abused her all the night until the morning: and when the day began to spring, they let her go.

26Then came the woman in the dawning of the day, and fell down at the door of the man's house where her lord was, till it was light.

27And her lord rose up in the morning, and opened the doors of the house, and went out to go his way; and, behold, the woman his concubine was fallen down at the door of the house, with her hands upon the threshold.

28And he said unto her, Up, and let us be going; but none answered: then he took her up upon the ass; and the man rose up, and gat him unto his place.

29And when he was come into his house, he took a knife, and laid hold on his concubine, and divided her, limb by limb, into twelve pieces, and sent her throughout all the borders of Israel.

30And it was so, that all that saw it said, There was no such deed done nor seen from the day that the children of Israel came up out of the land of Egypt unto this day: consider it, take counsel, and speak.

Chapter 20

1Then all the children of Israel went out, and the congregation was assembled as one man, from Dan even to Beer-sheba, with the land of Gilead, unto Yahweh at Mizpah.

2And the chiefs of all the people, even of all the tribes of Israel, presented themselves in the assembly of the people of God, four hundred thousand footmen that drew sword.

3(Now the children of Benjamin heard that the children of Israel were gone up to Mizpah.) And the children of Israel said, Tell us, how was this wickedness brought to pass?

4And the Levite, the husband of the woman that was murdered, answered and said, I came into Gibeah that belongeth to Benjamin, I and my concubine, to lodge.

5And the men of Gibeah rose against me, and beset the house round about me by night; me they thought to have slain, and my concubine they forced, and she is dead.

6And I took my concubine, and cut her in pieces, and sent her throughout all the country of the inheritance of Israel; for they have committed lewdness and folly in Israel.

7Behold, ye children of Israel, all of you, give here your advice and counsel.

8And all the people arose as one man, saying, We will not any of us go to his tent, neither will we any of us turn unto his house.

9But now this is the thing which we will do to Gibeah: we will go up against it by lot;

10and we will take ten men of a hundred throughout all the tribes of Israel, and a hundred of a thousand, and a thousand out of ten thousand, to fetch victuals for the people, that they may do, when they come to Gibeah of Benjamin, according to all the folly that they have wrought in Israel.

11So all the men of Israel were gathered against the city, knit together as one man.

12And the tribes of Israel sent men through all the tribe of Benjamin, saying, What wickedness is this that is come to pass among you?

13Now therefore deliver up the men, the base fellows, that are in Gibeah, that we may put them to death, and put away evil from Israel. But Benjamin would not hearken to the voice of their brethren the children of Israel.

14And the children of Benjamin gathered themselves together out of the cities unto Gibeah, to go out to battle against the children of Israel.

15And the children of Benjamin were numbered on that day out of the cities twenty and six thousand men that drew sword, besides the inhabitants of Gibeah, who were numbered seven hundred chosen men.

16Among all this people there were seven hundred chosen men lefthanded; every one could sling stones at a hair-breadth, and not miss.

17And the men of Israel, besides Benjamin, were numbered four hundred thousand men that drew sword: all these were men of war.

18And the children of Israel arose, and went up to Beth-el, and asked counsel of God; and they said, Who shall go up for us first to battle against the children of Benjamin? And Yahweh said, Judah shall go up first.

19And the children of Israel rose up in the morning, and encamped against Gibeah.

20And the men of Israel went out to battle against Benjamin; and the men of Israel set the battle in array against them at Gibeah.

21And the children of Benjamin came forth out of Gibeah, and destroyed down to the ground of the Israelites on that day twenty and two thousand men.

22And the people, the men of Israel, encouraged themselves, and set the battle again in array in the place where they set themselves in array the first day.

23And the children of Israel went up and wept before Yahweh until even; and they asked of Yahweh, saying, Shall I again draw nigh to battle against the children of Benjamin my brother? And Yahweh said, Go up against him.

24And the children of Israel came near against the children of Benjamin the second day.

25And Benjamin went forth against them out of Gibeah the second day, and destroyed down to the ground of the children of Israel again eighteen thousand men; all these drew the sword.

26Then all the children of Israel, and all the people, went up, and came unto Beth-el, and wept, and sat there before Yahweh, and fasted that day until even; and they offered burnt-offerings and peace-offerings before Yahweh.

27And the children of Israel asked of Yahweh (for the ark of the covenant of God was there in those days,

28and Phinehas, the son of Eleazar, the son of Aaron, stood before it in those days), saying, Shall I yet again go out to battle against the children of Benjamin my brother, or shall I cease? And Yahweh said, Go up; for to-morrow I will deliver him into thy hand.

29And Israel set liers-in-wait against Gibeah round about.

30And the children of Israel went up against the children of Benjamin on the third day, and set themselves in array against Gibeah, as at other times.

31And the children of Benjamin went out against the people, and were drawn away from the city; and they began to smite and kill of the people, as at other times, in the highways, of which one goeth up to Beth-el, and the other to Gibeah, in the field, about thirty men of Israel.

32And the children of Benjamin said, They are smitten down before us, as at the first. But the children of Israel said, Let us flee, and draw them away from the city unto the highways.

33And all the men of Israel rose up out of their place, and set themselves in array at Baal-tamar: and the liers-in-wait of Israel brake forth out of their place, even out of Maareh-geba.

34And there came over against Gibeah ten thousand chosen men out of all Israel, and the battle was sore; but they knew not that evil was close upon them.

35And Yahweh smote Benjamin before Israel; and the children of Israel destroyed of Benjamin that day twenty and five thousand and a hundred men: all these drew the sword.

36So the children of Benjamin saw that they were smitten; for the men of Israel gave place to Benjamin, because they trusted unto the liers-in-wait whom they had set against Gibeah.

37And the liers-in-wait hasted, and rushed upon Gibeah; and the liers-in-wait drew themselves along, and smote all the city with the edge of the sword.

38Now the appointed sign between the men of Israel and the liers-in-wait was, that they should make a great cloud of smoke rise up out of the city.

39And the men of Israel turned in the battle, and Benjamin began to smite and kill of the men of Israel about thirty persons; for they said, Surely they are smitten down before us, as in the first battle.

40But when the cloud began to arise up out of the city in a pillar of smoke, the Benjamites looked behind them; and, behold, the whole of the city went up in smoke to heaven.

41And the men of Israel turned, and the men of Benjamin were dismayed; for they saw that evil was come upon them.

42Therefore they turned their backs before the men of Israel unto the way of the wilderness; but the battle followed hard after them; and they that came out of the cities destroyed them in the midst thereof.

43They inclosed the Benjamites round about, and chased them, and trod them down at their resting-place, as far as over against Gibeah toward the sunrising.

44And there fell of Benjamin eighteen thousand men; all these were men of valor.

45And they turned and fled toward the wilderness unto the rock of Rimmon: and they gleaned of them in the highways five thousand men, and followed hard after them unto Gidom, and smote of them two thousand men.

46So that all who fell that day of Benjamin were twenty and five thousand men that drew the sword; all these were men of valor.

47But six hundred men turned and fled toward the wilderness unto the rock of Rimmon, and abode in the rock of Rimmon four months.

48And the men of Israel turned again upon the children of Benjamin, and smote them with the edge of the sword, both the entire city, and the cattle, and all that they found: moreover all the cities which they found they set on fire.

Chapter 21

1Now the men of Israel had sworn in Mizpah, saying, There shall not any of us give his daughter unto Benjamin to wife.

2And the people came to Beth-el, and sat there till even before God, and lifted up their voices, and wept sore.

3And they said, O Yahweh, the God of Israel, why is this come to pass in Israel, that there should be to-day one tribe lacking in Israel?

4And it came to pass on the morrow, that the people rose early, and built there an altar, and offered burnt-offerings and peace-offerings.

5And the children of Israel said, Who is there among all the tribes of Israel that came not up in the assembly unto Yahweh? For they had made a great oath concerning him that came not up unto Yahweh to Mizpah, saying, He shall surely be put to death.

6And the children of Israel repented them for Benjamin their brother, and said, There is one tribe cut off from Israel this day.

7How shall we do for wives for them that remain, seeing we have sworn by Yahweh that we will not give them of our daughters to wives?

8And they said, What one is there of the tribes of Israel that came not up unto Yahweh to Mizpah? And, behold, there came none to the camp from Jabesh-gilead to the assembly.

9For when the people were numbered, behold, there were none of the inhabitants of Jabesh-gilead there.

10And the congregation sent thither twelve thousand men of the valiantest, and commanded them, saying, Go and smite the inhabitants of Jabesh-gilead with the edge of the sword, with the women and the little ones.

11And this is the thing that ye shall do: ye shall utterly destroy every male, and every woman that hath lain by man.

12And they found among the inhabitants of Jabesh-gilead four hundred young virgins, that had not known man by lying with him; and they brought them unto the camp to Shiloh, which is in the land of Canaan.

13And the whole congregation sent and spake to the children of Benjamin that were in the rock of Rimmon, and proclaimed peace unto them.

14And Benjamin returned at that time; and they gave them the women whom they had saved alive of the women of Jabesh-gilead: and yet so they sufficed them not.

15And the people repented them for Benjamin, because that Yahweh had made a breach in the tribes of Israel.

16Then the elders of the congregation said, How shall we do for wives for them that remain, seeing the women are destroyed out of Benjamin?

17And they said, There must be an inheritance for them that are escaped of Benjamin, that a tribe be not blotted out from Israel.

18Howbeit we may not give them wives of our daughters, for the children of Israel had sworn, saying, Cursed be he that giveth a wife to Benjamin.

19And they said, Behold, there is a feast of Yahweh from year to year in Shiloh, which is on the north of Beth-el, on the east side of the highway that goeth up from Beth-el to Shechem, and on the south of Lebonah.

20And they commanded the children of Benjamin, saying, Go and lie in wait in the vineyards,

21and see, and, behold, if the daughters of Shiloh come out to dance in the dances, then come ye out of the vineyards, and catch you every man his wife of the daughters of Shiloh, and go to the land of Benjamin.

22And it shall be, when their fathers or their brethren come to complain unto us, that we will say unto them, Grant them graciously unto us, because we took not for each man of them his wife in battle, neither did ye give them unto them, else would ye now be guilty.

23And the children of Benjamin did so, and took them wives, according to their number, of them that danced, whom they carried off: and they went and returned unto their inheritance, and built the cities, and dwelt in them.

24And the children of Israel departed thence at that time, every man to his tribe and to his family, and they went out from thence every man to his inheritance.

25In those days there was no king in Israel: every man did that which was right in his own eyes.

The Book of Ruth

Chapter 1

1And it came to pass in the days when the judges judged, that there was a famine in the land. And a certain man of Bethlehem-judah went to sojourn in the country of Moab, he, and his wife, and his two sons.

2And the name of the man was Elimelech, and the name of his wife Naomi, and the name of his two sons Mahlon and Chilion, Ephrathites of Bethlehem-judah. And they came into the country of Moab, and continued there.

3And Elimelech, Naomi's husband, died; and she was left, and her two sons.

4And they took them wives of the women of Moab; the name of the one was Orpah, and the name of the other Ruth: and they dwelt there about ten years.

5And Mahlon and Chilion died both of them; and the woman was left of her two children and of her husband.

6Then she arose with her daughters-in-law, that she might return from the country of Moab: for she had heard in the country of Moab how that Yahweh had visited his people in giving them bread.

7And she went forth out of the place where she was, and her two daughters-in-law with her; and they went on the way to return unto the land of Judah.

8And Naomi said unto her two daughters-in-law, Go, return each of you to her mother's house: Yahweh deal kindly with you, as ye have dealt with the dead, and with me.

9Yahweh grant you that ye may find rest, each of you in the house of her husband. Then she kissed them, and they lifted up their voice, and wept.

10And they said unto her, Nay, but we will return with thee unto thy people.

11And Naomi said, Turn again, my daughters: why will ye go with me? have I yet sons in my womb, that they may be your husbands?

12Turn again, my daughters, go your way; for I am too old to have a husband. If I should say, I have hope, if I should even have a husband to-night, and should also bear sons;

13would ye therefore tarry till they were grown? would ye therefore stay from having husbands? nay, my daughters, for it grieveth me much for your sakes, for the hand of Yahweh is gone forth against me.

14And they lifted up their voice, and wept again: and Orpah kissed her mother-in-law, but Ruth clave unto her.

15And she said, Behold, thy sister-in-law is gone back unto her people, and unto her god: return thou after thy sister-in-law.

16And Ruth said, Entreat me not to leave thee, and to return from following after thee, for whither thou goest, I will go; and where thou lodgest, I will lodge; thy people shall be my people, and thy God my God;

17where thou diest, will I die, and there will I be buried: Yahweh do so to me, and more also, if aught but death part thee and me.

18And when she saw that she was stedfastly minded to go with her, she left off speaking unto her.

19So they two went until they came to Bethlehem. And it came to pass, when they were come to Bethlehem, that all the city was moved about them, and the women said, Is this Naomi?

20And she said unto them, Call me not Naomi, call me Mara; for the Almighty hath dealt very bitterly with me.

21I went out full, and Yahweh hath brought me home again empty; why call ye me Naomi, seeing Yahweh hath testified against me, and the Almighty hath afflicted me?

22So Naomi returned, and Ruth the Moabitess, her daughter-in-law, with her, who returned out of the country of Moab: and they came to Bethlehem in the beginning of barley harvest.

Chapter 2

1And Naomi had a kinsman of her husband's, a mighty man of wealth, of the family of Elimelech, and his name was Boaz.

2And Ruth the Moabitess said unto Naomi, Let me now go to the field, and glean among the ears of grain after him in whose sight I shall find favor. And she said unto her, Go, my daughter.

3And she went, and came and gleaned in the field after the reapers: and her hap was to light on the portion of the field belonging unto Boaz, who was of the family of Elimelech.

4And, behold, Boaz came from Bethlehem, and said unto the reapers, Yahweh be with you. And they answered him, Yahweh bless thee.

5Then said Boaz unto his servant that was set over the reapers, Whose damsel is this?

6And the servant that was set over the reapers answered and said, It is the Moabitish damsel that came back with Naomi out of the country of Moab:

7And she said, Let me glean, I pray you, and gather after the reapers among the sheaves. So she came, and hath continued even from the morning until now, save that she tarried a little in the house.

8Then said Boaz unto Ruth, Hearest thou not, my daughter? Go not to glean in another field, neither pass from hence, but abide here fast by my maidens.

9Let thine eyes be on the field that they do reap, and go thou after them: have I not charged the young men that they shall not touch thee? and when thou art athirst, go unto the vessels, and drink of that which the young men have drawn.

10Then she fell on her face, and bowed herself to the ground, and said unto him, Why have I found favor in thy sight, that thou shouldest take knowledge of me, seeing I am a foreigner?

11And Boaz answered and said unto her, It hath fully been showed me, all that thou hast done unto thy mother-in-law since the death of thy husband; and how thou hast left thy father and thy mother, and the land of thy nativity, and art come unto a people that thou knewest not heretofore.

12Yahweh recompense thy work, and a full reward be given thee of Yahweh, the God of Israel, under whose wings thou art come to take refuge.

13Then she said, Let me find favor in thy sight, my lord, for that thou hast comforted me, and for that thou hast spoken kindly unto thy handmaid, though I be not as one of thy handmaidens.

14And at meal-time Boaz said unto her, Come hither, and eat of the bread, and dip thy morsel in the vinegar. And she sat beside the reapers, and they reached her parched grain, and she did eat, and was sufficed, and left thereof.

15And when she was risen up to glean, Boaz commanded his young men, saying, Let her glean even among the sheaves, and reproach her not.

16And also pull out some for her from the bundles, and leave it, and let her glean, and rebuke her not.

17So she gleaned in the field until even; and she beat out that which she had gleaned, and it was about an ephah of barley.

18And she took it up, and went into the city; and her mother-in-law saw what she had gleaned: and she brought forth and gave to her that which she had left after she was sufficed.

19And her mother-in-law said unto her, Where hast thou gleaned to-day? and where hast thou wrought? blessed be he that did take knowledge of thee. And she showed her mother-in-law with whom she had wrought, and said, The man's name with whom I wrought to-day is Boaz.

20And Naomi said unto her daughter-in-law, Blessed be he of Yahweh, who hath not left off his kindness to the living and to the dead. And Naomi said unto her, The man is nigh of kin unto us, one of our near kinsmen.

21And Ruth the Moabitess said, Yea, he said unto me, Thou shalt keep fast by my young men, until they have ended all my harvest.

22And Naomi said unto Ruth her daughter-in-law, It is good, my daughter, that thou go out with his maidens, and that they meet thee not in any other field.

23So she kept fast by the maidens of Boaz, to glean unto the end of barley harvest and of wheat harvest; and she dwelt with her mother-in-law.

Chapter 3

1And Naomi her mother-in-law said unto her, My daughter, shall I not seek rest for thee, that it may be well with thee?

2And now is not Boaz our kinsman, with whose maidens thou wast? Behold, he winnoweth barley to-night in the threshing-floor.

3Wash thyself therefore, and anoint thee, and put thy raiment upon thee, and get thee down to the threshing-floor, but make not thyself known unto the man, until he shall have done eating and drinking.

4And it shall be, when he lieth down, that thou shalt mark the place where he shall lie, and thou shalt go in, and uncover his feet, and lay thee down; and he will tell thee what thou shalt do.

5And she said unto her, All that thou sayest I will do.

6And she went down unto the threshing-floor, and did according to all that her mother-in-law bade her.

7And when Boaz had eaten and drunk, and his heart was merry, he went to lie down at the end of the heap of grain: and she came softly, and uncovered his feet, and laid her down.

8And it came to pass at midnight, that the man was afraid, and turned himself; and, behold, a woman lay at his feet.

9And he said, Who art thou? And she answered, I am Ruth thy handmaid: spread therefore thy skirt over thy handmaid; for thou art a near kinsman.

10And he said, Blessed be thou of Yahweh, my daughter: thou hast showed more kindness in the latter end than at the beginning, inasmuch as thou followedst not young men, whether poor or rich.

11And now, my daughter, fear not; I will do to thee all that thou sayest; for all the city of my people doth know that thou art a worthy woman.

12And now it is true that I am a near kinsman; howbeit there is a kinsman nearer than I.

13Tarry this night, and it shall be in the morning, that if he will perform unto thee the part of a kinsman, well; let him do the kinsman's part: but if he will not do the part of a kinsman to thee, then will I do the part of a kinsman to thee, as Yahweh liveth: lie down until the morning.

14And she lay at his feet until the morning. And she rose up before one could discern another. For he said, Let it not be known that the woman came to the threshing-floor.

15And he said, Bring the mantle that is upon thee, and hold it; and she held it; and he measured six measures of barley, and laid it on her: and he went into the city.

16And when she came to her mother-in-law, she said, Who art thou, my daughter? And she told her all that the man had done to her.

17And she said, These six measures of barley gave he me; for he said, Go not empty unto thy mother-in-law.

18Then said she, Sit still, my daughter, until thou know how the matter will fall; for the man will not rest, until he have finished the thing this day.

Chapter 4

1Now Boaz went up to the gate, and sat him down there: and, behold, the near kinsman of whom Boaz spake came by; unto whom he said, Ho, such a one! turn aside, sit down here. And he turned aside, and sat down.

2And he took ten men of the elders of the city, and said, Sit ye down here. And they sat down.

3And he said unto the near kinsman, Naomi, that is come again out of the country of Moab, selleth the parcel of land, which was our brother Elimelech's:

4And I thought to disclose it unto thee, saying, Buy it before them that sit here, and before the elders of my people. If thou wilt redeem it, redeem it: but if

Ruth

thou wilt not redeem it, then tell me, that I may know; for there is none to redeem it besides thee; and I am after thee. And he said, I will redeem it.

5Then said Boaz, What day thou buyest the field of the hand of Naomi, thou must buy it also of Ruth the Moabitess, the wife of the dead, to raise up the name of the dead upon his inheritance.

6And the near kinsman said, I cannot redeem it for myself, lest I mar mine own inheritance: take thou my right of redemption on thee; for I cannot redeem it.

7Now this was the custom in former time in Israel concerning redeeming and concerning exchanging, to confirm all things: a man drew off his shoe, and gave it to his neighbor; and this was the manner of attestation in Israel.

8So the near kinsman said unto Boaz, Buy it for thyself. And he drew off his shoe.

9And Boaz said unto the elders, and unto all the people, Ye are witnesses this day, that I have bought all that was Elimelech's, and all that was Chilion's and Mahlon's, of the hand of Naomi.

10Moreover Ruth the Moabitess, the wife of Mahlon, have I purchased to be my wife, to raise up the name of the dead upon his inheritance, that the name of the dead be not cut off from among his brethren, and from the gate of his place: ye are witnesses this day.

11And all the people that were in the gate, and the elders, said, We are witnesses. Yahweh make the woman that is come into thy house like Rachel and like Leah, which two did build the house of Israel: and do thou worthily in Ephrathah, and be famous in Bethlehem:

12and let thy house be like the house of Perez, whom Tamar bare unto Judah, of the seed which Yahweh shall give thee of this young woman.

13So Boaz took Ruth, and she became his wife; and he went in unto her, and Yahweh gave her conception, and she bare a son.

14And the women said unto Naomi, Blessed be Yahweh, who hath not left thee this day without a near kinsman; and let his name be famous in Israel.

15And he shall be unto thee a restorer of life, and a nourisher of thine old age, for thy daughter-in-law, who loveth thee, who is better to thee than seven sons, hath borne him.

16And Naomi took the child, and laid it in her bosom, and became nurse unto it.

17And the women her neighbors gave it a name, saying, There is a son born to Naomi; and they called his name Obed: he is the father of Jesse, the father of David.

18Now these are the generations of Perez: Perez begat Hezron,

19and Hezron begat Ram, and Ram begat Amminadab,

20and Amminadab begat Nahshon, and Nahshon begat Salmon,

21and Salmon begat Boaz, and Boaz begat Obed,

22and Obed begat Jesse, and Jesse begat David.

The First Book of Samuel

Chapter 1

1 Now there was a certain man of Ramathaim-zophim, of the hill-country of Ephraim, and his name was Elkanah, the son of Jeroham, the son of Elihu, the son of Tohu, the son of Zuph, an Ephraimite:

2 and he had two wives; the name of the one was Hannah, and the name of other Peninnah: and Peninnah had children, but Hannah had no children.

3 And this man went up out of his city from year to year to worship and to sacrifice unto Yahweh of hosts in Shiloh. And the two sons of Eli, Hophni and Phinehas, priests unto Yahweh, were there.

4 And when the day came that Elkanah sacrificed, he gave to Peninnah his wife, and to all her sons and her daughters, portions:

5 but unto Hannah he gave a double portion; for he loved Hannah, but Yahweh had shut up her womb.

6 And her rival provoked her sore, to make her fret, because Yahweh had shut up her womb.

7 And as he did so year by year, when she went up to the house of Yahweh, so she provoked her; therefore she wept, and did not eat.

8 And Elkanah her husband said unto her, Hannah, why weepest thou? and why eatest thou not? and why is thy heart grieved? am not I better to thee than ten sons?

9 So Hannah rose up after they had eaten in Shiloh, and after they had drunk. Now Eli the priest was sitting upon his seat by the door-post of the temple of Yahweh.

10 And she was in bitterness of soul, and prayed unto Yahweh, and wept sore.

11 And she vowed a vow, and said, O Yahweh of hosts, if thou wilt indeed look on the affliction of thy handmaid, and remember me, and not forget thy handmaid, but wilt give unto thy handmaid a man-child, then I will give him unto Yahweh all the days of his life, and there shall no razor come upon his head.

12 And it came to pass, as she continued praying before Yahweh, that Eli marked her mouth.

13 Now Hannah, she spake in her heart; only her lips moved, but her voice was not heard: therefore Eli thought she had been drunken.

14 And Eli said unto her, How long wilt thou be drunken? put away thy wine from thee.

15 And Hannah answered and said, No, my lord, I am a woman of a sorrowful spirit: I have drunk neither wine nor strong drink, but I poured out my soul before Yahweh.

16 Count not thy handmaid for a wicked woman; for out of the abundance of my complaint and my provocation have I spoken hitherto.

17 Then Eli answered and said, Go in peace; and the God of Israel grant thy petition that thou hast asked of him.

18 And she said, Let thy handmaid find favor in thy sight. So the woman went her way, and did eat; and her countenance was no more sad.

19 And they rose up in the morning early, and worshipped before Yahweh, and returned, and came to their house to Ramah: and Elkanah knew Hannah his wife; and Yahweh remembered her.

20 And it came to pass, when the time was come about, that Hannah conceived, and bare a son; and she called his name Samuel, saying, Because I have asked him of Yahweh.

21 And the man Elkanah, and all his house, went up to offer unto Yahweh the yearly sacrifice, and his vow.

22 But Hannah went not up; for she said unto her husband, I will not go up until the child be weaned; and then I will bring him, that he may appear before Yahweh, and there abide for ever.

23 And Elkanah her husband said unto her, Do what seemeth thee good; tarry until thou have weaned him; only Yahweh establish his word. So the woman tarried and gave her son suck, until she weaned him.

24 And when she had weaned him, she took him up with her, with three bullocks, and one ephah of meal, and a bottle of wine, and brought him unto the house of Yahweh in Shiloh: and the child was young.

25 And they slew the bullock, and brought the child to Eli.

26 And she said, Oh, my lord, as thy soul liveth, my lord, I am the woman that stood by thee here, praying unto Yahweh.

27 For this child I prayed; and Yahweh hath given me my petition which I asked of him:

28 therefore also I have granted him to Yahweh; as long as he liveth he is granted to Yahweh. And he worshipped Yahweh there.

Chapter 2

1 And Hannah prayed, and said:
My heart exulteth in Yahweh;
My horn is exalted in Yahweh;
My mouth is enlarged over mine enemies;
Because I rejoice in thy salvation.
2 There is none holy as Yahweh;
For there is none besides thee,
Neither is there any rock like our God.
3 Talk no more so exceeding proudly;
Let not arrogancy come out of your mouth;
For Yahweh is a God of knowledge,
And by him actions are weighed.
4 The bows of the mighty men are broken;
And they that stumbled are girded with strength.
5 They that were full have hired out themselves for bread;
And they that were hungry have ceased to hunger:
Yea, the barren hath borne seven;
And she that hath many children languisheth.
6 Yahweh killeth, and maketh alive:
He bringeth down to Sheol, and bringeth up.
7 Yahweh maketh poor, and maketh rich:
He bringeth low, he also lifteth up.
8 He raiseth up the poor out of the dust,
He lifteth up the needy from the dunghill,
To make them sit with princes,
And inherit the throne of glory:
For the pillars of the earth are Yahweh's,
And he hath set the world upon them.
9 He will keep the feet of his holy ones;
But the wicked shall be put to silence in darkness;
For by strength shall no man prevail.
10 They that strive with Yahweh shall be broken to pieces;
Against them will he thunder in heaven:
Yahweh will judge the ends of the earth;
And he will give strength unto his king,
And exalt the horn of his anointed.

11 And Elkanah went to Ramah to his house. And the child did minister unto Yahweh before Eli the priest.

12 Now the sons of Eli were base men; they knew not Yahweh.

13 And the custom of the priests with the people was, that, when any man offered sacrifice, the priest's servant came, while the flesh was boiling, with a flesh-hook of three teeth in his hand;

14 and he struck it into the pan, or kettle, or caldron, or pot; all that the flesh-hook brought up the priest took therewith. So they did in Shiloh unto all the Israelites that came thither.

15 Yea, before they burnt the fat, the priest's servant came, and said to the man that sacrificed, Give flesh to roast for the priest; for he will not have boiled flesh of thee, but raw.

16 And if the man said unto him, They will surely burn the fat first, and then take as much as thy soul desireth; then he would say, Nay, but thou shalt give it me now: and if not, I will take it by force.

17 And the sin of the young men was very great before Yahweh; for the men despised the offering of Yahweh.

18 But Samuel ministered before Yahweh, being a child, girded with a linen ephod.

19 Moreover his mother made him a little robe, and brought it to him from year to year, when she came up with her husband to offer the yearly sacrifice.

20 And Eli blessed Elkanah and his wife, and said, Yahweh give thee seed of this woman for the petition which was asked of Yahweh. And they went unto their own home.

21 And Yahweh visited Hannah, and she conceived, and bare three sons and two daughters. And the child Samuel grew before Yahweh.

22 Now Eli was very old; and he heard all that his sons did unto all Israel, and how that they lay with the women that did service at the door of the tent of meeting.

23 And he said unto them, Why do ye such things? for I hear of your evil dealings from all this people.

24 Nay, my sons; for it is no good report that I hear: ye make Yahweh's people to transgress.

25 If one man sin against another, God shall judge him; but if a man sin against Yahweh, who shall entreat for him? Notwithstanding, they hearkened not unto the voice of their father, because Yahweh was minded to slay them.

26 And the child Samuel grew on, and increased in favor both with Yahweh, and also with men.

27 And there came a man of God unto Eli, and said unto him, Thus saith Yahweh, Did I reveal myself unto the house of thy father, when they were in Egypt in bondage to Pharaoh's house?

28 and did I choose him out of all the tribes of Israel to be my priest, to go up unto mine altar, to burn incense, to wear an ephod before me? and did I give unto the house of thy father all the offerings of the children of Israel made by fire?

29 Wherefore kick ye at my sacrifice and at mine offering, which I have commanded in my habitation, and honorest thy sons above me, to make yourselves fat with the chiefest of all the offerings of Israel my people?

30 Therefore Yahweh, the God of Israel, saith, I said indeed that thy house, and the house of thy father, should walk before me for ever: but now Yahweh saith, Be it far from me; for them that honor me I will honor, and they that despise me shall be lightly esteemed.

31 Behold, the days come, that I will cut off thine arm, and the arm of thy father's house, that there shall not be an old man in thy house.

32 And thou shalt behold the affliction of my habitation, in all the wealth which God shall give Israel; and there shall not be an old man in thy house for ever.

33 And the man of thine, whom I shall not cut off from mine altar, shall be to consume thine eyes, and to grieve thy heart; and all the increase of thy house shall die in the flower of their age.

34 And this shall be the sign unto thee, that shall come upon thy two sons, on Hophni and Phinehas: in one day they shall die both of them.

35 And I will raise me up a faithful priest, that shall do according to that which is in my heart and in my mind: and I will build him a sure house; and he shall walk before mine anointed for ever.

36 And it shall come to pass, that every one that is left in thy house shall

First Samuel

come and bow down to him for a piece of silver and a loaf of bread, and shall say, Put me, I pray thee, into one of the priests' offices, that I may eat a morsel of bread.

Chapter 3

1And the child Samuel ministered unto Yahweh before Eli. And the word of Yahweh was precious in those days; there was no frequent vision.

2And it came to pass at that time, when Eli was laid down in his place (now his eyes had begun to wax dim, so that he could not see),

3and the lamp of God was not yet gone out, and Samuel was laid down to sleep, in the temple of Yahweh, where the ark of God was;

4that Yahweh called Samuel; and he said, Here am I.

5And he ran unto Eli, and said, Here am I; for thou calledst me. And he said, I called not; lie down again. And he went and lay down.

6And Yahweh called yet again, Samuel. And Samuel arose and went to Eli, and said, Here am I; for thou calledst me. And he answered, I called not, my son; lie down again.

7Now Samuel did not yet know Yahweh, neither was the word of Yahweh yet revealed unto him.

8And Yahweh called Samuel again the third time. And he arose and went to Eli, and said, Here am I; for thou calledst me. And Eli perceived that Yahweh had called the child.

9Therefore Eli said unto Samuel, Go, lie down: and it shall be, if he call thee, that thou shalt say, Speak, Yahweh; for thy servant heareth. So Samuel went and lay down in his place.

10And Yahweh came, and stood, and called as at other times, Samuel, Samuel. Then Samuel said, Speak; for thy servant heareth.

11And Yahweh said to Samuel, Behold, I will do a thing in Israel, at which both the ears of every one that heareth it shall tingle.

12In that day I will perform against Eli all that I have spoken concerning his house, from the beginning even unto the end.

13For I have told him that I will judge his house for ever, for the iniquity which he knew, because his sons did bring a curse upon themselves, and he restrained them not.

14And therefore I have sworn unto the house of Eli, that the iniquity of Eli's house shall not be expiated with sacrifice nor offering for ever.

15And Samuel lay until the morning, and opened the doors of the house of Yahweh. And Samuel feared to show Eli the vision.

16Then Eli called Samuel, and said, Samuel, my son. And he said, Here am I.

17And he said, What is the thing that Yahweh hath spoken unto thee? I pray thee, hide it not from me: God do so to thee, and more also, if thou hide anything from me of all the things that he spake unto thee.

18And Samuel told him every whit, and hid nothing from him. And he said, It is Yahweh: let him do what seemeth him good.

19And Samuel grew, and Yahweh was with him, and did let none of his words fall to the ground.

20And all Israel from Dan even to Beer-sheba knew that Samuel was established to be a prophet of Yahweh.

21And Yahweh appeared again in Shiloh; for Yahweh revealed himself to Samuel in Shiloh by the word of Yahweh.

Chapter 4

1And the word of Samuel came to all Israel.

Now Israel went out against the Philistines to battle, and encamped beside Eben-ezer: and the Philistines encamped in Aphek.

2And the Philistines put themselves in array against Israel: and when they joined battle, Israel was smitten before the Philistines; and they slew of the army in the field about four thousand men.

3And when the people were come into the camp, the elders of Israel said, Wherefore hath Yahweh smitten us to-day before the Philistines? Let us fetch the ark of the covenant of Yahweh out of Shiloh unto us, that it may come among us, and save us out of the hand of our enemies.

4So the people sent to Shiloh; and they brought from thence the ark of the covenant of Yahweh of hosts, who sitteth above the cherubim: and the two sons of Eli, Hophni and Phinehas, were there with the ark of the covenant of God.

5And when the ark of the covenant of Yahweh came into the camp, all Israel shouted with a great shout, so that the earth rang again.

6And when the Philistines heard the noise of the shout, they said, What meaneth the noise of this great shout in the camp of the Hebrews? And they understood that the ark of Yahweh was come into the camp.

7And the Philistines were afraid, for they said, God is come into the camp. And they said, Woe unto us! for there hath not been such a thing heretofore.

8Woe unto us! who shall deliver us out of the hand of these mighty gods? these are the gods that smote the Egyptians with all manner of plagues in the wilderness.

9Be strong, and quit yourselves like men, O ye Philistines, that ye be not servants unto the Hebrews, as they have been to you: quit yourselves like men, and fight.

10And the Philistines fought, and Israel was smitten, and they fled every man to his tent: and there was a very great slaughter; for there fell of Israel thirty thousand footmen.

11And the ark of God was taken; and the two sons of Eli, Hophni and Phinehas, were slain.

12And there ran a man of Benjamin out of the army, and came to Shiloh the same day, with his clothes rent, and with earth upon his head.

13And when he came, lo, Eli was sitting upon his seat by the wayside watching; for his heart trembled for the ark of God. And when the man came into the city, and told it, all the city cried out.

14And when Eli heard the noise of the crying, he said, What meaneth the noise of this tumult? And the man hasted, and came and told Eli.

15Now Eli was ninety and eight years old; and his eyes were set, so that he could not see.

16And the man said unto Eli, I am he that came out of the army, and I fled to-day out of the army. And he said, How went the matter, my son?

17And he that brought the tidings answered and said, Israel is fled before the Philistines, and there hath been also a great slaughter among the people, and thy two sons also, Hophni and Phinehas, are dead, and the ark of God is taken.

18And it came to pass, when he made mention of the ark of God, that Eli feel from off his seat backward by the side of the gate; and his neck brake, and he died: for he was an old man, and heavy. And he had judged Israel forty years.

19And his daughter-in-law, Phinehas' wife, was with child, near to be delivered: and when she heard the tidings that the ark of God was taken, and that her father-in-law and her husband were dead, she bowed herself and brought forth; for her pains came upon her.

20And about the time of her death the women that stood by her said unto her, Fear not; for thou hast brought forth a son. But she answered not, neither did she regard it.

21And she named the child Ichabod, saying, The glory is departed from Israel; because the ark of God was taken, and because of her father-in-law and her husband.

22And she said, The glory is departed from Israel; for the ark of God is taken.

Chapter 5

1Now the Philistines had taken the ark of God, and they brought it from Eben-ezer unto Ashdod.

2And the Philistines took the ark of God, and brought it into the house of Dagon, and set it by Dagon.

3And when they of Ashdod arose early on the morrow, behold, Dagon was fallen upon his face to the ground before the ark of Yahweh. And they took Dagon, and set him in his place again.

4And when they arose early on the morrow morning, behold, Dagon was fallen upon his face to the ground before the ark of Yahweh; and the head of Dagon and both the palms of his hands lay cut off upon the threshold; only the stump of Dagon was left to him.

5Therefore neither the priests of Dagon, nor any that come into Dagon's house, tread on the threshold of Dagon in Ashdod, unto this day.

6But the hand of Yahweh was heavy upon them of Ashdod, and he destroyed them, and smote them with tumors, even Ashdod and the borders thereof.

7And when the men of Ashdod saw that it was so, they said, The ark of the God of Israel shall not abide with us; for his hand is sore upon us, and upon Dagon our god.

8They sent therefore and gathered all the lords of the Philistines unto them, and said, What shall we do with the ark of the God of Israel? And they answered, Let the ark of the God of Israel be carried about unto Gath. And they carried the ark of the God of Israel thither.

9And it was so, that, after they had carried it about, the hand of Yahweh was against the city with a very great discomfiture: and he smote the men of the city, both small and great; and tumors brake out upon them.

10So they sent the ark of God to Ekron. And it came to pass, as the ark of God came to Ekron, that the Ekronites cried out, saying, They have brought about the ark of the God of Israel to us, to slay us and our people.

11They sent therefore and gathered together all the lords of the Philistines, and they said, Send away the ark of the God of Israel, and let it go again to its own place, that is slay us not, and our people. For there was a deadly discomfiture throughout all the city; the hand of God was very heavy there.

12And the men that died not were smitten with the tumors; and the cry of the city went up to heaven.

Chapter 6

1And the ark of Yahweh was in the country of the Philistines seven months.

2And the Philistines called for the priests and the diviners, saying, What shall we do with the ark of Yahweh? show us wherewith we shall sent it to its place.

3And they said, If ye send away the ark of the God of Israel, send it not empty; but by all means return him a trespass-offering: then ye shall be healed, and it shall be known to you why his hand is not removed from you.

4Then said they, What shall be the trespass-offering which we shall return to him? And they said, Five golden tumors, and five golden mice, according to the number of the lords of the Philistines; for one plague was on you all, and on your lords.

5Wherefore ye shall make images of your tumors, and images of your mice that mar the land; and ye shall give glory unto the God of Israel: peradventure he will lighten his hand from off you, and from off your gods, and from off your land.

6Wherefore then do ye harden your hearts, as the Egyptians and Pharaoh hardened their hearts? When he had wrought wonderfully among them, did they not let the people go, and they departed?

7Now therefore take and prepare you a new cart, and two milch kine, on which there hath come no yoke, and tie the kine to the cart, and bring their calves home from them;

8and take the ark of Yahweh, and lay it upon the cart; and put the jewels of gold, which ye return him for a trespass-offering, in a coffer by the side thereof; and send it away, that it may go.

9And see; if it goeth up by the way of its own border to Beth-shemesh, then he hath done us this great evil: but if not, then we shall know that it is not his hand that smote us; it was a chance that happened to us.

10And the men did so, and took two milch kine, and tied them to the cart, and shut up their calves at home;

11and they put the ark of Yahweh upon the cart, and the coffer with the mice of gold and the images of their tumors.

12And the kine took the straight way by the way to Beth-shemesh; they went along the highway, lowing as they went, and turned not aside to the right hand or to the left; and the lords of the Philistines went after them unto the border of Beth-shemesh.

13And they of Beth-shemesh were reaping their wheat harvest in the valley; and they lifted up their eyes, and saw the ark, and rejoiced to see it.

14And the cart came into the field of Joshua the Beth-shemite, and stood there, where there was a great stone: and they clave the wood of the cart, and offered up the kine for a burnt-offering unto Yahweh.

15And the Levites took down the ark of Yahweh, and the coffer that was with it, wherein the jewels of gold were, and put them on the great stone: and the men of Beth-shemesh offered burnt-offerings and sacrificed sacrifices the same day unto Yahweh.

16And when the five lords of the Philistines had seen it, they returned to Ekron the same day.

17And these are the golden tumors which the Philistines returned for a trespass-offering unto Yahweh: for Ashdod one, for Gaza one, for Ashkelon one, for Gath one, for Ekron one;

18and the golden mice, according to the number of all the cities of the Philistines belonging to the five lords, both of fortified cities and of country villages, even unto the great stone, whereon they set down the ark of Yahweh, which stone remaineth unto this day in the field of Joshua the Beth-shemite.

19And he smote of the men of Beth-shemesh, because they had looked into the ark of Yahweh, he smote of the people seventy men, and fifty thousand men; and the people mourned, because Yahweh had smitten the people with a great slaughter.

20And the men of Beth-shemesh said, Who is able to stand before Yahweh, this holy God? and to whom shall he go up from us?

21And they sent messengers to the inhabitants of Kiriath-jearim, saying, The Philistines have brought back the ark of Yahweh; come ye down, and fetch it up to you.

Chapter 7

1And the men of Kiriath-jearim came, and fetched up the ark of Yahweh, and brought it into the house of Abinadab in the hill, and sanctified Eleazar his son to keep the ark of Yahweh.

2And it came to pass, from the day that the ark abode in Kiriath-jearim, that the time was long; for it was twenty years: and all the house of Israel lamented after Yahweh.

3And Samuel spake unto all the house of Israel, saying, If ye do return unto Yahweh with all your heart, then put away the foreign gods and the Ashtaroth from among you, and direct your hearts unto Yahweh, and serve him only; and he will deliver you out of the hand of the Philistines.

4Then the children of Israel did put away the Baalim and the Ashtaroth, and served Yahweh only.

5And Samuel said, Gather all Israel to Mizpah, and I will pray for you unto Yahweh.

6And they gathered together to Mizpah, and drew water, and poured it out before Yahweh, and fasted on that day, and said there, We have sinned against Yahweh. And Samuel judged the children of Israel in Mizpah.

7And when the Philistines heard that the children of Israel were gathered together to Mizpah, the lords of the Philistines went up against Israel. And when the children of Israel heard it, they were afraid of the Philistines.

8And the children of Israel said to Samuel, Cease not to cry unto Yahweh our God for us, that he will save us out of the hand of the Philistines.

9And Samuel took a sucking lamb, and offered it for a whole burnt-offering unto Yahweh: and Samuel cried unto Yahweh for Israel; and Yahweh answered him.

10And as Samuel was offering up the burnt-offering, the Philistines drew near to battle against Israel; but Yahweh thundered with a great thunder on that day upon the Philistines, and discomfited them; and they were smitten down before Israel.

11And the men of Israel went out of Mizpah, and pursued the Philistines, and smote them, until they came under Beth-car.

12Then Samuel took a stone, and set it between Mizpah and Shen, and called the name of it Eben-ezer, saying, Hitherto hath Yahweh helped us.

13So the Philistines were subdued, and they came no more within the border of Israel: and the hand of Yahweh was against the Philistines all the days of Samuel.

14And the cities which the Philistines had taken from Israel were restored to Israel, from Ekron even unto Gath: and the border thereof did Israel deliver out of the hand of the Philistines. And there was peace between Israel and the Amorites.

15And Samuel judged Israel all the days of his life.

16And he went from year to year in circuit to Beth-el and Gilgal, and Mizpah; and he judged Israel in all those places.

17And his return was to Ramah, for there was his house; and there he judged Israel: and he built there an altar unto Yahweh.

Chapter 8

1And it came to pass, when Samuel was old, that he made his sons judges over Israel.

2Now the name of his first-born was Joel; and the name of his second, Abijah: they were judges in Beer-sheba.

3And his sons walked not in his ways, but turned aside after lucre, and took bribes, and perverted justice.

4Then all the elders of Israel gathered themselves together, and came to Samuel unto Ramah;

5and they said unto him, Behold, thou art old, and thy sons walk not in thy ways: now make us a king to judge us like all the nations.

6But the thing displeased Samuel, when they said, Give us a king to judge us. And Samuel prayed unto Yahweh.

7And Yahweh said unto Samuel, Hearken unto the voice of the people in all that they say unto thee; for they have not rejected thee, but they have rejected me, that I should not be king over them.

8According to all the works which they have done since the day that I brought them up out of Egypt even unto this day, in that they have forsaken me, and served other gods, so do they also unto thee.

9Now therefore hearken unto their voice: howbeit thou shalt protest solemnly unto them, and shalt show them the manner of the king that shall reign over them.

10And Samuel told all the words of Yahweh unto the people that asked of him a king.

11And he said, This will be the manner of the king that shall reign over you: he will take your sons, and appoint them unto him, for his chariots, and to be his horsemen; and they shall run before his chariots;

12and he will appoint them unto him for captains of thousands, and captains of fifties; and he will set some to plow his ground, and to reap his harvest, and to make his instruments of war, and the instruments of his chariots.

13And he will take your daughters to be perfumers, and to be cooks, and to be bakers.

14And he will take your fields, and your vineyards, and your oliveyards, even the best of them, and give them to his servants.

15And he will take the tenth of your seed, and of your vineyards, and give to his officers, and to his servants.

16And he will take your men-servants, and your maid-servants, and your goodliest young men, and your asses, and put them to his work.

17He will take the tenth of your flocks: and ye shall be his servants.

18And ye shall cry out in that day because of your king whom ye shall have chosen you; and Yahweh will not answer you in that day.

19But the people refused to hearken unto the voice of Samuel; and they said, Nay: but we will have a king over us,

20that we also may be like all the nations, and that our king may judge us, and go out before us, and fight our battles.

21And Samuel heard all the words of the people, and he rehearsed them in the ears of Yahweh.

22And Yahweh said to Samuel, Hearken unto their voice, and make them a king. And Samuel said unto the men of Israel, Go ye every man unto his city.

Chapter 9

1Now there was a man of Benjamin, whose name was Kish, the son of Abiel, the son of Zeror, the son of Becorath, the son of Aphiah, the son of a Benjamite, a mighty man of valor.

2And he had a son, whose name was Saul, a young man and a goodly: and there was not among the children of Israel a goodlier person than he: from his shoulders and upward he was higher than any of the people.

3And the asses of Kish, Saul's father, were lost. And Kish said to Saul his son, Take now one of the servants with thee, and arise, go seek the asses.

4And he passed through the hill-country of Ephraim, and passed through the land of Shalishah, but they found them not: then they passed through the land of Shaalim, and there they were not: and he passed through the land of the Benjamites, but they found them not.

5When they were come to the land of Zuph, Saul said to his servant that was with him, Come, and let us return, lest my father leave off caring for the asses, and be anxious for us.

6And he said unto him, Behold now, there is in this city a man of God, and he is a man that is held in honor; all that he saith cometh surely to pass: now let us go thither; peradventure he can tell us concerning our journey whereon we go.

7Then said Saul to his servant, But, behold, if we go, what shall we bring the man? for the bread is spent in our vessels, and there is not a present to bring to the man of God: what have we?

8And the servant answered Saul again, and said, Behold, I have in my hand the fourth part of a shekel of silver: that will I give to the man of God, to tell us our way.

9(Beforetime in Israel, when a man went to inquire of God, thus he said, Come, and let us go to the seer; for he that is now called a Prophet was beforetime called a Seer.)

10Then said Saul to his servant, Well said; come, let us go. So they went unto the city where the man of God was.

11As they went up the ascent to the city, they found young maidens going out to draw water, and said unto them, Is the seer here?

12And they answered them, and said, He is; behold, he is before thee: make haste now, for he is come to-day into the city; for the people have a sacrifice to-day in the high place:

13as soon as ye are come into the city, ye shall straightway find him, before he goeth up to the high place to eat; for the people will not eat until he come, because he doth bless the sacrifice; and afterwards they eat that are bidden. Now

First Samuel

therefore get you up; for at this time ye shall find him.

14 And they went up to the city; and as they came within the city, behold, Samuel came out toward them, to go up to the high place.

15 Now Yahweh had revealed unto Samuel a day before Saul came, saying,

16 To-morrow about this time I will send thee a man out of the land of Benjamin, and thou shalt anoint him to be prince over my people Israel; and he shall save my people out of the hand of the Philistines: for I have looked upon my people, because their cry is come unto me.

17 And when Samuel saw Saul, Yahweh said unto him, Behold, the man of whom I spake to thee! this same shall have authority over my people.

18 Then Saul drew near to Samuel in the gate, and said, Tell me, I pray thee, where the seer's house is.

19 And Samuel answered Saul, and said, I am the seer; go up before me unto the high place, for ye shall eat with me to-day: and in the morning I will let thee go, and will tell thee all that is in thy heart.

20 And as for thine asses that were lost three days ago, set not they mind on them; for they are found. And for whom is all that is desirable in Israel? Is it not for thee, and for all thy father's house?

21 And Saul answered and said, Am not I a Benjamite, of the smallest of the tribes of Israel? and my family the least of all the families of the tribe of Benjamin? wherefore then speakest thou to me after this manner?

22 And Samuel took Saul and his servant, and brought them into the guest-chamber, and made them sit in the chiefest place among them that were bidden, who were about thirty persons.

23 And Samuel said unto the cook, Bring the portion which I gave thee, of which I said unto thee, Set it by thee.

24 And the cook took up the thigh, and that which was upon it, and set it before Saul. And Samuel said, Behold, that which hath been reserved! set it before thee and eat; because unto the appointed time hath it been kept for thee, for I said, I have invited the people. So Saul did eat with Samuel that day.

25 And when they were come down from the high place into the city, he communed with Saul upon the housetop.

26 And they arose early: and it came to pass about the spring of the day, that Samuel called to Saul on the housetop, saying, Up, that I may send thee away. And Saul arose, and they went out both of them, he and Samuel, abroad.

27 As they were going down at the end of the city, Samuel said to Saul, Bid the servant pass on before us (and he passed on), but stand thou still first, that I may cause thee to hear the word of God.

Chapter 10

1 Then Samuel took the vial of oil, and poured it upon his head, and kissed him, and said, Is it not that Yahweh hath anointed thee to be prince over his inheritance?

2 When thou art departed from me to-day, then thou shalt find two men by Rachel's sepulchre, in the border of Benjamin at Zelzah; and they will say unto thee, The asses which thou wentest to seek are found; and, lo, thy father hath left off caring for the asses, and is anxious for you, saying, What shall I do for my son?

3 Then shalt thou go on forward from thence, and thou shalt come to the oak of Tabor; and there shall meet thee there three men going up to God to Beth-el, one carrying three kids, and another carrying three loaves of bread, and another carrying a bottle of wine:

4 and they will salute thee, and give thee two loaves of bread, which thou shalt receive of their hand.

5 After that thou shalt come to the hill of God, where is the garrison of the Philistines: and it shall come to pass, when thou art come thither to the city, that thou shalt meet a band of prophets coming down from the high place with a psaltery, and a timbrel, and a pipe, and a harp, before them; and they will be prophesying:

6 and the Spirit of Yahweh will come mightily upon thee, and thou shalt prophesy with them, and shalt be turned into another man.

7 And let it be, when these signs are come unto thee, that thou do as occasion shall serve thee; for God is with thee.

8 And thou shalt go down before me to Gilgal; and, behold, I will come down unto thee, to offer burnt-offerings, and to sacrifice sacrifices of peace-offerings: seven days shalt thou tarry, till I come unto thee, and show thee what thou shalt do.

9 And it was so, that, when he had turned his back to go from Samuel, God gave him another heart: and all those signs came to pass that day.

10 And when they came thither to the hill, behold, a band of prophets met him; and the Spirit of God came mightily upon him, and he prophesied among them.

11 And it came to pass, when all that knew him beforetime saw that, behold, he prophesied with the prophets, then the people said one to another, What is this that is come unto the son of Kish? Is Saul also among the prophets?

12 And one of the same place answered and said, And who is their father? Therefore it became a proverb, Is Saul also among the prophets?

13 And when he had made an end of prophesying, he came to the high place.

14 And Saul's uncle said unto him and to his servant, Whither went ye? And he said, To seek the asses; and when we saw that they were not found, we came to Samuel.

15 And Saul's uncle said, Tell me, I pray thee, what Samuel said unto you.

16 And Saul said unto his uncle, He told us plainly that the asses were found. But concerning the matter of the kingdom, whereof Samuel spake, he told him not.

17 And Samuel called the people together unto Yahweh to Mizpah;

18 and he said unto the children of Israel, Thus saith Yahweh, the God of Israel, I brought up Israel out of Egypt, and I delivered you out of the hand of the Egyptians, and out of the hand of all the kingdoms that oppressed you:

19 but ye have this day rejected your God, who himself saveth you out of all your calamities and your distresses; and ye have said unto him, Nay, but set a king over us. Now therefore present yourselves before Yahweh by your tribes, and by your thousands.

20 So Samuel brought all the tribes of Israel near, and the tribe of Benjamin was taken.

21 And he brought the tribe of Benjamin near by their families; and the family of the Matrites was taken; and Saul the son of Kish was taken: but when they sought him, he could not be found.

22 Therefore they asked of Yahweh further, Is there yet a man to come hither? And Yahweh answered, Behold, he hath hid himself among the baggage.

23 And they ran and fetched him thence; and when he stood among the people, he was higher than any of the people from his shoulders and upward.

24 And Samuel said to all the people, See ye him whom Yahweh hath chosen, that there is none like him along all the people? And all the people shouted, and said, Long live the king.

25 Then Samuel told the people the manner of the kingdom, and wrote it in a book, and laid it up before Yahweh. And Samuel sent all the people away, every man to his house.

26 And Saul also went to his house to Gibeah; and there went with him the host, whose hearts God had touched.

27 But certain worthless fellows said, How shall this man save us? And they despised him, and brought him no present. But he held his peace.

Chapter 11

1 Then Nahash the Ammonite came up, and encamped against Jabesh-gilead: and all the men of Jabesh said unto Nahash, Make a covenant with us, and we will serve thee.

2 And Nahash the Ammonite said unto them, On this condition will I make it with you, that all your right eyes be put out; and I will lay it for a reproach upon all Israel.

3 And the elders of Jabesh said unto him, Give us seven days' respite, that we may send messengers unto all the borders of Israel; and then, if there be none to save us, we will come out to thee.

4 Then came the messengers to Gibeah of Saul, and spake these words in the ears of the people: and all the people lifted up their voice, and wept.

5 And, behold, Saul came following the oxen out of the field; and Saul said, What aileth the people that they weep? And they told him the words of the men of Jabesh.

6 And the Spirit of God came mightily upon Saul when he heard those words, and his anger was kindled greatly.

7 And he took a yoke of oxen, and cut them in pieces, and sent them throughout all the borders of Israel by the hand of messengers, saying, Whosoever cometh not forth after Saul and after Samuel, so shall it be done unto his oxen. And the dread of Yahweh fell on the people, and they came out as one man.

8 And he numbered them in Bezek; and the children of Israel were three hundred thousand, and the men of Judah thirty thousand.

9 And they said unto the messengers that came, Thus shall ye say unto the men of Jabesh-gilead, To-morrow, by the time the sun is hot, ye shall have deliverance. And the messengers came and told the men of Jabesh; and they were glad.

10 Therefore the men of Jabesh said, To-morrow we will come out unto you, and ye shall do with us all that seemeth good unto you.

11 And it was so on the morrow, that Saul put the people in three companies; and they came into the midst of the camp in the morning watch, and smote the Ammonites until the heat of the day: and it came to pass, that they that remained were scattered, so that not two of them were left together.

12 And the people said unto Samuel, Who is he that said, Shall Saul reign over us? bring the men, that we may put them to death.

13 And Saul said, There shall not a man be put to death this day; for to-day Yahweh hath wrought deliverance in Israel.

14 Then said Samuel to the people, Come, and let us go to Gilgal, and renew the kingdom there.

15 And all the people went to Gilgal; and there they made Saul king before Yahweh in Gilgal; and there they offered sacrifices of peace-offerings before Yahweh; and there Saul and all the men of Israel rejoiced greatly.

Chapter 12

1 And Samuel said unto all Israel, Behold, I have hearkened unto your voice in all that ye said unto me, and have made a king over you.

2 And now, behold, the king walketh before you; and I am old and grayheaded; and, behold, my sons are with you: and I have walked before you from my youth unto this day.

3 Here I am: witness against me before Yahweh, and before his anointed: whose ox have I taken? or whose ass have I taken? or whom have I defrauded? whom have I oppressed? or of whose hand have I taken a ransom to blind mine eyes therewith? and I will restore it you.

4 And they said, Thou hast not defrauded us, nor oppressed us, neither hast thou taken aught of any man's hand.

5 And he said unto them, Yahweh is witness against you, and his anointed is witness this day, that ye have not found aught in my hand. And they said, He is witness.

6 And Samuel said unto the people, It is Yahweh that appointed Moses and Aaron, and that brought your fathers up out of the land of Egypt.

7 Now therefore stand still, that I may plead with you before Yahweh concerning all the righteous acts of Yahweh, which he did to you and to your fathers.

8 When Jacob was come into Egypt, and your fathers cried unto Yahweh, then Yahweh sent Moses and Aaron, who brought forth your fathers out of Egypt,

and made them to dwell in this place.

9But they forgat Yahweh their God; and he sold them into the hand of Sisera, captain of the host of Hazor, and into the hand of the Philistines, and into the hand of the king of Moab; and they fought against them.

10And they cried unto Yahweh, and said, We have sinned, because we have forsaken Yahweh, and have served the Baalim and the Ashtaroth: but now deliver us out of the hand of our enemies, and we will serve thee.

11And Yahweh sent Jerubbaal, and Bedan, and Jephthah, and Samuel, and delivered you out of the hand of your enemies on every side; and ye dwelt in safety.

12And when ye saw that Nahash the king of the children of Ammon came against you, ye said unto me, Nay, but a king shall reign over us; when Yahweh your God was your king.

13Now therefore behold the king whom ye have chosen, and whom ye have asked for: and, behold, Yahweh hath set a king over you.

14If ye will fear Yahweh, and serve him, and hearken unto his voice, and not rebel against the commandment of Yahweh, and both ye and also the king that reigneth over you be followers of Yahweh your God, well:

15but if ye will not hearken unto the voice of Yahweh, but rebel against the commandment of Yahweh, then will the hand of Yahweh be against you, as it was against your fathers.

16Now therefore stand still and see this great thing, which Yahweh will do before your eyes.

17Is it not wheat harvest to-day? I will call unto Yahweh, that he may send thunder and rain; and ye shall know and see that your wickedness is great, which ye have done in the sight of Yahweh, in asking you a king.

18So Samuel called unto Yahweh; and Yahweh sent thunder and rain that day: and all the people greatly feared Yahweh and Samuel.

19And all the people said unto Samuel, Pray for thy servants unto Yahweh thy God, that we die not; for we have added unto all our sins this evil, to ask us a king.

20And Samuel said unto the people, Fear not; ye have indeed done all this evil; yet turn not aside from following Yahweh, but serve Yahweh with all your heart;

21and turn ye not aside; for then would ye go after vain things which cannot profit nor deliver, for they are vain.

22For Yahweh will not forsake his people for his great name's sake, because it hath pleased Yahweh to make you a people unto himself.

23Moreover as for me, far be it from me that I should sin against Yahweh in ceasing to pray for you: but I will instruct you in the good and the right way.

24Only fear Yahweh, and serve him in truth with all your heart; for consider how great things he hath done for you.

25But if ye shall still do wickedly, ye shall be consumed, both ye and your king.

Chapter 13

1Saul was forty years old when he began to reign; and when he had reigned two years over Israel,

2Saul chose him three thousand men of Israel, whereof two thousand were with Saul in Michmash and in the mount of Beth-el, and a thousand were with Jonathan in Gibeah of Benjamin: and the rest of the people he sent every man to his tent.

3And Jonathan smote the garrison of the Philistines that was in Geba: and the Philistines heard of it. And Saul blew the trumpet throughout all the land, saying, Let the Hebrews hear.

4And all Israel heard say that Saul had smitten the garrison of the Philistines, and also that Israel was had in abomination with the Philistines. And the people were gathered together after Saul to Gilgal.

5And the Philistines assembled themselves together to fight with Israel, thirty thousand chariots, and six thousand horsemen, and people as the sand which is on the sea-shore in multitude: and they came up, and encamped in Michmash, eastward of Beth-aven.

6When the men of Israel saw that they were in a strait (for the people were distressed), then the people did hide themselves in caves, and in thickets, and in rocks, and in coverts, and in pits.

7Now some of the Hebrews had gone over the Jordan to the land of Gad and Gilead; but as for Saul, he was yet in Gilgal, and all the people followed him trembling.

8And he tarried seven days, according to the set time that Samuel had appointed: but Samuel came not to Gilgal; and the people were scattered from him.

9And Saul said, Bring hither the burnt-offering to me, and the peace-offerings. And he offered the burnt-offering.

10And it came to pass that, as soon as he had made an end of offering the burnt-offering, behold, Samuel came; and Saul went out to meet him, that he might salute him.

11And Samuel said, What hast thou done? And Saul said, Because I saw that the people were scattered from me, and that thou camest not within the days appointed, and that the Philistines assembled themselves together at Michmash;

12therefore said I, Now will the Philistines come down upon me to Gilgal, and I have not entreated the favor of Yahweh: I forced myself therefore, and offered the burnt-offering.

13And Samuel said to Saul, Thou hast done foolishly; thou hast not kept the commandment of Yahweh thy God, which he commanded thee: for now would Yahweh have established thy kingdom upon Israel for ever.

14But now thy kingdom shall not continue: Yahweh hath sought him a man after his own heart, and Yahweh hath appointed him to be prince over his people, because thou hast not kept that which Yahweh commanded thee.

15And Samuel arose, and gat him up from Gilgal unto Gibeah of Benjamin.

And Saul numbered the people that were present with him, about six hundred men.

16And Saul, and Jonathan his son, and the people that were present with them, abode in Geba of Benjamin: but the Philistines encamped in Michmash.

17And the spoilers came out of the camp of the Philistines in three companies: one company turned unto the way that leadeth to Ophrah, unto the land of Shual;

18and another company turned the way to Beth-horon; and another company turned the way of the border that looketh down upon the valley of Zeboim toward the wilderness.

19Now there was no smith found throughout all the land of Israel; for the Philistines said, Lest the Hebrews make them swords or spears:

20but all the Israelites went down to the Philistines, to sharpen every man his share, and his coulter, and his axe, and his mattock;

21yet they had a file for the mattocks, and for the coulters, and for the forks, and for the axes, and to set the goads.

22So it came to pass in the day of battle, that there was neither sword nor spear found in the hand of any of the people that were with Saul and Jonathan: but with Saul and with Jonathan his son was there found.

23And the garrison of the Philistines went out unto the pass of Michmash.

Chapter 14

1Now it fell upon a day, that Jonathan the son of Saul said unto the young man that bare his armor, Come, and let us go over to the Philistines' garrison, that is on yonder side. But he told not his father.

2And Saul abode in the uttermost part of Gibeah under the pomegranate-tree which is in Migron: and the people that were with him were about six hundred men;

3and Ahijah, the son of Ahitub, Ichabod's brother, the son of Phinehas, the son of Eli, the priest of Yahweh in Shiloh, wearing an ephod. And the people knew not that Jonathan was gone.

4And between the passes, by which Jonathan sought to go over unto the Philistines' garrison, there was a rocky crag on the one side, and a rocky crag on the other side: and the name of the one was Bozez, and the name of the other Seneh.

5The one crag rose up on the north in front of Michmash, and the other on the south in front of Geba.

6And Jonathan said to the young man that bare his armor, Come, and let us go over unto the garrison of these uncircumcised: it may be that Yahweh will work for us; for there is no restraint to Yahweh to save by many or by few.

7And his armorbearer said unto him, Do all that is in thy heart: turn thee, behold, I am with thee according to thy heart.

8Then said Jonathan, Behold, we will pass over unto the men, and we will disclose ourselves unto them.

9If they say thus unto us, Tarry until we come to you; then we will stand still in our place, and will not go up unto them.

10But if they say thus, Come up unto us; then we will go up; for Yahweh hath delivered them into our hand: and this shall be the sign unto us.

11And both of them disclosed themselves unto the garrison of the Philistines: and the Philistines said, Behold, the Hebrews come forth out of the holes where they had hid themselves.

12And the men of the garrison answered Jonathan and his armorbearer, and said, Come up to us, and we will show you a thing. And Jonathan said unto his armorbearer, Come up after me; for Yahweh hath delivered them into the hand of Israel.

13And Jonathan climbed up upon his hands and upon his feet, and his armorbearer after him: and they fell before Jonathan; and his armorbearer slew them after him.

14And that first slaughter, which Jonathan and his armorbearer made, was about twenty men, within as it were half a furrow's length in an acre of land.

15And there was a trembling in the camp, in the field, and among all the people; the garrison, and the spoilers, they also trembled; and the earth quaked: so there was an exceeding great trembling.

16And the watchmen of Saul in Gibeah of Benjamin looked; and, behold, the multitude melted away, and they went hither and thither.

17Then said Saul unto the people that were with him, Number now, and see who is gone from us. And when they had numbered, behold, Jonathan and his armorbearer were not there.

18And Saul said unto Ahijah, Bring hither the ark of God. For the ark of God was there at that time with the children of Israel.

19And it came to pass, while Saul talked unto the priest, that the tumult that was in the camp of the Philistines went on and increased: and Saul said unto the priest, Withdraw thy hand.

20And Saul and all the people that were with him were gathered together, and came to the battle: and, behold, every man's sword was against his fellow, and there was a very great discomfiture.

21Now the Hebrews that were with the Philistines as beforetime, and that went up with them into the camp, from the country round about, even they also turned to be with the Israelites that were with Saul and Jonathan.

22Likewise all the men of Israel that had hid themselves in the hill-country of Ephraim, when they heard that the Philistines fled, even they also followed hard after them in the battle.

23So Yahweh saved Israel that day: and the battle passed over by Beth-aven.

24And the men of Israel were distressed that day; for Saul had adjured the people, saying, Cursed be the man that eateth any food until it be evening, and I be avenged on mine enemies. So none of the people tasted food.

25And all the people came into the forest; and there was honey upon the ground.

First Samuel

26And when the people were come unto the forest, behold, the honey dropped: but no man put his hand to his mouth; for the people feared the oath.

27But Jonathan heard not when his father charged the people with the oath: wherefore he put forth the end of the rod that was in his hand, and dipped it in the honeycomb, and put his hand to his mouth; and his eyes were enlightened.

28Then answered one of the people, and said, Thy father straitly charged the people with an oath, saying, Cursed be the man that eateth food this day. And the people were faint.

29Then said Jonathan, My father hath troubled the land: see, I pray you, how mine eyes have been enlightened, because I tasted a little of this honey.

30How much more, if haply the people had eaten freely to-day of the spoil of their enemies which they found? for now hath there been no great slaughter among the Philistines.

31And they smote of the Philistines that day from Michmash to Aijalon. And the people were very faint;

32and the people flew upon the spoil, and took sheep, and oxen, and calves, and slew them on the ground; and the people did eat them with the blood.

33Then they told Saul, saying, Behold, the people sin against Yahweh, in that they eat with the blood. And he said, ye have dealt treacherously: roll a great stone unto me this day.

34And Saul said, Disperse yourselves among the people, and say unto them, Bring me hither every man his ox, and every man his sheep, and slay them here, and eat; and sin not against Yahweh in eating with the blood. And all the people brought every man his ox with him that night, and slew them there.

35And Saul built an altar unto Yahweh: the same was the first altar that he built unto Yahweh.

36And Saul said, Let us go down after the Philistines by night, and take spoil among them until the morning light, and let us not leave a man of them. And they said, Do whatsoever seemeth good unto thee. Then said the priest, Let us draw near hither unto God.

37And Saul asked counsel of God, Shall I go down after the Philistines? wilt thou deliver them into the hand of Israel? But he answered him not that day.

38And Saul said, Draw nigh hither, all ye chiefs of the people; and know and see wherein this sin hath been this day.

39For, as Yahweh liveth, who saveth Israel, though it be in Jonathan my son, he shall surely die. But there was not a man among all the people that answered him.

40Then said he unto all Israel, Be ye on one side, and I and Jonathan my son will be on the other side. And the people said unto Saul, Do what seemeth good unto thee.

41Therefore Saul said unto Yahweh, the God of Israel, Show the right. And Jonathan and Saul were taken by lot; but the people escaped.

42And Saul said, Cast lots between me and Jonathan my son. And Jonathan was taken.

43Then Saul said to Jonathan, Tell me what thou hast done. And Jonathan told him, and said, I did certainly taste a little honey with the end of the rod that was in my hand; and, lo, I must die.

44And Saul said, God do so and more also; for thou shalt surely die, Jonathan.

45And the people said unto Saul, Shall Jonathan die, who hath wrought this great salvation in Israel? Far from it: as Yahweh liveth, there shall not one hair of his head fall to the ground; for he hath wrought with God this day. So the people rescued Jonathan, that he died not.

46Then Saul went up from following the Philistines; and the Philistines went to their own place.

47Now when Saul had taken the kingdom over Israel, he fought against all his enemies on every side, against Moab, and against the children of Ammon, and against Edom, and against the kings of Zobah, and against the Philistines: and whithersoever he turned himself, he put them to the worse.

48And he did valiantly, and smote the Amalekites, and delivered Israel out of the hands of them that despoiled them.

49Now the sons of Saul were Jonathan, and Ishvi, and Malchishua; and the names of his two daughters were these: the name of the first-born Merab, and the name of the younger Michal:

50and the name of Saul's wife was Ahinoam the daughter of Ahimaaz. And the name of the captain of his host was Abner the son of Ner, Saul's uncle.

51And Kish was the father of Saul; and Ner the father of Abner was the son of Abiel.

52And there was sore war against the Philistines all the days of Saul: and when Saul saw any mighty man, or any valiant man, he took him unto him.

Chapter 15

1And Samuel said unto Saul, Yahweh sent me to anoint thee to be king over his people, over Israel: now therefore hearken thou unto the voice of the words of Yahweh.

2Thus saith Yahweh of hosts, I have marked that which Amalek did to Israel, how he set himself against him in the way, when he came up out of Egypt.

3Now go and smite Amalek, and utterly destroy all that they have, and spare them not; but slay both man and woman, infant and suckling, ox and sheep, camel and ass.

4And Saul summoned the people, and numbered them in Telaim, two hundred thousand footmen, and ten thousand men of Judah.

5And Saul came to the city of Amalek, and laid wait in the valley.

6And Saul said unto the Kenites, Go, depart, get you down from among the Amalekites, lest I destroy you with them; for ye showed kindness to all the children of Israel, when they came up out of Egypt. So the Kenites departed from among the Amalekites.

7And Saul smote the Amalekites, from Havilah as thou goest to Shur, that is before Egypt.

8And he took Agag the king of the Amalekites alive, and utterly destroyed all the people with the edge of the sword.

9But Saul and the people spared Agag, and the best of the sheep, and of the oxen, and of the fatlings, and the lambs, and all that was good, and would not utterly destroy them: but everything that was vile and refuse, that they destroyed utterly.

10Then came the word of Yahweh unto Samuel, saying,

11It repenteth me that I have set up Saul to be king; for he is turned back from following me, and hath not performed my commandments. And Samuel was wroth; and he cried unto Yahweh all night.

12And Samuel rose early to meet Saul in the morning; and it was told Samuel, saying, Saul came to Carmel, and, behold, he set him up a monument, and turned, and passed on, and went down to Gilgal.

13And Samuel came to Saul; and Saul said unto him, Blessed be thou of Yahweh: I have performed the commandment of Yahweh.

14And Samuel said, What meaneth then this bleating of the sheep in mine ears, and the lowing of the oxen which I hear?

15And Saul said, They have brought them from the Amalekites: for the people spared the best of the sheep and of the oxen, to sacrifice unto Yahweh thy God; and the rest we have utterly destroyed.

16Then Samuel said unto Saul, Stay, and I will tell thee what Yahweh hath said to me this night. And he said unto him, Say on.

17And Samuel said, Though thou wast little in thine own sight, wast thou not made the head of the tribes of Israel? And Yahweh anointed thee king over Israel;

18and Yahweh sent thee on a journey, and said, Go, and utterly destroy the sinners the Amalekites, and fight against them until they be consumed.

19Wherefore then didst thou not obey the voice of Yahweh, but didst fly upon the spoil, and didst that which was evil in the sight of Yahweh?

20And Saul said unto Samuel, Yea, I have obeyed the voice of Yahweh, and have gone the way which Yahweh sent me, and have brought Agag the king of Amalek, and have utterly destroyed the Amalekites.

21But the people took of the spoil, sheep and oxen, the chief of the devoted things, to sacrifice unto Yahweh thy God in Gilgal.

22And Samuel said, Hath Yahweh as great delight in burnt-offerings and sacrifices, as in obeying the voice of Yahweh? Behold, to obey is better than sacrifice, and to hearken than the fat of rams.

23For rebellion is as the sin of witchcraft, and stubbornness is as idolatry and teraphim. Because thou hast rejected the word of Yahweh, he hath also rejected thee from being king.

24And Saul said unto Samuel, I have sinned; for I have transgressed the commandment of Yahweh, and thy words, because I feared the people, and obeyed their voice.

25Now therefore, I pray thee, pardon my sin, and turn again with me, that I may worship Yahweh.

26And Samuel said unto Saul, I will not return with thee; for thou hast rejected the word of Yahweh, and Yahweh hath rejected thee from being king over Israel.

27And as Samuel turned about to go away, Saul laid hold upon the skirt of his robe, and it rent.

28And Samuel said unto him, Yahweh hath rent the kingdom of Israel from thee this day, and hath given it to a neighbor of thine, that is better than thou.

29And also the Strength of Israel will not lie nor repent; for he is not a man, that he should repent.

30Then he said, I have sinned: yet honor me now, I pray thee, before the elders of my people, and before Israel, and turn again with me, that I may worship Yahweh thy God.

31So Samuel turned again after Saul; and Saul worshipped Yahweh.

32Then said Samuel, Bring ye hither to me Agag the king of the Amalekites. And Agag came unto him cheerfully. And Agag said, Surely the bitterness of death is past.

33And Samuel said, As thy sword hath made women childless, so shall thy mother be childless among women. And Samuel hewed Agag in pieces before Yahweh in Gilgal.

34Then Samuel went to Ramah; and Saul went up to his house to Gibeah of Saul.

35And Samuel came no more to see Saul until the day of his death; for Samuel mourned for Saul: and Yahweh repented that he had made Saul king over Israel.

Chapter 16

1And Yahweh said unto Samuel, How long wilt thou mourn for Saul, seeing I have rejected him from being king over Israel? fill thy horn with oil, and go: I will send thee to Jesse the Beth-lehemite; for I have provided me a king among his sons.

2And Samuel said, How can I go? if Saul hear it, he will kill me. And Yahweh said, Take a heifer with thee, and say, I am come to sacrifice to Yahweh.

3And call Jesse to the sacrifice, and I will show thee what thou shalt do: and thou shalt anoint unto me him whom I name unto thee.

4And Samuel did that which Yahweh spake, and came to Beth-lehem. And the elders of the city came to meet him trembling, and said, Comest thou peaceably?

5And he said, Peaceably; I am come to sacrifice unto Yahweh: sanctify yourselves, and come with me to the sacrifice. And he sanctified Jesse and his sons, and called them to the sacrifice.

6And it came to pass, when they were come, that he looked on Eliab, and said, Surely Yahweh's anointed is before him.

7But Yahweh said unto Samuel, Look not on his countenance, or on the height of his stature; because I have rejected him: for Yahweh seeth not as man seeth; for man looketh on the outward appearance, but Yahweh looketh on the heart.

8Then Jesse called Abinadab, and made him pass before Samuel. And he said, Neither hath Yahweh chosen this.

9Then Jesse made Shammah to pass by. And he said, Neither hath Yahweh chosen this.

10And Jesse made seven of his sons to pass before Samuel. And Samuel said unto Jesse, Yahweh hath not chosen these.

11And Samuel said unto Jesse, Are here all thy children? And he said, There remaineth yet the youngest, and, behold, he is keeping the sheep. And Samuel said unto Jesse, Send and fetch him; for we will not sit down till he come hither.

12And he sent, and brought him in. Now he was ruddy, and withal of a beautiful countenance, and goodly to look upon. And Yahweh said, Arise, anoint him; for this is he.

13Then Samuel took the horn of oil, and anointed him in the midst of his brethren: and the Spirit of Yahweh came mightily upon David from that day forward. So Samuel rose up, and went to Ramah.

14Now the Spirit of Yahweh departed from Saul, and an evil spirit from Yahweh troubled him.

15And Saul's servants said unto him, Behold now, an evil spirit from God troubleth thee.

16Let our lord now command thy servants, that are before thee, to seek out a man who is a skilful player on the harp: and it shall come to pass, when the evil spirit from God is upon thee, that he shall play with his hand, and thou shalt be well.

17And Saul said unto his servants, Provide me now a man that can play well, and bring him to me.

18Then answered one of the young men, and said, Behold, I have seen a son of Jesse the Beth-lehemite, that is skilful in playing, and a mighty man of valor, and a man of war, and prudent in speech, and a comely person; and Yahweh is with him.

19Wherefore Saul sent messengers unto Jesse, and said, Send me David thy son, who is with the sheep.

20And Jesse took an ass laden with bread, and a bottle of wine, and a kid, and sent them by David his son unto Saul.

21And David came to Saul, and stood before him: and he loved him greatly; and he became his armorbearer.

22And Saul sent to Jesse, saying, Let David, I pray thee, stand before me; for he hath found favor in my sight.

23And it came to pass, when the evil spirit from God was upon Saul, that David took the harp, and played with his hand: so Saul was refreshed, and was well, and the evil spirit departed from him.

Chapter 17

1Now the Philistines gathered together their armies to battle; and they were gathered together at Socoh, which belongeth to Judah, and encamped between Socoh and Azekah, in Ephes-dammim.

2And Saul and the men of Israel were gathered together, and encamped in the vale of Elah, and set the battle in array against the Philistines.

3And the Philistines stood on the mountain on the one side, and Israel stood on the mountain on the other side: and there was a valley between them.

4And there went out a champion out of the camp of the Philistines, named Goliath, of Gath, whose height was six cubits and a span.

5And he had a helmet of brass upon his head, and he was clad with a coat of mail; and the weight of the coat was five thousand shekels of brass.

6And he had greaves of brass upon his legs, and a javelin of brass between his shoulders.

7And the staff of his spear was like a weaver's beam; and his spear's head weighed six hundred shekels of iron: and his shield-bearer went before him.

8And he stood and cried unto the armies of Israel, and said unto them, Why are ye come out to set your battle in array? am not I a Philistine, and ye servants to Saul? choose you a man for you, and let him come down to me.

9If he be able to fight with me, and kill me, then will we be your servants; but if I prevail against him, and kill him, then shall ye be our servants, and serve us.

10And the Philistine said, I defy the armies of Israel this day; give me a man, that we may fight together.

11And when Saul and all Israel heard those words of the Philistine, they were dismayed, and greatly afraid.

12Now David was the son of that Ephrathite of Beth-lehem-judah, whose name was Jesse; and he had eight sons: and the man was an old man in the days of Saul, stricken in years among men.

13And the three eldest sons of Jesse had gone after Saul to the battle: and the names of his three sons that went to the battle were Eliab the first-born, and next unto him Abinadab, and the third Shammah.

14And David was the youngest; and the three eldest followed Saul.

15Now David went to and fro from Saul to feed his father's sheep at Beth-lehem.

16And the Philistine drew near morning and evening, and presented himself forty days.

17And Jesse said unto David his son, Take now for thy brethren an ephah of this parched grain, and these ten loaves, and carry them quickly to the camp to thy brethren;

18and bring these ten cheeses unto the captain of their thousand, and look how thy brethren fare, and take their pledge.

19Now Saul, and they, and all the men of Israel, were in the vale of Elah, fighting with the Philistines.

20And David rose up early in the morning, and left the sheep with a keeper, and took, and went, as Jesse had commanded him; and he came to the place of the wagons, as the host which was going forth to the fight shouted for the battle.

21And Israel and the Philistines put the battle in array, army against army.

22And David left his baggage in the hand of the keeper of the baggage, and ran to the army, and came and saluted his brethren.

23And as he talked with them, behold, there came up the champion, the Philistine of Gath, Goliath by name, out of the ranks of the Philistines, and spake according to the same words: and David heard them.

24And all the men of Israel, when they saw the man, fled from him, and were sore afraid.

25And the men of Israel said, Have ye seen this man that is come up? surely to defy Israel is he come up: and it shall be, that the man who killeth him, the king will enrich him with great riches, and will give him his daughter, and make his father's house free in Israel.

26And David spake to the men that stood by him, saying, What shall be done to the man that killeth this Philistine, and taketh away the reproach from Israel? for who is this uncircumcised Philistine, that he should defy the armies of the living God?

27And the people answered him after this manner, saying, So shall it be done to the man that killeth him.

28And Eliab his eldest brother heard when he spake unto the men; and Eliab's anger was kindled against David, and he said, Why art thou come down? and with whom hast thou left those few sheep in the wilderness? I know thy pride, and the naughtiness of thy heart; for thou art come down that thou mightest see the battle.

29And David said, What have I now done? Is there not a cause?

30And he turned away from him toward another, and spake after the same manner: and the people answered him again after the former manner.

31And when the words were heard which David spake, they rehearsed them before Saul; and he sent for him.

32And David said to Saul, Let no man's heart fail because of him; thy servant will go and fight with this Philistine.

33And Saul said to David, Thou art not able to go against this Philistine to fight with him; for thou art but a youth, and he a man of war from his youth.

34And David said unto Saul, Thy servant was keeping his father's sheep; and when there came a lion, or a bear, and took a lamb out of the flock,

35I went out after him, and smote him, and delivered it out of his mouth; and when he arose against me, I caught him by his beard, and smote him, and slew him.

36Thy servant smote both the lion and the bear: and this uncircumcised Philistine shall be as one of them, seeing he hath defied the armies of the living God.

37And David said, Yahweh that delivered me out of the paw of the lion, and out of the paw of the bear, he will deliver me out of the hand of this Philistine. And Saul said unto David, Go, and Yahweh shall be with thee.

38And Saul clad David with his apparel, and he put a helmet of brass upon his head, and he clad him with a coat of mail.

39And David girded his sword upon his apparel, and he assayed to go; for he had not proved it. And David said unto Saul, I cannot go with these; for I have not proved them. And David put them off him.

40And he took his staff in his hand, and chose him five smooth stones out of the brook, and put them in the shepherd's bag which he had, even in his wallet; and his sling was in his hand: and he drew near to the Philistine.

41And the Philistine came on and drew near unto David; and the man that bare the shield went before him.

42And when the Philistine looked about, and saw David, he disdained him; for he was but a youth, and ruddy, and withal of a fair countenance.

43And the Philistine said unto David, Am I a dog, that thou comest to me with staves? And the Philistine cursed David by his gods.

44And the Philistine said to David, Come to me, and I will give thy flesh unto the birds of the heavens, and to the beasts of the field.

45Then said David to the Philistine, Thou comest to me with a sword, and with a spear, and with a javelin: but I come to thee in the name of Yahweh of hosts, the God of the armies of Israel, whom thou hast defied.

46This day will Yahweh deliver thee into my hand; and I will smite thee, and take thy head from off thee; and I will give the dead bodies of the host of the Philistines this day unto the birds of the heavens, and to the wild beasts of the earth; that all the earth may know that there is a God in Israel,

47and that all this assembly may know that Yahweh saveth not with sword and spear: for the battle is Yahweh's, and he will give you into our hand.

48And it came to pass, when the Philistine arose, and came and drew nigh to meet David, that David hastened, and ran toward the army to meet the Philistine.

49And David put his hand in his bag, and took thence a stone, and slang it, and smote the Philistine in his forehead; and the stone sank into his forehead, and he fell upon his face to the earth.

50So David prevailed over the Philistine with a sling and with a stone, and smote the Philistine, and slew him; but there was no sword in the hand of David.

51Then David ran, and stood over the Philistine, and took his sword, and drew it out of the sheath thereof, and slew him, and cut off his head therewith. And when the Philistines saw that their champion was dead, they fled.

52And the men of Israel and of Judah arose, and shouted, and pursued the Philistines, until thou comest to Gai, and to the gates of Ekron. And the wounded of the Philistines fell down by the way to Shaaraim, even unto Gath, and unto Ekron.

53And the children of Israel returned from chasing after the Philistines, and they plundered their camp.

54And David took the head of the Philistine, and brought it to Jerusalem; but he put his armor in his tent.

55And when Saul saw David go forth against the Philistine, he said unto Abner, the captain of the host, Abner, whose son is this youth? And Abner said,

First Samuel

As thy soul liveth, O king, I cannot tell.

56And the king said, Inquire thou whose son the stripling is.

57And as David returned from the slaughter of the Philistine, Abner took him, and brought him before Saul with the head of the Philistine in his hand.

58And Saul said to him, Whose son art thou, thou young man? And David answered, I am the son of thy servant Jesse the Beth-lehemite.

Chapter 18

1And it came to pass, when he had made an end of speaking unto Saul, that the soul of Jonathan was knit with the soul of David, and Jonathan loved him as his own soul.

2And Saul took him that day, and would let him go no more home to his father's house.

3Then Jonathan and David made a covenant, because he loved him as his own soul.

4And Jonathan stripped himself of the robe that was upon him, and gave it to David, and his apparel, even to his sword, and to his bow, and to his girdle.

5And David went out whithersoever Saul sent him, and behaved himself wisely: and Saul set him over the men of war, and it was good in the sight of all the people, and also in the sight of Saul's servants.

6And it came to pass as they came, when David returned from the slaughter of the Philistine, that the women came out of all the cities of Israel, singing and dancing, to meet king Saul, with timbrels, with joy, and with instruments of music.

7And the women sang one to another as they played, and said,
Saul hath slain his thousands,
And David his ten thousands.

8And Saul was very wroth, and this saying displeased him; and he said, They have ascribed unto David ten thousands, and to me they have ascribed but thousands: and what can he have more but the kingdom?

9And Saul eyed David from that day and forward.

10And it came to pass on the morrow, that an evil spirit from God came mightily upon Saul, and he prophesied in the midst of the house: and David played with his hand, as he did day by day. And Saul had his spear in his hand;

11and Saul cast the spear; for he said, I will smite David even to the wall. And David avoided out of his presence twice.

12And Saul was afraid of David, because Yahweh was with him, and was departed from Saul.

13Therefore Saul removed him from him, and made him his captain over a thousand; and he went out and came in before the people.

14And David behaved himself wisely in all his ways; and Yahweh was with him.

15And when Saul saw that he behaved himself very wisely, he stood in awe of him.

16But all Israel and Judah loved David; for he went out and came in before them.

17And Saul said to David, Behold, my elder daughter Merab, her will I give thee to wife: only be thou valiant for me, and fight Yahweh's battles. For Saul said, Let not my hand be upon him, but let the hand of the Philistines be upon him.

18And David said unto Saul, Who am I, and what is my life, or my father's family in Israel, that I should be son-in-law to the king?

19But it came to pass at the time when Merab, Saul's daughter, should have been given to David, that she was given unto Adriel the Meholathite to wife.

20And Michal, Saul's daughter, loved David: and they told Saul, and the thing pleased him.

21And Saul said, I will give him her, that she may be a snare to him, and that the hand of the Philistines may be against him. Wherefore Saul said to David, Thou shalt this day be my son-in-law a second time.

22And Saul commanded his servants, saying, Commune with David secretly, and say, Behold, the king hath delight in thee, and all his servants love thee: now therefore be the king's son-in-law.

23And Saul's servants spake those words in the ears of David. And David said, Seemeth it to you a light thing to be the king's son-in-law, seeing that I am a poor man, and lightly esteemed?

24And the servants of Saul told him, saying, On this manner spake David.

25And Saul said, Thus shall ye say to David, The king desireth not any dowry, but a hundred foreskins of the Philistines, to be avenged of the king's enemies. Now Saul thought to make David fall by the hand of the Philistines.

26And when his servants told David these words, it pleased David well to be the king's son-in-law. And the days were not expired;

27and David arose and went, he and his men, and slew of the Philistines two hundred men; and David brought their foreskins, and they gave them in full number to the king, that he might be the king's son-in-law. And Saul gave him Michal his daughter to wife.

28And Saul saw and knew that Yahweh was with David; and Michal, Saul's daughter, loved him.

29And Saul was yet the more afraid of David; and Saul was David's enemy continually.

30Then the princes of the Philistines went forth: and it came to pass, as often as they went forth, that David behaved himself more wisely than all the servants of Saul; so that his name was much set by.

Chapter 19

1And Saul spake to Jonathan his son, and to all his servants, that they should slay David. But Jonathan, Saul's son, delighted much in David.

2And Jonathan told David, saying, Saul my father seeketh to slay thee: now therefore, I pray thee, take heed to thyself in the morning, and abide in a secret place, and hide thyself:

3and I will go out and stand beside my father in the field where thou art, and I will commune with my father of thee; and if I see aught, I will tell thee.

4And Jonathan spake good of David unto Saul his father, and said unto him, Let not the king sin against his servant, against David; because he hath not sinned against thee, and because his works have been to thee-ward very good:

5for he put his life in his hand, and smote the Philistine, and Yahweh wrought a great victory for all Israel: thou sawest it, and didst rejoice; wherefore then wilt thou sin against innocent blood, to slay David without a cause?

6And Saul hearkened unto the voice of Jonathan: and Saul sware, As Yahweh liveth, he shall not be put to death.

7And Jonathan called David, and Jonathan showed him all those things. And Jonathan brought David to Saul, and he was in his presence, as beforetime.

8And there was war again: and David went out, and fought with the Philistines, and slew them with a great slaughter; and they fled before him.

9And an evil spirit from Yahweh was upon Saul, as he sat in his house with his spear in his hand; and David was playing with his hand.

10And Saul sought to smite David even to the wall with the spear; but he slipped away out of Saul's presence, and he smote the spear into the wall: and David fled, and escaped that night.

11And Saul sent messengers unto David's house, to watch him, and to slay him in the morning: and Michal, David's wife, told him, saying, If thou save not thy life to-night, to-morrow thou wilt be slain.

12So Michal let David down through the window: and he went, and fled, and escaped.

13And Michal took the teraphim, and laid it in the bed, and put a pillow of goats' hair at the head thereof, and covered it with the clothes.

14And when Saul sent messengers to take David, she said, He is sick.

15And Saul sent the messengers to see David, saying, Bring him up to me in the bed, that I may slay him.

16And when the messengers came in, behold, the teraphim was in the bed, with the pillow of goats' hair at the head thereof.

17And Saul said unto Michal, Why hast thou deceived me thus, and let mine enemy go, so that he is escaped? And Michal answered Saul, He said unto me, Let me go; why should I kill thee?

18Now David fled, and escaped, and came to Samuel to Ramah, and told him all that Saul had done to him. And he and Samuel went and dwelt in Naioth.

19And it was told Saul, saying, Behold, David is at Naioth in Ramah.

20And Saul sent messengers to take David: and when they saw the company of the prophets prophesying, and Samuel standing as head over them, the Spirit of God came upon the messengers of Saul, and they also prophesied.

21And when it was told Saul, he sent other messengers, and they also prophesied. And Saul sent messengers again the third time, and they also prophesied.

22Then went he also to Ramah, and came to the great well that is in Secu: and he asked and said, Where are Samuel and David? And one said, Behold, they are at Naioth in Ramah.

23And he went thither to Naioth in Ramah: and the Spirit of God came upon him also, and he went on, and prophesied, until he came to Naioth in Ramah.

24And he also stripped off his clothes, and he also prophesied before Samuel, and lay down naked all that day and all that night. Wherefore they say, Is Saul also among the prophets?

Chapter 20

1And David fled from Naioth in Ramah, and came and said before Jonathan, What have I done? what is mine iniquity? and what is my sin before thy father, that he seeketh my life?

2And he said unto him, Far from it; thou shalt not die: behold, my father doeth nothing either great or small, but that he discloseth it unto me; and why should my father hide this thing from me? it is not so.

3And David sware moreover, and said, Thy father knoweth well that I have found favor in thine eyes; and he saith, Let not Jonathan know this, lest he be grieved: but truly as Yahweh liveth, and as thy soul liveth, there is but a step between me and death.

4Then said Jonathan unto David, Whatsoever thy soul desireth, I will even do it for thee.

5And David said unto Jonathan, Behold, to-morrow is the new moon, and I should not fail to sit with the king at meat: but let me go, that I may hide myself in the field unto the third day at even.

6If thy father miss me at all, then say, David earnestly asked leave of me that he might run to Beth-lehem his city; for it is the yearly sacrifice there for all the family.

7If he say thus, It is well; thy servant shall have peace: but if he be wroth, then know that evil is determined by him.

8Therefore deal kindly with thy servant; for thou hast brought thy servant into a covenant of Yahweh with thee: but if there be in me iniquity, slay me thyself; for why shouldest thou bring me to thy father?

9And Jonathan said, Far be it from thee; for if I should at all know that evil were determined by my father to come upon thee, then would not I tell it thee?

10Then said David to Jonathan, Who shall tell me if perchance thy father answer thee roughly?

11And Jonathan said unto David, Come, and let us go out into the field. And they went out both of them into the field.

12And Jonathan said unto David, Yahweh, the God of Israel, be witness: when I have sounded my father about this time to-morrow, or the third day, behold, if there be good toward David, shall I not then send unto thee, and disclose it unto thee?

13Yahweh do so to Jonathan, and more also, should it please my father to do thee evil, if I disclose it not unto thee, and send thee away, that thou mayest go in peace: and Yahweh be with thee, as he hath been with my father.

14And thou shalt not only while yet I live show me the lovingkindness of

Yahweh, that I die not;

¹⁵but also thou shalt not cut off thy kindness from my house for ever; no, not when Yahweh hath cut off the enemies of David every one from the face of the earth.

¹⁶So Jonathan made a covenant with the house of David, saying, And Yahweh will require it at the hand of David's enemies.

¹⁷And Jonathan caused David to swear again, for the love that he had to him; for he loved him as he loved his own soul.

¹⁸Then Jonathan said unto him, To-morrow is the new moon: and thou wilt be missed, because thy seat will be empty.

¹⁹And when thou hast stayed three days, thou shalt go down quickly, and come to the place where thou didst hide thyself when the business was in hand, and shalt remain by the stone Ezel.

²⁰And I will shoot three arrows on the side thereof, as though I shot at a mark.

²¹And, behold, I will send the lad, saying, Go, find the arrows. If I say unto the lad, Behold, the arrows are on this side of thee; take them, and come; for there is peace to thee and no hurt, as Yahweh liveth.

²²But if I say thus unto the boy, Behold, the arrows are beyond thee; go thy way; for Yahweh hath sent thee away.

²³And as touching the matter which thou and I have spoken of, behold, Yahweh is between thee and me for ever.

²⁴So David hid himself in the field: and when the new moon was come, the king sat him down to eat food.

²⁵And the king sat upon his seat, as at other times, even upon the seat by the wall; and Jonathan stood up, and Abner sat by Saul's side: but David's place was empty.

²⁶Nevertheless Saul spake not anything that day: for he thought, Something hath befallen him, he is not clean; surely he is not clean.

²⁷And it came to pass on the morrow after the new moon, which was the second day, that David's place was empty: and Saul said unto Jonathan his son, Wherefore cometh not the son of Jesse to meat, neither yesterday, nor to-day?

²⁸And Jonathan answered Saul, David earnestly asked leave of me to go to Beth-lehem:

²⁹and he said, Let me go, I pray thee; for our family hath a sacrifice in the city; and my brother, he hath commanded me to be there: and now, if I have found favor in thine eyes, let me get away, I pray thee, and see my brethren. Therefore he is not come unto the king's table.

³⁰Then Saul's anger was kindled against Jonathan, and he said unto him, Thou son of a perverse rebellious woman, do not I know that thou hast chosen the son of Jesse to thine own shame, and unto the shame of thy mother's nakedness?

³¹For as long as the son of Jesse liveth upon the ground, thou shalt not be established, nor thy kingdom. Wherefore now send and fetch him unto me, for he shall surely die.

³²And Jonathan answered Saul his father, and said unto him, Wherefore should he be put to death? what hath he done?

³³And Saul cast his spear at him to smite him; whereby Jonathan knew that is was determined of his father to put David to death.

³⁴So Jonathan arose from the table in fierce anger, and did eat no food the second day of the month; for he was grieved for David, because his father had done him shame.

³⁵And it came to pass in the morning, that Jonathan went out into the field at the time appointed with David, and a little lad with him.

³⁶And he said unto his lad, Run, find now the arrows which I shoot. And as the lad ran, he shot an arrow beyond him.

³⁷And when the lad was come to the place of the arrow which Jonathan had shot, Jonathan cried after the lad, and said, Is not the arrow beyond thee?

³⁸And Jonathan cried after the lad, Make speed, haste, stay not. And Jonathan's lad gathered up the arrows, and came to his master.

³⁹But the lad knew not anything: only Jonathan and David knew the matter.

⁴⁰And Jonathan gave his weapons unto his lad, and said unto him, Go, carry them to the city.

⁴¹And as soon as the lad was gone, David arose out of a place toward the South, and fell on his face to the ground, and bowed himself three times: and they kissed one another, and wept one with another, until David exceeded.

⁴²And Jonathan said to David, Go in peace, forasmuch as we have sworn both of us in the name of Yahweh, saying, Yahweh shall be between me and thee, and between my seed and thy seed, for ever. And he arose and departed: and Jonathan went into the city.

Chapter 21

¹Then came David to Nob to Ahimelech the priest: and Ahimelech came to meet David trembling, and said unto him, Why art thou alone, and no man with thee?

²And David said unto Ahimelech the priest, The king hath commanded me a business, and hath said unto me, Let no man know anything of the business whereabout I send thee, and what I have commanded thee: and I have appointed the young men to such and such a place.

³Now therefore what is under thy hand? give me five loaves of bread in my hand, or whatsoever there is present.

⁴And the priest answered David, and said, There is no common bread under my hand, but there is holy bread; if only the young men have kept themselves from women.

⁵And David answered the priest, and said unto him, Of a truth women have been kept from us about these three days; when I came out, the vessels of the young men were holy, though it was but a common journey; how much more then to-day shall their vessels be holy?

⁶So the priest gave him holy bread; for there was no bread there but the showbread, that was taken from before Yahweh, to put hot bread in the day when it was taken away.

⁷Now a certain man of the servants of Saul was there that day, detained before Yahweh; and his name was Doeg the Edomite, the chiefest of the herdsmen that belonged to Saul.

⁸And David said unto Ahimelech, And is there not here under thy hand spear or sword? for I have neither brought my sword nor my weapons with me, because the king's business required haste.

⁹And the priest said, The sword of Goliath the Philistine, whom thou slewest in the vale of Elah, behold, it is here wrapped in a cloth behind the ephod: if thou wilt take that, take it; for there is no other save that here. And David said, There is none like that; give it me.

¹⁰And David arose, and fled that day for fear of Saul, and went to Achish the king of Gath.

¹¹And the servants of Achish said unto him, Is not this David the king of the land? did they not sing one to another of him in dances, saying,
Saul hath slain his thousands,
And David his ten thousands?

¹²And David laid up these words in his heart, and was sore afraid of Achish the king of Gath.

¹³And he changed his behavior before them, and feigned himself mad in their hands, and scrabbled on the doors of the gate, and let his spittle fall down upon his beard.

¹⁴Then said Achish unto his servants, Lo, ye see the man is mad; wherefore then have ye brought him to me?

¹⁵Do I lack madmen, that ye have brought this fellow to play the madman in my presence? shall this fellow come into my house?

Chapter 22

¹David therefore departed thence, and escaped to the cave of Adullam: and when his brethren and all his father's house heard it, they went down thither to him.

²And every one that was in distress, and every one that was in debt, and every one that was discontented, gathered themselves unto him; and he became captain over them: and there were with him about four hundred men.

³And David went thence to Mizpeh of Moab: and he said unto the king of Moab, Let my father and my mother, I pray thee, come forth, and be with you, till I know what God will do for me.

⁴And he brought them before the king of Moab: and they dwelt with him all the while that David was in the stronghold.

⁵And the prophet Gad said unto David, Abide not in the stronghold; depart, and get thee into the land of Judah. Then David departed, and came into the forest of Hereth.

⁶And Saul heard that David was discovered, and the men that were with him: now Saul was sitting in Gibeah, under the tamarisk-tree in Ramah, with his spear in his hand, and all his servants were standing about him.

⁷And Saul said unto his servants that stood about him, Hear now, ye Benjamites; will the son of Jesse give every one of you fields and vineyards, will he make you all captains of thousands and captains of hundreds,

⁸that all of you have conspired against me, and there is none that discloseth to me when my son maketh a league with the son of Jesse, and there is none of you that is sorry for me, or discloseth unto me that my son hath stirred up my servant against me, to lie in wait, as at this day?

⁹Then answered Doeg the Edomite, who stood by the servants of Saul, and said, I saw the son of Jesse coming to Nob, to Ahimelech the son of Ahitub.

¹⁰And he inquired of Yahweh for him, and gave him victuals, and gave him the sword of Goliath the Philistine.

¹¹Then the king sent to call Ahimelech the priest, the son of Ahitub, and all his father's house, the priests that were in Nob: and they came all of them to the king.

¹²And Saul said, Hear now, thou son of Ahitub. And he answered, Here I am, my lord.

¹³And Saul said unto him, Why have ye conspired against me, thou and the son of Jesse, in that thou hast given him bread, and a sword, and hast inquired of God for him, that he should rise against me, to lie in wait, as at this day?

¹⁴Then Ahimelech answered the king, and said, And who among all thy servants is so faithful as David, who is the king's son-in-law, and is taken into thy council, and is honorable in thy house?

¹⁵Have I to-day begun to inquire of God for him? be it far from me: let not the king impute anything unto his servant, nor to all the house of my father; for thy servant knoweth nothing of all this, less or more.

¹⁶And the king said, Thou shalt surely die, Ahimelech, thou, and all thy father's house.

¹⁷And the king said unto the guard that stood about him, Turn, and slay the priests of Yahweh; because their hand also is with David, and because they knew that he fled, and did not disclose it to me. But the servants of the king would not put forth their hand to fall upon the priests of Yahweh.

¹⁸And the king said to Doeg, Turn thou, and fall upon the priests. And Doeg the Edomite turned, and he fell upon the priests, and he slew on that day fourscore and five persons that did wear a linen ephod.

¹⁹And Nob, the city of the priests, smote he with the edge of the sword, both men and women, children and sucklings, and oxen and asses and sheep, with the edge of the sword.

²⁰And one of the sons of Ahimelech, the son of Ahitub, named Abiathar, escaped, and fled after David.

²¹And Abiathar told David that Saul had slain Yahweh's priests.

²²And David said unto Abiathar, I knew on that day, when Doeg the Edomite was there, that he would surely tell Saul: I have occasioned the death of all the persons of thy father's house.

²³Abide thou with me, fear not; for he that seeketh my life seeketh thy life:

First Samuel

for with me thou shalt be in safeguard.

Chapter 23

1And they told David, saying, Behold, the Philistines are fighting against Keilah, and are robbing the threshing-floors.

2Therefore David inquired of Yahweh, saying, Shall I go and smite these Philistines? And Yahweh said unto David, Go, and smite the Philistines, and save Keilah.

3And David's men said unto him, Behold, we are afraid here in Judah: how much more then if we go to Keilah against the armies of the Philistines?

4Then David inquired of Yahweh yet again. And Yahweh answered him, and said, Arise, go down to Keilah; for I will deliver the Philistines into thy hand.

5And David and his men went to Keilah, and fought with the Philistines, and brought away their cattle, and slew them with a great slaughter. So David save the inhabitants of Keilah.

6And it came to pass, when Abiathar the son of Ahimelech fled to David to Keilah, that he came down with an ephod in his hand.

7And it was told Saul that David was come to Keilah. And Saul said, God hath delivered him into my hand; for he is shut in, by entering into a town that hath gates and bars.

8And Saul summoned all the people to war, to go down to Keilah, to besiege David and his men.

9And David knew that Saul was devising mischief against him; and he said to Abiathar the priest, Bring hither the ephod.

10Then said David, O Yahweh, the God of Israel, thy servant hath surely heard that Saul seeketh to come to Keilah, to destroy the city for my sake.

11Will the men of Keilah deliver me up into his hand? will Saul come down, as thy servant hath heard? O Yahweh, the God of Israel, I beseech thee, tell thy servant. And Yahweh said, He will come down.

12Then said David, Will the men of Keilah deliver up to me and my men into the hand of Saul? And Yahweh said, They will deliver thee up.

13Then David and his men, who were about six hundred, arose and departed out of Keilah, and went whithersoever they could go. And it was told Saul that David was escaped from Keilah; and he forbare to go forth.

14And David abode in the wilderness in the strongholds, and remained in the hill-country in the wilderness of Ziph. And Saul sought him every day, but God delivered him not into his hand.

15And David saw that Saul was come out to seek his life: and David was in the wilderness of Ziph in the wood.

16And Jonathan, Saul's son, arose, and went to David into the wood, and strengthened his hand in God.

17And he said unto him, Fear not; for the hand of Saul my father shall not find thee; and thou shalt be king over Israel, and I shall be next unto thee; and that also Saul my father knoweth.

18And they two made a covenant before Yahweh: and David abode in the wood, and Jonathan went to his house.

19Then came up the Ziphites to Saul to Gibeah, saying, Doth not David hide himself with us in the strongholds in the wood, in the hill of Hachilah, which is on the south of the desert?

20Now therefore, O king, come down, according to all the desire of thy soul to come down; and our part shall be to deliver him up into the king's hand.

21And Saul said, Blessed be ye of Yahweh; for ye have had compassion on me.

22Go, I pray you, make yet more sure, and know and see his place where his haunt is, and who hath seen him there; for it is told me that he dealeth very subtly.

23See therefore, and take knowledge of all the lurking-places where he hideth himself, and come ye again to me of a certainty, and I will go with you: and it shall come to pass, if he be in the land, that I will search him out among all the thousands of Judah.

24And they arose, and went to Ziph before Saul: but David and his men were in the wilderness of Maon, in the Arabah on the south of the desert.

25And Saul and his men went to seek him. And they told David: wherefore he came down to the rock, and abode in the wilderness of Maon. And when Saul heard that, he pursued after David in the wilderness of Maon.

26And Saul went on this side of the mountain, and David and his men on that side of the mountain: and David made haste to get away for fear of Saul; for Saul and his men compassed David and his men round about to take them.

27But there came a messenger unto Saul, saying, Haste thee, and come; for the Philistines have made a raid upon the land.

28So Saul returned from pursuing after David, and went against the Philistines: therefore they called that place Sela-hammahlekoth.

29And David went up from thence, and dwelt in the strongholds of En-gedi.

Chapter 24

1And it came to pass, when Saul was returned from following the Philistines, that it was told him, saying, Behold, David is in the wilderness of En-gedi.

2Then Saul took three thousand chosen men out of all Israel, and went to seek David and his men upon the rocks of the wild goats.

3And he came to the sheepcotes by the way, where was a cave; and Saul went in to cover his feet. Now David and his men were abiding in the innermost parts of the cave.

4And the men of David said unto him, Behold, the day of which Yahweh said unto thee, Behold, I will deliver thine enemy into thy hand, and thou shalt do to him as it shall seem good unto thee. Then David arose, and cut off the skirt of Saul's robe privily.

5And it came to pass afterward, that David's heart smote him, because he had cut off Saul's skirt.

6And he said unto his men, Yahweh forbid that I should do this thing unto my lord, Yahweh's anointed, to put forth my hand against him, seeing he is Yahweh's anointed.

7So David checked his men with these words, and suffered them not to rise against Saul. And Saul rose up out of the cave, and went on his way.

8David also arose afterward, and went out of the cave, and cried after Saul, saying, My lord the king. And when Saul looked behind him, David bowed with his face to the earth, and did obeisance.

9And David said to Saul, Wherefore hearkenest thou to men's words, saying, Behold, David seeketh thy hurt?

10Behold, this day thine eyes have seen how that Yahweh had delivered thee to-day into my hand in the cave: and some bade me kill thee; but mine eye spared thee; and I said, I will not put forth my hand against my lord; for he is Yahweh's anointed.

11Moreover, my father, see, yea, see the skirt of thy robe in my hand; for in that I cut off the skirt of thy robe, and killed thee not, know thou and see that there is neither evil nor transgression in my hand, and I have not sinned against thee, though thou huntest after my life to take it.

12Yahweh judge between me and thee, and Yahweh avenge me of thee; but my hand shall not be upon thee.

13As saith the proverb of the ancients, Out of the wicked cometh forth wickedness; but my hand shall not be upon thee.

14After whom is the king of Israel come out? after whom dost thou pursue? after a dead dog, after a flea.

15Yahweh therefore be judge, and give sentence between me and thee, and see, and plead my cause, and deliver me out of thy hand.

16And it came to pass, when David had made an end of speaking these words unto Saul, that Saul said, Is this thy voice, my son David? And Saul lifted up his voice, and wept.

17And he said to David, Thou art more righteous than I; for thou hast rendered unto me good, whereas I have rendered unto thee evil.

18And thou hast declared this day how that thou hast dealt well with me, forasmuch as when Yahweh had delivered me up into thy hand, thou killedst me not.

19For if a man find his enemy, will he let him go well away? wherefore Yahweh reward thee good for that which thou hast done unto me this day.

20And now, behold, I know that thou shalt surely be king, and that the kingdom of Israel shall be established in thy hand.

21Swear now therefore unto me by Yahweh, that thou wilt not cut off my seed after me, and that thou wilt not destroy my name out of my father's house.

22And David sware unto Saul. And Saul went home; but David and his men gat them up unto the stronghold.

Chapter 25

1And Samuel died; and all Israel gathered themselves together, and lamented him, and buried him in his house at Ramah. And David arose, and went down to the wilderness of Paran.

2And there was a man in Maon, whose possessions were in Carmel; and the man was very great, and he had three thousand sheep, and a thousand goats: and he was shearing his sheep in Carmel.

3Now the name of the man was Nabal; and the name of his wife Abigail; and the woman was of good understanding, and of a beautiful countenance: but the man was churlish and evil in his doings; and he was of the house of Caleb.

4And David heard in the wilderness that Nabal was shearing his sheep.

5And David sent ten young men, and David said unto the young men, Get you up to Carmel, and go to Nabal, and greet him in my name:

6and thus shall ye say to him that liveth in prosperity, Peace be unto thee, and peace be to thy house, and peace be unto all that thou hast.

7And now I have heard that thou hast shearers: thy shepherds have now been with us, and we did them no hurt, neither was there aught missing unto them, all the while they were in Carmel.

8Ask thy young men, and they will tell thee: wherefore let the young men find favor in thine eyes; for we come in a good day: give, I pray thee, whatsoever cometh to thy hand, unto thy servants, and to thy son David.

9And when David's young men came, they spake to Nabal according to all those words in the name of David, and ceased.

10And Nabal answered David's servants, and said, Who is David? and who is the son of Jesse? there are many servants now-a-days that break away every man from his master.

11Shall I then take my bread, and my water, and my flesh that I have killed for my shearers, and give it unto men of whom I know not whence they are?

12So David's young men turned on their way, and went back, and came and told him according to all these words.

13And David said unto his men, Gird ye on every man his sword. And they girded on every man his sword; and David also girded on his sword: and there went up after David about four hundred men; and two hundred abode by the baggage.

14But one of the young men told Abigail, Nabal's wife, saying, Behold, David sent messengers out of the wilderness to salute our master; and he railed at them.

15But the men were very good unto us, and we were not hurt, neither missed we anything, as long as we went with them, when we were in the fields:

16they were a wall unto us both by night and by day, all the while we were with them keeping the sheep.

17Now therefore know and consider what thou wilt do; for evil is determined against our master, and against all his house: for he is such a worthless fellow, that one cannot speak to him.

18Then Abigail made haste, and took two hundred loaves, and two bottles of wine, and five sheep ready dressed, and five measures of parched grain, and a hundred clusters of raisins, and two hundred cakes of figs, and laid them on asses.

19And she said unto her young men, Go on before me; behold, I come after you. But she told not her husband Nabal.

20And it was so, as she rode on her ass, and came down by the covert of the mountain, that, behold, David and his men came down toward her; and she met them.

21Now David had said, Surely in vain have I kept all that this fellow hath in the wilderness, so that nothing was missed of all that pertained unto him: and he hath returned me evil for good.

22God do so unto the enemies of David, and more also, if I leave of all that pertain to him by the morning light so much as one man-child.

23And when Abigail saw David, she hasted, and alighted from her ass, and fell before David on her face, and bowed herself to the ground.

24And she fell at his feet, and said, Upon me, my lord, upon me be the iniquity; and let thy handmaid, I pray thee, speak in thine ears, and hear thou the words of thy handmaid.

25Let not my lord, I pray thee, regard this worthless fellow, even Nabal; for as his name is, so is he; Nabal is his name, and folly is with him: but I thy handmaid saw not the young men of my lord, whom thou didst send.

26Now therefore, my lord, as Yahweh liveth, and as thy soul liveth, seeing Yahweh hath withholden thee from bloodguiltiness, and from avenging thyself with thine own hand, now therefore let thine enemies, and them that seek evil to my lord, be as Nabal.

27And now this present which thy servant hath brought unto my lord, let it be given unto the young men that follow my lord.

28Forgive, I pray thee, the trespass of thy handmaid: for Yahweh will certainly make my lord a sure house, because my lord fighteth the battles of Yahweh; and evil shall not be found in thee all thy days.

29And though men be risen up to pursue thee, and to seek thy soul, yet the soul of my lord shall be bound in the bundle of life with Yahweh thy God; and the souls of thine enemies, them shall he sling out, as from the hollow of a sling.

30And it shall come to pass, when Yahweh shall have done to my lord according to all the good that he hath spoken concerning thee, and shall have appointed thee prince over Israel,

31that this shall be no grief unto thee, nor offence of heart unto my lord, either that thou hast shed blood without cause, or that my lord hath avenged himself. And when Yahweh shall have dealt well with my lord, then remember thy handmaid.

32And David said to Abigail, Blessed be Yahweh, the God of Israel, who sent thee this day to meet me:

33and blessed be thy discretion, and blessed be thou, that hast kept me this day from bloodguiltiness, and from avenging myself with mine own hand.

34For in very deed, as Yahweh, the God of Israel, liveth, who hath withholden me from hurting thee, except thou hadst hasted and come to meet me, surely there had not been left unto Nabal by the morning light so much as one man-child.

35So David received of her hand that which she had brought him: and he said unto her, Go up in peace to thy house; see, I have hearkened to thy voice, and have accepted thy person.

36And Abigail came to Nabal; and, behold, he held a feast in his house, like the feast of a king; and Nabal's heart was merry within him, for he was very drunken: wherefore she told him nothing, less or more, until the morning light.

37And it came to pass in the morning, when the wine was gone out of Nabal, that his wife told him these things, and his heart died within him, and he became as a stone.

38And it came to pass about ten days after, that Yahweh smote Nabal, so that he died.

39And when David heard that Nabal was dead, he said, Blessed be Yahweh, that hath pleaded the cause of my reproach from the hand of Nabal, and hath kept back his servant from evil: and the evil-doing of Nabal hath Yahweh returned upon his own head. And David sent and spake concerning Abigail, to take her to him to wife.

40And when the servants of David were come to Abigail to Carmel, they spake unto her, saying, David hath sent us unto thee, to take thee to him to wife.

41And she arose, and bowed herself with her face to the earth, and said, Behold, thy handmaid is a servant to wash the feet of the servants of my lord.

42And Abigail hasted, and arose, and rode upon an ass, with five damsels of hers that followed her; and she went after the messengers of David, and became his wife.

43David also took Ahinoam of Jezreel; and they became both of them his wives.

44Now Saul had given Michal his daughter, David's wife, to Palti the son of Laish, who was of Gallim.

Chapter 26

1And the Ziphites came unto Saul to Gibeah, saying, Doth not David hide himself in the hill of Hachilah, which is before the desert?

2Then Saul arose, and went down to the wilderness of Ziph, having three thousand chosen men of Israel with him, to seek David in the wilderness of Ziph.

3And Saul encamped in the hill of Hachilah, which is before the desert, by the way. But David abode in the wilderness, and he saw that Saul came after him into the wilderness.

4David therefore sent out spies, and understood that Saul was come of a certainty.

5And David arose, and came to the place where Saul had encamped; and David beheld the place where Saul lay, and Abner the son of Ner, the captain of his host: and Saul lay within the place of the wagons, and the people were encamped round about him.

6Then answered David and said to Ahimelech the Hittite, and to Abishai the son of Zeruiah, brother to Joab, saying, Who will go down with me to Saul to the camp? And Abishai said, I will go down with thee.

7So David and Abishai came to the people by night: and, behold, Saul lay sleeping within the place of the wagons, with his spear stuck in the ground at his head; and Abner and the people lay round about him.

8Then said Abishai to David, God hath delivered up thine enemy into thy hand this day: now therefore let me smite him, I pray thee, with the spear to the earth at one stroke, and I will not smite him the second time.

9And David said to Abishai, Destroy him not; for who can put forth his hand against Yahweh's anointed, and be guiltless?

10And David said, As Yahweh liveth, Yahweh will smite him; or his day shall come to die; or he shall go down into battle and perish.

11Yahweh forbid that I should put forth my hand against Yahweh's anointed: but now take, I pray thee, the spear that is at his head, and the cruse of water, and let us go.

12So David took the spear and the cruse of water from Saul's head; and they gat them away: and no man saw it, nor knew it, neither did any awake; for they were all asleep, because a deep sleep from Yahweh was fallen upon them.

13Then David went over to the other side, and stood on the top of the mountain afar off; a great space being between them;

14and David cried to the people, and to Abner the son of Ner, saying, Answerest thou not, Abner? Then Abner answered and said, Who art thou that criest to the king?

15And David said to Abner, Art not thou a valiant man? and who is like to thee in Israel? wherefore then hast thou not kept watch over thy lord the king? for there came one of the people in to destroy the king thy lord.

16This thing is not good that thou hast done. As Yahweh liveth, ye are worthy to die, because ye have not kept watch over your lord, Yahweh's anointed. And now see where the king's spear is, and the cruse of water that was at his head.

17And Saul knew David's voice, and said, Is this thy voice, my son David? And David said, It is my voice, my lord, O king.

18And he said, Wherefore doth my lord pursue after his servant? for what have I done? or what evil is in my hand?

19Now therefore, I pray thee, let my lord the king hear the words of his servant. If it be Yahweh that hath stirred thee up against me, let him accept an offering: but if it be the children of men, cursed be they before Yahweh: for they have driven me out this day that I should not cleave unto the inheritance of Yahweh, saying, Go, serve other gods.

20Now therefore, let not my blood fall to the earth away from the presence of Yahweh: for the king of Israel is come out to seek a flea, as when one doth hunt a partridge in the mountains.

21Then said Saul, I have sinned: return, my son David; for I will no more do thee harm, because my life was precious in thine eyes this day: behold, I have played the fool, and have erred exceedingly.

22And David answered and said, Behold the spear, O king! let then one of the young men come over and fetch it.

23And Yahweh will render to every man his righteousness and his faithfulness; forasmuch as Yahweh delivered thee into my hand to-day, and I would not put forth my hand against Yahweh's anointed.

24And, behold, as thy life was much set by this day in mine eyes, so let my life be much set by in the eyes of Yahweh, and let him deliver me out of all tribulation.

25Then Saul said to David, Blessed be thou, my son David: thou shalt both do mightily, and shalt surely prevail. So David went his way, and Saul returned to his place.

Chapter 27

1And David said in his heart, I shall now perish one day by the hand of Saul: there is nothing better for me than that I should escape into the land of the Philistines; and Saul will despair of me, to seek me any more in all the borders of Israel: so shall I escape out of his hand.

2And David arose, and passed over, he and the six hundred men that were with him, unto Achish the son of Maoch, king of Gath.

3And David dwelt with Achish at Gath, he and his men, every man with his household, even David with his two wives, Ahinoam the Jezreelitess, and Abigail the Carmelitess, Nabal's wife.

4And it was told Saul that David was fled to Gath: and he sought no more again for him.

5And David said unto Achish, If now I have found favor in thine eyes, let them give me a place in one of the cities in the country, that I may dwell there: for why should thy servant dwell in the royal city with thee?

6Then Achish gave him Ziklag that day: wherefore Ziklag pertaineth unto the kings of Judah unto this day.

7And the number of the days that David dwelt in the country of the Philistines was a full year and four months.

8And David and his men went up, and made a raid upon the Geshurites, and the Girzites, and the Amalekites; for those nations were the inhabitants of the land, who were of old, as thou goest to Shur, even unto the land of Egypt.

9And David smote the land, and saved neither man nor woman alive, and took away the sheep, and the oxen, and the asses, and the camels, and the apparel; and he returned, and came to Achish.

10And Achish said, Against whom have ye made a raid to-day? And David said, Against the South of Judah, and against the South of the Jerahmeelites, and against the South of the Kenites.

11And David saved neither man nor woman alive, to bring them to Gath, saying, Lest they should tell of us, saying, So did David, and so hath been his manner all the while he hath dwelt in the country of the Philistines.

12And Achish believed David, saying, He hath made his people Israel utterly to abhor him; therefore he shall be my servant for ever.

First Samuel

Chapter 28

1 And it came to pass in those days, that the Philistines gathered their hosts together for warfare, to fight with Israel. And Achish said unto David, Know thou assuredly, that thou shalt go out with me in the host, thou and thy men.

2 And David said to Achish, Therefore thou shalt know what thy servant will do. And Achish said to David, Therefore will I make thee keeper of my head for ever.

3 Now Samuel was dead, and all Israel had lamented him, and buried him in Ramah, even in his own city. And Saul had put away those that had familiar spirits, and the wizards, out of the land.

4 And the Philistines gathered themselves together, and came and encamped in Shunem: and Saul gathered all Israel together, and they encamped in Gilboa.

5 And when Saul saw the host of the Philistines, he was afraid, and his heart trembled greatly.

6 And when Saul inquired of Yahweh, Yahweh answered him not, neither by dreams, nor by Urim, nor by prophets.

7 Then said Saul unto his servants, Seek me a woman that hath a familiar spirit, that I may go to her, and inquire of her. And his servants said to him, Behold, there is a woman that hath a familiar spirit at En-dor.

8 And Saul disguised himself, and put on other raiment, and went, he and two men with him, and they came to the woman by night: and he said, Divine unto me, I pray thee, by the familiar spirit, and bring me up whomsoever I shall name unto thee.

9 And the woman said unto him, Behold, thou knowest what Saul hath done, how he hath cut off those that have familiar spirits, and the wizards, out of the land: wherefore then layest thou a snare for my life, to cause me to die?

10 And Saul sware to her by Yahweh, saying, As Yahweh liveth, there shall no punishment happen to thee for this thing.

11 Then said the woman, Whom shall I bring up unto thee? And he said, Bring me up Samuel.

12 And when the woman saw Samuel, she cried with a loud voice; and the woman spake to Saul, saying, Why hast thou deceived me? for thou art Saul.

13 And the king said unto her, Be not afraid: for what seest thou? And the woman said unto Saul, I see a god coming up out of the earth.

14 And he said unto her, What form is he of? And she said, An old man cometh up; and he is covered with a robe. And Saul perceived that it was Samuel, and he bowed with his face to the ground, and did obeisance.

15 And Samuel said to Saul, Why hast thou disquieted me, to bring me up? And Saul answered, I am sore distressed; for the Philistines make war against me, and God is departed from me, and answereth me no more, neither by prophets, nor by dreams: therefore I have called thee, that thou mayest make known unto me what I shall do.

16 And Samuel said, Wherefore then dost thou ask of me, seeing Yahweh is departed from thee, and is become thine adversary?

17 And Yahweh hath done unto thee, as he spake by me: and Yahweh hath rent the kingdom out of thy hand, and given it to thy neighbor, even to David.

18 Because thou obeyedst not the voice of Yahweh, and didst not execute his fierce wrath upon Amalek, therefore hath Yahweh done this thing unto thee this day.

19 Moreover Yahweh will deliver Israel also with thee into the hand of the Philistines; and to-morrow shalt thou and thy sons be with me: Yahweh will deliver the host of Israel also into the hand of the Philistines.

20 Then Saul fell straightway his full length upon the earth, and was sore afraid, because of the words of Samuel: and there was no strength in him; for he had eaten no bread all the day, nor all the night.

21 And the woman came unto Saul, and saw that he was sore troubled, and said unto him, Behold, thy handmaid hath hearkened unto thy voice, and I have put my life in my hand, and have hearkened unto thy words which thou spakest unto me.

22 Now therefore, I pray thee, hearken thou also unto the voice of thy handmaid, and let me set a morsel of bread before thee; and eat, that thou mayest have strength, when thou goest on thy way.

23 But he refused, and said, I will not eat. But his servants, together with the woman, constrained him; and he hearkened unto their voice. So he arose from the earth, and sat upon the bed.

24 And the woman had a fatted calf in the house; and she hasted, and killed it; and she took flour, and kneaded it, and did bake unleavened bread thereof:

25 and she brought it before Saul, and before his servants; and they did eat. Then they rose up, and went away that night.

Chapter 29

1 Now the Philistines gathered together all their hosts to Aphek: and the Israelites encamped by the fountain which is in Jezreel.

2 And the lords of the Philistines passed on by hundreds, and by thousands; and David and his men passed on in the rearward with Achish.

3 Then said the princes of the Philistines, What do these Hebrews here? And Achish said unto the princes of the Philistines, Is not this David, the servant of Saul the king of Israel, who hath been with me these days, or rather these years, and I have found no fault in him since he fell away unto me unto this day?

4 But he princes of the Philistines were wroth with him; and the princes of the Philistines said unto him, Make the man return, that he may go back to his place where thou hast appointed him, and let him not go down with us to battle, lest in the battle he become an adversary to us: for wherewith should this fellow reconcile himself unto his lord? should it not be with the heads of these men?

5 Is not this David, of whom they sang one to another in dances, saying,
Saul hath slain his thousands,
And David his ten thousands?

6 Then Achish called David, and said unto him, As Yahweh liveth, thou hast been upright, and thy going out and thy coming in with me in the host is good in my sight; for I have not found evil in thee since the day of thy coming unto me unto this day: nevertheless the lords favor thee not.

7 Wherefore now return, and go in peace, that thou displease not the lords of the Philistines.

8 And David said unto Achish, But what have I done? and what hast thou found in thy servant so long as I have been before thee unto this day, that I may not go and fight against the enemies of my lord the king?

9 And Achish answered and said to David, I know that thou art good in my sight, as an angel of God: notwithstanding the princes of the Philistines have said, He shall not go up with us to the battle.

10 Wherefore now rise up early in the morning with the servants of thy lord that are come with thee; and as soon as ye are up early in the morning, and have light, depart.

11 So David rose up early, he and his men, to depart in the morning, to return into the land of the Philistines. And the Philistines went up to Jezreel.

Chapter 30

1 And it came to pass, when David and his men were come to Ziklag on the third day, that the Amalekites had made a raid upon the South, and upon Ziklag, and had smitten Ziklag, and burned it with fire,

2 and had taken captive the women and all that were therein, both small and great: they slew not any, but carried them off, and went their way.

3 And when David and his men came to the city, behold, it was burned with fire; and their wives, and their sons, and their daughters, were taken captive.

4 Then David and the people that were with him lifted up their voice and wept, until they had no more power to weep.

5 And David's two wives were taken captive, Ahinoam the Jezreelitess, and Abigail the wife of Nabal the Carmelite.

6 And David was greatly distressed; for the people spake of stoning him, because the soul of all the people was grieved, every man for his sons and for his daughters: but David strengthened himself in Yahweh his God.

7 And David said to Abiathar the priest, the son of Ahimelech, I pray thee, bring me hither the ephod. And Abiathar brought thither the ephod to David.

8 And David inquired of Yahweh, saying, If I pursue after this troop, shall I overtake them? And he answered him, Pursue; for thou shalt surely overtake them, and shalt without fail recover all.

9 So David went, he and the six hundred men that were with him, and came to the brook Besor, where those that were left behind stayed.

10 But David pursued, he and four hundred men; for two hundred stayed behind, who were so faint that they could not go over the brook Besor.

11 And they found an Egyptian in the field, and brought him to David, and gave him bread, and he did eat; and they gave him water to drink.

12 And they gave him a piece of a cake of figs, and two clusters of raisins: and when he had eaten, his spirit came again to him; for he had eaten no bread, nor drunk any water, three days and three nights.

13 And David said unto him, To whom belongest thou? and whence art thou? And he said, I am a young man of Egypt, servant to an Amalekite; and my master left me, because three days ago I fell sick.

14 We made a raid upon the South of the Cherethites, and upon that which belongeth to Judah, and upon the South of Caleb; and we burned Ziklag with fire.

15 And David said to him, Wilt thou bring me down to this troop? And he said, Swear unto me by God, that thou wilt neither kill me, nor deliver me up into the hands of my master, and I will bring thee down to this troop.

16 And when he had brought him down, behold, they were spread abroad over all the ground, eating and drinking, and dancing, because of all the great spoil that they had taken out of the land of the Philistines, and out of the land of Judah.

17 And David smote them from the twilight even unto the evening of the next day: and there escaped not a man of them, save four hundred young men, who rode upon camels and fled.

18 And David recovered all that the Amalekites had taken; and David rescued his two wives.

19 And there was nothing lacking to them, neither small nor great, neither sons nor daughters, neither spoil, nor anything that they had taken to them: David brought back all.

20 And David took all the flocks and the herds, which they drove before those other cattle, and said, This is David's spoil.

21 And David came to the two hundred men, who were so faint that they could not follow David, whom also they had made to abide at the brook Besor; and they went forth to meet David, and to meet the people that were with him: and when David came near to the people, he saluted them.

22 Then answered all the wicked men and base fellows, of those that went with David, and said, Because they went not with us, we will not give them aught of the spoil that we have recovered, save to every man his wife and his children, that he may lead them away, and depart.

23 Then said David, Ye shall not do so, my brethren, with that which Yahweh hath given unto us, who hath preserved us, and delivered the troop that came against us into our hand.

24 And who will hearken unto you in this matter? for as his share is that goeth down to the battle, so shall his share be that tarrieth by the baggage: they shall share alike.

25 And it was so from that day forward, that he made it a statute and an ordinance for Israel unto this day.

26 And when David came to Ziklag, he sent of the spoil unto the elders of Judah, even to his friends, saying, Behold, a present for you of the spoil of the enemies of Yahweh:

27 To them that were in Beth-el, and to them that were in Ramoth of the South, and to them that were in Jattir,

28 and to them that were in Aroer, and to them that were in Siphmoth, and to

them that were in Eshtemoa,

29and to them that were in Racal, and to them that were in the cities of the Jerahmeelites, and to them that were in the cities of the Kenites,

30and to them that were in Hormah, and to them that were in Bor-ashan, and to them that were in Athach,

31and to them that were in Hebron, and to all the places where David himself and his men were wont to haunt.

Chapter 31

1Now the Philistines fought against Israel: and the men of Israel fled from before the Philistines, and fell down slain in mount Gilboa.

2And the Philistines followed hard upon Saul and upon his sons; and the Philistines slew Jonathan, and Abinadab, and Malchishua, the sons of Saul.

3And the battle went sore against Saul, and the archers overtook him; and he was greatly distressed by reason of the archers.

4Then said Saul to his armorbearer, Draw thy sword, and thrust me through therewith, lest these uncircumcised come and thrust me through, and abuse me. But his armorbearer would not; for he was sore afraid. Therefore Saul took his sword, and fell upon it.

5And when his armorbearer saw that Saul was dead, he likewise fell upon his sword, and died with him.

6So Saul died, and his three sons, and his armorbearer, and all his men, that same day together.

7And when the men of Israel that were on the other side of the valley, and they that were beyond the Jordan, saw that the men of Israel fled, and that Saul and his sons were dead, they forsook the cities, and fled; and the Philistines came and dwelt in them.

8And it came to pass on the morrow, when the Philistines came to strip the slain, that they found Saul and his three sons fallen in mount Gilboa.

9And they cut off his head, and stripped off his armor, and sent into the land of the Philistines round about, to carry the tidings unto the house of their idols, and to the people.

10And they put his armor in the house of the Ashtaroth; and they fastened his body to the wall of Beth-shan.

11And when the inhabitants of Jabesh-gilead heard concerning him that which the Philistines had done to Saul,

12all the valiant men arose, and went all night, and took the body of Saul and the bodies of his sons from the wall of Beth-shan; and they came to Jabesh, and burnt them there.

13And they took their bones, and buried them under the tamarisk-tree in Jabesh, and fasted seven days.

Second Samuel
The Second Book of Samuel

Chapter 1

1And it came to pass after the death of Saul, when David was returned from the slaughter of the Amalekites, and David had abode two days in Ziklag;

2it came to pass on the third day, that, behold, a man came out of the camp from Saul, with his clothes rent, and earth upon his head: and so it was, when he came to David, that he fell to the earth, and did obeisance.

3And David said unto him, From whence comest thou? And he said unto him, Out of the camp of Israel am I escaped.

4And David said unto him, How went the matter? I pray thee, tell me. And he answered, The people are fled from the battle, and many of the people also are fallen and dead; and Saul and Jonathan his son are dead also.

5And David said unto the young man that told him, How knowest thou that Saul and Jonathan his son are dead?

6And the young man that told him said, As I happened by chance upon mount Gilboa, behold, Saul was leaning upon his spear; and, lo, the chariots and the horsemen followed hard after him.

7And when he looked behind him, he saw me, and called unto me. And I answered, Here am I.

8And he said unto me, Who art thou? And I answered him, I am an Amalekite.

9And he said unto me, Stand, I pray thee, beside me, and slay me; for anguish hath taken hold of me, because my life is yet whole in me.

10So I stood beside him, and slew him, because I was sure that he could not live after that he was fallen: and I took the crown that was upon his head, and the bracelet that was on his arm, and have brought them hither unto my lord.

11Then David took hold on his clothes, and rent them; and likewise all the men that were with him:

12and they mourned, and wept, and fasted until even, for Saul, and for Jonathan his son, and for the people of Yahweh, and for the house of Israel; because they were fallen by the sword.

13And David said unto the young man that told him, Whence art thou? And he answered, I am the son of a sojourner, an Amalekite.

14And David said unto him, How wast thou not afraid to put forth thy hand to destroy Yahweh's anointed?

15And David called one of the young men, and said, Go near, and fall upon him. And he smote him, so that he died.

16And David said unto him, Thy blood be upon thy head; for thy mouth hath testified against thee, saying, I have slain Yahweh's anointed.

17And David lamented with this lamentation over Saul and over Jonathan his son

18(and he bade them teach the children of Judah the song of the bow: behold, it is written in the book of Jashar):

19Thy glory, O Israel, is slain upon thy high places!
How are the mighty fallen!
20Tell it not in Gath,
Publish it not in the streets of Ashkelon;
Lest the daughters of the Philistines rejoice,
Lest the daughters of the uncircumcised triumph.
21Ye mountains of Gilboa,
Let there be no dew nor rain upon you, neither fields of offerings:
For there the shield of the mighty was vilely cast away,
The shield of Saul, not anointed with oil.
22From the blood of the slain, from the fat of the mighty,
The bow of Jonathan turned not back,
And the sword of Saul returned not empty.
23Saul and Jonathan were lovely and pleasant in their lives,
And in their death they were not divided:
They were swifter than eagles,
They were stronger than lions.
24Ye daughters of Israel, weep over Saul,
Who clothed you in scarlet delicately,
Who put ornaments of gold upon your apparel.
25How are the mighty fallen in the midst of the battle!
Jonathan is slain upon thy high places.
26I am distressed for thee, my brother Jonathan:
Very pleasant hast thou been unto me:
Thy love to me was wonderful,
Passing the love of women.
27How are the mighty fallen,
And the weapons of war perished!

Chapter 2

1And it came to pass after this, that David inquired of Yahweh, saying, Shall I go up into any of the cities of Judah? And Yahweh said unto him, Go up. And David said, Whither shall I go up? And he said, Unto Hebron.

2So David went up thither, and his two wives also, Ahinoam the Jezreelitess, and Abigail the wife of Nabal the Carmelite.

3And his men that were with him did David bring up, every man with his household: and they dwelt in the cities of Hebron.

4And the men of Judah came, and there they anointed David king over the house of Judah.

And they told David, saying, The men of Jabesh-gilead were they that buried Saul.

5And David sent messengers unto the men of Jabesh-gilead, and said unto them, Blessed be ye of Yahweh, that ye have showed this kindness unto your lord, even unto Saul, and have buried him.

6And now Yahweh show lovingkindness and truth unto you: and I also will requite you this kindness, because ye have done this thing.

7Now therefore let your hands be strong, and be ye valiant; for Saul your lord is dead, and also the house of Judah have anointed me king over them.

8Now Abner the son of Ner, captain of Saul's host, had taken Ish-bosheth the son of Saul, and brought him over to Mahanaim;

9and he made him king over Gilead, and over the Ashurites, and over Jezreel, and over Ephraim, and over Benjamin, and over all Israel.

10Ish-bosheth, Saul's son, was forty years old when he began to reign over Israel, and he reigned two years. But the house of Judah followed David.

11And the time that David was king in Hebron over the house of Judah was seven years and six months.

12And Abner the son of Ner, and the servants of Ish-bosheth the son of Saul, went out from Mahanaim to Gibeon.

13And Joab the son of Zeruiah, and the servants of David, went out, and met them by the pool of Gibeon; and they sat down, the one on the one side of the pool, and the other on the other side of the pool.

14And Abner said to Joab, Let the young men, I pray thee, arise and play before us. And Joab said, Let them arise.

15Then they arose and went over by number: twelve for Benjamin, and for Ish-bosheth the son of Saul, and twelve of the servants of David.

16And they caught every one his fellow by the head, and thrust his sword in his fellow's side; so they fell down together: wherefore that place was called Helkath-hazzurim, which is in Gibeon.

17And the battle was very sore that day: and Abner was beaten, and the men of Israel, before the servants of David.

18And the three sons of Zeruiah were there, Joab, and Abishai, and Asahel: and Asahel was as light of foot as a wild roe.

19And Asahel pursued after Abner; and in going he turned not to the right hand nor to the left from following Abner.

20Then Abner looked behind him, and said, Is it thou, Asahel? And he answered, It is I.

21And Abner said to him, Turn thee aside to thy right hand or to thy left, and lay thee hold on one of the young men, and take thee his armor. But Asahel would not turn aside from following him.

22And Abner said again to Asahel, Turn thee aside from following me: wherefore should I smite thee to the ground? how then should I hold up my face to Joab thy brother?

23Howbeit he refused to turn aside: wherefore Abner with the hinder end of the spear smote him in the body, so that the spear came out behind him; and he fell down there, and died in the same place: and it came to pass, that as many as came to the place where Asahel fell down and died stood still.

24But Joab and Abishai pursued after Abner: and the sun went down when they were come to the hill of Ammah, that lieth before Giah by the way of the wilderness of Gibeon.

25And the children of Benjamin gathered themselves together after Abner, and became one band, and stood on the top of a hill.

26Then Abner called to Joab, and said, Shall the sword devour for ever? knowest thou not that it will be bitterness in the latter end? how long shall it be then, ere thou bid the people return from following their brethren?

27And Joab said, As God liveth, if thou hadst not spoken, surely then in the morning the people had gone away, nor followed every one his brother.

28So Joab blew the trumpet; and all the people stood still, and pursued after Israel no more, neither fought they any more.

29And Abner and his men went all that night through the Arabah; and they passed over the Jordan, and went through all Bithron, and came to Mahanaim.

30And Joab returned from following Abner: and when he had gathered all the people together, there lacked of David's servants nineteen men and Asahel.

31But the servants of David had smitten of Benjamin, and of Abner's men, so that three hundred and threescore men died.

32And they took up Asahel, and buried him in the sepulchre of his father, which was in Beth-lehem. And Joab and his men went all night, and the day brake upon them at Hebron.

Chapter 3

1Now there was long war between the house of Saul and the house of David: and David waxed stronger and stronger, but the house of Saul waxed weaker and weaker.

2And unto David were sons born in Hebron: and his first-born was Amnon, of Ahinoam the Jezreelitess;

3and his second, Chileab, of Abigail the wife of Nabal the Carmelite; and the third, Absalom the son of Maacah the daughter of Talmai king of Geshur;

4and the fourth, Adonijah the son of Haggith; and the fifth, Shephatiah the son of Abital;

5and the sixth, Ithream, of Eglah, David's wife. These were born to David in Hebron.

6And it came to pass, while there was war between the house of Saul and the house of David, that Abner made himself strong in the house of Saul.

7Now Saul had a concubine, whose name was Rizpah, the daughter of Aiah: and Ish-bosheth said to Abner, Wherefore hast thou gone in unto my father's concubine?

8Then was Abner very wroth for the words of Ish-bosheth, and said, Am I a dog's head that belongeth to Judah? This day do I show kindness unto the house of Saul thy father, to his brethren, and to his friends, and have not delivered thee into the hand of David; and yet thou chargest me this day with a fault concerning this woman.

9God do so to Abner, and more also, if, as Yahweh hath sworn to David, I do not even so to him;

10to transfer the kingdom from the house of Saul, and to set up the throne of David over Israel and over Judah, from Dan even to Beer-sheba.

11And he could not answer Abner another word, because he feared him.

12And Abner sent messengers to David on his behalf, saying, Whose is the land? saying also, Make thy league with me, and, behold, my hand shall be with thee, to bring about all Israel unto thee.

13And he said, Well; I will make a league with thee; but one thing I require of thee: that is, thou shalt not see my face, except thou first bring Michal, Saul's daughter, when thou comest to see my face.

14And David sent messengers to Ish-bosheth, Saul's son, saying, Deliver me my wife Michal, whom I betrothed to me for a hundred foreskins of the Philistines.

15And Ish-bosheth sent, and took her from her husband, even from Paltiel the son of Laish.

16And her husband went with her, weeping as he went, and followed her to Bahurim. Then said Abner unto him, Go, return: and he returned.

17And Abner had communication with the elders of Israel, saying, In times past ye sought for David to be king over you;

18now then do it; for Yahweh hath spoken of David, saying, By the hand of my servant David I will save my people Israel out of the hand of the Philistines, and out of the hand of all their enemies.

19And Abner also spake in the ears of Benjamin: and Abner went also to speak in the ears of David in Hebron all that seemed good to Israel, and to the whole house of Benjamin.

20So Abner came to David to Hebron, and twenty men with him. And David made Abner and the men that were with him a feast.

21And Abner said unto David, I will arise and go, and will gather all Israel unto my lord the king, that they may make a covenant with thee, and that thou mayest reign over all that thy soul desireth. And David sent Abner away; and he went in peace.

22And, behold, the servants of David and Joab came from a foray, and brought in a great spoil with them: but Abner was not with David in Hebron; for he had sent him away, and he was gone in peace.

23When Joab and all the host that was with him were come, they told Joab, saying, Abner the son of Ner came to the king, and he hath sent him away, and he is gone in peace.

24Then Joab came to the king, and said, What hast thou done? behold, Abner came unto thee; why is it that thou hast sent him away, and he is quite gone?

25Thou knowest Abner the son of Ner, that he came to deceive thee, and to know thy going out and thy coming in, and to know all that thou doest.

26And when Joab was come out from David, he sent messengers after Abner, and they brought him back from the well of Sirah: but David knew it not.

27And when Abner was returned to Hebron, Joab took him aside into the midst of the gate to speak with him quietly, and smote him there in the body, so that he died, for the blood of Asahel his brother.

28And afterward, when David heard it, he said, I and my kingdom are guiltless before Yahweh for ever of the blood of Abner the son of Ner:

29let it fall upon the head of Joab, and upon all his father's house; and let there not fail from the house of Joab one that hath an issue, or that is a leper, or that leaneth on a staff, or that falleth by the sword, or that lacketh bread.

30So Joab and Abishai his brother slew Abner, because he had killed their brother Asahel at Gibeon in the battle.

31And David said to Joab, and to all the people that were with him, Rend your clothes, and gird you with sackcloth, and mourn before Abner. And king David followed the bier.

32And they buried Abner in Hebron: and the king lifted up his voice, and wept at the grave of Abner; and all the people wept.

33And the king lamented for Abner, and said,
Should Abner die as a fool dieth?

34Thy hands were not bound, nor thy feet put into fetters:
As a man falleth before the children of iniquity, so didst thou fall.
And all the people wept again over him.

35And all the people came to cause David to eat bread while it was yet day; but David sware, saying, God do so to me, and more also, if I taste bread, or aught else, till the sun be down.

36And all the people took notice of it, and it pleased them; as whatsoever the king did pleased all the people.

37So all the people and all Israel understood that day that it was not of the king to slay Abner the son of Ner.

38And the king said unto his servants, Know ye not that there is a prince and a great man fallen this day in Israel?

39And I am this day weak, though anointed king; and these men the sons of Zeruiah are too hard for me: Yahweh reward the evil-doer according to his wickedness.

Chapter 4

1And when Ish-bosheth, Saul's son, heard that Abner was dead in Hebron, his hands became feeble, and all the Israelites were troubled.

2And Ish-bosheth, Saul's son, had two men that were captains of bands: the name of the one was Baanah, and the name of the other Rechab, the sons of Rimmon the Beerothite, of the children of Benjamin (for Beeroth also is reckoned to Benjamin:

3and the Beerothites fled to Gittaim, and have been sojourners there until this day).

4Now Jonathan, Saul's son, had a son that was lame of his feet. He was five years old when the tidings came of Saul and Jonathan out of Jezreel; and his nurse took him up, and fled: and it came to pass, as she made haste to flee, that he fell, and became lame. And his name was Mephibosheth.

5And the sons of Rimmon the Beerothite, Rechab and Baanah, went, and came about the heat of the day to the house of Ish-bosheth, as he took his rest at noon.

6And they came thither into the midst of the house, as though they would have fetched wheat; and they smote him in the body: and Rechab and Baanah his brother escaped.

7Now when they came into the house, as he lay on his bed in his bedchamber, they smote him, and slew him, and beheaded him, and took his head, and went by the way of the Arabah all night.

8And they brought the head of Ish-bosheth unto David to Hebron, and said to the king, Behold, the head of Ish-bosheth, the son of Saul, thine enemy, who sought thy life; and Yahweh hath avenged my lord the king this day of Saul, and of his seed.

9And David answered Rechab and Baanah his brother, the sons of Rimmon the Beerothite, and said unto them, As Yahweh liveth, who hath redeemed my soul out of all adversity,

10when one told me, saying, Behold, Saul is dead, thinking to have brought good tidings, I took hold of him, and slew him in Ziklag, which was the reward I gave him for his tidings.

11How much more, when wicked men have slain a righteous person in his own house upon his bed, shall I not now require his blood of your hand, and take you away from the earth?

12And David commanded his young men, and they slew them, and cut off their hands and their feet, and hanged them up beside the pool in Hebron. But they took the head of Ish-bosheth, and buried it in the grave of Abner in Hebron.

Chapter 5

1Then came all the tribes of Israel to David unto Hebron, and spake, saying, Behold, we are thy bone and thy flesh.

2In times past, when Saul was king over us, it was thou that leddest out and broughtest in Israel: and Yahweh said to thee, Thou shalt be shepherd of my people Israel, and thou shalt be prince over Israel.

3So all the elders of Israel came to the king to Hebron; and king David made a covenant with them in Hebron before Yahweh: and they anointed David king over Israel.

4David was thirty years old when he began to reign, and he reigned forty years.

5In Hebron he reigned over Judah seven years and six months; and in Jerusalem he reigned thirty and three years over all Israel and Judah.

6And the king and his men went to Jerusalem against the Jebusites, the inhabitants of the land, who spake unto David, saying, Except thou take away the blind and the lame, thou shalt not come in hither; thinking, David cannot come in hither.

7Nevertheless David took the stronghold of Zion; the same is the city of David.

8And David said on that day, Whosoever smiteth the Jebusites, let him get up to the watercourse, and smite the lame and the blind, that are hated of David's soul. Wherefore they say, There are the blind and the lame; he cannot come into the house.

9And David dwelt in the stronghold, and called it the city of David. And David built round about from Millo and inward.

10And David waxed greater and greater; for Yahweh, the God of hosts, was with him.

11And Hiram king of Tyre sent messengers to David, and cedar-trees, and carpenters, and masons; and they built David a house.

12And David perceived that Yahweh had established him king over Israel, and that he had exalted his kingdom for his people Israel's sake.

13And David took him more concubines and wives out of Jerusalem, after he was come from Hebron; and there were yet sons and daughters born to David.

14And these are the names of those that were born unto him in Jerusalem: Shammua, and Shobab, and Nathan, and Solomon,

15and Ibhar, and Elishua, and Nepheg, and Japhia,

16and Elishama, and Eliada, and Eliphelet.

17And when the Philistines heard that they had anointed David king over Israel, all the Philistines went up to seek David; and David heard of it, and went down to the stronghold.

18Now the Philistines had come and spread themselves in the valley of Rephaim.

19And David inquired of Yahweh, saying, Shall I go up against the Philistines? wilt thou deliver them into my hand? And Yahweh said unto David, Go up; for I will certainly deliver the Philistines into thy hand.

20And David came to Baal-perazim, and David smote them there; and he said, Yahweh hath broken mine enemies before me, like the breach of waters. Therefore he called the name of that place Baal-perazim.

21And they left their images there; and David and his men took them away.

22And the Philistines came up yet again, and spread themselves in the valley of Rephaim.

23And when David inquired of Yahweh, he said, Thou shalt not go up: make a circuit behind them, and come upon them over against the mulberry-trees.

24And it shall be, when thou hearest the sound of marching in the tops of the mulberry-trees, that then thou shalt bestir thyself; for then is Yahweh gone out before thee to smite the host of the Philistines.

25And David did so, as Yahweh commanded him, and smote the Philistines from Geba until thou come to Gezer.

Second Samuel

Chapter 6

¹And David again gathered together all the chosen men of Israel, thirty thousand.

²And David arose, and went with all the people that were with him, from Baale-judah, to bring up from thence the ark of God, which is called by the Name, even the name of Yahweh of hosts that sitteth above the cherubim.

³And they set the ark of God upon a new cart, and brought it out of the house of Abinadab that was in the hill: and Uzzah and Ahio, the sons of Abinadab, drove the new cart.

⁴And they brought it out of the house of Abinadab, which was in the hill, with the ark of God: and Ahio went before the ark.

⁵And David and all the house of Israel played before Yahweh with all manner of instruments made of fir-wood, and with harps, and with psalteries, and with timbrels, and with castanets, and with cymbals.

⁶And when they came to the threshing-floor of Nacon, Uzzah put forth his hand to the ark of God, and took hold of it; for the oxen stumbled.

⁷And the anger of Yahweh was kindled against Uzzah; and God smote him there for his error; and there he died by the ark of God.

⁸And David was displeased, because Yahweh had broken forth upon Uzzah; and he called that place Perez-uzzah, unto this day.

⁹And David was afraid of Yahweh that day; and he said, How shall the ark of Yahweh come unto me?

¹⁰So David would not remove the ark of Yahweh unto him into the city of David; but David carried it aside into the house of Obed-edom the Gittite.

¹¹And the ark of Yahweh remained in the house of Obed-edom the Gittite three months: and Yahweh blessed Obed-edom, and all his house.

¹²And it was told king David, saying, Yahweh hath blessed the house of Obed-edom, and all that pertaineth unto him, because of the ark of God. And David went and brought up the ark of God from the house of Obed-edom into the city of David with joy.

¹³And it was so, that, when they that bare the ark of Yahweh had gone six paces, he sacrificed an ox and a fatling.

¹⁴And David danced before Yahweh with all his might; and David was girded with a linen ephod.

¹⁵So David and all the house of Israel brought up the ark of Yahweh with shouting, and with the sound of the trumpet.

¹⁶And it was so, as the ark of Yahweh came into the city of David, that Michal the daughter of Saul looked out at the window, and saw king David leaping and dancing before Yahweh; and she despised him in her heart.

¹⁷And they brought in the ark of Yahweh, and set it in its place, in the midst of the tent that David had pitched for it; and David offered burnt-offerings and peace-offerings before Yahweh.

¹⁸And when David had made an end of offering the burnt-offering and the peace-offerings, he blessed the people in the name of Yahweh of hosts.

¹⁹And he dealt among all the people, even among the whole multitude of Israel, both to men and women, to every one a cake of bread, and a portion of flesh, and a cake of raisins. So all the people departed every one to his house.

²⁰Then David returned to bless his household. And Michal the daughter of Saul came out to meet David, and said, How glorious was the king of Israel to-day, who uncovered himself to-day in the eyes of the handmaids of his servants, as one of the vain fellows shamelessly uncovereth himself!

²¹And David said unto Michal, It was before Yahweh, who chose me above thy father, and above all his house, to appoint me prince over the people of Yahweh, over Israel: therefore will I play before Yahweh.

²²And I will be yet more vile than this, and will be base in mine own sight: but of the handmaids of whom thou hast spoken, of them shall I be had in honor.

²³And Michal the daughter of Saul had no child unto the day of her death.

Chapter 7

¹And it came to pass, when the king dwelt in his house, and Yahweh had given him rest from all his enemies round about,

²that the king said unto Nathan the prophet, See now, I dwell in a house of cedar, but the ark of God dwelleth within curtains.

³And Nathan said to the king, Go, do all that is in thy heart; for Yahweh is with thee.

⁴And it came to pass the same night, that the word of Yahweh came unto Nathan, saying,

⁵Go and tell my servant David, Thus saith Yahweh, Shalt thou build me a house for me to dwell in?

⁶for I have not dwelt in a house since the day that I brought up the children of Israel out of Egypt, even to this day, but have walked in a tent and in a tabernacle.

⁷In all places wherein I have walked with all the children of Israel, spake I a word with any of the tribes of Israel, whom I commanded to be shepherd of my people Israel, saying, Why have ye not built me a house of cedar?

⁸Now therefore thus shalt thou say unto my servant David, Thus saith Yahweh of hosts, I took thee from the sheepcote, from following the sheep, that thou shouldest be prince over my people, over Israel;

⁹and I have been with thee whithersoever thou wentest, and have cut off all thine enemies from before thee; and I will make thee a great name, like unto the name of the great ones that are in the earth.

¹⁰And I will appoint a place for my people Israel, and will plant them, that they may dwell in their own place, and be moved no more; neither shall the children of wickedness afflict them any more, as at the first,

¹¹and as from the day that I commanded judges to be over my people Israel; and I will cause thee to rest from all thine enemies. Moreover Yahweh telleth thee that Yahweh will make thee a house.

¹²When thy days are fulfilled, and thou shalt sleep with thy fathers, I will set up thy seed after thee, that shall proceed out of thy bowels, and I will establish his kingdom.

¹³He shall build a house for my name, and I will establish the throne of his kingdom for ever.

¹⁴I will be his father, and he shall be my son: if he commit iniquity, I will chasten him with the rod of men, and with the stripes of the children of men;

¹⁵but my lovingkindness shall not depart from him, as I took it from Saul, whom I put away before thee.

¹⁶And thy house and thy kingdom shall be made sure for ever before thee: thy throne shall be established for ever.

¹⁷According to all these words, and according to all this vision, so did Nathan speak unto David.

¹⁸Then David the king went in, and sat before Yahweh; and he said, Who am I, O Lord Yahweh, and what is my house, that thou hast brought me thus far?

¹⁹And this was yet a small thing in thine eyes, O Lord Yahweh; but thou hast spoken also of thy servant's house for a great while to come; and this too after the manner of men, O Lord Yahweh!

²⁰And what can David say more unto thee? for thou knowest thy servant, O Lord Yahweh.

²¹For thy word's sake, and according to thine own heart, hast thou wrought all this greatness, to make thy servant know it.

²²Wherefore thou art great, O Yahweh God: for there is none like thee, neither is there any God besides thee, according to all that we have heard with our ears.

²³And what one nation in the earth is like thy people, even like Israel, whom God went to redeem unto himself for a people, and to make him a name, and to do great things for you, and terrible things for thy land, before thy people, whom thou redeemest to thee out of Egypt, from the nations and their gods?

²⁴And thou didst establish to thyself thy people Israel to be a people unto thee for ever; and thou, Yahweh, becamest their God.

²⁵And now, O Yahweh God, the word that thou hast spoken concerning thy servant, and concerning his house, confirm thou it for ever, and do as thou hast spoken.

²⁶And let thy name be magnified for ever, saying, Yahweh of hosts is God over Israel; and the house of thy servant David shall be established before thee.

²⁷For thou, O Yahweh of hosts, the God of Israel, hast revealed to thy servant, saying, I will build thee a house: therefore hath thy servant found in his heart to pray this prayer unto thee.

²⁸And now, O Lord Yahweh, thou art God, and thy words are truth, and thou hast promised this good thing unto thy servant:

²⁹now therefore let it please thee to bless the house of thy servant, that it may continue for ever before thee; for thou, O Lord Yahweh, hast spoken it: and with thy blessing let the house of thy servant be blessed for ever.

Chapter 8

¹And after this it came to pass, that David smote the Philistines, and subdued them: and David took the bridle of the mother city out of the hand of the Philistines.

²And he smote Moab, and measured them with the line, making them to lie down on the ground; and he measured two lines to put to death, and one full line to keep alive. And the Moabites became servants to David, and brought tribute.

³David smote also Hadadezer the son of Rehob, king of Zobah, as he went to recover his dominion at the River.

⁴And David took from him a thousand and seven hundred horsemen, and twenty thousand footmen: and David hocked all the chariot horses, but reserved of them for a hundred chariots.

⁵And when the Syrians of Damascus came to succor Hadadezer king of Zobah, David smote of the Syrians two and twenty thousand men.

⁶Then David put garrisons in Syria of Damascus; and the Syrians became servants to David, and brought tribute. And Yahweh gave victory to David whithersoever he went.

⁷And David took the shields of gold that were on the servants of Hadadezer, and brought them to Jerusalem.

⁸And from Betah and from Berothai, cities of Hadadezer, king David took exceeding much brass.

⁹And when Toi king of Hamath heard that David had smitten all the host of Hadadezer,

¹⁰then Toi sent Joram his son unto king David, to salute him, and to bless him, because he had fought against Hadadezer and smitten him: for Hadadezer had wars with Toi. And Joram brought with him vessels of silver, and vessels of gold, and vessels of brass:

¹¹These also did king David dedicate unto Yahweh, with the silver and gold that he dedicated of all the nations which he subdued;

¹²of Syria, and of Moab, and of the children of Ammon, and of the Philistines, and of Amalek, and of the spoil of Hadadezer, son of Rehob, king of Zobah.

¹³And David gat him a name when he returned from smiting the Syrians in the Valley of Salt, even eighteen thousand men.

¹⁴And he put garrisons in Edom; throughout all Edom put he garrisons, and all the Edomites became servants to David. And Yahweh gave victory to David whithersoever he went.

¹⁵And David reigned over all Israel; and David executed justice and righteousness unto all his people.

¹⁶And Joab the son of Zeruiah was over the host; and Jehoshaphat the son of Ahilud was recorder;

¹⁷and Zadok the son of Ahitub, and Ahimelech the son of Abiathar, were priests; and Seraiah was scribe;

¹⁸and Benaiah the son of Jehoiada was over the Cherethites and the Pelethites; and David's sons were chief ministers.

Chapter 9

1And David said, Is there yet any that is left of the house of Saul, that I may show him kindness for Jonathan's sake?

2And there was of the house of Saul a servant whose name was Ziba, and they called him unto David; and the king said unto him, Art thou Ziba? And he said, Thy servant is he.

3And the king said, Is there not yet any of the house of Saul, that I may show the kindness of God unto him? And Ziba said unto the king, Jonathan hath yet a son, who is lame of his feet.

4And the king said unto him, Where is he? And Ziba said unto the king, Behold, he is in the house of Machir the son of Ammiel, in Lo-debar.

5Then king David sent, and fetched him out of the house of Machir the son of Ammiel, from Lo-debar.

6And Mephibosheth, the son of Jonathan, the son of Saul, came unto David, and fell on his face, and did obeisance. And David said, Mephibosheth. And he answered, Behold, thy servant!

7And David said unto him, Fear not; for I will surely show thee kindness for Jonathan thy father's sake, and will restore thee all the land of Saul thy father; and thou shalt eat bread at my table continually.

8And he did obeisance, and said, What is thy servant, that thou shouldest look upon such a dead dog as I am?

9Then the king called to Ziba, Saul's servant, and said unto him, All that pertained to Saul and to all his house have I given unto thy master's son.

10And thou shalt till the land for him, thou, and thy sons, and thy servants; and thou shalt bring in the fruits, that thy master's son may have bread to eat: but Mephibosheth thy master's son shall eat bread alway at my table. Now Ziba had fifteen sons and twenty servants.

11Then said Ziba unto the king, According to all that my lord the king commandeth his servant, so shall thy servant do. As for Mephibosheth, said the king, he shall eat at my table, as one of the king's sons.

12And Mephibosheth had a young son, whose name was Mica. And all that dwelt in the house of Ziba were servants unto Mephibosheth.

13So Mephibosheth dwelt in Jerusalem; for he did eat continually at the king's table. And he was lame in both his feet.

Chapter 10

1And it came to pass after this, that the king of the children of Ammon died, and Hanun his son reigned in his stead.

2And David said, I will show kindness unto Hanun the son of Nahash, as his father showed kindness unto me. So David sent by his servants to comfort him concerning his father. And David's servants came into the land of the children of Ammon.

3But the princes of the children of Ammon said unto Hanun their lord, Thinkest thou that David doth honor thy father, in that he hath sent comforters unto thee? hath not David sent his servants unto thee to search the city, and to spy it out, and to overthrow it?

4So Hanun took David's servants, and shaved off the one half of their beards, and cut off their garments in the middle, even to their buttocks, and sent them away.

5When they told it unto David, he sent to meet them; for the men were greatly ashamed. And the king said, Tarry at Jericho until your beards be grown, and then return.

6And when the children of Ammon saw that they were become odious to David, the children of Ammon sent and hired the Syrians of Beth-rehob, and the Syrians of Zobah, twenty thousand footmen, and the king of Maacah with a thousand men, and the men of Tob twelve thousand men.

7And when David heard of it, he sent Joab, and all the host of the mighty men.

8And the children of Ammon came out, and put the battle in array at the entrance of the gate: and the Syrians of Zobah and of Rehob, and the men of Tob and Maacah, were by themselves in the field.

9Now when Joab saw that the battle was set against him before and behind, he chose of all the choice men of Israel, and put them in array against the Syrians:

10And the rest of the people he committed into the hand of Abishai his brother; and he put them in array against the children of Ammon.

11And he said, If the Syrians be too strong for me, then thou shalt help me; but if the children of Ammon be too strong for thee, then I will come and help thee.

12Be of good courage, and let us play the man for our people, and for the cities of our God: and Yahweh do that which seemeth him good.

13So Joab and the people that were with him drew nigh unto the battle against the Syrians: and they fled before him.

14And when the children of Ammon saw that the Syrians were fled, they likewise fled before Abishai, and entered into the city. Then Joab returned from the children of Ammon, and came to Jerusalem.

15And when the Syrians saw that they were put to the worse before Israel, they gathered themselves together.

16And Hadarezer sent, and brought out the Syrians that were beyond the River: and they came to Helam, with Shobach the captain of the host of Hadarezer at their head.

17And it was told David; and he gathered all Israel together, and passed over the Jordan, and came to Helam. And the Syrians set themselves in array against David, and fought with him.

18And the Syrians fled before Israel; and David slew of the Syrians the men of seven hundred chariots, and forty thousand horsemen, and smote Shobach the captain of their host, so that he died there.

19And when all the kings that were servants to Hadarezer saw that they were put to the worse before Israel, they made peace with Israel, and served them. So the Syrians feared to help the children of Ammon any more.

Chapter 11

1And it came to pass, at the return of the year, at the time when kings go out to battle, that David sent Joab, and his servants with him, and all Israel; and they destroyed the children of Ammon, and besieged Rabbah. But David tarried at Jerusalem.

2And it came to pass at eventide, that David arose from off his bed, and walked upon the roof of the king's house: and from the roof he saw a woman bathing; and the woman was very beautiful to look upon.

3And David send and inquired after the woman. And one said, Is not this Bath-sheba, the daughter of Eliam, the wife of Uriah the Hittite?

4And David sent messengers, and took her; and she came in unto him, and he lay with her (for she was purified from her uncleanness); and she returned unto her house.

5And the woman conceived; and she sent and told David, and said, I am with child.

6And David sent to Joab, saying, Send me Uriah the Hittite. And Joab sent Uriah to David.

7And when Uriah was come unto him, David asked of him how Joab did, and how the people fared, and how the war prospered.

8And David said to Uriah, Go down to thy house, and wash thy feet. And Uriah departed out of the king's house, and there followed him a mess of food from the king.

9But Uriah slept at the door of the king's house with all the servants of his lord, and went not down to his house.

10And when they had told David, saying, Uriah went not down unto his house, David said unto Uriah, Art thou not come from a journey? wherefore didst thou not go down unto thy house?

11And Uriah said unto David, The ark, and Israel, and Judah, abide in booths; and my lord Joab, and the servants of my lord, are encamped in the open field; shall I then go into my house, to eat and to drink, and to lie with my wife? as thou livest, and as thy soul liveth, I will not do this thing.

12And David said to Uriah, Tarry here to-day also, and to-morrow I will let thee depart. So Uriah abode in Jerusalem that day, and the morrow.

13And when David had called him, he did eat and drink before him; and he made him drunk: and at even he went out to lie on his bed with the servants of his lord, but went not down to his house.

14And it came to pass in the morning, that David wrote a letter to Joab, and sent it by the hand of Uriah.

15And he wrote in the letter, saying, Set ye Uriah in the forefront of the hottest battle, and retire ye from him, that he may be smitten, and die.

16And it came to pass, when Joab kept watch upon the city, that he assigned Uriah unto the place where he knew that valiant men were.

17And the men of the city went out, and fought with Joab: and there fell some of the people, even of the servants of David; and Uriah the Hittite died also.

18Then Joab sent and told David all the things concerning the war;

19and he charged the messenger, saying, When thou hast made an end of telling all the things concerning the war unto the king,

20it shall be that, if the king's wrath arise, and he say unto thee, Wherefore went ye so nigh unto the city to fight? knew ye not that they would shoot from the wall?

21who smote Abimelech the son of Jerubbesheth? did not a woman cast an upper millstone upon him from the wall, so that he died at Thebez? why went ye so nigh the wall? then shalt thou say, Thy servant Uriah the Hittite is dead also.

22So the messenger went, and came and showed David all that Joab had sent him for.

23And the messenger said unto David, The men prevailed against us, and came out unto us into the field, and we were upon them even unto the entrance of the gate.

24And the shooters shot at thy servants from off the wall; and some of the king's servants are dead, and thy servant Uriah the Hittite is dead also.

25Then David said unto the messenger, Thus shalt thou say unto Joab, Let not this thing displease thee, for the sword devoureth one as well as another; make thy battle more strong against the city, and overthrow it: and encourage thou him.

26And when the wife of Uriah heard that Uriah her husband was dead, she made lamentation for her husband.

27And when the mourning was past, David sent and took her home to his house, and she became his wife, and bare him a son. But the thing that David had done displeased Yahweh.

Chapter 12

1And Yahweh sent Nathan unto David. And he came unto him, and said unto him, There were two men in one city; the one rich, and the other poor.

2The rich man had exceeding many flocks and herds;

3but the poor man had nothing, save one little ewe lamb, which he had bought and nourished up: and it grew up together with him, and with his children; it did eat of his own morsel, and drank of his own cup, and lay in his bosom, and was unto him as a daughter.

4And there came a traveller unto the rich man, and he spared to take of his own flock and of his own herd, to dress for the wayfaring man that was come unto him, but took the poor man's lamb, and dressed it for the man that was come to him.

5And David's anger was greatly kindled against the man; and he said to Nathan, As Yahweh liveth, the man that hath done this is worthy to die:

6and he shall restore the lamb fourfold, because he did this thing, and because he had no pity.

7And Nathan said to David, Thou art the man. Thus saith Yahweh, the God

Second Samuel

of Israel, I anointed thee king over Israel, and I delivered thee out of the hand of Saul;

8and I gave thee thy master's house, and thy master's wives into thy bosom, and gave thee the house of Israel and of Judah; and if that had been too little, I would have added unto thee such and such things.

9Wherefore hast thou despised the word of Yahweh, to do that which is evil in his sight? thou hast smitten Uriah the Hittite with the sword, and hast taken his wife to be thy wife, and hast slain him with the sword of the children of Ammon.

10Now therefore the sword shall never depart from thy house, because thou hast despised me, and hast taken the wife of Uriah the Hittite to be thy wife.

11Thus saith Yahweh, Behold, I will raise up evil against thee out of thine own house; and I will take thy wives before thine eyes, and give them unto thy neighbor, and he shall lie with thy wives in the sight of this sun.

12For thou didst it secretly: but I will do this thing before all Israel, and before the sun.

13And David said unto Nathan, I have sinned against Yahweh. And Nathan said unto David, Yahweh also hath put away thy sin; thou shalt not die.

14Howbeit, because by this deed thou hast given great occasion to the enemies of Yahweh to blaspheme, the child also that is born unto thee shall surely die.

15And Nathan departed unto his house.

And Yahweh struck the child that Uriah's wife bare unto David, and it was very sick.

16David therefore besought God for the child; and David fasted, and went in, and lay all night upon the earth.

17And the elders of his house arose, and stood beside him, to raise him up from the earth: but he would not, neither did he eat bread with them.

18And it came to pass on the seventh day, that the child died. And the servants of David feared to tell him that the child was dead; for they said, Behold, while the child was yet alive, we spake unto him, and he hearkened not unto our voice: how will he then vex himself, if we tell him that the child is dead!

19But when David saw that his servants were whispering together, David perceived that the child was dead; and David said unto his servants, Is the child dead? And they said, He is dead.

20Then David arose from the earth, and washed, and anointed himself, and changed his apparel; and he came into the house of Yahweh, and worshipped: then he came to his own house; and when he required, they set bread before him, and he did eat.

21Then said his servants unto him, What thing is this that thou hast done? thou didst fast and weep for the child, while it was alive; but when the child was dead, thou didst rise and eat bread.

22And he said, While the child was yet alive, I fasted and wept: for I said, Who knoweth whether Yahweh will not be gracious to me, that the child may live?

23But now he is dead, wherefore should I fast? can I bring him back again? I shall go to him, but he will not return to me.

24And David comforted Bath-sheba his wife, and went in unto her, and lay with her: and she bare a son, and he called his name Solomon. And Yahweh loved him;

25and he sent by the hand of Nathan the prophet; and he called his name Jedidiah, for Yahweh's sake.

26Now Joab fought against Rabbah of the children of Ammon, and took the royal city.

27And Joab sent messengers to David, and said, I have fought against Rabbah; yea, I have taken the city of waters.

28Now therefore gather the rest of the people together, and encamp against the city, and take it; lest I take the city, and it be called after my name.

29And David gathered all the people together, and went to Rabbah, and fought against it, and took it.

30And he took the crown of their king from off his head; and the weight thereof was a talent of gold, and in it were precious stones; and it was set on David's head. And he brought forth the spoil of the city, exceeding much.

31And he brought forth the people that were therein, and put them under saws, and under harrows of iron, and under axes of iron, and made them pass through the brickkiln: and thus did he unto all the cities of the children of Ammon. And David and all the people returned unto Jerusalem.

Chapter 13

1And it came to pass after this, that Absalom the son of David had a fair sister, whose name was Tamar; and Amnon the son of David loved her.

2And Amnon was so vexed that he fell sick because of his sister Tamar; for she was a virgin; and it seemed hard to Amnon to do anything unto her.

3But Amnon had a friend, whose name was Jonadab, the son of Shimeah, David's brother; and Jonadab was a very subtle man.

4And he said unto him, Why, O son of the king, art thou thus lean from day to day? wilt thou not tell me? And Amnon said unto him, I love Tamar, my brother Absalom's sister.

5And Jonadab said unto him, Lay thee down on thy bed, and feign thyself sick: and when thy father cometh to see thee, say unto him, Let my sister Tamar come, I pray thee, and give me bread to eat, and dress the food in my sight, that I may see it, and eat it from her hand.

6So Amnon lay down, and feigned himself sick: and when the king was come to see him, Amnon said unto the king, Let her sister Tamar come, I pray thee, and make me a couple of cakes in my sight, that I may eat from her hand.

7Then David sent home to Tamar, saying, Go now to thy brother Amnon's house, and dress him food.

8So Tamar went to her brother Amnon's house; and he was laid down. And she took dough, and kneaded it, and made cakes in his sight, and did bake the cakes.

9And she took the pan, and poured them out before him; but he refused to eat. And Amnon said, Have out all men from me. And they went out every man from him.

10And Amnon said unto Tamar, Bring the food into the chamber, that I may eat from thy hand. And Tamar took the cakes which she had made, and brought them into the chamber to Amnon her brother.

11And when she had brought them near unto him to eat, he took hold of her, and said unto her, Come, lie with me, my sister.

12And she answered him, Nay, my brother, do not force me; for no such thing ought to be done in Israel: do not thou this folly.

13And I, whither shall I carry my shame? and as for thee, thou wilt be as one of the fools in Israel. Now therefore, I pray thee, speak unto the king; for he will not withhold me from thee.

14Howbeit he would not hearken unto her voice; but being stronger than she, he forced her, and lay with her.

15Then Amnon hated her with exceeding great hatred; for the hatred wherewith he hated her was greater than the love wherewith he had loved her. And Amnon said unto her, Arise, be gone.

16And she said unto him, Not so, because this great wrong in putting me forth is worse than the other that thou didst unto me. But he would not hearken unto her.

17Then he called his servant that ministered unto him, and said, Put now this woman out from me, and bolt the door after her.

18And she had a garment of divers colors upon her; for with such robes were the king's daughters that were virgins apparelled. Then his servant brought her out, and bolted the door after her.

19And Tamar put ashes on her head, and rent her garment of divers colors that was on her; and she laid her hand on her head, and went her way, crying aloud as she went.

20And Absalom her brother said unto her, Hath Amnon thy brother been with thee? but now hold thy peace, my sister: he is thy brother; take not this thing to heart. So Tamar remained desolate in her brother Absalom's house.

21But when king David heard of all these things, he was very wroth.

22And Absalom spake unto Amnon neither good nor bad; for Absalom hated Amnon, because he had forced his sister Tamar.

23And it came to pass after two full years, that Absalom had sheep-shearers in Baal-hazor, which is beside Ephraim: and Absalom invited all the king's sons.

24And Absalom came to the king, and said, Behold now, thy servant hath sheep-shearers; let the king, I pray thee, and his servants go with thy servant.

25And the king said to Absalom, Nay, my son, let us not all go, lest we be burdensome unto thee. And he pressed him: howbeit he would not go, but blessed him.

26Then said Absalom, If not, I pray thee, let my brother Amnon go with us. And the king said unto him, Why should he go with thee?

27But Absalom pressed him, and he let Amnon and all the king's sons go with him.

28And Absalom commanded his servants, saying, Mark ye now, when Amnon's heart is merry with wine; and when I say unto you, Smite Amnon, then kill him; fear not; have not I commanded you? be courageous, and be valiant.

29And the servants of Absalom did unto Amnon as Absalom had commanded. Then all the king's sons arose, and every man gat him up upon his mule, and fled.

30And it came to pass, while they were in the way, that the tidings came to David, saying, Absalom hath slain all the king's sons, and there is not one of them left.

31Then the king arose, and rent his garments, and lay on the earth; and all his servants stood by with their clothes rent.

32And Jonadab, the son of Shimeah, David's brother, answered and said, Let not my lord suppose that they have killed all the young men the king's sons; for Amnon only is dead: for by the appointment of Absalom this hath been determined from the day that he forced his sister Tamar.

33Now therefore let not my lord the king take the thing to his heart, to think that all the king's sons are dead; for Amnon only is dead.

34But Absalom fled. And the young man that kept the watch lifted up his eyes, and looked, and, behold, there came much people by the way of the hill-side behind him.

35And Jonadab said unto the king, Behold, the king's sons are come: as thy servant said, so it is.

36And it came to pass, as soon as he had made an end of speaking, that, behold, the king's sons came, and lifted up their voice, and wept: and the king also and all his servants wept very sore.

37But Absalom fled, and went to Talmai the son of Ammihur, king of Geshur. And David mourned for his son every day.

38So Absalom fled, and went to Geshur, and was there three years.

39And the soul of king David longed to go forth unto Absalom: for he was comforted concerning Amnon, seeing he was dead.

Chapter 14

1Now Joab the son of Zeruiah perceived that the king's heart was toward Absalom.

2And Joab sent to Tekoa, and fetched thence a wise woman, and said unto her, I pray thee, feign thyself to be a mourner, and put on mourning apparel, I pray thee, and anoint not thyself with oil, but be as a woman that hath a long time mourned for the dead:

3and go in to the king, and speak on this manner unto him. So Joab put the words in her mouth.

4And when the woman of Tekoa spake to the king, she fell on her face to the ground, and did obeisance, and said, Help, O king.

5And the king said unto her, What aileth thee? And she answered, Of a truth

I am a widow, and my husband is dead.

6And thy handmaid had two sons, and they two strove together in the field, and there was none to part them, but the one smote the other, and killed him.

7And, behold, the whole family is risen against thy handmaid, and they say, Deliver him that smote his brother, that we may kill him for the life of his brother whom he slew, and so destroy the heir also. Thus will they quench my coal which is left, and will leave to my husband neither name nor remainder upon the face of the earth.

8And the king said unto the woman, Go to thy house, and I will give charge concerning thee.

9And the woman of Tekoa said unto the king, My lord, O king, the iniquity be on me, and on my father's house; and the king and his throne be guiltless.

10And the king said, Whosoever saith aught unto thee, bring him to me, and he shall not touch thee any more.

11Then said she, I pray thee, let the king remember Yahweh thy God, that the avenger of blood destroy not any more, lest they destroy my son. And he said, As Yahweh liveth, there shall not one hair of thy son fall to the earth.

12Then the woman said, Let thy handmaid, I pray thee, speak a word unto my lord the king. And he said, Say on.

13And the woman said, Wherefore then hast thou devised such a thing against the people of God? for in speaking this word the king is as one that is guilty, in that the king doth not fetch home again his banished one.

14For we must needs die, and are as water split on the ground, which cannot be gathered up again; neither doth God take away life, but deviseth means, that he that is banished be not an outcast from him.

15Now therefore seeing that I am come to speak this word unto my lord the king, it is because the people have made me afraid: and thy handmaid said, I will now speak unto the king; it may be that the king will perform the request of his servant.

16For the king will hear, to deliver his servant out of the hand of the man that would destroy me and my son together out of the inheritance of God.

17Then thy handmaid said, Let, I pray thee, the word of my lord the king be comfortable; for as an angel of God, so is my lord the king to discern good and bad: and Yahweh thy God be with thee.

18Then the king answered and said unto the woman, Hide not from me, I pray thee, aught that I shall ask thee. And the woman said, Let my lord the king now speak.

19And the king said, Is the hand of Joab with thee in all this? And the woman answered and said, As thy soul liveth, my lord the king, none can turn to the right hand or to the left from aught that my lord the king hath spoken; for thy servant Joab, he bade me, and he put all these words in the mouth of thy handmaid;

20to change the face of the matter hath thy servant Joab done this thing: and my lord is wise, according to the wisdom of an angel of God, to know all things that are in the earth.

21And the king said unto Joab, Behold now, I have done this thing: go therefore, bring the young man Absalom back.

22And Joab fell to the ground on his face, and did obeisance, and blessed the king: and Joab said, To-day thy servant knoweth that I have found favor in thy sight, my lord, O king, in that the king hath performed the request of his servant.

23So Joab arose and went to Geshur, and brought Absalom to Jerusalem.

24And the king said, Let him turn to his own house, but let him not see my face. So Absalom turned to his own house, and saw not the king's face.

25Now in all Israel there was none to be so much praised as Absalom for his beauty: from the sole of his foot even to the crown of his head there was no blemish in him.

26And when he cut the hair of his head (now it was at every year's end that he cut it; because it was heavy on him, therefore he cut it); he weighed the hair of his head at two hundred shekels, after the king's weight.

27And unto Absalom there were born three sons, and one daughter, whose name was Tamar: she was a woman of a fair countenance.

28And Absalom dwelt two full years in Jerusalem; and he saw not the king's face.

29Then Absalom sent for Joab, to send him to the king; but he would not come to him: and he sent again a second time, but he would not come.

30Therefore he said unto his servants, See, Joab's field is near mine, and he hath barley there; go and set it on fire. And Absalom's servants set the field on fire.

31Then Joab arose, and came to Absalom unto his house, and said unto him, Wherefore have thy servants set my field on fire?

32And Absalom answered Joab, Behold, I sent unto thee, saying, Come hither, that I may send thee to the king, to say, Wherefore am I come from Geshur? it were better for me to be there still. Now therefore let me see the king's face; and if there be iniquity in me, let him kill me.

33So Joab came to the king, and told him; and when he had called for Absalom, he came to the king, and bowed himself on his face to the ground before the king: and the king kissed Absalom.

Chapter 15

1And it came to pass after this, that Absalom prepared him a chariot and horses, and fifty men to run before him.

2And Absalom rose up early, and stood beside the way of the gate: and it was so, that, when any man had a suit which should come to the king for judgment, then Absalom called unto him, and said, Of what city art thou? And he said, Thy servant is of one of the tribes of Israel.

3And Absalom said unto him, See, thy matters are good and right; but there is no man deputed of the king to hear thee.

4Absalom said moreover, Oh that I were made judge in the land, that every man who hath any suit or cause might come unto me, and I would do him justice!

5And it was so, that, when any man came nigh to do him obeisance, he put forth his hand, and took hold of him, and kissed him.

6And on this manner did Absalom to all Israel that came to the king for judgment: so Absalom stole the hearts of the men of Israel.

7And it came to pass at the end of forty years, that Absalom said unto the king, I pray thee, let me go and pay my vow, which I have vowed unto Yahweh, in Hebron.

8For thy servant vowed a vow while I abode at Geshur in Syria, saying, If Yahweh shall indeed bring me again to Jerusalem, then I will serve Yahweh.

9And the king said unto him, Go in peace. So he arose, and went to Hebron.

10But Absalom sent spies throughout all the tribes of Israel, saying, As soon as ye hear the sound of the trumpet, then ye shall say, Absalom is king in Hebron.

11And with Absalom went two hundred men out of Jerusalem, that were invited, and went in their simplicity; and they knew not anything.

12And Absalom sent for Ahithophel the Gilonite, David's counsellor, from his city, even from Giloh, while he was offering the sacrifices. And the conspiracy was strong; for the people increased continually with Absalom.

13And there came a messenger to David, saying, The hearts of the men of Israel are after Absalom.

14And David said unto all his servants that were with him at Jerusalem, Arise, and let us flee; for else none of us shall escape from Absalom: make speed to depart, lest he overtake us quickly, and bring down evil upon us, and smite the city with the edge of the sword.

15And the king's servants said unto the king, Behold, thy servants are ready to do whatsoever my lord the king shall choose.

16And the king went forth, and all his household after him. And the king left ten women, that were concubines, to keep the house.

17And the king went forth, and all the people after him; and they tarried in Beth-merhak.

18And all his servants passed on beside him; and all the Cherethites, and all the Pelethites, and all the Gittites, six hundred men that came after him from Gath, passed on before the king.

19Then said the king to Ittai the Gittite, Wherefore goest thou also with us? return, and abide with the king: for thou art a foreigner, and also an exile; return to thine own place.

20Whereas thou camest but yesterday, should I this day make thee go up and down with us, seeing I go whither I may? return thou, and take back thy brethren; mercy and truth be with thee.

21And Ittai answered the king, and said, As Yahweh liveth, and as my lord the king liveth, surely in what place my lord the king shall be, whether for death or for life, even there also will thy servant be.

22And David said to Ittai, Go and pass over. And Ittai the Gittite passed over, and all his men, and all the little ones that were with him.

23And all the country wept with a loud voice, and all the people passed over: the king also himself passed over the brook Kidron, and all the people passed over, toward the way of the wilderness.

24And, lo, Zadok also came, and all the Levites with him, bearing the ark of the covenant of God; and they set down the ark of God; and Abiathar went up, until all the people had done passing out of the city.

25And the king said unto Zadok, Carry back the ark of God into the city: if I shall find favor in the eyes of Yahweh, he will bring me again, and show me both it, and his habitation:

26but if he say thus, I have no delight in thee; behold, here am I, let him do to me as seemeth good unto him.

27The king said also unto Zadok the priest, Art thou not a seer? return into the city in peace, and your two sons with you, Ahimaaz thy son, and Jonathan the son of Abiathar.

28See, I will tarry at the fords of the wilderness, until there come word from you to certify me.

29Zadok therefore and Abiathar carried the ark of God again to Jerusalem: and they abode there.

30And David went up by the ascent of the mount of Olives, and wept as he went up; and he had his head covered, and went barefoot: and all the people that were with him covered every man his head, and they went up, weeping as they went up.

31And one told David, saying, Ahithophel is among the conspirators with Absalom. And David said, O Yahweh, I pray thee, turn the counsel of Ahithophel into foolishness.

32And it came to pass, that, when David was come to the top of the ascent, where God was worshipped, behold, Hushai the Archite came to meet him with his coat rent, and earth upon his head.

33And David said unto him, If thou passest on with me, then thou wilt be a burden unto me:

34but if thou return to the city, and say unto Absalom, I will be thy servant, O king; as I have been thy father's servant in time past, so will I now be thy servant; then wilt thou defeat for me the counsel of Ahithophel.

35And hast thou not there with thee Zadok and Abiathar the priests? therefore it shall be, that what thing soever thou shalt hear out of the king's house, thou shalt tell it to Zadok and Abiathar the priests.

36Behold, they have there with them their two sons, Ahimaaz, Zadok's son, and Jonathan, Abiathar's son; and by them ye shall send unto me everything that ye shall hear.

37So Hushai, David's friend, came into the city; and Absalom came into Jerusalem.

Second Samuel

Chapter 16

¹And when David was a little past the top of the ascent, behold, Ziba the servant of Mephibosheth met him, with a couple of asses saddled, and upon them two hundred loaves of bread, and a hundred clusters of raisins, and a hundred of summer fruits, and a bottle of wine.

²And the king said unto Ziba, What meanest thou by these? And Ziba said, The asses are for the king's household to ride on; and the bread and summer fruit for the young men to eat; and the wine, that such as are faint in the wilderness may drink.

³And the king said, And where is thy master's son? And Ziba said unto the king, Behold, he abideth at Jerusalem; for he said, To-day will the house of Israel restore me the kingdom of my father.

⁴Then said the king to Ziba, Behold, thine is all that pertaineth unto Mephibosheth. And Ziba said, I do obeisance; let me find favor in thy sight, my lord, O king.

⁵And when king David came to Bahurim, behold, there came out thence a man of the family of the house of Saul, whose name was Shimei, the son of Gera; he came out, and cursed still as he came.

⁶And he cast stones at David, and at all the servants of king David: and all the people and all the mighty men were on his right hand and on his left.

⁷And thus said Shimei when he cursed, Begone, begone, thou man of blood, and base fellow:

⁸Yahweh hath returned upon thee all the blood of the house of Saul, in whose stead thou hast reigned; and Yahweh hath delivered the kingdom into the hand of Absalom thy son; and, behold, thou art taken in thine own mischief, because thou art a man of blood.

⁹Then said Abishai the son of Zeruiah unto the king, Why should this dead dog curse my lord the king? let me go over, I pray thee, and take off his head.

¹⁰And the king said, What have I to do with you, ye sons of Zeruiah? Because he curseth, and because Yahweh hath said unto him, Curse David; who then shall say, Wherefore hast thou done so?

¹¹And David said to Abishai, and to all his servants, Behold, my son, who came forth from my bowels, seeketh my life: how much more may this Benjamite now do it? let him alone, and let him curse; for Yahweh hath bidden him.

¹²It may be that Yahweh will look on the wrong done unto me, and that Yahweh will requite me good for his cursing of me this day.

¹³So David and his men went by the way; and Shimei went along on the hill-side over against him, and cursed as he went, and threw stones at him, and cast dust.

¹⁴And the king, and all the people that were with him, came weary; and he refreshed himself there.

¹⁵And Absalom, and all the people, the men of Israel, came to Jerusalem, and Ahithophel with him.

¹⁶And it came to pass, when Hushai the Archite, David's friend, was come unto Absalom, that Hushai said unto Absalom, Long live the king, Long live the king.

¹⁷And Absalom said to Hushai, Is this thy kindness to thy friend? why wentest thou not with thy friend?

¹⁸And Hushai said unto Absalom, Nay; but whom Yahweh, and this people, and all the men of Israel have chosen, his will I be, and with him will I abide.

¹⁹And again, whom should I serve? should I not serve in the presence of his son? as I have served in thy father's presence, so will I be in thy presence.

²⁰Then said Absalom to Ahithophel, Give your counsel what we shall do.

²¹And Ahithophel said unto Absalom, Go in unto thy father's concubines, that he hath left to keep the house; and all Israel will hear that thou art abhorred of thy father: then will the hands of all that are with thee be strong.

²²So they spread Absalom a tent upon the top of the house; and Absalom went in unto his father's concubines in the sight of all Israel.

²³And the counsel of Ahithophel, which he gave in those days, was as if a man inquired at the oracle of God: so was all the counsel of Ahithophel both with David and with Absalom.

Chapter 17

¹Moreover Ahithophel said unto Absalom, Let me now choose out twelve thousand men, and I will arise and pursue after David this night:

²and I will come upon him while he is weary and weak-handed, and will make him afraid; and all the people that are with him shall flee; and I will smite the king only;

³and I will bring back all the people unto thee: the man whom thou seekest is as if all returned: so all the people shall be in peace.

⁴And the saying pleased Absalom well, and all the elders of Israel.

⁵Then said Absalom, Call now Hushai the Archite also, and let us hear likewise what he saith.

⁶And when Hushai was come to Absalom, Absalom spake unto him, saying, Ahithophel hath spoken after this manner: shall we do after his saying? if not, speak thou.

⁷And Hushai said unto Absalom, The counsel that Ahithophel hath given this time is not good.

⁸Hushai said moreover, Thou knowest thy father and his men, that they are mighty men, and they are chafed in their minds, as a bear robbed of her whelps in the field; and thy father is a man of war, and will not lodge with the people.

⁹Behold, he is hid now in some pit, or in some other place: and it will come to pass, when some of them are fallen at the first, that whosoever heareth it will say, There is a slaughter among the people that follow Absalom.

¹⁰And even he that is valiant, whose heart is as the heart of a lion, will utterly melt; for all Israel knoweth that thy father is a mighty man, and they that are with him are valiant men.

¹¹But I counsel that all Israel be gathered together unto thee, from Dan even to Beer-sheba, as the sand that is by the sea for multitude; and that thou go to battle in thine own person.

¹²So shall we come upon him in some place where he shall be found, and we will light upon him as the dew falleth on the ground; and of him and of all the men that are with him we will not leave so much as one.

¹³Moreover, if he be gotten into a city, then shall all Israel bring ropes to that city, and we will draw it into the river, until there be not one small stone found there.

¹⁴And Absalom and all the men of Israel said, The counsel of Hushai the Archite is better than the counsel of Ahithophel. For Yahweh had ordained to defeat the good counsel of Ahithophel, to the intent that Yahweh might bring evil upon Absalom.

¹⁵Then said Hushai unto Zadok and to Abiathar the priests, Thus and thus did Ahithophel counsel Absalom and the elders of Israel; and thus and thus have I counselled.

¹⁶Now therefore send quickly, and tell David, saying, Lodge not this night at the fords of the wilderness, but by all means pass over; lest the king be swallowed up, and all the people that are with him.

¹⁷Now Jonathan and Ahimaaz were staying by En-rogel; and a maid-servant used to go and tell them; and they went and told king David: for they might not be seen to come into the city.

¹⁸But a lad saw them, and told Absalom: and they went both of them away quickly, and came to the house of a man in Bahurim, who had a well in his court; and they went down thither.

¹⁹And the woman took and spread the covering over the well's mouth, and strewed bruised grain thereon; and nothing was known.

²⁰And Absalom's servants came to the woman to the house; and they said, Where are Ahimaaz and Jonathan? And the woman said unto them, They are gone over the brook of water. And when they had sought and could not find them, they returned to Jerusalem.

²¹And it came to pass, after they were departed, that they came up out of the well, and went and told king David; and they said unto David, Arise ye, and pass quickly over the water; for thus hath Ahithophel counselled against you.

²²Then David arose, and all the people that were with him, and they passed over the Jordan: by the morning light there lacked not one of them that was not gone over the Jordan.

²³And when Ahithophel saw that his counsel was not followed, he saddled his ass, and arose, and gat him home, unto his city, and set his house in order, and hanged himself; and he died, and was buried in the sepulchre of his father.

²⁴Then David came to Mahanaim. And Absalom passed over the Jordan, he and all the men of Israel with him.

²⁵And Absalom set Amasa over the host instead of Joab. Now Amasa was the son of a man, whose name was Ithra the Israelite, that went in to Abigal the daughter of Nahash, sister to Zeruiah, Joab's mother.

²⁶And Israel and Absalom encamped in the land of Gilead.

²⁷And it came to pass, when David was come to Mahanaim, that Shobi the son of Nahash of Rabbah of the children of Ammon, and Machir the son of Ammiel of Lodebar, and Barzillai the Gileadite of Rogelim,

²⁸brought beds, and basins, and earthen vessels, and wheat, and barley, and meal, and parched grain, and beans, and lentils, and parched pulse,

²⁹and honey, and butter, and sheep, and cheese of the herd, for David, and for the people that were with him, to eat: for they said, The people are hungry, and weary, and thirsty, in the wilderness.

Chapter 18

¹And David numbered the people that were with him, and set captains of thousands and captains of hundreds over them.

²And David sent forth the people, a third part under the hand of Joab, and a third part under the hand of Abishai the son of Zeruiah, Joab's brother, and a third part under the hand of Ittai the Gittite. And the king said unto the people, I will surely go forth with you myself also.

³But the people said, Thou shalt not go forth: for if we flee away, they will not care for us; neither if half of us die, will they care for us: but thou art worth ten thousand of us; therefore now it is better that thou be ready to succor us out of the city.

⁴And the king said unto them, What seemeth you best I will do. And the king stood by the gate-side, and all the people went out by hundreds and by thousands.

⁵And the king commanded Joab and Abishai and Ittai, saying, Deal gently for my sake with the young man, even with Absalom. And all the people heard when the king gave all the captains charge concerning Absalom.

⁶So the people went out into the field against Israel: and the battle was in the forest of Ephraim.

⁷And the people of Israel were smitten there before the servants of David, and there was a great slaughter there that day of twenty thousand men.

⁸For the battle was there spread over the face of all the country; and the forest devoured more people that day than the sword devoured.

⁹And Absalom chanced to meet the servants of David. And Absalom was riding upon his mule, and the mule went under the thick boughs of a great oak, and his head caught hold of the oak, and he was taken up between heaven and earth; and the mule that was under him went on.

¹⁰And a certain man saw it, and told Joab, and said, Behold, I saw Absalom hanging in an oak.

¹¹And Joab said unto the man that told him, And, behold, thou sawest it, and why didst thou not smite him there to the ground? and I would have given thee ten pieces of silver, and a girdle.

¹²And the man said unto Joab, Though I should receive a thousand pieces of silver in my hand, yet would I not put forth my hand against the king's son; for in our hearing the king charged thee and Abishai and Ittai, saying, Beware that none

touch the young man Absalom.

13Otherwise if I had dealt falsely against his life (and there is no matter hid from the king), then thou thyself wouldest have set thyself against me.

14Then said Joab, I may not tarry thus with thee. And he took three darts in his hand, and thrust them through the heart of Absalom, while he was yet alive in the midst of the oak.

15And ten young men that bare Joab's armor compassed about and smote Absalom, and slew him.

16And Joab blew the trumpet, and the people returned from pursuing after Israel; for Joab held back the people.

17And they took Absalom, and cast him into the great pit in the forest, and raised over him a very great heap of stones: and all Israel fled every one to his tent.

18Now Absalom in his lifetime had taken and reared up for himself the pillar, which is in the king's dale; for he said, I have no son to keep my name in remembrance: and he called the pillar after his own name; and it is called Absalom's monument, unto this day.

19Then said Ahimaaz the son of Zadok, Let me now run, and bear the king tidings, how that Yahweh hath avenged him of his enemies.

20And Joab said unto him, Thou shalt not be the bearer of tidings this day, but thou shalt bear tidings another day; but this day thou shalt bear no tidings, because the king's son is dead.

21Then said Joab to the Cushite, Go, tell the king what thou hast seen. And the Cushite bowed himself unto Joab, and ran.

22Then said Ahimaaz the son of Zadok yet again to Joab, But come what may, let me, I pray thee, also run after the Cushite. And Joab said, Wherefore wilt thou run, my son, seeing that thou wilt have no reward for the tidings?

23But come what may, said he, I will run. And he said unto him, Run. Then Ahimaaz ran by the way of the Plain, and outran the Cushite.

24Now David was sitting between the two gates: and the watchman went up to the roof of the gate unto the wall, and lifted up his eyes, and looked, and, behold, a man running alone.

25And the watchman cried, and told the king. And the king said, If he be alone, there is tidings in his mouth. And he came apace, and drew near.

26And the watchman saw another man running; and the watchman called unto the porter, and said, Behold, another man running alone. And the king said, He also bringeth tidings.

27And the watchman said, I think the running of the foremost is like the running of Ahimaaz the son of Zadok. And the king said, He is a good man, and cometh with good tidings.

28And Ahimaaz called, and said unto the king, All is well. And he bowed himself before the king with his face to the earth, and said, Blessed be Yahweh thy God, who hath delivered up the men that lifted up their hand against my lord the king.

29And the king said, Is it well with the young man Absalom? And Ahimaaz answered, When Joab sent the king's servant, even me thy servant, I saw a great tumult, but I knew not what it was.

30And the king said, Turn aside, and stand here. And he turned aside, and stood still.

31And, behold, the Cushite came; and the Cushite said, Tidings for my lord the king; for Yahweh hath avenged thee this day of all them that rose up against thee.

32And the king said unto the Cushite, Is it well with the young man Absalom? And the Cushite answered, The enemies of my lord the king, and all that rise up against thee to do thee hurt, be as that young man is.

33And the king was much moved, and went up to the chamber over the gate, and wept: and as he went, thus he said, O my son Absalom, my son, my son Absalom! would I had died for thee, O Absalom, my son, my son!

Chapter 19

1And it was told Joab, Behold, the king weepeth and mourneth for Absalom.

2And the victory that day was turned into mourning unto all the people; for the people heard say that day, The king grieveth for his son.

3And the people gat them by stealth that day into the city, as people that are ashamed steal away when they flee in battle.

4And the king covered his face, and the king cried with a loud voice, O my son Absalom, O Absalom, my son, my son!

5And Joab came into the house to the king, and said, Thou hast shamed this day the faces of all thy servants, who this day have saved thy life, and the lives of thy sons and of thy daughters, and the lives of thy wives, and the lives of thy concubines;

6in that thou lovest them that hate thee, and hatest them that love thee. For thou hast declared this day, that princes and servants are nought unto thee: for this day I perceive, that if Absalom had lived, and all we had died this day, then it had pleased thee well.

7Now therefore arise, go forth, and speak comfortably unto thy servants; for I swear by Yahweh, if thou go not forth, there will not tarry a man with thee this night: and that will be worse unto thee than all the evil that hath befallen thee from thy youth until now.

8Then the king arose, and sat in the gate. And they told unto all the people, saying, Behold, the king is sitting in the gate: and all the people came before the king.

Now Israel had fled every man to his tent.

9And all the people were at strife throughout all the tribes of Israel, saying, The king delivered us out of the hand of our enemies, and he saved us out of the hand of the Philistines; and now he is fled out of the land from Absalom.

10And Absalom, whom we anointed over us, is dead in battle. Now therefore why speak ye not a word of bringing the king back?

11And king David sent to Zadok and to Abiathar the priests, saying, Speak unto the elders of Judah, saying, Why are ye the last to bring the king back to his house? seeing the speech of all Israel is come to the king, to bring him to his house.

12Ye are my brethren, ye are my bone and my flesh: wherefore then are ye the last to bring back the king?

13And say ye to Amasa, Art thou not my bone and my flesh? God do so to me, and more also, if thou be not captain of the host before me continually in the room of Joab.

14And he bowed the heart of all the men of Judah, even as the heart of one man; so that they sent unto the king, saying, Return thou, and all thy servants.

15So the king returned, and came to the Jordan. And Judah came to Gilgal, to go to meet the king, to bring the king over the Jordan.

16And Shimei the son of Gera, the Benjamite, who was of Bahurim, hasted and came down with the men of Judah to meet king David.

17And there were a thousand men of Benjamin with him, and Ziba the servant of the house of Saul, and his fifteen sons and his twenty servants with him; and they went through the Jordan in the presence of the king.

18And there went over a ferry-boat to bring over the king's household, and to do what he thought good. And Shimei the son of Gera fell down before the king, when he was come over the Jordan.

19And he said unto the king, Let not my lord impute iniquity unto me, neither do thou remember that which thy servant did perversely the day that my lord the king went out of Jerusalem, that the king should take it to his heart.

20For thy servant doth know that I have sinned: therefore, behold, I am come this day the first of all the house of Joseph to go down to meet my lord the king.

21But Abishai the son of Zeruiah answered and said, Shall not Shimei be put to death for this, because he cursed Yahweh's anointed?

22And David said, What have I to do with you, ye sons of Zeruiah, that ye should this day be adversaries unto me? shall there any man be put to death this day in Israel? for do not I know that I am this day king over Israel?

23And the king said unto Shimei, Thou shalt not die. And the king sware unto him.

24And Mephibosheth the son of Saul came down to meet the king; and he had neither dressed his feet, nor trimmed his beard, nor washed his clothes, from the day the king departed until the day he came home in peace.

25And it came to pass, when he was come to Jerusalem to meet the king, that the king said unto him, Wherefore wentest not thou with me, Mephibosheth?

26And he answered, My lord, O king, my servant deceived me: for thy servant said, I will saddle me an ass, that I may ride thereon, and go with the king; because thy servant is lame.

27And he hath slandered thy servant unto my lord the king; but my lord the king is as an angel of God: do therefore what is good in thine eyes.

28For all my father's house were but dead men before my lord the king; yet didst thou set thy servant among them that did eat at thine own table. What right therefore have I yet that I should cry any more unto the king?

29And the king said unto him, Why speakest thou any more of thy matters? I say, Thou and Ziba divide the land.

30And Mephibosheth said unto the king, yea, let him take all, forasmuch as my lord the king is come in peace unto his own house.

31And Barzillai the Gileadite came down from Rogelim; and he went over the Jordan with the king, to conduct him over the Jordan.

32Now Barzillai was a very aged man, even fourscore years old: and he had provided the king with sustenance while he lay at Mahanaim; for he was a very great man.

33And the king said unto Barzillai, Come thou over with me, and I will sustain thee with me in Jerusalem.

34And Barzillai said unto the king, How many are the days of the years of my life, that I should go up with the king unto Jerusalem?

35I am this day fourscore years old: can I discern between good and bad? can thy servant taste what I eat or what I drink? can I hear any more the voice of singing men and singing women? wherefore then should thy servant be yet a burden unto my lord the king?

36Thy servant would but just go over the Jordan with the king: and why should the king recompense it me with such a reward?

37Let thy servant, I pray thee, turn back again, that I may die in mine own city, by the grave of my father and my mother. But behold, thy servant Chimham; let him go over with my lord the king; and do to him what shall seem good unto thee.

38And the king answered, Chimham shall go over with me, and I will do to him that which shall seem good unto thee: and whatsoever thou shalt require of me, that will I do for thee.

39And all the people went over the Jordan, and the king went over: and the king kissed Barzillai, and blessed him; and he returned unto his own place.

40So the king went over to Gilgal, and Chimham went over with him: and all the people of Judah brought the king over, and also half the people of Israel.

41And, behold, all the men of Israel came to the king, and said unto the king, Why have our brethren the men of Judah stolen thee away, and brought the king, and his household, over the Jordan, and all David's men with him?

42And all the men of Judah answered the men of Israel, Because the king is near of kin to us: wherefore then are ye angry for this matter? have we eaten at all at the king's cost? or hath he given us any gift?

43And the men of Israel answered the men of Judah, and said, We have ten parts in the king, and we have also more right in David than ye: why then did ye despise us, that our advice should not be first had in bringing back our king? And the words of the men of Judah were fiercer than the words of the men of Israel.

Second Samuel
Chapter 20

1And there happened to be there a base fellow, whose name was Sheba, the son of Bichri, a Benjamite: and he blew the trumpet, and said, We have no portion in David, neither have we inheritance in the son of Jesse: every man to his tents, O Israel.

2So all the men of Israel went up from following David, and followed Sheba the son of Bichri; but the men of Judah clave unto their king, from the Jordan even to Jerusalem.

3And David came to his house at Jerusalem; and the king took the ten women his concubines, whom he had left to keep the house, and put them in ward, and provided them with sustenance, but went not in unto them. So they were shut up unto the day of their death, living in widowhood.

4Then said the king to Amasa, Call me the men of Judah together within three days, and be thou here present.

5So Amasa went to call the men of Judah together; but he tarried longer than the set time which he had appointed him.

6And David said to Abishai, Now will Sheba the son of Bichri do us more harm than did Absalom: take thou thy lord's servants, and pursue after him, lest he get him fortified cities, and escape out of our sight.

7And there went out after him Joab's men, and the Cherethites and the Pelethites, and all the mighty men; and they went out of Jerusalem, to pursue after Sheba the son of Bichri.

8When they were at the great stone which is in Gibeon, Amasa came to meet them. And Joab was girded with his apparel of war that he had put on, and thereon was a girdle with a sword fastened upon his loins in the sheath thereof; and as he went forth it fell out.

9And Joab said to Amasa, Is it well with thee, my brother? And Joab took Amasa by the beard with his right hand to kiss him.

10But Amasa took no heed to the sword that was in Joab's hand: so he smote him therewith in the body, and shed out his bowels to the ground, and struck him not again; and he died.

And Joab and Abishai his brother pursued after Sheba the son of Bichri.

11And there stood by him one of Joab's young men, and said, He that favoreth Joab, and he that is for David, let him follow Joab.

12And Amasa lay wallowing in his blood in the midst of the highway. And when the man saw that all the people stood still, he carried Amasa out of the highway into the field, and cast a garment over him, when he saw that every one that came by him stood still.

13When he was removed out of the highway, all the people went on after Joab, to pursue after Sheba the son of Bichri.

14And he went through all the tribes of Israel unto Abel, and to Beth-maacah, and all the Berites: and they were gathered together, and went also after him.

15And they came and besieged him in Abel of Beth-maacah, and they cast up a mound against the city, and it stood against the rampart; and all the people that were with Joab battered the wall, to throw it down.

16Then cried a wise woman out of the city, Hear, hear; say, I pray you, unto Joab, Come near hither, that I may speak with thee.

17And he came near unto her; and the woman said, Art thou Joab? And he answered, I am. Then she said unto him, Hear the words of thy handmaid. And he answered, I do hear.

18Then she spake, saying, They were wont to speak in old time, saying, They shall surely ask counsel at Abel: and so they ended the matter.

19I am of them that are peaceable and faithful in Israel: thou seekest to destroy a city and a mother in Israel: why wilt thou swallow up the inheritance of Yahweh?

20And Joab answered and said, Far be it, far be it from me, that I should swallow up or destroy.

21The matter is not so: but a man of the hill-country of Ephraim, Sheba the son of Bichri by name, hath lifted up his hand against the king, even against David; deliver him only, and I will depart from the city. And the woman said unto Joab, Behold, his head shall be thrown to thee over the wall.

22Then the woman went unto all the people in her wisdom. And they cut off the head of Sheba the son of Bichri, and threw it out to Joab. And he blew the trumpet, and they were dispersed from the city, every man to his tent. And Joab returned to Jerusalem unto the king.

23Now Joab was over all the host of Israel; and Benaiah the son of Jehoiada was over the Cherethites and over the Pelethites;

24and Adoram was over the men subject to taskwork; and Jehoshaphat the son of Ahilud was the recorder;

25and Sheva was scribe; and Zadok and Abiathar were priests;

26and also Ira the Jairite was chief minister unto David.

Chapter 21

1And there was a famine in the days of David three years, year after year; and David sought the face of Yahweh. And Yahweh said, It is for Saul, and for his bloody house, because he put to death the Gibeonites.

2And the king called the Gibeonites, and said unto them (now the Gibeonites were not of the children of Israel, but of the remnant of the Amorites; and the children of Israel had sworn unto them: and Saul sought to slay them in his zeal for the children of Israel and Judah);

3And David said unto the Gibeonites, What shall I do for you? and wherewith shall I make atonement, that ye may bless the inheritance of Yahweh?

4And the Gibeonites said unto him, It is no matter of silver or gold between us and Saul, or his house; neither is it for us to put any man to death in Israel. And he said, What ye shall say, that will I do for you.

5And they said unto the king, The man that consumed us, and that devised against us, that we should be destroyed from remaining in any of the borders of Israel,

6let seven men of his sons be delivered unto us, and we will hang them up unto Yahweh in Gibeah of Saul, the chosen of Yahweh. And the king said, I will give them.

7But the king spared Mephibosheth, the son of Jonathan the son of Saul, because of Yahweh's oath that was between them, between David and Jonathan the son of Saul.

8But the king took the two sons of Rizpah the daughter of Aiah, whom she bare unto Saul, Armoni and Mephibosheth; and the five sons of Michal the daughter of Saul, whom she bare to Adriel the son of Barzillai the Meholathite:

9And he delivered them into the hands of the Gibeonites, and they hanged them in the mountain before Yahweh, and they fell all seven together. And they were put to death in the days of harvest, in the first days, at the beginning of barley harvest.

10And Rizpah the daughter of Aiah took sackcloth, and spread it for her upon the rock, from the beginning of harvest until water was poured upon them from heaven; and she suffered neither the birds of the heavens to rest on them by day, nor the beasts of the field by night.

11And it was told David what Rizpah the daughter of Aiah, the concubine of Saul, had done.

12And David went and took the bones of Saul and the bones of Jonathan his son from the men of Jabesh-gilead, who had stolen them from the street of Beth-shan, where the Philistines had hanged them, in the day that the Philistines slew Saul in Gilboa;

13and he brought up from thence the bones of Saul and the bones of Jonathan his son: and they gathered the bones of them that were hanged.

14And they buried the bones of Saul and Jonathan his son in the country of Benjamin in Zela, in the sepulchre of Kish his father: and they performed all that the king commanded. And after that God was entreated for the land.

15And the Philistines had war again with Israel; and David went down, and his servants with him, and fought against the Philistines. And David waxed faint;

16and Ishbibenob, who was of the sons of the giant, the weight of whose spear was three hundred shekels of brass in weight, he being girded with a new sword, thought to have slain David.

17But Abishai the son of Zeruiah succored him, and smote the Philistine, and killed him. Then the men of David sware unto him, saying, Thou shalt go no more out with us to battle, that thou quench not the lamp of Israel.

18And it came to pass after this, that there was again war with the Philistines at Gob: then Sibbecai the Hushathite slew Saph, who was of the sons of the giant.

19And there was again war with the Philistines at Gob; and Elhanan the son of Jaareoregim the Beth-lehemite slew Goliath the Gittite, the staff of whose spear was like a weaver's beam.

20And there was again war at Gath, where was a man of great stature, that had on every hand six fingers, and on every foot six toes, four and twenty in number; and he also was born to the giant.

21And when he defied Israel, Jonathan the son of Shimei, David's brother, slew him.

22These four were born to the giant in Gath; and they fell by the hand of David, and by the hand of his servants.

Chapter 22

1And David spake unto Yahweh the words of this song in the day that Yahweh delivered him out of the hand of all his enemies, and out of the hand of Saul:

2and he said,
Yahweh is my rock, and my fortress, and my deliverer, even mine;
3God, my rock, in him will I take refuge;
My shield, and the horn of my salvation, my high tower, and my refuge;
My saviour, thou savest me from violence.
4I will call upon Yahweh, who is worthy to be praised:
So shall I be saved from mine enemies.
5For the waves of death compassed me;
The floods of ungodliness made me afraid:
6The cords of Sheol were round about me;
The snares of death came upon me.
7In my distress I called upon Yahweh;
Yea, I called unto my God:
And he heard my voice out of his temple,
And my cry came into his ears.
8Then the earth shook and trembled,
The foundations of heaven quaked
And were shaken, because he was wroth.
9There went up a smoke out of his nostrils,
And fire out of his mouth devoured:
Coals were kindled by it.
10He bowed the heavens also, and came down;
And thick darkness was under his feet.
11And he rode upon a cherub, and did fly;
Yea, he was seen upon the wings of the wind.
12And he made darkness pavilions round about him,
Gathering of waters, thick clouds of the skies.
13At the brightness before him
Coals of fire were kindled.
14Yahweh thundered from heaven,
And the Most High uttered his voice.
15And he sent out arrows, and scattered them;
Lightning, and discomfited them.
16Then the channels of the sea appeared,

The foundations of the world were laid bare,
By the rebuke of Yahweh,
At the blast of the breath of his nostrils.
17He sent from on high, he took me;
He drew me out of many waters;
18He delivered me from my strong enemy,
From them that hated me; for they were too mighty for me.
19They came upon me in the day of my calamity;
But Yahweh was my stay.
20He brought me forth also into a large place;
He delivered me, because he delighted in me.
21Yahweh rewarded me according to my righteousness;
According to the cleanness of my hands hath he recompensed me.
22For I have kept the ways of Yahweh,
And have not wickedly departed from my God.
23For all his ordinances were before me;
And as for his statutes, I did not depart from them.
24I was also perfect toward him;
And I kept myself from mine iniquity.
25Therefore hath Yahweh recompensed me according to my righteousness,
According to my cleanness in his eyesight.
26With the merciful thou wilt show thyself merciful;
With the perfect man thou wilt show thyself perfect;
27With the pure thou wilt show thyself pure;
And with the perverse thou wilt show thyself froward.
28And the afflicted people thou wilt save;
But thine eyes are upon the haughty, that thou mayest bring them down.
29For thou art my lamp, O Yahweh;
And Yahweh will lighten my darkness.
30For by thee I run upon a troop;
By my God do I leap over a wall.
31As for God, his way is perfect:
The word of Yahweh is tried;
He is a shield unto all them that take refuge in him.
32For who is God, save Yahweh?
And who is a rock, save our God?
33God is my strong fortress;
And he guideth the perfect in his way.
34He maketh his feet like hinds' feet,
And setteth me upon my high places.
35He teacheth my hands to war,
So that mine arms do bend a bow of brass.
36Thou hast also given me the shield of thy salvation;
And thy gentleness hath made me great.
37Thou hast enlarged my steps under me;
And my feet have not slipped.
38I have pursued mine enemies, and destroyed them;
Neither did I turn again till they were consumed.
39And I have consumed them, and smitten them through, so that they cannot arise;
Yea, they are fallen under my feet.
40For thou hast girded me with strength unto the battle;
Thou hast subdued under me those that rose up against me.
41Thou hast also made mine enemies turn their backs unto me,
That I might cut off them that hate me.
42They looked, but there was none to save;
Even unto Yahweh, but he answered them not.
43Then did I beat them small as the dust of the earth,
I did crush them as the mire of the streets, and did spread them abroad.
44Thou also hast delivered me from the strivings of my people;
Thou hast kept me to be the head of the nations:
A people whom I have not known shall serve me.
45The foreigners shall submit themselves unto me:
As soon as they hear of me, they shall obey me.
46The foreigners shall fade away,
And shall come trembling out of their close places.
47Yahweh liveth; And blessed be my rock;
And exalted be God, the rock of my salvation;
48Even the God that executeth vengeance for me,
And that bringeth down peoples under me,
49And that bringeth me forth from mine enemies:
Yea, thou liftest me up above them that rise up against me;
Thou deliverest me from the violent man.
50Therefore I will give thanks unto thee, O Yahweh, among the nations,
And will sing praises unto thy name.
51Great deliverance giveth he to his king,
And showeth lovingkindness to his anointed,
To David and to his seed, for evermore.

Chapter 23

1Now these are the last words of David.
David the son of Jesse saith,
And the man who was raised on high saith,
The anointed of the God of Jacob,
And the sweet psalmist of Israel:
2The Spirit of Yahweh spake by me,
And his word was upon my tongue.
3The God of Israel said,
The Rock of Israel spake to me:
One that ruleth over men righteously,
That ruleth in the fear of God,
4He shall be as the light of the morning, when the sun riseth,
A morning without clouds,
When the tender grass springeth out of the earth,
Through clear shining after rain.
5Verily my house is not so with God;
Yet he hath made with me an everlasting covenant,
Ordered in all things, and sure:
For it is all my salvation, and all my desire,
Although he maketh it not to grow.
6But the ungodly shall be all of them as thorns to be thrust away,
Because they cannot be taken with the hand
7But the man that toucheth them
Must be armed with iron and the staff of a spear:
And they shall be utterly burned with fire in their place

8These are the names of the mighty men whom David had: Josheb-basshebeth a Tahchemonite, chief of the captains; the same was Adino the Eznite, against eight hundred slain at one time.

9And after him was Eleazar the son of Dodai the son of an Ahohite, one of the three mighty men with David, when they defied the Philistines that were there gathered together to battle, and the men of Israel were gone away.

10He arose, and smote the Philistines until his hand was weary, and his hand clave unto the sword; and Yahweh wrought a great victory that day; and the people returned after him only to take spoil.

11And after him was Shammah the son of Agee a Hararite. And the Philistines were gathered together into a troop, where was a plot of ground full of lentils; and the people fled from the Philistines.

12But he stood in the midst of the plot, and defended it, and slew the Philistines; and Yahweh wrought a great victory.

13And three of the thirty chief men went down, and came to David in the harvest time unto the cave of Adullam; and the troop of the Philistines was encamped in the valley of Rephaim.

14And David was then in the stronghold; and the garrison of the Philistines was then in Beth-lehem.

15And David longed, and said, Oh that one would give me water to drink of the well of Beth-lehem, which is by the gate!

16And the three mighty men brake through the host of the Philistines, and drew water out of the well of Beth-lehem, that was by the gate, and took it, and brought it to David: but he would not drink thereof, but poured it out unto Yahweh.

17And he said, Be it far from me, O Yahweh, that I should do this: shall I drink the blood of the men that went in jeopardy of their lives? therefore he would not drink it. These things did the three mighty men.

18And Abishai, the brother of Joab, the son of Zeruiah, was chief of the three. And he lifted up his spear against three hundred and slew them, and had a name among the three.

19Was he not most honorable of the three? therefore he was made their captain: howbeit he attained not unto the first three.

20And Benaiah the son of Jehoiada, the son of a valiant man of Kabzeel, who had done mighty deeds, he slew the two sons of Ariel of Moab: he went down also and slew a lion in the midst of a pit in time of snow.

21And he slew an Egyptian, a goodly man: and the Egyptian had a spear in his hand; but he went down to him with a staff, and plucked the spear out of the Egyptian's hand, and slew him with his own spear.

22These things did Benaiah the son of Jehoiada, and had a name among the three mighty men.

23He was more honorable than the thirty, but he attained not to the first three. And David set him over his guard.

24Asahel the brother of Joab was one of the thirty; Elhanan the son of Dodo of Beth-lehem,
25Shammah the Harodite, Elika the Harodite,
26Helez the Paltite, Ira the son of Ikkesh the Tekoite,
27Abiezer the Anathothite, Mebunnai the Hushathite,
28Zalmon the Ahohite, Maharai the Netophathite,
29Heleb the son of Baanah the Netophathite, Ittai the son of Ribai of Gibeah of the children of Benjamin,
30Benaiah a Pirathonite, Hiddai of the brooks of Gaash.
31Abialbon the Arbathite, Azmaveth the Barhumite,
32Eliahba the Shaalbonite, the sons of Jashen, Jonathan,
33Shammah the Hararite, Ahiam the son of Sharar the Ararite,
34Eliphelet the son of Ahasbai, the son of the Maacathite, Eliam the son of Ahithophel the Gilonite,
35Hezro the Carmelite, Paarai the Arbite,
36Igal the son of Nathan of Zobah, Bani the Gadite,
37Zelek the Ammonite, Naharai the Beerothite, armorbearers to Joab the son of Zeruiah,
38Ira the Ithrite, Gareb the Ithrite,
39Uriah the Hittite: thirty and seven in all.

Chapter 24

1And again the anger of Yahweh was kindled against Israel, and he moved David against them, saying, Go, number Israel and Judah.

2And the king said to Joab the captain of the host, who was with him, Go now to and fro through all the tribes of Israel, from Dan even to Beer-sheba, and number ye the people, that I may know the sum of the people.

3And Joab said unto the king, Now Yahweh thy God add unto the people, how many soever they may be, a hundredfold; and may the eyes of my lord the king see it: but why doth my lord the king delight in this thing?

Second Samuel

4Notwithstanding, the king's word prevailed against Joab, and against the captains of the host. And Joab and the captains of the host went out from the presence of the king, to number the people of Israel.

5And they passed over the Jordan, and encamped in Aroer, on the right side of the city that is in the middle of the valley of Gad, and unto Jazer:

6then they came to Gilead, and to the land of Tahtim-hodshi; and they came to Dan-jaan, and round about to Sidon,

7and came to the stronghold of Tyre, and to all the cities of the Hivites, and of the Canaanites; and they went out to the south of Judah, at Beer-sheba.

8So when they had gone to and from through all the land, they came to Jerusalem at the end of nine months and twenty days.

9And Joab gave up the sum of the numbering of the people unto the king: and there were in Israel eight hundred thousand valiant men that drew the sword; and the men of Judah were five hundred thousand men.

10And David's heart smote him after that he had numbered the people. And David said unto Yahweh, I have sinned greatly in that which I have done: but now, O Yahweh, put away, I beseech thee, the iniquity of thy servant; for I have done very foolishly.

11And when David rose up in the morning, the word of Yahweh came unto the prophet Gad, David's seer, saying,

12Go and speak unto David, Thus saith Yahweh, I offer thee three things: choose thee one of them, that I may do it unto thee.

13So Gad came to David, and told him, and said unto him, Shall seven years of famine come unto thee in thy land? or wilt thou flee three months before thy foes while they pursue thee? or shall there be three days' pestilence in thy land? now advise thee, and consider what answer I shall return to him that sent me.

14And David said unto Gad, I am in a great strait: let us fall now into the hand of Yahweh; for his mercies are great; and let me not fall into the hand of man.

15So Yahweh sent a pestilence upon Israel from the morning even to the time appointed; and there died of the people from Dan even to Beer-sheba seventy thousand men.

16And when the angel stretched out his hand toward Jerusalem to destroy it, Yahweh repented him of the evil, and said to the angel that destroyed the people, It is enough; now stay thy hand. And the angel of Yahweh was by the threshing-floor of Araunah the Jebusite.

17And David spake unto Yahweh when he saw the angel that smote the people, and said, Lo, I have sinned, and I have done perversely; but these sheep, what have they done? let thy hand, I pray thee, be against me, and against my father's house.

18And Gad came that day to David, and said unto him, Go up, rear an altar unto Yahweh in the threshing-floor of Araunah the Jebusite.

19And David went up according to the saying of Gad, as Yahweh commanded.

20And Araunah looked forth, and saw the king and his servants coming on toward him: and Araunah went out, and bowed himself before the king with his face to the ground.

21And Araunah said, Wherefore is my lord the king come to his servant? And David said, To buy the threshing-floor of thee, to build an altar unto Yahweh, that the plague may be stayed from the people.

22And Araunah said unto David, Let my lord the king take and offer up what seemeth good unto him: behold, the oxen for the burnt-offering, and the threshing instruments and the yokes of the oxen for the wood:

23all this, O king, doth Araunah give unto the king. And Araunah said unto the king, Yahweh thy God accept thee.

24And the king said unto Araunah, Nay; but I will verily buy it of thee at a price. Neither will I offer burnt-offerings unto Yahweh my God which cost me nothing. So David bought the threshing-floor and the oxen for fifty shekels of silver.

25And David built there an altar unto Yahweh, and offered burnt-offerings and peace-offerings. So Yahweh was entreated for the land, and the plague was stayed from Israel.

The First Book of the Kings

Chapter 1

¹Now king David was old and stricken in years; and they covered him with clothes, but he gat no heat.

²Wherefore his servants said unto him, Let there be sought for my lord the king a young virgin: and let her stand before the king, and cherish him; and let her lie in thy bosom, that my lord the king may get heat.

³So they sought for a fair damsel throughout all the borders of Israel, and found Abishag the Shunammite, and brought her to the king.

⁴And the damsel was very fair; and she cherished the king, and ministered to him; but the king knew her not.

⁵Then Adonijah the son of Haggith exalted himself, saying, I will be king: and he prepared him chariots and horsemen, and fifty men to run before him.

⁶And his father had not displeased him at any time in saying, Why hast thou done so? and he was also a very goodly man; and he was born after Absalom.

⁷And he conferred with Joab the son of Zeruiah, and with Abiathar the priest: and they following Adonijah helped him.

⁸But Zadok the priest, and Benaiah the son of Jehoiada, and Nathan the prophet, and Shimei, and Rei, and the mighty men that belonged to David, were not with Adonijah.

⁹And Adonijah slew sheep and oxen and fatlings by the stone of Zoheleth, which is beside En-rogel; and he called all his brethren, the king's sons, and all the men of Judah, the king's servants:

¹⁰but Nathan the prophet, and Benaiah, and the mighty men, and Solomon his brother, he called not.

¹¹Then Nathan spake unto Bath-sheba the mother of Solomon, saying, Hast thou not heard that Adonijah the son of Haggith doth reign, and David our lord knoweth it not?

¹²Now therefore come, let me, I pray thee, give thee counsel, that thou mayest save thine own life, and the life of thy son Solomon.

¹³Go and get thee in unto king David, and say unto him, Didst not thou, my lord, O king, swear unto thy handmaid, saying, Assuredly Solomon thy son shall reign after me, and he shall sit upon my throne? why then doth Adonijah reign?

¹⁴Behold, while thou yet talkest there with the king, I also will come in after thee, and confirm thy words.

¹⁵And Bath-sheba went in unto the king into the chamber: and the king was very old; and Abishag the Shunammite was ministering unto the king.

¹⁶And Bath-sheba bowed, and did obeisance unto the king. And the king said, What wouldest thou?

¹⁷And she said unto him, My lord, thou swarest by Yahweh thy God unto thy handmaid, saying, Assuredly Solomon thy son shall reign after me, and he shall sit upon my throne.

¹⁸And now, behold, Adonijah reigneth; and thou, my lord the king, knowest it not:

¹⁹and he hath slain oxen and fatlings and sheep in abundance, and hath called all the sons of the king, and Abiathar the priest, and Joab the captain of the host; but Solomon thy servant hath he not called.

²⁰And thou, my lord the king, the eyes of all Israel are upon thee, that thou shouldest tell them who shall sit on the throne of my lord the king after him.

²¹Otherwise it will come to pass, when my lord the king shall sleep with his fathers, that I and my son Solomon shall be counted offenders.

²²And, lo, while she yet talked with the king, Nathan the prophet came in.

²³And they told the king, saying, Behold, Nathan the prophet. And when he was come in before the king, he bowed himself before the king with his face to the ground.

²⁴And Nathan said, My lord, O king, hast thou said, Adonijah shall reign after me, and he shall sit upon my throne?

²⁵For he is gone down this day, and hath slain oxen and fatlings and sheep in abundance, and hath called all the king's sons, and the captains of the host, and Abiathar the priest; and, behold, they are eating and drinking before him, and say, Long live king Adonijah.

²⁶But me, even me thy servant, and Zadok the priest, and Benaiah the son of Jehoiada, and thy servant Solomon, hath he not called.

²⁷Is this thing done by my lord the king, and thou hast not showed unto thy servants who should sit on the throne of my lord the king after him?

²⁸Then king David answered and said, Call to me Bath-sheba. And she came into the king's presence, and stood before the king.

²⁹And the king sware, and said, As Yahweh liveth, who hath redeemed my soul out of all adversity,

³⁰verily as I sware unto thee by Yahweh, the God of Israel, saying, Assuredly Solomon thy son shall reign after me, and he shall sit upon my throne in my stead; verily so will I do this day.

³¹Then Bath-sheba bowed with her face to the earth, and did obeisance to the king, and said, Let my lord king David live for ever.

³²And king David said, Call to me Zadok the priest, and Nathan the prophet, and Benaiah the son of Jehoiada. And they came before the king.

³³And the king said unto them, Take with you the servants of your lord, and cause Solomon my son to ride upon mine own mule, and bring him down to Gihon:

³⁴and let Zadok the priest and Nathan the prophet anoint him there king over Israel; and blow ye the trumpet, and say, Long live king Solomon.

³⁵Then ye shall come up after him, and he shall come and sit upon my throne; for he shall be king in my stead; and I have appointed him to be prince over Israel and over Judah.

³⁶And Benaiah the son of Jehoiada answered the king, and said, Amen: Yahweh, the God of my lord the king, say so too.

³⁷As Yahweh hath been with my lord the king, even so be he with Solomon, and make his throne greater than the throne of my lord king David.

³⁸So Zadok the priest, and Nathan the prophet, and Benaiah the son of Jehoiada, and the Cherethites and the Pelethites, went down, and caused Solomon to ride upon king David's mule, and brought him to Gihon.

³⁹And Zadok the priest took the horn of oil out of the Tent, and anointed Solomon. And they blew the trumpet; and all the people said, Long live king Solomon.

⁴⁰And all the people came up after him, and the people piped with pipes, and rejoiced with great joy, so that the earth rent with the sound of them.

⁴¹And Adonijah and all the guests that were with him heard it as they had made an end of eating. And when Joab heard the sound of the trumpet, he said, Wherefore is this noise of the city being in an uproar?

⁴²While he yet spake, behold, Jonathan the son of Abiathar the priest came: and Adonijah said, Come in; for thou art a worthy man, and bringest good tidings.

⁴³And Jonathan answered and said to Adonijah, Verily our lord king David hath made Solomon king:

⁴⁴and the king hath sent with him Zadok the priest, and Nathan the prophet, and Benaiah the son of Jehoiada, and the Cherethites and the Pelethites; and they have caused him to ride upon the king's mule;

⁴⁵and Zadok the priest and Nathan the prophet have anointed him king in Gihon; and they are come up from thence rejoicing, so that the city rang again. This is the noise that ye have heard.

⁴⁶And also Solomon sitteth on the throne of the kingdom.

⁴⁷And moreover the king's servants came to bless our lord king David, saying, Thy God make the name of Solomon better than thy name, and make his throne greater than thy throne: and the king bowed himself upon the bed.

⁴⁸And also thus said the king, Blessed be Yahweh, the God of Israel, who hath given one to sit on my throne this day, mine eyes even seeing it.

⁴⁹And all the guests of Adonijah were afraid, and rose up, and went every man his way.

⁵⁰And Adonijah feared because of Solomon; and he arose, and went, and caught hold on the horns of the altar.

⁵¹And it was told Solomon, saying, Behold, Adonijah feareth king Solomon; for, lo, he hath laid hold on the horns of the altar, saying, Let king Solomon swear unto me first that he will not slay his servant with the sword.

⁵²And Solomon said, If he shall show himself a worthy man, there shall not a hair of him fall to the earth; but if wickedness be found in him, he shall die.

⁵³So king Solomon sent, and they brought him down from the altar. And he came and did obeisance to king Solomon; and Solomon said unto him, Go to thy house.

Chapter 2

¹Now the days of David drew nigh that he should die; and he charged Solomon his son, saying,

²I am going the way of all the earth: be thou strong therefore, and show thyself a man;

³and keep the charge of Yahweh thy God, to walk in his ways, to keep his statutes, and his commandments, and his ordinances, and his testimonies, according to that which is written in the law of Moses, that thou mayest prosper in all that thou doest, and whithersoever thou turnest thyself.

⁴That Yahweh may establish his word which he spake concerning me, saying, If thy children take heed to their way, to walk before me in truth with all their heart and with all their soul, there shall not fail thee (said he) a man on the throne of Israel.

⁵Moreover thou knowest also what Joab the son of Zeruiah did unto me, even what he did to the two captains of the hosts of Israel, unto Abner the son of Ner, and unto Amasa the son of Jether, whom he slew, and shed the blood of war in peace, and put the blood of war upon his girdle that was about his loins, and in his shoes that were on his feet.

⁶Do therefore according to thy wisdom, and let not his hoar head go down to Sheol in peace.

⁷But show kindness unto the sons of Barzillai the Gileadite, and let them be of those that eat at thy table; for so they came to me when I fled from Absalom thy brother.

⁸And, behold, there is with thee Shimei the son of Gera, the Benjamite, of Bahurim, who cursed me with a grievous curse in the day when I went to Mahanaim; but he came down to meet me at the Jordan, and I sware to him by Yahweh, saying, I will not put thee to death with the sword.

⁹Now therefore hold him not guiltless, for thou art a wise man; and thou wilt know what thou oughtest to do unto him, and thou shalt bring his hoar head down to Sheol with blood.

¹⁰And David slept with his fathers, and was buried in the city of David.

¹¹And the days that David reigned over Israel were forty years; seven years reigned he in Hebron, and thirty and three years reigned he in Jerusalem.

¹²And Solomon sat upon the throne of David his father; and his kingdom was established greatly.

¹³Then Adonijah the son of Haggith came to Bath-sheba the mother of Solomon. And she said, Comest thou peaceably? And he said, Peaceably.

¹⁴He said moreover, I have somewhat to say unto thee. And she said, Say on.

¹⁵And he said, Thou knowest that the kingdom was mine, and that all Israel set their faces on me, that I should reign: howbeit the kingdom is turned about, and is become my brother's; for it was his from Yahweh.

¹⁶And now I ask one petition of thee; deny me not. And she said unto him,

First Kings
Say on.

17And he said, Speak, I pray thee, unto Solomon the king (for he will not say thee nay), that he give me Abishag the Shunammite to wife.

18And Bath-sheba said, Well; I will speak for thee unto the king.

19Bath-sheba therefore went unto king Solomon, to speak unto him for Adonijah. And the king rose up to meet her, and bowed himself unto her, and sat down on his throne, and caused a throne to be set for the king's mother; and she sat on his right hand.

20Then she said, I ask one small petition of thee; deny me not. And the king said unto her, Ask on, my mother; for I will not deny thee.

21And she said, Let Abishag the Shunammite be given to Adonijah thy brother to wife.

22And king Solomon answered and said unto his mother, And why dost thou ask Abishag the Shunammite for Adonijah? ask for him the kingdom also; for he is mine elder brother; even for him, and for Abiathar the priest, and for Joab the son of Zeruiah.

23Then king Solomon sware by Yahweh, saying, God do so to me, and more also, if Adonijah hath not spoken this word against his own life.

24Now therefore as Yahweh liveth, who hath established me, and set me on the throne of David my father, and who hath made me a house, as he promised, surely Adonijah shall be put to death this day.

25And king Solomon sent by Benaiah the son of Jehoiada; and he fell upon him, so that he died.

26And unto Abiathar the priest said the king, Get thee to Anathoth, unto thine own fields; for thou art worthy of death: but I will not at this time put thee to death, because thou barest the ark of the Lord Yahweh before David my father, and because thou wast afflicted in all wherein my father was afflicted.

27So Solomon thrust out Abiathar from being priest unto Yahweh, that he might fulfil the word of Yahweh, which he spake concerning the house of Eli in Shiloh.

28And the tidings came to Joab; for Joab had turned after Adonijah, though he turned not after Absalom. And Joab fled unto the Tent of Yahweh, and caught hold on the horns of the altar.

29And it was told king Solomon, Joab is fled unto the Tent of Yahweh, and, behold, he is by the altar. Then Solomon sent Benaiah the son of Jehoiada, saying, Go, fall upon him.

30And Benaiah came to the Tent of Yahweh, and said unto him, Thus saith the king, Come forth. And he said, Nay; but I will die here. And Benaiah brought the king word again, saying, Thus said Joab, and thus he answered me.

31And the king said unto him, Do as he hath said, and fall upon him, and bury him; that thou mayest take away the blood, which Joab shed without cause, from me and from my father's house.

32And Yahweh will return his blood upon his own head, because he fell upon two men more righteous and better than he, and slew them with the sword, and my father David knew it not, to wit, Abner the son of Ner, captain of the host of Israel, and Amasa the son of Jether, captain of the host of Judah.

33So shall their blood return upon the head of Joab, and upon the head of his seed for ever: but unto David, and unto his seed, and unto his house, and unto his throne, shall there be peace for ever from Yahweh.

34Then Benaiah the son of Jehoiada went up, and fell upon him, and slew him; and he was buried in his own house in the wilderness.

35And the king put Benaiah the son of Jehoiada in his room over the host; and Zadok the priest did the king put in the room of Abiathar.

36And the king sent and called for Shimei, and said unto him, Build thee a house in Jerusalem, and dwell there, and go not forth thence any whither.

37For on the day thou goest out, and passest over the brook Kidron, know thou for certain that thou shalt surely die: thy blood shall be upon thine own head.

38And Shimei said unto the king, The saying is good: as my lord the king hath said, so will thy servant do. And Shimei dwelt in Jerusalem many days.

39And it came to pass at the end of three years, that two of the servants of Shimei ran away unto Achish, son of Maacah, king of Gath. And they told Shimei, saying, Behold, thy servants are in Gath.

40And Shimei arose, and saddled his ass, and went to Gath to Achish, to seek his servants; and Shimei went, and brought his servants from Gath.

41And it was told Solomon that Shimei had gone from Jerusalem to Gath, and was come again.

42And the king sent and called for Shimei, and said unto him, Did I not adjure thee by Yahweh, and protest unto thee, saying, Know for certain, that on the day thou goest out, and walkest abroad any whither, thou shalt surely die? and thou saidst unto me, The saying that I have heard is good.

43Why then hast thou not kept the oath of Yahweh, and the commandment that I have charged thee with?

44The king said moreover to Shimei, Thou knowest all the wickedness which thy heart is privy to, that thou didst to David my father: therefore Yahweh shall return thy wickedness upon thine own head.

45But king Solomon shall be blessed, and the throne of David shall be established before Yahweh for ever.

46So the king commanded Benaiah the son of Jehoiada; and he went out, and fell upon him, so that he died. And the kingdom was established in the hand of Solomon.

Chapter 3

1And Solomon made affinity with Pharaoh king of Egypt, and took Pharaoh's daughter, and brought her into the city of David, until he had made an end of building his own house, and the house of Yahweh, and the wall of Jerusalem round about.

2Only the people sacrificed in the high places, because there was no house built for the name of Yahweh until those days.

3And Solomon loved Yahweh, walking in the statutes of David his father: only he sacrificed and burnt incense in the high places.

4And the king went to Gibeon to sacrifice there; for that was the great high place: a thousand burnt-offerings did Solomon offer upon that altar.

5In Gibeon Yahweh appeared to Solomon in a dream by night; and God said, Ask what I shall give thee.

6And Solomon said, Thou hast showed unto thy servant David my father great lovingkindness, according as he walked before thee in truth, and in righteousness, and in uprightness of heart with thee; and thou hast kept for him this great lovingkindness, that thou hast given him a son to sit on his throne, as it is this day.

7And now, O Yahweh my God, thou hast made thy servant king instead of David my father: and I am but a little child; I know not how to go out or come in.

8And thy servant is in the midst of thy people which thou hast chosen, a great people, that cannot be numbered nor counted for multitude.

9Give thy servant therefore an understanding heart to judge thy people, that I may discern between good and evil; for who is able to judge this thy great people?

10And the speech pleased the Lord, that Solomon had asked this thing.

11And God said unto him, Because thou hast asked this thing, and hast not asked for thyself long life, neither hast asked riches for thyself, nor hast asked the life of thine enemies, but hast asked for thyself understanding to discern justice;

12behold, I have done according to thy word: lo, I have given thee a wise and an understanding heart; so that there hath been none like thee before thee, neither after thee shall any arise like unto thee.

13And I have also given thee that which thou hast not asked, both riches and honor, so that there shall not be any among the kings like unto thee, all thy days.

14And if thou wilt walk in my ways, to keep my statutes and my commandments, as thy father David did walk, then I will lengthen thy days.

15And Solomon awoke; and, behold, it was a dream: and he came to Jerusalem, and stood before the ark of the covenant of Yahweh, and offered up burnt-offerings, and offered peace-offerings, and made a feast to all his servants.

16Then there came two women that were harlots, unto the king, and stood before him.

17And the one woman said, Oh, my lord, I and this woman dwell in one house; and I was delivered of a child with her in the house.

18And it came to pass the third day after I was delivered, that this woman was delivered also; and we were together; there was no stranger with us in the house, save we two in the house.

19And this woman's child died in the night, because she lay upon it.

20And she arose at midnight, and took my son from beside me, while thy handmaid slept, and laid it in her bosom, and laid her dead child in my bosom.

21And when I rose in the morning to give my child suck, behold, it was dead; but when I had looked at it in the morning, behold, it was not my son, whom I did bear.

22And the other woman said, Nay; but the living is my son, and the dead is thy son. And this said, No; but the dead is thy son, and the living is my son. Thus they spake before the king.

23Then said the king, The one saith, This is my son that liveth, and thy son is the dead: and the other saith, Nay; but thy son is the dead, and my son is the living.

24And the king said, Fetch me a sword. And they brought a sword before the king.

25And the king said, Divide the living child in two, and give half to the one, and half to the other.

26Then spake the woman whose the living child was unto the king, for her heart yearned over her son, and she said, Oh, my lord, give her the living child, and in no wise slay it. But the other said, It shall be neither mine nor thine; divide it.

27Then the king answered and said, Give her the living child, and in no wise slay it: she is the mother thereof.

28And all Israel heard of the judgment which the king had judged; and they feared the king: for they saw that the wisdom of God was in him, to do justice.

Chapter 4

1And king Solomon was king over all Israel.

2And these were the princes whom he had: Azariah the son of Zadok, the priest;

3Elihoreph and Ahijah, the sons of Shisha, scribes; Jehoshaphat the son of Ahilud, the recorder;

4and Benaiah the son of Jehoiada was over the host; and Zadok and Abiathar were priests;

5and Azariah the son of Nathan was over the officers; and Zabud the son of Nathan was chief minister, and the king's friend;

6and Ahishar was over the household; and Adoniram the son of Abda was over the men subject to taskwork.

7And Solomon had twelve officers over all Israel, who provided victuals for the king and his household: each man had to make provision for a month in the year.

8And these are their names: Ben-hur, in the hill-country of Ephraim;

9Ben-deker, in Makaz, and in Shaalbim, and Beth-shemesh, and Elon-beth-hanan;

10Ben-hesed, in Arubboth (to him pertained Socoh, and all the land of Hepher);

11Ben-abinadab, in all the height of Dor (he had Taphath the daughter of Solomon to wife);

12Baana the son of Ahilud, in Taanach and Megiddo, and all Beth-shean which is beside Zarethan, beneath Jezreel, from Beth-shean to Abel-meholah, as far as beyond Jokmeam;

13Ben-geber, in Ramoth-gilead (to him pertained the towns of Jair the son of Manasseh, which are in Gilead; even to him pertained the region of Argob, which is in Bashan, threescore great cities with walls and brazen bars);

14Ahinadab the son of Iddo, in Mahanaim;

15Ahimaaz, in Naphtali (he also took Basemath the daughter of Solomon to wife);

16Baana the son of Hushai, in Asher and Bealoth;

17Jehoshaphat the son of Paruah, in Issachar;

18Shimei the son of Ela, in Benjamin;

19Geber the son of Uri, in the land of Gilead, the country of Sihon king of the Amorites and of Og king of Bashan; and he was the only officer that was in the land.

20Judah and Israel were many as the sand which is by the sea in multitude, eating and drinking and making merry.

21And Solomon ruled over all the kingdoms from the River unto the land of the Philistines, and unto the border of Egypt: they brought tribute, and served Solomon all the days of his life.

22And Solomon's provision for one day was thirty measures of fine flour, and threescore measures of meal,

23ten fat oxen, and twenty oxen out of the pastures, and a hundred sheep, besides harts, and gazelles, and roebucks, and fatted fowl.

24For he had dominion over all the region on this side the River, from Tiphsah even to Gaza, over all the kings on this side the River: and he had peace on all sides round about him.

25And Judah and Israel dwelt safely, every man under his vine and under his fig-tree, from Dan even to Beer-sheba, all the days of Solomon.

26And Solomon had forty thousand stalls of horses for his chariots, and twelve thousand horsemen.

27And those officers provided victuals for king Solomon, and for all that came unto king Solomon's table, every man in his month; they let nothing be lacking.

28Barley also and straw for the horses and swift steeds brought they unto the place where the officers were, every man according to his charge.

29And God gave Solomon wisdom and understanding exceeding much, and largeness of heart, even as the sand that is on the sea-shore.

30And Solomon's wisdom excelled the wisdom of all the children of the east, and all the wisdom of Egypt.

31For he was wiser than all men; than Ethan the Ezrahite, and Heman, and Calcol, and Darda, the sons of Mahol: and his fame was in all the nations round about.

32And he spake three thousand proverbs; and his songs were a thousand and five.

33And he spake of trees, from the cedar that is in Lebanon even unto the hyssop that springeth out of the wall; he spake also of beasts, and of birds, and of creeping things, and of fishes.

34And there came of all peoples to hear the wisdom of Solomon, from all kings of the earth, who had heard of his wisdom.

Chapter 5

1And Hiram king of Tyre sent his servants unto Solomon; for he had heard that they had anointed him king in the room of his father: for Hiram was ever a lover of David.

2And Solomon sent to Hiram, saying,

3Thou knowest how that David my father could not build a house for the name of Yahweh his God for the wars which were about him on every side, until Yahweh put them under the soles of his feet.

4But now Yahweh my God hath given me rest on every side; there is neither adversary, nor evil occurrence.

5And, behold, I purpose to build a house for the name of Yahweh my God, as Yahweh spake unto David my father, saying, Thy son, whom I will set upon thy throne in thy room, he shall build the house for my name.

6Now therefore command thou that they cut me cedar-trees out of Lebanon; and my servants shall be with thy servants; and I will give thee hire for thy servants according to all that thou shalt say: for thou knowest that there is not among us any that knoweth how to cut timber like unto the Sidonians.

7And it came to pass, when Hiram heard the words of Solomon, that he rejoiced greatly, and said, Blessed be Yahweh this day, who hath given unto David a wise son over this great people.

8And Hiram sent to Solomon, saying, I have heard the message which thou hast sent unto me: I will do all thy desire concerning timber of cedar, and concerning timber of fir.

9My servants shall bring them down from Lebanon unto the sea; and I will make them into rafts to go by sea unto the place that thou shalt appoint me, and will cause them to be broken up there, and thou shalt receive them; and thou shalt accomplish my desire, in giving food for my household.

10So Hiram gave Solomon timber of cedar and timber of fir according to all his desire.

11And Solomon gave Hiram twenty thousand measures of wheat for food to his household, and twenty measures of pure oil: thus gave Solomon to Hiram year by year.

12And Yahweh gave Solomon wisdom, as he promised him; and there was peace between Hiram and Solomon; and they two made a league together.

13And king Solomon raised a levy out of all Israel; and the levy was thirty thousand men.

14And he sent them to Lebanon, ten thousand a month by courses; a month they were in Lebanon, and two months at home; and Adoniram was over the men subject to taskwork.

15And Solomon had threescore and ten thousand that bare burdens, and fourscore thousand that were hewers in the mountains;

16besides Solomon's chief officers that were over the work, three thousand and three hundred, who bare rule over the people that wrought in the work.

17And the king commanded, and they hewed out great stones, costly stones, to lay the foundation of the house with wrought stone.

18And Solomon's builders and Hiram's builders and the Gebalites did fashion them, and prepared the timber and the stones to build the house.

Chapter 6

1And it came to pass in the four hundred and eightieth year after the children of Israel were come out of the land of Egypt, in the fourth year of Solomon's reign over Israel, in the month Ziv, which is the second month, that he began to build the house of Yahweh.

2And the house which king Solomon built for Yahweh, the length thereof was threescore cubits, and the breadth thereof twenty cubits, and the height thereof thirty cubits.

3And the porch before the temple of the house, twenty cubits was the length thereof, according to the breadth of the house; and ten cubits was the breadth thereof before the house.

4And for the house he made windows of fixed lattice-work.

5And against the wall of the house he built stories round about, against the walls of the house round about, both of the temple and of the oracle; and he made side-chambers round about.

6The nethermost story was five cubits broad, and the middle was six cubits broad, and the third was seven cubits broad; for on the outside he made offsets in the wall of the house round about, that the beams should not have hold in the walls of the house.

7And the house, when it was in building, was built of stone made ready at the quarry; and there was neither hammer nor axe nor any tool of iron heard in the house, while it was in building.

8The door for the middle side-chambers was in the right side of the house: and they went up by winding stairs into the middle story, and out of the middle into the third.

9So he built the house, and finished it; and he covered the house with beams and planks of cedar.

10And he built the stories against all the house, each five cubits high: and they rested on the house with timber of cedar.

11And the word of Yahweh came to Solomon, saying,

12Concerning this house which thou art building, if thou wilt walk in my statutes, and execute mine ordinances, and keep all my commandments to walk in them; then will I establish my word with thee, which I spake unto David thy father.

13And I will dwell among the children of Israel, and will not forsake my people Israel.

14So Solomon built the house, and finished it.

15And he built the walls of the house within with boards of cedar: from the floor of the house unto the walls of the ceiling, he covered them on the inside with wood; and he covered the floor of the house with boards of fir.

16And he built twenty cubits on the hinder part of the house with boards of cedar from the floor unto the walls of the ceiling: he built them for it within, for an oracle, even for the most holy place.

17And the house, that is, the temple before the oracle, was forty cubits long.

18And there was cedar on the house within, carved with knops and open flowers: all was cedar; there was no stone seen.

19And he prepared an oracle in the midst of the house within, to set there the ark of the covenant of Yahweh.

20And within the oracle was a space of twenty cubits in length, and twenty cubits in breadth, and twenty cubits in the height thereof; and he overlaid it with pure gold: and he covered the altar with cedar.

21So Solomon overlaid the house within with pure gold: and he drew chains of gold across before the oracle; and he overlaid it with gold.

22And the whole house he overlaid with gold, until all the house was finished: also the whole altar that belonged to the oracle he overlaid with gold.

23And in the oracle he made two cherubim of olive-wood, each ten cubits high.

24And five cubits was the one wing of the cherub, and five cubits the other wing of the cherub: from the uttermost part of the one wing unto the uttermost part of the other were ten cubits.

25And the other cherub was ten cubits: both the cherubim were of one measure and one form.

26The height of the one cherub was ten cubits, and so was it of the other cherub.

27And he set the cherubim within the inner house; and the wings of the cherubim were stretched forth, so that the wing of the one touched the one wall, and the wing of the other cherub touched the other wall; and their wings touched one another in the midst of the house.

28And he overlaid the cherubim with gold.

29And he carved all the walls of the house round about with carved figures of cherubim and palm-trees and open flowers, within and without.

30And the floor of the house he overlaid with gold, within and without.

31And for the entrance of the oracle he made doors of olive-wood: the lintel and door-posts were a fifth part of the wall.

32So he made two doors of olive-wood; and he carved upon them carvings of cherubim and palm-trees and open flowers, and overlaid them with gold; and he spread the gold upon the cherubim, and upon the palm-trees.

33So also made he for the entrance of the temple door-posts of olive-wood, out of a fourth part of the wall;

34and two doors of fir-wood: the two leaves of the one door were folding, and the two leaves of the other door were folding.

35And he carved thereon cherubim and palm-trees and open flowers; and he overlaid them with gold fitted upon the graven work.

First Kings

36And he built the inner court with three courses of hewn stone, and a course of cedar beams.

37In the fourth year was the foundation of the house of Yahweh laid, in the month Ziv.

38And in the eleventh year, in the month Bul, which is the eighth month, was the house finished throughout all the parts thereof, and according to all the fashion of it. So was he seven years in building it.

Chapter 7

1And Solomon was building his own house thirteen years, and he finished all his house.

2For he built the house of the forest of Lebanon; the length thereof was a hundred cubits, and the breadth thereof fifty cubits, and the height thereof thirty cubits, upon four rows of cedar pillars, with cedar beams upon the pillars.

3And it was covered with cedar above over the forty and five beams, that were upon the pillars; fifteen in a row.

4And there were beams in three rows, and window was over against window in three ranks.

5And all the doors and posts were made square with beams: and window was over against window in three ranks.

6And he made the porch of pillars; the length thereof was fifty cubits, and the breadth thereof thirty cubits; and a porch before them; and pillars and a threshold before them.

7And he made the porch of the throne where he was to judge, even the porch of judgment: and it was covered with cedar from floor to floor.

8And his house where he was to dwell, the other court within the porch, was of the like work. He made also a house for Pharaoh's daughter (whom Solomon had taken to wife), like unto this porch.

9All these were of costly stones, even of hewn stone, according to measure, sawed with saws, within and without, even from the foundation unto the coping, and so on the outside unto the great court.

10And the foundation was of costly stones, even great stones, stones of ten cubits, and stones of eight cubits.

11And above were costly stones, even hewn stone, according to measure, and cedar-wood.

12And the great court round about had three courses of hewn stone, and a course of cedar beams; like as the inner court of the house of Yahweh, and the porch of the house.

13And king Solomon sent and fetched Hiram out of Tyre.

14He was the son of a widow of the tribe of Naphtali, and his father was a man of Tyre, a worker in brass; and he was filled with wisdom and understanding and skill, to work all works in brass. And he came to king Solomon, and wrought all his work.

15For he fashioned the two pillars of brass, eighteen cubits high apiece: and a line of twelve cubits compassed either of them about.

16And he made two capitals of molten brass, to set upon the tops of the pillars: the height of the one capital was five cubits, and the height of the other capital was five cubits.

17There were nets of checker-work, and wreaths of chain-work, for the capitals which were upon the top of the pillars; seven for the one capital, and seven for the other capital.

18So he made the pillars; and there were two rows round about upon the one network, to cover the capitals that were upon the top of the pillars: and so did he for the other capital.

19And the capitals that were upon the top of the pillars in the porch were of lily-work, four cubits.

20And there were capitals above also upon the two pillars, close by the belly which was beside the network: and the pomegranates were two hundred, in rows round about upon the other capital.

21And he set up the pillars at the porch of the temple: and he set up the right pillar, and called the name thereof Jachin; and he set up the left pillar, and called the name thereof Boaz.

22And upon the top of the pillars was lily-work: so was the work of the pillars finished.

23And he made the molten sea of ten cubits from brim to brim, round in compass, and the height thereof was five cubits; and a line of thirty cubits compassed it round about.

24And under the brim of it round about there were knops which did compass it, for ten cubits, compassing the sea round about: the knops were in two rows, cast when it was cast.

25It stood upon twelve oxen, three looking toward the north, and three looking toward the west, and three looking toward the south, and three looking toward the east; and the sea was set upon them above, and all their hinder parts were inward.

26And it was a handbreadth thick: and the brim thereof was wrought like the brim of a cup, like the flower of a lily: it held two thousand baths.

27And he made the ten bases of brass: four cubits was the length of one base, and four cubits the breadth thereof, and three cubits the height of it.

28And the work of the bases was on this manner: they had panels; and there were panels between the ledges;

29and on the panels that were between the ledges were lions, oxen, and cherubim; and upon the ledges there was a pedestal above; and beneath the lions and oxen were wreaths of hanging work.

30And every base had four brazen wheels, and axles of brass; and the four feet thereof had undersetters: beneath the laver were the undersetters molten, with wreaths at the side of each.

31And the mouth of it within the capital and above was a cubit: and the mouth thereof was round after the work of a pedestal, a cubit and a half; and also upon the mouth of it were gravings, and their panels were foursquare, not round.

32And the four wheels were underneath the panels; and the axletrees of the wheels were in the base: and the height of a wheel was a cubit and half a cubit.

33And the work of the wheels was like the work of a chariot wheel: their axletrees, and their felloes, and their spokes, and their naves, were all molten.

34And there were four undersetters at the four corners of each base: the undersetters thereof were of the base itself.

35And in the top of the base was there a round compass half a cubit high; and on the top of the base the stays thereof and the panels thereof were of the same.

36And on the plates of the stays thereof, and on the panels thereof, he graved cherubim, lions, and palm-trees, according to the space of each, with wreaths round about.

37After this manner he made the ten bases: all of them had one casting, one measure, and one form.

38And he made ten lavers of brass: one laver contained forty baths; and every laver was four cubits; and upon very one of the ten bases one laver.

39And he set the bases, five on the right side of the house, and five on the left side of the house: and he set the sea on the right side of the house eastward, toward the south.

40And Hiram made the lavers, and the shovels, and the basins. So Hiram made an end of doing all the work that he wrought for king Solomon in the house of Yahweh:

41the two pillars, and the two bowls of the capitals that were on the top of the pillars; and the two networks to cover the two bowls of the capitals that were on the top of the pillars;

42and the four hundred pomegranates for the two networks; two rows of pomegranates for each network, to cover the two bowls of the capitals that were upon the pillars;

43and the ten bases, and the ten lavers on the bases;

44and the one sea, and the twelve oxen under the sea;

45and the pots, and the shovels, and the basins: even all these vessels, which Hiram made for king Solomon, in the house of Yahweh, were of burnished brass.

46In the plain of the Jordan did the king cast them, in the clay ground between Succoth and Zarethan.

47And Solomon left all the vessels unweighed, because they were exceeding many: the weight of the brass could not be found out.

48And Solomon made all the vessels that were in the house of Yahweh: the golden altar, and the table whereupon the showbread was, of gold;

49and the candlesticks, five on the right side, and five on the left, before the oracle, of pure gold; and the flowers, and the lamps, and the tongs, of gold;

50and the cups, and the snuffers, and the basins, and the spoons, and the firepans, of pure gold; and the hinges, both for the doors of the inner house, the most holy place, and for the doors of the house, to wit, of the temple, of gold.

51Thus all the work that king Solomon wrought in the house of Yahweh was finished. And Solomon brought in the things which David his father had dedicated, even the silver, and the gold, and the vessels, and put them in the treasuries of the house of Yahweh.

Chapter 8

1Then Solomon assembled the elders of Israel, and all the heads of the tribes, the princes of the fathers' houses of the children of Israel, unto king Solomon in Jerusalem, to bring up the ark of the covenant of Yahweh out of the city of David, which is Zion.

2And all the men of Israel assembled themselves unto king Solomon at the feast, in the month Ethanim, which is the seventh month.

3And all the elders of Israel came, and the priests took up the ark.

4And they brought up the ark of Yahweh, and the tent of meeting, and all the holy vessels that were in the Tent; even these did the priests and the Levites bring up.

5And king Solomon and all the congregation of Israel, that were assembled unto him, were with him before the ark, sacrificing sheep and oxen, that could not be counted nor numbered for multitude.

6And the priests brought in the ark of the covenant of Yahweh unto its place, into the oracle of the house, to the most holy place, even under the wings of the cherubim.

7For the cherubim spread forth their wings over the place of the ark, and the cherubim covered the ark and the staves thereof above.

8And the staves were so long that the ends of the staves were seen from the holy place before the oracle; but they were not seen without: and there they are unto this day.

9There was nothing in the ark save the two tables of stone which Moses put there at Horeb, when Yahweh made a covenant with the children of Israel, when they came out of the land of Egypt.

10And it came to pass, when the priests were come out of the holy place, that the cloud filled the house of Yahweh,

11so that the priests could not stand to minister by reason of the cloud; for the glory of Yahweh filled the house of Yahweh.

12Then spake Solomon, Yahweh hath said that he would dwell in the thick darkness.

13I have surely built thee a house of habitation, a place for thee to dwell in for ever.

14And the king turned his face about, and blessed all the assembly of Israel: and all the assembly of Israel stood.

15And he said, Blessed be Yahweh, the God of Israel, who spake with his mouth unto David thy father, and hath with his hand fulfilled it, saying,

16Since the day that I brought forth my people Israel out of Egypt, I chose no city out of all the tribes of Israel to build a house, that my name might be there; but I chose David to be over my people Israel.

17Now it was in the heart of David my father to build a house for the name of Yahweh, the God of Israel.

18But Yahweh said unto David my father, Whereas it was in thy heart to build a house for my name, thou didst well that it was in thy heart:

19nevertheless thou shalt not build the house; but thy son that shall come forth out of thy loins, he shall build the house for my name.

20And Yahweh hath established his word that he spake; for I am risen up in the room of David my father, and sit on the throne of Israel, as Yahweh promised, and have built the house for the name of Yahweh, the God of Israel.

21And there have I set a place for the ark, wherein is the covenant of Yahweh, which he made with our fathers, when he brought them out of the land of Egypt.

22And Solomon stood before the altar of Yahweh in the presence of all the assembly of Israel, and spread forth his hands toward heaven;

23and he said, O Yahweh, the God of Israel, there is no God like thee, in heaven above, or on earth beneath; who keepest covenant and lovingkindness with thy servants, that walk before thee with all their heart;

24who hast kept with thy servant David my father that which thou didst promise him: yea, thou spakest with thy mouth, and hast fulfilled it with thy hand, as it is this day.

25Now therefore, O Yahweh, the God of Israel, keep with thy servant David my father that which thou hast promised him, saying, There shall not fail thee a man in my sight to sit on the throne of Israel, if only thy children take heed to their way, to walk before me as thou hast walked before me.

26Now therefore, O God of Israel, let thy word, I pray thee, be verified, which thou spakest unto thy servant David my father.

27But will God in very deed dwell on the earth? behold, heaven and the heaven of heavens cannot contain thee; how much less this house that I have builded!

28Yet have thou respect unto the prayer of thy servant, and to his supplication, O Yahweh my God, to hearken unto the cry and to the prayer which thy servant prayeth before thee this day;

29that thine eyes may be open toward this house night and day, even toward the place whereof thou hast said, My name shall be there; to hearken unto the prayer which thy servant shall pray toward this place.

30And hearken thou to the supplication of thy servant, and of thy people Israel, when they shall pray toward this place: yea, hear thou in heaven thy dwelling-place; and when thou hearest, forgive.

31If a man sin against his neighbor, and an oath be laid upon him to cause him to swear, and he come and swear before thine altar in this house;

32then hear thou in heaven, and do, and judge thy servants, condemning the wicked, to bring his way upon his own head, and justifying the righteous, to give him according to his righteousness.

33When thy people Israel are smitten down before the enemy, because they have sinned against thee; if they turn again to thee, and confess thy name, and pray and make supplication unto thee in this house:

34then hear thou in heaven, and forgive the sin of thy people Israel, and bring them again unto the land which thou gavest unto their fathers.

35When heaven is shut up, and there is no rain, because they have sinned against thee; if they pray toward this place, and confess thy name, and turn from their sin, when thou dost afflict them:

36then hear thou in heaven, and forgive the sin of thy servants, and of thy people Israel, when thou teachest them the good way wherein they should walk; and send rain upon thy land, which thou hast given to thy people for an inheritance.

37If there be in the land famine, if there be pestilence, if there be blasting or mildew, locust or caterpillar; if their enemy besiege them in the land of their cities; whatsoever plague, whatsoever sickness there be;

38what prayer and supplication soever be made by any man, or by all thy people Israel, who shall know every man the plague of his own heart, and spread forth his hands toward this house:

39then hear thou in heaven thy dwelling-place, and forgive, and do, and render unto every man according to all his ways, whose heart thou knowest; (for thou, even thou only, knowest the hearts of all the children of men;)

40that they may fear thee all the days that they live in the land which thou gavest unto our fathers.

41Moreover concerning the foreigner, that is not of thy people Israel, when he shall come out of a far country for thy name's sake

42(for they shall hear of thy great name, and of thy mighty hand, and of thine outstretched arm); when he shall come and pray toward this house;

43hear thou in heaven thy dwelling-place, and do according to all that the foreigner calleth to thee for; that all the peoples of the earth may know thy name, to fear thee, as doth thy people Israel, and that they may know that this house which I have built is called by my name.

44If thy people go out to battle against their enemy, by whatsoever way thou shalt send them, and they pray unto Yahweh toward the city which thou hast chosen, and toward the house which I have built for thy name;

45then hear thou in heaven their prayer and their supplication, and maintain their cause.

46If they sin against thee (for there is no man that sinneth not), and thou be angry with them, and deliver them to the enemy, so that they carry them away captive unto the land of the enemy, far off or near;

47yet if they shall bethink themselves in the land whither they are carried captive, and turn again, and make supplication unto thee in the land of them that carried them captive, saying, We have sinned, and have done perversely, we have dealt wickedly;

48if they return unto thee with all their heart and with all their soul in the land of their enemies, who carried them captive, and pray unto thee toward their land, which thou gavest unto their fathers, the city which thou hast chosen, and the house which I have built for thy name:

49then hear thou their prayer and their supplication in heaven thy dwelling-place, and maintain their cause;

50and forgive thy people who have sinned against thee, and all their transgressions wherein they have transgressed against thee; and give them compassion before those who carried them captive, that they may have compassion on them

51(for they are thy people, and thine inheritance, which thou broughtest forth out of Egypt, from the midst of the furnace of iron);

52that thine eyes may be open unto the supplication of thy servant, and unto the supplication of thy people Israel, to hearken unto them whensoever they cry unto thee.

53For thou didst separate them from among all the peoples of the earth, to be thine inheritance, as thou spakest by Moses thy servant, when thou broughtest our fathers out of Egypt, O Lord Yahweh.

54And it was so, that, when Solomon had made an end of praying all this prayer and supplication unto Yahweh, he arose from before the altar of Yahweh, from kneeling on his knees with his hands spread forth toward heaven.

55And he stood, and blessed all the assembly of Israel with a loud voice, saying,

56Blessed be Yahweh, that hath given rest unto his people Israel, according to all that he promised: there hath not failed one word of all his good promise, which he promised by Moses his servant.

57Yahweh our God be with us, as he was with our fathers: let him not leave us, nor forsake us;

58that he may incline our hearts unto him, to walk in all his ways, and to keep his commandments, and his statutes, and his ordinances, which he commanded our fathers.

59And let these my words, wherewith I have made supplication before Yahweh, be nigh unto Yahweh our God day and night, that he maintain the cause of his servant, and the cause of his people Israel, as every day shall require;

60that all the peoples of the earth may know that Yahweh, he is God; there is none else.

61Let your heart therefore be perfect with Yahweh our God, to walk in his statutes, and to keep his commandments, as at this day.

62And the king, and all Israel with him, offered sacrifice before Yahweh.

63And Solomon offered for the sacrifice of peace-offerings, which he offered unto Yahweh, two and twenty thousand oxen, and a hundred and twenty thousand sheep. So the king and all the children of Israel dedicated the house of Yahweh.

64The same day did the king hallow the middle of the court that was before the house of Yahweh; for there he offered the burnt-offering, and the meal-offering, and the fat of the peace-offerings, because the brazen altar that was before Yahweh was too little to receive the burnt-offering, and the meal-offering, and the fat of the peace-offerings.

65So Solomon held the feast at that time, and all Israel with him, a great assembly, from the entrance of Hamath unto the brook of Egypt, before Yahweh our God, seven days and seven days, even fourteen days.

66On the eighth day he sent the people away; and they blessed the king, and went unto their tents joyful and glad of heart for all the goodness that Yahweh had showed unto David his servant, and to Israel his people.

Chapter 9

1And it came to pass, when Solomon had finished the building of the house of Yahweh, and the king's house, and all Solomon's desire which he was pleased to do,

2that Yahweh appeared to Solomon the second time, as he had appeared unto him at Gibeon.

3And Yahweh said unto him, I have heard thy prayer and thy supplication, that thou hast made before me: I have hallowed this house, which thou hast built, to put my name there for ever; and mine eyes and my heart shall be there perpetually.

4And as for thee, if thou wilt walk before me, as David thy father walked, in integrity of heart, and in uprightness, to do according to all that I have commanded thee, and wilt keep my statutes and mine ordinances;

5then I will establish the throne of thy kingdom over Israel for ever, according as I promised to David thy father, saying, There shall not fail thee a man upon the throne of Israel.

6But if ye shall turn away from following me, ye or your children, and not keep my commandments and my statutes which I have set before you, but shall go and serve other gods, and worship them;

7then will I cut off Israel out of the land which I have given them; and this house, which I have hallowed for my name, will I cast out of my sight; and Israel shall be a proverb and a byword among all peoples.

8And though this house is so high, yet shall every one that passeth by it be astonished, and shall hiss; and they shall say, Why hath Yahweh done thus unto this land, and to this house?

9and they shall answer, Because they forsook Yahweh their God, who brought forth their fathers out of the land of Egypt, and laid hold on other gods, and worshipped them, and served them: therefore hath Yahweh brought all this evil upon them.

10And it came to pass at the end of twenty years, wherein Solomon had built the two houses, the house of Yahweh and the king's house

11(now Hiram the king of Tyre had furnished Solomon with cedar-trees and fir-trees, and with gold, according to all his desire), that then king Solomon gave Hiram twenty cities in the land of Galilee.

12And Hiram came out from Tyre to see the cities which Solomon had given him; and they pleased him not.

13And he said, What cities are these which thou hast given me, my brother? And he called them the land of Cabul unto this day.

First Kings

14 And Hiram sent to the king sixscore talents of gold.

15 And this is the reason of the levy which king Solomon raised, to build the house of Yahweh, and his own house, and Millo, and the wall of Jerusalem, and Hazor, and Megiddo, and Gezer.

16 Pharaoh king of Egypt had gone up, and taken Gezer, and burnt it with fire, and slain the Canaanites that dwelt in the city, and given it for a portion unto his daughter, Solomon's wife.

17 And Solomon built Gezer, and Beth-horon the nether,

18 and Baalath, and Tamar in the wilderness, in the land,

19 and all the store-cities that Solomon had, and the cities for his chariots, and the cities for his horsemen, and that which Solomon desired to build for his pleasure in Jerusalem, and in Lebanon, and in all the land of his dominion.

20 As for all the people that were left of the Amorites, the Hittites, the Perizzites, the Hivites, and the Jebusites, who were not of the children of Israel;

21 their children that were left after them in the land, whom the children of Israel were not able utterly to destroy, of them did Solomon raise a levy of bondservants unto this day.

22 But of the children of Israel did Solomon make no bondservants; but they were the men of war, and his servants, and his princes, and his captains, and rulers of his chariots and of his horsemen.

23 These were the chief officers that were over Solomon's work, five hundred and fifty, who bare rule over the people that wrought in the work.

24 But Pharaoh's daughter came up out of the city of David unto her house which Solomon had built for her: then did he build Millo.

25 And three times a year did Solomon offer burnt-offerings and peace-offerings upon the altar which he built unto Yahweh, burning incense therewith, upon the altar that was before Yahweh. So he finished the house.

26 And king Solomon made a navy of ships in Ezion-geber, which is beside Eloth, on the shore of the Red Sea, in the land of Edom.

27 And Hiram sent in the navy his servants, shipmen that had knowledge of the sea, with the servants of Solomon.

28 And they came to Ophir, and fetched from thence gold, four hundred and twenty talents, and brought it to king Solomon.

Chapter 10

1 And when the queen of Sheba heard of the fame of Solomon concerning the name of Yahweh, she came to prove him with hard questions.

2 And she came to Jerusalem with a very great train, with camels that bare spices, and very much gold, and precious stones; and when she was come to Solomon, she communed with him of all that was in her heart.

3 And Solomon told her all her questions: there was not anything hid from the king which he told her not.

4 And when the queen of Sheba had seen all the wisdom of Solomon, and the house that he had built,

5 and the food of his table, and the sitting of his servants, and the attendance of his ministers, and their apparel, and his cupbearers, and his ascent by which he went up unto the house of Yahweh; there was no more spirit in her.

6 And she said to the king, It was a true report that I heard in mine own land of thine acts, and of thy wisdom.

7 Howbeit I believed not the words, until I came, and mine eyes had seen it: and, behold, the half was not told me; thy wisdom and prosperity exceed the fame which I heard.

8 Happy are thy men, happy are these thy servants, that stand continually before thee, and that hear thy wisdom.

9 Blessed be Yahweh thy God, who delighted in thee, to set thee on the throne of Israel: because Yahweh loved Israel for ever, therefore made he thee king, to do justice and righteousness.

10 And she gave the king a hundred and twenty talents of gold, and of spices very great store, and precious stones: there came no more such abundance of spices as these which the queen of Sheba gave to king Solomon.

11 And the navy also of Hiram, that brought gold from Ophir, brought in from Ophir great plenty of almug-trees and precious stones.

12 And the king made of the almug-trees pillars for the house of Yahweh, and for the king's house, harps also and psalteries for the singers: there came no such almug-trees, nor were seen, unto this day.

13 And king Solomon gave to the queen of Sheba all her desire, whatsoever she asked, besides that which Solomon gave her of his royal bounty. So she turned, and went to her own land, she and her servants.

14 Now the weight of gold that came to Solomon in one year was six hundred threescore and six talents of gold,

15 besides that which the traders brought, and the traffic of the merchants, and of all the kings of the mingled people, and of the governors of the country.

16 And king Solomon made two hundred bucklers of beaten gold; six hundred shekels of gold went to one buckler.

17 And he made three hundred shields of beaten gold; three pounds of gold went to one shield: and the king put them in the house of the forest of Lebanon.

18 Moreover the king made a great throne of ivory, and overlaid it with the finest gold.

19 There were six steps to the throne, and the top of the throne was round behind; and there were stays on either side by the place of the seat, and two lions standing beside the stays.

20 And twelve lions stood there on the one side and on the other upon the six steps: there was not the like made in any kingdom.

21 And all king Solomon's drinking vessels were of gold, and all the vessels of the house of the forest of Lebanon were of pure gold: none were of silver; it was nothing accounted of in the days of Solomon.

22 For the king had at sea a navy of Tarshish with the navy of Hiram: once every three years came the navy of Tarshish, bringing gold, and silver, ivory, and apes, and peacocks.

23 So king Solomon exceeded all the kings of the earth in riches and in wisdom.

24 And all the earth sought the presence of Solomon, to hear his wisdom, which God had put in his heart.

25 And they brought every man his tribute, vessels of silver, and vessels of gold, and raiment, and armor, and spices, horses, and mules, a rate year by year.

26 And Solomon gathered together chariots and horsemen: and he had a thousand and four hundred chariots, and twelve thousand horsemen, that he bestowed in the chariot cities, and with the king at Jerusalem.

27 And the king made silver to be in Jerusalem as stones, and cedars made he to be as the sycomore-trees that are in the lowland, for abundance.

28 And the horses which Solomon had were brought out of Egypt; and the king's merchants received them in droves, each drove at a price.

29 And a chariot came up and went out of Egypt for six hundred shekels of silver, and a horse for a hundred and fifty; and so for all the kings of the Hittites, and for the kings of Syria, did they bring them out by their means.

Chapter 11

1 Now king Solomon loved many foreign women, together with the daughter of Pharaoh, women of the Moabites, Ammonites, Edomites, Sidonians, and Hittites;

2 of the nations concerning which Yahweh said unto the children of Israel, Ye shall not go among them, neither shall they come among you; for surely they will turn away your heart after their gods: Solomon clave unto these in love.

3 And he had seven hundred wives, princesses, and three hundred concubines; and his wives turned away his heart.

4 For it came to pass, when Solomon was old, that his wives turned away his heart after other gods; and his heart was not perfect with Yahweh his God, as was the heart of David his father.

5 For Solomon went after Ashtoreth the goddess of the Sidonians, and after Milcom the abomination of the Ammonites.

6 And Solomon did that which was evil in the sight of Yahweh, and went not fully after Yahweh, as did David his father.

7 Then did Solomon build a high place for Chemosh the abomination of Moab, in the mount that is before Jerusalem, and for Molech the abomination of the children of Ammon.

8 And so did he for all his foreign wives, who burnt incense and sacrificed unto their gods.

9 And Yahweh was angry with Solomon, because his heart was turned away from Yahweh, the God of Israel, who had appeared unto him twice,

10 and had commanded him concerning this thing, that he should not go after other gods: but he kept not that which Yahweh commanded.

11 Wherefore Yahweh said unto Solomon, Forasmuch as this is done of thee, and thou hast not kept my covenant and my statutes, which I have commanded thee, I will surely rend the kingdom from thee, and will give it to thy servant.

12 Notwithstanding in thy days I will not do it, for David thy father's sake: but I will rend it out of the hand of thy son.

13 Howbeit I will not rend away all the kingdom; but I will give one tribe to thy son, for David my servant's sake, and for Jerusalem's sake which I have chosen.

14 And Yahweh raised up an adversary unto Solomon, Hadad the Edomite: he was of the king's seed in Edom.

15 For it came to pass, when David was in Edom, and Joab the captain of the host was gone up to bury the slain, and had smitten every male in Edom

16 (for Joab and all Israel remained there six months, until he had cut off every male in Edom);

17 that Hadad fled, he and certain Edomites of his father's servants with him, to go into Egypt, Hadad being yet a little child.

18 And they arose out of Midian, and came to Paran; and they took men with them out of Paran, and they came to Egypt, unto Pharaoh king of Egypt, who gave him a house, and appointed him victuals, and gave him land.

19 And Hadad found great favor in the sight of Pharaoh, so that he gave him to wife the sister of his own wife, the sister of Tahpenes the queen.

20 And the sister of Tahpenes bare him Genubath his son, whom Tahpenes weaned in Pharaoh's house; and Genubath was in Pharaoh's house among the sons of Pharaoh.

21 And when Hadad heard in Egypt that David slept with his fathers, and that Joab the captain of the host was dead, Hadad said to Pharaoh, Let me depart, that I may go to mine own country.

22 Then Pharaoh said unto him, But what hast thou lacked with me, that, behold, thou seekest to go to thine own country? And he answered, Nothing: howbeit only let me depart.

23 And God raised up another adversary unto him, Rezon the son of Eliada, who had fled from his lord Hadadezer king of Zobah.

24 And he gathered men unto him, and became captain over a troop, when David slew them of Zobah: and they went to Damascus, and dwelt therein, and reigned in Damascus.

25 And he was an adversary to Israel all the days of Solomon, besides the mischief that Hadad did: and he abhorred Israel, and reigned over Syria.

26 And Jeroboam the son of Nebat, an Ephraimite of Zeredah, a servant of Solomon, whose mother's name was Zeruah, a widow, he also lifted up his hand against the king.

27 And this was the reason why he lifted up his hand against the king: Solomon built Millo, and repaired the breach of the city of David his father.

28 And the man Jeroboam was a mighty man of valor; and Solomon saw the young man that he was industrious, and he gave him charge over all the labor of the house of Joseph.

29 And it came to pass at that time, when Jeroboam went out of Jerusalem, that the prophet Ahijah the Shilonite found him in the way; now Ahijah had clad

himself with a new garment; and they two were alone in the field.

³⁰And Ahijah laid hold of the new garment that was on him, and rent it in twelve pieces.

³¹And he said to Jeroboam, Take thee ten pieces; for thus saith Yahweh, the God of Israel, Behold, I will rend the kingdom out of the hand of Solomon, and will give ten tribes to thee

³²(but he shall have one tribe, for my servant David's sake and for Jerusalem's sake, the city which I have chosen out of all the tribes of Israel);

³³because that they have forsaken me, and have worshipped Ashtoreth the goddess of the Sidonians, Chemosh the god of Moab, and Milcom the god of the children of Ammon; and they have not walked in my ways, to do that which is right in mine eyes, and to keep my statutes and mine ordinances, as did David his father.

³⁴Howbeit I will not take the whole kingdom out of his hand; but I will make him prince all the days of his life, for David my servant's sake whom I chose, who kept my commandments and my statutes;

³⁵but I will take the kingdom out of his son's hand, and will give it unto thee, even ten tribes.

³⁶And unto his son will I give one tribe, that David my servant may have a lamp alway before me in Jerusalem, the city which I have chosen me to put my name there.

³⁷And I will take thee, and thou shalt reign according to all that thy soul desireth, and shalt be king over Israel.

³⁸And it shall be, if thou wilt hearken unto all that I command thee, and wilt walk in my ways, and do that which is right in mine eyes, to keep my statutes and my commandments, as David my servant did; that I will be with thee, and will build thee a sure house, as I built for David, and will give Israel unto thee.

³⁹And I will for this afflict the seed of David, but not for ever.

⁴⁰Solomon sought therefore to kill Jeroboam; but Jeroboam arose, and fled into Egypt, unto Shishak king of Egypt, and was in Egypt until the death of Solomon.

⁴¹Now the rest of the acts of Solomon, and all that he did, and his wisdom, are they not written in the book of the acts of Solomon?

⁴²And the time that Solomon reigned in Jerusalem over all Israel was forty years.

⁴³And Solomon slept with his fathers, and was buried in the city of David his father: and Rehoboam his son reigned in his stead.

Chapter 12

¹And Rehoboam went to Shechem: for all Israel were come to Shechem to make him king.

²And it came to pass, when Jeroboam the son of Nebat heard of it (for he was yet in Egypt, whither he had fled from the presence of king Solomon, and Jeroboam dwelt in Egypt,

³and they sent and called him), that Jeroboam and all the assembly of Israel came, and spake unto Rehoboam, saying,

⁴Thy father made our yoke grievous: now therefore make thou the grievous service of thy father, and his heavy yoke which he put upon us, lighter, and we will serve thee.

⁵And he said unto them, Depart yet for three days, then come again to me. And the people departed.

⁶And king Rehoboam took counsel with the old men, that had stood before Solomon his father while he yet lived, saying, What counsel give ye me to return answer to this people?

⁷And they spake unto him, saying, If thou wilt be a servant unto this people this day, and wilt serve them, and answer them, and speak good words to them, then they will be thy servants for ever.

⁸But he forsook the counsel of the old men which they had given him, and took counsel with the young men that were grown up with him, that stood before him.

⁹And he said unto them, What counsel give ye, that we may return answer to this people, who have spoken to me, saying, Make the yoke that thy father put upon us lighter?

¹⁰And the young men that were grown up with him spake unto him, saying, Thus shalt thou say unto this people that spake unto thee, saying, Thy father made our yoke heavy, but make thou it lighter unto us; thus shalt thou speak unto them, My little finger is thicker than my father's loins.

¹¹And now whereas my father did lade you with a heavy yoke, I will add to your yoke: my father chastised you with whips, but I will chastise you with scorpions.

¹²So Jeroboam and all the people came to Rehoboam the third day, as the king bade, saying, Come to me again the third day.

¹³And the king answered the people roughly, and forsook the counsel of the old men which they had given him,

¹⁴and spake to them after the counsel of the young men, saying, My father made your yoke heavy, but I will add to your yoke: my father chastised you with whips, but I will chastise you with scorpions.

¹⁵So the king hearkened not unto the people; for it was a thing brought about of Yahweh, that he might establish his word, which Yahweh spake by Ahijah the Shilonite to Jeroboam the son of Nebat.

¹⁶And when all Israel saw that the king hearkened not unto them, the people answered the king, saying, What portion have we in David? neither have we inheritance in the son of Jesse: to your tents, O Israel: now see to thine own house, David. So Israel departed unto their tents.

¹⁷But as for the children of Israel that dwelt in the cities of Judah, Rehoboam reigned over them.

¹⁸Then king Rehoboam sent Adoram, who was over the men subject to taskwork; and all Israel stoned him to death with stones. And king Rehoboam made speed to get him up to his chariot, to flee to Jerusalem.

¹⁹So Israel rebelled against the house of David unto this day.

²⁰And it came to pass, when all Israel heard that Jeroboam was returned, that they sent and called him unto the congregation, and made him king over all Israel: there was none that followed the house of David, but the tribe of Judah only.

²¹And when Rehoboam was come to Jerusalem, he assembled all the house of Judah, and the tribe of Benjamin, a hundred and fourscore thousand chosen men, that were warriors, to fight against the house of Israel, to bring the kingdom again to Rehoboam the son of Solomon.

²²But the word of God came unto Shemaiah the man of God, saying,

²³Speak unto Rehoboam the son of Solomon, king of Judah, and unto all the house of Judah and Benjamin, and to the rest of the people, saying,

²⁴Thus saith Yahweh, Ye shall not go up, nor fight against your brethren the children of Israel: return every man to his house; for this thing is of me. So they hearkened unto the word of Yahweh, and returned and went their way, according to the word of Yahweh.

²⁵Then Jeroboam built Shechem in the hill-country of Ephraim, and dwelt therein; and he went out from thence, and built Penuel.

²⁶And Jeroboam said in his heart, Now will the kingdom return to the house of David:

²⁷if this people go up to offer sacrifices in the house of Yahweh at Jerusalem, then will the heart of this people turn again unto their lord, even unto Rehoboam king of Judah; and they will kill me, and return to Rehoboam king of Judah.

²⁸Whereupon the king took counsel, and made two calves of gold; and he said unto them, It is too much for you to go up to Jerusalem: behold thy gods, O Israel, which brought thee up out of the land of Egypt.

²⁹And he set the one in Beth-el, and the other put he in Dan.

³⁰And this thing became a sin; for the people went to worship before the one, even unto Dan.

³¹And he made houses of high places, and made priests from among all the people, that were not of the sons of Levi.

³²And Jeroboam ordained a feast in the eighth month, on the fifteenth day of the month, like unto the feast that is in Judah, and he went up unto the altar; so did he in Beth-el, sacrificing unto the calves that he had made: and he placed in Beth-el the priests of the high places that he had made.

³³And he went up unto the altar which he had made in Beth-el on the fifteenth day in the eighth month, even in the month which he had devised of his own heart: and he ordained a feast for the children of Israel, and went up unto the altar, to burn incense.

Chapter 13

¹And, behold, there came a man of God out of Judah by the word of Yahweh unto Beth-el: and Jeroboam was standing by the altar to burn incense.

²And he cried against the altar by the word of Yahweh, and said, O altar, altar, thus saith Yahweh: Behold, a son shall be born unto the house of David, Josiah by name; and upon thee shall he sacrifice the priests of the high places that burn incense upon thee, and men's bones shall they burn upon thee.

³And he gave a sign the same day, saying, This is the sign which Yahweh hath spoken: Behold, the altar shall be rent, and the ashes that are upon it shall be poured out.

⁴And it came to pass, when the king heard the saying of the man of God, which he cried against the altar in Beth-el, that Jeroboam put forth his hand from the altar, saying, Lay hold on him. And his hand, which he put forth against him, dried up, so that he could not draw it back again to him.

⁵The altar also was rent, and the ashes poured out from the altar, according to the sign which the man of God had given by the word of Yahweh.

⁶And the king answered and said unto the man of God, Entreat now the favor of Yahweh thy God, and pray for me, that my hand may be restored me again. And the man of God entreated Yahweh, and the king's hand was restored him again, and became as it was before.

⁷And the king said unto the man of God, Come home with me, and refresh thyself, and I will give thee a reward.

⁸And the man of God said unto the king, If thou wilt give me half thy house, I will not go in with thee, neither will I eat bread nor drink water in this place;

⁹for so was it charged me by the word of Yahweh, saying, Thou shalt eat no bread, nor drink water, neither return by the way that thou camest.

¹⁰So he went another way, and returned not by the way that he came to Beth-el.

¹¹Now there dwelt an old prophet in Beth-el; and one of his sons came and told him all the works that the man of God had done that day in Beth-el: the words which he had spoken unto the king, them also they told unto their father.

¹²And their father said unto them, What way went he? Now his sons had seen what way the man of God went, that came from Judah.

¹³And he said unto his sons, Saddle me the ass. So they saddled him the ass; and he rode thereon.

¹⁴And he went after the man of God, and found him sitting under an oak; and he said unto him, Art thou the man of God that camest from Judah? And he said, I am.

¹⁵Then he said unto him, Come home with me, and eat bread.

¹⁶And he said, I may not return with thee, nor go in with thee; neither will I eat bread nor drink water with thee in this place:

¹⁷for it was said to me by the word of Yahweh, Thou shalt eat no bread nor drink water there, nor turn again to go by the way that thou camest.

¹⁸And he said unto him, I also am a prophet as thou art; and an angel spake unto me by the word of Yahweh, saying, Bring him back with thee into thy house, that he may eat bread and drink water. But he lied unto him.

¹⁹So he went back with him, and did eat bread in his house, and drank

First Kings

water.

20And it came to pass, as they sat at the table, that the word of Yahweh came unto the prophet that brought him back;

21and he cried unto the man of God that came from Judah, saying, Thus saith Yahweh, Forasmuch as thou hast been disobedient unto the mouth of Yahweh, and hast not kept the commandment which Yahweh thy God commanded thee,

22but camest back, and hast eaten bread and drunk water in the place of which he said to thee, Eat no bread, and drink no water; thy body shall not come unto the sepulchre of thy fathers.

23And it came to pass, after he had eaten bread, and after he had drunk, that he saddled for him the ass, to wit, for the prophet whom he had brought back.

24And when he was gone, a lion met him by the way, and slew him: and his body was cast in the way, and the ass stood by it; the lion also stood by the body.

25And, behold, men passed by, and saw the body cast in the way, and the lion standing by the body; and they came and told it in the city where the old prophet dwelt.

26And when the prophet that brought him back from the way heard thereof, he said, It is the man of God, who was disobedient unto the mouth of Yahweh: therefore Yahweh hath delivered him unto the lion, which hath torn him, and slain him, according to the word of Yahweh, which he spake unto him.

27And he spake to his sons, saying, Saddle me the ass. And they saddled it.

28And he went and found his body cast in the way, and the ass and the lion standing by the body: the lion had not eaten the body, nor torn the ass.

29And the prophet took up the body of the man of God, and laid it upon the ass, and brought it back; and he came to the city of the old prophet, to mourn, and to bury him.

30And he laid his body in his own grave; and they mourned over him, saying, Alas, my brother!

31And it came to pass, after he had buried him, that he spake to his sons, saying, When I am dead, then bury me in the sepulchre wherein the man of God is buried; lay my bones beside his bones.

32For the saying which he cried by the word of Yahweh against the altar in Beth-el, and against all the houses of the high places which are in the cities of Samaria, shall surely come to pass.

33After this thing Jeroboam returned not from his evil way, but made again from among all the people priests of the high places: whosoever would, he consecrated him, that there might be priests of the high places.

34And this thing became sin unto the house of Jeroboam, even to cut it off, and to destroy it from off the face of the earth.

Chapter 14

1At that time Abijah the son of Jeroboam fell sick.

2And Jeroboam said to his wife, Arise, I pray thee, and disguise thyself, that thou be not known to be the wife of Jeroboam; and get thee to Shiloh: behold, there is Ahijah the prophet, who spake concerning me that I should be king over this people.

3And take with thee ten loaves, and cakes, and a cruse of honey, and go to him: he will tell thee what shall become of the child.

4And Jeroboam's wife did so, and arose, and went to Shiloh, and came to the house of Ahijah. Now Ahijah could not see; for his eyes were set by reason of his age.

5And Yahweh said unto Ahijah, Behold, the wife of Jeroboam cometh to inquire of thee concerning her son; for he is sick: thus and thus shalt thou say unto her; for it will be, when she cometh in, that she will feign herself to be another woman.

6And it was so, when Ahijah heard the sound of her feet, as she came in at the door, that he said, Come in, thou wife of Jeroboam; why feignest thou thyself to be another? for I am sent to thee with heavy tidings.

7Go, tell Jeroboam, Thus saith Yahweh, the God of Israel: Forasmuch as I exalted thee from among the people, and made thee prince over my people Israel,

8and rent the kingdom away from the house of David, and gave it thee; and yet thou hast not been as my servant David, who kept my commandments, and who followed me with all his heart, to do that only which was right in mine eyes,

9but hast done evil above all that were before thee, and hast gone and made thee other gods, and molten images, to provoke me to anger, and hast cast me behind thy back:

10therefore, behold, I will bring evil upon the house of Jeroboam, and will cut off from Jeroboam every man-child, him that is shut up and him that is left at large in Israel, and will utterly sweep away the house of Jeroboam, as a man sweepeth away dung, till it be all gone.

11Him that dieth of Jeroboam in the city shall the dogs eat; and him that dieth in the field shall the birds of the heavens eat: for Yahweh hath spoken it.

12Arise thou therefore, get thee to thy house: and when thy feet enter into the city, the child shall die.

13And all Israel shall mourn for him, and bury him; for he only of Jeroboam shall come to the grave, because in him there is found some good thing toward Yahweh, the God of Israel, in the house of Jeroboam.

14Moreover Yahweh will raise him up a king over Israel, who shall cut off the house of Jeroboam that day: but what? even now.

15For Yahweh will smite Israel, as a reed is shaken in the water; and he will root up Israel out of this good land which he gave to their fathers, and will scatter them beyond the River, because they have made their Asherim, provoking Yahweh to anger.

16And he will give Israel up because of the sins of Jeroboam, which he hath sinned, and wherewith he hath made Israel to sin.

17And Jeroboam's wife arose, and departed, and came to Tirzah: and as she came to the threshold of the house, the child died.

18And all Israel buried him, and mourned for him, according to the word of Yahweh, which he spake by his servant Ahijah the prophet.

19And the rest of the acts of Jeroboam, how he warred, and how he reigned, behold, they are written in the book of the chronicles of the kings of Israel.

20And the days which Jeroboam reigned were two and twenty years: and he slept with his fathers, and Nadab his son reigned in his stead.

21And Rehoboam the son of Solomon reigned in Judah. Rehoboam was forty and one years old when he began to reign, and he reigned seventeen years in Jerusalem, the city which Yahweh had chosen out of all the tribes of Israel, to put his name there: and his mother's name was Naamah the Ammonitess.

22And Judah did that which was evil in the sight of Yahweh, and they provoked him to jealousy with their sins which they committed, above all that their fathers had done.

23For they also built them high places, and pillars, and Asherim, on every high hill, and under every green tree;

24and there were also sodomites in the land: they did according to all the abominations of the nations which Yahweh drove out before the children of Israel.

25And it came to pass in the fifth year of king Rehoboam, that Shishak king of Egypt came up against Jerusalem;

26and he took away the treasures of the house of Yahweh, and the treasures of the king's house; he even took away all: and he took away all the shields of gold which Solomon had made.

27And king Rehoboam made in their stead shields of brass, and committed them to the hands of the captains of the guard, who kept the door of the king's house.

28And it was so, that, as oft as the king went into the house of Yahweh, the guard bare them, and brought them back into the guard-chamber.

29Now the rest of the acts of Rehoboam, and all that he did, are they not written in the book of the chronicles of the kings of Judah?

30And there was war between Rehoboam and Jeroboam continually.

31And Rehoboam slept with his fathers, and was buried with his fathers in the city of David: and his mother's name was Naamah the Ammonitess. And Abijam his son reigned in his stead.

Chapter 15

1Now in the eighteenth year of king Jeroboam the son of Nebat began Abijam to reign over Judah.

2Three years reigned he in Jerusalem: and his mother's name was Maacah the daughter of Abishalom.

3And he walked in all the sins of his father, which he had done before him; and his heart was not perfect with Yahweh his God, as the heart of David his father.

4Nevertheless for David's sake did Yahweh his God give him a lamp in Jerusalem, to set up his son after him, and to establish Jerusalem;

5because David did that which was right in the eyes of Yahweh, and turned not aside from anything that he commanded him all the days of his life, save only in the matter of Uriah the Hittite.

6Now there was war between Rehoboam and Jeroboam all the days of his life.

7And the rest of the acts of Abijam, and all that he did, are they not written in the book of the chronicles of the kings of Judah? And there was war between Abijam and Jeroboam.

8And Abijam slept with his fathers; and they buried him in the city of David: and Asa his son reigned in his stead.

9And in the twentieth year of Jeroboam king of Israel began Asa to reign over Judah.

10And forty and one years reigned he in Jerusalem: and his mother's name was Maacah the daughter of Abishalom.

11And Asa did that which was right in the eyes of Yahweh, as did David his father.

12And he put away the sodomites out of the land, and removed all the idols that his fathers had made.

13And also Maacah his mother he removed from being queen, because she had made an abominable image for an Asherah; and Asa cut down her image, and burnt it at the brook Kidron.

14But the high places were not taken away: nevertheless the heart of Asa was perfect with Yahweh all his days.

15And he brought into the house of Yahweh the things that his father had dedicated, and the things that himself had dedicated, silver, and gold, and vessels.

16And there was war between Asa and Baasha king of Israel all their days.

17And Baasha king of Israel went up against Judah, and built Ramah, that he might not suffer any one to go out or come in to Asa king of Judah.

18Then Asa took all the silver and the gold that were left in the treasures of the house of Yahweh, and the treasures of the king's house, and delivered them into the hand of his servants; and king Asa sent them to Ben-hadad, the son of Tabrimmon, the son of Hezion, king of Syria, that dwelt at Damascus, saying,

19There is a league between me and thee, between my father and thy father: behold, I have sent unto thee a present of silver and gold; go, break thy league with Baasha king of Israel, that he may depart from me.

20And Ben-hadad hearkened unto king Asa, and sent the captains of his armies against the cities of Israel, and smote Ijon, and Dan, and Abel-beth-maacah, and all Chinneroth, with all the land of Naphtali.

21And it came to pass, when Baasha heard thereof, that he left off building Ramah, and dwelt in Tirzah.

22Then king Asa made a proclamation unto all Judah; none was exempted: and they carried away the stones of Ramah, and the timber thereof, wherewith Baasha had builded; and king Asa built therewith Geba of Benjamin, and Mizpah.

23Now the rest of all the acts of Asa, and all his might, and all that he did, and the cities which he built, are they not written in the book of the chronicles of the kings of Judah? But in the time of his old age he was diseased in his feet.

24And Asa slept with his fathers, and was buried with his fathers in the city of David his father; and Jehoshaphat his son reigned in his stead.

25And Nadab the son of Jeroboam began to reign over Israel in the second year of Asa king of Judah; and he reigned over Israel two years.

26And he did that which was evil in the sight of Yahweh, and walked in the way of his father, and in his sin wherewith he made Israel to sin.

27And Baasha the son of Ahijah, of the house of Issachar, conspired against him; and Baasha smote him at Gibbethon, which belonged to the Philistines; for Nadab and all Israel were laying siege to Gibbethon.

28Even in the third year of Asa king of Judah did Baasha slay him, and reigned in his stead.

29And it came to pass that, as soon as he was king, he smote all the house of Jeroboam: he left not to Jeroboam any that breathed, until he had destroyed him; according unto the saying of Yahweh, which he spake by his servant Ahijah the Shilonite;

30for the sins of Jeroboam which he sinned, and wherewith he made Israel to sin, because of his provocation wherewith he provoked Yahweh, the God of Israel, to anger.

31Now the rest of the acts of Nadab, and all that he did, are they not written in the book of the chronicles of the kings of Israel?

32And there was war between Asa and Baasha king of Israel all their days.

33In the third year of Asa king of Judah began Baasha the son of Ahijah to reign over all Israel in Tirzah, and reigned twenty and four years.

34And he did that which was evil in the sight of Yahweh, and walked in the way of Jeroboam, and in his sin wherewith he made Israel to sin.

Chapter 16

1And the word of Yahweh came to Jehu the son of Hanani against Baasha, saying,

2Forasmuch as I exalted thee out of the dust, and made thee prince over my people Israel, and thou hast walked in the way of Jeroboam, and hast made my people Israel to sin, to provoke me to anger with their sins;

3behold, I will utterly sweep away Baasha and his house; and I will make thy house like the house of Jeroboam the son of Nebat.

4Him that dieth of Baasha in the city shall the dogs eat; and him that dieth of his in the field shall the birds of the heavens eat.

5Now the rest of the acts of Baasha, and what he did, and his might, are they not written in the book of the chronicles of the kings of Israel?

6And Baasha slept with his fathers, and was buried in Tirzah; and Elah his son reigned in his stead.

7And moreover by the prophet Jehu the son of Hanani came the word of Yahweh against Baasha, and against his house, both because of all the evil that he did in the sight of Yahweh, to provoke him to anger with the work of his hands, in being like the house of Jeroboam, and because he smote him.

8In the twenty and sixth year of Asa king of Judah began Elah the son of Baasha to reign over Israel in Tirzah, and reigned two years.

9And his servant Zimri, captain of half his chariots, conspired against him. Now he was in Tirzah, drinking himself drunk in the house of Arza, who was over the household in Tirzah:

10and Zimri went in and smote him, and killed him, in the twenty and seventh year of Asa king of Judah, and reigned in his stead.

11And it came to pass, when he began to reign, as soon as he sat on his throne, that he smote all the house of Baasha: he left him not a single man-child, neither of his kinsfolks, nor of his friends.

12Thus did Zimri destroy all the house of Baasha, according to the word of Yahweh, which he spake against Baasha by Jehu the prophet,

13for all the sins of Baasha, and the sins of Elah his son, which they sinned, and wherewith they made Israel to sin, to provoke Yahweh, the God of Israel, to anger with their vanities.

14Now the rest of the acts of Elah, and all that he did, are they not written in the book of the chronicles of the kings of Israel?

15In the twenty and seventh year of Asa king of Judah did Zimri reign seven days in Tirzah. Now the people were encamped against Gibbethon, which belonged to the Philistines.

16And the people that were encamped heard say, Zimri hath conspired, and hath also smitten the king: wherefore all Israel made Omri, the captain of the host, king over Israel that day in the camp.

17And Omri went up from Gibbethon, and all Israel with him, and they besieged Tirzah.

18And it came to pass, when Zimri saw that the city was taken, that he went into the castle of the king's house, and burnt the king's house over him with fire, and died,

19for his sins which he sinned in doing that which was evil in the sight of Yahweh, in walking in the way of Jeroboam, and in his sin which he did, to make Israel to sin.

20Now the rest of the acts of Zimri, and his treason that he wrought, are they not written in the book of the chronicles of the kings of Israel?

21Then were the people of Israel divided into two parts: half of the people followed Tibni the son of Ginath, to make him king; and half followed Omri.

22But the people that followed Omri prevailed against the people that followed Tibni the son of Ginath: so Tibni died, and Omri reigned.

23In the thirty and first year of Asa king of Judah began Omri to reign over Israel, and reigned twelve years: six years reigned he in Tirzah.

24And he bought the hill Samaria of Shemer for two talents of silver; and he built on the hill, and called the name of the city which he built, after the name of Shemer, the owner of the hill, Samaria.

25And Omri did that which was evil in the sight of Yahweh, and dealt wickedly above all that were before him.

26For he walked in all the way of Jeroboam the son of Nebat, and in his sins wherewith he made Israel to sin, to provoke Yahweh, the God of Israel, to anger with their vanities.

27Now the rest of the acts of Omri which he did, and his might that he showed, are they not written in the book of the chronicles of the kings of Israel?

28So Omri slept with his fathers, and was buried in Samaria; and Ahab his son reigned in his stead.

29And in the thirty and eighth year of Asa king of Judah began Ahab the son of Omri to reign over Israel: and Ahab the son of Omri reigned over Israel in Samaria twenty and two years.

30And Ahab the son of Omri did that which was evil in the sight of Yahweh above all that were before him.

31And it came to pass, as if it had been a light thing for him to walk in the sins of Jeroboam the son of Nebat, that he took to wife Jezebel the daughter of Ethbaal king of the Sidonians, and went and served Baal, and worshipped him.

32And he reared up an altar for Baal in the house of Baal, which he had built in Samaria.

33And Ahab made the Asherah; and Ahab did yet more to provoke Yahweh, the God of Israel, to anger than all the kings of Israel that were before him.

34In his days did Hiel the Beth-elite build Jericho: he laid the foundation thereof with the loss of Abiram his first-born, and set up the gates thereof with the loss of his youngest son Segub, according to the word of Yahweh, which he spake by Joshua the son of Nun.

Chapter 17

1And Elijah the Tishbite, who was of the sojourners of Gilead, said unto Ahab, As Yahweh, the God of Israel, liveth, before whom I stand, there shall not be dew nor rain these years, but according to my word.

2And the word of Yahweh came unto him, saying,

3Get thee hence, and turn thee eastward, and hide thyself by the brook Cherith, that is before the Jordan.

4And it shall be, that thou shalt drink of the brook; and I have commanded the ravens to feed thee there.

5So he went and did according unto the word of Yahweh; for he went and dwelt by the brook Cherith, that is before the Jordan.

6And the ravens brought him bread and flesh in the morning, and bread and flesh in the evening; and he drank of the brook.

7And it came to pass after a while, that the brook dried up, because there was no rain in the land.

8And the word of Yahweh came unto him, saying,

9Arise, get thee to Zarephath, which belongeth to Sidon, and dwell there: behold, I have commanded a widow there to sustain thee.

10So he arose and went to Zarephath; and when he came to the gate of the city, behold, a widow was there gathering sticks: and he called to her, and said, Fetch me, I pray thee, a little water in a vessel, that I may drink.

11And as she was going to fetch it, he called to her, and said, Bring me, I pray thee, a morsel of bread in thy hand.

12And she said, As Yahweh thy God liveth, I have not a cake, but a handful of meal in the jar, and a little oil in the cruse: and, behold, I am gathering two sticks, that I may go in and dress it for me and my son, that we may eat it, and die.

13And Elijah said unto her, Fear not; go and do as thou hast said; but make me thereof a little cake first, and bring it forth unto me, and afterward make for thee and for thy son.

14For thus saith Yahweh, the God of Israel, The jar of meal shall not waste, neither shall the cruse of oil fail, until the day that Yahweh sendeth rain upon the earth.

15And she went and did according to the saying of Elijah: and she, and he, and her house, did eat many days.

16The jar of meal wasted not, neither did the cruse of oil fail, according to the word of Yahweh, which he spake by Elijah.

17And it came to pass after these things, that the son of the woman, the mistress of the house, fell sick; and his sickness was so sore, that there was no breath left in him.

18And she said unto Elijah, What have I to do with thee, O thou man of God? thou art come unto me to bring my sin to remembrance, and to slay my son!

19And he said unto her, Give me thy son. And he took him out of her bosom, and carried him up into the chamber, where he abode, and laid him upon his own bed.

20And he cried unto Yahweh, and said, O Yahweh my God, hast thou also brought evil upon the widow with whom I sojourn, by slaying her son?

21And he stretched himself upon the child three times, and cried unto Yahweh, and said, O Yahweh my God, I pray thee, let this child's soul come into him again.

22And Yahweh hearkened unto the voice of Elijah; and the soul of the child came into him again, and he revived.

23And Elijah took the child, and brought him down out of the chamber into the house, and delivered him unto his mother; and Elijah said, See, thy son liveth.

24And the woman said to Elijah, Now I know that thou art a man of God, and that the word of Yahweh in thy mouth is truth.

Chapter 18

1And it came to pass after many days, that the word of Yahweh came to Elijah, in the third year, saying, Go, show thyself unto Ahab; and I will send rain upon the earth.

2And Elijah went to show himself unto Ahab. And the famine was sore in Samaria.

3And Ahab called Obadiah, who was over the household. (Now Obadiah feared Yahweh greatly:

4for it was so, when Jezebel cut off the prophets of Yahweh, that Obadiah

First Kings

took a hundred prophets, and hid them by fifty in a cave, and fed them with bread and water.)

5And Ahab said unto Obadiah, Go through the land, unto all the fountains of water, and unto all the brooks: peradventure we may find grass and save the horses and mules alive, that we lose not all the beasts.

6So they divided the land between them to pass throughout it: Ahab went one way by himself, and Obadiah went another way by himself.

7And as Obadiah was in the way, behold, Elijah met him: and he knew him, and fell on his face, and said, Is it thou, my lord Elijah?

8And he answered him, It is I: go, tell thy lord, Behold, Elijah is here.

9And he said, Wherein have I sinned, that thou wouldest deliver thy servant into the hand of Ahab, to slay me?

10As Yahweh thy God liveth, there is no nation or kingdom, whither my lord hath not sent to seek thee: and when they said, He is not here, he took an oath of the kingdom and nation, that they found thee not.

11And now thou sayest, Go, tell thy lord, Behold, Elijah is here.

12And it will come to pass, as soon as I am gone from thee, that the Spirit of Yahweh will carry thee whither I know not; and so when I come and tell Ahab, and he cannot find thee, he will slay me: but I thy servant fear Yahweh from my youth.

13Was it not told my lord what I did when Jezebel slew the prophets of Yahweh, how I hid a hundred men of Yahweh's prophets by fifty in a cave, and fed them with bread and water?

14And now thou sayest, Go, tell thy lord, Behold, Elijah is here; and he will slay me.

15And Elijah said, As Yahweh of hosts liveth, before whom I stand, I will surely show myself unto him to-day.

16So Obadiah went to meet Ahab, and told him; and Ahab went to meet Elijah.

17And it came to pass, when Ahab saw Elijah, that Ahab said unto him, Is it thou, thou troubler of Israel?

18And he answered, I have not troubled Israel; but thou, and thy father's house, in that ye have forsaken the commandments of Yahweh, and thou hast followed the Baalim.

19Now therefore send, and gather to me all Israel unto mount Carmel, and the prophets of Baal four hundred and fifty, and the prophets of the Asherah four hundred, that eat at Jezebel's table.

20So Ahab sent unto all the children of Israel, and gathered the prophets together unto mount Carmel.

21And Elijah came near unto all the people, and said, How long go ye limping between the two sides? if Yahweh be God, follow him; but if Baal, then follow him. And the people answered him not a word.

22Then said Elijah unto the people, I, even I only, am left a prophet of Yahweh; but Baal's prophets are four hundred and fifty men.

23Let them therefore give us two bullocks; and let them choose one bullock for themselves, and cut it in pieces, and lay it on the wood, and put no fire under; and I will dress the other bullock, and lay it on the wood, and put no fire under.

24And call ye on the name of your god, and I will call on the name of Yahweh; and the God that answereth by fire, let him be God. And all the people answered and said, It is well spoken.

25And Elijah said unto the prophets of Baal, Choose you one bullock for yourselves, and dress it first; for ye are many; and call on the name of your god, but put no fire under.

26And they took the bullock which was given them, and they dressed it, and called on the name of Baal from morning even until noon, saying, O Baal, hear us. But there was no voice, nor any that answered. And they leaped about the altar which was made.

27And it came to pass at noon, that Elijah mocked them, and said, Cry aloud; for he is a god: either he is musing, or he is gone aside, or he is on a journey, or peradventure he sleepeth and must be awaked.

28And they cried aloud, and cut themselves after their manner with knives and lances, till the blood gushed out upon them.

29And it was so, when midday was past, that they prophesied until the time of the offering of the evening oblation; but there was neither voice, nor any to answer, nor any that regarded.

30And Elijah said unto all the people, Come near unto me; and all the people came near unto him. And he repaired the altar of Yahweh that was thrown down.

31And Elijah took twelve stones, according to the number of the tribes of the sons of Jacob, unto whom the word of Yahweh came, saying, Israel shall be thy name.

32And with the stones he built an altar in the name of Yahweh; and he made a trench about the altar, as great as would contain two measures of seed.

33And he put the wood in order, and cut the bullock in pieces, and laid it on the wood. And he said, Fill four jars with water, and pour it on the burnt-offering, and on the wood.

34And he said, Do it the second time; and they did it the second time. And he said, Do it the third time; and they did it the third time.

35And the water ran round about the altar; and he filled the trench also with water.

36And it came to pass at the time of the offering of the evening oblation, that Elijah the prophet came near, and said, O Yahweh, the God of Abraham, of Isaac, and of Israel, let it be known this day that thou art God in Israel, and that I am thy servant, and that I have done all these things at thy word.

37Hear me, O Yahweh, hear me, that this people may know that thou, Yahweh, art God, and that thou hast turned their heart back again.

38Then the fire of Yahweh fell, and consumed the burnt-offering, and the wood, and the stones, and the dust, and licked up the water that was in the trench.

39And when all the people saw it, they fell on their faces: and they said, Yahweh, he is God; Yahweh, he is God.

40And Elijah said unto them, Take the prophets of Baal; let not one of them escape. And they took them; and Elijah brought them down to the brook Kishon, and slew them there.

41And Elijah said unto Ahab, Get thee up, eat and drink; for there is the sound of abundance of rain.

42So Ahab went up to eat and to drink. And Elijah went up to the top of Carmel; and he bowed himself down upon the earth, and put his face between his knees.

43And he said to his servant, Go up now, look toward the sea. And he went up, and looked, and said, There is nothing. And he said, Go again seven times.

44And it came to pass at the seventh time, that he said, Behold, there ariseth a cloud out of the sea, as small as a man's hand. And he said, Go up, say unto Ahab, Make ready thy chariot, and get thee down, that the rain stop thee not.

45And it came to pass in a little while, that the heavens grew black with clouds and wind, and there was a great rain. And Ahab rode, and went to Jezreel:

46and the hand of Yahweh was on Elijah; and he girded up his loins, and ran before Ahab to the entrance of Jezreel.

Chapter 19

1And Ahab told Jezebel all that Elijah had done, and withal how he had slain all the prophets with the sword.

2Then Jezebel send a messenger unto Elijah, saying, So let the gods do to me, and more also, if I make not thy life as the life of one of them by to-morrow about this time.

3And when he saw that, he arose, and went for his life, and came to Beer-sheba, which belongeth to Judah, and left his servant there.

4But he himself went a day's journey into the wilderness, and came and sat down under a juniper-tree: and he requested for himself that he might die, and said, It is enough; now, O Yahweh, take away my life; for I am not better than my fathers.

5And he lay down and slept under a juniper-tree; and, behold, an angel touched him, and said unto him, Arise and eat.

6And he looked, and, behold, there was at his head a cake baken on the coals, and a cruse of water. And he did eat and drink, and laid him down again.

7And the angel of Yahweh came again the second time, and touched him, and said, Arise and eat, because the journey is too great for thee.

8And he arose, and did eat and drink, and went in the strength of that food forty days and forty nights unto Horeb the mount of God.

9And he came thither unto a cave, and lodged there; and, behold, the word of Yahweh came to him, and he said unto him, What doest thou here, Elijah?

10And he said, I have been very jealous for Yahweh, the God of hosts; for the children of Israel have forsaken thy covenant, thrown down thine altars, and slain thy prophets with the sword: and I, even I only, am left; and they seek my life, to take it away.

11And he said, Go forth, and stand upon the mount before Yahweh. And, behold, Yahweh passed by, and a great and strong wind rent the mountains, and brake in pieces the rocks before Yahweh; but Yahweh was not in the wind: and after the wind an earthquake; but Yahweh was not in the earthquake:

12and after the earthquake a fire; but Yahweh was not in the fire: and after the fire a still small voice.

13And it was so, when Elijah heard it, that he wrapped his face in his mantle, and went out, and stood in the entrance of the cave. And, behold, there came a voice unto him, and said, What doest thou here, Elijah?

14And he said, I have been very jealous for Yahweh, the God of hosts; for the children of Israel have forsaken thy covenant, thrown down thine altars, and slain thy prophets with the sword; and I, even I only, am left; and they seek my life, to take it away.

15And Yahweh said unto him, Go, return on thy way to the wilderness of Damascus: and when thou comest, thou shalt anoint Hazael to be king over Syria;

16and Jehu the son of Nimshi shalt thou anoint to be king over Israel; and Elisha the son of Shaphat of Abel-meholah shalt thou anoint to be prophet in thy room.

17And it shall come to pass, that him that escapeth from the sword of Hazael shall Jehu slay; and him that escapeth from the sword of Jehu shall Elisha slay.

18Yet will I leave me seven thousand in Israel, all the knees which have not bowed unto Baal, and every mouth which hath not kissed him.

19So he departed thence, and found Elisha the son of Shaphat, who was plowing, with twelve yoke of oxen before him, and he with the twelfth: and Elijah passed over unto him, and cast his mantle upon him.

20And he left the oxen, and ran after Elijah, and said, Let me, I pray thee, kiss my father and my mother, and then I will follow thee. And he said unto him, Go back again; for what have I done to thee?

21And he returned from following him, and took the yoke of oxen, and slew them, and boiled their flesh with the instruments of the oxen, and gave unto the people, and they did eat. Then he arose, and went after Elijah, and ministered unto him.

Chapter 20

1And Ben-hadad the king of Syria gathered all his host together; and there were thirty and two kings with him, and horses and chariots: and he went up and besieged Samaria, and fought against it.

2And he sent messengers to Ahab king of Israel, into the city, and said unto him, Thus saith Ben-hadad,

3Thy silver and thy gold is mine; thy wives also and thy children, even the goodliest, are mine.

4And the king of Israel answered and said, It is according to thy saying, my lord, O king; I am thine, and all that I have.

5And the messengers came again, and said, Thus speaketh Ben-hadad, saying, I sent indeed unto thee, saying, Thou shalt deliver me thy silver, and thy gold, and thy wives, and thy children;

6but I will send my servants unto thee to-morrow about this time, and they shall search thy house, and the houses of thy servants; and it shall be, that whatsoever is pleasant in thine eyes, they shall put it in their hand, and take it away.

7Then the king of Israel called all the elders of the land, and said, Mark, I pray you, and see how this man seeketh mischief: for he sent unto me for my wives, and for my children, and for my silver, and for my gold; and I denied him not.

8And all the elders and all the people said unto him, Hearken thou not, neither consent.

9Wherefore he said unto the messengers of Ben-hadad, Tell my lord the king, All that thou didst send for to thy servant at the first I will do; but this thing I may not do. And the messengers departed, and brought him word again.

10And Ben-hadad sent unto him, and said, The gods do so unto me, and more also, if the dust of Samaria shall suffice for handfuls for all the people that follow me.

11And the king of Israel answered and said, Tell him, Let not him that girdeth on his armor boast himself as he that putteth it off.

12And it came to pass, when Ben-hadad heard this message, as he was drinking, he and the kings, in the pavilions, that he said unto his servants, Set yourselves in array. And they set themselves in array against the city.

13And, behold, a prophet came near unto Ahab king of Israel, and said, Thus saith Yahweh, Hast thou seen all this great multitude? behold, I will deliver it into thy hand this day; and thou shalt know that I am Yahweh.

14And Ahab said, By whom? And he said, Thus saith Yahweh, By the young men of the princes of the provinces. Then he said, Who shall begin the battle? And he answered, Thou.

15Then he mustered the young men of the princes of the provinces, and they were two hundred and thirty-two: and after them he mustered all the people, even all the children of Israel, being seven thousand.

16And they went out at noon. But Ben-hadad was drinking himself drunk in the pavilions, he and the kings, the thirty and two kings that helped him.

17And the young men of the princes of the provinces went out first; and Ben-hadad sent out, and they told him, saying, There are men come out from Samaria.

18And he said, Whether they are come out for peace, take them alive, or whether they are come out for war, taken them alive.

19So these went out of the city, the young men of the princes of the provinces, and the army which followed them.

20And they slew every one his man; and the Syrians fled, and Israel pursued them: and Ben-hadad the king of Syria escaped on a horse with horsemen.

21And the king of Israel went out, and smote the horses and chariots, and slew the Syrians with a great slaughter.

22And the prophet came near to the king of Israel, and said unto him, Go, strengthen thyself, and mark, and see what thou doest; for at the return of the year the king of Syria will come up against thee.

23And the servants of the king of Syria said unto him, Their god is a god of the hills; therefore they were stronger than we: but let us fight against them in the plain, and surely we shall be stronger than they.

24And do this thing: take the kings away, every man out of his place, and put captains in their room;

25and number thee an army, like the army that thou hast lost, horse for horse, and chariot for chariot; and we will fight against them in the plain, and surely we shall be stronger than they. And he hearkened unto their voice, and did so.

26And it came to pass at the return of the year, that Ben-hadad mustered the Syrians, and went up to Aphek, to fight against Israel.

27And the children of Israel were mustered, and were victualled, and went against them: and the children of Israel encamped before them like two little flocks of kids; but the Syrians filled the country.

28And a man of God came near and spake unto the king of Israel, and said, Thus saith Yahweh, Because the Syrians have said, Yahweh is a god of the hills, but he is not a god of the valleys; therefore will I deliver all this great multitude into thy hand, and ye shall know that I am Yahweh.

29And they encamped one over against the other seven days. And so it was, that in the seventh day the battle was joined; and the children of Israel slew of the Syrians a hundred thousand footmen in one day.

30But the rest fled to Aphek, into the city; and the wall fell upon twenty and seven thousand men that were left. And Ben-hadad fled, and came into the city, into an inner chamber.

31And his servants said unto him, Behold now, we have heard that the kings of the house of Israel are merciful kings: let us, we pray thee, put sackcloth on our loins, and ropes upon our heads, and go out to the king of Israel: peradventure he will save thy life.

32So they girded sackcloth on their loins, and put ropes on their heads, and came to the king of Israel, and said, Thy servant Ben-hadad saith, I pray thee, let me live. And he said, Is he yet alive? he is my brother.

33Now the men observed diligently, and hasted to catch whether it were his mind; and they said, Thy brother Ben-hadad. Then he said, Go ye, bring him. Then Ben-hadad came forth to him; and he caused him to come up into the chariot.

34And Ben-hadad said unto him, The cities which my father took from thy father I will restore; and thou shalt make streets for thee in Damascus, as my father made in Samaria. And I, said Ahab, will let thee go with this covenant. So he made a covenant with him, and let him go.

35And a certain man of the sons of the prophets said unto his fellow by the word of Yahweh, Smite me, I pray thee. And the man refused to smite him.

36Then said he unto him, Because thou hast not obeyed the voice of Yahweh, behold, as soon as thou art departed from me, a lion shall slay thee. And as soon as he was departed from him, a lion found him, and slew him.

37Then he found another man, and said, Smite me, I pray thee. And the man smote him, smiting and wounding him.

38So the prophet departed, and waited for the king by the way, and disguised himself with his headband over his eyes.

39And as the king passed by, he cried unto the king; and he said, Thy servant went out into the midst of the battle; and, behold, a man turned aside, and brought a man unto me, and said, Keep this man: if by any means he be missing, then shall thy life be for his life, or else thou shalt pay a talent of silver.

40And as thy servant was busy here and there, he was gone. And the king of Israel said unto him, So shall thy judgment be; thyself hast decided it.

41And he hasted, and took the headband away from his eyes; and the king of Israel discerned him that he was of the prophets.

42And he said unto him, Thus saith Yahweh, Because thou hast let go out of thy hand the man whom I had devoted to destruction, therefore thy life shall go for his life, and thy people for his people.

43And the king of Israel went to his house heavy and displeased, and came to Samaria.

Chapter 21

1And it came to pass after these things, that Naboth the Jezreelite had a vineyard, which was in Jezreel, hard by the palace of Ahab king of Samaria.

2And Ahab spake unto Naboth, saying, Give me thy vineyard, that I may have it for a garden of herbs, because it is near unto my house; and I will give thee for it a better vineyard than it: or, if it seem good to thee, I will give thee the worth of it in money.

3And Naboth said to Ahab, Yahweh forbid it me, that I should give the inheritance of my fathers unto thee.

4And Ahab came into his house heavy and displeased because of the word which Naboth the Jezreelite had spoken to him; for he had said, I will not give thee the inheritance of my fathers. And he laid him down upon his bed, and turned away his face, and would eat no bread.

5But Jezebel his wife came to him, and said unto him, Why is thy spirit so sad, that thou eatest no bread?

6And he said unto her, Because I spake unto Naboth the Jezreelite, and said unto him, Give me thy vineyard for money; or else, if it please thee, I will give thee another vineyard for it: and he answered, I will not give thee my vineyard.

7And Jezebel his wife said unto him, Dost thou now govern the kingdom of Israel? arise, and eat bread, and let thy heart be merry: I will give thee the vineyard of Naboth the Jezreelite.

8So she wrote letters in Ahab's name, and sealed them with his seal, and sent the letters unto the elders and to the nobles that were in his city, and that dwelt with Naboth.

9And she wrote in the letters, saying, Proclaim a fast, and set Naboth on high among the people:

10and set two men, base fellows, before him, and let them bear witness against him, saying, Thou didst curse God and the king. And then carry him out, and stone him to death.

11And the men of his city, even the elders and the nobles who dwelt in his city, did as Jezebel had sent unto them, according as it was written in the letters which she had sent unto them.

12They proclaimed a fast, and set Naboth on high among the people.

13And the two men, the base fellows, came in and sat before him: and the base fellows bare witness against him, even against Naboth, in the presence of the people, saying, Naboth did curse God and the king. Then they carried him forth out of the city, and stoned him to death with stones.

14Then they sent to Jezebel, saying, Naboth is stoned, and is dead.

15And it came to pass, when Jezebel heard that Naboth was stoned, and was dead, that Jezebel said to Ahab, Arise, take possession of the vineyard of Naboth the Jezreelite, which he refused to give thee for money; for Naboth is not alive, but dead.

16And it came to pass, when Ahab heard that Naboth was dead, that Ahab rose up to go down to the vineyard of Naboth the Jezreelite, to take possession of it.

17And the word of Yahweh came to Elijah the Tishbite, saying,

18Arise, go down to meet Ahab king of Israel, who dwelleth in Samaria: behold, he is in the vineyard of Naboth, whither he is gone down to take possession of it.

19And thou shalt speak unto him, saying, Thus saith Yahweh, Hast thou killed and also taken possession? And thou shalt speak unto him, saying, Thus saith Yahweh, In the place where dogs licked the blood of Naboth shall dogs lick thy blood, even thine.

20And Ahab said to Elijah, Hast thou found me, O mine enemy? And he answered, I have found thee, because thou hast sold thyself to do that which is evil in the sight of Yahweh.

21Behold, I will bring evil upon thee, and will utterly sweep thee away and will cut off from Ahab every man-child, and him that is shut up and him that is left at large in Israel:

22and I will make thy house like the house of Jeroboam the son of Nebat, and like the house of Baasha the son of Ahijah for the provocation wherewith thou hast provoked me to anger, and hast made Israel to sin.

23And of Jezebel also spake Yahweh, saying, The dogs shall eat Jezebel by the rampart of Jezreel.

24Him that dieth of Ahab in the city the dogs shall eat; and him that dieth in the field shall the birds of the heavens eat.

25(But there was none like unto Ahab, who did sell himself to do that which

First Kings

was evil in the sight of Yahweh, whom Jezebel his wife stirred up.

26And he did very abominably in following idols, according to all that the Amorites did, whom Yahweh cast out before the children of Israel.)

27And it came to pass, when Ahab heard those words, that he rent his clothes, and put sackcloth upon his flesh, and fasted, and lay in sackcloth, and went softly.

28And the word of Yahweh came to Elijah the Tishbite, saying,

29Seest thou how Ahab humbleth himself before me? because he humbleth himself before me, I will not bring the evil in his days; but in his son's days will I bring the evil upon his house.

Chapter 22

1And they continued three years without war between Syria and Israel.

2And it came to pass in the third year, that Jehoshaphat the king of Judah came down to the king of Israel.

3And the king of Israel said unto his servants, Know ye that Ramoth-gilead is ours, and we are still, and take it not out of the hand of the king of Syria?

4And he said unto Jehoshaphat, Wilt thou go with me to battle to Ramoth-gilead? And Jehoshaphat said to the king of Israel, I am as thou art, my people as thy people, my horses as thy horses.

5And Jehoshaphat said unto the king of Israel, Inquire first, I pray thee, for the word of Yahweh.

6Then the king of Israel gathered the prophets together, about four hundred men, and said unto them, Shall I go against Ramoth-gilead to battle, or shall I forbear? And they said, Go up; for the Lord will deliver it into the hand of the king.

7But Jehoshaphat said, Is there not here a prophet of Yahweh besides, that we may inquire of him?

8And the king of Israel said unto Jehoshaphat, there is yet one man by whom we may inquire of Yahweh, Micaiah the son of Imlah: but I hate him; for he doth not prophesy good concerning me, but evil. And Jehoshaphat said, Let not the king say so.

9Then the king of Israel called an officer, and said, Fetch quickly Micaiah the son of Imlah.

10Now the king of Israel and Jehoshaphat the king of Judah were sitting each on his throne, arrayed in their robes, in an open place at the entrance of the gate of Samaria; and all the prophets were prophesying before them.

11And Zedekiah the son of Chenaanah made him horns of iron, and said, Thus saith Yahweh, With these shalt thou push the Syrians, until they be consumed.

12And all the prophets prophesied so, saying, Go up to Ramoth-gilead, and prosper; for Yahweh will deliver it into the hand of the king.

13And the messenger that went to call Micaiah spake unto him, saying, Behold now, the words of the prophets declare good unto the king with one mouth: let thy word, I pray thee, be like the word of one of them, and speak thou good.

14And Micaiah said, As Yahweh liveth, what Yahweh saith unto me, that will I speak.

15And when he was come to the king, the king said unto him, Micaiah, shall we go to Ramoth-gilead to battle, or shall we forbear? And he answered him, Go up and prosper; and Yahweh will deliver it into the hand of the king.

16And the king said unto him, How many times shall I adjure thee that thou speak unto me nothing but the truth in the name of Yahweh?

17And he said, I saw all Israel scattered upon the mountains, as sheep that have no shepherd: and Yahweh said, These have no master; let them return every man to his house in peace.

18And the king of Israel said to Jehoshaphat, Did I not tell thee that he would not prophesy good concerning me, but evil?

19And Micaiah said, Therefore hear thou the word of Yahweh: I saw Yahweh sitting on his throne, and all the host of heaven standing by him on his right hand and on his left.

20And Yahweh said, Who shall entice Ahab, that he may go up and fall at Ramoth-gilead? And one said on this manner; and another said on that manner.

21And there came forth a spirit, and stood before Yahweh, and said, I will entice him.

22And Yahweh said unto him, Wherewith? And he said, I will go forth, and will be a lying spirit in the mouth of all his prophets. And he said, Thou shalt entice him, and shalt prevail also: go forth, and do so.

23Now therefore, behold, Yahweh hath put a lying spirit in the mouth of all these thy prophets; and Yahweh hath spoken evil concerning thee.

24Then Zedekiah the son of Chenaanah came near, and smote Micaiah on the cheek, and said, Which way went the Spirit of Yahweh from me to speak unto thee?

25And Micaiah said, Behold, thou shalt see on that day, when thou shalt go into an inner chamber to hide thyself.

26And the king of Israel said, Take Micaiah, and carry him back unto Amon the governor of the city, and to Joash the king's son;

27and say, Thus saith the king, Put this fellow in the prison, and feed him with bread of affliction and with water of affliction, until I come in peace.

28And Micaiah said, If thou return at all in peace, Yahweh hath not spoken by me. And he said, Hear, ye peoples, all of you.

29So the king of Israel and Jehoshaphat the king of Judah went up to Ramoth-gilead.

30And the king of Israel said unto Jehoshaphat, I will disguise myself, and go into the battle; but put thou on thy robes. And the king of Israel disguised himself, and went into the battle.

31Now the king of Syria had commanded the thirty and two captains of his chariots, saying, Fight neither with small nor great, save only with the king of Israel.

32And it came to pass, when the captains of the chariots saw Jehoshaphat, that they said, Surely it is the king of Israel; and they turned aside to fight against him: and Jehoshaphat cried out.

33And it came to pass, when the captains of the chariots saw that it was not the king of Israel, that they turned back from pursuing him.

34And a certain man drew his bow at a venture, and smote the king of Israel between the joints of the armor: wherefore he said unto the driver of his chariot, Turn thy hand, and carry me out of the host; for I am sore wounded.

35And the battle increased that day: and the king was stayed up in his chariot against the Syrians, and died at even; and the blood ran out of the wound into the bottom of the chariot.

36And there went a cry throughout the host about the going down of the sun, saying, Every man to his city, and every man to his country.

37So the king died, and was brought to Samaria; and they buried the king in Samaria.

38And they washed the chariot by the pool of Samaria; and the dogs licked up his blood (now the harlots washed themselves there); according unto the word of Yahweh which he spake.

39Now the rest of the acts of Ahab, and all that he did, and the ivory house which he built, and all the cities that he built, are they not written in the book of the chronicles of the kings of Israel?

40So Ahab slept with his fathers; and Ahaziah his son reigned in his stead.

41And Jehoshaphat the son of Asa began to reign over Judah in the fourth year of Ahab king of Israel.

42Jehoshaphat was thirty and five years old when he began to reign; and he reigned twenty and five years in Jerusalem. And his mother's name was Azubah the daughter of Shilhi.

43And he walked in all the way of Asa his father; He turned not aside from it, doing that which was right in the eyes of Yahweh: howbeit the high places were not taken away; the people still sacrificed and burnt incense in the high places.

44And Jehoshaphat made peace with the king of Israel.

45Now the rest of the acts of Jehoshaphat, and his might that he showed, and how he warred, are they not written in the book of the chronicles of the kings of Judah?

46And the remnant of the sodomites, that remained in the days of his father Asa, he put away out of the land.

47And there was no king in Edom: a deputy was king.

48Jehoshaphat made ships of Tarshish to go to Ophir for gold: but they went not; for the ships were broken at Ezion-geber.

49Then said Ahaziah the son of Ahab unto Jehoshaphat, Let my servants go with thy servants in the ships. But Jehoshaphat would not.

50And Jehoshaphat slept with his fathers, and was buried with his fathers in the city of David his father; And Jehoram his son reigned in his stead.

51Ahaziah the son of Ahab began to reign over Israel in Samaria in the seventeenth year of Jehoshaphat king of Judah, and he reigned two years over Israel.

52And he did that which was evil in the sight of Yahweh, and walked in the way of his father, and in the way of his mother, and in the way of Jeroboam the son of Nebat, wherein he made Israel to sin.

53And he served Baal, and worshipped him, and provoked to anger Yahweh, the God of Israel, according to all that his father had done.

The Second Book of the Kings

Chapter 1

¹And Moab rebelled against Israel after the death of Ahab.

²And Ahaziah fell down through the lattice in his upper chamber that was in Samaria, and was sick: and he sent messengers, and said unto them, Go, inquire of Baal-zebub, the god of Ekron, whether I shall recover of this sickness.

³But the angel of Yahweh said to Elijah the Tishbite, Arise, go up to meet the messengers of the king of Samaria, and say unto them, Is it because there is no God in Israel, that ye go to inquire of Baal-zebub, the god of Ekron?

⁴Now therefore thus saith Yahweh, Thou shalt not come down from the bed whither thou art gone up, but shalt surely die. And Elijah departed.

⁵And the messengers returned unto him, and he said unto them, Why is it that ye are returned?

⁶And they said unto him, There came up a man to meet us, and said unto us, Go, turn again unto the king that sent you, and say unto him, Thus saith Yahweh, Is it because there is no God in Israel, that thou sendest to inquire of Baal-zebub, the god of Ekron? therefore thou shalt not come down from the bed whither thou art gone up, but shalt surely die.

⁷And he said unto them, What manner of man was he that came up to meet you, and told you these words?

⁸And they answered him, He was a hairy man, and girt with a girdle of leather about his loins. And he said, It is Elijah the Tishbite.

⁹Then the king sent unto him a captain of fifty with his fifty. And he went up to him: and, behold, he was sitting on the top of the hill. And he spake unto him, O man of God, the king hath said, Come down.

¹⁰And Elijah answered and said to the captain of fifty, If I be a man of God, let fire come down from heaven, and consume thee and thy fifty. And there came down fire from heaven, and consumed him and his fifty.

¹¹And again he sent unto him another captain of fifty and his fifty. And he answered and said unto him, O man of God, thus hath the king said, Come down quickly.

¹²And Elijah answered and said unto them, If I be a man of God, let fire come down from heaven, and consume thee and thy fifty. And the fire of God came down from heaven, and consumed him and his fifty.

¹³And again he sent the captain of a third fifty with his fifty. And the third captain of fifty went up, and came and fell on his knees before Elijah, and besought him, and said unto him, O man of God, I pray thee, let my life, and the life of these fifty thy servants, be precious in thy sight.

¹⁴Behold, there came fire down from heaven, and consumed the two former captains of fifty with their fifties; but now let my life be precious in thy sight.

¹⁵And the angel of Yahweh said unto Elijah, Go down with him: be not afraid of him. And he arose, and went down with him unto the king.

¹⁶And he said unto him, Thus saith Yahweh, Forasmuch as thou hast sent messengers to inquire of Baal-zebub, the god of Ekron, is it because there is no God in Israel to inquire of his word? therefore thou shalt not come down from the bed whither thou art gone up, but shalt surely die.

¹⁷So he died according to the word of Yahweh which Elijah had spoken. And Jehoram began to reign in his stead in the second year of Jehoram the son of Jehoshaphat king of Judah; because he had no son.

¹⁸Now the rest of the acts of Ahaziah which he did, are they not written in the book of the chronicles of the kings of Israel?

Chapter 2

¹And it came to pass, when Yahweh would take up Elijah by a whirlwind into heaven, that Elijah went with Elisha from Gilgal.

²And Elijah said unto Elisha, Tarry here, I pray thee; for Yahweh hath sent me as far as Beth-el. And Elisha said, As Yahweh liveth, and as thy soul liveth, I will not leave thee. So they went down to Beth-el.

³And the sons of the prophets that were at Beth-el came forth to Elisha, and said unto him, Knowest thou that Yahweh will take away thy master from thy head to-day? And he said, Yea, I know it; hold ye your peace.

⁴And Elijah said unto him, Elisha, tarry here, I pray thee; for Yahweh hath sent me to Jericho. And he said, As Yahweh liveth, and as thy soul liveth, I will not leave thee. So they came to Jericho.

⁵And the sons of the prophets that were at Jericho came near to Elisha, and said unto him, Knowest thou that Yahweh will take away thy master from thy head to-day? And he answered, Yea, I know it; hold ye your peace.

⁶And Elijah said unto him, Tarry here, I pray thee; for Yahweh hath sent me to the Jordan. And he said, As Yahweh liveth, and as thy soul liveth, I will not leave thee. And they two went on.

⁷And fifty men of the sons of the prophets went, and stood over against them afar off: and they two stood by the Jordan.

⁸And Elijah took his mantle, and wrapped it together, and smote the waters, and they were divided hither and thither, so that they two went over on dry ground.

⁹And it came to pass, when they were gone over, that Elijah said unto Elisha, Ask what I shall do for thee, before I am taken from thee. And Elisha said, I pray thee, let a double portion of thy spirit be upon me.

¹⁰And he said, Thou hast asked a hard thing: nevertheless, if thou see me when I am taken from thee, it shall be so unto thee; but if not, it shall not be so.

¹¹And it came to pass, as they still went on, and talked, that, behold, there appeared a chariot of fire, and horses of fire, which parted them both asunder; and Elijah went up by a whirlwind into heaven.

¹²And Elisha saw it, and he cried, My father, my father, the chariots of Israel and the horsemen thereof! And he saw him no more: and he took hold of his own clothes, and rent them in two pieces.

¹³He took up also the mantle of Elijah that fell from him, and went back, and stood by the bank of the Jordan.

¹⁴And he took up the mantle of Elijah that fell from him, and smote the waters, and said, Where is Yahweh, the God of Elijah? and when he also had smitten the waters, they were divided hither and thither; and Elisha went over.

¹⁵And when the sons of the prophets that were at Jericho over against him saw him, they said, The spirit of Elijah doth rest on Elisha. And they came to meet him, and bowed themselves to the ground before him.

¹⁶And they said unto him, Behold now, there are with thy servants fifty strong men; let them go, we pray thee, and seek thy master, lest the Spirit of Yahweh hath taken him up, and cast him upon some mountain, or into some valley. And he said, Ye shall not send.

¹⁷And when they urged him till he was ashamed, he said, Send. They sent therefore fifty men; and they sought three days, but found him not.

¹⁸And they came back to him, while he tarried at Jericho; and he said unto them, Did I not say unto you, Go not?

¹⁹And the men of the city said unto Elisha, Behold, we pray thee, the situation of this city is pleasant, as my lord seeth: but the water is bad, and the land miscarrieth.

²⁰And he said, Bring me a new cruse, and put salt therein. And they brought it to him.

²¹And he went forth unto the spring of the waters, and cast salt therein, and said, Thus saith Yahweh, I have healed these waters; there shall not be from thence any more death or miscarrying.

²²So the waters were healed unto this day, according to the word of Elisha which he spake.

²³And he went up from thence unto Beth-el; and as he was going up by the way, there came forth young lads out of the city, and mocked him, and said unto him, Go up, thou baldhead; go up, thou baldhead.

²⁴And he looked behind him and saw them, and cursed them in the name of Yahweh. And there came forth two she-bears out of the wood, and tare forty and two lads of them.

²⁵And he went from thence to mount Carmel, and from thence he returned to Samaria.

Chapter 3

¹Now Jehoram the son of Ahab began to reign over Israel in Samaria in the eighteenth year of Jehoshaphat king of Judah, and reigned twelve years.

²And he did that which was evil in the sight of Yahweh, but not like his father, and like his mother; for he put away the pillar of Baal that his father had made.

³Nevertheless he cleaved unto the sins of Jeroboam the son of Nebat, wherewith he made Israel to sin; he departed not therefrom.

⁴Now Mesha king of Moab was a sheep-master; and he rendered unto the king of Israel the wool of a hundred thousand lambs, and of a hundred thousand rams.

⁵But it came to pass, when Ahab was dead, that the king of Moab rebelled against the king of Israel.

⁶And king Jehoram went out of Samaria at that time, and mustered all Israel.

⁷And he went and sent to Jehoshaphat the king of Judah, saying, The king of Moab hath rebelled against me: wilt thou go with me against Moab to battle? And he said, I will go up: I am as thou art, my people as thy people, my horses as thy horses.

⁸And he said, Which way shall we go up? And he answered, The way of the wilderness of Edom.

⁹So the king of Israel went, and the king of Judah, and the king of Edom; and they made a circuit of seven days' journey: and there was no water for the host, nor for the beasts that followed them.

¹⁰And the king of Israel said, Alas! for Yahweh hath called these three kings together to deliver them into the hand of Moab.

¹¹But Jehoshaphat said, Is there not here a prophet of Yahweh, that we may inquire of Yahweh by him? And one of the king of Israel's servants answered and said, Elisha the son of Shaphat is here, who poured water on the hands of Elijah.

¹²And Jehoshaphat said, The word of Yahweh is with him. So the king of Israel and Jehoshaphat and the king of Edom went down to him.

¹³And Elisha said unto the king of Israel, What have I to do with thee? get thee to the prophets of thy father, and to the prophets of thy mother. And the king of Israel said unto him, Nay; for Yahweh hath called these three kings together to deliver them into the hand of Moab.

¹⁴And Elisha said, As Yahweh of hosts liveth, before whom I stand, surely, were it not that I regard the presence of Jehoshaphat the king of Judah, I would not look toward thee, nor see thee.

¹⁵But now bring me a minstrel. And it came to pass, when the minstrel played, that the hand of Yahweh came upon him.

¹⁶And he said, Thus saith Yahweh, Make this valley full of trenches.

¹⁷For thus saith Yahweh, Ye shall not see wind, neither shall ye see rain; yet that valley shall be filled with water, and ye shall drink, both ye and your cattle and your beasts.

¹⁸And this is but a light thing in the sight of Yahweh: he will also deliver the Moabites into your hand.

¹⁹And ye shall smite every fortified city, and every choice city, and shall fell every good tree, and stop all fountains of water, and mar every good piece of land with stones.

Second Kings

20And it came to pass in the morning, about the time of offering the oblation, that, behold, there came water by the way of Edom, and the country was filled with water.

21Now when all the Moabites heard that the kings were come up to fight against them, they gathered themselves together, all that were able to put on armor, and upward, and stood on the border.

22And they rose up early in the morning, and the sun shone upon the water, and the Moabites saw the water over against them as red as blood:

23and they said, This is blood; the kings are surely destroyed, and they have smitten each man his fellow: now therefore, Moab, to the spoil.

24And when they came to the camp of Israel, the Israelites rose up and smote the Moabites, so that they fled before them; and they went forward into the land smiting the Moabites.

25And they beat down the cities; and on every good piece of land they cast every man his stone, and filled it; and they stopped all the fountains of water, and felled all the good trees, until in Kir-haresheth only they left the stones thereof; howbeit the slingers went about it, and smote it.

26And when the king of Moab saw that the battle was too sore for him, he took with him seven hundred men that drew sword, to break through unto the king of Edom; but they could not.

27Then he took his eldest son that should have reigned in his stead, and offered him for a burnt-offering upon the wall. And there was great wrath against Israel: and they departed from him, and returned to their own land.

Chapter 4

1Now there cried a certain woman of the wives of the sons of the prophets unto Elisha, saying, Thy servant my husband is dead; and thou knowest that thy servant did fear Yahweh: and the creditor is come to take unto him my two children to be bondmen.

2And Elisha said unto her, What shall I do for thee? tell me; what hast thou in the house? And she said, Thy handmaid hath not anything in the house, save a pot of oil.

3Then he said, Go, borrow thee vessels abroad of all thy neighbors, even empty vessels; borrow not a few.

4And thou shalt go in, and shut the door upon thee and upon thy sons, and pour out into all those vessels; and thou shalt set aside that which is full.

5So she went from him, and shut the door upon her and upon her sons; they brought the vessels to her, and she poured out.

6And it came to pass, when the vessels were full, that she said unto her son, Bring me yet a vessel. And he said unto her, There is not a vessel more. And the oil stayed.

7Then she came and told the man of God. And he said, Go, sell the oil, and pay thy debt, and live thou and thy sons of the rest.

8And it fell on a day, that Elisha passed to Shunem, where was a great woman; and she constrained him to eat bread. And so it was, that as oft as he passed by, he turned in thither to eat bread.

9And she said unto her husband, Behold now, I perceive that this is a holy man of God, that passeth by us continually.

10Let us make, I pray thee, a little chamber on the wall; and let us set for him there a bed, and a table, and a seat, and a candlestick: and it shall be, when he cometh to us, that he shall turn in thither.

11And it fell on a day, that he came thither, and he turned into the chamber and lay there.

12And he said to Gehazi his servant, Call this Shunammite. And when he had called her, she stood before him.

13And he said unto him, Say now unto her, Behold, thou hast been careful for us with all this care; what is to be done for thee? wouldest thou be spoken for to the king, or to the captain of the host? And she answered, I dwell among mine own people.

14And he said, What then is to be done for her? And Gehazi answered, Verily she hath no son, and her husband is old.

15And he said, Call her. And when he had called her, she stood in the door.

16And he said, At this season, when the time cometh round, thou shalt embrace a son. And she said, Nay, my lord, thou man of God, do not lie unto thy handmaid.

17And the woman conceived, and bare a son at that season, when the time came round, as Elisha had said unto her.

18And when the child was grown, it fell on a day, that he went out to his father to the reapers.

19And he said unto his father, My head, my head. And he said to his servant, Carry him to his mother.

20And when he had taken him, and brought him to his mother, he sat on her knees till noon, and then died.

21And she went up and laid him on the bed of the man of God, and shut the door upon him, and went out.

22And she called unto her husband, and said, Send me, I pray thee, one of the servants, and one of the asses, that I may run to the man of God, and come again.

23And he said, Wherefore wilt thou go to him to-day? it is neither new moon nor sabbath. And she said, It shall be well.

24Then she saddled an ass, and said to her servant, Drive, and go forward; slacken me not the riding, except I bid thee.

25So she went, and came unto the man of God to mount Carmel. And it came to pass, when the man of God saw her afar off, that he said to Gehazi his servant, Behold, yonder is the Shunammite:

26run, I pray thee, now to meet her, and say unto her, Is it well with thee? is it well with thy husband? is it well with the child? And she answered, It is well.

27And when she came to the man of God to the hill, she caught hold of his feet. And Gehazi came near to thrust her away; but the man of God said, Let her alone: for her soul is vexed within her; and Yahweh hath hid it from me, and hath not told me.

28Then she said, Did I desire a son of my lord? did I not say, Do not deceive me?

29Then he said to Gehazi, Gird up thy loins, and take my staff in thy hand, and go thy way: if thou meet any man, salute him not; and if any salute thee, answer him not again: and lay my staff upon the face of the child.

30And the mother of the child said, As Yahweh liveth, and as thy soul liveth, I will not leave thee. And he arose, and followed her.

31And Gehazi passed on before them, and laid the staff upon the face of the child; but there was neither voice, nor hearing. Wherefore he returned to meet him, and told him, saying, The child is not awaked.

32And when Elisha was come into the house, behold, the child was dead, and laid upon his bed.

33He went in therefore, and shut the door upon them twain, and prayed unto Yahweh.

34And he went up, and lay upon the child, and put his mouth upon his mouth, and his eyes upon his eyes, and his hands upon his hands: and he stretched himself upon him; and the flesh of the child waxed warm.

35Then he returned, and walked in the house once to and fro; and went up, and stretched himself upon him: and the child sneezed seven times, and the child opened his eyes.

36And he called Gehazi, and said, Call this Shunammite. So he called her. And when she was come in unto him, he said, Take up thy son.

37Then she went in, and fell at his feet, and bowed herself to the ground; and she took up her son, and went out.

38And Elisha came again to Gilgal. And there was a dearth in the land; and the sons of the prophets were sitting before him; and he said unto his servant, Set on the great pot, and boil pottage for the sons of the prophets.

39And one went out into the field to gather herbs, and found a wild vine, and gathered thereof wild gourds his lap full, and came and shred them into the pot of pottage; for they knew them not.

40So they poured out for the men to eat. And it came to pass, as they were eating of the pottage, that they cried out, and said, O man of God, there is death in the pot. And they could not eat thereof.

41But he said, Then bring meal. And he cast it into the pot; and he said, Pour out for the people, that they may eat. And there was no harm in the pot.

42And there came a man from Baal-shalishah, and brought the man of God bread of the first-fruits, twenty loaves of barley, and fresh ears of grain in his sack. And he said, Give unto the people, that they may eat.

43And his servant said, What, should I set this before a hundred men? But he said, Give the people, that they may eat; for thus saith Yahweh, They shall eat, and shall leave thereof.

44So he set it before them, and they did eat, and left thereof, according to the word of Yahweh.

Chapter 5

1Now Naaman, captain of the host of the king of Syria, was a great man with his master, and honorable, because by him Yahweh had given victory unto Syria: he was also a mighty man of valor, but he was a leper.

2And the Syrians had gone out in bands, and had brought away captive out of the land of Israel a little maiden; and she waited on Naaman's wife.

3And she said unto her mistress, Would that my lord were with the prophet that is in Samaria! then would he recover him of his leprosy.

4And one went in, and told his lord, saying, Thus and thus said the maiden that is of the land of Israel.

5And the king of Syria said, Go now, and I will send a letter unto the king of Israel. And he departed, and took with him ten talents of silver, and six thousand pieces of gold, and ten changes of raiment.

6And he brought the letter to the king of Israel, saying, And now when this letter is come unto thee, behold, I have sent Naaman my servant to thee, that thou mayest recover him of his leprosy.

7And it came to pass, when the king of Israel had read the letter, that he rent his clothes, and said, Am I God, to kill and to make alive, that this man doth send unto me to recover a man of his leprosy? but consider, I pray you, and see how he seeketh a quarrel against me.

8And it was so, when Elisha the man of God heard that the king of Israel had rent his clothes, that he sent to the king, saying, Wherefore hast thou rent thy clothes? let him come now to me, and he shall know that there is a prophet in Israel.

9So Naaman came with his horses and with his chariots, and stood at the door of the house of Elisha.

10And Elisha sent a messenger unto him, saying, Go and wash in the Jordan seven times, and thy flesh shall come again to thee, and thou shalt be clean.

11But Naaman was wroth, and went away, and said, Behold, I thought, He will surely come out to me, and stand, and call on the name of Yahweh his God, and wave his hand over the place, and recover the leper.

12Are not Abanah and Pharpar, the rivers of Damascus, better than all the waters of Israel? may I not wash in them, and be clean? So he turned and went away in a rage.

13And his servants came near, and spake unto him, and said, My father, if the prophet had bid thee do some great thing, wouldest thou not have done it? how much rather then, when he saith to thee, Wash, and be clean?

14Then went he down, and dipped himself seven times in the Jordan, according to the saying of the man of God; and his flesh came again like unto the flesh of a little child, and he was clean.

15And he returned to the man of God, he and all his company, and came, and stood before him; and he said, Behold now, I know that there is no God in all the earth, but in Israel: now therefore, I pray thee, take a present of thy servant.

16But he said, As Yahweh liveth, before whom I stand, I will receive none. And he urged him to take it; but he refused.

17And Naaman said, If not, yet, I pray thee, let there be given to thy servant two mules' burden of earth; for thy servant will henceforth offer neither burnt-offering nor sacrifice unto other gods, but unto Yahweh.

18In this thing Yahweh pardon thy servant: when my master goeth into the house of Rimmon to worship there, and he leaneth on my hand, and I bow myself in the house of Rimmon, when I bow myself in the house of Rimmon, Yahweh pardon thy servant in this thing.

19And he said unto him, Go in peace. So he departed from him a little way.

20But Gehazi the servant of Elisha the man of God, said, Behold, my master hath spared this Naaman the Syrian, in not receiving at his hands that which he brought: as Yahweh liveth, I will run after him, and take somewhat of him.

21So Gehazi followed after Naaman. And when Naaman saw one running after him, he alighted from the chariot to meet him, and said, Is all well?

22And he said, All is well. My master hath sent me, saying, Behold, even now there are come to me from the hill-country of Ephraim two young men of the sons of the prophets; give them, I pray thee, a talent of silver, and two changes of raiment.

23And Naaman said, Be pleased to take two talents. And he urged him, and bound two talents of silver in two bags, with two changes of raiment, and laid them upon two of his servants; and they bare them before him.

24And when he came to the hill, he took them from their hand, and bestowed them in the house; and he let the men go, and they departed.

25But he went in, and stood before his master. And Elisha said unto him, Whence comest thou, Gehazi? And he said, Thy servant went no whither.

26And he said unto him, Went not my heart with thee, when the man turned from his chariot to meet thee? Is it a time to receive money, and to receive garments, and oliveyards and vineyards, and sheep and oxen, and men-servants and maid-servants?

27The leprosy therefore of Naaman shall cleave unto thee, and unto thy seed for ever. And he went out from his presence a leper as white as snow.

Chapter 6

1And the sons of the prophets said unto Elisha, Behold now, the place where we dwell before thee is too strait for us.

2Let us go, we pray thee, unto the Jordan, and take thence every man a beam, and let us make us a place there, where we may dwell. And he answered, Go ye.

3And one said, Be pleased, I pray thee, to go with thy servants. And he answered, I will go.

4So he went with them. And when they came to the Jordan, they cut down wood.

5But as one was felling a beam, the axe-head fell into the water; and he cried, and said, Alas, my master! for it was borrowed.

6And the man of God said, Where fell it? And he showed him the place. And he cut down a stick, and cast it in thither, and made the iron to swim.

7And he said, Take it up to thee. So he put out his hand, and took it.

8Now the king of Syria was warring against Israel; and he took counsel with his servants, saying, In such and such a place shall be my camp.

9And the man of God sent unto the king of Israel, saying, Beware that thou pass not such a place; for thither the Syrians are coming down.

10And the king of Israel sent to the place which the man of God told him and warned him of; and he saved himself there, not once nor twice.

11And the heart of the king of Syria was sore troubled for this thing; and he called his servants, and said unto them, Will ye not show me which of us is for the king of Israel?

12And one of his servants said, Nay, my lord, O king; but Elisha, the prophet that is in Israel, telleth the king of Israel the words that thou speakest in thy bedchamber.

13And he said, Go and see where he is, that I may send and fetch him. And it was told him, saying, Behold, he is in Dothan.

14Therefore sent he thither horses, and chariots, and a great host: and they came by night, and compassed the city about.

15And when the servant of the man of God was risen early, and gone forth, behold, a host with horses and chariots was round about the city. And his servant said unto him, Alas, my master! how shall we do?

16And he answered, Fear not; for they that are with us are more than they that are with them.

17And Elisha prayed, and said, Yahweh, I pray thee, open his eyes, that he may see. And Yahweh opened the eyes of the young man; and he saw: and, behold, the mountain was full of horses and chariots of fire round about Elisha.

18And when they came down to him, Elisha prayed unto Yahweh, and said, Smite this people, I pray thee, with blindness. And he smote them with blindness according to the word of Elisha.

19And Elisha said unto them, This is not the way, neither is this the city: follow me, and I will bring you to the man whom ye seek. And he led them to Samaria.

20And it came to pass, when they were come into Samaria, that Elisha said, Yahweh, open the eyes of these men, that they may see. And Yahweh opened their eyes, and they saw; and, behold, they were in the midst of Samaria.

21And the king of Israel said unto Elisha, when he saw them, My father, shall I smite them? shall I smite them?

22And he answered, Thou shalt not smite them: wouldest thou smite those whom thou hast taken captive with thy sword and with thy bow? set bread and water before them, that they may eat and drink, and go to their master.

23And he prepared great provision for them; and when they had eaten and drunk, he sent them away, and they went to their master. And the bands of Syria came no more into the land of Israel.

24And it came to pass after this, that Benhadad king of Syria gathered all his host, and went up, and besieged Samaria.

25And there was a great famine in Samaria: and, behold, they besieged it, until an ass's head was sold for fourscore pieces of silver, and the fourth part of a kab of dove's dung for five pieces of silver.

26And as the king of Israel was passing by upon the wall, there cried a woman unto him, saying, Help, my lord, O king.

27And he said, If Yahweh do not help thee, whence shall I help thee? out of the threshing-floor, or out of the winepress?

28And the king said unto her, What aileth thee? And she answered, This woman said unto me, Give thy son, that we may eat him to-day, and we will eat my son to-morrow.

29So we boiled my son, and did eat him: and I said unto her on the next day, Give thy son, that we may eat him; and she hath hid her son.

30And it came to pass, when the king heard the words of the woman, that he rent his clothes (now he was passing by upon the wall); and the people looked, and, behold, he had sackcloth within upon his flesh.

31Then he said, God do so to me, and more also, if the head of Elisha the son of Shaphat shall stand on him this day.

32But Elisha was sitting in his house, and the elders were sitting with him; and the king sent a man from before him: but ere the messenger came to him, he said to the elders, See ye how this son of a murderer hath sent to take away my head? look, when the messenger cometh, shut the door, and hold the door fast against him: is not the sound of his master's feet behind him?

33And while he was yet talking with them, behold, the messenger came down unto him: and he said, Behold, this evil is of Yahweh; why should I wait for Yahweh any longer?

Chapter 7

1And Elisha said, Hear ye the word of Yahweh: thus saith Yahweh, To-morrow about this time shall a measure of fine flour be sold for a shekel, and two measures of barley for a shekel, in the gate of Samaria.

2Then the captain on whose hand the king leaned answered the man of God, and said, Behold, if Yahweh should make windows in heaven, might this thing be? And he said, Behold, thou shalt see it with thine eyes, but shalt not eat thereof.

3Now there were four leprous men at the entrance of the gate: and they said one to another, Why sit we here until we die?

4If we say, We will enter into the city, then the famine is in the city, and we shall die there; and if we sit still here, we die also. Now therefore come, and let us fall unto the host of the Syrians: if they save us alive, we shall live; and if they kill us, we shall but die.

5And they rose up in the twilight, to go unto the camp of the Syrians; and when they were come to the outermost part of the camp of the Syrians, behold, there was no man there.

6For the Lord had made the host of the Syrians to hear a noise of chariots, and a noise of horses, even the noise of a great host: and they said one to another, Lo, the king of Israel hath hired against us the kings of the Hittites, and the kings of the Egyptians, to come upon us.

7Wherefore they arose and fled in the twilight, and left their tents, and their horses, and their asses, even the camp as it was, and fled for their life.

8And when these lepers came to the outermost part of the camp, they went into one tent, and did eat and drink, and carried thence silver, and gold, and raiment, and went and hid it; and they came back, and entered into another tent, and carried thence also, and went and hid it.

9Then they said one to another, We do not well; this day is a day of good tidings, and we hold our peace: if we tarry till the morning light, punishment will overtake us; now therefore come, let us go and tell the king's household.

10So they came and called unto the porter of the city; and they told them, saying, We came to the camp of the Syrians, and, behold, there was no man there, neither voice of man, but the horses tied, and the asses tied, and the tents as they were.

11And he called the porters; and they told it to the king's household within.

12And the king arose in the night, and said unto his servants, I will now show you what the Syrians have done to us. They know that we are hungry; therefore are they gone out of the camp to hide themselves in the field, saying, When they come out of the city, we shall take them alive, and get into the city.

13And one of his servants answered and said, Let some take, I pray thee, five of the horses that remain, which are left in the city (behold, they are as all the multitude of Israel that are left in it; behold, they are as all the multitude of Israel that are consumed); and let us send and see.

14They took therefore two chariots with horses; and the king sent after the host of the Syrians, saying, Go and see.

15And they went after them unto the Jordan: and, lo, all the way was full of garments and vessels, which the Syrians had cast away in their haste. And the messengers returned, and told the king.

16And the people went out, and plundered the camp of the Syrians. So a measure of fine flour was sold for a shekel, and two measures of barley for a shekel, according to the word of Yahweh.

17And the king appointed the captain on whose hand he leaned to have the charge of the gate: and the people trod upon him in the gate, and he died as the man of God had said, who spake when the king came down to him.

18And it came to pass, as the man of God had spoken to the king, saying, Two measures of barley for a shekel, and a measure of fine flour for a shekel, shall be to-morrow about this time in the gate of Samaria;

19and that captain answered the man of God, and said, Now, behold, if Yahweh should make windows in heaven, might such a thing be? and he said, Behold, thou shalt see it with thine eyes, but shalt not eat thereof:

20it came to pass even so unto him; for the people trod upon him in the gate, and he died.

Second Kings
Chapter 8

¹Now Elisha had spoken unto the woman, whose son he had restored to life, saying, Arise, and go thou and thy household, and sojourn wheresoever thou canst sojourn: for Yahweh hath called for a famine; and it shall also come upon the land seven years.

²And the woman arose, and did according to the word of the man of God; and she went with her household, and sojourned in the land of the Philistines seven years.

³And it came to pass at the seven years' end, that the woman returned out of the land of the Philistines: and she went forth to cry unto the king for her house and for her land.

⁴Now the king was talking with Gehazi the servant of the man of God, saying, Tell me, I pray thee, all the great things that Elisha hath done.

⁵And it came to pass, as he was telling the king how he had restored to life him that was dead, that, behold, the woman, whose son he had restored to life, cried to the king for her house and for her land. And Gehazi said, My lord, O king, this is the woman, and this is her son, whom Elisha restored to life.

⁶And when the king asked the woman, she told him. So the king appointed unto her a certain officer, saying, Restore all that was hers, and all the fruits of the field since the day that she left the land, even until now.

⁷And Elisha came to Damascus; and Benhadad the king of Syria was sick; and it was told him, saying, The man of God is come hither.

⁸And the king said unto Hazael, Take a present in thy hand, and go, meet the man of God, and inquire of Yahweh by him, saying, Shall I recover of this sickness?

⁹So Hazael went to meet him, and took a present with him, even of every good thing of Damascus, forty camels' burden, and came and stood before him, and said, Thy son Benhadad king of Syria hath sent me to thee, saying, Shall I recover of this sickness?

¹⁰And Elisha said unto him, Go, say unto him, Thou shalt surely recover; howbeit Yahweh hath showed me that he shall surely die.

¹¹And he settled his countenance stedfastly upon him, until he was ashamed: and the man of God wept.

¹²And Hazael said, Why weepeth my lord? And he answered, Because I know the evil that thou wilt do unto the children of Israel: their strongholds wilt thou set on fire, and their young men wilt thou slay with the sword, and wilt dash in pieces their little ones, and rip up their women with child.

¹³And Hazael said, But what is thy servant, who is but a dog, that he should do this great thing? And Elisha answered, Yahweh hath showed me that thou shalt be king over Syria.

¹⁴Then he departed from Elisha, and came to his master; who said to him, What said Elisha to thee? And he answered, He told me that thou wouldest surely recover.

¹⁵And it came to pass on the morrow, that he took the coverlet, and dipped it in water, and spread it on his face, so that he died: and Hazael reigned in his stead.

¹⁶And in the fifth year of Joram the son of Ahab king of Israel, Jehoshaphat being then king of Judah, Jehoram the son of Jehoshaphat king of Judah began to reign.

¹⁷Thirty and two years old was he when he began to reign; and he reigned eight years in Jerusalem.

¹⁸And he walked in the way of the kings of Israel, as did the house of Ahab: for he had the daughter of Ahab to wife; and he did that which was evil in the sight of Yahweh.

¹⁹Howbeit Yahweh would not destroy Judah, for David his servant's sake, as he promised him to give unto him a lamp for his children alway.

²⁰In his days Edom revolted from under the hand of Judah, and made a king over themselves.

²¹Then Joram passed over to Zair, and all his chariots with him: and he rose up by night, and smote the Edomites that compassed him about, and the captains of the chariots; and the people fled to their tents.

²²So Edom revolted from under the hand of Judah unto this day. Then did Libnah revolt at the same time.

²³And the rest of the acts of Joram, and all that he did, are they not written in the book of the chronicles of the kings of Judah?

²⁴And Joram slept with his fathers, and was buried with his fathers in the city of David; and Ahaziah his son reigned in his stead.

²⁵In the twelfth year of Joram the son of Ahab king of Israel did Ahaziah the son of Jehoram king of Judah begin to reign.

²⁶Two and twenty years old was Ahaziah when he began to reign; and he reigned one year in Jerusalem. And his mother's name was Athaliah the daughter of Omri king of Israel.

²⁷And he walked in the way of the house of Ahab, and did that which was evil in the sight of Yahweh, as did the house of Ahab; for he was the son-in-law of the house of Ahab.

²⁸And he went with Joram the son of Ahab to war against Hazael king of Syria at Ramoth-gilead: and the Syrians wounded Joram.

²⁹And king Joram returned to be healed in Jezreel of the wounds which the Syrians had given him at Ramah, when he fought against Hazael king of Syria. And Ahaziah the son of Jehoram king of Judah went down to see Joram the son of Ahab in Jezreel, because he was sick.

Chapter 9

¹And Elisha the prophet called one of the sons of the prophets, and said unto him, Gird up thy loins, and take this vial of oil in thy hand, and go to Ramoth-gilead.

²And when thou comest thither, look out there Jehu the son of Jehoshaphat the son of Nimshi, and go in, and make him arise up from among his brethren, and carry him to an inner chamber.

³Then take the vial of oil, and pour it on his head, and say, Thus saith Yahweh, I have anointed thee king over Israel. Then open the door, and flee, and tarry not.

⁴So the young man, even the young man the prophet, went to Ramoth-gilead.

⁵And when he came, behold, the captains of the host were sitting; and he said, I have an errand to thee, O captain. And Jehu said, Unto which of us all? And he said, To thee, O captain.

⁶And he arose, and went into the house; and he poured the oil on his head, and said unto him, Thus saith Yahweh, the God of Israel, I have anointed thee king over the people of Yahweh, even over Israel.

⁷And thou shalt smite the house of Ahab thy master, that I may avenge the blood of my servants the prophets, and the blood of all the servants of Yahweh, at the hand of Jezebel.

⁸For the whole house of Ahab shall perish; and I will cut off from Ahab every man-child, and him that is shut up and him that is left at large in Israel.

⁹And I will make the house of Ahab like the house of Jeroboam the son of Nebat, and like the house of Baasha the son of Ahijah.

¹⁰And the dogs shall eat Jezebel in the portion of Jezreel, and there shall be none to bury her. And he opened the door, and fled.

¹¹Then Jehu came forth to the servants of his lord: and one said unto him, Is all well? wherefore came this mad fellow to thee? And he said unto them, Ye know the man and what his talk was.

¹²And they said, It is false; tell us now. And he said, Thus and thus spake he to me, saying, Thus saith Yahweh, I have anointed thee king over Israel.

¹³Then they hasted, and took every man his garment, and put it under him on the top of the stairs, and blew the trumpet, saying, Jehu is king.

¹⁴So Jehu the son of Jehoshaphat the son of Nimshi conspired against Joram. (Now Joram was keeping Ramoth-gilead, he and all Israel, because of Hazael king of Syria;

¹⁵but king Joram was returned to be healed in Jezreel of the wounds which the Syrians had given him, when he fought with Hazael king of Syria.) And Jehu said, If this be your mind, then let none escape and go forth out of the city, to go to tell it in Jezreel.

¹⁶So Jehu rode in a chariot, and went to Jezreel; for Joram lay there. And Ahaziah king of Judah was come down to see Joram.

¹⁷Now the watchman was standing on the tower in Jezreel, and he spied the company of Jehu as he came, and said, I see a company. And Joram said, Take a horseman, and send to meet them, and let him say, Is it peace?

¹⁸So there went one on horseback to meet him, and said, Thus saith the king, Is it peace? And Jehu said, What hast thou to do with peace? turn thee behind me. And the watchman told, saying, The messenger came to them, but he cometh not back.

¹⁹Then he sent out a second on horseback, who came to them, and said, Thus saith the king, Is it peace? And Jehu answered, What hast thou to do with peace? turn thee behind me.

²⁰And the watchman told, saying, He came even unto them, and cometh not back: and the driving is like the driving of Jehu the son of Nimshi; for he driveth furiously.

²¹And Joram said, Make ready. And they made ready his chariot. And Joram king of Israel and Ahaziah king of Judah went out, each in his chariot, and they went out to meet Jehu, and found him in the portion of Naboth the Jezreelite.

²²And it came to pass, when Joram saw Jehu, that he said, Is it peace, Jehu? And he answered, What peace, so long as the whoredoms of thy mother Jezebel and her witchcrafts are so many?

²³And Joram turned his hands, and fled, and said to Ahaziah, There is treachery, O Ahaziah.

²⁴And Jehu drew his bow with his full strength, and smote Joram between his arms; and the arrow went out at his heart, and he sunk down in his chariot.

²⁵Then said Jehu to Bidkar his captain, Take up, and cast him in the portion of the field of Naboth the Jezreelite; for remember how that, when I and thou rode together after Ahab his father, Yahweh laid this burden upon him:

²⁶Surely I have seen yesterday the blood of Naboth, and the blood of his sons, saith Yahweh; and I will requite thee in this plat, saith Yahweh. Now therefore take and cast him into the plat of ground, according to the word of Yahweh.

²⁷But when Ahaziah the king of Judah saw this, he fled by the way of the garden-house. And Jehu followed after him, and said, Smite him also in the chariot: and they smote him at the ascent of Gur, which is by Ibleam. And he fled to Megiddo, and died there.

²⁸And his servants carried him in a chariot to Jerusalem, and buried him in his sepulchre with his fathers in the city of David.

²⁹And in the eleventh year of Joram the son of Ahab began Ahaziah to reign over Judah.

³⁰And when Jehu was come to Jezreel, Jezebel heard of it; and she painted her eyes, and attired her head, and looked out at the window.

³¹And as Jehu entered in at the gate, she said, Is it peace, thou Zimri, thy master's murderer?

³²And he lifted up his face to the window, and said, Who is on my side? who? And there looked out to him two or three eunuchs.

³³And he said, Throw her down. So they threw her down; and some of her blood was sprinkled on the wall, and on the horses: and he trod her under foot.

³⁴And when he was come in, he did eat and drink; and he said, See now to this cursed woman, and bury her; for she is a king's daughter.

³⁵And they went to bury her; but they found no more of her than the skull, and the feet, and the palms of her hands.

³⁶Wherefore they came back, and told him. And he said, This is the word of Yahweh, which he spake by his servant Elijah the Tishbite, saying, In the portion

of Jezreel shall the dogs eat the flesh of Jezebel;

37and the body of Jezebel shall be as dung upon the face of the field in the portion of Jezreel, so that they shall not say, This is Jezebel.

Chapter 10

1Now Ahab had seventy sons in Samaria. And Jehu wrote letters, and sent to Samaria, unto the rulers of Jezreel, even the elders, and unto them that brought up the sons of Ahab, saying,

2And now as soon as this letter cometh to you, seeing your master's sons are with you, and there are with you chariots and horses, a fortified city also, and armor;

3look ye out the best and meetest of your master's sons, and set him on his father's throne, and fight for your master's house.

4But they were exceedingly afraid, and said, Behold, the two kings stood not before him: how then shall we stand?

5And he that was over the household, and he that was over the city, the elders also, and they that brought up the children, sent to Jehu, saying, We are thy servants, and will do all that thou shalt bid us; we will not make any man king: do thou that which is good in thine eyes.

6Then he wrote a letter the second time to them, saying, If ye be on my side, and if ye will hearken unto my voice, take ye the heads of the men your master's sons, and come to me to Jezreel by to-morrow this time. Now the king's sons, being seventy persons, were with the great men of the city, who brought them up.

7And it came to pass, when the letter came to them, that they took the king's sons, and slew them, even seventy persons, and put their heads in baskets, and sent them unto him to Jezreel.

8And there came a messenger, and told him, saying, They have brought the heads of the king's sons. And he said, Lay ye them in two heaps at the entrance of the gate until the morning.

9And it came to pass in the morning, that he went out, and stood, and said to all the people, Ye are righteous: behold, I conspired against my master, and slew him; but who smote all these?

10Know now that there shall fall unto the earth nothing of the word of Yahweh, which Yahweh spake concerning the house of Ahab: for Yahweh hath done that which he spake by his servant Elijah.

11So Jehu smote all that remained of the house of Ahab in Jezreel, and all his great men, and his familiar friends, and his priests, until he left him none remaining.

12And he arose and departed, and went to Samaria. And as he was at the shearing-house of the shepherds in the way,

13Jehu met with the brethren of Ahaziah king of Judah, and said, Who are ye? And they answered, We are the brethren of Ahaziah: and we go down to salute the children of the king and the children of the queen.

14And he said, Take them alive. And they took them alive, and slew them at the pit of the shearing-house, even two and forty men; neither left he any of them.

15And when he was departed thence, he lighted on Jehonadab the son of Rechab coming to meet him; and he saluted him, and said to him, Is thy heart right, as my heart is with thy heart? And Jehonadab answered, It is. If it be, give me thy hand. And he gave him his hand; and he took him up to him into the chariot.

16And he said, Come with me, and see my zeal for Yahweh. So they made him ride in his chariot.

17And when he came to Samaria, he smote all that remained unto Ahab in Samaria, till he had destroyed him, according to the word of Yahweh, which he spake to Elijah.

18And Jehu gathered all the people together, and said unto them, Ahab served Baal a little; but Jehu will serve him much.

19Now therefore call unto me all the prophets of Baal, all his worshippers, and all his priests; let none be wanting: for I have a great sacrifice to do to Baal; whosoever shall be wanting, he shall not live. But Jehu did it in subtlety, to the intent that he might destroy the worshippers of Baal.

20And Jehu said, Sanctify a solemn assembly for Baal. And they proclaimed it.

21And Jehu sent through all Israel: and all the worshippers of Baal came, so that there was not a man left that came not. And they came into the house of Baal; and the house of Baal was filled from one end to another.

22And he said unto him that was over the vestry, Bring forth vestments for all the worshippers of Baal. And he brought them forth vestments.

23And Jehu went, and Jehonadab the son of Rechab, into the house of Baal; and he said unto the worshippers of Baal, Search, and look that there be here with you none of the servants of Yahweh, but the worshippers of Baal only.

24And they went in to offer sacrifices and burnt-offerings. Now Jehu had appointed him fourscore men without, and said, If any of the men whom I bring into your hands escape, he that letteth him go, his life shall be for the life of him.

25And it came to pass, as soon as he had made an end of offering the burnt-offering, that Jehu said to the guard and to the captains, Go in, and slay them; let none come forth. And they smote them with the edge of the sword; and the guard and the captains cast them out, and went to the city of the house of Baal.

26And they brought forth the pillars that were in the house of Baal, and burned them.

27And they brake down the pillar of Baal, and brake down the house of Baal, and made it a draught-house, unto this day.

28Thus Jehu destroyed Baal out of Israel.

29Howbeit from the sins of Jeroboam the son of Nebat, wherewith he made Israel to sin, Jehu departed not from after them, to wit, the golden calves that were in Beth-el, and that were in Dan.

30And Yahweh said unto Jehu, Because thou hast done well in executing that which is right in mine eyes, and hast done unto the house of Ahab according to all that was in my heart, thy sons of the fourth generation shall sit on the throne of Israel.

31But Jehu took no heed to walk in the law of Yahweh, the God of Israel, with all his heart: he departed not from the sins of Jeroboam, wherewith he made Israel to sin.

32In those days Yahweh began to cut off from Israel: and Hazael smote them in all the borders of Israel;

33from the Jordan eastward, all the land of Gilead, the Gadites, and the Reubenites, and the Manassites, from Aroer, which is by the valley of the Arnon, even Gilead and Bashan.

34Now the rest of the acts of Jehu, and all that he did, and all his might, are they not written in the book of the chronicles of the kings of Israel?

35And Jehu slept with his fathers; and they buried him in Samaria. And Jehoahaz his son reigned in his stead.

36And the time that Jehu reigned over Israel in Samaria was twenty and eight years.

Chapter 11

1Now when Athaliah the mother of Ahaziah saw that her son was dead, she arose and destroyed all the seed royal.

2But Jehosheba, the daughter of king Joram, sister of Ahaziah, took Joash the son of Ahaziah, and stole him away from among the king's sons that were slain, even him and his nurse, and put them in the bedchamber; and they hid him from Athaliah, so that he was not slain;

3And he was with her hid in the house of Yahweh six years. And Athaliah reigned over the land.

4And in the seventh year Jehoiada sent and fetched the captains over hundreds of the Carites and of the guard, and brought them to him into the house of Yahweh; and he made a covenant with them, and took an oath of them in the house of Yahweh, and showed them the king's son.

5And he commanded them, saying, This is the thing that ye shall do: a third part of you, that come in on the sabbath, shall be keepers of the watch of the king's house;

6And a third part shall be at the gate Sur; and a third part at the gate behind the guard: so shall ye keep the watch of the house, and be a barrier.

7And the two companies of you, even all that go forth on the sabbath, shall keep the watch of the house of Yahweh about the king.

8And ye shall compass the king round about, every man with his weapons in his hand; and he that cometh within the ranks, let him be slain: and be ye with the king when he goeth out, and when he cometh in.

9And the captains over hundreds did according to all that Jehoiada the priest commanded; and they took every man his men, those that were to come in on the sabbath, with those that were to go out on the sabbath, and came to Jehoiada the priest.

10And the priest delivered to the captains over hundreds the spears and shields that had been king David's, which were in the house of Yahweh.

11And the guard stood, every man with his weapons in his hand, from the right side of the house to the left side of the house, along by the altar and the house, by the king round about.

12Then he brought out the king's son, and put the crown upon him, and gave him the testimony; and they made him king, and anointed him; and they clapped their hands, and said, Long live the king.

13And when Athaliah heard the noise of the guard and of the people, she came to the people into the house of Yahweh:

14and she looked, and, behold, the king stood by the pillar, as the manner was, and the captains and the trumpets by the king; and all the people of the land rejoiced, and blew trumpets. Then Athaliah rent her clothes, and cried, Treason! treason!

15And Jehoiada the priest commanded the captains of hundreds that were set over the host, and said unto them, Have her forth between the ranks; and him that followeth her slay with the sword. For the priest said, Let her not be slain in the house of Yahweh.

16So they made way for her; and she went by the way of the horses' entry to the king's house: and there was she slain.

17And Jehoiada made a covenant between Yahweh and the king and the people, that they should be Yahweh's people; between the king also and the people.

18And all the people of the land went to the house of Baal, and brake it down; his altars and his images brake they in pieces thoroughly, and slew Mattan the priest of Baal before the altars. And the priest appointed officers over the house of Yahweh.

19And he took the captains over hundreds, and the Carites, and the guard, and all the people of the land; and they brought down the king from the house of Yahweh, and came by the way of the gate of the guard unto the king's house. And he sat on the throne of the kings.

20So all the people of the land rejoiced, and the city was quiet. And Athaliah they had slain with the sword at the king's house.

21Jehoash was seven years old when he began to reign.

Chapter 12

1In the seventh year of Jehu began Jehoash to reign; and he reigned forty years in Jerusalem: and his mother's name was Zibiah of Beer-sheba.

2And Jehoash did that which was right in the eyes of Yahweh all his days wherein Jehoiada the priest instructed him.

3Howbeit the high places were not taken away; the people still sacrificed and burnt incense in the high places.

4And Jehoash said to the priests, All the money of the hallowed things that is brought into the house of Yahweh, in current money, the money of the persons for whom each man is rated, and all the money that it cometh into any man's heart

Second Kings

to bring into the house of Yahweh,

5let the priests take it to them, every man from his acquaintance; and they shall repair the breaches of the house, wheresoever any breach shall be found.

6But it was so, that in the three and twentieth year of king Jehoash the priests had not repaired the breaches of the house.

7Then king Jehoash called for Jehoiada the priest, and for the other priests, and said unto them, Why repair ye not the breaches of the house? now therefore take no more money from your acquaintance, but deliver it for the breaches of the house.

8And the priests consented that they should take no more money from the people, neither repair the breaches of the house.

9But Jehoiada the priest took a chest, and bored a hole in the lid of it, and set it beside the altar, on the right side as one cometh into the house of Yahweh: and the priests that kept the threshold put therein all the money that was brought into the house of Yahweh.

10And it was so, when they saw that there was much money in the chest, that the king's scribe and the high priest came up, and they put up in bags and counted the money that was found in the house of Yahweh.

11And they gave the money that was weighed out into the hands of them that did the work, that had the oversight of the house of Yahweh: and they paid it out to the carpenters and the builders, that wrought upon the house of Yahweh,

12and to the masons and the hewers of stone, and for buying timber and hewn stone to repair the breaches of the house of Yahweh, and for all that was laid out for the house to repair it.

13But there were not made for the house of Yahweh cups of silver, snuffers, basins, trumpets, any vessels of gold, or vessels of silver, of the money that was brought into the house of Yahweh;

14for they gave that to them that did the work, and repaired therewith the house of Yahweh.

15Moreover they reckoned not with the men, into whose hand they delivered the money to give to them that did the work; for they dealt faithfully.

16The money for the trespass-offerings, and the money for the sin-offerings, was not brought into the house of Yahweh: it was the priests'.

17Then Hazael king of Syria went up, and fought against Gath, and took it; and Hazael set his face to go up to Jerusalem.

18And Jehoash king of Judah took all the hallowed things that Jehoshaphat and Jehoram and Ahaziah, his fathers, kings of Judah, had dedicated, and his own hallowed things, and all the gold that was found in the treasures of the house of Yahweh, and of the king's house, and sent it to Hazael king of Syria: and he went away from Jerusalem.

19Now the rest of the acts of Joash, and all that he did, are they not written in the book of the chronicles of the kings of Judah?

20And his servants arose, and made a conspiracy, and smote Joash at the house of Millo, on the way that goeth down to Silla.

21For Jozacar the son of Shimeath, and Jehozabad the son of Shomer, his servants, smote him, and he died; and they buried him with his fathers in the city of David: and Amaziah his son reigned in his stead.

Chapter 13

1In the three and twentieth year of Joash the son of Ahaziah, king of Judah, Jehoahaz the son of Jehu began to reign over Israel in Samaria, and reigned seventeen years.

2And he did that which was evil in the sight of Yahweh, and followed the sins of Jeroboam the son of Nebat, wherewith he made Israel to sin; he departed not therefrom.

3And the anger of Yahweh was kindled against Israel, and he delivered them into the hand of Hazael king of Syria, and into the hand of Benhadad the son of Hazael, continually.

4And Jehoahaz besought Yahweh, and Yahweh hearkened unto him; for he saw the oppression of Israel, how that the king of Syria oppressed them.

5(And Yahweh gave Israel a saviour, so that they went out from under the hand of the Syrians; and the children of Israel dwelt in their tents as beforetime.

6Nevertheless they departed not from the sins of the house of Jeroboam, wherewith he made Israel to sin, but walked therein: and there remained the Asherah also in Samaria.)

7For he left not to Jehoahaz of the people save fifty horsemen, and ten chariots, and ten thousand footmen; for the king of Syria destroyed them, and made them like the dust in threshing.

8Now the rest of the acts of Jehoahaz, and all that he did, and his might, are they not written in the book of the chronicles of the kings of Israel?

9And Jehoahaz slept with his fathers; and they buried him in Samaria: and Joash his son reigned in his stead.

10In the thirty and seventh year of Joash king of Judah began Jehoash the son of Jehoahaz to reign over Israel in Samaria, and reigned sixteen years.

11And he did that which was evil in the sight of Yahweh; he departed not from all the sins of Jeroboam the son of Nebat, wherewith he made Israel to sin; but he walked therein.

12Now the rest of the acts of Joash, and all that he did, and his might wherewith he fought against Amaziah king of Judah, are they not written in the book of the chronicles of the kings of Israel?

13And Joash slept with his fathers; and Jeroboam sat upon his throne: and Joash was buried in Samaria with the kings of Israel.

14Now Elisha was fallen sick of his sickness whereof he died: and Joash the king of Israel came down unto him, and wept over him, and said, My father, my father, the chariots of Israel and the horsemen thereof!

15And Elisha said unto him, Take bow and arrows; and he took unto him bow and arrows.

16And he said to the king of Israel, Put thy hand upon the bow; and he put his hand upon it. And Elisha laid his hands upon the king's hands.

17And he said, Open the window eastward; and he opened it. Then Elisha said, Shoot; and he shot. And he said, Yahweh's arrow of victory, even the arrow of victory over Syria; for thou shalt smite the Syrians in Aphek, till thou have consumed them.

18And he said, Take the arrows; and he took them. And he said unto the king of Israel, Smite upon the ground; and he smote thrice, and stayed.

19And the man of God was wroth with him, and said, Thou shouldest have smitten five or six times: then hadst thou smitten Syria till thou hadst consumed it, whereas now thou shalt smite Syria but thrice.

20And Elisha died, and they buried him. Now the bands of the Moabites invaded the land at the coming in of the year.

21And it came to pass, as they were burying a man, that, behold, they spied a band; and they cast the man into the sepulchre of Elisha: and as soon as the man touched the bones of Elisha, he revived, and stood up on his feet.

22And Hazael king of Syria oppressed Israel all the days of Jehoahaz.

23But Yahweh was gracious unto them, and had compassion on them, and had respect unto them, because of his covenant with Abraham, Isaac, and Jacob, and would not destroy them, neither cast he them from his presence as yet.

24And Hazael king of Syria died; and Benhadad his son reigned in his stead.

25And Jehoash the son of Jehoahaz took again out of the hand of Benhadad the son of Hazael the cities which he had taken out of the hand of Jehoahaz his father by war. Three times did Joash smite him, and recovered the cities of Israel.

Chapter 14

1In the second year of Joash son of Joahaz king of Israel began Amaziah the son of Joash king of Judah to reign.

2He was twenty and five years old when he began to reign; and he reigned twenty and nine years in Jerusalem: and his mother's name was Jehoaddin of Jerusalem.

3And he did that which was right in the eyes of Yahweh, yet not like David his father: he did according to all that Joash his father had done.

4Howbeit the high places were not taken away: the people still sacrificed and burnt incense in the high places.

5And it came to pass, as soon as the kingdom was established in his hand, that he slew his servants who had slain the king his father:

6but the children of the murderers he put not to death; according to that which is written in the book of the law of Moses, as Yahweh commanded, saying, The fathers shall not be put to death for the children, nor the children be put to death for the fathers; but every man shall die for his own sin.

7He slew of Edom in the Valley of Salt ten thousand, and took Sela by war, and called the name of it Joktheel, unto this day.

8Then Amaziah sent messengers to Jehoash, the son of Jehoahaz son of Jehu, king of Israel, saying, Come, let us look one another in the face.

9And Jehoash the king of Israel sent to Amaziah king of Judah, saying, The thistle that was in Lebanon sent to the cedar that was in Lebanon, saying, Give thy daughter to my son to wife: and there passed by a wild beast that was in Lebanon, and trod down the thistle.

10Thou hast indeed smitten Edom, and thy heart hath lifted thee up: glory thereof, and abide at home; for why shouldest thou meddle to thy hurt, that thou shouldest fall, even thou, and Judah with thee?

11But Amaziah would not hear. So Jehoash king of Israel went up; and he and Amaziah king of Judah looked one another in the face at Beth-shemesh, which belongeth to Judah.

12And Judah was put to the worse before Israel; and they fled every man to his tent.

13And Jehoash king of Israel took Amaziah king of Judah, the son of Jehoash the son of Ahaziah, at Beth-shemesh, and came to Jerusalem, and brake down the wall of Jerusalem from the gate of Ephraim unto the corner gate, four hundred cubits.

14And he took all the gold and silver, and all the vessels that were found in the house of Yahweh, and in the treasures of the king's house, the hostages also, and returned to Samaria.

15Now the rest of the acts of Jehoash which he did, and his might, and how he fought with Amaziah king of Judah, are they not written in the book of the chronicles of the kings of Israel?

16And Jehoash slept with his fathers, and was buried in Samaria with the kings of Israel; and Jeroboam his son reigned in his stead.

17And Amaziah the son of Joash king of Judah lived after the death of Jehoash son of Jehoahaz king of Israel fifteen years.

18Now the rest of the acts of Amaziah, are they not written in the book of the chronicles of the kings of Judah?

19And they made a conspiracy against him in Jerusalem; and he fled to Lachish: but they sent after him to Lachish, and slew him there.

20And they brought him upon horses; and he was buried at Jerusalem with his fathers in the city of David.

21And all the people of Judah took Azariah, who was sixteen years old, and made him king in the room of his father Amaziah.

22He built Elath, and restored it to Judah, after that the king slept with his fathers.

23In the fifteenth year of Amaziah the son of Joash king of Judah Jeroboam the son of Joash king of Israel began to reign in Samaria, and reigned forty and one years.

24And he did that which was evil in the sight of Yahweh: he departed not from all the sins of Jeroboam the son of Nebat, who made Israel to sin.

25He restored the border of Israel from the entrance of Hamath unto the sea of the Arabah, according to the word of Yahweh, the God of Israel, which he spake by his servant Jonah the son of Amittai, the prophet, who was of Gath-hepher.

26For Yahweh saw the affliction of Israel, that it was very bitter; for there was none shut up nor left at large, neither was there any helper for Israel.

27And Yahweh said not that he would blot out the name of Israel from under heaven; but he saved them by the hand of Jeroboam the son of Joash.

28Now the rest of the acts of Jeroboam, and all that he did, and his might, how he warred, and how he recovered Damascus, and Hamath, which had belonged to Judah, for Israel, are they not written in the book of the chronicles of the kings of Israel?

29And Jeroboam slept with his fathers, even with the kings of Israel; and Zechariah his son reigned in his stead.

Chapter 15

1In the twenty and seventh year of Jeroboam king of Israel began Azariah son of Amaziah king of Judah to reign.

2Sixteen years old was he when he began to reign; and he reigned two and fifty years in Jerusalem: and his mother's name was Jecoliah of Jerusalem.

3And he did that which was right in the eyes of Yahweh, according to all that his father Amaziah had done.

4Howbeit the high places were not taken away: the people still sacrificed and burnt incense in the high places.

5And Yahweh smote the king, so that he was a leper unto the day of his death, and dwelt in a separate house. And Jotham the king's son was over the household, judging the people of the land.

6Now the rest of the acts of Azariah, and all that he did, are they not written in the book of the chronicles of the kings of Judah?

7And Azariah slept with his fathers; and they buried him with his fathers in the city of David: and Jotham his son reigned in his stead.

8In the thirty and eighth year of Azariah king of Judah did Zechariah the son of Jeroboam reign over Israel in Samaria six months.

9And he did that which was evil in the sight of Yahweh, as his fathers had done: he departed not from the sins of Jeroboam the son of Nebat, wherewith he made Israel to sin.

10And Shallum the son of Jabesh conspired against him, and smote him before the people, and slew him, and reigned in his stead.

11Now the rest of the acts of Zechariah, behold, they are written in the book of the chronicles of the kings of Israel.

12This was the word of Yahweh which he spake unto Jehu, saying, Thy sons to the fourth generation shall sit upon the throne of Israel. And so it came to pass.

13Shallum the son of Jabesh began to reign in the nine and thirtieth year of Uzziah king of Judah; and he reigned the space of a month in Samaria.

14And Menahem the son of Gadi went up from Tirzah, and came to Samaria, and smote Shallum the son of Jabesh in Samaria, and slew him, and reigned in his stead.

15Now the rest of the acts of Shallum, and his conspiracy which he made, behold, they are written in the book of the chronicles of the kings of Israel.

16Then Menahem smote Tiphsah, and all that were therein, and the borders thereof, from Tirzah: because they opened not to him, therefore he smote it; and all the women therein that were with child he ripped up.

17In the nine and thirtieth year of Azariah king of Judah began Menahem the son of Gadi to reign over Israel, and reigned ten years in Samaria.

18And he did that which was evil in the sight of Yahweh: he departed not all his days from the sins of Jeroboam the son of Nebat, wherewith he made Israel to sin.

19There came against the land Pul the king of Assyria; and Menahem gave Pul a thousand talents of silver, that his hand might be with him to confirm the kingdom in his hand.

20And Menahem exacted the money of Israel, even of all the mighty men of wealth, of each man fifty shekels of silver, to give to the king of Assyria. So the king of Assyria turned back, and stayed not there in the land.

21Now the rest of the acts of Menahem, and all that he did, are they not written in the book of the chronicles of the kings of Israel?

22And Menahem slept with his fathers; and Pekahiah his son reigned in his stead.

23In the fiftieth year of Azariah king of Judah Pekahiah the son of Menahem began to reign over Israel in Samaria, and reigned two years.

24And he did that which was evil in the sight of Yahweh: he departed not from the sins of Jeroboam the son of Nebat, wherewith he made Israel to sin.

25And Pekah the son of Remaliah, his captain, conspired against him, and smote him in Samaria, in the castle of the king's house, with Argob and Arieh; and with him were fifty men of the Gileadites: and he slew him, and reigned in his stead.

26Now the rest of the acts of Pekahiah, and all that he did, behold, they are written in the book of the chronicles of the kings of Israel.

27In the two and fiftieth year of Azariah king of Judah Pekah the son of Remaliah began to reign over Israel in Samaria, and reigned twenty years.

28And he did that which was evil in the sight of Yahweh: he departed not from the sins of Jeroboam the son of Nebat, wherewith he made Israel to sin.

29In the days of Pekah king of Israel came Tiglath-pileser king of Assyria, and took Ijon, and Abel-beth-maacah, and Janoah, and Kedesh, and Hazor, and Gilead, and Galilee, all the land of Naphtali; and he carried them captive to Assyria.

30And Hoshea the son of Elah made a conspiracy against Pekah the son of Remaliah, and smote him, and slew him, and reigned in his stead, in the twentieth year of Jotham the son of Uzziah.

31Now the rest of the acts of Pekah, and all that he did, behold, they are written in the book of the chronicles of the kings of Israel.

32In the second year of Pekah the son of Remaliah king of Israel began Jotham the son of Uzziah king of Judah to reign.

33Five and twenty years old was he when he began to reign; and he reigned sixteen years in Jerusalem: and his mother's name was Jerusha the daughter of Zadok.

34And he did that which was right in the eyes of Yahweh; he did according to all that his father Uzziah had done.

35Howbeit the high places were not taken away: the people still sacrificed and burned incense in the high places. He built the upper gate of the house of Yahweh.

36Now the rest of the acts of Jotham, and all that he did, are they not written in the book of the chronicles of the kings of Judah?

37In those days Yahweh began to send against Judah Rezin the king of Syria, and Pekah the son of Remaliah.

38And Jotham slept with his fathers, and was buried with his fathers in the city of David his father: and Ahaz his son reigned in his stead.

Chapter 16

1In the seventeenth year of Pekah the son of Remaliah Ahaz the son of Jotham king of Judah began to reign.

2Twenty years old was Ahaz when he began to reign; and he reigned sixteen years in Jerusalem: and he did not that which was right in the eyes of Yahweh his God, like David his father.

3But he walked in the way of the kings of Israel, yea, and made his son to pass through the fire, according to the abominations of the nations, whom Yahweh cast out from before the children of Israel.

4And he sacrificed and burnt incense in the high places, and on the hills, and under every green tree.

5Then Rezin king of Syria and Pekah son of Remaliah king of Israel came up to Jerusalem to war: and they besieged Ahaz, but could not overcome him.

6At that time Rezin king of Syria recovered Elath to Syria, and drove the Jews from Elath; and the Syrians came to Elath, and dwelt there, unto this day.

7So Ahaz sent messengers to Tiglath-pileser king of Assyria, saying, I am thy servant and thy son: come up, and save me out of the hand of the king of Syria, and out of the hand of the king of Israel, who rise up against me.

8And Ahaz took the silver and gold that was found in the house of Yahweh, and in the treasures of the king's house, and sent it for a present to the king of Assyria.

9And the king of Assyria hearkened unto him; and the king of Assyria went up against Damascus, and took it, and carried the people of it captive to Kir, and slew Rezin.

10And king Ahaz went to Damascus to meet Tiglath-pileser king of Assyria, and saw the altar that was at Damascus; and king Ahaz sent to Urijah the priest the fashion of the altar, and the pattern of it, according to all the workmanship thereof.

11And Urijah the priest built an altar: according to all that king Ahaz had sent from Damascus, so did Urijah the priest make it against the coming of king Ahaz from Damascus.

12And when the king was come from Damascus, the king saw the altar: and the king drew near unto the altar, and offered thereon.

13And he burnt his burnt-offering and his meal-offering, and poured his drink-offering, and sprinkled the blood of his peace-offerings, upon the altar.

14And the brazen altar, which was before Yahweh, he brought from the forefront of the house, from between his altar and the house of Yahweh, and put it on the north side of his altar.

15And king Ahaz commanded Urijah the priest, saying, Upon the great altar burn the morning burnt-offering, and the evening meal-offering, and the king's burnt-offering, and his meal-offering, with the burnt-offering of all the people of the land, and their meal-offering, and their drink-offerings; and sprinkle upon it all the blood of the burnt-offering, and all the blood of the sacrifice: but the brazen altar shall be for me to inquire by.

16Thus did Urijah the priest, according to all that king Ahaz commanded.

17And king Ahaz cut off the panels of the bases, and removed the laver from off them, and took down the sea from off the brazen oxen that were under it, and put it upon a pavement of stone.

18And the covered way for the sabbath that they had built in the house, and the king's entry without, turned he unto the house of Yahweh, because of the king of Assyria.

19Now the rest of the acts of Ahaz which he did, are they not written in the book of the chronicles of the kings of Judah?

20And Ahaz slept with his fathers, and was buried with his fathers in the city of David: and Hezekiah his son reigned in his stead.

Chapter 17

1In the twelfth year of Ahaz king of Judah began Hoshea the son of Elah to reign in Samaria over Israel, and reigned nine years.

2And he did that which was evil in the sight of Yahweh, yet not as the kings of Israel that were before him.

3Against him came up Shalmaneser king of Assyria; and Hoshea became his servant, and brought him tribute.

4And the king of Assyria found conspiracy in Hoshea; for he had sent messengers to So king of Egypt, and offered no tribute to the king of Assyria, as he had done year by year: therefore the king of Assyria shut him up, and bound him in prison.

5Then the king of Assyria came up throughout all the land, and went up to Samaria, and besieged it three years.

6In the ninth year of Hoshea the king of Assyria took Samaria, and carried Israel away unto Assyria, and placed them in Halah, and on the Habor, the river of Gozan, and in the cities of the Medes.

7And it was so, because the children of Israel had sinned against Yahweh their God, who brought them up out of the land of Egypt from under the hand of Pharaoh king of Egypt, and had feared other gods,

Second Kings

8and walked in the statutes of the nations, whom Yahweh cast out from before the children of Israel, and of the kings of Israel, which they made.

9And the children of Israel did secretly things that were not right against Yahweh their God: and they built them high places in all their cities, from the tower of the watchmen to the fortified city;

10and they set them up pillars and Asherim upon every high hill, and under every green tree;

11and there they burnt incense in all the high places, as did the nations whom Yahweh carried away before them; and they wrought wicked things to provoke Yahweh to anger;

12and they served idols, whereof Yahweh had said unto them, Ye shall not do this thing.

13Yet Yahweh testified unto Israel, and unto Judah, by every prophet, and every seer, saying, Turn ye from your evil ways, and keep my commandments and my statutes, according to all the law which I commanded your fathers, and which I sent to you by my servants the prophets.

14Notwithstanding, they would not hear, but hardened their neck, like to the neck of their fathers, who believed not in Yahweh their God.

15And they rejected his statutes, and his covenant that he made with their fathers, and his testimonies which he testified unto them; and they followed vanity, and became vain, and went after the nations that were round about them, concerning whom Yahweh had charged them that they should not do like them.

16And they forsook all the commandments of Yahweh their God, and made them molten images, even two calves, and made an Asherah, and worshipped all the host of heaven, and served Baal.

17And they caused their sons and their daughters to pass through the fire, and used divination and enchantments, and sold themselves to do that which was evil in the sight of Yahweh, to provoke him to anger.

18Therefore Yahweh was very angry with Israel, and removed them out of his sight: there was none left but the tribe of Judah only.

19Also Judah kept not the commandments of Yahweh their God, but walked in the statutes of Israel which they made.

20And Yahweh rejected all the seed of Israel, and afflicted them, and delivered them into the hand of spoilers, until he had cast them out of his sight.

21For he rent Israel from the house of David; and they made Jeroboam the son of Nebat king: and Jeroboam drove Israel from following Yahweh, and made them sin a great sin.

22And the children of Israel walked in all the sins of Jeroboam which he did; they departed not from them;

23until Yahweh removed Israel out of his sight, as he spake by all his servants the prophets. So Israel was carried away out of their own land to Assyria unto this day.

24And the king of Assyria brought men from Babylon, and from Cuthah, and from Avva, and from Hamath and Sepharvaim, and placed them in the cities of Samaria instead of the children of Israel; and they possessed Samaria, and dwelt in the cities thereof.

25And so it was, at the beginning of their dwelling there, that they feared not Yahweh: therefore Yahweh sent lions among them, which killed some of them.

26Wherefore they spake to the king of Assyria, saying, The nations which thou hast carried away, and placed in the cities of Samaria, know not the law of the god of the land: therefore he hath sent lions among them, and, behold, they slay them, because they know not the law of the god of the land.

27Then the king of Assyria commanded, saying, Carry thither one of the priests whom ye brought from thence; and let them go and dwell there, and let him teach them the law of the god of the land.

28So one of the priests whom they had carried away from Samaria came and dwelt in Beth-el, and taught them how they should fear Yahweh.

29Howbeit every nation made gods of their own, and put them in the houses of the high places which the Samaritans had made, every nation in their cities wherein they dwelt.

30And the men of Babylon made Succoth-benoth, and the men of Cuth made Nergal, and the men of Hamath made Ashima,

31and the Avvites made Nibhaz and Tartak; and the Sepharvites burnt their children in the fire to Adrammelech and Anammelech, the gods of Sepharvaim.

32So they feared Yahweh, and made unto them from among themselves priests of the high places, who sacrificed for them in the houses of the high places.

33They feared Yahweh, and served their own gods, after the manner of the nations from among whom they had been carried away.

34Unto this day they do after the former manner: they fear not Yahweh, neither do they after their statutes, or after their ordinances, or after the law or after the commandment which Yahweh commanded the children of Jacob, whom he named Israel;

35with whom Yahweh had made a covenant, and charged them, saying, Ye shall not fear other gods, nor bow yourselves to them, nor serve them, nor sacrifice to them:

36but Yahweh, who brought you up out of the land of Egypt with great power and with an outstretched arm, him shall ye fear, and unto him shall ye bow yourselves, and to him shall ye sacrifice:

37and the statutes and the ordinances, and the law and the commandment, which he wrote for you, ye shall observe to do for evermore; and ye shall not fear other gods:

38and the covenant that I have made with you ye shall not forget; neither shall ye fear other gods:

39but Yahweh your God shall ye fear; and he will deliver you out of the hand of all your enemies.

40Howbeit they did not hearken, but they did after their former manner.

41So these nations feared Yahweh, and served their graven images; their children likewise, and their children's children, as did their fathers, so do they unto this day.

Chapter 18

1Now it came to pass in the third year of Hoshea son of Elah king of Israel, that Hezekiah the son of Ahaz king of Judah began to reign.

2Twenty and five years old was he when he began to reign; and he reigned twenty and nine years in Jerusalem: and his mother's name was Abi the daughter of Zechariah.

3And he did that which was right in the eyes of Yahweh, according to all that David his father had done.

4He removed the high places, and brake the pillars, and cut down the Asherah: and he brake in pieces the brazen serpent that Moses had made; for unto those days the children of Israel did burn incense to it; and he called it Nehushtan.

5He trusted in Yahweh, the God of Israel; so that after him was none like him among all the kings of Judah, nor among them that were before him.

6For he clave to Yahweh; he departed not from following him, but kept his commandments, which Yahweh commanded Moses.

7And Yahweh was with him; whithersoever he went forth he prospered: and he rebelled against the king of Assyria, and served him not.

8He smote the Philistines unto Gaza and the borders thereof, from the tower of the watchmen to the fortified city.

9And it came to pass in the fourth year of king Hezekiah, which was the seventh year of Hoshea son of Elah king of Israel, that Shalmaneser king of Assyria came up against Samaria, and besieged it.

10And at the end of three years they took it: in the sixth year of Hezekiah, which was the ninth year of Hoshea king of Israel, Samaria was taken.

11And the king of Assyria carried Israel away unto Assyria, and put them in Halah, and on the Habor, the river of Gozan, and in the cities of the Medes,

12because they obeyed not the voice of Yahweh their God, but transgressed his covenant, even all that Moses the servant of Yahweh commanded, and would not hear it, nor do it.

13Now in the fourteenth year of king Hezekiah did Sennacherib king of Assyria come up against all the fortified cities of Judah, and took them.

14And Hezekiah king of Judah sent to the king of Assyria to Lachish, saying, I have offended; return from me: that which thou puttest on me will I bear. And the king of Assyria appointed unto Hezekiah king of Judah three hundred talents of silver and thirty talents of gold.

15And Hezekiah gave him all the silver that was found in the house of Yahweh, and in the treasures of the king's house.

16At that time did Hezekiah cut off the gold from the doors of the temple of Yahweh, and from the pillars which Hezekiah king of Judah had overlaid, and gave it to the king of Assyria.

17And the king of Assyria sent Tartan and Rab-saris and Rabshakeh from Lachish to king Hezekiah with a great army unto Jerusalem. And they went up and came to Jerusalem. And when they were come up, they came and stood by the conduit of the upper pool, which is in the highway of the fuller's field.

18And when they had called to the king, there came out to them Eliakim the son of Hilkiah, who was over the household, and Shebnah the scribe, and Joah the son of Asaph the recorder.

19And Rabshakeh said unto them, Say ye now to Hezekiah, Thus saith the great king, the king of Assyria, What confidence is this wherein thou trustest?

20Thou sayest (but they are but vain words), There is counsel and strength for the war. Now on whom dost thou trust, that thou hast rebelled against me?

21Now, behold, thou trustest upon the staff of this bruised reed, even upon Egypt; whereon if a man lean, it will go into his hand, and pierce it: so is Pharaoh king of Egypt unto all that trust on him.

22But if ye say unto me, We trust in Yahweh our God; is not that he, whose high places and whose altars Hezekiah hath taken away, and hath said to Judah and to Jerusalem, Ye shall worship before this altar in Jerusalem?

23Now therefore, I pray thee, give pledges to my master the king of Assyria, and I will give thee two thousand horses, if thou be able on thy part to set riders upon them.

24How then canst thou turn away the face of one captain of the least of my master's servants, and put thy trust on Egypt for chariots and for horsemen?

25Am I now come up without Yahweh against this place to destroy it? Yahweh said unto me, Go up against this land, and destroy it.

26Then said Eliakim the son of Hilkiah, and Shebnah, and Joah, unto Rabshakeh, Speak, I pray thee, to thy servants in the Syrian language; for we understand it: and speak not with us in the Jews' language, in the ears of the people that are on the wall.

27But Rabshakeh said unto them, Hath my master sent me to thy master, and to thee, to speak these words? hath he not sent me to the men that sit on the wall, to eat their own dung, and to drink their own water with you?

28Then Rabshakeh stood, and cried with a loud voice in the Jews' language, and spake, saying, Hear ye the word of the great king, the king of Assyria.

29Thus saith the king, Let not Hezekiah deceive you; for he will not be able to deliver you out of his hand:

30neither let Hezekiah make you trust in Yahweh, saying, Yahweh will surely deliver us, and this city shall not be given into the hand of the king of Assyria.

31Hearken not to Hezekiah: for thus saith the king of Assyria, Make your peace with me, and come out to me; and eat ye every one of his vine, and every one of his fig-tree, and drink ye every one the waters of his own cistern;

32Until I come and take you away to a land like your own land, a land of grain and new wine, a land of bread and vineyards, a land of olive-trees and of honey, that ye may live, and not die: and hearken not unto Hezekiah, when he persuadeth you, saying, Yahweh will deliver us.

33Hath any of the gods of the nations ever delivered his land out of the hand of the king of Assyria?

34Where are the gods of Hamath, and of Arpad? where are the gods of Sepharvaim, of Hena, and Ivvah? have they delivered Samaria out of my hand?

35Who are they among all the gods of the countries, that have delivered their country out of my hand, that Yahweh should deliver Jerusalem out of my hand?

36But the people held their peace, and answered him not a word; for the king's commandment was, saying, Answer him not.

37Then came Eliakim the son of Hilkiah, who was over the household, and Shebna the scribe, and Joah the son of Asaph the recorder, to Hezekiah with their clothes rent, and told him the words of Rabshakeh.

Chapter 19

1And it came to pass, when king Hezekiah heard it, that he rent his clothes, and covered himself with sackcloth, and went into the house of Yahweh.

2And he sent Eliakim, who was over the household, and Shebna the scribe, and the elders of the priests, covered with sackcloth, unto Isaiah the prophet the son of Amoz.

3And they said unto him, Thus saith Hezekiah, This day is a day of trouble, and of rebuke, and of contumely; for the children are come to the birth, and there is not strength to bring forth.

4It may be Yahweh thy God will hear all the words of Rabshakeh, whom the king of Assyria his master hath sent to defy the living God, and will rebuke the words which Yahweh thy God hath heard: wherefore lift up thy prayer for the remnant that is left.

5So the servants of king Hezekiah came to Isaiah.

6And Isaiah said unto them, Thus shall ye say to your master, Thus saith Yahweh, Be not afraid of the words that thou hast heard, wherewith the servants of the king of Assyria have blasphemed me.

7Behold, I will put a spirit in him, and he shall hear tidings, and shall return to his own land; and I will cause him to fall by the sword in his own land.

8So Rabshakeh returned, and found the king of Assyria warring against Libnah; for he had heard that he was departed from Lachish.

9And when he heard say of Tirhakah king of Ethiopia, Behold, he is come out to fight against thee, he sent messengers again unto Hezekiah, saying,

10Thus shall ye speak to Hezekiah king of Judah, saying, Let not thy God in whom thou trustest deceive thee, saying, Jerusalem shall not be given into the hand of the king of Assyria.

11Behold, thou hast heard what the kings of Assyria have done to all lands, by destroying them utterly: and shalt thou be delivered?

12Have the gods of the nations delivered them, which my fathers have destroyed, Gozan, and Haran, and Rezeph, and the children of Eden that were in Telassar?

13Where is the king of Hamath, and the king of Arpad, and the king of the city of Sepharvaim, of Hena, and Ivvah?

14And Hezekiah received the letter from the hand of the messengers, and read it; and Hezekiah went up unto the house of Yahweh, and spread it before Yahweh.

15And Hezekiah prayed before Yahweh, and said, O Yahweh, the God of Israel, that sittest above the cherubim, thou art the God, even thou alone, of all the kingdoms of the earth; thou hast made heaven and earth.

16Incline thine ear, O Yahweh, and hear; open thine eyes, O Yahweh, and see; and hear the words of Sennacherib, wherewith he hath sent him to defy the living God.

17Of a truth, Yahweh, the kings of Assyria have laid waste the nations and their lands,

18and have cast their gods into the fire; for they were no gods, but the work of men's hands, wood and stone; therefore they have destroyed them.

19Now therefore, O Yahweh our God, save thou us, I beseech thee, out of his hand, that all the kingdoms of the earth may know that thou Yahweh art God alone.

20Then Isaiah the son of Amoz sent to Hezekiah, saying, Thus saith Yahweh, the God of Israel, Whereas thou hast prayed to me against Sennacherib king of Assyria, I have heard thee.

21This is the word that Yahweh hath spoken concerning him: The virgin daughter of Zion hath despised thee and laughed thee to scorn; the daughter of Jerusalem hath shaken her head at thee.

22Whom hast thou defied and blasphemed? and against whom hast thou exalted thy voice and lifted up thine eyes on high? even against the Holy One of Israel.

23By thy messengers thou hast defied the Lord, and hast said, With the multitude of my chariots am I come up to the height of the mountains, to the innermost parts of Lebanon; and I will cut down the tall cedars thereof, and the choice fir-trees thereof; and I will enter into his farthest lodging-place, the forest of his fruitful field.

24I have digged and drunk strange waters, and with the sole of my feet will I dry up all the rivers of Egypt.

25Hast thou not heard how I have done it long ago, and formed it of ancient times? now have I brought it to pass, that it should be thine to lay waste fortified cities into ruinous heaps.

26Therefore their inhabitants were of small power, they were dismayed and confounded; they were as the grass of the field, and as the green herb, as the grass on the housetops, and as grain blasted before it is grown up.

27But I know thy sitting down, and thy going out, and thy coming in, and thy raging against me.

28Because of thy raging against me, and because thine arrogancy is come up into mine ears, therefore will I put my hook in thy nose, and my bridle in thy lips, and I will turn thee back by the way by which thou camest.

29And this shall be the sign unto thee: Ye shall eat this year that which groweth of itself, and in the second year that which springeth of the same; and in the third year sow ye, and reap, and plant vineyards, and eat the fruit thereof.

30And the remnant that is escaped of the house of Judah shall again take root downward, and bear fruit upward.

31For out of Jerusalem shall go forth a remnant, and out of mount Zion they that shall escape: the zeal of Yahweh shall perform this.

32Therefore thus saith Yahweh concerning the king of Assyria, He shall not come unto this city, nor shoot an arrow there, neither shall he come before it with shield, nor cast up a mound against it.

33By the way that he came, by the same shall he return, and he shall not come unto this city, saith Yahweh.

34For I will defend this city to save it, for mine own sake, and for my servant David's sake.

35And it came to pass that night, that the angel of Yahweh went forth, and smote in the camp of the Assyrians a hundred fourscore and five thousand: and when men arose early in the morning, behold, these were all dead bodies.

36So Sennacherib king of Assyria departed, and went and returned, and dwelt at Nineveh.

37And it came to pass, as he was worshipping in the house of Nisroch his god, that Adrammelech and Sharezer smote him with the sword: and they escaped into the land of Ararat. And Esar-haddon his son reigned in his stead.

Chapter 20

1In those days was Hezekiah sick unto death. And Isaiah the prophet the son of Amoz came to him, and said unto him, Thus saith Yahweh, Set thy house in order: for thou shalt die, and not live.

2Then he turned his face to the wall, and prayed unto Yahweh, saying,

3Remember now, O Yahweh, I beseech thee, how I have walked before thee in truth and with a perfect heart, and have done that which is good in thy sight. And Hezekiah wept sore.

4And it came to pass, before Isaiah was gone out into the middle part of the city, that the word of Yahweh came to him, saying,

5Turn back, and say to Hezekiah the prince of my people, Thus saith Yahweh, the God of David thy father, I have heard thy prayer, I have seen thy tears: behold, I will heal thee; on the third day thou shalt go up unto the house of Yahweh.

6And I will add unto thy days fifteen years; and I will deliver thee and this city out of the hand of the king of Assyria; and I will defend this city for mine own sake, and for my servant David's sake.

7And Isaiah said, Take a cake of figs. And they took and laid it on the boil, and he recovered.

8And Hezekiah said unto Isaiah, What shall be the sign that Yahweh will heal me, and that I shall go up unto the house of Yahweh the third day?

9And Isaiah said, This shall be the sign unto thee from Yahweh, that Yahweh will do the thing that he hath spoken: shall the shadow go forward ten steps, or go back ten steps?

10And Hezekiah answered, It is a light thing for the shadow to decline ten steps: nay, but let the shadow return backward ten steps.

11And Isaiah the prophet cried unto Yahweh; and he brought the shadow ten steps backward, by which it had gone down on the dial of Ahaz.

12At that time Berodach-baladan the son of Baladan, king of Babylon, sent letters and a present unto Hezekiah; for he had heard that Hezekiah had been sick.

13And Hezekiah hearkened unto them, and showed them all the house of his precious things, the silver, and the gold, and the spices, and the precious oil, and the house of his armor, and all that was found in his treasures: there was nothing in his house, nor in all his dominion, that Hezekiah showed them not.

14Then came Isaiah the prophet unto king Hezekiah, and said unto him, What said these men? and from whence came they unto thee? And Hezekiah said, They are come from a far country, even from Babylon.

15And he said, What have they seen in thy house? And Hezekiah answered, All that is in my house have they seen: there is nothing among my treasures that I have not showed them.

16And Isaiah said unto Hezekiah, Hear the word of Yahweh.

17Behold, the days come, that all that is in thy house, and that which thy fathers have laid up in store unto this day, shall be carried to Babylon: nothing shall be left, saith Yahweh.

18And of thy sons that shall issue from thee, whom thou shalt beget, shall they take away; and they shall be eunuchs in the palace of the king of Babylon.

19Then said Hezekiah unto Isaiah, Good is the word of Yahweh which thou hast spoken. He said moreover, Is it not so, if peace and truth shall be in my days?

20Now the rest of the acts of Hezekiah, and all his might, and how he made the pool, and the conduit, and brought water into the city, are they not written in the book of the chronicles of the kings of Judah?

21And Hezekiah slept with his fathers; and Manasseh his son reigned in his stead.

Chapter 21

1Manasseh was twelve years old when he began to reign; and he reigned five and fifty years in Jerusalem: and his mother's name was Hephzibah.

2And he did that which was evil in the sight of Yahweh, after the abominations of the nations whom Yahweh cast out before the children of Israel.

3For he built again the high places which Hezekiah his father had destroyed; and he reared up altars for Baal, and made an Asherah, as did Ahab king of Israel, and worshipped all the host of heaven, and served them.

4And he built altars in the house of Yahweh, whereof Yahweh said, In Jerusalem will I put my name.

5And he built altars for all the host of heaven in the two courts of the house of Yahweh.

6And he made his son to pass through the fire, and practised augury, and used enchantments, and dealt with them that had familiar spirits, and with wizards: he wrought much evil in the sight of Yahweh, to provoke him to anger.

7And he set the graven image of Asherah, that he had made, in the house of which Yahweh said to David and to Solomon his son, In this house, and in Jerusalem, which I have chosen out of all the tribes of Israel, will I put my name for ever;

8neither will I cause the feet of Israel to wander any more out of the land which I gave their fathers, if only they will observe to do according to all that I have commanded them, and according to all the law that my servant Moses commanded them.

9But they hearkened not: and Manasseh seduced them to do that which is evil more than did the nations whom Yahweh destroyed before the children of Israel.

10And Yahweh spake by his servants the prophets, saying,

11Because Manasseh king of Judah hath done these abominations, and hath done wickedly above all that the Amorites did, that were before him, and hath made Judah also to sin with his idols;

12therefore thus saith Yahweh, the God of Israel, Behold, I bring such evil upon Jerusalem and Judah, that whosoever heareth of it, both his ears shall tingle.

13And I will stretch over Jerusalem the line of Samaria, and the plummet of the house of Ahab; and I will wipe Jerusalem as a man wipeth a dish, wiping it and turning it upside down.

14And I will cast off the remnant of mine inheritance, and deliver them into the hand of their enemies; and they shall become a prey and a spoil to all their enemies;

15because they have done that which is evil in my sight, and have provoked me to anger, since the day their fathers came forth out of Egypt, even unto this day.

16Moreover Manasseh shed innocent blood very much, till he had filled Jerusalem from one end to another; besides his sin wherewith he made Judah to sin, in doing that which was evil in the sight of Yahweh.

17Now the rest of the acts of Manasseh, and all that he did, and his sin that he sinned, are they not written in the book of the chronicles of the kings of Judah?

18And Manasseh slept with his fathers, and was buried in the garden of his own house, in the garden of Uzza: and Amon his son reigned in his stead.

19Amon was twenty and two years old when he began to reign; and he reigned two years in Jerusalem: and his mother's name was Meshullemeth the daughter of Haruz of Jotbah.

20And he did that which was evil in the sight of Yahweh, as did Manasseh his father.

21And he walked in all the way that his father walked in, and served the idols that his father served, and worshipped them:

22and he forsook Yahweh, the God of his fathers, and walked not in the way of Yahweh.

23And the servants of Amon conspired against him, and put the king to death in his own house.

24But the people of the land slew all them that had conspired against king Amon; and the people of the land made Josiah his son king in his stead.

25Now the rest of the acts of Amon which he did, are they not written in the book of the chronicles of the kings of Judah?

26And he was buried in his sepulchre in the garden of Uzza: and Josiah his son reigned in his stead.

Chapter 22

1Josiah was eight years old when he began to reign; and he reigned thirty and one years in Jerusalem: and his mother's name was Jedidah the daughter of Adaiah of Bozkath.

2And he did that which was right in the eyes of Yahweh, and walked in all the way of David his father, and turned not aside to the right hand or to the left.

3And it came to pass in the eighteenth year of king Josiah, that the king sent Shaphan, the son of Azaliah the son of Meshullam, the scribe, to the house of Yahweh, saying,

4Go up to Hilkiah the high priest, that he may sum the money which is brought into the house of Yahweh, which the keepers of the threshold have gathered of the people:

5and let them deliver it into the hand of the workmen that have the oversight of the house of Yahweh; and let them give it to the workmen that are in the house of Yahweh, to repair the breaches of the house,

6unto the carpenters, and to the builders, and to the masons, and for buying timber and hewn stone to repair the house.

7Howbeit there was no reckoning made with them of the money that was delivered into their hand; for they dealt faithfully.

8And Hilkiah the high priest said unto Shaphan the scribe, I have found the book of the law in the house of Yahweh. And Hilkiah delivered the book to Shaphan, and he read it.

9And Shaphan the scribe came to the king, and brought the king word again, and said, Thy servants have emptied out the money that was found in the house, and have delivered it into the hand of the workmen that have the oversight of the house of Yahweh.

10And Shaphan the scribe told the king, saying, Hilkiah the priest hath delivered me a book. And Shaphan read it before the king.

11And it came to pass, when the king had heard the words of the book of the law, that he rent his clothes.

12And the king commanded Hilkiah the priest, and Ahikam the son of Shaphan, and Achbor the son of Micaiah, and Shaphan the scribe, and Asaiah the king's servant, saying,

13Go ye, inquire of Yahweh for me, and for the people, and for all Judah, concerning the words of this book that is found; for great is the wrath of Yahweh that is kindled against us, because our fathers have not hearkened unto the words of this book, to do according unto all that which is written concerning us.

14So Hilkiah the priest, and Ahikam, and Achbor, and Shaphan, and Asaiah, went unto Huldah the prophetess, the wife of Shallum the son of Tikvah, the son of Harhas, keeper of the wardrobe (now she dwelt in Jerusalem in the second quarter); and they communed with her.

15And she said unto them, Thus saith Yahweh, the God of Israel: Tell ye the man that sent you unto me,

16Thus saith Yahweh, Behold, I will bring evil upon this place, and upon the inhabitants thereof, even all the words of the book which the king of Judah hath read.

17Because they have forsaken me, and have burned incense unto other gods, that they might provoke me to anger with all the work of their hands, therefore my wrath shall be kindled against this place, and it shall not be quenched.

18But unto the king of Judah, who sent you to inquire of Yahweh, thus shall ye say to him, Thus saith Yahweh, the God of Israel: As touching the words which thou hast heard,

19because thy heart was tender, and thou didst humble thyself before Yahweh, when thou heardest what I spake against this place, and against the inhabitants thereof, that they should become a desolation and a curse, and hast rent thy clothes, and wept before me; I also have heard thee, saith Yahweh.

20Therefore, behold, I will gather thee to thy fathers, and thou shalt be gathered to thy grave in peace, neither shall thine eyes see all the evil which I will bring upon this place. And they brought the king word again.

Chapter 23

1And the king sent, and they gathered unto him all the elders of Judah and of Jerusalem.

2And the king went up to the house of Yahweh, and all the men of Judah and all the inhabitants of Jerusalem with him, and the priests, and the prophets, and all the people, both small and great: and he read in their ears all the words of the book of the covenant which was found in the house of Yahweh.

3And the king stood by the pillar, and made a covenant before Yahweh, to walk after Yahweh, and to keep his commandments, and his testimonies, and his statutes, with all his heart, and all his soul, to confirm the words of this covenant that were written in this book: and all the people stood to the covenant.

4And the king commanded Hilkiah the high priest, and the priests of the second order, and the keepers of the threshold, to bring forth out of the temple of Yahweh all the vessels that were made for Baal, and for the Asherah, and for all the host of heaven, and he burned them without Jerusalem in the fields of the Kidron, and carried the ashes of them unto Beth-el.

5And he put down the idolatrous priests, whom the kings of Judah had ordained to burn incense in the high places in the cities of Judah, and in the places round about Jerusalem; them also that burned incense unto Baal, to the sun, and to the moon, and to the planets, and to all the host of heaven.

6And he brought out the Asherah from the house of Yahweh, without Jerusalem, unto the brook Kidron, and burned it at the brook Kidron, and beat it to dust, and cast the dust thereof upon the graves of the common people.

7And he brake down the houses of the sodomites, that were in the house of Yahweh, where the women wove hangings for the Asherah.

8And he brought all the priests out of the cities of Judah, and defiled the high places where the priests had burned incense, from Geba to Beer-sheba; and he brake down the high places of the gates that were at the entrance of the gate of Joshua the governor of the city, which were on a man's left hand at the gate of the city.

9Nevertheless the priests of the high places came not up to the altar of Yahweh in Jerusalem, but they did eat unleavened bread among their brethren.

10And he defiled Topheth, which is in the valley of the children of Hinnom, that no man might make his son or his daughter to pass through the fire to Molech.

11And he took away the horses that the kings of Judah had given to the sun, at the entrance of the house of Yahweh, by the chamber of Nathan-melech the chamberlain, which was in the precincts; and he burned the chariots of the sun with fire.

12And the altars that were on the roof of the upper chamber of Ahaz, which the kings of Judah had made, and the altars which Manasseh had made in the two courts of the house of Yahweh, did the king break down, and beat them down from thence, and cast the dust of them into the brook Kidron.

13And the high places that were before Jerusalem, which were on the right hand of the mount of corruption, which Solomon the king of Israel had builded for Ashtoreth the abomination of the Sidonians, and for Chemosh the abomination of Moab, and for Milcom the abomination of the children of Ammon, did the king defile.

14And he brake in pieces the pillars, and cut down the Asherim, and filled their places with the bones of men.

15Moreover the altar that was at Beth-el, and the high place which Jeroboam the son of Nebat, who made Israel to sin, had made, even that altar and the high place he brake down; and he burned the high place and beat it to dust, and burned the Asherah.

16And as Josiah turned himself, he spied the sepulchres that were there in the mount; and he sent, and took the bones out of the sepulchres, and burned them upon the altar, and defiled it, according to the word of Yahweh which the man of God proclaimed, who proclaimed these things.

17Then he said, What monument is that which I see? And the men of the city told him, It is the sepulchre of the man of God, who came from Judah, and proclaimed these things that thou hast done against the altar of Beth-el.

18And he said, Let him be; let no man move his bones. So they let his bones alone, with the bones of the prophet that came out of Samaria.

19And all the houses also of the high places that were in the cities of Samaria, which the kings of Israel had made to provoke Yahweh to anger, Josiah took away, and did to them according to all the acts that he had done in Beth-el.

20And he slew all the priests of the high places that were there, upon the altars, and burned men's bones upon them; and he returned to Jerusalem.

21And the king commanded all the people, saying, Keep the passover unto Yahweh your God, as it is written in this book of the covenant.

22Surely there was not kept such a passover from the days of the judges that judged Israel, nor in all the days of the kings of Israel, nor of the kings of Judah;

23but in the eighteenth year of king Josiah was this passover kept to Yahweh in Jerusalem.

24Moreover them that had familiar spirits, and the wizards, and the teraphim, and the idols, and all the abominations that were seen in the land of Judah and in Jerusalem, did Josiah put away, that he might confirm the words of the law which were written in the book that Hilkiah the priest found in the house of Yahweh.

25And like unto him was there no king before him, that turned to Yahweh with all his heart, and with all his soul, and with all his might, according to all the law of Moses; neither after him arose there any like him.

26Notwithstanding, Yahweh turned not from the fierceness of his great wrath, wherewith his anger was kindled against Judah, because of all the provocations wherewith Manasseh had provoked him.

27And Yahweh said, I will remove Judah also out of my sight, as I have removed Israel, and I will cast off this city which I have chosen, even Jerusalem, and the house of which I said, My name shall be there.

28Now the rest of the acts of Josiah, and all that he did, are they not written in the book of the chronicles of the kings of Judah?

29In his days Pharaoh-necoh king of Egypt went up against the king of Assyria to the river Euphrates: and king Josiah went against him; and Pharaoh-necoh slew him at Megiddo, when he had seen him.

30And his servants carried him in a chariot dead from Megiddo, and brought him to Jerusalem, and buried him in his own sepulchre. And the people of the land took Jehoahaz the son of Josiah, and anointed him, and made him king in his father's stead.

31Jehoahaz was twenty and three years old when he began to reign; and he reigned three months in Jerusalem: and his mother's name was Hamutal the daughter of Jeremiah of Libnah.

32And he did that which was evil in the sight of Yahweh, according to all that his fathers had done.

33And Pharaoh-necoh put him in bonds at Riblah in the land of Hamath, that he might not reign in Jerusalem; and put the land to a tribute of a hundred talents of silver, and a talent of gold.

34And Pharaoh-necoh made Eliakim the son of Josiah king in the room of Josiah his father, and changed his name to Jehoiakim: but he took Jehoahaz away; and he came to Egypt, and died there.

35And Jehoiakim gave the silver and the gold to Pharaoh; but he taxed the land to give the money according to the commandment of Pharaoh: he exacted the silver and the gold of the people of the land, of every one according to his taxation, to give it unto Pharaoh-necoh.

36Jehoiakim was twenty and five years old when he began to reign; and he reigned eleven years in Jerusalem: and his mother's name was Zebidah the daughter of Pedaiah of Rumah.

37And he did that which was evil in the sight of Yahweh, according to all that his fathers had done.

Chapter 24

1In his days Nebuchadnezzar king of Babylon came up, and Jehoiakim became his servant three years: then he turned and rebelled against him.

2And Yahweh sent against him bands of the Chaldeans, and bands of the Syrians, and bands of the Moabites, and bands of the children of Ammon, and sent them against Judah to destroy it, according to the word of Yahweh, which he spake by his servants the prophets.

3Surely at the commandment of Yahweh came this upon Judah, to remove them out of his sight, for the sins of Manasseh, according to all that he did,

4and also for the innocent blood that he shed; for he filled Jerusalem with innocent blood: and Yahweh would not pardon.

5Now the rest of the acts of Jehoiakim, and all that he did, are they not written in the book of the chronicles of the kings of Judah?

6So Jehoiakim slept with his fathers; and Jehoiachin his son reigned in his stead.

7And the king of Egypt came not again any more out of his land; for the king of Babylon had taken, from the brook of Egypt unto the river Euphrates, all that pertained to the king of Egypt.

8Jehoiachin was eighteen years old when he began to reign; and he reigned in Jerusalem three months: and his mother's name was Nehushta the daughter of Elnathan of Jerusalem.

9And he did that which was evil in the sight of Yahweh, according to all that his father had done.

10At that time the servants of Nebuchadnezzar king of Babylon came up to Jerusalem, and the city was besieged.

11And Nebuchadnezzar king of Babylon came unto the city, while his servants were besieging it;

12and Jehoiachin the king of Judah went out to the king of Babylon, he, and his mother, and his servants, and his princes, and his officers: and the king of Babylon took him in the eighth year of his reign.

13And he carried out thence all the treasures of the house of Yahweh, and the treasures of the king's house, and cut in pieces all the vessels of gold, which Solomon king of Israel had made in the temple of Yahweh, as Yahweh had said.

14And he carried away all Jerusalem, and all the princes, and all the mighty men of valor, even ten thousand captives, and all the craftsmen and the smiths; none remained, save the poorest sort of the people of the land.

15And he carried away Jehoiachin to Babylon; and the king's mother, and the king's wives, and his officers, and the chief men of the land, carried he into captivity from Jerusalem to Babylon.

16And all the men of might, even seven thousand, and the craftsmen and the smiths a thousand, all of them strong and apt for war, even them the king of Babylon brought captive to Babylon.

17And the king of Babylon made Mattaniah, Jehoiachin's father's brother, king is his stead, and changed his name to Zedekiah.

18Zedekiah was twenty and one years old when he began to reign; and he reigned eleven years in Jerusalem: and his mother's name was Hamutal the daughter of Jeremiah of Libnah.

19And he did that which was evil in the sight of Yahweh, according to all that Jehoiakim had done.

20For through the anger of Yahweh did it come to pass in Jerusalem and Judah, until he had cast them out from his presence. And Zedekiah rebelled against the king of Babylon.

Chapter 25

1And it came to pass in the ninth year of his reign, in the tenth month, in the tenth day of the month, that Nebuchadnezzar king of Babylon came, he and all his army, against Jerusalem, and encamped against it; and they built forts against it round about.

2So the city was besieged unto the eleventh year of king Zedekiah.

3On the ninth day of the fourth month the famine was sore in the city, so that there was no bread for the people of the land.

4Then a breach was made in the city, and all the men of war fled by night by the way of the gate between the two walls, which was by the king's garden (now the Chaldeans were against the city round about); and the king went by the way of the Arabah.

5But the army of the Chaldeans pursued after the king, and overtook him in the plains of Jericho; and all his army was scattered from him.

6Then they took the king, and carried him up unto the king of Babylon to Riblah; and they gave judgment upon him.

7And they slew the sons of Zedekiah before his eyes, and put out the eyes of Zedekiah, and bound him in fetters, and carried him to Babylon.

8Now in the fifth month, on the seventh day of the month, which was the nineteenth year of king Nebuchadnezzar, king of Babylon, came Nebuzaradan the captain of the guard, a servant of the king of Babylon, unto Jerusalem.

9And he burnt the house of Yahweh, and the king's house; and all the houses of Jerusalem, even every great house, burnt he with fire.

10And all the army of the Chaldeans, that were with the captain of the guard, brake down the walls of Jerusalem round about.

11And the residue of the people that were left in the city, and those that fell away, that fell to the king of Babylon, and the residue of the multitude, did Nebuzaradan the captain of the guard carry away captive.

12But the captain of the guard left of the poorest of the land to be vinedressers and husbandmen.

13And the pillars of brass that were in the house of Yahweh, and the bases and the brazen sea that were in the house of Yahweh, did the Chaldeans break in pieces, and carried the brass of them to Babylon.

14And the pots, and the shovels, and the snuffers, and the spoons, and all the vessels of brass wherewith they ministered, took they away.

15And the firepans, and the basins, that which was of gold, in gold, and that which was of silver, in silver, the captain of the guard took away.

16The two pillars, the one sea, and the bases, which Solomon had made for the house of Yahweh, the brass of all these vessels was without weight.

17The height of the one pillar was eighteen cubits, and a capital of brass was upon it; and the height of the capital was three cubits, with network and pomegranates upon the capital round about, all of brass: and like unto these had the second pillar with network.

18And the captain of the guard took Seraiah the chief priest, and Zephaniah the second priest, and the three keepers of the threshold:

19and out of the city he took an officer that was set over the men of war; and five men of them that saw the king's face, who were found in the city; and the scribe, the captain of the host, who mustered the people of the land; and threescore men of the people of the land, that were found in the city.

20And Nebuzaradan the captain of the guard took them, and brought them to the king of Babylon to Riblah.

21And the king of Babylon smote them, and put them to death at Riblah in the land of Hamath. So Judah was carried away captive out of his land.

22And as for the people that were left in the land of Judah, whom Nebuchadnezzar king of Babylon had left, even over them he made Gedaliah the son of Ahikam, the son of Shaphan, governor.

23Now when all the captains of the forces, they and their men, heard that the king of Babylon had made Gedaliah governor, they came to Gedaliah to Mizpah, even Ishmael the son of Nethaniah, and Johanan the son of Kareah, and Seraiah the son of Tanhumeth the Netophathite, and Jaazaniah the son of the Maacathite, they and their men.

24And Gedaliah sware to them and to their men, and said unto them, Fear not because of the servants of the Chaldeans: dwell in the land, and serve the king of Babylon, and it shall be well with you.

25But it came to pass in the seventh month, that Ishmael the son of Nethaniah, the son of Elishama, of the seed royal, came, and ten men with him, and smote Gedaliah, so that he died, and the Jews and the Chaldeans that were with him at Mizpah.

26And all the people, both small and great, and the captains of the forces, arose, and came to Egypt; for they were afraid of the Chaldeans.

27And it came to pass in the seven and thirtieth year of the captivity of Jehoiachin king of Judah, in the twelfth month, on the seven and twentieth day of the month, that Evil-merodach king of Babylon, in the year that he began to reign,

Second Kings

did lift up the head of Jehoiachin king of Judah out of prison; 28and he spake kindly to him, and set his throne above the throne of the kings that were with him in Babylon, 29and changed his prison garments. And Jehoiachin did eat bread before him continually all the days of his life: 30and for his allowance, there was a continual allowance given him of the king, every day a portion, all the days of his life.

The First Book of the Chronicles

Chapter 1

1 Adam, Seth, Enosh,
2 Kenan, Mahalalel, Jared,
3 Enoch, Methuselah, Lamech,
4 Noah, Shem, Ham, and Japheth.
5 The sons of Japheth: Gomer, and Magog, and Madai, and Javan, and Tubal, and Meshech, and Tiras.
6 And the sons of Gomer: Ashkenaz, and Diphath, and Togarmah.
7 And the sons of Javan: Elishah, and Tarshish, Kittim, and Rodanim.
8 The sons of Ham: Cush, and Mizraim, Put, and Canaan.
9 And the sons of Cush: Seba, and Havilah, and Sabta, and Raama, and Sabteca. And the sons of Raamah: Sheba, and Dedan.
10 And Cush begat Nimrod; he began to be a mighty one in the earth.
11 And Mizraim begat Ludim, and Anamim, and Lehabim, and Naphtuhim,
12 and Pathrusim, and Casluhim (from whence came the Philistines), and Caphtorim.
13 And Canaan begat Sidon his first-born, and Heth,
14 and the Jebusite, and the Amorite, and the Girgashite,
15 and the Hivite, and the Arkite, and the Sinite,
16 and the Arvadite, and the Zemarite, and the Hamathite.
17 The sons of Shem: Elam, and Asshur, and Arpachshad, and Lud, and Aram, and Uz, and Hul, and Gether, and Meshech.
18 And Arpachshad begat Shelah, and Shelah begat Eber.
19 And unto Eber were born two sons: the name of the one was Peleg; for in his days the earth was divided; and his brother's name was Joktan.
20 And Joktan begat Almodad, and Sheleph, and Hazarmaveth, and Jerah,
21 and Hadoram, and Uzal, and Diklah,
22 and Ebal, and Abimael, and Sheba,
23 and Ophir, and Havilah, and Jobab. All these were the sons of Joktan.
24 Shem, Arpachshad, Shelah,
25 Eber, Peleg, Reu,
26 Serug, Nahor, Terah,
27 Abram (the same is Abraham).
28 The sons of Abraham: Isaac, and Ishmael.
29 These are their generations: the first-born of Ishmael, Nebaioth; then Kedar, and Adbeel, and Mibsam,
30 Mishma, and Dumah, Massa, Hadad, and Tema,
31 Jetur, Naphish, and Kedemah. These are the sons of Ishmael.
32 And the sons of Keturah, Abraham's concubine: she bare Zimran, and Jokshan, and Medan, and Midian, and Ishbak, and Shuah. And the sons of Jokshan: Sheba, and Dedan.
33 And the sons of Midian: Ephah, and Epher, and Hanoch, and Abida, and Eldaah. All these were the sons of Keturah.
34 And Abraham begat Isaac. The sons of Isaac: Esau, and Israel.
35 The sons of Esau: Eliphaz, Reuel, and Jeush, and Jalam, and Korah.
36 The sons of Eliphaz: Teman, and Omar, Zephi, and Gatam, Kenaz, and Timna, and Amalek.
37 The sons of Reuel: Nahath, Zerah, Shammah, and Mizzah.
38 And the sons of Seir: Lotan, and Shobal, and Zibeon, and Anah, and Dishon, and Ezer, and Dishan.
39 And the sons of Lotan: Hori, and Homam; and Timna was Lotan's sister.
40 The sons of Shobal: Alian, and Manahath, and Ebal, Shephi, and Onam. And the sons of Zibeon: Aiah, and Anah.
41 The sons of Anah: Dishon. And the sons of Dishon: Hamran, and Eshban, and Ithran, and Cheran.
42 The sons of Ezer: Bilhan, and Zaavan, Jaakan. The sons of Dishan: Uz, and Aran.
43 Now these are the kings that reigned in the land of Edom, before there reigned any king over the children of Israel: Bela the son of Beor; and the name of his city was Dinhabah.
44 And Bela died, and Jobab the son of Zerah of Bozrah reigned in his stead.
45 And Jobab died, and Husham of the land of the Temanites reigned in his stead.
46 And Husham died, and Hadad the son of Bedad, who smote Midian in the field of Moab, reigned in his stead; and the name of his city was Avith.
47 And Hadad died, and Samlah of Masrekah reigned in his stead.
48 And Samlah died, and Shaul of Rehoboth by the River reigned in his stead.
49 And Shaul died, and Baal-hanan the son of Achbor reigned in his stead.
50 And Baal-hanan died, and Hadad reigned in his stead; and the name of his city was Pai: and his wife's name was Mehetabel, the daughter of Matred, the daughter of Me-zahab.
51 And Hadad died.
And the chiefs of Edom were: chief Timna, chief Aliah, chief Jetheth,
52 chief Oholibamah, chief Elah, chief Pinon,
53 chief Kenaz, chief Teman, chief Mibzar,
54 chief Magdiel, chief Iram. These are the chiefs of Edom.

Chapter 2

1 These are the sons of Israel: Reuben, Simeon, Levi, and Judah, Issachar, and Zebulun,
2 Dan, Joseph, and Benjamin, Naphtali, Gad, and Asher.
3 The sons of Judah: Er, and Onan, and Shelah; which three were born unto him of Shua's daughter the Canaanitess. And Er, Judah's first-born, was wicked in the sight of Yahweh; and he slew him.
4 And Tamar his daughter-in-law bare him Perez and Zerah. All the sons of Judah were five.
5 The sons of Perez: Hezron, and Hamul.
6 And the sons of Zerah: Zimri, and Ethan, and Heman, and Calcol, and Dara; five of them in all.
7 And the sons of Carmi: Achar, the troubler of Israel, who committed a trespass in the devoted thing.
8 And the sons of Ethan: Azariah.
9 The sons also of Hezron, that were born unto him: Jerahmeel, and Ram, and Chelubai.
10 And Ram begat Amminadab, and Amminadab begat Nahshon, prince of the children of Judah;
11 and Nahshon begat Salma, and Salma begat Boaz,
12 and Boaz begat Obed, and Obed begat Jesse;
13 and Jesse begat his first-born Eliab, and Abinadab the second, and Shimea the third,
14 Nethanel the fourth, Raddai the fifth,
15 Ozem the sixth, David the seventh;
16 and their sisters were Zeruiah and Abigail. And the sons of Zeruiah: Abishai, and Joab, and Asahel, three.
17 And Abigail bare Amasa; and the father of Amasa was Jether the Ishmaelite.
18 And Caleb the son of Hezron begat children of Azubah his wife, and of Jerioth; and these were her sons: Jesher, and Shobab, and Ardon.
19 And Azubah died, and Caleb took unto him Ephrath, who bare him Hur.
20 And Hur begat Uri, and Uri begat Bezalel.
21 And afterward Hezron went in to the daughter of Machir the father of Gilead, whom he took to wife when he was threescore years old; and she bare him Segub.
22 And Segub begat Jair, who had three and twenty cities in the land of Gilead.
23 And Geshur and Aram took the towns of Jair from them, with Kenath, and the villages thereof, even threescore cities. All these were the sons of Machir the father of Gilead.
24 And after that Hezron was dead in Caleb-ephrathah, then Abijah Hezron's wife bare him Ashhur the father of Tekoa.
25 And the sons of Jerahmeel the first-born of Hezron were Ram the first-born, and Bunah, and Oren, and Ozem, Ahijah.
26 And Jerahmeel had another wife, whose name was Atarah; she was the mother of Onam.
27 And the sons of Ram the first-born of Jerahmeel were Maaz, and Jamin, and Eker.
28 And the sons of Onam were Shammai, and Jada. And the sons of Shammai: Nadab, and Abishur.
29 And the name of the wife of Abishur was Abihail; and she bare him Ahban, and Molid.
30 And the sons of Nadab: Seled, and Appaim; but Seled died without children.
31 And the sons of Appaim: Ishi. And the sons of Ishi: Sheshan. And the sons of Sheshan: Ahlai.
32 And the sons of Jada the brother of Shammai: Jether, and Jonathan; and Jether died without children.
33 And the sons of Jonathan: Peleth, and Zaza. These were the sons of Jerahmeel.
34 Now Sheshan had no sons, but daughters. And Sheshan had a servant, an Egyptian, whose name was Jarha.
35 And Sheshan gave his daughter to Jarha his servant to wife; and she bare him Attai.
36 And Attai begat Nathan, and Nathan begat Zabad,
37 and Zabad begat Ephlal, and Ephlal begat Obed,
38 and Obed begat Jehu, and Jehu begat Azariah,
39 and Azariah begat Helez, and Helez begat Eleasah,
40 and Eleasah begat Sismai, and Sismai begat Shallum,
41 and Shallum begat Jekamiah, and Jekamiah begat Elishama.
42 And the sons of Caleb the brother of Jerahmeel were Mesha his first-born, who was the father of Ziph; and the sons of Mareshah the father of Hebron.
43 And the sons of Hebron: Korah, and Tappuah, and Rekem, and Shema.
44 And Shema begat Raham, the father of Jorkeam; and Rekem begat Shammai.
45 And the son of Shammai was Maon; and Maon was the father of Beth-zur.
46 And Ephah, Caleb's concubine, bare Haran, and Moza, and Gazez; and Haran begat Gazez.
47 And the sons of Jahdai: Regem, and Jotham, and Geshan, and Pelet, and Ephah, and Shaaph.
48 Maacah, Caleb's concubine, bare Sheber and Tirhanah.
49 She bare also Shaaph the father of Madmannah, Sheva the father of Machbena, and the father of Gibea; and the daughter of Caleb was Achsah.
50 These were the sons of Caleb, the son of Hur, the first-born of Ephrathah: Shobal the father of Kiriath-jearim,
51 Salma the father of Beth-lehem, Hareph the father of Beth-gader.
52 And Shobal the father of Kiriath-jearim had sons: Haroeh, half of the Menuhoth.
53 And the families of Kiriath-jearim: The Ithrites, and the Puthites, and the Shumathites, and the Mishraites; of them came the Zorathites and the Eshtaolites.

First Chronicles

54The sons of Salma: Beth-lehem, and the Netophathites, Atroth-beth-joab, and half of the Manahathites, the Zorites.

55And the families of scribes that dwelt at Jabez: the Tirathites, the Shimeathites, the Sucathites. These are the Kenites that came of Hammath, the father of the house of Rechab.

Chapter 3

1Now these were the sons of David, that were born unto him in Hebron: the first-born, Amnon, of Ahinoam the Jezreelitess; the second, Daniel, of Abigail the Carmelitess;

2the third, Absalom the son of Maacah the daughter of Talmai king of Geshur; the fourth, Adonijah the son of Haggith;

3the fifth, Shephatiah of Abital; the sixth, Ithream by Eglah his wife:

4six were born unto him in Hebron; and there he reigned seven years and six months. And in Jerusalem he reigned thirty and three years;

5and these were born unto him in Jerusalem: Shimea, and Shobab, and Nathan, and Solomon, four, of Bath-shua the daughter of Ammiel;

6and Ibhar, and Elishama, and Eliphelet,

7and Nogah, and Nepheg, and Japhia,

8and Elishama, and Eliada, and Eliphelet, nine.

9All these were the sons of David, besides the sons of the concubines; and Tamar was their sister.

10And Solomon's son was Rehoboam, Abijah his son, Asa his son, Jehoshaphat his son,

11Joram his son, Ahaziah his son, Joash his son,

12Amaziah his son, Azariah his son, Jotham his son,

13Ahaz his son, Hezekiah his son, Manasseh his son,

14Amon his son, Josiah his son.

15And the sons of Josiah: the first-born Johanan, the second Jehoiakim, the third Zedekiah, the fourth Shallum.

16And the sons of Jehoiakim: Jeconiah his son, Zedekiah his son.

17And the sons of Jeconiah, the captive: Shealtiel his son,

18and Malchiram, and Pedaiah, and Shenazzar, Jekamiah, Hoshama, and Nedabiah.

19And the sons of Pedaiah: Zerubbabel, and Shimei. And the sons of Zerubbabel: Meshullam, and Hananiah; and Shelomith was their sister;

20and Hashubah, and Ohel, and Berechiah, and Hasadiah, Jushab-hesed, five.

21And the sons of Hananiah: Pelatiah, and Jeshaiah; the sons of Rephaiah, the sons of Arnan, the sons of Obadiah, the sons of Shecaniah.

22And the sons of Shecaniah: Shemaiah. And the sons of Shemaiah: Hattush, and Igal, and Bariah, and Neariah, and Shaphat, six.

23And the sons of Neariah: Elioenai, and Hizkiah, and Azrikam, three.

24And the sons of Elioenai: Hodaviah, and Eliashib, and Pelaiah, and Akkub, and Johanan, and Delaiah, and Anani, seven.

Chapter 4

1The sons of Judah: Perez, Hezron, and Carmi, and Hur, and Shobal.

2And Reaiah the son of Shobal begat Jahath; and Jahath begat Ahumai and Lahad. These are the families of the Zorathites.

3And these were the sons of the father of Etam: Jezreel, and Ishma, and Idbash; and the name of their sister was Hazzelelponi;

4and Penuel the father of Gedor, and Ezer the father of Hushah. These are the sons of Hur, the first-born of Ephrathah, the father of Beth-lehem.

5And Ashhur the father of Tekoa had two wives, Helah and Naarah.

6And Naarah bare him Ahuzzam, and Hepher, and Temeni, and Haahashtari. These were the sons of Naarah.

7And the sons of Helah were Zereth, Izhar, and Ethnan.

8And Hakkoz begat Anub, and Zobebah, and the families of Aharhel the son of Harum.

9And Jabez was more honorable than his brethren: and his mother called his name Jabez, saying, Because I bare him with sorrow.

10And Jabez called on the God of Israel, saying, Oh that thou wouldest bless me indeed, and enlarge my border, and that thy hand might be with me, and that thou wouldest keep me from evil, that it be not to my sorrow! And God granted him that which he requested.

11And Chelub the brother of Shuhah begat Mehir, who was the father of Eshton.

12And Eshton begat Beth-rapha, and Paseah, and Tehinnah the father of Ir-nahash. These are the men of Recah.

13And the sons of Kenaz: Othniel, and Seraiah. And the sons of Othniel: Hathath.

14And Meonothai begat Ophrah: and Seraiah begat Joab the father of Ge-harashim; for they were craftsmen.

15And the sons of Caleb the son of Jephunneh: Iru, Elah, and Naam; and the sons of Elah; and Kenaz.

16And the sons of Jehallelel: Ziph, and Ziphah, Tiria, and Asarel.

17And the sons of Ezrah: Jether, and Mered, and Epher, and Jalon; and she bare Miriam, and Shammai, and Ishbah the father of Eshtemoa.

18And his wife the Jewess bare Jered the father of Gedor, and Heber the father of Soco, and Jekuthiel the father of Zanoah. And these are the sons of Bithiah the daughter of Pharaoh, whom Mered took.

19And the sons of the wife of Hodiah, the sister of Naham, were the father of Keilah the Garmite, and Eshtemoa the Maacathite.

20And the sons of Shimon: Amnon, and Rinnah, Ben-hanan, and Tilon. And the sons of Ishi: Zoheth, and Ben-zoheth.

21The sons of Shelah the son of Judah: Er the father of Lecah, and Laadah the father of Mareshah, and the families of the house of them that wrought fine linen, of the house of Ashbea;

22and Jokim, and the men of Cozeba, and Joash, and Saraph, who had dominion in Moab, and Jashubilehem. And the records are ancient.

23These were the potters, and the inhabitants of Netaim and Gederah: there they dwelt with the king for his work.

24The sons of Simeon: Nemuel, and Jamin, Jarib, Zerah, Shaul;

25Shallum his son, Mibsam his son, Mishma his son.

26And the sons of Mishma: Hammuel his son, Zaccur his son, Shimei his son.

27And Shimei had sixteen sons and six daughters; but his brethren had not many children, neither did all their family multiply like to the children of Judah.

28And they dwelt at Beer-sheba, and Moladah, and Hazarshual,

29and at Bilhah, and at Ezem, and at Tolad,

30and at Bethuel, and at Hormah, and at Ziklag,

31and at Beth-marcaboth, and Hazar-susim, and at Beth-biri, and at Shaaraim. These were their cities unto the reign of David.

32And their villages were Etam, and Ain, Rimmon, and Tochen, and Ashan, five cities;

33and all their villages that were round about the same cities, unto Baal. These were their habitations, and they have their genealogy.

34And Meshobab, and Jamlech, and Joshah the son of Amaziah,

35and Joel, and Jehu the son of Joshibiah, the son of Seraiah, the son of Asiel,

36and Elioenai, and Jaakobah, and Jeshohaiah, and Asaiah, and Adiel, and Jesimiel, and Benaiah,

37and Ziza the son of Shiphi, the son of Allon, the son of Jedaiah, the son of Shimri, the son of Shemaiah-

38these mentioned by name were princes in their families: and their fathers' houses increased greatly.

39And they went to the entrance of Gedor, even unto the east side of the valley, to seek pasture for their flocks.

40And they found fat pasture and good, and the land was wide, and quiet, and peaceable; for they that dwelt there aforetime were of Ham.

41And these written by name came in the days of Hezekiah king of Judah, and smote their tents, and the Meunim that were found there, and destroyed them utterly unto this day, and dwelt in their stead; because there was pasture there for their flocks.

42And some of them, even of the sons of Simeon, five hundred men, went to mount Seir, having for their captains Pelatiah, and Neariah, and Rephaiah, and Uzziel, the sons of Ishi.

43And they smote the remnant of the Amalekites that escaped, and have dwelt there unto this day.

Chapter 5

1And the sons of Reuben the first-born of Israel (for he was the first-born; but, forasmuch as he defiled his father's couch, his birthright was given unto the sons of Joseph the son of Israel; and the genealogy is not to be reckoned after the birthright.

2For Judah prevailed above his brethren, and of him came the prince; but the birthright was Joseph's:)

3the sons of Reuben the first-born of Israel: Hanoch, and Pallu, Hezron, and Carmi.

4The sons of Joel: Shemaiah his son, Gog his son, Shimei his son,

5Micah his son, Reaiah his son, Baal his son,

6Beerah his son, whom Tilgath-pilneser king of Assyria carried away captive: he was prince of the Reubenites.

7And his brethren by their families, when the genealogy of their generations was reckoned: the chief, Jeiel, and Zechariah,

8and Bela the son of Azaz, the son of Shema, the son of Joel, who dwelt in Aroer, even unto Nebo and Baal-meon:

9and eastward he dwelt even unto the entrance of the wilderness from the river Euphrates, because their cattle were multiplied in the land of Gilead.

10And in the days of Saul, they made war with the Hagrites, who fell by their hand; and they dwelt in their tents throughout all the land east of Gilead.

11And the sons of Gad dwelt over against them, in the land of Bashan unto Salecah:

12Joel the chief, and Shapham the second, and Janai, and Shaphat in Bashan.

13And their brethren of their fathers' houses: Michael, and Meshullam, and Sheba, and Jorai, and Jacan, and Zia, and Eber, seven.

14These were the sons of Abihail, the son of Huri, the son of Jaroah, the son of Gilead, the son of Michael, the son of Jeshishai, the son of Jahdo, the son of Buz;

15Ahi the son of Abdiel, the son of Guni, chief of their fathers' houses.

16And they dwelt in Gilead in Bashan, and in its towns, and in all the suburbs of Sharon, as far as their borders.

17All these were reckoned by genealogies in the days of Jotham king of Judah, and in the days of Jeroboam king of Israel.

18The sons of Reuben, and the Gadites, and the half-tribe of Manasseh, of valiant men, men able to bear buckler and sword, and to shoot with bow, and skilful in war, were forty and four thousand seven hundred and threescore, that were able to go forth to war.

19And they made war with the Hagrites, with Jetur, and Naphish, and Nodab.

20And they were helped against them, and the Hagrites were delivered into their hand, and all that were with them; for they cried to God in the battle, and he was entreated of them, because they put their trust in him.

21And they took away their cattle; of their camels fifty thousand, and of sheep two hundred and fifty thousand, and of asses two thousand, and of men a hundred thousand.

22For there fell many slain, because the war was of God. And they dwelt in their stead until the captivity.

23And the children of the half-tribe of Manasseh dwelt in the land: they increased from Bashan unto Baal-hermon and Senir and mount Hermon.

24And these were the heads of their fathers' houses: even Epher, and Ishi, and Eliel, and Azriel, and Jeremiah, and Hodaviah, and Jahdiel, mighty men of valor, famous men, heads of their fathers' houses.

25And they trespassed against the God of their fathers, and played the harlot after the gods of the peoples of the land, whom God destroyed before them.

26And the God of Israel stirred up the spirit of Pul king of Assyria, and the spirit of Tilgath-pilneser king of Assyria, and he carried them away, even the Reubenites, and the Gadites, and the half-tribe of Manasseh, and brought them unto Halah, and Habor, and Hara, and to the river of Gozan, unto this day.

Chapter 6

1The sons of Levi: Gershon, Kohath, and Merari.

2And the sons of Kohath: Amram, Izhar, and Hebron, and Uzziel.

3And the children of Amram: Aaron, and Moses, and Miriam. And the sons of Aaron: Nadab, and Abihu, Eleazar, and Ithamar.

4Eleazar begat Phinehas, Phinehas begat Abishua,

5and Abishua begat Bukki, and Bukki begat Uzzi,

6and Uzzi begat Zerahiah, and Zerahiah begat Meraioth,

7Meraioth begat Amariah, and Amariah begat Ahitub,

8and Ahitub begat Zadok, and Zadok begat Ahimaaz,

9and Ahimaaz begat Azariah, and Azariah begat Johanan,

10and Johanan begat Azariah, (he it is that executed the priest's office in the house that Solomon built in Jerusalem),

11and Azariah begat Amariah, and Amariah begat Ahitub,

12and Ahitub begat Zadok, and Zadok begat Shallum,

13and Shallum begat Hilkiah, and Hilkiah begat Azariah,

14and Azariah begat Seraiah, and Seraiah begat Jehozadak;

15And Jehozadak went into captivity, when Yahweh carried away Judah and Jerusalem by the hand of Nebuchadnezzar.

16The sons of Levi: Gershom, Kohath, and Merari.

17And these are the names of the sons of Gershom: Libni and Shimei.

18And the sons of Kohath were Amram, and Izhar, and Hebron, and Uzziel.

19The sons of Merari: Mahli and Mushi. And these are the families of the Levites according to their fathers' houses.

20Of Gershom: Libni his son, Jahath his son, Zimmah his son,

21Joah his son, Iddo his son, Zerah his son, Jeatherai his son.

22The sons of Kohath: Amminadab his son, Korah his son, Assir his son,

23Elkanah his son, and Ebiasaph his son, and Assir his son,

24Tahath his son, Uriel his son, Uzziah his son, and Shaul his son.

25And the sons of Elkanah: Amasai, and Ahimoth.

26As for Elkanah, the sons of Elkanah: Zophai his son, and Nahath his son,

27Eliab his son, Jeroham his son, Elkanah his son.

28And the sons of Samuel: the first-born Joel, and the second Abijah.

29The sons of Merari: Mahli, Libni his son, Shimei his son, Uzzah his son,

30Shimea his son, Haggiah his son, Asaiah his son.

31And these are they whom David set over the service of song in the house of Yahweh, after that the ark had rest.

32And they ministered with song before the tabernacle of the tent of meeting, until Solomon had built the house of Yahweh in Jerusalem: and they waited on their office according to their order.

33And these are they that waited, and their sons. Of the sons of the Kohathites: Heman the singer, the son of Joel, the son of Samuel,

34the son of Elkanah, the son of Jeroham, the son of Eliel, the son of Toah,

35the son of Zuph, the son of Elkanah, the son of Mahath, the son of Amasai,

36the son of Elkanah, the son of Joel, the son of Azariah, the son of Zephaniah,

37the son of Tahath, the son of Assir, the son of Ebiasaph, the son of Korah,

38the son of Izhar, the son of Kohath, the son of Levi, the son of Israel.

39And his brother Asaph, who stood on his right hand, even Asaph the son of Berechiah, the son of Shimea,

40the son of Michael, the son of Baaseiah, the son of Malchijah,

41the son of Ethni, the son of Zerah, the son of Adaiah,

42the son of Ethan, the son of Zimmah, the son of Shimei,

43the son of Jahath, the son of Gershom, the son of Levi.

44And on the left hand their brethren the sons of Merari: Ethan the son of Kishi, the son of Abdi, the son of Malluch,

45the son of Hashabiah, the son of Amaziah, the son of Hilkiah,

46the son of Amzi, the son of Bani, the son of Shemer,

47the son of Mahli, the son of Mushi, the son of Merari, the son of Levi.

48And their brethren the Levites were appointed for all the service of the tabernacle of the house of God.

49But Aaron and his sons offered upon the altar of burnt-offering, and upon the altar of incense, for all the work of the most holy place, and to make atonement for Israel, according to all that Moses the servant of God had commanded.

50And these are the sons of Aaron: Eleazar his son, Phinehas his son, Abishua his son,

51Bukki his son, Uzzi his son, Zerahiah his son,

52Meraioth his son, Amariah his son, Ahitub his son,

53Zadok his son, Ahimaaz his son.

54Now these are their dwelling-places according to their encampments in their borders: to the sons of Aaron, of the families of the Kohathites (for theirs was the first lot),

55to them they gave Hebron in the land of Judah, and the suburbs thereof round about it;

56but the fields of the city, and the villages thereof, they gave to Caleb the son of Jephunneh.

57And to the sons of Aaron they gave the cities of refuge, Hebron; Libnah also with its suburbs, and Jattir, and Eshtemoa with its suburbs,

58and Hilen with its suburbs, Debir with its suburbs,

59and Ashan with its suburbs, and Beth-shemesh with its suburbs;

60and out of the tribe of Benjamin, Geba with its suburbs, and Allemeth with its suburbs, and Anathoth with its suburbs. All their cities throughout their families were thirteen cities.

61And unto the rest of the sons of Kohath were given by lot, out of the family of the tribe, out of the half-tribe, the half of Manasseh, ten cities.

62And to the sons of Gershom, according to their families, out of the tribe of Issachar, and out of the tribe of Asher, and out of the tribe of Naphtali, and out of the tribe of Manasseh in Bashan, thirteen cities.

63Unto the sons of Merari were given by lot, according to their families, out of the tribe of Reuben, and out of the tribe of Gad, and out of the tribe of Zebulun, twelve cities.

64And the children of Israel gave to the Levites the cities with their suburbs.

65And they gave by lot out of the tribe of the children of Judah, and out of the tribe of the children of Simeon, and out of the tribe of the children of Benjamin, these cities which are mentioned by name.

66And some of the families of the sons of Kohath had cities of their borders out of the tribe of Ephraim.

67And they gave unto them the cities of refuge, Shechem in the hill-country of Ephraim with its suburbs; Gezer also with its suburbs,

68and Jokmeam with its suburbs, and Beth-horon with its suburbs,

69and Aijalon with its suburbs, and Gath-rimmon with its suburbs;

70and out of the half-tribe of Manasseh, Aner with its suburbs, and Bileam with its suburbs, for the rest of the family of the sons of Kohath.

71Unto the sons of Gershom were given, out of the family of the half-tribe of Manasseh, Golan in Bashan with its suburbs, and Ashtaroth with its suburbs;

72and out of the tribe of Issachar, Kedesh with its suburbs, Daberath with its suburbs,

73and Ramoth with its suburbs, and Anem with its suburbs;

74and out of the tribe of Asher, Mashal with its suburbs, and Abdon with its suburbs,

75and Hukok with its suburbs, and Rehob with its suburbs;

76and out of the tribe of Naphtali, Kedesh in Galilee with its suburbs, and Hammon with its suburbs, and Kiriathaim with its suburbs.

77Unto the rest of the Levites, the sons of Merari, were given, out of the tribe of Zebulun, Rimmono with its suburbs, Tabor with its suburbs;

78and beyond the Jordan at Jericho, on the east side of the Jordan, were given them, out of the tribe of Reuben, Bezer in the wilderness with its suburbs, and Jahzah with its suburbs,

79and Kedemoth with its suburbs, and Mephaath with its suburbs;

80and out of the tribe of Gad, Ramoth in Gilead with its suburbs, and Mahanaim with its suburbs,

81and Heshbon with its suburbs, and Jazer with its suburbs.

Chapter 7

1And of the sons of Issachar: Tola, and Puah, Jashub, and Shimron, four.

2And the sons of Tola: Uzzi, and Rephaiah, and Jeriel, and Jahmai, and Ibsam, and Shemuel, heads of their fathers' houses, to wit, of Tola; mighty men of valor in their generations: their number in the days of David was two and twenty thousand and six hundred.

3And the sons of Uzzi: Izrahiah. And the sons of Izrahiah: Michael, and Obadiah, and Joel, Isshiah, five; all of them chief men.

4And with them, by their generations, after their fathers' houses, were bands of the host for war, six and thirty thousand; for they had many wives and sons.

5And their brethren among all the families of Issachar, mighty men of valor, reckoned in all by genealogy, were fourscore and seven thousand.

6The sons of Benjamin: Bela, and Becher, and Jediael, three.

7And the sons of Bela: Ezbon, and Uzzi, and Uzziel, and Jerimoth, and Iri, five; heads of fathers' houses, mighty men of valor; and they were reckoned by genealogy twenty and two thousand and thirty and four.

8And the sons of Becher: Zemirah, and Joash, and Eliezer, and Elioenai, and Omri, and Jeremoth, and Abijah, and Anathoth, and Alemeth. All these were the sons of Becher.

9And they were reckoned by genealogy, after their generations, heads of their fathers' houses, mighty men of valor, twenty thousand and two hundred.

10And the sons of Jediael: Bilhan. And the sons of Bilhan: Jeush, and Benjamin, and Ehud, and Chenaanah, and Zethan, and Tarshish, and Ahishahar.

11All these were sons of Jediael, according to the heads of their fathers' houses, mighty men of valor, seventeen thousand and two hundred, that were able to go forth in the host for war.

12Shuppim also, and Huppim, the sons of Ir, Hushim, the sons of Aher.

13The sons of Naphtali: Jahziel, and Guni, and Jezer, and Shallum, the sons of Bilhah.

14The sons of Manasseh: Asriel, whom his concubine the Aramitess bare: she bare Machir the father of Gilead:

15and Machir took a wife of Huppim and Shuppim, whose sister's name was Maacah; and the name of the second was Zelophehad: and Zelophehad had daughters.

16And Maacah the wife of Machir bare a son, and she called his name Peresh; and the name of his brother was Sheresh; and his sons were Ulam and Rakem.

17And the sons of Ulam: Bedan. These were the sons of Gilead the son of

First Chronicles

Machir, the son of Manasseh.

18 And his sister Hammolecheth bare Ishhod, and Abiezer, and Mahlah.

19 And the sons of Shemida were Ahian, and Shechem, and Likhi, and Aniam.

20 And the sons of Ephraim: Shuthelah, and Bered his son, and Tahath his son, and Eleadah his son, and Tahath his son,

21 and Zabad his son, and Shuthelah his son, and Ezer, and Elead, whom the men of Gath that were born in the land slew, because they came down to take away their cattle.

22 And Ephraim their father mourned many days, and his brethren came to comfort him.

23 And he went in to his wife, and she conceived, and bare a son, and he called his name Beriah, because it went evil with his house.

24 And his daughter was Sheerah, who built Beth-horon the nether and the upper, and Uzzen-sheerah.

25 And Rephah was his son, and Resheph, and Telah his son, and Tahan his son,

26 Ladan his son, Ammihud his son, Elishama his son,

27 Nun his son, Joshua his son.

28 And their possessions and habitations were Beth-el and the towns thereof; and eastward Naaran, and westward Gezer, with the towns thereof; Shechem also and the towns thereof, unto Azzah and the towns thereof;

29 and by the borders of the children of Manasseh, Beth-shean and its towns, Taanach and its towns, Megiddo and its towns, Dor and its towns. In these dwelt the children of Joseph the son of Israel.

30 The sons of Asher: Imnah, and Ishvah, and Ishvi, and Beriah, and Serah their sister.

31 And the sons of Beriah: Heber, and Malchiel, who was the father of Birzaith.

32 And Heber begat Japhlet, and Shomer, and Hotham, and Shua their sister.

33 And the sons of Japhlet: Pasach, and Bimhal, and Ashvath. These are the children of Japhlet.

34 And the sons of Shemer: Ahi, and Rohgah, Jehubbah, and Aram.

35 And the sons of Helem his brother: Zophah, and Imna, and Shelesh, and Amal.

36 The sons of Zophah: Suah, and Harnepher, and Shual, and Beri, and Imrah,

37 Bezer, and Hod, and Shamma, and Shilshah, and Ithran, and Beera.

38 And the sons of Jether: Jephunneh, and Pispa, and Ara.

39 And the sons of Ulla: Arah, and Hanniel, and Rizia.

40 All these were the children of Asher, heads of the fathers' houses, choice and mighty men of valor, chief of the princes. And the number of them reckoned by genealogy for service in war was twenty and six thousand men.

Chapter 8

1 And Benjamin begat Bela his first-born, Ashbel the second, and Aharah the third,

2 Nohah the fourth, and Rapha the fifth.

3 And Bela had sons: Addar, and Gera, and Abihud,

4 and Abishua, and Naaman, and Ahoah,

5 and Gera, and Shephuphan, and Huram.

6 And these are the sons of Ehud: these are the heads of fathers' houses of the inhabitants of Geba, and they carried them captive to Manahath:

7 and Naaman, and Ahijah, and Gera, he carried them captive: and he begat Uzza and Ahihud.

8 And Shaharaim begat children in the field of Moab, after he had sent them away; Hushim and Baara were his wives.

9 And he begat of Hodesh his wife, Jobab, and Zibia, and Mesha, and Malcam,

10 and Jeuz, and Shachia, and Mirmah. These were his sons, heads of fathers' houses.

11 And of Hushim he begat Abitub and Elpaal.

12 And the sons of Elpaal: Eber, and Misham, and Shemed, who built Ono and Lod, with the towns thereof;

13 and Beriah, and Shema, who were heads of fathers' houses of the inhabitants of Aijalon, who put to flight the inhabitants of Gath;

14 and Ahio, Shashak, and Jeremoth,

15 and Zebadiah, and Arad, and Eder,

16 and Michael, and Ishpah, and Joha, the sons of Beriah,

17 and Zebadiah, and Meshullam, and Hizki, and Heber,

18 and Ishmerai, and Izliah, and Jobab, the sons of Elpaal,

19 and Jakim, and Zichri, and Zabdi,

20 and Elienai, and Zillethai, and Eliel,

21 and Adaiah, and Beraiah, and Shimrath, the sons of Shimei,

22 and Ishpan, and Eber, and Eliel,

23 and Abdon, and Zichri, and Hanan,

24 and Hananiah, and Elam, and Anthothijah,

25 and Iphdeiah, and Penuel, the sons of Shashak,

26 and Shamsherai, and Shehariah, and Athaliah,

27 and Jaareshiah, and Elijah, and Zichri, the sons of Jeroham.

28 These were heads of fathers' houses throughout their generations, chief men: these dwelt in Jerusalem.

29 And in Gibeon there dwelt the father of Gibeon, Jeiel, whose wife's name was Maacah;

30 and his first-born son Abdon, and Zur, and Kish, and Baal, and Nadab,

31 and Gedor, and Ahio, and Zecher.

32 And Mikloth begat Shimeah. And they also dwelt with their brethren in Jerusalem, over against their brethren.

33 And Ner begat Kish; and Kish begat Saul; and Saul begat Jonathan, and Malchi-shua, and Abinadab, and Eshbaal.

34 And the son of Jonathan was Merib-baal; and Merib-baal begat Micah.

35 And the sons of Micah: Pithon, and Melech, and Tarea, and Ahaz.

36 And Ahaz begat Jehoaddah; and Jehoaddah begat Alemeth, and Azmaveth, and Zimri; and Zimri begat Moza.

37 And Moza begat Binea; Raphah was his son, Eleasah his son, Azel his son.

38 And Azel had six sons, whose names are these: Azrikam, Bocheru, and Ishmael, and Sheariah, and Obadiah, and Hanan. All these were the sons of Azel.

39 And the sons of Eshek his brother: Ulam his first-born, Jeush the second, and Eliphelet the third.

40 And the sons of Ulam were mighty men of valor, archers, and had many sons, and sons' sons, a hundred and fifty. All these were of the sons of Benjamin.

Chapter 9

1 So all Israel were reckoned by genealogies; and, behold, they are written in the book of the kings of Israel: and Judah was carried away captive to Babylon for their transgression.

2 Now the first inhabitants that dwelt in their possessions in their cities were Israel, the priests, the Levites, and the Nethinim.

3 And in Jerusalem dwelt of the children of Judah, and of the children of Benjamin, and of the children of Ephraim and Manasseh:

4 Uthai the son of Ammihud, the son of Omri, the son of Imri, the son of Bani, of the children of Perez the son of Judah.

5 And of the Shilonites: Asaiah the first-born, and his sons.

6 And of the sons of Zerah: Jeuel, and their brethren, six hundred and ninety.

7 And of the sons of Benjamin: Sallu the son of Meshullam, the son of Hodaviah, the son of Hassenuah,

8 and Ibneiah the son of Jeroham, and Elah the son of Uzzi, the son of Michri, and Meshullam the son of Shephatiah, the son of Reuel, the son of Ibnijah;

9 and their brethren, according to their generations, nine hundred and fifty and six. All these men were heads of fathers' houses by their fathers' houses.

10 And of the priests: Jedaiah, and Jehoiarib, Jachin,

11 and Azariah the son of Hilkiah, the son of Meshullam, the son of Zadok, the son of Meraioth, the son of Ahitub, the ruler of the house of God;

12 and Adaiah the son of Jeroham, the son of Pashhur, the son of Malchijah, and Maasai the son of Adiel, the son of Jahzerah, the son of Meshullam, the son of Meshillemith, the son of Immer;

13 and their brethren, heads of their fathers' houses, a thousand and seven hundred and threescore; very able men for the work of the service of the house of God.

14 And of the Levites: Shemaiah the son of Hasshub, the son of Azrikam, the son of Hashabiah, of the sons of Merari;

15 and Bakbakkar, Heresh, and Galal, and Mattaniah the son of Mica, the son of Zichri, the son of Asaph,

16 and Obadiah the son of Shemaiah, the son of Galal, the son of Jeduthun, and Berechiah the son of Asa, the son of Elkanah, that dwelt in the villages of the Netophathites.

17 And the porters: Shallum, and Akkub, and Talmon, and Ahiman, and their brethren (Shallum was the chief),

18 who hitherto waited in the king's gate eastward: they were the porters for the camp of the children of Levi.

19 And Shallum the son of Kore, the son of Ebiasaph, the son of Korah, and his brethren, of his father's house, the Korahites, were over the work of the service, keepers of the thresholds of the tent: and their fathers had been over the camp of Yahweh, keepers of the entry.

20 And Phinehas the son of Eleazar was ruler over them in time past, and Yahweh was with him.

21 Zechariah the son of Meshelemiah was porter of the door of the tent of meeting.

22 All these that were chosen to be porters in the thresholds were two hundred and twelve. These were reckoned by genealogy in their villages, whom David and Samuel the seer did ordain in their office of trust.

23 So they and their children had the oversight of the gates of the house of Yahweh, even the house of the tent, by wards.

24 On the four sides were the porters, toward the east, west, north, and south.

25 And their brethren, in their villages, were to come in every seven days from time to time to be with them:

26 for the four chief porters, who were Levites, were in an office of trust, and were over the chambers and over the treasuries in the house of God.

27 And they lodged round about the house of God, because the charge thereof was upon them; and to them pertained the opening thereof morning by morning.

28 And certain of them had charge of the vessels of service; for by count were these brought in and by count were these taken out.

29 Some of them also were appointed over the furniture, and over all the vessels of the sanctuary, and over the fine flour, and the wine, and the oil, and the frankincense, and the spices.

30 And some of the sons of the priests prepared the confection of the spices.

31 And Mattithiah, one of the Levites, who was the first-born of Shallum the Korahite, had the office of trust over the things that were baked in pans.

32 And some of their brethren, of the sons of the Kohathites, were over the showbread, to prepare it every sabbath.

33 And these are the singers, heads of fathers' houses of the Levites, who dwelt in the chambers and were free from other service; for they were employed in their work day and night.

34 These were heads of fathers' houses of the Levites, throughout their generations, chief men: these dwelt at Jerusalem.

35And in Gibeon there dwelt the father of Gibeon, Jeiel, whose wife's name was Maacah:
36and his first-born son Abdon, and Zur, and Kish, and Baal, and Ner, and Nadab,
37and Gedor, and Ahio, and Zechariah, and Mikloth.
38And Mikloth begat Shimeam. And they also dwelt with their brethren in Jerusalem, over against their brethren.
39And Ner begat Kish; and Kish begat Saul; and Saul begat Jonathan, and Malchishua, and Abinadab, and Eshbaal.
40And the son of Jonathan was Merib-baal; and Merib-baal begat Micah.
41And the sons of Micah: Pithon, and Melech, and Tahrea, and Ahaz.
42And Ahaz begat Jarah; and Jarah begat Alemeth, and Azmaveth, and Zimri; and Zimri begat Moza;
43and Moza begat Binea; and Rephaiah his son, Eleasah his son, Azel his son.
44And Azel had six sons, whose names are these: Azrikam, Bocheru, and Ishmael, and Sheariah, and Obadiah, and Hanan: these were the sons of Azel.

Chapter 10

1Now the Philistines fought against Israel: and the men of Israel fled from before the Philistines, and fell down slain in mount Gilboa.
2And the Philistines followed hard after Saul and after his sons; and the Philistines slew Jonathan, and Abinadab, and Malchi-shua, the sons of Saul.
3And the battle went sore against Saul, and the archers overtook him; and he was distressed by reason of the archers.
4Then said Saul unto his armor-bearer, Draw thy sword, and thrust me through therewith, lest these uncircumcised come and abuse me. But his armor-bearer would not; for he was sore afraid. Therefore Saul took his sword, and fell upon it.
5And when his armor-bearer saw that Saul was dead, he likewise fell upon his sword, and died.
6So Saul died, and his three sons; and all his house died together.
7And when all the men of Israel that were in the valley saw that they fled, and that Saul and his sons were dead, they forsook their cities, and fled; and the Philistines came and dwelt in them.
8And it came to pass on the morrow, when the Philistines came to strip the slain, that they found Saul and his sons fallen in mount Gilboa.
9And they stripped him, and took his head, and his armor, and sent into the land of the Philistines round about, to carry the tidings unto their idols, and to the people.
10And they put his armor in the house of their gods, and fastened his head in the house of Dagon.
11And when all Jabesh-gilead heard all that the Philistines had done to Saul,
12all the valiant men arose, and took away the body of Saul, and the bodies of his sons, and brought them to Jabesh, and buried their bones under the oak in Jabesh, and fasted seven days.
13So Saul died for his trespass which he committed against Yahweh, because of the word of Yahweh, which he kept not; and also for that he asked counsel of one that had a familiar spirit, to inquire thereby,
14and inquired not of Yahweh: therefore he slew him, and turned the kingdom unto David the son of Jesse.

Chapter 11

1Then all Israel gathered themselves to David unto Hebron, saying, Behold, we are thy bone and thy flesh.
2In times past, even when Saul was king, it was thou that leddest out and broughtest in Israel: and Yahweh thy God said unto thee, Thou shalt be shepherd of my people Israel, and thou shalt be prince over my people Israel.
3So all the elders of Israel came to the king to Hebron; and David made a covenant with them in Hebron before Yahweh; and they anointed David king over Israel, according to the word of Yahweh by Samuel.
4And David and all Israel went to Jerusalem (the same is Jebus); and the Jebusites, the inhabitants of the land, were there.
5And the inhabitants of Jebus said to David, Thou shalt not come in hither. Nevertheless David took the stronghold of Zion; the same is the city of David.
6And David said, Whosoever smiteth the Jebusites first shall be chief and captain. And Joab the son of Zeruiah went up first, and was made chief.
7And David dwelt in the stronghold; therefore they called it the city of David.
8And he built the city round about, from Millo even round about; and Joab repaired the rest of the city.
9And David waxed greater and greater; for Yahweh of hosts was with him.
10Now these are the chief of the mighty men whom David had, who showed themselves strong with him in his kingdom, together with all Israel, to make him king, according to the word of Yahweh concerning Israel.
11And this is the number of the mighty men whom David had: Jashobeam, the son of a Hachmonite, the chief of the thirty; he lifted up his spear against three hundred and slew them at one time.
12And after him was Eleazar the son of Dodo, the Ahohite, who was one of the three mighty men.
13He was with David at Pasdammim, and there the Philistines were gathered together to battle, where was a plot of ground full of barley; and the people fled from before the Philistines.
14And they stood in the midst of the plot, and defended it, and slew the Philistines; and Yahweh saved them by a great victory.
15And three of the thirty chief men went down to the rock to David, into the cave of Adullam; and the host of the Philistines were encamped in the valley of Rephaim.
16And David was then in the stronghold, and the garrison of the Philistines was then in Beth-lehem.
17And David longed, and said, Oh that one would give me water to drink of the well of Beth-lehem, which is by the gate!
18And the three brake through the host of the Philistines, and drew water out of the well of Beth-lehem, that was by the gate, and took it, and brought it to David: but David would not drink thereof, but poured it out unto Yahweh,
19and said, My God forbid it me, that I should do this: shall I drink the blood of these men that have put their lives in jeopardy? for with the jeopardy of their lives they brought it. Therefore he would not drink it. These things did the three mighty men.
20And Abishai, the brother of Joab, he was chief of the three; for he lifted up his spear against three hundred and slew them, and had a name among the three.
21Of the three, he was more honorable than the two, and was made their captain: howbeit he attained not to the first three.
22Benaiah the son of Jehoiada, the son of a valiant man of Kabzeel, who had done mighty deeds, he slew the two sons of Ariel of Moab: he went down also and slew a lion in the midst of a pit in time of snow.
23And he slew an Egyptian, a man of great stature, five cubits high; and in the Egyptian's hand was a spear like a weaver's beam; and he went down to him with a staff, and plucked the spear out of the Egyptian's hand, and slew him with his own spear.
24These things did Benaiah the son of Jehoiada, and had a name among the three mighty men.
25Behold, he was more honorable than the thirty, but he attained not to the first three: and David set him over his guard.
26Also the mighty men of the armies: Asahel the brother of Joab, Elhanan the son of Dodo of Beth-lehem,
27Shammoth the Harorite, Helez the Pelonite,
28Ira the son of Ikkesh the Tekoite, Abiezer the Anathothite,
29Sibbecai the Hushathite, Ilai the Ahohite,
30Maharai the Netophathite, Heled the son of Baanah the Netophathite,
31Ithai the son of Ribai of Gibeah of the children of Benjamin, Benaiah the Pirathonite,
32Hurai of the brooks of Gaash, Abiel the Arbathite,
33Azmaveth the Baharumite, Eliahba the Shaalbonite,
34the sons of Hashem the Gizonite, Jonathan the son of Shagee the Hararite,
35Ahiam the son of Sacar the Hararite, Eliphal the son of Ur,
36Hepher the Mecherathite, Ahijah the Pelonite,
37Hezro the Carmelite, Naarai the son of Ezbai,
38Joel the brother of Nathan, Mibhar the son of Hagri,
39Zelek the Ammonite, Naharai the Berothite, the armorbearer of Joab the son of Zeruiah,
40Ira the Ithrite, Gareb the Ithrite,
41Uriah the Hittite, Zabad the son of Ahlai,
42Adina the son of Shiza the Reubenite, a chief of the Reubenites, and thirty with him,
43Hanan the son of Maacah, and Joshaphat the Mithnite,
44Uzzia the Ashterathite, Shama and Jeiel the sons of Hotham the Aroerite,
45Jediael the son of Shimri, and Joha his brother, the Tizite,
46Eliel the Mahavite, and Jeribai, and Joshaviah, the sons of Elnaam, and Ithmah the Moabite,
47Eliel, and Obed, and Jaasiel the Mezobaite.

Chapter 12

1Now these are they that came to David to Ziklag, while he yet kept himself close because of Saul the son of Kish; and they were among the mighty men, his helpers in war.
2They were armed with bows, and could use both the right hand and the left in slinging stones and in shooting arrows from the bow: they were of Saul's brethren of Benjamin.
3The chief was Ahiezer; then Joash, the sons of Shemaah the Gibeathite, and Jeziel, and Pelet, the sons of Azmaveth, and Beracah, and Jehu the Anathothite,
4and Ishmaiah the Gibeonite, a mighty man among the thirty, and over the thirty, and Jeremiah, and Jahaziel, and Johanan, and Jozabad the Gederathite,
5Eluzai, and Jerimoth, and Bealiah, and Shemariah, and Shephatiah the Haruphite,
6Elkanah, and Isshiah, and Azarel, and Joezer, and Jashobeam, the Korahites,
7and Joelah, and Zebadiah, the sons of Jeroham of Gedor.
8And of the Gadites there separated themselves unto David to the stronghold in the wilderness, mighty men of valor, men trained for war, that could handle shield and spear; whose faces were like the faces of lions, and they were as swift as the roes upon the mountains;
9Ezer the chief, Obadiah the second, Eliab the third,
10Mishmannah the fourth, Jeremiah the fifth,
11Attai the sixth, Eliel the seventh,
12Johanan the eighth, Elzabad the ninth,
13Jeremiah the tenth, Machbannai the eleventh.
14These of the sons of Gad were captains of the host: he that was least was equal to a hundred, and the greatest to a thousand.
15These are they that went over the Jordan in the first month, when it had overflowed all its banks; and they put to flight all them of the valleys, both toward the east, and toward the west.
16And there came of the children of Benjamin and Judah to the stronghold unto David.
17And David went out to meet them, and answered and said unto them, If ye

First Chronicles

be come peaceably unto me to help me, my heart shall be knit unto you; but if ye be come to betray me to mine adversaries, seeing there is no wrong in my hands, the God of our fathers look thereon, and rebuke it.

18Then the Spirit came upon Amasai, who was chief of the thirty, and he said, Thine are we, David, and on thy side, thou son of Jesse: peace, peace be unto thee, and peace be to thy helpers; for thy God helpeth thee. Then David received them, and made them captains of the band.

19Of Manasseh also there fell away some to David, when he came with the Philistines against Saul to battle: but they helped them not; for the lords of the Philistines upon advisement sent him away, saying, He will fall away to his master Saul to the jeopardy of our heads.

20As he went to Ziklag, there fell to him of Manasseh, Adnah, and Jozabad, and Jediael, and Michael, and Jozabad, and Elihu, and Zillethai, captains of thousands that were of Manasseh.

21And they helped David against the band of rovers: for they were all mighty men of valor, and were captains in the host.

22For from day to day men came to David to help him, until there was a great host, like the host of God.

23And these are the numbers of the heads of them that were armed for war, who came to David to Hebron, to turn the kingdom of Saul to him, according to the word of Yahweh.

24The children of Judah that bare shield and spear were six thousand and eight hundred, armed for war.

25Of the children of Simeon, mighty men of valor for the war, seven thousand and one hundred.

26Of the children of Levi four thousand and six hundred.

27And Jehoiada was the leader of the house of Aaron; and with him were three thousand and seven hundred,

28and Zadok, a young man mighty of valor, and of his father's house twenty and two captains.

29And of the children of Benjamin, the brethren of Saul, three thousand: for hitherto the greatest part of them had kept their allegiance to the house of Saul.

30And of the children of Ephraim twenty thousand and eight hundred, mighty men of valor, famous men in their fathers' houses.

31And of the half-tribe of Manasseh eighteen thousand, who were mentioned by name, to come and make David king.

32And of the children of Issachar, men that had understanding of the times, to know what Israel ought to do, the heads of them were two hundred; and all their brethren were at their commandment.

33Of Zebulun, such as were able to go out in the host, that could set the battle in array, with all manner of instruments of war, fifty thousand, and that could order the battle array, and were not of double heart.

34And of Naphtali a thousand captains, and with them with shield and spear thirty and seven thousand.

35And of the Danites that could set the battle in array, twenty and eight thousand and six hundred.

36And of Asher, such as were able to go out in the host, that could set the battle in array, forty thousand.

37And on the other side of the Jordan, of the Reubenites, and the Gadites, and of the half-tribe of Manasseh, with all manner of instruments of war for the battle, a hundred and twenty thousand.

38All these being men of war, that could order the battle array, came with a perfect heart to Hebron, to make David king over all Israel: and all the rest also of Israel were of one heart to make David king.

39And they were there with David three days, eating and drinking; for their brethren had made preparation for them.

40Moreover they that were nigh unto them, even as far as Issachar and Zebulun and Naphtali, brought bread on asses, and on camels, and on mules, and on oxen, victuals of meal, cakes of figs, and clusters of raisins, and wine, and oil, and oxen, and sheep in abundance: for there was joy in Israel.

Chapter 13

1And David consulted with the captains of thousands and of hundreds, even with every leader.

2And David said unto all the assembly of Israel, If it seem good unto you, and if it be of Yahweh our God, let us send abroad every where unto our brethren that are left in all the land of Israel, with whom the priests and Levites are in their cities that have suburbs, that they may gather themselves unto us;

3and let us bring again the ark of our God to us: for we sought not unto it in the days of Saul.

4And all the assembly said that they would do so; for the thing was right in the eyes of all the people.

5So David assembled all Israel together, from the Shihor the brook of Egypt even unto the entrance of Hamath, to bring the ark of God from Kiriath-jearim.

6And David went up, and all Israel, to Baalah, that is, to Kiriath-jearim, which belonged to Judah, to bring up from thence the ark of God Yahweh that sitteth above the cherubim, that is called by the Name.

7And they carried the ark of God upon a new cart, and brought it out of the house of Abinadab: and Uzza and Ahio drove the cart.

8And David and all Israel played before God with all their might, even with songs, and with harps, and with psalteries, and with timbrels, and with cymbals, and with trumpets.

9And when they came unto the threshing-floor of Chidon, Uzza put forth his hand to hold the ark; for the oxen stumbled.

10And the anger of Yahweh was kindled against Uzza, and he smote him, because he put forth his hand to the ark; and there he died before God.

11And David was displeased, because Yahweh had broken forth upon Uzza; and he called that place Perez-uzza, unto this day.

12And David was afraid of God that day, saying, How shall I bring the ark of God home to me?

13So David removed not the ark unto him into the city of David, but carried it aside into the house of Obed-edom the Gittite.

14And the ark of God remained with the family of Obed-edom in his house three months: and Yahweh blessed the house of Obed-edom, and all that he had.

Chapter 14

1And Hiram king of Tyre sent messengers to David, and cedar-trees, and masons, and carpenters, to build him a house.

2And David perceived that Yahweh had established him king over Israel; for his kingdom was exalted on high, for his people Israel's sake.

3And David took more wives at Jerusalem; and David begat more sons and daughters.

4And these are the names of the children whom he had in Jerusalem: Shammua, and Shobab, Nathan, and Solomon,

5and Ibhar, and Elishua, and Elpelet,

6and Nogah, and Nepheg, and Japhia,

7and Elishama, and Beeliada, and Eliphelet.

8And when the Philistines heard that David was anointed king over all Israel, all the Philistines went up to seek David: and David heard of it, and went out against them.

9Now the Philistines had come and made a raid in the valley of Rephaim.

10And David inquired of God, saying, Shall I go up against the Philistines? and wilt thou deliver them into my hand? And Yahweh said unto him, Go up; for I will deliver them into thy hand.

11So they came up to Baal-perazim, and David smote them there; and David said, God hath broken mine enemies by my hand, like the breach of waters. Therefore they called the name of that place Baal-perazim.

12And they left their gods there; and David gave commandment, and they were burned with fire.

13And the Philistines yet again made a raid in the valley.

14And David inquired again of God; and God said unto him, Thou shalt not go up after them: turn away from them, and come upon them over against the mulberry-trees.

15And it shall be, when thou hearest the sound of marching in the tops of the mulberry-trees, that then thou shalt go out to battle; for God is gone out before thee to smite the host of the Philistines.

16And David did as God commanded him: and they smote the host of the Philistines from Gibeon even to Gezer.

17And the fame of David went out into all lands; and Yahweh brought the fear of him upon all nations.

Chapter 15

1And David made him houses in the city of David; and he prepared a place for the ark of God, and pitched for it a tent.

2Then David said, None ought to carry the ark of God but the Levites: for them hath Yahweh chosen to carry the ark of God, and to minister unto him for ever.

3And David assembled all Israel at Jerusalem, to bring up the ark of Yahweh unto its place, which he had prepared for it.

4And David gathered together the sons of Aaron, and the Levites:

5of the sons of Kohath, Uriel the chief, and his brethren a hundred and twenty;

6of the sons of Merari, Asaiah the chief, and his brethren two hundred and twenty;

7of the sons of Gershom, Joel the chief, and his brethren a hundred and thirty;

8of the sons of Elizaphan, Shemaiah the chief, and his brethren two hundred;

9of the sons of Hebron, Eliel the chief, and his brethren fourscore;

10of the sons of Uzziel, Amminadab the chief, and his brethren a hundred and twelve.

11And David called for Zadok and Abiathar the priests, and for the Levites, for Uriel, Asaiah, and Joel, Shemaiah, and Eliel, and Amminadab,

12and said unto them, Ye are the heads of the fathers' houses of the Levites: sanctify yourselves, both ye and your brethren, that ye may bring up the ark of Yahweh, the God of Israel, unto the place that I have prepared for it.

13For because ye bare it not at the first, Yahweh our God made a breach upon us, for that we sought him not according to the ordinance.

14So the priests and the Levites sanctified themselves to bring up the ark of Yahweh, the God of Israel.

15And the children of the Levites bare the ark of God upon their shoulders with the staves thereon, as Moses commanded according to the word of Yahweh.

16And David spake to the chief of the Levites to appoint their brethren the singers, with instruments of music, psalteries and harps and cymbals, sounding aloud and lifting up the voice with joy.

17So the Levites appointed Heman the son of Joel; and of his brethren, Asaph the son of Berechiah; and of the sons of Merari their brethren, Ethan the son of Kushaiah;

18and with them their brethren of the second degree, Zechariah, Ben, and Jaaziel, and Shemiramoth, and Jehiel, and Unni, Eliab, and Benaiah, and Maaseiah, and Mattithiah, and Eliphelehu, and Mikneiah, and Obed-edom, and Jeiel, the doorkeepers.

19So the singers, Heman, Asaph, and Ethan, were appointed with cymbals of brass to sound aloud;

20and Zechariah, and Aziel, and Shemiramoth, and Jehiel, and Unni, and Eliab, and Maaseiah, and Benaiah, with psalteries set to Alamoth;

21and Mattithiah, and Eliphelehu, and Mikneiah, and Obed-edom, and Jeiel, and Azaziah, with harps set to the Sheminith, to lead.

22And Chenaniah, chief of the Levites, was over the song: he instructed about the song, because he was skilful.

23And Berechiah and Elkanah were doorkeepers for the ark.

24And Shebaniah, and Joshaphat, and Nethanel, and Amasai, and Zechariah, and Benaiah, and Eliezer, the priests, did blow the trumpets before the ark of God: and Obed-edom and Jehiah were doorkeepers for the ark.

25So David, and the elders of Israel, and the captains over thousands, went to bring up the ark of the covenant of Yahweh out of the house of Obed-edom with joy.

26And it came to pass, when God helped the Levites that bare the ark of the covenant of Yahweh, that they sacrificed seven bullocks and seven rams.

27And David was clothed with a robe of fine linen, and all the Levites that bare the ark, and the singers, and Chenaniah the master of the song with the singers; and David had upon him an ephod of linen.

28Thus all Israel brought up the ark of the covenant of Yahweh with shouting, and with sound of the cornet, and with trumpets, and with cymbals, sounding aloud with psalteries and harps.

29And it came to pass, as the ark of the covenant of Yahweh came to the city of David, that Michal the daughter of Saul looked out at the window, and saw king David dancing and playing; and she despised him in her heart.

Chapter 16

1And they brought in the ark of God, and set it in the midst of the tent that David had pitched for it: and they offered burnt-offerings and peace-offerings before God.

2And when David had made an end of offering the burnt-offering and the peace-offerings, he blessed the people in the name of Yahweh.

3And he dealt to every one of Israel, both man and woman, to every one a loaf of bread, and a portion of flesh, and a cake of raisins.

4And he appointed certain of the Levites to minister before the ark of Yahweh, and to celebrate and to thank and praise Yahweh, the God of Israel:

5Asaph the chief, and second to him Zechariah, Jeiel, and Shemiramoth, and Jehiel, and Mattithiah, and Eliab, and Benaiah, and Obed-edom, and Jeiel, with psalteries and with harps; and Asaph with cymbals, sounding aloud;.

6and Benaiah and Jahaziel the priests with trumpets continually, before the ark of the covenant of God.

7Then on that day did David first ordain to give thanks unto Yahweh, by the hand of Asaph and his brethren.

8O give thanks unto Yahweh, call upon his name;
Make known his doings among the peoples.
9Sing unto him, sing praises unto him;
Talk ye of all his marvellous works.
10Glory ye in his holy name;
Let the heart of them rejoice that seek Yahweh.
11Seek ye Yahweh and his strength;
Seek his face evermore.
12Remember his marvellous works that he hath done,
His wonders, and the judgments of his mouth,
13O ye seed of Israel his servant,
Ye children of Jacob, his chosen ones.
14He is Yahweh our God;
His judgments are in all the earth.
15Remember his covenant for ever,
The word which he commanded to a thousand generations,
16The covenant which he made with Abraham,
And his oath unto Isaac,
17And confirmed the same unto Jacob for a statute,
To Israel for an everlasting covenant,
18Saying, Unto thee will I give the land of Canaan,
The lot of your inheritance;
19When ye were but a few men in number,
Yea, very few, and sojourners in it;
20And they went about from nation to nation,
And from one kingdom to another people.
21He suffered no man to do them wrong;
Yea, he reproved kings for their sakes,
22Saying, Touch not mine anointed ones,
And do my prophets no harm.
23Sing unto Yahweh, all the earth;
Show forth his salvation from day to day.
24Declare his glory among the nations,
His marvellous works among all the peoples.
25For great is Yahweh, and greatly to be praised:
He also is to be feared above all gods.
26For all the gods of the peoples are idols:
But Yahweh made the heavens.
27Honor and majesty are before him:
Strength and gladness are in his place.
28Ascribe unto Yahweh, ye kindreds of the peoples,
Ascribe unto Yahweh glory and strength;
29Ascribe unto Yahweh the glory due unto his name:
Bring an offering, and come before him;
Worship Yahweh in holy array.
30Tremble before him, all the earth:
The world also is established that it cannot be moved.
31Let the heavens be glad, and let the earth rejoice;
And let them say among the nations, Yahweh reigneth.
32Let the sea roar, and the fulness thereof;
Let the field exult, and all that is therein;
33Then shall the trees of the wood sing for joy before Yahweh;
For he cometh to judge the earth.
34O give thanks unto Yahweh; for he is good;
For his lovingkindness endureth for ever.
35And say ye, Save us, O God of our salvation,
And gather us together and deliver us from the nations,
To give thanks unto thy holy name,
And to triumph in thy praise.
36Blessed be Yahweh, the God of Israel,
From everlasting even to everlasting.
And all the people said, Amen, and praised Yahweh.

37So he left there, before the ark of the covenant of Yahweh, Asaph and his brethren, to minister before the ark continually, as every day's work required;

38and Obed-edom with their brethren, threescore and eight; Obed-edom also the son of Jeduthun and Hosah to be doorkeepers;

39and Zadok the priest, and his brethren the priests, before the tabernacle of Yahweh in the high place that was at Gibeon,

40to offer burnt-offerings unto Yahweh upon the altar of burnt-offering continually morning and evening, even according to all that is written in the law of Yahweh, which he commanded unto Israel;

41and with them Heman and Jeduthun, and the rest that were chosen, who were mentioned by name, to give thanks to Yahweh, because his lovingkindness endureth for ever;

42and with them Heman and Jeduthun with trumpets and cymbals for those that should sound aloud, and with instruments for the songs of God; and the sons of Jeduthun to be at the gate.

43And all the people departed every man to his house: and David returned to bless his house.

Chapter 17

1And it came to pass, when David dwelt in his house, that David said to Nathan the prophet, Lo, I dwell in a house of cedar, but the ark of the covenant of Yahweh dwelleth under curtains.

2And Nathan said unto David, Do all that is in thy heart; for God is with thee.

3And it came to pass the same night, that the word of God came to Nathan, saying,

4Go and tell David my servant, Thus saith Yahweh, Thou shalt not build me a house to dwell in:

5for I have not dwelt in a house since the day that I brought up Israel, unto this day, but have gone from tent to tent, and from one tabernacle to another.

6In all places wherein I have walked with all Israel, spake I a word with any of the judges of Israel, whom I commanded to be shepherd of my people, saying, Why have ye not built me a house of cedar?

7Now therefore thus shalt thou say unto my servant David, Thus saith Yahweh of hosts, I took thee from the sheepcote, from following the sheep, that thou shouldest be prince over my people Israel:

8and I have been with thee whithersoever thou hast gone, and have cut off all thine enemies from before thee; and I will make thee a name, like unto the name of the great ones that are in the earth.

9And I will appoint a place for my people Israel, and will plant them, that they may dwell in their own place, and be moved no more; neither shall the children of wickedness waste them any more, as at the first,

10and as from the day that I commanded judges to be over my people Israel; and I will subdue all thine enemies. Moreover I tell thee that Yahweh will build thee a house.

11And it shall come to pass, when thy days are fulfilled that thou must go to be with thy fathers, that I will set up thy seed after thee, who shall be of thy sons; and I will establish his kingdom.

12He shall build me a house, and I will establish his throne for ever.

13I will be his father, and he shall be my son: and I will not take my lovingkindness away from him, as I took it from him that was before thee;

14but I will settle him in my house and in my kingdom for ever; and his throne shall be established for ever.

15According to all these words, and according to all this vision, so did Nathan speak unto David.

16Then David the king went in, and sat before Yahweh; and he said, Who am I, O Yahweh God, and what is my house, that thou hast brought me thus far?

17And this was a small thing in thine eyes, O God; but thou hast spoken of thy servant's house for a great while to come, and hast regarded me according to the estate of a man of high degree, O Yahweh God.

18What can David say yet more unto thee concerning the honor which is done to thy servant? for thou knowest thy servant.

19O Yahweh, for thy servant's sake, and according to thine own heart, hast thou wrought all this greatness, to make known all these great things.

20O Yahweh, there is none like thee, neither is there any God besides thee, according to all that we have heard with our ears.

21And what one nation in the earth is like thy people Israel, whom God went to redeem unto himself for a people, to make thee a name by great and terrible things, in driving out nations from before thy people, whom thou redeemest out of Egypt?

22For thy people Israel didst thou make thine own people for ever; and thou, Yahweh, becamest their God.

23And now, O Yahweh, let the word that thou hast spoken concerning thy servant, and concerning his house, be established for ever, and do as thou hast spoken.

24And let thy name be established and magnified for ever, saying, Yahweh of hosts is the God of Israel, even a God to Israel: and the house of David thy servant is established before thee.

25For thou, O my God, hast revealed to thy servant that thou wilt build him a house: therefore hath thy servant found in his heart to pray before thee.

26And now, O Yahweh, thou art God, and hast promised this good thing unto thy servant:

27and now it hath pleased thee to bless the house of thy servant, that it may continue for ever before thee: for thou, O Yahweh, hast blessed, and it is blessed for ever.

Chapter 18

1And after this it came to pass, that David smote the Philistines, and subdued them, and took Gath and its towns out of the hand of the Philistines.

2And he smote Moab; and the Moabites became servants to David, and brought tribute.

3And David smote Hadarezer king of Zobah unto Hamath, as he went to establish his dominion by the river Euphrates.

4And David took from him a thousand chariots, and seven thousand horsemen, and twenty thousand footmen; and David hocked all the chariot horses, but reserved of them for a hundred chariots.

5And when the Syrians of Damascus came to succor Hadarezer king of Zobah, David smote of the Syrians two and twenty thousand men.

6Then David put garrisons in Syria of Damascus; and the Syrians became servants to David, and brought tribute. And Yahweh gave victory to David whithersoever he went.

7And David took the shields of gold that were on the servants of Hadarezer, and brought them to Jerusalem.

8And from Tibhath and from Cun, cities of Hadarezer, David took very much brass, wherewith Solomon made the brazen sea, and the pillars, and the vessels of brass.

9And when Tou king of Hamath heard that David had smitten all the host of Hadarezer king of Zobah,

10he sent Hadoram his son to king David, to salute him, and to bless him, because he had fought against Hadarezer and smitten him; (for Hadarezer had wars with Tou;) and he had with him all manner of vessels of gold and silver and brass.

11These also did king David dedicate unto Yahweh, with the silver and the gold that he carried away from all the nations; from Edom, and from Moab, and from the children of Ammon, and from the Philistines, and from Amalek.

12Moreover Abishai the son of Zeruiah smote of the Edomites in the Valley of Salt eighteen thousand.

13And he put garrisons in Edom; and all the Edomites became servants to David. And Yahweh gave victory to David whithersoever he went.

14And David reigned over all Israel; and he executed justice and righteousness unto all his people.

15And Joab the son of Zeruiah was over the host; and Jehoshaphat the son of Ahilud was recorder;

16and Zadok the son of Ahitub, and Abimelech the son of Abiathar, were priests; and Shavsha was scribe;

17and Benaiah the son of Jehoiada was over the Cherethites and the Pelethites; and the sons of David were chief about the king.

Chapter 19

1And it came to pass after this, that Nahash the king of the children of Ammon died, and his son reigned in his stead.

2And David said, I will show kindness unto Hanun the son of Nahash, because his father showed kindness to me. So David sent messengers to comfort him concerning his father. And David's servants came into the land of the children of Ammon to Hanun, to comfort him.

3But the princes of the children of Ammon said to Hanun, Thinkest thou that David doth honor thy father, in that he hath sent comforters unto thee? are not his servants come unto thee to search, and to overthrow, and to spy out the land?

4So Hanun took David's servants, and shaved them, and cut off their garments in the middle, even to their buttocks, and sent them away.

5Then there went certain persons, and told David how the men were served. And he sent to meet them; for the men were greatly ashamed. And the king said, Tarry at Jericho until your beards be grown, and then return.

6And when the children of Ammon saw that they had made themselves odious to David, Hanun and the children of Ammon sent a thousand talents of silver to hire them chariots and horsemen out of Mesopotamia, and out of Arammaacah, and out of Zobah.

7So they hired them thirty and two thousand chariots, and the king of Maacah and his people, who came and encamped before Medeba. And the children of Ammon gathered themselves together from their cities, and came to battle.

8And when David heard of it, he sent Joab, and all the host of the mighty men.

9And the children of Ammon came out, and put the battle in array at the gate of the city: and the kings that were come were by themselves in the field.

10Now when Joab saw that the battle was set against him before and behind, he chose of all the choice men of Israel, and put them in array against the Syrians.

11And the rest of the people he committed into the hand of Abishai his brother; and they put themselves in array against the children of Ammon.

12And he said, If the Syrians be too strong for me, then thou shalt help me; but if the children of Ammon be too strong for thee, then I will help thee.

13Be of good courage, and let us play the man for our people, and for the cities of our God: and Yahweh do that which seemeth him good.

14So Joab and the people that were with him drew nigh before the Syrians unto the battle; and they fled before him.

15And when the children of Ammon saw that the Syrians were fled, they likewise fled before Abishai his brother, and entered into the city. Then Joab came to Jerusalem.

16And when the Syrians saw that they were put to the worse before Israel, they sent messengers, and drew forth the Syrians that were beyond the River, with Shophach the captain of the host of Hadarezer at their head.

17And it was told David; and he gathered all Israel together, and passed over the Jordan, and came upon them, and set the battle in array against them. So when David had put the battle in array against the Syrians, they fought with him.

18And the Syrians fled before Israel; and David slew of the Syrians the men of seven thousand chariots, and forty thousand footmen, and killed Shophach the captain of the host.

19And when the servants of Hadarezer saw that they were put to the worse before Israel, they made peace with David, and served him: neither would the Syrians help the children of Ammon any more.

Chapter 20

1And it came to pass, at the time of the return of the year, at the time when kings go out to battle, that Joab led forth the army, and wasted the country of the children of Ammon, and came and besieged Rabbah. But David tarried at Jerusalem. And Joab smote Rabbah, and overthrew it.

2And David took the crown of their king from off his head, and found it to weigh a talent of gold, and there were precious stones in it; and it was set upon David's head: and he brought forth the spoil of the city, exceeding much.

3And he brought forth the people that were therein, and cut them with saws, and with harrows of iron, and with axes. And thus did David unto all the cities of the children of Ammon. And David and all the people returned to Jerusalem.

4And it came to pass after this, that there arose war at Gezer with the Philistines: then Sibbecai the Hushathite slew Sippai, of the sons of the giant; and they were subdued.

5And there was again war with the Philistines; and Elhanan the son of Jair slew Lahmi the brother of Goliath the Gittite, the staff of whose spear was like a weaver's beam.

6And there was again war at Gath, where was a man of great stature, whose fingers and toes were four and twenty, six on each hand, and six on each foot; and he also was born unto the giant.

7And when he defied Israel, Jonathan the son of Shimea David's brother slew him.

8These were born unto the giant in Gath; and they fell by the hand of David, and by the hand of his servants.

Chapter 21

1And Satan stood up against Israel, and moved David to number Israel.

2And David said to Joab and to the princes of the people, Go, number Israel from Beer-sheba even to Dan; and bring me word, that I may know the sum of them.

3And Joab said, Yahweh make his people a hundred times as many as they are: but, my lord the king, are they not all my lord's servants? why doth my lord require this thing? why will he be a cause of guilt unto Israel?

4Nevertheless the king's word prevailed against Joab. Wherefore Joab departed, and went throughout all Israel, and came to Jerusalem.

5And Joab gave up the sum of the numbering of the people unto David. And all they of Israel were a thousand thousand and a hundred thousand men that drew sword: and Judah was four hundred threescore and ten thousand men that drew sword.

6But Levi and Benjamin counted he not among them; for the king's word was abominable to Joab.

7And God was displeased with this thing; therefore he smote Israel.

8And David said unto God, I have sinned greatly, in that I have done this thing: but now, put away, I beseech thee, the iniquity of thy servant; for I have done very foolishly.

9And Yahweh spake unto Gad, David's seer, saying,

10Go and speak unto David, saying, Thus saith Yahweh, I offer thee three things: choose thee one of them, that I may do it unto thee.

11So Gad came to David, and said unto him, Thus saith Yahweh, Take which thou wilt:

12either three years of famine; or three months to be consumed before thy foes, while the sword of thine enemies overtaketh thee; or else three days the sword of Yahweh, even pestilence in the land, and the angel of Yahweh destroying throughout all the borders of Israel. Now therefore consider what answer I shall return to him that sent me.

13And David said unto Gad, I am in a great strait: let me fall, I pray, into the hand of Yahweh; for very great are his mercies: and let me not fall into the hand of man.

14So Yahweh sent a pestilence upon Israel; and there fell of Israel seventy thousand men.

15And God sent an angel unto Jerusalem to destroy it: and as he was about to destroy, Yahweh beheld, and he repented him of the evil, and said to the destroying angel, It is enough; now stay thy hand. And the angel of Yahweh was standing by the threshing-floor of Ornan the Jebusite.

16And David lifted up his eyes, and saw the angel of Yahweh standing between earth and heaven, having a drawn sword in his hand stretched out over Jerusalem. Then David and the elders, clothed in sackcloth, fell upon their faces.

17And David said unto God, Is it not I that commanded the people to be numbered? even I it is that have sinned and done very wickedly; but these sheep, what have they done? let thy hand, I pray thee, O Yahweh my God, be against me, and against my father's house; but not against thy people, that they should be plagued.

18Then the angel of Yahweh commanded Gad to say to David, that David should go up, and rear an altar unto Yahweh in the threshing-floor of Ornan the Jebusite.

19And David went up at the saying of Gad, which he spake in the name of Yahweh.

20And Ornan turned back, and saw the angel; and his four sons that were with him hid themselves. Now Ornan was threshing wheat.

21And as David came to Ornan, Ornan looked and saw David, and went out of the threshing-floor, and bowed himself to David with his face to the ground.

22Then David said to Ornan, Give me the place of this threshing-floor, that I may build thereon an altar unto Yahweh: for the full price shalt thou give it me, that the plague may be stayed from the people.

23And Ornan said unto David, Take it to thee, and let my lord the king do that which is good in his eyes: lo, I give thee the oxen for burnt-offerings, and the threshing instruments for wood, and the wheat for the meal-offering; I give it all.

24And king David said to Ornan, Nay; but I will verily buy it for the full price: for I will not take that which is thine for Yahweh, nor offer a burnt-offering without cost.

25So David gave to Ornan for the place six hundred shekels of gold by weight.

26And David built there an altar unto Yahweh, and offered burnt-offerings and peace-offerings, and called upon Yahweh; and he answered him from heaven by fire upon the altar of burnt-offering.

27And Yahweh commanded the angel; and he put up his sword again into the sheath thereof.

28At that time, when David saw that Yahweh had answered him in the threshing-floor of Ornan the Jebusite, then he sacrificed there.

29For the tabernacle of Yahweh, which Moses made in the wilderness, and the altar of burnt-offering, were at that time in the high place at Gibeon.

30But David could not go before it to inquire of God; for he was afraid because of the sword of the angel of Yahweh.

Chapter 22

1Then David said, This is the house of Yahweh God, and this is the altar of burnt-offering for Israel.

2And David commanded to gather together the sojourners that were in the land of Israel; and he set masons to hew wrought stones to build the house of God.

3And David prepared iron in abundance for the nails for the doors of the gates, and for the couplings; and brass in abundance without weight;

4and cedar-trees without number: for the Sidonians and they of Tyre brought cedar-trees in abundance to David.

5And David said, Solomon my son is young and tender, and the house that is to be builded for Yahweh must be exceeding magnificent, of fame and of glory throughout all countries: I will therefore make preparation for it. So David prepared abundantly before his death.

6Then he called for Solomon his son, and charged him to build a house for Yahweh, the God of Israel.

7And David said to Solomon his son, As for me, it was in my heart to build a house unto the name of Yahweh my God.

8But the word of Yahweh came to me, saying, Thou hast shed blood abundantly, and hast made great wars: thou shalt not build a house unto my name, because thou hast shed much blood upon the earth in my sight.

9Behold, a son shall be born to thee, who shall be a man of rest; and I will give him rest from all his enemies round about; for his name shall be Solomon, and I will give peace and quietness unto Israel in his days:

10he shall build a house for my name; and he shall be my son, and I will be his father; and I will establish the throne of his kingdom over Israel for ever.

11Now, my son, Yahweh be with thee; and prosper thou, and build the house of Yahweh thy God, as he hath spoken concerning thee.

12Only Yahweh give thee discretion and understanding, and give thee charge concerning Israel; that so thou mayest keep the law of Yahweh thy God.

13Then shalt thou prosper, if thou observe to do the statutes and the ordinances which Yahweh charged Moses with concerning Israel: be strong, and of good courage; fear not, neither be dismayed.

14Now, behold, in my affliction I have prepared for the house of Yahweh a hundred thousand talents of gold, and a thousand thousand talents of silver, and of brass and iron without weight; for it is in abundance: timber also and stone have I prepared; and thou mayest add thereto.

15Moreover there are workmen with thee in abundance, hewers and workers of stone and timber, and all men that are skilful in every manner of work:

16of the gold, the silver, and the brass, and the iron, there is no number. Arise and be doing, and Yahweh be with thee.

17David also commanded all the princes of Israel to help Solomon his son, saying,

18Is not Yahweh your God with you? and hath he not given you rest on every side? for he hath delivered the inhabitants of the land into my hand; and the land is subdued before Yahweh, and before his people.

19Now set your heart and your soul to seek after Yahweh your God; arise therefore, and build ye the sanctuary of Yahweh God, to bring the ark of the covenant of Yahweh, and the holy vessels of God, into the house that is to be built to the name of Yahweh.

Chapter 23

1Now David was old and full of days; and he made Solomon his son king over Israel.

2And he gathered together all the princes of Israel, with the priests and the Levites.

3And the Levites were numbered from thirty years old and upward: and their number by their polls, man by man, was thirty and eight thousand.

4Of these, twenty and four thousand were to oversee the work of the house of Yahweh; and six thousand were officers and judges;

5and four thousand were doorkeepers; and four thousand praised Yahweh with the instruments which I made, said David, to praise therewith.

6And David divided them into courses according to the sons of Levi: Gershon, Kohath, and Merari.

7Of the Gershonites: Ladan and Shimei.

8The sons of Ladan: Jehiel the chief, and Zetham, and Joel, three.

9The sons of Shimei: Shelomoth, and Haziel, and Haran, three. These were the heads of the fathers' houses of Ladan.

10And the sons of Shimei: Jahath, Zina, and Jeush, and Beriah. These four were the sons of Shimei.

11And Jahath was the chief, and Zizah the second: but Jeush and Beriah had not many sons; therefore they became a fathers' house in one reckoning.

12The sons of Kohath: Amram, Izhar, Hebron, and Uzziel, four.

13The sons of Amram: Aaron and Moses; and Aaron was separated, that he should sanctify the most holy things, he and his sons, for ever, to burn incense before Yahweh, to minister unto him, and to bless in his name, for ever.

14But as for Moses the man of God, his sons were named among the tribe of Levi.

15The sons of Moses: Gershom and Eliezer.

16The sons of Gershom: Shebuel the chief.

17And the sons of Eliezer were: Rehabiah the chief, and Eliezer had no other sons; but the sons of Rehabiah were very many.

18The sons of Izhar: Shelomith the chief.

19The sons of Hebron: Jeriah the chief, Amariah the second, Jahaziel the third, and Jekameam the fourth.

20The sons of Uzziel: Micah the chief, and Isshiah the second.

21The sons of Merari: Mahli and Mushi. The sons of Mahli: Eleazar and Kish.

22And Eleazar died, and had no sons, but daughters only: and their brethren the sons of Kish took them to wife.

23The sons of Mushi: Mahli, and Eder, and Jeremoth, three.

24These were the sons of Levi after their fathers' houses, even the heads of the fathers' houses of those of them that were counted, in the number of names by their polls, who did the work for the service of the house of Yahweh, from twenty years old and upward.

25For David said, Yahweh, the God of Israel, hath given rest unto his people; and he dwelleth in Jerusalem for ever:

26and also the Levites shall no more have need to carry the tabernacle and all the vessels of it for the service thereof.

27For by the last words of David the sons of Levi were numbered, from twenty years old and upward.

28For their office was to wait on the sons of Aaron for the service of the house of Yahweh, in the courts, and in the chambers, and in the purifying of all holy things, even the work of the service of the house of God;

29for the showbread also, and for the fine flour for a meal-offering, whether of unleavened wafers, or of that which is baked in the pan, or of that which is soaked, and for all manner of measure and size;

30and to stand every morning to thank and praise Yahweh, and likewise at even;

31and to offer all burnt-offerings unto Yahweh, on the sabbaths, on the new moons, and on the set feasts, in number according to the ordinance concerning them, continually before Yahweh;

32and that they should keep the charge of the tent of meeting, and the charge of the holy place, and the charge of the sons of Aaron their brethren, for the service of the house of Yahweh.

Chapter 24

1And the courses of the sons of Aaron were these. The sons of Aaron: Nadab and Abihu, Eleazar and Ithamar.

2But Nadab and Abihu died before their father, and had no children: therefore Eleazar and Ithamar executed the priest's office.

3And David with Zadok of the sons of Eleazar, and Ahimelech of the sons of Ithamar, divided them according to their ordering in their service.

4And there were more chief men found of the sons of Eleazar than of the sons of Ithamar; and thus were they divided: of the sons of Eleazar there were sixteen, heads of fathers' houses; and of the sons of Ithamar, according to their fathers' houses, eight.

5Thus were they divided by lot, one sort with another; for there were princes of the sanctuary, and princes of God, both of the sons of Eleazar, and of the sons of Ithamar.

6And Shemaiah the son of Nethanel the scribe, who was of the Levites, wrote them in the presence of the king, and the princes, and Zadok the priest, and Ahimelech the son of Abiathar, and the heads of the fathers' houses of the priests and of the Levites; one fathers' house being taken for Eleazar, and one taken for Ithamar.

7Now the first lot came forth to Jehoiarib, the second to Jedaiah,

8the third to Harim, the fourth to Seorim,

9the fifth to Malchijah, the sixth to Mijamin,

10the seventh to Hakkoz, the eighth to Abijah,

11the ninth to Jeshua, the tenth to Shecaniah,

12the eleventh to Eliashib, the twelfth to Jakim,

13the thirteenth to Huppah, the fourteenth to Jeshebeab,

14the fifteenth to Bilgah, the sixteenth to Immer,

15the seventeenth to Hezir, the eighteenth to Happizzez,

16the nineteenth to Pethahiah, the twentieth to Jehezkel,

17the one and twentieth to Jachin, the two and twentieth to Gamul,

First Chronicles

18the three and twentieth to Delaiah, the four and twentieth to Maaziah.

19This was the ordering of them in their service, to come into the house of Yahweh according to the ordinance given unto them by Aaron their father, as Yahweh, the God of Israel, had commanded him.

20And of the rest of the sons of Levi: of the sons of Amram, Shubael; of the sons of Shubael, Jehdeiah.

21Of Rehabiah: of the sons of Rehabiah, Isshiah the chief.

22Of the Izharites, Shelomoth; of the sons of Shelomoth, Jahath.

23And the sons of Hebron: Jeriah the chief, Amariah the second, Jahaziel the third, Jekameam the fourth.

24The sons of Uzziel, Micah; of the sons of Micah, Shamir.

25The brother of Micah, Isshiah; of the sons of Isshiah, Zechariah.

26The sons of Merari: Mahli and Mushi; the sons of Jaaziah: Beno.

27The sons of Merari: of Jaaziah, Beno, and Shoham, and Zaccur, and Ibri.

28Of Mahli: Eleazar, who had no sons.

29Of Kish; the sons of Kish: Jerahmeel.

30And the sons of Mushi: Mahli, and Eder, and Jerimoth. These were the sons of the Levites after their fathers' houses.

31These likewise cast lots even as their brethren the sons of Aaron in the presence of David the king, and Zadok, and Ahimelech, and the heads of the fathers' houses of the priests and of the Levites; the fathers' houses of the chief even as those of his younger brother.

Chapter 25

1Moreover David and the captains of the host set apart for the service certain of the sons of Asaph, and of Heman, and of Jeduthun, who should prophesy with harps, with psalteries, and with cymbals: and the number of them that did the work according to their service was:

2of the sons of Asaph: Zaccur, and Joseph, and Nethaniah, and Asharelah, the sons of Asaph, under the hand of Asaph, who prophesied after the order of the king.

3Of Jeduthun; the sons of Jeduthun: Gedaliah, and Zeri, and Jeshaiah, Hashabiah, and Mattithiah, six, under the hands of their father Jeduthun with the harp, who prophesied in giving thanks and praising Yahweh.

4Of Heman; the sons of Heman: Bukkiah, Mattaniah, Uzziel, Shebuel, and Jerimoth, Hananiah, Hanani, Eliathah, Giddalti, and Romamti-ezer, Joshbekashah, Mallothi, Hothir, Mahazioth.

5All these were the sons of Heman the king's seer in the words of God, to lift up the horn. And God gave to Heman fourteen sons and three daughters.

6All these were under the hands of their father for song in the house of Yahweh, with cymbals, psalteries, and harps, for the service of the house of God; Asaph, Jeduthun, and Heman being under the order of the king.

7And the number of them, with their brethren that were instructed in singing unto Yahweh, even all that were skilful, was two hundred fourscore and eight.

8And they cast lots for their offices, all alike, as well the small as the great, the teacher as the scholar.

9Now the first lot came forth for Asaph to Joseph: the second to Gedaliah; he and his brethren and sons were twelve:

10the third to Zaccur, his sons and his brethren, twelve:

11the fourth to Izri, his sons and his brethren, twelve:

12the fifth to Nethaniah, his sons and his brethren, twelve:

13the sixth to Bukkiah, his sons and his brethren, twelve:

14the seventh to Jesharelah, his sons and his brethren, twelve:

15the eighth to Jeshaiah, his sons and his brethren, twelve:

16the ninth to Mattaniah, his sons and his brethren, twelve:

17the tenth to Shimei, his sons and his brethren, twelve:

18the eleventh to Azarel, his sons and his brethren, twelve:

19the twelfth to Hashabiah, his sons and his brethren, twelve:

20for the thirteenth, Shubael, his sons and his brethren, twelve:

21for the fourteenth, Mattithiah, his sons and his brethren, twelve:

22for the fifteenth to Jeremoth, his sons and his brethren, twelve:

23for the sixteenth to Hananiah, his sons and his brethren, twelve:

24for the seventeenth to Joshbekashah, his sons and his brethren, twelve:

25for the eighteenth to Hanani, his sons and his brethren, twelve:

26for the nineteenth to Mallothi, his sons and his brethren, twelve:

27for the twentieth to Eliathah, his sons and his brethren, twelve:

28for the one and twentieth to Hothir, his sons and his brethren, twelve:

29for the two and twentieth to Giddalti, his sons and his brethren, twelve:

30for the three and twentieth to Mahazioth, his sons and his brethren, twelve:

31for the four and twentieth to Romamtiezer, his sons and his brethren, twelve.

Chapter 26

1For the courses of the doorkeepers: of the Korahites, Meshelemiah the son of Kore, of the sons of Asaph.

2And Meshelemiah had sons: Zechariah the first-born, Jediael the second, Zebadiah the third, Jathniel the fourth;

3Elam the fifth, Jehohanan the sixth, Eliehoenai the seventh.

4And Obed-edom had sons: Shemaiah the first-born, Jehozabad the second, Joah the third, and Sacar the fourth, and Nethanel the fifth,

5Ammiel the sixth, Issachar the seventh, Peullethai the eighth; for God blessed him.

6Also unto Shemaiah his son were sons born, that ruled over the house of their father; for they were mighty men of valor.

7The sons of Shemaiah: Othni, and Rephael, and Obed, Elzabad, whose brethren were valiant men, Elihu, and Semachiah.

8All these were of the sons of Obed-edom: they and their sons and their brethren, able men in strength for the service; threescore and two of Obed-edom.

9And Meshelemiah had sons and brethren, valiant men, eighteen.

10Also Hosah, of the children of Merari, had sons: Shimri the chief, (for though he was not the first-born, yet his father made him chief),

11Hilkiah the second, Tebaliah the third, Zechariah the fourth: all the sons and brethren of Hosah were thirteen.

12Of these were the courses of the doorkeepers, even of the chief men, having offices like their brethren, to minister in the house of Yahweh.

13And they cast lots, as well the small as the great, according to their fathers' houses, for every gate.

14And the lot eastward fell to Shelemiah. Then for Zechariah his son, a discreet counsellor, they cast lots; and his lot came out northward.

15To Obed-edom southward; and to his sons the store-house.

16To Shuppim and Hosah westward, by the gate of Shallecheth, at the causeway that goeth up, watch against watch.

17Eastward were six Levites, northward four a day, southward four a day, and for the store-house two and two.

18For Parbar westward, four at the causeway, and two at Parbar.

19These were the courses of the doorkeepers; of the sons of the Korahites, and of the sons of Merari.

20And of the Levites, Ahijah was over the treasures of the house of God, and over the treasures of the dedicated things.

21The sons of Ladan, the sons of the Gershonites belonging to Ladan, the heads of the fathers' houses belonging to Ladan the Gershonite: Jehieli.

22The sons of Jehieli: Zetham, and Joel his brother, over the treasures of the house of Yahweh.

23Of the Amramites, of the Izharites, of the Hebronites, of the Uzzielites:

24and Shebuel the son of Gershom, the son of Moses, was ruler over the treasures.

25And his brethren: of Eliezer came Rehabiah his son, and Jeshaiah his son, and Joram his son, and Zichri his son, and Shelomoth his son.

26This Shelomoth and his brethren were over all the treasures of the dedicated things, which David the king, and the heads of the fathers' houses, the captains over thousands and hundreds, and the captains of the host, had dedicated.

27Out of the spoil won in battles did they dedicate to repair the house of Yahweh.

28And all that Samuel the seer, and Saul the son of Kish, and Abner the son of Ner, and Joab the son of Zeruiah, had dedicated, whosoever had dedicated anything, it was under the hand of Shelomoth, and of his brethren.

29Of the Izharites, Chenaniah and his sons were for the outward business over Israel, for officers and judges.

30Of the Hebronites, Hashabiah and his brethren, men of valor, a thousand and seven hundred, had the oversight of Israel beyond the Jordan westward, for all the business of Yahweh, and for the service of the king.

31Of the Hebronites was Jerijah the chief, even of the Hebronites, according to their generations by fathers' houses. In the fortieth year of the reign of David they were sought for, and there were found among them mighty men of valor at Jazer of Gilead.

32And his brethren, men of valor, were two thousand and seven hundred, heads of fathers' houses, whom king David made overseers over the Reubenites, and the Gadites, and the half-tribe of the Manassites, for every matter pertaining to God, and for the affairs of the king.

Chapter 27

1Now the children of Israel after their number, to wit, the heads of fathers' houses and the captains of thousands and of hundreds, and their officers that served the king, in any matter of the courses which came in and went out month by month throughout all the months of the year-of every course were twenty and four thousand.

2Over the first course for the first month was Jashobeam the son of Zabdiel: and in his course were twenty and four thousand.

3He was of the children of Perez, the chief of all the captains of the host for the first month.

4And over the course of the second month was Dodai the Ahohite, and his course; and Mikloth the ruler: and in his course were twenty and four thousand.

5The third captain of the host for the third month was Benaiah, the son of Jehoiada the priest, chief: and in his course were twenty and four thousand.

6This is that Benaiah, who was the mighty man of the thirty, and over the thirty: and of his course was Ammizabad his son.

7The fourth captain for the fourth month was Asahel the brother of Joab, and Zebadiah his son after him: and in his course were twenty and four thousand.

8The fifth captain for this fifth month was Shamhuth the Izrahite: and in his course were twenty and four thousand.

9The sixth captain for the sixth month was Ira the son of Ikkesh the Tekoite: and in his course were twenty and four thousand.

10The seventh captain for the seventh month was Helez the Pelonite, of the children of Ephraim: and in his course were twenty and four thousand.

11The eighth captain for the eighth month was Sibbecai the Hushathite, of the Zerahites: and in his course were twenty and four thousand.

12The ninth captain for the ninth month was Abiezer the Anathothite, of the Benjamites: and in his course were twenty and four thousand.

13The tenth captain for the tenth month was Maharai the Netophathite, of the Zerahites: and in his course were twenty and four thousand.

14The eleventh captain for the eleventh month was Benaiah the Pirathonite, of the children of Ephraim: and in his course were twenty and four thousand.

15The twelfth captain for the twelfth month was Heldai the Netophathite, of Othniel: and in his course were twenty and four thousand.

16Furthermore over the tribes of Israel: of the Reubenites was Eliezer the son of Zichri the ruler: of the Simeonites, Shephatiah the son of Maacah:

17of Levi, Hashabiah the son of Kemuel: of Aaron, Zadok:

18of Judah, Elihu, one of the brethren of David: of Issachar, Omri the son of Michael:

19of Zebulun, Ishmaiah the son of Obadiah: of Naphtali, Jeremoth the son of Azriel:

20of the children of Ephraim, Hoshea the son of Azaziah: of the half-tribe of Manasseh, Joel the son of Pedaiah:

21of the half-tribe of Manasseh in Gilead, Iddo the son of Zechariah: of Benjamin, Jaasiel the son of Abner:

22of Dan, Azarel the son of Jeroham. These were the captains of the tribes of Israel.

23But David took not the number of them from twenty years old and under, because Yahweh had said he would increase Israel like to the stars of heaven.

24Joab the son of Zeruiah began to number, but finished not; and there came wrath for this upon Israel; neither was the number put into the account in the chronicles of king David.

25And over the king's treasures was Azmaveth the son of Adiel: and over the treasures in the fields, in the cities, and in the villages, and in the castles, was Jonathan the son of Uzziah:

26And over them that did the work of the field for tillage of the ground was Ezri the son of Chelub:

27and over the vineyards was Shimei the Ramathite: and over the increase of the vineyards for the wine-cellars was Zabdi the Shiphmite:

28and over the olive-trees and the sycomore-trees that were in the lowland was Baal-hanan the Gederite: and over the cellars of oil was Joash:

29and over the herds that fed in Sharon was Shitrai the Sharonite: and over the herds that were in the valleys was Shaphat the son of Adlai:

30and over the camels was Obil the Ishmaelite: and over the asses was Jehdeiah the Meronothite: and over the flocks was Jaziz the Hagrite.

31All these were the rulers of the substance which was king David's.

32Also Jonathan, David's uncle, was a counsellor, a man of understanding, and a scribe: and Jehiel the son of Hachmoni was with the king's sons:

33And Ahithophel was the king's counsellor: and Hushai the Archite was the king's friend:

34and after Ahithophel was Jehoiada the son of Benaiah, and Abiathar: and the captain of the king's host was Joab.

Chapter 28

1And David assembled all the princes of Israel, the princes of the tribes, and the captains of the companies that served the king by course, and the captains of thousands, and the captains of hundreds, and the rulers over all the substance and possessions of the king and of his sons, with the officers, and the mighty men, even all the mighty men of valor, unto Jerusalem.

2Then David the king stood up upon his feet, and said, Hear me, my brethren, and my people: as for me, it was in my heart to build a house of rest for the ark of the covenant of Yahweh, and for the footstool of our God; and I had made ready for the building.

3But God said unto me, Thou shalt not build a house for my name, because thou art a man of war, and hast shed blood.

4Howbeit Yahweh, the God of Israel, chose me out of all the house of my father to be king over Israel for ever: for he hath chosen Judah to be prince; and in the house of Judah, the house of my father; and among the sons of my father he took pleasure in me to make me king over all Israel;

5And of all my sons (for Yahweh hath given me many sons), he hath chosen Solomon my son to sit upon the throne of the kingdom of Yahweh over Israel.

6And he said unto me, Solomon thy son, he shall build my house and my courts; for I have chosen him to be my son, and I will be his father.

7And I will establish his kingdom for ever, if he be constant to do my commandments and mine ordinances, as at this day.

8Now therefore, in the sight of all Israel, the assembly of Yahweh, and in the audience of our God, observe and seek out all the commandments of Yahweh your God; that ye may possess this good land, and leave it for an inheritance to your children after you for ever.

9And thou, Solomon my son, know thou the God of thy father, and serve him with a perfect heart and with a willing mind; for Yahweh searcheth all hearts, and understandeth all the imaginations of the thoughts: if thou seek him, he will be found of thee; but if thou forsake him, he will cast thee off for ever.

10Take heed now; for Yahweh hath chosen thee to build a house for the sanctuary: be strong, and do it.

11Then David gave to Solomon his son the pattern of the porch of the temple, and of the houses thereof, and of the treasuries thereof, and of the upper rooms thereof, and of the inner chambers thereof, and of the place of the mercy-seat;

12and the pattern of all that he had by the Spirit, for the courts of the house of Yahweh, and for all the chambers round about, for the treasuries of the house of God, and for the treasuries of the dedicated things;

13also for the courses of the priests and the Levites, and for all the work of the service of the house of Yahweh, and for all the vessels of service in the house of Yahweh;

14of gold by weight for the vessels of gold, for all vessels of every kind of service; of silver for all the vessels of silver by weight, for all vessels of every kind of service;

15by weight also for the candlesticks of gold, and for the lamps thereof, of gold, by weight for every candlestick and for the lamps thereof; and for the candlesticks of silver, silver by weight for every candlestick and for the lamps thereof, according to the use of every candlestick;

16and the gold by weight for the tables of showbread, for every table; and silver for the tables of silver;

17and the flesh-hooks, and the basins, and the cups, of pure gold; and for the golden bowls by weight for every bowl; and for the silver bowls by weight for every bowl;

18and for the altar of incense refined gold by weight; and gold for the pattern of the chariot, even the cherubim, that spread out their wings, and covered the ark of the covenant of Yahweh.

19All this, said David, have I been made to understand in writing from the hand of Yahweh, even all the works of this pattern.

20And David said to Solomon his son, Be strong and of good courage, and do it: fear not, nor be dismayed; for Yahweh God, even my God, is with thee; he will not fail thee, nor forsake thee, until all the work for the service of the house of Yahweh be finished.

21And, behold, there are the courses of the priests and the Levites, for all the service of the house of God: and there shall be with thee in all manner of work every willing man that hath skill, for any manner of service: also the captains and all the people will be wholly at thy commandment.

Chapter 29

1And David the king said unto all the assembly, Solomon my son, whom alone God hath chosen, is yet young and tender, and the work is great; for the palace is not for man, but for Yahweh God.

2Now I have prepared with all my might for the house of my God the gold for the things of gold, and the silver for the things of silver, and the brass for the things of brass, the iron for the things of iron, and wood for the things of wood; onyx stones, and stones to be set, stones for inlaid work, and of divers colors, and all manner of precious stones, and marble stones in abundance.

3Moreover also, because I have set my affection on the house of my God, seeing that I have a treasure of mine own of gold and silver, I give it unto the house of my God, over and above all that I have prepared for the holy house,

4even three thousand talents of gold, of the gold of Ophir, and seven thousand talents of refined silver, wherewith to overlay the walls of the houses;

5of gold for the things of gold, and of silver for the things of silver, and for all manner of work to be made by the hands of artificers. Who then offereth willingly to consecrate himself this day unto Yahweh?

6Then the princes of the fathers' houses, and the princes of the tribes of Israel, and the captains of thousands and of hundreds, with the rulers over the king's work, offered willingly;

7and they gave for the service of the house of God of gold five thousand talents and ten thousand darics, and of silver ten thousand talents, and of brass eighteen thousand talents, and of iron a hundred thousand talents.

8And they with whom precious stones were found gave them to the treasure of the house of Yahweh, under the hand of Jehiel the Gershonite.

9Then the people rejoiced, for that they offered willingly, because with a perfect heart they offered willingly to Yahweh: and David the king also rejoiced with great joy.

10Wherefore David blessed Yahweh before all the assembly; and David said, Blessed be thou, O Yahweh, the God of Israel our father, for ever and ever.

11Thine, O Yahweh, is the greatness, and the power, and the glory, and the victory, and the majesty: for all that is in the heavens and in the earth is thine; thine is the kingdom, O Yahweh, and thou art exalted as head above all.

12Both riches and honor come of thee, and thou rulest over all; and in thy hand is power and might; and in thy hand it is to make great, and to give strength unto all.

13Now therefore, our God, we thank thee, and praise thy glorious name.

14But who am I, and what is my people, that we should be able to offer so willingly after this sort? for all things come of thee, and of thine own have we given thee.

15For we are strangers before thee, and sojourners, as all our fathers were: our days on the earth are as a shadow, and there is no abiding.

16O Yahweh our God, all this store that we have prepared to build thee a house for thy holy name cometh of thy hand, and is all thine own.

17I know also, my God, that thou triest the heart, and hast pleasure in uprightness. As for me, in the uprightness of my heart I have willingly offered all these things: and now have I seen with joy thy people, that are present here, offer willingly unto thee.

18O Yahweh, the God of Abraham, of Isaac, and of Israel, our fathers, keep this for ever in the imagination of the thoughts of the heart of thy people, and prepare their heart unto thee;

19and give unto Solomon my son a perfect heart, to keep thy commandments, thy testimonies, and thy statutes, and to do all these things, and to build the palace, for which I have made provision.

20And David said to all the assembly, Now bless Yahweh your God. And all the assembly blessed Yahweh, the God of their fathers, and bowed down their heads, and worshipped Yahweh, and the king.

21And they sacrificed sacrifices unto Yahweh, and offered burnt-offerings unto Yahweh, on the morrow after that day, even a thousand bullocks, a thousand rams, and a thousand lambs, with their drink-offerings, and sacrifices in abundance for all Israel,

22and did eat and drink before Yahweh on that day with great gladness.

And they made Solomon the son of David king the second time, and anointed him unto Yahweh to be prince, and Zadok to be priest.

23Then Solomon sat on the throne of Yahweh as king instead of David his father, and prospered; and all Israel obeyed him.

24And all the princes, and the mighty men, and all the sons likewise of king David, submitted themselves unto Solomon the king.

25And Yahweh magnified Solomon exceedingly in the sight of all Israel, and bestowed upon him such royal majesty as had not been on any king before him in Israel.

26Now David the son of Jesse reigned over all Israel.

27And the time that he reigned over Israel was forty years; seven years

First Chronicles
reigned he in Hebron, and thirty and three years reigned he in Jerusalem.

²⁸And he died in a good old age, full of days, riches, and honor: and Solomon his son reigned in his stead.

²⁹Now the acts of David the king, first and last, behold, they are written in the history of Samuel the seer, and in the history of Nathan the prophet, and in the history of Gad the seer,

³⁰with all his reign and his might, and the times that went over him, and over Israel, and over all the kingdoms of the countries.

The Second Book of the Chronicles

Chapter 1

1 And Solomon the son of David was strengthened in his kingdom, and Yahweh his God was with him, and magnified him exceedingly.

2 And Solomon spake unto all Israel, to the captains of thousands and of hundreds, and to the judges, and to every prince in all Israel, the heads of the fathers' houses.

3 So Solomon, and all the assembly with him, went to the high place that was at Gibeon; for there was the tent of meeting of God, which Moses the servant of Yahweh had made in the wilderness.

4 But the ark of God had David brought up from Kiriath-jearim to the place that David had prepared for it; for he had pitched a tent for it at Jerusalem.

5 Moreover the brazen altar, that Bezalel the son of Uri, the son of Hur, had made, was there before the tabernacle of Yahweh: and Solomon and the assembly sought unto it.

6 And Solomon went up thither to the brazen altar before Yahweh, which was at the tent of meeting, and offered a thousand burnt-offerings upon it.

7 In that night did God appear unto Solomon, and said unto him, Ask what I shall give thee.

8 And Solomon said unto God, Thou hast showed great lovingkindness unto David my father, and hast made me king in his stead.

9 Now, O Yahweh God, let thy promise unto David my father be established; for thou hast made me king over a people like the dust of the earth in multitude.

10 Give me now wisdom and knowledge, that I may go out and come in before this people; for who can judge this thy people, that is so great?

11 And God said to Solomon, Because this was in thy heart, and thou hast not asked riches, wealth, or honor, nor the life of them that hate thee, neither yet hast asked long life; but hast asked wisdom and knowledge for thyself, that thou mayest judge my people, over whom I have made thee king:

12 wisdom and knowledge is granted unto thee; and I will give thee riches, and wealth, and honor, such as none of the kings have had that have been before thee; neither shall there any after thee have the like.

13 So Solomon came from the high place that was at Gibeon, from before the tent of meeting, unto Jerusalem; and he reigned over Israel.

14 And Solomon gathered chariots and horsemen: and he had a thousand and four hundred chariots, and twelve thousand horsemen, that he placed in the chariot cities, and with the king at Jerusalem.

15 And the king made silver and gold to be in Jerusalem as stones, and cedars made he to be as the sycomore-trees that are in the lowland, for abundance.

16 And the horses which Solomon had were brought out of Egypt; the king's merchants received them in droves, each drove at a price.

17 And they fetched up and brought out of Egypt a chariot for six hundred shekels of silver, and a horse for a hundred and fifty: and so for all the kings of the Hittites, and the kings of Syria, did they bring them out by their means.

Chapter 2

1 Now Solomon purposed to build a house for the name of Yahweh, and a house for his kingdom.

2 And Solomon counted out threescore and ten thousand men to bear burdens, and fourscore thousand men that were hewers in the mountains, and three thousand and six hundred to oversee them.

3 And Solomon sent to Huram the king of Tyre, saying, As thou didst deal with David my father, and didst send him cedars to build him a house to dwell therein, even so deal with me.

4 Behold, I am about to build a house for the name of Yahweh my God, to dedicate it to him, and to burn before him incense of sweet spices, and for the continual showbread, and for the burnt-offerings morning and evening, on the sabbaths, and on the new moons, and on the set feasts of Yahweh our God. This is an ordinance for ever to Israel.

5 And the house which I build is great; for great is our God above all gods.

6 But who is able to build him a house, seeing heaven and the heaven of heavens cannot contain him? who am I then, that I should build him a house, save only to burn incense before him?

7 Now therefore send me a man skilful to work in gold, and in silver, and in brass, and in iron, and in purple, and crimson, and blue, and that knoweth how to grave all manner of gravings, to be with the skilful men that are with me in Judah and in Jerusalem, whom David my father did provide.

8 Send me also cedar-trees, fir-trees, and algum-trees, out of Lebanon; for I know that thy servants know how to cut timber in Lebanon: and, behold, my servants shall be with thy servants,

9 even to prepare me timber in abundance; for the house which I am about to build shall be great and wonderful.

10 And, behold, I will give to thy servants, the hewers that cut timber, twenty thousand measures of beaten wheat, and twenty thousand measures of barley, and twenty thousand baths of wine, and twenty thousand baths of oil.

11 Then Huram the king of Tyre answered in writing, which he sent to Solomon, Because Yahweh loveth his people, he hath made thee king over them.

12 Huram said moreover, Blessed be Yahweh, the God of Israel, that made heaven and earth, who hath given to David the king a wise son, endued with discretion and understanding, that should build a house for Yahweh, and a house for his kingdom.

13 And now I have sent a skilful man, endued with understanding, of Huram my father's,

14 the son of a woman of the daughters of Dan; and his father was a man of Tyre, skilful to work in gold, and in silver, in brass, in iron, in stone, and in timber, in purple, in blue, and in fine linen, and in crimson, also to grave any manner of graving, and to devise any device; that there may be a place appointed unto him with thy skilful men, and with the skilful men of my lord David thy father.

15 Now therefore the wheat and the barley, the oil and the wine, which my lord hath spoken of, let him send unto his servants:

16 and we will cut wood out of Lebanon, as much as thou shalt need; and we will bring it to thee in floats by sea to Joppa; and thou shalt carry it up to Jerusalem.

17 And Solomon numbered all the sojourners that were in the land of Israel, after the numbering wherewith David his father had numbered them; and they were found a hundred and fifty thousand and three thousand and six hundred.

18 And he set threescore and ten thousand of them to bear burdens, and fourscore thousand that were hewers in the mountains, and three thousand and six hundred overseers to set the people at work.

Chapter 3

1 Then Solomon began to build the house of Yahweh at Jerusalem on mount Moriah, where Yahweh appeared unto David his father, which he made ready in the place that David had appointed, in the threshing-floor of Ornan the Jebusite.

2 And he began to build in the second day of the second month, in the fourth year of his reign.

3 Now these are the foundations which Solomon laid for the building of the house of God. The length by cubits after the first measure was threescore cubits, and the breadth twenty cubits.

4 And the porch that was before the house, the length of it, according to the breadth of the house, was twenty cubits, and the height a hundred and twenty; and he overlaid it within with pure gold.

5 And the greater house he ceiled with fir-wood, which he overlaid with fine gold, and wrought thereon palm-trees and chains.

6 And he garnished the house with precious stones for beauty: and the gold was gold of Parvaim.

7 He overlaid also the house, the beams, the thresholds, and the walls thereof, and the doors thereof, with gold; and graved cherubim on the walls.

8 And he made the most holy house: the length thereof, according to the breadth of the house, was twenty cubits, and the breadth thereof twenty cubits; and he overlaid it with fine gold, amounting to six hundred talents.

9 And the weight of the nails was fifty shekels of gold. And he overlaid the upper chambers with gold.

10 And in the most holy house he made two cherubim of image work; and they overlaid them with gold.

11 And the wings of the cherubim were twenty cubits long: the wing of the one cherub was five cubits, reaching to the wall of the house; and the other wing was likewise five cubits, reaching to the wing of the other cherub.

12 And the wing of the other cherub was five cubits, reaching to the wall of the house; and the other wing was five cubits also, joining to the wing of the other cherub.

13 The wings of these cherubim spread themselves forth twenty cubits: and they stood on their feet, and their faces were toward the house.

14 And he made the veil of blue, and purple, and crimson, and fine linen, and wrought cherubim thereon.

15 Also he made before the house two pillars of thirty and five cubits high, and the capital that was on the top of each of them was five cubits.

16 And he made chains in the oracle, and put them on the tops of the pillars; and he made a hundred pomegranates, and put them on the chains.

17 And he set up the pillars before the temple, one on the right hand, and the other on the left; and called the name of that on the right hand Jachin, and the name of that on the left Boaz.

Chapter 4

1 Moreover he made an altar of brass, twenty cubits the length thereof, and twenty cubits the breadth thereof, and ten cubits the height thereof.

2 Also he made the molten sea of ten cubits from brim to brim, round in compass; and the height thereof was five cubits; and a line of thirty cubits compassed it round about.

3 And under it was the likeness of oxen, which did compass it round about, for ten cubits, compassing the sea round about. The oxen were in two rows, cast when it was cast.

4 It stood upon twelve oxen, three looking toward the north, and three looking toward the west, and three looking toward the south, and three looking toward the east: and the sea was set upon them above, and all their hinder parts were inward.

5 And it was a handbreadth thick; and the brim thereof was wrought like the brim of a cup, like the flower of a lily: it received and held three thousand baths.

6 He made also ten lavers, and put five on the right hand, and five on the left, to wash in them; such things as belonged to the burnt-offering they washed in them; but the sea was for the priests to wash in.

7 And he made the ten candlesticks of gold according to the ordinance concerning them; and he set them in the temple, five on the right hand, and five on the left.

8 He made also ten tables, and placed them in the temple, five on the right side, and five on the left. And he made a hundred basins of gold.

9 Furthermore he made the court of the priests, and the great court, and doors for the court, and overlaid the doors of them with brass.

10 And he set the sea on the right side of the house eastward, toward the

Second Chronicles

11And Huram made the pots, and the shovels, and the basins. So Huram made an end of doing the work that he wrought for king Solomon in the house of God:

12the two pillars, and the bowls, and the two capitals which were on the top of the pillars, and the two networks to cover the two bowls of the capitals that were on the top of the pillars,

13and the four hundred pomegranates for the two networks; two rows of pomegranates for each network, to cover the two bowls of the capitals that were upon the pillars.

14He made also the bases, and the lavers made he upon the bases;

15one sea, and the twelve oxen under it.

16The pots also, and the shovels, and the flesh-hooks, and all the vessels thereof, did Huram his father make for king Solomon for the house of Yahweh of bright brass.

17In the plain of the Jordan did the king cast them, in the clay ground between Succoth and Zeredah.

18Thus Solomon made all these vessels in great abundance: for the weight of the brass could not be found out.

19And Solomon made all the vessels that were in the house of God, the golden altar also, and the tables whereon was the showbread;

20and the candlesticks with their lamps, to burn according to the ordinance before the oracle, of pure gold;

21and the flowers, and the lamps, and the tongs, of gold, and that perfect gold;

22and the snuffers, and the basins, and the spoons, and the firepans, of pure gold: and as for the entry of the house, the inner doors thereof for the most holy place, and the doors of the house, to wit, of the temple, were of gold.

Chapter 5

1Thus all the work that Solomon wrought for the house of Yahweh was finished. And Solomon brought in the things that David his father had dedicated, even the silver, and the gold, and all the vessels, and put them in the treasuries of the house of God.

2Then Solomon assembled the elders of Israel, and all the heads of the tribes, the princes of the fathers' houses of the children of Israel, unto Jerusalem, to bring up the ark of the covenant of Yahweh out of the city of David, which is Zion.

3nd all the men of Israel assembled themselves unto the king at the feast, which was in the seventh month.

4And all the elders of Israel came: and the Levites took up the ark;

5and they brought up the ark, and the tent of meeting, and all the holy vessels that were in the Tent; these did the priests the Levites bring up.

6And king Solomon and all the congregation of Israel, that were assembled unto him, were before the ark, sacrificing sheep and oxen, that could not be counted nor numbered for multitude.

7And the priests brought in the ark of the covenant of Yahweh unto its place, into the oracle of the house, to the most holy place, even under the wings of the cherubim.

8For the cherubim spread forth their wings over the place of the ark, and the cherubim covered the ark and the staves thereof above.

9And the staves were so long that the ends of the staves were seen from the ark before the oracle; but they were not seen without: and there it is unto this day.

10There was nothing in the ark save the two tables which Moses put there at Horeb, when Yahweh made a covenant with the children of Israel, when they came out of Egypt.

11And it came to pass, when the priests were come out of the holy place, (for all the priests that were present had sanctified themselves, and did not keep their courses;

12also the Levites who were the singers, all of them, even Asaph, Heman, Jeduthun, and their sons and their brethren, arrayed in fine linen, with cymbals and psalteries and harps, stood at the east end of the altar, and with them a hundred and twenty priests sounding with trumpets;)

13it came to pass, when the trumpeters and singers were as one, to make one sound to be heard in praising and thanking Yahweh; and when they lifted up their voice with the trumpets and cymbals and instruments of music, and praised Yahweh, saying, For he is good; for his lovingkindness endureth for ever; that then the house was filled with a cloud, even the house of Yahweh,

14so that the priests could not stand to minister by reason of the cloud: for the glory of Yahweh filled the house of God.

Chapter 6

1Then spake Solomon, Yahweh hath said that he would dwell in the thick darkness.

2But I have built thee a house of habitation, and a place for thee to dwell in for ever.

3And the king turned his face, and blessed all the assembly of Israel: and all the assembly of Israel stood.

4And he said, Blessed be Yahweh, the God of Israel, who spake with his mouth unto David my father, and hath with his hands fulfilled it, saying,

5Since the day that I brought forth my people out of the land of Egypt, I chose no city out of all the tribes of Israel to build a house in, that my name might be there; neither chose I any man to be prince over my people Israel:

6but I have chosen Jerusalem, that my name might be there; and have chosen David to be over my people Israel.

7Now it was in the heart of David my father to build a house for the name of Yahweh, the God of Israel.

8But Yahweh said unto David my father, Whereas it was in thy heart to build a house for my name, thou didst well that it was in thy heart:

9nevertheless thou shalt not build the house; but thy son that shall come forth out of thy loins, he shall build the house for my name.

10And Yahweh hath performed his word that he spake; for I am risen up in the room of David my father, and sit on the throne of Israel, as Yahweh promised, and have built the house for the name of Yahweh, the God of Israel.

11And there have I set the ark, wherein is the covenant of Yahweh, which he made with the children of Israel.

12And he stood before the altar of Yahweh in the presence of all the assembly of Israel, and spread forth his hands

13(for Solomon had made a brazen scaffold, five cubits long, and five cubits broad, and three cubits high, and had set it in the midst of the court; and upon it he stood, and kneeled down upon his knees before all the assembly of Israel, and spread forth his hands toward heaven;)

14and he said, O Yahweh, the God of Israel, there is no God like thee, in heaven, or on earth; who keepest covenant and lovingkindness with thy servants, that walk before thee with all their heart;

15who hast kept with thy servant David my father that which thou didst promise him: yea, thou spakest with thy mouth, and hast fulfilled it with thy hand, as it is this day.

16Now therefore, O Yahweh, the God of Israel, keep with thy servant David my father that which thou hast promised him, saying, There shall not fail thee a man in my sight to sit on the throne of Israel, if only thy children take heed to their way, to walk in my law as thou hast walked before me.

17Now therefore, O Yahweh, the God of Israel, let thy word be verified, which thou spakest unto thy servant David.

18But will God in very deed dwell with men on the earth? behold, heaven and the heaven of heavens cannot contain thee; how much less this house which I have builded!

19Yet have thou respect unto the prayer of thy servant, and to his supplication, O Yahweh my God, to hearken unto the cry and to the prayer which thy servant prayeth before thee;

20that thine eyes may be open toward this house day and night, even toward the place whereof thou hast said that thou wouldest put thy name there; to hearken unto the prayer which thy servant shall pray toward this place.

21And hearken thou to the supplications of thy servant, and of thy people Israel, when they shall pray toward this place: yea, hear thou from thy dwelling-place, even from heaven; and when thou hearest forgive.

22If a man sin against his neighbor, and an oath be laid upon him to cause him to swear, and he come and swear before thine altar in this house;

23then hear thou from heaven, and do, and judge thy servants, requiting the wicked, to bring his way upon his own head; and justifying the righteous, to give him according to his righteousness.

24And if thy people Israel be smitten down before the enemy, because they have sinned against thee, and shall turn again and confess thy name, and pray and make supplication before thee in this house;

25then hear thou from heaven, and forgive the sin of thy people Israel, and bring them again unto the land which thou gavest to them and to their fathers.

26When the heavens are shut up, and there is no rain, because they have sinned against thee; if they pray toward this place, and confess thy name, and turn from their sin, when thou dost afflict them:

27then hear thou in heaven, and forgive the sin of thy servants, and of thy people Israel, when thou teachest them the good way wherein they should walk; and send rain upon thy land, which thou hast given to thy people for an inheritance.

28If there be in the land famine, if there be pestilence, if there be blasting or mildew, locust or caterpillar; if their enemies besiege them in the land of their cities; whatsoever plague or whatsoever sickness there be;

29what prayer and supplication soever be made by any man, or by all thy people Israel, who shall know every man his own plague and his own sorrow, and shall spread forth his hands toward this house:

30then hear thou from heaven thy dwelling-place and forgive, and render unto every man according to all his ways, whose heart thou knowest; (for thou, even thou only, knowest the hearts of the children of men;)

31that they may fear thee, to walk in thy ways, so long as they live in the land which thou gavest unto our fathers.

32Moreover concerning the foreigner, that is not of thy people Israel, when he shall come from a far country for thy great name's sake, and thy mighty hand, and thine outstretched arm; when they shall come and pray toward this house:

33then hear thou from heaven, even from thy dwelling-place, and do according to all that the foreigner calleth to thee for; that all the peoples of the earth may know thy name, and fear thee, as doth thy people Israel, and that they may know that this house which I have built is called by thy name.

34If thy people go out to battle against their enemies, by whatsoever way thou shalt send them, and they pray unto thee toward this city which thou hast chosen, and the house which I have built for thy name;

35then hear thou from heaven their prayer and their supplication, and maintain their cause.

36If they sin against thee (for there is no man that sinneth not), and thou be angry with them, and deliver them to the enemy, so that they carry them away captive unto a land far off or near;

37yet if they shall bethink themselves in the land whither they are carried captive, and turn again, and make supplication unto thee in the land of their captivity, saying, We have sinned, we have done perversely, and have dealt wickedly;

38if they return unto thee with all their heart and with all their soul in the land of their captivity, whither they have carried them captive, and pray toward their land, which thou gavest unto their fathers, and the city which thou hast chosen, and toward the house which I have built for thy name:

39then hear thou from heaven, even from thy dwelling-place, their prayer and their supplications, and maintain their cause, and forgive thy people who have sinned against thee.

40Now, O my God, let, I beseech thee, thine eyes be open, and let thine ears be attent, unto the prayer that is made in this place.

41Now therefore arise, O Yahweh God, into thy resting-place, thou, and the ark of thy strength: let thy priests, O Yahweh God, be clothed with salvation, and let thy saints rejoice in goodness.

42O Yahweh God, turn not away the face of thine anointed: remember thy lovingkindnesses to David thy servant.

Chapter 7

1Now when Solomon had made an end of praying, the fire came down from heaven, and consumed the burnt-offering and the sacrifices; and the glory of Yahweh filled the house.

2And the priests could not enter into the house of Yahweh, because the glory of Yahweh filled Yahweh's house.

3And all the children of Israel looked on, when the fire came down, and the glory of Yahweh was upon the house; and they bowed themselves with their faces to the ground upon the pavement, and worshipped, and gave thanks unto Yahweh, saying, For he is good; for his lovingkindness endureth for ever.

4Then the king and all the people offered sacrifice before Yahweh.

5And king Solomon offered a sacrifice of twenty and two thousand oxen, and a hundred and twenty thousand sheep. So the king and all the people dedicated the house of God.

6And the priests stood, according to their offices; the Levites also with instruments of music of Yahweh, which David the king had made to give thanks unto Yahweh, (for his lovingkindness endureth for ever,) when David praised by their ministry: and the priests sounded trumpets before them; and all Israel stood.

7Moreover Solomon hallowed the middle of the court that was before the house of Yahweh; for there he offered the burnt-offerings, and the fat of the peace-offerings, because the brazen altar which Solomon had made was not able to receive the burnt-offering, and the meal-offering, and the fat.

8So Solomon held the feast at that time seven days, and all Israel with him, a very great assembly, from the entrance of Hamath unto the brook of Egypt.

9And on the eighth day they held a solemn assembly: for they kept the dedication of the altar seven days, and the feast seven days.

10And on the three and twentieth day of the seventh month he sent the people away unto their tents, joyful and glad of heart for the goodness that Yahweh had showed unto David, and to Solomon, and to Israel his people.

11Thus Solomon finished the house of Yahweh, and the king's house: and all that came into Solomon's heart to make in the house of Yahweh, and in his own house, he prosperously effected.

12And Yahweh appeared to Solomon by night, and said unto him, I have heard thy prayer, and have chosen this place to myself for a house of sacrifice.

13If I shut up the heavens so that there is no rain, or if I command the locust to devour the land, or if I send pestilence among my people;

14if my people, who are called by my name, shall humble themselves, and pray, and seek my face, and turn from their wicked ways; then will I hear from heaven, and will forgive their sin, and will heal their land.

15Now mine eyes shall be open, and mine ears attent, unto the prayer that is made in this place.

16For now have I chosen and hallowed this house, that my name may be there for ever; and mine eyes and my heart shall be there perpetually.

17And as for thee, if thou wilt walk before me as David thy father walked, and do according to all that I have commanded thee, and wilt keep my statutes and mine ordinances;

18then I will establish the throne of thy kingdom, according as I covenanted with David thy father, saying, There shall not fail thee a man to be ruler in Israel.

19But if ye turn away, and forsake my statutes and my commandments which I have set before you, and shall go and serve other gods, and worship them;

20then will I pluck them up by the roots out of my land which I have given them; and this house, which I have hallowed for my name, will I cast out of my sight, and I will make it a proverb and a byword among all peoples.

21And this house, which is so high, every one that passeth by it shall be astonished, and shall say, Why hath Yahweh done thus unto this land, and to this house?

22And they shall answer, Because they forsook Yahweh, the God of their fathers, who brought them forth out of the land of Egypt, and laid hold on other gods, and worshipped them, and served them: therefore hath he brought all this evil upon them.

Chapter 8

1And it came to pass at the end of twenty years, wherein Solomon had built the house of Yahweh, and his own house,

2that the cities which Huram had given to Solomon, Solomon built them, and caused the children of Israel to dwell there.

3And Solomon went to Hamath-zobah, and prevailed against it.

4And he built Tadmor in the wilderness, and all the store-cities, which he built in Hamath.

5Also he built Beth-horon the upper, and Beth-horon the nether, fortified cities, with walls, gates, and bars;

6and Baalath, and all the store-cities that Solomon had, and all the cities for his chariots, and the cities for his horsemen, and all that Solomon desired to build for his pleasure in Jerusalem, and in Lebanon, and in all the land of his dominion.

7As for all the people that were left of the Hittites, and the Amorites, and the Perizzites, and the Hivites, and the Jebusites, that were not of Israel;

8of their children that were left after them in the land, whom the children of Israel consumed not, of them did Solomon raise a levy of bondservants unto this day.

9But of the children of Israel did Solomon make no servants for his work; but they were men of war, and chief of his captains, and rulers of his chariots and of his horsemen.

10And these were the chief officers of king Solomon, even two hundred and fifty, that bare rule over the people.

11And Solomon brought up the daughter of Pharaoh out of the city of David unto the house that he had built for her; for he said, My wife shall not dwell in the house of David king of Israel, because the places are holy, whereunto the ark of Yahweh hath come.

12Then Solomon offered burnt-offerings unto Yahweh on the altar of Yahweh, which he had built before the porch,

13even as the duty of every day required, offering according to the commandment of Moses, on the sabbaths, and on the new moons, and on the set feasts, three times in the year, even in the feast of unleavened bread, and in the feast of weeks, and in the feast of tabernacles.

14And he appointed, according to the ordinance of David his father, the courses of the priests to their service, and the Levites to their offices, to praise, and to minister before the priests, as the duty of every day required; the doorkeepers also by their courses at every gate: for so had David the man of God commanded.

15And they departed not from the commandment of the king unto the priests and Levites concerning any matter, or concerning the treasures.

16Now all the work of Solomon was prepared unto the day of the foundation of the house of Yahweh, and until it was finished. So the house of Yahweh was completed.

17Then went Solomon to Ezion-geber, and to Eloth, on the seashore in the land of Edom.

18And Huram sent him by the hands of his servants ships, and servants that had knowledge of the sea; and they came with the servants of Solomon to Ophir, and fetched from thence four hundred and fifty talents of gold, and brought them to king Solomon.

Chapter 9

1And when the queen of Sheba heard of the fame of Solomon, she came to prove Solomon with hard questions at Jerusalem, with a very great train, and camels that bare spices, and gold in abundance, and precious stones: and when she was come to Solomon, she communed with him of all that was in her heart.

2And Solomon told her all her questions; and there was not anything hid from Solomon which he told her not.

3And when the queen of Sheba had seen the wisdom of Solomon, and the house that he had built,

4and the food of his table, and the sitting of his servants, and the attendance of his ministers, and their apparel, his cupbearers also, and their apparel, and his ascent by which he went up unto the house of Yahweh; there was no more spirit in her.

5And she said to the king, It was a true report that I heard in mine own land of thine acts, and of thy wisdom.

6Howbeit I believed not their words, until I came, and mine eyes had seen it; and, behold, the half of the greatness of thy wisdom was not told me: thou exceedest the fame that I heard.

7Happy are thy men, and happy are these thy servants, that stand continually before thee, and hear thy wisdom.

8Blessed be Yahweh thy God, who delighted in thee, to set thee on his throne, to be king for Yahweh thy God: because thy God loved Israel, to establish them for ever, therefore made he thee king over them, to do justice and righteousness.

9And she gave the king a hundred and twenty talents of gold, and spices in great abundance, and precious stones: neither was there any such spice as the queen of Sheba gave to king Solomon.

10And the servants also of Huram, and the servants of Solomon, that brought gold from Ophir, brought algum-trees and precious stones.

11And the king made of the algum-trees terraces for the house of Yahweh, and for the king's house, and harps and psalteries for the singers: and there were none such seen before in the land of Judah.

12And king Solomon gave to the queen of Sheba all her desire, whatsoever she asked, besides that which she had brought unto the king. So she turned, and went to her own land, she and her servants.

13Now the weight of gold that came to Solomon in one year was six hundred and threescore and six talents of gold,

14besides that which the traders and merchants brought: and all the kings of Arabia and the governors of the country brought gold and silver to Solomon.

15And king Solomon made two hundred bucklers of beaten gold; six hundred shekels of beaten gold went to one buckler.

16And he made three hundred shields of beaten gold; three hundred shekels of gold went to one shield: and the king put them in the house of the forest of Lebanon.

17Moreover the king made a great throne of ivory, and overlaid it with pure gold.

18nd there were six steps to the throne, with a footstool of gold, which were fastened to the throne, and stays on either side by the place of the seat, and two lions standing beside the stays.

19And twelve lions stood there on the one side and on the other upon the six steps: there was not the like made in any kingdom.

20And all king Solomon's drinking vessels were of gold, and all the vessels of the house of the forest of Lebanon were of pure gold: silver was nothing accounted of in the days of Solomon.

21For the king had ships that went to Tarshish with the servants of Huram; once every three years came the ships of Tarshish, bringing gold, and silver, ivory,

Second Chronicles

and apes, and peacocks.

22So king Solomon exceeded all the kings of the earth in riches and wisdom.

23And all the kings of the earth sought the presence of Solomon, to hear his wisdom, which God had put in his heart.

24And they brought every man his tribute, vessels of silver, and vessels of gold, and raiment, armor, and spices, horses, and mules, a rate year by year.

25And Solomon had four thousand stalls for horses and chariots, and twelve thousand horsemen, that he bestowed in the chariot cities, and with the king at Jerusalem.

26And he ruled over all the kings from the River even unto the land of the Philistines, and to the border of Egypt.

27And the king made silver to be in Jerusalem as stones, and cedars made he to be as the sycomore-trees that are in the lowland, for abundance.

28And they brought horses for Solomon out of Egypt, and out of all lands.

29Now the rest of the acts of Solomon, first and last, are they not written in the history of Nathan the prophet, and in the prophecy of Ahijah the Shilonite, and in the visions of Iddo the seer concerning Jeroboam the son of Nebat?

30And Solomon reigned in Jerusalem over all Israel forty years.

31And Solomon slept with his fathers, and he was buried in the city of David his father: and Rehoboam his son reigned in his stead.

Chapter 10

1And Rehoboam went to Shechem; for all Israel were come to Shechem to make him king.

2And it came to pass, when Jeroboam the son of Nebat heard of it, (for he was in Egypt, whither he had fled from the presence of king Solomon,) that Jeroboam returned out of Egypt.

3And they sent and called him; and Jeroboam and all Israel came, and they spake to Rehoboam, saying,

4Thy father made our yoke grievous: now therefore make thou the grievous service of thy father, and his heavy yoke which he put upon us, lighter, and we will serve thee.

5And he said unto them, Come again unto me after three days. And the people departed.

6And king Rehoboam took counsel with the old men, that had stood before Solomon his father while he yet lived, saying, What counsel give ye me to return answer to this people?

7And they spake unto him, saying, If thou be kind to this people, and please them, and speak good words to them, then they will be thy servants for ever.

8But he forsook the counsel of the old men which they had given him, and took counsel with the young men that were grown up with him, that stood before him.

9And he said unto them, What counsel give ye, that we may return answer to this people, who have spoken to me, saying, Make the yoke that thy father did put upon us lighter?

10And the young men that were grown up with him spake unto him, saying, Thus shalt thou say unto the people that spake unto thee, saying, Thy father made our yoke heavy, but make thou it lighter unto us; thus shalt thou say unto them, My little finger is thicker than my father's loins.

11And now whereas my father did lade you with a heavy yoke, I will add to your yoke: my father chastised you with whips, but I will chastise you with scorpions.

12So Jeroboam and all the people came to Rehoboam the third day, as the king bade, saying, Come to me again the third day.

13And the king answered them roughly; and king Rehoboam forsook the counsel of the old men,

14and spake to them after the counsel of the young men, saying, My father made your yoke heavy, but I will add thereto: my father chastised you with whips, but I will chastise you with scorpions.

15So the king hearkened not unto the people; for it was brought about of God, that Yahweh might establish his word, which he spake by Ahijah the Shilonite to Jeroboam the son of Nebat.

16And when all Israel saw that the king hearkened not unto them, the people answered the king, saying, What portion have we in David? neither have we inheritance in the son of Jesse: every man to your tents, O Israel: now see to thine own house, David. So all Israel departed unto their tents.

17But as for the children of Israel that dwelt in the cities of Judah, Rehoboam reigned over them.

18Then king Rehoboam sent Hadoram, who was over the men subject to taskwork; and the children of Israel stoned him to death with stones. And king Rehoboam made speed to get him up to his chariot, to flee to Jerusalem.

19So Israel rebelled against the house of David unto this day.

Chapter 11

1And when Rehoboam was come to Jerusalem, he assembled the house of Judah and Benjamin, a hundred and fourscore thousand chosen men, that were warriors, to fight against Israel, to bring the kingdom again to Rehoboam.

2But the word of Yahweh came to Shemaiah the man of God, saying,

3Speak unto Rehoboam the son of Solomon, king of Judah, and to all Israel in Judah and Benjamin, saying,

4Thus saith Yahweh, Ye shall not go up, nor fight against your brethren: return every man to his house; for this thing is of me. So they hearkened unto the words of Yahweh, and returned from going against Jeroboam.

5And Rehoboam dwelt in Jerusalem, and built cities for defence in Judah.

6He built Beth-lehem, and Etam, and Tekoa,

7And Beth-zur, and Soco, and Adullam,

8and Gath, and Mareshah, and Ziph,

9and Adoraim, and Lachish, and Azekah,

10and Zorah, and Aijalon, and Hebron, which are in Judah and in Benjamin, fortified cities.

11And he fortified the strongholds, and put captains in them, and stores of victuals, and oil and wine.

12And in every city he put shields and spears, and made them exceeding strong. And Judah and Benjamin belonged to him.

13And the priests and the Levites that were in all Israel resorted to him out of all their border.

14For the Levites left their suburbs and their possession, and came to Judah and Jerusalem: for Jeroboam and his sons cast them off, that they should not execute the priest's office unto Yahweh;

15and he appointed him priests for the high places, and for the he-goats, and for the calves which he had made.

16And after them, out of all the tribes of Israel, such as set their hearts to seek Yahweh, the God of Israel, came to Jerusalem to sacrifice unto Yahweh, the God of their fathers.

17So they strengthened the kingdom of Judah, and made Rehoboam the son of Solomon strong, three years; for they walked three years in the way of David and Solomon.

18And Rehoboam took him a wife, Mahalath the daughter of Jerimoth the son of David, and of Abihail the daughter of Eliab the son of Jesse;

19and she bare him sons: Jeush, and Shemariah, and Zaham.

20And after her he took Maacah the daughter of Absalom; and she bare him Abijah, and Attai, and Ziza, and Shelomith.

21And Rehoboam loved Maacah the daughter of Absalom above all his wives and his concubines: (for he took eighteen wives, and threescore concubines, and begat twenty and eight sons and threescore daughters.)

22And Rehoboam appointed Abijah the son of Maacah to be chief, even the prince among his brethren; for he was minded to make him king.

23And he dealt wisely, and dispersed of all his sons throughout all the lands of Judah and Benjamin, unto every fortified city: and he gave them victuals in abundance. And he sought for them many wives.

Chapter 12

1And it came to pass, when the kingdom of Rehoboam was established, and he was strong, that he forsook the law of Yahweh, and all Israel with him.

2And it came to pass in the fifth year of king Rehoboam, that Shishak king of Egypt came up against Jerusalem, because they had trespassed against Yahweh,

3with twelve hundred chariots, and threescore thousand horsemen. And the people were without number that came with him out of Egypt: the Lubim, the Sukkiim, and the Ethiopians.

4And he took the fortified cities which pertained to Judah, and came unto Jerusalem.

5Now Shemaiah the prophet came to Rehoboam, and to the princes of Judah, that were gathered together to Jerusalem because of Shishak, and said unto them, Thus saith Yahweh, Ye have forsaken me, therefore have I also left you in the hand of Shishak.

6Then the princes of Israel and the king humbled themselves; and they said, Yahweh is righteous.

7And when Yahweh saw that they humbled themselves, the word of Yahweh came to Shemaiah, saying, They have humbled themselves: I will not destroy them; but I will grant them some deliverance, and my wrath shall not be poured out upon Jerusalem by the hand of Shishak.

8Nevertheless they shall be his servants, that they may know my service, and the service of the kingdoms of the countries.

9So Shishak king of Egypt came up against Jerusalem, and took away the treasures of the house of Yahweh, and the treasures of the king's house: he took all away: he took away also the shields of gold which Solomon had made.

10And king Rehoboam made in their stead shields of brass, and committed them to the hands of the captains of the guard, that kept the door of the king's house.

11And it was so, that, as oft as the king entered into the house of Yahweh, the guard came and bare them, and brought them back into the guard-chamber.

12And when he humbled himself, the wrath of Yahweh turned from him, so as not to destroy him altogether: and moreover in Judah there were good things found.

13So king Rehoboam strengthened himself in Jerusalem, and reigned: for Rehoboam was forty and one years old when he began to reign, and he reigned seventeen years in Jerusalem, the city which Yahweh had chosen out of all the tribes of Israel, to put his name there: and his mother's name was Naamah the Ammonitess.

14And he did that which was evil, because he set not his heart to seek Yahweh.

15Now the acts of Rehoboam, first and last, are they not written in the histories of Shemaiah the prophet and of Iddo the seer, after the manner of genealogies? And there were wars between Rehoboam and Jeroboam continually.

16And Rehoboam slept with his fathers, and was buried in the city of David: and Abijah his son reigned in his stead.

Chapter 13

1In the eighteenth year of king Jeroboam began Abijah to reign over Judah.

2Three years reigned he in Jerusalem: and his mother's name was Micaiah the daughter of Uriel of Gibeah. And there was war between Abijah and Jeroboam.

3And Abijah joined battle with an army of valiant men of war, even four hundred thousand chosen men: and Jeroboam set the battle in array against him with eight hundred thousand chosen men, who were mighty men of valor.

⁴And Abijah stood up upon mount Zemaraim, which is in the hill-country of Ephraim, and said, Hear me, O Jeroboam and all Israel:
⁵Ought ye not to know that Yahweh, the God of Israel, gave the kingdom over Israel to David for ever, even to him and to his sons by a covenant of salt?
⁶Yet Jeroboam the son of Nebat, the servant of Solomon the son of David, rose up, and rebelled against his lord.
⁷And there were gathered unto him worthless men, base fellows, that strengthened themselves against Rehoboam the son of Solomon, when Rehoboam was young and tender-hearted, and could not withstand them.
⁸And now ye think to withstand the kingdom of Yahweh in the hand of the sons of David; and ye are a great multitude, and there are with you the golden calves which Jeroboam made you for gods.
⁹Have ye not driven out the priests of Yahweh, the sons of Aaron, and the Levites, and made you priests after the manner of the peoples of other lands? so that whosoever cometh to consecrate himself with a young bullock and seven rams, the same may be a priest of them that are no gods.
¹⁰But as for us, Yahweh is our God, and we have not forsaken him; and we have priests ministering unto Yahweh, the sons of Aaron, and the Levites in their work:
¹¹and they burn unto Yahweh every morning and every evening burnt-offerings and sweet incense: the showbread also set they in order upon the pure table; and the candlestick of gold with the lamps thereof, to burn every evening: for we keep the charge of Yahweh our God; but ye have forsaken him.
¹²And, behold, God is with us at our head, and his priests with the trumpets of alarm to sound an alarm against you. O children of Israel, fight ye not against Yahweh, the God of your fathers; for ye shall not prosper.
¹³But Jeroboam caused an ambushment to come about behind them: so they were before Judah, and the ambushment was behind them.
¹⁴And when Judah looked back, behold, the battle was before and behind them; and they cried unto Yahweh, and the priests sounded with the trumpets.
¹⁵Then the men of Judah gave a shout: and as the men of Judah shouted, it came to pass, that God smote Jeroboam and all Israel before Abijah and Judah.
¹⁶And the children of Israel fled before Judah; and God delivered them into their hand.
¹⁷And Abijah and his people slew them with a great slaughter: so there fell down slain of Israel five hundred thousand chosen men.
¹⁸Thus the children of Israel were brought under at that time, and the children of Judah prevailed, because they relied upon Yahweh, the God of their fathers.
¹⁹And Abijah pursued after Jeroboam, and took cities from him, Beth-el with the towns thereof, and Jeshanah with the towns thereof, and Ephron with the towns thereof.
²⁰Neither did Jeroboam recover strength again in the days of Abijah: and Yahweh smote him, and he died.
²¹But Abijah waxed mighty, and took unto himself fourteen wives, and begat twenty and two sons, and sixteen daughters.
²²And the rest of the acts of Abijah, and his ways, and his sayings, are written in the commentary of the prophet Iddo.

Chapter 14

¹So Abijah slept with his fathers, and they buried him in the city of David; and Asa his son reigned in his stead. In his days the land was quiet ten years.
²And Asa did that which was good and right in the eyes of Yahweh his God:
³for he took away the foreign altars, and the high places, and brake down the pillars, and hewed down the Asherim,
⁴and commanded Judah to seek Yahweh, the God of their fathers, and to do the law and the commandment.
⁵Also he took away out of all the cities of Judah the high places and the sun-images: and the kingdom was quiet before him.
⁶And he built fortified cities in Judah; for the land was quiet, and he had no war in those years, because Yahweh had given him rest.
⁷For he said unto Judah, Let us build these cities, and make about them walls, and towers, gates, and bars; the land is yet before us, because we have sought Yahweh our God; we have sought him, and he hath given us rest on every side. So they built and prospered.
⁸And Asa had an army that bare bucklers and spears, out of Judah three hundred thousand; and out of Benjamin, that bare shields and drew bows, two hundred and fourscore thousand: all these were mighty men of valor.
⁹And there came out against them Zerah the Ethiopian with an army of a thousand thousand, and three hundred chariots; and he came unto Mareshah.
¹⁰Then Asa went out to meet him, and they set the battle in array in the valley of Zephathah at Mareshah.
¹¹And Asa cried unto Yahweh his God, and said, Yahweh, there is none besides thee to help, between the mighty and him that hath no strength: help us, O Yahweh our God; for we rely on thee, and in thy name are we come against this multitude. O Yahweh, thou art our God; let not man prevail against thee.
¹²So Yahweh smote the Ethiopians before Asa, and before Judah; and the Ethiopians fled.
¹³And Asa and the people that were with him pursued them unto Gerar: and there fell of the Ethiopians so many that they could not recover themselves; for they were destroyed before Yahweh, and before his host; and they carried away very much booty.
¹⁴And they smote all the cities round about Gerar; for the fear of Yahweh came upon them: and they despoiled all the cities; for there was much spoil in them.
¹⁵They smote also the tents of cattle, and carried away sheep in abundance, and camels, and returned to Jerusalem.

Chapter 15

¹And the Spirit of God came upon Azariah the son of Oded:
²and he went out to meet Asa, and said unto him, Hear ye me, Asa, and all Judah and Benjamin: Yahweh is with you, while ye are with him; and if ye seek him, he will be found of you; but if ye forsake him, he will forsake you.
³Now for a long season Israel was without the true God, and without a teaching priest, and without law:
⁴But when in their distress they turned unto Yahweh, the God of Israel, and sought him, he was found of them.
⁵And in those times there was no peace to him that went out, nor to him that came in; but great vexations were upon all the inhabitants of the lands.
⁶And they were broken in pieces, nation against nation, and city against city; for God did vex them with all adversity.
⁷But be ye strong, and let not your hands be slack; for your work shall be rewarded.
⁸And when Asa heard these words, and the prophecy of Oded the prophet, he took courage, and put away the abominations out of all the land of Judah and Benjamin, and out of the cities which he had taken from the hill-country of Ephraim; and he renewed the altar of Yahweh, that was before the porch of Yahweh.
⁹And he gathered all Judah and Benjamin, and them that sojourned with them out of Ephraim and Manasseh, and out of Simeon: for they fell to him out of Israel in abundance, when they saw that Yahweh his God was with him.
¹⁰So they gathered themselves together at Jerusalem in the third month, in the fifteenth year of the reign of Asa.
¹¹And they sacrificed unto Yahweh in that day, of the spoil which they had brought, seven hundred oxen and seven thousand sheep.
¹²And they entered into the covenant to seek Yahweh, the God of their fathers, with all their heart and with all their soul;
¹³and that whosoever would not seek Yahweh, the God of Israel, should be put to death, whether small or great, whether man or woman.
¹⁴And they sware unto Yahweh with a loud voice, and with shouting, and with trumpets, and with cornets.
¹⁵And all Judah rejoiced at the oath; for they had sworn with all their heart, and sought him with their whole desire; and he was found of them: and Yahweh gave them rest round about.
¹⁶And also Maacah, the mother of Asa the king, he removed from being queen, because she had made an abominable image for an Asherah; and Asa cut down her image, and made dust of it, and burnt it at the brook Kidron.
¹⁷But the high places were not taken away out of Israel: nevertheless the heart of Asa was perfect all his days.
¹⁸And he brought into the house of God the things that his father had dedicated, and that he himself had dedicated, silver, and gold, and vessels.
¹⁹And there was no more war unto the five and thirtieth year of the reign of Asa.

Chapter 16

¹In the six and thirtieth year of the reign of Asa, Baasha king of Israel went up against Judah, and built Ramah, that he might not suffer any one to go out or come in to Asa king of Judah.
²Then Asa brought out silver and gold out of the treasures of the house of Yahweh and of the king's house, and sent to Ben-hadad king of Syria, that dwelt at Damascus, saying,
³There is a league between me and thee, as there was between my father and thy father: behold, I have sent thee silver and gold; go, break thy league with Baasha king of Israel, that he may depart from me.
⁴And Ben-hadad hearkened unto king Asa, and sent the captains of his armies against the cities of Israel; and they smote Ijon, and Dan, and Abel-maim, and all the store-cities of Naphtali.
⁵And it came to pass, when Baasha heard thereof, that he left off building Ramah, and let his work cease.
⁶Then Asa the king took all Judah; and they carried away the stones of Ramah, and the timber thereof, wherewith Baasha had builded; and he built therewith Geba and Mizpah.
⁷And at that time Hanani the seer came to Asa king of Judah, and said unto him, Because thou hast relied on the king of Syria, and hast not relied on Yahweh thy God, therefore is the host of the king of Syria escaped out of thy hand.
⁸Were not the Ethiopians and the Lubim a huge host, with chariots and horsemen exceeding many? yet, because thou didst rely on Yahweh, he delivered them into thy hand.
⁹For the eyes of Yahweh run to and fro throughout the whole earth, to show himself strong in the behalf of them whose heart is perfect toward him. Herein thou hast done foolishly; for from henceforth thou shalt have wars.
¹⁰Then Asa was wroth with the seer, and put him in the prison-house; for he was in a rage with him because of this thing. And Asa oppressed some of the people at the same time.
¹¹And, behold, the acts of Asa, first and last, lo, they are written in the book of the kings of Judah and Israel.
¹²And in the thirty and ninth year of his reign Asa was diseased in his feet; his disease was exceeding great: yet in his disease he sought not to Yahweh, but to the physicians.
¹³And Asa slept with his fathers, and died in the one and fortieth year of his reign.
¹⁴And they buried him in his own sepulchres, which he had hewn out for himself in the city of David, and laid him in the bed which was filled with sweet odors and divers kinds of spices prepared by the perfumers' art: and they made a very great burning for him.

Second Chronicles

Chapter 17

¹And Jehoshaphat his son reigned in his stead, and strengthened himself against Israel.

²And he placed forces in all the fortified cities of Judah, and set garrisons in the land of Judah, and in the cities of Ephraim, which Asa his father had taken.

³And Yahweh was with Jehoshaphat, because he walked in the first ways of his father David, and sought not unto the Baalim,

⁴but sought to the God of his father, and walked in his commandments, and not after the doings of Israel.

⁵Therefore Yahweh established the kingdom in his hand; and all Judah brought to Jehoshaphat tribute; and he had riches and honor in abundance.

⁶And his heart was lifted up in the ways of Yahweh: and furthermore he took away the high places and the Asherim out of Judah.

⁷Also in the third year of his reign he sent his princes, even Ben-hail, and Obadiah, and Zechariah, and Nethanel, and Micaiah, to teach in the cities of Judah;

⁸and with them the Levites, even Shemaiah, and Nethaniah, and Zebadiah, and Asahel, and Shemiramoth, and Jehonathan, and Adonijah, and Tobijah, and Tob-adonijah, the Levites; and with them Elishama and Jehoram, the priests.

⁹And they taught in Judah, having the book of the law of Yahweh with them; and they went about throughout all the cities of Judah, and taught among the people.

¹⁰And the fear of Yahweh fell upon all the kingdoms of the lands that were round about Judah, so that they made no war against Jehoshaphat.

¹¹And some of the Philistines brought Jehoshaphat presents, and silver for tribute; the Arabians also brought him flocks, seven thousand and seven hundred rams, and seven thousand and seven hundred he-goats.

¹²And Jehoshaphat waxed great exceedingly; and he built in Judah castles and cities of store.

¹³And he had many works in the cities of Judah; and men of war, mighty men of valor, in Jerusalem.

¹⁴And this was the numbering of them according to their fathers' houses: Of Judah, the captains of thousands: Adnah the captain, and with him mighty men of valor three hundred thousand;

¹⁵and next to him Jehohanan the captain, and with him two hundred and fourscore thousand;

¹⁶and next to him Amasiah the son of Zichri, who willingly offered himself unto Yahweh; and with him two hundred thousand mighty men of valor.

¹⁷And of Benjamin: Eliada a mighty man of valor, and with him two hundred thousand armed with bow and shield;

¹⁸and next to him Jehozabad and with him a hundred and fourscore thousand ready prepared for war.

¹⁹These were they that waited on the king, besides those whom the king put in the fortified cities throughout all Judah.

Chapter 18

¹Now Jehoshaphat had riches and honor in abundance; and he joined affinity with Ahab.

²And after certain years he went down to Ahab to Samaria. And Ahab killed sheep and oxen for him in abundance, and for the people that were with him, and moved him to go up with him to Ramoth-gilead.

³And Ahab king of Israel said unto Jehoshaphat king of Judah, Wilt thou go with me to Ramoth-gilead? And he answered him, I am as thou art, and my people as thy people; and we will be with thee in the war.

⁴And Jehoshaphat said unto the king of Israel, Inquire first, I pray thee, for the word of Yahweh.

⁵Then the king of Israel gathered the prophets together, four hundred men, and said unto them, Shall we go to Ramoth-gilead to battle, or shall I forbear? And they said, Go up; for God will deliver it into the hand of the king.

⁶But Jehoshaphat said, Is there not here a prophet of Yahweh besides, that we may inquire of him?

⁷And the king of Israel said unto Jehoshaphat, There is yet one man by whom we may inquire of Yahweh: but I hate him; for he never prophesieth good concerning me, but always evil: the same is Micaiah the son of Imla. And Jehoshaphat said, Let not the king say so.

⁸Then the king of Israel called an officer, and said, Fetch quickly Micaiah the son of Imla.

⁹Now the king of Israel and Jehoshaphat the king of Judah sat each on his throne, arrayed in their robes, and they were sitting in an open place at the entrance of the gate of Samaria; and all the prophets were prophesying before them.

¹⁰And Zedekiah the son of Chenaanah made him horns of iron, and said, Thus saith Yahweh, With these shalt thou push the Syrians, until they be consumed.

¹¹And all the prophets prophesied so, saying, Go up to Ramoth-gilead, and prosper; for Yahweh will deliver it into the hand of the king.

¹²And the messenger that went to call Micaiah spake to him, saying, Behold, the words of the prophets declare good to the king with one mouth: let thy word therefore, I pray thee, be like one of theirs, and speak thou good.

¹³And Micaiah said, As Yahweh liveth, what my God saith, that will I speak.

¹⁴And when he was come to the king, the king said unto him, Micaiah, shall we go to Ramoth-gilead to battle, or shall I forbear? And he said, Go ye up, and prosper; and they shall be delivered into your hand.

¹⁵And the king said to him, How many times shall I adjure thee that thou speak unto me nothing but the truth in the name of Yahweh?

¹⁶And he said, I saw all Israel scattered upon the mountains, as sheep that have no shepherd: and Yahweh said, These have no master; let them return every man to his house in peace.

¹⁷And the king of Israel said to Jehoshaphat, Did I not tell thee that he would not prophesy good concerning me, but evil?

¹⁸And Micaiah said, Therefore hear ye the word of Yahweh: I saw Yahweh sitting upon his throne, and all the host of heaven standing on his right hand and on his left.

¹⁹And Yahweh said, Who shall entice Ahab king of Israel, that he may go up and fall at Ramoth-gilead? And one spake saying after this manner, and another saying after that manner.

²⁰And there came forth a spirit, and stood before Yahweh, and said, I will entice him. And Yahweh said unto him, Wherewith?

²¹And he said, I will go forth, and will be a lying spirit in the mouth of all his prophets. And he said, Thou shalt entice him, and shalt prevail also: go forth, and do so.

²²Now therefore, behold, Yahweh hath put a lying spirit in the mouth of these thy prophets; and Yahweh hath spoken evil concerning thee.

²³Then Zedekiah the son of Chenaanah came near, and smote Micaiah upon the cheek, and said, Which way went the Spirit of Yahweh from me to speak unto thee?

²⁴And Micaiah said, Behold, thou shalt see on that day, when thou shalt go into an inner chamber to hide thyself.

²⁵And the king of Israel said, Take ye Micaiah, and carry him back unto Amon the governor of the city, and to Joash the king's son;

²⁶and say, Thus saith the king, Put this fellow in the prison, and feed him with bread of affliction and with water of affliction, until I return in peace.

²⁷And Micaiah said, If thou return at all in peace, Yahweh hath not spoken by me. And he said, Hear, ye peoples, all of you.

²⁸So the king of Israel and Jehoshaphat the king of Judah went up to Ramoth-gilead.

²⁹And the king of Israel said unto Jehoshaphat, I will disguise myself, and go into the battle; but put thou on thy robes. So the king of Israel disguised himself; and they went into the battle.

³⁰Now the king of Syria had commanded the captains of his chariots, saying, Fight neither with small nor great, save only with the king of Israel.

³¹And it came to pass, when the captains of the chariots saw Jehoshaphat, that they said, It is the king of Israel. Therefore they turned about to fight against him: but Jehoshaphat cried out, and Yahweh helped him; and God moved them to depart from him.

³²And it came to pass, when the captains of the chariots saw that it was not the king of Israel, that they turned back from pursuing him.

³³And a certain man drew his bow at a venture, and smote the king of Israel between the joints of the armor: wherefore he said to the driver of the chariot, Turn thy hand, and carry me out of the host; for I am sore wounded.

³⁴And the battle increased that day: howbeit the king of Israel stayed himself up in his chariot against the Syrians until the even; and about the time of the going down of the sun he died.

Chapter 19

¹And Jehoshaphat the king of Judah returned to his house in peace to Jerusalem.

²And Jehu the son of Hanani the seer went out to meet him, and said to king Jehoshaphat, Shouldest thou help the wicked, and love them that hate Yahweh? for this thing wrath is upon thee from before Yahweh.

³Nevertheless there are good things found in thee, in that thou hast put away the Asheroth out of the land, and hast set thy heart to seek God.

⁴And Jehoshaphat dwelt at Jerusalem: and he went out again among the people from Beer-sheba to the hill-country of Ephraim, and brought them back unto Yahweh, the God of their fathers.

⁵And he set judges in the land throughout all the fortified cities of Judah, city by city,

⁶and said to the judges, Consider what ye do: for ye judge not for man, but for Yahweh; and he is with you in the judgment.

⁷Now therefore let the fear of Yahweh be upon you; take heed and do it: for there is no iniquity with Yahweh our God, nor respect of persons, nor taking of bribes.

⁸Moreover in Jerusalem did Jehoshaphat set of the Levites and the priests, and of the heads of the fathers' houses of Israel, for the judgment of Yahweh, and for controversies. And they returned to Jerusalem.

⁹And he charged them, saying, Thus shall ye do in the fear of Yahweh, faithfully, and with a perfect heart.

¹⁰And whensoever any controversy shall come to you from your brethren that dwell in their cities, between blood and blood, between law and commandment, statutes and ordinances, ye shall warn them, that they be not guilty towards Yahweh, and so wrath come upon you and upon your brethren: this do, and ye shall not be guilty.

¹¹And, behold, Amariah the chief priest is over you in all matters of Yahweh; and Zebadiah the son of Ishmael, the ruler of the house of Judah, in all the king's matters: also the Levites shall be officers before you. Deal courageously, and Yahweh be with the good.

Chapter 20

¹And it came to pass after this, that the children of Moab, and the children of Ammon, and with them some of the Ammonites, came against Jehoshaphat to battle.

²Then there came some that told Jehoshaphat, saying, There cometh a great multitude against thee from beyond the sea from Syria; and, behold, they are in Hazazon-tamar (the same is En-gedi).

³And Jehoshaphat feared, and set himself to seek unto Yahweh; and he

proclaimed a fast throughout all Judah.

4And Judah gathered themselves together, to seek help of Yahweh: even out of all the cities of Judah they came to seek Yahweh.

5And Jehoshaphat stood in the assembly of Judah and Jerusalem, in the house of Yahweh, before the new court;

6and he said, O Yahweh, the God of our fathers, art not thou God in heaven? and art not thou ruler over all the kingdoms of the nations? and in thy hand is power and might, so that none is able to withstand thee.

7Didst not thou, O our God, drive out the inhabitants of this land before thy people Israel, and give it to the seed of Abraham thy friend for ever?

8And they dwelt therein, and have built thee a sanctuary therein for thy name, saying,

9If evil come upon us, the sword, judgment, or pestilence, or famine, we will stand before this house, and before thee, (for thy name is in this house,) and cry unto thee in our affliction, and thou wilt hear and save.

10And now, behold, the children of Ammon and Moab and mount Seir, whom thou wouldest not let Israel invade, when they came out of the land of Egypt, but they turned aside from them, and destroyed them not;

11behold, how they reward us, to come to cast us out of thy possession, which thou hast given us to inherit.

12O our God, wilt thou not judge them? for we have no might against this great company that cometh against us; neither know we what to do: but our eyes are upon thee.

13And all Judah stood before Yahweh, with their little ones, their wives, and their children.

14Then upon Jahaziel the son of Zechariah, the son of Benaiah, the son of Jeiel, the son of Mattaniah, the Levite, of the sons of Asaph, came the Spirit of Yahweh in the midst of the assembly;

15and he said, Hearken ye, all Judah, and ye inhabitants of Jerusalem, and thou king Jehoshaphat: Thus saith Yahweh unto you, Fear not ye, neither be dismayed by reason of this great multitude; for the battle is not yours, but God's.

16To-morrow go ye down against them: behold, they come up by the ascent of Ziz; and ye shall find them at the end of the valley, before the wilderness of Jeruel.

17Ye shall not need to fight in this battle: set yourselves, stand ye still, and see the salvation of Yahweh with you, O Judah and Jerusalem; fear not, nor be dismayed: to-morrow go out against them: for Yahweh is with you.

18And Jehoshaphat bowed his head with his face to the ground; and all Judah and the inhabitants of Jerusalem fell down before Yahweh, worshipping Yahweh.

19And the Levites, of the children of the Kohathites and of the children of the Korahites, stood up to praise Yahweh, the God of Israel, with an exceeding loud voice.

20And they rose early in the morning, and went forth into the wilderness of Tekoa: and as they went forth, Jehoshaphat stood and said, Hear me, O Judah, and ye inhabitants of Jerusalem: believe in Yahweh your God, so shall ye be established; believe his prophets, so shall ye prosper.

21And when he had taken counsel with the people, he appointed them that should sing unto Yahweh, and give praise in holy array, as they went out before the army, and say, Give thanks unto Yahweh; for his lovingkindness endureth for ever.

22And when they began to sing and to praise, Yahweh set liers-in-wait against the children of Ammon, Moab, and mount Seir, that were come against Judah; and they were smitten.

23For the children of Ammon and Moab stood up against the inhabitants of mount Seir, utterly to slay and destroy them: and when they had made an end of the inhabitants of Seir, every one helped to destroy another.

24And when Judah came to the watch-tower of the wilderness, they looked upon the multitude; and, behold, they were dead bodies fallen to the earth, and there were none that escaped.

25And when Jehoshaphat and his people came to take the spoil of them, they found among them in abundance both riches and dead bodies, and precious jewels, which they stripped off for themselves, more than they could carry away: and they were three days in taking the spoil, it was so much.

26And on the fourth day they assembled themselves in the valley of Beracah; for there they blessed Yahweh: therefore the name of that place was called The valley of Beracah unto this day.

27Then they returned, every man of Judah and Jerusalem, and Jehoshaphat in the forefront of them, to go again to Jerusalem with joy; for Yahweh had made them to rejoice over their enemies.

28And they came to Jerusalem with psalteries and harps and trumpets unto the house of Yahweh.

29And the fear of God was on all the kingdoms of the countries, when they heard that Yahweh fought against the enemies of Israel.

30So the realm of Jehoshaphat was quiet; for his God gave him rest round about.

31And Jehoshaphat reigned over Judah: he was thirty and five years old when he began to reign; and he reigned twenty and five years in Jerusalem: and his mother's name was Azubah the daughter of Shilhi.

32And he walked in the way of Asa his father, and turned not aside from it, doing that which was right in the eyes of Yahweh.

33Howbeit the high places were not taken away; neither as yet had the people set their hearts unto the God of their fathers.

34Now the rest of the acts of Jehoshaphat, first and last, behold, they are written in the history of Jehu the son of Hanani, which is inserted in the book of the kings of Israel.

35And after this did Jehoshaphat king of Judah join himself with Ahaziah king of Israel; the same did very wickedly:

36and he joined himself with him to make ships to go to Tarshish; and they made the ships in Ezion-geber.

37Then Eliezer the son of Dodavahu of Mareshah prophesied against Jehoshaphat, saying, Because thou hast joined thyself with Ahaziah, Yahweh hath destroyed thy works. And the ships were broken, so that they were not able to go to Tarshish.

Chapter 21

1And Jehoshaphat slept with his fathers, and was buried with his fathers in the city of David: and Jehoram his son reigned in his stead.

2And he had brethren, the sons of Jehoshaphat: Azariah, and Jehiel, and Zechariah, and Azariah, and Michael, and Shephatiah; all these were the sons of Jehoshaphat king of Israel.

3And their father gave them great gifts, of silver, and of gold, and of precious things, with fortified cities in Judah: but the kingdom gave he to Jehoram, because he was the first-born.

4Now when Jehoram was risen up over the kingdom of his father, and had strengthened himself, he slew all his brethren with the sword, and divers also of the princes of Israel.

5Jehoram was thirty and two years old when he began to reign; and he reigned eight years in Jerusalem.

6And he walked in the way of the kings of Israel, as did the house of Ahab; for he had the daughter of Ahab to wife: and he did that which was evil in the sight of Yahweh.

7Howbeit Yahweh would not destroy the house of David, because of the covenant that he had made with David, and as he promised to give a lamp to him and to his children alway.

8In his days Edom revolted from under the hand of Judah, and made a king over themselves.

9Then Jehoram passed over with his captains, and all his chariots with him: and he rose up by night, and smote the Edomites that compassed him about, and the captains of the chariots.

10So Edom revolted from under the hand of Judah unto this day: then did Libnah revolt at the same time from under his hand, because he had forsaken Yahweh, the God of his fathers.

11Moreover he made high places in the mountains of Judah, and made the inhabitants of Jerusalem to play the harlot, and led Judah astray.

12And there came a writing to him from Elijah the prophet, saying, Thus saith Yahweh, the God of David thy father, Because thou hast not walked in the ways of Jehoshaphat thy father, nor in the ways of Asa king of Judah,

13but hast walked in the way of the kings of Israel, and hast made Judah and the inhabitants of Jerusalem to play the harlot, like as the house of Ahab did, and also hast slain thy brethren of thy father's house, who were better than thyself:

14behold, Yahweh will smite with a great plague thy people, and thy children, and thy wives, and all thy substance;

15and thou shalt have great sickness by disease of thy bowels, until thy bowels fall out by reason of the sickness, day by day.

16And Yahweh stirred up against Jehoram the spirit of the Philistines, and of the Arabians that are beside the Ethiopians:

17and they came up against Judah, and brake into it, and carried away all the substance that was found in the king's house, and his sons also, and his wives; so that there was never a son left him, save Jehoahaz, the youngest of his sons.

18And after all this Yahweh smote him in his bowels with an incurable disease.

19And it came to pass, in process of time, at the end of two years, that his bowels fell out by reason of his sickness, and he died of sore diseases. And his people made no burning for him, like the burning of his fathers.

20Thirty and two years old was he when he began to reign, and he reigned in Jerusalem eight years: and he departed without being desired; and they buried him in the city of David, but not in the sepulchres of the kings.

Chapter 22

1And the inhabitants of Jerusalem made Ahaziah his youngest son king in his stead; for the band of men that came with the Arabians to the camp had slain all the eldest. So Ahaziah the son of Jehoram king of Judah reigned.

2Forty and two years old was Ahaziah when he began to reign; and he reigned one year in Jerusalem: and his mother's name was Athaliah the daughter of Omri.

3He also walked in the ways of the house of Ahab; for his mother was his counsellor to do wickedly.

4And he did that which was evil in the sight of Yahweh, as did the house of Ahab; for they were his counsellors after the death of his father, to his destruction.

5He walked also after their counsel, and went with Jehoram the son of Ahab king of Israel to war against Hazael king of Syria at Ramoth-gilead: and the Syrians wounded Joram.

6And he returned to be healed in Jezreel of the wounds which they had given him at Ramah, when he fought against Hazael king of Syria. And Azariah the son of Jehoram king of Judah went down to see Jehoram the son of Ahab in Jezreel, because he was sick.

7Now the destruction of Ahaziah was of God, in that he went unto Joram: for when he was come, he went out with Jehoram against Jehu the son of Nimshi, whom Yahweh had anointed to cut off the house of Ahab.

8And it came to pass, when Jehu was executing judgment upon the house of Ahab, that he found the princes of Judah, and the sons of the brethren of Ahaziah, ministering to Ahaziah, and slew them.

9And he sought Ahaziah, and they caught him (now he was hiding in Samaria), and they brought him to Jehu, and slew him; and they buried him, for they said, He is the son of Jehoshaphat, who sought Yahweh with all his heart. And the house of Ahaziah had no power to hold the kingdom.

10Now when Athaliah the mother of Ahaziah saw that her son was dead, she arose and destroyed all the seed royal of the house of Judah.

11But Jehoshabeath, the daughter of the king, took Joash the son of Ahaziah, and stole him away from among the king's sons that were slain, and put him and his nurse in the bedchamber. So Jehoshabeath, the daughter of king Jehoram, the wife of Jehoiada the priest (for she was the sister of Ahaziah), hid him from Athaliah, so that she slew him not.

12And he was with them hid in the house of God six years: and Athaliah reigned over the land.

Chapter 23

1And in the seventh year Jehoiada strengthened himself, and took the captains of hundreds, Azariah the son of Jeroham, and Ishmael the son of Jehohanan, and Azariah the son of Obed, and Maaseiah the son of Adaiah, and Elishaphat the son of Zichri, into covenant with him.

2And they went about in Judah, and gathered the Levites out of all the cities of Judah, and the heads of fathers' houses of Israel, and they came to Jerusalem.

3And all the assembly made a covenant with the king in the house of God. And he said unto them, Behold, the king's son shall reign, as Yahweh hath spoken concerning the sons of David.

4This is the thing that ye shall do: a third part of you, that come in on the sabbath, of the priests and of the Levites, shall be porters of the thresholds;

5and a third part shall be at the king's house; and a third part at the gate of the foundation: and all the people shall be in the courts of the house of Yahweh.

6But let none come into the house of Yahweh, save the priests, and they that minister of the Levites; they shall come in, for they are holy: but all the people shall keep the charge of Yahweh.

7And the Levites shall compass the king round about, every man with his weapons in his hand; and whosoever cometh into the house, let him be slain: and be ye with the king when he cometh in, and when he goeth out.

8So the Levites and all Judah did according to all that Jehoiada the priest commanded: and they took every man his men, those that were to come in on the sabbath; with those that were to go out on the sabbath; for Jehoiada the priest dismissed not the courses.

9And Jehoiada the priest delivered to the captains of hundreds the spears, and bucklers, and shields, that had been king David's, which were in the house of God.

10And he set all the people, every man with his weapon in his hand, from the right side of the house to the left side of the house, along by the altar and the house, by the king round about.

11Then they brought out the king's son, and put the crown upon him, and gave him the testimony, and made him king: and Jehoiada and his sons anointed him; and they said, Long live the king.

12And when Athaliah heard the noise of the people running and praising the king, she came to the people into the house of Yahweh:

13and she looked, and, behold, the king stood by his pillar at the entrance, and the captains and the trumpets by the king; and all the people of the land rejoiced, and blew trumpets; the singers also played on instruments of music, and led the singing of praise. Then Athaliah rent her clothes, and said, Treason! treason!

14And Jehoiada the priest brought out the captains of hundreds that were set over the host, and said unto them, Have her forth between the ranks; and whoso followeth her, let him be slain with the sword: for the priest said, Slay her not in the house of Yahweh.

15So they made way for her; and she went to the entrance of the horse gate to the king's house: and they slew her there.

16And Jehoiada made a covenant between himself, and all the people, and the king, that they should be Yahweh's people.

17And all the people went to the house of Baal, and brake it down, and brake his altars and his images in pieces, and slew Mattan the priest of Baal before the altars.

18And Jehoiada appointed the officers of the house of Yahweh under the hand of the priests the Levites, whom David had distributed in the house of Yahweh, to offer the burnt-offerings of Yahweh, as it is written in the law of Moses, with rejoicing and with singing, according to the order of David.

19And he set the porters at the gates of the house of Yahweh, that none that was unclean in anything should enter in.

20And he took the captains of hundreds, and the nobles, and the governors of the people, and all the people of the land, and brought down the king from the house of Yahweh: and they came through the upper gate unto the king's house, and set the king upon the throne of the kingdom.

21So all the people of the land rejoiced, and the city was quiet. And Athaliah they had slain with the sword.

Chapter 24

1Joash was seven years old when he began to reign; and he reigned forty years in Jerusalem: and his mother's name was Zibiah, of Beer-sheba.

2And Joash did that which was right in the eyes of Yahweh all the days of Jehoiada the priest.

3And Jehoiada took for him two wives; and he begat sons and daughters.

4And it came to pass after this, that Joash was minded to restore the house of Yahweh.

5And he gathered together the priests and the Levites, and said to them, Go out unto the cities of Judah, and gather of all Israel money to repair the house of your God from year to year; and see that ye hasten the matter. Howbeit the Levites hastened it not.

6And the king called for Jehoiada the chief, and said unto him, Why hast thou not required of the Levites to bring in out of Judah and out of Jerusalem the tax of Moses the servant of Yahweh, and of the assembly of Israel, for the tent of the testimony?

7For the sons of Athaliah, that wicked woman, had broken up the house of God; and also all the dedicated things of the house of Yahweh did they bestow upon the Baalim.

8So the king commanded, and they made a chest, and set it without at the gate of the house of Yahweh.

9And they made a proclamation through Judah and Jerusalem, to bring in for Yahweh the tax that Moses the servant of God laid upon Israel in the wilderness.

10And all the princes and all the people rejoiced, and brought in, and cast into the chest, until they had made an end.

11And it was so, that, at what time the chest was brought unto the king's officers by the hand of the Levites, and when they saw that there was much money, the king's scribe and the chief priest's officer came and emptied the chest, and took it, and carried it to its place again. Thus they did day by day, and gathered money in abundance.

12And the king and Jehoiada gave it to such as did the work of the service of the house of Yahweh; and they hired masons and carpenters to restore the house of Yahweh, and also such as wrought iron and brass to repair the house of Yahweh.

13So the workmen wrought, and the work of repairing went forward in their hands, and they set up the house of God in its state, and strengthened it.

14And when they had made an end, they brought the rest of the money before the king and Jehoiada, whereof were made vessels for the house of Yahweh, even vessels wherewith to minister and to offer, and spoons, and vessels of gold and silver. And they offered burnt-offerings in the house of Yahweh continually all the days of Jehoiada.

15But Jehoiada waxed old and was full of days, and he died; a hundred and thirty years old was he when he died.

16And they buried him in the city of David among the kings, because he had done good in Israel, and toward God and his house.

17Now after the death of Jehoiada came the princes of Judah, and made obeisance to the king. Then the king hearkened unto them.

18And they forsook the house of Yahweh, the God of their fathers, and served the Asherim and the idols: and wrath came upon Judah and Jerusalem for this their guiltiness.

19Yet he sent prophets to them, to bring them again unto Yahweh; and they testified against them: but they would not give ear.

20And the Spirit of God came upon Zechariah the son of Jehoiada the priest; and he stood above the people, and said unto them, Thus saith God, Why transgress ye the commandments of Yahweh, so that ye cannot prosper? because ye have forsaken Yahweh, he hath also forsaken you.

21And they conspired against him, and stoned him with stones at the commandment of the king in the court of the house of Yahweh.

22Thus Joash the king remembered not the kindness which Jehoiada his father had done to him, but slew his son. And when he died, he said, Yahweh look upon it, and require it.

23And it came to pass at the end of the year, that the army of the Syrians came up against him: and they came to Judah and Jerusalem, and destroyed all the princes of the people from among the people, and sent all the spoil of them unto the king of Damascus.

24For the army of the Syrians came with a small company of men; and Yahweh delivered a very great host into their hand, because they had forsaken Yahweh, the God of their fathers. So they executed judgment upon Joash.

25And when they were departed for him (for they left him very sick), his own servants conspired against him for the blood of the sons of Jehoiada the priest, and slew him on his bed, and he died; and they buried him in the city of David, but they buried him not in the sepulchres of the kings.

26And these are they that conspired against him: Zabad the son of Shimeath the Ammonitess, and Jehozabad the son of Shimrith the Moabitess.

27Now concerning his sons, and the greatness of the burdens laid upon him, and the rebuilding of the house of God, behold, they are written in the commentary of the book of the kings. And Amaziah his son reigned in his stead.

Chapter 25

1Amaziah was twenty and five years old when he began to reign; and he reigned twenty and nine years in Jerusalem: and his mother's name was Jehoaddan, of Jerusalem.

2And he did that which was right in the eyes of Yahweh, but not with a perfect heart.

3Now it came to pass, when the kingdom was established unto him, that he slew his servants that had killed the king his father.

4But he put not their children to death, but did according to that which is written in the law in the book of Moses, as Yahweh commanded, saying, The fathers shall not die for the children, neither shall the children die for the fathers; but every man shall die for his own sin.

5Moreover Amaziah gathered Judah together, and ordered them according to their fathers' houses, under captains of thousands and captains of hundreds, even all Judah and Benjamin: and he numbered them from twenty years old and upward, and found them three hundred thousand chosen men, able to go forth to war, that could handle spear and shield.

6He hired also a hundred thousand mighty men of valor out of Israel for a hundred talents of silver.

7But there came a man of God to him, saying, O king, let not the army of Israel go with thee; for Yahweh is not with Israel, to wit, with all the children of Ephraim.

8But if thou wilt go, do valiantly, be strong for the battle: God will cast thee down before the enemy; for God hath power to help, and to cast down.

9And Amaziah said to the man of God, But what shall we do for the hundred talents which I have given to the army of Israel? And the man of God answered, Yahweh is able to give thee much more than this.

10Then Amaziah separated them, to wit, the army that was come to him out of Ephraim, to go home again: wherefore their anger was greatly kindled against Judah, and they returned home in fierce anger.

11And Amaziah took courage, and led forth his people, and went to the Valley of Salt, and smote of the children of Seir ten thousand.

12And other ten thousand did the children of Judah carry away alive, and brought them to the top of the rock, and cast them down from the top of the rock, so that they all were broken in pieces.

13But the men of the army whom Amaziah sent back, that they should not go with him to battle, fell upon the cities of Judah, from Samaria even unto Beth-horon, and smote of them three thousand, and took much spoil.

14Now it came to pass, after that Amaziah was come from the slaughter of the Edomites, that he brought the gods of the children of Seir, and set them up to be his gods, and bowed down himself before them, and burned incense unto them.

15Wherefore the anger of Yahweh was kindled against Amaziah, and he sent unto him a prophet, who said unto him, Why hast thou sought after the gods of the people, which have not delivered their own people out of thy hand?

16And it came to pass, as he talked with him, that the king said unto him, Have we made thee of the king's counsel? forbear; why shouldest thou be smitten? Then the prophet forbare, and said, I know that God hath determined to destroy thee, because thou hast done this, and hast not hearkened unto my counsel.

17Then Amaziah king of Judah took advice, and sent to Joash, the son of Jehoahaz the son of Jehu, king of Israel, saying, Come, let us look one another in the face.

18And Joash king of Israel sent to Amaziah king of Judah, saying, The thistle that was in Lebanon sent to the cedar that was in Lebanon, saying, Give thy daughter to my son to wife: and there passed by a wild beast that was in Lebanon, and trod down the thistle.

19Thou sayest, Lo, thou hast smitten Edom; and thy heart lifteth thee up to boast: abide now at home; why shouldest thou meddle to thy hurt, that thou shouldest fall, even thou, and Judah with thee?

20But Amaziah would not hear; for it was of God, that he might deliver them into the hand of their enemies, because they had sought after the gods of Edom.

21So Joash king of Israel went up; and he and Amaziah king of Judah looked one another in the face at Beth-shemesh, which belongeth to Judah.

22And Judah was put to the worse before Israel; and they fled every man to his tent.

23And Joash king of Israel took Amaziah king of Judah, the son of Joash the son of Jehoahaz, at Beth-shemesh, and brought him to Jerusalem, and brake down the wall of Jerusalem from the gate of Ephraim unto the corner gate, four hundred cubits.

24And he took all the gold and silver, and all the vessels that were found in the house of God with Obed-edom, and the treasures of the king's house, the hostages also, and returned to Samaria.

25And Amaziah the son of Joash king of Judah lived after the death of Joash son of Jehoahaz king of Israel fifteen years.

26Now the rest of the acts of Amaziah, first and last, behold, are they not written in the book of the kings of Judah and Israel?

27Now from the time that Amaziah did turn away from following Yahweh they made a conspiracy against him in Jerusalem; and he fled to Lachish: but they sent after him to Lachish, and slew him there.

28And they brought him upon horses, and buried him with his fathers in the city of Judah.

Chapter 26

1And all the people of Judah took Uzziah, who was sixteen years old, and made him king in the room of his father Amaziah.

2He built Eloth, and restored it to Judah, after that the king slept with his fathers.

3Sixteen years old was Uzziah when he began to reign; and he reigned fifty and two years in Jerusalem: and his mother's name was Jechiliah, of Jerusalem.

4And he did that which was right in the eyes of Yahweh, according to all that his father Amaziah had done.

5And he set himself to seek God in the days of Zechariah, who had understanding in the vision of God: and as long as he sought Yahweh, God made him to prosper.

6And he went forth and warred against the Philistines, and brake down the wall of Gath, and the wall of Jabneh, and the wall of Ashdod; and he built cities in the country of Ashdod, and among the Philistines.

7And God helped him against the Philistines, and against the Arabians that dwelt in Gur-baal, and the Meunim.

8And the Ammonites gave tribute to Uzziah: and his name spread abroad even to the entrance of Egypt; for he waxed exceeding strong.

9Moreover Uzziah built towers in Jerusalem at the corner gate, and at the valley gate, and at the turning of the wall, and fortified them.

10And he built towers in the wilderness, and hewed out many cisterns, for he had much cattle; in the lowland also, and in the plain: and he had husbandmen and vinedressers in the mountains and in the fruitful fields; for he loved husbandry.

11Moreover Uzziah had an army of fighting men, that went out to war by bands, according to the number of their reckoning made by Jeiel the scribe and Maaseiah the officer, under the hand of Hananiah, one of the king's captains.

12The whole number of the heads of fathers' houses, even the mighty men of valor, was two thousand and six hundred.

13And under their hand was an army, three hundred thousand and seven thousand and five hundred, that made war with mighty power, to help the king against the enemy.

14And Uzziah prepared for them, even for all the host, shields, and spears, and helmets, and coats of mail, and bows, and stones for slinging.

15And he made in Jerusalem engines, invented by skilful men, to be on the towers and upon the battlements, wherewith to shoot arrows and great stones. And his name spread far abroad; for he was marvellously helped, till he was strong.

16But when he was strong, his heart was lifted up, so that he did corruptly, and he trespassed against Yahweh his God; for he went into the temple of Yahweh to burn incense upon the altar of incense.

17And Azariah the priest went in after him, and with him fourscore priests of Yahweh, that were valiant men:

18and they withstood Uzziah the king, and said unto him, It pertaineth not unto thee, Uzziah, to burn incense unto Yahweh, but to the priests the sons of Aaron, that are consecrated to burn incense: go out of the sanctuary; for thou hast trespassed; neither shall it be for thine honor from Yahweh God.

19Then Uzziah was wroth; and he had a censer in his hand to burn incense; and while he was wroth with the priests, the leprosy brake forth in his forehead before the priests in the house of Yahweh, beside the altar of incense.

20And Azariah the chief priest, and all the priests, looked upon him, and, behold, he was leprous in his forehead, and they thrust him out quickly from thence; yea, himself hasted also to go out, because Yahweh had smitten him.

21And Uzziah the king was a leper unto the day of his death, and dwelt in a separate house, being a leper; for he was cut off from the house of Yahweh: and Jotham his son was over the king's house, judging the people of the land.

22Now the rest of the acts of Uzziah, first and last, did Isaiah the prophet, the son of Amoz, write.

23So Uzziah slept with his fathers; and they buried him with his fathers in the field of burial which belonged to the kings; for they said, He is a leper: and Jotham his son reigned in his stead.

Chapter 27

1Jotham was twenty and five years old when he began to reign; and he reigned sixteen years in Jerusalem: and his mother's name was Jerushah the daughter of Zadok.

2And he did that which was right in the eyes of Yahweh, according to all that his father Uzziah had done: howbeit he entered not into the temple of Yahweh. And the people did yet corruptly.

3He built the upper gate of the house of Yahweh, and on the wall of Ophel he built much.

4Moreover he built cities in the hill-country of Judah, and in the forests he built castles and towers.

5He fought also with the king of the children of Ammon, and prevailed against them. And the children of Ammon gave him the same year a hundred talents of silver, and ten thousand measures of wheat, and ten thousand of barley. So much did the children of Ammon render unto him, in the second year also, and in the third.

6So Jotham became mighty, because he ordered his ways before Yahweh his God.

7Now the rest of the acts of Jotham, and all his wars, and his ways, behold, they are written in the book of the kings of Israel and Judah.

8He was five and twenty years old when he began to reign, and reigned sixteen years in Jerusalem.

9And Jotham slept with his fathers, and they buried him in the city of David: and Ahaz his son reigned in his stead.

Chapter 28

1Ahaz was twenty years old when he began to reign; and he reigned sixteen years in Jerusalem: and he did not that which was right in the eyes of Yahweh, like David his father;

2but he walked in the ways of the kings of Israel, and made also molten images for the Baalim.

3Moreover he burnt incense in the valley of the son of Hinnom, and burnt his children in the fire, according to the abominations of the nations whom Yahweh cast out before the children of Israel.

4And he sacrificed and burnt incense in the high places, and on the hills, and under every green tree.

5Wherefore Yahweh his God delivered him into the hand of the king of Syria; and they smote him, and carried away of his a great multitude of captives, and brought them to Damascus. And he was also delivered into the hand of the king of Israel, who smote him with a great slaughter.

6For Pekah the son of Remaliah slew in Judah a hundred and twenty thousand in one day, all of them valiant men; because they had forsaken Yahweh, the God of their fathers.

7And Zichri, a mighty man of Ephraim, slew Maaseiah the king's son, and Azrikam the ruler of the house, and Elkanah that was next to the king.

8And the children of Israel carried away captive of their brethren two hundred thousand, women, sons, and daughters, and took also away much spoil from them, and brought the spoil to Samaria.

9But a prophet of Yahweh was there, whose name was Oded: and he went out to meet the host that came to Samaria, and said unto them, Behold, because Yahweh, the God of your fathers, was wroth with Judah, he hath delivered them into your hand, and ye have slain them in a rage which hath reached up to heaven.

10And now ye purpose to keep under the children of Judah and Jerusalem for bondmen and bondwomen unto you: but are there not even with you trespasses of your own against Yahweh your God?

11Now hear me therefore, and send back the captives, that ye have taken captive of your brethren; for the fierce wrath of Yahweh is upon you.

Second Chronicles

12Then certain of the heads of the children of Ephraim, Azariah the son of Johanan, Berechiah the son of Meshillemoth, and Jehizkiah the son of Shallum, and Amasa the son of Hadlai, stood up against them that came from the war,

13and said unto them, Ye shall not bring in the captives hither: for ye purpose that which will bring upon us a trespass against Yahweh, to add unto our sins and to our trespass; for our trespass is great, and there is fierce wrath against Israel.

14So the armed men left the captives and the spoil before the princes and all the assembly.

15And the men that have been mentioned by name rose up, and took the captives, and with the spoil clothed all that were naked among them, and arrayed them, and shod them, and gave them to eat and to drink, and anointed them, and carried all the feeble of them upon asses, and brought them to Jericho, the city of palm-trees, unto their brethren: then they returned to Samaria.

16At that time did king Ahaz send unto the kings of Assyria to help him.

17For again the Edomites had come and smitten Judah, and carried away captives.

18The Philistines also had invaded the cities of the lowland, and of the South of Judah, and had taken Beth-shemesh, and Aijalon, and Gederoth, and Soco with the towns thereof, and Timnah with the towns thereof, Gimzo also and the towns thereof: and they dwelt there.

19For Yahweh brought Judah low because of Ahaz king of Israel; for he had dealt wantonly in Judah, and trespassed sore against Yahweh.

20And Tilgath-pilneser king of Assyria came unto him, and distressed him, but strengthened him not.

21For Ahaz took away a portion out of the house of Yahweh, and out of the house of the king and of the princes, and gave it unto the king of Assyria: but it helped him not.

22And in the time of his distress did he trespass yet more against Yahweh, this same king Ahaz.

23For he sacrificed unto the gods of Damascus, which smote him; and he said, Because the gods of the kings of Syria helped them, therefore will I sacrifice to them, that they may help me. But they were the ruin of him, and of all Israel.

24And Ahaz gathered together the vessels of the house of God, and cut in pieces the vessels of the house of God, and shut up the doors of the house of Yahweh; and he made him altars in every corner of Jerusalem.

25And in every city of Judah he made high places to burn incense unto other gods, and provoked to anger Yahweh, the God of his fathers.

26Now the rest of his acts, and all his ways, first and last, behold, they are written in the book of the kings of Judah and Israel.

27And Ahaz slept with his fathers, and they buried him in the city, even in Jerusalem; for they brought him not into the sepulchres of the kings of Israel: and Hezekiah his son reigned in his stead.

Chapter 29

1Hezekiah began to reign when he was five and twenty years old; and he reigned nine and twenty years in Jerusalem: and his mother's name was Abijah, the daughter of Zechariah.

2And he did that which was right in the eyes of Yahweh, according to all that David his father had done.

3He in the first year of his reign, in the first month, opened the doors of the house of Yahweh, and repaired them.

4And he brought in the priests and the Levites, and gathered them together into the broad place on the east,

5and said unto them, Hear me, ye Levites; now sanctify yourselves, and sanctify the house of Yahweh, the God of your fathers, and carry forth the filthiness out of the holy place.

6For our fathers have trespassed, and done that which was evil in the sight of Yahweh our God, and have forsaken him, and have turned away their faces from the habitation of Yahweh, and turned their backs.

7Also they have shut up the doors of the porch, and put out the lamps, and have not burned incense nor offered burnt-offerings in the holy place unto the God of Israel.

8Wherefore the wrath of Yahweh was upon Judah and Jerusalem, and he hath delivered them to be tossed to and fro, to be an astonishment, and a hissing, as ye see with your eyes.

9For, lo, our fathers have fallen by the sword, and our sons and our daughters and our wives are in captivity for this.

10Now it is in my heart to make a covenant with Yahweh, the God of Israel, that his fierce anger may turn away from us.

11My sons, be not now negligent; for Yahweh hath chosen you to stand before him, to minister unto him, and that ye should be his ministers, and burn incense.

12Then the Levites arose, Mahath, the son of Amasai, and Joel the son of Azariah, of the sons of the Kohathites; and of the sons of Merari, Kish the son of Abdi, and Azariah the son of Jehallelel; and of the Gershonites, Joah the son of Zimmah, and Eden the son of Joah;

13and of the sons of Elizaphan, Shimri and Jeuel; and of the sons of Asaph, Zechariah and Mattaniah;

14and of the sons of Heman, Jehuel and Shimei; and of the sons of Jeduthun, Shemaiah and Uzziel.

15And they gathered their brethren, and sanctified themselves, and went in, according to the commandment of the king by the words of Yahweh, to cleanse the house of Yahweh.

16And the priests went in unto the inner part of the house of Yahweh, to cleanse it, and brought out all the uncleanness that they found in the temple of Yahweh into the court of the house of Yahweh. And the Levites took it, to carry it out abroad to the brook Kidron.

17Now they began on the first day of the first month to sanctify, and on the eighth day of the month came they to the porch of Yahweh; and they sanctified the house of Yahweh in eight days: and on the sixteenth day of the first month they made an end.

18Then they went in to Hezekiah the king within the palace, and said, We have cleansed all the house of Yahweh, and the altar of burnt-offering, with all the vessels thereof, and the table of showbread, with all the vessels thereof.

19Moreover all the vessels, which king Ahaz in his reign did cast away when he trespassed, have we prepared and sanctified; and, behold, they are before the altar of Yahweh.

20Then Hezekiah the king arose early, and gathered the princes of the city, and went up to the house of Yahweh.

21And they brought seven bullocks, and seven rams, and seven lambs, and seven he-goats, for a sin-offering for the kingdom and for the sanctuary and for Judah. And he commanded the priests the sons of Aaron to offer them on the altar of Yahweh.

22So they killed the bullocks, and the priests received the blood, and sprinkled it on the altar: and they killed the rams, and sprinkled the blood upon the altar: they killed also the lambs, and sprinkled the blood upon the altar.

23And they brought near the he-goats for the sin-offering before the king and the assembly; and they laid their hands upon them:

24and the priests killed them, and they made a sin-offering with their blood upon the altar, to make atonement for all Israel; for the king commanded that the burnt-offering and the sin-offering should be made for all Israel.

25And he set the Levites in the house of Yahweh with cymbals, with psalteries, and with harps, according to the commandment of David, and of Gad the king's seer, and Nathan the prophet; for the commandment was of Yahweh by his prophets.

26And the Levites stood with the instruments of David, and the priests with the trumpets.

27And Hezekiah commanded to offer the burnt-offering upon the altar. And when the burnt-offering began, the song of Yahweh began also, and the trumpets, together with the instruments of David king of Israel.

28And all the assembly worshipped, and the singers sang, and the trumpeters sounded; all this continued until the burnt-offering was finished.

29And when they had made an end of offering, the king and all that were present with him bowed themselves and worshipped.

30Moreover Hezekiah the king and the princes commanded the Levites to sing praises unto Yahweh with the words of David, and of Asaph the seer. And they sang praises with gladness, and they bowed their heads and worshipped.

31Then Hezekiah answered and said, Now ye have consecrated yourselves unto Yahweh; come near and bring sacrifices and thank-offerings into the house of Yahweh. And the assembly brought in sacrifices and thank-offerings; and as many as were of a willing heart brought burnt-offerings.

32And the number of the burnt-offerings which the assembly brought was threescore and ten bullocks, a hundred rams, and two hundred lambs: all these were for a burnt-offering to Yahweh.

33And the consecrated things were six hundred oxen and three thousand sheep.

34But the priests were too few, so that they could not flay all the burnt-offerings: wherefore their brethren the Levites did help them, till the work was ended, and until the priests had sanctified themselves; for the Levites were more upright in heart to sanctify themselves than the priests.

35And also the burnt-offerings were in abundance, with the fat of the peace-offerings, and with the drink-offerings for every burnt-offering. So the service of the house of Yahweh was set in order.

36And Hezekiah rejoiced, and all the people, because of that which God had prepared for the people: for the thing was done suddenly.

Chapter 30

1And Hezekiah sent to all Israel and Judah, and wrote letters also to Ephraim and Manasseh, that they should come to the house of Yahweh at Jerusalem, to keep the passover unto Yahweh, the God of Israel.

2For the king had taken counsel, and his princes, and all the assembly in Jerusalem, to keep the passover in the second month.

3For they could not keep it at that time, because the priests had not sanctified themselves in sufficient number, neither had the people gathered themselves together to Jerusalem.

4And the thing was right in the eyes of the king and of all the assembly.

5So they established a decree to make proclamation throughout all Israel, from Beer-sheba even to Dan, that they should come to keep the passover unto Yahweh, the God of Israel, at Jerusalem: for they had not kept it in great numbers in such sort as it is written.

6So the posts went with the letters from the king and his princes throughout all Israel and Judah, and according to the commandment of the king, saying, Ye children of Israel, turn again unto Yahweh, the God of Abraham, Isaac, and Israel, that he may return to the remnant that are escaped of you out of the hand of the kings of Assyria.

7And be not ye like your fathers, and like your brethren, who trespassed against Yahweh, the God of their fathers, so that he gave them up to desolation, as ye see.

8Now be ye not stiffnecked, as your fathers were; but yield yourselves unto Yahweh, and enter into his sanctuary, which he hath sanctified for ever, and serve Yahweh your God, that his fierce anger may turn away from you.

9For if ye turn again unto Yahweh, your brethren and your children shall find compassion before them that led them captive, and shall come again into this land: for Yahweh your God is gracious and merciful, and will not turn away his face from you, if ye return unto him.

10So the posts passed from city to city through the country of Ephraim and Manasseh, even unto Zebulun: but they laughed them to scorn, and mocked them.

11Nevertheless certain men of Asher and Manasseh and of Zebulun humbled themselves, and came to Jerusalem.

12Also upon Judah came the hand of God to give them one heart, to do the commandment of the king and of the princes by the word of Yahweh.

13And there assembled at Jerusalem much people to keep the feast of unleavened bread in the second month, a very great assembly.

14And they arose and took away the altars that were in Jerusalem, and all the altars for incense took they away, and cast them into the brook Kidron.

15Then they killed the passover on the fourteenth day of the second month: and the priests and the Levites were ashamed, and sanctified themselves, and brought burnt-offerings into the house of Yahweh.

16And they stood in their place after their order, according to the law of Moses the man of God: the priests sprinkled the blood which they received of the hand of the Levites.

17For there were many in the assembly that had not sanctified themselves: therefore the Levites had the charge of killing the passovers for every one that was not clean, to sanctify them unto Yahweh.

18For a multitude of the people, even many of Ephraim and Manasseh, Issachar and Zebulun, had not cleansed themselves, yet did they eat the passover otherwise than it is written. For Hezekiah had prayed for them, saying, The good Yahweh pardon every one

19that setteth his heart to seek God, Yahweh, the God of his fathers, though he be not cleansed according to the purification of the sanctuary.

20And Yahweh hearkened to Hezekiah, and healed the people.

21And the children of Israel that were present at Jerusalem kept the feast of unleavened bread seven days with great gladness; and the Levites and the priests praised Yahweh day by day, singing with loud instruments unto Yahweh.

22And Hezekiah spake comfortably unto all the Levites that had good understanding in the service of Yahweh. So they did eat throughout the feast for the seven days, offering sacrifices of peace-offerings, and making confession to Yahweh, the God of their fathers.

23And the whole assembly took counsel to keep other seven days; and they kept other seven days with gladness.

24For Hezekiah king of Judah did give to the assembly for offerings a thousand bullocks and seven thousand sheep; and the princes gave to the assembly a thousand bullocks and ten thousand sheep: and a great number of priests sanctified themselves.

25And all the assembly of Judah, with the priests and the Levites, and all the assembly that came out of Israel, and the sojourners that came out of the land of Israel, and that dwelt in Judah, rejoiced.

26So there was great joy in Jerusalem; for since the time of Solomon the son of David king of Israel there was not the like in Jerusalem.

27Then the priests the Levites arose and blessed the people: and their voice was heard, and their prayer came up to his holy habitation, even unto heaven.

Chapter 31

1Now when all this was finished, all Israel that were present went out to the cities of Judah, and brake in pieces the pillars, and hewed down the Asherim, and brake down the high places and the altars out of all Judah and Benjamin, in Ephraim also and Manasseh, until they had destroyed them all. Then all the children of Israel returned, every man to his possession, into their own cities.

2And Hezekiah appointed the courses of the priests and the Levites after their courses, every man according to his service, both the priests and the Levites, for burnt-offerings and for peace-offerings, to minister, and to give thanks, and to praise in the gates of the camp of Yahweh.

3He appointed also the king's portion of his substance for the burnt-offerings, to wit, for the morning and evening burnt-offerings, and the burnt-offerings for the sabbaths, and for the new moons, and for the set feasts, as it is written in the law of Yahweh.

4Moreover he commanded the people that dwelt in Jerusalem to give the portion of the priests and the Levites, that they might give themselves to the law of Yahweh.

5And as soon as the commandment came abroad, the children of Israel gave in abundance the first-fruits of grain, new wine, and oil, and honey, and of all the increase of the field; and the tithe of all things brought they in abundantly.

6And the children of Israel and Judah, that dwelt in the cities of Judah, they also brought in the tithe of oxen and sheep, and the tithe of dedicated things which were consecrated unto Yahweh their God, and laid them by heaps.

7In the third month they began to lay the foundation of the heaps, and finished them in the seventh month.

8And when Hezekiah and the princes came and saw the heaps, they blessed Yahweh, and his people Israel.

9Then Hezekiah questioned the priests and the Levites concerning the heaps.

10And Azariah the chief priest, of the house of Zadok, answered him and said, Since the people began to bring the oblations into the house of Yahweh, we have eaten and had enough, and have left plenty: for Yahweh hath blessed his people; and that which is left is this great store.

11Then Hezekiah commanded to prepare chambers in the house of Yahweh; and they prepared them.

12And they brought in the oblations and the tithes and the dedicated things faithfully: and over them Conaniah the Levite was ruler, and Shimei his brother was second.

13And Jehiel, and Azaziah, and Nahath, and Asahel, and Jerimoth, and Jozabad, and Eliel, and Ismachiah, and Mahath, and Benaiah, were overseers under the hand of Conaniah and Shimei his brother, by the appointment of Hezekiah the king, and Azariah the ruler of the house of God.

14And Kore the son of Imnah the Levite, the porter at the east gate, was over the freewill-offerings of God, to distribute the oblations of Yahweh, and the most holy things.

15And under him were Eden, and Miniamin, and Jeshua, and Shemaiah, Amariah, and Shecaniah, in the cities of the priests, in their office of trust, to give to their brethren by courses, as well to the great as to the small:

16besides them that were reckoned by genealogy of males, from three years old and upward, even every one that entered into the house of Yahweh, as the duty of every day required, for their service in their offices according to their courses;

17and them that were reckoned by genealogy of the priests by their fathers' houses, and the Levites from twenty years old and upward, in their offices by their courses;

18and them that were reckoned by genealogy of all their little ones, their wives, and their sons, and their daughters, through all the congregation: for in their office of trust they sanctified themselves in holiness.

19Also for the sons of Aaron the priests, that were in the fields of the suburbs of their cities, in every city, there were men that were mentioned by name, to give portions to all the males among the priests, and to all that were reckoned by genealogy among the Levites.

20And thus did Hezekiah throughout all Judah; and he wrought that which was good and right and faithful before Yahweh his God.

21And in every work that he began in the service of the house of God, and in the law, and in the commandments, to seek his God, he did it with all his heart, and prospered.

Chapter 32

1After these things, and this faithfulness, Sennacherib king of Assyria came, and entered into Judah, and encamped against the fortified cities, and thought to win them for himself.

2And when Hezekiah saw that Sennacherib was come, and that he was purposed to fight against Jerusalem,

3he took counsel with his princes and his mighty men to stop the waters of the fountains which were without the city; and they helped him.

4So there was gathered much people together, and they stopped all the fountains, and the brook that flowed through the midst of the land, saying, Why should the kings of Assyria come, and find much water?

5And he took courage, and built up all the wall that was broken down, and raised it up to the towers, and the other wall without, and strengthened Millo in the city of David, and made weapons and shields in abundance.

6And he set captains of war over the people, and gathered them together to him in the broad place at the gate of the city, and spake comfortably to them, saying,

7Be strong and of good courage, be not afraid nor dismayed for the king of Assyria, nor for all the multitude that is with him; for there is a greater with us than with him:

8with him is an arm of flesh; but with us is Yahweh our God to help us, and to fight our battles. And the people rested themselves upon the words of Hezekiah king of Judah.

9After this did Sennacherib king of Assyria send his servants to Jerusalem, (now he was before Lachish, and all his power with him,) unto Hezekiah king of Judah, and unto all Judah that were at Jerusalem, saying,

10Thus saith Sennacherib king of Assyria, Whereon do ye trust, that ye abide the siege in Jerusalem?

11Doth not Hezekiah persuade you, to give you over to die by famine and by thirst, saying, Yahweh our God will deliver us out of the hand of the king of Assyria?

12Hath not the same Hezekiah taken away his high places and his altars, and commanded Judah and Jerusalem, saying, Ye shall worship before one altar, and upon it shall ye burn incense?

13Know ye not what I and my fathers have done unto all the peoples of the lands? Were the gods of the nations of the lands in any wise able to deliver their land out of my hand?

14Who was there among all the gods of those nations which my fathers utterly destroyed, that could deliver his people out of my hand, that your God should be able to deliver you out of my hand?

15Now therefore let not Hezekiah deceive you, nor persuade you after this manner, neither believe ye him; for no god of any nation or kingdom was able to deliver his people out of my hand, and out of the hand of my fathers: how much less shall your God deliver you out of my hand?

16And his servants spake yet more against Yahweh God, and against his servant Hezekiah.

17He wrote also letters, to rail on Yahweh, the God of Israel, and to speak against him, saying, As the gods of the nations of the lands, which have not delivered their people out of my hand, so shall not the God of Hezekiah deliver his people out of my hand.

18And they cried with a loud voice in the Jews' language unto the people of Jerusalem that were on the wall, to affright them, and to trouble them; that they might take the city.

19And they spake of the God of Jerusalem, as of the gods of the peoples of the earth, which are the work of men's hands.

20And Hezekiah the king, and Isaiah the prophet the son of Amoz, prayed because of this, and cried to heaven.

21And Yahweh sent an angel, who cut off all the mighty men of valor, and the leaders and captains, in the camp of the king of Assyria. So he returned with shame of face to his own land. And when he was come into the house of his god, they that came forth from his own bowels slew him there with the sword.

22Thus Yahweh saved Hezekiah and the inhabitants of Jerusalem from the hand of Sennacherib the king of Assyria, and from the hand of all others, and guided them on every side.

23And many brought gifts unto Yahweh to Jerusalem, and precious things to Hezekiah king of Judah; so that he was exalted in the sight of all nations from thenceforth.

24In those days Hezekiah was sick even unto death: and he prayed unto Yahweh; and he spake unto him, and gave him a sign.

25But Hezekiah rendered not again according to the benefit done unto him; for his heart was lifted up: therefore there was wrath upon him, and upon Judah and Jerusalem.

26Notwithstanding Hezekiah humbled himself for the pride of his heart, both he and the inhabitants of Jerusalem, so that the wrath of Yahweh came not upon them in the days of Hezekiah.

27And Hezekiah had exceeding much riches and honor: and he provided him treasuries for silver, and for gold, and for precious stones, and for spices, and for shields, and for all manner of goodly vessels;

28store-houses also for the increase of grain and new wine and oil; and stalls for all manner of beasts, and flocks in folds.

29Moreover he provided him cities, and possessions of flocks and herds in abundance; for God had given him very much substance.

30This same Hezekiah also stopped the upper spring of the waters of Gihon, and brought them straight down on the west side of the city of David. And Hezekiah prospered in all his works.

31Howbeit in the business of the ambassadors of the princes of Babylon, who sent unto him to inquire of the wonder that was done in the land, God left him, to try him, that he might know all that was in his heart.

32Now the rest of the acts of Hezekiah, and his good deeds, behold, they are written in the vision of Isaiah the prophet the son of Amoz, in the book of the kings of Judah and Israel.

33And Hezekiah slept with his fathers, and they buried him in the ascent of the sepulchres of the sons of David: and all Judah and the inhabitants of Jerusalem did him honor at his death. And Manasseh his son reigned in his stead.

Chapter 33

1Manasseh was twelve years old when he began to reign; and he reigned fifty and five years in Jerusalem.

2And he did that which was evil in the sight of Yahweh, after the abominations of the nations whom Yahweh cast out before the children of Israel.

3For he built again the high places which Hezekiah his father had broken down; and he reared up altars for the Baalim, and made Asheroth, and worshipped all the host of heaven, and served them.

4And he built altars in the house of Yahweh, whereof Yahweh said, In Jerusalem shall my name be for ever.

5And he built altars for all the host of heaven in the two courts of the house of Yahweh.

6He also made his children to pass through the fire in the valley of the son of Hinnom; and he practised augury, and used enchantments, and practised sorcery, and dealt with them that had familiar spirits, and with wizards: he wrought much evil in the sight of Yahweh, to provoke him to anger.

7And he set the graven image of the idol, which he had made, in the house of God, of which God said to David and to Solomon his son, In this house, and in Jerusalem, which I have chosen out of all the tribes of Israel, will I put my name for ever:

8neither will I any more remove the foot of Israel from off the land which I have appointed for your fathers, if only they will observe to do all that I have commanded them, even all the law and the statutes and the ordinances given by Moses.

9And Manasseh seduced Judah and the inhabitants of Jerusalem, so that they did evil more than did the nations whom Yahweh destroyed before the children of Israel.

10And Yahweh spake to Manasseh, and to his people; but they gave no heed.

11Wherefore Yahweh brought upon them the captains of the host of the king of Assyria, who took Manasseh in chains, and bound him with fetters, and carried him to Babylon.

12And when he was in distress, he besought Yahweh his God, and humbled himself greatly before the God of his fathers.

13And he prayed unto him; and he was entreated of him, and heard his supplication, and brought him again to Jerusalem into his kingdom. Then Manasseh knew that Yahweh he was God.

14Now after this he built an outer wall to the city of David, on the west side of Gihon, in the valley, even to the entrance at the fish gate; and he compassed Ophel about with it, and raised it up to a very great height: and he put valiant captains in all the fortified cities of Judah.

15And he took away the foreign gods, and the idol out of the house of Yahweh, and all the altars that he had built in the mount of the house of Yahweh, and in Jerusalem, and cast them out of the city.

16And he built up the altar of Yahweh, and offered thereon sacrifices of peace-offerings and of thanksgiving, and commanded Judah to serve Yahweh, the God of Israel.

17Nevertheless the people sacrificed still in the high places, but only unto Yahweh their God.

18Now the rest of the acts of Manasseh, and his prayer unto his God, and the words of the seers that spake to him in the name of Yahweh, the God of Israel, behold, they are written among the acts of the kings of Israel.

19His prayer also, and how God was entreated of him, and all his sin and his trespass, and the places wherein he built high places, and set up the Asherim and the graven images, before he humbled himself: behold, they are written in the history of Hozai.

20So Manasseh slept with his fathers, and they buried him in his own house: and Amon his son reigned in his stead.

21Amon was twenty and two years old when he began to reign; and he reigned two years in Jerusalem.

22And he did that which was evil in the sight of Yahweh, as did Manasseh his father; and Amon sacrificed unto all the graven images which Manasseh his father had made, and served them.

23And he humbled not himself before Yahweh, as Manasseh his father had humbled himself; but this same Amon trespassed more and more.

24And his servants conspired against him, and put him to death in his own house.

25But the people of the land slew all them that had conspired against king Amon; and the people of the land made Josiah his son king in his stead.

Chapter 34

1Josiah was eight years old when he began to reign; and he reigned thirty and one years in Jerusalem.

2And he did that which was right in the eyes of Yahweh, and walked in the ways of David his father, and turned not aside to the right hand or to the left.

3For in the eighth year of his reign, while he was yet young, he began to seek after the God of David his father; and in the twelfth year he began to purge Judah and Jerusalem from the high places, and the Asherim, and the graven images, and the molten images.

4And they brake down the altars of the Baalim in his presence; and the sun-images that were on high above them he hewed down; and the Asherim, and the graven images, and the molten images, he brake in pieces, and made dust of them, and strewed it upon the graves of them that had sacrificed unto them.

5And he burnt the bones of the priests upon their altars, and purged Judah and Jerusalem.

6And so did he in the cities of Manasseh and Ephraim and Simeon, even unto Naphtali, in their ruins round about.

7And he brake down the altars, and beat the Asherim and the graven images into powder, and hewed down all the sun-images throughout all the land of Israel, and returned to Jerusalem.

8Now in the eighteenth year of his reign, when he had purged the land and the house, he sent Shaphan the son of Azaliah, and Maaseiah the governor of the city, and Joah the son of Joahaz the recorder, to repair the house of Yahweh his God.

9And they came to Hilkiah the high priest, and delivered the money that was brought into the house of God, which the Levites, the keepers of the threshold, had gathered of the hand of Manasseh and Ephraim, and of all the remnant of Israel, and of all Judah and Benjamin, and of the inhabitants of Jerusalem.

10And they delivered it into the hand of the workmen that had the oversight of the house of Yahweh; and the workmen that wrought in the house of Yahweh gave it to mend and repair the house;

11even to the carpenters and to the builders gave they it, to buy hewn stone, and timber for couplings, and to make beams for the houses which the kings of Judah had destroyed.

12And the men did the work faithfully: and the overseers of them were Jahath and Obadiah, the Levites, of the sons of Merari; and Zechariah and Meshullam, of the sons of the Kohathites, to set it forward; and others of the Levites, all that were skilful with instruments of music.

13Also they were over the bearers of burdens, and set forward all that did the work in every manner of service: and of the Levites there were scribes, and officers, and porters.

14And when they brought out the money that was brought into the house of Yahweh, Hilkiah the priest found the book of the law of Yahweh given by Moses.

15And Hilkiah answered and said to Shaphan the scribe, I have found the book of the law in the house of Yahweh. And Hilkiah delivered the book to Shaphan.

16And Shaphan carried the book to the king, and moreover brought back word to the king, saying, All that was committed to thy servants, they are doing.

17And they have emptied out the money that was found in the house of Yahweh, and have delivered it into the hand of the overseers, and into the hand of the workmen.

18And Shaphan the scribe told the king, saying, Hilkiah the priest hath delivered me a book. And Shaphan read therein before the king.

19And it came to pass, when the king had heard the words of the law, that he rent his clothes.

20And the king commanded Hilkiah, and Ahikam the son of Shaphan, and Abdon the son of Micah, and Shaphan the scribe, and Asaiah the king's servant, saying,

21Go ye, inquire of Yahweh for me, and for them that are left in Israel and in Judah, concerning the words of the book that is found; for great is the wrath of Yahweh that is poured out upon us, because our fathers have not kept the word of Yahweh, to do according unto all that is written in this book.

22So Hilkiah, and they whom the king had commanded, went to Huldah the prophetess, the wife of Shallum the son of Tokhath, the son of Hasrah, keeper of the wardrobe; (now she dwelt in Jerusalem in the second quarter;) and they spake to her to that effect.

23And she said unto them, Thus saith Yahweh, the God of Israel: Tell ye the man that sent you unto me,

24Thus saith Yahweh, Behold, I will bring evil upon this place, and upon the inhabitants thereof, even all the curses that are written in the book which they have read before the king of Judah.

25Because they have forsaken me, and have burned incense unto other gods, that they might provoke me to anger with all the works of their hands; therefore is my wrath poured out upon this place, and it shall not be quenched.

26But unto the king of Judah, who sent you to inquire of Yahweh, thus shall ye say to him, Thus saith Yahweh, the God of Israel: As touching the words which thou hast heard,

27because thy heart was tender, and thou didst humble thyself before God, when thou heardest his words against this place, and against the inhabitants thereof, and hast humbled thyself before me, and hast rent thy clothes, and wept before me; I also have heard thee, saith Yahweh.

28Behold, I will gather thee to thy fathers, and thou shalt be gathered to thy grave in peace, neither shall thine eyes see all the evil that I will bring upon this place, and upon the inhabitants thereof. And they brought back word to the king.

29Then the king sent and gathered together all the elders of Judah and Jerusalem.

30And the king went up to the house of Yahweh, and all the men of Judah and the inhabitants of Jerusalem, and the priests, and the Levites, and all the people, both great and small: and he read in their ears all the words of the book of the covenant that was found in the house of Yahweh.

31And the king stood in his place, and made a covenant before Yahweh, to walk after Yahweh, and to keep his commandments, and his testimonies, and his statutes, with all his heart, and with all his soul, to perform the words of the covenant that were written in this book.

32And he caused all that were found in Jerusalem and Benjamin to stand to it. And the inhabitants of Jerusalem did according to the covenant of God, the God of their fathers.

33And Josiah took away all the abominations out of all the countries that pertained to the children of Israel, and made all that were found in Israel to serve, even to serve Yahweh their God. All his days they departed not from following Yahweh, the God of their fathers.

Chapter 35

1And Josiah kept a passover unto Yahweh in Jerusalem: and they killed the passover on the fourteenth day of the first month.

2And he set the priests in their offices, and encouraged them to the service of the house of Yahweh.

3And he said unto the Levites that taught all Israel, that were holy unto Yahweh, Put the holy ark in the house which Solomon the son of David king of Israel did build; there shall no more be a burden upon your shoulders: now serve Yahweh your God, and his people Israel.

4And prepare yourselves after your fathers' houses by your courses, according to the writing of David king of Israel, and according to the writing of Solomon his son.

5And stand in the holy place according to the divisions of the fathers' houses of your brethren the children of the people, and let there be for each a portion of a fathers' house of the Levites.

6And kill the passover, and sanctify yourselves, and prepare for your brethren, to do according to the word of Yahweh by Moses.

7And Josiah gave to the children of the people, of the flock, lambs and kids, all of them for the passover-offerings, unto all that were present, to the number of thirty thousand, and three thousand bullocks: these were of the king's substance.

8And his princes gave for a freewill-offering unto the people, to the priests, and to the Levites. Hilkiah and Zechariah and Jehiel, the rulers of the house of God, gave unto the priests for the passover-offerings two thousand and six hundred small cattle, and three hundred oxen.

9Conaniah also, and Shemaiah and Nethanel, his brethren, and Hashabiah and Jeiel and Jozabad, the chiefs of the Levites, gave unto the Levites for the passover-offerings five thousand small cattle, and five hundred oxen.

10So the service was prepared, and the priests stood in their place, and the Levites by their courses, according to the king's commandment.

11And they killed the passover, and the priests sprinkled the blood which they received of their hand, and the Levites flayed them.

12And they removed the burnt-offerings, that they might give them according to the divisions of the fathers' houses of the children of the people, to offer unto Yahweh, as it is written in the book of Moses. And so did they with the oxen.

13And they roasted the passover with fire according to the ordinance: and the holy offerings boiled they in pots, and in caldrons, and in pans, and carried them quickly to all the children of the people.

14And afterward they prepared for themselves, and for the priests, because the priests the sons of Aaron were busied in offering the burnt-offerings and the fat until night: therefore the Levites prepared for themselves, and for the priests the sons of Aaron.

15And the singers the sons of Asaph were in their place, according to the commandment of David, and Asaph, and Heman, and Jeduthun the king's seer; and the porters were at every gate: they needed not to depart from their service; for their brethren the Levites prepared for them.

16So all the service of Yahweh was prepared the same day, to keep the passover, and to offer burnt-offerings upon the altar of Yahweh, according to the commandment of king Josiah.

17And the children of Israel that were present kept the passover at that time, and the feast of unleavened bread seven days.

18And there was no passover like to that kept in Israel from the days of Samuel the prophet; neither did any of the kings of Israel keep such a passover as Josiah kept, and the priests, and the Levites, and all Judah and Israel that were present, and the inhabitants of Jerusalem.

19In the eighteenth year of the reign of Josiah was this passover kept.

20After all this, when Josiah had prepared the temple, Neco king of Egypt went up to fight against Carchemish by the Euphrates: and Josiah went out against him.

21But he sent ambassadors to him, saying, What have I to do with thee, thou king of Judah? I come not against thee this day, but against the house wherewith I have war; and God hath commanded me to make haste: forbear thee from meddling with God, who is with me, that he destroy thee not.

22Nevertheless Josiah would not turn his face from him, but disguised himself, that he might fight with him, and hearkened not unto the words of Neco from the mouth of God, and came to fight in the valley of Megiddo.

23And the archers shot at king Josiah; and the king said to his servants, Have me away; for I am sore wounded.

24So his servants took him out of the chariot, and put him in the second chariot that he had, and brought him to Jerusalem; and he died, and was buried in the sepulchres of his fathers. And all Judah and Jerusalem mourned for Josiah.

25And Jeremiah lamented for Josiah: and all the singing men and singing women spake of Josiah in their lamentations unto this day; and they made them an ordinance in Israel: and, behold, they are written in the lamentations.

26Now the rest of the acts of Josiah, and his good deeds, according to that which is written in the law of Yahweh,

27and his acts, first and last, behold, they are written in the book of the kings of Israel and Judah.

Chapter 36

1Then the people of the land took Jehoahaz the son of Josiah, and made him king in his father's stead in Jerusalem.

2Joahaz was twenty and three years old when he began to reign; and he reigned three months in Jerusalem.

3And the king of Egypt deposed him at Jerusalem, and fined the land a hundred talents of silver and a talent of gold.

4And the king of Egypt made Eliakim his brother king over Judah and Jerusalem, and changed his name to Jehoiakim. And Neco took Joahaz his brother, and carried him to Egypt.

5Jehoiakim was twenty and five years old when he began to reign; and he reigned eleven years in Jerusalem: and he did that which was evil in the sight of Yahweh his God.

6Against him came up Nebuchadnezzar king of Babylon, and bound him in fetters, to carry him to Babylon.

7Nebuchadnezzar also carried of the vessels of the house of Yahweh to Babylon, and put them in his temple at Babylon.

8Now the rest of the acts of Jehoiakim, and his abominations which he did, and that which was found in him, behold, they are written in the book of the kings of Israel and Judah: and Jehoiachin his son reigned in his stead.

9Jehoiachin was eight years old when he began to reign; and he reigned three months and ten days in Jerusalem: and he did that which was evil in the sight of Yahweh.

10And at the return of the year king Nebuchadnezzar sent, and brought him to Babylon, with the goodly vessels of the house of Yahweh, and made Zedekiah his brother king over Judah and Jerusalem.

11Zedekiah was twenty and one years old when he began to reign; and he reigned eleven years in Jerusalem:

12and he did that which was evil in the sight of Yahweh his God; he humbled not himself before Jeremiah the prophet speaking from the mouth of Yahweh.

13And he also rebelled against king Nebuchadnezzar, who had made him swear by God: but he stiffened his neck, and hardened his heart against turning unto Yahweh, the God of Israel.

14Moreover all the chiefs of the priests, and the people, trespassed very greatly after all the abominations of the nations; and they polluted the house of Yahweh which he had hallowed in Jerusalem.

15And Yahweh, the God of their fathers, sent to them by his messengers, rising up early and sending, because he had compassion on his people, and on his dwelling-place:

16but they mocked the messengers of God, and despised his words, and scoffed at his prophets, until the wrath of Yahweh arose against his people, till there was no remedy.

17Therefore he brought upon them the king of the Chaldeans, who slew their young men with the sword in the house of their sanctuary, and had no compassion upon young man or virgin, old man or hoary-headed: he gave them all into his hand.

18And all the vessels of the house of God, great and small, and the treasures of the house of Yahweh, and the treasures of the king, and of his princes, all these he brought to Babylon.

19And they burnt the house of God, and brake down the wall of Jerusalem, and burnt all the palaces thereof with fire, and destroyed all the goodly vessels thereof.

20And them that had escaped from the sword carried he away to Babylon; and they were servants to him and his sons until the reign of the kingdom of Persia:

21to fulfil the word of Yahweh by the mouth of Jeremiah, until the land had enjoyed its sabbaths: for as long as it lay desolate it kept sabbath, to fulfil threescore and ten years.

22Now in the first year of Cyrus king of Persia, that the word of Yahweh by the mouth of Jeremiah might be accomplished, Yahweh stirred up the spirit of Cyrus king of Persia, so that he made a proclamation throughout all his kingdom, and put it also in writing, saying,

23Thus saith Cyrus king of Persia, All the kingdoms of the earth hath Yahweh, the God of heaven, given me; and he hath charged me to build him a house in Jerusalem, which is in Judah. Whosoever there is among you of all his people, Yahweh his God be with him, and let him go up.

Ezra

Chapter 1

1 Now in the first year of Cyrus king of Persia, that the word of Yahweh by the mouth of Jeremiah might be accomplished, Yahweh stirred up the spirit of Cyrus king of Persia, so that he made a proclamation throughout all his kingdom, and put it also in writing, saying,

2 Thus saith Cyrus king of Persia, All the kingdoms of the earth hath Yahweh, the God of heaven, given me; and he hath charged me to build him a house in Jerusalem, which is in Judah.

3 Whosoever there is among you of all his people, his God be with him, and let him go up to Jerusalem, which is in Judah, and build the house of Yahweh, the God of Israel (he is God), which is in Jerusalem.

4 And whosoever is left, in any place where he sojourneth, let the men of his place help him with silver, and with gold, and with goods, and with beasts, besides the freewill-offering for the house of God which is in Jerusalem.

5 Then rose up the heads of fathers' houses of Judah and Benjamin, and the priests, and the Levites, even all whose spirit God had stirred to go up to build the house of Yahweh which is in Jerusalem.

6 And all they that were round about them strengthened their hands with vessels of silver, with gold, with goods, and with beasts, and with precious things, besides all that was willingly offered.

7 Also Cyrus the king brought forth the vessels of the house of Yahweh, which Nebuchadnezzar had brought forth out of Jerusalem, and had put in the house of his gods;

8 even those did Cyrus king of Persia bring forth by the hand of Mithredath the treasurer, and numbered them unto Sheshbazzar, the prince of Judah.

9 And this is the number of them: thirty platters of gold, a thousand platters of silver, nine and twenty knives,

10 thirty bowls of gold, silver bowls of a second sort four hundred and ten, and other vessels a thousand.

11 All the vessels of gold and of silver were five thousand and four hundred. All these did Sheshbazzar bring up, when they of the captivity were brought up from Babylon unto Jerusalem.

Chapter 2

1 Now these are the children of the province, that went up out of the captivity of those that had been carried away, whom Nebuchadnezzar the king of Babylon had carried away unto Babylon, and that returned unto Jerusalem and Judah, every one unto his city;

2 who came with Zerubbabel, Jeshua, Nehemiah, Seraiah, Reelaiah, Mordecai, Bilshan, Mispar, Bigvai, Rehum, Baanah. The number of the men of the people of Israel:

3 The children of Parosh, two thousand a hundred seventy and two.

4 The children of Shephatiah, three hundred seventy and two.

5 The children of Arah, seven hundred seventy and five.

6 The children of Pahath-moab, of the children of Jeshua and Joab, two thousand eight hundred and twelve.

7 The children of Elam, a thousand two hundred fifty and four.

8 The children of Zattu, nine hundred forty and five.

9 The children of Zaccai, seven hundred and threescore.

10 The children of Bani, six hundred forty and two.

11 The children of Bebai, six hundred twenty and three.

12 The children of Azgad, a thousand two hundred twenty and two.

13 The children of Adonikam, six hundred sixty and six.

14 The children of Bigvai, two thousand fifty and six.

15 The children of Adin, four hundred fifty and four.

16 The children of Ater, of Hezekiah, ninety and eight.

17 The children of Bezai, three hundred twenty and three.

18 The children of Jorah, a hundred and twelve.

19 The children of Hashum, two hundred twenty and three.

20 The children of Gibbar, ninety and five.

21 The children of Beth-lehem, a hundred twenty and three.

22 The men of Netophah, fifty and six.

23 The men of Anathoth, a hundred twenty and eight.

24 The children of Azmaveth, forty and two.

25 The children of Kiriath-arim, Chephirah, and Beeroth, seven hundred and forty and three.

26 The children of Ramah and Geba, six hundred twenty and one.

27 The men of Michmas, a hundred twenty and two.

28 The men of Beth-el and Ai, two hundred twenty and three.

29 The children of Nebo, fifty and two.

30 The children of Magbish, a hundred fifty and six.

31 The children of the other Elam, a thousand two hundred fifty and four.

32 The children of Harim, three hundred and twenty.

33 The children of Lod, Hadid, and Ono, seven hundred twenty and five.

34 The children of Jericho, three hundred forty and five.

35 The children of Senaah, three thousand and six hundred and thirty.

36 The priests: the children of Jedaiah, of the house of Jeshua, nine hundred seventy and three.

37 The children of Immer, a thousand fifty and two.

38 The children of Pashhur, a thousand two hundred forty and seven.

39 The children of Harim, a thousand and seventeen.

40 The Levites: the children of Jeshua and Kadmiel, of the children of Hodaviah, seventy and four.

41 The singers: the children of Asaph, a hundred twenty and eight.

42 The children of the porters: the children of Shallum, the children of Ater, the children of Talmon, the children of Akkub, the children of Hatita, the children of Shobai, in all a hundred thirty and nine.

43 The Nethinim: the children of Ziha, the children of Hasupha, the children of Tabbaoth,

44 the children of Keros, the children of Siaha, the children of Padon,

45 the children of Lebanah, the children of Hagabah, the children of Akkub,

46 the children of Hagab, the children of Shamlai, the children of Hanan,

47 the children of Giddel, the children of Gahar, the children of Reaiah,

48 the children of Rezin, the children of Nekoda, the children of Gazzam,

49 the children of Uzza, the children of Paseah, the children of Besai,

50 the children of Asnah, the children of Meunim, the children of Nephisim,

51 the children of Bakbuk, the children of Hakupha, the children of Harhur,

52 the children of Bazluth, the children of Mehida, the children of Harsha,

53 the children of Barkos, the children of Sisera, the children of Temah,

54 the children of Neziah, the children of Hatipha.

55 The children of Solomon's servants: the children of Sotai, the children of Hassophereth, the children of Peruda,

56 the children of Jaalah, the children of Darkon, the children of Giddel,

57 the children of Shephatiah, the children of Hattil, the children of Pochereth-hazzebaim, the children of Ami.

58 All the Nethinim, and the children of Solomon's servants, were three hundred ninety and two.

59 And these were they that went up from Tel-melah, Tel-harsha, Cherub, Addan, and Immer; but they could not show their fathers' houses, and their seed, whether they were of Israel:

60 the children of Delaiah, the children of Tobiah, the children of Nekoda, six hundred fifty and two.

61 And of the children of the priests: the children of Habaiah, the children of Hakkoz, the children of Barzillai, who took a wife of the daughters of Barzillai the Gileadite, and was called after their name.

62 These sought their register among those that were reckoned by genealogy, but they were not found: therefore were they deemed polluted and put from the priesthood.

63 And the governor said unto them, that they should not eat of the most holy things, till there stood up a priest with Urim and with Thummim.

64 The whole assembly together was forty and two thousand three hundred and threescore,

65 besides their men-servants and their maid-servants, of whom there were seven thousand three hundred thirty and seven: and they had two hundred singing men and singing women.

66 Their horses were seven hundred thirty and six; their mules, two hundred forty and five;

67 their camels, four hundred thirty and five; their asses, six thousand seven hundred and twenty.

68 And some of the heads of fathers' houses, when they came to the house of Yahweh which is in Jerusalem, offered willingly for the house of God to set it up in its place:

69 they gave after their ability into the treasury of the work threescore and one thousand darics of gold, and five thousand pounds of silver, and one hundred priests' garments.

70 So the priests, and the Levites, and some of the people, and the singers, and the porters, and the Nethinim, dwelt in their cities, and all Israel in their cities.

Chapter 3

1 And when the seventh month was come, and the children of Israel were in the cities, the people gathered themselves together as one man to Jerusalem.

2 Then stood up Jeshua the son of Jozadak, and his brethren the priests, and Zerubbabel the son of Shealtiel, and his brethren, and builded the altar of the God of Israel, to offer burnt-offerings thereon, as it is written in the law of Moses the man of God.

3 And they set the altar upon its base; for fear was upon them because of the peoples of the countries: and they offered burnt-offerings thereon unto Yahweh, even burnt-offerings morning and evening.

4 And they kept the feast of tabernacles, as it is written, and offered the daily burnt-offerings by number, according to the ordinance, as the duty of every day required;

5 and afterward the continual burnt-offering, and the offerings of the new moons, and of all the set feasts of Yahweh that were consecrated, and of every one that willingly offered a freewill-offering unto Yahweh.

6 From the first day of the seventh month began they to offer burnt-offerings unto Yahweh: but the foundation of the temple of Yahweh was not yet laid.

7 They gave money also unto the masons, and to the carpenters; and food, and drink, and oil, unto them of Sidon, and to them of Tyre, to bring cedar-trees from Lebanon to the sea, unto Joppa, according to the grant that they had of Cyrus king of Persia.

8 Now in the second year of their coming unto the house of God at Jerusalem, in the second month, began Zerubbabel the son of Shealtiel, and Jeshua the son of Jozadak, and the rest of their brethren the priests and the Levites, and all they that were come out of the captivity unto Jerusalem, and appointed the Levites, from twenty years old and upward, to have the oversight of the work of the house of Yahweh.

9 Then stood Jeshua with his sons and his brethren, Kadmiel and his sons, the sons of Judah, together, to have the oversight of the workmen in the house of God: the sons of Henadad, with their sons and their brethren the Levites.

10 And when the builders laid the foundation of the temple of Yahweh, they

set the priests in their apparel with trumpets, and the Levites the sons of Asaph with cymbals, to praise Yahweh, after the order of David king of Israel;

11And they sang one to another in praising and giving thanks unto Yahweh, saying, For he is good, for his lovingkindness endureth for ever toward Israel. And all the people shouted with a great shout, when they praised Yahweh, because the foundation of the house of Yahweh was laid.

12But many of the priests and Levites and heads of fathers' houses, the old men that had seen the first house, when the foundation of this house was laid before their eyes, wept with a loud voice; and many shouted aloud for joy:

13so that the people could not discern the noise of the shout of joy from the noise of the weeping of the people; for the people shouted with a loud shout, and the noise was heard afar off.

Chapter 4

4 1Now when the adversaries of Judah and Benjamin heard that the children of the captivity were building a temple unto Yahweh, the God of Israel;

2then they drew near to Zerubbabel, and to the heads of fathers' houses, and said unto them, Let us build with you; for we seek your God, as ye do; and we sacrifice unto him since the days of Esar-haddon king of Assyria, who brought us up hither.

3But Zerubbabel, and Jeshua, and the rest of the heads of fathers' houses of Israel, said unto them, Ye have nothing to do with us in building a house unto our God; but we ourselves together will build unto Yahweh, the God of Israel, as king Cyrus the king of Persia hath commanded us.

4Then the people of the land weakened the hands of the people of Judah, and troubled them in building,

5and hired counsellors against them, to frustrate their purpose, all the days of Cyrus king of Persia, even until the reign of Darius king of Persia.

6And in the reign of Ahasuerus, in the beginning of his reign, wrote they an accusation against the inhabitants of Judah and Jerusalem.

7And in the days of Artaxerxes wrote Bishlam, Mithredath, Tabeel, and the rest of his companions, unto Artaxerxes king of Persia; and the writing of the letter was written in the Syrian character, and set forth in the Syrian tongue.

8Rehum the chancellor and Shimshai the scribe wrote a letter against Jerusalem to Artaxerxes the king in this sort:

9then wrote Rehum the chancellor, and Shimshai the scribe, and the rest of their companions, the Dinaites, and the Apharsathchites, the Tarpelites, the Apharsites, the Archevites, the Babylonians, the Shushanchites, the Dehaites, the Elamites,

10and the rest of the nations whom the great and noble Osnappar brought over, and set in the city of Samaria, and in the rest of the country beyond the River, and so forth.

11This is the copy of the letter that they sent unto Artaxerxes the king: Thy servants the men beyond the River, and so forth.

12Be it known unto the king, that the Jews that came up from thee are come to us unto Jerusalem; they are building the rebellious and the bad city, and have finished the walls, and repaired the foundations.

13Be it known now unto the king, that, if this city be builded, and the walls finished, they will not pay tribute, custom, or toll, and in the end it will be hurtful unto the kings.

14Now because we eat the salt of the palace, and it is not meet for us to see the king's dishonor, therefore have we sent and certified the king;

15that search may be made in the book of the records of thy fathers: so shalt thou find in the book of the records, and know that this city is a rebellious city, and hurtful unto kings and provinces, and that they have moved sedition within the same of old time; for which cause was this city laid waste.

16We certify the king that, if this city be builded, and the walls finished, by this means thou shalt have no portion beyond the River.

17Then sent the king an answer unto Rehum the chancellor, and to Shimshai the scribe, and to the rest of their companions that dwell in Samaria, and in the rest of the country beyond the River: Peace, and so forth.

18The letter which ye sent unto us hath been plainly read before me.

19And I decreed, and search hath been made, and it is found that this city of old time hath made insurrection against kings, and that rebellion and sedition have been made therein.

20There have been mighty kings also over Jerusalem, who have ruled over all the country beyond the River; and tribute, custom, and toll, was paid unto them.

21Make ye now a decree to cause these men to cease, and that this city be not builded, until a decree shall be made by me.

22And take heed that ye be not slack herein: why should damage grow to the hurt of the kings?

23Then when the copy of king Artaxerxes' letter was read before Rehum, and Shimshai the scribe, and their companions, they went in haste to Jerusalem unto the Jews, and made them to cease by force and power.

24Then ceased the work of the house of God which is at Jerusalem; and it ceased until the second year of the reign of Darius king of Persia.

Chapter 5

5 1Now the prophets, Haggai the prophet, and Zechariah the son of Iddo, prophesied unto the Jews that were in Judah and Jerusalem; in the name of the God of Israel prophesied they unto them.

2Then rose up Zerubbabel the son of Shealtiel, and Jeshua the son of Jozadak, and began to build the house of God which is at Jerusalem; and with them were the prophets of God, helping them.

3At the same time came to them Tattenai, the governor beyond the River, and Shethar-bozenai, and their companions, and said thus unto them, Who gave you a decree to build this house, and to finish this wall?

4Then we told them after this manner, what the names of the men were that were making this building.

5But the eye of their God was upon the elders of the Jews, and they did not make them cease, till the matter should come to Darius, and then answer should be returned by letter concerning it.

6The copy of the letter that Tattenai, the governor beyond the River, and Shethar-bozenai, and his companions the Apharsachites, who were beyond the River, sent unto Darius the king;

7they sent a letter unto him, wherein was written thus: Unto Darius the king, all peace.

8Be it known unto the king, that we went into the province of Judah, to the house of the great God, which is builded with great stones, and timber is laid in the walls; and this work goeth on with diligence and prospereth in their hands.

9Then asked we those elders, and said unto them thus, Who gave you a decree to build this house, and to finish this wall?

10We asked them their names also, to certify thee, that we might write the names of the men that were at the head of them.

11And thus they returned us answer, saying, We are the servants of the God of heaven and earth, and are building the house that was builded these many years ago, which a great king of Israel builded and finished.

12But after that our fathers had provoked the God of heaven unto wrath, he gave them into the hand of Nebuchadnezzar king of Babylon, the Chaldean, who destroyed this house, and carried the people away into Babylon.

13But in the first year of Cyrus king of Babylon, Cyrus the king made a decree to build this house of God.

14And the gold and silver vessels also of the house of God, which Nebuchadnezzar took out of the temple that was in Jerusalem, and brought into the temple of Babylon, those did Cyrus the king take out of the temple of Babylon, and they were delivered unto one whose name was Sheshbazzar, whom he had made governor;

15and he said unto him, Take these vessels, go, put them in the temple that is in Jerusalem, and let the house of God be builded in its place.

16Then came the same Sheshbazzar, and laid the foundations of the house of God which is in Jerusalem: and since that time even until now hath it been in building, and yet it is not completed.

17Now therefore, if it seem good to the king, let there be search made in the king's treasure-house, which is there at Babylon, whether it be so, that a decree was made of Cyrus the king to build this house of God at Jerusalem; and let the king send his pleasure to us concerning this matter.

Chapter 6

6 1Then Darius the king made a decree, and search was made in the house of the archives, where the treasures were laid up in Babylon.

2And there was found at Achmetha, in the palace that is in the province of Media, a roll, and therein was thus written for a record:

3In the first year of Cyrus the king, Cyrus the king made a decree: Concerning the house of God at Jerusalem, let the house be builded, the place where they offer sacrifices, and let the foundations thereof be strongly laid; the height thereof threescore cubits, and the breadth thereof threescore cubits;

4with three courses of great stones, and a course of new timber: and let the expenses be given out of the king's house.

5And also let the gold and silver vessels of the house of God, which Nebuchadnezzar took forth out of the temple which is at Jerusalem, and brought unto Babylon, be restored, and brought again unto the temple which is at Jerusalem, every one to its place; and thou shalt put them in the house of God.

6Now therefore, Tattenai, governor beyond the River, Shethar-bozenai, and your companions the Apharsachites, who are beyond the River, be ye far from thence:

7let the work of this house of God alone; let the governor of the Jews and the elders of the Jews build this house of God in its place.

8Moreover I make a decree what ye shall do to these elders of the Jews for the building of this house of God: that of the king's goods, even of the tribute beyond the River, expenses be given with all diligence unto these men, that they be not hindered.

9And that which they have need of, both young bullocks, and rams, and lambs, for burnt-offerings to the God of heaven; also wheat, salt, wine, and oil, according to the word of the priests that are at Jerusalem, let it be given them day by day without fail;

10that they may offer sacrifices of sweet savor unto the God of heaven, and pray for the life of the king, and of his sons.

11Also I have made a decree, that whosoever shall alter this word, let a beam be pulled out from his house, and let him be lifted up and fastened thereon; and let his house be made a dunghill for this:

12and the God that hath caused his name to dwell there overthrow all kings and peoples that shall put forth their hand to alter the same, to destroy this house of God which is at Jerusalem. I Darius have made a decree; let it be done with all diligence.

13Then Tattenai, the governor beyond the River, Shethar-bozenai, and their companions, because that Darius the king had sent, did accordingly with all diligence.

14And the elders of the Jews builded and prospered, through the prophesying of Haggai the prophet and Zechariah the son of Iddo. And they builded and finished it, according to the commandment of the God of Israel, and according to the decree of Cyrus, and Darius, and Artaxerxes king of Persia.

15And this house was finished on the third day of the month Adar, which was in the sixth year of the reign of Darius the king.

16And the children of Israel, the priests, and the Levites, and the rest of the children of the captivity, kept the dedication of this house of God with joy.

17And they offered at the dedication of this house of God a hundred

Ezra

bullocks, two hundred rams, four hundred lambs; and for a sin-offering for all Israel, twelve he-goats, according to the number of the tribes of Israel.

18And they set the priests in their divisions, and the Levites in their courses, for the service of God, which is at Jerusalem; as it is written in the book of Moses.

19And the children of the captivity kept the passover upon the fourteenth day of the first month.

20For the priests and the Levites had purified themselves together; all of them were pure: and they killed the passover for all the children of the captivity, and for their brethren the priests, and for themselves.

21And the children of Israel that were come again out of the captivity, and all such as had separated themselves unto them from the filthiness of the nations of the land, to seek Yahweh, the God of Israel, did eat,

22and kept the feast of unleavened bread seven days with joy: for Yahweh had made them joyful, and had turned the heart of the king of Assyria unto them, to strengthen their hands in the work of the house of God, the God of Israel.

Chapter 7

1Now after these things, in the reign of Artaxerxes king of Persia, Ezra the son of Seraiah, the son of Azariah, the son of Hilkiah,

2the son of Shallum, the son of Zadok, the son of Ahitub,

3the son of Amariah, the son of Azariah, the son of Meraioth,

4the son of Zerahiah, the son of Uzzi, the son of Bukki,

5the son of Abishua, the son of Phinehas, the son of Eleazar, the son of Aaron the chief priest;

6this Ezra went up from Babylon: and he was a ready scribe in the law of Moses, which Yahweh, the God of Israel, had given; and the king granted him all his request, according to the hand of Yahweh his God upon him.

7And there went up some of the children of Israel, and of the priests, and the Levites, and the singers, and the porters, and the Nethinim, unto Jerusalem, in the seventh year of Artaxerxes the king.

8And he came to Jerusalem in the fifth month, which was in the seventh year of the king.

9For upon the first day of the first month began he to go up from Babylon; and on the first day of the fifth month came he to Jerusalem, according to the good hand of his God upon him.

10For Ezra had set his heart to seek the law of Yahweh, and to do it, and to teach in Israel statutes and ordinances.

11Now this is the copy of the letter that the king Artaxerxes gave unto Ezra the priest, the scribe, even the scribe of the words of the commandments of Yahweh, and of his statutes to Israel:

12Artaxerxes, king of kings, unto Ezra the priest, the scribe of the law of the God of heaven, perfect and so forth.

13I make a decree, that all they of the people of Israel, and their priests and the Levites, in my realm, that are minded of their own free will to go to Jerusalem, go with thee.

14Forasmuch as thou art sent of the king and his seven counsellors, to inquire concerning Judah and Jerusalem, according to the law of thy God which is in thy hand,

15and to carry the silver and gold, which the king and his counsellors have freely offered unto the God of Israel, whose habitation is in Jerusalem,

16and all the silver and gold that thou shalt find in all the province of Babylon, with the freewill-offering of the people, and of the priests, offering willingly for the house of their God which is in Jerusalem;

17therefore thou shalt with all diligence buy with this money bullocks, rams, lambs, with their meal-offerings and their drink-offerings, and shalt offer them upon the altar of the house of your God which is in Jerusalem.

18And whatsoever shall seem good to thee and to thy brethren to do with the rest of the silver and the gold, that do ye after the will of your God.

19And the vessels that are given thee for the service of the house of thy God, deliver thou before the God of Jerusalem.

20And whatsoever more shall be needful for the house of thy God, which thou shalt have occasion to bestow, bestow it out of the king's treasure-house.

21And I, even I Artaxerxes the king, do make a decree to all the treasurers that are beyond the River, that whatsoever Ezra the priest, the scribe of the law of the God of heaven, shall require of you, it be done with all diligence,

22unto a hundred talents of silver, and to a hundred measures of wheat, and to a hundred baths of wine, and to a hundred baths of oil, and salt without prescribing how much.

23Whatsoever is commanded by the God of heaven, let it be done exactly for the house of the God of heaven; for why should there be wrath against the realm of the king and his sons?

24Also we certify you, that touching any of the priests and Levites, the singers, porters, Nethinim, or servants of this house of God, it shall not be lawful to impose tribute, custom, or toll, upon them.

25And thou, Ezra, after the wisdom of thy God that is in thy hand, appoint magistrates and judges, who may judge all the people that are beyond the River, all such as know the laws of thy God; and teach ye him that knoweth them not.

26And whosoever will not do the law of thy God, and the law of the king, let judgment be executed upon him with all diligence, whether it be unto death, or to banishment, or to confiscation of goods, or to imprisonment.

27Blessed be Yahweh, the God of our fathers, who hath put such a thing as this in the king's heart, to beautify the house of Yahweh which is in Jerusalem;

28and hath extended lovingkindness unto me before the king, and his counsellors, and before all the king's mighty princes. And I was strengthened according to the hand of Yahweh my God upon me, and I gathered together out of Israel chief men to go up with me.

Chapter 8

1Now these are the heads of their fathers' houses, and this is the genealogy of them that went up with me from Babylon, in the reign of Artaxerxes the king:

2Of the sons of Phinehas, Gershom. Of the sons of Ithamar, Daniel. Of the sons of David, Hattush.

3Of the sons of Shecaniah, of the sons of Parosh, Zechariah; and with him were reckoned by genealogy of the males a hundred and fifty.

4Of the sons of Pahath-moab, Eliehoenai the son of Zerahiah; and with him two hundred males.

5Of the sons of Shecaniah, the son of Jahaziel; and with him three hundred males.

6And of the sons of Adin, Ebed the son of Jonathan; and with him fifty males.

7And of the sons of Elam, Jeshaiah the son of Athaliah; and with him seventy males.

8And of the sons of Shephatiah, Zebadiah the son of Michael; and with him fourscore males.

9Of the sons of Joab, Obadiah the son of Jehiel; and with him two hundred and eighteen males.

10And of the sons of Shelomith, the son of Josiphiah; and with him a hundred and threescore males.

11And of the sons of Bebai, Zechariah the son of Bebai; and with him twenty and eight males.

12And of the sons of Azgad, Johanan the son of Hakkatan; and with him a hundred and ten males.

13And of the sons of Adonikam, that were the last; and these are their names: Eliphelet, Jeuel, and Shemaiah; and with them threescore males.

14And of the sons of Bigvai, Uthai and Zabbud; and with them seventy males.

15And I gathered them together to the river that runneth to Ahava; and there we encamped three days: and I viewed the people, and the priests, and found there none of the sons of Levi.

16Then sent I for Eliezer, for Ariel, for Shemaiah, and for Elnathan, and for Jarib, and for Elnathan, and for Nathan, and for Zechariah, and for Meshullam, chief men; also for Joiarib, and for Elnathan, who were teachers.

17And I sent them forth unto Iddo the chief at the place Casiphia; and I told them what they should say unto Iddo, and his brethren the Nethinim, at the place Casiphia, that they should bring unto us ministers for the house of our God.

18And according to the good hand of our God upon us they brought us a man of discretion, of the sons of Mahli, the son of Levi, the son of Israel; and Sherebiah, with his sons and his brethren, eighteen;

19and Hashabiah, and with him Jeshaiah of the sons of Merari, his brethren and their sons, twenty;

20and of the Nethinim, whom David and the princes had given for the service of the Levites, two hundred and twenty Nethinim: all of them were mentioned by name.

21Then I proclaimed a fast there, at the river Ahava, that we might humble ourselves before our God, to seek of him a straight way for us, and for our little ones, and for all our substance.

22For I was ashamed to ask of the king a band of soldiers and horsemen to help us against the enemy in the way, because we had spoken unto the king, saying, The hand of our God is upon all them that seek him, for good; but his power and his wrath is against all them that forsake him.

23So we fasted and besought our God for this: and he was entreated of us.

24Then I set apart twelve of the chiefs of the priests, even Sherebiah, Hashabiah, and ten of their brethren with them,

25and weighed unto them the silver, and the gold, and the vessels, even the offering for the house of our God, which the king, and his counsellors, and his princes, and all Israel there present, had offered:

26I weighed into their hand six hundred and fifty talents of silver, and silver vessels a hundred talents; of gold a hundred talents;

27and twenty bowls of gold, of a thousand darics; and two vessels of fine bright brass, precious as gold.

28And I said unto them, Ye are holy unto Yahweh, and the vessels are holy; and the silver and the gold are a freewill-offering unto Yahweh, the God of your fathers.

29Watch ye, and keep them, until ye weigh them before the chiefs of the priests and the Levites, and the princes of the fathers' houses of Israel, at Jerusalem, in the chambers of the house of Yahweh.

30So the priests and the Levites received the weight of the silver and the gold, and the vessels, to bring them to Jerusalem unto the house of our God.

31Then we departed from the river Ahava on the twelfth day of the first month, to go unto Jerusalem: and the hand of our God was upon us, and he delivered us from the hand of the enemy and the lier-in-wait by the way.

32And we came to Jerusalem, and abode there three days.

33And on the fourth day the silver and the gold and the vessels were weighed in the house of our God into the hand of Meremoth the son of Uriah the priest; and with him was Eleazar the son of Phinehas; and with them was Jozabad the son of Jeshua, and Noadiah the son of Binnui, the Levite;

34the whole by number and by weight: and all the weight was written at that time.

35The children of the captivity, that were come out of exile, offered burnt-offerings unto the God of Israel, twelve bullocks for all Israel, ninety and six rams, seventy and seven lambs, twelve he-goats for a sin-offering: all this was a burnt-offering unto Yahweh.

36And they delivered the king's commissions unto the king's satraps, and to the governors beyond the River: and they furthered the people and the house of God.

Chapter 9

1Now when these things were done, the princes drew near unto me, saying, The people of Israel, and the priests and the Levites, have not separated themselves from the peoples of the lands, doing according to their abominations, even of the Canaanites, the Hittites, the Perizzites, the Jebusites, the Ammonites, the Moabites, the Egyptians, and the Amorites.

2For they have taken of their daughters for themselves and for their sons, so that the holy seed have mingled themselves with the peoples of the lands: yea, the hand of the princes and rulers hath been chief in this trespass.

3And when I heard this thing, I rent my garment and my robe, and plucked off the hair of my head and of my beard, and sat down confounded.

4Then were assembled unto me every one that trembled at the words of the God of Israel, because of the trespass of them of the captivity; and I sat confounded until the evening oblation.

5And at the evening oblation I arose up from my humiliation, even with my garment and my robe rent; and I fell upon my knees, and spread out my hands unto Yahweh my God;

6and I said, O my God, I am ashamed and blush to lift up my face to thee, my God; for our iniquities are increased over our head, and our guiltiness is grown up unto the heavens.

7Since the days of our fathers we have been exceeding guilty unto this day; and for our iniquities have we, our kings, and our priests, been delivered into the hand of the kings of the lands, to the sword, to captivity, and to plunder, and to confusion of face, as it is this day.

8And now for a little moment grace hath been showed from Yahweh our God, to leave us a remnant to escape, and to give us a nail in his holy place, that our God may lighten our eyes, and give us a little reviving in our bondage.

9For we are bondmen; yet our God hath not forsaken us in our bondage, but hath extended lovingkindness unto us in the sight of the kings of Persia, to give us a reviving, to set up the house of our God, and to repair the ruins thereof, and to give us a wall in Judah and in Jerusalem.

10And now, O our God, what shall we say after this? for we have forsaken thy commandments,

11which thou hast commanded by thy servants the prophets, saying, The land, unto which ye go to possess it, is an unclean land through the uncleanness of the peoples of the lands, through their abominations, which have filled it from one end to another with their filthiness:

12now therefore give not your daughters unto their sons, neither take their daughters unto your sons, nor seek their peace or their prosperity for ever; that ye may be strong, and eat the good of the land, and leave it for an inheritance to your children for ever.

13And after all that is come upon us for our evil deeds, and for our great guilt, seeing that thou our God hast punished us less than our iniquities deserve, and hast given us such a remnant,

14shall we again break thy commandments, and join in affinity with the peoples that do these abominations? wouldest not thou be angry with us till thou hadst consumed us, so that there should be no remnant, nor any to escape?

15O Yahweh, the God of Israel, thou art righteous; for we are left a remnant that is escaped, as it is this day: behold, we are before thee in our guiltiness; for none can stand before thee because of this.

Chapter 10

1Now while Ezra prayed and made confession, weeping and casting himself down before the house of God, there was gathered together unto him out of Israel a very great assembly of men and women and children; for the people wept very sore.

2And Shecaniah the son of Jehiel, one of the sons of Elam, answered and said unto Ezra, We have trespassed against our God, and have married foreign women of the peoples of the land: yet now there is hope for Israel concerning this thing.

3Now therefore let us make a covenant with our God to put away all the wives, and such as are born of them, according to the counsel of my lord, and of those that tremble at the commandment of our God; and let it be done according to the law.

4Arise; for the matter belongeth unto thee, and we are with thee: be of good courage, and do it.

5Then arose Ezra, and made the chiefs of the priests, the Levites, and all Israel, to swear that they would do according to this word. So they sware.

6Then Ezra rose up from before the house of God, and went into the chamber of Jehohanan the son of Eliashib: and when he came thither, he did eat no bread, nor drink water; for he mourned because of the trespass of them of the captivity.

7And they made proclamation throughout Judah and Jerusalem unto all the children of the captivity, that they should gather themselves together unto Jerusalem;

8and that whosoever came not within three days, according to the counsel of the princes and the elders, all his substance should be forfeited, and himself separated from the assembly of the captivity.

9Then all the men of Judah and Benjamin gathered themselves together unto Jerusalem within the three days; it was the ninth month, on the twentieth day of the month: and all the people sat in the broad place before the house of God, trembling because of this matter, and for the great rain.

10And Ezra the priest stood up, and said unto them, Ye have trespassed, and have married foreign women, to increase the guilt of Israel.

11Now therefore make confession unto Yahweh, the God of your fathers, and do his pleasure; and separate yourselves from the peoples of the land, and from the foreign women.

12Then all the assembly answered and said with a loud voice, As thou hast said concerning us, so must we do.

13But the people are many, and it is a time of much rain, and we are not able to stand without: neither is this a work of one day or two; for we have greatly transgressed in this matter.

14Let now our princes be appointed for all the assembly, and let all them that are in our cities that have married foreign women come at appointed times, and with them the elders of every city, and the judges thereof, until the fierce wrath of our God be turned from us, until this matter be despatched.

15Only Jonathan the son of Asahel and Jahzeiah the son of Tikvah stood up against this matter: and Meshullam and Shabbethai the Levite helped them.

16And the children of the captivity did so. And Ezra the priest, with certain heads of fathers' houses, after their fathers' houses, and all of them by their names, were set apart; and they sat down in the first day of the tenth month to examine the matter.

17And they made an end with all the men that had married foreign women by the first day of the first month.

18And among the sons of the priests there were found that had married foreign women: namely, of the sons of Jeshua, the son of Jozadak, and his brethren, Maaseiah, and Eliezer, and Jarib, and Gedaliah.

19And they gave their hand that they would put away their wives; and being guilty, they offered a ram of the flock for their guilt.

20And of the sons of Immer: Hanani and Zebadiah.

21And of the sons of Harim: Maaseiah, and Elijah, and Shemaiah, and Jehiel, and Uzziah.

22And of the sons of Pashhur: Elioenai, Maaseiah, Ishmael, Nethanel, Jozabad, and Elasah.

23And of the Levites: Jozabad, and Shimei, and Kelaiah (the same is Kelita), Pethahiah, Judah, and Eliezer.

24And of the singers: Eliashib. And of the porters: Shallum, and Telem, and Uri.

25And of Israel: Of the sons of Parosh: Ramiah, and Izziah, and Malchijah, and Mijamin, and Eleazar, and Malchijah, and Benaiah.

26And of the sons of Elam: Mattaniah, Zechariah, and Jehiel, and Abdi, and Jeremoth, and Elijah.

27And of the sons of Zattu: Elioenai, Eliashib, Mattaniah, and Jeremoth, and Zabad, and Aziza.

28And of the sons of Bebai: Jehohanan, Hananiah, Zabbai, Athlai.

29And of the sons of Bani: Meshullam, Malluch, and Adaiah, Jashub, and Sheal, Jeremoth.

30And of the sons of Pahath-moab: Adna, and Chelal, Benaiah, Maaseiah, Mattaniah, Bezalel, and Binnui, and Manasseh.

31And of the sons of Harim: Eliezer, Isshijah, Malchijah, Shemaiah, Shimeon,

32Benjamin, Malluch, Shemariah.

33Of the sons of Hashum: Mattenai, Mattattah, Zabad, Eliphelet, Jeremai, Manasseh, Shimei.

34Of the sons of Bani: Maadai, Amram, and Uel,

35Benaiah, Bedeiah, Cheluhi,

36Vaniah, Meremoth, Eliashib,

37Mattaniah, Mattenai, and Jaasu,

38and Bani, and Binnui, Shimei,

39and Shelemiah, and Nathan, and Adaiah,

40Machnadebai, Shashai, Sharai,

41Azarel, and Shelemiah, Shemariah,

42Shallum, Amariah, Joseph.

43Of the sons of Nebo: Jeiel, Mattithiah, Zabad, Zebina, Iddo, and Joel, Benaiah.

44All these had taken foreign wives; and some of them had wives by whom they had children.

Nehemiah
The Book of Nehemiah

Chapter 1

1The words of Nehemiah the son of Hacaliah. Now it came to pass in the month Chislev, in the twentieth year, as I was in Shushan the palace,

2that Hanani, one of my brethren, came, he and certain men out of Judah; and I asked them concerning the Jews that had escaped, that were left of the captivity, and concerning Jerusalem.

3And they said unto me, The remnant that are left of the captivity there in the province are in great affliction and reproach: the wall of Jerusalem also is broken down, and the gates thereof are burned with fire.

4And it came to pass, when I heard these words, that I sat down and wept, and mourned certain days; and I fasted and prayed before the God of heaven,

5and said, I beseech thee, O Yahweh, the God of heaven, the great and terrible God, that keepeth covenant and lovingkindness with them that love him and keep his commandments.

6Let thine ear now be attentive, and thine eyes open, that thou mayest hearken unto the prayer of thy servant, which I pray before thee at this time, day and night, for the children of Israel thy servants while I confess the sins of the children of Israel, which we have sinned against thee. Yea, I and my father's house have sinned:

7we have dealt very corruptly against thee, and have not kept the commandments, nor the statutes, nor the ordinances, which thou commandedst thy servant Moses.

8Remember, I beseech thee, the word that thou commandedst thy servant Moses, saying, If ye trespass, I will scatter you abroad among the peoples:

9but if ye return unto me, and keep my commandments and do them, though your outcasts were in the uttermost part of the heavens, yet will I gather them from thence, and will bring them unto the place that I have chosen, to cause my name to dwell there.

10Now these are thy servants and thy people, whom thou hast redeemed by thy great power, and by thy strong hand.

11O Lord, I beseech thee, let now thine ear be attentive to the prayer of thy servant, and to the prayer of thy servants, who delight to fear thy name; and prosper, I pray thee, thy servant this day, and grant him mercy in the sight of this man. Now I was cupbearer to the king.

Chapter 2

1And it came to pass in the month Nisan, in the twentieth year of Artaxerxes the king, when wine was before him, that I took up the wine, and gave it unto the king. Now I had not been beforetime sad in his presence.

2And the king said unto me, Why is thy countenance sad, seeing thou art not sick? this is nothing else but sorrow of heart. Then I was very sore afraid.

3And I said unto the king, Let the king live for ever: why should not my countenance be sad, when the city, the place of my fathers' sepulchres, lieth waste, and the gates thereof are consumed with fire?

4Then the king said unto me, For what dost thou make request? So I prayed to the God of heaven.

5And I said unto the king, If it please the king, and if thy servant have found favor in thy sight, that thou wouldest send me unto Judah, unto the city of my fathers' sepulchres, that I may build it.

6And the king said unto me (the queen also sitting by him,) For how long shall thy journey be? and when wilt thou return? So it pleased the king to send me; and I set him a time.

7Moreover I said unto the king, If it please the king, let letters be given me to the governors beyond the River, that they may let me pass through till I come unto Judah;

8and a letter unto Asaph the keeper of the king's forest, that he may give me timber to make beams for the gates of the castle which appertaineth to the house, and for the wall of the city, and for the house that I shall enter into. And the king granted me, according to the good hand of my God upon me.

9Then I came to the governors beyond the River, and gave them the king's letters. Now the king had sent with me captains of the army and horsemen.

10And when Sanballat the Horonite, and Tobiah the servant, the Ammonite, heard of it, it grieved them exceedingly, for that there was come a man to seek the welfare of the children of Israel.

11So I came to Jerusalem, and was there three days.

12And I arose in the night, I and some few men with me; neither told I any man what my God put into my heart to do for Jerusalem; neither was there any beast with me, save the beast that I rode upon.

13And I went out by night by the valley gate, even toward the jackal's well, and to the dung gate, and viewed the walls of Jerusalem, which were broken down, and the gates thereof were consumed with fire.

14Then I went on to the fountain gate and to the king's pool: but there was no place for the beast that was under me to pass.

15Then went I up in the night by the brook, and viewed the wall; and I turned back, and entered by the valley gate, and so returned.

16And the rulers knew not whither I went, or what I did; neither had I as yet told it to the Jews, nor to the priests, nor to the nobles, nor to the rulers, nor to the rest that did the work.

17Then said I unto them, Ye see the evil case that we are in, how Jerusalem lieth waste, and the gates thereof are burned with fire: come, and let us build up the wall of Jerusalem, that we be no more a reproach.

18And I told them of the hand of my God which was good upon me, as also of the king's words that he had spoken unto me. And they said, Let us rise up and build. So they strengthened their hands for the good work.

19But when Sanballat the Horonite, and Tobiah the servant, the Ammonite, and Geshem the Arabian, heard it, they laughed us to scorn, and despised us, and said, What is this thing that ye do? will ye rebel against the king?

20Then answered I them, and said unto them, The God of heaven, he will prosper us; therefore we his servants will arise and build: but ye have no portion, nor right, nor memorial, in Jerusalem.

Chapter 3

1Then Eliashib the high priest rose up with his brethren the priests, and they builded the sheep gate; they sanctified it, and set up the doors of it; even unto the tower of Hammeah they sanctified it, unto the tower of Hananel.

2And next unto him builded the men of Jericho. And next to them builded Zaccur the son of Imri.

3And the fish gate did the sons of Hassenaah build; they laid the beams thereof, and set up the doors thereof, the bolts thereof, and the bars thereof.

4And next unto them repaired Meremoth the son of Uriah, the son of Hakkoz. And next unto them repaired Meshullam the son of Berechiah, the son of Meshezabel. And next unto them repaired Zadok the son of Baana.

5And next unto them the Tekoites repaired; but their nobles put not their necks to the work of their lord.

6And the old gate repaired Joiada the son of Paseah and Meshullam the son of Besodeiah; they laid the beams thereof, and set up the doors thereof, and the bolts thereof, and the bars thereof.

7And next unto them repaired Melatiah the Gibeonite, and Jadon the Meronothite, the men of Gibeon, and of Mizpah, that appertained to the throne of the governor beyond the River.

8Next unto him repaired Uzziel the son of Harhaiah, goldsmiths. And next unto him repaired Hananiah one of the perfumers, and they fortified Jerusalem even unto the broad wall.

9And next unto them repaired Rephaiah the son of Hur, the ruler of half the district of Jerusalem.

10And next unto them repaired Jedaiah the son of Harumaph, over against his house. And next unto him repaired Hattush the son of Hashabneiah.

11Malchijah the son of Harim, and Hasshub the son of Pahath-moab, repaired another portion, and the tower of the furnaces.

12And next unto him repaired Shallum the son of Hallohesh, the ruler of half the district of Jerusalem, he and his daughters.

13The valley gate repaired Hanun, and the inhabitants of Zanoah; they built it, and set up the doors thereof, the bolts thereof, and the bars thereof, and a thousand cubits of the wall unto the dung gate.

14And the dung gate repaired Malchijah the son of Rechab, the ruler of the district of Beth-haccherem; he built it, and set up the doors thereof, the bolts thereof, and the bars thereof.

15And the fountain gate repaired Shallun the son of Colhozeh, the ruler of the district of Mizpah; he built it, and covered it, and set up the doors thereof, the bolts thereof, and the bars thereof, and the wall of the pool of Shelah by the king's garden, even unto the stairs that go down from the city of David.

16After him repaired Nehemiah the son of Azbuk, the ruler of half the district of Beth-zur, unto the place over against the sepulchres of David, and unto the pool that was made, and unto the house of the mighty men.

17After him repaired the Levites, Rehum the son of Bani. Next unto him repaired Hashabiah, the ruler of half the district of Keilah, for his district.

18After him repaired their brethren, Bavvai the son of Henadad, the ruler of half the district of Keilah.

19And next to him repaired Ezer the son of Jeshua, the ruler of Mizpah, another portion, over against the ascent to the armory at the turning of the wall.

20After him Baruch the son of Zabbai earnestly repaired another portion, from the turning of the wall unto the door of the house of Eliashib the high priest.

21After him repaired Meremoth the son of Uriah the son of Hakkoz another portion, from the door of the house of Eliashib even to the end of the house of Eliashib.

22And after him repaired the priests, the men of the Plain.

23After them repaired Benjamin and Hasshub over against their house. After them repaired Azariah the son of Maaseiah the son of Ananiah beside his own house.

24After him repaired Binnui the son of Henadad another portion, from the house of Azariah unto the turning of the wall, and unto the corner.

25Palal the son of Uzai repaired over against the turning of the wall, and the tower that standeth out from the upper house of the king, which is by the court of the guard. After him Pedaiah the son of Parosh repaired.

26(Now the Nethinim dwelt in Ophel, unto the place over against the water gate toward the east, and the tower that standeth out.)

27After him the Tekoites repaired another portion, over against the great tower that standeth out, and unto the wall of Ophel.

28Above the horse gate repaired the priests, every one over against his own house.

29After them repaired Zadok the son of Immer over against his own house. And after him repaired Shemaiah the son of Shecaniah, the keeper of the east gate.

30After him repaired Hananiah the son of Shelemiah, and Hanun the sixth son of Zalaph, another portion. After him repaired Meshullam the son of Berechiah over against his chamber.

31After him repaired Malchijah one of the goldsmiths unto the house of the Nethinim, and of the merchants, over against the gate of Hammiphkad, and to the ascent of the corner.

32And between the ascent of the corner and the sheep gate repaired the goldsmiths and the merchants.

Chapter 4

¹But it came to pass that, when Sanballat heard that we were building the wall, he was wroth, and took great indignation, and mocked the Jews.

²And he spake before his brethren and the army of Samaria, and said, What are these feeble Jews doing? will they fortify themselves? will they sacrifice? will they make an end in a day? will they revive the stones out of the heaps of rubbish, seeing they are burned?

³Now Tobiah the Ammonite was by him, and he said, Even that which they are building, if a fox go up, he shall break down their stone wall.

⁴Hear, O our God; for we are despised: and turn back their reproach upon their own head, and give them up for a spoil in a land of captivity;

⁵and cover not their iniquity, and let not their sin be blotted out from before thee; for they have provoked thee to anger before the builders.

⁶So we built the wall; and all the wall was joined together unto half the height thereof: for the people had a mind to work.

⁷But it came to pass that, when Sanballat, and Tobiah, and the Arabians, and the Ammonites, and the Ashdodites, heard that the repairing of the walls of Jerusalem went forward, and that the breaches began to be stopped, then they were very wroth;

⁸and they conspired all of them together to come and fight against Jerusalem, and to cause confusion therein.

⁹But we made our prayer unto our God, and set a watch against them day and night, because of them.

¹⁰And Judah said, The strength of the bearers of burdens is decayed, and there is much rubbish; so that we are not able to build the wall.

¹¹And our adversaries said, They shall not know, neither see, till we come into the midst of them, and slay them, and cause the work to cease.

¹²And it came to pass that, when the Jews that dwelt by them came, they said unto us ten times from all places, Ye must return unto us.

¹³Therefore set I in the lowest parts of the space behind the wall, in the open places, I set there the people after their families with their swords, their spears, and their bows.

¹⁴And I looked, and rose up, and said unto the nobles, and to the rulers, and to the rest of the people, Be not ye afraid of them: remember the Lord, who is great and terrible, and fight for your brethren, your sons, and your daughters, your wives, and your houses.

¹⁵And it came to pass, when our enemies heard that it was known unto us, and God had brought their counsel to nought, that we returned all of us to the wall, every one unto his work.

¹⁶And it came to pass from that time forth, that half of my servants wrought in the work, and half of them held the spears, the shields, and the bows, and the coats of mail; and the rulers were behind all the house of Judah.

¹⁷They all builded the wall and they that bare burdens laded themselves; every one with one of his hands wrought in the work, and with the other held his weapon;

¹⁸and the builders, every one had his sword girded by his side, and so builded. And he that sounded the trumpet was by me.

¹⁹And I said unto the nobles, and to the rulers and to the rest of the people, The work is great and large, and we are separated upon the wall, one far from another:

²⁰in what place soever ye hear the sound of the trumpet, resort ye thither unto us; our God will fight for us.

²¹So we wrought in the work: and half of them held the spears from the rising of the morning till the stars appeared.

²²Likewise at the same time said I unto the people, Let every one with his servant lodge within Jerusalem, that in the night they may be a guard to us, and may labor in the day.

²³So neither I, nor my brethren, nor my servants, nor the men of the guard that followed me, none of us put off our clothes, every one went with his weapon to the water.

Chapter 5

¹Then there arose a great cry of the people and of their wives against their brethren the Jews.

²For there were that said, We, our sons and our daughters, are many: let us get grain, that we may eat and live.

³Some also there were that said, We are mortgaging our fields, and our vineyards, and our houses: let us get grain, because of the dearth.

⁴There were also that said, We have borrowed money for the king's tribute upon our fields and our vineyards.

⁵Yet now our flesh is as the flesh of our brethren, our children as their children: and, lo, we bring into bondage our sons and our daughters to be servants, and some of our daughters are brought into bondage already: neither is it in our power to help it; for other men have our fields and our vineyards.

⁶And I was very angry when I heard their cry and these words.

⁷Then I consulted with myself, and contended with the nobles and the rulers, and said unto them, Ye exact usury, every one of his brother. And I held a great assembly against them.

⁸And I said unto them, We after our ability have redeemed our brethren the Jews, that were sold unto the nations; and would ye even sell your brethren, and should they be sold unto us? Then held they their peace, and found never a word.

⁹Also I said, The thing that ye do is not good: ought ye not to walk in the fear of our God, because of the reproach of the nations our enemies?

¹⁰And I likewise, my brethren and my servants, do lend them money and grain. I pray you, let us leave off this usury.

¹¹Restore, I pray you, to them, even this day, their fields, their vineyards, their oliveyards, and their houses, also the hundredth part of the money, and of the grain, the new wine, and the oil, that ye exact of them.

¹²Then said they, We will restore them, and will require nothing of them; so will we do, even as thou sayest. Then I called the priests, and took an oath of them, that they would do according to this promise.

¹³Also I shook out my lap, and said, So God shake out every man from his house, and from his labor, that performeth not this promise; even thus be he shaken out, and emptied. And all the assembly said, Amen, and praised Yahweh. And the people did according to this promise.

¹⁴Moreover from the time that I was appointed to be their governor in the land of Judah, from the twentieth year even unto the two and thirtieth year of Artaxerxes the king, that is, twelve years, I and my brethren have not eaten the bread of the governor.

¹⁵But the former governors that were before me were chargeable unto the people, and took of them bread and wine, besides forty shekels of silver; yea, even their servants bare rule over the people: but so did not I, because of the fear of God.

¹⁶Yea, also I continued in the work of this wall, neither bought we any land: and all my servants were gathered thither unto the work.

¹⁷Moreover there were at my table, of the Jews and the rulers, a hundred and fifty men, besides those that came unto us from among the nations that were round about us.

¹⁸Now that which was prepared for one day was one ox and six choice sheep; also fowls were prepared for me, and once in ten days store of all sorts of wine: yet for all this I demanded not the bread of the governor, because the bondage was heavy upon this people.

¹⁹Remember unto me, O my God, for good, all that I have done for this people.

Chapter 6

¹Now it came to pass, when it was reported to Sanballat and Tobiah, and to Geshem the Arabian, and unto the rest of our enemies, that I had builded the wall, and that there was no breach left therein; (though even unto that time I had not set up the doors in the gates;)

²that Sanballat and Geshem sent unto me, saying, Come, let us meet together in one of the villages in the plain of Ono. But they thought to do me mischief.

³And I sent messengers unto them, saying, I am doing a great work, so that I cannot come down: why should the work cease, whilst I leave it, and come down to you?

⁴And they sent unto me four times after this sort; and I answered them after the same manner.

⁵Then sent Sanballat his servant unto me in like manner the fifth time with an open letter in his hand,

⁶wherein was written, It is reported among the nations, and Gashmu saith it, that thou and the Jews think to rebel; for which cause thou art building the wall: and thou wouldest be their king, according to these words.

⁷And thou hast also appointed prophets to preach of thee at Jerusalem, saying, There is a king in Judah: and now shall it be reported to the king according to these words. Come now therefore, and let us take counsel together.

⁸Then I sent unto him, saying, There are no such things done as thou sayest, but thou feignest them out of thine own heart.

⁹For they all would have made us afraid, saying, Their hands shall be weakened from the work, that it be not done. But now, O God, strengthen thou my hands.

¹⁰And I went unto the house of Shemaiah the son of Delaiah the son of Mehetabel, who was shut up; and he said, Let us meet together in the house of God, within the temple, and let us shut the doors of the temple: for they will come to slay thee; yea, in the night will they come to slay thee.

¹¹And I said, Should such a man as I flee? and who is there, that, being such as I, would go into the temple to save his life? I will not go in.

¹²And I discerned, and, lo, God had not sent him; but he pronounced this prophecy against me: and Tobiah and Sanballat had hired him.

¹³For this cause was he hired, that I should be afraid, and do so, and sin, and that they might have matter for an evil report, that they might reproach me.

¹⁴Remember, O my God, Tobiah and Sanballat according to these their works, and also the prophetess Noadiah, and the rest of the prophets, that would have put me in fear.

¹⁵So the wall was finished in the twenty and fifth day of the month Elul, in fifty and two days.

¹⁶And it came to pass, when all our enemies heard thereof, that all the nations that were about us feared, and were much cast down in their own eyes; for they perceived that this work was wrought of our God.

¹⁷Moreover in those days the nobles of Judah sent many letters unto Tobiah, and the letters of Tobiah came unto them.

¹⁸For there were many in Judah sworn unto him, because he was the son-in-law of Shecaniah the son of Arah; and his son Jehohanan had taken the daughter of Meshullam the son of Berechiah to wife.

¹⁹Also they spake of his good deeds before me, and reported my words to him. And Tobiah sent letters to put me in fear.

Chapter 7

¹Now it came to pass, when the wall was built, and I had set up the doors, and the porters and the singers and the Levites were appointed,

²that I gave my brother Hanani, and Hananiah the governor of the castle, charge over Jerusalem; for he was a faithful man, and feared God above many.

³And I said unto them, Let not the gates of Jerusalem be opened until the sun be hot; and while they stand on guard, let them shut the doors, and bar ye them: and appoint watches of the inhabitants of Jerusalem, every one in his watch, and every one to be over against his house.

Nehemiah

4Now the city was wide and large; but the people were few therein; and the houses were not builded.

5And my God put into my heart to gather together the nobles, and the rulers, and the people, that they might be reckoned by genealogy. And I found the book of the genealogy of them that came up at the first, and I found written therein:

6These are the children of the province, that went up out of the captivity of those that had been carried away, whom Nebuchadnezzar the king of Babylon had carried away, and that returned unto Jerusalem and to Judah, every one unto his city;

7who came with Zerubbabel, Jeshua, Nehemiah, Azariah, Raamiah, Nahamani, Mordecai, Bilshan, Mispereth, Bigvai, Nehum, Baanah. The number of the men of the people of Israel:

8The children of Parosh, two thousand a hundred and seventy and two.
9The children of Shephatiah, three hundred seventy and two.
10The children of Arah, six hundred fifty and two.
11The children of Pahath-moab, of the children of Jeshua and Joab, two thousand and eight hundred and eighteen.
12The children of Elam, a thousand two hundred fifty and four.
13The children of Zattu, eight hundred forty and five.
14The children of Zaccai, seven hundred and threescore.
15The children of Binnui, six hundred forty and eight.
16The children of Bebai, six hundred twenty and eight.
17The children of Azgad, two thousand three hundred twenty and two.
18The children of Adonikam, six hundred threescore and seven.
19The children of Bigvai, two thousand threescore and seven.
20The children of Adin, six hundred fifty and five.
21The children of Ater, of Hezekiah, ninety and eight.
22The children of Hashum, three hundred twenty and eight.
23The children of Bezai, three hundred twenty and four.
24The children of Hariph, a hundred and twelve.
25The children of Gibeon, ninety and five.
26The men of Bethlehem and Netophah, a hundred fourscore and eight.
27The men of Anathoth, a hundred twenty and eight.
28The men of Beth-azmaveth, forty and two.
29The men of Kiriath-jearim, Chephirah, and Beeroth, seven hundred forty and three.
30The men of Ramah and Geba, six hundred twenty and one.
31The men of Michmas, a hundred and twenty and two.
32The men of Beth-el and Ai, a hundred twenty and three.
33The men of the other Nebo, fifty and two.
34The children of the other Elam, a thousand two hundred fifty and four.
35The children of Harim, three hundred and twenty.
36The children of Jericho, three hundred forty and five.
37The children of Lod, Hadid, and Ono, seven hundred twenty and one.
38The children of Senaah, three thousand nine hundred and thirty.
39The priests: The children of Jedaiah, of the house of Jeshua, nine hundred seventy and three.
40The children of Immer, a thousand fifty and two.
41The children of Pashhur, a thousand two hundred forty and seven.
42The children of Harim, a thousand and seventeen.
43The Levites: the children of Jeshua, of Kadmiel, of the children of Hodevah, seventy and four.
44The singers: the children of Asaph, a hundred forty and eight.
45The porters: the children of Shallum, the children of Ater, the children of Talmon, the children of Akkub, the children of Hatita, the children of Shobai, a hundred thirty and eight.
46The Nethinim: the children of Ziha, the children of Hasupha, the children of Tabbaoth,
47the children of Keros, the children of Sia, the children of Padon,
48the children of Lebana, the children of Hagaba, the children of Salmai,
49the children of Hanan, the children of Giddel, the children of Gahar,
50the children of Reaiah, the children of Rezin, the children of Nekoda,
51the children of Gazzam, the children of Uzza, the children of Paseah.
52The children of Besai, the children of Meunim, the children of Nephushesim,
53the children of Bakbuk, the children of Hakupha, the children of Harhur,
54the children of Bazlith, the children of Mehida, the children of Harsha,
55the children of Barkos, the children of Sisera, the children of Temah,
56the children of Neziah, the children of Hatipha.
57The children of Solomon's servants: the children of Sotai, the children of Sophereth, the children of Perida,
58the children of Jaala, the children of Darkon, the children of Giddel,
59the children of Shephatiah, the children of Hattil, the children of Pochereth-hazzebaim, the children of Amon.
60All the Nethinim, and the children of Solomon's servants, were three hundred ninety and two.

61And these were they that went up from Tel-melah, Tel-harsha, Cherub, Addon, and Immer; but they could not show their fathers' houses, nor their seed, whether they were of Israel:

62The children of Delaiah, the children of Tobiah, the children of Nekoda, six hundred forty and two.

63And of the priests: the children of Hobaiah, the children of Hakkoz, the children of Barzillai, who took a wife of the daughters of Barzillai the Gileadite, and was called after their name.

64These sought their register among those that were reckoned by genealogy, but it was not found: therefore were they deemed polluted and put from the priesthood.

65And the governor said unto them, that they should not eat of the most holy things, till there stood up a priest with Urim and Thummim.

66The whole assembly together was forty and two thousand three hundred and threescore,

67besides their men-servants and their maid-servants, of whom there were seven thousand three hundred thirty and seven: and they had two hundred forty and five singing men and singing women.

68Their horses were seven hundred thirty and six; their mules, two hundred forty and five;

69their camels, four hundred thirty and five; their asses, six thousand seven hundred and twenty.

70And some from among the heads of fathers' houses gave unto the work. The governor gave to the treasury a thousand darics of gold, fifty basins, five hundred and thirty priests' garments.

71And some of the heads of fathers' houses gave into the treasury of the work twenty thousand darics of gold, and two thousand and two hundred pounds of silver.

72And that which the rest of the people gave was twenty thousand darics of gold, and two thousand pounds of silver, and threescore and seven priests' garments.

73So the priests, and the Levites, and the porters, and the singers, and some of the people, and the Nethinim, and all Israel, dwelt in their cities. And when the seventh month was come, the children of Israel were in their cities.

Chapter 8

1And all the people gathered themselves together as one man into the broad place that was before the water gate; and they spake unto Ezra the scribe to bring the book of the law of Moses, which Yahweh had commanded to Israel.

2And Ezra the priest brought the law before the assembly, both men and women, and all that could hear with understanding, upon the first day of the seventh month.

3And he read therein before the broad place that was before the water gate from early morning until midday, in the presence of the men and the women, and of those that could understand; and the ears of all the people were attentive unto the book of the law.

4And Ezra the scribe stood upon a pulpit of wood, which they had made for the purpose; and beside him stood Mattithiah, and Shema, and Anaiah, and Uriah, and Hilkiah, and Maaseiah, on his right hand; and on his left hand, Pedaiah, and Mishael, and Malchijah, and Hashum, and Hashbaddanah, Zechariah, and Meshullam.

5And Ezra opened the book in the sight of all the people; (for he was above all the people;) and when he opened it, all the people stood up:

6and Ezra blessed Yahweh, the great God. And all the people answered, Amen, Amen, with the lifting up of their hands: and they bowed their heads, and worshipped Yahweh with their faces to the ground.

7Also Jeshua, and Bani, and Sherebiah, Jamin, Akkub, Shabbethai, Hodiah, Maaseiah, Kelita, Azariah, Jozabad, Hanan, Pelaiah, and the Levites, caused the people to understand the law: and the people stood in their place.

8And they read in the book, in the law of God, distinctly; and they gave the sense, so that they understood the reading.

9And Nehemiah, who was the governor, and Ezra the priest the scribe, and the Levites that taught the people, said unto all the people, This day is holy unto Yahweh your God; mourn not, nor weep. For all the people wept, when they heard the words of the law.

10Then he said unto them, Go your way, eat the fat, and drink the sweet, and send portions unto him for whom nothing is prepared; for this day is holy unto our Lord: neither be ye grieved; for the joy of Yahweh is your strength.

11So the Levites stilled all the people, saying, Hold your peace, for the day is holy; neither be ye grieved.

12And all the people went their way to eat, and to drink, and to send portions, and to make great mirth, because they had understood the words that were declared unto them.

13And on the second day were gathered together the heads of fathers' houses of all the people, the priests, and the Levites, unto Ezra the scribe, even to give attention to the words of the law.

14And they found written in the law, how that Yahweh had commanded by Moses, that the children of Israel should dwell in booths in the feast of the seventh month;

15and that they should publish and proclaim in all their cities, and in Jerusalem, saying, Go forth unto the mount, and fetch olive branches, and branches of wild olive, and myrtle branches, and palm branches, and branches of thick trees, to make booths, as it is written.

16So the people went forth, and brought them, and made themselves booths, every one upon the roof of his house, and in their courts, and in the courts of the house of God, and in the broad place of the water gate, and in the broad place of the gate of Ephraim.

17And all the assembly of them that were come again out of the captivity made booths, and dwelt in the booths; for since the days of Jeshua the son of Nun unto that day had not the children of Israel done so. And there was very great gladness.

18Also day by day, from the first day unto the last day, he read in the book of the law of God. And they kept the feast seven days; and on the eighth day was a solemn assembly, according unto the ordinance.

Chapter 9

1Now in the twenty and fourth day of this month the children of Israel were assembled with fasting, and with sackcloth, and earth upon them.

2And the seed of Israel separated themselves from all foreigners, and stood and confessed their sins, and the iniquities of their fathers.

3And they stood up in their place, and read in the book of the law of

Yahweh their God a fourth part of the day; and another fourth part they confessed, and worshipped Yahweh their God.

4Then stood up upon the stairs of the Levites, Jeshua, and Bani, Kadmiel, Shebaniah, Bunni, Sherebiah, Bani, and Chenani, and cried with a loud voice unto Yahweh their God.

5Then the Levites, Jeshua, and Kadmiel, Bani, Hashabneiah, Sherebiah, Hodiah, Shebaniah, and Pethahiah, said, Stand up and bless Yahweh your God from everlasting to everlasting; and blessed be thy glorious name, which is exalted above all blessing and praise.

6Thou art Yahweh, even thou alone; thou hast made heaven, the heaven of heavens, with all their host, the earth and all things that are thereon, the seas and all that is in them, and thou preservest them all; and the host of heaven worshippeth thee.

7Thou art Yahweh the God, who didst choose Abram, and broughtest him forth out of Ur of the Chaldees, and gavest him the name of Abraham,

8and foundest his heart faithful before thee, and madest a covenant with him to give the land of the Canaanite, the Hittite, the Amorite, and the Perizzite, and the Jebusite, and the Girgashite, to give it unto his seed, and hast performed thy words; for thou art righteous.

9And thou sawest the affliction of our fathers in Egypt, and heardest their cry by the Red Sea,

10and showedst signs and wonders upon Pharaoh, and on all his servants, and on all the people of his land; for thou knewest that they dealt proudly against them, and didst get thee a name, as it is this day.

11And thou didst divide the sea before them, so that they went through the midst of the sea on the dry land; and their pursuers thou didst cast into the depths, as a stone into the mighty waters.

12Moreover in a pillar of cloud thou leddest them by day; and in a pillar of fire by night, to give them light in the way wherein they should go.

13Thou camest down also upon mount Sinai, and spakest with them from heaven, and gavest them right ordinances and true laws, good statutes and commandments,

14and madest known unto them thy holy sabbath, and commandedst them commandments, and statutes, and a law, by Moses thy servant,

15and gavest them bread from heaven for their hunger, and broughtest forth water for them out of the rock for their thirst, and commandedst them that they should go in to possess the land which thou hadst sworn to give them.

16But they and our fathers dealt proudly and hardened their neck, and hearkened not to thy commandments,

17and refused to obey, neither were mindful of thy wonders that thou didst among them, but hardened their neck, and in their rebellion appointed a captain to return to their bondage. But thou art a God ready to pardon, gracious and merciful, slow to anger, and abundant in lovingkindness, and forsookest them not.

18Yea, when they had made them a molten calf, and said, This is thy God that brought thee up out of Egypt, and had wrought great provocations;

19yet thou in thy manifold mercies forsookest them not in the wilderness: the pillar of cloud departed not from over them by day, to lead them in the way; neither the pillar of fire by night, to show them light, and the way wherein they should go.

20Thou gavest also thy good Spirit to instruct them, and withheldest not thy manna from their mouth, and gavest them water for their thirst.

21Yea, forty years didst thou sustain them in the wilderness, and they lacked nothing; their clothes waxed not old, and their feet swelled not.

22Moreover thou gavest them kingdoms and peoples, which thou didst allot after their portions: so they possessed the land of Sihon, even the land of the king of Heshbon, and the land of Og king of Bashan.

23Their children also multipliedst thou as the stars of heaven, and broughtest them into the land concerning which thou didst say to their fathers, that they should go in to possess it.

24So the children went in and possessed the land, and thou subduedst before them the inhabitants of the land, the Canaanites, and gavest them into their hands, with their kings, and the peoples of the land, that they might do with them as they would.

25And they took fortified cities, and a fat land, and possessed houses full of all good things, cisterns hewn out, vineyards, and oliveyards, and fruit-trees in abundance: so they did eat, and were filled, and became fat, and delighted themselves in thy great goodness.

26Nevertheless they were disobedient, and rebelled against thee, and cast thy law behind their back, and slew thy prophets that testified against them to turn them again unto thee, and they wrought great provocations.

27Therefore thou deliveredst them into the hand of their adversaries, who distressed them: and in the time of their trouble, when they cried unto thee, thou heardest from heaven; and according to thy manifold mercies thou gavest them saviours who saved them out of the hand of their adversaries.

28But after they had rest, they did evil again before thee; therefore leftest thou them in the hand of their enemies, so that they had the dominion over them: yet when they returned, and cried unto thee, thou heardest from heaven; and many times didst thou deliver them according to thy mercies,

29and testifiedst against them, that thou mightest bring them again unto thy law. Yet they dealt proudly, and hearkened not unto thy commandments, but sinned against thine ordinances, (which if a man do, he shall live in them,) and withdrew the shoulder, and hardened their neck, and would not hear.

30Yet many years didst thou bear with them, and testifiedst against them by thy Spirit through thy prophets: yet would they not give ear: therefore gavest thou them into the hand of the peoples of the lands.

31Nevertheless in thy manifold mercies thou didst not make a full end of them, nor forsake them; for thou art a gracious and merciful God.

32Now therefore, our God, the great, the mighty, and the terrible God, who keepest covenant and lovingkindness, let not all the travail seem little before thee, that hath come upon us, on our kings, on our princes, and on our priests, and on our prophets, and on our fathers, and on all thy people, since the time of the kings of Assyria unto this day.

33Howbeit thou art just in all that is come upon us; for thou hast dealt truly, but we have done wickedly;

34neither have our kings, our princes, our priests, nor our fathers, kept thy law, nor hearkened unto thy commandments and thy testimonies wherewith thou didst testify against them.

35For they have not served thee in their kingdom, and in thy great goodness that thou gavest them, and in the large and fat land which thou gavest before them, neither turned they from their wicked works.

36Behold, we are servants this day, and as for the land that thou gavest unto our fathers to eat the fruit thereof and the good thereof, behold, we are servants in it.

37And it yieldeth much increase unto the kings whom thou hast set over us because of our sins: also they have power over our bodies, and over our cattle, at their pleasure, and we are in great distress.

38And yet for all this we make a sure covenant, and write it; and our princes, our Levites, and our priests, seal unto it.

Chapter 10

1Now those that sealed were: Nehemiah the governor, the son of Hacaliah, and Zedekiah,

2Seraiah, Azariah, Jeremiah,

3Pashhur, Amariah, Malchijah,

4Hattush, Shebaniah, Malluch,

5Harim, Meremoth, Obadiah,

6Daniel, Ginnethon, Baruch,

7Meshullam, Abijah, Mijamin,

8Maaziah, Bilgai, Shemaiah; these were the priests.

9And the Levites: namely, Jeshua the son of Azaniah, Binnui of the sons of Henadad, Kadmiel;

10and their brethren, Shebaniah, Hodiah, Kelita, Pelaiah, Hanan,

11Mica, Rehob, Hashabiah,

12Zaccur, Sherebiah, Shebaniah,

13Hodiah, Bani, Beninu.

14The chiefs of the people: Parosh, Pahath-moab, Elam, Zattu, Bani,

15Bunni, Azgad, Bebai,

16Adonijah, Bigvai, Adin,

17Ater, Hezekiah, Azzur,

18Hodiah, Hashum, Bezai,

19Hariph, Anathoth, Nobai,

20Magpiash, Meshullam, Hezir,

21Meshezabel, Zadok, Jaddua,

22Pelatiah, Hanan, Anaiah,

23Hoshea, Hananiah, Hasshub,

24Hallohesh, Pilha, Shobek,

25Rehum, Hashabnah, Maaseiah,

26and Ahiah, Hanan, Anan,

27Malluch, Harim, Baanah.

28And the rest of the people, the priests, the Levites, the porters, the singers, the Nethinim, and all they that had separated themselves from the peoples of the lands unto the law of God, their wives, their sons, and their daughters, every one that had knowledge, and understanding;

29They clave to their brethren, their nobles, and entered into a curse, and into an oath, to walk in God's law, which was given by Moses the servant of God, and to observe and do all the commandments of Yahweh our Lord, and his ordinances and his statutes;

30and that we would not give our daughters unto the peoples of the land, nor take their daughters for our sons;

31and if the peoples of the land bring wares or any grain on the sabbath day to sell, that we would not buy of them on the sabbath, or on a holy day; and that we would forego the seventh year, and the exaction of every debt.

32Also we made ordinances for us, to charge ourselves yearly with the third part of a shekel for the service of the house of our God;

33for the showbread, and for the continual meal-offering, and for the continual burnt-offering, for the sabbaths, for the new moons, for the set feasts, and for the holy things, and for the sin-offerings to make atonement for Israel, and for all the work of the house of our God.

34And we cast lots, the priests, the Levites, and the people, for the wood-offering, to bring it into the house of our God, according to our fathers' houses, at times appointed, year by year, to burn upon the altar of Yahweh our God, as it is written in the law;

35and to bring the first-fruits of our ground, and the first-fruits of all fruit of all manner of trees, year by year, unto the house of Yahweh;

36also the first-born of our sons, and of our cattle, as it is written in the law, and the firstlings of our herds and of our flocks, to bring to the house of our God, unto the priests that minister in the house of our God;

37and that we should bring the first-fruits of our dough, and our heave-offerings, and the fruit of all manner of trees, the new wine and the oil, unto the priests, to the chambers of the house of our God; and the tithes of our ground unto the Levites; for they, the Levites, take the tithes in all the cities of our tillage.

38And the priest the son of Aaron shall be with the Levites, when the Levites take tithes: and the Levites shall bring up the tithe of the tithes unto the house of our God, to the chambers, into the treasure-house.

39For the children of Israel and the children of Levi shall bring the heave-offering of the grain, of the new wine, and of the oil, unto the chambers, where are the vessels of the sanctuary, and the priests that minister, and the porters, and the singers: and we will not forsake the house of our God.

Nehemiah
Chapter 11

1And the princes of the people dwelt in Jerusalem: the rest of the people also cast lots, to bring one of ten to dwell in Jerusalem the holy city, and nine parts in the other cities.

2And the people blessed all the men that willingly offered themselves to dwell in Jerusalem.

3Now these are the chiefs of the province that dwelt in Jerusalem: but in the cities of Judah dwelt every one in his possession in their cities, to wit, Israel, the priests, and the Levites, and the Nethinim, and the children of Solomon's servants.

4And in Jerusalem dwelt certain of the children of Judah, and of the children of Benjamin. Of the children of Judah: Athaiah the son of Uzziah, the son of Zechariah, the son of Amariah, the son of Shephatiah, the son of Mahalalel, of the children of Perez;

5and Maaseiah the son of Baruch, the son of Colhozeh, the son of Hazaiah, the son of Adaiah, the son of Joiarib, the son of Zechariah, the son of the Shilonite.

6All the sons of Perez that dwelt in Jerusalem were four hundred threescore and eight valiant men.

7And these are the sons of Benjamin: Sallu the son of Meshullam, the son of Joed, the son of Pedaiah, the son of Kolaiah, the son of Maaseiah, the son of Ithiel, the son of Jeshaiah.

8And after him Gabbai, Sallai, nine hundred twenty and eight.

9And Joel the son of Zichri was their overseer; and Judah the son of Hassenuah was second over the city.

10Of the priests: Jedaiah the son of Joiarib, Jachin,

11Seraiah the son of Hilkiah, the son of Meshullam, the son of Zadok, the son of Meraioth, the son of Ahitub, the ruler of the house of God,

12and their brethren that did the work of the house, eight hundred twenty and two; and Adaiah the son of Jeroham, the son of Pelaliah, the son of Amzi, the son of Zechariah, the son of Pashhur, the son of Malchijah,

13and his brethren, chiefs of fathers' houses, two hundred forty and two; and Amashsai the son of Azarel, the son of Ahzai, the son of Meshillemoth, the son of Immer,

14and their brethren, mighty men of valor, a hundred twenty and eight; and their overseer was Zabdiel, the son of Haggedolim.

15And of the Levites: Shemaiah the son of Hasshub, the son of Azrikam, the son of Hashabiah, the son of Bunni;

16and Shabbethai and Jozabad, of the chiefs of the Levites, who had the oversight of the outward business of the house of God;

17and Mattaniah the son of Mica, the son of Zabdi, the son of Asaph, who was the chief to begin the thanksgiving in prayer, and Bakbukiah, the second among his brethren; and Abda the son of Shammua, the son of Galal, the son of Jeduthun.

18All the Levites in the holy city were two hundred fourscore and four.

19Moreover the porters, Akkub, Talmon, and their brethren, that kept watch at the gates, were a hundred seventy and two.

20And the residue of Israel, of the priests, the Levites, were in all the cities of Judah, every one in his inheritance.

21But the Nethinim dwelt in Ophel: and Ziha and Gishpa were over the Nethinim.

22The overseer also of the Levites at Jerusalem was Uzzi the son of Bani, the son of Hashabiah, the son of Mattaniah, the son of Mica, of the sons of Asaph, the singers, over the business of the house of God.

23For there was a commandment from the king concerning them, and a settled provision for the singers, as every day required.

24And Pethahiah the son of Meshezabel, of the children of Zerah the son of Judah, was at the king's hand in all matters concerning the people.

25And as for the villages, with their fields, some of the children of Judah dwelt in Kiriath-arba and the towns thereof, and in Dibon and the towns thereof, and in Jekabzeel and the villages thereof,

26and in Jeshua, and in Moladah, and Beth-pelet,

27and in Hazar-shual, and in Beer-sheba and the towns thereof,

28and in Ziklag, and in Meconah and in the towns thereof,

29and in En-rimmon, and in Zorah, and in Jarmuth,

30Zanoah, Adullam, and their villages, Lachish and the fields thereof, Azekah and the towns thereof. So they encamped from Beer-sheba unto the valley of Hinnom.

31The children of Benjamin also dwelt from Geba onward, at Michmash and Aija, and at Beth-el and the towns thereof,

32at Anathoth, Nob, Ananiah,

33Hazor, Ramah, Gittaim,

34Hadid, Zeboim, Neballat,

35Lod, and Ono, the valley of craftsmen.

36And of the Levites, certain courses in Judah were joined to Benjamin.

Chapter 12

1Now these are the priests and the Levites that went up with Zerubbabel the son of Shealtiel, and Jeshua: Seraiah, Jeremiah, Ezra,

2Amariah, Malluch, Hattush,

3Shecaniah, Rehum, Meremoth,

4Iddo, Ginnethoi, Abijah,

5Mijamin, Maadiah, Bilgah,

6Shemaiah, and Joiarib, Jedaiah.

7Sallu, Amok, Hilkiah, Jedaiah. These were the chiefs of the priests and of their brethren in the days of Jeshua.

8Moreover the Levites: Jeshua, Binnui, Kadmiel, Sherebiah, Judah, and Mattaniah, who was over the thanksgiving, he and his brethren.

9Also Bakbukiah and Unno, their brethren, were over against them according to their offices.

10And Jeshua begat Joiakim, and Joiakim begat Eliashib, and Eliashib begat Joiada,

11and Joiada begat Jonathan, and Jonathan begat Jaddua.

12And in the days of Joiakim were priests, heads of fathers' houses: of Seraiah, Meraiah; of Jeremiah, Hananiah;

13of Ezra, Meshullam; of Amariah, Jehohanan;

14of Malluchi, Jonathan; of Shebaniah, Joseph;

15of Harim, Adna; of Meraioth, Helkai;

16of Iddo, Zechariah; of Ginnethon, Meshullam;

17of Abijah, Zichri; of Miniamin, of Moadiah, Piltai;

18of Bilgah, Shammua; of Shemaiah, Jehonathan;

19and of Joiarib, Mattenai; of Jedaiah, Uzzi;

20of Sallai, Kallai; of Amok, Eber;

21of Hilkiah, Hashabiah; of Jedaiah, Nethanel.

22As for the Levites, in the days of Eliashib, Joiada, and Johanan, and Jaddua, there were recorded the heads of fathers' houses; also the priests, in the reign of Darius the Persian.

23The sons of Levi, heads of fathers' houses, were written in the book of the chronicles, even until the days of Johanan the son of Eliashib.

24And the chiefs of the Levites: Hashabiah, Sherebiah, and Jeshua the son of Kadmiel, with their brethren over against them, to praise and give thanks, according to the commandment of David the man of God, watch next to watch.

25Mattaniah, and Bakbukiah, Obadiah, Meshullam, Talmon, Akkub, were porters keeping the watch at the store-houses of the gates.

26These were in the days of Joiakim the son of Jeshua, the son of Jozadak, and in the days of Nehemiah the governor, and of Ezra the priest the scribe.

27And at the dedication of the wall of Jerusalem they sought the Levites out of all their places, to bring them to Jerusalem, to keep the dedication with gladness, both with thanksgivings, and with singing, with cymbals, psalteries, and with harps.

28And the sons of the singers gathered themselves together, both out of the plain round about Jerusalem, and from the villages of the Netophathites;

29also from Beth-gilgal, and out of the fields of Geba and Azmaveth: for the singers had builded them villages round about Jerusalem.

30And the priests and the Levites purified themselves; and they purified the people, and the gates, and the wall.

31Then I brought up the princes of Judah upon the wall, and appointed two great companies that gave thanks and went in procession; whereof one went on the right hand upon the wall toward the dung gate:

32and after them went Hoshaiah, and half of the princes of Judah,

33and Azariah, Ezra, and Meshullam,

34Judah, and Benjamin, and Shemaiah, and Jeremiah,

35and certain of the priests' sons with trumpets: Zechariah the son of Jonathan, the son of Shemaiah, the son of Mattaniah, the son of Micaiah, the son of Zaccur, the son of Asaph;

36and his brethren, Shemaiah, and Azarel, Milalai, Gilalai, Maai, Nethanel, and Judah, Hanani, with the musical instruments of David the man of God; and Ezra the scribe was before them.

37And by the fountain gate, and straight before them, they went up by the stairs of the city of David, at the ascent of the wall, above the house of David, even unto the water gate eastward.

38And the other company of them that gave thanks went to meet them, and I after them, with the half of the people, upon the wall, above the tower of the furnaces, even unto the broad wall,

39and above the gate of Ephraim, and by the old gate, and by the fish gate, and the tower of Hananel, and the tower of Hammeah, even unto the sheep gate: and they stood still in the gate of the guard.

40So stood the two companies of them that gave thanks in the house of God, and I, and the half of the rulers with me;

41and the priests, Eliakim, Maaseiah, Miniamin, Micaiah, Elioenai, Zechariah, and Hananiah, with trumpets;

42and Maaseiah, and Shemaiah, and Eleazar, and Uzzi, and Jehohanan, and Malchijah, and Elam, and Ezer. And the singers sang loud, with Jezrahiah their overseer.

43And they offered great sacrifices that day, and rejoiced; for God had made them rejoice with great joy; and the women also and the children rejoiced: so that the joy of Jerusalem was heard even afar off.

44And on that day were men appointed over the chambers for the treasures, for the heave-offerings, for the first-fruits, and for the tithes, to gather into them, according to the fields of the cities, the portions appointed by the law for the priests and Levites: for Judah rejoiced for the priests and for the Levites that waited.

45And they kept the charge of their God, and the charge of the purification, and so did the singers and the porters, according to the commandment of David, and of Solomon his son.

46For in the days of David and Asaph of old there was a chief of the singers, and songs of praise and thanksgiving unto God.

47And all Israel in the days of Zerubbabel, and in the days of Nehemiah, gave the portions of the singers and the porters, as every day required: and they set apart that which was for the Levites; and the Levites set apart that which was for the sons of Aaron.

Chapter 13

1On that day they read in the book of Moses in the audience of the people; and therein was found written, that an Ammonite and a Moabite should not enter into the assembly of God for ever,

2because they met not the children of Israel with bread and with water, but hired Balaam against them, to curse them: howbeit our God turned the curse into a blessing.

3And it came to pass, when they had heard the law, that they separated from Israel all the mixed multitude.

4Now before this, Eliashib the priest, who was appointed over the chambers of the house of our God, being allied unto Tobiah,

5had prepared for him a great chamber, where aforetime they laid the meal-offerings, the frankincense, and the vessels, and the tithes of the grain, the new wine, and the oil, which were given by commandment to the Levites, and the singers, and the porters; and the heave-offerings for the priests.

6But in all this time I was not at Jerusalem; for in the two and thirtieth year of Artaxerxes king of Babylon I went unto the king: and after certain days asked I leave of the king,

7and I came to Jerusalem, and understood the evil that Eliashib had done for Tobiah, in preparing him a chamber in the courts of the house of God.

8And it grieved me sore: therefore I cast forth all the household stuff of Tobiah out of the chamber.

9Then I commanded, and they cleansed the chambers: and thither brought I again the vessels of the house of God, with the meal-offerings and the frankincense.

10And I perceived that the portions of the Levites had not been given them; so that the Levites and the singers, that did the work, were fled every one to his field.

11Then contended I with the rulers, and said, Why is the house of God forsaken? And I gathered them together, and set them in their place.

12Then brought all Judah the tithe of the grain and the new wine and the oil unto the treasuries.

13And I made treasurers over the treasuries, Shelemiah the priest, and Zadok the scribe, and of the Levites, Pedaiah: and next to them was Hanan the son of Zaccur, the son of Mattaniah; for they were counted faithful, and their business was to distribute unto their brethren.

14Remember me, O my God, concerning this, and wipe not out my good deeds that I have done for the house of my God, and for the observances thereof.

15In those days saw I in Judah some men treading wine-presses on the sabbath, and bringing in sheaves, and lading asses therewith; as also wine, grapes, and figs, and all manner of burdens, which they brought into Jerusalem on the sabbath day: and I testified against them in the day wherein they sold victuals.

16There dwelt men of Tyre also therein, who brought in fish, and all manner of wares, and sold on the sabbath unto the children of Judah, and in Jerusalem.

17Then I contended with the nobles of Judah, and said unto them, What evil thing is this that ye do, and profane the sabbath day?

18Did not your fathers thus, and did not our God bring all this evil upon us, and upon this city? yet ye bring more wrath upon Israel by profaning the sabbath.

19And it came to pass that, when the gates of Jerusalem began to be dark before the sabbath, I commanded that the doors should be shut, and commanded that they should not be opened till after the sabbath: and some of my servants set I over the gates, that there should no burden be brought in on the sabbath day.

20So the merchants and sellers of all kind of wares lodged without Jerusalem once or twice.

21Then I testified against them, and said unto them, Why lodge ye about the wall? if ye do so again, I will lay hands on you. From that time forth came they no more on the sabbath.

22And I commanded the Levites that they should purify themselves, and that they should come and keep the gates, to sanctify the sabbath day. Remember unto me, O my God, this also, and spare me according to the greatness of thy lovingkindness.

23In those days also saw I the Jews that had married women of Ashdod, of Ammon, and of Moab:

24and their children spake half in the speech of Ashdod, and could not speak in the Jews' language, but according to the language of each people.

25And I contended with them, and cursed them, and smote certain of them, and plucked off their hair, and made them swear by God, saying, Ye shall not give your daughters unto their sons, nor take their daughters for your sons, or for yourselves.

26Did not Solomon king of Israel sin by these things? yet among many nations was there no king like him, and he was beloved of his God, and God made him king over all Israel: nevertheless even him did foreign women cause to sin.

27Shall we then hearken unto you to do all this great evil, to trespass against our God in marrying foreign women?

28And one of the sons of Joiada, the son of Eliashib the high priest, was son-in-law to Sanballat the Horonite: therefore I chased him from me.

29Remember them, O my God, because they have defiled the priesthood, and the covenant of the priesthood, and of the Levites.

30Thus cleansed I them from all foreigners, and appointed charges for the priests and for the Levites, every one in his work;

31and for the wood-offering, at times appointed, and for the first-fruits. Remember me, O my God, for good.

Esther
The Book of Esther

Chapter 1

1Now it came to pass in the days of Ahasuerus (this is Ahasuerus who reigned from India even unto Ethiopia, over a hundred and seven and twenty provinces),

2that in those days, when the king Ahasuerus sat on the throne of his kingdom, which was in Shushan the palace,

3in the third year of his reign, he made a feast unto all his princes and his servants; the power of Persia and Media, the nobles and princes of the provinces, being before him;

4when he showed the riches of his glorious kingdom and the honor of his excellent majesty many days, even a hundred and fourscore days.

5And when these days were fulfilled, the king made a feast unto all the people that were present in Shushan the palace, both great and small, seven days, in the court of the garden of the king's palace.

6There were hangings of white cloth, of green, and of blue, fastened with cords of fine linen and purple to silver rings and pillars of marble: the couches were of gold and silver, upon a pavement of red, and white, and yellow, and black marble.

7And they gave them drink in vessels of gold (the vessels being diverse one from another), and royal wine in abundance, according to the bounty of the king.

8And the drinking was according to the law; none could compel: for so the king had appointed to all the officers of his house, that they should do according to every man's pleasure.

9Also Vashti the queen made a feast for the women in the royal house which belonged to king Ahasuerus.

10On the seventh day, when the heart of the king was merry with wine, he commanded Mehuman, Biztha, Harbona, Bigtha, and Abagtha, Zethar, and Carcas, the seven chamberlains that ministered in the presence of Ahasuerus the king,

11to bring Vashti the queen before the king with the crown royal, to show the peoples and the princes her beauty; for she was fair to look on.

12But the queen Vashti refused to come at the king's commandment by the chamberlains: therefore was the king very wroth, and his anger burned in him.

13Then the king said to the wise men, who knew the times, (for so was the king's manner toward all that knew law and judgment;

14and the next unto him were Carshena, Shethar, Admatha, Tarshish, Meres, Marsena, and Memucan, the seven princes of Persia and Media, who saw the king's face, and sat first in the kingdom),

15What shall we do unto the queen Vashti according to law, because she hath not done the bidding of the king Ahasuerus by the chamberlains?

16And Memucan answered before the king and the princes, Vashti the queen hath not done wrong to the king only, but also to all the princes, and to all the peoples that are in all the provinces of the king Ahasuerus.

17For this deed of the queen will come abroad unto all women, to make their husbands contemptible in their eyes, when it shall be reported, The king Ahasuerus commanded Vashti the queen to be brought in before him, but she came not.

18And this day will the princesses of Persia and Media who have heard of the deed of the queen say the like unto all the king's princes. So will there arise much contempt and wrath.

19If it please the king, let there go forth a royal commandment from him, and let it be written among the laws of the Persians and the Medes, that it be not altered, that Vashti come no more before king Ahasuerus; and let the king give her royal estate unto another that is better than she.

20And when the king's decree which he shall make shall be published throughout all his kingdom (for it is great), all the wives will give to their husbands honor, both to great and small.

21And the saying pleased the king and the princes; and the king did according to the word of Memucan:

22for he sent letters into all the king's provinces, into every province according to the writing thereof, and to every people after their language, that every man should bear rule in his own house, and should speak according to the language of his people.

Chapter 2

1After these things, when the wrath of king Ahasuerus was pacified, he remembered Vashti, and what she had done, and what was decreed against her.

2Then said the king's servants that ministered unto him, Let there be fair young virgins sought for the king:

3and let the king appoint officers in all the provinces of his kingdom, that they may gather together all the fair young virgins unto Shushan the palace, to the house of the women, unto the custody of Hegai the king's chamberlain, keeper of the women; and let their things for purification be given them;

4and let the maiden that pleaseth the king be queen instead of Vashti. And the thing pleased the king; and he did so.

5There was a certain Jew in Shushan the palace, whose name was Mordecai, the son of Jair, the son of Shimei, the son of Kish, a Benjamite,

6who had been carried away from Jerusalem with the captives that had been carried away with Jeconiah king of Judah, whom Nebuchadnezzar the king of Babylon had carried away.

7And he brought up Hadassah, that is, Esther, his uncle's daughter: for she had neither father nor mother, and the maiden was fair and beautiful; and when her father and mother were dead, Mordecai took her for his own daughter.

8So it came to pass, when the king's commandment and his decree was heard, and when many maidens were gathered together unto Shushan the palace, unto the custody of Hegai, that Esther was taken into the king's house, to the custody of Hegai, keeper of the women.

9And the maiden pleased him, and she obtained kindness of him; and he speedily gave her her things for purification, with her portions, and the seven maidens who were meet to be given her out of the king's house: and he removed her and her maidens to the best place of the house of the women.

10Esther had not made known her people nor her kindred; for Mordecai had charged her that she should not make it known.

11And Mordecai walked every day before the court of the women's house, to know how Esther did, and what would become of her.

12Now when the turn of every maiden was come to go in to king Ahasuerus, after that it had been done to her according to the law for the women twelve months (for so were the days of their purifications accomplished, to wit, six months with oil of myrrh, and six months with sweet odors and with the things for the purifying of the women),

13then in this wise came the maiden unto the king: whatsoever she desired was given her to go with her out of the house of the women unto the king's house.

14In the evening she went, and on the morrow she returned into the second house of the women, to the custody of Shaashgaz, the king's chamberlain, who kept the concubines: she came in unto the king no more, except the king delighted in her, and she were called by name.

15Now when the turn of Esther, the daughter of Abihail the uncle of Mordecai, who had taken her for his daughter, was come to go in unto the king, she required nothing but what Hegai the king's chamberlain, the keeper of the women, appointed. And Esther obtained favor in the sight of all them that looked upon her.

16So Esther was taken unto king Ahasuerus into his house royal in the tenth month, which is the month Tebeth, in the seventh year of his reign.

17And the king loved Esther above all the women, and she obtained favor and kindness in his sight more than all the virgins; so that he set the royal crown upon her head, and made her queen instead of Vashti.

18Then the king made a great feast unto all his princes and his servants, even Esther's feast; and he made a release to the provinces, and gave gifts, according to the bounty of the king.

19And when the virgins were gathered together the second time, then Mordecai was sitting in the king's gate.

20Esther had not yet made known her kindred nor her people; as Mordecai had charged her: for Esther did the commandment of Mordecai, like as when she was brought up with him.

21In those days, while Mordecai was sitting in the king's gate, two of the king's chamberlains, Bigthan and Teresh, of those that kept the threshold, were wroth, and sought to lay hands on the king Ahasuerus.

22And the thing became known to Mordecai, who showed it unto Esther the queen; and Esther told the king thereof in Mordecai's name.

23And when inquisition was made of the matter, and it was found to be so, they were both hanged on a tree: and it was written in the book of the chronicles before the king.

Chapter 3

1After these things did king Ahasuerus promote Haman the son of Hammedatha the Agagite, and advanced him, and set his seat above all the princes that were with him.

2And all the king's servants, that were in the king's gate, bowed down, and did reverence to Haman; for the king had so commanded concerning him. But Mordecai bowed not down, nor did him reverence.

3Then the king's servants, that were in the king's gate, said unto Mordecai, Why transgressest thou the king's commandment?

4Now it came to pass, when they spake daily unto him, and he hearkened not unto them, that they told Haman, to see whether Mordecai's matters would stand: for he had told them that he was a Jew.

5And when Haman saw that Mordecai bowed not down, nor did him reverence, then was Haman full of wrath.

6But he thought scorn to lay hands on Mordecai alone; for they had made known to him the people of Mordecai: wherefore Haman sought to destroy all the Jews that were throughout the whole kingdom of Ahasuerus, even the people of Mordecai.

7In the first month, which is the month Nisan, in the twelfth year of king Ahasuerus, they cast Pur, that is, the lot, before Haman from day to day, and from month to month, to the twelfth month, which is the month Adar.

8And Haman said unto king Ahasuerus, There is a certain people scattered abroad and dispersed among the peoples in all the provinces of thy kingdom; and their laws are diverse from those of every people; neither keep they the king's laws: therefore it is not for the king's profit to suffer them.

9If it please the king, let it be written that they be destroyed: and I will pay ten thousand talents of silver into the hands of those that have the charge of the king's business, to bring it into the king's treasuries.

10And the king took his ring from his hand, and gave it unto Haman the son of Hammedatha the Agagite, the Jews' enemy.

11And the king said unto Haman, The silver is given to thee, the people also, to do with them as it seemeth good to thee.

12Then were the king's scribes called in the first month, on the thirteenth day thereof; and there was written according to all that Haman commanded unto the king's satraps, and to the governors that were over every province, and to the princes of every people, to every province according to the writing thereof, and to every people after their language; in the name of king Ahasuerus was it written, and it was sealed with the king's ring.

13And letters were sent by posts into all the king's provinces, to destroy, to slay, and to cause to perish, all Jews, both young and old, little children and women, in one day, even upon the thirteenth day of the twelfth month, which is the month Adar, and to take the spoil of them for a prey.

14A copy of the writing, that the decree should be given out in every province, was published unto all the peoples, that they should be ready against that day.

15The posts went forth in haste by the king's commandment, and the decree was given out in Shushan the palace. And the king and Haman sat down to drink; but the city of Shushan was perplexed.

Chapter 4

1Now when Mordecai knew all that was done, Mordecai rent his clothes, and put on sackcloth with ashes, and went out into the midst of the city, and cried with a loud and a bitter cry;

2and he came even before the king's gate: for none might enter within the king's gate clothed with sackcloth.

3And in every province, whithersoever the king's commandment and his decree came, there was great mourning among the Jews, and fasting, and weeping, and wailing; and many lay in sackcloth and ashes.

4And Esther's maidens and her chamberlains came and told it her; and the queen was exceedingly grieved: and she sent raiment to clothe Mordecai, and to take his sackcloth from off him; but he received it not.

5Then called Esther for Hathach, one of the king's chamberlains, whom he had appointed to attend upon her, and charged him to go to Mordecai, to know what this was, and why it was.

6So Hathach went forth to Mordecai unto the broad place of the city, which was before the king's gate.

7And Mordecai told him of all that had happened unto him, and the exact sum of the money that Haman had promised to pay to the king's treasuries for the Jews, to destroy them.

8Also he gave him the copy of the writing of the decree that was given out in Shushan to destroy them, to show it unto Esther, and to declare it unto her, and to charge her that she should go in unto the king, to make supplication unto him, and to make request before him, for her people.

9And Hathach came and told Esther the words of Mordecai.

10Then Esther spake unto Hathach, and gave him a message unto Mordecai saying:

11All the king's servants, and the people of the king's provinces, do know, that whosoever, whether man or woman, shall come unto the king into the inner court, who is not called, there is one law for him, that he be put to death, except those to whom the king shall hold out the golden sceptre, that he may live: but I have not been called to come in unto the king these thirty days.

12And they told to Mordecai Esther's words.

13Then Mordecai bade them return answer unto Esther, Think not with thyself that thou shalt escape in the king's house, more than all the Jews.

14For if thou altogether holdest thy peace at this time, then will relief and deliverance arise to the Jews from another place, but thou and thy father's house will perish: and who knoweth whether thou art not come to the kingdom for such a time as this?

15Then Esther bade them return answer unto Mordecai,

16Go, gather together all the Jews that are present in Shushan, and fast ye for me, and neither eat nor drink three days, night or day: I also and my maidens will fast in like manner; and so will I go in unto the king, which is not according to the law: and if I perish, I perish.

17So Mordecai went his way, and did according to all that Esther had commanded him.

Chapter 5

1Now it came to pass on the third day, that Esther put on her royal apparel, and stood in the inner court of the king's house, over against the king's house: and the king sat upon his royal throne in the royal house, over against the entrance of the house.

2And it was so, when the king saw Esther the queen standing in the court, that she obtained favor in his sight; and the king held out to Esther the golden sceptre that was in his hand. So Esther drew near, and touched the top of the sceptre.

3Then said the king unto her, What wilt thou, queen Esther? and what is thy request? it shall be given thee even to the half of the kingdom.

4And Esther said, If it seem good unto the king, let the king and Haman come this day unto the banquet that I have prepared for him.

5Then the king said, Cause Haman to make haste, that it may be done as Esther hath said. So the king and Haman came to the banquet that Esther had prepared.

6And the king said unto Esther at the banquet of wine, What is thy petition? and it shall be granted thee: and what is thy request? even to the half of the kingdom it shall be performed.

7Then answered Esther, and said, My petition and my request is:

8if I have found favor in the sight of the king, and if it please the king to grant my petition, and to perform my request, let the king and Haman come to the banquet that I shall prepare for them, and I will do to-morrow as the king hath said.

9Then went Haman forth that day joyful and glad of heart: but when Haman saw Mordecai in the king's gate, that he stood not up nor moved for him, he was filled with wrath against Mordecai.

10Nevertheless Haman refrained himself, and went home; and he sent and fetched his friends and Zeresh his wife.

11And Haman recounted unto them the glory of his riches, and the multitude of his children, and all the things wherein the king had promoted him, and how he had advanced him above the princes and servants of the king.

12Haman said moreover, Yea, Esther the queen did let no man come in with the king unto the banquet that she had prepared but myself; and to-morrow also am I invited by her together with the king.

13Yet all this availeth me nothing, so long as I see Mordecai the Jew sitting at the king's gate.

14Then said Zeresh his wife and all his friends unto him, Let a gallows be made fifty cubits high, and in the morning speak thou unto the king that Mordecai may be hanged thereon: then go thou in merrily with the king unto the banquet. And the thing pleased Haman; and he caused the gallows to be made.

Chapter 6

1On that night could not the king sleep; and he commanded to bring the book of records of the chronicles, and they were read before the king.

2And it was found written, that Mordecai had told of Bigthana and Teresh, two of the king's chamberlains, of those that kept the threshold, who had sought to lay hands on the king Ahasuerus.

3And the king said, What honor and dignity hath been bestowed on Mordecai for this? Then said the king's servants that ministered unto him, There is nothing done for him.

4And the king said, Who is in the court? Now Haman was come into the outward court of the king's house, to speak unto the king to hang Mordecai on the gallows that he had prepared for him.

5And the king's servants said unto him, Behold, Haman standeth in the court. And the king said, Let him come in.

6So Haman came in. And the king said unto him, What shall be done unto the man whom the king delighteth to honor? Now Haman said in his heart, To whom would the king delight to do honor more than to myself?

7And Haman said unto the king, For the man whom the king delighteth to honor,

8let royal apparel be brought which the king useth to wear, and the horse that the king rideth upon, and on the head of which a crown royal is set:

9and let the apparel and the horse be delivered to the hand of one of the king's most noble princes, that they may array the man therewith whom the king delighteth to honor, and cause him to ride on horseback through the street of the city, and proclaim before him, Thus shall it be done to the man whom the king delighteth to honor.

10Then the king said to Haman, Make haste, and take the apparel and the horse, as thou hast said, and do even so to Mordecai the Jew, that sitteth at the king's gate: let nothing fail of all that thou hast spoken.

11Then took Haman the apparel and the horse, and arrayed Mordecai, and caused him to ride through the street of the city, and proclaimed before him, Thus shall it be done unto the man whom the king delighteth to honor.

12And Mordecai came again to the king's gate. But Haman hasted to his house, mourning and having his head covered.

13And Haman recounted unto Zeresh his wife and all his friends everything that had befallen him. Then said his wise men and Zeresh his wife unto him, If Mordecai, before whom thou hast begun to fall, be of the seed of the Jews, thou shalt not prevail against him, but shalt surely fall before him.

14While they were yet talking with him, came the king's chamberlains, and hasted to bring Haman unto the banquet that Esther had prepared.

Chapter 7

1So the king and Haman came to banquet with Esther the queen.

2And the king said again unto Esther on the second day at the banquet of wine, What is thy petition, queen Esther? and it shall be granted thee: and what is thy request? even to the half of the kingdom it shall be performed.

3Then Esther the queen answered and said, If I have found favor in thy sight, O king, and if it please the king, let my life be given me at my petition, and my people at my request:

4for we are sold, I and my people, to be destroyed, to be slain, and to perish. But if we had been sold for bondmen and bondwomen, I had held my peace, although the adversary could not have compensated for the king's damage.

5Then spake the king Ahasuerus and said unto Esther the queen, Who is he, and where is he, that durst presume in his heart to do so?

6And Esther said, An adversary and an enemy, even this wicked Haman. Then Haman was afraid before the king and the queen.

7And the king arose in his wrath from the banquet of wine and went into the palace garden: and Haman stood up to make request for his life to Esther the queen; for he saw that there was evil determined against him by the king.

8Then the king returned out of the palace garden into the place of the banquet of wine; and Haman was fallen upon the couch whereon Esther was. Then said the king, Will he even force the queen before me in the house? As the word went out of the king's mouth, they covered Haman's face.

9Then said Harbonah, one of the chamberlains that were before the king, Behold also, the gallows fifty cubits high, which Haman hath made for Mordecai, who spake good for the king, standeth in the house of Haman. And the king said, Hang him thereon.

10So they hanged Haman on the gallows that he had prepared for Mordecai. Then was the king's wrath pacified.

Esther
Chapter 8

1On that day did the king Ahasuerus give the house of Haman the Jews' enemy unto Esther the queen. And Mordecai came before the king; for Esther had told what he was unto her.

2And the king took off his ring, which he had taken from Haman, and gave it unto Mordecai. And Esther set Mordecai over the house of Haman.

3And Esther spake yet again before the king, and fell down at his feet, and besought him with tears to put away the mischief of Haman the Agagite, and his device that he had devised against the Jews.

4Then the king held out to Esther the golden sceptre. So Esther arose, and stood before the king.

5And she said, If it please the king, and if I have found favor in his sight, and the thing seem right before the king, and I be pleasing in his eyes, let it be written to reverse the letters devised by Haman, the son of Hammedatha the Agagite, which he wrote to destroy the Jews that are in all the king's provinces:

6for how can I endure to see the evil that shall come unto my people? or how can I endure to see the destruction of my kindred?

7Then the king Ahasuerus said unto Esther the queen and to Mordecai the Jew, Behold, I have given Esther the house of Haman, and him they have hanged upon the gallows, because he laid his hand upon the Jews.

8Write ye also to the Jews, as it pleaseth you, in the king's name, and seal it with the king's ring; for the writing which is written in the king's name, and sealed with the king's ring, may no man reverse.

9Then were the king's scribes called at that time, in the third month Sivan, on the three and twentieth day thereof; and it was written according to all that Mordecai commanded unto the Jews, and to the satraps, and the governors and princes of the provinces which are from India unto Ethiopia, a hundred twenty and seven provinces, unto every province according to the writing thereof, and unto every people after their language, and to the Jews according to their writing, and according to their language.

10And he wrote the name of king Ahasuerus, and sealed it with the king's ring, and sent letters by post on horseback, riding on swift steeds that were used in the king's service, bred of the stud;

11wherein the king granted the Jews that were in every city to gather themselves together, and to stand for their life, to destroy, to slay, and to cause to perish, all the power of the people and province that would assault them, their little ones and women, and to take the spoil of them for a prey,

12upon one day in all the provinces of king Ahasuerus, namely, upon the thirteenth day of the twelfth month, which is the month Adar.

13A copy of the writing, that the decree should be given out in every province, was published unto all the peoples, and that the Jews should be ready against that day to avenge themselves on their enemies.

14So the posts that rode upon swift steeds that were used in the king's service went out, being hastened and pressed on by the king's commandment; and the decree was given out in Shushan the palace.

15And Mordecai went forth from the presence of the king in royal apparel of blue and white, and with a great crown of gold, and with a robe of fine linen and purple: and the city of Shushan shouted and was glad.

16The Jews had light and gladness, and joy and honor.

17And in every province, and in every city, whithersoever the king's commandment and his decree came, the Jews had gladness and joy, a feast and a good day. And many from among the peoples of the land became Jews; for the fear of the Jews was fallen upon them.

Chapter 9

1Now in the twelfth month, which is the month Adar, on the thirteenth day of the same, when the king's commandment and his decree drew near to be put in execution, on the day that the enemies of the Jews hoped to have rule over them, (whereas it was turned to the contrary, that the Jews had rule over them that hated them,)

2the Jews gathered themselves together in their cities throughout all the provinces of the king Ahasuerus, to lay hand on such as sought their hurt: and no man could withstand them; for the fear of them was fallen upon all the peoples.

3And all the princes of the provinces, and the satraps, and the governors, and they that did the king's business, helped the Jews; because the fear of Mordecai was fallen upon them.

4For Mordecai was great in the king's house, and his fame went forth throughout all the provinces; for the man Mordecai waxed greater and greater.

5And the Jews smote all their enemies with the stroke of the sword, and with slaughter and destruction, and did what they would unto them that hated them.

6And in Shushan the palace the Jews slew and destroyed five hundred men.

7And Parshandatha, and Dalphon, and Aspatha,

8and Poratha, and Adalia, and Aridatha,

9and Parmashta, and Arisai, and Aridai, and Vaizatha,

10the ten sons of Haman the son of Hammedatha, the Jew's enemy, slew they; but on the spoil they laid not their hand.

11On that day the number of those that were slain in Shushan the palace was brought before the king.

12And the king said unto Esther the queen, The Jews have slain and destroyed five hundred men in Shushan the palace, and the ten sons of Haman; what then have they done in the rest of the king's provinces! Now what is thy petition? and it shall be granted thee: or what is thy request further? and it shall be done.

13Then said Esther, If it please the king, let it be granted to the Jews that are in Shushan to do to-morrow also according unto this day's decree, and let Haman's ten sons be hanged upon the gallows.

14And the king commanded it so to be done: and a decree was given out in Shushan; and they hanged Haman's ten sons.

15And the Jews that were in Shushan gathered themselves together on the fourteenth day also of the month Adar, and slew three hundred men in Shushan; but on the spoil they laid not their hand.

16And the other Jews that were in the king's provinces gathered themselves together, and stood for their lives, and had rest from their enemies, and slew of them that hated them seventy and five thousand; but on the spoil they laid not their hand.

17This was done on the thirteenth day of the month Adar; and on the fourteenth day of the same they rested, and made it a day of feasting and gladness.

18But the Jews that were in Shushan assembled together on the thirteenth day thereof, and on the fourteenth thereof; and on the fifteenth day of the same they rested, and made it a day of feasting and gladness.

19Therefore do the Jews of the villages, that dwell in the unwalled towns, make the fourteenth day of the month Adar a day of gladness and feasting, and a good day, and of sending portions one to another.

20And Mordecai wrote these things, and sent letters unto all the Jews that were in all the provinces of the king Ahasuerus, both nigh and far,

21to enjoin them that they should keep the fourteenth day of the month Adar, and the fifteenth day of the same, yearly,

22as the days wherein the Jews had rest from their enemies, and the month which was turned unto them from sorrow to gladness, and from mourning into a good day; that they should make them days of feasting and gladness, and of sending portions one to another, and gifts to the poor.

23And the Jews undertook to do as they had begun, and as Mordecai had written unto them;

24because Haman the son of Hammedatha, the Agagite, the enemy of all the Jews, had plotted against the Jews to destroy them, and had cast Pur, that is the lot, to consume them, and to destroy them;

25but when the matter came before the king, he commanded by letters that his wicked device, which he had devised against the Jews, should return upon his own head, and that he and his sons should be hanged on the gallows.

26Wherefore they called these days Purim, after the name of Pur. Therefore because of all the words of this letter, and of that which they had seen concerning this matter, and that which had come unto them,

27the Jews ordained, and took upon them, and upon their seed, and upon all such as joined themselves unto them, so that it should not fail, that they would keep these two days according to the writing thereof, and according to the appointed time thereof, every year;

28and that these days should be remembered and kept throughout every generation, every family, every province, and every city; and that these days of Purim should not fail from among the Jews, nor the remembrance of them perish from their seed.

29Then Esther the queen, the daughter of Abihail, and Mordecai the Jew, wrote with all authority to confirm this second letter of Purim.

30And he sent letters unto all the Jews, to the hundred twenty and seven provinces of the kingdom of Ahasuerus, with words of peace and truth,

31to confirm these days of Purim in their appointed times, according as Mordecai the Jew and Esther the queen had enjoined them, and as they had ordained for themselves and for their seed, in the matter of the fastings and their cry.

32And the commandment of Esther confirmed these matters of Purim; and it was written in the book.

Chapter 10

1And the king Ahasuerus laid a tribute upon the land, and upon the isles of the sea.

2And all the acts of his power and of his might, and the full account of the greatness of Mordecai, whereunto the king advanced him, are they not written in the book of the chronicles of the kings of Media and Persia?

3For Mordecai the Jew was next unto king Ahasuerus, and great among the Jews, and accepted of the multitude of his brethren, seeking the good of his people, and speaking peace to all his seed.

The Book of Job

Chapter 1

1There was a man in the land of Uz, whose name was Job; and that man was perfect and upright, and one that feared God, and turned away from evil.

2And there were born unto him seven sons and three daughters.

3His substance also was seven thousand sheep, and three thousand camels, and five hundred yoke of oxen, and five hundred she-asses, and a very great household; so that this man was the greatest of all the children of the east.

4And his sons went and held a feast in the house of each one upon his day; and they sent and called for their three sisters to eat and to drink with them.

5And it was so, when the days of their feasting were gone about, that Job sent and sanctified them, and rose up early in the morning, and offered burnt-offerings according to the number of them all: for Job said, It may be that my sons have sinned, and renounced God in their hearts. Thus did Job continually.

6Now it came to pass on the day when the sons of God came to present themselves before Yahweh, that Satan also came among them.

7And Yahweh said unto Satan, Whence comest thou? Then Satan answered Yahweh, and said, From going to and fro in the earth, and from walking up and down in it.

8And Yahweh said unto Satan, Hast thou considered my servant Job? for there is none like him in the earth, a perfect and an upright man, one that feareth God, and turneth away from evil.

9Then Satan answered Yahweh, and said, Doth Job fear God for nought?

10Hast not thou made a hedge about him, and about his house, and about all that he hath, on every side? thou hast blessed the work of his hands, and his substance is increased in the land.

11But put forth thy hand now, and touch all that he hath, and he will renounce thee to thy face.

12And Yahweh said unto Satan, Behold, all that he hath is in thy power; only upon himself put not forth thy hand. So Satan went forth from the presence of Yahweh.

13And it fell on a day when his sons and his daughters were eating and drinking wine in their eldest brother's house,

14that there came a messenger unto Job, and said, The oxen were plowing, and the asses feeding beside them;

15and the Sabeans fell upon them, and took them away: yea, they have slain the servants with the edge of the sword; and I only am escaped alone to tell thee.

16While he was yet speaking, there came also another, and said, The fire of God is fallen from heaven, and hath burned up the sheep and the servants, and consumed them; and I only am escaped alone to tell thee.

17While he was yet speaking, there came also another, and said, The Chaldeans made three bands, and fell upon the camels, and have taken them away, yea, and slain the servants with the edge of the sword; and I only am escaped alone to tell thee.

18While he was yet speaking, there came also another, and said, Thy sons and thy daughters were eating and drinking wine in their eldest brother's house;

19and, behold, there came a great wind from the wilderness, and smote the four corners of the house, and it fell upon the young men, and they are dead; and I only am escaped alone to tell thee.

20Then Job arose, and rent his robe, and shaved his head, and fell down upon the ground, and worshipped;

21and he said, Naked came I out of my mother's womb, and naked shall I return thither: Yahweh gave, and Yahweh hath taken away; blessed be the name of Yahweh.

22In all this Job sinned not, nor charged God foolishly.

Chapter 2

1Again it came to pass on the day when the sons of God came to present themselves before Yahweh, that Satan came also among them to present himself before Yahweh.

2And Yahweh said unto Satan, From whence comest thou? And Satan answered Yahweh, and said, From going to and fro in the earth, and from walking up and down in it.

3And Yahweh said unto Satan, Hast thou considered my servant Job? for there is none like him in the earth, a perfect and an upright man, one that feareth God, and turneth away from evil: and he still holdeth fast his integrity, although thou movedst me against him, to destroy him without cause.

4And Satan answered Yahweh, and said, Skin for skin, yea, all that a man hath will he give for his life.

5But put forth thy hand now, and touch his bone and his flesh, and he will renounce thee to thy face.

6And Yahweh said unto Satan, Behold, he is in thy hand; only spare his life.

7So Satan went forth from the presence of Yahweh, and smote Job with sore boils from the sole of his foot unto his crown.

8And he took him a potsherd to scrape himself therewith; and he sat among the ashes.

9Then said his wife unto him, Dost thou still hold fast thine integrity? renounce God, and die.

10But he said unto her, Thou speakest as one of the foolish women speaketh. What? shall we receive good at the hand of God, and shall we not receive evil? In all this did not Job sin with his lips.

11Now when Job's three friends heard of all this evil that was come upon him, they came every one from his own place: Eliphaz the Temanite, and Bildad the Shuhite, and Zophar the Naamathite, and they made an appointment together to come to bemoan him and to comfort him.

12And when they lifted up their eyes afar off, and knew him not, they lifted up their voice, and wept; and they rent every one his robe, and sprinkled dust upon their heads toward heaven.

13So they sat down with him upon the ground seven days and seven nights, and none spake a word unto him: for they saw that his grief was very great.

Chapter 3

1After this opened Job his mouth, and cursed his day.

2And Job answered and said:

3Let the day perish wherein I was born,
And the night which said, There is a man-child conceived.
4Let that day be darkness;
Let not God from above seek for it,
Neither let the light shine upon it.
5Let darkness and the shadow of death claim it for their own;
Let a cloud dwell upon it;
Let all that maketh black the day terrify it.
6As for that night, let thick darkness seize upon it:
Let it not rejoice among the days of the year;
Let it not come into the number of the months.
7Lo, let that night be barren;
Let no joyful voice come therein.
8Let them curse it that curse the day,
Who are ready to rouse up leviathan.
9Let the stars of the twilight thereof be dark:
Let it look for light, but have none;
Neither let it behold the eyelids of the morning:
10Because it shut not up the doors of my mother's womb,
Nor hid trouble from mine eyes.
11Why died I not from the womb?
Why did I not give up the ghost when my mother bare me?
12Why did the knees receive me?
Or why the breast, that I should suck?
13For now should I have lain down and been quiet;
I should have slept; then had I been at rest,
14With kings and counsellors of the earth,
Who built up waste places for themselves;
15Or with princes that had gold,
Who filled their houses with silver:
16Or as a hidden untimely birth I had not been,
As infants that never saw light.
17There the wicked cease from troubling;
And there the weary are at rest.
18There the prisoners are at ease together;
They hear not the voice of the taskmaster.
19The small and the great are there:
And the servant is free from his master.
20Wherefore is light given to him that is in misery,
And life unto the bitter in soul;
21Who long for death, but it cometh not,
And dig for it more than for hid treasures;
22Who rejoice exceedingly,
And are glad, when they can find the grave?
23Why is light given to a man whose way is hid,
And whom God hath hedged in?
24For my sighing cometh before I eat,
And my groanings are poured out like water.
25For the thing which I fear cometh upon me,
And that which I am afraid of cometh unto me.
26I am not at ease, neither am I quiet, neither have I rest;
But trouble cometh.

Chapter 4

1Then answered Eliphaz the Temanite, and said,

2If one assay to commune with thee, wilt thou be grieved?
But who can withhold himself from speaking?
3Behold, thou hast instructed many,
And thou hast strengthened the weak hands.
4Thy words have upholden him that was falling,
And thou hast made firm the feeble knees.
5But now it is come unto thee, and thou faintest;
It toucheth thee, and thou art troubled.
6Is not thy fear of God thy confidence,
And the integrity of thy ways thy hope?
7Remember, I pray thee, who ever perished, being innocent?
Or where were the upright cut off?
8According as I have seen, they that plow iniquity,
And sow trouble, reap the same.
9By the breath of God they perish,
And by the blast of his anger are they consumed.
10The roaring of the lion, and the voice of the fierce lion,
And the teeth of the young lions, are broken.
11The old lion perisheth for lack of prey,
And the whelps of the lioness are scattered abroad.
12Now a thing was secretly brought to me,
And mine ear received a whisper thereof.

Job

13 In thoughts from the visions of the night,
When deep sleep falleth on men,
14 Fear came upon me, and trembling,
Which made all my bones to shake.
15 Then a spirit passed before my face;
The hair of my flesh stood up.
16 It stood still, but I could not discern the appearance thereof;
A form was before mine eyes:
There was silence, and I heard a voice, saying,
17 Shall mortal man be more just than God?
Shall a man be more pure than his Maker?
18 Behold, he putteth no trust in his servants;
And his angels he chargeth with folly:
19 How much more them that dwell in houses of clay,
Whose foundation is in the dust,
Who are crushed before the moth!
20 Betwixt morning and evening they are destroyed:
They perish for ever without any regarding it.
21 Is not their tent-cord plucked up within them?
They die, and that without wisdom.

Chapter 5

1 Call now; is there any that will answer thee?
And to which of the holy ones wilt thou turn?
2 For vexation killeth the foolish man,
And jealousy slayeth the silly one.
3 I have seen the foolish taking root:
But suddenly I cursed his habitation.
4 His children are far from safety,
And they are crushed in the gate,
Neither is there any to deliver them:
5 Whose harvest the hungry eateth up,
And taketh it even out of the thorns;
And the snare gapeth for their substance.
6 For affliction cometh not forth from the dust,
Neither doth trouble spring out of the ground;
7 But man is born unto trouble,
As the sparks fly upward.
8 But as for me, I would seek unto God,
And unto God would I commit my cause;
9 Who doeth great things and unsearchable,
Marvellous things without number:
10 Who giveth rain upon the earth,
And sendeth waters upon the fields;
11 So that he setteth up on high those that are low,
And those that mourn are exalted to safety.
12 He frustrateth the devices of the crafty,
So that their hands cannot perform their enterprise.
13 He taketh the wise in their own craftiness;
And the counsel of the cunning is carried headlong.
14 They meet with darkness in the day-time,
And grope at noonday as in the night.
15 But he saveth from the sword of their mouth,
Even the needy from the hand of the mighty.
16 So the poor hath hope,
And iniquity stoppeth her mouth.
17 Behold, happy is the man whom God correcteth:
Therefore despise not thou the chastening of the Almighty.
18 For he maketh sore, and bindeth up;
He woundeth, and his hands make whole.
19 He will deliver thee in six troubles;
Yea, in seven there shall no evil touch thee.
20 In famine he will redeem thee from death;
And in war from the power of the sword.
21 Thou shalt be hid from the scourge of the tongue;
Neither shalt thou be afraid of destruction when it cometh.
22 At destruction and dearth thou shalt laugh;
Neither shalt thou be afraid of the beasts of the earth.
23 For thou shalt be in league with the stones of the field;
And the beasts of the field shall be at peace with thee.
24 And thou shalt know that thy tent is in peace;
And thou shalt visit thy fold, and shall miss nothing.
25 Thou shalt know also that thy seed shall be great,
And thine offspring as the grass of the earth.
26 Thou shalt come to thy grave in a full age,
Like as a shock of grain cometh in in its season.
27 Lo this, we have searched it, so it is;
Hear it, and know thou it for thy good.

Chapter 6

1 Then Job answered and said,
2 Oh that my vexation were but weighed,
And all my calamity laid in the balances!
3 For now it would be heavier than the sand of the seas:
Therefore have my words been rash.
4 For the arrows of the Almighty are within me,
The poison whereof my spirit drinketh up:
The terrors of God do set themselves in array against me.
5 Doth the wild ass bray when he hath grass?
Or loweth the ox over his fodder?
6 Can that which hath no savor be eaten without salt?
Or is there any taste in the white of an egg?
7 My soul refuseth to touch them;
They are as loathsome food to me.
8 Oh that I might have my request;
And that God would grant me the thing that I long for!
9 Even that it would please God to crush me;
That he would let loose his hand, and cut me off!
10 And be it still my consolation,
Yea, let me exult in pain that spareth not,
That I have not denied the words of the Holy One.
11 What is my strength, that I should wait?
And what is mine end, that I should be patient?
12 Is my strength the strength of stones?
Or is my flesh of brass?
13 Is it not that I have no help in me,
And that wisdom is driven quite from me?
14 To him that is ready to faint kindness should be showed from his friend;
Even to him that forsaketh the fear of the Almighty.
15 My brethren have dealt deceitfully as a brook,
As the channel of brooks that pass away;
16 Which are black by reason of the ice,
And wherein the snow hideth itself:
17 What time they wax warm, they vanish;
When it is hot, they are consumed out of their place.
18 The caravans that travel by the way of them turn aside;
They go up into the waste, and perish.
19 The caravans of Tema looked,
The companies of Sheba waited for them.
20 They were put to shame because they had hoped;
They came thither, and were confounded.
21 For now ye are nothing;
Ye see a terror, and are afraid.
22 Did I say, Give unto me?
Or, Offer a present for me of your substance?
23 Or, Deliver me from the adversary's hand?
Or, Redeem me from the hand of the oppressors?
24 Teach me, and I will hold my peace;
And cause me to understand wherein I have erred.
25 How forcible are words of uprightness!
But your reproof, what doth it reprove?
26 Do ye think to reprove words,
Seeing that the speeches of one that is desperate are as wind?
27 Yea, ye would cast lots upon the fatherless,
And make merchandise of your friend.
28 Now therefore be pleased to look upon me;
For surely I shall not lie to your face.
29 Return, I pray you, let there be no injustice;
Yea, return again, my cause is righteous.
30 Is there injustice on my tongue?
Cannot my taste discern mischievous things?

Chapter 7

1 Is there not a warfare to man upon earth?
And are not his days like the days of a hireling?
2 As a servant that earnestly desireth the shadow,
And as a hireling that looketh for his wages:
3 So am I made to possess months of misery,
And wearisome nights are appointed to me.
4 When I lie down, I say,
When shall I arise, and the night be gone?
And I am full of tossings to and fro unto the dawning of the day.
5 My flesh is clothed with worms and clods of dust;
My skin closeth up, and breaketh out afresh.
6 My days are swifter than a weaver's shuttle,
And are spent without hope.
7 Oh remember that my life is a breath:
Mine eye shall no more see good.
8 The eye of him that seeth me shall behold me no more;
Thine eyes shall be upon me, but I shall not be.
9 As the cloud is consumed and vanisheth away,
So he that goeth down to Sheol shall come up no more.
10 He shall return no more to his house,
Neither shall his place know him any more.
11 Therefore I will not refrain my mouth;
I will speak in the anguish of my spirit;
I will complain in the bitterness of my soul.
12 Am I a sea, or a sea-monster,
That thou settest a watch over me?
13 When I say, My bed shall comfort me,
My couch shall ease my complaint;
14 Then thou scarest me with dreams,
And terrifiest me through visions:
15 So that my soul chooseth strangling,
And death rather than these my bones.
16 I loathe my life; I would not live alway:
Let me alone; for my days are vanity.

17What is man, that thou shouldest magnify him,
And that thou shouldest set thy mind upon him,
18And that thou shouldest visit him every morning,
And try him every moment?
19How long wilt thou not look away from me,
Nor let me alone till I swallow down my spittle?
20If I have sinned, what do I unto thee, O thou watcher of men?
Why hast thou set me as a mark for thee,
So that I am a burden to myself?
21And why dost thou not pardon my transgression, and take away mine iniquity?
For now shall I lie down in the dust;
And thou wilt seek me diligently, but I shall not be.

Chapter 8

1Then answered Bildad the Shuhite, and said,
2How long wilt thou speak these things?
And how long shall the words of thy mouth be like a mighty wind?
3Doth God pervert justice?
Or doth the Almighty pervert righteousness?
4If thy children have sinned against him,
And he hath delivered them into the hand of their transgression;
5If thou wouldest seek diligently unto God,
And make thy supplication to the Almighty;
6If thou wert pure and upright;
Surely now he would awake for thee,
And make the habitation of thy righteousness prosperous.
7And though thy beginning was small,
Yet thy latter end would greatly increase.
8For inquire, I pray thee, of the former age,
And apply thyself to that which their fathers have searched out:
9(For we are but of yesterday, and know nothing,
Because our days upon earth are a shadow);
10Shall not they teach thee, and tell thee,
And utter words out of their heart?
11Can the rush grow up without mire?
Can the flag grow without water?
12Whilst it is yet in its greenness, and not cut down,
It withereth before any other herb.
13So are the paths of all that forget God;
And the hope of the godless man shall perish:
14Whose confidence shall break in sunder,
And whose trust is a spider's web.
15He shall lean upon his house, but it shall not stand:
He shall hold fast thereby, but it shall not endure.
16He is green before the sun,
And his shoots go forth over his garden.
17His roots are wrapped about the stone-heap,
He beholdeth the place of stones.
18If he be destroyed from his place,
Then it shall deny him, saying, I have not seen thee.
19Behold, this is the joy of his way;
And out of the earth shall others spring.
20Behold, God will not cast away a perfect man,
Neither will he uphold the evil-doers.
21He will yet fill thy mouth with laughter,
And thy lips with shouting.
22They that hate thee shall be clothed with shame;
And the tent of the wicked shall be no more.

Chapter 9

1Then Job answered and said,
2Of a truth I know that it is so:
But how can man be just with God?
3If he be pleased to contend with him,
He cannot answer him one of a thousand.
4He is wise in heart, and mighty in strength:
Who hath hardened himself against him, and prospered?-
5Him that removeth the mountains, and they know it not,
When he overturneth them in his anger;
6That shaketh the earth out of its place,
And the pillars thereof tremble;
7That commandeth the sun, and it riseth not,
And sealeth up the stars;
8That alone stretcheth out the heavens,
And treadeth upon the waves of the sea;
9That maketh the Bear, Orion, and the Pleiades,
And the chambers of the south;
10That doeth great things past finding out,
Yea, marvellous things without number.
11Lo, he goeth by me, and I see him not:
He passeth on also, but I perceive him not.
12Behold, he seizeth the prey, who can hinder him?
Who will say unto him, What doest thou?
13God will not withdraw his anger;
The helpers of Rahab do stoop under him.
14How much less shall I answer him,
And choose out my words to reason with him?
15Whom, though I were righteous, yet would I not answer;
I would make supplication to my judge.
16If I had called, and he had answered me,
Yet would I not believe that he hearkened unto my voice.
17For he breaketh me with a tempest,
And multiplieth my wounds without cause.
18He will not suffer me to take my breath,
But filleth me with bitterness.
19If we speak of strength, lo, he is mighty!
And if of justice, Who, saith he, will summon me?
20Though I be righteous, mine own mouth shall condemn me:
Though I be perfect, it shall prove me perverse.
21I am perfect; I regard not myself;
I despise my life.
22It is all one; therefore I say,
He destroyeth the perfect and the wicked.
23If the scourge slay suddenly,
He will mock at the trial of the innocent.
24The earth is given into the hand of the wicked;
He covereth the faces of the judges thereof:
If it be not he, who then is it?
25Now my days are swifter than a post:
They flee away, they see no good,
26They are passed away as the swift ships;
As the eagle that swoopeth on the prey.
27If I say, I will forget my complaint,
I will put off my sad countenance, and be of good cheer;
28I am afraid of all my sorrows,
I know that thou wilt not hold me innocent.
29I shall be condemned;
Why then do I labor in vain?
30If I wash myself with snow water,
And make my hands never so clean;
31Yet wilt thou plunge me in the ditch,
And mine own clothes shall abhor me.
32For he is not a man, as I am, that I should answer him,
That we should come together in judgment.
33There is no umpire betwixt us,
That might lay his hand upon us both.
34Let him take his rod away from me,
And let not his terror make me afraid:
35Then would I speak, and not fear him;
For I am not so in myself.

Chapter 10

1My soul is weary of my life;
I will give free course to my complaint;
I will speak in the bitterness of my soul.
2I will say unto God, Do not condemn me;
Show me wherefore thou contendest with me.
3Is it good unto thee that thou shouldest oppress,
That thou shouldest despise the work of thy hands,
And shine upon the counsel of the wicked?
4Hast thou eyes of flesh?
Or seest thou as man seeth?
5Are thy days as the days of man,
Or thy years as man's days,
6That thou inquirest after mine iniquity,
And searchest after my sin,
7Although thou knowest that I am not wicked,
And there is none that can deliver out of thy hand?
8Thy hands have framed me and fashioned me
Together round about; yet thou dost destroy me.
9Remember, I beseech thee, that thou hast fashioned me as clay;
And wilt thou bring me into dust again?
10Hast thou not poured me out as milk,
And curdled me like cheese?
11Thou hast clothed me with skin and flesh,
And knit me together with bones and sinews.
12Thou hast granted me life and lovingkindness;
And thy visitation hath preserved my spirit.
13Yet these things thou didst hide in thy heart;
I know that this is with thee:
14If I sin, then thou markest me,
And thou wilt not acquit me from mine iniquity.
15If I be wicked, woe unto me;
And if I be righteous, yet shall I not lift up my head;
Being filled with ignominy,
And looking upon mine affliction.
16And if my head exalt itself, thou huntest me as a lion;
And again thou showest thyself marvellous upon me.
17Thou renewest thy witnesses against me,
And increasest thine indignation upon me:
Changes and warfare are with me.
18Wherefore then hast thou brought me forth out of the womb?
I had given up the ghost, and no eye had seen me.
19I should have been as though I had not been;
I should have been carried from the womb to the grave.
20Are not my days few? cease then,

And let me alone, that I may take comfort a little,
21Before I go whence I shall not return,
Even to the land of darkness and of the shadow of death;
22The land dark as midnight,
The land of the shadow of death, without any order,
And where the light is as midnight.

Chapter 11

1Then answered Zophar the Naamathite, and said,
2Should not the multitude of words be answered?
And should a man full of talk be justified?
3Should thy boastings make men hold their peace?
And when thou mockest, shall no man make thee ashamed?
4For thou sayest, My doctrine is pure,
And I am clean in thine eyes.
5But oh that God would speak,
And open his lips against thee,
6And that he would show thee the secrets of wisdom!
For he is manifold in understanding.
Know therefore that God exacteth of thee less than thine iniquity deserveth.
7Canst thou by searching find out God?
Canst thou find out the Almighty unto perfection?
8It is high as heaven; what canst thou do?
Deeper than Sheol; what canst thou know?
9The measure thereof is longer than the earth,
And broader than the sea.
10If he pass through, and shut up,
And all unto judgment, then who can hinder him?
11For he knoweth false men;
He seeth iniquity also, even though he consider it not.
12But vain man is void of understanding,
Yea, man is born as a wild ass's colt.
13If thou set thy heart aright,
And stretch out thy hands toward him;
14If iniquity be in thy hand, put it far away,
And let not unrighteousness dwell in thy tents.
15Surely then shalt thou lift up thy face without spot;
Yea, thou shalt be stedfast, and shalt not fear:
16For thou shalt forget thy misery;
Thou shalt remember it as waters that are passed away,
17And thy life shall be clearer than the noonday;
Though there be darkness, it shall be as the morning.
18And thou shalt be secure, because there is hope;
Yea, thou shalt search about thee, and shalt take thy rest in safety.
19Also thou shalt lie down, and none shall make thee afraid;
Yea, many shall make suit unto thee.
20But the eyes of the wicked shall fail,
And they shall have no way to flee;
And their hope shall be the giving up of the ghost.

Chapter 12

1Then Job answered and said,
2No doubt but ye are the people,
And wisdom shall die with you.
3But I have understanding as well as you;
I am not inferior to you:
Yea, who knoweth not such things as these?
4I am as one that is a laughing-stock to his neighbor,
I who called upon God, and he answered:
The just, the perfect man is a laughing-stock.
5In the thought of him that is at ease there is contempt for misfortune;
It is ready for them whose foot slippeth.
6The tents of robbers prosper,
And they that provoke God are secure;
Into whose hand God bringeth abundantly.
7But ask now the beasts, and they shall teach thee;
And the birds of the heavens, and they shall tell thee:
8Or speak to the earth, and it shall teach thee;
And the fishes of the sea shall declare unto thee.
9Who knoweth not in all these,
That the hand of Yahweh hath wrought this,
10In whose hand is the soul of every living thing,
And the breath of all mankind?
11Doth not the ear try words,
Even as the palate tasteth its food?
12With aged men is wisdom,
And in length of days understanding.
13With God is wisdom and might;
He hath counsel and understanding.
14Behold, he breaketh down, and it cannot be built again;
He shutteth up a man, and there can be no opening.
15Behold, he withholdeth the waters, and they dry up;
Again, he sendeth them out, and they overturn the earth.
16With him is strength and wisdom;
The deceived and the deceiver are his.
17He leadeth counsellors away stripped,
And judges maketh he fools.
18He looseth the bond of kings,
And he bindeth their loins with a girdle.
19He leadeth priests away stripped,
And overthroweth the mighty.
20He removeth the speech of the trusty,
And taketh away the understanding of the elders.
21He poureth contempt upon princes,
And looseth the belt of the strong.
22He uncovereth deep things out of darkness,
And bringeth out to light the shadow of death.
23He increaseth the nations, and he destroyeth them:
He enlargeth the nations, and he leadeth them captive.
24He taketh away understanding from the chiefs of the people of the earth,
And causeth them to wander in a wilderness where there is no way.
25They grope in the dark without light;
And he maketh them to stagger like a drunken man.

Chapter 13

1Lo, mine eye hath seen all this,
Mine ear hath heard and understood it.
2What ye know, the same do I know also:
I am not inferior unto you.
3Surely I would speak to the Almighty,
And I desire to reason with God.
4But ye are forgers of lies;
Ye are all physicians of no value.
5Oh that ye would altogether hold your peace!
And it would be your wisdom.
6Hear now my reasoning,
And hearken to the pleadings of my lips.
7Will ye speak unrighteously for God,
And talk deceitfully for him?
8Will ye show partiality to him?
Will ye contend for God?
9Is it good that he should search you out?
Or as one deceiveth a man, will ye deceive him?
10He will surely reprove you
If ye do secretly show partiality.
11Shall not his majesty make you afraid,
And his dread fall upon you?
12Your memorable sayings are proverbs of ashes,
Your defences are defences of clay.
13Hold your peace, let me alone, that I may speak;
And let come on me what will.
14Wherefore should I take my flesh in my teeth,
And put my life in my hand?
15Behold, he will slay me; I have no hope:
Nevertheless I will maintain my ways before him.
16This also shall be my salvation,
That a godless man shall not come before him.
17Hear diligently my speech,
And let my declaration be in your ears.
18Behold now, I have set my cause in order;
I know that I am righteous.
19Who is he that will contend with me?
For then would I hold my peace and give up the ghost.
20Only do not two things unto me;
Then will I not hide myself from thy face:
21Withdraw thy hand far from me;
And let not thy terror make me afraid.
22Then call thou, and I will answer;
Or let me speak, and answer thou me.
23How many are mine iniquities and sins?
Make me to know my transgression and my sin.
24Wherefore hidest thou thy face,
And holdest me for thine enemy?
25Wilt thou harass a driven leaf?
And wilt thou pursue the dry stubble?
26For thou writest bitter things against me,
And makest me to inherit the iniquities of my youth:
27Thou puttest my feet also in the stocks,
And markest all my paths;
Thou settest a bound to the soles of my feet:
28Though I am like a rotten thing that consumeth,
Like a garment that is moth-eaten.

Chapter 14

1Man, that is born of a woman,
Is of few days, and full of trouble.
2He cometh forth like a flower, and is cut down:
He fleeth also as a shadow, and continueth not.
3And dost thou open thine eyes upon such a one,
And bringest me into judgment with thee?
4Who can bring a clean thing out of an unclean? not one.
5Seeing his days are determined,
The number of his months is with thee,
And thou hast appointed his bounds that he cannot pass;
6Look away from him, that he may rest,
Till he shall accomplish, as a hireling, his day.

7For there is hope of a tree,
If it be cut down, that it will sprout again,
And that the tender branch thereof will not cease.
8Though the root thereof wax old in the earth,
And the stock thereof die in the ground;
9Yet through the scent of water it will bud,
And put forth boughs like a plant.
10But man dieth, and is laid low:
Yea, man giveth up the ghost, and where is he?
11As the waters fail from the sea,
And the river wasteth and drieth up;
12So man lieth down and riseth not:
Till the heavens be no more, they shall not awake,
Nor be roused out of their sleep.
13Oh that thou wouldest hide me in Sheol,
That thou wouldest keep me secret, until thy wrath be past,
That thou wouldest appoint me a set time, and remember me!
14If a man die, shall he live again?
All the days of my warfare would I wait,
Till my release should come.
15Thou wouldest call, and I would answer thee:
Thou wouldest have a desire to the work of thy hands.
16But now thou numberest my steps:
Dost thou not watch over my sin?
17My transgression is sealed up in a bag,
And thou fastenest up mine iniquity.
18But the mountain falling cometh to nought;
And the rock is removed out of its place;
19The waters wear the stones;
The overflowings thereof wash away the dust of the earth:
So thou destroyest the hope of man.
20Thou prevailest for ever against him, and he passeth;
Thou changest his countenance, and sendest him away.
21His sons come to honor, and he knoweth it not;
And they are brought low, but he perceiveth it not of them.
22But his flesh upon him hath pain,
And his soul within him mourneth.

Chapter 15

1Then answered Eliphaz the Temanite, and said,
2Should a wise man make answer with vain knowledge,
And fill himself with the east wind?
3Should he reason with unprofitable talk,
Or with speeches wherewith he can do no good?
4Yea, thou doest away with fear,
And hinderest devotion before God.
5For thine iniquity teacheth thy mouth,
And thou choosest the tongue of the crafty.
6Thine own mouth condemneth thee, and not I;
Yea, thine own lips testify against thee.
7Art thou the first man that was born?
Or wast thou brought forth before the hills?
8Hast thou heard the secret counsel of God?
And dost thou limit wisdom to thyself?
9What knowest thou, that we know not?
What understandest thou, which is not in us?
10With us are both the gray-headed and the very aged men,
Much elder than thy father.
11Are the consolations of God too small for thee,
Even the word that is gentle toward thee?
12Why doth thy heart carry thee away?
And why do thine eyes flash,
13That against God thou turnest thy spirit,
And lettest words go out of thy mouth?
14What is man, that he should be clean?
And he that is born of a woman, that he should be righteous?
15Behold, he putteth no trust in his holy ones;
Yea, the heavens are not clean in his sight:
16How much less one that is abominable and corrupt,
A man that drinketh iniquity like water!
17I will show thee, hear thou me;
And that which I have seen I will declare:
18(Which wise men have told
From their fathers, and have not hid it;
19Unto whom alone the land was given,
And no stranger passed among them):
20The wicked man travaileth with pain all his days,
Even the number of years that are laid up for the oppressor.
21A sound of terrors is in his ears;
In prosperity the destroyer shall come upon him.
22He believeth not that he shall return out of darkness,
And he is waited for of the sword.
23He wandereth abroad for bread, saying, Where is it?
He knoweth that the day of darkness is ready at his hand.
24Distress and anguish make him afraid;
They prevail against him, as a king ready to the battle.
25Because he hath stretched out his hand against God,
And behaveth himself proudly against the Almighty;
26He runneth upon him with a stiff neck,
With the thick bosses of his bucklers;
27Because he hath covered his face with his fatness,
And gathered fat upon his loins;
28And he hath dwelt in desolate cities,
In houses which no man inhabited,
Which were ready to become heaps;
29He shall not be rich, neither shall his substance continue,
Neither shall their possessions be extended on the earth.
30He shall not depart out of darkness;
The flame shall dry up his branches,
And by the breath of God's mouth shall he go away.
31Let him not trust in vanity, deceiving himself;
For vanity shall be his recompense.
32It shall be accomplished before his time,
And his branch shall not be green.
33He shall shake off his unripe grape as the vine,
And shall cast off his flower as the olive-tree.
34For the company of the godless shall be barren,
And fire shall consume the tents of bribery.
35They conceive mischief, and bring forth iniquity,
And their heart prepareth deceit.

Chapter 16

1Then Job answered and said,
2I have heard many such things:
Miserable comforters are ye all.
3Shall vain words have an end?
Or what provoketh thee that thou answerest?
4I also could speak as ye do;
If your soul were in my soul's stead,
I could join words together against you,
And shake my head at you.
5But I would strengthen you with my mouth,
And the solace of my lips would assuage your grief.
6Though I speak, my grief is not assuaged;
And though I forbear, what am I eased?
7But now he hath made me weary:
Thou hast made desolate all my company.
8And thou hast laid fast hold on me, which is a witness against me:
And my leanness riseth up against me,
It testifieth to my face.
9He hath torn me in his wrath, and persecuted me;
He hath gnashed upon me with his teeth:
Mine adversary sharpeneth his eyes upon me.
10They have gaped upon me with their mouth;
They have smitten me upon the cheek reproachfully:
They gather themselves together against me.
11God delivereth me to the ungodly,
And casteth me into the hands of the wicked.
12I was at ease, and he brake me asunder;
Yea, he hath taken me by the neck, and dashed me to pieces:
He hath also set me up for his mark.
13His archers compass me round about;
He cleaveth my reins asunder, and doth not spare;
He poureth out my gall upon the ground.
14He breaketh me with breach upon breach;
He runneth upon me like a giant.
15I have sewed sackcloth upon my skin,
And have laid my horn in the dust.
16My face is red with weeping,
And on my eyelids is the shadow of death;
17Although there is no violence in my hands,
And my prayer is pure.
18O earth, cover not thou my blood,
And let my cry have no resting-place.
19Even now, behold, my witness is in heaven,
And he that voucheth for me is on high.
20My friends scoff at me;
But mine eye poureth out tears unto God,
21That he would maintain the right of a man with God,
And of a son of man with his neighbor!
22For when a few years are come,
I shall go the way whence I shall not return.

Chapter 17

1My spirit is consumed, my days are extinct,
The grave is ready for me.
2Surely there are mockers with me,
And mine eye dwelleth upon their provocation.
3Give now a pledge, be surety for me with thyself;
Who is there that will strike hands with me?
4For thou hast hid their heart from understanding:
Therefore shalt thou not exalt them.
5He that denounceth his friends for a prey,
Even the eyes of his children shall fail.
6But he hath made me a byword of the people;
And they spit in my face.
7Mine eye also is dim by reason of sorrow,

And all my members are as a shadow.
8Upright men shall be astonished at this,
And the innocent shall stir up himself against the godless.
9Yet shall the righteous hold on his way,
And he that hath clean hands shall wax stronger and stronger.
10But as for you all, come on now again;
And I shall not find a wise man among you.
11My days are past, my purposes are broken off,
Even the thoughts of my heart.
12They change the night into day:
The light, say they, is near unto the darkness.
13If I look for Sheol as my house;
If I have spread my couch in the darkness;
14If I have said to corruption, Thou art my father;
To the worm, Thou art my mother, and my sister;
15Where then is my hope?
And as for my hope, who shall see it?
16It shall go down to the bars of Sheol,
When once there is rest in the dust.

Chapter 18

1Then answered Bildad the Shuhite, and said,
2How long will ye hunt for words?
Consider, and afterwards we will speak.
3Wherefore are we counted as beasts,
And are become unclean in your sight?
4Thou that tearest thyself in thine anger,
Shall the earth be forsaken for thee?
Or shall the rock be removed out of its place?
5Yea, the light of the wicked shall be put out,
And the spark of his fire shall not shine.
6The light shall be dark in his tent,
And his lamp above him shall be put out.
7The steps of his strength shall be straitened,
And his own counsel shall cast him down.
8For he is cast into a net by his own feet,
And he walketh upon the toils.
9A gin shall take him by the heel,
And a snare shall lay hold on him.
10A noose is hid for him in the ground,
And a trap for him in the way.
11Terrors shall make him afraid on every side,
And shall chase him at his heels.
12His strength shall be hunger-bitten,
And calamity shall be ready at his side.
13The members of his body shall be devoured,
Yea, the first-born of death shall devour his members.
14He shall be rooted out of his tent where he trusteth;
And he shall be brought to the king of terrors.
15There shall dwell in his tent that which is none of his:
Brimstone shall be scattered upon his habitation.
16His roots shall be dried up beneath,
And above shall his branch be cut off.
17His remembrance shall perish from the earth,
And he shall have no name in the street.
18He shall be driven from light into darkness,
And chased out of the world.
19He shall have neither son nor son's son among his people,
Nor any remaining where he sojourned.
20They that come after shall be astonished at his day,
As they that went before were affrighted.
21Surely such are the dwellings of the unrighteous,
And this is the place of him that knoweth not God.

Chapter 19

1Then Job answered and said,
2How long will ye vex my soul,
And break me in pieces with words?
3These ten times have ye reproached me:
Ye are not ashamed that ye deal hardly with me.
4And be it indeed that I have erred,
Mine error remaineth with myself.
5If indeed ye will magnify yourselves against me,
And plead against me my reproach;
6Know now that God hath subverted me in my cause,
And hath compassed me with his net.
7Behold, I cry out of wrong, but I am not heard:
I cry for help, but there is no justice.
8He hath walled up my way that I cannot pass,
And hath set darkness in my paths.
9He hath stripped me of my glory,
And taken the crown from my head.
10He hath broken me down on every side, and I am gone;
And my hope hath he plucked up like a tree.
11He hath also kindled his wrath against me,
And he counteth me unto him as one of his adversaries.
12His troops come on together,
And cast up their way against me,
And encamp round about my tent.
13He hath put my brethren far from me,
And mine acquaintance are wholly estranged from me.
14My kinsfolk have failed,
And my familiar friends have forgotten me.
15They that dwell in my house, and my maids, count me for a stranger;
I am an alien in their sight.
16I call unto my servant, and he giveth me no answer,
Though I entreat him with my mouth.
17My breath is strange to my wife,
And my supplication to the children of mine own mother.
18Even young children despise me;
If I arise, they speak against me.
19All my familiar friends abhor me,
And they whom I loved are turned against me.
20My bone cleaveth to my skin and to my flesh,
And I am escaped with the skin of my teeth.
21Have pity upon me, have pity upon me, O ye my friends;
For the hand of God hath touched me.
22Why do ye persecute me as God,
And are not satisfied with my flesh?
23Oh that my words were now written!
Oh that they were inscribed in a book!
24That with an iron pen and lead
They were graven in the rock for ever!
25But as for me I know that my Redeemer liveth,
And at last he will stand up upon the earth:
26And after my skin, even this body, is destroyed,
Then without my flesh shall I see God;
27Whom I, even I, shall see, on my side,
And mine eyes shall behold, and not as a stranger.
My heart is consumed within me.
28If ye say, How we will persecute him!
And that the root of the matter is found in me;
29Be ye afraid of the sword:
For wrath bringeth the punishments of the sword,
That ye may know there is a judgment.

Chapter 20

1Then answered Zophar the Naamathite, and said,
2Therefore do my thoughts give answer to me,
Even by reason of my haste that is in me.
3I have heard the reproof which putteth me to shame;
And the spirit of my understanding answereth me.
4Knowest thou not this of old time,
Since man was placed upon earth,
5That the triumphing of the wicked is short,
And the joy of the godless but for a moment?
6Though his height mount up to the heavens,
And his head reach unto the clouds;
7Yet he shall perish for ever like his own dung:
They that have seen him shall say, Where is he?
8He shall fly away as a dream, and shall not be found:
Yea, he shall be chased away as a vision of the night.
9The eye which saw him shall see him no more;
Neither shall his place any more behold him.
10His children shall seek the favor of the poor,
And his hands shall give back his wealth.
11His bones are full of his youth,
But it shall lie down with him in the dust.
12Though wickedness be sweet in his mouth,
Though he hide it under his tongue,
13Though he spare it, and will not let it go,
But keep it still within his mouth;
14Yet his food in his bowels is turned,
It is the gall of asps within him.
15He hath swallowed down riches, and he shall vomit them up again;
God will cast them out of his belly.
16He shall suck the poison of asps:
The viper's tongue shall slay him.
17He shall not look upon the rivers,
The flowing streams of honey and butter.
18That which he labored for shall he restore, and shall not swallow it down;
According to the substance that he hath gotten, he shall not rejoice.
19For he hath oppressed and forsaken the poor;
He hath violently taken away a house, and he shall not build it up.
20Because he knew no quietness within him,
He shall not save aught of that wherein he delighteth.
21There was nothing left that he devoured not;
Therefore his prosperity shall not endure.
22In the fulness of his sufficiency he shall be in straits:
The hand of every one that is in misery shall come upon him.
23When he is about to fill his belly, God will cast the fierceness of his wrath upon him,
And will rain it upon him while he is eating.
24He shall flee from the iron weapon,
And the bow of brass shall strike him through.
25He draweth it forth, and it cometh out of his body;
Yea, the glittering point cometh out of his gall:

Terrors are upon him.
26All darkness is laid up for his treasures:
A fire not blown by man shall devour him;
It shall consume that which is left in his tent.
27The heavens shall reveal his iniquity,
And the earth shall rise up against him.
28The increase of his house shall depart;
His goods shall flow away in the day of his wrath.
29This is the portion of a wicked man from God,
And the heritage appointed unto him by God.

Chapter 21

1Then Job answered and said,
2Hear diligently my speech;
And let this be your consolations.
3Suffer me, and I also will speak;
And after that I have spoken, mock on.
4As for me, is my complaint to man?
And why should I not be impatient?
5Mark me, and be astonished,
And lay your hand upon your mouth.
6Even when I remember I am troubled,
And horror taketh hold on my flesh.
7Wherefore do the wicked live,
Become old, yea, wax mighty in power?
8Their seed is established with them in their sight,
And their offspring before their eyes.
9Their houses are safe from fear,
Neither is the rod of God upon them.
10Their bull gendereth, and faileth not;
Their cow calveth, and casteth not her calf.
11They send forth their little ones like a flock,
And their children dance.
12They sing to the timbrel and harp,
And rejoice at the sound of the pipe.
13They spend their days in prosperity,
And in a moment they go down to Sheol.
14And they say unto God, Depart from us;
For we desire not the knowledge of thy ways.
15What is the Almighty, that we should serve him?
And what profit should we have, if we pray unto him?
16Lo, their prosperity is not in their hand:
The counsel of the wicked is far from me.
17How oft is it that the lamp of the wicked is put out?
That their calamity cometh upon them?
That God distributeth sorrows in his anger?
18That they are as stubble before the wind,
And as chaff that the storm carrieth away?
19Ye say, God layeth up his iniquity for his children.
Let him recompense it unto himself, that he may know it:
20Let his own eyes see his destruction,
And let him drink of the wrath of the Almighty.
21For what careth he for his house after him,
When the number of his months is cut off?
22Shall any teach God knowledge,
Seeing he judgeth those that are high?
23One dieth in his full strength,
Being wholly at ease and quiet:
24His pails are full of milk,
And the marrow of his bones is moistened.
25And another dieth in bitterness of soul,
And never tasteth of good.
26They lie down alike in the dust,
And the worm covereth them.
27Behold, I know your thoughts,
And the devices wherewith ye would wrong me.
28For ye say, Where is the house of the prince?
And where is the tent wherein the wicked dwelt?
29Have ye not asked wayfaring men?
And do ye not know their evidences,
30That the evil man is reserved to the day of calamity?
That they are led forth to the day of wrath?
31Who shall declare his way to his face?
And who shall repay him what he hath done?
32Yet shall he be borne to the grave,
And men shall keep watch over the tomb.
33The clods of the valley shall be sweet unto him,
And all men shall draw after him,
As there were innumerable before him.
34How then comfort ye me in vain,
Seeing in your answers there remaineth only falsehood?

Chapter 22

1Then answered Eliphaz the Temanite, and said,
2Can a man be profitable unto God?
Surely he that is wise is profitable unto himself.
3Is it any pleasure to the Almighty, that thou art righteous?
Or is it gain to him, that thou makest thy ways perfect?
4Is it for thy fear of him that he reproveth thee,
That he entereth with thee into judgment?
5Is not thy wickedness great?
Neither is there any end to thine iniquities.
6For thou hast taken pledges of thy brother for nought,
And stripped the naked of their clothing.
7Thou hast not given water to the weary to drink,
And thou hast withholden bread from the hungry.
8But as for the mighty man, he had the earth;
And the honorable man, he dwelt in it.
9Thou hast sent widows away empty,
And the arms of the fatherless have been broken.
10Therefore snares are round about thee,
And sudden fear troubleth thee,
11Or darkness, so that thou canst not see,
And abundance of waters cover thee.
12Is not God in the height of heaven?
And behold the height of the stars, how high they are!
13And thou sayest, What doth God know?
Can he judge through the thick darkness?
14Thick clouds are a covering to him, so that he seeth not;
And he walketh on the vault of heaven.
15Wilt thou keep the old way
Which wicked men have trodden?
16Who were snatched away before their time,
Whose foundation was poured out as a stream,
17Who said unto God, Depart from us;
And, What can the Almighty do for us?
18Yet he filled their houses with good things:
But the counsel of the wicked is far from me.
19The righteous see it, and are glad;
And the innocent laugh them to scorn,
20Saying, Surely they that did rise up against us are cut off,
And the remnant of them the fire hath consumed.
21Acquaint now thyself with him, and be at peace:
Thereby good shall come unto thee.
22Receive, I pray thee, the law from his mouth,
And lay up his words in thy heart.
23If thou return to the Almighty, thou shalt be built up,
If thou put away unrighteousness far from thy tents.
24And lay thou thy treasure in the dust,
And the gold of Ophir among the stones of the brooks;
25And the Almighty will be thy treasure,
And precious silver unto thee.
26For then shalt thou delight thyself in the Almighty,
And shalt lift up thy face unto God.
27Thou shalt make thy prayer unto him, and he will hear thee;
And thou shalt pay thy vows.
28Thou shalt also decree a thing, and it shall be established unto thee;
And light shall shine upon thy ways.
29When they cast thee down, thou shalt say, There is lifting up;
And the humble person he will save.
30He will deliver even him that is not innocent:
Yea, he shall be delivered through the cleanness of thy hands.

Chapter 23

1Then Job answered and said,
2Even to-day is my complaint rebellious:
My stroke is heavier than my groaning.
3Oh that I knew where I might find him!
That I might come even to his seat!
4I would set my cause in order before him,
And fill my mouth with arguments.
5I would know the words which he would answer me,
And understand what he would say unto me.
6Would he contend with me in the greatness of his power?
Nay; but he would give heed unto me.
7There the upright might reason with him;
So should I be delivered for ever from my judge.
8Behold, I go forward, but he is not there;
And backward, but I cannot perceive him;
9On the left hand, when he doth work, but I cannot behold him;
He hideth himself on the right hand, that I cannot see him.
10But he knoweth the way that I take;
When he hath tried me, I shall come forth as gold.
11My foot hath held fast to his steps;
His way have I kept, and turned not aside.
12I have not gone back from the commandment of his lips;
I have treasured up the words of his mouth more than my necessary food.
13But he is in one mind, and who can turn him?
And what his soul desireth, even that he doeth.
14For he performeth that which is appointed for me:
And many such things are with him.
15Therefore am I terrified at his presence;
When I consider, I am afraid of him.
16For God hath made my heart faint,
And the Almighty hath terrified me;
17Because I was not cut off before the darkness,
Neither did he cover the thick darkness from my face.

Job

Chapter 24

1 Why are times not laid up by the Almighty?
And why do not they that know him see his days?
2 There are that remove the landmarks;
They violently take away flocks, and feed them.
3 They drive away the ass of the fatherless;
They take the widow's ox for a pledge.
4 They turn the needy out of the way:
The poor of the earth all hide themselves.
5 Behold, as wild asses in the desert
They go forth to their work, seeking diligently for food;
The wilderness yieldeth them bread for their children.
6 They cut their provender in the field;
And they glean the vintage of the wicked.
7 They lie all night naked without clothing,
And have no covering in the cold.
8 They are wet with the showers of the mountains,
And embrace the rock for want of a shelter.
9 There are that pluck the fatherless from the breast,
And take a pledge of the poor:
10 So that they go about naked without clothing,
And being hungry they carry the sheaves.
11 They make oil within the walls of these men;
They tread their winepresses, and suffer thirst.
12 From out of the populous city men groan,
And the soul of the wounded crieth out:
Yet God regardeth not the folly.
13 These are of them that rebel against the light;
They know not the ways thereof,
Nor abide in the paths thereof.
14 The murderer riseth with the light;
He killeth the poor and needy;
And in the night he is as a thief.
15 The eye also of the adulterer waiteth for the twilight,
Saying, No eye shall see me:
And he disguiseth his face.
16 In the dark they dig through houses:
They shut themselves up in the day-time;
They know not the light.
17 For the morning is to all of them as thick darkness;
For they know the terrors of the thick darkness.
18 Swiftly they pass away upon the face of the waters;
Their portion is cursed in the earth:
They turn not into the way of the vineyards.
19 Drought and heat consume the snow waters:
So doth Sheol those that have sinned.
20 The womb shall forget him;
The worm shall feed sweetly on him;
He shall be no more remembered;
And unrighteousness shall be broken as a tree.
21 He devoureth the barren that beareth not,
And doeth not good to the widow.
22 Yet God preserveth the mighty by his power:
He riseth up that hath no assurance of life.
23 God giveth them to be in security, and they rest thereon;
And his eyes are upon their ways.
24 They are exalted; yet a little while, and they are gone;
Yea, they are brought low, they are taken out of the way as all others,
And are cut off as the tops of the ears of grain.
25 And if it be not so now, who will prove me a liar,
And make my speech nothing worth?

Chapter 25

1 Then answered Bildad the Shuhite, and said,
2 Dominion and fear are with him;
He maketh peace in his high places.
3 Is there any number of his armies?
And upon whom doth not his light arise?
4 How then can man be just with God?
Or how can he be clean that is born of a woman?
5 Behold, even the moon hath no brightness,
And the stars are not pure in his sight:
6 How much less man, that is a worm!
And the son of man, that is a worm!

Chapter 26

1 Then Job answered and said,
2 How hast thou helped him that is without power!
How hast thou saved the arm that hath no strength!
3 How hast thou counselled him that hath no wisdom,
And plentifully declared sound knowledge!
4 To whom hast thou uttered words?
And whose spirit came forth from thee?
5 They that are deceased tremble
Beneath the waters and the inhabitants thereof.
6 Sheol is naked before God,
And Abaddon hath no covering.
7 He stretcheth out the north over empty space,
And hangeth the earth upon nothing.
8 He bindeth up the waters in his thick clouds;
And the cloud is not rent under them.
9 He incloseth the face of his throne,
And spreadeth his cloud upon it.
10 He hath described a boundary upon the face of the waters,
Unto the confines of light and darkness.
11 The pillars of heaven tremble
And are astonished at his rebuke.
12 He stirreth up the sea with his power,
And by his understanding he smiteth through Rahab.
13 By his Spirit the heavens are garnished;
His hand hath pierced the swift serpent.
14 Lo, these are but the outskirts of his ways:
And how small a whisper do we hear of him!
But the thunder of his power who can understand?

Chapter 27

1 And Job again took up his parable, and said,
2 As God liveth, who hath taken away my right,
And the Almighty, who hath vexed my soul:
3 (For my life is yet whole in me,
And the spirit of God is in my nostrils);
4 Surely my lips shall not speak unrighteousness,
Neither shall my tongue utter deceit.
5 Far be it from me that I should justify you:
Till I die I will not put away mine integrity from me.
6 My righteousness I hold fast, and will not let it go:
My heart shall not reproach me so long as I live.
7 Let mine enemy be as the wicked,
And let him that riseth up against me be as the unrighteous.
8 For what is the hope of the godless, though he get him gain,
When God taketh away his soul?
9 Will God hear his cry,
When trouble cometh upon him?
10 Will he delight himself in the Almighty,
And call upon God at all times?
11 I will teach you concerning the hand of God;
That which is with the Almighty will I not conceal.
12 Behold, all ye yourselves have seen it;
Why then are ye become altogether vain?
13 This is the portion of a wicked man with God,
And the heritage of oppressors, which they receive from the Almighty:
14 If his children be multiplied, it is for the sword;
And his offspring shall not be satisfied with bread.
15 Those that remain of him shall be buried in death,
And his widows shall make no lamentation.
16 Though he heap up silver as the dust,
And prepare raiment as the clay;
17 He may prepare it, but the just shall put it on,
And the innocent shall divide the silver.
18 He buildeth his house as the moth,
And as a booth which the keeper maketh.
19 He lieth down rich, but he shall not be gathered to his fathers;
He openeth his eyes, and he is not.
20 Terrors overtake him like waters;
A tempest stealeth him away in the night.
21 The east wind carrieth him away, and he departeth;
And it sweepeth him out of his place.
22 For God shall hurl at him, and not spare:
He would fain flee out of his hand.
23 Men shall clap their hands at him,
And shall hiss him out of his place.

Chapter 28

1 Surely there is a mine for silver,
And a place for gold which they refine.
2 Iron is taken out of the earth,
And copper is molten out of the stone.
3 Man setteth an end to darkness,
And searcheth out, to the furthest bound,
The stones of obscurity and of thick darkness.
4 He breaketh open a shaft away from where men sojourn;
They are forgotten of the foot;
They hang afar from men, they swing to and fro.
5 As for the earth, out of it cometh bread;
And underneath it is turned up as it were by fire.
6 The stones thereof are the place of sapphires,
And it hath dust of gold.
7 That path no bird of prey knoweth,
Neither hath the falcon's eye seen it:
8 The proud beasts have not trodden it,
Nor hath the fierce lion passed thereby.
9 He putteth forth his hand upon the flinty rock;
He overturneth the mountains by the roots.
10 He cutteth out channels among the rocks;
And his eye seeth every precious thing.
11 He bindeth the streams that they trickle not;

And the thing that is hid bringeth he forth to light.
12But where shall wisdom be found?
And where is the place of understanding?
13Man knoweth not the price thereof;
Neither is it found in the land of the living.
14The deep saith, It is not in me;
And the sea saith, It is not with me.
15It cannot be gotten for gold,
Neither shall silver be weighed for the price thereof.
16It cannot be valued with the gold of Ophir,
With the precious onyx, or the sapphire.
17Gold and glass cannot equal it,
Neither shall it be exchanged for jewels of fine gold.
18No mention shall be made of coral or of crystal:
Yea, the price of wisdom is above rubies.
19The topaz of Ethiopia shall not equal it,
Neither shall it be valued with pure gold.
20Whence then cometh wisdom?
And where is the place of understanding?
21Seeing it is hid from the eyes of all living,
And kept close from the birds of the heavens.
22Destruction and Death say,
We have heard a rumor thereof with our ears.
23God understandeth the way thereof,
And he knoweth the place thereof.
24For he looketh to the ends of the earth,
And seeth under the whole heaven;
25To make a weight for the wind;
Yea, he meteth out the waters by measure.
26When he made a decree for the rain,
And a way for the lightning of the thunder;
27Then did he see it, and declare it;
He established it, yea, and searched it out.
28And unto man he said,
Behold, the fear of the Lord, that is wisdom;
And to depart from evil is understanding.

Chapter 29

1And Job again took up his parable, and said,
2Oh that I were as in the months of old,
As in the days when God watched over me;
3When his lamp shined upon my head,
And by his light I walked through darkness;
4As I was in the ripeness of my days,
When the friendship of God was upon my tent;
5When the Almighty was yet with me,
And my children were about me;
6When my steps were washed with butter,
And the rock poured me out streams of oil!
7When I went forth to the gate unto the city,
When I prepared my seat in the street,
8The young men saw me and hid themselves,
And the aged rose up and stood;
9The princes refrained from talking,
And laid their hand on their mouth;
10The voice of the nobles was hushed,
And their tongue cleaved to the roof of their mouth.
11For when the ear heard me, then it blessed me;
And when the eye saw me, it gave witness unto me:
12Because I delivered the poor that cried,
The fatherless also, that had none to help him.
13The blessing of him that was ready to perish came upon me;
And I caused the widow's heart to sing for joy.
14I put on righteousness, and it clothed me:
My justice was as a robe and a diadem.
15I was eyes to the blind,
And feet was I to the lame.
16I was a father to the needy:
And the cause of him that I knew not I searched out.
17And I brake the jaws of the unrighteous,
And plucked the prey out of his teeth.
18Then I said, I shall die in my nest,
And I shall multiply my days as the sand:
19My root is spread out to the waters,
And the dew lieth all night upon my branch;
20My glory is fresh in me,
And my bow is renewed in my hand.
21Unto me men gave ear, and waited,
And kept silence for my counsel.
22After my words they spake not again;
And my speech distilled upon them.
23And they waited for me as for the rain;
And they opened their mouth wide as for the latter rain.
24I smiled on them, when they had no confidence;
And the light of my countenance they cast not down.
25I chose out their way, and sat as chief,
And dwelt as a king in the army,
As one that comforteth the mourners.

Chapter 30

1But now they that are younger than I have me in derision,
Whose fathers I disdained to set with the dogs of my flock.
2Yea, the strength of their hands, whereto should it profit me?
Men in whom ripe age is perished.
3They are gaunt with want and famine;
They gnaw the dry ground, in the gloom of wasteness and desolation.
4They pluck salt-wort by the bushes;
And the roots of the broom are their food.
5They are driven forth from the midst of men;
They cry after them as after a thief;
6So that they dwell in frightful valleys,
In holes of the earth and of the rocks.
7Among the bushes they bray;
Under the nettles they are gathered together.
8They are children of fools, yea, children of base men;
They were scourged out of the land.
9And now I am become their song,
Yea, I am a byword unto them.
10They abhor me, they stand aloof from me,
And spare not to spit in my face.
11For he hath loosed his cord, and afflicted me;
And they have cast off the bridle before me.
12Upon my right hand rise the rabble;
They thrust aside my feet,
And they cast up against me their ways of destruction.
13They mar my path,
They set forward my calamity,
Even men that have no helper.
14As through a wide breach they come:
In the midst of the ruin they roll themselves upon me.
15Terrors are turned upon me;
They chase mine honor as the wind;
And my welfare is passed away as a cloud.
16And now my soul is poured out within me;
Days of affliction have taken hold upon me.
17In the night season my bones are pierced in me,
And the pains that gnaw me take no rest.
18By God's great force is my garment disfigured;
It bindeth me about as the collar of my coat.
19He hath cast me into the mire,
And I am become like dust and ashes.
20I cry unto thee, and thou dost not answer me:
I stand up, and thou gazest at me.
21Thou art turned to be cruel to me;
With the might of thy hand thou persecutest me.
22Thou liftest me up to the wind, thou causest me to ride upon it;
And thou dissolvest me in the storm.
23For I know that thou wilt bring me to death,
And to the house appointed for all living.
24Howbeit doth not one stretch out the hand in his fall?
Or in his calamity therefore cry for help?
25Did not I weep for him that was in trouble?
Was not my soul grieved for the needy?
26When I looked for good, then evil came;
And when I waited for light, there came darkness.
27My heart is troubled, and resteth not;
Days of affliction are come upon me.
28I go mourning without the sun:
I stand up in the assembly, and cry for help.
29I am a brother to jackals,
And a companion to ostriches.
30My skin is black, and falleth from me,
And my bones are burned with heat.
31Therefore is my harp turned to mourning,
And my pipe into the voice of them that weep.

Chapter 31

1I made a covenant with mine eyes;
How then should I look upon a virgin?
2For what is the portion from God above,
And the heritage from the Almighty on high?
3Is it not calamity to the unrighteous,
And disaster to the workers of iniquity?
4Doth not he see my ways,
And number all my steps?
5If I have walked with falsehood,
And my foot hath hasted to deceit
6(Let me be weighed in an even balance,
That God may know mine integrity);
7If my step hath turned out of the way,
And my heart walked after mine eyes,
And if any spot hath cleaved to my hands:
8Then let me sow, and let another eat;
Yea, let the produce of my field be rooted out.
9If my heart hath been enticed unto a woman,
And I have laid wait at my neighbor's door;
10Then let my wife grind unto another,

And let others bow down upon her.
11 For that were a heinous crime;
Yea, it were an iniquity to be punished by the judges:
12 For it is a fire that consumeth unto Destruction,
And would root out all mine increase.
13 If I have despised the cause of my man-servant or of my maid-servant,
When they contended with me;
14 What then shall I do when God riseth up?
And when he visiteth, what shall I answer him?
15 Did not he that made me in the womb make him?
And did not one fashion us in the womb?
16 If I have withheld the poor from their desire,
Or have caused the eyes of the widow to fail,
17 Or have eaten my morsel alone,
And the fatherless hath not eaten thereof
18 (Nay, from my youth he grew up with me as with a father,
And her have I guided from my mother's womb);
19 If I have seen any perish for want of clothing,
Or that the needy had no covering;
20 If his loins have not blessed me,
And if he hath not been warmed with the fleece of my sheep;
21 If I have lifted up my hand against the fatherless,
Because I saw my help in the gate:
22 Then let my shoulder fall from the shoulder-blade,
And mine arm be broken from the bone.
23 For calamity from God is a terror to me,
And by reason of his majesty I can do nothing.
24 If I have made gold my hope,
And have said to the fine gold, Thou art my confidence;
25 If I have rejoiced because my wealth was great,
And because my hand had gotten much;
26 If I have beheld the sun when it shined,
Or the moon walking in brightness,
27 And my heart hath been secretly enticed,
And my mouth hath kissed my hand:
28 This also were an iniquity to be punished by the judges;
For I should have denied the God that is above.
29 If I have rejoiced at the destruction of him that hated me,
Or lifted up myself when evil found him;
30 (Yea, I have not suffered by mouth to sin
By asking his life with a curse);
31 If the men of my tent have not said,
Who can find one that hath not been filled with his meat?
32 (The sojourner hath not lodged in the street;
But I have opened my doors to the traveller);
33 If like Adam I have covered my transgressions,
By hiding mine iniquity in my bosom,
34 Because I feared the great multitude,
And the contempt of families terrified me,
So that I kept silence, and went not out of the door-
35 Oh that I had one to hear me!
(Lo, here is my signature, let the Almighty answer me);
And that I had the indictment which mine adversary hath written!
36 Surely I would carry it upon my shoulder;
I would bind it unto me as a crown;
37 I would declare unto him the number of my steps;
As a prince would I go near unto him.
38 If my land crieth out against me,
And the furrows thereof weep together;
39 If I have eaten the fruits thereof without money,
Or have caused the owners thereof to lose their life:
40 Let thistles grow instead of wheat,
And cockle instead of barley.
The words of Job are ended.

Chapter 32

1 So these three men ceased to answer Job, because he was righteous in his own eyes.
2 Then was kindled the wrath of Elihu the son of Barachel the Buzite, of the family of Ram: against Job was his wrath kindled, because he justified himself rather than God.
3 Also against his three friends was his wrath kindled, because they had found no answer, and yet had condemned Job.
4 Now Elihu had waited to speak unto Job, because they were elder than he.
5 And when Elihu saw that there was no answer in the mouth of these three men, his wrath was kindled.
6 And Elihu the son of Barachel the Buzite answered and said,
I am young, and ye are very old;
Wherefore I held back, and durst not show you mine opinion.
7 I said, Days should speak,
And multitude of years should teach wisdom.
8 But there is a spirit in man,
And the breath of the Almighty giveth them understanding.
9 It is not the great that are wise,
Nor the aged that understand justice.
10 Therefore I said, Hearken to me;
I also will show mine opinion.
11 Behold, I waited for your words,
I listened for your reasonings,
Whilst ye searched out what to say.
12 Yea, I attended unto you,
And, behold, there was none that convinced Job,
Or that answered his words, among you.
13 Beware lest ye say, We have found wisdom;
God may vanquish him, not man:
14 For he hath not directed his words against me;
Neither will I answer him with your speeches.
15 They are amazed, they answer no more:
They have not a word to say.
16 And shall I wait, because they speak not,
Because they stand still, and answer no more?
17 I also will answer my part,
I also will show mine opinion.
18 For I am full of words;
The spirit within me constraineth me.
19 Behold, my breast is as wine which hath no vent;
Like new wine-skins it is ready to burst.
20 I will speak, that I may be refreshed;
I will open my lips and answer.
21 Let me not, I pray you, respect any man's person;
Neither will I give flattering titles unto any man.
22 For I know not to give flattering titles;
Else would my Maker soon take me away.

Chapter 33

1 Howbeit, Job, I pray thee, hear my speech,
And hearken to all my words.
2 Behold now, I have opened my mouth;
My tongue hath spoken in my mouth.
3 My words shall utter the uprightness of my heart;
And that which my lips know they shall speak sincerely.
4 The Spirit of God hath made me,
And the breath of the Almighty giveth me life.
5 If thou canst, answer thou me;
Set thy words in order before me, stand forth.
6 Behold, I am toward God even as thou art:
I also am formed out of the clay.
7 Behold, my terror shall not make thee afraid,
Neither shall my pressure be heavy upon thee.
8 Surely thou hast spoken in my hearing,
And I have heard the voice of thy words, saying,
9 I am clean, without transgression;
I am innocent, neither is there iniquity in me:
10 Behold, he findeth occasions against me,
He counteth me for his enemy:
11 He putteth my feet in the stocks,
He marketh all my paths.
12 Behold, I will answer thee, in this thou art not just;
For God is greater than man.
13 Why dost thou strive against him,
For that he giveth not account of any of his matters?
14 For God speaketh once,
Yea twice, though man regardeth it not.
15 In a dream, in a vision of the night,
When deep sleep falleth upon men,
In slumberings upon the bed;
16 Then he openeth the ears of men,
And sealeth their instruction,
17 That he may withdraw man from his purpose,
And hide pride from man;
18 He keepeth back his soul from the pit,
And his life from perishing by the sword.
19 He is chastened also with pain upon his bed,
And with continual strife in his bones;
20 So that his life abhorreth bread,
And his soul dainty food.
21 His flesh is consumed away, that it cannot be seen;
And his bones that were not seen stick out.
22 Yea, his soul draweth near unto the pit,
And his life to the destroyers.
23 If there be with him an angel,
An interpreter, one among a thousand,
To show unto man what is right for him;
24 Then God is gracious unto him, and saith,
Deliver him from going down to the pit,
I have found a ransom.
25 His flesh shall be fresher than a child's;
He returneth to the days of his youth.
26 He prayeth unto God, and he is favorable unto him,
So that he seeth his face with joy:
And he restoreth unto man his righteousness.
27 He singeth before men, and saith,
I have sinned, and perverted that which was right,
And it profited me not:
28 He hath redeemed my soul from going into the pit,
And my life shall behold the light.
29 Lo, all these things doth God work,
Twice, yea thrice, with a man,

30To bring back his soul from the pit,
That he may be enlightened with the light of the living.
31Mark well, O Job, hearken unto me:
Hold thy peace, and I will speak.
32If thou hast anything to say, answer me:
Speak, for I desire to justify thee.
33If not, hearken thou unto me:
Hold thy peace, and I will teach thee wisdom.

Chapter 34

1Moreover Elihu answered and said,
2Hear my words, ye wise men;
And give ear unto me, ye that have knowledge.
3For the ear trieth words,
As the palate tasteth food.
4Let us choose for us that which is right:
Let us know among ourselves what is good.
5For Job hath said, I am righteous,
And God hath taken away my right:
6Notwithstanding my right I am accounted a liar;
My wound is incurable, though I am without transgression.
7What man is like Job,
Who drinketh up scoffing like water,
8Who goeth in company with the workers of iniquity,
And walketh with wicked men?
9For he hath said, It profiteth a man nothing
That he should delight himself with God.
10Therefore hearken unto me, ye men of understanding:
Far be it from God, that he should do wickedness,
And from the Almighty, that he should commit iniquity.
11For the work of a man will he render unto him,
And cause every man to find according to his ways.
12Yea, of a surety, God will not do wickedly,
Neither will the Almighty pervert justice.
13Who gave him a charge over the earth?
Or who hath disposed the whole world?
14If he set his heart upon himself,
If he gather unto himself his spirit and his breath;
15All flesh shall perish together,
And man shall turn again unto dust.
16If now thou hast understanding, hear this:
Hearken to the voice of my words.
17Shall even one that hateth justice govern?
And wilt thou condemn him that is righteous and mighty?-
18Him that saith to a king, Thou art vile,
Or to nobles, Ye are wicked;
19That respecteth not the persons of princes,
Nor regardeth the rich more than the poor;
For they all are the work of his hands.
20In a moment they die, even at midnight;
The people are shaken and pass away,
And the mighty are taken away without hand.
21For his eyes are upon the ways of a man,
And he seeth all his goings.
22There is no darkness, nor thick gloom,
Where the workers of iniquity may hide themselves.
23For he needeth not further to consider a man,
That he should go before God in judgment.
24He breaketh in pieces mighty men in ways past finding out,
And setteth others in their stead.
25Therefore he taketh knowledge of their works;
And he overturneth them in the night, so that they are destroyed.
26He striketh them as wicked men
In the open sight of others;
27Because they turned aside from following him,
And would not have regard in any of his ways:
28So that they caused the cry of the poor to come unto him,
And he heard the cry of the afflicted.
29When he giveth quietness, who then can condemn?
And when he hideth his face, who then can behold him?
Alike whether it be done unto a nation, or unto a man:
30That the godless man reign not,
That there be none to ensnare the people.
31For hath any said unto God,
I have borne chastisement, I will not offend any more:
32That which I see not teach thou me:
If I have done iniquity, I will do it no more?
33Shall his recompense be as thou wilt, that thou refusest it?
For thou must choose, and not I:
Therefore speak what thou knowest.
34Men of understanding will say unto me,
Yea, every wise man that heareth me:
35Job speaketh without knowledge,
And his words are without wisdom.
36Would that Job were tried unto the end,
Because of his answering like wicked men.
37For he addeth rebellion unto his sin;
He clappeth his hands among us,
And multiplieth his words against God.

Chapter 35

1Moreover Elihu answered and said,
2Thinkest thou this to be thy right,
Or sayest thou, My righteousness is more than God's,
3That thou sayest, What advantage will it be unto thee?
And, What profit shall I have, more than if I had sinned?
4I will answer thee,
And thy companions with thee.
5Look unto the heavens, and see;
And behold the skies, which are higher than thou.
6If thou hast sinned, what effectest thou against him?
And if thy transgressions be multiplied, what doest thou unto him?
7If thou be righteous, what givest thou him?
Or what receiveth he of thy hand?
8Thy wickedness may hurt a man as thou art;
And thy righteousness may profit a son of man.
9By reason of the multitude of oppressions they cry out;
They cry for help by reason of the arm of the mighty.
10But none saith, Where is God my Maker,
Who giveth songs in the night,
11Who teacheth us more than the beasts of the earth,
And maketh us wiser than the birds of the heavens?
12There they cry, but none giveth answer,
Because of the pride of evil men.
13Surely God will not hear an empty cry,
Neither will the Almighty regard it.
14How much less when thou sayest thou beholdest him not,
The cause is before him, and thou waitest for him!
15But now, because he hath not visited in his anger,
Neither doth he greatly regard arrogance;
16Therefore doth Job open his mouth in vanity;
He multiplieth words without knowledge.

Chapter 36

1Elihu also proceeded, and said,
2Suffer me a little, and I will show thee;
For I have yet somewhat to say on God's behalf.
3I will fetch my knowledge from afar,
And will ascribe righteousness to my Maker.
4For truly my words are not false:
One that is perfect in knowledge is with thee.
5Behold, God is mighty, and despiseth not any:
He is mighty in strength of understanding.
6He preserveth not the life of the wicked,
But giveth to the afflicted their right.
7He withdraweth not his eyes from the righteous:
But with kings upon the throne
He setteth them for ever, and they are exalted.
8And if they be bound in fetters,
And be taken in the cords of afflictions;
9Then he showeth them their work,
And their transgressions, that they have behaved themselves proudly.
10He openeth also their ear to instruction,
And commandeth that they return from iniquity.
11If they hearken and serve him,
They shall spend their days in prosperity,
And their years in pleasures.
12But if they hearken not, they shall perish by the sword,
And they shall die without knowledge.
13But they that are godless in heart lay up anger:
They cry not for help when he bindeth them.
14They die in youth,
And their life perisheth among the unclean.
15He delivereth the afflicted by their affliction,
And openeth their ear in oppression.
16Yea, he would have allured thee out of distress
Into a broad place, where there is no straitness;
And that which is set on thy table would be full of fatness.
17But thou art full of the judgment of the wicked:
Judgment and justice take hold on thee.
18For let not wrath stir thee up against chastisements;
Neither let the greatness of the ransom turn thee aside.
19Will thy cry avail, that thou be not in distress,
Or all the forces of thy strength?
20Desire not the night,
When peoples are cut off in their place.
21Take heed, regard not iniquity:
For this hast thou chosen rather than affliction.
22Behold, God doeth loftily in his power:
Who is a teacher like unto him?
23Who hath enjoined him his way?
Or who can say, Thou hast wrought unrighteousness?
24Remember that thou magnify his work,
Whereof men have sung.
25All men have looked thereon;
Man beholdeth it afar off.
26Behold, God is great, and we know him not;
The number of his years is unsearchable.

27For he draweth up the drops of water,
Which distil in rain from his vapor,
28Which the skies pour down
And drop upon man abundantly.
29Yea, can any understand the spreadings of the clouds,
The thunderings of his pavilion?
30Behold, he spreadeth his light around him;
And he covereth the bottom of the sea.
31For by these he judgeth the peoples;
He giveth food in abundance.
32He covereth his hands with the lightning,
And giveth it a charge that it strike the mark.
33The noise thereof telleth concerning him,
The cattle also concerning the storm that cometh up.

Chapter 37

1Yea, at this my heart trembleth,
And is moved out of its place.
2Hear, oh, hear the noise of his voice,
And the sound that goeth out of his mouth.
3He sendeth it forth under the whole heaven,
And his lightening unto the ends of the earth.
4After it a voice roareth;
He thundereth with the voice of his majesty;
And he restraineth not the lightnings when his voice is heard.
5God thundereth marvellously with his voice;
Great things doeth he, which we cannot comprehend.
6For he saith to the snow, Fall thou on the earth;
Likewise to the shower of rain,
And to the showers of his mighty rain.
7He sealeth up the hand of every man,
That all men whom he hath made may know it.
8Then the beasts go into coverts,
And remain in their dens.
9Out of the chamber of the south cometh the storm,
And cold out of the north.
10By the breath of God ice is given;
And the breadth of the waters is straitened.
11Yea, he ladeth the thick cloud with moisture;
He spreadeth abroad the cloud of his lightning:
12And it is turned round about by his guidance,
That they may do whatsoever he commandeth them
Upon the face of the habitable world,
13Whether it be for correction, or for his land,
Or for lovingkindness, that he cause it to come.
14Hearken unto this, O Job:
Stand still, and consider the wondrous works of God.
15Dost thou know how God layeth his charge upon them,
And causeth the lightning of his cloud to shine?
16Dost thou know the balancings of the clouds,
The wondrous works of him who is perfect in knowledge?
17How thy garments are warm,
When the earth is still by reason of the south wind?
18Canst thou with him spread out the sky,
Which is strong as a molten mirror?
19Teach us what we shall say unto him;
For we cannot set our speech in order by reason of darkness.
20Shall it be told him that I would speak?
Or should a man wish that he were swallowed up?
21And now men see not the light which is bright in the skies;
But the wind passeth, and cleareth them.
22Out of the north cometh golden splendor:
God hath upon him terrible majesty.
23Touching the Almighty, we cannot find him out
He is excellent in power;
And in justice and plenteous righteousness he will not afflict.
24Men do therefore fear him:
He regardeth not any that are wise of heart.

Chapter 38

1Then Yahweh answered Job out of the whirlwind, and said,
2Who is this that darkeneth counsel
By words without knowledge?
3Gird up now thy loins like a man;
For I will demand of thee, and declare thou unto me.
4Where wast thou when I laid the foundations of the earth?
Declare, if thou hast understanding.
5Who determined the measures thereof, if thou knowest?
Or who stretched the line upon it?
6Whereupon were the foundations thereof fastened?
Or who laid the corner-stone thereof,
7When the morning stars sang together,
And all the sons of God shouted for joy?
8Or who shut up the sea with doors,
When it brake forth, as if it had issued out of the womb;
9When I made clouds the garment thereof,
And thick darkness a swaddling-band for it,
10And marked out for it my bound,
And set bars and doors,
11And said, Hitherto shalt thou come, but no further;
And here shall thy proud waves be stayed?
12Hast thou commanded the morning since thy days began,
And caused the dayspring to know its place;
13That it might take hold of the ends of the earth,
And the wicked be shaken out of it?
14It is changed as clay under the seal;
And all things stand forth as a garment:
15And from the wicked their light is withholden,
And the high arm is broken.
16Hast thou entered into the springs of the sea?
Or hast thou walked in the recesses of the deep?
17Have the gates of death been revealed unto thee?
Or hast thou seen the gates of the shadow of death?
18Hast thou comprehended the earth in its breadth?
Declare, if thou knowest it all.
19Where is the way to the dwelling of light?
And as for darkness, where is the place thereof,
20That thou shouldest take it to the bound thereof,
And that thou shouldest discern the paths to the house thereof?
21Doubtless, thou knowest, for thou wast then born,
And the number of thy days is great!
22Hast thou entered the treasuries of the snow,
Or hast thou seen the treasuries of the hail,
23Which I have reserved against the time of trouble,
Against the day of battle and war?
24By what way is the light parted,
Or the east wind scattered upon the earth?
25Who hath cleft a channel for the waterflood,
Or the way for the lightning of the thunder;
26To cause it to rain on a land where no man is;
On the wilderness, wherein there is no man;
27To satisfy the waste and desolate ground,
And to cause the tender grass to spring forth?
28Hath the rain a father?
Or who hath begotten the drops of dew?
29Out of whose womb came the ice?
And the hoary frost of heaven, who hath gendered it?
30The waters hide themselves and become like stone,
And the face of the deep is frozen.
31Canst thou bind the cluster of the Pleiades,
Or loose the bands of Orion?
32Canst thou lead forth the Mazzaroth in their season?
Or canst thou guide the Bear with her train?
33Knowest thou the ordinances of the heavens?
Canst thou establish the dominion thereof in the earth?
34Canst thou lift up thy voice to the clouds,
That abundance of waters may cover thee?
35Canst thou send forth lightnings, that they may go,
And say unto thee, Here we are?
36Who hath put wisdom in the inward parts?
Or who hath given understanding to the mind?
37Who can number the clouds by wisdom?
Or who can pour out the bottles of heaven,
38When the dust runneth into a mass,
And the clods cleave fast together?
39Canst thou hunt the prey for the lioness,
Or satisfy the appetite of the young lions,
40When they couch in their dens,
And abide in the covert to lie in wait?
41Who provideth for the raven his prey,
When his young ones cry unto God,
And wander for lack of food?

Chapter 39

1Knowest thou the time when the wild goats of the rock bring forth?
Or canst thou mark when the hinds do calve?
2Canst thou number the months that they fulfil?
Or knowest thou the time when they bring forth?
3They bow themselves, they bring forth their young,
They cast out their pains.
4Their young ones become strong, they grow up in the open field;
They go forth, and return not again.
5Who hath sent out the wild ass free?
Or who hath loosed the bonds of the swift ass,
6Whose home I have made the wilderness,
And the salt land his dwelling-place?
7He scorneth the tumult of the city,
Neither heareth he the shoutings of the driver.
8The range of the mountains is his pasture,
And he searcheth after every green thing.
9Will the wild-ox be content to serve thee?
Or will he abide by thy crib?
10Canst thou bind the wild-ox with his band in the furrow?
Or will he harrow the valleys after thee?
11Wilt thou trust him, because his strength is great?
Or wilt thou leave to him thy labor?
12Wilt thou confide in him, that he will bring home thy seed,

And gather the grain of thy threshing-floor?
13 The wings of the ostrich wave proudly;
But are they the pinions and plumage of love?
14 For she leaveth her eggs on the earth,
And warmeth them in the dust,
15 And forgetteth that the foot may crush them,
Or that the wild beast may trample them.
16 She dealeth hardly with her young ones, as if they were not hers:
Though her labor be in vain, she is without fear;
17 Because God hath deprived her of wisdom,
Neither hath he imparted to her understanding.
18 What time she lifteth up herself on high,
She scorneth the horse and his rider.
19 Hast thou given the horse his might?
Hast thou clothed his neck with the quivering mane?
20 Hast thou made him to leap as a locust?
The glory of his snorting is terrible.
21 He paweth in the valley, and rejoiceth in his strength:
He goeth out to meet the armed men.
22 He mocketh at fear, and is not dismayed;
Neither turneth he back from the sword.
23 The quiver rattleth against him,
The flashing spear and the javelin.
24 He swalloweth the ground with fierceness and rage;
Neither believeth he that it is the voice of the trumpet.
25 As oft as the trumpet soundeth he saith, Aha!
And he smelleth the battle afar off,
The thunder of the captains, and the shouting.
26 Is it by thy wisdom that the hawk soareth,
(And) stretcheth her wings toward the south?
27 Is it at thy command that the eagle mounteth up,
And maketh her nest on high?
28 On the cliff she dwelleth, and maketh her home,
Upon the point of the cliff, and the stronghold.
29 From thence she spieth out the prey;
Her eyes behold it afar off.
30 Her young ones also suck up blood:
And where the slain are, there is she.

Chapter 40

1 Moreover Yahweh answered Job, and said,
2 Shall he that cavilleth contend with the Almighty?
He that argueth with God, let him answer it.
3 Then Job answered Yahweh, and said,
4 Behold, I am of small account; What shall I answer thee?
I lay my hand upon my mouth.
5 Once have I spoken, and I will not answer;
Yea, twice, but I will proceed no further.
6 Then Yahweh answered Job out of the whirlwind, and said,
7 Gird up thy loins now like a man:
I will demand of thee, and declare thou unto me.
8 Wilt thou even annul my judgment?
Wilt thou condemn me, that thou mayest be justified?
9 Or hast thou an arm like God?
And canst thou thunder with a voice like him?
10 Deck thyself now with excellency and dignity;
And array thyself with honor and majesty.
11 Pour forth the overflowings of thine anger;
And look upon every one that is proud, and abase him.
12 Look on every one that is proud, and bring him low;
And tread down the wicked where they stand.
13 Hide them in the dust together;
Bind their faces in the hidden place.
14 Then will I also confess of thee
That thine own right hand can save thee.
15 Behold now, behemoth, which I made as well as thee;
He eateth grass as an ox.
16 Lo now, his strength is in his loins,
And his force is in the muscles of his belly.
17 He moveth his tail like a cedar:
The sinews of his thighs are knit together.
18 His bones are as tubes of brass;
His limbs are like bars of iron.
19 He is the chief of the ways of God:
He only that made him giveth him his sword.
20 Surely the mountains bring him forth food,
Where all the beasts of the field do play.
21 He lieth under the lotus-trees,
In the covert of the reed, and the fen.
22 The lotus-trees cover him with their shade;
The willows of the brook compass him about.
23 Behold, if a river overflow, he trembleth not;
He is confident, though a Jordan swell even to his mouth.
24 Shall any take him when he is on the watch,
Or pierce through his nose with a snare?

Chapter 41

1 Canst thou draw out leviathan with a fishhook?
Or press down his tongue with a cord?
2 Canst thou put a rope into his nose?
Or pierce his jaw through with a hook?
3 Will he make many supplications unto thee?
Or will he speak soft words unto thee?
4 Will he make a covenant with thee,
That thou shouldest take him for a servant for ever?
5 Wilt thou play with him as with a bird?
Or wilt thou bind him for thy maidens?
6 Will the bands of fishermen make traffic of him?
Will they part him among the merchants?
7 Canst thou fill his skin with barbed irons,
Or his head with fish-spears?
8 Lay thy hand upon him;
Remember the battle, and do so no more.
9 Behold, the hope of him is in vain:
Will not one be cast down even at the sight of him?
10 None is so fierce that he dare stir him up;
Who then is he that can stand before me?
11 Who hath first given unto me, that I should repay him?
Whatsoever is under the whole heaven is mine.
12 I will not keep silence concerning his limbs,
Nor his mighty strength, nor his goodly frame.
13 Who can strip off his outer garment?
Who shall come within his jaws?
14 Who can open the doors of his face?
Round about his teeth is terror.
15 His strong scales are his pride,
Shut up together as with a close seal.
16 One is so near to another,
That no air can come between them.
17 They are joined one to another;
They stick together, so that they cannot be sundered.
18 His sneezings flash forth light,
And his eyes are like the eyelids of the morning.
19 Out of his mouth go burning torches,
And sparks of fire leap forth.
20 Out of his nostrils a smoke goeth,
As of a boiling pot and burning rushes.
21 His breath kindleth coals,
And a flame goeth forth from his mouth.
22 In his neck abideth strength,
And terror danceth before him.
23 The flakes of his flesh are joined together:
They are firm upon him; they cannot be moved.
24 His heart is as firm as a stone;
Yea, firm as the nether millstone.
25 When he raiseth himself up, the mighty are afraid:
By reason of consternation they are beside themselves.
26 If one lay at him with the sword, it cannot avail;
Nor the spear, the dart, nor the pointed shaft.
27 He counteth iron as straw,
And brass as rotten wood.
28 The arrow cannot make him flee:
Sling-stones are turned with him into stubble.
29 Clubs are counted as stubble:
He laugheth at the rushing of the javelin.
30 His underparts are like sharp potsherds:
He spreadeth as it were a threshing-wain upon the mire.
31 He maketh the deep to boil like a pot:
He maketh the sea like a pot of ointment.
32 He maketh a path to shine after him;
One would think the deep to be hoary.
33 Upon earth there is not his like,
That is made without fear.
34 He beholdeth everything that is high:
He is king over all the sons of pride.

Chapter 42

1 Then Job answered Yahweh, and said,
2 I know that thou canst do all things,
And that no purpose of thine can be restrained.
3 Who is this that hideth counsel without knowledge?
Therefore have I uttered that which I understood not,
Things too wonderful for me, which I knew not.
4 Hear, I beseech thee, and I will speak;
I will demand of thee, and declare thou unto me.
5 I had heard of thee by the hearing of the ear;
But now mine eye seeth thee:
6 Wherefore I abhor myself,
And repent in dust and ashes.
7 And it was so, that, after Yahweh had spoken these words unto Job, Yahweh said to Eliphaz the Temanite, My wrath is kindled against thee, and against thy two friends; for ye have not spoken of me the thing that is right, as my servant Job hath.
8 Now therefore, take unto you seven bullocks and seven rams, and go to my

Job

servant Job, and offer up for yourselves a burnt-offering; and my servant Job shall pray for you; for him will I accept, that I deal not with you after your folly; for ye have not spoken of me the thing that is right, as my servant Job hath.

9So Eliphaz the Temanite and Bildad the Shuhite and Zophar the Naamathite went, and did according as Yahweh commanded them: and Yahweh accepted Job.

10And Yahweh turned the captivity of Job, when he prayed for his friends: and Yahweh gave Job twice as much as he had before.

11Then came there unto him all his brethren, and all his sisters, and all they that had been of his acquaintance before, and did eat bread with him in his house: and they bemoaned him, and comforted him concerning all the evil that Yahweh had brought upon him: every man also gave him a piece of money, and every one a ring of gold.

12So Yahweh blessed the latter end of Job more than his beginning: And he had fourteen thousand sheep, and six thousand camels, and a thousand yoke of oxen, and a thousand she-asses.

13He had also seven sons and three daughters.

14And he called the name of the first, Jemimah: and the name of the second, Keziah; and the name of the third, Keren-happuch.

15And in all the land were no women found so fair as the daughters of Job: and their father gave them inheritance among their brethren.

16And after this Job lived a hundred and forty years, and saw his sons, and his sons' sons, even four generations.

17So Job died, being old and full of days.

The Book of Psalms

Book I

Chapter 1

1Blessed is the man that walketh not in the counsel of the wicked,
Nor standeth in the way of sinners,
Nor sitteth in the seat of scoffers:
2But his delight is in the law of Yahweh;
And on his law doth he meditate day and night.
3And he shall be like a tree planted by the streams of water,
That bringeth forth its fruit in its season,
Whose leaf also doth not wither;
And whatsoever he doeth shall prosper.
4The wicked are not so,
But are like the chaff which the wind driveth away.
5Therefore the wicked shall not stand in the judgment,
Nor sinners in the congregation of the righteous.
6For Yahweh knoweth the way of the righteous;
But the way of the wicked shall perish.

Chapter 2

1Why do the nations rage,
And the peoples meditate a vain thing?
2The kings of the earth set themselves,
And the rulers take counsel together,
Against Yahweh, and against his anointed, saying,
3Let us break their bonds asunder,
And cast away their cords from us.
4He that sitteth in the heavens will laugh:
The Lord will have them in derision.
5Then will he speak unto them in his wrath,
And vex them in his sore displeasure:
6Yet I have set my king
Upon my holy hill of Zion.
7I will tell of the decree:
Yahweh said unto me, Thou art my son;
This day have I begotten thee.
8Ask of me, and I will give thee the nations for thine inheritance,
And the uttermost parts of the earth for thy possession.
9Thou shalt break them with a rod of iron;
Thou shalt dash them in pieces like a potter's vessel.
10Now therefore be wise, O ye kings:
Be instructed, ye judges of the earth.
11Serve Yahweh with fear,
And rejoice with trembling.
12Kiss the son, lest he be angry, and ye perish in the way,
For his wrath will soon be kindled.
Blessed are all they that take refuge in him.

Chapter 3

A Psalm of David, when he fled from Absalom his son.
1Yahweh, how are mine adversaries increased!
Many are they that rise up against me.
2Many there are that say of my soul,
There is no help for him in God.
Selah
3But thou, O Yahweh, art a shield about me;
My glory and the lifter up of my head.
4I cry unto Yahweh with my voice,
And he answereth me out of his holy hill.
Selah
5I laid me down and slept;
I awaked; for Yahweh sustaineth me.
6I will not be afraid of ten thousands of the people
That have set themselves against me round about.
7Arise, O Yahweh; save me, O my God:
For thou hast smitten all mine enemies upon the cheek bone;
Thou hast broken the teeth of the wicked.
8Salvation belongeth unto Yahweh:
Thy blessing be upon thy people.
Selah

Chapter 4

For the Chief Musician; on stringed instruments. A Psalm of David.
1Answer me when I call, O God of my righteousness;
Thou hast set me at large when I was in distress:
Have mercy upon me, and hear my prayer.
2O ye sons of men, how long shall my glory be turned into dishonor?
How long will ye love vanity, and seek after falsehood?
Selah
3But know that Yahweh hath set apart for himself him that is godly:
Yahweh will hear when I call unto him.
4Stand in awe, and sin not:
Commune with your own heart upon your bed, and be still.
Selah
5Offer the sacrifices of righteousness,
And put your trust in Yahweh.
6Many there are that say, Who will show us any good?
Yahweh, lift thou up the light of thy countenance upon us.
7Thou hast put gladness in my heart,
More than they have when their grain and their new wine are increased.
8In peace will I both lay me down and sleep;
For thou, Yahweh, alone makest me dwell in safety.

Chapter 5

For the Chief Musician; with the Nehiloth. A Psalm of David.
1Give ear to my words, O Yahweh,
Consider my meditation.
2Hearken unto the voice of my cry, my King, and my God;
For unto thee do I pray.
3O Yahweh, in the morning shalt thou hear my voice;
In the morning will I order my prayer unto thee, and will keep watch.
4For thou art not a God that hath pleasure in wickedness:
Evil shall not sojourn with thee.
5The arrogant shall not stand in thy sight:
Thou hatest all workers of iniquity.
6Thou wilt destroy them that speak lies:
Yahweh abhorreth the blood-thirsty and deceitful man.
7But as for me, in the abundance of thy lovingkindness will I come into thy house:
In thy fear will I worship toward thy holy temple.
8Lead me, O Yahweh, in thy righteousness because of mine enemies;
Make thy way straight before my face.
9For there is no faithfulness in their mouth;
Their inward part is very wickedness;
Their throat is an open sepulchre;
They flatter with their tongue.
10Hold them guilty, O God;
Let them fall by their own counsels;
Thrust them out in the multitude of their transgressions;
For they have rebelled against thee.
11But let all those that take refuge in thee rejoice,
Let them ever shout for joy, because thou defendest them:
Let them also that love thy name be joyful in thee.
12For thou wilt bless the righteous;
O Yahweh, thou wilt compass him with favor as with a shield.

Chapter 6

For the Chief Musician; on stringed instruments, set to the Sheminith. A Psalm of David.
1O Yahweh, rebuke me not in thine anger,
Neither chasten me in thy hot displeasure.
2Have mercy upon me, O Yahweh; for I am withered away:
O Yahweh, heal me; for my bones are troubled.
3My soul also is sore troubled:
And thou, O Yahweh, how long?
4Return, O Yahweh, deliver my soul:
Save me for thy lovingkindness' sake.
5For in death there is no remembrance of thee:
In Sheol who shall give thee thanks?
6I am weary with my groaning;
Every night make I my bed to swim;
I water my couch with my tears.
7Mine eye wasteth away because of grief;
It waxeth old because of all mine adversaries.
8Depart from me, all ye workers of iniquity;
For Yahweh hath heard the voice of my weeping.
9Yahweh hath heard my supplication;
Yahweh will receive my prayer.
10All mine enemies shall be put to shame and sore troubled:
They shall turn back, they shall be put to shame suddenly.

Chapter 7

Shiggaion of David, which he sang unto Jehova, concerning the words of Cush a Benjamite.
1O Yahweh my God, in thee do I take refuge:
Save me from all them that pursue me, and deliver me,
2Lest they tear my soul like a lion,
Rending it in pieces, while there is none to deliver.
3O Yahweh my God, if I have done this;
If there be iniquity in my hands;
4If I have rewarded evil unto him that was at peace with me;
(Yea, I have delivered him that without cause was mine adversary;)
5Let the enemy pursue my soul, and overtake it;
Yea, let him tread my life down to the earth,
And lay my glory in the dust.
Selah
6Arise, O Yahweh, in thine anger;
Lift up thyself against the rage of mine adversaries,
And awake for me; thou hast commanded judgment.

Psalms

7And let the congregation of the peoples compass thee about;
And over them return thou on high.
8Yahweh ministereth judgment to the peoples:
Judge me, O Yahweh, according to my righteousness, and to mine integrity that is in me.
9O let the wickedness of the wicked come to an end, but establish thou the righteous:
For the righteous God trieth the minds and hearts.
10My shield is with God,
Who saveth the upright in heart.
11God is a righteous judge,
Yea, a God that hath indignation every day.
12If a man turn not, he will whet his sword;
He hath bent his bow, and made it ready.
13He hath also prepared for him the instruments of death;
He maketh his arrows fiery shafts.
14Behold, he travaileth with iniquity;
Yea, he hath conceived mischief, and brought forth falsehood.
15He hath made a pit, and digged it,
And is fallen into the ditch which he made.
16His mischief shall return upon his own head,
And his violence shall come down upon his own pate.
17I will give thanks unto Yahweh according to his righteousness,
And will sing praise to the name of Yahweh Most High.

Chapter 8

For the Chief Musician; set to the Gittith. A Psalm of David.
1O Yahweh, our Lord, How excellent is thy name in all the earth,
Who hast set thy glory upon the heavens!
2Out of the mouth of babes and sucklings hast thou established strength,
Because of thine adversaries,
That thou mightest still the enemy and the avenger.
3When I consider thy heavens, the work of thy fingers,
The moon and the stars, which thou hast ordained;
4What is man, that thou art mindful of him?
And the son of man, that thou visitest him?
5For thou hast made him but little lower than aGod,
And crownest him with glory and honor.
6Thou makest him to have dominion over the works of thy hands;
Thou hast put all things under his feet:
7All sheep and oxen,
Yea, and the beasts of the field,
8The birds of the heavens, and the fish of the sea,
Whatsoever passeth through the paths of the seas.
9O Yahweh, our Lord,
How excellent is thy name in all the earth!

Chapter 9

For the Chief Musician; set to Muthlabben. A Psalm of David.
1I will give thanks unto Yahweh with my whole heart;
I will show forth all thy marvellous works.
2I will be glad and exult in thee;
I will sing praise to thy name, O thou Most High.
3When mine enemies turn back,
They stumble and perish at thy presence.
4For thou hast maintained my right and my cause;
Thou sittest in the throne judging righteously.
5Thou hast rebuked the nations, thou hast destroyed the wicked;
Thou hast blotted out their name for ever and ever.
6The enemy are come to an end, they are desolate for ever;
And the cities which thou hast overthrown,
The very remembrance of them is perished.
7But Yahweh sitteth as king for ever:
He hath prepared his throne for judgment;
8And he will judge the world in righteousness,
He will minister judgment to the peoples in uprightness.
9Yahweh also will be a high tower for the oppressed,
A high tower in times of trouble;
10And they that know thy name will put their trust in thee;
For thou, Yahweh, hast not forsaken them that seek thee.
11Sing praises to Yahweh, who dwelleth in Zion:
Declare among the people his doings.
12For he that maketh inquisition for blood remembereth them;
He forgetteth not the cry of the poor.
13Have mercy upon me, O Yahweh;
Behold my affliction which I suffer of them that hate me,
Thou that liftest me up from the gates of death;
14That I may show forth all thy praise.
In the gates of the daughter of Zion
I will rejoice in thy salvation.
15The nations are sunk down in the pit that they made:
In the net which they hid is their own foot taken.
16Yahweh hath made himself known, he hath executed judgment:
The wicked is snared in the work of his own hands.
Higgaion. Selah
17The wicked shall be turned back unto Sheol,
Even all the nations that forget God.
18For the needy shall not alway be forgotten,
Nor the expectation of the poor perish for ever.
19Arise, O Yahweh; let not man prevail:
Let the nations be judged in thy sight.
20Put them in fear, O Yahweh:
Let the nations know themselves to be but men.
Selah

Chapter 10

1Why standest thou afar off, O Yahweh?
Why hidest thou thyself in times of trouble?
2In the pride of the wicked the poor is hotly pursued;
Let them be taken in the devices that they have conceived.
3For the wicked boasteth of his heart's desire,
And the covetous renounceth, yea, contemneth Yahweh.
4The wicked, in the pride of his countenance, saith, He will not require it.
All his thoughts are, There is no God.
5His ways are firm at all times;
Thy judgments are far above out of his sight:
As for all his adversaries, he puffeth at them.
6He saith in his heart, I shall not be moved;
To all generations I shall not be in adversity.
7His mouth is full of cursing and deceit and oppression:
Under his tongue is mischief and iniquity.
8He sitteth in the lurking-places of the villages;
In the secret places doth he murder the innocent;
His eyes are privily set against the helpless.
9He lurketh in secret as a lion in his covert;
He lieth in wait to catch the poor:
He doth catch the poor, when he draweth him in his net.
10He croucheth, he boweth down,
And the helpless fall by his strong ones.
11He saith in his heart, God hath forgotten;
He hideth his face; he will never see it.
12Arise, O Yahweh; O God, lift up thy hand:
Forget not the poor.
13Wherefore doth the wicked contemn God,
And say in his heart, Thou wilt not require it?
14Thou hast seen it; for thou beholdest mischief and spite, to requite it with thy hand:
The helpless committeth himself unto thee;
Thou hast been the helper of the fatherless.
15Break thou the arm of the wicked;
And as for the evil man, seek out his wickedness till thou find none.
16Yahweh is King for ever and ever:
The nations are perished out of his land.
17Yahweh, thou hast heard the desire of the meek:
Thou wilt prepare their heart, thou wilt cause thine ear to hear;
18To judge the fatherless and the oppressed,
That man who is of the earth may be terrible no more.

Chapter 11

For the Chief Musician. A Psalm of David.
1In Yahweh do I take refuge:
How say ye to my soul,
Flee as a bird to your mountain;
2For, lo, the wicked bend the bow,
They make ready their arrow upon the string,
That they may shoot in darkness at the upright in heart;
3If the foundations be destroyed,
What can the righteous do?
4Yahweh is in his holy temple;
Yahweh, his throne is in heaven;
His eyes behold, his eyelids try, the children of men.
5Yahweh trieth the righteous;
But the wicked and him that loveth violence his soul hateth.
6Upon the wicked he will rain snares;
Fire and brimstone and burning wind shall be the portion of their cup.
7For Yahweh is righteous; he loveth righteousness:
The upright shall behold his face.

Chapter 12

For the Chief Musician; set to the Sheminith. A Psalm of David.
1Help, Yahweh; for the godly man ceaseth;
For the faithful fail from among the children of men.
2They speak falsehood every one with his neighbor:
With flattering lip, and with a double heart, do they speak.
3Yahweh will cut off all flattering lips,
The tongue that speaketh great things;
4Who have said, With our tongue will we prevail;
Our lips are our own: who is lord over us?
5Because of the oppression of the poor, because of the sighing of the needy,
Now will I arise, saith Yahweh;
I will set him in the safety he panteth for.
6The words of Yahweh are pure words;
As silver tried in a furnace on the earth,
Purified seven times.
7Thou wilt keep them, O Yahweh,
Thou wilt preserve them from this generation for ever.

⁸The wicked walk on every side,
When vileness is exalted among the sons of men.

Chapter 13

For the Chief Musician. A Psalm of David.
¹How long, O Yahweh? wilt thou forget me for ever?
How long wilt thou hide thy face from me?
²How long shall I take counsel in my soul,
Having sorrow in my heart all the day?
How long shall mine enemy be exalted over me?
³Consider and answer me, O Yahweh my God:
Lighten mine eyes, lest I sleep the sleep of death;
⁴Lest mine enemy say, I have prevailed against him;
Lest mine adversaries rejoice when I am moved.
⁵But I have trusted in thy lovingkindness;
My heart shall rejoice in thy salvation.
⁶I will sing unto Yahweh,
Because he hath dealt bountifully with me.

Chapter 14

For the Chief Musician. A Psalm of David.
¹The fool hath said in his heart, There is no God.
They are corrupt, they have done abominable works;
There is none that doeth good.
²Yahweh looked down from heaven upon the children of men,
To see if there were any that did understand,
That did seek after God.
³They are all gone aside; they are together become filthy;
There is none that doeth good, no, not one.
⁴Have all the workers of iniquity no knowledge,
Who eat up my people as they eat bread,
And call not upon Yahweh?
⁵There were they in great fear;
For God is in the generation of the righteous.
⁶Ye put to shame the counsel of the poor,
Because Yahweh is his refuge.
⁷Oh that the salvation of Israel were come out of Zion!
When Yahweh bringeth back the captivity of his people,
Then shall Jacob rejoice, and Israel shall be glad.

Chapter 15

A Psalm of David.
¹Yahweh, who shall sojourn in thy tabernacle?
Who shall dwell in thy holy hill?
²He that walketh uprightly, and worketh righteousness,
And speaketh truth in his heart;
³He that slandereth not with his tongue,
Nor doeth evil to his friend,
Nor taketh up a reproach against his neighbor;
⁴In whose eyes a reprobate is despised,
But who honoreth them that fear Yahweh;
He that sweareth to his own hurt, and changeth not;
⁵He that putteth not out his money to interest,
Nor taketh reward against the innocent.
He that doeth these things shall never be moved.

Chapter 16

Michtam of David.
¹Preserve me, O God; for in thee do I take refuge.
²O my soul, thou hast said unto Yahweh, Thou art my Lord:
I have no good beyond thee.
³As for the saints that are in the earth,
They are the excellent in whom is all my delight.
⁴Their sorrows shall be multiplied that give gifts for another god:
Their drink-offerings of blood will I not offer,
Nor take their names upon my lips.
⁵Yahweh is the portion of mine inheritance and of my cup:
Thou maintainest my lot.
⁶The lines are fallen unto me in pleasant places;
Yea, I have a goodly heritage.
⁷I will bless Yahweh, who hath given me counsel;
Yea, my heart instructeth me in the night seasons.
⁸I have set Yahweh always before me:
Because he is at my right hand, I shall not be moved.
⁹Therefore my heart is glad, and my glory rejoiceth;
My flesh also shall dwell in safety.
¹⁰For thou wilt not leave my soul to Sheol;
Neither wilt thou suffer thy holy one to see corruption.
¹¹Thou wilt show me the path of life:
In thy presence is fulness of joy;
In thy right hand there are pleasures for evermore.

Chapter 17

A Prayer of David.
¹Hear the right, O Yahweh, attend unto my cry;
Give ear unto my prayer, that goeth not out of feigned lips.
²Let my sentence come forth from thy presence;
Let thine eyes look upon equity.
³Thou hast proved my heart; thou hast visited me in the night;
Thou hast tried me, and findest nothing;
I am purposed that my mouth shall not transgress.
⁴As for the works of men, by the word of thy lips
I have kept me from the ways of the violent.
⁵My steps have held fast to thy paths,
My feet have not slipped.
⁶I have called upon thee, for thou wilt answer me, O God:
Incline thine ear unto me, and hear my speech.
⁷Show thy marvellous lovingkindness,
O thou that savest by thy right hand them that take refuge in thee
From those that rise up against them.
⁸Keep me as the apple of the eye;
Hide me under the shadow of thy wings,
⁹From the wicked that oppress me,
My deadly enemies, that compass me about.
¹⁰They are inclosed in their own fat:
With their mouth they speak proudly.
¹¹They have now compassed us in our steps;
They set their eyes to cast us down to the earth.
¹²He is like a lion that is greedy of his prey,
And as it were a young lion lurking in secret places.
¹³Arise, O Yahweh,
Confront him, cast him down:
Deliver my soul from the wicked by thy sword;
¹⁴From men by thy hand, O Yahweh,
From men of the world, whose portion is in this life,
And whose belly thou fillest with thy treasure:
They are satisfied with children,
And leave the rest of their substance to their babes.
¹⁵As for me, I shall behold thy face in righteousness;
I shall be satisfied, when I awake, with beholding thy form.

Chapter 18

For the Chief Musician. A Psalm of David the servant of Yahweh, who spake unto Yahweh the words of this song in the day that Yahweh delivered him from the hand of all his enemies, and from the hand of Saul: and he said,
¹I love thee, O Yahweh, my strength.
²Yahweh is my rock, and my fortress, and my deliverer;
My God, my rock, in whom I will take refuge;
My shield, and the horn of my salvation, my high tower.
³I will call upon Yahweh, who is worthy to be praised:
So shall I be saved from mine enemies.
⁴The cords of death compassed me,
And the floods of ungodliness made me afraid.
⁵The cords of Sheol were round about me;
The snares of death came upon me.
⁶In my distress I called upon Yahweh,
And cried unto my God:
He heard my voice out of his temple,
And my cry before him came into his ears.
⁷Then the earth shook and trembled;
The foundations also of the mountains quaked
And were shaken, because he was wroth.
⁸There went up a smoke out of his nostrils,
And fire out of his mouth devoured:
Coals were kindled by it.
⁹He bowed the heavens also, and came down;
And thick darkness was under his feet.
¹⁰And he rode upon a cherub, and did fly;
Yea, he soared upon the wings of the wind.
¹¹He made darkness his hiding-place, his pavilion round about him,
Darkness of waters, thick clouds of the skies.
¹²At the brightness before him his thick clouds passed,
Hailstones and coals of fire.
¹³Yahweh also thundered in the heavens,
And the Most High uttered his voice,
Hailstones and coals of fire.
¹⁴And he sent out his arrows, and scattered them;
Yea, lightnings manifold, and discomfited them.
¹⁵Then the channels of waters appeared,
And the foundations of the world were laid bare,
At thy rebuke, O Yahweh,
At the blast of the breath of thy nostrils.
¹⁶He sent from on high, he took me;
He drew me out of many waters.
¹⁷He delivered me from my strong enemy,
And from them that hated me; for they were too mighty for me.
¹⁸They came upon me in the day of my calamity;
But Yahweh was my stay.
¹⁹He brought me forth also into a large place;
He delivered me, because he delighted in me.
²⁰Yahweh hath rewarded me according to my righteousness;
According to the cleanness of my hands hath he recompensed me.
²¹For I have kept the ways of Yahweh,
And have not wickedly departed from my God.
²²For all his ordinances were before me,
And I put not away his statutes from me.
²³I was also perfect with him,

Psalms

And I kept myself from mine iniquity.
24Therefore hath Yahweh recompensed me according to my righteousness,
According to the cleanness of my hands in his eyesight.
25With the merciful thou wilt show thyself merciful;
With the perfect man thou wilt show thyself perfect;
26With the pure thou wilt show thyself pure;
And with the perverse thou wilt show thyself froward.
27For thou wilt save the afflicted people;
But the haughty eyes thou wilt bring down.
28For thou wilt light my lamp;
Yahweh my God will lighten my darkness.
29For by thee I run upon a troop;
And by my God do I leap over a wall.
30As for God, his way is perfect:
The word of Yahweh is tried;
He is a shield unto all them that take refuge in him.
31For who is God, save Yahweh?
And who is a rock, besides our God,
32The God that girdeth me with strength,
And maketh my way perfect?
33He maketh my feet like hinds' feet:
And setteth me upon my high places.
34He teacheth my hands to war;
So that mine arms do bend a bow of brass.
35Thou hast also given me the shield of thy salvation;
And thy right hand hath holden me up,
And thy gentleness hath made me great.
36Thou hast enlarged my steps under me,
And my feet have not slipped.
37I will pursue mine enemies, and overtake them;
Neither will I turn again till they are consumed.
38I will smite them through, so that they shall not be able to rise:
They shall fall under my feet.
39For thou hast girded me with strength unto the battle:
Thou hast subdued under me those that rose up against me.
40Thou hast also made mine enemies turn their backs unto me,
That I might cut off them that hate me.
41They cried, but there was none to save;
Even unto Yahweh, but he answered them not.
42Then did I beat them small as the dust before the wind;
I did cast them out as the mire of the streets.
43Thou hast delivered me from the strivings of the people;
Thou hast made me the head of the nations:
A people whom I have not known shall serve me.
44As soon as they hear of me they shall obey me;
The foreigners shall submit themselves unto me.
45The foreigners shall fade away,
And shall come trembling out of their close places.
46Yahweh liveth; and blessed be my rock;
And exalted be the God of my salvation:
47Even the God that executeth vengeance for me,
And subdueth peoples under me.
48He rescueth me from mine enemies;
Yea, thou liftest me up above them that rise up against me;
Thou deliverest me from the violent man.
49Therefore I will give thanks unto thee, O Yahweh, among the nations,
And will sing praises unto thy name.
50Great deliverance giveth he to his king,
And showeth lovingkindness to his anointed,
To David and to his seed, for evermore.

Chapter 19

For the Chief Musician. A Psalm of David.
1The heavens declare the glory of God;
And the firmament showeth his handiwork.
2Day unto day uttereth speech,
And night unto night showeth knowledge.
3There is no speech nor language;
Their voice is not heard.
4Their line is gone out through all the earth,
And their words to the end of the world.
In them hath he set a tabernacle for the sun,
5Which is as a bridegroom coming out of his chamber,
And rejoiceth as a strong man to run his course.
6His going forth is from the end of the heavens,
And his circuit unto the ends of it;
And there is nothing hid from the heat thereof.
7The law of Yahweh is perfect, restoring the soul:
The testimony of Yahweh is sure, making wise the simple.
8The precepts of Yahweh are right, rejoicing the heart:
The commandment of Yahweh is pure, enlightening the eyes.
9The fear of Yahweh is clean, enduring for ever:
The ordinances of Yahweh are true, and righteous altogether.
10More to be desired are they than gold, yea, than much fine gold;
Sweeter also than honey and the droppings of the honeycomb.
11Moreover by them is thy servant warned;
In keeping them there is great reward.
12Who can discern his errors?
Clear thou me from hidden faults.
13Keep back thy servant also from presumptuous sins;
Let them not have dominion over me:
Then shall I be upright,
And I shall be clear from great transgression.
14Let the words of my mouth and the meditation of my heart
Be acceptable in thy sight,
O Yahweh, my rock, and my redeemer.

Chapter 20

For the Chief Musician. A Psalm of David.
1Yahweh answer thee in the day of trouble;
The name of the God of Jacob set thee up on high;
2Send thee help from the sanctuary,
And strengthen thee out of Zion;
3Remember all thy offerings,
And accept thy burnt-sacrifice;
Selah
4Grant thee thy heart's desire,
And fulfil all thy counsel.
5We will triumph in thy salvation,
And in the name of our God we will set up our banners:
Yahweh fulfil all thy petitions.
6Now know I that Yahweh saveth his anointed;
He will answer him from his holy heaven
With the saving strength of his right hand.
7Some trust in chariots, and some in horses;
But we will make mention of the name of Yahweh our God.
8They are bowed down and fallen;
But we are risen, and stand upright.
9Save, Yahweh:
Let the King answer us when we call.

Chapter 21

For the Chief Musician. A Psalm of David.
1The king shall joy in thy strength, O Yahweh;
And in thy salvation how greatly shall he rejoice!
2Thou hast given him his heart's desire,
And hast not withholden the request of his lips.
Selah
3For thou meetest him with the blessings of goodness:
Thou settest a crown of fine gold on his head.
4He asked life of thee, thou gavest it him,
Even length of days for ever and ever.
5His glory is great in thy salvation:
Honor and majesty dost thou lay upon him.
6For thou makest him most blessed for ever:
Thou makest him glad with joy in thy presence.
7For the king trusteth in Yahweh;
And through the lovingkindness of the Most High he shall not be moved.
8Thy hand will find out all thine enemies;
Thy right hand will find out those that hate thee.
9Thou wilt make them as a fiery furnace in the time of thine anger:
Yahweh will swallow them up in his wrath,
And the fire shall devour them.
10Their fruit wilt thou destroy from the earth,
And their seed from among the children of men.
11For they intended evil against thee;
They conceived a device which they are not able to perform.
12For thou wilt make them turn their back;
Thou wilt make ready with thy bowstrings against their face.
13Be thou exalted, O Yahweh, in thy strength:
So will we sing and praise thy power.

Chapter 22

For the Chief Musician; set to aAijaleth hash-Shahar. A Psalm of David.
1My God, my God, why hast thou forsaken me?
Why art thou so far from helping me, and from the words of my groaning?
2O my God, I cry in the daytime, but thou answerest not;
And in the night season, and am not silent.
3But thou art holy,
O thou that inhabitest the praises of Israel.
4Our fathers trusted in thee:
They trusted, and thou didst deliver them.
5They cried unto thee, and were delivered:
They trusted in thee, and were not put to shame.
6But I am a worm, and no man;
A reproach of men, and despised of the people.
7All they that see me laugh me to scorn:
They shoot out the lip, they shake the head, saying,
8Commit thyself unto Yahweh;
Let him deliver him:
Let him rescue him, seeing he delighteth in him.
9But thou art he that took me out of the womb;
Thou didst make me trust when I was upon my mother's breasts.
10I was cast upon thee from the womb;
Thou art my God since my mother bare me.
11Be not far from me; for trouble is near;
For there is none to help.

12Many bulls have compassed me;
Strong bulls of Bashan have beset me round.
13They gape upon me with their mouth,
As a ravening and a roaring lion.
14I am poured out like water,
And all my bones are out of joint:
My heart is like wax;
It is melted within me.
15My strength is dried up like a potsherd;
And my tongue cleaveth to my jaws;
And thou hast brought me into the dust of death.
16For dogs have compassed me:
A company of evil-doers have inclosed me;
They pierced my hands and my feet.
17I may count all my bones;
They look and stare upon me.
18They part my garments among them,
And upon my vesture do they cast lots.
19But be not thou far off, O Yahweh;
O thou my succor, haste thee to help me.
20Deliver my soul from the sword,
My darling from the power of the dog.
21Save me from the lion's mouth;
Yea, from the horns of the wild-oxen thou hast answered me.
22I will declare thy name unto my brethren:
In the midst of the assembly will I praise thee.
23Ye that fear Yahweh, praise him;
All ye the seed of Jacob, glorify him;
And stand in awe of him, all ye the seed of Israel.
24For he hath not despised nor abhorred the affliction of the afflicted;
Neither hath he hid his face from him;
But when he cried unto him, he heard.
25Of thee cometh my praise in the great assembly:
I will pay my vows before them that fear him.
26The meek shall eat and be satisfied;
They shall praise Yahweh that seek after him:
Let your heart live for ever.
27All the ends of the earth shall remember and turn unto Yahweh;
And all the kindreds of the nations shall worship before thee.
28For the kingdom is Yahweh's;
And he is the ruler over the nations.
29All the fat ones of the earth shall eat and worship:
All they that go down to the dust shall bow before him,
Even he that cannot keep his soul alive.
30A seed shall serve him;
It shall be told of the Lord unto the next generation.
31They shall come and shall declare his righteousness
Unto a people that shall be born, that he hath done it.

Chapter 23
A Psalm of David.
1Yahweh is my shepherd; I shall not want.
2He maketh me to lie down in green pastures;
He leadeth me beside still waters.
3He restoreth my soul:
He guideth me in the paths of righteousness for his name's sake.
4Yea, thou I walk through the valley of the shadow of death,
I will fear no evil; for thou art with me;
Thy rod and thy staff, they comfort me.
5Thou preparest a table before me in the presence of mine enemies:
Thou hast anointed my head with oil;
My cup runneth over.
6Surely goodness and lovingkindness shall follow me all the days of my life;
And I shall dwell in the house of Yahweh for ever.

Chapter 24
A Psalm of David.
1The earth is Yahweh's, and the fulness thereof;
The world, and they that dwell therein.
2For he hath founded it upon the seas,
And established it upon the floods.
3Who shall ascend into the hill of Yahweh?
And who shall stand in his holy place?
4He that hath clean hands, and a pure heart;
Who hath not lifted up his soul unto falsehood,
And hath not sworn deceitfully.
5He shall receive a blessing from Yahweh,
And righteousness from the God of his salvation.
6This is the generation of them that seek after him,
That seek thy face, even Jacob.
Selah
7Lift up your heads, O ye gates;
And be ye lifted up, ye everlasting doors:
And the King of glory will come in.
8Who is the King of glory?
Yahweh strong and mighty,
Yahweh mighty in battle.
9Lift up your heads, O ye gates;
Yea, lift them up, ye everlasting doors:
And the King of glory will come in.
10Who is this King of glory?
Yahweh of hosts,
He is the King of glory.
Selah

Chapter 25
A Psalm of David.
1Unto thee, O Yahweh, do I lift up my soul.
2O my God, in thee have I trusted,
Let me not be put to shame;
Let not mine enemies triumph over me.
3Yea, none that wait for thee shall be put to shame:
They shall be put to shame that deal treacherously without cause.
4Show me thy ways, O Yahweh;
Teach me thy paths.
5Guide me in thy truth, and teach me;
For thou art the God of my salvation;
For thee do I wait all the day.
6Remember, O Yahweh, thy tender mercies and thy lovingkindness;
For they have been ever of old.
7Remember not the sins of my youth, nor my transgressions:
According to thy lovingkindness remember thou me,
For thy goodness' sake, O Yahweh.
8Good and upright is Yahweh:
Therefore will he instruct sinners in the way.
9The meek will he guide in justice;
And the meek will he teach his way.
10All the paths of Yahweh are lovingkindness and truth
Unto such as keep his covenant and his testimonies.
11For thy name's sake, O Yahweh,
Pardon mine iniquity, for it is great.
12What man is he that feareth Yahweh?
Him shall he instruct in the way that he shall choose.
13His soul shall dwell at ease;
And his seed shall inherit the land.
14The friendship of Yahweh is with them that fear him;
And he will show them his covenant.
15Mine eyes are ever toward Yahweh;
For he will pluck my feet out of the net.
16Turn thee unto me, and have mercy upon me;
For I am desolate and afflicted.
17The troubles of my heart are enlarged:
Oh bring thou me out of my distresses.
18Consider mine affliction and my travail;
And forgive all my sins.
19Consider mine enemies, for they are many;
And they hate me with cruel hatred.
20Oh keep my soul, and deliver me:
Let me not be put to shame, for I take refuge in thee.
21Let integrity and uprightness preserve me,
For I wait for thee.
22Redeem Israel, O God,
Out all of his troubles.

Chapter 26
A Psalm of David.
1Judge me, O Yahweh, for I have walked in mine integrity:
I have trusted also in Yahweh without wavering.
2Examine me, O Yahweh, and prove me;
Try my heart and my mind.
3For thy lovingkindness is before mine eyes;
And I have walked in thy truth.
4I have not sat with men of falsehood;
Neither will I go in with dissemblers.
5I hate the assembly of evil-doers,
And will not sit with the wicked.
6I will wash my hands in innocency:
So will I compass thine altar, O Yahweh;
7That I may make the voice of thanksgiving to be heard,
And tell of all thy wondrous works.
8Yahweh, I love the habitation of thy house,
And the place where thy glory dwelleth.
9Gather not my soul with sinners,
Nor my life with men of blood;
10In whose hands is wickedness,
And their right hand is full of bribes.
11But as for me, I will walk in mine integrity:
Redeem me, and be merciful unto me.
12My foot standeth in an even place:
In the congregations will I bless Yahweh.

Psalms

Chapter 27

A Psalm of David.

1Yahweh is my light and my salvation;
Whom shall I fear?
Yahweh is the strength of my life;
Of whom shall I be afraid?
2When evil-doers came upon me to eat up my flesh,
Even mine adversaries and my foes, they stumbled and fell.
3Though a host should encamp against me,
My heart shall not fear:
Though war should rise against me,
Even then will I be confident.
4One thing have I asked of Yahweh, that will I seek after;
That I may dwell in the house of Yahweh all the days of my life,
To behold the beauty of Yahweh,
And to inquire in his temple.
5For in the day of trouble he will keep me secretly in his pavilion:
In the covert of his tabernacle will he hide me;
He will lift me up upon a rock.
6And now shall my head be lifted up above mine enemies round about me.
And I will offer in his tabernacle sacrifices of joy;
I will sing, yea, I will sing praises unto Yahweh.
7Hear, O Yahweh, when I cry with my voice:
Have mercy also upon me, and answer me.
8When thou saidst, Seek ye my face;
My heart said unto thee,
Thy face, Yahweh, will I seek.
9Hide not thy face from me;
Put not thy servant away in anger:
Thou hast been my help;
Cast me not off, neither forsake me, O God of my salvation.
10When my father and my mother forsake me,
Then Yahweh will take me up.
11Teach me thy way, O Yahweh;
And lead me in a plain path,
Because of mine enemies.
12Deliver me not over unto the will of mine adversaries:
For false witnesses are risen up against me,
And such as breathe out cruelty.
13I had fainted, unless I had believed to see the goodness of Yahweh
In the land of the living.
14Wait for Yahweh:
Be strong, and let thy heart take courage;
Yea, wait thou for Yahweh.

Chapter 28

A Psalm of David.

1Unto thee, O Yahweh, will I call:
My rock, be not thou deaf unto me;
Lest, if thou be silent unto me,
I become like them that go down into the pit.
2Hear the voice of my supplications, when I cry unto thee,
When I lift up my hands toward thy holy oracle.
3Draw me not away with the wicked,
And with the workers of iniquity;
That speak peace with their neighbors,
But mischief is in their hearts.
4Give them according to their work, and according to the wickedness of their doings:
Give them after the operation of their hands;
Render to them their desert.
5Because they regard not the works of Yahweh,
Nor the operation of his hands,
He will break them down and not build them up.
6Blessed be Yahweh,
Because he hath heard the voice of my supplications.
7Yahweh is my strength and my shield;
My heart hath trusted in him, and I am helped:
Therefore my heart greatly rejoiceth;
And with my song will I praise him.
8Yahweh is their strength,
And he is a stronghold of salvation to his anointed.
9Save thy people, and bless thine inheritance:
Be their shepherd also, and bear them up for ever.

Chapter 29

A Psalm of David.

1Ascribe unto Yahweh, O ye sons of the mighty,
Ascribe unto Yahweh glory and strength.
2Ascribe unto Yahweh the glory due unto his name;
Worship Yahweh in holy array.
3The voice of Yahweh is upon the waters:
The God of glory thundereth,
Even Yahweh upon many waters.
4The voice of Yahweh is powerful;
The voice of Yahweh is full of majesty.
5The voice of Yahweh breaketh the cedars;
Yea, Yahweh breaketh in pieces the cedars of Lebanon.
6He maketh them also to skip like a calf;
Lebanon and Sirion like a young wild-ox.
7The voice of Yahweh cleaveth the flames of fire.
8The voice of Yahweh shaketh the wilderness;
Yahweh shaketh the wilderness of Kadesh.
9The voice of Yahweh maketh the hinds to calve,
And strippeth the forests bare:
And in his temple everything saith, Glory.
10Yahweh sat as King at the Flood;
Yea, Yahweh sitteth as King for ever.
11Yahweh will give strength unto his people;
Yahweh will bless his people with peace.

Chapter 30

A Psalm; a Song at the Dedication of the House. A Psalm of David.

1I will extol thee, O Yahweh; for thou hast raised me up,
And hast not made my foes to rejoice over me.
2O Yahweh my God,
I cried unto thee, and thou hast healed me.
3O Yahweh, thou hast brought up my soul from Sheol;
Thou hast kept me alive, that I should not go down to the pit.
4Sing praise unto Yahweh, O ye saints of his,
And give thanks to his holy memorial name.
5For his anger is but for a moment;
His favor is for a life-time:
Weeping may tarry for the night,
But joy cometh in the morning.
6As for me, I said in my prosperity,
I shall never be moved.
7Thou, Yahweh, of thy favor hadst made my mountain to stand strong:
Thou didst hide thy face; I was troubled.
8I cried to thee, O Yahweh;
And unto Yahweh made supplication:
9What profit is there in my blood, when I go down to the pit?
Shall the dust praise thee? shall it declare thy truth?
10Hear, O Yahweh, and have mercy upon me:
Yahweh, be thou my helper.
11Thou hast turned for me my mourning into dancing;
Thou hast loosed my sackcloth, and girded me with gladness;
12To the end that my glory may sing praise to thee, and not be silent.
O Yahweh my God, I will give thanks unto thee for ever.

Chapter 31

For the Chief Musician. A Psalm of David.

1In thee, O Yahweh, do I take refuge;
Let me never be put to shame:
Deliver me in thy righteousness.
2Bow down thine ear unto me; deliver me speedily:
Be thou to me a strong rock,
A house of defence to save me.
3For thou art my rock and my fortress;
Therefore for thy name's sake lead me and guide me.
4Pluck me out of the net that they have laid privily for me;
For thou art my stronghold.
5Into thy hand I commend my spirit:
Thou hast redeemed me, O Yahweh, thou God of truth.
6I hate them that regard lying vanities;
But I trust in Yahweh.
7I will be glad and rejoice in thy lovingkindness;
For thou hast seen my affliction;
Thou hast known my soul in adversities;
8And thou hast not shut me up into the hand of the enemy;
Thou hast set my feet in a large place.
9Have mercy upon me, O Yahweh, for I am in distress:
Mine eye wasteth away with grief, yea, my soul and my body.
10For my life is spent with sorrow,
And my years with sighing:
My strength faileth because of mine iniquity,
And my bones are wasted away.
11Because of all mine adversaries I am become a reproach,
Yea, unto my neighbors exceedingly,
And a fear to mine acquaintance:
They that did see me without fled from me.
12I am forgotten as a dead man out of mind:
I am like a broken vessel.
13For I have heard the defaming of many,
Terror on every side:
While they took counsel together against me,
They devised to take away my life.
14But I trusted in thee, O Yahweh:
I said, Thou art my God.
15My times are in thy hand:
Deliver me from the hand of mine enemies, and from them that persecute me.
16Make thy face to shine upon thy servant:
Save me in thy lovingkindness.
17Let me not be put to shame, O Yahweh; for I have called upon thee:
Let the wicked be put to shame, let them be silent in Sheol.

18Let the lying lips be dumb,
Which speak against the righteous insolently,
With pride and contempt.
19Oh how great is thy goodness,
Which thou hast laid up for them that fear thee,
Which thou hast wrought for them that take refuge in thee,
Before the sons of men!
20In the covert of thy presence wilt thou hide them from the plottings of man:
Thou wilt keep them secretly in a pavilion from the strife of tongues.
21Blessed be Yahweh;
For he hath showed me his marvellous lovingkindness in a strong city.
22As for me, I said in my haste,
I am cut off from before thine eyes:
Nevertheless thou heardest the voice of my supplications
When I cried unto thee.
23Oh love Yahweh, all ye his saints:
Yahweh preserveth the faithful,
And plentifully rewardeth him that dealeth proudly.
24Be strong, and let your heart take courage,
All ye that hope in Yahweh.

Chapter 32

A Psalm of David. Maschil.
1Blessed is he whose transgression is forgiven,
Whose sin is covered.
2Blessed is the man unto whom Yahweh imputeth not iniquity,
And in whose spirit there is no guile.
3When I kept silence, my bones wasted away
Through my groaning all the day long.
4For day and night thy hand was heavy upon me:
My moisture was changed as with the drought of summer.
Selah
5I acknowledged my sin unto thee,
And mine iniquity did I not hide:
I said, I will confess my transgressions unto Yahweh;
And thou forgavest the iniquity of my sin.
Selah
6For this let every one that is godly pray unto thee in a time when thou mayest be found:
Surely when the great waters overflow they shall not reach unto him.
7Thou art my hiding-place; thou wilt preserve me from trouble;
Thou wilt compass me about with songs of deliverance.
Selah
8I will instruct thee and teach thee in the way which thou shalt go:
I will counsel thee with mine eye upon thee.
9Be ye not as the horse, or as the mule, which have no understanding;
Whose trappings must be bit and bridle to hold them in,
Else they will not come near unto thee.
10Many sorrows shall be to the wicked;
But he that trusteth in Yahweh, lovingkindness shall compass him about.
11Be glad in Yahweh, and rejoice, ye righteous;
And shout for joy, all ye that are upright in heart.

Chapter 33

1Rejoice in Yahweh, O ye righteous:
Praise is comely for the upright.
2Give thanks unto Yahweh with the harp:
Sing praises unto him with the psaltery of ten strings.
3Sing unto him a new song;
Play skilfully with a loud noise.
4For the word of Yahweh is right;
And all his work is done in faithfulness.
5He loveth righteousness and justice:
The earth is full of the lovingkindness of Yahweh.
6By the word of Yahweh were the heavens made,
And all the host of them by the breath of his mouth.
7He gathereth the waters of the sea together as a heap:
He layeth up the deeps in store-houses.
8Let all the earth fear Yahweh:
Let all the inhabitants of the world stand in awe of him.
9For he spake, and it was done;
He commanded, and it stood fast.
10Yahweh bringeth the counsel of the nations to nought;
He maketh the thoughts of the peoples to be of no effect.
11The counsel of Yahweh standeth fast for ever,
The thoughts of his heart to all generations.
12Blessed is the nation whose God is Yahweh,
The people whom he hath chosen for his own inheritance.
13Yahweh looketh from heaven;
He beholdeth all the sons of men;
14From the place of his habitation he looketh forth
Upon all the inhabitants of the earth,
15He that fashioneth the hearts of them all,
That considereth all their works.
16There is no king saved by the multitude of a host:
A mighty man is not delivered by great strength.
17A horse is a vain thing for safety;
Neither doth he deliver any by his great power.
18Behold, the eye of Yahweh is upon them that fear him,
Upon them that hope in his lovingkindness;
19To deliver their soul from death,
And to keep them alive in famine.
20Our soul hath waited for Yahweh:
He is our help and our shield.
21For our heart shall rejoice in him,
Because we have trusted in his holy name.
22Let thy lovingkindness, O Yahweh, be upon us,
According as we have hoped in thee.

Chapter 34

A Psalm of David; when he changed his behavior before Abimelech, who drove him away, and he departed.
1I will bless Yahweh at all times:
His praise shall continually be in my mouth.
2My soul shall make her boast in Yahweh:
The meek shall hear thereof, and be glad.
3Oh magnify Yahweh with me,
And let us exalt his name together.
4I sought Yahweh, and he answered me,
And delivered me from all my fears.
5They looked unto him, and were radiant;
And their faces shall never be confounded.
6This poor man cried, and Yahweh heard him,
And saved him out of all his troubles.
7The angel of Yahweh encampeth round about them that fear him,
And delivereth them.
8Oh taste and see that Yahweh is good:
Blessed is the man that taketh refuge in him.
9Oh fear Yahweh, ye his saints;
For there is no want to them that fear him.
10The young lions do lack, and suffer hunger;
But they that seek Yahweh shall not want any good thing.
11Come, ye children, hearken unto me:
I will teach you the fear of Yahweh.
12What man is he that desireth life,
And loveth many days, that he may see good?
13Keep thy tongue from evil,
And thy lips from speaking guile.
14Depart from evil, and do good;
Seek peace, and pursue it.
15The eyes of Yahweh are toward the righteous,
And his ears are open unto their cry.
16The face of Yahweh is against them that do evil,
To cut off the remembrance of them from the earth.
17The righteous cried, and Yahweh heard,
And delivered them out of all their troubles.
18Yahweh is nigh unto them that are of a broken heart,
And saveth such as are of a contrite spirit.
19Many are the afflictions of the righteous;
But Yahweh delivereth him out of them all.
20He keepeth all his bones:
Not one of them is broken.
21Evil shall slay the wicked;
And they that hate the righteous shall be condemned.
22Yahweh redeemeth the soul of his servants;
And none of them that take refuge in him shall be condemned.

Chapter 35

A Psalm of David.
1Strive thou, O Yahweh, with them that strive with me:
Fight thou against them that fight against me.
2Take hold of shield and buckler,
And stand up for my help.
3Draw out also the spear, and stop the way against them that pursue me:
Say unto my soul, I am thy salvation.
4Let them be put to shame and brought to dishonor that seek after my soul:
Let them be turned back and confounded that devise my hurt.
5Let them be as chaff before the wind,
And the angel of Yahweh driving them on.
6Let their way be dark and slippery,
And the angel of Yahweh pursuing them.
7For without cause have they hid for me their net in a pit;
Without cause have they digged a pit for my soul.
8Let destruction come upon him unawares;
And let his net that he hath hid catch himself:
With destruction let him fall therein.
9And my soul shall be joyful in Yahweh:
It shall rejoice in his salvation.
10All my bones shall say, Yahweh, who is like unto thee,
Who deliverest the poor from him that is too strong for him,
Yea, the poor and the needy from him that robbeth him?
11Unrighteous witnesses rise up;
They ask me of things that I know not.
12They reward me evil for good,
To the bereaving of my soul.

Psalms

13 But as for me, when they were sick, my clothing was sackcloth:
I afflicted my soul with fasting;
And my prayer returned into mine own bosom.
14 I behaved myself as though it had been my friend or my brother:
I bowed down mourning, as one that bewaileth his mother.
15 But in mine adversity they rejoiced, and gathered themselves together:
The abjects gathered themselves together against me, and I knew it not;
They did tear me, and ceased not:
16 Like the profane mockers in feasts,
They gnashed upon me with their teeth.
17 Lord, how long wilt thou look on?
Rescue my soul from their destructions,
My darling from the lions.
18 I will give thee thanks in the great assembly:
I will praise thee among much people.
19 Let not them that are mine enemies wrongfully rejoice over me;
Neither let them wink with the eye that hate me without a cause.
20 For they speak not peace;
But they devise deceitful words against them that are quiet in the land.
21 Yea, they opened their mouth wide against me;
They said, Aha, aha, our eye hath seen it.
22 Thou hast seen it, O Yahweh; keep not silence:
O Lord, be not far from me.
23 Stir up thyself, and awake to the justice due unto me,
Even unto my cause, my God and my Lord.
24 Judge me, O Yahweh my God, according to thy righteousness;
And let them not rejoice over me.
25 Let them not say in their heart, Aha, so would we have it:
Let them not say, We have swallowed him up.
26 Let them be put to shame and confounded together that rejoice at my hurt:
Let them be clothed with shame and dishonor that magnify themselves against me.
27 Let them shout for joy, and be glad, that favor my righteous cause:
Yea, let them say continually, Yahweh be magnified,
Who hath pleasure in the prosperity of his servant.
28 And my tongue shall talk of thy righteousness
And of thy praise all the day long.

Chapter 36

For the Chief Musician. A Psalm of David the servant of Yahweh.
1 The transgression of the wicked saith within my heart,
There is no fear of God before his eyes.
2 For he flattereth himself in his own eyes,
That his iniquity will not be found out and be hated.
3 The words of his mouth are iniquity and deceit:
He hath ceased to be wise and to do good.
4 He deviseth iniquity upon his bed;
He setteth himself in a way that is not good;
He abhorreth not evil.
5 Thy lovingkindness, O Yahweh, is in the heavens;
Thy faithfulness reacheth unto the skies.
6 Thy righteousness is like the mountains of God;
Thy judgments are a great deep:
O Yahweh, thou preservest man and beast.
7 How precious is thy lovingkindness, O God!
And the children of men take refuge under the shadow of thy wings.
8 They shall be abundantly satisfied with the fatness of thy house;
And thou wilt make them drink of the river of thy pleasures.
9 For with thee is the fountain of life:
In thy light shall we see light.
10 Oh continue thy lovingkindness unto them that know thee,
And thy righteousness to the upright in heart.
11 Let not the foot of pride come against me,
And let not the hand of the wicked drive me away.
12 There are the workers of iniquity fallen:
They are thrust down, and shall not be able to rise.

Chapter 37

A Psalm of David.
1 Fret not thyself because of evil-doers,
Neither be thou envious against them that work unrighteousness.
2 For they shall soon be cut down like the grass,
And wither as the green herb.
3 Trust in Yahweh, and do good;
Dwell in the land, and feed on his faithfulness.
4 Delight thyself also in Yahweh;
And he will give thee the desires of thy heart.
5 Commit thy way unto Yahweh;
Trust also in him, and he will bring it to pass.
6 And he will make thy righteousness to go forth as the light,
And thy justice as the noon-day.
7 Rest in Yahweh, and wait patiently for him:
Fret not thyself because of him who prospereth in his way,
Because of the man who bringeth wicked devices to pass.
8 Cease from anger, and forsake wrath:
Fret not thyself, it tendeth only to evil-doing.
9 For evil-doers shall be cut off;
But those that wait for Yahweh, they shall inherit the land.
10 For yet a little while, and the wicked shall not be:
Yea, thou shalt diligently consider his place, and he shall not be.
11 But the meek shall inherit the land,
And shall delight themselves in the abundance of peace.
12 The wicked plotteth against the just,
And gnasheth upon him with his teeth.
13 The Lord will laugh at him;
For he seeth that his day is coming.
14 The wicked have drawn out the sword, and have bent their bow,
To cast down the poor and needy,
To slay such as are upright in the way.
15 Their sword shall enter into their own heart,
And their bows shall be broken.
16 Better is a little that the righteous hath
Than the abundance of many wicked.
17 For the arms of the wicked shall be broken;
But Yahweh upholdeth the righteous.
18 Yahweh knoweth the days of the perfect;
And their inheritance shall be for ever.
19 They shall not be put to shame in the time of evil;
And in the days of famine they shall be satisfied.
20 But the wicked shall perish,
And the enemies of Yahweh shall be as the fat of lambs:
They shall consume;
In smoke shall they consume away.
21 The wicked borroweth, and payeth not again;
But the righteous dealeth graciously, and giveth.
22 For such as are blessed of him shall inherit the land;
And they that are cursed of him shall be cut off.
23 A man's goings are established of Yahweh;
And he delighteth in his way.
24 Though he fall, he shall not be utterly cast down;
For Yahweh upholdeth him with his hand.
25 I have been young, and now am old;
Yet have I not seen the righteous forsaken,
Nor his seed begging bread.
26 All the day long he dealeth graciously, and lendeth;
And his seed is blessed.
27 Depart from evil, and do good;
And dwell for evermore.
28 For Yahweh loveth justice,
And forsaketh not his saints;
They are preserved for ever:
But the seed of the wicked shall be cut off.
29 The righteous shall inherit the land,
And dwell therein for ever.
30 The mouth of the righteous talketh of wisdom,
And his tongue speaketh justice.
31 The law of his God is in his heart;
None of his steps shall slide.
32 The wicked watcheth the righteous,
And seeketh to slay him.
33 Yahweh will not leave him in his hand,
Nor condemn him when he is judged.
34 Wait for Yahweh, and keep his way,
And he will exalt thee to inherit the land:
When the wicked are cut off, thou shalt see it.
35 I have seen the wicked in great power,
And spreading himself like a green tree in its native soil.
36 But one passed by, and, lo, he was not:
Yea, I sought him, but he could not be found.
37 Mark the perfect man, and behold the upright;
For there is a happy end to the man of peace.
38 As for transgressors, they shall be destroyed together;
The end of the wicked shall be cut off.
39 But the salvation of the righteous is of Yahweh;
He is their stronghold in the time of trouble.
40 And Yahweh helpeth them, and rescueth them;
He rescueth them from the wicked, and saveth them,
Because they have taken refuge in him.

Chapter 38

A Psalm of David, to bring to remembrance.
1 O Yahweh, rebuke me not in thy wrath;
Neither chasten me in thy hot displeasure.
2 For thine arrows stick fast in me,
And thy hand presseth me sore.
3 There is no soundness in my flesh because of thine indignation;
Neither is there any health in my bones because of my sin.
4 For mine iniquities are gone over my head:
As a heavy burden they are too heavy for me.
5 My wounds are loathsome and corrupt,
Because of my foolishness.
6 I am pained and bowed down greatly;
I go mourning all the day long.
7 For my loins are filled with burning;
And there is no soundness in my flesh.
8 I am faint and sore bruised:
I have groaned by reason of the disquietness of my heart.

9Lord, all my desire is before thee;
And my groaning is not hid from thee.
10My heart throbbeth, my strength faileth me:
As for the light of mine eyes, it also is gone from me.
11My lovers and my friends stand aloof from my plague;
And my kinsmen stand afar off.
12They also that seek after my life lay snares for me;
And they that seek my hurt speak mischievous things,
And meditate deceits all the day long.
13But I, as a deaf man, hear not;
And I am as a dumb man that openeth not his mouth.
14Yea, I am as a man that heareth not,
And in whose mouth are no reproofs.
15For in thee, O Yahweh, do I hope:
Thou wilt answer, O Lord my God.
16For I said, Lest they rejoice over me:
When my foot slippeth, they magnify themselves against me.
17For I am ready to fall,
And my sorrow is continually before me.
18For I will declare mine iniquity; I will be sorry for my sin.
19But mine enemies are lively, and are strong;
And they that hate me wrongfully are multiplied.
20They also that render evil for good
Are adversaries unto me, because I follow the thing that is good.
21Forsake me not, O Yahweh:
O my God, be not far from me.
22Make haste to help me,
O Lord, my salvation.

Chapter 39

For the Chief Musician, Jeduthun. A Psalm of David.
1I said, I will take heed to my ways,
That I sin not with my tongue:
I will keep my mouth with a bridle,
While the wicked is before me.
2I was dumb with silence, I held my peace, even from good;
And my sorrow was stirred.
3My heart was hot within me;
While I was musing the fire burned:
Then spake I with my tongue:
4Yahweh, make me to know mine end,
And the measure of my days, what it is;
Let me know how frail I am.
5Behold, thou hast made my days as handbreadths;
And my life-time is as nothing before thee:
Surely every man at his best estate is altogether vanity.
Selah
6Surely every man walketh in a vain show;
Surely they are disquieted in vain:
He heapeth up riches, and knoweth not who shall gather them.
7And now, Lord, what wait I for?
My hope is in thee.
8Deliver me from all my transgressions:
Make me not the reproach of the foolish.
9I was dumb, I opened not my mouth;
Because thou didst it.
10Remove thy stroke away from me:
I am consumed by the blow of thy hand.
11When thou with rebukes dost correct man for iniquity,
Thou makest his beauty to consume away like a moth;
Surely every man is vanity.
Selah
12Hear my prayer, O Yahweh, and give ear unto my cry;
Hold not thy peace at my tears:
For I am a stranger with thee,
A sojourner, as all my fathers were.
13Oh spare me, that I may recover strength,
Before I go hence, and be no more.

Chapter 40

For the Chief Musician. A Psalm of David.
1I waited patiently for Yahweh;
And he inclined unto me, and heard my cry.
2He brought me up also out of a horrible pit, out of the miry clay;
And he set my feet upon a rock, and established my goings.
3And he hath put a new song in my mouth, even praise unto our God:
Many shall see it, and fear,
And shall trust in Yahweh.
4Blessed is the man that maketh Yahweh his trust,
And respecteth not the proud, nor such as turn aside to lies.
5Many, O Yahweh my God, are the wonderful works which thou hast done,
And thy thoughts which are to us-ward;
They cannot be set in order unto thee;
If I would declare and speak of them,
They are more than can be numbered.
6Sacrifice and offering thou hast no delight in;
Mine ears hast thou opened:
Burnt-offering and sin-offering hast thou not required.
7Then said I, Lo, I am come;
In the roll of the book it is written of me:
8I delight to do thy will, O my God;
Yea, thy law is within my heart.
9I have proclaimed glad tidings of righteousness in the great assembly;
Lo, I will not refrain my lips,
O Yahweh, thou knowest.
10I have not hid thy righteousness within my heart;
I have declared thy faithfulness and thy salvation;
I have not concealed thy lovingkindness and thy truth from the great assembly.
11Withhold not thou thy tender mercies from me, O Yahweh;
Let thy lovingkindness and thy truth continually preserve me.
12For innumerable evils have compassed me about;
Mine iniquities have overtaken me, so that I am not able to look up;
They are more than the hairs of my head;
And my heart hath failed me.
13Be pleased, O Yahweh, to deliver me:
Make haste to help me, O Yahweh.
14Let them be put to shame and confounded together
That seek after my soul to destroy it:
Let them be turned backward and brought to dishonor
That delight in my hurt.
15Let them be desolate by reason of their shame
That say unto me, Aha, aha.
16Let all those that seek thee rejoice and be glad in thee:
Let such as love thy salvation say continually,
Yahweh be magnified.
17But I am poor and needy;
Yet the Lord thinketh upon me:
Thou art my help and my deliverer;
Make no tarrying, O my God.

Chapter 41

For the Chief Musician. A Psalm of David.
1Blessed is he that considereth the poor:
Yahweh will deliver him in the day of evil.
2Yahweh will preserve him, and keep him alive,
And he shall be blessed upon the earth;
And deliver not thou him unto the will of his enemies.
3Yahweh will support him upon the couch of languishing:
Thou makest all his bed in his sickness.
4I said, O Yahweh, have mercy upon me:
Heal my soul; for I have sinned against thee.
5Mine enemies speak evil against me, saying,
When will he die, and his name perish?
6And if he come to see me, he speaketh falsehood;
His heart gathereth iniquity to itself:
When he goeth abroad, he telleth it.
7All that hate me whisper together against me;
Against me do they devise my hurt.
8An evil disease, say they, cleaveth fast unto him;
And now that he lieth he shall rise up no more.
9Yea, mine own familiar friend, in whom I trusted,
Who did eat of my bread,
Hath lifted up his heel against me.
10But thou, O Yahweh, have mercy upon me, and raise me up,
That I may requite them.
11By this I know that thou delightest in me,
Because mine enemy doth not triumph over me.
12And as for me, thou upholdest me in mine integrity,
And settest me before thy face for ever.
13Blessed be Yahweh, the God of Israel,
From everlasting and to everlasting.
Amen, and Amen.

Book II

Chapter 42

For the Chief Musician. Maschil of the sons of Korah.
1As the hart panteth after the water brooks,
So panteth my soul after thee, O God.
2My soul thirsteth for God, for the living God:
When shall I come and appear before God?
3My tears have been my food day and night,
While they continually say unto me, Where is thy God?
4These things I remember, and pour out my soul within me,
How I went with the throng, and led them to the house of God,
With the voice of joy and praise, a multitude keeping holyday.
5Why art thou cast down, O my soul?
And why art thou disquieted within me?
Hope thou in God; for I shall yet praise him
For the help of his countenance.
6O my God, my soul is cast down within me:
Therefore do I remember thee from the land of the Jordan,
And the Hermons, from the hill Mizar.
7Deep calleth unto deep at the noise of thy waterfalls:
All thy waves and thy billows are gone over me.

8Yet Yahweh will command his lovingkindness in the day-time;
And in the night his song shall be with me,
Even a prayer unto the God of my life.
9I will say unto God my rock, Why hast thou forgotten me?
Why go I mourning because of the oppression of the enemy?
10As with a sword in my bones, mine adversaries reproach me,
While they continually say unto me, Where is thy God?
11Why art thou cast down, O my soul?
And why art thou disquieted within me?
Hope thou in God; for I shall yet praise him,
Who is the help of my countenance, and my God.

Chapter 43

1Judge me, O God, and plead my cause against an ungodly nation:
Oh deliver me from the deceitful and unjust man.
2For thou art the God of my strength; why hast thou cast me off?
Why go I mourning because of the oppression of the enemy?
3Oh send out thy light and thy truth; let them lead me:
Let them bring me unto thy holy hill,
And to thy tabernacles.
4Then will I go unto the altar of God,
Unto God my exceeding joy;
And upon the harp will I praise thee, O God, my God.
5Why art thou cast down, O my soul?
And why art thou disquieted within me?
Hope thou in God; for I shall yet praise him,
Who is the help of my countenance, and my God.

Chapter 44

For the Chief Musician. A Psalm of the sons of Korah. Maschil.
1We have heard with our ears, O God,
Our fathers have told us,
What work thou didst in their days,
In the days of old.
2Thou didst drive out the nations with thy hand;
But them thou didst plant:
Thou didst afflict the peoples;
But them thou didst spread abroad.
3For they gat not the land in possession by their own sword,
Neither did their own arm save them;
But thy right hand, and thine arm, and the light of thy countenance,
Because thou wast favorable unto them.
4Thou art my King, O God:
Command deliverance for Jacob.
5Through thee will we push down our adversaries:
Through thy name will we tread them under that rise up against us.
6For I will not trust in my bow,
Neither shall my sword save me.
7But thou hast saved us from our adversaries,
And hast put them to shame that hate us.
8In God have we made our boast all the day long,
And we will give thanks unto thy name for ever.
Selah
9But now thou hast cast us off, and brought us to dishonor,
And goest not forth with our hosts.
10Thou makest us to turn back from the adversary;
And they that hate us take spoil for themselves.
11Thou hast made us like sheep appointed for food,
And hast scattered us among the nations.
12Thou sellest thy people for nought,
And hast not increased thy wealth by their price.
13Thou makest us a reproach to our neighbors,
A scoffing and a derision to them that are round about us.
14Thou makest us a byword among the nations,
A shaking of the head among the peoples.
15All the day long is my dishonor before me,
And the shame of my face hath covered me,
16For the voice of him that reproacheth and blasphemeth,
By reason of the enemy and the avenger.
17All this is come upon us;
Yet have we not forgotten thee,
Neither have we dealt falsely in thy covenant.
18Our heart is not turned back,
Neither have our steps declined from thy way,
19That thou hast sore broken us in the place of jackals,
And covered us with the shadow of death.
20If we have forgotten the name of our God,
Or spread forth our hands to a strange god;
21Will not God search this out?
For he knoweth the secrets of the heart.
22Yea, for thy sake are we killed all the day long;
We are accounted as sheep for the slaughter.
23Awake, why sleepest thou, O Lord?
Arise, cast us not off for ever.
24Wherefore hidest thou thy face,
And forgettest our affliction and our oppression?
25For our soul is bowed down to the dust:
Our body cleaveth unto the earth.
26Rise up for our help,
And redeem us for thy lovingkindness' sake.

Chapter 45

For the Chief Musician; set to aShoshannim. A Psalm of the sons of Korah. Maschil. A Song of loves.
1My heart overfloweth with a goodly matter;
I speak the things which I have made touching the king:
My tongue is the pen of a ready writer.
2Thou art fairer than the children of men;
Grace is poured into thy lips:
Therefore God hath blessed thee for ever.
3Gird thy sword upon thy thigh, O mighty one,
Thy glory and thy majesty.
4And in thy majesty ride on prosperously,
Because of truth and meekness and righteousness:
And thy right hand shall teach thee terrible things.
5Thine arrows are sharp;
The peoples fall under thee;
They are in the heart of the king's enemies.
6Thy throne, O God, is for ever and ever:
A sceptre of equity is the sceptre of thy kingdom.
7Thou hast loved righteousness, and hated wickedness:
Therefore God, thy God, hath anointed thee
With the oil of gladness above thy fellows.
8All thy garments smell of myrrh, and aloes, and cassia;
Out of ivory palaces stringed instruments have made thee glad.
9Kings' daughters are among thy honorable women:
At thy right hand doth stand the queen in gold of Ophir.
10Hearken, O daughter, and consider, and incline thine ear;
Forget also thine own people, and thy father's house:
11So will the king desire thy beauty;
For he is thy lord; and reverence him.
12And the daughter of Tyre shall be there with a gift;
The rich among the people shall entreat thy favor.
13The king's daughter within the palace is all glorious:
Her clothing is inwrought with gold.
14She shall be led unto the king in broidered work:
The virgins her companions that follow her
Shall be brought unto thee.
15With gladness and rejoicing shall they be led:
They shall enter into the king's palace.
16Instead of thy fathers shall be thy children,
Whom thou shalt make princes in all the earth.
17I will make thy name to be remembered in all generations:
Therefore shall the peoples give thee thanks for ever and ever.

Chapter 46

For the Chief Musician. A Psalm of the sons of Korah; set to Alamoth. A Song.
1God is our refuge and strength,
A very present help in trouble.
2Therefore will we not fear, though the earth do change,
And though the mountains be shaken into the heart of the seas;
3Though the waters thereof roar and be troubled,
Though the mountains tremble with the swelling thereof.
Selah
4There is a river, the streams whereof make glad the city of God,
The holy place of the tabernacles of the Most High.
5God is in the midst of her; she shall not be moved:
God will help her, and that right early.
6The nations raged, the kingdoms were moved:
He uttered his voice, the earth melted.
7Yahweh of hosts is with us;
The God of Jacob is our refuge.
Selah
8Come, behold the works of Yahweh,
What desolations he hath made in the earth.
9He maketh wars to cease unto the end of the earth;
He breaketh the bow, and cutteth the spear in sunder;
He burneth the chariots in the fire.
10Be still, and know that I am God:
I will be exalted among the nations, I will be exalted in the earth.
11Yahweh of hosts is with us;
The God of Jacob is our refuge.
Selah

Chapter 47

For the Chief Musician. A Psalm of the sons of Korah.
1Oh clap your hands, all ye peoples;
Shout unto God with the voice of triumph.
2For Yahweh Most High is terrible;
He is a great King over all the earth.
3He subdueth peoples under us,
And nations under our feet.
4He chooseth our inheritance for us,
The glory of Jacob whom he loved.
Selah

⁵God is gone up with a shout,
Yahweh with the sound of a trumpet.
⁶Sing praise to God, sing praises:
Sing praises unto our King, sing praises.
⁷For God is the King of all the earth:
Sing ye praises with understanding.
⁸God reigneth over the nations:
God sitteth upon his holy throne.
⁹The princes of the peoples are gathered together
To be the people of the God of Abraham:
For the shields of the earth belong unto God;
He is greatly exalted.

Chapter 48

A Song; a Psalm of the sons of Korah.
¹Great is Yahweh, and greatly to be praised,
In the city of our God, in his holy mountain.
²Beautiful in elevation, the joy of the whole earth,
Is mount Zion, on the sides of the north,
The city of the great King.
³God hath made himself known in her palaces for a refuge.
⁴For, lo, the kings assembled themselves,
They passed by together.
⁵They saw it, then were they amazed;
They were dismayed, they hasted away.
⁶Trembling took hold of them there,
Pain, as of a woman in travail.
⁷With the east wind
Thou breakest the ships of Tarshish.
⁸As we have heard, so have we seen
In the city of Yahweh of hosts, in the city of our God:
God will establish it for ever.
Selah
⁹We have thought on thy lovingkindness, O God,
In the midst of thy temple.
¹⁰As is thy name, O God,
So is thy praise unto the ends of the earth:
Thy right hand is full of righteousness.
¹¹Let mount Zion be glad,
Let the daughters of Judah rejoice,
Because of thy judgments.
¹²Walk about Zion, and go round about her;
Number the towers thereof;
¹³Mark ye well her bulwarks;
Consider her palaces:
That ye may tell it to the generation following.
¹⁴For this God is our God for ever and ever:
He will be our guide even unto death.

Chapter 49

For the Chief Musician. A Psalm of the sons of Korah.
¹Hear this, all ye peoples;
Give ear, all ye inhabitants of the world,
²Both low and high,
Rich and poor together.
³My mouth shall speak wisdom;
And the meditation of my heart shall be of understanding.
⁴I will incline mine ear to a parable:
I will open my dark saying upon the harp.
⁵Wherefore should I fear in the days of evil,
When iniquity at my heels compasseth me about?
⁶They that trust in their wealth,
And boast themselves in the multitude of their riches;
⁷None of them can by any means redeem his brother,
Nor give to God a ransom for him;
⁸(For the redemption of their life is costly,
And it faileth for ever;)
⁹That he should still live alway,
That he should not see corruption.
¹⁰For he shall see it. Wise men die;
The fool and the brutish alike perish,
And leave their wealth to others.
¹¹Their inward thought is, that their houses shall continue for ever,
And their dwelling-places to all generations;
They call their lands after their own names.
¹²But man being in honor abideth not:
He is like the beasts that perish.
¹³This their way is their folly:
Yet after them men approve their sayings.
Selah
¹⁴They are appointed as a flock for Sheol;
Death shall be their shepherd;
And the upright shall have dominion over them in the morning;
And their beauty shall be for Sheol to consume,
That there be no habitation for it.
¹⁵But God will redeem my soul from the power of Sheol;
For he will receive me.
Selah
¹⁶Be not thou afraid when one is made rich,
When the glory of his house is increased.
¹⁷For when he dieth he shall carry nothing away;
His glory shall not descend after him.
¹⁸Though while he lived he blessed his soul
(And men praise thee, when thou doest well to thyself,)
¹⁹He shall go to the generation of his fathers;
They shall never see the light.
²⁰Man that is in honor, and understandeth not,
Is like the beasts that perish.

Chapter 50

A Psalm of Asaph.
¹The Mighty One, God, Yahweh, hath spoken,
And called the earth from the rising of the sun unto the going down thereof.
²Out of Zion, the perfection of beauty,
God hath shined forth.
³Our God cometh, and doth not keep silence:
A fire devoureth before him,
And it is very tempestuous round about him.
⁴He calleth to the heavens above,
And to the earth, that he may judge his people:
⁵Gather my saints together unto me,
Those that have made a covenant with me by sacrifice.
⁶And the heavens shall declare his righteousness;
For God is judge himself.
Selah
⁷Hear, O my people, and I will speak;
O Israel, and I will testify unto thee:
I am God, even thy God.
⁸I will not reprove thee for thy sacrifices;
And thy burnt-offerings are continually before me.
⁹I will take no bullock out of thy house,
Nor he-goats out of thy folds.
¹⁰For every beast of the forest is mine,
And the cattle upon a thousand hills.
¹¹I know all the birds of the mountains;
And the wild beasts of the field are mine.
¹²If I were hungry, I would not tell thee;
For the world is mine, and the fulness thereof.
¹³Will I eat the flesh of bulls,
Or drink the blood of goats?
¹⁴Offer unto God the sacrifice of thanksgiving;
And pay thy vows unto the Most High:
¹⁵And call upon me in the day of trouble;
I will deliver thee, and thou shalt glorify me.
¹⁶But unto the wicked God saith,
What hast thou to do to declare my statutes,
And that thou hast taken my covenant in thy mouth,
¹⁷Seeing thou hatest instruction,
And castest my words behind thee?
¹⁸When thou sawest a thief, thou consentedst with him,
And hast been partaker with adulterers.
¹⁹Thou givest thy mouth to evil,
And thy tongue frameth deceit.
²⁰Thou sittest and speakest against thy brother;
Thou slanderest thine own mother's son.
²¹These things hast thou done, and I kept silence;
Thou thoughtest that I was altogether such a one as thyself:
But I will reprove thee, and set them in order before thine eyes.
²²Now consider this, ye that forget God,
Lest I tear you in pieces, and there be none to deliver:
²³Whoso offereth the sacrifice of thanksgiving glorifieth me;
And to him that ordereth his way aright
Will I show the salvation of God.

Chapter 51

For the Chief Musician. A Psalm of David; when Nathan the prophet came unto him, after he had gone in to Bathsheba.
¹Have mercy upon me, O God, according to thy lovingkindness:
According to the multitude of thy tender mercies blot out my transgressions.
²Wash me thoroughly from mine iniquity,
And cleanse me from my sin.
³For I know my transgressions;
And my sin is ever before me.
⁴Against thee, thee only, have I sinned,
And done that which is evil in thy sight;
That thou mayest be justified when thou speakest,
And be clear when thou judgest.
⁵Behold, I was brought forth in iniquity;
And in sin did my mother conceive me.
⁶Behold, thou desirest truth in the inward parts;
And in the hidden part thou wilt make me to know wisdom.
⁷Purify me with hyssop, and I shall be clean:
Wash me, and I shall be whiter than snow.
⁸Make me to hear joy and gladness,
That the bones which thou hast broken may rejoice.
⁹Hide thy face from my sins,

Psalms

And blot out all mine iniquities.
10Create in me a clean heart, O God;
And renew a right spirit within me.
11Cast me not away from thy presence;
And take not thy holy Spirit from me.
12Restore unto me the joy of thy salvation;
And uphold me with a willing spirit.
13Then will I teach transgressors thy ways;
And sinners shall be converted unto thee.
14Deliver me from bloodguiltiness, O God, thou God of my salvation;
And my tongue shall sing aloud of thy righteousness.
15O Lord, open thou my lips;
And my mouth shall show forth thy praise.
16For thou delightest not in sacrifice; else would I give it:
Thou hast no pleasure in burnt-offering.
17The sacrifices of God are a broken spirit:
A broken and contrite heart, O God, thou wilt not despise.
18Do good in thy good pleasure unto Zion:
Build thou the walls of Jerusalem.
19Then will thou delight in the sacrifices of righteousness,
In burnt-offering and in whole burnt-offering:
Then will they offer bullocks upon thine altar.

Chapter 52

For the Chief Musician. Maschil of David; when Doeg the Edomite came and told Saul, and said unto him, David is come to the house of Abimelech.
1Why boastest thou thyself in mischief, O mighty man?
The lovingkindness of God endureth continually.
2Thy tongue deviseth very wickedness,
Like a sharp razor, working deceitfully.
3Thou lovest evil more than good,
And lying rather than to speak righteousness.
Selah
4Thou lovest all devouring words,
thou deceitful tongue.
5God will likewise destroy thee for ever;
He will take thee up, and pluck thee out of thy tent,
And root thee out of the land of the living.
Selah
6The righteous also shall see it, and fear,
And shall laugh at him, saying,
7Lo, this is the man that made not God his strength,
But trusted in the abundance of his riches,
And strengthened himself in his wickedness.
8But as for me, I am like a green olive-tree in the house of God:
I trust in the lovingkindness of God for ever and ever.
9I will give thee thanks for ever, because thou hast done it;
And I will hope in thy name, for it is good, in the presence of thy saints.

Chapter 53

For the Chief Musician; set to Mahalath. Maschil of David.
1The fool hath said in his heart, There is no God.
Corrupt are they, and have done abominable iniquity;
There is none that doeth good.
2God looked down from heaven upon the children of men,
To see if there were any that did understand,
That did seek after God.
3Every one of them is gone back; they are together become filthy;
There is none that doeth good, no, not one.
4Have the workers of iniquity no knowledge,
Who eat up my people as they eat bread,
And call not upon God?
5There were they in great fear, where no fear was;
For God hath scattered the bones of him that encampeth against thee:
Thou hast put them to shame, because of God hath rejected them.
6Oh that the salvation of Israel were come out of Zion!
When God bringeth back the captivity of his people,
Then shall Jacob rejoice, and Israel shall be glad.

Chapter 54

For the Chief Musician; on stringed instruments. Maschil of David; when the Ziphites came and said to Saul, Doth not David hide himself with us?
1Save me, O God, by thy name,
And judge me in thy might.
2Hear my prayer, O God;
Give ear to the words of my mouth.
3For strangers are risen up against me,
And violent men have sought after my soul:
They have not set God before them.
Selah
4Behold, God is my helper:
The Lord is of them that uphold my soul.
5He will requite the evil unto mine enemies:
Destroy thou them in thy truth.
6With a freewill-offering will I sacrifice unto thee:
I will give thanks unto thy name, O Yahweh, for it is good.
7For he hath delivered me out of all trouble;
And mine eye hath seen my desire upon mine enemies.

Chapter 55

For the Chief Musician; on stringed instruments. Maschil of David.
1Give ear to my prayer, O God;
And hide not thyself from my supplication.
2Attend unto me, and answer me:
I am restless in my complaint, and moan,
3Because of the voice of the enemy,
Because of the oppression of the wicked;
For they cast iniquity upon me,
And in anger they persecute me.
4My heart is sore pained within me:
And the terrors of death are fallen upon me.
5Fearfulness and trembling are come upon me,
And horror hath overwhelmed me.
6And I said, Oh that I had wings like a dove!
Then would I fly away, and be at rest.
7Lo, then would I wander far off,
I would lodge in the wilderness.
Selah
8I would haste me to a shelter
From the stormy wind and tempest.
9Destroy, O Lord, and divide their tongue;
For I have seen violence and strife in the city.
10Day and night they go about it upon the walls thereof:
Iniquity also and mischief are in the midst of it.
11Wickedness is in the midst thereof:
Oppression and guile depart not from its streets.
12For it was not an enemy that reproached me;
Then I could have borne it:
Neither was it he that hated me that did magnify himself against me;
Then I would have hid myself from him:
13But it was thou, a man mine equal,
My companion, and my familiar friend.
14We took sweet counsel together;
We walked in the house of God with the throng.
15Let death come suddenly upon them,
Let them go down alive into Sheol;
For wickedness is in their dwelling, in the midst of them.
16As for me, I will call upon God;
And Yahweh will save me.
17Evening, and morning, and at noonday, will I complain, and moan;
And he will hear my voice.
18He hath redeemed my soul in peace from the battle that was against me;
For they were many that strove with me.
19God will hear, and answer them,
Even he that abideth of old,
Selah
The men who have no changes,
And who fear not God.
20He hath put forth his hands against such as were at peace with him:
He hath profaned his covenant.
21His mouth was smooth as butter,
But his heart was war:
His words were softer than oil,
Yet were they drawn swords.
22Cast thy burden upon Yahweh, and he will sustain thee:
He will never suffer the righteous to be moved.
23But thou, O God, wilt bring them down into the pit of destruction:
Bloodthirsty and deceitful men shall not live out half their days;
But I will trust in thee.

Chapter 56

For the Chief Musician; set to aJonath elem rehokim. A Psalm of David. Michtam: when the Philistines took him in Gath.
1Be merciful unto me, O God; for man would swallow me up:
All the day long he fighting oppresseth me.
2Mine enemies would swallow me up all the day long;
For they are many that fight proudly against me.
3What time I am afraid,
I will put my trust in thee.
4In God (I will praise his word),
In God have I put my trust, I will not be afraid;
What can flesh do unto me?
5All the day long they wrest my words:
All their thoughts are against me for evil.
6They gather themselves together, they hide themselves,
They mark my steps,
Even as they have waited for my soul.
7Shall they escape by iniquity?
In anger cast down the peoples, O God.
8Thou numberest my wanderings:
Put thou my tears into thy bottle;
Are they not in thy book?
9Then shall mine enemies turn back in the day that I call:
This I know, that God is for me.
10In God (I will praise his word),
In Yahweh (I will praise his word),
11In God have I put my trust, I will not be afraid;

What can man do unto me?
12Thy vows are upon me, O God:
I will render thank-offerings unto thee.
13For thou hast delivered my soul from death:
Hast thou not delivered my feet from falling,
That I may walk before God
In the light of the living?

Chapter 57

For the Chief Musician; set to Al-tash-heth. A Psalm of David. Michtam; when he fled from Saul, in the cave.
1Be merciful unto me, O God, be merciful unto me;
For my soul taketh refuge in thee:
Yea, in the shadow of thy wings will I take refuge,
Until these calamities be overpast.
2I will cry unto God Most High,
Unto God that performeth all things for me.
3He will send from heaven, and save me,
When he that would swallow me up reproacheth;
Selah
God will send forth his lovingkindness and his truth.
4My soul is among lions;
I lie among them that are set on fire,
Even the sons of men, whose teeth are spears and arrows,
And their tongue a sharp sword.
5Be thou exalted, O God, above the heavens;
Let thy glory be above all the earth.
6They have prepared a net for my steps;
My soul is bowed down:
They have digged a pit before me;
They are fallen into the midst thereof themselves.
Selah
7My heart is fixed, O God, my heart is fixed:
I will sing, yea, I will sing praises.
8Awake up, my glory; awake, psaltery and harp:
I myself will awake right early.
9I will give thanks unto thee, O Lord, among the peoples:
I will sing praises unto thee among the nations.
10For thy lovingkindness is great unto the heavens,
And thy truth unto the skies.
11Be thou exalted, O God, above the heavens;
Let thy glory be above all the earth.

Chapter 58

For the Chief Musician; set to Al-tashheth. A Psalm of David. Michtam.
1Do ye indeed in silence speak righteousness?
Do ye judge uprightly, O ye sons of men?
2Nay, in heart ye work wickedness;
Ye weigh out the violence of your hands in the earth.
3The wicked are estranged from the womb:
They go astray as soon as they are born, speaking lies.
4Their poison is like the poison of a serpent:
They are like the deaf adder that stoppeth her ear,
5Which hearkeneth not to the voice of charmers,
Charming never so wisely.
6Break their teeth, O God, in their mouth:
Break out the great teeth of the young lions, O Yahweh.
7Let them melt away as water that runneth apace:
When he aimeth his arrows, let them be as though they were cut off.
8Let them be as a snail which melteth and passeth away,
Like the untimely birth of a woman, that hath not seen the sun.
9Before your pots can feel the thorns,
He will take them away with a whirlwind, the green and the burning alike.
10The righteous shall rejoice when he seeth the vengeance:
He shall wash his feet in the blood of the wicked;
11So that men shall say, Verily there is a reward for the righteous:
Verily there is a God that judgeth in the earth.

Chapter 59

For the Chief Musician; set to Al-tashheth. A Psalm of David. Michtam; when Saul sent, and they watched the house to kill him.
1Deliver me from mine enemies, O my God:
Set me on high from them that rise up against me.
2Deliver me from the workers of iniquity,
And save me from the bloodthirsty men.
3For, lo, they lie in wait for my soul;
The mighty gather themselves together against me:
Not for my transgression, nor for my sin, O Yahweh.
4They run and prepare themselves without my fault:
Awake thou to help me, and behold.
5Even thou, O Yahweh God of hosts, the God of Israel,
Arise to visit all the nations:
Be not merciful to any wicked transgressors.
Selah
6They return at evening, they howl like a dog,
And go round about the city.
7Behold, they belch out with their mouth;
Swords are in their lips:
For who, say they, doth hear?
8But thou, O Yahweh, wilt laugh at them;
Thou wilt have all the nations in derision.
9Because of his strength I will give heed unto thee;
For God is my high tower.
10My God with his lovingkindness will meet me:
God will let me see my desire upon mine enemies.
11Slay them not, lest my people forget:
Scatter them by thy power, and bring them down,
O Lord our shield.
12For the sin of their mouth, and the words of their lips,
Let them even be taken in their pride,
And for cursing and lying which they speak.
13Consume them in wrath, consume them, so that they shall be no more:
And let them know that God ruleth in Jacob,
Unto the ends of the earth.
Selah
14And at evening let them return, let them howl like a dog,
And go round about the city.
15They shall wander up and down for food,
And tarry all night if they be not satisfied.
16But I will sing of thy strength;
Yea, I will sing aloud of thy lovingkindness in the morning:
For thou hast been my high tower,
And a refuge in the day of my distress.
17Unto thee, O my strength, will I sing praises:
For God is my high tower, the God of my mercy.

Chapter 60

For the Chief Musician; set to aShushan Eduth. Michtam of David, to teach; and when he strove with Aram-naharaim and with Aram-zobah, and Joab returned, and smote of Edom in the Valley of Salt twelve thousand.
60 1O God thou hast cast us off, thou hast broken us down;
Thou hast been angry; oh restore us again.
2Thou hast made the land to tremble; thou hast rent it:
Heal the breaches thereof; for it shaketh.
3Thou hast showed thy people hard things:
Thou hast made us to drink the wine of staggering.
4Thou hast given a banner to them that fear thee,
That it may be displayed because of the truth.
Selah
5That thy beloved may be delivered,
Save with thy right hand, and answer us.
6God hath spoken in his holiness: I will exult;
I will divide Shechem, and mete out the valley of Succoth.
7Gilead is mine, and Manasseh is mine;
Ephraim also is the defence of my head;
Judah is my sceptre.
8Moab is my washpot;
Upon Edom will I cast my shoe:
Philistia, shout thou because of me.
9Who will bring me into the strong city?
Who hath led me unto Edom?
10Hast not thou, O God, cast us off?
And thou goest not forth, O God, with our hosts.
11Give us help against the adversary;
For vain is the help of man.
12Through God we shall do valiantly;
For he it is that will tread down our adversaries.

Chapter 61

For the Chief Musician; on a stringed instrument. A Psalm of David.
1Hear my cry, O God;
Attend unto my prayer.
2From the end of the earth will I call unto thee, when my heart ais overwhelmed:
Lead me to athe rock that is higher than I.
3For thou hast been a refuge for me,
A strong tower from the enemy.
4I will dwell in thy tabernacle for ever:
I will take refuge in the covert of thy wings.
Selah
5For thou, O God, hast heard my vows:
Thou hast given me the heritage of those that fear thy name.
6Thou wilt prolong the king's life;
His years shall be as many generations.
7He shall abide before God for ever:
Oh prepare lovingkindness and truth, that they may preserve him.
8So will I sing praise unto thy name for ever,
That I may daily perform my vows.

Chapter 62

For the Chief Musician; after the manner of Jeduthan. A Psalm of David.
1My soul waiteth in silence for God only:
From him cometh my salvation.
2He only is my rock and my salvation:
He is my high tower; I shall not be greatly moved.
3How long will ye set upon a man,

That ye may slay him, all of you,
Like a leaning wall, like a tottering fence?
4They only consult to thrust him down from his dignity;
They delight in lies;
They bless with their mouth, but they curse inwardly.
Selah
5My soul, wait thou in silence for God only;
For my expectation is from him.
6He only is my rock and my salvation:
He is my high tower; I shall not be moved.
7With God is my salvation and my glory:
The rock of my strength, and my refuge, is in God.
8Trust in him at all times, ye people;
Pour out your heart before him:
God is a refuge for us.
Selah
9Surely men of low degree are vanity, and men of high degree are a lie:
In the balances they will go up;
They are together lighter than vanity.
10Trust not in oppression,
And become not vain in robbery:
If riches increase, set not your heart thereon.
11God hath spoken once,
Twice have I heard this,
That power belongeth unto God.
12Also unto thee, O Lord, belongeth lovingkindness;
For thou renderest to every man according to his work.

Chapter 63

A Psalm of David when he was in the wilderness of Judah.
1O God, thou art my God; earnestly will I seek thee:
My soul thirsteth for thee, my flesh longeth for thee,
In a dry and weary land, where no water is.
2So have I looked upon thee in the sanctuary,
To see thy power and thy glory.
3Because thy lovingkindness is better than life,
My lips shall praise thee.
4So will I bless thee while I live:
I will lift up my hands in thy name.
5My soul shall be satisfied as with marrow and fatness;
And my mouth shall praise thee with joyful lips;
6When I remember thee upon my bed,
And meditate on thee in the night-watches.
7For thou hast been my help,
And in the shadow of thy wings will I rejoice.
8My soul followeth hard after thee:
Thy right hand upholdeth me.
9But those that seek my soul, to destroy it,
Shall go into the lower parts of the earth.
10They shall be given over to the power of the sword:
They shall be a portion for foxes.
11But the king shall rejoice in God:
Every one that sweareth by him shall glory;
For the mouth of them that speak lies shall be stopped.

Chapter 64

For the Chief Musician. A Psalm of David.
1Hear my voice, O God, in my complaint:
Preserve my life from fear of the enemy.
2Hide me from the secret counsel of evil-doers,
From the tumult of the workers of iniquity;
3Who have whet their tongue like a sword,
And have aimed their arrows, even bitter words,
4That they may shoot in secret places at the perfect:
Suddenly do they shoot at him, and fear not.
5They encourage themselves in an evil purpose;
They commune of laying snares privily;
They say, Who will see them?
6They search out iniquities;
We have accomplished, say they, a diligent search:
And the inward thought and the heart of every one is deep.
7But God will shoot at them;
With an arrow suddenly shall they be wounded.
8So they shall be made to stumble, their own tongue being against them:
All that see them shall wag the head.
9And all men shall fear;
And they shall declare the work of God,
And shall wisely consider of his doing.
10The righteous shall be glad in Yahweh, and shall take refuge in him;
And all the upright in heart shall glory.

Chapter 65

For the Chief Musician. A Psalm. A song of David.
1Praise waiteth for thee, O God, in Zion;
And unto thee shall the vow be performed.
2O thou that hearest prayer,
Unto thee shall all flesh come.
3Iniquities prevail against me:
As for our transgressions, thou wilt forgive them.
4Blessed is the man whom thou choosest, and causest to approach unto thee,
That he may dwell in thy courts:
We shall be satisfied with the goodness of thy house,
Thy holy temple.
5By terrible things thou wilt answer us in righteousness,
Oh God of our salvation,
Thou that art the confidence of all the ends of the earth,
And of them that are afar off upon the sea:
6Who by his strength setteth fast the mountains,
Being girded about with might;
7Who stilleth the roaring of the seas,
The roaring of their waves,
And the tumult of the peoples.
8They also that dwell in the uttermost parts are afraid at thy tokens:
Thou makest the outgoings of the morning and evening to rejoice.
9Thou visitest the earth, and waterest it,
Thou greatly enrichest it;
The river of God is full of water:
Thou providest them grain, when thou hast so prepared the earth.
10Thou waterest its furrows abundantly;
Thou settlest the ridges thereof:
Thou makest it soft with showers;
Thou blessest the springing thereof.
11Thou crownest the year with thy goodness;
And thy paths drop fatness.
12They drop upon the pastures of the wilderness;
And the hills are girded with joy.
13The pastures are clothed with flocks;
The valleys also are covered over with grain;
They shout for joy, they also sing.

Chapter 66

For the Chief Musician. A song, a Psalm.
1Make a joyful noise unto God, all the earth:
2Sing forth the glory of his name:
Make his praise glorious.
3Say unto God, How terrible are thy works!
Through the greatness of thy power shall thine enemies submit themselves unto thee.
4All the earth shall worship thee,
And shall sing unto thee;
They shall sing to thy name.
Selah
5Come, and see the works of God;
He is terrible in his doing toward the children of men.
6He turned the sea into dry land;
They went through the river on foot:
There did we rejoice in him.
7He ruleth by his might for ever;
His eyes observe the nations:
Let not the rebellious exalt themselves.
Selah
8Oh bless our God, ye peoples,
And make the voice of his praise to be heard;
9Who holdeth our soul in life,
And suffereth not our feet to be moved.
10For thou, O God, hast proved us:
Thou hast tried us, as silver is tried.
11Thou broughtest us into the net;
Thou layedst a sore burden upon our loins.
12Thou didst cause men to ride over our heads;
We went through fire and through water;
But thou broughtest us out into a wealthy place.
13I will come into thy house with burnt-offerings;
I will pay thee my vows,
14Which my lips uttered,
And my mouth spake, when I was in distress.
15I will offer unto thee burnt-offerings of fatlings,
With the incense of rams;
I will offer bullocks with goats.
Selah
16Come, and hear, all ye that fear God,
And I will declare what he hath done for my soul.
17I cried unto him with my mouth,
And he was extolled with my tongue.
18If I regard iniquity in my heart,
The Lord will not hear:
19But verily God hath heard;
He hath attended to the voice of my prayer.
20Blessed be God,
Who hath not turned away my prayer,
Nor his lovingkindness from me.

Chapter 67

For the Chief Musician; on stringed instruments. A Psalm, a song.

1God be merciful unto us, and bless us,
And cause his face to shine upon us;
Selah
2That thy way may be known upon earth,
Thy salvation among all nations.
3Let the peoples praise thee, O God;
Let all the peoples apraise thee.
4Oh let the nations be glad and sing for joy;
For thou wilt judge the peoples with equity,
And govern the nations upon earth.
Selah
5Let the peoples praise thee, O God;
Let all the peoples praise thee.
6The earth hath yielded its increase:
God, even our own God, will bless us.
7God will bless us;
And all the ends of the earth shall fear him.

Chapter 68

For the Chief Musician; A Psalm of David, a song.

1Let God arise, let his enemies be scattered;
Let them also that hate him flee before him.
2As smoke is driven away, so drive them away:
As wax melteth before the fire,
So let the wicked perish at the presence of God.
3But let the righteous be glad; let them exult before God:
Yea, let them rejoice with gladness.
4Sing unto God, sing praises to his name:
Cast up a highway for him that rideth through the deserts;
His name is Yahweh; and exult ye before him.
5A father of the fatherless, and a judge of the widows,
Is God in his holy habitation.
6God setteth the solitary in families:
He bringeth out the prisoners into prosperity;
But the rebellious dwell in a parched land.
7O God, when thou wentest forth before thy people,
When thou didst march through the wilderness;
Selah
8The earth trembled,
The heavens also dropped rain at the presence of God:
Yon Sinai trembled at the presence of God, the God of Israel.
9Thou, O God, didst send a plentiful rain,
Thou didst confirm thine inheritance, when it was weary.
10Thy congregation dwelt therein:
Thou, O God, didst prepare of thy goodness for the poor.
11The Lord giveth the word:
The women that publish the tidings are a great host.
12Kings of armies flee, they flee;
And she that tarrieth at home divideth the spoil.
13When ye lie among the sheepfolds,
It is as the wings of a dove covered with silver,
And her pinions with yellow gold.
14When the Almighty scattered kings therein,
It was as when it snoweth in Zalmon.
15A mountain of God is the mountain of Bashan;
A high mountain is the mountain of Bashan.
16Why look ye askance, ye high mountains,
At the mountain which God hath desired for his abode?
Yea, Yahweh will dwell in it for ever.
17The chariots of God are twenty thousand, even thousands upon thousands;
The Lord is among them, as in Sinai, in the sanctuary.
18Thou hast ascended on high, thou hast led away captives;
Thou hast received gifts among men,
Yea, among the rebellious also, that Yahweh God might dwell with them.
19Blessed be the Lord, who daily beareth our burden,
Even the God who is our salvation.
Selah
20God is unto us a God of deliverances;
And unto Yahweh the Lord belongeth escape from death.
21But God will smite through the head of his enemies,
The hairy scalp of such a one as goeth on still in his guiltiness.
22The Lord said, I will bring again from Bashan,
I will bring them again from the depths of the sea;
23That thou mayest crush them, dipping thy foot in blood,
That the tongue of thy dogs may have its portion from thine enemies.
24They have seen thy goings, O God,
Even the goings of my God, my King, into the sanctuary.
25The singers went before, the minstrels followed after,
In the midst of the damsels playing with timbrels.
26Bless ye God in the congregations,
Even the Lord, ye that are of the fountain of Israel.
27There is little Benjamin their ruler,
The princes of Judah and their council,
The princes of Zebulun, the princes of Naphtali.
28Thy God hath commanded thy strength:
Strengthen, O God, that which thou hast wrought for us.
29Because of thy temple at Jerusalem
Kings shall bring presents unto thee.
30Rebuke the wild beast of the reeds,
The multitude of the bulls, with the calves of the peoples,
Trampling under foot the pieces of silver:
He hath scattered the peoples that delight in war.
31Princes shall come out of Egypt;
Ethiopia shall haste to stretch out her hands unto God.
32Sing unto God, ye kingdoms of the earth;
Oh sing praises unto the Lord;
Selah
33To him that rideth upon the heaven of heavens, which are of old;
Lo, he uttereth his voice, a mighty voice.
34Ascribe ye strength unto God:
His excellency is over Israel,
And his strength is in the skies.
35O God, thou art terrible out of thy holy places:
The God of Israel, he giveth strength and power unto his people.
Blessed be God.

Chapter 69

For the Chief Musician; set to aShoshanim. A Psalm of David.

1Save me, O God;
For the waters are come in unto my soul.
2I sink in deep mire, where there is no standing:
I am come into deep waters, where the floods overflow me.
3I am weary with my crying; my throat is dried:
Mine eyes fail while I wait for my God.
4They that hate me without a cause are more than the hairs of my head:
They that would cut me off, being mine enemies wrongfully, are mighty:
That which I took not away I have to restore.
5O God, thou knowest my foolishness;
And my sins are not hid from thee.
6Let not them that wait for thee be put to shame through me, O Lord Yahweh of hosts:
Let not those that seek thee be brought to dishonor through me, O God of Israel.
7Because for thy sake I have borne reproach;
Shame hath covered my face.
8I am become a stranger unto my brethren,
And an alien unto my mother's children.
9For the zeal of thy house hath eaten me up;
And the reproaches of them that reproach thee are fallen upon me.
10When I wept, and chastened my soul with fasting,
That was to my reproach.
11When I made sackcloth my clothing,
I became a byword unto them.
12They that sit in the gate talk of me;
And I am the song of the drunkards.
13But as for me, my prayer is unto thee, O Yahweh, in an acceptable time:
O God, in the abundance of thy lovingkindness,
Answer me in the truth of thy salvation.
14Deliver me out of the mire, and let me not sink:
Let me be delivered from them that hate me, and out of the deep waters.
15Let not the waterflood overwhelm me,
Neither let the deep shallow me up;
And let not the pit shut its mouth upon me.
16Answer me, O Yahweh; for thy lovingkindness is good:
According to the multitude of thy tender mercies turn thou unto me.
17And hide not thy face from thy servant;
For I am in distress; answer me speedily.
18Draw nigh unto my soul, and redeem it:
Ransom me because of mine enemies.
19Thou knowest my reproach, and my shame, and my dishonor:
Mine adversaries are all before thee.
20Reproach hath broken my heart; and I am full of heaviness:
And I looked for some to take pity, but there was none;
And for comforters, but I found none.
21They gave me also gall for my food;
And in my thirst they gave me vinegar to drink.
22Let their table before them become a snare;
And when they are in peace, let it become a trap.
23Let their eyes be darkened, so that they cannot see;
And make their loins continually to shake.
24Pour out thine indignation upon them,
And let the fierceness of thine anger overtake them.
25Let their habitation be desolate;
Let none dwell in their tents.
26For they persecute him whom thou hast smitten;
And they tell of the sorrow of those whom thou hast wounded.
27Add iniquity unto their iniquity;
And let them not come into thy righteousness.
28Let them be blotted out of the book of life,
And not be written with the righteous.
29But I am poor and sorrowful:
Let thy salvation, O God, set me up on high.
30I will praise the name of God with a song,
And will magnify him with thanksgiving.
31And it will please Yahweh better than an ox,

Psalms

Or a bullock that hath horns and hoofs.
32The meek have seen it, and are glad:
Ye that seek after God, let your heart live.
33For Yahweh heareth the needy,
And despiseth not his prisoners.
34Let heaven and earth praise him,
The seas, and everything that moveth therein.
35For God will save Zion, and build the cities of Judah;
And they shall abide there, and have it in possession.
36The seed also of his servants shall inherit it;
And they that love his name shall dwell therein.

Chapter 70

For the Chief Musician. A Psalm of David; ato bring to remembrance.
1Make haste, O God, to deliver me;
Make haste to help me, O Yahweh.
2Let them be put to shame and confounded
That seek after my soul:
Let them be turned backward and brought to dishonor
That delight in my hurt.
3Let them be turned back by reason of their shame
That say, Aha, aha.
4Let all those that seek thee rejoice and be glad in thee;
And let such as love thy salvation say continually,
Let God be magnified.
5But I am poor and needy;
Make haste unto me, O God:
Thou art my help and my deliverer;
O Yahweh, make no tarrying.

Chapter 71

1In thee, O Yahweh, do I take refuge:
Let me never be put to shame.
2Deliver me in thy righteousness, and rescue me;
Bow down thine ear unto me, and save me.
3Be thou to me a rock of habitation, whereunto I may continually resort:
Thou hast given commandment to save me;
For thou art my rock and my fortress.
4Rescue me, O my God, out of the hand of the wicked,
Out of the hand of the unrighteous and cruel man.
5For thou art my hope, O Lord Yahweh:
Thou art my trust from my youth.
6By thee have I been holden up from the womb;
Thou art he that took me out of my mother's bowels:
My praise shall be continually of thee.
7I am as a wonder unto many;
But thou art my strong refuge.
8My mouth shall be filled with thy praise,
And with thy honor all the day.
9Cast me not off in the time of old age;
Forsake me not when my strength faileth.
10For mine enemies speak concerning me;
And they that watch for my soul take counsel together,
11Saying, God hath forsaken him:
Pursue and take him; for there is none to deliver.
12O God, be not far from me;
O my God, make haste to help me.
13Let them be put to shame and consumed that are adversaries to my soul;
Let them be covered with reproach and dishonor that seek my hurt.
14But I will hope continually,
And will praise thee yet more and more.
15My mouth shall tell of thy righteousness,
And of thy salvation all the day;
For I know not the numbers thereof.
16I will come with the mighty acts of the Lord Yahweh:
I will make mention of thy righteousness, even of thine only.
17O God, thou hast taught me from my youth;
And hitherto have I declared thy wondrous works.
18Yea, even when I am old and grayheaded, O God, forsake me not,
Until I have declared thy strength unto the next generation,
Thy might to every one that is to come.
19Thy righteousness also, O God, is very high;
Thou who hast done great things, O God, who is like unto thee?
20Thou, who hast showed us many and sore troubles,
Wilt quicken us again,
And wilt bring us up again from the depths of the earth.
21Increase thou my greatness,
And turn again and comfort me.
22I will also praise thee with the psaltery,
Even thy truth, O my God:
Unto thee will I sing praises with the harp,
O thou Holy One of Israel.
23My lips shall shout for joy when I sing praises unto thee;
And my soul, which thou hast redeemed.
24My tongue also shall talk of thy righteousness all the day long;
For they are put to shame, for they are confounded, that seek my hurt.

Chapter 72

A Psalm of Solomon.
1Give the king thy judgments, O God,
And thy righteousness unto the king's son.
2aHe will judge thy people with righteousness,
And thy poor with justice.
3The mountains shall bring peace to the people,
And the hills, in righteousness.
4He will judge the poor of the people,
He will save the children of the needy,
And will break in pieces the oppressor.
5They shall fear thee while the sun endureth,
And so long as the moon, throughout all generations.
6He will come down like rain upon the mown grass,
As showers that water the earth.
7In his days shall the righteous flourish,
And abundance of peace, till the moon be no more.
8He shall have dominion also from sea to sea,
And from the River unto the ends of the earth.
9They that dwell in the wilderness shall bow before him;
And his enemies shall lick the dust.
10The kings of Tarshish and of the isles shall render tribute:
The kings of Sheba and Seba shall offer gifts.
11Yea, all kings shall fall down before him;
All nations shall serve him.
12For he will deliver the needy when he crieth,
And the poor, that hath no helper.
13He will have pity on the poor and needy,
And the souls of the needy he will save.
14He will redeem their soul from oppression and violence;
And precious will their blood be in his sight:
15And they shall live; and to him shall be given of the gold of Sheba:
And men shall pray for him continually;
They shall bless him all the day long.
16There shall be abundance of grain in the earth upon the top of the mountains;
The fruit thereof shall shake like Lebanon:
And they of the city shall flourish like grass of the earth.
17His name shall endure for ever;
His name shall be continued as long as the sun:
And men shall be blessed in him;
All nations shall call him happy.
18Blessed be Yahweh God, the God of Israel,
Who only doeth wondrous things:
19And blessed be his glorious name for ever;
And let the whole earth be filled with his glory.
Amen, and Amen.
20The prayers of David the son of Jesse are ended.

BOOK III

Chapter 73

A Psalm of Asaph.
1Surely God is good to Israel,
Even to such as are pure in heart.
2But as for me, my feet were almost gone;
My steps had well nigh slipped.
3For I was envious at the arrogant,
When I saw the prosperity of the wicked.
4For there are no pangs in their death;
But their strength is firm.
5They are not in trouble as other men;
Neither are they plagued like other men.
6Therefore pride is as a chain about their neck;
Violence covereth them as a garment.
7Their eyes stand out with fatness:
They have more than heart could wish.
8They scoff, and in wickedness utter oppression:
They speak loftily.
9They have set their mouth in the heavens,
And their tongue walketh through the earth.
10Therefore his people return hither:
And waters of a full cup are drained by them.
11And they say, How doth God know?
And is there knowledge in the Most High?
12Behold, these are the wicked;
And, being alway at ease, they increase in riches.
13Surely in vain have I cleansed my heart,
And washed my hands in innocency;
14For all the day long have I been plagued,
And achastened every morning.
15If I had said, I will speak thus;
Behold, I had dealt treacherously with the generation of thy children.
16When I thought how I might know this,
It was too painful for me;
17Until I went into the sanctuary of God,
And considered their latter end.
18Surely thou settest them in slippery places:

Thou castest them down to destruction.
19How are they become a desolation in a moment!
They are utterly consumed with terrors.
20As a dream when one awaketh,
So, O Lord, when thou awakest, thou wilt despise their image.
21For my soul was grieved,
And I was pricked in my heart:
22So brutish was I, and ignorant;
I was as a beast before thee.
23Nevertheless I am continually with thee:
Thou hast holden my right hand.
24Thou wilt guide me with thy counsel,
And afterward receive me to glory.
25Whom have I in heaven but thee?
And there is none upon earth that I desire besides thee.
26My flesh and my heart faileth;
But God is the strength of my heart and my portion for ever.
27For, lo, they that are far from thee shall perish:
Thou hast destroyed all them that play the harlot, departing from thee.
28But it is good for me to draw near unto God:
I have made the Lord Yahweh my refuge,
That I may tell of all thy works.

Chapter 74

Maschil of Asaph.
1O God, why hast thou cast us off for ever?
Why doth thine anger smoke against the sheep of thy pasture?
2Remember thy congregation, which thou hast gotten of old,
Which thou hast redeemed to be the tribe of thine inheritance;
And mount Zion, wherein thou hast dwelt.
3Lift up thy feet unto the perpetual ruins,
All the evil that the enemy hath done in the sanctuary.
4Thine adversaries have roared in the midst of thine assembly;
They have set up their ensigns for signs.
5They seemed as men that lifted up
Axes upon a thicket of trees.
6And now all the carved work thereof
They break down with hatchet and hammers.
7They have set thy sanctuary on fire;
They have profaned the dwelling-place of thy name by casting it to the ground.
8They said in their heart, Let us make havoc of them altogether:
They have burned up all the asynagogues of God in the land.
9We see not our signs:
There is no more any prophet;
Neither is there among us any that knoweth how long.
10How long, O God, shall the adversary reproach?
Shall the enemy blaspheme thy name for ever?
11Why drawest thou back thy hand, even thy right hand?
Pluck it out of thy bosom and consume them.
12Yet God is my King of old,
Working salvation in the midst of the earth.
13Thou didst divide the sea by thy strength:
Thou brakest the heads of the sea-monsters in the waters.
14Thou brakest the heads of leviathan in pieces;
Thou gavest him to be food to the people inhabiting the wilderness.
15Thou didst cleave fountain and flood:
Thou driedst up mighty rivers.
16The day is thine, the night also is thine:
Thou hast prepared the light and the sun.
17Thou hast set all the borders of the earth:
Thou hast made summer and winter.
18Remember this, that the enemy hath reproached, O Yahweh,
And that a foolish people hath blasphemed thy name.
19Oh deliver not the soul of thy turtle-dove unto the wild beast:
Forget not the life of thy poor for ever.
20Have respect unto the covenant;
For the dark places of the earth are full of the habitations of violence.
21Oh let not the oppressed return ashamed:
Let the poor and needy praise thy name.
22Arise, O God, plead thine own cause:
Remember how the foolish man reproacheth thee all the day.
23Forget not the voice of thine adversaries:
The tumult of those that rise up against thee ascendeth continually.

Chapter 75

For the Chief Musician; set to Al-tash-heth. A Psalm of Asaph; a song.
1We give thanks unto thee, O God;
We give thanks, for thy name is near:
Men tell of thy wondrous works.
2When I shall afind the set time, I will judge uprightly.
3aThe earth and all the inhabitants thereof are dissolved:
I have aset up the pillars of it.
Selah
4I said unto the aarrogant, Deal not arrogantly;
And to the wicked, Lift not up the horn:
5Lift not up your horn on high;
Speak not awith a stiff neck.
6For neither from the east, nor from the west,
Nor yet afrom the asouth, cometh lifting up.
7But God is the judge:
He putteth down one, and lifteth up another.
8For in the hand of Yahweh there is a cup, and the wine afoameth;
It is full of mixture, and he poureth out of the same:
Surely the dregs thereof, all the wicked of the earth shall drain them, and drink them.
9But I will declare for ever,
I will sing praises to the God of Jacob.
10All the horns of the wicked also will I cut off;
But the horns of the righteous shall be lifted up.

Chapter 76

For the Chief Musician; on stringed instruments. A Psalm of Asaph, a song.
1In Judah is God known:
His name is great in Israel.
2In Salem also is his tabernacle,
And his adwelling-place in Zion.
3There he brake the aarrows of the bow;
The shield, and the sword, and the battle.
Selah
4Glorious art thou and excellent,
aFrom the mountains of prey.
5The stouthearted are made a spoil,
They have slept their sleep;
And none of the men of might have found their hands.
6At thy rebuke, O God of Jacob,
Both chariot and horse are cast into a deep sleep.
7Thou, even thou, art to be feared;
And who may stand in thy sight when once thou art angry?
8Thou didst cause sentence to be heard from heaven;
The earth feared, and was still,
9When God arose to judgment,
To save all the meek of the earth.
Selah
10Surely the wrath of man shall praise thee:
The residue of wrath shalt thou agird upon thee.
11Vow, and pay unto Yahweh your God:
Let all that are round about him bring presents unto him that ought to be feared.
12He will cut off the spirit of princes:
He is terrible to the kings of the earth.

Chapter 77

For the Chief Musician; after the manner of Jeduthan. A Psalm of Asaph.
1I will cry unto God with my voice,
Even unto God with my voice; and he will give ear unto me.
2In the day of my trouble I sought the Lord:
My hand was stretched out in the night, and slacked not;
My soul refused to be comforted.
3I remember God, and am disquieted:
I complain, and my spirit is aoverwhelmed.
Selah
4Thou holdest mine eyes watching:
I am so troubled that I cannot speak.
5I have considered the days of old,
The years of ancient times.
6I call to remembrance my song in the night:
I commune with mine own heart;
And my spirit maketh diligent search.
7Will the Lord cast off for ever?
And will he be favorable no more?
8Is his lovingkindness clean gone for ever?
Doth his promise fail for evermore?
9Hath God forgotten to be gracious?
Hath he in anger shut up his tender mercies?
Selah
10And I said, This is my infirmity;
But I will remember the years of the right hand of the Most High.
11I will make mention of the deeds of aYahweh;
For I will remember thy wonders of old.
12I will meditate also upon all thy work,
And muse on thy doings.
13Thy way, O God, is ain the sanctuary:
Who is a great god like unto God?
14Thou art the God that doest wonders:
Thou hast made known thy strength among the peoples.
15Thou hast with thine arm redeemed thy people,
The sons of Jacob and Joseph.
Selah
16The waters saw thee, O God;
The waters saw thee, they awere afraid:
The depths also trembled.
17The clouds poured out water;
The skies sent out a sound:
Thine arrows also went abroad.
18The voice of thy thunder was in the whirlwind;

Psalms

The lightnings lightened the world:
The earth trembled and shook.
19Thy way was in the sea,
And thy paths in the great waters,
And thy footsteps were not known.
20Thou leddest thy people like a flock,
By the hand of Moses and Aaron.

Chapter 78

Maschil of Asaph.
1Give ear, O my people, to my alaw:
Incline your ears to the words of my mouth.
2I will open my mouth in a parable;
I will utter dark sayings of old,
3Which we have heard and known,
And our fathers have told us.
4We will not hide them from their children,
Telling to the generation to come the praises of Yahweh,
And his strength, and his wondrous works that he hath done.
5For he established a testimony in Jacob,
And appointed a law in Israel,
Which he commanded our fathers,
That they should make them known to their children;
6That the generation to come might know them, even the children that should be born;
Who should arise and tell them to their children,
7That they might set their hope in God,
And not forget the works of God,
But keep his commandments,
8And might not be as their fathers,
A stubborn and rebellious generation,
A generation athat set not their heart aright,
And whose spirit was not stedfast with God.
9The children of Ephraim, being armed and carrying bows,
Turned back in the day of battle.
10They kept not the covenant of God,
And refused to walk in his law;
11And they forgat his doings,
And his wondrous works that he had showed them.
12Marvellous things did he in the sight of their fathers,
In the land of Egypt, in the field of Zoan.
13He clave the sea, and caused them to pass through;
And he made the waters to stand as a heap.
14In the day-time also he led them with a cloud,
And all the night with a light of fire.
15He clave rocks in the wilderness,
And gave them drink abundantly as out of the depths.
16He brought streams also out of the rock,
And caused waters to run down like rivers.
17Yet went they on still to sin against him,
To rebel against the Most High in the adesert.
18And they tempted God in their heart
By asking food aaccording to their desire.
19Yea, they spake against God;
They said, Can God prepare a table in the wilderness?
20Behold, he smote the rock, so that waters gushed out,
And streams overflowed;
Can he give bread also?
Will he provide flesh for his people?
21Therefore Yahweh heard, and was wroth;
And a fire was kindled against Jacob,
And anger also went up against Israel;
22Because they believed not in God,
And trusted not in his salvation.
23Yet he commanded the skies above,
And opened the doors of heaven;
24And he rained down manna upon them to eat,
And gave them afood from heaven.
25aMan did eat the bread of the mighty:
He sent them food to the full.
26He acaused the east wind to blow in the heavens;
And by his power he guided the south wind.
27He rained flesh also upon them as the dust,
And winged birds as the sand of the seas:
28And he let it fall in the midst of their camp,
Round about their habitations.
29So they did eat, and were well filled;
And he gave them their own desire.
30They were not estranged from that which they desired,
Their food was yet in their mouths,
31When the anger of God went up against them,
And slew of the fattest of them,
And smote down the young men of Israel.
32For all this they sinned still,
And believed not in his wondrous works.
33Therefore their days did he consume in vanity,
And their years in terror.
34When he slew them, then they inquired after him;
And they returned and sought God earnestly.
35And they remembered that God was their rock,
And the Most High God their redeemer.
36But they flattered him with their mouth,
And lied unto him with their tongue.
37For their heart was not aright with him,
Neither were they faithful in his covenant.
38But he, being merciful, forgave their iniquity, and destroyed them not:
Yea, many a time turned he his anger away,
And did not stir up all his wrath.
39And he remembered that they were but flesh,
A wind that passeth away, and cometh not again.
40How oft did they rebel against him in the wilderness,
And grieve him in the desert!
41And they turned again and tempted God,
And aprovoked the Holy One of Israel.
42They remember not his hand,
Nor the day when he redeemed them from the adversary;
43How he set his signs in Egypt,
And his wonders in the field of Zoan,
44And turned their rivers into blood,
And their streams, so that they could not drink.
45He sent among them swarms of flies, which devoured them;
And frogs, which destroyed them.
46He gave also their increase unto the caterpillar,
And their labor unto the locust.
47He adestroyed their vines with hail,
And their sycomore-trees with afrost.
48He gave over their cattle also to the hail,
And their flocks to hot thunderbolts.
49He cast upon them the fierceness of his anger,
Wrath, and indignation, and trouble,
aA band of angels of evil.
50He amade a path for his anger;
He spared not their soul from death,
But gave atheir life over to the pestilence,
51And smote all the first-born in Egypt,
The achief of their strength in the tents of Ham.
52But he led forth his own people like sheep,
And guided them in the wilderness like a flock.
53And he led them safely, so that they feared not;
But the sea overwhelmed their enemies.
54And he brought them to the border of his sanctuary,
To this amountain, which his right hand had gotten.
55He drove out the nations also before them,
And allotted them for an inheritance by line,
And made the tribes of Israel to dwell in their tents.
56Yet they tempted and rebelled against the Most High God,
And kept not his testimonies;
57But turned back, and dealt treacherously like their fathers:
They were turned aside like a deceitful bow.
58For they provoked him to anger with their high places,
And moved him to jealousy with their graven images.
59When God heard this, he was wroth,
And greatly abhorred Israel;
60So that he forsook the tabernacle of Shiloh,
The tent which he placed among men;
61And delivered his strength into captivity,
And his glory into the adversary's hand.
62He gave his people over also unto the sword,
And was wroth with his inheritance.
63Fire devoured their young men;
And their virgins had no marriage-song.
64Their priests fell by the sword;
And their widows made no lamentation.
65Then the Lord awaked as one out of sleep,
Like a mighty man that shouteth by reason of wine.
66And he smote his adversaries backward:
He put them to a perpetual reproach.
67Moreover he refused the tent of Joseph,
And chose not the tribe of Ephraim,
68But chose the tribe of Judah,
The mount Zion which he loved.
69And he built his sanctuary like the heights,
Like the earth which he hath established for ever.
70He chose David also his servant,
And took him from the sheepfolds:
71From following the ewes that have their young he brought him,
To be the shepherd of Jacob his people, and Israel his inheritance.
72So he was their shepherd according to the integrity of his heart,
And guided them by the skilfulness of his hands.

Chapter 79

A Psalm of Asaph.
1O God, the nations are come into thine inheritance;
Thy holy temple have they defiled;
They have laid Jerusalem in heaps.
2The dead bodies of thy servants have they given to be food unto the birds of the heavens,
The flesh of thy saints unto the beasts of the earth.

3Their blood have they shed like water round about Jerusalem;
And there was none to bury them.
4We are become a reproach to our neighbors,
A scoffing and derision to them that are round about us.
5How long, O Yahweh? wilt thou be angry for ever?
Shall thy jealousy burn like fire?
6Pour out thy wrath upon the nations that know thee not,
And upon the kingdoms that call not upon thy name.
7For they have devoured Jacob,
And laid waste his habitation.
8Remember not against us the iniquities of our forefathers:
Let thy tender mercies speedily meet us;
For we are brought very low.
9Help us, O God of our salvation, for the glory of thy name;
And deliver us, and aforgive our sins, for thy name's sake.
10Wherefore should the nations say, Where is their God?
Let the avenging of the blood of thy servants which is shed
Be known among the nations in our sight.
11Let the sighing of the prisoner come before thee:
According to the greatness aof thy power preserve thou athose that are appointed to death;
12And render unto our neighbors sevenfold into their bosom
Their reproach, wherewith they have reproached thee, O Lord.
13So we thy people and sheep of thy pasture
Will give thee thanks for ever:
We will show forth thy praise to all generations.

Chapter 80

For the Chief Musician, set to aShoshanim Eduth.. A Psalm of Asaph.
1Give ear, O Shepherd of Israel,
Thou that leadest Joseph like a flock;
Thou that asittest above the cherubim, shine forth.
2Before Ephraim and Benjamin and Manasseh, stir up thy might,
And come to save us.
3aTurn us again, O God;
And cause thy face to shine, and we shall be saved.
4O Yahweh God of hosts,
How long awilt thou be angry against the prayer of thy people?
5Thou hast fed them with the bread of tears,
And given them tears to drink in large measure.
6Thou makest us a strife unto our neighbors;
And our enemies laugh among themselves.
7Turn us again, O God of hosts;
And cause thy face to shine, and we shall be saved.
8Thou broughtest a vine out of Egypt:
Thou didst drive out the nations, and plantedst it.
9Thou preparedst room before it,
And it took deep root, and filled the land.
10The mountains were covered with the shadow of it,
And athe boughs thereof were like acedars of God.
11It sent out its branches unto the sea,
And its shoots unto the River.
12Why hast thou broken down its walls,
So that all they that pass by the way do pluck it?
13The boar out of the wood doth ravage it,
And the wild beasts of the field feed on it.
14Turn again, we beseech thee, O God of hosts:
Look down from heaven, and behold, and visit this vine,
15And athe stock which thy right hand planted,
And the abranch that thou madest strong for thyself.
16It is burned with fire, it is cut down:
They perish at the rebuke of thy countenance.
17Let thy hand be upon the man of thy right hand,
Upon the son of man whom thou madest strong for thyself.
18So shall we not go back from thee:
Quicken thou us, and we will call upon thy name.
19aTurn us again, O Yahweh God of hosts;
Cause thy face to shine, and we shall be saved.

Chapter 81

For the Chief Musician; set to the Gittith. A Psalm of Asaph.
1Sing aloud unto God our strength:
Make a joyful noise unto the God of Jacob.
2Raise a song, and abring hither the timbrel,
The pleasant harp with the psaltery.
3Blow the trumpet at the new moon,
At the full moon, on our feast-day.
4For it is a statute for Israel,
An ordinance of the God of Jacob.
5He appointed it in Joseph for a testimony,
When he went out aover the land of Egypt,
Where I heard aa language that I knew not.
6I removed his shoulder from the burden:
His hands were freed from the basket.
7Thou calledst in trouble, and I delivered thee;
I answered thee in the secret place of thunder;
I proved thee at the waters of Meribah.
Selah

8Hear, O my people, and I will testify unto thee:
O Israel, if thou wouldest hearken unto me!
9There shall no strange god be in thee;
Neither shalt thou worship any foreign god.
10I am Yahweh thy God,
Who brought thee up out of the land of Egypt:
Open thy mouth wide, and I will fill it.
11But my people hearkened not to my voice;
And Israel would none of me.
12So I let them go after the stubbornness of their heart,
That they might walk in their own counsels.
13Oh that my people would hearken unto me,
That Israel would walk in my ways!
14I would soon subdue their enemies,
And turn my hand against their adversaries.
15The haters of Yahweh should asubmit themselves unto him:
But their time should endure for ever.
16He would feed them also with the afinest of the wheat;
And with honey out of the rock would I satisfy thee.

Chapter 82

A Psalm of Asaph.
1God standeth in the congregation of God;
He judgeth among the gods.
2How long will ye judge unjustly,
And respect the persons of the wicked?
Selah
3Judge the apoor and fatherless:
Do justice to the afflicted and destitute.
4Rescue the poor and needy:
Deliver them out of the hand of the wicked.
5They know not, neither do they understand;
They walk to and fro in darkness:
All the foundations of the earth are shaken.
6I said, Ye are gods,
And all of you sons of the Most High.
7Nevertheless ye shall die like men,
And fall like one of the princes.
8Arise, O God, judge the earth;
For thou shalt inherit all the nations.

Chapter 83

A song. A Psalm of Asaph.
1O God, keep not thou silence:
Hold not thy peace, and be not still, O God.
2For, lo, thine enemies make a tumult;
And they that hate thee have lifted up the head.
3Thy take crafty counsel against thy people,
And consult together against thy hidden ones.
4They have said, Come, and let us cut them off from being a nation;
That the name of Israel may be no more in remembrance.
5For they have consulted together with one consent;
Against thee do they make a covenant:
6The tents of Edom and the Ishmaelites;
Moab, and the Hagarenes;
7Gebal, and Ammon, and Amalek;
Philistia with the inhabitants of Tyre:
8Assyria also is joined with them;
They have ahelped the children of Lot.
Selah
9Do thou unto them as unto Midian,
As to Sisera, as to Jabin, at the river Kishon;
10Who perished at Endor,
Who became as dung for the earth.
11Make their nobles like Oreb and Zeeb;
Yea, all their princes like Zebah and Zalmunna;
12Who said, Let us take to ourselves in possession
The ahabitations of God.
13O my God, make them like the whirling dust;
As stubble before the wind.
14As the fire that burneth the forest,
And as the flame that setteth the mountains on fire,
15So pursue them with thy tempest,
And terrify them with thy storm.
16Fill their faces with confusion,
That they may seek thy name, O Yahweh.
17Let them be put to shame and dismayed for ever;
Yea, let them be confounded and perish;
18That they may know that athou alone, whose name is Yahweh,
Art the Most High over all the earth.

Chapter 84

For the Chief Musician; set to the Gittith. A Psalm of the sons of Korah.
1How aamiable are thy tabernacles,
O Yahweh of hosts!
2My soul longeth, yea, even fainteth for the courts of Yahweh;
My heart and my flesh acry out unto the living God.
3Yea, the sparrow hath found her a house,

And the swallow a nest for herself, where she may lay her young,
Even thine altars, O Yahweh of hosts,
My King, and my God.
4Blessed are they that dwell in thy house:
They will be still praising thee.
Selah
5Blessed is the man whose strength is in thee;
In whose heart are the highways to Zion.
6Passing through the valley of aWeeping they make it a place of springs;
Yea, the early rain covereth it with blessings.
7They go from strength to strength;
Every one of them appeareth before God in Zion.
8O Yahweh God of hosts, hear my prayer;
Give ear, O God of Jacob.
Selah
9aBehold, O God our shield,
And look upon the face of thine anointed.
10For a day in thy courts is better than a thousand.
I had rather abe a doorkeeper in the house of my God,
Than to dwell in the tents of wickedness.
11For Yahweh God is a sun and a shield:
Yahweh will give grace and glory;
No good thing will he withhold from them that walk uprightly.
12O Yahweh of hosts,
Blessed is the man that trusteth in thee.

Chapter 85

For the Chief Musician. A Psalm of the sons of Korah.
1Yahweh, thou hast been favorable unto thy land;
Thou hast abrought back the captivity of Jacob.
2Thou hast forgiven the iniquity of thy people;
Thou hast covered all their sin.
Selah
3Thou hast taken away all thy wrath;
Thou hast turned thyself from the fierceness of thine anger.
4aTurn us, O God of our salvation,
And cause thine indignation toward us to cease.
5Wilt thou be angry with us for ever?
Wilt thou draw out thine anger to all generations?
6Wilt thou not quicken us again,
That thy people may rejoice in thee?
7Show us thy lovingkindness, O Yahweh,
And grant us thy salvation.
8I will hear what God Yahweh will speak;
For he will speak peace unto his people, and to his saints:
But let them not turn again to folly.
9Surely his salvation is nigh them that fear him,
That glory may dwell in our land.
10Mercy and truth are met together;
Righteousness and peace have kissed each other.
11Truth springeth out of the earth;
And righteousness hath looked down from heaven.
12Yea, Yahweh will give that which is good;
And our land shall yield its increase.
13Righteousness shall go before him,
And shall amake his footsteps a way to walk in.

Chapter 86

A Prayer of David
1Bow down thine ear, O Yahweh, and answer me;
For I am poor and needy.
2Preserve my soul; for I am godly:
O thou my God, save thy servant that trusteth in thee.
3Be merciful unto me, O Lord;
For unto thee do I cry all the day long.
4Rejoice the soul of thy servant;
For unto thee, O Lord, do I lift up my soul.
5For thou, Lord, art good, and ready to forgive,
And abundant in lovingkindness unto all them that call upon thee.
6Give ear, O Yahweh, unto my prayer;
And hearken unto the voice of my supplications.
7In the day of my trouble I will call upon thee;
For thou wilt answer me.
8There is none like unto thee among the gods, O Lord;
Neither are there any works like unto thy works.
9All nations whom thou hast made shall come and worship before thee, O Lord;
And they shall glorify thy name.
10For thou art great, and doest wondrous things:
Thou art God alone.
11Teach me thy way, O Yahweh; I will walk in thy truth:
Unite my heart to fear thy name.
12I will praise thee, O Lord my God, with my whole heart;
And I will glorify thy name for evermore.
13For great is thy lovingkindness toward me;
And thou hast delivered my soul from the lowest Sheol.
14O God, the proud are risen up against me,
And a company of violent men have sought after my soul,
And have not set thee before them.
15But thou, O Lord, art a God merciful and gracious,
Slow to anger, and abundant in lovingkindness and truth.
16Oh turn unto me, and ahave mercy upon me;
Give thy strength unto thy servant,
And save the son of thy handmaid.
17Show me a token for good,
That they who hate me may see it, and be put to shame,
Because thou, Yahweh, hast helped me, and comforted me.

Chapter 87

A Psalm of the sons of Korah; a Song.
1aHis foundation is in the holy mountains.
2Yahweh loveth the gates of Zion
More than all the dwellings of Jacob.
3Glorious things are spoken of thee, O city of God.
Selah
4I will make mention of aRahab and Babylon as among them that know me:
Behold, Philistia, and Tyre, with aEthiopia:
This one was born there.
5Yea, of Zion it shall be said, This one and that one was born in her;
And the Most High himself will establish her.
6Yahweh will count, when he writeth up the peoples,
This one was born there.
Selah
7They that sing as well as athey that dance shall say,
All my fountains are in thee.

Chapter 88

A Song, a Psalm of the sons of Korah; for the Chief Musician; set to Mahalath aLeannoth. Maschil of Heman the Ezrahite.
1O Yahweh, the God of my salvation,
I have cried day and night before thee.
2Let my prayer enter into thy presence;
Incline thine ear unto my cry.
3For my soul is full of troubles,
And my life draweth nigh unto Sheol.
4I am reckoned with them that go down into the pit;
I am as a man that hath no help,
5Cast aoff among the dead,
Like the slain that lie in the grave,
Whom thou rememberest no more,
And they are cut off from thy hand.
6Thou hast laid me in the lowest pit,
In dark places, in the deeps.
7Thy wrath lieth hard upon me,
And thou hast afflicted me with all thy waves.
Selah
8Thou hast put mine acquaintance far from me;
Thou hast made me an abomination unto them:
I am shut up, and I cannot come forth.
9Mine eye wasteth away by reason of affliction:
I have called daily upon thee, O Yahweh;
I have spread forth my hands unto thee.
10Wilt thou show wonders to the dead?
Shall athey that are deceased arise and praise thee?
Selah
11Shall thy lovingkindness be declared in the grave?
Or thy faithfulness in aDestruction?
12Shall thy wonders be known in the dark?
And thy righteousness in the land of forgetfulness?
13But unto thee, O Yahweh, have I cried;
And in the morning shall my prayer come before thee.
14Yahweh, why castest thou off my soul?
Why hidest thou thy face from me?
15I am afflicted and ready to die from my youth up:
While I suffer thy terrors I am distracted.
16Thy fierce wrath is gone over me;
Thy terrors have cut me off.
17They came round about me like water all the day long;
They compassed me about together.
18Lover and friend hast thou put far from me,
And mine acquaintance ainto darkness.

Chapter 89

Maschil of Ethan the Ezrahite.
1I will sing of the lovingkindness of Yahweh for ever:
With my mouth will I make known thy faithfulness to all generations.
2For I have said, Mercy shall be built up for ever;
Thy faithfulness wilt thou establish in the very heavens.
3I have made a covenant with my chosen,
I have sworn unto David my servant:
4Thy seed will I establish for ever,
And build up thy throne to all generations.
Selah
5And the heavens shall praise thy wonders, O Yahweh;
Thy faithfulness also in the assembly of the holy ones.
6For who in the skies can be compared unto Yahweh?

Who among the asons of the amighty is like unto Yahweh,
7A God very terrible in the council of the holy ones,
And to be feared above all them that are round about him?
8O Yahweh God of hosts,
Who is a mighty one, like unto thee, O aYahweh?
And thy faithfulness is round about thee.
9Thou rulest the pride of the sea:
When the waves thereof arise, thou stillest them.
10Thou hast broken Rahab in pieces, as one that is slain;
Thou hast scattered thine enemies with the arm of thy strength.
11The heavens are thine, the earth also is thine:
The world and the fulness thereof, thou hast founded them.
12The north and the south, thou hast created them:
Tabor and Hermon rejoice in thy name.
13Thou hast aa mighty arm;
Strong is thy hand, and high is thy right hand.
14Righteousness and justice are the foundation of thy throne:
Lovingkindness and truth go before thy face.
15Blessed is the people that know the ajoyful sound:
They walk, O Yahweh, in the light of thy countenance.
16In thy name do they rejoice all the day;
And in thy righteousness are they exalted.
17For thou art the glory of their strength;
And in thy favor aour horn shall be exalted.
18For our shield belongeth unto Yahweh;
aAnd our king to the Holy One of Israel.
19Then thou spakest in vision to thy asaints,
And saidst, I have laid help upon one that is mighty;
I have exalted one chosen out of the people.
20I have found David my servant;
With my holy oil have I anointed him:
21With whom my hand shall be established,
Mine arm also shall strengthen him.
22The enemy shall not aexact from him,
Nor the son of wickedness afflict him.
23And I will beat down his adversaries before him,
And smite them that hate him.
24But my faithfulness and my lovingkindness shall be with him;
And in my name shall his horn be exalted.
25I will set his hand also on the sea,
And his right hand on the rivers.
26He shall cry unto me, Thou art my Father,
My God, and the rock of my salvation.
27I also will make him my first-born,
The highest of the kings of the earth.
28My lovingkindness will I keep for him for evermore;
And my covenant shall astand fast with him.
29His seed also will I make to endure for ever,
And his throne as the days of heaven.
30If his children forsake my law,
And walk not in mine ordinances;
31If they abreak my statutes,
And keep not my commandments;
32Then will I visit their transgression with the rod,
And their iniquity with stripes.
33But my lovingkindness will I not utterly take from him,
Nor suffer my faithfulness to fail.
34My covenant will I not break,
Nor alter the thing that is gone out of my lips.
35 aOnce have I sworn by my holiness:
I will not lie unto David:
36His seed shall endure for ever,
And his throne as the sun before me.
37 aIt shall be established for ever as the moon,
aAnd as the faithful witness in the sky.
Selah
38But thou hast cast off and rejected,
Thou hast been wroth with thine anointed.
39Thou hast abhorred the covenant of thy servant:
Thou hast profaned his crown by casting it to the ground.
40Thou hast broken down all his hedges;
Thou hast brought his strongholds to ruin.
41All that pass by the way rob him:
He is become a reproach to his neighbors.
42Thou hast exalted the right hand of his adversaries;
Thou hast made all his enemies to rejoice.
43Yea, thou turnest back the edge of his sword,
And hast not made him to stand in the battle.
44Thou hast made his brightness to cease,
And cast his throne down to the ground.
45The days of his youth hast thou shortened:
Thou hast covered him with shame.
Selah
46How long, O Yahweh? wilt thou hide thyself for ever?
How long shall thy wrath burn like fire?
47Oh remember how short my time is:
For what vanity hast thou created all the children of men!
48What man is he that shall live and not see death,
That shall deliver his soul from the apower of Sheol?
Selah
49Lord, where are thy former lovingkindnesses,
Which thou swarest unto David in thy faithfulness?
50Remember, Lord, the reproach of thy servants;
How I do bear in my bosom the reproach of all the amighty peoples,
51Wherewith thine enemies have reproached, O Yahweh,
Wherewith they have reproached the footsteps of thine anointed.
52Blessed be Yahweh for evermore.
Amen, and Amen.

BOOK IV

Chapter 90

A Prayer of Moses the man of God.
1Lord, thou hast been our dwelling-place
In all generations.
2Before the mountains were brought forth,
Or ever thou ahadst formed the earth and the world,
Even from everlasting to everlasting, thou art God.
3Thou turnest man to adestruction,
And sayest, Return, ye children of men.
4For a thousand years in thy sight
Are but as yesterday awhen it is past,
And as a watch in the night.
5Thou carriest them away as with a flood; they are as a sleep:
In the morning they are like grass which groweth up.
6In the morning it flourisheth, and groweth up;
In the evening it is cut down, and withereth.
7For we are consumed in thine anger,
And in thy wrath are we troubled.
8Thou hast set our iniquities before thee,
Our secret sins in the light of thy countenance.
9For all our days are passed away in thy wrath:
We bring our years to an end as aa sigh.
10The days of our years are threescore years and ten,
Or even by reason of strength fourscore years;
Yet is their pride but labor and sorrow;
For it is soon gone, and we fly away.
11Who knoweth the power of thine anger,
And thy wrath according to the fear that is due unto thee?
12So teach us to number our days,
That we may get us a heart of wisdom.
13Return, O Yahweh; how long?
And let it repent thee concerning thy servants.
14Oh satisfy us in the morning with thy lovingkindness,
That we may rejoice and be glad all our days.
15Make us glad according to the days wherein thou hast afflicted us,
And the years wherein we have seen evil.
16Let thy work appear unto thy servants,
And thy glory upon their children.
17And let the afavor of the Lord our God be upon us;
And establish thou the work of our hands upon us;
Yea, the work of our hands establish thou it.

Chapter 91

1He that dwelleth in the secret place of the Most High
aShall abide under the shadow of the Almighty.
2I will say of Yahweh, He is my refuge and my fortress;
My God, in whom I trust.
3For he will deliver thee from the snare of the fowler,
And from the deadly pestilence.
4He will cover thee with his pinions,
And under his wings shalt thou take refuge:
His truth is a shield and a buckler.
5Thou shalt not be afraid for the terror by night,
Nor for the arrow that flieth by day;
6For the pestilence that walketh in darkness,
Nor for the destruction that wasteth at noonday.
7A thousand shall fall at thy side,
And ten thousand at thy right hand;
But it shall not come nigh thee.
8Only with thine eyes shalt thou behold,
And see the reward of the wicked.
9 aFor thou, O Yahweh, art my refuge!
Thou hast made the Most High thy habitation;
10There shall no evil befall thee,
Neither shall any plague come nigh thy tent.
11For he will give his angels charge over thee,
To keep thee in all thy ways.
12They shall bear thee up in their hands,
Lest thou dash thy foot against a stone.
13Thou shalt tread upon the lion and adder:
The young lion and the serpent shalt thou trample under foot.
14Because he hath set his love upon me, therefore will I deliver him:
I will set him on high, because he hath known my name.
15He shall call upon me, and I will answer him;
I will be with him in trouble:
I will deliver him, and honor him.

Psalms

16With long life will I satisfy him,
And show him my salvation.

Chapter 92

A Psalm, a Song for the sabbath day.
1It is a good thing to give thanks unto Yahweh,
And to sing praises unto thy name, O Most High;
2To show forth thy lovingkindness in the morning,
And thy faithfulness every night,
3With an instrument of ten strings, and with the psaltery;
With a solemn sound upon the harp.
4For thou, Yahweh, hast made me glad through thy work:
I will triumph in the works of thy hands.
5How great are thy works, O Yahweh!
Thy thoughts are very deep.
6A brutish man knoweth not;
Neither doth a fool understand this:
7When the wicked spring as the grass,
And when all the workers of iniquity do flourish;
It is that they shall be destroyed for ever.
8But thou, O Yahweh, art on high for evermore.
9For, lo, thine enemies, O Yahweh,
For, lo, thine enemies shall perish;
All the workers of iniquity shall be scattered.
10But my horn hast thou exalted like the horn of the wild-ox:
I am anointed with fresh oil.
11Mine eye also hath seen my desire on amine enemies,
Mine ears have heard my desire of the evil-doers that rise up against me.
12The righteous shall flourish like the palm-tree:
He shall grow like a cedar in Lebanon.
13They are planted in the house of Yahweh;
They shall flourish in the courts of our God.
14They shall still bring forth fruit in old age;
They shall be full of sap and green:
15To show that Yahweh is upright;
He is my rock, and there is no unrighteousness in him.

Chapter 93

1Yahweh reigneth; he is clothed with majesty;
Yahweh is clothed with strength; he hath girded himself therewith:
The world also is established, that it cannot be moved.
2Thy throne is established of old:
Thou art from everlasting.
3The floods have lifted up, O Yahweh,
The floods have lifted up their voice;
The floods lift up their awaves.
4Above the voices of many waters,
The mighty breakers of the sea,
Yahweh on high is mighty.
5Thy testimonies are very sure:
Holiness becometh thy house,
O Yahweh, for evermore.

Chapter 94

1O Yahweh, thou God to whom vengeance belongeth,
Thou God to whom vengeance belongeth, shine forth.
2Lift up thyself, thou judge of the earth:
Render to the proud their desert.
3Yahweh, how long shall the wicked,
How long shall the wicked triumph?
4They prate, they speak arrogantly:
All the workers of iniquity boast themselves.
5They break in pieces thy people, O Yahweh,
And afflict thy heritage.
6They slay the widow and the sojourner,
And murder the fatherless.
7And they say, aYahweh will not see,
Neither will the God of Jacob consider.
8Consider, ye brutish among the people;
And ye fools, when will ye be wise?
9He that planted the ear, shall he not hear?
He that formed the eye, shall he not see?
10He that achastiseth the nations, shall not he correct,
Even he that teacheth man knowledge?
11Yahweh knoweth the thoughts of man,
aThat they are avanity.
12Blessed is the man whom thou chastenest, O Yahweh,
And teachest out of thy law;
13That thou mayest give him rest from the days of adversity,
Until the pit be digged for the wicked.
14For Yahweh will not cast off his people,
Neither will he forsake his inheritance.
15For judgment shall return unto righteousness,
And all the upright in heart shall follow it.
16Who will rise up for me against the evil-doers?
Who will stand up for me against the workers of iniquity?
17Unless Yahweh had been my help,
My soul had soon dwelt in silence.
18When I said, My foot slippeth;
Thy lovingkindness, O Yahweh, held me up.
19In the multitude of my athoughts within me Thy comforts delight my soul.
20Shall the athrone of wickedness have fellowship with thee,
Which frameth mischief by statute?
21They gather themselves together against the soul of the righteous,
And condemn the innocent blood.
22But Yahweh hath been my high tower,
And my God the rock of my refuge.
23And he hath brought upon them their own iniquity,
And will cut them off in their own wickedness;
Yahweh our God will cut them off.

Chapter 95

1Oh come, let us sing unto Yahweh;
Let us make a joyful noise to the rock of our salvation.
2Let us come before his presence with thanksgiving;
Let us make a joyful noise unto him with psalms.
3For Yahweh is a great God,
And a great King above all gods.
4In his hand are the deep places of the earth;
The aheights of the mountains are his also.
5The sea is his, and he made it;
And his hands formed the dry land.
6Oh come, let us worship and bow down;
Let us kneel before Yahweh our Maker:
7For he is our God,
And we are the people of his pasture, and the sheep of his hand.
To-day, aoh that ye would hear his voice!
8Harden not your heart, as at aMeribah,
As in the day of aMassah in the wilderness;
9When your fathers tempted me,
Proved me, and saw my work.
10Forty years long was I grieved with that generation,
And said, It is a people that do err in their heart,
And they have not known my ways:
11Wherefore I sware in my wrath,
That they should not enter into my rest.

Chapter 96

1Oh sing unto Yahweh a new song:
Sing unto Yahweh, all the earth.
2Sing unto Yahweh, bless his name;
Show forth his salvation from day to day.
3Declare his glory among the nations,
His marvellous works among all the peoples.
4For great is Yahweh, and greatly to be praised:
He is to be feared above all gods.
5For all the gods of the peoples are aidols;
But Yahweh made the heavens.
6Honor and majesty are before him;
Strength and beauty are in his sanctuary.
7Ascribe unto Yahweh, ye kindreds of the peoples,
Ascribe unto Yahweh glory and strength.
8Ascribe unto Yahweh the glory due unto his name:
Bring an offering, and come into his courts.
9Oh worship Yahweh ain holy array:
Tremble before him, all the earth.
10Say among the nations, Yahweh reigneth:
The world also is established that it cannot be moved:
He will judge the peoples with equity.
11Let the heavens be glad, and let the earth rejoice;
Let the sea roar, and the fulness thereof;
12Let the field exult, and all that is therein;
Then shall all the trees of the wood sing for joy
13Before Yahweh; for he cometh,
For he cometh to judge the earth:
He will judge the world with righteousness,
And the peoples awith his truth.

Chapter 97

1Yahweh reigneth; let the earth rejoice;
Let the multitude of isles be glad.
2Clouds and darkness are round about him:
Righteousness and justice are the foundation of his throne.
3A fire goeth before him,
And burneth up his adversaries round about.
4His lightnings lightened the world:
The earth saw, and trembled.
5The mountains melted like wax at the presence of Yahweh,
At the presence of the Lord of the whole earth.
6The heavens declare his righteousness,
And all the peoples have seen his glory.
7Let all them be put to shame that serve graven images,
That boast themselves of idols:
Worship him, all ye gods.
8Zion heard and was glad,

And the daughters of Judah rejoiced,
Because of thy judgments, O Yahweh.
9For thou, Yahweh, art most high above all the earth:
Thou art exalted far above all gods.
10O ye that love Yahweh, hate evil:
He preserveth the souls of his saints;
He delivereth them out of the hand of the wicked.
11Light is sown for the righteous,
And gladness for the upright in heart.
12Be glad in Yahweh, ye righteous;
And give thanks to his holy memorial name.

Chapter 98

A Psalm.
1Oh sing unto Yahweh a new song;
For he hath done marvellous things:
His right hand, and his holy arm, hath wrought salvation for him.
2Yahweh hath made known his salvation:
His righteousness hath he openly showed in the sight of the nations.
3He hath remembered his lovingkindness and his faithfulness toward the house of Israel:
All the ends of the earth have seen the salvation of our God.
4Make a joyful noise unto Yahweh, all the earth:
Break forth and sing for joy, yea, sing praises.
5Sing praises unto Yahweh with the harp;
With the harp and the voice of melody.
6With trumpets and sound of cornet
Make a joyful noise before the King, Yahweh.
7Let the sea roar, and the fulness thereof;
The world, and they that dwell therein;
8Let the floods clap their hands;
Let the hills sing for joy together
9Before Yahweh; for he cometh to judge the earth:
He will judge the world with righteousness,
And the peoples with equity.

Chapter 99

1Yahweh reigneth; let the peoples tremble:
He asitteth above the cherubim; let the earth be moved.
2Yahweh is great in Zion;
And he is high above all the peoples.
3Let them praise thy great and terrible name:
Holy is he.
4The king's strength also loveth justice;
Thou dost establish equity;
Thou executest justice and righteousness in Jacob.
5Exalt ye Yahweh our God,
And worship at his footstool:
Holy is he.
6Moses and Aaron among his priests,
And Samuel among them that call upon his name;
They called upon Yahweh, and he answered them.
7He spake unto them in the pillar of cloud:
They kept his testimonies,
And the statute that he gave them.
8Thou answeredst them, O Yahweh our God:
Thou wast a God that forgavest them,
Though thou tookest vengeance of their doings.
9Exalt ye Yahweh our God,
And worship at his holy hill;
For Yahweh our God is holy.

Chapter 100

A Psalm aof thanksgiving.
1Make a joyful noise unto Yahweh, aall ye lands.
2Serve Yahweh with gladness:
Come before his presence with singing.
3Know ye that Yahweh, he is God:
It is he that hath made us, aand we are his;
We are his people, and the sheep of his pasture.
4Enter into his gates with athanksgiving,
And into his courts with praise:
Give thanks unto him, and bless his name.
5For Yahweh is good; his lovingkindness endureth for ever,
And his faithfulness unto all generations.

Chapter 101

A Psalm of David.
1I will sing of lovingkindness and justice:
Unto thee, O Yahweh, I will sing praises.
2I will abehave myself wisely in a perfect way:
Oh when wilt thou come unto me?
I will walk within my house awith a perfect heart.
3I will set no base thing before mine eyes:
I hate athe work of them that turn aside;
It shall not cleave unto me.
4A perverse heart shall depart from me:
I will know no aevil thing.
5Whoso privily slandereth his neighbor, him will I destroy:
Him that hath a high look and a proud heart will I not suffer.
6Mine eyes shall be upon the faithful of the land, that they may dwell with me:
He that walketh in a perfect way, he shall minister unto me.
7He that worketh deceit shall not dwell within my house:
He that speaketh falsehood shall not be established before mine eyes.
8Morning by morning will I destroy all the wicked of the land;
To cut off all the workers of iniquity from the city of Yahweh.

Chapter 102

A Prayer of the afflicted, when he is aoverwhelmed, and poureth out his complaint before Yahweh.
1Hear my prayer, O Yahweh,
And let my cry come unto thee.
2Hide not thy face from me in the day of my distress:
Incline thine ear unto me;
In the day when I call answer me speedily.
3For my days consume away alike smoke,
And my bones are burned aas a firebrand.
4My heart is smitten like grass, and withered;
For I forget to eat my bread.
5By reason of the voice of my groaning
My bones cleave to my flesh.
6I am like a pelican of the wilderness;
I am become as an owl of the waste places.
7I watch, and am become like a sparrow
That is alone upon the house-top.
8Mine enemies reproach me all the day;
They that are mad against me do curse by me.
9For I have eaten ashes like bread,
And mingled my drink with weeping,
10Because of thine indignation and thy wrath:
For thou hast taken me up, and cast me away.
11My days are like a shadow that adeclineth;
And I am withered like grass.
12But thou, O Yahweh, awilt abide for ever;
And thy memorial name unto all generations.
13Thou wilt arise, and have mercy upon Zion;
For it is time to have pity upon her,
Yea, the set time is come.
14For thy servants take pleasure in her stones,
And have pity upon her dust.
15So the nations shall fear the name of Yahweh,
And all the kings of the earth thy glory.
16For Yahweh hath built up Zion;
He hath appeared in his glory.
17He hath regarded the prayer of the destitute,
And hath not despised their prayer.
18This shall be written for the generation to come;
And a people which shall be created shall praise aYahweh.
19For he hath looked down from the height of his sanctuary;
From heaven did Yahweh behold the earth;
20To hear the sighing of the prisoner;
To loose athose that are appointed to death;
21That men may declare the name of Yahweh in Zion,
And his praise in Jerusalem;
22When the peoples are gathered together,
And the kingdoms, to serve Yahweh.
23He aweakened my strength in the way;
He shortened my days.
24I said, O my God, take me not away in the midst of my days:
Thy years are throughout all generations.
25Of old didst thou lay the foundation of the earth;
And the heavens are the work of thy hands.
26They shall perish, but thou shalt endure;
Yea, all of them shall wax old like a garment;
As a vesture shalt thou change them, and they shall be changed:
27But thou art the same,
And thy years shall have no end.
28The children of thy servants shall continue,
And their seed shall be established before thee.

Chapter 103

A Psalm of David.
1Bless Yahweh, O my soul;
And all that is within me, bless his holy name.
2Bless Yahweh, O my soul,
And forget not all his benefits:
3Who forgiveth all thine iniquities;
Who healeth all thy diseases;
4Who redeemeth thy life from adestruction;
Who crowneth thee with lovingkindness and tender mercies;
5Who satisfieth athy desire with good things,
So that thy youth is renewed like the eagle.
6Yahweh executeth righteous acts,
And judgments for all that are oppressed.
7He made known his ways unto Moses,

Psalms

His doings unto the children of Israel.
8Yahweh is merciful and gracious,
Slow to anger, and abundant in lovingkindness.
9He will not always chide;
Neither will he keep his anger for ever.
10He hath not dealt with us after our sins,
Nor rewarded us after our iniquities.
11For as the heavens are high above the earth,
So great is his lovingkindness toward them that fear him.
12As far as the east is from the west,
So far hath he removed our transgressions from us.
13Like as a father pitieth his children,
So Yahweh pitieth them that fear him.
14For he knoweth our frame;
He remembereth that we are dust.
15As for man, his days are as grass;
As a flower of the field, so he flourisheth.
16For the wind passeth over it, and it is gone;
And the place thereof shall know it no more.
17But the lovingkindness of Yahweh is from everlasting to everlasting upon them that fear him,
And his righteousness unto children's children;
18To such as keep his covenant,
And to those that remember his precepts to do them.
19Yahweh hath established his throne in the heavens;
And his kingdom ruleth over all.
20Bless Yahweh, ye his angels,
That are mighty in strength, that fulfil his word,
Hearkening unto the voice of his word.
21Bless Yahweh, all ye his hosts,
Ye ministers of his, that do his pleasure.
22Bless Yahweh, all ye his works,
In all places of his dominion:
Bless Yahweh, O my soul.

Chapter 104

1Bless Yahweh, O my soul.
O Yahweh my God, thou art very great;
Thou art clothed with honor and majesty:
2Who coverest thyself with light as with a garment;
Who stretchest out the heavens like a curtain;
3Who layeth the beams of his chambers in the waters;
Who maketh the clouds his chariot;
Who walketh upon the wings of the wind;
4Who maketh awinds his messengers;
Flames of fire his ministers;
5 aWho laid the foundations of the earth,
That it should not be moved for ever.
6Thou coveredst it with the deep as with a vesture;
The waters stood above the mountains.
7At thy rebuke they fled;
At the voice of thy thunder they hasted away
8 a(The mountains rose, the valleys sank down)
Unto the place which thou hadst founded for them.
9Thou hast set a bound that they may not pass over;
That they turn not again to cover the earth.
10He sendeth forth springs into the valleys;
They run among the mountains;
11They give drink to every beast of the field;
The wild asses quench their thirst.
12By them the birds of the heavens have their habitation;
They asing among the branches.
13He watereth the mountains from his chambers:
The earth is filled with the fruit of thy works.
14He causeth the grass to grow for the cattle,
And herb for the aservice of man;
That he may bring forth afood out of the earth,
15And wine that maketh glad the heart of man,
aAnd oil to make his face to shine,
And bread that strengtheneth man's heart.
16The trees of Yahweh are filled with moisture,
The cedars of Lebanon, which he hath planted;
17Where the birds make their nests:
As for the stork, the fir-trees are her house.
18The high mountains are for the wild goats;
The rocks are a refuge for the conies.
19He appointed the moon for seasons:
The sun knoweth his going down.
20Thou makest darkness, and it is night,
Wherein all the beasts of the forest creep forth.
21The young lions roar after their prey,
And seek their food from God.
22The sun ariseth, they get them away,
And lay them down in their dens.
23Man goeth forth unto his work
And to his labor until the evening.
24O Yahweh, how manifold are thy works!
In wisdom hast thou made them all:
The earth is full of thy ariches.

25Yonder is the sea, great and wide,
Wherein are things creeping innumerable,
Both small and great beasts.
26There go the ships;
There is leviathan, whom thou hast formed to play atherein.
27These wait all for thee,
That thou mayest give them their food in due season.
28Thou givest unto them, they gather;
Thou openest thy hand, they are satisfied with good.
29Thou hidest thy face, they are troubled;
Thou atakest away their breath, they die,
And return to their dust.
30Thou sendest forth thy Spirit, they are created;
And thou renewest the face of the ground.
31Let the glory of Yahweh endure for ever;
Let Yahweh rejoice in his works:
32Who looketh on the earth, and it trembleth;
He toucheth the mountains, and they smoke.
33I will sing unto Yahweh as long as I live:
I will sing praise to my God while I have any being.
34Let thy meditation be sweet unto him:
I will rejoice in Yahweh.
35Let sinners be consumed out of the earth.
And let the wicked be no more.
Bless Yahweh, O my soul.
aPraise ye Yahweh.

Chapter 105

1Oh give thanks unto Yahweh, call upon his name;
Make known among the peoples his doings.
2Sing unto him, sing praises unto him;
aTalk ye of all his marvelous works.
3Glory ye in his holy name:
Let the heart of them rejoice that seek Yahweh.
4Seek ye Yahweh and his strength;
Seek his face evermore.
5Remember his marvellous works that he hath done,
His wonders, and the judgments of his mouth,
6O ye seed of Abraham his servant,
Ye children of Jacob, his chosen ones.
7He is Yahweh our God:
His judgments are in all the earth.
8He hath remembered his covenant for ever,
The word which he commanded to a thousand generations,
9The covenant which he made with Abraham,
And his oath unto Isaac,
10And confirmed the same unto Jacob for a statute,
To Israel for an everlasting covenant,
11Saying, Unto thee will I give the land of Canaan,
The alot of your inheritance;
12When they were but a few men in number,
Yea, very few, and sojourners in it.
13And they went about from nation to nation,
From one kingdom to another people.
14He suffered no man to do them wrong;
Yea, he reproved kings for their sakes,
15Saying, Touch not mine anointed ones,
And do my prophets no harm.
16And he called for a famine upon the land;
He brake the whole staff of bread.
17He sent a man before them;
Joseph was sold for a servant:
18His feet they hurt with fetters:
aHe was laid in chains of iron,
19Until the time that his word came to pass,
The word of Yahweh tried him.
20The king sent and loosed him;
Even the ruler of peoples, and let him go free.
21He made him lord of his house,
And ruler of all his substance;
22To bind his princes at his pleasure,
And teach his elders wisdom.
23Israel also came into Egypt;
And Jacob sojourned in the land of Ham.
24And he increased his people greatly,
And made them stronger than their adversaries.
25He turned their heart to hate his people,
To deal subtly with his servants.
26He sent Moses his servant,
And Aaron whom he had chosen.
27They set among them ahis signs,
And wonders in the land of Ham.
28He sent darkness, and made it dark;
And they rebelled not against his words.
29He turned their waters into blood,
And slew their fish.
30Their land swarmed with frogs In the chambers of their kings.
31He spake, and there came swarms of flies,
And lice in all their borders.

32He gave them hail for rain,
And flaming fire in their land.
33He smote their vines also and their fig-trees,
And brake the trees of their borders.
34He spake, and the locust came,
And the grasshopper, and that without number,
35And did eat up every herb in their land,
And did eat up the fruit of their ground.
36He smote also all the first-born in their land,
The achief of all their strength.
37And he brought them forth with silver and gold;
And there was anot one feeble person among his tribes.
38Egypt was glad when they departed;
For the fear of them had fallen upon them.
39He spread a cloud for a covering,
And fire to give light in the night.
40They asked, and he brought quails,
And satisfied them with the bread of heaven.
41He opened the rock, and waters gushed out;
They ran in the dry places like a river.
42For he remembered his holy word,
And Abraham his servant.
43And he brought forth his people with joy,
And his chosen with singing.
44And he gave them the lands of the nations;
And they took the labor of the peoples in possession:
45That they might keep his statutes,
And observe his laws.
aPraise ye Yahweh.

Chapter 106

1 aPraise ye Yahweh.
Oh give thanks unto Yahweh; for he is good;
For his lovingkindness endureth forever.
2Who can utter the mighty acts of Yahweh,
Or show forth all his praise?
3Blessed are they that keep justice,
And he that doeth righteousness at all times.
4Remember me, O Yahweh, with the favor that thou bearest unto thy people;
Oh visit me with thy salvation,
5That I may see the prosperity of thy chosen,
That I may rejoice in the gladness of thy nation,
That I may glory with thine inheritance.
6We have sinned with our fathers,
We have committed iniquity, we have done wickedly.
7Our fathers understood not thy wonders in Egypt;
They remembered not the multitude of thy lovingkindnesses,
But were rebellious at the sea, even at the Red Sea.
8Nevertheless he saved them for his name's sake,
That he might make his mighty power to be known.
9He rebuked the Red Sea also, and it was dried up:
So he led them through the depths, as through a awilderness.
10And he saved them from the hand of him that hated them,
And redeemed them from the hand of the enemy.
11And the waters covered their adversaries;
There was not one of them left.
12Then believed they his words;
They sang his praise.
13They soon forgat his works;
They waited not for his counsel,
14But lusted exceedingly in the wilderness,
And tempted God in the desert.
15And he gave them their request,
But sent leanness into their soul.
16They envied Moses also in the camp,
And Aaron the asaint of Yahweh.
17The earth opened and swallowed up Dathan,
And covered the company of Abiram.
18And a fire was kindled in their company;
The flame burned up the wicked.
19They made a calf in Horeb,
And worshipped a molten image.
20Thus they changed their glory
For the likeness of an ox that eateth grass.
21They forgat God their Saviour,
Who had done great things in Egypt,
22Wondrous works in the land of Ham,
And terrible things by the Red Sea.
23Therefore he said that he would destroy them,
Had not Moses his chosen stood before him in the breach,
To turn away his wrath, lest he should destroy them.
24Yea, they despised the pleasant land,
They believed not his word,
25But murmured in their tents,
And hearkened not unto the voice of Yahweh.
26Therefore he asware unto them,
That he would aoverthrow them in the wilderness,
27And that he would overthrow their seed among the nations,
And scatter them in the lands.
28They joined themselves also unto Baal-peor,
And ate the sacrifices of the dead.
29Thus they provoked him to anger with their doings;
And the plague brake in upon them.
30Then stood up Phinehas, and executed judgment;
And so the plague was stayed.
31And that was reckoned unto him for righteousness,
Unto all generations for evermore.
32They angered him also at the waters of aMeribah,
So that it went ill with Moses for their sakes;
33Because they were rebellious against his spirit,
And he spake unadvisedly with his lips.
34They did not destroy the peoples,
As Yahweh commanded them,
35But mingled themselves with the nations,
And learned their works,
36And served their idols,
Which became a snare unto them.
37Yea, they sacrificed their sons and their daughters unto demons,
38And shed innocent blood,
Even the blood of their sons and of their daughters,
Whom they sacrificed unto the idols of Canaan;
And the land was polluted with blood.
39Thus were they defiled with their works,
And played the harlot in their doings.
40Therefore was the wrath of Yahweh kindled against his people,
And he abhorred his inheritance.
41And he gave them into the hand of the nations;
And they that hated them ruled over them.
42Their enemies also oppressed them,
And they were brought into subjection under their hand.
43Many times did he deliver them;
But they were rebellious in their counsel,
And were brought low in their iniquity.
44Nevertheless he regarded their distress,
When he heard their cry:
45And he remembered for them his covenant,
And repented according to the multitude of his lovingkindnesses.
46He made them also to be pitied
Of all those that carried them captive.
47Save us, O Yahweh our God,
And gather us from among the nations,
To give thanks unto thy holy name,
And to triumph in thy praise.
48Blessed be Yahweh, the God of Israel,
From everlasting even to everlasting.
And let all the people say, Amen.
aPraise ye Yahweh.

BOOK V

Chapter 107

1O give thanks unto Yahweh;
For he is good;
For his lovingkindness endureth for ever.
2Let the redeemed of Yahweh say so,
Whom he hath redeemed from the hand of the adversary,
3And gathered out of the lands,
From the east and from the west,
From the north and afrom the south.
4They wandered in the wilderness in a desert way;
They found no city of habitation.
5Hungry and thirsty,
Their soul fainted in them.
6Then they cried unto Yahweh in their trouble,
And he delivered them out of their distresses,
7He led them also by a straight way,
That they might go to a city of habitation.
8Oh that men would praise Yahweh for his lovingkindness,
And for his wonderful works to the children of men!
9For he satisfieth the longing soul,
And the hungry soul he filleth with good.
10Such as sat in darkness and in the shadow of death,
Being bound in affliction and iron,
11Because they rebelled against the words of God,
And contemned the counsel of the Most High:
12Therefore he brought down their heart with labor;
They fell down, and there was none to help.
13Then they cried unto Yahweh in their trouble,
And he saved them out of their distresses.
14He brought them out of darkness and the shadow of death,
And brake their bonds in sunder.
15Oh that men would praise Yahweh for his lovingkindness,
And for his wonderful works to the children of men!
16For he hath broken the gates of brass,
And cut the bars of iron in sunder.
17Fools because of atheir transgression,

Psalms

And because of their iniquities, are afflicted.
18Their soul abhorreth all manner of food;
And they draw near unto the gates of death.
19Then they cry unto Yahweh in their trouble,
And he saveth them out of their distresses.
20He sendeth his word, and healeth them,
And delivereth them from their adestructions.
21Oh that men would praise Yahweh for his lovingkindness,
And for his wonderful works to the children of men!
22And let them offer the sacrifices of thanksgiving,
And declare his works with singing.
23They that go down to the sea in ships,
That do business in great waters;
24These see the works of Yahweh,
And his wonders in the deep.
25For he commandeth, and raiseth the stormy wind,
Which lifteth up the waves thereof.
26They mount up to the heavens, they go down again to the depths:
Their soul melteth away because of trouble.
27They reel to and fro, and stagger like a drunken man,
And aare at their wits' end.
28Then they cry unto Yahweh in their trouble,
And he bringeth them out of their distresses.
29He maketh the storm a calm,
So that the waves thereof are still.
30Then are they glad because they are quiet;
So he bringeth them unto their desired haven.
31Oh that men would praise Yahweh for his lovingkindness,
And for his wonderful works to the children of men!
32Let them exalt him also in the assembly of the people,
And praise him in the seat of the elders.
33He turneth rivers into a wilderness,
And watersprings into a thirsty ground;
34A fruitful land into a salt desert,
For the wickedness of them that dwell therein.
35He turneth a wilderness into a pool of water,
And a dry land into watersprings.
36And there he maketh the hungry to dwell,
That they may prepare a city of habitation,
37And sow fields, and plant vineyards,
And get them fruits of increase.
38He blesseth them also, so that they are multiplied greatly;
And he suffereth not their cattle to decrease.
39Again, they are diminished and bowed down
Through oppression, trouble, and sorrow.
40He poureth contempt upon princes,
And causeth them to wander in the waste, where there is no way.
41Yet setteth he the needy on high from affliction,
And maketh him families like a flock.
42The upright shall see it, and be glad;
And all iniquity shall stop her mouth.
43Whoso is wise will give heed to these things;
And they will consider the lovingkindnesses of Yahweh.

Chapter 108

A Song, A Psalm of David.
1My heart is fixed, O God; I will sing, yea,
I will sing praises, even with my glory.
2Awake, psaltery and harp:
I myself will aawake right early.
3I will give thanks unto thee, O Yahweh, among the peoples;
And I will sing praises unto thee among the nations.
4For thy lovingkindness is great above the heavens;
And thy truth reacheth unto the skies.
5Be thou exalted, O God, above the heavens,
And thy glory above all the earth.
6That thy beloved may be delivered,
Save with thy right hand, and answer aus.
7God hath spoken in his holiness: I will exult;
I will divide Shechem, and mete out the valley of Succoth.
8Gilead is mine; Manasseh is mine;
Ephraim also is the defence of my head;
Judah is my asceptre.
9Moab is my washpot;
aUpon Edom will I cast my shoe;
Over Philistia will I shout.
10Who will bring me into the fortified city?
Who ahath led me unto Edom?
11 aHast not thou cast us off, O God?
And thou goest not forth, O God, with our hosts.
12Give us help against the adversary;
For vain is the help of man.
13Through God we shall do valiantly:
For he it is that will tread down our adversaries.

Chapter 109

For the Chief Musicion. A Psalm of David.
1Hold not thy peace, O God of my praise;
2For the mouth of the wicked and the mouth of deceit have they opened against me:
They have spoken aunto me with a lying tongue.
3They have compassed me about also with words of hatred,
And fought against me without a cause.
4For my love they are my adversaries:
But I give myself unto prayer.
5And they have arewarded me evil for good,
And hatred for my love.
6Set thou a wicked man over him;
And let aan adversary stand at his right hand.
7When he is judged, let him come forth guilty;
And let his prayer abe turned into sin.
8Let his days be few;
And let another take his office.
9Let his children be fatherless,
And his wife a widow.
10Let his children be vagabonds, and beg;
And let them seek their bread aout of their desolate places.
11Let the extortioner acatch all that he hath;
And let strangers make spoil of his labor.
12Let there be none to aextend kindness unto him;
Neither let there be any to have pity on his fatherless children.
13Let his posterity be cut off;
In the generation following let their name be blotted out.
14Let the iniquity of his fathers be remembered with Yahweh;
And let not the sin of his mother be blotted out.
15Let them be before Yahweh continually,
That he may cut off the memory of them from the earth;
16Because he remembered not to show kindness,
But persecuted the poor and needy man,
And the broken in heart, to slay them.
17Yea, he loved cursing, and it came unto him;
And he delighted not in blessing, and it was far from him.
18He clothed himself also with cursing as with his garment,
And it came into his inward parts like water,
And like oil into his bones.
19Let it be unto him as the raiment wherewith he covereth himself,
And for the girdle wherewith he is girded continually.
20This is the reward of mine adversaries from Yahweh,
And of them that speak evil against my soul.
21But deal thou with me, O Yahweh the Lord, for thy name's sake:
Because thy lovingkindness is good, deliver thou me;
22For I am poor and needy,
And my heart is wounded within me.
23I am gone like the shadow when it adeclineth:
I am tossed up and down as the locust.
24My knees aare weak through fasting;
And my flesh faileth of fatness.
25I am become also a reproach unto them:
When they see me, they shake their head.
26Help me, O Yahweh my God;
Oh save me according to thy lovingkindness:
27That they may know that this is thy hand;
That thou, Yahweh, hast done it.
28Let them curse, but bless thou:
When they arise, they shall be put to shame,
But thy servant shall rejoice.
29 aLet mine adversaries be clothed with dishonor,
And let them cover themselves with their own shame as with a robe.
30I will give great thanks unto Yahweh with my mouth;
Yea, I will praise him among the multitude.
31For he will stand at the right hand of the needy,
To save him from them that judge his soul.

Chapter 110

A Psalm of David.
1Yahweh saith unto my Lord, Sit thou at my right hand,
Until I make thine enemies thy footstool.
2Yahweh will asend forth the arod of thy strength out of Zion:
Rule thou in the midst of thine enemies.
3Thy people aoffer themselves willingly
In the day of thy apower, ain holy array:
Out of the womb of the morning
aThou hast the dew of thy youth.
4Yahweh hath sworn, and will not repent:
Thou art a priest for ever
After the aorder of Melchizedek.
5The Lord at thy right hand
aWill strike through kings in the day of his wrath.
6He will judge among the nations,
aHe awill fill the places with dead bodies;
He awill strike through the head ain many countries.
7He will drink of the brook in the way:
Therefore will he lift up the head.

Chapter 111

1 aPraise ye Yahweh.
I will give thanks unto Yahweh with my whole heart,
In the council of the upright, and in the congregation.
2 The works of Yahweh are great,
Sought out of all them that have pleasure therein.
3 His work is honor and majesty;
And his righteousness endureth for ever.
4 He hath made his wonderful works to be remembered:
Yahweh is gracious and merciful.
5 He hath given afood unto them that fear him:
He will ever be mindful of his covenant.
6 He hath showed his people the power of his works,
In giving them the heritage of the nations.
7 The works of his hands are truth and justice;
All his precepts are sure.
8 They are established for ever and ever;
They are adone in truth and uprightness.
9 He hath sent redemption unto his people;
He hath commanded his covenant for ever:
Holy and reverend is his name.
10 The fear of Yahweh is the beginning of wisdom;
aA good understanding have all they that do ahis commandments:
His praise endureth for ever.

Chapter 112

1 aPraise ye Yahweh.
Blessed is the man that feareth Yahweh,
That delighteth greatly in his commandments.
2 His seed shall be mighty upon earth:
The generation of the upright shall be blessed.
3 Wealth and riches are in his house;
And his righteousness endureth for ever.
4 Unto the upright there ariseth light in the darkness:
He is gracious, and merciful, and righteous.
5 Well is it with the man that dealeth graciously and lendeth;
He shall maintain his cause in judgment.
6 For he shall never be moved;
The righteous shall be had in everlasting remembrance.
7 He shall not be afraid of evil tidings:
His heart is fixed, trusting in Yahweh.
8 His heart is established, he shall not be afraid,
Until he see his desire upon his adversaries.
9 He hath dispersed, he hath given to the needy;
His righteousness endureth for ever:
His horn shall be exalted with honor.
10 The wicked shall see it, and be grieved;
He shall gnash with his teeth, and melt away:
The desire of the wicked shall perish.

Chapter 113

1 Praise ye Yahweh.
Praise, O ye servants of Yahweh,
Praise the name of Yahweh.
2 Blessed be the name of Yahweh
From this time forth and for evermore.
3 From the rising of the sun unto the going down of the same
Yahweh's name is to be praised.
4 Yahweh is high above all nations,
And his glory above the heavens.
5 Who is like unto Yahweh our God,
That hath his seat on high,
6 That humbleth himself ato behold
The things that are in heaven and in the earth?
7 He raiseth up the poor out of the dust,
And lifteth up the needy from the dunghill;
8 That he may set him with princes,
Even with the princes of his people.
9 He maketh the barren woman to keep house,
And to be a joyful mother of children.
Praise ye Yahweh.

Chapter 114

1 When Israel went forth out of Egypt,
The house of Jacob from a people of strange language;
2 Judah became his sanctuary,
Israel his dominion.
3 The sea saw it, and fled;
The Jordan was driven back.
4 The mountains skipped like rams,
The little hills like lambs.
5 What aileth thee, O thou sea, that thou fleest?
Thou Jordan, that thou turnest back?
6 Ye mountains, that ye skip like rams;
Ye little hills, like lambs?
7 Tremble, thou earth, at the presence of the Lord,
At the presence of the God of Jacob,
8 Who turned the rock into a pool of water,
The flint into a fountain of waters.

Chapter 115

1 Not unto us, O Yahweh, not unto us,
But unto thy name give glory,
For thy lovingkindness, and for thy truth's sake.
2 Wherefore should the nations say,
Where is now their God?
3 But our God is in the heavens:
He hath done whatsoever he pleased.
4 Their idols are silver and gold,
The work of men's hands.
5 They have mouths, but they speak not;
Eyes have they, but they see not;
6 They have ears, but they hear not;
Noses have they, but they smell not;
7 They have hands, but they handle not;
Feet have they, but they walk not;
Neither speak they through their throat.
8 They that make them shall be like unto them;
Yea, every one that trusteth in them.
9 O Israel, trust thou in Yahweh:
He is their help and their shield.
10 O house of Aaron, trust ye in Yahweh:
He is their help and their shield.
11 Ye that fear Yahweh, trust in Yahweh:
He is their help and their shield.
12 Yahweh hath been mindful of us; he will bless us:
He will bless the house of Israel;
He will bless the house of Aaron.
13 He will bless them that fear Yahweh,
Both small and great.
14 Yahweh increase you more and more,
You and your children.
15 Blessed are ye of Yahweh,
Who made heaven and earth.
16 The heavens are the heavens of Yahweh;
But the earth hath he given to the children of men.
17 The dead praise not Yahweh,
Neither any that go down into silence;
18 But we will bless Yahweh
From this time forth and for evermore.
aPraise ye Yahweh.

Chapter 116

1 I love Yahweh, because he heareth
My voice and my supplications.
2 Because he hath inclined his ear unto me,
Therefore will I call upon him as long as I live.
3 The cords of death compassed me,
And the pains of Sheol agat hold upon me:
I found trouble and sorrow.
4 Then called I upon the name of Yahweh:
O Yahweh, I beseech thee, deliver my soul.
5 Gracious is Yahweh, and righteous;
Yea, our God is merciful.
6 Yahweh preserveth the simple:
I was brought low, and he saved me.
7 Return unto thy rest, O my soul;
For Yahweh hath dealt bountifully with thee.
8 For thou hast delivered my soul from death,
Mine eyes from tears,
And my feet from falling.
9 I will walk before Yahweh
In the land of the living.
10 I abelieve, for I will speak:
I was greatly afflicted:
11 I said in my ahaste,
All men are liars.
12 What shall I render unto Yahweh
For all his benefits toward me?
13 I will take the cup of salvation,
And call upon the name of Yahweh.
14 I will pay my vows unto Yahweh,
Yea, in the presence of all his people.
15 Precious in the sight of Yahweh
Is the death of his saints.
16 O Yahweh, truly I am thy servant:
I am thy servant, the son of thy handmaid;
Thou hast loosed my bonds.
17 I will offer to thee the sacrifice of thanksgiving,
And will call upon the name of Yahweh.
18 I will pay my vows unto Yahweh,
Yea, in the presence of all his people,
19 In the courts of Yahweh's house,
In the midst of thee, O Jerusalem.
aPraise ye Yahweh.

Psalms

Chapter 117

1 O praise Yahweh, all ye nations;
Laud him, all ye peoples.
2 For his lovingkindness is great toward us;
And the truth of Yahweh endureth for ever.
aPraise ye Yahweh.

Chapter 118

1 Oh give thanks unto Yahweh; for he is good;
For his lovingkindness endureth for ever.
2 Let Israel now say,
That his lovingkindness endureth for ever.
3 Let the house of Aaron now say,
That his lovingkindness endureth for ever.
4 Let them now that fear Yahweh say,
That his lovingkindness endureth for ever.
5 Out of my distress I called upon aYahweh:
aYahweh answered me and set me in a large place.
6 Yahweh is on my side; I will not fear:
What can man do unto me?
7 Yahweh is on my side among them that help me:
Therefore shall I see my desire upon them that hate me.
8 It is better to take refuge in Yahweh
Than to put confidence in man.
9 It is better to take refuge in Yahweh
Than to put confidence in princes.
10 All nations compassed me about:
In the name of Yahweh I will cut them off.
11 They compassed me about; yea, they compassed me about:
In the name of Yahweh I will cut them off.
12 They compassed me about like bees;
They are quenched as the fire of thorns:
In the name of Yahweh I will cut them off.
13 Thou didst thrust sore at me that I might fall;
But Yahweh helped me.
14 Yahweh is my strength and song;
And he is become my salvation.
15 The voice of rejoicing and salvation is in the tents of the righteous:
The right hand of Yahweh doeth valiantly.
16 The right hand of Yahweh is exalted:
The right hand of Yahweh doeth valiantly.
17 I shall not die, but live,
And declare the works of Yahweh.
18 aYahweh hath chastened me sore;
But he hath not given me over unto death.
19 Open to me the gates of righteousness:
I will enter into them, I will give thanks unto Yahweh.
20 This is the gate of Yahweh;
The righteous shall enter into it.
21 I will give thanks unto thee; for thou hast answered me,
And art become my salvation.
22 The stone which the builders rejected Is become the head of the corner.
23 This is aYahweh's doing;
It is marvellous in our eyes.
24 This is the day which Yahweh hath made;
We will rejoice and be glad in it.
25 Save now, we beseech thee, O Yahweh:
O Yahweh, we beseech thee, send now prosperity.
26 Blessed be he that acometh in the name of Yahweh:
We have blessed you out of the house of Yahweh.
27 Yahweh is God, and he hath given us light:
Bind the sacrifice with cords, even unto the horns of the altar.
28 Thou art my God, and I will give thanks unto thee:
Thou art my God, I will exalt thee.
29 Oh give thanks unto Yahweh; for he is good;
For his lovingkindness endureth for ever.

Chapter 119

ALEPH.

119 1 Blessed are they that are aperfect in the way,
Who walk in the law of Yahweh.
2 Blessed are they that keep his testimonies,
That seek him with the whole heart.
3 Yea, they do no unrighteousness;
They walk in his ways.
4 Thou hast commanded us thy precepts,
That we should observe them diligently.
5 Oh that my ways were established
To observe thy statutes!
6 Then shall I not be put to shame,
When I have respect unto all thy commandments.
7 I will give thanks unto thee with uprightness of heart,
When I learn thy righteous judgments.
8 I will observe thy statutes:
Oh forsake me not utterly.

BETH.

9 Wherewith shall a young man cleanse his way?
By taking heed thereto according to thy word.
10 With my whole heart have I sought thee:
Oh let me not wander from thy commandments.
11 Thy word have I laid up in my heart,
That I might not sin against thee.
12 Blessed art thou, O Yahweh:
Teach me thy statutes.
13 With my lips have I declared
All the ordinances of thy mouth.
14 I have rejoiced in the way of thy testimonies,
As much as in all riches.
15 I will meditate on thy precepts,
And have respect unto thy ways.
16 I will delight myself in thy statutes:
I will not forget thy word.

GIMEL.

17 Deal bountifully with thy servant, that I may live;
So will I observe thy word.
18 Open thou mine eyes, that I may behold
Wondrous things out of thy law.
19 I am a sojourner in the earth:
Hide not thy commandments from me.
20 My soul breaketh for the longing
That it hath unto thine ordinances at all times.
21 Thou hast rebuked the proud athat are cursed,
That do wander from thy commandments.
22 Take away from me reproach and contempt;
For I have kept thy testimonies.
23 Princes also sat and talked against me;
But thy servant did meditate on thy statutes.
24 Thy testimonies also are my delight
And amy counsellors.

DALETH.

25 My soul cleaveth unto the dust:
Quicken thou me according to thy word.
26 I declared my ways, and thou answeredst me:
Teach me thy statutes.
27 Make me to understand the way of thy precepts:
So shall I meditate on thy wondrous works.
28 My soul amelteth for heaviness:
Strengthen thou me according unto thy word.
29 Remove from me the way of falsehood;
And grant me thy law graciously.
30 I have chosen the way of faithfulness:
Thine ordinances have I set before me.
31 I cleave unto thy testimonies:
O Yahweh, put me not to shame.
32 I will run the way of thy commandments,
When thou shalt enlarge my heart.

HE.

33 Teach me, O Yahweh, the way of thy statutes;
And I shall keep it unto the end.
34 Give me understanding, and I shall keep thy law;
Yea, I shall observe it with my whole heart.
35 Make me to go in the path of thy commandments;
For therein do I delight.
36 Incline my heart unto thy testimonies,
And not to covetousness.
37 Turn away mine eyes from beholding vanity,
And quicken me in thy ways.
38 Confirm unto thy servant thy word,
aWhich is in order unto the fear of thee.
39 Turn away my reproach whereof I am afraid;
For thine ordinances are good.
40 Behold, I have longed after thy precepts:
Quicken me in thy righteousness.

VAV.

41 Let thy lovingkindnesses also come unto me, O Yahweh,
Even thy salvation, according to thy word.
42 So shall I have an answer for him that reproacheth me;
For I trust in thy word.
43 And take not the word of truth utterly out of my mouth;
For I have hoped in thine ordinances.
44 So shall I observe thy law continually
For ever and ever.
45 And I shall walk at liberty;
For I have sought thy precepts.
46 I will also speak of thy testimonies before kings,
And shall not be put to shame.
47 And I will delight myself in thy commandments,
Which I have loved.
48 I will lift up my hands also unto thy commandments, which I have loved;
And I will meditate on thy statutes.

ZAYIN.
49Remember the word unto thy servant,
Because thou hast made me to hope.
50This is my comfort in my affliction;
aFor thy word hath quickened me.
51The proud have had me greatly in derision:
Yet have I not swerved from thy law.
52I have remembered thine ordinances of old, O Yahweh,
And have comforted myself.
53 aHot indignation hath taken hold upon me,
Because of the wicked that forsake thy law.
54Thy statutes have been my songs
In the house of my pilgrimage.
55I have remembered thy name, O Yahweh, in the night,
And have observed thy law.
56This I have had,
Because I have kept thy precepts.

HHETH.
57 Yahweh is my portion:
I have said that I would observe thy words.
58I entreated thy favor with my whole heart:
Be merciful unto me according to thy word.
59I thought on my ways,
And turned my feet unto thy testimonies.
60I made haste, and delayed not,
To observe thy commandments.
61The cords of the wicked have wrapped me round;
But I have not forgotten thy law.
62At midnight I will rise to give thanks unto thee
Because of thy righteous ordinances.
63I am a companion of all them that fear thee,
And of them that observe thy precepts.
64The earth, O Yahweh, is full of thy lovingkindness:
Teach me thy statutes.

TETH.
65Thou hast dealt well with thy servant,
O Yahweh, according unto thy word.
66Teach me good judgment and knowledge;
For I have believed in thy commandments.
67Before I was afflicted I went astray;
But now I observe thy word.
68Thou art good, and doest good;
Teach me thy statutes.
69The proud have forged a lie against me:
With my whole heart will I keep thy precepts.
70Their heart is as fat as grease;
But I delight in thy law.
71It is good for me that I have been afflicted;
That I may learn thy statutes.
72The law of thy mouth is better unto me
Than thousands of gold and silver.

YODH.
73Thy hands have made me and afashioned me:
Give me understanding, that I may learn thy commandments.
74They that fear thee shall see me and be glad,
Because I have hoped in thy word.
75I know, O Yahweh, that thy judgments are righteous,
And that in faithfulness thou hast afflicted me.
76Let, I pray thee, thy lovingkindness be for my comfort,
According to thy word unto thy servant.
77Let thy tender mercies come unto me, that I may live;
For thy law is my delight.
78Let the proud be put to shame;
For they have overthrown me awrongfully:
But I will meditate on thy precepts.
79Let those that fear thee turn unto me,
aAnd they shall know thy testimonies.
80Let my heart be perfect in thy statutes,
That I be not put to shame.

KAPH.
81My soul fainteth for thy salvation;
But I hope in thy word.
82Mine eyes fail for thy word,
While I say, When wilt thou comfort me?
83For I am become like a wine-skin in the smoke;
Yet do I not forget thy statutes.
84How many are the days of thy servant?
When wilt thou execute judgment on them that persecute me?
85The proud have digged pits for me,
Who are not according to thy law.
86All thy commandments are faithful:
They persecute me wrongfully; help thou me.
87They had almost consumed me upon earth;
But I forsook not thy precepts.

LAMEDH.
88Quicken me after thy lovingkindness;
So shall I observe the testimony of thy mouth.
89For ever, O Yahweh,
Thy word is settled in heaven.
90Thy faithfulness is unto all generations:
Thou hast established the earth, and it abideth.
91 aThey abide this day according to thine ordinances;
For all things are thy servants.
92Unless thy law had been my delight,
I should then have perished in mine affliction.
93I will never forget thy precepts;
For with them thou hast quickened me.
94I am thine, save me;
For I have sought thy precepts.
95The wicked have waited for me, to destroy me;
But I will consider thy testimonies.

MEM.
96I have seen an end of all perfection;
But thy commandment is exceeding broad.
97Oh how love I thy law!
It is my meditation all the day.
98 aThy commandments make me wiser than mine enemies;
For they are ever with me.
99I have more understanding than all my teachers;
For thy testimonies are my meditation.
100I understand more than the aged,
Because I have kept thy precepts.
101I have refrained my feet from every evil way,
That I might observe thy word.
102I have not turned aside from thine ordinances;
For thou hast taught me.
103How sweet are thy words unto my ataste!
Yea, sweeter than honey to my mouth!
104Through thy precepts I get understanding:
Therefore I hate every false way.

NUN.
105Thy word is a lamp unto my feet,
And light unto my path.
106I have sworn, and have confirmed it,
That I will observe thy righteous ordinances.
107I am afflicted very much:
Quicken me, O Yahweh, according unto thy word.
108Accept, I beseech thee, the freewill-offerings of my mouth, O Yahweh,
And teach me thine ordinances.
109My soul is continually in my hand;
Yet do I not forget thy law.
110The wicked have laid a snare for me;
Yet have I not gone astray from thy precepts.
111Thy testimonies have I taken as a heritage for ever;
For they are the rejoicing of my heart.
112I have inclined my heart to perform thy statutes
For ever, even unto the end.

SAMEKH:
113I hate them that are of a double mind;
But thy law do I love.
114Thou art my hiding-place and my shield:
I hope in thy word.
115Depart from me, ye evil-doers,
That I may keep the commandments of my God.
116Uphold me according unto thy word, that I may live;
And let me not be ashamed of my hope.
117Hold thou me up, and I shall be safe,
And shall have respect unto thy statutes continually.
118Thou hast set at nought all them that err from thy statutes;
For their deceit is afalsehood.
119Thou aputtest away all the wicked of the earth like dross:
Therefore I love thy testimonies.
120My flesh trembleth for fear of thee;
And I am afraid of thy judgments.

AYIN.
121I have done justice and righteousness:
Leave me not to mine oppressors.
122Be surety for thy servant for good:
Let not the proud oppress me.
123Mine eyes fail for thy salvation,
And for thy righteous word.
124Deal with thy servant according unto thy lovingkindness,
And teach me thy statutes.
125I am thy servant; give me understanding,
That I may know thy testimonies.
126It is time for Yahweh to work;
For they have made void thy law.
127Therefore I love thy commandments

Psalms

Above gold, yea, above fine gold.
128 Therefore I esteem all thy precepts concerning all things to be right;
And I hate every false way.

PE.

129 Thy testimonies are wonderful;
Therefore doth my soul keep them.
130 The opening of thy words giveth light;
It giveth understanding unto the simple.
131 I opened wide my mouth, and panted;
For I longed for thy commandments.
132 Turn thee unto me, and have mercy upon me,
As thou usest to do unto those that love thy name.
133 Establish my footsteps in thy word;
And let not any iniquity have dominion over me.
134 Redeem me from the oppression of man:
So will I observe thy precepts.
135 Make thy face to shine upon thy servant;
And teach me thy statutes.
136 Streams of water run down mine eyes,
Because they observe not thy law.

TSADHE.

137 Righteous art thou, O Yahweh,
And upright aare thy judgments.
138 Thou hast commanded thy testimonies in righteousness
And very faithfulness.
139 My zeal hath aconsumed me,
Because mine adversaries have forgotten thy words.
140 Thy word is very apure;
Therefore thy servant loveth it.
141 I am small and despised;
Yet do I not forget thy precepts.
142 Thy righteousness is an everlasting righteousness,
And thy law is truth.
143 Trouble and anguish have ataken hold on me;
Yet thy commandments are my delight.
144 Thy testimonies are righteous for ever:
Give me understanding, and I shall live.

QOPH.

145 I have called with my whole heart; answer me, O Yahweh:
I will keep thy statutes.
146 I have called unto thee; save me,
And I shall observe thy testimonies.
147 I anticipated the dawning of the morning, and cried:
I hoped in thy words.
148 Mine eyes anticipated the night-watches,
That I might meditate on thy word.
149 Hear my voice according unto thy lovingkindness:
Quicken me, O Yahweh, aaccording to thine ordinances.
150 They draw nigh athat follow after wickedness;
They are far from thy law.
151 Thou art nigh, O Yahweh;
And all thy commandments are truth.
152 Of old have I known from thy testimonies,
That thou hast founded them for ever.

RESH.

153 Consider mine affliction, and deliver me;
For I do not forget thy law.
154 Plead thou my cause, and redeem me:
Quicken me according to thy word.
155 Salvation is far from the wicked;
For they seek not thy statutes.
156 Great are thy tender mercies, O Yahweh:
Quicken me according to thine ordinances.
157 Many are my persecutors and mine adversaries;
Yet have I not swerved from thy testimonies.
158 I beheld the treacherous, and awas grieved,
Because they observe not thy word.
159 Consider how I love thy precepts:
Quicken me, O Yahweh, according to thy lovingkindness.
160 The sum of thy word is truth;
And every one of thy righteous ordinances endureth for ever.

SHIN.

161 Princes have persecuted me without a cause;
But my heart standeth in awe of thy words.
162 I rejoice at thy word,
As one that findeth great spoil.
163 I hate and abhor falsehood;
But thy law do I love.
164 Seven times a day do I praise thee,
Because of thy righteous ordinances.
165 Great peace have they that love thy law;
And they have no occasion of stumbling.
166 I have hoped for thy salvation, O Yahweh,
And have done thy commandments.

167 My soul hath observed thy testimonies;
And I love them exceedingly.
168 I have observed thy precepts and thy testimonies;
For all my ways are before thee.

TAV.

169 Let my cry come near before thee, O Yahweh:
Give me understanding according to thy word.
170 Let my supplication come before thee:
Deliver me according to thy word.
171 Let my lips utter praise;
For thou teachest me thy statutes.
172 Let my tongue sing of thy word;
For all thy commandments are righteousness.
173 Let thy hand be ready to help me;
For I have chosen thy precepts.
174 I have longed for thy salvation, O Yahweh;
And thy law is my delight.
175 Let my soul live, and it shall praise thee;
And let thine ordinances help me.
176 I have gone astray like a lost sheep;
Seek thy servant;
For I do not forget thy commandments.

Chapter 120

A Song of Ascents.
1 In my distress I cried unto Yahweh,
And he answered me.
2 Deliver my soul, O Yahweh, from lying lips,
And from a deceitful tongue.
3 What shall be given unto thee, and what shall be done more unto thee,
Thou deceitful tongue?
4 aSharp arrows of the mighty,
With coals of ajuniper.
5 Woe is me, that I sojourn in Meshech,
That I dwell among the tents of Kedar!
6 My soul hath long had her dwelling
With him that hateth peace.
7 I am for peace:
But when I speak, they are for war.

Chapter 121

A Song of Ascents.
1 I will lift up mine eyes unto the mountains:
From whence shall my help come?
2 My help cometh from Yahweh,
Who made heaven and earth.
3 aHe will not suffer thy foot to be moved:
He that keepeth thee will not slumber.
4 Behold, he that keepeth Israel
Will neither slumber nor sleep.
5 Yahweh is thy keeper:
Yahweh is thy shade upon thy right hand.
6 The sun shall not smite thee by day,
Nor the moon by night.
7 Yahweh will keep thee from all evil;
He will keep thy soul.
8 Yahweh will keep thy going out and thy coming in
From this time forth and for evermore.

Chapter 122

A Song of Ascents; of David.
1 I was glad when they said unto me,
Let us go unto the house of Yahweh.
2 Our feet aare standing
Within thy gates, O Jerusalem.
3 Jerusalem, that art builded
As a city that is compact together;
4 Whither the tribes go up, even the tribes of aYahweh,
For aan ordinance for Israel,
To give thanks unto the name of Yahweh.
5 For there aare set thrones for judgment,
The thrones of the house of David.
6 aPray for the peace of Jerusalem:
aThey shall prosper that love thee.
7 Peace be within thy walls,
And prosperity within thy palaces.
8 For my brethren and companions' sakes,
I will now say, Peace be within thee.
9 For the sake of the house of Yahweh our God
I will seek thy good.

Chapter 123

A Song of Ascents.
1 Unto thee do I lift up mine eyes,
O thou that sittest in the heavens.
2 Behold, as the eyes of servants look unto the hand of their master,
As the eyes of a maid unto the hand of her mistress;

So our eyes look unto Yahweh our God,
Until he have mercy upon us.
3Have mercy upon us, O Yahweh, have mercy upon us;
For we are exceedingly filled with contempt.
4Our soul is exceedingly filled
With the scoffing of those that are at ease,
And with the contempt of the proud.

Chapter 124
A Song of Ascents; of David.
1If it had not been Yahweh who was on our side,
Let Israel now say,
2If it had not been Yahweh who was on our side,
When men rose up against us;
3Then they had swallowed us up alive,
When their wrath was kindled against us;
4Then the waters had overwhelmed us,
The stream had gone over our soul;
5Then the proud waters had gone over our soul.
6Blessed be Yahweh,
Who hath not given us as a prey to their teeth.
7Our soul is escaped as a bird out of the snare of the fowlers:
The snare is broken, and we are escaped.
8Our help is in the name of Yahweh,
Who made heaven and earth.

Chapter 125
A Song of Ascents.
1They that trust in Yahweh
Are as mount Zion, which cannot be moved, but abideth for ever.
2As the mountains are round about Jerusalem,
So Yahweh is round about his people
From this time forth and for evermore.
3For the sceptre of wickedness shall not rest upon the lot of the righteous;
That the righteous put not forth their hands unto iniquity.
4Do good, O Yahweh, unto those that are good,
And to them that are upright in their hearts.
5But as for such as turn aside unto their crooked ways,
Yahweh will lead them forth with the workers of iniquity.
Peace be upon Israel.

Chapter 126
A Song of Ascents.
1When Yahweh brought back those that returned to Zion,
We were like unto them that dream.
2Then was our mouth filled with laughter,
And our tongue with singing:
Then said they among the nations,
Yahweh hath done great things for them.
3Yahweh hath done great things for us,
Whereof we are glad.
4Turn again our captivity, O Yahweh,
As the streams in the South.
5They that sow in tears shall reap in joy.
6He that goeth forth and weepeth, abearing seed for sowing,
Shall doubtless come again with joy, bringing his sheaves with him.

Chapter 127
A Song of Ascents; of Solomon.
1Except Yahweh build the house,
They labor in vain that build it:
Except Yahweh keep the city,
The watchman waketh but in vain.
2It is vain for you to rise up early,
To take rest late,
To eat the bread of toil;
For so he giveth unto his beloved asleep.
3Lo, children are a heritage of Yahweh;
And the fruit of the womb is his reward.
4As arrows in the hand of a mighty man,
So are the children of youth.
5Happy is the man that hath his quiver full of them:
They shall not be put to shame,
When they speak with their enemies in the gate.

Chapter 128
A Song of Ascents.
1Blessed is every one that feareth Yahweh,
That walketh in his ways.
2For thou shalt eat the labor of thy hands:
Happy shalt thou be, and it shall be well with thee.
3Thy wife shall be as a fruitful vine,
In the innermost parts of thy house;
Thy children like olive plants,
Round about thy table.
4Behold, thus shall the man be blessed
That feareth Yahweh.
5Yahweh bless thee out of Zion:
And see thou the good of Jerusalem all the days of thy life.
6Yea, see thou thy children's children.
aPeace be upon Israel.

Chapter 129
A Song of Ascents.
1 aMany a time have they afflicted me from my youth up,
Let Israel now say,
2Many a time have they afflicted me from my youth up:
Yet they have not prevailed against me.
3The plowers plowed upon my back;
They made long their furrows.
4Yahweh is righteous:
He hath cut asunder the cords of the wicked.
5Let them be put to shame and turned backward,
All they that hate Zion.
6Let them be as the grass upon the housetops,
Which withereth before it agroweth up;
7Wherewith the reaper filleth not his hand,
Nor he that bindeth sheaves his bosom.
8Neither do they that go by say,
The blessing of Yahweh be upon you;
We bless you in the name of Yahweh.

Chapter 130
A Song of Ascents.
1Out of the depths have I cried unto thee, O Yahweh.
2Lord, hear my voice:
Let thine ears be attentive
To the voice of my supplications.
3If thou, Yahweh, shouldest mark iniquities,
O Lord, who could stand?
4But there is forgiveness with thee,
That thou mayest be feared.
5I wait for Yahweh, my soul doth wait,
And in his word do I hope.
6My soul waiteth for the Lord
More than watchmen wait for the morning;
Yea, more than watchmen for the morning.
7O Israel, hope in Yahweh;
For with Yahweh there is lovingkindness,
And with him is plenteous redemption.
8And he will redeem Israel
From all his iniquities.

Chapter 131
A Song of Ascents; of David.
1Yahweh, my heart is not haughty, nor mine eyes lofty;
Neither do I exercise myself in great matters,
Or in things too wonderful for me.
2Surely I have stilled and quieted my soul;
Like a weaned child with his mother,
Like a weaned child is my soul within me.
3O Israel, hope in Yahweh
From this time forth and for evermore.

Chapter 132
A Song of Ascents.
1Yahweh, remember for David
All his affliction;
2How he sware unto Yahweh,
And vowed unto the Mighty One of Jacob:
3Surely I will not come into the tabernacle of my house,
Nor go up into my bed;
4I will not give sleep to mine eyes,
Or slumber to mine eyelids;
5Until I find out a place for Yahweh,
A tabernacle for the Mighty One of Jacob.
6Lo, we heard of it in Ephrathah:
We found it in the field of the wood.
7We will go into his tabernacles;
We will worship at his footstool.
8Arise, O Yahweh, into thy resting-place;
Thou, and the ark of thy strength.
9Let thy priest be clothed with righteousness;
And let thy saints shout for joy.
10For thy servant David's sake
Turn not away the face of thine anointed.
11Yahweh hath sworn unto David in truth;
He will not turn from it:
Of the fruit of thy body will I set upon thy throne.
12If thy children will keep my covenant
And my testimony that I shall teach them,
Their children also shall sit upon thy throne for evermore.
13For Yahweh hath chosen Zion;
He hath desired it for his habitation.
14This is my resting-place for ever:
Here will I dwell; for I have desired it.

Psalms

15I will abundantly bless her provision:
I will satisfy her poor with bread.
16Her priests also will I clothe with salvation;
And her saints shall shout aloud for joy.
17There will I make the horn of David to bud:
I have ordained a lamp for mine anointed.
18His enemies will I clothe with shame;
But upon himself shall his crown flourish.

Chapter 133

A Song of Ascents; of David.
1Behold, how good and how pleasant it is
For brethren to dwell together in unity!
2It is like the precious oil upon the head,
That ran down upon the beard,
Even Aaron's beard;
That came down upon the skirt of his garments;
3Like the dew of Hermon,
That cometh down upon the mountains of Zion:
For there Yahweh commanded the blessing,
Even life for evermore.

Chapter 134

A Song of Ascents.
1Behold, bless ye Yahweh, all ye servants of Yahweh,
That by night stand in the house of Yahweh.
2Lift up your hands to the sanctuary,
And bless ye Yahweh.
3Yahweh bless thee out of Zion;
Even he that made heaven and earth.

Chapter 135

1Praise ye Yahweh.
Praise ye the name of Yahweh;
Praise him, O ye servants of Yahweh,
2Ye that stand in the house of Yahweh,
In the courts of the house of our God.
3Praise ye Yahweh; for Yahweh is good:
Sing praises unto his name; for it is pleasant.
4For Yahweh hath chosen Jacob unto himself,
And Israel for his own possession.
5For I know that Yahweh is great,
And that our Lord is above all gods.
6Whatsoever Yahweh pleased, that hath he done,
In heaven and in earth, in the seas and in all deeps;
7Who causeth the vapors to ascend from the ends of the earth;
Who maketh lightnings for the rain;
Who bringeth forth the wind out of his treasuries;
8Who smote the first-born of Egypt,
Both of man and beast;
9Who sent signs and wonders into the midst of thee, O Egypt,
Upon Pharaoh, and upon all his servants;
10Who smote many nations,
And slew mighty kings,
11Sihon king of the Amorites,
And Og king of Bashan,
And all the kingdoms of Canaan,
12And gave their land for a heritage,
A heritage unto Israel his people.
13Thy name, O Yahweh, endureth for ever;
Thy memorial name, O Yahweh, throughout all generations.
14For Yahweh will judge his people,
And repent himself concerning his servants.
15The idols of the nations are silver and gold,
The work of men's hands.
16They have mouths, but they speak not;
Eyes have they, but they see not;
17They have ears, but they hear not;
Neither is there any breath in their mouths.
18They that make them shall be like unto them;
Yea, every one that trusteth in them.
19O house of Israel, bless ye Yahweh:
O house of Aaron, bless ye Yahweh:
20O house of Levi, bless ye Yahweh:
Ye that fear Yahweh, bless ye Yahweh.
21Blessed be Yahweh out of Zion,
Who dwelleth at Jerusalem.
Praise ye Yahweh.

Chapter 136

1Oh give thanks unto Yahweh; for he is good;
For his lovingkindness endureth for ever.
2Oh give thanks unto the God of gods;
For his lovingkindness endureth for ever.
3Oh give thanks unto the Lord of lords;
For his lovingkindness endureth for ever:
4To him who alone doeth great wonders;
For his lovingkindness endureth for ever:
5To him that by understanding made the heavens;
For his lovingkindness endureth for ever:
6To him that spread forth the earth above the waters;
For his lovingkindness endureth for ever:
7To him that made great lights;
For his lovingkindness endureth for ever:
8The sun to rule by day;
For his lovingkindness endureth for ever;
9The moon and stars to rule by night;
For his lovingkindness endureth for ever:
10To him that smote Egypt in their first-born;
For his lovingkindness endureth for ever;
11And brought out Israel from among them;
For his lovingkindness endureth for ever;
12With a strong hand, and with an outstretched arm;
For his lovingkindness endureth for ever:
13To him that divided the Red Sea in sunder;
For his lovingkindness endureth for ever;
14And made Israel to pass through the midst of it;
For his lovingkindness endureth for ever:
15But overthrew Pharaoh and his host in the Red Sea;
For his lovingkindness endureth for ever:
16To him that led his people through the wilderness;
For his lovingkindness endureth for ever:
17To him that smote great kings;
For his lovingkindness endureth for ever;
18And slew famous kings;
For his lovingkindness endureth for ever:
19Sihon king of the Amorites;
For his lovingkindness endureth forever;
20And Og king of Bashan;
For his lovingkindness endureth for ever;
21And gave their land for a heritage;
For his lovingkindness endureth for ever;
22Even a heritage unto Israel his servant;
For his lovingkindness endureth for ever:
23Who remembered us in our low estate;
For his lovingkindness endureth for ever:
24And hath delivered us from our adversaries;
For his lovingkindness endureth for ever:
25Who giveth food to all flesh;
For his lovingkindness endureth for ever.
26Oh give thanks unto the God of heaven;
For his lovingkindness endureth for ever.

Chapter 137

1By the rivers of Babylon,
There we sat down, yea, we wept,
When we remembered Zion.
2Upon the willows in the midst thereof We hanged up our harps.
3For there they that led us captive required of us songs,
And they that wasted us required of us mirth, saying,
Sing us one of the songs of Zion.
4How shall we sing Yahweh's song
In a foreign land?
5If I forget thee, O Jerusalem,
Let my right hand forget her skill.
6Let my tongue cleave to the roof of my mouth,
If I remember thee not;
If I prefer not Jerusalem
Above my chief joy.
7Remember, O Yahweh, against the children of Edom
The day of Jerusalem;
Who said, Rase it, rase it,
Even to the foundation thereof.
8O daughter of Babylon, that art to be destroyed,
Happy shall he be, that rewardeth thee
As thou hast served us.
9Happy shall he be, that taketh and dasheth thy little ones
Against the rock.

Chapter 138

A Psalm of David.
1I will give thee thanks with my whole heart:
Before the gods will I sing praises unto thee.
2I will worship toward thy holy temple,
And give thanks unto thy name for thy lovingkindness and for thy truth:
For thou hast magnified thy word above all thy name.
3In the day that I called thou answeredst me,
Thou didst encourage me with strength in my soul.
4All the kings of the earth shall give thee thanks, O Yahweh,
For they have heard the words of thy mouth.
5Yea, they shall sing of the ways of Yahweh;
For great is the glory of Yahweh.
6For though Yahweh is high, yet hath he respect unto the lowly;
But the haughty he knoweth from afar.
7Though I walk in the midst of trouble, thou wilt revive me;
Thou wilt stretch forth thy hand against the wrath of mine enemies,

And thy right hand will save me.
8Yahweh will perfect that which concerneth me:
Thy lovingkindness, O Yahweh, endureth for ever;
Forsake not the works of thine own hands.

Chapter 139

For the Chief Musician. A Psalm of David.
1O Yahweh, thou hast searched me, and known me.
2Thou knowest my downsitting and mine uprising;
Thou understandest my thought afar off.
3Thou searchest out my path and my lying down,
And art acquainted with all my ways.
4For there is not a word in my tongue,
But, lo, O Yahweh, thou knowest it altogether.
5Thou hast beset me behind and before,
And laid thy hand upon me.
6Such knowledge is too wonderful for me;
It is high, I cannot attain unto it.
7Whither shall I go from thy Spirit?
Or whither shall I flee from thy presence?
8If I ascend up into heaven, thou art there:
If I make my bed in Sheol, behold, thou art there.
9If I take the wings of the morning,
And dwell in the uttermost parts of the sea;
10Even there shall thy hand lead me,
And thy right hand shall hold me.
11If I say, Surely the darkness shall overwhelm me,
And the light about me shall be night;
12Even the darkness hideth not from thee,
But the night shineth as the day:
The darkness and the light are both alike to thee.
13For thou didst form my inward parts:
Thou didst cover me in my mother's womb.
14I will give thanks unto thee; for I am fearfully and wonderfully made:
Wonderful are thy works;
And that my soul knoweth right well.
15My frame was not hidden from thee,
When I was made in secret,
And curiously wrought in the lowest parts of the earth.
16Thine eyes did see mine unformed substance;
And in thy book they were all written,
Even the days that were ordained for me,
When as yet there was none of them.
17How precious also are thy thoughts unto me, O God!
How great is the sum of them!
18If I should count them, they are more in number than the sand:
When I awake, I am still with thee.
19Surely thou wilt slay the wicked, O God:
Depart from me therefore, ye bloodthirsty men.
20For they speak against thee wickedly,
And thine enemies take thy name in vain.
21Do not I hate them, O Yahweh, that hate thee?
And am not I grieved with those that rise up against thee?
22I hate them with perfect hatred:
They are become mine enemies.
23Search me, O God, and know my heart:
Try me, and know my thoughts;
24And see if there be any wicked way in me,
And lead me in the way everlasting.

Chapter 140

For the Chief Musician. A Psalm of David.
1Deliver me, O Yahweh, from the evil man;
Preserve me from the violent man:
2Who devise mischiefs in their heart;
Continually do they gather themselves together for war.
3They have sharpened their tongue like a serpent;
Adders' poison is under their lips.
Selah
4Keep me, O Yahweh, from the hands of the wicked;
Preserve me from the violent man:
Who have purposed to thrust aside my steps.
5The proud have hid a snare for me, and cords;
They have spread a net by the wayside;
They have set gins for me.
Selah
6I said unto Yahweh, Thou art my God:
Give ear unto the voice of my supplications, O Yahweh.
7O Yahweh the Lord, the strength of my salvation,
Thou hast covered my head in the day of battle.
8Grant not, O Yahweh, the desires of the wicked;
Further not his evil device, lest they exalt themselves.
Selah
9As for the head of those that compass me about,
Let the mischief of their own lips cover them.
10Let burning coals fall upon them:
Let them be cast into the fire,
Into deep pits, whence they shall not rise.
11An evil speaker shall not be established in the earth:
Evil shall hunt the violent man to overthrow him.
12I know that Yahweh will maintain the cause of the afflicted,
And justice for the needy.
13Surely the righteous shall give thanks unto thy name:
The upright shall dwell in thy presence.

Chapter 141

A Psalm of David.
1Yahweh, I have called upon thee; make haste unto me:
Give ear unto my voice, when I call unto thee.
2Let my prayer be set forth as incense before thee;
The lifting up of my hands as the evening sacrifice.
3Set a watch, O Yahweh, before my mouth;
Keep the door of my lips.
4Incline not my heart to any evil thing,
To practise deeds of wickedness
With men that work iniquity:
And let me not eat of their dainties.
5Let the righteous smite me, it shall be a kindness;
And let him reprove me, it shall be as oil upon the head;
Let not my head refuse it:
For even in their wickedness shall my prayer continue.
6Their judges are thrown down by the sides of the rock;
And they shall hear my words; for they are sweet.
7As when one ploweth and cleaveth the earth,
Our bones are scattered at the mouth of Sheol.
8For mine eyes are unto thee, O Yahweh the Lord:
In thee do I take refuge; leave not my soul destitute.
9Keep me from the snare which they have laid for me,
And from the gins of the workers of iniquity.
10Let the wicked fall into their own nets,
Whilst that I withal escape.

Chapter 142

Maschil of David, when he was in the cave; a Prayer.
1I cry with my voice unto Yahweh;
With my voice unto Yahweh do I make supplication.
2I pour out my complaint before him;
I show before him my trouble.
3When my spirit was overwhelmed within me,
Thou knewest my path.
In the way wherein I walk
Have they hidden a snare for me.
4Look on my right hand, and see;
For there is no man that knoweth me:
Refuge hath failed me;
No man careth for my soul.
5I cried unto thee, O Yahweh;
I said, Thou art my refuge,
My portion in the land of the living.
6Attend unto my cry;
For I am brought very low:
Deliver me from my persecutors;
For they are stronger than I.
7Bring my soul out of prison,
That I may give thanks unto thy name:
The righteous shall compass me about;
For thou wilt deal bountifully with me.

Chapter 143

A Psalm of David.
1Hear my prayer, O Yahweh; give ear to my supplications:
In thy faithfulness answer me, and in thy righteousness.
2And enter not into judgment with thy servant;
For in thy sight no man living is righteous.
3For the enemy hath persecuted my soul;
He hath smitten my life down to the ground:
He hath made me to dwell in dark places, as those that have been long dead.
4Therefore is my spirit overwhelmed within me;
My heart within me is desolate.
5I remember the days of old;
I meditate on all thy doings;
I muse on the work of thy hands.
6I spread forth my hands unto thee:
My soul thirsteth after thee, as a weary land.
Selah
7Make haste to answer me, O Yahweh; my spirit faileth:
Hide not thy face from me,
Lest I become like them that go down into the pit.
8Cause me to hear thy lovingkindness in the morning;
For in thee do I trust:
Cause me to know the way wherein I should walk;
For I lift up my soul unto thee.
9Deliver me, O Yahweh, from mine enemies:
I flee unto thee to hide me.
10Teach me to do thy will;
For thou art my God:

Psalms

Thy Spirit is good;
Lead me in the land of uprightness.
11Quicken me, O Yahweh, for thy name's sake:
In thy righteousness bring my soul out of trouble.
12And in thy lovingkindness cut off mine enemies,
And destroy all them that afflict my soul;
For I am thy servant.

Chapter 144

A Psalm of David.
1Blessed be Yahweh my rock,
Who teacheth my hands to war,
And my fingers to fight:
2My lovingkindness, and my fortress,
My high tower, and my deliverer;
My shield, and he in whom I take refuge;
Who subdueth my people under me.
3Yahweh, what is man, that thou takest knowledge of him?
Or the son of man, that thou makest account of him?
4Man is like to vanity:
His days are as a shadow that passeth away.
5Bow thy heavens, O Yahweh, and come down:
Touch the mountains, and they shall smoke.
6Cast forth lightning, and scatter them;
Send out thine arrows, and discomfit them.
7Stretch forth thy hand from above;
Rescue me, and deliver me out of great waters,
Out of the hand of aliens;
8Whose mouth speaketh deceit,
And whose right hand is a right hand of falsehood.
9I will sing a new song unto thee, O God:
Upon a psaltery of ten strings will I sing praises unto thee.
10Thou art he that giveth salvation unto kings;
Who rescueth David his servant from the hurtful sword.
11Rescue me, and deliver me out of the hand of aliens,
Whose mouth speaketh deceit,
And whose right hand is a right hand of falsehood.
12When our sons shall be as plants grown up in their youth,
And our daughters as corner-stones hewn after the fashion of a palace;
13When our garners are full, affording all manner of store,
And our sheep bring forth thousands and ten thousands in our fields;
14When our oxen are well laden;
When there is no breaking in, and no going forth,
And no outcry in our streets:
15Happy is the people that is in such a case;
Yea, happy is the people whose God is Yahweh:

Chapter 145

A Psalm of praise; of David.
1I will extol thee, my God, O King;
And I will bless thy name for ever and ever.
2Every day will I bless thee;
And I will praise thy name for ever and ever.
3Great is Yahweh, and greatly to be praised;
And his greatness is unsearchable.
4One generation shall laud thy works to another,
And shall declare thy mighty acts.
5Of the glorious majesty of thine honor,
And of thy wondrous works, will I meditate.
6And men shall speak of the might of thy terrible acts;
And I will declare thy greatness.
7They shall utter the memory of thy great goodness,
And shall sing of thy righteousness.
8Yahweh is gracious, and merciful;
Slow to anger, and of great lovingkindness.
9Yahweh is good to all;
And his tender mercies are over all his works.
10All thy works shall give thanks unto thee, O Yahweh;
And thy saints shall bless thee.
11They shall speak of the glory of thy kingdom,
And talk of thy power;
12To make known to the sons of men his mighty acts,
And the glory of the majesty of his kingdom.
13Thy kingdom is an everlasting kingdom,
And thy dominion endureth throughout all generations.
14Yahweh upholdeth all that fall,
And raiseth up all those that are bowed down.
15The eyes of all wait for thee;
And thou givest them their food in due season.
16Thou openest thy hand,
And satisfiest the desire of every living thing.
17Yahweh is righteous in all his ways,
And gracious in all his works.
18Yahweh is nigh unto all them that call upon him,
To all that call upon him in truth.
19He will fulfil the desire of them that fear him;
He also will hear their cry and will save them.
20Yahweh preserveth all them that love him;
But all the wicked will he destroy.
21My mouth shall speak the praise of Yahweh;
And let all flesh bless his holy name for ever and ever.

Chapter 146

1Praise ye Yahweh.
Praise Yahweh, O my soul.
2While I live will I praise Yahweh:
I will sing praises unto my God while I have any being.
3Put not your trust in princes,
Nor in the son of man, in whom there is no help.
4His breath goeth forth, he returneth to his earth;
In that very day his thoughts perish.
5Happy is he that hath the God of Jacob for his help,
Whose hope is in Yahweh his God:
6Who made heaven and earth,
The sea, and all that in them is;
Who keepeth truth for ever;
7Who executeth justice for the oppressed;
Who giveth food to the hungry.
Yahweh looseth the prisoners;
8Yahweh openeth the eyes of the blind;
Yahweh raiseth up them that are bowed down;
Yahweh loveth the righteous;
9Yahweh preserveth the sojourners;
He upholdeth the fatherless and widow;
But the way of the wicked he turneth upside down.
10Yahweh will reign for ever,
Thy God, O Zion, unto all generations.
Praise ye Yahweh.

Chapter 147

1Praise ye Yahweh;
For it is good to sing praises unto our God;
For it is pleasant, and praise is comely.
2Yahweh doth build up Jerusalem;
He gathereth together the outcasts of Israel.
3He healeth the broken in heart,
And bindeth up their wounds.
4He counteth the number of the stars;
He calleth them all by their names.
5Great is our Lord, and mighty in power;
His understanding is infinite.
6Yahweh upholdeth the meek:
He bringeth the wicked down to the ground.
7Sing unto Yahweh with thanksgiving;
Sing praises upon the harp unto our God,
8Who covereth the heavens with clouds,
Who prepareth rain for the earth,
Who maketh grass to grow upon the mountains.
9He giveth to the beast his food,
And to the young ravens which cry.
10He delighteth not in the strength of the horse:
He taketh no pleasure in the legs of a man.
11Yahweh taketh pleasure in them that fear him,
In those that hope in his lovingkindness.
12Praise Yahweh, O Jerusalem;
Praise thy God, O Zion.
13For he hath strengthened the bars of thy gates;
He hath blessed thy children within thee.
14He maketh peace in thy borders;
He filleth thee with the finest of the wheat.
15He sendeth out his commandment upon earth;
His word runneth very swiftly.
16He giveth snow like wool;
He scattereth the hoar-frost like ashes.
17He casteth forth his ice like morsels:
Who can stand before his cold?
18He sendeth out his word, and melteth them:
He causeth his wind to blow, and the waters flow.
19He showeth his word unto Jacob,
His statutes and his ordinances unto Israel.
20He hath not dealt so with any nation;
And as for his ordinances, they have not known them.
Praise ye Yahweh.

Chapter 148

1Praise ye Yahweh.
Praise ye Yahweh from the heavens:
Praise him in the heights.
2Praise ye him, all his angels:
Praise ye him, all his host.
3Praise ye him, sun and moon:
Praise him, all ye stars of light.
4Praise him, ye heavens of heavens,
And ye waters that are above the heavens.
5Let them praise the name of Yahweh;
For he commanded, and they were created.

6He hath also established them for ever and ever:
He hath made a decree which shall not pass away.
7Praise Yahweh from the earth,
Ye sea-monsters, and all deeps.
8Fire and hail, snow and vapor;
Stormy wind, fulfilling his word;
9Mountains and all hills;
Fruitful trees and all cedars;
10Beasts and all cattle;
Creeping things and flying birds;
11Kings of the earth and all peoples;
Princes and all judges of the earth;
12Both young men and virgins;
Old men and children:
13Let them praise the name of Yahweh;
For his name alone is exalted;
His glory is above the earth and the heavens.
14And he hath lifted up the horn of his people,
The praise of all his saints;
Even of the children of Israel, a people near unto him.
Praise ye Yahweh.

Chapter 149
1Praise ye Yahweh.
Sing unto Yahweh a new song,
And his praise in the assembly of the saints.
2Let Israel rejoice in him that made him:
Let the children of Zion be joyful in their King.
3Let them praise his name in the dance:
Let them sing praises unto him with timbrel and harp.
4For Yahweh taketh pleasure in his people:
He will beautify the meek with salvation.
5Let the saints exult in glory:
Let them sing for joy upon their beds.
6Let the high praises of God be in their mouth,
And a two-edged sword in their hand;
7To execute vengeance upon the nations,
And punishments upon the peoples;
8To bind their kings with chains,
And their nobles with fetters of iron;
9To execute upon them the judgment written:
This honor have all his saints.
Praise ye Yahweh.

Chapter 150
1Praise ye Yahweh.
Praise God in his sanctuary:
Praise him in the firmament of his power.
2Praise him for his mighty acts:
Praise him according to his excellent greatness.
3Praise him with trumpet sound:
Praise him with psaltery and harp.
4Praise him with timbrel and dance:
Praise him with stringed instruments and pipe.
5Praise him with loud cymbals:
Praise him with high sounding cymbals.
6Let everything that hath breath praise Yahweh.
Praise ye Yahweh.

The Proverbs

Chapter 1

1 The proverbs of Solomon the son of David, king of Israel:
2 To know wisdom and instruction;
To discern the words of understanding;
3 To receive instruction in wise dealing,
In righteousness and justice and equity;
4 To give prudence to the simple,
To the young man knowledge and discretion:
5 That the wise man may hear, and increase in learning;
And that the man of understanding may attain unto sound counsels:
6 To understand a proverb, and a figure,
The words of the wise, and their dark sayings.
7 The fear of Yahweh is the beginning of knowledge;
But the foolish despise wisdom and instruction.
8 My son, hear the instruction of thy father,
And forsake not the law of thy mother:
9 For they shall be a chaplet of grace unto thy head,
And chains about thy neck.
10 My son, if sinners entice thee, Consent thou not.
11 If they say, Come with us,
Let us lay wait for blood;
Let us lurk privily for the innocent without cause;
12 Let us swallow them up alive as Sheol,
And whole, as those that go down into the pit;
13 We shall find all precious substance;
We shall fill our houses with spoil;
14 Thou shalt cast thy lot among us;
We will all have one purse:
15 My son, walk not thou in the way with them;
Refrain thy foot from their path:
16 For their feet run to evil,
And they make haste to shed blood.
17 For in vain is the net spread
In the sight of any bird:
18 And these lay wait for their own blood;
They lurk privily for their own lives.
19 So are the ways of every one that is greedy of gain;
It taketh away the life of the owners thereof.
20 Wisdom crieth aloud in the street;
She uttereth her voice in the broad places;
21 She crieth in the chief place of concourse;
At the entrance of the gates,
In the city, she uttereth her words:
22 How long, ye simple ones, will ye love simplicity?
And scoffers delight them in scoffing,
And fools hate knowledge?
23 Turn you at my reproof:
Behold, I will pour out my spirit upon you;
I will make known my words unto you.
24 Because I have called, and ye have refused;
I have stretched out my hand, and no man hath regarded;
25 But ye have set at nought all my counsel,
And would none of my reproof:
26 I also will laugh in the day of your calamity;
I will mock when your fear cometh;
27 When your fear cometh as a storm,
And your calamity cometh on as a whirlwind;
When distress and anguish come upon you.
28 Then will they call upon me, but I will not answer;
They will seek me diligently, but they shall not find me:
29 For that they hated knowledge,
And did not choose the fear of Yahweh:
30 They would none of my counsel;
They despised all my reproof.
31 Therefore shall they eat of the fruit of their own way,
And be filled with their own devices.
32 For the backsliding of the simple shall slay them,
And the careless ease of fools shall destroy them.
33 But whoso hearkeneth unto me shall dwell securely,
And shall be quiet without fear of evil.

Chapter 2

1 My son, if thou wilt receive my words,
And lay up my commandments with thee;
2 So as to incline thine ear unto wisdom,
And apply thy heart to understanding;
3 Yea, if thou cry after discernment,
And lift up thy voice for understanding;
4 If thou seek her as silver,
And search for her as for hid treasures:
5 Then shalt thou understand the fear of Yahweh,
And find the knowledge of God.
6 For Yahweh giveth wisdom;
Out of his mouth cometh knowledge and understanding:
7 He layeth up sound wisdom for the upright;
He is a shield to them that walk in integrity;
8 That he may guard the paths of justice,
And preserve the way of his saints.
9 Then shalt thou understand righteousness and justice,
And equity, yea, every good path.
10 For wisdom shall enter into thy heart,
And knowledge shall be pleasant unto thy soul;
11 Discretion shall watch over thee;
Understanding shall keep thee:
12 To deliver thee from the way of evil,
From the men that speak perverse things;
13 Who forsake the paths of uprightness,
To walk in the ways of darkness;
14 Who rejoice to do evil,
And delight in the perverseness of evil;
15 Who are crooked in their ways,
And wayward in their paths:
16 To deliver thee from the strange woman,
Even from the foreigner that flattereth with her words;
17 That forsaketh the friend of her youth,
And forgetteth the covenant of her God:
18 For her house inclineth unto death,
And her paths unto the dead;
19 None that go unto her return again,
Neither do they attain unto the paths of life:
20 That thou mayest walk in the way of good men,
And keep the paths of the righteous.
21 For the upright shall dwell in the land,
And the perfect shall remain in it.
22 But the wicked shall be cut off from the land,
And the treacherous shall be rooted out of it.

Chapter 3

1 My son, forget not my law;
But let thy heart keep my commandments:
2 For length of days, and years of life,
And peace, will they add to thee.
3 Let not kindness and truth forsake thee:
Bind them about thy neck;
Write them upon the tablet of thy heart:
4 So shalt thou find favor and good understanding
In the sight of God and man.
5 Trust in Yahweh with all thy heart,
And lean not upon thine own understanding:
6 In all thy ways acknowledge him,
And he will direct thy paths.
7 Be not wise in thine own eyes;
Fear Yahweh, and depart from evil:
8 It will be health to thy navel,
And marrow to thy bones.
9 Honor Yahweh with thy substance,
And with the first-fruits of all thine increase:
10 So shall thy barns be filled with plenty,
And thy vats shall overflow with new wine.
11 My son, despise not the chastening of Yahweh;
Neither be weary of his reproof:
12 For whom Yahweh loveth he reproveth;
Even as a father the son in whom he delighteth.
13 Happy is the man that findeth wisdom,
And the man that getteth understanding.
14 For the gaining of it is better than the gaining of silver,
And the profit thereof than fine gold.
15 She is more precious than rubies:
And none of the things thou canst desire are to be compared unto her.
16 Length of days is in her right hand;
In her left hand are riches and honor.
17 Her ways are ways of pleasantness,
And all her paths are peace.
18 She is a tree of life to them that lay hold upon her:
And happy is every one that retaineth her.
19 Yahweh by wisdom founded the earth;
By understanding he established the heavens.
20 By his knowledge the depths were broken up,
And the skies drop down the dew.
21 My son, let them not depart from thine eyes;
Keep sound wisdom and discretion:
22 So shall they be life unto thy soul,
And grace to thy neck.
23 Then shalt thou walk in thy way securely,
And thy foot shall not stumble.
24 When thou liest down, thou shalt not be afraid:
Yea, thou shalt lie down, and thy sleep shall be sweet.
25 Be not afraid of sudden fear,
Neither of the desolation of the wicked, when it cometh:
26 For Yahweh will be thy confidence,

And will keep thy foot from being taken.
27Withhold not good from them to whom it is due,
When it is in the power of thy hand to do it.
28Say not unto thy neighbor, Go, and come again,
And to-morrow I will give;
When thou hast it by thee.
29Devise not evil against thy neighbor,
Seeing he dwelleth securely by thee.
30Strive not with a man without cause,
If he have done thee no harm.
31Envy thou not the man of violence,
And choose none of his ways.
32For the perverse is an abomination to Yahweh;
But his friendship is with the upright.
33The curse of Yahweh is in the house of the wicked;
But he blesseth the habitation of the righteous.
34Surely he scoffeth at the scoffers;
But he giveth grace unto the lowly.
35The wise shall inherit glory;
But shame shall be the promotion of fools.

Chapter 4

1Hear, my sons, the instruction of a father,
And attend to know understanding:
2For I give you good doctrine;
Forsake ye not my law.
3For I was a son unto my father,
Tender and only beloved in the sight of my mother.
4And he taught me, and said unto me:
Let thy heart retain my words;
Keep my commandments, and live;
5Get wisdom, get understanding;
Forget not, neither decline from the words of my mouth;
6Forsake her not, and she will preserve thee;
Love her, and she will keep thee.
7Wisdom is the principal thing; therefore get wisdom;
Yea, with all thy getting get understanding.
8Exalt her, and she will promote thee;
She will bring thee to honor, when thou dost embrace her.
9She will give to thy head a chaplet of grace;
A crown of beauty will she deliver to thee.
10Hear, O my son, and receive my sayings;
And the years of thy life shall be many.
11I have taught thee in the way of wisdom;
I have led thee in paths of uprightness.
12When thou goest, thy steps shall not be straitened;
And if thou runnest, thou shalt not stumble.
13Take fast hold of instruction; let her not go:
Keep her; for she is thy life.
14Enter not into the path of the wicked,
And walk not in the way of evil men.
15Avoid it, pass not by it;
Turn from it, and pass on.
16For they sleep not, except they do evil;
And their sleep is taken away, unless they cause some to fall.
17For they eat the bread of wickedness,
And drink the wine of violence.
18But the path of the righteous is as the dawning light,
That shineth more and more unto the perfect day.
19The way of the wicked is as darkness;
They know not at what they stumble.
20My son, attend to my words;
Incline thine ear unto my sayings.
21Let them not depart from thine eyes;
Keep them in the midst of thy heart.
22For they are life unto those that find them,
And health to all their flesh.
23Keep thy heart with all diligence;
For out of it are the issues of life.
24Put away from thee a wayward mouth,
And perverse lips put far from thee.
25Let thine eyes look right on,
And let thine eyelids look straight before thee.
26Make level the path of thy feet,
And let all thy ways be established.
27Turn not to the right hand nor to the left:
Remove thy foot from evil.

Chapter 5

1My son, attend unto my wisdom;
Incline thine ear to my understanding:
2That thou mayest preserve discretion,
And that thy lips may keep knowledge.
3For the lips of a strange woman drop honey,
And her mouth is smoother than oil:
4But in the end she is bitter as wormwood,
Sharp as a two-edged sword.
5Her feet go down to death;
Her steps take hold on Sheol;
6So that she findeth not the level path of life:
Her ways are unstable, and she knoweth it not.
7Now therefore, my sons, hearken unto me,
And depart not from the words of my mouth.
8Remove thy way far from her,
And come not nigh the door of her house;
9Lest thou give thine honor unto others,
And thy years unto the cruel;
10Lest strangers be filled with thy strength,
And thy labors be in the house of an alien,
11And thou mourn at thy latter end,
When thy flesh and thy body are consumed,
12And say, How have I hated instruction,
And my heart despised reproof;
13Neither have I obeyed the voice of my teachers,
Nor inclined mine ear to them that instructed me!
14I was well-nigh in all evil
In the midst of the assembly and congregation.
15Drink waters out of thine own cistern,
And running waters out of thine own well.
16Should thy springs be dispersed abroad,
And streams of water in the streets?
17Let them be for thyself alone,
And not for strangers with thee.
18Let thy fountain be blessed;
And rejoice in the wife of thy youth.
19As a loving hind and a pleasant doe,
Let her breasts satisfy thee at all times;
And be thou ravished always with her love.
20For why shouldest thou, my son, be ravished with a strange woman,
And embrace the bosom of a foreigner?
21For the ways of man are before the eyes of Yahweh;
And he maketh level all his paths.
22His own iniquities shall take the wicked,
And he shall be holden with the cords of his sin.
23He shall die for lack of instruction;
And in the greatness of his folly he shall go astray.

Chapter 6

1My son, if thou art become surety for thy neighbor,
If thou hast stricken thy hands for a stranger;
2Thou art snared with the words of thy mouth,
Thou art taken with the words of thy mouth.
3Do this now, my son, and deliver thyself,
Seeing thou art come into the hand of thy neighbor:
Go, humble thyself, and importune thy neighbor;
4Give not sleep to thine eyes,
Nor slumber to thine eyelids;
5Deliver thyself as a roe from the hand of the hunter,
And as a bird from the hand of the fowler.
6Go to the ant, thou sluggard;
Consider her ways, and be wise:
7Which having no chief,
Overseer, or ruler,
8Provideth her bread in the summer,
And gathereth her food in the harvest.
9How long wilt thou sleep, O sluggard?
When wilt thou arise out of thy sleep?
10Yet a little sleep, a little slumber,
A little folding of the hands to sleep:
11So shall thy poverty come as a robber,
And thy want as an armed man.
12A worthless person, a man of iniquity,
Is he that walketh with a perverse mouth;
13That winketh with his eyes, that speaketh with his feet,
That maketh signs with his fingers;
14In whose heart is perverseness,
Who deviseth evil continually,
Who soweth discord.
15Therefore shall his calamity come suddenly;
On a sudden shall he be broken, and that without remedy.
16There are six things which Yahweh hateth;
Yea, seven which are an abomination unto him:
17Haughty eyes, a lying tongue,
And hands that shed innocent blood;
18A heart that deviseth wicked purposes,
Feet that are swift in running to mischief,
19A false witness that uttereth lies,
And he that soweth discord among brethren.
20My son, keep the commandment of thy father,
And forsake not the law of thy mother;
21Bind them continually upon thy heart;
Tie them about thy neck.
22When thou walkest, it shall lead thee;
When thou sleepest, it shall watch over thee;
And when thou awakest, it shall talk with thee.
23For the commandment is a lamp; and the law is light;
And reproofs of instruction are the way of life:

Proverbs

24 To keep thee from the evil woman,
From the flattery of the foreigner's tongue.
25 Lust not after her beauty in thy heart;
Neither let her take thee with her eyelids.
26 For on account of a harlot a man is brought to a piece of bread;
And the adulteress hunteth for the precious life.
27 Can a man take fire in his bosom,
And his clothes not be burned?
28 Or can one walk upon hot coals,
And his feet not be scorched?
29 So he that goeth in to his neighbor's wife;
Whosoever toucheth her shall not be unpunished.
30 Men do not despise a thief, if he steal
To satisfy himself when he is hungry:
31 But if he be found, he shall restore sevenfold;
He shall give all the substance of his house.
32 He that committeth adultery with a woman is void of understanding:
He doeth it who would destroy his own soul.
33 Wounds and dishonor shall he get;
And his reproach shall not be wiped away.
34 For jealousy is the rage of a man;
And he will not spare in the day of vengeance.
35 He will not regard any ransom;
Neither will he rest content, though thou givest many gifts.

Chapter 7

1 My son, keep my words,
And lay up my commandments with thee.
2 Keep my commandments and live;
And my law as the apple of thine eye.
3 Bind them upon thy fingers;
Write them upon the tablet of thy heart.
4 Say unto wisdom, Thou art my sister;
And call understanding thy kinswoman.
5 That they may keep thee from the strange woman,
From the foreigner that flattereth with her words.
6 For at the window of my house
I looked forth through my lattice;
7 And I beheld among the simple ones,
I discerned among the youths,
A young man void of understanding,
8 Passing through the street near her corner;
And he went the way to her house,
9 In the twilight, in the evening of the day,
In the middle of the night and in the darkness.
10 And, behold, there met him a woman
With the attire of a harlot, and wily of heart.
11 She is clamorous and wilful;
Her feet abide not in her house:
12 Now she is in the streets, now in the broad places,
And lieth in wait at every corner.
13 So she caught him, and kissed him,
And with an impudent face she said unto him:
14 Sacrifices of peace-offerings are with me;
This day have I paid my vows.
15 Therefore came I forth to meet thee,
Diligently to seek thy face, and I have found thee.
16 I have spread my couch with carpets of tapestry,
With striped cloths of the yarn of Egypt.
17 I have perfumed my bed
With myrrh, aloes, and cinnamon.
18 Come, let us take our fill of love until the morning;
Let us solace ourselves with loves.
19 For the man is not at home;
He is gone a long journey:
20 He hath taken a bag of money with him;
He will come home at the full moon.
21 With her much fair speech she causeth him to yield;
With the flattering of her lips she forceth him along.
22 He goeth after her straightway,
As an ox goeth to the slaughter,
Or as one in fetters to the correction of the fool;
23 Till an arrow strike through his liver;
As a bird hasteth to the snare,
And knoweth not that it is for his life.
24 Now therefore, my sons, hearken unto me,
And attend to the words of my mouth.
25 Let not thy heart decline to her ways;
Go not astray in her paths.
26 For she hath cast down many wounded:
Yea, all her slain are a mighty host.
27 Her house is the way to Sheol,
Going down to the chambers of death.

Chapter 8

1 Doth not wisdom cry,
And understanding put forth her voice?
2 On the top of high places by the way,
Where the paths meet, she standeth;
3 Beside the gates, at the entry of the city,
At the coming in at the doors, she crieth aloud:
4 Unto you, O men, I call;
And my voice is to the sons of men.
5 O ye simple, understand prudence;
And, ye fools, be of an understanding heart.
6 Hear, for I will speak excellent things;
And the opening of my lips shall be right things.
7 For my mouth shall utter truth;
And wickedness is an abomination to my lips.
8 All the words of my mouth are in righteousness;
There is nothing crooked or perverse in them.
9 They are all plain to him that understandeth,
And right to them that find knowledge.
10 Receive my instruction, and not silver;
And knowledge rather than choice gold.
11 For wisdom is better than rubies;
And all the things that may be desired are not to be compared unto it.
12 I wisdom have made prudence my dwelling,
And find out knowledge and discretion.
13 The fear of Yahweh is to hate evil:
Pride, and arrogancy, and the evil way,
And the perverse mouth, do I hate.
14 Counsel is mine, and sound knowledge:
I am understanding; I have might.
15 By me kings reign,
And princes decree justice.
16 By me princes rule,
And nobles, even all the judges of the earth.
17 I love them that love me;
And those that seek me diligently shall find me.
18 Riches and honor are with me;
Yea, durable wealth and righteousness.
19 My fruit is better than gold, yea, than fine gold;
And my revenue than choice silver.
20 I walk in the way of righteousness,
In the midst of the paths of justice;
21 That I may cause those that love me to inherit substance,
And that I may fill their treasuries.
22 Yahweh possessed me in the beginning of his way,
Before his works of old.
23 I was set up from everlasting, from the beginning,
Before the earth was.
24 When there were no depths, I was brought forth,
When there were no fountains abounding with water.
25 Before the mountains were settled,
Before the hills was I brought forth;
26 While as yet he had not made the earth, nor the fields,
Nor the beginning of the dust of the world.
27 When he established the heavens, I was there;
When he set a circle upon the face of the deep,
28 When he made firm the skies above,
When the fountains of the deep became strong,
29 When he gave to the sea its bound,
That the waters should not transgress his commandment,
When he marked out the foundations of the earth;
30 Then I was by him, as a master workman;
And I was daily his delight,
Rejoicing always before him,
31 Rejoicing in his habitable earth;
And my delight was with the sons of men.
32 Now therefore, my sons, hearken unto me;
For blessed are they that keep my ways.
33 Hear instruction, and be wise,
And refuse it not.
34 Blessed is the man that heareth me,
Watching daily at my gates,
Waiting at the posts of my doors.
35 For whoso findeth me findeth life,
And shall obtain favor of Yahweh.
36 But he that sinneth against me wrongeth his own soul:
All they that hate me love death.

Chapter 9

1 Wisdom hath builded her house;
She hath hewn out her seven pillars:
2 She hath killed her beasts;
She hath mingled her wine;
She hath also furnished her table:
3 She hath sent forth her maidens;
She crieth upon the highest places of the city:
4 Whoso is simple, let him turn in hither;
As for him that is void of understanding, she saith to him,

⁵Come, eat ye of my bread,
And drink of the wine which I have mingled.
⁶Leave off, ye simple ones, and live;
And walk in the way of understanding.
⁷He that correcteth a scoffer getteth to himself reviling;
And he that reproveth a wicked man getteth himself a blot.
⁸Reprove not a scoffer, lest he hate thee:
Reprove a wise man, and he will love thee.
⁹Give instruction to a wise man, and he will be yet wiser:
Teach a righteous man, and he will increase in learning.
¹⁰The fear of Yahweh is the beginning of wisdom;
And the knowledge of the Holy One is understanding.
¹¹For by me thy days shall be multiplied,
And the years of thy life shall be increased.
¹²If thou art wise, thou art wise for thyself;
And if thou scoffest, thou alone shalt bear it.
¹³The foolish woman is clamorous;
She is simple, and knoweth nothing.
¹⁴And she sitteth at the door of her house,
On a seat in the high places of the city,
¹⁵To call to them that pass by,
Who go right on their ways:
¹⁶Whoso is simple, let him turn in hither;
And as for him that is void of understanding, she saith to him,
¹⁷Stolen waters are sweet,
And bread eaten in secret is pleasant.
¹⁸But he knoweth not that the dead are there;
That her guests are in the depths of Sheol.

Chapter 10

¹The proverbs of Solomon.
A wise son maketh a glad father;
But a foolish son is the heaviness of his mother.
²Treasures of wickedness profit nothing;
But righteousness delivereth from death.
³Yahweh will not suffer the soul of the righteous to famish;
But he thrusteth away the desire of the wicked.
⁴He becometh poor that worketh with a slack hand;
But the hand of the diligent maketh rich.
⁵He that gathereth in summer is a wise son;
But he that sleepeth in harvest is a son that causeth shame.
⁶Blessings are upon the head of the righteous;
But violence covereth the mouth of the wicked.
⁷The memory of the righteous is blessed;
But the name of the wicked shall rot.
⁸The wise in heart will receive commandments;
But a prating fool shall fall.
⁹He that walketh uprightly walketh surely;
But he that perverteth his ways shall be known.
¹⁰He that winketh with the eye causeth sorrow;
But a prating fool shall fall.
¹¹The mouth of the righteous is a fountain of life;
But violence covereth the mouth of the wicked.
¹²Hatred stirreth up strifes;
But love covereth all transgressions.
¹³In the lips of him that hath discernment wisdom is found;
But a rod is for the back of him that is void of understanding.
¹⁴Wise men lay up knowledge;
But the mouth of the foolish is a present destruction.
¹⁵The rich man's wealth is his strong city;
The destruction of the poor is their poverty.
¹⁶The labor of the righteous tendeth to life;
The increase of the wicked, to sin.
¹⁷He is in the way of life that heedeth correction;
But he that forsaketh reproof erreth.
¹⁸He that hideth hatred is of lying lips;
And he that uttereth a slander is a fool.
¹⁹In the multitude of words there wanteth not transgression;
But he that refraineth his lips doeth wisely.
²⁰The tongue of the righteous is as choice silver:
The heart of the wicked is little worth.
²¹The lips of the righteous feed many;
But the foolish die for lack of understanding.
²²The blessing of Yahweh, it maketh rich;
And he addeth no sorrow therewith.
²³It is as sport to a fool to do wickedness;
And so is wisdom to a man of understanding.
²⁴The fear of the wicked, it shall come upon him;
And the desire of the righteous shall be granted.
²⁵When the whirlwind passeth, the wicked is no more;
But the righteous is an everlasting foundation.
²⁶As vinegar to the teeth, and as smoke to the eyes,
So is the sluggard to them that send him.
²⁷The fear of Yahweh prolongeth days;
But the years of the wicked shall be shortened.
²⁸The hope of the righteous shall be gladness;
But the expectation of the wicked shall perish.
²⁹The way of Yahweh is a stronghold to the upright;
But it is a destruction to the workers of iniquity.
³⁰The righteous shall never be removed;
But the wicked shall not dwell in the land.
³¹The mouth of the righteous bringeth forth wisdom;
But the perverse tongue shall be cut off.
³²The lips of the righteous know what is acceptable;
But the mouth of the wicked speaketh perverseness.

Chapter 11

¹A false balance is an abomination to Yahweh;
But a just weight is his delight.
²When pride cometh, then cometh shame;
But with the lowly is wisdom.
³The integrity of the upright shall guide them;
But the perverseness of the treacherous shall destroy them.
⁴Riches profit not in the day of wrath;
But righteousness delivereth from death.
⁵The righteousness of the perfect shall direct his way;
But the wicked shall fall by his own wickedness.
⁶The righteousness of the upright shall deliver them;
But the treacherous shall be taken in their own iniquity.
⁷When a wicked man dieth, his expectation shall perish;
And the hope of iniquity perisheth.
⁸The righteous is delivered out of trouble,
And the wicked cometh in his stead.
⁹With his mouth the godless man destroyeth his neighbor;
But through knowledge shall the righteous be delivered.
¹⁰When it goeth well with the righteous, the city rejoiceth;
And when the wicked perish, there is shouting.
¹¹By the blessing of the upright the city is exalted;
But it is overthrown by the mouth of the wicked.
¹²He that despiseth his neighbor is void of wisdom;
But a man of understanding holdeth his peace.
¹³He that goeth about as a tale-bearer revealeth secrets;
But he that is of a faithful spirit concealeth a matter.
¹⁴Where no wise guidance is, the people falleth;
But in the multitude of counsellors there is safety.
¹⁵He that is surety for a stranger shall smart for it;
But he that hateth suretyship is secure.
¹⁶A gracious woman obtaineth honor;
And violent men obtain riches.
¹⁷The merciful man doeth good to his own soul;
But he that is cruel troubleth his own flesh.
¹⁸The wicked earneth deceitful wages;
But he that soweth righteousness hath a sure reward.
¹⁹He that is stedfast in righteousness shall attain unto life;
And he that pursueth evil doeth it to his own death.
²⁰They that are perverse in heart are an abomination to Yahweh;
But such as are perfect in their way are his delight.
²¹Though hand join in hand, the evil man shall not be unpunished;
But the seed of the righteous shall be delivered.
²²As a ring of gold in a swine's snout,
So is a fair woman that is without discretion.
²³The desire of the righteous is only good;
But the expectation of the wicked is wrath.
²⁴There is that scattereth, and increaseth yet more;
And there is that withholdeth more than is meet, but it tendeth only to want.
²⁵The liberal soul shall be made fat;
And he that watereth shall be watered also himself.
²⁶He that withholdeth grain, the people shall curse him;
But blessing shall be upon the head of him that selleth it.
²⁷He that diligently seeketh good seeketh favor;
But he that searcheth after evil, it shall come unto him.
²⁸He that trusteth in his riches shall fall;
But the righteous shall flourish as the green leaf.
²⁹He that troubleth his own house shall inherit the wind;
And the foolish shall be servant to the wise of heart.
³⁰The fruit of the righteous is a tree of life;
And he that is wise winneth souls.
³¹Behold, the righteous shall be recompensed in the earth:
How much more the wicked and the sinner!

Chapter 12

¹Whoso loveth correction loveth knowledge;
But he that hateth reproof is brutish.
²A good man shall obtain favor of Yahweh;
But a man of wicked devices will he condemn.
³A man shall not be established by wickedness;
But the root of the righteous shall not be moved.
⁴A worthy woman is the crown of her husband;
But she that maketh ashamed is as rottenness in his bones.
⁵The thoughts of the righteous are just;
But the counsels of the wicked are deceit.
⁶The words of the wicked are of lying in wait for blood;
But the mouth of the upright shall deliver them.
⁷The wicked are overthrown, and are not;
But the house of the righteous shall stand.
⁸A man shall be commended according to his wisdom;

But he that is of a perverse heart shall be despised.
9Better is he that is lightly esteemed, and hath a servant,
Than he that honoreth himself, and lacketh bread.
10A righteous man regardeth the life of his beast;
But the tender mercies of the wicked are cruel.
11He that tilleth his land shall have plenty of bread;
But he that followeth after vain persons is void of understanding.
12The wicked desireth the net of evil men;
But the root of the righteous yieldeth fruit.
13In the transgression of the lips is a snare to the evil man;
But the righteous shall come out of trouble.
14A man shall be satisfied with good by the fruit of his mouth;
And the doings of a man's hands shall be rendered unto him.
15The way of a fool is right in his own eyes;
But he that is wise hearkeneth unto counsel.
16A fool's vexation is presently known;
But a prudent man concealeth shame.
17He that uttereth truth showeth forth righteousness;
But a false witness, deceit.
18There is that speaketh rashly like the piercings of a sword;
But the tongue of the wise is health.
19The lip of truth shall be established for ever;
But a lying tongue is but for a moment.
20Deceit is in the heart of them that devise evil;
But to the counsellors of peace is joy.
21There shall no mischief happen to the righteous;
But the wicked shall be filled with evil.
22Lying lips are an abomination to Yahweh;
But they that deal truly are his delight.
23A prudent man concealeth knowledge;
But the heart of fools proclaimeth foolishness.
24The hand of the diligent shall bear rule;
But the slothful shall be put under taskwork.
25Heaviness in the heart of a man maketh it stoop;
But a good word maketh it glad.
26The righteous is a guide to his neighbor;
But the way of the wicked causeth them to err.
27The slothful man roasteth not that which he took in hunting;
But the precious substance of men is to the diligent.
28In the way of righteousness is life;
And in the pathway thereof there is no death.

Chapter 13

1A wise son heareth his father's instruction;
But a scoffer heareth not rebuke.
2A man shall eat good by the fruit of his mouth;
But the soul of the treacherous shall eat violence.
3He that guardeth his mouth keepeth his life;
But he that openeth wide his lips shall have destruction.
4The soul of the sluggard desireth, and hath nothing;
But the soul of the diligent shall be made fat.
5A righteous man hateth lying;
But a wicked man is loathsome, and cometh to shame.
6Righteousness guardeth him that is upright in the way;
But wickedness overthroweth the sinner.
7There is that maketh himself rich, yet hath nothing:
There is that maketh himself poor, yet hath great wealth.
8The ransom of a man's life is his riches;
But the poor heareth no threatening.
9The light of the righteous rejoiceth;
But the lamp of the wicked shall be put out.
10By pride cometh only contention;
But with the well-advised is wisdom.
11Wealth gotten by vanity shall be diminished;
But he that gathereth by labor shall have increase.
12Hope deferred maketh the heart sick;
But when the desire cometh, it is a tree of life.
13Whoso despiseth the word bringeth destruction on himself;
But he that feareth the commandment shall be rewarded.
14The law of the wise is a fountain of life,
That one may depart from the snares of death.
15Good understanding giveth favor;
But the way of the transgressor is hard.
16Every prudent man worketh with knowledge;
But a fool flaunteth his folly.
17A wicked messenger falleth into evil;
But a faithful ambassador is health.
18Poverty and shame shall be to him that refuseth correction;
But he that regardeth reproof shall be honored.
19The desire accomplished is sweet to the soul;
But it is an abomination to fools to depart from evil.
20Walk with wise men, and thou shalt be wise;
But the companion of fools shall smart for it.
21Evil pursueth sinners;
But the righteous shall be recompensed with good.
22A good man leaveth an inheritance to his children's children;
And the wealth of the sinner is laid up for the righteous.
23Much food is in the tillage of the poor;
But there is that is destroyed by reason of injustice.
24He that spareth his rod hateth his son;
But he that loveth him chasteneth him betimes.
25The righteous eateth to the satisfying of his soul;
But the belly of the wicked shall want.

Chapter 14

1Every wise woman buildeth her house;
But the foolish plucketh it down with her own hands.
2He that walketh in his uprightness feareth Yahweh;
But he that is perverse in his ways despiseth him.
3In the mouth of the foolish is a rod for his pride;
But the lips of the wise shall preserve them.
4Where no oxen are, the crib is clean;
But much increase is by the strength of the ox.
5A faithful witness will not lie;
But a false witness uttereth lies.
6A scoffer seeketh wisdom, and findeth it not;
But knowledge is easy unto him that hath understanding.
7Go into the presence of a foolish man,
And thou shalt not perceive in him the lips of knowledge.
8The wisdom of the prudent is to understand his way;
But the folly of fools is deceit.
9A trespass-offering mocketh fools;
But among the upright there is good will.
10The heart knoweth its own bitterness;
And a stranger doth not intermeddle with its joy.
11The house of the wicked shall be overthrown;
But the tent of the upright shall flourish.
12There is a way which seemeth right unto a man;
But the end thereof are the ways of death.
13Even in laughter the heart is sorrowful;
And the end of mirth is heaviness.
14The backslider in heart shall be filled with his own ways;
And a good man shall be satisfied from himself.
15The simple believeth every word;
But the prudent man looketh well to his going.
16A wise man feareth, and departeth from evil;
But the fool beareth himself insolently, and is confident.
17He that is soon angry will deal foolishly;
And a man of wicked devices is hated.
18The simple inherit folly;
But the prudent are crowned with knowledge.
19The evil bow down before the good;
And the wicked, at the gates of the righteous.
20The poor is hated even of his own neighbor;
But the rich hath many friends.
21He that despiseth his neighbor sinneth;
But he that hath pity on the poor, happy is he.
22Do they not err that devise evil?
But mercy and truth shall be to them that devise good.
23In all labor there is profit;
But the talk of the lips tendeth only to penury.
24The crown of the wise is their riches;
But the folly of fools is only folly.
25A true witness delivereth souls;
But he that uttereth lies causeth deceit.
26In the fear of Yahweh is strong confidence;
And his children shall have a place of refuge.
27The fear of Yahweh is a fountain of life,
That one may depart from the snares of death.
28In the multitude of people is the king's glory;
But in the want of people is the destruction of the prince.
29He that is slow to anger is of great understanding;
But he that is hasty of spirit exalteth folly.
30A tranquil heart is the life of the flesh;
But envy is the rottenness of the bones.
31He that oppresseth the poor reproacheth his Maker;
But he that hath mercy on the needy honoreth him.
32The wicked is thrust down in his evil-doing;
But the righteous hath a refuge in his death.
33Wisdom resteth in the heart of him that hath understanding;
But that which is in the inward part of fools is made known.
34Righteousness exalteth a nation;
But sin is a reproach to any people.
35The king's favor is toward a servant that dealeth wisely;
But his wrath will be against him that causeth shame.

Chapter 15

1A soft answer turneth away wrath;
But a grievous word stirreth up anger.
2The tongue of the wise uttereth knowledge aright;
But the mouth of fools poureth out folly.
3The eyes of Yahweh are in every place,
Keeping watch upon the evil and the good.
4A gentle tongue is a tree of life;
But perverseness therein is a breaking of the spirit.
5A fool despiseth his father's correction;
But he that regardeth reproof getteth prudence.

6In the house of the righteous is much treasure;
But in the revenues of the wicked is trouble.
7The lips of the wise disperse knowledge;
But the heart of the foolish doeth not so.
8The sacrifice of the wicked is an abomination to Yahweh;
But the prayer of the upright is his delight.
9The way of the wicked is an abomination to Yahweh;
But he loveth him that followeth after righteousness.
10There is grievous correction for him that forsaketh the way;
And he that hateth reproof shall die.
11Sheol and Abaddon are before Yahweh:
How much more then the hearts of the children of men!
12A scoffer loveth not to be reproved;
He will not go unto the wise.
13A glad heart maketh a cheerful countenance;
But by sorrow of heart the spirit is broken.
14The heart of him that hath understanding seeketh knowledge;
But the mouth of fools feedeth on folly.
15All the days of the afflicted are evil;
But he that is of a cheerful heart hath a continual feast.
16Better is little, with the fear of Yahweh,
Than great treasure and trouble therewith.
17Better is a dinner of herbs, where love is,
Than a stalled ox and hatred therewith.
18A wrathful man stirreth up contention;
But he that is slow to anger appeaseth strife.
19The way of the sluggard is as a hedge of thorns;
But the path of the upright is made a highway.
20A wise son maketh a glad father;
But a foolish man despiseth his mother.
21Folly is joy to him that is void of wisdom;
But a man of understanding maketh straight his going.
22Where there is no counsel, purposes are disappointed;
But in the multitude of counsellors they are established.
23A man hath joy in the answer of his mouth;
And a word in due season, how good is it!
24To the wise the way of life goeth upward,
That he may depart from Sheol beneath.
25Yahweh will root up the house of the proud;
But he will establish the border of the widow.
26Evil devices are an abomination to Yahweh;
But pleasant words are pure.
27He that is greedy of gain troubleth his own house;
But he that hateth bribes shall live.
28The heart of the righteous studieth to answer;
But the mouth of the wicked poureth out evil things.
29Yahweh is far from the wicked;
But he heareth the prayer of the righteous.
30The light of the eyes rejoiceth the heart;
And good tidings make the bones fat.
31The ear that hearkeneth to the reproof of life
Shall abide among the wise.
32He that refuseth correction despiseth his own soul;
But he that hearkeneth to reproof getteth understanding.
33The fear of Yahweh is the instruction of wisdom;
And before honor goeth humility.

Chapter 16

1The plans of the heart belong to man;
But the answer of the tongue is from Yahweh.
2All the ways of a man are clean in his own eyes;
But Yahweh weigheth the spirits.
3Commit thy works unto Yahweh,
And thy purposes shall be established.
4Yahweh hath made everything for its own end;
Yea, even the wicked for the day of evil.
5Every one that is proud in heart is an abomination to Yahweh:
Though hand join in hand, he shall not be unpunished.
6By mercy and truth iniquity is atoned for;
And by the fear of Yahweh men depart from evil.
7When a man's ways please Yahweh,
He maketh even his enemies to be at peace with him.
8Better is a little, with righteousness,
Than great revenues with injustice.
9A man's heart deviseth his way;
But Yahweh directeth his steps.
10A divine sentence is in the lips of the king;
His mouth shall not transgress in judgment.
11A just balance and scales are Yahweh's;
All the weights of the bag are his work.
12It is an abomination to kings to commit wickedness;
For the throne is established by righteousness.
13Righteous lips are the delight of kings;
And they love him that speaketh right.
14The wrath of a king is as messengers of death;
But a wise man will pacify it.
15In the light of the king's countenance is life;
And his favor is as a cloud of the latter rain.
16How much better is it to get wisdom than gold!
Yea, to get understanding is rather to be chosen than silver.
17The highway of the upright is to depart from evil:
He that keepeth his way preserveth his soul.
18Pride goeth before destruction,
And a haughty spirit before a fall.
19Better it is to be of a lowly spirit with the poor,
Than to divide the spoil with the proud.
20He that giveth heed unto the word shall find good;
And whoso trusteth in Yahweh, happy is he.
21The wise in heart shall be called prudent;
And the sweetness of the lips increaseth learning.
22Understanding is a well-spring of life unto him that hath it;
But the correction of fools is their folly.
23The heart of the wise instructeth his mouth,
And addeth learning to his lips.
24Pleasant words are as a honeycomb,
Sweet to the soul, and health to the bones.
25There is a way which seemeth right unto a man,
But the end thereof are the ways of death.
26The appetite of the laboring man laboreth for him;
For his mouth urgeth him thereto.
27A worthless man deviseth mischief;
And in his lips there is as a scorching fire.
28A perverse man scattereth abroad strife;
And a whisperer separateth chief friends.
29A man of violence enticeth his neighbor,
And leadeth him in a way that is not good.
30He that shutteth his eyes, it is to devise perverse things:
He that compresseth his lips bringeth evil to pass.
31The hoary head is a crown of glory;
It shall be found in the way of righteousness.
32He that is slow to anger is better than the mighty;
And he that ruleth his spirit, than he that taketh a city.
33The lot is cast into the lap;
But the whole disposing thereof is of Yahweh.

Chapter 17

1Better is a dry morsel, and quietness therewith,
Than a house full of feasting with strife.
2A servant that dealeth wisely shall have rule over a son that causeth shame,
And shall have part in the inheritance among the brethren.
3The refining pot is for silver, and the furnace for gold;
But Yahweh trieth the hearts.
4An evil-doer giveth heed to wicked lips;
And a liar giveth ear to a mischievous tongue.
5Whoso mocketh the poor reproacheth his Maker;
And he that is glad at calamity shall not be unpunished.
6Children's children are the crown of old men;
And the glory of children are their fathers.
7Excellent speech becometh not a fool;
Much less do lying lips a prince.
8A bribe is as a precious stone in the eyes of him that hath it;
Whithersoever it turneth, it prospereth.
9He that covereth a transgression seeketh love;
But he that harpeth on a matter separateth chief friends.
10A rebuke entereth deeper into one that hath understanding
Than a hundred stripes into a fool.
11An evil man seeketh only rebellion;
Therefore a cruel messenger shall be sent against him.
12Let a bear robbed of her whelps meet a man,
Rather than a fool in his folly.
13Whoso rewardeth evil for good,
Evil shall not depart from his house.
14The beginning of strife is as when one letteth out water:
Therefore leave off contention, before there is quarrelling.
15He that justifieth the wicked, and he that condemneth the righteous,
Both of them alike are an abomination to Yahweh.
16Wherefore is there a price in the hand of a fool to buy wisdom,
Seeing he hath no understanding?
17A friend loveth at all times;
And a brother is born for adversity.
18A man void of understanding striketh hands,
And becometh surety in the presence of his neighbor.
19He loveth transgression that loveth strife:
He that raiseth high his gate seeketh destruction.
20He that hath a wayward heart findeth no good;
And he that hath a perverse tongue falleth into mischief.
21He that begetteth a fool doeth it to his sorrow;
And the father of a fool hath no joy.
22A cheerful heart is a good medicine;
But a broken spirit drieth up the bones.
23A wicked man receiveth a bribe out of the bosom,
To pervert the ways of justice.
24Wisdom is before the face of him that hath understanding;
But the eyes of a fool are in the ends of the earth.
25A foolish son is a grief to his father,
And bitterness to her that bare him.
26Also to punish the righteous is not good,
Nor to smite the noble for their uprightness.

Chapter 18

1 He that separateth himself seeketh his own desire,
And rageth against all sound wisdom.
2 A fool hath no delight in understanding,
But only that his heart may reveal itself.
3 When the wicked cometh, there cometh also contempt,
And with ignominy cometh reproach.
4 The words of a man's mouth are as deep waters;
The wellspring of wisdom is as a flowing brook.
5 To respect the person of the wicked is not good,
Nor to turn aside the righteous in judgment.
6 A fool's lips enter into contention,
And his mouth calleth for stripes.
7 A fool's mouth is his destruction,
And his lips are the snare of his soul.
8 The words of a whisperer are as dainty morsels,
And they go down into the innermost parts.
9 He also that is slack in his work
Is brother to him that is a destroyer.
10 The name of Yahweh is a strong tower;
The righteous runneth into it, and is safe.
11 The rich man's wealth is his strong city,
And as a high wall in his own imagination.
12 Before destruction the heart of man is haughty;
And before honor goeth humility.
13 He that giveth answer before he heareth,
It is folly and shame unto him.
14 The spirit of a man will sustain his infirmity;
But a broken spirit who can bear?
15 The heart of the prudent getteth knowledge;
And the ear of the wise seeketh knowledge.
16 A man's gift maketh room for him,
And bringeth him before great men.
17 He that pleadeth his cause first seemeth just;
But his neighbor cometh and searcheth him out.
18 The lot causeth contentions to cease,
And parteth between the mighty.
19 A brother offended is harder to be won than a strong city;
And such contentions are like the bars of a castle.
20 A man's belly shall be filled with the fruit of his mouth;
With the increase of his lips shall he be satisfied.
21 Death and life are in the power of the tongue;
And they that love it shall eat the fruit thereof.
22 Whoso findeth a wife findeth a good thing,
And obtaineth favor of Yahweh.
23 The poor useth entreaties;
But the rich answereth roughly.
24 He that maketh many friends doeth it to his own destruction;
But there is a friend that sticketh closer than a brother.

Chapter 19

1 Better is the poor that walketh in his integrity
Than he that is perverse in his lips and is a fool.
2 Also, that the soul be without knowledge is not good;
And he that hasteth with his feet sinneth.
3 The foolishness of man subverteth his way;
And his heart fretteth against Yahweh.
4 Wealth addeth many friends;
But the poor is separated from his friend.
5 A false witness shall not be unpunished;
And he that uttereth lies shall not escape.
6 Many will entreat the favor of the liberal man;
And every man is a friend to him that giveth gifts.
7 All the brethren of the poor do hate him;
How much more do his friends go far from him!
He pursueth them with words, but they are gone.
8 He that getteth wisdom loveth his own soul:
He that keepeth understanding shall find good.
9 A false witness shall not be unpunished;
And he that uttereth lies shall perish.
10 Delicate living is not seemly for a fool;
Much less for a servant to have rule over princes.
11 The discretion of a man maketh him slow to anger;
And it is his glory to pass over a transgression.
12 The king's wrath is as the roaring of a lion;
But his favor is as dew upon the grass.
13 A foolish son is the calamity of his father;
And the contentions of a wife are a continual dropping.
14 House and riches are an inheritance from fathers;
But a prudent wife is from Yahweh.
15 Slothfulness casteth into a deep sleep;
And the idle soul shall suffer hunger.
16 He that keepeth the commandment keepeth his soul;
But he that is careless of his ways shall die.
17 He that hath pity upon the poor lendeth unto Yahweh,
And his good deed will he pay him again.
18 Chasten thy son, seeing there is hope;
and set not thy heart on his destruction.
19 A man of great wrath shall bear the penalty;
For if thou deliver him, thou must do it yet again.
20 Hear counsel, and receive instruction,
That thou mayest be wise in thy latter end.
21 There are many devices in a man's heart;
But the counsel of Yahweh, that shall stand.
22 That which maketh a man to be desired is his kindness;
And a poor man is better than a liar.
23 The fear of Yahweh tendeth to life;
And he that hath it shall abide satisfied;
He shall not be visited with evil.
24 The sluggard burieth his hand in the dish,
And will not so much as bring it to his mouth again.
25 Smite a scoffer, and the simple will learn prudence;
And reprove one that hath understanding, and he will understand knowledge.
26 He that doeth violence to his father, and chaseth away his mother,
Is a son that causeth shame and bringeth reproach.
27 Cease, my son, to hear instruction
Only to err from the words of knowledge.
28 A worthless witness mocketh at justice;
And the mouth of the wicked swalloweth iniquity.
29 Judgments are prepared for scoffers,
And stripes for the back of fools.

Chapter 20

1 Wine is a mocker, strong drink a brawler;
And whosoever erreth thereby is not wise.
2 The terror of a king is as the roaring of a lion:
He that provoketh him to anger sinneth against his own life.
3 It is an honor for a man to keep aloof from strife;
But every fool will be quarrelling.
4 The sluggard will not plow by reason of the winter;
Therefore he shall beg in harvest, and have nothing.
5 Counsel in the heart of man is like deep water;
But a man of understanding will draw it out.
6 Most men will proclaim every one his own kindness;
But a faithful man who can find?
7 A righteous man that walketh in his integrity,
Blessed are his children after him.
8 A king that sitteth on the throne of judgment
Scattereth away all evil with his eyes.
9 Who can say, I have made my heart clean,
I am pure from my sin?
10 Diverse weights, and diverse measures,
Both of them alike are an abomination to Yahweh.
11 Even a child maketh himself known by his doings,
Whether his work be pure, and whether it be right.
12 The hearing ear, and the seeing eye,
Yahweh hath made even both of them.
13 Love not sleep, lest thou come to poverty;
Open thine eyes, and thou shalt be satisfied with bread.
14 It is bad, it is bad, saith the buyer;
But when he is gone his way, then he boasteth.
15 There is gold, and abundance of rubies;
But the lips of knowledge are a precious jewel.
16 Take his garment that is surety for a stranger;
And hold him in pledge that is surety for foreigners.
17 Bread of falsehood is sweet to a man;
But afterwards his mouth shall be filled with gravel.
18 Every purpose is established by counsel;
And by wise guidance make thou war.
19 He that goeth about as a tale-bearer revealeth secrets;
Therefore company not with him that openeth wide his lips.
20 Whoso curseth his father or his mother,
His lamp shall be put out in blackness of darkness.
21 An inheritance may be gotten hastily at the beginning;
But the end thereof shall not be blessed.
22 Say not thou, I will recompense evil:
Wait for Yahweh, and he will save thee.
23 Diverse weights are an abomination to Yahweh;
And a false balance is not good.
24 A man's goings are of Yahweh;
How then can man understand his way?
25 It is a snare to a man rashly to say, It is holy,
And after vows to make inquiry.
26 A wise king winnoweth the wicked,
And bringeth the threshing-wheel over them.
27 The spirit of man is the lamp of Yahweh,
Searching all his innermost parts.
28 Kindness and truth preserve the king;
And his throne is upholden by kindness.
29 The glory of young men is their strength;
And the beauty of old men is the hoary head.

30Stripes that wound cleanse away evil;
And strokes reach the innermost parts.

Chapter 21

1The king's heart is in the hand of Yahweh as the watercourses:
He turneth it whithersoever he will.
2Every way of a man is right in his own eyes;
But Yahweh weigheth the hearts.
3To do righteousness and justice
Is more acceptable to Yahweh than sacrifice.
4A high look, and a proud heart,
Even the lamp of the wicked, is sin.
5The thoughts of the diligent tend only to plenteousness;
But every one that is hasty hasteth only to want.
6The getting of treasures by a lying tongue
Is a vapor driven to and fro by them that seek death.
7The violence of the wicked shall sweep them away,
Because they refuse to do justice.
8The way of him that is laden with guilt is exceeding crooked;
But as for the pure, his work is right.
9It is better to dwell in the corner of the housetop,
Than with a contentious woman in a wide house.
10The soul of the wicked desireth evil:
His neighbor findeth no favor in his eyes.
11When the scoffer is punished, the simple is made wise;
And when the wise is instructed, he receiveth knowledge.
12The righteous man considereth the house of the wicked,
How the wicked are overthrown to their ruin.
13Whoso stoppeth his ears at the cry of the poor,
He also shall cry, but shall not be heard.
14A gift in secret pacifieth anger;
And a present in the bosom, strong wrath.
15It is joy to the righteous to do justice;
But it is a destruction to the workers of iniquity.
16The man that wandereth out of the way of understanding
Shall rest in the assembly of the dead.
17He that loveth pleasure shall be a poor man:
He that loveth wine and oil shall not be rich.
18The wicked is a ransom for the righteous;
And the treacherous cometh in the stead of the upright.
19It is better to dwell in a desert land,
Than with a contentious and fretful woman.
20There is precious treasure and oil in the dwelling of the wise;
But a foolish man swalloweth it up.
21He that followeth after righteousness and kindness
Findeth life, righteousness, and honor.
22A wise man scaleth the city of the mighty,
And bringeth down the strength of the confidence thereof.
23Whoso keepeth his mouth and his tongue
Keepeth his soul from troubles.
24The proud and haughty man, scoffer is his name;
He worketh in the arrogance of pride.
25The desire of the sluggard killeth him;
For his hands refuse to labor.
26There is that coveteth greedily all the day long;
But the righteous giveth and withholdeth not.
27The sacrifice of the wicked is an abomination:
How much more, when he bringeth it with a wicked mind!
28A false witness shall perish;
But the man that heareth shall speak so as to endure.
29A wicked man hardeneth his face;
But as for the upright, he establisheth his ways.
30There is no wisdom nor understanding
Nor counsel against Yahweh.
31The horse is prepared against the day of battle;
But victory is of Yahweh.

Chapter 22

1A good name is rather to be chosen than great riches,
And loving favor rather than silver and gold.
2The rich and the poor meet together:
Yahweh is the maker of them all.
3A prudent man seeth the evil, and hideth himself;
But the simple pass on, and suffer for it.
4The reward of humility and the fear of Yahweh
Is riches, and honor, and life.
5Thorns and snares are in the way of the perverse:
He that keepeth his soul shall be far from them.
6Train up a child in the way he should go,
And even when he is old he will not depart from it.
7The rich ruleth over the poor;
And the borrower is servant to the lender.
8He that soweth iniquity shall reap calamity;
And the rod of his wrath shall fail.
9He that hath a bountiful eye shall be blessed;
For he giveth of his bread to the poor.
10Cast out the scoffer, and contention will go out;
Yea, strife and ignominy will cease.
11He that loveth pureness of heart,
For the grace of his lips the king will be his friend.
12The eyes of Yahweh preserve him that hath knowledge;
But he overthroweth the words of the treacherous man.
13The sluggard saith, There is a lion without:
I shall be slain in the streets.
14The mouth of strange women is a deep pit:
He that is abhorred of Yahweh shall fall therein.
15Foolishness is bound up in the heart of a child;
But the rod of correction shall drive it far from him.
16He that oppresseth the poor to increase his gain,
And he that giveth to the rich, shall come only to want.
17Incline thine ear, and hear the words of the wise,
And apply thy heart unto my knowledge.
18For it is a pleasant thing if thou keep them within thee,
If they be established together upon thy lips.
19That thy trust may be in Yahweh,
I have made them known to thee this day, even to thee.
20Have not I written unto thee excellent things
Of counsels and knowledge,
21To make thee know the certainty of the words of truth,
That thou mayest carry back words of truth to them that send thee?
22Rob not the poor, because he is poor;
Neither oppress the afflicted in the gate:
23For Yahweh will plead their cause,
And despoil of life those that despoil them.
24Make no friendship with a man that is given to anger;
And with a wrathful man thou shalt not go:
25Lest thou learn this ways,
And get a snare to thy soul.
26Be thou not one of them that strike hands,
Or of them that are sureties for debts.
27If thou hast not wherewith to pay,
Why should he take away thy bed from under thee?
28Remove not the ancient landmark,
Which thy fathers have set.
29Seest thou a man diligent in his business? he shall stand before kings;
He shall not stand before mean men.

Chapter 23

1When thou sittest to eat with a ruler,
Consider diligently him that is before thee;
2And put a knife to thy throat,
If thou be a man given to appetite.
3Be not desirous of his dainties;
Seeing they are deceitful food.
4Weary not thyself to be rich;
Cease from thine own wisdom.
5Wilt thou set thine eyes upon that which is not?
For riches certainly make themselves wings,
Like an eagle that flieth toward heaven.
6Eat thou not the bread of him that hath an evil eye,
Neither desire thou his dainties:
7For as he thinketh within himself, so is he:
Eat and drink, saith he to thee;
But his heart is not with thee.
8The morsel which thou hast eaten shalt thou vomit up,
And lose thy sweet words.
9Speak not in the hearing of a fool;
For he will despise the wisdom of thy words.
10Remove not the ancient landmark;
And enter not into the fields of the fatherless:
11For their Redeemer is strong;
He will plead their cause against thee.
12Apply thy heart unto instruction,
And thine ears to the words of knowledge.
13Withhold not correction from the child;
For if thou beat him with the rod, he will not die.
14Thou shalt beat him with the rod,
And shalt deliver his soul from Sheol.
15My son, if thy heart be wise,
My heart will be glad, even mine:
16Yea, my heart will rejoice,
When thy lips speak right things.
17Let not thy heart envy sinners;
But be thou in the fear of Yahweh all the day long:
18For surely there is a reward;
And thy hope shall not be cut off.
19Hear thou, my son, and be wise,
And guide thy heart in the way.
20Be not among winebibbers,
Among gluttonous eaters of flesh:
21For the drunkard and the glutton shall come to poverty;
And drowsiness will clothe a man with rags.
22Hearken unto thy father that begat thee,
And despise not thy mother when she is old.
23Buy the truth, and sell it not;
Yea, wisdom, and instruction, and understanding.
24The father of the righteous will greatly rejoice;

And he that begetteth a wise child will have joy of him.
25Let thy father and thy mother be glad,
And let her that bare thee rejoice.
26My son, give me thy heart;
And let thine eyes delight in my ways.
27For a harlot is a deep ditch;
And a foreign woman is a narrow pit.
28Yea, she lieth in wait as a robber,
And increaseth the treacherous among men.
29Who hath woe? who hath sorrow? who hath contentions?
Who hath complaining? who hath wounds without cause?
Who hath redness of eyes?
30They that tarry long at the wine;
They that go to seek out mixed wine.
31Look not thou upon the wine when it is red,
When it sparkleth in the cup,
When it goeth down smoothly:
32At the last it biteth like a serpent,
And stingeth like an adder.
33Thine eyes shall behold strange things,
And thy heart shall utter perverse things.
34Yea, thou shalt be as he that lieth down in the midst of the sea,
Or as he that lieth upon the top of a mast.
35They have stricken me, shalt thou say, and I was not hurt;
They have beaten me, and I felt it not:
When shall I awake? I will seek it yet again.

Chapter 24

1Be not thou envious against evil men;
Neither desire to be with them:
2For their heart studieth oppression,
And their lips talk of mischief.
3Through wisdom is a house builded;
And by understanding it is established;
4And by knowledge are the chambers filled
With all precious and pleasant riches.
5A wise man is strong;
Yea, a man of knowledge increaseth might
6For by wise guidance thou shalt make thy war;
And in the multitude of counsellors there is safety.
7Wisdom is too high for a fool:
He openeth not his mouth in the gate.
8He that deviseth to do evil,
Men shall call him a mischief-maker.
9The thought of foolishness is sin;
And the scoffer is an abomination to men.
10If thou faint in the day of adversity,
Thy strength is small.
11Deliver them that are carried away unto death,
And those that are ready to be slain see that thou hold back.
12If thou sayest, Behold, we knew not this;
Doth not he that weigheth the hearts consider it?
And he that keepeth thy soul, doth not he know it?
And shall not he render to every man according to his work?
13My son, eat thou honey, for it is good;
And the droppings of the honeycomb, which are sweet to thy taste:
14So shalt thou know wisdom to be unto thy soul;
If thou hast found it, then shall there be a reward,
And thy hope shall not be cut off.
15Lay not wait, O wicked man, against the habitation of the righteous;
Destroy not his resting-place:
16For a righteous man falleth seven times, and riseth up again;
But the wicked are overthrown by calamity.
17Rejoice not when thine enemy falleth,
And let not thy heart be glad when he is overthrown;
18Lest Yahweh see it, and it displease him,
And he turn away his wrath from him.
19Fret not thyself because of evil-doers;
Neither be thou envious at the wicked:
20For there shall be no reward to the evil man;
The lamp of the wicked shall be put out.
21My son, fear thou Yahweh and the king;
And company not with them that are given to change:
22For their calamity shall rise suddenly;
And the destruction from them both, who knoweth it?
23These also are sayings of the wise.
To have respect of persons in judgment is not good.
24He that saith unto the wicked, Thou art righteous;
Peoples shall curse him, nations shall abhor him:
25But to them that rebuke him shall be delight,
And a good blessing shall come upon them.
26He kisseth the lips
Who giveth a right answer.
27Prepare thy work without,
And make it ready for thee in the field;
And afterwards build thy house.
28Be not a witness against thy neighbor without cause;
And deceive not with thy lips.
29Say not, I will do so to him as he hath done to me;
I will render to the man according to his work.
30I went by the field of the sluggard,
And by the vineyard of the man void of understanding;
31And, lo, it was all grown over with thorns,
The face thereof was covered with nettles,
And the stone wall thereof was broken down.
32Then I beheld, and considered well;
I saw, and received instruction:
33Yet a little sleep, a little slumber,
A little folding of the hands to sleep;
34So shall thy poverty come as a robber,
And thy want as an armed man.

Chapter 25

1These also are proverbs of Solomon, which the men of Hezekiah king of Judah copied out.
2It is the glory of God to conceal a thing;
But the glory of kings is to search out a matter.
3As the heavens for height, and the earth for depth,
So the heart of kings is unsearchable.
4Take away the dross from the silver,
And there cometh forth a vessel for the refiner:
5Take away the wicked from before the king,
And his throne shall be established in righteousness.
6Put not thyself forward in the presence of the king,
And stand not in the place of great men:
7For better is it that it be said unto thee, Come up hither,
Than that thou shouldest be put lower in the presence of the prince,
Whom thine eyes have seen.
8Go not forth hastily to strive,
Lest thou know not what to do in the end thereof,
When thy neighbor hath put thee to shame.
9Debate thy cause with thy neighbor himself,
And disclose not the secret of another;
10Lest he that heareth it revile thee,
And thine infamy turn not away.
11A word fitly spoken
Is like apples of gold in network of silver.
12As an ear-ring of gold, and an ornament of fine gold,
So is a wise reprover upon an obedient ear.
13As the cold of snow in the time of harvest,
So is a faithful messenger to them that send him;
For he refresheth the soul of his masters.
14As clouds and wind without rain,
So is he that boasteth himself of his gifts falsely.
15By long forbearing is a ruler persuaded,
And a soft tongue breaketh the bone.
16Hast thou found honey? eat so much as is sufficient for thee,
Lest thou be filled therewith, and vomit it.
17Let thy foot be seldom in thy neighbor's house,
Lest he be weary of thee, and hate thee.
18A man that beareth false witness against his neighbor
Is a maul, and a sword, and a sharp arrow.
19Confidence in an unfaithful man in time of trouble
Is like a broken tooth, and a foot out of joint.
20As one that taketh off a garment in cold weather, and as vinegar upon soda,
So is he that singeth songs to a heavy heart.
21If thine enemy be hungry, give him bread to eat;
And if he be thirsty, give him water to drink:
22For thou wilt heap coals of fire upon his head,
And Yahweh will reward thee.
23The north wind bringeth forth rain:
So doth a backbiting tongue an angry countenance.
24It is better to dwell in the corner of the housetop,
Than with a contentious woman in a wide house.
25As cold waters to a thirsty soul,
So is good news from a far country.
26As a troubled fountain, and a corrupted spring,
So is a righteous man that giveth way before the wicked.
27It is not good to eat much honey:
So for men to search out their own glory is grievous.
28He whose spirit is without restraint
Is like a city that is broken down and without walls.

Chapter 26

1As snow in summer, and as rain in harvest,
So honor is not seemly for a fool.
2As the sparrow in her wandering, as the swallow in her flying,
So the curse that is causeless alighteth not.
3A whip for the horse, a bridle for the ass,
And a rod for the back of fools.
4Answer not a fool according to his folly,
Lest thou also be like unto him.
5Answer a fool according to his folly,
Lest he be wise in his own conceit.
6He that sendeth a message by the hand of a fool
Cutteth off his own feet, and drinketh in damage.

7The legs of the lame hang loose:
So is a parable in the mouth of fools.
8As one that bindeth a stone in a sling,
So is he that giveth honor to a fool.
9As a thorn that goeth up into the hand of a drunkard,
So is a parable in the mouth of fools.
10As an archer that woundeth all,
So is he that hireth a fool and he that hireth them that pass by.
11As a dog that returneth to his vomit,
So is a fool that repeateth his folly.
12Seest thou a man wise in his own conceit?
There is more hope of a fool than of him.
13The sluggard saith, There is a lion in the way;
A lion is in the streets.
14As the door turneth upon its hinges,
So doth the sluggard upon his bed.
15The sluggard burieth his hand in the dish;
It wearieth him to bring it again to his mouth.
16The sluggard is wiser in his own conceit
Than seven men that can render a reason.
17He that passeth by, and vexeth himself with strife belonging not to him,
Is like one that taketh a dog by the ears.
18As a madman who casteth firebrands,
Arrows, and death,
19So is the man that deceiveth his neighbor,
And saith, Am not I in sport?
20For lack of wood the fire goeth out;
And where there is no whisperer, contention ceaseth.
21As coals are to hot embers, and wood to fire,
So is a contentious man to inflame strife.
22The words of a whisperer are as dainty morsels,
And they go down into the innermost parts.
23Fervent lips and a wicked heart
Are like an earthen vessel overlaid with silver dross.
24He that hateth dissembleth with his lips;
But he layeth up deceit within him:
25When he speaketh fair, believe him not;
For there are seven abominations in his heart:
26Though his hatred cover itself with guile,
His wickedness shall be openly showed before the assembly.
27Whoso diggeth a pit shall fall therein;
And he that rolleth a stone, it shall return upon him.
28A lying tongue hateth those whom it hath wounded;
And a flattering mouth worketh ruin.

Chapter 27

1Boast not thyself of tomorrow;
For thou knowest not what a day may bring forth.
2Let another man praise thee, and not thine own mouth;
A stranger, and not thine own lips.
3A stone is heavy, and the sand weighty;
But a fool's vexation is heavier than they both.
4Wrath is cruel, and anger is overwhelming;
But who is able to stand before jealousy?
5Better is open rebuke
Than love that is hidden.
6Faithful are the wounds of a friend;
But the kisses of an enemy are profuse.
7The full soul loatheth a honeycomb;
But to the hungry soul every bitter thing is sweet.
8As a bird that wandereth from her nest,
So is a man that wandereth from his place.
9Oil and perfume rejoice the heart;
So doth the sweetness of a man's friend that cometh of hearty counsel.
10Thine own friend, and thy father's friend, forsake not;
And go not to thy brother's house in the day of thy calamity:
Better is a neighbor that is near than a brother far off.
11My son, be wise, and make my heart glad,
That I may answer him that reproacheth me.
12A prudent man seeth the evil, and hideth himself;
But the simple pass on, and suffer for it.
13Take his garment that is surety for a stranger,
And hold him in pledge that is surety for a foreign woman.
14He that blesseth his friend with a loud voice, rising early in the morning,
It shall be counted a curse to him.
15A continual dropping in a very rainy day
And a contentious woman are alike:
16He that would restrain her restraineth the wind;
And his right hand encountereth oil.
17Iron sharpeneth iron;
So a man sharpeneth the countenance of his friend.
18Whoso keepeth the fig-tree shall eat the fruit thereof;
And he that regardeth his master shall be honored.
19As in water face answereth to face,
So the heart of man to man.
20Sheol and Abaddon are never satisfied;
And the eyes of man are never satisfied.
21The refining pot is for silver, and the furnace for gold;
And a man is tried by his praise.
22Though thou shouldest bray a fool in a mortar with a pestle along with bruised grain,
Yet will not his foolishness depart from him.
23Be thou diligent to know the state of thy flocks,
And look well to thy herds:
24For riches are not for ever:
And doth the crown endure unto all generations?
25The hay is carried, and the tender grass showeth itself,
And the herbs of the mountains are gathered in.
26The lambs are for thy clothing,
And the goats are the price of the field;
27And there will be goats' milk enough for thy food, for the food of thy household,
And maintenance for thy maidens.

Chapter 28

1The wicked flee when no man pursueth;
But the righteous are bold as a lion.
2For the transgression of a land many are the princes thereof;
But by men of understanding and knowledge the state thereof shall be prolonged.
3A needy man that oppresseth the poor
Is like a sweeping rain which leaveth no food.
4They that forsake the law praise the wicked;
But such as keep the law contend with them.
5Evil men understand not justice;
But they that seek Yahweh understand all things.
6Better is the poor that walketh in his integrity,
Than he that is perverse in his ways, though he be rich.
7Whoso keepeth the law is a wise son;
But he that is a companion of gluttons shameth his father.
8He that augmenteth his substance by interest and increase,
Gathereth it for him that hath pity on the poor.
9He that turneth away his ear from hearing the law,
Even his prayer is an abomination.
10Whoso causeth the upright to go astray in an evil way,
He shall fall himself into his own pit;
But the perfect shall inherit good.
11The rich man is wise in his own conceit;
But the poor that hath understanding searcheth him out.
12When the righteous triumph, there is great glory;
But when the wicked rise, men hide themselves.
13He that covereth his transgressions shall not prosper:
But whoso confesseth and forsaketh them shall obtain mercy.
14Happy is the man that feareth alway;
But he that hardeneth his heart shall fall into mischief.
15As a roaring lion, and a ranging bear,
So is a wicked ruler over a poor people.
16The prince that lacketh understanding is also a great oppressor;
But he that hateth covetousness shall prolong his days.
17A man that is laden with the blood of any person
Shall flee unto the pit; let no man stay him.
18Whoso walketh uprightly shall be delivered;
But he that is perverse in his ways shall fall at once.
19He that tilleth his land shall have plenty of bread;
But he that followeth after vain persons shall have poverty enough.
20A faithful man shall abound with blessings;
But he that maketh haste to be rich shall not be unpunished.
21To have respect of persons is not good;
Neither that a man should transgress for a piece of bread.
22he that hath an evil eye hasteth after riches,
And knoweth not that want shall come upon him.
23He that rebuketh a man shall afterward find more favor
Than he that flattereth with the tongue.
24Whoso robbeth his father or his mother, and saith, It is no transgression,
The same is the companion of a destroyer.
25He that is of a greedy spirit stirreth up strife;
But he that putteth his trust in Yahweh shall be made fat.
26He that trusteth in his own heart is a fool;
But whoso walketh wisely, he shall be delivered.
27He that giveth unto the poor shall not lack;
But he that hideth his eyes shall have many a curse.
28When the wicked rise, men hide themselves;
But when they perish, the righteous increase.

Chapter 29

1He that being often reproved hardeneth his neck
Shall suddenly be destroyed, and that without remedy.
2When the righteous are increased, the people rejoice;
But when a wicked man beareth rule, the people sigh.
3Whoso loveth wisdom rejoiceth his father;
But he that keepeth company with harlots wasteth his substance.
4The king by justice establisheth the land;
But he that exacteth gifts overthroweth it.
5A man that flattereth his neighbor
Spreadeth a net for his steps.
6In the transgression of an evil man there is a snare;
But the righteous doth sing and rejoice.

Proverbs

7 The righteous taketh knowledge of the cause of the poor;
The wicked hath not understanding to know it.
8 Scoffers set a city in a flame;
But wise men turn away wrath.
9 If a wise man hath a controversy with a foolish man,
Whether he be angry or laugh, there will be no rest.
10 The bloodthirsty hate him that is perfect;
And as for the upright, they seek his life.
11 A fool uttereth all his anger;
But a wise man keepeth it back and stilleth it.
12 If a ruler hearkeneth to falsehood,
All his servants are wicked.
13 The poor man and the oppressor meet together;
Yahweh lighteneth the eyes of them both.
14 The king that faithfully judgeth the poor,
His throne shall be established for ever.
15 The rod and reproof give wisdom;
But a child left to himself causeth shame to his mother.
16 When the wicked are increased, transgression increaseth;
But the righteous shall look upon their fall.
17 Correct thy son, and he will give thee rest;
Yea, he will give delight unto thy soul.
18 Where there is no vision, the people cast off restraint;
But he that keepeth the law, happy is he.
19 A servant will not be corrected by words;
For though he understand, he will not give heed.
20 Seest thou a man that is hasty in his words?
There is more hope of a fool than of him.
21 He that delicately bringeth up his servant from a child
Shall have him become a son at the last.
22 An angry man stirreth up strife,
And a wrathful man aboundeth in transgression.
23 A man's pride shall bring him low;
But he that is of a lowly spirit shall obtain honor.
24 Whoso is partner with a thief hateth his own soul;
He heareth the adjuration and uttereth nothing.
25 The fear of man bringeth a snare;
But whoso putteth his trust in Yahweh shall be safe.
26 Many seek the ruler's favor;
But a man's judgment cometh from Yahweh.
27 An unjust man is an abomination to the righteous;
And he that is upright in the way is an abomination to the wicked.

Chapter 30

1 The words of Agur the son of Jakeh; The oracle.
The man saith unto Ithiel, unto Ithiel and Ucal:
2 Surely I am more brutish than any man,
And have not the understanding of a man;
3 And I have not learned wisdom,
Neither have I the knowledge of the Holy One.
4 Who hath ascended up into heaven, and descended?
Who hath gathered the wind in his fists?
Who hath bound the waters in his garment?
Who hath established all the ends of the earth?
What is his name, and what is his son's name, if thou knowest?
5 Every word of God is tried:
He is a shield unto them that take refuge in him.
6 Add thou not unto his words,
Lest he reprove thee, and thou be found a liar.
7 Two things have I asked of thee;
Deny me them not before I die:
8 Remove far from me falsehood and lies;
Give me neither poverty nor riches;
Feed me with the food that is needful for me:
9 Lest I be full, and deny thee, and say, Who is Yahweh?
Or lest I be poor, and steal,
And use profanely the name of my God.
10 Slander not a servant unto his master,
Lest he curse thee, and thou be held guilty.
11 There is a generation that curse their father,
And bless not their mother.
12 There is a generation that are pure in their own eyes,
And yet are not washed from their filthiness.
13 There is a generation, oh how lofty are their eyes!
And their eyelids are lifted up.
14 There is a generation whose teeth are as swords, and their jaw teeth as knives,
To devour the poor from off the earth, and the needy from among men.
15 The horseleach hath two daughters, crying, Give, give.
There are three things that are never satisfied,
Yea, four that say not, Enough:
16 Sheol; and the barren womb;
The earth that is not satisfied with water;
And the fire that saith not, Enough.
17 The eye that mocketh at his father,
And despiseth to obey his mother,
The ravens of the valley shall pick it out,
And the young eagles shall eat it.
18 There are three things which are too wonderful for me,
Yea, four which I know not:
19 The way of an eagle in the air;
The way of a serpent upon a rock;
The way of a ship in the midst of the sea;
And the way of a man with a maiden.
20 So is the way of an adulterous woman;
She eateth, and wipeth her mouth,
And saith, I have done no wickedness.
21 For three things the earth doth tremble,
And for four, which it cannot bear:
22 For a servant when he is king;
And a fool when he is filled with food;
23 For an odious woman when she is married;
And a handmaid that is heir to her mistress.
24 There are four things which are little upon the earth,
But they are exceeding wise:
25 The ants are a people not strong,
Yet they provide their food in the summer;
26 The conies are but a feeble folk,
Yet make they their houses in the rocks;
27 The locusts have no king,
Yet go they forth all of them by bands;
28 The lizard taketh hold with her hands,
Yet is she in kings' palaces.
29 There are three things which are stately in their march,
Yea, four which are stately in going:
30 The lion, which is mightiest among beasts,
And turneth not away for any;
31 The greyhound; the he-goat also;
And the king against whom there is no rising up.
32 If thou hast done foolishly in lifting up thyself,
Or if thou hast thought evil,
Lay thy hand upon thy mouth.
33 For the churning of milk bringeth forth butter,
And the wringing of the nose bringeth forth blood;
So the forcing of wrath bringeth forth strife.

Chapter 31

1 The words of king Lemuel; the oracle which his mother taught him.
2 What, my son? and what, O son of my womb?
And what, O son of my vows?
3 Give not thy strength unto women,
Nor thy ways to that which destroyeth kings.
4 It is not for kings, O Lemuel, it is not for kings to drink wine;
Nor for princes to say, Where is strong drink?
5 Lest they drink, and forget the law,
And pervert the justice due to any that is afflicted.
6 Give strong drink unto him that is ready to perish,
And wine unto the bitter in soul:
7 Let him drink, and forget his poverty,
And remember his misery no more.
8 Open thy mouth for the dumb,
In the cause of all such as are left desolate.
9 Open thy mouth, judge righteously,
And minister justice to the poor and needy.
10 A worthy woman who can find?
For her price is far above rubies.
11 The heart of her husband trusteth in her,
And he shall have no lack of gain.
12 She doeth him good and not evil
All the days of her life.
13 She seeketh wool and flax,
And worketh willingly with her hands.
14 She is like the merchant-ships;
She bringeth her bread from afar.
15 She riseth also while it is yet night,
And giveth food to her household,
And their task to her maidens.
16 She considereth a field, and buyeth it;
With the fruit of her hands she planteth a vineyard.
17 She girdeth her loins with strength,
And maketh strong her arms.
18 She perceiveth that her merchandise is profitable:
Her lamp goeth not out by night.
19 She layeth her hands to the distaff,
And her hands hold the spindle.
20 She stretcheth out her hand to the poor;
Yea, she reacheth forth her hands to the needy.
21 She is not afraid of the snow for her household;
For all her household are clothed with scarlet.
22 She maketh for herself carpets of tapestry;
Her clothing is fine linen and purple.
23 Her husband is known in the gates,
When he sitteth among the elders of the land.
24 She maketh linen garments and selleth them,
And delivereth girdles unto the merchant.
25 Strength and dignity are her clothing;
And she laugheth at the time to come.
26 She openeth her mouth with wisdom;

And the law of kindness is on her tongue.
27She looketh well to the ways of her household,
And eateth not the bread of idleness.
28Her children rise up, and call her blessed;
Her husband also, and he praiseth her, saying:
29Many daughters have done worthily,
But thou excellest them all.
30Grace is deceitful, and beauty is vain;
But a woman that feareth Yahweh, she shall be praised.
31Give her of the fruit of her hands;
And let her works praise her in the gates.

Ecclesiastes or, The Preacher

Chapter 1

1The words of the Preacher, the son of David, king in Jerusalem.
2Vanity of vanities, saith the Preacher; vanity of vanities, all is vanity.
3What profit hath man of all his labor wherein he laboreth under the sun?
4One generation goeth, and another generation cometh; but the earth abideth for ever.
5The sun also ariseth, and the sun goeth down, and hasteth to its place where it ariseth.
6The wind goeth toward the south, and turneth about unto the north; it turneth about continually in its course, and the wind returneth again to its circuits.
7All the rivers run into the sea, yet the sea is not full; unto the place whither the rivers go, thither they go again.
8All things are full of weariness; man cannot utter it: the eye is not satisfied with seeing, nor the ear filled with hearing.
9That which hath been is that which shall be; and that which hath been done is that which shall be done: and there is no new thing under the sun.
10Is there a thing whereof it may be said, See, this is new? it hath been long ago, in the ages which were before us.
11There is no remembrance of the former generations; neither shall there be any remembrance of the latter generations that are to come, among those that shall come after.
12I the Preacher was king over Israel in Jerusalem.
13And I applied my heart to seek and to search out by wisdom concerning all that is done under heaven: it is a sore travail that God hath given to the sons of men to be exercised therewith.
14I have seen all the works that are done under the sun; and, behold, all is vanity and a striving after wind.
15That which is crooked cannot be made straight; and that which is wanting cannot be numbered.
16I communed with mine own hear, saying, Lo, I have gotten me great wisdom above all that were before me in Jerusalem; yea, my heart hath had great experience of wisdom and knowledge.
17And I applied my heart to know wisdom, and to know madness and folly: I perceived that this also was a striving after wind.
18For in much wisdom is much grief; and he that increaseth knowledge increaseth sorrow.

Chapter 2

1I said in my heart, Come now, I will prove thee with mirth; therefore enjoy pleasure: and, behold, this also was vanity.
2I said of laughter, It is mad; and of mirth, What doeth it?
3I searched in my heart how to cheer my flesh with wine, my heart yet guiding me with wisdom, and how to lay hold on folly, till I might see what it was good for the sons of men that they should do under heaven all the days of their life.
4I made me great works; I builded me houses; I planted me vineyards;
5I made me gardens and parks, and I planted trees in them of all kinds of fruit;
6I made me pools of water, to water therefrom the forest where trees were reared;
7I bought men-servants and maid-servants, and had servants born in my house; also I had great possessions of herds and flocks, above all that were before me in Jerusalem;
8I gathered me also silver and gold, and the treasure of kings and of the provinces; I gat me men-singers and women-singers, and the delights of the sons of men, musical instruments, and that of all sorts.
9So I was great, and increased more than all that were before me in Jerusalem: also my wisdom remained with me.
10And whatsoever mine eyes desired I kept not from them; I withheld not my heart from any joy; for my heart rejoiced because of all my labor; and this was my portion from all my labor.
11Then I looked on all the works that my hands had wrought, and on the labor that I had labored to do; and, behold, all was vanity and a striving after wind, and there was no profit under the sun.
12And I turned myself to behold wisdom, and madness, and folly: for what can the man do that cometh after the king? even that which hath been done long ago.
13Then I saw that wisdom excelleth folly, as far as light excelleth darkness.
14The wise man's eyes are in his head, and the fool walketh in darkness: and yet I perceived that one event happeneth to them all.
15Then said I in my heart, As it happeneth to the fool, so will it happen even to me; and why was I then more wise? Then said I in my heart, that this also is vanity.
16For of the wise man, even as of the fool, there is no remembrance for ever; seeing that in the days to come all will have been long forgotten. And how doth the wise man die even as the fool!
17So I hated life, because the work that is wrought under the sun was grievous unto me; for all is vanity and a striving after wind.
18And I hated all my labor wherein I labored under the sun, seeing that I must leave it unto the man that shall be after me.
19And who knoweth whether he will be a wise man or a fool? yet will he have rule over all my labor wherein I have labored, and wherein I have showed myself wise under the sun. This also is vanity.
20Therefore I turned about to cause my heart to despair concerning all the labor wherein I had labored under the sun.
21For there is a man whose labor is with wisdom, and with knowledge, and with skilfulness; yet to a man that hath not labored therein shall he leave it for his portion. This also is vanity and a great evil.
22For what hath a man of all his labor, and of the striving of his heart, wherein he laboreth under the sun?
23For all his days are but sorrows, and his travail is grief; yea, even in the night his heart taketh no rest. This also is vanity.
24There is nothing better for a man than that he should eat and drink, and make his soul enjoy good in his labor. This also I saw, that it is from the hand of God.
25For who can eat, or who can have enjoyment, more than I?
26For to the man that pleaseth him God giveth wisdom, and knowledge, and joy; but to the sinner he giveth travail, to gather and to heap up, that he may give to him that pleaseth God. This also is vanity and a striving after wind.

Chapter 3

1For everything there is a season, and a time for very purpose under heaven:
2a time to be born, and a time to die; a time to plant, and a time to pluck up that which is planted;
3a time to kill, and a time to heal; a time to break down, and a time to build up;
4a time to weep, and a time to laugh; a time to mourn, and a time to dance;
5a time to cast away stones, and a time to gather stones together; a time to embrace, and a time to refrain from embracing;
6a time to seek, and a time to lose; a time to keep, and a time to cast away;
7a time to rend, and a time to sew; a time to keep silence, and a time to speak;
8a time to love, and a time to hate; a time for war, and a time for peace.
9What profit hath he that worketh in that wherein he laboreth?
10I have seen the travail which God hath given to the sons of men to be exercised therewith.
11He hath made everything beautiful in its time: also he hath set eternity in their heart, yet so that man cannot find out the work that God hath done from the beginning even to the end.
12I know that there is nothing better for them, than to rejoice, and to do good so long as they live.
13And also that every man should eat and drink, and enjoy good in all his labor, is the gift of God.
14I know that, whatsoever God doeth, it shall be for ever: nothing can be put to it, nor anything taken from it; and God hath done it, that men should fear before him.
15That which is hath been long ago; and that which is to be hath long ago been: and God seeketh again that which is passed away.
16And moreover I saw under the sun, in the place of justice, that wickedness was there; and in the place of righteousness, that wickedness was there.
17I said in my heart, God will judge the righteous and the wicked; for there is a time there for every purpose and for every work.
18I said in my heart, It is because of the sons of men, that God may prove them, and that they may see that they themselves are but as beasts.
19For that which befalleth the sons of men befalleth beasts; even one thing befalleth them: as the one dieth, so dieth the other; yea, they have all one breath; and man hath no preeminence above the beasts: for all is vanity.
20All go unto one place; all are of the dust, and all turn to dust again.
21Who knoweth the spirit of man, whether it goeth upward, and the spirit of the beast, whether it goeth downward to the earth?
22Wherefore I saw that there is nothing better, than that a man should rejoice in his works; for that is his portion: for who shall bring him back to see what shall be after him?

Chapter 4

1Then I returned and saw all the oppressions that are done under the sun: and, behold, the tears of such as were oppressed, and they had no comforter; and on the side of their oppressors there was power; but they had no comforter.
2Wherefore I praised the dead that have been long dead more than the living that are yet alive;
3yea, better than them both did I esteem him that hath not yet been, who hath not seen the evil work that is done under the sun.
4Then I saw all labor and every skilful work, that for this a man is envied of his neighbor. This also is vanity and a striving after wind.
5The fool foldeth his hands together, and eateth his own flesh.
6Better is a handful, with quietness, than two handfuls with labor and striving after wind.
7Then I returned and saw vanity under the sun.
8There is one that is alone, and he hath not a second; yea, he hath neither son nor brother; yet is there no end of all his labor, neither are his eyes satisfied with riches. For whom then, saith he, do I labor, and deprive my soul of good? This also is vanity, yea, it is a sore travail.
9Two are better than one, because they have a good reward for their labor.
10For if they fall, the one will lift up his fellow; but woe to him that is alone when he falleth, and hath not another to lift him up.
11Again, if two lie together, then they have warmth; but how can one be warm alone?
12And if a man prevail against him that is alone, two shall withstand him; and a threefold cord is not quickly broken.
13Better is a poor and wise youth than an old and foolish king, who

knoweth not how to receive admonition any more.

14For out of prison he came forth to be king; yea, even in his kingdom he was born poor.

15I saw all the living that walk under the sun, that they were with the youth, the second, that stood up in his stead.

16There was no end of all the people, even of all them over whom he was: yet they that come after shall not rejoice in him. Surely this also is vanity and a striving after wind.

Chapter 5

1Keep thy foot when thou goest to the house of God; for to draw nigh to hear is better than to give the sacrifice of fools: for they know not that they do evil.

2Be not rash with thy mouth, and let not thy heart be hasty to utter anything before God; for God is in heaven, and thou upon earth: therefore let thy words be few.

3For a dream cometh with a multitude of business, and a fool's voice with a multitude of words.

4When thou vowest a vow unto God, defer not to pay it; for he hath no pleasure in fools: pay that which thou vowest.

5Better is it that thou shouldest not vow, than that thou shouldest vow and not pay.

6Suffer not thy mouth to cause thy flesh to sin; neither say thou before the angel, that is was an error: wherefore should God be angry at thy voice, and destroy the work of thy hands?

7For in the multitude of dreams there are vanities, and in many words: but fear thou God.

8If thou seest the oppression of the poor, and the violent taking away of justice and righteousness in a province, marvel not at the matter: for one higher than the high regardeth; and there are higher than they.

9Moreover the profit of the earth is for all: the king himself is served by the field.

10He that loveth silver shall not be satisfied with silver; nor he that loveth abundance, with increase: this also is vanity.

11When goods increase, they are increased that eat them; and what advantage is there to the owner thereof, save the beholding of them with his eyes?

12The sleep of a laboring man is sweet, whether he eat little or much; but the fulness of the rich will not suffer him to sleep.

13There is a grievous evil which I have seen under the sun, namely, riches kept by the owner thereof to his hurt:

14and those riches perish by evil adventure; and if he hath begotten a son, there is nothing in his hand.

15As he came forth from his mother's womb, naked shall he go again as he came, and shall take nothing for his labor, which he may carry away in his hand.

16And this also is a grievous evil, that in all points as he came, so shall he go: and what profit hath he that laboreth for the wind?

17All his days also he eateth in darkness, and he is sore vexed, and hath sickness and wrath.

18Behold, that which I have seen to be good and to be comely is for one to eat and to drink, and to enjoy good in all his labor, wherein he laboreth under the sun, all the days of his life which God hath given him: for this is his portion.

19Every man also to whom God hath given riches and wealth, and hath given him power to eat thereof, and to take his portion, and to rejoice in his labor- this is the gift of God.

20For he shall not much remember the days of his life; because God answereth him in the joy of his heart.

Chapter 6

1There is an evil which I have seen under the sun, and it is heavy upon men:

2a man to whom God giveth riches, wealth, and honor, so that he lacketh nothing for his soul of all that he desireth, yet God giveth him not power to eat thereof, but an alien eateth it; this is vanity, and it is an evil disease.

3If a man beget a hundred children, and live many years, so that the days of his years are many, but his soul be not filled with good, and moreover he have no burial; I say, that an untimely birth is better than he:

4for it cometh in vanity, and departeth in darkness, and the name thereof is covered with darkness;

5moreover it hath not seen the sun nor known it; this hath rest rather than the other:

6yea, though he live a thousand years twice told, and yet enjoy no good, do not all go to one place?

7All the labor of man is for his mouth, and yet the appetite is not filled.

8For what advantage hath the wise more than the fool? or what hath the poor man, that knoweth how to walk before the living?

9Better is the sight of the eyes than the wandering of the desire: this also is vanity and a striving after wind.

10Whatsoever hath been, the name thereof was given long ago; and it is know what man is; neither can he contend with him that is mightier than he.

11Seeing there are many things that increase vanity, what is man the better?

12For who knoweth what is good for man in his life, all the days of his vain life which he spendeth as a shadow? for who can tell a man what shall be after him under the sun?

Chapter 7

1A good name is better than precious oil; and the day of death, than the day of one's birth.

2It is better to go to the house of mourning than to go to the house of feasting: for that is the end of all men; and the living will lay it to his heart.

3Sorrow is better than laughter; for by the sadness of the countenance the heart is made glad.

4The heart of the wise is in the house of mourning; but the heart of fools is in the house of mirth.

5It is better to hear the rebuke of the wise, than for a man to hear the song of fools.

6For as the crackling of thorns under a pot, so is the laughter of the fool: this also is vanity.

7Surely extortion maketh the wise man foolish; and a bribe destroyeth the understanding.

8Better is the end of a thing than the beginning thereof; and the patient in spirit is better than the proud in spirit.

9Be not hasty in thy spirit to be angry; for anger resteth in the bosom of fools.

10Say not thou, What is the cause that the former days were better than these? for thou dost not inquire wisely concerning this.

11Wisdom is as good as an inheritance; yea, more excellent is it for them that see the sun.

12For wisdom is a defence, even as money is a defence; but the excellency of knowledge is, that wisdom preserveth the life of him that hath it.

13Consider the work of God: for who can make that straight, which he hath made crooked?

14In the day of prosperity be joyful, and in the day of adversity consider; yea, God hath made the one side by side with the other, to the end that man should not find out anything that shall be after him.

15All this have I seen in my days of vanity: there is a righteous man that perisheth in his righteousness, and there is a wicked man that prolongeth his life in his evil-doing.

16Be not righteous overmuch; neither make thyself overwise: why shouldest thou destroy thyself?

17Be not overmuch wicked, neither be thou foolish: why shouldest thou die before thy time?

18It is good that thou shouldest take hold of this; yea, also from that withdraw not thy hand: for he that feareth God shall come forth from them all.

19Wisdom is a strength to the wise man more than ten rulers that are in a city.

20Surely there is not a righteous man upon earth, that doeth good, and sinneth not.

21Also take not heed unto all words that are spoken, lest thou hear thy servant curse thee;

22for oftentimes also thine own heart knoweth that thou thyself likewise hast cursed others.

23All this have I proved in wisdom: I said, I will be wise; but it was far from me.

24That which is, is far off and exceeding deep; who can find it out?

25I turned about, and my heart was set to know and to search out, and to seek wisdom and the reason of things, and to know that wickedness is folly, and that foolishness is madness.

26And I find more bitter than death the woman whose heart is snares and nets, and whose hands are bands: whoso pleaseth God shall escape from her; but the sinner shall be taken by her.

27Behold, this have I found, saith the Preacher, laying one thing to another, to find out the account;

28which my soul still seeketh, but I have not found: one man among a thousand have I found; but a woman among all those have I not found.

29Behold, this only have I found: that God made man upright; but they have sought out many inventions.

Chapter 8

1Who is as the wise man? and who knoweth the interpretation of a thing? A man's wisdom maketh his face to shine, and the hardness of his face is changed.

2I counsel thee, Keep the king's command, and that in regard of the oath of God.

3Be not hasty to go out of his presence; persist not in an evil thing: for he doeth whatsoever pleaseth him.

4For the king's word hath power; and who may say unto him, What doest thou?

5Whoso keepeth the commandment shall know no evil thing; and a wise man's heart discerneth time and judgment:

6for to every purpose there is a time and judgment; because the misery of man is great upon him:

7for he knoweth not that which shall be; for who can tell him how it shall be?

8There is no man that hath power over the spirit to retain the spirit; neither hath he power over the day of death; and there is no discharge in war: neither shall wickedness deliver him that is given to it.

9All this have I seen, and applied my heart unto every work that is done under the sun: there is a time wherein one man hath power over another to his hurt.

10So I saw the wicked buried, and they came to the grave; and they that had done right went away from the holy place, and were forgotten in the city: this also is vanity.

11Because sentence against an evil work is not executed speedily, therefore the heart of the sons of men is fully set in them to do evil.

12Though a sinner do evil a hundred times, and prolong his days, yet surely I know that it shall be well with them that fear God, that fear before him:

13but it shall not be well with the wicked, neither shall he prolong his days, which are as a shadow; because he feareth not before God.

14There is a vanity which is done upon the earth, that there are righteous men unto whom it happeneth according to the work of the wicked; again, there are wicked men to whom it happeneth according to the work of the righteous: I said that this also is vanity.

15Then I commended mirth, because a man hath no better thing under the sun, than to eat, and to drink, and to be joyful: for that shall abide with him in his labor all the days of his life which God hath given him under the sun.

16When I applied my heart to know wisdom, and to see the business that is done upon the earth (for also there is that neither day nor night seeth sleep with his eyes),

17then I beheld all the work of God, that man cannot find out the work that is done under the sun: because however much a man labor to seek it out, yet he shall not find it; yea moreover, though a wise man think to know it, yet shall he not be able to find it.

Chapter 9

1For all this I laid to my heart, even to explore all this: that the righteous, and the wise, and their works, are in the hand of God; whether it be love or hatred, man knoweth it not; all is before them.

2All things come alike to all: there is one event to the righteous and to the wicked; to the good and to the clean and to the unclean; to him that sacrificeth and to him that sacrificeth not; as is the good, so is the sinner; and he that sweareth, as he that feareth an oath.

3This is an evil in all that is done under the sun, that there is one event unto all: yea also, the heart of the sons of men is full of evil, and madness is in their heart while they live, and after that they go to the dead.

4For to him that is joined with all the living there is hope; for a living dog is better than a dead lion.

5For the living know that they shall die: but the dead know not anything, neither have they any more a reward; for the memory of them is forgotten.

6As well their love, as their hatred and their envy, is perished long ago; neither have they any more a portion for ever in anything that is done under the sun.

7Go thy way, eat thy bread with joy, and drink thy wine with a merry heart; for God hath already accepted thy works.

8Let thy garments be always white; and let not thy head lack oil.

9Live joyfully with the wife whom thou lovest all the days of thy life of vanity, which he hath given thee under the sun, all thy days of vanity: for that is thy portion in life, and in thy labor wherein thou laborest under the sun.

10Whatsoever thy hand findeth to do, do it with thy might; for there is no work, nor device, nor knowledge, nor wisdom, in Sheol, whither thou goest.

11I returned, and saw under the sun, that the race is not to the swift, nor the battle to the strong, neither yet bread to the wise, nor yet riches to men of understanding, nor yet favor to men of skill; but time and chance happeneth to them all.

12For man also knoweth not his time: as the fishes that are taken in an evil net, and as the birds that are caught in the snare, even so are the sons of men snared in an evil time, when it falleth suddenly upon them.

13I have also seen wisdom under the sun on this wise, and it seemed great unto me:

14There was a little city, and few men within it; and there came a great king against it, and besieged it, and built great bulwarks against it.

15Now there was found in it a poor wise man, and he by his wisdom delivered the city; yet no man remembered that same poor man.

16Then said I, Wisdom is better than strength: nevertheless the poor man's wisdom is despised, and his words are not heard.

17The words of the wise heard in quiet are better than the cry of him that ruleth among fools.

18Wisdom is better than weapons of war; but one sinner destroyeth much good.

Chapter 10

1Dead flies cause the oil of the perfumer to send forth an evil odor; so doth a little folly outweigh wisdom and honor.

2A wise man's heart is at his right hand; but a fool's heart at his left.

3Yea also, when the fool walketh by the way, his understanding faileth him, and he saith to every one that he is a fool.

4If the spirit of the ruler rise up against thee, leave not thy place; for gentleness allayeth great offences.

5There is an evil which I have seen under the sun, as it were an error which proceedeth from the ruler:

6folly is set in great dignity, and the rich sit in a low place.

7I have seen servants upon horses, and princes walking like servants upon the earth.

8He that diggeth a pit shall fall into it; and whoso breaketh through a wall, a serpent shall bite him.

9Whoso heweth out stones shall be hurt therewith; and he that cleaveth wood is endangered thereby.

10If the iron be blunt, and one do not whet the edge, then must he put to more strength: but wisdom is profitable to direct.

11If the serpent bite before it is charmed, then is there no advantage in the charmer.

12The words of a wise man's mouth are gracious; but the lips of a fool will swallow up himself.

13The beginning of the words of his mouth is foolishness; and the end of his talk is mischievous madness.

14A fool also multiplieth words: yet man knoweth not what shall be; and that which shall be after him, who can tell him?

15The labor of fools wearieth every one of them; for he knoweth not how to go to the city.

16Woe to thee, O land, when thy king is a child, and thy princes eat in the morning!

17Happy art thou, O land, when thy king is the son of nobles, and thy princes eat in due season, for strength, and not for drunkenness!

18By slothfulness the roof sinketh in; and through idleness of the hands the house leaketh.

19A feast is made for laughter, and wine maketh glad the life; and money answereth all things.

20Revile not the king, no, not in thy thought; and revile not the rich in thy bedchamber: for a bird of the heavens shall carry the voice, and that which hath wings shall tell the matter.

Chapter 11

1Cast thy bread upon the waters; for thou shalt find it after many days.

2Give a portion to seven, yea, even unto eight; for thou knowest not what evil shall be upon the earth.

3If the clouds be full of rain, they empty themselves upon the earth; and if a tree fall toward the south, or toward the north, in the place where the tree falleth, there shall it be.

4He that observeth the wind shall not sow; and he that regardeth the clouds shall not reap.

5As thou knowest not what is the way of the wind, nor how the bones do grow in the womb of her that is with child; even so thou knowest not the work of God who doeth all.

6In the morning sow thy seed, and in the evening withhold not thy hand; for thou knowest not which shall prosper, whether this or that, or whether they both shall be alike good.

7Truly the light is sweet, and a pleasant thing it is for the eyes to behold the sun.

8Yea, if a man live many years, let him rejoice in them all; but let him remember the days of darkness, for they shall be many. All that cometh is vanity.

9Rejoice, O young man, in thy youth, and let thy heart cheer thee in the days of thy youth, and walk in the ways of thy heart, and in the sight of thine eyes; but know thou, that for all these things God will bring thee into judgment.

10Therefore remove sorrow from thy heart, and put away evil from thy flesh; for youth and the dawn of life are vanity.

Chapter 12

1Remember also thy Creator in the days of thy youth, before the evil days come, and the years draw nigh, when thou shalt say, I have no pleasure in them;

2before the sun, and the light, and the moon, and the stars, are darkened, and the clouds return after the rain;

3in the day when the keepers of the house shall tremble, and the strong men shall bow themselves, and the grinders cease because they are few, and those that look out of the windows shall be darkened,

4and the doors shall be shut in the street; when the sound of the grinding is low, and one shall rise up at the voice of a bird, and all the daughters of music shall be brought low;

5yea, they shall be afraid of that which is high, and terrors shall be in the way; and the almond-tree shall blossom, and the grasshopper shall be a burden, and desire shall fail; because man goeth to his everlasting home, and the mourners go about the streets:

6before the silver cord is loosed, or the golden bowl is broken, or the pitcher is broken at the fountain, or the wheel broken at the cistern,

7and the dust returneth to the earth as it was, and the spirit returneth unto God who gave it.

8Vanity of vanities, saith the Preacher; all is vanity.

9And further, because the Preacher was wise, he still taught the people knowledge; yea, he pondered, and sought out, and set in order many proverbs.

10The Preacher sought to find out acceptable words, and that which was written uprightly, even words of truth.

11The words of the wise are as goads; and as nails well fastened are the words of the masters of assemblies, which are given from one shepherd.

12And furthermore, my son, be admonished: of making many books there is no end; and much study is a weariness of the flesh.

13This is the end of the matter; all hath been heard: fear God, and keep his commandments; for this is the whole duty of man.

14For God will bring every work into judgment, with every hidden thing, whether it be good, or whether it be evil.

The Song of Songs, Which is Solomon's

Chapter 1
1The Song of songs, which is Solomon's.
2Let him kiss me with the kisses of his mouth;
For thy love is better than wine.
3Thine oils have a goodly fragrance;
Thy name is as oil poured forth;
Therefore do the virgins love thee.
4Draw me; we will run after thee:
The king hath brought me into his chambers;
We will be glad and rejoice in thee;
We will make mention of thy love more than of wine:
Rightly do they love thee.
5I am black, but comely,
Oh ye daughters of Jerusalem,
As the tents of Kedar,
As the curtains of Solomon.
6Look not upon me, because I am swarthy,
Because the sun hath scorched me.
My mother's sons were incensed against me;
They made me keeper of the vineyards;
But mine own vineyard have I not kept.
7Tell me, O thou whom my soul loveth,
Where thou feedest thy flock,
Where thou makest it to rest at noon:
For why should I be as one that is veiled
Beside the flocks of thy companions?
8If thou know not, O thou fairest among women,
Go thy way forth by the footsteps of the flock,
And feed thy kids beside the shepherds' tents.
9I have compared thee, O my love,
To a steed in Pharaoh's chariots.
10Thy cheeks are comely with plaits of hair,
Thy neck with strings of jewels.
11We will make thee plaits of gold
With studs of silver.
12While the king sat at his table,
My spikenard sent forth its fragrance.
13My beloved is unto me as a bundle of myrrh,
That lieth betwixt my breasts.
14My beloved is unto me as a cluster of henna-flowers
In the vineyards of En-gedi.
15Behold, thou art fair, my love;
Behold thou art fair;
Thine eyes are as doves.
16Behold, thou art fair, my beloved, yea, pleasant:
Also our couch is green.
17The beams of our house are cedars,
And our rafters are firs.

Chapter 2
1I am a rose of Sharon,
A lily of the valleys.
2As a lily among thorns,
So is my love among the daughters.
3As the apple-tree among the trees of the wood,
So is my beloved among the sons.
I sat down under his shadow with great delight,
And his fruit was sweet to my taste.
4He brought me to the banqueting-house,
And his banner over me was love.
5Stay ye me with raisins, refresh me with apples;
For I am sick from love.
6His left hand is under my head,
And his right hand doth embrace me.
7I adjure you, O daughters of Jerusalem,
By the roes, or by the hinds of the field,
That ye stir not up, nor awake my love,
Until he please.
8The voice of my beloved! behold, he cometh,
Leaping upon the mountains,
Skipping upon the hills.
9My beloved is like a roe or a young hart:
Behold, he standeth behind our wall;
He looketh in at the windows;
He glanceth through the lattice.
10My beloved spake, and said unto me,
Rise up, my love, my fair one, and come away.
11For, lo, the winter is past;
The rain is over and gone;
12The flowers appear on the earth;
The time of the singing of birds is come,
And the voice of the turtle-dove is heard in our land;
13The fig-tree ripeneth her green figs,
And the vines are in blossom;
They give forth their fragrance.
Arise, my love, my fair one, and come away.
14O my dove, that art in the clefts of the rock,
In the covert of the steep place,
Let me see thy countenance,
Let me hear thy voice;
For sweet is thy voice, and thy countenance is comely.
15Take us the foxes, the little foxes,
That spoil the vineyards;
For our vineyards are in blossom.
16My beloved is mine, and I am his:
He feedeth his flock among the lilies.
17Until the day be cool, and the shadows flee away,
Turn, my beloved, and be thou like a roe or a young hart
Upon the mountains of Bether.

Chapter 3
1By night on my bed
I sought him whom my soul loveth:
I sought him, but I found him not.
2I said, I will rise now, and go about the city;
In the streets and in the broad ways
I will seek him whom my soul loveth:
I sought him, but I found him not.
3The watchmen that go about the city found me;
To whom I said, Saw ye him whom my soul loveth?
4It was but a little that I passed from them,
When I found him whom my soul loveth:
I held him, and would not let him go,
Until I had brought him into my mother's house,
And into the chamber of her that conceived me.
5I adjure you, O daughters of Jerusalem,
By the roes, or by the hinds of the field,
That ye stir not up, nor awake my love,
Until he please.
6Who is this that cometh up from the wilderness
Like pillars of smoke,
Perfumed with myrrh and frankincense,
With all powders of the merchant?
7Behold, it is the litter of Solomon;
Threescore mighty men are about it,
Of the mighty men of Israel.
8They all handle the sword, and are expert in war:
Every man hath his sword upon his thigh,
Because of fear in the night.
9King Solomon made himself a palanquin
Of the wood of Lebanon.
10He made the pillars thereof of silver,
The bottom thereof of gold, the seat of it of purple,
The midst thereof being paved with love,
From the daughters of Jerusalem.
11Go forth, O ye daughters of Zion, and behold king Solomon,
With the crown wherewith his mother hath crowned him
In the day of his espousals,
And in the day of the gladness of his heart.

Chapter 4
1Behold, thou art fair, my love; behold, thou art fair;
Thine eyes are as doves behind thy veil.
Thy hair is as a flock of goats,
That lie along the side of mount Gilead.
2Thy teeth are like a flock of ewes that are newly shorn,
Which are come up from the washing,
Whereof every one hath twins,
And none is bereaved among them.
3Thy lips are like a thread of scarlet,
And thy mouth is comely.
Thy temples are like a piece of a pomegranate
Behind thy veil.
4Thy neck is like the tower of David builded for an armory,
Whereon there hang a thousand bucklers,
All the shields of the mighty men.
5Thy two breasts are like two fawns
That are twins of a roe,
Which feed among the lilies.
6Until the day be cool, and the shadows flee away,
I will get me to the mountain of myrrh,
And to the hill of frankincense.
7Thou art all fair, my love;
And there is no spot in thee.
8Come with me from Lebanon, my bride,
With me from Lebanon:
Look from the top of Amana,
From the top of Senir and Hermon,
From the lions' dens,
From the mountains of the leopards.

9 Thou hast ravished my heart, my sister, my bride;
Thou hast ravished my heart with one of thine eyes,
With one chain of thy neck.
10 How fair is thy love, my sister, my bride!
How much better is thy love than wine!
And the fragrance of thine oils than all manner of spices!
11 Thy lips, O my bride, drop as the honeycomb:
Honey and milk are under thy tongue;
And the smell of thy garments is like the smell of Lebanon.
12 A garden shut up is my sister, my bride;
A spring shut up, a fountain sealed.
13 Thy shoots are an orchard of pomegranates, with precious fruits;
Henna with spikenard plants,
14 Spikenard and saffron,
Calamus and cinnamon, with all trees of frankincense;
Myrrh and aloes, with all the chief spices.
15 Thou art a fountain of gardens,
A well of living waters,
And flowing streams from Lebanon.
16 Awake, O north wind; and come, thou south;
Blow upon my garden, that the spices thereof may flow out.
Let my beloved come into his garden,
And eat his precious fruits.

Chapter 5

1 I am come into my garden, my sister, my bride:
I have gathered my myrrh with my spice;
I have eaten my honeycomb with my honey;
I have drunk my wine with my milk.
Eat, O friends;
Drink, yea, drink abundantly, O beloved.
2 I was asleep, but my heart waked:
It is the voice of my beloved that knocketh, saying,
Open to me, my sister, my love, my dove, my undefiled;
For my head is filled with dew,
My locks with the drops of the night.
3 I have put off my garment; how shall I put it on?
I have washed my feet; how shall I defile them?
4 My beloved put in his hand by the hole of the door,
And my heart was moved for him.
5 I rose up to open to my beloved;
And my hands droppeth with myrrh,
And my fingers with liquid myrrh,
Upon the handles of the bolt.
6 I opened to my beloved;
But my beloved had withdrawn himself, and was gone.
My soul had failed me when he spake:
I sought him, but I could not find him;
I called him, but he gave me no answer.
7 The watchmen that go about the city found me,
They smote me, they wounded me;
The keepers of the walls took away my mantle from me.
8 I adjure you, O daughters of Jerusalem,
If ye find my beloved,
That ye tell him, that I am sick from love.
9 What is thy beloved more than another beloved,
O thou fairest among women?
What is thy beloved more than another beloved,
That thou dost so adjure us?
10 My beloved is white and ruddy,
The chiefest among ten thousand.
11 His head is as the most fine gold;
His locks are bushy, and black as a raven.
12 His eyes are like doves beside the water-brooks,
Washed with milk, and fitly set.
13 His cheeks are as a bed of spices,
As banks of sweet herbs:
His lips are as lilies, dropping liquid myrrh.
14 His hands are as rings of gold set with beryl:
His body is as ivory work overlaid with sapphires.
15 His legs are as pillars of marble, set upon sockets of fine gold:
His aspect is like Lebanon, excellent as the cedars.
16 His mouth is most sweet;
Yea, he is altogether lovely.
This is my beloved, and this is my friend,
O daughters of Jerusalem.

Chapter 6

1 Whither is thy beloved gone,
O thou fairest among women?
Whither hath thy beloved turned him,
That we may seek him with thee?
2 My beloved is gone down to his garden,
To the beds of spices,
To feed in the gardens, and to gather lilies.
3 I am my beloved's, and my beloved is mine;
He feedeth his flock among the lilies.
4 Thou art fair, O my love, as Tirzah,
Comely as Jerusalem,
Terrible as an army with banners.
5 Turn away thine eyes from me,
For they have overcome me.
Thy hair is as a flock of goats,
That lie along the side of Gilead.
6 Thy teeth are like a flock of ewes,
Which are come up from the washing;
Whereof every one hath twins,
And none is bereaved among them.
7 Thy temples are like a piece of a pomegranate
Behind thy veil.
8 There are threescore queens, and fourscore concubines,
And virgins without number.
9 My dove, my undefiled, is but one;
She is the only one of her mother;
She is the choice one of her that bare her.
The daughters saw her, and called her blessed;
Yea, the queens and the concubines, and they praised her.
10 Who is she that looketh forth as the morning,
Fair as the moon,
Clear as the sun,
Terrible as an army with banners?
11 I went down into the garden of nuts,
To see the green plants of the valley,
To see whether the vine budded,
And the pomegranates were in flower.
12 Before I was aware, my soul set me
Among the chariots of my princely people.
13 Return, return, O Shulammite;
Return, return, that we may look upon thee.
Why will ye look upon the Shulammite,
As upon the dance of Mahanaim?

Chapter 7

1 How beautiful are thy feet in sandals, O prince's daughter!
Thy rounded thighs are like jewels,
The work of the hands of a skilful workman.
2 Thy body is like a round goblet,
Wherein no mingled wine is wanting:
Thy waist is like a heap of wheat
Set about with lilies.
3 Thy two breasts are like two fawns
That are twins of a roe.
4 Thy neck is like the tower of ivory;
Thine eyes as the pools in Heshbon,
By the gate of Bath-rabbim;
Thy nose is like the tower of Lebanon
Which looketh toward Damascus.
5 Thy head upon thee is like Carmel,
And the hair of thy head like purple;
The king is held captive in the tresses thereof.
6 How fair and how pleasant art thou,
O love, for delights!
7 This thy stature is like to a palm-tree,
And thy breasts to its clusters.
8 I said, I will climb up into the palm-tree,
I will take hold of the branches thereof:
Let thy breasts be as clusters of the vine,
And the smell of thy breath like apples,
9 And thy mouth like the best wine,
That goeth down smoothly for my beloved,
Gliding through the lips of those that are asleep.
10 I am my beloved's;
And his desire is toward me.
11 Come, my beloved, let us go forth into the field;
Let us lodge in the villages.
12 Let us get up early to the vineyards;
Let us see whether the vine hath budded,
And its blossom is open,
And the pomegranates are in flower:
There will I give thee my love.
13 The mandrakes give forth fragrance;
And at our doors are all manner of precious fruits, new and old,
Which I have laid up for thee, O my beloved.

Chapter 8

1 Oh that thou wert as my brother,
That sucked the breasts of my mother!
When I should find thee without, I would kiss thee;
Yea, and none would despise me.
2 I would lead thee, and bring thee into my mother's house,
Who would instruct me;
I would cause thee to drink of spiced wine,
Of the juice of my pomegranate.
3 His left hand should be under my head,
And his right hand should embrace me.
4 I adjure you, O daughters of Jerusalem,

That ye stir not up, nor awake my love,
Until he please.
5Who is this that cometh up from the wilderness,
Leaning upon her beloved?
Under the apple-tree I awakened thee:
There thy mother was in travail with thee,
There was she in travail that brought thee forth.
6Set me as a seal upon thy heart,
As a seal upon thine arm:
For love is strong as death;
Jealousy is cruel as Sheol;
The flashes thereof are flashes of fire,
A very flame of Yahweh.
7Many waters cannot quench love,
Neither can floods drown it:
If a man would give all the substance of his house for love,
He would utterly be contemned.
8We have a little sister,
And she hath no breasts:
What shall we do for our sister
In the day when she shall be spoken for?
9If she be a wall,
We will build upon her a turret of silver:
And if she be a door,
We will inclose her with boards of cedar.
10I am a wall, and my breasts like the towers thereof
Then was I in his eyes as one that found peace.
11Solomon had a vineyard at Baal-hamon;
He let out the vineyard unto keepers;
Every one for the fruit thereof was to bring a thousand pieces of silver.
12My vineyard, which is mine, is before me:
Thou, O Solomon, shalt have the thousand,
And those that keep the fruit thereof two hundred.
13Thou that dwellest in the gardens,
The companions hearken for thy voice:
Cause me to hear it.
14Make haste, my beloved,
And be thou like to a roe or to a young hart
Upon the mountains of spices.

Isaiah
The Book of the Prophet Isaiah

Chapter 1

1The vision of Isaiah the son of Amoz, which he saw concerning Judah and Jerusalem, in the days of Uzziah, Jotham, Ahaz, and Hezekiah, kings of Judah.

2Hear, O heavens, and give ear, O earth; for Yahweh hath spoken: I have nourished and brought up children, and they have rebelled against me.

3The ox knoweth his owner, and the ass his master's crib; but Israel doth not know, my people doth not consider.

4Ah sinful nation, a people laden with iniquity, a seed of evil-doers, children that deal corruptly! they have forsaken Yahweh, they have despised the Holy One of Israel, they are estranged and gone backward.

5Why will ye be still stricken, that ye revolt more and more? the whole head is sick, and the whole heart faint.

6From the sole of the foot even unto the head there is no soundness in it; but wounds, and bruises, and fresh stripes: they have not been closed, neither bound up, neither mollified with oil.

7Your country is desolate; your cities are burned with fire; your land, strangers devour it in your presence, and it is desolate, as overthrown by strangers.

8And the daughter of Zion is left as a booth in a vineyard, as a lodge in a garden of cucumbers, as a besieged city.

9Except Yahweh of hosts had left unto us a very small remnant, we should have been as Sodom, we should have been like unto Gomorrah.

10Hear the word of Yahweh, ye rulers of Sodom; give ear unto the law of our God, ye people of Gomorrah.

11What unto me is the multitude of your sacrifices? saith Yahweh: I have had enough of the burnt-offerings of rams, and the fat of fed beasts; and I delight not in the blood of bullocks, or of lambs, or of he-goats.

12When ye come to appear before me, who hath required this at your hand, to trample my courts?

13Bring no more vain oblations; incense is an abomination unto me; new moon and sabbath, the calling of assemblies,- I cannot away with iniquity and the solemn meeting.

14Your new moons and your appointed feasts my soul hateth; they are a trouble unto me; I am weary of bearing them.

15And when ye spread forth your hands, I will hide mine eyes from you; yea, when ye make many prayers, I will not hear: your hands are full of blood.

16Wash you, make you clean; put away the evil of your doings from before mine eyes; cease to do evil;

17learn to do well; seek justice, relieve the oppressed, judge the fatherless, plead for the widow.

18Come now, and let us reason together, saith Yahweh: though your sins be as scarlet, they shall be as white as snow; though they be red like crimson, they shall be as wool.

19If ye be willing and obedient, ye shall eat the good of the land:

20but if ye refuse and rebel, ye shall be devoured with the sword; for the mouth of Yahweh hath spoken it.

21How is the faithful city become a harlot! she that was full of justice! righteousness lodged in her, but now murderers.

22Thy silver is become dross, thy wine mixed with water.

23Thy princes are rebellious, and companions of thieves; every one loveth bribes, and followeth after rewards: they judge not the fatherless, neither doth the cause of the widow come unto them.

24Therefore saith the Lord, Yahweh of hosts, the Mighty One of Israel, Ah, I will ease me of mine adversaries, and avenge me of mine enemies;

25and I will turn my hand upon thee, and thoroughly purge away thy dross, and will take away all thy tin;

26and I will restore thy judges as at the first, and thy counsellors as at the beginning: afterward thou shalt be called The city of righteousness, a faithful town.

27Zion shall be redeemed with justice, and her converts with righteousness.

28But the destruction of transgressors and sinners shall be together, and they that forsake Yahweh shall be consumed.

29For they shall be ashamed of the oaks which ye have desired, and ye shall be confounded for the gardens that ye have chosen.

30For ye shall be as an oak whose leaf fadeth, and as a garden that hath no water.

31And the strong shall be as tow, and his work as a spark; and they shall both burn together, and none shall quench them.

Chapter 2

1The word that Isaiah the son of Amoz saw concerning Judah and Jerusalem.

2And it shall come to pass in the latter days, that the mountain of Yahweh's house shall be established on the top of the mountains, and shall be exalted above the hills; and all nations shall flow unto it.

3And many peoples shall go and say, Come ye, and let us go up to the mountain of Yahweh, to the house of the God of Jacob; and he will teach us of his ways, and we will walk in his paths: for out of Zion shall go forth the law, and the word of Yahweh from Jerusalem.

4And he will judge between the nations, and will decide concerning many peoples; and they shall beat their swords into plowshares, and their spears into pruning-hooks; nation shall not lift up sword against nation, neither shall they learn war any more.

5O house of Jacob, come ye, and let us walk in the light of Yahweh.

6For thou hast forsaken thy people the house of Jacob, because they are filled with customs from the east, and are soothsayers like the Philistines, and they strike hands with the children of foreigners.

7And their land is full of silver and gold, neither is there any end of their treasures; their land also is full of horses, neither is there any end of their chariots.

8Their land also is full of idols; they worship the work of their own hands, that which their own fingers have made.

9And the mean man is bowed down, and the great man is brought low: therefore forgive them not.

10Enter into the rock, and hide thee in the dust, from before the terror of Yahweh, and from the glory of his majesty.

11The lofty looks of man shall be brought low, and the haughtiness of men shall be bowed down, and Yahweh alone shall be exalted in that day.

12For there shall be a day of Yahweh of hosts upon all that is proud and haughty, and upon all that is lifted up; and it shall be brought low;

13and upon all the cedars of Lebanon, that are high and lifted up, and upon all the oaks of Bashan,

14and upon all the high mountains, and upon all the hills that are lifted up,

15and upon every lofty tower, and upon every fortified wall,

16and upon all the ships of Tarshish, and upon all pleasant imagery.

17And the loftiness of man shall be bowed down, and the haughtiness of men shall be brought low; and Yahweh alone shall be exalted in that day.

18And the idols shall utterly pass away.

19And men shall go into the caves of the rocks, and into the holes of the earth, from before the terror of Yahweh, and from the glory of his majesty, when he ariseth to shake mightily the earth.

20In that day men shall cast away their idols of silver, and their idols of gold, which have been made for them to worship, to the moles and to the bats;

21to go into the caverns of the rocks, and into the clefts of the ragged rocks, from before the terror of Yahweh, and from the glory of his majesty, when he ariseth to shake mightily the earth.

22Cease ye from man, whose breath is in his nostrils; for wherein is he to be accounted of?

Chapter 3

1For, behold, the Lord, Yahweh of hosts, doth take away from Jerusalem and from Judah stay and staff, the whole stay of bread, and the whole stay of water;

2the mighty man, and the man of war; the judge, and the prophet, and the diviner, and the elder;

3the captain of fifty, and the honorable man, and the counsellor, and the expert artificer, and the skilful enchanter.

4And I will give children to be their princes, and babes shall rule over them.

5And the people shall be oppressed, every one by another, and every one by his neighbor: the child shall behave himself proudly against the old man, and the base against the honorable.

6When a man shall take hold of his brother in the house of his father, saying, Thou hast clothing, be thou our ruler, and let this ruin be under thy hand;

7in that day shall he lift up his voice, saying, I will not be a healer; for in my house is neither bread nor clothing: ye shall not make me ruler of the people.

8For Jerusalem is ruined, and Judah is fallen; because their tongue and their doings are against Yahweh, to provoke the eyes of his glory.

9The show of their countenance doth witness against them; and they declare their sin as Sodom, they hide it not. Woe unto their soul! for they have done evil unto themselves.

10Say ye of the righteous, that it shall be well with him; for they shall eat the fruit of their doings.

11Woe unto the wicked! it shall be ill with him; for what his hands have done shall be done unto him.

12As for my people, children are their oppressors, and women rule over them. O my people, they that lead thee cause thee to err, and destroy the way of thy paths.

13Yahweh standeth up to contend, and standeth to judge the peoples.

14Yahweh will enter into judgment with the elders of his people, and the princes thereof: It is ye that have eaten up the vineyard; the spoil of the poor is in your houses:

15what mean ye that ye crush my people, and grind the face of the poor? saith the Lord, Yahweh of hosts.

16Moreover Yahweh said, Because the daughters of Zion are haughty, and walk with outstretched necks and wanton eyes, walking and mincing as they go, and making a tinkling with their feet;

17therefore the Lord will smite with a scab the crown of the head of the daughters of Zion, and Yahweh will lay bare their secret parts.

18In that day the Lord will take away the beauty of their anklets, and the cauls, and the crescents;

19the pendants, and the bracelets, and the mufflers;

20the headtires, and the ankle chains, and the sashes, and the perfume-boxes, and the amulets;

21the rings, and the nose-jewels;

22the festival robes, and the mantles, and the shawls, and the satchels;

23the hand-mirrors, and the fine linen, and the turbans, and the veils.

24And it shall come to pass, that instead of sweet spices there shall be rottenness; and instead of a girdle, a rope; and instead of well set hair, baldness; and instead of a robe, a girding of sackcloth; branding instead of beauty.

25Thy men shall fall by the sword, and thy mighty in the war.

26And her gates shall lament and mourn; and she shall be desolate and sit upon the ground.

Chapter 4

1And seven women shall take hold of one man in that day, saying, We will eat our own bread, and wear our own apparel: only let us be called by thy name; take thou away our reproach.

2In that day shall the branch of Yahweh be beautiful and glorious, and the fruit of the land shall be excellent and comely for them that are escaped of Israel.

3And it shall come to pass, that he that is left in Zion, and he that remaineth in Jerusalem, shall be called holy, even every one that is written among the living in Jerusalem;

4when the Lord shall have washed away the filth of the daughters of Zion, and shall have purged the blood of Jerusalem from the midst thereof, by the spirit of justice, and by the spirit of burning.

5And Yahweh will create over the whole habitation of mount Zion, and over her assemblies, a cloud and smoke by day, and the shining of a flaming fire by night; for over all the glory shall be spread a covering.

6And there shall be a pavilion for a shade in the day-time from the heat, and for a refuge and for a covert from storm and from rain.

Chapter 5

1Let me sing for my wellbeloved a song of my beloved touching his vineyard. My wellbeloved had a vineyard in a very fruitful hill:

2and he digged it, and gathered out the stones thereof, and planted it with the choicest vine, and built a tower in the midst of it, and also hewed out a winepress therein: and he looked that it should bring forth grapes, and it brought forth wild grapes.

3And now, O inhabitants of Jerusalem and men of Judah, judge, I pray you, betwixt me and my vineyard.

4What could have been done more to my vineyard, that I have not done in it? wherefore, when I looked that it should bring forth grapes, brought it forth wild grapes?

5And now I will tell you what I will do to my vineyard: I will take away the hedge thereof, and it shall be eaten up; I will break down the wall thereof, and it shall be trodden down:

6and I will lay it waste; it shall not be pruned nor hoed; but there shall come up briers and thorns: I will also command the clouds that they rain no rain upon it.

7For the vineyard of Yahweh of hosts is the house of Israel, and the men of Judah his pleasant plant: and he looked for justice, but, behold, oppression; for righteousness, but, behold, a cry.

8Woe unto them that join house to house, that lay field to field, till there be no room, and ye be made to dwell alone in the midst of the land!

9In mine ears saith Yahweh of hosts, Of a truth many houses shall be desolate, even great and fair, without inhabitant.

10For ten acres of vineyard shall yield one bath, and a homer of seed shall yield but an ephah.

11Woe unto them that rise up early in the morning, that they may follow strong drink; that tarry late into the night, till wine inflame them!

12And the harp and the lute, the tabret and the pipe, and wine, are in their feasts; but they regard not the work of Yahweh, neither have they considered the operation of his hands.

13Therefore my people are gone into captivity for lack of knowledge; and their honorable men are famished, and their multitude are parched with thirst.

14Therefore Sheol hath enlarged its desire, and opened its mouth without measure; and their glory, and their multitude, and their pomp, and he that rejoiceth among them, descend into it.

15And the mean man is bowed down, and the great man is humbled, and the eyes of the lofty are humbled:

16but Yahweh of hosts is exalted in justice, and God the Holy One is sanctified in righteousness.

17Then shall the lambs feed as in their pasture, and the waste places of the fat ones shall wanderers eat.

18Woe unto them that draw iniquity with cords of falsehood, and sin as it were with a cart rope;

19that say, Let him make speed, let him hasten his work, that we may see it; and let the counsel of the Holy One of Israel draw nigh and come, that we may know it!

20Woe unto them that call evil good, and good evil; that put darkness for light, and light for darkness; that put bitter for sweet, and sweet for bitter!

21Woe unto them that are wise in their own eyes, and prudent in their own sight!

22Woe unto them that are mighty to drink wine, and men of strength to mingle strong drink;

23that justify the wicked for a bribe, and take away the righteousness of the righteous from him!

24Therefore as the tongue of fire devoureth the stubble, and as the dry grass sinketh down in the flame, so their root shall be as rottenness, and their blossom shall go up as dust; because they have rejected the law of Yahweh of hosts, and despised the word of the Holy One of Israel.

25Therefore is the anger of Yahweh kindled against his people, and he hath stretched forth his hand against them, and hath smitten them; and the mountains tremble, and their dead bodies are as refuse in the midst of the streets. For all this his anger is not turned away, but his hand is stretched out still.

26And he will lift up an ensign to the nations from far, and will hiss for them from the end of the earth; and, behold, they shall come with speed swiftly.

27None shall be weary nor stumble among them; none shall slumber nor sleep; neither shall the girdle of their loins be loosed, nor the latchet of their shoes be broken:

28whose arrows are sharp, and all their bows bent; their horses' hoofs shall be accounted as flint, and their wheels as a whirlwind:

29their roaring shall be like a lioness, they shall roar like young lions; yea, they shall roar, and lay hold of the prey, and carry it away safe, and there shall be none to deliver.

30And they shall roar against them in that day like the roaring of the sea: and if one look unto the land, behold, darkness and distress; and the light is darkened in the clouds thereof.

Chapter 6

1In the year that king Uzziah died I saw the Lord sitting upon a throne, high and lifted up; and his train filled the temple.

2Above him stood the seraphim: each one had six wings; with twain he covered his face, and with twain he covered his feet, and with twain he did fly.

3And one cried unto another, and said, Holy, holy, holy, is Yahweh of hosts: the whole earth is full of his glory.

4And the foundations of the thresholds shook at the voice of him that cried, and the house was filled with smoke.

5Then said I, Woe is me! for I am undone; because I am a man of unclean lips, and I dwell in the midst of a people of unclean lips: for mine eyes have seen the King, Yahweh of hosts.

6Then flew one of the seraphim unto me, having a live coal in his hand, which he had taken with the tongs from off the altar:

7and he touched my mouth with it, and said, Lo, this hath touched thy lips; and thine iniquity is taken away, and thy sin forgiven.

8And I heard the voice of the Lord, saying, Whom shall I send, and who will go for us? Then I said, Here am I; send me.

9And he said, Go, and tell this people, Hear ye indeed, but understand not; and see ye indeed, but perceive not.

10Make the heart of this people fat, and make their ears heavy, and shut their eyes; lest they see with their eyes, and hear with their ears, and understand with their heart, and turn again, and be healed.

11Then said I, Lord, how long? And he answered, Until cities be waste without inhabitant, and houses without man, and the land become utterly waste,

12and Yahweh have removed men far away, and the forsaken places be many in the midst of the land.

13And if there be yet a tenth in it, it also shall in turn be eaten up: as a terebinth, and as an oak, whose stock remaineth, when they are felled; so the holy seed is the stock thereof.

Chapter 7

1And it came to pass in the days of Ahaz the son of Jotham, the son of Uzziah, king of Judah, that Rezin the king of Syria, and Pekah the son of Remaliah, king of Israel, went up to Jerusalem to war against it, but could not prevail against it.

2And it was told the house of David, saying, Syria is confederate with Ephraim. And his heart trembled, and the heart of his people, as the trees of the forest tremble with the wind.

3Then said Yahweh unto Isaiah, Go forth now to meet Ahaz, thou, and Shear-jashub thy son, at the end of the conduit of the upper pool, in the highway of the fuller's field;

4and say unto him, Take heed, and be quiet; fear not, neither let thy heart be faint, because of these two tails of smoking firebrands, for the fierce anger of Rezin and Syria, and of the son of Remaliah.

5Because Syria, Ephraim, and the son of Remaliah, have purposed evil against thee, saying,

6Let us go up against Judah, and vex it, and let us make a breach therein for us, and set up a king in the midst of it, even the son of Tabeel;

7thus saith the Lord Yahweh, It shall not stand, neither shall it come to pass.

8For the head of Syria is Damascus, and the head of Damascus is Rezin; and within threescore and five years shall Ephraim be broken in pieces, so that is shall not be a people:

9and the head of Ephraim is Samaria, and the head of Samaria is Remaliah's son. If ye will not believe, surely ye shall not be established.

10And Yahweh spake again unto Ahaz, saying,

11Ask thee a sign of Yahweh thy God; ask it either in the depth, or in the height above.

12But Ahaz said, I will not ask, neither will I tempt Yahweh.

13And he said, Hear ye now, O house of David; Is it a small thing for you to weary men, that ye will weary my God also?

14Therefore the Lord himself will give you a sign: behold, a virgin shall conceive, and bear a son, and shall call his name Immanuel.

15Butter and honey shall he eat, when he knoweth to refuse the evil, and choose the good.

16For before the child shall know to refuse the evil, and choose the good, the land whose two kings thou abhorrest shall be forsaken.

17Yahweh will bring upon thee, and upon thy people, and upon thy father's house, days that have not come, from the day that Ephraim departed from Judah-even the king of Assyria.

18And it shall come to pass in that day, that Yahweh will hiss for the fly that is in the uttermost part of the rivers of Egypt, and for the bee that is in the land of Assyria.

19And they shall come, and shall rest all of them in the desolate valleys, and in the clefts of the rocks, and upon all thorn-hedges, and upon all pastures.

20In that day will the Lord shave with a razor that is hired in the parts beyond the River, even with the king of Assyria, the head and the hair of the feet; and it shall also consume the beard.

21And it shall come to pass in that day, that a man shall keep alive a young cow, and two sheep;

22and it shall come to pass, that because of the abundance of milk which

Isaiah

they shall give he shall eat butter: for butter and honey shall every one eat that is left in the midst of the land.

23And it shall come to pass in that day, that every place, where there were a thousand vines at a thousand silverlings, shall be for briers and thorns.

24With arrows and with bow shall one come thither, because all the land shall be briers and thorns.

25And all the hills that were digged with the mattock, thou shalt not come thither for fear of briers and thorns; but it shall be for the sending forth of oxen, and for the treading of sheep.

Chapter 8

1And Yahweh said unto me, Take thee a great tablet, and write upon it with the pen of a man, For Maher-shalal-hash-baz;

2and I will take unto me faithful witnesses to record, Uriah the priest, and Zechariah the son of Jeberechiah.

3And I went unto the prophetess; and she conceived, and bare a son. Then said Yahweh unto me, Call his name Maher-shalal-hash-baz.

4For before the child shall have knowledge to cry, My father, and, My mother, the riches of Damascus and the spoil of Samaria shall be carried away before the king of Assyria.

5And Yahweh spake unto me yet again, saying,

6Forasmuch as this people have refused the waters of Shiloah that go softly, and rejoice in Rezin and Remaliah's son;

7now therefore, behold, the Lord bringeth up upon them the waters of the River, strong and many, even the king of Assyria and all his glory: and it shall come up over all its channels, and go over all its banks;

8and it shall sweep onward into Judah; it shall overflow and pass through; it shall reach even to the neck; and the stretching out of its wings shall fill the breadth of thy land, O Immanuel.

9Make an uproar, O ye peoples, and be broken in pieces; and give ear, all ye of far countries: gird yourselves, and be broken in pieces; gird yourselves, and be broken in pieces.

10Take counsel together, and it shall be brought to nought; speak the word, and it shall not stand: for God is with us.

11For Yahweh spake thus to me with a strong hand, and instructed me not to walk in the way of this people, saying,

12Say ye not, A conspiracy, concerning all whereof this people shall say, A conspiracy; neither fear ye their fear, nor be in dread thereof.

13Yahweh of hosts, him shall ye sanctify; and let him be your fear, and let him be your dread.

14And he shall be for a sanctuary; but for a stone of stumbling and for a rock of offence to both the houses of Israel, for a gin and for a snare to the inhabitants of Jerusalem.

15And many shall stumble thereon, and fall, and be broken, and be snared, and be taken.

16Bind thou up the testimony, seal the law among my disciples.

17And I will wait for Yahweh, that hideth his face from the house of Jacob, and I will look for him.

18Behold, I and the children whom Yahweh hath given me are for signs and for wonders in Israel from Yahweh of hosts, who dwelleth in mount Zion.

19And when they shall say unto you, Seek unto them that have familiar spirits and unto the wizards, that chirp and that mutter: should not a people seek unto their God? on behalf of the living should they seek unto the dead?

20To the law and to the testimony! if they speak not according to this word, surely there is no morning for them.

21And they shall pass through it, sore distressed and hungry; and it shall come to pass that, when they shall be hungry, they shall fret themselves, and curse by their king and by their God, and turn their faces upward:

22and they shall look unto the earth, and behold, distress and darkness, the gloom of anguish; and into thick darkness they shall be driven away.

Chapter 9

1But there shall be no gloom to her that was in anguish. In the former time he brought into contempt the land of Zebulun and the land of Naphtali; but in the latter time hath he made it glorious, by the way of the sea, beyond the Jordan, Galilee of the nations.

2The people that walked in darkness have seen a great light: they that dwelt in the land of the shadow of death, upon them hath the light shined.

3Thou hast multiplied the nation, thou hast increased their joy: they joy before thee according to the joy in harvest, as men rejoice when they divide the spoil.

4For the yoke of his burden, and the staff of his shoulder, the rod of his oppressor, thou hast broken as in the day of Midian.

5For all the armor of the armed man in the tumult, and the garments rolled in blood, shall be for burning, for fuel of fire.

6For unto us a child is born, unto us a son is given; and the government shall be upon his shoulder: and his name shall be called Wonderful, Counsellor, Mighty God, Everlasting Father, Prince of Peace.

7Of the increase of his government and of peace there shall be no end, upon the throne of David, and upon his kingdom, to establish it, and to uphold it with justice and with righteousness from henceforth even for ever. The zeal of Yahweh of hosts will perform this.

8The Lord sent a word into Jacob, and it hath lighted upon Israel.

9And all the people shall know, even Ephraim and the inhabitant of Samaria, that say in pride and in stoutness of heart,

10The bricks are fallen, but we will build with hewn stone; the sycomores are cut down, but we will put cedars in their place.

11Therefore Yahweh will set up on high against him the adversaries of Rezin, and will stir up his enemies,

12the Syrians before, and the Philistines behind; and they shall devour Israel with open mouth. For all this his anger is not turned away, but his hand is stretched out still.

13Yet the people have not turned unto him that smote them, neither have they sought Yahweh of hosts.

14Therefore Yahweh will cut off from Israel head and tail, palm-branch and rush, in one day.

15The elder and the honorable man, he is the head; and the prophet that teacheth lies, he is the tail.

16For they that lead this people cause them to err; and they that are led of them are destroyed.

17Therefore the Lord will not rejoice over their young men, neither will he have compassion on their fatherless and widows; for every one is profane and an evil-doer, and every mouth speaketh folly. For all this his anger is not turned away, but his hand is stretched out still.

18For wickedness burneth as the fire; it devoureth the briers and thorns; yea, it kindleth in the thickets of the forest, and they roll upward in a column of smoke.

19Through the wrath of Yahweh of hosts is the land burnt up; and the people are as the fuel of fire: no man spareth his brother.

20And one shall snatch on the right hand, and be hungry; and he shall eat on the left hand, and they shall not be satisfied: they shall eat every man the flesh of his own arm:

21Manasseh, Ephraim; and Ephraim, Manasseh; and they together shall be against Judah. For all this his anger is not turned away, but his hand is stretched out still.

Chapter 10

1Woe unto them that decree unrighteous decrees, and to the writers that write perverseness;

2to turn aside the needy from justice, and to rob the poor of my people of their right, that widows may be their spoil, and that they may make the fatherless their prey!

3And what will ye do in the day of visitation, and in the desolation which shall come from far? to whom will ye flee for help? and where will ye leave your glory?

4They shall only bow down under the prisoners, and shall fall under the slain. For all this his anger is not turned away, but his hand is stretched out still.

5Ho Assyrian, the rod of mine anger, the staff in whose hand is mine indignation!

6I will send him against a profane nation, and against the people of my wrath will I give him a charge, to take the spoil, and to take the prey, and to tread them down like the mire of the streets.

7Howbeit he meaneth not so, neither doth his heart think so; but it is in his heart to destroy, and to cut off nations not a few.

8For he saith, Are not my princes all of them kings?

9Is not Calno as Carchemish? is not Hamath as Arpad? is not Samaria as Damascus?

10As my hand hath found the kingdoms of the idols, whose graven images did excel them of Jerusalem and of Samaria;

11shall I not, as I have done unto Samaria and her idols, so do to Jerusalem and her idols?

12Wherefore it shall come to pass, that, when the Lord hath performed his whole work upon mount Zion and on Jerusalem, I will punish the fruit of the stout heart of the king of Assyria, and the glory of his high looks.

13For he hath said, By the strength of my hand I have done it, and by my wisdom; for I have understanding: and I have removed the bounds of the peoples, and have robbed their treasures, and like a valiant man I have brought down them that sit on thrones:

14and my hand hath found as a nest the riches of the peoples; and as one gathereth eggs that are forsaken, have I gathered all the earth: and there was none that moved the wing, or that opened the mouth, or chirped.

15Shall the axe boast itself against him that heweth therewith? shall the saw magnify itself against him that wieldeth it? as if a rod should wield them that lift it up, or as if a staff should lift up him that is not wood.

16Therefore will the Lord, Yahweh of hosts, send among his fat ones leanness; and under his glory there shall be kindled a burning like the burning of fire.

17And the light of Israel will be for a fire, and his Holy One for a flame; and it will burn and devour his thorns and his briers in one day.

18And he will consume the glory of his forest, and of his fruitful field, both soul and body: and it shall be as when a standard-bearer fainteth.

19And the remnant of the trees of his forest shall be few, so that a child may write them.

20And it shall come to pass in that day, that the remnant of Israel, and they that are escaped of the house of Jacob, shall no more again lean upon him that smote them, but shall lean upon Yahweh, the Holy One of Israel, in truth.

21A remnant shall return, even the remnant of Jacob, unto the mighty God.

22For though thy people, Israel, be as the sand of the sea, only a remnant of them shall return: a destruction is determined, overflowing with righteousness.

23For a full end, and that determined, will the Lord, Yahweh of hosts, make in the midst of all the earth.

24Therefore thus saith the Lord, Yahweh of hosts, O my people that dwellest in Zion, be not afraid of the Assyrian, though he smite thee with the rod, and lift up his staff against thee, after the manner of Egypt.

25For yet a very little while, and the indignation against thee shall be accomplished, and mine anger shall be directed to his destruction.

26And Yahweh of hosts will stir up against him a scourge, as in the slaughter of Midian at the rock of Oreb: and his rod will be over the sea, and he will lift it up after the manner of Egypt.

27And it shall come to pass in that day, that his burden shall depart from off thy shoulder, and his yoke from off thy neck, and the yoke shall be destroyed by reason of fatness.

28He is come to Aiath, he is passed through Migron; at Michmash he layeth up his baggage;

29they are gone over the pass; they have taken up their lodging at Geba; Ramah trembleth; Gibeah of Saul is fled.

30Cry aloud with thy voice, O daughter of Gallim! hearken, O Laishah! O thou poor Anathoth!

31Madmenah is a fugitive; the inhabitants of Gebim flee for safety.

32This very day shall he halt at Nob: he shaketh his hand at the mount of the daughter of Zion, the hill of Jerusalem.

33Behold, the Lord, Yahweh of hosts, will lop the boughs with terror: and the high of stature shall be hewn down, and the lofty shall be brought low.

34And he will cut down the thickets of the forest with iron, and Lebanon shall fall by a mighty one.

Chapter 11

1And there shall come forth a shoot out of the stock of Jesse, and a branch out of his roots shall bear fruit.

2And the Spirit of Yahweh shall rest upon him, the spirit of wisdom and understanding, the spirit of counsel and might, the spirit of knowledge and of the fear of Yahweh.

3And his delight shall be in the fear of Yahweh; and he shall not judge after the sight of his eyes, neither decide after the hearing of his ears;

4but with righteousness shall he judge the poor, and decide with equity for the meek of the earth; and he shall smite the earth with the rod of his mouth; and with the breath of his lips shall he slay the wicked.

5And righteousness shall be the girdle of his waist, and faithfulness the girdle of his loins.

6And the wolf shall dwell with the lamb, and the leopard shall lie down with the kid; and the calf and the young lion and the fatling together; and a little child shall lead them.

7And the cow and the bear shall feed; their young ones shall lie down together; and the lion shall eat straw like the ox.

8And the sucking child shall play on the hole of the asp, and the weaned child shall put his hand on the adder's den.

9They shall not hurt nor destroy in all my holy mountain; for the earth shall be full of the knowledge of Yahweh, as the waters cover the sea.

10And it shall come to pass in that day, that the root of Jesse, that standeth for an ensign of the peoples, unto him shall the nations seek; and his resting-place shall be glorious.

11And it shall come to pass in that day, that the Lord will set his hand again the second time to recover the remnant of his people, that shall remain, from Assyria, and from Egypt, and from Pathros, and from Cush, and from Elam, and from Shinar, and from Hamath, and from the islands of the sea.

12And he will set up an ensign for the nations, and will assemble the outcasts of Israel, and gather together the dispersed of Judah from the four corners of the earth.

13The envy also of Ephraim shall depart, and they that vex Judah shall be cut off: Ephraim shall not envy Judah, and Judah shall not vex Ephraim.

14And they shall fly down upon the shoulder of the Philistines on the west; together shall they despoil the children of the east: they shall put forth their hand upon Edom and Moab; and the children of Ammon shall obey them.

15And Yahweh will utterly destroy the tongue of the Egyptian sea; and with his scorching wind will he wave his hand over the River, and will smite it into seven streams, and cause men to march over dryshod.

16And there shall be a highway for the remnant of his people, that shall remain, from Assyria; like as there was for Israel in the day that he came up out of the land of Egypt.

Chapter 12

1And in that day thou shalt say, I will give thanks unto thee, O Yahweh; for though thou wast angry with me, thine anger is turned away and thou comfortest me.

2Behold, God is my salvation; I will trust, and will not be afraid; for Yahweh, even Yahweh, is my strength and song; and he is become my salvation.

3Therefore with joy shall ye draw water out of the wells of salvation.

4And in that day shall ye say, Give thanks unto Yahweh, call upon his name, declare his doings among the peoples, make mention that his name is exalted.

5Sing unto Yahweh; for he hath done excellent things: let this be known in all the earth.

6Cry aloud and shout, thou inhabitant of Zion; for great in the midst of thee is the Holy One of Israel.

Chapter 13

1The burden of Babylon, which Isaiah the son of Amoz did see.

2Set ye up an ensign upon the bare mountain, lift up the voice unto them, wave the hand, that they may go into the gates of the nobles.

3I have commanded my consecrated ones, yea, I have called my mighty men for mine anger, even my proudly exulting ones.

4The noise of a multitude in the mountains, as of a great people! the noise of a tumult of the kingdoms of the nations gathered together! Yahweh of hosts is mustering the host for the battle.

5They come from a far country, from the uttermost part of heaven, even Yahweh, and the weapons of his indignation, to destroy the whole land.

6Wail ye; for the day of Yahweh is at hand; as destruction from the Almighty shall it come.

7Therefore shall all hands be feeble, and every heart of man shall melt:

8and they shall be dismayed; pangs and sorrows shall take hold of them; they shall be in pain as a woman in travail: they shall look in amazement one at another; their faces shall be faces of flame.

9Behold, the day of Yahweh cometh, cruel, with wrath and fierce anger; to make the land a desolation, and to destroy the sinners thereof out of it.

10For the stars of heaven and the constellations thereof shall not give their light; the sun shall be darkened in its going forth, and the moon shall not cause its light to shine.

11And I will punish the world for their evil, and the wicked for their iniquity: and I will cause the arrogancy of the proud to cease, and will lay low the haughtiness of the terrible.

12I will make a man more rare than fine gold, even a man than the pure gold of Ophir.

13Therefore I will make the heavens to tremble, and the earth shall be shaken out of its place, in the wrath of Yahweh of hosts, and in the day of his fierce anger.

14And it shall come to pass, that as the chased roe, and as sheep that no man gathereth, they shall turn every man to his own people, and shall flee every man to his own land.

15Every one that is found shall be thrust through; and every one that is taken shall fall by the sword.

16Their infants also shall be dashed in pieces before their eyes; their houses shall be rifled, and their wives ravished.

17Behold, I will stir up the Medes against them, who shall not regard silver, and as for gold, they shall not delight in it.

18And their bows shall dash the young men in pieces; and they shall have no pity on the fruit of the womb; their eye shall not spare children.

19And Babylon, the glory of kingdoms, the beauty of the Chaldeans' pride, shall be as when God overthrew Sodom and Gomorrah.

20It shall never be inhabited, neither shall it be dwelt in from generation to generation: neither shall the Arabian pitch tent there; neither shall shepherds make their flocks to lie down there.

21But wild beasts of the desert shall lie there; and their houses shall be full of doleful creatures; and ostriches shall dwell there, and wild goats shall dance there.

22And wolves shall cry in their castles, and jackals in the pleasant palaces: and her time is near to come, and her days shall not be prolonged.

Chapter 14

1For Yahweh will have compassion on Jacob, and will yet choose Israel, and set them in their own land: and the sojourner shall join himself with them, and they shall cleave to the house of Jacob.

2And the peoples shall take them, and bring them to their place; and the house of Israel shall possess them in the land of Yahweh for servants and for handmaids: and they shall take them captive whose captives they were; and they shall rule over their oppressors.

3And it shall come to pass in the day that Yahweh shall give thee rest from thy sorrow, and from thy trouble, and from the hard service wherein thou wast made to serve,

4that thou shalt take up this parable against the king of Babylon, and say, How hath the oppressor ceased! the golden city ceased!

5Yahweh hath broken the staff of the wicked, the sceptre of the rulers;

6that smote the peoples in wrath with a continual stroke, that ruled the nations in anger, with a persecution that none restrained.

7The whole earth is at rest, and is quiet: they break forth into singing.

8Yea, the fir-trees rejoice at thee, and the cedars of Lebanon, saying, Since thou art laid low, no hewer is come up against us.

9Sheol from beneath is moved for thee to meet thee at thy coming; it stirreth up the dead for thee, even all the chief ones of the earth; it hath raised up from their thrones all the kings of the nations.

10All they shall answer and say unto thee, Art thou also become weak as we? art thou become like unto us?

11Thy pomp is brought down to Sheol, and the noise of thy viols: the worm is spread under thee, and worms cover thee.

12How art thou fallen from heaven, O day-star, son of the morning! how art thou cut down to the ground, that didst lay low the nations!

13And thou saidst in thy heart, I will ascend into heaven, I will exalt my throne above the stars of God; and I will sit upon the mount of congregation, in the uttermost parts of the north;

14I will ascend above the heights of the clouds; I will make myself like the Most High.

15Yet thou shalt be brought down to Sheol, to the uttermost parts of the pit.

16They that see thee shall gaze at thee, they shall consider thee, saying, Is this the man that made the earth to tremble, that did shake kingdoms;

17that made the world as a wilderness, and overthrew the cities thereof; that let not loose his prisoners to their home?

18All the kings of the nations, all of them, sleep in glory, every one in his own house.

19But thou art cast forth away from thy sepulchre like an abominable branch, clothed with the slain, that are thrust through with the sword, that go down to the stones of the pit; as a dead body trodden under foot.

20Thou shalt not be joined with them in burial, because thou hast destroyed thy land, thou hast slain thy people; the seed of evil-doers shall not be named for ever.

21Prepare ye slaughter for his children for the iniquity of their fathers, that they rise not up, and possess the earth, and fill the face of the world with cities.

Isaiah

22And I will rise up against them, saith Yahweh of hosts, and cut off from Babylon name and remnant, and son and son's son, saith Yahweh.

23I will also make it a possession for the porcupine, and pools of water: and I will sweep it with the besom of destruction, saith Yahweh of hosts.

24Yahweh of hosts hath sworn, saying, Surely, as I have thought, so shall it come to pass; and as I have purposed, so shall it stand:

25that I will break the Assyrian in my land, and upon my mountains tread him under foot: then shall his yoke depart from off them, and his burden depart from off their shoulder.

26This is the purpose that is purposed upon the whole earth; and this is the hand that is stretched out upon all the nations.

27For Yahweh of hosts hath purposed, and who shall annul it? and his hand is stretched out, and who shall turn it back?

28In the year that king Ahaz died was this burden.

29Rejoice not, O Philistia, all of thee, because the rod that smote thee is broken; for out of the serpent's root shall come forth an adder, and his fruit shall be a fiery flying serpent.

30And the first-born of the poor shall feed, and the needy shall lie down in safety; and I will kill thy root with famine, and thy remnant shall be slain.

31Howl, O gate; cry, O city; thou art melted away, O Philistia, all of thee; for there cometh a smoke out of the north, and there is no straggler in his ranks.

32What then shall one answer the messengers of the nation? That Yahweh hath founded Zion, and in her shall the afflicted of his people take refuge.

Chapter 15

1The burden of Moab. For in a night Ar of Moab is laid waste, and brought to nought; for in a night Kir of Moab is laid waste, and brought to nought.

2They are gone up to Bayith, and to Dibon, to the high places, to weep: Moab waileth over Nebo, and over Medeba; on all their heads is baldness, every beard is cut off.

3In their streets they gird themselves with sackcloth; on their housetops, and in their broad places, every one waileth, weeping abundantly.

4And Heshbon crieth out, and Elealeh; their voice is heard even unto Jahaz: therefore the armed men of Moab cry aloud; his soul trembleth within him.

5My heart crieth out for Moab; her nobles flee unto Zoar, to Eglath-shelishi-yah: for by the ascent of Luhith with weeping they go up; for in the way of Horonaim they raise up a cry of destruction.

6For the waters of Nimrim shall be desolate; for the grass is withered away, the tender grass faileth, there is no green thing.

7Therefore the abundance they have gotten, and that which they have laid up, shall they carry away over the brook of the willows.

8For the cry is gone round about the borders of Moab; the wailing thereof unto Eglaim, and the wailing thereof unto Beer-elim.

9For the waters of Dimon are full of blood; for I will bring yet more upon Dimon, a lion upon them of Moab that escape, and upon the remnant of the land.

Chapter 16

1Send ye the lambs for the ruler of the land from Selah to the wilderness, unto the mount of the daughter of Zion.

2For it shall be that, as wandering birds, as a scattered nest, so shall the daughters of Moab be at the fords of the Arnon.

3Give counsel, execute justice; make thy shade as the night in the midst of the noonday; hide the outcasts; betray not the fugitive.

4Let mine outcasts dwell with thee; as for Moab, be thou a covert to him from the face of the destroyer. For the extortioner is brought to nought, destruction ceaseth, the oppressors are consumed out of the land.

5And a throne shall be established in lovingkindness; and one shall sit thereon in truth, in the tent of David, judging, and seeking justice, and swift to do righteousness.

6We have heard of the pride of Moab, that he is very proud; even of his arrogancy, and his pride, and his wrath; his boastings are nought.

7Therefore shall Moab wail for Moab, every one shall wail: for the raisin-cakes of Kir-hareseth shall ye mourn, utterly stricken.

8For the fields of Heshbon languish, and the vine of Sibmah; the lords of the nations have broken down the choice branches thereof, which reached even unto Jazer, which wandered into the wilderness; its shoots were spread abroad, they passed over the sea.

9Therefore I will weep with the weeping of Jazer for the vine of Sibmah; I will water thee with my tears, O Heshbon, and Elealeh: for upon thy summer fruits and upon thy harvest the battle shout is fallen.

10And gladness is taken away, and joy out of the fruitful field; and in the vineyards there shall be no singing, neither joyful noise: no treader shall tread out wine in the presses; I have made the vintage shout to cease.

11Wherefore my heart soundeth like a harp for Moab, and mine inward parts for Kir-heres.

12And it shall come to pass, when Moab presenteth himself, when he wearieth himself upon the high place, and shall come to his sanctuary to pray, that he shall not prevail.

13This is the word that Yahweh spake concerning Moab in time past.

14But now Yahweh hath spoken, saying, Within three years, as the years of a hireling, the glory of Moab shall be brought into contempt, with all his great multitude; and the remnant shall be very small and of no account.

Chapter 17

1The burden of Damascus. Behold, Damascus is taken away from being a city, and it shall be a ruinous heap.

2The cities of Aroer are forsaken; they shall be for flocks, which shall lie down, and none shall make them afraid.

3And the fortress shall cease from Ephraim, and the kingdom from Damascus, and the remnant of Syria; they shall be as the glory of the children of Israel, saith Yahweh of hosts.

4And it shall come to pass in that day, that the glory of Jacob shall be made thin, and the fatness of his flesh shall wax lean.

5And it shall be as when the harvestman gathereth the standing grain, and his arm reapeth the ears; yea, it shall be as when one gleaneth ears in the valley of Rephaim.

6Yet there shall be left therein gleanings, as the shaking of an olive-tree, two or three berries in the top of the uppermost bough, four or five in the outmost branches of a fruitful tree, saith Yahweh, the God of Israel.

7In that day shall men look unto their Maker, and their eyes shall have respect to the Holy One of Israel.

8And they shall not look to the altars, the work of their hands; neither shall they have respect to that which their fingers have made, either the Asherim, or the sun-images.

9In that day shall their strong cities be as the forsaken places in the wood and on the mountain top, which were forsaken from before the children of Israel; and it shall be a desolation.

10For thou hast forgotten the God of thy salvation, and hast not been mindful of the rock of thy strength; therefore thou plantest pleasant plants, and settest it with strange slips.

11In the day of thy planting thou hedgest it in, and in the morning thou makest thy seed to blossom; but the harvest fleeth away in the day of grief and of desperate sorrow.

12Ah, the uproar of many peoples, that roar like the roaring of the seas; and the rushing of nations, that rush like the rushing of mighty waters!

13The nations shall rush like the rushing of many waters: but he shall rebuke them, and they shall flee far off, and shall be chased as the chaff of the mountains before the wind, and like the whirling dust before the storm.

14At eventide, behold, terror; and before the morning they are not. This is the portion of them that despoil us, and the lot of them that rob us.

Chapter 18

1Ah, the land of the rustling of wings, which is beyond the rivers of Ethiopia;

2that sendeth ambassadors by the sea, and in vessels of papyrus upon the waters, saying, Go, ye swift messengers, to a nation tall and smooth, to a people terrible from their beginning onward, a nation that meteth out and treadeth down, whose land the rivers divide!

3All ye inhabitants of the world, and ye dwellers on the earth, when an ensign is lifted up on the mountains, see ye; and when the trumpet is blown, hear ye.

4For thus hath Yahweh said unto me, I will be still, and I will behold in my dwelling-place, like clear heat in sunshine, like a cloud of dew in the heat of harvest.

5For before the harvest, when the blossom is over, and the flower becometh a ripening grape, he will cut off the sprigs with pruning-hooks, and the spreading branches will he take away and cut down.

6They shall be left together unto the ravenous birds of the mountains, and to the beasts of the earth; and the ravenous birds shall summer upon them, and all the beasts of the earth shall winter upon them.

7In that time shall a present be brought unto Yahweh of hosts from a people tall and smooth, even from a people terrible from their beginning onward, a nation that meteth out and treadeth down, whose land the rivers divide, to the place of the name of Yahweh of hosts, the mount Zion.

Chapter 19

1The burden of Egypt. Behold, Yahweh rideth upon a swift cloud, and cometh unto Egypt: and the idols of Egypt shall tremble at his presence; and the heart of Egypt shall melt in the midst of it.

2And I will stir up the Egyptians against the Egyptians: and they shall fight every one against his brother, and every one against his neighbor; city against city, and kingdom against kingdom.

3And the spirit of Egypt shall fail in the midst of it; and I will destroy the counsel thereof: and they shall seek unto the idols, and to the charmers, and to them that have familiar spirits, and to the wizards.

4And I will give over the Egyptians into the hand of a cruel lord; and a fierce king shall rule over them, saith the Lord, Yahweh of hosts.

5And the waters shall fail from the sea, and the river shall be wasted and become dry.

6And the rivers shall become foul; the streams of Egypt shall be diminished and dried up; the reeds and flags shall wither away.

7The meadows by the Nile, by the brink of the Nile, and all the sown fields of the Nile, shall become dry, be driven away, and be no more.

8And the fishers shall lament, and all they that cast angle into the Nile shall mourn, and they that spread nets upon the waters shall languish.

9Moreover they that work in combed flax, and they that weave white cloth, shall be confounded.

10And the pillars of Egypt shall be broken in pieces; all they that work for hire shall be grieved in soul.

11The princes of Zoan are utterly foolish; the counsel of the wisest counsellors of Pharaoh is become brutish: how say ye unto Pharaoh, I am the son of the wise, the son of ancient kings?

¹²Where then are thy wise men? and let them tell thee now; and let them know what Yahweh of hosts hath purposed concerning Egypt.

¹³The princes of Zoan are become fools, the princes of Memphis are deceived; they have caused Egypt to go astray, that are the corner-stone of her tribes.

¹⁴Yahweh hath mingled a spirit of perverseness in the midst of her; and they have caused Egypt to go astray in every work thereof, as a drunken man staggereth in his vomit.

¹⁵Neither shall there be for Egypt any work, which head or tail, palm-branch or rush, may do.

¹⁶In that day shall the Egyptians be like unto women; and they shall tremble and fear because of the shaking of the hand of Yahweh of hosts, which he shaketh over them.

¹⁷And the land of Judah shall become a terror unto Egypt; every one to whom mention is made thereof shall be afraid, because of the purpose of Yahweh of hosts, which he purposeth against it.

¹⁸In that day there shall be five cities in the land of Egypt that speak the language of Canaan, and swear to Yahweh of hosts; one shall be called The city of destruction.

¹⁹In that day shall there be an altar to Yahweh in the midst of the land of Egypt, and a pillar at the border thereof to Yahweh.

²⁰And it shall be for a sign and for a witness unto Yahweh of hosts in the land of Egypt; for they shall cry unto Yahweh because of oppressors, and he will send them a saviour, and a defender, and he will deliver them.

²¹And Yahweh shall be known to Egypt, and the Egyptians shall know Yahweh in that day; yea, they shall worship with sacrifice and oblation, and shall vow a vow unto Yahweh, and shall perform it.

²²And Yahweh will smite Egypt, smiting and healing; and they shall return unto Yahweh, and he will be entreated of them, and will heal them.

²³In that day shall there be a highway out of Egypt to Assyria, and the Assyrian shall come into Egypt, and the Egyptian into Assyria; and the Egyptians shall worship with the Assyrians.

²⁴In that day shall Israel be the third with Egypt and with Assyria, a blessing in the midst of the earth;

²⁵for that Yahweh of hosts hath blessed them, saying, Blessed be Egypt my people, and Assyria the work of my hands, and Israel mine inheritance.

Chapter 20

¹In the year that Tartan came unto Ashdod, when Sargon the king of Assyria sent him, and he fought against Ashdod and took it;

²at that time Yahweh spake by Isaiah the son of Amoz, saying, Go, and loose the sackcloth from off thy loins, and put thy shoe from off thy foot. And he did so, walking naked and barefoot.

³And Yahweh said, Like as my servant Isaiah hath walked naked and barefoot three years for a sign and a wonder concerning Egypt and concerning Ethiopia;

⁴so shall the king of Assyria lead away the captives of Egypt, and the exiles of Ethiopia, young and old, naked and barefoot, and with buttocks uncovered, to the shame of Egypt.

⁵And they shall be dismayed and confounded, because of Ethiopia their expectation, and of Egypt their glory.

⁶And the inhabitant of this coast-land shall say in that day, Behold, such is our expectation, whither we fled for help to be delivered from the king of Assyria: and we, how shall we escape?

Chapter 21

¹The burden of the wilderness of the sea. As whirlwinds in the South sweep through, it cometh from the wilderness, from a terrible land.

²A grievous vision is declared unto me; the treacherous man dealeth treacherously, and the destroyer destroyeth. Go up, O Elam; besiege, O Media; all the sighing thereof have I made to cease.

³Therefore are my loins filled with anguish; pangs have taken hold upon me, as the pangs of a woman in travail: I am pained so that I cannot hear; I am dismayed so that I cannot see.

⁴My heart fluttereth, horror hath affrighted me; the twilight that I desired hath been turned into trembling unto me.

⁵They prepare the table, they set the watch, they eat, they drink: rise up, ye princes, anoint the shield.

⁶For thus hath the Lord said unto me, Go, set a watchman: let him declare what he seeth:

⁷and when he seeth a troop, horsemen in pairs, a troop of asses, a troop of camels, he shall hearken diligently with much heed.

⁸And he cried as a lion: O Lord, I stand continually upon the watch-tower in the day-time, and am set in my ward whole nights;

⁹and, behold, here cometh a troop of men, horsemen in pairs. And he answered and said, Fallen, fallen is Babylon; and all the graven images of her gods are broken unto the ground.

¹⁰O thou my threshing, and the grain of my floor! that which I have heard from Yahweh of hosts, the God of Israel, have I declared unto you.

¹¹The burden of Dumah. One calleth unto me out of Seir, Watchman, what of the night? Watchman, what of the night?

¹²The watchman said, The morning cometh, and also the night: if ye will inquire, inquire ye: turn ye, come.

¹³The burden upon Arabia. In the forest in Arabia shall ye lodge, O ye caravans of Dedanites.

¹⁴Unto him that was thirsty they brought water; the inhabitants of the land of Tema did meet the fugitives with their bread.

¹⁵For they fled away from the swords, from the drawn sword, and from the bent bow, and from the grievousness of war.

¹⁶For thus hath the Lord said unto me, Within a year, according to the years of a hireling, all the glory of Kedar shall fail;

¹⁷and the residue of the number of the archers, the mighty men of the children of Kedar, shall be few; for Yahweh, the God of Israel, hath spoken it.

Chapter 22

¹The burden of the valley of vision. What aileth thee now, that thou art wholly gone up to the housetops?

²O thou that art full of shoutings, a tumultuous city, a joyous town; thy slain are not slain with the sword, neither are they dead in battle.

³All thy rulers fled away together, they were bound by the archers; all that were found of thee were bound together; they fled afar off.

⁴Therefore said I, Look away from me, I will weep bitterly; labor not to comfort me for the destruction of the daughter of my people.

⁵For it is a day of discomfiture, and of treading down, and of perplexity, from the Lord, Yahweh of hosts, in the valley of vision; a breaking down of the walls, and a crying to the mountains.

⁶And Elam bare the quiver, with chariots of men and horsemen; and Kir uncovered the shield.

⁷And it came to pass, that thy choicest valleys were full of chariots, and the horsemen set themselves in array at the gate.

⁸And he took away the covering of Judah; and thou didst look in that day to the armor in the house of the forest.

⁹And ye saw the breaches of the city of David, that they were many; and ye gathered together the waters of the lower pool;

¹⁰and ye numbered the houses of Jerusalem, and ye brake down the houses to fortify the wall;

¹¹ye made also a reservoir between the two walls for the water of the old pool. But ye looked not unto him that had done this, neither had ye respect unto him that purposed it long ago.

¹²And in that day did the Lord, Yahweh of hosts, call to weeping, and to mourning, and to baldness, and to girding with sackcloth:

¹³and behold, joy and gladness, slaying oxen and killing sheep, eating flesh and drinking wine: let us eat and drink, for to-morrow we shall die.

¹⁴And Yahweh of hosts revealed himself in mine ears, Surely this iniquity shall not be forgiven you till ye die, saith the Lord, Yahweh of hosts.

¹⁵Thus saith the Lord, Yahweh of hosts, Go, get thee unto this treasurer, even unto Shebna, who is over the house, and say,

¹⁶What doest thou here? and whom has thou here, that thou hast hewed thee out here a sepulchre? hewing him out a sepulchre on high, graving a habitation for himself in the rock!

¹⁷Behold, Yahweh, like a strong man, will hurl thee away violently; yea, he will wrap thee up closely.

¹⁸He will surely wind thee round and round, and toss thee like a ball into a large country; there shalt thou die, and there shall be the chariots of thy glory, thou shame of thy lord's house.

¹⁹And I will thrust thee from thine office; and from thy station shalt thou be pulled down.

²⁰And it shall come to pass in that day, that I will call my servant Eliakim the son of Hilkiah:

²¹and I will cloth him with thy robe, and strengthen him with thy girdle, and I will commit thy government into his hand; and he shall be a father to the inhabitants of Jerusalem, and to the house of Judah.

²²And the key of the house of David will I lay upon his shoulder; and he shall open, and none shall shut; and he shall shut, and none shall open.

²³And I will fasten him as a nail in a sure place; and he shall be for a throne of glory to his father's house.

²⁴And they shall hang upon him all the glory of his father's house, the offspring and the issue, every small vessel, from the cups even to all the flagons.

²⁵In that day, saith Yahweh of hosts, shall the nail that was fastened in a sure place give way; and it shall be hewn down, and fall; and the burden that was upon it shall be cut off; for Yahweh hath spoken it.

Chapter 23

¹The burden of Tyre. Howl, ye ships of Tarshish; for it is laid waste, so that there is no house, no entering in: from the land of Kittim it is revealed to them.

²Be still, ye inhabitants of the coast, thou whom the merchants of Sidon, that pass over the sea, have replenished.

³And on great waters the seed of the Shihor, the harvest of the Nile, was her revenue; and she was the mart of nations.

⁴Be thou ashamed, O Sidon; for the sea hath spoken, the stronghold of the sea, saying, I have not travailed, nor brought forth, neither have I nourished young men, nor brought up virgins.

⁵When the report cometh to Egypt, they shall be sorely pained at the report of Tyre.

⁶Pass ye over to Tarshish; wail, ye inhabitants of the coast.

⁷Is this your joyous city, whose antiquity is of ancient days, whose feet carried her afar off to sojourn?

⁸Who hath purposed this against Tyre, the bestower of crowns, whose merchants are princes, whose traffickers are the honorable of the earth?

⁹Yahweh of hosts hath purposed it, to stain the pride of all glory, to bring into contempt all the honorable of the earth.

¹⁰Pass through thy land as the Nile, O daughter of Tarshish; there is no restraint any more.

¹¹He hath stretched out his hand over the sea, he hath shaken the kingdoms: Yahweh hath given commandment concerning Canaan, to destroy the strongholds

Isaiah

thereof.

12And he said, Thou shalt no more rejoice, O thou oppressed virgin daughter of Sidon: arise, pass over to Kittim; even there shalt thou have no rest.

13Behold, the land of the Chaldeans: this people was not; the Assyrian founded it for them that dwell in the wilderness; they set up their towers; they overthrew the palaces thereof; they made it a ruin.

14Howl, ye ships of Tarshish; for your stronghold is laid waste.

15And it shall come to pass in that day, that Tyre shall be forgotten seventy years, according to the days of one king: after the end of seventy years it shall be unto Tyre as in the song of the harlot.

16Take a harp, go about the city, thou harlot that hast been forgotten; make sweet melody, sing many songs, that thou mayest be remembered.

17And it shall come to pass after the end of seventy years, that Yahweh will visit Tyre, and she shall return to her hire, and shall play the harlot with all the kingdoms of the world upon the face of the earth.

18And her merchandise and her hire shall be holiness to Yahweh: it shall not be treasured nor laid up; for her merchandise shall be for them that dwell before Yahweh, to eat sufficiently, and for durable clothing.

Chapter 24

1Behold, Yahweh maketh the earth empty, and maketh it waste, and turneth it upside down, and scattereth abroad the inhabitants thereof.

2And it shall be, as with the people, so with the priest; as with the servant, so with his master; as with the maid, so with her mistress; as with the buyer, so with the seller; as with the creditor, so with the debtor; as with the taker of interest, so with the giver of interest to him.

3The earth shall be utterly emptied, and utterly laid waste; for Yahweh hath spoken this word.

4The earth mourneth and fadeth away, the world languisheth and fadeth away, the lofty people of the earth do languish.

5The earth also is polluted under the inhabitants thereof; because they have transgressed the laws, violated the statutes, broken the everlasting covenant.

6Therefore hath the curse devoured the earth, and they that dwell therein are found guilty: therefore the inhabitants of the earth are burned, and few men left.

7The new wine mourneth, the vine languisheth, all the merry-hearted do sigh.

8The mirth of tabrets ceaseth, the noise of them that rejoice endeth, the joy of the harp ceaseth.

9They shall not drink wine with a song; strong drink shall be bitter to them that drink it.

10The waste city is broken down; every house is shut up, that no man may come in.

11There is a crying in the streets because of the wine; all joy is darkened, the mirth of the land is gone.

12In the city is left desolation, and the gate is smitten with destruction.

13For thus shall it be in the midst of the earth among the peoples, as the shaking of an olive-tree, as the gleanings when the vintage is done.

14These shall lift up their voice, they shall shout; for the majesty of Yahweh they cry aloud from the sea.

15Wherefore glorify ye Yahweh in the east, even the name of Yahweh, the God of Israel, in the isles of the sea.

16From the uttermost part of the earth have we heard songs: Glory to the righteous. But I said, I pine away, I pine away, woe is me! the treacherous have dealt treacherously; yea, the treacherous have dealt very treacherously.

17Fear, and the pit, and the snare, are upon thee, O inhabitant of the earth.

18And it shall come to pass, that he who fleeth from the noise of the fear shall fall into the pit; and he that cometh up out of the midst of the pit shall be taken in the snare: for the windows on high are opened, and the foundations of the earth tremble.

19The earth is utterly broken, the earth is rent asunder, the earth is shaken violently.

20The earth shall stagger like a drunken man, and shall sway to and fro like a hammock; and the transgression thereof shall be heavy upon it, and it shall fall, and not rise again.

21And it shall come to pass in that day, that Yahweh will punish the host of the high ones on high, and the kings of the earth upon the earth.

22And they shall be gathered together, as prisoners are gathered in the pit, and shall be shut up in the prison; and after many days shall they be visited.

23Then the moon shall be confounded, and the sun ashamed; for Yahweh of hosts will reign in mount Zion, and in Jerusalem; and before his elders shall be glory.

Chapter 25

1O Yahweh, thou art my God; I will exalt thee, I will praise thy name; for thou hast done wonderful things, even counsels of old, in faithfulness and truth.

2For thou hast made of a city a heap, of a fortified city a ruin, a palace of strangers to be no city; it shall never be built.

3Therefore shall a strong people glorify thee; a city of terrible nations shall fear thee.

4For thou hast been a stronghold to the poor, a stronghold to the needy in his distress, a refuge from the storm, a shade from the heat, when the blast of the terrible ones is as a storm against the wall.

5As the heat in a dry place wilt thou bring down the noise of strangers; as the heat by the shade of a cloud, the song of the terrible ones shall be brought low.

6And in this mountain will Yahweh of hosts make unto all peoples a feast of fat things, a feast of wines on the lees, of fat things full of marrow, of wines on the lees well refined.

7And he will destroy in this mountain the face of the covering that covereth all peoples, and the veil that is spread over all nations.

8He hath swallowed up death for ever; and the Lord Yahweh will wipe away tears from off all faces; and the reproach of his people will he take away from off all the earth: for Yahweh hath spoken it.

9And it shall be said in that day, Lo, this is our God; we have waited for him, and he will save us: this is Yahweh; we have waited for him, we will be glad and rejoice in his salvation.

10For in this mountain will the hand of Yahweh rest; and Moab shall be trodden down in his place, even as straw is trodden down in the water of the dung-hill.

11And he shall spread forth his hands in the midst thereof, as he that swimmeth spreadeth forth his hands to swim; but Yahweh will lay low his pride together with the craft of his hands.

12And the high fortress of thy walls hath he brought down, laid low, and brought to the ground, even to the dust.

Chapter 26

1In that day shall this song be sung in the land of Judah: we have a strong city; salvation will he appoint for walls and bulwarks.

2Open ye the gates, that the righteous nation which keepeth faith may enter in.

3Thou wilt keep him in perfect peace, whose mind is stayed on thee; because he trusteth in thee.

4Trust ye in Yahweh for ever; for in Yahweh, even Yahweh, is an everlasting rock.

5For he hath brought down them that dwell on high, the lofty city: he layeth it low, he layeth it low even to the ground; he bringeth it even to the dust.

6The foot shall tread it down; even the feet of the poor, and the steps of the needy.

7The way of the just is uprightness: thou that art upright dost direct the path of the just.

8Yea, in the way of thy judgments, O Yahweh, have we waited for thee; to thy name, even to thy memorial name, is the desire of our soul.

9With my soul have I desired thee in the night; yea, with my spirit within me will I seek thee earnestly: for when thy judgments are in the earth, the inhabitants of the world learn righteousness.

10Let favor be showed to the wicked, yet will he not learn righteousness; in the land of uprightness will he deal wrongfully, and will not behold the majesty of Yahweh.

11Yahweh, thy hand is lifted up, yet they see not: but they shall see thy zeal for the people, and be put to shame; yea, fire shall devour thine adversaries.

12Yahweh, thou wilt ordain peace for us; for thou hast also wrought all our works for us.

13O Yahweh our God, other lords besides thee have had dominion over us; but by thee only will we make mention of thy name.

14They are dead, they shall not live; they are deceased, they shall not rise: therefore hast thou visited and destroyed them, and made all remembrance of them to perish.

15Thou hast increased the nation, O Yahweh, thou hast increased the nation; thou art glorified; thou hast enlarged all the borders of the land.

16Yahweh, in trouble have they visited thee; they poured out a prayer when thy chastening was upon them.

17Like as a woman with child, that draweth near the time of her delivery, is in pain and crieth out in her pangs; so we have been before thee, O Yahweh.

18We have been with child, we have been in pain, we have as it were brought forth wind; we have not wrought any deliverance in the earth; neither have the inhabitants of the world fallen.

19Thy dead shall live; my dead bodies shall arise. Awake and sing, ye that dwell in the dust; for thy dew is as the dew of herbs, and the earth shall cast forth the dead.

20Come, my people, enter thou into thy chambers, and shut thy doors about thee: hide thyself for a little moment, until the indignation be overpast.

21For, behold, Yahweh cometh forth out of his place to punish the inhabitants of the earth for their iniquity: the earth also shall disclose her blood, and shall no more cover her slain.

Chapter 27

1In that day Yahweh with his hard and great and strong sword will punish leviathan the swift serpent, and leviathan the crooked serpent; and he will slay the monster that is in the sea.

2In that day: A vineyard of wine, sing ye unto it.

3I Yahweh am its keeper; I will water it every moment: lest any hurt it, I will keep it night and day.

4Wrath is not in me: would that the briers and thorns were against me in battle! I would march upon them, I would burn them together.

5Or else let him take hold of my strength, that he may make peace with me; yea, let him make peace with me.

6In days to come shall Jacob take root; Israel shall blossom and bud; and they shall fill the face of the world with fruit.

7Hath he smitten them as he smote those that smote them? or are they slain according to the slaughter of them that were slain by them?

8In measure, when thou sendest them away, thou dost contend with them; he hath removed them with his rough blast in the day of the east wind.

9Therefore by this shall the iniquity of Jacob be forgiven, and this is all the fruit of taking away his sin: that he maketh all the stones of the altar as chalkstones that are beaten in sunder, so that the Asherim and the sun-images shall rise no more.

10For the fortified city is solitary, a habitation deserted and forsaken, like the wilderness: there shall the calf feed, and there shall he lie down, and consume the branches thereof.

11When the boughs thereof are withered, they shall be broken off; the women shall come, and set them on fire; for it is a people of no understanding: therefore he that made them will not have compassion upon them, and he that formed them will show them no favor.

12And it shall come to pass in that day, that Yahweh will beat off his fruit from the flood of the River unto the brook of Egypt; and ye shall be gathered one by one, O ye children of Israel.

13And it shall come to pass in that day, that a great trumpet shall be blown; and they shall come that were ready to perish in the land of Assyria, and they that were outcasts in the land of Egypt; and they shall worship Yahweh in the holy mountain at Jerusalem.

Chapter 28

1Woe to the crown of pride of the drunkards of Ephraim, and to the fading flower of his glorious beauty, which is on the head of the fat valley of them that are overcome with wine!

2Behold, the Lord hath a mighty and strong one; as a tempest of hail, a destroying storm, as a tempest of mighty waters overflowing, will he cast down to the earth with the hand.

3The crown of pride of the drunkards of Ephraim shall be trodden under foot:

4and the fading flower of his glorious beauty, which is on the head of the fat valley, shall be as the first-ripe fig before the summer; which when he that looketh upon it seeth, while it is yet in his hand he eateth it up.

5In that day will Yahweh of hosts become a crown of glory, and a diadem of beauty, unto the residue of his people;

6and a spirit of justice to him that sitteth in judgment, and strength to them that turn back the battle at the gate.

7And even these reel with wine, and stagger with strong drink; the priest and the prophet reel with strong drink, they are swallowed up of wine, they stagger with strong drink; they err in vision, they stumble in judgment.

8For all tables are full of vomit and filthiness, so that there is no place clean.

9Whom will he teach knowledge? and whom will he make to understand the message? them that are weaned from the milk, and drawn from the breasts?

10For it is precept upon precept, precept upon precept; line upon line, line upon line; here a little, there a little.

11Nay, but by men of strange lips and with another tongue will he speak to this people;

12to whom he said, This is the rest, give ye rest to him that is weary; and this is the refreshing: yet they would not hear.

13Therefore shall the word of Yahweh be unto them precept upon precept, precept upon precept; line upon line, line upon line; here a little, there a little; that they may go, and fall backward, and be broken, and snared, and taken.

14Wherefore hear the word of Yahweh, ye scoffers, that rule this people that is in Jerusalem:

15Because ye have said, We have made a covenant with death, and with Sheol are we at agreement; when the overflowing scourge shall pass through, it shall not come unto us; for we have made lies our refuge, and under falsehood have we hid ourselves:

16therefore thus saith the Lord Yahweh, Behold, I lay in Zion for a foundation a stone, a tried stone, a precious corner-stone of sure foundation: he that believeth shall not be in haste.

17And I will make justice the line, and righteousness the plummet; and the hail shall sweep away the refuge of lies, and the waters shall overflow the hiding-place.

18And your covenant with death shall be annulled, and your agreement with Sheol shall not stand; when the overflowing scourge shall pass through, then ye shall be trodden down by it.

19As often as it passeth through, it shall take you; for morning by morning shall it pass through, by day and by night: and it shall be nought but terror to understand the message.

20For the bed is shorter than that a man can stretch himself on it; and the covering narrower than that he can wrap himself in it.

21For Yahweh will rise up as in mount Perazim, he will be wroth as in the valley of Gibeon; that he may do his work, his strange work, and bring to pass his act, his strange act.

22Now therefore be ye not scoffers, lest your bonds be made strong; for a decree of destruction have I heard from the Lord, Yahweh of hosts, upon the whole earth.

23Give ye ear, and hear my voice; hearken, and hear my speech.

24Doth he that ploweth to sow plow continually? doth he continually open and harrow his ground?

25When he hath levelled the face thereof, doth he not cast abroad the fitches, and scatter the cummin, and put in the wheat in rows, and the barley in the appointed place, and the spelt in the border thereof?

26For his God doth instruct him aright, and doth teach him.

27For the fitches are not threshed with a sharp threshing instrument, neither is a cart wheel turned about upon the cummin; but the fitches are beaten out with a staff, and the cummin with a rod.

28Bread grain is ground; for he will not be always threshing it: and though the wheel of his cart and his horses scatter it, he doth not grind it.

29This also cometh forth from Yahweh of hosts, who is wonderful in counsel, and excellent in wisdom.

Chapter 29

1Ho Ariel, Ariel, the city where David encamped! add ye year to year; let the feasts come round:

2then will I distress Ariel, and there shall be mourning and lamentation; and she shall be unto me as Ariel.

3And I will encamp against thee round about, and will lay siege against thee with posted troops, and I will raise siege works against thee.

4And thou shalt be brought down, and shalt speak out of the ground, and thy speech shall be low out of the dust; and thy voice shall be as of one that hath a familiar spirit, out of the ground, and thy speech shall whisper out of the dust.

5But the multitude of thy foes shall be like small dust, and the multitude of the terrible ones as chaff that passeth away: yea, it shall be in an instant suddenly.

6She shall be visited of Yahweh of hosts with thunder, and with earthquake, and great noise, with whirlwind and tempest, and the flame of a devouring fire.

7And the multitude of all the nations that fight against Ariel, even all that fight against her and her stronghold, and that distress her, shall be as a dream, a vision of the night.

8And it shall be as when a hungry man dreameth, and, behold, he eateth; but he awaketh, and his soul is empty: or as when a thirsty man dreameth, and, behold, he drinketh; but he awaketh, and, behold, he is faint, and his soul hath appetite: so shall the multitude of all the nations be, that fight against mount Zion.

9Tarry ye and wonder; take your pleasure and be blind: they are drunken, but not with wine; they stagger, but not with strong drink.

10For Yahweh hath poured out upon you the spirit of deep sleep, and hath closed your eyes, the prophets; and your heads, the seers, hath he covered.

11And all vision is become unto you as the words of a book that is sealed, which men deliver to one that is learned, saying, Read this, I pray thee; and he saith, I cannot, for it is sealed:

12and the book is delivered to him that is not learned, saying, Read this, I pray thee; and he saith, I am not learned.

13And the Lord said, Forasmuch as this people draw nigh unto me, and with their mouth and with their lips to honor me, but have removed their heart far from me, and their fear of me is a commandment of men which hath been taught them;

14therefore, behold, I will proceed to do a marvellous work among this people, even a marvellous work and a wonder; and the wisdom of their wise men shall perish, and the understanding of their prudent men shall be hid.

15Woe unto them that hide deep their counsel from Yahweh, and whose works are in the dark, and that say, Who seeth us? and who knoweth us?

16Ye turn things upside down! Shall the potter be esteemed as clay; that the thing made should say of him that made it, He made me not; or the thing formed say of him that formed it, He hath no understanding?

17Is it not yet a very little while, and Lebanon shall be turned into a fruitful field, and the fruitful field shall be esteemed as a forest?

18And in that day shall the deaf hear the words of the book, and the eyes of the blind shall see out of obscurity and out of darkness.

19The meek also shall increase their joy in Yahweh, and the poor among men shall rejoice in the Holy One of Israel.

20For the terrible one is brought to nought, and the scoffer ceaseth, and all they that watch for iniquity are cut off;

21that make a man an offender in his cause, and lay a snare for him that reproveth in the gate, and turn aside the just with a thing of nought.

22Therefore thus saith Yahweh, who redeemed Abraham, concerning the house of Jacob: Jacob shall not now be ashamed, neither shall his face now wax pale.

23But when he seeth his children, the work of my hands, in the midst of him, they shall sanctify my name; yea, they shall sanctify the Holy One of Jacob, and shall stand in awe of the God of Israel.

24They also that err in spirit shall come to understanding, and they that murmur shall receive instruction.

Chapter 30

1Woe to the rebellious children, saith Yahweh, that take counsel, but not of me; and that make a league, but not of my Spirit, that they may add sin to sin,

2that set out to go down into Egypt, and have not asked at my mouth; to strengthen themselves in the strength of Pharaoh, and to take refuge in the shadow of Egypt!

3Therefore shall the strength of Pharaoh be your shame, and the refuge in the shadow of Egypt your confusion.

4For their princes are at Zoan, and their ambassadors are come to Hanes.

5They shall all be ashamed because of a people that cannot profit them, that are not a help nor profit, but a shame, and also a reproach.

6The burden of the beasts of the South. Through the land of trouble and anguish, from whence come the lioness and the lion, the viper and fiery flying serpent, they carry their riches upon the shoulders of young asses, and their treasures upon the humps of camels, to a people that shall not profit them.

7For Egypt helpeth in vain, and to no purpose: therefore have I called her Rahab that sitteth still.

8Now go, write it before them on a tablet, and inscribe it in a book, that it may be for the time to come for ever and ever.

9For it is a rebellious people, lying children, children that will not hear the law of Yahweh;

10that say to the seers, See not; and to the prophets, Prophesy not unto us right things, speak unto us smooth things, prophesy deceits,

11get you out of the way, turn aside out of the path, cause the Holy One of Israel to cease from before us.

12Wherefore thus saith the Holy One of Israel, Because ye despise this word, and trust in oppression and perverseness, and rely thereon;

13therefore this iniquity shall be to you as a breach ready to fall, swelling

Isaiah

out in a high wall, whose breaking cometh suddenly in an instant.

14And he shall break it as a potter's vessel is broken, breaking it in pieces without sparing; so that there shall not be found among the pieces thereof a sherd wherewith to take fire from the hearth, or to dip up water out of the cistern.

15For thus said the Lord Yahweh, the Holy One of Israel, In returning and rest shall ye be saved; in quietness and in confidence shall be your strength. And ye would not:

16but ye said, No, for we will flee upon horses; therefore shall ye flee: and, We will ride upon the swift; therefore shall they that pursue you be swift.

17One thousand shall flee at the threat of one; at the threat of five shall ye flee: till ye be left as a beacon upon the top of a mountain, and as an ensign on a hill.

18And therefore will Yahweh wait, that he may be gracious unto you; and therefore will he be exalted, that he may have mercy upon you: for Yahweh is a God of justice; blessed are all they that wait for him.

19For the people shall dwell in Zion at Jerusalem; thou shalt weep no more; he will surely be gracious unto thee at the voice of thy cry; when he shall hear, he will answer thee.

20And though the Lord give you the bread of adversity and the water of affliction, yet shall not thy teachers be hidden anymore, but thine eyes shall see thy teachers;

21and thine ears shall hear a word behind thee, saying, This is the way, walk ye in it; when ye turn to the right hand, and when ye turn to the left.

22And ye shall defile the overlaying of thy graven images of silver, and the plating of thy molten images of gold: thou shalt cast them away as an unclean thing; thou shalt say unto it, Get thee hence.

23And he will give the rain for thy seed, wherewith thou shalt sow the ground; and bread of the increase of the ground, and it shall be fat and plenteous. In that day shall thy cattle feed in large pastures;

24the oxen likewise and the young asses that till the ground shall eat savory provender, which hath been winnowed with the shovel and with the fork.

25And there shall be upon every lofty mountain, and upon every high hill, brooks and streams of waters, in the day of the great slaughter, when the towers fall.

26Moreover the light of the moon shall be as the light of the sun, and the light of the sun shall be sevenfold, as the light of seven days, in the day that Yahweh bindeth up the hurt of his people, and healeth the stroke of their wound.

27Behold, the name of Yahweh cometh from far, burning with his anger, and in thick rising smoke: his lips are full of indignation, and his tongue is as a devouring fire;

28and his breath is as an overflowing stream, that reacheth even unto the neck, to sift the nations with the sieve of destruction: and a bridle that causeth to err shall be in the jaws of the peoples.

29Ye shall have a song as in the night when a holy feast is kept; and gladness of heart, as when one goeth with a pipe to come unto the mountain of Yahweh, to the Rock of Israel.

30And Yahweh will cause his glorious voice to be heard, and will show the lighting down of his arm, with the indignation of his anger, and the flame of a devouring fire, with a blast, and tempest, and hailstones.

31For through the voice of Yahweh shall the Assyrian be dismayed; with his rod will he smite him.

32And every stroke of the appointed staff, which Yahweh shall lay upon him, shall be with the sound of tabrets and harps; and in battles with the brandishing of his arm will he fight with them.

33For a Topheth is prepared of old; yea, for the king it is made ready; he hath made it deep and large; the pile thereof is fire and much wood; the breath of Yahweh, like a stream of brimstone, doth kindle it.

Chapter 31

1Woe to them that go down to Egypt for help, and rely on horses, and trust in chariots because they are many, and in horsemen because they are very strong, but they look not unto the Holy One of Israel, neither seek Yahweh!

2Yet he also is wise, and will bring evil, and will not call back his words, but will arise against the house of the evil-doers, and against the help of them that work iniquity.

3Now the Egyptians are men, and not God; and their horses flesh, and not spirit: and when Yahweh shall stretch out his hand, both he that helpeth shall stumble, and he that is helped shall fall, and they all shall be consumed together.

4For thus saith Yahweh unto me, As the lion and the young lion growling over his prey, if a multitude of shepherds be called forth against him, will not be dismayed at their voice, nor abase himself for the noise of them: so will Yahweh of hosts come down to fight upon mount Zion, and upon the hill thereof.

5As birds hovering, so will Yahweh of hosts protect Jerusalem; he will protect and deliver it, he will pass over and preserve it.

6Turn ye unto him from whom ye have deeply revolted, O children of Israel.

7For in that day they shall cast away every man his idols of silver, and his idols of gold, which your own hands have made unto you for a sin.

8And the Assyrian shall fall by the sword, not of man; and the sword, not of men, shall devour him; and he shall flee from the sword, and his young men shall become subject to taskwork.

9And his rock shall pass away by reason of terror, and his princes shall be dismayed at the ensign, saith Yahweh, whose fire is in Zion, and his furnace in Jerusalem.

Chapter 32

1Behold, a king shall reign in righteousness, and princes shall rule in justice.

2And a man shall be as a hiding-place from the wind, and a covert from the tempest, as streams of water in a dry place, as the shade of a great rock in a weary land.

3And the eyes of them that see shall not be dim, and the ears of them that hear shall hearken.

4And the heart of the rash shall understand knowledge, and the tongue of the stammerers shall be ready to speak plainly.

5The fool shall be no more called noble, nor the churl said to be bountiful.

6For the fool will speak folly, and his heart will work iniquity, to practise profaneness, and to utter error against Yahweh, to make empty the soul of the hungry, and to cause the drink of the thirsty to fail.

7And the instruments of the churl are evil: he deviseth wicked devices to destroy the meek with lying words, even when the needy speaketh right.

8But the noble deviseth noble things; and in noble things shall he continue.

9Rise up, ye women that are at ease, and hear my voice; ye careless daughters, give ear unto my speech.

10For days beyond a year shall ye be troubled, ye careless women; for the vintage shall fail, the ingathering shall not come.

11Tremble, ye women that are at ease; be troubled, ye careless ones; strip you, and make you bare, and gird sackcloth upon your loins.

12They shall smite upon the breasts for the pleasant fields, for the fruitful vine.

13Upon the land of my people shall come up thorns and briers; yea, upon all the houses of joy in the joyous city.

14For the palace shall be forsaken; the populous city shall be deserted; the hill and the watch-tower shall be for dens for ever, a joy of wild asses, a pasture of flocks;

15until the Spirit be poured upon us from on high, and the wilderness become a fruitful field, and the fruitful field be esteemed as a forest.

16Then justice shall dwell in the wilderness; and righteousness shall abide in the fruitful field.

17And the work of righteousness shall be peace; and the effect of righteousness, quietness and confidence for ever.

18And my people shall abide in a peaceable habitation, and in safe dwellings, and in quiet resting-places.

19But it shall hail in the downfall of the forest; and the city shall be utterly laid low.

20Blessed are yet that sow beside all waters, that send forth the feet of the ox and the ass.

Chapter 33

1Woe to thee that destroyest, and thou wast not destroyed; and dealest treacherously, and they dealt not treacherously with thee! When thou hast ceased to destroy, thou shalt be destroyed; and when thou hast made an end of dealing treacherously, they shall deal treacherously with thee.

2O Yahweh, be gracious unto us; we have waited for thee: be thou our arm every morning, our salvation also in the time of trouble.

3At the noise of the tumult the peoples are fled; at the lifting up of thyself the nations are scattered.

4And your spoil shall be gathered as the caterpillar gathereth: as locusts leap shall men leap upon it.

5Yahweh is exalted; for he dwelleth on high: he hath filled Zion with justice and righteousness.

6And there shall be stability in thy times, abundance of salvation, wisdom, and knowledge: the fear of Yahweh is thy treasure.

7Behold, their valiant ones cry without; the ambassadors of peace weep bitterly.

8The highways lie waste, the wayfaring man ceaseth: the enemy hath broken the covenant, he hath despised the cities, he regardeth not man.

9The land mourneth and languisheth; Lebanon is confounded and withereth away; Sharon is like a desert; and Bashan and Carmel shake off their leaves.

10Now will I arise, saith Yahweh; now will I lift up myself; now will I be exalted.

11Ye shall conceive chaff, ye shall bring forth stubble: your breath is a fire that shall devour you.

12And the peoples shall be as the burnings of lime, as thorns cut down, that are burned in the fire.

13Hear, ye that are far off, what I have done; and, ye that are near, acknowledge my might.

14The sinners in Zion are afraid; trembling hath seized the godless ones: Who among us can dwell with the devouring fire? who among us can dwell with everlasting burnings?

15He that walketh righteously, and speaketh uprightly; he that despiseth the gain of oppressions, that shaketh his hands from taking a bribe, that stoppeth his ears from hearing of blood, and shutteth his eyes from looking upon evil:

16He shall dwell on high; his place of defence shall be the munitions of rocks; his bread shall be given him; his waters shall be sure.

17Thine eyes shall see the king in his beauty: they shall behold a land that reacheth afar.

18Thy heart shall muse on the terror: Where is he that counted, where is he that weighed the tribute? where is he that counted the towers?

19Thou shalt not see the fierce people, a people of a deep speech that thou canst not comprehend, of a strange tongue that thou canst not understand.

20Look upon Zion, the city of our solemnities: thine eyes shall see Jerusalem a quiet habitation, a tent that shall not be removed, the stakes whereof shall never be plucked up, neither shall any of the cords thereof be broken.

21But there Yahweh will be with us in majesty, a place of broad rivers and streams, wherein shall go no galley with oars, neither shall gallant ship pass thereby.

22For Yahweh is our judge, Yahweh is our lawgiver, Yahweh is our king; he will save us.

23Thy tacklings are loosed; they could not strengthen the foot of their mast, they could not spread the sail: then was the prey of a great spoil divided; the lame took the prey.

24And the inhabitant shall not say, I am sick: the people that dwell therein shall be forgiven their iniquity.

Chapter 34

1Come near, ye nations, to hear; and hearken, ye peoples: let the earth hear, and the fulness thereof; the world, and all things that come forth from it.

2For Yahweh hath indignation against all the nations, and wrath against all their host: he hath utterly destroyed them, he hath delivered them to the slaughter.

3Their slain also shall be cast out, and the stench of their dead bodies shall come up; and the mountains shall be melted with their blood.

4And all the host of heaven shall be dissolved, and the heavens shall be rolled together as a scroll; and all their host shall fade away, as the leaf fadeth from off the vine, and as a fading leaf from the fig-tree.

5For my sword hath drunk its fill in heaven: behold, it shall come down upon Edom, and upon the people of my curse, to judgment.

6The sword of Yahweh is filled with blood, it is made fat with fatness, with the blood of lambs and goats, with the fat of the kidneys of rams; for Yahweh hath a sacrifice in Bozrah, and a great slaughter in the land of Edom.

7And the wild-oxen shall come down with them, and the bullocks with the bulls: and their land shall be drunken with blood, and their dust made fat with fatness.

8For Yahweh hath a day of vengeance, a year of recompense for the cause of Zion.

9And the streams of Edom shall be turned into pitch, and the dust thereof into brimstone, and the land thereof shall become burning pitch.

10It shall not be quenched night nor day; the smoke thereof shall go up for ever; from generation to generation it shall lie waste; none shall pass through it for ever and ever.

11But the pelican and the porcupine shall possess it; and the owl and the raven shall dwell therein: and he will stretch over it the line of confusion, and the plummet of emptiness.

12They shall call the nobles thereof to the kingdom, but none shall be there; and all its princes shall be nothing.

13And thorns shall come up in its palaces, nettles and thistles in the fortresses thereof; and it shall be a habitation of jackals, a court for ostriches.

14And the wild beasts of the desert shall meet with the wolves, and the wild goat shall cry to his fellow; yea, the night-monster shall settle there, and shall find her a place of rest.

15There shall the dart-snake make her nest, and lay, and hatch, and gather under her shade; yea, there shall the kites be gathered, every one with her mate.

16Seek ye out of the book of Yahweh, and read: no one of these shall be missing, none shall want her mate; for my mouth, it hath commanded, and his Spirit, it hath gathered them.

17And he hath cast the lot for them, and his hand hath divided it unto them by line: they shall possess it for ever; from generation to generation shall they dwell therein.

Chapter 35

1The wilderness and the dry land shall be glad; and the desert shall rejoice, and blossom as the rose.

2It shall blossom abundantly, and rejoice even with joy and singing; the glory of Lebanon shall be given unto it, the excellency of Carmel and Sharon: they shall see the glory of Yahweh, the excellency of our God.

3Strengthen ye the weak hands, and confirm the feeble knees.

4Say to them that are of a fearful heart, Be strong, fear not: behold, your God will come with vengeance, with the recompense of God; he will come and save you.

5Then the eyes of the blind shall be opened, and the ears of the deaf shall be unstopped.

6Then shall the lame man leap as a hart, and the tongue of the dumb shall sing; for in the wilderness shall waters break out, and streams in the desert.

7And the glowing sand shall become a pool, and the thirsty ground springs of water: in the habitation of jackals, where they lay, shall be grass with reeds and rushes.

8And a highway shall be there, and a way, and it shall be called The way of holiness; the unclean shall not pass over it; but it shall be for the redeemed: the wayfaring men, yea fools, shall not err therein.

9No lion shall be there, nor shall any ravenous beast go up thereon; they shall not be found there; but the redeemed shall walk there:

10and the ransomed of Yahweh shall return, and come with singing unto Zion; and everlasting joy shall be upon their heads: they shall obtain gladness and joy, and sorrow and sighing shall flee away.

Chapter 36

1Now it came to pass in the fourteenth year of king Hezekiah, that Sennacherib king of Assyria came up against all the fortified cities of Judah, and took them.

2And the king of Assyria sent Rabshakeh from Lachish to Jerusalem unto king Hezekiah with a great army. And he stood by the conduit of the upper pool in the highway of the fuller's field.

3Then came forth unto him Eliakim the son of Hilkiah, who was over the household, and Shebna the scribe, and Joah, the son of Asaph, the recorder.

4And Rabshakeh said unto them, Say ye now to Hezekiah, Thus saith the great king, the king of Assyria, What confidence is this wherein thou trustest?

5I say, thy counsel and strength for the war are but vain words: now on whom dost thou trust, that thou hast rebelled against me?

6Behold, thou trustest upon the staff of this bruised reed, even upon Egypt, whereon if a man lean, it will go into his hand, and pierce it: so is Pharaoh king of Egypt to all that trust on him.

7But if thou say unto me, We trust in Yahweh our God: is not that he, whose high places and whose altars Hezekiah hath taken away, and hath said to Judah and to Jerusalem, Ye shall worship before this altar?

8Now therefore, I pray thee, give pledges to my master the king of Assyria, and I will give thee two thousand horses, if thou be able on thy part to set riders upon them.

9How then canst thou turn away the face of one captain of the least of my master's servants, and put thy trust on Egypt for chariots and for horsemen?

10And am I now come up without Yahweh against this land to destroy it? Yahweh said unto me, Go up against this land, and destroy it.

11Then said Eliakim and Shebna and Joah unto Rabshakeh, Speak, I pray thee, unto thy servants in the Syrian language; for we understand it: and speak not to us in the Jews' language, in the ears of the people that are on the wall.

12But Rabshakeh said, Hath my master sent me to thy master, and to thee, to speak these words? hath he not sent me to the men that sit upon the wall, to eat their own dung, and to drink their own water with you?

13Then Rabshakeh stood, and cried with a loud voice in the Jews' language, and said, Hear ye the words of the great king, the king of Assyria.

14Thus saith the king, Let not Hezekiah deceive you; for he will not be able to deliver you:

15neither let Hezekiah make you trust in Yahweh, saying, Yahweh will surely deliver us; this city shall not be given into the hand of the king of Assyria.

16Hearken not to Hezekiah: for thus saith the king of Assyria, Make your peace with me, and come out to me; and eat ye every one of his vine, and every one of his fig-tree, and drink ye every one the waters of his own cistern;

17until I come and take you away to a land like your own land, a land of grain and new wine, a land of bread and vineyards.

18Beware lest Hezekiah persuade you, saying, Yahweh will deliver us. Hath any of the gods of the nations delivered his land out of the hand of the king of Assyria?

19Where are the gods of Hamath and Arpad? where are the gods of Sepharvaim? and have they delivered Samaria out of my hand?

20Who are they among all the gods of these countries, that have delivered their country out of my hand, that Yahweh should deliver Jerusalem out of my hand?

21But they held their peace, and answered him not a word; for the king's commandment was, saying, Answer him not.

22Then came Eliakim the son of Hilkiah, that was over the household, and Shebna the scribe, and Joah, the son of Asaph, the recorder, to Hezekiah with their clothes rent, and told him the words of Rabshakeh.

Chapter 37

1And it came to pass, when king Hezekiah heard it, that he rent his clothes, and covered himself with sackcloth, and went into the house of Yahweh.

2And he sent Eliakim, who was over the household, and Shebna the scribe, and the elders of the priests, covered with sackcloth, unto Isaiah the prophet the son of Amoz.

3And they said unto him, Thus saith Hezekiah, This day is a day of trouble, and of rebuke, and of contumely; for the children are come to the birth, and there is not strength to bring forth.

4It may be Yahweh thy God will hear the words of Rabshakeh, whom the king of Assyria his master hath sent to defy the living God, and will rebuke the words which Yahweh thy God hath heard: wherefore lift up thy prayer for the remnant that is left.

5So the servants of king Hezekiah came to Isaiah.

6And Isaiah said unto them, Thus shall ye say to your master, Thus saith Yahweh, Be not afraid of the words that thou hast heard, wherewith the servants of the king of Assyria have blasphemed me.

7Behold, I will put a spirit in him, and he shall hear tidings, and shall return unto his own land; and I will cause him to fall by the sword in his own land.

8So Rabshakeh returned, and found the king of Assyria warring against Libnah; for he had heard that he was departed from Lachish.

9And he heard say concerning Tirhakah king of Ethiopia, He is come out to fight against thee. And when he heard it, he sent messengers to Hezekiah, saying,

10Thus shall ye speak to Hezekiah king of Judah, saying, Let not thy God in whom thou trustest deceive thee, saying, Jerusalem shall not be given into the hand of the king of Assyria.

11Behold, thou hast heard what the kings of Assyria have done to all lands, by destroying them utterly: and shalt thou be delivered?

12Have the gods of the nations delivered them, which my fathers have destroyed, Gozan, and Haran, and Rezeph, and the children of Eden that were in Telassar?

13Where is the king of Hamath, and the king of Arpad, and the king of the city of Sepharvaim, of Hena, and Ivvah?

14And Hezekiah received the letter from the hand of the messengers, and read it; and Hezekiah went up unto the house of Yahweh, and spread it before Yahweh.

15And Hezekiah prayed unto Yahweh, saying,

16O Yahweh of hosts, the God of Israel, that sittest above the cherubim, thou art the God, even thou alone, of all the kingdoms of the earth; thou hast made

Isaiah

heaven and earth.

17Incline thine ear, O Yahweh, and hear; open thine eyes, O Yahweh, and see; and hear all the words of Sennacherib, who hath sent to defy the living God.

18Of a truth, Yahweh, the kings of Assyria have laid waste all the countries, and their land,

19and have cast their gods into the fire: for they were no gods, but the work of men's hands, wood and stone; therefore they have destroyed them.

20Now therefore, O Yahweh our God, save us from his hand, that all the kingdoms of the earth may know that thou art Yahweh, even thou only.

21Then Isaiah the son of Amoz sent unto Hezekiah, saying, Thus saith Yahweh, the God of Israel, Whereas thou hast prayed to me against Sennacherib king of Assyria,

22this is the word which Yahweh hath spoken concerning him: The virgin daughter of Zion hath despised thee and laughed thee to scorn; the daughter of Jerusalem hath shaken her head at thee.

23Whom hast thou defied and blasphemed? and against whom hast thou exalted thy voice and lifted up thine eyes on high? even against the Holy One of Israel.

24By thy servants hast thou defied the Lord, and hast said, With the multitude of my chariots am I come up to the height of the mountains, to the innermost parts of Lebanon; and I will cut down the tall cedars thereof, and the choice fir-trees thereof; and I will enter into its farthest height, the forest of its fruitful field;

25I have digged and drunk water, and with the sole of my feet will I dry up all the rivers of Egypt.

26Hast thou not heard how I have done it long ago, and formed it of ancient times? now have I brought it to pass, that it should be thine to lay waste fortified cities into ruinous heaps.

27Therefore their inhabitants were of small power, they were dismayed and confounded; they were as the grass of the field, and as the green herb, as the grass on the housetops, and as a field of grain before it is grown up.

28But I know thy sitting down, and thy going out, and thy coming in, and thy raging against me.

29Because of thy raging against me, and because thine arrogancy is come up into mine ears, therefore will I put my hook in thy nose, and my bridle in thy lips, and I will turn thee back by the way by which thou camest.

30And this shall be the sign unto thee: ye shall eat this year that which groweth of itself, and in the second year that which springeth of the same; and in the third year sow ye, and reap, and plant vineyards, and eat the fruit thereof.

31And the remnant that is escaped of the house of Judah shall again take root downward, and bear fruit upward.

32For out of Jerusalem shall go forth a remnant, and out of mount Zion they that shall escape. The zeal of Yahweh of hosts will perform this.

33Therefore thus saith Yahweh concerning the king of Assyria, He shall not come unto this city, nor shoot an arrow there, neither shall he come before it with shield, nor cast up a mound against it.

34By the way that he came, by the same shall he return, and he shall not come unto this city, saith Yahweh.

35For I will defend this city to save it, for mine own sake, and for my servant David's sake.

36And the angel of Yahweh went forth, and smote in the camp of the Assyrians a hundred and fourscore and five thousand; and when men arose early in the morning, behold, these were all dead bodies.

37So Sennacherib king of Assyria departed, and went and returned, and dwelt at Nineveh.

38And it came to pass, as he was worshipping in the house of Nisroch his god, that Adrammelech and Sharezer his sons smote him with the sword; and they escaped into the land of Ararat. And Esar-haddon his son reigned in his stead.

Chapter 38

1In those days was Hezekiah sick unto death. And Isaiah the prophet the son of Amoz came to him, and said unto him, Thus saith Yahweh, Set thy house in order; for thou shalt die, and not live.

2Then Hezekiah turned his face to the wall, and prayed unto Yahweh,

3and said, Remember now, O Yahweh, I beseech thee, how I have walked before thee in truth and with a perfect heart, and have done that which is good in thy sight. And Hezekiah wept sore.

4Then came the word of Yahweh to Isaiah, saying,

5Go, and say to Hezekiah, Thus saith Yahweh, the God of David thy father, I have heard thy prayer, I have seen thy tears: behold, I will add unto thy days fifteen years.

6And I will deliver thee and this city out of the hand of the king of Assyria; and I will defend this city.

7And this shall be the sign unto thee from Yahweh, that Yahweh will do this thing that he hath spoken:

8behold, I will cause the shadow on the steps, which is gone down on the dial of Ahaz with the sun, to return backward ten steps. So the sun returned ten steps on the dial whereon it was gone down.

9The writing of Hezekiah king of Judah, when he had been sick, and was recovered of his sickness.

10I said, In the noontide of my days I shall go into the gates of Sheol:
I am deprived of the residue of my years.

11I said, I shall not see Yahweh, even Yahweh in the land of the living:
I shall behold man no more with the inhabitants of the world.

12My dwelling is removed, and is carried away from me as a shepherd's tent:
I have rolled up, like a weaver, my life; he will cut me off from the loom:
From day even to night wilt thou make an end of me.

13I quieted myself until morning; as a lion, so he breaketh all my bones:
From day even to night wilt thou make an end of me.

14Like a swallow or a crane, so did I chatter;
I did moan as a dove; mine eyes fail with looking upward:
O Lord, I am oppressed, be thou my surety.

15What shall I say? he hath both spoken unto me, and himself hath done it:
I shall go softly all my years because of the bitterness of my soul.

16O Lord, by these things men live;
And wholly therein is the life of my spirit:
Wherefore recover thou me, and make me to live.

17Behold, it was for my peace that I had great bitterness:
But thou hast in love to my soul delivered it from the pit of corruption;
For thou hast cast all my sins behind thy back.

18For Sheol cannot praise thee, death cannot celebrate thee:
They that go down into the pit cannot hope for thy truth.

19The living, the living, he shall praise thee, as I do this day:
The father to the children shall make known thy truth.

20Yahweh is ready to save me:
Therefore we will sing my songs with stringed instruments
All the days of our life in the house of Yahweh.

21Now Isaiah had said, Let them take a cake of figs, and lay it for a plaster upon the boil, and he shall recover.

22Hezekiah also had said, What is the sign that I shall go up to the house of Yahweh?

Chapter 39

1At that time Merodach-baladan the son of Baladan, king of Babylon, sent letters and a present to Hezekiah; for he heard that he had been sick, and was recovered.

2And Hezekiah was glad of them, and showed them the house of his precious things, the silver, and the gold, and the spices, and the precious oil, and all the house of his armor, and all that was found in his treasures: there was nothing in his house, nor in all his dominion, that Hezekiah showed them not.

3Then came Isaiah the prophet unto king Hezekiah, and said unto him, What said these men? and from whence came they unto thee? And Hezekiah said, They are come from a far country unto me, even from Babylon.

4Then said he, What have they seen in thy house? And Hezekiah answered, All that is in my house have they seen: there is nothing among my treasures that I have not showed them.

5Then said Isaiah to Hezekiah, Hear the word of Yahweh of hosts:

6Behold, the days are coming, when all that is in thy house, and that which thy fathers have laid up in store until this day, shall be carried to Babylon: nothing shall be left, saith Yahweh.

7And of thy sons that shall issue from thee, whom thou shalt beget, shall they take away; and they shall be eunuchs in the palace of the king of Babylon.

8Then said Hezekiah unto Isaiah, Good is the word of Yahweh which thou hast spoken. He said moreover, For there shall be peace and truth in my days.

Chapter 40

1Comfort ye, comfort ye my people, saith your God.

2Speak ye comfortably to Jerusalem; and cry unto her, that her warfare is accomplished, that her iniquity is pardoned, that she hath received of Yahweh's hand double for all her sins.

3The voice of one that crieth, Prepare ye in the wilderness the way of Yahweh; make level in the desert a highway for our God.

4Every valley shall be exalted, and every mountain and hill shall be made low; and the uneven shall be made level, and the rough places a plain:

5and the glory of Yahweh shall be revealed, and all flesh shall see it together; for the mouth of Yahweh hath spoken it.

6The voice of one saying, Cry. And one said, What shall I cry? All flesh is grass, and all the goodliness thereof is as the flower of the field.

7The grass withereth, the flower fadeth, because the breath of Yahweh bloweth upon it; surely the people is grass.

8The grass withereth, the flower fadeth; but the word of our God shall stand forever.

9O thou that tellest good tidings to Zion, get thee up on a high mountain; O thou that tellest good tidings to Jerusalem, lift up thy voice with strength; lift it up, be not afraid; say unto the cities of Judah, Behold, your God!

10Behold, the Lord Yahweh will come as a mighty one, and his arm will rule for him: Behold, his reward is with him, and his recompense before him.

11He will feed his flock like a shepherd, he will gather the lambs in his arm, and carry them in his bosom, and will gently lead those that have their young.

12Who hath measured the waters in the hollow of his hand, and meted out heaven with the span, and comprehended the dust of the earth in a measure, and weighed the mountains in scales, and the hills in a balance?

13Who hath directed the Spirit of Yahweh, or being his counsellor hath taught him?

14With whom took he counsel, and who instructed him, and taught him in the path of justice, and taught him knowledge, and showed to him the way of understanding?

15Behold, the nations are as a drop of a bucket, and are accounted as the small dust of the balance: Behold, he taketh up the isles as a very little thing.

16And Lebanon is not sufficient to burn, nor the beasts thereof sufficient for a burnt-offering.

17All the nations are as nothing before him; they are accounted by him as less than nothing, and vanity.

18To whom then will ye liken God? or what likeness will ye compare unto him?

19The image, a workman hath cast it, and the goldsmith overlayeth it with gold, and casteth for it silver chains.

20He that is too impoverished for such an oblation chooseth a tree that will not rot; he seeketh unto him a skilful workman to set up a graven image, that shall not be moved.

21Have ye not known? have yet not heard? hath it not been told you from the beginning? have ye not understood from the foundations of the earth?

22It is he that sitteth above the circle of the earth, and the inhabitants thereof are as grasshoppers; that stretcheth out the heavens as a curtain, and spreadeth them out as a tent to dwell in;

23that bringeth princes to nothing; that maketh the judges of the earth as vanity.

24Yea, they have not been planted; yea, they have not been sown; yea, their stock hath not taken root in the earth: moreover he bloweth upon them, and they wither, and the whirlwind taketh them away as stubble.

25To whom then will ye liken me, that I should be equal to him? saith the Holy One.

26Lift up your eyes on high, and see who hath created these, that bringeth out their host by number; he calleth them all by name; by the greatness of his might, and for that he is strong in power, not one is lacking.

27Why sayest thou, O Jacob, and speakest, O Israel, My way is hid from Yahweh, and the justice due to me is passed away from my God?

28Hast thou not known? hast thou not heard? The everlasting God, Yahweh, the Creator of the ends of the earth, fainteth not, neither is weary; there is no searching of his understanding.

29He giveth power to the faint; and to him that hath no might he increaseth strength.

30Even the youths shall faint and be weary, and the young men shall utterly fall:

31but they that wait for Yahweh shall renew their strength; they shall mount up with wings as eagles; they shall run, and not be weary; they shall walk, and not faint.

Chapter 41

1Keep silence before me, O islands; and let the peoples renew their strength: let them come near; then let them speak; let us come near together to judgment.

2Who hath raised up one from the east, whom he calleth in righteousness to his foot? he giveth nations before him, and maketh him rule over kings; he giveth them as the dust to his sword, as the driven stubble to his bow.

3He pursueth them, and passeth on safely, even by a way that he had not gone with his feet.

4Who hath wrought and done it, calling the generations from the beginning? I, Yahweh, the first, and with the last, I am he.

5The isles have seen, and fear; the ends of the earth tremble; they draw near, and come.

6They help every one his neighbor; and every one saith to his brother, Be of good courage.

7So the carpenter encourageth the goldsmith, and he that smootheth with the hammer him that smiteth the anvil, saying of the soldering, It is good; and he fasteneth it with nails, that it should not be moved.

8But thou, Israel, my servant, Jacob whom I have chosen, the seed of Abraham my friend,

9thou whom I have taken hold of from the ends of the earth, and called from the corners thereof, and said unto thee, Thou art my servant, I have chosen thee and not cast thee away;

10Fear thou not, for I am with thee; be not dismayed, for I am thy God; I will strengthen thee; yea, I will help thee; yea, I will uphold thee with the right hand of my righteousness.

11Behold, all they that are incensed against thee shall be put to shame and confounded: they that strive with thee shall be as nothing, and shall perish.

12Thou shalt seek them, and shalt not find them, even them that contend with thee: they that war against thee shall be as nothing, and as a thing of nought.

13For I, Yahweh thy God, will hold thy right hand, saying unto thee, Fear not; I will help thee.

14Fear not, thou worm Jacob, and ye men of Israel; I will help thee, saith Yahweh, and thy Redeemer is the Holy One of Israel.

15Behold, I have made thee to be a new sharp threshing instrument having teeth; thou shalt thresh the mountains, and beat them small, and shalt make the hills as chaff.

16Thou shalt winnow them, and the wind shall carry them away, and the whirlwind shall scatter them; and thou shalt rejoice in Yahweh, thou shalt glory in the Holy One of Israel.

17The poor and needy seek water, and there is none, and their tongue faileth for thirst; I, Yahweh, will answer them, I, the God of Israel, will not forsake them.

18I will open rivers on the bare heights, and fountains in the midst of the valleys; I will make the wilderness a pool of water, and the dry land springs of water.

19I will put in the wilderness the cedar, the acacia, and the myrtle, and the oil-tree; I will set in the desert the fir-tree, the pine, and the box-tree together:

20that they may see, and know, and consider, and understand together, that the hand of Yahweh hath done this, and the Holy One of Israel hath created it.

21Produce your cause, saith Yahweh; bring forth your strong reasons, saith the King of Jacob.

22Let them bring forth, and declare unto us what shall happen: declare ye the former things, what they are, that we may consider them, and know the latter end of them; or show us things to come.

23Declare the things that are to come hereafter, that we may know that ye are gods: yea, do good, or do evil, that we may be dismayed, and behold it together.

24Behold, ye are of nothing, and your work is of nought; an abomination is he that chooseth you.

25I have raised up one from the north, and he is come; from the rising of the sun one that calleth upon my name: and he shall come upon rulers as upon mortar, and as the potter treadeth clay.

26Who hath declared it from the beginning, that we may know? and beforetime, that we may say, He is right? yea, there is none that declareth, yea, there is none that showeth, yea, there is none that heareth your words.

27I am the first that saith unto Zion, Behold, behold them; and I will give to Jerusalem one that bringeth good tidings.

28And when I look, there is no man: even among them there is no counsellor, that, when I ask of them, can answer a word.

29Behold, all of them, their works are vanity and nought; their molten images are wind and confusion.

Chapter 42

1Behold, my servant, whom I uphold; my chosen, in whom my soul delighteth: I have put my Spirit upon him; he will bring forth justice to the Gentiles.

2He will not cry, nor lift up his voice, nor cause it to be heard in the street.

3A bruised reed will he not break, and a dimly burning wick will he not quench: he will bring forth justice in truth.

4He will not fail nor be discouraged, till he have set justice in the earth; and the isles shall wait for his law.

5Thus saith God Yahweh, he that created the heavens, and stretched them forth; he that spread abroad the earth and that which cometh out of it; he that giveth breath unto the people upon it, and spirit to them that walk therein:

6I, Yahweh, have called thee in righteousness, and will hold thy hand, and will keep thee, and give thee for a covenant of the people, for a light of the Gentiles;

7to open the blind eyes, to bring out the prisoners from the dungeon, and them that sit in darkness out of the prison-house.

8I am Yahweh, that is my name; and my glory will I not give to another, neither my praise unto graven images.

9Behold, the former things are come to pass, and new things do I declare; before they spring forth I tell you of them.

10Sing unto Yahweh a new song, and his praise from the end of the earth; ye that go down to the sea, and all that is therein, the isles, and the inhabitants thereof.

11Let the wilderness and the cities thereof lift up their voice, the villages that Kedar doth inhabit; let the inhabitants of Sela sing, let them shout from the top of the mountains.

12Let them give glory unto Yahweh, and declare his praise in the islands.

13Yahweh will go forth as a mighty man; he will stir up his zeal like a man of war: he will cry, yea, he will shout aloud; he will do mightily against his enemies.

14I have long time holden my peace; I have been still, and refrained myself: now will I cry out like a travailing woman; I will gasp and pant together.

15I will lay waste mountains and hills, and dry up all their herbs; and I will make the rivers islands, and will dry up the pools.

16And I will bring the blind by a way that they know not; in paths that they know not will I lead them; I will make darkness light before them, and crooked places straight. These things will I do, and I will not forsake them.

17They shall be turned back, they shall be utterly put to shame, that trust in graven images, that say unto molten images, Ye are our gods.

18Hear, ye deaf; and look, ye blind, that ye may see.

19Who is blind, but my servant? or deaf, as my messenger that I send? who is blind as he that is at peace with me, and blind as Yahweh's servant?

20Thou seest many things, but thou observest not; his ears are open, but he heareth not.

21It pleased Yahweh, for his righteousness' sake, to magnify the law, and make it honorable.

22But this is a people robbed and plundered; they are all of them snared in holes, and they are hid in prison-houses: they are for a prey, and none delivereth; for a spoil, and none saith, Restore.

23Who is there among you that will give ear to this? that will hearken and hear for the time to come?

24Who gave Jacob for a spoil, and Israel to the robbers? did not Yahweh? he against whom we have sinned, and in whose ways they would not walk, neither were they obedient unto his law.

25Therefore he poured upon him the fierceness of his anger, and the strength of battle; and it set him on fire round about, yet he knew not; and it burned him, yet he laid it not to heart.

Chapter 43

1But now thus saith Yahweh that created thee, O Jacob, and he that formed thee, O Israel: Fear not, for I have redeemed thee; I have called thee by thy name, thou art mine.

2When thou passest through the waters, I will be with thee; and through the rivers, they shall not overflow thee: when thou walkest through the fire, thou shalt not be burned, neither shall the flame kindle upon thee.

3For I am Yahweh thy God, the Holy One of Israel, thy Saviour; I have given Egypt as thy ransom, Ethiopia and Seba in thy stead.

4Since thou hast been precious in my sight, and honorable, and I have loved thee; therefore will I give men in thy stead, and peoples instead of thy life.

5Fear not; for I am with thee: I will bring thy seed from the east, and gather thee from the west;

6I will say to the north, Give up; and to the south, Keep not back; bring my sons from far, and my daughters from the end of the earth;

Isaiah

7every one that is called by my name, and whom I have created for my glory, whom I have formed, yea, whom I have made.

8Bring forth the blind people that have eyes, and the deaf that have ears.

9Let all the nations be gathered together, and let the peoples be assembled: who among them can declare this, and show us former things? let them bring their witnesses, that they may be justified; or let them hear, and say, It is truth.

10Ye are my witnesses, saith Yahweh, and my servant whom I have chosen; that ye may know and believe me, and understand that I am he: before me there was no God formed, neither shall there be after me.

11I, even I, am Yahweh; and besides me there is no saviour.

12I have declared, and I have saved, and I have showed; and there was no strange god among you: therefore ye are my witnesses, saith Yahweh, and I am God.

13Yea, since the day was I am he; and there is none that can deliver out of my hand: I will work, and who can hinder it?

14Thus saith Yahweh, your Redeemer, the Holy One of Israel: For your sake I have sent to Babylon, and I will bring down all of them as fugitives, even the Chaldeans, in the ships of their rejoicing.

15I am Yahweh, your Holy One, the Creator of Israel, your King.

16Thus saith Yahweh, who maketh a way in the sea, and a path in the mighty waters;

17who bringeth forth the chariot and horse, the army and the mighty man (they lie down together, they shall not rise; they are extinct, they are quenched as a wick):

18Remember ye not the former things, neither consider the things of old.

19Behold, I will do a new thing; now shall it spring forth; shall ye not know it? I will even make a way in the wilderness, and rivers in the desert.

20The beasts of the field shall honor me, the jackals and the ostriches; because I give waters in the wilderness, and rivers in the desert, to give drink to my people, my chosen,

21the people which I formed for myself, that they might set forth my praise.

22Yet thou hast not called upon me, O Jacob; but thou hast been weary of me, O Israel.

23Thou hast not brought me of thy sheep for burnt-offerings; neither hast thou honored me with thy sacrifices. I have not burdened thee with offerings, nor wearied thee with frankincense.

24Thou hast bought me no sweet cane with money, neither hast thou filled me with the fat of thy sacrifices; but thou hast burdened me with thy sins, thou hast wearied me with thine iniquities.

25I, even I, am he that blotteth out thy transgressions for mine own sake; and I will not remember thy sins.

26Put me in remembrance; let us plead together: set thou forth thy cause, that thou mayest be justified.

27Thy first father sinned, and thy teachers have transgressed against me.

28Therefore I will profane the princes of the sanctuary; and I will make Jacob a curse, and Israel a reviling.

Chapter 44

1Yet now hear, O Jacob my servant, and Israel, who I have chosen:

2Thus saith Yahweh that made thee, and formed thee from the womb, who will help thee: Fear not, O Jacob my servant; and thou, Jeshurun, whom I have chosen.

3For I will pour water upon him that is thirsty, and streams upon the dry ground; I will pour my Spirit upon thy seed, and my blessing upon thine offspring:

4and they shall spring up among the grass, as willows by the watercourses.

5One shall say, I am Yahweh's; and another shall call himself by the name of Jacob; and another shall subscribe with his hand unto Yahweh, and surname himself by the name of Israel.

6Thus saith Yahweh, the King of Israel, and his Redeemer, Yahweh of hosts: I am the first, and I am the last; and besides me there is no God.

7And who, as I, shall call, and shall declare it, and set it in order for me, since I established the ancient people? and the things that are coming, and that shall come to pass, let them declare.

8Fear ye not, neither be afraid: have I not declared unto thee of old, and showed it? and ye are my witnesses. Is there a God besides me? yea, there is no Rock; I know not any.

9They that fashion a graven image are all of them vanity; and the things that they delight in shall not profit; and their own witnesses see not, nor know: that they may be put to shame.

10Who hath fashioned a god, or molten an image that is profitable for nothing?

11Behold, all his fellows shall be put to shame; and the workmen, they are of men: let them all be gathered together, let them stand up; they shall fear, they shall be put to shame together.

12The smith maketh an axe, and worketh in the coals, and fashioneth it with hammers, and worketh it with his strong arm: yea, he is hungry, and his strength faileth; he drinketh no water, and is faint.

13The carpenter stretcheth out a line; he marketh it out with a pencil; he shapeth it with planes, and he marketh it out with the compasses, and shapeth it after the figure of a man, according to the beauty of a man, to dwell in a house.

14He heweth him down cedars, and taketh the holm-tree and the oak, and strengtheneth for himself one among the trees of the forest: he planteth a fir-tree, and the rain doth nourish it.

15Then shall it be for a man to burn; and he taketh thereof, and warmeth himself; yea, he kindleth it, and baketh bread: yea, he maketh a god, and worshippeth it; he maketh it a graven image, and falleth down thereto.

16He burneth part thereof in the fire; with part thereof he eateth flesh; he roasteth roast, and is satisfied; yea, he warmeth himself, and saith, Aha, I am warm, I have seen the fire.

17And the residue thereof he maketh a god, even his graven image; he falleth down unto it and worshippeth, and prayeth unto it, and saith, Deliver me; for thou art my god.

18They know not, neither do they consider: for he hath shut their eyes, that they cannot see; and their hearts, that they cannot understand.

19And none calleth to mind, neither is there knowledge nor understanding to say, I have burned part of it in the fire; yea, also I have baked bread upon the coals thereof; I have roasted flesh and eaten it: and shall I make the residue thereof an abomination? shall I fall down to the stock of a tree?

20He feedeth on ashes; a deceived heart hath turned him aside; and he cannot deliver his soul, nor say, Is there not a lie in my right hand?

21Remember these things, O Jacob, and Israel; for thou art my servant: I have formed thee; thou art my servant: O Israel, thou shalt not be forgotten of me.

22I have blotted out, as a thick cloud, thy transgressions, and, as a cloud, thy sins: return unto me; for I have redeemed thee.

23Sing, O ye heavens, for Yahweh hath done it; shout, ye lower parts of the earth; break forth into singing, ye mountains, O forest, and every tree therein: for Yahweh hath redeemed Jacob, and will glorify himself in Israel.

24Thus saith Yahweh, thy Redeemer, and he that formed thee from the womb: I am Yahweh, that maketh all things; that stretcheth forth the heavens alone; that spreadeth abroad the earth (who is with me?);

25that frustrateth the signs of the liars, and maketh diviners mad; that turneth wise men backward, and maketh their knowledge foolish;

26that confirmeth the word of his servant, and performeth the counsel of his messengers; that saith of Jerusalem, She shall be inhabited; and of the cities of Judah, They shall be built, and I will raise up the waste places thereof;

27that saith to the deep, Be dry, and I will dry up thy rivers;

28That saith of Cyrus, He is my shepherd, and shall perform all my pleasure, even saying of Jerusalem, She shall be built; and of the temple, Thy foundation shall be laid.

Chapter 45

1Thus saith Yahweh to his anointed, to Cyrus, whose right hand I have holden, to subdue nations before him, and I will loose the loins of kings; to open the doors before him, and the gates shall not be shut:

2I will go before thee, and make the rough places smooth; I will break in pieces the doors of brass, and cut in sunder the bars of iron;

3and I will give thee the treasures of darkness, and hidden riches of secret places, that thou mayest know that it is I, Yahweh, who call thee by thy name, even the God of Israel.

4For Jacob my servant's sake, and Israel my chosen, I have called thee by thy name: I have surnamed thee, though thou hast not known me.

5I am Yahweh, and there is none else; besides me there is no God. I will gird thee, though thou hast not known me;

6that they may know from the rising of the sun, and from the west, that there is none besides me: I am Yahweh, and there is none else.

7I form the light, and create darkness; I make peace, and create evil. I am Yahweh, that doeth all these things.

8Distil, ye heavens, from above, and let the skies pour down righteousness: let the earth open, that it may bring forth salvation, and let it cause righteousness to spring up together; I, Yahweh, have created it.

9Woe unto him that striveth with his Maker! a potsherd among the potsherds of the earth! Shall the clay say to him that fashioneth it, What makest thou? or thy work, He hath no hands?

10Woe unto him that saith unto a father, What begettest thou? or to a woman, With what travailest thou?

11Thus saith Yahweh, the Holy One of Israel, and his Maker: Ask me of the things that are to come; concerning my sons, and concerning the work of my hands, command ye me.

12I have made the earth, and created man upon it: I, even my hands, have stretched out the heavens; and all their host have I commanded.

13I have raised him up in righteousness, and I will make straight all his ways: he shall build my city, and he shall let my exiles go free, not for price nor reward, saith Yahweh of hosts.

14Thus saith Yahweh, The labor of Egypt, and the merchandise of Ethiopia, and the Sabeans, men of stature, shall come over unto thee, and they shall be thine: they shall go after thee, in chains they shall come over; and they shall fall down unto thee, they shall make supplication unto thee, saying, Surely God is in thee; and there is none else, there is no God.

15Verily thou art a God that hidest thyself, O God of Israel, the Saviour.

16They shall be put to shame, yea, confounded, all of them; they shall go into confusion together that are makers of idols.

17But Israel shall be saved by Yahweh with an everlasting salvation: ye shall not be put to shame nor confounded world without end.

18For thus saith Yahweh that created the heavens, the God that formed the earth and made it, that established it and created it not a waste, that formed it to be inhabited: I am Yahweh, and there is none else.

19I have not spoken in secret, in a place of the land of darkness; I said not unto the seed of Jacob, Seek ye me in vain: I, Yahweh, speak righteousness, I declare things that are right.

20Assemble yourselves and come; draw near together, ye that are escaped of the nations: they have no knowledge that carry the wood of their graven image, and pray unto a god that cannot save.

21Declare ye, and bring it forth; yea, let them take counsel together: who hath showed this from ancient time? who hath declared it of old? have not I, Yahweh? and there is no God else besides me, a just God and a Saviour; there is none besides me.

22Look unto me, and be ye saved, all the ends of the earth; for I am God, and there is none else.

23By myself have I sworn, the word is gone forth from my mouth in righteousness, and shall not return, that unto me every knee shall bow, every tongue shall swear.

24Only in Yahweh, it is said of me, is righteousness and strength; even to him shall men come; and all they that were incensed against him shall be put to shame.

25In Yahweh shall all the seed of Israel be justified, and shall glory.

Chapter 46

1Bel boweth down, Nebo stoopeth; their idols are upon the beasts, and upon the cattle: the things that ye carried about are made a load, a burden to the weary beast.

2They stoop, they bow down together; they could not deliver the burden, but themselves are gone into captivity.

3Hearken unto me, O house of Jacob, and all the remnant of the house of Israel, that have been borne by me from their birth, that have been carried from the womb;

4and even to old age I am he, and even to hoar hairs will I carry you; I have made, and I will bear; yea, I will carry, and will deliver.

5To whom will ye like me, and make me equal, and compare me, that we may be like?

6Such as lavish gold out of the bag, and weigh silver in the balance, they hire a goldsmith, and he maketh it a god; they fall down, yea, they worship.

7They bear it upon the shoulder, they carry it, and set it in its place, and it standeth, from its place shall it not remove: yea, one may cry unto it, yet can it not answer, nor save him out of his trouble.

8Remember this, and show yourselves men; bring it again to mind, O ye transgressors.

9Remember the former things of old: for I am God, and there is none else; I am God, and there is none like me;

10declaring the end from the beginning, and from ancient times things that are not yet done; saying, My counsel shall stand, and I will do all my pleasure;

11calling a ravenous bird from the east, the man of my counsel from a far country; yea, I have spoken, I will also bring it to pass; I have purposed, I will also do it.

12Hearken unto me, ye stout-hearted, that are far from righteousness:

13I bring near my righteousness, it shall not be far off, and my salvation shall not tarry; and I will place salvation in Zion for Israel my glory.

Chapter 47

1Come down, and sit in the dust, O virgin daughter of Babylon; sit on the ground without a throne, O daughter of the Chaldeans: for thou shalt no more be called tender and delicate.

2Take the millstones, and grind meal; remove thy veil, strip off the train, uncover the leg, pass through the rivers.

3Thy nakedness shall be uncovered, yea, thy shame shall be seen: I will take vengeance, and will spare no man.

4Our Redeemer, Yahweh of hosts is his name, the Holy One of Israel.

5Sit thou silent, and get thee into darkness, O daughter of the Chaldeans; for thou shalt no more be called The mistress of kingdoms.

6I was wroth with my people, I profaned mine inheritance, and gave them into thy hand: thou didst show them no mercy; upon the aged hast thou very heavily laid thy yoke.

7And thou saidst, I shall be mistress for ever; so that thou didst not lay these things to thy heart, neither didst remember the latter end thereof.

8Now therefore hear this, thou that art given to pleasures, that sittest securely, that sayest in thy heart, I am, and there is none else besides me; I shall not sit as a widow, neither shall I know the loss of children;

9but these two things shall come to thee in a moment in one day, the loss of children, and widowhood; in their full measure shall they come upon thee, in the multitude of thy sorceries, and the great abundance of thine enchantments.

10For thou hast trusted in thy wickedness; thou hast said, None seeth me; thy wisdom and thy knowledge, it hath perverted thee, and thou hast said in thy heart, I am, and there is none else besides me.

11Therefore shall evil come upon thee; thou shalt not know the dawning thereof: and mischief shall fall upon thee; thou shalt not be able to put it away: and desolation shall come upon thee suddenly, which thou knowest not.

12Stand now with thine enchantments, and with the multitude of thy sorceries, wherein thou hast labored from thy youth; if so be thou shalt be able to profit, if so be thou mayest prevail.

13Thou art wearied in the multitude of thy counsels: let now the astrologers, the star-gazers, the monthly prognosticators, stand up, and save thee from the things that shall come upon thee.

14Behold, they shall be as stubble; the fire shall burn them; they shall not deliver themselves from the power of the flame: it shall not be a coal to warm at, nor a fire to sit before.

15Thus shall the things be unto thee wherein thou hast labored: they that have trafficked with thee from thy youth shall wander every one to his quarter; there shall be none to save thee.

Chapter 48

1Hear ye this, O house of Jacob, who are called by the name of Israel, and are come forth out of the waters of Judah; who swear by the name of Yahweh, and make mention of the God of Israel, but not in truth, nor in righteousness

2(for they call themselves of the holy city, and stay themselves upon the God of Israel; Yahweh of hosts is his name):

3I have declared the former things of old; yea, they went forth out of my mouth, and I showed them: suddenly I did them, and they came to pass.

4Because I knew that thou art obstinate, and thy neck is an iron sinew, and thy brow brass;

5therefore I have declared it to thee from of old; before it came to pass I showed it thee; lest thou shouldest say, Mine idol hath done them, and my graven image, and my molten image, hath commanded them.

6Thou hast heard it; behold all this; and ye, will ye not declare it? I have showed thee new things from this time, even hidden things, which thou hast not known.

7They are created now, and not from of old; and before this day thou heardest them not; lest thou shouldest say, Behold, I knew them.

8Yea, thou heardest not; yea, thou knewest not; yea, from of old thine ear was not opened: for I knew that thou didst deal very treacherously, and wast called a transgressor from the womb.

9For my name's sake will I defer mine anger, and for my praise will I refrain for thee, that I cut thee not off.

10Behold, I have refined thee, but not as silver; I have chosen thee in the furnace of affliction.

11For mine own sake, for mine own sake, will I do it; for how should my name be profaned? and my glory will I not give to another.

12Hearken unto me, O Jacob, and Israel my called: I am he; I am the first, I also am the last.

13Yea, my hand hath laid the foundation of the earth, and my right hand hath spread out the heavens: when I call unto them, they stand up together.

14Assemble yourselves, all ye, and hear; who among them hath declared these things? He whom Yahweh loveth shall perform his pleasure on Babylon, and his arm shall be on the Chaldeans.

15I, even I, have spoken; yea, I have called him; I have brought him, and he shall make his way prosperous.

16Come ye near unto me, hear ye this; from the beginning I have not spoken in secret; from the time that it was, there am I: and now the Lord Yahweh hath sent me, and his Spirit.

17Thus saith Yahweh, thy Redeemer, the Holy One of Israel: I am Yahweh thy God, who teacheth thee to profit, who leadeth thee by the way that thou shouldest go.

18Oh that thou hadst hearkened to my commandments! then had thy peace been as a river, and thy righteousness as the waves of the sea:

19thy seed also had been as the sand, and the offspring of thy bowels like the grains thereof: his name would not be cut off nor destroyed from before me.

20Go ye forth from Babylon, flee ye from the Chaldeans; with a voice of singing declare ye, tell this, utter it even to the end of the earth: say ye, Yahweh hath redeemed his servant Jacob.

21And they thirsted not when he led them through the deserts; he caused the waters to flow out of the rock for them; he clave the rock also, and the waters gushed out.

22There is no peace, saith Yahweh, to the wicked.

Chapter 49

1Listen, O isles, unto me; and hearken, ye peoples, from far: Yahweh hath called me from the womb; from the bowels of my mother hath he made mention of my name:

2and he hath made my mouth like a sharp sword; in the shadow of his hand hath he hid me: and he hath made me a polished shaft; in his quiver hath he kept me close:

3and he said unto me, Thou art my servant; Israel, in whom I will be glorified.

4But I said, I have labored in vain, I have spent my strength for nought and vanity; yet surely the justice due to me is with Yahweh, and my recompense with my God.

5And now saith Yahweh that formed me from the womb to be his servant, to bring Jacob again to him, and that Israel be gathered unto him (for I am honorable in the eyes of Yahweh, and my God is become my strength);

6yea, he saith, It is too light a thing that thou shouldest be my servant to raise up the tribes of Jacob, and to restore the preserved of Israel: I will also give thee for a light to the Gentiles, that thou mayest be my salvation unto the end of the earth.

7Thus saith Yahweh, the Redeemer of Israel, and his Holy One, to him whom man despiseth, to him whom the nation abhorreth, to a servant of rulers: Kings shall see and arise; princes, and they shall worship; because of Yahweh that is faithful, even the Holy One of Israel, who hath chosen thee.

8Thus saith Yahweh, In an acceptable time have I answered thee, and in a day of salvation have I helped thee; and I will preserve thee, and give thee for a covenant of the people, to raise up the land, to make them inherit the desolate heritages:

9saying to them that are bound, Go forth; to them that are in darkness, Show yourselves. They shall feed in the ways, and on all bare heights shall be their pasture.

10They shall not hunger nor thirst; neither shall the heat nor sun smite them: for he that hath mercy on them will lead them, even by springs of water will he guide them.

11And I will make all my mountains a way, and my highways shall be exalted.

12Lo, these shall come from far; and, lo, these from the north and from the west; and these from the land of Sinim.

13Sing, O heavens; and be joyful, O earth; and break forth into singing, O mountains: for Yahweh hath comforted his people, and will have compassion upon his afflicted.

14But Zion said, Yahweh hath forsaken me, and the Lord hath forgotten me.

15Can a woman forget her sucking child, that she should not have compassion on the son of her womb? yea, these may forget, yet will not I forget

Isaiah

thee.

16 Behold, I have graven thee upon the palms of my hands; thy walls are continually before me.

17 Thy children make haste; thy destroyers and they that made thee waste shall go forth from thee.

18 Lift up thine eyes round about, and behold: all these gather themselves together, and come to thee. As I live, saith Yahweh, thou shalt surely clothe thee with them all as with an ornament, and gird thyself with them, like a bride.

19 For, as for thy waste and thy desolate places, and thy land that hath been destroyed, surely now shalt thou be too strait for the inhabitants, and they that swallowed thee up shall be far away.

20 The children of thy bereavement shall yet say in thine ears, The place is too strait for me; give place to me that I may dwell.

21 Then shalt thou say in thy heart, Who hath begotten me these, seeing I have been bereaved of my children, and am solitary, an exile, and wandering to and fro? and who hath brought up these? Behold, I was left alone; these, where were they?

22 Thus saith the Lord Yahweh, Behold, I will lift up my hand to the nations, and set up my ensign to the peoples; and they shall bring thy sons in their bosom, and thy daughters shall be carried upon their shoulders.

23 And kings shall be thy nursing fathers, and their queens thy nursing mothers: they shall bow down to thee with their faces to the earth, and lick the dust of thy feet; and thou shalt know that I am Yahweh; and they that wait for me shall not be put to shame.

24 Shall the prey be taken from the mighty, or the lawful captives be delivered?

25 But thus saith Yahweh, Even the captives of the mighty shall be taken away, and the prey of the terrible shall be delivered; for I will contend with him that contendeth with thee, and I will save thy children.

26 And I will feed them that oppress thee with their own flesh; and they shall be drunken with their own blood, as with sweet wine: and all flesh shall know that I, Yahweh, am thy Saviour, and thy Redeemer, the Mighty One of Jacob.

Chapter 50

1 Thus saith Yahweh, Where is the bill of your mother's divorcement, wherewith I have put her away? or which of my creditors is it to whom I have sold you? Behold, for your iniquities were ye sold, and for your transgressions was your mother put away.

2 Wherefore, when I came, was there no man? when I called, was there none to answer? Is my hand shortened at all, that it cannot redeem? or have I no power to deliver? Behold, at my rebuke I dry up the sea, I make the rivers a wilderness: their fish stink, because there is no water, and die for thirst.

3 I clothe the heavens with blackness, and I make sackcloth their covering.

4 The Lord Yahweh hath given me the tongue of them that are taught, that I may know how to sustain with words him that is weary: he wakeneth morning by morning, he wakeneth mine ear to hear as they that are taught.

5 The Lord Yahweh hath opened mine ear, and I was not rebellious, neither turned away backward.

6 I gave my back to the smiters, and my cheeks to them that plucked off the hair; I hid not my face from shame and spitting.

7 For the Lord Yahweh will help me; therefore have I not been confounded: therefore have I set my face like a flint, and I know that I shall not be put to shame.

8 He is near that justifieth me; who will contend with me? let us stand up together: who is mine adversary? let him come near to me.

9 Behold, the Lord Yahweh will help me; who is he that shall condemn me? behold, all they shall wax old as a garment, the moth shall eat them up.

10 Who is among you that feareth Yahweh, that obeyeth the voice of his servant? he that walketh in darkness, and hath no light, let him trust in the name of Yahweh, and rely upon his God.

11 Behold, all ye that kindle a fire, that gird yourselves about with firebrands; walk ye in the flame of your fire, and among the brands that ye have kindled. This shall ye have of my hand; ye shall lie down in sorrow.

Chapter 51

1 Hearken to me, ye that follow after righteousness, ye that seek Yahweh: look unto the rock whence ye were hewn, and to the hold of the pit whence ye were digged.

2 Look unto Abraham your father, and unto Sarah that bare you; for when he was but one I called him, and I blessed him, and made him many.

3 For Yahweh hath comforted Zion; he hath comforted all her waste places, and hath made her wilderness like Eden, and her desert like the garden of Yahweh; joy and gladness shall be found therein, thanksgiving, and the voice of melody.

4 Attend unto me, O my people; and give ear unto me, O my nation: for a law shall go forth from me, and I will establish my justice for a light of the peoples.

5 My righteousness is near, my salvation is gone forth, and mine arms shall judge the peoples; the isles shall wait for me, and on mine arm shall they trust.

6 Lift up your eyes to the heavens, and look upon the earth beneath; for the heavens shall vanish away like smoke, and the earth shall wax old like a garment; and they that dwell therein shall die in like manner: but my salvation shall be for ever, and my righteousness shall not be abolished.

7 Hearken unto me, ye that know righteousness, the people in whose heart is my law; fear ye not the reproach of men, neither be ye dismayed at their revilings.

8 For the moth shall eat them up like a garment, and the worm shall eat them like wool; but my righteousness shall be for ever, and my salvation unto all generations.

9 Awake, awake, put on strength, O arm of Yahweh; awake, as in the days of old, the generations of ancient times. Is it not thou that didst cut Rahab in pieces, that didst pierce the monster?

10 Is it not thou that driedst up the sea, the waters of the great deep; that madest the depths of the sea a way for the redeemed to pass over?

11 And the ransomed of Yahweh shall return, and come with singing unto Zion; and everlasting joy shall be upon their heads: they shall obtain gladness and joy; and sorrow and sighing shall flee away.

12 I, even I, am he that comforteth you: who art thou, that thou art afraid of man that shall die, and of the son of man that shall be made as grass;

13 and hast forgotten Yahweh thy Maker, that stretched forth the heavens, and laid the foundations of the earth; and fearest continually all the day because of the fury of the oppressor, when he maketh ready to destroy? and where is the fury of the oppressor?

14 The captive exile shall speedily be loosed; and he shall not die and go down into the pit, neither shall his bread fail.

15 For I am Yahweh thy God, who stirreth up the sea, so that the waves thereof roar: Yahweh of hosts is his name.

16 And I have put my words in thy mouth, and have covered thee in the shadow of my hand, that I may plant the heavens, and lay the foundations of the earth, and say unto Zion, Thou art my people.

17 Awake, awake, stand up, O Jerusalem, that hast drunk at the hand of Yahweh the cup of his wrath; thou hast drunken the bowl of the cup of staggering, and drained it.

18 There is none to guide her among all the sons whom she hath brought forth; neither is there any that taketh her by the hand among all the sons that she hath brought up.

19 These two things are befallen thee, who shall bemoan thee? desolation and destruction, and the famine and the sword; how shall I comfort thee?

20 Thy sons have fainted, they lie at the head of all the streets, as an antelope in a net; they are full of the wrath of Yahweh, the rebuke of thy God.

21 Therefore hear now this, thou afflicted, and drunken, but now with wine:

22 Thus saith thy Lord Yahweh, and thy God that pleadeth the cause of his people, Behold, I have taken out of thy hand the cup of staggering, even the bowl of the cup of my wrath; thou shalt no more drink it again:

23 and I will put it into the hand of them that afflict thee, that have said to thy soul, Bow down, that we may go over; and thou hast laid thy back as the ground, and as the street, to them that go over.

Chapter 52

1 Awake, awake, put on thy strength, O Zion; put on thy beautiful garments, O Jerusalem, the holy city: for henceforth there shall no more come into thee the uncircumcised and the unclean.

2 Shake thyself from the dust; arise, sit on thy throne, O Jerusalem: loose thyself from the bonds of thy neck, O captive daughter of Zion.

3 For thus saith Yahweh, Ye were sold for nought; and ye shall be redeemed without money.

4 For thus saith the Lord Yahweh, My people went down at the first into Egypt to sojourn there: and the Assyrian hath oppressed them without cause.

5 Now therefore, what do I here, saith Yahweh, seeing that my people is taken away for nought? they that rule over them do howl, saith Yahweh, and my name continually all the day is blasphemed.

6 Therefore my people shall know my name: therefore they shall know in that day that I am he that doth speak; behold, it is I.

7 How beautiful upon the mountains are the feet of him that bringeth good tidings, that publisheth peace, that bringeth good tidings of good, that publisheth salvation, that saith unto Zion, Thy God reigneth!

8 The voice of thy watchmen! they lift up the voice, together do they sing; for they shall see eye to eye, when Yahweh returneth to Zion.

9 Break forth into joy, sing together, ye waste places of Jerusalem; for Yahweh hath comforted his people, he hath redeemed Jerusalem.

10 Yahweh hath made bare his holy arm in the eyes of all the nations; and all the ends of the earth have seen the salvation of our God.

11 Depart ye, depart ye, go ye out from thence, touch no unclean thing; go ye out of the midst of her; cleanse yourselves, ye that bear the vessels of Yahweh.

12 For ye shall not go out in haste, neither shall ye go by flight: for Yahweh will go before you; and the God of Israel will be your rearward.

13 Behold, my servant shall deal wisely, he shall be exalted and lifted up, and shall be very high.

14 Like as many were astonished at thee (his visage was so marred more than any man, and his form more than the sons of men),

15 so shall he sprinkle many nations; kings shall shut their mouths at him: for that which had not been told them shall they see; and that which they had not heard shall they understand.

Chapter 53

1 Who hath believed our message? and to whom hath the arm of Yahweh been revealed?

2 For he grew up before him as a tender plant, and as a root out of a dry ground: he hath no form nor comeliness; and when we see him, there is no beauty that we should desire him.

3 He was despised, and rejected of men; a man of sorrows, and acquainted with grief: and as one from whom men hide their face he was despised; and we esteemed him not.

4 Surely he hath borne our griefs, and carried our sorrows; yet we did esteem him stricken, smitten of God, and afflicted.

5 But he was wounded for our transgressions, he was bruised for our iniquities; the chastisement of our peace was upon him; and with his stripes we are healed.

⁶All we like sheep have gone astray; we have turned every one to his own way; and Yahweh hath laid on him the iniquity of us all.

⁷He was oppressed, yet when he was afflicted he opened not his mouth; as a lamb that is led to the slaughter, and as a sheep that before its shearers is dumb, so he opened not his mouth.

⁸By oppression and judgment he was taken away; and as for his generation, who among them considered that he was cut off out of the land of the living for the transgression of my people to whom the stroke was due?

⁹And they made his grave with the wicked, and with a rich man in his death; although he had done no violence, neither was any deceit in his mouth.

¹⁰Yet it pleased Yahweh to bruise him; he hath put him to grief: when thou shalt make his soul an offering for sin, he shall see his seed, he shall prolong his days, and the pleasure of Yahweh shall prosper in his hand.

¹¹He shall see of the travail of his soul, and shall be satisfied: by the knowledge of himself shall my righteous servant justify many; and he shall bear their iniquities.

¹²Therefore will I divide him a portion with the great, and he shall divide the spoil with the strong; because he poured out his soul unto death, and was numbered with the transgressors: yet he bare the sin of many, and made intercession for the transgressors.

Chapter 54

¹Sing, O barren, thou that didst not bear; break forth into singing, and cry aloud, thou that didst not travail with child: for more are the children of the desolate than the children of the married wife, saith Yahweh.

²Enlarge the place of thy tent, and let them stretch forth the curtains of thy habitations; spare not: lengthen thy cords, and strengthen thy stakes.

³For thou shalt spread aboard on the right hand and on the left; and thy seed shall possess the nations, and make the desolate cities to be inhabited.

⁴Fear not; for thou shalt not be ashamed: neither be thou confounded; for thou shalt not be put to shame: for thou shalt forget the shame of thy youth; and the reproach of thy widowhood shalt thou remember no more.

⁵For thy Maker is thy husband; Yahweh of hosts is his name: and the Holy One of Israel is thy Redeemer; the God of the whole earth shall he be called.

⁶For Yahweh hath called thee as a wife forsaken and grieved in spirit, even a wife of youth, when she is cast off, saith thy God.

⁷For a small moment have I forsaken thee; but with great mercies will I gather thee.

⁸In overflowing wrath I hid my face from thee for a moment; but with everlasting lovingkindness will I have mercy on thee, saith Yahweh thy Redeemer.

⁹For this is as the waters of Noah unto me; for as I have sworn that the waters of Noah shall no more go over the earth, so have I sworn that I will not be wroth with thee, nor rebuke thee.

¹⁰For the mountains may depart, and the hills be removed; but my lovingkindness shall not depart from thee, neither shall my covenant of peace be removed, saith Yahweh that hath mercy on thee.

¹¹O thou afflicted, tossed with tempest, and not comforted, behold, I will set thy stones in fair colors, and lay thy foundations with sapphires.

¹²And I will make thy pinnacles of rubies, and thy gates of carbuncles, and all thy border of precious stones.

¹³And all thy children shall be taught of Yahweh; and great shall be the peace of thy children.

¹⁴In righteousness shalt thou be established: thou shalt be far from oppression, for thou shalt not fear; and from terror, for it shall not come near thee.

¹⁵Behold, they may gather together, but not by me: whosoever shall gather together against thee shall fall because of thee.

¹⁶Behold, I have created the smith that bloweth the fire of coals, and bringeth forth a weapon for his work; and I have created the waster to destroy.

¹⁷No weapon that is formed against thee shall prosper; and every tongue that shall rise against thee in judgment thou shalt condemn. This is the heritage of the servants of Yahweh, and their righteousness which is of me, saith Yahweh.

Chapter 55

¹Ho, every one that thirsteth, come ye to the waters, and he that hath no money; come ye, buy, and eat; yea, come, buy wine and milk without money and without price.

²Wherefore do ye spend money for that which is not bread? and your labor for that which satisfieth not? hearken diligently unto me, and eat ye that which is good, and let your soul delight itself in fatness.

³Incline your ear, and come unto me; hear, and your soul shall live: and I will make an everlasting covenant with you, even the sure mercies of David.

⁴Behold, I have given him for a witness to the peoples, a leader and commander to the peoples.

⁵Behold, thou shalt call a nation that thou knowest not; and a nation that knew not thee shall run unto thee, because of Yahweh thy God, and for the Holy One of Israel; for he hath glorified thee.

⁶Seek ye Yahweh while he may be found; call ye upon him while he is near:

⁷let the wicked forsake his way, and the unrighteous man his thoughts; and let him return unto Yahweh, and he will have mercy upon him; and to our God, for he will abundantly pardon.

⁸For my thoughts are not your thoughts, neither are your ways my ways, saith Yahweh.

⁹For as the heavens are higher than the earth, so are my ways higher than your ways, and my thoughts than your thoughts.

¹⁰For as the rain cometh down and the snow from heaven, and returneth not thither, but watereth the earth, and maketh it bring forth and bud, and giveth seed to the sower and bread to the eater;

¹¹so shall my word be that goeth forth out of my mouth: it shall not return unto me void, but it shall accomplish that which I please, and it shall prosper in the thing whereto I sent it.

¹²For ye shall go out with joy, and be led forth with peace: the mountains and the hills shall break forth before you into singing; and all the trees of the fields shall clap their hands.

¹³Instead of the thorn shall come up the fir-tree; and instead of the brier shall come up the myrtle-tree: and it shall be to Yahweh for a name, for an everlasting sign that shall not be cut off.

Chapter 56

¹Thus saith Yahweh, Keep ye justice, and do righteousness; for my salvation is near to come, and my righteousness to be revealed.

²Blessed is the man that doeth this, and the son of man that holdeth it fast; that keepeth the sabbath from profaning it, and keepeth his hand from doing any evil.

³Neither let the foreigner, that hath joined himself to Yahweh, speak, saying, Yahweh will surely separate me from his people; neither let the eunuch say, Behold, I am a dry tree.

⁴For thus saith Yahweh of the eunuchs that keep my sabbaths, and choose the things that please me, and hold fast my covenant:

⁵Unto them will I give in my house and within my walls a memorial and a name better than of sons and of daughters; I will give them an everlasting name, that shall not be cut off.

⁶Also the foreigners that join themselves to Yahweh, to minister unto him, and to love the name of Yahweh, to be his servants, every one that keepeth the sabbath from profaning it, and holdeth fast my covenant;

⁷even them will I bring to my holy mountain, and make them joyful in my house of prayer: their burnt-offerings and their sacrifices shall be accepted upon mine altar; for my house shall be called a house of prayer for all peoples.

⁸The Lord Yahweh, who gathereth the outcasts of Israel, saith, Yet will I gather others to him, besides his own that are gathered.

⁹All ye beasts of the field, come to devour, yea, all ye beasts in the forest.

¹⁰His watchmen are blind, they are all without knowledge; they are all dumb dogs, they cannot bark; dreaming, lying down, loving to slumber.

¹¹Yea, the dogs are greedy, they can never have enough; and these are shepherds that cannot understand: they have all turned to their own way, each one to his gain, from every quarter.

¹²Come ye, say they, I will fetch wine, and we will fill ourselves with strong drink; and to-morrow shall be as this day, a day great beyond measure.

Chapter 57

¹The righteous perisheth, and no man layeth it to heart; and merciful men are taken away, none considering that the righteous is taken away from the evil to come.

²He entereth into peace; they rest in their beds, each one that walketh in his uprightness.

³But draw near hither, ye sons of the sorceress, the seed of the adulterer and the harlot.

⁴Against whom do ye sport yourselves? against whom make ye a wide mouth, and put out the tongue? are ye not children of transgression, a seed of falsehood,

⁵ye that inflame yourselves among the oaks, under every green tree; that slay the children in the valleys, under the clefts of the rocks?

⁶Among the smooth stones of the valley is thy portion; they, they are thy lot; even to them hast thou poured a drink-offering, thou hast offered an oblation. Shall I be appeased for these things?

⁷Upon a high and lofty mountain hast thou set thy bed; thither also wentest thou up to offer sacrifice.

⁸And behind the doors and the posts hast thou set up thy memorial: for thou hast uncovered thyself to another than me, and art gone up; thou hast enlarged thy bed, and made thee a covenant with them: thou lovedst their bed where thou sawest it.

⁹And thou wentest to the king with oil, and didst increase thy perfumes, and didst send thine ambassadors far off, and didst debase thyself even unto Sheol.

¹⁰Thou wast wearied with the length of thy way; yet saidst thou not, It is in vain: thou didst find a quickening of thy strength; therefore thou wast not faint.

¹¹And of whom hast thou been afraid and in fear, that thou liest, and hast not remembered me, nor laid it to thy heart? have not I held my peace even of long time, and thou fearest me not?

¹²I will declare thy righteousness; and as for thy works, they shall not profit thee.

¹³When thou criest, let them that thou hast gathered deliver thee; but the wind shall take them, a breath shall carry them all away: but he that taketh refuge in me shall possess the land, and shall inherit my holy mountain.

¹⁴And he will say, Cast ye up, cast ye up, prepare the way, take up the stumbling-block out of the way of my people.

¹⁵For thus saith the high and lofty One that inhabiteth eternity, whose name is Holy: I dwell in the high and holy place, with him also that is of a contrite and humble spirit, to revive the spirit of the humble, and to revive the heart of the contrite.

¹⁶For I will not contend for ever, neither will I be always wroth; for the spirit would faint before me, and the souls that I have made.

¹⁷For the iniquity of his covetousness was I wroth, and smote him; I hid my face and was wroth; and he went on backsliding in the way of his heart.

¹⁸I have seen his ways, and will heal him: I will lead him also, and restore comforts unto him and to his mourners.

¹⁹I create the fruit of the lips: Peace, peace, to him that is far off and to him that is near, saith Yahweh; and I will heal him.

Isaiah

20But the wicked are like the troubled sea; for it cannot rest, and its waters cast up mire and dirt.

21There is no peace, saith my God, to the wicked.

Chapter 58

1Cry aloud, spare not, lift up thy voice like a trumpet, and declare unto my people their transgression, and to the house of Jacob their sins.

2Yet they seek me daily, and delight to know my ways: as a nation that did righteousness, and forsook not the ordinance of their God, they ask of me righteous judgments; they delight to draw near unto God.

3Wherefore have we fasted, say they, and thou seest not? wherefore have we afflicted our soul, and thou takest no knowledge? Behold, in the day of your fast ye find your own pleasure, and exact all your labors.

4Behold, ye fast for strife and contention, and to smite with the fist of wickedness: ye fast not this day so as to make your voice to be heard on high.

5Is such the fast that I have chosen? the day for a man to afflict his soul? Is it to bow down his head as a rush, and to spread sackcloth and ashes under him? wilt thou call this a fast, and an acceptable day to Yahweh?

6Is not this the fast that I have chosen: to loose the bonds of wickedness, to undo the bands of the yoke, and to let the oppressed go free, and that ye break every yoke?

7Is it not to deal thy bread to the hungry, and that thou bring the poor that are cast out to thy house? when thou seest the naked, that thou cover him; and that thou hide not thyself from thine own flesh?

8Then shall thy light break forth as the morning, and thy healing shall spring forth speedily; and thy righteousness shall go before thee; the glory of Yahweh shall by thy rearward.

9Then shalt thou call, and Yahweh will answer; thou shalt cry, and he will say, Here I am. If thou take away from the midst of thee the yoke, the putting forth of the finger, and speaking wickedly;

10and if thou draw out thy soul to the hungry, and satisfy the afflicted soul: then shall thy light rise in darkness, and thine obscurity be as the noonday;

11and Yahweh will guide thee continually, and satisfy thy soul in dry places, and make strong thy bones; and thou shalt be like a watered garden, and like a spring of water, whose waters fail not.

12And they that shall be of thee shall build the old waste places; thou shalt raise up the foundations of many generations; and thou shalt be called The repairer of the breach, The restorer of paths to dwell in.

13If thou turn away thy foot from the sabbath, from doing thy pleasure on my holy day; and call the sabbath a delight, and the holy of Yahweh honorable; and shalt honor it, not doing thine own ways, nor finding thine own pleasure, nor speaking thine own words:

14then shalt thou delight thyself in Yahweh; and I will make thee to ride upon the high places of the earth; and I will feed thee with the heritage of Jacob thy father: for the mouth of Yahweh hath spoken it.

Chapter 59

1Behold, Yahweh's hand is not shortened, that it cannot save; neither his ear heavy, that it cannot hear:

2but your iniquities have separated between you and your God, and your sins have hid his face from you, so that he will not hear.

3For your hands are defiled with blood, and your fingers with iniquity; your lips have spoken lies, your tongue muttereth wickedness.

4None sueth in righteousness, and none pleadeth in truth: they trust in vanity, and speak lies; they conceive mischief, and bring forth iniquity.

5They hatch adders' eggs, and weave the spider's web: he that eateth of their eggs dieth; and that which is crushed breaketh out into a viper.

6Their webs shall not become garments, neither shall they cover themselves with their works: their works are works of iniquity, and the act of violence is in their hands.

7Their feet run to evil, and they make haste to shed innocent blood: their thoughts are thoughts of iniquity; desolation and destruction are in their paths.

8The way of peace they know not; and there is no justice in their goings: they have made them crooked paths; whosoever goeth therein doth not know peace.

9Therefore is justice far from us, neither doth righteousness overtake us: we look for light, but, behold, darkness; for brightness, but we walk in obscurity.

10We grope for the wall like the blind; yea, we grope as they that have no eyes: we stumble at noonday as in the twilight; among them that are lusty we are as dead men.

11We roar all like bears, and moan sore like doves: we look for justice, but there is none; for salvation, but it is far off from us.

12For our transgressions are multiplied before thee, and our sins testify against us; for our transgressions are with us, and as for our iniquities, we know them:

13transgressing and denying Yahweh, and turning away from following our God, speaking oppression and revolt, conceiving and uttering from the heart words of falsehood.

14And justice is turned away backward, and righteousness standeth afar off; for truth is fallen in the street, and uprightness cannot enter.

15Yea, truth is lacking; and he that departeth from evil maketh himself a prey. And Yahweh saw it, and it displeased him that there was no justice.

16And he saw that there was no man, and wondered that there was no intercessor: therefore his own arm brought salvation unto him; and his righteousness, it upheld him.

17And he put on righteousness as a breastplate, and a helmet of salvation upon his head; and he put on garments of vengeance for clothing, and was clad with zeal as a mantle.

18According to their deeds, accordingly he will repay, wrath to his adversaries, recompense to his enemies; to the islands he will repay recompense.

19So shall they fear the name of Yahweh from the west, and his glory from the rising of the sun; for he will come as a rushing stream, which the breath of Yahweh driveth.

20And a Redeemer will come to Zion, and unto them that turn from transgression in Jacob, saith Yahweh.

21And as for me, this is my covenant with them, saith Yahweh: my Spirit that is upon thee, and my words which I have put in thy mouth, shall not depart out of thy mouth, nor out of the mouth of thy seed, nor out of the mouth of thy seed's seed, saith Yahweh, from henceforth and for ever.

Chapter 60

1Arise, shine; for thy light is come, and the glory of Yahweh is risen upon thee.

2For, behold, darkness shall cover the earth, and gross darkness the peoples; but Yahweh will arise upon thee, and his glory shall be seen upon thee.

3And nations shall come to thy light, and kings to the brightness of thy rising.

4Lift up thine eyes round about, and see: they all gather themselves together, they come to thee; thy sons shall come from far, and thy daughters shall be carried in the arms.

5Then thou shalt see and be radiant, and thy heart shall thrill and be enlarged; because the abundance of the sea shall be turned unto thee, the wealth of the nations shall come unto thee.

6The multitude of camels shall cover thee, the dromedaries of Midian and Ephah; all they from Sheba shall come; they shall bring gold and frankincense, and shall proclaim the praises of Yahweh.

7All the flocks of Kedar shall be gathered together unto thee, the rams of Nebaioth shall minister unto thee; they shall come up with acceptance on mine altar; and I will glorify the house of my glory.

8Who are these that fly as a cloud, and as the doves to their windows?

9Surely the isles shall wait for me, and the ships of Tarshish first, to bring thy sons from far, their silver and their gold with them, for the name of Yahweh thy God, and for the Holy One of Israel, because he hath glorified thee.

10And foreigners shall build up thy walls, and their kings shall minister unto thee: for in my wrath I smote thee, but in my favor have I had mercy on thee.

11Thy gates also shall be open continually; they shall not be shut day nor night; that men may bring unto thee the wealth of the nations, and their kings led captive.

12For that nation and kingdom that will not serve thee shall perish; yea, those nations shall be utterly wasted.

13The glory of Lebanon shall come unto thee, the fir-tree, the pine, and the box-tree together, to beautify the place of my sanctuary; and I will make the place of my feet glorious.

14And the sons of them that afflicted thee shall come bending unto thee; and all they that despised thee shall bow themselves down at the soles of thy feet; and they shall call thee The city of Yahweh, The Zion of the Holy One of Israel.

15Whereas thou hast been forsaken and hated, so that no man passed through thee, I will make thee an eternal excellency, a joy of many generations.

16Thou shalt also suck the milk of the nations, and shalt suck the breast of kings; and thou shalt know that I, Yahweh, am thy Saviour, and thy Redeemer, the Mighty One of Jacob.

17For brass I will bring gold, and for iron I will bring silver, and for wood brass, and for stones iron. I will also make thy officers peace, and thine exactors righteousness.

18Violence shall no more be heard in thy land, desolation nor destruction within thy borders; but thou shalt call thy walls Salvation, and thy gates Praise.

19The sun shall be no more thy light by day; neither for brightness shall the moon give light unto thee: but Yahweh will be unto thee an everlasting light, and thy God thy glory.

20Thy sun shall no more go down, neither shall thy moon withdraw itself; for Yahweh will be thine everlasting light, and the days of thy mourning shall be ended.

21Thy people also shall be all righteous; they shall inherit the land for ever, the branch of my planting, the work of my hands, that I may be glorified.

22The little one shall become a thousand, and the small one a strong nation; I, Yahweh, will hasten it in its time.

Chapter 61

1The Spirit of the Lord Yahweh is upon me; because Yahweh hath anointed me to preach good tidings unto the meek; he hath sent me to bind up the broken-hearted, to proclaim liberty to the captives, and the opening of the prison to them that are bound;

2to proclaim the year of Yahweh's favor, and the day of vengeance of our God; to comfort all that mourn;

3to appoint unto them that mourn in Zion, to give unto them a garland for ashes, the oil of joy for mourning, the garment of praise for the spirit of heaviness; that they may be called trees of righteousness, the planting of Yahweh, that he may be glorified.

4And they shall build the old wastes, they shall raise up the former desolations, and they shall repair the waste cities, the desolations of many generations.

5And strangers shall stand and feed your flocks, and foreigners shall be your plowmen and your vine-dressers.

6But ye shall be named the priests of Yahweh; men shall call you the ministers of our God: ye shall eat the wealth of the nations, and in their glory shall ye boast yourselves.

7Instead of your shame ye shall have double; and instead of dishonor they shall rejoice in their portion: therefore in their land they shall possess double; everlasting joy shall be unto them.

8For I, Yahweh, love justice, I hate robbery with iniquity; and I will give them their recompense in truth, and I will make an everlasting covenant with them.

9And their seed shall be known among the nations, and their offspring among the peoples; all that see them shall acknowledge them, that they are the seed which Yahweh hath blessed.

10I will greatly rejoice in Yahweh, my soul shall be joyful in my God; for he hath clothed me with the garments of salvation, he hath covered me with the robe of righteousness, as a bridegroom decketh himself with a garland, and as a bride adorneth herself with her jewels.

11For as the earth bringeth forth its bud, and as the garden causeth the things that are sown in it to spring forth; so the Lord Yahweh will cause righteousness and praise to spring forth before all the nations.

Chapter 62

1For Zion's sake will I not hold my peace, and for Jerusalem's sake I will not rest, until her righteousness go forth as brightness, and her salvation as a lamp that burneth.

2And the nations shall see thy righteousness, and all kings thy glory, and thou shalt be called by a new name, which the mouth of Yahweh shall name.

3Thou shalt also be a crown of beauty in the hand of Yahweh, and a royal diadem in the hand of thy God.

4Thou shalt no more be termed Forsaken; neither shall thy land any more be termed Desolate: but thou shalt be called Hephzi-bah, and thy land Beulah; for Yahweh delighteth in thee, and thy land shall be married.

5For as a young man marrieth a virgin, so shall thy sons marry thee; and as the bridegroom rejoiceth over the bride, so shall thy God rejoice over thee.

6I have set watchmen upon thy walls, O Jerusalem; they shall never hold their peace day nor night: ye that are Yahweh's remembrancers, take ye no rest,

7and give him no rest, till he establish, and till he make Jerusalem a praise in the earth.

8Yahweh hath sworn by his right hand, and by the arm of his strength, Surely I will no more give thy grain to be food for thine enemies; and foreigners shall not drink thy new wine, for which thou hast labored:

9but they that have garnered it shall eat it, and praise Yahweh; and they that have gathered it shall drink it in the courts of my sanctuary.

10Go through, go through the gates; prepare ye the way of the people; cast up, cast up the highway; gather out the stones; lift up an ensign for the peoples.

11Behold, Yahweh hath proclaimed unto the end of the earth, Say ye to the daughter of Zion, Behold, thy salvation cometh; behold, his reward is with him, and his recompense before him.

12And they shall call them The holy people, The redeemed of Yahweh: and thou shalt be called Sought out, A city not forsaken.

Chapter 63

1Who is this that cometh from Edom, with dyed garments from Bozrah? this that is glorious in his apparel, marching in the greatness of his strength? I that speak in righteousness, mighty to save.

2Wherefore art thou red in thine apparel, and thy garments like him that treadeth in the winevat?

3I have trodden the winepress alone; and of the peoples there was no man with me: yea, I trod them in mine anger, and trampled them in my wrath; and their lifeblood is sprinkled upon my garments, and I have stained all my raiment.

4For the day of vengeance was in my heart, and the year of my redeemed is come.

5And I looked, and there was none to help; and I wondered that there was none to uphold: therefore mine own arm brought salvation unto me; and my wrath, it upheld me.

6And I trod down the peoples in mine anger, and made them drunk in my wrath, and I poured out their lifeblood on the earth.

7I will make mention of the lovingkindnesses of Yahweh, and the praises of Yahweh, according to all that Yahweh hath bestowed on us, and the great goodness toward the house of Israel, which he hath bestowed on them according to his mercies, and according to the multitude of his lovingkindnesses.

8For he said, Surely, they are my people, children that will not deal falsely: so he was their Saviour.

9In all their affliction he was afflicted, and the angel of his presence saved them: in his love and in his pity he redeemed them; and he bare them, and carried them all the days of old.

10But they rebelled, and grieved his holy Spirit: therefore he was turned to be their enemy, and himself fought against them.

11Then he remembered the days of old, Moses and his people, saying, Where is he that brought them up out of the sea with the shepherds of his flock? where is he that put his holy Spirit in the midst of them?

12that caused his glorious arm to go at the right hand of Moses? that divided the waters before them, to make himself an everlasting name?

13that led them through the depths, as a horse in the wilderness, so that they stumbled not?

14As the cattle that go down into the valley, the Spirit of Yahweh caused them to rest; so didst thou lead thy people, to make thyself a glorious name.

15Look down from heaven, and behold from the habitation of thy holiness and of thy glory: where are thy zeal and thy mighty acts? the yearning of thy heart and thy compassions are restrained toward me.

16For thou art our Father, though Abraham knoweth us not, and Israel doth not acknowledge us: thou, O Yahweh, art our Father; our Redeemer from everlasting is thy name.

17O Yahweh, why dost thou make us to err from thy ways, and hardenest our heart from thy fear? Return for thy servants' sake, the tribes of thine inheritance.

18Thy holy people possessed it but a little while: our adversaries have trodden down thy sanctuary.

19We are become as they over whom thou never barest rule, as they that were not called by thy name.

Chapter 64

1Oh that thou wouldest rend the heavens, that thou wouldest come down, that the mountains might quake at thy presence,

2as when fire kindleth the brushwood, and the fire causeth the waters to boil; to make thy name known to thine adversaries, that the nations may tremble at thy presence!

3When thou didst terrible things which we looked not for, thou camest down, the mountains quaked at thy presence.

4For from of old men have not heard, nor perceived by the ear, neither hath the eye seen a God besides thee, who worketh for him that waiteth for him.

5Thou meetest him that rejoiceth and worketh righteousness, those that remember thee in thy ways: behold, thou wast wroth, and we sinned: in them have we been of long time; and shall we be saved?

6For we are all become as one that is unclean, and all our righteousnesses are as a polluted garment: and we all do fade as a leaf; and our iniquities, like the wind, take us away.

7And there is none that calleth upon thy name, that stirreth up himself to take hold of thee; for thou hast hid thy face from us, and hast consumed us by means of our iniquities.

8But now, O Yahweh, thou art our Father; we are the clay, and thou our potter; and we all are the work of thy hand.

9Be not wroth very sore, O Yahweh, neither remember iniquity for ever: behold, look, we beseech thee, we are all thy people.

10Thy holy cities are become a wilderness, Zion is become a wilderness, Jerusalem a desolation.

11Our holy and our beautiful house, where our fathers praised thee, is burned with fire; and all our pleasant places are laid waste.

12Wilt thou refrain thyself for these things, O Yahweh? wilt thou hold thy peace, and afflict us very sore?

Chapter 65

1I am inquired of by them that asked not for me; I am found of them that sought me not: I said, Behold me, behold me, unto a nation that was not called by my name.

2I have spread out my hands all the day unto a rebellious people, that walk in a way that is not good, after their own thoughts;

3a people that provoke me to my face continually, sacrificing in gardens, and burning incense upon bricks;

4that sit among the graves, and lodge in the secret places; that eat swine's flesh, and broth of abominable things is in their vessels;

5that say, Stand by thyself, come not near to me, for I am holier than thou. These are a smoke in my nose, a fire that burneth all the day.

6Behold, it is written before me: I will not keep silence, but will recompense, yea, I will recompense into their bosom,

7your own iniquities, and the iniquities of your fathers together, saith Yahweh, that have burned incense upon the mountains, and blasphemed me upon the hills; therefore will I first measure their work into their bosom.

8Thus saith Yahweh, As the new wine is found in the cluster, and one saith, Destroy it not, for a blessing is in it: so will I do for my servants' sake, that I may not destroy them all.

9And I will bring forth a seed out of Jacob, and out of Judah an inheritor of my mountains; and my chosen shall inherit it, and my servants shall dwell there.

10And Sharon shall be a fold of flocks, and the valley of Achor a place for herds to lie down in, for my people that have sought me.

11But ye that forsake Yahweh, that forget my holy mountain, that prepare a table for Fortune, and that fill up mingled wine unto Destiny;

12I will destine you to the sword, and ye shall all bow down to the slaughter; because when I called, ye did not answer; when I spake, ye did not hear; but ye did that which was evil in mine eyes, and chose that wherein I delighted not.

13Therefore thus saith the Lord Yahweh, Behold, my servants shall eat, but ye shall be hungry; behold, my servants shall drink, but ye shall be thirsty; behold, my servants shall rejoice, but ye shall be put to shame;

14behold, my servants shall sing for joy of heart, but ye shall cry for sorrow of heart, and shall wail for vexation of spirit.

15And ye shall leave your name for a curse unto my chosen; and the Lord Yahweh will slay thee; and he will call his servants by another name:

16so that he who blesseth himself in the earth shall bless himself in the God of truth; and he that sweareth in the earth shall swear by the God of truth; because the former troubles are forgotten, and because they are hid from mine eyes.

17For, behold, I create new heavens and a new earth; and the former things shall not be remembered, nor come into mind.

18But be ye glad and rejoice for ever in that which I create; for, behold, I create Jerusalem a rejoicing, and her people a joy.

19And I will rejoice in Jerusalem, and joy in my people; and there shall be heard in her no more the voice of weeping and the voice of crying.

20There shall be no more thence an infant of days, nor an old man that hath not filled his days; for the child shall die a hundred years old, and the sinner being a hundred years old shall be accursed.

Isaiah

21And they shall build houses, and inhabit them; and they shall plant vineyards, and eat the fruit of them.

22They shall not build, and another inhabit; they shall not plant, and another eat: for as the days of a tree shall be the days of my people, and my chosen shall long enjoy the work of their hands.

23They shall not labor in vain, nor bring forth for calamity; for they are the seed of the blessed of Yahweh, and their offspring with them.

24And it shall come to pass that, before they call, I will answer; and while they are yet speaking, I will hear.

25The wolf and the lamb shall feed together, and the lion shall eat straw like the ox; and dust shall be the serpent's food. They shall not hurt nor destroy in all my holy mountain, saith Yahweh.

Chapter 66

1Thus saith Yahweh, Heaven is my throne, and the earth is my footstool: what manner of house will ye build unto me? and what place shall be my rest?

2For all these things hath my hand made, and so all these things came to be, saith Yahweh: but to this man will I look, even to him that is poor and of a contrite spirit, and that trembleth at my word.

3He that killeth an ox is as he that slayeth a man; he that sacrificeth a lamb, as he that breaketh a dog's neck; he that offereth an oblation, as he that offereth swine's blood; he that burneth frankincense, as he that blesseth an idol. Yea, they have chosen their own ways, and their soul delighteth in their abominations:

4I also will choose their delusions, and will bring their fears upon them; because when I called, none did answer; when I spake, they did not hear: but they did that which was evil in mine eyes, and chose that wherein I delighted not.

5Hear the word of Yahweh, ye that tremble at his word: Your brethren that hate you, that cast you out for my name's sake, have said, Let Yahweh be glorified, that we may see your joy; but it is they that shall be put to shame.

6A voice of tumult from the city, a voice from the temple, a voice of Yahweh that rendereth recompense to his enemies.

7Before she travailed, she brought forth; before her pain came, she was delivered of a man-child.

8Who hath heard such a thing? who hath seen such things? Shall a land be born in one day? shall a nation be brought forth at once? for as soon as Zion travailed, she brought forth her children.

9Shall I bring to the birth, and not cause to bring forth? saith Yahweh: shall I that cause to bring forth shut the womb? saith thy God.

10Rejoice ye with Jerusalem, and be glad for her, all ye that love her: rejoice for joy with her, all ye that mourn over her;

11that ye may suck and be satisfied with the breasts of her consolations; that ye may milk out, and be delighted with the abundance of her glory.

12For thus saith Yahweh, Behold, I will extend peace to her like a river, and the glory of the nations like an overflowing stream: and ye shall suck thereof; ye shall be borne upon the side, and shall be dandled upon the knees.

13As one whom his mother comforteth, so will I comfort you; and ye shall be comforted in Jerusalem.

14And ye shall see it, and your heart shall rejoice, and your bones shall flourish like the tender grass: and the hand of Yahweh shall be known toward his servants; and he will have indignation against his enemies.

15For, behold, Yahweh will come with fire, and his chariots shall be like the whirlwind; to render his anger with fierceness, and his rebuke with flames of fire.

16For by fire will Yahweh execute judgment, and by his sword, upon all flesh; and the slain of Yahweh shall be many.

17They that sanctify themselves and purify themselves to go unto the gardens, behind one in the midst, eating swine's flesh, and the abomination, and the mouse, they shall come to an end together, saith Yahweh.

18For I know their works and their thoughts: the time cometh, that I will gather all nations and tongues; and they shall come, and shall see my glory.

19And I will set a sign among them, and I will send such as escape of them unto the nations, to Tarshish, Pul, and Lud, that draw the bow, to Tubal and Javan, to the isles afar off, that have not heard my fame, neither have seen my glory; and they shall declare my glory among the nations.

20And they shall bring all your brethren out of all the nations for an oblation unto Yahweh, upon horses, and in chariots, and in litters, and upon mules, and upon dromedaries, to my holy mountain Jerusalem, saith Yahweh, as the children of Israel bring their oblation in a clean vessel into the house of Yahweh.

21And of them also will I take for priests and for Levites, saith Yahweh.

22For as the new heavens and the new earth, which I will make, shall remain before me, saith Yahweh, so shall your seed and your name remain.

23And it shall come to pass, that from one new moon to another, and from one sabbath to another, shall all flesh come to worship before me, saith Yahweh.

24And they shall go forth, and look upon the dead bodies of the men that have transgressed against me: for their worm shall not die, neither shall their fire be quenched; and they shall be an abhorring unto all flesh.

The Book of the Prophet Jeremiah

Chapter 1

1The words of Jeremiah the son of Hilkiah, of the priests that were in Anathoth in the land of Benjamin:

2to whom the word of Yahweh came in the days of Josiah the son of Amon, king of Judah, in the thirteenth year of his reign.

3It came also in the days of Jehoiakim the son of Josiah, king of Judah, unto the end of the eleventh year of Zedekiah, the son of Josiah, king of Judah, unto the carrying away of Jerusalem captive in the fifth month.

4Now the word of Yahweh came unto me, saying,

5Before I formed thee in the belly I knew thee, and before thou camest forth out of the womb I sanctified thee; I have appointed thee a prophet unto the nations.

6Then said I, Ah, Lord Yahweh! behold, I know not how to speak; for I am a child.

7But Yahweh said unto me, Say not, I am a child; for to whomsoever I shall send thee thou shalt go, and whatsoever I shall command thee thou shalt speak.

8Be not afraid because of them; for I am with thee to deliver thee, saith Yahweh.

9Then Yahweh put forth his hand, and touched my mouth; and Yahweh said unto me, Behold, I have put my words in thy mouth:

10see, I have this day set thee over the nations and over the kingdoms, to pluck up and to break down and to destroy and to overthrow, to build and to plant.

11Moreover the word of Yahweh came unto me, saying, Jeremiah, what seest thou? And I said, I see a rod of an almond-tree.

12Then said Yahweh unto me, Thou hast well seen: for I watch over my word to perform it.

13And the word of Yahweh came unto me the second time, saying, What seest thou? And I said, I see a boiling caldron; and the face thereof is from the north.

14Then Yahweh said unto me, Out of the north evil shall break forth upon all the inhabitants of the land.

15For, lo, I will call all the families of the kingdoms of the north, saith Yahweh; and they shall come, and they shall set every one his throne at the entrance of the gates of Jerusalem, and against all the walls thereof round about, and against all the cities of Judah.

16And I will utter my judgments against them touching all their wickedness, in that they have forsaken me, and have burned incense unto other gods, and worshipped the works of their own hands.

17Thou therefore gird up thy loins, and arise, and speak unto them all that I command thee: be not dismayed at them, lest I dismay thee before them.

18For, behold, I have made thee this day a fortified city, and an iron pillar, and brazen walls, against the whole land, against the kings of Judah, against the princes thereof, against the priests thereof, and against the people of the land.

19And they shall fight against thee; but they shall not prevail against thee: for I am with thee, saith Yahweh, to deliver thee.

Chapter 2

1And the word of Yahweh came to me, saying,

2Go, and cry in the ears of Jerusalem, saying, Thus saith Yahweh, I remember for thee the kindness of thy youth, the love of thine espousals; how thou wentest after me in the wilderness, in a land that was not sown.

3Israel was holiness unto Yahweh, the first-fruits of his increase: all that devour him shall be held guilty; evil shall come upon them, saith Yahweh.

4Hear ye the word of Yahweh, O house of Jacob, and all the families of the house of Israel:

5thus saith Yahweh, What unrighteousness have your fathers found in me, that they are gone far from me, and have walked after vanity, and are become vain?

6Neither said they, Where is Yahweh that brought us up out of the land of Egypt, that led us through the wilderness, through a land of deserts and of pits, through a land of drought and of the shadow of death, through a land that none passed through, and where no man dwelt?

7And I brought you into a plentiful land, to eat the fruit thereof and the goodness thereof; but when ye entered, ye defiled my land, and made my heritage an abomination.

8The priests said not, Where is Yahweh? and they that handle the law knew me not: the rulers also transgressed against me, and the prophets prophesied by Baal, and walked after things that do not profit.

9Wherefore I will yet contend with you, saith Yahweh, and with your children's children will I contend.

10For pass over to the isles of Kittim, and see; and send unto Kedar, and consider diligently; and see if there hath been such a thing.

11Hath a nation changed its gods, which yet are no gods? but my people have changed their glory for that which doth not profit.

12Be astonished, O ye heavens, at this, and be horribly afraid, be ye very desolate, saith Yahweh.

13For my people have committed two evils: they have forsaken me, the fountain of living waters, and hewed them out cisterns, broken cisterns, that can hold no water.

14Is Israel a servant? is he a home-born slave? why is he become a prey?

15The young lions have roared upon him, and yelled; and they have made his land waste: his cities are burned up, without inhabitant.

16The children also of Memphis and Tahpanhes have broken the crown of thy head.

17Hast thou not procured this unto thyself, in that thou hast forsaken Yahweh thy God, when he led thee by the way?

18And now what hast thou to do in the way to Egypt, to drink the waters of the Shihor? or what hast thou to do in the way to Assyria, to drink the waters of the River?

19Thine own wickedness shall correct thee, and thy backslidings shall reprove thee: know therefore and see that it is an evil thing and a bitter, that thou hast forsaken Yahweh thy God, and that my fear is not in thee, saith the Lord, Yahweh of hosts.

20For of old time I have broken thy yoke, and burst thy bonds; and thou saidst, I will not serve; for upon every high hill and under every green tree thou didst bow thyself, playing the harlot.

21Yet I had planted thee a noble vine, wholly a right seed: how then art thou turned into the degenerate branches of a foreign vine unto me?

22For though thou wash thee with lye, and take thee much soap, yet thine iniquity is marked before me, saith the Lord Yahweh.

23How canst thou say, I am not defiled, I have not gone after the Baalim? see thy way in the valley, know what thou hast done: thou art a swift dromedary traversing her ways;

24a wild ass used to the wilderness, that snuffeth up the wind in her desire; in her occasion who can turn her away? all they that seek her will not weary themselves; in her month they shall find her.

25Withhold thy foot from being unshod, and thy throat from thirst: but thou saidst, It is in vain; no, for I have loved strangers, and after them will I go.

26As the thief is ashamed when he is found, so is the house of Israel ashamed; they, their kings, their princes, and their priests, and their prophets;

27who say to a stock, Thou art my father; and to a stone, Thou hast brought me forth: for they have turned their back unto me, and not their face; but in the time of their trouble they will say, Arise, and save us.

28But where are thy gods that thou hast made thee? let them arise, if they can save thee in the time of thy trouble: for according to the number of thy cities are thy gods, O Judah.

29Wherefore will ye contend with me? ye all have transgressed against me, saith Yahweh.

30In vain have I smitten your children; they received no correction: your own sword hath devoured your prophets, like a destroying lion.

31O generation, see ye the word of Yahweh. Have I been a wilderness unto Israel? or a land of thick darkness? wherefore say my people, We are broken loose; we will come no more unto thee?

32Can a virgin forget her ornaments, or a bride her attire? yet my people have forgotten me days without number.

33How trimmest thou thy way to seek love! therefore even the wicked women hast thou taught thy ways.

34Also in thy skirts is found the blood of the souls of the innocent poor: thou didst not find them breaking in; but it is because of all these things.

35Yet thou saidst, I am innocent; surely his anger is turned away from me. Behold, I will enter into judgment with thee, because thou sayest, I have not sinned.

36Why gaddest thou about so much to change thy way? thou shalt be ashamed of Egypt also, as thou wast ashamed of Assyria.

37From thence also shalt thou go forth, with thy hands upon thy head: for Yahweh hath rejected those in whom thou trustest, and thou shalt not prosper with them.

Chapter 3

1They say, If a man put away his wife, and she go from him, and become another man's, will he return unto her again? will not that land be greatly polluted? But thou hast played the harlot with many lovers; yet return again to me, saith Yahweh.

2Lift up thine eyes unto the bare heights, and see; where hast thou not been lain with? By the ways hast thou sat for them, as an Arabian in the wilderness; and thou hast polluted the land with thy whoredoms and with thy wickedness.

3Therefore the showers have been withholden, and there hath been no latter rain; yet thou hast a harlot's forehead, thou refusedst to be ashamed.

4Wilt thou not from this time cry unto me, My Father, thou art the guide of my youth?

5Will he retain his anger for ever? will he keep it to the end? Behold, thou hast spoken and hast done evil things, and hast had thy way.

6Moreover Yahweh said unto me in the days of Josiah the king, Hast thou seen that which backsliding Israel hath done? she is gone up upon every high mountain and under every green tree, and there hath played the harlot.

7And I said after she had done all these things, She will return unto me; but she returned not: and her treacherous sister Judah saw it.

8And I saw, when, for this very cause that backsliding Israel had committed adultery, I had put her away and given her a bill of divorcement, yet treacherous Judah her sister feared not; but she also went and played the harlot.

9And it came to pass through the lightness of her whoredom, that the land was polluted, and she committed adultery with stones and with stocks.

10And yet for all this her treacherous sister Judah hath not returned unto me with her whole heart, but feignedly, saith Yahweh.

11And Yahweh said unto me, Backsliding Israel hath showed herself more righteous than treacherous Judah.

12Go, and proclaim these words toward the north, and say, Return, thou backsliding Israel, saith Yahweh; I will not look in anger upon you; for I am merciful, saith Yahweh, I will not keep anger for ever.

13Only acknowledge thine iniquity, that thou hast transgressed against Yahweh thy God, and hast scattered thy ways to the strangers under every green

Jeremiah

tree, and ye have not obeyed my voice, saith Yahweh.

14Return, O backsliding children, saith Yahweh; for I am a husband unto you: and I will take you one of a city, and two of a family, and I will bring you to Zion:

15and I will give you shepherds according to my heart, who shall feed you with knowledge and understanding.

16And it shall come to pass, when ye are multiplied and increased in the land, in those days, saith Yahweh, they shall say no more, The ark of the covenant of Yahweh; neither shall it come to mind; neither shall they remember it; neither shall they miss it; neither shall it be made any more.

17At that time they shall call Jerusalem the throne of Yahweh; and all the nations shall be gathered unto it, to the name of Yahweh, to Jerusalem: neither shall they walk any more after the stubbornness of their evil heart.

18In those days the house of Judah shall walk with the house of Israel, and they shall come together out of the land of the north to the land that I gave for an inheritance unto your fathers.

19But I said, How I will put thee among the children, and give thee a pleasant land, a goodly heritage of the hosts of the nations! and I said, Ye shall call me My Father, and shall not turn away from following me.

20Surely as a wife treacherously departeth from her husband, so have ye dealt treacherously with me, O house of Israel, saith Yahweh.

21A voice is heard upon the bare heights, the weeping and the supplications of the children of Israel; because they have perverted their way, they have forgotten Yahweh their God.

22Return, ye backsliding children, I will heal your backslidings. Behold, we are come unto thee; for thou art Yahweh our God.

23Truly in vain is the help that is looked for from the hills, the tumult on the mountains: truly in Yahweh our God is the salvation of Israel.

24But the shameful thing hath devoured the labor of our fathers from our youth, their flocks and their herds, their sons and their daughters.

25Let us lie down in our shame, and let our confusion cover us; for we have sinned against Yahweh our God, we and our fathers, from our youth even unto this day; and we have not obeyed the voice of Yahweh our God.

Chapter 4

1If thou wilt return, O Israel, saith Yahweh, if thou wilt return unto me, and if thou wilt put away thine abominations out of my sight; then shalt thou not be removed;

2and thou shalt swear, As Yahweh liveth, in truth, in justice, and in righteousness; and the nations shall bless themselves in him, and in him shall they glory.

3For thus saith Yahweh to the men of Judah and to Jerusalem, Break up your fallow ground, and sow not among thorns.

4Circumcise yourselves to Yahweh, and take away the foreskins of your heart, ye men of Judah and inhabitants of Jerusalem; lest my wrath go forth like fire, and burn so that none can quench it, because of the evil of your doings.

5Declare ye in Judah, and publish in Jerusalem; and say, Blow ye the trumpet in the land: cry aloud and say, Assemble yourselves, and let us go into the fortified cities.

6Set up a standard toward Zion: flee for safety, stay not; for I will bring evil from the north, and a great destruction.

7A lion is gone up from his thicket, and a destroyer of nations; he is on his way, he is gone forth from his place, to make thy land desolate, that thy cities be laid waste, without inhabitant.

8For this gird you with sackcloth, lament and wail; for the fierce anger of Yahweh is not turned back from us.

9And it shall come to pass at that day, saith Yahweh, that the heart of the king shall perish, and the heart of the princes; and the priests shall be astonished, and the prophets shall wonder.

10Then said I, Ah, Lord Yahweh! surely thou hast greatly deceived this people and Jerusalem, saying, Ye shall have peace; whereas the sword reacheth unto the life.

11At that time shall it be said to this people and to Jerusalem, A hot wind from the bare heights in the wilderness toward the daughter of my people, not to winnow, nor to cleanse;

12a full wind from these shall come for me: now will I also utter judgments against them.

13Behold, he shall come up as clouds, and his chariots shall be as the whirlwind: his horses are swifter than eagles. Woe unto us! for we are ruined.

14O Jerusalem, wash thy heart from wickedness, that thou mayest be saved. How long shall thine evil thoughts lodge within thee?

15For a voice declareth from Dan, and publisheth evil from the hills of Ephraim:

16make ye mention to the nations; behold, publish against Jerusalem, that watchers come from a far country, and give out their voice against the cities of Judah.

17As keepers of a field are they against her round about, because she hath been rebellious against me, saith Yahweh.

18Thy way and thy doings have procured these things unto thee; this is thy wickedness; for it is bitter, for it reacheth unto thy heart.

19My anguish, my anguish! I am pained at my very heart; my heart is disquieted in me; I cannot hold my peace; because thou hast heard, O my soul, the sound of the trumpet, the alarm of war.

20Destruction upon destruction is cried; for the whole land is laid waste: suddenly are my tents destroyed, and my curtains in a moment.

21How long shall I see the standard, and hear the sound of the trumpet?

22For my people are foolish, they know me not; they are sottish children, and they have no understanding; they are wise to do evil, but to do good they have no knowledge.

23I beheld the earth, and, lo, it was waste and void; and the heavens, and they had no light.

24I beheld the mountains, and, lo, they trembled, and all the hills moved to and fro.

25I beheld, and, lo, there was no man, and all the birds of the heavens were fled.

26I beheld, and, lo, the fruitful field was a wilderness, and all the cities thereof were broken down at the presence of Yahweh, and before his fierce anger.

27For thus saith Yahweh, The whole land shall be a desolation; yet will I not make a full end.

28For this shall the earth mourn, and the heavens above be black; because I have spoken it, I have purposed it, and I have not repented, neither will I turn back from it.

29Every city fleeth for the noise of the horsemen and bowmen; they go into the thickets, and climb up upon the rocks: every city is forsaken, and not a man dwelleth therein.

30And thou, when thou art made desolate, what wilt thou do? Though thou clothest thyself with scarlet, though thou deckest thee with ornaments of gold, though thou enlargest thine eyes with paint, in vain dost thou make thyself fair; thy lovers despise thee, they seek thy life.

31For I have heard a voice as of a woman in travail, the anguish as of her that bringeth forth her first child, the voice of the daughter of Zion, that gaspeth for breath, that spreadeth her hands, saying, Woe is me now! for my soul fainteth before the murderers.

Chapter 5

1Run ye to and fro through the streets of Jerusalem, and see now, and know, and seek in the broad places thereof, if ye can find a man, if there be any that doeth justly, that seeketh truth; and I will pardon her.

2And though they say, As Yahweh liveth; surely they swear falsely.

3O Yahweh, do not thine eyes look upon truth? thou hast stricken them, but they were not grieved; thou hast consumed them, but they have refused to receive correction: they have made their faces harder than a rock; they have refused to return.

4Then I said, Surely these are poor; they are foolish; for they know not the way of Yahweh, nor the law of their God:

5I will get me unto the great men, and will speak unto them; for they know the way of Yahweh, and the law of their God. But these with one accord have broken the yoke, and burst the bonds.

6Wherefore a lion out of the forest shall slay them, a wolf of the evenings shall destroy them, a leopard shall watch against their cities; every one that goeth out thence shall be torn in pieces; because their transgressions are many, and their backslidings are increased.

7How can I pardon thee? thy children have forsaken me, and sworn by them that are no gods: when I had fed them to the full, they committed adultery, and assembled themselves in troops at the harlots' houses.

8They were as fed horses roaming at large; every one neighed after his neighbor's wife.

9Shall I not visit for these things? saith Yahweh; and shall not my soul be avenged on such a nation as this?

10Go ye up upon her walls, and destroy; but make not a full end: take away her branches; for they are not Yahweh's.

11For the house of Israel and the house of Judah have dealt very treacherously against me, saith Yahweh.

12They have denied Yahweh, and said, It is not he; neither shall evil come upon us; neither shall we see sword nor famine:

13and the prophets shall become wind, and the word is not in them: thus shall it be done unto them.

14Wherefore thus saith Yahweh, the God of hosts, Because ye speak this word, behold, I will make my words in thy mouth fire, and this people wood, and it shall devour them.

15Lo, I will bring a nation upon you from far, O house of Israel, saith Yahweh: it is a mighty nation, it is an ancient nation, a nation whose language thou knowest not, neither understandest what they say.

16Their quiver is an open sepulchre, they are all mighty men.

17And they shall eat up thy harvest, and thy bread, which thy sons and thy daughters should eat; they shall eat up thy flocks and thy herds; they shall eat up thy vines and thy fig-trees; they shall beat down thy fortified cities, wherein thou trustest, with the sword.

18But even in those days, saith Yahweh, I will not make a full end with you.

19And it shall come to pass, when ye shall say, Wherefore hath Yahweh our God done all these things unto us? then shalt thou say unto them, Like as ye have forsaken me, and served foreign gods in your land, so shall ye serve strangers in a land that is not yours.

20Declare ye this in the house of Jacob, and publish it in Judah, saying,

21Hear now this, O foolish people, and without understanding; that have eyes, and see not; that have ears, and hear not:

22Fear ye not me? saith Yahweh: will ye not tremble at my presence, who have placed the sand for the bound of the sea, by a perpetual decree, that it cannot pass it? and though the waves thereof toss themselves, yet can they not prevail; though they roar, yet can they not pass over it.

23But this people hath a revolting and a rebellious heart; they are revolted and gone.

24Neither say they in their heart, Let us now fear Yahweh our God, that giveth rain, both the former and the latter, in its season; that preserveth unto us the appointed weeks of the harvest.

25Your iniquities have turned away these things, and your sins have withholden good from you.

26For among my people are found wicked men: they watch, as fowlers lie in wait; they set a trap, they catch men.

27As a cage is full of birds, so are their houses full of deceit: therefore they are become great, and waxed rich.

28They are waxed fat, they shine: yea, they overpass in deeds of wickedness; they plead not the cause, the cause of the fatherless, that they may prosper; and the right of the needy do they not judge.

29Shall I not visit for these things? saith Yahweh; shall not my soul be avenged on such a nation as this?

30A wonderful and horrible thing is come to pass in the land:

31the prophets prophesy falsely, and the priests bear rule by their means; and my people love to have it so: and what will ye do in the end thereof?

Chapter 6

1Flee for safety, ye children of Benjamin, out of the midst of Jerusalem, and blow the trumpet in Tekoa, and raise up a signal on Beth-haccherem; for evil looketh forth from the north, and a great destruction.

2The comely and delicate one, the daughter of Zion, will I cut off.

3Shepherds with their flocks shall come unto her; they shall pitch their tents against her round about; they shall feed every one in his place.

4Prepare ye war against her; arise, and let us go up at noon. Woe unto us! for the day declineth, for the shadows of the evening are stretched out.

5Arise, and let us go up by night, and let us destroy her palaces.

6For thus hath Yahweh of hosts said, Hew ye down trees, and cast up a mound against Jerusalem: this is the city to be visited; she is wholly oppression in the midst of her.

7As a well casteth forth its waters, so she casteth forth her wickedness: violence and destruction is heard in her; before me continually is sickness and wounds.

8Be thou instructed, O Jerusalem, lest my soul be alienated from thee; lest I make thee a desolation, a land not inhabited.

9Thus saith Yahweh of hosts, They shall thoroughly glean the remnant of Israel as a vine: turn again thy hand as a grape-gatherer into the baskets.

10To whom shall I speak and testify, that they may hear? behold, their ear is uncircumcised, and they cannot hearken: behold, the word of Yahweh is become unto them a reproach; they have no delight in it.

11Therefore I am full of the wrath of Yahweh; I am weary with holding in: pour it out upon the children in the street, and upon the assembly of young men together; for even the husband with the wife shall be taken, the aged with him that is full of days.

12And their houses shall be turned unto others, their fields and their wives together; for I will stretch out my hand upon the inhabitants of the land, saith Yahweh.

13For from the least of them even unto the greatest of them every one is given to covetousness; and from the prophet even unto the priest every one dealeth falsely.

14They have healed also the hurt of my people slightly, saying, Peace, peace; when there is no peace.

15Were they ashamed when they had committed abomination? nay, they were not at all ashamed, neither could they blush: therefore they shall fall among them that fall; at the time that I visit them they shall be cast down, saith Yahweh.

16Thus saith Yahweh, Stand ye in the ways and see, and ask for the old paths, where is the good way; and walk therein, and ye shall find rest for your souls: but they said, We will not walk therein.

17And I set watchmen over you, saying, Hearken to the sound of the trumpet; but they said, We will not hearken.

18Therefore hear, ye nations, and know, O congregation, what is among them.

19Hear, O earth: behold, I will bring evil upon this people, even the fruit of their thoughts, because they have not hearkened unto my words; and as for my law, they have rejected it.

20To what purpose cometh there to me frankincense from Sheba, and the sweet cane from a far country? your burnt-offerings are not acceptable, nor your sacrifices pleasing unto me.

21Therefore thus saith Yahweh, Behold, I will lay stumbling-blocks before this people; and the fathers and the sons together shall stumble against them; the neighbor and his friend shall perish.

22Thus saith Yahweh, Behold, a people cometh from the north country; and a great nation shall be stirred up from the uttermost parts of the earth.

23They lay hold on bow and spear; they are cruel, and have no mercy; their voice roareth like the sea, and they ride upon horses, every one set in array, as a man to the battle, against thee, O daughter of Zion.

24We have heard the report thereof; our hands wax feeble: anguish hath taken hold of us, and pangs as of a woman in travail.

25Go not forth into the field, nor walk by the way; for the sword of the enemy, and terror, are on every side.

26O daughter of my people, gird thee with sackcloth, and wallow thyself in ashes: make thee mourning, as for an only son, most bitter lamentation; for the destroyer shall suddenly come upon us.

27I have made thee a trier and a fortress among my people; that thou mayest know and try their way.

28They are all grievous revolters, going about with slanders; they are brass and iron: they all of them deal corruptly.

29The bellows blow fiercely; the lead is consumed of the fire: in vain do they go on refining; for the wicked are not plucked away.

30Refuse silver shall men them, because Yahweh hath rejected them.

Chapter 7

1The word that came to Jeremiah from Yahweh, saying,

2Stand in the gate of Yahweh's house, and proclaim there this word, and say, Hear the word of Yahweh, all ye of Judah, that enter in at these gates to worship Yahweh.

3Thus saith Yahweh of hosts, the God of Israel, Amend your ways and your doings, and I will cause you to dwell in this place.

4Trust ye not in lying words, saying, The temple of Yahweh, the temple of Yahweh, the temple of Yahweh, are these.

5For if ye thoroughly amend your ways and your doings; if ye thoroughly execute justice between a man and his neighbor;

6if ye oppress not the sojourner, the fatherless, and the widow, and shed not innocent blood in this place, neither walk after other gods to your own hurt:

7then will I cause you to dwell in this place, in the land that I gave to your fathers, from of old even for evermore.

8Behold, ye trust in lying words, that cannot profit.

9Will ye steal, murder, and commit adultery, and swear falsely, and burn incense unto Baal, and walk after other gods that ye have not known,

10and come and stand before me in this house, which is called by my name, and say, We are delivered; that ye may do all these abominations?

11Is this house, which is called by my name, become a den of robbers in your eyes? Behold, I, even I, have seen it, saith Yahweh.

12But go ye now unto my place which was in Shiloh, where I caused my name to dwell at the first, and see what I did to it for the wickedness of my people Israel.

13And now, because ye have done all these works, saith Yahweh, and I spake unto you, rising up early and speaking, but ye heard not; and I called you, but ye answered not:

14therefore will I do unto the house which is called by my name, wherein ye trust, and unto the place which I gave to you and to your fathers, as I did to Shiloh.

15And I will cast you out of my sight, as I have cast out all your brethren, even the whole seed of Ephraim.

16Therefore pray not thou for this people, neither lift up cry nor prayer for them, neither make intercession to me; for I will not hear thee.

17Seest thou not what they do in the cities of Judah and in the streets of Jerusalem?

18The children gather wood, and the fathers kindle the fire, and the women knead the dough, to make cakes to the queen of heaven, and to pour out drink-offerings unto other gods, that they may provoke me to anger.

19Do they provoke me to anger? saith Yahweh; do they not provoke themselves, to the confusion of their own faces?

20Therefore thus saith the Lord Yahweh: Behold, mine anger and my wrath shall be poured out upon this place, upon man, and upon beast, and upon the trees of the field, and upon the fruit of the ground; and it shall burn, and shall not be quenched.

21Thus saith Yahweh of hosts, the God of Israel: Add your burnt-offerings unto your sacrifices, and eat ye flesh.

22For I spake not unto your fathers, nor commanded them in the day that I brought them out of the land of Egypt, concerning burnt-offerings or sacrifices:

23but this thing I commanded them, saying, Hearken unto my voice, and I will be your God, and ye shall be my people; and walk ye in all the way that I command you, that it may be well with you.

24But they hearkened not, nor inclined their ear, but walked in their own counsels and in the stubbornness of their evil heart, and went backward, and not forward.

25Since the day that your fathers came forth out of the land of Egypt unto this day, I have sent unto you all my servants the prophets, daily rising up early and sending them:

26yet they hearkened not unto me, nor inclined their ear, but made their neck stiff: they did worse than their fathers.

27And thou shalt speak all these words unto them; but they will not hearken to thee: thou shalt also call unto them; but they will not answer thee.

28And thou shalt say unto them, This is the nation that hath not hearkened to the voice of Yahweh their God, nor received instruction: truth is perished, and is cut off from their mouth.

29Cut off thy hair, O Jerusalem, and cast it away, and take up a lamentation on the bare heights; for Yahweh hath rejected and forsaken the generation of his wrath.

30For the children of Judah have done that which is evil in my sight, saith Yahweh: they have set their abominations in the house which is called by my name, to defile it.

31And they have built the high places of Topheth, which is in the valley of the son of Hinnom, to burn their sons and their daughters in the fire; which I commanded not, neither came it into my mind.

32Therefore, behold, the days come, saith Yahweh, that it shall no more be called Topheth, nor The valley of the son of Hinnom, but The valley of Slaughter: for they shall bury in Topheth, till there be no place to bury.

33And the dead bodies of this people shall be food for the birds of the heavens, and for the beasts of the earth; and none shall frighten them away.

34Then will I cause to cease from the cities of Judah, and from the streets of Jerusalem, the voice of mirth and the voice of gladness, the voice of the bridegroom and the voice of the bride; for the land shall become a waste.

Jeremiah
Chapter 8

¹At that time, saith Yahweh, they shall bring out the bones of the kings of Judah, and the bones of his princes, and the bones of the priests, and the bones of the prophets, and the bones of the inhabitants of Jerusalem, out of their graves;

²and they shall spread them before the sun, and the moon, and all the host of heaven, which they have loved, and which they have served, and after which they have walked, and which they have sought, and which they have worshipped: they shall not be gathered, nor be buried, they shall be for dung upon the face of the earth.

³And death shall be chosen rather than life by all the residue that remain of this evil family, that remain in all the places whither I have driven them, saith Yahweh of hosts.

⁴Moreover thou shalt say unto them, Thus saith Yahweh: Shall men fall, and not rise up again? Shall one turn away, and not return?

⁵Why then is this people of Jerusalem slidden back by a perpetual backsliding? they hold fast deceit, they refuse to return.

⁶I hearkened and heard, but they spake not aright: no man repenteth him of his wickedness, saying, What have I done? every one turneth to his course, as a horse that rusheth headlong in the battle.

⁷Yea, the stork in the heavens knoweth her appointed times; and the turtle-dove and the swallow and the crane observe the time of their coming; but my people know not the law of Yahweh.

⁸How do ye say, We are wise, and the law of Yahweh is with us? But, behold, the false pen of the scribes hath wrought falsely.

⁹The wise men are put to shame, they are dismayed and taken: lo, they have rejected the word of Yahweh; and what manner of wisdom is in them?

¹⁰Therefore will I give their wives unto others, and their fields to them that shall possess them: for every one from the least even unto the greatest is given to covetousness; from the prophet even unto the priest every one dealeth falsely.

¹¹And they have healed the hurt of the daughter of my people slightly, saying, Peace, peace; when there is no peace.

¹²Were they ashamed when they had committed abomination? nay, they were not at all ashamed, neither could they blush: therefore shall they fall among them that fall; in the time of their visitation they shall be cast down, saith Yahweh.

¹³I will utterly consume them, saith Yahweh: there shall be no grapes on the vine, nor figs on the fig-tree, and the leaf shall fade; and the things that I have given them shall pass away from them.

¹⁴Why do we sit still? assemble yourselves, and let us enter into the fortified cities, and let us be silent there; for Yahweh our God hath put us to silence, and given us water of gall to drink, because we have sinned against Yahweh.

¹⁵We looked for peace, but no good came; and for a time of healing, and, behold, dismay!

¹⁶The snorting of his horses is heard from Dan: at the sound of the neighing of his strong ones the whole land trembleth; for they are come, and have devoured the land and all that is in it; the city and those that dwell therein.

¹⁷For, behold, I will send serpents, adders, among you, which will not be charmed; and they shall bite you, saith Yahweh.

¹⁸Oh that I could comfort myself against sorrow! my heart is faint within me.

¹⁹Behold, the voice of the cry of the daughter of my people from a land that is very far off: is not Yahweh in Zion? is not her King in her? Why have they provoked me to anger with their graven images, and with foreign vanities?

²⁰The harvest is past, the summer is ended, and we are not saved.

²¹For the hurt of the daughter of my people am I hurt: I mourn; dismay hath taken hold on me.

²²Is there no balm in Gilead? is there no physician there? why then is not the health of the daughter of my people recovered?

Chapter 9

¹Oh that my head were waters, and mine eyes a fountain of tears, that I might weep day and night for the slain of the daughter of my people!

²Oh that I had in the wilderness a lodging-place of wayfaring men; that I might leave my people, and go from them! for they are all adulterers, an assembly of treacherous men.

³And they bend their tongue, as it were their bow, for falsehood; and they are grown strong in the land, but not for truth: for they proceed from evil to evil, and they know not me, saith Yahweh.

⁴Take ye heed every one of his neighbor, and trust ye not in any brother; for every brother will utterly supplant, and every neighbor will go about with slanders.

⁵And they will deceive every one his neighbor, and will not speak the truth: they have taught their tongue to speak lies; they weary themselves to commit iniquity.

⁶Thy habitation is in the midst of deceit; through deceit they refuse to know me, saith Yahweh.

⁷Therefore thus saith Yahweh of hosts, Behold, I will melt them, and try them; for how else should I do, because of the daughter of my people?

⁸Their tongue is a deadly arrow; it speaketh deceit: one speaketh peaceably to his neighbor with his mouth, but in his heart he layeth wait for him.

⁹Shall I not visit them for these things? saith Yahweh; shall not my soul be avenged on such a nation as this?

¹⁰For the mountains will I take up a weeping and wailing, and for the pastures of the wilderness a lamentation, because they are burned up, so that none passeth through; neither can men hear the voice of the cattle; both the birds of the heavens and the beasts are fled, they are gone.

¹¹And I will make Jerusalem heaps, a dwelling-place of jackals; and I will make the cities of Judah a desolation, without inhabitant.

¹²Who is the wise man, that may understand this? and who is he to whom the mouth of Yahweh hath spoken, that he may declare it? wherefore is the land perished and burned up like a wilderness, so that none passeth through?

¹³And Yahweh saith, Because they have forsaken my law which I set before them, and have not obeyed my voice, neither walked therein,

¹⁴but have walked after the stubbornness of their own heart, and after the Baalim, which their fathers taught them;

¹⁵therefore thus saith Yahweh of hosts, the God of Israel, Behold, I will feed them, even this people, with wormwood, and give them water of gall to drink.

¹⁶I will scatter them also among the nations, whom neither they nor their fathers have known; and I will send the sword after them, till I have consumed them.

¹⁷Thus saith Yahweh of hosts, Consider ye, and call for the mourning women, that they may come; and send for the skilful women, that they may come:

¹⁸and let them make haste, and take up a wailing for us, that our eyes may run down with tears, and our eyelids gush out with waters.

¹⁹For a voice of wailing is heard out of Zion, How are we ruined! we are greatly confounded, because we have forsaken the land, because they have cast down our dwellings.

²⁰Yet hear the word of Yahweh, O ye women, and let your ear receive the word of his mouth; and teach your daughters wailing, and every one her neighbor lamentation.

²¹For death is come up into our windows, it is entered into our palaces; to cut off the children from without, and the young men from the streets.

²²Speak, Thus saith Yahweh, The dead bodies of men shall fall as dung upon the open field, and as the handful after the harvestman; and none shall gather them.

²³Thus saith Yahweh, Let not the wise man glory in his wisdom, neither let the mighty man glory in his might, let not the rich man glory in his riches;

²⁴but let him that glorieth glory in this, that he hath understanding, and knoweth me, that I am Yahweh who exerciseth lovingkindness, justice, and righteousness, in the earth: for in these things I delight, saith Yahweh.

²⁵Behold, the days come, saith Yahweh, that I will punish all them that are circumcised in their uncircumcision:

²⁶Egypt, and Judah, and Edom, and the children of Ammon, and Moab, and all that have the corners of their hair cut off, that dwell in the wilderness; for all the nations are uncircumcised, and all the house of Israel are uncircumcised in heart.

Chapter 10

¹Hear ye the word which Yahweh speaketh unto you, O house of Israel:

²thus saith Yahweh, Learn not the way of the nations, and be not dismayed at the signs of heaven; for the nations are dismayed at them.

³For the customs of the peoples are vanity; for one cutteth a tree out of the forest, the work of the hands of the workman with the axe.

⁴They deck it with silver and with gold; they fasten it with nails and with hammers, that it move not.

⁵They are like a palm-tree, of turned work, and speak not: they must needs be borne, because they cannot go. Be not afraid of them; for they cannot do evil, neither is it in them to do good.

⁶There is none like unto thee, O Yahweh; thou art great, and thy name is great in might.

⁷Who should not fear thee, O King of the nations? for to thee doth it appertain; forasmuch among all the wise men of the nations, and in all their royal estate, there is none like unto thee.

⁸But they are together brutish and foolish: the instruction of idols! it is but a stock.

⁹There is silver beaten into plates, which is brought from Tarshish, and gold from Uphaz, the work of the artificer and of the hands of the goldsmith; blue and purple for their clothing; they are all the work of skilful men.

¹⁰But Yahweh is the true God; he is the living God, and an everlasting King: at his wrath the earth trembleth, and the nations are not able to abide his indignation.

¹¹Thus shall ye say unto them, The gods that have not made the heavens and the earth, these shall perish from the earth, and from under the heavens.

¹²He hath made the earth by his power, he hath established the world by his wisdom, and by his understanding hath he stretched out the heavens:

¹³when he uttereth his voice, there is a tumult of waters in the heavens, and he causeth the vapors to ascend from the ends of the earth; he maketh lightnings for the rain, and bringeth forth the wind out of his treasuries.

¹⁴Every man is become brutish and is without knowledge; every goldsmith is put to shame by his graven image; for his molten image is falsehood, and there is no breath in them.

¹⁵They are vanity, a work of delusion: in the time of their visitation they shall perish.

¹⁶The portion of Jacob is not like these; for he is the former of all things; and Israel is the tribe of his inheritance: Yahweh of hosts is his name.

¹⁷Gather up thy wares out of the land, O thou that abidest in the siege.

¹⁸For thus saith Yahweh, Behold, I will sling out the inhabitants of the land at this time, and will distress them, that they may feel it.

¹⁹Woe is me because of my hurt! my wound is grievous: but I said, Truly this is my grief, and I must bear it.

²⁰My tent is destroyed, and all my cords are broken: my children are gone forth from me, and they are not: there is none to spread my tent any more, and to set up my curtains.

²¹For the shepherds are become brutish, and have not inquired of Yahweh: therefore they have not prospered, and all their flocks are scattered.

²²The voice of tidings, behold, it cometh, and a great commotion out of the north country, to make the cities of Judah a desolation, a dwelling-place of jackals.

23O Yahweh, I know that the way of man is not in himself: it is not in man that walketh to direct his steps.

24O Yahweh, correct me, but in measure: not in thine anger, lest thou bring me to nothing.

25Pour out thy wrath upon the nations that know thee not, and upon the families that call not on thy name: for they have devoured Jacob, yea, they have devoured him and consumed him, and have laid waste his habitation.

Chapter 11

1The word that came to Jeremiah from Yahweh, saying,

2Hear ye the words of this covenant, and speak unto the men of Judah, and to the inhabitants of Jerusalem;

3and say thou unto them, Thus saith Yahweh, the God of Israel: Cursed be the man that heareth not the words of this covenant,

4which I commanded your fathers in the day that I brought them forth out of the land of Egypt, out of the iron furnace, saying, Obey my voice, and do them, according to all which I command you: so shall ye be my people, and I will be your God;

5that I may establish the oath which I sware unto your fathers, to give them a land flowing with milk and honey, as at this day. Then answered I, and said, Amen, O Yahweh.

6And Yahweh said unto me, Proclaim all these words in the cities of Judah, and in the streets of Jerusalem, saying, Hear ye the words of this covenant, and do them.

7For I earnestly protested unto your fathers in the day that I brought them up out of the land of Egypt, even unto this day, rising early and protesting, saying, Obey my voice.

8Yet they obeyed not, nor inclined their ear, but walked every one in the stubbornness of their evil heart: therefore I brought upon them all the words of this covenant, which I commanded them to do, but they did them not.

9And Yahweh said unto me, A conspiracy is found among the men of Judah, and among the inhabitants of Jerusalem.

10They are turned back to the iniquities of their forefathers, who refused to hear my words; and they are gone after other gods to serve them: the house of Israel and the house of Judah have broken my covenant which I made with their fathers.

11Therefore thus saith Yahweh, Behold, I will bring evil upon them, which they shall not be able to escape; and they shall cry unto me, but I will not hearken unto them.

12Then shall the cities of Judah and the inhabitants of Jerusalem go and cry unto the gods unto which they offer incense: but they will not save them at all in the time of their trouble.

13For according to the number of thy cities are thy gods, O Judah; and according to the number of the streets of Jerusalem have ye set up altars to the shameful thing, even altars to burn incense unto Baal.

14Therefore pray not thou for this people, neither lift up cry nor prayer for them; for I will not hear them in the time that they cry unto me because of their trouble.

15What hath my beloved to do in my house, seeing she hath wrought lewdness with many, and the holy flesh is passed from thee? when thou doest evil, then thou rejoicest.

16Yahweh called thy name, A green olive-tree, fair with goodly fruit: with the noise of a great tumult he hath kindled fire upon it, and the branches of it are broken.

17For Yahweh of hosts, who planted thee, hath pronounced evil against thee, because of the evil of the house of Israel and of the house of Judah, which they have wrought for themselves in provoking me to anger by offering incense unto Baal.

18And Yahweh gave me knowledge of it, and I knew it: then thou showedst me their doings.

19But I was like a gentle lamb that is led to the slaughter; and I knew not that they had devised devices against me, saying, Let us destroy the tree with the fruit thereof, and let us cut him off from the land of the living, that his name may be no more remembered.

20But, O Yahweh of hosts, who judgest righteously, who triest the heart and the mind, I shall see thy vengeance on them; for unto thee have I revealed my cause.

21Therefore thus saith Yahweh concerning the men of Anathoth, that seek thy life, saying, Thou shalt not prophesy in the name of Yahweh, that thou die not by our hand;

22therefore thus saith Yahweh of hosts, Behold, I will punish them: the young men shall die by the sword; their sons and their daughters shall die by famine;

23and there shall be no remnant unto them: for I will bring evil upon the men of Anathoth, even the year of their visitation.

Chapter 12

1Righteous art thou, O Yahweh, when I contend with thee; yet would I reason the cause with thee: wherefore doth the way of the wicked prosper? wherefore are all they at ease that deal very treacherously?

2Thou hast planted them, yea, they have taken root; they grow, yea, they bring forth fruit: thou art near in their mouth, and far from their heart.

3But thou, O Yahweh, knowest me; thou seest me, and triest my heart toward thee: pull them out like sheep for the slaughter, and prepare them for the day of slaughter.

4How long shall the land mourn, and the herbs of the whole country wither? for the wickedness of them that dwell therein, the beasts are consumed, and the birds; because they said, He shall not see our latter end.

5If thou hast run with the footmen, and they have wearied thee, then how canst thou contend with horses? and though in a land of peace thou art secure, yet how wilt thou do in the pride of the Jordan?

6For even thy brethren, and the house of thy father, even they have dealt treacherously with thee; even they have cried aloud after thee: believe them not, though they speak fair words unto thee.

7I have forsaken my house, I have cast off my heritage; I have given the dearly beloved of my soul into the hand of her enemies.

8My heritage is become unto me as a lion in the forest: she hath uttered her voice against me; therefore I have hated her.

9Is my heritage unto me as a speckled bird of prey? are the birds of prey against her round about? go ye, assemble all the beasts of the field, bring them to devour.

10Many shepherds have destroyed my vineyard, they have trodden my portion under foot, they have made my pleasant portion a desolate wilderness.

11They have made it a desolation; it mourneth unto me, being desolate; the whole land is made desolate, because no man layeth it to heart.

12Destroyers are come upon all the bare heights in the wilderness; for the sword of Yahweh devoureth from the one end of the land even to the other end of the land: no flesh hath peace.

13They have sown wheat, and have reaped thorns; they have put themselves to pain, and profit nothing: and ye shall be ashamed of your fruits, because of the fierce anger of Yahweh.

14Thus saith Yahweh against all mine evil neighbors, that touch the inheritance which I have caused my people Israel to inherit: behold, I will pluck them up from off their land, and will pluck up the house of Judah from among them.

15And it shall come to pass, after that I have plucked them up, I will return and have compassion on them; and I will bring them again, every man to his heritage, and every man to his land.

16And it shall come to pass, if they will diligently learn the ways of my people, to swear by my name, As Yahweh liveth; even as they taught my people to swear by Baal; then shall they be built up in the midst of my people.

17But if they will not hear, then will I pluck up that nation, plucking up and destroying it, saith Yahweh.

Chapter 13

1Thus saith Yahweh unto me, Go, and buy thee a linen girdle, and put it upon thy loins, and put it not in water.

2So I bought a girdle according to the word of Yahweh, and put it upon my loins.

3And the word of Yahweh came unto me the second time, saying,

4Take the girdle that thou hast bought, which is upon thy loins, and arise, go to the Euphrates, and hide it there in a cleft of the rock.

5So I went, and hid it by the Euphrates, as Yahweh commanded me.

6And it came to pass after many days, that Yahweh said unto me, Arise, go to the Euphrates, and take the girdle from thence, which I commanded thee to hide there.

7Then I went to the Euphrates, and digged, and took the girdle from the place where I had hid it; and, behold, the girdle was marred, it was profitable for nothing.

8Then the word of Yahweh came unto me, saying,

9Thus saith Yahweh, After this manner will I mar the pride of Judah, and the great pride of Jerusalem.

10This evil people, that refuse to hear my words, that walk in the stubbornness of their heart, and are gone after other gods to serve them, and to worship them, shall even be as this girdle, which is profitable for nothing.

11For as the girdle cleaveth to the loins of a man, so have I caused to cleave unto me the whole house of Israel and the whole house of Judah, saith Yahweh; that they may be unto me for a people, and for a name, and for a praise, and for a glory: but they would not hear.

12Therefore thou shalt speak unto them this word: Thus saith Yahweh, the God of Israel, Every bottle shall be filled with wine: and they shall say unto thee, Do we not certainly know that every bottle shall be filled with wine?

13Then shalt thou say unto them, Thus saith Yahweh, Behold, I will fill all the inhabitants of this land, even the kings that sit upon David's throne, and the priests, and the prophets, and all the inhabitants of Jerusalem, with drunkenness.

14And I will dash them one against another, even the fathers and the sons together, saith Yahweh: I will not pity, nor spare, nor have compassion, that I should not destroy them.

15Hear ye, and give ear; be not proud; for Yahweh hath spoken.

16Give glory to Yahweh your God, before he cause darkness, and before your feet stumble upon the dark mountains, and, while ye look for light, he turn it into the shadow of death, and make it gross darkness.

17But if ye will not hear it, my soul shall weep in secret for your pride; and mine eye shall weep sore, and run down with tears, because Yahweh's flock is taken captive.

18Say thou unto the king and to the queen-mother, Humble yourselves, sit down; for your headtires are come down, even the crown of your glory.

19The cities of the South are shut up, and there is none to open them: Judah is carried away captive, all of it; it is wholly carried away captive.

20Lift up your eyes, and behold them that come from the north: where is the flock that was given thee, thy beautiful flock?

21What wilt thou say, when he shall set over thee as head those whom thou hast thyself taught to be friends to thee? shall not sorrows take hold of thee, as of a woman in travail?

22And if thou say in thy heart, Wherefore are these things come upon me? for the greatness of thine iniquity are thy skirts uncovered, and thy heels suffer violence.

Jeremiah

23Can the Ethiopian change his skin, or the leopard his spots? then may ye also do good, that are accustomed to do evil.

24Therefore will I scatter them, as the stubble that passeth away, by the wind of the wilderness.

25This is thy lot, the portion measured unto thee from me, saith Yahweh; because thou hast forgotten me, and trusted in falsehood.

26Therefore will I also uncover thy skirts upon thy face, and thy shame shall appear.

27I have seen thine abominations, even thine adulteries, and thy neighings, the lewdness of thy whoredom, on the hills in the field. Woe unto thee, O Jerusalem! thou wilt not be made clean; how long shall it yet be?

Chapter 14

1The word of Yahweh that came to Jeremiah concerning the drought.

2Judah mourneth, and the gates thereof languish, they sit in black upon the ground; and the cry of Jerusalem is gone up.

3And their nobles send their little ones to the waters: they come to the cisterns, and find no water; they return with their vessels empty; they are put to shame and confounded, and cover their heads.

4Because of the ground which is cracked, for that no rain hath been in the land, the plowmen are put to shame, they cover their heads.

5Yea, the hind also in the field calveth, and forsaketh her young, because there is no grass.

6And the wild asses stand on the bare heights, they pant for air like jackals; their eyes fail, because there is no herbage.

7Though our iniquities testify against us, work thou for thy name's sake, O Yahweh; for our backslidings are many; we have sinned against thee.

8O thou hope of Israel, the Saviour thereof in the time of trouble, why shouldest thou be as a sojourner in the land, and as a wayfaring man that turneth aside to tarry for a night?

9Why shouldest thou be as a man affrighted, as a mighty man that cannot save? yet thou, O Yahweh, art in the midst of us, and we are called by thy name; leave us not.

10Thus saith Yahweh unto this people, Even so have they loved to wander; they have not refrained their feet: therefore Yahweh doth not accept them; now will he remember their iniquity, and visit their sins.

11And Yahweh said unto me, Pray not for this people for their good.

12When they fast, I will not hear their cry; and when they offer burnt-offering and meal-offering, I will not accept them; but I will consume them by the sword, and by the famine, and by the pestilence.

13Then said I, Ah, Lord Yahweh! behold, the prophets say unto them, Ye shall not see the sword, neither shall ye have famine; but I will give you assured peace in this place.

14Then Yahweh said unto me, The prophets prophesy lies in my name; I sent them not, neither have I commanded them, neither spake I unto them: they prophesy unto you a lying vision, and divination, and a thing of nought, and the deceit of their own heart.

15Therefore thus saith Yahweh concerning the prophets that prophesy in my name, and I sent them not, yet they say, Sword and famine shall not be in this land: By sword and famine shall those prophets be consumed.

16And the people to whom they prophesy shall be cast out in the streets of Jerusalem because of the famine and the sword; and they shall have none to bury them-them, their wives, nor their sons, nor their daughters: for I will pour their wickedness upon them.

17And thou shalt say this word unto them, Let mine eyes run down with tears night and day, and let them not cease; for the virgin daughter of my people is broken with a great breach, with a very grievous wound.

18If I go forth into the field, then, behold, the slain with the sword! and if I enter into the city, then, behold, they that are sick with famine! for both the prophet and the priest go about in the land, and have no knowledge.

19Hast thou utterly rejected Judah? hath thy soul loathed Zion? why hast thou smitten us, and there is no healing for us? We looked for peace, but no good came; and for a time of healing, and, behold, dismay!

20We acknowledge, O Yahweh, our wickedness, and the iniquity of our fathers; for we have sinned against thee.

21Do not abhor us, for thy name's sake; do not disgrace the throne of thy glory: remember, break not thy covenant with us.

22Are there any among the vanities of the nations that can cause rain? or can the heavens give showers? art not thou he, O Yahweh our God? therefore we will wait for thee; for thou hast made all these things.

Chapter 15

1Then said Yahweh unto me, Though Moses and Samuel stood before me, yet my mind would not be toward this people: cast them out of my sight, and let them go forth.

2And it shall come to pass, when they say unto thee, Whither shall we go forth? then thou shalt tell them, Thus saith Yahweh: Such as are for death, to death; and such as are for the sword, to the sword; and such as are for the famine, to the famine; and such as are for captivity, to captivity.

3And I will appoint over them four kinds, saith Yahweh: the sword to slay, and the dogs to tear, and the birds of the heavens, and the beasts of the earth, to devour and to destroy.

4And I will cause them to be tossed to and fro among all the kingdoms of the earth, because of Manasseh, the son of Hezekiah, king of Judah, for that which he did in Jerusalem.

5For who will have pity upon thee, O Jerusalem? or who will bemoan thee? or who will turn aside to ask of thy welfare?

6Thou hast rejected me, saith Yahweh, thou art gone backward: therefore have I stretched out my hand against thee, and destroyed thee; I am weary with repenting.

7And I have winnowed them with a fan in the gates of the land; I have bereaved them of children, I have destroyed my people; they returned not from their ways.

8Their widows are increased to me above the sand of the seas; I have brought upon them against the mother of the young men a destroyer at noonday: I have caused anguish and terrors to fall upon her suddenly.

9She that hath borne seven languisheth; she hath given up the ghost; her sun is gone down while it was yet day; she hath been put to shame and confounded: and the residue of them will I deliver to the sword before their enemies, saith Yahweh.

10Woe is me, my mother, that thou hast borne me a man of strife and a man of contention to the whole earth! I have not lent, neither have men lent to me; yet every one of them doth curse me.

11Yahweh said, Verily I will strengthen thee for good; verily I will cause the enemy to make supplication unto thee in the time of evil and in the time of affliction.

12Can one break iron, even iron from the north, and brass?

13Thy substance and thy treasures will I give for a spoil without price, and that for all thy sins, even in all thy borders.

14And I will make them to pass with thine enemies into a land which thou knowest not; for a fire is kindled in mine anger, which shall burn upon you.

15O Yahweh, thou knowest; remember me, and visit me, and avenge me of my persecutors; take me not away in thy longsuffering: know that for thy sake I have suffered reproach.

16Thy words were found, and I did eat them; and thy words were unto me a joy and the rejoicing of my heart: for I am called by thy name, O Yahweh, God of hosts.

17I sat not in the assembly of them that make merry, nor rejoiced; I sat alone because of thy hand; for thou hast filled me with indignation.

18Why is my pain perpetual, and my wound incurable, which refuseth to be healed? wilt thou indeed be unto me as a deceitful brook, as waters that fail?

19Therefore thus saith Yahweh, If thou return, then will I bring thee again, that thou mayest stand before me; and if thou take forth the precious from the vile, thou shalt be as my mouth: they shall return unto thee, but thou shalt not return unto them.

20And I will make thee unto this people a fortified brazen wall; and they shall fight against thee, but they shall not prevail against thee; for I am with thee to save thee and to deliver thee, saith Yahweh.

21And I will deliver thee out of the hand of the wicked, and I will redeem thee out of the hand of the terrible.

Chapter 16

1The word of Yahweh came also unto me, saying,

2Thou shalt not take thee a wife, neither shalt thou have sons or daughters, in this place.

3For thus saith Yahweh concerning the sons and concerning the daughters that are born in this place, and concerning their mothers that bare them, and concerning their fathers that begat them in this land:

4They shall die grievous deaths: they shall not be lamented, neither shall they be buried; they shall be as dung upon the face of the ground; and they shall be consumed by the sword, and by famine; and their dead bodies shall be food for the birds of the heavens, and for the beasts of the earth.

5For thus saith Yahweh, Enter not into the house of mourning, neither go to lament, neither bemoan them; for I have taken away my peace from this people, saith Yahweh, even lovingkindness and tender mercies.

6Both great and small shall die in this land; they shall not be buried, neither shall men lament for them, nor cut themselves, nor make themselves bald for them;

7neither shall men break bread for them in mourning, to comfort them for the dead; neither shall men give them the cup of consolation to drink for their father or for their mother.

8And thou shalt not go into the house of feasting to sit with them, to eat and to drink.

9For thus saith Yahweh of hosts, the God of Israel: Behold, I will cause to cease out of this place, before your eyes and in your days, the voice of mirth and the voice of gladness, the voice of the bridegroom and the voice of the bride.

10And it shall come to pass, when thou shalt show this people all these words, and they shall say unto thee, Wherefore hath Yahweh pronounced all this great evil against us? or what is our iniquity? or what is our sin that we have committed against Yahweh our God?

11Then shalt thou say unto them, Because your fathers have forsaken me, saith Yahweh, and have walked after other gods, and have served them, and have worshipped them, and have forsaken me, and have not kept my law;

12and ye have done evil more than your fathers; for, behold, ye walk every one after the stubbornness of his evil heart, so that ye hearken not unto me:

13therefore will I cast you forth out of this land into the land that ye have not known, neither ye nor your fathers; and there shall ye serve other gods day and night; for I will show you no favor.

14Therefore, behold, the days come, saith Yahweh, that it shall no more be said, As Yahweh liveth, that brought up the children of Israel out of the land of Egypt;

15but, As Yahweh liveth, that brought up the children of Israel from the land of the north, and from all the countries whither he had driven them. And I will bring them again into their land that I gave unto their fathers.

16Behold, I will send for many fishers, saith Yahweh, and they shall fish them up; and afterward I will send for many hunters, and they shall hunt them from every mountain, and from every hill, and out of the clefts of the rocks.

17For mine eyes are upon all their ways; they are not hid from my face, neither is their iniquity concealed from mine eyes.

18And first I will recompense their iniquity and their sin double, because they have polluted my land with the carcasses of their detestable things, and have filled mine inheritance with their abominations.

19O Yahweh, my strength, and my stronghold, and my refuge in the day of affliction, unto thee shall the nations come from the ends of the earth, and shall say, Our fathers have inherited nought but lies, even vanity and things wherein there is no profit.

20Shall a man make unto himself gods, which yet are no gods?

21Therefore, behold, I will cause them to know, this once will I cause them to know my hand and my might; and they shall know that my name is Yahweh.

Chapter 17.

1The sin of Judah is written with a pen of iron, and with the point of a diamond: it is graven upon the tablet of their heart, and upon the horns of your altars;

2whilst their children remember their altars and their Asherim by the green trees upon the high hills.

3O my mountain in the field, I will give thy substance and all thy treasures for a spoil, and thy high places, because of sin, throughout all thy borders.

4And thou, even of thyself, shalt discontinue from thy heritage that I gave thee; and I will cause thee to serve thine enemies in the land which thou knowest not: for ye have kindled a fire in mine anger which shall burn for ever.

5Thus saith Yahweh: Cursed is the man that trusteth in man, and maketh flesh his arm, and whose heart departeth from Yahweh.

6For he shall be like the heath in the desert, and shall not see when good cometh, but shall inhabit the parched places in the wilderness, a salt land and not inhabited.

7Blessed is the man that trusteth in Yahweh, and whose trust Yahweh is.

8For he shall be as a tree planted by the waters, that spreadeth out its roots by the river, and shall not fear when heat cometh, but its leaf shall be green; and shall not be careful in the year of drought, neither shall cease from yielding fruit.

9The heart is deceitful above all things, and it is exceedingly corrupt: who can know it?

10I, Yahweh, search the mind, I try the heart, even to give every man according to his ways, according to the fruit of his doings.

11As the partridge that sitteth on eggs which she hath not laid, so is he that getteth riches, and not by right; in the midst of his days they shall leave him, and at his end he shall be a fool.

12A glorious throne, set on high from the beginning, is the place of our sanctuary.

13O Yahweh, the hope of Israel, all that forsake thee shall be put to shame. They that depart from me shall be written in the earth, because they have forsaken Yahweh, the fountain of living waters.

14Heal me, O Yahweh, and I shall be healed; save me, and I shall be saved: for thou art my praise.

15Behold, they say unto me, Where is the word of Yahweh? let it come now.

16As for me, I have not hastened from being a shepherd after thee; neither have I desired the woeful day; thou knowest: that which came out of my lips was before thy face.

17Be not a terror unto me: thou art my refuge in the day of evil.

18Let them be put to shame that persecute me, but let not me be put to shame; let them be dismayed, but let not me be dismayed; bring upon them the day of evil, and destroy them with double destruction.

19Thus said Yahweh unto me: Go, and stand in the gate of the children of the people, whereby the kings of Judah come in, and by which they go out, and in all the gates of Jerusalem;

20and say unto them, Hear ye the word of Yahweh, ye kings of Judah, and all Judah, and all the inhabitants of Jerusalem, that enter in by these gates:

21Thus saith Yahweh, Take heed to yourselves, and bear no burden on the sabbath day, nor bring it in by the gates of Jerusalem;

22neither carry forth a burden out of your houses on the sabbath day, neither do ye any work: but hallow ye the sabbath day, as I commanded your fathers.

23But they hearkened not, neither inclined their ear, but made their neck stiff, that they might not hear, and might not receive instruction.

24And it shall come to pass, if ye diligently hearken unto me, saith Yahweh, to bring in no burden through the gates of this city on the sabbath day, but to hallow the sabbath day, to do no work therein;

25then shall there enter in by the gates of this city kings and princes sitting upon the throne of David, riding in chariots and on horses, they, and their princes, the men of Judah, and the inhabitants of Jerusalem; and this city shall remain for ever.

26And they shall come from the cities of Judah, and from the places round about Jerusalem, and from the land of Benjamin, and from the lowland, and from the hill-country, and from the South, bringing burnt-offerings, and sacrifices, and meal-offerings, and frankincense, and bringing sacrifices of thanksgiving, unto the house of Yahweh.

27But if ye will not hearken unto me to hallow the sabbath day, and not to bear a burden and enter in at the gates of Jerusalem on the sabbath day; then will I kindle a fire in the gates thereof, and it shall devour the palaces of Jerusalem, and it shall not be quenched.

Chapter 18

1The word which came to Jeremiah from Yahweh, saying,

2Arise, and go down to the potter's house, and there I will cause thee to hear my words.

3Then I went down to the potter's house, and, behold, he was making a work on the wheels.

4And when the vessel that he made of the clay was marred in the hand of the potter, he made it again another vessel, as seemed good to the potter to make it.

5Then the word of Yahweh came to me, saying,

6O house of Israel, cannot I do with you as this potter? saith Yahweh. Behold, as the clay in the potter's hand, so are ye in my hand, O house of Israel.

7At what instant I shall speak concerning a nation, and concerning a kingdom, to pluck up and to break down and to destroy it;

8if that nation, concerning which I have spoken, turn from their evil, I will repent of the evil that I thought to do unto them.

9And at what instant I shall speak concerning a nation, and concerning a kingdom, to build and to plant it;

10if they do that which is evil in my sight, that they obey not my voice, then I will repent of the good, wherewith I said I would benefit them.

11Now therefore, speak to the men of Judah, and to the inhabitants of Jerusalem, saying, Thus saith Yahweh: Behold, I frame evil against you, and devise a device against you: return ye now every one from his evil way, and amend your ways and your doings.

12But they say, It is in vain; for we will walk after our own devices, and we will do every one after the stubbornness of his evil heart.

13Therefore thus saith Yahweh: Ask ye now among the nations, who hath heard such things; the virgin of Israel hath done a very horrible thing.

14Shall the snow of Lebanon fail from the rock of the field? or shall the cold waters that flow down from afar be dried up?

15For my people have forgotten me, they have burned incense to false gods; and they have been made to stumble in their ways, in the ancient paths, to walk in bypaths, in a way not cast up;

16to make their land an astonishment, and a perpetual hissing; every one that passeth thereby shall be astonished, and shake his head.

17I will scatter them as with an east wind before the enemy; I will show them the back, and not the face, in the day of their calamity.

18Then said they, Come, and let us devise devices against Jeremiah; for the law shall not perish from the priest, nor counsel from the wise, nor the word from the prophet. Come, and let us smite him with the tongue, and let us not give heed to any of his words.

19Give heed to me, O Yahweh, and hearken to the voice of them that contend with me.

20Shall evil be recompensed for good? for they have digged a pit for my soul. Remember how I stood before thee to speak good for them, to turn away thy wrath from them.

21Therefore deliver up their children to the famine, and give them over to the power of the sword; and let their wives become childless, and widows; and let their men be slain of death, and their young men smitten of the sword in battle.

22Let a cry be heard from their houses, when thou shalt bring a troop suddenly upon them; for they have digged a pit to take me, and hid snares for my feet.

23Yet, Yahweh, thou knowest all their counsel against me to slay me; forgive not their iniquity, neither blot out their sin from thy sight; but let them be overthrown before thee; deal thou with them in the time of thine anger.

Chapter 19

1Thus said Yahweh, Go, and buy a potter's earthen bottle, and take of the elders of the people, and of the elders of the priests;

2and go forth unto the valley of the son of Hinnom, which is by the entry of the gate Harsith, and proclaim there the words that I shall tell thee;

3and say, Hear ye the word of Yahweh, O kings of Judah, and inhabitants of Jerusalem: thus saith Yahweh of hosts, the God of Israel, Behold, I will bring evil upon this place, which whosoever heareth, his ears shall tingle.

4Because they have forsaken me, and have estranged this place, and have burned incense in it unto other gods, that they knew not, they and their fathers and the kings of Judah; and have filled this place with the blood of innocents;

5and have built the high places of Baal, to burn their sons in the fire for burnt-offerings unto Baal; which I commanded not, nor spake it, neither came it into my mind:

6therefore, behold, the days come, saith Yahweh, that this place shall no more be called Topheth, nor The valley of the son of Hinnom, but The valley of Slaughter.

7And I will make void the counsel of Judah and Jerusalem in this place; and I will cause them to fall by the sword before their enemies, and by the hand of them that seek their life: and their dead bodies will I give to be food for the birds of the heavens, and for the beasts of the earth.

8And I will make this city an astonishment, and a hissing; every one that passeth thereby shall be astonished and hiss because of all the plagues thereof.

9And I will cause them to eat the flesh of their sons and the flesh of their daughters; and they shall eat every one the flesh of his friend, in the siege and in the distress, wherewith their enemies, and they that seek their life, shall distress them.

10Then shalt thou break the bottle in the sight of the men that go with thee,

11and shalt say unto them, Thus saith Yahweh of hosts: Even so will I break this people and this city, as one breaketh a potter's vessel, that cannot be made whole again; and they shall bury in Topheth, till there be no place to bury.

12Thus will I do unto this place, saith Yahweh, and to the inhabitants

Jeremiah

thereof, even making this city as Topheth;

13and the houses of Jerusalem, and the houses of the kings of Judah, which are defiled, shall be as the place of Topheth, even all the houses upon whose roofs they have burned incense unto all the host of heaven, and have poured out drink-offerings unto other gods.

14Then came Jeremiah from Topheth, whither Yahweh had sent him to prophesy; and he stood in the court of Yahweh's house, and said to all the people:

15Thus saith Yahweh of hosts, the God of Israel, Behold, I will bring upon this city and upon all its towns all the evil that I have pronounced against it; because they have made their neck stiff, that they may not hear my words.

Chapter 20

1Now Pashhur, the son of Immer the priest, who was chief officer in the house of Yahweh, heard Jeremiah prophesying these things.

2Then Pashhur smote Jeremiah the prophet, and put him in the stocks that were in the upper gate of Benjamin, which was in the house of Yahweh.

3And it came to pass on the morrow, that Pashhur brought forth Jeremiah out of the stocks. Then said Jeremiah unto him, Yahweh hath not called thy name Pashhur, but Magor-missabib.

4For thus saith Yahweh, Behold, I will make thee a terror to thyself, and to all thy friends; and they shall fall by the sword of their enemies, and thine eyes shall behold it; and I will give all Judah into the hand of the king of Babylon, and he shall carry them captive to Babylon, and shall slay them with the sword.

5Moreover I will give all the riches of this city, and all the gains thereof, and all the precious things thereof, yea, all the treasures of the kings of Judah will I give into the hand of their enemies; and they shall make them a prey, and take them, and carry them to Babylon.

6And thou, Pashhur, and all that dwell in thy house shall go into captivity; and thou shalt come to Babylon, and there thou shalt die, and there shalt thou be buried, thou, and all thy friends, to whom thou hast prophesied falsely.

7O Yahweh, thou hast persuaded me, and I was persuaded; thou art stronger than I, and hast prevailed: I am become a laughing-stock all the day, every one mocketh me.

8For as often as I speak, I cry out; I cry, Violence and destruction! because the word of Yahweh is made a reproach unto me, and a derision, all the day.

9And if I say, I will not make mention of him, nor speak any more in his name, then there is in my heart as it were a burning fire shut up in my bones, and I am weary with forbearing, and I cannot contain.

10For I have heard the defaming of many, terror on every side. Denounce, and we will denounce him, say all my familiar friends, they that watch for my fall; peradventure he will be persuaded, and we shall prevail against him, and we shall take our revenge on him.

11But Yahweh is with me as a mighty one and a terrible: therefore my persecutors shall stumble, and they shall not prevail; they shall be utterly put to shame, because they have not dealt wisely, even with an everlasting dishonor which shall never be forgotten.

12But, O Yahweh of hosts, that triest the righteous, that seest the heart and the mind, let me see thy vengeance on them; for unto thee have I revealed my cause.

13Sing unto Yahweh, praise ye Yahweh; for he hath delivered the soul of the needy from the hand of evil-doers.

14Cursed be the day wherein I was born: let not the day wherein my mother bare me be blessed.

15Cursed be the man who brought tidings to my father, saying, A man-child is born unto thee; making him very glad.

16And let that man be as the cities which Yahweh overthrew, and repented not: and let him hear a cry in the morning, and shouting at noontime;

17because he slew me not from the womb; and so my mother would have been my grave, and her womb always great.

18Wherefore came I forth out of the womb to see labor and sorrow, that my days should be consumed with shame?

Chapter 21

1The word which came unto Jeremiah from Yahweh, when king Zedekiah sent unto him Pashhur the son of Malchijah, and Zephaniah the son of Maaseiah, the priest, saying,

2Inquire, I pray thee, of Yahweh for us; for Nebuchadrezzar king of Babylon maketh war against us: peradventure Yahweh will deal with us according to all his wondrous works, that he may go up from us.

3Then said Jeremiah unto them, Thus shall ye say to Zedekiah:

4Thus saith Yahweh, the God of Israel, Behold, I will turn back the weapons of war that are in your hands, wherewith ye fight against the king of Babylon, and against the Chaldeans that besiege you, without the walls; and I will gather them into the midst of this city.

5And I myself will fight against you with an outstretched hand and with a strong arm, even in anger, and in wrath, and in great indignation.

6And I will smite the inhabitants of this city, both man and beast: they shall die of a great pestilence.

7And afterward, saith Yahweh, I will deliver Zedekiah king of Judah, and his servants, and the people, even such as are left in this city from the pestilence, from the sword, and from the famine, into the hand of Nebuchadrezzar king of Babylon, and into the hand of their enemies, and into the hand of those that seek their life: and he shall smite them with the edge of the sword; he shall not spare them, neither have pity, nor have mercy.

8And unto this people thou shalt say, Thus saith Yahweh: Behold, I set before you the way of life and the way of death.

9He that abideth in this city shall die by the sword, and by the famine, and by the pestilence; but he that goeth out, and passeth over to the Chaldeans that besiege you, he shall live, and his life shall be unto him for a prey.

10For I have set my face upon this city for evil, and not for good, saith Yahweh: it shall be given into the hand of the king of Babylon, and he shall burn it with fire.

11And touching the house of the king of Judah, hear ye the word of Yahweh:

12O house of David, thus saith Yahweh, Execute justice in the morning, and deliver him that is robbed out of the hand of the oppressor, lest my wrath go forth like fire, and burn so that none can quench it, because of the evil of your doings.

13Behold, I am against thee, O inhabitant of the valley, and of the rock of the plain, saith Yahweh; you that say, Who shall come down against us? or who shall enter into our habitations?

14And I will punish you according to the fruit of your doings, saith Yahweh; and I will kindle a fire in her forest, and it shall devour all that is round about her.

Chapter 22

1Thus said Yahweh: Go down to the house of the king of Judah, and speak there this word,

2And say, Hear the word of Yahweh, O king of Judah, that sittest upon the throne of David, thou, and thy servants, and thy people that enter in by these gates.

3Thus saith Yahweh: Execute ye justice and righteousness, and deliver him that is robbed out of the hand of the oppressor: and do no wrong, do no violence, to the sojourner, the fatherless, nor the widow; neither shed innocent blood in this place.

4For if ye do this thing indeed, then shall there enter in by the gates of this house kings sitting upon the throne of David, riding in chariots and on horses, he, and his servants, and his people.

5But if ye will not hear these words, I swear by myself, saith Yahweh, that this house shall become a desolation.

6For thus saith Yahweh concerning the house of the king of Judah: Thou art Gilead unto me, and the head of Lebanon; yet surely I will make thee a wilderness, and cities which are not inhabited.

7And I will prepare destroyers against thee, every one with his weapons; and they shall cut down thy choice cedars, and cast them into the fire.

8And many nations shall pass by this city, and they shall say every man to his neighbor, Wherefore hath Yahweh done thus unto this great city?

9Then they shall answer, Because they forsook the covenant of Yahweh their God, and worshipped other gods, and served them.

10Weep ye not for the dead, neither bemoan him; but weep sore for him that goeth away; for he shall return no more, nor see his native country.

11For thus saith Yahweh touching Shallum the son of Josiah, king of Judah, who reigned instead of Josiah his father, and who went forth out of this place: He shall not return thither any more.

12But in the place whither they have led him captive, there shall he die, and he shall see this land no more.

13Woe unto him that buildeth his house by unrighteousness, and his chambers by injustice; that useth his neighbor's service without wages, and giveth him not his hire;

14that saith, I will build me a wide house and spacious chambers, and cutteth him out windows; and it is ceiled with cedar, and painted with vermilion.

15Shalt thou reign, because thou strivest to excel in cedar? Did not thy father eat and drink, and do justice and righteousness? then it was well with him.

16He judged the cause of the poor and needy; then it was well. Was not this to know me? saith Yahweh.

17But thine eyes and thy heart are not but for thy covetousness, and for shedding innocent blood, and for oppression, and for violence, to do it.

18Therefore thus saith Yahweh concerning Jehoiakim the son of Josiah, king of Judah: they shall not lament for him, saying, Ah my brother! or, Ah sister! They shall not lament for him, saying Ah lord! or, Ah his glory!

19He shall be buried with the burial of an ass, drawn and cast forth beyond the gates of Jerusalem.

20Go up to Lebanon, and cry; and lift up thy voice in Bashan, and cry from Abarim; for all thy lovers are destroyed.

21I spake unto thee in thy prosperity; but thou saidst, I will not hear. This hath been thy manner from thy youth, that thou obeyedst not my voice.

22The wind shall feed all thy shepherds, and thy lovers shall go into captivity: surely then shalt thou be ashamed and confounded for all thy wickedness.

23O inhabitant of Lebanon, that makest thy nest in the cedars, how greatly to be pitied shalt thou be when pangs come upon thee, the pain as of a woman in travail!

24As I live, saith Yahweh, though Coniah the son of Jehoiakim king of Judah were the signet upon my right hand, yet would I pluck thee thence;

25and I will give thee into the hand of them that seek thy life, and into the hand of them of whom thou art afraid, even into the hand of Nebuchadrezzar king of Babylon, and into the hand of the Chaldeans.

26And I will cast thee out, and thy mother that bare thee, into another country, where ye were not born; and there shall ye die.

27But to the land whereunto their soul longeth to return, thither shall they not return.

28Is this man Coniah a despised broken vessel? is he a vessel wherein none delighteth? wherefore are they cast out, he and his seed, and are cast into the land which they know not?

29O earth, earth, earth, hear the word of Yahweh.

30Thus saith Yahweh, Write ye this man childless, a man that shall not prosper in his days; for no more shall a man of his seed prosper, sitting upon the throne of David, and ruling in Judah.

Chapter 23

1Woe unto the shepherds that destroy and scatter the sheep of my pasture! saith Yahweh.

2Therefore thus saith Yahweh, the God of Israel, against the shepherds that feed my people: Ye have scattered my flock, and driven them away, and have not visited them; behold, I will visit upon you the evil of your doings, saith Yahweh.

3And I will gather the remnant of my flock out of all the countries whither I have driven them, and will bring them again to their folds; and they shall be fruitful and multiply.

4And I will set up shepherds over them, who shall feed them; and they shall fear no more, nor be dismayed, neither shall any be lacking, saith Yahweh.

5Behold, the days come, saith Yahweh, that I will raise unto David a righteous Branch, and he shall reign as king and deal wisely, and shall execute justice and righteousness in the land.

6In his days Judah shall be saved, and Israel shall dwell safely; and this is his name whereby he shall be called: Yahweh our righteousness.

7Therefore, behold, the days come, saith Yahweh, that they shall no more say, As Yahweh liveth, who brought up the children of Israel out of the land of Egypt,

8but, As Yahweh liveth, who brought up and who led the seed of the house of Israel out of the north country, and from all the countries whither I had driven them. And they shall dwell in their own land.

9Concerning the prophets. My heart within me is broken, all my bones shake; I am like a drunken man, and like a man whom wine hath overcome, because of Yahweh, and because of his holy words.

10For the land is full of adulterers; for because of swearing the land mourneth; the pastures of the wilderness are dried up. And their course is evil, and their might is not right;

11for both prophet and priest are profane; yea, in my house have I found their wickedness, saith Yahweh.

12Wherefore their way shall be unto them as slippery places in the darkness: they shall be driven on, and fall therein; for I will bring evil upon them, even the year of their visitation, saith Yahweh.

13And I have seen folly in the prophets of Samaria; they prophesied by Baal, and caused my people Israel to err.

14In the prophets of Jerusalem also I have seen a horrible thing: they commit adultery, and walk in lies; and they strengthen the hands of evil-doers, so that none doth return from his wickedness: they are all of them become unto me as Sodom, and the inhabitants thereof as Gomorrah.

15Therefore thus saith Yahweh of hosts concerning the prophets: Behold, I will feed them with wormwood, and make them drink the water of gall; for from the prophets of Jerusalem is ungodliness gone forth into all the land.

16Thus saith Yahweh of hosts, Hearken not unto the words of the prophets that prophesy unto you: they teach you vanity; they speak a vision of their own heart, and not out of the mouth of Yahweh.

17They say continually unto them that despise me, Yahweh hath said, Ye shall have peace; and unto every one that walketh in the stubbornness of his own heart they say, No evil shall come upon you.

18For who hath stood in the council of Yahweh, that he should perceive and hear his word? who hath marked my word, and heard it?

19Behold, the tempest of Yahweh, even his wrath, is gone forth, yea, a whirling tempest: it shall burst upon the head of the wicked.

20The anger of Yahweh shall not return, until he have executed, and till he have performed the intents of his heart: in the latter days ye shall understand it perfectly.

21I sent not these prophets, yet they ran: I spake not unto them, yet they prophesied.

22But if they had stood in my council, then had they caused my people to hear my words, and had turned them from their evil way, and from the evil of their doings.

23Am I a God at hand, saith Yahweh, and not a God afar off?

24Can any hide himself in secret places so that I shall not see him? saith Yahweh. Do not I fill heaven and earth? saith Yahweh.

25I have heard what the prophets have said, that prophesy lies in my name, saying, I have dreamed, I have dreamed.

26How long shall this be in the heart of the prophets that prophesy lies, even the prophets of the deceit of their own heart?

27that think to cause my people to forget my name by their dreams which they tell every man to his neighbor, as their fathers forgat my name for Baal.

28The prophet that hath a dream, let him tell a dream; and he that hath my word, let him speak my word faithfully. What is the straw to the wheat? saith Yahweh.

29Is not my word like fire? saith Yahweh; and like a hammer that breaketh the rock in pieces?

30Therefore, behold, I am against the prophets, saith Yahweh, that steal my words every one from his neighbor.

31Behold, I am against the prophets, saith Yahweh, that use their tongues, and say, He saith.

32Behold, I am against them that prophesy lying dreams, saith Yahweh, and do tell them, and cause my people to err by their lies, and by their vain boasting: yet I sent them not, nor commanded them; neither do they profit this people at all, saith Yahweh.

33And when this people, or the prophet, or a priest, shall ask thee, saying, What is the burden of Yahweh? then shalt thou say unto them, What burden! I will cast you off, saith Yahweh.

34And as for the prophet, and the priest, and the people, that shall say, The burden of Yahweh, I will even punish that man and his house.

35Thus shall ye say every one to his neighbor, and every one to his brother, What hath Yahweh answered? and, What hath Yahweh spoken?

36And the burden of Yahweh shall ye mention no more: for every man's own word shall be his burden; for ye have perverted the words of the living God, of Yahweh of hosts our God.

37Thus shalt thou say to the prophet, What hath Yahweh answered thee? and, What hath Yahweh spoken?

38But if ye say, The burden of Yahweh; therefore thus saith Yahweh: Because ye say this word, The burden of Yahweh, and I have sent unto you, saying, Ye shall not say, The burden of Yahweh;

39therefore, behold, I will utterly forget you, and I will cast you off, and the city that I gave unto you and to your fathers, away from my presence:

40and I will bring an everlasting reproach upon you, and a perpetual shame, which shall not be forgotten.

Chapter 24

1Yahweh showed me, and, behold, two baskets of figs set before the temple of Yahweh, after that Nebuchadrezzar king of Babylon had carried away captive Jeconiah the son of Jehoiakim, king of Judah, and the princes of Judah, with the craftsmen and smiths, from Jerusalem, and had brought them to Babylon.

2One basket had very good figs, like the figs that are first-ripe; and the other basket had very bad figs, which could not be eaten, they were so bad.

3Then said Yahweh unto me, What seest thou, Jeremiah? And I said, Figs; the good figs, very good; and the bad, very bad, that cannot be eaten, they are so bad.

4And the word of Yahweh came unto me, saying,

5Thus saith Yahweh, the God of Israel: Like these good figs, so will I regard the captives of Judah, whom I have sent out of this place into the land of the Chaldeans, for good.

6For I will set mine eyes upon them for good, and I will bring them again to this land: and I will build them, and not pull them down; and I will plant them, and not pluck them up.

7And I will give them a heart to know me, that I am Yahweh: and they shall be my people, and I will be their God; for they shall return unto me with their whole heart.

8And as the bad figs, which cannot be eaten, they are so bad, surely thus saith Yahweh, So will I give up Zedekiah the king of Judah, and his princes, and the residue of Jerusalem, that remain in this land, and them that dwell in the land of Egypt,

9I will even give them up to be tossed to and fro among all the kingdoms of the earth for evil; to be a reproach and a proverb, a taunt and a curse, in all places whither I shall drive them.

10And I will send the sword, the famine, and the pestilence, among them, till they be consumed from off the land that I gave unto them and to their fathers.

Chapter 25

1The word that came to Jeremiah concerning all the people of Judah, in the fourth year of Jehoiakim the son of Josiah, king of Judah (the same was the first year of Nebuchadrezzar king of Babylon,)

2which Jeremiah the prophet spake unto all the people of Judah, and to all the inhabitants of Jerusalem, saying:

3From the thirteenth year of Josiah the son of Amon, king of Judah, even unto this day, these three and twenty years, the word of Yahweh hath come unto me, and I have spoken unto you, rising up early and speaking; but ye have not hearkened.

4And Yahweh hath sent unto you all his servants the prophets, rising up early and sending them, (but ye have not hearkened, nor inclined your ear to hear,)

5saying, Return ye now every one from his evil way, and from the evil of your doings, and dwell in the land that Yahweh hath given unto you and to your fathers, from of old and even for evermore;

6and go not after other gods to serve them, and to worship them, and provoke me not to anger with the work of your hands; and I will do you no hurt.

7Yet ye have not hearkened unto me, saith Yahweh; that ye may provoke me to anger with the work of your hands to your own hurt.

8Therefore thus saith Yahweh of hosts: Because ye have not heard my words,

9behold, I will send and take all the families of the north, saith Yahweh, and I will send unto Nebuchadrezzar the king of Babylon, my servant, and will bring them against this land, and against the inhabitants thereof, and against all these nations round about; and I will utterly destroy them, and make them an astonishment, and a hissing, and perpetual desolations.

10Moreover I will take from them the voice of mirth and the voice of gladness, the voice of the bridegroom and the voice of the bride, the sound of the millstones, and the light of the lamp.

11And this whole land shall be a desolation, and an astonishment; and these nations shall serve the king of Babylon seventy years.

12And it shall come to pass, when seventy years are accomplished, that I will punish the king of Babylon, and that nation, saith Yahweh, for their iniquity, and the land of the Chaldeans; and I will make it desolate for ever.

13And I will bring upon that land all my words which I have pronounced against it, even all that is written in this book, which Jeremiah hath prophesied against all the nations.

14For many nations and great kings shall make bondmen of them, even of them; and I will recompense them according to their deeds, and according to the work of their hands.

15For thus saith Yahweh, the God of Israel, unto me: take this cup of the wine of wrath at my hand, and cause all the nations, to whom I send thee, to drink it.

16And they shall drink, and reel to and fro, and be mad, because of the sword that I will send among them.

Jeremiah

17Then took I the cup at Yahweh's hand, and made all the nations to drink, unto whom Yahweh had sent me:

18to wit, Jerusalem, and the cities of Judah, and the kings thereof, and the princes thereof, to make them a desolation, an astonishment, a hissing, and a curse, as it is this day;

19Pharaoh king of Egypt, and his servants, and his princes, and all his people;

20and all the mingled people, and all the kings of the land of the Uz, and all the kings of the Philistines, and Ashkelon, and Gaza, and Ekron, and the remnant of Ashdod;

21Edom, and Moab, and the children of Ammon;

22and all the kings of Tyre, and all the kings of Sidon, and the kings of the isle which is beyond the sea;

23Dedan, and Tema, and Buz, and all that have the corners of their hair cut off;

24and all the kings of Arabia, and all the kings of the mingled people that dwell in the wilderness;

25and all the kings of Zimri, and all the kings of Elam, and all the kings of the Medes;

26and all the kings of the north, far and near, one with another; and all the kingdoms of the world, which are upon the face of the earth: and the king of Sheshach shall drink after them.

27And thou shalt say unto them, Thus saith Yahweh of hosts, the God of Israel: Drink ye, and be drunken, and spew, and fall, and rise no more, because of the sword which I will send among you.

28And it shall be, if they refuse to take the cup at thy hand to drink, then shalt thou say unto them, Thus saith Yahweh of hosts: Ye shall surely drink.

29For, lo, I begin to work evil at the city which is called by my name; and should ye be utterly unpunished? Ye shall not be unpunished; for I will call for a sword upon all the inhabitants of the earth, saith Yahweh of hosts.

30Therefore prophesy thou against them all these words, and say unto them, Yahweh will roar from on high, and utter his voice from his holy habitation; he will mightily roar against his fold; he will give a shout, as they that tread the grapes, against all the inhabitants of the earth.

31A noise shall come even to the end of the earth; for Yahweh hath a controversy with the nations; he will enter into judgment with all flesh: as for the wicked, he will give them to the sword, saith Yahweh.

32Thus saith Yahweh of hosts, Behold, evil shall go forth from nation to nation, and a great tempest shall be raised up from the uttermost parts of the earth.

33And the slain of Yahweh shall be at that day from one end of the earth even to the other end of the earth: they shall not be lamented, neither gathered, nor buried; they shall be dung upon the face of the ground.

34Wail, ye shepherds, and cry; and wallow in ashes, ye principal of the flock; for the days of your slaughter and of your dispersions are fully come, and ye shall fall like a goodly vessel.

35And the shepherds shall have no way to flee, nor the principal of the flock to escape.

36A voice of the cry of the shepherds, and the wailing of the principal of the flock! for Yahweh layeth waste their pasture.

37And the peaceable folds are brought to silence because of the fierce anger of Yahweh.

38He hath left his covert, as the lion; for their land is become an astonishment because of the fierceness of the oppressing sword, and because of his fierce anger.

Chapter 26

1In the beginning of the reign of Jehoiakim the son of Josiah, king of Judah, came this word from Yahweh, saying,

2Thus saith Yahweh: Stand in the court of Yahweh's house, and speak unto all the cities of Judah, which come to worship in Yahweh's house, all the words that I command thee to speak unto them; diminish not a word.

3It may be they will hearken, and turn every man from his evil way; that I may repent me of the evil which I purpose to do unto them because of the evil of their doings.

4And thou shalt say unto them, Thus saith Yahweh: If ye will not hearken to me, to walk in my law, which I have set before you,

5to hearken to the words of my servants the prophets, whom I send unto you, even rising up early and sending them, but ye have not hearkened;

6then will I make this house like Shiloh, and will make this city a curse to all the nations of the earth.

7And the priests and the prophets and all the people heard Jeremiah speaking these words in the house of Yahweh.

8And it came to pass, when Jeremiah had made an end of speaking all that Yahweh had commanded him to speak unto all the people, that the priests and the prophets and all the people laid hold on him, saying, Thou shalt surely die.

9Why hast thou prophesied in the name of Yahweh, saying, This house shall be like Shiloh, and this city shall be desolate, without inhabitant? And all the people were gathered unto Jeremiah in the house of Yahweh.

10And when the princes of Judah heard these things, they came up from the king's house unto the house of Yahweh; and they sat in the entry of the new gate of Yahweh's house.

11Then spake the priests and the prophets unto the princes and to all the people, saying, This man is worthy of death; for he hath prophesied against this city, as ye have heard with your ears.

12Then spake Jeremiah unto all the princes and to all the people, saying, Yahweh sent me to prophesy against this house and against this city all the words that ye have heard.

13Now therefore amend your ways and your doings, and obey the voice of Yahweh your God; and Yahweh will repent him of the evil that he hath pronounced against you.

14But as for me, behold, I am in your hand: do with me as is good and right in your eyes.

15Only know ye for certain that, if ye put me to death, ye will bring innocent blood upon yourselves, and upon this city, and upon the inhabitants thereof; for of a truth Yahweh hath sent me unto you to speak all these words in your ears.

16Then said the princes and all the people unto the priests and to the prophets: This man is not worthy of death; for he hath spoken to us in the name of Yahweh our God.

17Then rose up certain of the elders of the land, and spake to all the assembly of the people, saying,

18Micah the Morashtite prophesied in the days of Hezekiah king of Judah; and he spake to all the people of Judah, saying, Thus saith Yahweh of hosts: Zion shall be plowed as a field, and Jerusalem shall become heaps, and the mountain of the house as the high places of a forest.

19Did Hezekiah king of Judah and all Judah put him to death? did he not fear Yahweh, and entreat the favor of Yahweh, and Yahweh repented him of the evil which he had pronounced against them? Thus should we commit great evil against our own souls.

20And there was also a man that prophesied in the name of Yahweh, Uriah the son of Shemaiah of Kiriath-jearim; and he prophesied against this city and against this land according to all the words of Jeremiah:

21and when Jehoiakim the king, with all his mighty-men, and all the princes, heard his words, the king sought to put him to death; but when Uriah heard it, he was afraid, and fled, and went into Egypt:

22and Jehoiakim the king sent men into Egypt, namely, Elnathan the son of Achbor, and certain men with him, into Egypt:

23and they fetched forth Uriah out of Egypt, and brought him unto Jehoiakim the king, who slew him with the sword, and cast his dead body into the graves of the common people.

24But the hand of Ahikam the son of Shaphan was with Jeremiah, that they should not give him into the hand of the people to put him to death.

Chapter 27

1In the beginning of the reign of Jehoiakim the son of Josiah, king of Judah, came this word unto Jeremiah from Yahweh, saying,

2Thus saith Yahweh to me: Make thee bonds and bars, and put them upon thy neck;

3and send them to the king of Edom, and to the king of Moab, and to the king of the children of Ammon, and to the king of Tyre, and to the king of Sidon, by the hand of the messengers that come to Jerusalem unto Zedekiah king of Judah;

4and give them a charge unto their masters, saying, Thus saith Yahweh of hosts, the God of Israel, Thus shall ye say unto your masters:

5I have made the earth, the men and the beasts that are upon the face of the earth, by my great power and by my outstretched arm; and I give it unto whom it seemeth right unto me.

6And now have I given all these lands into the hand of Nebuchadnezzar the king of Babylon, my servant; and the beasts of the field also have I given him to serve him.

7And all the nations shall serve him, and his son, and his son's son, until the time of his own land come: and then many nations and great kings shall make him their bondman.

8And it shall come to pass, that the nation and the kingdom which will not serve the same Nebuchadnezzar king of Babylon, and that will not put their neck under the yoke of the king of Babylon, that nation will I punish, saith Yahweh, with the sword, and with the famine, and with the pestilence, until I have consumed them by his hand.

9But as for you, hearken ye not to your prophets, nor to your diviners, nor to your dreams, nor to your soothsayers, nor to your sorcerers, that speak unto you, saying, Ye shall not serve the king of Babylon:

10for they prophesy a lie unto you, to remove you far from your land, and that I should drive you out, and ye should perish.

11But the nation that shall bring their neck under the yoke of the king of Babylon, and serve him, that nation will I let remain in their own land, saith Yahweh; and they shall till it, and dwell therein.

12And I spake to Zedekiah king of Judah according to all these words, saying, Bring your necks under the yoke of the king of Babylon, and serve him and his people, and live.

13Why will ye die, thou and thy people, by the sword, by the famine, and by the pestilence, as Yahweh hath spoken concerning the nation that will not serve the king of Babylon?

14And hearken not unto the words of the prophets that speak unto you, saying, Ye shall not serve the king of Babylon; for they prophesy a lie unto you.

15For I have not sent them, saith Yahweh, but they prophesy falsely in my name; that I may drive you out, and that ye may perish, ye, and the prophets that prophesy unto you.

16Also I spake to the priests and to all this people, saying, Thus saith Yahweh: Hearken not to the words of your prophets that prophesy unto you, saying, Behold, the vessels of Yahweh's house shall now shortly be brought again from Babylon; for they prophesy a lie unto you.

17Hearken not unto them; serve the king of Babylon, and live: wherefore should this city become a desolation?

18But if they be prophets, and if the word of Yahweh be with them, let them now make intercession to Yahweh of hosts, that the vessels which are left in the house of Yahweh, and in the house of the king of Judah, and at Jerusalem, go not to Babylon.

19For thus saith Yahweh of hosts concerning the pillars, and concerning the sea, and concerning the bases, and concerning the residue of the vessels that are left in this city,

20which Nebuchadnezzar king of Babylon took not, when he carried away captive Jeconiah the son of Jehoiakim, king of Judah, from Jerusalem to Babylon, and all the nobles of Judah and Jerusalem;

21yea, thus saith Yahweh of hosts, the God of Israel, concerning the vessels that are left in the house of Yahweh, and in the house of the king of Judah, and at Jerusalem:

22They shall be carried to Babylon, and there shall they be, until the day that I visit them, saith Yahweh; then will I bring them up, and restore them to this place.

Chapter 28

1And it came to pass the same year, in the beginning of the reign of Zedekiah king of Judah, in the fourth year, in the fifth month, that Hananiah the son of Azzur, the prophet, who was of Gibeon, spake unto me in the house of Yahweh, in the presence of the priests and of all the people, saying,

2Thus speaketh Yahweh of hosts, the God of Israel, saying, I have broken the yoke of the king of Babylon.

3Within two full years will I bring again into this place all the vessels of Yahweh's house, that Nebuchadnezzar king of Babylon took away from this place, and carried to Babylon.

4and I will bring again to this place Jeconiah the son of Jehoiakim, king of Judah, with all the captives of Judah, that went to Babylon, saith Yahweh; for I will break the yoke of the king of Babylon.

5Then the prophet Jeremiah said unto the prophet Hananiah in the presence of the priests, and in the presence of all the people that stood in the house of Yahweh,

6even the prophet Jeremiah said, Amen: Yahweh do so; Yahweh perform thy words which thou hast prophesied, to bring again the vessels of Yahweh's house, and all them of the captivity, from Babylon unto this place.

7Nevertheless hear thou now this word that I speak in thine ears, and in the ears of all the people:

8The prophets that have been before me and before thee of old prophesied against many countries, and against great kingdoms, of war, and of evil, and of pestilence.

9The prophet that prophesieth of peace, when the word of the prophet shall come to pass, then shall the prophet be known, that Yahweh hath truly sent him.

10Then Hananiah the prophet took the bar from off the prophet Jeremiah's neck, and brake it.

11And Hananiah spake in the presence of all the people, saying, Thus saith Yahweh: Even so will I break the yoke of Nebuchadnezzar king of Babylon within two full years from off the neck of all the nations. And the prophet Jeremiah went his way.

12Then the word of Yahweh came unto Jeremiah, after that Hananiah the prophet had broken the bar from off the neck of the prophet Jeremiah, saying,

13Go, and tell Hananiah, saying, Thus saith Yahweh: Thou hast broken the bars of wood; but thou hast made in their stead bars of iron.

14For thus saith Yahweh of hosts, the God of Israel: I have put a yoke of iron upon the neck of all these nations, that they may served Nebuchadnezzar king of Babylon; and they shall serve him: and I have given him the beasts of the field also.

15Then said the prophet Jeremiah unto Hananiah the prophet, Hear now, Hananiah: Yahweh hath not sent thee; but thou makest this people to trust in a lie.

16Therefore thus saith Yahweh, Behold, I will send thee away from off the face of the earth: this year thou shalt die, because thou hast spoken rebellion against Yahweh.

17So Hananiah the prophet died the same year in the seventh month.

Chapter 29

1Now these are the words of the letter that Jeremiah the prophet sent from Jerusalem unto the residue of the elders of the captivity, and to the priests, and to the prophets, and to all the people, whom Nebuchadnezzar had carried away captive from Jerusalem to Babylon,

2(after that Jeconiah the king, and the queen-mother, and the eunuchs, and the princes of Judah and Jerusalem, and the craftsmen, and the smiths, were departed from Jerusalem,)

3by the hand of Elasah the son of Shaphan, and Gemariah the son of Hilkiah, (whom Zedekiah king of Judah sent unto Babylon to Nebuchadnezzar king of Babylon,) saying,

4Thus saith Yahweh of hosts, the God of Israel, unto all the captivity, whom I have caused to be carried away captive from Jerusalem unto Babylon:

5Build ye houses, and dwell in them; and plant gardens, and eat the fruit of them.

6Take ye wives, and beget sons and daughters; and take wives for your sons, and give your daughters to husbands, that they may bear sons and daughters; and multiply ye there, and be not diminished.

7And seek the peace of the city whither I have caused you to be carried away captive, and pray unto Yahweh for it; for in the peace thereof shall ye have peace.

8For thus saith Yahweh of hosts, the God of Israel: Let not your prophets that are in the midst of you, and your diviners, deceive you; neither hearken ye to your dreams which ye cause to be dreamed.

9For they prophesy falsely unto you in my name: I have not sent them, saith Yahweh.

10For thus saith Yahweh, After seventy years are accomplished for Babylon, I will visit you, and perform my good word toward you, in causing you to return to this place.

11For I know the thoughts that I think toward you, saith Yahweh, thoughts of peace, and not of evil, to give you hope in your latter end.

12And ye shall call upon me, and ye shall go and pray unto me, and I will hearken unto you.

13And ye shall seek me, and find me, when ye shall search for me with all your heart.

14And I will be found of you, saith Yahweh, and I will turn again your captivity, and I will gather you from all the nations, and from all the places wither I have driven you, saith Yahweh; and I will bring you again unto the place whence I caused you to be carried away captive.

15Because ye have said, Yahweh hath raised us up prophets in Babylon;

16thus saith Yahweh concerning the king that sitteth upon the throne of David, and concerning all the people that dwell in this city, your brethren that are not gone forth with you into captivity;

17thus saith Yahweh of hosts; Behold, I will send upon them the sword, the famine, and the pestilence, and will make them like vile figs, that cannot be eaten, they are so bad.

18And I will pursue after them with the sword, with the famine, and with the pestilence, and will deliver them to be tossed to and fro among all the kingdoms of the earth, to be an execration, and an astonishment, and a hissing, and a reproach, among all the nations whither I have driven them;

19because they have not hearkened to my words, saith Yahweh, wherewith I sent unto them my servants the prophets, rising up early and sending them; but ye would not hear, saith Yahweh.

20Hear ye therefore the word of Yahweh, all ye of the captivity, whom I have sent away from Jerusalem to Babylon.

21Thus saith Yahweh of hosts, the God of Israel, concerning Ahab the son of Kolaiah, and concerning Zedekiah the son of Maaseiah, who prophesy a lie unto you in my name: Behold, I will deliver them into the hand of Nebuchadrezzar king of Babylon; and he shall slay them before your eyes;

22and of them shall be taken up a curse by all the captives of Judah that are in Babylon, saying, Yahweh make thee like Zedekiah and like Ahab, whom the king of Babylon roasted in the fire;

23because they have wrought folly in Israel, and have committed adultery with their neighbors' wives, and have spoken words in my name falsely, which I commanded them not; and I am he that knoweth, and am witness, saith Yahweh.

24And concerning Shemaiah the Nehelamite thou shalt speak, saying,

25Thus speaketh Yahweh of hosts, the God of Israel, saying, Because thou hast sent letters in thine own name unto all the people that are at Jerusalem, and to Zephaniah the son of Maaseiah, the priest, and to all the priests, saying,

26Yahweh hath made thee priest in the stead of Jehoiada the priest, that there may be officers in the house of Yahweh, for every man that is mad, and maketh himself a prophet, that thou shouldest put him in the stocks and in shackles.

27Now therefore, why hast thou not rebuked Jeremiah of Anathoth, who maketh himself a prophet to you,

28forasmuch as he hath sent unto us in Babylon, saying, The captivity is long: build ye houses, and dwell in them; and plant gardens, and eat the fruit of them?

29And Zephaniah the priest read this letter in the ears of Jeremiah the prophet.

30Then came the word of Yahweh unto Jeremiah, saying,

31Send to all them of the captivity, saying, Thus saith Yahweh concerning Shemaiah the Nehelamite: Because that Shemaiah hath prophesied unto you, and I sent him not, and he hath caused you to trust in a lie;

32therefore thus saith Yahweh, Behold, I will punish Shemaiah the Nehelamite, and his seed; he shall not have a man to dwell among this people, neither shall he behold the good that I will do unto my people, saith Yahweh, because he hath spoken rebellion against Yahweh.

Chapter 30

1The word that came to Jeremiah from Yahweh, saying,

2Thus speaketh Yahweh, the God of Israel, saying, Write thee all the words that I have spoken unto thee in a book.

3For, lo, the days come, saith Yahweh, that I will turn again the captivity of my people Israel and Judah, saith Yahweh; and I will cause them to return to the land that I gave to their fathers, and they shall possess it.

4And these are the words that Yahweh spake concerning Israel and concerning Judah.

5For thus saith Yahweh: We have heard a voice of trembling, of fear, and not of peace.

6Ask ye now, and see whether a man doth travail with child: wherefore do I see every man with his hands on his loins, as a woman in travail, and all faces are turned into paleness?

7Alas! for that day is great, so that none is like it: it is even the time of Jacob's trouble; but he shall be saved out of it.

8And it shall come to pass in that day, saith Yahweh of hosts, that I will break his yoke from off thy neck, and will burst thy bonds; and strangers shall no more make him their bondman;

9but they shall serve Yahweh their God, and David their king, whom I will raise up unto them.

10Therefore fear thou not, O Jacob my servant, saith Yahweh; neither be dismayed, O Israel: for, lo, I will save thee from afar, and thy seed from the land of their captivity; and Jacob shall return, and shall be quiet and at ease, and none shall make him afraid.

11For I am with thee, saith Yahweh, to save thee: for I will make a full end of all the nations whither I have scattered thee, but I will not make a full end of thee; but I will correct thee in measure, and will in no wise leave thee unpunished.

12For thus saith Yahweh, Thy hurt is incurable, and thy wound grievous.

Jeremiah

13There is none to plead thy cause, that thou mayest be bound up: thou hast no healing medicines.

14All thy lovers have forgotten thee; they seek thee not: for I have wounded thee with the wound of an enemy, with the chastisement of a cruel one, for the greatness of thine iniquity, because thy sins were increased.

15Why criest thou for thy hurt? thy pain is incurable: for the greatness of thine iniquity, because thy sins were increased, I have done these things unto thee.

16Therefore all they that devour thee shall be devoured; and all thine adversaries, every one of them, shall go into captivity; and they that despoil thee shall be a spoil, and all that prey upon thee will I give for a prey.

17For I will restore health unto thee, and I will heal thee of thy wounds, saith Yahweh; because they have called thee an outcast, saying, It is Zion, whom no man seeketh after.

18Thus saith Yahweh: Behold, I will turn again the captivity of Jacob's tents, and have compassion on his dwelling-places; and the city shall be builded upon its own hill, and the palace shall be inhabited after its own manner.

19And out of them shall proceed thanksgiving and the voice of them that make merry: and I will multiply them, and they shall not be few; I will also glorify them, and they shall not be small.

20Their children also shall be as aforetime, and their congregation shall be established before me; and I will punish all that oppress them.

21And their prince shall be of themselves, and their ruler shall proceed from the midst of them; and I will cause him to draw near, and he shall approach unto me: for who is he that hath had boldness to approach unto me? saith Yahweh.

22And ye shall be my people, and I will be your God.

23Behold, the tempest of Yahweh, even his wrath, is gone forth, a sweeping tempest: it shall burst upon the head of the wicked.

24The fierce anger of Yahweh shall not return, until he have executed, and till he have performed the intents of his heart: in the latter days ye shall understand it.

Chapter 31

1At that time, saith Yahweh, will I be the God of all the families of Israel, and they shall be my people.

2Thus saith Yahweh, The people that were left of the sword found favor in the wilderness; even Israel, when I went to cause him to rest.

3Yahweh appeared of old unto me, saying, Yea, I have loved thee with an everlasting love: therefore with lovingkindness have I drawn thee.

4Again will I build thee, and thou shalt be built, O virgin of Israel: again shalt thou be adorned with thy tabrets, and shalt go forth in the dances of them that make merry.

5Again shalt thou plant vineyards upon the mountains of Samaria; the planters shall plant, and shall enjoy the fruit thereof.

6For there shall be a day, that the watchmen upon the hills of Ephraim shall cry, Arise ye, and let us go up to Zion unto Yahweh our God.

7For thus saith Yahweh, Sing with gladness for Jacob, and shout for the chief of the nations: publish ye, praise ye, and say, O Yahweh, save thy people, the remnant of Israel.

8Behold, I will bring them from the north country, and gather them from the uttermost parts of the earth, and with them the blind and the lame, the woman with child and her that travaileth with child together: a great company shall they return hither.

9They shall come with weeping; and with supplications will I lead them: I will cause them to walk by rivers of waters, in a straight way wherein they shall not stumble; for I am a father to Israel, and Ephraim is my first-born.

10Hear the word of Yahweh, O ye nations, and declare it in the isles afar off; and say, He that scattered Israel will gather him, and keep him, as shepherd doth his flock.

11For Yahweh hath ransomed Jacob, and redeemed him from the hand of him that was stronger than he.

12And they shall come and sing in the height of Zion, and shall flow unto the goodness of Yahweh, to the grain, and to the new wine, and to the oil, and to the young of the flock and of the herd: and their soul shall be as a watered garden; and they shall not sorrow any more at all.

13Then shall the virgin rejoice in the dance, and the young men and the old together; for I will turn their mourning into joy, and will comfort them, and make them rejoice from their sorrow.

14And I will satiate the soul of the priests with fatness, and my people shall be satisfied with my goodness, saith Yahweh.

15Thus saith Yahweh: A voice is heard in Ramah, lamentatión, and bitter weeping, Rachel weeping for her children; she refuseth to be comforted for her children, because they are not.

16Thus saith Yahweh: Refrain thy voice from weeping, and thine eyes from tears; for thy work shall be rewarded, saith Yahweh; and they shall come again from the land of the enemy.

17And there is hope for thy latter end, saith Yahweh; and thy children shall come again to their own border.

18I have surely heard Ephraim bemoaning himself thus, Thou hast chastised me, and I was chastised, as a calf unaccustomed to the yoke: turn thou me, and I shall be turned; for thou art Yahweh my God.

19Surely after that I was turned, I repented; and after that I was instructed, I smote upon my thigh: I was ashamed, yea, even confounded, because I did bear the reproach of my youth.

20Is Ephraim my dear son? is he a darling child? for as often as I speak against him, I do earnestly remember him still: therefore my heart yearneth for him; I will surely have mercy upon him, saith Yahweh.

21Set thee up waymarks, make thee guide-posts; set thy heart toward the highway, even the way by which thou wentest: turn again, O virgin of Israel, turn again to these thy cities.

22How long wilt thou go hither and thither, O thou backsliding daughter? for Yahweh hath created a new thing in the earth: a woman shall encompass a man.

23Thus saith Yahweh of hosts, the God of Israel, Yet again shall they use this speech in the land of Judah and in the cities thereof, when I shall bring again their captivity: Yahweh bless thee, O habitation of righteousness, O mountain of holiness.

24And Judah and all the cities thereof shall dwell therein together, the husbandmen, and they that go about with flocks.

25For I have satiated the weary soul, and every sorrowful soul have I replenished.

26Upon this I awaked, and beheld; and my sleep was sweet unto me.

27Behold, the days come, saith Yahweh, that I will sow the house of Israel and the house of Judah with the seed of man, and with the seed of beast.

28And it shall come to pass that, like as I have watched over them to pluck up and to break down and to overthrow and to destroy and to afflict, so will I watch over them to build and to plant, saith Yahweh.

29In those days they shall say no more, The fathers have eaten sour grapes, and the children's teeth are set on edge.

30But every one shall die for his own iniquity: every man that eateth the sour grapes, his teeth shall be set on edge.

31Behold, the days come, saith Yahweh, that I will make a new covenant with the house of Israel, and with the house of Judah:

32not according to the covenant that I made with their fathers in the day that I took them by the hand to bring them out of the land of Egypt; which my covenant they brake, although I was a husband unto them, saith Yahweh.

33But this is the covenant that I will make with the house of Israel after those days, saith Yahweh: I will put my law in their inward parts, and in their heart will I write it; and I will be their God, and they shall be my people:

34and they shall teach no more every man his neighbor, and every man his brother, saying, Know Yahweh; for they shall all know me, from the least of them unto the greatest of them, saith Yahweh: for I will forgive their iniquity, and their sin will I remember no more.

35Thus saith Yahweh, who giveth the sun for a light by day, and the ordinances of the moon and of the stars for a light by night, who stirreth up the sea, so that the waves thereof roar; Yahweh of hosts is his name:

36If these ordinances depart from before me, saith Yahweh, then the seed of Israel also shall cease from being a nation before me for ever.

37Thus saith Yahweh: If heaven above can be measured, and the foundations of the earth searched out beneath, then will I also cast off all the seed of Israel for all that they have done, saith Yahweh.

38Behold, the days come, saith Yahweh, that the city shall be built to Yahweh from the tower of Hananel unto the gate of the corner.

39And the measuring line shall go out further straight onward unto the hill Gareb, and shall turn about unto Goah.

40And the whole valley of the dead bodies and of the ashes, and all the fields unto the brook Kidron, unto the corner of the horse gate toward the east, shall be holy unto Yahweh; it shall not be plucked up, nor thrown down any more for ever.

Chapter 32

1The word that came to Jeremiah from Yahweh in the tenth year of Zedekiah king of Judah, which was the eighteenth year of Nebuchadrezzar.

2Now at that time the king of Babylon's army was besieging Jerusalem; and Jeremiah the prophet was shut up in the court of the guard, which was in the king of Judah's house.

3For Zedekiah king of Judah had shut him up, saying, Wherefore dost thou prophesy, and say, Thus saith Yahweh, Behold, I will give this city into the hand of the king of Babylon, and he shall take it;

4and Zedekiah king of Judah shall not escape out of the hand of the Chaldeans, but shall surely be delivered into the hand of the king of Babylon, and shall speak with him mouth to mouth, and his eyes shall behold his eyes;

5and he shall bring Zedekiah to Babylon, and there shall he be until I visit him, saith Yahweh: though ye fight with the Chaldeans, ye shall not prosper?

6And Jeremiah said, The word of Yahweh came unto me, saying,

7Behold, Hanamel the son of Shallum thine uncle shall come unto thee, saying, Buy thee my field that is in Anathoth; for the right of redemption is thine to buy it.

8So Hanamel mine uncle's son came to me in the court of the guard according to the word of Yahweh, and said unto me, Buy my field, I pray thee, that is in Anathoth, which is in the land of Benjamin; for the right of inheritance is thine, and the redemption is thine; buy it for thyself. Then I knew that this was the word of Yahweh.

9And I bought the field that was in Anathoth of Hanamel mine uncle's son, and weighed him the money, even seventeen shekels of silver.

10And I subscribed the deed, and sealed it, and called witnesses, and weighed him the money in the balances.

11So I took the deed of the purchase, both that which was sealed, according to the law and custom, and that which was open:

12and I delivered the deed of the purchase unto Baruch the son of Neriah, the son of Mahseiah, in the presence of Hanamel mine uncle's son, and in the presence of the witnesses that subscribed the deed of the purchase, before all the Jews that sat in the court of the guard.

13And I charged Baruch before them, saying,

14Thus saith Yahweh of hosts, the God of Israel: Take these deeds, this deed of the purchase which is sealed, and this deed which is open, and put them in an earthen vessel; that they may continue many days.

15For thus saith Yahweh of hosts, the God of Israel: Houses and fields and vineyards shall yet again be bought in this land.

¹⁶Now after I had delivered the deed of the purchase unto Baruch the son of Neriah, I prayed unto Yahweh, saying,

¹⁷Ah Lord Yahweh! behold, thou hast made the heavens and the earth by thy great power and by thine outstretched arm; there is nothing too hard for thee,

¹⁸who showest lovingkindness unto thousands, and recompensest the iniquity of the fathers into the bosom of their children after them; the great, the mighty God, Yahweh of hosts is his name;

¹⁹great in counsel, and mighty in work; whose eyes are open upon all the ways of the sons of men, to give every one according to his ways, and according to the fruit of his doings;

²⁰who didst set signs and wonders in the land of Egypt, even unto this day, both in Israel and among other men; and madest thee a name, as at this day;

²¹and didst bring forth thy people Israel out of the land of Egypt with signs, and with wonders, and with a strong hand, and with an outstretched arm, and with great terror;

²²and gavest them this land, which thou didst swear to their fathers to give them, a land flowing with milk and honey;

²³and they came in, and possessed it, but they obeyed not thy voice, neither walked in thy law; they have done nothing of all that thou commandedst them to do: therefore thou hast caused all this evil to come upon them.

²⁴Behold, the mounds, they are come unto the city to take it; and the city is given into the hand of the Chaldeans that fight against it, because of the sword, and of the famine, and of the pestilence; and what thou hast spoken is come to pass; and, behold, thou seest it.

²⁵And thou hast said unto me, O Lord Yahweh, Buy thee the field for money, and call witnesses; whereas the city is given into the hand of the Chaldeans.

²⁶Then came the word of Yahweh unto Jeremiah, saying,

²⁷Behold, I am Yahweh, the God of all flesh: is there anything too hard for me?

²⁸Therefore thus saith Yahweh: Behold, I will give this city into the hand of the Chaldeans, and into the hand of Nebuchadrezzar king of Babylon, and he shall take it:

²⁹and the Chaldeans, that fight against this city, shall come and set this city on fire, and burn it, with the houses, upon whose roofs they have offered incense unto Baal, and poured out drink-offerings unto other gods, to provoke me to anger.

³⁰For the children of Israel and the children of Judah have done only that which was evil in my sight from their youth; for the children of Israel have only provoked me to anger with the work of their hands, saith Yahweh.

³¹For this city hath been to me a provocation of mine anger and of my wrath from the day that they built it even unto this day; that I should remove it from before my face,

³²because of all the evil of the children of Israel and of the children of Judah, which they have done to provoke me to anger, they, their kings, their princes, their priests, and their prophets, and the men of Judah, and the inhabitants of Jerusalem.

³³And they have turned unto me the back, and not the face: and though I taught them, rising up early and teaching them, yet they have not hearkened to receive instruction.

³⁴But they set their abominations in the house which is called by my name, to defile it.

³⁵And they built the high places of Baal, which are in the valley of the son of Hinnom, to cause their sons and their daughters to pass through the fire unto Molech; which I commanded them not, neither came it into my mind, that they should do this abomination, to cause Judah to sin.

³⁶And now therefore thus saith Yahweh, the God of Israel, concerning this city, whereof ye say, It is given into the hand of the king of Babylon by the sword, and by the famine, and by the pestilence:

³⁷Behold, I will gather them out of all the countries, whither I have driven them in mine anger, and in my wrath, and in great indignation; and I will bring them again unto this place, and I will cause them to dwell safely:

³⁸and they shall be my people, and I will be their God:

³⁹and I will give them one heart and one way, that they may fear me for ever, for the good of them, and of their children after them:

⁴⁰and I will make an everlasting covenant with them, that I will not turn away from following them, to do them good; and I will put my fear in their hearts, that they may not depart from me.

⁴¹Yea, I will rejoice over them to do them good, and I will plant them in this land assuredly with my whole heart and with my whole soul.

⁴²For thus saith Yahweh: Like as I have brought all this great evil upon this people, so will I bring upon them all the good that I have promised them.

⁴³And fields shall be bought in this land, whereof ye say, It is desolate, without man or beast; it is given into the hand of the Chaldeans.

⁴⁴Men shall buy fields for money, and subscribe the deeds, and seal them, and call witnesses, in the land of Benjamin, and in the places about Jerusalem, and in the cities of Judah, and in the cities of the hill-country, and in the cities of the lowland, and in the cities of the South: for I will cause their captivity to return, saith Yahweh.

Chapter 33

¹Moreover the word of Yahweh came unto Jeremiah the second time, while he was yet shut up in the court of the guard, saying,

²Thus saith Yahweh that doeth it, Yahweh that formeth it to establish it; Yahweh is his name:

³Call unto me, and I will answer thee, and will show thee great things, and difficult, which thou knowest not.

⁴For thus saith Yahweh, the God of Israel, concerning the houses of this city, and concerning the houses of the kings of Judah, which are broken down to make a defence against the mounds and against the sword;

⁵while men come to fight with the Chaldeans, and to fill them with the dead bodies of men, whom I have slain in mine anger and in my wrath, and for all whose wickedness I have hid my face from this city:

⁶Behold, I will bring it health and cure, and I will cure them; and I will reveal unto them abundance of peace and truth.

⁷And I will cause the captivity of Judah and the captivity of Israel to return, and will build them, as at the first.

⁸And I will cleanse them from all their iniquity, whereby they have sinned against me; and I will pardon all their iniquities, whereby they have sinned against me, and whereby they have transgressed against me.

⁹And this city shall be to me for a name of joy, for a praise and for a glory, before all the nations of the earth, which shall hear all the good that I do unto them, and shall fear and tremble for all the good and for all the peace that I procure unto it.

¹⁰Thus saith Yahweh: Yet again there shall be heard in this place, whereof ye say, It is waste, without man and without beast, even in the cities of Judah, and in the streets of Jerusalem, that are desolate, without man and without inhabitant and without beast,

¹¹the voice of joy and the voice of gladness, the voice of the bridegroom and the voice of the bride, the voice of them that say, Give thanks to Yahweh of hosts, for Yahweh is good, for his lovingkindness endureth for ever; and of them that bring sacrifices of thanksgiving into the house of Yahweh. For I will cause the captivity of the land to return as at the first, saith Yahweh.

¹²Thus saith Yahweh of hosts: Yet again shall there be in this place, which is waste, without man and without beast, and in all the cities thereof, a habitation of shepherds causing their flocks to lie down.

¹³In the cities of the hill-country, in the cities of the lowland, and in the cities of the South, and in the land of Benjamin, and in the places about Jerusalem, and in the cities of Judah, shall the flocks again pass under the hands of him that numbereth them, saith Yahweh.

¹⁴Behold, the days come, saith Yahweh, that I will perform that good word which I have spoken concerning the house of Israel and concerning the house of Judah.

¹⁵In those days, and at that time, will I cause a Branch of righteousness to grow up unto David; and he shall execute justice and righteousness in the land.

¹⁶In those days shall Judah be saved, and Jerusalem shall dwell safely; and this is the name whereby she shall be called: Yahweh our righteousness.

¹⁷For thus saith Yahweh: David shall never want a man to sit upon the throne of the house of Israel;

¹⁸neither shall the priests the Levites want a man before me to offer burnt-offerings, and to burn meal-offerings, and to do sacrifice continually.

¹⁹And the word of Yahweh came unto Jeremiah, saying,

²⁰Thus saith Yahweh: If ye can break my covenant of the day, and my covenant of the night, so that there shall not be day and night in their season;

²¹then may also my covenant be broken with David my servant, that he shall not have a son to reign upon his throne; and with the Levites the priests, my ministers.

²²As the host of heaven cannot be numbered, neither the sand of the sea measured; so will I multiply the seed of David my servant, and the Levites that minister unto me.

²³And the word of Yahweh came to Jeremiah, saying,

²⁴Considerest thou not what this people have spoken, saying, The two families which Yahweh did choose, he hath cast them off? thus do they despise my people, that they should be no more a nation before them.

²⁵Thus saith Yahweh: If my covenant of day and night stand not, if I have not appointed the ordinances of heaven and earth;

²⁶then will I also cast away the seed of Jacob, and of David my servant, so that I will not take of his seed to be rulers over the seed of Abraham, Isaac, and Jacob: for I will cause their captivity to return, and will have mercy on them.

Chapter 34

¹The word which came unto Jeremiah from Yahweh, when Nebuchadnezzar king of Babylon, and all his army, and all the kingdoms of the earth that were under his dominion, and all the peoples, were fighting against Jerusalem, and against all the cities thereof, saying,

²Thus saith Yahweh, the God of Israel, Go, and speak to Zedekiah king of Judah, and tell him, Thus saith Yahweh, Behold, I will give this city into the hand of the king of Babylon, and he shall burn it with fire:

³and thou shalt not escape out of his hand, but shalt surely be taken, and delivered into his hand; and thine eyes shall behold the eyes of the king of Babylon, and he shall speak with thee mouth to mouth, and thou shalt go to Babylon.

⁴Yet hear the word of Yahweh, O Zedekiah king of Judah: thus saith Yahweh concerning thee, Thou shalt not die by the sword;

⁵thou shalt die in peace; and with the burnings of thy fathers, the former kings that were before thee, so shall they make a burning for thee; and they shall lament thee, saying, Ah Lord! for I have spoken the word, saith Yahweh.

⁶Then Jeremiah the prophet spake all these words unto Zedekiah king of Judah in Jerusalem,

⁷when the king of Babylon's army was fighting against Jerusalem, and against all the cities of Judah that were left, against Lachish and against Azekah; for these alone remained of the cities of Judah as fortified cities.

⁸The word that came unto Jeremiah from Yahweh, after that the king Zedekiah had made a covenant with all the people that were at Jerusalem, to proclaim liberty unto them;

⁹that every man should let his man-servant, and every man his maid-servant, that is a Hebrew or a Hebrewess, go free; that none should make bondmen of them, to wit, of a Jew his brother.

¹⁰And all the princes and all the people obeyed, that had entered into the

Jeremiah

covenant, that every one should let his man-servant, and every one his maid-servant, go free, that none should make bondmen of them any more; they obeyed, and let them go:

11but afterwards they turned, and caused the servants and the handmaids, whom they had let go free, to return, and brought them into subjection for servants and for handmaids.

12Therefore the word of Yahweh came to Jeremiah from Yahweh, saying,

13Thus saith Yahweh, the God of Israel: I made a covenant with your fathers in the day that I brought them forth out of the land of Egypt, out of the house of bondage, saying,

14At the end of seven years ye shall let go every man his brother that is a Hebrew, that hath been sold unto thee, and hath served thee six years, thou shalt let him go free from thee: but your fathers hearkened not unto me, neither inclined their ear.

15And ye were now turned, and had done that which is right in mine eyes, in proclaiming liberty every man to his neighbor; and ye had made a covenant before me in the house which is called by my name:

16but ye turned and profaned my name, and caused every man his servant, and every man his handmaid, whom ye had let go free at their pleasure, to return; and ye brought them into subjection, to be unto you for servants and for handmaids.

17Therefore thus saith Yahweh: ye have not hearkened unto me, to proclaim liberty, every man to his brother, and every man to his neighbor: behold, I proclaim unto you a liberty, saith Yahweh, to the sword, to the pestilence, and to the famine; and I will make you to be tossed to and fro among all the kingdoms of the earth.

18And I will give the men that have transgressed my covenant, that have not performed the words of the covenant which they made before me, when they cut the calf in twain and passed between the parts thereof;

19the princes of Judah, and the princes of Jerusalem, the eunuchs, and the priests, and all the people of the land, that passed between the parts of the calf;

20I will even give them into the hand of their enemies, and into the hand of them that seek their life; and their dead bodies shall be for food unto the birds of the heavens, and to the beasts of the earth.

21And Zedekiah king of Judah and his princes will I give into the hand of their enemies, and into the hand of them that seek their life, and into the hand of the king of Babylon's army, that are gone away from you.

22Behold, I will command, saith Yahweh, and cause them to return to this city; and they shall fight against it, and take it, and burn it with fire: and I will make the cities of Judah a desolation, without inhabitant.

Chapter 35

1The word which came unto Jeremiah from Yahweh in the days of Jehoiakim the son of Josiah, king of Judah, saying,

2Go unto the house of the Rechabites, and speak unto them, and bring them into the house of Yahweh, into one of the chambers, and give them wine to drink.

3Then I took Jaazaniah the son of Jeremiah, the son of Habazziniah, and his brethren, and all his sons, and the whole house of the Rechabites;

4and I brought them into the house of Yahweh, into the chamber of the sons of Hanan the son of Igdaliah, the man of God, which was by the chamber of the princes, which was above the chamber of Maaseiah the son of Shallum, the keeper of the threshold.

5And I set before the sons of the house of the Rechabites bowls full of wine, and cups; and I said unto them, Drink ye wine.

6But they said, We will drink no wine; for Jonadab the son of Rechab, our father, commanded us, saying, Ye shall drink no wine, neither ye, nor your sons, for ever:

7neither shall ye build house, nor sow seed, nor plant vineyard, nor have any; but all your days ye shall dwell in tents; that ye may live many days in the land wherein ye sojourn.

8And we have obeyed the voice of Jonadab the son of Rechab, our father, in all that he charged us, to drink no wine all our days, we, our wives, our sons, or our daughters;

9nor to build houses for us to dwell in; neither have we vineyard, nor field, nor seed.

10but we have dwelt in tents, and have obeyed, and done according to all that Jonadab our father commanded us.

11But it came to pass, when Nebuchadrezzar king of Babylon came up into the land, that we said, Come, and let us go to Jerusalem for fear of the army of the Chaldeans, and for fear of the army of the Syrians; so we dwell at Jerusalem.

12Then came the word of Yahweh unto Jeremiah, saying,

13Thus saith Yahweh of hosts, the God of Israel: Go, and say to the men of Judah and the inhabitants of Jerusalem, Will ye not receive instruction to hearken to my words? saith Yahweh.

14The words of Jonadab the son of Rechab, that he commanded his sons, not to drink wine, are performed; and unto this day they drink none, for they obey their father's commandment: but I have spoken unto you, rising up early and speaking; and ye have not hearkened unto me.

15I have sent also unto you all my servants the prophets, rising up early and sending them, saying, Return ye now every man from his evil way, and amend your doings, and go not after other gods to serve them, and ye shall dwell in the land which I have given to you and to your fathers: but ye have not inclined your ear, nor hearkened unto me.

16Forasmuch as the sons of Jonadab the son of Rechab have performed the commandment of their father which he commanded them, but this people hath not hearkened unto me;

17therefore thus saith Yahweh, the God of hosts, the God of Israel: Behold, I will bring upon Judah and upon all the inhabitants of Jerusalem all the evil that I have pronounced against them; because I have spoken unto them, but they have not heard; and I have called unto them, but they have not answered.

18And Jeremiah said unto the house of the Rechabites, Thus saith Yahweh of hosts, the God of Israel: Because ye have obeyed the commandment of Jonadab your father, and kept all his precepts, and done according unto all that he commanded you;

19therefore thus saith Yahweh of hosts, the God of Israel: Jonadab the son of Rechab shall not want a man to stand before me for ever.

Chapter 36

1And it came to pass in the fourth year of Jehoiakim the son of Josiah, king of Judah, that this word came unto Jeremiah from Yahweh, saying,

2Take thee a roll of a book, and write therein all the words that I have spoken unto thee against Israel, and against Judah, and against all the nations, from the day I spake unto thee, from the days of Josiah, even unto this day.

3It may be that the house of Judah will hear all the evil which I purpose to do unto them; that they may return every man from his evil way; that I may forgive their iniquity and their sin.

4Then Jeremiah called Baruch the son of Neriah; and Baruch wrote from the mouth of Jeremiah all the words of Yahweh, which he had spoken unto him, upon a roll of a book.

5And Jeremiah commanded Baruch, saying, I am shut up; I cannot go into the house of Yahweh:

6therefore go thou, and read in the roll, which thou hast written from my mouth, the words of Yahweh in the ears of the people in Yahweh's house upon the fast-day; and also thou shalt read them in the ears of all Judah that come out of their cities.

7It may be they will present their supplication before Yahweh, and will return every one from his evil way; for great is the anger and the wrath that Yahweh hath pronounced against this people.

8And Baruch the son of Neriah did according to all that Jeremiah the prophet commanded him, reading in the book the words of Yahweh in Yahweh's house.

9Now it came to pass in the fifth year of Jehoiakim the son of Josiah, king of Judah, in the ninth month, that all the people in Jerusalem, and all the people that came from the cities of Judah unto Jerusalem, proclaimed a fast before Yahweh.

10Then read Baruch in the book the words of Jeremiah in the house of Yahweh, in the chamber of Gemariah the son of Shaphan, the scribe, in the upper court, at the entry of the new gate of Yahweh's house, in the ears of all the people.

11And when Micaiah the son of Gemariah, the son of Shaphan, had heard out of the book all the words of Yahweh,

12he went down into the king's house, into the scribe's chamber: and, lo, all the princes were sitting there, to wit, Elishama the scribe, and Delaiah the son of Shemaiah, and Elnathan the son of Achbor, and Gemariah the son of Shaphan, and Zedekiah the son of Hananiah, and all the princes.

13Then Micaiah declared unto them all the words that he had heard, when Baruch read the book in the ears of the people.

14Therefore all the princes sent Jehudi the son of Nethaniah, the son of Shelemiah, the son of Cushi, unto Baruch, saying, Take in thy hand the roll wherein thou hast read in the ears of the people, and come. So Baruch the son of Neriah took the roll in his hand, and came unto them.

15And they said unto him, Sit down now, and read it in our ears. So Baruch read it in their ears.

16Now it came to pass, when they had heard all the words, they turned in fear one toward another, and said unto Baruch, We will surely tell the king of all these words.

17And they asked Baruch, saying, Tell us now, How didst thou write all these words at his mouth?

18Then Baruch answered them, He pronounced all these words unto me with his mouth, and I wrote them with ink in the book.

19Then said the princes unto Baruch, Go, hide thee, thou and Jeremiah; and let no man know where ye are.

20And they went in to the king into the court; but they had laid up the roll in the chamber of Elishama the scribe; and they told all the words in the ears of the king.

21So the king sent Jehudi to fetch the roll; and he took it out of the chamber of Elishama the scribe. And Jehudi read it in the ears of the king, and in the ears of all the princes that stood beside the king.

22Now the king was sitting in the winter-house in the ninth month: and there was a fire in the brazier burning before him.

23And it came to pass, when Jehudi had read three or four leaves, that the king cut it with the penknife, and cast it into the fire that was in the brazier, until all the roll was consumed in the fire that was in the brazier.

24And they were not afraid, nor rent their garments, neither the king, nor any of his servants that heard all these words.

25Moreover Elnathan and Delaiah and Gemariah had made intercession to the king that he would not burn the roll; but he would not hear them.

26And the king commanded Jerahmeel the king's son, and Seraiah the son of Azriel, and Shelemiah the son of Abdeel, to take Baruch the scribe and Jeremiah the prophet; but Yahweh hid them.

27Then the word of Yahweh came to Jeremiah, after that the king had burned the roll, and the words which Baruch wrote at the mouth of Jeremiah, saying,

28Take thee again another roll, and write in it all the former words that were in the first roll, which Jehoiakim the king of Judah hath burned.

29And concerning Jehoiakim king of Judah thou shalt say, Thus saith Yahweh: Thou hast burned this roll, saying, Why hast thou written therein, saying, The king of Babylon shall certainly come and destroy this land, and shall cause to cease from thence man and beast?

30Therefore thus saith Yahweh concerning Jehoiakim king of Judah: He shall have none to sit upon the throne of David; and his dead body shall be cast out in the day to the heat, and in the night to the frost.

31And I will punish him and his seed and his servants for their iniquity; and I will bring upon them, and upon the inhabitants of Jerusalem, and upon the men of Judah, all the evil that I have pronounced against them, but they hearkened not.

32Then took Jeremiah another roll, and gave it to Baruch the scribe, the son of Neriah, who wrote therein from the mouth of Jeremiah all the words of the book which Jehoiakim king of Judah had burned in the fire; and there were added besides unto them many like words.

Chapter 37

1And Zedekiah the son of Josiah reigned as king, instead of Coniah the son of Jehoiakim, whom Nebuchadrezzar king of Babylon made king in the land of Judah.

2But neither he, nor his servants, nor the people of the land, did hearken unto the words of Yahweh, which he spake by the prophet Jeremiah.

3And Zedekiah the king sent Jehucal the son of Shelemiah, and Zephaniah the son of Maaseiah, the priest, to the prophet Jeremiah, saying, Pray now unto Yahweh our God for us.

4Now Jeremiah came in and went out among the people; for they had not put him into prison.

5And Pharaoh's army was come forth out of Egypt; and when the Chaldeans that were besieging Jerusalem heard tidings of them, they brake up from Jerusalem.

6Then came the word of Yahweh unto the prophet Jeremiah, saying,

7Thus saith Yahweh, the God of Israel, Thus shall ye say to the king of Judah, that sent you unto me to inquire of me: Behold, Pharaoh's army, which is come forth to help you, shall return to Egypt into their own land.

8And the Chaldeans shall come again, and fight against this city; and they shall take it, and burn it with fire.

9Thus saith Yahweh, Deceive not yourselves, saying, The Chaldeans shall surely depart from us; for they shall not depart.

10For though ye had smitten the whole army of the Chaldeans that fight against you, and there remained but wounded men among them, yea would they rise up every man in his tent, and burn this city with fire.

11And it came to pass that, when the army of the Chaldeans was broken up from Jerusalem for fear of Pharaoh's army,

12then Jeremiah went forth out of Jerusalem to go into the land of Benjamin, to receive his portion there, in the midst of the people.

13And when he was in the gate of Benjamin, a captain of the ward was there, whose name was Irijah, the son of Shelemiah, the son of Hananiah; and he laid hold on Jeremiah the prophet, saying, Thou art falling away to the Chaldeans.

14Then said Jeremiah, It is false; I am not falling away to the Chaldeans. But he hearkened not to him; so Irijah laid hold on Jeremiah, and brought him to the princes.

15And the princes were wroth with Jeremiah, and smote him, and put him in prison in the house of Jonathan the scribe; for they had made that the prison.

16When Jeremiah was come into the dungeon-house, and into the cells, and Jeremiah had remained there many days;

17Then Zedekiah the king sent, and fetched him: and the king asked him secretly in his house, and said, Is there any word from Yahweh? And Jeremiah said, There is. He said also, Thou shalt be delivered into the hand of the king of Babylon.

18Moreover Jeremiah said unto king Zedekiah, Wherein have I sinned against thee, or against thy servants, or against this people, that ye have put me in prison?

19Where now are your prophets that prophesied unto you, saying, The king of Babylon shall not come against you, nor against this land?

20And now hear, I pray thee, O my lord the king: let my supplication, I pray thee, be presented before thee, that thou cause me not to return to the house of Jonathan the scribe, lest I die there.

21Then Zedekiah the king commanded, and they committed Jeremiah into the court of the guard; and they gave him daily a loaf of bread out of the bakers' street, until all the bread in the city was spent. Thus Jeremiah remained in the court of the guard.

Chapter 38

1And Shephatiah the son of Mattan, and Gedaliah the son of Pashhur, and Jucal the son of Shelemiah, and Pashhur the son of Malchijah, heard the words that Jeremiah spake unto all the people, saying,

2Thus saith Yahweh, He that abideth in this city shall die by the sword, by the famine, and by the pestilence; but he that goeth forth to the Chaldeans shall live, and his life shall be unto him for a prey, and he shall live.

3Thus saith Yahweh, This city shall surely be given into the hand of the army of the king of Babylon, and he shall take it.

4Then the princes said unto the king, Let this man, we pray thee, be put to death; forasmuch as he weakeneth the hands of the men of war that remain in this city, and the hands of all the people, in speaking such words unto them: for this man seeketh not the welfare of this people, but the hurt.

5And Zedekiah the king said, Behold, he is in your hand; for the king is not he that can do anything against you.

6Then took they Jeremiah, and cast him into the dungeon of Malchijah the king's son, that was in the court of the guard: and they let down Jeremiah with cords. And in the dungeon there was no water, but mire; and Jeremiah sank in the mire.

7Now when Ebed-melech the Ethiopian, a eunuch, who was in the king's house, heard that they had put Jeremiah in the dungeon (the king then sitting in the gate of Benjamin,)

8Ebed-melech went forth out of the king's house, and spake to the king, saying,

9My lord the king, these men have done evil in all that they have done to Jeremiah the prophet, whom they have cast into the dungeon; and he is like to die in the place where he is, because of the famine; for there is no more bread in the city.

10Then the king commanded Ebed-melech the Ethiopian, saying, Take from hence thirty men with thee, and take up Jeremiah the prophet out of the dungeon, before he die.

11So Ebed-melech took the men with him, and went into the house of the king under the treasury, and took thence rags and worn-out garments, and let them down by cords into the dungeon to Jeremiah.

12And Ebed-melech the Ethiopian said unto Jeremiah, Put now these rags and worn-out garments under thine armholes under the cords. And Jeremiah did so.

13So they drew up Jeremiah with the cords, and took him up out of the dungeon: and Jeremiah remained in the court of the guard.

14Then Zedekiah the king sent, and took Jeremiah the prophet unto him into the third entry that is in the house of Yahweh: and the king said unto Jeremiah, I will ask thee a thing; hide nothing from me.

15Then Jeremiah said unto Zedekiah, If I declare it unto thee, wilt thou not surely put me to death? and if I give thee counsel, thou wilt not hearken unto me.

16So Zedekiah the king sware secretly unto Jeremiah, saying, As Yahweh liveth, that made us this soul, I will not put thee to death, neither will I give thee into the hand of these men that seek thy life.

17Then said Jeremiah unto Zedekiah, Thus saith Yahweh, the God of hosts, the God of Israel: If thou wilt go forth unto the king of Babylon's princes, then thy soul shall live, and this city shall not be burned with fire; and thou shalt live, and thy house.

18But if thou wilt not go forth to the king of Babylon's princes, then shall this city be given into the hand of the Chaldeans, and they shall burn it with fire, and thou shalt not escape out of their hand.

19And Zedekiah the king said unto Jeremiah, I am afraid of the Jews that are fallen away to the Chaldeans, lest they deliver me into their hand, and they mock me.

20But Jeremiah said, They shall not deliver thee. Obey, I beseech thee, the voice of Yahweh, in that which I speak unto thee: so it shall be well with thee, and thy soul shall live.

21But if thou refuse to go forth, this is the word that Yahweh hath showed me:

22behold, all the women that are left in the king of Judah's house shall be brought forth to the king of Babylon's princes, and those women shall say, Thy familiar friends have set thee on, and have prevailed over thee: now that thy feet are sunk in the mire, they are turned away back.

23And they shall bring out all thy wives and thy children to the Chaldeans; and thou shalt not escape out of their hand, but shalt be taken by the hand of the king of Babylon: and thou shalt cause this city to be burned with fire.

24Then said Zedekiah unto Jeremiah, Let no man know of these words, and thou shalt not die.

25But if the princes hear that I have talked with thee, and they come unto thee, and say unto thee, Declare unto us now what thou hast said unto the king; hide it not from us, and we will not put thee to death; also what the king said unto thee:

26then thou shalt say unto them, I presented my supplication before the king, that he would not cause me to return to Jonathan's house, to die there.

27Then came all the princes unto Jeremiah, and asked him; and he told them according to all these words that the king had commanded. So they left off speaking with him; for the matter was not perceived.

28So Jeremiah abode in the court of the guard until the day that Jerusalem was taken.

Chapter 39

1And it came to pass when Jerusalem was taken, (in the ninth year of Zedekiah king of Judah, in the tenth month, came Nebuchadrezzar king of Babylon and all his army against Jerusalem, and besieged it;

2in the eleventh year of Zedekiah, in the fourth month, the ninth day of the month, a breach was made in the city,)

3that all the princes of the king of Babylon came in, and sat in the middle gate, to wit, Nergal-sharezer, Samgar-nebo, Sarsechim, Rab-saris, Nergal-sharezer, Rab-mag, with all the rest of the princes of the king of Babylon.

4And it came to pass that, when Zedekiah the king of Judah and all the men of war saw them, then they fled, and went forth out of the city by night, by the way of the king's garden, through the gate betwixt the two walls; and he went out toward the Arabah.

5But the army of the Chaldeans pursued after them, and overtook Zedekiah in the plains of Jericho: and when they had taken him, they brought him up to Nebuchadrezzar king of Babylon to Riblah in the land of Hamath; and he gave judgment upon him.

6Then the king of Babylon slew the sons of Zedekiah in Riblah before his eyes: also the king of Babylon slew all the nobles of Judah.

7Moreover he put out Zedekiah's eyes, and bound him in fetters, to carry him to Babylon.

8And the Chaldeans burned the king's house, and the houses of the people, with fire, and brake down the walls of Jerusalem.

9Then Nebuzaradan the captain of the guard carried away captive into Babylon the residue of the people that remained in the city, the deserters also that fell away to him, and the residue of the people that remained.

10But Nebuzaradan the captain of the guard left of the poor of the people, that had nothing, in the land of Judah, and gave them vineyards and fields at the same time.

11Now Nebuchadrezzar king of Babylon gave charge concerning Jeremiah to Nebuzaradan the captain of the guard, saying,

12Take him, and look well to him, and do him no harm; but do unto him even as he shall say unto thee.

13So Nebuzaradan the captain of the guard sent, and Nebushazban, Rab-saris, and Nergal-sharezer, Rab-mag, and all the chief officers of the king of Babylon;

14they sent, and took Jeremiah out of the court of the guard, and committed him unto Gedaliah the son of Ahikam, the son of Shaphan, that he should carry him home: so he dwelt among the people.

15Now the word of Yahweh came unto Jeremiah, while he was shut up in the court of the guard, saying,

16Go, and speak to Ebed-melech the Ethiopian, saying, Thus saith Yahweh of hosts, the God of Israel: Behold, I will bring my words upon this city for evil, and not for good; and they shall be accomplished before thee in that day.

17But I will deliver thee in that day, saith Yahweh; and thou shalt not be given into the hand of the men of whom thou art afraid.

18For I will surely save thee, and thou shalt not fall by the sword, but thy life shall be for a prey unto thee; because thou hast put thy trust in me, saith Yahweh.

Chapter 40

1The word which came to Jeremiah from Yahweh, after that Nebuzaradan the captain of the guard had let him go from Ramah, when he had taken him being bound in chains among all the captives of Jerusalem and Judah, that were carried away captive unto Babylon.

2And the captain of the guard took Jeremiah, and said unto him, Yahweh thy God pronounced this evil upon this place;

3and Yahweh hath brought it, and done according as he spake: because ye have sinned against Yahweh, and have not obeyed his voice, therefore this thing is come upon you.

4And now, behold, I loose thee this day from the chains which are upon thy hand. If it seem good unto thee to come with me into Babylon, come, and I will look well unto thee; but if it seem ill unto thee to come with me into Babylon, forbear: behold, all the land is before thee; whither it seemeth good and right unto thee to go, thither go.

5Now while he was not yet gone back, Go back then, said he, to Gedaliah the son of Ahikam, the son of Shaphan, whom the king of Babylon hath made governor over the cities of Judah, and dwell with him among the people; or go wheresoever it seemeth right unto thee to go. So the captain of the guard gave him victuals and a present, and let him go.

6Then went Jeremiah unto Gedaliah the son of Ahikam to Mizpah, and dwelt with him among the people that were left in the land.

7Now when all the captains of the forces that were in the fields, even they and their men, heard that the king of Babylon had made Gedaliah the son of Ahikam governor in the land, and had committed unto him men, and women, and children, and of the poorest of the land, of them that were not carried away captive to Babylon;

8then they came to Gedaliah to Mizpah, to wit, Ishmael the son of Nethaniah, and Johanan and Jonathan the sons of Kareah, and Seraiah the son of Tanhumeth, and the sons of Ephai the Netophathite, and Jezaniah the son of the Maacathite, they and their men.

9And Gedaliah the son of Ahikam the son of Shaphan sware unto them and to their men, saying, Fear not to serve the Chaldeans: dwell in the land, and serve the king of Babylon, and it shall be well with you.

10As for me, behold, I will dwell at Mizpah, to stand before the Chaldeans that shall come unto us: but ye, gather ye wine and summer fruits and oil, and put them in your vessels, and dwell in your cities that ye have taken.

11Likewise when all the Jews that were in Moab, and among the children of Ammon, and in Edom, and that were in all the countries, heard that the king of Babylon had left a remnant of Judah, and that he had set over them Gedaliah the son of Ahikam, the son of Shaphan;

12then all the Jews returned out of all places whither they were driven, and came to the land of Judah, to Gedaliah, unto Mizpah, and gathered wine and summer fruits very much.

13Moreover Johanan the son of Kareah, and all the captains of the forces that were in the fields, came to Gedaliah to Mizpah,

14and said unto him, Dost thou know that Baalis the king of the children of Ammon hath sent Ishmael the son of Nethaniah to take thy life? But Gedaliah the son of Ahikam believed them not.

15Then Johanan the son of Kareah spake to Gedaliah in Mizpah secretly, saying, Let me go, I pray thee, and I will slay Ishmael the son of Nethaniah, and no man shall know it: wherefore should he take thy life, that all the Jews that are gathered unto thee should be scattered, and the remnant of Judah perish?

16But Gedaliah the son of Ahikam said unto Johanan the son of Kareah, Thou shalt not do this thing; for thou speakest falsely of Ishmael.

Chapter 41

1Now it came to pass in the seventh month, that Ishmael the son of Nethaniah, the son of Elishama, of the seed royal and one of the chief officers of the king, and ten men with him, came unto Gedaliah the son of Ahikam to Mizpah; and there they did eat bread together in Mizpah.

2Then arose Ishmael the son of Nethaniah, and the ten men that were with him, and smote Gedaliah the son of Ahikam the son of Shaphan with the sword, and slew him, whom the king of Babylon had made governor over the land.

3Ishmael also slew all the Jews that were with him, to wit, with Gedaliah, at Mizpah, and the Chaldeans that were found there, the men of war.

4And it came to pass the second day after he had slain Gedaliah, and no man knew it,

5that there came men from Shechem, from Shiloh, and from Samaria, even fourscore men, having their beards shaven and their clothes rent, and having cut themselves, with meal-offerings and frankincense in their hand, to bring them to the house of Yahweh.

6And Ishmael the son of Nethaniah went forth from Mizpah to meet them, weeping all along as he went: and it came to pass, as he met them, he said unto them, Come to Gedaliah the son of Ahikam.

7And it was so, when they came into the midst of the city, that Ishmael the son of Nethaniah slew them, and cast them into the midst of the pit, he, and the men that were with him.

8But ten men were found among them that said unto Ishmael, Slay us not; for we have stores hidden in the field, of wheat, and of barley, and of oil, and of honey. So he forbare, and slew them not among their brethren.

9Now the pit wherein Ishmael cast all the dead bodies of the men whom he had slain, by the side of Gedaliah (the same was that which Asa the king had made for fear of Baasha king of Israel,) Ishmael the son of Nethaniah filled it with them that were slain.

10Then Ishmael carried away captive all the residue of the people that were in Mizpah, even the king's daughters, and all the people that remained in Mizpah, whom Nebuzaradan the captain of the guard had committed to Gedaliah the son of Ahikam; Ishmael the son of Nethaniah carried them away captive, and departed to go over to the children of Ammon.

11But when Johanan the son of Kareah, and all the captains of the forces that were with him, heard of all the evil that Ishmael the son of Nethaniah had done,

12then they took all the men, and went to fight with Ishmael the son of Nethaniah, and found him by the great waters that are in Gibeon.

13Now it came to pass that, when all the people that were with Ishmael saw Johanan the son of Kareah, and all the captains of the forces that were with him, then they were glad.

14So all the people that Ishmael had carried away captive from Mizpah turned about and came back, and went unto Johanan the son of Kareah.

15But Ishmael the son of Nethaniah escaped from Johanan with eight men, and went to the children of Ammon.

16Then took Johanan the son of Kareah, and all the captains of the forces that were with him, all the remnant of the people whom he had recovered from Ishmael the son of Nethaniah, from Mizpah, after that he had slain Gedaliah the son of Ahikam, to wit, the men of war, and the women, and the children, and the eunuchs, whom he had brought back from Gibeon.

17and they departed, and dwelt in Geruth Chimham, which is by Beth-lehem, to go to enter into Egypt,

18because of the Chaldeans; for they were afraid of them, because Ishmael the son of Nethaniah had slain Gedaliah the son of Ahikam, whom the king of Babylon made governor over the land.

Chapter 42

1Then all the captains of the forces, and Johanan the son of Kareah, and Jezaniah the son of Hoshaiah, and all the people from the least even unto the greatest, came near,

2and said unto Jeremiah the prophet, Let, we pray thee, our supplication be presented before thee, and pray for us unto Yahweh thy God, even for all this remnant; for we are left but a few of many, as thine eyes do behold us:

3that Yahweh thy God may show us the way wherein we should walk, and the thing that we should do.

4Then Jeremiah the prophet said unto them, I have heard you; behold, I will pray unto Yahweh your God according to your words; and it shall come to pass that whatsoever thing Yahweh shall answer you, I will declare it unto you; I will keep nothing back from you.

5Then they said to Jeremiah, Yahweh be a true and faithful witness amongst us, if we do not according to all the word wherewith Yahweh thy God shall send thee to us.

6Whether it be good, or whether it be evil, we will obey the voice of Yahweh our God, to whom we send thee; that it may be well with us, when we obey the voice of Yahweh our God.

7And it came to pass after ten days, that the word of Yahweh came unto Jeremiah.

8Then called he Johanan the son of Kareah, and all the captains of the forces that were with him, and all the people from the least even to the greatest,

9and said unto them, Thus saith Yahweh, the God of Israel, unto whom ye sent me to present your supplication before him:

10If ye will still abide in this land, then will I build you, and not pull you down, and I will plant you, and not pluck you up; for I repent me of the evil that I have done unto you.

11Be not afraid of the king of Babylon, of whom ye are afraid; be not afraid of him, saith Yahweh: for I am with you to save you, and to deliver you from his hand.

12And I will grant you mercy, that he may have mercy upon you, and cause you to return to your own land.

13But if ye say, We will not dwell in this land; so that ye obey not the voice of Yahweh your God,

14saying, No; but we will go into the land of Egypt, where we shall see no war, nor hear the sound of the trumpet, nor have hunger of bread; and there will we dwell:

15now therefore hear ye the word of Yahweh, O remnant of Judah: Thus saith Yahweh of hosts, the God of Israel, If ye indeed set your faces to enter into Egypt, and go to sojourn there;

16then it shall come to pass, that the sword, which ye fear, shall overtake you there in the land of Egypt; and the famine, whereof ye are afraid, shall follow hard after you there in Egypt; and there ye shall die.

17So shall it be with all the men that set their faces to go into Egypt to sojourn there: they shall die by the sword, by the famine, and by the pestilence; and none of them shall remain or escape from the evil that I will bring upon them.

18For thus saith Yahweh of hosts, the God of Israel: As mine anger and my wrath hath been poured forth upon the inhabitants of Jerusalem, so shall my wrath be poured forth upon you, when ye shall enter into Egypt; and ye shall be an execration, and an astonishment, and a curse, and a reproach; and ye shall see this place no more.

19Yahweh hath spoken concerning you, O remnant of Judah, Go ye not into Egypt: know certainly that I have testified unto you this day.

20For ye have dealt deceitfully against your own souls; for ye sent me unto Yahweh your God, saying, Pray for us unto Yahweh our God; and according unto all that Yahweh our God shall say, so declare unto us, and we will do it:

21and I have this day declared it to you; but ye have not obeyed the voice of Yahweh your God in anything for which he hath sent me unto you.

22Now therefore know certainly that ye shall die by the sword, by the famine, and by the pestilence, in the place whither ye desire to go to sojourn there:

Chapter 43

1And it came to pass that, when Jeremiah had made an end of speaking unto all the people all the words of Yahweh their God, wherewith Yahweh their God had sent him to them, even all these words,

2then spake Azariah the son of Hoshaiah, and Johanan the son of Kareah, and all the proud men, saying unto Jeremiah, Thou speakest falsely: Yahweh our God hath not sent thee to say, Ye shall not go into Egypt to sojourn there;

3but Baruch the son of Neriah setteth thee on against us, to deliver us into the hand of the Chaldeans, that they may put us to death, and carry us away captive to Babylon.

4So Johanan the son of Kareah, and all the captains of the forces, and all the people, obeyed not the voice of Yahweh, to dwell in the land of Judah.

5But Johanan the son of Kareah, and all the captains of the forces, took all the remnant of Judah, that were returned from all the nations whither they had been driven, to sojourn in the land of Judah;

6the men, and the women, and the children, and the king's daughters, and every person that Nebuzaradan the captain of the guard had left with Gedaliah the son of Ahikam, the son of Shaphan; and Jeremiah the prophet, and Baruch the son of Neriah;

7and they came into the land of Egypt; for they obeyed not the voice of Yahweh: and they came unto Tahpanhes.

8Then came the word of Yahweh unto Jeremiah in Tahpanhes, saying,

9Take great stones in thy hand, and hide them in mortar in the brickwork, which is at the entry of Pharaoh's house in Tahpanhes, in the sight of the men of Judah;

10and say unto them, Thus saith Yahweh of hosts, the God of Israel: Behold, I will send and take Nebuchadrezzar the king of Babylon, my servant, and will set his throne upon these stones that I have hid; and he shall spread his royal pavilion over them.

11And he shall come, and shall smite the land of Egypt; such as are for death shall be given to death, and such as are for captivity to captivity, and such as are for the sword to the sword.

12And I will kindle a fire in the houses of the gods of Egypt; and he shall burn them, and carry them away captive: and he shall array himself with the land of Egypt, as a shepherd putteth on his garment; and he shall go forth from thence in peace.

13He shall also break the pillars of Beth-shemesh, that is in the land of Egypt; and the houses of the gods of Egypt shall he burn with fire.

Chapter 44

1The word that came to Jeremiah concerning all the Jews that dwelt in the land of Egypt, that dwelt at Migdol, and at Tahpanhes, and at Memphis, and in the country of Pathros, saying,

2Thus saith Yahweh of hosts, the God of Israel: Ye have seen all the evil that I have brought upon Jerusalem, and upon all the cities of Judah; and, behold, this day they are a desolation, and no man dwelleth therein,

3because of their wickedness which they have committed to provoke me to anger, in that they went to burn incense, and to serve other gods, that they knew not, neither they, nor ye, nor your fathers.

4Howbeit I sent unto you all my servants the prophets, rising up early and sending them, saying, Oh, do not this abominable thing that I hate.

5But they hearkened not, nor inclined their ear to turn from their wickedness, to burn no incense unto other gods.

6Wherefore my wrath and mine anger was poured forth, and was kindled in the cities of Judah and in the streets of Jerusalem; and they are wasted and desolate, as it is this day.

7Therefore now thus saith Yahweh, the God of hosts, the God of Israel: Wherefore commit ye this great evil against your own souls, to cut off from you man and woman, infant and suckling, out of the midst of Judah, to leave you none remaining;

8in that ye provoke me unto anger with the works of your hands, burning incense unto other gods in the land of Egypt, whither ye are gone to sojourn; that ye may be cut off, and that ye may be a curse and a reproach among all the nations of the earth?

9Have ye forgotten the wickedness of your fathers, and the wickedness of the kings of Judah, and the wickedness of their wives, and your own wickedness, and the wickedness of your wives which they committed in the land of Judah, and in the streets of Jerusalem?

10They are not humbled even unto this day, neither have they feared, nor walked in my law, nor in my statutes, that I set before you and before your fathers.

11Therefore thus saith Yahweh of hosts, the God of Israel: Behold, I will set my face against you for evil, even to cut off all Judah.

12And I will take the remnant of Judah, that have set their faces to go into the land of Egypt to sojourn there, and they shall all be consumed; in the land of Egypt shall they fall; they shall be consumed by the sword and by the famine; they shall die, from the least even unto the greatest, by the sword and by the famine; and they shall be an execration, and an astonishment, and a curse, and a reproach.

13For I will punish them that dwell in the land of Egypt, as I have punished Jerusalem, by the sword, by the famine, and by the pestilence;

14so that none of the remnant of Judah, that are gone into the land of Egypt to sojourn there, shall escape or be left, to return into the land of Judah, to which they have a desire to return to dwell there: for none shall return save such as shall escape.

15Then all the men who knew that their wives burned incense unto other gods, and all the women that stood by, a great assembly, even all the people that dwelt in the land of Egypt, in Pathros, answered Jeremiah, saying,

16As for the word that thou hast spoken unto us in the name of Yahweh, we will not hearken unto thee.

17But we will certainly perform every word that is gone forth out of our mouth, to burn incense unto the queen of heaven, and to pour out drink-offerings unto her, as we have done, we and our fathers, our kings and our princes, in the cities of Judah, and in the streets of Jerusalem; for then had we plenty of victuals, and were well, and saw no evil.

18But since we left off burning incense to the queen of heaven, and pouring out drink-offerings unto her, we have wanted all things, and have been consumed by the sword and by the famine.

19And when we burned incense to the queen of heaven, and poured out drink-offerings unto her, did we make her cakes to worship her, and pour out drink-offerings unto her, without our husbands?

20Then Jeremiah said unto all the people, to the men, and to the women, even to all the people that had given him that answer, saying,

21The incense that ye burned in the cities of Judah, and in the streets of Jerusalem, ye and your fathers, your kings and your princes, and the people of the land, did not Yahweh remember them, and came it not into his mind?

22so that Yahweh could not longer bear, because of the evil of your doings, and because of the abominations which ye have committed; therefore is your land become a desolation, and an astonishment, and a curse, without inhabitant, as it is this day.

23Because ye have burned incense, and because ye have sinned against Yahweh, and have not obeyed the voice of Yahweh, nor walked in his law, nor in his statutes, nor in his testimonies; therefore this evil is happened unto you, as it is this day.

24Moreover Jeremiah said unto all the people, and to all the women, Hear the word of Yahweh, all Judah that are in the land of Egypt:

25Thus saith Yahweh of hosts, the God of Israel, saying, Ye and your wives have both spoken with your mouths, and with your hands have fulfilled it, saying, We will surely perform our vows that we have vowed, to burn incense to the queen of heaven, and to pour out drink-offerings unto her: establish then your vows, and perform your vows.

26Therefore hear ye the word of Yahweh, all Judah that dwell in the land of Egypt: Behold, I have sworn by my great name, saith Yahweh, that my name shall no more be named in the mouth of any man of Judah in all the land of Egypt, saying, As the Lord Yahweh liveth.

27Behold, I watch over them for evil, and not for good; and all the men of Judah that are in the land of Egypt shall be consumed by the sword and by the famine, until there be an end of them.

28And they that escape the sword shall return out of the land of Egypt into the land of Judah, few in number; and all the remnant of Judah, that are gone into the land of Egypt to sojourn there, shall know whose word shall stand, mine, or theirs.

29And this shall be the sign unto you, saith Yahweh, that I will punish you in this place, that ye may know that my words shall surely stand against you for evil:

30Thus saith Yahweh, Behold, I will give Pharaoh Hophra king of Egypt into the hand of his enemies, and into the hand of them that seek his life; as I gave Zedekiah king of Judah into the hand of Nebuchadrezzar king of Babylon, who was his enemy, and sought his life.

Chapter 45

1The word that Jeremiah the prophet spake unto Baruch the son of Neriah, when he wrote these word in a book at the mouth of Jeremiah, in the fourth year of Jehoiakim the son of Josiah, king of Judah, saying,

2Thus saith Yahweh, the God of Israel, unto thee, O Baruch:

3Thou didst say, Woe is me now! for Yahweh hath added sorrow to my pain; I am weary with my groaning, and I find no rest.

4Thus shalt thou say unto him, Thus saith Yahweh: Behold, that which I have built will I break down, and that which I have planted I will pluck up; and this in the whole land.

5And seekest thou great things for thyself? seek them not; for, behold, I will bring evil upon all flesh, saith Yahweh; but thy life will I give unto thee for a prey in all places whither thou goest.

Jeremiah
Chapter 46
¹The word of Yahweh which came to Jeremiah the prophet concerning the nations.

²Of Egypt: concerning the army of Pharaoh-neco king of Egypt, which was by the river Euphrates in Carchemish, which Nebuchadrezzar king of Babylon smote in the fourth year of Jehoiakim the son of Josiah, king of Judah.

³Prepare ye the buckler and shield, and draw near to battle.

⁴Harness the horses, and get up, ye horsemen, and stand forth with your helmets; furbish the spears, put on the coats of mail.

⁵Wherefore have I seen it? they are dismayed and are turned backward; and their mighty ones are beaten down, and are fled apace, and look not back: terror is on every side, saith Yahweh.

⁶Let not the swift flee away, nor the mighty man escape; in the north by the river Euphrates have they stumbled and fallen.

⁷Who is this that riseth up like the Nile, whose waters toss themselves like the rivers?

⁸Egypt riseth up like the Nile, and his waters toss themselves like the rivers: and he saith, I will rise up, I will cover the earth; I will destroy cities and the inhabitants thereof.

⁹Go up, ye horses; and rage, ye chariots; and let the mighty men go forth: Cush and Put, that handle the shield; and the Ludim, that handle and bend the bow.

¹⁰For that day is a day of the Lord, Yahweh of hosts, a day of vengeance, that he may avenge him of his adversaries: and the sword shall devour and be satiate, and shall drink its fill of their blood; for the Lord, Yahweh of hosts, hath a sacrifice in the north country by the river Euphrates.

¹¹Go up into Gilead, and take balm, O virgin daughter of Egypt: in vain dost thou use many medicines; there is no healing for thee.

¹²The nations have heard of thy shame, and the earth is full of thy cry: for the mighty man hath stumbled against the mighty, they are fallen both of them together.

¹³The word that Yahweh spake to Jeremiah the prophet, how that Nebuchadrezzar king of Babylon should come and smite the land of Egypt.

¹⁴Declare ye in Egypt, and publish in Migdol, and publish in Memphis and in Tahpanhes: say ye, Stand forth, and prepare thee; for the sword hath devoured round about thee.

¹⁵Why are thy strong ones swept away? they stood not, because Yahweh did drive them.

¹⁶He made many to stumble, yea, they fell one upon another: and they said, Arise, and let us go again to our own people, and to the land of our nativity, from the oppressing sword.

¹⁷They cried there, Pharaoh king of Egypt is but a noise; he hath let the appointed time pass by.

¹⁸As I live, saith the King, whose name is Yahweh of hosts, surely like Tabor among the mountains, and like Carmel by the sea, so shall he come.

¹⁹O thou daughter that dwellest in Egypt, furnish thyself to go into captivity; for Memphis shall become a desolation, and shall be burnt up, without inhabitant.

²⁰Egypt is a very fair heifer; but destruction out of the north is come, it is come.

²¹Also her hired men in the midst of her are like calves of the stall; for they also are turned back, they are fled away together, they did not stand: for the day of their calamity is come upon them, the time of their visitation.

²²The sound thereof shall go like the serpent; for they shall march with an army, and come against her with axes, as hewers of wood.

²³They shall cut down her forest, saith Yahweh, though it cannot be searched; because they are more than the locusts, and are innumerable.

²⁴The daughter of Egypt shall be put to shame; she shall be delivered into the hand of the people of the north.

²⁵Yahweh of hosts, the God of Israel, saith: Behold, I will punish Amon of No, and Pharaoh, and Egypt, with her gods, and her kings; even Pharaoh, and them that trust in him:

²⁶and I will deliver them into the hand of those that seek their lives, and into the hand of Nebuchadrezzar king of Babylon, and into the hand of his servants; and afterwards it shall be inhabited, as in the days of old, saith Yahweh.

²⁷But fear not thou, O Jacob my servant, neither be dismayed, O Israel: for, lo, I will save thee from afar, and thy seed from the land of their captivity; and Jacob shall return, and shall be quiet and at ease, and none shall make him afraid.

²⁸Fear not thou, O Jacob my servant, saith Yahweh; for I am with thee: for I will make a full end of all the nations whither I have driven thee; but I will not make a full end of thee, but I will correct thee in measure, and will in no wise leave thee unpunished.

Chapter 47
¹The word of Yahweh that came to Jeremiah the prophet concerning the Philistines, before that Pharaoh smote Gaza.

²Thus saith Yahweh: Behold, waters rise up out of the north, and shall become an overflowing stream, and shall overflow the land and all that is therein, the city and them that dwell therein; and the men shall cry, and all the inhabitants of the land shall wail.

³At the noise of the stamping of the hoofs of his strong ones, at the rushing of his chariots, at the rumbling of his wheels, the fathers look not back to their children for feebleness of hands;

⁴because of the day that cometh to destroy all the Philistines, to cut off from Tyre and Sidon every helper that remaineth: for Yahweh will destroy the Philistines, the remnant of the isle of Caphtor.

⁵Baldness is come upon Gaza; Ashkelon is brought to nought, the remnant of their valley: how long wilt thou cut thyself?

⁶O thou sword of Yahweh, how long will it be ere thou be quiet? put up thyself into thy scabbard; rest, and be still.

⁷How canst thou be quiet, seeing Yahweh hath given thee a charge? Against Ashkelon, and against the sea-shore, there hath he appointed it.

Chapter 48
¹Of Moab. Thus saith Yahweh of hosts, the God of Israel: Woe unto Nebo! for it is laid waste; Kiriathaim is put to shame, it is taken; Misgab is put to shame and broken down.

²The praise of Moab is no more; in Heshbon they have devised evil against her: Come, and let us cut her off from being a nation. Thou also, O Madmen, shalt be brought to silence: the sword shall pursue thee.

³The sound of a cry from Horonaim, desolation and great destruction!

⁴Moab is destroyed; her little ones have caused a cry to be heard.

⁵For by the ascent of Luhith with continual weeping shall they go up; for at the descent of Horonaim they have heard the distress of the cry of destruction.

⁶Flee, save your lives, and be like the heath in the wilderness.

⁷For, because thou hast trusted in thy works and in thy treasures, thou also shalt be taken: and Chemosh shall go forth into captivity, his priests and his princes together.

⁸And the destroyer shall come upon every city, and no city shall escape; the valley also shall perish, and the plain shall be destroyed; as Yahweh hath spoken.

⁹Give wings unto Moab, that she may fly and get her away: and her cities shall become a desolation, without any to dwell therein.

¹⁰Cursed be he that doeth the work of Yahweh negligently; and cursed be he that keepeth back his sword from blood.

¹¹Moab hath been at ease from his youth, and he hath settled on his lees, and hath not been emptied from vessel to vessel, neither hath he gone into captivity: therefore his taste remaineth in him, and his scent is not changed.

¹²Therefore, behold, the days come, saith Yahweh, that I will send unto him them that pour off, and they shall pour him off; and they shall empty his vessels, and break their bottles in pieces.

¹³And Moab shall be ashamed of Chemosh, as the house of Israel was ashamed of Beth-el their confidence.

¹⁴How say ye, We are mighty men, and valiant men for the war?

¹⁵Moab is laid waste, and they are gone up into his cities, and his chosen young men are gone down to the slaughter, saith the King, whose name is Yahweh of hosts.

¹⁶The calamity of Moab is near to come, and his affliction hasteth fast.

¹⁷All ye that are round about him, bemoan him, and all ye that know his name; say, How is the strong staff broken, the beautiful rod!

¹⁸O thou daughter that dwellest in Dibon, come down from thy glory, and sit in thirst; for the destroyer of Moab is come up against thee, he hath destroyed thy strongholds.

¹⁹O inhabitant of Aroer, stand by the way, and watch: ask him that fleeth, and her that escapeth; say, What hath been done?

²⁰Moab is put to shame; for it is broken down: wail and cry; tell ye it by the Arnon, that Moab is laid waste.

²¹And judgment is come upon the plain country, upon Holon, and upon Jahzah, and upon Mephaath,

²²and upon Dibon, and upon Nebo, and upon Beth-diblathaim,

²³and upon Kiriathaim, and upon Beth-gamul, and upon Beth-meon,

²⁴and upon Kerioth, and upon Bozrah, and upon all the cities of the land of Moab, far or near.

²⁵The horn of Moab is cut off, and his arm is broken, saith Yahweh.

²⁶Make ye him drunken; for he magnified himself against Yahweh: and Moab shall wallow in his vomit, and he also shall be in derision.

²⁷For was not Israel a derision unto thee? was he found among thieves? for as often as thou speakest of him, thou waggest the head.

²⁸O ye inhabitants of Moab, leave the cities, and dwell in the rock; and be like the dove that maketh her nest over the mouth of the abyss.

²⁹We have heard of the pride of Moab, that he is very proud; his loftiness, and his pride, and his arrogancy, and the haughtiness of his heart.

³⁰I know his wrath, saith Yahweh, that it is nought; his boastings have wrought nothing.

³¹Therefore will I wail for Moab; yea, I will cry out for all Moab: for the men of Kir-heres shall they mourn.

³²With more than the weeping of Jazer will I weep for thee, O vine of Sibmah: thy branches passed over the sea, they reached even to the sea of Jazer: upon thy summer fruits and upon thy vintage the destroyer is fallen.

³³And gladness and joy is taken away from the fruitful field and from the land of Moab; and I have caused wine to cease from the winepresses: none shall tread with shouting; the shouting shall be no shouting.

³⁴From the cry of Heshbon even unto Elealeh, even unto Jahaz have they uttered their voice, from Zoar even unto Horonaim, to Eglath-shelishiyah: for the waters of Nimrim also shall become desolate.

³⁵Moreover I will cause to cease in Moab, saith Yahweh, him that offereth in the high place, and him that burneth incense to his gods.

³⁶Therefore my heart soundeth for Moab like pipes, and my heart soundeth like pipes for the men of Kir-heres: therefore the abundance that he hath gotten is perished.

³⁷For every head is bald, and every beard clipped: upon all the hands are cuttings, and upon the loins sackcloth.

³⁸On all the housetops of Moab and in the streets thereof there is lamentation every where; for I have broken Moab like a vessel wherein none delighteth, saith Yahweh.

³⁹How is it broken down! how do they wail! how hath Moab turned the back with shame! so shall Moab become a derision and a terror to all that are round about him.

40For thus saith Yahweh: Behold, he shall fly as an eagle, and shall spread out his wings against Moab.

41Kerioth is taken, and the strongholds are seized, and the heart of the mighty men of Moab at that day shall be as the heart of a woman in her pangs.

42And Moab shall be destroyed from being a people, because he hath magnified himself against Yahweh.

43Fear, and the pit, and the snare, are upon thee, O inhabitant of Moab, saith Yahweh.

44He that fleeth from the fear shall fall into the pit; and he that getteth up out of the pit shall be taken in the snare: for I will bring upon him, even upon Moab, the year of their visitation, saith Yahweh.

45They that fled stand without strength under the shadow of Heshbon; for a fire is gone forth out of Heshbon, and a flame from the midst of Sihon, and hath devoured the corner of Moab, and the crown of the head of the tumultuous ones.

46Woe unto thee, O Moab! the people of Chemosh is undone; for thy sons are taken away captive, and thy daughters into captivity.

47Yet will I bring back the captivity of Moab in the latter days, saith Yahweh. Thus far is the judgment of Moab.

Chapter 49

1Of the children of Ammon. Thus saith Yahweh: Hath Israel no sons? hath he no heir? why then doth Malcam possess Gad, and his people well in the cities thereof?

2Therefore, behold, the days come, saith Yahweh, that I will cause an alarm of war to be heard against Rabbah of the children of Ammon; and it shall become a desolate heap, and her daughters shall be burned with fire: then shall Israel possess them that did possess him, saith Yahweh.

3Wail, O Heshbon, for Ai is laid waste; cry, ye daughters of Rabbah, gird you with sackcloth: lament, and run to and fro among the fences; for Malcam shall go into captivity, his priests and his princes together.

4Wherefore gloriest thou in the valleys, thy flowing valley, O backsliding daughter? that trusted in her treasures, saying, Who shall come unto me?

5Behold, I will bring a fear upon thee, saith the Lord, Yahweh of hosts, from all that are round about thee; and ye shall be driven out every man right forth, and there shall be none to gather together the fugitives.

6But afterward I will bring back the captivity of the children of Ammon, saith Yahweh.

7Of Edom. Thus saith Yahweh of hosts: Is wisdom no more in Teman? is counsel perished from the prudent? is their wisdom vanished?

8Flee ye, turn back, dwell in the depths, O inhabitants of Dedan; for I will bring the calamity of Esau upon him, the time that I shall visit him.

9If grape-gatherers came to thee, would they not leave some gleaning grapes? if thieves by night, would they not destroy till they had enough?

10But I have made Esau bare, I have uncovered his secret places, and he shall not be able to hide himself: his seed is destroyed, and his brethren, and his neighbors; and he is not.

11Leave thy fatherless children, I will preserve them alive; and let thy widows trust in me.

12For thus saith Yahweh: Behold, they to whom it pertained not to drink of the cup shall assuredly drink; and art thou he that shall altogether go unpunished? thou shalt not go unpunished, but thou shalt surely drink.

13For I have sworn by myself, saith Yahweh, that Bozrah shall become an astonishment, a reproach, a waste, and a curse; and all the cities thereof shall be perpetual wastes.

14I have heard tidings from Yahweh, and an ambassador is sent among the nations, saying, Gather yourselves together, and come against her, and rise up to the battle.

15For, behold, I have made thee small among the nations, and despised among men.

16As for thy terribleness, the pride of thy heart hath deceived thee, O thou that dwellest in the clefts of the rock, that holdest the height of the hill: though thou shouldest make thy nest as high as the eagle, I will bring thee down from thence, saith Yahweh.

17And Edom shall become an astonishment: every one that passeth by it shall be astonished, and shall hiss at all the plagues thereof.

18As in the overthrow of Sodom and Gomorrah and the neighbor cities thereof, saith Yahweh, no man shall dwell there, neither shall any son of man sojourn therein.

19Behold, he shall come up like a lion from the pride of the Jordan against the strong habitation: for I will suddenly make them run away from it; and whoso is chosen, him will I appoint over it: for who is like me? and who will appoint me a time? and who is the shepherd that will stand before me?

20Therefore hear ye the counsel of Yahweh, that he hath taken against Edom; and his purposes, that he hath purposed against the inhabitants of Teman: Surely they shall drag them away, even the little ones of the flock; surely he shall make their habitation desolate over them.

21The earth trembleth at the noise of their fall; there is a cry, the noise whereof is heard in the Red Sea.

22Behold, he shall come up and fly as the eagle, and spread out his wings against Bozrah: and the heart of the mighty men of Edom at that day shall be as the heart of a woman in her pangs.

23Of Damascus. Hamath is confounded, and Arpad; for they have heard evil tidings, they are melted away: there is sorrow on the sea; it cannot be quiet.

24Damascus is waxed feeble, she turneth herself to flee, and trembling hath seized on her: anguish and sorrows have taken hold of her, as of a woman in travail.

25How is the city of praise not forsaken, the city of my joy?

26Therefore her young men shall fall in her streets, and all the men of war shall be brought to silence in that day, saith Yahweh of hosts.

27And I will kindle a fire in the wall of Damascus, and it shall devour the palaces of Ben-hadad.

28Of Kedar, and of the kingdoms of Hazor, which Nebuchadrezzar king of Babylon smote. Thus saith Yahweh: Arise ye, go up to Kedar, and destroy the children of the east.

29Their tents and their flocks shall they take; they shall carry away for themselves their curtains, and all their vessels, and their camels; and they shall cry unto them, Terror on every side!

30Flee ye, wander far off, dwell in the depths, O ye inhabitants of Hazor, saith Yahweh; for Nebuchadrezzar king of Babylon hath taken counsel against you, and hath conceived a purpose against you.

31Arise, get you up unto a nation that is at ease, that dwelleth without care, saith Yahweh; that have neither gates nor bars, that dwell alone.

32And their camels shall be a booty, and the multitude of their cattle a spoil: and I will scatter unto all winds them that have the corners of their hair cut off; and I will bring their calamity from every side of them, saith Yahweh.

33And Hazor shall be a dwelling-place of jackals, a desolation for ever: no man shall dwell there, neither shall any son of man sojourn therein.

34The word of Yahweh that came to Jeremiah the prophet concerning Elam, in the beginning of the reign of Zedekiah king of Judah, saying,

35Thus saith Yahweh of hosts: Behold, I will break the bow of Elam, the chief of their might.

36And upon Elam will I bring the four winds from the four quarters of heaven, and will scatter them toward all those winds; and there shall be no nation whither the outcasts of Elam shall not come.

37And I will cause Elam to be dismayed before their enemies, and before them that seek their life; and I will bring evil upon them, even my fierce anger, saith Yahweh; and I will send the sword after them, till I have consumed them;

38and I will set my throne in Elam, and will destroy from thence king and princes, saith Yahweh.

39But it shall come to pass in the latter days, that I will bring back the captivity of Elam, saith Yahweh.

Chapter 50

1The word that Yahweh spake concerning Babylon, concerning the land of the Chaldeans, by Jeremiah the prophet.

2Declare ye among the nations and publish, and set up a standard; publish, and conceal not: say, Babylon is taken, Bel is put to shame, Merodach is dismayed; her images are put to shame, her idols are dismayed.

3For out of the north there cometh up a nation against her, which shall make her land desolate, and none shall dwell therein: they are fled, they are gone, both man and beast.

4In those days, and in that time, saith Yahweh, the children of Israel shall come, they and the children of Judah together; they shall go on their way weeping, and shall seek Yahweh their God.

5They shall inquire concerning Zion with their faces thitherward, saying, Come ye, and join yourselves to Yahweh in an everlasting covenant that shall not be forgotten.

6My people have been lost sheep: their shepherds have caused them to go astray; they have turned them away on the mountains; they have gone from mountain to hill; they have forgotten their resting-place.

7All that found them have devoured them; and their adversaries said, We are not guilty, because they have sinned against Yahweh, the habitation of righteousness, even Yahweh, the hope of their fathers.

8Flee out of the midst of Babylon, and go forth out of the land of the Chaldeans, and be as the he-goats before the flocks.

9For, lo, I will stir up and cause to come up against Babylon a company of great nations from the north country; and they shall set themselves in array against her; from thence she shall be taken: their arrows shall be as of an expert mighty man; none shall return in vain.

10And Chaldea shall be a prey: all that prey upon her shall be satisfied, saith Yahweh.

11Because ye are glad, because ye rejoice, O ye that plunder my heritage, because ye are wanton as a heifer that treadeth out the grain, and neigh as strong horses;

12your mother shall be utterly put to shame; she that bare you shall be confounded: behold, she shall be the hindermost of the nations, a wilderness, a dry land, and a desert.

13Because of the wrath of Yahweh she shall not be inhabited, but she shall be wholly desolate: every one that goeth by Babylon shall be astonished, and hiss at all her plagues.

14Set yourselves in array against Babylon round about, all ye that bend the bow; shoot at her, spare no arrows: for she hath sinned against Yahweh.

15Shout against her round about: she hath submitted herself; her bulwarks are fallen, her walls are thrown down; for it is the vengeance of Yahweh: take vengeance upon her; as she hath done, do unto her.

16Cut off the sower from Babylon, and him that handleth the sickle in the time of harvest: for fear of the oppressing sword they shall turn every one to his people, and they shall flee every one to his own land.

17Israel is a hunted sheep; the lions have driven him away: first, the king of Assyria devoured him; and now at last Nebuchadrezzar king of Babylon hath broken his bones.

18Therefore thus saith Yahweh of hosts, the God of Israel: Behold, I will punish the king of Babylon and his land, as I have punished the king of Assyria.

19And I will bring Israel again to his pasture, and he shall feed on Carmel and Bashan, and his soul shall be satisfied upon the hills of Ephraim and in Gilead.

20In those days, and in that time, saith Yahweh, the iniquity of Israel shall be sought for, and there shall be none; and the sins of Judah, and they shall not be found: for I will pardon them whom I leave as a remnant.

Jeremiah

21Go up against the land of Merathaim, even against it, and against the inhabitants of Pekod: slay and utterly destroy after them, saith Yahweh, and do according to all that I have commanded thee.

22A sound of battle is in the land, and of great destruction.

23How is the hammer of the whole earth cut asunder and broken! how is Babylon become a desolation among the nations!

24I have laid a snare for thee, and thou art also taken, O Babylon, and thou wast not aware: thou art found, and also caught, because thou hast striven against Yahweh.

25Yahweh hath opened his armory, and hath brought forth the weapons of his indignation; for the Lord, Yahweh of hosts, hath a work to do in the land of the Chaldeans.

26Come against her from the utmost border; open her store-houses; cast her up as heaps, and destroy her utterly; let nothing of her be left.

27Slay all her bullocks; let them go down to the slaughter: woe unto them! for their day is come, the time of their visitation.

28The voice of them that flee and escape out of the land of Babylon, to declare in Zion the vengeance of Yahweh our God, the vengeance of his temple.

29Call together the archers against Babylon, all them that bend the bow; encamp against her round about; let none thereof escape: recompense her according to her work; according to all that she hath done, do unto her; for she hath been proud against Yahweh, against the Holy One of Israel.

30Therefore shall her young men fall in her streets, and all her men of war shall be brought to silence in that day, saith Yahweh.

31Behold, I am against thee, O thou proud one, saith the Lord, Yahweh of hosts; for thy day is come, the time that I will visit thee.

32And the proud one shall stumble and fall, and none shall raise him up; and I will kindle a fire in his cities, and it shall devour all that are round about him.

33Thus saith Yahweh of hosts: The children of Israel and the children of Judah are oppressed together; and all that took them captive hold them fast; they refuse to let them go.

34Their Redeemer is strong; Yahweh of hosts is his name: he will thoroughly plead their cause, that he may give rest to the earth, and disquiet the inhabitants of Babylon.

35A sword is upon the Chaldeans, saith Yahweh, and upon the inhabitants of Babylon, and upon her princes, and upon her wise men.

36A sword is upon the boasters, and they shall become fools; a sword is upon her mighty men, and they shall be dismayed.

37A sword is upon their horses, and upon their chariots, and upon all the mingled people that are in the midst of her; and they shall become as women: a sword is upon her treasures, and they shall be robbed.

38A drought is upon her waters, and they shall be dried up; for it is a land of graven images, and they are mad over idols.

39Therefore the wild beasts of the desert with the wolves shall dwell there, and the ostriches shall dwell therein: and it shall be no more inhabited for ever; neither shall it be dwelt in from generation to generation.

40As when God overthrew Sodom and Gomorrah and the neighbor cities thereof, saith Yahweh, so shall no man dwell there, neither shall any son of man sojourn therein.

41Behold, a people cometh from the north; and a great nation and many kings shall be stirred up from the uttermost parts of the earth.

42They lay hold on bow and spear; they are cruel, and have no mercy; their voice roareth like the sea; and they ride upon horses, every one set in array, as a man to the battle, against thee, O daughter of Babylon.

43The king of Babylon hath heard the tidings of them, and his hands wax feeble: anguish hath taken hold of him, and pangs as of a woman in travail.

44Behold, the enemy shall come up like a lion from the pride of the Jordan against the strong habitation: for I will suddenly make them run away from it; and whoso is chosen, him will I appoint over it: for who is like me? and who will appoint me a time? and who is the shepherd that can stand before me?

45Therefore hear ye the counsel of Yahweh, that he hath taken against Babylon; and his purposes, that he hath purposed against the land of the Chaldeans: Surely they shall drag them away, even the little ones of the flock; surely he shall make their habitation desolate over them.

46At the noise of the taking of Babylon the earth trembleth, and the cry is heard among the nations.

Chapter 51

1Thus saith Yahweh: Behold, I will raise up against Babylon, and against them that dwell in Leb-kamai, a destroying wind.

2And I will send unto Babylon strangers, that shall winnow her; and they shall empty her land: for in the day of trouble they shall be against her round about.

3Against him that bendeth let the archer bend his bow, and against him that lifteth himself up in his coat of mail: and spare ye not her young men; destroy ye utterly all her host.

4And they shall fall down slain in the land of the Chaldeans, and thrust through in her streets.

5For Israel is not forsaken, nor Judah, of his God, of Yahweh of hosts; though their land is full of guilt against the Holy One of Israel.

6Flee out of the midst of Babylon, and save every man his life; be not cut off in her iniquity: for it is the time of Yahweh's vengeance; he will render unto her a recompense.

7Babylon hath been a golden cup in Yahweh's hand, that made all the earth drunken: the nations have drunk of her wine; therefore the nations are mad.

8Babylon is suddenly fallen and destroyed: wail for her; take balm for her pain, if so be she may be healed.

9We would have healed Babylon, but she is not healed: forsake her, and let us go every one into his own country; for her judgment reacheth unto heaven, and is lifted up even to the skies.

10Yahweh hath brought forth our righteousness: come, and let us declare in Zion the work of Yahweh our God.

11Make sharp the arrows; hold firm the shields: Yahweh hath stirred up the spirit of the kings of the Medes; because his purpose is against Babylon, to destroy it: for it is the vengeance of Yahweh, the vengeance of his temple.

12Set up a standard against the walls of Babylon, make the watch strong, set the watchmen, prepare the ambushes; for Yahweh hath both purposed and done that which he spake concerning the inhabitants of Babylon.

13O thou that dwellest upon many waters, abundant in treasures, thine end is come, the measure of thy covetousness.

14Yahweh of hosts hath sworn by himself, saying, Surely I will fill thee with men, as with the canker-worm; and they shall lift up a shout against thee.

15He hath made the earth by his power, he hath established the world by his wisdom, and by his understanding hath he stretched out the heavens:

16when he uttereth his voice, there is a tumult of waters in the heavens, and he causeth the vapors to ascend from the ends of the earth; he maketh lightnings for the rain, and bringeth forth the wind out of his treasuries.

17Every man is become brutish and is without knowledge; every goldsmith is put to shame by his image; for his molten image is falsehood, and there is no breath in them.

18They are vanity, a work of delusion: in the time of their visitation they shall perish.

19The portion of Jacob is not like these; for he is the former of all things; and Israel is the tribe of his inheritance: Yahweh of hosts is his name.

20Thou art my battle-axe and weapons of war: and with thee will I break in pieces the nations; and with thee will I destroy kingdoms;

21and with thee will I break in pieces the horse and his rider;

22and with thee will I break in pieces the chariot and him that rideth therein; and with thee will I break in pieces man and woman; and with thee will I break in pieces the old man and the youth; and with thee will I break in pieces the young man and the virgin;

23and with thee will I break in pieces the shepherd and his flock; and with thee will I break in pieces the husbandman and his yoke of oxen; and with thee will I break in pieces governors and deputies.

24And I will render unto Babylon and to all the inhabitants of Chaldea all their evil that they have done in Zion in your sight, saith Yahweh.

25Behold, I am against thee, O destroying mountain, saith Yahweh, which destroyest all the earth; and I will stretch out my hand upon thee, and roll thee down from the rocks, and will make thee a burnt mountain.

26And they shall not take of thee a stone for a corner, nor a stone for foundations; but thou shalt be desolate for ever, saith Yahweh.

27Set ye up a standard in the land, blow the trumpet among the nations, prepare the nations against her, call together against her the kingdoms of Ararat, Minni, and Ashkenaz: appoint a marshal against her; cause the horses to come up as the rough canker-worm.

28Prepare against her the nations, the kings of the Medes, the governors thereof, and all the deputies thereof, and all the land of their dominion.

29And the land trembleth and is in pain; for the purposes of Yahweh against Babylon do stand, to make the land of Babylon a desolation, without inhabitant.

30The mighty men of Babylon have forborne to fight, they remain in their strongholds; their might hath failed; they are become as women: her dwelling-places are set on fire; her bars are broken.

31One post shall run to meet another, and one messenger to meet another, to show the king of Babylon that his city is taken on every quarter:

32and the passages are seized, and the reeds they have burned with fire, and the men of war are affrighted.

33For thus saith Yahweh of hosts, the God of Israel: The daughter of Babylon is like a threshing-floor at the time when it is trodden; yet a little while, and the time of harvest shall come for her.

34Nebuchadrezzar the king of Babylon hath devoured me, he hath crushed me, he hath made me an empty vessel, he hath, like a monster, swallowed me up, he hath filled his maw with my delicacies; he hath cast me out.

35The violence done to me and to my flesh be upon Babylon, shall the inhabitant of Zion say; and, My blood be upon the inhabitants of Chaldea, shall Jerusalem say.

36Therefore thus saith Yahweh: Behold, I will plead thy cause, and take vengeance for thee; and I will dry up her sea, and make her fountain dry.

37And Babylon shall become heaps, a dwelling-place for jackals, an astonishment, and a hissing, without inhabitant.

38They shall roar together like young lions; they shall growl as lions' whelps.

39When they are heated, I will make their feast, and I will make them drunken, that they may rejoice, and sleep a perpetual sleep, and not wake, saith Yahweh.

40I will bring them down like lambs to the slaughter, like rams with he-goats.

41How is Sheshach taken! and the praise of the whole earth seized! how is Babylon become a desolation among the nations!

42The sea is come up upon Babylon; she is covered with the multitude of the waves thereof.

43Her cities are become a desolation, a dry land, and a desert, a land wherein no man dwelleth, neither doth any son of man pass thereby.

44And I will execute judgment upon Bel in Babylon, and I will bring forth out of his mouth that which he hath swallowed up; and the nations shall not flow any more unto him: yea, the wall of Babylon shall fall.

45My people, go ye out of the midst of her, and save yourselves every man from the fierce anger of Yahweh.

46And let not your heart faint, neither fear ye for the tidings that shall be heard in the land; for tidings shall come one year, and after that in another year shall come tidings, and violence in the land, ruler against ruler.

47Therefore, behold, the days come, that I will execute judgment upon the graven images of Babylon; and her whole land shall be confounded; and all her slain shall fall in the midst of her.

48Then the heavens and the earth, and all that is therein, shall sing for joy over Babylon; for the destroyers shall come unto her from the north, saith Yahweh.

49As Babylon hath caused the slain of Israel to fall, so at Babylon shall fall the slain of all the land.

50Ye that have escaped the sword, go ye, stand not still; remember Yahweh from afar, and let Jerusalem come into your mind.

51We are confounded, because we have heard reproach; confusion hath covered our faces: for strangers are come into the sanctuaries of Yahweh's house.

52Wherefore, behold, the days come, saith Yahweh, that I will execute judgment upon her graven images; and through all her land the wounded shall groan.

53Though Babylon should mount up to heaven, and though she should fortify the height of her strength, yet from me shall destroyers come unto her, saith Yahweh.

54The sound of a cry from Babylon, and of great destruction from the land of the Chaldeans!

55For Yahweh layeth Babylon waste, and destroyeth out of her the great voice; and their waves roar like many waters; the noise of their voice is uttered:

56for the destroyer is come upon her, even upon Babylon, and her mighty men are taken, their bows are broken in pieces; for Yahweh is a God of recompenses, he will surely requite.

57And I will make drunk her princes and her wise men, her governors and her deputies, and her mighty men; and they shall sleep a perpetual sleep, and not wake, saith the King, whose name is Yahweh of hosts.

58Thus saith Yahweh of hosts: The broad walls of Babylon shall be utterly overthrown, and her high gates shall be burned with fire; and the peoples shall labor for vanity, and the nations for the fire; and they shall be weary.

59The word which Jeremiah the prophet commanded Seraiah the son of Neriah, the son of Mahseiah, when he went with Zedekiah the king of Judah to Babylon in the fourth year of his reign. Now Seraiah was chief chamberlain.

60And Jeremiah wrote in a book all the evil that should come upon Babylon, even all these words that are written concerning Babylon.

61And Jeremiah said to Seraiah, When thou comest to Babylon, then see that thou read all these words,

62and say, O Yahweh, thou hast spoken concerning this place, to cut it off, that none shall dwell therein, neither man nor beast, but that it shall be desolate for ever.

63And it shall be, when thou hast made an end of reading this book, that thou shalt bind a stone to it, and cast it into the midst of the Euphrates:

64and thou shalt say, Thus shall Babylon sink, and shall not rise again because of the evil that I will bring upon her; and they shall be weary. Thus far are the words of Jeremiah.

Chapter 52

1Zedekiah was one and twenty years old when he began to reign; and he reigned eleven years in Jerusalem: and his mother's name was Hamutal the daughter of Jeremiah of Libnah.

2And he did that which was evil in the sight of Yahweh, according to all that Jehoiakim had done.

3For through the anger of Yahweh did it come to pass in Jerusalem and Judah, until he had cast them out from his presence. And Zedekiah rebelled against the king of Babylon.

4And it came to pass in the ninth year of his reign, in the tenth month, in the tenth day of the month, that Nebuchadrezzar king of Babylon came, he and all his army, against Jerusalem, and encamped against it; and they built forts against it round about.

5So the city was besieged unto the eleventh year of king Zedekiah.

6In the fourth month, in the ninth day of the month, the famine was sore in the city, so that there was no bread for the people of the land.

7Then a breach was made in the city, and all the men of war fled, and went forth out of the city by night by the way of the gate between the two walls, which was by the king's garden; (now the Chaldeans were against the city round about;) and they went toward the Arabah.

8But the army of the Chaldeans pursued after the king, and overtook Zedekiah in the plains of Jericho; and all his army was scattered from him.

9Then they took the king, and carried him up unto the king of Babylon to Riblah in the land of Hamath; and he gave judgment upon him.

10And the king of Babylon slew the sons of Zedekiah before his eyes: he slew also all the princes of Judah in Riblah.

11And he put out the eyes of Zedekiah; and the king of Babylon bound him in fetters, and carried him to Babylon, and put him in prison till the day of his death.

12Now in the fifth month, in the tenth day of the month, which was the nineteenth year of king Nebuchadrezzar, king of Babylon, came Nebuzaradan the captain of the guard, who stood before the king of Babylon, into Jerusalem:

13and he burned the house of Yahweh, and the king's house; and all the houses of Jerusalem, even every great house, burned he with fire.

14And all the army of the Chaldeans, that were with the captain of the guard, brake down all the walls of Jerusalem round about.

15Then Nebuzaradan the captain of the guard carried away captive of the poorest of the people, and the residue of the people that were left in the city, and those that fell away, that fell to the king of Babylon, and the residue of the multitude.

16But Nebuzaradan the captain of the guard left of the poorest of the land to be vinedressers and husbandmen.

17And the pillars of brass that were in the house of Yahweh, and the bases and the brazen sea that were in the house of Yahweh, did the Chaldeans break in pieces, and carried all the brass of them to Babylon.

18The pots also, and the shovels, and the snuffers, and the basins, and the spoons, and all the vessels of brass wherewith they ministered, took they away.

19And the cups, and the firepans, and the basins, and the pots, and the candlesticks, and the spoons, and the bowls-that which was of gold, in gold, and that which was of silver, in silver,- the captain of the guard took away.

20The two pillars, the one sea, and the twelve brazen bulls that were under the bases, which king Solomon had made for the house of Yahweh-the brass of all these vessels was without weight.

21And as for the pillars, the height of the one pillar was eighteen cubits; and a line of twelve cubits did compass it; and the thickness thereof was four fingers: it was hollow.

22And a capital of brass was upon it; and the height of the one capital was five cubits, with network and pomegranates upon the capital round about, all of brass: and the second pillar also had like unto these, and pomegranates.

23And there were ninety and six pomegranates on the sides; all the pomegranates were a hundred upon the network round about.

24And the captain of the guard took Seraiah the chief priest, and Zephaniah the second priest, and the three keepers of the threshold:

25and out of the city he took an officer that was set over the men of war; and seven men of them that saw the king's face, that were found in the city; and the scribe of the captain of the host, who mustered the people of the land; and threescore men of the people of the land, that were found in the midst of the city.

26And Nebuzaradan the captain of the guard took them, and brought them to the king of Babylon to Riblah.

27And the king of Babylon smote them, and put them to death at Riblah in the land of Hamath. So Judah was carried away captive out of his land.

28This is the people whom Nebuchadrezzar carried away captive: in the seventh year three thousand Jews and three and twenty;

29in the eighteenth year of Nebuchadrezzar he carried away captive from Jerusalem eight hundred thirty and two persons;

30in the three and twentieth year of Nebuchadrezzar Nebuzaradan the captain of the guard carried away captive of the Jews seven hundred forty and five persons: all the persons were four thousand and six hundred.

31And it came to pass in the seven and thirtieth year of the captivity of Jehoiachin king of Judah, in the twelfth month, in the five and twentieth day of the month, that Evil-merodach king of Babylon, in the first year of his reign, lifted up the head of Jehoiachin king of Judah, and brought him forth out of prison;

32and he spake kindly to him, and set his throne above the throne of the kings that were with him in Babylon,

33and changed his prison garments. And Jehoiachin did eat bread before him continually all the days of his life:

34and for his allowance, there was a continual allowance given him by the king of Babylon, every day a portion until the day of his death, all the days of his life.

Lamentations
The Lamentations of Jeremiah

Chapter 1

1 How doth the city sit solitary, that was full of people!
She is become as a widow, that was great among the nations!
She that was a princess among the provinces is become tributary!
2 She weepeth sore in the night, and her tears are on her cheeks;
Among all her lovers she hath none to comfort her:
All her friends have dealt treacherously with her; they are become her enemies.
3 Judah is gone into captivity because of affliction, and because of great servitude:
She dwelleth among the nations, she findeth no rest:
All her persecutors overtook her within the straits.
4 The ways of Zion do mourn, because none come to the solemn assembly;
All her gates are desolate, her priests do sigh:
Her virgins are afflicted, and she herself is in bitterness.
5 Her adversaries are become the head, her enemies prosper;
For Yahweh hath afflicted her for the multitude of her transgressions:
Her young children are gone into captivity before the adversary.
6 And from the daughter of Zion all her majesty is departed:
Her princes are become like harts that find no pasture,
And they are gone without strength before the pursuer.
7 Jerusalem remembereth in the days of her affliction and of her miseries all her pleasant things that were from the days of old:
When her people fell into the hand of the adversary, and none did help her,
The adversaries saw her, they did mock at her desolations.
8 Jerusalem hath grievously sinned; therefore she is become as an unclean thing;
All that honored her despise her, because they have seen her nakedness:
Yea, she sigheth, and turneth backward.
9 Her filthiness was in her skirts; she remembered not her latter end;
Therefore is she come down wonderfully; she hath no comforter:
Behold, O Yahweh, my affliction; for the enemy hath magnified himself.
10 The adversary hath spread out his hand upon all her pleasant things:
For she hath seen that the nations are entered into her sanctuary,
Concerning whom thou didst command that they should not enter into thine assembly.
11 All her people sigh, they seek bread;
They have given their pleasant things for food to refresh the soul:
See, O Yahweh, and behold; for I am become abject.
12 Is it nothing to you, all ye that pass by?
Behold, and see if there be any sorrow like unto my sorrow, which is brought upon me,
Wherewith Yahweh hath afflicted me in the day of his fierce anger.
13 From on high hath he sent fire into my bones, and it prevaileth against them;
He hath spread a net for my feet, he hath turned me back:
He hath made me desolate and faint all the day.
14 The yoke of my transgressions is bound by his hand;
They are knit together, they are come up upon my neck; he hath made my strength to fail:
The Lord hath delivered me into their hands, against whom I am not able to stand.
15 The Lord hath set at nought all my mighty men in the midst of me;
He hath called a solemn assembly against me to crush my young men:
The Lord hath trodden as in a winepress the virgin daughter of Judah.
16 For these things I weep; mine eye, mine eye runneth down with water;
Because the comforter that should refresh my soul is far from me:
My children are desolate, because the enemy hath prevailed.
17 Zion spreadeth forth her hands; there is none to comfort her;
Yahweh hath commanded concerning Jacob, that they that are round about him should be his adversaries:
Jerusalem is among them as an unclean thing.
18 Yahweh is righteous; for I have rebelled against his commandment:
Hear, I pray you, all ye peoples, and behold my sorrow:
My virgins and my young men are gone into captivity.
19 I called for my lovers, but they deceived me:
My priests and mine elders gave up the ghost in the city,
While they sought them food to refresh their souls.
20 Behold, O Yahweh; for I am in distress; my heart is troubled;
My heart is turned within me; for I have grievously rebelled:
Abroad the sword bereaveth, at home there is as death.
21 They have heard that I sigh; there is none to comfort me;
All mine enemies have heard of my trouble; they are glad that thou hast done it:
Thou wilt bring the day that thou hast proclaimed, and they shall be like unto me.
22 Let all their wickedness come before thee;
And do unto them, as thou hast done unto me for all my transgressions:
For my sighs are many, and my heart is faint.

Chapter 2

1 How hath the Lord covered the daughter of Zion with a cloud in his anger!
He hath cast down from heaven unto the earth the beauty of Israel,
And hath not remembered his footstool in the day of his anger.
2 The Lord hath swallowed up all the habitations of Jacob, and hath not pitied:
He hath thrown down in his wrath the strongholds of the daughter of Judah;
He hath brought them down to the ground; he hath profaned the kingdom and the princes thereof.
3 He hath cut off in fierce anger all the horn of Israel;
He hath drawn back his right hand from before the enemy:
And he hath burned up Jacob like a flaming fire, which devoureth round about.
4 He hath bent his bow like an enemy, he hath stood with his right hand as an adversary,
And hath slain all that were pleasant to the eye:
In the tent of the daughter of Zion he hath poured out his wrath like fire.
5 The Lord is become as an enemy, he hath swallowed up Israel;
He hath swallowed up all her palaces, he hath destroyed his strongholds;
And he hath multiplied in the daughter of Judah mourning and lamentation.
6 And he hath violently taken away his tabernacle, as if it were of a garden; he hath destroyed his place of assembly:
Yahweh hath caused solemn assembly and sabbath to be forgotten in Zion,
And hath despised in the indignation of his anger the king and the priest.
7 The Lord hath cast off his altar, he hath abhorred his sanctuary;
He hath given up into the hand of the enemy the walls of her palaces:
They have made a noise in the house of Yahweh, as in the day of a solemn assembly.
8 Yahweh hath purposed to destroy the wall of the daughter of Zion;
He hath stretched out the line, he hath not withdrawn his hand from destroying;
And he hath made the rampart and wall to lament; they languish together.
9 Her gates are sunk into the ground; he hath destroyed and broken her bars:
Her king and her princes are among the nations where the law is not;
Yea, her prophets find no vision from Yahweh.
10 The elders of the daughter of Zion sit upon the ground, they keep silence;
They have cast up dust upon their heads; they have girded themselves with sackcloth:
The virgins of Jerusalem hang down their heads to the ground.
11 Mine eyes do fail with tears, my heart is troubled;
My liver is poured upon the earth, because of the destruction of the daughter of my people,
Because the young children and the sucklings swoon in the streets of the city.
12 They say to their mothers, Where is grain and wine?
When they swoon as the wounded in the streets of the city,
When their soul is poured out into their mothers' bosom.
13 What shall I testify unto thee? what shall I liken to thee, O daughter of Jerusalem?
What shall I compare to thee, that I may comfort thee, O virgin daughter of Zion?
For thy breach is great like the sea: who can heal thee?
14 Thy prophets have seen for thee false and foolish visions;
And they have not uncovered thine iniquity, to bring back thy captivity,
But have seen for thee false oracles and causes of banishment.
15 All that pass by clap their hands at thee;
They hiss and wag their head at the daughter of Jerusalem, saying,
Is this the city that men called The perfection of beauty, The joy of the whole earth?
16 All thine enemies have opened their mouth wide against thee;
They hiss and gnash the teeth; they say, We have swallowed her up;
Certainly this is the day that we looked for; we have found, we have seen it.
17 Yahweh hath done that which he purposed; he hath fulfilled his word that he commanded in the days of old;
He hath thrown down, and hath not pitied:
And he hath caused the enemy to rejoice over thee; he hath exalted the horn of thine adversaries.
18 Their heart cried unto the Lord:
O wall of the daughter of Zion, let tears run down like a river day and night;
Give thyself no respite; let not the apple of thine eye cease.
19 Arise, cry out in the night, at the beginning of the watches;
Pour out thy heart like water before the face of the Lord:
Lift up thy hands toward him for the life of thy young children, that faint for hunger at the head of every street.
20 See, O Yahweh, and behold to whom thou hast done thus!
Shall the women eat their fruit, the children that are dandled in the hands?
Shall the priest and the prophet be slain in the sanctuary of the Lord?
21 The youth and the old man lie on the ground in the streets;
My virgins and my young men are fallen by the sword;
Thou hast slain them in the day of thine anger; thou hast slaughtered, and not pitied.
22 Thou hast called, as in the day of a solemn assembly, my terrors on every side;
And there was none that escaped or remained in the day of Yahweh's anger:
Those that I have dandled and brought up hath mine enemy consumed.

Chapter 3

1 I am the man that hath seen affliction by the rod of his wrath.
2 He hath led me and caused me to walk in darkness, and not in light.
3 Surely against me he turneth his hand again and again all the day.
4 My flesh and my skin hath he made old; he hath broken my bones.
5 He hath builded against me, and compassed me with gall and travail.
6 He hath made me to dwell in dark places, as those that have been long dead.
7 He hath walled me about, that I cannot go forth; he hath made my chain heavy.
8 Yea, when I cry, and call for help, he shutteth out my prayer.
9 He hath walled up my ways with hewn stone; he hath made my paths crooked.
10 He is unto me as a bear lying in wait, as a lion in secret places.
11 He hath turned aside my ways, and pulled me in pieces; he hath made me desolate.
12 He hath bent his bow, and set me as a mark for the arrow.
13 He hath caused the shafts of his quiver to enter into my reins.
14 I am become a derision to all my people, and their song all the day.
15 He hath filled me with bitterness, he hath sated me with wormwood.
16 He hath also broken my teeth with gravel stones; he hath covered me with ashes.
17 And thou hast removed my soul far off from peace; I forgat prosperity.
18 And I said, My strength is perished, and mine expectation from Yahweh.
19 Remember mine affliction and my misery, the wormwood and the gall.
20 My soul hath them still in remembrance, and is bowed down within me.
21 This I recall to my mind; therefore have I hope.
22 It is of Yahweh's lovingkindnesses that we are not consumed, because his compassions fail not.
23 They are new every morning; great is thy faithfulness.
24 Yahweh is my portion, saith my soul; therefore will I hope in him.
25 Yahweh is good unto them that wait for him, to the soul that seeketh him.
26 It is good that a man should hope and quietly wait for the salvation of Yahweh.
27 It is good for a man that he bear the yoke in his youth.
28 Let him sit alone and keep silence, because he hath laid it upon him.
29 Let him put his mouth in the dust, if so be there may be hope.
30 Let him give his cheek to him that smiteth him; let him be filled full with reproach.
31 For the Lord will not cast off for ever.
32 For though he cause grief, yet will he have compassion according to the multitude of his lovingkindnesses.
33 For he doth not afflict willingly, nor grieve the children of men.
34 To crush under foot all the prisoners of the earth,
35 To turn aside the right of a man before the face of the Most High,
36 To subvert a man in his cause, the Lord approveth not.
37 Who is he that saith, and it cometh to pass, when the Lord commandeth it not?
38 Out of the mouth of the Most High cometh there not evil and good?
39 Wherefore doth a living man complain, a man for the punishment of his sins?
40 Let us search and try our ways, and turn again to Yahweh.
41 Let us lift up our heart with our hands unto God in the heavens.
42 We have transgressed and have rebelled; thou hast not pardoned.
43 Thou hast covered with anger and pursued us; thou hast slain, thou hast not pitied.
44 Thou hast covered thyself with a cloud, so that no prayer can pass through.
45 Thou hast made us an off-scouring and refuse in the midst of the peoples.
46 All our enemies have opened their mouth wide against us.
47 Fear and the pit are come upon us, devastation and destruction.
48 Mine eye runneth down with streams of water, for the destruction of the daughter of my people.
49 Mine eye poureth down, and ceaseth not, without any intermission,
50 Till Yahweh look down, and behold from heaven.
51 Mine eye affecteth my soul, because of all the daughters of my city.
52 They have chased me sore like a bird, they that are mine enemies without cause.
53 They have cut off my life in the dungeon, and have cast a stone upon me.
54 Waters flowed over my head; I said, I am cut off.
55 I called upon thy name, O Yahweh, out of the lowest dungeon.
56 Thou heardest my voice; hide not thine ear at my breathing, at my cry.
57 Thou drewest near in the day that I called upon thee; thou saidst, Fear not.
58 O Lord, thou hast pleaded the causes of my soul; thou hast redeemed my life.
59 O Yahweh, thou hast seen my wrong; judge thou my cause.
60 Thou hast seen all their vengeance and all their devices against me.
61 Thou hast heard their reproach, O Yahweh, and all their devices against me,
62 The lips of those that rose up against me, and their device against me all the day.
63 Behold thou their sitting down, and their rising up; I am their song.
64 Thou wilt render unto them a recompense, O Yahweh, according to the work of their hands.
65 Thou wilt give them hardness of heart, thy curse unto them.
66 Thou wilt pursue them in anger, and destroy them from under the heavens of Yahweh.

Chapter 4

1 How is the gold become dim! how is the most pure gold changed!
The stones of the sanctuary are poured out at the head of every street.
2 The precious sons of Zion, comparable to fine gold,
How are they esteemed as earthen pitchers, the work of the hands of the potter!
3 Even the jackals draw out the breast, they give suck to their young ones:
The daughter of my people is become cruel, like the ostriches in the wilderness.
4 The tongue of the sucking child cleaveth to the roof of his mouth for thirst:
The young children ask bread, and no man breaketh it unto them.
5 They that did feed delicately are desolate in the streets:
They that were brought up in scarlet embrace dunghills.
6 For the iniquity of the daughter of my people is greater than the sin of Sodom,
That was overthrown as in a moment, and no hands were laid upon her.
7 Her nobles were purer than snow, they were whiter than milk;
They were more ruddy in body than rubies, their polishing was as of sapphire.
8 Their visage is blacker than a coal; they are not known in the streets:
Their skin cleaveth to their bones; it is withered, it is become like a stick.
9 They that are slain with the sword are better than they that are slain with hunger;
For these pine away, stricken through, for want of the fruits of the field.
10 The hands of the pitiful women have boiled their own children;
They were their food in the destruction of the daughter of my people.
11 Yahweh hath accomplished his wrath, he hath poured out his fierce anger;
And he hath kindled a fire in Zion, which hath devoured the foundations thereof.
12 The kings of the earth believed not, neither all the inhabitants of the world,
That the adversary and the enemy would enter into the gates of Jerusalem.
13 It is because of the sins of her prophets, and the iniquities of her priests,
That have shed the blood of the just in the midst of her.
14 They wander as blind men in the streets, they are polluted with blood,
So that men cannot touch their garments.
15 Depart ye, they cried unto them, Unclean! depart, depart, touch not!
When they fled away and wandered, men said among the nations, They shall no more sojourn here.
16 The anger of Yahweh hath scattered them; he will no more regard them:
They respected not the persons of the priests, they favored not the elders.
17 Our eyes do yet fail in looking for our vain help:
In our watching we have watched for a nation that could not save.
18 They hunt our steps, so that we cannot go in our streets:
Our end is near, our days are fulfilled; for our end is come.
19 Our pursuers were swifter than the eagles of the heavens:
They chased us upon the mountains, they laid wait for us in the wilderness.
20 The breath of our nostrils, the anointed of Yahweh, was taken in their pits;
Of whom we said, Under his shadow we shall live among the nations.
21 Rejoice and be glad, O daughter of Edom, that dwellest in the land of Uz:
The cup shall pass through unto thee also; thou shalt be drunken, and shalt make thyself naked.
22 The punishment of thine iniquity is accomplished, O daughter of Zion; he will no more carry thee away into captivity:
He will visit thine iniquity, O daughter of Edom; he will uncover thy sins.

Chapter 5

1 Remember, O Yahweh, what is come upon us:
Behold, and see our reproach.
2 Our inheritance is turned unto strangers,
Our houses unto aliens.
3 We are orphans and fatherless;
Our mothers are as widows.
4 We have drunken our water for money;
Our wood is sold unto us.
5 Our pursuers are upon our necks:
We are weary, and have no rest.
6 We have given the hand to the Egyptians,
And to the Assyrians, to be satisfied with bread.
7 Our fathers sinned, and are not;
And we have borne their iniquities.
8 Servants rule over us:
There is none to deliver us out of their hand.
9 We get our bread at the peril of our lives,
Because of the sword of the wilderness.
10 Our skin is black like an oven,
Because of the burning heat of famine.
11 They ravished the women in Zion,
The virgins in the cities of Judah.
12 Princes were hanged up by their hand:
The faces of elders were not honored.
13 The young men bare the mill;
And the children stumbled under the wood.
14 The elders have ceased from the gate,
The young men from their music.
15 The joy of our heart is ceased;

Lamentations

Our dance is turned into mourning.
16 The crown is fallen from our head:
Woe unto us! for we have sinned.
17 For this our heart is faint;
For these things our eyes are dim;
18 For the mountain of Zion, which is desolate:
The foxes walk upon it.
19 Thou, O Yahweh, abidest for ever;
Thy throne is from generation to generation.
20 Wherefore dost thou forget us for ever,
And forsake us so long time?
21 Turn thou us unto thee, O Yahweh, and we shall be turned;
Renew our days as of old.
22 But thou hast utterly rejected us;
Thou art very wroth against us.

The Book of the Prophet Ezekiel

Chapter 1

¹Now it came to pass in the thirtieth year, in the fourth month, in the fifth day of the month, as I was among the captives by the river Chebar, that the heavens were opened, and I saw visions of God.

²In the fifth day of the month, which was the fifth year of king Jehoiachin's captivity,

³the word of Yahweh came expressly unto Ezekiel the priest, the son of Buzi, in the land of the Chaldeans by the river Chebar; and the hand of Yahweh was there upon him.

⁴And I looked, and, behold, a stormy wind came out of the north, a great cloud, with a fire infolding itself, and a brightness round about it, and out of the midst thereof as it were glowing metal, out of the midst of the fire.

⁵And out of the midst thereof came the likeness of four living creatures. And this was their appearance: they had the likeness of a man.

⁶And every one had four faces, and every one of them had four wings.

⁷And their feet were straight feet; and the sole of their feet was like the sole of a calf's foot; and they sparkled like burnished brass.

⁸And they had the hands of a man under their wings on their four sides; and they four had their faces and their wings thus:

⁹their wings were joined one to another; they turned not when they went; they went every one straight forward.

¹⁰As for the likeness of their faces, they had the face of a man; and they four had the face of a lion on the right side; and they four had the face of an ox on the left side; they four had also the face of an eagle.

¹¹And their faces and their wings were separate above; two wings of every one were joined one to another, and two covered their bodies.

¹²And they went every one straight forward: whither the spirit was to go, they went; they turned not when they went.

¹³As for the likeness of the living creatures, their appearance was like burning coals of fire, like the appearance of torches: the fire went up and down among the living creatures; and the fire was bright, and out of the fire went forth lightning.

¹⁴And the living creatures ran and returned as the appearance of a flash of lightning.

¹⁵Now as I beheld the living creatures, behold, one wheel upon the earth beside the living creatures, for each of the four faces thereof.

¹⁶The appearance of the wheels and their work was like unto a beryl: and they four had one likeness; and their appearance and their work was as it were a wheel within a wheel.

¹⁷When they went, they went in their four directions: they turned not when they went.

¹⁸As for their rims, they were high and dreadful; and they four had their rims full of eyes round about.

¹⁹And when the living creatures went, the wheels went beside them; and when the living creatures were lifted up from the earth, the wheels were lifted up.

²⁰Whithersoever the spirit was to go, they went; thither was the spirit to go: and the wheels were lifted up beside them; for the spirit of the living creature was in the wheels.

²¹When those went, these went; and when those stood, these stood; and when those were lifted up from the earth, the wheels were lifted up beside them: for the spirit of the living creature was in the wheels.

²²And over the head of the living creature there was the likeness of a firmament, like the terrible crystal to look upon, stretched forth over their heads above.

²³And under the firmament were their wings straight, the one toward the other: every one had two which covered on this side, and every one had two which covered on that side, their bodies.

²⁴And when they went, I heard the noise of their wings like the noise of great waters, like the voice of the Almighty, a noise of tumult like the noise of a host: when they stood, they let down their wings.

²⁵And there was a voice above the firmament that was over their heads: when they stood, they let down their wings.

²⁶And above the firmament that was over their heads was the likeness of a throne, as the appearance of a sapphire stone; and upon the likeness of the throne was a likeness as the appearance of a man upon it above.

²⁷And I saw as it were glowing metal, as the appearance of fire within it round about, from the appearance of his loins and upward; and from the appearance of his loins and downward I saw as it were the appearance of fire, and there was brightness round about him.

²⁸As the appearance of the bow that is in the cloud in the day of rain, so was the appearance of the brightness round about. This was the appearance of the likeness of the glory of Yahweh. And when I saw it, I fell upon my face, and I heard a voice of one that spake.

Chapter 2

¹And he said unto me, Son of man, stand upon thy feet, and I will speak with thee.

²And the Spirit entered into me when he spake unto me, and set me upon my feet; and I heard him that spake unto me.

³And he said unto me, Son of man, I send thee to the children of Israel, to nations that are rebellious, which have rebelled against me: they and their fathers have transgressed against me even unto this very day.

⁴And the children are impudent and stiffhearted: I do sent thee unto them; and thou shalt say unto them, Thus saith the Lord Yahweh.

⁵And they, whether they will hear, or whether they will forbear, (for they are a rebellious house,) yet shall know that there hath been a prophet among them.

⁶And thou, son of man, be not afraid of them, neither be afraid of their words, though briers and thorns are with thee, and thou dost dwell among scorpions: be not afraid of their words, nor be dismayed at their looks, though they are a rebellious house.

⁷And thou shalt speak my words unto them, whether they will hear, or whether they will forbear; for they are most rebellious.

⁸But thou, son of man, hear what I say unto thee; be not thou rebellious like that rebellious house: open thy mouth, and eat that which I give thee.

⁹And when I looked, behold, a hand was put forth unto me; and, lo, a roll of a book was therein;

¹⁰And he spread it before me: and it was written within and without; and there were written therein lamentations, and mourning, and woe.

Chapter 3

¹And he said unto me, Son of man, eat that which thou findest; eat this roll, and go, speak unto the house of Israel.

²So I opened my mouth, and he caused me to eat the roll.

³And he said unto me, Son of man, cause thy belly to eat, and fill thy bowels with this roll that I give thee. Then did I eat it; and it was in my mouth as honey for sweetness.

⁴And he said unto me, Son of man, go, get thee unto the house of Israel, and speak with my words unto them.

⁵For thou art not sent to a people of a strange speech and of a hard language, but to the house of Israel;

⁶not to many peoples of a strange speech and of a hard language, whose words thou canst not understand. Surely, if I sent thee to them, they would hearken unto thee.

⁷But the house of Israel will not hearken unto thee; for they will not hearken unto me: for all the house of Israel are of hard forehead and of a stiff heart.

⁸Behold, I have made thy face hard against their faces, and thy forehead hard against their foreheads.

⁹As an adamant harder than flint have I made thy forehead: fear them not, neither be dismayed at their looks, though they are a rebellious house.

¹⁰Moreover he said unto me, Son of man, all my words that I shall speak unto thee receive in thy heart, and hear with thine ears.

¹¹And go, get thee to them of the captivity, unto the children of thy people, and speak unto them, and tell them, Thus saith the Lord Yahweh; whether they will hear, or whether they will forbear.

¹²Then the Spirit lifted me up, and I heard behind me the voice of a great rushing, saying, Blessed be the glory of Yahweh from his place.

¹³And I heard the noise of the wings of the living creatures as they touched one another, and the noise of the wheels beside them, even the noise of a great rushing.

¹⁴So the Spirit lifted me up, and took me away; and I went in bitterness, in the heat of my spirit; and the hand of Yahweh was strong upon me.

¹⁵Then I came to them of the captivity at Tel-abib, that dwelt by the river Chebar, and to where they dwelt; and I sat there overwhelmed among them seven days.

¹⁶And it came to pass at the end of seven days, that the word of Yahweh came unto me, saying,

¹⁷Son of man, I have made thee a watchman unto the house of Israel: therefore hear the word at my mouth, and give them warning from me.

¹⁸When I say unto the wicked, Thou shalt surely die; and thou givest him not warning, nor speakest to warn the wicked from his wicked way, to save his life; the same wicked man shall die in his iniquity; but his blood will I require at thy hand.

¹⁹Yet if thou warn the wicked, and he turn not from his wickedness, nor from his wicked way, he shall die in his iniquity; but thou hast delivered thy soul.

²⁰Again, when a righteous man doth turn from his righteousness, and commit iniquity, and I lay a stumblingblock before him, he shall die: because thou hast not given him warning, he shall die in his sin, and his righteous deeds which he hath done shall not be remembered; but his blood will I require at thy hand.

²¹Nevertheless if thou warn the righteous man, that the righteous sin not, and he doth not sin, he shall surely live, because he took warning; and thou hast delivered thy soul.

²²And the hand of Yahweh was there upon me; and he said unto me, Arise, go forth into the plain, and I will there talk with thee.

²³Then I arose, and went forth into the plain: and, behold, the glory of Yahweh stood there, as the glory which I saw by the river Chebar; and I fell on my face.

²⁴Then the Spirit entered into me, and set me upon my feet; and he spake with me, and said unto me, Go, shut thyself within thy house.

²⁵But thou, son of man, behold, they shall lay bands upon thee, and shall bind thee with them, and thou shalt not go out among them:

²⁶and I will make thy tongue cleave to the roof of thy mouth, that thou shalt be dumb, and shalt not be to them a reprover; for they are a rebellious house.

²⁷But when I speak with thee, I will open thy mouth, and thou shalt say unto them, Thus saith the Lord Yahweh: He that heareth, let him hear; and he that forbeareth, let him forbear: for they are a rebellious house.

Ezekiel

Chapter 4

¹Thou also, son of man, take thee a tile, and lay it before thee, and portray upon it a city, even Jerusalem:

²and lay siege against it, and build forts against it, and cast up a mound against it; set camps also against it, and plant battering rams against it round about.

³And take thou unto thee an iron pan, and set it for a wall of iron between thee and the city: and set thy face toward it, and it shall be besieged, and thou shalt lay siege against it. This shall be a sign to the house of Israel.

⁴Moreover lie thou upon thy left side, and lay the iniquity of the house of Israel upon it; according to the number of the days that thou shalt lie upon it, thou shalt bear their iniquity.

⁵For I have appointed the years of their iniquity to be unto thee a number of days, even three hundred and ninety days: so shalt thou bear the iniquity of the house of Israel.

⁶And again, when thou hast accomplished these, thou shalt lie on thy right side, and shalt bear the iniquity of the house of Judah: forty days, each day for a year, have I appointed it unto thee.

⁷And thou shalt set thy face toward the siege of Jerusalem, with thine arm uncovered; and thou shalt prophesy against it.

⁸And, behold, I lay bands upon thee, and thou shalt not turn thee from one side to the other, till thou hast accomplished the days of thy siege.

⁹Take thou also unto thee wheat, and barley, and beans, and lentils, and millet, and spelt, and put them in one vessel, and make thee bread thereof; according to the number of the days that thou shalt lie upon thy side, even three hundred and ninety days, shalt thou eat thereof.

¹⁰And thy food which thou shalt eat shall be by weight, twenty shekels a day: from time to time shalt thou eat it.

¹¹And thou shalt drink water by measure, the sixth part of a hin: from time to time shalt thou drink.

¹²And thou shalt eat it as barley cakes, and thou shalt bake it in their sight with dung that cometh out of man.

¹³And Yahweh said, Even thus shall the children of Israel eat their bread unclean, among the nations whither I will drive them.

¹⁴Then said I, Ah Lord Yahweh! behold, my soul hath not been polluted; for from my youth up even till now have I not eaten of that which dieth of itself, or is torn of beasts; neither came there abominable flesh into my mouth.

¹⁵Then he said unto me, See, I have given thee cow's dung for man's dung, and thou shalt prepare thy bread thereon.

¹⁶Moreover he said unto me, Son of man, behold, I will break the staff of bread in Jerusalem: and they shall eat bread by weight, and with fearfulness; and they shall drink water by measure, and in dismay:

¹⁷that they may want bread and water, and be dismayed one with another, and pine away in their iniquity.

Chapter 5

¹And thou, son of man, take thee a sharp sword; as a barber's razor shalt thou take it unto thee, and shalt cause it to pass upon thy head and upon thy beard: then take thee balances to weigh, and divide the hair.

²A third part shalt thou burn in the fire in the midst of the city, when the days of the siege are fulfilled; and thou shalt take a third part, and smite with the sword round about it; and a third part thou shalt scatter to the wind, and I will draw out a sword after them.

³And thou shalt take thereof a few in number, and bind them in thy skirts.

⁴And of these again shalt thou take, and cast them into the midst of the fire, and burn them in the fire; therefrom shall a fire come forth into all the house of Israel.

⁵Thus saith the Lord Yahweh: This is Jerusalem; I have set her in the midst of the nations, and countries are round about her.

⁶And she hath rebelled against mine ordinances in doing wickedness more than the nations, and against my statutes more than the countries that are round about her; for they have rejected mine ordinances, and as for my statutes, they have not walked in them.

⁷Therefore thus saith the Lord Yahweh: Because ye are turbulent more than the nations that are round about you, and have not walked in my statutes, neither have kept mine ordinances, neither have done after the ordinances of the nations that are round about you;

⁸therefore thus saith the Lord Yahweh: Behold, I, even I, am against thee; and I will execute judgments in the midst of thee in the sight of the nations.

⁹And I will do in thee that which I have not done, and whereunto I will not do any more the like, because of all thine abominations.

¹⁰Therefore the fathers shall eat the sons in the midst of thee, and the sons shall eat their fathers; and I will execute judgments on thee; and the whole remnant of thee will I scatter unto all the winds.

¹¹Wherefore, as I live, saith the Lord Yahweh, surely, because thou hast defiled my sanctuary with all thy detestable things, and with all thine abominations, therefore will I also diminish thee; neither shall mine eye spare, and I also will have no pity.

¹²A third part of thee shall die with the pestilence, and with famine shall they be consumed in the midst of thee; and a third part shall fall by the sword round about thee; and a third part I will scatter unto all the winds, and will draw out a sword after them.

¹³Thus shall mine anger be accomplished, and I will cause my wrath toward them to rest, and I shall be comforted; and they shall know that I, Yahweh, have spoken in my zeal, when I have accomplished my wrath upon them.

¹⁴Moreover I will make thee a desolation and a reproach among the nations that are round about thee, in the sight of all that pass by.

¹⁵So it shall be a reproach and a taunt, an instruction and an astonishment, unto the nations that are round about thee, when I shall execute judgments on thee in anger and in wrath, and in wrathful rebukes; (I, Yahweh, have spoken it;)

¹⁶when I shall send upon them the evil arrows of famine, that are for destruction, which I will send to destroy you: and I will increase the famine upon you, and will break your staff of bread;

¹⁷and I will send upon you famine and evil beasts, and they shall bereave thee; and pestilence and blood shall pass through thee; and I will bring the sword upon thee: I, Yahweh, have spoken it.

Chapter 6

¹And the word of Yahweh came unto me, saying,

²Son of man, set thy face toward the mountains of Israel, and prophesy unto them,

³and say, Ye mountains of Israel, hear the word of the Lord Yahweh: Thus saith the Lord Yahweh to the mountains and to the hills, to the watercourses and to the valleys: Behold, I, even I, will bring a sword upon you, and I will destroy your high places.

⁴And your altars shall become desolate, and your sun-images shall be broken; and I will cast down your slain men before your idols.

⁵And I will lay the dead bodies of the children of Israel before their idols; and I will scatter your bones round about your altars.

⁶In all your dwelling-places the cities shall be laid waste, and the high places shall be desolate; that your altars may be laid waste and made desolate, and your idols may be broken and cease, and your sun-images may be hewn down, and your works may be abolished.

⁷And the slain shall fall in the midst of you, and ye shall know that I am Yahweh.

⁸Yet will I leave a remnant, in that ye shall have some that escape the sword among the nations, when ye shall be scattered through the countries.

⁹And those of you that escape shall remember me among the nations whither they shall be carried captive, how that I have been broken with their lewd heart, which hath departed from me, and with their eyes, which play the harlot after their idols: and they shall loathe themselves in their own sight for the evils which they have committed in all their abominations.

¹⁰And they shall know that I am Yahweh: I have not said in vain that I would do this evil unto them.

¹¹Thus saith the Lord Yahweh: Smite with thy hand, and stamp with thy foot, and say, Alas! because of all the evil abominations of the house of Israel; for they shall fall by the sword, by the famine, and by the pestilence.

¹²He that is far off shall die of the pestilence; and he that is near shall fall by the sword; and he that remaineth and is besieged shall die by the famine: thus will I accomplish my wrath upon them.

¹³And ye shall know that I am Yahweh, when their slain men shall be among their idols round about their altars, upon every high hill, on all the tops of the mountains, and under every green tree, and under every thick oak, the places where they offered sweet savor to all their idols.

¹⁴And I will stretch out my hand upon them, and make the land desolate and waste, from the wilderness toward Diblah, throughout all their habitations: and they shall know that I am Yahweh.

Chapter 7

¹Moreover the word of Yahweh came unto me, saying,

²And thou, son of man, thus saith the Lord Yahweh unto the land of Israel, An end: the end is come upon the four corners of the land.

³Now is the end upon thee, and I will send mine anger upon thee, and will judge thee according to thy ways; and I will bring upon thee all thine abominations.

⁴And mine eye shall not spare thee, neither will I have pity; but I will bring thy ways upon thee, and thine abominations shall be in the midst of thee: and ye shall know that I am Yahweh.

⁵Thus saith the Lord Yahweh: An evil, an only evil; behold, it cometh.

⁶An end is come, the end is come; it awaketh against thee; behold, it cometh.

⁷Thy doom is come unto thee, O inhabitant of the land: the time is come, the day is near, a day of tumult, and not of joyful shouting, upon the mountains.

⁸Now will I shortly pour out my wrath upon thee, and accomplish mine anger against thee, and will judge thee according to thy ways; and I will bring upon thee all thine abominations.

⁹And mine eye shall not spare, neither will I have pity: I will bring upon thee according to thy ways; and thine abominations shall be in the midst of thee; and ye shall know that I, Yahweh, do smite.

¹⁰Behold, the day, behold, it cometh: thy doom is gone forth; the rod hath blossomed, pride hath budded.

¹¹Violence is risen up into a rod of wickedness; none of them shall remain, nor of their multitude, nor of their wealth: neither shall there be eminency among them.

¹²The time is come, the day draweth near: let not the buyer rejoice, nor the seller mourn; for wrath is upon all the multitude thereof.

¹³For the seller shall not return to that which is sold, although they be yet alive: for the vision is touching the whole multitude thereof, none shall return; neither shall any strengthen himself in the iniquity of his life.

¹⁴They have blown the trumpet, and have made all ready; but none goeth to the battle; for my wrath is upon all the multitude thereof.

¹⁵The sword is without, and the pestilence and the famine within: he that is in the field shall die with the sword: and he that is in the city, famine and pestilence shall devour him.

¹⁶But those of them that escape shall escape, and shall be on the mountains like doves of the valleys, all of them moaning, every one in his iniquity.

17All hands shall be feeble, and all knees shall be weak as water.

18They shall also gird themselves with sackcloth, and horror shall cover them; and shame shall be upon all faces, and baldness upon all their heads.

19They shall cast their silver in the streets, and their gold shall be as an unclean thing; their silver and their gold shall not be able to deliver them in the day of the wrath of Yahweh: they shall not satisfy their souls, neither fill their bowels; because it hath been the stumblingblock of their iniquity.

20As for the beauty of his ornament, he set it in majesty; but they made the images of their abominations and their detestable things therein: therefore have I made it unto them as an unclean thing.

21And I will give it into the hands of the strangers for a prey, and to the wicked of the earth for a spoil; and they shall profane it.

22My face will I turn also from them, and they shall profane my secret place; and robbers shall enter into it, and profane it.

23Make the chain; for the land is full of bloody crimes, and the city is full of violence.

24Wherefore I will bring the worst of the nations, and they shall possess their houses: I will also make the pride of the strong to cease; and their holy places shall be profaned.

25Destruction cometh; and they shall seek peace, and there shall be none.

26Mischief shall come upon mischief, and rumor shall be upon rumor; and they shall seek a vision of the prophet; but the law shall perish from the priest, and counsel from the elders.

27The king shall mourn, and the prince shall be clothed with desolation, and the hands of the people of the land shall be troubled: I will do unto them after their way, and according to their deserts will I judge them; and they shall know that I am Yahweh.

Chapter 8

1And it came to pass in the sixth year, in the sixth month, in the fifth day of the month, as I sat in my house, and the elders of Judah sat before me, that the hand of the Lord Yahweh fell there upon me.

2Then I beheld, and, lo, a likeness as the appearance of fire; from the appearance of his loins and downward, fire; and from his loins and upward, as the appearance of brightness, as it were glowing metal.

3And he put forth the form of a hand, and took me by a lock of my head; and the Spirit lifted me up between earth and heaven, and brought me in the visions of God to Jerusalem, to the door of the gate of the inner court that looketh toward the north; where was the seat of the image of jealousy, which provoketh to jealousy.

4And, behold, the glory of the God of Israel was there, according to the appearance that I saw in the plain.

5Then said he unto me, Son of man, lift up thine eyes now the way toward the north. So I lifted up mine eyes the way toward the north, and behold, northward of the gate of the altar this image of jealousy in the entry.

6And he said unto me, Son of man, seest thou what they do? even the great abominations that the house of Israel do commit here, that I should go far off from my sanctuary? but thou shalt again see yet other great abominations.

7And he brought me to the door of the court; and when I looked, behold, a hole in the wall.

8Then said he unto me, Son of man, dig now in the wall: and when I had digged in the wall, behold, a door.

9And he said unto me, Go in, and see the wicked abominations that they do here.

10So I went in and saw; and behold, every form of creeping things, and abominable beasts, and all the idols of the house of Israel, portrayed upon the wall round about.

11And there stood before them seventy men of the elders of the house of Israel; and in the midst of them stood Jaazaniah the son of Shaphan, every man with his censer in his hand; and the odor of the cloud of incense went up.

12Then said he unto me, Son of man, hast thou seen what the elders of the house of Israel do in the dark, every man in his chambers of imagery? for they say, Yahweh seeth us not; Yahweh hath forsaken the land.

13He said also unto me, Thou shalt again see yet other great abominations which they do.

14Then he brought me to the door of the gate of Yahweh's house which was toward the north; and behold, there sat the women weeping for Tammuz.

15Then said he unto me, Hast thou seen this, O son of man? thou shalt again see yet greater abominations than these.

16And he brought me into the inner court of Yahweh's house; and behold, at the door of the temple of Yahweh, between the porch and the altar, were about five and twenty men, with their backs toward the temple of Yahweh, and their faces toward the east; and they were worshipping the sun toward the east.

17Then he said unto me, Hast thou seen this, O son of man? Is it a light thing to the house of Judah that they commit the abominations which they commit here? for they have filled the land with violence, and have turned again to provoke me to anger: and, lo, they put the branch to their nose.

18Therefore will I also deal in wrath; mine eye shall not spare, neither will I have pity; and though they cry in mine ears with a loud voice, yet will I not hear them.

Chapter 9

1Then he cried in mine ears with a loud voice, saying, Cause ye them that have charge over the city to draw near, every man with his destroying weapon in his hand.

2And behold, six men came from the way of the upper gate, which lieth toward the north, every man with his slaughter weapon in his hand; and one man in the midst of them clothed in linen, with a writer's inkhorn by his side. And they went in, and stood beside the brazen altar.

3And the glory of the God of Israel was gone up from the cherub, whereupon it was, to the threshold of the house: and he called to the man clothed in linen, who had the writer's inkhorn by his side.

4And Yahweh said unto him, Go through the midst of the city, through the midst of Jerusalem, and set a mark upon the foreheads of the men that sigh and that cry over all the abominations that are done in the midst thereof.

5And to the others he said in my hearing, Go ye through the city after him, and smite: let not your eye spare, neither have ye pity;

6slay utterly the old man, the young man and the virgin, and little children and women; but come not near any man upon whom is the mark: and begin at my sanctuary. Then they began at the old men that were before the house.

7And he said unto them, Defile the house, and fill the courts with the slain: go ye forth. And they went forth, and smote in the city.

8And it came to pass, while they were smiting, and I was left, that I fell upon my face, and cried, and said, Ah Lord Yahweh! wilt thou destroy all the residue of Israel in thy pouring out of thy wrath upon Jerusalem?

9Then said he unto me, The iniquity of the house of Israel and Judah is exceeding great, and the land is full of blood, and the city full of wrestling of judgment: for they say, Yahweh hath forsaken the land, and Yahweh seeth not.

10And as for me also, mine eye shall not spare, neither will I have pity, but I will bring their way upon their head.

11And behold, the man clothed in linen, who had the inkhorn by his side, reported the matter, saying, I have done as thou hast commanded me.

Chapter 10

1Then I looked, and behold, in the firmament that was over the head of the cherubim there appeared above them as it were a sapphire stone, as the appearance of the likeness of a throne.

2And he spake unto the man clothed in linen, and said, Go in between the whirling wheels, even under the cherub, and fill both thy hands with coals of fire from between the cherubim, and scatter them over the city. And he went in in my sight.

3Now the cherubim stood on the right side of the house, when the man went in; and the cloud filled the inner court.

4And the glory of Yahweh mounted up from the cherub, and stood over the threshold of the house; and the house was filled with the cloud, and the court was full of the brightness of Yahweh's glory.

5And the sound of the wings of the cherubim was heard even to the outer court, as the voice of God Almighty when he speaketh.

6And it came to pass, when he commanded the man clothed in linen, saying, Take fire from between the whirling wheels, from between the cherubim, that he went in, and stood beside a wheel.

7And the cherub stretched forth his hand from between the cherubim unto the fire that was between the cherubim, and took thereof, and put it into the hands of him that was clothed in linen, who took it and went out.

8And there appeared in the cherubim the form of a man's hand under their wings.

9And I looked, and behold, four wheels beside the cherubim, one wheel beside one cherub, and another wheel beside another cherub; and the appearance of the wheels was like unto a beryl stone.

10And as for their appearance, they four had one likeness, as if a wheel have been within a wheel.

11When they went, they went in their four directions: they turned not as they went, but to the place whither the head looked they followed it; they turned not as they went.

12And their whole body, and their backs, and their hands, and their wings, and the wheels, were full of eyes round about, even the wheels that they four had.

13As for the wheels, they were called in my hearing, the whirling wheels.

14And every one had four faces: the first face was the face of the cherub, and the second face was the face of a man, and the third face the face of a lion, and the fourth the face of an eagle.

15And the cherubim mounted up: this is the living creature that I saw by the river Chebar.

16And when the cherubim went, the wheels went beside them; and when the cherubim lifted up their wings to mount up from the earth, the wheels also turned not from beside them.

17When they stood, these stood; and when they mounted up, these mounted up with them: for the spirit of the living creature was in them.

18And the glory of Yahweh went forth from over the threshold of the house, and stood over the cherubim.

19And the cherubim lifted up their wings, and mounted up from the earth in my sight when they went forth, and the wheels beside them: and they stood at the door of the east gate of Yahweh's house; and the glory of the God of Israel was over them above.

20This is the living creature that I saw under the God of Israel by the river Chebar; and I knew that they were cherubim.

21Every one had four faces, and every one four wings; and the likeness of the hands of a man was under their wings.

22And as for the likeness of their faces, they were the faces which I saw by the river Chebar, their appearances and themselves; they went every one straight forward.

Ezekiel

Chapter 11

1Moreover the Spirit lifted me up, and brought me unto the east gate of Yahweh's house, which looketh eastward: and behold, at the door of the gate five and twenty men; and I saw in the midst of them Jaazaniah the son of Azzur, and Pelatiah the son of Benaiah, princes of the people.

2And he said unto me, Son of man, these are the men that devise iniquity, and that give wicked counsel in this city;

3that say, The time is not near to build houses: this city is the caldron, and we are the flesh.

4Therefore prophesy against them, prophesy, O son of man.

5And the Spirit of Yahweh fell upon me, and he said unto me, Speak, Thus saith Yahweh: Thus have ye said, O house of Israel; for I know the things that come into your mind.

6Ye have multiplied your slain in this city, and ye have filled the streets thereof with the slain.

7Therefore thus saith the Lord Yahweh: Your slain whom ye have laid in the midst of it, they are the flesh, and this city is the caldron; but ye shall be brought forth out of the midst of it.

8Ye have feared the sword; and I will bring the sword upon you, saith the Lord Yahweh.

9And I will bring you forth out of the midst thereof, and deliver you into the hands of strangers, and will execute judgments among you.

10Ye shall fall by the sword; I will judge you in the border of Israel; and ye shall know that I am Yahweh.

11This city shall not be your caldron, neither shall ye be the flesh in the midst thereof; I will judge you in the border of Israel;

12and ye shall know that I am Yahweh: for ye have not walked in my statutes, neither have ye executed mine ordinances, but have done after the ordinances of the nations that are round about you.

13And it came to pass, when I prophesied, that Pelatiah the son of Benaiah died. Then fell I down upon my face, and cried with a loud voice, and said, Ah Lord Yahweh! wilt thou make a full end of the remnant of Israel?

14And the word of Yahweh came unto me, saying,

15Son of man, thy brethren, even thy brethren, the men of thy kindred, and all the house of Israel, all of them, are they unto whom the inhabitants of Jerusalem have said, Get you far from Yahweh; unto us is this land given for a possession.

16Therefore say, Thus saith the Lord Yahweh: Whereas I have removed them far off among the nations, and whereas I have scattered them among the countries, yet will I be to them a sanctuary for a little while in the countries where they are come.

17Therefore say, Thus saith the Lord Yahweh: I will gather you from the peoples, and assemble you out of the countries where ye have been scattered, and I will give you the land of Israel.

18And they shall come thither, and they shall take away all the detestable things thereof and all the abominations thereof from thence.

19And I will give them one heart, and I will put a new spirit within you; and I will take the stony heart out of their flesh, and will give them a heart of flesh;

20that they may walk in my statutes, and keep mine ordinances, and do them: and they shall be my people, and I will be their God.

21But as for them whose heart walketh after the heart of their detestable things and their abominations, I will bring their way upon their own heads, saith the Lord Yahweh.

22Then did the cherubim lift up their wings, and the wheels were beside them; and the glory of the God of Israel was over them above.

23And the glory of Yahweh went up from the midst of the city, and stood upon the mountain which is on the east side of the city.

24And the Spirit lifted me up, and brought me in the vision by the Spirit of God into Chaldea, to them of the captivity. So the vision that I had seen went up from me.

25Then I spake unto them of the captivity all the things that Yahweh had showed me.

Chapter 12

1The word of Yahweh also came unto me, saying,

2Son of man, thou dwellest in the midst of the rebellious house, that have eyes to see, and see not, that have ears to hear, and hear not; for they are a rebellious house.

3Therefore, thou son of man, prepare thee stuff for removing, and remove by day in their sight; and thou shalt remove from thy place to another place in their sight: it may be they will consider, though they are a rebellious house.

4And thou shalt bring forth thy stuff by day in their sight, as stuff for removing; and thou shalt go forth thyself at even in their sight, as when men go forth into exile.

5Dig thou through the wall in their sight, and carry out thereby.

6In their sight shalt thou bear it upon thy shoulder, and carry it forth in the dark; thou shalt cover thy face, that thou see not the land: for I have set thee for a sign unto the house of Israel.

7And I did so as I was commanded: I brought forth my stuff by day, as stuff for removing, and in the even I digged through the wall with my hand; I brought it forth in the dark, and bare it upon my shoulder in their sight.

8And in the morning came the word of Yahweh unto me, saying,

9Son of man, hath not the house of Israel, the rebellious house, said unto thee, What doest thou?

10Say thou unto them, Thus saith the Lord Yahweh: This burden concerneth the prince in Jerusalem, and all the house of Israel among whom they are.

11Say, I am your sign: like as I have done, so shall it be done unto them; they shall go into exile, into captivity.

12And the prince that is among them shall bear upon his shoulder in the dark, and shall go forth: they shall dig through the wall to carry out thereby: he shall cover his face, because he shall not see the land with his eyes.

13My net also will I spread upon him, and he shall be taken in my snare; and I will bring him to Babylon to the land of the Chaldeans; yet shall he not see it, though he shall die there.

14And I will scatter toward every wind all that are round about him to help him, and all his bands; and I will draw out the sword after them.

15And they shall know that I am Yahweh, when I shall disperse them among the nations, and scatter them through the countries.

16But I will leave a few men of them from the sword, from the famine, and from the pestilence; that they may declare all their abominations among the nations whither they come; and they shall know that I am Yahweh.

17Moreover the word of Yahweh came to me, saying,

18Son of man, eat thy bread with quaking, and drink thy water with trembling and with fearfulness;

19and say unto the people of the land, Thus saith the Lord Yahweh concerning the inhabitants of Jerusalem, and the land of Israel: They shall eat their bread with fearfulness, and drink their water in dismay, that her land may be desolate, and despoiled of all that is therein, because of the violence of all them that dwell therein.

20And the cities that are inhabited shall be laid waste, and the land shall be a desolation; and ye shall know that I am Yahweh.

21And the word of Yahweh came unto me, saying,

22Son of man, what is this proverb that ye have in the land of Israel, saying, The days are prolonged, and every vision faileth?

23Tell them therefore, Thus saith the Lord Yahweh: I will make this proverb to cease, and they shall no more use it as a proverb in Israel; but say unto them, The days are at hand, and the fulfilment of every vision.

24For there shall be no more any false vision nor flattering divination within the house of Israel.

25For I am Yahweh; I will speak, and the word that I shall speak shall be performed; it shall be no more deferred: for in your days, O rebellious house, will I speak the word, and will perform it, saith the Lord Yahweh.

26Again the word of Yahweh came to me, saying,

27Son of man, behold, they of the house of Israel say, The vision that he seeth is for many day to come, and he prophesieth of times that are far off.

28Therefore say unto them, Thus saith the Lord Yahweh: There shall none of my words be deferred any more, but the word which I shall speak shall be performed, saith the Lord Yahweh.

Chapter 13

1And the word of Yahweh came unto me, saying,

2Son of man, prophesy against the prophets of Israel that prophesy, and say thou unto them that prophesy out of their own heart, Hear ye the word of Yahweh:

3Thus saith the Lord Yahweh, Woe unto the foolish prophets, that follow their own spirit, and have seen nothing!

4O Israel, thy prophets have been like foxes in the waste places.

5Ye have not gone up into the gaps, neither built up the wall for the house of Israel, to stand in the battle in the day of Yahweh.

6They have seen falsehood and lying divination, that say, Yahweh saith; but Yahweh hath not sent them: and they have made men to hope that the word would be confirmed.

7Have ye not seen a false vision, and have ye not spoken a lying divination, in that ye say, Yahweh saith; albeit I have not spoken?

8Therefore thus saith the Lord Yahweh: Because ye have spoken falsehood, and seen lies, therefore, behold, I am against you, saith the Lord Yahweh.

9And my hand shall be against the prophets that see false visions, and that divine lies: they shall not be in the council of my people, neither shall they be written in the writing of the house of Israel, neither shall they enter into the land of Israel; and ye shall know that I am the Lord Yahweh.

10Because, even because they have seduced my people, saying, Peace; and there is no peace; and when one buildeth up a wall, behold, they daub it with untempered mortar;

11say unto them that daub it with untempered mortar, that it shall fall: there shall be an overflowing shower; and ye, O great hailstones, shall fall; and a stormy wind shall rend it.

12Lo, when the wall is fallen, shall it not be said unto you, Where is the daubing wherewith ye have daubed it?

13Therefore thus saith the Lord Yahweh: I will even rend it with a stormy wind in my wrath; and there shall be an overflowing shower in mine anger, and great hailstones in wrath to consume it.

14So will I break down the wall that ye have daubed with untempered mortar, and bring it down to the ground, so that the foundation thereof shall be uncovered; and it shall fall, and ye shall be consumed in the midst thereof: and ye shall know that I am Yahweh.

15Thus will I accomplish my wrath upon the wall, and upon them that have daubed it with untempered mortar; and I will say unto you, The wall is no more, neither they that daubed it;

16to wit, the prophets of Israel that prophesy concerning Jerusalem, and that see visions of peace for her, and there is no peace, saith the Lord Yahweh.

17And thou, son of man, set thy face against the daughters of thy people, that prophesy out of their own heart; and prophesy thou against them,

18and say, Thus saith the Lord Yahweh: Woe to the women that sew pillows upon all elbows, and make kerchiefs for the head of persons of every stature to hunt souls! Will ye hunt the souls of my people, and save souls alive for yourselves?

19And ye have profaned me among my people for handfuls of barley and for pieces of bread, to slay the souls that should not die, and to save the souls alive that should not live, by your lying to my people that hearken unto lies.

20Wherefore thus saith the Lord Yahweh: Behold, I am against your pillows, wherewith ye there hunt the souls to make them fly, and I will tear them from your arms; and I will let the souls go, even the souls that ye hunt to make them fly.

21Your kerchiefs also will I tear, and deliver my people out of your hand, and they shall be no more in your hand to be hunted; and ye shall know that I am Yahweh.

22Because with lies ye have grieved the heart of the righteous, whom I have not made sad; and strengthened the hands of the wicked, that he should not return from his wicked way, and be saved alive:

23Therefore ye shall no more see false visions, nor divine divinations: and I will deliver my people out of your hand; and ye shall know that I am Yahweh.

Chapter 14

1Then came certain of the elders of Israel unto me, and sat before me.

2And the word of Yahweh came unto me, saying,

3Son of man, these men have taken their idols into their heart, and put the stumblingblock of their iniquity before their face: should I be inquired of at all by them?

4Therefore speak unto them, and say unto them, Thus saith the Lord Yahweh: Every man of the house of Israel that taketh his idols into his heart, and putteth the stumblingblock of his iniquity before his face, and cometh to the prophet; I Yahweh will answer him therein according to the multitude of his idols;

5that I may take the house of Israel in their own heart, because they are all estranged from me through their idols.

6Therefore say unto the house of Israel, Thus saith the Lord Yahweh: Return ye, and turn yourselves from your idols; and turn away your faces from all your abominations.

7For every one of the house of Israel, or of the strangers that sojourn in Israel, that separateth himself from me, and taketh his idols into his heart, and putteth the stumblingblock of his iniquity before his face, and cometh to the prophet to inquire for himself of me; I Yahweh will answer him by myself:

8and I will set my face against that man, and will make him an astonishment, for a sign and a proverb, and I will cut him off from the midst of my people; and ye shall know that I am Yahweh.

9And if the prophet be deceived and speak a word, I, Yahweh, have deceived that prophet, and I will stretch out my hand upon him, and will destroy him from the midst of my people Israel.

10And they shall bear their iniquity: the iniquity of the prophet shall be even as the iniquity of him that seeketh unto him;

11that the house of Israel may go no more astray from me, neither defile themselves any more with all their transgressions; but that they may be my people, and I may be their God, saith the Lord Yahweh.

12And the word of Yahweh came unto me, saying,

13Son of man, when a land sinneth against me by committing a trespass, and I stretch out my hand upon it, and break the staff of the bread thereof, and send famine upon it, and cut off from it man and beast;

14though these three men, Noah, Daniel, and Job, were in it, they should deliver but their own souls by their righteousness, saith the Lord Yahweh.

15If I cause evil beasts to pass through the land, and they ravage it, and it be made desolate, so that no man may pass through because of the beasts;

16though these three men were in it, as I live, saith the Lord Yahweh, they should deliver neither sons nor daughters; they only should be delivered, but the land should be desolate.

17Or if I bring a sword upon that land, and say, Sword, go through the land; so that I cut off from it man and beast;

18though these three men were in it, as I live, saith the Lord Yahweh, they should deliver neither sons nor daughters, but they only should be delivered themselves.

19Or if I send a pestilence into that land, and pour out my wrath upon it in blood, to cut off from it man and beast;

20though Noah, Daniel, and Job, were in it, as I live, saith the Lord Yahweh, they should deliver neither son nor daughter; they should but deliver their own souls by their righteousness.

21For thus saith the Lord Yahweh: How much more when I send my four sore judgments upon Jerusalem, the sword, and the famine, and the evil beasts, and the pestilence, to cut off from it man and beast!

22Yet, behold, therein shall be left a remnant that shall be carried forth, both sons and daughters: behold, they shall come forth unto you, and ye shall see their way and their doings; and ye shall be comforted concerning the evil that I have brought upon Jerusalem, even concerning all that I have brought upon it.

23And they shall comfort you, when ye see their way and their doings; and ye shall know that I have not done without cause all that I have done in it, saith the Lord Yahweh.

Chapter 15

1And the word of Yahweh came unto me, saying,

2Son of man, what is the vine-tree more than any tree, the vine-branch which is among the trees of the forest?

3Shall wood be taken thereof to make any work? or will men take a pin of it to hang any vessel thereon?

4Behold, it is cast into the fire for fuel; the fire hath devoured both the ends of it, and the midst of it is burned: is it profitable for any work?

5Behold, when it was whole, it was meet for no work: how much less, when the fire hath devoured it, and it is burned, shall it yet be meet for any work!

6Therefore thus saith the Lord Yahweh: As the vine-tree among the trees of the forest, which I have given to the fire for fuel, so will I give the inhabitants of Jerusalem.

7And I will set my face against them; they shall go forth from the fire, but the fire shall devour them; and ye shall know that I am Yahweh, when I set my face against them.

8And I will make the land desolate, because they have committed a trespass, saith the Lord Yahweh.

Chapter 16

1Again the word of Yahweh came unto me, saying,

2Son of man, cause Jerusalem to know her abominations;

3and say, Thus saith the Lord Yahweh unto Jerusalem: Thy birth and thy nativity is of the land of the Canaanite; the Amorite was thy father, and thy mother was a Hittite.

4And as for thy nativity, in the day thou wast born thy navel was not cut, neither wast thou washed in water to cleanse thee; thou wast not salted at all, nor swaddled at all.

5No eye pitied thee, to do any of these things unto thee, to have compassion upon thee; but thou wast cast out in the open field, for that thy person was abhorred, in the day that thou wast born.

6And when I passed by thee, and saw thee weltering in thy blood, I said unto thee, Though thou art in thy blood, live; yea, I said unto thee, Though thou art in thy blood, live.

7I caused thee to multiply as that which groweth in the field, and thou didst increase and wax great, and thou attainedst to excellent ornament; thy breasts were fashioned, and thy hair was grown; yet thou wast naked and bare.

8Now when I passed by thee, and looked upon thee, behold, thy time was the time of love; and I spread my skirt over thee, and covered thy nakedness: yea, I sware unto thee, and entered into a covenant with thee, saith the Lord Yahweh, and thou becamest mine.

9Then washed I thee with water; yea, I thoroughly washed away thy blood from thee, and I anointed thee with oil.

10I clothed thee also with broidered work, and shod thee with sealskin, and I girded thee about with fine linen, and covered thee with silk.

11And I decked thee with ornaments, and I put bracelets upon thy hands, and a chain on thy neck.

12And I put a ring upon thy nose, and ear-rings in thine ears, and a beautiful crown upon thy head.

13Thus wast thou decked with gold and silver; and thy raiment was of fine linen, and silk, and broidered work; thou didst eat fine flour, and honey, and oil; and thou wast exceeding beautiful, and thou didst prosper unto royal estate.

14And thy renown went forth among the nations for thy beauty; for it was perfect, through my majesty which I had put upon thee, saith the Lord Yahweh.

15But thou didst trust in thy beauty, and playedst the harlot because of thy renown, and pouredst out thy whoredoms on every one that passed by; his it was.

16And thou didst take of thy garments, and madest for thee high places decked with divers colors, and playedst the harlot upon them: the like things shall not come, neither shall it be so.

17Thou didst also take thy fair jewels of my gold and of my silver, which I had given thee, and madest for thee images of men, and didst play the harlot with them;

18and thou tookest thy broidered garments, and coveredst them, and didst set mine oil and mine incense before them.

19My bread also which I gave thee, fine flour, and oil, and honey, wherewith I fed thee, thou didst even set it before them for a sweet savor; and thus it was, saith the Lord Yahweh.

20Moreover thou hast taken thy sons and thy daughters, whom thou hast borne unto me, and these hast thou sacrificed unto them to be devoured. Were thy whoredoms a small matter,

21that thou hast slain my children, and delivered them up, in causing them to pass through the fire unto them?

22And in all thine abominations and thy whoredoms thou hast not remembered the days of thy youth, when thou wast naked and bare, and wast weltering in thy blood.

23And it is come to pass after all thy wickedness, (woe, woe unto thee! saith the Lord Yahweh,)

24that thou hast built unto thee a vaulted place, and hast made thee a lofty place in every street.

25Thou hast built thy lofty place at the head of every way, and hast made thy beauty an abomination, and hast opened thy feet to every one that passed by, and multiplied thy whoredom.

26Thou hast also committed fornication with the Egyptians, thy neighbors, great of flesh; and hast multiplied thy whoredom, to provoke me to anger.

27Behold therefore, I have stretched out my hand over thee, and have diminished thine ordinary food, and delivered thee unto the will of them that hate thee, the daughters of the Philistines, that are ashamed of thy lewd way.

28Thou hast played the harlot also with the Assyrians, because thou wast insatiable; yea, thou hast played the harlot with them, and yet thou wast not satisfied.

29Thou hast moreover multiplied thy whoredom unto the land of traffic, unto Chaldea; and yet thou wast not satisfied herewith.

30How weak is thy heart, saith the Lord Yahweh, seeing thou doest all these things, the work of an impudent harlot;

31in that thou buildest thy vaulted place at the head of every way, and makest thy lofty place in every street, and hast not been as a harlot, in that thou scornest hire.

32A wife that committeth adultery! that taketh strangers instead of her husband!

33They give gifts to all harlots; but thou givest thy gifts to all thy lovers, and bribest them, that they may come unto thee on every side for thy whoredoms.

34And thou art different from other women in thy whoredoms, in that none followeth thee to play the harlot; and whereas thou givest hire, and no hire is given unto thee, therefore thou art different.

35Wherefore, O harlot, hear the word of Yahweh:

36Thus saith the Lord Yahweh, Because thy filthiness was poured out, and thy nakedness uncovered through thy whoredoms with thy lovers; and because of all the idols of thy abominations, and for the blood of thy children, that thou didst give unto them;

37therefore behold, I will gather all thy lovers, with whom thou hast taken pleasure, and all them that thou hast loved, with all them that thou hast hated; I will even gather them against thee on every side, and will uncover thy nakedness unto them, that they may see all thy nakedness.

38And I will judge thee, as women that break wedlock and shed blood are judged; and I will bring upon thee the blood of wrath and jealousy.

39I will also give thee into their hand, and they shall throw down thy vaulted place, and break down thy lofty places; and they shall strip thee of thy clothes, and take thy fair jewels; and they shall leave thee naked and bare.

40They shall also bring up a company against thee, and they shall stone thee with stones, and thrust thee through with their swords.

41And they shall burn thy houses with fire, and execute judgments upon thee in the sight of many women; and I will cause thee to cease from playing the harlot, and thou shalt also give no hire any more.

42So will I cause my wrath toward thee to rest, and my jealousy shall depart from thee, and I will be quiet, and will be no more angry.

43Because thou hast not remembered the days of thy youth, but hast raged against me in all these things; therefore, behold, I also will bring thy way upon thy head, saith the Lord Yahweh: and thou shalt not commit this lewdness with all thine abominations.

44Behold, every one that useth proverbs shall use this proverb against thee, saying, As is the mother, so is her daughter.

45Thou art the daughter of thy mother, that loatheth her husband and her children; and thou art the sister of thy sisters, who loathed their husbands and their children: your mother was a Hittite, and your father an Amorite.

46And thine elder sister is Samaria, that dwelleth at thy left hand, she and her daughters; and thy younger sister, that dwelleth at thy right hand, is Sodom and her daughters.

47Yet hast thou not walked in their ways, nor done after their abominations; but, as if that were a very little thing, thou wast more corrupt than they in all thy ways.

48As I live, saith the Lord Yahweh, Sodom thy sister hath not done, she nor her daughters, as thou hast done, thou and thy daughters.

49Behold, this was the iniquity of thy sister Sodom: pride, fulness of bread, and prosperous ease was in her and in her daughters; neither did she strengthen the hand of the poor and needy.

50And they were haughty, and committed abomination before me: therefore I took them away as I saw good.

51Neither hath Samaria committed half of thy sins; but thou hast multiplied thine abominations more than they, and hast justified thy sisters by all thine abominations which thou hast done.

52Thou also, bear thou thine own shame, in that thou hast given judgment for thy sisters; through thy sins that thou hast committed more abominable than they, they are more righteous that thou: yea, be thou also confounded, and bear thy shame, in that thou hast justified thy sisters.

53And I will turn again their captivity, the captivity of Sodom and her daughters, and the captivity of Samaria and her daughters, and the captivity of thy captives in the midst of them;

54that thou mayest bear thine own shame, and mayest be ashamed because of all that thou hast done, in that thou art a comfort unto them.

55And thy sisters, Sodom and her daughters, shall return to their former estate; and Samaria and her daughters shall return to their former estate; and thou and thy daughters shall return to your former estate.

56For thy sister Sodom was not mentioned by thy mouth in the day of thy pride,

57before thy wickedness was uncovered, as at the time of the reproach of the daughters of Syria, and of all that are round about her, the daughters of the Philistines, that do despite unto thee round about.

58Thou hast borne thy lewdness and thine abominations, saith Yahweh.

59For thus saith the Lord Yahweh: I will also deal with thee as thou hast done, who hast despised the oath in breaking the covenant.

60Nevertheless I will remember my covenant with thee in the days of thy youth, and I will establish unto thee an everlasting covenant.

61Then shalt thou remember thy ways, and be ashamed, when thou shalt receive thy sisters, thine elder sisters and thy younger; and I will give them unto thee for daughters, but not by thy covenant.

62And I will establish my covenant with thee; and thou shalt know that I am Yahweh;

63that thou mayest remember, and be confounded, and never open thy mouth any more, because of thy shame, when I have forgiven thee all that thou hast done, saith the Lord Yahweh.

Chapter 17

1And the word of Yahweh came unto me, saying,

2Son of man, put forth a riddle, and speak a parable unto the house of Israel;

3and say, Thus saith the Lord Yahweh: A great eagle with great wings and long pinions, full of feathers, which had divers colors, came unto Lebanon, and took the top of the cedar:

4he cropped off the topmost of the young twigs thereof, and carried it unto a land of traffic; he set it in a city of merchants.

5He took also of the seed of the land, and planted it in a fruitful soil; he placed it beside many waters; he set it as a willow-tree.

6And it grew, and became a spreading vine of low stature, whose branches turned toward him, and the roots thereof were under him: so it became a vine, and brought forth branches, and shot forth sprigs.

7There was also another great eagle with great wings and many feathers: and, behold, this vine did bend its roots toward him, and shot forth its branches toward him, from the beds of its plantation, that he might water it.

8It was planted in a good soil by many waters, that it might bring forth branches, and that it might bear fruit, that it might be a goodly vine.

9Say thou, Thus saith the Lord Yahweh: Shall it prosper? shall he not pull up the roots thereof, and cut off the fruit thereof, that it may wither; that all its fresh springing leaves may wither? and not by a strong arm or much people can it be raised from the roots thereof.

10Yea, behold, being planted, shall it prosper? shall it not utterly wither, when the east wind toucheth it? it shall wither in the beds where it grew.

11Moreover the word of Yahweh came unto me, saying,

12Say now to the rebellious house, Know ye not what these things mean? tell them, Behold, the king of Babylon came to Jerusalem, and took the king thereof, and the princes thereof, and brought them to him to Babylon:

13and he took of the seed royal, and made a covenant with him; he also brought him under an oath, and took away the mighty of the land;

14that the kingdom might be base, that it might not lift itself up, but that by keeping his covenant it might stand.

15But he rebelled against him in sending his ambassadors into Egypt, that they might give him horses and much people. Shall he prosper? shall he escape that doeth such things? shall he break the covenant, and yet escape?

16As I live, saith the Lord Yahweh, surely in the place where the king dwelleth that made him king, whose oath he despised, and whose covenant he brake, even with him in the midst of Babylon he shall die.

17Neither shall Pharaoh with his mighty army and great company help him in the war, when they cast up mounds and build forts, to cut off many persons.

18For he hath despised the oath by breaking the covenant; and behold, he had given his hand, and yet hath done all these things; he shall not escape.

19Therefore thus saith the Lord Yahweh: As I live, surely mine oath that he hath despised, and my covenant that he hath broken, I will even bring it upon his own head.

20And I will spread my net upon him, and he shall be taken in my snare, and I will bring him to Babylon, and will enter into judgment with him there for his trespass that he hath trespassed against me.

21And all his fugitives in all his bands shall fall by the sword, and they that remain shall be scattered toward every wind: and ye shall know that I, Yahweh, have spoken it.

22Thus saith the Lord Yahweh: I will also take of the lofty top of the cedar, and will set it; I will crop off from the topmost of its young twigs a tender one, and I will plant it upon a high and lofty mountain:

23in the mountain of the height of Israel will I plant it; and it shall bring forth boughs, and bear fruit, and be a goodly cedar: and under it shall dwell all birds of every wing; in the shade of the branches thereof shall they dwell.

24And all the trees of the field shall know that I, Yahweh, have brought down the high tree, have exalted the low tree, have dried up the green tree, and have made the dry tree to flourish; I, Yahweh, have spoken and have done it.

Chapter 18

1The word of Yahweh came unto me again, saying,

2What mean ye, that ye use this proverb concerning the land of Israel, saying, The fathers have eaten sour grapes, and the children's teeth are set on edge?

3As I live, saith the Lord Yahweh, ye shall not have occasion any more to use this proverb in Israel.

4Behold, all souls are mine; as the soul of the father, so also the soul of the son is mine: the soul that sinneth, it shall die.

5But if a man be just, and do that which is lawful and right,

6and hath not eaten upon the mountains, neither hath lifted up his eyes to the idols of the house of Israel, neither hath defiled his neighbor's wife, neither hath come near to a woman in her impurity,

7and hath not wronged any, but hath restored to the debtor his pledge, hath taken nought by robbery, hath given his bread to the hungry, and hath covered the naked with a garment;

8he that hath not given forth upon interest, neither hath taken any increase, that hath withdrawn his hand from iniquity, hath executed true justice between man and man,

9hath walked in my statutes, and hath kept mine ordinances, to deal truly; he is just, he shall surely live, saith the Lord Yahweh.

10If he beget a son that is a robber, a shedder of blood, and that doeth any one of these things,

11and that doeth not any of those duties, but even hath eaten upon the mountains, and defiled his neighbor's wife,

12hath wronged the poor and needy, hath taken by robbery, hath not restored the pledge, and hath lifted up his eyes to the idols, hath committed abomination,

13hath given forth upon interest, and hath taken increase; shall he then live? he shall not live: he hath done all these abominations; he shall surely die; his blood shall be upon him.

14Now, lo, if he beget a son, that seeth all his father's sins, which he hath done, and feareth, and doeth not such like;

15that hath not eaten upon the mountains, neither hath lifted up his eyes to the idols of the house of Israel, hath not defiled his neighbor's wife,

16neither hath wronged any, hath not taken aught to pledge, neither hath taken by robbery, but hath given his bread to the hungry, and hath covered the naked with a garment;

17that hath withdrawn his hand from the poor, that hath not received interest nor increase, hath executed mine ordinances, hath walked in my statutes; he shall not die for the iniquity of his father, he shall surely live.

18As for his father, because he cruelly oppressed, robbed his brother, and did that which is not good among his people, behold, he shall die in his iniquity.

19Yet say ye, Wherefore doth not the son bear the iniquity of the father? when the son hath done that which is lawful and right, and hath kept all my statutes, and hath done them, he shall surely live.

20The soul that sinneth, it shall die: the son shall not bear the iniquity of the father, neither shall the father bear the iniquity of the son; the righteousness of the righteous shall be upon him, and the wickedness of the wicked shall be upon him.

21But if the wicked turn from all his sins that he hath committed, and keep all my statutes, and do that which is lawful and right, he shall surely live, he shall not die.

22None of his transgressions that he hath committed shall be remembered against him: in his righteousness that he hath done he shall live.

23Have I any pleasure in the death of the wicked? saith the Lord Yahweh; and not rather that he should return from his way, and live?

24But when the righteous turneth away from his righteousness, and committeth iniquity, and doeth according to all the abominations that the wicked man doeth, shall he live? None of his righteous deeds that he hath done shall be remembered: in his trespass that he hath trespassed, and in his sin that he hath sinned, in them shall he die.

25Yet ye say, The way of the Lord is not equal. Hear now, O house of Israel: Is not my way equal? are not your ways unequal?

26When the righteous man turneth away from his righteousness, and committeth iniquity, and dieth therein; in his iniquity that he hath done shall he die.

27Again, when the wicked man turneth away from his wickedness that he hath committed, and doeth that which is lawful and right, he shall save his soul alive.

28Because he considereth, and turneth away from all his transgressions that he hath committed, he shall surely live, he shall not die.

29Yet saith the house of Israel, The way of the Lord is not equal. O house of Israel, are not my ways equal? are not your ways unequal?

30Therefore I will judge you, O house of Israel, every one according to his ways, saith the Lord Yahweh. Return ye, and turn yourselves from all your transgressions; so iniquity shall not be your ruin.

31Cast away from you all your transgressions, wherein ye have transgressed; and make you a new heart and a new spirit: for why will ye die, O house of Israel?

32For I have no pleasure in the death of him that dieth, saith the Lord Yahweh: wherefore turn yourselves, and live.

Chapter 19

1Moreover, take thou up a lamentation for the princes of Israel,

2and say, What was thy mother? A lioness: she couched among lions, in the midst of the young lions she nourished her whelps.

3And she brought up one of her whelps: he became a young lion, and he learned to catch the prey; he devoured men.

4The nations also heard of him; he was taken in their pit; and they brought him with hooks unto the land of Egypt.

5Now when she saw that she had waited, and her hope was lost, then she took another of her whelps, and made him a young lion.

6And he went up and down among the lions; he became a young lion, and he learned to catch the prey; he devoured men.

7And he knew their palaces, and laid waste their cities; and the land was desolate, and the fulness thereof, because of the noise of his roaring.

8Then the nations set against him on every side from the provinces; and they spread their net over him; he was taken in their pit.

9And they put him in a cage with hooks, and brought him to the king of Babylon; they brought him into strongholds, that his voice should no more be heard upon the mountains of Israel.

10Thy mother was like a vine, in thy blood, planted by the waters: it was fruitful and full of branches by reason of many waters.

11And it had strong rods for the sceptres of them that bare rule, and their stature was exalted among the thick boughs, and they were seen in their height with the multitude of their branches.

12But it was plucked up in fury, it was cast down to the ground, and the east wind dried up its fruit: its strong rods were broken off and withered; the fire consumed them.

13And now it is planted in the wilderness, in a dry and thirsty land.

14And fire is gone out of the rods of its branches, it hath devoured its fruit, so that there is in it no strong rod to be a sceptre to rule. This is a lamentation, and shall be for a lamentation.

Chapter 20

1And it came to pass in the seventh year, in the fifth month, the tenth day of the month, that certain of the elders of Israel came to inquire of Yahweh, and sat before me.

2And the word of Yahweh came unto me, saying,

3Son of man, speak unto the elders of Israel, and say unto them, Thus saith the Lord Yahweh: Is it to inquire of me that ye are come? As I live, saith the Lord Yahweh, I will not be inquired of by you.

4Wilt thou judge them, son of man, wilt thou judge them? Cause them to know the abominations of their fathers;

5and say unto them, Thus saith the Lord Yahweh: In the day when I chose Israel, and sware unto the seed of the house of Jacob, and made myself known unto them in the land of Egypt, when I sware unto them, saying, I am Yahweh your God;

6in that day I sware unto them, to bring them forth out of the land of Egypt into a land that I had searched out for them, flowing with milk and honey, which is the glory of all lands.

7And I said unto them, Cast ye away every man the abominations of his eyes, and defile not yourselves with the idols of Egypt; I am Yahweh your God.

8But they rebelled against me, and would not hearken unto me; they did not every man cast away the abominations of their eyes, neither did they forsake the idols of Egypt. Then I said I would pour out my wrath upon them, to accomplish my anger against them in the midst of the land of Egypt.

9But I wrought for my name's sake, that it should not be profaned in the sight of the nations, among which they were, in whose sight I made myself known unto them, in bringing them forth out of the land of Egypt.

10So I caused them to go forth out of the land of Egypt, and brought them into the wilderness.

11And I gave them my statutes, and showed them mine ordinances, which if a man do, he shall live in them.

12Moreover also I gave them my sabbaths, to be a sign between me and them, that they might know that I am Yahweh that sanctifieth them.

13But the house of Israel rebelled against me in the wilderness: they walked not in my statutes, and they rejected mine ordinances, which if a man keep, he shall live in them; and my sabbaths they greatly profaned. Then I said I would pour out my wrath upon them in the wilderness, to consume them.

14But I wrought for my name's sake, that it should not be profaned in the sight of the nations, in whose sight I brought them out.

15Moreover also I sware unto them in the wilderness, that I would not bring them into the land which I had given them, flowing with milk and honey, which is the glory of all lands;

16because they rejected mine ordinances, and walked not in my statutes, and profaned my sabbaths: for their heart went after their idols.

17Nevertheless mine eye spared them, and I destroyed them not, neither did I make a full end of them in the wilderness.

18And I said unto their children in the wilderness, Walk ye not in the statutes of your fathers, neither observe their ordinances, nor defile yourselves with their idols.

19I am Yahweh your God: walk in my statutes, and keep mine ordinances, and do them;

20and hallow my sabbaths; and they shall be a sign between me and you, that ye may know that I am Yahweh your God.

21But the children rebelled against me; they walked not in my statutes, neither kept mine ordinances to do them, which if a man do, he shall live in them; they profaned my sabbaths. Then I said I would pour out my wrath upon them, to accomplish my anger against them in the wilderness.

22Nevertheless I withdrew my hand, and wrought for my name's sake, that it should not be profaned in the sight of the nations, in whose sight I brought them forth.

23Moreover I sware unto them in the wilderness, that I would scatter them among the nations, and disperse them through the countries;

24because they had not executed mine ordinances, but had rejected my statutes, and had profaned my sabbaths, and their eyes were after their fathers' idols.

25Moreover also I gave them statutes that were not good, and ordinances wherein they should not live;

26and I polluted them in their own gifts, in that they caused to pass through the fire all that openeth the womb, that I might make them desolate, to the end that they might know that I am Yahweh.

27Therefore, son of man, speak unto the house of Israel, and say unto them, Thus saith the Lord Yahweh: In this moreover have your fathers blasphemed me, in that they have committed a trespass against me.

28For when I had brought them into the land, which I sware to give unto them, then they saw every high hill, and every thick tree, and they offered there their sacrifices, and there they presented the provocation of their offering; there also they made their sweet savor, and they poured out there their drink-offerings.

29Then I said unto them, What meaneth the high place whereunto ye go? So the name thereof is called Bamah unto this day.

30Wherefore say unto the house of Israel, Thus saith the Lord Yahweh: Do ye pollute yourselves after the manner of your fathers? and play ye the harlot after their abominations?

31and when ye offer your gifts, when ye make your sons to pass through the fire, do ye pollute yourselves with all your idols unto this day? and shall I be inquired of by you, O house of Israel? As I live, saith the Lord Yahweh, I will not be inquired of by you;

32and that which cometh into your mind shall not be at all, in that ye say, We will be as the nations, as the families of the countries, to serve wood and stone.

33As I live, saith the Lord Yahweh, surely with a mighty hand, and with an outstretched arm, and with wrath poured out, will I be king over you:

34and I will bring you out from the peoples, and will gather you out of the countries wherein ye are scattered, with a mighty hand, and with an outstretched arm, and with wrath poured out;

35and I will bring you into the wilderness of the peoples, and there will I enter into judgment with you face to face.

36Like as I entered into judgment with your fathers in the wilderness of the land of Egypt, so will I enter into judgment with you, saith the Lord Yahweh.

37And I will cause you to pass under the rod, and I will bring you into the bond of the covenant;

38and I will purge out from among you the rebels, and them that transgress

Ezekiel

against me; I will bring them forth out of the land where they sojourn, but they shall not enter into the land of Israel: and ye shall know that I am Yahweh.

39As for you, O house of Israel, thus saith the Lord Yahweh: Go ye, serve every one his idols, and hereafter also, if ye will not hearken unto me; but my holy name shall ye no more profane with your gifts, and with your idols.

40For in my holy mountain, in the mountain of the height of Israel, saith the Lord Yahweh, there shall all the house of Israel, all of them, serve me in the land: there will I accept them, and there will I require your offerings, and the first-fruits of your oblations, with all your holy things.

41As a sweet savor will I accept you, when I bring you out from the peoples, and gather you out of the countries wherein ye have been scattered; and I will be sanctified in you in the sight of the nations.

42And ye shall know that I am Yahweh, when I shall bring you into the land of Israel, into the country which I sware to give unto your fathers.

43And there shall ye remember your ways, and all your doings, wherein ye have polluted yourselves; and ye shall loathe yourselves in your own sight for all your evils that ye have committed.

44And ye shall know that I am Yahweh, when I have dealt with you for my name's sake, not according to your evil ways, nor according to your corrupt doings, O ye house of Israel, saith the Lord Yahweh.

45And the word of Yahweh came unto me, saying,

46Son of man, set thy face toward the south, and drop thy word toward the south, and prophesy against the forest of the field in the South;

47and say to the forest of the South, Hear the word of Yahweh: Thus saith the Lord Yahweh, Behold, I will kindle a fire in thee, and it shall devour every green tree in thee, and every dry tree: the flaming flame shall not be quenched, and all faces from the south to the north shall be burnt thereby.

48And all flesh shall see that I, Yahweh, have kindled it; it shall not be quenched.

49Then said I, Ah Lord Yahweh! they say of me, Is he not a speaker of parables?

Chapter 21

1And the word of Yahweh came unto me, saying,

2Son of man, set thy face toward Jerusalem, and drop thy word toward the sanctuaries, and prophesy against the land of Israel;

3and say to the land of Israel, Thus saith Yahweh: Behold, I am against thee, and will draw forth my sword out of its sheath, and will cut off from thee the righteous and the wicked.

4Seeing then that I will cut off from thee the righteous and the wicked, therefore shall my sword go forth out of its sheath against all flesh from the south to the north:

5and all flesh shall know that I, Yahweh, have drawn forth my sword out of its sheath; it shall not return any more.

6Sigh therefore, thou son of man; with the breaking of thy loins and with bitterness shalt thou sigh before their eyes.

7And it shall be, when they say unto thee, Wherefore sighest thou? that thou shalt say, Because of the tidings, for it cometh; and every heart shall melt, and all hands shall be feeble, and every spirit shall faint, and all knees shall be weak as water: behold, it cometh, and it shall be done, saith the Lord Yahweh.

8And the word of Yahweh came unto me, saying,

9Son of man, prophesy, and say, Thus saith Yahweh: Say, A sword, a sword, it is sharpened, and also furbished;

10it is sharpened that it may make a slaughter; it is furbished that it may be as lightning: shall we then make mirth? the rod of my son, it contemneth every tree.

11And it is given to be furbished, that it may be handled: the sword, it is sharpened, yea, it is furbished, to give it into the hand of the slayer.

12Cry and wail, son of man; for it is upon my people, it is upon all the princes of Israel: they are delivered over to the sword with my people; smite therefore upon thy thigh.

13For there is a trial; and what if even the rod that contemneth shall be no more? saith the Lord Yahweh.

14Thou therefore, son of man, prophesy, and smite thy hands together; and let the sword be doubled the third time, the sword of the deadly wounded: it is the sword of the great one that is deadly wounded, which entereth into their chambers.

15I have set the threatening sword against all their gates, that their heart may melt, and their stumblings be multiplied: ah! it is made as lightning, it is pointed for slaughter.

16Gather thee together, go to the right, set thyself in array, go to the left, whithersoever thy face is set.

17I will also smite my hands together, and I will cause my wrath to rest: I, Yahweh, have spoken it.

18The word of Yahweh came unto me again, saying,

19Also, thou son of man, appoint thee two ways, that the sword of the king of Babylon may come; they twain shall come forth out of one land: and mark out a place, mark it out at the head of the way to the city.

20Thou shalt appoint a way for the sword to come to Rabbah of the children of Ammon, and to Judah in Jerusalem the fortified.

21For the king of Babylon stood at the parting of the way, at the head of the two ways, to use divination: he shook the arrows to and fro, he consulted the teraphim, he looked in the liver.

22In his right hand was the divination for Jerusalem, to set battering rams, to open the mouth in the slaughter, to lift up the voice with shouting, to set battering rams against the gates, to cast up mounds, to build forts.

23And it shall be unto them as a false divination in their sight, who have sworn oaths unto them; but he bringeth iniquity to remembrance, that they may be taken.

24Therefore thus saith the Lord Yahweh: Because ye have made your iniquity to be remembered, in that your transgressions are uncovered, so that in all your doings your sins do appear; because that ye are come to remembrance, ye shall be taken with the hand.

25And thou, O deadly wounded wicked one, the prince of Israel, whose day is come, in the time of the iniquity of the end,

26thus saith the Lord Yahweh: Remove the mitre, and take off the crown; this shall be no more the same; exalt that which is low, and abase that which is high.

27I will overturn, overturn, overturn it: this also shall be no more, until he come whose right it is; and I will give it him.

28And thou, son of man, prophesy, and say, Thus saith the Lord Yahweh concerning the children of Ammon, and concerning their reproach; and say thou, A sword, a sword is drawn, for the slaughter it is furbished, to cause it to devour, that it may be as lightning;

29while they see for thee false visions, while they divine lies unto thee, to lay thee upon the necks of the wicked that are deadly wounded, whose day is come in the time of the iniquity of the end.

30Cause it to return into its sheath. In the place where thou wast created, in the land of thy birth, will I judge thee.

31And I will pour out mine indignation upon thee; I will blow upon thee with the fire of my wrath; and I will deliver thee into the hand of brutish men, skilful to destroy.

32Thou shalt be for fuel to the fire; thy blood shall be in the midst of the land; thou shalt be no more remembered: for I, Yahweh, have spoken it.

Chapter 22

1Moreover the word of Yahweh came unto me, saying,

2And thou, son of man, wilt thou judge, wilt thou judge the bloody city? then cause her to know all her abominations.

3And thou shalt say, Thus saith the Lord Yahweh: A city that sheddeth blood in the midst of her, that her time may come, and that maketh idols against herself to defile her!

4Thou art become guilty in thy blood that thou hast shed, and art defiled in thine idols which thou hast made; and thou hast caused thy days to draw near, and art come even unto thy years: therefore have I made thee a reproach unto the nations, and a mocking to all the countries.

5Those that are near, and those that are far from thee, shall mock thee, thou infamous one and full of tumult.

6Behold, the princes of Israel, every one according to his power, have been in thee to shed blood.

7In thee have they set light by father and mother; in the midst of thee have they dealt by oppression with the sojourner; in thee have they wronged the fatherless and the widow.

8Thou hast despised my holy things, and hast profaned my sabbaths.

9Slanderous men have been in thee to shed blood; and in thee they have eaten upon the mountains: in the midst of thee they have committed lewdness.

10In thee have they uncovered their fathers' nakedness; in thee have they humbled her that was unclean in her impurity.

11And one hath committed abomination with his neighbor's wife; and another hath lewdly defiled his daughter-in-law; and another in thee hath humbled his sister, his father's daughter.

12In thee have they taken bribes to shed blood; thou hast taken interest and increase, and thou hast greedily gained of thy neighbors by oppression, and hast forgotten me, saith the Lord Yahweh.

13Behold, therefore, I have smitten my hand at thy dishonest gain which thou hast made, and at thy blood which hath been in the midst of thee.

14Can thy heart endure, or can thy hands be strong, in the days that I shall deal with thee? I, Yahweh, have spoken it, and will do it.

15And I will scatter thee among the nations, and disperse thee through the countries; and I will consume thy filthiness out of thee.

16And thou shalt be profaned in thyself, in the sight of the nations; and thou shalt know that I am Yahweh.

17And the word of Yahweh came unto me, saying,

18Son of man, the house of Israel is become dross unto me: all of them are brass and tin and iron and lead, in the midst of the furnace; they are the dross of silver.

19Therefore thus saith the Lord Yahweh: Because ye are all become dross, therefore, behold, I will gather you into the midst of Jerusalem.

20As they gather silver and brass and iron and lead and tin into the midst of the furnace, to blow the fire upon it, to melt it; so will I gather you in mine anger and in my wrath, and I will lay you there, and melt you.

21Yea, I will gather you, and blow upon you with the fire of my wrath, and ye shall be melted in the midst thereof.

22As silver is melted in the midst of the furnace, so shall ye be melted in the midst thereof; and ye shall know that I, Yahweh, have poured out my wrath upon you.

23And the word of Yahweh came unto me, saying,

24Son of man, say unto her, Thou art a land that is not cleansed, nor rained upon in the day of indignation.

25There is a conspiracy of her prophets in the midst thereof, like a roaring lion ravening the prey: they have devoured souls; they take treasure and precious things; they have made her widows many in the midst thereof.

26Her priests have done violence to my law, and have profaned my holy things: they have made no distinction between the holy and the common, neither have they caused men to discern between the unclean and the clean, and have hid their eyes from my sabbaths, and I am profaned among them.

27Her princes in the midst thereof are like wolves ravening the prey, to shed blood, and to destroy souls, that they may get dishonest gain.

28And her prophets have daubed for them with untempered mortar, seeing false visions, and divining lies unto them, saying, Thus saith the Lord Yahweh, when Yahweh hath not spoken.

29The people of the land have used oppression, and exercised robbery; yea, they have vexed the poor and needy, and have oppressed the sojourner wrongfully.

30And I sought for a man among them, that should build up the wall, and stand in the gap before me for the land, that I should not destroy it; but I found none.

31Therefore have I poured out mine indignation upon them; I have consumed them with the fire of my wrath: their own way have I brought upon their heads, saith the Lord Yahweh.

Chapter 23

1The word of Yahweh came again unto me, saying,

2Son of man, there were two women, the daughters of one mother:

3and they played the harlot in Egypt; they played the harlot in their youth; there were their breasts pressed, and there was handled the bosom of their virginity.

4And the names of them were Oholah the elder, and Oholibah her sister: and they became mine, and they bare sons and daughters. And as for their names, Samaria is Oholah, and Jerusalem Oholibah.

5And Oholah played the harlot when she was mine; and she doted on her lovers, on the Assyrians her neighbors,

6who were clothed with blue, governors and rulers, all of them desirable young men, horsemen riding upon horses.

7And she bestowed her whoredoms upon them, the choicest men of Assyria all of them; and on whomsoever she doted, with all their idols she defiled herself.

8Neither hath she left her whoredoms since the days of Egypt; for in her youth they lay with her, and they handled the bosom of her virginity; and they poured out their whoredom upon her.

9Wherefore I delivered her into the hand of her lovers, into the hand of the Assyrians, upon whom she doted.

10These uncovered her nakedness; they took her sons and her daughters; and her they slew with the sword: and she became a byword among women; for they executed judgments upon her.

11And her sister Oholibah saw this, yet was she more corrupt in her doting than she, and in her whoredoms which were more than the whoredoms of her sister.

12She doted upon the Assyrians, governors and rulers, her neighbors, clothed most gorgeously, horsemen riding upon horses, all of them desirable young men.

13And I saw that she was defiled; they both took one way.

14And she increased her whoredoms; for she saw men portrayed upon the wall, the images of the Chaldeans portrayed with vermilion,

15girded with girdles upon their loins, with flowing turbans upon their heads, all of them princes to look upon, after the likeness of the Babylonians in Chaldea, the land of their nativity.

16And as soon as she saw them she doted upon them, and sent messengers unto them into Chaldea.

17And the Babylonians came to her into the bed of love, and they defiled her with their whoredom, and she was polluted with them, and her soul was alienated from them.

18So she uncovered her whoredoms, and uncovered her nakedness: then my soul was alienated from her, like as my soul was alienated from her sister.

19Yet she multiplied her whoredoms, remembering the days of her youth, wherein she had played the harlot in the land of Egypt.

20And she doted upon their paramours, whose flesh is as the flesh of asses, and whose issue is like the issue of horses.

21Thus thou calledst to remembrance the lewdness of thy youth, in the handling of thy bosom by the Egyptians for the breasts of thy youth.

22Therefore, O Oholibah, thus saith the Lord Yahweh: Behold, I will raise up thy lovers against thee, from whom thy soul is alienated, and I will bring them against thee on every side:

23the Babylonians and all the Chaldeans, Pekod and Shoa and Koa, and all the Assyrians with them; desirable young men, governors and rulers all of them, princes and men of renown, all of them riding upon horses.

24And they shall come against thee with weapons, chariots, and wagons, and with a company of peoples; they shall set themselves against thee with buckler and shield and helmet round about; and I will commit the judgment unto them, and they shall judge thee according to their judgments.

25And I will set my jealousy against thee, and they shall deal with thee in fury; they shall take away thy nose and thine ears; and thy residue shall fall by the sword: they shall take thy sons and thy daughters; and thy residue shall be devoured by the fire.

26They shall also strip thee of thy clothes, and take away thy fair jewels.

27Thus will I make thy lewdness to cease from thee, and thy whoredom brought from the land of Egypt; so that thou shalt not lift up thine eyes unto them, nor remember Egypt any more.

28For thus saith the Lord Yahweh: Behold, I will deliver thee into the hand of them whom thou hatest, into the hand of them from whom thy soul is alienated:

29and they shall deal with thee in hatred, and shall take away all thy labor, and shall leave thee naked and bare: and the nakedness of thy whoredoms shall be uncovered, both thy lewdness and thy whoredoms.

30These things shall be done unto thee, for that thou hast played the harlot after the nations, and because thou art polluted with their idols.

31Thou hast walked in the way of thy sister; therefore will I give her cup into thy hand.

32Thus saith the Lord Yahweh: Thou shalt drink of thy sister's cup, which is deep and large; thou shalt be laughed to scorn and had in derision; it containeth much.

33Thou shalt be filled with drunkenness and sorrow, with the cup of astonishment and desolation, with the cup of thy sister Samaria.

34Thou shalt even drink it and drain it out, and thou shalt gnaw the sherds thereof, and shalt tear thy breasts; for I have spoken it, saith the Lord Yahweh.

35Therefore thus saith the Lord Yahweh: Because thou hast forgotten me, and cast me behind thy back, therefore bear thou also thy lewdness and thy whoredoms.

36Yahweh said moreover unto me: Son of man, wilt thou judge Oholah and Oholibah? then declare unto them their abominations.

37For they have committed adultery, and blood is in their hands; and with their idols have they committed adultery; and they have also caused their sons, whom they bare unto me, to pass through the fire unto them to be devoured.

38Moreover this they have done unto me: they have defiled my sanctuary in the same day, and have profaned my sabbaths.

39For when they had slain their children to their idols, then they came the same day into my sanctuary to profane it; and, lo, thus have they done in the midst of my house.

40And furthermore ye have sent for men that come from far, unto whom a messenger was sent, and, lo, they came; for whom thou didst wash thyself, paint thine eyes, and deck thyself with ornaments,

41and sit upon a stately bed, with a table prepared before it, whereupon thou didst set mine incense and mine oil.

42And the voice of a multitude being at ease was with her: and with men of the common sort were brought drunkards from the wilderness; and they put bracelets upon the hands of them twain, and beautiful crowns upon their heads.

43Then said I of her that was old in adulteries, Now will they play the harlot with her, and she with them.

44And they went in unto her, as they go in unto a harlot: so went they in unto Oholah and unto Oholibah, the lewd women.

45And righteous men, they shall judge them with the judgment of adulteresses, and with the judgment of women that shed blood; because they are adulteresses, and blood is in their hands.

46For thus saith the Lord Yahweh: I will bring up a company against them, and will give them to be tossed to and fro and robbed.

47And the company shall stone them with stones, and despatch them with their swords; they shall slay their sons and their daughters, and burn up their houses with fire.

48Thus will I cause lewdness to cease out of the land, that all women may be taught not to do after your lewdness.

49And they shall recompense your lewdness upon you, and ye shall bear the sins of your idols; and ye shall know that I am the Lord Yahweh.

Chapter 24

1Again, in the ninth year, in the tenth month, in the tenth day of the month, the word of Yahweh came unto me, saying,

2Son of man, write thee the name of the day, even of this selfsame day: the king of Babylon drew close unto Jerusalem this selfsame day.

3And utter a parable unto the rebellious house, and say unto them, Thus saith the Lord Yahweh, Set on the caldron, set it on, and also pour water into it:

4gather the pieces thereof into it, even every good piece, the thigh, and the shoulder; fill it with the choice bones.

5Take the choice of the flock, and also a pile of wood for the bones under the caldron; make it boil well; yea, let the bones thereof be boiled in the midst of it.

6Wherefore thus saith the Lord Yahweh: Woe to the bloody city, to the caldron whose rust is therein, and whose rust is not gone out of it! take out of it piece after piece; No lot is fallen upon it.

7For her blood is in the midst of her; she set it upon the bare rock; she poured it not upon the ground, to cover it with dust.

8That it may cause wrath to come up to take vengeance, I have set her blood upon the bare rock, that it should not be covered.

9Therefore thus saith the Lord Yahweh: Woe to the bloody city! I also will make the pile great.

10Heap on the wood, make the fire hot, boil well the flesh, and make thick the broth, and let the bones be burned.

11Then set it empty upon the coals thereof, that it may be hot, and the brass thereof may burn, and that the filthiness of it may be molten in it, that the rust of it may be consumed.

12She hath wearied herself with toil; yet her great rust goeth not forth out of her; her rust goeth not forth by fire.

13In thy filthiness is lewdness: because I have cleansed thee and thou wast not cleansed, thou shalt not be cleansed from thy filthiness any more, till I have caused my wrath toward thee to rest.

14I, Yahweh, have spoken it: it shall come to pass, and I will do it: I will not go back, neither will I spare, neither will I repent; according to thy ways, and according to thy doings, shall they judge thee, saith the Lord Yahweh.

15Also the word of Yahweh came unto me, saying,

16Son of man, behold, I take away from thee the desire of thine eyes with a stroke: yet thou shalt neither mourn nor weep, neither shall thy tears run down.

17Sigh, but not aloud, make no mourning for the dead; bind thy headtire upon thee, and put thy shoes upon thy feet, and cover not thy lips, and eat not the bread of men.

18So I spake unto the people in the morning; and at even my wife died; and I did in the morning as I was commanded.

19And the people said unto me, Wilt thou not tell us what these things are to us, that thou doest so?

20Then I said unto them, The word of Yahweh came unto me, saying,

21Speak unto the house of Israel, Thus saith the Lord Yahweh: Behold, I will profane my sanctuary, the pride of your power, the desire of your eyes, and

Ezekiel

that which your soul pitieth; and your sons and your daughters whom ye have left behind shall fall by the sword.

22And ye shall do as I have done: ye shall not cover your lips, nor eat the bread of men.

23And your tires shall be upon your heads, and your shoes upon your feet: ye shall not mourn nor weep; but ye shall pine away in your iniquities, and moan one toward another.

24Thus shall Ezekiel be unto you a sign; according to all that he hath done shall ye do: when this cometh, then shall ye know that I am the Lord Yahweh.

25And thou, son of man, shall it not be in the day when I take from them their strength, the joy of their glory, the desire of their eyes, and that whereupon they set their heart, their sons and their daughters,

26that in that day he that escapeth shall come unto thee, to cause thee to hear it with thine ears?

27In that day shall thy mouth be opened to him that is escaped, and thou shalt speak, and be no more dumb: so shalt thou be a sign unto them; and they shall know that I am Yahweh.

Chapter 25

1And the word of Yahweh came unto me, saying,

2Son of man, set thy face toward the children of Ammon, and prophesy against them:

3and say unto the children of Ammon, Hear the word of the Lord Yahweh: Thus saith the Lord Yahweh, Because thou saidst, Aha, against my sanctuary, when it was profaned; and against the land of Israel, when it was made desolate; and against the house of Judah, when they went into captivity;

4therefore, behold, I will deliver thee to the children of the east for a possession, and they shall set their encampments in thee, and make their dwellings in thee; they shall eat thy fruit, and they shall drink thy milk.

5And I will make Rabbah a stable for camels, and the children of Ammon a couching-place for flocks: and ye shall know that I am Yahweh.

6For thus saith the Lord Yahweh: Because thou hast clapped thy hands, and stamped with the feet, and rejoiced with all the despite of thy soul against the land of Israel;

7therefore, behold, I have stretched out my hand upon thee, and will deliver thee for a spoil to the nations; and I will cut thee off from the peoples, and I will cause thee to perish out of the countries: I will destroy thee; and thou shalt know that I am Yahweh.

8Thus saith the Lord Yahweh: Because that Moab and Seir do say, Behold, the house of Judah is like unto all the nations;

9therefore, behold, I will open the side of Moab from the cities, from his cities which are on his frontiers, the glory of the country, Beth-jeshimoth, Baal-meon, and Kiriathaim,

10unto the children of the east, to go against the children of Ammon; and I will give them for a possession, that the children of Ammon may not be remembered among the nations.

11and I will execute judgments upon Moab; and they shall know that I am Yahweh.

12Thus saith the Lord Yahweh: Because that Edom hath dealt against the house of Judah by taking vengeance, and hath greatly offended, and revenged himself upon them;

13therefore thus saith the Lord Yahweh, I will stretch out my hand upon Edom, and will cut off man and beast from it; and I will make it desolate from Teman; even unto Dedan shall they fall by the sword.

14And I will lay my vengeance upon Edom by the hand of my people Israel; and they shall do in Edom according to mine anger and according to my wrath; and they shall know my vengeance, saith the Lord Yahweh.

15Thus saith the Lord Yahweh: Because the Philistines have dealt by revenge, and have taken vengeance with despite of soul to destroy with perpetual enmity;

16therefore thus saith the Lord Yahweh, Behold, I will stretch out my hand upon the Philistines, and I will cut off the Cherethites, and destroy the remnant of the sea coast.

17And I will execute great vengeance upon them with wrathful rebukes; and they shall know that I am Yahweh, when I shall lay my vengeance upon them.

Chapter 26

1And it came to pass in the eleventh year, in the first day of the month, that the word of Yahweh came unto me, saying,

2Son of man, because that Tyre hath said against Jerusalem, Aha, she is broken that was the gate of the peoples; she is turned unto me; I shall be replenished, now that she is laid waste:

3therefore thus saith the Lord Yahweh, Behold, I am against thee, O Tyre, and will cause many nations to come up against thee, as the sea causeth its waves to come up.

4And they shall destroy the walls of Tyre, and break down her towers: I will also scrape her dust from her, and make her a bare rock.

5She shall be a place for the spreading of nets in the midst of the sea; for I have spoken it, saith the Lord Yahweh; and she shall become a spoil to the nations.

6And her daughters that are in the field shall be slain with the sword: and they shall know that I am Yahweh.

7For thus saith the Lord Yahweh: Behold, I will bring upon Tyre Nebuchadrezzar king of Babylon, king of kings, from the north, with horses, and with chariots, and with horsemen, and a company, and much people.

8He shall slay with the sword thy daughters in the field; and he shall make forts against thee, and cast up a mound against thee, and raise up the buckler against thee.

9And he shall set his battering engines against thy walls, and with his axes he shall break down thy towers.

10By reason of the abundance of his horses their dust shall cover thee: thy walls shall shake at the noise of the horsemen, and of the wagons, and of the chariots, when he shall enter into thy gates, as men enter into a city wherein is made a breach.

11With the hoofs of his horses shall he tread down all thy streets; he shall slay thy people with the sword; and the pillars of thy strength shall go down to the ground.

12And they shall make a spoil of thy riches, and make a prey of thy merchandise; and they shall break down thy walls, and destroy thy pleasant houses; and they shall lay thy stones and thy timber and thy dust in the midst of the waters.

13And I will cause the noise of thy songs to cease; and the sound of thy harps shall be no more heard.

14And I will make thee a bare rock; thou shalt be a place for the spreading of nets; thou shalt be built no more: for I Yahweh have spoken it, saith the Lord Yahweh.

15Thus saith the Lord Yahweh to Tyre: shall not the isles shake at the sound of thy fall, when the wounded groan, when the slaughter is made in the midst of thee?

16Then all the princes of the sea shall come down from their thrones, and lay aside their robes, and strip off their broidered garments: they shall clothe themselves with trembling; they shall sit upon the ground, and shall tremble every moment, and be astonished at thee.

17And they shall take up a lamentation over thee, and say to thee, How art thou destroyed, that wast inhabited by seafaring men, the renowned city, that was strong in the sea, she and her inhabitants, that caused their terror to be on all that dwelt there!

18Now shall the isles tremble in the day of thy fall; yea, the isles that are in the sea shall be dismayed at thy departure.

19For thus saith the Lord Yahweh: When I shall make thee a desolate city, like the cities that are not inhabited; when I shall bring up the deep upon thee, and the great waters shall cover thee;

20then will I bring thee down with them that descend into the pit, to the people of old time, and will make thee to dwell in the nether parts of the earth, in the places that are desolate of old, with them that go down to the pit, that thou be not inhabited; and I will set glory in the land of the living:

21I will make thee a terror, and thou shalt no more have any being; though thou be sought for, yet shalt thou never be found again, saith the Lord Yahweh.

Chapter 27

1The word of Yahweh came again unto me, saying,

2And thou, son of man, take up a lamentation over Tyre;

3and say unto Tyre, O thou that dwellest at the entry of the sea, that art the merchant of the peoples unto many isles, thus saith the Lord Yahweh: Thou, O Tyre, hast said, I am perfect in beauty.

4Thy borders are in the heart of the seas; thy builders have perfected thy beauty.

5They have made all thy planks of fir-trees from Senir; they have taken a cedar from Lebanon to make a mast for thee.

6Of the oaks of Bashan have they made thine oars; they have made thy benches of ivory inlaid in boxwood, from the isles of Kittim.

7Of fine linen with broidered work from Egypt was thy sail, that it might be to thee for an ensign; blue and purple from the isles of Elishah was thine awning.

8The inhabitants of Sidon and Arvad were thy rowers: thy wise men, O Tyre, were in thee, they were thy pilots.

9The old men of Gebal and the wise men thereof were in thee thy calkers: all the ships of the sea with their mariners were in thee to deal in thy merchandise.

10Persia and Lud and Put were in thine army, thy men of war: they hanged the shield and helmet in thee; they set forth thy comeliness.

11The men of Arvad with thine army were upon thy walls round about, and valorous men were in thy towers; they hanged their shields upon thy walls round about; they have perfected thy beauty.

12Tarshish was thy merchant by reason of the multitude of all kinds of riches; with silver, iron, tin, and lead, they traded for thy wares.

13Javan, Tubal, and Meshech, they were thy traffickers; they traded the persons of men and vessels of brass for thy merchandise.

14They of the house of Togarmah traded for thy wares with horses and war-horses and mules.

15The men of Dedan were thy traffickers; many isles were the mart of thy hand: they brought thee in exchange horns of ivory and ebony.

16Syria was thy merchant by reason of the multitude of thy handiworks: they traded for thy wares with emeralds, purple, and broidered work, and fine linen, and coral, and rubies.

17Judah, and the land of Israel, they were thy traffickers: they traded for thy merchandise wheat of Minnith, and pannag, and honey, and oil, and balm.

18Damascus was thy merchant for the multitude of thy handiworks, by reason of the multitude of all kinds of riches, with the wine of Helbon, and white wool.

19Vedan and Javan traded with yarn for thy wares: bright iron, cassia, and calamus, were among thy merchandise.

20Dedan was thy trafficker in precious cloths for riding.

21Arabia, and all the princes of Kedar, they were the merchants of thy hand; in lambs, and rams, and goats, in these were they thy merchants.

22The traffickers of Sheba and Raamah, they were thy traffickers; they traded for thy wares with the chief of all spices, and with all precious stones, and gold.

23Haran and Canneh and Eden, the traffickers of Sheba, Asshur and

Chilmad, were thy traffickers.

24These were thy traffickers in choice wares, in wrappings of blue and broidered work, and in chests of rich apparel, bound with cords and made of cedar, among thy merchandise.

25The ships of Tarshish were thy caravans for thy merchandise: and thou wast replenished, and made very glorious in the heart of the seas.

26Thy rowers have brought thee into great waters: the east wind hath broken thee in the heart of the seas.

27Thy riches, and thy wares, thy merchandise, thy mariners, and thy pilots, thy calkers, and the dealers in thy merchandise, and all thy men of war, that are in thee, with all thy company which is in the midst of thee, shall fall into the heart of the seas in the day of thy ruin.

28At the sound of the cry of thy pilots the suburbs shall shake.

29And all that handled the oar, the mariners, and all the pilots of the sea, shall come down from their ships; they shall stand upon the land,

30and shall cause their voice to be heard over thee, and shall cry bitterly, and shall cast up dust upon their heads, they shall wallow themselves in the ashes:

31and they shall make themselves bald for thee, and gird them with sackcloth, and they shall weep for thee in bitterness of soul with bitter mourning.

32And in their wailing they shall take up a lamentation for thee, and lament over thee, saying, Who is there like Tyre, like her that is brought to silence in the midst of the sea?

33When thy wares went forth out of the seas, thou filledst many peoples; thou didst enrich the kings of the earth with the multitude of thy riches and of thy merchandise.

34In the time that thou wast broken by the seas in the depths of the waters, thy merchandise and all thy company did fall in the midst of thee.

35All the inhabitants of the isles are astonished at thee, and their kings are horribly afraid; they are troubled in their countenance.

36The merchants among the peoples hiss at thee; thou art become a terror, and thou shalt nevermore have any being.

Chapter 28

1The word of Yahweh came again unto me, saying,

2Son of man, say unto the prince of Tyre, Thus saith the Lord Yahweh: Because thy heart is lifted up, and thou hast said, I am a god, I sit in the seat of God, in the midst of the seas; yet thou art man, and not God, though thou didst set thy heart as the heart of God;-

3behold, thou art wiser than Daniel; there is no secret that is hidden from thee;

4by thy wisdom and by thine understanding thou hast gotten thee riches, and hast gotten gold and silver into thy treasuries;

5by thy great wisdom and by thy traffic hast thou increased thy riches, and thy heart is lifted up because of thy riches;-

6therefore thus saith the Lord Yahweh: Because thou hast set thy heart as the heart of God,

7therefore, behold, I will bring strangers upon thee, the terrible of the nations; and they shall draw their swords against the beauty of thy wisdom, and they shall defile thy brightness.

8They shall bring thee down to the pit; and thou shalt die the death of them that are slain, in the heart of the seas.

9Wilt thou yet say before him that slayeth thee, I am God? but thou art man, and not God, in the hand of him that woundeth thee.

10Thou shalt die the death of the uncircumcised by the hand of strangers: for I have spoken it, saith the Lord Yahweh.

11Moreover the word of Yahweh came unto me, saying,

12Son of man, take up a lamentation over the king of Tyre, and say unto him, Thus saith the Lord Yahweh: Thou sealest up the sum, full of wisdom, and perfect in beauty.

13Thou wast in Eden, the garden of God; every precious stone was thy covering, the sardius, the topaz, and the diamond, the beryl, the onyx, and the jasper, the sapphire, the emerald, and the carbuncle, and gold: the workmanship of thy tabrets and of thy pipes was in thee; in the day that thou wast created they were prepared.

14Thou wast the anointed cherub that covereth: and I set thee, so that thou wast upon the holy mountain of God; thou hast walked up and down in the midst of the stones of fire.

15Thou wast perfect in thy ways from the day that thou wast created, till unrighteousness was found in thee.

16By the abundance of thy traffic they filled the midst of thee with violence, and thou hast sinned: therefore have I cast thee as profane out of the mountain of God; and I have destroyed thee, O covering cherub, from the midst of the stones of fire.

17Thy heart was lifted up because of thy beauty; thou hast corrupted thy wisdom by reason of thy brightness: I have cast thee to the ground; I have laid thee before kings, that they may behold thee.

18By the multitude of thine iniquities, in the unrighteousness of thy traffic, thou hast profaned thy sanctuaries; therefore have I brought forth a fire from the midst of thee; it hath devoured thee, and I have turned thee to ashes upon the earth in the sight of all them that behold thee.

19All they that know thee among the peoples shall be astonished at thee: thou art become a terror, and thou shalt nevermore have any being.

20And the word of Yahweh came unto me, saying,

21Son of man, set thy face toward Sidon, and prophesy against it,

22and say, Thus saith the Lord Yahweh: Behold, I am against thee, O Sidon; and I will be glorified in the midst of thee; and they shall know that I am Yahweh, when I shall have executed judgments in her, and shall be sanctified in her.

23For I will send pestilence into her, and blood into her streets; and the wounded shall fall in the midst of her, with the sword upon her on every side; and they shall know that I am Yahweh.

24And there shall be no more a pricking brier unto the house of Israel, nor a hurting thorn of any that are round about them, that did despite unto them; and they shall know that I am the Lord Yahweh.

25Thus saith the Lord Yahweh: When I shall have gathered the house of Israel from the peoples among whom they are scattered, and shall be sanctified in them in the sight of the nations, then shall they dwell in their own land which I gave to my servant Jacob.

26And they shall dwell securely therein; yea, they shall build houses, and plant vineyards, and shall dwell securely, when I have executed judgments upon all those that do them despite round about them; and they shall know that I am Yahweh their God.

Chapter 29

1In the tenth year, in the tenth month, in the twelfth day of the month, the word of Yahweh came unto me, saying,

2Son of man, set thy face against Pharaoh king of Egypt, and prophesy against him, and against all Egypt;

3speak, and say, Thus saith the Lord Yahweh: Behold, I am against thee, Pharaoh king of Egypt, the great monster that lieth in the midst of his rivers, that hath said, My river is mine own, and I have made it for myself.

4And I will put hooks in thy jaws, and I will cause the fish of thy rivers to stick unto thy scales; and I will bring thee up out of the midst of thy rivers, with all the fish of thy rivers which stick unto thy scales.

5And I will cast thee forth into the wilderness, thee and all the fish of thy rivers: thou shalt fall upon the open field; thou shalt not be brought together, nor gathered; I have given thee for food to the beasts of the earth and to the birds of the heavens.

6And all the inhabitants of Egypt shall know that I am Yahweh, because they have been a staff of reed to the house of Israel.

7When they took hold of thee by thy hand, thou didst break, and didst rend all their shoulders; and when they leaned upon thee, thou brakest, and madest all their loins to be at a stand.

8Therefore thus saith the Lord Yahweh: Behold, I will bring a sword upon thee, and will cut off from thee man and beast.

9And the land of Egypt shall be a desolation and a waste; and they shall know that I am Yahweh. Because he hath said, The river is mine, and I have made it;

10therefore, behold, I am against thee, and against thy rivers, and I will make the land of Egypt an utter waste and desolation, from the tower of Seveneh even unto the border of Ethiopia.

11No foot of man shall pass through it, nor foot of beast shall pass through it, neither shall it be inhabited forty years.

12And I will make the land of Egypt a desolation in the midst of the countries that are desolate; and her cities among the cities that are laid waste shall be a desolation forty years; and I will scatter the Egyptians among the nations, and will disperse them through the countries.

13For thus saith the Lord Yahweh: At the end of forty years will I gather the Egyptians from the peoples whither they were scattered;

14and I will bring back the captivity of Egypt, and will cause them to return into the land of Pathros, into the land of their birth; and they shall be there a base kingdom.

15It shall be the basest of the kingdoms; neither shall it any more lift itself up above the nations: and I will diminish them, that they shall no more rule over the nations.

16And it shall be no more the confidence of the house of Israel, bringing iniquity to remembrance, when they turn to look after them: and they shall know that I am the Lord Yahweh.

17And it came to pass in the seven and twentieth year, in the first month, in the first day of the month, the word of Yahweh came unto me, saying,

18Son of man, Nebuchadrezzar king of Babylon caused his army to serve a great service against Tyre: every head was made bald, and every shoulder was worn; yet had he no wages, nor his army, from Tyre, for the service that he had served against it.

19Therefore thus saith the Lord Yahweh: Behold, I will give the land of Egypt unto Nebuchadrezzar king of Babylon; and he shall carry off her multitude, and take her spoil, and take her prey; and it shall be the wages for his army.

20I have given him the land of Egypt as his recompense for which he served, because they wrought for me, saith the Lord Yahweh.

21In that day will I cause a horn to bud forth unto the house of Israel, and I will give thee the opening of the mouth in the midst of them; and they shall know that I am Yahweh.

Chapter 30

30 1The word of Yahweh came again unto me, saying,

2Son of man, prophesy, and say, Thus saith the Lord Yahweh: Wail ye, Alas for the day!

3For the day is near, even the day of Yahweh is near; it shall be a day of clouds, a time of the nations.

4And a sword shall come upon Egypt, and anguish shall be in Ethiopia, when the slain shall fall in Egypt; and they shall take away her multitude, and her foundations shall be broken down.

5Ethiopia, and Put, and Lud, and all the mingled people, and Cub, and the children of the land that is in league, shall fall with them by the sword.

6Thus saith Yahweh: They also that uphold Egypt shall fall; and the pride of her power shall come down: from the tower of Seveneh shall they fall in it by the sword, saith the Lord Yahweh.

7And they shall be desolate in the midst of the countries that are desolate;

Ezekiel

and her cities shall be in the midst of the cities that are wasted.

8And they shall know at I am Yahweh, when I have set a fire in Egypt, and all her helpers are destroyed.

9In that day shall messengers go forth from before me in ships to make the careless Ethiopians afraid; and there shall be anguish upon them, as in the day of Egypt; for, lo, it cometh.

10Thus saith the Lord Yahweh: I will also make the multitude of Egypt to cease, by the hand of Nebuchadrezzar king of Babylon.

11He and his people with him, the terrible of the nations, shall be brought in to destroy the land; and they shall draw their swords against Egypt, and fill the land with the slain.

12And I will make the rivers dry, and will sell the land into the hand of evil men; and I will make the land desolate, and all that is therein, by the hand of strangers: I, Yahweh, have spoken it.

13Thus saith the Lord Yahweh: I will also destroy the idols, and I will cause the images to cease from Memphis; and there shall be no more a prince from the land of Egypt: and I will put a fear in the land of Egypt.

14And I will make Pathros desolate, and will set a fire in Zoan, and will execute judgments upon No.

15And I will pour my wrath upon Sin, the stronghold of Egypt; and I will cut off the multitude of No.

16And I will set a fire in Egypt: Sin shall be in great anguish, and No shall be broken up; and Memphis shall have adversaries in the day-time.

17The young men of Aven and of Pibeseth shall fall by the sword; and these cities shall go into captivity.

18At Tehaphnehes also the day shall withdraw itself, when I shall break there the yokes of Egypt, and the pride of her power shall cease in her: as for her, a cloud shall cover her, and her daughters shall go into captivity.

19Thus will I execute judgments upon Egypt; and they shall know that I am Yahweh.

20And it came to pass in the eleventh year, in the first month, in the seventh day of the month, that the word of Yahweh came unto me, saying,

21Son of man, I have broken the arm of Pharaoh king of Egypt; and, lo, it hath not been bound up, to apply healing medicines, to put a bandage to bind it, that it be strong to hold the sword.

22Therefore thus saith the Lord Yahweh: Behold, I am against Pharaoh king of Egypt, and will break his arms, the strong arm, and that which was broken; and I will cause the sword to fall out of his hand.

23And I will scatter the Egyptians among the nations, and will disperse them through the countries.

24And I will strengthen the arms of the king of Babylon, and put my sword in his hand: but I will break the arms of Pharaoh, and he shall groan before him with the groanings of a deadly wounded man.

25And I will hold up the arms of the king of Babylon; and the arms of Pharaoh shall fall down; and they shall know that I am Yahweh, when I shall put my sword into the hand of the king of Babylon, and he shall stretch it out upon the land of Egypt.

26And I will scatter the Egyptians among the nations, and disperse them through the countries; and they shall know that I am Yahweh.

Chapter 31

1And it came to pass in the eleventh year, in the third month, in the first day of the month, that the word of Yahweh came unto me, saying,

2Son of man, say unto Pharaoh king of Egypt, and to his multitude: Whom art thou like in thy greatness?

3Behold, the Assyrian was a cedar in Lebanon with fair branches, and with a forest-like shade, and of high stature; and its top was among the thick boughs.

4The waters nourished it, the deep made it to grow: the rivers thereof ran round about its plantation; and it sent out its channels unto all the trees of the field.

5Therefore its stature was exalted above all the trees of the field; and its boughs were multiplied, and its branches became long by reason of many waters, when it shot them forth.

6All the birds of the heavens made their nests in its boughs; and under its branches did all the beasts of the field bring forth their young; and under its shadow dwelt all great nations.

7Thus was it fair in its greatness, in the length of its branches; for its root was by many waters.

8The cedars in the garden of God could not hide it; the fir-trees were not like its boughs, and the plane-trees were not as its branches; nor was any tree in the garden of God like unto it in its beauty.

9I made it fair by the multitude of its branches, so that all the trees of Eden, that were in the garden of God, envied it.

10Therefore thus said the Lord Yahweh: Because thou art exalted in stature, and he hath set his top among the thick boughs, and his heart is lifted up in his height;

11I will even deliver him into the hand of the mighty one of the nations; he shall surely deal with him; I have driven him out for his wickedness.

12And strangers, the terrible of the nations, have cut him off, and have left him: upon the mountains and in all the valleys his branches are fallen, and his boughs are broken by all the watercourses of the land; and all the peoples of the earth are gone down from his shadow, and have left him.

13Upon his ruin all the birds of the heavens shall dwell, and all the beasts of the field shall be upon his branches;

14to the end that none of all the trees by the waters exalt themselves in their stature, neither set their top among the thick boughs, nor that their mighty ones stand up on their height, even all that drink water: for they are all delivered unto death, to the nether parts of the earth, in the midst of the children of men, with them that go down to the pit.

15Thus saith the Lord Yahweh: In the day when he went down to Sheol I caused a mourning: I covered the deep for him, and I restrained the rivers thereof; and the great waters were stayed; and I caused Lebanon to mourn for him, and all the trees of the field fainted for him.

16I made the nations to shake at the sound of his fall, when I cast him down to Sheol with them that descend into the pit; and all the trees of Eden, the choice and best of Lebanon, all that drink water, were comforted in the nether parts of the earth.

17They also went down into Sheol with him unto them that are slain by the sword; yea, they that were his arm, that dwelt under his shadow in the midst of the nations.

18To whom art thou thus like in glory and in greatness among the trees of Eden? yet shalt thou be brought down with the trees of Eden unto the nether parts of the earth: thou shalt lie in the midst of the uncircumcised, with them that are slain by the sword. This is Pharaoh and all his multitude, saith the Lord Yahweh.

Chapter 32

1And it came to pass in the twelfth year, in the twelfth month, in the first day of the month, that the word of Yahweh came unto me, saying,

2Son of man, take up a lamentation over Pharaoh king of Egypt, and say unto him, Thou wast likened unto a young lion of the nations: yet art thou as a monster in the seas; and thou didst break forth with thy rivers, and troubledst the waters with thy feet, and fouledst their rivers.

3Thus saith the Lord Yahweh: I will spread out my net upon thee with a company of many peoples; and they shall bring thee up in my net.

4And I will leave thee upon the land, I will cast thee forth upon the open field, and will cause all the birds of the heavens to settle upon thee, and I will satisfy the beasts of the whole earth with thee.

5And I will lay thy flesh upon the mountains, and fill the valleys with thy height.

6I will also water with thy blood the land wherein thou swimmest, even to the mountains; and the watercourses shall be full of thee.

7And when I shall extinguish thee, I will cover the heavens, and make the stars thereof dark; I will cover the sun with a cloud, and the moon shall not give its light.

8All the bright lights of heaven will I make dark over thee, and set darkness upon thy land, saith the Lord Yahweh.

9I will also vex the hearts of many peoples, when I shall bring thy destruction among the nations, into the countries which thou hast not known.

10Yea, I will make many peoples amazed at thee, and their kings shall be horribly afraid for thee, when I shall brandish my sword before them; and they shall tremble at every moment, every man for his own life, in the day of thy fall.

11For thus saith the Lord Yahweh: The sword of the king of Babylon shall come upon thee.

12By the swords of the mighty will I cause thy multitude to fall; the terrible of the nations are they all: and they shall bring to nought the pride of Egypt, and all the multitude thereof shall be destroyed.

13I will destroy also all the beasts thereof from beside many waters; neither shall the foot of man trouble them any more, nor the hoofs of beasts trouble them.

14Then will I make their waters clear, and cause their rivers to run like oil, saith the Lord Yahweh.

15When I shall make the land of Egypt desolate and waste, a land destitute of that whereof it was full, when I shall smite all them that dwell therein, then shall they know that I am Yahweh.

16This is the lamentation wherewith they shall lament; the daughters of the nations shall lament therewith; over Egypt, and over all her multitude, shall they lament therewith, saith the Lord Yahweh.

17It came to pass also in the twelfth year, in the fifteenth day of the month, that the word of Yahweh came unto me, saying,

18Son of man, wail for the multitude of Egypt, and cast them down, even her, and the daughters of the famous nations, unto the nether parts of the earth, with them that go down into the pit.

19Whom dost thou pass in beauty? go down, and be thou laid with the uncircumcised.

20They shall fall in the midst of them that are slain by the sword: she is delivered to the sword; draw her away and all her multitudes.

21The strong among the mighty shall speak to him out of the midst of Sheol with them that help him: they are gone down, they lie still, even the uncircumcised, slain by the sword.

22Asshur is there and all her company; her graves are round about her; all of them slain, fallen by the sword;

23whose graves are set in the uttermost parts of the pit, and her company is round about her grave; all of them slain, fallen by the sword, who caused terror in the land of the living.

24There is Elam and all her multitude round about her grave; all of them slain, fallen by the sword, who are gone down uncircumcised into the nether parts of the earth, who caused their terror in the land of the living, and have borne their shame with them that go down to the pit.

25They have set her a bed in the midst of the slain with all her multitude; her graves are round about her; all of them uncircumcised, slain by the sword; for their terror was caused in the land of the living, and they have borne their shame with them that go down to the pit: he is put in the midst of them that are slain.

26There is Meshech, Tubal, and all their multitude; their graves are round about them; all of them uncircumcised, slain by the sword; for they caused their terror in the land of the living.

27And they shall not lie with the mighty that are fallen of the uncircumcised, that are gone down to Sheol with their weapons of war, and have laid their swords under their heads, and their iniquities are upon their bones; for they were the terror of the mighty in the land of the living.

28But thou shalt be broken in the midst of the uncircumcised, and shalt lie with them that are slain by the sword.

29There is Edom, her kings and all her princes, who in their might are laid with them that are slain by the sword: they shall lie with the uncircumcised, and with them that go down to the pit.

30There are the princes of the north, all of them, and all the Sidonians, who are gone down with the slain; in the terror which they caused by their might they are put to shame; and they lie uncircumcised with them that are slain by the sword, and bear their shame with them that go down to the pit.

31Pharaoh shall see them, and shall be comforted over all his multitude, even Pharaoh and all his army, slain by the sword, saith the Lord Yahweh.

32For I have put his terror in the land of the living; and he shall be laid in the midst of the uncircumcised, with them that are slain by the sword, even Pharaoh and all his multitude, saith the Lord Yahweh.

Chapter 33

1And the word of Yahweh came unto me, saying,

2Son of man, speak to the children of thy people, and say unto them, When I bring the sword upon a land, and the people of the land take a man from among them, and set him for their watchman;

3if, when he seeth the sword come upon the land, he blow the trumpet, and warn the people;

4then whosoever heareth the sound of the trumpet, and taketh not warning, if the sword come, and take him away, his blood shall be upon his own head.

5He heard the sound of the trumpet, and took not warning; his blood shall be upon him; whereas if he had taken warning, he would have delivered his soul.

6But if the watchman see the sword come, and blow not the trumpet, and the people be not warned, and the sword come, and take any person from among them; he is taken away in his iniquity, but his blood will I require at the watchman's hand.

7So thou, son of man, I have set thee a watchman unto the house of Israel; therefore hear the word at my mouth, and give them warning from me.

8When I say unto the wicked, O wicked man, thou shalt surely die, and thou dost not speak to warn the wicked from his way; that wicked man shall die in his iniquity, but his blood will I require at thy hand.

9Nevertheless, if thou warn the wicked of his way to turn from it, and he turn not from his way; he shall die in his iniquity, but thou hast delivered thy soul.

10And thou, son of man, say unto the house of Israel: Thus ye speak, saying, Our transgressions and our sins are upon us, and we pine away in them; how then can we live?

11Say unto them, As I live, saith the Lord Yahweh, I have no pleasure in the death of the wicked; but that the wicked turn from his way and live: turn ye, turn ye from your evil ways; for why will ye die, O house of Israel?

12And thou, son of man, say unto the children of thy people, The righteousness of the righteous shall not deliver him in the day of his transgression; and as for the wickedness of the wicked, he shall not fall thereby in the day that he turneth from his wickedness; neither shall he that is righteous be able to live thereby in the day that he sinneth.

13When I say to the righteous, that he shall surely live; if he trust to his righteousness, and commit iniquity, none of his righteous deeds shall be remembered; but in his iniquity that he hath committed, therein shall he die.

14Again, when I say unto the wicked, Thou shalt surely die; if he turn from his sin, and do that which is lawful and right;

15if the wicked restore the pledge, give again that which he had taken by robbery, walk in the statutes of life, committing no iniquity; he shall surely live, he shall not die.

16None of his sins that he hath committed shall be remembered against him: he hath done that which is lawful and right; he shall surely live.

17Yet the children of thy people say, The way of the Lord is not equal: but as for them, their way is not equal.

18When the righteous turneth from his righteousness, and committeth iniquity, he shall even die therein.

19And when the wicked turneth from his wickedness, and doeth that which is lawful and right, he shall live thereby.

20Yet ye say, The way of the Lord is not equal. O house of Israel, I will judge you every one after his ways.

21And it came to pass in the twelfth year of our captivity, in the tenth month, in the fifth day of the month, that one that had escaped out of Jerusalem came unto me, saying, The city is smitten.

22Now the hand of Yahweh had been upon me in the evening, before he that was escaped came; and he had opened my mouth, until he came to me in the morning; and my mouth was opened, and I was no more dumb.

23And the word of Yahweh came unto me, saying,

24Son of man, they that inhabit those waste places in the land of Israel speak, saying, Abraham was one, and he inherited the land: but we are many; the land is given us for inheritance.

25Wherefore say unto them, Thus saith the Lord Yahweh: Ye eat with the blood, and lift up your eyes unto your idols, and shed blood: and shall ye possess the land?

26Ye stand upon your sword, ye work abomination, and ye defile every one his neighbor's wife: and shall ye possess the land?

27Thus shalt thou say unto them, Thus saith the Lord Yahweh: As I live, surely they that are in the waste places shall fall by the sword; and him that is in the open field will I give to the beasts to be devoured; and they that are in the strongholds and in the caves shall die of the pestilence.

28And I will make the land a desolation and an astonishment; and the pride of her power shall cease; and the mountains of Israel shall be desolate, so that none shall pass through.

29Then shall they know that I am Yahweh, when I have made the land a desolation and an astonishment, because of all their abominations which they have committed.

30And as for thee, son of man, the children of thy people talk of thee by the walls and in the doors of the houses, and speak one to another, every one to his brother, saying, Come, I pray you, and hear what is the word that cometh forth from Yahweh.

31And they come unto thee as the people cometh, and they sit before thee as my people, and they hear thy words, but do them not; for with their mouth they show much love, but their heart goeth after their gain.

32And, lo, thou art unto them as a very lovely song of one that hath a pleasant voice, and can play well on an instrument; for they hear thy words, but they do them not.

33And when this cometh to pass, (behold, it cometh,) then shall they know that a prophet hath been among them.

Chapter 34

1And the word of Yahweh came unto me, saying,

2Son of man, prophesy against the shepherds of Israel, prophesy, and say unto them, even to the shepherds, Thus saith the Lord Yahweh: Woe unto the shepherds of Israel that do feed themselves! should not the shepherds feed the sheep?

3Ye eat the fat, and ye clothe you with the wool, ye kill the fatlings; but ye feed not the sheep.

4The diseased have ye not strengthened, neither have ye healed that which was sick, neither have ye bound up that which was broken, neither have ye brought back that which was driven away, neither have ye sought that which was lost; but with force and with rigor have ye ruled over them.

5And they were scattered, because there was no shepherd; and they became food to all the beasts of the field, and were scattered.

6My sheep wandered through all the mountains, and upon every high hill: yea, my sheep were scattered upon all the face of the earth; and there was none that did search or seek after them.

7Therefore, ye shepherds, hear the word of Yahweh:

8As I live, saith the Lord Yahweh, surely forasmuch as my sheep became a prey, and my sheep became food to all the beasts of the field, because there was no shepherd, neither did my shepherds search for my sheep, but the shepherds fed themselves, and fed not my sheep;

9therefore, ye shepherds, hear the word of Yahweh:

10Thus saith the Lord Yahweh: Behold, I am against the shepherds; and I will require my sheep at their hand, and cause them to cease from feeding the sheep; neither shall the shepherds feed themselves any more; and I will deliver my sheep from their mouth, that they may not be food for them.

11For thus saith the Lord Yahweh: Behold, I myself, even I, will search for my sheep, and will seek them out.

12As a shepherd seeketh out his flock in the day that he is among his sheep that are scattered abroad, so will I seek out my sheep; and I will deliver them out of all places whither they have been scattered in the cloudy and dark day.

13And I will bring them out from the peoples, and gather them from the countries, and will bring them into their own land; and I will feed them upon the mountains of Israel, by the watercourses, and in all the inhabited places of the country.

14I will feed them with good pasture; and upon the mountains of the height of Israel shall their fold be: there shall they lie down in a good fold; and on fat pasture shall they feed upon the mountains of Israel.

15I myself will be the shepherd of my sheep, and I will cause them to lie down, saith the Lord Yahweh.

16I will seek that which was lost, and will bring back that which was driven away, and will bind up that which was broken, and will strengthen that which was sick: but the fat and the strong I will destroy; I will feed them in justice.

17And as for you, O my flock, thus saith the Lord Yahweh: Behold, I judge between sheep and sheep, the rams and the he-goats.

18Seemeth it a small thing unto you to have fed upon the good pasture, but ye must tread down with your feet the residue of your pasture? and to have drunk of the clear waters, but ye must foul the residue with your feet?

19And as for my sheep, they eat that which ye have trodden with your feet, and they drink that which ye have fouled with your feet.

20Therefore thus saith the Lord Yahweh unto them: Behold, I, even I, will judge between the fat sheep and the lean sheep.

21Because ye thrust with side and with shoulder, and push all the diseased with your horns, till ye have scattered them abroad;

22therefore will I save my flock, and they shall no more be a prey; and I will judge between sheep and sheep.

23And I will set up one shepherd over them, and he shall feed them, even my servant David; he shall feed them, and he shall be their shepherd.

24And I, Yahweh, will be their God, and my servant David prince among them; I, Yahweh, have spoken it.

25And I will make with them a covenant of peace, and will cause evil beasts to cease out of the land; and they shall dwell securely in the wilderness, and sleep in the woods.

26And I will make them and the places round about my hill a blessing; and I will cause the shower to come down in its season; there shall be showers of blessing.

27And the tree of the field shall yield its fruit, and the earth shall yield its increase, and they shall be secure in their land; and they shall know that I am Yahweh, when I have broken the bars of their yoke, and have delivered them out of the hand of those that made bondmen of them.

28And they shall no more be a prey to the nations, neither shall the beasts of the earth devour them; but they shall dwell securely, and none shall make them afraid.

29And I will raise up unto them a plantation for renown, and they shall be

Ezekiel

no more consumed with famine in the land, neither bear the shame of the nations any more.

30And they shall know that I, Yahweh, their God am with them, and that they, the house of Israel, are my people, saith the Lord Yahweh.

31And ye my sheep, the sheep of my pasture, are men, and I am your God, saith the Lord Yahweh.

Chapter 35

1Moreover the word of Yahweh came unto me, saying,

2Son of man, set thy face against mount Seir, and prophesy against it,

3and say unto it, Thus saith the Lord Yahweh: Behold, I am against thee, O mount Seir, and I will stretch out my hand against thee, and I will make thee a desolation and an astonishment.

4I will lay thy cities waste, and thou shalt be desolate; and thou shalt know that I am Yahweh.

5Because thou hast had a perpetual enmity, and hast given over the children of Israel to the power of the sword in the time of their calamity, in the time of the iniquity of the end;

6therefore, as I live, saith the Lord Yahweh, I will prepare thee unto blood, and blood shall pursue thee: since thou hast not hated blood, therefore blood shall pursue thee.

7Thus will I make mount Seir an astonishment and a desolation; and I will cut off from it him that passeth through and him that returneth.

8And I will fill its mountains with its slain: in thy hills and in thy valleys and in all thy watercourses shall they fall that are slain with the sword.

9I will make thee a perpetual desolation, and thy cities shall not be inhabited; and ye shall know that I am Yahweh.

10Because thou hast said, These two nations and these two countries shall be mine, and we will possess it; whereas Yahweh was there:

11therefore, as I live, saith the Lord Yahweh, I will do according to thine anger, and according to thine envy which thou hast showed out of thy hatred against them; and I will make myself known among them, when I shall judge thee.

12And thou shalt know that I, Yahweh, have heard all thy revilings which thou hast spoken against the mountains of Israel, saying, They are laid desolate, they are given us to devour.

13And ye have magnified yourselves against me with your mouth, and have multiplied your words against me: I have heard it.

14Thus saith the Lord Yahweh: When the whole earth rejoiceth, I will make thee desolate.

15As thou didst rejoice over the inheritance of the house of Israel, because it was desolate, so will I do unto thee: thou shalt be desolate, O mount Seir, and all Edom, even all of it; and they shall know that I am Yahweh.

Chapter 36

1And thou, son of man, prophesy unto the mountains of Israel, and say, Ye mountains of Israel, hear the word of Yahweh.

2Thus saith the Lord Yahweh: Because the enemy hath said against you, Aha! and, The ancient high places are ours in possession;

3therefore prophesy, and say, Thus saith the Lord Yahweh: Because, even because they have made you desolate, and swallowed you up on every side, that ye might be a possession unto the residue of the nations, and ye are taken up in the lips of talkers, and the evil report of the people;

4therefore, ye mountains of Israel, hear the word of the Lord Yahweh: Thus saith the Lord Yahweh to the mountains and to the hills, to the watercourses and to the valleys, to the desolate wastes and to the cities that are forsaken, which are become a prey and derision to the residue of the nations that are round about;

5therefore thus saith the Lord Yahweh: Surely in the fire of my jealousy have I spoken against the residue of the nations, and against all Edom, that have appointed my land unto themselves for a possession with the joy of all their heart, with despite of soul, to cast it out for a prey.

6Therefore prophesy concerning the land of Israel, and say unto the mountains and to the hills, to the watercourses and to the valleys, Thus saith the Lord Yahweh: Behold, I have spoken in my jealousy and in my wrath, because ye have borne the shame of the nations:

7therefore thus saith the Lord Yahweh: I have sworn, saying, Surely the nations that are round about you, they shall bear their shame.

8But ye, O mountains of Israel, ye shall shoot forth your branches, and yield your fruit to my people Israel; for they are at hand to come.

9For, behold, I am for you, and I will turn into you, and ye shall be tilled and sown;

10and I will multiply men upon you, all the house of Israel, even all of it; and the cities shall be inhabited, and the waste places shall be builded;

11and I will multiply upon you man and beast; and they shall increase and be fruitful; and I will cause you to be inhabited after your former estate, and will do better unto you than at your beginnings: and ye shall know that I am Yahweh.

12Yea, I will cause men to walk upon you, even my people Israel; and they shall possess thee, and thou shalt be their inheritance, and thou shalt no more henceforth bereave them of children.

13Thus saith the Lord Yahweh: Because they say unto you, Thou land art a devourer of men, and hast been a bereaver of thy nation;

14therefore thou shalt devour men no more, neither bereave thy nation any more, saith the Lord Yahweh.

15neither will I let thee hear any more the shame of the nations, neither shalt thou bear the reproach of the peoples any more, neither shalt thou cause thy nation to stumble any more, saith the Lord Yahweh.

16Moreover the word of Yahweh came unto me, saying,

17Son of man, when the house of Israel dwelt in their own land, they defiled it by their way and by their doings: their way before me was as the uncleanness of a woman in her impurity.

18Wherefore I poured out my wrath upon them for the blood which they had poured out upon the land, and because they had defiled it with their idols;

19and I scattered them among the nations, and they were dispersed through the countries: according to their way and according to their doings I judged them.

20And when they came unto the nations, whither they went, they profaned my holy name; in that men said of them, These are the people of Yahweh, and are gone forth out of his land.

21But I had regard for my holy name, which the house of Israel had profaned among the nations, whither they went.

22Therefore say unto the house of Israel, Thus saith the Lord Yahweh: I do not this for your sake, O house of Israel, but for my holy name, which ye have profaned among the nations, whither ye went.

23And I will sanctify my great name, which hath been profaned among the nations, which ye have profaned in the midst of them; and the nations shall know that I am Yahweh, saith the Lord Yahweh, when I shall be sanctified in you before their eyes.

24For I will take you from among the nations, and gather you out of all the countries, and will bring you into your own land.

25And I will sprinkle clean water upon you, and ye shall be clean: from all your filthiness, and from all your idols, will I cleanse you.

26A new heart also will I give you, and a new spirit will I put within you; and I will take away the stony heart out of your flesh, and I will give you a heart of flesh.

27And I will put my Spirit within you, and cause you to walk in my statutes, and ye shall keep mine ordinances, and do them.

28And ye shall dwell in the land that I gave to your fathers; and ye shall be my people, and I will be your God.

29And I will save you from all your uncleannesses: and I will call for the grain, and will multiply it, and lay no famine upon you.

30And I will multiply the fruit of the tree, and the increase of the field, that ye may receive no more the reproach of famine among the nations.

31Then shall ye remember your evil ways, and your doings that were not good; and ye shall loathe yourselves in your own sight for your iniquities and for your abominations.

32Nor for your sake do I this, saith the Lord Yahweh, be it known unto you: be ashamed and confounded for your ways, O house of Israel.

33Thus saith the Lord Yahweh: In the day that I cleanse you from all your iniquities, I will cause the cities to be inhabited, and the waste places shall be builded.

34And the land that was desolate shall be tilled, whereas it was a desolation in the sight of all that passed by.

35And they shall say, This land that was desolate is become like the garden of Eden; and the waste and desolate and ruined cities are fortified and inhabited.

36Then the nations that are left round about you shall know that I, Yahweh, have builded the ruined places, and planted that which was desolate: I, Yahweh, have spoken it, and I will do it.

37Thus saith the Lord Yahweh: For this, moreover, will I be inquired of by the house of Israel, to do it for them: I will increase them with men like a flock.

38As the flock for sacrifice, as the flock of Jerusalem in her appointed feasts, so shall the waste cities be filled with flocks of men; and they shall know that I am Yahweh.

Chapter 37

1The hand of Yahweh was upon me, and he brought me out in the Spirit of Yahweh, and set me down in the midst of the valley; and it was full of bones.

2And he caused me to pass by them round about: and, behold, there were very many in the open valley; and, lo, they were very dry.

3And he said unto me, Son of man, can these bones live? And I answered, O Lord Yahweh, thou knowest.

4Again he said unto me, Prophesy over these bones, and say unto them, O ye dry bones, hear the word of Yahweh.

5Thus saith the Lord Yahweh unto these bones: Behold, I will cause breath to enter into you, and ye shall live.

6And I will lay sinews upon you, and will bring up flesh upon you, and cover you with skin, and put breath in you, and ye shall live; and ye shall know that I am Yahweh.

7So I prophesied as I was commanded: and as I prophesied, there was a noise, and, behold, an earthquake; and the bones came together, bone to its bone.

8And I beheld, and, lo, there were sinews upon them, and flesh came up, and skin covered them above; but there was no breath in them.

9Then said he unto me, Prophesy unto the wind, prophesy, son of man, and say to the wind, Thus saith the Lord Yahweh: Come from the four winds, O breath, and breathe upon these slain, that they may live.

10So I prophesied as he commanded me, and the breath came into them, and they lived, and stood up upon their feet, an exceeding great army.

11Then he said unto me, Son of man, these bones are the whole house of Israel: behold, they say, Our bones are dried up, and our hope is lost; we are clean cut off.

12Therefore prophesy, and say unto them, Thus saith the Lord Yahweh: Behold, I will open your graves, and cause you to come up out of your graves, O my people; and I will bring you into the land of Israel.

13And ye shall know that I am Yahweh, when I have opened your graves, and caused you to come up out of your graves, O my people.

14And I will put my Spirit in you, and ye shall live, and I will place you in your own land: and ye shall know that I, Yahweh, have spoken it and performed it, saith Yahweh.

15The word of Yahweh came again unto me, saying,

16And thou, son of man, take thee one stick, and write upon it, For Judah, and for the children of Israel his companions: then take another stick, and write upon it, For Joseph, the stick of Ephraim, and for all the house of Israel his companions:

17and join them for thee one to another into one stick, that they may become one in thy hand.

18And when the children of thy people shall speak unto thee, saying, Wilt thou not show us what thou meanest by these?

19say unto them, Thus saith the Lord Yahweh: Behold, I will take the stick of Joseph, which is in the hand of Ephraim, and the tribes of Israel his companions; and I will put them with it, even with the stick of Judah, and make them one stick, and they shall be one in my hand.

20And the sticks whereon thou writest shall be in thy hand before their eyes.

21And say unto them, Thus saith the Lord Yahweh: Behold, I will take the children of Israel from among the nations, whither they are gone, and will gather them on every side, and bring them into their own land:

22And I will make them one nation in the land, upon the mountains of Israel; and one king shall be king to them all; and they shall be no more two nations, neither shall they be divided into two kingdoms any more at all;

23neither shall they defile themselves any more with their idols, nor with their detestable things, nor with any of their transgressions; but I will save them out of all their dwelling-places, wherein they have sinned, and will cleanse them: so shall they be my people, and I will be their God.

24And my servant David shall be king over them; and they all shall have one shepherd: they shall also walk in mine ordinances, and observe my statutes, and do them.

25And they shall dwell in the land that I have given unto Jacob my servant, wherein your fathers dwelt; and they shall dwell therein, they, and their children, and their children's children, for ever: and David my servant shall be their prince for ever.

26Moreover I will make a covenant of peace with them; it shall be an everlasting covenant with them; and I will place them, and multiply them, and will set my sanctuary in the midst of them for evermore.

27My tabernacle also shall be with them; and I will be their God, and they shall be my people.

28And the nations shall know that I am Yahweh that sanctifieth Israel, when my sanctuary shall be in the midst of them for evermore.

Chapter 38

1And the word of Yahweh came unto me, saying,

2Son of man, set thy face toward Gog, of the land of Magog, the prince of Rosh, Meshech, and Tubal, and prophesy against him,

3and say, Thus saith the Lord Yahweh: Behold, I am against thee, O Gog, prince of Rosh, Meshech, and Tubal:

4and I will turn thee about, and put hooks into thy jaws, and I will bring thee forth, and all thine army, horses and horsemen, all of them clothed in full armor, a great company with buckler and shield, all of them handling swords;

5Persia, Cush, and Put with them, all of them with shield and helmet;

6Gomer, and all his hordes; the house of Togarmah in the uttermost parts of the north, and all his hordes; even many peoples with thee.

7Be thou prepared, yea, prepare thyself, thou, and all thy companies that are assembled unto thee, and be thou a guard unto them.

8After many days thou shalt be visited: in the latter years thou shalt come into the land that is brought back from the sword, that is gathered out of many peoples, upon the mountains of Israel, which have been a continual waste; but it is brought forth out of the peoples, and they shall dwell securely, all of them.

9And thou shalt ascend, thou shalt come like a storm, thou shalt be like a cloud to cover the land, thou, and all thy hordes, and many peoples with thee.

10Thus saith the Lord Yahweh: It shall come to pass in that day, that things shall come into thy mind, and thou shalt devise an evil device:

11and thou shalt say, I will go up to the land of unwalled villages; I will go to them that are at rest, that dwell securely, all of them dwelling without walls, and having neither bars nor gates;

12to take the spoil and to take the prey; to turn thy hand against the waste places that are now inhabited, and against the people that are gathered out of the nations, that have gotten cattle and goods, that dwell in the middle of the earth.

13Sheba, and Dedan, and the merchants of Tarshish, with all the young lions thereof, shall say unto thee, Art thou come to take the spoil? hast thou assembled thy company to take the prey? to carry away silver and gold, to take away cattle and goods, to take great spoil?

14Therefore, son of man, prophesy, and say unto Gog, Thus saith the Lord Yahweh: In that day when my people Israel dwelleth securely, shalt thou not know it?

15And thou shalt come from thy place out of the uttermost parts of the north, thou, and many peoples with thee, all of them riding upon horses, a great company and a mighty army;

16and thou shalt come up against my people Israel, as a cloud to cover the land: it shall come to pass in the latter days, that I will bring thee against my land, that the nations may know me, when I shall be sanctified in thee, O Gog, before their eyes.

17Thus saith the Lord Yahweh: Art thou he of whom I spake in old time by my servants the prophets of Israel, that prophesied in those days for many years that I would bring thee against them?

18And it shall come to pass in that day, when Gog shall come against the land of Israel, saith the Lord Yahweh, that my wrath shall come up into my nostrils.

19For in my jealousy and in the fire of my wrath have I spoken, Surely in that day there shall be a great shaking in the land of Israel;

20so that the fishes of the sea, and the birds of the heavens, and the beasts of the field, and all creeping things that creep upon the earth, and all the men that are upon the face of the earth, shall shake at my presence, and the mountains shall be thrown down, and the steep places shall fall, and every wall shall fall to the ground.

21And I will call for a sword against him unto all my mountains, saith the Lord Yahweh: every man's sword shall be against his brother.

22And with pestilence and with blood will I enter into judgment with him; and I will rain upon him, and upon his hordes, and upon the many peoples that are with him, an overflowing shower, and great hailstones, fire, and brimstone.

23And I will magnify myself, and sanctify myself, and I will make myself known in the eyes of many nations; and they shall know that I am Yahweh.

Chapter 39

1And thou, son of man, prophesy against Gog, and say, Thus saith the Lord Yahweh: Behold, I am against thee, O Gog, prince of Rosh, Meshech, and Tubal:

2and I will turn thee about, and will lead thee on, and will cause thee to come up from the uttermost parts of the north; and I will bring thee upon the mountains of Israel;

3and I will smite thy bow out of thy left hand, and will cause thine arrows to fall out of thy right hand.

4Thou shalt fall upon the mountains of Israel, thou, and all thy hordes, and the peoples that are with thee: I will give thee unto the ravenous birds of every sort, and to the beasts of the field to be devoured.

5Thou shalt fall upon the open field; for I have spoken it, saith the Lord Yahweh.

6And I will send a fire on Magog, and on them that dwell securely in the isles; and they shall know that I am Yahweh.

7And my holy name will I make known in the midst of my people Israel; neither will I suffer my holy name to be profaned any more: and the nations shall know that I am Yahweh, the Holy One in Israel.

8Behold, it cometh, and it shall be done, saith the Lord Yahweh; this is the day whereof I have spoken.

9And they that dwell in the cities of Israel shall go forth, and shall make fires of the weapons and burn them, both the shields and the bucklers, the bows and the arrows, and the handstaves, and the spears, and they shall make fires of them seven years;

10so that they shall take no wood out of the field, neither cut down any out of the forests; for they shall make fires of the weapons; and they shall plunder those that plundered them, and rob those that robbed them, saith the Lord Yahweh.

11And it shall come to pass in that day, that I will give unto Gog a place for burial in Israel, the valley of them that pass through on the east of the sea; and it shall stop them that pass through: and there shall they bury Gog and all his multitude; and they shall call it The valley of Hamon-gog.

12And seven months shall the house of Israel be burying them, that they may cleanse the land.

13Yea, all the people of the land shall bury them; and it shall be to them a renown in the day that I shall be glorified, saith the Lord Yahweh.

14And they shall set apart men of continual employment, that shall pass through the land, and, with them that pass through, those that bury them that remain upon the face of the land, to cleanse it: after the end of seven months shall they search.

15And they that pass through the land shall pass through; and when any seeth a man's bone, then shall he set up a sign by it, till the buriers have buried it in the valley of Hamon-gog.

16And Hamonah shall also be the name of a city. Thus shall they cleanse the land.

17And thou, son of man, thus saith the Lord Yahweh: Speak unto the birds of every sort, and to every beast of the field, Assemble yourselves, and come; gather yourselves on every side to my sacrifice that I do sacrifice for you, even a great sacrifice upon the mountains of Israel, that ye may eat flesh and drink blood.

18Ye shall eat the flesh of the mighty, and drink the blood of the princes of the earth, of rams, of lambs, and of goats, of bullocks, all of them fatlings of Bashan.

19And ye shall eat fat till ye be full, and drink blood till ye be drunken, of my sacrifice which I have sacrificed for you.

20And ye shall be filled at my table with horses and chariots, with mighty men, and with all men of war, saith the Lord Yahweh.

21And I will set my glory among the nations; and all the nations shall see my judgment that I have executed, and my hand that I have laid upon them.

22So the house of Israel shall know that I am Yahweh their God, from that day and forward.

23And the nations shall know that the house of Israel went into captivity for their iniquity; because they trespassed against me, and I hid my face from them: so I gave them into the hand of their adversaries, and they fell all of them by the sword.

24According to their uncleanness and according to their transgressions did I unto them; and I hid my face from them.

25Therefore thus saith the Lord Yahweh: Now will I bring back the captivity of Jacob, and have mercy upon the whole house of Israel; and I will be jealous for my holy name.

26And they shall bear their shame, and all their trespasses whereby they have trespassed against me, when they shall dwell securely in their land, and none shall make them afraid;

27when I have brought them back from the peoples, and gathered them out of their enemies' lands, and am sanctified in them in the sight of many nations.

28And they shall know that I am Yahweh their God, in that I caused them to go into captivity among the nations, and have gathered them unto their own land; and I will leave none of them any more there;

29neither will I hide my face any more from them; for I have poured out my Spirit upon the house of Israel, saith the Lord Yahweh.

Ezekiel
Chapter 40

¹In the five and twentieth year of our captivity, in the beginning of the year, in the tenth day of the month, in the fourteenth year after that the city was smitten, in the selfsame day, the hand of Yahweh was upon me, and he brought me thither.

²In the visions of God brought he me into the land of Israel, and set me down upon a very high mountain, whereon was as it were the frame of a city on the south.

³And he brought me thither; and, behold, there was a man, whose appearance was like the appearance of brass, with a line of flax in his hand, and a measuring reed; and he stood in the gate.

⁴And the man said unto me, Son of man, behold with thine eyes, and hear with thine ears, and set thy heart upon all that I shall show thee; for, to the intent that I may show them unto thee, art thou brought hither: declare all that thou seest to the house of Israel.

⁵And, behold, a wall on the outside of the house round about, and in the man's hand a measuring reed six cubits long, of a cubit and a handbreadth each: so he measured the thickness of the building, one reed; and the height, one reed.

⁶Then came he unto the gate which looketh toward the east, and went up the steps thereof: and he measured the threshold of the gate, one reed broad; and the other threshold, one reed broad.

⁷And every lodge was one reed long, and one reed broad; and the space between the lodges was five cubits; and the threshold of the gate by the porch of the gate toward the house was one reed.

⁸He measured also the porch of the gate toward the house, one reed.

⁹Then measured he the porch of the gate, eight cubits; and the posts thereof, two cubits; and the porch of the gate was toward the house.

¹⁰And the lodges of the gate eastward were three on this side, and three on that side; they three were of one measure: and the posts had one measure on this side and on that side.

¹¹And he measured the breadth of the opening of the gate, ten cubits; and the length of the gate, thirteen cubits;

¹²and a border before the lodges, one cubit on this side, and a border, one cubit on that side; and the lodges, six cubits on this side, and six cubits on that side.

¹³And he measured the gate from the roof of the one lodge to the roof of the other, a breadth of five and twenty cubits; door against door.

¹⁴He made also posts, threescore cubits; and the court reached unto the posts, round about the gate.

¹⁵And from the forefront of the gate at the entrance unto the forefront of the inner porch of the gate were fifty cubits.

¹⁶And there were closed windows to the lodges, and to their posts within the gate round about, and likewise to the arches; and windows were round about inward; and upon each post were palm-trees.

¹⁷Then brought he me into the outer court; and, lo, there were chambers and a pavement, made for the court round about: thirty chambers were upon the pavement.

¹⁸And the pavement was by the side of the gates, answerable unto the length of the gates, even the lower pavement.

¹⁹Then he measured the breadth from the forefront of the lower gate unto the forefront of the inner court without, a hundred cubits, both on the east and on the north.

²⁰And the gate of the outer court whose prospect is toward the north, he measured the length thereof and the breadth thereof.

²¹And the lodges thereof were three on this side and three on that side; and the posts thereof and the arches thereof were after the measure of the first gate: the length thereof was fifty cubits, and the breadth five and twenty cubits.

²²And the windows thereof, and the arches thereof, and the palm-trees thereof, were after the measure of the gate whose prospect is toward the east; and they went up unto it by seven steps; and the arches thereof were before them.

²³And there was a gate to the inner court over against the other gate, both on the north and on the east; and he measured from gate to gate a hundred cubits.

²⁴And he led me toward the south; and, behold, a gate toward the south: and he measured the posts thereof and the arches thereof according to these measures.

²⁵And there were windows in it and in the arches thereof round about, like those windows: the length was fifty cubits, and the breadth five and twenty cubits.

²⁶And there were seven steps to go up to it, and the arches thereof were before them; and it had palm-trees, one on this side, and another on that side, upon the posts thereof.

²⁷And there was a gate to the inner court toward the south: and he measured from gate to gate toward the south a hundred cubits.

²⁸Then he brought me to the inner court by the south gate: and he measured the south gate according to these measures;

²⁹and the lodges thereof, and the posts thereof, and the arches thereof, according to these measures: and there were windows in it and in the arches thereof round about; it was fifty cubits long, and five and twenty cubits broad.

³⁰And there were arches round about, five and twenty cubits long, and five cubits broad.

³¹And the arches thereof were toward the outer court; and palm-trees were upon the posts thereof: and the ascent to it had eight steps.

³²And he brought me into the inner court toward the east: and he measured the gate according to these measures;

³³and the lodges thereof, and the posts thereof, and the arches thereof, according to these measures: and there were windows therein and in the arches thereof round about; it was fifty cubits long, and five and twenty cubits broad.

³⁴And the arches thereof were toward the outer court; and palm-trees were upon the posts thereof, on this side, and on that side: and the ascent to it had eight steps.

³⁵And he brought me to the north gate: and he measured it according to these measures;

³⁶the lodges thereof, the posts thereof, and the arches thereof: and there were windows therein round about; the length was fifty cubits, and the breadth five and twenty cubits.

³⁷And the posts thereof were toward the outer court; and palm-trees were upon the posts thereof, on this side, and on that side: and the ascent to it had eight steps.

³⁸And a chamber with the door thereof was by the posts at the gates; there they washed the burnt-offering.

³⁹And in the porch of the gate were two tables on this side, and two tables on that side, to slay thereon the burnt-offering and the sin-offering and the trespass-offering.

⁴⁰And on the one side without, as one goeth up to the entry of the gate toward the north, were two tables; and on the other side, which belonged to the porch of the gate, were two tables.

⁴¹Four tables were on this side, and four tables on that side, by the side of the gate; eight tables, whereupon they slew the sacrifices.

⁴²And there were four tables for the burnt-offering, of hewn stone, a cubit and a half long, and a cubit and a half broad, and one cubit high; whereupon they laid the instruments wherewith they slew the burnt-offering and the sacrifice.

⁴³And the hooks, a handbreadth long, were fastened within round about: and upon the tables was the flesh of the oblation.

⁴⁴And without the inner gate were chambers for the singers in the inner court, which was at the side of the north gate; and their prospect was toward the south; one at the side of the east gate having the prospect toward the north.

⁴⁵And he said unto me, This chamber, whose prospect is toward the south, is for the priests, the keepers of the charge of the house;

⁴⁶and the chamber whose prospect is toward the north is for the priests, the keepers of the charge of the altar: these are the sons of Zadok, who from among the sons of Levi come near to Yahweh to minister unto him.

⁴⁷And he measured the court, a hundred cubits long, and a hundred cubits broad, foursquare; and the altar was before the house.

⁴⁸Then he brought me to the porch of the house, and measured each post of the porch, five cubits on this side, and five cubits on that side: and the breadth of the gate was three cubits on this side, and three cubits on that side.

⁴⁹The length of the porch was twenty cubits, and the breadth eleven cubits; even by the steps whereby they went up to it: and there were pillars by the posts, one on this side, and another on that side.

Chapter 41

¹And he brought me to the temple, and measured the posts, six cubits broad on the one side, and six cubits broad on the other side, which was the breadth of the tabernacle.

²And the breadth of the entrance was ten cubits; and the sides of the entrance were five cubits on the one side, and five cubits on the other side: and he measured the length thereof, forty cubits, and the breadth, twenty cubits.

³Then went he inward, and measured each post of the entrance, two cubits; and the entrance, six cubits; and the breadth of the entrance, seven cubits.

⁴And he measured the length thereof, twenty cubits, and the breadth, twenty cubits, before the temple: and he said unto me, This is the most holy place.

⁵Then he measured the wall of the house, six cubits; and the breadth of every side-chamber, four cubits, round about the house on every side.

⁶And the side-chambers were in three stories, one over another, and thirty in order; and they entered into the wall which belonged to the house for the side-chambers round about, that they might have hold therein, and not have hold in the wall of the house.

⁷And the side-chambers were broader as they encompassed the house higher and higher; for the encompassing of the house went higher and higher round about the house: therefore the breadth of the house continued upward; and so one went up from the lowest chamber to the highest by the middle chamber.

⁸I saw also that the house had a raised basement round about: the foundations of the side-chambers were a full reed of six great cubits.

⁹The thickness of the wall, which was for the side-chambers, on the outside, was five cubits: and that which was left was the place of the side-chambers that belonged to the house.

¹⁰And between the chambers was a breadth of twenty cubits round about the house on every side.

¹¹And the doors of the side-chambers were toward the place that was left, one door toward the north, and another door toward the south: and the breadth of the place that was left was five cubits round about.

¹²And the building that was before the separate place at the side toward the west was seventy cubits broad; and the wall of the building was five cubits thick round about, and the length thereof ninety cubits.

¹³So he measured the house, a hundred cubits long; and the separate place, and the building, with the walls thereof, a hundred cubits long;

¹⁴also the breadth of the face of the house, and of the separate place toward the east, a hundred cubits.

¹⁵And he measured the length of the building before the separate place which was at the back thereof, and the galleries thereof on the one side and on the other side, a hundred cubits; and the inner temple, and the porches of the court;

¹⁶the thresholds, and the closed windows, and the galleries round about on their three stories, over against the threshold, ceiled with wood round about, and from the ground up to the windows, (now the windows were covered),

¹⁷to the space above the door, even unto the inner house, and without, and by all the wall round about within and without, by measure.

¹⁸And it was made with cherubim and palm-trees; and a palm-tree was between cherub and cherub, and every cherub had two faces;

¹⁹so that there was the face of a man toward the palm-tree on the one side, and the face of a young lion toward the palm-tree on the other side. thus was it made through all the house round about:

20from the ground unto above the door were cherubim and palm-trees made: thus was the wall of the temple.

21As for the temple, the door-posts were squared; and as for the face of the sanctuary, the appearance thereof was as the appearance of the temple.

22The altar was of wood, three cubits high, and the length thereof two cubits; and the corners thereof, and the length thereof, and the walls thereof, were of wood: and he said unto me, This is the table that is before Yahweh.

23And the temple and the sanctuary had two doors.

24And the doors had two leaves apiece, two turning leaves: two leaves for the one door, and two leaves for the other.

25And there were made on them, on the doors of the temple, cherubim and palm-trees, like as were made upon the walls; and there was a threshold of wood upon the face of the porch without.

26And there were closed windows and palm-trees on the one side and on the other side, on the sides of the porch: thus were the side-chambers of the house, and the thresholds.

Chapter 42

1Then he brought me forth into the outer court, the way toward the north: and he brought me into the chamber that was over against the separate place, and which was over against the building toward the north.

2Before the length of a hundred cubits was the north door, and the breadth was fifty cubits.

3Over against the twenty cubits which belonged to the inner court, and over against the pavement which belonged to the outer court, was gallery against gallery in the third story.

4And before the chambers was a walk of ten cubits' breadth inward, a way of one cubit; and their doors were toward the north.

5Now the upper chambers were shorter; for the galleries took away from these, more than from the lower and the middlemost, in the building.

6For they were in three stories, and they had not pillars as the pillars of the courts: therefore the uppermost was straitened more than the lowest and the middlemost from the ground.

7And the wall that was without by the side of the chambers, toward the outer court before the chambers, the length thereof was fifty cubits.

8For the length of the chambers that were in the outer court was fifty cubits: and, lo, before the temple were a hundred cubits.

9And from under these chambers was the entry on the east side, as one goeth into them from the outer court.

10In the thickness of the wall of the court toward the east, before the separate place, and before the building, there were chambers.

11And the way before them was like the appearance of the way of the chambers which were toward the north; according to their length so was their breadth: and all their egresses were both according to their fashions, and according to their doors.

12And according to the doors of the chambers that were toward the south was a door at the head of the way, even the way directly before the wall toward the east, as one entereth into them.

13Then said he unto me, The north chambers and the south chambers, which are before the separate place, they are the holy chambers, where the priests that are near unto Yahweh shall eat the most holy things: there shall they lay the most holy things, and the meal-offering, and the sin-offering, and the trespass-offering; for the place is holy.

14When the priests enter in, then shall they not go out of the holy place into the outer court, but there they shall lay their garments wherein they minister; for they are holy: and they shall put on other garments, and shall approach to that which pertaineth to the people.

15Now when he had made an end of measuring the inner house, he brought me forth by the way of the gate whose prospect is toward the east, and measured it round about.

16He measured on the east side with the measuring reed five hundred reeds, with the measuring reed round about.

17He measured on the north side five hundred reeds with the measuring reed round about.

18He measured on the south side five hundred reeds with the measuring reed.

19He turned about to the west side, and measured five hundred reeds with the measuring reed.

20He measured it on the four sides: it had a wall round about, the length five hundred, and the breadth five hundred, to make a separation between that which was holy and that which was common.

Chapter 43

1Afterward he brought me to the gate, even the gate that looketh toward the east.

2And, behold, the glory of the God of Israel came from the way of the east: and his voice was like the sound of many waters; and the earth shined with his glory.

3And it was according to the appearance of the vision which I saw, even according to the vision that I saw when I came to destroy the city; and the visions were like the vision that I saw by the river Chebar; and I fell upon my face.

4And the glory of Yahweh came into the house by the way of the gate whose prospect is toward the east.

5And the Spirit took me up, and brought me into the inner court; and, behold, the glory of Yahweh filled the house.

6And I heard one speaking unto me out of the house; and a man stood by me.

7And he said unto me, Son of man, this is the place of my throne, and the place of the soles of my feet, where I will dwell in the midst of the children of Israel for ever. And the house of Israel shall no more defile my holy name, neither they, nor their kings, by their whoredom, and by the dead bodies of their kings in their high places;

8in their setting of their threshold by my threshold, and their door-post beside my door-post, and there was but the wall between me and them; and they have defiled my holy name by their abominations which they have committed: wherefore I have consumed them in mine anger.

9Now let them put away their whoredom, and the dead bodies of their kings, far from me; and I will dwell in the midst of them for ever.

10Thou, son of man, show the house to the house of Israel, that they may be ashamed of their iniquities; and let them measure the pattern.

11And if they be ashamed of all that they have done, make known unto them the form of the house, and the fashion thereof, and the egresses thereof, and the entrances thereof, and all the forms thereof, and all the ordinances thereof, and all the forms thereof, and all the laws thereof; and write it in their sight; that they may keep the whole form thereof, and all the ordinances thereof, and do them.

12This is the law of the house: upon the top of the mountain the whole limit thereof round about shall be most holy. Behold, this is the law of the house.

13And these are the measures of the altar by cubits (the cubit is a cubit and a handbreadth): the bottom shall be a cubit, and the breadth a cubit, and the border thereof by the edge thereof round about a span; and this shall be the base of the altar.

14And from the bottom upon the ground to the lower ledge shall be two cubits, and the breadth one cubit; and from the lesser ledge to the greater ledge shall be four cubits, and the breadth a cubit.

15And the upper altar shall be four cubits; and from the altar hearth and upward there shall be four horns.

16And the altar hearth shall be twelve cubits long by twelve broad, square in the four sides thereof.

17And the ledge shall be fourteen cubits long by fourteen broad in the four sides thereof; and the border about it shall be half a cubit; and the bottom thereof shall be a cubit round about; and the steps thereof shall look toward the east.

18And he said unto me, Son of man, thus saith the Lord Yahweh: These are the ordinances of the altar in the day when they shall make it, to offer burnt-offerings thereon, and to sprinkle blood thereon.

19Thou shalt give to the priests the Levites that are of the seed of Zadok, who are near unto me, to minister unto me, saith the Lord Yahweh, a young bullock for a sin-offering.

20And thou shalt take of the blood thereof, and put it on the four horns of it, and on the four corners of the ledge, and upon the border round about: thus shalt thou cleanse it and make atonement for it.

21Thou shalt also take the bullock of the sin-offering, and it shall be burnt in the appointed place of the house, without the sanctuary.

22And on the second day thou shalt offer a he-goat without blemish for a sin-offering; and they shall cleanse the altar, as they did cleanse it with the bullock.

23When thou hast made an end of cleansing it, thou shalt offer a young bullock without blemish, and a ram out of the flock without blemish.

24And thou shalt bring them near before Yahweh, and the priests shall cast salt upon them, and they shall offer them up for a burnt-offering unto Yahweh.

25Seven days shalt thou prepare every day a goat for a sin-offering: they shall also prepare a young bullock, and a ram out of the flock, without blemish.

26Seven days shall they make atonement for the altar and purify it; so shall they consecrate it.

27And when they have accomplished the days, it shall be that upon the eighth day, and forward, the priests shall make your burnt-offerings upon the altar, and your peace-offerings; and I will accept you, saith the Lord Yahweh.

Chapter 44

1Then he brought me back by the way of the outer gate of the sanctuary, which looketh toward the east; and it was shut.

2And Yahweh said unto me, This gate shall be shut; it shall not be opened, neither shall any man enter in by it; for Yahweh, the God of Israel, hath entered in by it; therefore it shall be shut.

3As for the prince, he shall sit therein as prince to eat bread before Yahweh; he shall enter by the way of the porch of the gate, and shall go out by the way of the same.

4Then he brought me by the way of the north gate before the house; and I looked, and, behold, the glory of Yahweh filled the house of Yahweh: and I fell upon my face.

5And Yahweh said unto me, Son of man, mark well, and behold with thine eyes, and hear with thine ears all that I say unto thee concerning all the ordinances of the house of Yahweh, and all the laws thereof; and mark well the entrance of the house, with every egress of the sanctuary.

6And thou shalt say to the rebellious, even to the house of Israel, Thus saith the Lord Yahweh: O ye house of Israel, let it suffice you of all your abominations,

7in that ye have brought in foreigners, uncircumcised in heart and uncircumcised in flesh, to be in my sanctuary, to profane it, even my house, when ye offer my bread, the fat and the blood, and they have broken my covenant, to add unto all your abominations.

8And ye have not kept the charge of my holy things; but ye have set keepers of my charge in my sanctuary for yourselves.

9Thus saith the Lord Yahweh, No foreigner, uncircumcised in heart and uncircumcised in flesh, shall enter into my sanctuary, of any foreigners that are among the children of Israel.

10But the Levites that went far from me, when Israel went astray, that went astray from me after their idols, they shall bear their iniquity.

11Yet they shall be ministers in my sanctuary, having oversight at the gates

Ezekiel

of the house, and ministering in the house: they shall slay the burnt-offering and the sacrifice for the people, and they shall stand before them to minister unto them.

12Because they ministered unto them before their idols, and became a stumblingblock of iniquity unto the house of Israel; therefore have I lifted up my hand against them, saith the Lord Yahweh, and they shall bear their iniquity.

13And they shall not come near unto me, to execute the office of priest unto me, nor to come near to any of my holy things, unto the things that are most holy; but they shall bear their shame, and their abominations which they have committed.

14Yet will I make them keepers of the charge of the house, for all the service thereof, and for all that shall be done therein.

15But the priests the Levites, the sons of Zadok, that kept the charge of my sanctuary when the children of Israel went astray from me, they shall come near to me to minister unto me; and they shall stand before me to offer unto me the fat and the blood, saith the Lord Yahweh.

16they shall enter into my sanctuary, and they shall come near to my table, to minister unto me, and they shall keep my charge.

17And it shall be that, when they enter in at the gates of the inner court, they shall be clothed with linen garments; and no wool shall come upon them, while they minister in the gates of the inner court, and within.

18They shall have linen tires upon their heads, and shall have linen breeches upon their loins; they shall not gird themselves with anything that causeth sweat.

19And when they go forth into the outer court, even into the outer court to the people, they shall put off their garments wherein they minister, and lay them in the holy chambers; and they shall put on other garments, that they sanctify not the people with their garments.

20Neither shall they shave their heads, nor suffer their locks to grow long; they shall only cut off the hair of their heads.

21Neither shall any of the priests drink wine, when they enter into the inner court.

22Neither shall they take for their wives a widow, nor her that is put away; but they shall take virgins of the seed of the house of Israel, or a widow that is the widow of a priest.

23And they shall teach my people the difference between the holy and the common, and cause them to discern between the unclean and the clean.

24And in a controversy they shall stand to judge; according to mine ordinances shall they judge it: and they shall keep my laws and my statutes in all my appointed feasts; and they shall hallow my sabbaths.

25And they shall go in to no dead person to defile themselves; but for father, or for mother, or for son, or for daughter, for brother, or for sister that hath had no husband, they may defile themselves.

26And after he is cleansed, they shall reckon unto him seven days.

27And in the day that he goeth into the sanctuary, into the inner court, to minister in the sanctuary, he shall offer his sin-offering, saith the Lord Yahweh.

28And they shall have an inheritance: I am their inheritance; and ye shall give them no possession in Israel; I am their possession.

29They shall eat the meal-offering, and the sin-offering, and the trespass-offering; and every devoted thing in Israel shall be theirs.

30And the first of all the first-fruits of every thing, and every oblation of everything, of all your oblations, shall be for the priest: ye shall also give unto the priests the first of your dough, to cause a blessing to rest on thy house.

31The priests shall not eat of anything that dieth of itself, or is torn, whether it be bird or beast.

Chapter 45

1Moreover, when ye shall divide by lot the land for inheritance, ye shall offer an oblation unto Yahweh, a holy portion of the land; the length shall be the length of five and twenty thousand reeds, and the breadth shall be ten thousand: it shall be holy in all the border thereof round about.

2Of this there shall be for the holy place five hundred in length by five hundred in breadth, square round about; and fifty cubits for the suburbs thereof round about.

3And of this measure shalt thou measure a length of five and twenty thousand, and a breadth of ten thousand: and in it shall be the sanctuary, which is most holy.

4It is a holy portion of the land; it shall be for the priests, the ministers of the sanctuary, that come near to minister unto Yahweh; and it shall be a place for their houses, and a holy place for the sanctuary.

5And five and twenty thousand in length, and ten thousand in breadth, shall be unto the Levites, the ministers of the house, for a possession unto themselves, for twenty chambers.

6And ye shall appoint the possession of the city five thousand broad, and five and twenty thousand long, side by side with the oblation of the holy portion: it shall be for the whole house of Israel.

7And whatsoever is for the prince shall be on the one side and on the other side of the holy oblation and of the possession of the city, in front of the holy oblation and in front of the possession of the city, on the west side westward, and on the east side eastward; and in length answerable unto one of the portions, from the west border unto the east border.

8In the land it shall be to him for a possession in Israel: and my princes shall no more oppress my people; but they shall give the land to the house of Israel according to their tribes.

9Thus saith the Lord Yahweh: Let it suffice you, O princes of Israel: remove violence and spoil, and execute justice and righteousness; take away your exactions from my people, saith the Lord Yahweh.

10Ye shall have just balances, and a just ephah, and a just bath.

11The ephah and the bath shall be of one measure, that the bath may contain the tenth part of a homer, and the ephah the tenth part of a homer: the measure thereof shall be after the homer.

12And the shekel shall be twenty gerahs; twenty shekels, five and twenty shekels, fifteen shekels, shall be your maneh.

13This is the oblation that ye shall offer: the sixth part of an ephah from a homer of wheat; and ye shall give the sixth part of an ephah from a homer of barley;

14and the set portion of oil, of the bath of oil, the tenth part of a bath out of the cor, which is ten baths, even a homer; (for ten baths are a homer;)

15and one lamb of the flock, out of two hundred, from the well-watered pastures of Israel; -for a meal-offering, and for a burnt-offering, and for peace-offerings, to make atonement for them, saith the Lord Yahweh.

16All the people of the land shall give unto this oblation for the prince in Israel.

17And it shall be the prince's part to give the burnt-offerings, and the meal-offerings, and the drink-offerings, in the feasts, and on the new moons, and on the sabbaths, in all the appointed feasts of the house of Israel: he shall prepare the sin-offering, and the meal-offering, and the burnt-offering, and the peace-offerings, to make atonement for the house of Israel.

18Thus saith the Lord Yahweh: In the first month, in the first day of the month, thou shalt take a young bullock without blemish; and thou shalt cleanse the sanctuary.

19And the priest shall take of the blood of the sin-offering, and put it upon the door-posts of the house, and upon the four corners of the ledge of the altar, and upon the posts of the gate of the inner court.

20And so thou shalt do on the seventh day of the month for every one that erreth, and for him that is simple: so shall ye make atonement for the house.

21In the first month, in the fourteenth day of the month, ye shall have the passover, a feast of seven days; unleavened bread shall be eaten.

22And upon that day shall the prince prepare for himself and for all the people of the land a bullock for a sin-offering.

23And the seven days of the feast he shall prepare a burnt-offering to Yahweh, seven bullocks and seven rams without blemish daily the seven days; and a he-goat daily for a sin-offering.

24And he shall prepare a meal-offering, an ephah for a bullock, and an ephah for a ram, and a hin of oil to an ephah.

25In the seventh month, in the fifteenth day of the month, in the feast, shall he do the like the seven days; according to the sin-offering, according to the burnt-offering, and according to the meal-offering, and according to the oil.

Chapter 46

1Thus saith the Lord Yahweh: The gate of the inner court that looketh toward the east shall be shut the six working days; but on the sabbath day it shall be opened, and on the day of the new moon it shall be opened.

2And the prince shall enter by the way of the porch of the gate without, and shall stand by the post of the gate; and the priests shall prepare his burnt-offering and his peace-offerings, and he shall worship at the threshold of the gate: then he shall go forth; but the gate shall not be shut until the evening.

3And the people of the land shall worship at the door of that gate before Yahweh on the sabbaths and on the new moons.

4And the burnt-offering that the prince shall offer unto Yahweh shall be on the sabbath day six lambs without blemish and a ram without blemish;

5and the meal-offering shall be an ephah for the ram, and the meal-offering for the lambs as he is able to give, and a hin of oil to an ephah.

6And on the day of the new moon it shall be a young bullock without blemish, and six lambs, and a ram; they shall be without blemish:

7and he shall prepare a meal-offering, an ephah for the bullock, and an ephah for the ram, and for the lambs according as he is able, and a hin of oil to an ephah.

8And when the prince shall enter, he shall go in by the way of the porch of the gate, and he shall go forth by the way thereof.

9But when the people of the land shall come before Yahweh in the appointed feasts, he that entereth by the way of the north gate to worship shall go forth by the way of the south gate; and he that entereth by the way of the south gate shall go forth by the way of the north gate: he shall not return by the way of the gate whereby he came in, but shall go forth straight before him.

10And the prince, when they go in, shall go in in the midst of them; and when they go forth, they shall go forth together.

11And in the feasts and in the solemnities the meal-offering shall be an ephah for a bullock, and an ephah for a ram, and for the lambs as he is able to give, and a hin of oil to an ephah.

12And when the prince shall prepare a freewill-offering, a burnt-offering or peace-offerings as a freewill-offering unto Yahweh, one shall open for him the gate that looketh toward the east; and he shall prepare his burnt-offering and his peace-offerings, as he doth on the sabbath day: then he shall go forth; and after his going forth one shall shut the gate.

13And thou shalt prepare a lamb a year old without blemish for a burnt-offering unto Yahweh daily: morning by morning shalt thou prepare it.

14And thou shalt prepare a meal-offering with it morning by morning, the sixth part of an ephah, and the third part of a hin of oil, to moisten the fine flour; a meal-offering unto Yahweh continually by a perpetual ordinance.

15Thus shall they prepare the lamb, and the meal-offering, and the oil, morning by morning, for a continual burnt-offering.

16Thus saith the Lord Yahweh: If the prince give a gift unto any of his sons, it is his inheritance, it shall belong to his sons; it is their possession by inheritance.

17But if he give of his inheritance a gift to one of his servants, it shall be his to the year of liberty; then it shall return to the prince; but as for his inheritance, it shall be for his sons.

18Moreover the prince shall not take of the people's inheritance, to thrust them out of their possession; he shall give inheritance to his sons out of his own possession, that my people be not scattered every man from his possession.

¹⁹Then he brought me through the entry, which was at the side of the gate, into the holy chambers for the priests, which looked toward the north: and, behold, there was a place on the hinder part westward.

²⁰And he said unto me, This is the place where the priests shall boil the trespass-offering and the sin-offering, and where they shall bake the meal-offering; that they bring them not forth into the outer court, to sanctify the people.

²¹Then he brought me forth into the outer court, and caused me to pass by the four corners of the court; and, behold, in every corner of the court there was a court.

²²In the four corners of the court there were courts inclosed, forty cubits long and thirty broad: these four in the corners were of one measure.

²³And there was a wall round about in them, round about the four, and boiling-places were made under the walls round about.

²⁴Then said he unto me, These are the boiling-houses, where the ministers of the house shall boil the sacrifice of the people.

Chapter 47

¹And he brought me back unto the door of the house; and, behold, waters issued out from under the threshold of the house eastward; (for the forefront of the house was toward the east;) and the waters came down from under, from the right side of the house, on the south of the altar.

²Then he brought me out by the way of the gate northward, and led me round by the way without unto the outer gate, by the way of the gate that looketh toward the east; and, behold, there ran out waters on the right side.

³When the man went forth eastward with the line in his hand, he measured a thousand cubits, and he caused me to pass through the waters, waters that were to the ankles.

⁴Again he measured a thousand, and caused me to pass through the waters, waters that were to the knees. Again he measured a thousand, and caused me to pass through the waters, waters that were to the loins.

⁵Afterward he measured a thousand; and it was a river that I could not pass through; for the waters were risen, waters to swim in, a river that could not be passed through.

⁶And he said unto me, Son of man, hast thou seen this? Then he brought me, and caused me to return to the bank of the river.

⁷Now when I had returned, behold, upon the bank of the river were very many trees on the one side and on the other.

⁸Then said he unto me, These waters issue forth toward the eastern region, and shall go down into the Arabah; and they shall go toward the sea; into the sea shall the waters go which were made to issue forth; and the waters shall be healed.

⁹And it shall come to pass, that every living creature which swarmeth, in every place whither the rivers come, shall live; and there shall be a very great multitude of fish; for these waters are come thither, and the waters of the sea shall be healed, and everything shall live whithersoever the river cometh.

¹⁰And it shall come to pass, that fishers shall stand by it: from En-gedi even unto En-eglaim shall be a place for the spreading of nets; their fish shall be after their kinds, as the fish of the great sea, exceeding many.

¹¹But the miry places thereof, and the marshes thereof, shall not be healed; they shall be given up to salt.

¹²And by the river upon the bank thereof, on this side and on that side, shall grow every tree for food, whose leaf shall not whither, neither shall the fruit thereof fail: it shall bring forth new fruit every month, because the waters thereof issue out of the sanctuary; and the fruit thereof shall be for food, and the leaf thereof for healing.

¹³Thus saith the Lord Yahweh: This shall be the border, whereby ye shall divide the land for inheritance according to the twelve tribes of Israel: Joseph shall have two portions.

¹⁴And ye shall inherit it, one as well as another; for I sware to give it unto your fathers: and this land shall fall unto you for inheritance.

¹⁵And this shall be the border of the land: On the north side, from the great sea, by the way of Hethlon, unto the entrance of Zedad;

¹⁶Hamath, Berothah, Sibraim, which is between the border of Damascus and the border of Hamath; Hazer-hatticon, which is by the border of Hauran.

¹⁷And the border from the sea, shall be Hazar-enon at the border of Damascus; and on the north northward is the border of Hamath. This is the north side.

¹⁸And the east side, between Hauran and Damascus and Gilead, and the land of Israel, shall be the Jordan; from the north border unto the east sea shall ye measure. This is the east side.

¹⁹And the south side southward shall be from Tamar as far as the waters of Meriboth-kadesh, to the brook of Egypt, unto the great sea. This is the south side southward.

²⁰And the west side shall be the great sea, from the south border as far as over against the entrance of Hamath. This is the west side.

²¹So shall ye divide this land unto you according to the tribes of Israel.

²²And it shall come to pass, that ye shall divide it by lot for an inheritance unto you and to the strangers that sojourn among you, who shall beget children among you; and they shall be unto you as the home-born among the children of Israel; they shall have inheritance with you among the tribes of Israel.

²³And it shall come to pass, that in what tribe the stranger sojourneth, there shall ye give him his inheritance, saith the Lord Yahweh.

Chapter 48

¹Now these are the names of the tribes: From the north end, beside the way of Hethlon to the entrance of Hamath, Hazar-enan at the border of Damascus, northward beside Hamath, (and they shall have their sides east and west,) Dan, one portion.

²And by the border of Dan, from the east side unto the west side, Asher, one portion.

³And by the border of Asher, from the east side even unto the west side, Naphtali, one portion.

⁴And by the border of Naphtali, from the east side unto the west side, Manasseh, one portion.

⁵And by the border of Manasseh, from the east side unto the west side, Ephraim, one portion.

⁶And by the border of Ephraim, from the east side even unto the west side, Reuben, one portion.

⁷And by the border of Reuben, from the east side unto the west side, Judah, one portion.

⁸And by the border of Judah, from the east side unto the west side, shall be the oblation which ye shall offer, five and twenty thousand reeds in breadth, and in length as one of the portions, from the east side unto the west side: and the sanctuary shall be in the midst of it.

⁹The oblation that ye shall offer unto Yahweh shall be five and twenty thousand reeds in length, and ten thousand in breadth.

¹⁰And for these, even for the priests, shall be the holy oblation: toward the north five and twenty thousand in length, and toward the west ten thousand in breadth, and toward the east ten thousand in breadth, and toward the south five and twenty thousand in length: and the sanctuary of Yahweh shall be in the midst thereof.

¹¹It shall be for the priests that are sanctified of the sons of Zadok, that have kept my charge, that went not astray when the children of Israel went astray, as the Levites went astray.

¹²And it shall be unto them an oblation from the oblation of the land, a thing most holy, by the border of the Levites.

¹³And answerable unto the border of the priests, the Levites shall have five and twenty thousand in length, and ten thousand in breadth: all the length shall be five and twenty thousand, and the breadth ten thousand.

¹⁴And they shall sell none of it, nor exchange it, nor shall the first-fruits of the land be alienated; for it is holy unto Yahweh.

¹⁵And the five thousand that are left in the breadth, in front of the five and twenty thousand, shall be for common use, for the city, for dwelling and for suburbs; and the city shall be in the midst thereof.

¹⁶And these shall be the measures thereof: the north side four thousand and five hundred, and the south side four thousand and five hundred, and on the east side four thousand and five hundred, and the west side four thousand and five hundred.

¹⁷And the city shall have suburbs: toward the north two hundred and fifty, and toward the south two hundred and fifty, and toward the east two hundred and fifty, and toward the west two hundred and fifty.

¹⁸And the residue in the length, answerable unto the holy oblation, shall be ten thousand eastward, and ten thousand westward; and it shall be answerable unto the holy oblation; and the increase thereof shall be for food unto them that labor in the city.

¹⁹And they that labor in the city, out of all the tribes of Israel, shall till it.

²⁰All the oblation shall be five and twenty thousand by five and twenty thousand: ye shall offer the holy oblation four-square, with the possession of the city.

²¹And the residue shall be for the prince, on the one side and on the other of the holy oblation and of the possession of the city; in front of the five and twenty thousand of the oblation toward the east border, and westward in front of the five and twenty thousand toward the west border, answerable unto the portions, it shall be for the prince: and the holy oblation and the sanctuary of the house shall be in the midst thereof.

²²Moreover from the possession of the Levites, and from the possession of the city, being in the midst of that which is the prince's, between the border of Judah and the border of Benjamin, it shall be for the prince.

²³And as for the rest of the tribes: from the east side unto the west side, Benjamin, one portion.

²⁴And by the border of Benjamin, from the east side unto the west side, Simeon, one portion.

²⁵And by the border of Simeon, from the east side unto the west side, Issachar, one portion.

²⁶And by the border of Issachar, from the east side unto the west side, Zebulun, one portion.

²⁷And by the border of Zebulun, from the east side unto the west side, Gad, one portion.

²⁸And by the border of Gad, at the south side southward, the border shall be even from Tamar unto the waters of Meribath-kadesh, to the brook of Egypt, unto the great sea.

²⁹This is the land which ye shall divide by lot unto the tribes of Israel for inheritance, and these are their several portions, saith the Lord Yahweh.

³⁰And these are the egresses of the city: On the north side four thousand and five hundred reeds by measure;

³¹and the gates of the city shall be after the names of the tribes of Israel, three gates northward: the gate of Reuben, one; the gate of Judah, one; the gate of Levi, one.

³²And at the east side four thousand and five hundred reeds, and three gates: even the gate of Joseph, one; the gate of Benjamin, one; the gate of Dan, one.

³³And at the south side four thousand and five hundred reeds by measure, and three gates: the gate of Simeon, one; the gate of Issachar, one; the gate of Zebulun, one.

³⁴At the west side four thousand and five hundred reeds, with their three gates: the gate of Gad, one; the gate of Asher, one; the gate of Naphtali, one.

³⁵It shall be eighteen thousand reeds round about: and the name of the city from that day shall be, Yahweh is there.

The Book of Daniel

Chapter 1

1 In the third year of the reign of Jehoiakim king of Judah came Nebuchadnezzar king of Babylon unto Jerusalem, and besieged it.

2 And the Lord gave Jehoiakim king of Judah into his hand, with part of the vessels of the house of God; and he carried them into the land of Shinar to the house of his god: and he brought the vessels into the treasure-house of his god.

3 And the king spake unto Ashpenaz the master of his eunuchs, that he should bring in certain of the children of Israel, even of the seed royal and of the nobles;

4 youths in whom was no blemish, but well-favored, and skilful in all wisdom, and endued with knowledge, and understanding science, and such as had ability to stand in the king's palace; and that he should teach them the learning and the tongue of the Chaldeans.

5 And the king appointed for them a daily portion of the king's dainties, and of the wine which he drank, and that they should be nourished three years; that at the end thereof they should stand before the king.

6 Now among these were, of the children of Judah, Daniel, Hananiah, Mishael, and Azariah.

7 And the prince of the eunuchs gave names unto them: unto Daniel he gave the name of Belteshazzar; and to Hananiah, of Shadrach; and to Mishael, of Meshach; and to Azariah, of Abed-nego.

8 But Daniel purposed in his heart that he would not defile himself with the king's dainties, nor with the wine which he drank: therefore he requested of the prince of the eunuchs that he might not defile himself.

9 Now God made Daniel to find kindness and compassion in the sight of the prince of the eunuchs.

10 And the prince of the eunuchs said unto Daniel, I fear my lord the king, who hath appointed your food and your drink: for why should he see your faces worse looking than the youths that are of your own age? so would ye endanger my head with the king.

11 Then said Daniel to the steward whom the prince of the eunuchs had appointed over Daniel, Hananiah, Mishael, and Azariah:

12 Prove thy servants, I beseech thee, ten days; and let them give us pulse to eat, and water to drink.

13 Then let our countenances be looked upon before thee, and the countenance of the youths that eat of the king's dainties; and as thou seest, deal with thy servants.

14 So he hearkened unto them in this matter, and proved them ten days.

15 And at the end of ten days their countenances appeared fairer, and they were fatter in flesh, than all the youths that did eat of the king's dainties.

16 So the steward took away their dainties, and the wine that they should drink, and gave them pulse.

17 Now as for these four youths, God gave them knowledge and skill in all learning and wisdom: and Daniel had understanding in all visions and dreams.

18 And at the end of the days which the king had appointed for bringing them in, the prince of the eunuchs brought them in before Nebuchadnezzar.

19 And the king communed with them; and among them all was found none like Daniel, Hananiah, Mishael, and Azariah: therefore stood they before the king.

20 And in every matter of wisdom and understanding, concerning which the king inquired of them, he found them ten times better than all the magicians and enchanters that were in all his realm.

21 And Daniel continued even unto the first year of king Cyrus.

Chapter 2

1 And in the second year of the reign of Nebuchadnezzar, Nebuchadnezzar dreamed dreams; and his spirit was troubled, and his sleep went from him.

2 Then the king commanded to call the magicians, and the enchanters, and the sorcerers, and the Chaldeans, to tell the king his dreams. So they came in and stood before the king.

3 And the king said unto them, I have dreamed a dream, and my spirit is troubled to know the dream.

4 Then spake the Chaldeans to the king in the Syrian language, O king, live for ever: tell thy servants the dream, and we will show the interpretation.

5 The king answered and said to the Chaldeans, The thing is gone from me: if ye make not known unto me the dream and the interpretation thereof, ye shall be cut in pieces, and your houses shall be made a dunghill.

6 But if ye show the dream and the interpretation thereof, ye shall receive of me gifts and rewards and great honor: therefore show me the dream and the interpretation thereof.

7 They answered the second time and said, Let the king tell his servants the dream, and we will show the interpretation.

8 The king answered and said, I know of a certainty that ye would gain time, because ye see the thing is gone from me.

9 But if ye make not known unto me the dream, there is but one law for you; for ye have prepared lying and corrupt words to speak before me, till the time be changed: therefore tell me the dream, and I shall know that ye can show me the interpretation thereof.

10 The Chaldeans answered before the king, and said, There is not a man upon the earth that can show the king's matter, forasmuch as no king, lord, or ruler, hath asked such a thing of any magician, or enchanter, or Chaldean.

11 And it is a rare thing that the king requireth, and there is no other that can show it before the king, except the gods, whose dwelling is not with flesh.

12 For this cause the king was angry and very furious, and commanded to destroy all the wise men of Babylon.

13 So the decree went forth, and the wise men were to be slain; and they sought Daniel and his companions to be slain.

14 Then Daniel returned answer with counsel and prudence to Arioch the captain of the king's guard, who was gone forth to slay the wise men of Babylon;

15 he answered and said to Arioch the king's captain, Wherefore is the decree so urgent from the king? Then Arioch made the thing known to Daniel.

16 And Daniel went in, and desired of the king that he would appoint him a time, and he would show the king the interpretation.

17 Then Daniel went to his house, and made the thing known to Hananiah, Mishael, and Azariah, his companions:

18 that they would desire mercies of the God of heaven concerning this secret; that Daniel and his companions should not perish with the rest of the wise men of Babylon.

19 Then was the secret revealed unto Daniel in a vision of the night. Then Daniel blessed the God of heaven.

20 Daniel answered and said, Blessed be the name of God for ever and ever; for wisdom and might are his.

21 And he changeth the times and the seasons; he removeth kings, and setteth up kings; he giveth wisdom unto the wise, and knowledge to them that have understanding;

22 he revealeth the deep and secret things; he knoweth what is in the darkness, and the light dwelleth with him.

23 I thank thee, and praise thee, O thou God of my fathers, who hast given me wisdom and might, and hast now made known unto me what we desired of thee; for thou hast made known unto us the king's matter.

24 Therefore Daniel went in unto Arioch, whom the king had appointed to destroy the wise men of Babylon; he went and said thus unto him: Destroy not the wise men of Babylon; bring me in before the king, and I will show unto the king the interpretation.

25 Then Arioch brought in Daniel before the king in haste, and said thus unto him, I have found a man of the children of the captivity of Judah, that will make known unto the king the interpretation.

26 The king answered and said to Daniel, whose name was Belteshazzar, Art thou able to make known unto me the dream which I have seen, and the interpretation thereof?

27 Daniel answered before the king, and said, The secret which the king hath demanded can neither wise men, enchanters, magicians, nor soothsayers, show unto the king;

28 but there is a God in heaven that revealeth secrets, and he hath made known to the king Nebuchadnezzar what shall be in the latter days. Thy dream, and the visions of thy head upon thy bed, are these:

29 as for thee, O king, thy thoughts came into thy mind upon thy bed, what should come to pass hereafter; and he that revealeth secrets hath made known to thee what shall come to pass.

30 But as for me, this secret is not revealed to me for any wisdom that I have more than any living, but to the intent that the interpretation may be made known to the king, and that thou mayest know the thoughts of thy heart.

31 Thou, O king, sawest, and, behold, a great image. This image, which was mighty, and whose brightness was excellent, stood before thee; and the aspect thereof was terrible.

32 As for this image, its head was of fine gold, its breast and its arms of silver, its belly and its thighs of brass,

33 its legs of iron, its feet part of iron, and part of clay.

34 Thou sawest till that a stone was cut out without hands, which smote the image upon its feet that were of iron and clay, and brake them in pieces.

35 Then was the iron, the clay, the brass, the silver, and the gold, broken in pieces together, and became like the chaff of the summer threshing-floors; and the wind carried them away, so that no place was found for them: and the stone that smote the image became a great mountain, and filled the whole earth.

36 This is the dream; and we will tell the interpretation thereof before the king.

37 Thou, O king, art king of kings, unto whom the God of heaven hath given the kingdom, the power, and the strength, and the glory;

38 and wheresoever the children of men dwell, the beasts of the field and the birds of the heavens hath he given into thy hand, and hath made thee to rule over them all: thou art the head of gold.

39 And after thee shall arise another kingdom inferior to thee; and another third kingdom of brass, which shall bear rule over all the earth.

40 And the fourth kingdom shall be strong as iron, forasmuch as iron breaketh in pieces and subdueth all things; and as iron that crusheth all these, shall it break in pieces and crush.

41 And whereas thou sawest the feet and toes, part of potters' clay, and part of iron, it shall be a divided kingdom; but there shall be in it of the strength of the iron, forasmuch as thou sawest the iron mixed with miry clay.

42 And as the toes of the feet were part of iron, and part of clay, so the kingdom shall be partly strong, and partly broken.

43 And whereas thou sawest the iron mixed with miry clay, they shall mingle themselves with the seed of men; but they shall not cleave one to another, even as iron doth not mingle with clay.

44 And in the days of those kings shall the God of heaven set up a kingdom which shall never be destroyed, nor shall the sovereignty thereof be left to another people; but it shall break in pieces and consume all these kingdoms, and it shall stand for ever.

45 Forasmuch as thou sawest that a stone was cut out of the mountain without hands, and that it brake in pieces the iron, the brass, the clay, the silver, and the gold; the great God hath made known to the king what shall come to pass hereafter: and the dream is certain, and the interpretation thereof sure.

46Then the king Nebuchadnezzar fell upon his face, and worshipped Daniel, and commanded that they should offer an oblation and sweet odors unto him.

47The king answered unto Daniel, and said, Of a truth your God is the God of gods, and the Lord of kings, and a revealer of secrets, seeing thou hast been able to reveal this secret.

48Then the king made Daniel great, and gave him many great gifts, and made him to rule over the whole province of Babylon, and to be chief governor over all the wise men of Babylon.

49And Daniel requested of the king, and he appointed Shadrach, Meshach, and Abed-nego, over the affairs of the province of Babylon: but Daniel was in the gate of the king.

Chapter 3

1Nebuchadnezzar the king made an image of gold, whose height was threescore cubits, and the breadth thereof six cubits: he set it up in the plain of Dura, in the province of Babylon.

2Then Nebuchadnezzar the king sent to gather together the satraps, the deputies, and the governors, the judges, the treasurers, the counsellors, the sheriffs, and all the rulers of the provinces, to come to the dedication of the image which Nebuchadnezzar the king had set up.

3Then the satraps, the deputies, and the governors, the judges, the treasurers, the counsellors, the sheriffs, and all the rulers of the provinces, were gathered together unto the dedication of the image that Nebuchadnezzar the king had set up; and they stood before the image that Nebuchadnezzar had set up.

4Then the herald cried aloud, To you it is commanded, O peoples, nations, and languages,

5that at what time ye hear the sound of the cornet, flute, harp, sackbut, psaltery, dulcimer, and all kinds of music, ye fall down and worship the golden image that Nebuchadnezzar the king hath set up;

6and whoso falleth not down and worshippeth shall the same hour be cast into the midst of a burning fiery furnace.

7Therefore at that time, when all the peoples heard the sound of the cornet, flute, harp, sackbut, psaltery, and all kinds of music, all the peoples, the nations, and the languages, fell down and worshipped the golden image that Nebuchadnezzar the king had set up.

8Wherefore at that time certain Chaldeans came near, and brought accusation against the Jews.

9They answered and said to Nebuchadnezzar the king, O king, live for ever.

10Thou, O king, hast made a decree, that every man that shall hear the sound of the cornet, flute, harp, sackbut, psaltery, and dulcimer, and all kinds of music, shall fall down and worship the golden image;

11and whoso falleth not down and worshippeth, shall be cast into the midst of a burning fiery furnace.

12There are certain Jews whom thou hast appointed over the affairs of the province of Babylon: Shadrach, Meshach, and Abed-nego; these men, O king, have not regarded thee: they serve not thy gods, nor worship the golden image which thou hast set up.

13Then Nebuchadnezzar in his rage and fury commanded to bring Shadrach, Meshach, and Abed-nego. Then they brought these men before the king.

14Nebuchadnezzar answered and said unto them, Is it of purpose, O Shadrach, Meshach, and Abed-nego, that ye serve not my god, nor worship the golden image which I have set up?

15Now if ye be ready that at what time ye hear the sound of the cornet, flute, harp, sackbut, psaltery, and dulcimer, and all kinds of music, ye fall down and worship the image which I have made, well: but if ye worship not, ye shall be cast the same hour into the midst of a burning fiery furnace; and who is that god that shall deliver you out of my hands?

16Shadrach, Meshach, and Abed-nego answered and said to the king, O Nebuchadnezzar, we have no need to answer thee in this matter.

17If it be so, our God whom we serve is able to deliver us from the burning fiery furnace; and he will deliver us out of thy hand, O king.

18But if not, be it known unto thee, O king, that we will not serve thy gods, nor worship the golden image which thou hast set up.

19Then was Nebuchadnezzar full of fury, and the form of his visage was changed against Shadrach, Meshach, and Abed-nego: therefore he spake, and commanded that they should heat the furnace seven times more than it was wont to be heated.

20And he commanded certain mighty men that were in his army to bind Shadrach, Meshach, and Abed-nego, and to cast them into the burning fiery furnace.

21Then these men were bound in their hosen, their tunics, and their mantles, and their other garments, and were cast into the midst of the burning fiery furnace.

22Therefore because the king's commandment was urgent, and the furnace exceeding hot, the flame of the fire slew those men that took up Shadrach, Meshach, and Abed-nego.

23And these three men, Shadrach, Meshach, and Abed-nego, fell down bound into the midst of the burning fiery furnace.

24Then Nebuchadnezzar the king was astonished, and rose up in haste: he spake and said unto his counsellors, Did not we cast three men bound into the midst of the fire? They answered and said unto the king, True, O king.

25He answered and said, Lo, I see four men loose, walking in the midst of the fire, and they have no hurt; and the aspect of the fourth is like a son of the gods.

26Then Nebuchadnezzar came near to the mouth of the burning fiery furnace: he spake and said, Shadrach, Meshach, and Abed-nego, ye servants of the Most High God, come forth, and come hither. Then Shadrach, Meshach, and Abed-nego came forth out of the midst of the fire.

27And the satraps, the deputies, and the governors, and the king's counsellors, being gathered together, saw these men, that the fire had no power upon their bodies, nor was the hair of their head singed, neither were their hosen changed, nor had the smell of fire passed on them.

28Nebuchadnezzar spake and said, Blessed be the God of Shadrach, Meshach, and Abed-nego, who hath sent his angel, and delivered his servants that trusted in him, and have changed the king's word, and have yielded their bodies, that they might not serve nor worship any god, except their own God.

29Therefore I make a decree, that every people, nation, and language, which speak anything amiss against the God of Shadrach, Meshach, and Abed-nego, shall be cut in pieces, and their houses shall be made a dunghill; because there is no other god that is able to deliver after this sort.

30Then the king promoted Shadrach, Meshach, and Abed-nego in the province of Babylon.

Chapter 4

1Nebuchadnezzar the king, unto all the peoples, nations, and languages, that dwell in all the earth: Peace be multiplied unto you.

2It hath seemed good unto me to show the signs and wonders that the Most High God hath wrought toward me.

3How great are his signs! and how mighty are his wonders! his kingdom is an everlasting kingdom, and his dominion is from generation to generation.

4I, Nebuchadnezzar, was at rest in my house, and flourishing in my palace.

5I saw a dream which made me afraid; and the thoughts upon my bed and the visions of my head troubled me.

6Therefore made I a decree to bring in all the wise men of Babylon before me, that they might make known unto me the interpretation of the dream.

7Then came in the magicians, the enchanters, the Chaldeans, and the soothsayers; and I told the dream before them; but they did not make known unto me the interpretation thereof.

8But at the last Daniel came in before me, whose name was Belteshazzar, according to the name of my god, and in whom is the spirit of the holy gods: and I told the dream before him, saying,

9O Belteshazzar, master of the magicians, because I know that the spirit of the holy gods is in thee, and no secret troubleth thee, tell me the visions of my dream that I have seen, and the interpretation thereof.

10Thus were the visions of my head upon my bed: I saw, and, behold, a tree in the midst of the earth; and the height thereof was great.

11The tree grew, and was strong, and the height thereof reached unto heaven, and the sight thereof to the end of all the earth.

12The leaves thereof were fair, and the fruit thereof much, and in it was food for all: the beasts of the field had shadow under it, and the birds of the heavens dwelt in the branches thereof, and all flesh was fed from it.

13I saw in the visions of my head upon my bed, and, behold, a watcher and a holy one came down from heaven.

14He cried aloud, and said thus, Hew down the tree, and cut off its branches, shake off its leaves, and scatter its fruit: let the beasts get away from under it, and the fowls from its branches.

15Nevertheless leave the stump of its roots in the earth, even with a band of iron and brass, in the tender grass of the field; and let it be wet with the dew of heaven: and let his portion be with the beasts in the grass of the earth:

16let his heart be changed from man's, and let a beast's heart be given unto him; and let seven times pass over him.

17The sentence is by the decree of the watchers, and the demand by the word of the holy ones; to the intent that the living may know that the Most High ruleth in the kingdom of men, and giveth it to whomsoever he will, and setteth up over it the lowest of men.

18This dream I, king Nebuchadnezzar, have seen; and thou, O Belteshazzar, declare the interpretation, forasmuch as all the wise men of my kingdom are not able to make known unto me the interpretation; but thou art able; for the spirit of the holy gods is in thee.

19Then Daniel, whose name was Belteshazzar, was stricken dumb for a while, and his thoughts troubled him. The king answered and said, Belteshazzar, let not the dream, or the interpretation, trouble thee. Belteshazzar answered and said, My lord, the dream be to them that hate thee, and the interpretation thereof to thine adversaries.

20The tree that thou sawest, which grew, and was strong, whose height reached unto heaven, and the sight thereof to all the earth;

21whose leaves were fair, and the fruit thereof much, and in it was food for all; under which the beasts of the field dwelt, and upon whose branches the birds of the heavens had their habitation:

22it is thou, O king, that art grown and become strong; for thy greatness is grown, and reacheth unto heaven, and thy dominion to the end of the earth.

23And whereas the king saw a watcher and a holy one coming down from heaven, and saying, Hew down the tree, and destroy it; nevertheless leave the stump of the roots thereof in the earth, even with a band of iron and brass, in the tender grass of the field, and let it be wet with the dew of heaven: and let his portion be with the beasts of the field, till seven times pass over him;

24this is the interpretation, O king, and it is the decree of the Most High, which is come upon my lord the king:

25that thou shalt be driven from men, and thy dwelling shall be with the beasts of the field, and thou shalt be made to eat grass as oxen, and shalt be wet with the dew of heaven, and seven times shall pass over thee; till thou know that the Most High ruleth in the kingdom of men, and giveth it to whomsoever he will.

26And whereas they commanded to leave the stump of the roots of the tree; thy kingdom shall be sure unto thee, after that thou shalt have known that the heavens do rule.

27Wherefore, O king, let my counsel be acceptable unto thee, and break off thy sins by righteousness, and thine iniquities by showing mercy to the poor; if there may be a lengthening of thy tranquillity.

28All this came upon the king Nebuchadnezzar.

Daniel

29At the end of twelve months he was walking in the royal palace of Babylon.

30The king spake and said, Is not this great Babylon, which I have built for the royal dwelling-place, by the might of my power and for the glory of my majesty?

31While the word was in the king's mouth, there fell a voice from heaven, saying, O king Nebuchadnezzar, to thee it is spoken: The kingdom is departed from thee:

32and thou shalt be driven from men; and thy dwelling shall be with the beasts of the field; thou shalt be made to eat grass as oxen; and seven times shall pass over thee; until thou know that the Most High ruleth in the kingdom of men, and giveth it to whomsoever he will.

33The same hour was the thing fulfilled upon Nebuchadnezzar: and he was driven from men, and did eat grass as oxen, and his body was wet with the dew of heaven, till his hair was grown like eagles' feathers, and his nails like birds' claws.

34And at the end of the days I, Nebuchadnezzar, lifted up mine eyes unto heaven, and mine understanding returned unto me, and I blessed the Most High, and I praised and honored him that liveth for ever; for his dominion is an everlasting dominion, and his kingdom from generation to generation.

35And all the inhabitants of the earth are reputed as nothing; and he doeth according to his will in the army of heaven, and among the inhabitants of the earth; and none can stay his hand, or say unto him, What doest thou?

36At the same time mine understanding returned unto me; and for the glory of my kingdom, my majesty and brightness returned unto me; and my counsellors and my lords sought unto me; and I was established in my kingdom, and excellent greatness was added unto me.

37Now I, Nebuchadnezzar, praise and extol and honor the King of heaven; for all his works are truth, and his ways justice; and those that walk in pride he is able to abase.

Chapter 5

1Belshazzar the king made a great feast to a thousand of his lords, and drank wine before the thousand.

2Belshazzar, while he tasted the wine, commanded to bring the golden and silver vessels which Nebuchadnezzar his father had taken out of the temple which was in Jerusalem; that the king and his lords, his wives and his concubines, might drink therefrom.

3Then they brought the golden vessels that were taken out of the temple of the house of God which was at Jerusalem; and the king and his lords, his wives and his concubines, drank from them.

4They drank wine, and praised the gods of gold, and of silver, of brass, of iron, of wood, and of stone.

5In the same hour came forth the fingers of a man's hand, and wrote over against the candlestick upon the plaster of the wall of the king's palace: and the king saw the part of the hand that wrote.

6Then the king's countenance was changed in him, and his thoughts troubled him; and the joints of his loins were loosed, and his knees smote one against another.

7The king cried aloud to bring in the enchanters, the Chaldeans, and the soothsayers. The king spake and said to the wise men of Babylon, Whosoever shall read this writing, and show me the interpretation thereof, shall be clothed with purple, and have a chain of gold about his neck, and shall be the third ruler in the kingdom.

8Then came in all the king's wise men; but they could not read the writing, nor make known to the king the interpretation.

9Then was king Belshazzar greatly troubled, and his countenance was changed in him, and his lords were perplexed.

10Now the queen by reason of the words of the king and his lords came into the banquet house: the queen spake and said, O king, live forever; let not thy thoughts trouble thee, nor let thy countenance be changed.

11There is a man in thy kingdom, in whom is the spirit of the holy gods; and in the days of thy father light and understanding and wisdom, like the wisdom of the gods, were found in him; and the king Nebuchadnezzar thy father, the king, I say, thy father, made him master of the magicians, enchanters, Chaldeans, and soothsayers;

12forasmuch as an excellent spirit, and knowledge, and understanding, interpreting of dreams, and showing of dark sentences, and dissolving of doubts, were found in the same Daniel, whom the king named Belteshazzar. Now let Daniel be called, and he will show the interpretation.

13Then was Daniel brought in before the king. The king spake and said unto Daniel, Art thou that Daniel, who art of the children of the captivity of Judah, whom the king my father brought out of Judah?

14I have heard of thee, that the spirit of the gods is in thee, and that light and understanding and excellent wisdom are found in thee.

15And now the wise men, the enchanters, have been brought in before me, that they should read this writing, and make known unto me the interpretation thereof; but they could not show the interpretation of the thing.

16But I have heard of thee, that thou canst give interpretations, and dissolve doubts; now if thou canst read the writing, and make known to me the interpretation thereof, thou shalt be clothed with purple, and have a chain of gold about thy neck, and shalt be the third ruler in the kingdom.

17Then Daniel answered and said before the king, Let thy gifts be to thyself, and give thy rewards to another; nevertheless I will read the writing unto the king, and make known to him the interpretation.

18O thou king, the Most High God gave Nebuchadnezzar thy father the kingdom, and greatness, and glory, and majesty:

19and because of the greatness that he gave him, all the peoples, nations, and languages trembled and feared before him: whom he would he slew, and whom he would he kept alive; and whom he would he raised up, and whom he would he put down.

20But when his heart was lifted up, and his spirit was hardened so that he dealt proudly, he was deposed from his kingly throne, and they took his glory from him:

21and he was driven from the sons of men, and his heart was made like the beasts', and his dwelling was with the wild asses; he was fed with grass like oxen, and his body was wet with the dew of heaven; until he knew that the Most High God ruleth in the kingdom of men, and that he setteth up over it whomsoever he will.

22And thou his son, O Belshazzar, hast not humbled thy heart, though thou knewest all this,

23but hast lifted up thyself against the Lord of heaven; and they have brought the vessels of his house before thee, and thou and thy lords, thy wives and thy concubines, have drunk wine from them; and thou hast praised the gods of silver and gold, of brass, iron, wood, and stone, which see not, nor hear, nor know; and the God in whose hand thy breath is, and whose are all thy ways, hast thou not glorified.

24Then was the part of the hand sent from before him, and this writing was inscribed.

25And this is the writing that was inscribed: MENE, MENE, TEKEL, UPHARSIN.

26This is the interpretation of the thing: MENE; God hath numbered thy kingdom, and brought it to an end;

27TEKEL; thou art weighed in the balances, and art found wanting.

28PERES; thy kingdom is divided, and given to the Medes and Persians.

29Then commanded Belshazzar, and they clothed Daniel with purple, and put a chain of gold about his neck, and made proclamation concerning him, that he should be the third ruler in the kingdom.

30In that night Belshazzar the Chaldean King was slain.

31And Darius the Mede received the kingdom, being about threescore and two years old.

Chapter 6

1It pleased Darius to set over the kingdom a hundred and twenty satraps, who should be throughout the whole kingdom;

2and over them three presidents, of whom Daniel was one; that these satraps might give account unto them, and that the king should have no damage.

3Then this Daniel was distinguished above the presidents and the satraps, because an excellent spirit was in him; and the king thought to set him over the whole realm.

4Then the presidents and the satraps sought to find occasion against Daniel as touching the kingdom; but they could find no occasion nor fault, forasmuch as he was faithful, neither was there any error or fault found in him.

5Then said these men, We shall not find any occasion against this Daniel, except we find it against him concerning the law of his God.

6Then these presidents and satraps assembled together to the king, and said thus unto him, King Darius, live for ever.

7All the presidents of the kingdom, the deputies and the satraps, the counsellors and the governors, have consulted together to establish a royal statute, and to make a strong interdict, that whosoever shall ask a petition of any god or man for thirty days, save of thee, O king, he shall be cast into the den of lions.

8Now, O king, establish the interdict, and sign the writing, that it be not changed, according to the law of the Medes and Persians, which altereth not.

9Wherefore king Darius signed the writing and the interdict.

10And when Daniel knew that the writing was signed, he went into his house (now his windows were open in his chamber toward Jerusalem) and he kneeled upon his knees three times a day, and prayed, and gave thanks before his God, as he did aforetime.

11Then these men assembled together, and found Daniel making petition and supplication before his God.

12Then they came near, and spake before the king concerning the king's interdict: Hast thou not signed an interdict, that every man that shall make petition unto any god or man within thirty days, save unto thee, O king, shall be cast into the den of lions? The king answered and said, The thing is true, according to the law of the Medes and Persians, which altereth not.

13Then answered they and said before the king, That Daniel, who is of the children of the captivity of Judah, regardeth not thee, O king, nor the interdict that thou hast signed, but maketh his petition three times a day.

14Then the king, when he heard these words, was sore displeased, and set his heart on Daniel to deliver him; and he labored till the going down of the sun to rescue him.

15Then these men assembled together unto the king, and said unto the king, Know, O king, that it is a law of the Medes and Persians, that no interdict nor statute which the king establisheth may be changed.

16Then the king commanded, and they brought Daniel, and cast him into the den of lions. Now the king spake and said unto Daniel, Thy God whom thou servest continually, he will deliver thee.

17And a stone was brought, and laid upon the mouth of the den; and the king sealed it with his own signet, and with the signet of his lords; that nothing might be changed concerning Daniel.

18Then the king went to his palace, and passed the night fasting; neither were instruments of music brought before him: and his sleep fled from him.

19Then the king arose very early in the morning, and went in haste unto the den of lions.

20And when he came near unto the den to Daniel, he cried with a lamentable voice; the king spake and said to Daniel, O Daniel, servant of the living God, is thy God, whom thou servest continually, able to deliver thee from the lions?

21Then said Daniel unto the king, O king, live for ever.

22My God hath sent his angel, and hath shut the lions' mouths, and they have not hurt me; forasmuch as before him innocency was found in me; and also before thee, O king, have I done no hurt.

23Then was the king exceeding glad, and commanded that they should take Daniel up out of the den. So Daniel was taken up out of the den, and no manner of hurt was found upon him, because he had trusted in his God.

24And the king commanded, and they brought those men that had accused Daniel, and they cast them into the den of lions, them, their children, and their wives; and the lions had the mastery of them, and brake all their bones in pieces, before they came to the bottom of the den.

25Then king Darius wrote unto all the peoples, nations, and languages, that dwell in all the earth: Peace be multiplied unto you.

26I make a decree, that in all the dominion of my kingdom men tremble and fear before the God of Daniel; for he is the living God, and stedfast for ever, And his kingdom that which shall not be destroyed; and his dominion shall be even unto the end.

27He delivereth and rescueth, and he worketh signs and wonders in heaven and in earth, who hath delivered Daniel from the power of the lions.

28So this Daniel prospered in the reign of Darius, and in the reign of Cyrus the Persian.

Chapter 7

1In the first year of Belshazzar king of Babylon Daniel had a dream and visions of his head upon his bed: then he wrote the dream and told the sum of the matters.

2Daniel spake and said, I saw in my vision by night, and, behold, the four winds of heaven brake forth upon the great sea.

3And four great beasts came up from the sea, diverse one from another.

4The first was like a lion, and had eagle's wings: I beheld till the wings thereof were plucked, and it was lifted up from the earth, and made to stand upon two feet as a man; and a man's heart was given to it.

5And, behold, another beast, a second, like to a bear; and it was raised up on one side, and three ribs were in its mouth between its teeth: and they said thus unto it, Arise, devour much flesh.

6After this I beheld, and, lo, another, like a leopard, which had upon its back four wings of a bird; the beast had also four heads; and dominion was given to it.

7After this I saw in the night-visions, and, behold, a fourth beast, terrible and powerful, and strong exceedingly; and it had great iron teeth; it devoured and brake in pieces, and stamped the residue with its feet: and it was diverse from all the beasts that were before it; and it had ten horns.

8I considered the horns, and, behold, there came up among them another horn, a little one, before which three of the first horns were plucked up by the roots: and, behold, in this horn were eyes like the eyes of a man, and a mouth speaking great things.

9I beheld till thrones were placed, and one that was ancient of days did sit: his raiment was white as snow, and the hair of his head like pure wool; his throne was fiery flames, and the wheels thereof burning fire.

10A fiery stream issued and came forth from before him: thousands of thousands ministered unto him, and ten thousand times ten thousand stood before him: the judgment was set, and the books were opened.

11I beheld at that time because of the voice of the great words which the horn spake; I beheld even till the beast was slain, and its body destroyed, and it was given to be burned with fire.

12And as for the rest of the beasts, their dominion was taken away: yet their lives were prolonged for a season and a time.

13I saw in the night-visions, and, behold, there came with the clouds of heaven one like unto a son of man, and he came even to the ancient of days, and they brought him near before him.

14And there was given him dominion, and glory, and a kingdom, that all the peoples, nations, and languages should serve him: his dominion is an everlasting dominion, which shall not pass away, and his kingdom that which shall not be destroyed.

15As for me, Daniel, my spirit was grieved in the midst of my body, and the visions of my head troubled me.

16I came near unto one of them that stood by, and asked him the truth concerning all this. So he told me, and made me know the interpretation of the things.

17These great beasts, which are four, are four kings, that shall arise out of the earth.

18But the saints of the Most High shall receive the kingdom, and possess the kingdom for ever, even for ever and ever.

19Then I desired to know the truth concerning the fourth beast, which was diverse from all of them, exceeding terrible, whose teeth were of iron, and its nails of brass; which devoured, brake in pieces, and stamped the residue with its feet;

20and concerning the ten horns that were on its head, and the other horn which came up, and before which three fell, even that horn that had eyes, and a mouth that spake great things, whose look was more stout than its fellows.

21I beheld, and the same horn made war with the saints, and prevailed against them;

22until the ancient of days came, and judgment was given to the saints of the Most High, and the time came that the saints possessed the kingdom.

23Thus he said, The fourth beast shall be a fourth kingdom upon earth, which shall be diverse from all the kingdoms, and shall devour the whole earth, and shall tread it down, and break it in pieces.

24And as for the ten horns, out of this kingdom shall ten kings arise: and another shall arise after them; and he shall be diverse from the former, and he shall put down three kings.

25And he shall speak words against the Most High, and shall wear out the saints of the Most High; and he shall think to change the times and the law; and they shall be given into his hand until a time and times and half a time.

26But the judgment shall be set, and they shall take away his dominion, to consume and to destroy it unto the end.

27And the kingdom and the dominion, and the greatness of the kingdoms under the whole heaven, shall be given to the people of the saints of the Most High: his kingdom is an everlasting kingdom, and all dominions shall serve and obey him.

28Here is the end of the matter. As for me, Daniel, my thoughts much troubled me, and my countenance was changed in me: but I kept the matter in my heart.

Chapter 8

1In the third year of the reign of king Belshazzar a vision appeared unto me, even unto me, Daniel, after that which appeared unto me at the first.

2And I saw in the vision; now it was so, that when I saw, I was in Shushan the palace, which is in the province of Elam; and I saw in the vision, and I was by the river Ulai.

3Then I lifted up mine eyes, and saw, and, behold, there stood before the river a ram which had two horns: and the two horns were high; but one was higher than the other, and the higher came up last.

4I saw the ram pushing westward, and northward, and southward; and no beasts could stand before him, neither was there any that could deliver out of his hand; but he did according to his will, and magnified himself.

5And as I was considering, behold, a he-goat came from the west over the face of the whole earth, and touched not the ground: and the goat had a notable horn between his eyes.

6And he came to the ram that had the two horns, which I saw standing before the river, and ran upon him in the fury of his power.

7And I saw him come close unto the ram, and he was moved with anger against him, and smote the ram, and brake his two horns; and there was no power in the ram to stand before him; but he cast him down to the ground, and trampled upon him; and there was none that could deliver the ram out of his hand.

8And the he-goat magnified himself exceedingly: and when he was strong, the great horn was broken; and instead of it there came up four notable horns toward the four winds of heaven.

9And out of one of them came forth a little horn, which waxed exceeding great, toward the south, and toward the east, and toward the glorious land.

10And it waxed great, even to the host of heaven; and some of the host and of the stars it cast down to the ground, and trampled upon them.

11Yea, it magnified itself, even to the prince of the host; and it took away from him the continual burnt-offering, and the place of his sanctuary was cast down.

12And the host was given over to it together with the continual burnt-offering through transgression; and it cast down truth to the ground, and it did its pleasure and prospered.

13Then I heard a holy one speaking; and another holy one said unto that certain one who spake, How long shall be the vision concerning the continual burnt-offering, and the transgression that maketh desolate, to give both the sanctuary and the host to be trodden under foot?

14And he said unto me, Unto two thousand and three hundred evenings and mornings; then shall the sanctuary be cleansed.

15And it came to pass, when I, even I Daniel, had seen the vision, that I sought to understand it; and, behold, there stood before me as the appearance of a man.

16And I heard a man's voice between the banks of the Ulai, which called, and said, Gabriel, make this man to understand the vision.

17So he came near where I stood; and when he came, I was affrighted, and fell upon my face: but he said unto me, Understand, O son of man; for the vision belongeth to the time of the end.

18Now as he was speaking with me, I fell into a deep sleep with my face toward the ground; but he touched me, and set me upright.

19And he said, Behold, I will make thee know what shall be in the latter time of the indignation; for it belongeth to the appointed time of the end.

20The ram which thou sawest, that had the two horns, they are the kings of Media and Persia.

21And the rough he-goat is the king of Greece: and the great horn that is between his eyes is the first king.

22And as for that which was broken, in the place whereof four stood up, four kingdoms shall stand up out of the nation, but not with his power.

23And in the latter time of their kingdom, when the transgressors are come to the full, a king of fierce countenance, and understanding dark sentences, shall stand up.

24And his power shall be mighty, but not by his own power; and he shall destroy wonderfully, and shall prosper and do his pleasure; and he shall destroy the mighty ones and the holy people.

25And through his policy he shall cause craft to prosper in his hand; and he shall magnify himself in his heart, and in their security shall he destroy many: he shall also stand up against the prince of princes; but he shall be broken without hand.

26And the vision of the evenings and mornings which hath been told is true: but shut thou up the vision; for it belongeth to many days to come.

27And I, Daniel, fainted, and was sick certain days; then I rose up, and did the king's business: and I wondered at the vision, but none understood it.

Daniel
Chapter 9

1In the first year of Darius the son of Ahasuerus, of the seed of the Medes, who was made king over the realm of the Chaldeans,

2in the first year of his reign I, Daniel, understood by the books the number of the years whereof the word of Yahweh came to Jeremiah the prophet, for the accomplishing of the desolations of Jerusalem, even seventy years.

3And I set my face unto the Lord God, to seek by prayer and supplications, with fasting and sackcloth and ashes.

4And I prayed unto Yahweh my God, and made confession, and said, Oh, Lord, the great and dreadful God, who keepeth covenant and lovingkindness with them that love him and keep his commandments,

5we have sinned, and have dealt perversely, and have done wickedly, and have rebelled, even turning aside from thy precepts and from thine ordinances;

6neither have we hearkened unto thy servants the prophets, that spake in thy name to our kings, our princes, and our fathers, and to all the people of the land.

7O Lord, righteousness belongeth unto thee, but unto us confusion of face, as at this day; to the men of Judah, and to the inhabitants of Jerusalem, and unto all Israel, that are near, and that are far off, through all the countries whither thou hast driven them, because of their trespass that they have trespassed against thee.

8O Lord, to us belongeth confusion of face, to our kings, to our princes, and to our fathers, because we have sinned against thee.

9To the Lord our God belong mercies and forgivenesses; for we have rebelled against him;

10neither have we obeyed the voice of Yahweh our God, to walk in his laws, which he set before us by his servants the prophets.

11Yea, all Israel have transgressed thy law, even turning aside, that they should not obey thy voice: therefore hath the curse been poured out upon us, and the oath that is written in the law of Moses the servant of God; for we have sinned against him.

12And he hath confirmed his words, which he spake against us, and against our judges that judged us, by bringing upon us a great evil; for under the whole heaven hath not been done as hath been done upon Jerusalem.

13As it is written in the law of Moses, all this evil is come upon us: yet have we not entreated the favor of Yahweh our God, that we should turn from our iniquities, and have discernment in thy truth.

14Therefore hath Yahweh watched over the evil, and brought it upon us; for Yahweh our God is righteous in all his works which he doeth, and we have not obeyed his voice.

15And now, O Lord our God, that hast brought thy people forth out of the land of Egypt with a mighty hand, and hast gotten thee renown, as at this day; we have sinned, we have done wickedly.

16O Lord, according to all thy righteousness, let thine anger and thy wrath, I pray thee, be turned away from thy city Jerusalem, thy holy mountain; because for our sins, and for the iniquities of our fathers, Jerusalem and thy people are become a reproach to all that are round about us.

17Now therefore, O our God, hearken unto the prayer of thy servant, and to his supplications, and cause thy face to shine upon thy sanctuary that is desolate, for the Lord's sake.

18O my God, incline thine ear, and hear; open thine eyes, and behold our desolations, and the city which is called by thy name: for we do not present our supplications before thee for our righteousness, but for thy great mercies' sake.

19O Lord, hear; O Lord, forgive; O Lord, hearken and do; defer not, for thine own sake, O my God, because thy city and thy people are called by thy name.

20And while I was speaking, and praying, and confessing my sin and the sin of my people Israel, and presenting my supplication before Yahweh my God for the holy mountain of my God;

21yea, while I was speaking in prayer, the man Gabriel, whom I had seen in the vision at the beginning, being caused to fly swiftly, touched me about the time of the evening oblation.

22And he instructed me, and talked with me, and said, O Daniel, I am now come forth to give thee wisdom and understanding.

23At the beginning of thy supplications the commandment went forth, and I am come to tell thee; for thou art greatly beloved: therefore consider the matter, and understand the vision.

24Seventy weeks are decreed upon thy people and upon thy holy city, to finish transgression, and to make an end of sins, and to make reconciliation for iniquity, and to bring in everlasting righteousness, and to seal up vision and prophecy, and to anoint the most holy.

25Know therefore and discern, that from the going forth of the commandment to restore and to build Jerusalem unto the anointed one, the prince, shall be seven weeks, and threescore and two weeks: it shall be built again, with street and moat, even in troublous times.

26And after the threescore and two weeks shall the anointed one be cut off, and shall have nothing: and the people of the prince that shall come shall destroy the city and the sanctuary; and the end thereof shall be with a flood, and even unto the end shall be war; desolations are determined.

27And he shall make a firm covenant with many for one week: and in the midst of the week he shall cause the sacrifice and the oblation to cease; and upon the wing of abominations shall come one that maketh desolate; and even unto the full end, and that determined, shall wrath be poured out upon the desolate.

Chapter 10

1In the third year of Cyrus king of Persia a thing was revealed unto Daniel, whose name was called Belteshazzar; and the thing was true, even a great warfare: and he understood the thing, and had understanding of the vision.

2In those days I, Daniel, was mourning three whole weeks.

3I ate no pleasant bread, neither came flesh nor wine into my mouth, neither did I anoint myself at all, till three whole weeks were fulfilled.

4And in the four and twentieth day of the first month, as I was by the side of the great river, which is Hiddekel,

5I lifted up mine eyes, and looked, and, behold, a man clothed in linen, whose loins were girded with pure gold of Uphaz:

6his body also was like the beryl, and his face as the appearance of lightning, and his eyes as flaming torches, and his arms and his feet like unto burnished brass, and the voice of his words like the voice of a multitude.

7And I, Daniel, alone saw the vision; for the men that were with me saw not the vision; but a great quaking fell upon them, and they fled to hide themselves.

8So I was left alone, and saw this great vision, and there remained no strength in me; for my comeliness was turned in me into corruption, and I retained no strength.

9Yet heard I the voice of his words; and when I heard the voice of his words, then was I fallen into a deep sleep on my face, with my face toward the ground.

10And, behold, a hand touched me, which set me upon my knees and upon the palms of my hands.

11And he said unto me, O Daniel, thou man greatly beloved, understand the words that I speak unto thee, and stand upright; for unto thee am I now sent. And when he had spoken this word unto me, I stood trembling.

12Then said he unto me, Fear not, Daniel; for from the first day that thou didst set thy heart to understand, and to humble thyself before thy God, thy words were heard: and I am come for thy words' sake.

13But the prince of the kingdom of Persia withstood me one and twenty days; but, lo, Michael, one of the chief princes, came to help me: and I remained there with the kings of Persia.

14Now I am come to make thee understand what shall befall thy people in the latter days; for the vision is yet for many days:

15and when he had spoken unto me according to these words, I set my face toward the ground, and was dumb.

16And, behold, one in the likeness of the sons of men touched my lips: then I opened my mouth, and spake and said unto him that stood before me, O my lord, by reason of the vision my sorrows are turned upon me, and I retain no strength.

17For how can the servant of this my lord talk with this my lord? for as for me, straightway there remained no strength in me, neither was there breath left in me.

18Then there touched me again one like the appearance of a man, and he strengthened me.

19And he said, O man greatly beloved, fear not: peace be unto thee, be strong, yea, be strong. And when he spake unto me, I was strengthened, and said, Let my lord speak; for thou hast strengthened me.

20Then said he, Knowest thou wherefore I am come unto thee? and now will I return to fight with the prince of Persia: and when I go forth, lo, the prince of Greece shall come.

21But I will tell thee that which is inscribed in the writing of truth: and there is none that holdeth with me against these, but Michael your prince.

Chapter 11

1And as for me, in the first year of Darius the Mede, I stood up to confirm and strengthen him.

2And now will I show thee the truth. Behold, there shall stand up yet three kings in Persia; and the fourth shall be far richer than they all: and when he is waxed strong through his riches, he shall stir up all against the realm of Greece.

3And a mighty king shall stand up, that shall rule with great dominion, and do according to his will.

4And when he shall stand up, his kingdom shall be broken, and shall be divided toward the four winds of heaven, but not to his posterity, nor according to his dominion wherewith he ruled; for his kingdom shall be plucked up, even for others besides these.

5And the king of the south shall be strong, and one of his princes; and he shall be strong above him, and have dominion; his dominion shall be a great dominion.

6And at the end of years they shall join themselves together; and the daughter of the king of the south shall come to the king of the north to make an agreement: but she shall not retain the strength of her arm; neither shall he stand, nor his arm; but she shall be given up, and they that brought her, and he that begat her, and he that strengthened her in those times.

7But out of a shoot from her roots shall one stand up in his place, who shall come unto the army, and shall enter into the fortress of the king of the north, and shall deal against them, and shall prevail.

8And also their gods, with their molten images, and with their goodly vessels of silver and of gold, shall he carry captive into Egypt; and he shall refrain some years from the king of the north.

9And he shall come into the realm of the king of the south, but he shall return into his own land.

10And his sons shall war, and shall assemble a multitude of great forces, which shall come on, and overflow, and pass through; and they shall return and war, even to his fortress.

11And the king of the south shall be moved with anger, and shall come forth and fight with him, even with the king of the north; and he shall set forth a great multitude, and the multitude shall be given into his hand.

12And the multitude shall be lifted up, and his heart shall be exalted; and he shall cast down tens of thousands, but he shall not prevail.

13And the king of the north shall return, and shall set forth a multitude greater than the former; and he shall come on at the end of the times, even of years, with a great army and with much substance.

14And in those times there shall many stand up against the king of the south: also the children of the violent among thy people shall lift themselves up to establish the vision; but they shall fall.

¹⁵So the king of the north shall come, and cast up a mound, and take a well-fortified city: and the forces of the south shall not stand, neither his chosen people, neither shall there be any strength to stand.

¹⁶But he that cometh against him shall do according to his own will, and none shall stand before him; and he shall stand in the glorious land, and in his hand shall be destruction.

¹⁷And he shall set his face to come with the strength of his whole kingdom, and with him equitable conditions; and he shall perform them: and he shall give him the daughter of women, to corrupt her; but she shall not stand, neither be for him.

¹⁸After this shall he turn his face unto the isles, and shall take many: but a prince shall cause the reproach offered by him to cease; yea, moreover, he shall cause his reproach to turn upon him.

¹⁹Then shall he turn his face toward the fortresses of his own land; but he shall stumble and fall, and shall not be found.

²⁰Then shall stand up in his place one that shall cause an exactor to pass through the glory of the kingdom; but within few days he shall be destroyed, neither in anger, nor in battle.

²¹And in his place shall stand up a contemptible person, to whom they had not given the honor of the kingdom: but he shall come in time of security, and shall obtain the kingdom by flatteries.

²²And the overwhelming forces shall be overwhelmed from before him, and shall be broken; yea, also the prince of the covenant.

²³And after the league made with him he shall work deceitfully; for he shall come up, and shall become strong, with a small people.

²⁴In time of security shall he come even upon the fattest places of the province; and he shall do that which his fathers have not done, nor his fathers' fathers; he shall scatter among them prey, and spoil, and substance: yea, he shall devise his devices against the strongholds, even for a time.

²⁵And he shall stir up his power and his courage against the king of the south with a great army; and the king of the south shall war in battle with an exceeding great and mighty army; but he shall not stand; for they shall devise devices against him.

²⁶Yea, they that eat of his dainties shall destroy him, and his army shall overflow; and many shall fall down slain.

²⁷And as for both these kings, their hearts shall be to do mischief, and they shall speak lies at one table: but it shall not prosper; for yet the end shall be at the time appointed.

²⁸Then shall he return into his land with great substance; and his heart shall be against the holy covenant; and he shall do his pleasure, and return to his own land.

²⁹At the time appointed he shall return, and come into the south; but it shall not be in the latter time as it was in the former.

³⁰For ships of Kittim shall come against him; therefore he shall be grieved, and shall return, and have indignation against the holy covenant, and shall do his pleasure: he shall even return, and have regard unto them that forsake the holy covenant.

³¹And forces shall stand on his part, and they shall profane the sanctuary, even the fortress, and shall take away the continual burnt-offering, and they shall set up the abomination that maketh desolate.

³²And such as do wickedly against the covenant shall he pervert by flatteries; but the people that know their God shall be strong, and do exploits.

³³And they that are wise among the people shall instruct many; yet they shall fall by the sword and by flame, by captivity and by spoil, many days.

³⁴Now when they shall fall, they shall be helped with a little help; but many shall join themselves unto them with flatteries.

³⁵And some of them that are wise shall fall, to refine them, and to purify, and to make them white, even to the time of the end: because it is yet for the time appointed.

³⁶And the king shall do according to his will; and he shall exalt himself, and magnify himself above every god, and shall speak marvellous things against the God of gods; and he shall prosper till the indignation be accomplished; for that which is determined shall be done.

³⁷Neither shall he regard the gods of his fathers, nor the desire of women, nor regard any god; for he shall magnify himself above all.

³⁸But in his place shall he honor the god of fortresses; and a god whom his fathers knew not shall he honor with gold, and silver, and with precious stones, and pleasant things.

³⁹And he shall deal with the strongest fortresses by the help of a foreign god: whosoever acknowledgeth him he will increase with glory; and he shall cause them to rule over many, and shall divide the land for a price.

⁴⁰And at the time of the end shall the king of the south contend with him; and the king of the north shall come against him like a whirlwind, with chariots, and with horsemen, and with many ships; and he shall enter into the countries, and shall overflow and pass through.

⁴¹He shall enter also into the glorious land, and many countries shall be overthrown; but these shall be delivered out of his hand: Edom, and Moab, and the chief of the children of Ammon.

⁴²He shall stretch forth his hand also upon the countries; and the land of Egypt shall not escape.

⁴³But he shall have power over the treasures of gold and of silver, and over all the precious things of Egypt; and the Libyans and the Ethiopians shall be at his steps.

⁴⁴But tidings out of the east and out of the north shall trouble him; and he shall go forth with great fury to destroy and utterly to sweep away many.

⁴⁵And he shall plant the tents of his palace between the sea and the glorious holy mountain; yet he shall come to his end, and none shall help him.

Chapter 12

¹And at that time shall Michael stand up, the great prince who standeth for the children of thy people; and there shall be a time of trouble, such as never was since there was a nation even to that same time: and at that time thy people shall be delivered, every one that shall be found written in the book.

²And many of them that sleep in the dust of the earth shall awake, some to everlasting life, and some to shame and everlasting contempt.

³And they that are wise shall shine as the brightness of the firmament; and they that turn many to righteousness as the stars for ever and ever.

⁴But thou, O Daniel, shut up the words, and seal the book, even to the time of the end: many shall run to and fro, and knowledge shall be increased.

⁵Then I, Daniel, looked, and, behold, there stood other two, the one on the brink of the river on this side, and the other on the brink of the river on that side.

⁶And one said to the man clothed in linen, who was above the waters of the river, How long shall it be to the end of these wonders?

⁷And I heard the man clothed in linen, who was above the waters of the river, when he held up his right hand and his left hand unto heaven, and sware by him that liveth for ever that it shall be for a time, times, and a half; and when they have made an end of breaking in pieces the power of the holy people, all these things shall be finished.

⁸And I heard, but I understood not: then said I, O my lord, what shall be the issue of these things?

⁹And he said, Go thy way, Daniel; for the words are shut up and sealed till the time of the end.

¹⁰Many shall purify themselves, and make themselves white, and be refined; but the wicked shall do wickedly; and none of the wicked shall understand; but they that are wise shall understand.

¹¹And from the time that the continual burnt-offering shall be taken away, and the abomination that maketh desolate set up, there shall be a thousand two hundred and ninety days.

¹²Blessed is he that waiteth, and cometh to the thousand three hundred and five and thirty days.

¹³But go thou thy way till the end be; for thou shalt rest, and shalt stand in thy lot, at the end of the days.

Hosea

Chapter 1

1 The word of Yahweh that came unto Hosea the son of Beeri, in the days of Uzziah, Jotham, Ahaz, and Hezekiah, kings of Judah, and in the days of Jeroboam the son of Joash, king of Israel.

2 When Yahweh spake at the first by Hosea, Yahweh said unto Hosea, Go, take unto thee a wife of whoredom and children of whoredom; for the land doth commit great whoredom, departing from Yahweh.

3 So he went and took Gomer the daughter of Diblaim; and she conceived, and bare him a son.

4 And Yahweh said unto him, Call his name Jezreel; for yet a little while, and I will avenge the blood of Jezreel upon the house of Jehu, and will cause the kingdom of the house of Israel to cease.

5 And it shall come to pass at that day, that I will break the bow of Israel in the valley of Jezreel.

6 And she conceived again, and bare a daughter. And Yahweh said unto him, Call her name Lo-ruhamah; for I will no more have mercy upon the house of Israel, that I should in any wise pardon them.

7 But I will have mercy upon the house of Judah, and will save them by Yahweh their God, and will not save them by bow, nor by sword, nor by battle, by horses, nor by horsemen.

8 Now when she had weaned Lo-ruhamah, she conceived, and bare a son.

9 And Yahweh said, Call his name Lo-ammi; for ye are not my people, and I will not be your God.

10 Yet the number of the children of Israel shall be as the sand of the sea, which cannot be measured nor numbered; and it shall come to pass that, in the place where it was said unto them, Ye are not my people, it shall be said unto them, Ye are the sons of the living God.

11 And the children of Judah and the children of Israel shall be gathered together, and they shall appoint themselves one head, and shall go up from the land; for great shall be the day of Jezreel.

Chapter 2

1 Say ye unto your brethren, Ammi; and to your sisters, Ruhamah.

2 Contend with your mother, contend; for she is not my wife, neither am I her husband; and let her put away her whoredoms from her face, and her adulteries from between her breasts;

3 lest I strip her naked, and set her as in the day that she was born, and make her as a wilderness, and set her like a dry land, and slay her with thirst.

4 Yea, upon her children will I have no mercy; for they are children of whoredom;

5 for their mother hath played the harlot; she that conceived them hath done shamefully; for she said, I will go after my lovers, that give me my bread and my water, my wool and my flax, mine oil and my drink.

6 Therefore, behold, I will hedge up thy way with thorns, and I will build a wall against her, that she shall not find her paths.

7 And she shall follow after her lovers, but she shall not overtake them; and she shall seek them, but shall not find them: then shall she say, I will go and return to my first husband; for then was it better with me than now.

8 For she did not know that I gave her the grain, and the new wine, and the oil, and multiplied unto her silver and gold, which they used for Baal.

9 Therefore will I take back my grain in the time thereof, and my new wine in the season thereof, and will pluck away my wool and my flax which should have covered her nakedness.

10 And now will I uncover her lewdness in the sight of her lovers, and none shall deliver her out of my hand.

11 I will also cause all her mirth to cease, her feasts, her new moons, and her sabbaths, and all her solemn assemblies.

12 And I will lay waste her vines and her fig-trees, whereof she hath said, These are my hire that my lovers have given me; and I will make them a forest, and the beasts of the field shall eat them.

13 And I will visit upon her the days of the Baalim, unto which she burned incense, when she decked herself with her earrings and her jewels, and went after her lovers, and forgat me, saith Yahweh.

14 Therefore, behold, I will allure her, and bring her into the wilderness, and speak comfortably unto her.

15 And I will give her her vineyards from thence, and the valley of Achor for a door of hope; and she shall make answer there, as in the days of her youth, and as in the day when she came up out of the land of Egypt.

16 And it shall be at that day, saith Yahweh, that thou shalt call me Ishi, and shalt call me no more Baali.

17 For I will take away the names of the Baalim out of her mouth, and they shall no more be mentioned by their name.

18 And in that day will I make a covenant for them with the beasts of the field, and with the birds of the heavens, and with the creeping things of the ground: and I will break the bow and the sword and the battle out of the land, and will make them to lie down safely.

19 And I will betroth thee unto me for ever; yea, I will betroth thee unto me in righteousness, and in justice, and in lovingkindness, and in mercies.

20 I will even betroth thee unto me in faithfulness; and thou shalt know Yahweh.

21 And it shall come to pass in that day, I will answer, saith Yahweh, I will answer the heavens, and they shall answer the earth;

22 and the earth shall answer the grain, and the new wine, and the oil; and they shall answer Jezreel.

23 And I will sow her unto me in the earth; and I will have mercy upon her that had not obtained mercy; and I will say to them that were not my people, Thou art my people; and they shall say, Thou art my God.

Chapter 3

1 And Yahweh said unto me, Go again, love a woman beloved of her friend, and an adulteress, even as Yahweh loveth the children of Israel, though they turn unto other gods, and love cakes of raisins.

2 So I bought her to me for fifteen pieces of silver, and a homer of barley, and a half-homer of barley;

3 and I said unto her, Thou shalt abide for me many days; thou shalt not play the harlot, and thou shalt not be any man's wife: so will I also be toward thee.

4 For the children of Israel shall abide many days without king, and without prince, and without sacrifice, and without pillar, and without ephod or teraphim:

5 afterward shall the children of Israel return, and seek Yahweh their God, and David their king, and shall come with fear unto Yahweh and to his goodness in the latter days.

Chapter 4

1 Hear the word of Yahweh, ye children of Israel; for Yahweh hath a controversy with the inhabitants of the land, because there is no truth, nor goodness, nor knowledge of God in the land.

2 There is nought but swearing and breaking faith, and killing, and stealing, and committing adultery; they break out, and blood toucheth blood.

3 Therefore shall the land mourn, and every one that dwelleth therein shall languish, with the beasts of the field and the birds of the heavens; yea, the fishes of the sea also shall be taken away.

4 Yet let no man strive, neither let any man reprove; for thy people are as they that strive with the priest.

5 And thou shalt stumble in the day, and the prophet also shall stumble with thee in the night; and I will destroy thy mother.

6 My people are destroyed for lack of knowledge: because thou hast rejected knowledge, I will also reject thee, that thou shalt be no priest to me: seeing thou hast forgotten the law of thy God, I also will forget thy children.

7 As they were multiplied, so they sinned against me: I will change their glory into shame.

8 They feed on the sin of my people, and set their heart on their iniquity.

9 And it shall be, like people, like priest; and I will punish them for their ways, and will requite them their doings.

10 And they shall eat, and not have enough; they shall play the harlot, and shall not increase; because they have left off taking heed to Yahweh.

11 Whoredom and wine and new wine take away the understanding.

12 My people ask counsel at their stock, and their staff declareth unto them; for the spirit of whoredom hath caused them to err, and they have played the harlot, departing from under their God.

13 They sacrifice upon the tops of the mountains, and burn incense upon the hills, under oaks and poplars and terebinths, because the shadow thereof is good: therefore your daughters play the harlot, and your brides commit adultery.

14 I will not punish your daughters when they play the harlot, nor your brides when they commit adultery; for the men themselves go apart with harlots, and they sacrifice with the prostitutes; and the people that doth not understand shall be overthrown.

15 Though thou, Israel, play the harlot, yet let not Judah offend; and come not ye unto Gilgal, neither go ye up to Beth-aven, nor swear, As Yahweh liveth.

16 For Israel hath behaved himself stubbornly, like a stubborn heifer: now will Yahweh feed them as a lamb in a large place.

17 Ephraim is joined to idols; let him alone.

18 Their drink is become sour; they play the harlot continually; her rulers dearly love shame.

19 The wind hath wrapped her up in its wings; and they shall be put to shame because of their sacrifices.

Chapter 5

1 Hear this, O ye priests, and hearken, O house of Israel, and give ear, O house of the king; for unto you pertaineth the judgment; for ye have been a snare at Mizpah, and a net spread upon Tabor.

2 And the revolters are gone deep in making slaughter; but I am a rebuker of them all.

3 I know Ephraim, and Israel is not hid from me; for now, O Ephraim, thou hast played the harlot, Israel is defiled.

4 Their doings will not suffer them to turn unto their God; for the spirit of whoredom is within them, and they know not Yahweh.

5 And the pride of Israel doth testify to his face: therefore Israel and Ephraim shall stumble in their iniquity; Judah also shall stumble with them.

6 They shall go with their flocks and with their herds to seek Yahweh; but they shall not find him: he hath withdrawn himself from them.

7 They have dealt treacherously against Yahweh; for they have borne strange children: now shall the new moon devour them with their fields.

8 Blow ye the cornet in Gibeah, and the trumpet in Ramah: sound an alarm at Beth-aven; behind thee, O Benjamin.

9 Ephraim shall become a desolation in the day of rebuke: among the tribes of Israel have I made known that which shall surely be.

10 The princes of Judah are like them that remove the landmark: I will pour out my wrath upon them like water.

11 Ephraim is oppressed, he is crushed in judgment; because he was content to walk after man's command.

12Therefore am I unto Ephraim as a moth, and to the house of Judah as rottenness.

13When Ephraim saw his sickness, and Judah saw his wound, then went Ephraim to Assyria, and sent to king Jareb: but he is not able to heal you, neither will he cure you of your wound.

14For I will be unto Ephraim as a lion, and as a young lion to the house of Judah: I, even I, will tear and go away; I will carry off, and there shall be none to deliver.

15I will go and return to my place, till they acknowledge their offence, and seek my face: in their affliction they will seek me earnestly.

Chapter 6

1Come, and let us return unto Yahweh; for he hath torn, and he will heal us; he hath smitten, and he will bind us up.

2After two days will he revive us: on the third day he will raise us up, and we shall live before him.

3And let us know, let us follow on to know Yahweh: his going forth is sure as the morning; and he will come unto us as the rain, as the latter rain that watereth the earth.

4O Ephraim, what shall I do unto thee? O Judah, what shall I do unto thee? for your goodness is as a morning cloud, and as the dew that goeth early away.

5Therefore have I hewed them by the prophets; I have slain them by the words of my mouth: and thy judgments are as the light that goeth forth.

6For I desire goodness, and not sacrifice; and the knowledge of God more than burnt-offerings.

7But they like Adam have transgressed the covenant: there have they dealt treacherously against me.

8Gilead is a city of them that work iniquity; it is stained with blood.

9And as troops of robbers wait for a man, so the company of priests murder in the way toward Shechem; yea, they have committed lewdness.

10In the house of Israel I have seen a horrible thing: there whoredom is found in Ephraim, Israel is defiled.

11Also, O Judah, there is a harvest appointed for thee, when I bring back the captivity of my people.

Chapter 7

1When I would heal Israel, then is the iniquity of Ephraim uncovered, and the wickedness of Samaria; for they commit falsehood, and the thief entereth in, and the troop of robbers ravageth without.

2And they consider not in their hearts that I remember all their wickedness: now have their own doings beset them about; they are before my face.

3They make the king glad with their wickedness, and the princes with their lies.

4They are all adulterers; they are as an oven heated by the baker; he ceaseth to stir the fire, from the kneading of the dough, until it be leavened.

5On the day of our king the princes made themselves sick with the heat of wine; he stretched out his hand with scoffers.

6For they have made ready their heart like an oven, while they lie in wait: their baker sleepeth all the night; in the morning it burneth as a flaming fire.

7They are all hot as an oven, and devour their judges; all their kings are fallen: there is none among them that calleth unto me.

8Ephraim, he mixeth himself among the peoples; Ephraim is a cake not turned.

9Strangers have devoured his strength, and he knoweth it not: yea, gray hairs are here and there upon him, and he knoweth it not.

10And the pride of Israel doth testify to his face: yet they have not returned unto Yahweh their God, nor sought him, for all this.

11And Ephraim is like a silly dove, without understanding: they call unto Egypt, they go to Assyria.

12When they shall go, I will spread my net upon them; I will bring them down as the birds of the heavens; I will chastise them, as their congregation hath heard.

13Woe unto them! for they have wandered from me; destruction unto them! for they have trespassed against me: though I would redeem them, yet they have spoken lies against me.

14And they have not cried unto me with their heart, but they howl upon their beds: they assemble themselves for grain and new wine; they rebel against me.

15Though I have taught and strengthened their arms, yet do they devise mischief against me.

16They return, but not to him that is on high; they are like a deceitful bow; their princes shall fall by the sword for the rage of their tongue: this shall be their derision in the land of Egypt.

Chapter 8

1Set the trumpet to thy mouth. As an eagle he cometh against the house of Yahweh, because they have transgressed my covenant, and trespassed against my law.

2They shall cry unto me, My God, we Israel know thee.

3Israel hath cast off that which is good: the enemy shall pursue him.

4They have set up kings, but not by me; they have made princes, and I knew it not: of their silver and their gold have they made them idols, that they may be cut off.

5He hath cast off thy calf, O Samaria; mine anger is kindled against them: how long will it be ere they attain to innocency?

6For from Israel is even this; the workman made it, and it is no God; yea, the calf of Samaria shall be broken in pieces.

7For they sow the wind, and they shall reap the whirlwind: he hath no standing grain; the blade shall yield no meal; if so be it yield, strangers shall swallow it up.

8Israel is swallowed up: now are they among the nations as a vessel wherein none delighteth.

9For they are gone up to Assyria, like a wild ass alone by himself: Ephraim hath hired lovers.

10Yea, though they hire among the nations, now will I gather them; and they begin to be diminished by reason of the burden of the king of princes.

11Because Ephraim hath multiplied altars for sinning, altars have been unto him for sinning.

12I wrote for him the ten thousand things of my law; but they are counted as a strange thing.

13As for the sacrifices of mine offerings, they sacrifice flesh and eat it; but Yahweh accepteth them not: now will he remember their iniquity, and visit their sins; they shall return to Egypt.

14For Israel hath forgotten his Maker, and builded palaces; and Judah hath multiplied fortified cities: but I will send a fire upon his cities, and it shall devour the castles thereof.

Chapter 9

1Rejoice not, O Israel, for joy, like the peoples; for thou hast played the harlot, departing from thy God; thou hast loved hire upon every grain-floor.

2The threshing-floor and the winepress shall not feed them, and the new wine shall fail her.

3They shall not dwell in Yahweh's land; but Ephraim shall return to Egypt, and they shall eat unclean food in Assyria.

4They shall not pour out wine-offerings to Yahweh, neither shall they be pleasing unto him: their sacrifices shall be unto them as the bread of mourners; all that eat thereof shall be polluted; for their bread shall be for their appetite; it shall not come into the house of Yahweh.

5What will ye do in the day of solemn assembly, and in the day of the feast of Yahweh?

6For, lo, they are gone away from destruction; yet Egypt shall gather them up, Memphis shall bury them; their pleasant things of silver, nettles shall possess them; thorns shall be in their tents.

7The days of visitation are come, the days of recompense are come; Israel shall know it: the prophet is a fool, the man that hath the spirit is mad, for the abundance of thine iniquity, and because the enmity is great.

8Ephraim was a watchman with my God: as for the prophet, a fowler's snare is in all his ways, and enmity in the house of his God.

9They have deeply corrupted themselves, as in the days of Gibeah: he will remember their iniquity, he will visit their sins.

10I found Israel like grapes in the wilderness; I saw your fathers as the first-ripe in the fig-tree at its first season: but they came to Baal-peor, and consecrated themselves unto the shameful thing, and became abominable like that which they loved.

11As for Ephraim, their glory shall fly away like a bird: there shall be no birth, and none with child, and no conception.

12Though they bring up their children, yet will I bereave them, so that not a man shall be left: yea, woe also to them when I depart from them!

13Ephraim, like as I have seen Tyre, is planted in a pleasant place: but Ephraim shall bring out his children to the slayer.

14Give them, O Yahweh-what wilt thou give? give them a miscarrying womb and dry breasts.

15All their wickedness is in Gilgal; for there I hated them: because of the wickedness of their doings I will drive them out of my house; I will love them no more; all their princes are revolters.

16Ephraim is smitten, their root is dried up, they shall bear no fruit: yea, though they bring forth, yet will I slay the beloved fruit of their womb.

17My God will cast them away, because they did not hearken unto him; and they shall be wanderers among the nations.

Chapter 10

1Israel is a luxuriant vine, that putteth forth his fruit: according to the abundance of his fruit he hath multiplied his altars; according to the goodness of their land they have made goodly pillars.

2Their heart is divided; now shall they be found guilty: he will smite their altars, he will destroy their pillars.

3Surely now shall they say, We have no king; for we fear not Yahweh; and the king, what can he do for us?

4They speak vain words, swearing falsely in making covenants: therefore judgment springeth up as hemlock in the furrows of the field.

5The inhabitants of Samaria shall be in terror for the calves of Beth-aven; for the people thereof shall mourn over it, and the priests thereof that rejoiced over it, for the glory thereof, because it is departed from it.

6It also shall be carried unto Assyria for a present to king Jareb: Ephraim shall receive shame, and Israel shall be ashamed of his own counsel.

7As for Samaria, her king is cut off, as foam upon the water.

8The high places also of Aven, the sin of Israel, shall be destroyed: the thorn and the thistle shall come up on their altars; and they shall say to the mountains, Cover us; and to the hills, Fall on us.

9O Israel, thou hast sinned from the days of Gibeah: there they stood; the battle against the children of iniquity doth not overtake them in Gibeah.

10When it is my desire, I will chastise them; and the peoples shall be gathered against them, when they are bound to their two transgressions.

11And Ephraim is a heifer that is taught, that loveth to tread out the grain; but I have passed over upon her fair neck: I will set a rider on Ephraim; Judah shall plow, Jacob shall break his clods.

12Sow to yourselves in righteousness, reap according to kindness; break up your fallow ground; for it is time to seek Yahweh, till he come and rain righteousness upon you.

13Ye have plowed wickedness, ye have reaped iniquity; ye have eaten the fruit of lies; for thou didst trust in thy way, in the multitude of thy mighty men.

14Therefore shall a tumult arise among thy people, and all thy fortresses shall be destroyed, as Shalman destroyed Beth-arbel in the day of battle: the mother was dashed in pieces with her children.

15So shall Beth-el do unto you because of your great wickedness: at daybreak shall the king of Israel be utterly cut off.

Chapter 11

1When Israel was a child, then I loved him, and called my son out of Egypt.

2The more the prophets called them, the more they went from them: they sacrificed unto the Baalim, and burned incense to graven images.

3Yet I taught Ephraim to walk; I took them on my arms; but they knew not that I healed them.

4I drew them with cords of a man, with bands of love; and I was to them as they that lift up the yoke on their jaws; and I laid food before them.

5They shall not return into the land of Egypt; but the Assyrian shall be their king, because they refused to return to me.

6And the sword shall fall upon their cities, and shall consume their bars, and devour them, because of their own counsels.

7And my people are bent on backsliding from me: though they call them to him that is on high, none at all will exalt him.

8How shall I give thee up, Ephraim? how shall I cast thee off, Israel? how shall I make thee as Admah? how shall I set thee as Zeboiim? my heart is turned within me, my compassions are kindled together.

9I will not execute the fierceness of mine anger, I will not return to destroy Ephraim: for I am God, and not man; the Holy One in the midst of thee; and I will not come in wrath.

10They shall walk after Yahweh, who will roar like a lion; for he will roar, and the children shall come trembling from the west.

11They shall come trembling as a bird out of Egypt, and as a dove out of the land of Assyria; and I will make them to dwell in their houses, saith Yahweh.

12Ephraim compasseth me about with falsehood, and the house of Israel with deceit; but Judah yet ruleth with God, and is faithful with the Holy One.

Chapter 12

1Ephraim feedeth on wind, and followeth after the east wind: he continually multiplieth lies and desolation; and they make a covenant with Assyria, and oil is carried into Egypt.

2Yahweh hath also a controversy with Judah, and will punish Jacob according to his ways; according to his doings will he recompense him.

3In the womb he took his brother by the heel; and in his manhood he had power with God:

4yea, he had power over the angel, and prevailed; he wept, and made supplication unto him: he found him at Beth-el, and there he spake with us,

5even Yahweh, the God of hosts; Yahweh is his memorial name.

6Therefore turn thou to thy God: keep kindness and justice, and wait for thy God continually.

7He is a trafficker, the balances of deceit are in his hand: he loveth to oppress.

8And Ephraim said, Surely I am become rich, I have found me wealth: in all my labors they shall find in me no iniquity that were sin.

9But I am Yahweh thy God from the land of Egypt; I will yet again make thee to dwell in tents, as in the days of the solemn feast.

10I have also spoken unto the prophets, and I have multiplied visions; and by the ministry of the prophets have I used similitudes.

11Is Gilead iniquity? they are altogether false; in Gilgal they sacrifice bullocks; yea, their altars are as heaps in the furrows of the field.

12And Jacob fled into the field of Aram, and Israel served for a wife, and for a wife he kept sheep.

13And by a prophet Yahweh brought Israel up out of Egypt, and by a prophet was he preserved.

14Ephraim hath provoked to anger most bitterly: therefore shall his blood be left upon him, and his reproach shall his Lord return unto him.

Chapter 13

1When Ephraim spake, there was trembling; he exalted himself in Israel; but when he offended in Baal, he died.

2And now they sin more and more, and have made them molten images of their silver, even idols according to their own understanding, all of them the work of the craftsmen: they say of them, Let the men that sacrifice kiss the calves.

3Therefore they shall be as the morning cloud, and as the dew that passeth early away, as the chaff that is driven with the whirlwind out of the threshing-floor, and as the smoke out of the chimney.

4Yet I am Yahweh thy God from the land of Egypt; and thou shalt know no god but me, and besides me there is no saviour.

5I did know thee in the wilderness, in the land of great drought.

6According to their pasture, so were they filled; they were filled, and their heart was exalted: therefore have they forgotten me.

7Therefore am I unto them as a lion; as a leopard will I watch by the way;

8I will meet them as a bear that is bereaved of her whelps, and will rend the caul of their heart; and there will I devour them like a lioness; the wild beast shall tear them.

9It is thy destruction, O Israel, that thou art against me, against thy help.

10Where now is thy king, that he may save thee in all thy cities? and thy judges, of whom thou saidst, Give me a king and princes?

11I have given thee a king in mine anger, and have taken him away in my wrath.

12The iniquity of Ephraim is bound up; his sin is laid up in store.

13The sorrows of a travailing woman shall come upon him: he is an unwise son; for it is time he should not tarry in the place of the breaking forth of children.

14I will ransom them from the power of Sheol; I will redeem them from death: O death, where are thy plagues? O Sheol, where is thy destruction? repentance shall be hid from mine eyes.

15Though he be fruitful among his brethren, an east wind shall come, the breath of Yahweh coming up from the wilderness; and his spring shall become dry, and his fountain shall be dried up: he shall make spoil of the treasure of all goodly vessels.

16Samaria shall bear her guilt; for she hath rebelled against her God: they shall fall by the sword; their infants shall be dashed in pieces, and their women with child shall be ripped up.

Chapter 14

1O Israel, return unto Yahweh thy God; for thou hast fallen by thine iniquity.

2Take with you words, and return unto Yahweh: say unto him, Take away all iniquity, and accept that which is good: so will we render as bullocks the offering of our lips.

3Assyria shall not save us; we will not ride upon horses; neither will we say any more to the work of our hands, Ye are our gods; for in thee the fatherless findeth mercy.

4I will heal their backsliding, I will love them freely; for mine anger is turned away from him.

5I will be as the dew unto Israel; he shall blossom as the lily, and cast forth his roots as Lebanon.

6His branches shall spread, and his beauty shall be as the olive-tree, and his smell as Lebanon.

7They that dwell under his shadow shall return; they shall revive as the grain, and blossom as the vine: the scent thereof shall be as the wine of Lebanon.

8Ephraim shall say, What have I to do any more with idols? I have answered, and will regard him: I am like a green fir-tree; from me is thy fruit found.

9Who is wise, that he may understand these things? prudent, that he may know them? for the ways of Yahweh are right, and the just shall walk in them; but transgressors shall fall therein.

Joel

Chapter 1

¹The word of Yahweh that came to Joel the son of Pethuel.

²Hear this, ye old men, and give ear, all ye inhabitants of the land. Hath this been in your days, or in the days of your fathers?

³Tell ye your children of it, and let your children tell their children, and their children another generation.

⁴That which the palmer-worm hath left hath the locust eaten; and that which the locust hath left hath the canker-worm eaten; and that which the canker-worm hath left hath the caterpillar eaten.

⁵Awake, ye drunkards, and weep; and wail, all ye drinkers of wine, because of the sweet wine; for it is cut off from your mouth.

⁶For a nation is come up upon my land, strong, and without number; his teeth are the teeth of a lion, and he hath the jaw-teeth of a lioness.

⁷He hath laid my vine waste, and barked my fig-tree: he hath made it clean bare, and cast it away; the branches thereof are made white.

⁸Lament like a virgin girded with sackcloth for the husband of her youth.

⁹The meal-offering and the drink-offering are cut off from the house of Yahweh; the priests, Yahweh's ministers, mourn.

¹⁰The field is laid waste, the land mourneth; for the grain is destroyed, the new wine is dried up, the oil languisheth.

¹¹Be confounded, O ye husbandmen, wail, O ye vinedressers, for the wheat and for the barley; for the harvest of the field is perished.

¹²The vine is withered, and the fig-tree languisheth; the pomegranate-tree, the palm-tree also, and the apple-tree, even all the trees of the field are withered: for joy is withered away from the sons of men.

¹³Gird yourselves with sackcloth, and lament, ye priests; wail, ye ministers of the altar; come, lie all night in sackcloth, ye ministers of my God: for the meal-offering and the drink-offering are withholden from the house of your God.

¹⁴Sanctify a fast, call a solemn assembly, gather the old men and all the inhabitants of the land unto the house of Yahweh your God, and cry unto Yahweh.

¹⁵Alas for the day! for the day of Yahweh is at hand, and as destruction from the Almighty shall it come.

¹⁶Is not the food cut off before our eyes, yea, joy and gladness from the house of our God?

¹⁷The seeds rot under their clods; the garners are laid desolate, the barns are broken down; for the grain is withered.

¹⁸How do the beasts groan! the herds of cattle are perplexed, because they have no pasture; yea, the flocks of sheep are made desolate.

¹⁹O Yahweh, to thee do I cry; for the fire hath devoured the pastures of the wilderness, and the flame hath burned all the trees of the field.

²⁰Yea, the beasts of the field pant unto thee; for the water brooks are dried up, and the fire hath devoured the pastures of the wilderness.

Chapter 2

¹Blow ye the trumpet in Zion, and sound an alarm in my holy mountain; let all the inhabitants of the land tremble: for the day of Yahweh cometh, for it is nigh at hand;

²a day of darkness and gloominess, a day of clouds and thick darkness, as the dawn spread upon the mountains; a great people and a strong; there hath not been ever the like, neither shall be any more after them, even to the years of many generations.

³A fire devoureth before them; and behind them a flame burneth: the land is as the garden of Eden before them, and behind them a desolate wilderness; yea, and none hath escaped them.

⁴The appearance of them is as the appearance of horses; and as horsemen, so do they run.

⁵Like the noise of chariots on the tops of the mountains do they leap, like the noise of a flame of fire that devoureth the stubble, as a strong people set in battle array.

⁶At their presence the peoples are in anguish; all faces are waxed pale.

⁷They run like mighty men; they climb the wall like men of war; and they march every one on his ways, and they break not their ranks.

⁸Neither doth one thrust another; they march every one in his path; and they burst through the weapons, and break not off their course.

⁹They leap upon the city; they run upon the wall; they climb up into the houses; they enter in at the windows like a thief.

¹⁰The earth quaketh before them; the heavens tremble; the sun and the moon are darkened, and the stars withdraw their shining.

¹¹And Yahweh uttereth his voice before his army; for his camp is very great; for he is strong that executeth his word; for the day of Yahweh is great and very terrible; and who can abide it?

¹²Yet even now, saith Yahweh, turn ye unto me with all your heart, and with fasting, and with weeping, and with mourning:

¹³and rend your heart, and not your garments, and turn unto Yahweh your God; for he is gracious and merciful, slow to anger, and abundant in lovingkindness, and repenteth him of the evil.

¹⁴Who knoweth whether he will not turn and repent, and leave a blessing behind him, even a meal-offering and a drink-offering unto Yahweh your God?

¹⁵Blow the trumpet in Zion, sanctify a fast, call a solemn assembly;

¹⁶gather the people, sanctify the assembly, assemble the old men, gather the children, and those that suck the breasts; let the bridegroom go forth from his chamber, and the bride out of her closet.

¹⁷Let the priests, the ministers of Yahweh, weep between the porch and the altar, and let them say, Spare thy people, O Yahweh, and give not thy heritage to reproach, that the nations should rule over them: wherefore should they say among the peoples, Where is their God?

¹⁸Then was Yahweh jealous for his land, and had pity on his people.

¹⁹And Yahweh answered and said unto his people, Behold, I will send you grain, and new wine, and oil, and ye shall be satisfied therewith; and I will no more make you a reproach among the nations;

²⁰but I will remove far off from you the northern army, and will drive it into a land barren and desolate, its forepart into the eastern sea, and its hinder part into the western sea; and its stench shall come up, and its ill savor shall come up, because it hath done great things.

²¹Fear not, O land, be glad and rejoice; for Yahweh hath done great things.

²²Be not afraid, ye beasts of the field; for the pastures of the wilderness do spring, for the tree beareth its fruit, the fig-tree and the vine do yield their strength.

²³Be glad then, ye children of Zion, and rejoice in Yahweh your God; for he giveth you the former rain in just measure, and he causeth to come down for you the rain, the former rain and the latter rain, in the first month.

²⁴And the floors shall be full of wheat, and the vats shall overflow with new wine and oil.

²⁵And I will restore to you the years that the locust hath eaten, the canker-worm, and the caterpillar, and the palmer-worm, my great army which I sent among you.

²⁶And ye shall eat in plenty and be satisfied, and shall praise the name of Yahweh your God, that hath dealt wondrously with you; and my people shall never be put to shame.

²⁷And ye shall know that I am in the midst of Israel, and that I am Yahweh your God, and there is none else; and my people shall never be put to shame.

²⁸And it shall come to pass afterward, that I will pour out my Spirit upon all flesh; and your sons and your daughters shall prophesy, your old men shall dream dreams, your young men shall see visions:

²⁹and also upon the servants and upon the handmaids in those days will I pour out my Spirit.

³⁰And I will show wonders in the heavens and in the earth: blood, and fire, and pillars of smoke.

³¹The sun shall be turned into darkness, and the moon into blood, before the great and terrible day of Yahweh cometh.

³²And it shall come to pass, that whosoever shall call on the name of Yahweh shall be delivered; for in mount Zion and in Jerusalem there shall be those that escape, as Yahweh hath said, and among the remnant those whom Yahweh doth call.

Chapter 3

¹For, behold, in those days, and in that time, when I shall bring back the captivity of Judah and Jerusalem,

²I will gather all nations, and will bring them down into the valley of Jehoshaphat; and I will execute judgment upon them there for my people and for my heritage Israel, whom they have scattered among the nations: and they have parted my land,

³and have cast lots for my people, and have given a boy for a harlot, and sold a girl for wine, that they may drink.

⁴Yea, and what are ye to me, O Tyre, and Sidon, and all the regions of Philistia? will ye render me a recompense? and if ye recompense me, swiftly and speedily will I return your recompense upon your own head.

⁵Forasmuch as ye have taken my silver and my gold, and have carried into your temples my goodly precious things,

⁶and have sold the children of Judah and the children of Jerusalem unto the sons of the Grecians, that ye may remove them far from their border;

⁷behold, I will stir them up out of the place whither ye have sold them, and will return your recompense upon your own head;

⁸and I will sell your sons and your daughters into the hand of the children of Judah, and they shall sell them to the men of Sheba, to a nation far off: for Yahweh hath spoken it.

⁹Proclaim ye this among the nations; prepare war; stir up the mighty men; let all the men of war draw near, let them come up.

¹⁰Beat your plowshares into swords, and your pruning-hooks into spears: let the weak say, I am strong.

¹¹Haste ye, and come, all ye nations round about, and gather yourselves together: thither cause thy mighty ones to come down, O Yahweh.

¹²Let the nations bestir themselves, and come up to the valley of Jehoshaphat; for there will I sit to judge all the nations round about.

¹³Put ye in the sickle; for the harvest is ripe: come, tread ye; for the winepress is full, the vats overflow; for their wickedness is great.

¹⁴Multitudes, multitudes in the valley of decision! for the day of Yahweh is near in the valley of decision.

¹⁵The sun and the moon are darkened, and the stars withdraw their shining.

¹⁶And Yahweh will roar from Zion, and utter his voice from Jerusalem; and the heavens and the earth shall shake: but Yahweh will be a refuge unto his people, and a stronghold to the children of Israel.

¹⁷So shall ye know that I am Yahweh your God, dwelling in Zion my holy mountain: then shall Jerusalem be holy, and there shall no strangers pass through her any more.

¹⁸And it shall come to pass in that day, that the mountains shall drop down sweet wine, and the hills shall flow with milk, and all the brooks of Judah shall flow with waters; and a fountain shall come forth from the house of Yahweh, and shall water the valley of Shittim.

Joel

19 Egypt shall be a desolation, and Edom shall be a desolate wilderness, for the violence done to the children of Judah, because they have shed innocent blood in their land.

20 But Judah shall abide for ever, and Jerusalem from generation to generation.

21 And I will cleanse their blood, that I have not cleansed: for Yahweh dwelleth in Zion.

Amos

Chapter 1

1The words of Amos, who was among the herdsmen of Tekoa, which he saw concerning Israel in the days of Uzziah king of Judah, and in the days of Jeroboam the son of Joash king of Israel, two years before the earthquake.

2And he said, Yahweh will roar from Zion, and utter his voice from Jerusalem; and the pastures of the shepherds shall mourn, and the top of Carmel shall wither.

3Thus saith Yahweh: For three transgressions of Damascus, yea, for four, I will not turn away the punishment thereof; because they have threshed Gilead with threshing instruments of iron:

4but I will send a fire into the house of Hazael, and it shall devour the palaces of Ben-hadad.

5And I will break the bar of Damascus, and cut off the inhabitant from the valley of Aven, and him that holdeth the sceptre from the house of Eden; and the people of Syria shall go into captivity unto Kir, saith Yahweh.

6Thus saith Yahweh: For three transgressions of Gaza, yea, for four, I will not turn away the punishment thereof; because they carried away captive the whole people, to deliver them up to Edom:

7but I will send a fire on the wall of Gaza, and it shall devour the palaces thereof.

8And I will cut off the inhabitant from Ashdod, and him that holdeth the sceptre from Ashkelon; and I will turn my hand against Ekron; and the remnant of the Philistines shall perish, saith the Lord Yahweh.

9Thus saith Yahweh: For three transgressions of Tyre, yea, for four, I will not turn away the punishment thereof; because they delivered up the whole people to Edom, and remembered not the brotherly covenant:

10but I will send a fire on the wall of Tyre, and it shall devour the palaces thereof.

11Thus saith Yahweh: For three transgressions of Edom, yea, for four, I will not turn away the punishment thereof; because he did pursue his brother with the sword, and did cast off all pity, and his anger did tear perpetually, and he kept his wrath for ever:

12but I will send a fire upon Teman, and it shall devour the palaces of Bozrah.

13Thus saith Yahweh: For three transgressions of the children of Ammon, yea, for four, I will not turn away the punishment thereof; because they have ripped up the women with child of Gilead, that they may enlarge their border.

14But I will kindle a fire in the wall of Rabbah, and it shall devour the palaces thereof, with shouting in the day of battle, with a tempest in the day of the whirlwind;

15and their king shall go into captivity, he and his princes together, saith Yahweh.

Chapter 2

1Thus saith Yahweh: For three transgressions of Moab, yea, for four, I will not turn away the punishment thereof; because he burned the bones of the king of Edom into lime:

2but I will send a fire upon Moab, and it shall devour the palaces of Kerioth; and Moab shall die with tumult, with shouting, and with the sound of the trumpet;

3and I will cut off the judge from the midst thereof, and will slay all the princes thereof with him, saith Yahweh.

4Thus saith Yahweh: For three transgressions of Judah, yea, for four, I will not turn away the punishment thereof; because they have rejected the law of Yahweh, and have not kept his statutes, and their lies have caused them to err, after which their fathers did walk:

5but I will send a fire upon Judah, and it shall devour the palaces of Jerusalem.

6Thus saith Yahweh: For three transgressions of Israel, yea, for four, I will not turn away the punishment thereof; because they have sold the righteous for silver, and the needy for a pair of shoes:

7they that pant after the dust of the earth on the head of the poor, and turn aside the way of the meek: and a man and his father go unto the same maiden, to profane my holy name:

8and they lay themselves down beside every altar upon clothes taken in pledge; and in the house of their God they drink the wine of such as have been fined.

9Yet destroyed I the Amorite before them, whose height was like the height of the cedars, and he was strong as the oaks; yet I destroyed his fruit from above, and his roots from beneath.

10Also I brought you up out of the land of Egypt, and led you forty years in the wilderness, to possess the land of the Amorite.

11And I raised up of your sons for prophets, and of your young men for Nazirites. Is it not even thus, O ye children of Israel? saith Yahweh.

12But ye gave the Nazirites wine to drink, and commanded the prophets, saying, Prophesy not.

13Behold, I will press you in your place, as a cart presseth that is full of sheaves.

14And flight shall perish from the swift; and the strong shall not strengthen his force; neither shall the mighty deliver himself;

15neither shall he stand that handleth the bow; and he that is swift of foot shall not deliver himself; neither shall he that rideth the horse deliver himself;

16and he that is courageous among the mighty shall flee away naked in that day, saith Yahweh.

Chapter 3

1Hear this word that Yahweh hath spoken against you, O children of Israel, against the whole family which I brought up out of the land of Egypt, saying,

2You only have I known of all the families of the earth: therefore I will visit upon you all your iniquities.

3Shall two walk together, except they have agreed?

4Will a lion roar in the forest, when he hath no prey? will a young lion cry out of his den, if he have taken nothing?

5Can a bird fall in a snare upon the earth, where no gin is set for him? shall a snare spring up from the ground, and have taken nothing at all?

6Shall the trumpet be blown in a city, and the people not be afraid? shall evil befall a city, and Yahweh hath not done it?

7Surely the Lord Yahweh will do nothing, except he reveal his secret unto his servants the prophets.

8The lion hath roared; who will not fear? The Lord Yahweh hath spoken; who can but prophesy?

9Publish ye in the palaces at Ashdod, and in the palaces in the land of Egypt, and say, Assemble yourselves upon the mountains of Samaria, and behold what great tumults are therein, and what oppressions in the midst thereof.

10For they know not to do right, saith Yahweh, who store up violence and robbery in their palaces.

11Therefore thus saith the Lord Yahweh: An adversary there shall be, even round about the land; and he shall bring down thy strength from thee, and thy palaces shall be plundered.

12Thus saith Yahweh: As the shepherd rescueth out of the mouth of the lion two legs, or a piece of an ear, so shall the children of Israel be rescued that sit in Samaria in the corner of a couch, and on the silken cushions of a bed.

13Hear ye, and testify against the house of Jacob, saith the Lord Yahweh, the God of hosts.

14For in the day that I shall visit the transgressions of Israel upon him, I will also visit the altars of Beth-el; and the horns of the altar shall be cut off, and fall to the ground.

15And I will smite the winter-house with the summer-house; and the houses of ivory shall perish, and the great houses shall have an end, saith Yahweh.

Chapter 4

1Hear this word, ye kine of Bashan, that are in the mountain of Samaria, that oppress the poor, that crush the needy, that say unto their lords, Bring, and let us drink.

2The Lord Yahweh hath sworn by his holiness, that, lo, the days shall come upon you, that they shall take you away with hooks, and your residue with fish-hooks.

3And ye shall go out at the breaches, every one straight before her; and ye shall cast yourselves into Harmon, saith Yahweh.

4Come to Beth-el, and transgress; to Gilgal, and multiply transgression; and bring your sacrifices every morning, and your tithes every three days;

5and offer a sacrifice of thanksgiving of that which is leavened, and proclaim freewill-offerings and publish them: for this pleaseth you, O ye children of Israel, saith the Lord Yahweh.

6And I also have given you cleanness of teeth in all your cities, and want of bread in all your places; yet have ye not returned unto me, saith Yahweh.

7And I also have withholden the rain from you, when there were yet three months to the harvest; and I caused it to rain upon one city, and caused it not to rain upon another city: one piece was rained upon, and the piece whereupon it rained not withered.

8So two or three cities wandered unto one city to drink water, and were not satisfied: yet have ye not returned unto me, saith Yahweh.

9I have smitten you with blasting and mildew: the multitude of your gardens and your vineyards and your fig-trees and your olive-trees hath the palmer-worm devoured: yet have ye not returned unto me, saith Yahweh.

10I have sent among you the pestilence after the manner of Egypt: your young men have I slain with the sword, and have carried away your horses; and I have made the stench of your camp to come up even into your nostrils: yet have ye not returned unto me, saith Yahweh.

11I have overthrown cities among you, as when God overthrew Sodom and Gomorrah, and ye were as a brand plucked out of the burning: yet have ye not returned unto me, saith Yahweh.

12Therefore thus will I do unto thee, O Israel; and because I will do this unto thee, prepare to meet thy God, O Israel.

13For, lo, he that formeth the mountains, and createth the wind, and declareth unto man what is his thought; that maketh the morning darkness, and treadeth upon the high places of the Earth-Yahweh, the God of hosts, is his name.

Chapter 5

1Hear ye this word which I take up for a lamentation over you, O house of Israel.

2The virgin of Israel is fallen; she shall no more rise: she is cast down upon her land; there is none to raise her up.

3For thus saith the Lord Yahweh: The city that went forth a thousand shall have a hundred left, and that which went forth a hundred shall have ten left, to the house of Israel.

4For thus saith Yahweh unto the house of Israel, Seek ye me, and ye shall live;

5but seek not Beth-el, nor enter into Gilgal, and pass not to Beer-sheba: for Gilgal shall surely go into captivity, and Beth-el shall come to nought.

Amos

6Seek Yahweh, and ye shall live; lest he break out like fire in the house of Joseph, and it devour, and there be none to quench it in Beth-el.

7Ye who turn justice to wormwood, and cast down righteousness to the earth,

8seek him that maketh the Pleiades and Orion, and turneth the shadow of death into the morning, and maketh the day dark with night; that calleth for the waters of the sea, and poureth them out upon the face of the earth (Yahweh is his name);

9that bringeth sudden destruction upon the strong, so that destruction cometh upon the fortress.

10They hate him that reproveth in the gate, and they abhor him that speaketh uprightly.

11Forasmuch therefore as ye trample upon the poor, and take exactions from him of wheat: ye have built houses of hewn stone, but ye shall not dwell in them; ye have planted pleasant vineyards, but ye shall not drink the wine thereof.

12For I know how manifold are your transgressions, and how mighty are your sins-ye that afflict the just, that take a bribe, and that turn aside the needy in the gate from their right.

13Therefore he that is prudent shall keep silence in such a time; for it is an evil time.

14Seek good, and not evil, that ye may live; and so Yahweh, the God of hosts, will be with you, as ye say.

15Hate the evil, and love the good, and establish justice in the gate: it may be that Yahweh, the God of hosts, will be gracious unto the remnant of Joseph.

16Therefore thus saith Yahweh, the God of hosts, the Lord: Wailing shall be in all the broad ways; and they shall say in all the streets, Alas! Alas! and they shall call the husbandman to mourning, and such as are skilful in lamentation to wailing.

17And in all vineyards shall be wailing; for I will pass through the midst of thee, saith Yahweh.

18Woe unto you that desire the day of Yahweh! Wherefore would ye have the day of Yahweh? It is darkness, and not light.

19As if a man did flee from a lion, and a bear met him; or went into the house and leaned his hand on the wall, and a serpent bit him.

20Shall not the day of Yahweh be darkness, and not light? even very dark, and no brightness in it?

21I hate, I despise your feasts, and I will take no delight in your solemn assemblies.

22Yea, though ye offer me your burnt-offerings and meal-offerings, I will not accept them; neither will I regard the peace-offerings of your fat beasts.

23Take thou away from me the noise of thy songs; for I will not hear the melody of thy viols.

24But let justice roll down as waters, and righteousness as a mighty stream.

25Did ye bring unto me sacrifices and offerings in the wilderness forty years, O house of Israel?

26Yea, ye have borne the tabernacle of your king and the shrine of your images, the star of your god, which ye made to yourselves.

27Therefore will I cause you to go into captivity beyond Damascus, saith Yahweh, whose name is the God of hosts.

Chapter 6

1Woe to them that are at ease in Zion, and to them that are secure in the mountain of Samaria, the notable men of the chief of the nations, to whom the house of Israel come!

2Pass ye unto Calneh, and see; and from thence go ye to Hamath the great; then go down to Gath of the Philistines: are they better than these kingdoms? or is their border greater than your border?

3-ye that put far away the evil day, and cause the seat of violence to come near;

4that lie upon beds of ivory, and stretch themselves upon their couches, and eat the lambs out of the flock, and the calves out of the midst of the stall;

5that sing idle songs to the sound of the viol; that invent for themselves instruments of music, like David;

6that drink wine in bowls, and anoint themselves with the chief oils; but they are not grieved for the affliction of Joseph.

7Therefore shall they now go captive with the first that go captive; and the revelry of them that stretched themselves shall pass away.

8The Lord Yahweh hath sworn by himself, saith Yahweh, the God of hosts: I abhor the excellency of Jacob, and hate his palaces; therefore will I deliver up the city with all that is therein.

9And it shall come to pass, if there remain ten men in one house, that they shall die.

10And when a man's uncle shall take him up, even he that burneth him, to bring out the bones out of the house, and shall say unto him that is in the innermost parts of the house, Is there yet any with thee? and he shall say, No; then shall he say, Hold thy peace; for we may not make mention of the name of Yahweh.

11For, behold, Yahweh commandeth, and the great house shall be smitten with breaches, and the little house with clefts.

12Shall horses run upon the rock? will one plow there with oxen? that ye have turned justice into gall, and the fruit of righteousness into wormwood;

13ye that rejoice in a thing of nought, that say, Have we not taken to us horns by our own strength?

14For, behold, I will raise up against you a nation, O house of Israel, saith Yahweh, the God of hosts; and they shall afflict you from the entrance of Hamath unto the brook of the Arabah.

Chapter 7

1Thus the Lord Yahweh showed me: and, behold, he formed locusts in the beginning of the shooting up of the latter growth; and, lo, it was the latter growth after the king's mowings.

2And it came to pass that, when they made an end of eating the grass of the land, then I said, O Lord Yahweh, forgive, I beseech thee: how shall Jacob stand? for he is small.

3Yahweh repented concerning this: It shall not be, saith Yahweh.

4Thus the Lord Yahweh showed me: and, behold, the Lord Yahweh called to content by fire; and it devoured the great deep, and would have eaten up the land.

5Then said I, O Lord Yahweh, cease, I beseech thee: how shall Jacob stand? for he is small.

6Yahweh repented concerning this: this also shall not be, saith the Lord Yahweh.

7Thus he showed me: and, behold, the Lord stood beside a wall made by a plumb-line, with a plumb-line in his hand.

8And Yahweh said unto me, Amos, what seest thou? And I said, A plumb-line. Then said the Lord, Behold, I will set a plumb-line in the midst of my people Israel; I will not again pass by them any more;

9and the high places of Isaac shall be desolate, and the sanctuaries of Israel shall be laid waste; and I will rise against the house of Jeroboam with the sword.

10Then Amaziah the priest of Beth-el sent to Jeroboam king of Israel, saying, Amos hath conspired against thee in the midst of the house of Israel: the land is not able to bear all his words.

11For thus Amos saith, Jeroboam shall die by the sword, and Israel shall surely be led away captive out of his land.

12Also Amaziah said unto Amos, O thou seer, go, flee thou away into the land of Judah, and there eat bread, and prophesy there:

13but prophesy not again any more at Beth-el; for it is the king's sanctuary, and it is a royal house.

14Then answered Amos, and said to Amaziah, I was no prophet, neither was I a prophet's son; but I was a herdsman, and a dresser of sycomore-trees:

15and Yahweh took me from following the flock, and Yahweh said unto me, Go, prophesy unto my people Israel.

16Now therefore hear thou the word of Yahweh: Thou sayest, Prophesy not against Israel, and drop not thy word against the house of Isaac;

17therefore thus saith Yahweh: Thy wife shall be a harlot in the city, and thy sons and thy daughters shall fall by the sword, and thy land shall be divided by line; and thou thyself shalt die in a land that is unclean, and Israel shall surely be led away captive out of his land.

Chapter 8

1Thus the Lord Yahweh showed me: and, behold, a basket of summer fruit.

2And he said, Amos, what seest thou? And I said, A basket of summer fruit. Then said Yahweh unto me, The end is come upon my people Israel; I will not again pass by them any more.

3And the songs of the temple shall be wailings in that day, saith the Lord Yahweh: the dead bodies shall be many: in every place shall they cast them forth with silence.

4Hear this, O ye that would swallow up the needy, and cause the poor of the land to fail,

5saying, When will the new moon be gone, that we may sell grain? and the sabbath, that we may set forth wheat, making the ephah small, and the shekel great, and dealing falsely with balances of deceit;

6that we may buy the poor for silver, and the needy for a pair of shoes, and sell the refuse of the wheat?

7Yahweh hath sworn by the excellency of Jacob, Surely I will never forget any of their works.

8Shall not the land tremble for this, and every one mourn that dwelleth therein? yea, it shall rise up wholly like the River; and it shall be troubled and sink again, like the River of Egypt.

9And it shall come to pass in that day, saith the Lord Yahweh, that I will cause the sun to go down at noon, and I will darken the earth in the clear day.

10And I will turn your feasts into mourning, and all your songs into lamentation; and I will bring sackcloth upon all loins, and baldness upon every head; and I will make it as the mourning for an only son, and the end thereof as a bitter day.

11Behold, the days come, saith the Lord Yahweh, that I will send a famine in the land, not a famine of bread, nor a thirst for water, but of hearing the words of Yahweh.

12And they shall wander from sea to sea, and from the north even to the east; they shall run to and fro to seek the word of Yahweh, and shall not find it.

13In that day shall the fair virgins and the young men faint for thirst.

14They that swear by the sin of Samaria, and say, As thy god, O Dan, liveth; and, As the way of Beer-sheba liveth; they shall fall, and never rise up again.

Chapter 9

1I saw the Lord standing beside the altar: and he said, Smite the capitals, that the thresholds may shake; and break them in pieces on the head of all of them; and I will slay the last of them with the sword: there shall not one of them flee away, and there shall not one of them escape.

2Though they dig into Sheol, thence shall my hand take them; and though they climb up to heaven, thence will I bring them down.

3And though they hide themselves in the top of Carmel, I will search and take them out thence; and though they be hid from my sight in the bottom of the sea, thence will I command the serpent, and it shall bite them.

4And though they go into captivity before their enemies, thence will I command the sword, and it shall slay them: and I will set mine eyes upon them for evil, and not for good.

5For the Lord, Yahweh of hosts, is he that toucheth the land and it melteth, and all that dwell therein shall mourn; and it shall rise up wholly like the River, and shall sink again, like the River of Egypt;

6it is he that buildeth his chambers in the heavens, and hath founded his vault upon the earth; he that calleth for the waters of the sea, and poureth them out upon the face of the earth; Yahweh is his name.

7Are ye not as the children of the Ethiopians unto me, O children of Israel? saith Yahweh. Have not I brought up Israel out of the land of Egypt, and the Philistines from Caphtor, and the Syrians from Kir?

8Behold, the eyes of the Lord Yahweh are upon the sinful kingdom, and I will destroy it from off the face of the earth; save that I will not utterly destroy the house of Jacob, saith Yahweh.

9For, lo, I will command, and I will sift the house of Israel among all the nations, like as grain is sifted in a sieve, yet shall not the least kernel fall upon the earth.

10All the sinners of my people shall die by the sword, who say, The evil shall not overtake nor meet us.

11In that day will I raise up the tabernacle of David that is fallen, and close up the breaches thereof; and I will raise up its ruins, and I will build it as in the days of old;

12that they may possess the remnant of Edom, and all the nations that are called by my name, saith Yahweh that doeth this.

13Behold, the days come, saith Yahweh, that the plowman shall overtake the reaper, and the treader of grapes him that soweth seed; and the mountains shall drop sweet wine, and all the hills shall melt.

14And I will bring back the captivity of my people Israel, and they shall build the waste cities, and inhabit them; and they shall plant vineyards, and drink the wine thereof; they shall also make gardens, and eat the fruit of them.

15And I will plant them upon their land, and they shall no more be plucked up out of their land which I have given them, saith Yahweh thy God.

Obadiah

¹The vision of Obadiah. Thus saith the Lord Yahweh concerning Edom: We have heard tidings from Yahweh, and an ambassador is sent among the nations, saying, Arise ye, and let us rise up against her in battle.

²Behold, I have made thee small among the nations: thou art greatly despised.

³The pride of thy heart hath deceived thee, O thou that dwellest in the clefts of the rock, whose habitation is high; that saith in his heart, Who shall bring me down to the ground?

⁴Though thou mount on high as the eagle, and though thy nest be set among the stars, I will bring thee down from thence, saith Yahweh.

⁵If thieves came to thee, if robbers by night (how art thou cut off!), would they not steal only till they had enough? if grape-gatherers came to thee, would they not leave some gleaning grapes?

⁶How are the things of Esau searched! how are his hidden treasures sought out!

⁷All the men of thy confederacy have brought thee on thy way, even to the border: the men that were at peace with thee have deceived thee, and prevailed against thee; they that eat thy bread lay a snare under thee: there is no understanding in him.

⁸Shall I not in that day, saith Yahweh, destroy the wise men out of Edom, and understanding out of the mount of Esau?

⁹And thy mighty men, O Teman, shall be dismayed, to the end that every one may be cut off from the mount of Esau by slaughter.

¹⁰For the violence done to thy brother Jacob, shame shall cover thee, and thou shalt be cut off for ever.

¹¹In the day that thou stoodest on the other side, in the day that strangers carried away his substance, and foreigners entered into his gates, and cast lots upon Jerusalem, even thou wast as one of them.

¹²But look not thou on the day of thy brother in the day of his disaster, and rejoice not over the children of Judah in the day of their destruction; neither speak proudly in the day of distress.

¹³Enter not into the gate of my people in the day of their calamity; yea, look not thou on their affliction in the day of their calamity, neither lay ye hands on their substance in the day of their calamity.

¹⁴And stand thou not in the crossway, to cut off those of his that escape; and deliver not up those of his that remain in the day of distress.

¹⁵For the day of Yahweh is near upon all the nations: as thou hast done, it shall be done unto thee; thy dealing shall return upon thine own head.

¹⁶For as ye have drunk upon my holy mountain, so shall all the nations drink continually; yea, they shall drink, and swallow down, and shall be as though they had not been.

¹⁷But in mount Zion there shall be those that escape, and it shall be holy; and the house of Jacob shall possess their possessions.

¹⁸And the house of Jacob shall be a fire, and the house of Joseph a flame, and the house of Esau for stubble, and they shall burn among them, and devour them; and there shall not be any remaining to the house of Esau; for Yahweh hath spoken it.

¹⁹And they of the South shall possess the mount of Esau, and they of the lowland the Philistines; and they shall possess the field of Ephraim, and the field of Samaria; and Benjamin shall possess Gilead.

²⁰And the captives of this host of the children of Israel, that are among the Canaanites, shall possess even unto Zarephath; and the captives of Jerusalem, that are in Sepharad, shall possess the cities of the South.

²¹And saviours shall come up on mount Zion to judge the mount of Esau; and the kingdom shall be Yahweh's.

Jonah

Chapter 1

¹Now the word of Yahweh came unto Jonah the son of Amittai, saying,
²Arise, go to Nineveh, that great city, and cry against it; for their wickedness is come up before me.
³But Jonah rose up to flee unto Tarshish from the presence of Yahweh; and he went down to Joppa, and found a ship going to Tarshish: so he paid the fare thereof, and went down into it, to go with them unto Tarshish from the presence of Yahweh.
⁴But Yahweh sent out a great wind upon the sea, and there was a mighty tempest on the sea, so that the ship was like to be broken.
⁵Then the mariners were afraid, and cried every man unto his god; and they cast forth the wares that were in the ship into the sea, to lighten it unto them. But Jonah was gone down into the innermost parts of the ship; and he lay, and was fast asleep.
⁶So the shipmaster came to him, and said unto him, What meanest thou, O sleeper? arise, call upon thy God, if so be that God will think upon us, that we perish not.
⁷And they said every one to his fellow, Come, and let us cast lots, that we may know for whose cause this evil is upon us. So they cast lots, and the lot fell upon Jonah.
⁸Then said they unto him, Tell us, we pray thee, for whose cause this evil is upon us; what is thine occupation? and whence comest thou? what is thy country? and of what people art thou?
⁹And he said unto them, I am a Hebrew; and I fear Yahweh, the God of heaven, who hath made the sea and the dry land.
¹⁰Then were the men exceedingly afraid, and said unto him, What is this that thou hast done? For the men knew that he was fleeing from the presence of Yahweh, because he had told them.
¹¹Then said they unto him, What shall we do unto thee, that the sea may be calm unto us? for the sea grew more and more tempestuous.
¹²And he said unto them, Take me up, and cast me forth into the sea; so shall the sea be calm unto you: for I know that for my sake this great tempest is upon you.
¹³Nevertheless the men rowed hard to get them back to the land; but they could not: for the sea grew more and more tempestuous against them.
¹⁴Wherefore they cried unto Yahweh, and said, We beseech thee, O Yahweh, we beseech thee, let us not perish for this man's life, and lay not upon us innocent blood; for thou, O Yahweh, hast done as it pleased thee.
¹⁵So they took up Jonah, and cast him forth into the sea; and the sea ceased from its raging.
¹⁶Then the men feared Yahweh exceedingly; and they offered a sacrifice unto Yahweh, and made vows.
¹⁷And Yahweh prepared a great fish to swallow up Jonah; and Jonah was in the belly of the fish three days and three nights.

Chapter 2

¹Then Jonah prayed unto Yahweh his God out of the fish's belly.
²And he said, I called by reason of mine affliction unto Yahweh, And he answered me; Out of the belly of Sheol cried I, And thou heardest my voice.
³For thou didst cast me into the depth, in the heart of the seas, And the flood was round about me; All thy waves and thy billows passed over me.
⁴And I said, I am cast out from before thine eyes; Yet I will look again toward thy holy temple.
⁵The waters compassed me about, even to the soul; The deep was round about me; The weeds were wrapped about my head.
⁶I went down to the bottoms of the mountains; The earth with its bars closed upon me for ever: Yet hast thou brought up my life from the pit, O Yahweh my God.
⁷When my soul fainted within me, I remembered Yahweh; And my prayer came in unto thee, into thy holy temple.
⁸They that regard lying vanities Forsake their own mercy.
⁹But I will sacrifice unto thee with the voice of thanksgiving; I will pay that which I have vowed. Salvation is of Yahweh.
¹⁰And Yahweh spake unto the fish, and it vomited out Jonah upon the dry land.

Chapter 3

¹And the word of Yahweh came unto Jonah the second time, saying,
²Arise, go unto Nineveh, that great city, and preach unto it the preaching that I bid thee.
³So Jonah arose, and went unto Nineveh, according to the word of Yahweh. Now Nineveh was an exceeding great city, of three days' journey.
⁴And Jonah began to enter into the city a day's journey, and he cried, and said, Yet forty days, and Nineveh shall be overthrown.
⁵And the people of Nineveh believed God; and they proclaimed a fast, and put on sackcloth, from the greatest of them even to the least of them.
⁶And the tidings reached the king of Nineveh, and he arose from his throne, and laid his robe from him, and covered him with sackcloth, and sat in ashes.
⁷And he made proclamation and published through Nineveh by the decree of the king and his nobles, saying, Let neither man nor beast, herd nor flock, taste anything; let them not feed, nor drink water;
⁸but let them be covered with sackcloth, both man and beast, and let them cry mightily unto God: yea, let them turn every one from his evil way, and from the violence that is in his hands.
⁹Who knoweth whether God will not turn and repent, and turn away from his fierce anger, that we perish not?
¹⁰And God saw their works, that they turned from their evil way; and God repented of the evil which he said he would do unto them; and he did it not.

Chapter 4

¹But it displeased Jonah exceedingly, and he was angry.
²And he prayed unto Yahweh, and said, I pray thee, O Yahweh, was not this my saying, when I was yet in my country? Therefore I hasted to flee unto Tarshish; for I knew that thou art a gracious God, and merciful, slow to anger, and abundant in lovingkindness, and repentest thee of the evil.
³Therefore now, O Yahweh, take, I beseech thee, my life from me; for it is better for me to die than to live.
⁴And Yahweh said, Doest thou well to be angry?
⁵Then Jonah went out of the city, and sat on the east side of the city, and there made him a booth, and sat under it in the shade, till he might see what would become of the city.
⁶And Yahweh God prepared a gourd, and made it to come up over Jonah, that it might be a shade over his head, to deliver him from his evil case. So Jonah was exceeding glad because of the gourd.
⁷But God prepared a worm when the morning rose the next day, and it smote the gourd, that it withered.
⁸And it came to pass, when the sun arose, that God prepared a sultry east wind; and the sun beat upon the head of Jonah, that he fainted, and requested for himself that he might die, and said, It is better for me to die than to live.
⁹And God said to Jonah, Doest thou well to be angry for the gourd? And he said, I do well to be angry, even unto death.
¹⁰And Yahweh said, Thou hast had regard for the gourd, for which thou hast not labored, neither madest it grow; which came up in a night, and perished in a night:
¹¹and should not I have regard for Nineveh, that great city, wherein are more than sixscore thousand persons that cannot discern between their right hand and their left hand; and also much cattle?

Micah

Chapter 1

1The word of Yahweh that came to Micah the Morashtite in the days of Jotham, Ahaz, and Hezekiah, kings of Judah, which he saw concerning Samaria and Jerusalem.

2Hear, ye peoples, all of you: hearken, O earth, and all that therein is: and let the Lord Yahweh be witness against you, the Lord from his holy temple.

3For, behold, Yahweh cometh forth out of his place, and will come down, and tread upon the high places of the earth.

4And the mountains shall be melted under him, and the valleys shall be cleft, as wax before the fire, as waters that are poured down a steep place.

5For the transgression of Jacob is all this, and for the sins of the house of Israel. What is the transgression of Jacob? is it not Samaria? and what are the high places of Judah? are they not Jerusalem?

6Therefore I will make Samaria as a heap of the field, and as places for planting vineyards; and I will pour down the stones thereof into the valley, and I will uncover the foundations thereof.

7And all her graven images shall be beaten to pieces, and all her hires shall be burned with fire, and all her idols will I lay desolate; for of the hire of a harlot hath she gathered them, and unto the hire of a harlot shall they return.

8For this will I lament and wail; I will go stripped and naked; I will make a wailing like the jackals, and a lamentation like the ostriches.

9For her wounds are incurable; for it is come even unto Judah; it reacheth unto the gate of my people, even to Jerusalem.

10Tell it not in Gath, weep not at all: at Beth-le-aphrah have I rolled myself in the dust.

11Pass away, O inhabitant of Shaphir, in nakedness and shame: the inhabitant of Zaanan is not come forth; the wailing of Beth-ezel shall take from you the stay thereof.

12For the inhabitant of Maroth waiteth anxiously for good, because evil is come down from Yahweh unto the gate of Jerusalem.

13Bind the chariot to the swift steed, O inhabitant of Lachish: she was the beginning of sin to the daughter of Zion; for the transgressions of Israel were found in thee.

14Therefore shalt thou give a parting gift to Moresheth-gath: the houses of Achzib shall be a deceitful thing unto the kings of Israel.

15I will yet bring unto thee, O inhabitant of Mareshah, him that shall possess thee: the glory of Israel shall come even unto Adullam.

16Make thee bald, and cut off thy hair for the children of thy delight: enlarge thy baldness as the eagle; for they are gone into captivity from thee.

Chapter 2

1Woe to them that devise iniquity and work evil upon their beds! when the morning is light, they practise it, because it is in the power of their hand.

2And they covet fields, and seize them; and houses, and take them away: and they oppress a man and his house, even a man and his heritage.

3Therefore thus saith Yahweh: Behold, against this family do I devise an evil, from which ye shall not remove your necks, neither shall ye walk haughtily; for it is an evil time.

4In that day shall they take up a parable against you, and lament with a doleful lamentation, and say, We are utterly ruined: he changeth the portion of my people: how doth he remove it from me! to the rebellious he divideth our fields.

5Therefore thou shalt have none that shall cast the line by lot in the assembly of Yahweh.

6Prophesy ye not, thus they prophesy. They shall not prophesy to these: reproaches shall not depart.

7Shall it be said, O house of Jacob, Is the Spirit of Yahweh straitened? are these his doings? Do not my words do good to him that walketh uprightly?

8But of late my people is risen up as an enemy: ye strip the robe from off the garment from them that pass by securely as men averse from war.

9The women of my people ye cast out from their pleasant houses; from their young children ye take away my glory for ever.

10Arise ye, and depart; for this is not your resting-place; because of uncleanness that destroyeth, even with a grievous destruction.

11If a man walking in a spirit of falsehood do lie, saying, I will prophesy unto thee of wine and of strong drink; he shall even be the prophet of this people.

12I will surely assemble, O Jacob, all of thee; I will surely gather the remnant of Israel; I will put them together as the sheep of Bozrah, as a flock in the midst of their pasture; they shall make great noise by reason of the multitude of men.

13The breaker is gone up before them: they have broken forth and passed on to the gate, and are gone out threat; and their king is passed on before them, and Yahweh at the head of them.

Chapter 3

1And I said, Hear, I pray you, ye heads of Jacob, and rulers of the house of Israel: is it not for you to know justice?

2ye who hate the good, and love the evil; who pluck off their skin from off them, and their flesh from off their bones;

3who also eat the flesh of my people, and flay their skin from off them, and break their bones, and chop them in pieces, as for the pot, and as flesh within the caldron.

4Then shall they cry unto Yahweh, but he will not answer them; yea, he will hide his face from them at that time, according as they have wrought evil in their doings.

5Thus saith Yahweh concerning the prophets that make my people to err; that bite with their teeth, and cry, Peace; and whoso putteth not into their mouths, they even prepare war against him:

6Therefore it shall be night unto you, that ye shall have no vision; and it shall be dark unto you, that ye shall not divine; and the sun shall go down upon the prophets, and the day shall be black over them.

7And the seers shall be put to shame, and the diviners confounded; yea, they shall all cover their lips; for there is no answer of God.

8But as for me, I am full of power by the Spirit of Yahweh, and of judgment, and of might, to declare unto Jacob his transgression, and to Israel his sin.

9Hear this, I pray you, ye heads of the house of Jacob, and rulers of the house of Israel, that abhor justice, and pervert all equity.

10They build up Zion with blood, and Jerusalem with iniquity.

11The heads thereof judge for reward, and the priests thereof teach for hire, and the prophets thereof divine for money: yet they lean upon Yahweh, and say, Is not Yahweh in the midst of us? no evil shall come upon us.

12Therefore shall Zion for your sake be plowed as a field, and Jerusalem shall become heaps, and the mountain of the house as the high places of a forest.

Chapter 4

1But in the latter days it shall come to pass, that the mountain of Yahweh's house shall be established on the top of the mountains, and it shall be exalted above the hills; and peoples shall flow unto it.

2And many nations shall go and say, Come ye, and let us go up to the mountain of Yahweh, and to the house of the God of Jacob; and he will teach us of his ways, and we will walk in his paths. For out of Zion shall go forth the law, and the word of Yahweh from Jerusalem;

3and he will judge between many peoples, and will decide concerning strong nations afar off: and they shall beat their swords into plowshares, and their spears into pruning-hooks; nation shall not lift up sword against nation, neither shall they learn war any more.

4But they shall sit every man under his vine and under his fig-tree; and none shall make them afraid: for the mouth of Yahweh of hosts hath spoken it.

5For all the peoples walk every one in the name of his god; and we will walk in the name of Yahweh our God for ever and ever.

6In that day, saith Yahweh, will I assemble that which is lame, and I will gather that which is driven away, and that which I have afflicted;

7and I will make that which was lame a remnant, and that which was cast far off a strong nation: and Yahweh will reign over them in mount Zion from henceforth even for ever.

8And thou, O tower of the flock, the hill of the daughter of Zion, unto thee shall it come, yea, the former dominion shall come, the kingdom of the daughter of Jerusalem.

9Now why dost thou cry out aloud? Is there no king in thee, is thy counsellor perished, that pangs have taken hold of thee as of a woman in travail?

10Be in pain, and labor to bring forth, O daughter of Zion, like a woman in travail; for now shalt thou go forth out of the city, and shalt dwell in the field, and shalt come even unto Babylon: there shalt thou be rescued; there will Yahweh redeem thee from the hand of thine enemies.

11And now many nations are assembled against thee, that say, Let her be defiled, and let our eye see our desire upon Zion.

12But they know not the thoughts of Yahweh, neither understand they his counsel; for he hath gathered them as the sheaves to the threshing-floor.

13Arise and thresh, O daughter of Zion; for I will make thy horn iron, and I will make thy hoofs brass; and thou shalt beat in pieces many peoples: and I will devote their gain unto Yahweh, and their substance unto the Lord of the whole earth.

Chapter 5

1Now shalt thou gather thyself in troops, O daughter of troops: he hath laid siege against us; they shall smite the judge of Israel with a rod upon the cheek.

2But thou, Beth-lehem Ephrathah, which art little to be among the thousands of Judah, out of thee shall one come forth unto me that is to be ruler in Israel; whose goings forth are of old, from everlasting.

3Therefore will he give them up, until the time that she who travaileth hath brought forth: then the residue of his brethren shall return unto the children of Israel.

4And he shall stand, and shall feed his flock in the strength of Yahweh, in the majesty of the name of Yahweh his God: and they shall abide; for now shall he be great unto the ends of the earth.

5And this man shall be our peace. When the Assyrian shall come into our land, and when he shall tread in our palaces, then shall we raise against him seven shepherds, and eight principal men.

6And they shall waste the land of Assyria with the sword, and the land of Nimrod in the entrances thereof: and he shall deliver us from the Assyrian, when he cometh into our land, and when he treadeth within our border.

7And the remnant of Jacob shall be in the midst of many peoples as dew from Yahweh, as showers upon the grass, that tarry not for man, nor wait for the sons of men.

8And the remnant of Jacob shall be among the nations, in the midst of many peoples, as a lion among the beasts of the forest, as a young lion among the flocks of sheep; who, if he go through, treadeth down and teareth in pieces, and there is none to deliver.

9Let thy hand be lifted up above thine adversaries, and let all thine enemies be cut off.

10And it shall come to pass in that day, saith Yahweh, that I will cut off thy horses out of the midst of thee, and will destroy thy chariots:
11and I will cut off the cities of thy land, and will throw down all thy strongholds.
12And I will cut off witchcrafts out of thy hand; and thou shalt have no more soothsayers:
13and I will cut off thy graven images and thy pillars out of the midst of thee; and thou shalt no more worship the work of thy hands;
14and I will pluck up thine Asherim out of the midst of thee; and I will destroy thy cities.
15And I will execute vengeance in anger and wrath upon the nations which hearkened not.

Chapter 6

1Hear ye now what Yahweh saith: Arise, contend thou before the mountains, and let the hills hear thy voice.
2Hear, O ye mountains, Yahweh's controversy, and ye enduring foundations of the earth; for Yahweh hath a controversy with his people, and he will contend with Israel.
3O my people, what have I done unto thee? and wherein have I wearied thee? testify against me.
4For I brought thee up out of the land of Egypt, and redeemed thee out of the house of bondage; and I sent before thee Moses, Aaron, and Miriam.
5O my people, remember now what Balak king of Moab devised, and what Balaam the son of Beor answered him; remember from Shittim unto Gilgal, that ye may know the righteous acts of Yahweh.
6Wherewith shall I come before Yahweh, and bow myself before the high God? shall I come before him with burnt-offerings, with calves a year old?
7will Yahweh be pleased with thousands of rams, or with ten thousands of rivers of oil? shall I give my first-born for my transgression, the fruit of my body for the sin of my soul?
8He hath showed thee, O man, what is good; and what doth Yahweh require of thee, but to do justly, and to love kindness, and to walk humbly with thy God?
9The voice of Yahweh crieth unto the city, and the man of wisdom will see thy name: hear ye the rod, and who hath appointed it.
10Are there yet treasures of wickedness in the house of the wicked, and a scant measure that is abominable?
11Shall I be pure with wicked balances, and with a bag of deceitful weights?
12For the rich men thereof are full of violence, and the inhabitants thereof have spoken lies, and their tongue is deceitful in their mouth.
13Therefore I also have smitten thee with a grievous wound; I have made thee desolate because of thy sins.
14Thou shalt eat, but not be satisfied; and thy humiliation shall be in the midst of thee: and thou shalt put away, but shalt not save; and that which thou savest will I give up to the sword.
15Thou shalt sow, but shalt not reap; thou shalt tread the olives, but shalt not anoint thee with oil; and the vintage, but shalt not drink the wine.
16For the statutes of Omri are kept, and all the works of the house of Ahab, and ye walk in their counsels; that I may make thee a desolation, and the inhabitants thereof a hissing: and ye shall bear the reproach of my people.

Chapter 7

1Woe is me! for I am as when they have gathered the summer fruits, as the grape gleanings of the vintage: there is no cluster to eat; my soul desireth the first-ripe fig.
2The godly man is perished out of the earth, and there is none upright among men: they all lie in wait for blood; they hunt every man his brother with a net.
3Their hands are upon that which is evil to do it diligently; the prince asketh, and the judge is ready for a reward; and the great man, he uttereth the evil desire of his soul: thus they weave it together.
4The best of them is as a brier; the most upright is worse than a thorn hedge: the day of thy watchmen, even thy visitation, is come; now shall be their perplexity.
5Trust ye not in a neighbor; put ye not confidence in a friend; keep the doors of thy mouth from her that lieth in thy bosom.
6For the son dishonoreth the father, the daughter riseth up against her mother, the daughter-in-law against her mother-in-law; a man's enemies are the men of his own house.
7But as for me, I will look unto Yahweh; I will wait for the God of my salvation: my God will hear me.
8Rejoice not against me, O mine enemy: when I fall, I shall arise; when I sit in darkness, Yahweh will be a light unto me.
9I will bear the indignation of Yahweh, because I have sinned against him, until he plead my cause, and execute judgment for me: he will bring me forth to the light, and I shall behold his righteousness.
10Then mine enemy shall see it, and shame shall cover her who said unto me, Where is Yahweh thy God? Mine eyes shall see my desire upon her; now shall she be trodden down as the mire of the streets.
11A day for building thy walls! in that day shall the decree be far removed.
12In that day shall they come unto thee from Assyria and the cities of Egypt, and from Egypt even to the River, and from sea to sea, and from mountain to mountain.
13Yet shall the land be desolate because of them that dwell therein, for the fruit of their doings.
14Feed thy people with thy rod, the flock of thy heritage, which dwell solitarily, in the forest in the midst of Carmel: let them feed in Bashan and Gilead, as in the days of old.
15As in the days of thy coming forth out of the land of Egypt will I show unto them marvellous things.
16The nations shall see and be ashamed of all their might; they shall lay their hand upon their mouth; their ears shall be deaf.
17They shall lick the dust like a serpent; like crawling things of the earth they shall come trembling out of their close places; they shall come with fear unto Yahweh our God, and shall be afraid because of thee.
18Who is a God like unto thee, that pardoneth iniquity, and passeth over the transgression of the remnant of his heritage? he retaineth not his anger for ever, because he delighteth in lovingkindness.
19He will again have compassion upon us; he will tread our iniquities under foot; and thou wilt cast all their sins into the depths of the sea.
20Thou wilt perform the truth to Jacob, and the lovingkindness to Abraham, which thou hast sworn unto our fathers from the days of old.

Nahum

Chapter 1

1 The burden of Nineveh. The book of the vision of Nahum the Elkoshite.

2 Yahweh is a jealous God and avengeth; Yahweh avengeth and is full of wrath; Yahweh taketh vengeance on his adversaries, and he reserveth wrath for his enemies.

3 Yahweh is slow to anger, and great in power, and will by no means clear the guilty: Yahweh hath his way in the whirlwind and in the storm, and the clouds are the dust of his feet.

4 He rebuketh the sea, and maketh it dry, and drieth up all the rivers: Bashan languisheth, and Carmel; and the flower of Lebanon languisheth.

5 The mountains quake at him, and the hills melt; and the earth is upheaved at his presence, yea, the world, and all that dwell therein.

6 Who can stand before his indignation? and who can abide in the fierceness of his anger? his wrath is poured out like fire, and the rocks are broken asunder by him.

7 Yahweh is good, a stronghold in the day of trouble; and he knoweth them that take refuge in him.

8 But with an over-running flood he will make a full end of her place, and will pursue his enemies into darkness.

9 What do ye devise against Yahweh? he will make a full end; affliction shall not rise up the second time.

10 For entangled like thorns, and drunken as with their drink, they are consumed utterly as dry stubble.

11 There is one gone forth out of thee, that deviseth evil against Yahweh, that counselleth wickedness.

12 Thus saith Yahweh: Though they be in full strength, and likewise many, even so shall they be cut down, and he shall pass away. Though I have afflicted thee, I will afflict thee no more.

13 And now will I break his yoke from off thee, and will burst thy bonds in sunder.

14 And Yahweh hath given commandment concerning thee, that no more of thy name be sown: out of the house of thy gods will I cut off the graven image and the molten image; I will make thy grave; for thou art vile.

15 Behold, upon the mountains the feet of him that bringeth good tidings, that publisheth peace! Keep thy feasts, O Judah, perform thy vows; for the wicked one shall no more pass through thee; he is utterly cut off.

Chapter 2

1 He that dasheth in pieces is come up against thee: keep the fortress, watch the way, make thy loins strong, fortify thy power mightily.

2 For Yahweh restoreth the excellency of Jacob, as the excellency of Israel; for the emptiers have emptied them out, and destroyed their vine-branches.

3 The shield of his mighty men is made red, the valiant men are in scarlet: the chariots flash with steel in the day of his preparation, and the cypress spears are brandished.

4 The chariots rage in the streets; they rush to and fro in the broad ways: the appearance of them is like torches; they run like the lightnings.

5 He remembereth his nobles: they stumble in their march; they make haste to the wall thereof, and the mantelet is prepared.

6 The gates of the rivers are opened, and the palace is dissolved.

7 And it is decreed: she is uncovered, she is carried away; and her handmaids moan as with the voice of doves, beating upon their breasts.

8 But Nineveh hath been from of old like a pool of water: yet they flee away. Stand, stand, they cry; but none looketh back.

9 Take ye the spoil of silver, take the spoil of gold; for there is no end of the store, the glory of all goodly furniture.

10 She is empty, and void, and waste; and the heart melteth, and the knees smite together, and anguish is in all loins, and the faces of them all are waxed pale.

11 Where is the den of the lions, and the feeding-place of the young lions, where the lion and the lioness walked, the lion's whelp, and none made them afraid?

12 The lion did tear in pieces enough for his whelps, and strangled for his lionesses, and filled his caves with prey, and his dens with ravin.

13 Behold, I am against thee, saith Yahweh of hosts, and I will burn her chariots in the smoke, and the sword shall devour thy young lions; and I will cut off thy prey from the earth, and the voice of thy messengers shall no more be heard.

Chapter 3

1 Woe to the bloody city! it is all full of lies and rapine; the prey departeth not.

2 The noise of the whip, and the noise of the rattling of wheels, and prancing horses, and bounding chariots,

3 the horseman mounting, and the flashing sword, and the glittering spear, and a multitude of slain, and a great heap of corpses, and there is no end of the bodies; they stumble upon their bodies;-

4 because of the multitude of the whoredoms of the well-favored harlot, the mistress of witchcrafts, that selleth nations through her whoredoms, and families through her witchcrafts.

5 Behold, I am against thee, saith Yahweh of hosts, and I will uncover thy skirts upon thy face; and I will show the nations thy nakedness, and the kingdoms thy shame.

6 And I will cast abominable filth upon thee, and make thee vile, and will set thee as a gazing-stock.

7 And it shall come to pass, that all they that look upon thee shall flee from thee, and say, Nineveh is laid waste: who will bemoan her? whence shall I seek comforters for thee?

8 Art thou better than No-amon, that was situate among the rivers, that had the waters round about her; whose rampart was the sea, and her wall was of the sea?

9 Ethiopia and Egypt were her strength, and it was infinite; Put and Lubim were thy helpers.

10 Yet was she carried away, she went into captivity; her young children also were dashed in pieces at the head of all the streets; and they cast lots for her honorable men, and all her great men were bound in chains.

11 Thou also shalt be drunken; thou shalt be hid; thou also shalt seek a stronghold because of the enemy.

12 All thy fortresses shall be like fig-trees with the first-ripe figs: if they be shaken, they fall into the mouth of the eater.

13 Behold, thy people in the midst of thee are women; the gates of thy land are set wide open unto thine enemies: the fire hath devoured thy bars.

14 Draw thee water for the siege; strengthen thy fortresses; go into the clay, and tread the mortar; make strong the brickkiln.

15 There shall the fire devour thee; the sword shall cut thee off; it shall devour thee like the canker-worm: make thyself many as the canker-worm; make thyself many as the locust.

16 Thou hast multiplied thy merchants above the stars of heaven: the canker-worm ravageth, and fleeth away.

17 Thy princes are as the locusts, and thy marshals as the swarms of grasshoppers, which encamp in the hedges in the cold day, but when the sun ariseth they flee away, and their place is not known where they are.

18 Thy shepherds slumber, O king of Assyria; thy nobles are at rest; thy people are scattered upon the mountains, and there is none to gather them.

19 There is no assuaging of thy hurt: thy wound is grievous: all that hear the report of thee clap their hands over thee; for upon whom hath not thy wickedness passed continually?

Habakkuk

Chapter 1

1 The burden which Habakkuk the prophet did see.

2 O Yahweh, how long shall I cry, and thou wilt not hear? I cry out unto thee of violence, and thou wilt not save.

3 Why dost thou show me iniquity, and look upon perverseness? for destruction and violence are before me; and there is strife, and contention riseth up.

4 Therefore the law is slacked, and justice doth never go forth; for the wicked doth compass about the righteous; therefore justice goeth forth perverted.

5 Behold ye among the nations, and look, and wonder marvellously; for I am working a work in your days, which ye will not believe though it be told you.

6 For, lo, I raise up the Chaldeans, that bitter and hasty nation, that march through the breadth of the earth, to possess dwelling-places that are not theirs.

7 They are terrible and dreadful; their judgment and their dignity proceed from themselves.

8 Their horses also are swifter than leopards, and are more fierce than the evening wolves; and their horsemen press proudly on: yea, their horsemen come from far; they fly as an eagle that hasteth to devour.

9 They come all of them for violence; the set of their faces is forwards; and they gather captives as the sand.

10 Yea, he scoffeth at kings, and princes are a derision unto him; he derideth every stronghold; for he heapeth up dust, and taketh it.

11 Then shall he sweep by as a wind, and shall pass over, and be guilty, even he whose might is his god.

12 Art not thou from everlasting, O Yahweh my God, my Holy One? we shall not die. O Yahweh, thou hast ordained him for judgment; and thou, O Rock, hast established him for correction.

13 Thou that art of purer eyes than to behold evil, and that canst not look on perverseness, wherefore lookest thou upon them that deal treacherously, and holdest thy peace when the wicked swalloweth up the man that is more righteous than he;

14 and makest men as the fishes of the sea, as the creeping things, that have no ruler over them?

15 He taketh up all of them with the angle, he catcheth them in his net, and gathereth them in his drag: therefore he rejoiceth and is glad.

16 Therefore he sacrificeth unto his net, and burneth incense unto his drag; because by them his portion is fat, and his food plenteous.

17 Shall he therefore empty his net, and spare not to slay the nations continually?

Chapter 2

1 I will stand upon my watch, and set me upon the tower, and will look forth to see what he will speak with me, and what I shall answer concerning my complaint.

2 And Yahweh answered me, and said, Write the vision, and make it plain upon tablets, that he may run that readeth it.

3 For the vision is yet for the appointed time, and it hasteth toward the end, and shall not lie: though it tarry, wait for it; because it will surely come, it will not delay.

4 Behold, his soul is puffed up, it is not upright in him; but the righteous shall live by his faith.

5 Yea, moreover, wine is treacherous, a haughty man, that keepeth not at home; who enlargeth his desire as Sheol, and he is as death, and cannot be satisfied, but gathereth unto him all nations, and heapeth unto him all peoples.

6 Shall not all these take up a parable against him, and a taunting proverb against him, and say, Woe to him that increaseth that which is not his! how long? and that ladeth himself with pledges!

7 Shall they not rise up suddenly that shall bite thee, and awake that shall vex thee, and thou shalt be for booty unto them?

8 Because thou hast plundered many nations, all the remnant of the peoples shall plunder thee, because of men's blood, and for the violence done to the land, to the city and to all that dwell therein.

9 Woe to him that getteth an evil gain for his house, that he may set his nest on high, that he may be delivered from the hand of evil!

10 Thou hast devised shame to thy house, by cutting off many peoples, and hast sinned against thy soul.

11 For the stone shall cry out of the wall, and the beam out of the timber shall answer it.

12 Woe to him that buildeth a town with blood, and establisheth a city by iniquity!

13 Behold, is it not of Yahweh of hosts that the peoples labor for the fire, and the nations weary themselves for vanity?

14 For the earth shall be filled with the knowledge of the glory of Yahweh, as the waters cover the sea.

15 Woe unto him that giveth his neighbor drink, to thee that addest thy venom, and makest him drunken also, that thou mayest look on their nakedness!

16 Thou art filled with shame, and not glory: drink thou also, and be as one uncircumcised; the cup of Yahweh's right hand shall come round unto thee, and foul shame shall be upon thy glory.

17 For the violence done to Lebanon shall cover thee, and the destruction of the beasts, which made them afraid; because of men's blood, and for the violence done to the land, to the city and to all that dwell therein.

18 What profiteth the graven image, that the maker thereof hath graven it; the molten image, even the teacher of lies, that he that fashioneth its form trusteth therein, to make dumb idols?

19 Woe unto him that saith to the wood, Awake; to the dumb stone, Arise! Shall this teach? Behold, it is overlaid with gold and silver, and there is no breath at all in the midst of it.

20 But Yahweh is in his holy temple: let all the earth keep silence before him.

Chapter 3

1 A prayer of Habakkuk the prophet, set to Shigionoth.

2 O Yahweh, I have heard the report of thee, and am afraid:
O Yahweh, revive thy work in the midst of the years;
In the midst of the years make it known;
In wrath remember mercy.

3 God came from Teman,
And the Holy One from mount Paran.
Selah.
His glory covered the heavens,
And the earth was full of his praise.

4 And his brightness was as the light;
He had rays coming forth from his hand;
And there was the hiding of his power.

5 Before him went the pestilence,
And fiery bolts went forth at his feet.

6 He stood, and measured the earth;
He beheld, and drove asunder the nations;
And the eternal mountains were scattered;
The everlasting hills did bow;
His goings were as of old.

7 I saw the tents of Cushan in affliction;
The curtains of the land of Midian did tremble.

8 Was Yahweh displeased with the rivers?
Was thine anger against the rivers,
Or thy wrath against the sea,
That thou didst ride upon thy horses,
Upon thy chariots of salvation?

9 Thy bow was made quite bare;
The oaths to the tribes were a sure word.
Selah.
Thou didst cleave the earth with rivers.

10 The mountains saw thee, and were afraid;
The tempest of waters passed by;
The deep uttered its voice,
And lifted up its hands on high.

11 The sun and moon stood still in their habitation,
At the light of thine arrows as they went,
At the shining of thy glittering spear.

12 Thou didst march though the land in indignation;
Thou didst thresh the nations in anger.

13 Thou wentest forth for the salvation of thy people,
For the salvation of thine anointed;
Thou woundest the head out of the house of the wicked man,
Laying bare the foundation even unto the neck.
Selah.

14 Thou didst pierce with his own staves the head of his warriors:
They came as a whirlwind to scatter me;
Their rejoicing was as to devour the poor secretly.

15 Thou didst tread the sea with thy horses,
The heap of mighty waters.

16 I heard, and my body trembled,
My lips quivered at the voice;
Rottenness entereth into my bones, and I tremble in my place;
Because I must wait quietly for the day of trouble,
For the coming up of the people that invadeth us.

17 For though the fig-tree shall not flourish,
Neither shall fruit be in the vines;
The labor of the olive shall fail,
And the fields shall yield no food;
The flock shall be cut off from the fold,
And there shall be no herd in the stalls:

18 Yet I will rejoice in Yahweh,
I will joy in the God of my salvation.

19 Yahweh, the Lord, is my strength;
And he maketh my feet like hinds' feet,
And will make me to walk upon my high places.

Zephaniah

Chapter 1

1The word of Yahweh which came unto Zephaniah the son of Cushi, the son of Gedaliah, the son of Amariah, the son of Hezekiah, in the days of Josiah the son of Amon, king of Judah.

2I will utterly consume all things from off the face of the ground, saith Yahweh.

3I will consume man and beast; I will consume the birds of the heavens, and the fishes of the sea, and the stumblingblocks with the wicked; and I will cut off man from off the face of the ground, saith Yahweh.

4And I will stretch out my hand upon Judah, and upon all the inhabitants of Jerusalem; and I will cut off the remnant of Baal from this place, and the name of the Chemarim with the priests;

5and them that worship the host of heaven upon the housetops; and them that worship, that swear to Yahweh and swear by Malcam;

6and them that are turned back from following Yahweh; and those that have not sought Yahweh, nor inquired after him.

7Hold thy peace at the presence of the Lord Yahweh; for the day of Yahweh is at hand: for Yahweh hath prepared a sacrifice, he hath consecrated his guests.

8And it shall come to pass in the day of Yahweh's sacrifice, that I will punish the princes, and the king's sons, and all such as are clothed with foreign apparel.

9And in that day I will punish all those that leap over the threshold, that fill their master's house with violence and deceit.

10And in that day, saith Yahweh, there shall be the noise of a cry from the fish gate, and a wailing from the second quarter, and a great crashing from the hills.

11Wail, ye inhabitants of Maktesh; for all the people of Canaan are undone; all they that were laden with silver are cut off.

12And it shall come to pass at that time, that I will search Jerusalem with lamps; and I will punish the men that are settled on their lees, that say in their heart, Yahweh will not do good, neither will he do evil.

13And their wealth shall become a spoil, and their houses a desolation: yea, they shall build houses, but shall not inhabit them; and they shall plant vineyards, but shall not drink the wine thereof.

14The great day of Yahweh is near, it is near and hasteth greatly, even the voice of the day of Yahweh; the mighty man crieth there bitterly.

15That day is a day of wrath, a day of trouble and distress, a day of wasteness and desolation, a day of darkness and gloominess, a day of clouds and thick darkness,

16a day of the trumpet and alarm, against the fortified cities, and against the high battlements.

17And I will bring distress upon men, that they shall walk like blind men, because they have sinned against Yahweh; and their blood shall be poured out as dust, and their flesh as dung.

18Neither their silver nor their gold shall be able to deliver them in the day of Yahweh's wrath; but the whole land shall be devoured by the fire of his jealousy: for he will make an end, yea, a terrible end, of all them that dwell in the land.

Chapter 2

1Gather yourselves together, yea, gather together, O nation that hath no shame;

2before the decree bring forth, before the day pass as the chaff, before the fierce anger of Yahweh come upon you, before the day of Yahweh's anger come upon you.

3Seek ye Yahweh, all ye meek of the earth, that have kept his ordinances; seek righteousness, seek meekness: it may be ye will be hid in the day of Yahweh's anger.

4For Gaza shall be forsaken, and Ashkelon a desolation; they shall drive out Ashdod at noonday, and Ekron shall be rooted up.

5Woe unto the inhabitants of the sea-coast, the nation of the Cherethites! The word of Yahweh is against you, O Canaan, the land of the Philistines; I will destroy thee, that there shall be no inhabitant.

6And the sea-coast shall be pastures, with cottages for shepherds and folds for flocks.

7And the coast shall be for the remnant of the house of Judah; they shall feed their flocks thereupon; in the houses of Ashkelon shall they lie down in the evening; for Yahweh their God will visit them, and bring back their captivity.

8I have heard the reproach of Moab, and the revilings of the children of Ammon, wherewith they have reproached my people, and magnified themselves against their border.

9Therefore as I live, saith Yahweh of hosts, the God of Israel, Surely Moab shall be as Sodom, and the children of Ammon as Gomorrah, a possession of nettles, and saltpits, and a perpetual desolation: the residue of my people shall make a prey of them, and the remnant of my nation shall inherit them.

10This shall they have for their pride, because they have reproached and magnified themselves against the people of Yahweh of hosts.

11Yahweh will be terrible unto them; for he will famish all the gods of the earth; and men shall worship him, every one from his place, even all the isles of the nations.

12Ye Ethiopians also, ye shall be slain by my sword.

13And he will stretch out his hand against the north, and destroy Assyria, and will make Nineveh a desolation, and dry like the wilderness.

14And herds shall lie down in the midst of her, all the beasts of the nations: both the pelican and the porcupine shall lodge in the capitals thereof; their voice shall sing in the windows; desolation shall be in the thresholds: for he hath laid bare the cedar-work.

15This is the joyous city that dwelt carelessly, that said in her heart, I am, and there is none besides me: how is she become a desolation, a place for beasts to lie down in! every one that passeth by her shall hiss, and wag his hand.

Chapter 3

1Woe to her that is rebellious and polluted! to the oppressing city!

2She obeyed not the voice; she received not correction; she trusted not in Yahweh; she drew not near to her God.

3Her princes in the midst of her are roaring lions; her judges are evening wolves; they leave nothing till the morrow.

4Her prophets are light and treacherous persons; her priests have profaned the sanctuary, they have done violence to the law.

5Yahweh in the midst of her is righteous; he will not do iniquity; every morning doth he bring his justice to light, he faileth not; but the unjust knoweth no shame.

6I have cut off nations; their battlements are desolate; I have made their streets waste, so that none passeth by; their cities are destroyed, so that there is no man, so that there is no inhabitant.

7I said, Only fear thou me; receive correction; so her dwelling shall not be cut off, according to all that I have appointed concerning her: but they rose early and corrupted all their doings.

8Therefore wait ye for me, saith Yahweh, until the day that I rise up to the prey; for my determination is to gather the nations, that I may assemble the kingdoms, to pour upon them mine indignation, even all my fierce anger; for all the earth shall be devoured with the fire of my jealousy.

9For then will I turn to the peoples of a pure language, that they may all call upon the name of Yahweh, to serve him with one consent.

10From beyond the rivers of Ethiopia my suppliants, even the daughter of my dispersed, shall bring mine offering.

11In that day shalt thou not be put to shame for all thy doings, wherein thou hast transgressed against me; for then I will take away out of the midst of thee thy proudly exulting ones, and thou shalt no more be haughty in my holy mountain.

12But I will leave in the midst of thee an afflicted and poor people, and they shall take refuge in the name of Yahweh.

13The remnant of Israel shall not do iniquity, nor speak lies; neither shall a deceitful tongue be found in their mouth; for they shall feed and lie down, and none shall make them afraid.

14Sing, O daughter of Zion; shout, O Israel; be glad and rejoice with all the heart, O daughter of Jerusalem.

15Yahweh hath taken away thy judgments, he hath cast out thine enemy: the King of Israel, even Yahweh, is in the midst of thee; thou shalt not fear evil any more.

16In that day it shall be said to Jerusalem, Fear thou not; O Zion, let not thy hands be slack.

17Yahweh thy God is in the midst of thee, a mighty one who will save; he will rejoice over thee with joy; he will rest in his love; he will joy over thee with singing.

18I will gather them that sorrow for the solemn assembly, who were of thee; to whom the burden upon her was a reproach.

19Behold, at that time I will deal with all them that afflict thee; and I will save that which is lame, and gather that which was driven away; and I will make them a praise and a name, whose shame hath been in all the earth.

20At that time will I bring you in, and at that time will I gather you; for I will make you a name and a praise among all the peoples of the earth, when I bring back your captivity before your eyes, saith Yahweh.

Haggai

Chapter 1

1In the second year of Darius the king, in the sixth month, in the first day of the month, came the word of Yahweh by Haggai the prophet unto Zerubbabel the son of Shealtiel, governor of Judah, and to Joshua the son of Jehozadak, the high priest, saying,

2Thus speaketh Yahweh of hosts, saying, This people say, It is not the time for us to come, the time for Yahweh's house to be built.

3Then came the word of Yahweh by Haggai the prophet, saying,

4Is it a time for you yourselves to dwell in your ceiled houses, while this house lieth waste?

5Now therefore thus saith Yahweh of hosts: Consider your ways.

6Ye have sown much, and bring in little; ye eat, but ye have not enough; ye drink, but ye are not filled with drink; ye clothe you, but there is none warm; and he that earneth wages earneth wages to put it into a bag with holes.

7Thus saith Yahweh of hosts: Consider your ways.

8Go up to the mountain, and bring wood, and build the house; and I will take pleasure in it, and I will be glorified, saith Yahweh.

9Ye looked for much, and, lo, it came to little; and when ye brought it home, I did blow upon it. Why? saith Yahweh of hosts. Because of my house that lieth waste, while ye run every man to his own house.

10Therefore for your sake the heavens withhold the dew, and the earth withholdeth its fruit.

11And I called for a drought upon the land, and upon the mountains, and upon the grain, and upon the new wine, and upon the oil, and upon that which the ground bringeth forth, and upon men, and upon cattle, and upon all the labor of the hands.

12Then Zerubbabel the son of Shealtiel, and Joshua the son of Jehozadak, the high priest, with all the remnant of the people, obeyed the voice of Yahweh their God, and the words of Haggai the prophet, as Yahweh their God had sent him; and the people did fear before Yahweh.

13Then spake Haggai Yahweh's messenger in Yahweh's message unto the people, saying, I am with you, saith Yahweh.

14And Yahweh stirred up the spirit of Zerubbabel the son of Shealtiel, governor of Judah, and the spirit of Joshua the son of Jehozadak, the high priest, and the spirit of all the remnant of the people; and they came and did work on the house of Yahweh of hosts, their God,

15in the four and twentieth day of the month, in the sixth month, in the second year of Darius the king.

Chapter 2

1In the seventh month, in the one and twentieth day of the month, came the word of Yahweh by Haggai the prophet, saying,

2Speak now to Zerubbabel the son of Shealtiel, governor of Judah, and to Joshua the son of Jehozadak, the high priest, and to the remnant of the people, saying,

3Who is left among you that saw this house in its former glory? and how do ye see it now? is it not in your eyes as nothing?

4Yet now be strong, O Zerubbabel, saith Yahweh; and be strong, O Joshua, son of Jehozadak, the high priest; and be strong, all ye people of the land, saith Yahweh, and work: for I am with you, saith Yahweh of hosts,

5according to the word that I covenanted with you when ye came out of Egypt, and my Spirit abode among you: fear ye not.

6For thus saith Yahweh of hosts: Yet once, it is a little while, and I will shake the heavens, and the earth, and the sea, and the dry land;

7and I will shake all nations; and the precious things of all nations shall come; and I will fill this house with glory, saith Yahweh of hosts.

8The silver is mine, and the gold is mine, saith Yahweh of hosts.

9The latter glory of this house shall be greater than the former, saith Yahweh of hosts; and in this place will I give peace, saith Yahweh of hosts.

10In the four and twentieth day of the ninth month, in the second year of Darius, came the word of Yahweh by Haggai the prophet, saying,

11Thus saith Yahweh of hosts: Ask now the priests concerning the law, saying,

12If one bear holy flesh in the skirt of his garment, and with his skirt do touch bread, or pottage, or wine, or oil, or any food, shall it become holy? And the priests answered and said, No.

13Then said Haggai, If one that is unclean by reason of a dead body touch any of these, shall it be unclean? And the priests answered and said, It shall be unclean.

14Then answered Haggai and said, So is this people, and so is this nation before me, saith Yahweh; and so is every work of their hands; and that which they offer there is unclean.

15And now, I pray you, consider from this day and backward, before a stone was laid upon a stone in the temple of Yahweh.

16Through all that time, when one came to a heap of twenty measures, there were but ten; when one came to the winevat to draw out fifty vessels, there were but twenty.

17I smote you with blasting and with mildew and with hail in all the work of your hands; yet ye turned not to me, saith Yahweh.

18Consider, I pray you, from this day and backward, from the four and twentieth day of the ninth month, since the day that the foundation of Yahweh's temple was laid, consider it.

19Is the seed yet in the barn? yea, the vine, and the fig-tree, and the pomegranate, and the olive-tree have not brought forth; from this day will I bless you.

20And the word of Yahweh came the second time unto Haggai in the four and twentieth day of the month, saying,

21Speak to Zerubbabel, governor of Judah, saying, I will shake the heavens and the earth;

22and I will overthrow the throne of kingdoms; and I will destroy the strength of the kingdoms of the nations; and I will overthrow the chariots, and those that ride in them; and the horses and their riders shall come down, every one by the sword of his brother.

23In that day, saith Yahweh of hosts, will I take thee, O Zerubbabel, my servant, the son of Shealtiel, saith Yahweh, and will make thee as a signet; for I have chosen thee, saith Yahweh of hosts.

Zechariah

Chapter 1

1In the eighth month, in the second year of Darius, came the word of Yahweh unto Zechariah the son of Berechiah, the son of Iddo, the prophet, saying,

2Yahweh was sore displeased with your fathers.

3Therefore say thou unto them, Thus saith Yahweh of hosts: Return unto me, saith Yahweh of hosts, and I will return unto you, saith Yahweh of hosts.

4Be ye not as your fathers, unto whom the former prophets cried, saying, Thus saith Yahweh of hosts, Return ye now from your evil ways, and from your evil doings: but they did not hear, nor hearken unto me, saith Yahweh.

5Your fathers, where are they? and the prophets, do they live for ever?

6But my words and my statutes, which I commanded my servants the prophets, did they not overtake your fathers? and they turned and said, Like as Yahweh of hosts thought to do unto us, according to our ways, and according to our doings, so hath he dealt with us.

7Upon the four and twentieth day of the eleventh month, which is the month Shebat, in the second year of Darius, came the word of Yahweh unto Zechariah the son of Berechiah, the son of Iddo, the prophet, saying,

8I saw in the night, and, behold, a man riding upon a red horse, and he stood among the myrtle-trees that were in the bottom; and behind him there were horses, red, sorrel, and white.

9Then said I, O my lord, what are these? And the angel that talked with me said unto me, I will show thee what these are.

10And the man that stood among the myrtle-trees answered and said, These are they whom Yahweh hath sent to walk to and fro through the earth.

11And they answered the angel of Yahweh that stood among the myrtle-trees, and said, We have walked to and fro through the earth, and, behold, all the earth sitteth still, and is at rest.

12Then the angel of Yahweh answered and said, O Yahweh of hosts, how long wilt thou not have mercy on Jerusalem and on the cities of Judah, against which thou hast had indignation these threescore and ten years?

13And Yahweh answered the angel that talked with me with good words, even comfortable words.

14So the angel that talked with me said unto me, Cry thou, saying, Thus saith Yahweh of hosts: I am jealous for Jerusalem and for Zion with a great jealousy.

15And I am very sore displeased with the nations that are at ease; for I was but a little displeased, and they helped forward the affliction.

16Therefore thus saith Yahweh: I am returned to Jerusalem with mercies; my house shall be built in it, saith Yahweh of hosts, and a line shall be stretched forth over Jerusalem.

17Cry yet again, saying, Thus saith Yahweh of hosts: My cities shall yet overflow with prosperity; and Yahweh shall yet comfort Zion, and shall yet choose Jerusalem.

18And I lifted up mine eyes, and saw, and, behold, four horns.

19And I said unto the angel that talked with me, What are these? And he answered me, These are the horns which have scattered Judah, Israel, and Jerusalem.

20And Yahweh showed me four smiths.

21Then said I, What come these to do? And he spake, saying, These are the horns which scattered Judah, so that no man did lift up his head; but these are come to terrify them, to cast down the horns of the nations, which lifted up their horn against the land of Judah to scatter it.

Chapter 2

1And I lifted up mine eyes, and saw, and, behold, a man with a measuring line in his hand.

2Then said I, Whither goest thou? And he said unto me, To measure Jerusalem, to see what is the breadth thereof, and what is the length thereof.

3And, behold, the angel that talked with me went forth, and another angel went out to meet him,

4and said unto him, Run, speak to this young man, saying, Jerusalem shall be inhabited as villages without walls, by reason of the multitude of men and cattle therein.

5For I, saith Yahweh, will be unto her a wall of fire round about, and I will be the glory in the midst of her.

6Ho, ho, flee from the land of the north, saith Yahweh; for I have spread you abroad as the four winds of the heavens, saith Yahweh.

7Ho Zion, escape, thou that dwellest with the daughter of Babylon.

8For thus saith Yahweh of hosts: After glory hath he sent me unto the nations which plundered you; for he that toucheth you toucheth the apple of his eye.

9For, behold, I will shake my hand over them, and they shall be a spoil to those that served them; and ye shall know that Yahweh of hosts hath sent me.

10Sing and rejoice, O daughter of Zion; for, lo, I come, and I will dwell in the midst of thee, saith Yahweh.

11And many nations shall join themselves to Yahweh in that day, and shall be my people; and I will dwell in the midst of thee, and thou shalt know that Yahweh of hosts has sent me unto thee.

12And Yahweh shall inherit Judah as his portion in the holy land, and shall yet choose Jerusalem.

13Be silent, all flesh, before Yahweh; for he is waked up out of his holy habitation.

Chapter 3

1And he showed me Joshua the high priest standing before the angel of Yahweh, and Satan standing at his right hand to be his adversary.

2And Yahweh said unto Satan, Yahweh rebuke thee, O Satan; yea, Yahweh that hath chosen Jerusalem rebuke thee: is not this a brand plucked out of the fire?

3Now Joshua was clothed with filthy garments, and was standing before the angel.

4And he answered and spake unto those that stood before him, saying, Take the filthy garments from off him. And unto him he said, Behold, I have caused thine iniquity to pass from thee, and I will clothe thee with rich apparel.

5And I said, Let them set a clean mitre upon his head. So they set a clean mitre upon his head, and clothed him with garments; and the angel of Yahweh was standing by.

6And the angel of Yahweh protested unto Joshua, saying,

7Thus saith Yahweh of hosts: If thou wilt walk in my ways, and if thou wilt keep my charge, then thou also shalt judge my house, and shalt also keep my courts, and I will give thee a place of access among these that stand by.

8Hear now, O Joshua the high priest, thou and thy fellows that sit before thee; for they are men that are a sign: for, behold, I will bring forth my servant the Branch.

9For, behold, the stone that I have set before Joshua; upon one stone are seven eyes: behold, I will engrave the graving thereof, saith Yahweh of hosts, and I will remove the iniquity of that land in one day.

10In that day, saith Yahweh of hosts, shall ye invite every man his neighbor under the vine and under the fig-tree.

Chapter 4

1And the angel that talked with me came again, and waked me, as a man that is wakened out of his sleep.

2And he said unto me, What seest thou? And I said, I have seen, and, behold, a candlestick all of gold, with its bowl upon the top of it, and its seven lamps thereon; there are seven pipes to each of the lamps, which are upon the top thereof;

3and two olive-trees by it, one upon the right side of the bowl, and the other upon the left side thereof.

4And I answered and spake to the angel that talked with me, saying, What are these, my lord?

5Then the angel that talked with me answered and said unto me, Knowest thou not what these are? And I said, No, my lord.

6Then he answered and spake unto me, saying, This is the word of Yahweh unto Zerubbabel, saying, Not by might, nor by power, but by my Spirit, saith Yahweh of hosts.

7Who art thou, O great mountain? before Zerubbabel thou shalt become a plain; and he shall bring forth the top stone with shoutings of Grace, grace, unto it.

8Moreover the word of Yahweh came unto me, saying,

9The hands of Zerubbabel have laid the foundation of this house; his hands shall also finish it; and thou shalt know that Yahweh of hosts hath sent me unto you.

10For who hath despised the day of small things? for these seven shall rejoice, and shall see the plummet in the hand of Zerubbabel; these are the eyes of Yahweh, which run to and fro through the whole earth.

11Then answered I, and said unto him, What are these two olive-trees upon the right side of the candlestick and upon the left side thereof?

12And I answered the second time, and said unto him, What are these two olive-branches, which are beside the two golden spouts, that empty the golden oil out of themselves?

13And he answered me and said, Knowest thou not what these are? And I said, No, my lord.

14Then said he, These are the two anointed ones, that stand by the Lord of the whole earth.

Chapter 5

1Then again I lifted up mine eyes, and saw, and, behold, a flying roll.

2And he said unto me, What seest thou? And I answered, I see a flying roll; the length thereof is twenty cubits, and the breadth thereof ten cubits.

3Then said he unto me, This is the curse that goeth forth over the face of the whole land: for every one that stealeth shall be cut off on the one side according to it; and every one that sweareth shall be cut off on the other side according to it.

4I will cause it to go forth, saith Yahweh of hosts, and it shall enter into the house of the thief, and into the house of him that sweareth falsely by my name; and it shall abide in the midst of his house, and shall consume it with the timber thereof and the stones thereof.

5Then the angel that talked with me went forth, and said unto me, Lift up now thine eyes, and see what is this that goeth forth.

6And I said, What is it? And he said, This is the ephah that goeth forth. He said moreover, This is their appearance in all the land

7(and, behold, there was lifted up a talent of lead); and this is a woman sitting in the midst of the ephah.

8And he said, This is Wickedness: and he cast her down into the midst of the ephah; and he cast the weight of lead upon the mouth thereof.

9Then lifted I up mine eyes, and saw, and, behold, there came forth two women, and the wind was in their wings; now they had wings like the wings of a stork; and they lifted up the ephah between earth and heaven.

10Then said I to the angel that talked with me, Whither do these bear the ephah?

11And he said unto me, To build her a house in the land of Shinar: and when it is prepared, she shall be set there in her own place.

Chapter 6

1And again I lifted up mine eyes, and saw, and, behold, there came four chariots out from between two mountains; and the mountains were mountains of brass.

2In the first chariot were red horses; and in the second chariot black horses;

3and in the third chariot white horses; and in the fourth chariot grizzled strong horses.

4Then I answered and said unto the angel that talked with me, What are these, my lord?

5And the angel answered and said unto me, These are the four winds of heaven, which go forth from standing before the Lord of all the earth.

6The chariot wherein are the black horses goeth forth toward the north country; and the white went forth after them; and the grizzled went forth toward the south country.

7And the strong went forth, and sought to go that they might walk to and fro through the earth: and he said, Get you hence, walk to and fro through the earth. So they walked to and fro through the earth.

8Then cried he to me, and spake unto me, saying, Behold, they that go toward the north country have quieted my spirit in the north country.

9And the word of Yahweh came unto me, saying,

10Take of them of the captivity, even of Heldai, of Tobijah, and of Jedaiah; and come thou the same day, and go into the house of Josiah the son of Zephaniah, whither they are come from Babylon;

11yea, take of them silver and gold, and make crowns, and set them upon the head of Joshua the son of Jehozadak, the high priest;

12and speak unto him, saying, Thus speaketh Yahweh of hosts, saying, Behold, the man whose name is the Branch: and he shall grow up out of his place; and he shall build the temple of Yahweh;

13even he shall build the temple of Yahweh; and he shall bear the glory, and shall sit and rule upon his throne; and he shall be a priest upon his throne; and the counsel of peace shall be between them both.

14And the crowns shall be to Helem, and to Tobijah, and to Jedaiah, and to Hen the son of Zephaniah, for a memorial in the temple of Yahweh.

15And they that are far off shall come and build in the temple of Yahweh; and ye shall know that Yahweh of hosts hath sent me unto you. And this shall come to pass, if ye will diligently obey the voice of Yahweh your God.

Chapter 7

1And it came to pass in the fourth year of king Darius, that the word of Yahweh came unto Zechariah in the fourth day of the ninth month, even in Chislev.

2Now they of Beth-el had sent Sharezer and Regem-melech, and their men, to entreat the favor of Yahweh,

3and to speak unto the priests of the house of Yahweh of hosts, and to the prophets, saying, Should I weep in the fifth month, separating myself, as I have done these so many years?

4Then came the word of Yahweh of hosts unto me, saying,

5Speak unto all the people of the land, and to the priests, saying, When ye fasted and mourned in the fifth and in the seventh month, even these seventy years, did ye at all fast unto me, even to me?

6And when ye eat, and when ye drink, do not ye eat for yourselves, and drink for yourselves?

7Should ye not hear the words which Yahweh cried by the former prophets, when Jerusalem was inhabited and in prosperity, and the cities thereof round about her, and the South and the lowland were inhabited?

8And the word of Yahweh came unto Zechariah, saying,

9Thus hath Yahweh of hosts spoken, saying, Execute true judgment, and show kindness and compassion every man to his brother;

10and oppress not the widow, nor the fatherless, the sojourner, nor the poor; and let none of you devise evil against his brother in your heart.

11But they refused to hearken, and pulled away the shoulder, and stopped their ears, that they might not hear.

12Yea, they made their hearts as an adamant stone, lest they should hear the law, and the words which Yahweh of hosts had sent by his Spirit by the former prophets: therefore there came great wrath from Yahweh of hosts.

13And it is come to pass that, as he cried, and they would not hear, so they shall cry, and I will not hear, said Yahweh of hosts;

14but I will scatter them with a whirlwind among all the nations which they have not known. Thus the land was desolate after them, so that no man passed through nor returned: for they laid the pleasant land desolate.

Chapter 8

1And the word of Yahweh of hosts came to me, saying,

2Thus saith Yahweh of hosts: I am jealous for Zion with great jealousy, and I am jealous for her with great wrath.

3Thus saith Yahweh: I am returned unto Zion, and will dwell in the midst of Jerusalem: and Jerusalem shall be called The city of truth; and the mountain of Yahweh of hosts, The holy mountain.

4Thus saith Yahweh of hosts: There shall yet old men and old women dwell in the streets of Jerusalem, every man with his staff in his hand for very age.

5And the streets of the city shall be full of boys and girls playing in the streets thereof.

6Thus saith Yahweh of hosts: If it be marvellous in the eyes of the remnant of this people in those days, should it also be marvellous in mine eyes? saith Yahweh of hosts.

7Thus saith Yahweh of hosts: Behold, I will save my people from the east country, and from the west country;

8and I will bring them, and they shall dwell in the midst of Jerusalem; and they shall be my people, and I will be their God, in truth and in righteousness.

9Thus saith Yahweh of hosts: Let your hands be strong, ye that hear in these days these words from the mouth of the prophets that were in the day that the foundation of the house of Yahweh of hosts was laid, even the temple, that it might be built.

10For before those days there was no hire for man, nor any hire for beast; neither was there any peace to him that went out or came in, because of the adversary: for I set all men every one against his neighbor.

11But now I will not be unto the remnant of this people as in the former days, saith Yahweh of hosts.

12For there shall be the seed of peace; the vine shall give its fruit, and the ground shall give its increase, and the heavens shall give their dew; and I will cause the remnant of this people to inherit all these things.

13And it shall come to pass that, as ye were a curse among the nations, O house of Judah and house of Israel, so will I save you, and ye shall be a blessing. Fear not, but let your hands be strong.

14For thus saith Yahweh of hosts: As I thought to do evil unto you, when your fathers provoked me to wrath, saith Yahweh of hosts, and I repented not;

15so again have I thought in these days to do good unto Jerusalem and to the house of Judah: fear ye not.

16These are the things that ye shall do: speak ye every man the truth with his neighbor; execute the judgment of truth and peace in your gates;

17and let none of you devise evil in your hearts against his neighbor; and love no false oath: for all these are things that I hate, saith Yahweh.

18And the word of Yahweh of hosts came unto me, saying,

19Thus saith Yahweh of hosts: The fast of the fourth month, and the fast of the fifth, and the fast of the seventh, and the fast of the tenth, shall be to the house of Judah joy and gladness, and cheerful feasts; therefore love truth and peace.

20Thus saith Yahweh of hosts: It shall yet come to pass, that there shall come peoples, and the inhabitants of many cities;

21and the inhabitants of one city shall go to another, saying, Let us go speedily to entreat the favor of Yahweh, and to seek Yahweh of hosts: I will go also.

22Yea, many peoples and strong nations shall come to seek Yahweh of hosts in Jerusalem, and to entreat the favor of Yahweh.

23Thus saith Yahweh of hosts: In those days it shall come to pass, that ten men shall take hold, out of all the languages of the nations, they shall take hold of the skirt of him that is a Jew, saying, We will go with you, for we have heard that God is with you.

Chapter 9

1The burden of the word of Yahweh upon the land of Hadrach, and Damascus shall be its resting-place (for the eye of man and of all the tribes of Israel is toward Yahweh);

2and Hamath, also, which bordereth thereon; Tyre and Sidon, because they are very wise.

3And Tyre did build herself a stronghold, and heaped up silver as the dust, and fine gold as the mire of the streets.

4Behold, the Lord will dispossess her, and he will smite her power in the sea; and she shall be devoured with fire.

5Ashkelon shall see it, and fear; Gaza also, and shall be sore pained; and Ekron, for her expectation shall be put to shame; and the king shall perish from Gaza, and Ashkelon shall not be inhabited.

6And a bastard shall dwell in Ashdod, and I will cut off the pride of the Philistines.

7And I will take away his blood out of his mouth, and his abominations from between his teeth; and he also shall be a remnant for our God; and he shall be as a chieftain in Judah, and Ekron as a Jebusite.

8And I will encamp about my house against the army, that none pass through or return; and no oppressor shall pass through them any more: for now have I seen with mine eyes.

9Rejoice greatly, O daughter of Zion; shout, O daughter of Jerusalem: behold, thy king cometh unto thee; he is just, and having salvation; lowly, and riding upon an ass, even upon a colt the foal of an ass.

10And I will cut off the chariot from Ephraim, and the horse from Jerusalem; and the battle bow shall be cut off; and he shall speak peace unto the nations: and his dominion shall be from sea to sea, and from the River to the ends of the earth.

11As for thee also, because of the blood of thy covenant I have set free thy prisoners from the pit wherein is no water.

12Turn you to the stronghold, ye prisoners of hope: even to-day do I declare that I will render double unto thee.

13For I have bent Judah for me, I have filled the bow with Ephraim; and I will stir up thy sons, O Zion, against thy sons, O Greece, and will make thee as the sword of a mighty man.

14And Yahweh shall be seen over them; and his arrow shall go forth as the lightning; and the Lord Yahweh will blow the trumpet, and will go with whirlwinds of the south.

15Yahweh of hosts will defend them; and they shall devour, and shall tread down the sling-stones; and they shall drink, and make a noise as through wine; and they shall be filled like bowls, like the corners of the altar.

16And Yahweh their God will save them in that day as the flock of his people; for they shall be as the stones of a crown, lifted on high over his land.

17For how great is his goodness, and how great is his beauty! grain shall make the young men flourish, and new wine the virgins.

Zechariah
Chapter 10

¹Ask ye of Yahweh rain in the time of the latter rain, even of Yahweh that maketh lightnings; and he will give them showers of rain, to every one grass in the field.

²For the teraphim have spoken vanity, and the diviners have seen a lie; and they have told false dreams, they comfort in vain: therefore they go their way like sheep, they are afflicted, because there is no shepherd.

³Mine anger is kindled against the shepherds, and I will punish the he-goats; for Yahweh of hosts hath visited his flock, the house of Judah, and will make them as his goodly horse in the battle.

⁴From him shall come forth the corner-stone, from him the nail, from him the battle bow, from him every ruler together.

⁵And they shall be as mighty men, treading down their enemies in the mire of the streets in the battle; and they shall fight, because Yahweh is with them; and the riders on horses shall be confounded.

⁶And I will strengthen the house of Judah, and I will save the house of Joseph, and I will bring them back; for I have mercy upon them; and they shall be as though I had not cast them off: for I am Yahweh their God, and I will hear them.

⁷And they of Ephraim shall be like a mighty man, and their heart shall rejoice as through wine; yea, their children shall see it, and rejoice; their heart shall be glad in Yahweh.

⁸I will hiss for them, and gather them; for I have redeemed them; and they shall increase as they have increased.

⁹And I will sow them among the peoples; and they shall remember me in far countries; and they shall live with their children, and shall return.

¹⁰I will bring them again also out of the land of Egypt, and gather them out of Assyria; and I will bring them into the land of Gilead and Lebanon; and place shall not be found for them.

¹¹And he will pass through the sea of affliction, and will smite the waves in the sea, and all the depths of the Nile shall dry up; and the pride of Assyria shall be brought down, and the sceptre of Egypt shall depart.

¹²And I will strengthen them in Yahweh; and they shall walk up and down in his name, saith Yahweh.

Chapter 11

¹Open thy doors, O Lebanon, that the fire may devour thy cedars.

²Wail, O fir-tree, for the cedar is fallen, because the goodly ones are destroyed: wail, O ye oaks of Bashan, for the strong forest is come down.

³A voice of the wailing of the shepherds! for their glory is destroyed: a voice of the roaring of young lions! for the pride of the Jordan is laid waste.

⁴Thus said Yahweh my God: Feed the flock of slaughter;

⁵whose possessors slay them, and hold themselves not guilty; and they that sell them say, Blessed be Yahweh, for I am rich; and their own shepherds pity them not.

⁶For I will no more pity the inhabitants of the land, saith Yahweh; but, lo, I will deliver the men every one into his neighbor's hand, and into the hand of his king; and they shall smite the land, and out of their hand I will not deliver them.

⁷So I fed the flock of slaughter, verily the poor of the flock. And I took unto me two staves; the one I called Beauty, and the other I called Bands; and I fed the flock.

⁸And I cut off the three shepherds in one month; for my soul was weary of them, and their soul also loathed me.

⁹Then said I, I will not feed you: that which dieth, let it die; and that which is to be cut off, let it be cut off; and let them that are left eat every one the flesh of another.

¹⁰And I took my staff Beauty, and cut it asunder, that I might break my covenant which I had made with all the peoples.

¹¹And it was broken in that day; and thus the poor of the flock that gave heed unto me knew that it was the word of Yahweh.

¹²And I said unto them, If ye think good, give me my hire; and if not, forbear. So they weighed for my hire thirty pieces of silver.

¹³And Yahweh said unto me, Cast it unto the potter, the goodly price that I was prized at by them. And I took the thirty pieces of silver, and cast them unto the potter, in the house of Yahweh.

¹⁴Then I cut asunder mine other staff, even Bands, that I might break the brotherhood between Judah and Israel.

¹⁵And Yahweh said unto me, Take unto thee yet again the instruments of a foolish shepherd.

¹⁶For, lo, I will raise up a shepherd in the land, who will not visit those that are cut off, neither will seek those that are scattered, nor heal that which is broken, nor feed that which is sound; but he will eat the flesh of the fat sheep, and will tear their hoofs in pieces.

¹⁷Woe to the worthless shepherd that leaveth the flock! the sword shall be upon his arm, and upon his right eye: his arm shall be clean dried up, and his right eye shall be utterlydarkened.

Chapter 12

¹The burden of the word of Yahweh concerning Israel. Thus saith Yahweh, who stretcheth forth the heavens, and layeth the foundation of the earth, and formeth the spirit of man within him:

²behold, I will make Jerusalem a cup of reeling unto all the peoples round about, and upon Judah also shall it be in the siege against Jerusalem.

³And it shall come to pass in that day, that I will make Jerusalem a burdensome stone for all the peoples; all that burden themselves with it shall be sore wounded; and all the nations of the earth shall be gathered together against it.

⁴In that day, saith Yahweh, I will smite every horse with terror, and his rider with madness; and I will open mine eyes upon the house of Judah, and will smite every horse of the peoples with blindness.

⁵And the chieftains of Judah shall say in their heart, The inhabitants of Jerusalem are my strength in Yahweh of hosts their God.

⁶In that day will I make the chieftains of Judah like a pan of fire among wood, and like a flaming torch among sheaves; and they shall devour all the peoples round about, on the right hand and on the left; and they of Jerusalem shall yet again dwell in their own place, even in Jerusalem.

⁷Yahweh also shall save the tents of Judah first, that the glory of the house of David and the glory of the inhabitants of Jerusalem be not magnified above Judah.

⁸In that day shall Yahweh defend the inhabitants of Jerusalem: and he that is feeble among them at that day shall be as David; and the house of David shall be as God, as the angel of Yahweh before them.

⁹And it shall come to pass in that day, that I will seek to destroy all the nations that come against Jerusalem.

¹⁰And I will pour upon the house of David, and upon the inhabitants of Jerusalem, the spirit of grace and of supplication; and they shall look unto me whom they have pierced; and they shall mourn for him, as one mourneth for his only son, and shall be in bitterness for him, as one that is in bitterness for his first-born.

¹¹In that day shall there be a great mourning in Jerusalem, as the mourning of Hadadrimmon in the valley of Megiddon.

¹²And the land shall mourn, every family apart; the family of the house of David apart, and their wives apart; the family of the house of Nathan apart, and their wives apart;

¹³the family of the house of Levi apart, and their wives apart; the family of the Shimeites apart, and their wives apart;

¹⁴all the families that remain, every family apart, and their wives apart.

Chapter 13

¹In that day there shall be a fountain opened to the house of David and to the inhabitants of Jerusalem, for sin and for uncleanness.

²And it shall come to pass in that day, saith Yahweh of hosts, that I will cut off the names of the idols out of the land, and they shall no more be remembered; and also I will cause the prophets and the unclean spirit to pass out of the land.

³And it shall come to pass that, when any shall yet prophesy, then his father and his mother that begat him shall say unto him, Thou shalt not live; for thou speakest lies in the name of Yahweh; and his father and his mother that begat him shall thrust him through when he prophesieth.

⁴And it shall come to pass in that day, that the prophets shall be ashamed every one of his vision, when he prophesieth; neither shall they wear a hairy mantle to deceive:

⁵but he shall say, I am no prophet, I am a tiller of the ground; for I have been made a bondman from my youth.

⁶And one shall say unto him, What are these wounds between thine arms? Then he shall answer, Those with which I was wounded in the house of my friends.

⁷Awake, O sword, against my shepherd, and against the man that is my fellow, saith Yahweh of hosts: smite the shepherd, and the sheep shall be scattered; and I will turn my hand upon the little ones.

⁸And it shall come to pass, that in all the land, saith Yahweh, two parts therein shall be cut off and die; but the third shall be left therein.

⁹And I will bring the third part into the fire, and will refine them as silver is refined, and will try them as gold is tried. They shall call on my name, and I will hear them: I will say, It is my people; and they shall say, Yahweh is my God.

Chapter 14

¹Behold, a day of Yahweh cometh, when thy spoil shall be divided in the midst of thee.

²For I will gather all nations against Jerusalem to battle; and the city shall be taken, and the houses rifled, and the women ravished; and half of the city shall go forth into captivity, and the residue of the people shall not be cut off from the city.

³Then shall Yahweh go forth, and fight against those nations, as when he fought in the day of battle.

⁴And his feet shall stand in that day upon the mount of Olives, which is before Jerusalem on the east; and the mount of Olives shall be cleft in the midst thereof toward the east and toward the west, and there shall be a very great valley; and half of the mountain shall remove toward the north, and half of it toward the south.

⁵And ye shall flee by the valley of my mountains; for the valley of the mountains shall reach unto Azel; yea, ye shall flee, like as ye fled from before the earthquake in the days of Uzziah king of Judah; and Yahweh my God shall come, and all the holy ones with thee.

⁶And it shall come to pass in that day, that there shall not be light; the bright ones shall withdraw themselves:

⁷but it shall be one day which is known unto Yahweh; not day, and not night; but it shall come to pass, that at evening time there shall be light.

⁸And it shall come to pass in that day, that living waters shall go out from Jerusalem; half of them toward the eastern sea, and half of them toward the western sea: in summer and in winter shall it be.

⁹And Yahweh shall be King over all the earth: in that day shall Yahweh be one, and his name one.

¹⁰All the land shall be made like the Arabah, from Geba to Rimmon south of Jerusalem; and she shall be lifted up, and shall dwell in her place, from Benjamin's gate unto the place of the first gate, unto the corner gate, and from the tower of Hananel unto the king's wine-presses.

¹¹And men shall dwell therein, and there shall be no more curse; but

Jerusalem shall dwell safely.

12And this shall be the plague wherewith Yahweh will smite all the peoples that have warred against Jerusalem: their flesh shall consume away while they stand upon their feet, and their eyes shall consume away in their sockets, and their tongue shall consume away in their mouth.

13And it shall come to pass in that day, that a great tumult from Yahweh shall be among them; and they shall lay hold every one on the hand of his neighbor, and his hand shall rise up against the hand of his neighbor.

14And Judah also shall fight at Jerusalem; and the wealth of all the nations round about shall be gathered together, gold, and silver, and apparel, in great abundance.

15And so shall be the plague of the horse, of the mule, of the camel, and of the ass, and of all the beasts that shall be in those camps, as that plague.

16And it shall come to pass, that every one that is left of all the nations that came against Jerusalem shall go up from year to year to worship the King, Yahweh of hosts, and to keep the feast of tabernacles.

17And it shall be, that whoso of all the families of the earth goeth not up unto Jerusalem to worship the King, Yahweh of hosts, upon them there shall be no rain.

18And if the family of Egypt go not up, and come not, neither shall it be upon them; there shall be the plague wherewith Yahweh will smite the nations that go not up to keep the feast of tabernacles.

19This shall be the punishment of Egypt, and the punishment of all the nations that go not up to keep the feast of tabernacles.

20In that day shall there be upon the bells of the horses, HOLY UNTO YAHWEH; and the pots in Yahweh's house shall be like the bowls before the altar.

21Yea, every pot in Jerusalem and in Judah shall be holy unto Yahweh of hosts; and all they that sacrifice shall come and take of them, and boil therein: and in that day there shall be no more a Canaanite in the house of Yahweh of hosts.

Malachi

Chapter 1

¹The burden of the word of Yahweh to Israel by Malachi.

²I have loved you, saith Yahweh. Yet ye say, Wherein hast thou loved us? Was not Esau Jacob's brother, saith Yahweh: yet I loved Jacob;

³but Esau I hated, and made his mountains a desolation, and gave his heritage to the jackals of the wilderness.

⁴Whereas Edom saith, We are beaten down, but we will return and build the waste places; thus saith Yahweh of hosts, They shall build, but I will throw down; and men shall call them The border of wickedness, and The people against whom Yahweh hath indignation for ever.

⁵And your eyes shall see, and ye shall say, Yahweh be magnified beyond the border of Israel.

⁶A son honoreth his father, and a servant his master: if then I am a father, where is mine honor? and if I am a master, where is my fear? saith Yahweh of hosts unto you, O priests, that despise my name. And ye say, Wherein have we despised thy name?

⁷Ye offer polluted bread upon mine altar. And ye say, Wherein have we polluted thee? In that ye say, The table of Yahweh is contemptible.

⁸And when ye offer the blind for sacrifice, it is no evil! and when ye offer the lame and sick, it is no evil! Present it now unto thy governor; will he be pleased with thee? or will he accept thy person? saith Yahweh of hosts.

⁹And now, I pray you, entreat the favor of God, that he may be gracious unto us: this hath been by your means: will he accept any of your persons? saith Yahweh of hosts.

¹⁰Oh that there were one among you that would shut the doors, that ye might not kindle fire on mine altar in vain! I have no pleasure in you, saith Yahweh of hosts, neither will I accept an offering at your hand.

¹¹For from the rising of the sun even unto the going down of the same my name shall be great among the Gentiles; and in every place incense shall be offered unto my name, and a pure offering: for my name shall be great among the Gentiles, saith Yahweh of hosts.

¹²But ye profane it, in that ye say, The table of Yahweh is polluted, and the fruit thereof, even its food, is contemptible.

¹³Ye say also, Behold, what a weariness is it! and ye have snuffed at it, saith Yahweh of hosts; and ye have brought that which was taken by violence, and the lame, and the sick; thus ye bring the offering: should I accept this at your hand? saith Yahweh.

¹⁴But cursed be the deceiver, who hath in his flock a male, and voweth, and sacrificeth unto the Lord a blemished thing; for I am a great King, saith Yahweh of hosts, and my name is terrible among the Gentiles.

Chapter 2

¹And now, O ye priests, this commandment is for you.

²If ye will not hear, and if ye will not lay it to heart, to give glory unto my name, saith Yahweh of hosts, then will I send the curse upon you, and I will curse your blessings; yea, I have cursed them already, because ye do not lay it to heart.

³Behold, I will rebuke your seed, and will spread dung upon your faces, even the dung of your feasts; and ye shall be taken away with it.

⁴And ye shall know that I have sent this commandment unto you, that my covenant may be with Levi, saith Yahweh of hosts.

⁵My covenant was with him of life and peace; and I gave them to him that he might fear; and he feared me, and stood in awe of my name.

⁶The law of truth was in his mouth, and unrighteousness was not found in his lips: he walked with me in peace and uprightness, and turned many away from iniquity.

⁷For the priest's lips should keep knowledge, and they should seek the law at his mouth; for he is the messenger of Yahweh of hosts.

⁸But ye are turned aside out of the way; ye have caused many to stumble in the law; ye have corrupted the covenant of Levi, saith Yahweh of hosts.

⁹Therefore have I also made you contemptible and base before all the people, according as ye have not kept my ways, but have had respect of persons in the law.

¹⁰Have we not all one father? hath not one God created us? why do we deal treacherously every man against his brother, profaning the covenant of our fathers?

¹¹Judah hath dealt treacherously, and an abomination is committed in Israel and in Jerusalem; for Judah hath profaned the holiness of Yahweh which he loveth, and hath married the daughter of a foreign god.

¹²Yahweh will cut off, to the man that doeth this, him that waketh and him that answereth, out of the tents of Jacob, and him that offereth an offering unto Yahweh of hosts.

¹³And this again ye do: ye cover the altar of Yahweh with tears, with weeping, and with sighing, insomuch that he regardeth not the offering any more, neither receiveth it with good will at your hand.

¹⁴Yet ye say, Wherefore? Because Yahweh hath been witness between thee and the wife of thy youth, against whom thou hast dealt treacherously, though she is thy companion, and the wife of thy covenant.

¹⁵And did he not make one, although he had the residue of the Spirit? And wherefore one? He sought a godly seed. Therefore take heed to your spirit, and let none deal treacherously against the wife of his youth.

¹⁶For I hate putting away, saith Yahweh, the God of Israel, and him that covereth his garment with violence, saith Yahweh of hosts: therefore take heed to your spirit, that ye deal not treacherously.

¹⁷Ye have wearied Yahweh with your words. Yet ye say, Wherein have we wearied him? In that ye say, Every one that doeth evil is good in the sight of Yahweh, and he delighteth in them; or where is the God of justice?

Chapter 3

¹Behold, I send my messenger, and he shall prepare the way before me: and the Lord, whom ye seek, will suddenly come to his temple; and the messenger of the covenant, whom ye desire, behold, he cometh, saith Yahweh of hosts.

²But who can abide the day of his coming? and who shall stand when he appeareth? for he is like a refiner's fire, and like fuller's soap:

³and he will sit as a refiner and purifier of silver, and he will purify the sons of Levi, and refine them as gold and silver; and they shall offer unto Yahweh offerings in righteousness.

⁴Then shall the offering of Judah and Jerusalem be pleasant unto Yahweh, as in the days of old, and as in ancient years.

⁵And I will come near to you to judgment; and I will be a swift witness against the sorcerers, and against the adulterers, and against the false swearers, and against those that oppress the hireling in his wages, the widow, and the fatherless, and that turn aside the sojourner from his right, and fear not me, saith Yahweh of hosts.

⁶For I, Yahweh, change not; therefore ye, O sons of Jacob, are not consumed.

⁷From the days of your fathers ye have turned aside from mine ordinances, and have not kept them. Return unto me, and I will return unto you, saith Yahweh of hosts. But ye say, Wherein shall we return?

⁸Will a man rob God? yet ye rob me. But ye say, Wherein have we robbed thee? In tithes and offerings.

⁹Ye are cursed with the curse; for ye rob me, even this whole nation.

¹⁰Bring ye the whole tithe into the store-house, that there may be food in my house, and prove me now herewith, saith Yahweh of hosts, if I will not open you the windows of heaven, and pour you out a blessing, that there shall not be room enough to receive it.

¹¹And I will rebuke the devourer for your sakes, and he shall not destroy the fruits of your ground; neither shall your vine cast its fruit before the time in the field, saith Yahweh of hosts.

¹²And all nations shall call you happy; for ye shall be a delightsome land, saith Yahweh of hosts.

¹³Your words have been stout against me, saith Yahweh. Yet ye say, What have we spoken against thee?

¹⁴Ye have said, It is vain to serve God; and what profit is it that we have kept his charge, and that we have walked mournfully before Yahweh of hosts?

¹⁵And now we call the proud happy; yea, they that work wickedness are built up; yea, they tempt God, and escape.

¹⁶Then they that feared Yahweh spake one with another; and Yahweh hearkened, and heard, and a book of remembrance was written before him, for them that feared Yahweh, and that thought upon his name.

¹⁷And they shall be mine, saith Yahweh of hosts, even mine own possession, in the day that I make; and I will spare them, as a man spareth his own son that serveth him.

¹⁸Then shall ye return and discern between the righteous and the wicked, between him that serveth God and him that serveth him not.

Chapter 4

¹For, behold, the day cometh, it burneth as a furnace; and all the proud, and all that work wickedness, shall be stubble; and the day that cometh shall burn them up, saith Yahweh of hosts, that it shall leave them neither root nor branch.

²But unto you that fear my name shall the sun of righteousness arise with healing in its wings; and ye shall go forth, and gambol as calves of the stall.

³And ye shall tread down the wicked; for they shall be ashes under the soles of your feet in the day that I make, saith Yahweh of hosts.

⁴Remember ye the law of Moses my servant, which I commanded unto him in Horeb for all Israel, even statutes and ordinances.

⁵Behold, I will send you Elijah the prophet before the great and terrible day of Yahweh come.

⁶And he shall turn the heart of the fathers to the children, and the heart of the children to their fathers; lest I come and smite the earth with a curse.

New Testament

The Gospel According to St. Matthew

Chapter 1

1The book of the generation of Jesus Christ, the son of David, the son of Abraham.

2Abraham begat Isaac; and Isaac begat Jacob; and Jacob begat Judah and his brethren;

3and Judah begat Perez and Zerah of Tamar; and Perez begat Hezron; and Hezron begat Ram;

4and Ram begat Amminadab; and Amminadab begat Nahshon; and Nahshon begat Salmon;

5and Salmon begat Boaz of Rahab; and Boaz begat Obed of Ruth; and Obed begat Jesse;

6and Jesse begat David the king.

And David begat Solomon of her that had been the wife of Uriah;

7and Solomon begat Rehoboam; and Rehoboam begat Abijah; and Abijah begat Asa;

8and Asa begat Jehoshaphat; and Jehoshaphat begat Joram; and Joram begat Uzziah;

9and Uzziah begat Jotham; and Jotham begat Ahaz; and Ahaz begat Hezekiah;

10and Hezekiah begat Manasseh; and Manasseh begat Amon; and Amon begat Josiah;

11and Josiah begat Jechoniah and his brethren, at the time of the carrying away to Babylon.

12And after the carrying away to Babylon, Jechoniah begat Shealtiel; and Shealtiel begat Zerubbabel;

13and Zerubbabel begat Abiud; and Abiud begat Eliakim; and Eliakim begat Azor;

14and Azor begat Sadoc; and Sadoc begat Achim; and Achim begat Eliud;

15and Eliud begat Eleazar; and Eleazar begat Matthan; and Matthan begat Jacob;

16and Jacob begat Joseph the husband of Mary, of whom was born Jesus, who is called Christ.

17So all the generations from Abraham unto David are fourteen generations; and from David unto the carrying away to Babylon fourteen generations; and from the carrying away to Babylon unto the Christ fourteen generations.

18Now the birth of Jesus Christ was on this wise: When his mother Mary had been betrothed to Joseph, before they came together she was found with child of the Holy Spirit.

19And Joseph her husband, being a righteous man, and not willing to make her a public example, was minded to put her away privily.

20But when he thought on these things, behold, an angel of the Lord appeared unto him in a dream, saying, Joseph, thou son of David, fear not to take unto thee Mary thy wife: for that which is conceived in her is of the Holy Spirit.

21And she shall bring forth a son; and thou shalt call his name JESUS; for it is he that shall save his people from their sins.

22Now all this is come to pass, that it might be fulfilled which was spoken by the Lord through the prophet, saying,

23Behold, the virgin shall be with child, and shall bring forth a son,
And they shall call his name Immanuel;
which is, being interpreted, God with us.

24And Joseph arose from his sleep, and did as the angel of the Lord commanded him, and took unto him his wife;

25and knew her not till she had brought forth a son: and he called his name JESUS.

Chapter 2

1Now when Jesus was born in Bethlehem of Judaea in the days of Herod the king, behold, Wise-men from the east came to Jerusalem, saying,

2Where is he that is born King of the Jews? for we saw his star in the east, and are come to worship him.

3And when Herod the king heard it, he was troubled, and all Jerusalem with him.

4And gathering together all the chief priests and scribes of the people, he inquired of them where the Christ should be born.

5And they said unto him, In Bethlehem of Judaea: for thus it is written through the prophet,

6And thou Bethlehem, land of Judah,
Art in no wise least among the princes of Judah:
For out of thee shall come forth a governor,
Who shall be shepherd of my people Israel.

7Then Herod privily called the Wise-men, and learned of them exactly what time the star appeared.

8And he sent them to Bethlehem, and said, Go and search out exactly concerning the young child; and when ye have found him, bring me word, that I also may come and worship him.

9And they, having heard the king, went their way; and lo, the star, which they saw in the east, went before them, till it came and stood over where the young child was.

10And when they saw the star, they rejoiced with exceeding great joy.

11And they came into the house and saw the young child with Mary his mother; and they fell down and worshipped him; and opening their treasures they offered unto him gifts, gold and frankincense and myrrh.

12And being warned of God in a dream that they should not return to Herod, they departed into their own country another way.

13Now when they were departed, behold, an angel of the Lord appeareth to Joseph in a dream, saying, Arise and take the young child and his mother, and flee into Egypt, and be thou there until I tell thee: for Herod will seek the young child to destroy him.

14And he arose and took the young child and his mother by night, and departed into Egypt;

15and was there until the death of Herod: that it might be fulfilled which was spoken by the Lord through the prophet, saying, Out of Egypt did I call my son.

16Then Herod, when he saw that he was mocked of the Wise-men, was exceeding wroth, and sent forth, and slew all the male children that were in Bethlehem, and in all the borders thereof, from two years old and under, according to the time which he had exactly learned of the Wise-men.

17Then was fulfilled that which was spoken through Jeremiah the prophet, saying,

18A voice was heard in Ramah,
Weeping and great mourning,
Rachel weeping for her children;
And she would not be comforted, because they are not.

19But when Herod was dead, behold, an angel of the Lord appeareth in a dream to Joseph in Egypt, saying,

20Arise and take the young child and his mother, and go into the land of Israel: for they are dead that sought the young child's life.

21And he arose and took the young child and his mother, and came into the land of Israel.

22But when he heard that Archelaus was reigning over Judaea in the room of his father Herod, he was afraid to go thither; and being warned of God in a dream, he withdrew into the parts of Galilee,

23and came and dwelt in a city called Nazareth; that it might be fulfilled which was spoken through the prophets, that he should be called a Nazarene.

Chapter 3

1And in those days cometh John the Baptist, preaching in the wilderness of Judaea, saying,

2Repent ye; for the kingdom of heaven is at hand.

3For this is he that was spoken of through Isaiah the prophet, saying,
The voice of one crying in the wilderness,
Make ye ready the way of the Lord,
Make his paths straight.

4Now John himself had his raiment of camel's hair, and a leathern girdle about his loins; and his food was locusts and wild honey.

5Then went out unto him Jerusalem, and all Judaea, and all the region round about the Jordan;

6and they were baptized of him in the river Jordan, confessing their sins.

7But when he saw many of the Pharisees and Sadducees coming to his baptism, he said unto them, Ye offspring of vipers, who warned you to flee from the wrath to come?

8Bring forth therefore fruit worthy of repentance:

9and think not to say within yourselves, We have Abraham to our father: for I say unto you, that God is able of these stones to raise up children unto Abraham.

10And even now the axe lieth at the root of the trees: every tree therefore that bringeth not forth good fruit is hewn down, and cast into the fire.

11I indeed baptize you in water unto repentance: but he that cometh after me is mightier than I, whose shoes I am not worthy to bear: he shall baptize you in the Holy Spirit and in fire:

12whose fan is in his hand, and he will thoroughly cleanse his threshing-floor; and he will gather his wheat into the garner, but the chaff he will burn up with unquenchable fire.

13Then cometh Jesus from Galilee to the Jordan unto John, to be baptized of him.

14But John would have hindered him, saying, I have need to be baptized of thee, and comest thou to me?

15But Jesus answering said unto him, Suffer it now: for thus it becometh us to fulfil all righteousness. Then he suffereth him.

16And Jesus when he was baptized, went up straightway from the water: and lo, the heavens were opened unto him, and he saw the Spirit of God descending as a dove, and coming upon him;

17and lo, a voice out of the heavens, saying, This is my beloved Son, in whom I am well pleased.

Chapter 4

1Then was Jesus led up of the Spirit into the wilderness to be tempted of the devil.

2And when he had fasted forty days and forty nights, he afterward hungered.

3And the tempter came and said unto him, If thou art the Son of God, command that these stones become bread.

4But he answered and said, It is written, Man shall not live by bread alone,

Matthew

but by every word that proceedeth out of the mouth of God.

5 Then the devil taketh him into the holy city; and he set him on the pinnacle of the temple,

6 and saith unto him, If thou art the Son of God, cast thyself down: for it is written,

He shall give his angels charge concerning thee:

and,

On their hands they shall bear thee up,

Lest haply thou dash thy foot against a stone.

7 Jesus said unto him, Again it is written, Thou shalt not make trial of the Lord thy God.

8 Again, the devil taketh him unto an exceeding high mountain, and showeth him all the kingdoms of the world, and the glory of them;

9 and he said unto him, All these things will I give thee, if thou wilt fall down and worship me.

10 Then saith Jesus unto him, Get thee hence, Satan: for it is written, Thou shalt worship the Lord thy God, and him only shalt thou serve.

11 Then the devil leaveth him; and behold, angels came and ministered unto him.

12 Now when he heard that John was delivered up, he withdrew into Galilee;

13 and leaving Nazareth, he came and dwelt in Capernaum, which is by the sea, in the borders of Zebulun and Naphtali:

14 that it might be fulfilled which was spoken through Isaiah the prophet, saying,

15 The land of Zebulun and the land of Naphtali,

Toward the sea, beyond the Jordan,

Galilee of the Gentiles,

16 The people that sat in darkness

Saw a great light,

And to them that sat in the region and shadow of death,

To them did light spring up.

17 From that time began Jesus to preach, and to say, Repent ye; for the kingdom of heaven is at hand.

18 And walking by the sea of Galilee, he saw two brethren, Simon who is called Peter, and Andrew his brother, casting a net into the sea; for they were fishers.

19 And he saith unto them, Come ye after me, and I will make you fishers of men.

20 And they straightway left the nets, and followed him.

21 And going on from thence he saw two other brethren, James the son of Zebedee, and John his brother, in the boat with Zebedee their father, mending their nets; and he called them.

22 And they straightway left the boat and their father, and followed him.

23 And Jesus went about in all Galilee, teaching in their synagogues, and preaching the gospel of the kingdom, and healing all manner of disease and all manner of sickness among the people.

24 And the report of him went forth into all Syria: and they brought unto him all that were sick, holden with divers diseases and torments, possessed with demons, and epileptic, and palsied; and he healed them.

25 And there followed him great multitudes from Galilee and Decapolis and Jerusalem and Judaea and from beyond the Jordan.

Chapter 5

1 And seeing the multitudes, he went up into the mountain: and when he had sat down, his disciples came unto him:

2 and he opened his mouth and taught them, saying,

3 Blessed are the poor in spirit: for theirs is the kingdom of heaven.

4 Blessed are they that mourn: for they shall be comforted.

5 Blessed are the meek: for they shall inherit the earth.

6 Blessed are they that hunger and thirst after righteousness: for they shall be filled.

7 Blessed are the merciful: for they shall obtain mercy.

8 Blessed are the pure in heart: for they shall see God.

9 Blessed are the peacemakers: for they shall be called sons of God.

10 Blessed are they that have been persecuted for righteousness' sake: for theirs is the kingdom of heaven.

11 Blessed are ye when men shall reproach you, and persecute you, and say all manner of evil against you falsely, for my sake.

12 Rejoice, and be exceeding glad: for great is your reward in heaven: for so persecuted they the prophets that were before you.

13 Ye are the salt of the earth: but if the salt have lost its savor, wherewith shall it be salted? it is thenceforth good for nothing, but to be cast out and trodden under foot of men.

14 Ye are the light of the world. A city set on a hill cannot be hid.

15 Neither do men light a lamp, and put it under the bushel, but on the stand; and it shineth unto all that are in the house.

16 Even so let your light shine before men; that they may see your good works, and glorify your Father who is in heaven.

17 Think not that I came to destroy the law or the prophets: I came not to destroy, but to fulfil.

18 For verily I say unto you, Till heaven and earth pass away, one jot or one tittle shall in no wise pass away from the law, till all things be accomplished.

19 Whosoever therefore shall break one of these least commandments, and shall teach men so, shall be called least in the kingdom of heaven: but whosoever shall do and teach them, he shall be called great in the kingdom of heaven.

20 For I say unto you, that except your righteousness shall exceed the righteousness of the scribes and Pharisees, ye shall in no wise enter into the kingdom of heaven.

21 Ye have heard that it was said to them of old time, Thou shalt not kill; and whosoever shall kill shall be in danger of the judgment:

22 but I say unto you, that every one who is angry with his brother shall be in danger of the judgment; and whosoever shall say to his brother, Raca, shall be in danger of the council; and whosoever shall say, Thou fool, shall be in danger of the hell of fire.

23 If therefore thou art offering thy gift at the altar, and there rememberest that thy brother hath aught against thee,

24 leave there thy gift before the altar, and go thy way, first be reconciled to thy brother, and then come and offer thy gift.

25 Agree with thine adversary quickly, while thou art with him in the way; lest haply the adversary deliver thee to the judge, and the judge deliver thee to the officer, and thou be cast into prison.

26 Verily I say unto thee, thou shalt by no means come out thence, till thou have paid the last farthing.

27 Ye have heard that it was said, Thou shalt not commit adultery:

28 but I say unto you, that every one that looketh on a woman to lust after her hath committed adultery with her already in his heart.

29 And if thy right eye causeth thee to stumble, pluck it out, and cast it from thee: for it is profitable for thee that one of thy members should perish, and not thy whole body be cast into hell.

30 And if thy right hand causeth thee to stumble, cut it off, and cast it from thee: for it is profitable for thee that one of thy members should perish, and not thy whole body go into hell.

31 It was said also, Whosoever shall put away his wife, let him give her a writing of divorcement:

32 but I say unto you, that every one that putteth away his wife, saving for the cause of fornication, maketh her an adulteress: and whosoever shall marry her when she is put away committeth adultery.

33 Again, ye have heard that it was said to them of old time, Thou shalt not forswear thyself, but shalt perform unto the Lord thine oaths:

34 but I say unto you, swear not at all; neither by the heaven, for it is the throne of God;

35 nor by the earth, for it is the footstool of his feet; nor by Jerusalem, for it is the city of the great King.

36 Neither shalt thou swear by thy head, for thou canst not make one hair white or black.

37 But let your speech be, Yea, yea; Nay, nay: and whatsoever is more than these is of the evil one.

38 Ye have heard that it was said, An eye for an eye, and a tooth for a tooth:

39 but I say unto you, resist not him that is evil: but whosoever smiteth thee on thy right cheek, turn to him the other also.

40 And if any man would go to law with thee, and take away thy coat, let him have thy cloak also.

41 And whosoever shall compel thee to go one mile, go with him two.

42 Give to him that asketh thee, and from him that would borrow of thee turn not thou away.

43 Ye have heard that it was said, Thou shalt love thy neighbor, and hate thine enemy:

44 but I say unto you, love your enemies, and pray for them that persecute you;

45 that ye may be sons of your Father who is in heaven: for he maketh his sun to rise on the evil and the good, and sendeth rain on the just and the unjust.

46 For if ye love them that love you, what reward have ye? do not even the publicans the same?

47 And if ye salute your brethren only, what do ye more than others? do not even the Gentiles the same?

48 Ye therefore shall be perfect, as your heavenly Father is perfect.

Chapter 6

1 Take heed that ye do not your righteousness before men, to be seen of them: else ye have no reward with your Father who is in heaven.

2 When therefore thou doest alms, sound not a trumpet before thee, as the hypocrites do in the synagogues and in the streets, that they may have glory of men. Verily I say unto you, They have received their reward.

3 But when thou doest alms, let not thy left hand know what thy right hand doeth:

4 that thine alms may be in secret: and thy Father who seeth in secret shall recompense thee.

5 And when ye pray, ye shall not be as the hypocrites: for they love to stand and pray in the synagogues and in the corners of the streets, that they may be seen of men. Verily I say unto you, They have received their reward.

6 But thou, when thou prayest, enter into thine inner chamber, and having shut thy door, pray to thy Father who is in secret, and thy Father who seeth in secret shall recompense thee.

7 And in praying use not vain repetitions, as the Gentiles do: for they think that they shall be heard for their much speaking.

8 Be not therefore like unto them: for your Father knoweth what things ye have need of, before ye ask him.

9 After this manner therefore pray ye. Our Father who art in heaven, Hallowed be thy name.

10 Thy kingdom come. Thy will be done, as in heaven, so on earth.

11 Give us this day our daily bread.

12 And forgive us our debts, as we also have forgiven our debtors.

13 And bring us not into temptation, but deliver us from the evil one.

14 For if ye forgive men their trespasses, your heavenly Father will also forgive you.

15 But if ye forgive not men their trespasses, neither will your Father forgive your trespasses.

16 Moreover when ye fast, be not, as the hypocrites, of a sad countenance:

for they disfigure their faces, that they may be seen of men to fast. Verily I say unto you, They have received their reward.

17But thou, when thou fastest, anoint thy head, and wash thy face;
18that thou be not seen of men to fast, but of thy Father who is in secret: and thy Father, who seeth in secret, shall recompense thee.
19Lay not up for yourselves treasures upon the earth, where moth and rust consume, and where thieves break through and steal:
20but lay up for yourselves treasures in heaven, where neither moth nor rust doth consume, and where thieves do not break through nor steal:
21for where thy treasure is, there will thy heart be also.
22The lamp of the body is the eye: if therefore thine eye be single, thy whole body shall be full of light.
23But if thine eye be evil, thy whole body shall be full of darkness. If therefore the light that is in thee be darkness, how great is the darkness!
24No man can serve two masters; for either he will hate the one, and love the other; or else he will hold to one, and despise the other. Ye cannot serve God and mammon.
25Therefore I say unto you, be not anxious for your life, what ye shall eat, or what ye shall drink; nor yet for your body, what ye shall put on. Is not the life more than the food, and the body than the raiment?
26Behold the birds of the heaven, that they sow not, neither do they reap, nor gather into barns; and your heavenly Father feedeth them. Are not ye of much more value then they?
27And which of you by being anxious can add one cubit unto the measure of his life?
28And why are ye anxious concerning raiment? Consider the lilies of the field, how they grow; they toil not, neither do they spin:
29yet I say unto you, that even Solomon in all his glory was not arrayed like one of these.
30But if God doth so clothe the grass of the field, which to-day is, and to-morrow is cast into the oven, shall he not much more clothe you, O ye of little faith?
31Be not therefore anxious, saying, What shall we eat? or, What shall we drink? or, Wherewithal shall we be clothed?
32For after all these things do the Gentiles seek; for your heavenly Father knoweth that ye have need of all these things.
33But seek ye first his kingdom, and his righteousness; and all these things shall be added unto you.
34Be not therefore anxious for the morrow: for the morrow will be anxious for itself. Sufficient unto the day is the evil thereof.

Chapter 7

1Judge not, that ye be not judged.
2For with what judgment ye judge, ye shall be judged: and with what measure ye mete, it shall be measured unto you.
3And why beholdest thou the mote that is in thy brother's eye, but considerest not the beam that is in thine own eye?
4Or how wilt thou say to thy brother, Let me cast out the mote out of thine eye; and lo, the beam is in thine own eye?
5Thou hypocrite, cast out first the beam out of thine own eye; and then shalt thou see clearly to cast out the mote out of thy brother's eye.
6Give not that which is holy unto the dogs, neither cast your pearls before the swine, lest haply they trample them under their feet, and turn and rend you.
7Ask, and it shall be given you; seek, and ye shall find; knock, and it shall be opened unto you:
8for every one that asketh receiveth; and he that seeketh findeth; and to him that knocketh it shall be opened.
9Or what man is there of you, who, if his son shall ask him for a loaf, will give him a stone;
10or if he shall ask for a fish, will give him a serpent?
11If ye then, being evil, know how to give good gifts unto your children, how much more shall your Father who is in heaven give good things to them that ask him?
12All things therefore whatsoever ye would that men should do unto you, even so do ye also unto them: for this is the law and the prophets.
13Enter ye in by the narrow gate: for wide is the gate, and broad is the way, that leadeth to destruction, and many are they that enter in thereby.
14For narrow is the gate, and straitened the way, that leadeth unto life, and few are they that find it.
15Beware of false prophets, who come to you in sheep's clothing, but inwardly are ravening wolves.
16By their fruits ye shall know them. Do men gather grapes of thorns, or figs of thistles?
17Even so every good tree bringeth forth good fruit; but the corrupt tree bringeth forth evil fruit.
18A good tree cannot bring forth evil fruit, neither can a corrupt tree bring forth good fruit.
19Every tree that bringeth not forth good fruit is hewn down, and cast into the fire.
20Therefore by their fruits ye shall know them.
21Not every one that saith unto me, Lord, Lord, shall enter into the kingdom of heaven; but he that doeth the will of my Father who is in heaven.
22Many will say to me in that day, Lord, Lord, did we not prophesy by thy name, and by thy name cast out demons, and by thy name do many mighty works?
23And then will I profess unto them, I never knew you: depart from me, ye that work iniquity.
24Every one therefore that heareth these words of mine, and doeth them, shall be likened unto a wise man, who built his house upon the rock:
25and the rain descended, and the floods came, and the winds blew, and beat upon that house; and if fell not: for it was founded upon the rock.
26And every one that heareth these words of mine, and doeth them not, shall be likened unto a foolish man, who built his house upon the sand:
27and the rain descended, and the floods came, and the winds blew, and smote upon that house; and it fell: and great was the fall thereof.
28And it came to pass, when Jesus had finished these words, the multitudes were astonished at his teaching:
29for he taught them as one having authority, and not as their scribes.

Chapter 8

1And when he was come down from the mountain, great multitudes followed him.
2And behold, there came to him a leper and worshipped him, saying, Lord, if thou wilt, thou canst make me clean.
3And he stretched forth his hand, and touched him, saying, I will; be thou made clean. And straightway his leprosy was cleansed.
4And Jesus saith unto him, See thou tell no man; but go, show thyself to the priest, and offer the gift that Moses commanded, for a testimony unto them.
5And when he was entered into Capernaum, there came unto him a centurion, beseeching him,
6and saying, Lord, my servant lieth in the house sick of the palsy, grievously tormented.
7And he saith unto him, I will come and heal him.
8And the centurion answered and said, Lord, I am not worthy that thou shouldest come under my roof; but only say the word, and my servant shall be healed.
9For I also am a man under authority, having under myself soldiers: and I say to this one, Go, and he goeth; and to another, Come, and he cometh; and to my servant, Do this, and he doeth it.
10And when Jesus heard it, he marvelled, and said to them that followed, Verily I say unto you, I have not found so great faith, no, not in Israel.
11And I say unto you, that many shall come from the east and the west, and shall sit down with Abraham, and Isaac, and Jacob, in the kingdom of heaven:
12but the sons of the kingdom shall be cast forth into the outer darkness: there shall be the weeping and the gnashing of teeth.
13And Jesus said unto the centurion, Go thy way; as thou hast believed, so be it done unto thee. And the servant was healed in that hour.
14And when Jesus was come into Peter's house, he saw his wife's mother lying sick of a fever.
15And he touched her hand, and the fever left her; and she arose, and ministered unto him.
16And when even was come, they brought unto him many possessed with demons: and he cast out the spirits with a word, and healed all that were sick:
17that it might be fulfilled which was spoken through Isaiah the prophet, saying: Himself took our infirmities, and bare our diseases.
18Now when Jesus saw great multitudes about him, he gave commandments to depart unto the other side.
19And there came a scribe, and said unto him, Teacher, I will follow thee whithersoever thou goest.
20And Jesus saith unto him, The foxes have holes, and the birds of the heaven have nests; but the Son of man hath not where to lay his head.
21And another of the disciples said unto him, Lord, suffer me first to go and bury my father.
22But Jesus saith unto him, Follow me; and leave the dead to bury their own dead.
23And when he was entered into a boat, his disciples followed him.
24And behold, there arose a great tempest in the sea, insomuch that the boat was covered with the waves: but he was asleep.
25And they came to him, and awoke him, saying, Save, Lord; we perish.
26And he saith unto them, Why are ye fearful, O ye of little faith? Then he arose, and rebuked the winds and the sea; and there was a great calm.
27And the men marvelled, saying, What manner of man is this, that even the winds and the sea obey him?
28And when he was come to the other side into the country of the Gadarenes, there met him two possessed with demons, coming forth out of the tombs, exceeding fierce, so that no man could pass by that way.
29And behold, they cried out, saying, What have we to do with thee, thou Son of God? art thou come hither to torment us before the time?
30Now there was afar off from them a herd of many swine feeding.
31And the demons besought him, saying, If thou cast us out, send us away into the herd of swine.
32And he said unto them, Go. And they came out, and went into the swine: and behold, the whole herd rushed down the steep into the sea, and perished in the waters.
33And they that fed them fled, and went away into the city, and told everything, and what was befallen to them that were possessed with demons.
34And behold, all the city came out to meet Jesus: and when they saw him, they besought him that he would depart from their borders.

Chapter 9

1And he entered into a boat, and crossed over, and came into his own city.
2And behold, they brought to him a man sick of the palsy, lying on a bed: and Jesus seeing their faith said unto the sick of the palsy, Son, be of good cheer; thy sins are forgiven.
3And behold, certain of the scribes said within themselves, This man blasphemeth.
4And Jesus knowing their thoughts said, Wherefore think ye evil in your hearts?

Matthew

5For which is easier, to say, Thy sins are forgiven; or to say, Arise, and walk?

6But that ye may know that the Son of man hath authority on earth to forgive sins (then saith he to the sick of the palsy), Arise, and take up thy bed, and go up unto thy house.

7And he arose, and departed to his house.

8But when the multitudes saw it, they were afraid, and glorified God, who had given such authority unto men.

9And as Jesus passed by from thence, he saw a man, called Matthew, sitting at the place of toll: and he saith unto him, Follow me. And he arose, and followed him.

10And it came to pass, as he sat at meat in the house, behold, many publicans and sinners came and sat down with Jesus and his disciples.

11And when the Pharisees saw it, they said unto his disciples, Why eateth your Teacher with the publicans and sinners?

12But when he heard it, he said, They that are whole have no need of a physician, but they that are sick.

13But go ye and learn what this meaneth, I desire mercy, and not sacrifice, for I came not to call the righteous, but sinners.

14Then come to him the disciples of John, saying, Why do we and the Pharisees fast oft, but thy disciples fast not?

15And Jesus said unto them, Can the sons of the bridechamber mourn, as long as the bridegroom is with them? but the days will come, when the bridegroom shall be taken away from them, and then will they fast.

16And no man putteth a piece of undressed cloth upon an old garment; for that which should fill it up taketh from the garment, and a worse rent is made.

17Neither do men put new wine into old wine-skins: else the skins burst, and the wine is spilled, and the skins perish: but they put new wine into fresh wine-skins, and both are preserved.

18While he spake these things unto them, behold, there came a ruler, and worshipped him, saying, My daughter is even now dead: but come and lay thy hand upon her, and she shall live.

19And Jesus arose, and followed him, and so did his disciples.

20And behold, a woman, who had an issue of blood twelve years, came behind him, and touched the border of his garment:

21for she said within herself, If I do but touch his garment, I shall be made whole.

22But Jesus turning and seeing her said, Daughter, be of good cheer; thy faith hath made thee whole. And the woman was made whole from that hour.

23And when Jesus came into the ruler's house, and saw the flute-players, and the crowd making a tumult,

24he said, Give place: for the damsel is not dead, but sleepeth. And they laughed him to scorn.

25But when the crowd was put forth, he entered in, and took her by the hand; and the damsel arose.

26And the fame hereof went forth into all that land.

27And as Jesus passed by from thence, two blind men followed him, crying out, and saying, Have mercy on us, thou son of David.

28And when he was come into the house, the blind men came to him: and Jesus saith unto them, Believe ye that I am able to do this? They say unto him, Yea, Lord.

29Then touched he their eyes, saying, According to your faith be it done unto you.

30And their eyes were opened. And Jesus strictly charged them, saying, See that no man know it.

31But they went forth, and spread abroad his fame in all that land.

32And as they went forth, behold, there was brought to him a dumb man possessed with a demon.

33And when the demon was cast out, the dumb man spake: and the multitudes marvelled, saying, It was never so seen in Israel.

34But the Pharisees said, By the prince of the demons casteth he out demons.

35And Jesus went about all the cities and the villages, teaching in their synagogues, and preaching the gospel of the kingdom, and healing all manner of disease and all manner of sickness.

36But when he saw the multitudes, he was moved with compassion for them, because they were distressed and scattered, as sheep not having a shepherd.

37Then saith he unto his disciples, The harvest indeed is plenteous, but the laborers are few.

38Pray ye therefore the Lord of the harvest, that he send forth laborers into his harvest.

Chapter 10

1And he called unto him his twelve disciples, and gave them authority over unclean spirits, to cast them out, and to heal all manner of disease and all manner of sickness.

2Now the names of the twelve apostles are these: The first, Simon, who is called Peter, and Andrew his brother; James the son of Zebedee, and John his brother;

3Philip, and Bartholomew; Thomas, and Matthew the publican; James the son of Alphaeus, and Thaddaeus;

4Simon the Cananaean, and Judas Iscariot, who also betrayed him.

5These twelve Jesus sent forth, and charged them, saying, Go not into any way of the Gentiles, and enter not into any city of the Samaritans:

6but go rather to the lost sheep of the house of Israel.

7And as ye go, preach, saying, The kingdom of heaven is at hand.

8Heal the sick, raise the dead, cleanse the lepers, cast out demons: freely ye received, freely give.

9Get you no gold, nor silver, nor brass in your purses;

10no wallet for your journey, neither two coats, nor shoes, nor staff: for the laborer is worthy of his food.

11And into whatsoever city or village ye shall enter, search out who in it is worthy; and there abide till ye go forth.

12And as ye enter into the house, salute it.

13And if the house be worthy, let your peace come upon it: but if it be not worthy, let your peace return to you.

14And whosoever shall not receive you, nor hear your words, as ye go forth out of that house or that city, shake off the dust of your feet.

15Verily I say unto you, It shall be more tolerable for the land of Sodom and Gomorrah in the day of judgment, than for that city.

16Behold, I send you forth as sheep in the midst of wolves: be ye therefore wise as serpents, and harmless as doves.

17But beware of men: for they will deliver you up to councils, and in theirs synagogues they will scourge you;

18yea and before governors and kings shall ye be brought for my sake, for a testimony to them and to the Gentiles.

19But when they deliver you up, be not anxious how or what ye shall speak: for it shall be given you in that hour what ye shall speak.

20For it is not ye that speak, but the Spirit of your Father that speaketh in you.

21And brother shall deliver up brother to death, and the father his child: and children shall rise up against parents, and cause them to be put to death.

22And ye shall be hated of all men for my name's sake: but he that endureth to the end, the same shall be saved.

23But when they persecute you in this city, flee into the next: for verily I say unto you, Ye shall not have gone through the cities of Israel, till the Son of man be come.

24A disciple is not above his teacher, nor a servant above his lord.

25It is enough for the disciple that he be as his teacher, and the servant as his lord. If they have called the master of the house Beelzebub, how much more them of his household!

26Fear them not therefore: for there is nothing covered, that shall not be revealed; and hid, that shall not be known.

27What I tell you in the darkness, speak ye in the light; and what ye hear in the ear, proclaim upon the house-tops.

28And be not afraid of them that kill the body, but are not able to kill the soul: but rather fear him who is able to destroy both soul and body in hell.

29Are not two sparrows sold for a penny? and not one of them shall fall on the ground without your Father:

30but the very hairs of your head are all numbered.

31Fear not therefore: ye are of more value than many sparrows.

32Every one therefore who shall confess me before men, him will I also confess before my Father who is in heaven.

33But whosoever shall deny me before men, him will I also deny before my Father who is in heaven.

34Think not that I came to send peace on the earth: I came not to send peace, but a sword.

35For I came to set a man at variance against his father, and the daughter against her mother, and the daughter in law against her mother in law:

36and a man's foes shall be they of his own household.

37He that loveth father or mother more than me is not worthy of me; and he that loveth son or daughter more than me is not worthy of me.

38And he that doth not take his cross and follow after me, is not worthy of me.

39He that findeth his life shall lose it; and he that loseth his life for my sake shall find it.

40He that receiveth you receiveth me, and he that receiveth me receiveth him that sent me.

41He that receiveth a prophet in the name of a prophet shall receive a prophet's reward: and he that receiveth a righteous man in the name of a righteous man shall receive a righteous man's reward.

42And whosoever shall give to drink unto one of these little ones a cup of cold water only, in the name of a disciple, verily I say unto you he shall in no wise lose his reward.

Chapter 11

1And it came to pass when Jesus had finished commanding his twelve disciples, he departed thence to teach and preach in their cities.

2Now when John heard in the prison the works of the Christ, he sent by his disciples

3and said unto him, Art thou he that cometh, or look we for another?

4And Jesus answered and said unto them, Go and tell John the things which ye hear and see:

5the blind receive their sight, and the lame walk, the lepers are cleansed, and the deaf hear, and the dead are raised up, and the poor have good tidings preached to them.

6And blessed is he, whosoever shall find no occasion of stumbling in me.

7And as these went their way, Jesus began to say unto the multitudes concerning John, What went ye out into the wilderness to behold? a reed shaken with the wind?

8But what went ye out to see? a man clothed in soft raiment? Behold, they that wear soft raiment are in king's houses.

9But wherefore went ye out? to see a prophet? Yea, I say unto you, and much more than a prophet.

10This is he, of whom it is written,

Behold, I send my messenger before thy face,

Who shall prepare thy way before thee.

11Verily I say unto you, Among them that are born of women there hath not arisen a greater than John the Baptist: yet he that is but little in the kingdom of heaven is greater than he.

12And from the days of John the Baptist until now the kingdom of heaven suffereth violence, and men of violence take it by force.

13For all the prophets and the law prophesied until John.

14And if ye are willing to receive it, this is Elijah, that is to come.

15He that hath ears to hear, let him hear.

16But whereunto shall I liken this generation? It is like unto children sitting in the marketplaces, who call unto their fellows

17and say, We piped unto you, and ye did not dance; we wailed, and ye did not mourn.

18For John came neither eating nor drinking, and they say, He hath a demon.

19The Son of man came eating and drinking, and they say, Behold, a gluttonous man and a winebibber, a friend of publicans and sinners! And wisdom is justified by her works.

20Then began he to upbraid the cities wherein most of his mighty works were done, because they repented not.

21Woe unto thee, Chorazin! woe unto thee, Bethsaida! for if the mighty works had been done in Tyre and Sidon which were done in you, they would have repented long ago in sackcloth and ashes.

22But I say unto you, it shall be more tolerable for Tyre and Sidon in the day of judgment than for you.

23And thou, Capernaum, shalt thou be exalted unto heaven? thou shalt go down unto Hades: for if the mighty works had been done in Sodom which were done in thee, it would have remained until this day.

24But I say unto you that it shall be more tolerable for the land of Sodom in the day of judgment, than for thee.

25At that season Jesus answered and said, I thank thee, O Father, Lord of heaven and earth, that thou didst hide these things from the wise and understanding, and didst reveal them unto babes:

26yea, Father, for so it was well-pleasing in thy sight.

27All things have been delivered unto me of my Father: and no one knoweth the Son, save the Father; neither doth any know the Father, save the Son, and he to whomsoever the Son willeth to reveal him.

28Come unto me, all ye that labor and are heavy laden, and I will give you rest.

29Take my yoke upon you, and learn of me; for I am meek and lowly in heart: and ye shall find rest unto your souls.

30For my yoke is easy, and my burden is light.

Chapter 12

1At that season Jesus went on the sabbath day through the grainfields; and his disciples were hungry and began to pluck ears and to eat.

2But the Pharisees, when they saw it, said unto him, Behold, thy disciples do that which it is not lawful to do upon the sabbath.

3But he said unto them, Have ye not read what David did, when he was hungry, and they that were with him;

4how he entered into the house of God, and ate the showbread, which it was not lawful for him to eat, neither for them that were with him, but only for the priests?

5Or have ye not read in the law, that on the sabbath day the priests in the temple profane the sabbath, and are guiltless?

6But I say unto you, that one greater than the temple is here.

7But if ye had known what this meaneth, I desire mercy, and not sacrifice, ye would not have condemned the guiltless.

8For the Son of man is lord of the sabbath.

9And he departed thence, and went into their synagogue:

10and behold, a man having a withered hand. And they asked him, saying, Is it lawful to heal on the sabbath day? that they might accuse him.

11And he said unto them, What man shall there be of you, that shall have one sheep, and if this fall into a pit on the sabbath day, will he not lay hold on it, and lift it out?

12How much then is a man of more value than a sheep! Wherefore it is lawful to do good on the sabbath day.

13Then saith he to the man, Stretch forth thy hand. And he stretched it forth; and it was restored whole, as the other.

14But the Pharisees went out, and took counsel against him, how they might destroy him.

15And Jesus perceiving it withdrew from thence: and many followed him; and he healed them all,

16and charged them that they should not make him known:

17that it might be fulfilled which was spoken through Isaiah the prophet, saying,

18Behold, my servant whom I have chosen;
My beloved in whom my soul is well pleased:
I will put my Spirit upon him,
And he shall declare judgment to the Gentiles.

19He shall not strive, nor cry aloud;
Neither shall any one hear his voice in the streets.

20A bruised reed shall he not break,
And smoking flax shall he not quench,
Till he send forth judgment unto victory.

21And in his name shall the Gentiles hope.

22Then was brought unto him one possessed with a demon, blind and dumb: and he healed him, insomuch that the dumb man spake and saw.

23And all the multitudes were amazed, and said, Can this be the son of David?

24But when the Pharisees heard it, they said, This man doth not cast out demons, but by Beelzebub the prince of the demons.

25And knowing their thoughts he said unto them, Every kingdom divided against itself is brought to desolation; and every city or house divided against itself shall not stand:

26and if Satan casteth out Satan, he is divided against himself; how then shall his kingdom stand?

27And if I by Beelzebub cast out demons, by whom do your sons cast them out? therefore shall they be your judges.

28But if I by the Spirit of God cast out demons, then is the kingdom of God come upon you.

29Or how can one enter into the house of the strong man, and spoil his goods, except he first bind the strong man? and then he will spoil his house.

30He that is not with me is against me, and he that gathereth not with me scattereth.

31Therefore I say unto you, Every sin and blasphemy shall be forgiven unto men; but the blasphemy against the Spirit shall not be forgiven.

32And whosoever shall speak a word against the Son of man, it shall be forgiven him; but whosoever shall speak against the Holy Spirit, it shall not be forgiven him, neither in this world, nor in that which is to come.

33Either make the tree good, and its fruit good; or make the tree corrupt, and its fruit corrupt: for the tree is known by its fruit.

34Ye offspring of vipers, how can ye, being evil, speak good things? for out of the abundance of the heart the mouth speaketh.

35The good man out of his good treasure bringeth forth good things: and the evil man out of his evil treasure bringeth forth evil things.

36And I say unto you, that every idle word that men shall speak, they shall give account thereof in the day of judgment.

37For by thy words thou shalt be justified, and by thy words thou shalt be condemned.

38Then certain of the scribes and Pharisees answered him, saying, Teacher, we would see a sign from thee.

39But he answered and said unto them, An evil and adulterous generation seeketh after a sign; and there shall no sign be given it but the sign of Jonah the prophet:

40for as Jonah was three days and three nights in the belly of the whale; so shall the Son of man be three days and three nights in the heart of the earth.

41The men of Nineveh shall stand up in the judgment with this generation, and shall condemn it: for they repented at the preaching of Jonah; and behold, a greater than Jonah is here.

42The queen of the south shall rise up in the judgment with this generation, and shall condemn it: for she came from the ends of the earth to hear the wisdom of Solomon; and behold, a greater than Solomon is here.

43But the unclean spirit, when he is gone out of the man, passeth through waterless places, seeking rest, and findeth it not.

44Then he saith, I will return into my house whence I came out; and when he is come, he findeth it empty, swept, and garnished.

45Then goeth he, and taketh with himself seven other spirits more evil than himself, and they enter in and dwell there: and the last state of that man becometh worse than the first. Even so shall it be also unto this evil generation.

46While he was yet speaking to the multitudes, behold, his mother and his brethren stood without, seeking to speak to him.

47And one said unto him, Behold, thy mother and thy brethren stand without, seeking to speak to thee.

48But he answered and said unto him that told him, Who is my mother? and who are my brethren?

49And he stretched forth his hand towards his disciples, and said, Behold, my mother and my brethren!

50For whosoever shall do the will of my Father who is in heaven, he is my brother, and sister, and mother.

Chapter 13

1On that day went Jesus out of the house, and sat by the sea side.

2And there were gathered unto him great multitudes, so that he entered into a boat, and sat; and all the multitude stood on the beach.

3And he spake to them many things in parables, saying, Behold, the sower went forth to sow;

4and as he sowed, some seeds fell by the way side, and the birds came and devoured them:

5and others fell upon the rocky places, where they had not much earth: and straightway they sprang up, because they had no deepness of earth:

6and when the sun was risen, they were scorched; and because they had no root, they withered away.

7And others fell upon the thorns; and the thorns grew up and choked them:

8and others fell upon the good ground, and yielded fruit, some a hundredfold, some sixty, some thirty.

9He that hath ears, let him hear.

10And the disciples came, and said unto him, Why speakest thou unto them in parables?

11And he answered and said unto them, Unto you it is given to know the mysteries of the kingdom of heaven, but to them it is not given.

12For whosoever hath, to him shall be given, and he shall have abundance: but whosoever hath not, from him shall be taken away even that which he hath.

13Therefore speak I to them in parables; because seeing they see not, and hearing they hear not, neither do they understand.

14And unto them is fulfilled the prophecy of Isaiah, which saith,
By hearing ye shall hear, and shall in no wise understand;
And seeing ye shall see, and shall in no wise perceive:

15For this people's heart is waxed gross,
And their ears are dull of hearing,

Matthew

And their eyes they have closed;
Lest haply they should perceive with their eyes,
And hear with their ears,
And understand with their heart,
And should turn again,
And I should heal them.

16But blessed are your eyes, for they see; and your ears, for they hear.

17For verily I say unto you, that many prophets and righteous men desired to see the things which ye see, and saw them not; and to hear the things which ye hear, and heard them not.

18Hear then ye the parable of the sower.

19When any one heareth the word of the kingdom, and understandeth it not, then cometh the evil one, and snatcheth away that which hath been sown in his heart. This is he that was sown by the way side.

20And he that was sown upon the rocky places, this is he that heareth the word, and straightway with joy receiveth it;

21yet hath he not root in himself, but endureth for a while; and when tribulation or persecution ariseth because of the word, straightway he stumbleth.

22And he that was sown among the thorns, this is he that heareth the word; and the care of the world, and the deceitfulness of riches, choke the word, and he becometh unfruitful.

23And he that was sown upon the good ground, this is he that heareth the word, and understandeth it; who verily beareth fruit, and bringeth forth, some a hundredfold, some sixty, some thirty.

24Another parable set he before them, saying, The kingdom of heaven is likened unto a man that sowed good seed in his field:

25but while men slept, his enemy came and sowed tares also among the wheat, and went away.

26But when the blade sprang up and brought forth fruit, then appeared the tares also.

27And the servants of the householder came and said unto him, Sir, didst thou not sow good seed in thy field? whence then hath it tares?

28And he said unto them, An enemy hath done this. And the servants say unto him, Wilt thou then that we go and gather them up?

29But he saith, Nay; lest haply while ye gather up the tares, ye root up the wheat with them.

30Let both grow together until the harvest: and in the time of the harvest I will say to the reapers, Gather up first the tares, and bind them in bundles to burn them; but gather the wheat into my barn.

31Another parable set he before them, saying, The kingdom of heaven is like unto a grain of mustard seed, which a man took, and sowed in his field:

32which indeed is less than all seeds; but when it is grown, it is greater than the herbs, and becometh a tree, so that the birds of the heaven come and lodge in the branches thereof.

33Another parable spake he unto them; The kingdom of heaven is like unto leaven, which a woman took, and hid in three measures of meal, till it was all leavened.

34All these things spake Jesus in parables unto the multitudes; and without a parable spake he nothing unto them:

35that it might be fulfilled which was spoken through the prophet, saying,
I will open my mouth in parables;
I will utter things hidden from the foundation of the world.

36Then he left the multitudes, and went into the house: and his disciples came unto him, saying, Explain unto us the parable of the tares of the field.

37And he answered and said, He that soweth the good seed is the Son of man;

38and the field is the world; and the good seed, these are the sons of the kingdom; and the tares are the sons of the evil one;

39and the enemy that sowed them is the devil: and the harvest is the end of the world; and the reapers are angels.

40As therefore the tares are gathered up and burned with fire; so shall it be in the end of the world.

41The Son of man shall send forth his angels, and they shall gather out of his kingdom all things that cause stumbling, and them that do iniquity,

42and shall cast them into the furnace of fire: there shall be the weeping and the gnashing of teeth.

43Then shall the righteous shine forth as the sun in the kingdom of their Father. He that hath ears, let him hear.

44The kingdom of heaven is like unto a treasure hidden in the field; which a man found, and hid; and in his joy he goeth and selleth all that he hath, and buyeth that field.

45Again, the kingdom of heaven is like unto a man that is a merchant seeking goodly pearls:

46and having found one pearl of great price, he went and sold all that he had, and bought it.

47Again, the kingdom of heaven is like unto a net, that was cast into the sea, and gathered of every kind:

48which, when it was filled, they drew up on the beach; and they sat down, and gathered the good into vessels, but the bad they cast away.

49So shall it be in the end of the world: the angels shall come forth, and sever the wicked from among the righteous,

50and shall cast them into the furnace of fire: there shall be the weeping and the gnashing of teeth.

51Have ye understood all these things? They say unto him, Yea.

52And he said unto them, Therefore every scribe who hath been made a disciple to the kingdom of heaven is like unto a man that is a householder, who bringeth forth out of his treasure things new and old.

53And it came to pass, when Jesus had finished these parables, he departed thence.

54And coming into his own country he taught them in their synagogue, insomuch that they were astonished, and said, Whence hath this man this wisdom, and these mighty works?

55Is not this the carpenter's son? is not his mother called Mary? and his brethren, James, and Joseph, and Simon, and Judas?

56And his sisters, are they not all with us? Whence then hath this man all these things?

57And they were offended in him. But Jesus said unto them, A prophet is not without honor, save in his own country, and in his own house.

58And he did not many mighty works there because of their unbelief.

Chapter 14

1At that season Herod the tetrarch heard the report concerning Jesus,

2and said unto his servants, This is John the Baptist; he is risen from the dead; and therefore do these powers work in him.

3For Herod had laid hold on John, and bound him, and put him in prison for the sake of Herodias, his brother Philip's wife.

4For John said unto him, It is not lawful for thee to have her.

5And when he would have put him to death, he feared the multitude, because they counted him as a prophet.

6But when Herod's birthday came, the daughter of Herodias danced in the midst, and pleased Herod.

7Whereupon he promised with an oath to give her whatsoever she should ask.

8And she, being put forward by her mother, saith, Give me here on a platter the head of John the Baptist.

9And the king was grieved; but for the sake of his oaths, and of them that sat at meat with him, he commanded it to be given;

10and he sent and beheaded John in the prison.

11And his head was brought on a platter, and given to the damsel: and she brought it to her mother.

12And his disciples came, and took up the corpse, and buried him; and they went and told Jesus.

13Now when Jesus heard it, he withdrew from thence in a boat, to a desert place apart: and when the multitudes heard thereof, they followed him on foot from the cities.

14And he came forth, and saw a great multitude, and he had compassion on them, and healed their sick.

15And when even was come, the disciples came to him, saying, The place is desert, and the time is already past; send the multitudes away, that they may go into the villages, and buy themselves food.

16But Jesus said unto them, They have no need to go away; give ye them to eat.

17And they say unto him, We have here but five loaves, and two fishes.

18And he said, Bring them hither to me.

19And he commanded the multitudes to sit down on the grass; and he took the five loaves, and the two fishes, and looking up to heaven, he blessed, and brake and gave the loaves to the disciples, and the disciples to the multitudes.

20And they all ate, and were filled: and they took up that which remained over of the broken pieces, twelve baskets full.

21And they that did eat were about five thousand men, besides women and children.

22And straightway he constrained the disciples to enter into the boat, and to go before him unto the other side, till he should send the multitudes away.

23And after he had sent the multitudes away, he went up into the mountain apart to pray: and when even was come, he was there alone.

24But the boat was now in the midst of the sea, distressed by the waves; for the wind was contrary.

25And in the fourth watch of the night he came unto them, walking upon the sea.

26And when the disciples saw him walking on the sea, they were troubled, saying, It is a ghost; and they cried out for fear.

27But straightway Jesus spake unto them, saying Be of good cheer; it is I; be not afraid.

28And Peter answered him and said, Lord, if it be thou, bid me come unto them upon the waters.

29And he said, Come. And Peter went down from the boat, and walked upon the waters to come to Jesus.

30But when he saw the wind, he was afraid; and beginning to sink, he cried out, saying, Lord, save me.

31And immediately Jesus stretched forth his hand, and took hold of him, and saith unto him, O thou of little faith, wherefore didst thou doubt?

32And when they were gone up into the boat, the wind ceased.

33And they that were in the boat worshipped him, saying, Of a truth thou art the Son of God.

34And when they had crossed over, they came to the land, unto Gennesaret.

35And when the men of that place knew him, they sent into all that region round about, and brought unto him all that were sick,

36and they besought him that they might only touch the border of his garment: and as many as touched were made whole.

Chapter 15

1Then there come to Jesus from Jerusalem Pharisees and scribes, saying,

2Why do thy disciples transgress the tradition of the elders? for they wash not their hands when they eat bread.

3And he answered and said unto them, Why do ye also transgress the commandment of God because of your tradition?

4For God said, Honor thy father and thy mother: and, He that speaketh evil of father or mother, let him die the death.

5But ye say, whosoever shall say to his father or his mother, That wherewith thou mightest have been profited by me is given to God;

6he shall not honor his father. And ye have made void the word of God because of your tradition.

7Ye hypocrites, well did Isaiah prophesy of you, saying,

8This people honoreth me with their lips;
But their heart is far from me.

9But in vain do they worship me,
Teaching as their doctrines the precepts of men.

10And he called to him the multitude, and said unto them, Hear, and understand:

11Not that which entereth into the mouth defileth the man; but that which proceedeth out of the mouth, this defileth the man.

12Then came the disciples, and said unto him, Knowest thou that the Pharisees were offended, when they heard this saying?

13But he answered and said, Every plant which my heavenly Father planted not, shall be rooted up.

14Let them alone: they are blind guides. And if the blind guide the blind, both shall fall into a pit.

15And Peter answered and said unto him, Declare unto us the parable.

16And he said, Are ye also even yet without understanding?

17Perceive ye not, that whatsoever goeth into the mouth passeth into the belly, and is cast out into the draught?

18But the things which proceed out of the mouth come forth out of the heart; and they defile the man.

19For out of the heart come forth evil thoughts, murders, adulteries, fornications, thefts, false witness, railings:

20these are the things which defile the man; but to eat with unwashen hands defileth not the man.

21And Jesus went out thence, and withdrew into the parts of Tyre and Sidon.

22And behold, a Canaanitish woman came out from those borders, and cried, saying, Have mercy on me, O Lord, thou son of David; my daughter is grievously vexed with a demon.

23But he answered her not a word. And his disciples came and besought him, saying, Send her away; for she crieth after us.

24But he answered and said, I was not sent but unto the lost sheep of the house of Israel.

25But she came and worshipped him, saying, Lord, help me.

26And he answered and said, It is not meet to take the children's bread and cast it to the dogs.

27But she said, Yea, Lord: for even the dogs eat of the crumbs which fall from their masters' table.

28Then Jesus answered and said unto her, O woman, great is thy faith: be it done unto thee even as thou wilt. And her daughter was healed from that hour.

29And Jesus departed thence, and came nigh unto the sea of Galilee; and he went up into the mountain, and sat there.

30And there came unto him great multitudes, having with them the lame, blind, dumb, maimed, and many others, and they cast them down at this feet; and he healed them:

31insomuch that the multitude wondered, when they saw the dumb speaking, the maimed whole, and lame walking, and the blind seeing: and they glorified the God of Israel.

32And Jesus called unto him his disciples, and said, I have compassion on the multitude, because they continue with me now three days and have nothing to eat: and I would not send them away fasting, lest haply they faint on the way.

33And the disciples say unto him, Whence should we have so many loaves in a desert place as to fill so great a multitude?

34And Jesus said unto them, How many loaves have ye? And they said, Seven, and a few small fishes.

35And he commanded the multitude to sit down on the ground;

36and he took the seven loaves and the fishes; and he gave thanks and brake, and gave to the disciples, and the disciples to the multitudes.

37And they all ate, and were filled: and they took up that which remained over of the broken pieces, seven baskets full.

38And they that did eat were four thousand men, besides women and children.

39And he sent away the multitudes, and entered into the boat, and came into the borders of Magadan.

Chapter 16

1And the Pharisees and Sadducees came, and trying him asked him to show them a sign from heaven.

2But he answered and said unto them, When it is evening, ye say, It will be fair weather: for the heaven is red.

3And in the morning, It will be foul weather to-day: for the heaven is red and lowering. Ye know how to discern the face of the heaven; but ye cannot discern the signs of the times.

4An evil and adulterous generation seeketh after a sign; and there shall no sign be given unto it, but the sign of Jonah. And he left them, and departed.

5And the disciples came to the other side and forgot to take bread.

6And Jesus said unto them, Take heed and beware of the leaven of the Pharisees and Sadducees.

7And they reasoned among themselves, saying, We took no bread.

8And Jesus perceiving it said, O ye of little faith, why reason ye among yourselves, because ye have no bread?

9Do ye not yet perceive, neither remember the five loaves of the five thousand, and how many baskets ye took up?

10Neither the seven loaves of the four thousand, and how many baskets ye took up?

11How is it that ye do not perceive that I spake not to you concerning bread? But beware of the leaven of the Pharisees and Sadducees.

12Then understood they that he bade them not beware of the leaven of bread, but of the teaching of the Pharisees and Sadducees.

13Now when Jesus came into the parts of Caesarea Philippi, he asked his disciples, saying, Who do men say that the Son of man is?

14And they said, Some say John the Baptist; some, Elijah; and others, Jeremiah, or one of the prophets.

15He saith unto them, But who say ye that I am?

16And Simon Peter answered and said, Thou art the Christ, the Son of the living God.

17And Jesus answered and said unto him, Blessed art thou, Simon Bar-jonah: for flesh and blood hath not revealed it unto thee, but my Father who is in heaven.

18And I also say unto thee, that thou art Peter, and upon this rock I will build my church; and the gates of Hades shall not prevail against it.

19I will give unto thee the keys of the kingdom of heaven: and whatsoever thou shalt bind on earth shall be bound in heaven; and whatsoever thou shalt loose on earth shall be loosed in heaven.

20Then charged he the disciples that they should tell no man that he was the Christ.

21From that time began Jesus to show unto his disciples, that he must go unto Jerusalem, and suffer many things of the elders and chief priests and scribes, and be killed, and the third day be raised up.

22And Peter took him, and began to rebuke him, saying, Be it far from thee, Lord: this shall never be unto thee.

23But he turned, and said unto Peter, Get thee behind me, Satan: thou art a stumbling-block unto me: for thou mindest not the things of God, but the things of men.

24Then said Jesus unto his disciples, If any man would come after me, let him deny himself, and take up his cross, and follow me.

25For whosoever would save his life shall lose it: and whosoever shall lose his life for my sake shall find it.

26For what shall a man be profited, if he shall gain the whole world, and forfeit his life? or what shall a man give in exchange for his life?

27For the Son of man shall come in the glory of his Father with his angels; and then shall he render unto every man according to his deeds.

28Verily I say unto you, there are some of them that stand here, who shall in no wise taste of death, till they see the Son of man coming in his kingdom.

Chapter 17

1And after six days Jesus taketh with him Peter, and James, and John his brother, and bringeth them up into a high mountain apart:

2and he was transfigured before them; and his face did shine as the sun, and his garments became white as the light.

3And behold, there appeared unto them Moses and Elijah talking with him.

4And Peter answered, and said unto Jesus, Lord, it is good for us to be here: if thou wilt, I will make here three tabernacles; one for thee, and one for Moses, and one for Elijah.

5While he was yet speaking, behold, a bright cloud overshadowed them: and behold, a voice out of the cloud, saying, This is my beloved Son, in whom I am well pleased; hear ye him.

6And when the disciples heard it, they fell on their face, and were sore afraid.

7And Jesus came and touched them and said, Arise, and be not afraid.

8And lifting up their eyes, they saw no one, save Jesus only.

9And as they were coming down from the mountain, Jesus commanded them, saying, Tell the vision to no man, until the Son of man be risen from the dead.

10And his disciples asked him, saying, Why then say the scribes that Elijah must first come?

11And he answered and said, Elijah indeed cometh, and shall restore all things:

12but I say unto you, that Elijah is come already, and they knew him not, but did unto him whatsoever they would. Even so shall the Son of man also suffer of them.

13Then understood the disciples that he spake unto them of John the Baptist.

14And when they were come to the multitude, there came to him a man, kneeling to him, saying,

15Lord, have mercy on my son: for he is epileptic, and suffereth grievously; for oft-times he falleth into the fire, and off-times into the water.

16And I brought him to thy disciples, and they could not cure him.

17And Jesus answered and said, O faithless and perverse generation, how long shall I be with you? how long shall I bear with you? bring him hither to me.

18And Jesus rebuked him; and the demon went out of him: and the boy was cured from that hour.

19Then came the disciples to Jesus apart, and said, Why could not we cast it out?

20And he saith unto them, Because of your little faith: for verily I say unto you, If ye have faith as a grain of mustard seed, ye shall say unto this mountain, Remove hence to yonder place; and it shall remove; and nothing shall be impossible unto you.

21But this kind goeth not out save by prayer and fasting.

22And while they abode in Galilee, Jesus said unto them, The Son of man shall be delivered up into the hands of men;

23and they shall kill him, and the third day he shall be raised up. And they were exceeding sorry.

Matthew

24And when they were come to Capernaum, they that received the half-shekel came to Peter, and said, Doth not your teacher pay the half-shekel?

25He saith, Yea. And when he came into the house, Jesus spake first to him, saying, What thinkest thou, Simon? the kings of the earth, from whom do they receive toll or tribute? from their sons, or from strangers?

26And when he said, From strangers, Jesus said unto him, Therefore the sons are free.

27But, lest we cause them to stumble, go thou to the sea, and cast a hook, and take up the fish that first cometh up; and when thou hast opened his mouth, thou shalt find a shekel: that take, and give unto them for me and thee.

Chapter 18

1In that hour came the disciples unto Jesus, saying, Who then is greatest in the kingdom of heaven?

2And he called to him a little child, and set him in the midst of them,

3and said, Verily I say unto you, Except ye turn, and become as little children, ye shall in no wise enter into the kingdom of heaven.

4Whosoever therefore shall humble himself as this little child, the same is the greatest in the kingdom of heaven.

5And whoso shall receive one such little child in my name receiveth me:

6But whoso shall cause one of these little ones that believe on me to stumble, it is profitable for him that a great millstone should be hanged about his neck, and that he should be sunk in the depth of the sea.

7Woe unto the world because of occasions of stumbling! for it must needs be that the occasions come; but woe to that man through whom the occasion cometh!

8And if thy hand or thy foot causeth thee to stumble, cut it off, and cast it from thee: it is good for thee to enter into life maimed or halt, rather than having two hands or two feet to be cast into the eternal fire.

9And if thine eye causeth thee to stumble, pluck it out, and cast it from thee: it is good for thee to enter into life with one eye, rather than having two eyes to be cast into the hell of fire.

10See that ye despise not one of these little ones; for I say unto you, that in heaven their angels do always behold the face of my Father who is in heaven.

11For the Son of man came to save that which was lost.

12How think ye? if any man have a hundred sheep, and one of them be gone astray, doth he not leave the ninety and nine, and go unto the mountains, and seek that which goeth astray?

13And if so be that he find it, verily I say unto you, he rejoiceth over it more than over the ninety and nine which have not gone astray.

14Even so it is not the will of your Father who is in heaven, that one of these little ones should perish.

15And if thy brother sin against thee, go, show him his fault between thee and him alone: if he hear thee, thou hast gained thy brother.

16But if he hear thee not, take with thee one or two more, that at the mouth of two witnesses or three every word may be established.

17And if he refuse to hear them, tell it unto the church: and if he refuse to hear the church also, let him be unto thee as the Gentile and the publican.

18Verily I say unto you, what things soever ye shall bind on earth shall be bound in heaven; and what things soever ye shall loose on earth shall be loosed in heaven.

19Again I say unto you, that if two of you shall agree on earth as touching anything that they shall ask, it shall be done for them of my Father who is in heaven.

20For where two or three are gathered together in my name, there am I in the midst of them.

21Then came Peter and said to him, Lord, how oft shall my brother sin against me, and I forgive him? until seven times?

22Jesus saith unto him, I say not unto thee, Until seven times; but, Until seventy times seven.

23Therefore is the kingdom of heaven likened unto a certain king, who would make a reckoning with his servants.

24And when he had begun to reckon, one was brought unto him, that owed him ten thousand talents.

25But forasmuch as he had not wherewith to pay, his lord commanded him to be sold, and his wife, and children, and all that he had, and payment to be made.

26The servant therefore fell down and worshipped him, saying, Lord, have patience with me, and I will pay thee all.

27And the lord of that servant, being moved with compassion, released him, and forgave him the debt.

28But that servant went out, and found one of his fellow-servants, who owed him a hundred shillings: and he laid hold on him, and took him by the throat, saying, Pay what thou owest.

29So his fellow-servant fell down and besought him, saying, Have patience with me, and I will pay thee.

30And he would not: but went and cast him into prison, till he should pay that which was due.

31So when his fellow-servants saw what was done, they were exceeding sorry, and came and told unto their lord all that was done.

32Then his lord called him unto him, and saith to him, Thou wicked servant, I forgave thee all that debt, because thou besoughtest me:

33shouldest not thou also have had mercy on thy fellow-servant, even as I had mercy on thee?

34And his lord was wroth, and delivered him to the tormentors, till he should pay all that was due.

35So shall also my heavenly Father do unto you, if ye forgive not every one his brother from your hearts.

Chapter 19

1And it came to pass when Jesus had finished these words, he departed from Galilee, and came into the borders of Judaea beyond the Jordan;

2and great multitudes followed him; and he healed them there.

3And there came unto him Pharisees, trying him, and saying, Is it lawful for a man to put away his wife for every cause?

4And he answered and said, Have ye not read, that he who made them from the beginning made them male and female,

5and said, For this cause shall a man leave his father and mother, and shall cleave to his wife; and the two shall become one flesh?

6So that they are no more two, but one flesh. What therefore God hath joined together, let not man put asunder.

7They say unto him, Why then did Moses command to give a bill of divorcement, and to put her away?

8He saith unto them, Moses for your hardness of heart suffered you to put away your wives: but from the beginning it hath not been so.

9And I say unto you, Whosoever shall put away his wife, except for fornication, and shall marry another, committeth adultery: and he that marrieth her when she is put away committeth adultery.

10The disciples say unto him, If the case of the man is so with his wife, it is not expedient to marry.

11But he said unto them, Not all men can receive this saying, but they to whom it is given.

12For there are eunuchs, that were so born from their mother's womb: and there are eunuchs, that were made eunuchs by men: and there are eunuchs, that made themselves eunuchs for the kingdom of heaven's sake. He that is able to receive it, let him receive it.

13Then were there brought unto him little children, that he should lay his hands on them, and pray: and the disciples rebuked them.

14But Jesus said, Suffer the little children, and forbid them not, to come unto me: for to such belongeth the kingdom of heaven.

15And he laid his hands on them, and departed thence.

16And behold, one came to him and said, Teacher, what good thing shall I do, that I may have eternal life?

17And he said unto him, Why askest thou me concerning that which is good? One there is who is good: but if thou wouldest enter into life, keep the commandments.

18He saith unto him, Which? And Jesus said, Thou shalt not kill, Thou shalt not commit adultery, Thou shalt not steal, Thou shalt not bear false witness,

19Honor thy father and mother; and, Thou shalt love thy neighbor as thyself.

20The young man saith unto him, All these things have I observed: what lack I yet?

21Jesus said unto him, If thou wouldest be perfect, go, sell that which thou hast, and give to the poor, and thou shalt have treasure in heaven: and come, follow me.

22But when the young man heard the saying, he went away sorrowful; for he was one that had great possessions.

23And Jesus said unto his disciples, Verily I say unto you, It is hard for a rich man to enter into the kingdom of heaven.

24And again I say unto you, It is easier for a camel to go through a needle's eye, than for a rich man to enter into the kingdom of God.

25And when the disciples heard it, they were astonished exceedingly, saying, Who then can be saved?

26And Jesus looking upon them said to them, With men this is impossible; but with God all things are possible.

27Then answered Peter and said unto him, Lo, we have left all, and followed thee; what then shall we have?

28And Jesus said unto them, Verily I say unto you, that ye who have followed me, in the regeneration when the Son of man shall sit on the throne of his glory, ye also shall sit upon twelve thrones, judging the twelve tribes of Israel.

29And every one that hath left houses, or brethren, or sisters, or father, or mother, or children, or lands, for my name's sake, shall receive a hundredfold, and shall inherit eternal life.

30But many shall be last that are first; and first that are last.

Chapter 20

1For the kingdom of heaven is like unto a man that was a householder, who went out early in the morning to hire laborers into his vineyard.

2And when he had agreed with the laborers for a shilling a day, he sent them into his vineyard.

3And he went out about the third hour, and saw others standing in the marketplace idle;

4and to them he said, Go ye also into the vineyard, and whatsoever is right I will give you. And they went their way.

5Again he went out about the sixth and the ninth hour, and did likewise.

6And about the eleventh hour he went out, and found others standing; and he saith unto them, Why stand ye here all the day idle?

7They say unto him, Because no man hath hired us. He saith unto them, Go ye also into the vineyard.

8And when even was come, the lord of the vineyard saith unto his steward, Call the laborers, and pay them their hire, beginning from the last unto the first.

9And when they came that were hired about the eleventh hour, they received every man a shilling.

10And when the first came, they supposed that they would receive more; and they likewise received every man a shilling.

11And when they received it, they murmured against the householder,

12saying, These last have spent but one hour, and thou hast made them equal unto us, who have borne the burden of the day and the scorching heat.

13But he answered and said to one of them, Friend, I do thee no wrong: didst not thou agree with me for a shilling?

14Take up that which is thine, and go thy way; it is my will to give unto this last, even as unto thee.

15Is it not lawful for me to do what I will with mine own? or is thine eye evil, because I am good?

16So the last shall be first, and the first last.

17And as Jesus was going up to Jerusalem, he took the twelve disciples apart, and on the way he said unto them,

18Behold, we go up to Jerusalem; and the Son of man shall be delivered unto the chief priests and scribes; and they shall condemn him to death,

19and shall deliver him unto the Gentiles to mock, and to scourge, and to crucify: and the third day he shall be raised up.

20Then came to him the mother of the sons of Zebedee with her sons, worshipping him, and asking a certain thing of him.

21And he said unto her, What wouldest thou? She saith unto him, Command that these my two sons may sit, one on thy right hand, and one on thy left hand, in thy kingdom.

22But Jesus answered and said, Ye know not what ye ask. Are ye able to drink the cup that I am about to drink? They say unto him, We are able.

23He saith unto them, My cup indeed ye shall drink: but to sit on my right hand, and on my left hand, is not mine to give; but it is for them for whom it hath been prepared of my Father.

24And when the ten heard it, they were moved with indignation concerning the two brethren.

25But Jesus called them unto him, and said, Ye know that the rulers of the Gentiles lord it over them, and their great ones exercise authority over them.

26Not so shall it be among you: but whosoever would become great among you shall be your minister;

27and whosoever would be first among you shall be your servant:

28even as the Son of man came not to be ministered unto, but to minister, and to give his life a ransom for many.

29And as they went out from Jericho, a great multitude followed him.

30And behold, two blind men sitting by the way side, when they heard that Jesus was passing by, cried out, saying, Lord, have mercy on us, thou son of David.

31And the multitude rebuked them, that they should hold their peace: but they cried out the more, saying, Lord, have mercy on us, thou son of David.

32And Jesus stood still, and called them, and said, What will ye that I should do unto you?

33They say unto him, Lord, that our eyes may be opened.

34And Jesus, being moved with compassion, touched their eyes; and straightway they received their sight, and followed him.

Chapter 21

1And when they drew nigh unto Jerusalem, and came unto Bethphage, unto the mount of Olives, then Jesus sent two disciples,

2saying unto them, Go into the village that is over against you, and straightway ye shall find an ass tied, and a colt with her: loose them, and bring them unto me.

3And if any one say aught unto you, ye shall say, The Lord hath need of them; and straightway he will send them.

4Now this is come to pass, that it might be fulfilled which was spoken through the prophet, saying,

5Tell ye the daughter of Zion,
Behold, thy King cometh unto thee,
Meek, and riding upon an ass,
And upon a colt the foal of an ass.

6And the disciples went, and did even as Jesus appointed them,

7and brought the ass, and the colt, and put on them their garments; and he sat thereon.

8And the most part of the multitude spread their garments in the way; and others cut branches from the trees, and spread them in the way.

9And the multitudes that went before him, and that followed, cried, saying, Hosanna to the son of David: Blessed is he that cometh in the name of the Lord; Hosanna in the highest.

10And when he was come into Jerusalem, all the city was stirred, saying, Who is this?

11And the multitudes said, This is the prophet, Jesus, from Nazareth of Galilee.

12And Jesus entered into the temple of God, and cast out all them that sold and bought in the temple, and overthrew the tables of he money-changers, and the seats of them that sold the doves;

13and he saith unto them, It is written, My house shall be called a house of prayer: but ye make it a den of robbers.

14And the blind and the lame came to him in the temple; and he healed them.

15But when the chief priests and the scribes saw the wonderful things that he did, and the children that were crying in the temple and saying, Hosanna to the son of David; they were moved with indignation,

16and said unto him, Hearest thou what these are saying? And Jesus saith unto them, Yea: did ye never read, Out of the mouth of babes and sucklings thou has perfected praise?

17And he left them, and went forth out of the city to Bethany, and lodged there.

18Now in the morning as he returned to the city, he hungered.

19And seeing a fig tree by the way side, he came to it, and found nothing thereon, but leaves only; and he saith unto it, Let there be no fruit from thee henceforward for ever. And immediately the fig tree withered away.

20And when the disciples saw it, they marvelled, saying, How did the fig tree immediately wither away?

21And Jesus answered and said unto them, Verily I say unto you, If ye have faith, and doubt not, ye shall not only do what is done to the fig tree, but even if ye shall say unto this mountain, Be thou taken up and cast into the sea, it shall be done.

22And all things, whatsoever ye shall ask in prayer, believing, ye shall receive.

23And when he was come into the temple, the chief priests and the elders of the people came unto him as he was teaching, and said, By what authority doest thou these things? and who gave thee this authority?

24And Jesus answered and said unto them, I also will ask you one question, which if ye tell me, I likewise will tell you by what authority I do these things.

25The baptism of John, whence was it? from heaven or from men? And they reasoned with themselves, saying, If we shall say, From heaven; he will say unto us, Why then did ye not believe him?

26But if we shall say, From men; we fear the multitude; for all hold John as a prophet.

27And they answered Jesus, and said, We know not. He also said unto them, Neither tell I you by what authority I do these things.

28But what think ye? A man had two sons; and he came to the first, and said, Son, go work to-day in the vineyard.

29And he answered and said, I will not: but afterward he repented himself, and went.

30And he came to the second, and said likewise. And he answered and said, I go, sir: and went not.

31Which of the two did the will of his father? They say, The first. Jesus saith unto them, Verily I say unto you, that the publicans and the harlots go into the kingdom of God before you.

32For John came unto you in the way of righteousness, and ye believed him not; but the publicans and the harlots believed him: and ye, when ye saw it, did not even repent yourselves afterward, that ye might believe him.

33Hear another parable: There was a man that was a householder, who planted a vineyard, and set a hedge about it, and digged a winepress in it, and built a tower, and let it out to husbandmen, and went into another country.

34And when the season of the fruits drew near, he sent his servants to the husbandmen, to receive his fruits.

35And the husbandmen took his servants, and beat one, and killed another, and stoned another.

36Again, he sent other servants more than the first: and they did unto them in like manner.

37But afterward he sent unto them his son, saying, They will reverence my son.

38But the husbandmen, when they saw the son, said among themselves, This is the heir; come, let us kill him, and take his inheritance.

39And they took him, and cast him forth out of the vineyard, and killed him.

40When therefore the lord of the vineyard shall come, what will he do unto those husbandmen?

41They say unto him, He will miserably destroy those miserable men, and will let out the vineyard unto other husbandmen, who shall render him the fruits in their seasons.

42Jesus saith unto them, Did ye never read in the scriptures,
The stone which the builders rejected,
The same was made the head of the corner;
This was from the Lord,
And it is marvelous in our eyes?

43Therefore say I unto you, The kingdom of God shall be taken away from you, and shall be given to a nation bringing forth the fruits thereof.

44And he that falleth on this stone shall be broken to pieces: but on whomsoever it shall fall, it will scatter him as dust.

45And when the chief priests and the Pharisees heard his parables, they perceived that he spake of them.

46And when they sought to lay hold on him, they feared the multitudes, because they took him for a prophet.

Chapter 22

1And Jesus answered and spake again in parables unto them, saying,

2The kingdom of heaven is likened unto a certain king, who made a marriage feast for his son,

3and sent forth his servants to call them that were bidden to the marriage feast: and they would not come.

4Again he sent forth other servants, saying, Tell them that are bidden, Behold, I have made ready my dinner; my oxen and my fatlings are killed, and all things are ready: come to the marriage feast.

5But they made light of it, and went their ways, one to his own farm, another to his merchandise;

6and the rest laid hold on his servants, and treated them shamefully, and killed them.

7But the king was wroth; and he sent his armies, and destroyed those murderers, and burned their city.

8Then saith he to his servants, The wedding is ready, but they that were bidden were not worthy.

9Go ye therefore unto the partings of the highways, and as many as ye shall find, bid to the marriage feast.

10And those servants went out into the highways, and gathered together all as many as they found, both bad and good: and the wedding was filled with guests.

11But when the king came in to behold the guests, he saw there a man who had not on a wedding-garment:

12and he saith unto him, Friend, how camest thou in hither not having a

Matthew

wedding-garment? And he was speechless.

13Then the king said to the servants, Bind him hand and foot, and cast him out into the outer darkness; there shall be the weeping and the gnashing of teeth.

14For many are called, but few chosen.

15Then went the Pharisees, and took counsel how they might ensnare him in his talk.

16And they send to him their disciples, with the Herodians, saying, Teacher, we know that thou art true, and teachest the way of God in truth, and carest not for any one: for thou regardest not the person of men.

17Tell us therefore, What thinkest thou? Is it lawful to give tribute unto Caesar, or not?

18But Jesus perceived their wickedness, and said, Why make ye trial of me, ye hypocrites?

19Show me the tribute money. And they brought unto him a denarius.

20And he saith unto them, Whose is this image and superscription?

21They say unto him, Caesar's. Then saith he unto them, Render therefore unto Caesar the things that are Caesar's; and unto God the things that are God's.

22And when they heard it, they marvelled, and left him, and went away.

23On that day there came to him Sadducees, they that say that there is no resurrection: and they asked him,

24saying, Teacher, Moses said, If a man die, having no children, his brother shall marry his wife, and raise up seed unto his brother.

25Now there were with us seven brethren: and the first married and deceased, and having no seed left his wife unto his brother;

26in like manner the second also, and the third, unto the seventh.

27And after them all, the woman died.

28In the resurrection therefore whose wife shall she be of the seven? for they all had her.

29But Jesus answered and said unto them, Ye do err, not knowing the scriptures, nor the power of God.

30For in the resurrection they neither marry, nor are given in marriage, but are as angels in heaven.

31But as touching the resurrection of the dead, have ye not read that which was spoken unto you by God, saying,

32I am the God of Abraham, and the God of Isaac, and the God of Jacob? God is not the God of the dead, but of the living.

33And when the multitudes heard it, they were astonished at his teaching.

34But the Pharisees, when they heard that he had put the Sadducees to silence, gathered themselves together.

35And one of them, a lawyer, asked him a question, trying him:

36Teacher, which is the great commandment in the law?

37And he said unto him, Thou shalt love the Lord thy God with all thy heart, and with all thy soul, and with all thy mind.

38This is the great and first commandment.

39And a second like unto it is this, Thou shalt love thy neighbor as thyself.

40On these two commandments the whole law hangeth, and the prophets.

41Now while the Pharisees were gathered together, Jesus asked them a question,

42saying, What think ye of the Christ? whose son is he? They say unto him, The son of David.

43He saith unto them, How then doth David in the Spirit call him Lord, saying,

44The Lord said unto my Lord,
Sit thou on my right hand,
Till I put thine enemies underneath thy feet?

45If David then calleth him Lord, how is he his son?

46And no one was able to answer him a word, neither durst any man from that day forth ask him any more questions.

Chapter 23

1Then spake Jesus to the multitudes and to his disciples,

2saying, The scribes and the Pharisees sit on Moses seat:

3all things therefore whatsoever they bid you, these do and observe: but do not ye after their works; for they say, and do not.

4Yea, they bind heavy burdens and grievous to be borne, and lay them on men's shoulders; but they themselves will not move them with their finger.

5But all their works they do to be seen of men: for they make broad their phylacteries, and enlarge the borders of their garments,

6and love the chief place at feasts, and the chief seats in the synagogues,

7and the salutations in the marketplaces, and to be called of men, Rabbi.

8But be not ye called Rabbi: for one is your teacher, and all ye are brethren.

9And call no man your father on the earth: for one is your Father, even he who is in heaven.

10Neither be ye called masters: for one is your master, even the Christ.

11But he that is greatest among you shall be your servant.

12And whosoever shall exalt himself shall be humbled; and whosoever shall humble himself shall be exalted.

13But woe unto you, scribes and Pharisees, hypocrites! because ye shut the kingdom of heaven against men: for ye enter not in yourselves, neither suffer ye them that are entering in to enter

14Woe unto you, scribes and Pharisees, hypocrites! for ye devour widows' houses, even while for a pretence ye make long prayers: therefore ye shall receive greater condemnation.

15Woe unto you, scribes and Pharisees, hypocrites! for ye compass sea and land to make one proselyte; and when he is become so, ye make him twofold more a son of hell than yourselves.

16Woe unto you, ye blind guides, that say, Whosoever shall swear by the temple, it is nothing; but whosoever shall swear by the gold of the temple, he is a debtor.

17Ye fools and blind: for which is greater, the gold, or the temple that hath sanctified the gold?

18And, Whosoever shall swear by the altar, it is nothing; but whosoever shall swear by the gift that is upon it, he is a debtor.

19Ye blind: for which is greater, the gift, or the altar that sanctifieth the gift?

20He therefore that sweareth by the altar, sweareth by it, and by all things thereon.

21And he that sweareth by the temple, sweareth by it, and by him that dwelleth therein.

22And he that sweareth by the heaven, sweareth by the throne of God, and by him that sitteth thereon.

23Woe unto you, scribes and Pharisees, hypocrites! for ye tithe mint and anise and cummin, and have left undone the weightier matters of the law, justice, and mercy, and faith: but these ye ought to have done, and not to have left the other undone.

24Ye blind guides, that strain out the gnat, and swallow the camel!

25Woe unto you, scribes and Pharisees, hypocrites! for ye cleanse the outside of the cup and of the platter, but within they are full from extortion and excess.

26Thou blind Pharisee, cleanse first the inside of the cup and of the platter, that the outside thereof may become clean also.

27Woe unto you, scribes and Pharisees, hypocrites! for ye are like unto whited sepulchres, which outwardly appear beautiful, but inwardly are full of dead men's bones, and of all uncleanness.

28Even so ye also outwardly appear righteous unto men, but inwardly ye are full of hypocrisy and iniquity.

29Woe unto you, scribes and Pharisees, hypocrites! for ye build the sepulchres of the prophets, and garnish the tombs of the righteous,

30and say, If we had been in the days of our fathers, we should not have been partakers with them in the blood of the prophets.

31Wherefore ye witness to yourselves, that ye are sons of them that slew the prophets.

32Fill ye up then the measure of your fathers.

33Ye serpents, ye offspring of vipers, how shall ye escape the judgment of hell?

34Therefore, behold, I send unto you prophets, and wise men, and scribes: some of them shall ye kill and crucify; and some of them shall ye scourge in your synagogues, and persecute from city to city:

35that upon you may come all the righteous blood shed on the earth, from the blood of Abel the righteous unto the blood of Zachariah son of Barachiah, whom ye slew between the sanctuary and the altar.

36Verily I say unto you, All these things shall come upon this generation.

37O Jerusalem, Jerusalem, that killeth the prophets, and stoneth them that are sent unto her! how often would I have gathered thy children together, even as a hen gathereth her chickens under her wings, and ye would not!

38Behold, your house is left unto you desolate.

39For I say unto you, Ye shall not see me henceforth, till ye shall say, Blessed is he that cometh in the name of the Lord.

Chapter 24

1And Jesus went out from the temple, and was going on his way; and his disciples came to him to show him the buildings of the temple.

2But he answered and said unto them, See ye not all these things? verily I say unto you, There shall not be left here one stone upon another, that shall not be thrown down.

3And as he sat on the mount of Olives, the disciples came unto him privately, saying, Tell us, when shall these things be? and what shall be the sign of thy coming, and of the end of the world?

4And Jesus answered and said unto them, Take heed that no man lead you astray.

5For many shall come in my name, saying, I am the Christ; and shall lead many astray.

6And ye shall hear of wars and rumors of wars; see that ye be not troubled: for these things must needs come to pass; but the end is not yet.

7For nation shall rise against nation, and kingdom against kingdom; and there shall be famines and earthquakes in divers places.

8But all these things are the beginning of travail.

9Then shall they deliver you up unto tribulation, and shall kill you: and ye shall be hated of all the nations for my name's sake.

10And then shall many stumble, and shall deliver up one another, and shall hate one another.

11And many false prophets shall arise, and shall lead many astray.

12And because iniquity shall be multiplied, the love of the many shall wax cold.

13But he that endureth to the end, the same shall be saved.

14And this gospel of the kingdom shall be preached in the whole world for a testimony unto all the nations; and then shall the end come.

15When therefore ye see the abomination of desolation, which was spoken of through Daniel the prophet, standing in the holy place (let him that readeth understand),

16then let them that are in Judaea flee unto the mountains:

17let him that is on the housetop not go down to take out things that are in his house:

18and let him that is in the field not return back to take his cloak.

19But woe unto them that are with child and to them that give suck in those days!

20And pray ye that your flight be not in the winter, neither on a sabbath:

21for then shall be great tribulation, such as hath not been from the beginning of the world until now, no, nor ever shall be.

22And except those days had been shortened, no flesh would have been saved: but for the elect's sake those days shall be shortened.

23Then if any man shall say unto you, Lo, here is the Christ, or, Here; believe it not.

24For there shall arise false Christs, and false prophets, and shall show great signs and wonders; so as to lead astray, if possible, even the elect.

25Behold, I have told you beforehand.

26If therefore they shall say unto you, Behold, he is in the wilderness; go not forth: Behold, he is in the inner chambers; believe it not.

27For as the lightning cometh forth from the east, and is seen even unto the west; so shall be the coming of the Son of man.

28Wheresoever the carcase is, there will the eagles be gathered together.

29But immediately after the tribulation of those days the sun shall be darkened, and the moon shall not give her light, and the stars shall fall from heaven, and the powers of the heavens shall be shaken:

30and then shall appear the sign of the Son of man in heaven: and then shall all the tribes of the earth mourn, and they shall see the Son of man coming on the clouds of heaven with power and great glory.

31And he shall send forth his angels with a great sound of a trumpet, and they shall gather together his elect from the four winds, from one end of heaven to the other.

32Now from the fig tree learn her parable: when her branch is now become tender, and putteth forth its leaves, ye know that the summer is nigh;

33even so ye also, when ye see all these things, know ye that he is nigh, even at the doors.

34Verily I say unto you, This generation shall not pass away, till all these things be accomplished.

35Heaven and earth shall pass away, but my words shall not pass away.

36But of that day and hour knoweth no one, not even the angels of heaven, neither the Son, but the Father only.

37And as were the days of Noah, so shall be the coming of the Son of man.

38For as in those days which were before the flood they were eating and drinking, marrying and giving in marriage, until the day that Noah entered into the ark,

39and they knew not until the flood came, and took them all away; so shall be the coming of the Son of man.

40Then shall two men be in the field; one is taken, and one is left:

41two women shall be grinding at the mill; one is taken, and one is left.

42Watch therefore: for ye know not on what day your Lord cometh.

43But know this, that if the master of the house had known in what watch the thief was coming, he would have watched, and would not have suffered his house to be broken through.

44Therefore be ye also ready; for in an hour that ye think not the Son of man cometh.

45Who then is the faithful and wise servant, whom his lord hath set over his household, to give them their food in due season?

46Blessed is that servant, whom his lord when he cometh shall find so doing.

47Verily I say unto you, that he will set him over all that he hath.

48But if that evil servant shall say in his heart, My lord tarrieth;

49and shall begin to beat his fellow-servants, and shall eat and drink with the drunken;

50the lord of that servant shall come in a day when he expecteth not, and in an hour when he knoweth not,

51and shall cut him asunder, and appoint his portion with the hypocrites: there shall be the weeping and the gnashing of teeth.

Chapter 25

1Then shall the kingdom of heaven be likened unto ten virgins, who took their lamps, and went forth to meet the bridegroom.

2And five of them were foolish, and five were wise.

3For the foolish, when they took their lamps, took no oil with them:

4but the wise took oil in their vessels with their lamps.

5Now while the bridegroom tarried, they all slumbered and slept.

6But at midnight there is a cry, Behold, the bridegroom! Come ye forth to meet him.

7Then all those virgins arose, and trimmed their lamps.

8And the foolish said unto the wise, Give us of your oil; for our lamps are going out.

9But the wise answered, saying, Peradventure there will not be enough for us and you: go ye rather to them that sell, and buy for yourselves.

10And while they went away to buy, the bridegroom came; and they that were ready went in with him to the marriage feast: and the door was shut.

11Afterward came also the other virgins, saying, Lord, Lord, open to us.

12But he answered and said, Verily I say unto you, I know you not.

13Watch therefore, for ye know not the day nor the hour.

14For it is as when a man, going into another country, called his own servants, and delivered unto them his goods.

15And unto one he gave five talents, to another two, to another one; to each according to his several ability; and he went on his journey.

16Straightway he that received the five talents went and traded with them, and made other five talents.

17In like manner he also that received the two gained other two.

18But he that received the one went away and digged in the earth, and hid his lord's money.

19Now after a long time the lord of those servants cometh, and maketh a reckoning with them.

20And he that received the five talents came and brought other five talents, saying, Lord, thou deliveredst unto me five talents: lo, I have gained other five talents.

21His lord said unto him, Well done, good and faithful servant: thou hast been faithful over a few things, I will set thee over many things; enter thou into the joy of thy lord.

22And he also that received the two talents came and said, Lord, thou deliveredst unto me two talents: lo, I have gained other two talents.

23His lord said unto him, Well done, good and faithful servant: thou hast been faithful over a few things, I will set thee over many things; enter thou into the joy of thy lord.

24And he also that had received the one talent came and said, Lord, I knew thee that thou art a hard man, reaping where thou didst not sow, and gathering where thou didst not scatter;

25and I was afraid, and went away and hid thy talent in the earth: lo, thou hast thine own.

26But his lord answered and said unto him, Thou wicked and slothful servant, thou knewest that I reap where I sowed not, and gather where I did not scatter;

27thou oughtest therefore to have put my money to the bankers, and at my coming I should have received back mine own with interest.

28Take ye away therefore the talent from him, and give it unto him that hath the ten talents.

29For unto every one that hath shall be given, and he shall have abundance: but from him that hath not, even that which he hath shall be taken away.

30And cast ye out the unprofitable servant into the outer darkness: there shall be the weeping and the gnashing of teeth.

31But when the Son of man shall come in his glory, and all the angels with him, then shall he sit on the throne of his glory:

32and before him shall be gathered all the nations: and he shall separate them one from another, as the shepherd separateth the sheep from the goats;

33and he shall set the sheep on his right hand, but the goats on the left.

34Then shall the King say unto them on his right hand, Come, ye blessed of my Father, inherit the kingdom prepared for you from the foundation of the world:

35for I was hungry, and ye gave me to eat; I was thirsty, and ye gave me drink; I was a stranger, and ye took me in;

36naked, and ye clothed me; I was sick, and ye visited me; I was in prison, and ye came unto me.

37Then shall the righteous answer him, saying, Lord, when saw we thee hungry, and fed thee? or athirst, and gave thee drink?

38And when saw we thee a stranger, and took thee in? or naked, and clothed thee?

39And when saw we thee sick, or in prison, and came unto thee?

40And the King shall answer and say unto them, Verily I say unto you, Inasmuch as ye did it unto one of these my brethren, even these least, ye did it unto me.

41Then shall he say also unto them on the left hand, Depart from me, ye cursed, into the eternal fire which is prepared for the devil and his angels:

42for I was hungry, and ye did not give me to eat; I was thirsty, and ye gave me no drink;

43I was a stranger, and ye took me not in; naked, and ye clothed me not; sick, and in prison, and ye visited me not.

44Then shall they also answer, saying, Lord, when saw we thee hungry, or athirst, or a stranger, or naked, or sick, or in prison, and did not minister unto thee?

45Then shall he answer them, saying, Verily I say unto you, Inasmuch as ye did it not unto one of these least, ye did it not unto me.

46And these shall go away into eternal punishment: but the righteous into eternal life.

Chapter 26

1And it came to pass, when Jesus had finished all these words, he said unto his disciples,

2Ye know that after two days the passover cometh, and the Son of man is delivered up to be crucified.

3Then were gathered together the chief priests, and the elders of the people, unto the court of the high priest, who was called Caiaphas;

4and they took counsel together that they might take Jesus by subtlety, and kill him.

5But they said, Not during the feast, lest a tumult arise among people.

6Now when Jesus was in Bethany, in the house of Simon the leper,

7there came unto him a woman having an alabaster cruse of exceeding precious ointment, and she poured it upon his head, as he sat at meat.

8But when the disciples saw it, they had indignation, saying, To what purpose is this waste?

9For this ointment might have been sold for much, and given to the poor.

10But Jesus perceiving it said unto them, Why trouble ye the woman? for she hath wrought a good work upon me.

11For ye have the poor always with you; but me ye have not always.

12For in that she poured this ointment upon my body, she did it to prepare me for burial.

13Verily I say unto you, Wheresoever this gospel shall be preached in the whole world, that also which this woman hath done shall be spoken of for a memorial of her.

14Then one of the twelve, who was called Judas Iscariot, went unto the chief priests,

15and said, What are ye willing to give me, and I will deliver him unto you? And they weighed unto him thirty pieces of silver.

16And from that time he sought opportunity to deliver him unto them.

17Now on the first day of unleavened bread the disciples came to Jesus, saying, Where wilt thou that we make ready for thee to eat the passover?

18And he said, Go into the city to such a man, and say unto him, The

Matthew

Teacher saith, My time is at hand; I keep the passover at thy house with my disciples.

¹⁹And the disciples did as Jesus appointed them; and they made ready the passover.

²⁰Now when even was come, he was sitting at meat with the twelve disciples;

²¹and as they were eating, he said, Verily I say unto you, that one of you shall betray me.

²²And they were exceeding sorrowful, and began to say unto him every one, Is it I, Lord?

²³And he answered and said, He that dipped his hand with me in the dish, the same shall betray me.

²⁴The Son of man goeth, even as it is written of him: but woe unto that man through whom the Son of man is betrayed! good were it for that man if he had not been born.

²⁵And Judas, who betrayed him, answered and said, Is it I, Rabbi? He saith unto him, Thou hast said.

²⁶And as they were eating, Jesus took bread, and blessed, and brake it; and he gave to the disciples, and said, Take, eat; this is my body.

²⁷And he took a cup, and gave thanks, and gave to them, saying, Drink ye all of it;

²⁸for this is my blood of the covenant, which is poured out for many unto remission of sins.

²⁹But I say unto you, I shall not drink henceforth of this fruit of the vine, until that day when I drink it new with you in my Father's kingdom.

³⁰And when they had sung a hymn, they went out unto the mount of Olives.

³¹Then saith Jesus unto them, All ye shall be offended in me this night: for it is written, I will smite the shepherd, and the sheep of the flock shall be scattered abroad.

³²But after I am raised up, I will go before you into Galilee.

³³But Peter answered and said unto him, If all shall be offended in thee, I will never be offended.

³⁴Jesus said unto him, Verily I say unto thee, that this night, before the cock crow, thou shalt deny me thrice.

³⁵Peter saith unto him, Even if I must die with thee, yet will I not deny thee. Likewise also said all the disciples.

³⁶Then cometh Jesus with them unto a place called Gethsemane, and saith unto his disciples, Sit ye here, while I go yonder and pray.

³⁷And he took with him Peter and the two sons of Zebedee, and began to be sorrowful and sore troubled.

³⁸Then saith he unto them, My soul is exceeding sorrowful, even unto death: abide ye here, and watch with me.

³⁹And he went forward a little, and fell on his face, and prayed, saying, My Father, if it be possible, let this cup pass away from me: nevertheless, not as I will, but as thou wilt.

⁴⁰And he cometh unto the disciples, and findeth them sleeping, and saith unto Peter, What, could ye not watch with me one hour?

⁴¹Watch and pray, that ye enter not into temptation: the spirit indeed is willing, but the flesh is weak.

⁴²Again a second time he went away, and prayed, saying, My Father, if this cannot pass away, except I drink it, thy will be done.

⁴³And he came again and found them sleeping, for their eyes were heavy.

⁴⁴And he left them again, and went away, and prayed a third time, saying again the same words.

⁴⁵Then cometh he to the disciples, and saith unto them, Sleep on now, and take your rest: behold, the hour is at hand, and the Son of man is betrayed into the hands of sinners.

⁴⁶Arise, let us be going: behold, he is at hand that betrayeth me.

⁴⁷And while he yet spake, lo, Judas, one of the twelve, came, and with him a great multitude with swords and staves, from the chief priest and elders of the people.

⁴⁸Now he that betrayed him gave them a sign, saying, Whomsoever I shall kiss, that is he: take him.

⁴⁹And straightway he came to Jesus, and said, Hail, Rabbi; and kissed him.

⁵⁰And Jesus said unto him, Friend, do that for which thou art come. Then they came and laid hands on Jesus, and took him.

⁵¹And behold, one of them that were with Jesus stretched out his hand, and drew his sword, and smote the servant of the high priest, and struck off his ear.

⁵²Then saith Jesus unto him, Put up again thy sword into its place: for all they that take the sword shall perish with the sword.

⁵³Or thinkest thou that I cannot beseech my Father, and he shall even now send me more than twelve legions of angels?

⁵⁴How then should the scriptures be fulfilled that thus it must be?

⁵⁵In that hour said Jesus to the multitudes, Are ye come out as against a robber with swords and staves to seize me? I sat daily in the temple teaching, and ye took me not.

⁵⁶But all this is come to pass, that the scriptures of the prophets might be fulfilled. Then all the disciples left him, and fled.

⁵⁷And they that had taken Jesus led him away to the house of Caiaphas the high priest, where the scribes and the elders were gathered together.

⁵⁸But Peter followed him afar off, unto the court of the high priest, and entered in, and sat with the officers, to see the end.

⁵⁹Now the chief priests and the whole council sought false witness against Jesus, that they might put him to death;

⁶⁰and they found it not, though many false witnesses came. But afterward came two,

⁶¹and said, This man said, I am able to destroy the temple of God, and to build it in three days.

⁶²And the high priest stood up, and said unto him, Answerest thou nothing? what is it which these witness against thee?

⁶³But Jesus held his peace. And the high priest said unto him, I adjure thee by the living God, that thou tell us whether thou art the Christ, the Son of God.

⁶⁴Jesus said unto him, Thou hast said: nevertheless I say unto you, Henceforth ye shall see the Son of man sitting at the right hand of Power, and coming on the clouds of heaven.

⁶⁵Then the high priest rent his garments, saying, He hath spoken blasphemy: what further need have we of witnesses? behold, now ye have heard the blasphemy:

⁶⁶what think ye? They answered and said, He is worthy of death.

⁶⁷Then did they spit in his face and buffet him: and some smote him with the palms of their hands,

⁶⁸saying, Prophesy unto us, thou Christ: who is he that struck thee?

⁶⁹Now Peter was sitting without in the court: and a maid came unto him, saying, Thou also wast with Jesus the Galilaean.

⁷⁰But he denied before them all, saying, I know not what thou sayest.

⁷¹And when he was gone out into the porch, another maid saw him, and saith unto them that were there, This man also was with Jesus of Nazareth.

⁷²And again he denied with an oath, I know not the man.

⁷³And after a little while they that stood by came and said to Peter, Of a truth thou also art one of them; for thy speech maketh thee known.

⁷⁴Then began he to curse and to swear, I know not the man. And straightway the cock crew.

⁷⁵And Peter remembered the word which Jesus had said, Before the cock crow, thou shalt deny me thrice. And he went out, and wept bitterly.

Chapter 27

¹Now when morning was come, all the chief priests and the elders of the people took counsel against Jesus to put him to death:

²and they bound him, and led him away, and delivered him up to Pilate the governor.

³Then Judas, who betrayed him, when he saw that he was condemned, repented himself, and brought back the thirty pieces of silver to the chief priests and elders,

⁴saying, I have sinned in that I betrayed innocent blood. But they said, What is that to us? see thou to it.

⁵And he cast down the pieces of silver into the sanctuary, and departed; and he went away and hanged himself.

⁶And the chief priests took the pieces of silver, and said, It is not lawful to put them into the treasury, since it is the price of blood.

⁷And they took counsel, and bought with them the potter's field, to bury strangers in.

⁸Wherefore that field was called, the field of blood, unto this day.

⁹Then was fulfilled that which was spoken through Jeremiah the prophet, saying, And they took the thirty pieces of silver, the price of him that was priced, whom certain of the children of Israel did price;

¹⁰and they gave them for the potter's field, as the Lord appointed me.

¹¹Now Jesus stood before the governor: and the governor asked him, saying, Art thou the King of the Jews? And Jesus said unto him, Thou sayest.

¹²And when he was accused by the chief priests and elders, he answered nothing.

¹³Then saith Pilate unto him, Hearest thou not how many things they witness against thee?

¹⁴And he gave him no answer, not even to one word: insomuch that the governor marvelled greatly.

¹⁵Now at the feast the governor was wont to release unto the multitude one prisoner, whom they would.

¹⁶And they had then a notable prisoner, called Barabbas.

¹⁷When therefore they were gathered together, Pilate said unto them, Whom will ye that I release unto you? Barabbas, or Jesus who is called Christ?

¹⁸For he knew that for envy they had delivered him up.

¹⁹And while he was sitting on the judgment-seat, his wife sent unto him, saying, Have thou nothing to do with that righteous man; for I have suffered many things this day in a dream because of him.

²⁰Now the chief priests and the elders persuaded the multitudes that they should ask for Barabbas, and destroy Jesus.

²¹But the governor answered and said unto them, Which of the two will ye that I release unto you? And they said, Barabbas.

²²Pilate saith unto them, What then shall I do unto Jesus who is called Christ? They all say, Let him be crucified.

²³And he said, Why, what evil hath he done? But they cried out exceedingly, saying, Let him be crucified.

²⁴So when Pilate saw that he prevailed nothing, but rather that a tumult was arising, he took water, and washed his hands before the multitude, saying, I am innocent of the blood of this righteous man; see ye to it.

²⁵And all the people answered and said, His blood be on us, and on our children.

²⁶Then released he unto them Barabbas; but Jesus he scourged and delivered to be crucified.

²⁷Then the soldiers of the governor took Jesus into the Praetorium, and gathered unto him the whole band.

²⁸And they stripped him, and put on him a scarlet robe.

²⁹And they platted a crown of thorns and put it upon his head, and a reed in his right hand; and they kneeled down before him, and mocked him, saying, Hail, King of the Jews!

³⁰And they spat upon him, and took the reed and smote him on the head.

³¹And when they had mocked him, they took off from him the robe, and put on him his garments, and led him away to crucify him.

³²And as they came out, they found a man of Cyrene, Simon by name: him

they compelled to go with them, that he might bear his cross.

33And they were come unto a place called Golgotha, that is to say, The place of a skull,

34they gave him wine to drink mingled with gall: and when he had tasted it, he would not drink.

35And when they had crucified him, they parted his garments among them, casting lots;

36and they sat and watched him there.

37And they set up over his head his accusation written, THIS IS JESUS THE KING OF THE JEWS.

38Then are there crucified with him two robbers, one on the right hand and one on the left.

39And they that passed by railed on him, wagging their heads,

40and saying, Thou that destroyest the temple, and buildest it in three days, save thyself: if thou art the Son of God, come down from the cross.

41In like manner also the chief priests mocking him, with the scribes and elders, said,

42He saved others; himself he cannot save. He is the King of Israel; let him now come down from the cross, and we will believe on him.

43He trusteth on God; let him deliver him now, if he desireth him: for he said, I am the Son of God.

44And the robbers also that were crucified with him cast upon him the same reproach.

45Now from the sixth hour there was darkness over all the land until the ninth hour.

46And about the ninth hour Jesus cried with a loud voice, saying, Eli, Eli, lama sabachthani? that is, My God, my God, why hast thou forsaken me?

47And some of them stood there, when they heard it, said, This man calleth Elijah.

48And straightway one of them ran, and took a sponge, and filled it with vinegar, and put it on a reed, and gave him to drink.

49And the rest said, Let be; let us see whether Elijah cometh to save him.

50And Jesus cried again with a loud voice, and yielded up his spirit.

51And behold, the veil of the temple was rent in two from the top to the bottom; and the earth did quake; and the rocks were rent;

52and the tombs were opened; and many bodies of the saints that had fallen asleep were raised;

53and coming forth out of the tombs after his resurrection they entered into the holy city and appeared unto many.

54Now the centurion, and they that were with him watching Jesus, when they saw the earthquake, and the things that were done, feared exceedingly, saying, Truly this was the Son of God.

55And many women were there beholding from afar, who had followed Jesus from Galilee, ministering unto him:

56among whom was Mary Magdalene, and Mary the mother of James and Joses, and the mother of the sons of Zebedee.

57And when even was come, there came a rich man from Arimathaea, named Joseph, who also himself was Jesus' disciple:

58this man went to Pilate, and asked for the body of Jesus. Then Pilate commanded it to be given up.

59And Joseph took the body, and wrapped it in a clean linen cloth,

60and laid it in his own new tomb, which he had hewn out in the rock: and he rolled a great stone to the door of the tomb, and departed.

61And Mary Magdalene was there, and the other Mary, sitting over against the sepulchre.

62Now on the morrow, which is the day after the Preparation, the chief priests and the Pharisees were gathered together unto Pilate,

63saying, Sir, we remember that that deceiver said while he was yet alive, After three days I rise again.

64Command therefore that the sepulchre be made sure until the third day, lest haply his disciples come and steal him away, and say unto the people, He is risen from the dead: and the last error will be worse than the first.

65Pilate said unto them, Ye have a guard: go, make it as sure as ye can.

66So they went, and made the sepulchre sure, sealing the stone, the guard being with them.

Chapter 28

1Now late on the sabbath day, as it began to dawn toward the first day of the week, came Mary Magdalene and the other Mary to see the sepulchre.

2And behold, there was a great earthquake; for an angel of the Lord descended from heaven, and came and rolled away the stone, and sat upon it.

3His appearance was as lightning, and his raiment white as snow:

4and for fear of him the watchers did quake, and became as dead men.

5And the angel answered and said unto the women, Fear not ye; for I know that ye seek Jesus, who hath been crucified.

6He is not here; for he is risen, even as he said. Come, see the place where the Lord lay.

7And go quickly, and tell his disciples, He is risen from the dead; and lo, he goeth before you into Galilee; there shall ye see him: lo, I have told you.

8And they departed quickly from the tomb with fear and great joy, and ran to bring his disciples word.

9And behold, Jesus met them, saying, All hail. And they came and took hold of his feet, and worshipped him.

10Then saith Jesus unto them, Fear not: go tell my brethren that they depart into Galilee, and there shall they see me.

11Now while they were going, behold, some of the guard came into the city, and told unto the chief priests all the things that were come to pass.

12And when they were assembled with the elders, and had taken counsel, they gave much money unto the soldiers,

13saying, Say ye, His disciples came by night, and stole him away while we slept.

14And if this come to the governor's ears, we will persuade him, and rid you of care.

15So they took the money, and did as they were taught: and this saying was spread abroad among the Jews, and continueth until this day.

16But the eleven disciples went into Galilee, unto the mountain where Jesus had appointed them.

17And when they saw him, they worshipped him; but some doubted.

18And Jesus came to them and spake unto them, saying, All authority hath been given unto me in heaven and on earth.

19Go ye therefore, and make disciples of all the nations, baptizing them into the name of the Father and of the Son and of the Holy Spirit:

20teaching them to observe all things whatsoever I commanded you: and lo, I am with you always, even unto the end of the world.

Mark
The Gospel According to St. Mark

Chapter 1

1 The beginning of the gospel of Jesus Christ, the Son of God.

2 Even as it is written in Isaiah the prophet, Behold, I send my messenger before thy face, Who shall prepare thy way.

3 The voice of one crying in the wilderness, Make ye ready the way of the Lord, Make his paths straight;

4 John came, who baptized in the wilderness and preached the baptism of repentance unto remission of sins.

5 And there went out unto him all the country of Judaea, and all they of Jerusalem; And they were baptized of him in the river Jordan, confessing their sins.

6 And John was clothed with camel's hair, and had a leathern girdle about his loins, and did eat locusts and wild honey.

7 And he preached, saying, There cometh after me he that is mightier than I, the latchet of whose shoes I am not worthy to stoop down and unloose.

8 I baptized you in water; But he shall baptize you in the Holy Spirit.

9 And it came to pass in those days, that Jesus came from Nazareth of Galilee, and was baptized of John in the Jordan.

10 And straightway coming up out of the water, he saw the heavens rent asunder, and the Spirit as a dove descending upon him:

11 And a voice came out of the heavens, Thou art my beloved Son, in thee I am well pleased.

12 And straightway the Spirit driveth him forth into the wilderness.

13 And he was in the wilderness forty days tempted of Satan; And he was with the wild beasts; And the angels ministered unto him.

14 Now after John was delivered up, Jesus came into Galilee, preaching the gospel of God,

15 and saying, The time is fulfilled, and the kingdom of God is at hand: repent ye, and believe in the gospel.

16 And passing along by the sea of Galilee, he saw Simon and Andrew the brother of Simon casting a net in the sea; for they were fishers.

17 And Jesus said unto them, Come ye after me, and I will make you to become fishers of men.

18 And straightway they left the nets, and followed him.

19 And going on a little further, he saw James the son of Zebedee, and John his brother, who also were in the boat mending the nets.

20 And straightway he called them: and they left their father Zebedee in the boat with the hired servants, and went after him.

21 And they go into Capernaum; and straightway on the sabbath day he entered into the synagogue and taught.

22 And they were astonished at his teaching: For he taught them as having authority, and not as the scribes.

23 And straightway there was in their synagogue a man with an unclean spirit; and he cried out,

24 saying, What have we to do with thee, Jesus thou Nazarene? art thou come to destroy us? I know thee who thou art, the Holy One of God.

25 And Jesus rebuked him, saying, Hold thy peace, and come out of him.

26 And the unclean spirit, tearing him and crying with a loud voice, came out of him.

27 And they were all amazed, insomuch that they questioned among themselves, saying, What is this? a new teaching! with authority he commandeth even the unclean spirits, and they obey him.

28 And the report of him went out straightway everywhere into all the region of Galilee round about.

29 And straightway, when they were come out of the synagogue, they came into the house of Simon and Andrew, with James and John.

30 Now Simon's wife's mother lay sick of a fever; and straightway they tell him of her:

31 and he came and took her by the hand, and raised her up; and the fever left her, and she ministered unto them.

32 And at even, when the sun did set, they brought unto him all that were sick, and them that were possessed with demons.

33 And all the city was gathered together at the door.

34 And he healed many that were sick with divers diseases, and cast out many demons; and he suffered not the demons to speak, because they knew him.

35 And in the morning, a great while before day, he rose up and went out, and departed into a desert place, and there prayed.

36 And Simon and they that were with him followed after him;

37 and they found him, and say unto him, All are seeking thee.

38 And he saith unto them, Let us go elsewhere into the next towns, that I may preach there also; for to this end came I forth.

39 And he went into their synagogues throughout all Galilee, preaching and casting out demons.

40 And there cometh to him a leper, beseeching him, and kneeling down to him, and saying unto him, If thou wilt, thou canst make me clean.

41 And being moved with compassion, he stretched forth his hand, and touched him, and saith unto him, I will; be thou made clean.

42 And straightway the leprosy departed from him, and he was made clean.

43 And he strictly charged him, and straightway sent him out,

44 and saith unto him, See thou say nothing to any man: but go show thyself to the priest, and offer for thy cleansing the things which Moses commanded, for a testimony unto them.

45 But he went out, and began to publish it much, and to spread abroad the matter, insomuch that Jesus could no more openly enter into a city, but was without in desert places: and they came to him from every quarter.

Chapter 2

1 And when he entered again into Capernaum after some days, it was noised that he was in the house.

2 And many were gathered together, so that there was no longer room for them, no, not even about the door: and he spake the word unto them.

3 And they come, bringing unto him a man sick of the palsy, borne of four.

4 And when they could not come nigh unto him for the crowd, they uncovered the roof where he was: and when they had broken it up, they let down the bed whereon the sick of the palsy lay.

5 And Jesus seeing their faith saith unto the sick of the palsy, Son, thy sins are forgiven.

6 But there were certain of the scribes sitting there, and reasoning in their hearts,

7 Why doth this man thus speak? he blasphemeth: who can forgive sins but one, even God?

8 And straightway Jesus, perceiving in his spirit that they so reasoned within themselves, saith unto them, Why reason ye these things in your hearts?

9 Which is easier, to say to the sick of the palsy, Thy sins are forgiven; or to say, Arise, and take up thy bed, and walk?

10 But that ye may know that the Son of man hath authority on earth to forgive sins (he saith to the sick of the palsy),

11 I say unto thee, Arise, take up thy bed, and go unto thy house.

12 And he arose, and straightway took up the bed, and went forth before them all; insomuch that they were all amazed, and glorified God, saying, We never saw it on this fashion.

13 And he went forth again by the sea side; and all the multitude resorted unto him, and he taught them.

14 And as he passed by, he saw Levi the son of Alphaeus sitting at the place of toll, and he saith unto him, Follow me. And he arose and followed him.

15 And it came to pass, that he was sitting at meat in his house, and many publicans and sinners sat down with Jesus and his disciples: for there were many, and they followed him.

16 And the scribes of the Pharisees, when they saw that he was eating with the sinners and publicans, said unto his disciples, How is it that he eateth and drinketh with publicans and sinners?

17 And when Jesus heard it, he saith unto them, They that are whole have no need of a physician, but they that are sick: I came not to call the righteous, but sinners.

18 And John's disciples and the Pharisees were fasting: and they come and say unto him, Why do John's disciples and the disciples of the Pharisees fast, but thy disciples fast not?

19 And Jesus said unto them, Can the sons of the bridechamber fast, while the bridegroom is with them? as long as they have the bridegroom with them, they cannot fast.

20 But the days will come, when the bridegroom shall be taken away from them, and then will they fast in that day.

21 No man seweth a piece of undressed cloth on an old garment: else that which should fill it up taketh from it, the new from the old, and a worse rent is made.

22 And no man putteth new wine into old wineskins; else the wine will burst the skins, and the wine perisheth, and the skins: but they put new wine into fresh wine-skins.

23 And it came to pass, that he was going on the sabbath day through the grainfields; and his disciples began, as they went, to pluck the ears.

24 And the Pharisees said unto him, Behold, why do they on the sabbath day that which is not lawful?

25 And he said unto them, Did ye never read what David did, when he had need, and was hungry, he, and they that were with him?

26 How he entered into the house of God when Abiathar was high priest, and ate the showbread, which it is not lawful to eat save for the priests, and gave also to them that were with him?

27 And he said unto them, The sabbath was made for man, and not man for the sabbath:

28 so that the Son of man is lord even of the sabbath.

Chapter 3

1 And he entered again into the synagogue; and there was a man there who had his hand withered.

2 And they watched him, whether he would heal him on the sabbath day; that they might accuse him.

3 And he saith unto the man that had his hand withered, Stand forth.

4 And he saith unto them, Is it lawful on the sabbath day to do good, or to do harm? to save a life, or to kill? But they held their peace.

5 And when he had looked round about on them with anger, being grieved at the hardening of their heart, he saith unto the man, Stretch forth thy hand. And he stretched it forth; and his hand was restored.

6 And the Pharisees went out, and straightway with the Herodians took counsel against him, how they might destroy him.

7 And Jesus with his disciples withdrew to the sea: and a great multitude from Galilee followed; and from Judaea,

8 and from Jerusalem, and from Idumaea, and beyond the Jordan, and about Tyre and Sidon, a great multitude, hearing what great things he did, came unto him.

9 And he spake to his disciples, that a little boat should wait on him because of the crowd, lest they should throng him:

10for he had healed many; insomuch that as many as had plagues pressed upon him that they might touch him.

11And the unclean spirits, whensoever they beheld him, fell down before him, and cried, saying, Thou art the Son of God.

12And he charged them much that they should not make him known.

13And he goeth up into the mountain, and calleth unto him whom he himself would; and they went unto him.

14And he appointed twelve, that they might be with him, and that he might send them forth to preach,

15and to have authority to cast out demons:

16and Simon he surnamed Peter;

17and James the son of Zebedee, and John the brother of James; and them he surnamed Boanerges, which is, Sons of thunder:

18and Andrew, and Philip, and Bartholomew, and Matthew, and Thomas, and James the son of Alphaeus, and Thaddaeus, and Simon the Cananaean,

19and Judas Iscariot, who also betrayed him. And he cometh into a house.

20And the multitude cometh together again, so that they could not so much as eat bread.

21And when his friends heard it, they went out to lay hold on him: for they said, He is beside himself.

22And the scribes that came down from Jerusalem said, He hath Beelzebub, and, By the prince of the demons casteth he out the demons.

23And he called them unto him, and said unto them in parables, How can Satan cast out Satan?

24And if a kingdom be divided against itself, that kingdom cannot stand.

25And if a house be divided against itself, that house will not be able to stand.

26And if Satan hath rise up against himself, and is divided, he cannot stand, but hath an end.

27But no one can enter into the house of the strong man, and spoil his goods, except he first bind the strong man; and then he will spoil his house.

28Verily I say unto you, All their sins shall be forgiven unto the sons of men, and their blasphemies wherewith soever they shall blaspheme:

29but whosoever shall blaspheme against the Holy Spirit hath never forgiveness, but is guilty of an eternal sin:

30because they said, He hath an unclean spirit.

31And there come his mother and his brethren; and, standing without, they sent unto him, calling him.

32And a multitude was sitting about him; and they say unto him, Behold, thy mother and thy brethren without seek for thee.

33And he answereth them, and saith, Who is my mother and my brethren?

34And looking round on them that sat round about him, he saith, Behold, my mother and my brethren!

35For whosoever shall do the will of God, the same is my brother, and sister, and mother.

Chapter 4

1And again he began to teach by the sea side. And there is gathered unto him a very great multitude, so that he entered into a boat, and sat in the sea; and all the multitude were by the sea on the land.

2And he taught them many things in parables, and said unto them in his teaching,

3Hearken: Behold, the sower went forth to sow:

4and it came to pass, as he sowed, some seed fell by the way side, and the birds came and devoured it.

5And other fell on the rocky ground, where it had not much earth; and straightway it sprang up, because it had no deepness of earth:

6and when the sun was risen, it was scorched; and because it had no root, it withered away.

7And other fell among the thorns, and the thorns grew up, and choked it, and it yielded no fruit.

8And others fell into the good ground, and yielded fruit, growing up and increasing; and brought forth, thirtyfold, and sixtyfold, and a hundredfold.

9And he said, Who hath ears to hear, let him hear.

10And when he was alone, they that were about him with the twelve asked of him the parables.

11And he said unto them, Unto you is given the mystery of the kingdom of God: but unto them that are without, all things are done in parables:

12that seeing they may see, and not perceive; and hearing they may hear, and not understand; lest haply they should turn again, and it should be forgiven them.

13And he saith unto them, Know ye not this parable? and how shall ye know all the parables?

14The sower soweth the word.

15And these are they by the way side, where the word is sown; and when they have heard, straightway cometh Satan, and taketh away the word which hath been sown in them.

16And these in like manner are they that are sown upon the rocky places, who, when they have heard the word, straightway receive it with joy;

17and they have no root in themselves, but endure for a while; then, when tribulation or persecution ariseth because of the word, straightway they stumble.

18And others are they that are sown among the thorns; these are they that have heard the word,

19and the cares of the world, and the deceitfulness of riches, and the lusts of other things entering in, choke the word, and it becometh unfruitful.

20And those are they that were sown upon the good ground; such as hear the word, and accept it, and bear fruit, thirtyfold, and sixtyfold, and a hundredfold.

21And he said unto them, Is the lamp brought to be put under the bushel, or under the bed, and not to be put on the stand?

22For there is nothing hid, save that it should be manifested; neither was anything made secret, but that it should come to light.

23If any man hath ears to hear, let him hear.

24And he said unto them, Take heed what ye hear: with what measure ye mete it shall be measured unto you; and more shall be given unto you.

25For he that hath, to him shall be given: and he that hath not, from him shall be taken away even that which he hath.

26And he said, So is the kingdom of God, as if a man should cast seed upon the earth;

27and should sleep and rise night and day, and the seed should spring up and grow, he knoweth not how.

28The earth beareth fruit of herself; first the blade, then the ear, then the full grain in the ear.

29But when the fruit is ripe, straightway he putteth forth the sickle, because the harvest is come.

30And he said, How shall we liken the kingdom of God? or in what parable shall we set it forth?

31It is like a grain of mustard seed, which, when it is sown upon the earth, though it be less than all the seeds that are upon the earth,

32yet when it is sown, groweth up, and becometh greater than all the herbs, and putteth out great branches; so that the birds of the heaven can lodge under the shadow thereof.

33And with many such parables spake he the word unto them, as they were able to hear it;

34and without a parable spake he not unto them: but privately to his own disciples he expounded all things.

35And on that day, when even was come, he saith unto them, Let us go over unto the other side.

36And leaving the multitude, they take him with them, even as he was, in the boat. And other boats were with him.

37And there ariseth a great storm of wind, and the waves beat into the boat, insomuch that the boat was now filling.

38And he himself was in the stern, asleep on the cushion: and they awake him, and say unto him, Teacher, carest thou not that we perish?

39And he awoke, and rebuked the wind, and said unto the sea, Peace, be still. And the wind ceased, and there was a great calm.

40And he said unto them, Why are ye fearful? have ye not yet faith?

41And they feared exceedingly, and said one to another, Who then is this, that even the wind and the sea obey him?

Chapter 5

1And they came to the other side of the sea, into the country of the Gerasenes.

2And when he was come out of the boat, straightway there met him out of the tombs a man with an unclean spirit,

3who had his dwelling in the tombs: and no man could any more bind him, no, not with a chain;

4because that he had been often bound with fetters and chains, and the chains had been rent asunder by him, and the fetters broken in pieces: and no man had strength to tame him.

5And always, night and day, in the tombs and in the mountains, he was crying out, and cutting himself with stones.

6And when he saw Jesus from afar, he ran and worshipped him;

7and crying out with a loud voice, he saith, What have I to do with thee, Jesus, thou Son of the Most High God? I adjure thee by God, torment me not.

8For he said unto him, Come forth, thou unclean spirit, out of the man.

9And he asked him, What is thy name? And he saith unto him, My name is Legion; for we are many.

10And he besought him much that he would not send them away out of the country.

11Now there was there on the mountain side a great herd of swine feeding.

12And they besought him, saying, Send us into the swine, that we may enter into them.

13And he gave them leave. And the unclean spirits came out, and entered into the swine: and the herd rushed down the steep into the sea, in number about two thousand; and they were drowned in the sea.

14And they that fed them fled, and told it in the city, and in the country. And they came to see what it was that had come to pass.

15And they come to Jesus, and behold him that was possessed with demons sitting, clothed and in his right mind, even him that had the legion: and they were afraid.

16And they that saw it declared unto them how it befell him that was possessed with demons, and concerning the swine.

17And they began to beseech him to depart from their borders.

18And as he was entering into the boat, he that had been possessed with demons besought him that he might be with him.

19And he suffered him not, but saith unto him, Go to thy house unto thy friends, and tell them how great things the Lord hath done for thee, and how he had mercy on thee.

20And he went his way, and began to publish in Decapolis how great things Jesus had done for him: and all men marvelled.

21And when Jesus had crossed over again in the boat unto the other side, a great multitude was gathered unto him; and he was by the sea.

22And there cometh one of the rulers of the synagogue, Jairus by name; and seeing him, he falleth at his feet,

23and beseecheth him much, saying, My little daughter is at the point of death: I pray thee, that thou come and lay thy hands on her, that she may be made whole, and live.

24And he went with him; and a great multitude followed him, and they

Mark

thronged him.

25And a woman, who had an issue of blood twelve years,

26and had suffered many things of many physicians, and had spent all that she had, and was nothing bettered, but rather grew worse,

27having heard the things concerning Jesus, came in the crowd behind, and touched his garment.

28For she said, If I touch but his garments, I shall be made whole.

29And straightway the fountain of her blood was dried up; and she felt in her body that she was healed of her plague.

30And straightway Jesus, perceiving in himself that the power proceeding from him had gone forth, turned him about in the crowd, and said, Who touched my garments?

31And his disciples said unto him, Thou seest the multitude thronging thee, and sayest thou, Who touched me?

32And he looked round about to see her that had done this thing.

33But the woman fearing and trembling, knowing what had been done to her, came and fell down before him, and told him all the truth.

34And he said unto her, Daughter, thy faith hath made thee whole; go in peace, and be whole of thy plague.

35While he yet spake, they come from the ruler of the synagogue's house saying, Thy daughter is dead: why troublest thou the Teacher any further?

36But Jesus, not heeding the word spoken, saith unto the ruler of the synagogue, Fear not, only believe.

37And he suffered no man to follow with him, save Peter, and James, and John the brother of James.

38And they come to the house of the ruler of the synagogue; and he beholdeth a tumult, and many weeping and wailing greatly.

39And when he was entered in, he saith unto them, Why make ye a tumult, and weep? the child is not dead, but sleepeth.

40And they laughed him to scorn. But he, having put them all forth, taketh the father of the child and her mother and them that were with him, and goeth in where the child was.

41And taking the child by the hand, he saith unto her, Talitha cumi; which is, being interpreted, Damsel, I say unto thee, Arise.

42And straightway the damsel rose up, and walked; for she was twelve years old. And they were amazed straightway with a great amazement.

43And he charged them much that no man should know this: and he commanded that something should be given her to eat.

Chapter 6

1And he went out from thence; and he cometh into his own country; and his disciples follow him.

2And when the sabbath was come, he began to teach in the synagogue: and many hearing him were astonished, saying, Whence hath this man these things? and, What is the wisdom that is given unto this man, and what mean such mighty works wrought by his hands?

3Is not this the carpenter, the son of Mary, and brother of James, and Joses, and Judas, and Simon? and are not his sisters here with us? And they were offended in him.

4And Jesus said unto them, A prophet is not without honor, save in his own country, and among his own kin, and in his own house.

5And he could there do no mighty work, save that he laid his hands upon a few sick folk, and healed them.

6And he marvelled because of their unbelief. And he went round about the villages teaching.

7And he calleth unto him the twelve, and began to send them forth by two and two; and he gave them authority over the unclean spirits;

8and he charged them that they should take nothing for their journey, save a staff only; no bread, no wallet, no money in their purse;

9but to go shod with sandals: and, said he, put not on two coats.

10And he said unto them, Wheresoever ye enter into a house, there abide till ye depart thence.

11And whatsoever place shall not receive you, and they hear you not, as ye go forth thence, shake off the dust that is under your feet for a testimony unto them.

12And they went out, and preached that men should repent.

13And they cast out many demons, and anointed with oil many that were sick, and healed them.

14And king Herod heard thereof; for his name had become known: and he said, John the Baptizer is risen from the dead, and therefore do these powers work in him.

15But others said, It is Elijah. And others said, It is a prophet, even as one of the prophets.

16But Herod, when he heard thereof, said, John, whom I beheaded, he is risen.

17For Herod himself had sent forth and laid hold upon John, and bound him in prison for the sake of Herodias, his brother Philip's wife; for he had married her.

18For John said unto Herod, It is not lawful for thee to have thy brother's wife.

19And Herodias set herself against him, and desired to kill him; and she could not;

20for Herod feared John, knowing that he was a righteous and holy man, and kept him safe. And when he heard him, he was much perplexed; and he heard him gladly.

21And when a convenient day was come, that Herod on his birthday made a supper to his lords, and the high captains, and the chief men of Galilee;

22and when the daughter of Herodias herself came in and danced, she pleased Herod and them that sat at meat with him; and the king said unto the damsel, Ask of me whatsoever thou wilt, and I will give it thee.

23And he sware unto her, Whatsoever thou shalt ask of me, I will give it thee, unto the half of my kingdom.

24And she went out, and said unto her mother, What shall I ask? And she said, The head of John the Baptizer.

25And she came in straightway with haste unto the king, and asked, saying, I will that thou forthwith give me on a platter the head of John the Baptist.

26And the king was exceeding sorry; but for the sake of his oaths, and of them that sat at meat, he would not reject her.

27And straightway the king sent forth a soldier of his guard, and commanded to bring his head: and he went and beheaded him in the prison,

28and brought his head on a platter, and gave it to the damsel; and the damsel gave it to her mother.

29And when his disciples heard thereof, they came and took up his corpse, and laid it in a tomb.

30And the apostles gather themselves together unto Jesus; and they told him all things, whatsoever they had done, and whatsoever they had taught.

31And he saith unto them, Come ye yourselves apart into a desert place, and rest a while. For there were many coming and going, and they had no leisure so much as to eat.

32And they went away in the boat to a desert place apart.

33And the people saw them going, and many knew them, and they ran together there on foot from all the cities, and outwent them.

34And he came forth and saw a great multitude, and he had compassion on them, because they were as sheep not having a shepherd: and he began to teach them many things.

35And when the day was now far spent, his disciples came unto him, and said, The place is desert, and the day is now far spent;

36send them away, that they may go into the country and villages round about, and buy themselves somewhat to eat.

37But he answered and said unto them, Give ye them to eat. And they say unto him, Shall we go and buy two hundred shillings' worth of bread, and give them to eat?

38And he saith unto them, How many loaves have ye? go and see. And when they knew, they say, Five, and two fishes.

39And he commanded them that all should sit down by companies upon the green grass.

40And they sat down in ranks, by hundreds, and by fifties.

41And he took the five loaves and the two fishes, and looking up to heaven, he blessed, and brake the loaves; and he gave to the disciples to set before them; and the two fishes divided he among them all.

42And they all ate, and were filled.

43And they took up broken pieces, twelve basketfuls, and also of the fishes.

44And they that ate the loaves were five thousand men.

45And straightway he constrained his disciples to enter into the boat, and to go before him unto the other side to Bethsaida, while he himself sendeth the multitude away.

46And after he had taken leave of them, he departed into the mountain to pray.

47And when even was come, the boat was in the midst of the sea, and he alone on the land.

48And seeing them distressed in rowing, for the wind was contrary unto them, about the fourth watch of the night he cometh unto them, walking on the sea; and he would have passed by them:

49but they, when they saw him walking on the sea, supposed that it was a ghost, and cried out;

50for they all saw him, and were troubled. But he straightway spake with them, and saith unto them, Be of good cheer: it is I; be not afraid.

51And he went up unto them into the boat; and the wind ceased: and they were sore amazed in themselves;

52for they understood not concerning the loaves, but their heart was hardened.

53And when they had crossed over, they came to the land unto Gennesaret, and moored to the shore.

54And when they were come out of the boat, straightway the people knew him,

55and ran round about that whole region, and began to carry about on their beds those that were sick, where they heard he was.

56And wheresoever he entered, into villages, or into cities, or into the country, they laid the sick in the marketplaces, and besought him that they might touch if it were but the border of his garment: and as many as touched him were made whole.

Chapter 7

1And there are gathered together unto him the Pharisees, and certain of the scribes, who had come from Jerusalem,

2and had seen that some of his disciples ate their bread with defiled, that is, unwashen, hands.

3(For the Pharisees, and all the Jews, except they wash their hands diligently, eat not, holding the tradition of the elders;

4and when they come from the market-place, except they bathe themselves, they eat not; and many other things there are, which they have received to hold, washings of cups, and pots, and brasen vessels.)

5And the Pharisees and the scribes ask him, Why walk not thy disciples according to the tradition of the elders, but eat their bread with defiled hands?

6And he said unto them, Well did Isaiah prophesy of you hypocrites, as it is written,

This people honoreth me with their lips,

But their heart is far from me.

7But in vain do they worship me,

Teaching as their doctrines the precepts of men.

⁸Ye leave the commandment of God, and hold fast the tradition of men.

⁹And he said unto them, Full well do ye reject the commandment of God, that ye may keep your tradition.

¹⁰For Moses said, Honor thy father and thy mother; and, He that speaketh evil of father or mother, let him die the death:

¹¹but ye say, If a man shall say to his father or his mother, That wherewith thou mightest have been profited by me is Corban, that is to say, Given to God;

¹²ye no longer suffer him to do aught for his father or his mother;

¹³making void the word of God by your tradition, which ye have delivered: and many such like things ye do.

¹⁴And he called to him the multitude again, and said unto them, Hear me all of you, and understand:

¹⁵there is nothing from without the man, that going into him can defile him; but the things which proceed out of the man are those that defile the man.

¹⁶If any man hath ears to hear, let him hear.

¹⁷And when he was entered into the house from the multitude, his disciples asked of him the parable.

¹⁸And he saith unto them, Are ye so without understanding also? Perceive ye not, that whatsoever from without goeth into the man, it cannot defile him;

¹⁹because it goeth not into his heart, but into his belly, and goeth out into the draught? This he said, making all meats clean.

²⁰And he said, That which proceedeth out of the man, that defileth the man.

²¹For from within, out of the heart of men, evil thoughts proceed, fornications, thefts, murders, adulteries,

²²covetings, wickednesses, deceit, lasciviousness, an evil eye, railing, pride, foolishness:

²³all these evil things proceed from within, and defile the man.

²⁴And from thence he arose, and went away into the borders of Tyre and Sidon. And he entered into a house, and would have no man know it; and he could not be hid.

²⁵But straightway a woman, whose little daughter had an unclean spirit, having heard of him, came and fell down at his feet.

²⁶Now the woman was a Greek, a Syrophoenician by race. And she besought him that he would cast forth the demon out of her daughter.

²⁷And he said unto her, Let the children first be filled: for it is not meet to take the children's bread and cast it to the dogs.

²⁸But she answered and saith unto him, Yea, Lord; even the dogs under the table eat of the children's crumbs.

²⁹And he said unto her, For this saying go thy way; the demon is gone out of thy daughter.

³⁰And she went away unto her house, and found the child laid upon the bed, and the demon gone out.

³¹And again he went out from the borders of Tyre, and came through Sidon unto the sea of Galilee, through the midst of the borders of Decapolis.

³²And they bring unto him one that was deaf, and had an impediment in his speech; and they beseech him to lay his hand upon him.

³³And he took him aside from the multitude privately, and put his fingers into his ears, and he spat, and touched his tongue;

³⁴and looking up to heaven, he sighed, and saith unto him, Ephphatha, that is, Be opened.

³⁵And his ears were opened, and the bond of his tongue was loosed, and he spake plain.

³⁶And he charged them that they should tell no man: but the more he charged them, so much the more a great deal they published it.

³⁷And they were beyond measure astonished, saying, He hath done all things well; he maketh even the deaf to hear, and the dumb to speak.

Chapter 8

¹In those days, when there was again a great multitude, and they had nothing to eat, he called unto him his disciples, and saith unto them,

²I have compassion on the multitude, because they continue with me now three days, and have nothing to eat:

³and if I send them away fasting to their home, they will faint on the way; and some of them are come from far.

⁴And his disciples answered him, Whence shall one be able to fill these men with bread here in a desert place?

⁵And he asked them, How many loaves have ye? And they said, Seven.

⁶And he commandeth the multitude to sit down on the ground: and he took the seven loaves, and having given thanks, he brake, and gave to his disciples, to set before them; and they set them before the multitude.

⁷And they had a few small fishes: and having blessed them, he commanded to set these also before them.

⁸And they ate, and were filled: and they took up, of broken pieces that remained over, seven baskets.

⁹And they were about four thousand: and he sent them away.

¹⁰And straightway he entered into the boat with his disciples, and came into the parts of Dalmanutha.

¹¹And the Pharisees came forth, and began to question with him, seeking of him a sign from heaven, trying him.

¹²And he sighed deeply in his spirit, and saith, Why doth this generation seek a sign? verily I say unto you, There shall no sign be given unto this generation.

¹³And he left them, and again entering into the boat departed to the other side.

¹⁴And they forgot to take bread; and they had not in the boat with them more than one loaf.

¹⁵And he charged them, saying, Take heed, beware of the leaven of the Pharisees and the leaven of Herod.

¹⁶And they reasoned one with another, saying, We have no bread.

¹⁷And Jesus perceiving it saith unto them, Why reason ye, because ye have no bread? do ye not yet perceive, neither understand? have ye your heart hardened?

¹⁸Having eyes, see ye not? and having ears, hear ye not? and do ye not remember?

¹⁹When I brake the five loaves among the five thousand, how many baskets full of broken pieces took ye up? They say unto him, Twelve.

²⁰And when the seven among the four thousand, how many basketfuls of broken pieces took ye up? And they say unto him, Seven.

²¹And he said unto them, Do ye not yet understand?

²²And they come unto Bethsaida. And they bring to him a blind man, and beseech him to touch him.

²³And he took hold of the blind man by the hand, and brought him out of the village; and when he had spit on his eyes, and laid his hands upon him, he asked him, Seest thou aught?

²⁴And he looked up, and said, I see men; for I behold them as trees, walking.

²⁵Then again he laid his hands upon his eyes; and he looked stedfastly, and was restored, and saw all things clearly.

²⁶And he sent him away to his home, saying, Do not even enter into the village.

²⁷And Jesus went forth, and his disciples, into the villages of Caesarea Philippi: and on the way he asked his disciples, saying unto them, Who do men say that I am?

²⁸And they told him, saying, John the Baptist; and others, Elijah; but others, One of the prophets.

²⁹And he asked them, But who say ye that I am? Peter answereth and saith unto him, Thou art the Christ.

³⁰And he charged them that they should tell no man of him.

³¹And he began to teach them, that the Son of man must suffer many things, and be rejected by the elders, and the chief priests, and the scribes, and be killed, and after three days rise again.

³²And he spake the saying openly. And Peter took him, and began to rebuke him.

³³But he turning about, and seeing his disciples, rebuked Peter, and saith, Get thee behind me, Satan; for thou mindest not the things of God, but the things of men.

³⁴And he called unto him the multitude with his disciples, and said unto them, If any man would come after me, let him deny himself, and take up his cross, and follow me.

³⁵For whosoever would save his life shall lose it; and whosoever shall lose his life for my sake and the gospel's shall save it.

³⁶For what doth it profit a man, to gain the whole world, and forfeit his life?

³⁷For what should a man give in exchange for his life?

³⁸For whosoever shall be ashamed of me and of my words in this adulterous and sinful generation, the Son of man also shall be ashamed of him, when he cometh in the glory of his Father with the holy angels.

Chapter 9

¹And he said unto them, Verily I say unto you, There are some here of them that stand by, who shall in no wise taste of death, till they see the kingdom of God come with power.

²And after six days Jesus taketh with him Peter, and James, and John, and bringeth them up into a high mountain apart by themselves: and he was transfigured before them;

³and his garments became glistering, exceeding white, so as no fuller on earth can whiten them.

⁴And there appeared unto them Elijah with Moses: and they were talking with Jesus.

⁵And Peter answereth and saith to Jesus, Rabbi, it is good for us to be here: and let us make three tabernacles; one for thee, and one for Moses, and one for Elijah.

⁶For he knew not what to answer; for they became sore afraid.

⁷And there came a cloud overshadowing them: and there came a voice out of the cloud, This is my beloved Son: hear ye him.

⁸And suddenly looking round about, they saw no one any more, save Jesus only with themselves.

⁹And as they were coming down from the mountain, he charged them that they should tell no man what things they had seen, save when the Son of man should have risen again from the dead.

¹⁰And they kept the saying, questioning among themselves what the rising again from the dead should mean.

¹¹And they asked him, saying, How is it that the scribes say that Elijah must first come?

¹²And he said unto them, Elijah indeed cometh first, and restoreth all things; and how is it written of the Son of man, that he should suffer many things and be set at nought?

¹³But I say unto you, that Elijah is come, and they have also done unto him whatsoever they would, even as it is written of him.

¹⁴And when they came to the disciples, they saw a great multitude about them, and scribes questioning with them.

¹⁵And straightway all the multitude, when they saw him, were greatly amazed, and running to him saluted him.

¹⁶And he asked them, What question ye with them?

¹⁷And one of the multitude answered him, Teacher, I brought unto thee my son, who hath a dumb spirit;

¹⁸and wheresoever it taketh him, it dasheth him down: and he foameth, and grindeth his teeth, and pineth away: and I spake to thy disciples that they should

Mark

cast it out; and they were not able.

19And he answereth them and saith, O faithless generation, how long shall I be with you? how long shall I bear with you? bring him unto me.

20And they brought him unto him: and when he saw him, straightway the spirit tare him grievously; and he fell on the ground, and wallowed foaming.

21And he asked his father, How long time is it since this hath come unto him? And he said, From a child.

22And oft-times it hath cast him both into the fire and into the waters, to destroy him: but if thou canst do anything, have compassion on us, and help us.

23And Jesus said unto him, If thou canst! All things are possible to him that believeth.

24Straightway the father of the child cried out, and said, I believe; help thou mine unbelief.

25And when Jesus saw that a multitude came running together, he rebuked the unclean spirit, saying unto him, Thou dumb and deaf spirit, I command thee, come out of him, and enter no more into him.

26And having cried out, and torn him much, he came out: and the boy became as one dead; insomuch that the more part said, He is dead.

27But Jesus took him by the hand, and raised him up; and he arose.

28And when he was come into the house, his disciples asked him privately, How is it that we could not cast it out?

29And he said unto them, This kind can come out by nothing, save by prayer.

30And they went forth from thence, and passed through Galilee; and he would not that any man should know it.

31For he taught his disciples, and said unto them, The Son of man is delivered up into the hands of men, and they shall kill him; and when he is killed, after three days he shall rise again.

32But they understood not the saying, and were afraid to ask him.

33And they came to Capernaum: and when he was in the house he asked them, What were ye reasoning on the way?

34But they held their peace: for they had disputed one with another on the way, who was the greatest.

35And he sat down, and called the twelve; and he saith unto them, If any man would be first, he shall be last of all, and servant of all.

36And he took a little child, and set him in the midst of them: and taking him in his arms, he said unto them,

37Whosoever shall receive one of such little children in my name, receiveth me: and whosoever receiveth me, receiveth not me, but him that sent me.

38John said unto him, Teacher, we saw one casting out demons in thy name; and we forbade him, because he followed not us.

39But Jesus said, Forbid him not: for there is no man who shall do a mighty work in my name, and be able quickly to speak evil of me.

40For he that is not against us is for us.

41For whosoever shall give you a cup of water to drink, because ye are Christ's, verily I say unto you, he shall in no wise lose his reward.

42And whosoever shall cause one of these little ones that believe on me to stumble, it were better for him if a great millstone were hanged about his neck, and he were cast into the sea.

43And if thy hand cause thee to stumble, cut it off: it is good for thee to enter into life maimed, rather than having thy two hands to go into hell, into the unquenchable fire.

44where their worm dieth not, and the fire is not quenched.

45And if thy foot cause thee to stumble, cut it off: it is good for thee to enter into life halt, rather than having thy two feet to be cast into hell.

46where their worm dieth not, and the fire is not quenched.

47And if thine eye cause thee to stumble, cast it out: it is good for thee to enter into the kingdom of God with one eye, rather than having two eyes to be cast into hell;

48where their worm dieth not, and the fire is not quenched.

49For every one shall be salted with fire.

50Salt is good: but if the salt have lost its saltness, wherewith will ye season it? Have salt in yourselves, and be at peace one with another.

Chapter 10

1And he arose from thence and cometh into the borders of Judaea and beyond the Jordan: and multitudes come together unto him again; and, as he was wont, he taught them again.

2And there came unto him Pharisees, and asked him, Is it lawful for a man to put away his wife? trying him.

3And he answered and said unto them, What did Moses command you?

4And they said, Moses suffered to write a bill of divorcement, and to put her away.

5But Jesus said unto them, For your hardness of heart he wrote you this commandment.

6But from the beginning of the creation, Male and female made he them.

7For this cause shall a man leave his father and mother, and shall cleave to his wife;

8and the two shall become one flesh: so that they are no more two, but one flesh.

9What therefore God hath joined together, let not man put asunder.

10And in the house the disciples asked him again of this matter.

11And he saith unto them, Whosoever shall put away his wife, and marry another, committeth adultery against her:

12and if she herself shall put away her husband, and marry another, she committeth adultery.

13And they were bringing unto him little children, that he should touch them: and the disciples rebuked them.

14But when Jesus saw it, he was moved with indignation, and said unto them, Suffer the little children to come unto me; forbid them not: for to such belongeth the kingdom of God.

15Verily I say unto you, Whosoever shall not receive the kingdom of God as a little child, he shall in no wise enter therein.

16And he took them in his arms, and blessed them, laying his hands upon them.

17And as he was going forth into the way, there ran one to him, and kneeled to him, and asked him, Good Teacher, what shall I do that I may inherit eternal life?

18And Jesus said unto him, Why callest thou me good? none is good save one, even God.

19Thou knowest the commandments, Do not kill, Do not commit adultery, Do not steal, Do not bear false witness, Do not defraud, Honor thy father and mother.

20And he said unto him, Teacher, all these things have I observed from my youth.

21And Jesus looking upon him loved him, and said unto him, One thing thou lackest: go, sell whatsoever thou hast, and give to the poor, and thou shalt have treasure in heaven: and come, follow me.

22But his countenance fell at the saying, and he went away sorrowful: for he was one that had great possessions.

23And Jesus looked round about, and saith unto his disciples, How hardly shall they that have riches enter into the kingdom of God!

24And the disciples were amazed at his words. But Jesus answereth again, and saith unto them, Children, how hard is it for them that trust in riches to enter into the kingdom of God!

25It is easier for a camel to go through a needle's eye, than for a rich man to enter into the kingdom of God.

26And they were astonished exceedingly, saying unto him, Then who can be saved?

27Jesus looking upon them saith, With men it is impossible, but not with God: for all things are possible with God.

28Peter began to say unto him, Lo, we have left all, and have followed thee.

29Jesus said, Verily I say unto you, There is no man that hath left house, or brethren, or sisters, or mother, or father, or children, or lands, for my sake, and for the gospel's sake,

30but he shall receive a hundredfold now in this time, houses, and brethren, and sisters, and mothers, and children, and lands, with persecutions; and in the world to come eternal life.

31But many that are first shall be last; and the last first.

32And they were on the way, going up to Jerusalem; and Jesus was going before them: and they were amazed; and they that followed were afraid. And he took again the twelve, and began to tell them the things that were to happen unto him,

33saying, Behold, we go up to Jerusalem; and the Son of man shall be delivered unto the chief priests and the scribes; and they shall condemn him to death, and shall deliver him unto the Gentiles:

34and they shall mock him, and shall spit upon him, and shall scourge him, and shall kill him; and after three days he shall rise again.

35And there come near unto him James and John, the sons of Zebedee, saying unto him, Teacher, we would that thou shouldest do for us whatsoever we shall ask of thee.

36And he said unto them, What would ye that I should do for you?

37And they said unto him, Grant unto us that we may sit, one on thy right hand, and one on thy left hand, in thy glory.

38But Jesus said unto them, Ye know not what ye ask. Are ye able to drink the cup that I drink? or to be baptized with the baptism that I am baptized with?

39And they said unto him, We are able. And Jesus said unto them, The cup that I drink ye shall drink; and with the baptism that I am baptized withal shall ye be baptized:

40but to sit on my right hand or on my left hand is not mine to give; but it is for them for whom it hath been prepared.

41And when the ten heard it, they began to be moved with indignation concerning James and John.

42And Jesus called them to him, and saith unto them, Ye know that they who are accounted to rule over the Gentiles lord it over them; and their great ones exercise authority over them.

43But it is not so among you: but whosoever would become great among you, shall be your minister;

44and whosoever would be first among you, shall be servant of all.

45For the Son of man also came not to be ministered unto, but to minister, and to give his life a ransom for many.

46And they come to Jericho: and as he went out from Jericho, with his disciples and a great multitude, the son of Timaeus, Bartimaeus, a blind beggar, was sitting by the way side.

47And when he heard that it was Jesus the Nazarene, he began to cry out, and say, Jesus, thou son of David, have mercy on me.

48And many rebuked him, that he should hold his peace: but he cried out the more a great deal, Thou son of David, have mercy on me.

49And Jesus stood still, and said, Call ye him. And they call the blind man, saying unto him, Be of good cheer: rise, he calleth thee.

50And he, casting away his garment, sprang up, and came to Jesus.

51And Jesus answered him, and said, What wilt thou that I should do unto thee? And the blind man said unto him, Rabboni, that I may receive my sight.

52And Jesus said unto him, Go thy way; thy faith hath made thee whole. And straightway he received his sight, and followed him in the way.

Chapter 11

1And when they draw nigh unto Jerusalem, unto Bethphage and Bethany, at the mount of Olives, he sendeth two of his disciples,

2and saith unto them, Go your way into the village that is over against you: and straightway as ye enter into it, ye shall find a colt tied, whereon no man ever yet sat; loose him, and bring him.

3And if any one say unto you, Why do ye this? say ye, The Lord hath need of him; and straightway he will send him back hither.

4And they went away, and found a colt tied at the door without in the open street; and they loose him.

5And certain of them that stood there said unto them, What do ye, loosing the colt?

6And they said unto them even as Jesus had said: and they let them go.

7And they bring the colt unto Jesus, and cast on him their garments; and he sat upon him.

8And many spread their garments upon the way; and others branches, which they had cut from the fields.

9And they that went before, and they that followed, cried, Hosanna; Blessed is he that cometh in the name of the Lord:

10Blessed is the kingdom that cometh, the kingdom of our father David: Hosanna in the highest.

11And he entered into Jerusalem, into the temple; and when he had looked round about upon all things, it being now eventide, he went out unto Bethany with the twelve.

12And on the morrow, when they were come out from Bethany, he hungered.

13And seeing a fig tree afar off having leaves, he came, if haply he might find anything thereon: and when he came to it, he found nothing but leaves; for it was not the season of figs.

14And he answered and said unto it, No man eat fruit from thee henceforward for ever. And his disciples heard it.

15And they come to Jerusalem: and he entered into the temple, and began to cast out them that sold and them that bought in the temple, and overthrew the tables of the money-changers, and the seats of them that sold the doves;

16and he would not suffer that any man should carry a vessel through the temple.

17And he taught, and said unto them, Is it not written, My house shall be called a house of prayer for all the nations? but ye have made it a den of robbers.

18And the chief priests and the scribes heard it, and sought how they might destroy him: for they feared him, for all the multitude was astonished at his teaching.

19And every evening he went forth out of the city.

20And as they passed by in the morning, they saw the fig tree withered away from the roots.

21And Peter calling to remembrance saith unto him, Rabbi, behold, the fig tree which thou cursedst is withered away.

22And Jesus answering saith unto them, Have faith in God.

23Verily I say unto you, Whosoever shall say unto this mountain, Be thou taken up and cast into the sea; and shall not doubt in his heart, but shall believe that what he saith cometh to pass; he shall have it.

24Therefore I say unto you, All things whatsoever ye pray and ask for, believe that ye receive them, and ye shall have them.

25And whensoever ye stand praying, forgive, if ye have aught against any one; that your Father also who is in heaven may forgive you your trespasses.

26But if ye do not forgive, neither will your Father who is in heaven forgive your trespasses.

27And they come again to Jerusalem: and as he was walking in the temple, there come to him the chief priests, and the scribes, and the elders;

28and they said unto him, By what authority doest thou these things? or who gave thee this authority to do these things?

29And Jesus said unto them, I will ask of you one question, and answer me, and I will tell you by what authority I do these things.

30The baptism of John, was it from heaven, or from men? answer me.

31And they reasoned with themselves, saying, If we shall say, From heaven; He will say, Why then did ye not believe him?

32But should we say, From men--they feared the people: for all verily held John to be a prophet.

33And they answered Jesus and say, We know not. And Jesus saith unto them, Neither tell I you by what authority I do these things.

Chapter 12

1And he began to speak unto them in parables. A man planted a vineyard, and set a hedge about it, and digged a pit for the winepress, and built a tower, and let it out to husbandmen, and went into another country.

2And at the season he sent to the husbandmen a servant, that he might receive from the husbandmen of the fruits of the vineyard.

3And they took him, and beat him, and sent him away empty.

4And again he sent unto them another servant; and him they wounded in the head, and handled shamefully.

5And he sent another; and him they killed: and many others; beating some, and killing some.

6He had yet one, a beloved son: he sent him last unto them, saying, They will reverence my son.

7But those husbandmen said among themselves, This is the heir; come, let us kill him, and the inheritance shall be ours.

8And they took him, and killed him, and cast him forth out of the vineyard.

9What therefore will the lord of the vineyard do? he will come and destroy the husbandmen, and will give the vineyard unto others.

10Have ye not read even this scripture:
The stone which the builders rejected,
The same was made the head of the corner;

11This was from the Lord,
And it is marvellous in our eyes?

12And they sought to lay hold on him; and they feared the multitude; for they perceived that he spake the parable against them: and they left him, and went away.

13And they send unto him certain of the Pharisees and of the Herodians, that they might catch him in talk.

14And when they were come, they say unto him, Teacher, we know that thou art true, and carest not for any one; for thou regardest not the person of men, but of a truth teachest the way of God: Is it lawful to give tribute unto Caesar, or not?

15Shall we give, or shall we not give? But he, knowing their hypocrisy, said unto them, Why make ye trial of me? bring me a denarius, that I may see it.

16And they brought it. And he saith unto them, Whose is this image and superscription? And they said unto him, Caesar's.

17And Jesus said unto them, Render unto Caesar the things that are Caesar's, and unto God the things that are God's. And they marvelled greatly at him.

18And there come unto him Sadducees, who say that there is no resurrection; and they asked him, saying,

19Teacher, Moses wrote unto us, If a man's brother die, and leave a wife behind him, and leave no child, that his brother should take his wife, and raise up seed unto his brother.

20There were seven brethren: and the first took a wife, and dying left no seed;

21and the second took her, and died, leaving no seed behind him; and the third likewise;

22and the seven left no seed. Last of all the woman also died.

23In the resurrection whose wife shall she be of them? for the seven had her to wife.

24Jesus said unto them, Is it not for this cause that ye err, that ye know not the scriptures, nor the power of God?

25For when they shall rise from the dead, they neither marry, nor are given in marriage; but are as angels in heaven.

26But as touching the dead, that they are raised; have ye not read in the book of Moses, in the place concerning the Bush, how God spake unto him, saying, I am the God of Abraham, and the God of Isaac, and the God of Jacob?

27He is not the God of the dead, but of the living: ye do greatly err.

28And one of the scribes came, and heard them questioning together, and knowing that he had answered them well, asked him, What commandment is the first of all?

29Jesus answered, The first is, Hear, O Israel; The Lord our God, the Lord is one:

30and thou shalt love the Lord thy God with all thy heart, and with all thy soul, and with all thy mind, and with all thy strength.

31The second is this, Thou shalt love thy neighbor as thyself. There is none other commandment greater than these.

32And the scribe said unto him, Of a truth, Teacher, thou hast well said that he is one; and there is none other but he:

33and to love him with all the heart, and with all the understanding, and with all the strength, and to love his neighbor as himself, is much more than all whole burnt-offerings and sacrifices.

34And when Jesus saw that he answered discreetly, he said unto him, Thou art not far from the kingdom of God. And no man after that durst ask him any question.

35And Jesus answered and said, as he taught in the temple, How say the scribes that the Christ is the son of David?

36David himself said in the Holy Spirit,
The Lord said unto my Lord,
Sit thou on my right hand,
Till I make thine enemies the footstool of thy feet.

37David himself calleth him Lord; and whence is he his son? And the common people heard him gladly.

38And in his teaching he said, Beware of the scribes, who desire to walk in long robes, and to have salutations in the marketplaces,

39and chief seats in the synagogues, and chief places at feasts:

40they that devour widows' houses, and for a pretence make long prayers; these shall receive greater condemnation.

41And he sat down over against the treasury, and beheld how the multitude cast money into the treasury: and many that were rich cast in much.

42And there came a poor widow, and she cast in two mites, which make a farthing.

43And he called unto him his disciples, and said unto them, Verily I say unto you, This poor widow cast in more than all they that are casting into the treasury:

44for they all did cast in of their superfluity; but she of her want did cast in all that she had, even all her living.

Chapter 13

1And as he went forth out of the temple, one of his disciples saith unto him, Teacher, behold, what manner of stones and what manner of buildings!

2And Jesus said unto him, Seest thou these great buildings? there shall not be left here one stone upon another, which shall not be thrown down.

3And as he sat on the mount of Olives over against the temple, Peter and James and John and Andrew asked him privately,

4Tell us, when shall these things be? and what shall be the sign when these things are all about to be accomplished?

Mark

5And Jesus began to say unto them, Take heed that no man lead you astray.
6Many shall come in my name, saying, I am he; and shall lead many astray.
7And when ye shall hear of wars and rumors of wars, be not troubled: these things must needs come to pass; but the end is not yet.
8For nation shall rise against nation, and kingdom against kingdom; there shall be earthquakes in divers places; there shall be famines: these things are the beginning of travail.
9But take ye heed to yourselves: for they shall deliver you up to councils; and in synagogues shall ye be beaten; and before governors and kings shall ye stand for my sake, for a testimony unto them.
10And the gospel must first be preached unto all the nations.
11And when they lead you to judgment, and deliver you up, be not anxious beforehand what ye shall speak: but whatsoever shall be given you in that hour, that speak ye; for it is not ye that speak, but the Holy Spirit.
12And brother shall deliver up brother to death, and the father his child; and children shall rise up against parents, and cause them to be put to death.
13And ye shall be hated of all men for my name's sake: but he that endureth to the end, the same shall be saved.
14But when ye see the abomination of desolation standing where he ought not (let him that readeth understand), then let them that are in Judaea flee unto the mountains:
15and let him that is on the housetop not go down, nor enter in, to take anything out his house:
16and let him that is in the field not return back to take his cloak.
17But woe unto them that are with child and to them that give suck in those days!
18And pray ye that it be not in the winter.
19For those days shall be tribulation, such as there hath not been the like from the beginning of the creation which God created until now, and never shall be.
20And except the Lord had shortened the days, no flesh would have been saved; but for the elect's sake, whom he chose, he shortened the days.
21And then if any man shall say unto you, Lo, here is the Christ; or, Lo, there; believe it not:
22for there shall arise false Christs and false prophets, and shall show signs and wonders, that they may lead astray, if possible, the elect.
23But take ye heed: behold, I have told you all things beforehand.
24But in those days, after that tribulation, the sun shall be darkened, and the moon shall not give her light,
25and the stars shall be falling from heaven, and the powers that are in the heavens shall be shaken.
26And then shall they see the Son of man coming in clouds with great power and glory.
27And then shall he send forth the angels, and shall gather together his elect from the four winds, from the uttermost part of the earth to the uttermost part of heaven.
28Now from the fig tree learn her parable: when her branch is now become tender, and putteth forth its leaves, ye know that the summer is nigh;
29even so ye also, when ye see these things coming to pass, know ye that he is nigh, even at the doors.
30Verily I say unto you, This generation shall not pass away, until all these things be accomplished.
31Heaven and earth shall pass away: but my words shall not pass away.
32But of that day or that hour knoweth no one, not even the angels in heaven, neither the Son, but the Father.
33Take ye heed, watch and pray: for ye know not when the time is.
34It is as when a man, sojourning in another country, having left his house, and given authority to his servants, to each one his work, commanded also the porter to watch.
35Watch therefore: for ye know not when the lord of the house cometh, whether at even, or at midnight, or at cockcrowing, or in the morning;
36lest coming suddenly he find you sleeping.
37And what I say unto you I say unto all, Watch.

Chapter 14

1Now after two days was the feast of the passover and the unleavened bread: and the chief priests and the scribes sought how they might take him with subtlety, and kill him:
2for they said, Not during the feast, lest haply there shall be a tumult of the people.
3And while he was in Bethany in the house of Simon the leper, as he sat at meat, there came a woman having an alabaster cruse of ointment of pure nard very costly; and she brake the cruse, and poured it over his head.
4But there were some that had indignation among themselves, saying, To what purpose hath this waste of the ointment been made?
5For this ointment might have been sold for above three hundred shillings, and given to the poor. And they murmured against her.
6But Jesus said, Let her alone; why trouble ye her? she hath wrought a good work on me.
7For ye have the poor always with you, and whensoever ye will ye can do them good: but me ye have not always.
8She hath done what she could; she hath anointed my body beforehand for the burying.
9And verily I say unto you, Wheresoever the gospel shall be preached throughout the whole world, that also which this woman hath done shall be spoken of for a memorial of her.
10And Judas Iscariot, he that was one of the twelve, went away unto the chief priests, that he might deliver him unto them.
11And they, when they heard it, were glad, and promised to give him money. And he sought how he might conveniently deliver him unto them.
12And on the first day of unleavened bread, when they sacrificed the passover, his disciples say unto him, Where wilt thou that we go and make ready that thou mayest eat the passover?
13And he sendeth two of his disciples, and saith unto them, Go into the city, and there shall meet you a man bearing a pitcher of water: follow him;
14and wheresoever he shall enter in, say to the master of the house, The Teacher saith, Where is my guest-chamber, where I shall eat the passover with my disciples?
15And he will himself show you a large upper room furnished and ready: and there make ready for us.
16And the disciples went forth, and came into the city, and found as he had said unto them: and they made ready the passover.
17And when it was evening he cometh with the twelve.
18And as they sat and were eating, Jesus said, Verily I say unto you, One of you shall betray me, even he that eateth with me.
19They began to be sorrowful, and to say unto him one by one, Is it I?
20And he said unto them, It is one of the twelve, he that dippeth with me in the dish.
21For the Son of man goeth, even as it is written of him: but woe unto that man through whom the Son of man is betrayed! good were it for that man if he had not been born.
22And as they were eating, he took bread, and when he had blessed, he brake it, and gave to them, and said, Take ye: this is my body.
23And he took a cup, and when he had given thanks, he gave to them: and they all drank of it.
24And he said unto them, This is my blood of the covenant, which is poured out for many.
25Verily I say unto you, I shall no more drink of the fruit of the vine, until that day when I drink it new in the kingdom of God.
26And when they had sung a hymn, they went out unto the mount of Olives.
27And Jesus saith unto them, All ye shall be offended: for it is written, I will smite the shepherd, and the sheep shall be scattered abroad.
28Howbeit, after I am raised up, I will go before you into Galilee.
29But Peter said unto him, Although all shall be offended, yet will not I.
30And Jesus saith unto him, Verily I say unto thee, that thou to-day, even this night, before the cock crow twice, shalt deny me thrice.
31But he spake exceedingly vehemently, If I must die with thee, I will not deny thee. And in like manner also said they all.
32And they come unto a place which was named Gethsemane: and he saith unto his disciples, Sit ye here, while I pray.
33And he taketh with him Peter and James and John, and began to be greatly amazed, and sore troubled.
34And he saith unto them, My soul is exceeding sorrowful even unto death: abide ye here, and watch.
35And he went forward a little, and fell on the ground, and prayed that, if it were possible, the hour might pass away from him.
36And he said, Abba, Father, all things are possible unto thee; remove this cup from me: howbeit not what I will, but what thou wilt.
37And he cometh, and findeth them sleeping, and saith unto Peter, Simon, sleepest thou? couldest thou not watch one hour?
38Watch and pray, that ye enter not into temptation: the spirit indeed is willing, but the flesh is weak.
39And again he went away, and prayed, saying the same words.
40And again he came, and found them sleeping, for their eyes were very heavy; and they knew not what to answer him.
41And he cometh the third time, and saith unto them, Sleep on now, and take your rest: it is enough; the hour is come; behold, the Son of man is betrayed into the hands of sinners.
42Arise, let us be going: behold, he that betrayeth me is at hand.
43And straightway, while he yet spake, cometh Judas, one of the twelve, and with him a multitude with swords and staves, from the chief priests and the scribes and the elders.
44Now he that betrayed him had given them a token, saying, Whomsoever I shall kiss, that is he; take him, and lead him away safely.
45And when he was come, straightway he came to him, and saith, Rabbi; and kissed him.
46And they laid hands on him, and took him.
47But a certain one of them that stood by drew his sword, and smote the servant of the high priest, and struck off his ear.
48And Jesus answered and said unto them, Are ye come out, as against a robber, with swords and staves to seize me?
49I was daily with you in the temple teaching, and ye took me not: but this is done that the scriptures might be fulfilled.
50And they all left him, and fled.
51And a certain young man followed with him, having a linen cloth cast about him, over his naked body: and they lay hold on him;
52but he left the linen cloth, and fled naked.
53And they led Jesus away to the high priest: and there come together with him all the chief priests and the elders and the scribes.
54And Peter had followed him afar off, even within, into the court of the high priest; and he was sitting with the officers, and warming himself in the light of the fire.
55Now the chief priests and the whole council sought witness against Jesus to put him to death; and found it not.
56For many bare false witness against him, and their witness agreed not together.
57And there stood up certain, and bare false witness against him, saying,
58We heard him say, I will destroy this temple that is made with hands, and

in three days I will build another made without hands.

59And not even so did their witness agree together.

60And the high priest stood up in the midst, and asked Jesus, saying, Answerest thou nothing? what is it which these witness against thee?

61But he held his peace, and answered nothing. Again the high priest asked him, and saith unto him, Art thou the Christ, the Son of the Blessed?

62And Jesus said, I am: and ye shall see the Son of man sitting at the right hand of Power, and coming with the clouds of heaven.

63And the high priest rent his clothes, and saith, What further need have we of witnesses?

64Ye have heard the blasphemy: what think ye? And they all condemned him to be worthy of death.

65And some began to spit on him, and to cover his face, and to buffet him, and to say unto him, Prophesy: and the officers received him with blows of their hands.

66And as Peter was beneath in the court, there cometh one of the maids of the high priest;

67and seeing Peter warming himself, she looked upon him, and saith, Thou also wast with the Nazarene, even Jesus.

68But he denied, saying, I neither know, nor understand what thou sayest: and he went out into the porch; and the cock crew.

69And the maid saw him, and began again to say to them that stood by, This is one of them.

70But he again denied it. And after a little while again they that stood by said to Peter, of a truth thou art one of them; for thou art a Galilaean.

71But he began to curse, and to swear, I know not this man of whom ye speak.

72And straightway the second time the cock crew. And Peter called to mind the word, how that Jesus said unto him, Before the cock crow twice, thou shalt deny me thrice. And when he thought thereon, he wept.

Chapter 15

1And straightway in the morning the chief priests with the elders and scribes, and the whole council, held a consultation, and bound Jesus, and carried him away, and delivered him up to Pilate.

2And Pilate asked him, Art thou the King of the Jews? And he answering saith unto him, Thou sayest.

3And the chief priests accused him of many things.

4And Pilate again asked him, saying, Answerest thou nothing? behold how many things they accuse thee of.

5But Jesus no more answered anything; insomuch that Pilate marvelled.

6Now at the feast he used to release unto them one prisoner, whom they asked of him.

7And there was one called Barabbas, lying bound with them that had made insurrection, men who in the insurrection had committed murder.

8And the multitude went up and began to ask him to do as he was wont to do unto them.

9And Pilate answered them, saying, Will ye that I release unto you the King of the Jews?

10For he perceived that for envy the chief priests had delivered him up.

11But the chief priests stirred up the multitude, that he should rather release Barabbas unto them.

12And Pilate again answered and said unto them, What then shall I do unto him whom ye call the King of the Jews?

13And they cried out again, Crucify him.

14And Pilate said unto them, Why, what evil hath he done? But they cried out exceedingly, Crucify him.

15And Pilate, wishing to content the multitude, released unto them Barabbas, and delivered Jesus, when he had scourged him, to be crucified.

16And the soldiers led him away within the court, which is the Praetorium; and they call together the whole band.

17And they clothe him with purple, and platting a crown of thorns, they put it on him;

18and they began to salute him, Hail, King of the Jews!

19And they smote his head with a reed, and spat upon him, and bowing their knees worshipped him.

20And when they had mocked him, they took off from him the purple, and put on him his garments. And they lead him out to crucify him.

21And they compel one passing by, Simon of Cyrene, coming from the country, the father of Alexander and Rufus, to go with them, that he might bear his cross.

22And they bring him unto the place Golgotha, which is, being interpreted, The place of a skull.

23And they offered him wine mingled with myrrh: but he received it not.

24And they crucify him, and part his garments among them, casting lots upon them, what each should take.

25And it was the third hour, and they crucified him.

26And the superscription of his accusation was written over, THE KING OF THE JEWS.

27And with him they crucify two robbers; one on his right hand, and one on his left.

28And the scripture was fulfilled, which saith, And he was reckoned with transgressors.

29And they that passed by railed on him, wagging their heads, and saying, Ha! Thou that destroyest the temple, and buildest it in three days,

30save thyself, and come down from the cross.

31In like manner also the chief priests mocking him among themselves with the scribes said, He saved others; himself he cannot save.

32Let the Christ, the King of Israel, now come down from the cross, that we may see and believe. And they that were crucified with him reproached him.

33And when the sixth hour was come, there was darkness over the whole land until the ninth hour.

34And at the ninth hour Jesus cried with a loud voice, Eloi, Eloi, lama sabachthani? which is, being interpreted, My God, my God, why hast thou forsaken me?

35And some of them that stood by, when they heard it, said, Behold, he calleth Elijah.

36And one ran, and filling a sponge full of vinegar, put it on a reed, and gave him to drink, saying, Let be; let us see whether Elijah cometh to take him down.

37And Jesus uttered a loud voice, and gave up the ghost.

38And the veil of the temple was rent in two from the top to the bottom.

39And when the centurion, who stood by over against him, saw that he so gave up the ghost, he said, Truly this man was the Son of God.

40And there were also women beholding from afar: among whom were both Mary Magdalene, and Mary the mother of James the less and of Joses, and Salome;

41who, when he was in Galilee, followed him, and ministered unto him; and many other women that came up with him unto Jerusalem.

42And when even was now come, because it was the Preparation, that is, the day before the sabbath,

43there came Joseph of Arimathaea, a councillor of honorable estate, who also himself was looking for the kingdom of God; and he boldly went in unto Pilate, and asked for the body of Jesus.

44And Pilate marvelled if he were already dead: and calling unto him the centurion, he asked him whether he had been any while dead.

45And when he learned it of the centurion, he granted the corpse to Joseph.

46And he bought a linen cloth, and taking him down, wound him in the linen cloth, and laid him in a tomb which had been hewn out of a rock; and he rolled a stone against the door of the tomb.

47And Mary Magdalene and Mary the mother of Joses beheld where he was laid.

Chapter 16

1And when the sabbath was past, Mary Magdalene, and Mary the mother of James, and Salome, bought spices, that they might come and anoint him.

2And very early on the first day of the week, they come to the tomb when the sun was risen.

3And they were saying among themselves, Who shall roll us away the stone from the door of the tomb?

4and looking up, they see that the stone is rolled back: for it was exceeding great.

5And entering into the tomb, they saw a young man sitting on the right side, arrayed in a white robe; and they were amazed.

6And he saith unto them, Be not amazed: ye seek Jesus, the Nazarene, who hath been crucified: he is risen; he is not here: behold, the place where they laid him!

7But go, tell his disciples and Peter, He goeth before you into Galilee: there shall ye see him, as he said unto you.

8And they went out, and fled from the tomb; for trembling and astonishment had come upon them: and they said nothing to any one; for they were afraid.

9Now when he was risen early on the first day of the week, he appeared first to Mary Magdalene, from whom he had cast out seven demons.

10She went and told them that had been with him, as they mourned and wept.

11And they, when they heard that he was alive, and had been seen of her, disbelieved.

12And after these things he was manifested in another form unto two of them, as they walked, on their way into the country.

13And they went away and told it unto the rest: neither believed they them.

14And afterward he was manifested unto the eleven themselves as they sat at meat; and he upbraided them with their unbelief and hardness of heart, because they believed not them that had seen him after he was risen.

15And he said unto them, Go ye into all the world, and preach the gospel to the whole creation.

16He that believeth and is baptized shall be saved; but he that disbelieveth shall be condemned.

17And these signs shall accompany them that believe: in my name shall they cast out demons; they shall speak with new tongues;

18they shall take up serpents, and if they drink any deadly thing, it shall in no wise hurt them; they shall lay hands on the sick, and they shall recover.

19So then the Lord Jesus, after he had spoken unto them, was received up into heaven, and sat down at the right hand of God.

20And they went forth, and preached everywhere, the Lord working with them, and confirming the word by the signs that followed. Amen.

Luke

The Gospel According to St. Luke

Chapter 1

1Forasmuch as many have taken in hand to draw up a narrative concerning those matters which have been fulfilled among us,

2even as they delivered them unto us, who from the beginning were eyewitnesses and ministers of the word,

3it seemed good to me also, having traced the course of all things accurately from the first, to write unto thee in order, most excellent Theophilus;

4that thou mightest know the certainty concerning the things wherein thou wast instructed.

5There was in the days of Herod, king of Judaea, a certain priest named Zacharias, of the course of Abijah: and he had a wife of the daughters of Aaron, and her name was Elisabeth.

6And they were both righteous before God, walking in all the commandments and ordinances of the Lord blameless.

7And they had no child, because that Elisabeth was barren, and they both were now well stricken in years.

8Now it came to pass, while he executed the priest's office before God in the order of his course,

9according to the custom of the priest's office, his lot was to enter into the temple of the Lord and burn incense.

10And the whole multitude of the people were praying without at the hour of incense.

11And there appeared unto him an angel of the Lord standing on the right side of altar of incense.

12And Zacharias was troubled when he saw him, and fear fell upon him.

13But the angel said unto him, Fear not, Zacharias: because thy supplication is heard, and thy wife Elisabeth shall bear thee a son, and thou shalt call his name John.

14And thou shalt have joy and gladness; and many shall rejoice at his birth.

15For he shall be great in the sight of the Lord, and he shall drink no wine nor strong drink; and he shall be filled with the Holy Spirit, even from his mother's womb.

16And many of the children of Israel shall be turn unto the Lord their God.

17And he shall go before his face in the spirit and power of Elijah, to turn the hearts of the fathers to the children, and the disobedient to walk in the wisdom of the just; to make ready for the Lord a people prepared for him.

18And Zacharias said unto the angel, Whereby shall I know this? for I am an old man, and my wife well stricken in years.

19And the angel answering said unto him, I am Gabriel, that stand in the presence of God; and I was sent to speak unto thee, and to bring thee these good tidings.

20And behold, thou shalt be silent and not able to speak, until the day that these things shall come to pass, because thou believedst not my words, which shall be fulfilled in their season.

21And the people were waiting for Zacharias, and they marvelled while he tarried in the temple.

22And when he came out, he could not speak unto them: and they perceived that he had seen a vision in the temple: and he continued making signs unto them, and remained dumb.

23And it came to pass, when the days of his ministration were fulfilled, he departed unto his house.

24And after these days Elisabeth his wife conceived; and she hid herself five months, saying,

25Thus hath the Lord done unto me in the days wherein he looked upon me, to take away my reproach among men.

26Now in the sixth month the angel Gabriel was sent from God unto a city of Galilee, named Nazareth,

27to a virgin betrothed to a man whose name was Joseph, of the house of David; and the virgin's name was Mary.

28And he came in unto her, and said, Hail, thou that art highly favored, the Lord is with thee.

29But she was greatly troubled at the saying, and cast in her mind what manner of salutation this might be.

30And the angel said unto her, Fear not, Mary: for thou hast found favor with God.

31And behold, thou shalt conceive in thy womb, and bring forth a son, and shalt call his name JESUS.

32He shall be great, and shall be called the Son of the Most High: and the Lord God shall give unto him the throne of his father David:

33and he shall reign over the house of Jacob for ever; and of his kingdom there shall be no end.

34And Mary said unto the angel, How shall this be, seeing I know not a man?

35And the angel answered and said unto her, The Holy Spirit shall come upon thee, and the power of the Most High shall overshadow thee: wherefore also the holy thing which is begotten shall be called the Son of God.

36And behold, Elisabeth thy kinswoman, she also hath conceived a son in her old age; and this is the sixth month with her that was called barren.

37For no word from God shall be void of power.

38And Mary said, Behold, the handmaid of the Lord; be it unto me according to thy word. And the angel departed from her.

39And Mary arose in these days and went into the hill country with haste, into a city of Judah;

40and entered into the house of Zacharias and saluted Elisabeth.

41And it came to pass, when Elisabeth heard the salutation of Mary, the babe leaped in her womb; and Elisabeth was filled with the Holy Spirit;

42and she lifted up her voice with a loud cry, and said, Blessed art thou among women, and blessed is the fruit of thy womb.

43And whence is this to me, that the mother of my Lord should come unto me?

44For behold, when the voice of thy salutation came into mine ears, the babe leaped in my womb for joy.

45And blessed is she that believed; for there shall be a fulfilment of the things which have been spoken to her from the Lord.

46And Mary said,
My soul doth magnify the Lord,

47And my spirit hath rejoiced in God my Saviour.

48For he hath looked upon the low estate of his handmaid:
For behold, from henceforth all generations shall call me blessed.

49For he that is mighty hath done to me great things;
And holy is his name.

50And his mercy is unto generations and generations
On them that fear him.

51He hath showed strength with his arm;
He hath scattered the proud in the imagination of their heart.

52He hath put down princes from their thrones,
And hath exalted them of low degree.

53The hungry he hath filled with good things;
And the rich he hath sent empty away.

54He hath given help to Israel his servant,
That he might remember mercy

55(As he spake unto our fathers)
Toward Abraham and his seed for ever.

56And Mary abode with her about three months, and returned unto her house.

57Now Elisabeth's time was fulfilled that she should be delivered; and she brought forth a son.

58And her neighbors and her kinsfolk heard that the Lord had magnified his mercy towards her; and they rejoiced with her.

59And it came to pass on the eighth day, that they came to circumcise the child; and they would have called him Zacharias, after the name of the father.

60And his mother answered and said, Not so; but he shall be called John.

61And they said unto her, There is none of thy kindred that is called by this name.

62And they made signs to his father, what he would have him called.

63And he asked for a writing tablet, and wrote, saying, His name is John. And they marvelled all.

64And his mouth was opened immediately, and his tongue loosed, and he spake, blessing God.

65And fear came on all that dwelt round about them: and all these sayings were noised abroad throughout all the hill country of Judaea.

66And all that heard them laid them up in their heart, saying, What then shall this child be? For the hand of the Lord was with him.

67And his father Zacharias was filled with the Holy Spirit, and prophesied, saying,

68Blessed be the Lord, the God of Israel;
For he hath visited and wrought redemption for his people,

69And hath raised up a horn of salvation for us
In the house of his servant David

70(As he spake by the mouth of his holy prophets that have been from of old),

71Salvation from our enemies, and from the hand of all that hate us;

72To show mercy towards, our fathers,
And to remember his holy covenant;

73The oath which he spake unto Abraham our father,

74To grant unto us that we being delivered out of the hand of our enemies
Should serve him without fear,

75In holiness and righteousness before him all our days.

76Yea and thou, child, shalt be called the prophet of the Most High:
For thou shalt go before the face of the Lord to make ready his ways;

77To give knowledge of salvation unto his people
In the remission of their sins,

78Because of the tender mercy of our God,
Whereby the dayspring from on high shall visit us,

79To shine upon them that sit in darkness and the shadow of death;
To guide our feet into the way of peace.

80And the child grew, and waxed strong in spirit, and was in the deserts till the day of his showing unto Israel.

Chapter 2

1Now it came to pass in those days, there went out a decree from Caesar Augustus, that all the world should be enrolled.

2This was the first enrolment made when Quirinius was governor of Syria.

3And all went to enrol themselves, every one to his own city.

4And Joseph also went up from Galilee, out of the city of Nazareth, into Judaea, to the city of David, which is called Bethlehem, because he was of the house and family of David;

5to enrol himself with Mary, who was betrothed to him, being great with child.

6And it came to pass, while they were there, the days were fulfilled that she should be delivered.

7And she brought forth her firstborn son; and she wrapped him in swaddling clothes, and laid him in a manger, because there was no room for them in the inn.

8And there were shepherds in the same country abiding in the field, and keeping watch by night over their flock.

9And an angel of the Lord stood by them, and the glory of the Lord shone round about them: and they were sore afraid.

10And the angel said unto them, Be not afraid; for behold, I bring you good tidings of great joy which shall be to all the people:

11for there is born to you this day in the city of David a Saviour, who is Christ the Lord.

12And this is the sign unto you: Ye shall find a babe wrapped in swaddling clothes, and lying in a manger.

13And suddenly there was with the angel a multitude of the heavenly host praising God, and saying,

14Glory to God in the highest,
And on earth peace among men in whom he is well pleased.

15And it came to pass, when the angels went away from them into heaven, the shepherds said one to another, Let us now go even unto Bethlehem, and see this thing that is come to pass, which the Lord hath made known unto us.

16And they came with haste, and found both Mary and Joseph, and the babe lying in the manger.

17And when they saw it, they made known concerning the saying which was spoken to them about this child.

18And all that heard it wondered at the things which were spoken unto them by the shepherds.

19But Mary kept all these sayings, pondering them in her heart.

20And the shepherds returned, glorifying and praising God for all the things that they had heard and seen, even as it was spoken unto them.

21And when eight days were fulfilled for circumcising him, his name was called JESUS, which was so called by the angel before he was conceived in the womb.

22And when the days of their purification according to the law of Moses were fulfilled, they brought him up to Jerusalem, to present him to the Lord

23(as it is written in the law of the Lord, Every male that openeth the womb shall be called holy to the Lord),

24and to offer a sacrifice according to that which is said in the law of the Lord, A pair of turtledoves, or two young pigeons.

25And behold, there was a man in Jerusalem whose name was Simeon; and this man was righteous and devout, looking for the consolation of Israel: and the Holy Spirit was upon him.

26And it had been revealed unto him by the Holy Spirit, that he should not see death, before he had seen the Lord's Christ.

27And he came in the Spirit into the temple: and when the parents brought in the child Jesus, that they might do concerning him after the custom of the law,

28then he received him into his arms, and blessed God, and said,

29Now lettest thou thy servant depart, Lord,
According to thy word, in peace;

30For mine eyes have seen thy salvation,

31Which thou hast prepared before the face of all peoples;

32A light for revelation to the Gentiles,
And the glory of thy people Israel.

33And his father and his mother were marvelling at the things which were spoken concerning him;

34and Simeon blessed them, and said unto Mary his mother, Behold, this child is set for the falling and the rising of many in Israel; and for a sign which is spoken against;

35yea and a sword shall pierce through thine own soul; that thoughts out of many hearts may be revealed.

36And there was one Anna, a prophetess, the daughter of Phanuel, of the tribe of Asher (she was of a great age, having lived with a husband seven years from her virginity,

37and she had been a widow even unto fourscore and four years), who departed not from the temple, worshipping with fastings and supplications night and day.

38And coming up at that very hour she gave thanks unto God, and spake of him to all them that were looking for the redemption of Jerusalem.

39And when they had accomplished all things that were according to the law of the Lord, they returned into Galilee, to their own city Nazareth.

40And the child grew, and waxed strong, filled with wisdom: and the grace of God was upon him.

41And his parents went every year to Jerusalem at the feast of the passover.

42And when he was twelve years old, they went up after the custom of the feast;

43and when they had fulfilled the days, as they were returning, the boy Jesus tarried behind in Jerusalem; and his parents knew it not;

44but supposing him to be in the company, they went a day's journey; and they sought for him among their kinsfolk and acquaintance:

45and when they found him not, they returned to Jerusalem, seeking for him.

46And it came to pass, after three days they found him in the temple, sitting in the midst of the teachers, both hearing them, and asking them questions:

47and all that heard him were amazed at his understanding and his answers.

48And when they saw him, they were astonished; and his mother said unto him, Son, why hast thou thus dealt with us? behold, thy father and I sought thee sorrowing.

49And he said unto them, How is it that ye sought me? knew ye not that I must be in my Father's house?

50And they understood not the saying which he spake unto them.

51And he went down with them, and came to Nazareth; and he was subject unto them: and his mother kept all these sayings in her heart.

52And Jesus advanced in wisdom and stature, and in favor with God and men.

Chapter 3

1Now in the fifteenth year of the reign of Tiberius Caesar, Pontius Pilate being governor of Judaea, and Herod being tetrarch of Galilee, and his brother Philip tetrarch of the region of Ituraea and Trachonitis, and Lysanias tetrarch of Abilene,

2in the highpriesthood of Annas and Caiaphas, the word of God came unto John the son of Zacharias in the wilderness.

3And he came into all the region round about the Jordan, preaching the baptism of repentance unto remission of sins;

4as it is written in the book of the words of Isaiah the prophet, The voice of one crying in the wilderness, Make ye ready the way of the Lord, Make his paths straight.

5Every valley shall be filled, And every mountain and hill shall be brought low; And the crooked shall become straight, And the rough ways smooth;

6And all flesh shall see the salvation of God.

7He said therefore to the multitudes that went out to be baptized of him, Ye offspring of vipers, who warned you to flee from the wrath to come?

8Bring forth therefore fruits worthy of repentance, and begin not to say within yourselves, We have Abraham to our father: for I say unto you, that God is able of these stones to raise up children unto Abraham.

9And even now the axe also lieth at the root of the trees: every tree therefore that bringeth not forth good fruit is hewn down, and cast into the fire.

10And the multitudes asked him, saying, What then must we do?

11And he answered and said unto them, He that hath two coats, let him impart to him that hath none; and he that hath food, let him do likewise.

12And there came also publicans to be baptized, and they said unto him, Teacher, what must we do?

13And he said unto them, Extort no more than that which is appointed you.

14And soldiers also asked him, saying, And we, what must we do? And he said unto them, Extort from no man by violence, neither accuse any one wrongfully; and be content with your wages.

15And as the people were in expectation, and all men reasoned in their hearts concerning John, whether haply he were the Christ;

16John answered, saying unto them all, I indeed baptize you with water; but there cometh he that is mightier than I, the latchet of whose shoes I am not worthy to unloose: he shall baptize you in the Holy Spirit and in fire:

17whose fan is in his hand, thoroughly to cleanse his threshing-floor, and to gather the wheat into his garner; but the chaff he will burn up with unquenchable fire.

18With many other exhortations therefore preached he good tidings unto the people;

19but Herod the tetrarch, being reproved by him for Herodias his brother's wife, and for all the evil things which Herod had done,

20added this also to them all, that he shut up John in prison.

21Now it came to pass, when all the people were baptized, that, Jesus also having been baptized, and praying, the heaven was opened,

22and the Holy Spirit descended in a bodily form, as a dove, upon him, and a voice came out of heaven, Thou art my beloved Son; in thee I am well pleased.

23And Jesus himself, when he began to teach, was about thirty years of age, being the son (as was supposed) of Joseph, the son of Heli,

24the son of Matthat, the son of Levi, the son of Melchi, the son of Jannai, the son of Joseph,

25the son of Mattathias, the son of Amos, the son of Nahum, the son of Esli, the son of Naggai,

26the son of Maath, the son of Mattathias, the son of Semein, the son of Josech, the son of Joda,

27the son of Joanan, the son of Rhesa, the son of Zerubbabel, the son of Shealtiel, the son of Neri,

28the son of Melchi, the son of Addi, the son of Cosam, the son of Elmadam, the son of Er,

29the son of Jesus, the son of Eliezer, the son of Jorim, the son of Matthat, the son of Levi,

30the son of Symeon, the son of Judas, the son of Joseph, the son of Jonam, the son of Eliakim,

31the son of Melea, the son of Menna, the son of Mattatha, the son of Nathan, the son of David,

32the son of Jesse, the son of Obed, the son of Boaz, the son of Salmon, the son of Nahshon,

33the son of Amminadab, the son of Arni, the son of Hezron, the son of Perez, the son of Judah,

34the son of Jacob, the son of Isaac, the son of Abraham, the son of Terah, the son of Nahor,

35the son of Serug, the son of Reu, the son of Peleg, the son of Eber, the son of Shelah,

36the son of Cainan, the son of Arphaxad, the son of Shem, the son of Noah, the son of Lamech,

37the son of Methuselah, the son of Enoch, the son of Jared, the son of Mahalaleel, the son of Cainan,

38the son of Enos, the son of Seth, the son of Adam, the son of God.

Luke
Chapter 4

1And Jesus, full of the Holy Spirit, returned from the Jordan, and was led in the Spirit in the wilderness

2during forty days, being tempted of the devil. And he did eat nothing in those days: and when they were completed, he hungered.

3And the devil said unto him, if thou art the Son of God, command this stone that it become bread.

4And Jesus answered unto him, It is written, Man shall not live by bread alone.

5And he led him up, and showed him all the kingdoms of the world in a moment of time.

6And the devil said unto him, To thee will I give all this authority, and the glory of them: for it hath been delivered unto me; and to whomsoever I will I give it.

7If thou therefore wilt worship before me, it shall all be thine.

8And Jesus answered and said unto him, It is written, Thou shalt worship the Lord thy God, and him only shalt thou serve.

9And he led him to Jerusalem, and set him on the pinnacle of the temple, and said unto him, If thou art the Son of God, cast thyself down from hence:

10for it is written,
He shall give his angels charge concerning thee, to guard thee:

11and,
On their hands they shall bear thee up,
Lest haply thou dash thy foot against a stone.

12And Jesus answering said unto him, It is said, Thou shalt not make trial of the Lord thy God.

13And when the devil had completed every temptation, he departed from him for a season.

14And Jesus returned in the power of the Spirit into Galilee: and a fame went out concerning him through all the region round about.

15And he taught in their synagogues, being glorified of all.

16And he came to Nazareth, where he had been brought up: and he entered, as his custom was, into the synagogue on the sabbath day, and stood up to read.

17And there was delivered unto him the book of the prophet Isaiah. And he opened the book, and found the place where it was written,

18The Spirit of the Lord is upon me,
Because he anointed me to preach good tidings to the poor:
He hath sent me to proclaim release to the captives,
And recovering of sight to the blind,
To set at liberty them that are bruised,

19To proclaim the acceptable year of the Lord.

20And he closed the book, and gave it back to the attendant, and sat down: and the eyes of all in the synagogue were fastened on him.

21And he began to say unto them, To-day hath this scripture been fulfilled in your ears.

22And all bare him witness, and wondered at the words of grace which proceeded out of his mouth: and they said, Is not this Joseph's son?

23And he said unto them, Doubtless ye will say unto me this parable, Physician, heal thyself: whatsoever we have heard done at Capernaum, do also here in thine own country.

24And he said, Verily I say unto you, No prophet is acceptable in his own country.

25But of a truth I say unto you, There were many widows in Israel in the days of Elijah, when the heaven was shut up three years and six months, when there came a great famine over all the land;

26and unto none of them was Elijah sent, but only to Zarephath, in the land of Sidon, unto a woman that was a widow.

27And there were many lepers in Israel in the time of Elisha the prophet; and none of them was cleansed, but only Naaman the Syrian.

28And they were all filled with wrath in the synagogue, as they heard these things;

29and they rose up, and cast him forth out of the city, and led him unto the brow of the hill whereon their city was built, that they might throw him down headlong.

30But he passing through the midst of them went his way.

31And he came down to Capernaum, a city of Galilee. And he was teaching them on the sabbath day:

32and they were astonished at his teaching; for his word was with authority.

33And in the synagogue there was a man, that had a spirit of an unclean demon; and he cried out with a loud voice,

34Ah! what have we to do with thee, Jesus thou Nazarene? art thou come to destroy us? I know thee who thou art, the Holy One of God.

35And Jesus rebuked him, saying, Hold thy peace, and come out of him. And when the demon had thrown him down in the midst, he came out of him, having done him no hurt.

36And amazement came upon all, and they spake together, one with another, saying, What is this word? for with authority and power he commandeth the unclean spirits, and they come out.

37And there went forth a rumor concerning him into every place of the region round about.

38And he rose up from the synagogue, and entered into the house of Simon. And Simon's wife's mother was holden with a great fever; and they besought him for her.

39And he stood over her, and rebuked the fever; and it left her: and immediately she rose up and ministered unto them.

40And when the sun was setting, all they that had any sick with divers diseases brought them unto him; and he laid his hands on every one of them, and healed them.

41And demons also came out from many, crying out, and saying, Thou art the Son of God. And rebuking them, he suffered them not to speak, because they knew that he was the Christ.

42And when it was day, he came out and went into a desert place: and the multitudes sought after him, and came unto him, and would have stayed him, that he should not go from them.

43But he said unto them, I must preach the good tidings of the kingdom of God to the other cities also: for therefore was I sent.

44And he was preaching in the synagogues of Galilee.

Chapter 5

1Now it came to pass, while the multitude pressed upon him and heard the word of God, that he was standing by the lake of Gennesaret;

2and he saw two boats standing by the lake: but the fishermen had gone out of them, and were washing their nets.

3And he entered into one of the boats, which was Simon's, and asked him to put out a little from the land. And he sat down and taught the multitudes out of the boat.

4And when he had left speaking, he said unto Simon, Put out into the deep, and let down your nets for a draught.

5And Simon answered and said, Master, we toiled all night, and took nothing: but at thy word I will let down the nets.

6And when they had done this, they inclosed a great multitude of fishes; and their nets were breaking;

7and they beckoned unto their partners in the other boat, that they should come and help them. And they came, and filled both the boats, so that they began to sink.

8But Simon Peter, when he saw it, fell down at Jesus' knees, saying, Depart from me; for I am a sinful man, O Lord.

9For he was amazed, and all that were with him, at the draught of the fishes which they had taken;

10and so were also James and John, sons of Zebedee, who were partners with Simon. And Jesus said unto Simon, Fear not; from henceforth thou shalt catch men.

11And when they had brought their boats to land, they left all, and followed him.

12And it came to pass, while he was in one of the cities, behold, a man full of leprosy: and when he saw Jesus, he fell on his face, and besought him, saying, Lord, if thou wilt, thou canst make me clean.

13And he stretched forth his hand, and touched him, saying, I will; be thou made clean. And straightway the leprosy departed from him.

14And he charged him to tell no man: but go thy way, and show thyself to the priest, and offer for thy cleansing, according as Moses commanded, for a testimony unto them.

15But so much the more went abroad the report concerning him: and great multitudes came together to hear, and to be healed of their infirmities.

16But he withdrew himself in the deserts, and prayed.

17And it came to pass on one of those days, that he was teaching; and there were Pharisees and doctors of the law sitting by, who were come out of every village of Galilee and Judaea and Jerusalem: and the power of the Lord was with him to heal.

18And behold, men bring on a bed a man that was palsied: and they sought to bring him in, and to lay him before him.

19And not finding by what way they might bring him in because of the multitude, they went up to the housetop, and let him down through the tiles with his couch into the midst before Jesus.

20And seeing their faith, he said, Man, thy sins are forgiven thee.

21And the scribes and the Pharisees began to reason, saying, Who is this that speaketh blasphemies? Who can forgive sins, but God alone?

22But Jesus perceiving their reasonings, answered and said unto them, Why reason ye in your hearts?

23Which is easier, to say, Thy sins are forgiven thee; or to say, Arise and walk?

24But that ye may know that the Son of man hath authority on earth to forgive sins (he said unto him that was palsied), I say unto thee, Arise, and take up thy couch, and go unto thy house.

25And immediately he rose up before them, and took up that whereon he lay, and departed to his house, glorifying God.

26And amazement took hold on all, and they glorified God; and they were filled with fear, saying, We have seen strange things to-day.

27And after these things he went forth, and beheld a publican, named Levi, sitting at the place of toll, and said unto him, Follow me.

28And he forsook all, and rose up and followed him.

29And Levi made him a great feast in his house: and there was a great multitude of publicans and of others that were sitting at meat with them.

30And the Pharisees and their scribes murmured against his disciples, saying, Why do ye eat and drink with the publicans and sinners?

31And Jesus answering said unto them, They that are in health have no need of a physician; but they that are sick.

32I am not come to call the righteous but sinners to repentance.

33And they said unto him, The disciples of John fast often, and make supplications; likewise also the disciples of the Pharisees; but thine eat and drink.

34And Jesus said unto them, Can ye make the sons of the bride-chamber fast, while the bridegroom is with them?

35But the days will come; and when the bridegroom shall be taken away from them, then will they fast in those days.

36And he spake also a parable unto them: No man rendeth a piece from a new garment and putteth it upon an old garment; else he will rend the new, and also the piece from the new will not agree with the old.

37And no man putteth new wine into old wine-skins; else the new wine will burst the skins, and itself will be spilled, and the skins will perish.

38But new wine must be put into fresh wine-skins.

39And no man having drunk old wine desireth new; for he saith, The old is good.

Chapter 6

1Now it came to pass on a sabbath, that he was going through the grainfields; and his disciples plucked the ears, and did eat, rubbing them in their hands.

2But certain of the Pharisees said, Why do ye that which it is not lawful to do on the sabbath day?

3And Jesus answering them said, Have ye not read even this, what David did, when he was hungry, he, and they that were with him;

4how he entered into the house of God, and took and ate the showbread, and gave also to them that were with him; which it is not lawful to eat save for the priests alone?

5And he said unto them, The Son of man is lord of the sabbath.

6And it came to pass on another sabbath, that he entered into the synagogue and taught: and there was a man there, and his right hand was withered.

7And the scribes and the Pharisees watched him, whether he would heal on the sabbath; that they might find how to accuse him.

8But he knew their thoughts; and he said to the man that had his hand withered, Rise up, and stand forth in the midst. And he arose and stood forth.

9And Jesus said unto them, I ask you, Is it lawful on the sabbath to do good, or to do harm? to save a life, or to destroy it?

10And he looked round about on them all, and said unto him, Stretch forth thy hand. And he did so: and his hand was restored.

11But they were filled with madness; and communed one with another what they might do to Jesus.

12And it came to pass in these days, that he went out into the mountain to pray; and he continued all night in prayer to God.

13And when it was day, he called his disciples; and he chose from them twelve, whom also he named apostles:

14Simon, whom he also named Peter, and Andrew his brother, and James and John, and Philip and Bartholomew,

15and Matthew and Thomas, and James the son of Alphaeus, and Simon who was called the Zealot,

16and Judas the son of James, and Judas Iscariot, who became a traitor;

17and he came down with them, and stood on a level place, and a great multitude of his disciples, and a great number of the people from all Judaea and Jerusalem, and the sea coast of Tyre and Sidon, who came to hear him, and to be healed of their diseases;

18and they that were troubled with unclean spirits were healed.

19And all the multitude sought to touch him; for power came forth from him, and healed them all.

20And he lifted up his eyes on his disciples, and said, Blessed are ye poor: for yours is the kingdom of God.

21Blessed are ye that hunger now: for ye shall be filled. Blessed are ye that weep now: for ye shall laugh.

22Blessed are ye, when men shall hate you, and when they shall separate you from their company, and reproach you, and cast out your name as evil, for the Son of man's sake.

23Rejoice in that day, and leap for joy: for behold, your reward is great in heaven; for in the same manner did their fathers unto the prophets.

24But woe unto you that are rich! for ye have received your consolation.

25Woe unto you, ye that are full now! for ye shall hunger. Woe unto you, ye that laugh now! for ye shall mourn and weep.

26Woe unto you, when all men shall speak well of you! for in the same manner did their fathers to the false prophets.

27But I say unto you that hear, Love your enemies, do good to them that hate you,

28bless them that curse you, pray for them that despitefully use you.

29To him that smiteth thee on the one cheek offer also the other; and from him that taketh away thy cloak withhold not thy coat also.

30Give to every one that asketh thee; and of him that taketh away thy goods ask them not again.

31And as ye would that men should do to you, do ye also to them likewise.

32And if ye love them that love you, what thank have ye? for even sinners love those that love them.

33And if ye do good to them that do good to you, what thank have ye? for even sinners do the same.

34And if ye lend to them of whom ye hope to receive, what thank have ye? even sinners lend to sinners, to receive again as much.

35But love your enemies, and do them good, and lend, never despairing; and your reward shall be great, and ye shall be sons of the Most High: for he is kind toward the unthankful and evil.

36Be ye merciful, even as your Father is merciful.

37And judge not, and ye shall not be judged: and condemn not, and ye shall not be condemned: release, and ye shall be released:

38give, and it shall be given unto you; good measure, pressed down, shaken together, running over, shall they give into your bosom. For with what measure ye mete it shall be measured to you again.

39And he spake also a parable unto them, Can the blind guide the blind? shall they not both fall into a pit?

40The disciple is not above his teacher: but every one when he is perfected shall be as his teacher.

41And why beholdest thou the mote that is in thy brother's eye, but considerest not the beam that is in thine own eye?

42Or how canst thou say to thy brother, Brother, let me cast out the mote that is in thine eye, when thou thyself beholdest not the beam that is in thine own eye? Thou hypocrite, cast out first the beam out of thine own eye, and then shalt thou see clearly to cast out the mote that is in thy brother's eye.

43For there is no good tree that bringeth forth corrupt fruit; nor again a corrupt tree that bringeth forth good fruit.

44For each tree is known by its own fruit. For of thorns men do not gather figs, nor of a bramble bush gather they grapes.

45The good man out of the good treasure of his heart bringeth forth that which is good; and the evil man out of the evil treasure bringeth forth that which is evil: for out of the abundance of the heart his mouth speaketh.

46And why call ye me, Lord, Lord, and do not the things which I say?

47Every one that cometh unto me, and heareth my words, and doeth them, I will show you to whom he is like:

48he is like a man building a house, who digged and went deep, and laid a foundation upon the rock: and when a flood arose, the stream brake against that house, and could not shake it: because it had been well builded.

49But he that heareth, and doeth not, is like a man that built a house upon the earth without a foundation; against which the stream brake, and straightway it fell in; and the ruin of that house was great.

Chapter 7

1After he had ended all his sayings in the ears of the people, he entered into Capernaum.

2And a certain centurion's servant, who was dear unto him, was sick and at the point of death.

3And when he heard concerning Jesus, he sent unto him elders of the Jews, asking him that he would come and save his servant.

4And they, when they came to Jesus, besought him earnestly, saying, He is worthy that thou shouldest do this for him;

5for he loveth our nation, and himself built us our synagogue.

6And Jesus went with them. And when he was now not far from the house, the centurion sent friends to him, saying unto him, Lord, trouble not thyself; for I am not worthy that thou shouldest come under my roof:

7wherefore neither thought I myself worthy to come unto thee: but say the word, and my servant shall be healed.

8For I also am a man set under authority, having under myself soldiers: and I say to this one, Go, and he goeth; and to another, Come, and he cometh; and to my servant, Do this, and he doeth it.

9And when Jesus heard these things, he marvelled at him, and turned and said unto the multitude that followed him, I say unto you, I have not found so great faith, no, not in Israel.

10And they that were sent, returning to the house, found the servant whole.

11And it came to pass soon afterwards, that he went to a city called Nain; and his disciples went with him, and a great multitude.

12Now when he drew near to the gate of the city, behold, there was carried out one that was dead, the only son of his mother, and she was a widow: and much people of the city was with her.

13And when the Lord saw her, he had compassion on her, and said unto her, Weep not.

14And he came nigh and touched the bier: and the bearers stood still. And he said, Young man, I say unto thee, Arise.

15And he that was dead sat up, and began to speak. And he gave him to his mother.

16And fear took hold on all: and they glorified God, saying, A great prophet is arisen among us: and, God hath visited his people.

17And this report went forth concerning him in the whole of Judaea, and all the region round about.

18And the disciples of John told him of all these things.

19And John calling unto him two of his disciples sent them to the Lord, saying, Art thou he that cometh, or look we for another?

20And when the men were come unto him, they said, John the Baptist hath sent us unto thee, saying, Art thou he that cometh, or look we for another?

21In that hour he cured many of diseases and plagues and evil spirits; and on many that were blind he bestowed sight.

22And he answered and said unto them, Go and tell John the things which ye have seen and heard; the blind receive their sight, the lame walk, the lepers are cleansed, and the deaf hear, the dead are raised up, the poor have good tidings preached to them.

23And blessed is he, whosoever shall find no occasion of stumbling in me.

24And when the messengers of John were departed, he began to say unto the multitudes concerning John, What went ye out into the wilderness to behold? a reed shaken with the wind?

25But what went ye out to see? a man clothed in soft raiment? Behold, they that are gorgeously apparelled, and live delicately, are in kings' courts.

26But what went ye out to see? a prophet? Yea, I say unto you, and much more than a prophet.

27This is he of whom it is written,
Behold, I send my messenger before thy face,
Who shall prepare thy way before thee.

28I say unto you, Among them that are born of women there is none greater than John: yet he that is but little in the kingdom of God is greater than he.

29And all the people when they heard, and the publicans, justified God, being baptized with the baptism of John.

30But the Pharisees and the lawyers rejected for themselves the counsel of God, being not baptized of him.

31Whereunto then shall I liken the men of this generation, and to what are they like?

32They are like unto children that sit in the marketplace, and call one to another; who say, We piped unto you, and ye did not dance; we wailed, and ye did

Luke

not weep.

33For John the Baptist is come eating no bread nor drinking wine; and ye say, He hath a demon.

34The Son of man is come eating and drinking; and ye say, Behold, a gluttonous man, and a winebibber, a friend of publicans and sinners!

35And wisdom is justified of all her children.

36And one of the Pharisees desired him that he would eat with him. And he entered into the Pharisee's house, and sat down to meat.

37And behold, a woman who was in the city, a sinner; and when she knew that he was sitting at meat in the Pharisee's house, she brought an alabaster cruse of ointment,

38and standing behind at his feet, weeping, she began to wet his feet with her tears, and wiped them with the hair of her head, and kissed his feet, and anointed them with the ointment.

39Now when the Pharisee that had bidden him saw it, he spake within himself, saying, This man, if he were a prophet, would have perceived who and what manner of woman this is that toucheth him, that she is a sinner.

40And Jesus answering said unto him, Simon, I have somewhat to say unto thee. And he saith, Teacher, say on.

41A certain lender had two debtors: the one owed five hundred shillings, and the other fifty.

42When they had not wherewith to pay, he forgave them both. Which of them therefore will love him most?

43Simon answered and said, He, I suppose, to whom he forgave the most. And he said unto him, Thou hast rightly judged.

44And turning to the woman, he said unto Simon, Seest thou this woman? I entered into thy house, thou gavest me no water for my feet: but she hath wetted my feet with her tears, and wiped them with her hair.

45Thou gavest me no kiss: but she, since the time I came in, hath not ceased to kiss my feet.

46My head with oil thou didst not anoint: but she hath anointed my feet with ointment.

47Wherefore I say unto thee, Her sins, which are many, are forgiven; for she loved much: but to whom little is forgiven, the same loveth little.

48And he said unto her, Thy sins are forgiven.

49And they that sat at meat with him began to say within themselves, Who is this that even forgiveth sins?

50And he said unto the woman, Thy faith hath saved thee; go in peace.

Chapter 8

1And it came to pass soon afterwards, that he went about through cities and villages, preaching and bringing the good tidings of the kingdom of God, and with him the twelve,

2and certain women who had been healed of evil spirits and infirmities: Mary that was called Magdalene, from whom seven demons had gone out,

3and Joanna the wife of Chuzas Herod's steward, and Susanna, and many others, who ministered unto them of their substance.

4And when a great multitude came together, and they of every city resorted unto him, he spake by a parable:

5The sower went forth to sow his seed: and as he sowed, some fell by the way side; and it was trodden under foot, and the birds of the heaven devoured it.

6And other fell on the rock; and as soon as it grew, it withered away, because it had no moisture.

7And other fell amidst the thorns; and the thorns grew with it, and choked it.

8And other fell into the good ground, and grew, and brought forth fruit a hundredfold. As he said these things, he cried, He that hath ears to hear, let him hear.

9And his disciples asked him what this parable might be.

10And he said, Unto you it is given to know the mysteries of the kingdom of God: but to the rest in parables; that seeing they may not see, and hearing they may not understand.

11Now the parable is this: The seed is the word of God.

12And those by the way side are they that have heard; then cometh the devil, and taketh away the word from their heart, that they may not believe and be saved.

13And those on the rock are they who, when they have heard, receive the word with joy; and these have no root, who for a while believe, and in time of temptation fall away.

14And that which fell among the thorns, these are they that have heard, and as they go on their way they are choked with cares and riches and pleasures of this life, and bring no fruit to perfection.

15And that in the good ground, these are such as in an honest and good heart, having heard the word, hold it fast, and bring forth fruit with patience.

16And no man, when he hath lighted a lamp, covereth it with a vessel, or putteth it under a bed; but putteth it on a stand, that they that enter in may see the light.

17For nothing is hid, that shall not be made manifest; nor anything secret, that shall not be known and come to light.

18Take heed therefore how ye hear: for whosoever hath, to him shall be given; and whosoever hath not, from him shall be taken away even that which he thinketh he hath.

19And there came to him his mother and brethren, and they could not come at him for the crowd.

20And it was told him, Thy mother and thy brethren stand without, desiring to see thee.

21But he answered and said unto them, My mother and my brethren are these that hear the word of God, and do it.

22Now it came to pass on one of those days, that he entered into a boat, himself and his disciples; and he said unto them, Let us go over unto the other side of the lake: and they launched forth.

23But as they sailed he fell asleep: and there came down a storm of wind on the lake; and they were filling with water, and were in jeopardy.

24And they came to him, and awoke him, saying, Master, master, we perish. And he awoke, and rebuked the wind and the raging of the water: and they ceased, and there was a calm.

25And he said unto them, Where is your faith? And being afraid they marvelled, saying one to another, Who then is this, that he commandeth even the winds and the water, and they obey him?

26And they arrived at the country of the Gerasenes, which is over against Galilee.

27And when he was come forth upon the land, there met him a certain man out of the city, who had demons; and for a long time he had worn no clothes, and abode not in any house, but in the tombs.

28And when he saw Jesus, he cried out, and fell down before him, and with a loud voice said, What have I to do with thee, Jesus, thou Son of the Most High God? I beseech thee, torment me not.

29For he was commanding the unclean spirit to come out from the man. For oftentimes it had seized him: and he was kept under guard, and bound with chains and fetters; and breaking the bands asunder, he was driven of the demon into the deserts.

30And Jesus asked him, What is thy name? And he said, Legion; for many demons were entered into him.

31And they entreated him that he would not command them to depart into the abyss.

32Now there was there a herd of many swine feeding on the mountain: and they entreated him that he would give them leave to enter into them. And he gave them leave.

33And the demons came out from the man, and entered into the swine: and the herd rushed down the steep into the lake, and were drowned.

34And when they that fed them saw what had come to pass, they fled, and told it in the city and in the country.

35And they went out to see what had come to pass; and they came to Jesus, and found the man, from whom the demons were gone out, sitting, clothed and in his right mind, at the feet of Jesus: and they were afraid.

36And they that saw it told them how he that was possessed with demons was made whole.

37And all the people of the country of the Gerasenes round about asked him to depart from them, for they were holden with great fear: and he entered into a boat, and returned.

38But the man from whom the demons were gone out prayed him that he might be with him: but he sent him away, saying,

39Return to thy house, and declare how great things God hath done for thee. And he went his way, publishing throughout the whole city how great things Jesus had done for him.

40And as Jesus returned, the multitude welcomed him; for they were all waiting for him.

41And behold, there came a man named Jairus, and he was a ruler of the synagogue: and he fell down at Jesus' feet, and besought him to come into his house;

42for he had an only daughter, about twelve years of age, and she was dying. But as he went the multitudes thronged him.

43And a woman having an issue of blood twelve years, who had spent all her living upon physicians, and could not be healed of any,

44came behind him, and touched the border of his garment: and immediately the issue of her blood stanched.

45And Jesus said, Who is it that touched me? And when all denied, Peter said, and they that were with him, Master, the multitudes press thee and crush thee.

46But Jesus said, Some one did touch me; for I perceived that power had gone forth from me.

47And when the woman saw that she was not hid, she came trembling, and falling down before him declared in the presence of all the people for what cause she touched him, and how she was healed immediately.

48And he said unto her, Daughter, thy faith hath made thee whole; go in peace.

49While he yet spake, there cometh one from the ruler of the synagogue's house, saying, Thy daughter is dead; trouble not the Teacher.

50But Jesus hearing it, answered him, Fear not: only believe, and she shall be made whole.

51And when he came to the house, he suffered not any man to enter in with him, save Peter, and John, and James, and the father of the maiden and her mother.

52And all were weeping, and bewailing her: but he said, Weep not; for she is not dead, but sleepeth.

53And they laughed him to scorn, knowing that she was dead.

54But he, taking her by the hand, called, saying, Maiden, arise.

55And her spirit returned, and she rose up immediately: and he commanded that something be given her to eat.

56And her parents were amazed: but he charged them to tell no man what had been done.

Chapter 9

1And he called the twelve together, and gave them power and authority over all demons, and to cure diseases.

2And he sent them forth to preach the kingdom of God, and to heal the sick.

3And he said unto them, Take nothing for your journey, neither staff, nor wallet, nor bread, nor money; neither have two coats.

4And into whatsoever house ye enter, there abide, and thence depart.

5And as many as receive you not, when ye depart from that city, shake off the dust from your feet for a testimony against them.

6And they departed, and went throughout the villages, preaching the gospel, and healing everywhere.

7Now Herod the tetrarch heard of all that was done: and he was much perplexed, because that it was said by some, that John was risen from the dead;

8and by some, that Elijah had appeared; and by others, that one of the old prophets was risen again.

9And Herod said, John I beheaded: but who is this, about whom I hear such things? And he sought to see him.

10And the apostles, when they were returned, declared unto him what things they had done. And he took them, and withdrew apart to a city called Bethsaida.

11But the multitudes perceiving it followed him: and he welcomed them, and spake to them of the kingdom of God, and them that had need of healing he cured.

12And the day began to wear away; and the twelve came, and said unto him, Send the multitude away, that they may go into the villages and country round about, and lodge, and get provisions: for we are here in a desert place.

13But he said unto them, Give ye them to eat. And they said, We have no more than five loaves and two fishes; except we should go and buy food for all this people.

14For they were about five thousand men. And he said unto his disciples, Make them sit down in companies, about fifty each.

15And they did so, and made them all sit down.

16And he took the five loaves and the two fishes, and looking up to heaven, he blessed them, and brake; and gave to the disciples to set before the multitude.

17And they ate, and were all filled: and there was taken up that which remained over to them of broken pieces, twelve baskets.

18And it came to pass, as he was praying apart, the disciples were with him: and he asked them, saying, Who do the multitudes say that I am?

19And they answering said, John the Baptist; but others say, Elijah; and others, that one of the old prophets is risen again.

20And he said unto them, But who say ye that I am? And Peter answering said, The Christ of God.

21But he charged them, and commanded them to tell this to no man;

22saying, The Son of man must suffer many things, and be rejected of the elders and chief priests and scribes, and be killed, and the third day be raised up.

23And he said unto all, If any man would come after me, let him deny himself, and take up his cross daily, and follow me.

24For whosoever would save his life shall lose it; but whosoever shall lose his life for my sake, the same shall save it.

25For what is a man profited, if he gain the whole world, and lose or forfeit his own self?

26For whosoever shall be ashamed of me and of my words, of him shall the Son of man be ashamed, when he cometh in his own glory, and the glory of the Father, and of the holy angels.

27But I tell you of a truth, There are some of them that stand here, who shall in no wise taste of death, till they see the kingdom of God.

28And it came to pass about eight days after these sayings, that he took with him Peter and John and James, and went up into the mountain to pray.

29And as he was praying, the fashion of his countenance was altered, and his raiment became white and dazzling.

30And behold, there talked with him two men, who were Moses and Elijah;

31who appeared in glory, and spake of his decease which he was about to accomplish at Jerusalem.

32Now Peter and they that were with him were heavy with sleep: but when they were fully awake, they saw his glory, and the two men that stood with him.

33And it came to pass, as they were parting from him, Peter said unto Jesus, Master, it is good for us to be here: and let us make three tabernacles; one for thee, and one for Moses, and one for Elijah: not knowing what he said.

34And while he said these things, there came a cloud, and overshadowed them: and they feared as they entered into the cloud.

35And a voice came out of the cloud, saying, This is my Son, my chosen: hear ye him.

36And when the voice came, Jesus was found alone. And they held their peace, and told no man in those days any of the things which they had seen.

37And it came to pass, on the next day, when they were come down from the mountain, a great multitude met him.

38And behold, a man from the multitude cried, saying, Teacher, I beseech thee to look upon my son; for he is mine only child:

39and behold, a spirit taketh him, and he suddenly crieth out; and it teareth him that he foameth, and it hardly departeth from him, bruising him sorely.

40And I besought thy disciples to cast it out; and they could not.

41And Jesus answered and said, O faithless and perverse generation, how long shall I be with you, and bear with you? bring hither thy son.

42And as he was yet a coming, the demon dashed him down, and tare him grievously. But Jesus rebuked the unclean spirit, and healed the boy, and gave him back to his father.

43And they were all astonished at the majesty of God. But while all were marvelling at all the things which he did, he said unto his disciples,

44Let these words sink into your ears: for the Son of man shall be delivered up into the hands of men.

45But they understood not this saying, and it was concealed from them, that they should not perceive it; and they were afraid to ask him about this saying.

46And there arose a reasoning among them, which of them was the greatest.

47But when Jesus saw the reasoning of their heart, he took a little child, and set him by his side,

48and said unto them, Whosoever shall receive this little child in my name receiveth me: and whosoever shall receive me receiveth him that sent me: for he that is least among you all, the same is great.

49And John answered and said, Master, we saw one casting out demons in thy name; and we forbade him, because he followeth not with us.

50But Jesus said unto him, Forbid him not: for he that is not against you is for you.

51And it came to pass, when the days were well-nigh come that he should be received up, he stedfastly set his face to go to Jerusalem,

52and sent messengers before his face: and they went, and entered into a village of the Samaritans, to make ready for him.

53And they did not receive him, because his face was as though he were going to Jerusalem.

54And when his disciples James and John saw this, they said, Lord, wilt thou that we bid fire to come down from heaven, and consume them?

55But he turned, and rebuked them.

56And they went to another village.

57And as they went on the way, a certain man said unto him, I will follow thee whithersoever thou goest.

58And Jesus said unto him, The foxes have holes, and the birds of the heaven have nests; but the Son of man hath not where to lay his head.

59And he said unto another, Follow me. But he said, Lord, suffer me first to go and bury my father.

60But he said unto him, Leave the dead to bury their own dead; but go thou and publish abroad the kingdom of God.

61And another also said, I will follow thee, Lord; but first suffer me to bid farewell to them that are at my house.

62But Jesus said unto him, No man, having put his hand to the plow, and looking back, is fit for the kingdom of God.

Chapter 10

1Now after these things the Lord appointed seventy others, and sent them two and two before his face into every city and place, whither he himself was about to come.

2And he said unto them, The harvest indeed is plenteous, but the laborers are few: pray ye therefore the Lord of the harvest, that he send forth laborers into his harvest.

3Go your ways; behold, I send you forth as lambs in the midst of wolves.

4Carry no purse, no wallet, no shoes; and salute no man on the way.

5And into whatsoever house ye shall enter, first say, Peace be to this house.

6And if a son of peace be there, your peace shall rest upon him: but if not, it shall turn to you again.

7And in that same house remain, eating and drinking such things as they give: for the laborer is worthy of his hire. Go not from house to house.

8And into whatsoever city ye enter, and they receive you, eat such things as are set before you:

9and heal the sick that are therein, and say unto them, The kingdom of God is come nigh unto you.

10But into whatsoever city ye shall enter, and they receive you not, go out into the streets thereof and say,

11Even the dust from your city, that cleaveth to our feet, we wipe off against you: nevertheless know this, that the kingdom of God is come nigh.

12I say unto you, it shall be more tolerable in that day for Sodom, than for that city.

13Woe unto thee, Chorazin! woe unto thee, Bethsaida! for if the mighty works had been done in Tyre and Sidon, which were done in you, they would have repented long ago, sitting in sackcloth and ashes.

14But it shall be more tolerable for Tyre and Sidon in the judgment, than for you.

15And thou, Capernaum, shalt thou be exalted unto heaven? thou shalt be brought down unto Hades.

16He that heareth you heareth me; and he that rejecteth you rejecteth me; and he that rejecteth me rejecteth him that sent me.

17And the seventy returned with joy, saying, Lord, even the demons are subject unto us in thy name.

18And he said unto them, I beheld Satan fallen as lightning from heaven.

19Behold, I have given you authority to tread upon serpents and scorpions, and over all the power of the enemy: and nothing shall in any wise hurt you.

20Nevertheless in this rejoice not, that the spirits are subject unto you; but rejoice that your names are written in heaven.

21In that same hour he rejoiced in the Holy Spirit, and said, I thank thee, O Father, Lord of heaven and earth, that thou didst hide these things from the wise and understanding, and didst reveal them unto babes: yea, Father; for so it was well-pleasing in thy sight.

22All things have been delivered unto me of my Father: and no one knoweth who the Son is, save the Father; and who the Father is, save the Son, and he to whomsoever the Son willeth to reveal him.

23And turning to the disciples, he said privately, Blessed are the eyes which see the things that ye see:

24for I say unto you, that many prophets and kings desired to see the things which ye see, and saw them not; and to hear the things which ye hear, and heard them not.

25And behold, a certain lawyer stood up and made trial of him, saying, Teacher, what shall I do to inherit eternal life?

26And he said unto him, What is written in the law? how readest thou?

27And he answering said, Thou shalt love the Lord thy God with all thy heart, and with all thy soul, and with all thy strength, and with all thy mind; and thy neighbor as thyself.

28And he said unto him, Thou hast answered right: this do, and thou shalt live.

29But he, desiring to justify himself, said unto Jesus, And who is my neighbor?

Luke

30Jesus made answer and said, A certain man was going down from Jerusalem to Jericho; and he fell among robbers, who both stripped him and beat him, and departed, leaving him half dead.

31And by chance a certain priest was going down that way: and when he saw him, he passed by on the other side.

32And in like manner a Levite also, when he came to the place, and saw him, passed by on the other side.

33But a certain Samaritan, as he journeyed, came where he was: and when he saw him, he was moved with compassion,

34and came to him, and bound up his wounds, pouring on them oil and wine; and he set him on his own beast, and brought him to an inn, and took care of him.

35And on the morrow he took out two shillings, and gave them to the host, and said, Take care of him; and whatsoever thou spendest more, I, when I come back again, will repay thee.

36Which of these three, thinkest thou, proved neighbor unto him that fell among the robbers?

37And he said, He that showed mercy on him. And Jesus said unto him, Go, and do thou likewise.

38Now as they went on their way, he entered into a certain village: and a certain woman named Martha received him into her house.

39And she had a sister called Mary, who also sat at the Lord's feet, and heard his word.

40But Martha was cumbered about much serving; and she came up to him, and said, Lord, dost thou not care that my sister did leave me to serve alone? bid her therefore that she help me.

41But the Lord answered and said unto her, Martha, Martha, thou art anxious and troubled about many things:

42but one thing is needful: for Mary hath chosen the good part, which shall not be taken away from her.

Chapter 11

1And it came to pass, as he was praying in a certain place, that when he ceased, one of his disciples said unto him, Lord, teach us to pray, even as John also taught his disciples.

2And he said unto them, When ye pray, say, Father, Hallowed be thy name. Thy kingdom come.

3Give us day by day our daily bread.

4And forgive us our sins; for we ourselves also forgive every one that is indebted to us. And bring us not into temptation.

5And he said unto them, Which of you shall have a friend, and shall go unto him at midnight, and say to him, Friend, lend me three loaves;

6for a friend of mine is come to me from a journey, and I have nothing to set before him;

7and he from within shall answer and say, Trouble me not: the door is now shut, and my children are with me in bed; I cannot rise and give thee?

8I say unto you, Though he will not rise and give him because he is his friend, yet because of his importunity he will arise and give him as many as he needeth.

9And I say unto you, Ask, and it shall be given you; seek, and ye shall find; knock, and it shall be opened unto you.

10For every one that asketh receiveth; and he that seeketh findeth; and to him that knocketh it shall be opened.

11And of which of you that is a father shall his son ask a loaf, and he give him a stone? or a fish, and he for a fish give him a serpent?

12Or if he shall ask an egg, will he give him a scorpion?

13If ye then, being evil, know how to give good gifts unto your children, how much more shall your heavenly Father give the Holy Spirit to them that ask him?

14And he was casting out a demon that was dumb. And it came to pass, when the demon was gone out, the dumb man spake; and the multitudes marvelled.

15But some of them said, By Beelzebub the prince of the demons casteth he out demons.

16And others, trying him, sought of him a sign from heaven.

17But he, knowing their thoughts, said unto them, Every kingdom divided against itself is brought to desolation; and a house divided against a house falleth.

18And if Satan also is divided against himself, how shall his kingdom stand? because ye say that I cast out demons by Beelzebub.

19And if I by Beelzebub cast out demons, by whom do your sons cast them out? therefore shall they be your judges.

20But if I by the finger of God cast out demons, then is the kingdom of God come upon you.

21When the strong man fully armed guardeth his own court, his goods are in peace:

22but when a stronger than he shall come upon him, and overcome him, he taketh from him his whole armor wherein he trusted, and divideth his spoils.

23He that is not with me is against me; and he that gathereth not with me scattereth.

24The unclean spirit when he is gone out of the man, passeth through waterless places, seeking rest, and finding none, he saith, I will turn back unto my house whence I came out.

25And when he is come, he findeth it swept and garnished.

26Then goeth he, and taketh to him seven other spirits more evil than himself; and they enter in and dwell there: and the last state of that man becometh worse than the first.

27And it came to pass, as he said these things, a certain woman out of the multitude lifted up her voice, and said unto him, Blessed is the womb that bare thee, and the breasts which thou didst suck.

28But he said, Yea rather, blessed are they that hear the word of God, and keep it.

29And when the multitudes were gathering together unto him, he began to say, This generation is an evil generation: it seeketh after a sign; and there shall no sign be given to it but the sign of Jonah.

30For even as Jonah became a sign unto the Ninevites, so shall also the Son of man be to this generation.

31The queen of the south shall rise up in the judgment with the men of this generation, and shall condemn them: for she came from the ends of the earth to hear the wisdom of Solomon; and behold, a greater than Solomon is here.

32The men of Nineveh shall stand up in the judgment with this generation, and shall condemn it: for they repented at the preaching of Jonah; and behold, a greater than Jonah is here.

33No man, when he hath lighted a lamp, putteth it in a cellar, neither under the bushel, but on the stand, that they which enter in may see the light.

34The lamp of thy body is thine eye: when thine eye is single, thy whole body also is full of light; but when it is evil, thy body also is full of darkness.

35Look therefore whether the light that is in thee be not darkness.

36If therefore thy whole body be full of light, having no part dark, it shall be wholly full of light, as when the lamp with its bright shining doth give thee light.

37Now as he spake, a Pharisee asketh him to dine with him: and he went in, and sat down to meat.

38And when the Pharisee saw it, he marvelled that he had not first bathed himself before dinner.

39And the Lord said unto him, Now ye the Pharisees cleanse the outside of the cup and of the platter; but your inward part is full of extortion and wickedness.

40Ye foolish ones, did not he that made the outside make the inside also?

41But give for alms those things which are within; and behold, all things are clean unto you.

42But woe unto you Pharisees! for ye tithe mint and rue and every herb, and pass over justice and the love of God: but these ought ye to have done, and not to leave the other undone.

43Woe unto you Pharisees! for ye love the chief seats in the synagogues, and the salutations in the marketplaces.

44Woe unto you! for ye are as the tombs which appear not, and the men that walk over them know it not.

45And one of the lawyers answering saith unto him, Teacher, in saying this thou reproachest us also.

46And he said, Woe unto you lawyers also! for ye load men with burdens grievous to be borne, and ye yourselves touch not the burdens with one of your fingers.

47Woe unto you! for ye build the tombs of the prophets, and your fathers killed them.

48So ye are witnesses and consent unto the works of your fathers: for they killed them, and ye build their tombs.

49Therefore also said the wisdom of God, I will send unto them prophets and apostles; and some of them they shall kill and persecute;

50that the blood of all the prophets, which was shed from the foundation of the world, may be required of this generation;

51from the blood of Abel unto the blood of Zachariah, who perished between the altar and the sanctuary: yea, I say unto you, it shall be required of this generation.

52Woe unto you lawyers! for ye took away the key of knowledge: ye entered not in yourselves, and them that were entering in ye hindered.

53And when he was come out from thence, the scribes and the Pharisees began to press upon him vehemently, and to provoke him to speak of many things;

54laying wait for him, to catch something out of his mouth.

Chapter 12

1In the mean time, when the many thousands of the multitude were gathered together, insomuch that they trod one upon another, he began to say unto his disciples first of all, Beware ye of the leaven of the Pharisees, which is hypocrisy.

2But there is nothing covered up, that shall not be revealed; and hid, that shall not be known.

3Wherefore whatsoever ye have said in the darkness shall be heard in the light; and what ye have spoken in the ear in the inner chambers shall be proclaimed upon the housetops.

4And I say unto you my friends, Be not afraid of them that kill the body, and after that have no more that they can do.

5But I will warn you whom ye shall fear: Fear him, who after he hath killed hath power to cast into hell; yea, I say unto you, Fear him.

6Are not five sparrows sold for two pence? and not one of them is forgotten in the sight of God.

7But the very hairs of your head are all numbered. Fear not: ye are of more value than many sparrows.

8And I say unto you, Every one who shall confess me before men, him shall the Son of man also confess before the angels of God:

9but he that denieth me in the presence of men shall be denied in the presence of the angels of God.

10And every one who shall speak a word against the Son of man, it shall be forgiven him: but unto him that blasphemeth against the Holy Spirit it shall not be forgiven.

11And when they bring you before the synagogues, and the rulers, and the authorities, be not anxious how or what ye shall answer, or what ye shall say:

12for the Holy Spirit shall teach you in that very hour what ye ought to say.

13And one out of the multitude said unto him, Teacher, bid my brother divide the inheritance with me.

14But he said unto him, Man, who made me a judge or a divider over you?

15And he said unto them, Take heed, and keep yourselves from all covetousness: for a man's life consisteth not in the abundance of the things which he possesseth.

16And he spake a parable unto them, saying, The ground of a certain rich man brought forth plentifully:

17and he reasoned within himself, saying, What shall I do, because I have not where to bestow my fruits?

18And he said, This will I do: I will pull down my barns, and build greater; and there will I bestow all my grain and my goods.

19And I will say to my soul, Soul, thou hast much goods laid up for many years; take thine ease, eat, drink, be merry.

20But God said unto him, Thou foolish one, this night is thy soul required of thee; and the things which thou hast prepared, whose shall they be?

21So is he that layeth up treasure for himself, and is not rich toward God.

22And he said unto his disciples, Therefore I say unto you, Be not anxious for your life, what ye shall eat; nor yet for your body, what ye shall put on.

23For the life is more than the food, and the body than the raiment.

24Consider the ravens, that they sow not, neither reap; which have no store-chamber nor barn; and God feedeth them: of how much more value are ye than the birds!

25And which of you by being anxious can add a cubit unto the measure of his life?

26If then ye are not able to do even that which is least, why are ye anxious concerning the rest?

27Consider the lilies, how they grow: they toil not, neither do they spin; yet I say unto you, Even Solomon in all his glory was not arrayed like one of these.

28But if God doth so clothe the grass in the field, which to-day is, and to-morrow is cast into the oven; how much more shall he clothe you, O ye of little faith?

29And seek not ye what ye shall eat, and what ye shall drink, neither be ye of doubtful mind.

30For all these things do the nations of the world seek after: but your Father knoweth that ye have need of these things.

31Yet seek ye his kingdom, and these things shall be added unto you.

32Fear not, little flock; for it is your Father's good pleasure to give you the kingdom.

33Sell that which ye have, and give alms; make for yourselves purses which wax not old, a treasure in the heavens that faileth not, where no thief draweth near, neither moth destroyeth.

34For where your treasure is, there will your heart be also.

35Let your loins be girded about, and your lamps burning;

36and be ye yourselves like unto men looking for their lord, when he shall return from the marriage feast; that, when he cometh and knocketh, they may straightway open unto him.

37Blessed are those servants, whom the lord when he cometh shall find watching: verily I say unto you, that he shall gird himself, and make them sit down to meat, and shall come and serve them.

38And if he shall come in the second watch, and if in the third, and find them so blessed are those servants.

39But know this, that if the master of the house had known in what hour the thief was coming, he would have watched, and not have left his house to be broken through.

40Be ye also ready: for in an hour that ye think not the Son of man cometh.

41And Peter said, Lord, speakest thou this parable unto us, or even unto all?

42And the Lord said, Who then is the faithful and wise steward, whom his lord shall set over his household, to give them their portion of food in due season?

43Blessed is that servant, whom his lord when he cometh shall find so doing.

44Of a truth I say unto you, that he will set him over all that he hath.

45But if that servant shall say in his heart, My lord delayeth his coming; and shall begin to beat the menservants and the maidservants, and to eat and drink, and to be drunken;

46the lord of that servant shall come in a day when he expecteth not, and in an hour when he knoweth not, and shall cut him asunder, and appoint his portion with the unfaithful.

47And that servant, who knew his lord's will, and made not ready, nor did according to his will, shall be beaten with many stripes;

48but he that knew not, and did things worthy of stripes, shall be beaten with few stripes. And to whomsoever much is given, of him shall much be required: and to whom they commit much, of him will they ask the more.

49I came to cast fire upon the earth; and what do I desire, if it is already kindled?

50But I have a baptism to be baptized with; and how am I straitened till it be accomplished!

51Think ye that I am come to give peace in the earth? I tell you, Nay; but rather division:

52for there shall be from henceforth five in one house divided, three against two, and two against three.

53They shall be divided, father against son, and son against father; mother against daughter, and daughter against her mother; mother in law against her daughter in law, and daughter in law against her mother in law.

54And he said to the multitudes also, When ye see a cloud rising in the west, straightway ye say, There cometh a shower; and so it cometh to pass.

55And when ye see a south wind blowing, ye say, There will be a scorching heat; and it cometh to pass.

56Ye hypocrites, ye know how to interpret the face of the earth and the heaven; but how is it that ye know not how to interpret this time?

57And why even of yourselves judge ye not what is right?

58For as thou art going with thine adversary before the magistrate, on the way give diligence to be quit of him; lest haply he drag thee unto the judge, and the judge shall deliver thee to the officer, and the officer shall cast thee into prison.

59I say unto thee, Thou shalt by no means come out thence, till thou have paid the very last mite.

Chapter 13

1Now there were some present at that very season who told him of the Galilaeans, whose blood Pilate had mingled with their sacrifices.

2And he answered and said unto them, Think ye that these Galilaeans were sinners above all the Galilaeans, because they have suffered these things?

3I tell you, Nay: but, except ye repent, ye shall all in like manner perish.

4Or those eighteen, upon whom the tower in Siloam fell, and killed them, think ye that they were offenders above all the men that dwell in Jerusalem?

5I tell you, Nay: but, except ye repent, ye shall all likewise perish.

6And he spake this parable; A certain man had a fig tree planted in his vineyard; and he came seeking fruit thereon, and found none.

7And he said unto the vinedresser, Behold, these three years I come seeking fruit on this fig tree, and find none: cut it down; why doth it also cumber the ground?

8And he answering saith unto him, Lord, let it alone this year also, till I shall dig about it, and dung it:

9and if it bear fruit thenceforth, well; but if not, thou shalt cut it down.

10And he was teaching in one of the synagogues on the sabbath day.

11And behold, a woman that had a spirit of infirmity eighteen years; and she was bowed together, and could in no wise lift herself up.

12And when Jesus saw her, he called her, and said to her, Woman, thou art loosed from thine infirmity.

13And he laid his hands upon her: and immediately she was made straight, and glorified God.

14And the ruler of the synagogue, being moved with indignation because Jesus had healed on the sabbath, answered and said to the multitude, There are six days in which men ought to work: in them therefore come and be healed, and not on the day of the sabbath.

15But the Lord answered him, and said, Ye hypocrites, doth not each one of you on the sabbath loose his ox or his ass from the stall, and lead him away to watering?

16And ought not this woman, being a daughter of Abraham, whom Satan had bound, lo, these eighteen years, to have been loosed from this bond on the day of the sabbath?

17And as he said these things, all his adversaries were put to shame: and all the multitude rejoiced for all the glorious things that were done by him.

18He said therefore, Unto what is the kingdom of God like? and whereunto shall I liken it?

19It is like unto a grain of mustard seed, which a man took, and cast into his own garden; and it grew, and became a tree; and the birds of the heaven lodged in the branches thereof.

20And again he said, Whereunto shall I liken the kingdom of God?

21It is like unto leaven, which a woman took and hid in three measures of meal, till it was all leavened.

22And he went on his way through cities and villages, teaching, and journeying on unto Jerusalem.

23And one said unto him, Lord, are they few that are saved? And he said unto them,

24Strive to enter in by the narrow door: for many, I say unto you, shall seek to enter in, and shall not be able.

25When once the master of the house is risen up, and hath shut to the door, and ye begin to stand without, and to knock at the door, saying, Lord, open to us; and he shall answer and say to you, I know you not whence ye are;

26then shall ye begin to say, We did eat and drink in thy presence, and thou didst teach in our streets;

27and he shall say, I tell you, I know not whence ye are; depart from me, all ye workers of iniquity.

28There shall be the weeping and the gnashing of teeth, when ye shall see Abraham, and Isaac, and Jacob, and all the prophets, in the kingdom of God, and yourselves cast forth without.

29And they shall come from the east and west, and from the north and south, and shall sit down in the kingdom of God.

30And behold, there are last who shall be first, and there are first who shall be last.

31In that very hour there came certain Pharisees, saying to him, Get thee out, and go hence: for Herod would fain kill thee.

32And he said unto them, Go and say to that fox, Behold, I cast out demons and perform cures to-day and to-morrow, and the third day I am perfected.

33Nevertheless I must go on my way to-day and to-morrow and the day following: for it cannot be that a prophet perish out of Jerusalem.

34O Jerusalem, Jerusalem, that killeth the prophets, and stoneth them that are sent unto her! how often would I have gathered thy children together, even as a hen gathereth her own brood under her wings, and ye would not!

35Behold, your house is left unto you desolate: and I say unto you, Ye shall not see me, until ye shall say, Blessed is he that cometh in the name of the Lord.

Chapter 14

1And it came to pass, when he went into the house of one of the rulers of the Pharisees on a sabbath to eat bread, that they were watching him.

2And behold, there was before him a certain man that had the dropsy.

3And Jesus answering spake unto the lawyers and Pharisees, saying, Is it lawful to heal on the sabbath, or not?

4But they held their peace. And he took him, and healed him, and let him go.

Luke

5And he said unto them, Which of you shall have an ass or an ox fallen into a well, and will not straightway draw him up on a sabbath day?

6And they could not answer again unto these things.

7And he spake a parable unto those that were bidden, when he marked how they chose out the chief seats; saying unto them,

8When thou art bidden of any man to a marriage feast, sit not down in the chief seat; lest haply a more honorable man than thou be bidden of him;

9and he that bade thee and him shall come and say to thee, Give this man place; and then thou shalt begin with shame to take the lowest place.

10But when thou art bidden, go and sit down in the lowest place; that when he that hath bidden thee cometh, he may say to thee, Friend, go up higher: then shalt thou have glory in the presence of all that sit at meat with thee.

11For everyone that exalteth himself shall be humbled; and he that humbleth himself shall be exalted.

12And he said to him also that had bidden him, When thou makest a dinner or a supper, call not thy friends, nor thy brethren, nor thy kinsmen, nor rich neighbors; lest haply they also bid thee again, and a recompense be made thee.

13But when thou makest a feast, bid the poor, the maimed, the lame, the blind:

14and thou shalt be blessed; because they have not wherewith to recompense thee: for thou shalt be recompensed in the resurrection of the just.

15And when one of them that sat at meat with him heard these things, he said unto him, Blessed is he that shall eat bread in the kingdom of God.

16But he said unto him, A certain man made a great supper; and he bade many:

17and he sent forth his servant at supper time to say to them that were bidden, Come; for all things are now ready.

18And they all with one consent began to make excuse. The first said unto him, I have bought a field, and I must needs go out and see it; I pray thee have me excused.

19And another said, I have bought five yoke of oxen, and I go to prove them; I pray thee have me excused.

20And another said, I have married a wife, and therefore I cannot come.

21And the servant came, and told his lord these things. Then the master of the house being angry said to his servant, Go out quickly into the streets and lanes of the city, and bring in hither the poor and maimed and blind and lame.

22And the servant said, Lord, what thou didst command is done, and yet there is room.

23And the lord said unto the servant, Go out into the highways and hedges, and constrain them to come in, that my house may be filled.

24For I say unto you, that none of those men that were bidden shall taste of my supper.

25Now there went with him great multitudes: and he turned, and said unto them,

26If any man cometh unto me, and hateth not his own father, and mother, and wife, and children, and brethren, and sisters, yea, and his own life also, he cannot be my disciple.

27Whosoever doth not bear his own cross, and come after me, cannot be my disciple.

28For which of you, desiring to build a tower, doth not first sit down and count the cost, whether he have wherewith to complete it?

29Lest haply, when he hath laid a foundation, and is not able to finish, all that behold begin to mock him,

30saying, This man began to build, and was not able to finish.

31Or what king, as he goeth to encounter another king in war, will not sit down first and take counsel whether he is able with ten thousand to meet him that cometh against him with twenty thousand?

32Or else, while the other is yet a great way off, he sendeth an ambassage, and asketh conditions of peace.

33So therefore whosoever he be of you that renounceth not all that he hath, he cannot be my disciple.

34Salt therefore is good: but if even the salt have lost its savor, wherewith shall it be seasoned?

35It is fit neither for the land nor for the dunghill: men cast it out. He that hath ears to hear, let him hear.

Chapter 15

1Now all the publicans and sinners were drawing near unto him to hear him.

2And both the Pharisees and the scribes murmured, saying, This man receiveth sinners, and eateth with them.

3And he spake unto them this parable, saying,

4What man of you, having a hundred sheep, and having lost one of them, doth not leave the ninety and nine in the wilderness, and go after that which is lost, until he find it?

5And when he hath found it, he layeth it on his shoulders, rejoicing.

6And when he cometh home, he calleth together his friends and his neighbors, saying unto them, Rejoice with me, for I have found my sheep which was lost.

7I say unto you, that even so there shall be joy in heaven over one sinner that repenteth, more than over ninety and nine righteous persons, who need no repentance.

8Or what woman having ten pieces of silver, if she lose one piece, doth not light a lamp, and sweep the house, and seek diligently until she find it?

9And when she hath found it, she calleth together her friends and neighbors, saying, Rejoice with me, for I have found the piece which I had lost.

10Even so, I say unto you, there is joy in the presence of the angels of God over one sinner that repenteth.

11And he said, A certain man had two sons:

12and the younger of them said to his father, Father, give me the portion of thy substance that falleth to me. And he divided unto them his living.

13And not many days after, the younger son gathered all together and took his journey into a far country; and there he wasted his substance with riotous living.

14And when he had spent all, there arose a mighty famine in that country; and he began to be in want.

15And he went and joined himself to one of the citizens of that country; and he sent him into his fields to feed swine.

16And he would fain have filled his belly with the husks that the swine did eat: and no man gave unto him.

17But when he came to himself he said, How many hired servants of my father's have bread enough and to spare, and I perish here with hunger!

18I will arise and go to my father, and will say unto him, Father, I have sinned against heaven, and in thy sight:

19I am no more worthy to be called your son: make me as one of thy hired servants.

20And he arose, and came to his father. But while he was yet afar off, his father saw him, and was moved with compassion, and ran, and fell on his neck, and kissed him.

21And the son said unto him, Father, I have sinned against heaven, and in thy sight: I am no more worthy to be called thy son.

22But the father said to his servants, Bring forth quickly the best robe, and put it on him; and put a ring on his hand, and shoes on his feet:

23and bring the fatted calf, and kill it, and let us eat, and make merry:

24for this my son was dead, and is alive again; he was lost, and is found. And they began to be merry.

25Now his elder son was in the field: and as he came and drew nigh to the house, he heard music and dancing.

26And he called to him one of the servants, and inquired what these things might be.

27And he said unto him, Thy brother is come; and thy father hath killed the fatted calf, because he hath received him safe and sound.

28But he was angry, and would not go in: and his father came out, and entreated him.

29But he answered and said to his father, Lo, these many years do I serve thee, and I never transgressed a commandment of thine; and yet thou never gavest me a kid, that I might make merry with my friends:

30but when this thy son came, who hath devoured thy living with harlots, thou killedst for him the fatted calf.

31And he said unto him, Son, thou art ever with me, and all that is mine is thine.

32But it was meet to make merry and be glad: for this thy brother was dead, and is alive again; and was lost, and is found.

Chapter 16

1And he said also unto the disciples, There was a certain rich man, who had a steward; and the same was accused unto him that he was wasting his goods.

2And he called him, and said unto him, What is this that I hear of thee? render the account of thy stewardship; for thou canst be no longer steward.

3And the steward said within himself, What shall I do, seeing that my lord taketh away the stewardship from me? I have not strength to dig; to beg I am ashamed.

4I am resolved what to do, that, when I am put out of the stewardship, they may receive me into their houses.

5And calling to him each one of his lord's debtors, he said to the first, How much owest thou unto my lord?

6And he said, A hundred measures of oil. And he said unto him, Take thy bond, and sit down quickly and write fifty.

7Then said he to another, And how much owest thou? And he said, A hundred measures of wheat. He saith unto him, Take thy bond, and write fourscore.

8And his lord commended the unrighteous steward because he had done wisely: for the sons of this world are for their own generation wiser than the sons of the light.

9And I say unto you, Make to yourselves friends by means of the mammon of unrighteousness; that, when it shall fail, they may receive you into the eternal tabernacles.

10He that is faithful in a very little is faithful also in much: and he that is unrighteous in a very little is unrighteous also in much.

11If therefore ye have not been faithful in the unrighteous mammon, who will commit to your trust the true riches?

12And if ye have not been faithful in that which is another's, who will give you that which is your own?

13No servant can serve two masters: for either he will hate the one, and love the other; or else he will hold to one, and despise the other. Ye cannot serve God and mammon.

14And the Pharisees, who were lovers of money, heard all these things; and they scoffed at him.

15And he said unto them, Ye are they that justify yourselves in the sight of men; but God knoweth your hearts: for that which is exalted among men is an abomination in the sight of God.

16The law and the prophets were until John: from that time the gospel of the kingdom of God is preached, and every man entereth violently into it.

17But it is easier for heaven and earth to pass away, than for one tittle of the law to fall.

18Every one that putteth away his wife, and marrieth another, committeth adultery: and he that marrieth one that is put away from a husband committeth adultery.

19Now there was a certain rich man, and he was clothed in purple and fine linen, faring sumptuously every day:

20and a certain beggar named Lazarus was laid at his gate, full of sores,

21and desiring to be fed with the crumbs that fell from the rich man's table; yea, even the dogs come and licked his sores.

22And it came to pass, that the beggar died, and that he was carried away by the angels into Abraham's bosom: and the rich man also died, and was buried.

23And in Hades he lifted up his eyes, being in torments, and seeth Abraham afar off, and Lazarus in his bosom.

24And he cried and said, Father Abraham, have mercy on me, and send Lazarus, that he may dip the tip of his finger in water, and cool my tongue; for I am in anguish in this flame.

25But Abraham said, Son, remember that thou in thy lifetime receivedst thy good things, and Lazarus in like manner evil things: but now here he is comforted and thou art in anguish.

26And besides all this, between us and you there is a great gulf fixed, that they that would pass from hence to you may not be able, and that none may cross over from thence to us.

27And he said, I pray thee therefore, father, that thou wouldest send him to my father's house;

28for I have five brethren; that he may testify unto them, lest they also come into this place of torment.

29But Abraham saith, They have Moses and the prophets; let them hear them.

30And he said, Nay, father Abraham: but if one go to them from the dead, they will repent.

31And he said unto him, If they hear not Moses and the prophets, neither will they be persuaded, if one rise from the dead.

Chapter 17

1And he said unto his disciples, It is impossible but that occasions of stumbling should come; but woe unto him, through whom they come!

2It were well for him if a millstone were hanged about his neck, and he were thrown into the sea, rather than that he should cause one of these little ones to stumble.

3Take heed to yourselves: if thy brother sin, rebuke him; and if he repent, forgive him.

4And if he sin against thee seven times in the day, and seven times turn again to thee, saying, I repent; thou shalt forgive him.

5And the apostles said unto the Lord, Increase our faith.

6And the Lord said, If ye had faith as a grain of mustard seed, ye would say unto this sycamine tree, Be thou rooted up, and be thou planted in the sea; and it would obey you.

7But who is there of you, having a servant plowing or keeping sheep, that will say unto him, when he is come in from the field, Come straightway and sit down to meat;

8and will not rather say unto him, Make ready wherewith I may sup, and gird thyself, and serve me, till I have eaten and drunken; and afterward thou shalt eat and drink?

9Doth he thank the servant because he did the things that were commanded?

10Even so ye also, when ye shall have done all the things that are commanded you, say, We are unprofitable servants; we have done that which it was our duty to do.

11And it came to pass, as they were on their way to Jerusalem, that he was passing along the borders of Samaria and Galilee.

12And as he entered into a certain village, there met him ten men that were lepers, who stood afar off:

13and they lifted up their voices, saying, Jesus, Master, have mercy on us.

14And when he saw them, he said unto them, Go and show yourselves unto the priests. And it came to pass, as they went, they were cleansed.

15And one of them, when he saw that he was healed, turned back, with a loud voice glorifying God;

16and he fell upon his face at his feet, giving him thanks: and he was a Samaritan.

17And Jesus answering said, Were not the ten cleansed? but where are the nine?

18Were there none found that returned to give glory to God, save this stranger?

19And he said unto him, Arise, and go thy way: thy faith hath made thee whole.

20And being asked by the Pharisees, when the kingdom of God cometh, he answered them and said, The kingdom of God cometh not with observation:

21neither shall they say, Lo, here! or, There! for lo, the kingdom of God is within you.

22And he said unto the disciples, The days will come, when ye shall desire to see one of the days of the Son of man, and ye shall not see it.

23And they shall say to you, Lo, there! Lo, here! go not away, nor follow after them:

24for as the lightning, when it lighteneth out of the one part under the heaven, shineth unto the other part under heaven; so shall the Son of man be in his day.

25But first must he suffer many things and be rejected of this generation.

26And as it came to pass in the days of Noah, even so shall it be also in the days of the Son of man.

27They ate, they drank, they married, they were given in marriage, until the day that Noah entered into the ark, and the flood came, and destroyed them all.

28Likewise even as it came to pass in the days of Lot; they ate, they drank, they bought, they sold, they planted, they builded;

29but in the day that Lot went out from Sodom it rained fire and brimstone from heaven, and destroyed them all:

30after the same manner shall it be in the day that the Son of man is revealed.

31In that day, he that shall be on the housetop, and his goods in the house, let him not go down to take them away: and let him that is in the field likewise not return back.

32Remember Lot's wife.

33Whosoever shall seek to gain his life shall lose it: but whosoever shall lose his life shall preserve it.

34I say unto you, In that night there shall be two men on one bed; the one shall be taken, and the other shall be left.

35There shall be two women grinding together; the one shall be taken, and the other shall be left.

36There shall be two men in the field; the one shall be taken, and the other shall be left.

37And they answering say unto him, Where, Lord? And he said unto them, Where the body is, thither will the eagles also be gathered together.

Chapter 18

1And he spake a parable unto them to the end that they ought always to pray, and not to faint;

2saying, There was in a city a judge, who feared not God, and regarded not man:

3and there was a widow in that city; and she came oft unto him, saying, Avenge me of mine adversary.

4And he would not for a while: but afterward he said within himself, Though I fear not God, nor regard man;

5yet because this widow troubleth me, I will avenge her, lest she wear me out by her continual coming.

6And the Lord said, Hear what the unrighteous judge saith.

7And shall not God avenge his elect, that cry to him day and night, and yet he is longsuffering over them?

8I say unto you, that he will avenge them speedily. Nevertheless, when the Son of man cometh, shall he find faith on the earth?

9And he spake also this parable unto certain who trusted in themselves that they were righteous, and set all others at nought:

10Two men went up into the temple to pray; the one a Pharisee, and the other a publican.

11The Pharisee stood and prayed thus with himself, God, I thank thee, that I am not as the rest of men, extortioners, unjust, adulterers, or even as this publican.

12I fast twice in the week; I give tithes of all that I get.

13But the publican, standing afar off, would not lift up so much as his eyes unto heaven, but smote his breast, saying, God, be thou merciful to me a sinner.

14I say unto you, This man went down to his house justified rather than the other: for every one that exalteth himself shall be humbled; but he that humbleth himself shall be exalted.

15And they were bringing unto him also their babes, that he should touch them: but when the disciples saw it, they rebuked them.

16But Jesus called them unto him, saying, Suffer the little children to come unto me, and forbid them not: for to such belongeth the kingdom of God.

17Verily I say unto you, Whosoever shall not receive the kingdom of God as a little child, he shall in no wise enter therein.

18And a certain ruler asked him, saying, Good Teacher, what shall I do to inherit eternal life?

19And Jesus said unto him, Why callest thou me good? none is good, save one, even God.

20Thou knowest the commandments, Do not commit adultery, Do not kill, Do not steal, Do not bear false witness, Honor thy father and mother.

21And he said, All these things have I observed from my youth up.

22And when Jesus heard it, he said unto him, One thing thou lackest yet: sell all that thou hast, and distribute unto the poor, and thou shalt have treasure in heaven: and come, follow me.

23But when he heard these things, he became exceeding sorrowful; for he was very rich.

24And Jesus seeing him said, How hardly shall they that have riches enter into the kingdom of God!

25For it is easier for a camel to enter in through a needle's eye, than for a rich man to enter into the kingdom of God.

26And they that heard it said, Then who can be saved?

27But he said, The things which are impossible with men are possible with God.

28And Peter said, Lo, we have left our own, and followed thee.

29And he said unto them, Verily I say unto you, There is no man that hath left house, or wife, or brethren, or parents, or children, for the kingdom of God's sake,

30who shall not receive manifold more in this time, and in the world to come eternal life.

31And he took unto him the twelve, and said unto them, Behold, we go up to Jerusalem, and all the things that are written through the prophets shall be accomplished unto the Son of man.

32For he shall be delivered up unto the Gentiles, and shall be mocked, and shamefully treated, and spit upon:

33and they shall scourge and kill him: and the third day he shall rise again.

34And they understood none of these things; and this saying was hid from them, and they perceived not the things that were said.

35And it came to pass, as he drew nigh unto Jericho, a certain blind man sat by the way side begging:

36and hearing a multitude going by, he inquired what this meant.

37And they told him that Jesus of Nazareth passeth by.

38And he cried, saying, Jesus, thou son of David, have mercy on me.

Luke

39And they that went before rebuked him, that he should hold his peace: but he cried out the more a great deal, Thou son of David, have mercy on me.

40And Jesus stood, and commanded him to be brought unto him: and when he was come near, he asked him,

41What wilt thou that I should do unto thee? And he said, Lord, that I may receive my sight.

42And Jesus said unto him, Receive thy sight; thy faith hath made thee whole.

43And immediately he received his sight, and followed him, glorifying God: and all the people, when they saw it, gave praise unto God.

Chapter 19

1And he entered and was passing through Jericho.

2And behold, a man called by name Zacchaeus; and he was a chief publican, and he was rich.

3And he sought to see Jesus who he was; and could not for the crowd, because he was little of stature.

4And he ran on before, and climbed up into a sycomore tree to see him: for he was to pass that way.

5And when Jesus came to the place, he looked up, and said unto him, Zacchaeus, make haste, and come down; for to-day I must abide at thy house.

6And he made haste, and came down, and received him joyfully.

7And when they saw it, they all murmured, saying, He is gone in to lodge with a man that is a sinner.

8And Zacchaeus stood, and said unto the Lord, Behold, Lord, the half of my goods I give to the poor; and if I have wrongfully exacted aught of any man, I restore fourfold.

9And Jesus said unto him, To-day is salvation come to this house, forasmuch as he also is a son of Abraham.

10For the Son of man came to seek and to save that which was lost.

11And as they heard these things, he added and spake a parable, because he was nigh to Jerusalem, and because they supposed that the kingdom of God was immediately to appear.

12He said therefore, A certain nobleman went into a far country, to receive for himself a kingdom, and to return.

13And he called ten servants of his, and gave them ten pounds, and said unto them, Trade ye herewith till I come.

14But his citizens hated him, and sent an ambassage after him, saying, We will not that this man reign over us.

15And it came to pass, when he was come back again, having received the kingdom, that he commanded these servants, unto whom he had given the money, to be called to him, that he might know what they had gained by trading.

16And the first came before him, saying, Lord, thy pound hath made ten pounds more.

17And he said unto him, Well done, thou good servant: because thou wast found faithful in a very little, have thou authority over ten cities.

18And the second came, saying, Thy pound, Lord, hath made five pounds.

19And he said unto him also, Be thou also over five cities.

20And another came, saying, Lord, behold, here is thy pound, which I kept laid up in a napkin:

21for I feared thee, because thou art an austere man: thou takest up that which thou layedst not down, and reapest that which thou didst not sow.

22He saith unto him, Out of thine own mouth will I judge thee, thou wicked servant. Thou knewest that I am an austere man, taking up that which I laid not down, and reaping that which I did not sow;

23then wherefore gavest thou not my money into the bank, and I at my coming should have required it with interest?

24And he said unto them that stood by, Take away from him the pound, and give it unto him that hath the ten pounds.

25And they said unto him, Lord, he hath ten pounds.

26I say unto you, that unto every one that hath shall be given; but from him that hath not, even that which he hath shall be taken away from him.

27But these mine enemies, that would not that I should reign over them, bring hither, and slay them before me.

28And when he had thus spoken, he went on before, going up to Jerusalem.

29And it came to pass, when he drew nigh unto Bethphage and Bethany, at the mount that is called Olivet, he sent two of the disciples,

30saying, Go your way into the village over against you; in which ye enter ye shall find a colt tied, whereon no man ever yet sat: loose him, and bring him.

31And if any one ask you, Why do ye loose him? thus shall ye say, The Lord hath need of him.

32And they that were sent went away, and found even as he had said unto them.

33And as they were loosing the colt, the owners thereof said unto them, Why loose ye the colt?

34And they said, The Lord hath need of him.

35And they brought him to Jesus: and they threw their garments upon the colt, and set Jesus thereon.

36And as he went, they spread their garments in the way.

37And as he was now drawing nigh, even at the descent of the mount of Olives, the whole multitude of the disciples began to rejoice and praise God with a loud voice for all the mighty works which they had seen;

38saying, Blessed is the King that cometh in the name of the Lord: peace in heaven, and glory in the highest.

39And some of the Pharisees from the multitude said unto him, Teacher, rebuke thy disciples.

40And he answered and said, I tell you that, if these shall hold their peace, the stones will cry out.

41And when he drew nigh, he saw the city and wept over it,

42saying, If thou hadst known in this day, even thou, the things which belong unto peace! but now they are hid from thine eyes.

43For the days shall come upon thee, when thine enemies shall cast up a bank about thee, and compass thee round, and keep thee in on every side,

44and shall dash thee to the ground, and thy children within thee; and they shall not leave in thee one stone upon another; because thou knewest not the time of thy visitation.

45And he entered into the temple, and began to cast out them that sold,

46saying unto them, It is written, And my house shall be a house of prayer: but ye have made it a den of robbers.

47And he was teaching daily in the temple. But the chief priests and the scribes and the principal men of the people sought to destroy him:

48and they could not find what they might do; for the people all hung upon him, listening.

Chapter 20

1And it came to pass, on one of the days, as he was teaching the people in the temple, and preaching the gospel, there came upon him the chief priests and the scribes with the elders;

2and they spake, saying unto him, Tell us: By what authority doest thou these things? or who is he that gave thee this authority?

3And he answered and said unto them, I also will ask you a question; and tell me:

4The baptism of John, was it from heaven, or from men?

5And they reasoned with themselves, saying, If we shall say, From heaven; he will say, Why did ye not believe him?

6But if we shall say, From men; all the people will stone us: for they are persuaded that John was a prophet.

7And they answered, that they knew not whence it was.

8And Jesus said unto them, Neither tell I you by what authority I do these things.

9And he began to speak unto the people this parable: A man planted a vineyard, and let it out to husbandmen, and went into another country for a long time.

10And at the season he sent unto the husbandmen a servant, that they should give him of the fruit of the vineyard: but the husbandmen beat him, and sent him away empty.

11And he sent yet another servant: and him also they beat, and handled him shamefully, and sent him away empty.

12And he sent yet a third: and him also they wounded, and cast him forth.

13And the lord of the vineyard said, What shall I do? I will send my beloved son; it may be they will reverence him.

14But when the husbandmen saw him, they reasoned one with another, saying, This is the heir; let us kill him, that the inheritance may be ours.

15And they cast him forth out of the vineyard, and killed him. What therefore will the lord of the vineyard do unto them?

16He will come and destroy these husbandmen, and will give the vineyard unto others. And when they heard it, they said, God forbid.

17But he looked upon them, and said, What then is this that is written,
The stone which the builders rejected,
The same was made the head of the corner?

18Every one that falleth on that stone shall be broken to pieces; but on whomsoever it shall fall, it will scatter him as dust.

19And the scribes and the chief priests sought to lay hands on him in that very hour; and they feared the people: for they perceived that he spake this parable against them.

20And they watched him, and sent forth spies, who feigned themselves to be righteous, that they might take hold of his speech, so as to deliver him up to the rule and to the authority of the governor.

21And they asked him, saying, Teacher, we know that thou sayest and teachest rightly, and acceptest not the person of any, but of a truth teachest the way of God:

22Is it lawful for us to give tribute unto Caesar, or not?

23But he perceived their craftiness, and said unto them,

24Show me a denarius. Whose image and superscription hath it? And they said, Caesar's.

25And he said unto them, Then render unto Caesar the things that are Caesar's, and unto God the things that are God's.

26And they were not able to take hold of the saying before the people: and they marvelled at his answer, and held their peace.

27And there came to him certain of the Sadducees, they that say that there is no resurrection;

28and they asked him, saying, Teacher, Moses wrote unto us, that if a man's brother die, having a wife, and he be childless, his brother should take the wife, and raise up seed unto his brother.

29There were therefore seven brethren: and the first took a wife, and died childless;

30and the second:

31and the third took her; and likewise the seven also left no children, and died.

32Afterward the woman also died.

33In the resurrection therefore whose wife of them shall she be? for the seven had her to wife.

34And Jesus said unto them, The sons of this world marry, and are given in marriage:

35but they that are accounted worthy to attain to that world, and the resurrection from the dead, neither marry, nor are given in marriage:

36for neither can they die any more: for they are equal unto the angels; and are sons of God, being sons of the resurrection.

37But that the dead are raised, even Moses showed, in the place concerning the Bush, when he calleth the Lord the God of Abraham, and the God of Isaac, and the God of Jacob.

38Now he is not the God of the dead, but of the living: for all live unto him.

39And certain of the scribes answering said, Teacher, thou hast well said.

40For they durst not any more ask him any question.

41And he said unto them, How say they that the Christ is David's son?

42For David himself saith in the book of Psalms,

The Lord said unto my Lord,

Sit thou on my right hand,

43Till I make thine enemies the footstool of thy feet.

44David therefore calleth him Lord, and how is he his son?

45And in the hearing of all the people he said unto his disciples,

46Beware of the scribes, who desire to walk in long robes, and love salutations in the marketplaces, and chief seats in the synagogues, and chief places at feasts;

47who devour widows' houses, and for a pretence make long prayers: these shall receive greater condemnation.

Chapter 21

1And he looked up, and saw the rich men that were casting their gifts into the treasury.

2And he saw a certain poor widow casting in thither two mites.

3And he said, Of a truth I say unto you, This poor widow cast in more than they all:

4for all these did of their superfluity cast in unto the gifts; but she of her want did cast in all the living that she had.

5And as some spake of the temple, how it was adorned with goodly stones and offerings, he said,

6As for these things which ye behold, the days will come, in which there shall not be left here one stone upon another, that shall not be thrown down.

7And they asked him, saying, Teacher, when therefore shall these things be? and what shall be the sign when these things are about to come to pass?

8And he said, Take heed that ye be not led astray: for many shall come in my name, saying, I am he; and, The time is at hand: go ye not after them.

9And when ye shall hear of wars and tumults, be not terrified: for these things must needs come to pass first; but the end is not immediately.

10Then said he unto them, Nation shall rise against nation, and kingdom against kingdom;

11and there shall be great earthquakes, and in divers places famines and pestilences; and there shall be terrors and great signs from heaven.

12But before all these things, they shall lay their hands on you, and shall persecute you, delivering you up to the synagogues and prisons, bringing you before kings and governors for my name's sake.

13It shall turn out unto you for a testimony.

14Settle it therefore in your hearts, not to meditate beforehand how to answer:

15for I will give you a mouth and wisdom, which all your adversaries shall not be able to withstand or to gainsay.

16But ye shall be delivered up even by parents, and brethren, and kinsfolk, and friends; and some of you shall they cause to be put to death.

17And ye shall be hated of all men for my name's sake.

18And not a hair of your head shall perish.

19In your patience ye shall win your souls.

20But when ye see Jerusalem compassed with armies, then know that her desolation is at hand.

21Then let them that are in Judaea flee unto the mountains; and let them that are in the midst of her depart out; and let not them that are in the country enter therein.

22For these are days of vengeance, that all things which are written may be fulfilled.

23Woe unto them that are with child and to them that give suck in those days! for there shall be great distress upon the land, and wrath unto this people.

24And they shall fall by the edge of the sword, and shall be led captive into all the nations: and Jerusalem shall be trodden down of the Gentiles, until the times of the Gentiles be fulfilled.

25And there shall be signs in sun and moon and stars; and upon the earth distress of nations, in perplexity for the roaring of the sea and the billows;

26men fainting for fear, and for expectation of the things which are coming on the world: for the powers of the heavens shall be shaken.

27And then shall they see the Son of man coming in a cloud with power and great glory.

28But when these things begin to come to pass, look up, and lift up your heads; because your redemption draweth nigh.

29And he spake to them a parable: Behold the fig tree, and all the trees:

30when they now shoot forth, ye see it and know of your own selves that the summer is now nigh.

31Even so ye also, when ye see these things coming to pass, know ye that the kingdom of God is nigh.

32Verily I say unto you, This generation shall not pass away, till all things be accomplished.

33Heaven and earth shall pass away: but my words shall not pass away.

34But take heed to yourselves, lest haply your hearts be overcharged with surfeiting, and drunkenness, and cares of this life, and that day come on you suddenly as a snare:

35for so shall it come upon all them that dwell on the face of all the earth.

36But watch ye at every season, making supplication, that ye may prevail to escape all these things that shall come to pass, and to stand before the Son of man.

37And every day he was teaching in the temple; and every night he went out, and lodged in the mount that is called Olivet.

38And all the people came early in the morning to him in the temple, to hear him.

Chapter 22

1Now the feast of unleavened bread drew nigh, which is called the Passover.

2And the chief priests and the scribes sought how they might put him to death; for they feared the people.

3And Satan entered into Judas who was called Iscariot, being of the number of the twelve.

4And he went away, and communed with the chief priests and captains, how he might deliver him unto them.

5And they were glad, and covenanted to give him money.

6And he consented, and sought opportunity to deliver him unto them in the absence of the multitude.

7And the day of unleavened bread came, on which the passover must be sacrificed.

8And he sent Peter and John, saying, Go and make ready for us the passover, that we may eat.

9And they said unto him, Where wilt thou that we make ready?

10And he said unto them, Behold, when ye are entered into the city, there shall meet you a man bearing a pitcher of water; follow him into the house whereinto he goeth.

11And ye shall say unto the master of the house, The Teacher saith unto thee, Where is the guestchamber, where I shall eat the passover with my disciples?

12And he will show you a large upper room furnished: there make ready.

13And they went, and found as he had said unto them: and they made ready the passover.

14And when the hour was come, he sat down, and the apostles with him.

15And he said unto them, With desire I have desired to eat this passover with you before I suffer:

16for I say unto you, I shall not eat it, until it be fulfilled in the kingdom of God.

17And he received a cup, and when he had given thanks, he said, Take this, and divide it among yourselves:

18for I say unto you, I shall not drink from henceforth of the fruit of the vine, until the kingdom of God shall come.

19And he took bread, and when he had given thanks, he brake it, and gave to them, saying, This is my body which is given for you: this do in remembrance of me.

20And the cup in like manner after supper, saying, This cup is the new covenant in my blood, even that which is poured out for you.

21But behold, the hand of him that betrayeth me is with me on the table.

22For the Son of man indeed goeth, as it hath been determined: but woe unto that man through whom he is betrayed!

23And they began to question among themselves, which of them it was that should do this thing.

24And there arose also a contention among them, which of them was accounted to be greatest.

25And he said unto them, The kings of the Gentiles have lordship over them; and they that have authority over them are called Benefactors.

26But ye shall not be so: but he that is the greater among you, let him become as the younger; and he that is chief, as he that doth serve.

27For which is greater, he that sitteth at meat, or he that serveth? is not he that sitteth at meat? but I am in the midst of you as he that serveth.

28But ye are they that have continued with me in my temptations;

29and I appoint unto you a kingdom, even as my Father appointed unto me,

30that ye may eat and drink at my table in my kingdom; and ye shall sit on thrones judging the twelve tribes of Israel.

31Simon, Simon, behold, Satan asked to have you, that he might sift you as wheat:

32but I made supplication for thee, that thy faith fail not; and do thou, when once thou hast turned again, establish thy brethren.

33And he said unto him, Lord, with thee I am ready to go both to prison and to death.

34And he said, I tell thee, Peter, the cock shall not crow this day, until thou shalt thrice deny that thou knowest me.

35And he said unto them, When I sent you forth without purse, and wallet, and shoes, lacked ye anything? And they said, Nothing.

36And he said unto them, But now, he that hath a purse, let him take it, and likewise a wallet; and he that hath none, let him sell his cloak, and buy a sword.

37For I say unto you, that this which is written must be fulfilled in me, And he was reckoned with transgressors: for that which concerneth me hath fulfilment.

38And they said, Lord, behold, here are two swords. And he said unto them, It is enough.

39And he came out, and went, as his custom was, unto the mount of Olives; and the disciples also followed him.

40And when he was at the place, he said unto them, Pray that ye enter not into temptation.

41And he was parted from them about a stone's cast; and he kneeled down and prayed,

42saying, Father, if thou be willing, remove this cup from me: nevertheless not my will, but thine, be done.

43And there appeared unto him an angel from heaven, strengthening him.

44And being in an agony he prayed more earnestly; and his sweat became as it were great drops of blood falling down upon the ground.

45And when he rose up from his prayer, he came unto the disciples, and found them sleeping for sorrow,

Luke

46and said unto them, Why sleep ye? rise and pray, that ye enter not into temptation.

47While he yet spake, behold, a multitude, and he that was called Judas, one of the twelve, went before them; and he drew near unto Jesus to kiss him.

48But Jesus said unto him, Judas, betrayest thou the Son of man with a kiss?

49And when they that were about him saw what would follow, they said, Lord, shall we smite with the sword?

50And a certain one of them smote the servant of the high priest, and struck off his right ear.

51But Jesus answered and said, Suffer ye them thus far. And he touched his ear, and healed him.

52And Jesus said unto the chief priests, and captains of the temple, and elders, that were come against him, Are ye come out, as against a robber, with swords and staves?

53When I was daily with you in the temple, ye stretched not forth your hands against me: but this is your hour, and the power of darkness.

54And they seized him, and led him away, and brought him into the high priest's house. But Peter followed afar off.

55And when they had kindled a fire in the midst of the court, and had sat down together, Peter sat in the midst of them.

56And a certain maid seeing him as he sat in the light of the fire, and looking stedfastly upon him, said, This man also was with him.

57But he denied, saying, Woman, I know him not.

58And after a little while another saw him, and said, Thou also art one of them. But Peter said, Man, I am not.

59And after the space of about one hour another confidently affirmed, saying, Of a truth this man also was with him; for he is a Galilaean.

60But Peter said, Man, I know not what thou sayest. And immediately, while he yet spake, the cock crew.

61And the Lord turned, and looked upon Peter. And Peter remembered the word of the Lord, how that he said unto him, Before the cock crow this day thou shalt deny me thrice.

62And he went out, and wept bitterly.

63And the men that held Jesus mocked him, and beat him.

64And they blindfolded him, and asked him, saying, Prophesy: who is he that struck thee?

65And many other things spake they against him, reviling him.

66And as soon as it was day, the assembly of the elders of the people was gathered together, both chief priests and scribes; and they led him away into their council, saying,

67If thou art the Christ, tell us. But he said unto them, If I tell you, ye will not believe:

68and if I ask you, ye will not answer.

69But from henceforth shall the Son of man be seated at the right hand of the power of God.

70And they all said, Art thou then the Son of God? And he said unto them, Ye say that I am.

71And they said, What further need have we of witness? for we ourselves have heard from his own mouth.

Chapter 23

1And the whole company of them rose up, and brought him before Pilate.

2And they began to accuse him, saying, We found this man perverting our nation, and forbidding to give tribute to Caesar, and saying that he himself is Christ a king.

3And Pilate asked him, saying, Art thou the King of the Jews? And he answered him and said, Thou sayest.

4And Pilate said unto the chief priests and the multitudes, I find no fault in this man.

5But they were the more urgent, saying, He stirreth up the people, teaching throughout all Judaea, and beginning from Galilee even unto this place.

6But when Pilate heard it, he asked whether the man were a Galilaean.

7And when he knew that he was of Herod's jurisdiction, he sent him unto Herod, who himself also was at Jerusalem in these days.

8Now when Herod saw Jesus, he was exceeding glad: for he was of a long time desirous to see him, because he had heard concerning him; and he hoped to see some miracle done by him.

9And he questioned him in many words; but he answered him nothing.

10And the chief priests and the scribes stood, vehemently accusing him.

11And Herod with his soldiers set him at nought, and mocked him, and arraying him in gorgeous apparel sent him back to Pilate.

12And Herod and Pilate became friends with each other that very day: for before they were at enmity between themselves.

13And Pilate called together the chief priests and the rulers and the people,

14and said unto them, Ye brought unto me this man, as one that perverteth the people: and behold, I, having examined him before you, found no fault in this man touching those things whereof ye accuse him:

15no, nor yet Herod: for he sent him back unto us; and behold, nothing worthy of death hath been done by him.

16I will therefore chastise him, and release him.

17Now he must needs release unto them at the feast one prisoner.

18But they cried out all together, saying, Away with this man, and release unto us Barabbas: --

19one who for a certain insurrection made in the city, and for murder, was cast into prison.

20And Pilate spake unto them again, desiring to release Jesus;

21but they shouted, saying, Crucify, crucify him.

22And he said unto them the third time, Why, what evil hath this man done? I have found no cause of death in him: I will therefore chastise him and release him.

23But they were urgent with loud voices, asking that he might be crucified. And their voices prevailed.

24And Pilate gave sentence that what they asked for should be done.

25And he released him that for insurrection and murder had been cast into prison, whom they asked for; but Jesus he delivered up to their will.

26And when they led him away, they laid hold upon one Simon of Cyrene, coming from the country, and laid on him the cross, to bear it after Jesus.

27And there followed him a great multitude of the people, and of women who bewailed and lamented him.

28But Jesus turning unto them said, Daughters of Jerusalem, weep not for me, but weep for yourselves, and for your children.

29For behold, the days are coming, in which they shall say, Blessed are the barren, and the wombs that never bare, and the breasts that never gave suck.

30Then shall they begin to say to the mountains, Fall on us; and to the hills, Cover us.

31For if they do these things in the green tree, what shall be done in the dry?

32And there were also two others, malefactors, led with him to be put to death.

33And when they came unto the place which is called The skull, there they crucified him, and the malefactors, one on the right hand and the other on the left.

34And Jesus said, Father, forgive them; for they know not what they do. And parting his garments among them, they cast lots.

35And the people stood beholding. And the rulers also scoffed at him, saying, He saved others; let him save himself, if this is the Christ of God, his chosen.

36And the soldiers also mocked him, coming to him, offering him vinegar,

37and saying, If thou art the King of the Jews, save thyself.

38And there was also a superscription over him, THIS IS THE KING OF THE JEWS.

39And one of the malefactors that were hanged railed on him, saying, Art not thou the Christ? save thyself and us.

40But the other answered, and rebuking him said, Dost thou not even fear God, seeing thou art in the same condemnation?

41And we indeed justly; for we receive the due reward of our deeds: but this man hath done nothing amiss.

42And he said, Jesus, remember me when thou comest in thy kingdom.

43And he said unto him, Verily I say unto thee, To-day shalt thou be with me in Paradise.

44And it was now about the sixth hour, and a darkness came over the whole land until the ninth hour,

45the sun's light failing: and the veil of the temple was rent in the midst.

46And Jesus, crying with a loud voice, said, Father, into thy hands I commend my spirit: and having said this, he gave up the ghost.

47And when the centurion saw what was done, he glorified God, saying, Certainly this was a righteous man.

48And all the multitudes that came together to this sight, when they beheld the things that were done, returned smiting their breasts.

49And all his acquaintance, and the women that followed with him from Galilee, stood afar off, seeing these things.

50And behold, a man named Joseph, who was a councillor, a good and righteous man

51(he had not consented to their counsel and deed), a man of Arimathaea, a city of the Jews, who was looking for the kingdom of God:

52this man went to Pilate, and asked for the body of Jesus.

53And he took it down, and wrapped it in a linen cloth, and laid him in a tomb that was hewn in stone, where never man had yet lain.

54And it was the day of the Preparation, and the sabbath drew on.

55And the women, who had come with him out of Galilee, followed after, and beheld the tomb, and how his body was laid.

56And they returned, and prepared spices and ointments. And on the sabbath they rested according to the commandment.

Chapter 24

1But on the first day of the week, at early dawn, they came unto the tomb, bringing the spices which they had prepared.

2And they found the stone rolled away from the tomb.

3And they entered in, and found not the body of the Lord Jesus.

4And it came to pass, while they were perplexed thereabout, behold, two men stood by them in dazzling apparel:

5and as they were affrighted and bowed down their faces to the earth, they said unto them, Why seek ye the living among the dead?

6He is not here, but is risen: remember how he spake unto you when he was yet in Galilee,

7saying that the Son of man must be delivered up into the hands of sinful men, and be crucified, and the third day rise again.

8And they remembered his words,

9and returned from the tomb, and told all these things to the eleven, and to all the rest.

10Now they were Mary Magdalene, and Joanna, and Mary the mother of James: and the other women with them told these things unto the apostles.

11And these words appeared in their sight as idle talk; and they disbelieved them.

12But Peter arose, and ran unto the tomb; and stooping and looking in, he seeth the linen cloths by themselves; and he departed to his home, wondering at that which was come to pass.

13And behold, two of them were going that very day to a village named Emmaus, which was threescore furlongs from Jerusalem.

14And they communed with each other of all these things which had happened.

¹⁵And it came to pass, while they communed and questioned together, that Jesus himself drew near, and went with them.

¹⁶But their eyes were holden that they should not know him.

¹⁷And he said unto them, What communications are these that ye have one with another, as ye walk? And they stood still, looking sad.

¹⁸And one of them, named Cleopas, answering said unto him, Dost thou alone sojourn in Jerusalem and not know the things which are come to pass there in these days?

¹⁹And he said unto them, What things? And they said unto him, The things concerning Jesus the Nazarene, who was a prophet mighty in deed and word before God and all the people:

²⁰and how the chief priests and our rulers delivered him up to be condemned to death, and crucified him.

²¹But we hoped that it was he who should redeem Israel. Yea and besides all this, it is now the third day since these things came to pass.

²²Moreover certain women of our company amazed us, having been early at the tomb;

²³and when they found not his body, they came, saying, that they had also seen a vision of angels, who said that he was alive.

²⁴And certain of them that were with us went to the tomb, and found it even so as the women had said: but him they saw not.

²⁵And he said unto them, O foolish men, and slow of heart to believe in all that the prophets have spoken!

²⁶Behooved it not the Christ to suffer these things, and to enter into his glory?

²⁷And beginning from Moses and from all the prophets, he interpreted to them in all the scriptures the things concerning himself.

²⁸And they drew nigh unto the village, whither they were going: and he made as though he would go further.

²⁹And they constrained him, saying, Abide with us; for it is toward evening, and the day is now far spent. And he went in to abide with them.

³⁰And it came to pass, when he had sat down with them to meat, he took the bread and blessed; and breaking it he gave to them.

³¹And their eyes were opened, and they knew him; and he vanished out of their sight.

³²And they said one to another, Was not our heart burning within us, while he spake to us in the way, while he opened to us the scriptures?

³³And they rose up that very hour, and returned to Jerusalem, and found the eleven gathered together, and them that were with them,

³⁴saying, The Lord is risen indeed, and hath appeared to Simon.

³⁵And they rehearsed the things that happened in the way, and how he was known of them in the breaking of the bread.

³⁶And as they spake these things, he himself stood in the midst of them, and saith unto them, Peace be unto you.

³⁷But they were terrified and affrighted, and supposed that they beheld a spirit.

³⁸And he said unto them, Why are ye troubled? and wherefore do questionings arise in your heart?

³⁹See my hands and my feet, that it is I myself: handle me, and see; for a spirit hath not flesh and bones, as ye behold me having.

⁴⁰And when he had said this, he showed them his hands and his feet.

⁴¹And while they still disbelieved for joy, and wondered, he said unto them, Have ye here anything to eat?

⁴²And they gave him a piece of a broiled fish.

⁴³And he took it, and ate before them.

⁴⁴And he said unto them, These are my words which I spake unto you, while I was yet with you, that all things must needs be fulfilled, which are written in the law of Moses, and the prophets, and the psalms, concerning me.

⁴⁵Then opened he their mind, that they might understand the scriptures;

⁴⁶and he said unto them, Thus it is written, that the Christ should suffer, and rise again from the dead the third day;

⁴⁷and that repentance and remission of sins should be preached in his name unto all the nations, beginning from Jerusalem.

⁴⁸Ye are witnesses of these things.

⁴⁹And behold, I send forth the promise of my Father upon you: but tarry ye in the city, until ye be clothed with power from on high.

⁵⁰And he led them out until they were over against Bethany: and he lifted up his hands, and blessed them.

⁵¹And it came to pass, while he blessed them, he parted from them, and was carried up into heaven.

⁵²And they worshipped him, and returned to Jerusalem with great joy:

⁵³and were continually in the temple, blessing God.

John
The Gospel According to St. John

Chapter 1

1In the beginning was the Word, and the Word was with God, and the Word was God.

2The same was in the beginning with God.

3All things were made through him; and without him was not anything made that hath been made.

4In him was life; and the life was the light of men.

5And the light shineth in the darkness; and the darkness apprehended it not.

6There came a man, sent from God, whose name was John.

7The same came for witness, that he might bear witness of the light, that all might believe through him.

8He was not the light, but came that he might bear witness of the light.

9There was the true light, even the light which lighteth every man, coming into the world.

10He was in the world, and the world was made through him, and the world knew him not.

11He came unto his own, and they that were his own received him not.

12But as many as received him, to them gave he the right to become children of God, even to them that believe on his name:

13who were born, not of blood, nor of the will of the flesh, nor of the will of man, but of God.

14And the Word became flesh, and dwelt among us (and we beheld his glory, glory as of the only begotten from the Father), full of grace and truth.

15John beareth witness of him, and crieth, saying, This was he of whom I said, He that cometh after me is become before me: for he was before me.

16For of his fulness we all received, and grace for grace.

17For the law was given through Moses; grace and truth came through Jesus Christ.

18No man hath seen God at any time; the only begotten Son, who is in the bosom of the Father, he hath declared him.

19And this is the witness of John, when the Jews sent unto him from Jerusalem priests and Levites to ask him, Who art thou?

20And he confessed, and denied not; and he confessed, I am not the Christ.

21And they asked him, What then? Art thou Elijah? And he saith, I am not. Art thou the prophet? And he answered, No.

22They said therefore unto him, Who art thou? that we may give an answer to them that sent us. What sayest thou of thyself?

23He said, I am the voice of one crying in the wilderness, Make straight the way of the Lord, as said Isaiah the prophet.

24And they had been sent from the Pharisees.

25And they asked him, and said unto him, Why then baptizest thou, if thou art not the Christ, neither Elijah, neither the prophet?

26John answered them, saying, I baptize in water: in the midst of you standeth one whom ye know not,

27even he that cometh after me, the latchet of whose shoe I am not worthy to unloose.

28These things were done in Bethany beyond the Jordan, where John was baptizing.

29On the morrow he seeth Jesus coming unto him, and saith, Behold, the Lamb of God, that taketh away the sin of the world!

30This is he of whom I said, After me cometh a man who is become before me: for he was before me.

31And I knew him not; but that he should be made manifest to Israel, for this cause came I baptizing in water.

32And John bare witness, saying, I have beheld the Spirit descending as a dove out of heaven; and it abode upon him.

33And I knew him not: but he that sent me to baptize in water, he said unto me, Upon whomsoever thou shalt see the Spirit descending, and abiding upon him, the same is he that baptizeth in the Holy Spirit.

34And I have seen, and have borne witness that this is the Son of God.

35Again on the morrow John was standing, and two of his disciples;

36and he looked upon Jesus as he walked, and saith, Behold, the Lamb of God!

37And the two disciples heard him speak, and they followed Jesus.

38And Jesus turned, and beheld them following, and saith unto them, What seek ye? And they said unto him, Rabbi (which is to say, being interpreted, Teacher), where abidest thou?

39He saith unto them, Come, and ye shall see. They came therefore and saw where he abode; and they abode with him that day: it was about the tenth hour.

40One of the two that heard John speak, and followed him, was Andrew, Simon Peter's brother.

41He findeth first his own brother Simon, and saith unto him, We have found the Messiah (which is, being interpreted, Christ).

42He brought him unto Jesus. Jesus looked upon him, and said, Thou art Simon the son of John: thou shalt be called Cephas (which is by interpretation, Peter).

43On the morrow he was minded to go forth into Galilee, and he findeth Philip: and Jesus saith unto him, Follow me.

44Now Philip was from Bethsaida, of the city of Andrew and Peter.

45Philip findeth Nathanael, and saith unto him, We have found him, of whom Moses in the law, and the prophets, wrote, Jesus of Nazareth, the son of Joseph.

46And Nathanael said unto him, Can any good thing come out of Nazareth? Philip saith unto him, Come and see.

47Jesus saw Nathanael coming to him, and saith of him, Behold, an Israelite indeed, in whom is no guile!

48Nathanael saith unto him, Whence knowest thou me? Jesus answered and said unto him, Before Philip called thee, when thou wast under the fig tree, I saw thee.

49Nathanael answered him, Rabbi, thou art the Son of God; thou art King of Israel.

50Jesus answered and said unto him, Because I said unto thee, I saw thee underneath the fig tree, believest thou? thou shalt see greater things than these.

51And he saith unto him, Verily, verily, I say unto you, Ye shall see the heaven opened, and the angels of God ascending and descending upon the Son of man.

Chapter 2

1And the third day there was a marriage in Cana of Galilee; and the mother of Jesus was there:

2and Jesus also was bidden, and his disciples, to the marriage.

3And when the wine failed, the mother of Jesus saith unto him, They have no wine.

4And Jesus saith unto her, Woman, what have I to do with thee? mine hour is not yet come.

5His mother saith unto the servants, Whatsoever he saith unto you, do it.

6Now there were six waterpots of stone set there after the Jews' manner of purifying, containing two or three firkins apiece.

7Jesus saith unto them, Fill the waterpots with water. And they filled them up to the brim.

8And he saith unto them, Draw out now, and bear unto the ruler of the feast. And they bare it.

9And when the ruler of the feast tasted the water now become wine, and knew not whence it was (but the servants that had drawn the water knew), the ruler of the feast calleth the bridegroom,

10and saith unto him, Every man setteth on first the good wine; and when men have drunk freely, then that which is worse: thou hast kept the good wine until now.

11This beginning of his signs did Jesus in Cana of Galilee, and manifested his glory; and his disciples believed on him.

12After this he went down to Capernaum, he, and his mother, and his brethren, and his disciples; and there they abode not many days.

13And the passover of the Jews was at hand, and Jesus went up to Jerusalem.

14And he found in the temple those that sold oxen and sheep and doves, and the changers of money sitting:

15and he made a scourge of cords, and cast all out of the temple, both the sheep and the oxen; and he poured out the changers' money, and overthrew their tables;

16and to them that sold the doves he said, Take these things hence; make not my Father's house a house of merchandise.

17His disciples remembered that it was written, Zeal for thy house shall eat me up.

18The Jews therefore answered and said unto him, What sign showest thou unto us, seeing that thou doest these things?

19Jesus answered and said unto them, Destroy this temple, and in three days I will raise it up.

20The Jews therefore said, Forty and six years was this temple in building, and wilt thou raise it up in three days?

21But he spake of the temple of his body.

22When therefore he was raised from the dead, his disciples remembered that he spake this; and they believed the scripture, and the word which Jesus had said.

23Now when he was in Jerusalem at the passover, during the feast, many believed on his name, beholding his signs which he did.

24But Jesus did not trust himself unto them, for that he knew all men,

25and because he needed not that any one should bear witness concerning man; for he himself knew what was in man.

Chapter 3

1Now there was a man of the Pharisees, named Nicodemus, a ruler of the Jews:

2the same came unto him by night, and said to him, Rabbi, we know that thou art a teacher come from God; for no one can do these signs that thou doest, except God be with him.

3Jesus answered and said unto him, Verily, verily, I say unto thee, Except one be born anew, he cannot see the kingdom of God.

4Nicodemus saith unto him, How can a man be born when he is old? can he enter a second time into his mother's womb, and be born?

5Jesus answered, Verily, verily, I say unto thee, Except one be born of water and the Spirit, he cannot enter into the kingdom of God!

6That which is born of the flesh is flesh; and that which is born of the Spirit is spirit.

7Marvel not that I said unto thee, Ye must be born anew.

8The wind bloweth where it will, and thou hearest the voice thereof, but knowest not whence it cometh, and whither it goeth: so is every one that is born of the Spirit.

9Nicodemus answered and said unto him, How can these things be?

10Jesus answered and said unto him, Art thou the teacher of Israel, and understandest not these things?

11Verily, verily, I say unto thee, We speak that which we know, and bear witness of that which we have seen; and ye receive not our witness.

12If I told you earthly things and ye believe not, how shall ye believe if I tell you heavenly things?

13And no one hath ascended into heaven, but he that descended out of heaven, even the Son of man, who is in heaven.

14And as Moses lifted up the serpent in the wilderness, even so must the Son of man be lifted up;

15that whosoever believeth may in him have eternal life.

16For God so loved the world, that he gave his only begotten Son, that whosoever believeth on him should not perish, but have eternal life.

17For God sent not the Son into the world to judge the world; but that the world should be saved through him.

18He that believeth on him is not judged: he that believeth not hath been judged already, because he hath not believed on the name of the only begotten Son of God.

19And this is the judgment, that the light is come into the world, and men loved the darkness rather than the light; for their works were evil.

20For every one that doeth evil hateth the light, and cometh not to the light, lest his works should be reproved.

21But he that doeth the truth cometh to the light, that his works may be made manifest, that they have been wrought in God.

22After these things came Jesus and his disciples into the land of Judea; and there he tarried with them, and baptized.

23And John also was baptizing in Enon near to Salim, because there was much water there: and they came, and were baptized.

24For John was not yet cast into prison.

25There arose therefore a questioning on the part of John's disciples with a Jew about purifying.

26And they came unto John, and said to him, Rabbi, he that was with thee beyond the Jordan, to whom thou hast borne witness, behold, the same baptizeth, and all men come to him.

27John answered and said, A man can receive nothing, except it have been given him from heaven.

28Ye yourselves bear me witness, that I said, I am not the Christ, but, that I am sent before him.

29He that hath the bride is the bridegroom: but the friend of the bridegroom, that standeth and heareth him, rejoiceth greatly because of the bridegroom's voice: this my joy therefore is made full.

30He must increase, but I must decrease.

31He that cometh from above is above all: he that is of the earth is of the earth, and of the earth he speaketh: he that cometh from heaven is above all.

32What he hath seen and heard, of that he beareth witness; and no man receiveth his witness.

33He that hath received his witness hath set his seal to this, that God is true.

34For he whom God hath sent speaketh the words of God: for he giveth not the Spirit by measure.

35The Father loveth the Son, and hath given all things into his hand.

36He that believeth on the Son hath eternal life; but he that obeyeth not the Son shall not see life, but the wrath of God abideth on him.

Chapter 4

1When therefore the Lord knew that the Pharisees had heard that Jesus was making and baptizing more disciples than John

2(although Jesus himself baptized not, but his disciples),

3he left Judea, and departed again into Galilee.

4And he must needs pass through Samaria.

5So he cometh to a city of Samaria, called Sychar, near to the parcel of ground that Jacob gave to his son Joseph:

6and Jacob's well was there. Jesus therefore, being wearied with his journey, sat thus by the well. It was about the sixth hour.

7There cometh a woman of Samaria to draw water: Jesus saith unto her, Give me to drink.

8For his disciples were gone away into the city to buy food.

9The Samaritan woman therefore saith unto him, How is it that thou, being a Jew, askest drink of me, who am a Samaritan woman? (For Jews have no dealings with Samaritans.)

10Jesus answered and said unto her, If thou knewest the gift of God, and who it is that saith to thee, Give me to drink; thou wouldest have asked of him, and he would have given thee living water.

11The woman saith unto him, Sir, thou hast nothing to draw with, and the well is deep: whence then hast thou that living water?

12Art thou greater than our father Jacob, who gave us the well, and drank thereof himself, and his sons, and his cattle?

13Jesus answered and said unto her, Every one that drinketh of this water shall thirst again:

14but whosoever drinketh of the water that I shall give him shall never thirst; but the water that I shall give him shall become in him a well of water springing up unto eternal life.

15The woman saith unto him, Sir, give me this water, that I thirst not, neither come all the way hither to draw.

16Jesus saith unto her, Go, call thy husband, and come hither.

17The woman answered and said unto him, I have no husband. Jesus saith unto her, Thou saidst well, I have no husband:

18for thou hast had five husbands; and he whom thou now hast is not thy husband: this hast thou said truly.

19The woman saith unto him, Sir, I perceive that thou art a prophet.

20Our fathers worshipped in this mountain; and ye say, that in Jerusalem is the place where men ought to worship.

21Jesus saith unto her, Woman, believe me, the hour cometh, when neither in this mountain, nor in Jerusalem, shall ye worship the Father.

22Ye worship that which ye know not: we worship that which we know; for salvation is from the Jews.

23But the hour cometh, and now is, when the true worshippers shall worship the Father in spirit and truth: for such doth the Father seek to be his worshippers.

24God is a Spirit: and they that worship him must worship in spirit and truth.

25The woman saith unto him, I know that Messiah cometh (he that is called Christ): when he is come, he will declare unto us all things.

26Jesus saith unto her, I that speak unto thee am he.

27And upon this came his disciples; and they marvelled that he was speaking with a woman; yet no man said, What seekest thou? or, Why speakest thou with her?

28So the woman left her waterpot, and went away into the city, and saith to the people,

29Come, see a man, who told me all things that ever I did: can this be the Christ?

30They went out of the city, and were coming to him.

31In the mean while the disciples prayed him, saying, Rabbi, eat.

32But he said unto them, I have meat to eat that ye know not.

33The disciples therefore said one to another, Hath any man brought him aught to eat?

34Jesus saith unto them, My meat is to do the will of him that sent me, and to accomplish his work.

35Say not ye, There are yet four months, and then cometh the harvest? behold, I say unto you, Lift up your eyes, and look on the fields, that they are white already unto harvest.

36He that reapeth receiveth wages, and gathereth fruit unto life eternal; that he that soweth and he that reapeth may rejoice together.

37For herein is the saying true, One soweth, and another reapeth.

38I sent you to reap that whereon ye have not labored: others have labored, and ye are entered into their labor.

39And from that city many of the Samaritans believed on him because of the word of the woman, who testified, He told me all things that ever I did.

40So when the Samaritans came unto him, they besought him to abide with them: and he abode there two days.

41And many more believed because of his word;

42and they said to the woman, Now we believe, not because of thy speaking: for we have heard for ourselves, and know that this is indeed the Saviour of the world.

43And after the two days he went forth from thence into Galilee.

44For Jesus himself testified, that a prophet hath no honor in his own country.

45So when he came into Galilee, the Galilaeans received him, having seen all the things that he did in Jerusalem at the feast: for they also went unto the feast.

46He came therefore again unto Cana of Galilee, where he made the water wine. And there was a certain nobleman, whose son was sick at Capernaum.

47When he heard that Jesus was come out of Judaea into Galilee, he went unto him, and besought him that he would come down, and heal his son; for he was at the point of death.

48Jesus therefore said unto him, Except ye see signs and wonders, ye will in no wise believe.

49The nobleman saith unto him, Sir, come down ere my child die.

50Jesus saith unto him, Go thy way; thy son liveth. The man believed the word that Jesus spake unto him, and he went his way.

51And as he was now going down, his servants met him, saying, that his son lived.

52So he inquired of them the hour when he began to amend. They said therefore unto him, Yesterday at the seventh hour the fever left him.

53So the father knew that it was at that hour in which Jesus said unto him, Thy son liveth: and himself believed, and his whole house.

54This is again the second sign that Jesus did, having come out of Judaea into Galilee.

Chapter 5

1After these things there was a feast of the Jews; and Jesus went up to Jerusalem.

2Now there is in Jerusalem by the sheep gate a pool, which is called in Hebrew Bethesda, having five porches.

3In these lay a multitude of them that were sick, blind, halt, withered, waiting for the moving of the water.

4for an angel of the Lord went down at certain seasons into the pool, and troubled the water: whosoever then first after the troubling of the waters stepped in was made whole, with whatsoever disease he was holden.

5And a certain man was there, who had been thirty and eight years in his infirmity.

6When Jesus saw him lying, and knew that he had been now a long time in that case, he saith unto him, Wouldest thou be made whole?

7The sick man answered him, Sir, I have no man, when the water is troubled, to put me into the pool: but while I am coming, another steppeth down before me.

8Jesus saith unto him, Arise, take up thy bed, and walk.

9And straightway the man was made whole, and took up his bed and walked. Now it was the sabbath on that day.

10So the Jews said unto him that was cured, It is the sabbath, and it is not lawful for thee to take up thy bed.

11But he answered them, He that made me whole, the same said unto me, Take up thy bed, and walk.

John

12They asked him, Who is the man that said unto thee, Take up thy bed, and walk?

13But he that was healed knew not who it was; for Jesus had conveyed himself away, a multitude being in the place.

14Afterward Jesus findeth him in the temple, and said unto him, Behold, thou art made whole: sin no more, lest a worse thing befall thee.

15The man went away, and told the Jews that it was Jesus who had made him whole.

16And for this cause the Jews persecuted Jesus, because he did these things on the sabbath.

17But Jesus answered them, My Father worketh even until now, and I work.

18For this cause therefore the Jews sought the more to kill him, because he not only brake the sabbath, but also called God his own Father, making himself equal with God.

19Jesus therefore answered and said unto them, Verily, verily, I say unto you, The Son can do nothing of himself, but what he seeth the Father doing: for what things soever he doeth, these the Son also doeth in like manner.

20For the Father loveth the Son, and showeth him all things that himself doeth: and greater works than these will he show him, that ye may marvel.

21For as the Father raiseth the dead and giveth them life, even so the Son also giveth life to whom he will.

22For neither doth the Father judge any man, but he hath given all judgment unto the Son;

23that all may honor the Son, even as they honor the Father. He that honoreth not the Son honoreth not the Father that sent him.

24Verily, verily, I say unto you, He that heareth my word, and believeth him that sent me, hath eternal life, and cometh not into judgment, but hath passed out of death into life.

25Verily, verily, I say unto you, The hour cometh, and now is, when the dead shall hear the voice of the Son of God; and they that hear shall live.

26For as the Father hath life in himself, even so gave he to the Son also to have life in himself:

27and he gave him authority to execute judgment, because he is a son of man.

28Marvel not at this: for the hour cometh, in which all that are in the tombs shall hear his voice,

29and shall come forth; they that have done good, unto the resurrection of life; and they that have done evil, unto the resurrection of judgment.

30I can of myself do nothing: as I hear, I judge: and my judgment is righteous; because I seek not mine own will, but the will of him that sent me.

31If I bear witness of myself, my witness is not true.

32It is another that beareth witness of me; and I know that the witness which he witnesseth of me is true.

33Ye have sent unto John, and he hath borne witness unto the truth.

34But the witness which I receive is not from man: howbeit I say these things, that ye may be saved.

35He was the lamp that burneth and shineth; and ye were willing to rejoice for a season in his light.

36But the witness which I have is greater than that of John; for the works which the Father hath given me to accomplish, the very works that I do, bear witness of me, that the Father hath sent me.

37And the Father that sent me, he hath borne witness of me. Ye have neither heard his voice at any time, nor seen his form.

38And ye have not his word abiding in you: for whom he sent, him ye believe not.

39Ye search the scriptures, because ye think that in them ye have eternal life; and these are they which bear witness of me;

40and ye will not come to me, that ye may have life.

41I receive not glory from men.

42But I know you, that ye have not the love of God in yourselves.

43I am come in my Father's name, and ye receive me not: if another shall come in his own name, him ye will receive.

44How can ye believe, who receive glory one of another, and the glory that cometh from the only God ye seek not?

45Think not that I will accuse you to the Father: there is one that accuseth you, even Moses, on whom ye have set your hope.

46For if ye believed Moses, ye would believe me; for he wrote of me.

47But if ye believe not his writings, how shall ye believe my words?

Chapter 6

1After these things Jesus went away to the other side of the sea of Galilee, which is the sea of Tiberias.

2And a great multitude followed him, because they beheld the signs which he did on them that were sick.

3And Jesus went up into the mountain, and there he sat with his disciples.

4Now the passover, the feast of the Jews, was at hand.

5Jesus therefore lifting up his eyes, and seeing that a great multitude cometh unto him, saith unto Philip, Whence are we to buy bread, that these may eat?

6And this he said to prove him: for he himself knew what he would do.

7Philip answered him, Two hundred shillings' worth of bread is not sufficient for them, that every one may take a little.

8One of his disciples, Andrew, Simon Peter's brother, saith unto him,

9There is a lad here, who hath five barley loaves, and two fishes: but what are these among so many?

10Jesus said, Make the people sit down. Now there was much grass in the place. So the men sat down, in number about five thousand.

11Jesus therefore took the loaves; and having given thanks, he distributed to them that were set down; likewise also of the fishes as much as they would.

12And when they were filled, he saith unto his disciples, Gather up the broken pieces which remain over, that nothing be lost.

13So they gathered them up, and filled twelve baskets with broken pieces from the five barley loaves, which remained over unto them that had eaten.

14When therefore the people saw the sign which he did, they said, This is of a truth the prophet that cometh into the world.

15Jesus therefore perceiving that they were about to come and take him by force, to make him king, withdrew again into the mountain himself alone.

16And when evening came, his disciples went down unto the sea;

17and they entered into a boat, and were going over the sea unto Capernaum. And it was now dark, and Jesus had not yet come to them.

18And the sea was rising by reason of a great wind that blew.

19When therefore they had rowed about five and twenty or thirty furlongs, they behold Jesus walking on the sea, and drawing nigh unto the boat: and they were afraid.

20But he saith unto them, It is I; be not afraid.

21They were willing therefore to receive him into the boat: and straightway the boat was at the land whither they were going.

22On the morrow the multitude that stood on the other side of the sea saw that there was no other boat there, save one, and that Jesus entered not with his disciples into the boat, but that his disciples went away alone

23(howbeit there came boats from Tiberias nigh unto the place where they ate the bread after the Lord had given thanks):

24when the multitude therefore saw that Jesus was not there, neither his disciples, they themselves got into the boats, and came to Capernaum, seeking Jesus.

25And when they found him on the other side of the sea, they said unto him, Rabbi, when camest thou hither?

26Jesus answered them and said, Verily, verily, I say unto you, Ye seek me, not because ye saw signs, but because ye ate of the loaves, and were filled.

27Work not for the food which perisheth, but for the food which abideth unto eternal life, which the Son of man shall give unto you: for him the Father, even God, hath sealed.

28They said therefore unto him, What must we do, that we may work the works of God?

29Jesus answered and said unto them, This is the work of God, that ye believe on him whom he hath sent.

30They said therefore unto him, What then doest thou for a sign, that we may see, and believe thee? what workest thou?

31Our fathers ate the manna in the wilderness; as it is written, He gave them bread out of heaven to eat.

32Jesus therefore said unto them, Verily, verily, I say unto you, It was not Moses that gave you the bread out of heaven; but my Father giveth you the true bread out of heaven.

33For the bread of God is that which cometh down out of heaven, and giveth life unto the world.

34They said therefore unto him, Lord, evermore give us this bread.

35Jesus said unto them. I am the bread of life: he that cometh to me shall not hunger, and he that believeth on me shall never thirst.

36But I said unto you, that ye have seen me, and yet believe not.

37All that which the Father giveth me shall come unto me; and him that cometh to me I will in no wise cast out.

38For I am come down from heaven, not to do mine own will, but the will of him that sent me.

39And this is the will of him that sent me, that of all that which he hath given me I should lose nothing, but should raise it up at the last day.

40For this is the will of my Father, that every one that beholdeth the Son, and believeth on him, should have eternal life; and I will raise him up at the last day.

41The Jews therefore murmured concerning him, because he said, I am the bread which came down out of heaven.

42And they said, Is not this Jesus, the son of Joseph, whose father and mother we know? how doth he now say, I am come down out of heaven?

43Jesus answered and said unto them, Murmur not among yourselves.

44No man can come to me, except the Father that sent me draw him: and I will raise him up in the last day.

45It is written in the prophets, And they shall all be taught of God. Every one that hath heard from the Father, and hath learned, cometh unto me.

46Not that any man hath seen the Father, save he that is from God, he hath seen the Father.

47Verily, verily, I say unto you, He that believeth hath eternal life.

48I am the bread of life.

49Your fathers ate the manna in the wilderness, and they died.

50This is the bread which cometh down out of heaven, that a man may eat thereof, and not die.

51I am the living bread which came down out of heaven: if any man eat of this bread, he shall live for ever: yea and the bread which I will give is my flesh, for the life of the world.

52The Jews therefore strove one with another, saying, How can this man give us his flesh to eat?

53Jesus therefore said unto them, Verily, verily, I say unto you, Except ye eat the flesh of the Son of man and drink his blood, ye have not life in yourselves.

54He that eateth my flesh and drinketh my blood hath eternal life: and I will raise him up at the last day.

55For my flesh is meat indeed, and my blood is drink indeed.

56He that eateth my flesh and drinketh my blood abideth in me, and I in him.

57As the living Father sent me, and I live because of the Father; so he that eateth me, he also shall live because of me.

58This is the bread which came down out of heaven: not as the fathers ate, and died; he that eateth this bread shall live for ever.

59These things said he in the synagogue, as he taught in Capernaum.

60Many therefore of his disciples, when they heard this, said, This is a hard saying; who can hear it?

61But Jesus knowing in himself that his disciples murmured at this, said unto them, Doth this cause you to stumble?

62What then if ye should behold the Son of man ascending where he was before?

63It is the spirit that giveth life; the flesh profiteth nothing: the words that I have spoken unto you are spirit, and are life.

64But there are some of you that believe not. For Jesus knew from the beginning who they were that believed not, and who it was that should betray him.

65And he said, For this cause have I said unto you, that no man can come unto me, except it be given unto him of the Father.

66Upon this many of his disciples went back, and walked no more with him.

67Jesus said therefore unto the twelve, Would ye also go away?

68Simon Peter answered him, Lord, to whom shall we go? thou hast the words of eternal life.

69And we have believed and know that thou art the Holy One of God.

70Jesus answered them, Did not I choose you the twelve, and one of you is a devil?

71Now he spake of Judas the son of Simon Iscariot, for he it was that should betray him, being one of the twelve.

Chapter 7

1And after these things Jesus walked in Galilee: for he would not walk in Judaea, because the Jews sought to kill him.

2Now the feast of the Jews, the feast of tabernacles, was at hand.

3His brethren therefore said unto him, Depart hence, and go into Judaea, that thy disciples also may behold thy works which thou doest.

4For no man doeth anything in secret, and himself seeketh to be known openly. If thou doest these things, manifest thyself to the world.

5For even his brethren did not believe on him.

6Jesus therefore saith unto them, My time is not yet come; but your time is always ready.

7The world cannot hate you; but me it hateth, because I testify of it, that its works are evil.

8Go ye up unto the feast: I go not up unto this feast; because my time is not yet fulfilled.

9And having said these things unto them, he abode still in Galilee.

10But when his brethren were gone up unto the feast, then went he also up, not publicly, but as it were in secret.

11The Jews therefore sought him at the feast, and said, Where is he?

12And there was much murmuring among the multitudes concerning him: some said, He is a good man; others said, Not so, but he leadeth the multitude astray.

13Yet no man spake openly of him for fear of the Jews.

14But when it was now the midst of the feast Jesus went up into the temple, and taught.

15The Jews therefore marvelled, saying, How knoweth this man letters, having never learned?

16Jesus therefore answered them and said, My teaching is not mine, but his that sent me.

17If any man willeth to do his will, he shall know of the teaching, whether it is of God, or whether I speak from myself.

18He that speaketh from himself seeketh his own glory: but he that seeketh the glory of him that sent him, the same is true, and no unrighteousness is in him.

19Did not Moses give you the law, and yet none of you doeth the law? Why seek ye to kill me?

20The multitude answered, Thou hast a demon: who seeketh to kill thee?

21Jesus answered and said unto them, I did one work, and ye all marvel because thereof.

22Moses hath given you circumcision (not that it is of Moses, but of the fathers); and on the sabbath ye circumcise a man.

23If a man receiveth circumcision on the sabbath, that the law of Moses may not be broken; are ye wroth with me, because I made a man every whit whole on the sabbath?

24Judge not according to appearance, but judge righteous judgment.

25Some therefore of them of Jerusalem said, Is not this he whom they seek to kill?

26And lo, he speaketh openly, and they say nothing unto him. Can it be that the rulers indeed know that this is the Christ?

27Howbeit we know this man whence he is: but when the Christ cometh, no one knoweth whence he is.

28Jesus therefore cried in the temple, teaching and saying, Ye both know me, and know whence I am; and I am not come of myself, but he that sent me is true, whom ye know not.

29I know him; because I am from him, and he sent me.

30They sought therefore to take him: and no man laid his hand on him, because his hour was not yet come.

31But of the multitude many believed on him; and they said, When the Christ shall come, will he do more signs than those which this man hath done?

32The Pharisees heard the multitude murmuring these things concerning him; and the chief priests and the Pharisees sent officers to take him.

33Jesus therefore said, Yet a little while am I with you, and I go unto him that sent me.

34Ye shall seek me, and shall not find me: and where I am, ye cannot come.

35The Jews therefore said among themselves, Whither will this man go that we shall not find him? will he go unto the Dispersion among the Greeks, and teach the Greeks?

36What is this word that he said, Ye shall seek me, and shall not find me; and where I am, ye cannot come?

37Now on the last day, the great day of the feast, Jesus stood and cried, saying, If any man thirst, let him come unto me and drink.

38He that believeth on me, as the scripture hath said, from within him shall flow rivers of living water.

39But this spake he of the Spirit, which they that believed on him were to receive: for the Spirit was not yet given; because Jesus was not yet glorified.

40Some of the multitude therefore, when they heard these words, said, This is of a truth the prophet.

41Others said, This is the Christ. But some said, What, doth the Christ come out of Galilee?

42Hath not the scripture said that the Christ cometh of the seed of David, and from Bethlehem, the village where David was?

43So there arose a division in the multitude because of him.

44And some of them would have taken him; but no man laid hands on him.

45The officers therefore came to the chief priests and Pharisees; and they said unto them, Why did ye not bring him?

46The officers answered, Never a man so spake.

47The Pharisees therefore answered them, Are ye also led astray?

48Hath any of the rulers believed on him, or of the Pharisees?

49But this multitude that knoweth not the law are accursed.

50Nicodemus saith unto them (he that came to him before, being one of them),

51Doth our law judge a man, except it first hear from himself and know what he doeth?

52They answered and said unto him, Art thou also of Galilee? Search, and see that out of Galilee ariseth no prophet.

53And they went every man unto his own house:

Chapter 8

1but Jesus went unto the mount of Olives.

2And early in the morning he came again into the temple, and all the people came unto him; and he sat down, and taught them.

3And the scribes and the Pharisees bring a woman taken in adultery; and having set her in the midst,

4they say unto him, Teacher, this woman hath been taken in adultery, in the very act.

5Now in the law Moses commanded us to stone such: what then sayest thou of her?

6And this they said, trying him, that they might have whereof to accuse him. But Jesus stooped down, and with his finger wrote on the ground.

7But when they continued asking him, he lifted up himself, and said unto them, He that is without sin among you, let him first cast a stone at her.

8And again he stooped down, and with his finger wrote on the ground.

9And they, when they heard it, went out one by one, beginning from the eldest, even unto the last: and Jesus was left alone, and the woman, where she was, in the midst.

10And Jesus lifted up himself, and said unto her, Woman, where are they? did no man condemn thee?

11And she said, No man, Lord. And Jesus said, Neither do I condemn thee: go thy way; from henceforth sin no more.

12Again therefore Jesus spake unto them, saying, I am the light of the world: he that followeth me shall not walk in the darkness, but shall have the light of life.

13The Pharisees therefore said unto him, Thou bearest witness of thyself; thy witness is not true.

14Jesus answered and said unto them, Even if I bear witness of myself, my witness is true; for I know whence I came, and whither I go; but ye know not whence I come, or whither I go.

15Ye judge after the flesh; I judge no man.

16Yea and if I judge, my judgment is true; for I am not alone, but I and the Father that sent me.

17Yea and in your law it is written, that the witness of two men is true.

18I am he that beareth witness of myself, and the Father that sent me beareth witness of me.

19They said therefore unto him, Where is thy Father? Jesus answered, Ye know neither me, nor my Father: if ye knew me, ye would know my Father also.

20These words spake he in the treasury, as he taught in the temple: and no man took him; because his hour was not yet come.

21He said therefore again unto them, I go away, and ye shall seek me, and shall die in your sin: whither I go, ye cannot come.

22The Jews therefore said, Will he kill himself, that he saith, Whither I go, ye cannot come?

23And he said unto them, Ye are from beneath; I am from above: ye are of this world; I am not of this world.

24I said therefore unto you, that ye shall die in your sins: for except ye believe that I am he, ye shall die in your sins.

25They said therefore unto him, Who art thou? Jesus said unto them, Even that which I have also spoken unto you from the beginning.

26I have many things to speak and to judge concerning you: howbeit he that sent me is true; and the things which I heard from him, these speak I unto the world.

27They perceived not that he spake to them of the Father.

28Jesus therefore said, When ye have lifted up the Son of man, then shall ye know that I am he, and that I do nothing of myself, but as the Father taught me, I speak these things.

29And he that sent me is with me; he hath not left me alone; for I do always

John

the things that are pleasing to him.

30 As he spake these things, many believed on him.

31 Jesus therefore said to those Jews that had believed him, If ye abide in my word, then are ye truly my disciples;

32 and ye shall know the truth, and the truth shall make you free.

33 They answered unto him, We are Abraham's seed, and have never yet been in bondage to any man: how sayest thou, Ye shall be made free?

34 Jesus answered them, Verily, verily, I say unto you, Every one that committeth sin is the bondservant of sin.

35 And the bondservant abideth not in the house for ever: the son abideth for ever.

36 If therefore the Son shall make you free, ye shall be free indeed.

37 I know that ye are Abraham's seed: yet ye seek to kill me, because my word hath not free course in you.

38 I speak the things which I have seen with my Father: and ye also do the things which ye heard from your father.

39 They answered and said unto him, Our father is Abraham. Jesus saith unto them, If ye were Abraham's children, ye would do the works of Abraham.

40 But now ye seek to kill me, a man that hath told you the truth, which I heard from God: this did not Abraham.

41 Ye do the works of your father. They said unto him, We were not born of fornication; we have one Father, even God.

42 Jesus said unto them, If God were your Father, ye would love me: for I came forth and am come from God; for neither have I come of myself, but he sent me.

43 Why do ye not understand my speech? Even because ye cannot hear my word.

44 Ye are of your father the devil, and the lusts of your father it is your will to do. He was a murderer from the beginning, and standeth not in the truth, because there is no truth in him. When he speaketh a lie, he speaketh of his own: for he is a liar, and the father thereof.

45 But because I say the truth, ye believe me not.

46 Which of you convicteth me of sin? If I say truth, why do ye not believe me?

47 He that is of God heareth the words of God: for this cause ye hear them not, because ye are not of God.

48 The Jews answered and said unto him, Say we not well that thou art a Samaritan, and hast a demon?

49 Jesus answered, I have not a demon; but I honor my Father, and ye dishonor me.

50 But I seek not mine own glory: there is one that seeketh and judgeth.

51 Verily, verily, I say unto you, If a man keep my word, he shall never see death.

52 The Jews said unto him, Now we know that thou hast a demon. Abraham died, and the prophets; and thou sayest, If a man keep my word, he shall never taste of death.

53 Art thou greater than our father Abraham, who died? and the prophets died: whom makest thou thyself?

54 Jesus answered, If I glorify myself, my glory is nothing: it is my Father that glorifieth me; of whom ye say, that he is your God;

55 and ye have not known him: but I know him; and if I should say, I know him not, I shall be like unto you, a liar: but I know him, and keep his word.

56 Your father Abraham rejoiced to see my day; and he saw it, and was glad.

57 The Jews therefore said unto him, Thou art not yet fifty years old, and hast thou seen Abraham?

58 Jesus said unto them, Verily, verily, I say unto you, Before Abraham was born, I am.

59 They took up stones therefore to cast at him: but Jesus hid himself, and went out of the temple.

Chapter 9

1 And as he passed by, he saw a man blind from his birth.

2 And his disciples asked him, saying, Rabbi, who sinned, this man, or his parents, that he should be born blind?

3 Jesus answered, Neither did this man sin, nor his parents: but that the works of God should be made manifest in him.

4 We must work the works of him that sent me, while it is day: the night cometh, when no man can work.

5 When I am in the world, I am the light of the world.

6 When he had thus spoken, he spat on the ground, and made clay of the spittle, and anointed his eyes with the clay,

7 and said unto him, Go, wash in the pool of Siloam (which is by interpretation, Sent). He went away therefore, and washed, and came seeing.

8 The neighbors therefore, and they that saw him aforetime, that he was a beggar, said, Is not this he that sat and begged?

9 Others said, It is he: others said, No, but he is like him. He said, I am he.

10 They said therefore unto him, How then were thine eyes opened?

11 He answered, The man that is called Jesus made clay, and anointed mine eyes, and said unto me, Go to Siloam, and wash: so I went away and washed, and I received sight.

12 And they said unto him, Where is he? He saith, I know not.

13 They bring to the Pharisees him that aforetime was blind.

14 Now it was the sabbath on the day when Jesus made the clay, and opened his eyes.

15 Again therefore the Pharisees also asked him how he received his sight. And he said unto them, He put clay upon mine eyes, and I washed, and I see.

16 Some therefore of the Pharisees said, This man is not from God, because he keepeth not the sabbath. But others said, How can a man that is a sinner do such signs? And there was division among them.

17 They say therefore unto the blind man again, What sayest thou of him, in that he opened thine eyes? And he said, He is a prophet.

18 The Jews therefore did not believe concerning him, that he had been blind, and had received his sight, until they called the parents of him that had received his sight,

19 and asked them, saying, Is this your son, who ye say was born blind? How then doth he now see?

20 His parents answered and said, We know that this is our son, and that he was born blind:

21 but how he now seeth, we know not; or who opened his eyes, we know not: ask him; he is of age; he shall speak for himself.

22 These things said his parents, because they feared the Jews: for the Jews had agreed already, that if any man should confess him to be Christ, he should be put out of the synagogue.

23 Therefore said his parents, He is of age; ask him.

24 So they called a second time the man that was blind, and said unto him, Give glory to God: we know that this man is a sinner.

25 He therefore answered, Whether he is a sinner, I know not: one thing I know, that, whereas I was blind, now I see.

26 They said therefore unto him, What did he to thee? How opened he thine eyes?

27 He answered them, I told you even now, and ye did not hear; wherefore would ye hear it again? would ye also become his disciples?

28 And they reviled him, and said, Thou art his disciple; but we are disciples of Moses.

29 We know that God hath spoken unto Moses: but as for this man, we know not whence he is.

30 The man answered and said unto them, Why, herein is the marvel, that ye know not whence he is, and yet he opened mine eyes.

31 We know that God heareth not sinners: but if any man be a worshipper of God, and do his will, him he heareth.

32 Since the world began it was never heard that any one opened the eyes of a man born blind.

33 If this man were not from God, he could do nothing.

34 They answered and said unto him, Thou wast altogether born in sins, and dost thou teach us? And they cast him out.

35 Jesus heard that they had cast him out; and finding him, he said, Dost thou believe on the Son of God?

36 He answered and said, And who is he, Lord, that I may believe on him?

37 Jesus said unto him, Thou hast both seen him, and he it is that speaketh with thee.

38 And he said, Lord, I believe. And he worshipped him.

39 And Jesus said, For judgment came I into this world, that they that see not may see; and that they that see may become blind.

40 Those of the Pharisees who were with him heard these things, and said unto him, Are we also blind?

41 Jesus said unto them, If ye were blind, ye would have no sin: but now ye say, We see: your sin remaineth.

Chapter 10

1 Verily, verily, I say unto you, He that entereth not by the door into the fold of the sheep, but climbeth up some other way, the same is a thief and a robber.

2 But he that entereth in by the door is the shepherd of the sheep.

3 To him the porter openeth; and the sheep hear his voice: and he calleth his own sheep by name, and leadeth them out.

4 When he hath put forth all his own, he goeth before them, and the sheep follow him: for they know his voice.

5 And a stranger will they not follow, but will flee from him: for they know not the voice of strangers.

6 This parable spake Jesus unto them: but they understood not what things they were which he spake unto them.

7 Jesus therefore said unto them again, Verily, verily, I say unto you, I am the door of the sheep.

8 All that came before me are thieves and robbers: but the sheep did not hear them.

9 I am the door; by me if any man enter in, he shall be saved, and shall go in and go out, and shall find pasture.

10 The thief cometh not, but that he may steal, and kill, and destroy: I came that they may have life, and may have it abundantly.

11 I am the good shepherd: the good shepherd layeth down his life for the sheep.

12 He that is a hireling, and not a shepherd, whose own the sheep are not, beholdeth the wolf coming, and leaveth the sheep, and fleeth, and the wolf snatcheth them, and scattereth them:

13 he fleeth because he is a hireling, and careth not for the sheep.

14 I am the good shepherd; and I know mine own, and mine own know me,

15 even as the Father knoweth me, and I know the Father; and I lay down my life for the sheep.

16 And other sheep I have, which are not of this fold: them also I must bring, and they shall hear my voice: and they shall become one flock, one shepherd.

17 Therefore doth the Father love me, because I lay down my life, that I may take it again.

18 No one taketh it away from me, but I lay it down of myself. I have power to lay it down, and I have power to take it again. This commandment received I from my Father.

19 There arose a division again among the Jews because of these words.

20 And many of them said, He hath a demon, and is mad; why hear ye him?

21 Others said, These are not the sayings of one possessed with a demon. Can a demon open the eyes of the blind?

22And it was the feast of the dedication at Jerusalem: 23it was winter; and Jesus was walking in the temple in Solomon's porch. 24The Jews therefore came round about him, and said unto him, How long dost thou hold us in suspense? If thou art the Christ, tell us plainly. 25Jesus answered them, I told you, and ye believe not: the works that I do in my Father's name, these bear witness of me. 26But ye believe not, because ye are not of my sheep. 27My sheep hear my voice, and I know them, and they follow me: 28and I give unto them eternal life; and they shall never perish, and no one shall snatch them out of my hand. 29My Father, who hath given them unto me, is greater than all; and no one is able to snatch them out of the Father's hand. 30I and the Father are one. 31The Jews took up stones again to stone him. 32Jesus answered them, Many good works have I showed you from the Father; for which of those works do ye stone me? 33The Jews answered him, For a good work we stone thee not, but for blasphemy; and because that thou, being a man, makest thyself God. 34Jesus answered them, Is it not written in your law, I said, ye are gods? 35If he called them gods, unto whom the word of God came (and the scripture cannot be broken), 36say ye of him, whom the Father sanctified and sent into the world, Thou blasphemest; because I said, I am the Son of God? 37If I do not the works of my Father, believe me not. 38But if I do them, though ye believe not me, believe the works: that ye may know and understand that the Father is in me, and I in the Father. 39They sought again to take him: and he went forth out of their hand. 40And he went away again beyond the Jordan into the place where John was at the first baptizing; and there he abode. 41And many came unto him; and they said, John indeed did no sign: but all things whatsoever John spake of this man were true. 42And many believed on him there.

Chapter 11

1Now a certain man was sick, Lazarus of Bethany, of the village of Mary and her sister Martha. 2And it was that Mary who anointed the Lord with ointment, and wiped his feet with her hair, whose brother Lazarus was sick. 3The sisters therefore sent unto him, saying, Lord, behold, he whom thou lovest is sick. 4But when Jesus heard it, he said, This sickness is not unto death, but for the glory of God, that the Son of God may be glorified thereby. 5Now Jesus loved Martha, and her sister, and Lazarus. 6When therefore he heard that he was sick, he abode at that time two days in the place where he was. 7Then after this he saith to the disciples, Let us go into Judaea again. 8The disciples say unto him, Rabbi, the Jews were but now seeking to stone thee; and goest thou thither again? 9Jesus answered, Are there not twelve hours in the day? If a man walk in the day, he stumbleth not, because he seeth the light of this world. 10But if a man walk in the night, he stumbleth, because the light is not in him. 11These things spake he: and after this he saith unto them, Our friend Lazarus is fallen asleep; but I go, that I may awake him out of sleep. 12The disciples therefore said unto him, Lord, if he is fallen asleep, he will recover. 13Now Jesus had spoken of his death: but they thought that he spake of taking rest in sleep. 14Then Jesus therefore said unto them plainly, Lazarus is dead. 15And I am glad for your sakes that I was not there, to the intent ye may believe; nevertheless let us go unto him. 16Thomas therefore, who is called Didymus, said unto his fellow-disciples, Let us also go, that we may die with him. 17So when Jesus came, he found that he had been in the tomb four days already. 18Now Bethany was nigh unto Jerusalem, about fifteen furlongs off; 19and many of the Jews had come to Martha and Mary, to console them concerning their brother. 20Martha therefore, when she heard that Jesus was coming, went and met him: but Mary still sat in the house. 21Martha therefore said unto Jesus, Lord, if thou hadst been here, my brother had not died. 22And even now I know that, whatsoever thou shalt ask of God, God will give thee. 23Jesus saith unto her, Thy brother shall rise again. 24Martha saith unto him, I know that he shall rise again in the resurrection at the last day. 25Jesus said unto her, I am the resurrection, and the life: he that believeth on me, though he die, yet shall he live; 26and whosoever liveth and believeth on me shall never die. Believest thou this? 27She saith unto him, Yea, Lord: I have believed that thou art the Christ, the Son of God, even he that cometh into the world. 28And when she had said this, she went away, and called Mary her sister secretly, saying, The Teacher is her, and calleth thee. 29And she, when she heard it, arose quickly, and went unto him. 30(Now Jesus was not yet come into the village, but was still in the place where Martha met him.) 31The Jews then who were with her in the house, and were consoling her, when they saw Mary, that she rose up quickly and went out, followed her, supposing that she was going unto the tomb to weep there. 32Mary therefore, when she came where Jesus was, and saw him, fell down at his feet, saying unto him, Lord, if thou hadst been here, my brother had not died. 33When Jesus therefore saw her weeping, and the Jews also weeping who came with her, he groaned in the spirit, and was troubled, 34and said, Where have ye laid him? They say unto him, Lord, come and see. 35Jesus wept. 36The Jews therefore said, Behold how he loved him! 37But some of them said, Could not this man, who opened the eyes of him that was blind, have caused that this man also should not die? 38Jesus therefore again groaning in himself cometh to the tomb. Now it was a cave, and a stone lay against it. 39Jesus saith, Take ye away the stone. Martha, the sister of him that was dead, saith unto him, Lord, by this time the body decayeth; for he hath been dead four days. 40Jesus saith unto her, Said I not unto thee, that, if thou believedst, thou shouldest see the glory of God? 41So they took away the stone. And Jesus lifted up his eyes, and said, Father, I thank thee that thou heardest me. 42And I knew that thou hearest me always: but because of the multitude that standeth around I said it, that they may believe that thou didst send me. 43And when he had thus spoken, he cried with a loud voice, Lazarus, come forth. 44He that was dead came forth, bound hand and foot with grave-clothes; and his face was bound about with a napkin. Jesus saith unto them, Loose him, and let him go. 45Many therefore of the Jews, who came to Mary and beheld that which he did, believed on him. 46But some of them went away to the Pharisees, and told them the things which Jesus had done. 47The chief priests therefore and the Pharisees gathered a council, and said, What do we? for this man doeth many signs. 48If we let him thus alone, all men will believe on him: and the Romans will come and take away both our place and our nation. 49But a certain one of them, Caiaphas, being high priest that year, said unto them, Ye know nothing at all, 50nor do ye take account that it is expedient for you that one man should die for the people, and that the whole nation perish not. 51Now this he said not of himself: but, being high priest that year, he prophesied that Jesus should die for the nation; 52and not for the nation only, but that he might also gather together into one the children of God that are scattered abroad. 53So from that day forth they took counsel that they might put him to death. 54Jesus therefore walked no more openly among the Jews, but departed thence into the country near to the wilderness, into a city called Ephraim; and there he tarried with the disciples. 55Now the passover of the Jews was at hand: and many went up to Jerusalem out of the country before the passover, to purify themselves. 56They sought therefore for Jesus, and spake one with another, as they stood in the temple, What think ye? That he will not come to the feast? 57Now the chief priests and the Pharisees had given commandment, that, if any man knew where he was, he should show it, that they might take him.

Chapter 12

1Jesus therefore six days before the passover came to Bethany, where Lazarus was, whom Jesus raised from the dead. 2So they made him a supper there: and Martha served; but Lazarus was one of them that sat at meat with him. 3Mary therefore took a pound of ointment of pure nard, very precious, and anointed the feet of Jesus, and wiped his feet with her hair: and the house was filled with the odor of the ointment. 4But Judas Iscariot, one of his disciples, that should betray him, saith, 5Why was not this ointment sold for three hundred shillings, and given to the poor? 6Now this he said, not because he cared for the poor; but because he was a thief, and having the bag took away what was put therein. 7Jesus therefore said, Suffer her to keep it against the day of my burying. 8For the poor ye have always with you; but me ye have not always. 9The common people therefore of the Jews learned that he was there: and they came, not for Jesus' sake only, but that they might see Lazarus also, whom he had raised from the dead. 10But the chief priests took counsel that they might put Lazarus also to death; 11because that by reason of him many of the Jews went away, and believed on Jesus. 12On the morrow a great multitude that had come to the feast, when they heard that Jesus was coming to Jerusalem, 13took the branches of the palm trees, and went forth to meet him, and cried out, Hosanna: Blessed is he that cometh in the name of the Lord, even the King of Israel. 14And Jesus, having found a young ass, sat thereon; as it is written, 15Fear not, daughter of Zion: behold, thy King cometh, sitting on an ass's colt. 16These things understood not his disciples at the first: but when Jesus was glorified, then remembered they that these things were written of him, and that they had done these things unto him.

John

17The multitude therefore that was with him when he called Lazarus out of the tomb, and raised him from the dead, bare witness.
18For this cause also the multitude went and met him, for that they heard that he had done this sign.
19The Pharisees therefore said among themselves, Behold how ye prevail nothing: lo, the world is gone after him.
20Now there were certain Greeks among those that went up to worship at the feast:
21these therefore came to Philip, who was of Bethsaida of Galilee, and asked him, saying, Sir, we would see Jesus.
22Philip cometh and telleth Andrew: Andrew cometh, and Philip, and they tell Jesus.
23And Jesus answereth them, saying, The hour is come, that the Son of man should be glorified.
24Verily, verily, I say unto you, Except a grain of wheat fall into the earth and die, it abideth by itself alone; but if it die, it beareth much fruit.
25He that loveth his life loseth it; and he that hateth his life in this world shall keep it unto life eternal.
26If any man serve me, let him follow me; and where I am, there shall also my servant be: if any man serve me, him will the Father honor.
27Now is my soul troubled; and what shall I say? Father, save me from this hour. But for this cause came I unto this hour.
28Father, glorify thy name. There came therefore a voice out of heaven, saying, I have both glorified it, and will glorify it again.
29The multitude therefore, that stood by, and heard it, said that it had thundered: others said, An angel hath spoken to him.
30Jesus answered and said, This voice hath not come for my sake, but for your sakes.
31Now is the judgment of this world: now shall the prince of this world be cast out.
32And I, if I be lifted up from the earth, will draw all men unto myself.
33But this he said, signifying by what manner of death he should die.
34The multitude therefore answered him, We have heard out of the law that the Christ abideth for ever: and how sayest thou, The Son of man must be lifted up? who is this Son of man?
35Jesus therefore said unto them, Yet a little while is the light among you. Walk while ye have the light, that darkness overtake you not: and he that walketh in the darkness knoweth not whither he goeth.
36While ye have the light, believe on the light, that ye may become sons of light. These things spake Jesus, and he departed and hid himself from them.
37But though he had done so many signs before them, yet they believed not on him:
38that the word of Isaiah the prophet might be fulfilled, which he spake, Lord, who hath believed our report?
And to whom hath the arm of the Lord been revealed?
39For this cause they could not believe, for that Isaiah said again,
40He hath blinded their eyes, and he hardened their heart;
Lest they should see with their eyes, and perceive with their heart,
And should turn,
And I should heal them.
41These things said Isaiah, because he saw his glory; and he spake of him.
42Nevertheless even of the rulers many believed on him; but because of the Pharisees they did not confess it, lest they should be put out of the synagogue:
43for they loved the glory that is of men more than the glory that is of God.
44And Jesus cried and said, He that believeth on me, believeth not on me, but on him that sent me.
45And he that beholdeth me beholdeth him that sent me.
46I am come a light into the world, that whosoever believeth on me may not abide in the darkness.
47And if any man hear my sayings, and keep them not, I judge him not: for I came not to judge the world, but to save the world.
48He that rejecteth me, and receiveth not my sayings, hath one that judgeth him: the word that I spake, the same shall judge him in the last day.
49For I spake not from myself; but the Father that sent me, he hath given me a commandment, what I should say, and what I should speak.
50And I know that his commandment is life eternal: the things therefore which I speak, even as the Father hath said unto me, so I speak.

Chapter 13

1Now before the feast of the passover, Jesus knowing that his hour was come that he should depart out of this world unto his Father, having loved his own that were in the world, he loved them unto the end.
2And during supper, the devil having already put into the heart of Judas Iscariot, Simon's son, to betray him,
3Jesus, knowing that the Father had given all the things into his hands, and that he came forth from God, and goeth unto God,
4riseth from supper, and layeth aside his garments; and he took a towel, and girded himself.
5Then he poureth water into the basin, and began to wash the disciples' feet, and to wipe them with the towel wherewith he was girded.
6So he cometh to Simon Peter. He saith unto him, Lord, dost thou wash my feet?
7Jesus answered and said unto him, What I do thou knowest not now; but thou shalt understand hereafter.
8Peter saith unto him, Thou shalt never wash my feet. Jesus answered him, If I wash thee not, thou hast no part with me.
9Simon Peter saith unto him, Lord, not my feet only, but also my hands and my head.
10Jesus saith to him, He that is bathed needeth not save to wash his feet, but is clean every whit: and ye are clean, but not all.
11For he knew him that should betray him; therefore said he, Ye are not all clean.
12So when he had washed their feet, and taken his garments, and sat down again, he said unto them, Know ye what I have done to you?
13Ye call me, Teacher, and, Lord: and ye say well; for so I am.
14If I then, the Lord and the Teacher, have washed your feet, ye also ought to wash one another's feet.
15For I have given you an example, that ye also should do as I have done to you.
16Verily, verily, I say unto you, a servant is not greater than his lord; neither one that is sent greater than he that sent him.
17If ye know these things, blessed are ye if ye do them.
18I speak not of you all: I know whom I have chosen: but that the scripture may be fulfilled: He that eateth my bread lifted up his heel against me.
19From henceforth I tell you before it come to pass, that, when it is come to pass, ye may believe that I am he.
20Verily, verily, I say unto you, he that receiveth whomsoever I send receiveth me; and he that receiveth me receiveth him that sent me.
21When Jesus had thus said, he was troubled in the spirit, and testified, and said, Verily, verily, I say unto you, that one of you shall betray me.
22The disciples looked one on another, doubting of whom he spake.
23There was at the table reclining in Jesus' bosom one of his disciples, whom Jesus loved.
24Simon Peter therefore beckoneth to him, and saith unto him, Tell us who it is of whom he speaketh.
25He leaning back, as he was, on Jesus' breast saith unto him, Lord, who is it?
26Jesus therefore answereth, He it is, for whom I shall dip the sop, and give it him. So when he had dipped the sop, he taketh and giveth it to Judas, the son of Simon Iscariot.
27And after the sop, then entered Satan into him. Jesus therefore saith unto him, What thou doest, do quickly.
28Now no man at the table knew for what intent he spake this unto him.
29For some thought, because Judas had the bag, that Jesus said unto him, Buy what things we have need of for the feast; or, that he should give something to the poor.
30He then having received the sop went out straightway: and it was night.
31When therefore he was gone out, Jesus saith, Now is the Son of man glorified, and God is glorified in him;
32and God shall glorify him in himself, and straightway shall he glorify him.
33Little children, yet a little while I am with you. Ye shall seek me: and as I said unto the Jews, Whither I go, ye cannot come; so now I say unto you.
34A new commandment I give unto you, that ye love one another; even as I have loved you, that ye also love one another.
35By this shall all men know that ye are my disciples, if ye have love one to another.
36Simon Peter saith unto him, Lord, whither goest thou? Jesus answered, Whither I go, thou canst not follow now; but thou shalt follow afterwards.
37Peter saith unto him, Lord, why cannot I follow thee even now? I will lay down my life for thee.
38Jesus answereth, Wilt thou lay down thy life for me? Verily, verily, I say unto thee, The cock shall not crow, till thou hast denied me thrice.

Chapter 14

1Let not your heart be troubled: believe in God, believe also in me.
2In my Father's house are many mansions; if it were not so, I would have told you; for I go to prepare a place for you.
3And if I go and prepare a place for you, I come again, and will receive you unto myself; that where I am, there ye may be also.
4And whither I go, ye know the way.
5Thomas saith unto him, Lord, we know not whither thou goest; how know we the way?
6Jesus saith unto him, I am the way, and the truth, and the life: no one cometh unto the Father, but by me.
7If ye had known me, ye would have known my Father also: from henceforth ye know him, and have seen him.
8Philip saith unto him, Lord, show us the Father, and it sufficeth us.
9Jesus saith unto him, Have I been so long time with you, and dost thou not know me, Philip? he that hath seen me hath seen the Father; how sayest thou, Show us the Father?
10Believest thou not that I am in the Father, and the Father in me? the words that I say unto you I speak not from myself: but the Father abiding in me doeth his works.
11Believe me that I am in the Father, and the Father in me: or else believe me for the very works' sake.
12Verily, verily, I say unto you, he that believeth on me, the works that I do shall he do also; and greater works than these shall he do; because I go unto the Father.
13And whatsoever ye shall ask in my name, that will I do, that the Father may be glorified in the Son.
14If ye shall ask anything in my name, that will I do.
15If ye love me, ye will keep my commandments.
16And I will pray the Father, and he shall give you another Comforter, that he may be with you for ever,
17even the Spirit of truth: whom the world cannot receive; for it beholdeth him not, neither knoweth him: ye know him; for he abideth with you, and shall be in you.

18I will not leave you desolate: I come unto you.
19Yet a little while, and the world beholdeth me no more; but ye behold me: because I live, ye shall live also.
20In that day ye shall know that I am in my Father, and ye in me, and I in you.
21He that hath my commandments, and keepeth them, he it is that loveth me: and he that loveth me shall be loved of my Father, and I will love him, and will manifest myself unto him.
22Judas (not Iscariot) saith unto him, Lord, what is come to pass that thou wilt manifest thyself unto us, and not unto the world?
23Jesus answered and said unto him, If a man love me, he will keep my word: and my Father will love him, and we will come unto him, and make our abode with him.
24He that loveth me not keepeth not my words: and the word which ye hear is not mine, but the Father's who sent me.
25These things have I spoken unto you, while yet abiding with you.
26But the Comforter, even the Holy Spirit, whom the Father will send in my name, he shall teach you all things, and bring to your remembrance all that I said unto you.
27Peace I leave with you; my peace I give unto you: not as the world giveth, give I unto you. Let not your heart be troubled, neither let it be fearful.
28Ye heard how I said to you, I go away, and I come unto you. If ye loved me, ye would have rejoiced, because I go unto the Father: for the Father is greater than I.
29And now I have told you before it come to pass, that, when it is come to pass, ye may believe.
30I will no more speak much with you, for the prince of the world cometh: and he hath nothing in me;
31but that the world may know that I love the Father, and as the Father gave me commandment, even so I do. Arise, let us go hence.

Chapter 15

1I am the true vine, and my Father is the husbandman.
2Every branch in me that beareth not fruit, he taketh it away: and every branch that beareth fruit, he cleanseth it, that it may bear more fruit.
3Already ye are clean because of the word which I have spoken unto you.
4Abide in me, and I in you. As the branch cannot bear fruit of itself, except it abide in the vine; so neither can ye, except ye abide in me.
5I am the vine, ye are the branches: He that abideth in me, and I in him, the same beareth much fruit: for apart from me ye can do nothing.
6If a man abide not in me, he is cast forth as a branch, and is withered; and they gather them, and cast them into the fire, and they are burned.
7If ye abide in me, and my words abide in you, ask whatsoever ye will, and it shall be done unto you.
8Herein is my Father glorified, that ye bear much fruit; and so shall ye be my disciples.
9Even as the Father hath loved me, I also have loved you: abide ye in my love.
10If ye keep my commandments, ye shall abide in my love; even as I have kept my Father's commandments, and abide in his love.
11These things have I spoken unto you, that my joy may be in you, and that your joy may be made full.
12This is my commandment, that ye love one another, even as I have loved you.
13Greater love hath no man than this, that a man lay down his life for his friends.
14Ye are my friends, if ye do the things which I command you.
15No longer do I call you servants; for the servant knoweth not what his lord doeth: but I have called you friends; for all things that I heard from my Father, I have made known unto you.
16Ye did not choose me, but I chose you, and appointed you, that ye should go and bear fruit, and that your fruit should abide: that whatsoever ye shall ask of the Father in my name, he may give it you.
17These things I command you, that ye may love one another.
18If the world hateth you, ye know that it hath hated me before it hated you.
19If ye were of the world, the world would love its own: but because ye are not of the world, but I chose you out of the world, therefore the world hateth you.
20Remember the word that I said unto you, A servant is not greater than his lord. If they persecuted me, they will also persecute you; if they kept my word, they will keep yours also.
21But all these things will they do unto you for my name's sake, because they know not him that sent me.
22If I had not come and spoken unto them, they had not had sin: but now they have no excuse for their sin.
23He that hateth me hateth my Father also.
24If I had not done among them the works which none other did, they had not had sin: but now have they both seen and hated both me and my Father.
25But this cometh to pass, that the word may be fulfilled that is written in their law, They hated me without a cause.
26But when the Comforter is come, whom I will send unto you from the Father, even the Spirit of truth, which proceedeth from the Father, he shall bear witness of me:
27and ye also bear witness, because ye have been with me from the beginning.

Chapter 16

1These things have I spoken unto you, that ye should not be caused to stumble.
2They shall put you out of the synagogues: yea, the hour cometh, that whosoever killeth you shall think that he offereth service unto God.
3And these things will they do, because they have not known the Father, nor me.
4But these things have I spoken unto you, that when their hour is come, ye may remember them, how that I told you. And these things I said not unto you from the beginning, because I was with you.
5But now I go unto him that sent me; and none of you asketh me, Whither goest thou?
6But because I have spoken these things unto you, sorrow hath filled your heart.
7Nevertheless I tell you the truth: It is expedient for you that I go away; for if I go not away, the Comforter will not come unto you; but if I go, I will send him unto you.
8And he, when he is come, will convict the world in respect of sin, and of righteousness, and of judgment:
9of sin, because they believe not on me;
10of righteousness, because I go to the Father, and ye behold me no more;
11of judgment, because the prince of this world hath been judged.
12I have yet many things to say unto you, but ye cannot bear them now.
13Howbeit when he, the Spirit of truth, is come, he shall guide you into all the truth: for he shall not speak from himself; but what things soever he shall hear, these shall he speak: and he shall declare unto you the things that are to come.
14He shall glorify me: for he shall take of mine, and shall declare it unto you.
15All things whatsoever the Father hath are mine: therefore said I, that he taketh of mine, and shall declare it unto you.
16A little while, and ye behold me no more; and again a little while, and ye shall see me.
17Some of his disciples therefore said one to another, What is this that he saith unto us, A little while, and ye behold me not; and again a little while, and ye shall see me: and, Because I go to the Father?
18They said therefore, What is this that he saith, A little while? We know not what he saith.
19Jesus perceived that they were desirous to ask him, and he said unto them, Do ye inquire among yourselves concerning this, that I said, A little while, and ye behold me not, and again a little while, and ye shall see me?
20Verily, verily, I say unto you, that ye shall weep and lament, but the world shall rejoice: ye shall be sorrowful, but your sorrow shall be turned into joy.
21A woman when she is in travail hath sorrow, because her hour is come: but when she is delivered of the child, she remembereth no more the anguish, for the joy that a man is born into the world.
22And ye therefore now have sorrow: but I will see you again, and your heart shall rejoice, and your joy no one taketh away from you.
23And in that day ye shall ask me no question. Verily, verily, I say unto you, if ye shall ask anything of the Father, he will give it you in my name.
24Hitherto have ye asked nothing in my name: ask, and ye shall receive, that your joy may be made full.
25These things have I spoken unto you in dark sayings: the hour cometh, when I shall no more speak unto you in dark sayings, but shall tell you plainly of the Father.
26In that day ye shall ask in my name: and I say not unto you, that I will pray the Father for you;
27for the Father himself loveth you, because ye have loved me, and have believed that I came forth from the Father.
28I came out from the Father, and am come into the world: again, I leave the world, and go unto the Father.
29His disciples say, Lo, now speakest thou plainly, and speakest no dark saying.
30Now know we that thou knowest all things, and needest not that any man should ask thee: by this we believe that thou camest forth from God.
31Jesus answered them, Do ye now believe?
32Behold, the hour cometh, yea, is come, that ye shall be scattered, every man to his own, and shall leave me alone: and yet I am not alone, because the Father is with me.
33These things have I spoken unto you, that in me ye may have peace. In the world ye have tribulation: but be of good cheer; I have overcome the world.

Chapter 17

1These things spake Jesus; and lifting up his eyes to heaven, he said, Father, the hour is come; glorify thy Son, that the son may glorify thee:
2even as thou gavest him authority over all flesh, that to all whom thou hast given him, he should give eternal life.
3And this is life eternal, that they should know thee the only true God, and him whom thou didst send, even Jesus Christ.
4I glorified thee on the earth, having accomplished the work which thou hast given me to do.
5And now, Father, glorify thou me with thine own self with the glory which I had with thee before the world was.
6I manifested thy name unto the men whom thou gavest me out of the world: thine they were, and thou gavest them to me; and they have kept thy word.
7Now they know that all things whatsoever thou hast given me are from thee:
8for the words which thou gavest me I have given unto them; and they received them, and knew of a truth that I came forth from thee, and they believed

John

that thou didst send me.

9I pray for them: I pray not for the world, but for those whom thou hast given me; for they are thine:

10and all things that are mine are thine, and thine are mine: and I am glorified in them.

11And I am no more in the world, and these are in the world, and I come to thee. Holy Father, keep them in thy name which thou hast given me, that they may be one, even as we are.

12While I was with them, I kept them in thy name which thou hast given me: and I guarded them, and not one of them perished, but the son of perdition; that the scripture might be fulfilled.

13But now I come to thee; and these things I speak in the world, that they may have my joy made full in themselves.

14I have given them thy word; and the world hated them, because they are not of the world, even as I am not of the world.

15I pray not that thou shouldest take them from the world, but that thou shouldest keep them from the evil one.

16They are not of the world even as I am not of the world.

17Sanctify them in the truth: thy word is truth.

18As thou didst send me into the world, even so sent I them into the world.

19And for their sakes I sanctify myself, that they themselves also may be sanctified in truth.

20Neither for these only do I pray, but for them also that believe on me through their word;

21that they may all be one; even as thou, Father, art in me, and I in thee, that they also may be in us: that the world may believe that thou didst send me.

22And the glory which thou hast given me I have given unto them; that they may be one, even as we are one;

23I in them, and thou in me, that they may be perfected into one; that the world may know that thou didst send me, and lovedst them, even as thou lovedst me.

24Father, I desire that they also whom thou hast given me be with me where I am, that they may behold my glory, which thou hast given me: for thou lovedst me before the foundation of the world.

25O righteous Father, the world knew thee not, but I knew thee; and these knew that thou didst send me;

26and I made known unto them thy name, and will make it known; that the love wherewith thou lovedst me may be in them, and I in them.

Chapter 18

1When Jesus had spoken these words, he went forth with his disciples over the brook Kidron, where was a garden, into which he entered, himself and his disciples.

2Now Judas also, who betrayed him, knew the place: for Jesus oft-times resorted thither with his disciples.

3Judas then, having received the band of soldiers, and officers from the chief priests and the Pharisees, cometh thither with lanterns and torches and weapons.

4Jesus therefore, knowing all the things that were coming upon him, went forth, and saith unto them, Whom seek ye?

5They answered him, Jesus of Nazareth. Jesus saith unto them, I am he. And Judas also, who betrayed him, was standing with them.

6When therefore he said unto them, I am he, they went backward, and fell to the ground.

7Again therefore he asked them, Whom seek ye? And they said, Jesus of Nazareth.

8Jesus answered, I told you that I am he; if therefore ye seek me, let these go their way:

9that the word might be fulfilled which he spake, Of those whom thou hast given me I lost not one.

10Simon Peter therefore having a sword drew it, and struck the high priest's servant, and cut off his right ear. Now the servant's name was Malchus.

11Jesus therefore said unto Peter, Put up the sword into the sheath: the cup which the Father hath given me, shall I not drink it?

12So the band and the chief captain, and the officers of the Jews, seized Jesus and bound him,

13and led him to Annas first; for he was father in law to Caiaphas, who was high priest that year.

14Now Caiaphas was he that gave counsel to the Jews, that it was expedient that one man should die for the people.

15And Simon Peter followed Jesus, and so did another disciple. Now that disciple was known unto the high priest, and entered in with Jesus into the court of the high priest;

16but Peter was standing at the door without. So the other disciple, who was known unto the high priest, went out and spake unto her that kept the door, and brought in Peter.

17The maid therefore that kept the door saith unto Peter, Art thou also one of this man's disciples? He saith, I am not.

18Now the servants and the officers were standing there, having made a fire of coals; for it was cold; and they were warming themselves: and Peter also was with them, standing and warming himself.

19The high priest therefore asked Jesus of his disciples, and of his teaching.

20Jesus answered him, I have spoken openly to the world; I ever taught in synagogues, and in the temple, where all the Jews come together; and in secret spake I nothing.

21Why askest thou me? Ask them that have heard me, what I spake unto them: behold, these know the things which I said.

22And when he had said this, one of the officers standing by struck Jesus with his hand, saying, Answerest thou the high priest so?

23Jesus answered him, If I have spoken evil, bear witness of the evil: but if well, why smitest thou me?

24Annas therefore sent him bound unto Caiaphas the high priest.

25Now Simon Peter was standing and warming himself. They said therefore unto him, Art thou also one of his disciples? He denied, and said, I am not.

26One of the servants of the high priest, being a kinsman of him whose ear Peter cut off, saith, Did not I see thee in the garden with him?

27Peter therefore denied again: and straightway the cock crew.

28They lead Jesus therefore from Caiaphas into the Praetorium: and it was early; and they themselves entered not into the Praetorium, that they might not be defiled, but might eat the passover.

29Pilate therefore went out unto them, and saith, What accusation bring ye against this man?

30They answered and said unto him, If this man were not an evildoer, we should not have delivered him up unto thee.

31Pilate therefore said unto them, Take him yourselves, and judge him according to your law. The Jews said unto him, It is not lawful for us to put any man to death:

32that the word of Jesus might be fulfilled, which he spake, signifying by what manner of death he should die.

33Pilate therefore entered again into the Praetorium, and called Jesus, and said unto him, Art thou the King of the Jews?

34Jesus answered, Sayest thou this of thyself, or did others tell it thee concerning me?

35Pilate answered, Am I a Jew? Thine own nation and the chief priests delivered thee unto me: what hast thou done?

36Jesus answered, My kingdom is not of this world: if my kingdom were of this world, then would my servants fight, that I should not be delivered to the Jews: but now is my kingdom not from hence.

37Pilate therefore said unto him, Art thou a king then? Jesus answered, Thou sayest that I am a king. To this end have I been born, and to this end am I come into the world, that I should bear witness unto the truth. Every one that is of the truth heareth my voice.

38Pilate saith unto him, What is truth? And when he had said this, he went out again unto the Jews, and saith unto them, I find no crime in him.

39But ye have a custom, that I should release unto you one at the passover: will ye therefore that I release unto you the King of the Jews?

40They cried out therefore again, saying, Not this man, but Barabbas. Now Barabbas was a robber.)

Chapter 19

1Then Pilate therefore took Jesus, and scourged him.

2And the soldiers platted a crown of thorns, and put it on his head, and arrayed him in a purple garment;

3and they came unto him, and said, Hail, King of the Jews! and they struck him with their hands.

4And Pilate went out again, and saith unto them, Behold, I bring him out to you, that ye may know that I find no crime in him.

5Jesus therefore came out, wearing the crown of thorns and the purple garment. And Pilate saith unto them, Behold, the man!

6When therefore the chief priests and the officers saw him, they cried out, saying, Crucify him, crucify him! Pilate saith unto them, Take him yourselves, and crucify him: for I find no crime in him.

7The Jews answered him, We have a law, and by that law he ought to die, because he made himself the Son of God.

8When Pilate therefore heard this saying, he was the more afraid;

9and he entered into the Praetorium again, and saith unto Jesus, Whence art thou? But Jesus gave him no answer.

10Pilate therefore saith unto him, Speakest thou not unto me? Knowest thou not that I have power to release thee, and have power to crucify thee?

11Jesus answered him, Thou wouldest have no power against me, except it were given thee from above: therefore he that delivered me unto thee hath greater sin.

12Upon this Pilate sought to release him: but the Jews cried out, saying, If thou release this man, thou art not Caesar's friend: every one that maketh himself a king speaketh against Caesar.

13When Pilate therefore heard these words, he brought Jesus out, and sat down on the judgment-seat at a place called The Pavement, but in Hebrew, Gabbatha.

14Now it was the Preparation of the passover: it was about the sixth hour. And he saith unto the Jews, Behold, your King!

15They therefore cried out, Away with him, away with him, crucify him! Pilate saith unto them, Shall I crucify your King? The chief priests answered, We have no king but Caesar.

16Then therefore he delivered him unto them to be crucified.

17They took Jesus therefore: and he went out, bearing the cross for himself, unto the place called The place of a skull, which is called in Hebrew, Golgotha:

18where they crucified him, and with him two others, on either side one, and Jesus in the midst.

19And Pilate wrote a title also, and put it on the cross. And there was written, JESUS OF NAZARETH, THE KING OF THE JEWS.

20This title therefore read many of the Jews, for the place where Jesus was crucified was nigh to the city; and it was written in Hebrew, and in Latin, and in Greek.

21The chief priests of the Jews therefore said to Pilate, Write not, The King of the Jews; but that he said, I am King of the Jews.

22Pilate answered, What I have written I have written.

23The soldiers therefore, when they had crucified Jesus, took his garments and made four parts, to every soldier a part; and also the coat: now the coat was without seam, woven from the top throughout.

24They said therefore one to another, Let us not rend it, but cast lots for it, whose it shall be: that the scripture might be fulfilled, which saith,

They parted my garments among them,
And upon my vesture did they cast lots.

25These things therefore the soldiers did. But there were standing by the cross of Jesus his mother, and his mother's sister, Mary the wife of Clopas, and Mary Magdalene.

26When Jesus therefore saw his mother, and the disciple standing by whom he loved, he saith unto his mother, Woman, behold thy son!

27Then saith he to the disciple, Behold, thy mother! And from that hour the disciple took her unto his own home.

28After this Jesus, knowing that all things are now finished, that the scripture might be accomplished, saith, I thirst.

29There was set there a vessel full of vinegar: so they put a sponge full of the vinegar upon hyssop, and brought it to his mouth.

30When Jesus therefore had received the vinegar, he said, It is finished: and he bowed his head, and gave up his spirit.

31The Jews therefore, because it was the Preparation, that the bodies should not remain on the cross upon the sabbath (for the day of that sabbath was a high day), asked of Pilate that their legs might be broken, and that they might be taken away.

32The soldiers therefore came, and brake the legs of the first, and of the other that was crucified with him:

33but when they came to Jesus, and saw that he was dead already, they brake not his legs:

34howbeit one of the soldiers with a spear pierced his side, and straightway there came out blood and water.

35And he that hath seen hath borne witness, and his witness is true: and he knoweth that he saith true, that ye also may believe.

36For these things came to pass, that the scripture might be fulfilled, A bone of him shall not be broken.

37And again another scripture saith, They shall look on him whom they pierced.

38And after these things Joseph of Arimathaea, being a disciple of Jesus, but secretly for fear of the Jews, asked of Pilate that he might take away the body of Jesus: and Pilate gave him leave. He came therefore, and took away his body.

39And there came also Nicodemus, he who at the first came to him by night, bringing a mixture of myrrh and aloes, about a hundred pounds.

40So they took the body of Jesus, and bound it in linen cloths with the spices, as the custom of the Jews is to bury.

41Now in the place where he was crucified there was a garden; and in the garden a new tomb wherein was never man yet laid.

42There then because of the Jews' Preparation (for the tomb was nigh at hand) they laid Jesus.

Chapter 20

1Now on the first day of the week cometh Mary Magdalene early, while it was yet dark, unto the tomb, and seeth the stone taken away from the tomb.

2She runneth therefore, and cometh to Simon Peter, and to the other disciple whom Jesus loved, and saith unto them, They have taken away the Lord out of the tomb, and we know not where they have laid him.

3Peter therefore went forth, and the other disciple, and they went toward the tomb.

4And they ran both together: and the other disciple outran Peter, and came first to the tomb;

5and stooping and looking in, he seeth the linen cloths lying; yet entered he not in.

6Simon Peter therefore also cometh, following him, and entered into the tomb; and he beholdeth the linen cloths lying,

7and the napkin, that was upon his head, not lying with the linen cloths, but rolled up in a place by itself.

8Then entered in therefore the other disciple also, who came first to the tomb, and he saw, and believed.

9For as yet they knew not the scripture, that he must rise from the dead.

10So the disciples went away again unto their own home.

11But Mary was standing without at the tomb weeping: so, as she wept, she stooped and looked into the tomb;

12and she beholdeth two angels in white sitting, one at the head, and one at the feet, where the body of Jesus had lain.

13And they say unto her, Woman, why weepest thou? She saith unto them, Because they have taken away my Lord, and I know not where they have laid him.

14When she had thus said, she turned herself back, and beholdeth Jesus standing, and knew not that it was Jesus.

15Jesus saith unto her, Woman, why weepest thou? whom seekest thou? She, supposing him to be the gardener, saith unto him, Sir, if thou hast borne him hence, tell me where thou hast laid him, and I will take him away.

16Jesus saith unto her, Mary. She turneth herself, and saith unto him in Hebrew, Rabboni; which is to say, Teacher.

17Jesus saith to her, Touch me not; for I am not yet ascended unto the Father: but go unto my brethren, and say to them, I ascend unto my Father and your Father, and my God and your God.

18Mary Magdalene cometh and telleth the disciples, I have seen the Lord; and that he had said these things unto her.

19When therefore it was evening, on that day, the first day of the week, and when the doors were shut where the disciples were, for fear of the Jews, Jesus came and stood in the midst, and saith unto them, Peace be unto you.

20And when he had said this, he showed unto them his hands and his side. The disciples therefore were glad, when they saw the Lord.

21Jesus therefore said to them again, Peace be unto you: as the Father hath sent me, even so send I you.

22And when he had said this, he breathed on them, and saith unto them, Receive ye the Holy Spirit:

23whose soever sins ye forgive, they are forgiven unto them; whose soever sins ye retain, they are retained.

24But Thomas, one of the twelve, called Didymus, was not with them when Jesus came.

25The other disciples therefore said unto him, We have seen the Lord. But he said unto them, Except I shall see in his hands the print of the nails, and put my hand into his side, I will not believe.

26And after eight days again his disciples were within, and Thomas with them. Jesus cometh, the doors being shut, and stood in the midst, and said, Peace be unto you.

27Then saith he to Thomas, Reach hither thy finger, and see my hands; and reach hither thy hand, and put it into my side: and be not faithless, but believing.

28Thomas answered and said unto him, My Lord and my God.

29Jesus saith unto him, Because thou hast seen me, thou hast believed: blessed are they that have not seen, and yet have believed.

30Many other signs therefore did Jesus in the presence of the disciples, which are not written in this book:

31but these are written, that ye may believe that Jesus is the Christ, the Son of God; and that believing ye may have life in his name.

Chapter 21

1After these things Jesus manifested himself again to the disciples at the sea of Tiberias; and he manifested himself on this wise.

2There was together Simon Peter, and Thomas called Didymus, and Nathanael of Cana in Galilee, and the sons of Zebedee, and two other of his disciples.

3Simon Peter saith unto them, I go a fishing. They say unto him, We also come with thee. They went forth, and entered into the boat; and that night they took nothing.

4But when day was now breaking, Jesus stood on the beach: yet the disciples knew not that it was Jesus.

5Jesus therefore saith unto them, Children, have ye aught to eat? They answered him, No.

6And he said unto them, Cast the net on the right side of the boat, and ye shall find. They cast therefore, and now they were not able to draw it for the multitude of fishes.

7That disciple therefore whom Jesus loved saith unto Peter, It is the Lord. So when Simon Peter heard that it was the Lord, he girt his coat about him (for he was naked), and cast himself into the sea.

8But the other disciples came in the little boat (for they were not far from the land, but about two hundred cubits off), dragging the net full of fishes.

9So when they got out upon the land, they see a fire of coals there, and fish laid thereon, and bread.

10Jesus saith unto them, Bring of the fish which ye have now taken.

11Simon Peter therefore went up, and drew the net to land, full of great fishes, a hundred and fifty and three: and for all there were so many, the net was not rent.

12Jesus saith unto them, Come and break your fast. And none of the disciples durst inquire of him, Who art thou? knowing that it was the Lord.

13Jesus cometh, and taketh the bread, and giveth them, and the fish likewise.

14This is now the third time that Jesus was manifested to the disciples, after that he was risen from the dead.

15So when they had broken their fast, Jesus saith to Simon Peter, Simon, son of John, lovest thou me more than these? He saith unto him, Yea, Lord; thou knowest that I love thee. He saith unto him, Feed my lambs.

16He saith to him again a second time, Simon, son of John, lovest thou me? He saith unto him, Yea, Lord; thou knowest that I love thee. He saith unto him, Tend my sheep.

17He saith unto him the third time, Simon, son of John, lovest thou me? Peter was grieved because he said unto him the third time, Lovest thou me? And he said unto him, Lord, thou knowest all things; thou knowest that I love thee. Jesus saith unto him, Feed my sheep.

18Verily, verily, I say unto thee, When thou wast young, thou girdedst thyself, and walkedst whither thou wouldest: but when thou shalt be old, thou shalt stretch forth thy hands, and another shall gird thee, and carry thee whither thou wouldest not.

19Now this he spake, signifying by what manner of death he should glorify God. And when he had spoken this, he saith unto him, Follow me.

20Peter, turning about, seeth the disciple whom Jesus loved following; who also leaned back on his breast at the supper, and said, Lord, who is he that betrayeth thee?

21Peter therefore seeing him saith to Jesus, Lord, and what shall this man do?

22Jesus saith unto him, If I will that he tarry till I come, what is that to thee? Follow thou me.

23This saying therefore went forth among the brethren, that that disciple should not die: yet Jesus said not unto him, that he should not die; but, If I will that he tarry till I come, what is that to thee?

24This is the disciple that beareth witness of these things, and wrote these things: and we know that his witness is true.

25And there are also many other things which Jesus did, the which if they should be written every one, I suppose that even the world itself would not contain the books that should be written.

The Acts of the Apostles

Chapter 1

1 The former treatise I made, O Theophilus, concerning all that Jesus began both to do and to teach,

2 until the day in which he was received up, after that he had given commandment through the Holy Spirit unto the apostles whom he had chosen:

3 To whom he also showed himself alive after his passion by many proofs, appearing unto them by the space of forty days, and speaking the things concerning the kingdom of God:

4 and, being assembled together with them, he charged them not to depart from Jerusalem, but to wait for the promise of the Father, which, said he, ye heard from me:

5 For John indeed baptized with water; but ye shall be baptized in the Holy Spirit not many days hence.

6 They therefore, when they were come together, asked him, saying, Lord, dost thou at this time restore the kingdom to Israel?

7 And he said unto them, It is not for you to know times or seasons, which the Father hath set within His own authority.

8 But ye shall receive power, when the Holy Spirit is come upon you: and ye shall be my witnesses both in Jerusalem, and in all Judaea and Samaria, and unto the uttermost part of the earth.

9 And when he had said these things, as they were looking, he was taken up; and a cloud received him out of their sight.

10 And while they were looking stedfastly into heaven as he went, behold, two men stood by them in white apparel;

11 who also said, Ye men of Galilee, why stand ye looking into heaven? this Jesus, who was received up from you into heaven shall so come in like manner as ye beheld him going into heaven.

12 Then returned they unto Jerusalem from the mount called Olivet, which is nigh unto Jerusalem, a Sabbath day's journey off.

13 And when they were come in, they went up into the upper chamber, where they were abiding; both Peter and John and James and Andrew, Philip and Thomas, Bartholomew and Matthew, James the son of Alphaeus, and Simon the Zealot, and Judas the son of James.

14 These all with one accord continued stedfastly in prayer, with the women, and Mary the mother of Jesus, and with his brethren.

15 And in these days Peter stood up in the midst of the brethren, and said (and there was a multitude of persons gathered together, about a hundred and twenty),

16 Brethren, it was needful that the Scripture should be fulfilled, which the Holy Spirit spake before by the mouth of David concerning Judas, who was guide to them that took Jesus.

17 For he was numbered among us, and received his portion in this ministry.

18 (Now this man obtained a field with the reward of his iniquity; and falling headlong, he burst asunder in the midst, and all his bowels gushed out.

19 And it became known to all the dwellers at Jerusalem; insomuch that in their language that field was called Akeldama, that is, The field of blood.)

20 For it is written in the book of Psalms,
Let his habitation be made desolate,
And let no man dwell therein:
and,
His office let another take.

21 Of the men therefore that have companied with us all the time that the Lord Jesus went in and went out among us,

22 beginning from the baptism of John, unto the day that he was received up from us, of these must one become a witness with us of his resurrection.

23 And they put forward two, Joseph called Barsabbas, who was surnamed Justus, and Matthias.

24 And they prayed, and said, Thou, Lord, who knowest the hearts of all men, show of these two the one whom thou hast chosen,

25 to take the place in this ministry and apostleship from which Judas fell away, that he might go to his own place.

26 And they gave lots for them; and the lot fell upon Matthias; and he was numbered with the eleven apostles.

Chapter 2

1 And when the day of Pentecost was now come, they were all together in one place.

2 And suddenly there came from heaven a sound as of the rushing of a mighty wind, and it filled all the house where they were sitting.

3 And there appeared unto them tongues parting asunder, like as of fire; and it sat upon each one of them.

4 And they were all filled with the Holy Spirit, and began to speak with other tongues, as the Spirit gave them utterance.

5 Now there were dwelling at Jerusalem Jews, devout men, from every nation under heaven.

6 And when this sound was heard, the multitude came together, and were confounded, because that every man heard them speaking in his own language.

7 And they were all amazed and marvelled, saying, Behold, are not all these that speak Galilaeans?

8 And how hear we, every man in our own language wherein we were born?

9 Parthians and Medes and Elamites, and the dwellers in Mesopotamia, in Judaea and Cappadocia, in Pontus and Asia,

10 in Phrygia and Pamphylia, in Egypt and the parts of Libya about Cyrene, and sojourners from Rome, both Jews and proselytes,

11 Cretans and Arabians, we hear them speaking in our tongues the mighty works of God.

12 And they were all amazed, and were perplexed, saying one to another, What meaneth this?

13 But others mocking said, They are filled with new wine.

14 But Peter, standing up with the eleven, lifted up his voice, and spake forth unto them, saying, Ye men of Judaea, and all ye that dwell at Jerusalem, be this known unto you, and give ear unto my words.

15 For these are not drunken, as ye suppose; seeing it is but the third hour of the day.

16 but this is that which hath been spoken through the prophet Joel:

17 And it shall be in the last days, saith God,
I will pour forth of my Spirit upon all flesh:
And your sons and your daughters shall prophesy,
And your young men shall see visions,
And your old men shall dream dreams:

18 Yea and on my servants and on my handmaidens in those days
Will I pour forth of my Spirit; and they shall prophesy.

19 And I will show wonders in the heaven above,
And signs on the earth beneath;
Blood, and fire, and vapor of smoke:

20 The sun shall be turned into darkness,
And the moon into blood,
Before the day of the Lord come,
That great and notable day.

21 And it shall be, that whosoever shall call on the name of the Lord shall be saved.

22 Ye men of Israel, hear these words: Jesus of Nazareth, a man approved of God unto you by mighty works and wonders and signs which God did by him in the midst of you, even as ye yourselves know;

23 him, being delivered up by the determinate counsel and foreknowledge of God, ye by the hand of lawless men did crucify and slay:

24 whom God raised up, having loosed the pangs of death: because it was not possible that he should be holden of it.

25 For David saith concerning him,
I beheld the Lord always before my face;
For he is on my right hand, that I should not be moved:

26 Therefore my heart was glad, and my tongue rejoiced;
Moreover my flesh also shall dwell in hope:

27 Because thou wilt not leave my soul unto Hades,
Neither wilt thou give thy Holy One to see corruption.

28 Thou madest known unto me the ways of life;
Thou shalt make me full of gladness with thy countenance.

29 Brethren, I may say unto you freely of the patriarch David, that he both died and was buried, and his tomb is with us unto this day.

30 Being therefore a prophet, and knowing that God had sworn with an oath to him, that of the fruit of his loins he would set one upon his throne;

31 he foreseeing this spake of the resurrection of the Christ, that neither was he left unto Hades, nor did his flesh see corruption.

32 This Jesus did God raise up, whereof we all are witnesses.

33 Being therefore by the right hand of God exalted, and having received of the Father the promise of the Holy Spirit, he hath poured forth this, which ye see and hear.

34 For David ascended not into the heavens: but he saith himself,
The Lord said unto my Lord, Sit thou on my right hand,

35 Till I make thine enemies the footstool of thy feet.

36 Let all the house of Israel therefore know assuredly, that God hath made him both Lord and Christ, this Jesus whom ye crucified.

37 Now when they heard this, they were pricked in their heart, and said unto Peter and the rest of the apostles, Brethren, what shall we do?

38 And Peter said unto them, Repent ye, and be baptized every one of you in the name of Jesus Christ unto the remission of your sins; and ye shall receive the gift of the Holy Spirit.

39 For to you is the promise, and to your children, and to all that are afar off, even as many as the Lord our God shall call unto him.

40 And with many other words he testified, and exhorted them, saying, Save yourselves from this crooked generation.

41 They then that received his word were baptized: and there were added unto them in that day about three thousand souls.

42 And they continued stedfastly in the apostles' teaching and fellowship, in the breaking of bread and the prayers.

43 And fear came upon every soul: and many wonders and signs were done through the apostles.

44 And all that believed were together, and had all things common;

45 and they sold their possessions and goods, and parted them to all, according as any man had need.

46 And day by day, continuing stedfastly with one accord in the temple, and breaking bread at home, they took their food with gladness and singleness of heart,

47 praising God, and having favor with all the people. And the Lord added to them day by day those that were saved.

Chapter 3

1Now Peter and John were going up into the temple at the hour of prayer, being the ninth hour.

2And a certain man that was lame from his mother's womb was carried, whom they laid daily at the door of the temple which is called Beautiful, to ask alms of them that entered into the temple;

3who seeing Peter and John about to go into the temple, asked to receive an alms.

4And Peter, fastening his eyes upon him, with John, said, Look on us.

5And he gave heed unto them, expecting to receive something from them.

6But Peter said, Silver and gold have I none; but what I have, that give I thee. In the name of Jesus Christ of Nazareth, walk.

7And he took him by the right hand, and raised him up: and immediately his feet and his ankle-bones received strength.

8And leaping up, he stood, and began to walk; and he entered with them into the temple, walking, and leaping, and praising God.

9And all the people saw him walking and praising God:

10and they took knowledge of him, that it was he that sat for alms at the Beautiful Gate of the temple; and they were filled with wonder and amazement at that which had happened unto him.

11And as he held Peter and John, all the people ran together unto them in the porch that is called Solomon's, greatly wondering.

12And when Peter saw it, he answered unto the people, Ye men of Israel, why marvel ye at this man? or why fasten ye your eyes on us, as though by our own power or godliness we had made him to walk?

13The God of Abraham, and of Isaac, and of Jacob, the God of our fathers, hath glorified his Servant Jesus; whom ye delivered up, and denied before the face of Pilate, when he had determined to release him.

14But ye denied the Holy and Righteous One, and asked for a murderer to be granted unto you,

15and killed the Prince of life; whom God raised from the dead; whereof we are witnesses.

16And by faith in his name hath his name made this man strong, whom ye behold and know: yea, the faith which is through him hath given him this perfect soundness in the presence of you all.

17And now, brethren, I know that in ignorance ye did it, as did also your rulers.

18But the things which God foreshowed by the mouth of all the prophets, that his Christ should suffer, he thus fulfilled.

19Repent ye therefore, and turn again, that your sins may be blotted out, that so there may come seasons of refreshing from the presence of the Lord;

20and that he may send the Christ who hath been appointed for you, even Jesus:

21whom the heaven must receive until the times of restoration of all things, whereof God spake by the mouth of His holy prophets that have been from of old.

22Moses indeed said, A prophet shall the Lord God raise up unto you from among your brethren, like unto me. To him shall ye hearken in all things whatsoever he shall speak unto you.

23And it shall be, that every soul that shall not hearken to that prophet, shall be utterly destroyed from among the people.

24Yea and all the prophets from Samuel and them that followed after, as many as have spoken, they also told of these days.

25Ye are the sons of the prophets, and of the covenant which God made with your fathers, saying unto Abraham, And in thy seed shall all the families of the earth be blessed.

26Unto you first God, having raised up his Servant, sent him to bless you, in turning away every one of you from your iniquities.

Chapter 4

1And as they spake unto the people, the priests and the captain of the temple and the Sadducees came upon them,

2being sore troubled because they taught the people, and proclaimed in Jesus the resurrection from the dead.

3And they laid hands on them, and put them in ward unto the morrow: for it was now eventide.

4But many of them that heard the word believed; and the number of the men came to be about five thousand.

5And it came to pass on the morrow, that their rulers and elders and scribes were gathered together in Jerusalem;

6and Annas the high priest was there, and Caiaphas, and John, and Alexander, and as many as were of the kindred of the high priest.

7And when they had set them in the midst, they inquired, By what power, or in what name, have ye done this?

8Then Peter, filled with the Holy Spirit, said unto them, Ye rulers of the people, and elders,

9if we this day are examined concerning a good deed done to an impotent man, by what means this man is made whole;

10be it known unto you all, and to all the people of Israel, that in the name of Jesus Christ of Nazareth, whom ye crucified, whom God raised from the dead, even in him doth this man stand here before you whole.

11He is the stone which was set at nought of you the builders, which was made the head of the corner.

12And in none other is there salvation: for neither is there any other name under heaven, that is given among men, wherein we must be saved.

13Now when they beheld the boldness of Peter and John, and had perceived that they were unlearned and ignorant men, they marvelled; and they took knowledge of them, that they had been with Jesus.

14And seeing the man that was healed standing with them, they could say nothing against it.

15But when they had commanded them to go aside out of the council, they conferred among themselves,

16saying, What shall we do to these men? for that indeed a notable miracle hath been wrought through them, is manifest to all that dwell in Jerusalem; and we cannot deny it.

17But that it spread no further among the people, let us threaten them, that they speak henceforth to no man in this name.

18And they called them, and charged them not to speak at all nor teach in the name of Jesus.

19But Peter and John answered and said unto them, Whether it is right in the sight of God to hearken unto you rather than unto God, judge ye:

20for we cannot but speak the things which we saw and heard.

21And they, when they had further threatened them, let them go, finding nothing how they might punish them, because of the people; for all men glorified God for that which was done.

22For the man was more than forty years old, on whom this miracle of healing was wrought.

23And being let go, they came to their own company, and reported all that the chief priests and the elders had said unto them.

24And they, when they heard it, lifted up their voice to God with one accord, and said, O Lord, thou that didst make the heaven and the earth and the sea, and all that in them is:

25who by the Holy Spirit, by the mouth of our father David thy servant, didst say,

Why did the Gentiles rage,

And the peoples imagine vain things?

26The kings of the earth set themselves in array,

And the rulers were gathered together,

Against the Lord, and against his Anointed:

27for of a truth in this city against thy holy Servant Jesus, whom thou didst anoint, both Herod and Pontius Pilate, with the Gentiles and the peoples of Israel, were gathered together,

28to do whatsoever thy hand and thy council foreordained to come to pass.

29And now, Lord, look upon their threatenings: and grant unto thy servants to speak thy word with all boldness,

30while thy stretchest forth thy hand to heal; and that signs and wonders may be done through the name of thy holy Servant Jesus.

31And when they had prayed, the place was shaken wherein they were gathered together; and they were all filled with the Holy Spirit, and they spake the word of God with boldness.

32And the multitude of them that believed were of one heart and soul: and not one of them said that aught of the things which he possessed was his own; but they had all things common.

33And with great power gave the apostles their witness of the resurrection of the Lord Jesus: and great grace was upon them all.

34For neither was there among them any that lacked: for as many as were possessors of lands or houses sold them, and brought the prices of the things that were sold,

35and laid them at the apostles' feet: and distribution was made unto each, according as any one had need.

36And Joseph, who by the apostles was surnamed Barnabas (which is, being interpreted, Son of exhortation), a Levite, a man of Cyprus by race,

37having a field, sold it, and brought the money and laid it at the apostles' feet.

Chapter 5

1But a certain man named Ananias, with Sapphira his wife, sold a possession,

2and kept back part of the price, his wife also being privy to it, and brought a certain part, and laid it at the apostles' feet.

3But Peter said, Ananias, why hath Satan filled thy heart to lie to the Holy Spirit, and to keep back part of the price of the land?

4While it remained, did it not remain thine own? and after it was sold, was it not in thy power? How is it that thou hast conceived this thing in thy heart? thou has not lied unto men, but unto God.

5And Ananias hearing these words fell down and gave up the ghost: and great fear came upon all that heard it.

6And the young men arose and wrapped him round, and they carried him out and buried him.

7And it was about the space of three hours after, when his wife, not knowing what was done, came in.

8And Peter answered unto her, Tell me whether ye sold the land for so much. And she said, Yea, for so much.

9But Peter said unto her, How is it that ye have agreed together to try the Spirit of the Lord? behold, the feet of them that have buried thy husband are at the door, and they shall carry thee out.

10And she fell down immediately at his feet, and gave up the ghost: and the young men came in and found her dead, and they carried her out and buried her by her husband.

11And great fear came upon the whole church, and upon all that heard these things.

12And by the hands of the apostles were many signs and wonders wrought among the people; and they were all with one accord in Solomon's porch.

13But of the rest durst no man join himself to them: howbeit the people magnified them;

14and believers were the more added to the Lord, multitudes both of them and women;

15insomuch that they even carried out the sick into the streets, and laid them

Acts

on beds and couches, that, as Peter came by, at the least his shadow might overshadow some one of them.

16 And there also came together the multitudes from the cities round about Jerusalem, bring sick folk, and them that were vexed with unclean spirits: and they were healed every one.

17 But the high priest rose up, and all they that were with him (which is the sect of the Sadducees), and they were filled with jealousy,

18 and laid hands on the apostles, and put them in public ward.

19 But an angel of the Lord by night opened the prison doors, and brought them out, and said,

20 Go ye, and stand and speak in the temple to the people all the words of this Life.

21 And when they heard this, they entered into the temple about daybreak, and taught. But the high priest came, and they that were with him, and called the council together, and all the senate of the children of Israel, and sent to the prison-house to have them brought.

22 But the officers that came found them not in the prison; and they returned, and told,

23 saying, The prison-house we found shut in all safety, and the keepers standing at the doors: but when we had opened, we found no man within.

24 Now when the captain of the temple and the chief priests heard these words, they were much perplexed concerning them whereunto this would grow.

25 And there came one and told them, Behold, the men whom ye put in the prison are in the temple standing and teaching the people.

26 Then went the captain with the officers, and brought them, but without violence; for they feared the people, lest they should be stoned.

27 And when they had brought them, they set them before the council. And the high priest asked them,

28 saying, We strictly charged you not to teach in this name: and behold, ye have filled Jerusalem with your teaching, and intend to bring this man's blood upon us.

29 But Peter and the apostles answered and said, We must obey God rather than men.

30 The God of our fathers raised up Jesus, whom ye slew, hanging him on a tree.

31 Him did God exalt with his right hand to be a Prince and a Saviour, to give repentance to Israel, and remission of sins.

32 And we are witnesses of these things; and so is the Holy Spirit, whom God hath given to them that obey him.

33 But they, when they heard this, were cut to the heart, and minded to slay them.

34 But there stood up one in the council, a Pharisee, named Gamaliel, a doctor of the law, had in honor of all the people, and commanded to put the men forth a little while.

35 And he said unto them, Ye men of Israel, take heed to yourselves as touching these men, what ye are about to do.

36 For before these days rose up Theudas, giving himself out to be somebody; to whom a number of men, about four hundred, joined themselves: who was slain; and all, as many as obeyed him, were dispersed, and came to nought.

37 After this man rose up Judas of Galilee in the days of the enrolment, and drew away some of the people after him: he also perished; and all, as many as obeyed him, were scattered abroad.

38 And now I say unto you, Refrain from these men, and let them alone: for if this counsel or this work be of men, it will be overthrown:

39 but if it is of God, ye will not be able to overthrow them; lest haply ye be found even to be fighting against God.

40 And to him they agreed: and when they had called the apostles unto them, they beat them and charged them not to speak in the name of Jesus, and let them go.

41 They therefore departed from the presence of the council, rejoicing that they were counted worthy to suffer dishonor for the Name.

42 And every day, in the temple and at home, they ceased not to teach and to preach Jesus as the Christ.

Chapter 6

1 Now in these days, when the number of the disciples was multiplying, there arose a murmuring of the Grecian Jews against the Hebrews, because their widows were neglected in the daily ministration.

2 And the twelve called the multitude of the disciples unto them, and said, It is not fit that we should forsake the word of God, and serve tables.

3 Look ye out therefore, brethren, from among you seven men of good report, full of the Spirit and of wisdom, whom we may appoint over this business.

4 But we will continue stedfastly in prayer, and in the ministry of the word.

5 And the saying pleased the whole multitude: and they chose Stephen, a man full of faith and of the Holy Spirit, and Philip, and Prochorus, and Nicanor, and Timon, and Parmenas, and Nicolaus a proselyte of Antioch;

6 whom they set before the apostles: and when they had prayed, they laid their hands upon them.

7 And the word of God increased; and the number of the disciples multiplied in Jerusalem exceedingly; and a great company of the priests were obedient to the faith.

8 And Stephen, full of grace and power, wrought great wonders and signs among the people.

9 But there arose certain of them that were of the synagogue called the synagogue of the Libertines, and of the Cyrenians, and of the Alexandrians, and of them of Cilicia and Asia, disputing with Stephen.

10 And they were not able to withstand the wisdom and the Spirit by which he spake.

11 Then they suborned men, who said, We have heard him speak blasphemous words against Moses, and against God.

12 And they stirred up the people, and the elders, and the scribes, and came upon him, and seized him, and brought him into the council,

13 and set up false witnesses, who said, This man ceaseth not to speak words against this holy place, and the law:

14 for we have heard him say, that this Jesus of Nazareth shall destroy this place, and shall change the customs which Moses delivered unto us.

15 And all that sat in the council, fastening their eyes on him, saw his face as it had been the face of an angel.

Chapter 7

1 And the high priest said, Are these things so?

2 And he said, Brethren and fathers, hearken: The God of glory appeared unto our father Abraham, when he was in Mesopotamia, before he dwelt in Haran,

3 and said unto him, Get thee out of thy land, and from thy kindred, and come into the land which I shall show thee.

4 Then came he out of the land of the Chaldaeans, and dwelt in Haran: and from thence, when his father was dead, God removed him into this land, wherein ye now dwell:

5 and he gave him none inheritance in it, no, not so much as to set his foot on: and he promised that he would give it to him in possession, and to his seed after him, when as yet he had no child.

6 And God spake on this wise, that his seed should sojourn in a strange land, and that they should bring them into bondage, and treat them ill, four hundred years.

7 And the nation to which they shall be in bondage will I judge, said God: and after that shall they come forth, and serve me in this place.

8 And he gave him the covenant of circumcision: and so Abraham begat Isaac, and circumcised him the eighth day; and Isaac begat Jacob, and Jacob the twelve patriarchs.

9 And the patriarchs, moved with jealousy against Joseph, sold him into Egypt: and God was with him,

10 and delivered him out of all his afflictions, and gave him favor and wisdom before Pharaoh king of Egypt; and he made him governor over Egypt and all his house.

11 Now there came a famine over all Egypt and Canaan, and great affliction: and our fathers found no sustenance.

12 But when Jacob heard that there was grain in Egypt, he sent forth our fathers the first time.

13 And at the second time Joseph was made known to his brethren; and Joseph's race became manifest unto Pharaoh.

14 And Joseph sent, and called to him Jacob his father, and all his kindred, threescore and fifteen souls.

15 And Jacob went down into Egypt; and he died, himself and our fathers;

16 and they were carried over unto Shechem, and laid in the tomb that Abraham bought for a price in silver of the sons of Hamor in Shechem.

17 But as the time of the promise drew nigh which God vouchsafed unto Abraham, the people grew and multiplied in Egypt,

18 till there arose another king over Egypt, who knew not Joseph.

19 The same dealt craftily with our race, and ill-treated our fathers, that they should cast out their babes to the end they might not live.

20 At which season Moses was born, and was exceeding fair; and he was nourished three months in his father's house.

21 and when he was cast out, Pharaoh's daughter took him up, and nourished him for her own son.

22 And Moses was instructed in all the wisdom of the Egyptians; and he was mighty in his words and works.

23 But when he was well-nigh forty years old, it came into his heart to visit his brethren the children of Israel.

24 And seeing one of them suffer wrong, he defended him, and avenged him that was oppressed, smiting the Egyptian:

25 and he supposed that his brethren understood that God by his hand was giving them deliverance; but they understood not.

26 And the day following he appeared unto them as they strove, and would have set them at one again, saying, Sirs, ye are brethren; why do ye wrong one to another?

27 But he that did his neighbor wrong thrust him away, saying, Who made thee a ruler and a judge over us?

28 Wouldest thou kill me, as thou killedst the Egyptian yesterday?

29 And Moses fled at this saying, and became a sojourner in the land of Midian, where he begat two sons.

30 And when forty years were fulfilled, an angel appeared to him in the wilderness of Mount Sinai, in a flame of fire in a bush.

31 And when Moses saw it, he wondered at the sight: and as he drew near to behold, there came a voice of the Lord,

32 I am the God of thy fathers, the God of Abraham, and of Isaac, and of Jacob. And Moses trembled, and durst not behold.

33 And the Lord said unto him, Loose the shoes from thy feet: for the place whereon thou standest is holy ground.

34 I have surely seen the affliction of my people that is in Egypt, and have heard their groaning, and I am come down to deliver them: and now come, I will send thee into Egypt.

35 This Moses whom they refused, saying, Who made thee a ruler and a judge? him hath God sent to be both a ruler and a deliverer with the hand of the angel that appeared to him in the bush.

36 This man led them forth, having wrought wonders and signs in Egypt, and in the Red Sea, and in the wilderness forty years.

37 This is that Moses, who said unto the children of Israel, A prophet shall

God raise up unto you from among your brethren, like unto me.

38This is he that was in the church in the wilderness with the angel that spake to him in the Mount Sinai, and with our fathers: who received living oracles to give unto us:

39to whom our fathers would not be obedient, but thrust him from them, and turned back in their hearts unto Egypt,

40saying unto Aaron, Make us gods that shall go before us: for as for this Moses, who led us forth out of the land of Egypt, we know not what is become of him.

41And they made a calf in those days, and brought a sacrifice unto the idol, and rejoiced in the works of their hands.

42But God turned, and gave them up to serve the host of heaven; as it is written in the book of the prophets,

Did ye offer unto me slain beasts and sacrifices
Forty years in the wilderness, O house of Israel?
43And ye took up the tabernacle of Moloch,
And the star of the god Rephan,
The figures which ye made to worship them:
And I will carry you away beyond Babylon.

44Our fathers had the tabernacle of the testimony in the wilderness, even as he appointed who spake unto Moses, that he should make it according to the figure that he had seen.

45Which also our fathers, in their turn, brought in with Joshua when they entered on the possession of the nations, that God thrust out before the face of our fathers, unto the days of David;

46who found favor in the sight of God, and asked to find a habitation for the God of Jacob.

47But Solomon built him a house.

48Howbeit the Most High dwelleth not in houses made with hands; as saith the prophet,

49The heaven is my throne,
And the earth the footstool of my feet:
What manner of house will ye build me? saith the Lord:
Or what is the place of my rest?
50Did not my hand make all these things?

51Ye stiffnecked and uncircumcised in heart and ears, ye do always resist the Holy Spirit: as your fathers did, so do ye.

52Which of the prophets did not your fathers persecute? and they killed them that showed before of the coming of the Righteous One; of whom ye have now become betrayers and murderers;

53ye who received the law as it was ordained by angels, and kept it not.

54Now when they heard these things, they were cut to the heart, and they gnashed on him with their teeth.

55But he, being full of the Holy Spirit, looked up stedfastly into heaven, and saw the glory of God, and Jesus standing on the right hand of God,

56and said, Behold, I see the heavens opened, and the Son of Man standing on the right hand of God.

57But they cried out with a loud voice, and stopped their ears, and rushed upon him with one accord;

58and they cast him out of the city, and stoned him: and the witnesses laid down their garments at the feet of a young man named Saul.

59And they stoned Stephen, calling upon the Lord, and saying, Lord Jesus, receive my spirit.

60And he kneeled down, and cried with a loud voice, Lord, lay not this sin to their charge. And when he had said this, he fell asleep.

Chapter 8

1And Saul was consenting unto his death. And there arose on that day a great persecution against the church which was in Jerusalem; and they were all scattered abroad throughout the regions of Judaea and Samaria, except the apostles.

2And devout men buried Stephen, and made great lamentation over him.

3But Saul laid waste the church, entering into every house, and dragging men and women committed them to prison.

4They therefore that were scattered abroad, went about preaching the word.

5And Philip went down to the city of Samaria, and proclaimed unto them the Christ.

6And the multitudes gave heed with one accord unto the things that were spoken by Philip, when they heard, and saw the signs which he did.

7For from many of those that had unclean spirits, they came out, crying with a loud voice: and many that were palsied, and that were lame, were healed.

8And there was much joy in that city.

9But there was a certain man, Simon by name, who beforetime in the city used sorcery, and amazed the people of Samaria, giving out that himself was some great one:

10to whom they all gave heed, from the least to the greatest, saying, This man is that power of God which is called Great.

11And they gave heed to him, because that of long time he had amazed them with his sorceries.

12But when they believed Philip preaching good tidings concerning the kingdom of God and the name of Jesus Christ, they were baptized, both men and women.

13And Simon also himself believed: and being baptized, he continued with Philip; and beholding signs and great miracles wrought, he was amazed.

14Now when the apostles that were at Jerusalem heard that Samaria had received the word of God, they sent unto them Peter and John:

15who, when they were come down, prayed for them, that they might receive the Holy Spirit:

16for as yet it was fallen upon none of them: only they had been baptized into the name of the Lord Jesus.

17Then laid they their hands on them, and they received the Holy Spirit.

18Now when Simon saw that through the laying on of the apostles' hands the Holy Spirit was given, he offered them money,

19saying, Give me also this power, that on whomsoever I lay my hands, he may receive the Holy Spirit.

20But Peter said unto him, Thy silver perish with thee, because thou hast thought to obtain the gift of God with money.

21Thou hast neither part nor lot in this matter: for thy heart is not right before God.

22Repent therefore of this thy wickedness, and pray the Lord, if perhaps the thought of thy heart shall be forgiven thee.

23For I see that thou art in the gall of bitterness and in the bond of iniquity.

24And Simon answered and said, Pray ye for me to the Lord, that none of the things which ye have spoken come upon me.

25They therefore, when they had testified and spoken the word of the Lord, returned to Jerusalem, and preached the gospel to many villages of the Samaritans.

26But an angel of the Lord spake unto Philip, saying, Arise, and go toward the south unto the way that goeth down from Jerusalem unto Gaza: the same is desert.

27And he arose and went: and behold, a man of Ethiopia, a eunuch of great authority under Candace, queen of the Ethiopians, who was over all her treasure, who had come to Jerusalem to worship;

28and he was returning and sitting in his chariot, and was reading the prophet Isaiah.

29And the Spirit said unto Philip, Go near, and join thyself to this chariot.

30And Philip ran to him, and heard him reading Isaiah the prophet, and said, Understandest thou what thou readest?

31And he said, How can I, except some one shall guide me? And he besought Philip to come up and sit with him.

32Now the passage of the Scripture which he was reading was this,

He was led as a sheep to the slaughter;
And as a lamb before his shearer is dumb,
So he openeth not his mouth:
33In his humiliation his judgment was taken away:
His generation who shall declare?
For his life is taken from the earth.

34And the eunuch answered Philip, and said, I pray thee, of whom speaketh the prophet this? of himself, or of some other?

35And Philip opened his mouth, and beginning from this Scripture, preached unto him Jesus.

36And as they went on the way, they came unto a certain water; and the eunuch saith, Behold, here is water; what doth hinder me to be baptized?

37And Philip said, If thou believest with all thy heart, thou mayest. And he answered and said, I believe that Jesus Christ is the Son of God.

38And he commanded the chariot to stand still: and they both went down into the water, both Philip and the eunuch, and he baptized him.

39And when they came up out of the water, the Spirit of the Lord caught away Philip; and the eunuch saw him no more, for he went on his way rejoicing.

40But Philip was found at Azotus: and passing through he preached the gospel to all the cities, till he came to Caesarea.

Chapter 9

1But Saul, yet breathing threatening and slaughter against the disciples of the Lord, went unto the high priest,

2and asked of him letters to Damascus unto the synagogues, that if he found any that were of the Way, whether men or women, he might bring them bound to Jerusalem.

3And as he journeyed, it came to pass that he drew nigh unto Damascus: and suddenly there shone round about him a light out of heaven:

4and he fell upon the earth, and heard a voice saying unto him, Saul, Saul, why persecutest thou me?

5And he said, Who art thou, Lord? And he said, I am Jesus whom thou persecutest:

6but rise, and enter into the city, and it shall be told thee what thou must do.

7And the men that journeyed with him stood speechless, hearing the voice, but beholding no man.

8And Saul arose from the earth; and when his eyes were opened, he saw nothing; and they led him by the hand, and brought him into Damascus.

9And he was three days without sight, and did neither eat nor drink.

10Now there was a certain disciple at Damascus, named Ananias; and the Lord said unto him in a vision, Ananias. And he said, Behold, I am here, Lord.

11And the Lord said unto him, Arise, and go to the street which is called Straight, and inquire in the house of Judas for one named Saul, a man of Tarsus: for behold, he prayeth;

12and he hath seen a man named Ananias coming in, and laying his hands on him, that he might receive his sight.

13But Ananias answered, Lord, I have heard from many of this man, how much evil he did to thy saints at Jerusalem:

14and here he hath authority from the chief priests to bind all that call upon thy name.

15But the Lord said unto him, Go thy way: for he is a chosen vessel unto me, to bear my name before the Gentiles and kings, and the children of Israel:

16for I will show him how many things he must suffer for my name's sake.

17And Ananias departed, and entered into the house; and laying his hands on him said, Brother Saul, the Lord, even Jesus, who appeared unto thee in the way which thou camest, hath sent me, that thou mayest receive thy sight, and be filled with the Holy Spirit.

18And straightway there fell from his eyes as it were scales, and he received

Acts

his sight; and he arose and was baptized;

19and he took food and was strengthened. And he was certain days with the disciples that were at Damascus.

20And straightway in the synagogues he proclaimed Jesus, that he is the Son of God.

21And all that heard him were amazed, and said, Is not this he that in Jerusalem made havoc of them that called on this name? and he had come hither for this intent, that he might bring them bound before the chief priests.

22But Saul increased the more in strength, and confounded the Jews that dwelt at Damascus, proving that this is the Christ.

23And when many days were fulfilled, the Jews took counsel together to kill him:

24but their plot became known to Saul. And they watched the gates also day and night that they might kill him:

25but his disciples took him by night, and let him down through the wall, lowering him in a basket.

26And when he was come to Jerusalem, he assayed to join himself to the disciples: and they were all afraid of him, not believing that he was a disciple.

27But Barnabas took him, and brought him to the apostles, and declared unto them how he had seen the Lord in the way, and that he had spoken to him, and how at Damascus he had preached boldly in the name of Jesus.

28And he was with them going in and going out at Jerusalem,

29preaching boldly in the name of the Lord: and he spake and disputed against the Grecian Jews; but they were seeking to kill him.

30And when the brethren knew it, they brought him down to Caesarea, and sent him forth to Tarsus.

31So the church throughout all Judaea and Galilee and Samaria had peace, being edified; and, walking in the fear of the Lord and in the comfort of the Holy Spirit, was multiplied.

32And it came to pass, as Peter went throughout all parts, he came down also to the saints that dwelt at Lydda.

33And there he found a certain man named Aeneas, who had kept his bed eight years; for he was palsied.

34And Peter said unto him, Aeneas, Jesus Christ healeth thee: arise and make thy bed. And straightway he arose.

35And all that dwelt at Lydda and in Sharon saw him, and they turned to the Lord.

36Now there was at Joppa a certain disciple named Tabitha, which by interpretation is called Dorcas: this woman was full of good works and almsdeeds which she did.

37And it came to pass in those days, that she fell sick, and died: and when they had washed her, they laid her in an upper chamber.

38And as Lydda was nigh unto Joppa, the disciples, hearing that Peter was there, sent two men unto him, entreating him, Delay not to come on unto us.

39And Peter arose and went with them. And when he was come, they brought him into the upper chamber: and all the widows stood by him weeping, and showing the coats and garments which Dorcas made, while she was with them.

40But Peter put them all forth, and kneeled down and prayed; and turning to the body, he said, Tabitha, arise. And she opened her eyes; and when she saw Peter, she sat up.

41And he gave her his hand, and raised her up; and calling the saints and widows, he presented her alive.

42And it became known throughout all Joppa: and many believed on the Lord.

43And it came to pass, that he abode many days in Joppa with one Simon a tanner.

Chapter 10

1Now there was a certain man in Caesarea, Cornelius by name, a centurion of the band called the Italian band,

2a devout man, and one that feared God with all his house, who gave much alms to the people, and prayed to God always.

3He saw in a vision openly, as it were about the ninth hour of the day, an angel of God coming in unto him, and saying to him, Cornelius.

4And he, fastening his eyes upon him, and being affrighted, said, What is it, Lord? And he said unto him, Thy prayers and thine alms are gone up for a memorial before God.

5And now send men to Joppa, and fetch one Simon, who is surnamed Peter:

6he lodgeth with one Simon a tanner, whose house is by the sea side.

7And when the angel that spake unto him was departed, he called two of his household-servants, and a devout soldier of them that waited on him continually;

8and having rehearsed all things unto them, he sent them to Joppa.

9Now on the morrow, as they were on their journey, and drew nigh unto the city, Peter went up upon the housetop to pray, about the sixth hour:

10and he became hungry, and desired to eat: but while they made ready, he fell into a trance;

11and he beholdeth the heaven opened, and a certain vessel descending, as it were a great sheet, let down by four corners upon the earth:

12wherein were all manner of fourfooted beasts and creeping things of the earth and birds of the heaven.

13And there came a voice to him, Rise, Peter; kill and eat.

14But Peter said, Not so, Lord; for I have never eaten anything that is common and unclean.

15And a voice came unto him again the second time, What God hath cleansed, make not thou common.

16And this was done thrice: and straightway the vessel was received up into heaven.

17Now while Peter was much perplexed in himself what the vision which he had seen might mean, behold, the men that were sent by Cornelius, having made inquiry for Simon's house, stood before the gate,

18and called and asked whether Simon, who was surnamed Peter, were lodging there.

19And while Peter thought on the vision, the Spirit said unto him, Behold, three men seek thee.

20But arise, and get thee down, and go with them, nothing doubting: for I have sent them.

21And Peter went down to the men, and said, Behold, I am he whom ye seek: what is the cause wherefore ye are come?

22And they said, Cornelius a centurion, a righteous man and one that feareth God, and well reported of by all the nation of the Jews, was warned of God by a holy angel to send for thee into his house, and to hear words from thee.

23So he called them in and lodged them. And on the morrow he arose and went forth with them, and certain of the brethren from Joppa accompanied him.

24And on the morrow they entered into Caesarea. And Cornelius was waiting for them, having called together his kinsmen and his near friends.

25And when it came to pass that Peter entered, Cornelius met him, and fell down at his feet, and worshipped him.

26But Peter raised him up, saying, Stand up; I myself also am a man.

27And as he talked with him, he went in, and findeth many come together:

28and he said unto them, Ye yourselves know how it is an unlawful thing for a man that is a Jew to join himself or come unto one of another nation; and yet unto me hath God showed that I should not call any man common or unclean:

29wherefore also I came without gainsaying, when I was sent for. I ask therefore with what intent ye sent for me.

30And Cornelius said, Four days ago, until this hour, I was keeping the ninth hour of prayer in my house; and behold, a man stood before me in bright apparel,

31and saith, Cornelius, thy prayer is heard, and thine alms are had in remembrance in the sight of God.

32Send therefore to Joppa, and call unto thee Simon, who is surnamed Peter; he lodgeth in the house of Simon a tanner, by the sea side.

33Forthwith therefore I sent to thee; and thou hast well done that thou art come. Now therefore we are all here present in the sight of God, to hear all things that have been commanded thee of the Lord.

34And Peter opened his mouth and said, Of a truth I perceive that God is no respecter of persons:

35but in every nation he that feareth him, and worketh righteousness, is acceptable to him.

36The word which he sent unto the children of Israel, preaching good tidings of peace by Jesus Christ (He is Lord of all.) --

37that saying ye yourselves know, which was published throughout all Judaea, beginning from Galilee, after the baptism which John preached;

38even Jesus of Nazareth, how God anointed him with the Holy Spirit and with power: who went about doing good, and healing all that were oppressed of the devil; for God was with him.

39And we are witnesses of all things which he did both in the country of the Jews, and in Jerusalem; whom also they slew, hanging him on a tree.

40Him God raised up the third day, and gave him to be made manifest,

41not to all the people, but unto witnesses that were chosen before of God, even to us, who ate and drank with him after he rose from the dead.

42And he charged us to preach unto the people, and to testify that this is he who is ordained of God to be the Judge of the living and the dead.

43To him bear all the prophets witness, that through his name every one that believeth on him shall receive remission of sins.

44While Peter yet spake these words, the Holy Spirit fell on all them that heard the word.

45And they of the circumcision that believed were amazed, as many as came with Peter, because that on the Gentiles also was poured out the gift of the Holy Spirit.

46For they heard them speak with tongues, and magnify God. Then answered Peter,

47Can any man forbid the water, that these should not be baptized, who have received the Holy Spirit as well as we?

48And he commanded them to be baptized in the name of Jesus Christ. Then prayed they him to tarry certain days.

Chapter 11

1Now the apostles and the brethren that were in Judaea heard that the Gentiles also had received the word of God.

2And when Peter was come up to Jerusalem, they that were of the circumcision contended with him,

3saying, Thou wentest in to men uncircumcised, and didst eat with them.

4But Peter began, and expounded the matter unto them in order, saying,

5I was in the city of Joppa praying: and in a trance I saw a vision, a certain vessel descending, as it were a great sheet let down from heaven by four corners; and it came even unto me:

6upon which when I had fastened mine eyes, I considered, and saw the fourfooted beasts of the earth and wild beasts and creeping things and birds of the heaven.

7And I heard also a voice saying unto me, Rise, Peter; kill and eat.

8But I said, Not so, Lord: for nothing common or unclean hath ever entered into my mouth.

9But a voice answered the second time out of heaven, What God hath cleansed, make not thou common.

10And this was done thrice: and all were drawn up again into heaven.

11And behold, forthwith three men stood before the house in which we were, having been sent from Caesarea unto me.

12And the Spirit bade me go with them, making no distinction. And these six brethren also accompanied me; and we entered into the man's house:

13and he told us how he had seen the angel standing in his house, and saying, Send to Joppa, and fetch Simon, whose surname is Peter;

14who shall speak unto thee words, whereby thou shalt be saved, thou and all thy house.

15And as I began to speak, the Holy Spirit fell on them, even as on us at the beginning.

16And I remembered the word of the Lord, how he said, John indeed baptized with water; but ye shall be baptized in the Holy Spirit.

17If then God gave unto them the like gift as he did also unto us, when we believed on the Lord Jesus Christ, who was I, that I could withstand God?

18And when they heard these things, they held their peace, and glorified God, saying, Then to the Gentiles also hath God granted repentance unto life.

19They therefore that were scattered abroad upon the tribulation that arose about Stephen travelled as far as Phoenicia, and Cyprus, and Antioch, speaking the word to none save only to Jews.

20But there were some of them, men of Cyprus and Cyrene, who, when they were come to Antioch, spake unto the Greeks also, preaching the Lord Jesus.

21And the hand of the Lord was with them: and a great number that believed turned unto the Lord.

22And the report concerning them came to the ears of the church which was in Jerusalem: and they sent forth Barnabas as far as Antioch:

23who, when he was come, and had seen the grace of God, was glad; and he exhorted them all, that with purpose of heart they would cleave unto the Lord:

24for he was a good man, and full of the Holy Spirit and of faith: and much people was added unto the Lord.

25And he went forth to Tarsus to seek for Saul;

26and when he had found him, he brought him unto Antioch. And it came to pass, that even for a whole year they were gathered together with the church, and taught much people, and that the disciples were called Christians first in Antioch.

27Now in these days there came down prophets from Jerusalem unto Antioch.

28And there stood up one of them named Agabus, and signified by the Spirit that there should be a great famine over all the world: which came to pass in the days of Claudius.

29And the disciples, every man according to his ability, determined to send relief unto the brethren that dwelt in Judea:

30which also they did, sending it to the elders by the hand of Barnabas and Saul.

Chapter 12

1Now about that time Herod the king put forth his hands to afflict certain of the church.

2And he killed James the brother of John with the sword.

3And when he saw that it pleased the Jews, he proceeded to seize Peter also. And those were the days of unleavened bread.

4And when he had taken him, he put him in prison, and delivered him to four quaternions of soldiers to guard him; intending after the Passover to bring him forth to the people.

5Peter therefore was kept in the prison: but prayer was made earnestly of the church unto God for him.

6And when Herod was about to bring him forth, the same night Peter was sleeping between two soldiers, bound with two chains: and guards before the door kept the prison.

7And behold, an angel of the Lord stood by him, and a light shined in the cell: and he smote Peter on the side, and awoke him, saying, Rise up quickly. And his chains fell off from his hands.

8And the angel said unto him, Gird thyself, and bind on thy sandals. And he did so. And he saith unto him, Cast thy garment about thee, and follow me.

9And he went out, and followed; and he knew not that it was true which was done by the angel, but thought he saw a vision.

10And when they were past the first and the second guard, they came unto the iron gate that leadeth into the city; which opened to them of its own accord: and they went out, and passed on through one street; and straightway the angel departed from him.

11And when Peter was come to himself, he said, Now I know of a truth, that the Lord hath sent forth his angel and delivered me out of the hand of Herod, and from all the expectation of the people of the Jews.

12And when he had considered the thing, he came to the house of Mary the mother of John whose surname was Mark; where many were gathered together and were praying.

13And when he knocked at the door of the gate, a maid came to answer, named Rhoda.

14And when she knew Peter's voice, she opened not the gate for joy, but ran in, and told that Peter stood before the gate.

15And they said unto her, Thou art mad. But she confidently affirmed that it was even so. And they said, It is his angel.

16But Peter continued knocking: and when they had opened, they saw him, and were amazed.

17But he, beckoning unto them with the hand to hold their peace, declared unto them how the Lord had brought him forth out of the prison. And he said, Tell these things unto James, and to the brethren. And he departed, and went to another place.

18Now as soon as it was day, there was no small stir among the soldiers, what was become of Peter.

19And when Herod had sought for him, and found him not, he examined the guards, and commanded that they should be put to death. And he went down from Judaea to Caesarea, and tarried there.

20Now he was highly displeased with them of Tyre and Sidon: and they came with one accord to him, and, having made Blastus the king's chamberlain their friend, they asked for peace, because their country was fed from the king's country.

21And upon a set day Herod arrayed himself in royal apparel, and sat on the throne, and made an oration unto them.

22And the people shouted, saying, The voice of a god, and not of a man.

23And immediately an angel of the Lord smote him, because he gave not God the glory: and he was eaten of worms, and gave up the ghost.

24But the word of God grew and multiplied.

25And Barnabas and Saul returned from Jerusalem, when they had fulfilled their ministration, taking with them John whose surname was Mark.

Chapter 13

1Now there were at Antioch, in the church that was there, prophets and teachers, Barnabas, and Symeon that was called Niger, and Lucius of Cyrene, and Manaen the foster-brother of Herod the tetrarch, and Saul.

2And as they ministered to the Lord, and fasted, the Holy Spirit said, Separate me Barnabas and Saul for the work whereunto I have called them.

3Then, when they had fasted and prayed and laid their hands on them, they sent them away.

4So they, being sent forth by the Holy Spirit, went down to Seleucia; and from thence they sailed to Cyprus.

5And when they were at Salamis, they proclaimed the word of God in the synagogues of the Jews: and they had also John as their attendant.

6And when they had gone through the whole island unto Paphos, they found a certain sorcerer, a false prophet, a Jew, whose name was Bar-jesus;

7who was with the proconsul, Sergius Paulus, a man of understanding. The same called unto him Barnabas and Saul, and sought to hear the word of God.

8But Elymas the sorcerer (for so is his name by interpretation) withstood them, seeking to turn aside the proconsul from the faith.

9But Saul, who is also called Paul, filled with the Holy Spirit, fastened his eyes on him,

10and said, O full of all guile and all villany, thou son of the devil, thou enemy of all righteousness, wilt thou not cease to pervert the right ways of the Lord?

11And now, behold, the hand of the Lord is upon thee, and thou shalt be blind, not seeing the sun for a season. And immediately there fell on him a mist and a darkness; and he went about seeking some to lead him by the hand.

12Then the proconsul, when he saw what was done, believed, being astonished at the teaching of the Lord.

13Now Paul and his company set sail from Paphos, and came to Perga in Pamphylia: and John departed from them and returned to Jerusalem.

14But they, passing through from Perga, came to Antioch of Pisidia; and they went into the synagogue on the sabbath day, and sat down.

15And after the reading of the law and the prophets the rulers of the synagogue sent unto them, saying, Brethren, if ye have any word of exhortation for the people, say on.

16And Paul stood up, and beckoning with the hand said, Men of Israel, and ye that fear God, hearken:

17The God of this people Israel chose our fathers, and exalted the people when they sojourned in the land of Egypt, and with a high arm led he them forth out of it.

18And for about the time of forty years as a nursing-father bare he them in the wilderness.

19And when he had destroyed seven nations in the land of Canaan, he gave them their land for an inheritance, for about four hundred and fifty years:

20and after these things he gave them judges until Samuel the prophet.

21And afterward they asked for a king: and God gave unto them Saul the son of Kish, a man of the tribe of Benjamin, for the space of forty years.

22And when he had removed him, he raised up David to be their king; to whom also he bare witness and said, I have found David the son of Jesse, a man after My heart, who shall do all My will.

23Of this man's seed hath God according to promise brought unto Israel a Saviour, Jesus;

24when John had first preached before his coming the baptism of repentance to all the people of Israel.

25And as John was fulfilling his course, he said, What suppose ye that I am? I am not he. But behold, there cometh one after me the shoes of whose feet I am not worthy to unloose.

26Brethren, children of the stock of Abraham, and those among you that fear God, to us is the word of this salvation sent forth.

27For they that dwell in Jerusalem, and their rulers, because they knew him not, nor the voices of the prophets which are read every sabbath, fulfilled them by condemning him.

28And though they found no cause of death in him, yet asked they of Pilate that he should be slain.

29And when they had fulfilled all things that were written of him, they took him down from the tree, and laid him in a tomb.

30But God raised him from the dead:

31and he was seen for many days of them that came up with him from Galilee to Jerusalem, who are now his witnesses unto the people.

32And we bring you good tidings of the promise made unto the fathers,

33that God hath fulfilled the same unto our children, in that he raised up Jesus; as also it is written in the second psalm, Thou art my Son, this day have I begotten thee.

34And as concerning that he raised him up from the dead, now no more to return to corruption, he hath spoken on this wise, I will give you the holy and sure blessings of David.

35Because he saith also in another psalm, Thou wilt not give Thy Holy One to see corruption.

36For David, after he had in his own generation served the counsel of God, fell asleep, and was laid unto his fathers, and saw corruption:

37but he whom God raised up saw no corruption.

38Be it known unto you therefore, brethren, that through this man is proclaimed unto you remission of sins:

39and by him every one that believeth is justified from all things, from which ye could not be justified by the law of Moses.

40Beware therefore, lest that come upon you which is spoken in the prophets:

41Behold, ye despisers, and wonder, and perish;
For I work a work in your days,
A work which ye shall in no wise believe, if one declare it unto you.

42And as they went out, they besought that these words might be spoken to them the next sabbath.

43Now when the synagogue broke up, many of the Jews and of the devout proselytes followed Paul and Barnabas; who, speaking to them, urged them to continue in the grace of God.

44And the next sabbath almost the whole city was gathered together to hear the word of God.

45But when the Jews saw the multitudes, they were filled with jealousy, and contradicted the things which were spoken by Paul, and blasphemed.

46And Paul and Barnabas spake out boldly, and said, It was necessary that the word of God should first be spoken to you. Seeing ye thrust it from you, and judge yourselves unworthy of eternal life, lo, we turn to the Gentiles.

47For so hath the Lord commanded us, saying,
I have set thee for a light of the Gentiles,
That thou shouldest be for salvation unto the uttermost part of the earth.

48And as the Gentiles heard this, they were glad, and glorified the word of God: and as many as were ordained to eternal life believed.

49And the word of the Lord was spread abroad throughout all the region.

50But the Jews urged on the devout women of honorable estate, and the chief men of the city, and stirred up a persecution against Paul and Barnabas, and cast them out of their borders.

51But they shook off the dust of their feet against them, and came unto Iconium.

52And the disciples were filled with joy with the Holy Spirit.

Chapter 14

1And it came to pass in Iconium that they entered together into the synagogue of the Jews, and so spake that a great multitude both of Jews and of Greeks believed.

2But the Jews that were disobedient stirred up the souls of the Gentiles, and made them evil affected against the brethren.

3Long time therefore they tarried there speaking boldly in the Lord, who bare witness unto the word of his grace, granting signs and wonders to be done by their hands.

4But the multitude of the city was divided; and part held with the Jews, and part with the apostles.

5And when there was made an onset both of the Gentiles and of the Jews with their rulers, to treat them shamefully and to stone them,

6they became aware of it, and fled unto the cities of Lycaonia, Lystra and Derbe, and the region round about:

7and there they preached the gospel.

8And at Lystra there sat a certain man, impotent in his feet, a cripple from his mother's womb, who never had walked.

9The same heard Paul speaking, who, fastening eyes upon him, and seeing that he had faith to be made whole,

10said with a loud voice, Stand upright on thy feet. And he leaped up and walked.

11And when the multitude saw what Paul had done, they lifted up their voice, saying in the speech of Lycaonia, The gods are come down to us in the likeness of men.

12And they called Barnabas, Jupiter; and Paul, Mercury, because he was the chief speaker.

13And the priest of Jupiter whose temple was before the city, brought oxen and garlands unto the gates, and would have done sacrifice with the multitudes.

14But when the apostles, Barnabas and Paul, heard of it, they rent their garments, and sprang forth among the multitude, crying out

15and saying, Sirs, why do ye these things? We also are men of like passions with you, and bring you good tidings, that ye should turn from these vain things unto a living God, who made the heaven and the earth and the sea, and all that in them is:

16who in the generations gone by suffered all the nations to walk in their own ways.

17And yet He left not himself without witness, in that he did good and gave you from heaven rains and fruitful seasons, filling your hearts with food and gladness.

18And with these sayings scarce restrained they the multitudes from doing sacrifice unto them.

19But there came Jews thither from Antioch and Iconium: and having persuaded the multitudes, they stoned Paul, and dragged him out of the city, supposing that he was dead.

20But as the disciples stood round about him, he rose up, and entered into the city: and on the morrow he went forth with Barnabas to Derbe.

21And when they had preached the gospel to that city, and had made many disciples, they returned to Lystra, and to Iconium, and to Antioch,

22confirming the souls of the disciples, exhorting them to continue in the faith, and that through many tribulations we must enter into the kingdom of God.

23And when they had appointed for them elders in every church, and had prayed with fasting, they commended them to the Lord, on whom they had believed.

24And they passed through Pisidia, and came to Pamphylia.

25And when they had spoken the word in Perga, they went down to Attalia;

26and thence they sailed to Antioch, from whence they had been committed to the grace of God for the work which they had fulfilled.

27And when they were come, and had gathered the church together, they rehearsed all things that God had done with them, and that he had opened a door of faith unto the Gentiles.

28And they tarried no little time with the disciples.

Chapter 15

1And certain men came down from Judaea and taught the brethren, saying, Except ye be circumcised after the custom of Moses, ye cannot be saved.

2And when Paul and Barnabas had no small dissension and questioning with them, the brethren appointed that Paul and Barnabas, and certain other of them, should go up to Jerusalem unto the apostles and elders about this question.

3They therefore, being brought on their way by the church, passed through both Phoenicia and Samaria, declaring the conversion of the Gentiles: and they caused great joy unto all the brethren.

4And when they were come to Jerusalem, they were received of the church and the apostles and the elders, and they rehearsed all things that God had done with them.

5But there rose up certain of the sect of the Pharisees who believed, saying, It is needful to circumcise them, and to charge them to keep the law of Moses.

6And the apostles and the elders were gathered together to consider of this matter.

7And when there had been much questioning, Peter rose up, and said unto them, Brethren, ye know that a good while ago God made choice among you, that by my mouth the Gentiles should hear the word of the gospel, and believe.

8And God, who knoweth the heart, bare them witness, giving them the Holy Spirit, even as he did unto us;

9and he made no distinction between us and them, cleansing their hearts by faith.

10Now therefore why make ye trial of God, that ye should put a yoke upon the neck of the disciples which neither our fathers nor we were able to bear?

11But we believe that we shall be saved through the grace of the Lord Jesus, in like manner as they.

12And all the multitude kept silence; and they hearkened unto Barnabas and Paul rehearsing what signs and wonders God had wrought among the Gentiles through them.

13And after they had held their peace, James answered, saying, Brethren, hearken unto me:

14Symeon hath rehearsed how first God visited the Gentiles, to take out of them a people for his name.

15And to this agree the words of the prophets; as it is written,

16After these things I will return,
And I will build again the tabernacle of David, which is fallen;
And I will build again the ruins thereof,
And I will set it up:

17That the residue of men may seek after the Lord,
And all the Gentiles, upon whom my name is called,

18Saith the Lord, who maketh these things known from of old.

19Wherefore my judgment is, that we trouble not them that from among the Gentiles turn to God;

20but that we write unto them, that they abstain from the pollutions of idols, and from fornication, and from what is strangled, and from blood.

21For Moses from generations of old hath in every city them that preach him, being read in the synagogues every sabbath.

22Then it seemed good to the apostles and the elders, with the whole church, to choose men out of their company, and send them to Antioch with Paul and Barnabas; namely, Judas called Barsabbas, and Silas, chief men among the brethren:

23and they wrote thus by them, The apostles and the elders, brethren, unto the brethren who are of the Gentiles in Antioch and Syria and Cilicia, greeting:

24Forasmuch as we have heard that certain who went out from us have troubled you with words, subverting your souls; to whom we gave no commandment;

25it seemed good unto us, having come to one accord, to choose out men and send them unto you with our beloved Barnabas and Paul,

26men that have hazarded their lives for the name of our Lord Jesus Christ.

27We have sent therefore Judas and Silas, who themselves also shall tell you the same things by word of mouth.

28For it seemed good to the Holy Spirit, and to us, to lay upon you no greater burden than these necessary things:

29that ye abstain from things sacrificed to idols, and from blood, and from things strangled, and from fornication; from which if ye keep yourselves, it shall be well with you. Fare ye well.

30So they, when they were dismissed, came down to Antioch; and having gathered the multitude together, they delivered the epistle.

31And when they had read it, they rejoiced for the consolation.

32And Judas and Silas, being themselves also prophets, exhorted the brethren with many words, and confirmed them.

33And after they had spent some time there, they were dismissed in peace from the brethren unto those that had sent them forth.

34But it seemed good unto Silas to abide there.

35But Paul and Barnabas tarried in Antioch, teaching and preaching the word of the Lord, with many others also.

36And after some days Paul said unto Barnabas, Let us return now and visit the brethren in every city wherein we proclaimed the word of the Lord, and see how they fare.

37And Barnabas was minded to take with them John also, who was called Mark.

38But Paul thought not good to take with them him who withdrew from them from Pamphylia, and went not with them to the work.

39And there arose a sharp contention, so that they parted asunder one from the other, and Barnabas took Mark with him, and sailed away unto Cyprus;

40but Paul choose Silas, and went forth, being commended by the brethren to the grace of the Lord.

41And he went through Syria and Cilicia, confirming the churches.

Chapter 16

1And he came also to Derbe and to Lystra: and behold, a certain disciple was there, named Timothy, the son of a Jewess that believed; but his father was a Greek.

2The same was well reported of by the brethren that were at Lystra and Iconium.

3Him would Paul have to go forth with him; and he took and circumcised him because of the Jews that were in those parts: for they all knew that his father was a Greek.

4And as they went on their way through the cities, they delivered them the decrees to keep which had been ordained of the apostles and elders that were at Jerusalem.

5So the churches were strengthened in the faith, and increased in number daily.

6And they went through the region of Phrygia and Galatia, having been forbidden of the Holy Spirit to speak the word in Asia;

7and when they were come over against Mysia, they assayed to go into Bithynia; and the Spirit of Jesus suffered them not;

8and passing by Mysia, they came down to Troas.

9And a vision appeared to Paul in the night: There was a man of Macedonia standing, beseeching him, and saying, Come over into Macedonia, and help us.

10And when he had seen the vision, straightway we sought to go forth into Macedonia, concluding that God had called us to preach the gospel to them.

11Setting sail therefore from Troas, we made a straight course to Samothrace, and the day following to Neapolis;

12and from thence to Philippi, which is a city of Macedonia, the first of the district, a Roman colony: and we were in this city tarrying certain days.

13And on the sabbath day we went forth without the gate by a river side, where we supposed there was a place of prayer; and we sat down, and spake unto the women that were come together.

14And a certain woman named Lydia, a seller of purple of the city of Thyatira, one that worshipped God, heard us: whose heart the Lord opened to give heed unto the things which were spoken by Paul.

15And when she was baptized, and her household, she besought us, saying, If ye have judged me to be faithful to the Lord, come into my house, and abide there. And she constrained us.

16And it came to pass, as we were going to the place of prayer, that a certain maid having a spirit of divination met us, who brought her masters much gain by soothsaying.

17The same following after Paul and us cried out, saying, These men are servants of the Most High God, who proclaim unto you the way of salvation.

18And this she did for many days. But Paul, being sore troubled, turned and said to the spirit, I charge thee in the name of Jesus Christ to come out of her. And it came out that very hour.

19But when her masters saw that the hope of their gain was gone, they laid hold on Paul and Silas, and dragged them into the marketplace before the rulers,

20and when they had brought them unto the magistrates, they said, These men, being Jews, do exceedingly trouble our city,

21and set forth customs which it is not lawful for us to receive, or to observe, being Romans.

22And the multitude rose up together against them: and the magistrates rent their garments off them, and commanded to beat them with rods.

23And when they had laid many stripes upon them, they cast them into prison, charging the jailor to keep them safely:

24who, having received such a charge, cast them into the inner prison, and made their feet fast in the stocks.

25But about midnight Paul and Silas were praying and singing hymns unto God, and the prisoners were listening to them;

26and suddenly there was a great earthquake, so that the foundations of the prison-house were shaken: and immediately all the doors were opened, and every one's bands were loosed.

27And the jailor, being roused out of sleep and seeing the prison doors open, drew his sword and was about to kill himself, supposing that the prisoners had escaped.

28But Paul cried with a loud voice, saying, Do thyself no harm: for we are all here.

29And he called for lights and sprang in, and, trembling for fear, fell down before Paul and Silas,

30and brought them out and said, Sirs, what must I do to be saved?

31And they said, Believe on the Lord Jesus, and thou shalt be saved, thou and thy house.

32And they spake the word of the Lord unto him, with all that were in his house.

33And he took them the same hour of the night, and washed their stripes; and was baptized, he and all his, immediately.

34And he brought them up into his house, and set food before them, and rejoiced greatly, with all his house, having believed in God.

35But when it was day, the magistrates sent the sergeants, saying, Let those men go.

36And the jailor reported the words to Paul, saying, The magistrates have sent to let you go: now therefore come forth, and go in peace.

37But Paul said unto them, They have beaten us publicly, uncondemned, men that are Romans, and have cast us into prison; and do they now cast us out privily? Nay verily; but let them come themselves and bring us out.

38And the sergeants reported these words unto the magistrates: and they feared when they heard that they were Romans;

39and they came and besought them; and when they had brought them out, they asked them to go away from the city.

40And they went out of the prison, and entered into the house of Lydia: and when they had seen the brethren, they comforted them, and departed.

Chapter 17

1Now when they had passed through Amphipolis and Apollonia, they came to Thessalonica, where was a synagogue of the Jews:

2and Paul, as his custom was, went in unto them, and for three sabbath days reasoned with them from the Scriptures,

3opening and alleging that it behooved the Christ to suffer, and to rise again from the dead; and that this Jesus, whom, said he, I proclaim unto you, is the Christ.

4And some of them were persuaded, and consorted with Paul and Silas, and of the devout Greeks a great multitude, and of the chief women not a few.

5But the Jews, being moved with jealousy, took unto them certain vile fellows of the rabble, and gathering a crowd, set the city on an uproar; and assaulting the house of Jason, they sought to bring them forth to the people.

6And when they found them not, they dragged Jason and certain brethren before the rulers of the city, crying, These that have turned the world upside down are come hither also;

7whom Jason hath received: and these all act contrary to the decrees of Caesar, saying that there is another king, one Jesus.

8And they troubled the multitude and the rulers of the city, when they heard these things.

9And when they had taken security from Jason and the rest, they let them go.

10And the brethren immediately sent away Paul and Silas by night unto Beroea: who when they were come thither went into the synagogue of the Jews.

11Now these were more noble than those in Thessalonica, in that they received the word with all readiness of the mind, examining the Scriptures daily, whether these things were so.

12Many of them therefore believed; also of the Greek women of honorable estate, and of men, not a few.

13But when the Jews of Thessalonica had knowledge that the word of God was proclaimed of Paul at Beroea also, they came thither likewise, stirring up and troubling the multitudes.

14And then immediately the brethren sent forth Paul to go as far as to the sea: and Silas and Timothy abode there still.

15But they that conducted Paul brought him as far as Athens: and receiving a commandment unto Silas and Timothy that they should come to him with all speed, they departed.

16Now while Paul waited for them at Athens, his spirit was provoked within him as he beheld the city full of idols.

17So he reasoned in the synagogue with Jews and the devout persons, and in the marketplace every day with them that met him.

18And certain also of the Epicurean and Stoic philosophers encountered him. And some said, What would this babbler say? others, He seemeth to be a setter forth of strange gods: because he preached Jesus and the resurrection.

19And they took hold of him, and brought him unto the Areopagus, saying, May we know what this new teaching is, which is spoken by thee?

20For thou bringest certain strange things to our ears: we would know therefore what these things mean.

21(Now all the Athenians and the strangers sojourning there spent their time in nothing else, but either to tell or to hear some new thing.)

22And Paul stood in the midst of the Areopagus, and said, Ye men of Athens, in all things, I perceive that ye are very religious.

23For as I passed along, and observed the objects of your worship, I found also an altar with this inscription, TO AN UNKNOWN GOD. What therefore ye worship in ignorance, this I set forth unto you.

24The God that made the world and all things therein, he, being Lord of heaven and earth, dwelleth not in temples made with hands;

25neither is he served by men's hands, as though he needed anything, seeing he himself giveth to all life, and breath, and all things;

26and he made of one every nation of men to dwell on all the face of the earth, having determined their appointed seasons, and the bounds of their habitation;

27that they should seek God, if haply they might feel after him and find him, though he is not far from each one of us:

28for in him we live, and move, and have our being; as certain even of your own poets have said, For we are also his offspring.

29Being then the offspring of God, we ought not to think that the Godhead is like unto gold, or silver, or stone, graven by art and device of man.

30The times of ignorance therefore God overlooked; but now he commandeth men that they should all everywhere repent:

31inasmuch as he hath appointed a day in which he will judge the world in righteousness by the man whom he hath ordained; whereof he hath given assurance unto all men, in that he hath raised him from the dead.

32Now when they heard of the resurrection of the dead, some mocked; but others said, We will hear thee concerning this yet again.

33Thus Paul went out from among them.

34But certain men clave unto him, and believed: among whom also was Dionysius the Areopagite, and a woman named Damaris, and others with them.

Chapter 18

1After these things he departed from Athens, and came to Corinth.

2And he found a certain Jew named Aquila, a man of Pontus by race, lately come from Italy, with his wife Priscilla, because Claudius had commanded all the Jews to depart from Rome: and he came unto them;

3and because he was of the same trade, he abode with them, and they wrought, for by their trade they were tentmakers.

4And he reasoned in the synagogue every sabbath, and persuaded Jews and Greeks.

5But when Silas and Timothy came down from Macedonia, Paul was constrained by the word, testifying to the Jews that Jesus was the Christ.

6And when they opposed themselves and blasphemed, he shook out his raiment and said unto them, Your blood be upon your own heads; I am clean: from henceforth I will go unto the Gentiles.

7And he departed thence, and went into the house of a certain man named Titus Justus, one that worshipped God, whose house joined hard to the synagogue.

8And Crispus, the ruler of the synagogue, believed in the Lord with all his house; and many of the Corinthians hearing believed, and were baptized.

9And the Lord said unto Paul in the night by a vision, Be not afraid, but speak and hold not thy peace:

10for I am with thee, and no man shall set on thee to harm thee: for I have much people in this city.

11And he dwelt there a year and six months, teaching the word of God among them.

12But when Gallio was proconsul of Achaia, the Jews with one accord rose up against Paul and brought him before the judgment-seat,

13saying, This man persuadeth men to worship God contrary to the law.

14But when Paul was about to open his mouth, Gallio said unto the Jews, If indeed it were a matter of wrong or of wicked villany, O ye Jews, reason would that I should bear with you:

15but if they are questions about words and names and your own law, look to it yourselves; I am not minded to be a judge of these matters.

16And he drove them from the judgment-seat.

17And they all laid hold on Sosthenes, the ruler of the synagogue, and beat him before the judgment-seat. And Gallio cared for none of these things.

18And Paul, having tarried after this yet many days, took his leave of the brethren, and sailed thence for Syria, and with him Priscilla and Aquila: having shorn his head in Cenchreae; for he had a vow.

19And they came to Ephesus, and he left them there: but he himself entered into the synagogue, and reasoned with the Jews.

20And when they asked him to abide a longer time, he consented not;

21but taking his leave of them, and saying, I will return again unto you if God will, he set sail from Ephesus.

22And when he had landed at Caesarea, he went up and saluted the church, and went down to Antioch.

23And having spent some time there, he departed, and went through the region of Galatia, and Phrygia, in order, establishing all the disciples.

24Now a certain Jew named Apollos, an Alexandrian by race, an eloquent man, came to Ephesus; and he was mighty in the scriptures.

25This man had been instructed in the way of the Lord; and being fervent in spirit, he spake and taught accurately the things concerning Jesus, knowing only the baptism of John:

26and he began to speak boldly in the synagogue. But when Priscilla and Aquila heard him, they took him unto them, and expounded unto him the way of God more accurately.

27And when he was minded to pass over into Achaia, the brethren encouraged him, and wrote to the disciples to receive him: and when he was come, he helped them much that had believed through grace;

28for he powerfully confuted the Jews, and that publicly, showing by the scriptures that Jesus was the Christ.

Chapter 19

1And it came to pass, that, while Apollos was at Corinth, Paul having passed through the upper country came to Ephesus, and found certain disciples:

2and he said unto them, Did ye receive the Holy Spirit when ye believed? And they said unto him, Nay, we did not so much as hear whether the Holy Spirit was given.

3And he said, Into what then were ye baptized? And they said, Into John's baptism.

4And Paul said, John baptized with the baptism of repentance, saying unto the people that they should believe on him that should come after him, that is, on Jesus.

5And when they heard this, they were baptized into the name of the Lord Jesus.

6And when Paul had laid his hands upon them, the Holy Spirit came on them; and they spake with tongues, and prophesied.

7And they were in all about twelve men.

8And he entered into the synagogue, and spake boldly for the space of three months, reasoning and persuading as to the things concerning the kingdom of God.

9But when some were hardened and disobedient, speaking evil of the Way before the multitude, he departed from them, and separated the disciples, reasoning daily in the school of Tyrannus.

10And this continued for the space of two years; so that all they that dwelt in Asia heard the word of the Lord, both Jews and Greeks.

11And God wrought special miracles by the hands of Paul:

12insomuch that unto the sick were carried away from his body handkerchiefs or aprons, and the evil spirits went out.

13But certain also of the strolling Jews, exorcists, took upon them to name over them that had the evil spirits the name of the Lord Jesus, saying, I adjure you by Jesus whom Paul preacheth.

14And there were seven sons of one Sceva, a Jew, a chief priest, who did this.

15And the evil spirit answered and said unto them, Jesus I know, and Paul I know, but who are ye?

16And the man in whom the evil spirit was leaped on them, and mastered both of them, and prevailed against them, so that they fled out of that house naked and wounded.

17And this became known to all, both Jews and Greeks, that dwelt at Ephesus; and fear fell upon them all, and the name of the Lord Jesus was magnified.

18Many also of them that had believed came, confessing, and declaring their deeds.

19And not a few of them that practised magical arts brought their books together and burned them in the sight of all; and they counted the price of them, and found it fifty thousand pieces of silver.

20So mightily grew the word of the Lord and prevailed.

21Now after these things were ended, Paul purposed in the spirit, when he had passed through Macedonia and Achaia, to go to Jerusalem, saying, After I have been there, I must also see Rome.

22And having sent into Macedonia two of them that ministered unto him, Timothy and Erastus, he himself stayed in Asia for a while.

23And about that time there arose no small stir concerning the Way.

24For a certain man named Demetrius, a silversmith, who made silver shrines of Diana, brought no little business unto the craftsmen;

25whom he gathered together, with the workmen of like occupation, and said, Sirs, ye know that by this business we have our wealth.

26And ye see and hear, that not alone at Ephesus, but almost throughout all Asia, this Paul hath persuaded and turned away much people, saying that they are no gods, that are made with hands:

27and not only is there danger that this our trade come into disrepute; but also that the temple of the great goddess Diana be made of no account, and that she should even be deposed from her magnificence whom all Asia and the world worshippeth.

28And when they heard this they were filled with wrath, and cried out, saying, Great is Diana of the Ephesus.

29And the city was filled with the confusion: and they rushed with one accord into the theatre, having seized Gaius and Aristarchus, men of Macedonia, Paul's companions in travel.

30And when Paul was minded to enter in unto the people, the disciples suffered him not.

31And certain also of the Asiarchs, being his friends, sent unto him and besought him not to adventure himself into the theatre.

32Some therefore cried one thing, and some another: for the assembly was in confusion; and the more part knew not wherefore they were come together.

33And they brought Alexander out of the multitude, the Jews putting him forward. And Alexander beckoned with the hand, and would have made a defense unto the people.

34But when they perceived that he was a Jew, all with one voice about the space of two hours cried out, Great is Diana of the Ephesians.

35And when the townclerk had quieted the multitude, he saith, Ye men of Ephesus, what man is there who knoweth not that the city of the Ephesians is temple-keeper of the great Diana, and of the image which fell down from Jupiter?

36Seeing then that these things cannot be gainsaid, ye ought to be quiet, and to do nothing rash.

37For ye have brought hither these men, who are neither robbers of temples nor blasphemers of our goddess.

38If therefore Demetrius, and the craftsmen that are with him, have a matter against any man, the courts are open, and there are proconsuls: let them accuse one another.

39But if ye seek anything about other matters, it shall be settled in the regular assembly.

40For indeed we are in danger to be accused concerning this day's riot, there being no cause for it: and as touching it we shall not be able to give account of this concourse.

41And when he had thus spoken, he dismissed the assembly.

Chapter 20

1And after the uproar ceased, Paul having sent for the disciples and exhorted them, took leave of them, and departed to go into Macedonia.

2And when he had gone through those parts, and had given them much exhortation, he came into Greece.

3And when he had spent three months there, and a plot was laid against him by Jews as he was about to set sail for Syria, he determined to return through Macedonia.

4And there accompanied him as far as Asia, Sopater of Beroea, the son of Pyrrhus; and of the Thessalonians, Aristarchus and Secundus; and Gaius of Derbe, and Timothy; and of Asia, Tychicus and Trophimus.

5But these had gone before, and were waiting for us at Troas.

6And we sailed away from Philippi after the days of unleavened bread, and came unto them to Troas in five days, where we tarried seven days.

7And upon the first day of the week, when we were gathered together to break bread, Paul discoursed with them, intending to depart on the morrow; and prolonged his speech until midnight.

8And there were many lights in the upper chamber where we were gathered together.

9And there sat in the window a certain young man named Eutychus, borne down with deep sleep; and as Paul discoursed yet longer, being borne down by his sleep he fell down from the third story, and was taken up dead.

10And Paul went down, and fell on him, and embracing him said, Make ye no ado; for his life is in him.

11And when he was gone up, and had broken the bread, and eaten, and had talked with them a long while, even till break of day, so he departed.

12And they brought the lad alive, and were not a little comforted.

13But we going before to the ship set sail for Assos, there intending to take in Paul: for so had he appointed, intending himself to go by land.

14And when he met us at Assos, we took him in, and came to Mitylene.

15And sailing from thence, we came the following day over against Chios; and the next day we touched at Samos; and the day after we came to Miletus.

16For Paul had determined to sail past Ephesus, that he might not have to spend time in Asia; for he was hastening, if it were possible for him, to be at Jerusalem the day of Pentecost.

17And from Miletus he sent to Ephesus, and called to him the elders of the church.

18And when they were come to him, he said unto them, Ye yourselves know, from the first day that I set foot in Asia, after what manner I was with you all the time,

19serving the Lord with all lowliness of mind, and with tears, and with trials which befell me by the plots of the Jews;

20how I shrank not from declaring unto you anything that was profitable, and teaching you publicly, and from house to house,

21testifying both to Jews and to Greeks repentance toward God, and faith toward our Lord Jesus Christ.

22And now, behold, I go bound in the spirit unto Jerusalem, not knowing the things that shall befall me there:

23save that the Holy Spirit testifieth unto me in every city, saying that bonds and afflictions abide me.

24But I hold not my life of any account as dear unto myself, so that I may accomplish my course, and the ministry which I received from the Lord Jesus, to testify the gospel of the grace of God.

25And now, behold, I know that ye all, among whom I went about preaching the kingdom, shall see my face no more.

26Wherefore I testify unto you this day, that I am pure from the blood of all men.

27For I shrank not from declaring unto you the whole counsel of God.

28Take heed unto yourselves, and to all the flock, in which the Holy Spirit hath made you bishops, to feed the church of the Lord which he purchased with his own blood.

29I know that after my departing grievous wolves shall enter in among you, not sparing the flock;

30and from among your own selves shall men arise, speaking perverse things, to draw away the disciples after them.

31Wherefore watch ye, remembering that by the space of three years I ceased not to admonish every one night and day with tears.

32And now I commend you to God, and to the word of his grace, which is able to build you up, and to give you the inheritance among all them that are sanctified.

33I coveted no man's silver, or gold, or apparel.

34Ye yourselves know that these hands ministered unto my necessities, and to them that were with me.

35In all things I gave you an example, that so laboring ye ought to help the weak, and to remember the words of the Lord Jesus, that he himself said, It is more blessed to give than to receive.

36And when he had thus spoken, he kneeled down and prayed with them all.

37And they all wept sore, and fell on Paul's neck and kissed him,

38sorrowing most of all for the word which he had spoken, that they should behold his face no more. And they brought him on his way unto the ship.

Chapter 21

1And when it came to pass that were parted from them and had set sail, we came with a straight course unto Cos, and the next day unto Rhodes, and from thence unto Patara:

2and having found a ship crossing over unto Phoenicia, we went aboard, and set sail.

3And when we had come in sight of Cyprus, leaving it on the left hand, we sailed unto Syria, and landed at Tyre; for there the ship was to unlade her burden.

4And having found the disciples, we tarried there seven days: and these said to Paul through the Spirit, that he should not set foot in Jerusalem.

5And when it came to pass that we had accomplished the days, we departed and went on our journey; and they all, with wives and children, brought us on our way till we were out of the city: and kneeling down on the beach, we prayed, and bade each other farewell;

6and we went on board the ship, but they returned home again.

7And when we had finished the voyage from Tyre, we arrived at Ptolemais; and we saluted the brethren, and abode with them one day.

8And on the morrow we departed, and came unto Caesarea: and entering into the house of Philip the evangelist, who was one of the seven, we abode with him.

9Now this man had four virgin daughters, who prophesied.

10And as we tarried there some days, there came down from Judaea a certain prophet, named Agabus.

11And coming to us, and taking Paul's girdle, he bound his own feet and hands, and said, Thus saith the Holy Spirit, So shall the Jews at Jerusalem bind the man that owneth this girdle, and shall deliver him into the hands of the Gentiles.

12And when we heard these things, both we and they of that place besought him not to go up to Jerusalem.

13Then Paul answered, What do ye, weeping and breaking my heart? for I am ready not to be bound only, but also to die at Jerusalem for the name of the Lord Jesus.

14And when he would not be persuaded, we ceased, saying, The will of the Lord be done.

15And after these days we took up our baggage and went up to Jerusalem.

16And there went with us also certain of the disciples from Caesarea, bringing with them one Mnason of Cyprus, an early disciple, with whom we should lodge.

17And when we were come to Jerusalem, the brethren received us gladly.

18And the day following Paul went in with us unto James; and all the elders were present.

19And when he had saluted them, he rehearsed one by one the things which God had wrought among the Gentiles through his ministry.

20And they, when they heard it, glorified God; and they said unto him, Thou seest, brother, how many thousands there are among the Jews of them that have believed; and they are all zealous for the law:

21and they have been informed concerning thee, that thou teachest all the Jews who are among the Gentiles to forsake Moses, telling them not to circumcise their children neither to walk after the customs.

22What is it therefore? They will certainly hear that thou art come.

23Do therefore this that we say to thee: We have four men that have a vow on them;

24these take, and purify thyself with them, and be at charges for them, that they may shave their heads: and all shall know that there is no truth in the things whereof they have been informed concerning thee; but that thou thyself also walkest orderly, keeping the law.

25But as touching the Gentiles that have believed, we wrote, giving judgment that they should keep themselves from things sacrificed to idols, and from blood, and from what is strangled, and from fornication.

26Then Paul took the men, and the next day purifying himself with them went into the temple, declaring the fulfilment of the days of purification, until the offering was offered for every one of them.

27And when the seven days were almost completed, the Jews from Asia, when they saw him in the temple, stirred up all the multitude and laid hands on him,

28crying out, Men of Israel, help: This is the man that teacheth all men everywhere against the people, and the law, and this place; and moreover he brought Greeks also into the temple, and hath defiled this holy place.

29For they had before seen with him in the city Trophimus the Ephesian, whom they supposed that Paul had brought into the temple.

30And all the city was moved, and the people ran together; and they laid hold on Paul, and dragged him out of the temple: and straightway the doors were shut.

31And as they were seeking to kill him, tidings came up to the chief captain of the band, that all Jerusalem was in confusion.

32And forthwith he took soldiers and centurions, and ran down upon them: and they, when they saw the chief captain and the soldiers, left off beating Paul.

33Then the chief captain came near, and laid hold on him, and commanded him to be bound with two chains; and inquired who he was, and what he had done.

34And some shouted one thing, some another, among the crowd: and when he could not know the certainty for the uproar, he commanded him to be brought into the castle.

35And when he came upon the stairs, so it was that he was borne of the soldiers for the violence of the crowd;

36for the multitude of the people followed after, crying out, Away with him.

37And as Paul was about to be brought into the castle, he saith unto the chief captain, May I say something unto thee? And he said, Dost thou know Greek?

38Art thou not then the Egyptian, who before these days stirred up to sedition and led out into the wilderness the four thousand men of the Assassins?

39But Paul said, I am a Jew, of Tarsus in Cilicia, a citizen of no mean city: and I beseech thee, give me leave to speak unto the people.

40And when he had given him leave, Paul, standing on the stairs, beckoned with the hand unto the people; and when there was made a great silence, he spake unto them in the Hebrew language, saying,

Chapter 22

1Brethren and fathers, hear ye the defence which I now make unto you.

2And when they heard that he spake unto them in the Hebrew language, they were the more quiet: and he saith,

3I am a Jew, born in Tarsus of Cilicia, but brought up in this city, at the feet of Gamaliel, instructed according to the strict manner of the law of our fathers, being zealous for God, even as ye all are this day:

4and I persecuted this Way unto the death, binding and delivering into prisons both men and women.

5As also the high priest doth bear me witness, and all the estate of the elders: from whom also I received letters unto the brethren, and journeyed to Damascus to bring them also that were there unto Jerusalem in bonds to be punished.

6And it came to pass, that, as I made my journey, and drew nigh unto Damascus, about noon, suddenly there shone from heaven a great light round about me.

Acts

7And I fell unto the ground, and heard a voice saying unto me, Saul, Saul, why persecutest thou me?

8And I answered, Who art thou, Lord? And he said unto me, I am Jesus of Nazareth, whom thou persecutest.

9And they that were with me beheld indeed the light, but they heard not the voice of him that spake to me.

10And I said, What shall I do, Lord? And the Lord said unto me, Arise, and go into Damascus; and there it shall be told thee of all things which are appointed for thee to do.

11And when I could not see for the glory of that light, being led by the hand of them that were with me I came into Damascus.

12And one Ananias, a devout man according to the law, well reported of by all the Jews that dwelt there,

13came unto me, and standing by me said unto me, Brother Saul, receive thy sight. And in that very hour I looked up on him.

14And he said, The God of our fathers hath appointed thee to know his will, and to see the Righteous One, and to hear a voice from his mouth.

15For thou shalt be a witness for him unto all men of what thou hast seen and heard.

16And now why tarriest thou? arise, and be baptized, and wash away thy sins, calling on his name.

17And it came to pass, that, when I had returned to Jerusalem, and while I prayed in the temple, I fell into a trance,

18and saw him saying unto me, Make haste, and get thee quickly out of Jerusalem; because they will not receive of thee testimony concerning me.

19And I said, Lord, they themselves know that I imprisoned and beat in every synagogue them that believed on thee:

20and when the blood of Stephen thy witness was shed, I also was standing by, and consenting, and keeping the garments of them that slew him.

21And he said unto me, Depart: for I will send thee forth far hence unto the Gentiles.

22And they gave him audience unto this word; and they lifted up their voice, and said, Away with such a fellow from the earth: for it is not fit that he should live.

23And as they cried out, and threw off their garments, and cast dust into the air,

24the chief captain commanded him be brought into the castle, bidding that he should be examined by scourging, that he might know for what cause they so shouted against him.

25And when they had tied him up with the thongs, Paul said unto the centurion that stood by, Is it lawful for you to scourge a man that is a Roman, and uncondemned?

26And when the centurion heard it, he went to the chief captain and told him, saying, What art thou about to do? for this man is a Roman.

27And the chief captain came and said unto him, Tell me, art thou a Roman? And he said, Yea.

28And the chief captain answered, With a great sum obtained I this citizenship. And Paul said, But I am a Roman born.

29They then that were about to examine him straightway departed from him: and the chief captain also was afraid when he knew that he was a Roman, and because he had bound him.

30But on the morrow, desiring to know the certainty wherefore he was accused of the Jews, he loosed him, and commanded the chief priests and all the council to come together, and brought Paul down and set him before them.

Chapter 23

1And Paul, looking stedfastly on the council, said, Brethren, I have lived before God in all good conscience until this day.

2And the high priest Ananias commanded them that stood by him to smite him on the mouth.

3Then said Paul unto him, God shall smite thee, thou whited wall: and sittest thou to judge me according to the law, and commandest me to be smitten contrary to the law?

4And they that stood by said, Revilest thou God's high priest?

5And Paul said, I knew not, brethren, that he was high priest: for it is written, Thou shalt not speak evil of a ruler of thy people.

6But when Paul perceived that the one part were Sadducees and the other Pharisees, he cried out in the council, Brethren, I am a Pharisee, a son of Pharisees: touching the hope and resurrection of the dead I am called in question.

7And when he had so said, there arose a dissension between the Pharisees and Sadducees; and the assembly was divided.

8For the Sadducees say that there is no resurrection, neither angel, nor spirit; but the Pharisees confess both.

9And there arose a great clamor: and some of the scribes of the Pharisees part stood up, and strove, saying, We find no evil in this man: and what if a spirit hath spoken to him, or an angel?

10And when there arose a great dissension, the chief captain, fearing lest Paul should be torn in pieces by them, commanded the soldiers to go down and take him by force from among them, and bring him into the castle.

11And the night following the Lord stood by him, and said, Be of good cheer: for as thou hast testified concerning me at Jerusalem, so must thou bear witness also at Rome.

12And when it was day, the Jews banded together, and bound themselves under a curse, saying that they would neither eat nor drink till they had killed Paul.

13And they were more than forty that made this conspiracy.

14And they came to the chief priests and the elders, and said, We have bound ourselves under a great curse, to taste nothing until we have killed Paul.

15Now therefore do ye with the council signify to the chief captain that he bring him down unto you, as though ye would judge of his case more exactly: and we, before he comes near, are ready to slay him.

16But Paul's sister's son heard of their lying in wait, and he came and entered into the castle and told Paul.

17And Paul called unto him one of the centurions, and said, Bring this young man unto the chief captain; for he hath something to tell him.

18So he took him, and brought him to the chief captain, and saith, Paul the prisoner called me unto him, and asked me to bring this young man unto thee, who hath something to say to thee.

19And the chief captain took him by the hand, and going aside asked him privately, What is it that thou hast to tell me?

20And he said, The Jews have agreed to ask thee to bring down Paul tomorrow unto the council, as though thou wouldest inquire somewhat more exactly concerning him.

21Do not thou therefore yield unto them: for there lie in wait for him of them more than forty men, who have bound themselves under a curse, neither to eat nor to drink till they have slain him: and now are they ready, looking for the promise from thee.

22So the chief captain let the young man go, charging him, Tell no man that thou hast signified these things to me.

23And he called unto him two of the centurions, and said, Make ready two hundred soldiers to go as far as Caesarea, and horsemen threescore and ten, and spearmen two hundred, at the third hour of the night:

24and he bade them provide beasts, that they might set Paul thereon, and bring him safe unto Felix the governor.

25And he wrote a letter after this form:

26Claudius Lysias unto the most excellent governor Felix, greeting.

27This man was seized by the Jews, and was about to be slain of them, when I came upon them with the soldiers and rescued him, having learned that he was a Roman.

28And desiring to know the cause wherefore they accused him, I brought him down unto their council:

29whom I found to be accused about questions of their law, but to have nothing laid to his charge worthy of death or of bonds.

30And when it was shown to me that there would be a plot against the man, I sent him to thee forthwith, charging his accusers also to speak against him before thee.

31So the soldiers, as it was commanded them, took Paul and brought him by night to Antipatris.

32But on the morrow they left the horsemen to go with him, and returned to the castle:

33and they, when they came to Caesarea and delivered the letter to the governor, presented Paul also before him.

34And when he had read it, he asked of what province he was; and when he understood that he was of Cilicia,

35I will hear thee fully, said he, when thine accusers also are come: and he commanded him to be kept in Herod's palace.

Chapter 24

1And after five days the high priest Ananias came down with certain elders, and with an orator, one Tertullus; and they informed the governor against Paul.

2And when he was called, Tertullus began to accuse him, saying, Seeing that by thee we enjoy much peace, and that by the providence evils are corrected for this nation,

3we accept it in all ways and in all places, most excellent Felix, with all thankfulness.

4But, that I be not further tedious unto thee, I entreat thee to hear us of thy clemency a few words.

5For we have found this man a pestilent fellow, and a mover of insurrections among all the Jews throughout the world, and a ringleader of the sect of the Nazarenes:

6who moreover assayed to profane the temple: on whom also we laid hold: and we would have judged him according to our law.

7But the chief captain Lysias came, and with great violence took him away out of our hands,

8commanding his accusers to come before thee. from whom thou wilt be able, by examining him thyself, to take knowledge of all these things whereof we accuse him.

9And the Jews also joined in the charge, affirming that these things were so.

10And when the governor had beckoned unto him to speak, Paul answered, Forasmuch as I know that thou hast been of many years a judge unto this nation, I cheerfully make my defense:

11Seeing that thou canst take knowledge that it is not more than twelve days since I went up to worship at Jerusalem:

12and neither in the temple did they find me disputing with any man or stirring up a crowd, nor in the synagogues, nor in the city.

13Neither can they prove to thee the things whereof they now accuse me.

14But this I confess unto thee, that after the Way which they call a sect, so serve I the God of our fathers, believing all things which are according to the law, and which are written in the prophets;

15having hope toward God, which these also themselves look for, that there shall be a resurrection both of the just and unjust.

16Herein I also exercise myself to have a conscience void of offence toward God and men always.

17Now after some years I came to bring alms to my nation, and offerings:

18amidst which they found me purified in the temple, with no crowd, nor yet with tumult: but there were certain Jews from Asia--

19who ought to have been here before thee, and to make accusation, if they had aught against me.

20Or else let these men themselves say what wrong-doing they found when

I stood before the council,

21except it be for this one voice, that I cried standing among them, Touching the resurrection of the dead I am called in question before you this day.

22But Felix, having more exact knowledge concerning the Way, deferred them, saying, When Lysias the chief captain shall come down, I will determine your matter.

23And he gave order to the centurion that he should be kept in charge, and should have indulgence; and not to forbid any of his friends to minister unto him.

24But after certain days, Felix came with Drusilla, his wife, who was a Jewess, and sent for Paul, and heard him concerning the faith in Christ Jesus.

25And as he reasoned of righteousness, and self-control, and the judgment to come, Felix was terrified, and answered, Go thy way for this time; and when I have a convenient season, I will call thee unto me.

26He hoped withal that money would be given him of Paul: wherefore also he sent for him the oftener, and communed with him.

27But when two years were fulfilled, Felix was succeeded by Porcius Festus; and desiring to gain favor with the Jews, Felix left Paul in bonds.

Chapter 25

1Festus therefore, having come into the province, after three days went up to Jerusalem from Caesarea.

2And the chief priests and the principal men of the Jews informed him against Paul; and they besought him,

3asking a favor against him, that he would send for him to Jerusalem; laying a plot to kill him on the way.

4Howbeit Festus answered, that Paul was kept in charge at Caesarea, and that he himself was about to depart thither shortly.

5Let them therefore, saith he, that are of power among you go down with me, and if there is anything amiss in the man, let them accuse him.

6And when he had tarried among them not more than eight or ten days, he went down unto Caesarea; and on the morrow he sat on the judgment-seat, and commanded Paul to be brought.

7And when he was come, the Jews that had come down from Jerusalem stood round about him, bringing against him many and grievous charges which they could not prove;

8while Paul said in his defense, Neither against the law of the Jews, nor against the temple, nor against Caesar, have I sinned at all.

9But Festus, desiring to gain favor with the Jews, answered Paul and said, Wilt thou go up to Jerusalem, and there be judged of these things before me?

10But Paul said, I am standing before Caesar's judgment-seat, where I ought to be judged: to the Jews have I done no wrong, as thou also very well knowest.

11If then I am a wrong-doer, and have committed anything worthy of death, I refuse not to die; but if none of those things is true whereof these accuse me, no man can give me up unto them. I appeal unto Caesar.

12Then Festus, when he had conferred with the council, answered, Thou hast appealed unto Caesar: unto Caesar shalt thou go.

13Now when certain days were passed, Agrippa the King and Bernice arrived at Caesarea, and saluted Festus.

14And as they tarried there many days, Festus laid Paul's case before the King, saying, There is a certain man left a prisoner by Felix;

15about whom, when I was at Jerusalem, the chief priests and the elders of the Jews informed me, asking for sentence against him.

16To whom I answered, that it is not the custom of the Romans to give up any man, before that the accused have the accusers face to face, and have had opportunity to make his defense concerning the matter laid against him.

17When therefore they were come together here, I made no delay, but on the next day sat on the judgment-seat, and commanded the man to be brought.

18Concerning whom, when the accusers stood up, they brought no charge of such evil things as I supposed;

19but had certain questions against him of their own religion, and of one Jesus, who was dead, whom Paul affirmed to be alive.

20And I, being perplexed how to inquire concerning these things, asked whether he would go to Jerusalem and there be judged of these matters.

21But when Paul had appealed to be kept for the decision of the emperor, I commanded him to be kept till I should send him to Caesar.

22And Agrippa said unto Festus, I also could wish to hear the man myself. To-morrow, saith he, thou shalt hear him.

23So on the morrow, when Agrippa was come, and Bernice, with great pomp, and they were entered into the place of hearing with the chief captains and principal men of the city, at the command of Festus Paul was brought in.

24And Festus saith, King Agrippa, and all men who are here present with us, ye behold this man, about whom all the multitude of the Jews made suit to me, both at Jerusalem and here, crying that he ought not to live any longer.

25But I found that he had committed nothing worthy of death: and as he himself appealed to the emperor I determined to send him.

26Of whom I have no certain thing to write unto my lord. Wherefore I have brought him forth before you, and specially before thee, king Agrippa, that, after examination had, I may have somewhat to write.

27For it seemeth to me unreasonable, in sending a prisoner, not withal to signify the charges against him.

Chapter 26

1And Agrippa said unto Paul, Thou art permitted to speak for thyself. Then Paul stretched forth his hand, and made his defence:

2I think myself happy, king Agrippa, that I am to make my defense before thee this day touching all the things whereof I am accused by the Jews:

3especially because thou art expert in all customs and questions which are among the Jews: wherefore I beseech thee to hear me patiently.

4My manner of life then from my youth up, which was from the beginning among mine own nation and at Jerusalem, know all the Jews;

5having knowledge of me from the first, if they be willing to testify, that after the straitest sect of our religion I lived a Pharisee.

6And now I stand here to be judged for the hope of the promise made of God unto our fathers;

7unto which promise our twelve tribes, earnestly serving God night and day, hope to attain. And concerning this hope I am accused by the Jews, O king!

8Why is it judged incredible with you, if God doth raise the dead?

9I verily thought with myself that I ought to do many things contrary to the name of Jesus of Nazareth.

10And this I also did in Jerusalem: and I both shut up many of the saints in prisons, having received authority from the chief priests, and when they were put to death I gave my vote against them.

11And punishing them oftentimes in all the synagogues, I strove to make them blaspheme; and being exceedingly mad against them, I persecuted them even unto foreign cities.

12Whereupon as I journeyed to Damascus with the authority and commission of the chief priests,

13at midday, O king, I saw on the way a light from heaven, above the brightness of the sun, shining round about me and them that journeyed with me.

14And when we were all fallen to the earth, I heard a voice saying unto me in the Hebrew language, Saul, Saul, why persecutest thou me? it is hard for thee to kick against the goad.

15And I said, Who art thou, Lord? And the Lord said, I am Jesus whom thou persecutest.

16But arise, and stand upon thy feet: for to this end have I appeared unto thee, to appoint thee a minister and a witness both of the things wherein thou hast seen me, and of the things wherein I will appear unto thee;

17delivering thee from the people, and from the Gentiles, unto whom I send thee,

18to open their eyes, that they may turn from darkness to light and from the power of Satan unto God, that they may receive remission of sins and an inheritance among them that are sanctified by faith in me.

19Wherefore, O king Agrippa, I was not disobedient unto the heavenly vision:

20but declared both to them of Damascus first and at Jerusalem, and throughout all the country of Judaea, and also to the Gentiles, that they should repent and turn to God, doing works worthy of repentance.

21For this cause the Jews seized me in the temple, and assayed to kill me.

22Having therefore obtained the help that is from God, I stand unto this day testifying both to small and great, saying nothing but what the prophets and Moses did say should come;

23how that the Christ must suffer, and how that he first by the resurrection of the dead should proclaim light both to the people and to the Gentiles.

24And as he thus made his defense, Festus saith with a loud voice, Paul, thou art mad; thy much learning is turning thee mad.

25But Paul saith, I am not mad, most excellent Festus; but speak forth words of truth and soberness.

26For the king knoweth of these things, unto whom also I speak freely: for I am persuaded that none of these things is hidden from him; for this hath not been done in a corner.

27King Agrippa, believest thou the prophets? I know that thou believest.

28And Agrippa said unto Paul, With but little persuasion thou wouldest fain make me a Christian.

29And Paul said, I would to God, that whether with little or with much, not thou only, but also all that hear me this day, might become such as I am, except these bonds.

30And the king rose up, and the governor, and Bernice, and they that sat with them:

31and when they had withdrawn, they spake one to another, saying, This man doeth nothing worthy of death or of bonds.

32And Agrippa said unto Festus, This man might have been set at liberty, if he had not appealed unto Caesar.

Chapter 27

1And when it was determined that we should sail for Italy, they delivered Paul and certain other prisoners to a centurion named Julius, of the Augustan band.

2And embarking in a ship of Adramyttium, which was about to sail unto the places on the coast of Asia, we put to sea, Aristarchus, a Macedonian of Thessalonica, being with us.

3And the next day we touched at Sidon: and Julius treated Paul kindly, and gave him leave to go unto his friends and refresh himself.

4And putting to sea from thence, we sailed under the lee of Cyprus, because the winds were contrary.

5And when we had sailed across the sea which is off Cilicia and Pamphylia, we came to Myra, a city of Lycia.

6And there the centurion found a ship of Alexandria sailing for Italy; and he put us therein.

7And when we had sailed slowly many days, and were come with difficulty over against Cnidus, the wind not further suffering us, we sailed under the lee of Crete, over against Salmone;

8and with difficulty coasting along it we came unto a certain place called Fair Havens; nigh whereunto was the city of Lasea.

9And when much time was spent, and the voyage was now dangerous, because the Fast was now already gone by, Paul admonished them,

10and said unto them, Sirs, I perceive that the voyage will be with injury and much loss, not only of the lading and the ship, but also of our lives.

Acts

11But the centurion gave more heed to the master and to the owner of the ship, than to those things which were spoken by Paul.

12And because the haven was not commodious to winter in, the more part advised to put to sea from thence, if by any means they could reach Phoenix, and winter there; which is a haven of Crete, looking northeast and south-east.

13And when the south wind blew softly, supposing that they had obtained their purpose, they weighed anchor and sailed along Crete, close in shore.

14But after no long time there beat down from it a tempestuous wind, which is called Euraquilo.

15and when the ship was caught, and could not face the wind, we gave way to it, and were driven.

16And running under the lee of a small island called Cauda, we were able, with difficulty, to secure the boat:

17and when they had hoisted it up, they used helps, under-girding the ship; and, fearing lest they should be cast upon the Syrtis, they lowered the gear, and so were driven.

18And as we labored exceedingly with the storm, the next day they began to throw the the freight overboard;

19and the third day they cast out with their own hands the tackling of the ship.

20And when neither sun nor stars shone upon us for many days, and no small tempest lay on us, all hope that we should be saved was now taken away.

21And when they had been long without food, then Paul stood forth in the midst of them, and said, Sirs, ye should have hearkened unto me, and not have set sail from Crete, and have gotten this injury and loss.

22And now I exhort you to be of good cheer; for there shall be no loss of life among you, but only of the ship.

23For there stood by me this night an angel of the God whose I am, whom also I serve,

24saying, Fear not, Paul; thou must stand before Caesar: and lo, God hath granted thee all them that sail with thee.

25Wherefore, sirs, be of good cheer: for I believe God, that it shall be even so as it hath been spoken unto me.

26But we must be cast upon a certain island.

27But when the fourteenth night was come, as we were driven to and fro in the sea of Adria, about midnight the sailors surmised that they were drawing near to some country:

28and they sounded, and found twenty fathoms; and after a little space, they sounded again, and found fifteen fathoms.

29And fearing lest haply we should be cast ashore on rocky ground, they let go four anchors from the stern, and wished for the day.

30And as the sailors were seeking to flee out of the ship, and had lowered the boat into the sea, under color as though they would lay out anchors from the foreship,

31Paul said to the centurion and to the soldiers, Except these abide in the ship, ye cannot be saved.

32Then the soldiers cut away the ropes of the boat, and let her fall off.

33And while the day was coming on, Paul besought them all to take some food, saying, This day is the fourteenth day that ye wait and continue fasting, having taken nothing.

34Wherefore I beseech you to take some food: for this is for your safety: for there shall not a hair perish from the head of any of you.

35And when he had said this, and had taken bread, he gave thanks to God in the presence of all; and he brake it, and began to eat.

36Then were they all of good cheer, and themselves also took food.

37And we were in all in the ship two hundred threescore and sixteen souls.

38And when they had eaten enough, they lightened the ship, throwing out the wheat into the sea.

39And when it was day, they knew not the land: but they perceived a certain bay with a beach, and they took counsel whether they could drive the ship upon it.

40And casting off the anchors, they left them in the sea, at the same time loosing the bands of the rudders; and hoisting up the foresail to the wind, they made for the beach.

41But lighting upon a place where two seas met, they ran the vessel aground; and the foreship struck and remained unmoveable, but the stern began to break up by the violence of the waves.

42And the soldiers' counsel was to kill the prisoners, lest any of them should swim out, and escape.

43But the centurion, desiring to save Paul, stayed them from their purpose; and commanded that they who could swim should cast themselves overboard, and get first to the land;

44and the rest, some on planks, and some on other things from the ship. And so it came to pass, that they all escaped safe to the land.

Chapter 28

1And when we were escaped, then we knew that the island was called Melita.

2And the barbarians showed us no common kindness; for they kindled a fire, and received us all, because of the present rain, and because of the cold.

3But when Paul had gathered a bundle of sticks and laid them on the fire, a viper came out by reason of the heat, and fastened on his hand.

4And when the barbarians saw the venomous creature hanging from his hand, they said one to another, No doubt this man is a murderer, whom, though he hath escaped from the sea, yet Justice hath not suffered to live.

5Howbeit he shook off the creature into the fire, and took no harm.

6But they expected that he would have swollen, or fallen down dead suddenly: but when they were long in expectation and beheld nothing amiss came to him, they changed their minds, and said that he was a god.

7Now in the neighborhood of that place were lands belonging to the chief man of the island, named Publius, who received us, and entertained us three days courteously.

8And it was so, that the father of Publius lay sick of fever and dysentery: unto whom Paul entered in, and prayed, and laying his hands on him healed him.

9And when this was done, the rest also that had diseases in the island came, and were cured:

10who also honored us with many honors; and when we sailed, they put on board such things as we needed.

11And after three months we set sail in a ship of Alexandria which had wintered in the island, whose sign was The Twin Brothers.

12And touching at Syracuse, we tarried there three days.

13And from thence we made a circuit, and arrived at Rhegium: and after one day a south wind sprang up, and on the second day we came to Puteoli;

14where we found brethren, and were entreated to tarry with them seven days: and so we came to Rome.

15And from thence the brethren, when they heard of us, came to meet us as far as The Market of Appius and The Three Taverns; whom when Paul saw, he thanked God, and took courage.

16And when we entered into Rome, Paul was suffered to abide by himself with the soldier that guarded him.

17And it came to pass, that after three days he called together those that were the chief of the Jews: and when they were come together, he said unto them, I, brethren, though I had done nothing against the people, or the customs of our fathers, yet was delivered prisoner from Jerusalem into the hands of the Romans:

18who, when they had examined me, desired to set me at liberty, because there was no cause of death in me.

19But when the Jews spake against it, I was constrained to appeal unto Caesar; not that I had aught whereof to accuse my nation.

20For this cause therefore did I entreat you to see and to speak with me: for because of the hope of Israel I am bound with this chain.

21And they said unto him, We neither received letters from Judaea concerning thee, nor did any of the brethren come hither and report or speak any harm of thee.

22But we desire to hear of thee what thou thinkest: for as concerning this sect, it is known to us that everywhere it is spoken against.

23And when they had appointed him a day, they came to him into his lodging in great number; to whom he expounded the matter, testifying the kingdom of God, and persuading them concerning Jesus, both from the law of Moses and from the prophets, from morning till evening.

24And some believed the things which were spoken, and some disbelieved.

25And when they agreed not among themselves, they departed after that Paul had spoken one word, Well spake The Holy Spirit through Isaiah the prophet unto your fathers,

26saying,

Go thou unto this people, and say,

By hearing ye shall hear, and shall in no wise understand;

And seeing ye shall see, and shall in no wise perceive:

27For this people's heart is waxed gross,

And their ears are dull of hearing,

And their eyes they have closed;

Lest, haply they should perceive with their eyes,

And hear with their ears,

And understand with their heart,

And should turn again,

And I should heal them.

28Be it known therefore unto you, that this salvation of God is sent unto the Gentiles: they will also hear.

29And when he had said these words, the Jews departed, having much disputing among themselves.

30And he abode two whole years in his own hired dwelling, and received all that went in unto him,

31preaching the kingdom of God, and teaching the things concerning the Lord Jesus Christ with all boldness, none forbidding him.

The Epistle of Paul the Apostle to the Romans

Chapter 1

1Paul, a servant of Jesus Christ, called to be an apostle, separated unto the gospel of God,

2which he promised afore through his prophets in the holy scriptures,

3concerning his Son, who was born of the seed of David according to the flesh,

4who was declared to be the Son of God with power, according to the spirit of holiness, by the resurrection from the dead; even Jesus Christ our Lord,

5through whom we received grace and apostleship, unto obedience of faith among all the nations, for his name's sake;

6among whom are ye also called to be Jesus Christ's:

7To all that are in Rome, beloved of God, called to be saints: Grace to you and peace from God our Father and the Lord Jesus Christ.

8First, I thank my God through Jesus Christ for you all, that your faith is proclaimed throughout the whole world.

9For God is my witness, whom I serve in my spirit in the gospel of his Son,. how unceasingly I make mention of you, always in my prayers

10making request, if by any means now at length I may be prospered by the will of God to come unto you.

11For I long to see you, that I may impart unto you some spiritual gift, to the end ye may be established;

12that is, that I with you may be comforted in you, each of us by the other's faith, both yours and mine.

13And I would not have you ignorant, brethren, that oftentimes I purposed to come unto you (and was hindered hitherto), that I might have some fruit in you also, even as in the rest of the Gentiles.

14I am debtor both to Greeks and to Barbarians, both to the wise and to the foolish.

15So, as much as in me is, I am ready to preach the gospel to you also that are in Rome.

16For I am not ashamed of the gospel: for it is the power of God unto salvation to every one that believeth; to the Jew first, and also to the Greek.

17For therein is revealed a righteousness of God from faith unto faith: as it is written, But the righteous shall live by faith.

18For the wrath of God is revealed from heaven against all ungodliness and unrighteousness of men, who hinder the truth in unrighteousness;

19because that which is known of God is manifest in them; for God manifested it unto them.

20For the invisible things of him since the creation of the world are clearly seen, being perceived through the things that are made, even his everlasting power and divinity; that they may be without excuse:

21because that, knowing God, they glorified him not as God, neither gave thanks; but became vain in their reasonings, and their senseless heart was darkened.

22Professing themselves to be wise, they became fools,

23and changed the glory of the incorruptible God for the likeness of an image of corruptible man, and of birds, and four-footed beasts, and creeping things.

24Wherefore God gave them up in the lusts of their hearts unto uncleanness, that their bodies should be dishonored among themselves:

25for that they exchanged the truth of God for a lie, and worshipped and served the creature rather than the Creator, who is blessed for ever. Amen.

26For this cause God gave them up unto vile passions: for their women changed the natural use into that which is against nature:

27and likewise also the men, leaving the natural use of the woman, burned in their lust one toward another, men with men working unseemliness, and receiving in themselves that recompense of their error which was due.

28And even as they refused to have God in their knowledge, God gave them up unto a reprobate mind, to do those things which are not fitting;

29being filled with all unrighteousness, wickedness, covetousness, maliciousness; full of envy, murder, strife, deceit, malignity; whisperers,

30backbiters, hateful to God, insolent, haughty, boastful, inventors of evil things, disobedient to parents,

31without understanding, covenant-breakers, without natural affection, unmerciful:

32who, knowing the ordinance of God, that they that practise such things are worthy of death, not only do the same, but also consent with them that practise them.

Chapter 2

1Wherefore thou art without excuse, O man, whosoever thou art that judgest: for wherein thou judges another, thou condemnest thyself; for thou that judgest dost practise the same things.

2And we know that the judgment of God is according to truth against them that practise such things.

3And reckonest thou this, O man, who judgest them that practise such things, and doest the same, that thou shalt escape the judgment of God?

4Or despisest thou the riches of his goodness and forbearance and longsuffering, not knowing that the goodness of God leadeth thee to repentance?

5but after thy hardness and impenitent heart treasurest up for thyself wrath in the day of wrath and revelation of the righteous judgment of God:

6who will render to every man according to his works:

7to them that by patience in well-doing seek for glory and honor and incorruption, eternal life:

8but unto them that are factious, and obey not the truth, but obey unrighteousness, shall be wrath and indignation,

9tribulation and anguish, upon every soul of man that worketh evil, of the Jew first, and also of the Greek;

10but glory and honor and peace to every man that worketh good, to the Jew first, and also to the Greek:

11for there is no respect of persons with God.

12For as many as have sinned without law shall also perish without the law: and as many as have sinned under the law shall be judged by the law;

13for not the hearers of the law are just before God, but the doers of the law shall be justified:

14(for when Gentiles that have not the law do by nature the things of the law, these, not having the law, are the law unto themselves;

15in that they show the work of the law written in their hearts, their conscience bearing witness therewith, and their thoughts one with another accusing or else excusing them);

16in the day when God shall judge the secrets of men, according to my gospel, by Jesus Christ.

17But if thou bearest the name of a Jew, and restest upon the law, and gloriest in God,

18and knowest his will, and approvest the things that are excellent, being instructed out of the law,

19and art confident that thou thyself art a guide of the blind, a light of them that are in darkness,

20a corrector of the foolish, a teacher of babes, having in the law the form of knowledge and of the truth;

21thou therefore that teachest another, teachest thou not thyself? thou that preachest a man should not steal, dost thou steal?

22thou that sayest a man should not commit adultery, dost thou commit adultery? thou that abhorrest idols, dost thou rob temples?

23thou who gloriest in the law, through thy transgression of the law dishonorest thou God?

24For the name of God is blasphemed among the Gentiles because of you, even as it is written.

25For circumcision indeed profiteth, if thou be a doer of the law: but if thou be a transgressor of the law, thy circumcision is become uncircumcision.

26If therefore the uncircumcision keep the ordinances of the law, shall not his uncircumcision be reckoned for circumcision?

27and shall not the uncircumcision which is by nature, if it fulfil the law, judge thee, who with the letter and circumcision art a transgressor of the law?

28For he is not a Jew who is one outwardly; neither is that circumcision which is outward in the flesh:

29but he is a Jew who is one inwardly; and circumcision is that of the heart, in the spirit not in the letter; whose praise is not of men, but of God.

Chapter 3

1What advantage then hath the Jew? or what is the profit of circumcision?

2Much every way: first of all, that they were intrusted with the oracles of God.

3For what if some were without faith? shall their want of faith make of none effect the faithfulness of God?

4God forbid: yea, let God be found true, but every man a liar; as it is written,

That thou mightest be justified in thy words,
And mightest prevail when thou comest into judgment.

5But if our righteousness commendeth the righteousness of God, what shall we say? Is God unrighteous who visiteth with wrath? (I speak after the manner of men.)

6God forbid: for then how shall God judge the world?

7But if the truth of God through my lie abounded unto his glory, why am I also still judged as a sinner?

8and why not (as we are slanderously reported, and as some affirm that we say), Let us do evil, that good may come? whose condemnation is just.

9What then? are we better than they? No, in no wise: for we before laid to the charge both of Jews and Greeks, that they are all under sin;

10as it is written,
There is none righteous, no, not one;
11There is none that understandeth,
There is none that seeketh after God;
12They have all turned aside, they are together become unprofitable;
There is none that doeth good, no, not, so much as one:
13Their throat is an open sepulchre;
With their tongues they have used deceit:
The poison of asps is under their lips:
14Whose mouth is full of cursing and bitterness:
15Their feet are swift to shed blood;
16Destruction and misery are in their ways;
17And the way of peace have they not known:
18There is no fear of God before their eyes.

19Now we know that what things soever the law saith, it speaketh to them that are under the law; that every mouth may be stopped, and all the world may be brought under the judgment of God:

20because by the works of the law shall no flesh be justified in his sight; for through the law cometh the knowledge of sin.

21But now apart from the law a righteousness of God hath been manifested, being witnessed by the law and the prophets;

22even the righteousness of God through faith in Jesus Christ unto all them that believe; for there is no distinction;

23for all have sinned, and fall short of the glory of God;

24being justified freely by his grace through the redemption that is in Christ Jesus:

25whom God set forth to be a propitiation, through faith, in his blood, to show his righteousness because of the passing over of the sins done aforetime, in the forbearance of God;

26for the showing, I say, of his righteousness at this present season: that he might himself be just, and the justifier of him that hath faith in Jesus.

27Where then is the glorying? It is excluded. By what manner of law? of works? Nay: but by a law of faith.

28We reckon therefore that a man is justified by faith apart from the works of the law.

29Or is God the God of Jews only? is he not the God of Gentiles also? Yea, of Gentiles also:

30if so be that God is one, and he shall justify the circumcision by faith, and the uncircumcision through faith.

31Do we then make the law of none effect through faith? God forbid: nay, we establish the law.

Chapter 4

1What then shall we say that Abraham, our forefather, hath found according to the flesh?

2For if Abraham was justified by works, he hath whereof to glory; but not toward God.

3For what saith the scripture? And Abraham believed God, and it was reckoned unto him for righteousness.

4Now to him that worketh, the reward is not reckoned as of grace, but as of debt.

5But to him that worketh not, but believeth on him that justifieth the ungodly, his faith is reckoned for righteousness.

6Even as David also pronounceth blessing upon the man, unto whom God reckoneth righteousness apart from works,

7saying,

Blessed are they whose iniquities are forgiven,

And whose sins are covered.

8Blessed is the man to whom, the Lord will not reckon sin.

9Is this blessing then pronounced upon the circumcision, or upon the uncircumcision also? for we say, To Abraham his faith was reckoned for righteousness.

10How then was it reckoned? when he was in circumcision, or in uncircumcision? Not in circumcision, but in uncircumcision:

11and he received the sign of circumcision, a seal of the righteousness of the faith which he had while he was in uncircumcision; that he might be the father of all them that believe, though they be in uncircumcision, that righteousness might be reckoned unto them;

12and the father of circumcision to them who not only are of the circumcision, but who also walk in the steps of that faith of our father Abraham which he had in uncircumcision.

13For not through the law was the promise to Abraham or to his seed that he should be heir of the world, but through the righteousness of faith.

14For if they that are of the law are heirs, faith is made void, and the promise is made of none effect:

15for the law worketh wrath; but where there is no law, neither is there transgression.

16For this cause it is of faith, that it may be according to grace; to the end that the promise may be sure to all the seed; not to that only which is of the law, but to that also which is of the faith of Abraham, who is the father of us all

17(as it is written, A father of many nations have I made thee) before him whom he believed, even God, who giveth life to the dead, and calleth the things that are not, as though they were.

18Who in hope believed against hope, to the end that he might become a father of many nations, according to that which had been spoken, So shall thy seed be.

19And without being weakened in faith he considered his own body now as good as dead (he being about a hundred years old), and the deadness of Sarah's womb;

20yet, looking unto the promise of God, he wavered not through unbelief, but waxed strong through faith, giving glory to God,

21and being fully assured that what he had promised, he was able also to perform.

22Wherefore also it was reckoned unto him for righteousness.

23Now it was not written for his sake alone, that it was reckoned unto him;

24but for our sake also, unto whom it shall be reckoned, who believe on him that raised Jesus our Lord from the dead,

25who was delivered up for our trespasses, and was raised for our justification.

Chapter 5

1Being therefore justified by faith, we have peace with God through our Lord Jesus Christ;

2through whom also we have had our access by faith into this grace wherein we stand; and we rejoice in hope of the glory of God.

3And not only so, but we also rejoice in our tribulations: knowing that tribulation worketh stedfastness;

4and stedfastness, approvedness; and approvedness, hope:

5and hope putteth not to shame; because the love of God hath been shed abroad in our hearts through the Holy Spirit which was given unto us.

6For while we were yet weak, in due season Christ died for the ungodly.

7For scarcely for a righteous man will one die: for peradventure for the good man some one would even dare to die.

8But God commendeth his own love toward us, in that, while we were yet sinners, Christ died for us.

9Much more then, being now justified by his blood, shall we be saved from the wrath of God through him.

10For if, while we were enemies, we were reconciled to God through the death of his Son, much more, being reconciled, shall we be saved by his life;

11and not only so, but we also rejoice in God through our Lord Jesus Christ, through whom we have now received the reconciliation.

12Therefore, as through one man sin entered into the world, and death through sin; and so death passed unto all men, for that all sinned:--

13for until the law sin was in the world; but sin is not imputed when there is no law.

14Nevertheless death reigned from Adam until Moses, even over them that had not sinned after the likeness of Adam's transgression, who is a figure of him that was to come.

15But not as the trespass, so also is the free gift. For if by the trespass of the one the many died, much more did the grace of God, and the gift by the grace of the one man, Jesus Christ, abound unto the many.

16And not as through one that sinned, so is the gift: for the judgment came of one unto condemnation, but the free gift came of many trespasses unto justification.

17For if, by the trespass of the one, death reigned through the one; much more shall they that receive the abundance of grace and of the gift of righteousness reign in life through the one, even Jesus Christ.

18So then as through one trespass the judgment came unto all men to condemnation; even so through one act of righteousness the free gift came unto all men to justification of life.

19For as through the one man's disobedience the many were made sinners, even so through the obedience of the one shall the many be made righteous.

20And the law came in besides, that the trespass might abound; but where sin abounded, grace did abound more exceedingly:

21that, as sin reigned in death, even so might grace reign through righteousness unto eternal life through Jesus Christ our Lord.

Chapter 6

1What shall we say then? Shall we continue in sin, that grace may abound?

2God forbid. We who died to sin, how shall we any longer live therein?

3Or are ye ignorant that all we who were baptized into Christ Jesus were baptized into his death?

4We were buried therefore with him through baptism unto death: that like as Christ was raised from the dead through the glory of the Father, so we also might walk in newness of life.

5For if we have become united with him in the likeness of his death, we shall be also in the likeness of his resurrection;

6knowing this, that our old man was crucified with him, that the body of sin might be done away, that so we should no longer be in bondage to sin;

7for he that hath died is justified from sin.

8But if we died with Christ, we believe that we shall also live with him;

9knowing that Christ being raised from the dead dieth no more; death no more hath dominion over him.

10For the death that he died, he died unto sin once: but the life that he liveth, he liveth unto God.

11Even so reckon ye also yourselves to be dead unto sin, but alive unto God in Christ Jesus.

12Let not sin therefore reign in your mortal body, that ye should obey the lusts thereof:

13neither present your members unto sin as instruments of unrighteousness; but present yourselves unto God, as alive from the dead, and your members as instruments of righteousness unto God.

14For sin shall not have dominion over you: for ye are not under law, but under grace.

15What then? shall we sin, because we are not under law, but under grace? God forbid.

16Know ye not, that to whom ye present yourselves as servants unto obedience, his servants ye are whom ye obey; whether of sin unto death, or of obedience unto righteousness?

17But thanks be to God, that, whereas ye were servants of sin, ye became obedient from the heart to that form of teaching whereunto ye were delivered;

18and being made free from sin, ye became servants of righteousness.

19I speak after the manner of men because of the infirmity of your flesh: for as ye presented your members as servants to uncleanness and to iniquity unto iniquity, even so now present your members as servants to righteousness unto sanctification.

20For when ye were servants of sin, ye were free in regard of righteousness.

21What fruit then had ye at that time in the things whereof ye are now ashamed? for the end of those things is death.

22But now being made free from sin and become servants to God, ye have your fruit unto sanctification, and the end eternal life.

23For the wages of sin is death; but the free gift of God is eternal life in Christ Jesus our Lord.

Chapter 7

1 Or are ye ignorant, brethren (for I speak to men who know the law), that the law hath dominion over a man for so long time as he liveth?

2 For the woman that hath a husband is bound by law to the husband while he liveth; but if the husband die, she is discharged from the law of the husband.

3 So then if, while the husband liveth, she be joined to another man, she shall be called an adulteress: but if the husband die, she is free from the law, so that she is no adulteress, though she be joined to another man.

4 Wherefore, my brethren, ye also were made dead to the law through the body of Christ; that ye should be joined to another, even to him who was raised from the dead, that we might bring forth fruit unto God.

5 For when we were in the flesh, the sinful passions, which were through the law, wrought in our members to bring forth fruit unto death.

6 But now we have been discharged from the law, having died to that wherein we were held; so that we serve in newness of the spirit, and not in oldness of the letter.

7 What shall we say then? Is the law sin? God forbid. Howbeit, I had not known sin, except through the law: for I had not known coveting, except the law had said, Thou shalt not covet:

8 but sin, finding occasion, wrought in me through the commandment all manner of coveting: for apart from the law sin is dead.

9 And I was alive apart from the law once: but when the commandment came, sin revived, and I died;

10 and the commandment, which was unto life, this I found to be unto death:

11 for sin, finding occasion, through the commandment beguiled me, and through it slew me.

12 So that the law is holy, and the commandment holy, and righteous, and good.

13 Did then that which is good become death unto me? God forbid. But sin, that it might be shown to be sin, by working death to me through that which is good; --that through the commandment sin might become exceeding sinful.

14 For we know that the law is spiritual: but I am carnal, sold under sin.

15 For that which I do I know not: for not what I would, that do I practise; but what I hate, that I do.

16 But if what I would not, that I do, I consent unto the law that it is good.

17 So now it is no more I that do it, but sin which dwelleth in me.

18 For I know that in me, that is, in my flesh, dwelleth no good thing: for to will is present with me, but to do that which is good is not.

19 For the good which I would I do not: but the evil which I would not, that I practise.

20 But if what I would not, that I do, it is no more I that do it, but sin which dwelleth in me.

21 I find then the law, that, to me who would do good, evil is present.

22 For I delight in the law of God after the inward man:

23 but I see a different law in my members, warring against the law of my mind, and bringing me into captivity under the law of sin which is in my members.

24 Wretched man that I am! who shall deliver me out of the body of this death?

25 I thank God through Jesus Christ our Lord. So then I of myself with the mind, indeed, serve the law of God; but with the flesh the law of sin.

Chapter 8

1 There is therefore now no condemnation to them that are in Christ Jesus.

2 For the law of the Spirit of life in Christ Jesus made me free from the law of sin and of death.

3 For what the law could not do, in that it was weak through the flesh, God, sending his own Son in the likeness of sinful flesh and for sin, condemned sin in the flesh:

4 that the ordinance of the law might be fulfilled in us, who walk not after the flesh, but after the Spirit.

5 For they that are after the flesh mind the things of the flesh; but they that are after the Spirit the things of the Spirit.

6 For the mind of the flesh is death; but the mind of the Spirit is life and peace:

7 because the mind of the flesh is enmity against God; for it is not subject to the law of God, neither indeed can it be:

8 and they that are in the flesh cannot please God.

9 But ye are not in the flesh but in the Spirit, if so be that the Spirit of God dwelleth in you. But if any man hath not the Spirit of Christ, he is none of his.

10 And if Christ is in you, the body is dead because of sin; but the spirit is life because of righteousness.

11 But if the Spirit of him that raised up Jesus from the dead dwelleth in you, he that raised up Christ Jesus from the dead shall give life also to your mortal bodies through his Spirit that dwelleth in you.

12 So then, brethren, we are debtors, not to the flesh, to live after the flesh:

13 for if ye live after the flesh, ye must die; but if by the Spirit ye put to death the deeds of the body, ye shall live.

14 For as many as are led by the Spirit of God, these are sons of God.

15 For ye received not the spirit of bondage again unto fear; but ye received the spirit of adoption, whereby we cry, Abba, Father.

16 The Spirit himself beareth witness with our spirit, that we are children of God:

17 and if children, then heirs; heirs of God, and joint-heirs with Christ; if so be that we suffer with him, that we may be also glorified with him.

18 For I reckon that the sufferings of this present time are not worthy to be compared with the glory which shall be revealed to us-ward.

19 For the earnest expectation of the creation waiteth for the revealing of the sons of God.

20 For the creation was subjected to vanity, not of its own will, but by reason of him who subjected it, in hope

21 that the creation itself also shall be delivered from the bondage of corruption into the liberty of the glory of the children of God.

22 For we know that the whole creation groaneth and travaileth in pain together until now.

23 And not only so, but ourselves also, who have the first-fruits of the Spirit, even we ourselves groan within ourselves, waiting for our adoption, to wit, the redemption of our body.

24 For in hope were we saved: but hope that is seen is not hope: for who hopeth for that which he seeth?

25 But if we hope for that which we see not, then do we with patience wait for it.

26 And in like manner the Spirit also helpeth our infirmity: for we know not how to pray as we ought; but the Spirit himself maketh intercession for us with groanings which cannot be uttered;

27 and he that searcheth the hearts knoweth what is the mind of the Spirit, because he maketh intercession for the saints according to the will of God.

28 And we know that to them that love God all things work together for good, even to them that are called according to his purpose.

29 For whom he foreknew, he also foreordained to be conformed to the image of his Son, that he might be the firstborn among many brethren:

30 and whom he foreordained, them he also called: and whom he called, them he also justified: and whom he justified, them he also glorified.

31 What then shall we say to these things? If God is for us, who is against us?

32 He that spared not his own Son, but delivered him up for us all, how shall he not also with him freely give us all things?

33 Who shall lay anything to the charge of God's elect? It is God that justifieth;

34 who is he that condemneth? It is Christ Jesus that died, yea rather, that was raised from the dead, who is at the right hand of God, who also maketh intercession for us.

35 Who shall separate us from the love of Christ? shall tribulation, or anguish, or persecution, or famine, or nakedness, or peril, or sword?

36 Even as it is written, For thy sake we are killed all the day long; We were accounted as sheep for the slaughter.

37 Nay, in all these things we are more than conquerors through him that loved us.

38 For I am persuaded, that neither death, nor life, nor angels, nor principalities, nor things present, nor things to come, nor powers,

39 nor height, nor depth, nor any other creature, shall be able to separate us from the love of God, which is in Christ Jesus our Lord.

Chapter 9

1 I say the truth in Christ, I lie not, my conscience bearing witness with me in the Holy Spirit,

2 that I have great sorrow and unceasing pain in my heart.

3 For I could wish that I myself were anathema from Christ for my brethren's sake, my kinsmen according to the flesh:

4 who are Israelites; whose is the adoption, and the glory, and the covenants, and the giving of the law, and the service of God, and the promises;

5 whose are the fathers, and of whom is Christ as concerning the flesh, who is over all, God blessed for ever. Amen.

6 But it is not as though the word of God hath come to nought. For they are not all Israel, that are of Israel:

7 neither, because they are Abraham's seed, are they all children: but, In Isaac shall thy seed be called.

8 That is, it is not the children of the flesh that are children of God; but the children of the promise are reckoned for a seed.

9 For this is a word of promise, According to this season will I come, and Sarah shall have a son.

10 And not only so; but Rebecca also having conceived by one, even by our father Isaac--

11 for the children being not yet born, neither having done anything good or bad, that the purpose of God according to election might stand, not of works, but of him that calleth,

12 it was said unto her, The elder shall serve the younger.

13 Even as it is written, Jacob I loved, but Esau I hated.

14 What shall we say then? Is there unrighteousness with God? God forbid.

15 For he saith to Moses, I will have mercy on whom I have mercy, and I will have compassion on whom I have compassion.

16 So then it is not of him that willeth, nor of him that runneth, but of God that hath mercy.

17 For the scripture saith unto Pharaoh, For this very purpose did I raise thee up, that I might show in thee my power, and that my name might be published abroad in all the earth.

18 So then he hath mercy on whom he will, and whom he will be hardeneth.

19 Thou wilt say then unto me, Why doth he still find fault? For who withstandeth his will?

20 Nay but, O man, who art thou that repliest against God? Shall the thing formed say to him that formed it, Why didst thou make me thus?

21 Or hath not the potter a right over the clay, from the same lump to make one part a vessel unto honor, and another unto dishonor?

22 What if God, willing to show his wrath, and to make his power known, endured with much longsuffering vessels of wrath fitted unto destruction:

23 and that he might make known the riches of his glory upon vessels of mercy, which he afore prepared unto glory,

24 even us, whom he also called, not from the Jews only, but also from the

Gentiles?

25As he saith also in Hosea,
I will call that my people, which was not my people;
And her beloved, that was not beloved.

26And it shall be, that in the place where it was said unto them, Ye are not my people,
There shall they be called sons of the living God.

27And Isaiah crieth concerning Israel, If the number of the children of Israel be as the sand of the sea, it is the remnant that shall be saved:

28for the Lord will execute his word upon the earth, finishing it and cutting it short.

29And, as Isaiah hath said before,
Except the Lord of Sabaoth had left us a seed,
We had become as Sodom, and had been made like unto Gomorrah.

30What shall we say then? That the Gentiles, who followed not after righteousness, attained to righteousness, even the righteousness which is of faith:

31but Israel, following after a law of righteousness, did not arrive at that law.

32Wherefore? Because they sought it not by faith, but as it were by works. They stumbled at the stone of stumbling;

33even as it is written,
Behold, I lay in Zion a stone of stumbling and a rock of offence:
And he that believeth on him shall not be put to shame.

Chapter 10

1Brethren, my heart's desire and my supplication to God is for them, that they may be saved.

2For I bear them witness that they have a zeal for God, but not according to knowledge.

3For being ignorant of God's righteousness, and seeking to establish their own, they did not subject themselves to the righteousness of God.

4For Christ is the end of the law unto righteousness to every one that believeth.

5For Moses writeth that the man that doeth the righteousness which is of the law shall live thereby.

6But the righteousness which is of faith saith thus, Say not in thy heart, Who shall ascend into heaven? (that is, to bring Christ down:)

7or, Who shall descend into the abyss? (That is, to bring Christ up from the dead.)

8But what saith it? The word is nigh thee, in thy mouth, and in thy heart: that is, the word of faith, which we preach:

9because if thou shalt confess with thy mouth Jesus as Lord, and shalt believe in thy heart that God raised him from the dead, thou shalt be saved:

10for with the heart man believeth unto righteousness; and with the mouth confession is made unto salvation.

11For the scripture saith, Whosoever believeth on him shall not be put to shame.

12For there is no distinction between Jew and Greek: for the same Lord is Lord of all, and is rich unto all that call upon him:

13for, Whosoever shall call upon the name of the Lord shall be saved.

14How then shall they call on him in whom they have not believed? and how shall they believe in him whom they have not heard? and how shall they hear without a preacher?

15and how shall they preach, except they be sent? even as it is written, How beautiful are the feet of them that bring glad tidings of good things!

16But they did not all hearken to the glad tidings. For Isaiah saith, Lord, who hath believed our report?

17So belief cometh of hearing, and hearing by the word of Christ.

18But I say, Did they not hear? Yea, verily,
Their sound went out into all the earth,
And their words unto the ends of the world.

19But I say, Did Israel not know? First Moses saith,
I will provoke you to jealousy with that which is no nation,
With a nation void of understanding will I anger you.

20And Isaiah is very bold, and saith,
I was found of them that sought me not;
I became manifest unto them that asked not of me.

21But as to Israel he saith, All the day long did I spread out my hands unto a disobedient and gainsaying people.

Chapter 11

1I say then, Did God cast off his people? God forbid. For I also am an Israelite, of the seed of Abraham, of the tribe of Benjamin.

2God did not cast off his people which he foreknew. Or know ye not what the scripture saith of Elijah? how he pleadeth with God against Israel:

3Lord, they have killed thy prophets, they have digged down thine altars; and I am left alone, and they seek my life.

4But what saith the answer of God unto him? I have left for myself seven thousand men, who have not bowed the knee to Baal.

5Even so then at this present time also there is a remnant according to the election of grace.

6But if it is by grace, it is no more of works: otherwise grace is no more grace.

7What then? that which Israel seeketh for, that he obtained not; but the election obtained it, and the rest were hardened:

8according as it is written, God gave them a spirit of stupor, eyes that they should not see, and ears that they should not hear, unto this very day.

9And David saith,
Let their table be made a snare, and a trap,
And a stumblingblock, and a recompense unto them:

10Let their eyes be darkened, that they may not see,
And bow thou down their back always.

11I say then, Did they stumble that they might fall? God forbid: but by their fall salvation is come unto the Gentiles, to provoke them to jealousy.

12Now if their fall, is the riches of the world, and their loss the riches of the Gentiles; how much more their fulness?

13But I speak to you that are Gentiles. Inasmuch then as I am an apostle of Gentiles, I glorify my ministry;

14if by any means I may provoke to jealousy them that are my flesh, and may save some of them.

15For if the casting away of them is the reconciling of the world, what shall the receiving of them be, but life from the dead?

16And if the firstfruit is holy, so is the lump: and if the root is holy, so are the branches.

17But if some of the branches were broken off, and thou, being a wild olive, wast grafted in among them, and didst become partaker with them of the root of the fatness of the olive tree;

18glory not over the branches: but if thou gloriest, it is not thou that bearest the root, but the root thee.

19Thou wilt say then, Branches were broken off, that I might be grafted in.

20Well; by their unbelief they were broken off, and thou standest by thy faith. Be not highminded, but fear:

21for if God spared not the natural branches, neither will he spare thee.

22Behold then the goodness and severity of God: toward them that fell, severity; but toward thee, God's goodness, if thou continue in his goodness: otherwise thou also shalt be cut off.

23And they also, if they continue not in their unbelief, shall be grafted in: for God is able to graft them in again.

24For if thou wast cut out of that which is by nature a wild olive tree, and wast grafted contrary to nature into a good olive tree; how much more shall these, which are the natural branches, be grafted into their own olive tree?

25For I would not, brethren, have you ignorant of this mystery, lest ye be wise in your own conceits, that a hardening in part hath befallen Israel, until the fulness of the Gentiles be come in;

26and so all Israel shall be saved: even as it is written,
There shall come out of Zion the Deliverer;
He shall turn away ungodliness from Jacob:

27And this is my covenant unto them,
When I shall take away their sins.

28As touching the gospel, they are enemies for your sake: but as touching the election, they are beloved for the fathers' sake.

29For the gifts and the calling of God are not repented of.

30For as ye in time past were disobedient to God, but now have obtained mercy by their disobedience,

31even so have these also now been disobedient, that by the mercy shown to you they also may now obtain mercy.

32For God hath shut up all unto disobedience, that he might have mercy upon all.

33O the depth of the riches both of the wisdom and the knowledge of God! how unsearchable are his judgments, and his ways past tracing out!

34For who hath known the mind of the Lord? or who hath been his counsellor?

35or who hath first given to him, and it shall be recompensed unto him again?

36For of him, and through him, and unto him, are all things. To him be the glory for ever. Amen.

Chapter 12

1I beseech you therefore, brethren, by the mercies of God, to present your bodies a living sacrifice, holy, acceptable to God, which is your spiritual service.

2And be not fashioned according to this world: but be ye transformed by the renewing of your mind, and ye may prove what is the good and acceptable and perfect will of God.

3For I say, through the grace that was given me, to every man that is among you, not to think of himself more highly than he ought to think; but to think as to think soberly, according as God hath dealt to each man a measure of faith.

4For even as we have many members in one body, and all the members have not the same office:

5so we, who are many, are one body in Christ, and severally members one of another.

6And having gifts differing according to the grace that was given to us, whether prophecy, let us prophesy according to the proportion of our faith;

7or ministry, let us give ourselves to our ministry; or he that teacheth, to his teaching;

8or he that exhorteth, to his exhorting: he that giveth, let him do it with liberality; he that ruleth, with diligence; he that showeth mercy, with cheerfulness.

9Let love be without hypocrisy. Abhor that which is evil; cleave to that which is good.

10In love of the brethren be tenderly affectioned one to another; in honor preferring one another;

11in diligence not slothful; fervent in spirit; serving the Lord;

12rejoicing in hope; patient in tribulation; continuing stedfastly in prayer;

13communicating to the necessities of the saints; given to hospitality.

14Bless them that persecute you; bless, and curse not.

15Rejoice with them that rejoice; weep with them that weep.

16Be of the same mind one toward another. Set not your mind on high things, but condescend to things that are lowly. Be not wise in your own conceits.

17Render to no man evil for evil. Take thought for things honorable in the sight of all men.

18If it be possible, as much as in you lieth, be at peace with all men.

19Avenge not yourselves, beloved, but give place unto the wrath of God: for it is written, Vengeance belongeth unto me; I will recompense, saith the Lord.

20But if thine enemy hunger, feed him; if he thirst, give him to drink: for in so doing thou shalt heap coals of fire upon his head.

21Be not overcome of evil, but overcome evil with good.

Chapter 13

1Let every soul be in subjection to the higher powers: for there is no power but of God; and the powers that be are ordained of God.

2Therefore he that resisteth the power, withstandeth the ordinance of God: and they that withstand shall receive to themselves judgment.

3For rulers are not a terror to the good work, but to the evil. And wouldest thou have no fear of the power? do that which is good, and thou shalt have praise from the same:

4for he is a minister of God to thee for good. But if thou do that which is evil, be afraid; for he beareth not the sword in vain: for he is a minister of God, an avenger for wrath to him that doeth evil.

5Wherefore ye must needs be in subjection, not only because of the wrath, but also for conscience' sake.

6For this cause ye pay tribute also; for they are ministers of God's service, attending continually upon this very thing.

7Render to all their dues: tribute to whom tribute is due; custom to whom custom; fear to whom fear; honor to whom honor.

8Owe no man anything, save to love one another: for he that loveth his neighbor hath fulfilled the law.

9For this, Thou shalt not commit adultery, Thou shalt not kill, Thou shalt not steal, Thou shalt not covet, and if there be any other commandment, it is summed up in this word, namely, Thou shalt love thy neighbor as thyself.

10Love worketh no ill to his neighbor: love therefore is the fulfilment of the law.

11And this, knowing the season, that already it is time for you to awake out of sleep: for now is salvation nearer to us than when we first believed.

12The night is far spent, and the day is at hand: let us therefore cast off the works of darkness, and let us put on the armor of light.

13Let us walk becomingly, as in the day; not in revelling and drunkenness, not in chambering and wantonness, not in strife and jealousy.

14But put ye on the Lord Jesus Christ, and make not provision for the flesh, to fulfil the lusts thereof.

Chapter 14

1But him that is weak in faith receive ye, yet not for decision of scruples.

2One man hath faith to eat all things: but he that is weak eateth herbs.

3Let not him that eateth set at nought him that eateth not; and let not him that eateth not judge him that eateth: for God hath received him.

4Who art thou that judgest the servant of another? to his own lord he standeth or falleth. Yea, he shall be made to stand; for the Lord hath power to make him stand.

5One man esteemeth one day above another: another esteemeth every day alike. Let each man be fully assured in his own mind.

6He that regardeth the day, regardeth it unto the Lord: and he that eateth, eateth unto the Lord, for he giveth God thanks; and he that eateth not, unto the Lord he eateth not, and giveth God thanks.

7For none of us liveth to himself, and none dieth to himself.

8For whether we live, we live unto the Lord; or whether we die, we die unto the Lord: whether we live therefore, or die, we are the Lord's.

9For to this end Christ died and lived again, that he might be Lord of both the dead and the living.

10But thou, why dost thou judge thy brother? or thou again, why dost thou set at nought thy brother? for we shall all stand before the judgment-seat of God.

11For it is written,
As I live, saith the Lord, to me every knee shall bow,
And every tongue shall confess to God.

12So then each one of us shall give account of himself to God.

13Let us not therefore judge one another any more: but judge ye this rather, that no man put a stumblingblock in his brother's way, or an occasion of falling.

14I know, and am persuaded in the Lord Jesus, that nothing is unclean of itself: save that to him who accounteth anything to be unclean, to him it is unclean.

15For if because of meat thy brother is grieved, thou walkest no longer in love. Destroy not with thy meat him for whom Christ died.

16Let not then your good be evil spoken of:

17for the kingdom of God is not eating and drinking, but righteousness and peace and joy in the Holy Spirit.

18For he that herein serveth Christ is well-pleasing to God, and approved of men.

19So then let us follow after things which make for peace, and things whereby we may edify one another.

20Overthrow not for meat's sake the work of God. All things indeed are clean; howbeit it is evil for that man who eateth with offence.

21It is good not to eat flesh, nor to drink wine, nor to do anything whereby thy brother stumbleth.

22The faith which thou hast, have thou to thyself before God. Happy is he that judgeth not himself in that which he approveth.

23But he that doubteth is condemned if he eat, because he eateth not of faith; and whatsoever is not of faith is sin.

Chapter 15

1Now we that are strong ought to bear the infirmities of the weak, and not to please ourselves.

2Let each one of us please his neighbor for that which is good, unto edifying.

3For Christ also pleased not himself; but, as it is written, The reproaches of them that reproached thee fell upon me.

4For whatsoever things were written aforetime were written for our learning, that through patience and through comfort of the scriptures we might have hope.

5Now the God of patience and of comfort grant you to be of the same mind one with another according to Christ Jesus:

6that with one accord ye may with one mouth glorify the God and Father of our Lord Jesus Christ.

7Wherefore receive ye one another, even as Christ also received you, to the glory of God.

8For I say that Christ hath been made a minister of the circumcision for the truth of God, that he might confirm the promises given unto the fathers,

9and that the Gentiles might glorify God for his mercy; as it is written,
Therefore will I give praise unto thee among the Gentiles,
And sing unto thy name.

10And again he saith,
Rejoice, ye Gentiles, with his people.

11And again,
Praise the Lord, all ye Gentiles;
And let all the peoples praise him.

12And again, Isaiah saith,
There shall be the root of Jesse,
And he that ariseth to rule over the Gentiles;
On him shall the Gentiles hope.

13Now the God of hope fill you with all joy and peace in believing, that ye may abound in hope, in the power of the Holy Spirit.

14And I myself also am persuaded of you, my brethren, that ye yourselves are full of goodness, filled with all knowledge, able also to admonish one another.

15But I write the more boldly unto you in some measure, as putting you again in remembrance, because of the grace that was given me of God,

16that I should be a minister of Christ Jesus unto the Gentiles, ministering the gospel of God, that the offering up of the Gentiles might be made acceptable, being sanctified by the Holy Spirit.

17I have therefore my glorifying in Christ Jesus in things pertaining to God.

18For I will not dare to speak of any things save those which Christ wrought through me, for the obedience of the Gentiles, by word and deed,

19in the power of signs and wonders, in the power of the Holy Spirit; so that from Jerusalem, and round about even unto Illyricum, I have fully preached the gospel of Christ;

20yea, making it my aim so to preach the gospel, not where Christ was already named, that I might not build upon another man's foundation;

21but, as it is written,
They shall see, to whom no tidings of him came,
And they who have not heard shall understand.

22Wherefore also I was hindered these many times from coming to you:

23but now, having no more any place in these regions, and having these many years a longing to come unto you,

24whensoever I go unto Spain (for I hope to see you in my journey, and to be brought on my way thitherward by you, if first in some measure I shall have been satisfied with your company)--

25but now, I say, I go unto Jerusalem, ministering unto the saints.

26For it hath been the good pleasure of Macedonia and Achaia to make a certain contribution for the poor among the saints that are at Jerusalem.

27Yea, it hath been their good pleasure; and their debtors they are. For if the Gentiles have been made partakers of their spiritual things, they owe it to them also to minister unto them in carnal things.

28When therefore I have accomplished this, and have sealed to them this fruit, I will go on by you unto Spain.

29And I know that, when I come unto you, I shall come in the fulness of the blessing of Christ.

30Now I beseech you, brethren, by our Lord Jesus Christ, and by the love of the Spirit, that ye strive together with me in your prayers to God for me;

31that I may be delivered from them that are disobedient in Judaea, and that my ministration which I have for Jerusalem may be acceptable to the saints;

32that I may come unto you in joy through the will of God, and together with you find rest.

33Now the God of peace be with you all. Amen.

Chapter 16

1I commend unto you Phoebe our sister, who is a servant of the church that is at Cenchreae:

2that ye receive her in the Lord, worthily of the saints, and that ye assist her in whatsoever matter she may have need of you: for she herself also hath been a helper of many, and of mine own self.

3Salute Prisca and Aquila my fellow-workers in Christ Jesus,

4who for my life laid down their own necks; unto whom not only I give thanks, but also all the churches of the Gentiles:

5and salute the church that is in their house. Salute Epaenetus my beloved, who is the first-fruits of Asia unto Christ.

6Salute Mary, who bestowed much labor on you.

7Salute Andronicus and Junias, my kinsmen, and my fellow-prisoners, who are of note among the apostles, who also have been in Christ before me.

Romans

8Salute Ampliatus my beloved in the Lord.

9Salute Urbanus our fellow-worker in Christ, and Stachys my beloved.

10Salute Apelles the approved in Christ. Salute them that are of the household of Aristobulus.

11Salute Herodion my kinsman. Salute them of the household of Narcissus, that are in the Lord.

12Salute Tryphaena and Tryphosa, who labor in the Lord. Salute Persis the beloved, who labored much in the Lord.

13Salute Rufus the chosen in the Lord, and his mother and mine.

14Salute Asyncritus, Phlegon, Hermes, Patrobas, Hermas, and the brethren that are with them.

15Salute Philologus and Julia, Nereus and his sister, and Olympas, and all the saints that are with them.

16Salute one another with a holy kiss. All the churches of Christ salute you.

17Now I beseech you, brethren, mark them that are causing the divisions and occasions of stumbling, contrary to the doctrine which ye learned: and turn away from them.

18For they that are such serve not our Lord Christ, but their own belly; and by their smooth and fair speech they beguile the hearts of the innocent.

19For your obedience is come abroad unto all men. I rejoice therefore over you: but I would have you wise unto that which is good, and simple unto that which is evil.

20And the God of peace shall bruise Satan under your feet shortly. The grace of our Lord Jesus Christ be with you.

21Timothy my fellow-worker saluteth you; and Lucius and Jason and Sosipater, my kinsmen.

22I Tertius, who write the epistle, salute you in the Lord.

23Gaius my host, and of the whole church, saluteth you. Erastus the treasurer of the city saluteth you, and Quartus the brother.

24The grace of our Lord Jesus Christ be with you all. Amen.

25Now to him that is able to establish you according to my gospel and the preaching of Jesus Christ, according to the revelation of the mystery which hath been kept in silence through times eternal,

26but now is manifested, and by the scriptures of the prophets, according to the commandment of the eternal God, is made known unto all the nations unto obedience of faith:

27to the only wise God, through Jesus Christ, to whom be the glory for ever. Amen.

The First Epistle of Paul the Apostle to the Corinthians

Chapter 1

1 Paul, called to be an apostle of Jesus Christ through the will of God, and Sosthenes our brother,

2 unto the church of God which is at Corinth, even them that are sanctified in Christ Jesus, called to be saints, with all that call upon the name of our Lord Jesus Christ in every place, their Lord and ours:

3 Grace to you and peace from God our Father and the Lord Jesus Christ.

4 I thank my God always concerning you, for the grace of God which was given you in Christ Jesus;

5 that in everything ye were enriched in him, in all utterance and all knowledge;

6 even as the testimony of Christ was confirmed in you:

7 so that ye come behind in no gift; waiting for the revelation of our Lord Jesus Christ;

8 who shall also confirm you unto the end, that ye be unreproveable in the day of our Lord Jesus Christ.

9 God is faithful, through whom ye were called into the fellowship of his Son Jesus Christ our Lord.

10 Now I beseech you, brethren, through the name of our Lord Jesus Christ, that ye all speak the same thing and that there be no divisions among you; but that ye be perfected together in the same mind and in the same judgment.

11 For it hath been signified unto me concerning you, my brethren, by them that are of the household of Chloe, that there are contentions among you.

12 Now this I mean, that each one of you saith, I am of Paul; and I of Apollos: and I of Cephas; and I of Christ.

13 Is Christ divided? was Paul crucified for you? or were ye baptized into the name of Paul?

14 I thank God that I baptized none of you, save Crispus and Gaius;

15 lest any man should say that ye were baptized into my name.

16 And I baptized also the household of Stephanas: besides, I know not whether I baptized any other.

17 For Christ sent me not to baptize, but to preach the gospel: not in wisdom of words, lest the cross of Christ should be made void.

18 For the word of the cross is to them that perish foolishness; but unto us who are saved it is the power of God.

19 For it is written,
I will destroy the wisdom of the wise,
And the discernment of the discerning will I bring to nought.

20 Where is the wise? where is the scribe? where is the disputer of this world? hath not God made foolish the wisdom of the world?

21 For seeing that in the wisdom of God the world through its wisdom knew not God, it was God's good pleasure through the foolishness of the preaching to save them that believe.

22 Seeing that Jews ask for signs, and Greeks seek after wisdom:

23 but we preach Christ crucified, unto Jews a stumblingblock, and unto Gentiles foolishness;

24 but unto them that are called, both Jews and Greeks, Christ the power of God, and the wisdom of God.

25 Because the foolishness of God is wiser than men; and the weakness of God is stronger than men.

26 For behold your calling, brethren, that not many wise after the flesh, not many mighty, not many noble, are called:

27 but God chose the foolish things of the world, that he might put to shame them that are wise; and God chose the weak things of the world, that he might put to shame the things that are strong;

28 and the base things of the world, and the things that are despised, did God choose, yea and the things that are not, that he might bring to nought the things that are:

29 that no flesh should glory before God.

30 But of him are ye in Christ Jesus, who was made unto us wisdom from God, and righteousness and sanctification, and redemption:

31 that, according as it is written, He that glorieth, let him glory in the Lord.

Chapter 2

1 And I, brethren, when I came unto you, came not with excellency of speech or of wisdom, proclaiming to you the testimony of God.

2 For I determined not to know anything among you, save Jesus Christ, and him crucified.

3 And I was with you in weakness, and in fear, and in much trembling.

4 And my speech and my preaching were not in persuasive words of wisdom, but in demonstration of the Spirit and of power:

5 that your faith should not stand in the wisdom of men, but in the power of God.

6 We speak wisdom, however, among them that are fullgrown: yet a wisdom not of this world, nor of the rulers of this world, who are coming to nought:

7 but we speak God's wisdom in a mystery, even the wisdom that hath been hidden, which God foreordained before the worlds unto our glory:

8 which none of the rulers of this world hath known: for had they known it, they would not have crucified the Lord of glory:

9 but as it is written,
Things which eye saw not, and ear heard not,
And which entered not into the heart of man,
Whatsoever things God prepared for them that love him.

10 But unto us God revealed them through the Spirit: for the Spirit searcheth all things, yea, the deep things of God.

11 For who among men knoweth the things of a man, save the spirit of the man, which is in him? even so the things of God none knoweth, save the Spirit of God.

12 But we received, not the spirit of the world, but the spirit which is from God; that we might know the things that were freely given to us of God.

13 Which things also we speak, not in words which man's wisdom teacheth, but which the Spirit teacheth; combining spiritual things with spiritual words.

14 Now the natural man receiveth not the things of the Spirit of God: for they are foolishness unto him; and he cannot know them, because they are spiritually judged.

15 But he that is spiritual judgeth all things, and he himself is judged of no man.

16 For who hath known the mind of the Lord, that he should instruct him? But we have the mind of Christ.

Chapter 3

1 And I, brethren, could not speak unto you as unto spiritual, but as unto carnal, as unto babes in Christ.

2 I fed you with milk, not with meat; for ye were not yet able to bear it: nay, not even now are ye able;

3 for ye are yet carnal: for whereas there is among you jealousy and strife, are ye not carnal, and do ye not walk after the manner of men?

4 For when one saith, I am of Paul; and another, I am of Apollos; are ye not men?

5 What then is Apollos? and what is Paul? Ministers through whom ye believed; and each as the Lord gave to him.

6 I planted, Apollos watered; but God gave the increase.

7 So then neither is he that planteth anything, neither he that watereth; but God that giveth the increase.

8 Now he that planteth and he that watereth are one: but each shall receive his own reward according to his own labor.

9 For we are God's fellow-workers: ye are God's husbandry, God's building.

10 According to the grace of God which was given unto me, as a wise masterbuilder I laid a foundation; and another buildeth thereon. But let each man take heed how he buildeth thereon.

11 For other foundation can no man lay than that which is laid, which is Jesus Christ.

12 But if any man buildeth on the foundation gold, silver, costly stones, wood, hay, stubble;

13 each man's work shall be made manifest: for the day shall declare it, because it is revealed in fire; and the fire itself shall prove each man's work of what sort it is.

14 If any man's work shall abide which he built thereon, he shall receive a reward.

15 If any man's work shall be burned, he shall suffer loss: but he himself shall be saved; yet so as through fire.

16 Know ye not that ye are a temple of God, and that the Spirit of God dwelleth in you?

17 If any man destroyeth the temple of God, him shall God destroy; for the temple of God is holy, and such are ye.

18 Let no man deceive himself. If any man thinketh that he is wise among you in this world, let him become a fool, that he may become wise.

19 For the wisdom of this world is foolishness with God. For it is written, He that taketh the wise in their craftiness:

20 and again, The Lord knoweth the reasonings of the wise that they are vain.

21 Wherefore let no one glory in men. For all things are yours;

22 whether Paul, or Apollos, or Cephas, or the world, or life, or death, or things present, or things to come; all are yours;

23 and ye are Christ's; and Christ is God's.

Chapter 4

1 Let a man so account of us, as of ministers of Christ, and stewards of the mysteries of God.

2 Here, moreover, it is required in stewards, that a man be found faithful.

3 But with me it is a very small thing that I should be judged of you, or of man's judgment: yea, I judge not mine own self.

4 For I know nothing against myself; yet am I not hereby justified: but he that judgeth me is the Lord.

5 Wherefore judge nothing before the time, until the Lord come, who will both bring to light the hidden things of darkness, and make manifest the counsels of the hearts; and then shall each man have his praise from God.

6 Now these things, brethren, I have in a figure transferred to myself and Apollos for your sakes; that in us ye might learn not to go beyond the things which are written; that no one of you be puffed up for the one against the other.

7 For who maketh thee to differ? and what hast thou that thou didst not receive? but if thou didst receive it, why dost thou glory as if thou hadst not received it?

8 Already are ye filled, already ye are become rich, ye have come to reign without us: yea and I would that ye did reign, that we also might reign with you.

9 For, I think, God hath set forth us the apostles last of all, as men doomed to death: for we are made a spectacle unto the world, both to angels and men.

10 We are fools for Christ's sake, but ye are wise in Christ; we are weak, but ye are strong; ye have glory, but we have dishonor.

11 Even unto this present hour we both hunger, and thirst, and are naked, and

First Corinthians

are buffeted, and have no certain dwelling-place;

12and we toil, working with our own hands: being reviled, we bless; being persecuted, we endure;

13being defamed, we entreat: we are made as the filth of the world, the offscouring of all things, even until now.

14I write not these things to shame you, but to admonish you as my beloved children.

15For though ye have ten thousand tutors in Christ, yet have ye not many fathers; for in Christ Jesus I begat you through the gospel.

16I beseech you therefore, be ye imitators of me.

17For this cause have I sent unto you Timothy, who is my beloved and faithful child in the Lord, who shall put you in remembrance of my ways which are in Christ, even as I teach everywhere in every church.

18Now some are puffed up, as though I were not coming to you.

19But I will come to you shortly, if the Lord will; and I will know, not the word of them that are puffed up, but the power.

20For the kingdom of God is not in word, but in power.

21What will ye? shall I come unto you with a rod, or in love and a spirit of gentleness?

Chapter 5

1It is actually reported that there is fornication among you, and such fornication as is not even among the Gentiles, that one of you hath his father's wife.

2And ye are puffed up, and did not rather mourn, that he that had done this deed might be taken away from among you.

3For I verily, being absent in body but present in spirit, have already as though I were present judged him that hath so wrought this thing,

4in the name of our Lord Jesus, ye being gathered together, and my spirit, with the power of our Lord Jesus,

5to deliver such a one unto Satan for the destruction of the flesh, that the spirit may be saved in the day of the Lord Jesus.

6Your glorying is not good. Know ye not that a little leaven leaveneth the whole lump?

7Purge out the old leaven, that ye may be a new lump, even as ye are unleavened. For our passover also hath been sacrificed, even Christ:

8wherefore let us keep the feast, not with old leaven, neither with the leaven of malice and wickedness, but with the unleavened bread of sincerity and truth.

9I wrote unto you in my epistle to have no company with fornicators;

10not at all meaning with the fornicators of this world, or with the covetous and extortioners, or with idolaters; for then must ye needs go out of the world:

11but as it is, I wrote unto you not to keep company, if any man that is named a brother be a fornicator, or covetous, or an idolater, or a reviler, or a drunkard, or an extortioner; with such a one no, not to eat.

12For what have I to do with judging them that are without? Do not ye judge them that are within?

13But them that are without God judgeth. Put away the wicked man from among yourselves.

Chapter 6

1Dare any of you, having a matter against his neighbor, go to law before the unrighteous, and not before the saints?

2Or know ye not that the saints shall judge the world? and if the world is judged by you, are ye unworthy to judge the smallest matters?

3Know ye not that we shall judge angels? how much more, things that pertain to this life?

4If then ye have to judge things pertaining to this life, do ye set them to judge who are of no account in the church?

5I say this to move you to shame. What, cannot there be found among you one wise man who shall be able to decide between his brethren,

6but brother goeth to law with brother, and that before unbelievers?

7Nay, already it is altogether a defect in you, that ye have lawsuits one with another. Why not rather take wrong? why not rather be defrauded?

8Nay, but ye yourselves do wrong, and defraud, and that your brethren.

9Or know ye not that the unrighteous shall not inherit the kingdom of God? Be not deceived: neither fornicators, nor idolaters, nor adulterers, nor effeminate, nor abusers of themselves with men,

10nor thieves, nor covetous, nor drunkards, nor revilers, nor extortioners, shall inherit the kingdom of God.

11And such were some of you: but ye were washed, but ye were sanctified, but ye were justified in the name of the Lord Jesus Christ, and in the Spirit of our God.

12All things are lawful for me; but not all things are expedient. All things are lawful for me; but I will not be brought under the power of any.

13Meats for the belly, and the belly for meats: but God shall bring to nought both it and them. But the body is not for fornication, but for the Lord; and the Lord for the body:

14and God both raised the Lord, and will raise up as through his power.

15Know ye not that your bodies are members of Christ? shall I then take away the members of Christ, and make them members of a harlot? God forbid.

16Or know ye not that he that is joined to a harlot is one body? for, The twain, saith he, shall become one flesh.

17But he that is joined unto the Lord is one spirit.

18Flee fornication. Every sin that a man doeth is without the body; but he that committeth fornication sinneth against his own body.

19Or know ye not that your body is a temple of the Holy Spirit which is in you, which ye have from God? and ye are not your own;

20for ye were bought with a price: glorify God therefore in your body.

Chapter 7

1Now concerning the things whereof ye wrote: It is good for a man not to touch a woman.

2But, because of fornications, let each man have his own wife, and let each woman have her own husband.

3Let the husband render unto the wife her due: and likewise also the wife unto the husband.

4The wife hath not power over her own body, but the husband: and likewise also the husband hath not power over his own body, but the wife.

5Defraud ye not one the other, except it be by consent for a season, that ye may give yourselves unto prayer, and may be together again, that Satan tempt you not because of your incontinency.

6But this I say by way of concession, not of commandment.

7Yet I would that all men were even as I myself. Howbeit each man hath his own gift from God, one after this manner, and another after that.

8But I say to the unmarried and to widows, It is good for them if they abide even as I.

9But if they have not continency, let them marry: for it is better to marry than to burn.

10But unto the married I give charge, yea not I, but the Lord, That the wife depart not from her husband

11(but should she depart, let her remain unmarried, or else be reconciled to her husband); and that the husband leave not his wife.

12But to the rest say I, not the Lord: If any brother hath an unbelieving wife, and she is content to dwell with him, let him not leave her.

13And the woman that hath an unbelieving husband, and he is content to dwell with her, let her not leave her husband.

14For the unbelieving husband is sanctified in the wife, and the unbelieving wife is sanctified in the brother: else were your children unclean; but now are they holy.

15Yet if the unbelieving departeth, let him depart: the brother or the sister is not under bondage in such cases: but God hath called us in peace.

16For how knowest thou, O wife, whether thou shalt save thy husband? Or how knowest thou, O husband, whether thou shalt save thy wife?

17Only, as the Lord hath distributed to each man, as God hath called each, so let him walk. And so ordain I in all the churches.

18Was any man called being circumcised? Let him not become uncircumcised. Hath any been called in uncircumcision? Let him not be circumcised.

19Circumcision is nothing, and uncircumcision is nothing; but the keeping of the commandments of God.

20Let each man abide in that calling wherein he was called.

21Wast thou called being a bondservant? Care not for it: nay, even if thou canst become free, use it rather.

22For he that was called in the Lord being a bondservant, is the Lord's freedman: likewise he that was called being free, is Christ's bondservant.

23Ye were bought with a price; become not bondservants of men.

24Brethren, let each man, wherein he was called, therein abide with God.

25Now concerning virgins I have no commandment of the Lord: but I give my judgment, as one that hath obtained mercy of the Lord to be trustworthy.

26I think therefore that this is good by reason of the distress that is upon us, namely, that it is good for a man to be as he is.

27Art thou bound unto a wife? Seek not to be loosed. Art thou loosed from a wife? Seek not a wife.

28But shouldest thou marry, thou hast not sinned; and if a virgin marry, she hath not sinned. Yet such shall have tribulation in the flesh: and I would spare you.

29But this I say, brethren, the time is shortened, that henceforth both those that have wives may be as though they had none;

30and those that weep, as though they wept not; and those that rejoice, as though they rejoiced not; and those that buy, as though they possessed not;

31and those that use the world, as not using it to the full: for the fashion of this world passeth away.

32But I would have you to be free from cares. He that is unmarried is careful for the things of the Lord, how he may please the Lord:

33but he that is married is careful for the things of the world, how he may please his wife,

34and is divided. So also the woman that is unmarried and the virgin is careful for the things of the Lord, that she may be holy both in body and in spirit: but she that is married is careful for the things of the world, how she may please her husband.

35And this I say for your own profit; not that I may cast a snare upon you, but for that which is seemly, and that ye may attend upon the Lord without distraction.

36But if any man thinketh that he behaveth himself unseemly toward his virgin daughter, if she be past the flower of her age, and if need so requireth, let him do what he will; he sinneth not; let them marry.

37But he that standeth stedfast in his heart, having no necessity, but hath power as touching his own heart, to keep his own virgin daughter, shall do well.

38So then both he that giveth his own virgin daughter in marriage doeth well; and he that giveth her not in marriage shall do better.

39A wife is bound for so long time as her husband liveth; but if the husband be dead, she is free to be married to whom she will; only in the Lord.

40But she is happier if she abide as she is, after my judgment: and I think that I also have the Spirit of God.

Chapter 8

1Now concerning things sacrificed to idols: We know that we all have knowledge. Knowledge puffeth up, but love edifieth.

2If any man thinketh that he knoweth anything, he knoweth not yet as he ought to know;

3but if any man loveth God, the same is known by him.

4Concerning therefore the eating of things sacrificed to idols, we know that no idol is anything in the world, and that there is no God but one.

5For though there be that are called gods, whether in heaven or on earth; as there are gods many, and lords many;

6yet to us there is one God, the Father, of whom are all things, and we unto him; and one Lord, Jesus Christ, through whom are all things, and we through him.

7Howbeit there is not in all men that knowledge: but some, being used until now to the idol, eat as of a thing sacrificed to an idol; and their conscience being weak is defiled.

8But food will not commend us to God: neither, if we eat not, are we the worse; nor, if we eat, are we the better.

9But take heed lest by any means this liberty of yours become a stumblingblock to the weak.

10For if a man see thee who hast knowledge sitting at meat in an idol's temple, will not his conscience, if he is weak, be emboldened to eat things sacrificed to idols?

11For through thy knowledge he that is weak perisheth, the brother for whose sake Christ died.

12And thus, sinning against the brethren, and wounding their conscience when it is weak, ye sin against Christ.

13Wherefore, if meat causeth my brother to stumble, I will eat no flesh for evermore, that I cause not my brother to stumble.

Chapter 9

1Am I not free? Am I not an apostle? Have I not seen Jesus our Lord? Are not ye my work in the Lord?

2If to others I am not an apostle, yet at least I am to you; for the seal of mine apostleship are ye in the Lord.

3My defence to them that examine me is this.

4Have we no right to eat and to drink?

5Have we no right to lead about a wife that is a believer, even as the rest of the apostles, and the brethren of the Lord, and Cephas?

6Or I only and Barnabas, have not a right to forbear working?

7What soldier ever serveth at his own charges? who planteth a vineyard, and eateth not the fruit thereof? Or who feedeth a flock, and eateth not of the milk of the flock?

8Do I speak these things after the manner of men? or saith not the law also the same?

9For it is written in the law of Moses, Thou shalt not muzzle the ox when he treadeth out the corn. Is it for the oxen that God careth,

10or saith he it assuredly for our sake? Yea, for our sake it was written: because he that ploweth ought to plow in hope, and he that thresheth, to thresh in hope of partaking.

11If we sowed unto you spiritual things, is it a great matter if we shall reap your carnal things?

12If others partake of this right over you, do not we yet more? Nevertheless we did not use this right; but we bear all things, that we may cause no hindrance to the gospel of Christ.

13Know ye not that they that minister about sacred things eat of the things of the temple, and they that wait upon the altar have their portion with the altar?

14Even so did the Lord ordain that they that proclaim the gospel should live of the gospel.

15But I have used none of these things: and I write not these things that it may be so done in my case; for it were good for me rather to die, than that any man should make my glorifying void.

16For if I preach the gospel, I have nothing to glory of; for necessity is laid upon me; for woe is unto me, if I preach not the gospel.

17For if I do this of mine own will, I have a reward: but if not of mine own will, I have a stewardship intrusted to me.

18What then is my reward? That, when I preach the gospel, I may make the gospel without charge, so as not to use to the full my right in the gospel.

19For though I was free from all men, I brought myself under bondage to all, that I might gain the more.

20And to the Jews I became as a Jew, that I might gain Jews; to them that are under the law, as under the law, not being myself under the law, that I might gain them that are under the law;

21to them that are without law, as without law, not being without law to God, but under law to Christ, that I might gain them that are without law.

22To the weak I became weak, that I might gain the weak: I am become all things to all men, that I may by all means save some.

23And I do all things for the gospel's sake, that I may be a joint partaker thereof.

24Know ye not that they that run in a race run all, but one receiveth the prize? Even so run; that ye may attain.

25And every man that striveth in the games exerciseth self-control in all things. Now they do it to receive a corruptible crown; but we an incorruptible.

26I therefore so run, as not uncertainly; so fight I, as not beating the air:

27but I buffet my body, and bring it into bondage: lest by any means, after that I have preached to others, I myself should be rejected.

Chapter 10

1For I would not, brethren, have you ignorant, that our fathers were all under the cloud, and all passed through the sea;

2and were all baptized unto Moses in the cloud and in the sea;

3and did all eat the same spiritual food;

4and did all drink the same spiritual drink: for they drank of a spiritual rock that followed them: and the rock was Christ.

5Howbeit with most of them God was not well pleased: for they were overthrown in the wilderness.

6Now these things were our examples, to the intent we should not lust after evil things, as they also lusted.

7Neither be ye idolaters, as were some of them; as it is written, The people sat down to eat and drink, and rose up to play.

8Neither let us commit fornication, as some of them committed, and fell in one day three and twenty thousand.

9Neither let us make trial of the Lord, as some of them made trial, and perished by the serpents.

10Neither murmur ye, as some of them murmured, and perished by the destroyer.

11Now these things happened unto them by way of example; and they were written for our admonition, upon whom the ends of the ages are come.

12Wherefore let him that thinketh he standeth take heed lest he fall.

13There hath no temptation taken you but such as man can bear: but God is faithful, who will not suffer you to be tempted above that ye are able; but will with the temptation make also the way of escape, that ye may be able to endure it.

14Wherefore, my beloved, flee from idolatry.

15I speak as to wise men; judge ye what I say.

16The cup of blessing which we bless, is it not a communion of the blood of Christ? The bread which we break, is it not a communion of the body of Christ?

17seeing that we, who are many, are one bread, one body: for we are all partake of the one bread.

18Behold Israel after the flesh: have not they that eat the sacrifices communion with the altar?

19What say I then? that a thing sacrificed to idols is anything, or that an idol is anything?

20But I say, that the things which the Gentiles sacrifice, they sacrifice to demons, and not to God: and I would not that ye should have communion with demons.

21Ye cannot drink the cup of the Lord, and the cup of demons: ye cannot partake of the table of the Lord, and of the table of demons.

22Or do we provoke the Lord to jealousy? are we stronger than he?

23All things are lawful; but not all things are expedient. All things are lawful; but not all things edify.

24Let no man seek his own, but each his neighbor's good.

25Whatsoever is sold in the shambles, eat, asking no question for conscience' sake,

26for the earth is the Lord's, and the fulness thereof.

27If one of them that believe not biddeth you to a feast, and ye are disposed to go; whatsoever is set before you, eat, asking no question for conscience' sake.

28But if any man say unto you, This hath been offered in sacrifice, eat not, for his sake that showed it, and for conscience sake:

29conscience, I say, not thine own, but the other's; for why is my liberty judged by another conscience?

30If I partake with thankfulness, why am I evil spoken of for that for which I give thanks?

31Whether therefore ye eat, or drink, or whatsoever ye do, do all to the glory of God.

32Give no occasions of stumbling, either to Jews, or to Greeks, or to the church of God:

33even as I also please all men in all things, not seeking mine own profit, but the profit of the many, that they may be saved.

Chapter 11

1Be ye imitators of me, even as I also am of Christ.

2Now I praise you that ye remember me in all things, and hold fast the traditions, even as I delivered them to you.

3But I would have you know, that the head of every man is Christ; and the head of the woman is the man; and the head of Christ is God.

4Every man praying or prophesying, having his head covered, dishonoreth his head.

5But every woman praying or prophesying with her head unveiled dishonoreth her head; for it is one and the same thing as if she were shaven.

6For if a woman is not veiled, let her also be shorn: but if it is a shame to a woman to be shorn or shaven, let her be veiled.

7For a man indeed ought not to have his head veiled, forasmuch as he is the image and glory of God: but the woman is the glory of the man.

8For the man is not of the woman; but the woman of the man:

9for neither was the man created for the woman; but the woman for the man:

10for this cause ought the woman to have a sign of authority on her head, because of the angels.

11Nevertheless, neither is the woman without the man, nor the man without the woman, in the Lord.

12For as the woman is of the man, so is the man also by the woman; but all things are of God.

13Judge ye in yourselves: is it seemly that a woman pray unto God unveiled?

First Corinthians

14Doth not even nature itself teach you, that, if a man have long hair, it is a dishonor to him?

15But if a woman have long hair, it is a glory to her: for her hair is given her for a covering.

16But if any man seemeth to be contentious, we have no such custom, neither the churches of God.

17But in giving you this charge, I praise you not, that ye come together not for the better but for the worse.

18For first of all, when ye come together in the church, I hear that divisions exist among you; and I partly believe it.

19For there must be also factions among you, that they that are approved may be made manifest among you.

20When therefore ye assemble yourselves together, it is not possible to eat the Lord's supper:

21for in your eating each one taketh before other his own supper; and one is hungry, and another is drunken.

22What, have ye not houses to eat and to drink in? or despise ye the church of God, and put them to shame that have not? What shall I say to you? shall I praise you? In this I praise you not.

23For I received of the Lord that which also I delivered unto you, that the Lord Jesus in the night in which he was betrayed took bread;

24and when he had given thanks, he brake it, and said, This is my body, which is for you: this do in remembrance of me.

25In like manner also the cup, after supper, saying, This cup is the new covenant in my blood: this do, as often as ye drink it, in remembrance of me.

26For as often as ye eat this bread, and drink the cup, ye proclaim the Lord's death till he come.

27Wherefore whosoever shall eat the bread or drink the cup of the Lord in an unworthy manner, shall be guilty of the body and the blood of the Lord.

28But let a man prove himself, and so let him eat of the bread, and drink of the cup.

29For he that eateth and drinketh, eateth and drinketh judgment unto himself, if he discern not the body.

30For this cause many among you are weak and sickly, and not a few sleep.

31But if we discerned ourselves, we should not be judged.

32But when we are judged, we are chastened of the Lord, that we may not be condemned with the world.

33Wherefore, my brethren, when ye come together to eat, wait one for another.

34If any man is hungry, let him eat at home; that your coming together be not unto judgment. And the rest will I set in order whensoever I come.

Chapter 12

1Now concerning spiritual gifts, brethren, I would not have you ignorant.

2Ye know that when ye were Gentiles ye were led away unto those dumb idols, howsoever ye might led.

3Wherefore I make known unto you, that no man speaking in the Spirit of God saith, Jesus is anathema; and no man can say, Jesus is Lord, but in the Holy Spirit.

4Now there are diversities of gifts, but the same Spirit.

5And there are diversities of ministrations, and the same Lord.

6And there are diversities of workings, but the same God, who worketh all things in all.

7But to each one is given the manifestation of the Spirit to profit withal.

8For to one is given through the Spirit the word of wisdom; and to another the word of knowledge, according to the same Spirit:

9to another faith, in the same Spirit; and to another gifts of healings, in the one Spirit;

10and to another workings of miracles; and to another prophecy; and to another discernings of spirits; to another divers kinds of tongues; and to another the interpretation of tongues:

11but all these worketh the one and the same Spirit, dividing to each one severally even as he will.

12For as the body is one, and hath many members, and all the members of the body, being many, are one body; so also is Christ.

13For in one Spirit were we all baptized into one body, whether Jews or Greeks, whether bond or free; and were all made to drink of one Spirit.

14For the body is not one member, but many.

15If the foot shall say, Because I am not the hand, I am not of the body; it is not therefore not of the body.

16And if the ear shall say, Because I am not the eye, I am not of the body; it is not therefore not of the body.

17If the whole body were an eye, where were the hearing? If the whole were hearing, where were the smelling?

18But now hath God set the members each one of them in the body, even as it pleased him.

19And if they were all one member, where were the body?

20But now they are many members, but one body.

21And the eye cannot say to the hand, I have no need of thee: or again the head to the feet, I have no need of you.

22Nay, much rather, those members of the body which seem to be more feeble are necessary:

23and those parts of the body, which we think to be less honorable, upon these we bestow more abundant honor; and our uncomely parts have more abundant comeliness;

24whereas our comely parts have no need: but God tempered the body together, giving more abundant honor to that part which lacked;

25that there should be no schism in the body; but that the members should have the same care one for another.

26And whether one member suffereth, all the members suffer with it; or one member is honored, all the members rejoice with it.

27Now ye are the body of Christ, and severally members thereof.

28And God hath set some in the church, first apostles, secondly prophets, thirdly teachers, then miracles, then gifts of healings, helps, governments, divers kinds of tongues.

29Are all apostles? are all prophets? are all teachers? are all workers of miracles?

30have all gifts of healings? do all speak with tongues? do all interpret?

31But desire earnestly the greater gifts. And moreover a most excellent way show I unto you.

Chapter 13

1If I speak with the tongues of men and of angels, but have not love, I am become sounding brass, or a clanging cymbal.

2And if I have the gift of prophecy, and know all mysteries and all knowledge; and if I have all faith, so as to remove mountains, but have not love, I am nothing.

3And if I bestow all my goods to feed the poor, and if I give my body to be burned, but have not love, it profiteth me nothing.

4Love suffereth long, and is kind; love envieth not; love vaunteth not itself, is not puffed up,

5doth not behave itself unseemly, seeketh not its own, is not provoked, taketh not account of evil;

6rejoiceth not in unrighteousness, but rejoiceth with the truth;

7beareth all things, believeth all things, hopeth all things, endureth all things.

8Love never faileth: but whether there be prophecies, they shall be done away; whether there be tongues, they shall cease; whether there be knowledge, it shall be done away.

9For we know in part, and we prophesy in part;

10but when that which is perfect is come, that which is in part shall be done away.

11When I was a child, I spake as a child, I felt as a child, I thought as a child: now that I am become a man, I have put away childish things.

12For now we see in a mirror, darkly; but then face to face: now I know in part; but then shall I know fully even as also I was fully known.

13But now abideth faith, hope, love, these three; and the greatest of these is love.

Chapter 14

1Follow after love; yet desire earnestly spiritual gifts, but rather that ye may prophesy.

2For he that speaketh in a tongue speaketh not unto men, but unto God; for no man understandeth; but in the spirit he speaketh mysteries.

3But he that prophesieth speaketh unto men edification, and exhortation, and consolation.

4He that speaketh in a tongue edifieth himself; but he that prophesieth edifieth the church.

5Now I would have you all speak with tongues, but rather that ye should prophesy: and greater is he that prophesieth than he that speaketh with tongues, except he interpret, that the church may receive edifying.

6But now, brethren, if I come unto you speaking with tongues, what shall I profit you, unless I speak to you either by way of revelation, or of knowledge, or of prophesying, or of teaching?

7Even things without life, giving a voice, whether pipe or harp, if they give not a distinction in the sounds, how shall it be known what is piped or harped?

8For if the trumpet give an uncertain voice, who shall prepare himself for war?

9So also ye, unless ye utter by the tongue speech easy to understood, how shall it be known what is spoken? for ye will be speaking into the air.

10There are, it may be, so many kinds of voices in the world, and no kind is without signification.

11If then I know not the meaning of the voice, I shall be to him that speaketh a barbarian, and he that speaketh will be a barbarian unto me.

12So also ye, since ye are zealous of spiritual gifts, seek that ye may abound unto the edifying of the church.

13Wherefore let him that speaketh in a tongue pray that he may interpret.

14For if I pray in a tongue, my spirit prayeth, but my understanding is unfruitful.

15What is it then? I will pray with the spirit, and I will pray with the understanding also: I will sing with the spirit, and I will sing with the understanding also.

16Else if thou bless with the spirit, how shall he that filleth the place of the unlearned say the Amen at thy giving of thanks, seeing he knoweth not what thou sayest?

17For thou verily givest thanks well, but the other is not edified.

18I thank God, I speak with tongues more than you all:

19howbeit in the church I had rather speak five words with my understanding, that I might instruct others also, than ten thousand words in a tongue.

20Brethren, be not children in mind: yet in malice be ye babes, but in mind be men.

21In the law it is written, By men of strange tongues and by the lips of strangers will I speak unto this people; and not even thus will they hear me, saith the Lord.

22Wherefore tongues are for a sign, not to them that believe, but to the unbelieving: but prophesying is for a sign, not to the unbelieving, but to them that believe.

23If therefore the whole church be assembled together and all speak with tongues, and there come in men unlearned or unbelieving, will they not say that ye are mad?

24But if all prophesy, and there come in one unbelieving or unlearned, he is reproved by all, he is judged by all;

25the secrets of his heart are made manifest; and so he will fall down on his face and worship God, declaring that God is among you indeed.

26What is it then, brethren? When ye come together, each one hath a psalm, hath a teaching, hath a revelation, hath a tongue, hath an interpretation. Let all things be done unto edifying.

27If any man speaketh in a tongue, let it be by two, or at the most three, and that in turn; and let one interpret:

28but if there be no interpreter, let him keep silence in the church; and let him speak to himself, and to God.

29And let the prophets speak by two or three, and let the others discern.

30But if a revelation be made to another sitting by, let the first keep silence.

31For ye all can prophesy one by one, that all may learn, and all may be exhorted;

32and the spirits of the prophets are subject to the prophets;

33for God is not a God of confusion, but of peace. As in all the churches of the saints,

34let the women keep silence in the churches: for it is not permitted unto them to speak; but let them be in subjection, as also saith the law.

35And if they would learn anything, let them ask their own husbands at home: for it is shameful for a woman to speak in the church.

36What? was it from you that the word of God went forth? or came it unto you alone?

37If any man thinketh himself to be a prophet, or spiritual, let him take knowledge of the things which I write unto you, that they are the commandment of the Lord.

38But if any man is ignorant, let him be ignorant.

39Wherefore, my brethren, desire earnestly to prophesy, and forbid not to speak with tongues.

40But let all things be done decently and in order.

Chapter 15

1Now I make known unto you brethren, the gospel which I preached unto you, which also ye received, wherein also ye stand,

2by which also ye are saved, if ye hold fast the word which I preached unto you, except ye believed in vain.

3For I delivered unto you first of all that which also I received: that Christ died for our sins according to the scriptures;

4and that he was buried; and that he hath been raised on the third day according to the scriptures;

5and that he appeared to Cephas; then to the twelve;

6then he appeared to above five hundred brethren at once, of whom the greater part remain until now, but some are fallen asleep.

7then he appeared to James; then to all the apostles;

8and last of all, as to the child untimely born, he appeared to me also.

9For I am the least of the apostles, that am not meet to be called an apostle, because I persecuted the church of God.

10But by the grace of God I am what I am: and his grace which was bestowed upon me was not found vain; but I labored more abundantly than they all: yet not I, but the grace of God which was with me.

11Whether then it be I or they, so we preach, and so ye believed.

12Now if Christ is preached that he hath been raised from the dead, how say some among you that there is no resurrection of the dead?

13But if there is no resurrection of the dead, neither hath Christ been raised:

14and if Christ hath not been raised, then is our preaching vain, your faith also is vain.

15Yea, we are found false witnesses of God; because we witnessed of God that he raised up Christ: whom he raised not up, if so be that the dead are not raised.

16For if the dead are not raised, neither hath Christ been raised:

17and if Christ hath not been raised, your faith is vain; ye are yet in your sins.

18Then they also that are fallen asleep in Christ have perished.

19If we have only hoped in Christ in this life, we are of all men most pitiable.

20But now hath Christ been raised from the dead, the firstfruits of them that are asleep.

21For since by man came death, by man came also the resurrection of the dead.

22For as in Adam all die, so also in Christ shall all be made alive.

23But each in his own order: Christ the firstfruits; then they that are Christ's, at his coming.

24Then cometh the end, when he shall deliver up the kingdom to God, even the Father; when he shall have abolished all rule and all authority and power.

25For he must reign, till he hath put all his enemies under his feet.

26The last enemy that shall be abolished is death.

27For, He put all things in subjection under his feet. But when he saith, All things are put in subjection, it is evident that he is excepted who did subject all things unto him.

28And when all things have been subjected unto him, then shall the Son also himself be subjected to him that did subject all things unto him, that God may be all in all.

29Else what shall they do that are baptized for the dead? If the dead are not raised at all, why then are they baptized for them?

30Why do we also stand in jeopardy every hour?

31I protest by that glorifying in you, brethren, which I have in Christ Jesus our Lord, I die daily.

32If after the manner of men I fought with beasts at Ephesus, what doth it profit me? If the dead are not raised, let us eat and drink, for to-morrow we die.

33Be not deceived: Evil companionships corrupt good morals.

34Awake to soberness righteously, and sin not; for some have no knowledge of God: I speak this to move you to shame.

35But some one will say, How are the dead raised? and with what manner of body do they come?

36Thou foolish one, that which thou thyself sowest is not quickened except it die:

37and that which thou sowest, thou sowest not the body that shall be, but a bare grain, it may chance of wheat, or of some other kind;

38but God giveth it a body even as it pleased him, and to each seed a body of its own.

39All flesh is not the same flesh: but there is one flesh of men, and another flesh of beasts, and another flesh of birds, and another of fishes.

40There are also celestial bodies, and bodies terrestrial: but the glory of the celestial is one, and the glory of the terrestrial is another.

41There is one glory of the sun, and another glory of the moon, and another glory of the stars; for one star differeth from another star in glory.

42So also is the resurrection of the dead. It is sown in corruption; it is raised in incorruption:

43it is sown in dishonor; it is raised in glory: it is sown in weakness; it is raised in power:

44it is sown a natural body; it is raised a spiritual body. If there is a natural body, there is also a spiritual body.

45So also it is written, The first man Adam became a living soul. The last Adam became a life-giving spirit.

46Howbeit that is not first which is spiritual, but that which is natural; then that which is spiritual.

47The first man is of the earth, earthy: the second man is of heaven.

48As is the earthy, such are they also that are earthy: and as is the heavenly, such are they also that are heavenly.

49And as we have borne the image of the earthy, we shall also bear the image of the heavenly.

50Now this I say, brethren, that flesh and blood cannot inherit the kingdom of God; neither doth corruption inherit incorruption.

51Behold, I tell you a mystery: We all shall not sleep, but we shall all be changed,

52in a moment, in the twinkling of an eye, at the last trump: for the trumpet shall sound, and the dead shall be raised incorruptible, and we shall be changed.

53For this corruptible must put on incorruption, and this mortal must put on immortality.

54But when this corruptible shall have put on incorruption, and this mortal shall have put on immortality, then shall come to pass the saying that is written, Death is swallowed up in victory.

55O death, where is thy victory? O death, where is thy sting?

56The sting of death is sin; and the power of sin is the law:

57but thanks be to God, who giveth us the victory through our Lord Jesus Christ.

58Wherefore, my beloved brethren, be ye stedfast, unmoveable, always abounding in the work of the Lord, forasmuch as ye know that your labor is not vain in the Lord.

Chapter 16

1Now concerning the collection for the saints, as I gave order to the churches of Galatia, so also do ye.

2Upon the first day of the week let each one of you lay by him in store, as he may prosper, that no collections be made when I come.

3And when I arrive, whomsoever ye shall approve, them will I send with letters to carry your bounty unto Jerusalem:

4and if it be meet for me to go also, they shall go with me.

5But I will come unto you, when I shall have passed through Macedonia; for I pass through Macedonia;

6but with you it may be that I shall abide, or even winter, that ye may set me forward on my journey whithersoever I go.

7For I do not wish to see you now by the way; for I hope to tarry a while with you, if the Lord permit.

8But I will tarry at Ephesus until Pentecost;

9for a great door and effectual is opened unto me, and there are many adversaries.

10Now if Timothy come, see that he be with you without fear; for he worketh the work of the Lord, as I also do:

11let no man therefore despise him. But set him forward on his journey in peace, that he may come unto me: for I expect him with the brethren.

12But as touching Apollos the brother, I besought him much to come unto you with the brethren: and it was not all his will to come now; but he will come when he shall have opportunity.

13Watch ye, stand fast in the faith, quit you like men, be strong.

14Let all that ye do be done in love.

15Now I beseech you, brethren (ye know the house of Stephanas, that it is the firstfruits of Achaia, and that they have set themselves to minister unto the saints),

16that ye also be in subjection unto such, and to every one that helpeth in the work and laboreth.

17And I rejoice at the coming of Stephanas and Fortunatus and Achaicus: for that which was lacking on your part they supplied.

First Corinthians

18 For they refreshed my spirit and yours: acknowledge ye therefore them that are such.

19 The churches of Asia salute you. Aquila and Prisca salute you much in the Lord, with the church that is in their house.

20 All the brethren salute you. Salute one another with a holy kiss.

21 The salutation of me Paul with mine own hand.

22 If any man loveth not the Lord, let him be anathema. Maranatha.

23 The grace of the Lord Jesus Christ be with you.

24 My love be with you all in Christ Jesus. Amen.

The Second Epistle of Paul the Apostle to the Corinthians

Chapter 1

¹Paul, an apostle of Christ Jesus through the will of God, and Timothy our brother, unto the church of God which is at Corinth, with all the saints that are in the whole of Achaia:

²Grace to you and peace from God our Father and the Lord Jesus Christ.

³Blessed be the God and Father of our Lord Jesus Christ, the Father of mercies and God of all comfort;

⁴who comforteth us in all our affliction, that we may be able to comfort them that are in any affliction, through the comfort wherewith we ourselves are comforted of God.

⁵For as the sufferings of Christ abound unto us, even so our comfort also aboundeth through Christ.

⁶But whether we are afflicted, it is for your comfort and salvation; or whether we are comforted, it is for your comfort, which worketh in the patient enduring of the same sufferings which we also suffer:

⁷and our hope for you is stedfast; knowing that, as ye are partakers of the sufferings, so also are ye of the comfort.

⁸For we would not have you ignorant, brethren, concerning our affliction which befell us in Asia, that we were weighed down exceedingly, beyond our power, insomuch that we despaired even of life:

⁹yea, we ourselves have had the sentence of death within ourselves, that we should not trust in ourselves, but in God who raiseth the dead:

¹⁰who delivered us out of so great a death, and will deliver: on whom we have set our hope that he will also still deliver us;

¹¹ye also helping together on our behalf by your supplication; that, for the gift bestowed upon us by means of many, thanks may be given by many persons on our behalf.

¹²For our glorifying is this, the testimony of our conscience, that in holiness and sincerity of God, not in fleshly wisdom but in the grace of God, we behaved ourselves in the world, and more abundantly to you-ward.

¹³For we write no other things unto you, than what ye read or even acknowledge, and I hope ye will acknowledge unto the end:

¹⁴as also ye did acknowledge us in part, that we are your glorying, even as ye also are ours, in the day of our Lord Jesus.

¹⁵And in this confidence I was minded to come first unto you, that ye might have a second benefit;

¹⁶and by you to pass into Macedonia, and again from Macedonia to come unto you, and of you to be set forward on my journey unto Judaea.

¹⁷When I therefore was thus minded, did I show fickleness? or the things that I purpose, do I purpose according to the flesh, that with me there should be the yea yea and the nay nay?

¹⁸But as God is faithful, our word toward you is not yea and nay.

¹⁹For the Son of God, Jesus Christ, who was preached among you by us, even by me and Silvanus and Timothy, was not yea and nay, but in him is yea.

²⁰For how many soever be the promises of God, in him is the yea: wherefore also through him is the Amen, unto the glory of God through us.

²¹Now he that establisheth us with you in Christ, and anointed us, is God;

²²who also sealed us, and gave us the earnest of the Spirit in our hearts.

²³But I call God for a witness upon my soul, that to spare you I forbare to come unto Corinth.

²⁴Not that we have lordship over your faith, but are helpers of your joy: for in faith ye stand fast.

Chapter 2

¹But I determined this for myself, that I would not come again to you with sorrow.

²For if I make you sorry, who then is he that maketh me glad but he that is made sorry by me?

³And I wrote this very thing, lest, when I came, I should have sorrow from them of whom I ought to rejoice; having confidence in you all, that my joy is the joy of you all.

⁴For out of much affliction and anguish of heart I wrote unto you with many tears; not that ye should be made sorry, but that ye might know the love that I have more abundantly unto you.

⁵But if any hath caused sorrow, he hath caused sorrow, not to me, but in part (that I press not too heavily) to you all.

⁶Sufficient to such a one is this punishment which was inflicted by the many;

⁷so that contrariwise ye should rather forgive him and comfort him, lest by any means such a one should be swallowed up with his overmuch sorrow.

⁸Wherefore I beseech you to confirm your love toward him.

⁹For to this end also did I write, that I might know the proof of you, whether ye are obedient in all things.

¹⁰But to whom ye forgive anything, I forgive also: for what I also have forgiven, if I have forgiven anything, for your sakes have I forgiven it in the presence of Christ;

¹¹that no advantage may be gained over us by Satan: for we are not ignorant of his devices.

¹²Now when I came to Troas for the gospel of Christ, and when a door was opened unto me in the Lord,

¹³I had no relief for my spirit, because I found not Titus my brother: but taking my leave of them, I went forth into Macedonia.

¹⁴But thanks be unto God, who always leadeth us in triumph in Christ, and maketh manifest through us the savor of his knowledge in every place.

¹⁵For we are a sweet savor of Christ unto God, in them that are saved, and in them that perish;

¹⁶to the one a savor from death unto death; to the other a savor from life unto life. And who is sufficient for these things?

¹⁷For we are not as the many, corrupting the word of God: but as of sincerity, but as of God, in the sight of God, speak we in Christ.

Chapter 3

¹Are we beginning again to commend ourselves? or need we, as do some, epistles of commendation to you or from you?

²Ye are our epistle, written in our hearts, known and read of all men;

³being made manifest that ye are an epistle of Christ, ministered by us, written not with ink, but with the Spirit of the living God; not in tables of stone, but in tables that are hearts of flesh.

⁴And such confidence have we through Christ to God-ward:

⁵not that we are sufficient of ourselves, to account anything as from ourselves; but our sufficiency is from God;

⁶who also made us sufficient as ministers of a new covenant; not of the letter, but of the spirit: for the letter killeth, but the spirit giveth life.

⁷But if the ministration of death, written, and engraven on stones, came with glory, so that the children of Israel could not look stedfastly upon the face of Moses for the glory of his face; which glory was passing away:

⁸how shall not rather the ministration of the spirit be with glory?

⁹For if the ministration of condemnation hath glory, much rather doth the ministration of righteousness exceed in glory.

¹⁰For verily that which hath been made glorious hath not been made glorious in this respect, by reason of the glory that surpasseth.

¹¹For if that which passeth away was with glory, much more that which remaineth is in glory.

¹²Having therefore such a hope, we use great boldness of speech,

¹³and are not as Moses, who put a veil upon his face, that the children of Israel should not look stedfastly on the end of that which was passing away:

¹⁴but their minds were hardened: for until this very day at the reading of the old covenant the same veil remaineth, it not being revealed to them that it is done away in Christ.

¹⁵But unto this day, whensoever Moses is read, a veil lieth upon their heart.

¹⁶But whensoever it shall turn to the Lord, the veil is taken away.

¹⁷Now the Lord is the Spirit: and where the Spirit of the Lord is, there is liberty.

¹⁸But we all, with unveiled face beholding as in a mirror the glory of the Lord, are transformed into the same image from glory to glory, even as from the Lord the Spirit.

Chapter 4

¹Therefore seeing we have this ministry, even as we obtained mercy, we faint not:

²but we have renounced the hidden things of shame, not walking in craftiness, nor handling the word of God deceitfully; but by the manifestation of the truth commending ourselves to every man's conscience in the sight of God.

³And even if our gospel is veiled, it is veiled in them that perish:

⁴in whom the god of this world hath blinded the minds of the unbelieving, that the light of the gospel of the glory of Christ, who is the image of God, should not dawn upon them.

⁵For we preach not ourselves, but Christ Jesus as Lord, and ourselves as your servants for Jesus' sake.

⁶Seeing it is God, that said, Light shall shine out of darkness, who shined in our hearts, to give the light of the knowledge of the glory of God in the face of Jesus Christ.

⁷But we have this treasure in earthen vessels, that the exceeding greatness of the power may be of God, and not from ourselves;

⁸we are pressed on every side, yet not straitened; perplexed, yet not unto despair;

⁹pursued, yet not forsaken; smitten down, yet not destroyed;

¹⁰always bearing about in the body the dying of Jesus, that the life also of Jesus may be manifested in our body.

¹¹For we who live are always delivered unto death for Jesus' sake, that the life also of Jesus may be manifested in our mortal flesh.

¹²So then death worketh in us, but life in you.

¹³But having the same spirit of faith, according to that which is written, I believed, and therefore did I speak; we also believe, and therefore also we speak;

¹⁴knowing that he that raised up the Lord Jesus shall raise up us also with Jesus, and shall present us with you.

¹⁵For all things are for your sakes, that the grace, being multiplied through the many, may cause the thanksgiving to abound unto the glory of God.

¹⁶Wherefore we faint not; but though our outward man is decaying, yet our inward man is renewed day by day.

¹⁷For our light affliction, which is for the moment, worketh for us more and more exceedingly an eternal weight of glory;

¹⁸while we look not at the things which are seen, but at the things which are not seen: for the things which are seen are temporal; but the things which are not seen are eternal.

Second Corinthians

Chapter 5

¹For we know that if the earthly house of our tabernacle be dissolved, we have a building from God, a house not made with hands, eternal, in the heavens.

²For verily in this we groan, longing to be clothed upon with our habitation which is from heaven:

³if so be that being clothed we shall not be found naked.

⁴For indeed we that are in this tabernacle do groan, being burdened; not for that we would be unclothed, but that we would be clothed upon, that what is mortal may be swallowed up of life.

⁵Now he that wrought us for this very thing is God, who gave unto us the earnest of the Spirit.

⁶Being therefore always of good courage, and knowing that, whilst we are at home in the body, we are absent from the Lord

⁷(for we walk by faith, not by sight);

⁸we are of good courage, I say, and are willing rather to be absent from the body, and to be at home with the Lord.

⁹Wherefore also we make it our aim, whether at home or absent, to be well-pleasing unto him.

¹⁰For we must all be made manifest before the judgment-seat of Christ; that each one may receive the things done in the body, according to what he hath done, whether it be good or bad.

¹¹Knowing therefore the fear of the Lord, we persuade men, but we are made manifest unto God; and I hope that we are made manifest also in your consciences.

¹²We are not again commending ourselves unto you, but speak as giving you occasion of glorying on our behalf, that ye may have wherewith to answer them that glory in appearance, and not in heart.

¹³For whether we are beside ourselves, it is unto God; or whether we are of sober mind, it is unto you.

¹⁴For the love of Christ constraineth us; because we thus judge, that one died for all, therefore all died;

¹⁵and he died for all, that they that live should no longer live unto themselves, but unto him who for their sakes died and rose again.

¹⁶Wherefore we henceforth know no man after the flesh: even though we have known Christ after the flesh, yet now we know him so no more.

¹⁷Wherefore if any man is in Christ, he is a new creature: the old things are passed away; behold, they are become new.

¹⁸But all things are of God, who reconciled us to himself through Christ, and gave unto us the ministry of reconciliation;

¹⁹to wit, that God was in Christ reconciling the world unto himself, not reckoning unto them their trespasses, and having committed unto us the word of reconciliation.

²⁰We are ambassadors therefore on behalf of Christ, as though God were entreating by us: we beseech you on behalf of Christ, be ye reconciled to God.

²¹Him who knew no sin he made to be sin on our behalf; that we might become the righteousness of God in him.

Chapter 6

¹And working together with him we entreat also that ye receive not the grace of God in vain

²(for he saith,
At an acceptable time I hearkened unto thee,
And in a day of salvation did I succor thee:
behold, now is the acceptable time; behold, now is the day of salvation):

³giving no occasion of stumbling in anything, that our ministration be not blamed;

⁴but in everything commending ourselves, as ministers of God, in much patience, in afflictions, in necessities, in distresses,

⁵in stripes, in imprisonments, in tumults, in labors, in watchings, in fastings;

⁶in pureness, in knowledge, in long suffering, in kindness, in the Holy Spirit, in love unfeigned,

⁷in the word of truth, in the power of God; by the armor of righteousness on the right hand and on the left,

⁸by glory and dishonor, by evil report and good report; as deceivers, and yet true;

⁹as unknown, and yet well known; as dying, and behold, we live; as chastened, and not killed;

¹⁰as sorrowful, yet always rejoicing; as poor, yet making many rich; as having nothing, and yet possessing all things.

¹¹Our mouth is open unto you, O Corinthians, our heart is enlarged.

¹²Ye are not straitened in us, but ye are straitened in your own affections.

¹³Now for a recompense in like kind (I speak as unto my children), be ye also enlarged.

¹⁴Be not unequally yoked with unbelievers: for what fellowship have righteousness and iniquity? or what communion hath light with darkness?

¹⁵And what concord hath Christ with Belial? or what portion hath a believer with an unbeliever?

¹⁶And what agreement hath a temple of God with idols? for we are a temple of the living God; even as God said, I will dwell in them, and walk in them; and I will be their God, and they shall be my people.

¹⁷Wherefore
Come ye out from among them, and be ye separate,
saith the Lord,
And touch no unclean thing;
And I will receive you,

¹⁸And will be to you a Father,
And ye shall be to me sons and daughters,
saith the Lord Almighty.

Chapter 7

¹Having therefore these promises, beloved, let us cleanse ourselves from all defilement of flesh and spirit, perfecting holiness in the fear of God.

²Open your hearts to us: we wronged no man, we corrupted no man, we took advantage of no man.

³I say it not to condemn you: for I have said before, that ye are in our hearts to die together and live together.

⁴Great is my boldness of speech toward you, great is my glorying on your behalf: I am filled with comfort, I overflow with joy in all our affliction.

⁵For even when we were come into Macedonia our flesh had no relief, but we were afflicted on every side; without were fightings, within were fears.

⁶Nevertheless he that comforteth the lowly, even God, comforted us by the coming of Titus;

⁷and not by his coming only, but also by the comfort wherewith he was comforted in you, while he told us your longing, your mourning, your zeal for me; so that I rejoiced yet more.

⁸For though I made you sorry with my epistle, I do not regret it: though I did regret it (for I see that that epistle made you sorry, though but for a season),

⁹I now rejoice, not that ye were made sorry, but that ye were made sorry unto repentance; for ye were made sorry after a godly sort, that ye might suffer loss by us in nothing.

¹⁰For godly sorrow worketh repentance unto salvation, a repentance which bringeth no regret: but the sorrow of the world worketh death.

¹¹For behold, this selfsame thing, that ye were made sorry after a godly sort, what earnest care it wrought in you, yea what clearing of yourselves, yea what indignation, yea what fear, yea what longing, yea what zeal, yea what avenging! In everything ye approved yourselves to be pure in the matter.

¹²So although I wrote unto you, I wrote not for his cause that did the wrong, nor for his cause that suffered the wrong, but that your earnest care for us might be made manifest unto you in the sight of God.

¹³Therefore we have been comforted: And in our comfort we joyed the more exceedingly for the joy of Titus, because his spirit hath been refreshed by you all.

¹⁴For if in anything I have gloried to him on your behalf, I was not put to shame; but as we spake all things to you in truth, so our glorying also which I made before Titus was found to be truth.

¹⁵And his affection is more abundantly toward you, while he remembereth the obedience of you all, how with fear and trembling ye received him.

¹⁶I rejoice that in everything I am of good courage concerning you.

Chapter 8

¹Moreover, brethren, we make known to you the grace of God which hath been given in the churches of Macedonia;

²how that in much proof of affliction the abundance of their joy and their deep poverty abounded unto the riches of their liberality.

³For according to their power, I bear witness, yea and beyond their power, they gave of their own accord,

⁴beseeching us with much entreaty in regard of this grace and the fellowship in the ministering to the saints:

⁵and this, not as we had hoped, but first they gave their own selves to the Lord, and to us through the will of God.

⁶Insomuch that we exhorted Titus, that as he made a beginning before, so he would also complete in you this grace also.

⁷But as ye abound in everything, in faith, and utterance, and knowledge, and in all earnestness, and in your love to us, see that ye abound in this grace also.

⁸I speak not by way of commandment, but as proving through the earnestness of others the sincerity also of your love.

⁹For ye know the grace of our Lord Jesus Christ, that, though he was rich, yet for your sakes he became poor, that ye through his poverty might become rich.

¹⁰And herein I give my judgment: for this is expedient for you, who were the first to make a beginning a year ago, not only to do, but also to will.

¹¹But now complete the doing also; that as there was the readiness to will, so there may be the completion also out of your ability.

¹²For if the readiness is there, it is acceptable according as a man hath, not according as he hath not.

¹³For I say not this that others may be eased and ye distressed;

¹⁴but by equality: your abundance being a supply at this present time for their want, that their abundance also may become a supply for your want; that there may be equality:

¹⁵as it is written, He that gathered much had nothing over; and he that gathered little had no lack.

¹⁶But thanks be to God, who putteth the same earnest care for you into the heart of Titus.

¹⁷For he accepted indeed our exhortation; but being himself very earnest, he went forth unto you of his own accord.

¹⁸And we have sent together with him the brother whose praise in the gospel is spread through all the churches;

¹⁹and not only so, but who was also appointed by the churches to travel with us in the matter of this grace, which is ministered by us to the glory of the Lord, and to show our readiness:

²⁰Avoiding this, that any man should blame us in the matter of this bounty which is ministered by us:

²¹for we take thought for things honorable, not only in the sight of the Lord, but also in the sight of men.

²²and we have sent with them our brother, whom we have many times proved earnest in many things, but now much more earnest, by reason of the great confidence which he hath in you.

23Whether any inquire about Titus, he is my partner and my fellow-worker to you-ward, or our brethren, they are the messengers of the churches, they are the glory of Christ.

24Show ye therefore unto them in the face of the churches the proof of your love, and of our glorying on your behalf.

Chapter 9

1For as touching the ministering to the saints, it is superfluous for me to write to you:

2for I know your readiness, of which I glory on your behalf to them of Macedonia, that Achaia hath been prepared for a year past; and your zeal hath stirred up very many of them.

3But I have sent the brethren, that our glorying on your behalf may not be made void in this respect; that, even as I said, ye may be prepared:

4lest by any means, if there come with me any of Macedonia and find you unprepared, we (that we say not, ye) should be put to shame in this confidence.

5I thought it necessary therefore to entreat the brethren, that they would go before unto you, and make up beforehand your aforepromised bounty, that the same might be ready as a matter of bounty, and not of extortion.

6But this I say, He that soweth sparingly shall reap also sparingly; and he that soweth bountifully shall reap also bountifully.

7Let each man do according as he hath purposed in his heart: not grudgingly, or of necessity: for God loveth a cheerful giver.

8And God is able to make all grace abound unto you; that ye, having always all sufficiency in everything, may abound unto every good work:

9as it is written,

He hath scattered abroad, he hath given to the poor;

His righteousness abideth for ever.

10And he that supplieth seed to the sower and bread for food, shall supply and multiply your seed for sowing, and increase the fruits of your righteousness:

11ye being enriched in everything unto all liberality, which worketh through us thanksgiving to God.

12For the ministration of this service not only filleth up the measure of the wants of the saints, but aboundeth also through many thanksgivings unto God;

13seeing that through the proving of you by this ministration they glorify God for the obedience of your confession unto the gospel of Christ, and for the liberality of your contribution unto them and unto all;

14while they themselves also, with supplication on your behalf, long after you by reason of the exceeding grace of God in you.

15Thanks be to God for his unspeakable gift.

Chapter 10

1Now I Paul myself entreat you by the meekness and gentleness of Christ, I who in your presence am lowly among you, but being absent am of good courage toward you:

2yea, I beseech you, that I may not when present show courage with the confidence wherewith I count to be bold against some, who count of us as if we walked according to the flesh.

3For though we walk in the flesh, we do not war according to the flesh

4(for the weapons of our warfare are not of the flesh, but mighty before God to the casting down of strongholds),

5casting down imaginations, and every high thing that is exalted against the knowledge of God, and bringing every thought into captivity to the obedience of Christ;

6and being in readiness to avenge all disobedience, when your obedience shall be made full.

7Ye look at the things that are before your face. If any man trusteth in himself that he is Christ's, let him consider this again with himself, that, even as he is Christ's, so also are we.

8For though I should glory somewhat abundantly concerning our authority (which the Lord gave for building you up, and not for casting you down), I shall not be put to shame:

9that I may not seem as if I would terrify you by my letters.

10For, His letters, they say, are weighty and strong; but his bodily presence is weak, and his speech of no account.

11Let such a one reckon this, that, what we are in word by letters when we are absent, such are we also in deed when we are present.

12For we are not bold to number or compare ourselves with certain of them that commend themselves: but they themselves, measuring themselves by themselves, and comparing themselves with themselves, are without understanding.

13But we will not glory beyond our measure, but according to the measure of the province which God apportioned to us as a measure, to reach even unto you.

14For we stretch not ourselves overmuch, as though we reached not unto you: for we came even as far as unto you in the gospel of Christ:

15not glorying beyond our measure, that is, in other men's labors; but having hope that, as your faith groweth, we shall be magnified in you according to our province unto further abundance,

16so as to preach the gospel even unto the parts beyond you, and not to glory in another's province in regard of things ready to our hand.

17But he that glorieth, let him glory in the Lord.

18For not he that commendeth himself is approved, but whom the Lord commendeth.

Chapter 11

1Would that ye could bear with me in a little foolishness: but indeed ye do bear with me.

2For I am jealous over you with a godly jealousy: for I espoused you to one husband, that I might present you as a pure virgin to Christ.

3But I fear, lest by any means, as the serpent beguiled Eve in his craftiness, your minds should be corrupted from the simplicity and the purity that is toward Christ.

4For if he that cometh preacheth another Jesus, whom we did not preach, or if ye receive a different spirit, which ye did not receive, or a different gospel, which ye did not accept, ye do well to bear with him.

5For I reckon that I am not a whit behind the very chiefest apostles.

6But though I be rude in speech, yet am I not in knowledge; nay, in every way have we made this manifest unto you in all things.

7Or did I commit a sin in abasing myself that ye might be exalted, because I preached to you the gospel of God for nought?

8I robbed other churches, taking wages of them that I might minister unto you;

9and when I was present with you and was in want, I was not a burden on any man; for the brethren, when they came from Macedonia, supplied the measure of my want; and in everything I kept myself from being burdensome unto you, and so will I keep myself.

10As the truth of Christ is in me, no man shall stop me of this glorying in the regions of Achaia.

11Wherefore? because I love you not? God knoweth.

12But what I do, that I will do, that I may cut off occasion from them that desire an occasion; that wherein they glory, they may be found even as we.

13For such men are false apostles, deceitful workers, fashioning themselves into apostles of Christ.

14And no marvel; for even Satan fashioneth himself into an angel of light.

15It is no great thing therefore if his ministers also fashion themselves as ministers of righteousness, whose end shall be according to their works.

16I say again, let no man think me foolish; but if ye do, yet as foolish receive me, that I also may glory a little.

17That which I speak, I speak not after the Lord, but as in foolishness, in this confidence of glorying.

18Seeing that many glory after the flesh, I will glory also.

19For ye bear with the foolish gladly, being wise yourselves.

20For ye bear with a man, if he bringeth you into bondage, if he devoureth you, if he taketh you captive, if he exalteth himself, if he smiteth you on the face.

21I speak by way of disparagement, as though we had been weak. Yet whereinsoever any is bold (I speak in foolishness), I am bold also.

22Are they Hebrews? so am I. Are they Israelites? so am I. Are they the seed of Abraham? so am I.

23Are they ministers of Christ? (I speak as one beside himself) I more; in labors more abundantly, in prisons more abundantly, in stripes above measure, in deaths oft.

24Of the Jews five times received I forty stripes save one.

25Thrice was I beaten with rods, once was I stoned, thrice I suffered shipwreck, a night and a day have I been in the deep;

26in journeyings often, in perils of rivers, in perils of robbers, in perils from my countrymen, in perils from the Gentiles, in perils in the city, in perils in the wilderness, in perils in the sea, in perils among false brethren;

27in labor and travail, in watchings often, in hunger and thirst, in fastings often, in cold and nakedness.

28Besides those things that are without, there is that which presseth upon me daily, anxiety for all the churches.

29Who is weak, and I am not weak? who is caused to stumble, and I burn not?

30If I must needs glory, I will glory of the things that concern my weakness.

31The God and Father of the Lord Jesus, he who is blessed for evermore knoweth that I lie not.

32In Damascus the governor under Aretas the king guarded the city of the Damascenes in order to take me:

33and through a window was I let down in a basket by the wall, and escaped his hands.

Chapter 12

1I must needs glory, though it is not expedient; but I will come to visions and revelations of the Lord.

2I know a man in Christ, fourteen years ago (whether in the body, I know not; or whether out of the body, I know not; God knoweth), such a one caught up even to the third heaven.

3And I know such a man (whether in the body, or apart from the body, I know not; God knoweth),

4how that he was caught up into Paradise, and heard unspeakable words, which it is not lawful for a man to utter.

5On behalf of such a one will I glory: but on mine own behalf I will not glory, save in my weaknesses.

6For if I should desire to glory, I shall not be foolish; for I shall speak the truth: but I forbear, lest any man should account of me above that which he seeth me to be, or heareth from me.

7And by reason of the exceeding greatness of the revelations, that I should not be exalted overmuch, there was given to me a thorn in the flesh, a messenger of Satan to buffet me, that I should not be exalted overmuch.

8Concerning this thing I besought the Lord thrice, that it might depart from me.

9And he hath said unto me, My grace is sufficient for thee: for my power is made perfect in weakness. Most gladly therefore will I rather glory in my weaknesses, that the power of Christ may rest upon me.

10Wherefore I take pleasure in weaknesses, in injuries, in necessities, in persecutions, in distresses, for Christ's sake: for when I am weak, then am I strong.

11I am become foolish: ye compelled me; for I ought to have been

Second Corinthians

commended of you: for in nothing was I behind the very chiefest apostles, though I am nothing.

12Truly the signs of an apostle were wrought among you in all patience, by signs and wonders and mighty works.

13For what is there wherein ye were made inferior to the rest of the churches, except it be that I myself was not a burden to you? forgive me this wrong.

14Behold, this is the third time I am ready to come to you; and I will not be a burden to you: for I seek not yours, but you: for the children ought not to lay up for the parents, but the parents for the children.

15And I will most gladly spend and be spent for your souls. If I love you more abundantly, am I loved the less?

16But be it so, I did not myself burden you; but, being crafty, I caught you with guile.

17Did I take advantage of you by any one of them whom I have sent unto you?

18I exhorted Titus, and I sent the brother with him. Did Titus take any advantage of you? walked we not in the same spirit? walked we not in the same steps?

19Ye think all this time that we are excusing ourselves unto you. In the sight of God speak we in Christ. But all things, beloved, are for your edifying.

20For I fear, lest by any means, when I come, I should find you not such as I would, and should myself be found of you such as ye would not; lest by any means there should be strife, jealousy, wraths, factions, backbitings, whisperings, swellings, tumults;

21lest again when I come my God should humble me before you, and I should mourn for many of them that have sinned heretofore, and repented not of the uncleanness and fornication and lasciviousness which they committed.

Chapter 13

1This is the third time I am coming to you. At the mouth of two witnesses or three shall every word established.

2I have said beforehand, and I do say beforehand, as when I was present the second time, so now, being absent, to them that have sinned heretofore, and to all the rest, that, if I come again, I will not spare;

3seeing that ye seek a proof of Christ that speaketh in me; who to you-ward is not weak, but is powerful in you:

4for he was crucified through weakness, yet he liveth through the power of God. For we also are weak in him, but we shall live with him through the power of God toward you.

5Try your own selves, whether ye are in the faith; prove your own selves. Or know ye not as to your own selves, that Jesus Christ is in you? unless indeed ye be reprobate.

6But I hope that ye shall know that we are not reprobate.

7Now we pray to God that ye do no evil; not that we may appear approved, but that ye may do that which is honorable, though we be as reprobate.

8For we can do nothing against the truth, but for the truth.

9For we rejoice, when we are weak, and ye are strong: this we also pray for, even your perfecting.

10For this cause I write these things while absent, that I may not when present deal sharply, according to the authority which the Lord gave me for building up, and not for casting down.

11Finally, brethren, farewell. Be perfected; be comforted; be of the same mind; live in peace: and the God of love and peace shall be with you.

12Salute one another with a holy kiss.

13All the saints salute you.

14The grace of the Lord Jesus Christ, and the love of God, and the communion of the Holy Spirit, be with you all.

The Epistle of Paul the Apostle to the Galatians

Chapter 1

1Paul, an apostle (not from men, neither through man, but through Jesus Christ, and God the Father, who raised him from the dead),

2and all the brethren that are with me, unto the churches of Galatia:

3Grace to you and peace from God the Father, and our Lord Jesus Christ,

4who gave himself for our sins, that he might deliver us out of this present evil world, according to the will of our God and Father:

5to whom be the glory for ever and ever. Amen.

6I marvel that ye are so quickly removing from him that called you in the grace of Christ unto a different gospel;

7which is not another gospel only there are some that trouble you, and would pervert the gospel of Christ.

8But though we, or an angel from heaven, should preach unto you any gospel other than that which we preached unto you, let him be anathema.

9As we have said before, so say I now again, if any man preacheth unto you any gospel other than that which ye received, let him be anathema.

10For am I now seeking the favor of men, or of God? or am I striving to please men? if I were still pleasing men, I should not be a servant of Christ.

11For I make known to you, brethren, as touching the gospel which was preached by me, that it is not after man.

12For neither did I receive it from man, nor was I taught it, but it came to me through revelation of Jesus Christ.

13For ye have heard of my manner of life in time past in the Jews' religion, how that beyond measure I persecuted the church of God, and made havoc of it:

14and I advanced in the Jews' religion beyond many of mine own age among my countrymen, being more exceedingly zealous for the traditions of my fathers.

15But when it was the good pleasure of God, who separated me, even from my mother's womb, and called me through his grace,

16to reveal his Son in me, that I might preach him among the Gentiles; straightway I conferred not with flesh and blood:

17neither went I up to Jerusalem to them that were apostles before me: but I went away into Arabia; and again I returned unto Damascus.

18Then after three years I went up to Jerusalem to visit Cephas, and tarried with him fifteen days.

19But other of the apostles saw I none, save James the Lord's brother.

20Now touching the things which I write unto you, behold, before God, I lie not.

21Then I came unto the regions of Syria and Cilicia.

22And I was still unknown by face unto the churches of Judaea which were in Christ:

23but they only heard say, He that once persecuted us now preacheth the faith of which he once made havoc;

24and they glorified God in me.

Chapter 2

1Then after the space of fourteen years I went up again to Jerusalem with Barnabas, taking Titus also with me.

2And I went up by revelation; and I laid before them the gospel which I preach among the Gentiles but privately before them who were of repute, lest by any means I should be running, or had run, in vain.

3But not even Titus who was with me, being a Greek, was compelled to be circumcised:

4and that because of the false brethren privily brought in, who came in privily to spy out our liberty which we have in Christ Jesus, that they might bring us into bondage:

5to whom we gave place in the way of subjection, no, not for an hour; that the truth of the gospel might continue with you.

6But from those who were reputed to be somewhat (whatsoever they were, it maketh no matter to me: God accepteth not man's person)-- they, I say, who were of repute imparted nothing to me:

7but contrariwise, when they saw that I had been intrusted with the gospel of the uncircumcision, even as Peter with the gospel of the circumcision

8(for he that wrought for Peter unto the apostleship of the circumcision wrought for me also unto the Gentiles);

9and when they perceived the grace that was given unto me, James and Cephas and John, they who were reputed to be pillars, gave to me and Barnabas the right hands of fellowship, that we should go unto the Gentiles, and they unto the circumcision;

10only they would that we should remember the poor; which very thing I was also zealous to do.

11But when Cephas came to Antioch, I resisted him to the face, because he stood condemned.

12For before that certain came from James, he ate with the Gentiles; but when they came, he drew back and separated himself, fearing them that were of the circumcision.

13And the rest of the Jews dissembled likewise with him; insomuch that even Barnabas was carried away with their dissimulation.

14But when I saw that they walked not uprightly according to the truth of the gospel, I said unto Cephas before them all, If thou, being a Jew, livest as do the Gentiles, and not as do the Jews, how compellest thou the Gentiles to live as do the Jews?

15We being Jews by nature, and not sinners of the Gentiles,

16yet knowing that a man is not justified by the works of the law but through faith in Jesus Christ, even we believed on Christ Jesus, that we might be justified by faith in Christ, and not by the works of the law: because by the works of the law shall no flesh be justified.

17But if, while we sought to be justified in Christ, we ourselves also were found sinners, is Christ a minister of sin? God forbid.

18For if I build up again those things which I destroyed, I prove myself a transgressor.

19For I through the law died unto the law, that I might live unto God.

20I have been crucified with Christ; and it is no longer I that live, but Christ living in me: and that life which I now live in the flesh I live in faith, the faith which is in the Son of God, who loved me, and gave himself up for me.

21I do not make void the grace of God: for if righteousness is through the law, then Christ died for nought.

Chapter 3

1O foolish Galatians, who did bewitch you, before whose eyes Jesus Christ was openly set forth crucified?

2This only would I learn from you. Received ye the Spirit by the works of the law, or by the hearing of faith?

3Are ye so foolish? having begun in the Spirit, are ye now perfected in the flesh?

4Did ye suffer so many things in vain? if it be indeed in vain.

5He therefore that supplieth to you the Spirit, and worketh miracles among you, doeth he it by the works of the law, or by the hearing of faith?

6Even as Abraham believed God, and it was reckoned unto him for righteousness.

7Know therefore that they that are of faith, the same are sons of Abraham.

8And the scripture, foreseeing that God would justify the Gentiles by faith, preached the gospel beforehand unto Abraham, saying, In thee shall all the nations be blessed.

9So then they that are of faith are blessed with the faithful Abraham.

10For as many as are of the works of the law are under a curse: for it is written, Cursed is every one who continueth not in all things that are written in the book of the law, to do them.

11Now that no man is justified by the law before God, is evident: for, The righteous shall live by faith;

12and the law is not of faith; but, He that doeth them shall live in them.

13Christ redeemed us from the curse of the law, having become a curse for us; for it is written, Cursed is every one that hangeth on a tree:

14that upon the Gentiles might come the blessing of Abraham in Christ Jesus; that we might receive the promise of the Spirit through faith.

15Brethren, I speak after the manner of men: Though it be but a man's covenant, yet when it hath been confirmed, no one maketh it void, or addeth thereto.

16Now to Abraham were the promises spoken, and to his seed. He saith not, And to seeds, as of many; but as of one, And to thy seed, which is Christ.

17Now this I say: A covenant confirmed beforehand by God, the law, which came four hundred and thirty years after, doth not disannul, so as to make the promise of none effect.

18For if the inheritance is of the law, it is no more of promise: but God hath granted it to Abraham by promise.

19What then is the law? It was added because of transgressions, till the seed should come to whom the promise hath been made; and it was ordained through angels by the hand of a mediator.

20Now a mediator is not a mediator of one; but God is one.

21Is the law then against the promises of God? God forbid: for if there had been a law given which could make alive, verily righteousness would have been of the law.

22But the scriptures shut up all things under sin, that the promise by faith in Jesus Christ might be given to them that believe.

23But before faith came, we were kept in ward under the law, shut up unto the faith which should afterwards be revealed.

24So that the law is become our tutor to bring us unto Christ, that we might be justified by faith.

25But now faith that is come, we are no longer under a tutor.

26For ye are all sons of God, through faith, in Christ Jesus.

27For as many of you as were baptized into Christ did put on Christ.

28There can be neither Jew nor Greek, there can be neither bond nor free, there can be no male and female; for ye all are one man in Christ Jesus.

29And if ye are Christ's, then are ye Abraham's seed, heirs according to promise.

Chapter 4

1But I say that so long as the heir is a child, he differeth nothing from a bondservant though he is lord of all;

2but is under guardians and stewards until the day appointed of the father.

3So we also, when we were children, were held in bondage under the rudiments of the world:

4but when the fulness of the time came, God sent forth his Son, born of a woman, born under the law,

5that he might redeem them that were under the law, that we might receive the adoption of sons.

6And because ye are sons, God sent forth the Spirit of his Son into our hearts, crying, Abba, Father.

7So that thou art no longer a bondservant, but a son; and if a son, then an heir through God.

Galatians

8Howbeit at that time, not knowing God, ye were in bondage to them that by nature are no gods:

9but now that ye have come to know God, or rather to be known by God, how turn ye back again to the weak and beggarly rudiments, whereunto ye desire to be in bondage over again?

10Ye observe days, and months, and seasons, and years.

11I am afraid of you, lest by any means I have bestowed labor upon you in vain.

12I beseech you, brethren, become as I am, for I also am become as ye are. Ye did me no wrong;

13but ye know that because of an infirmity of the flesh I preached the gospel unto you the first time:

14and that which was a temptation to you in my flesh ye despised not, nor rejected; but ye received me as an angel of God, even as Christ Jesus.

15Where then is that gratulation of yourselves? for I bear you witness, that, if possible, ye would have plucked out your eyes and given them to me.

16So then am I become your enemy, by telling you the truth?

17They zealously seek you in no good way; nay, they desire to shut you out, that ye may seek them.

18But it is good to be zealously sought in a good matter at all times, and not only when I am present with you.

19My little children, of whom I am again in travail until Christ be formed in you--

20but I could wish to be present with you now, and to change my tone; for I am perplexed about you.

21Tell me, ye that desire to be under the law, do ye not hear the law?

22For it is written, that Abraham had two sons, one by the handmaid, and one by the freewoman.

23Howbeit the son by the handmaid is born after the flesh; but the son by the freewoman is born through promise.

24Which things contain an allegory: for these women are two covenants; one from mount Sinai, bearing children unto bondage, which is Hagar.

25Now this Hagar is mount Sinai in Arabia and answereth to the Jerusalem that now is: for she is in bondage with her children.

26But the Jerusalem that is above is free, which is our mother.

27For it is written,
Rejoice, thou barren that bearest not;
Break forth and cry, thou that travailest not:
For more are the children of the desolate than of her that hath the husband.

28Now we, brethren, as Isaac was, are children of promise.

29But as then he that was born after the flesh persecuted him that was born after the Spirit, so also it is now.

30Howbeit what saith the scripture? Cast out the handmaid and her son: for the son of the handmaid shall not inherit with the son of the freewoman.

31Wherefore, brethren, we are not children of a handmaid, but of the freewoman.

Chapter 5

1For freedom did Christ set us free: stand fast therefore, and be not entangled again in a yoke of bondage.

2Behold, I Paul say unto you, that, if ye receive circumcision, Christ will profit you nothing.

3Yea, I testify again to every man that receiveth circumcision, that he is a debtor to do the whole law.

4Ye are severed from Christ, ye would be justified by the law; ye are fallen away from grace.

5For we through the Spirit by faith wait for the hope of righteousness.

6For in Christ Jesus neither circumcision availeth anything, nor uncircumcision; but faith working through love.

7Ye were running well; who hindered you that ye should not obey the truth?

8This persuasion came not of him that calleth you.

9A little leaven leaveneth the whole lump.

10I have confidence to you-ward in the Lord, that ye will be none otherwise minded: but he that troubleth you shall bear his judgment, whosoever he be.

11But I, brethren, if I still preach circumcision, why am I still persecuted? then hath the stumbling-block of the cross been done away.

12I would that they that unsettle you would even go beyond circumcision.

13For ye, brethren, were called for freedom; only use not your freedom for an occasion to the flesh, but through love be servants one to another.

14For the whole law is fulfilled in one word, even in this: Thou shalt love thy neighbor as thyself.

15But if ye bite and devour one another, take heed that ye be not consumed one of another.

16But I say, walk by the Spirit, and ye shall not fulfil the lust of the flesh.

17For the flesh lusteth against the Spirit, and the Spirit against the flesh; for these are contrary the one to the other; that ye may not do the things that ye would.

18But if ye are led by the Spirit, ye are not under the law.

19Now the works of the flesh are manifest, which are these: fornication, uncleanness, lasciviousness,

20idolatry, sorcery, enmities, strife, jealousies, wraths, factions, divisions, parties,

21envyings, drunkenness, revellings, and such like; of which I forewarn you, even as I did forewarn you, that they who practise such things shall not inherit the kingdom of God.

22But the fruit of the Spirit is love, joy, peace, longsuffering, kindness, goodness, faithfulness,

23meekness, self-control; against such there is no law.

24And they that are of Christ Jesus have crucified the flesh with the passions and the lusts thereof.

25If we live by the Spirit, by the Spirit let us also walk.

26Let us not become vainglorious, provoking one another, envying one another.

Chapter 6

1Brethren, even if a man be overtaken in any trespass, ye who are spiritual, restore such a one in a spirit of gentleness; looking to thyself, lest thou also be tempted.

2Bear ye one another's burdens, and so fulfil the law of Christ.

3For if a man thinketh himself to be something when he is nothing, he deceiveth himself.

4But let each man prove his own work, and then shall he have his glorying in regard of himself alone, and not of his neighbor.

5For each man shall bear his own burden.

6But let him that is taught in the word communicate unto him that teacheth in all good things.

7Be not deceived; God is not mocked: for whatsoever a man soweth, that shall he also reap.

8For he that soweth unto his own flesh shall of the flesh reap corruption; but he that soweth unto the Spirit shall of the Spirit reap eternal life.

9And let us not be weary in well-doing: for in due season we shall reap, if we faint not.

10So then, as we have opportunity, let us work that which is good toward all men, and especially toward them that are of the household of the faith.

11See with how large letters I write unto you with mine own hand.

12As many as desire to make a fair show in the flesh, they compel you to be circumcised; only that they may not be persecuted for the cross of Christ.

13For not even they who receive circumcision do themselves keep the law; but they desire to have you circumcised, that they may glory in your flesh.

14But far be it from me to glory, save in the cross of our Lord Jesus Christ, through which the world hath been crucified unto me, and I unto the world.

15For neither is circumcision anything, nor uncircumcision, but a new creature.

16And as many as shall walk by this rule, peace be upon them, and mercy, and upon the Israel of God.

17Henceforth, let no man trouble me; for I bear branded on my body the marks of Jesus.

18The grace of our Lord Jesus Christ be with your spirit, brethren. Amen.

The Epistle of Paul the Apostle to the Ephesians

Chapter 1

1Paul, an apostle of Christ Jesus through the will of God, to the saints that are at Ephesus, and the faithful in Christ Jesus:

2Grace to you and peace from God our Father and the Lord Jesus Christ.

3Blessed be the God and Father of our Lord Jesus Christ, who hath blessed us with every spiritual blessing in the heavenly places in Christ:

4even as he chose us in him before the foundation of the world, that we should be holy and without blemish before him in love:

5having foreordained us unto adoption as sons through Jesus Christ unto himself, according to the good pleasure of his will,

6to the praise of the glory of his grace, which he freely bestowed on us in the Beloved:

7in whom we have our redemption through his blood, the forgiveness of our trespasses, according to the riches of his grace,

8which he made to abound toward us in all wisdom and prudence,

9making known unto us the mystery of his will, according to his good pleasure which he purposed in him

10unto a dispensation of the fulness of the times, to sum up all things in Christ, the things in the heavens, and the things upon the earth; in him, I say,

11in whom also we were made a heritage, having been foreordained according to the purpose of him who worketh all things after the counsel of his will;

12to the end that we should be unto the praise of his glory, we who had before hoped in Christ:

13in whom ye also, having heard the word of the truth, the gospel of your salvation,-- in whom, having also believed, ye were sealed with the Holy Spirit of promise,

14which is an earnest of our inheritance, unto the redemption of God's own possession, unto the praise of his glory.

15For this cause I also, having heard of the faith in the Lord Jesus which is among you, and the love which ye show toward all the saints,

16cease not to give thanks for you, making mention of you in my prayers;

17that the God of our Lord Jesus Christ, the Father of glory, may give unto you a spirit of wisdom and revelation in the knowledge of him;

18having the eyes of your heart enlightened, that ye may know what is the hope of his calling, what the riches of the glory of his inheritance in the saints,

19and what the exceeding greatness of his power to us-ward who believe, according to that working of the strength of his might

20which he wrought in Christ, when he raised him from the dead, and made him to sit at his right hand in the heavenly places,

21far above all rule, and authority, and power, and dominion, and every name that is named, not only in this world, but also in that which is to come:

22and he put all things in subjection under his feet, and gave him to be head over all things to the church,

23which is his body, the fulness of him that filleth all in all.

Chapter 2

1And you did he make alive, when ye were dead through your trespasses and sins,

2wherein ye once walked according to the course of this world, according to the prince of the powers of the air, of the spirit that now worketh in the sons of disobedience;

3among whom we also all once lived in the lust of our flesh, doing the desires of the flesh and of the mind, and were by nature children of wrath, even as the rest:--

4but God, being rich in mercy, for his great love wherewith he loved us,

5even when we were dead through our trespasses, made us alive together with Christ (by grace have ye been saved),

6and raised us up with him, and made us to sit with him in the heavenly places, in Christ Jesus:

7that in the ages to come he might show the exceeding riches of his grace in kindness toward us in Christ Jesus:

8for by grace have ye been saved through faith; and that not of yourselves, it is the gift of God;

9not of works, that no man should glory.

10For we are his workmanship, created in Christ Jesus for good works, which God afore prepared that we should walk in them.

11Wherefore remember, that once ye, the Gentiles in the flesh, who are called Uncircumcision by that which is called Circumcision, in the flesh, made by hands;

12that ye were at that time separate from Christ, alienated from the commonwealth of Israel, and strangers from the covenants of the promise, having no hope and without God in the world.

13But now in Christ Jesus ye that once were far off are made nigh in the blood of Christ.

14For he is our peace, who made both one, and brake down the middle wall of partition,

15having abolished in the flesh the enmity, even the law of commandments contained in ordinances; that he might create in himself of the two one new man, so making peace;

16and might reconcile them both in one body unto God through the cross, having slain the enmity thereby:

17and he came and preached peace to you that were far off, and peace to them that were nigh:

18for through him we both have our access in one Spirit unto the Father.

19So then ye are no more strangers and sojourners, but ye are fellow-citizens with the saints, and of the household of God,

20being built upon the foundation of the apostles and prophets, Christ Jesus himself being the chief corner stone;

21in whom each several building, fitly framed together, groweth into a holy temple in the Lord;

22in whom ye also are builded together for a habitation of God in the Spirit.

Chapter 3

1For this cause I Paul, the prisoner of Christ Jesus in behalf of you Gentiles,--

2if so be that ye have heard of the dispensation of that grace of God which was given me to you-ward;

3how that by revelation was made known unto me the mystery, as I wrote before in few words,

4whereby, when ye read, ye can perceive my understanding in the mystery of Christ;

5which in other generation was not made known unto the sons of men, as it hath now been revealed unto his holy apostles and prophets in the Spirit;

6to wit, that the Gentiles are fellow-heirs, and fellow-members of the body, and fellow-partakers of the promise in Christ Jesus through the gospel,

7whereof I was made a minister, according to the gift of that grace of God which was given me according to the working of his power.

8Unto me, who am less than the least of all saints, was this grace given, to preach unto the Gentiles the unsearchable riches of Christ;

9and to make all men see what is the dispensation of the mystery which for ages hath been hid in God who created all things;

10to the intent that now unto the principalities and the powers in the heavenly places might be made known through the church the manifold wisdom of God,

11according to the eternal purpose which he purposed in Christ Jesus our Lord:

12in whom we have boldness and access in confidence through our faith in him.

13Wherefore I ask that ye may not faint at my tribulations for you, which are your glory.

14For this cause I bow my knees unto the Father,

15from whom every family in heaven and on earth is named,

16that he would grant you, according to the riches of his glory, that ye may be strengthened with power through his Spirit in the inward man;

17that Christ may dwell in your hearts through faith; to the end that ye, being rooted and grounded in love,

18may be strong to apprehend with all the saints what is the breadth and length and height and depth,

19and to know the love of Christ which passeth knowledge, that ye may be filled unto all the fulness of God.

20Now unto him that is able to do exceeding abundantly above all that we ask or think, according to the power that worketh in us,

21unto him be the glory in the church and in Christ Jesus unto all generations for ever and ever. Amen.

Chapter 4

1I therefore, the prisoner in the Lord, beseech you to walk worthily of the calling wherewith ye were called,

2with all lowliness and meekness, with longsuffering, forbearing one another in love;

3giving diligence to keep the unity of the Spirit in the bond of peace.

4There is one body, and one Spirit, even as also ye were called in one hope of your calling;

5one Lord, one faith, one baptism,

6one God and Father of all, who is over all, and through all, and in all.

7But unto each one of us was the grace given according to the measure of the gift of Christ.

8Wherefore he saith, When he ascended on high, he led captivity captive, And gave gifts unto men.

9(Now this, He ascended, what is it but that he also descended into the lower parts of the earth?

10He that descended is the same also that ascended far above all the heavens, that he might fill all things.)

11And he gave some to be apostles; and some, prophets; and some, evangelists; and some, pastors and teachers;

12for the perfecting of the saints, unto the work of ministering, unto the building up of the body of Christ:

13till we all attain unto the unity of the faith, and of the knowledge of the Son of God, unto a fullgrown man, unto the measure of the stature of the fulness of Christ:

14that we may be no longer children, tossed to and fro and carried about with every wind of doctrine, by the sleight of men, in craftiness, after the wiles of error;

15but speaking truth in love, we may grow up in all things into him, who is the head, even Christ;

16from whom all the body fitly framed and knit together through that which every joint supplieth, according to the working in due measure of each several part, maketh the increase of the body unto the building up of itself in love.

17This I say therefore, and testify in the Lord, that ye no longer walk as the

Ephesians

Gentiles also walk, in the vanity of their mind,

18being darkened in their understanding, alienated from the life of God, because of the ignorance that is in them, because of the hardening of their heart:

19who being past feeling gave themselves up to lasciviousness, to work all uncleanness with greediness.

20But ye did not so learn Christ;

21if so be that ye heard him, and were taught in him, even as truth is in Jesus:

22that ye put away, as concerning your former manner of life, the old man, that waxeth corrupt after the lusts of deceit;

23and that ye be renewed in the spirit of your mind,

24and put on the new man, that after God hath been created in righteousness and holiness of truth.

25Wherefore, putting away falsehood, speak ye truth each one with his neighbor: for we are members one of another.

26Be ye angry, and sin not: let not the sun go down upon your wrath:

27neither give place to the devil.

28Let him that stole steal no more: but rather let him labor, working with his hands the thing that is good, that he may have whereof to give to him that hath need.

29Let no corrupt speech proceed out of your mouth, but such as is good for edifying as the need may be, that it may give grace to them that hear.

30And grieve not the Holy Spirit of God, in whom ye were sealed unto the day of redemption.

31Let all bitterness, and wrath, and anger, and clamor, and railing, be put away from you, with all malice:

32and be ye kind one to another, tenderhearted, forgiving each other, even as God also in Christ forgave you.

Chapter 5

1Be ye therefore imitators of God, as beloved children;

2and walk in love, even as Christ also loved you, and gave himself up for us, an offering and a sacrifice to God for an odor of a sweet smell.

3But fornication, and all uncleanness, or covetousness, let it not even be named among you, as becometh saints;

4nor filthiness, nor foolish talking, or jesting, which are not befitting: but rather giving of thanks.

5For this ye know of a surety, that no fornicator, nor unclean person, nor covetous man, who is an idolater, hath any inheritance in the kingdom of Christ and God.

6Let no man deceive you with empty words: for because of these things cometh the wrath of God upon the sons of disobedience.

7Be not ye therefore partakers with them;

8For ye were once darkness, but are now light in the Lord: walk as children of light

9(for the fruit of the light is in all goodness and righteousness and truth),

10proving what is well-pleasing unto the Lord;

11and have no fellowship with the unfruitful works of darkness, but rather even reprove them;

12for the things which are done by them in secret it is a shame even to speak of.

13But all things when they are reproved are made manifest by the light: for everything that is made manifest is light.

14Wherefore he saith, Awake, thou that sleepest, and arise from the dead, and Christ shall shine upon thee.

15Look therefore carefully how ye walk, not as unwise, but as wise;

16redeeming the time, because the days are evil.

17Wherefore be ye not foolish, but understand what the will of the Lord is.

18And be not drunken with wine, wherein is riot, but be filled with the Spirit;

19speaking one to another in psalms and hymns and spiritual songs, singing and making melody with your heart to the Lord;

20giving thanks always for all things in the name of our Lord Jesus Christ to God, even the Father;

21subjecting yourselves one to another in the fear of Christ.

22Wives, be in subjection unto your own husbands, as unto the Lord.

23For the husband is the head of the wife, and Christ also is the head of the church, being himself the saviour of the body.

24But as the church is subject to Christ, so let the wives also be to their husbands in everything.

25Husbands, love your wives, even as Christ also loved the church, and gave himself up for it;

26that he might sanctify it, having cleansed it by the washing of water with the word,

27that he might present the church to himself a glorious church, not having spot or wrinkle or any such thing; but that it should be holy and without blemish.

28Even so ought husbands also to love their own wives as their own bodies. He that loveth his own wife loveth himself:

29for no man ever hated his own flesh; but nourisheth and cherisheth it, even as Christ also the church;

30because we are members of his body.

31For this cause shall a man leave his father and mother, and shall cleave to his wife; and the two shall become one flesh.

32This mystery is great: but I speak in regard of Christ and of the church.

33Nevertheless do ye also severally love each one his own wife even as himself; and let the wife see that she fear her husband.

Chapter 6

1Children, obey your parents in the Lord: for this is right.

2Honor thy father and mother (which is the first commandment with promise),

3that it may be well with thee, and thou mayest live long on the earth.

4And, ye fathers, provoke not your children to wrath: but nurture them in the chastening and admonition of the Lord.

5Servants, be obedient unto them that according to the flesh are your masters, with fear and trembling, in singleness of your heart, as unto Christ;

6not in the way of eyeservice, as men-pleasers; but as servants of Christ, doing the will of God from the heart;

7with good will doing service, as unto the Lord, and not unto men:

8knowing that whatsoever good thing each one doeth, the same shall he receive again from the Lord, whether he be bond or free.

9And, ye masters, do the same things unto them, and forbear threatening: knowing that he who is both their Master and yours is in heaven, and there is no respect of persons with him.

10Finally, be strong in the Lord, and in the strength of his might.

11Put on the whole armor of God, that ye may be able to stand against the wiles of the devil.

12For our wrestling is not against flesh and blood, but against the principalities, against the powers, against the world-rulers of this darkness, against the spiritual hosts of wickedness in the heavenly places.

13Wherefore take up the whole armor of God, that ye may be able to withstand in the evil day, and, having done all, to stand.

14Stand therefore, having girded your loins with truth, and having put on the breastplate of righteousness,

15and having shod your feet with the preparation of the gospel of peace;

16withal taking up the shield of faith, wherewith ye shall be able to quench all the fiery darts of the evil one.

17And take the helmet of salvation, and the sword of the Spirit, which is the word of God:

18with all prayer and supplication praying at all seasons in the Spirit, and watching thereunto in all perseverance and supplication for all the saints,

19And on my behalf, that utterance may be given unto me in opening my mouth, to make known with boldness the mystery of the gospel,

20for which I am an ambassador in chains; that in it I may speak boldly, as I ought to speak.

21But that ye also may know my affairs, how I do, Tychicus, the beloved brother and faithful minister in the Lord, shall make known to you all things:

22whom I have sent unto you for this very purpose, that ye may know our state, and that he may comfort your hearts.

23Peace be to the brethren, and love with faith, from God the Father and the Lord Jesus Christ.

24Grace be with all them that love our Lord Jesus Christ with a love incorruptible.

The Epistle of Paul the Apostle to the Philippians

Chapter 1

1 Paul and Timothy, servants of Christ Jesus, to all the saints in Christ Jesus that are at Philippi, with the bishops and deacons:

2 Grace to you and peace from God our Father and the Lord Jesus Christ.

3 I thank my God upon all my remembrance of you,

4 always in every supplication of mine on behalf of you all making my supplication with joy,

5 for your fellowship in furtherance of the gospel from the first day until now;

6 being confident of this very thing, that he who began a good work in you will perfect it until the day of Jesus Christ:

7 even as it is right for me to be thus minded on behalf of you all, because I have you in my heart, inasmuch as, both in my bonds and in the defence and confirmation of the gospel, ye all are partakers with me of grace.

8 For God is my witness, how I long after you all in the tender mercies of Christ Jesus.

9 And this I pray, that your love may abound yet more and more in knowledge and all discernment;

10 so that ye may approve the things that are excellent; that ye may be sincere and void of offence unto the day of Christ;

11 being filled with the fruits of righteousness, which are through Jesus Christ, unto the glory and praise of God.

12 Now I would have you know, brethren, that the things which happened unto me have fallen out rather unto the progress of the gospel;

13 so that my bonds became manifest in Christ throughout the whole praetorian guard, and to all the rest;

14 and that most of the brethren in the Lord, being confident through my bonds, are more abundantly bold to speak the word of God without fear.

15 Some indeed preach Christ even of envy and strife; and some also of good will:

16 the one do it of love, knowing that I am set for the defence of the gospel;

17 but the other proclaim Christ of faction, not sincerely, thinking to raise up affliction for me in my bonds.

18 What then? only that in every way, whether in pretence or in truth, Christ is proclaimed; and therein I rejoice, yea, and will rejoice.

19 For I know that this shall turn out to my salvation, through your supplication and the supply of the Spirit of Jesus Christ,

20 according to my earnest expectation and hope, that in nothing shall I be put to shame, but that with all boldness, as always, so now also Christ shall be magnified in my body, whether by life, or by death.

21 For to me to live is Christ, and to die is gain.

22 But if to live in the flesh, --if this shall bring fruit from my work, then what I shall choose I know not.

23 But I am in a strait betwixt the two, having the desire to depart and be with Christ; for it is very far better:

24 yet to abide in the flesh is more needful for your sake.

25 And having this confidence, I know that I shall abide, yea, and abide with you all, for your progress and joy in the faith;

26 that your glorying may abound in Christ Jesus in me through my presence with you again.

27 Only let your manner of life be worthy of the gospel of Christ: that, whether I come and see you and be absent, I may hear of your state, that ye stand fast in one spirit, with one soul striving for the faith of the gospel;

28 and in nothing affrighted by the adversaries: which is for them an evident token of perdition, but of your salvation, and that from God;

29 because to you it hath been granted in the behalf of Christ, not only to believe on him, but also to suffer in his behalf:

30 having the same conflict which ye saw in me, and now hear to be in me.

Chapter 2

1 If there is therefore any exhortation in Christ, if any consolation of love, if any fellowship of the Spirit, if any tender mercies and compassions,

2 make full my joy, that ye be of the same mind, having the same love, being of one accord, of one mind;

3 doing nothing through faction or through vainglory, but in lowliness of mind each counting other better than himself;

4 not looking each of you to his own things, but each of you also to the things of others.

5 Have this mind in you, which was also in Christ Jesus:

6 who, existing in the form of God, counted not the being on an equality with God a thing to be grasped,

7 but emptied himself, taking the form of a servant, being made in the likeness of men;

8 and being found in fashion as a man, he humbled himself, becoming obedient even unto death, yea, the death of the cross.

9 Wherefore also God highly exalted him, and gave unto him the name which is above every name;

10 that in the name of Jesus every knee should bow, of things in heaven and things on earth and things under the earth,

11 and that every tongue should confess that Jesus Christ is Lord, to the glory of God the Father.

12 So then, my beloved, even as ye have always obeyed, not as in my presence only, but now much more in my absence, work out your own salvation with fear and trembling;

13 for it is God who worketh in you both to will and to work, for his good pleasure.

14 Do all things without murmurings and questionings:

15 that ye may become blameless and harmless, children of God without blemish in the midst of a crooked and perverse generation, among whom ye are seen as lights in the world,

16 holding forth the word of life; that I may have whereof to glory in the day of Christ, that I did not run in vain neither labor in vain.

17 Yea, and if I am offered upon the sacrifice and service of your faith, I joy, and rejoice with you all:

18 and in the same manner do ye also joy, and rejoice with me.

19 But I hope in the Lord Jesus to send Timothy shortly unto you, that I also may be of good comfort, when I know your state.

20 For I have no man likeminded, who will care truly for your state.

21 For they all seek their own, not the things of Jesus Christ.

22 But ye know the proof of him, that, as a child serveth a father, so he served with me in furtherance of the gospel.

23 Him therefore I hope to send forthwith, so soon as I shall see how it will go with me:

24 but I trust in the Lord that I myself also shall come shortly.

25 But I counted it necessary to send to you Epaphroditus, my brother and fellow-worker and fellow-soldier, and your messenger and minister to my need;

26 since he longed after you all, and was sore troubled, because ye had heard that he was sick:

27 for indeed he was sick nigh unto death: but God had mercy on him; and not on him only, but on me also, that I might not have sorrow upon sorrow.

28 I have sent him therefore the more diligently, that, when ye see him again, ye may rejoice, and that I may be the less sorrowful.

29 Receive him therefore in the Lord with all joy; and hold such in honor:

30 because for the work of Christ he came nigh unto death, hazarding his life to supply that which was lacking in your service toward me.

Chapter 3

1 Finally, my brethren, rejoice in the Lord. To write the same things to you, to me indeed is not irksome, but for you it is safe.

2 Beware of the dogs, beware of the evil workers, beware of the concision:

3 for we are the circumcision, who worship by the Spirit of God, and glory in Christ Jesus, and have no confidence in the flesh:

4 though I myself might have confidence even in the flesh: if any other man thinketh to have confidence in the flesh, I yet more:

5 circumcised the eighth day, of the stock of Israel, of the tribe of Benjamin, a Hebrew of Hebrews; as touching the law, a Pharisee;

6 as touching zeal, persecuting the church; as touching the righteousness which is in the law, found blameless.

7 Howbeit what things were gain to me, these have I counted loss for Christ.

8 Yea verily, and I count all things to be loss for the excellency of the knowledge of Christ Jesus my Lord: for whom I suffered the loss of all things, and do count them but refuse, that I may gain Christ,

9 and be found in him, not having a righteousness of mine own, even that which is of the law, but that which is through faith in Christ, the righteousness which is from God by faith:

10 that I may know him, and the power of his resurrection, and the fellowship of his sufferings, becoming conformed unto his death;

11 if by any means I may attain unto the resurrection from the dead.

12 Not that I have already obtained, or am already made perfect: but I press on, if so be that I may lay hold on that for which also I was laid hold on by Christ Jesus.

13 Brethren, I could not myself yet to have laid hold: but one thing I do, forgetting the things which are behind, and stretching forward to the things which are before,

14 I press on toward the goal unto the prize of the high calling of God in Christ Jesus.

15 Let us therefore, as many as are perfect, be thus minded: and if in anything ye are otherwise minded, this also shall God reveal unto you:

16 only, whereunto we have attained, by that same rule let us walk.

17 Brethren, be ye imitators together of me, and mark them that so walk even as ye have us for an ensample.

18 For many walk, of whom I told you often, and now tell you even weeping, that they are the enemies of the cross of Christ:

19 whose end is perdition, whose god is the belly, and whose glory is in their shame, who mind earthly things.

20 For our citizenship is in heaven; whence also we wait for a Saviour, the Lord Jesus Christ:

21 who shall fashion anew the body of our humiliation, that it may be conformed to the body of his glory, according to the working whereby he is able even to subject all things unto himself.

Chapter 4

1 Wherefore, my brethren beloved and longed for, my joy and crown, so stand fast in the Lord, my beloved.

2 I exhort Euodia, and I exhort Syntyche, to be of the same mind in the Lord.

3 Yea, I beseech thee also, true yokefellow, help these women, for they labored with me in the gospel, with Clement also, and the rest of my fellow-workers, whose names are in the book of life.

4 Rejoice in the Lord always: again I will say, Rejoice.

5 Let your forbearance be known unto all men. The Lord is at hand.

Philippians

6In nothing be anxious; but in everything by prayer and supplication with thanksgiving let your requests be made known unto God.

7And the peace of God, which passeth all understanding, shall guard your hearts and your thoughts in Christ Jesus.

8Finally, brethren, whatsoever things are true, whatsoever things are honorable, whatsoever things are just, whatsoever things are pure, whatsoever things are lovely, whatsoever things are of good report; if there be any virtue, and if there be any praise, think on these things.

9The things which ye both learned and received and heard and saw in me, these things do: and the God of peace shall be with you.

10But I rejoice in the Lord greatly, that now at length ye have revived your thought for me; wherein ye did indeed take thought, but ye lacked opportunity.

11Not that I speak in respect of want: for I have learned, in whatsoever state I am, therein to be content.

12I know how to be abased, and I know also how to abound: in everything and in all things have I learned the secret both to be filled and to be hungry, both to abound and to be in want.

13I can do all things in him that strengtheneth me.

14Howbeit ye did well that ye had fellowship with my affliction.

15And ye yourselves also know, ye Philippians, that in the beginning of the gospel, when I departed from Macedonia, no church had fellowship with me in the matter of giving and receiving but ye only;

16for even in Thessalonica ye sent once and again unto my need.

17Not that I seek for the gift; but I seek for the fruit that increaseth to your account.

18But I have all things, and abound: I am filled, having received from Epaphroditus the things that came from you, and odor of a sweet smell, a sacrifice acceptable, well-pleasing to God.

19And my God shall supply every need of yours according to his riches in glory in Christ Jesus.

20Now unto our God and Father be the glory for ever and ever. Amen.

21Salute every saint in Christ Jesus. The brethren that are with me salute you.

22All the saints salute you, especially they that are of Caesar's household.

23The grace of the Lord Jesus Christ be with your spirit.

The Epistle of Paul the Apostle to the Colossians

Chapter 1

1Paul, an apostle of Christ Jesus through the will of God, and Timothy our brother,

2To the saints and faithful brethren in Christ that are at Colossae: Grace to you and peace from God our Father.

3We give thanks to God the Father of our Lord Jesus Christ, praying always for you,

4having heard of your faith in Christ Jesus, and of the love which ye have toward all the saints,

5because of the hope which is laid up for you in the heavens, whereof ye heard before in the word of the truth of the gospel,

6which is come unto you; even as it is also in all the world bearing fruit and increasing, as it doth in you also, since the day ye heard and knew the grace of God in truth;

7even as ye learned of Epaphras our beloved fellow-servant, who is a faithful minister of Christ on our behalf,

8who also declared unto us your love in the Spirit.

9For this cause we also, since the day we heard it, do not cease to pray and make request for you, that ye may be filled with the knowledge of his will in all spiritual wisdom and understanding,

10to walk worthily of the Lord unto all pleasing, bearing fruit in every good work, and increasing in the knowledge of God;

11strengthened with all power, according to the might of his glory, unto all patience and longsuffering with joy;

12giving thanks unto the Father, who made us meet to be partakers of the inheritance of the saints in light;

13who delivered us out of the power of darkness, and translated us into the kingdom of the Son of his love;

14in whom we have our redemption, the forgiveness of our sins:

15who is the image of the invisible God, the firstborn of all creation;

16for in him were all things created, in the heavens and upon the earth, things visible and things invisible, whether thrones or dominions or principalities or powers; all things have been created through him, and unto him;

17and he is before all things, and in him all things consist.

18And he is the head of the body, the church: who is the beginning, the firstborn from the dead; that in all things he might have the preeminence.

19For it was the good pleasure of the Father that in him should all the fulness dwell;

20and through him to reconcile all things unto himself, having made peace through the blood of his cross; through him, I say, whether things upon the earth, or things in the heavens.

21And you, being in time past alienated and enemies in your mind in your evil works,

22yet now hath he reconciled in the body of his flesh through death, to present you holy and without blemish and unproveable before him:

23if so be that ye continue in the faith, grounded and stedfast, and not moved away from the hope of the gospel which ye heard, which was preached in all creation under heaven; whereof I Paul was made a minister.

24Now I rejoice in my sufferings for your sake, and fill up on my part that which is lacking of the afflictions of Christ in my flesh for his body's sake, which is the church;

25whereof I was made a minister, according to the dispensation of God which was given me to you-ward, to fulfil the word of God,

26even the mystery which hath been hid for ages and generations: but now hath it been manifested to his saints,

27to whom God was pleased to make known what is the riches of the glory of this mystery among the Gentiles, which is Christ in you, the hope of glory:

28whom we proclaim, admonishing every man and teaching every man in all wisdom, that we may present every man perfect in Christ;

29whereunto I labor also, striving according to his working, which worketh in me mightily.

Chapter 2

1For I would have you know how greatly I strive for you, and for them at Laodicea, and for as many as have not seen my face in the flesh;

2that their hearts may be comforted, they being knit together in love, and unto all riches of the full assurance of understanding, that they may know the mystery of God, even Christ,

3in whom are all the treasures of wisdom and knowledge hidden.

4This I say, that no one may delude you with persuasiveness of speech.

5For though I am absent in the flesh, yet am I with you in the spirit, joying and beholding your order, and the stedfastness of your faith in Christ.

6As therefore ye received Christ Jesus the Lord, so walk in him,

7rooted and builded up in him, and established in your faith, even as ye were taught, abounding in thanksgiving.

8Take heed lest there shall be any one that maketh spoil of you through his philosophy and vain deceit, after the tradition of men, after the rudiments of the world, and not after Christ:

9for in him dwelleth all the fulness of the Godhead bodily,

10and in him ye are made full, who is the head of all principality and power:

11in whom ye were also circumcised with a circumcision not made with hands, in the putting off of the body of the flesh, in the circumcision of Christ;

12having been buried with him in baptism, wherein ye were also raised with him through faith in the working of God, who raised him from the dead.

13And you, being dead through your trespasses and the uncircumcision of your flesh, you, I say, did he make alive together with him, having forgiven us all our trespasses;

14having blotted out the bond written in ordinances that was against us, which was contrary to us: and he hath taken it out that way, nailing it to the cross;

15having despoiled the principalities and the powers, he made a show of them openly, triumphing over them in it.

16Let no man therefore judge you in meat, or in drink, or in respect of a feast day or a new moon or a sabbath day:

17which are a shadow of the things to come; but the body is Christ's.

18Let no man rob you of your prize by a voluntary humility and worshipping of the angels, dwelling in the things which he hath seen, vainly puffed up by his fleshly mind,

19and not holding fast the Head, from whom all the body, being supplied and knit together through the joints and bands, increasing with the increase of God.

20If ye died with Christ from the rudiments of the world, why, as though living in the world, do ye subject yourselves to ordinances,

21Handle not, nor taste, nor touch

22(all which things are to perish with the using), after the precepts and doctrines of men?

23Which things have indeed a show of wisdom in will-worship, and humility, and severity to the body; but are not of any value against the indulgence of the flesh.

Chapter 3

1If then ye were raised together with Christ, seek the things that are above, where Christ is, seated on the right hand of God.

2Set your mind on the things that are above, not on the things that are upon the earth.

3For ye died, and your life is hid with Christ in God.

4When Christ, who is our life, shall be manifested, then shall ye also with him be manifested in glory.

5Put to death therefore your members which are upon the earth: fornication, uncleanness, passion, evil desire, and covetousness, which is idolatry;

6for which things' sake cometh the wrath of God upon the sons of disobedience;

7wherein ye also once walked, when ye lived in these things;

8but now do ye also put them all away: anger, wrath, malice, railing, shameful speaking out of your mouth:

9lie not one to another; seeing that ye have put off the old man with his doings,

10and have put on the new man, that is being renewed unto knowledge after the image of him that created him:

11where there cannot be Greek and Jew, circumcision and uncircumcision, barbarian, Scythian, bondman, freeman; but Christ is all, and in all.

12Put on therefore, as God's elect, holy and beloved, a heart of compassion, kindness, lowliness, meekness, longsuffering;

13forbearing one another, and forgiving each other, if any man have a complaint against any; even as the Lord forgave you, so also do ye:

14and above all these things put on love, which is the bond of perfectness.

15And let the peace of Christ rule in your hearts, to the which also ye were called in one body; and be ye thankful.

16Let the word of Christ dwell in you richly; in all wisdom teaching and admonishing one another with psalms and hymns and spiritual songs, singing with grace in your hearts unto God.

17And whatsoever ye do, in word or in deed, do all in the name of the Lord Jesus, giving thanks to God the Father through him.

18Wives, be in subjection to your husbands, as is fitting in the Lord.

19Husbands, love your wives, and be not bitter against them.

20Children, obey your parents in all things, for this is well-pleasing in the Lord.

21Fathers, provoke not your children, that they be not discouraged.

22Servants, obey in all things them that are your masters according to the flesh; not with eye-service, as men-pleasers, but in singleness of heart, fearing the Lord:

23whatsoever ye do, work heartily, as unto the Lord, and not unto men;

24knowing that from the Lord ye shall receive the recompense of the inheritance: ye serve the Lord Christ.

25For he that doeth wrong shall receive again for the wrong that he hath done: and there is no respect of persons.

Chapter 4

1Masters, render unto your servants that which is just and equal; knowing that ye also have a Master in heaven.

2Continue stedfastly in prayer, watching therein with thanksgiving;

3withal praying for us also, that God may open unto us a door for the word, to speak the mystery of Christ, for which I am also in bonds;

4that I may make it manifest, as I ought to speak.

5Walk in wisdom toward them that are without, redeeming the time.

6Let your speech be always with grace, seasoned with salt, that ye may know how ye ought to answer each one.

7All my affairs shall Tychicus make known unto you, the beloved brother and faithful minister and fellow-servant in the Lord:

8whom I have sent you for this very purpose, that ye may know our state, and that he may comfort your hearts;

Colossians

9together with Onesimus, the faithful and beloved brother, who is one of you. They shall make known unto you all things that are done here.

10Aristarchus my fellow-prisoner saluteth you, and Mark, the cousin of Barnabas (touching whom ye received commandments; if he come unto you, receive him),

11and Jesus that is called Justus, who are of the circumcision: these only are my fellow-workers unto the kingdom of God, men that have been a comfort unto me.

12Epaphras, who is one of you, a servant of Christ Jesus, saluteth you, always striving for you in his prayers, that ye may stand perfect and fully assured in all the will of God.

13For I bear him witness, that he hath much labor for you, and for them in Laodicea, and for them in Hierapolis.

14Luke, the beloved physician, and Demas salute you.

15Salute the brethren that are in Laodicea, and Nymphas, and the church that is in their house.

16And when this epistle hath been read among you, cause that it be read also in the church of the Laodiceans; and that ye also read the epistle from Laodicea.

17And say to Archippus, Take heed to the ministry which thou hast received in the Lord, that thou fulfil it.

18The salutation of me Paul with mine own hand. Remember my bonds. Grace be with you.

The First Epistle of Paul to the Thessalonians

Chapter 1

1Paul, and Silvanus, and Timothy, unto the church of the Thessalonians in God the Father and the Lord Jesus Christ: Grace to you and peace.

2We give thanks to God always for you all, making mention of you in our prayers;

3remembering without ceasing your work of faith and labor of love and patience of hope in our Lord Jesus Christ, before our God and Father;

4knowing, brethren beloved of God, your election,

5how that our gospel came not unto you in word only, but also in power, and in the Holy Spirit, and in much assurance; even as ye know what manner of men we showed ourselves toward you for your sake.

6And ye became imitators of us, and of the Lord, having received the word in much affliction, with joy of the Holy Spirit;

7so that ye became an ensample to all that believe in Macedonia and in Achaia.

8For from you hath sounded forth the word of the Lord, not only in Macedonia and Achaia, but in every place your faith to God-ward is gone forth; so that we need not to speak anything.

9For they themselves report concerning us what manner of entering in we had unto you; and how ye turned unto God from idols, to serve a living and true God,

10and to wait for his Son from heaven, whom he raised from the dead, even Jesus, who delivereth us from the wrath to come.

Chapter 2

1For yourselves, brethren, know our entering in unto you, that it hath not been found vain:

2but having suffered before and been shamefully treated, as ye know, at Philippi, we waxed bold in our God to speak unto you the gospel of God in much conflict.

3For our exhortation is not of error, nor of uncleanness, nor in guile:

4but even as we have been approved of God to be intrusted with the gospel, so we speak; not as pleasing men, but God who proveth our hearts.

5For neither at any time were we found using words of flattery, as ye know, nor a cloak of covetousness, God is witness;

6nor seeking glory of men, neither from you nor from others, when we might have claimed authority as apostles of Christ.

7But we were gentle in the midst of you, as when a nurse cherisheth her own children:

8even so, being affectionately desirous of you, we were well pleased to impart unto you, not the gospel of God only, but also our own souls, because ye were become very dear to us.

9For ye remember, brethren, our labor and travail: working night and day, that we might not burden any of you, we preached unto you the gospel of God.

10Ye are witnesses, and God also, how holily and righteously and unblameably we behaved ourselves toward you that believe:

11as ye know how we dealt with each one of you, as a father with his own children, exhorting you, and encouraging you, and testifying,

12to the end that ye should walk worthily of God, who calleth you into his own kingdom and glory.

13And for this cause we also thank God without ceasing, that, when ye received from us the word of the message, even the word of God, ye accepted it not as the word of men, but, as it is in truth, the word of God, which also worketh in you that believe.

14For ye, brethren, became imitators of the churches of God which are in Judaea in Christ Jesus: for ye also suffered the same things of your own countrymen, even as they did of the Jews;

15who both killed the Lord Jesus and the prophets, and drove out us, and pleased not God, and are contrary to all men;

16forbidding us to speak to the Gentiles that they may be saved; to fill up their sins always: but the wrath is come upon them to the uttermost.

17But we, brethren, being bereaved of you for a short season, in presence not in heart, endeavored the more exceedingly to see your face with great desire:

18because we would fain have come unto you, I Paul once and again; and Satan hindered us.

19For what is our hope, or joy, or crown of glorying? Are not even ye, before our Lord Jesus at his coming?

20For ye are our glory and our joy.

Chapter 3

1Wherefore when we could no longer forbear, we thought it good to be left behind at Athens alone;

2and sent Timothy, our brother and God's minister in the gospel of Christ, to establish you, and to comfort you concerning your faith;

3that no man be moved by these afflictions; for yourselves know that hereunto we are appointed.

4For verily, when we were with you, we told you beforehand that we are to suffer affliction; even as it came to pass, and ye know.

5For this cause I also, when I could no longer forbear, sent that I might know your faith, lest by any means the tempter had tempted you, and our labor should be in vain.

6But when Timothy came even now unto us from you, and brought us glad tidings of your faith and love, and that ye have good remembrance of us always, longing to see us, even as we also to see you;

7for this cause, brethren, we were comforted over you in all our distress and affliction through your faith:

8for now we live, if ye stand fast in the Lord.

9For what thanksgiving can we render again unto God for you, for all the joy wherewith we joy for your sakes before our God;

10night and day praying exceedingly that we may see your face, and may perfect that which is lacking in your faith?

11Now may our God and Father himself, and our Lord Jesus, direct our way unto you:

12and the Lord make you to increase and abound in love one toward another, and toward all men, even as we also do toward you;

13to the end he may establish your hearts unblameable in holiness before our God and Father, at the coming of our Lord Jesus with all his saints.

Chapter 4

1Finally then, brethren, we beseech and exhort you in the Lord Jesus, that, as ye received of us how ye ought to walk and to please God, even as ye do walk, --that ye abound more and more.

2For ye know what charge we gave you through the Lord Jesus.

3For this is the will of God, even your sanctification, that ye abstain from fornication;

4that each one of you know how to possess himself of his own vessel in sanctification and honor,

5not in the passion of lust, even as the Gentiles who know not God;

6that no man transgress, and wrong his brother in the matter: because the Lord is an avenger in all these things, as also we forewarned you and testified.

7For God called us not for uncleanness, but in sanctification.

8Therefore he that rejecteth, rejecteth not man, but God, who giveth his Holy Spirit unto you.

9But concerning love of the brethren ye have no need that one write unto you: for ye yourselves are taught of God to love one another;

10for indeed ye do it toward all the brethren that are in all Macedonia. But we exhort you, brethren, that ye abound more and more;

11and that ye study to be quiet, and to do your own business, and to work with your hands, even as we charged you;

12that ye may walk becomingly toward them that are without, and may have need of nothing.

13But we would not have you ignorant, brethren, concerning them that fall asleep; that ye sorrow not, even as the rest, who have no hope.

14For if we believe that Jesus died and rose again, even so them also that are fallen asleep in Jesus will God bring with him.

15For this we say unto you by the word of the Lord, that we that are alive, that are left unto the coming of the Lord, shall in no wise precede them that are fallen asleep.

16For the Lord himself shall descend from heaven, with a shout, with the voice of the archangel, and with the trump of God: and the dead in Christ shall rise first;

17then we that are alive, that are left, shall together with them be caught up in the clouds, to meet the Lord in the air: and so shall we ever be with the Lord.

18Wherefore comfort one another with these words.

Chapter 5

1But concerning the times and the seasons, brethren, ye have no need that aught be written unto you.

2For yourselves know perfectly that the day of the Lord so cometh as a thief in the night.

3When they are saying, Peace and safety, then sudden destruction cometh upon them, as travail upon a woman with child; and they shall in no wise escape.

4But ye, brethren, are not in darkness, that that day should overtake you as a thief:

5for ye are all sons of light, and sons of the day: we are not of the night, nor of darkness;

6so then let us not sleep, as do the rest, but let us watch and be sober.

7For they that sleep sleep in the night: and they that are drunken are drunken in the night.

8But let us, since we are of the day, be sober, putting on the breastplate of faith and love; and for a helmet, the hope of salvation.

9For God appointed us not into wrath, but unto the obtaining of salvation through our Lord Jesus Christ,

10who died for us, that, whether we wake or sleep, we should live together with him.

11Wherefore exhort one another, and build each other up, even as also ye do.

12But we beseech you, brethren, to know them that labor among you, and are over you in the Lord, and admonish you;

13and to esteem them exceeding highly in love for their work's sake. Be at peace among yourselves.

14And we exhort you, brethren, admonish the disorderly, encourage the fainthearted, support the weak, be longsuffering toward all.

15See that none render unto any one evil for evil; but always follow after that which is good, one toward another, and toward all.

16Rejoice always;

17pray without ceasing;

18in everything give thanks: for this is the will of God in Christ Jesus to you-ward.

19Quench not the Spirit;

First Thessalonians

20 despise not prophesyings;
21 prove all things; hold fast that which is good;
22 abstain from every form of evil.
23 And the God of peace himself sanctify you wholly; and may your spirit and soul and body be preserved entire, without blame at the coming of our Lord Jesus Christ.
24 Faithful is he that calleth you, who will also do it.
25 Brethren, pray for us.
26 Salute all the brethren with a holy kiss.
27 I adjure you by the Lord that this epistle be read unto all the brethren.
28 The grace of our Lord Jesus Christ be with you.

The Second Epistle of Paul the Apostle to the Thessalonians

Chapter 1

¹Paul, and Silvanus, and Timothy, unto the church of the Thessalonians in God our Father and the Lord Jesus Christ;

²Grace to you and peace from God the Father and the Lord Jesus Christ.

³We are bound to give thanks to God always to you, brethren, even as it is meet, for that your faith growth exceedingly, and the love of each one of you all toward one another aboundeth;

⁴so that we ourselves glory in you in the churches of God for your patience and faith in all your persecutions and in the afflictions which ye endure;

⁵which is a manifest token of the righteous judgment of God; to the end that ye may be counted worthy of the kingdom of God, for which ye also suffer:

⁶if so be that it is righteous thing with God to recompense affliction to them that afflict you,

⁷and to you that are afflicted rest with us, at the revelation of the Lord Jesus from heaven with the angels of his power in flaming fire,

⁸rendering vengeance to them that know not God, and to them that obey not the gospel of our Lord Jesus:

⁹who shall suffer punishment, even eternal destruction from the face of the Lord and from the glory of his might,

¹⁰when he shall come to be glorified in his saints, and to be marvelled at in all them that believed (because our testimony unto you was believed) in that day.

¹¹To which end we also pray always for you, that our God may count you worthy of your calling, and fulfil every desire of goodness and every work of faith, with power;

¹²that the name of our Lord Jesus may be glorified in you, and ye in him, according to the grace of our God and the Lord Jesus Christ.

Chapter 2

¹Now we beseech you, brethren, touching the coming of our Lord Jesus Christ, and our gathering together unto him;

²to the end that ye be not quickly shaken from your mind, nor yet be troubled, either by spirit, or by word, or by epistle as from us, as that the day of the Lord is just at hand;

³let no man beguile you in any wise: for it will not be, except the falling away come first, and the man of sin be revealed, the son of perdition,

⁴he that opposeth and exalteth himself against all that is called God or that is worshipped; so that he sitteth in the temple of God, setting himself forth as God.

⁵Remember ye not, that, when I was yet with you, I told you these things?

⁶And now ye know that which restraineth, to the end that he may be revealed in his own season.

⁷For the mystery of lawlessness doth already work: only there is one that restraineth now, until he be taken out of the way.

⁸And then shall be revealed the lawless one, whom the Lord Jesus shall slay with the breath of his mouth, and bring to nought by the manifestation of his coming;

⁹even he, whose coming is according to the working of Satan with all power and signs and lying wonders,

¹⁰and with all deceit of unrighteousness for them that perish; because they received not the love of the truth, that they might be saved.

¹¹And for this cause God sendeth them a working of error, that they should believe a lie:

¹²that they all might be judged who believed not the truth, but had pleasure in unrighteousness.

¹³But we are bound to give thanks to God always for you, brethren beloved of the Lord, for that God chose you from the beginning unto salvation in sanctification of the Spirit and belief of the truth:

¹⁴whereunto he called you through our gospel, to the obtaining of the glory of our Lord Jesus Christ.

¹⁵So then, brethren, stand fast, and hold the traditions which ye were taught, whether by word, or by epistle of ours.

¹⁶Now our Lord Jesus Christ himself, and God our Father who loved us and gave us eternal comfort and good hope through grace,

¹⁷comfort your hearts and establish them in every good work and word.

Chapter 3

¹Finally, brethren, pray for us, that the word of the Lord may run and be glorified, even as also it is with you;

²and that we may be delivered from unreasonable and evil men; for all have not faith.

³But the Lord is faithful, who shall establish you, and guard you from the evil one.

⁴And we have confidence in the Lord touching you, that ye both do and will do the things which we command.

⁵And the Lord direct your hearts into the love of God, and into the patience of Christ.

⁶Now we command you, brethren, in the name of our Lord Jesus Christ, that ye withdraw yourselves from every brother that walketh disorderly, and not after the tradition which they received of us.

⁷For yourselves know how ye ought to imitate us: for we behaved not ourselves disorderly among you;

⁸neither did we eat bread for nought at any man's hand, but in labor and travail, working night and day, that we might not burden any of you:

⁹not because we have not the right, but to make ourselves an ensample unto you, that ye should imitate us.

¹⁰For even when we were with you, this we commanded you, If any will not work, neither let him eat.

¹¹For we hear of some that walk among you disorderly, that work not at all, but are busybodies.

¹²Now them that are such we command and exhort in the Lord Jesus Christ, that with quietness they work, and eat their own bread.

¹³But ye, brethren, be not weary in well-doing.

¹⁴And if any man obeyeth not our word by this epistle, note that man, that ye have no company with him, to the end that he may be ashamed.

¹⁵And yet count him not as an enemy, but admonish him as a brother.

¹⁶Now the Lord of peace himself give you peace at all times in all ways. The Lord be with you all.

¹⁷The salutation of me Paul with mine own hand, which is the token in every epistle: so I write.

¹⁸The grace of our Lord Jesus Christ be with you all.

The First Epistle of Paul the Apostle to Timothy

Chapter 1

¹Paul, an apostle of Christ Jesus according to the commandment of God our Saviour, and Christ Jesus our hope;

²unto Timothy, my true child in faith: Grace, mercy, peace, from God the Father and Christ Jesus our Lord.

³As I exhorted thee to tarry at Ephesus, when I was going into Macedonia, that thou mightest charge certain men not to teach a different doctrine,

⁴neither to give heed to fables and endless genealogies, which minister questionings, rather than a dispensation of God which is in faith; so do I now.

⁵But the end of the charge is love out of a pure heart and a good conscience and faith unfeigned:

⁶from which things some having swerved have turned aside unto vain talking;

⁷desiring to be teachers of the law, though they understand neither what they say, nor whereof they confidently affirm.

⁸But we know that the law is good, if a man use it lawfully,

⁹as knowing this, that law is not made for a righteous man, but for the lawless and unruly, for the ungodly and sinners, for the unholy and profane, for murderers of fathers and murderers of mothers, for manslayers,

¹⁰for fornicators, for abusers of themselves with men, for menstealers, for liars, for false swearers, and if there be any other thing contrary to the sound doctrine;

¹¹according to the gospel of the glory of the blessed God, which was committed to my trust.

¹²I thank him that enabled me, even Christ Jesus our Lord, for that he counted me faithful, appointing me to his service;

¹³though I was before a blasphemer, and a persecutor, and injurious: howbeit I obtained mercy, because I did it ignorantly in unbelief;

¹⁴and the grace of our Lord abounded exceedingly with faith and love which is in Christ Jesus.

¹⁵Faithful is the saying, and worthy of all acceptation, that Christ Jesus came into the world to save sinners; of whom I am chief:

¹⁶howbeit for this cause I obtained mercy, that in me as chief might Jesus Christ show forth all his longsuffering, for an ensample of them that should thereafter believe on him unto eternal life.

¹⁷Now unto the King eternal, immortal, invisible, the only God, be honor and glory forever and ever. Amen.

¹⁸This charge I commit unto thee, my child Timothy, according to the prophecies which led the way to thee, that by them thou mayest war the good warfare;

¹⁹holding faith and a good conscience; which some having thrust from them made shipwreck concerning the faith:

²⁰of whom is Hymenaeus and Alexander; whom I delivered unto Satan, that they might be taught not to blaspheme.

Chapter 2

¹I exhort therefore, first of all, that supplications, prayers, intercessions, thanksgivings, be made for all men;

²for kings and all that are in high place; that we may lead a tranquil and quiet life in all godliness and gravity.

³This is good and acceptable in the sight of God our Saviour;

⁴who would have all men to be saved, and come to the knowledge of the truth.

⁵For there is one God, one mediator also between God and men, himself man, Christ Jesus,

⁶who gave himself a ransom for all; the testimony to be borne in its own times;

⁷whereunto I was appointed a preacher and an apostle (I speak the truth, I lie not), a teacher of the Gentiles in faith and truth.

⁸I desire therefore that the men pray in every place, lifting up holy hands, without wrath and disputing.

⁹In like manner, that women adorn themselves in modest apparel, with shamefastness and sobriety; not with braided hair, and gold or pearls or costly raiment;

¹⁰but (which becometh women professing godliness) through good works.

¹¹Let a woman learn in quietness with all subjection.

¹²But I permit not a woman to teach, nor to have dominion over a man, but to be in quietness.

¹³For Adam was first formed, then Eve;

¹⁴and Adam was not beguiled, but the woman being beguiled hath fallen into transgression:

¹⁵but she shall be saved through her child-bearing, if they continue in faith and love and sanctification with sobriety.

Chapter 3

¹Faithful is the saying, If a man seeketh the office of a bishop, he desireth a good work.

²The bishop therefore must be without reproach, the husband of one wife, temperate, sober-minded, orderly, given to hospitality, apt to teach;

³no brawler, no striker; but gentle, not contentious, no lover of money;

⁴one that ruleth well his own house, having his children in subjection with all gravity;

⁵(but if a man knoweth not how to rule his own house, how shall he take care of the church of God?)

⁶not a novice, lest being puffed up he fall into the condemnation of the devil.

⁷Moreover he must have good testimony from them that are without; lest he fall into reproach and the snare of the devil.

⁸Deacons in like manner must be grave, not double-tongued, not given to much wine, not greedy of filthy lucre;

⁹holding the mystery of the faith in a pure conscience.

¹⁰And let these also first be proved; then let them serve as deacons, if they be blameless.

¹¹Women in like manner must be grave, not slanderers, temperate, faithful in all things.

¹²Let deacons be husbands of one wife, ruling their children and their own houses well.

¹³For they that have served well as deacons gain to themselves a good standing, and great boldness in the faith which is in Christ Jesus.

¹⁴These things write I unto thee, hoping to come unto thee shortly;

¹⁵but if I tarry long, that thou mayest know how men ought to behave themselves in the house of God, which is the church of the living God, the pillar and ground of the truth.

¹⁶And without controversy great is the mystery of godliness;
He who was manifested in the flesh,
Justified in the spirit,
Seen of angels,
Preached among the nations,
Believed on in the world,
Received up in glory.

Chapter 4

¹But the Spirit saith expressly, that in later times some shall fall away from the faith, giving heed to seducing spirits and doctrines of demons,

²through the hypocrisy of men that speak lies, branded in their own conscience as with a hot iron;

³forbidding to marry, and commanding to abstain from meats, which God created to be received with thanksgiving by them that believe and know the truth.

⁴For every creature of God is good, and nothing is to be rejected, if it be received with thanksgiving:

⁵for it is sanctified through the word of God and prayer.

⁶If thou put the brethren in mind of these things, thou shalt be a good minister of Christ Jesus, nourished in the words of the faith, and of the good doctrine which thou hast followed until now:

⁷but refuse profane and old wives' fables. And exercise thyself unto godliness:

⁸for bodily exercise is profitable for a little; but godliness is profitable for all things, having promise of the life which now is, and of that which is to come.

⁹Faithful is the saying, and worthy of all acceptation.

¹⁰For to this end we labor and strive, because we have our hope set on the living God, who is the Saviour of all men, specially of them that believe.

¹¹These things command and teach.

¹²Let no man despise thy youth; but be thou an ensample to them that believe, in word, in manner of life, in love, in faith, in purity.

¹³Till I come, give heed to reading, to exhortation, to teaching.

¹⁴Neglect not the gift that is in thee, which was given thee by prophecy, with the laying on of the hands of the presbytery.

¹⁵Be diligent in these things; give thyself wholly to them; that thy progress may be manifest unto all.

¹⁶Take heed to thyself, and to thy teaching. Continue in these things; for in doing this thou shalt save both thyself and them that hear thee.

Chapter 5

¹Rebuke not an elder, but exhort him as a father; the younger men as brethren:

²the elder women as mothers; the younger as sisters, in all purity.

³Honor widows that are widows indeed.

⁴But if any widow hath children or grandchildren, let them learn first to show piety towards their own family, and to requite their parents: for this is acceptable in the sight of God.

⁵Now she that is a widow indeed, and desolate, hath her hope set on God, and continueth in supplications and prayers night and day.

⁶But she that giveth herself to pleasure is dead while she liveth.

⁷These things also command, that they may be without reproach.

⁸But if any provideth not for his own, and specially his own household, he hath denied the faith, and is worse than an unbeliever.

⁹Let none be enrolled as a widow under threescore years old, having been the wife of one man,

¹⁰well reported of for good works; if she hath brought up children, if she hath used hospitality to strangers, if she hath washed the saints' feet, if she hath relieved the afflicted, if she hath diligently followed every good work.

¹¹But younger widows refuse: for when they have waxed wanton against Christ, they desire to marry;

¹²having condemnation, because they have rejected their first pledge.

¹³And withal they learn also to be idle, going about from house to house; and not only idle, but tattlers also and busybodies, speaking things which they ought not.

¹⁴I desire therefore that the younger widows marry, bear children, rule the household, give no occasion to the adversary for reviling:

¹⁵for already some are turned aside after Satan.

16If any woman that believeth hath widows, let her relieve them, and let not the church be burdened; that it may relieve them that are widows indeed.

17Let the elders that rule well be counted worthy of double honor, especially those who labor in the word and in teaching.

18For the scripture saith, Thou shalt not muzzle the ox when he treadeth out the corn. And, The laborer is worthy of his hire.

19Against an elder receive not an accusation, except at the mouth of two or three witnesses.

20Them that sin reprove in the sight of all, that the rest also may be in fear.

21I charge thee in the sight of God, and Christ Jesus, and the elect angels, that thou observe these things without prejudice, doing nothing by partiality.

22Lay hands hastily on no man, neither be partaker of other men's sins: keep thyself pure.

23Be no longer a drinker of water, but use a little wine for thy stomach's sake and thine often infirmities.

24Some men's sins are evident, going before unto judgment; and some men also they follow after.

25In like manner also there are good works that are evident; and such as are otherwise cannot be hid.

Chapter 6

1Let as many as are servants under the yoke count their own masters worthy of all honor, that the name of God and the doctrine be not blasphemed.

2And they that have believing masters, let them not despise them, because they are brethren; but let them serve them the rather, because they that partake of the benefit are believing and beloved. These things teach and exhort.

3If any man teacheth a different doctrine, and consenteth not to sound words, even the words of our Lord Jesus Christ, and to the doctrine which is according to godliness;

4he is puffed up, knowing nothing, but doting about questionings and disputes of words, whereof cometh envy, strife, railings, evil surmisings,

5wranglings of men corrupted in mind and bereft of the truth, supposing that godliness is a way of gain.

6But godliness with contentment is great gain:

7for we brought nothing into the world, for neither can we carry anything out;

8but having food and covering we shall be therewith content.

9But they that are minded to be rich fall into a temptation and a snare and many foolish and hurtful lusts, such as drown men in destruction and perdition.

10For the love of money is a root of all kinds of evil: which some reaching after have been led astray from the faith, and have pierced themselves through with many sorrows.

11But thou, O man of God, flee these things; and follow after righteousness, godliness, faith, love, patience, meekness.

12Fight the good fight of the faith, lay hold on the life eternal, whereunto thou wast called, and didst confess the good confession in the sight of many witnesses.

13I charge thee in the sight of God, who giveth life to all things, and of Christ Jesus, who before Pontius Pilate witnessed the good confession;

14that thou keep the commandment, without spot, without reproach, until the appearing of our Lord Jesus Christ:

15which in its own times he shall show, who is the blessed and only Potentate, the King of kings, and Lord of lords;

16who only hath immortality, dwelling in light unapproachable; whom no man hath seen, nor can see: to whom be honor and power eternal. Amen.

17Charge them that are rich in this present world, that they be not highminded, nor have their hope set on the uncertainty of riches, but on God, who giveth us richly all things to enjoy;

18that they do good, that they be rich in good works, that they be ready to distribute, willing to communicate;

19laying up in store for themselves a good foundation against the time to come, that they may lay hold on the life which is life indeed.

20O Timothy, guard that which is committed unto thee, turning away from the profane babblings and oppositions of the knowledge which is falsely so called;

21which some professing have erred concerning the faith. Grace be with you.

Second Timothy
The Second Epistle of Paul the Apostle to Timothy

Chapter 1

1Paul, an apostle of Christ Jesus through the will of God, according to the promise of the life which is in Christ Jesus,

2to Timothy, my beloved child: Grace, mercy, peace, from God the Father and Christ Jesus our Lord.

3I thank God, whom I serve from my forefathers in a pure conscience, how unceasing is my remembrance of thee in my supplications, night and day

4longing to see thee, remembering thy tears, that I may be filled with joy;

5having been reminded of the unfeigned faith that is in thee; which dwelt first in thy grandmother Lois, and thy mother Eunice; and, I am persuaded, in thee also.

6For which cause I put thee in remembrance that thou stir up the gift of God, which is in thee through the laying on of my hands.

7For God gave us not a spirit of fearfulness; but of power and love and discipline.

8Be not ashamed therefore of the testimony of our Lord, nor of me his prisoner: but suffer hardship with the gospel according to the power of God;

9who saved us, and called us with a holy calling, not according to our works, but according to his own purpose and grace, which was given us in Christ Jesus before times eternal,

10but hath now been manifested by the appearing of our Saviour Christ Jesus, who abolished death, and brought life and immortality to light through the gospel,

11whereunto I was appointed a preacher, and an apostle, and a teacher.

12For which cause I suffer also these things: yet I am not ashamed; for I know him whom I have believed, and I am persuaded that he is able to guard that which I have committed unto him against that day.

13Hold the pattern of sound words which thou hast heard from me, in faith and love which is in Christ Jesus.

14That good thing which was committed unto thee guard through the Holy Spirit which dwelleth in us.

15This thou knowest, that all that are in Asia turned away from me; of whom are Phygelus and Hermogenes.

16The Lord grant mercy unto the house of Onesiphorus: for he oft refreshed me, and was not ashamed of my chain;

17but, when he was in Rome, he sought me diligently, and found me

18(the Lord grant unto him to find mercy of the Lord in that day); and in how many things he ministered at Ephesus, thou knowest very well.

Chapter 2

1Thou therefore, my child, be strengthened in the grace that is in Christ Jesus.

2And the things which thou hast heard from me among many witnesses, the same commit thou to faithful men, who shall be able to teach others also.

3Suffer hardship with me, as a good soldier of Christ Jesus.

4No soldier on service entangleth himself in the affairs of this life; that he may please him who enrolled him as a soldier.

5And if also a man contend in the games, he is not crowded, except he have contended lawfully.

6The husbandmen that laboreth must be the first to partake of the fruits.

7Consider what I say; for the Lord shall give thee understanding in all things.

8Remember Jesus Christ, risen from the dead, of the seed of David, according to my gospel:

9wherein I suffer hardship unto bonds, as a malefactor; but the word of God is not bound.

10Therefore I endure all things for the elect's sake, that they also may obtain the salvation which is in Christ Jesus with eternal glory.

11Faithful is the saying: For if we died with him, we shall also live with him;

12if we endure, we shall also reign with him: if we shall deny him, he also will deny us:

13if we are faithless, he abideth faithful; for he cannot deny himself.

14Of these things put them in remembrance, charging them in the sight of the Lord, that they strive not about words, to no profit, to the subverting of them that hear.

15Give diligence to present thyself approved unto God, a workman that needeth not to be ashamed, handling aright the word of truth.

16But shun profane babblings: for they will proceed further in ungodliness,

17and their word will eat as doth a gangrene: or whom is Hymenaeus an Philetus;

18men who concerning the truth have erred, saying that the resurrection is past already, and overthrow the faith of some.

19Howbeit the firm foundation of God standeth, having this seal, The Lord knoweth them that are his: and, Let every one that nameth the name of the Lord depart from unrighteousness.

20Now in a great house there are not only vessels of gold and of silver, but also of wood and of earth; and some unto honor, and some unto dishonor.

21If a man therefore purge himself from these, he shall be a vessel unto honor, sanctified, meet for the master's use, prepared unto every good work.

22after righteousness, faith, love, pace, with them that call on the Lord out of a pure heart.

23But foolish and ignorant questionings refuse, knowing that they gender strifes.

24And the Lord's servant must not strive, but be gentle towards all, apt to teach, forbearing,

25in meekness correcting them that oppose themselves; if peradventure God may give them repentance unto the knowledge of the truth,

26and they may recover themselves out of the snare of the devil, having been taken captive by him unto his will.

Chapter 3

1But know this, that in the last days grievous times shall come.

2For men shall be lovers of self, lovers of money, boastful, haughty, railers, disobedient to parents, unthankful, unholy,

3without natural affection, implacable, slanderers, without self-control, fierce, no lovers of good,

4traitors, headstrong, puffed up, lovers of pleasure rather than lovers of God;

5holding a form of godliness, but having denied the power therefore. From these also turn away.

6For of these are they that creep into houses, and take captive silly women laden with sins, led away by divers lusts,

7ever learning, and never able to come to the knowledge of the truth.

8And even as Jannes and Jambres withstood Moses, so do these also withstand the truth. Men corrupted in mind, reprobate concerning the faith.

9But they shall proceed no further. For their folly shall be evident unto all men, as theirs also came to be.

10But thou didst follow my teaching, conduct, purpose, faith, longsuffering, love, patience,

11persecutions, sufferings. What things befell me at Antioch, at Iconium, at Lystra; what persecutions I endured. And out of them all the Lord delivered me.

12Yea, and all that would live godly in Christ Jesus shall suffer persecution.

13But evil men and impostors shall wax worse and worse, deceiving and being deceived.

14But abide thou in the things which thou hast learned and hast been assured of, knowing of whom thou hast learned them.

15And that from a babe thou hast known the sacred writings which are able to make thee wise unto salvation through faith which is in Christ Jesus.

16Every scripture inspired of God is also profitable for teaching, for reproof, for correction, for instruction which is in righteousness.

17That the man of God may be complete, furnished completely unto every good work.

Chapter 4

1I charge thee in the sight of God, and of Christ Jesus, who shall judge the living and the dead, and by his appearing and his kingdom:

2preach the word; be urgent in season, out of season; reprove, rebuke, exhort, with all longsuffering and teaching.

3For the time will come when they will not endure the sound doctrine; but, having itching ears, will heap to themselves teachers after their own lusts;

4and will turn away their ears from the truth, and turn aside unto fables.

5But be thou sober in all things, suffer hardship, do the work of an evangelist, fulfil thy ministry.

6For I am already being offered, and the time of my departure is come.

7I have fought the good fight, I have finished the course, I have kept the faith:

8henceforth there is laid up for me the crown of righteousness, which the Lord, the righteous judge, shall give to me at that day; and not to me only, but also to all them that have loved his appearing.

9Give diligence to come shortly unto me:

10for Demas forsook me, having loved this present world, and went to Thessalonica; Crescens to Galatia, Titus to Dalmatia.

11Only Luke is with me. Take Mark, and bring him with thee; for he is useful to me for ministering.

12But Tychicus I sent to Ephesus.

13The cloak that I left at Troas with Carpus, bring when thou comest, and the books, especially the parchments.

14Alexander the coppersmith did me much evil: the Lord will render to him according to his works:

15of whom do thou also beware; for he greatly withstood our words.

16At my first defence no one took my part, but all forsook me: may it not be laid to their account.

17But the Lord stood by me, and strengthened me; that through me the message might be fully proclaimed, and that all the Gentiles might hear: and I was delivered out of the mouth of the lion.

18The Lord will deliver me from every evil work, and will save me unto his heavenly kingdom: to whom be the glory forever and ever. Amen.

19Salute Prisca and Aquila, and the house of Onesiphorus.

20Erastus remained at Corinth: but Trophimus I left at Miletus sick.

21Give diligence to come before winter. Eubulus saluteth thee, and Pudens, and Linus, and Claudia, and all the brethren.

22The Lord be with thy spirit. Grace be with you.

The Epistle of Paul to Titus

Chapter 1

1 Paul, a servant of God, and an apostle of Jesus Christ, according to the faith of God's elect, and the knowledge of the truth which is according to godliness,

2 in hope of eternal life, which God, who cannot lie, promised before times eternal;

3 but in his own seasons manifested his word in the message, wherewith I was intrusted according to the commandment of God our Saviour;

4 to Titus, my true child after a common faith: Grace and peace from God the Father and Christ Jesus our Saviour.

5 For this cause left I thee in Crete, that thou shouldest set in order the things that were wanting, and appoint elders in every city, as I gave thee charge;

6 if any man is blameless, the husband of one wife, having children that believe, who are not accused of riot or unruly.

7 For the bishop must be blameless, as God's steward; not self-willed, not soon angry, no brawler, no striker, not greedy of filthy lucre;

8 but given to hospitality, as lover of good, sober-minded, just, holy, self-controlled;

9 holding to the faithful word which is according to the teaching, that he may be able to exhort in the sound doctrine, and to convict the gainsayers.

10 For there are many unruly men, vain talkers and deceivers, specially they of the circumcision,

11 whose mouths must be stopped; men who overthrow whole houses, teaching things which they ought not, for filthy lucre's sake.

12 One of themselves, a prophet of their own, said, Cretans are always liars, evil beasts, idle gluttons.

13 This testimony is true. For which cause reprove them sharply, that they may be sound in the faith,

14 not giving heed to Jewish fables, and commandments of men who turn away from the truth.

15 To the pure all things are pure: but to them that are defiled and unbelieving nothing is pure; but both their mind and their conscience are defiled.

16 They profess that they know God; but by their works they deny him, being abominable, and disobedient, and unto every good work reprobate.

Chapter 2

1 But speak thou the things which befit the sound doctrine:

2 that aged men be temperate, grave, sober-minded, sound in faith, in love, in patience:

3 that aged women likewise be reverent in demeanor, not slanderers nor enslaved to much wine, teachers of that which is good;

4 that they may train the young women to love their husbands, to love their children,

5 to be sober-minded, chaste, workers at home, kind, being in subjection to their own husbands, that the word of God be not blasphemed:

6 the younger men likewise exhort to be sober-minded:

7 in all things showing thyself an ensample of good works; in thy doctrine showing uncorruptness, gravity,

8 sound speech, that cannot be condemned; that he that is of the contrary part may be ashamed, having no evil thing to say of us.

9 Exhort servants to be in subjection to their own masters, and to be well-pleasing to them in all things; not gainsaying;

10 not purloining, but showing all good fidelity; that they may adorn the doctrine of God our Saviour in all things.

11 For the grace of God hath appeared, bringing salvation to all men,

12 instructing us, to the intent that, denying ungodliness and worldly lusts, we should live soberly and righteously and godly in this present world;

13 looking for the blessed hope and appearing of the glory of the great God and our Saviour Jesus Christ;

14 who gave himself for us, that he might redeem us from all iniquity, and purify unto himself a people for his own possession, zealous of good works.

15 These things speak and exhort and reprove with all authority. Let no man despise thee.

Chapter 3

1 Put them in mind to be in subjection to rulers, to authorities, to be obedient, to be ready unto every good work,

2 to speak evil of no man, not to be contentious, to be gentle, showing all meekness toward all men.

3 For we also once were foolish, disobedient, deceived, serving divers lusts and pleasures, living in malice and envy, hateful, hating one another.

4 But when the kindness of God our Saviour, and his love toward man, appeared,

5 not by works done in righteousness, which we did ourselves, but according to his mercy he saved us, through the washing of regeneration and renewing of the Holy Spirit,

6 which he poured out upon us richly, through Jesus Christ our Saviour;

7 that, being justified by his grace, we might be made heirs according to the hope of eternal life.

8 Faithful is the saying, and concerning these things I desire that thou affirm confidently, to the end that they who have believed God may be careful to maintain good works. These things are good and profitable unto men:

9 but shun foolish questionings, and genealogies, and strifes, and fightings about law; for they are unprofitable and vain.

10 A factious man after a first and second admonition refuse;

11 knowing that such a one is perverted, and sinneth, being self-condemned.

12 When I shall send Artemas unto thee, or Tychicus, give diligence to come unto me to Nicopolis: for there I have determined to winter.

13 Set forward Zenas the lawyer and Apollos on their journey diligently, that nothing be wanting unto them.

14 And let our people also learn to maintain good works for necessary uses, that they be not unfruitful.

15 All that are with me salute thee. Salute them that love us in faith. Grace be with you all.

The Epistle of Paul to Philemon

¹Paul, a prisoner of Christ Jesus, and Timothy our brother, to Philemon our beloved and fellow-worker,

²and to Apphia our sister, and to Archippus our fellow-soldier, and to the church in thy house:

³Grace to you and peace from God our Father and the Lord Jesus Christ.

⁴I thank my God always, making mention of thee in my prayers,

⁵hearing of thy love, and of the faith which thou hast toward the Lord Jesus, and toward all the saints;

⁶that the fellowship of thy faith may become effectual, in the knowledge of every good thing which is in you, unto Christ.

⁷For I had much joy and comfort in thy love, because the hearts of the saints have been refreshed through thee, brother.

⁸Wherefore, though I have all boldness in Christ to enjoin thee that which is befitting,

⁹yet for love's sake I rather beseech, being such a one as Paul the aged, and now a prisoner also of Christ Jesus:

¹⁰I beseech thee for my child, whom I have begotten in my bonds, Onesimus,

¹¹who once was unprofitable to thee, but now is profitable to thee and to me:

¹²whom I have sent back to thee in his own person, that is, my very heart:

¹³whom I would fain have kept with me, that in thy behalf he might minister unto me in the bonds of the gospel:

¹⁴but without thy mind I would do nothing; that thy goodness should not be as of necessity, but of free will.

¹⁵For perhaps he was therefore parted from thee for a season, that thou shouldest have him for ever;

¹⁶no longer as a servant, but more than a servant, a brother beloved, specially to me, but how much rather to thee, both in the flesh and in the Lord.

¹⁷If then thou countest me a partner, receive him as myself.

¹⁸But if he hath wronged the at all, or oweth thee aught, put that to mine account;

¹⁹I Paul write it with mine own hand, I will repay it: that I say not unto thee that thou owest to me even thine own self besides.

²⁰Yea, brother, let me have joy of thee in the Lord: refresh my heart in Christ.

²¹Having confidence in thine obedience I write unto thee, knowing that thou wilt do even beyond what I say.

²²But withal prepare me also a lodging: for I hope that through your prayers I shall be granted unto you.

²³Epaphras, my fellow-prisoner in Christ Jesus, saluteth thee;

²⁴and so do Mark, Aristarchus, Demas, Luke, my fellow-workers.

²⁵The grace of our Lord Jesus Christ be with your spirit. Amen.

The Epistle to the Hebrews

Chapter 1

¹God, having of old time spoken unto the fathers in the prophets by divers portions and in divers manners,

²hath at the end of these days spoken unto us in his Son, whom he appointed heir of all things, through whom also he made the worlds;

³who being the effulgence of his glory, and the very image of his substance, and upholding all things by the word of his power, when he had made purification of sins, sat down on the right hand of the Majesty on high;

⁴having become by so much better than the angels, as he hath inherited a more excellent name than they.

⁵For unto which of the angels said he at any time,
Thou art my Son,
This day have I begotten thee?
and again,
I will be to him a Father,
And he shall be to me a Son?

⁶And when he again bringeth in the firstborn into the world he saith, And let all the angels of God worship him.

⁷And of the angels he saith,
Who maketh his angels winds,
And his ministers a flame a fire:

⁸but of the Son he saith,
Thy throne, O God, is for ever and ever;
And the sceptre of uprightness is the sceptre of thy kingdom.

⁹Thou hast loved righteousness, and hated iniquity;
Therefore God, thy God, hath anointed thee
With the oil of gladness above thy fellows.

¹⁰And,
Thou, Lord, in the beginning didst lay the foundation of the earth,
And the heavens are the works of thy hands:

¹¹They shall perish; but thou continuest:
And they all shall wax old as doth a garment;

¹²And as a mantle shalt thou roll them up,
As a garment, and they shall be changed:
But thou art the same,
And thy years shall not fail.

¹³But of which of the angels hath he said at any time,
Sit thou on my right hand,
Till I make thine enemies the footstool of thy feet?

¹⁴Are they not all ministering spirits, sent forth to do service for the sake of them that shall inherit salvation?

Chapter 2

¹Therefore we ought to give the more earnest heed to the things that were heard, lest haply we drift away from them.

²For if the word spoken through angels proved stedfast, and every transgression and disobedience received a just recompense of reward;

³how shall we escape, if we neglect so great a salvation? which having at the first been spoken through the Lord, was confirmed unto us by them that heard;

⁴God also bearing witness with them, both by signs and wonders, and by manifold powers, and by gifts of the Holy Spirit, according to his own will.

⁵For not unto angels did he subject the world to come, whereof we speak.

⁶But one hath somewhere testified, saying,
What is man, that thou art mindful of him?
Or the son of man, that thou visitest him?

⁷Thou madest him a little lower than the angels;
Thou crownedst him with glory and honor,
And didst set him over the works of thy hands:

⁸Thou didst put all things in subjection under his feet.
For in that he subjected all things unto him, he left nothing that is not subject to him. But now we see not yet all things subjected to him.

⁹But we behold him who hath been made a little lower than the angels, even Jesus, because of the suffering of death crowned with glory and honor, that by the grace of God he should taste of death for every man.

¹⁰For it became him, for whom are all things, and through whom are all things, in bringing many sons unto glory, to make the author of their salvation perfect through sufferings.

¹¹For both he that sanctifieth and they that are sanctified are all of one: for which cause he is not ashamed to call them brethren,

¹²saying,
I will declare thy name unto my brethren,
In the midst of the congregation will I sing thy praise.

¹³And again, I will put my trust in him. And again, Behold, I and the children whom God hath given me.

¹⁴Since then the children are sharers in flesh and blood, he also himself in like manner partook of the same; that through death he might bring to nought him that had the power of death, that is, the devil;

¹⁵and might deliver all them who through fear of death were all their lifetime subject to bondage.

¹⁶For verily not to angels doth he give help, but he giveth help to the seed of Abraham.

¹⁷Wherefore it behooved him in all things to be made like unto his brethren, that he might become a merciful and faithful high priest in things pertaining to God, to make propitiation for the sins of the people.

¹⁸For in that he himself hath suffered being tempted, he is able to succor them that are tempted.

Chapter 3

¹Wherefore, holy brethren, partakers of a heavenly calling, consider the Apostle and High Priest of our confession, even Jesus;

²who was faithful to him that appointed him, as also was Moses in all his house.

³For he hath been counted worthy of more glory than Moses, by so much as he that built the house hath more honor than the house.

⁴For every house is builded by some one; but he that built all things is God.

⁵And Moses indeed was faithful in all his house as a servant, for a testimony of those things which were afterward to be spoken;

⁶but Christ as a son, over his house; whose house are we, if we hold fast our boldness and the glorying of our hope firm unto the end.

⁷Wherefore, even as the Holy Spirit saith,
To-day if ye shall hear his voice,

⁸Harden not your hearts, as in the provocation,
Like as in the day of the trial in the wilderness,

⁹Where your fathers tried me by proving me,
And saw my works forty years.

¹⁰Wherefore I was displeased with this generation,
And said, They do always err in their heart:
But they did not know my ways;

¹¹As I sware in my wrath,
They shall not enter into my rest.

¹²Take heed, brethren, lest haply there shall be in any one of you an evil heart of unbelief, in falling away from the living God:

¹³but exhort one another day by day, so long as it is called To-day; lest any one of you be hardened by the deceitfulness of sin:

¹⁴for we are become partakers of Christ, if we hold fast the beginning of our confidence firm unto the end:

¹⁵while it is said,
To-day if ye shall hear his voice,
Harden not your hearts, as in the provocation.

¹⁶For who, when they heard, did provoke? nay, did not all they that came out of Egypt by Moses?

¹⁷And with whom was he displeased forty years? was it not with them that sinned, whose bodies fell in the wilderness?

¹⁸And to whom sware he that they should not enter into his rest, but to them that were disobedient?

¹⁹And we see that they were not able to enter in because of unbelief.

Chapter 4

¹Let us fear therefore, lest haply, a promise being left of entering into his rest, any one of you should seem to have come short of it.

²For indeed we have had good tidings preached unto us, even as also they: but the word of hearing did not profit them, because it was not united by faith with them that heard.

³For we who have believed do enter into that rest; even as he hath said,
As I sware in my wrath,
They shall not enter into my rest:
although the works were finished from the foundation of the world.

⁴For he hath said somewhere of the seventh day on this wise, And God rested on the seventh day from all his works;

⁵and in this place again,
They shall not enter into my rest.

⁶Seeing therefore it remaineth that some should enter thereinto, and they to whom the good tidings were before preached failed to enter in because of disobedience,

⁷he again defineth a certain day, To-day, saying in David so long a time afterward (even as hath been said before),
To-day if ye shall hear his voice,
Harden not your hearts.

⁸For if Joshua had given them rest, he would not have spoken afterward of another day.

⁹There remaineth therefore a sabbath rest for the people of God.

¹⁰For he that is entered into his rest hath himself also rested from his works, as God did from his.

¹¹Let us therefore give diligence to enter into that rest, that no man fall after the same example of disobedience.

¹²For the word of God is living, and active, and sharper than any two-edged sword, and piercing even to the dividing of soul and spirit, of both joints and marrow, and quick to discern the thoughts and intents of the heart.

¹³And there is no creature that is not manifest in his sight: but all things are naked and laid open before the eyes of him with whom we have to do.

¹⁴Having then a great high priest, who hath passed through the heavens, Jesus the Son of God, let us hold fast our confession.

¹⁵For we have not a high priest that cannot be touched with the feeling of our infirmities; but one that hath been in all points tempted like as we are, yet without sin.

¹⁶Let us therefore draw near with boldness unto the throne of grace, that we may receive mercy, and may find grace to help us in time of need.

Hebrews

Chapter 5

1For every high priest, being taken from among men, is appointed for men in things pertaining to God, that he may offer both gifts and sacrifices for sins:

2who can bear gently with the ignorant and erring, for that he himself also is compassed with infirmity;

3and by reason thereof is bound, as for the people, so also for himself, to offer for sins.

4And no man taketh the honor unto himself, but when he is called of God, even as was Aaron.

5So Christ also glorified not himself to be made a high priest, but he that spake unto him,
Thou art my Son,
This day have I begotten thee:

6as he saith also in another place,
Thou art a priest for ever
After the order of Melchizedek.

7Who in the days of his flesh, having offered up prayers and supplications with strong crying and tears unto him that was able to save him from death, and having been heard for his godly fear,

8though he was a Son, yet learned obedience by the things which he suffered;

9and having been made perfect, he became unto all them that obey him the author of eternal salvation;

10named of God a high priest after the order of Melchizedek.

11Of whom we have many things to say, and hard of interpretation, seeing ye are become dull of hearing.

12For when by reason of the time ye ought to be teachers, ye have need again that some one teach you the rudiments of the first principles of the oracles of God; and are become such as have need of milk, and not of solid food.

13For every one that partaketh of milk is without experience of the word of righteousness; for he is a babe.

14But solid food is for fullgrown men, even those who by reason of use have their senses exercised to discern good and evil.

Chapter 6

1Wherefore leaving the doctrine of the first principles of Christ, let us press on unto perfection; not laying again a foundation of repentance from dead works, and of faith toward God,

2of the teaching of baptisms, and of laying on of hands, and of resurrection of the dead, and of eternal judgment.

3And this will we do, if God permit.

4For as touching those who were once enlightened and tasted of the heavenly gift, and were made partakers of the Holy Spirit,

5and tasted the good word of God, and the powers of the age to come,

6and then fell away, it is impossible to renew them again unto repentance; seeing they crucify to themselves the Son of God afresh, and put him to an open shame.

7For the land which hath drunk the rain that cometh oft upon it, and bringeth forth herbs meet for them for whose sake it is also tilled, receiveth blessing from God:

8but if it beareth thorns and thistles, it is rejected and nigh unto a curse; whose end is to be burned.

9But, beloved, we are persuaded better things of you, and things that accompany salvation, though we thus speak:

10for God is not unrighteous to forget your work and the love which ye showed toward his name, in that ye ministered unto the saints, and still do minister.

11And we desire that each one of you may show the same diligence unto the fulness of hope even to the end:

12that ye be not sluggish, but imitators of them who through faith and patience inherit the promises.

13For when God made promise to Abraham, since he could swear by none greater, he sware by himself,

14saying, Surely blessing I will bless thee, and multiplying I will multiply thee.

15And thus, having patiently endured, he obtained the promise.

16For men swear by the greater: and in every dispute of theirs the oath is final for confirmation.

17Wherein God, being minded to show more abundantly unto the heirs of the promise the immutability of his counsel, interposed with an oath;

18that by two immutable things, in which it is impossible for God to lie, we may have a strong encouragement, who have fled for refuge to lay hold of the hope set before us:

19which we have as an anchor of the soul, a hope both sure and stedfast and entering into that which is within the veil;

20whither as a forerunner Jesus entered for us, having become a high priest for ever after the order of Melchizedek.

Chapter 7

1For this Melchizedek, king of Salem, priest of God Most High, who met Abraham returning from the slaughter of the kings and blessed him,

2to whom also Abraham divided a tenth part of all (being first, by interpretation, King of righteousness, and then also King of Salem, which is King of peace;

3without father, without mother, without genealogy, having neither beginning of days nor end of life, but made like unto the Son of God), abideth a priest continually.

4Now consider how great this man was, unto whom Abraham, the patriarch, gave a tenth out of the chief spoils.

5And they indeed of the sons of Levi that receive the priest's office have commandment to take tithes of the people according to the law, that is, of their brethren, though these have come out of the loins of Abraham:

6but he whose genealogy is not counted from them hath taken tithes of Abraham, and hath blessed him that hath the promises.

7But without any dispute the less is blessed of the better.

8And here men that die receive tithes; but there one, of whom it is witnessed that he liveth.

9And, so to say, through Abraham even Levi, who receiveth tithes, hath paid tithes;

10for he was yet in the loins of his father, when Melchizedek met him.

11Now if there was perfection through the Levitical priesthood (for under it hath the people received the law), what further need was there that another priest should arise after the order of Melchizedek, and not be reckoned after the order of Aaron?

12For the priesthood being changed, there is made of necessity a change also of the law.

13For he of whom these things are said belongeth to another tribe, from which no man hath given attendance at the altar.

14For it is evident that our Lord hath sprung out of Judah; as to which tribe Moses spake nothing concerning priests.

15And what we say is yet more abundantly evident, if after the likeness of Melchizedek there ariseth another priest,

16who hath been made, not after the law of a carnal commandment, but after the power of an endless life:

17for it is witnessed of him,
Thou art a priest for ever
After the order of Melchizedek.

18For there is a disannulling of a foregoing commandment because of its weakness and unprofitableness

19(for the law made nothing perfect), and a bringing in thereupon of a better hope, through which we draw nigh unto God.

20And inasmuch as it is not without the taking of an oath

21(for they indeed have been made priests without an oath; but he with an oath by him that saith of him,
The Lord sware and will not repent himself,
Thou art a priest for ever);

22by so much also hath Jesus become the surety of a better covenant.

23And they indeed have been made priests many in number, because that by death they are hindered from continuing:

24but he, because he abideth for ever, hath his priesthood unchangeable.

25Wherefore also he is able to save to the uttermost them that draw near unto God through him, seeing he ever liveth to make intercession for them.

26For such a high priest became us, holy, guileless, undefiled, separated from sinners, and made higher than the heavens;

27who needeth not daily, like those high priests, to offer up sacrifices, first for his own sins, and then for the sins of the people: for this he did once for all, when he offered up himself.

28For the law appointeth men high priests, having infirmity; but the word of the oath, which was after the law, appointeth a Son, perfected for evermore.

Chapter 8

1Now in the things which we are saying the chief point is this: We have such a high priest, who sat down on the right hand of the throne of the Majesty in the heavens,

2a minister of the sanctuary, and of the true tabernacle, which the Lord pitched, not man.

3For every high priest is appointed to offer both gifts and sacrifices: wherefore it is necessary that this high priest also have somewhat to offer.

4Now if he were on earth, he would not be a priest at all, seeing there are those who offer the gifts according to the law;

5who serve that which is a copy and shadow of the heavenly things, even as Moses is warned of God when he is about to make the tabernacle: for, See, saith he, that thou make all things according to the pattern that was showed thee in the mount.

6But now hath he obtained a ministry the more excellent, by so much as he is also the mediator of a better covenant, which hath been enacted upon better promises.

7For if that first covenant had been faultless, then would no place have been sought for a second.

8For finding fault with them, he saith,
Behold, the days come, saith the Lord,
That I will make a new covenant with the house of Israel and with the house of Judah;

9Not according to the covenant that I made with their fathers
In the day that I took them by the hand to lead them forth out of the land of Egypt;
For they continued not in my covenant,
And I regarded them not, saith the Lord.

10For this is the covenant that I will make with the house of Israel
After those days, saith the Lord;
I will put my laws into their mind,
And on their heart also will I write them:
And I will be to them a God,
And they shall be to me a people:

11And they shall not teach every man his fellow-citizen,
And every man his brother, saying, Know the Lord:
For all shall know me,

From the least to the greatest of them.
12For I will be merciful to their iniquities,
And their sins will I remember no more.

13In that he saith, A new covenant he hath made the first old. But that which is becoming old and waxeth aged is nigh unto vanishing away.

Chapter 9

1Now even a first covenant had ordinances of divine service, and its sanctuary, a sanctuary of this world.

2For there was a tabernacle prepared, the first, wherein were the candlestick, and the table, and the showbread; which is called the Holy place.

3And after the second veil, the tabernacle which is called the Holy of holies;

4having a golden altar of incense, and the ark of the covenant overlaid round about with gold, wherein was a golden pot holding the manna, and Aaron's rod that budded, and the tables of the covenant;

5and above it cherubim of glory overshadowing the mercy-seat; of which things we cannot now speak severally.

6Now these things having been thus prepared, the priests go in continually into the first tabernacle, accomplishing the services;

7but into the second the high priest alone, once in the year, not without blood, which he offereth for himself, and for the errors of the people:

8the Holy Spirit this signifying, that the way into the holy place hath not yet been made manifest, while the first tabernacle is yet standing;

9which is a figure for the time present; according to which are offered both gifts and sacrifices that cannot, as touching the conscience, make the worshipper perfect,

10being only (with meats and drinks and divers washings) carnal ordinances, imposed until a time of reformation.

11But Christ having come a high priest of the good things to come, through the greater and more perfect tabernacle, not made with hands, that is to say, not of this creation,

12nor yet through the blood of goats and calves, but through his own blood, entered in once for all into the holy place, having obtained eternal redemption.

13For if the blood of goats and bulls, and the ashes of a heifer sprinkling them that have been defiled, sanctify unto the cleanness of the flesh:

14how much more shall the blood of Christ, who through the eternal Spirit offered himself without blemish unto God, cleanse your conscience from dead works to serve the living God?

15And for this cause he is the mediator of a new covenant, that a death having taken place for the redemption of the transgressions that were under the first covenant, they that have been called may receive the promise of the eternal inheritance.

16For where a testament is, there must of necessity be the death of him that made it.

17For a testament is of force where there hath been death: for it doth never avail while he that made it liveth.

18Wherefore even the first covenant hath not been dedicated without blood.

19For when every commandment had been spoken by Moses unto all the people according to the law, he took the blood of the calves and the goats, with water and scarlet wool and hyssop, and sprinkled both the book itself and all the people,

20saying, This is the blood of the covenant which God commanded to you-ward.

21Moreover the tabernacle and all the vessels of the ministry he sprinkled in like manner with the blood.

22And according to the law, I may almost say, all things are cleansed with blood, and apart from shedding of blood there is no remission.

23It was necessary therefore that the copies of the things in the heavens should be cleansed with these; but the heavenly things themselves with better sacrifices than these.

24For Christ entered not into a holy place made with hands, like in pattern to the true; but into heaven itself, now to appear before the face of God for us:

25nor yet that he should offer himself often, as the high priest entereth into the holy place year by year with blood not his own;

26else must he often have suffered since the foundation of the world: but now once at the end of the ages hath he been manifested to put away sin by the sacrifice of himself.

27And inasmuch as it is appointed unto men once to die, and after this cometh judgment;

28so Christ also, having been once offered to bear the sins of many, shall appear a second time, apart from sin, to them that wait for him, unto salvation.

Chapter 10

1For the law having a shadow of the good things to come, not the very image of the things, can never with the same sacrifices year by year, which they offer continually, make perfect them that draw nigh.

2Else would they not have ceased to be offered? because the worshippers, having been once cleansed, would have had no more consciousness of sins.

3But in those sacrifices there is a remembrance made of sins year by year.

4For it is impossible that the blood of bulls and goats should take away sins.

5Wherefore when he cometh into the world, he saith,
Sacrifice and offering thou wouldest not,
But a body didst thou prepare for me;

6In whole burnt offerings and sacrifices for sin thou hadst no pleasure:

7Then said I, Lo, I am come (In the roll of the book it is written of me)
To do thy will, O God.

8Saying above, Sacrifices and offerings and whole burnt offerings and sacrifices for sin thou wouldest not, neither hadst pleasure therein (the which are offered according to the law),

9then hath he said, Lo, I am come to do thy will. He taketh away the first, that he may establish the second.

10By which will we have been sanctified through the offering of the body of Jesus Christ once for all.

11And every priest indeed standeth day by day ministering and offering oftentimes the same sacrifices, the which can never take away sins:

12but he, when he had offered one sacrifice for sins for ever, sat down on the right hand of God;

13henceforth expecting till his enemies be made the footstool of his feet.

14For by one offering he hath perfected for ever them that are sanctified.

15And the Holy Spirit also beareth witness to us; for after he hath said,

16This is the covenant that I will make with them
After those days, saith the Lord:
I will put my laws on their heart,
And upon their mind also will I write them;

then saith he,

17And their sins and their iniquities will I remember no more.

18Now where remission of these is, there is no more offering for sin.

19Having therefore, brethren, boldness to enter into the holy place by the blood of Jesus,

20by the way which he dedicated for us, a new and living way, through the veil, that is to say, his flesh;

21and having a great priest over the house of God;

22let us draw near with a true heart in fulness of faith, having our hearts sprinkled from an evil conscience: and having our body washed with pure water,

23let us hold fast the confession of our hope that it waver not; for he is faithful that promised:

24and let us consider one another to provoke unto love and good works;

25not forsaking our own assembling together, as the custom of some is, but exhorting one another; and so much the more, as ye see the day drawing nigh.

26For if we sin wilfully after that we have received the knowledge of the truth, there remaineth no more a sacrifice for sins,

27but a certain fearful expectation of judgment, and a fierceness of fire which shall devour the adversaries.

28A man that hath set at nought Moses law dieth without compassion on the word of two or three witnesses:

29of how much sorer punishment, think ye, shall he be judged worthy, who hath trodden under foot the Son of God, and hath counted the blood of the covenant wherewith he was sanctified an unholy thing, and hath done despite unto the Spirit of grace?

30For we know him that said, Vengeance belongeth unto me, I will recompense. And again, The Lord shall judge his people.

31It is a fearful thing to fall into the hands of the living God.

32But call to remembrance the former days, in which, after ye were enlightened, ye endured a great conflict of sufferings;

33partly, being made a gazingstock both by reproaches and afflictions; and partly, becoming partakers with them that were so used.

34For ye both had compassion on them that were in bonds, and took joyfully the spoiling of your possessions, knowing that ye have for yourselves a better possession and an abiding one.

35Cast not away therefore your boldness, which hath great recompense of reward.

36For ye have need of patience, that, having done the will of God, ye may receive the promise.

37For yet a very little while,
He that cometh shall come, and shall not tarry.

38But my righteous one shall live by faith:
And if he shrink back, my soul hath no pleasure in him.

39But we are not of them that shrink back unto perdition; but of them that have faith unto the saving of the soul.

Chapter 11

1Now faith is assurance of things hoped for, a conviction of things not seen.

2For therein the elders had witness borne to them.

3By faith we understand that the worlds have been framed by the word of God, so that what is seen hath not been made out of things which appear.

4By faith Abel offered unto God a more excellent sacrifice than Cain, through which he had witness borne to him that he was righteous, God bearing witness in respect of his gifts: and through it he being dead yet speaketh.

5By faith Enoch was translated that he should not see death; and he was not found, because God translated him: for he hath had witness borne to him that before his translation he had been well-pleasing unto God:

6And without faith it is impossible to be well-pleasing unto him; for he that cometh to God must believe that he is, and that he is a rewarder of them that seek after him.

7By faith Noah, being warned of God concerning things not seen as yet, moved with godly fear, prepared an ark to the saving of his house; through which he condemned the world, and became heir of the righteousness which is according to faith.

8By faith Abraham, when he was called, obeyed to go out unto a place which he was to receive for an inheritance; and he went out, not knowing whither he went.

9By faith he became a sojourner in the land of promise, as in a land not his own, dwelling in tents, with Isaac and Jacob, the heirs with him of the same promise:

10for he looked for the city which hath the foundations, whose builder and maker is God.

11By faith even Sarah herself received power to conceive seed when she was past age, since she counted him faithful who had promised:

12wherefore also there sprang of one, and him as good as dead, so many as the stars of heaven in multitude, and as the sand, which is by the sea-shore, innumerable.

13These all died in faith, not having received the promises, but having seen them and greeted them from afar, and having confessed that they were strangers and pilgrims on the earth.

14For they that say such things make it manifest that they are seeking after a country of their own.

15And if indeed they had been mindful of that country from which they went out, they would have had opportunity to return.

16But now they desire a better country, that is, a heavenly: wherefore God is not ashamed of them, to be called their God; for he hath prepared for them a city.

17By faith Abraham, being tried, offered up Isaac: yea, he that had gladly received the promises was offering up his only begotten son;

18even he to whom it was said, In Isaac shall thy seed be called:

19accounting that God is able to raise up, even from the dead; from whence he did also in a figure receive him back.

20By faith Isaac blessed Jacob and Esau, even concerning things to come.

21By faith Jacob, when he was dying, blessed each of the sons of Joseph; and worshipped, leaning upon the top of his staff.

22By faith Joseph, when his end was nigh, made mention of the departure of the children of Israel; and gave commandment concerning his bones.

23By faith Moses, when he was born, was hid three months by his parents, because they saw he was a goodly child; and they were not afraid of the king's commandment.

24By faith Moses, when he was grown up, refused to be called the son of Pharaoh's daughter;

25choosing rather to share ill treatment with the people of God, than to enjoy the pleasures of sin for a season;

26accounting the reproach of Christ greater riches than the treasures of Egypt: for he looked unto the recompense of reward.

27By faith he forsook Egypt, not fearing the wrath of the king: for he endured, as seeing him who is invisible.

28By faith he kept the passover, and the sprinkling of the blood, that the destroyer of the firstborn should not touch them.

29By faith they passed through the Red sea as by dry land: which the Egyptians assaying to do were swallowed up.

30By faith the walls of Jericho fell down, after they had been compassed about for seven days.

31By faith Rahab the harlot perished not with them that were disobedient, having received the spies with peace.

32And what shall I more say? for the time will fail me if I tell of Gideon, Barak, Samson, Jephthah; of David and Samuel and the prophets:

33who through faith subdued kingdoms, wrought righteousness, obtained promises, stopped the mouths of lions,

34quenched the power of fire, escaped the edge of the sword, from weakness were made strong, waxed mighty in war, turned to flight armies of aliens.

35Women received their dead by a resurrection: and others were tortured, not accepting their deliverance; that they might obtain a better resurrection:

36and others had trial of mockings and scourgings, yea, moreover of bonds and imprisonment:

37they were stoned, they were sawn asunder, they were tempted, they were slain with the sword: they went about in sheepskins, in goatskins; being destitute, afflicted, ill-treated

38(of whom the world was not worthy), wandering in deserts and mountains and caves, and the holes of the earth.

39And these all, having had witness borne to them through their faith, received not the promise,

40God having provided some better thing concerning us, that apart from us they should not be made perfect.

Chapter 12

1Therefore let us also, seeing we are compassed about with so great a cloud of witnesses, lay aside every weight, and the sin which doth so easily beset us, and let us run with patience the race that is set before us,

2looking unto Jesus the author and perfecter of our faith, who for the joy that was set before him endured the cross, despising shame, and hath sat down at the right hand of the throne of God.

3For consider him that hath endured such gainsaying of sinners against himself, that ye wax not weary, fainting in your souls.

4Ye have not yet resisted unto blood, striving against sin:

5and ye have forgotten the exhortation which reasoneth with you as with sons,

My son, regard not lightly the chastening of the Lord,
Nor faint when thou art reproved of him;

6For whom the Lord loveth he chasteneth,
And scourgeth every son whom he receiveth.

7It is for chastening that ye endure; God dealeth with you as with sons; for what son is there whom his father chasteneth not?

8But if ye are without chastening, whereof all have been made partakers, then are ye bastards, and not sons.

9Furthermore, we had the fathers of our flesh to chasten us, and we gave them reverence: shall we not much rather be in subjection unto the Father of spirits, and live?

10For they indeed for a few days chastened us as seemed good to them; but he for our profit, that we may be partakers of his holiness.

11All chastening seemeth for the present to be not joyous but grievous; yet afterward it yieldeth peaceable fruit unto them that have been exercised thereby, even the fruit of righteousness.

12Wherefore lift up the hands that hang down, and the palsied knees;

13and make straight paths for your feet, that that which is lame be not turned out of the way, but rather be healed.

14Follow after peace with all men, and the sanctification without which no man shall see the Lord:

15looking carefully lest there be any man that falleth short of the grace of God; lest any root of bitterness springing up trouble you, and thereby the many be defiled;

16lest there be any fornication, or profane person, as Esau, who for one mess of meat sold his own birthright.

17For ye know that even when he afterward desired to inherit the blessing, he was rejected; for he found no place for a change of mind in his father, though he sought it diligently with tears.

18For ye are not come unto a mount that might be touched, and that burned with fire, and unto blackness, and darkness, and tempest,

19and the sound of a trumpet, and the voice of words; which voice they that heard entreated that no word more should be spoken unto them;

20for they could not endure that which was enjoined, If even a beast touch the mountain, it shall be stoned;

21and so fearful was the appearance, that Moses said, I exceedingly fear and quake:

22but ye are come unto mount Zion, and unto the city of the living God, the heavenly Jerusalem, and to innumerable hosts of angels,

23to the general assembly and church of the firstborn who are enrolled in heaven, and to God the Judge of all, and to the spirits of just men made perfect,

24and to Jesus the mediator of a new covenant, and to the blood of sprinkling that speaketh better than that of Abel.

25See that ye refuse not him that speaketh. For if they escaped not when they refused him that warned them on earth, much more shall not we escape who turn away from him that warneth from heaven:

26whose voice then shook the earth: but now he hath promised, saying, Yet once more will I make to tremble not the earth only, but also the heaven.

27And this word, Yet once more, signifieth the removing of those things that are shaken, as of things that have been made, that those things which are not shaken may remain.

28Wherefore, receiving a kingdom that cannot be shaken, let us have grace, whereby we may offer service well-pleasing to God with reverence and awe:

29for our God is a consuming fire.

Chapter 13

1Let love of the brethren continue.

2Forget not to show love unto strangers: for thereby some have entertained angels unawares.

3Remember them that are in bonds, as bound with them; them that are illtreated, as being yourselves also in the body.

4Let marriage be had in honor among all, and let the bed be undefiled: for fornicators and adulterers God will judge.

5Be ye free from the love of money; content with such things as ye have: for himself hath said, I will in no wise fail thee, neither will I in any wise forsake thee.

6So that with good courage we say,

The Lord is my helper; I will not fear:
What shall man do unto me?

7Remember them that had the rule over you, men that spake unto you the word of God; and considering the issue of their life, imitate their faith.

8Jesus Christ is the same yesterday and to-day, yea and for ever.

9Be not carried away by divers and strange teachings: for it is good that the heart be established by grace; not by meats, wherein they that occupied themselves were not profited.

10We have an altar, whereof they have no right to eat that serve the tabernacle.

11For the bodies of those beasts whose blood is brought into the holy place by the high priest as an offering for sin, are burned without the camp.

12Wherefore Jesus also, that he might sanctify the people through his own blood, suffered without the gate.

13Let us therefore go forth unto him without the camp, bearing his reproach.

14For we have not here an abiding city, but we seek after the city which is to come.

15Through him then let us offer up a sacrifice of praise to God continually, that is, the fruit of lips which make confession to his name.

16But to do good and to communicate forget not: for with such sacrifices God is well pleased.

17Obey them that have the rule over you, and submit to them: for they watch in behalf of your souls, as they that shall give account; that they may do this with joy, and not with grief: for this were unprofitable for you.

18Pray for us: for we are persuaded that we have a good conscience, desiring to live honorably in all things.

19And I exhort you the more exceedingly to do this, that I may be restored to you the sooner.

20Now the God of peace, who brought again from the dead the great shepherd of the sheep with the blood of an eternal covenant, even our Lord Jesus,

21make you perfect in every good thing to do his will, working in us that which is well-pleasing in his sight, through Jesus Christ; to whom be the glory for ever and ever. Amen.

²²But I exhort you, brethren, bear with the word of exhortation, for I have written unto you in few words.

²³Know ye that our brother Timothy hath been set at liberty; with whom, if he come shortly, I will see you.

²⁴Salute all them that have the rule over you, and all the saints. They of Italy salute you.

²⁵Grace be with you all. Amen.

James
The General Epistle of James

Chapter 1

1James, a servant of God and of the Lord Jesus Christ, to the twelve tribes which are of the Dispersion, greeting.

2Count it all joy, my brethren, when ye fall into manifold temptations;

3Knowing that the proving of your faith worketh patience.

4And let patience have its perfect work, that ye may be perfect and entire, lacking in nothing.

5But if any of you lacketh wisdom, let him ask of God, who giveth to all liberally and upbraideth not; and it shall be given him.

6But let him ask in faith, nothing doubting: for he that doubteth is like the surge of the sea driven by the wind and tossed.

7For let not that man think that he shall receive anything of the Lord;

8a doubleminded man, unstable in all his ways.

9But let the brother of low degree glory in his high estate:

10and the rich, in that he is made low: because as the flower of the grass he shall pass away.

11For the sun ariseth with the scorching wind, and withereth the grass: and the flower thereof falleth, and the grace of the fashion of it perisheth: so also shall the rich man fade away in his goings.

12Blessed is the man that endureth temptation; for when he hath been approved, he shall receive the crown of life, which the Lord promised to them that love him.

13Let no man say when he is tempted, I am tempted of God; for God cannot be tempted with evil, and he himself tempteth no man:

14but each man is tempted, when he is drawn away by his own lust, and enticed.

15Then the lust, when it hath conceived, beareth sin: and the sin, when it is fullgrown, bringeth forth death.

16Be not deceived, my beloved brethren.

17Every good gift and every perfect gift is from above, coming down from the Father of lights, with whom can be no variation, neither shadow that is cast by turning.

18Of his own will he brought us forth by the word of truth, that we should be a kind of firstfruits of his creatures.

19Ye know this, my beloved brethren. But let every man be swift to hear, slow to speak, slow to wrath:

20for the wrath of man worketh not the righteousness of God.

21Wherefore putting away all filthiness and overflowing of wickedness, receive with meekness the implanted word, which is able to save your souls.

22But be ye doers of the word, and not hearers only, deluding your own selves.

23For if any one is a hearer of the word and not a doer, he is like unto a man beholding his natural face in a mirror:

24for he beholdeth himself, and goeth away, and straightway forgetteth what manner of man he was.

25But he that looketh into the perfect law, the law of liberty, and so continueth, being not a hearer that forgetteth but a doer that worketh, this man shall be blessed in his doing.

26If any man thinketh himself to be religious, while he bridleth not his tongue but deceiveth his heart, this man's religion is vain.

27Pure religion and undefiled before our God and Father is this, to visit the fatherless and widows in their affliction, and to keep oneself unspotted from the world.

Chapter 2

1My brethren, hold not the faith of our Lord Jesus Christ, the Lord of glory, with respect of persons.

2For if there come into your synagogue a man with a gold ring, in fine clothing, and there come in also a poor man in vile clothing;

3and ye have regard to him that weareth the fine clothing, and say, Sit thou here in a good place; and ye say to the poor man, Stand thou there, or sit under my footstool;

4Do ye not make distinctions among yourselves, and become judges with evil thoughts?

5Hearken, my beloved brethren; did not God choose them that are poor as to the world to be rich in faith, and heirs of the kingdom which he promised to them that love him?

6But ye have dishonored the poor man. Do not the rich oppress you, and themselves drag you before the judgment-seats?

7Do not they blaspheme the honorable name by which ye are called?

8Howbeit if ye fulfil the royal law, according to the scripture, Thou shalt love thy neighbor as thyself, ye do well:

9but if ye have respect of persons, ye commit sin, being convicted by the law as transgressors.

10For whosoever shall keep the whole law, and yet stumble in one point, he is become guilty of all.

11For he that said, Do not commit adultery, said also, Do not kill. Now if thou dost not commit adultery, but killest, thou art become a transgressor of the law.

12So speak ye, and so do, as men that are to be judged by a law of liberty.

13For judgment is without mercy to him that hath showed no mercy: mercy glorieth against judgment.

14What doth it profit, my brethren, if a man say he hath faith, but have not works? can that faith save him?

15If a brother or sister be naked and in lack of daily food,

16and one of you say unto them, Go in peace, be ye warmed and filled; and yet ye give them not the things needful to the body; what doth it profit?

17Even so faith, if it have not works, is dead in itself.

18Yea, a man will say, Thou hast faith, and I have works: show me thy faith apart from thy works, and I by my works will show thee my faith.

19Thou believest that God is one; thou doest well: the demons also believe, and shudder.

20But wilt thou know, O vain man, that faith apart from works is barren?

21Was not Abraham our father justified by works, in that he offered up Isaac his son upon the altar?

22Thou seest that faith wrought with his works, and by works was faith made perfect;

23and the scripture was fulfilled which saith, And Abraham believed God, and it was reckoned unto him for righteousness; and he was called the friend of God.

24Ye see that by works a man is justified, and not only by faith.

25And in like manner was not also Rahab the harlot justified by works, in that she received the messengers, and sent them out another way?

26For as the body apart from the spirit is dead, even so faith apart from works is dead.

Chapter 3

1Be not many of you teachers, my brethren, knowing that we shall receive heavier judgment.

2For in many things we all stumble. If any stumbleth not in word, the same is a perfect man, able to bridle the whole body also.

3Now if we put the horses' bridles into their mouths that they may obey us, we turn about their whole body also.

4Behold, the ships also, though they are so great and are driven by rough winds, are yet turned about by a very small rudder, whither the impulse of the steersman willeth.

5So the tongue also is a little member, and boasteth great things. Behold, how much wood is kindled by how small a fire!

6And the tongue is a fire: the world of iniquity among our members is the tongue, which defileth the whole body, and setteth on fire the wheel of nature, and is set on fire by hell.

7For every kind of beasts and birds, of creeping things and things in the sea, is tamed, and hath been tamed by mankind.

8But the tongue can no man tame; it is a restless evil, it is full of deadly poison.

9Therewith bless we the Lord and Father; and therewith curse we men, who are made after the likeness of God:

10out of the same mouth cometh forth blessing and cursing. My brethren, these things ought not so to be.

11Doth the fountain send forth from the same opening sweet water and bitter?

12Can a fig tree, my brethren, yield olives, or a vine figs? Neither can salt water yield sweet.

13Who is wise and understanding among you? let him show by his good life his works in meekness of wisdom.

14But if ye have bitter jealousy and faction in your heart, glory not and lie not against the truth.

15This wisdom is not a wisdom that cometh down from above, but is earthly, sensual, devilish.

16For where jealousy and faction are, there is confusion and every vile deed.

17But the wisdom that is from above is first pure, then peaceable, gentle, easy to be entreated, full of mercy and good fruits, without variance, without hypocrisy.

18And the fruit of righteousness is sown in peace for them that make peace.

Chapter 4

1Whence come wars and whence come fightings among you? come they not hence, even of your pleasures that war in your members?

2Ye lust, and have not: ye kill, and covet, and cannot obtain: ye fight and war; ye have not, because ye ask not.

3Ye ask, and receive not, because ye ask amiss, that ye may spend it in your pleasures.

4Ye adulteresses, know ye not that the friendship of the world is enmity with God? Whosoever therefore would be a friend of the world maketh himself an enemy of God.

5Or think ye that the scripture speaketh in vain? Doth the spirit which he made to dwell in us long unto envying?

6But he giveth more grace. Wherefore the scripture saith, God resisteth the proud, but giveth grace to the humble.

7Be subject therefore unto God; but resist the devil, and he will flee from you.

8Draw nigh to God, and he will draw nigh to you. Cleanse your hands, ye sinners; and purify your hearts, ye doubleminded.

9Be afflicted, and mourn, and weep: let your laughter be turned to mourning, and your joy to heaviness.

10Humble yourselves in the sight of the Lord, and he shall exalt you.

11Speak not one against another, brethren. He that speaketh against a brother, or judgeth his brother, speaketh against the law, and judgeth the law: but if thou judgest the law, thou art not a doer of the law, but a judge.

12One only is the lawgiver and judge, even he who is able to save and to destroy: but who art thou that judgest thy neighbor?

¹³Come now, ye that say, To-day or to-morrow we will go into this city, and spend a year there, and trade, and get gain:

¹⁴whereas ye know not what shall be on the morrow. What is your life? For ye are a vapor, that appeareth for a little time, and then vanisheth away.

¹⁵For that ye ought to say, If the Lord will, we shall both live, and do this or that.

¹⁶But now ye glory in your vauntings: all such glorying is evil.

¹⁷To him therefore that knoweth to do good, and doeth it not, to him it is sin.

Chapter 5

¹Come now, ye rich, weep and howl for your miseries that are coming upon you.

²Your riches are corrupted, and your garments are moth-eaten.

³Your gold and your silver are rusted; and their rust shall be for a testimony against you, and shall eat your flesh as fire. Ye have laid up your treasure in the last days.

⁴Behold, the hire of the laborers who mowed your fields, which is of you kept back by fraud, crieth out: and the cries of them that reaped have entered into the ears of the Lord of Sabaoth.

⁵Ye have lived delicately on the earth, and taken your pleasure; ye have nourished your hearts in a day of slaughter.

⁶Ye have condemned, ye have killed the righteous one; he doth not resist you.

⁷Be patient therefore, brethren, until the coming of the Lord. Behold, the husbandman waiteth for the precious fruit of the earth, being patient over it, until it receive the early and latter rain.

⁸Be ye also patient; establish your hearts: for the coming of the Lord is at hand.

⁹Murmur not, brethren, one against another, that ye be not judged: behold, the judge standeth before the doors.

¹⁰Take, brethren, for an example of suffering and of patience, the prophets who spake in the name of the Lord.

¹¹Behold, we call them blessed that endured: ye have heard of the patience of Job, and have seen the end of the Lord, how that the Lord is full of pity, and merciful.

¹²But above all things, my brethren, swear not, neither by the heaven, nor by the earth, nor by any other oath: but let your yea be yea, and your nay, nay; that ye fall not under judgment.

¹³Is any among you suffering? Let him pray. Is any cheerful? Let him sing praise.

¹⁴Is any among you sick? Let him call for the elders of the church; and let them pray over him, anointing him with oil in the name of the Lord:

¹⁵and the prayer of faith shall save him that is sick, and the Lord shall raise him up; and if he have committed sins, it shall be forgiven him.

¹⁶Confess therefore your sins one to another, and pray one for another, that ye may be healed. The supplication of a righteous man availeth much in its working.

¹⁷Elijah was a man of like passions with us, and he prayed fervently that it might not rain; and it rained not on the earth for three years and six months.

¹⁸And he prayed again; and the heaven gave rain, and the earth brought forth her fruit.

¹⁹My brethren, if any among you err from the truth, and one convert him;

²⁰let him know, that he who converteth a sinner from the error of his way shall save a soul from death, and shall cover a multitude of sins.

First Peter
The First Epistle General of Peter

Chapter 1

1Peter, an apostle of Jesus Christ, to the elect who are sojourners of the Dispersion in Pontus, Galatia, Cappadocia, Asia, and Bithynia,

2according to the foreknowledge of God the Father, in sanctification of the Spirit, unto obedience and sprinkling of the blood of Jesus Christ: Grace to you and peace be multiplied.

3Blessed be the God and Father of our Lord Jesus Christ, who according to his great mercy begat us again unto a living hope by the resurrection of Jesus Christ from the dead,

4unto an inheritance incorruptible, and undefiled, and that fadeth not away, reserved in heaven for you,

5who by the power of God are guarded through faith unto a salvation ready to be revealed in the last time.

6Wherein ye greatly rejoice, though now for a little while, if need be, ye have been put to grief in manifold trials,

7that the proof of your faith, being more precious than gold that perisheth though it is proved by fire, may be found unto praise and glory and honor at the revelation of Jesus Christ:

8whom not having seen ye love; on whom, though now ye see him not, yet believing, ye rejoice greatly with joy unspeakable and full of glory:

9receiving the end of your faith, even the salvation of your souls.

10Concerning which salvation the prophets sought and searched diligently, who prophesied of the grace that should come unto you:

11searching what time or what manner of time the Spirit of Christ which was in them did point unto, when it testified beforehand the sufferings of Christ, and the glories that should follow them.

12To whom it was revealed, that not unto themselves, but unto you, did they minister these things, which now have been announced unto you through them that preached the gospel unto you by the Holy Spirit sent forth from heaven; which things angel desire to look into.

13Wherefore girding up the loins of your mind, be sober and set your hope perfectly on the grace that is to be brought unto you at the revelation of Jesus Christ;

14as children of obedience, not fashioning yourselves according to your former lusts in the time of your ignorance:

15but like as he who called you is holy, be ye yourselves also holy in all manner of living;

16because it is written, Ye shall be holy; for I am holy.

17And if ye call on him as Father, who without respect of persons judgeth according to each man's work, pass the time of your sojourning in fear:

18knowing that ye were redeemed, not with corruptible things, with silver or gold, from your vain manner of life handed down from your fathers;

19but with precious blood, as of a lamb without spot, even the blood of Christ:

20who was foreknown indeed before the foundation of the world, but was manifested at the end of times for your sake,

21who through him are believers in God, that raised him from the dead, and gave him glory; so that your faith and hope might be in God.

22Seeing ye have purified your souls in your obedience to the truth unto unfeigned love of the brethren, love one another from the heart fervently:

23having been begotten again, not of corruptible seed, but of incorruptible, through the word of God, which liveth and abideth.

24For, All flesh is as grass, And all the glory thereof as the flower of grass. The grass withereth, and the flower falleth:

25But the word of the Lord abideth for ever. And this is the word of good tidings which was preached unto you.

Chapter 2

1Putting away therefore all wickedness, and all guile, and hypocrisies, and envies, and all evil speakings,

2as newborn babes, long for the spiritual milk which is without guile, that ye may grow thereby unto salvation;

3if ye have tasted that the Lord is gracious:

4unto whom coming, a living stone, rejected indeed of men, but with God elect, precious,

5ye also, as living stones, are built up a spiritual house, to be a holy priesthood, to offer up spiritual sacrifices, acceptable to God through Jesus Christ.

6Because it is contained in scripture,
Behold, I lay in Zion a chief corner stone, elect, precious:
And he that believeth on him shall not be put to shame.

7For you therefore that believe is the preciousness: but for such as disbelieve,
The stone which the builders rejected,
The same was made the head of the corner;

8and,
A stone of stumbling, and a rock of offence;
for they stumble at the word, being disobedient: whereunto also they were appointed.

9But ye are a elect race, a royal priesthood, a holy nation, a people for God's own possession, that ye may show forth the excellencies of him who called you out of darkness into his marvellous light:

10who in time past were no people, but now are the people of God: who had not obtained mercy, but now have obtained mercy.

11Beloved, I beseech you as sojourners and pilgrims, to abstain from fleshly lust, which war against the soul;

12having your behavior seemly among the Gentiles; that, wherein they speak against you as evil-doers, they may by your good works, which they behold, glorify God in the day of visitation.

13Be subject to every ordinance of man for the Lord's sake: whether to the king, as supreme;

14or unto governors, as sent by him for vengeance on evil-doers and for praise to them that do well.

15For so is the will of God, that by well-doing ye should put to silence the ignorance of foolish men:

16as free, and not using your freedom for a cloak of wickedness, but as bondservants of God.

17Honor all men. Love the brotherhood. Fear God. Honor the king.

18Servants, be in subjection to your masters with all fear; not only to the good and gentle, but also to the froward.

19For this is acceptable, if for conscience toward God a man endureth griefs, suffering wrongfully.

20For what glory is it, if, when ye sin, and are buffeted for it, ye shall take it patiently? but if, when ye do well, and suffer for it, ye shall take it patiently, this is acceptable with God.

21For hereunto were ye called: because Christ also suffered for you, leaving you an example, that ye should follow his steps:

22who did no sin, neither was guile found in his mouth:

23who, when he was reviled, reviled not again; when he suffered threatened not; but committed himself to him that judgeth righteously:

24who his own self bare our sins in his body upon the tree, that we, having died unto sins, might live unto righteousness; by whose stripes ye were healed.

25For ye were going astray like sheep; but are now returned unto the Shepherd and Bishop of your souls.

Chapter 3

1In like manner, ye wives, be in subjection to your own husbands; that, even if any obey not the word, they may without the word be gained by the behavior of their wives;

2beholding your chaste behavior coupled with fear.

3Whose adorning let it not be the outward adorning of braiding the hair, and of wearing jewels of gold, or of putting on apparel,

4but let it be the hidden man of the heart, in the incorruptible apparel of a meek and quiet spirit, which is in the sight of God of great price.

5For after this manner aforetime the holy women also, who hoped in God, adorned themselves, being in subjection to their own husbands:

6as Sarah obeyed Abraham, calling him lord: whose children ye now are, if ye do well, and are not put in fear by any terror.

7Ye husbands, in like manner, dwell with your wives according to knowledge, giving honor unto the woman, as unto the weaker vessel, as being also joint-heirs of the grace of life; to the end that your prayers be not hindered.

8Finally, be ye all likeminded, compassionate, loving as brethren, tenderhearted, humbleminded:

9not rendering evil for evil, or reviling for reviling; but contrariwise blessing; for hereunto were ye called, that ye should inherit a blessing.

10For,
He that would love life,
And see good days,
Let him refrain his tongue from evil,
And his lips that they speak no guile:

11And let him turn away from evil, and do good;
Let him seek peace, and pursue it.

12For the eyes of the Lord are upon the righteous,
And his ears unto their supplication:
But the face of the Lord is upon them that do evil.

13And who is he that will harm you, if ye be zealous of that which is good?

14But even if ye should suffer for righteousness' sake, blessed are ye: and fear not their fear, neither be troubled;

15but sanctify in your hearts Christ as Lord: being ready always to give answer to every man that asketh you a reason concerning the hope that is in you, yet with meekness and fear:

16having a good conscience; that, wherein ye are spoken against, they may be put to shame who revile your good manner of life in Christ.

17For it is better, if the will of God should so will, that ye suffer for well-doing than for evil-doing.

18Because Christ also suffered for sins once, the righteous for the unrighteous, that he might bring us to God; being put to death in the flesh, but made alive in the spirit;

19in which also he went and preached unto the spirits in prison,

20that aforetime were disobedient, when the longsuffering of God waited in the days of Noah, while the ark was a preparing, wherein few, that is, eight souls, were saved through water:

21which also after a true likeness doth now save you, even baptism, not the putting away of the filth of the flesh, but the interrogation of a good conscience toward God, through the resurrection of Jesus Christ;

22who is one the right hand of God, having gone into heaven; angels and authorities and powers being made subject unto him.

Chapter 4

¹Forasmuch then as Christ suffered in the flesh, arm ye yourselves also with the same mind; for he that hath suffered in the flesh hath ceased from sin;

²that ye no longer should live the rest of your time in flesh to the lusts of men, but to the will of God.

³For the time past may suffice to have wrought the desire of the Gentiles, and to have walked in lasciviousness, lusts, winebibbings, revellings, carousings, and abominable idolatries:

⁴wherein they think strange that ye run not with them into the same excess of riot, speaking evil of you:

⁵who shall give account to him that is ready to judge the living and the dead.

⁶For unto this end was the gospel preached even to the dead, that they might be judged indeed according to men in the flesh, but live according to God in the spirit.

⁷But the end of all things is at hand: be ye therefore of sound mind, and be sober unto prayer:

⁸above all things being fervent in your love among yourselves; for love covereth a multitude of sins:

⁹using hospitality one to another without murmuring:

¹⁰according as each hath received a gift, ministering it among yourselves, as good stewards of the manifold grace of God;

¹¹if any man speaketh, speaking as it were oracles of God; is any man ministereth, ministering as of the strength which God supplieth: that in all things God may be glorified through Jesus Christ, whose is the glory and the dominion for ever and ever. Amen.

¹²Beloved, think it not strange concerning the fiery trial among you, which cometh upon you to prove you, as though a strange thing happened unto you:

¹³but insomuch as ye are partakers of Christ's sufferings, rejoice; that at the revelation of his glory also ye may rejoice with exceeding joy.

¹⁴If ye are reproached for the name of Christ, blessed are ye; because the Spirit of glory and the Spirit of God resteth upon you.

¹⁵For let none of you suffer as a murderer, or a thief, or an evil-doer, or as a meddler in other men's matters:

¹⁶but if a man suffer as a Christian, let him not be ashamed; but let him glorify God in this name.

¹⁷For the time is come for judgment to begin at the house of God: and if it begin first at us, what shall be the end of them that obey not the gospel of God?

¹⁸And if the righteous is scarcely saved, where shall the ungodly and sinner appear?

¹⁹Wherefore let them also that suffer according to the will of God commit their souls in well-doing unto a faithful Creator.

Chapter 5

¹The elders among you I exhort, who am a fellow-elder, and a witness of the sufferings of Christ, who am also a partaker of the glory that shall be revealed:

²Tend the flock of God which is among you, exercising the oversight, not of constraint, but willingly, according to the will of God; nor yet for filthy lucre, but of a ready mind;

³neither as lording it over the charge allotted to you, but making yourselves ensamples to the flock.

⁴And when the chief Shepherd shall be manifested, ye shall receive the crown of glory that fadeth not away.

⁵Likewise, ye younger, be subject unto the elder. Yea, all of you gird yourselves with humility, to serve one another: for God resisteth the proud, but giveth grace to the humble.

⁶Humble yourselves therefore under the mighty hand of God, that he may exalt you in due time;

⁷casting all your anxiety upon him, because he careth for you.

⁸Be sober, be watchful: your adversary the devil, as a roaring lion, walketh about, seeking whom he may devour,

⁹whom withstand stedfast in your faith, knowing that the same sufferings are accomplished in your brethren who are in the world.

¹⁰And the God of all grace, who called you unto his eternal glory in Christ, after that ye have suffered a little while, shall himself perfect, establish, strengthen you.

¹¹To him be the dominion for ever and ever. Amen.

¹²By Silvanus, our faithful brother, as I account him, I have written unto you briefly, exhorting, and testifying that this is the true grace of God. Stand ye fast therein.

¹³She that is in Babylon, elect together with you, saluteth you; and so doth Mark my son.

¹⁴Salute one another with a kiss of love. Peace be unto you all that are in Christ.

Second Peter
The Second Epistle General of Peter

Chapter 1

1 Simon Peter, a servant and apostle of Jesus Christ, to them that have obtained a like precious faith with us in the righteousness of our God and the Saviour Jesus Christ:

2 Grace to you and peace be multiplied in the knowledge of God and of Jesus our Lord;

3 seeing that his divine power hath granted unto us all things that pertain unto life and godliness, through the knowledge of him that called us by his own glory and virtue;

4 whereby he hath granted unto us his precious and exceeding great promises; that through these ye may become partakers of the divine nature, having escaped from the corruption that is in the world by lust.

5 Yea, and for this very cause adding on your part all diligence, in your faith supply virtue; and in your virtue knowledge;

6 and in your knowledge self-control; and in your self-control patience; and in your patience godliness;

7 and in your godliness brotherly kindness; and in your brotherly kindness love.

8 For if these things are yours and abound, they make you to be not idle nor unfruitful unto the knowledge of our Lord Jesus Christ.

9 For he that lacketh these things is blind, seeing only what is near, having forgotten the cleansing from his old sins.

10 Wherefore, brethren, give the more diligence to make your calling and election sure: for if ye do these things, ye shall never stumble:

11 for thus shall be richly supplied unto you the entrance into the eternal kingdom of our Lord and Saviour Jesus Christ.

12 Wherefore I shall be ready always to put you in remembrance of these things, though ye know them, and are established in the truth which is with you.

13 And I think it right, as long as I am in this tabernacle, to stir you up by putting you in remembrance;

14 knowing that the putting off of my tabernacle cometh swiftly, even as our Lord Jesus Christ signified unto me.

15 Yea, I will give diligence that at every time ye may be able after my decease to call these things to remembrance.

16 For we did not follow cunningly devised fables, when we made known unto you the power and coming of our Lord Jesus Christ, but we were eyewitnesses of his majesty.

17 For he received from God the Father honor and glory, when there was borne such a voice to him by the Majestic Glory, This is my beloved Son, in whom I am well pleased:

18 and this voice we ourselves heard borne out of heaven, when we were with him in the holy mount.

19 And we have the word of prophecy made more sure; whereunto ye do well that ye take heed, as unto a lamp shining in a dark place, until the day dawn, and the day-star arise in your hearts;

20 knowing this first, that no prophecy of scripture is of private interpretation.

21 For no prophecy ever came by the will of man: but men spake from God, being moved by the Holy Spirit.

Chapter 2

2 1 But there arose false prophets also among the people, as among you also there shall be false teachers, who shall privily bring in destructive heresies, denying even the Master that bought them, bringing upon themselves swift destruction.

2 And many shall follow their lascivious doings; by reason of whom the way of the truth shall be evil spoken of.

3 And in covetousness shall they with feigned words make merchandise of you: whose sentence now from of old lingereth not, and their destruction slumbereth not.

4 For if God spared not angels when they sinned, but cast them down to hell, and committed them to pits of darkness, to be reserved unto judgment;

5 and spared not the ancient world, but preserved Noah with seven others, a preacher of righteousness, when he brought a flood upon the world of the ungodly;

6 and turning the cities of Sodom and Gomorrah into ashes condemned them with an overthrow, having made them an example unto those that should live ungodly;

7 and delivered righteous Lot, sore distressed by the lascivious life of the wicked

8 (for that righteous man dwelling among them, in seeing and hearing, vexed his righteous soul from day to day with their lawless deeds):

9 the Lord knoweth how to deliver the godly out of temptation, and to keep the unrighteous under punishment unto the day of judgment;

10 but chiefly them that walk after the flesh in the lust of defilement, and despise dominion. Daring, self-willed, they tremble not to rail at dignities:

11 whereas angels, though greater in might and power, bring not a railing judgment against them before the Lord.

12 But these, as creatures without reason, born mere animals to be taken and destroyed, railing in matters whereof they are ignorant, shall in their destroying surely be destroyed;

13 suffering wrong as the hire of wrong-doing; men that count it pleasure to revel in the day-time, spots and blemishes, revelling in their deceivings while they feast with you;

14 having eyes full of adultery, and that cannot cease from sin; enticing unstedfast souls; having a heart exercised in covetousness; children of cursing;

15 forsaking the right way, they went astray, having followed the way of Balaam the son of Beor, who loved the hire of wrong-doing;

16 but he was rebuked for his own transgression: a dumb ass spake with man's voice and stayed the madness of the prophet.

17 These are springs without water, and mists driven by a storm; for whom the blackness of darkness hath been reserved.

18 For, uttering great swelling words of vanity, they entice in the lusts of the flesh, by lasciviousness, those who are just escaping from them that live in error;

19 promising them liberty, while they themselves are bondservants of corruption; for of whom a man is overcome, of the same is he also brought into bondage.

20 For if, after they have escaped the defilements of the world through the knowledge of the Lord and Saviour Jesus Christ, they are again entangled therein and overcome, the last state is become worse with them than the first.

21 For it were better for them not to have known the way of righteousness, than, after knowing it, to turn back from the holy commandment delivered unto them.

22 It has happened unto them according to the true proverb, The dog turning to his own vomit again, and the sow that had washed to wallowing in the mire.

Chapter 3

1 This is now, beloved, the second epistle that I write unto you; and in both of them I stir up your sincere mind by putting you in remembrance;

2 that ye should remember the words which were spoken before by the holy prophets, and the commandments of the Lord and Saviour through your apostles:

3 knowing this first, that in the last days mockers shall come with mockery, walking after their own lusts,

4 and saying, Where is the promise of his coming? for, from the day that the fathers fell asleep, all things continue as they were from the beginning of the creation.

5 For this they willfully forget, that there were heavens from of old, and an earth compacted out of water and amidst water, by the word of God;

6 by which means the world that then was, being overflowed with water, perished:

7 but the heavens that now are, and the earth, by the same word have been stored up for fire, being reserved against the day of judgment and destruction of ungodly men.

8 But forget not this one thing, beloved, that one day is with the Lord as a thousand years, and a thousand years as one day.

9 The Lord is not slack concerning his promise, as some count slackness; but is longsuffering to you-ward, not wishing that any should perish, but that all should come to repentance.

10 But the day of the Lord will come as a thief; in the which the heavens shall pass away with a great noise, and the elements shall be dissolved with fervent heat, and the earth and the works that are therein shall be burned up.

11 Seeing that these things are thus all to be dissolved, what manner of persons ought ye to be in all holy living and godliness,

12 looking for and earnestly desiring the coming of the day of God, by reason of which the heavens being on fire shall be dissolved, and the elements shall melt with fervent heat?

13 But, according to his promise, we look for new heavens and a new earth, wherein dwelleth righteousness.

14 Wherefore, beloved, seeing that ye look for these things, give diligence that ye may be found in peace, without spot and blameless in his sight.

15 And account that the longsuffering of our Lord is salvation; even as our beloved brother Paul also, according to the wisdom given to him, wrote unto you;

16 as also in all his epistles, speaking in them of these things; wherein are some things hard to be understood, which the ignorant and unstedfast wrest, as they do also the other scriptures, unto their own destruction.

17 Ye therefore, beloved, knowing these things beforehand, beware lest, being carried away with the error of the wicked, ye fall from your own stedfastness.

18 But grow in the grace and knowledge of our Lord and Saviour Jesus Christ. To him be the glory both now and for ever. Amen.

The First Epistle General of John

Chapter 1

1That which was from the beginning, that which we have heard, that which we have seen with our eyes, that which we beheld, and our hands handled, concerning the Word of life

2(and the life was manifested, and we have seen, and bear witness, and declare unto you the life, the eternal life, which was with the Father, and was manifested unto us);

3that which we have seen and heard declare we unto you also, that ye also may have fellowship with us: yea, and our fellowship is with the Father, and with his Son Jesus Christ:

4and these things we write, that our joy may be made full.

5And this is the message which we have heard from him and announce unto you, that God is light, and in him is no darkness at all.

6If we say that we have fellowship with him and walk in the darkness, we lie, and do not the truth:

7but if we walk in the light, as he is in the light, we have fellowship one with another, and the blood of Jesus his Son cleanseth us from all sin.

8If we say that we have no sin, we deceive ourselves, and the truth is not in us.

9If we confess our sins, he is faithful and righteous to forgive us our sins, and to cleanse us from all unrighteousness.

10If we say that we have not sinned, we make him a liar, and his word is not in us.

Chapter 2

1My little children, these things write I unto you that ye may not sin. And if any man sin, we have an Advocate with the Father, Jesus Christ the righteous:

2and he is the propitiation for our sins; and not for ours only, but also for the whole world.

3And hereby we know that we know him, if we keep his commandments.

4He that saith, I know him, and keepeth not his commandments, is a liar, and the truth is not in him;

5but whoso keepeth his word, in him verily hath the love of God been perfected. Hereby we know that we are in him:

6he that saith he abideth in him ought himself also to walk even as he walked.

7Beloved, no new commandment write I unto you, but an old commandment which ye had from the beginning: the old commandment is the word which ye heard.

8Again, a new commandment write I unto you, which thing is true in him and in you; because the darkness is passing away, and the true light already shineth.

9He that saith he is in the light and hateth his brother, is in the darkness even until now.

10He that loveth his brother abideth in the light, and there is no occasion of stumbling in him.

11But he that hateth his brother is in the darkness, and walketh in the darkness, and knoweth not whither he goeth, because the darkness hath blinded his eyes.

12I write unto you, my little children, because your sins are forgiven you for his name's sake.

13I write unto you, fathers, because ye know him who is from the beginning. I write unto you, young men, because ye have overcome the evil one. I have written unto you, little children, because ye know the Father.

14I have written unto you, fathers, because ye know him who is from the beginning. I have written unto you, young men, because ye are strong, and the word of God abideth in you, and ye have overcome the evil one.

15Love not the world, neither the things that are in the world. If any man love the world, the love of the Father is not in him.

16For all that is in the world, the lust of the flesh and the lust of the eyes and the vain glory of life, is not of the Father, but is of the world.

17And the world passeth away, and the lust thereof: but he that doeth the will of God abideth for ever.

18Little children, it is the last hour: and as ye heard that antichrist cometh, even now have there arisen many antichrists; whereby we know that it is the last hour.

19They went out from us, but they were not of us; for if they had been of us, they would have continued with us: but they went out, that they might be made manifest that they all are not of us.

20And ye have an anointing from the Holy One, and ye know all the things.

21I have not written unto you because ye know not the truth, but because ye know it, and because no lie is of the truth.

22Who is the liar but he that denieth that Jesus is the Christ? This is the antichrist, even he that denieth the Father and the Son.

23Whosoever denieth the Son, the same hath not the Father: he that confesseth the Son hath the Father also.

24As for you, let that abide in you which ye heard from the beginning. If that which ye heard from the beginning abide in you, ye also shall abide in the Son, and in the Father.

25And this is the promise which he promised us, even the life eternal.

26These things have I written unto you concerning them that would lead you astray.

27And as for you, the anointing which ye received of him abideth in you, and ye need not that any one teach you; but as his anointing teacheth you, concerning all things, and is true, and is no lie, and even as it taught you, ye abide in him.

28And now, my little children, abide in him; that, if he shall be manifested, we may have boldness, and not be ashamed before him at his coming.

29If ye know that he is righteous, ye know that every one also that doeth righteousness is begotten of him.

Chapter 3

1Behold what manner of love the Father hath bestowed upon us, that we should be called children of God; and such we are. For this cause the world knoweth us not, because it knew him not.

2Beloved, now are we children of God, and it is not yet made manifest what we shall be. We know that, if he shall be manifested, we shall be like him; for we shall see him even as he is.

3And every one that hath this hope set on him purifieth himself, even as he is pure.

4Every one that doeth sin doeth also lawlessness; and sin is lawlessness.

5And ye know that he was manifested to take away sins; and in him is no sin.

6Whosoever abideth in him sinneth not: whosoever sinneth hath not seen him, neither knoweth him.

7My little children, let no man lead you astray: he that doeth righteousness is righteous, even as he is righteous:

8he that doeth sin is of the devil; for the devil sinneth from the beginning. To this end was the Son of God manifested, that he might destroy the works of the devil.

9Whosoever is begotten of God doeth no sin, because his seed abideth in him; and he cannot sin, because he is begotten of God.

10In this the children of God are manifest, and the children of the devil: whosoever doeth not righteousness is not of God, neither he that loveth not his brother.

11For this is the message which ye heard from the beginning, that we should love one another:

12not as Cain was of the evil one, and slew his brother. And wherefore slew he him? Because his works were evil, and his brother's righteous.

13Marvel not, brethren, if the world hateth you.

14We know that we have passed out of death into life, because we love the brethren. He that loveth not abideth in death.

15Whosoever hateth his brother is a murderer: and ye know that no murderer hath eternal life abiding in him.

16Hereby know we love, because he laid down his life for us: and we ought to lay down our lives for the brethren.

17But whoso hath the world's goods, and beholdeth his brother in need, and shutteth up his compassion from him, how doth the love of God abide in him?

18My Little children, let us not love in word, neither with the tongue; but in deed and truth.

19Hereby shall we know that we are of the truth, and shall assure our heart before him:

20because if our heart condemn us, God is greater than our heart, and knoweth all things.

21Beloved, if our heart condemn us not, we have boldness toward God;

22and whatsoever we ask we receive of him, because we keep his commandments and do the things that are pleasing in his sight.

23And this is his commandment, that we should believe in the name of his Son Jesus Christ, and love one another, even as he gave us commandment.

24And he that keepeth his commandments abideth in him, and he in him. And hereby we know that he abideth in us, by the Spirit which he gave us.

Chapter 4

1Beloved, believe not every spirit, but prove the spirits, whether they are of God; because many false prophets are gone out into the world.

2Hereby know ye the Spirit of God: every spirit that confesseth that Jesus Christ is come in the flesh is of God:

3and every spirit that confesseth not Jesus is not of God: and this is the spirit of the antichrist, whereof ye have heard that it cometh; and now it is in the world already.

4Ye are of God, my little children, and have overcome them: because greater is he that is in you than he that is in the world.

5They are of the world: therefore speak they as of the world, and the world heareth them.

6We are of God: he that knoweth God heareth us; he who is not of God heareth us not. By this we know the spirit of truth, and the spirit of error.

7Beloved, let us love one another: for love is of God; and every one that loveth is begotten of God, and knoweth God.

8He that loveth not knoweth not God; for God is love.

9Herein was the love of God manifested in us, that God hath sent his only begotten Son into the world that we might live through him.

10Herein is love, not that we loved us, but that he loved us, and sent his Son to be the propitiation for our sins.

11Beloved, if God so loved us, we also ought to love one another.

12No man hath beheld God at any time: if we love one another, God abideth in us, and his love is perfected in us:

13hereby we know that we abide in him and he in us, because he hath given us of his Spirit.

14And we have beheld and bear witness that the Father hath sent the Son to be the Saviour of the world.

First John

15Whosoever shall confess that Jesus is the Son of God, God abideth in him, and he in God.

16And we know and have believed the love which God hath in us. God is love; and he that abideth in love abideth in God, and God abideth in him.

17Herein is love made perfect with us, that we may have boldness in the day of judgment; because as he is, even so are we in this world.

18There is no fear in love: but perfect love casteth out fear, because fear hath punishment; and he that feareth is not made perfect in love.

19We love, because he first loved us.

20If a man say, I love God, and hateth his brother, he is a liar: for he that loveth not his brother whom he hath seen, cannot love God whom he hath not seen.

21And this commandment have we from him, that he who loveth God love his brother also.

Chapter 5

1Whosoever believeth that Jesus is the Christ is begotten of God: and whosoever loveth him that begat loveth him also that is begotten of him.

2Hereby we know that we love the children of God, when we love God and do his commandments.

3For this is the love of God, that we keep his commandments: and his commandments are not grievous.

4For whatsoever is begotten of God overcometh the world: and this is the victory that hath overcome the world, even our faith.

5And who is he that overcometh the world, but he that believeth that Jesus is the Son of God?

6This is he that came by water and blood, even Jesus Christ; not with the water only, but with the water and with the blood.

7And it is the Spirit that beareth witness, because the Spirit is the truth.

8For there are three who bear witness, the Spirit, and the water, and the blood: and the three agree in one.

9If we receive the witness of men, the witness of God is greater: for the witness of God is this, that he hath borne witness concerning his Son.

10He that believeth on the Son of God hath the witness in him: he that believeth not God hath made him a liar; because he hath not believed in the witness that God hath borne concerning his Son.

11And the witness is this, that God gave unto us eternal life, and this life is in his Son.

12He that hath the Son hath the life; he that hath not the Son of God hath not the life.

13These things have I written unto you, that ye may know that ye have eternal life, even unto you that believe on the name of the Son of God.

14And this is the boldness which we have toward him, that, if we ask anything according to his will, he heareth us:

15and if we know that he heareth us whatsoever we ask, we know that we have the petitions which we have asked of him.

16If any man see his brother sinning a sin not unto death, he shall ask, and God will give him life for them that sin not unto death. There is a sin unto death: not concerning this do I say that he should make request.

17All unrighteousness is sin: and there is a sin not unto death.

18We know that whosoever is begotten of God sinneth not; but he that was begotten of God keepeth himself, and the evil one toucheth him not.

19We know that we are of God, and the whole world lieth in the evil one.

20And we know that the Son of God is come, and hath given us an understanding, that we know him that is true, and we are in him that is true, even in his Son Jesus Christ. This is the true God, and eternal life.

21My little children, guard yourselves from idols.

The Second Epistle of John

¹The elder unto the elect lady and her children, whom I love in truth; and not I only, but also all they that know the truth;

²for the truth's sake which abideth in us, and it shall be with us for ever:

³Grace, mercy, peace shall be with us, from God the Father, and from Jesus Christ, the Son of the Father, in truth and love.

⁴I rejoice greatly that I have found certain of thy children walking in truth, even as we received commandment from the Father.

⁵And now I beseech thee, lady, not as though I wrote to thee a new commandment, but that which we had from the beginning, that we love one another.

⁶And this is love, that we should walk after his commandments. This is the commandment, even as ye heard from the beginning, that ye should walk in it.

⁷For many deceivers are gone forth into the world, even they that confess not that Jesus Christ cometh in the flesh. This is the deceiver and the antichrist.

⁸Look to yourselves, that ye lose not the things which we have wrought, but that ye receive a full reward.

⁹Whosoever goeth onward and abideth not in the teaching of Christ, hath not God: he that abideth in the teaching, the same hath both the Father and the Son.

¹⁰If any one cometh unto you, and bringeth not this teaching, receive him not into your house, and give him no greeting:

¹¹for he that giveth him greeting partaketh in his evil works.

¹²Having many things to write unto you, I would not write them with paper and ink: but I hope to come unto you, and to speak face to face, that your joy may be made full.

¹³The children of thine elect sister salute thee.

Third John
The Third Epistle of John

¹The elder unto Gaius the beloved, whom I love in truth.

²Beloved, I pray that in all things thou mayest prosper and be in health, even as thy soul prospereth.

³For I rejoiced greatly, when brethren came and bare witness unto thy truth, even as thou walkest in truth.

⁴Greater joy have I none than this, to hear of my children walking in the truth.

⁵Beloved, thou doest a faithful work in whatsoever thou doest toward them that are brethren and strangers withal;

⁶who bare witness to thy love before the church: whom thou wilt do well to set forward on their journey worthily of God:

⁷because that for the sake of the Name they went forth, taking nothing of the Gentiles.

⁸We therefore ought to welcome such, that we may be fellow-workers for the truth.

⁹I wrote somewhat unto the church: but Diotrephes, who loveth to have the preeminence among them, receiveth us not.

¹⁰Therefore, if I come, I will bring to remembrance his works which he doeth, prating against us with wicked words: and not content therewith, neither doth he himself receive the brethren, and them that would he forbiddeth and casteth them out of the church.

¹¹Beloved, imitate not that which is evil, but that which is good. He that doeth good is of God: he that doeth evil hath not seen God.

¹²Demetrius hath the witness of all men, and of the truth itself: yea, we also bear witness: and thou knowest that our witness is true.

¹³I had many things to write unto thee, but I am unwilling to write them to thee with ink and pen:

¹⁴but I hope shortly to see thee, and we shall speak face to face. Peace be unto thee. The friends salute thee. Salute the friends by name.

The General Epistle of Jude

¹Jude, a servant of Jesus Christ, and brother of James, to them that are called, beloved in God the Father, and kept for Jesus Christ:

²Mercy unto you and peace and love be multiplied.

³Beloved, while I was giving all diligence to write unto you of our common salvation, I was constrained to write unto you exhorting you to contend earnestly for the faith which was once for all delivered unto the saints.

⁴For there are certain men crept in privily, even they who were of old written of beforehand unto this condemnation, ungodly men, turning the grace of our God into lasciviousness, and denying our only Master and Lord, Jesus Christ.

⁵Now I desire to put you in remembrance, though ye know all things once for all, that the Lord, having saved a people out of the land of Egypt, afterward destroyed them that believed not.

⁶And angels that kept not their own principality, but left their proper habitation, he hath kept in everlasting bonds under darkness unto the judgment of the great day.

⁷Even as Sodom and Gomorrah, and the cities about them, having in like manner with these given themselves over to fornication and gone after strange flesh, are set forth as an example, suffering the punishment of eternal fire.

⁸Yet in like manner these also in their dreamings defile the flesh, and set at nought dominion, and rail at dignities.

⁹But Michael the archangel, when contending with the devil he disputed about the body of Moses, durst not bring against him a railing judgment, but said, The Lord rebuke thee.

¹⁰But these rail at whatsoever things they know not: and what they understand naturally, like the creatures without reason, in these things are they destroyed.

¹¹Woe unto them! For they went in the way of Cain, and ran riotously in the error of Balaam for hire, and perished in the gainsaying of Korah.

¹²These are they who are hidden rocks in your love-feasts when they feast with you, shepherds that without fear feed themselves; clouds without water, carried along by winds; autumn leaves without fruit, twice dead, plucked up by the roots;

¹³Wild waves of the sea, foaming out their own shame; wandering stars, for whom the blackness of darkness hath been reserved forever.

¹⁴And to these also Enoch, the seventh from Adam, prophesied, saying, Behold, the Lord came with ten thousands of his holy ones,

¹⁵to execute judgment upon all, and to convict all the ungodly of all their works of ungodliness which they have ungodly wrought, and of all the hard things which ungodly sinners have spoken against him.

¹⁶These are murmurers, complainers, walking after their lusts (and their mouth speaketh great swelling words), showing respect of persons for the sake of advantage.

¹⁷But ye, beloved, remember ye the words which have been spoken before by the apostles of our Lord Jesus Christ;

¹⁸That they said to you, In the last time there shall be mockers, walking after their own ungodly lusts.

¹⁹These are they who make separations, sensual, having not the Spirit.

²⁰But ye, beloved, building up yourselves on your most holy faith, praying in the Holy Spirit,

²¹keep yourselves in the love of God, looking for the mercy of our Lord Jesus Christ unto eternal life.

²²And on some have mercy, who are in doubt;

²³and some save, snatching them out of the fire; and on some have mercy with fear; hating even the garment spotted by the flesh.

²⁴Now unto him that is able to guard you from stumbling, and to set you before the presence of his glory without blemish in exceeding joy,

²⁵to the only God our Saviour, through Jesus Christ our Lord, be glory, majesty, dominion and power, before all time, and now, and for evermore. Amen.

Revelation
The Revelation to St. John

Chapter 1

1The Revelation of Jesus Christ, which God gave him to show unto his servants, even the things which must shortly come to pass: and he sent and signified it by his angel unto his servant John;

2who bare witness of the word of God, and of the testimony of Jesus Christ, even of all things that he saw.

3Blessed is he that readeth, and they that hear the words of the prophecy, and keep the things that are written therein: for the time is at hand.

4John to the seven churches that are in Asia: Grace to you and peace, from him who is and who was and who is to come; and from the seven Spirits that are before his throne;

5and from Jesus Christ, who is the faithful witness, the firstborn of the dead, and the ruler of the kings of the earth. Unto him that loveth us, and loosed us from our sins by his blood;

6and he made us to be a kingdom, to be priests unto his God and Father; to him be the glory and the dominion for ever and ever. Amen.

7Behold, he cometh with the clouds; and every eye shall see him, and they that pierced him; and all the tribes of the earth shall mourn over him. Even so, Amen.

8I am the Alpha and the Omega, saith the Lord God, who is and who was and who is to come, the Almighty.

9I John, your brother and partaker with you in tribulation and kingdom and patience which are in Jesus, was in the isle that is called Patmos, for the word of God and the testimony of Jesus.

10I was in the Spirit on the Lord's day, and I heard behind me a great voice, as of a trumpet

11saying, What thou seest, write in a book and send it to the seven churches: unto Ephesus, and unto Smyrna, and unto Pergamum, and unto Thyatira, and unto Sardis, and unto Philadelphia, and unto Laodicea.

12And I turned to see the voice that spake with me. And having turned I saw seven golden candlesticks;

13and in the midst of the candlesticks one like unto a son of man, clothed with a garment down to the foot, and girt about at the breasts with a golden girdle.

14And his head and his hair were white as white wool, white as snow; and his eyes were as a flame of fire;

15and his feet like unto burnished brass, as if it had been refined in a furnace; and his voice as the voice of many waters.

16And he had in his right hand seven stars: and out of his mouth proceeded a sharp two-edged sword: and his countenance was as the sun shineth in his strength.

17And when I saw him, I fell at his feet as one dead. And he laid his right hand upon me, saying, Fear not; I am the first and the last,

18and the Living one; and I was dead, and behold, I am alive for evermore, and I have the keys of death and of Hades.

19Write therefore the things which thou sawest, and the things which are, and the things which shall come to pass hereafter;

20the mystery of the seven stars which thou sawest in my right hand, and the seven golden candlesticks. The seven stars are the angels of the seven churches: and the seven candlesticks are seven churches.

Chapter 2

1To the angel of the church in Ephesus write: These things saith he that holdeth the seven stars in his right hand, he that walketh in the midst of the seven golden candlesticks:

2I know thy works, and thy toil and patience, and that thou canst not bear evil men, and didst try them that call themselves apostles, and they are not, and didst find them false;

3and thou hast patience and didst bear for my name's sake, and hast not grown weary.

4But I have this against thee, that thou didst leave thy first love.

5Remember therefore whence thou art fallen, and repent and do the first works; or else I come to thee, and will move thy candlestick out of its place, except thou repent.

6But this thou hast, that thou hatest the works of the Nicolaitans, which I also hate.

7He that hath an ear, let him hear what the Spirit saith to the churches. To him that overcometh, to him will I give to eat of the tree of life, which is in the Paradise of God.

8And to the angel of the church in Smyrna write: These things saith the first and the last, who was dead, and lived again:

9I know thy tribulation, and thy poverty (but thou art rich), and the blasphemy of them that say they are Jews, and they art not, but are a synagogue of Satan.

10Fear not the things which thou art about to suffer: behold, the devil is about to cast some of you into prison, that ye may be tried; and ye shall have tribulation ten days. Be thou faithful unto death, and I will give thee the crown of life.

11He that hath an ear, let him hear what the Spirit saith to the churches. He that overcometh shall not be hurt of the second death.

12and to the angel of the church in Pergamum write: These things saith he that hath the sharp two-edged sword:

13I know where thou dwellest, even where Satan's throne is; and thou holdest fast my name, and didst not deny my faith, even in the days of Antipas my witness, my faithful one, who was killed among you, where Satan dwelleth.

14But I have a few things against thee, because thou hast there some that hold the teaching of Balaam, who taught Balak to cast a stumblingblock before the children of Israel, to eat things sacrificed to idols, and to commit fornication.

15So hast thou also some that hold the teaching of the Nicolaitans in like manner.

16Repent therefore; or else I come to thee quickly, and I will make war against them with the sword of my mouth.

17He that hath an ear, let him hear what the Spirit saith to the churches. To him that overcometh, to him will I give of the hidden manna, and I will give him a white stone, and upon the stone a new name written, which no one knoweth but he that receiveth it.

18And to the angel of the church in Thyatira write: These things saith the Son of God, who hath his eyes like a flame of fire, and his feet are like unto burnished brass:

19I know thy works, and thy love and faith and ministry and patience, and that thy last works are more than the first.

20But I have this against thee, that thou sufferest the woman Jezebel, who calleth herself a prophetess; and she teacheth and seduceth my servants to commit fornication, and to eat things sacrificed to idols.

21And I gave her time that she should repent; and she willeth not to repent of her fornication.

22Behold, I cast her into a bed, and them that commit adultery with her into great tribulation, except they repent of her works.

23And I will kill her children with death; and all the churches shall know that I am he that searcheth the reins and hearts: and I will give unto each one of you according to your works.

24But to you I say, to the rest that are in Thyatira, as many as have not this teaching, who know not the deep things of Satan, as they are wont to say; I cast upon you none other burden.

25Nevertheless that which ye have, hold fast till I come.

26And he that overcometh, and he that keepeth my works unto the end, to him will I give authority over the nations:

27and he shall rule them with a rod of iron, as the vessels of the potter are broken to shivers; as I also have received of my Father:

28and I will give him the morning star.

29He that hath an ear, let him hear what the Spirit saith to the churches.

Chapter 3

1And to the angel of the church in Sardis write: These things saith he that hath the seven Spirits of God, and the seven stars: I know thy works, that thou hast a name that thou livest, and thou art dead.

2Be thou watchful, and establish the things that remain, which were ready to die: for I have found no works of thine perfected before my God.

3Remember therefore how thou hast received and didst hear; and keep it, and repent. If therefore thou shalt not watch, I will come as a thief, and thou shalt not know what hour I will come upon thee.

4But thou hast a few names in Sardis that did not defile their garments: and they shall walk with me in white; for they are worthy.

5He that overcometh shall thus be arrayed in white garments; and I will in no wise blot his name out of the book of life, and I will confess his name before my Father, and before his angels.

6He that hath an ear, let him hear what the Spirit saith to the churches.

7And to the angel of the church in Philadelphia write: These things saith he that is holy, he that is true, he that hath the key of David, he that openeth and none shall shut, and that shutteth and none openeth:

8I know thy works (behold, I have set before thee a door opened, which none can shut), that thou hast a little power, and didst keep my word, and didst not deny my name.

9Behold, I give of the synagogue of Satan, of them that say they are Jews, and they are not, but do lie; behold, I will make them to come and worship before thy feet, and to know that I have loved thee.

10Because thou didst keep the word of my patience, I also will keep thee from the hour of trial, that hour which is to come upon the whole world, to try them that dwell upon the earth.

11I come quickly: hold fast that which thou hast, that no one take thy crown.

12He that overcometh, I will make him a pillar in the temple of my God, and he shall go out thence no more: and I will write upon him the name of my God, and the name of the city of my God, the new Jerusalem, which cometh down out of heaven from my God, and mine own new name.

13He that hath an ear, let him hear what the Spirit saith to the churches.

14And to the angel of the church in Laodicea write: These things saith the Amen, the faithful and true witness, the beginning of the creation of God:

15I know thy works, that thou art neither cold nor hot: I would thou wert cold or hot.

16So because thou art lukewarm, and neither hot nor cold, I will spew thee out of my mouth.

17Because thou sayest, I am rich, and have gotten riches, and have need of nothing; and knowest not that thou art the wretched one and miserable and poor and blind and naked:

18I counsel thee to buy of me gold refined by fire, that thou mayest become rich; and white garments, that thou mayest clothe thyself, and that the shame of thy nakedness be not made manifest; and eyesalve to anoint thine eyes, that thou mayest see.

19As many as I love, I reprove and chasten: be zealous therefore, and repent.

20Behold, I stand at the door and knock: if any man hear my voice and open the door, I will come in to him, and will sup with him, and he with me.

21He that overcometh, I will give to him to sit down with me in my throne, as I also overcame, and sat down with my Father in his throne.

22He that hath an ear, let him hear what the Spirit saith to the churches.

Chapter 4

1After these things I saw, and behold, a door opened in heaven, and the first voice that I heard, a voice as of a trumpet speaking with me, one saying, Come up hither, and I will show thee the things which must come to pass hereafter.

2Straightway I was in the Spirit: and behold, there was a throne set in heaven, and one sitting upon the throne;

3and he that sat was to look upon like a jasper stone and a sardius: and there was a rainbow round about the throne, like an emerald to look upon.

4And round about the throne were four and twenty thrones: and upon the thrones I saw four and twenty elders sitting, arrayed in white garments; and on their heads crowns of gold.

5And out of the throne proceed lightnings and voices and thunders. And there was seven lamps of fire burning before the throne, which are the seven Spirits of God;

6and before the throne, as it were a sea of glass like a crystal; and in the midst of the throne, and round about the throne, four living creatures full of eyes before and behind.

7And the first creature was like a lion, and the second creature like a calf, and the third creature had a face as of a man, and the fourth creature was like a flying eagle.

8and the four living creatures, having each one of them six wings, are full of eyes round about and within: and they have no rest day and night, saying,

Holy, holy, holy, is the Lord God, the Almighty, who was and who is and who is to come.

9And when the living creatures shall give glory and honor and thanks to him that sitteth on the throne, to him that liveth for ever and ever,

10the four and twenty elders shall fall down before him that sitteth on the throne, and shall worship him that liveth for ever and ever, and shall cast their crowns before the throne, saying,

11Worthy art thou, our Lord and our God, to receive the glory and the honor and the power: for thou didst create all things, and because of thy will they were, and were created.

Chapter 5

1And I saw in the right hand of him that sat on the throne a book written within and on the back, close sealed with seven seals.

2And I saw a strong angel proclaiming with a great voice, Who is worthy to open the book, and to loose the seals thereof?

3And no one in the heaven, or on the earth, or under the earth, was able to open the book, or to look thereon.

4And I wept much, because no one was found worthy to open the book, or to look thereon:

5and one of the elders saith unto me, Weep not; behold, the Lion that is of the tribe of Judah, the Root of David, hath overcome to open the book and the seven seals thereof.

6And I saw in the midst of the throne and of the four living creatures, and in the midst of the elders, a Lamb standing, as though it had been slain, having seven horns, and seven eyes, which are the seven Spirits of God, sent forth into all the earth.

7And he came, and he taketh it out of the right hand of him that sat on the throne.

8And when he had taken the book, the four living creatures and the four and twenty elders fell down before the Lamb, having each one a harp, and golden bowls full of incense, which are the prayers of the saints.

9And they sing a new song, saying,

Worthy art thou to take the book, and to open the seals thereof: for thou was slain, and didst purchase unto God with thy blood men of every tribe, and tongue, and people, and nation,

10and madest them to be unto our God a kingdom and priests; and they reign upon earth.

11And I saw, and I heard a voice of many angels round about the throne and the living creatures and the elders; and the number of them was ten thousand times ten thousand, and thousands of thousands;

12saying with a great voice,

Worthy is the Lamb that hath been slain to receive the power, and riches, and wisdom, and might and honor, and glory, and blessing.

13And every created thing which is in the heaven, and on the earth, and under the earth, and on the sea, and all things are in them, heard I saying,

Unto him that sitteth on the throne, and unto the Lamb, be the blessing, and the honor, and the glory, and the dominion, for ever and ever.

14And the four living creatures said, Amen. And the elders fell down and worshipped.

Chapter 6

1And I saw when the Lamb opened one of the seven seals, and I heard one of the four living creatures saying as with a voice of thunder, Come.

2And I saw, and behold, a white horse, and he that sat thereon had a bow; and there was given unto him a crown: and he came forth conquering, and to conquer.

3And when he opened the second seal, I heard the second living creature saying, Come.

4And another horse came forth, a red horse: and to him that sat thereon it was given to take peace from the earth, and that they should slay one another: and there was given unto him a great sword.

5And when he opened the third seal, I heard the third living creature saying, Come. And I saw, and behold, a black horse; and he that sat thereon had a balance in his hand.

6And I heard as it were a voice in the midst of the four living creatures saying, A measure of wheat for a shilling, and three measures of barley for a shilling; and the oil and the wine hurt thou not.

7And when he opened the fourth seal, I heard the voice of the fourth living creature saying, Come.

8And I saw, and behold, a pale horse: and he that sat upon him, his name was Death; and Hades followed with him. And there was given unto them authority over the fourth part of the earth, to kill with sword, and with famine, and with death, and by the wild beasts of the earth.

9And when he opened the fifth seal, I saw underneath the altar the souls of them that had been slain for the word of God, and for the testimony which they held:

10and they cried with a great voice, saying, How long, O Master, the holy and true, dost thou not judge and avenge our blood on them that dwell on the earth?

11And there was given them to each one a white robe; and it was said unto them, that they should rest yet for a little time, until their fellow-servants also and their brethren, who should be killed even as they were, should have fulfilled their course.

12And I saw when he opened the sixth seal, and there was a great earthquake; and the sun became black as sackcloth of hair, and the whole moon became as blood;

13and the stars of the heaven fell unto the earth, as a fig tree casteth her unripe figs when she is shaken of a great wind.

14And the heaven was removed as a scroll when it is rolled up; and every mountain and island were moved out of their places.

15And the kings of the earth, and the princes, and the chief captains, and the rich, and the strong, and every bondman and freeman, hid themselves in the caves and in the rocks of the mountains;

16and they say to the mountains and to the rocks, Fall on us, and hide us from the face of him that sitteth on the throne, and from the wrath of the Lamb:

17for the great day of their wrath is come; and who is able to stand?

Chapter 7

1After this I saw four angels standing at the four corners of the earth, holding the four winds of the earth, that no wind should blow on the earth, or on the sea, or upon any tree.

2And I saw another angel ascend from the sunrising, having the seal of the living God: and he cried with a great voice to the four angels to whom it was given to hurt the earth and the sea,

3saying, Hurt not the earth, neither the sea, nor the trees, till we shall have sealed the servants of our God on their foreheads.

4And I heard the number of them that were sealed, a hundred and forty and four thousand, sealed out of every tribe of the children of Israel:

5Of the tribe of Judah were sealed twelve thousand:
Of the tribe of Reuben twelve thousand;
Of the tribe of Gad twelve thousand;
6Of the tribe of Asher twelve thousand;
Of the tribe of Naphtali twelve thousand;
Of the tribe of Manasseh twelve thousand;
7Of the tribe of Simeon twelve thousand;
Of the tribe of Levi twelve thousand;
Of the tribe of Issachar twelve thousand;
8Of the tribe of Zebulun twelve thousand;
Of the tribe of Joseph twelve thousand;
Of the tribe of Benjamin were sealed twelve thousand.

9After these things I saw, and behold, a great multitude, which no man could number, out of every nation and of all tribes and peoples and tongues, standing before the throne and before the Lamb, arrayed in white robes, and palms in their hands;

10and they cry with a great voice, saying,

Salvation unto our God who sitteth on the throne, and unto the Lamb.

11And all the angels were standing round about the throne, and about the elders and the four living creatures; and they fell before the throne on their faces, and worshipped God,

12saying,

Amen: Blessing, and glory, and wisdom, and thanksgiving, and honor, and power, and might, be unto our God for ever and ever. Amen.

13And one of the elders answered, saying unto me, These that are arrayed in white robes, who are they, and whence came they?

14And I say unto him, My lord, thou knowest. And he said to me, These are they that come of the great tribulation, and they washed their robes, and made them white in the blood of the Lamb.

15Therefore are they before the throne of God; and they serve him day and night in his temple: and he that sitteth on the throne shall spread his tabernacle over them.

16They shall hunger no more, neither thirst any more; neither shall the sun strike upon them, nor any heat:

17for the Lamb that is in the midst of the throne shall be their shepherd, and shall guide them unto fountains of waters of life: and God shall wipe away every tear from their eyes.

Revelation

Chapter 8

1And when he opened the seventh seal, there followed a silence in heaven about the space of half an hour.

2And I saw the seven angels that stand before God; and there were given unto them seven trumpets.

3And another angel came and stood over the altar, having a golden censer; and there was given unto him much incense, that he should add it unto the prayers of all the saints upon the golden altar which was before the throne.

4And the smoke of the incense, with the prayers of the saints, went up before God out of the angel's hand.

5And the angel taketh the censer; and he filled it with the fire of the altar, and cast it upon the earth: and there followed thunders, and voices, and lightnings, and an earthquake.

6And the seven angels that had the seven trumpets prepared themselves to sound.

7And the first sounded, and there followed hail and fire, mingled with blood, and they were cast upon the earth: and the third part of the earth was burnt up, and the third part of the trees was burnt up, and all green grass was burnt up.

8And the second angel sounded, and as it were a great mountain burning with fire was cast into the sea: and the third part of the sea became blood;

9and there died the third part of the creatures which were in the sea, even they that had life; and the third part of the ships was destroyed.

10And the third angel sounded, and there fell from heaven a great star, burning as a torch, and it fell upon the third part of the rivers, and upon the fountains of the waters;

11and the name of the star is called Wormwood: and the third part of the waters became wormwood; and many men died of the waters, because they were made bitter.

12And the fourth angel sounded, and the third part of the sun was smitten, and the third part of the moon, and the third part of the stars; that the third part of them should be darkened, and the day should not shine for the third part of it, and the night in like manner.

13And I saw, and I heard an eagle, flying in mid heaven, saying with a great voice, Woe, woe, woe, for them that dwell on the earth, by reason of the other voices of the trumpet of the three angels, who are yet to sound.

Chapter 9

1And the fifth angel sounded, and I saw a star from heaven fallen unto the earth: and there was given to him the key of the pit of the abyss.

2And he opened the pit of the abyss; and there went up a smoke out of the pit, as the smoke of a great furnace; and the sun and the air were darkened by reason of the smoke of the pit.

3And out of the smoke came forth locusts upon the earth: and power was given them, as the scorpions of the earth have power.

4And it was said unto them that they should not hurt the grass of the earth, neither any green thing, neither any tree, but only such men as have not the seal of God on their foreheads.

5And it was given them that they should not kill them, but that they should be tormented five months: and their torment was as the torment of a scorpion, when it striketh a man.

6And in those days men shall seek death, and shall in no wise find it; and they shall desire to die, and death fleeth from them.

7And the shapes of the locusts were like unto horses prepared for war; and upon their heads as it were crowns like unto gold, and their faces were as men's faces.

8And they had hair as the hair of women, and their teeth were as teeth of lions.

9And they had breastplates, as it were breastplates of iron; and the sound of their wings was as the sound of chariots, of many horses rushing to war.

10And they have tails like unto scorpions, and stings; and in their tails is their power to hurt men five months.

11They have over them as king the angel of the abyss: his name in Hebrew is Abaddon, and in the Greek tongue he hath the name Apollyon.

12The first Woe is past: behold, there come yet two Woes hereafter.

13And the sixth angel sounded, and I heard a voice from the horns of the golden altar which is before God,

14one saying to the sixth angel that had one trumpet, Loose the four angels that are bound at the great river Euphrates.

15And the four angels were loosed, that had been prepared for the hour and day and month and year, that they should kill the third part of men.

16And the number of the armies of the horsemen was twice ten thousand times ten thousand: I heard the number of them.

17And thus I saw the horses in the vision, and them that sat on them, having breastplates as of fire and of hyacinth and of brimstone: and the heads of lions; and out of their mouths proceedeth fire and smoke and brimstone.

18By these three plagues was the third part of men killed, by the fire and the smoke and the brimstone, which proceeded out of their mouths.

19For the power of the horses is in their mouth, and in their tails: for their tails are like unto serpents, and have heads; and with them they hurt.

20And the rest of mankind, who were not killed with these plagues, repented not of the works of their hands, that they should not worship demons, and the idols of gold, and of silver, and of brass, and of stone, and of wood; which can neither see, nor hear, nor walk:

21and they repented not of their murders, nor of their sorceries, nor of their fornication, nor of their thefts.

Chapter 10

1And I saw another strong angel coming down out of heaven, arrayed with a cloud; and the rainbow was upon his head, and his face was as the sun, and his feet as pillars of fire;

2and he had in his hand a little book open: and he set his right foot upon the sea, and his left upon the earth;

3and he cried with a great voice, as a lion roareth: and when he cried, the seven thunders uttered their voices.

4And when the seven thunders uttered their voices, I was about to write: and I heard a voice from heaven saying, Seal up the things which the seven thunders uttered, and write them not.

5And the angel that I saw standing upon the sea and upon the earth lifted up his right hand to heaven,

6and sware by him that liveth for ever and ever, who created the heaven and the things that are therein, and the earth and the things that are therein, and the sea and the things that are therein, that there shall be delay no longer;

7but in the days of the voice of the seventh angel, when he is about to sound, then is finished the mystery of God, according to the good tidings which he declared to his servants the prophets.

8And the voice which I heard from heaven, I heard it again speaking with me, and saying, Go, take the book which is open in the hand of the angel that standeth upon the sea and upon the earth.

9And I went unto the angel, saying unto him that he should give me the little book. And he saith unto me, Take it, and eat it up; and it shall make thy belly bitter, but in thy mouth it shall be sweet as honey.

10And I took the little book out of the angel's hand, and ate it up; and it was in my mouth sweet as honey: and when I had eaten it, my belly was made bitter.

11And they say unto me, Thou must prophesy again over many peoples and nations and tongues and kings.

Chapter 11

1And there was given me a reed like unto a rod: and one said, Rise, and measure the temple of God, and the altar, and them that worship therein.

2And the court which is without the temple leave without, and measure it not; for it hath been given unto the nations: and the holy city shall they tread under foot forty and two months.

3And I will give unto my two witnesses, and they shall prophesy a thousand two hundred and threescore days, clothed in sackcloth.

4These are the two olive trees and the two candlesticks, standing before the Lord of the earth.

5And if any man desireth to hurt them, fire proceedeth out of their mouth and devoureth their enemies; and if any man shall desire to hurt them, in this manner must he be killed.

6These have the power to shut the heaven, that it rain not during the days of their prophecy: and they have power over the waters to turn them into blood, and to smite the earth with every plague, as often as they shall desire.

7And when they shall have finished their testimony, the beast that cometh up out of the abyss shall make war with them, and overcome them, and kill them.

8And their dead bodies lie in the street of the great city, which spiritually is called Sodom and Egypt, where also their Lord was crucified.

9And from among the peoples and tribes and tongues and nations do men look upon their dead bodies three days and a half, and suffer not their dead bodies to be laid in a tomb.

10And they that dwell on the earth rejoice over them, and make merry; and they shall send gifts one to another; because these two prophets tormented them that dwell on the earth.

11And after the three days and a half the breath of life from God entered into them, and they stood upon their feet; and great fear fell upon them that beheld them.

12And they heard a great voice from heaven saying unto them, Come up hither. And they went up into heaven in the cloud; and their enemies beheld them.

13And in that hour there was a great earthquake, and the tenth part of the city fell; and there were killed in the earthquake seven thousand persons: and the rest were affrighted, and gave glory to the God of heaven.

14The second Woe is past: behold, the third Woe cometh quickly.

15And the seventh angel sounded; and there followed great voices in heaven, and they said,

The kingdom of the world is become the kingdom of our Lord, and of his Christ: and he shall reign for ever and ever.

16And the four and twenty elders, who sit before God on their thrones, fell upon their faces and worshipped God,

17saying,

We give thee thanks, O Lord God, the Almighty, who art and who wast; because thou hast taken thy great power, and didst reign.

18And the nations were wroth, and thy wrath came, and the time of the dead to be judged, and the time to give their reward to thy servants the prophets, and to the saints, and to them that fear thy name, the small and the great; and to destroy them that destroy the earth.

19And there was opened the temple of God that is in heaven; and there was seen in his temple the ark of his covenant; and there followed lightnings, and voices, and thunders, and an earthquake, and great hail.

Chapter 12

1And a great sign was seen in heaven: a woman arrayed with the sun, and the moon under her feet, and upon her head a crown of twelve stars;

2and she was the child; and she crieth out, travailing in birth, and in pain to be delivered.

3And there was seen another sign in heaven: and behold, a great red dragon, having seven heads and ten horns, and upon his heads seven diadems,

4And his tail draweth the third part of the stars of heaven, and did cast them to the earth: and the dragon standeth before the woman that is about to be delivered, that when she is delivered he may devour her child.

5And she was delivered of a son, a man child, who is to rule all the nations with a rod of iron: and her child was caught up unto God, and unto his throne.

6And the woman fled into the wilderness, where she hath a place prepared of God, that there they may nourish her a thousand two hundred and threescore days.

7And there was war in heaven: Michael and his angels going forth to war with the dragon; and the dragon warred and his angels;

8And they prevailed not, neither was their place found any more in heaven.

9And the great dragon was cast down, the old serpent, he that is called the Devil and Satan, the deceiver of the whole world; he was cast down to the earth, and his angels were cast down with him.

10And I heard a great voice in heaven, saying, Now is come the salvation, and the power, and the kingdom of our God, and the authority of his Christ: for the accuser of our brethren is cast down, who accuseth them before our God day and night.

11And they overcame him because of the blood of the Lamb, and because of the word of their testimony; and they loved not their life even unto death.

12Therefore rejoice, O heavens, and ye that dwell in them. Woe for the earth and for the sea: because the devil is gone down unto you, having great wrath, knowing that he hath but a short time.

13And when the dragon saw that he was cast down to the earth, he persecuted the woman that brought forth the man child.

14And there were given to the woman the two wings of the great eagle, that she might fly into the wilderness unto her place, where she is nourished for a time, and times, and half a time, from the face of the serpent.

15And the serpent cast out of his mouth after the woman water as a river, that he might cause her to be carried away by the stream.

16And the earth helped the woman, and the earth opened her mouth and swallowed up the river which the dragon cast out of his mouth.

17And the dragon waxed wroth with the woman, and went away to make war with the rest of her seed, that keep the commandments of God, and hold the testimony of Jesus:

Chapter 13

1and he stood upon the sand of the sea. And I saw a beast coming up out of the sea, having ten horns, and seven heads, and on his horns ten diadems, and upon his heads names of blasphemy.

2And the beast which I saw was like unto a leopard, and his feet were as the feet of a bear, and his mouth as the mouth of a lion: and the dragon gave him his power, and his throne, and great authority.

3And I saw one of his heads as though it had been smitten unto death; and his death-stroke was healed: and the whole earth wondered after the beast;

4and they worshipped the dragon, because he gave his authority unto the beast; and they worshipped the beast, saying, Who is like unto the beast? And who is able to war with him?

5and there was given to him a mouth speaking great things and blasphemies; and there was given to him authority to continue forty and two months.

6And he opened his mouth for blasphemies against God, to blaspheme his name, and his tabernacle, even them that dwell in the heaven.

7And it was given unto him to make war with the saints, and to overcome them: and there was given to him authority over every tribe and people and tongue and nation.

8And all that dwell on the earth shall worship him, every one whose name hath not been written from the foundation of the world in the book of life of the Lamb that hath been slain.

9If any man hath an ear, let him hear.

10If any man is for captivity, into captivity he goeth: if any man shall kill with the sword, with the sword must he be killed. Here is the patience and the faith of the saints.

11And I saw another beast coming up out of the earth; and he had two horns like unto lamb, and he spake as a dragon.

12And he exerciseth all the authority of the first beast in his sight. And he maketh the earth and them dwell therein to worship the first beast, whose death-stroke was healed.

13And he doeth great signs, that he should even make fire to come down out of heaven upon the earth in the sight of men.

14And he deceiveth them that dwell on the earth by reason of the signs which it was given him to do in the sight of the beast; saying to them that dwell on the earth, that they should make an image to the beast who hath the stroke of the sword and lived.

15And it was given unto him to give breath to it, even to the image to the beast, that the image of the beast should both speak, and cause that as many as should not worship the image of the beast should be killed.

16And he causeth all, the small and the great, and the rich and the poor, and the free and the bond, that there be given them a mark on their right hand, or upon their forehead;

17and that no man should be able to buy or to sell, save he that hath the mark, even the name of the beast or the number of his name.

18Here is wisdom. He that hath understanding, let him count the number of the beast; for it is the number of a man: and his number is Six hundred and sixty and six.

Chapter 14

1And I saw, and behold, the Lamb standing on the mount Zion, and with him a hundred and forty and four thousand, having his name, and the name of his Father, written on their foreheads.

2And I heard a voice from heaven, as the voice of many waters, and as the voice of a great thunder: and the voice which I heard was as the voice of harpers harping with their harps:

3and they sing as it were a new song before the throne, and before the four living creatures and the elders: and no man could learn the song save the hundred and forty and four thousand, even they that had been purchased out of the earth.

4These are they that were not defiled with women; for they are virgins. These are they that follow the Lamb whithersoever he goeth. These were purchased from among men, to be the firstfruits unto God and unto the Lamb.

5And in their mouth was found no lie: they are without blemish.

6And I saw another angel flying in mid heaven, having eternal good tidings to proclaim unto them that dwell on the earth, and unto every nation and tribe and tongue and people;

7and he saith with a great voice, Fear God, and give him glory; for the hour of his judgment is come: and worship him that made the heaven and the earth and sea and fountains of waters.

8And another, a second angel, followed, saying, Fallen, fallen is Babylon the great, that hath made all the nations to drink of the wine of the wrath of her fornication.

9And another angel, a third, followed them, saying with a great voice, If any man worshippeth the beast and his image, and receiveth a mark on his forehead, or upon his hand,

10he also shall drink of the wine of the wrath of God, which is prepared unmixed in the cup of his anger; and he shall be tormented with fire and brimstone in the presence of the holy angels, and in the presence of the Lamb:

11and the smoke of their torment goeth up for ever and ever; and they have no rest day and night, they that worship the beast and his image, and whoso receiveth the mark of his name.

12Here is the patience of the saints, they that keep the commandments of God, and the faith of Jesus.

13And I heard the voice from heaven saying, Write, Blessed are the dead who die in the Lord from henceforth: yea, saith the Spirit, that they may rest from their labors; for their works follow with them.

14And I saw, and behold, a white cloud; and on the cloud I saw one sitting like unto a son of man, having on his head a golden crown, and in his hand sharp sickle.

15And another angel came out from the temple, crying with a great voice to him that sat on the cloud, Send forth thy sickle, and reap: for the hour to reap is come; for the harvest of the earth is ripe.

16And he that sat on the cloud cast his sickle upon the earth; and the earth was reaped.

17Another angel came out from the temple which is in heaven, he also having a sharp sickle.

18And another angel came out from the altar, he that hath power over fire; and he called with a great voice to him that had the sharp sickle, saying, Send forth thy sharp sickle, and gather the clusters of the vine of the earth; for her grapes are fully ripe.

19And the angel cast his sickle into the earth, and gathered the vintage of the earth, and cast it into the winepress, the great winepress, of the wrath of God.

20And the winepress are trodden without the city, and there came out blood from the winepress, even unto the bridles of the horses, as far as a thousand and six hundred furlongs.

Chapter 15

1And I saw another sign in heaven, great and marvellous, seven angels having seven plagues, which are the last, for in them is finished the wrath of God.

2And I saw as it were a sea of glass mingled with fire; and them that come off victorious from the beast, and from his image, and from the number of his name, standing by the sea of glass, having harps of God.

3And they sing the song of Moses the servant of God, and the song of the Lamb, saying,

Great and marvellous are thy works, O Lord God, the Almighty; righteous and true are thy ways, thou King of the ages.

4Who shall not fear, O Lord, and glorify thy name? for thou only art holy; for all the nations shall come and worship before thee; for thy righteous acts have been made manifest.

5And after these things I saw, and the temple of the tabernacle of the testimony in heaven was opened:

6and there came out from the temple the seven angels that had the seven plagues, arrayed with precious stone, pure and bright, and girt about their breasts with golden girdles.

7And one of the four living creatures gave unto the seven angels seven golden bowls full of the wrath of God, who liveth for ever and ever.

8And the temple was filled with smoke from the glory of God, and from his power; and none was able to enter into the temple, till the seven plagues of the seven angels should be finished.

Revelation

Chapter 16

1 And I heard a great voice out of the temple, saying to the seven angels, Go ye, and pour out the seven bowls of the wrath of God into the earth.

2 And the first went, and poured out his bowl into the earth; and it became a noisome and grievous sore upon the men that had the mark of the beast, and that worshipped his image.

3 And the second poured out his bowl into the sea; and it became blood as of a dead man; and every living soul died, even the things that were in the sea.

4 And the third poured out his bowl into the rivers and the fountains of the waters; and it became blood.

5 And I heard the angel of the waters saying, Righteous art thou, who art and who wast, thou Holy One, because thou didst thus judge:

6 for they poured out the blood of the saints and the prophets, and blood hast thou given them to drink: they are worthy.

7 And I heard the altar saying, Yea, O Lord God, the Almighty, true and righteous are thy judgments.

8 And the fourth poured out his bowl upon the sun; and it was given unto it to scorch men with fire.

9 And men were scorched men with great heat: and they blasphemed the name of God who hath the power over these plagues; and they repented not to give him glory.

10 And the fifth poured out his bowl upon the throne of the beast; and his kingdom was darkened; and they gnawed their tongues for pain,

11 and they blasphemed the God of heaven because of their pains and their sores; and they repented not of their works.

12 And the sixth poured out his bowl upon the great river, the river Euphrates; and the water thereof was dried up, that the way might by made ready for the kings that come from the sunrising.

13 And I saw coming out of the mouth of the dragon, and out of the mouth of the beast, and out of the mouth of the false prophet, three unclean spirits, as it were frogs:

14 for they are spirits of demons, working signs; which go forth unto the kings of the whole world, to gather them together unto the war of the great day of God, the Almighty.

15 (Behold, I come as a thief. Blessed is he that watcheth, and keepeth his garments, lest he walked naked, and they see his shame.)

16 And they gathered them together into the place which is called in Hebrew Har-magedon.

17 And the seventh poured out his bowl upon the air; and there came forth a great voice out of the temple, from the throne, saying, It is done:

18 and there were lightnings, and voices, and thunders; and there was a great earthquake, such as was not since there were men upon the earth, so great an earthquake, so mighty.

19 And the great city was divided into three parts, and the cities of the nations fell: and Babylon the great was remembered in the sight of God, to give unto her the cup of the wine of the fierceness of his wrath.

20 And every island fled away, and the mountains were not found.

21 And great hail, every stone about the weight of a talent, cometh down out of heaven upon men; and men blasphemed God because of the plague of the hail; for the plague thereof is exceeding great.

Chapter 17

1 And there came one of the seven angels that had the seven bowls, and spake with me, saying, Come hither, I will show thee the judgment of the great harlot that sitteth upon many waters;

2 with whom the kings of the earth committed fornication, and they that dwell in the earth were made drunken with the wine of her fornication.

3 And he carried me away in the Spirit into a wilderness: and I saw a woman sitting upon a scarlet-colored beast, full of names of blasphemy, having seven heads and ten horns.

4 And the woman was arrayed in purple and scarlet, and decked with gold and precious stone and pearls, having in her hand a golden cup full of abominations, even the unclean things of her fornication,

5 and upon her forehead a name written, MYSTERY, BABYLON THE GREAT, THE MOTHER OF THE HARLOTS AND OF THE ABOMINATIONS OF THE EARTH.

6 And I saw the woman drunken with the blood of the saints, and with the blood of the martyrs of Jesus. And when I saw her, I wondered with a great wonder.

7 And the angel said unto me, Wherefore didst thou wonder? I will tell thee the mystery of the woman, and of the beast that carrieth her, which hath the seven heads and the ten horns.

8 The beast that thou sawest was, and is not; and is about to come up out of the abyss, and to go into perdition. And they that dwell on the earth shall wonder, they whose name hath not been written in the book of life from the foundation of the world, when they behold the beast, how that he was, and is not, and shall come.

9 Here is the mind that hath wisdom. The seven heads are seven mountains, on which the woman sitteth:

10 and they are seven kings; the five are fallen, the one is, the other is not yet come; and when he cometh, he must continue a little while.

11 And the beast that was, and is not, is himself also an eighth, and is of the seven; and he goeth into perdition.

12 And the ten horns that thou sawest are ten kings, who have received no kingdom as yet; but they receive authority as kings, with the beast, for one hour.

13 These have one mind, and they give their power and authority unto the beast.

14 These shall war against the Lamb, and the Lamb shall overcome them, for he is Lord of lords, and King of kings; and they also shall overcome that are with him, called and chosen and faithful.

15 And he saith unto me, The waters which thou sawest, where the harlot sitteth, are peoples, and multitudes, and nations, and tongues.

16 And the ten horns which thou sawest, and the beast, these shall hate the harlot, and shall make her desolate and naked, and shall eat her flesh, and shall burn her utterly with fire.

17 For God did put in their hearts to do his mind, and to come to one mind, and to give their kingdom unto the beast, until the words of God should be accomplished.

18 And the woman whom thou sawest is the great city, which reigneth over the kings of the earth.

Chapter 18

1 After these things I saw another angel coming down out of heaven, having great authority; and the earth was lightened with his glory.

2 And he cried with a mighty voice, saying, Fallen, fallen is Babylon the great, and is become a habitation of demons, and a hold of every unclean spirit, and a hold of every unclean and hateful bird.

3 For by the wine of the wrath of her fornication all the nations are fallen; and the kings of the earth committed fornication with her, and the merchants of the earth waxed rich by the power of her wantonness.

4 And I heard another voice from heaven, saying, Come forth, my people, out of her, that ye have no fellowship with her sins, and that ye receive not of her plagues:

5 for her sins have reached even unto heaven, and God hath remembered her iniquities.

6 Render unto her even as she rendered, and double unto her the double according to her works: in the cup which she mingled, mingle unto her double.

7 How much soever she glorified herself, and waxed wanton, so much give her of torment and mourning: for she saith in her heart, I sit a queen, and am no widow, and shall in no wise see mourning.

8 Therefore in one day shall her plagues come, death, and mourning, and famine; and she shall be utterly burned with fire; for strong is the Lord God who judged her.

9 And the kings of the earth, who committed fornication and lived wantonly with her, shall weep and wail over her, when they look upon the smoke of her burning,

10 standing afar off for the fear of her torment, saying, Woe, woe, the great city, Babylon, the strong city! for in one hour is thy judgment come.

11 And the merchants of the earth weep and mourn over her, for no man buyeth their merchandise any more;

12 merchandise of gold, and silver, and precious stone, and pearls, and fine linen, and purple, and silk, and scarlet; and all thyine wood, and every vessel of ivory, and every vessel made of most precious wood, and of brass, and iron, and marble;

13 and cinnamon, and spice, and incense, and ointment, and frankincense, and wine, and oil, and fine flour, and wheat, and cattle, and sheep; and merchandise of horses and chariots and slaves; and souls of men.

14 And the fruits which thy soul lusted after are gone from thee, and all things that were dainty and sumptuous are perished from thee, and men shall find them no more at all.

15 The merchants of these things, who were made rich by her, shall stand afar off for the fear of her torment, weeping and mourning;

16 saying, Woe, woe, the great city, she that was arrayed in fine linen and purple and scarlet, and decked with gold and precious stone and pearl!

17 for in an hour so great riches is made desolate. And every shipmaster, and every one that saileth any wither, and mariners, and as many as gain their living by sea, stood afar off,

18 and cried out as they looked upon the smoke of her burning, saying, What city is like the great city?

19 And they cast dust on their heads, and cried, weeping and mourning, saying, Woe, woe, the great city, wherein all that had their ships in the sea were made rich by reason of her costliness! for in one hour is she made desolate.

20 Rejoice over her, thou heaven, and ye saints, and ye apostles, and ye prophets; for God hath judged your judgment on her.

21 And a strong angel took up a stone as it were a great millstone and cast it into the sea, saying, Thus with a mighty fall shall Babylon, the great city, be cast down, and shall be found no more at all.

22 And the voice of harpers and minstrels and flute-players and trumpeters shall be heard no more at all in thee; and no craftsman, of whatsoever craft, shall be found any more at all in thee; and the voice of a mill shall be heard no more at all in thee;

23 and the light of a lamp shall shine no more at all in thee; and the voice of the bridegroom and of the bride shall be heard no more at all in thee: for thy merchants were the princes of the earth; for with thy sorcery were all the nations deceived.

24 And in her was found the blood of prophets and of saints, and of all that have been slain upon the earth.

Chapter 19

1 After these things I heard as it were a great voice of a great multitude in heaven, saying,

Hallelujah; Salvation, and glory, and power, belong to our God:

2 for true and righteous are his judgments; for he hath judged the great harlot, her that corrupted the earth with her fornication, and he hath avenged the blood of his servants at her hand.

3 And a second time they say, Hallelujah. And her smoke goeth up for ever

and ever.

4And the four and twenty elders and the four living creatures fell down and worshipped God that sitteth on the throne, saying, Amen; Hallelujah.

5And a voice came forth from the throne, saying,

Give praise to our God, all ye his servants, ye that fear him, the small and the great.

6And I heard as it were the voice of a great multitude, and as the voice of many waters, and as the voice of mighty thunders, saying,

Hallelujah: for the Lord our God, the Almighty, reigneth.

7Let us rejoice and be exceeding glad, and let us give the glory unto him: for the marriage of the Lamb is come, and his wife hath made herself ready.

8And it was given unto her that she should array herself in fine linen, bright and pure: for the fine linen is the righteous acts of the saints.

9And he saith unto me, Write, Blessed are they that are bidden to the marriage supper of the Lamb. And he saith unto me, These are true words of God.

10And I fell down before his feet to worship him. And he saith unto me, See thou do it not: I am a fellow-servant with thee and with thy brethren that hold the testimony of Jesus: worship God; for the testimony of Jesus is the spirit of prophecy.

11And I saw the heaven opened; and behold, a white horse, and he that sat thereon called Faithful and True; and in righteous he doth judge and make war.

12And his eyes are a flame of fire, and upon his head are many diadems; and he hath a name written which no one knoweth but he himself.

13And he is arrayed in a garment sprinkled with blood: and his name is called The Word of God.

14And the armies which are in heaven followed him upon white horses, clothed in fine linen, white and pure.

15And out of his mouth proceedeth a sharp sword, that with it he should smite the nations: and he shall rule them with a rod of iron: and he treadeth the winepress of the fierceness of the wrath of God, the Almighty.

16And he hath on his garment and on his thigh a name written, KINGS OF KINGS, AND LORD OF LORDS.

17And I saw an angel standing in the sun; and he cried with a loud voice, saying to all the birds that fly in mid heaven, Come and be gathered together unto the great supper of God;

18that ye may eat the flesh of kings, and the flesh of captains, and the flesh of mighty men, and the flesh of horses and of them that sit thereon, and the flesh of all men, both free and bond, and small and great.

19And I saw the beast, and the kings of the earth, and their armies, gathered together to make war against him that sat upon the horse, and against his army.

20And the beast was taken, and with him the false prophet that wrought the signs in his sight, wherewith he deceived them that had received the mark of the beast and them that worshipped his image: they two were cast alive into the lake of fire that burneth with brimstone:

21and the rest were killed with the sword of him that sat upon the horse, even the sword which came forth out of his mouth: and all the birds were filled with their flesh.

Chapter 20

1And I saw an angel coming down out of heaven, having the key of the abyss and a great chain in his hand.

2And he laid hold on the dragon, the old serpent, which is the Devil and Satan, and bound him for a thousand years,

3and cast him into the abyss, and shut it, and sealed it over him, that he should deceive the nations no more, until the thousand years should be finished: after this he must be loosed for a little time.

4And I saw thrones, and they sat upon them, and judgment was given unto them: and I saw the souls of them that had been beheaded for the testimony of Jesus, and for the word of God, and such as worshipped not the beast, neither his image, and received not the mark upon their forehead and upon their hand; and they lived, and reigned with Christ a thousand years.

5The rest of the dead lived not until the thousand years should be finished. This is the first resurrection.

6Blessed and holy is he that hath part in the first resurrection: over these the second death hath no power; but they shall be priests of God and of Christ, and shall reign with him a thousand years.

7And when the thousand years are finished, Satan shall be loosed out of his prison,

8and shall come forth to deceive the nations which are in the four corners of the earth, Gog and Magog, to gather them together to the war: the number of whom is as the sand of the sea.

9And they went up over the breadth of the earth, and compassed the camp of the saints about, and the beloved city: and fire came down out of heaven, and devoured them.

10And the devil that deceived them was cast into the lake of fire and brimstone, where are also the beast and the false prophet; and they shall be tormented day and night for ever and ever.

11And I saw a great white throne, and him that sat upon it, from whose face the earth and the heaven fled away; and there was found no place for them.

12And I saw the dead, the great and the small, standing before the throne; and books were opened: and another book was opened, which is the book of life: and the dead were judged out of the things which were written in the books, according to their works.

13And the sea gave up the dead that were in it; and death and Hades gave up the dead that were in them: and they were judged every man according to their works.

14And death and Hades were cast into the lake of fire. This is the second death, even the lake of fire.

15And if any was not found written in the book of life, he was cast into the lake of fire.

Chapter 21

1And I saw a new heaven and a new earth: for the first heaven and the first earth are passed away; and the sea is no more.

2And I saw the holy city, new Jerusalem, coming down out of heaven of God, made ready as a bride adorned for her husband.

3And I heard a great voice out of the throne saying, Behold, the tabernacle of God is with men, and he shall dwell with them, and they shall be his peoples, and God himself shall be with them, and be their God:

4and he shall wipe away every tear from their eyes; and death shall be no more; neither shall there be mourning, nor crying, nor pain, any more: the first things are passed away.

5And he that sitteth on the throne said, Behold, I make all things new. And he saith, Write: for these words are faithful and true.

6And he said unto me, They are come to pass. I am the Alpha and the Omega, the beginning and the end. I will give unto him that is athirst of the fountain of the water of life freely.

7He that overcometh shall inherit these things; and I will be his God, and he shall be my son.

8But for the fearful, and unbelieving, and abominable, and murderers, and fornicators, and sorcerers, and idolaters, and all liars, their part shall be in the lake that burneth with fire and brimstone; which is the second death.

9And there came one of the seven angels who had the seven bowls, who were laden with the seven last plagues; and he spake with me, saying, Come hither, I will show thee the bride, the wife of the Lamb.

10And he carried me away in the Spirit to a mountain great and high, and showed me the holy city Jerusalem, coming down out of heaven from God,

11having the glory of God: her light was like unto a stone most precious, as it were a jasper stone, clear as crystal;

12having a wall great and high; having twelve gates, and at the gates twelve angels; and names written thereon, which are the names of the twelve tribes of the children of Israel:

13on the east were three gates; and on the north three gates; and on the south three gates; and on the west three gates.

14And the wall of the city had twelve foundations, and on them twelve names of the twelve apostles of the Lamb.

15And he that spake with me had for a measure a golden reed to measure the city, and the gates thereof, and the wall thereof.

16And the city lieth foursquare, and the length thereof is as great as the breadth: and he measured the city with the reed, twelve thousand furlongs: the length and the breadth and the height thereof are equal.

17And he measured the wall thereof, a hundred and forty and four cubits, according to the measure of a man, that is, of an angel.

18And the building of the wall thereof was jasper: and the city was pure gold, like unto pure glass.

19The foundations of the wall of the city were adorned with all manner of precious stones. The first foundation was jasper; the second, sapphire; the third, chalcedony; the fourth, emerald;

20the fifth, sardonyx; the sixth, sardius; the seventh, chrysolite; the eighth, beryl; the ninth, topaz; the tenth, chrysoprase; the eleventh, jacinth; the twelfth, amethyst.

21And the twelve gates were twelve pearls; each one of the several gates was of one pearl: and the street of the city was pure gold, as it were transparent glass.

22And I saw no temple therein: for the Lord God the Almighty, and the Lamb, are the temple thereof.

23And the city hath no need of the sun, neither of the moon, to shine upon it: for the glory of God did lighten it, and the lamp thereof is the Lamb.

24And the nations shall walk amidst the light thereof: and the kings of the earth bring their glory into it.

25And the gates thereof shall in no wise be shut by day (for there shall be no night there):

26and they shall bring the glory and the honor of the nations into it:

27and there shall in no wise enter into it anything unclean, or he that maketh an abomination and a lie: but only they that are written in the Lamb's book of life.

Chapter 22

1And he showed me a river of water of life, bright as crystal, proceeding out of the throne of God and of the Lamb,

2in the midst of the street thereof. And on this side of the river and on that was the tree of life, bearing twelve manner of fruits, yielding its fruit every month: and the leaves of the tree were for the healing of the nations.

3And there shall be no curse any more: and the throne of God and of the Lamb shall be therein: and his servants shall serve him;

4and they shall see his face; and his name shall be on their foreheads.

5And there shall be night no more; and they need no light of lamp, neither light of sun; for the Lord God shall give them light: and they shall reign for ever and ever.

6And he said unto me, These words are faithful and true: and the Lord, the God of the spirits of the prophets, sent his angels to show unto his servants the things which must shortly come to pass.

7And behold, I come quickly. Blessed is he that keepeth the words of the prophecy of this book.

8And I John am he that heard and saw these things. And when I heard and saw, I fell down to worship before the feet of the angel that showed me these things.

9And he saith unto me, See thou do it not: I am a fellow-servant with thee

Revelation

and with thy brethren the prophets, and with them that keep the words of this book: worship God.

10And he saith unto me, Seal not up the words of the prophecy of this book; for the time is at hand.

11He that is unrighteous, let him do unrighteousness still: and he that is filthy, let him be made filthy still: and he that is righteous, let him do righteousness still: and he that is holy, let him be made holy still.

12Behold, I come quickly; and my reward is with me, to render to each man according as his work is.

13I am the Alpha and the Omega, the first and the last, the beginning and the end.

14Blessed are they that wash their robes, that they may have the right to come to the tree of life, and may enter in by the gates into the city.

15Without are the dogs, and the sorcerers, and the fornicators, and the murderers, and the idolaters, and every one that loveth and maketh a lie.

16I Jesus have sent mine angel to testify unto you these things for the churches. I am the root and the offspring of David, the bright, the morning star.

17And the Spirit and the bride say, Come. And he that heareth, let him say, Come. And he that is athirst, let him come: he that will, let him take the water of life freely.

18I testify unto every man that heareth the words of the prophecy of this book, if any man shall add unto them, God shall add unto him the plagues which are written in this book:

19and if any man shall take away from the words of the book of this prophecy, God shall take away his part from the tree of life, and out of the holy city, which are written in this book.

20He who testifieth these things saith, Yea: I come quickly. Amen: come, Lord Jesus.

21The grace of the Lord Jesus be with the saints. Amen.

www.ingramcontent.com/pod-product-compliance
Lightning Source LLC
Chambersburg PA
CBHW060504300426
44112CB00017B/2544